HOLT McDOUGAL

The AMERICANS

correlated to the

New York State Learning Standards *and* New York State Core Curriculum

U.S. History and Government

CONTENTS

LESSONS WITH EMBEDDED NEW YORK LEARNING & CONTENT EXPECTATIONS

 Look for the New York symbol throughout this book. It highlights targeted learning and content expectations to help you master the state standards.

New York Reviewers

Julie Barker
Pittsford Central Schools
Pittsford, NY

Mark Chenault
West Side High School
New York, NY

Mike Harnick
Williamsville East High School
East Amherst, NY

Bryant Harris
Thurgood Marshall Academy
New York, NY

Amy Kantz
Williamsville East High School
East Amherst, NY

Lisa Kissinger
Shenendehowa East High School
Clifton Park, NY

Paul Lampe
Rochester City Schools
Rochester, NY

Nick Petraccione
Bethlehem High School
Delmar, NY

Mark Whitworth
Bronx Regional High School
Bronx, NY

New York State Standards

Throughout the United States History and Government course, you will study the people and events that helped to shape our country from prehistory to the present. To ensure successful study, you will follow the **New York State Learning Standards for Social Studies** and the more detailed standards outlined in the **New York State Social Studies Core Curriculum.**

This course will focus on Social Studies Learning Standard 1—History of the United States and New York. Standard 1 requires that you learn about the people, events, and ideas that have helped shape the history of the United States and the state of New York. Standard 1 is divided into four **Key Ideas.** These Key Ideas describe the information that you will be learning and the skills that you will be practicing. Each Key Idea is further divided into **Performance Indicators** (PI). These Performance Indicators identify what you must do to demonstrate proficiency within each Key Idea.

In addition to the Learning Standards, Key Ideas, and Performance Indicators, your study will be guided by a more detailed set of standards—the New York State Social Studies Core Curriculum. The Core Curriculum lists expectations for student mastery of content and skills for the United States History and Government course. The Core Curriculum is organized chronologically across seven historical units, each of which covers a specific period of history. Each unit lists particular content, concepts, themes, and connections to key people, places, and events in United States history and government.

State Capitol in Albany, New York

New York State Learning Standards

Standard 1—History of the United States and New York

Students will learn a variety of intellectual skills to demonstrate their understanding of major ideas, eras, themes, developments, and turning points in the history of the United States and New York.

KEY IDEA 1: The study of New York State and United States history requires an analysis of the development of American culture, its diversity and multicultural context, and the ways people are unified by many values, practices, and traditions.

1.1 Analyze the development of American culture, explaining how ideas, values, beliefs, and traditions have changed over time and how they united all Americans.

1.2 Describe the evolution of American democratic values and beliefs as expressed in the Declaration of Independence, the New York State Constitution, the United States Constitution, the Bill of Rights, and other important historical documents.

KEY IDEA 2: Important ideas, social and cultural values, beliefs, and traditions from New York State and United States history illustrate the connections and interactions of people and events across time and from a variety of perspectives.

2.1 Discuss several schemes for periodizing the history of New York State and the United States.

2.2 Develop and test hypotheses about important events, eras, or issues in New York State and United States history, setting clear and valid criteria for judging the importance and significance of these events, eras, or issues.

2.3 Compare and contrast the experiences of different groups in the United States.

2.4 Examine how the Constitution, United States law, and the rights of citizenship provide a major unifying factor in bringing together Americans from diverse roots and traditions.

2.5 Analyze the United States involvement in foreign affairs and a willingness to engage in international politics, examining the ideas and traditions leading to these foreign policies.

2.6 Compare and contrast the values exhibited and foreign policies implemented by the United States and other nations over time with those expressed in the United Nations Charter and international law.

Lower Manhattan, New York City

KEY IDEA 3: Study about the major social, political, economic, cultural, and religious developments in New York State and United States history involves learning about the important roles and contributions of individuals and groups.

PI 3.1 Compare and contrast the experiences of different ethnic, national, and religious groups, including Native American Indians, in the United States, explaining their contributions to American society and culture.

PI 3.2 Research and analyze the major themes and developments in New York State and United States history (e.g., colonization and settlement; Revolution and New National Period; immigration; expansion and reform era; Civil War and Reconstruction; the American labor movement; Great Depression; World Wars; contemporary United States).

PI 3.3 Prepare essays and oral reports about the important social, political, economic, scientific, technological, and cultural developments, issues, and events from New York State and United States history.

PI 3.4 Understand the interrelationships between world events and developments in New York State and the United States (e.g., causes for immigration, economic opportunities, human rights abuses, and tyranny versus freedom).

KEY IDEA 4: The skills of historical analysis include the ability to: explain the significance of historical evidence; weigh the importance, reliability, and validity of evidence; understand the concept of multiple causation; understand the importance of changing and competing interpretations of different historical developments.

PI 4.1 Analyze historical narratives about key events in New York State and United States history to identify the facts and evaluate the authors' perspectives.

PI 4.2 Consider different historians' analyses of the same event or development in United States history to understand how different viewpoints and/or frames of reference influence historical interpretations.

PI 4.3 Evaluate the validity and credibility of historical interpretations of important events or issues in New York State or United States history, revising these interpretations as new information is learned and other interpretations are developed. (Adapted from *National Standards for United States History*)

Adirondack State Park

New York State Core Curriculum

United States History and Government

UNIT ONE: Introduction

I. GEOGRAPHY

A. The physical/cultural setting in the Americas

  1. Size and location

  2. Major zones/areas

    a. Climate zones

    b. Vegetation zones

    c. Agricultural areas

    d. Natural resources

  3. Factors that shaped the identity of the United States

    a. Major mountain ranges

    b. Major river systems

    c. Great Plains

    d. Atlantic/Pacific oceans

    e. Coastlines

    f. Climate

    g. Abundance of natural resources

  4. Barriers to expansion/development

    a. Climate

    b. Mountain ranges

    c. Arid lands

    d. Great Plains

B. Role/influence of geography on historical/cultural development

  1. Influences on early Native American Indians

  2. Influence on colonization patterns and colonial development

  3. Territorial expansion

  4. Impact during wartime

  5. Effect of location on United States foreign policy

C. Geographic issues today

  1. Waste disposal

  2. Water/air pollution

  3. Shifting populations

  4. Energy usage

  5. Urban problems/challenges

D. Demographics

  1. Characteristics

    a. Gender

    b. Age

    c. Ethnicity

    d. Religion

    e. Economic variables

    f. Nature of household

    g. Marital status

  2. Immigration

  3. Migration

  4. Population relationships/trends since 1865

    a. Population growth

    b. Distribution

    c. Density

  5. Current issues

    a. Graying of America

    b. Effects of the baby boom generation

    c. Changing composition of populations

UNIT TWO: Constitutional Foundations for the United States Democratic Republic

I. THE CONSTITUTION: THE FOUNDATION OF AMERICAN SOCIETY

A. Historical foundations

  1. 17th- and 18th-century Enlightenment thought

    a. European intellectuals (Locke, Montesquieu, Voltaire, Rousseau)

    b. Key events (Magna Carta, habeas corpus, English Bill of Rights, Glorious Revolution)

Ossining, New York

2. The peoples and peopling of the American colonies (voluntary and involuntary)
   a. Native American Indians (relations between colonists and Native American Indians, trade, alliances, forced labor, warfare)
   b. Slave trade
   c. Varieties of immigrant motivation, ethnicities, and experiences
3. Colonial experience: political rights and mercantile relationships
   a. Colonial charters and self-government: Mayflower Compact, town meetings, House of Burgesses, local government, property rights, enforceable contracts, Albany Plan of Union
   b. Native American governmental systems
   c. Colonial slavery (evolution and variation of slavery in Chesapeake, South Carolina and Georgia, lower Mississippi Valley, middle colonies, and the North; slave resistance; influence of Africa and African-American culture upon colonial cultures; contradiction between slavery and emerging ideals of freedom and liberty)
   d. Freedom of the press: the Zenger case
   e. Salutary neglect, rights of English citizens in America
4. The Revolutionary War and the Declaration of Independence
   a. Causes of the Revolution
   b. Revolutionary ideology (republican principles natural rights)
   c. Revolutionary leaders: Benjamin Franklin, George Washington, John Adams, Samuel Adams, Patrick Henry
   d. Slavery, African-Americans, and the outcome of the American Revolution (African-American role in the Revolution, growth of the "free black" population)

5. New York State Constitution based on republican principles
   a. New York State Constitution
   b. State constitutions (ratification by the people, unicameral versus bicameral legislatures, branches of government)
   c. Guaranteeing religious liberty (disestablishment of churches, the growth of religious pluralism)
   d. The abolition of slavery in the North
6. Articles of Confederation
7. Northwest Ordinance
B. Constitutional Convention
   1. Representation and process
      a. Framers of the Constitution (James Madison)
      b. Plans of government (Virginia plan, New Jersey plan, Connecticut plan)
   2. Conflict and compromise: seeking effective institutions
      a. Protecting liberty against abuses or power
      b. Power separated and balanced
      c. The Constitution, slavery, and fear of tyrannical powers of government
   3. The document: structure of government
   4. Ratification
      a. The Federalist Papers—a New York activity with widespread influence
      b. The debate: Federalist and Anti-Federalist arguments
C. The Bill of Rights
D. Basic structure and function: three branches and their operation
E. Basic constitutional principles
   (1) national power—limits and potentials
   (2) federalism—balance between nation and state
   (3) the judiciary—interpreter of the Constitution or shaper of public policy
   (4) civil liberties—protecting individual liberties from governmental abuses; the balance between government and the individual
   (5) criminal procedures—the balance between the rights of the accused and protection of the community and victims
   (6) equality—its historic and present meaning as a constitutional value
   (7) the rights of women under the Constitution
   (8) the rights of ethnic and racial groups under the Constitution
   (9) Presidential power in wartime and in foreign affairs
   (10) the separation of powers and the capacity to govern
   (11) avenues of representation
   (12) property rights and economic policy
   (13) constitutional change and flexibility

Niagara Falls

F. Implementing the new constitutional principles

1. Creating domestic stability through sound financial policies: Hamilton's financial plans

2. Development of unwritten constitutional government under Washington, Adams, and Jefferson: cabinet, political parties, judicial review, executive and Congressional interpretation, lobbying; the Marshall Court (*Marbury* v. *Madison*, 1803, *McCulloch* v. *Maryland*, 1819, and *Gibbons* v. *Ogden*, 1824)

3. Establishing a stable political system
   a. The Federalist and Republican parties (philosophies of Hamilton and Jefferson)
   b. Suppressing dissent (the Whiskey Rebellion, the Alien and Sedition Acts)

4. Neutrality and national security, Washington through Monroe: foreign affairs, establishing boundaries
   a. Neutrality: A key element of American foreign policy—influence of geography
   b. A new nation in a world at war
   c. Economic pressures as a tool of diplomacy
   d. The failure of Republican diplomacy: War of 1812 (significance of the War for Native American Indians, Spain, the growth of industry)
   e. Monroe Doctrine

II. THE CONSTITUTION TESTED: NATIONALISM AND SECTIONALISM

A. Factors unifying the United States, 1789–1861
1. The first and second two-party systems
2. The market economy and interstate commerce
3. The Marshall Court

B. Constitutional stress and crisis
1. Developing sectional differences and philosophies of government
   a. The growth of urban and industrial patterns of life in the North
      (1) the transportation revolution (Erie Canal, rise of the port of New York, New York City's rise as a trade and manufacturing center)
      (2) the introduction of the factory system
      (3) working conditions
      (4) women and work
      (5) urban problems
   b. Middle-class and working-class life in the pre-Civil War North (families, gender roles, schooling, childhood, living conditions, status of free blacks)
   c. Foreign immigration and nativist reactions (Jews; Irish mass starvation, 1845–1850; Germans; 1848 refugees; Know Nothings)
   d. Patterns of Southern development (growth of cotton cultivation, movement into the Old Southwest, women on plantations)
   e. Life under slavery (slave laws; material conditions of life; women and children; religious and cultural expression; resistance)

2. Equal rights and justice: expansion of franchise; search for minority rights; expansion of slavery; abolitionist movement; the underground railroad; denial of Native American Indian rights and land ownership
   a. Political democratization: national political nominating convention, secret ballot
   b. The rise of mass politics (John Quincy Adams, Andrew Jackson, the spoils system, the bank war, Martin Van Buren)
   c. Native Americans
      (1) History of Indian relations from 1607
      (2) Native American cultural survival strategies (cultural adaptation, cultural revitalization movements, Pan-Indian movements, resistance)
      (3) The removal policy: *Worcester* v. *Georgia*, 1832
   d. The birth of the American reform tradition (religious and secular roots; public schools; care for the physically disabled and the mentally ill; the problems of poverty and crime; antislavery; women's rights movement)

3. The great constitutional debates: states' rights versus federal supremacy (nullification); efforts to address slavery issue (Missouri Compromise, Compromise of 1850, fugitive slave law, *Dred Scott* v. *Sanford*, 1857); preservation of the Union

C. Territorial expansion through diplomacy, migration, annexation, and war; Manifest Destiny
1. The Louisiana Purchase
2. Exploring and settling the West (explorers, Lewis and Clark expedition, naturalists, trappers and traders, trailblazers, missionaries, pioneers, the Mormon Church)
3. The Spanish, Mexican, and Native American West
4. Motives for and implications of expansion and western settlement
5. Politics of western expansion (Manifest Destiny, the Texas and Oregon questions, the Mexican War)
6. Impact of western expansion upon Mexicans and Native Americans

D. The Constitution in jeopardy: The American Civil War
1. United States society divided
   a. Party disintegration and realignment and sectional polarization (Kansas-Nebraska Act, disintegration of the Whig Party and the rise of the Republican Party, Dred Scott decision, John Brown's raid)

New York
state quarter

b. Abraham Lincoln, the secession crisis, and efforts at compromise (Lincoln-Douglas debates, election of 1860, secession, compromise plans, Fort Sumter)

2. Wartime actions

    a. Military strategy, major battles (Antietam, Gettysburg), and human toll

    b. Impact of war on home front (civil liberties during the Civil War, women's roles)

    c. Government policy during the war (wartime finances, creating a national currency, transcontinental railroad, Homestead Act)

    d. Lincoln and Emancipation (the Emancipation Proclamation, the Gettysburg Address, African-American participation in the Civil War, the 13th Amendment)

UNIT THREE: Industrialization of the United States

I. THE RECONSTRUCTED NATION

A. Reconstruction plans

    1. Lincoln's plan

    2. Congressional Reconstruction

    3. Post-Civil War amendments (13th, 14th, and 15th)

    4. Impeachment of Andrew Johnson

    5. The reconstructed nation and shifting relationships between the federal government, state governments, and individual citizens

B. The North

    1. Economic and technological impacts of the Civil War

    2. Expanding world markets

    3. Developing labor needs

C. The New South

    1. Agriculture: land and labor (sharecropping and tenant farming)

    2. Status of freedmen

        a. The economic, political, social, and educational experiences of formerly enslaved African-Americans

        b. From exclusion to segregation

    3. Struggle for political control in the New South

    4. Supreme Court interpretations of the 13th and 14th amendments (*Civil Rights Cases*, 1883)

    5. The emerging debate over "proper" role of African-Americans

D. End of Reconstruction

    1. Disputed election of 1876

    2. End of military occupation

    3. Restoration of white control in the South (1870s and 1880s) and abridgment of rights of freed African-Americans

    4. *Plessy* v. *Ferguson*, 1896: "separate but equal"

E. The Impact of the Civil War and Reconstruction: Summary

1. On political alignments

2. On the nature of citizenship

3. On federal-state relations

4. On the development of the North as an industrial power

5. On American society

II. THE RISE OF AMERICAN BUSINESS, INDUSTRY, AND LABOR, 1865–1920

A. Economic transformation and the "search for order"

    1. Business response to change: organize and rationalize

    2. Organizational responses

        a. From proprietorships and partnerships to the rise of monopolies

        b. Incorporation

        c. Capital concentration; consolidation

        d. Expanding markets: national and international

        e. Merchandising changes, department stores, mail order catalogs

B. Major areas of growth in business and industry

    1. Transportation: railroads and automobiles; urban transportation

    2. Building materials: steel

    3. Energy sources: coal, oil, electricity

    4. Communications: telegraph, telephone

C. Representative entrepreneurs: Case studies in concentrated wealth and effort (other personalities may be substituted; local examples of enterprise should also be used)

    1. John D. Rockefeller: oil; Andrew Carnegie: steel; Ford: auto

    2. Work ethic: Cotton Mather to Horatio Alger

    3. Conflict between public good and private gain, e.g., use of resources

D. New business and government practices: Popular and government responses

    1. Laissez-faire and government support; interpretation of 14th Amendment by Supreme Court

    2. Railroad "pooling"; rate inequities (*Wabash, St. Louis, and Pacific Railway* v. *Illinois*, 1886); railroad regulation: state and national ICC

    3. Competition and absorption; mergers and trusts; Sherman Antitrust Act, 1890 (*United States* v. *E.C. Knight*, 1895)

E. Labor's response to economic change: Organize

    1. Efforts at national labor unions: Knights of Labor (1869); AF of L (1881–1886); ILGWU (1900)

        a. "Bread and butter" objectives

        b. Unions and social issues (education)

        c. Attitudes toward immigrants, African-Americans, women

        d. Union leadership (Gompers, Debs)

2. Struggle and conflict
   a. Major strikes: gains and losses—Homestead, Pullman (*In Re Debs,* 1895), Lawrence
   b. Management's position
   c. Weapons or tactics employed in disputes between labor and management
   d. Attitude and role of government

F. Agrarian response to economic change: Organize and protest
   a. The Grange movement as agrarian protest
   b. Populism: a political response—William Jennings Bryan and the election of 1896
      (1) Case study: The Populists as a grass-roots political party
   c. National government response: Interstate Commerce Act, 1887

III. ADJUSTING SOCIETY TO INDUSTRIALISM: AMERICAN PEOPLE AND PLACES

A. Impact of industrialization
   1. Urban growth
      a. Attractions: jobs, education, culture, public education system
      b. Problems (slums, increased crime, inadequate water and sanitation services)
      c. Skyscrapers and elevators; tenements and walk-ups
      d. Social Darwinism, increased class division, conspicuous consumption, social conscience, philanthropy
   2. Work and workers
      a. Factories and people—immigrant patterns of settlement
      b. Geographic, economic, social, and political considerations
      c. Working conditions: "wage slavery"
      d. Living conditions: company towns and urban slums
      e. The Great Migration: The migration of African-Americans to the North
   3. Women, families, and work
      a. Traditional roles—Victorian ideal and reality
      b. Outside and inside their homes: double drudgery
      c. Jobs for domestics, laundresses, and textile workers; technology brought jobs as telephone operators and typists
      d. Emerging family patterns: two wage earners, broken homes
      e. Problems of child labor, elderly, disabled, and African-American women
         (1) Case study: child labor
      f. Role of religion in a pluralistic society
         (1) Religious tolerance develops slowly
         (2) Puritan beliefs and values influenced our historical development
         (3) Religion and party politics to 1896

4. The growing middle class (consumerism and its material benefits and effects)
5. Art and literature (Mark Twain and penny dailies)

B. Immigration, 1850–1924
   1. New sources: eastern/southern Europe; Asia—the "new ethnicity"
      a. Case studies: Italian immigration, Chinese immigration (1850–1924, West to East migration), Russian/Jewish immigration
   2. The impulses abroad
   3. The attractions here: labor shortages, liberty, and freedoms
   4. Urbanization: ghettos
   5. "Americanization" process
   6. Impacts on family, religion, education, and politics
   7. Contributions to American society
      a. Diversity of the United States population

C. Reactions to the "new" immigration
   1. Cultural pluralism: assimilation (Americanization), acculturation ("melting pot" or cultural pluralism), or both
   2. Nativist reactions: stereotyping and prejudice
      (1) Case study: Irish immigration
   3. Impact on African-Americans and other established minorities
   4. "Yellow Peril," West Coast restrictions
   5. Literacy testing, 1917
   6. The Red Scare
   7. Quota acts of 1921 and 1924

D. The frontier (1850–1890)
   1. Land west of the Mississippi
      a. Rolling plains and the Great American Desert
      b. Native American Indian nations; concept of oneness with the environment
      c. The Homestead Act, 1862, and the settlement of the West
   2. The impact of industrialization
      a. Improved transportation facilitated shipping of foodstuffs and migration of population
      b. Western migration of immigrants
      c. Potential for investment: development of key urban centers
   3. Native American Indians
      a. Pressures of advancing white settlement: differing views of land use and ownership
      b. Treaties and legal status
      c. The Indian wars: 1850–1900
      d. Legislating Indian life: reservations; Dawes Act (1887)
      e. Indian civil rights laws—legal status of Native American Indians,

1887–1970: citizenship, 1924; self-government, 1934; self-determination, 1970

UNIT FOUR: The Progressive Movement: Responses to the Challenges Brought about by Industrialization And Urbanization

I. REFORM IN AMERICA

A. Pressures for reform

  1. Progressives supported the use of government power for different reform purposes

  2. Effects of developing technologies and their social, ethical, and moral impacts

  3. Struggle for fair standards of business operation and working conditions (*Lochner* v. *New York,* 1905; *Muller* v. *Oregon,* 1908)

  4. Increasing inequities between wealth and poverty

  5. Rising power and influence of the middle class

B. Progress: Social and economic reform and consumer protection

  1. The "Muckrakers" and reform

    a. Magazine writers (Steffens, Tarbell)

    b. Novelists (Norris, Sinclair)

    c. Legislation (Pure Food and Drug Act, 1906, Meat Inspection Act, 1906)

  2. Other areas of concern

    a. Social settlement movement and the problems of poverty (Jacob Riis, Jane Addams)

    b. Women's rights and efforts for peace

      (1) The suffrage movement (Elizabeth Cady Stanton, Susan B. Anthony); Seneca Falls

      (2) Beginnings of fight for birth control (Margaret Sanger)

      (3) Peace movement

    c. The black movement and reform (Booker T. Washington and W.E.B. DuBois)

      (1) Formation of NAACP (1912)

      (2) Ida Wells (anti-lynching)

      (3) Marcus Garvey

    d. Temperance/prohibition

    e. Formation of Anti-Defamation League (1913)

C. Progressivism and government action

  1. Emerging Progressive movement: political reform

    (1) Influence of America's urban middle class

    a. Municipal and state reform

      (1) Municipal reform: response to urban problems

      (2) Sudden growth and needed services

    b. Progressive state reform: e.g., Wisconsin (Robert LaFollette); New York (Theodore Roosevelt); Massachusetts (initiative,

referendum, recall); economic, social, environmental reforms

  2. Theodore Roosevelt and the Square Deal

    a. The stewardship theory of the Presidency

    b. Legislation strengthening railroad regulation and consumer protection

    c. "Trust-busting" court cases (*Northern Securities Co.* v. *United States,* 1904); rule of reason: Standard Oil

  3. Conservation

    a. Theodore Roosevelt's concern for nature, land, and resources

    b. Federal legislation and projects: effects on states' limits

    c. Roles of Gifford Pinchot and John Muir

  4. Woodrow Wilson and the New Freedom

    a. Progressivism at its zenith; the 1912 election: Taft, Roosevelt, Wilson

    b. The Underwood Tariff and the graduated income tax

    c. Clayton Antitrust Act and the Federal Trade Commission

    d. The Federal Reserve System (monetary controls)

    e. Women's suffrage amendment

  5. World War I: effect on domestic reform

II. THE RISE OF AMERICAN POWER

A. An emerging global involvement

  1. From old diplomacy to new, 1865–1900

    a. Role of increased American power

      (1) Communications technology

      (2) American attitudes toward international role

      (3) Growth of naval power

    b. Perry and the "opening" of Japan (1854)

  2. Other Pacific overtures

    a. United States and China; the Chinese perspective (Boxer Rebellion)

    b. The Open-Door policy

    c. Acquisition of Hawaii

    d. Naval bases: Samoa

  3. Imperialism: the Spanish-American War

    a. Causes for war

    b. United States empire—Puerto Rico; Cuban protectorate (the Platt Amendment)

      (1) Acquisition of the Philippines: "the great debate"

      (2) Disposition of territories

      (3) Constitutional issues

  4. Latin American affairs

    a. Monroe Doctrine update (Roosevelt corollary): the view from Latin America

    b. West Indies protectorates ("the big stick")

    c. Panama Canal: acquisition and construction; Canal retrocession treaty

    d. Taft and dollar diplomacy

B. Restraint and involvement: 1914–1920

    1. United States involvement

        a. Efforts at neutrality and "preparedness"

        b. Causes of United States entry into World War I

        c. United States role in the war

        d. United States reaction to the Russian Revolution

C. Wartime constitutional issues

    1. War opposition and patriotism: the draft issue

    2. Espionage and Sedition acts

    3. *Schenck* v. *United States,* 1919; clear and present danger doctrine

    4. Red Scare, 1918–1919

D. The search for peace and arms control: 1914–1930

    1. The peace movement: Women's International League for Peace and Freedom

    2. War aims: The Fourteen Points

    3. Treaty of Versailles: Wilson's role

    4. League of Nations: Henry Cabot Lodge and the United States Senate rejection

    5. Washington Naval Disarmament Conference (1920s)

    6. Reparations and war debts (United States as a world banker)

    7. Kellogg-Briand Pact (1928)

    8. Establishment of the World Court

UNIT FIVE: At Home and Abroad: Prosperity and Depression, 1917–1940

I. WAR AND PROSPERITY: 1917–1929

A. Impact of war

    1. War's effects on gender roles, on African-Americans, and other minority groups

    2. Case study: Movement of African-Americans from the South to northern cities

    3. Return to "normalcy": 1918–1921

B. The twenties: Business boom or false prosperity?

    1. Post-World War I recession

    2. Avarice and scandal: Teapot Dome

    3. Coolidge prosperity; not for everyone

    4. Problems on the farm

        a. Expansion, mortgages, and advancing technology

        b. Farmers and minorities fail to share in economic benefit

    5. Speculative boom: the "big bull market"

C. Mass consumption and the clash of cultural values

    1. Mass consumption

        a. The automobile: new industries, products, and services

        b. Installment buying: consumer durable goods (appliances)

        c. Real estate boom and suburban development; its economic and geographic implications: decline of trolleys and trains, improvement of roads

            (1) The emergence of new regional, political, and economic units

        d. Entertainment: radio; motion pictures; advertising and cultural homogenization

    2. Constitutional and legal issues

        a. Threats to civil liberties: Red Scare, Ku Klux Klan, and Sacco and Vanzetti

        b. Prohibition (18th Amendment) and the Volstead Act: stimulus to crime, public attitudes, repeal (21st Amendment)

        c. Science, religion, and education: the Scopes trial (1925)

        d. Restrictions on immigration: closing the "golden door"

    3. Shifting cultural values

        a. Revolution in morals and manners: fads, flappers, and Freud

        b. Women's changing roles

            (1) Effect of World War I

            (2) Involvement in the political process: the 19th Amendment

            (3) Health and working conditions

            (4) Women in the workforce

            (5) Emerging role: emphasis on wife rather than mother

        c. The literary scene

            (1) Sinclair Lewis, Ernest Hemingway, Edith Wharton, Willa Cather, and F. Scott Fitzgerald

            (2) The Harlem Renaissance: Duke Ellington, Langston Hughes, Bessie Smith

Downtown New York harbor

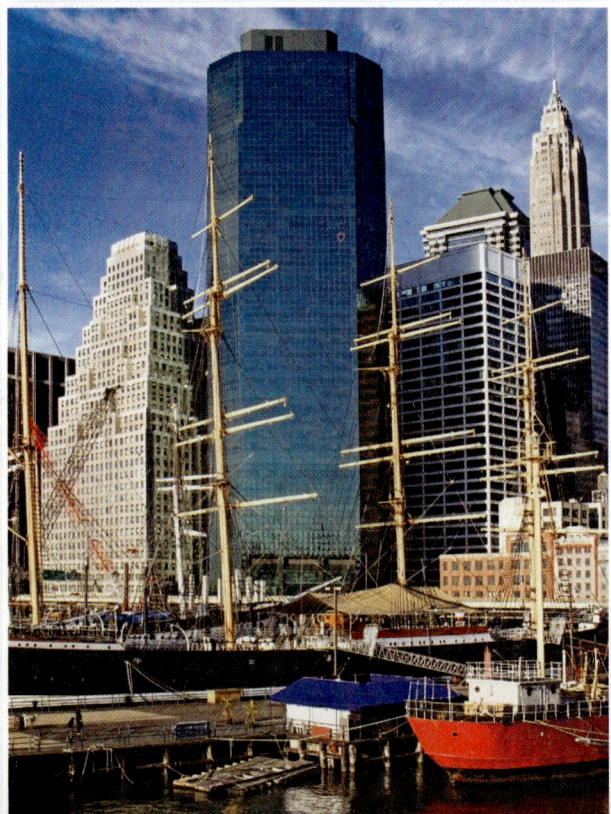

II. THE GREAT DEPRESSION

A. Onset of the Depression

  1. Weakness in the economy

    a. Overproduction/underconsumption (maldistribution of wealth)

    b. Overexpansion of credit (e.g., buying stock on margin)

  2. The stock market crash

    a. Worldwide nature—Growing financial interdependence

    b. Interdependent banking systems

    c. International trade

    d. Political repercussions

  3. The Hoover response

    a. Rugged individualism; "trickle down" economics

    b. Reconstruction Finance Corporation

  4. Unemployment, the Bonus Army, Hoovervilles; impact on women and minorities

B. Franklin D. Roosevelt and the New Deal: Relief, recovery, and reform programs

  1. Relief of human suffering

    a. Bank "holiday"; Emergency Banking Act

    b. Federal Emergency Relief Act

    c. Unemployment: WPA, PWA, CCC; troubling equity issues

  2. Recovery of the United States economy

    a. NRA: "codes of fair competition"

    b. Mortgage relief: HOLC, FHA

    c. First and second AAA, scarcity and parity

  3. Search for effective reform (program examples)

    a. Banking: Glass-Steagall Act (FDIC)

    b. Stock market: SEC

    c. Social Security

    d. Labor

      (1) Wagner Act (NLRB)

      (2) Labor Standards Act

  4. Labor's response: Formation of CIO

  5. Controversial aspects of the New Deal

    a. Constitutional issues

      (1) Supreme Court and the NRA(*Schechter Poultry Corp.* v. *United States,* 1935)

      (2) Supreme Court and the AAA

      (3) TVA: model yardstick or creeping socialism

    b. 1936 election "mandate"

    c. Roosevelt's "Court-packing" proposal: failure and success

    d. 1940: third-term controversy (the unwritten constitution)

    e. Passage of the 22nd Amendment (1951)

  6. The human factor

    a. FDR as communicator and his efforts to restore public confidence; press conferences, "fireside chats," and effective use of the radio

    b. Eleanor Roosevelt as the President's eyes and ears

    c. The Dust Bowl and the Okies

    d. The New Deal and women (Frances Perkins)

    e. The New Deal and minorities (shift in African-American vote): discriminatory results

    f. Indian Reorganization Act (1934)

  7. Culture of the Depression

    a. Literature: John Steinbeck and Langston Hughes

    b. Music: jazz, swing (big bands)

    c. Art: WPA, fine arts, Hollywood, comic books

  8. Opposition to the New Deal: Al Smith, Norman Thomas, Huey Long, Father Coughlin, Dr. Townsend

UNIT SIX: The United States in an Age of Global Crisis: Responsibility and Cooperation

I. PEACE IN PERIL: 1933–1950

A. Isolation and neutrality

  1. Causes of disillusion and pacifism

  2. Neutrality Acts of 1935–37

  3. Spanish Civil War: testing war technology and ideology

  4. FDR's "quarantine" speech (1937)

B. Failure of peace; triumph of aggression

  1. Aggressions of Japan, Germany, Italy: 1932–1940

  2. Appeasement: The Munich Conference (1938)

  3. German attack on Poland; start of World War II in Europe

  4. Gradual United States involvement

    a. Neutrality Act of 1939 ("cash and carry")

    b. Lend-Lease Act and 50 overage destroyers deal

    c. The moral dimension: The Atlantic Charter (August 1941)

C. The United States in World War II

  1. Pearl Harbor

  2. The human dimensions of the war

    a. The "arsenal of democracy" (feats of productivity)

    b. Role of women: WACs; Rosie the Riveter; return of the retired

    c. Mobilization: the draft; minority issues

    d. Financing the war: war bond drives; Hollywood goes to war

    e. Rationing

    f. Experiences of men and women in military service

  3. Allied strategy and leadership

    a. Assistance to Soviet Union

    b. Europe first

    c. A two-front war

  4. The atomic bomb

    a. The Manhattan Project (role of refugees)

b. Truman's decision to use the atomic bomb against Japan: Hiroshima and Nagasaki

c. United States occupation of Japan; the "MacArthur constitution"

d. Japanese war crime trials

5. The war's impact on minorities

    a. Incarceration of West Coast Japanese-Americans; Executive Order 9066; *Korematsu* v. *United States* (1944)

    b. Extent of racially integrated units in the military

    c. The Nazi Holocaust: United States and world reactions

    d. The Nuremberg war crimes trials; later trials of other Nazi criminals, e.g., Eichmann, Barbie

6. Demobilization

    a. Inflation and strikes

    b. The G.I. Bill; impact on education and housing

    c. Truman's Fair Deal

    d. Partisan problems with Congress

    e. Minorities continued to find it difficult to obtain fair practices in housing, employment, education

    f. Upset election of 1948; Truman versus Dewey

    g. Truman and civil rights

II. PEACE WITH PROBLEMS: 1945–1960

A. International peace efforts

1. Formation of the United Nations

2. United Nations Universal Declaration of Human Rights

    a. Eleanor Roosevelt's role

    b. Senate response

3. Displaced persons: refugee efforts

B. Expansion and containment: Europe

1. Summitry: Yalta and Potsdam, establishing "spheres of influence"

2. The Iron Curtain: Winston Churchill

3. Postwar uses for United States power

    a. The Truman Doctrine: Greece and Turkey

    b. The Marshall Plan

        (1) Aid for Europe

        (2) The Common Market

        (3) European Parliament

    c. Berlin airlift

    d. Formation of NATO alliance

C. Containment in Asia, Africa, and Latin America

1. The United States and Japan

    a. Separate peace treaty (1951)

    b. Reconstruction of Japan

2. The United States and China

    a. Rise to power of Mao Zedong and the People's Republic of China

    b. Chiang Kai-shek to Taiwan (1949)

3. USSR tests an A-bomb (1949)

4. The "hot war" in Asia: Korean War

    a. The Yalu River: China enters the war

    b. United Nations efforts: MacArthur, Truman, and "limited war"

    c. Stalemate and truce (1953)

5. Point four aid: Africa, Asia, Latin America

D. The Cold War at home

1. Truman and government loyalty checks Case studies: The Smith Act and the House Un-American Activities Committee (*Watkins* v. *United States,* 1957); the Alger Hiss case (1950); the Rosenberg trial (1950)

2. Loyalty and dissent: the case of Robert Oppenheimer

3. McCarthyism

4. Politics of the Cold War

    a. Loss of China

    b. Stalemate in Korea

    c. Truman's falling popularity

UNIT SEVEN: World in Uncertain Times: 1950–Present

I. TOWARD A POSTINDUSTRIAL WORLD: LIVING IN A GLOBAL AGE

A. Changes within the United States

1. Energy sources (nuclear power)

2. Materials (plastics, light metals)

3. Technology (computers)

4. Corporate structures (multinational corporations)

5. Nature of employment (agriculture to industry to service)

6. Problems (waste disposal, air/water pollution, growing energy usage, depleting resources, e.g., domestic oil supply)

II. CONTAINMENT AND CONSENSUS: 1945–1960

A. Review postwar events

1. Emerging power relationships: East/West; North/South; (haves/have-nots; developed/developing nations)

B. Eisenhower foreign policies

1. The end of the Korean War

2. John Foster Dulles, the domino theory and massive retaliation; brinkmanship posture

3. The H-bomb; atoms for peace

4. Summits and U-2s

5. Establishment of SEATO

6. Controversy: Aswan Dam and Suez Canal

7. Polish and Hungarian uprisings

8. Eisenhower Doctrine: intervention in Lebanon

9. Sputnik: initiating the space race

C. Domestic politics and constitutional issues

1. The Eisenhower peace
   a. Returning the United States to a peacetime economy
   b. Interstate Highway Act (1956)
   c. Suburbanization
   d. The Warren Court
2. Civil rights
   a. Jackie Robinson breaks the color barrier
   b. *Brown v. Board of Education of Topeka,* 1954
   c. Beginnings of modern civil rights movement
      (1) Rosa Parks and the Montgomery bus boycott
      (2) Little Rock: school desegregation
      (3) Segregation in public transportation ruled unconstitutional
      (4) Sit-ins: nonviolent tactic
      (5) Civil Rights Act of 1957

D. The people
   1. Prosperity and conservatism
      a. Postwar consumption: homes, autos, and television
      b. New educational opportunities: G.I. Bill
      c. The baby boom and its effects
   2. Migration and immigration
      a. Suburbanization: Levittowns
      b. Cities: declining
      c. New immigration patterns: Caribbean focus

III. DECADE OF CHANGE: 1960s

A. The Kennedy years
   1. The New Frontier: dreams and promises
      a. Civil rights actions
         (1) James Meredith at the University of Mississippi
         (2) Public career of Dr. Martin Luther King, Jr., Birmingham protest ("Letter from Birmingham Jail")
         (3) Assassination of Medgar Evers
         (4) March on Washington
   2. Foreign policy and Cold War crises
      a. Bay of Pigs invasion
      b. Vienna Summit/Berlin Wall
      c. Cuban missile crisis
      d. Laos and Vietnam
      e. Latin America and the Alliance for Progress
      f. Peace Corps
      g. Launching the race to the Moon
      h. Nuclear Test Ban Treaty 1963, 1967; Hot Line established
   3. Movement for rights of disabled citizens
      a. Background
         (1) Historic attitude that disabled were defective
         (2) Emergence of humanitarian view in 19th century, development of large institutions
         (3) Development of the concept of normalization; early-20th-century programs of education and training
      b. Kennedy administration, 1961–1963; beginning awareness, changing attitudes
         (1) President's Council on Mental Retardation
         (2) Special Olympics
      c. Litigation and legislation; 1960– present
         (1) Education of the Handicapped Act, 1966
         (2) Education for All Handicapped Children Act, 1971
         (3) Rehabilitation Act of 1973, Section 504
         (4) Americans with Disabilities Act, 1990
      d. Dependence to independence
         (1) Activism by disabled veterans
         (2) Deinstitutionalization
         (3) Mainstreaming
   4. Assassination in Dallas

B. Johnson and the Great Society
   1. Expanding on the Kennedy social programs
      a. War on poverty; VISTA
      b. Medicare
      c. Federal aid to education
      d. Environmental issues and concerns
   2. The Moon landing: the challenge of space exploration
   3. Continued demands for equality: civil rights movement
      a. Black protest, pride, and power
         (1) NAACP (National Association for the Advancement of Colored People): legal judicial leadership, Urban League
      b. Case studies
         (1) SNCC (Student Nonviolent Coordinating Committee): sit-in movement among college students
         (2) SCLC (Southern Christian Leadership Conference): promote nonviolent resistance, sit-ins, boycotts
         (3) CORE (Congress of Racial Equality): "Freedom Riders"
         (4) Testing of segregation laws
         (5) Others: Black Muslims; prominence of Malcolm X: advocating separation of races, separate state in the United States
         (6) Civil unrest: Watts riot, 1965, as example; Kerner Commission
         (7) Assassination of Malcolm X (February 1965)
      c. Legislative impact
         (1) Civil Rights Act of 1964 (*Heart of Atlanta Motel, Inc.* v. *United States,* 1964), modifications since 1964

(2) 24th Amendment (eliminating poll tax)

(3) Voting Rights Act, 1965

(4) Court decisions since 1948 upholding or modifying preferential treatment in employment; equal access to housing; travel and accommodations; voting rights; educational equity

(5) Fair Housing Act, 1968

4. Demands for equality: women

   a. The modern women's movement

     (1) Kennedy Commission and the Civil Rights Act, 1963–1964

     (2) NOW (1966) to present

   b. Issues

     (1) Shifting roles and images

     (2) Equal Rights Amendment (failure to ratify)

     (3) *Roe* v. *Wade,* 1973

     (4) Equality in the workplace: compensation, the glass ceiling

     (5) Increased focus on domestic abuse

5. Rising consciousness of Hispanic-Americans

   a. "Brown power" movement

   b. Organizing farm labor (Cesar Chavez)

   c. Cuban and Haitian immigration

   d. Increasing presence in American politics

6. Demands for equality: American Indian Movement (AIM) and other protests

   a. Occupation of Alcatraz

   b. The "long march"

   c. Wounded Knee, 1973

7. Rights of the accused

   a. *Mapp* v. *Ohio,* 1961

   b. *Gideon* v. *Wainwright,* 1963

   c. *Miranda* v. *Arizona,* 1966

8. Legislative reapportionment: *Baker* v. *Carr,* 1962

IV. THE LIMITS OF POWER: TURMOIL AT HOME AND ABROAD, 1965–1972

A. Vietnam: sacrifice and turmoil

1. The French-Indochinese War: early United States involvement; Truman, Eisenhower, and Kennedy policies (review how foreign policy is formulated)

2. United States and the spread of communism; domino theory; credibility of other United States commitments

3. Civil war in South Vietnam; concept of guerrilla warfare

4. LBJ and the Americanization of the war

   a. Fear of "losing" Vietnam

   b. Escalation and United States assumptions; Tet offensive

5. Student protests at home

   a. Draft protesters

   b. Political radicals: protests, Students for a Democratic Society (SDS), antiwar

   c. Cultural radicals: hippies and communalists

6. 1968: A year of turmoil

   a. President Johnson's decision not to seek reelection

   b. Assassinations of Dr. Martin Luther King, Jr. (April 1968) and Robert Kennedy (June 1968)

   c. The Democratic Convention; war protesters disrupt proceedings

   d. Impact of the Vietnam War on society

V. THE TREND TOWARD CONSERVATISM, 1972–1985

A. Nixon as President, 1969–1974

1. Domestic policies and events

   a. Modifications to Great Society programs (OSHA, Federal Energy Office, DEA, Clean Air Act, food stamps, revenue sharing)

   b. The Moon landing

   c. Environmental Protection Agency (1970)

   d. Self-determination for American Indians (1970)

   e. Ratification of the 26th Amendment (1971)

   f. Title IX – equal education access (1972)

2. Nixon's internationalism

   a. Henry Kissinger and realpolitik

     (1) Withdrawal from Vietnam and Cambodia; peace talks and signing of Paris Peace Accords (Pentagon papers, *New York Times* v. *United States,* 1971)

     (2) Nixon Doctrine

     (3) Opening to China

     (4) Détente: SALT and grain

3. The Presidency in crisis

   a. Resignation of Spiro Agnew

   b. Watergate affair and its constitutional implications

   c. *United States* v. *Nixon,* 1974

   d. The impeachment process and resignation

B. The Ford and Carter Presidencies

1. The appointive Presidency: Ford and Rockefeller (the constitutional aspects)

2. Domestic policy issues

   a. Pardon for Nixon and amnesty for draft evaders

   b. Oil crisis: shifting energy priorities

   c. Environmental concerns

     (1) Three Mile Island

     (2) Acid rain

     (3) Toxic waste

3. Foreign policy issues: the United States after Vietnam

   a. Fall of South Vietnam, 1975

   b. Oil crisis: Middle East in turmoil

   c. Middle East mediation: Camp David Accords

Lincoln Center

Countdown to the New York State Regents Exam

Social Studies Learning Standard 1 covers the history of the United States and New York. The Key Ideas and Performance Indicators (PI) for Standard 1 highlight the outstanding people and events and the fundamental concepts of United States and New York history. You are required to master these concepts for the United States History and Government Regents Exam. All high school students in New York must pass this exam to graduate.

Countdown to the New York State Regents Exam is your guide. This assessment workbook introduces you to the components of Standard 1 that you are required to master. Use this resource to help you learn and analyze the information presented in your United States history course.

Countdown to the New York State Regents Exam helps you by

- **Breaking down the learning.** This workbook examines a different key idea every week. A practice question is presented for each day of the week. Each question allows you to explore one or more performance indicators. In addition, there are two document-based questions at the end of the Countdown. These provide you with practice opportunities on an important feature of the Regents Exam.
- **Connecting the performance indicators and sample tasks to your United States history textbook.** References accompanying each question direct you to relevant material in your textbook. You can use these references to find answers and review important information.
- **Using different information sources.** Each section includes questions derived from maps, charts, graphic organizers, images, and primary sources. These questions expose you to different forms of historical documentation and require you to think about historical information in a variety of ways.
- **Giving you answers.** Countdown to the New York State Regents Exam includes an Answer Key against which you can check your mastery of United States and New York history.

KEY IDEA 3 Study about the major social, political, economic, cultural, and religious developments in New York State and United States history involves learning about the important roles and contributions of individuals and groups.

MONDAY PI 3.1

1 **The first Americans were most likely**
(Chapter 1.1)

(1) Aztecs

(2) Maya

(3) Anasazi

(4) hunter-gatherers from Asia

TUESDAY PI 3.1

2 **Before European colonization, North American indigenous peoples** *(Chapter 1.2)*

(1) established one vast culture in the American Northeast that slowly spread west

(2) formed large, clustered civilizations in the American Southwest and Northeast

(3) developed many distinct cultures with different languages, religious beliefs, and economic systems across the continent

(4) split into many small tribal units across the continent that traded peaceably and shared a common language and religious system

WEDNESDAY PI 3.2

3 **Which of the following European countries did not establish major settlements in North America?**
(Chapters 1.5, 2.1, 2.2)

(1) Spain

(2) Holland

(3) England

(4) Portugal

THURSDAY PI 3.2

4 **Rousseau's *The Social Contract***
(Chapter 4.2)

(1) sought to guarantee liberty by dividing the powers of government

(2) led to the growth of new Protestant denominations in the mid-1700s

(3) questioned the authority of any church to persecute those who did not accept its teachings

(4) held that if a government did not protect citizens and their rights, then citizens were justified in overthrowing it

FRIDAY PI 3.2, PI 3.3

It is not the cause of a poor printer, nor of New York alone, which you are now trying. No! It may in its consequences affect every freeman that lives under a British government on the mainland of America. It is the best Cause. It is the cause of liberty."
—Trial of John Peter Zenger, 1735

5 **What significant contribution did the trial of John Peter Zenger make to the development of American democratic values?**
(Chapter 3.1)

(1) It set a precedent for trial by jury.

(2) It set a precedent for freedom of the press.

(3) It set a precedent for freedom of religious worship.

(4) It set a precedent for criticism of colonial governments.

KEY IDEA 1 The study of New York State and United States history requires an analysis of the development of American culture, its diversity and multicultural context, and the ways people are unified by many values, practices, and traditions.

MONDAY
 PI 1.1, PI 1.2

1 **Colonists objected to the Stamp Act, the Townshend Acts, the Tea Act, and the Intolerable Acts because all of these**
(Chapter 4.1)

(1) led to a boycott of American goods

(2) resulted in less government involvement from Britain

(3) threatened the colonies' power of self-government

(4) jeopardized the colonists' security and ability to settle western lands

TUESDAY
 PI 1.1, PI 1.2

2 **From which of the following Enlightenment thinkers did the authors of the Declaration of Independence adopt many of their principles?**
(Chapter 4.2)

(1) John Locke

(2) Sir Isaac Newton

(3) Jonathan Edwards

(4) Jean-Jacques Rousseau

WEDNESDAY
 PI 1.2

3 **What does this cartoon illustrate?**
(Chapter 5.3)

(1) the American Revolution

(2) colonial resistance to British policies

(3) conflicts between colonists and Native Americans

(4) the struggle over ratification of the U.S. Constitution

THURSDAY
 PI 1.1, PI 1.2

4 **How does the First Amendment affect religious liberty in the United States?**
(Chapter 5.3)

(1) It gave states the power to regulate religion.

(2) It gives Congress the power to make laws regarding any religion or religious practice.

(3) It guarantees citizens the right to hold any religious belief and forbids the establishment of state churches.

(4) It guarantees citizens the right to hold any religious belief but gives states the right to establish official state churches.

FRIDAY
 PI 1.2

5 **What was the significance of *Marbury* v. *Madison*?**
(Chapter 6.3)

(1) It upheld the president's power to appoint judges.

(2) It led to the formation of new positions in the judiciary branch.

(3) It established the Supreme Court's right to declare a law unconstitutional.

(4) It established the Supreme Court's right to refuse presidential appointments.

KEY IDEA 3 Study about the major social, political, economic, cultural, and religious developments in New York State and United States history involves learning about the important roles and contributions of individuals and groups.

MONDAY

 P! 3.2, P! 3.4

> *The American continents … are henceforth not to be considered as subjects for future colonization by any European powers.*
> Monroe Doctrine, 1823

1 **The Monroe Doctrine was** *(Chapter 7.2)*

(1) an invitation for foreign colonization

(2) a policy of active U.S. involvement in Europe

(3) a plan for reorganizing the U.S. government

(4) an effort to keep the United States out of European affairs and European countries from colonizing the Americas

TUESDAY

 P! 3.2

2 **A Boston newspaper called James Monroe's presidency "the era of good feelings" because** *(Chapter 7.1)*

(1) the United States embraced a new spirit of isolationism

(2) it was characterized by economic growth and feelings of nationalism

(3) the administration focused on existing states, not expansion into new territories

(4) European nations and the United States entered into economic and diplomatic partnerships

WEDNESDAY

 P! 3.1, P! 3.2

3 **What was the significance of Andrew Jackson's policy toward Native Americans in the 1830s?** *(Chapter 7.3)*

(1) It contributed to the development of an independent Cherokee state.

(2) It led to the forced removal of thousands of Native Americans from the southeastern United States.

(3) It ended in a war that eliminated most of the Native American population east of the Mississippi River.

(4) It prompted a new series of treaties guaranteeing mutual respect and cooperation between Native Americans and the United States.

THURSDAY

 P! 3.2, P! 3.3

4 **The Industrial Revolution refers to a period from the mid-1700s to the mid-1800s when** *(Chapters 7.1)*

(1) cities in both the North and South grew at a faster rate

(2) American business owners rebelled against British business owners

(3) technological developments changed the way of life in both the North and the South

(4) agriculture and handcrafts gave way to machine production and manufacturing

FRIDAY

 P! 3.1

5 **The Second Great Awakening revived religious fervor by encouraging** *(Chapter 8.1)*

(1) people that their destiny lay in their own hands

(2) a return to traditional values and strict adherence to church rules

(3) the codification of Christian doctrine as law at all levels of government

(4) the establishment of new churches based on public displays of faith and denial of material wants

KEY IDEA 2 Important ideas, social and cultural values, beliefs, and traditions from New York State and United States history illustrate the connections and interactions of people and events across time and from a variety of perspectives.

MONDAY PI 2.2, PI 2.3

1 What effect did the Great Irish Famine have on the United States? *(Chapter 8.4)*

(1) United States citizens undertook a massive relief effort.

(2) More than 1 million Irish immigrated to the United States.

(3) Trade between Europe and the United States decreased by more than half.

(4) The United States government began using federal monies to provide foreign aid.

TUESDAY PI 2.1, PI 2.2

2 During the 1800s the United States underwent which two significant economic and social processes? *(Chapter 8.4)*

(1) revolution and expansion

(2) reformation and unionization

(3) militarization and privatization

(4) industrialization and urbanization

WEDNESDAY PI 2.2, PI 2.3

3 According to the map, routes along the Underground Railroad *(Chapter 10.2)*

(1) began in free states

(2) ran only from east to west

(3) originated in slave states

(4) led only to territories where slavery was permitted

THURSDAY PI 2.2

4 Manifest destiny can best be described as the belief that the United States *(Chapter 9.2)*

(1) had the right and obligation to spread across the entire continent

(2) was destined to advance freedom and democracy around the world

(3) had a mission to industrialize and advance capitalism around the world

(4) was entitled to oversee political and economic developments throughout the Western Hemisphere

FRIDAY PI 2.3

5 What group, founded by Joseph Smith, migrated west when its practices came under attack in the mid-1800s? *(Chapter 9.2)*

(1) Quakers

(2) Mormons

(3) Christians

(4) Seventh-Day Adventists

KEY IDEA 3 Study about the major social, political, economic, cultural, and religious developments in New York State and United States history involves learning about the important roles and contributions of individuals and groups.

MONDAY PI 3.1, PI 3.3

1 What significant social effect did the Kansas-Nebraska Act have on settlement in those territories? *(Chapter 10.2)*

(1) It caused a rapid decline in settlement.

(2) It contributed to a rapid growth in urbanization.

(3) It established a precedent for deciding the slavery issue peaceably by ballot.

(4) It led to violence between competing waves of proslavery and Free-Soil settlers.

TUESDAY PI 3.1, PI 3.3

2 Which of the following people led a raid on the U.S. arsenal at Harpers Ferry with the intention of starting a slave revolt? *(Chapter 10.4)*

(1) Dred Scott

(2) John Brown

(3) Preston Brooks

(4) Steven Douglas

WEDNESDAY PI 3.1, PI 3.3

3 This map illustrates the national split caused by Abraham Lincoln's election, which led to the *(Chapters 10.4, 11.1)*

(1) Freeport Doctrine

(2) call for a new election

(3) secession of southern states

(4) formation of the Republican party

Candidate	Political Affiliation	Electoral Votes	Popular Votes
Abraham Lincoln	Republican	180	1,868,452
John C. Breckinridge	Southern Democratic	72	847,953
John Bell	Constitutional Union	39	590,631
Stephen A. Douglas	Northern Democratic	12	1,375,157

Striped pattern shows state where electoral votes went to two candidates as indicated by the colors.

THURSDAY PI 3.1, PI 3.3

4 Which of the following groups of people did the Emancipation Proclamation free? *(Chapter 11.2)*

(1) enslaved persons in U.S. territories

(2) enslaved persons in other countries

(3) enslaved persons throughout the United States

(4) enslaved persons in areas in rebellion against the United States

FRIDAY PI 3.2, PI 3.3

5 What unconstitutional action did Abraham Lincoln take when he jailed critics of the war and the draft? *(Chapter 11.2)*

(1) Lincoln declared martial law.

(2) Lincoln suspended habeas corpus.

(3) Lincoln issued a declaration of war.

(4) Lincoln issued an executive order opposing the First Amendment.

WEEK 6

KEY IDEA 3 Study about the major social, political, economic, cultural, and religious developments in New York State and United States history involves learning about the important roles and contributions of individuals and groups.

MONDAY PI 3.1, PI 3.2

1 **During the Civil War people from the border states** *(Chapter 11.1)*

(1) remained neutral

(2) sided only with the Union

(3) sided only with the Confederacy

(4) fought for both the Union and the Confederacy

TUESDAY PI 3.2

2 **Early in 1865, before the end of the Civil War, Congress passed the Thirteenth Amendment to** *(Chapter 11.5)*

(1) abolish slavery

(2) establish the electoral college system

(3) grant citizenship to former enslaved persons

(4) guarantee former enslaved persons the right to vote

WEDNESDAY PI 3.1, PI 3.2

3 **In March 1865 the Freedmen's Bureau was established to** *(Chapter 12.1)*

(1) lead enslaved persons to freedom in the North

(2) advocate for civil rights on behalf of former enslaved persons

(3) help black and white southerners uprooted by the Civil War

(4) combat the influx of carpetbaggers and scalawags in the South

THURSDAY PI 3.2, PI 3.3

4 **What was the key difference between Reconstruction under Andrew Johnson and Reconstruction under Congress?** *(Chapter 12.1)*

(1) Johnson's Reconstruction ensured a role for freedmen in southern government.

(2) Congressional Reconstruction helped preserve the old Confederate power structure.

(3) Johnson's Reconstruction involved harsher penalties against the former Confederate states.

(4) Congressional Reconstruction made it more difficult for southern states to rejoin the Union.

FRIDAY PI 3.2, PI 3.3

5 **This image illustrates the shift in the Reconstruction South from** *(Chapter 12.2)*

(1) Democratic control to Republican control

(2) plantations to sharecropping and tenant farming

(3) industrialization to an emphasis on agricultural businesses

(4) an agrarian plantation system to a more diversified economy

KEY IDEA 3 Study about the major social, political, economic, cultural, and religious developments in New York State and United States history involves learning about the important roles and contributions of individuals and groups.

MONDAY
 PI 3.1, PI 3.2

1 **Americanization refers to** *(Chapter 13.1)*

(1) policies restricting interaction among Native American groups

(2) efforts by the U.S. government to remove Native Americans from U.S. territories

(3) practices meant to isolate Native Americans in cultural pockets on their reservations

(4) programs designed to dissolve Native American tribal identities and acculturate Native Americans

TUESDAY
 PI 3.1, PI 3.2

2 **Which of the following industries drew many people west in the mid-1800s?**

(Chapter 13.1)

(1) mining

(2) trading

(3) shipping

(4) manufacturing

WEDNESDAY
PI 3.1, PI 3.2

3 **In the late 1800s most of the railroad lines shown**

(Chapter 14.2)

(1) linked the United States and Canada

(2) were clustered in the Pacific Time Zone

(3) were clustered in the Central and Eastern Time Zones

(4) extended only as far west as places in the Mountain Time Zone

THURSDAY
 PI 3.2, PI 3.3

4 **Corporate trusts and monopolies, such as John D. Rockefeller's Standard Oil, were extensions of business practices grounded in** *(Chapter 14.3)*

(1) philanthropy

(2) mass marketing

(3) laissez-faire capitalism

(4) governmental regulation

FRIDAY
 PI 3.2, PI 3.3

5 **What effect did industrialization have on working conditions in the United States?**

(Chapter 14.3)

(1) Workers enjoyed income equality across classes.

(2) Laborers worked eight-hour days in well-paying jobs.

(3) Employers provided workers with benefits, such as sick leave.

(4) Workers labored long hours in poor conditions at low-paying jobs.

KEY IDEA 3 Study about the major social, political, economic, cultural, and religious developments in New York State and United States history involves learning about the important roles and contributions of individuals and groups.

MONDAY PI 3.1, PI 3.2

1 **In the late 1800s workers responded to poor conditions and wages by** *(Chapter 14.3)*

(1) creating blacklists

(2) organizing labor unions

(3) taking over control of factories

(4) pushing for anti-immigrant legislation

TUESDAY PI 3.2, PI 3.3

2 **All of the following inventions reshaped life in the late 1800s except** *(Chapter 14.1)*

(1) airplanes

(2) telephones

(3) typewriters

(4) electrical lighting

WEDNESDAY PI 3.1, PI 3.2

3 **This map shows how immigrants in the late 1800s changed the face of Chicago—and other cities—by**

(Chapter 15.1)

(1) pushing out earlier immigrants

(2) building cultural enclaves around the cities

(3) settling in ethnic neighborhoods within cities

(4) integrating into existing neighborhoods and adopting local customs

THURSDAY PI 3.1, PI 3.3

4 **In the late 1800s urban political machines often gained power by** *(Chapter 15.3)*

(1) changing to the gold standard

(2) offering jobs, housing, and other help to immigrants

(3) organizing labor leaders and reformers to combat corruption

(4) promising to reduce immigration and competition for jobs

FRIDAY PI 3.1, PI 3.3

5 **In the case *Plessy* v. *Ferguson*, the Supreme Court** *(Chapter 16.3)*

(1) legalized slavery in all U.S. territories

(2) overturned the "separate but equal" standard

(3) legalized segregation and established the "separate but equal" standard

(4) declared Jim Crow laws unconstitutional, which led to voting rights reform

KEY IDEA 1 The study of New York State and United States history requires an analysis of the development of American culture, its diversity and multicultural context, and the ways people are unified by many values, practices, and traditions.

MONDAY PI 1.1

1 Jacob Riis' photographs in *How the Other Half Lives* shocked many people in the early 1900s by revealing the

(Chapters 14.3, 15.2)

(1) conditions of urban poverty

(2) need for workplace reforms

(3) cultural practices of immigrants

(4) standard of living in western European nations

TUESDAY PI 1.2

2 The Seventeenth Amendment had an important effect on the American democratic process by *(Chapter 17.1)*

(1) reducing the voting age to 18

(2) introducing the electoral college

(3) guaranteeing all citizens the right to vote

(4) giving voters the power to elect their senators directly

WEDNESDAY PI 1.1, PI 1.2

3 This cartoon illustrates Theodore Roosevelt's determination to *(Chapter 17.3)*

(1) become president of the United States

(2) break up trusts that were not in the public interest

(3) persuade voters to embrace his Square Deal platform

(4) discourage competition by promoting de-regulation of business

NO MOLLY-CODDLING HERE

THURSDAY   PI 1.1

4 Upton Sinclair's *The Jungle* exposed

(Chapter 17.3)

(1) child labor in the textile industry

(2) child labor in the mining industry

(3) poor sanitation and unsafe working conditions in the meatpacking industry

(4) poor sanitation and unsafe working conditions in the iron and steel industry

FRIDAY PI 1.1, PI 1.2

5 In what year did women gain full voting rights? *(Chapter 17.5)*

(1) 1868

(2) 1896

(3) 1920

(4) 1965

KEY IDEA 2 Important ideas, social and cultural values, beliefs, and traditions from New York State and United States history illustrate the connections and interactions of people and events across time and from a variety of perspectives.

MONDAY

1 Secretary of State John Hay's Open Door Policy was meant to *(Chapter 18.3)*

(1) isolate China and its products from the rest of the world

(2) allow unrestricted Chinese immigration to the United States

(3) give the United States exclusive trading privileges with China

(4) give all nations, including the United States, equal trading rights in China

TUESDAY

2 The interests of the United States in Asia, Latin America, and the Pacific islands in the 1800s can best be described as *(Chapters 18.1, 18.2, 18.3)*

(1) diplomatic

(2) imperialist

(3) democratic

(4) commercial

WEDNESDAY

3 Both Theodore Roosevelt's "Big Stick" diplomacy and William Taft's dollar diplomacy were designed to *(Chapter 18.4)*

(1) help Cuba remain independent

(2) protect U.S. interests and influence in Latin America

(3) increase European intervention in Latin America

(4) establish permanent military bases in countries around the world

THURSDAY

4 In 1917 the United States entered World War I as a result of the *(Chapter 19.1)*

(1) British defeat at Gallipoli

(2) sinking of the *Lusitania*

(3) German invasion of Belgium

(4) sinking of three American merchant ships by German U-boats

FRIDAY

5 This poster, used by the Committee on Public Information to build and maintain support for the war effort, is an example of which of the following? *(Chapters 19.2, 19.3)*

(1) war bonds

(2) legislation

(3) propaganda

(4) executive order

KEY IDEA 2 Important ideas, social and cultural values, beliefs, and traditions from New York State and United States history illustrate the connections and interactions of people and events across time and from a variety of perspectives.

MONDAY
 PI 2.2

1 After World War I communism and other radical ideas that threatened American norms led to the Red Scare and

(Chapter 20.1)

(1) renewed confidence in labor unions

(2) the start of the Bolshevik Revolution

(3) an attack known as the Palmer Raids

(4) greater understanding between earlier and more recent immigrants

TUESDAY
 PI 2.2

2 Calvin Coolidge supported the ideas of

(Chapter 20.3)

(1) limiting big business and funding more public works projects

(2) promoting business and limiting government regulatory power

(3) increasing government oversight and strictly enforcing business regulations

(4) regulating business only when it conflicts with the public interest and supporting the nation's farmers

WEDNESDAY
 PI 2.2

3 This cartoon about the Scopes trial illustrates one of the most dramatic conflicts between supporters of the separation of church and state and

(Chapter 21.1)

(1) fundamentalism

(2) social Darwinism

(3) transcendentalism

(4) Protestant revivalism

GATHERING DATA FOR THE TENNESSEE TRIAL

THURSDAY
 PI 2.1, PI 2.3

4 All of the following were renowned figures during the Harlem Renaissance except

(Chapter 21.4)

(1) Billy Sunday

(2) Langston Hughes

(3) Zora Neale Hurston

(4) James Weldon Johnson

FRIDAY
 PI 2.2

5 In the 1920s the growth of radio, film, and the automobile contributed to the

(Chapter 21.3)

(1) Great Depression

(2) end of World War I

(3) suffrage movement

(4) development of a common American culture

KEY IDEA 3 Study about the major social, political, economic, cultural, and religious developments in New York State and United States history involves learning about the important roles and contributions of individuals and groups.

MONDAY
 PI 3.1, **PI** 3.2

1 **What potential issue does this chart illustrate?**

(Chapter 22.1)

(1) The distribution of wealth and income were well balanced.

(2) The boom of the Roaring Twenties hid great economic disparity.

(3) Only a small percentage of workers invested in the stock market.

(4) Few workers earned enough income to participate in the new consumer culture.

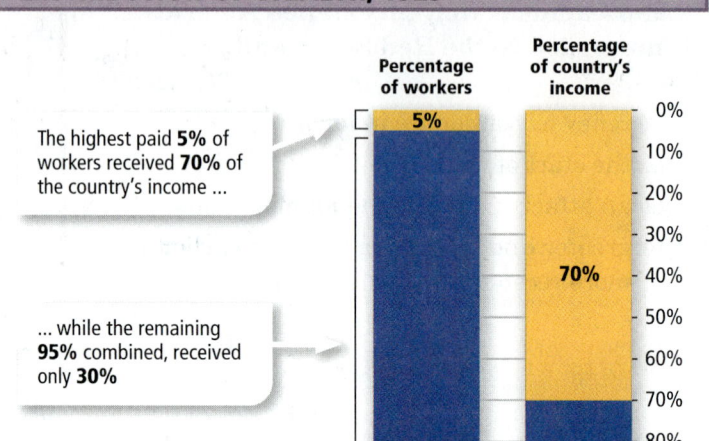

DISTRIBUTION OF WEALTH, 1929

The highest paid **5%** of workers received **70%** of the country's income …

… while the remaining **95%** combined, received only **30%**

Source: *Historical Statistics of the United States*

TUESDAY
 PI 3.2, **PI** 3.3

2 **Which of the following contributed to the Great Depression?** *(Chapter 22.1)*

(1) labor shortages

(2) the stock market boom

(3) business and farm foreclosures

(4) increases in consumer spending

WEDNESDAY
 PI 3.2

3 **Which of the following compounded the devastation of the Great Depression?**

(Chapter 22.2)

(1) World War II

(2) the Red Scare

(3) an influenza epidemic

(4) drought and dust storms in the Great Plains

THURSDAY
 PI 3.1, **PI** 3.2

4 **During the 1930s many people who lived in the Dust Bowl states** *(Chapter 22.2)*

(1) migrated east

(2) migrated west

(3) joined labor unions

(4) went to work on the railroads

FRIDAY
 PI 3.2, **PI** 3.3

5 **Henry Ford revolutionized the manufacturing industry by introducing which of the following?** *(Chapters 17.1, 20.3)*

(1) the automobile

(2) the assembly line

(3) welfare capitalism

(4) the concept of buying on credit

KEY IDEA 1 The study of New York State and United States history requires an analysis of the development of American culture, its diversity and multicultural context, and the ways people are unified by many values, practices, and traditions.

MONDAY PI 1.2

1 All of the following were part of Franklin Roosevelt's New Deal except the

(Chapter 23.1)

(1) Federal Securities Act

(2) Smoot-Hawley Tariff Act

(3) Civilian Conservation Corps

(4) Public Works Administration

TUESDAY PI 1.2

2 One major criticism of the New Deal was that the programs *(Chapter 23.1)*

(1) failed to alleviate unemployment

(2) gave too much power to the executive branch

(3) did not include provisions for banking reforms

(4) ceded too much federal decision-making to state governments

WEDNESDAY PI 1.1, PI 1.2

3 Social Security represented a major change in the relationship between the federal government and the citizenry because it *(Chapter 23.2)*

(1) restructured the federal tax system

(2) set up a national pension and healthcare system for all American workers

(3) provided immediate economic relief in the form of paid jobs on public works projects

(4) promised a government-funded pension and unemployment insurance for many American workers

THURSDAY PI 1.1

4 One key difference between the American Federation of Labor and the Committee for Industrial Organization was that the *(Chapter 23.2)*

(1) CIO represented the interests of unskilled workers

(2) AFL represented the interests of unskilled workers

(3) CIO won every confrontation with American business

(4) AFL represented unions organized across broad industries

FRIDAY PI 1.1, PI 1.2

5 This graph supports the statement that the 1935 National Labor Relations Act

(Chapter 23.2)

(1) helped increase union membership

(2) restricted workers' rights to organize

(3) encouraged company-sponsored unions

(4) discouraged the organizing of unions across industries

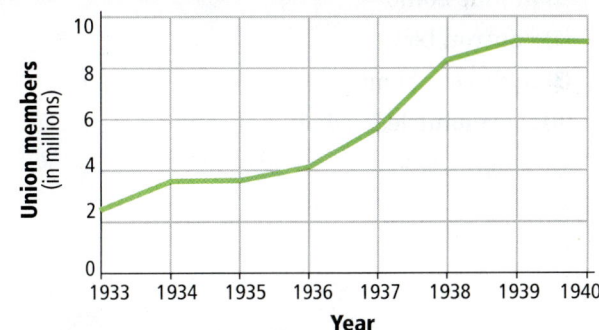

GROWTH OF UNION MEMBERSHIP, 1933–1940

Source: *Historical Statistics of the United States*

WEEK 14

 KEY IDEA 2 Important ideas, social and cultural values, beliefs, and traditions from New York State and United States history illustrate the connections and interactions of people and events across time and from a variety of perspectives.

MONDAY PI 2.2, PI 2.5

1 Which of the following events changed American public opinion in support of U.S. involvement in World War II?
(Chapter 24.5)

(1) Japan's invasion of China
(2) Italy's invasion of Ethiopia
(3) Japan's attack on Pearl Harbor
(4) the sinking of the USS *Reuben James*

TUESDAY PI 2.3, PI 2.6

2 During World War II, African Americans
(Chapters 25.1, 25.2)

(1) did not serve in the military
(2) served in the military in segregated units
(3) served in the military without discrimination
(4) served in the military in noncombat capacities only

WEDNESDAY PI 2.5, PI 2.6

3 After World War II the United States, Great Britain, France, and the Soviet Union organized which of the following bodies to deal with the Nazis responsible for the Holocaust?
(Chapter 25.3)

(1) United Nations
(2) Yalta Conference
(3) Nuremberg Trials
(4) Manhattan Project

THURSDAY PI 2.3, PI 2.4

4 Which of the following actions on the part of the United States conflicted with constitutional liberties?
(Chapter 25.4)

(1) the policy of food rationing
(2) the declaration of war on Japan
(3) the internment of Japanese Americans
(4) the bombing of Hiroshima and Nagasaki

FRIDAY PI 2.2, PI 2.5

5 This image shows a mushroom cloud from what new weapon used by the United States during World War II?
(Chapter 25.3)

(1) atomic bomb
(2) neutron bomb
(3) hydrogen bomb
(4) thermonuclear bomb

KEY IDEA 2 Important ideas, social and cultural values, beliefs, and traditions from New York State and United States history illustrate the connections and interactions of people and events across time and from a variety of perspectives.

MONDAY

1 Aid given by the United States under the Marshall Plan was part of a broader Cold War policy of *(Chapter 26.1)*

(1) détente

(2) containment

(3) brinkmanship

(4) dollar diplomacy

THE MARSHALL PLAN

Purpose: A U.S. financial aid program to rebuild the economies of European countries in order to create stable conditions for democratic governments.

Total amount of aid: $13.4 billion

Number of countries that received aid: 17

Countries that received the most aid: Great Britain, France, and Italy

TUESDAY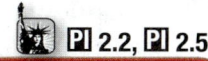

2 In 1949 twelve nations, including the United States, formed the North Atlantic Treaty Organization in reaction to the *(Chapter 26.1)*

(1) Korean War

(2) Cuban missile crisis

(3) Soviet blockade of Berlin

(4) formation of the Warsaw Pact

WEDNESDAY

3 After China fell to communism, some conservatives in Congress claimed that the U.S. government *(Chapter 26.2)*

(1) was riddled with Communist agents

(2) secretly backed Mao Zedong

(3) wanted Japan to retake China

(4) forced Chiang Kai-shek to abandon the mainland

THURSDAY

4 McCarthyism was empowered primarily by *(Chapter 26.3)*

(1) Ethel and Julius Rosenberg

(2) the public's fear of communism

(3) propaganda films made in Hollywood

(4) the conflict surrounding the Vietnam War

FRIDAY

5 In the 1950s President Eisenhower warned that the arms industry in the United States had *(Chapter 28.1)*

(1) adjusted slowly to the demands of modern war

(2) become a permanent, vast, military-industrial complex

(3) fallen behind the technological advancements of the Soviet arms industry

(4) focused too much on technological development and not enough on maintaining conventional arms

KEY IDEA 2 Important ideas, social and cultural values, beliefs, and traditions from New York State and United States history illustrate the connections and interactions of people and events across time and from a variety of perspectives.

MONDAY PI 2.1, PI 2.2

1 John F. Kennedy's presidency was largely dominated by a period of volatile international relations know as the *(Chapter 28.1)*

(1) Cold War

(2) Red Scare

(3) Iron Curtain

(4) Great Society

TUESDAY PI 2.5, PI 2.6

2 The Bay of Pigs invasion was orchestrated by the CIA to *(Chapter 28.1)*

(1) support the French in Vietnam

(2) overthrow Fidel Castro in Cuba

(3) regain control of the Suez Canal

(4) restore independence to South Korea

WEDNESDAY PI 2.3, PI 2.4

3 During the 1950s and 1960s, the Supreme Court under Chief Justice Earl Warren did all of the following except *(Chapter 28.3)*

(1) ban racial segregation in the nation's schools

(2) rule that legislative districts must have equal populations

(3) extend the Bill of Rights to cover the actions of state governments

(4) deny people the right to lawyers during routine police questioning

THURSDAY PI 2.5

4 President Kennedy's program that offered economic and technical assistance to Latin American countries was called the *(Chapter 28.2)*

(1) Great Society

(2) New Frontier

(3) Kennedy Action Plan

(4) Alliance for Progress

FRIDAY PI 2.2, PI 2.3

5 Which Great Society program provided housing for low-income Americans? *(Chapter 28.3)*

(1) Civil Rights Acts

(2) Voting Rights Act

(3) Omnibus Housing Act

(4) Economic Opportunity Act

MAJOR GREAT SOCIETY PROGRAMS

Year Enacted	Legislation	Purpose and Provisions
1964	Economic Opportunity Act	created the Job Corps, VISTA, and eight other programs to fight the "war on poverty"
1964	Tax Reduction Act	cut income tax rates up to 30%, with the greatest cuts going to lower-income
1964	Civil Rights Act	outlawed discrimination in housing, employment, and public accomodations; authorized federal government to enforce desegregation
1965	Elementary and Secondary School Act	provided aid to school systems based on number of students from low-income homes
1965	Social Security Amendments	established Medicare and Medicaid
1965	Voting Rights Act	ended the requirement that voters pass literacy tests and allowed federal supervision of voter registration
1965	Omnibus Housing Act	provided housing for low-income Americans
1965	Water Quality Act	required states to clean up rivers and lakes
1965	Higher Education Act	provided scholarships and low-interest loans for college students

KEY IDEA 3 Study about the major social, political, economic, cultural, and religious developments in New York State and United States history involves learning about the important roles and contributions of individuals and groups.

MONDAY PI 3.2

1 The arrest of Rosa Parks in 1955 led to integrated *(Chapter 29.1)*

(1) buses

(2) public schools

(3) universities and colleges

(4) lunch counters and restaurants

TUESDAY PI 3.1, PI 3.2

2 James Farmer of CORE and Martin Luther King Jr. of SCLC drew on what principle of Mohandas Gandhi when organizing the civil rights movement? *(Chapters 29.1, 29.2)*

(1) political action

(2) massive resistance

(3) nonviolent resistance

(4) public accommodations

WEDNESDAY PI 3.2

3 During what event in 1963 did Martin Luther King Jr. give his "I Have a Dream" speech? *(Chapter 29.2)*

(1) Selma march

(2) Freedom Rides

(3) March on Washington

(4) Birmingham campaign

THURSDAY PI 3.2

4 Lyndon Johnson strongly supported the Civil Rights Act of 1964, which *(Chapter 29.2)*

(1) made harming civil rights workers a federal crime

(2) eliminated the use of literacy tests for voting registration

(3) made segregation in institutions of higher education illegal

(4) banned discrimination in employment and in public accommodations

FRIDAY PI 3.2

5 The voter registration efforts of Freedom Summer of 1964 came in response to the passage of the *(Chapter 29.2)*

(1) Civil Rights Act

(2) Voting Rights Act

(3) Equal Rights Amendment

(4) Twenty-fourth Amendment

KEY IDEA 3 Study about the major social, political, economic, cultural, and religious developments in New York State and United States history involves learning about the important roles and contributions of individuals and groups.

MONDAY

1 In 1964 the Tonkin Gulf Resolution expanded presidential powers by
(Chapter 30.1)

(1) stripping Congress of its power to declare war

(2) giving the president the power to declare war even in peacetime

(3) making the president the commander-in-chief of the armed forces

(4) giving the president the power to make war in Southeast Asia without a declaration of war

TUESDAY

2 The Equal Rights Amendment (ERA), which passed Congress but failed to win ratification in enough states, promised
(Chapter 31.2)

(1) equal treatment of men and women only in the public sector

(2) equal opportunities for men and women only in the workplace

(3) equal treatment for men and women in all spheres of society

(4) equal opportunities for men and women only in institutions of higher education

WEDNESDAY

3 The American Indian Movement (AIM) and the larger Red Power movement were responses to the federal government's
(Chapter 31.1)

(1) termination policy

(2) urbanization policy

(3) Americanization policy

(4) Native American self-determination policy

THURSDAY

4 Which Latino leader became a national figure after heading a boycott of California grapes?
(Chapter 31.1)

(1) César Chávez

(2) Vine Deloria

(3) Joseph Montoya

(4) José Angel Gutiérrez

FRIDAY

5 To which movement are David Sanchez and the Brown Berets linked? *(Chapter 31.1)*

(1) labor movement

(2) Chicano movement

(3) Red Power movement

(4) Black Power movement

KEY IDEA 2 Important ideas, social and cultural values, beliefs, and traditions from New York State and United States history illustrate the connections and interactions of people and events across time and from a variety of perspectives.

MONDAY
 PI 2.3, PI 2.4

1 As president Richard Nixon supported and worked for all of the following except
(Chapter 32.1)

(1) economic reform

(2) forced desegregation

(3) social welfare programs

(4) environmental protections

TUESDAY
 PI 2.1, PI 2.6

2 Richard Nixon's presidency was characterized by a foreign policy primarily based on
(Chapter 32.1)

(1) détente

(2) glasnost

(3) containment

(4) shuttle diplomacy

WEDNESDAY
 PI 2.2

3 The political cartoon shows Richard Nixon hiding behind the seal of the President of the United States. This cartoon was symbolic of Nixon's attempt to protect himself during the Watergate scandal by invoking
(Chapter 32.2)

(1) executive privilege

(2) checks and balances

(3) presidential pardons

(4) the Fifth Amendment

Speaking of sanctuaries ...

THURSDAY
  PI 2.2

4 An accident at Three Mile Island in Pennsylvania brought attention to the
(Chapter 32.4)

(1) hazards of toxic waste

(2) need for energy conservation

(3) safety risks of nuclear power

(4) nation's dependence on fossil fuels

FRIDAY
 PI 2.1, PI 2.5

5 All of the following occurred during Jimmy Carter's presidency except the
(Chapter 32.3)

(1) SALT II talks

(2) Iran-Contra affair

(3) Camp David Accords

(4) Iranian hostage crisis

KEY IDEA 2 Important ideas, social and cultural values, beliefs, and traditions from New York State and United States history illustrate the connections and interactions of people and events across time and from a variety of perspectives.

MONDAY
 PI 2.2, PI 2.3

1 In the 1980s who became a hero of a growing movement known as the New Right? *(Chapter 33.1)*

(1) Ronald Reagan

(2) Gerald Ford

(3) Richard Nixon

(4) Jerry Falwell

TUESDAY
 PI 2.1, PI 2.2

2 The Reaganomics of the 1980s emphasized *(Chapter 33.2)*

(1) supply-side economics

(2) corporate tax increases

(3) reduced military spending

(4) more federal spending on social programs

WEDNESDAY
 PI 2.2, PI 2.6

And then I hear the noise. Pick, pick, pick. Chuck, chuck, chuck. Growing louder and louder as hundreds of hammers and chisels attack the wall, taking it down chip by chip. I laugh and laugh—and cry at the same time.

—BBC reporter Tim Weber, November 9, 1989

3 This quotation about the end of the Cold War refers to the *(Chapter 33.4)*

(1) velvet revolution

(2) fall of the Berlin Wall

(3) Soviet withdrawal from Afghanistan

(4) meltdown at the Chernobyl nuclear plant

THURSDAY
 PI 2.2, PI 2.5, PI 2.6

4 Which of the following statements best describes the United States' interest in Iraq's invasion of Kuwait? *(Chapter 33.4)*

(1) Iraq formed a nonmilitary buffer between Kuwait and Iran.

(2) Iraq had rich supplies of petroleum on which the United States depended.

(3) Kuwait had rich supplies of petroleum on which the United States depended.

(4) Iran, Iraq, and Kuwait were allies, making it difficult for the United States to choose sides.

FRIDAY
 PI 2.5, PI 2.6

5 The Iran-Contra scandal that plagued Ronald Reagan's second term as president involved an illegal scheme to raise money for guerrilla forces in *(Chapter 33.4)*

(1) Iran

(2) Panama

(3) Grenada

(4) Nicaragua

KEY IDEA 3 Study about the major social, political, economic, cultural, and religious developments in New York State and United States history involves learning about the important roles and contributions of individuals and groups.

MONDAY PI 3.2, PI 3.3

1 Which of the following contributed to a major Republican victory in the 1994 mid-term elections? *(Chapter 34.1)*

(1) welfare reform

(2) tax cuts

(3) Clinton's failed health-care plan

(4) Clinton's social security plan

TUESDAY PI 3.1, PI 3.3

2 Critics of the North American Free Trade Agreement contended primarily that *(Chapter 34.1)*

(1) trade between Mexico and the United States would decline

(2) Mexican immigration into the United States would increase

(3) American businesses would not be able to sell more goods in Mexico and Canada

(4) lower wages and fewer regulations in Mexican factories would drive American jobs to Mexico

WEDNESDAY PI 3.2, PI 3.3

3 The 2000 presidential election illustrated in this map ended with *(Chapter 34.1)*

(1) a narrow electoral victory for Al Gore

(2) an overwhelming electoral victory for Al Gore

(3) a narrow popular-vote victory for George W. Bush

(4) a narrow electoral victory for George W. Bush

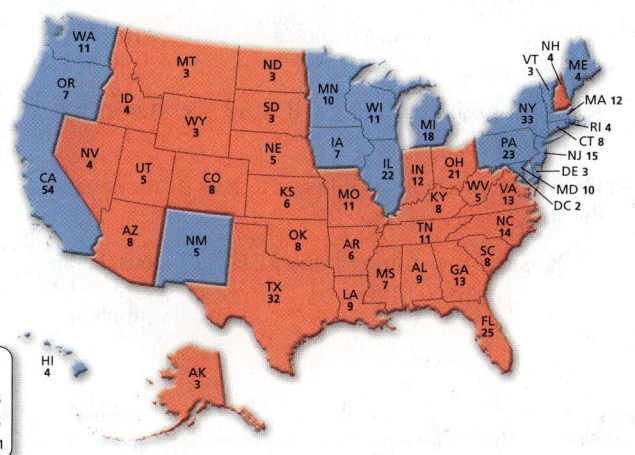

Candidate	Political Affiliation	Electoral Votes	Popular Votes
George W. Bush	Republican	271	50,455,156
Albert A. Gore	Democratic	266	50,992,335
TOTAL		537	105,396,641

THURSDAY PI 3.3, PI 3.4

4 The attacks on the World Trade Center on September 11, 2001, led to all of the following except *(Chapter 34.1, Epilogue 1)*

(1) war in Afghanistan

(2) passage of the USA PATRIOT Act

(3) a military alliance with the Taliban

(4) formation of the Department of Homeland Security

FRIDAY PI 3.2, PI 3.3

5 Which of the following might result from the graying of the American population? *(Epilogue 9)*

(1) declining work force

(2) failure of the Social Security system

(3) inadequate prescription drug coverage

(4) collapse of the private healthcare industry

KEY IDEA 2 Important ideas, social and cultural values, beliefs, and traditions from New York State and United States history illustrate the connections and interactions of people and events across time and from a variety of perspectives.

MONDAY PI 2.3

1 The Bracero Program   *(Chapter 27.4)*

(1) assimilated immigrants into American culture

(2) created a seasonal, circular migration pattern

(3) offered humanitarian protection to immigrants

(4) placed various limitations on U.S. immigration

TUESDAY PI 2.2

2 In the late 1990s, as enthusiasm for high-tech businesses grew, which technology-dominated index rose dramatically?
          (Chapter 34.2)

(1) NYSE

(2) NASDAQ

(3) DJIA

(4) CBOT

WEDNESDAY PI 2.2

3 What does this cartoon imply about the future of social security in America?
          (Epilogue 9)

(1) Age restrictions on social security will be lifted.

(2) An ongoing surplus will fund social security indefinitely.

(3) Social security will become less of an issue as Americans age.

(4) Most of the money behind social security eventually will dry up.

THURSDAY PI 2.2

4 The 1998 shootings at Columbine High School in Colorado focused attention on which of the following potential causes of violent crime?   *(Chapter 34.1)*

(1) human nature

(2) drugs and alcohol

(3) violence in the media

(4) race and class conflict

FRIDAY PI 2.3

5 Which of the following groups of people is least likely to interpret U.S. businesses moving their operations to other countries as a positive economic trend?
          (Chapter 34.2)

(1) investors

(2) foreign workers

(3) domestic workers

(4) market economists

ANSWER KEY

WEEK 1
1. (4)
2. (3)
3. (4)
4. (4)
5. (2)

WEEK 2
1. (3)
2. (1)
3. (4)
4. (3)
5. (3)

WEEK 3
1. (4)
2. (2)
3. (2)
4. (4)
5. (1)

WEEK 4
1. (2)
2. (4)
3. (3)
4. (1)
5. (2)

WEEK 5
1. (4)
2. (2)
3. (3)
4. (4)
5. (2)

WEEK 6
1. (4)
2. (1)
3. (3)
4. (4)
5. (4)

WEEK 7
1. (4)
2. (1)
3. (3)
4. (3)
5. (4)

WEEK 8
1. (2)
2. (1)
3. (3)
4. (2)
5. (3)

WEEK 9
1. (1)
2. (4)
3. (2)
4. (3)
5. (3)

WEEK 10
1. (4)
2. (2)
3. (2)
4. (4)
5. (3)

WEEK 11
1. (3)
2. (2)
3. (1)
4. (1)
5. (4)

WEEK 12
1. (2)
2. (3)
3. (4)
4. (2)
5. (2)

WEEK 13
1. (2)
2. (2)
3. (4)
4. (1)
5. (1)

WEEK 14
1. (3)
2. (2)
3. (3)
4. (3)
5. (1)

WEEK 15
1. (2)
2. (3)
3. (1)
4. (2)
5. (2)

WEEK 16
1. (1)
2. (2)
3. (4)
4. (4)
5. (3)

WEEK 17
1. (1)
2. (3)
3. (3)
4. (4)
5. (4)

WEEK 18
1. (4)
2. (3)
3. (1)
4. (1)
5. (2)

WEEK 19
1. (2)
2. (1)
3. (1)
4. (3)
5. (2)

WEEK 20
1. (1)
2. (1)
3. (2)
4. (3)
5. (4)

WEEK 21
1. (3)
2. (4)
3. (4)
4. (3)
5. (2)

WEEK 22
1. (2)
2. (2)
3. (4)
4. (3)
5. (3)

A **document-based question** focuses on several documents—both visual and written. These documents often are accompanied by short-answer questions. Students use their answers to these questions and information from the documents to write an essay on a specified subject.

Strategies

1. Carefully read the "Historical Context" section to get an indication of the issue addressed in the question.

2. Note the action words used in the "Task" section. These words will tell you exactly what the essay question requires.

3. Study and analyze each document. Think about how the documents are connected to the essay question. Take notes on your ideas.

4. Read and answer each of the document-specific questions.

1 **Historical Context** Rachel Carson's book *Silent Spring* (1962) awakened Americans to the issue of environmental pollution. Since that time, efforts have been made to protect the environment.

Task: Trace the progress on the environment made in the United States since the 1960s and consider the environmental challenges still facing the country today. 2

Part A: Short Answer

Directions: Study each document carefully and answer the questions that follow.

DOCUMENT 1 3

Recycling in the United States, 1970–2000

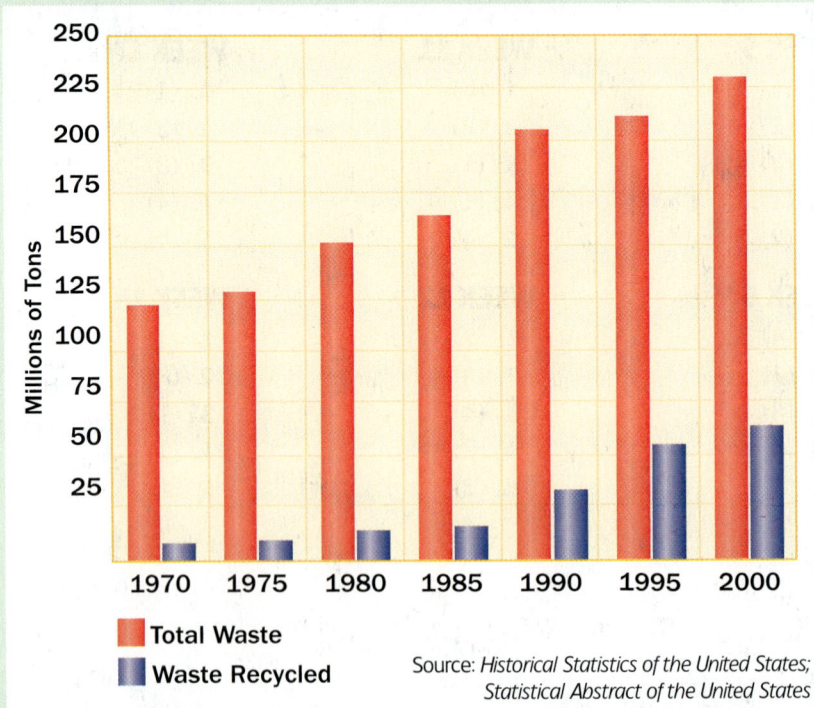

Source: *Historical Statistics of the United States; Statistical Abstract of the United States*

4 **What positive and negative trends does this graph show?**
The amount of waste recycled is increasing, but so, too, is total waste produced.

DOCUMENT 2

Solar Panels in Albuquerque, New Mexico

© Superstock RF/Superstock

What alternative energy source is shown in the photograph? Why has the United States sought alternatives to such traditional energy sources as oil and coal?
solar energy; because supply of fossil fuels is limited and because oil, coal, and nuclear energy all carry a pollution risk

DOCUMENT 3

Clean Water

> With the enactment of the Clean Water Act in 1972, the nation . . . made a new commitment to restore and maintain the chemical, physical, and biological integrity of [its] waters.
>
> America has honored its commitment to clean water. Since enactment of the Clean Water Act, the number of waters that are safe for fishing and swimming has doubled. National clean water standards stop billions of pounds of industrial pollution from flowing into waters each year. . . . Today, . . . many . . . water bodies that were once severely polluted are well on the way to recovery. . . .
>
> Despite impressive progress, many of the nation's rivers, lakes, and coastal waters do not meet water quality goals. [And] many waters that are now clean face [a] threat . . . from diverse pollution sources.
>
> —Clean Water Action Plan (EPA)

What impact has the Clean Water Act had on America's waterways?
Many bodies of water that once were polluted are clean or well on their way to recovery.

Part B: Essay

❺

Using information from the documents, your answers to the questions in Part A, and your knowledge of American history, write an essay in which you trace the progress on the environment made in the United States since the 1960s and consider the environmental challenges that still face the country today. ❻

❺ Carefully read the essay question. Then, write an outline for your essay.

❻ Write your essay. Be sure that it has an introductory paragraph that introduces your argument, main body paragraphs that explain it, and a concluding paragraph that restates your position. In your essay, include extracts or details from specific documents to support your ideas. Add other supporting facts or details that you know from your study of American history.

Essay Rubric The best essays will note such progress as cleaner water (Document 3), increased recycling (Document 1), and the search for energy alternatives that neither deplete the country's natural resources nor threaten the environment (Document 2). Essays should refer to such challenges as the increasing amount of waste produced (Document 1) and lingering pollution threats to the water (Document 3).

DOCUMENT-BASED QUESTIONS

Read the documents in Part A and answer the questions that follow each document. Then, read the directions for Part B and write your essay.

Historical Context: From 1929 to 1940, the United States suffered from a severe economic depression. Facing a damaged economy and a shaken public, President Franklin D. Roosevelt took action, creating a new role for the federal government.

Task: Describe how the role of the federal government changed during the Depression and discuss how that change continues to impact life in the United States today.

Part A: Short Answer

Directions: Study each document carefully and answer the questions that follow.

DOCUMENT 1

Federal Spending, 1925–1940

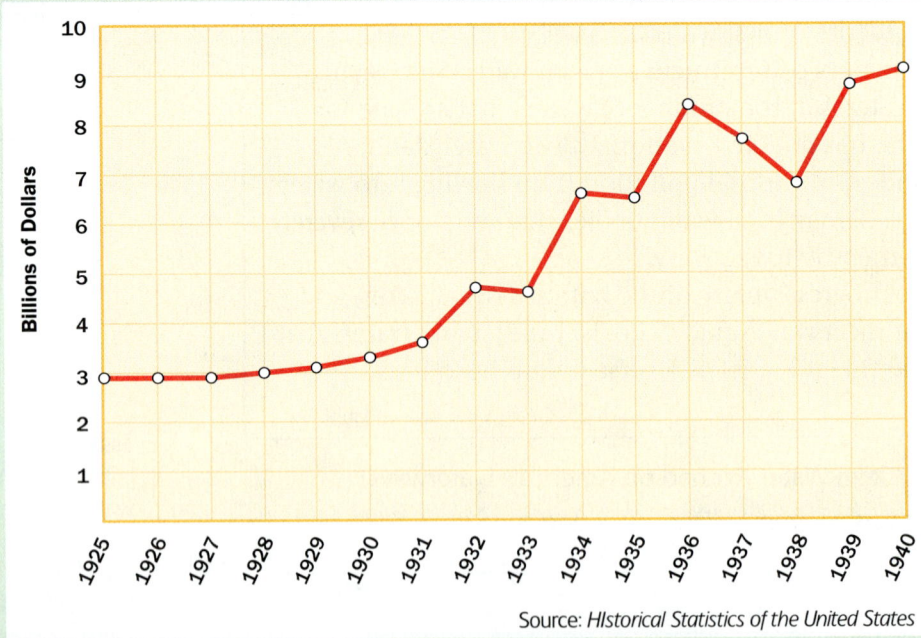

Source: *Historical Statistics of the United States*

President Franklin D. Roosevelt began introducing New Deal policies soon after taking office in 1933. What was the overall trend in federal spending in the New Deal years?

DOCUMENT 2

The Civilian Conservation Corps

THE NEW DEAL

THE OLD

THE BREAD LINE

© New York Daily News, L.P. reprinted–reproduced with permission

How does the "Old Deal" differ from the "New Deal"?

DOCUMENT 3

A Policy for Labor (1936)

Among the first items in this growing labor policy of the American government are the following:

1. That the government ought to do everything in its power to establish minimum basic standards for labor, below which competition should not be permitted to force standards of health, wages, or hours.

2. That the government ought to use its influence to bring about arrangements which will make possible peaceful settlements of controversies and relieve labor of the necessity of resorting to strikes to secure equitable conditions and the right to be heard.

—Secretary of Labor Frances Perkins,
"A National Labor Policy."

How did the National Labor Relations Act (1935) and the Fair Labor Standards Act (1938) put the New Deal labor policy into practice?

Part B: Essay

Using information from the documents, your answers to the questions in Part A, and your knowledge of American history, write an essay in which you describe how the role of the federal government changed during the Depression and discuss how that change continues to impact life in the United States today.

Excerpt from "A National Labor Policy" by Frances Perkins. The American Academy of Political and Social Sciences, 1936. Reprinted by permission.

A Review of New York History

Colonial New York

Reading Focus *As you read, think about what life might have been like for a colonial New Yorker.*

In 1609 Henry Hudson, sailing for the Dutch, explored the river that was soon named for him. Hudson's explorations led the Dutch government to claim New York. The Dutch named their colony New Netherland.

Europeans and Native Americans

Dutch traders were attracted to New Netherland by the abundance of valuable resources, especially fur. In 1624 the Dutch established Fort Orange, a fur-trading post on the Hudson River. The following year, Dutch settlers established New Amsterdam at the southern end of the island of Manhattan. From its earliest days, the city was home to a diverse mix of cultures—one visitor heard 18 different languages in the growing city. Outside of the towns, huge tracts of fertile land were granted to wealthy landowners called patroons, who then rented sections to farmers.

Eager to build an empire of its own, England conquered New Netherland in 1664, renaming the colony New York. The city of New Amsterdam became New York City, and Fort Orange was renamed Albany.

By 1700 a diverse mix of about 20,000 European settlers lived in the New York colony. In some ways, these colonists were similar to the Native Americans who also lived in New York. Cultural traditions and family ties were very important in both societies. Both developed systems of organizing communities and choosing leaders. Both worked to be as self-sufficient as possible.

Differences between Native Americans and colonists included the social roles of men and women in each community. Native American women had more influence than most women in colonial societies. In addition, Native groups owned land communally, while the colonists used a system of private ownership. Further, Native Americans and colonists spoke different languages and often the colonists used different names for Native Americans than the groups used for themselves. Dutch settlers, for example, named Algonquian groups according to nearby geographic features. Thus the Lenape people, who lived along the Delaware River, became known to Europeans as the Delaware.

KEY FACTS

- **1625** Dutch New Amsterdam is established on Manhattan.
- **1664** New Amsterdam is renamed New York by the English.
- **1763** The French and Indian War breaks out.
- **1776** The thirteen American colonies declare independence.

From Colony to State

New York continued to grow under British rule, with industries such as farming and shipbuilding gaining importance. By 1733 New York was one of 13 British colonies along the east coast of what is now the United States.

Declaring Independence

In the 1760s, Britain decided to raise the tax on American colonists. New Yorkers joined the protests that soon led to the American Revolution.

The Revolution created challenges for the new states. New Yorkers had to organize a new state government, recruit soldiers, help finance the war effort, and deal with issues such as slavery. Citizens were divided over

From Colony to State, 1625–1800

1647 Peter Stuyvesant becomes governor of New Netherland.

1688 A diverse mix of 20,000 European settlers lives in the New York colony.

1700 About 5,000 people live in New York City.

1625

1733

1625 The Dutch establish New Amsterdam on Manhzattan Island.

1664 The English conquer New Netherland and rename it New York.

Peter Stuyvesant was forced to surrender New Amsterdam to the English in 1664.

these important issues, as well as over support for the war. New York City, captured by the British in 1776, became a refuge for Loyalists. In other parts of the state, Loyalists were attacked or had their property confiscated.

New York and the Revolution

New York State witnessed many important battles during the war. In 1775 Patriots seized Fort Ticonderoga, capturing badly needed cannons for the Continental Army. The British invasion of New York in 1777 ended with an American victory at Saratoga—a victory that became known as the "turning point" of the war. New York also saw fierce fighting between Patriots and Native American groups, several of which sided with Britain.

When the war finally ended in 1783, many Loyalists fled to Canada. This migration changed the balance between British and French settlers in Canada, resulting in a strengthening of ties to Great Britain.

Participation in the struggle for independence changed the way New Yorkers thought about government. Many now expected to become active citizens in their government. Republican ideals, which emphasized the sharing of power, began to influence politics in the new state.

Forming New Governments

After declaring independence in July 1776, New Yorkers began work on a state constitution. Led by John Jay, Robert Livingston, and Gouverneur Morris, New York leaders completed drafting a New York constitution in 1777. The constitution, which included the text of the Declaration of Independence, was approved by representatives at the constitutional convention in Kingston, New York.

The plan of government was based on the principle of majority rule, with protections for the rights and liberties of the minority. A governor with limited authority served a three-year term. New York's legislature had two houses: the Senate and the Assembly. Senators served four-year terms, while Assembly members served a one-year term. New York's first system of state courts was also established by the constitution. The right

Revolutionary Battle Map of New York

New York Colony
Present-day boundary
Patriot victories
British victories

0   50   100 Miles
0   50   100 Kilometers
Projection: Albers Equal Area

CANADA

Lake Ontario

Fort Ticonderoga, July 1777

Freeman's Farm, September 1777

Saratoga, October 1777

NEW YORK   Albany

Hudson River

White Plains, October 1776

Fort Washington, November 1776

New York City   Long Island, August 1776

1733 New York is one of 13 British colonies in North America.

1754 The Albany Plan of Union provides a model for later plans of government.

1763 The British defeat the French in the French and Indian War.

1765 The Stamp Act Congress meets in New York City.

1775 The Patriots capture Fort Ticonderoga.

1776 The British occupy New York City during the American Revolution.

1777 The Americans win the Battle of Saratoga.

1733

1800

Anti–Stamp Act cartoon

to vote for elected leaders was limited to men who owned property. New York's new constitution was in effect from 1777 to 1822.

New York's early state government functioned fairly well—more smoothly, in fact, than the national government under the Articles of Confederation. For this reason, the New York constitution became a model for the new national plan of government.

New York and the U.S. Constitution

The national government under the Articles of Confederation was clearly unable to solve the young country's problems. In 1786 Alexander Hamilton of New York and leaders from other states met in Annapolis, Maryland, to discuss ways to improve the effectiveness of the national government. This meeting led to the Constitutional Convention the following year in Philadelphia. Hamilton influenced the debate in Philadelphia with his ideas for a powerful national government. The United States Constitution was completed and signed by delegates in September 1787.

The question of ratification sparked heated debate between Federalists, who supported the Constitution, and Antifederalists, who worried that it gave the federal government too much power. The Antifederalist cause was strong in New York. To combat this, Alexander Hamilton and John Jay joined James Madison of Virginia to write the *Federalist Papers*, a series of articles arguing in favor of ratification. First published in New York City newspapers, the *Federalist Papers* greatly influenced the debate in New York and other states. New York's ratification convention was held in Poughkeepsie in June 1788. The delegates approved the Constitution in a close vote of 30 to 27.

George Washington traveled to New York City, the new national capital, and was sworn in as president on April 30, 1789. Washington chose Alexander Hamilton as his secretary of the treasury.

George Washington

Forming New Governments, 1777–1800

George Clinton

1777 George Clinton is elected first governor of New York.

1777 New York's first state constitution is written.

1786 New York leaders attend the Annapolis Convention.

1787-1788 Alexander Hamilton and John Jay help write the *Federalist Papers*.

1789 George Washington is sworn in as president in New York City.

1788 Delegates to the Poughkeepsie Convention discuss New York's ratification of the Constitution.

1788 New York becomes the eleventh state to ratify the Constitution.

1777   1800

The Empire State

Reading Focus *As you read, notice how life changed for New Yorkers during the early and mid-1800s.*

At the time of the American Revolution, New York ranked just seventh in population among the original 13 states. By 1810, however, New York had the largest population in the nation and was among the leaders in manufacturing, transportation, and trade. Around that time, people began referring to New York as "the Empire State." The name comes from a quotation by George Washington, who called New York State "the seat of empire." Washington hoped the young nation would prosper as New York had done.

Transportation and Manufacturing

The Transportation Revolution of the 1800s was a major factor in New York's rapid rise. In 1807 Robert Fulton successfully tested his steamboat *Clermont* on the Hudson River. In 1825 the 363-mile Erie Canal was completed, connecting Buffalo, on Lake Erie, with Albany, on the Hudson River. The Erie Canal greatly lowered the cost of transporting goods from the Midwest to the East. Cities along the canal boomed, and New York City became the busiest port in the country. By 1850 a growing network of railroads replaced canals in importance. As canals had done, railroads lowered the cost of moving large quantities of goods between New York and other parts of the country.

Improvements in transportation helped farmers earn more money—money they wanted to spend on manufactured goods. New York cities became major manufacturing centers as the Industrial Revolution changed life in the United States. By 1860, for example, nearly half of the nation's clothing was being manufactured in New York City.

Lockport, on the Erie Canal

The Empire State, 1800–1835

1807 Robert Fulton's steamboat *Clermont* makes its first voyage.

1825 The Erie Canal opens.

1800

1810 New York City is the biggest city in the United States.

1810 New York State has the largest population of any state.

Sojourner Truth

1827 Sojourner Truth escapes from slavery to a New York farm.

1827 Slavery ends in New York State.

1831 New York's first railroad connects Albany and Schenectady.

1835

A Wave of Immigration

The rapid growth of American industry attracted millions of immigrants to the United States in the mid-1800s. Most entered the United States at the port of New York City. Many of them also settled in the city. In fact, New York City was not only the nation's largest city—it was also home to the nation's largest population of immigrants. By 1860, 48 percent of New York City's 1 million residents were foreign born.

This large wave of immigration led to tensions in New York, as in other states. The majority of New York's immigrants were Catholic. Prejudice toward Catholics sparked anti-immigrant feelings in some New Yorkers. Others worried they might lose their jobs to immigrants who would work for lower wages. Opponents of immigration, known as nativists, formed an organization known as the Know-Nothing Party, which briefly gained influence in New York politics in the 1850s.

New York City Population, 1800–1860

The population of New York City rose dramatically during the first half of the nineteenth century.

Reform Movements

Like many states, New York saw an expansion of voting rights during the Age of Jackson. An 1822 revision of the state constitution gave the vote to all white men who paid taxes. Black men, however, were still required to own property in order to vote.

As more New Yorkers became actively involved in the democratic process, many began participating in reform movements. A Protestant religious revival known as the Second Great Awakening inspired many reformers in New York. Revivals in central and western New York were so intense, this region became known as the "Burned-Over District" because of the heated sermons given.

In 1799 New York passed a law calling for the gradual abolition of slavery in the state. Slavery ended once and for all in 1827. Many New Yorkers were active in the movement to abolish slavery everywhere in

Reform Movements and the Civil War, 1820–1870

1845-1850 Hundreds of thousands of Irish immigrants settle in New York during the Irish potato famine.

Elizabeth Cady Stanton

1848 The first women's rights convention is held in Seneca Falls.

1820

1825-1835 The Second Great Awakening reaches its peak in western New York.

THE NORTH STAR.

Frederick Douglass' newspaper

1847 Frederick Douglass starts the abolitionist newspaper the *North Star* in Rochester.

1850 New York State leads the nation in manufacturing.

1850

New York textile mill in the mid-1800s

the United States. Frederick Douglass moved to Rochester, New York, where he began publishing the *North Star*, an abolitionist newspaper. Harriet Tubman, who escorted hundreds of slaves to freedom on the Underground Railroad, also moved to New York. Several important Underground Railroad routes passed through New York to Canada.

New Yorker Elizabeth Cady Stanton organized the nation's first women's rights convention, which was held in Seneca Falls, New York, in 1848. Stanton, along with Susan B. Anthony and other New York activists, helped lead a national campaign for women's property rights and voting rights.

New York and the Civil War

Although no Civil War battles were fought in New York, the war did bring conflict to the state. In July 1863, a massive riot broke out in New York City. The direct cause of the riot was the federal government's decision to begin drafting soldiers into the Union army. In a week of rioting, antidraft rioters attacked government buildings and African American neighborhoods. Almost 100 people were killed. Rioters caused more than $1.5 million of damage, including the destruction of an African American church and orphanage.

In July 1864 the government opened a large prisoner of war camp in Elmira, New York. More than 12,000 captured Confederate soldiers were held in Elmira. Prisoners were sent to Elmira from other overcrowded camps, but their situation did not improve. Conditions at the camp were largely unsanitary, and much-needed supplies rarely arrived despite the efforts of the camp's commander. Due to overcrowding and disease, about 25 percent of the prisoners in Elmira died.

New York sent 450,000 soldiers to the Civil War. More than 4,000 of these soldiers were African Americans. New York factories contributed to the Union victory by producing war supplies. The Union's most well-known ironclad warship, the *Monitor*, was built in a Brooklyn shipyard.

1860 Two-thirds of the nation's imports come through the Port of New York.
1860 The population of New York City reaches 1 million.

1864 A prisoner camp for captured Confederate soldiers opens at Elmira.

1868 The Fourteenth Amendment guarantees all citizens equal protection of the law.

1850

1857 Harriet Tubman moves to Auburn, New York, and continues working on the Underground Railroad.

1861 The Civil War begins.

1863 Draft riots break out in New York City.

1870 The Fifteenth Amendment gives African American men the right to vote.

1870

Harriet Tubman

The New York City draft riot

Industrial and Urban Growth

Reading Focus *As you read, draw conclusions about the changes that took place in New York during the late 1800s and early 1900s.*

The rise of corrupt political machines was a serious problem throughout New York in the years following the Civil War. Reformers, including lawyer Samuel J. Tilden, worked to fight political corruption. Known as an effective reformer, Tilden was elected governor of New York in 1874 and was chosen to be the Democratic candidate for president in 1876. Tilden faced Republican Rutherford B. Hayes in one of the most intensely disputed presidential elections in U.S. history. Though Tilden won the popular vote, the electoral vote was contested in several states. After weeks of bitter debate, Hayes was declared the winner.

New York Industry

New York's economy continued to grow in the second half of the 1800s. One major development was the increasing importance of the New York Stock Exchange, based on Wall Street in Manhattan. By selling shares on Wall Street, companies raised money to expand their businesses. New York City became the financial capital of the country, a position it still holds today.

New York entrepreneurs made key contributions to the nation's rapid industrial expansion. Cornelius Vanderbilt bought several railroad companies, consolidating them in an efficient network that made train travel faster and easier. George Eastman began selling Kodak cameras in 1888, making photography widely accessible. John D. Rockefeller built Standard Oil into a massive company that controlled 90 percent of the country's oil refining business by 1880. While the state's industries boomed, local farmers were

KEY FACTS

- **1882** The first electric power station opens in Manhattan.
- **1886** The Statue of Liberty opens.
- **1892** Ellis Island opens.

Industrial and Urban Growth, 1870–1920

John D. Rockefeller

1876 Samuel J. Tilden is defeated in the disputed presidential election.

1885 John D. Rockefeller opens his new Standard Oil headquarters in New York City.

1888 George Eastman begins selling Kodak cameras.

1870 — 1890

1882 Thomas Edison opens the nation's first electric power station in downtown Manhattan.

1886 The Statue of Liberty opens to the public.

The Statue of Liberty

Thomas Edison's Manhattan power station

unable to compete with the huge wheat and corn farms of the Midwest. Some New York farmers responded by diversifying their crops, producing dairy products, fruits, and vegetables.

New Immigrants

The Statue of Liberty, a gift from France, opened to the public in October 1886. This huge copper-covered statue on Liberty Island in New York Harbor became a symbol of American freedom and opportunity—the very things that were attracting millions of immigrants to the United States. For many of these immigrants, the first stop was the Ellis Island immigration station, which opened in 1892.

New Wave of Immigration

From the 1870s to the 1920s, more than 20 million immigrants arrived in this country. These immigrants became known as "new immigrants," to distinguish them from the "old immigrants" who had arrived in the mid-1800s. The new immigrants came largely from Italy, Austria-Hungary, Poland, Russia, and other parts of Eastern and Southern Europe. About 2 million Jews, escaping persecution at home, were part of this massive wave of immigration. Several hundred thousand French Canadians also came, often settling in northern New York and New England.

Arriving with little money, many immigrants crowded into poor urban neighborhoods throughout New York. Buffalo's Italian and Polish communities grew rapidly. New York City's Lower East Side was home to a variety of ethnic neighborhoods. Nearby Chinatown provided a haven for Chinese immigrants, who often faced discrimination in the United States.

Becoming American

Immigrants began the process of Americanization—adjusting to the language, economy, government, and traditions of the United States. While

Madame C. J. Walker

1900 The first electric bus begins running along New York City's Fifth Avenue.

1916 Entrepreneur Madame C. J. Walker moves to New York City.

1890

1920

1892 Ellis Island immigration station opens.

1880s–1920s Millions of immigrants settle in New York.

Immigrants arrive at Ellis Island

adapting to American life, immigrants also influenced their new country with their own cultures and traditions. The process of change that takes place when one culture comes in contact with another is known as acculturation.

City Life

By the year 1900, the population of New York State topped 7 million. More than half of the state's population lived in just four cities: New York City, Buffalo, Rochester, and Syracuse. New York's urban areas offered both exciting opportunities and serious challenges.

Urban Attractions

New York City was home to more than 3 million people in 1900, making it twice as big as the next-largest American city, Chicago. As the city grew, new types of construction helped improve city life. Skyscrapers, for example, made efficient use of crowded city streets. The Flatiron Building, opened in 1902, was one of the city's first skyscrapers. One of the innovations that made skyscrapers possible was the safety elevator, invented by Elisha Graves Otis in his Yonkers workshop. Another development that changed city life was the opening of the New York City subway in 1904. Subway lines eased crowding in lower Manhattan neighborhoods by allowing families to move farther from their jobs.

Urban Problems

One major problem facing New York was the continuing influence of corrupt political machines. New York City's Tammany Hall, led by Boss Tweed, used payoffs and bribes to influence both city and state government. Unhealthy living conditions in many urban neighborhoods presented another major challenge. Overcrowding, poor sanitation, disease, and crime were all common in areas like New York City's Lower East Side.

KEY FACTS

- **1882** New Yorkers hold the first Labor Day celebration.
- **1883** The Brooklyn Bridge is completed.
- **1901** Theodore Roosevelt is elected president.
- **1905** The Supreme Court hears *Lochner* v. *New York.*
- **1911** Fire breaks out at the Triangle Shirtwaist factory.
- **1917** New York women gain suffrage.

City Life and Reform, 1880–1920

New Yorker Theodore Roosevelt

1882 New York workers hold the nation's first Labor Day celebration.

1890 Jacob Riis publishes *How the Other Half Lives*, describing terrible living conditions in New York City tenements.

1901 Theodore Roosevelt becomes president.

1880

1902

1883 Construction of the Brooklyn Bridge is completed.

Brooklyn Bridge

1902 The Flatiron Building becomes one of New York City's first skyscrapers.

Progressive Reforms

A group of investigative reporters known as muckrakers wrote about political corruption, unhealthy living conditions, and other problems facing American society. By describing these issues to the public, muckrakers hoped to inspire change. In 1904, for example, New York City–based *McClure's Magazine* published Ida Tarbell's description of the unfair business practices of Rockefeller's Standard Oil Company.

Progressives

A reform movement known as the Progressive Movement began addressing many of these problems in the late 1800s and early 1900s. One of New York's leading Progressives was Theodore Roosevelt, who served as New York City police commissioner and state governor before serving as president from 1901 to 1909.

Progressives in New York government helped pass the Tenement House Act of 1901, which required tenements to have better plumbing and ventilation. New York State also took the lead in passing labor laws, including a law limiting bakers to a 10-hour workday. This law was challenged in the case *Lochner* v. *New York*, in which the Supreme Court overturned New York's labor law.

Labor and Suffrage

New York was also at the center of the labor and women's suffrage movements. New York workers established the holiday that became Labor Day when they held a huge parade in September 1882. In 1886 Samuel Gompers, a union leader at a New York City cigar factory, helped found the American Federation of Labor. Meanwhile, a new generation of suffrage activists continued the work of Elizabeth Cady Stanton and Susan B. Anthony, holding rallies around the state. Women gained the right to vote in New York in 1917. Three years later, the Nineteenth Amendment became law, granting the vote to all American women.

1905 In *Lochner* v. *New York* the Supreme Court overturns a New York law limiting working hours.

1917 Women gain the right to vote in New York State.

1902

1920

1904 Ida Tarbell publishes *The History of the Standard Oil Company.*

1904 The New York City subway opens.

1911 One hundred forty-six workers die in the Triangle Shirtwaist Factory fire.

1920 The Nineteenth Amendment becomes law.

New York City subway

Triangle Shirtwaist Factory

New York and the Modern World

Reading Focus *As you read, notice how history has affected the lives of modern New Yorkers.*

New York played a central role in the cultural life of the United States in the early 1900s. Babe Ruth, who began playing for the New York Yankees in 1920, helped make baseball a nationally popular sport. Lillian and Dorothy Gish and Rudolph Valentino were among the many movie stars who got their start in New York theaters.

Literature and Music

In the 1800s New York was home to some of the nation's most accomplished writers, including Washington Irving, Herman Melville, and Walt Whitman. In the early 1900s, Edith Wharton helped continue this tradition of great literature. Though she grew up in a time when women were discouraged from becoming serious writers, Wharton wrote dozens of successful short stories and novels—and in 1921 became the first woman to win the Pulitzer Prize for fiction.

Great literature was also being produced in New York City's Harlem, the largest African American neighborhood in the country. In the 1920s poet Langston Hughes was part of the creative movement known as the Harlem Renaissance. More than just a literary movement, the Harlem Renaissance witnessed a celebration of African American culture. The brilliant jazz composer and band leader Duke Ellington also moved to New York in the 1920s. People packed into New York City clubs to hear the exciting and innovative music that give this decade the nickname the Jazz Age.

KEY FACTS

- **1929** The stock market crashes.
- **1932** Franklin Roosevelt is elected president.
- **1941** The Japanese bomb Pearl Harbor.
- **1942** The Manhattan Project begins.

New York in a New Century, 1920–1950

1921 Edith Wharton's *The Age of Innocence* wins the Pulitzer Prize for fiction.

1923 Duke Ellington moves to New York City.

1926 Langston Hughes publishes his first book of poetry.

1932 Franklin D. Roosevelt is elected president.

1920

1935

1920 Babe Ruth begins playing for the New York Yankees.

1929 The stock market crash begins the Great Depression.

1931 The Empire State Building opens, standing as the tallest building in the world until 1954.

New York Yankee Babe Ruth

New York City's Empire State building

VARIETY
STAGE · BROADWAY · SCREEN
WALL ST. LAYS AN EGG

The Great Depression and the New Deal

During the boom years of the 1920s, people and business from all over the country invested heavily in the stock market. Americans dreamed of making a quick fortune on Wall Street. When the stock market crashed in 1929, the entire national economy crashed with it. Franklin D. Roosevelt was governor of New York during the start of the Great Depression. Roosevelt developed state government programs designed to help people through the hard times. These programs gained national attention, helping Roosevelt win the presidential election of 1932. As president, Roosevelt expanded the ideas he had tried in New York into the New Deal, a broad series of programs designed to battle the Great Depression.

World War II

Another of President Roosevelt's policy goals was to improve U.S. relations with Latin American countries. As part of what he called the Good Neighbor policy, Roosevelt announced that the United States would intervene less frequently in Latin American affairs.

Roosevelt's main foreign policy challenge was World War II. As it had done in previous wars, New York contributed more soldiers to the war effort than any other state. New York factories and shipyards pumped out supplies for the Allied armies. Another vital part of the war effort was the Manhattan Project, the American-led program to build an atomic bomb. It was named the Manhattan Project because scientists began working on the effort at Manhattan's Columbia University.

After World War II, world leaders formed the United Nations, which established its headquarters in New York City in 1946. Representing the United States at the UN, Eleanor Roosevelt headed the United Nations Commission on Human Rights. She helped draft the Universal Declaration of Human Rights, which was passed by the UN in 1948.

Atomic bomb

1942-1945 The Manhattan Project produces the world's first atomic bombs.

1946 The United Nations establishes its headquarters in New York City.

1947 Joe DiMaggio of the New York Yankees wins his third American League Most Valuable Player award.

1941

1950

1941 The United States enters World War II.

1946 Eleanor Roosevelt is chosen to lead the UN Commission on Human Rights.

Modern Issues and Challenges

The American economy boomed in the years after World War II, and life in New York continued to change. One significant development was the rapid growth of suburbs. Levittown, a 17,000-home suburban community on Long Island, became a model for other suburbs around the country.

Diversity in New York

On April 15, 1947, Jackie Robinson took the field for the Brooklyn Dodgers, ending decades of segregation in major-league baseball. In addition to becoming a Hall of Fame ballplayer, Robinson was as a key figure in the growing African American civil rights movement. Native Americans also struggled for their rights. The Onondaga, Oneida, and other Iroquois nations filed land claims, demanding the return of parts of their traditional lands in New York. Some of these land claims are still unresolved today.

In the 1960s, women who had been calling for equality since the founding of the nation and had won the right to vote in 1920, began a new movement to increase their rights. Many had grown dissatisfied with the expectation that they should be only wives and mothers. Women, like Bronx-born Bella Abzug, became vocal in the fight for equality. In 1970 Abzug ran for the U.S. House of Representatives on a platform of women's rights and peace. She won, becoming one of only 12 women in the House of Representatives.

The Vietnam Era

Bitter debate over the Vietnam War caused deep divisions in American society in the 1960s. Violent protests broke out in New York and in other parts of the nation. In 1968, for example, student protesters occupied several buildings on the campus of Columbia University in New York City. The police used force to remove the protesters. Some 700 students were arrested.

KEY FACTS

- **1947** Major-league baseball is integrated.
- **1969** The Woodstock festival is held.
- **1971** The Pentagon Papers are published.
- **2001** Terrorists destroy the World Trade Center.

Shirley Chisholm

Modern New York, 1945–today

1947 Jackie Robinson begins playing for the Brooklyn Dodgers, ending segregation in baseball.

1968 Shirley Chisholm becomes the first African American woman elected to the U.S. Congress.

1945

1971

1947 The suburb of Levittown is established on Long Island.

1969 The Woodstock festival is held on a New York farm.

1971 The *New York Times* begins publishing the Pentagon Papers.

Woodstock poster

Some young people protested mainstream American culture by forming a rebellious counterculture. In 1969 more than 300,000 people gathered at the Woodstock Music and Art Fair, held at a Bethel, New York, farm. Woodstock became a lasting symbol of the counterculture's idealistic spirit.

In June 1971, two years after Woodstock, the *New York Times* began publishing the Pentagon Papers. These secret U.S. government documents made it clear that government officials had been misleading the public about the progress of the Vietnam War. The Nixon Administration went to court to block publication of these documents, leading to the Supreme Court case *New York Times* v. *United States*. The Supreme Court ruled that the First Amendment protected the newspaper's right to publish the controversial documents.

September 11 and Beyond

As the 20th century came to a close, the United States faced challenges different from any the country had faced before. International terrorism was a growing danger in the 1990s. This reality was brought home to New Yorkers in February 1993, when terrorists exploded bombs beneath the World Trade Center in downtown Manhattan. Terrorists struck New York City again on September 11, 2001, crashing two hijacked jet planes into the Twin Towers of the World Trade Center. The towers were destroyed, and nearly 3,000 people were killed.

People from all over the state and country responded by pulling together to find ways to help. In the years since September 11, New York City has begun the long process of rebuilding. Rudolph Giuliani, who was mayor of New York at the time of the attacks, believes the city is even stronger today than it was before the attacks. "The city is more vital," he said, "the city is rebuilding, the city is even more diverse."

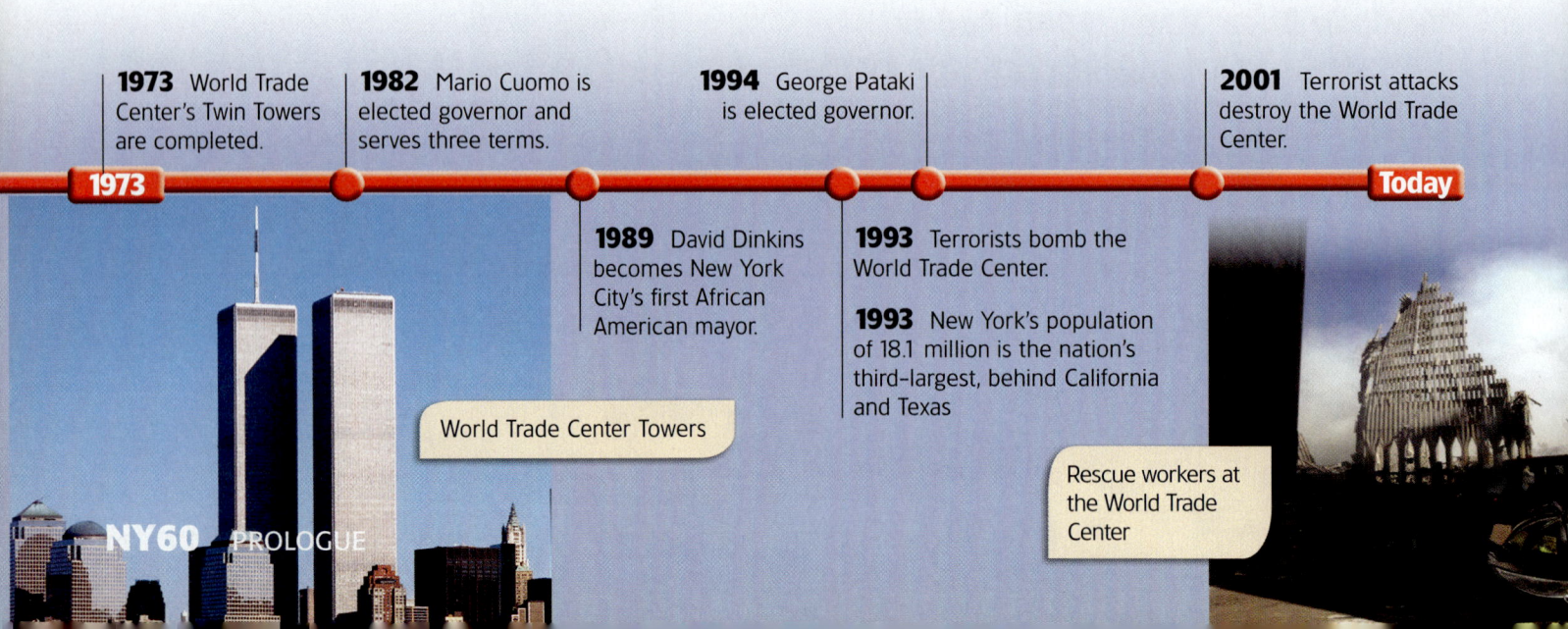

1973 World Trade Center's Twin Towers are completed.

1982 Mario Cuomo is elected governor and serves three terms.

1994 George Pataki is elected governor.

2001 Terrorist attacks destroy the World Trade Center.

1973 — Today

1989 David Dinkins becomes New York City's first African American mayor.

1993 Terrorists bomb the World Trade Center.

1993 New York's population of 18.1 million is the nation's third-largest, behind California and Texas

World Trade Center Towers

Rescue workers at the World Trade Center

New York: Physical

NEW YORK MAPS AND FACTS

NEW HAMPSHIRE

NEW YORK

VERMONT

MASSACHUSETTS

CONNECTICUT

ATLANTIC OCEAN

Long Island Sound

Long Island

Staten Island

NEW JERSEY

PENNSYLVANIA

CANADA

Lake Champlain

Saranac Lakes

St. Lawrence Champlain Lowland

St. Lawrence River

Highest Point:
Mt. Marcy
5,344 ft.
(1,629 m)

Lake Placid

Lake George

Adirondack Mountains

Panther Mountain
3,865 ft. (1,178 m)

Long Lake

Cranberry Lake

Great Sacandaga Lake

Hudson-Mohawk Lowland

Taconic Range

Hudson River

Huntersfield Mountain
3,423 ft. (1,043 m)

Catskill Mountains

Slide Mountain
4,204 ft. (1,281 m)

Shawangunk Mountains

APPALACHIAN MOUNTAINS

Mohawk River

Delaware River

Tug Hill

Oneida Lake

Chenango River

Susquehanna River

Allegheny Plateau

Great Lakes Plain

Finger Lakes

Genesee River

Erie Canal

Lake Ontario

Lake Erie

Chautauqua Lake

44°N

78°W

72°W

ELEVATION

Feet		Meters
13,120		4,000
6,560		2,000
1,640		500
655		200
(Sea level) 0		0 (Sea level)
Below sea level		Below sea level

0   25   50 Miles

0   25   50 Kilometers

Projection: Albers Equal Area

New York: Political

CANADA

VERMONT

NEW HAMPSHIRE

MASSACHUSETTS

CONNECTICUT

NEW JERSEY

PENNSYLVANIA

ATLANTIC OCEAN

Lake Champlain

Lake Ontario

Lake Erie

Long Island Sound

Lake George

Great Sacandaga Lake

Lake Pleasant

Oneida Lake

Finger Lakes

Chautauqua Lake

St. Lawrence River

Mohawk River

Hudson River

Adirondack Park

Catskill Park

Cities and places:
Malone, Plattsburgh, Elizabethtown, Canton, Watertown, Lowville, Hudson Falls, Lake George, Mechanicville, Troy, Ballston Spa, Schenectady, Albany, Hudson, Catskill, Kingston, Poughkeepsie, Carmel, Peekskill, White Plains, Yonkers, Bronx, New City, Newburgh, Goshen, Middletown, Monticello, Delhi, Cooperstown, Herkimer, Utica, Rome, Oneonta, Binghamton, Norwich, Cortland, Ithaca, Watkins Glen, Owego, Elmira, Bath, Penn Yan, Geneva, Ovid, Lyons, Canandaigua, Geneseo, Warsaw, Batavia, Albion, Rochester, Lockport, Buffalo, Hamburg, Niagara Falls, Mayville, Jamestown, Little Valley, Olean, Belmont, Oswego, Syracuse, Auburn, Wampsville, Oneonta, Staten Island, St. George, Brooklyn, Jamaica, Mineola, Riverhead, Long Island, NEW YORK CITY

Star — State capital — Albany

★ State capital
• Other cities

0   25   50 Miles
0   25   50 Kilometers
Projection: Albers Equal Area

72°W
78°W
44°N

N E W S

New York Governors

George Clinton (1777–1795)
John Jay (1795–1801)
George Clinton (1801–1804)
Morgan Lewis (1804–1807)
Daniel D. Tompkins (1807–1817)
John Tayler (1817)
De Witt Clinton (1817–1822)
Joseph C. Yates (1823–1824)
De Witt Clinton (1825–1828)
Nathaniel Pitcher (1828)
Martin Van Buren (1829)
Enos T. Throop (1829–1832)
William L. Marcy (1833–1838)
William H. Seward (1839–1842)
William C. Bouck (1843–1844)
Silas Wright (1845–1846)
John Young (1847–1848)
Hamilton Fish (1849–1850)
Washington Hunt (1851–1852)

Horatio Seymour (1853–1854)
Myron H. Clark (1855–1856)
John A. King (1857–1858)
Edwin D. Morgan (1859–1862)
Horatio Seymour (1863–1864)
Reuben E. Fenton (1865–1868)
John T. Hoffman (1869–1872)
John A. Dix (1873–1874)
Samuel J. Tilden (1875–1876)
Lucius Robinson (1877–1879)
Alonzo B. Cornell (1880–1882)
Grover Cleveland (1883–1884)
David B. Hill (1885–1891)
Roswell P. Flower (1892–1894)
Levi P. Morton (1895–1896)
Frank S. Black (1897–1898)
Theodore Roosevelt (1899–1900)
Benjamin B. Odell, Jr. (1901–1904)
Frank W. Higgins (1905–1906)

Charles E. Hughes (1907–1910)
Horace White (1910)
John A. Dix (1911–1912)
William Sulzer (1913)
Martin H. Glynn (1913–1914)
Charles S. Whitman (1915–1918)
Alfred E. Smith (1919–1920)
Nathan L. Miller (1921–1922)
Alfred E. Smith (1923–1928)
Franklin D. Roosevelt (1929–1932)
Herbert H. Lehman (1933–1942)
Charles Poletti (1942)
Thomas E. Dewey (1943–1954)
W. Averell Harriman (1955–1958)
Nelson A. Rockefeller (1959–1973)
Malcolm Wilson (1973–1974)
Hugh L. Carey (1975–1982)
Mario M. Cuomo (1983–1994)
George E. Pataki (1995– 2006)
Eliot L. Spitzer (2007–2008)
David A. Paterson (2008–2010)
Andrew M. Cuomo (2011–)

New York Government

Executive Branch

Carries out the laws and policies of state government

The Governor

- Elected by voters to a four-year term
- No term limits
- Appoints officials and some judges
- Can veto whole laws or items of laws regarding budgets

Lieutenant Governor

- Elected along with governor
- Various jobs include replacing governor should he or she leave office

The Cabinet

- Consists of officials appointed by governor
- Offers advice to governor on specific areas of knowledge

Legislative Branch

Makes state laws

Bicameral System

- Has two houses — State Senate and Assembly
- Both houses take part in lawmaking
- Legislature can override the governor's veto with a two-thirds vote in both houses

The State Senate

- 62 Senators
- Serve two-year terms
- No limit on number of terms

The Assembly

- 150 Assembly members
- Serve two-year terms
- No limit on number of terms

Judicial Branch

Decides conflicts and questions about the law

Trial Courts

- Hear civil and criminal cases
- Five divisions of superior courts

Appellate Courts

- Hear and determine appeals from the lower courts
- Four divisions of appellate courts

Circuit Courts

- Determines statewide principles of law in deciding specific lawsuits
- Focuses on broad issues of law, not individual factual disputes
- Has one Chief Judge and six Associate Judges
- Appointed by governor with approval of the Senate
- Serve 14-year terms

New York Facts

State tree	Sugar maple
State bird	Bluebird
State marine animal	Trout
State animal	Beaver
State insect	Ladybug
State fossil	Sea scorpion
State shell	Bay scallop
State flower	Rose
State fruit	Apple
Capital	Albany
Year of Statehood	1788 (11th State)
Nickname	The Empire State
Motto	Excelsior (Ever Upward)
Song	"I Love New York"
Highest Elevation	Mt. Marcy, 5,344 feet above sea level
Lowest Elevation	Sea level
Total Area	54,475 sq. miles
National Rank in Land Area	27
Total Coastline	1,850 miles (includes every bay & inlet on Long Island) 127 miles (Atlantic coastline only)
Largest City	New York City
Largest Lake	Lake Oneida
Number of Counties	62
Longest River	Hudson River
Population (2009 est.)	19,541,453
National Rank in Population	3
Length (North to South)	310 miles
Width (East to West)	440 miles [including Long Island]

The rose is the New York state flower.

New York state flag

New York

HOLT McDOUGAL

The AMERICANS

Gerald A. Danzer

J. Jorge Klor de Alva

Larry S. Krieger

Louis E. Wilson

Nancy Woloch

HISTORY

HOLT McDOUGAL

 HOUGHTON MIFFLIN HARCOURT

Authors and Consultants

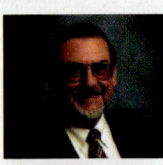

Gerald A. Danzer, Ph.D.
Gerald A. Danzer is Professor of History at the University of Illinois at Chicago. He served from 1992 to 1994 as Chair of the Council for Effective Teaching and Learning at UIC and was Director of the Chicago Neighborhood History Project. Dr. Danzer's area of specialization is historical geography, in which he has written *Discovering American History Through Maps and Views* and numerous other publications. Before entering university teaching, Dr. Danzer taught high school history in the Chicago area. Dr. Danzer received his Ph.D. in history from Northwestern University.

J. Jorge Klor de Alva, J.D. and Ph.D.
J. Jorge Klor de Alva is President of Apollo International, Inc., a global education provider. Formerly he was president of the University of Phoenix. Before that he was Class of 1940 Professor of Comparative Ethnic Studies and Anthropology at the University of California at Berkeley and former Professor of Anthropology at Princeton University. Dr. Klor de Alva's interests include interethnic relations, historical ethnography, and educational reform. His publications include *The Aztec Image of Self* and *Society and Interethnic Images: Discourse and Practice in the New World, 1492–1992*, as well as more than ten other books and more than seventy scholarly articles. Dr. Klor de Alva earned his J.D. from the University of California at Berkeley and his Ph.D. in history/anthropology from the University of California at Santa Cruz.

Larry S. Krieger, B.A., M.A., M.A.T.
Larry S. Krieger is the Social Studies Supervisor for Grades K–12 in Montgomery Township Public Schools in New Jersey. For 26 years he has been a world history teacher in public schools. He has also introduced many innovative in-service programs, such as "Putting the Story Back in History," and has co-authored several successful history textbooks. Mr. Krieger earned his B.A. and M.A.T. from the University of North Carolina and his M.A. from Wake Forest University.

Louis E. Wilson, Ph.D.
Louis E. Wilson is Associate Professor and from 1989 through 1998 was the Chair of the Afro-American and African Studies Department at Smith College. In 1999, Dr. Wilson was a Senior Fulbright History Professor at the University of Cape Town, South Africa. Previously Dr. Wilson was on the faculty at the University of Colorado, Boulder, and was a senior Fulbright Scholar at the University of Ghana, Legon. Dr. Wilson is the author of *The Krobo People of Ghana to 1892: A Political, Social, and Economic History* and *Genealogical and Militia Data on Blacks, Indians, and Mustees from Military American Revolutionary War Records*. He is also one of the authors of *Houghton Mifflin Social Studies*. Dr. Wilson is currently writing a book entitled *Forgotten Patriots: African Americans and Native Americans in the American Revolution from Rhode Island*. In 1991, Dr. Wilson received The Blackwell Fellowship and Prize as Outstanding Black New England Scholar. Dr. Wilson received his Ph.D. in history from the University of California at Los Angeles.

Nancy Woloch, Ph.D.
Nancy Woloch teaches history at Barnard College, where she has been on the faculty since 1988. Dr. Woloch's main scholarly interest is the history of women in the United States, and in this area she has published *Women and the American Experience* and *Early American Women: A Documentary History, 1600–1900*. She is also the author of *Muller v. Oregon* and the co-author of *The American Century*. Dr. Woloch was the recipient of two National Endowment for the Humanities Fellowships. She received her Ph.D. in history and American studies from Indiana University.

This book contains material written by **John S. Bowes** that originally appeared in *The Americans* © 1985 and © 1991.

Senior Consultant
Dr. Robert Dallek
Presidential historian and biographer
Washington, D.C.

Constitution Consultant
Melvin Dubnick
Professor of Political Science
Rutgers University, Trenton
Trenton, New Jersey

Contributing Writer
Miriam Greenblatt
Educational Writer and Consultant
Highland Park, Illinois

Multicultural Advisory Board
The multicultural advisers reviewed the manuscript for appropriateness content.

Pat A. Brown
Director of the Indianapolis Public Schools Office of African-Centered Multicultural Education
Indianapolis Public Schools
Indianapolis, Indiana

Ogle B. Duff
Associate Professor of English
University of Pittsburgh
Pittsburgh, Pennsylvania

Mary Ellen Maddox
Black Education Commission Director, Los Angeles Unified School District
Los Angeles, California

Jon Reyhner
Associate Professor and Coordinator of the Bilingual Multicultural Ed. Program
Northern Arizona University
Flagstaff, Arizona

Curtis L. Walker
Executive Officer, Office of Equity and Compliance
Pittsburgh Public Schools
Pittsburgh, Pennsylvania

Ruben Zepeda
Compliance Advisor, Language Acquisition and Curriculum Development
Los Angeles, California

Consultants and Reviewers

Content Consultants

The content consultants reviewed the manuscript for historical depth and accuracy and for clarity of presentation.

Catherine Clinton
Fellow of the W. E. B.
Du Bois Institute
Harvard University
Cambridge, Massachusetts

Theodore Karaminski
Professor of History
Loyola University
Chicago, Illinois

Joseph Kett
Professor of History
University of Virginia
Charlottesville, Virginia

Jack Rakove
Professor of History
Stanford University
Stanford, California

Harvard Sitkoff
Professor of History
University of New Hampshire
Durham, New Hampshire

Teacher Consultants

The following educators contributed ideas and activities for the program.

Edmund Austin
William Tennant High School
Warminster, Pennsylvania

William Brown
Retired,
Northeast High School
Philadelphia, Pennsylvania

Larry Bruno
Denby High School
Detroit, Michigan

Suzanne Cook
Scarborough High School
Houston, Texas

John Devine
Elgin High School
Elgin, Illinois

George Dyche
West Aurora High School
Aurora, Illinois

Steve Ellison
Petaluma High School
Petaluma, California

Betsy Fitzgerald
Erskine Academy
South China, Maine

Michael Fleming
Jupiter High School
Jupiter, Florida

Thomas J. Flynn
Turner High School
Kansas City, Kansas

Dominic Fruscello
West Genesee High School
Camillus, New York

Craig T. Grace
Lanier High School
West Austin, Texas

Cynthia M. Greene
Ridley High School
Folsom, Pennsylvania

Patti Harrold
Edmond Memorial High School
Edmond, Oklahoma

Korri Kinney
Meridian High School
Meridian, Idaho

Don A. Lee
Mira Mesa High School
San Diego, California

Dr. Carol D. McCree
DeBakey Health Prof.
High School
Houston, Texas

Harry McCown
Hazelwood West High School
Hazelwood, Missouri

Lou Morrison
Lake Weir High School
Ocala, Florida

Theresa C. Noonan
West Irondequoit High School
Rochester, New York

Gloria Remijio
Del Valle High School
El Paso, Texas

Diane M. Rodgers
Crooksville High School
Crooksville, Ohio

James Rosenberg
Retired, Crystal Lake South
High School
Crystal Lake, Illinois

John Seeley
Westminster High School
Westminster, California

Brenda G. Smith
Instructional Supervisor,
Social Studies, Colorado
Springs District 11
Colorado Springs, Colorado

Steve Smith
Clayton High School
Clayton, North Carolina

Ruby Thompson
Athens Drive High School
Raleigh, North Carolina

Linda Tillis
South Oak Cliff High School
Dallas, Texas

Mark A. Van Hecke
Anchor Bay High School
New Baltimore, Michigan

Joshua Weiner
Benson High School
Portland, Oregon

Teacher Review Panels

The following educators provided ongoing review during the development of prototypes, the table of contents, and key components of the program.

FLORIDA TEACHER PANEL

David Debs
Mandarin High School
Jacksonville, Florida

Ronald Eckstein
Hudson High School
Hudson, Florida

Sharman Feliciani
Land O'Lakes High School
Land O'Lakes, Florida

Flossie Gautier
Bay High School
Panama City, Florida

Glenn Hallick
Vanguard High School
Ocala, Florida

Mary Kenney
Astronaut High School
Titusville, Florida

Lou Morrison
Lake Weir High School
Ocala, Florida

Brenda Sims Palmer
Lehigh High School
Lehigh Acres, Florida

Marsee Perkins
Maynard Evans High School
Orlando, Florida

Kent Rettig
Pensacola High School
Pensacola, Florida

Jim Sutton
Edgewater High School
Orlando, Florida

ILLINOIS TEACHER PANEL

Rosemary Albright
Conant High School
Hoffman Estates, Illinois

Jeff Anhut
Wheaton Warrenville South
High School
Wheaton, Illinois

James Crider
Downers Grove South
High School
Downers Grove, Illinois

John Devine
Elgin High School
Elgin, Illinois

George Dyche
West Aurora High School
Aurora, Illinois

Diane Ring
St. Charles High School
St. Charles, Illinois

Jim Rosenberg
Crystal Lake South
High School
Crystal Lake, Illinois

Pam Zimmerman
Stevenson High School
Lincolnshire, Illinois

CALIFORNIA TEACHER PANEL

Elaine Deatherage
Hiram Johnson High School
Sacramento, California

Steve Ellison
Petaluma High School
Petaluma, California

Judy Horrigan
Moreno Valley High School
Moreno Valley, California

Don Lee
Mira Mesa High School
San Diego, California

Russom Mesfun
Fremont High School
Oakland, California

Randy Sanford
Hueneme High School
Oxnard, California

John Seeley
Westminster High School
Westminster, California

Kathleen Torosian
Herbert Hoover High School
Fresno, California

Glenda Watanabe
Banning High School
Los Angeles, California

TEXAS TEACHER PANEL

Patricia Brison
Bellaire High School
Houston, Texas

Brian Greeney
Stratford High School
Spring Branch, Texas

Jim Lee
Lamar High School
Arlington, Texas

Janie Maldonado
Lanier High School
Austin, Texas

Leonore Murray
Lubbock High School
Lubbock, Texas

Deborah Pennington
The Woodlands High School
Conroe, Texas

Gloria Remijio
Dell Valley High School
Yselta, Texas

H.V. Stafford
MacArthur High School
Aldine, Texas

Dawn Stapp
Lee Freshman High School
Midland, Texas

Manuscript Reviewers

The educators listed in the next column reviewed the prototype chapter and the manuscript of the entire book.

Arman Afshani
North Tonawanda High School
North Tonawanda, New York

Debra Brown
Eisenhower High School
Houston, Texas

Dianne Bumgarner
Ashbrook High School
Mt. Holly, North Carolina

Sherry Burgin
Garland High School
Garland, Texas

Maurice Bush
South Point High School
Crouse, North Carolina

(continued on R122)

Student Board

The following students reviewed prototype materials for the book.

John Afordakos
Chantilly High School
Fairfax County, Virginia

Marisha Cook
Rockford East High School
Rockford, Illinois

Matthew Cornejo
New Bedford High School
New Bedford, Massachusetts

(continued on R122)

HISTORY™ is the leading destination for revealing, award-winning, original non-fiction series and event-driven specials that connect history with viewers in an informative, immersive and entertaining manner across multiple platforms. HISTORY is part of A&E Television Networks (AETN), a joint venture of Hearst Corporation, Disney/ABC Television Group and NBC Universal, an award-winning, international media company that also includes, among others, A&E Network™, BIO™, and History International™.

HISTORY programming greatly appeals to educators and young people who are drawn into the visual stories our documentaries tell. Our Education Department has a long-standing record in providing teachers and students with curriculum resources that bring the past to life in the classroom. Our content covers a diverse variety of subjects, including American and world history, government, economics, the natural and applied sciences, arts, literature and the humanities, health and guidance, and even pop culture.

The HISTORY website, located at **www.history.com**, is the definitive historical online source that delivers entertaining and informative content featuring broadband video, interactive timelines, maps, games, podcasts and more.

"We strive to engage, inspire and encourage the love of learning..."

Since its founding in 1995, HISTORY has demonstrated a commitment to providing the highest quality resources for educators. We develop multimedia resources for K–12 schools, two- and four-year colleges, government agencies, and other organizations by drawing on the award-winning documentary programming of A&E Television Networks. We strive to engage, inspire and encourage the love of learning by connecting with students in an informative and compelling manner. To help achieve this goal, we have formed a partnership with Houghton Mifflin Harcourt.

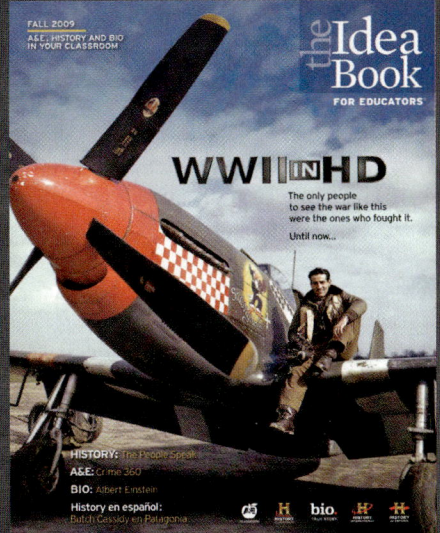

The Idea Book for Educators

Classroom resources that bring the past to life

Live webcasts

HISTORY Take a Veteran to School Day

In addition to premium video-based resources, **HISTORY** has extensive offerings for teachers, parents, and students to use in the classroom and in their in-home educational activities, including:

▶ *The Idea Book for Educators* is a biannual teacher's magazine, featuring guides and info on the latest happenings in history education to help keep teachers on the cutting edge.

▶ **HISTORY Classroom (www.history.com/classroom)** is an interactive website that serves as a portal for history educators nationwide. Streaming videos on topics ranging from the Roman aqueducts to the civil rights movement connect with classroom curricula.

▶ **HISTORY email newsletters** feature updates and supplements to our award-winning programming relevant to the classroom with links to teaching guides and video clips on a variety of topics, special offers, and more.

▶ **Live webcasts** are featured each year as schools tune in via streaming video.

▶ **HISTORY Take a Veteran to School Day** connects veterans with young people in our schools and communities nationwide.

In addition to **HOUGHTON MIFFLIN HARCOURT**, our partners include the *Library of Congress,* the *Smithsonian Institution, National History Day, The Gilder Lehrman Institute of American History,* the *Organization of American Historians,* and many more. HISTORY video is also featured in museums throughout America and in over 70 other historic sites worldwide.

American Beginnings to 1783

An advertisement for land in Virginia, page 45

William Franklin, page 103

Molly Pitcher portrayed in battle, page 117

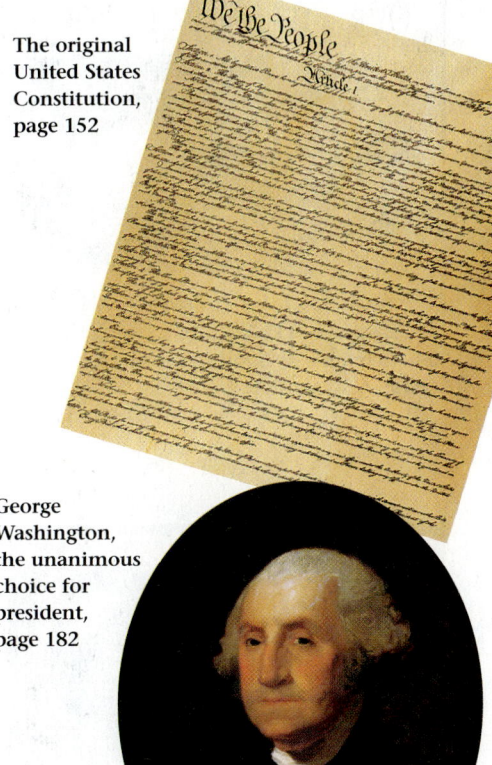

The original United States Constitution, page 152

George Washington, the unanimous choice for president, page 182

A decorative serving tray showing Vermont preacher Lemuel Haynes, page 241

1825–1877
An Era of Growth and Disunion

"OUR FIELD IS THE WORLD."

McCormick Harvesting Machine Co., Chicago.
ESTABLISHED 1831.

Rapid changes in farming encouraged westward expansion, page 279

Abraham Lincoln, before the presidency took its toll, page 324

Mother and daughter in Mt. Meigs, Alabama, page 388

UNIT 4

1877–1917

Migration and Industrialization

A Sioux man and woman, page 409

The first light bulb, page 438

Coney Island amusement park, page 498

1890–1920
Modern America Emerges

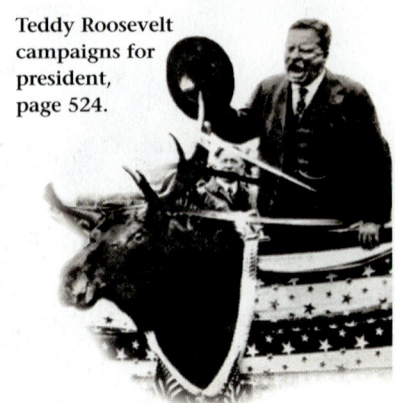

Teddy Roosevelt campaigns for president, page 524.

Uncle Sam rides upon two "hemispheres," page 557.

Eddie Rickenbacker and the First World War, page 587

UNIT 6

1919–1940

The 1920s and the Great Depression

"Big business" dances with Calvin Coolidge, page 632.

Zora Neale Hurston and the Harlem Renaissance, page 658

An unemployed man during the Great Depression, page 676

UNIT 8

1954–1975
Living with Great Turmoil

Kennedy and Johnson promise active leadership, page 876.

Jo Ann Gibson Robinson and the Bus Boycott, page 906

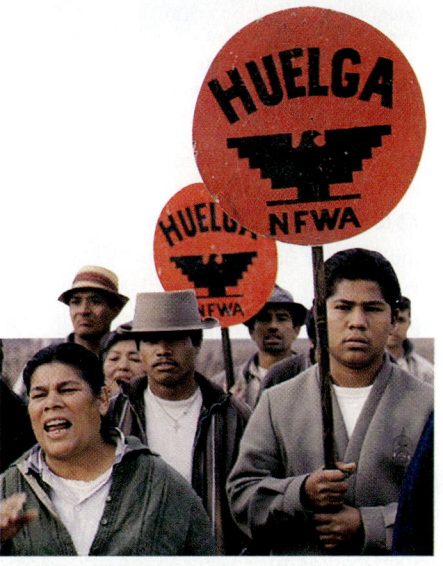

Farm workers protest, page 974.

Passage to a New Century

Tape-recorded conversations ensnare the Nixon White House, page 1012.

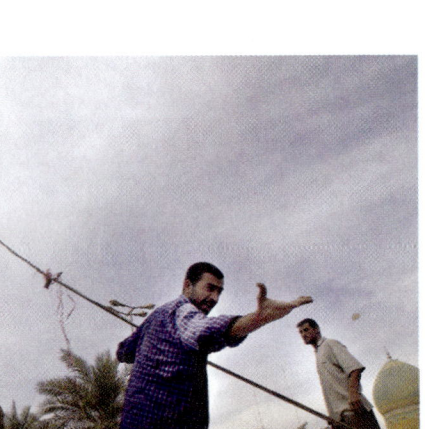

A statue of Saddam Hussein is toppled in Baghdad after the Iraqi dictator is overthrown, page 1105.

Available @ 🔽 hmhsocialstudies.com
• Strategies for Taking Standardized Tests
• Economics Handbook

The history of a nation is shaped as much by geography as by people and events. Paying attention to the following themes of geography can help you recognize when geographic forces are at work in the story of the United States.

LOCATION

Geographers speak of absolute location—the latitude and longitude of an area—and of relative location—where one area is in relation to another. In absolute terms, the city of San Francisco lies at 37°45' North latitude and 122°26' West longitude. This information allows you to pinpoint San Francisco on a map. In relative terms, San Francisco lies at the western edge of North America and looks out across the vast Pacific Ocean. This information helps explain San Francisco's history as a port city where people and ideas have come together.

Critical Thinking Locate your city or town on both a political and a physical map. How has location influenced the history of your city or town?

PLACE

Place, in geography, refers to what an area looks like in physical and human terms. An area's landforms, soil, climate, and resources are aspects of place. So are the numbers and cultures of the population. San Francisco's natural harbor has made the city an international port. It is connected to the American River—where gold was discovered in 1848. Its position along a major fault line has subjected it to periodic earthquakes, the most disastrous in 1906. During its history, San Francisco has attracted people from North America, Europe, Asia, and various Pacific islands, making its population one of the most diverse in the United States.

Critical Thinking What is unique about the place where you live and the people who live there? What past events contributed to its uniqueness?

REGION

Geographers use the idea of region to show what places in close proximity to one another have in common. As a part of the Pacific Coast region, San Francisco shares with Seattle, Washington, and Portland, Oregon, a mild, rainy climate and an economic interest in international shipping. As a part of California, San Francisco shares economic and environmental concerns of the state as a whole.

Critical Thinking To what region or regions does your area belong? How have the characteristics and concerns of your region changed over the last generation?

MOVEMENT

One place or region can influence another through the movement of people, materials, and even ideas. San Francisco has been the site of many important movements of people and cultures. It has been a port of entry for immigrants, many of them Asian. It also lies along the path that Spanish missionaries trod in their quest to convert native peoples.

Critical Thinking When and by what groups was your area settled? What trends in movement today may shape the future of your area?

HUMAN-ENVIRONMENT INTERACTION

Wherever people live, they affect the environment in the way they modify their natural surroundings. They build shelters and clear trees. They turn the earth inside out to extract its resources. People in the San Francisco Bay area have built bridges in order to move around more easily. People have also modified the bay itself, reducing its area by about one-third as they filled in tidelands for development.

Critical Thinking How have people in your area modified their surroundings? What consquences might these modifications have?

Themes in History

Among the important themes in U.S. history are the promise of technology, the rights enjoyed by Americans, and the roles of women in the 21st century. As you study U.S. history, you will encounter these and other themes again and again. The Americans *focuses on nine themes, described on these pages. What do you think are the important issues raised by each theme?*

DIVERSITY AND THE NATIONAL IDENTITY

E Pluribus Unum—From the Many, One. Pick up a dollar bill and you'll find this Latin motto on the Great Seal of the United States. From the first settlement, this has been a land of many peoples, cultures, and faiths. This mixing of ethnic, racial, and religious groups has produced a rich and uniquely American culture. It has also led to competition and conflict. Today, the United States is more diverse than ever, yet the nation's motto remains *E Pluribus Unum*. (See **Tracing Themes** on page 466.)

Critical Thinking How do you think America today is enriched by its diversity?

AMERICA IN WORLD AFFAIRS

From the earliest colonial times, the United States has been influenced by the events, people, and forms of government in other nations—and America has influenced world affairs. Today, relationships between the United States and other countries are more critical than ever, as modern communications and transportation have drawn the world closer together. As America continues to participate in world affairs, questions of trade, diplomacy, and regional conflict will grow in importance. (See **Tracing Themes** on page 610.)

Critical Thinking What do you think America's role in the world should be in the 21st century?

ECONOMIC OPPORTUNITY

America has always been a land of economic opportunity. Blessed with fertile land and abundant resources, this has been a country where anyone who has worked hard has had a chance to prosper. Indeed, American history is full of heartening "rags-to-riches" success stories. Just as inspiring are the heroic struggles of women and minorities who fought to improve their economic prospects. As your generation enters the work force, you and your friends will have the opportunity to write your own success stories. (See **Tracing Themes** on page 634.)

Critical Thinking What do you think are the most exciting economic opportunities for Americans today?

SCIENCE AND TECHNOLOGY

Americans have always had a deep respect for the power of science and technology to improve life. In the past two centuries, new inventions, new technologies, and scientific breakthroughs have transformed the United States—and continue to appear at a dizzying pace. Which ones will change your life? You can be sure that some will, and in ways that no one can yet predict. (See **Tracing Themes** on page 794.)

Critical Thinking How do you think science and technology will change American life in the 21st century?

WOMEN AND POLITICAL POWER

More than half of all Americans are women, but only recently have their contributions and concerns found their way into history books. American women have helped shape the social and political history of every era. In their private roles as wives and mothers, they have strengthened families and raised America's children. In their more public roles as workers, reformers, and crusaders for equal rights, they have attacked the nation's worst social ills and challenged barriers to women's full participation in American life. (See **Tracing Themes** on page 124.)

Critical Thinking What do you think is the most important goal for American women today?

IMMIGRATION AND MIGRATION

Seeking a better life seems to be part of the American character. This nation was first established by and has remained a magnet for immigrants. One out of every ten people living in the United States today was born in another country. Moreover, every year one out of every six Americans moves to a new address. (See **Tracing Themes** on page 1094.)

Critical Thinking Why do you think people continue to have the dream of immigrating to the United States?

STATES' RIGHTS

The power struggle between states and the federal government has caused controversy since the country's beginning. In 1861 the conflict led to the Civil War, in which Southern states acted upon the belief that they had the right to nullfy acts of the federal government and even to leave the Union if they chose to do so. Throughout the history of this country, state and federal governments have squared off on this and other constitutional issues. (See **Tracing Themes** on page 322.)

Critical Thinking When do you think a state has the right to challenge a federal law?

VOTING RIGHTS

When Americans first began their experiment with democracy, only white men with property could vote or hold office. Over the past two centuries, women, African Americans, and other groups have fought for and won the right to vote and participate in government. Today the challenge is getting people to exercise the right to vote. In 2000, only 50.7 percent of eligible voters cast ballots in the presidential election. (See **Tracing Themes** on page 174.)

Critical Thinking What do you think can be done to bring more Americans into the democratic process?

CIVIL RIGHTS

The American system of government is based on a simple but revolutionary idea: Every citizen has certain rights and liberties. Among them are the right to participate in government and to exercise such liberties as freedom of speech and worship. Deciding who should have what rights, how these rights should be exercised, and how to protect a person's civil rights is anything but easy. Defining and protecting our civil rights are not likely to get any easier. (See **Tracing Themes** on page 930.)

Critical Thinking What issue of civil rights do you think is most critical in the United States today?

UNIT 1

UNIT PROJECT

Letter to the Editor

As you read Unit 1, look for an
issue that interests you, such as
the effect of colonization on Native
Americans or the rights of
American colonists. Write a letter
to the editor in which you explain
your views. Your letter should
include reasons and facts.

The Landing of the Pilgrims,
by Samuel Bartoll (1825)

American Beginnings
to 1783

CHAPTER 1

THREE WORLDS MEET

Essential Question

How did their convergence affect the cultures of North America, Africa, and Europe?

 New York Standards

KEY IDEA 3 Study about the major social, political, economic, cultural, and religious developments in New York State and United States history involves learning about the important roles and contributions of individuals and groups.

SECTION 1: Peopling the Americas

SECTION 2: North American Societies Around 1492

SECTION 3: West African Societies Around 1492

SECTION 4: European Societies Around 1492

SECTION 5: Transatlantic Encounters

Native Americans watch for the arrival of a European ship.

c. 20,000 B.C. Asian peoples begin migrating to America across the Beringia land bridge.

c. 5000 B.C. Corn is raised as a domesticated crop in central Mexico.

1200 B.C. Olmec society, which created this colossal stone head, develops in what is now southern Mexico.

500 B.C. Adena culture begins building large earthen mounds in what is now southern Ohio.

200 B.C.– A.D. 400 Hopewell culture, which created this mica bird claw, flourishes in the Midwest.

AMERICAS
WORLD

1200 B.C.* **A.D.*** **500**

1020 B.C. Israel becomes a kingdom.

753 B.C. Rome is founded.

622 Muhammad founds Islam.

*B.C. corresponds to B.C.E., or "before the common era."
A.D. corresponds to C.E., or "common era."

INTERACT
WITH HISTORY

You live on a Caribbean island in the 15th century. Your society hunts game freely, grows crops of great variety, and trades actively with nearby cultures. Now you sense that your world is about to change; the ships you see approaching are like nothing you have encountered before.

Explore the Issues

- How would you react to a people whose appearance and language are unlike anything you have ever known?

- What can happen when one culture imposes its values on another?

1000 Viking Leif Ericson reaches what is now Newfoundland.

1492 Christopher Columbus first reaches America.

c. 1500 Iroquois League is formed.

1000

1500

1096 The Crusades begin.

1434 Portuguese begin West African slave trade.

1440 Johann Gutenberg develops printing press.

Peopling the Americas

MAIN IDEA	WHY IT MATTERS NOW	Terms & Names
In ancient times, migrating peoples settled the Americas, where their descendants developed complex societies.	Patterns of immigration have always shaped and continue to shape American history.	• nomadic • Hohokam • Olmec • Anasazi • Maya • Adena • Aztec • Hopewell • Inca • Mississippian

One American's Story

hmhsocialstudies.com
TAKING NOTES
Use the graphic organizer online to take notes on the early civilizations of the Americas.

Thomas Canby, a writer for *National Geographic* magazine, spent a year with archaeologists as they searched for clues about the earliest Americans. As Canby watched the archaeologists unearthing fragile artifacts, a long-lost world came into sharper focus.

A PERSONAL VOICE THOMAS CANBY

" What a wild world it was! To see it properly, we must board a time machine and travel back into the Ice Age. The northern half of North America has vanished, buried beneath ice sheets two miles thick. Stretching south to Kentucky, they buckle earth's crust with their weight. . . . Animals grow oversize. . . . Elephant-eating jaguars stand as tall as lions, beavers grow as big as bears, South American sloths as tall as giraffes. With arctic cold pushing so far southward, walrus bask on Virginia beaches, and musk-oxen graze from Maryland to California. "

—"The Search for the First Americans," *National Geographic*, Sept. 1979

▲ **Modern depiction of early Americans hunting the woolly mammoth around 20,000 B.C.**

This was the world of the first Americans—people who migrated to the Americas from another continent. Centuries later, a different kind of immigration to the Americas would bring together people from three complex societies: the Native American, the European, and the West African. The interaction of these three cultures helped create the present-day culture of the United States. However, it is with the ancient peoples of the Americas that the story of America actually begins.

Background
The Americas include two continents—North and South America. This huge land mass stretches some 10,000 miles from the Arctic Circle in the north to the waters around Antarctica in the south.

Ancient Peoples Come to the Americas

The first Americans may have arrived as early as 22,000 years ago. Ice Age glaciers had frozen vast quantities of the earth's water, lowering sea levels enough to expose a land bridge between Asia and Alaska. Ancient hunters trekked across the frozen land, now called Beringia, into North America.

HUNTING AND GATHERING Experts suspect that most of these ancient explorers came by foot. Some groups may have edged down the Pacific coast in boats fashioned from the bones and hides of animals—boats that are much like the kayaks used by modern-day Inuit.

The evidence suggests that the earliest Americans were big-game hunters. Their most challenging and rewarding prey was the woolly mammoth, which provided food, clothing, and bones for making shelters and tools.

As the Ice Age ended around 12,000 to 10,000 years ago, this hunting way of life also ended. Temperatures warmed, glaciers melted, and sea levels rose once again. Travel to the Americas by foot ceased as the ancient land bridge disappeared below the Bering Sea.

Over time, people switched to hunting smaller game, fishing, and gathering nuts, berries, and fruit along with grains, beans, and squash. While many ancient groups established settlements in North America, others continued south through what is now Mexico into South America. Wherever they went, the first Americans developed ways of life to suit their surroundings.

AGRICULTURE DEVELOPS Between 10,000 and 5,000 years ago, a revolution quietly took place in what is now central Mexico. There, people began to plant crops. Some archaeologists believe that maize (corn) was the first plant that ancient Americans developed for human use. Other plants followed—gourds, pumpkins, peppers, beans, and more. Eventually, agricultural techniques spread throughout the Americas.

The introduction of agriculture brought tremendous change. Agriculture made it possible for people to remain in one place and to store surplus food. As their surplus increased, people had more time to develop other skills. From this agricultural base evolved larger, more stable societies and increasingly complex cultures. However, some Native American cultures never adopted agriculture and remained **nomadic,** moving from place to place in search of food and water, while others mixed nomadic and non-nomadic lifestyles. **A**

Hunters roaming over 10,000 years ago in what is now southern Arizona may have used this large spearhead to kill a woolly mammoth.

MAIN IDEA

Analyzing Effects

A What were the effects of agriculture on the hunting and gathering peoples of the Americas?

Complex Societies Flourish in the Americas

Around 3,000 years ago, the first Americans began to form larger communities and build flourishing civilizations. A closer look at the more prominent of these societies reveals the diversity and complexity of the early American world.

Today, Alaska and Siberia are separated by the Bering Strait, a strip of sea only 55 miles wide. During the last Ice Age, glaciers moved south from the North Pole, freezing up the waters of the Bering Sea and exposing more land. This formed the Beringia land bridge, over which the earliest Americans probably migrated from Asia.
▼

The Great Serpent Mound, a giant effigy mound of the Adena culture

The 200-room Cliff Palace in Colorado, an Anasazi pueblo, or cliff dwelling

Cahokia, a center of the Mississippian culture, as it might have looked around 1150

ATLANTIC OCEAN

ADENA & HOPEWELL

Missouri R.
Cahokia

Ohio River

Colorado River

ANASAZI & HOHOKAM

MISSISSIPPIAN

Mississippi River

Moundville

30°N

One of the massive sculptures created by Olmec peoples

Gulf of Mexico

20°N

Tropic of Cancer

Chichén Itzá

Tenochtitlán

OLMEC

AZTEC

MAYA

The astronomical observatory in the Mayan city of Chichén Itzá

Artist's rendering of Tenochtitlán, the Aztec capital in the middle of Lake Texcoco

0   250   500 miles
0   250   500 kilometers

Timeline

1200	1000	800	600	400	200	0	200	400	600	800	1000	1200	1400	1600

B.C. | A.D.

OLMEC

ADENA & HOPEWELL

ANASAZI & HOHOKAM

MAYA

MISSISSIPPIAN

AZTEC

GEOGRAPHY SKILLBUILDER

1. **Region** Which river ran through the Mississippian, Adena, and Hopewell culture areas?
2. **Place** What do the cities of Chichén Itzá and Tenochtitlán reveal about the cultures that created them?

VIDEO
Secret Mounds of Pre-Historic America

hmhsocialstudies.com

EMPIRES OF MIDDLE AND SOUTH AMERICA Archaeologists believe that the first empire of the Americas emerged as early as 1200 B.C. in what is now southern Mexico. There the **Olmec** peoples created a thriving civilization in the humid rain forest along the coast of the Gulf of Mexico. Other civilizations appeared in the wake of the Olmec's mysterious collapse around 400 B.C. These included the **Maya,** who built a dynamic culture in Guatemala and the Yucatán Peninsula between A.D. 250 and 900, and the **Aztec,** who swept into the Valley of Mexico in the 1200s.

In South America the most prominent of these empire builders were the **Inca,** who around A.D. 1200 created a glittering empire that stretched nearly 2,500 miles along the mountainous western coast of South America.

MAIN IDEA

Summarizing
 What were some of the achievements of the early civilizations of the Americas?

These empires' achievements rivaled those of ancient cultures in other parts of the world. The peoples of these American empires built great cities and ceremonial centers, some with huge palaces, temple-topped pyramids, and central plazas. To record their histories, some of these civilizations invented forms of glyph writing—using symbols or images to express words and ideas. **B**

ANCIENT DESERT FARMERS As early as 3,000 years ago, several North American groups, including the **Hohokam** and the **Anasazi,** introduced crops into the arid deserts of the Southwest. Later, between 300 B.C. and A.D. 1400, each group established its own civilization. The Hohokam settled in the valleys of the Salt and Gila rivers in what is now central Arizona. The Anasazi took to the mesa tops, cliff sides, and canyon bottoms of the Four Corners region—an area where the present-day states of Utah, Colorado, Arizona, and New Mexico meet.

MOUND BUILDERS To the east of the Mississippi River, in a region extending from the Great Lakes to the Gulf of Mexico, another series of complex societies developed. There the **Adena,** the **Hopewell,** and the **Mississippian** societies excelled at trade and at building. Some Adena and Hopewell structures consisted of huge burial mounds filled with finely crafted objects. Other mounds were sculpted into effigies, or likenesses, of animals so large that they can be seen clearly only from the air. People of the Mississippian culture constructed gigantic pyramidal mounds.

Although societies such as the Mississippian and the Aztec still flourished when Christopher Columbus reached American shores in 1492, others had long since disappeared. Despite their fate, these early peoples were the ancestors of the many Native American groups that inhabited North America on the eve of its encounter with the European world.

HISTORICAL SPOTLIGHT

THE "OTHER" PYRAMIDS

The stone pyramids of Egypt, which were used as elaborate tombs for Egyptian kings more than 4,000 years ago, are some of today's most famous structures. However, they were not the only pyramids to tower over the ancient world.

On the American side of the Atlantic, the Maya built giant flat-topped pyramids with stairs leading to rooftop temples, where Mayan priests performed religious ceremonies.

Farther north, at Cahokia, in what is now Illinois, people of the Mississippian culture constructed more than 100 massive earthen mounds. The mounds served as tombs, temples, and foundations for elaborate homes. The largest of these mounds is Monk's Mound, which is 100 feet high and covers about 16 acres at its base.

SECTION 1 ASSESSMENT

1. TERMS & NAMES For each term or name, write a sentence explaining its significance.

- nomadic
- Olmec
- Maya
- Aztec
- Inca
- Hohokam
- Anasazi
- Adena
- Hopewell
- Mississippian

MAIN IDEA

2. TAKING NOTES
In a chart like the one below, list the early civilizations of the Americas. Include the approximate dates they flourished and their locations.

Civilization	Dates	Location

What are some similarities that you have noticed among these early civilizations?

CRITICAL THINKING

3. ANALYZING
How did the development of agriculture affect ancient societies in the Americas?

4. EVALUATING
Evaluate the achievements of the ancient cultures of the Americas. Which single accomplishment do you find most remarkable and why?

5. DRAWING CONCLUSIONS
Which ancient American empire do you think was most advanced? Support your choice with details from the text. **Think About:**

- the cultural achievements of each empire
- the characteristics of modern civilizations

SECTION 2

PI 3.1
CC Unit 1.I.A.2.a   CC Unit 1.I.A.2.b
CC Unit 1.I.A.2.c   CC Unit 2.I.A.2.b
CC Unit 2.I.A.3.b

North American Societies Around 1492

MAIN IDEA	WHY IT MATTERS NOW	Terms & Names
The varied landscapes of North America encouraged the diversity of Native American cultures.	Many modern Native American groups maintain ancient customs of their respective cultures.	• Kashaya Pomo • Iroquois • Kwakiutl • kinship • Pueblo • division of labor

One American's Story

hmhsocialstudies.com
TAKING NOTES

Use the graphic organizer online to take notes about North America's diverse societies.

Essie Parrish, a Native American storyteller and medicine woman, kept alive stories from a time when her people, the **Kashaya Pomo,** flourished along the northern California coast. She invited Robert Oswalt, an anthropologist, to time-travel with her to the 1540s. As Parrish spoke, the centuries rolled back.

▲ Dressed for a ceremony in the 1950s, spiritual leader Essie Parrish wears a feathered headdress and holds two bead-covered staffs.

A PERSONAL VOICE ESSIE PARRISH

" In the old days, before the white people came up here, there was a boat sailing on the ocean from the south. Because before that . . . [the Kashaya Pomo] had never seen a boat, they said, 'Our world must be coming to an end. Couldn't we do something? This big bird floating on the ocean is from somewhere, probably from up high. . . .' [T]hey promised Our Father [a feast] saying that destruction was upon them.

When they had done so, they watched [the ship] sail way up north and disappear. . . . They were saying that nothing had happened to them—the big bird person had sailed north-ward without doing anything—because of the promise of a feast. . . . Consequently they held a feast and a big dance. "

—quoted in *Kashaya Texts*

The event became part of the Kashaya Pomo's oral history. Stories like this have provided us with a broad picture of the Native American world before it came into contact with the world of European explorers and settlers.

Native Americans Live in Diverse Societies

The native groups of North America were as diverse as the environments in which they lived. The North American continent provided for many different ways of life, from nomadic to the kind of fixed, nonmigratory life of farming communities.

MAIN IDEA

Making Inferences

A How might California's varied landscapes have encouraged diverse ways of life?

CALIFORNIA Not one land, but many lands—that's how the Kashaya Pomo and other native peoples regarded the region that is now California. The land has a long coastline, a lush northwestern rain forest, and a parched southern desert.

The peoples of California adapted to these diverse settings. The Kashaya Pomo hunted waterfowl with slingshots and nets. To the north, the Yurok and Hupa searched the forests for acorns and fished in mountain streams. **A**

NORTHWEST COAST The waterways and forests of the northwest coast sustained large communities year-round. The sea was of prime importance. On a coastline that stretched from what is now southern Alaska to northern California, peoples such as the **Kwakiutl** (kwä′kē-ōot′l), Nootka, and Haida collected shellfish from the beaches and hunted the ocean for whales, sea otters, and seals.

Peoples such as the Kwakiutl decorated masks and boats with magnificent totems, symbols of the ancestral spirits that guided each family. Kwakiutl families also displayed their histories on huge totem poles set in front of their cedar-plank houses. A family's totems announced its wealth and status.

Leading Kwakiutl families also organized potlatches, elaborate ceremonies in which they gave away large quantities of their possessions. A family's reputation depended upon the size of its potlatch—that is, on how much wealth it gave away. A family might spend up to 12 years planning the event.

SOUTHWEST In the dry Southwest, the Pima and Pueblo tribes, descendants of the Hohokam and Anasazi, lived in a harsh environment. By 1300, the **Pueblo** and a related tribe, the Hopi, had left the cliff houses of their Anasazi ancestors. The Pueblo built new settlements near waterways such as the Rio Grande, where they could irrigate their farms. However, the Hopi and the Acoma continued to live near the cliffs and developed irrigation systems.

Vocabulary
adobe: a sun-dried brick of clay and straw

People lived in multistory houses made of adobe or stone and grew corn, beans, melons, and squash. Like their ancestors, they built underground kivas, or ceremonial chambers, for religious ceremonies and councils.

Science & Technology

FORENSIC RECONSTRUCTIONS

Artists are now able to recreate the facial features of ancient peoples. The appearance of Native Americans who died sometime between A.D. 1000 and 1400 have recently been reconstructed from skeletal remains. These remains, removed from a burial site in Virginia, have since been returned to the Monacan tribe. The reconstructions bear a remarkable resemblance to modern Monacans.

◄ The forensic artist first makes a plaster cast from the original skull. Then the artist uses clay to build up the facial features. Finally, the artist individualizes the head, based on clues about the subject's weight, muscularity, and environment.

The final reconstruction ► presents a close approximation of the person's original appearance.

SKILLBUILDER Interpreting Visual Sources
1. What strikes you most about these reconstructed faces?
2. How might forensic reconstructions contribute to our understanding of the past?

 SEE SKILLBUILDER HANDBOOK, PAGE R23.

The lyrics to the ritual songs they sang may have resembled the ones recalled by a Hopi chief named Lololomai at the start of the 1900s. "This is the song of the men from my kiva," Lololomai explained. "It tells how in my kiva the chief and his men are praying to make the corn to grow next year for all the people."

★ **A PERSONAL VOICE** LOLOLOMAI

" **Thus we, thus we**
The night along,
With happy hearts
Wish well one another.

In the chief's kiva
They, the fathers . . .
Plant the double ear—
Plant the perfect double corn-ear.
So the fields shall shine
With tassels white of perfect corn-ears.

Hither to them, hither come,
Rain that stands and cloud that rushes! "

—quoted in *The Indians' Book*

◄ This kachina doll represented the corn spirit in Hopi religious ceremonies.

EASTERN WOODLANDS The landscape of the Southwest contrasted sharply with the woodlands east of the Mississippi River. Here, hardwood forests stretched from the Great Lakes and the St. Lawrence River in the north to the Gulf of Mexico in the south.

The tribes that lived in the Eastern Woodlands had much in common. Native peoples like the **Iroquois** (ĭr′ə-kwoi′) built villages in forest clearings and blended agriculture with hunting and gathering. They traveled by foot or by canoe. Because of the vast supply of trees, most groups used woodworking tools to craft everything from snowshoes to canoes.

The peoples of the Eastern Woodlands also differed from one another in their languages, customs, and environments. In the Northeast, where winters could be long and harsh, people relied on wild animals for clothing and food. In the warmer Southeast, groups grew such crops as corn, squash, and beans. **B**

MAIN IDEA

Contrasting
B In what ways did food production differ among Native American societies?

Native Americans Share Cultural Patterns

Although no two Native American societies were alike, many did share certain cultural traits. Patterns of trade, attitudes toward land use, and certain religious beliefs and social values were common to many cultures.

TRADING NETWORKS Trade was one of the biggest factors in bringing Native American peoples into contact with one another. As tribes established permanent settlements, many of these settlements became well known for specific products or skills. The Nootka of the Northwest Coast mastered whaling. The Ojibwa of the upper Great Lakes collected wild rice. The Taos of the Southwest made pottery. These items, and many more, were traded both locally and long-distance.

An elaborate transcontinental trading network enabled one group to trade with another without direct contact. Traders passed along items from far-off, unfamiliar places. Intermediaries carried goods hundreds and sometimes thousands of miles from their source. So extensive was the network of forest trails and river roads that an English sailor named David Ingram claimed in 1568 to have walked along Native American trade routes all the way from Mexico to the Atlantic Coast. **C**

MAIN IDEA

Forming Generalizations
C In what ways did trade link Native Americans?

North American Cultures in the 1400s

hmhsocialstudies.com **INTERACTIVE MAP**

Tepees could be quickly dismantled and were well suited to the nomadic lifestyle of the Plains.

KWAKIUTL
NOOTKA

CHINOOK

NEZ PERCE

BLACKFOOT

ARIKARA

MANDAN

CROW

CREE

OJIBWA
(Chippewa)

OTTAWA

ALGONQUIN

SHOSHONE

KATO

KASHAYA
POMO

CHEYENNE

DAKOTA
(Sioux)

SAUK

HURON

POTAWATOMI

WAMPANOAG
PEQUOT
NARRAGANSETT

40°N

IOWA

ARAPAHO

PAWNEE

MIAMI

DELAWARE

SUSQUEHANNOCK

PAIUTE

UTE

KANSA

ILLINOIS

SHAWNEE

MONACAN

CHUMASH

30°N

HOPI

NAVAJO

KIOWA

OSAGE

POWHATAN

PIMA

ZUNI

PUEBLO

KIOWA-
APACHE

TUSCARORA

CHEROKEE

MESCALERO
APACHE

COMANCHE

CHICKASAW

CHOCTAW

HITCHITI

A longhouse of the Eastern Woodlands region.

JUMANO

TIMUCUA

Pueblos, built of sun-dried brick, or adobe, were characteristic dwellings of the Southwest.

HUICHOL

20°N

Gulf of
Mexico

Tropic of Cancer

TAINO

N
W E
S

MAYA

AZTEC

PACIFIC OCEAN

ATLANTIC OCEAN

Native American Trade

Before the arrival of Columbus, the trade routes of North America allowed goods to travel across the continent.

Group and Region	Goods Traded
Algonquin of the Eastern Woodlands	colored feathers, copper
Apaches of the Plains	meat, hides, salt
Navajo of the Southwest	pottery, blankets, crops
Kwakiutl of the Northwest Coast	fish oil
Ute of the Great Basin	hides, buffalo robes
Choctaw of the Southeast	deerskins, bear oil

GEOGRAPHY SKILLBUILDER
1. **Region** What does this map reveal about North America in the 1400s?
2. **Location** Why do you think some regions had more trade routes than others?

Subarctic	Southeastern
Northwest Coast	Southwest
California	Great Basin
Plateau	Mesoamerican
Plains	Caribbean
Eastern Woodlands	– – – Major trade routes

0   250   500 miles
0   250   500 kilometers

30°N

0°

Three Worlds Meet **11**

LAND USE Native Americans traded many things, but land was not one of them. They regarded the land as the source of life, not as a commodity to be sold. "We cannot sell the lives of men and animals," said one Blackfoot chief in the 1800s, "therefore we cannot sell this land." This attitude would lead to many clashes with the Europeans, who believed in private ownership of land.

Vocabulary
commodity: an article of trade or commerce

Native Americans disturbed the land only for the most important activities, such as food gathering or farming. A female shaman, or priestess, from the Wintu of California expressed this age-old respect for the land as she spoke to anthropologist Dorothy Lee.

> ### A PERSONAL VOICE WINTU WOMAN
> "When we dig roots, we make little holes. When we build houses, we make little holes. . . . We shake down acorns and pinenuts. We don't chop down the trees. We only use dead wood [for fires]. . . . But the white people plow up the ground, pull down the trees, [and. . . the] tree says, 'Don't. I am sore. Don't hurt me.' "
>
> —quoted in *Freedom and Culture*

RELIGIOUS BELIEFS Nearly all Native Americans thought of the natural world as filled with spirits. Past generations remained alive to guide the living. Every object—both living and non-living—possessed a voice that might be heard if one listened closely. "I hear what the ground says," remarked Young Chief of the Cayuses, who lived in what is now Washington and Oregon, in 1855. "The ground says, 'It is the Great Spirit that placed me here.' The Great Spirit tells me to take care of the Indians. . . " Some cultures believed in one supreme being, known as "Great Spirit," "Great Mystery," "the Creative Power," or "the Creator."

Native American Village Life

hmhsocialstudies.com INTERACTIVE

John White, one of the first English colonists to arrive in North America, made several drawings of Native American life in the Chesapeake region in 1585. The engraving shown here was copied from White's original drawing and published in 1590. The image shows the village life of the Secotan people, who lived near Roanoke Island, North Carolina.

A Agriculture
A Secotan guards the ripened corn crop to keep away hungry birds and animals. A tobacco field appears to the left of this field, and other corn fields and a pumpkin patch appear below it.

B Hunting
Men hunt for deer.

C The Home
Huts, whose sides can be rolled up for ventilation, are woven from thick plant stems.

D Social Life
Villagers prepare for a community feast. The fire for this feast appears up the path in the heart of the village.

E Religion
Residents dance around a circle of idols in a religious ceremony. Across the main path lies a prayer circle with fire.

SKILLBUILDER Analyzing Primary Sources
1. What Native American work activities are shown in this drawing?
2. Based on the drawing, what appear to be two significant daily concerns of the Secotan?

SOCIAL ORGANIZATION Bonds of **kinship,** or strong ties among family members, ensured the continuation of tribal customs. Elders instructed the young. In exchange, the young honored the elders and their departed ancestors.

The tasks assigned to men and women varied with each society. Among the Iroquois and Hopi, for example, women owned the household items, and families traced their ancestry from mother to grandmother to great-grandmother, and so on. In other Native American cultures, men owned the family possessions and traced their ancestry through their father's kin.

The **division of labor**—the assignment of tasks according to gender, age, or status—formed the basis of social order. Among the Kwakiutl, for example, slaves performed the most menial jobs, while nobles ensured that Kwakiutl law was obeyed.

The basic unit of organization among all Native American groups was the family, which included aunts, uncles, cousins, and other relatives. Some tribes further organized the families into clans, or groups of families descended from a common ancestor. Among the Iroquois, for example, members of a clan often lived together in huge bark-covered longhouses. All families participated in community decision making.

Not all Native American groups lived together for long periods of time. In societies in which people hunted and gathered, groups broke into smaller bands for hunting. On the plains, for example, families searched the grasslands for buffalo. Groups like these reunited only to celebrate important occasions. **D**

In the late 1400s, on the eve of the encounter with the Europeans, the rhythms of Native American life were well-established. No one could have imagined the changes that were about to transform the Native American societies.

MAIN IDEA

Comparing
D What similarities and differences existed among Native American social structures?

NOW & THEN

SCHEMITZUN

The sights and sounds of the Native American world come alive each August for several days on the Connecticut reservation of Mashantucket. Here, performers and visitors from nearly 500 Native American tribes meet under a massive tent for Schemitzun, the "World Championship of Song and Dance."

Schemitzun was traditionally a dance to celebrate the corn harvest. Today it has become an occasion for Native Americans to meet, share their art and culture, and celebrate their heritage.

SECTION 2 ASSESSMENT

1. **TERMS & NAMES** For each term or name, write a sentence explaining its significance.
   - Kashaya Pomo
   - Kwakiutl
   - Pueblo
   - Iroquois
   - kinship
   - division of labor

MAIN IDEA

2. **TAKING NOTES**
Copy an outline of North America like the one below. Then shade in the areas belonging to each of the following Native American cultures: Northwest Coast, Southwest, and Eastern Woodlands. Describe how each society adapted to its environment.

CRITICAL THINKING

3. **COMPARING**
In your opinion, were the differences between Native American groups greater than their similarities? Cite specific examples to support your answer. **Think About:**
   - adaptation to physical settings
   - the role of tradition
   - the variety of goods and languages encountered in trading

4. **SYNTHESIZING**
Describe the relationship between the individual and his or her social group in Native American society. Use details from the text to support your description.

5. **HYPOTHESIZING**
Why did Native American societies not wish to buy and sell land?

West African Societies Around 1492

MAIN IDEA	WHY IT MATTERS NOW	Terms & Names
West Africa in the 1400s was home to a variety of peoples and cultures.	Modern African Americans have strong ancestral ties to the people of West Africa.	• Islam • Benin • plantation • Kongo • Songhai • lineage • savanna

One African's Story

Leo Africanus was about 18 when he laid eyes on the renowned city of Timbuktu in the West African empire of Songhai. A Muslim born in Granada (in modern Spain) and raised in North Africa, Leo Africanus visited the city with his uncle, who was on a diplomatic mission to the emperor of Songhai. At the time of their journey in 1513, Songhai was one of the largest kingdoms in the world, and the emperor, Askia Muhammad, was rich and powerful. Leo Africanus later described the bustling prosperity of Timbuktu and its lively intellectual climate.

A PERSONAL VOICE LEO AFRICANUS

" Here are many shops of . . . merchants, and especially such as weave linen and cotton cloth. And hither do the Barbary [North African] merchants bring cloth of Europe. . . . Here are great store of doctors, judges, priests, and other learned men, that are bountifully maintained at the king's cost and charges, and hither are brought divers manuscripts or written books out of Barbary, which are sold for more money than any other merchandise. "

—*The History and Description of Africa Done into English* by John Pory

These ancient boards from Africa contain sayings from the Qur'an, the holy scripture of Islam.

Leo Africanus provides a glimpse of 16th-century West African life. From this region of Africa, and particularly from the West and West-Central coastal areas, would come millions of people brought to the Americas as slaves. These people would have a tremendous impact on American history and culture.

West Africa Connects with the Wider World

Although geographically isolated from Europe and Asia, West Africa by the 1400s had long been connected to the wider world through trade. For centuries, trade had brought into the region new goods, new ideas, and new beliefs, including those of the Islamic religion. Then, in the mid-1400s, the level of interaction with the world increased with the arrival of European traders on the West African coast.

THE SAHARA HIGHWAY The Timbuktu that Leo Africanus described was the hub of a well-established trading network that connected most of West Africa to the coastal ports of North Africa, and through these ports to markets in Europe and Asia. Leo Africanus and his uncle reached Timbuktu by following ancient trade routes across the Sahara desert. At the crossroads of this trade, cities such as Timbuktu, Gao, and Jenne became busy commercial centers. The empires that controlled these cities and trade routes grew wealthy and powerful.

Traders from North Africa brought more than goods across the Sahara—they also brought their Islamic faith. **Islam,** founded in Arabia in 622 by Muhammad, spread quickly across the Middle East and North Africa. By the 1200s, Islam had become the court religion of the large empire of Mali, and it was later embraced by the rulers of Songhai, including Askia Muhammad. Despite its official status, however, Islam did not yet have much influence over the daily lives and religious practices of most West Africans in the late 1400s. **Ⓐ**

THE PORTUGUESE ARRIVE The peoples of West Africa and Europe knew little of each other before the 1400s. This situation began to change as Portuguese mariners made trading contacts along the West African coast. By the 1470s, Portuguese traders had established an outpost on the West African coast near the large Akan goldfields, the source of much West African gold. Other trading outposts soon

HISTORICAL SPOTLIGHT

ISLAM

Like Judaism and Christianity, Islam is monotheistic, or based on the belief in one God. Islam was founded by Muhammad (about A.D. 570–632), who believed the angel Gabriel appeared to him and told him to preach a new religion to the Arabs. This religion became known as Islam, which in Arabic means "surrender" [to Allah]. (Allah is the Arabic name for God.) The followers of Islam are called Muslims, "those who submit to God's will."

The words that Muhammad claimed he had received from God were recorded in the Qur'an, the holy book of Islam.

West Africa in the 1400s

hmhsocialstudies.com **INTERACTIVE MAP**

Boundaries of West African kingdoms are shown at greatest extent.

- – – – Major trade routes
- Desert
- Savanna
- Rain forest

0   600   1,200 miles
0   600   1,200 kilometers

Algiers · Tunis · Tripoli · Mediterranean Sea · Alexandria · Cairo · Marrakesh · Sabha · Taghaza · In Salah · Ghat · S A H A R A · Nile R. · Red Sea · Walata · Timbuktu · Gao · Jenne · SONGHAI · HAUSA STATES · KANEM-BORNU · Kano · Niger R. · Bobo Dioulasso · Kong · Volta R. · OYO · Benue R. · Ife · Lagos · BENIN · AKAN · Gulf of Guinea · Príncipe · Equator · São Tomé · Congo R. · KONGO · Mbanza Kongo · Luanda · ATLANTIC OCEAN · 10°N · 0°

GEOGRAPHY SKILLBUILDER
1. **Human-Environment Interaction** What are the three climate zones of West Africa?
2. **Location** How did Songhai's location aid the growth of that kingdom?

followed. These early contacts between West Africans and Portuguese traders would have two significant consequences for West Africa and the Americas. First, direct trade between the Portuguese and the coastal peoples of West Africa bypassed the old trade routes across the Sahara and pulled the coastal region into a closer relationship with Europe. Second, the Portuguese began the European trade in West African slaves.

In the 1480s the Portuguese claimed two uninhabited islands off the African coast, Príncipe and São Tomé. Discovering that the soil and climate were perfect for growing sugar cane, they established large sugar plantations there. A **plantation** is a farm on which a single crop, usually one that requires much human labor, is grown on a large scale. To work these plantations, the Portuguese began importing slaves from the West African mainland.

At first this trade was limited to a small number of West Africans purchased from village chiefs, usually captives from rival groups. However, the success of the Portuguese slave plantations provided a model that would be reproduced on a larger scale in the Americas—including the British North American colonies. **B**

MAIN IDEA

Summarizing
B How did the Portuguese sugar plantations affect the course of history?

Three African Kingdoms Flourish

In the late 1400s, western Africa was a land of thriving trade, diverse cultures, and many rich and well-ordered states.

SONGHAI From about 600 to 1600, a succession of empires—first Ghana, then Mali, and beginning in the mid-1400s, **Songhai** (sông′hī′)—gained power and wealth by controlling the trans-Sahara trade. The rulers of these empires grew enormously rich by taxing the goods that passed through their realms.

With wealth flowing in from the north-south trade routes, the rulers of Songhai could raise large armies and conquer new territory. They could also build cities, administer laws, and support the arts and education. So it was with two great rulers of the Songhai. The first great king, Sunni Ali, who ruled from 1464 to 1492, made Songhai the largest West African empire in history. His military prowess became legendary—during his entire reign, he never lost a battle.

A desert caravan reaches the fabled Songhai city of Timbuktu.
▼

Another great ruler, Askia Muhammad, was a master organizer, a devout Muslim, and a scholar. He organized Songhai into administrative districts and appointed officials to govern, collect taxes, and regulate trade, agriculture, and fishing. Under his rule, Timbuktu regained its reputation as an important education center as it attracted scholars from all over the Islamic world.

At its height in the 1500s, Songhai's power extended across much of West Africa. However, it did not control the forest kingdoms. Songhai's cavalry might easily thunder across the **savanna,** the region of dry grassland, but it could not penetrate the belt of dense rain forest along the southern coast. Protected by the forest, peoples such as the Akan, Ibo, Edo, Ifi, Oyo, and Yoruba lived in kingdoms that thrived in the 1400s and 1500s.

BENIN Although the forests provided protection from conquest, they nevertheless allowed access for trade. Traders carried goods out of the forests or paddled them along the Niger River to the savanna. The brisk trade with Songhai and North Africa, and later with Portugal, helped the forest kingdoms grow. In the 1400s one of these kingdoms, **Benin,** dominated a large region around the Niger Delta. Leading the expansion was a powerful oba (ruler) named Ewuare. Stories that have been passed down to the present day recall Ewuare's triumphs in the mid-1400s.

★ **A PERSONAL VOICE** CHIEF JACOB EGHAREVBA

" He fought against and captured 201 towns and villages. . . . He took their rulers captive and he caused the people to pay tribute to him. He made good roads in Benin City. . . . In fact the town rose to importance and gained the name of city during his reign. It was he who had the innermost and greatest of the walls and ditches made round the city, and he also made powerful charms and had them buried at each of the nine gateways of the city so as to ward against any evil. "

—*A Short History of Benin*

Within this great walled city, Ewuare headed a highly organized government in which districts were governed by appointed chiefs. Through other appointed officials, the oba controlled trade and managed the metal-working industries such as goldsmithing and brass-smithing. He also exchanged ambassadors with Portugal in the late 1400s. Under the patronage of Ewuare and his successors, metalworkers produced stunning and sophisticated works of art, such as bronze sculptures and plaques. **C**

MAIN IDEA

Comparing

C How was the government in Benin similar to that of Askia Muhammad?

KONGO Within another stretch of rain forest, in West Central Africa, the powerful kingdom of **Kongo** arose on the lower Zaire (Congo) River. In the late 1400s, Kongo consisted of a series of small kingdoms ruled by a single leader called the Manikongo, who lived in what is today Angola. The Manikongo, who could be either a man or a woman, held kingdoms together by a system of royal marriages, taxes, and, when necessary, by war and tribute. By the 1470s, the Manikongo oversaw an empire estimated at over 4 million people.

The Bakongo, the people of Kongo, mined iron ore and produced well-wrought tools and weapons. They also wove palm leaf threads into fabric that reminded Europeans of velvet. The Portuguese sailors who first reached Kongo in 1483 were struck by the similarities between Kongo and their own world. Its system of government—a collection of provinces centralized under one strong king—resembled that of many European nations at the time.

▲ An unknown Yoruba artist in the kingdom of Ife produced this bronze head of a king in the 1100s. The highly developed bronze artistry of Ife was handed down to the kingdom of Benin, which arose later in the same area.

West African Culture

In the late 1400s the world of most West Africans was a local one. Most people lived in small villages, where life revolved around family, the community, and tradition. West African customs varied greatly but followed some common patterns. These patterns would influence the future interactions between Africans and Europeans and shape the experience of enslaved Africans in the Americas.

FAMILY AND GOVERNMENT Bonds of kinship—ties among people of the same **lineage,** or line of common descent—formed the basis of most aspects of life in rural West Africa. Some societies, such as the Akan, were matrilineal—that is, people traced their lineage through their mother's family. These lineage ties determined not only family loyalties but also inheritances and whom people could marry. Societies such as the Ibo also encouraged people to find a mate outside their lineage groups. These customs helped create a complex web of family alliances.

Within a family, age carried rank. The oldest living descendant of the group's common ancestor controlled family members and represented them in councils of the larger groups to which a family might belong. These larger groups shared a common language and history and often a common territory. One leader or chief might speak for the group as a whole. But this person rarely spoke without consulting a council of elders made up of the heads of individual extended families.

RELIGION Religion was important in all aspects of African life. Political leaders claimed authority on the basis of religion. For example, the ruler of the Ife kingdom claimed descent from the first person placed on earth by the "God of the Sky." Religious rituals were also central to the daily activities of farmers, hunters, and fishers. **D**

West Africans believed that nature was filled with spirits and perceived spiritual forces in both living and non-living objects. They also believed that the spirits of ancestors spoke to the village elders in dreams. Although West African peoples might worship a variety of ancestral spirits and lesser gods, most believed in a single creator. The Bakongo, for example, believed in *Nzambi ampungu*, a term that means the "creator of all things," and so understood the Christian or Muslim belief in a supreme god. However, the Bakongo and other cultures could not

MAIN IDEA

Hypothesizing
D Why did political leaders claim authority on the basis of religion?

Against the backdrop of centuries-old cliff dwellings built by their ancestors, modern-day Dogon elders in Mali carry out an ancient religious ritual.

© 1993 Chester Higgins, Jr.

understand the Christian and Muslim insistence that West Africans stop worshipping spirits, who were believed to carry out the Creator's work. Out of this difference grew many cultural conflicts.

LIVELIHOOD Throughout West Africa, people supported themselves by age-old methods of farming, herding, hunting, and fishing, and by mining and trading. Almost all groups believed in collective ownership of land. Individuals might farm the land, but it reverted to family or village ownership when not in use.

People on the dry savanna depended on rivers, such as the Niger, to nourish their crops and livestock. On the western coast, along the Senegal and Gambia rivers, farmers converted tangled mangrove swamps into rice fields. This grain—and the skills for growing it—would accompany West Africans to the Americas. **E**

USE OF SLAVE LABOR West Africans divided tasks by age and by social status. At the lowest rung in some societies were slaves. However, in Africa, people were not born into slavery, nor did slavery necessarily mean a lifetime of servitude. In Africa, slaves could escape their bondage in a number of ways. Sometimes they were adopted into or they married into the family they served. This was a very different kind of servitude from that which evolved in the Americas, where slavery continued from generation to generation and was based on race.

While slavery eventually came to dominate the interaction between Africans and Europeans, it was not the primary concern of the Portuguese sailors who first explored the African coast. At this time, in the late 1400s, a variety of political, social, and economic changes in Europe spurred rulers and adventurers to push outward into unexplored reaches of the ocean.

MAIN IDEA

Developing Historical Perspective

E What agricultural skills did West Africans bring to the Americas?

KENTE CLOTH

Today people of African descent all over the world value as a symbol of Africa the multicolored fabric known as kente cloth. For African Americans who choose to wear kente cloth or display it in their homes, the fabric serves as a tangible link to West African cultures from which their ancestors came.

Artisans of the Asante (Ashanti) people of modern Ghana have woven kente cloth for centuries. Working at looms, they produce long strips of cloth of complex designs and varying colors. These strips are then sewn together into a brilliant fabric that sparkles with reds, greens, blues, golds, and whatever other hues the weavers chose as dyes.

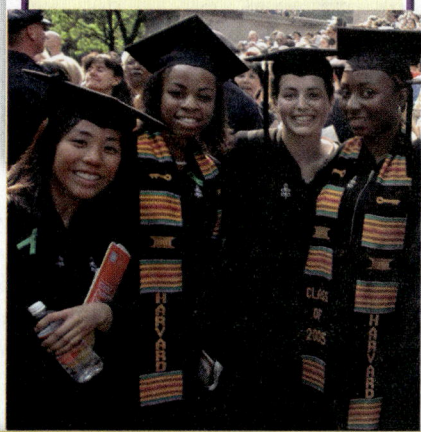

SECTION 3 ASSESSMENT

1. TERMS & NAMES For each term or name, write a sentence explaining its significance.

- Islam
- plantation
- Songhai
- savanna
- Benin
- Kongo
- lineage

MAIN IDEA

2. TAKING NOTES
Make an outline using the main topics shown below, and fill it in with factual details related to each topic.

> **I.** West Africa's Climate Zones
>
> **II.** West Africa's Major Geographical Features
>
> **III.** Three West African Kingdoms and Their Climate Zones

CRITICAL THINKING

3. ANALYZING CAUSES
What factors helped the trade system flourish in West Africa? Use evidence from the text to support your response. **Think About:**

- the geography of the region
- the kinds of goods exchanged
- the societies that emerged in West Africa

4. ANALYZING EFFECTS
What effects did Portuguese trade routes have on West Africa?

5. CONTRASTING
How did West African slavery differ from the kind of slavery that developed in the Americas?

PI 3.4

European Societies Around 1492

MAIN IDEA	WHY IT MATTERS NOW	Terms & Names
Political, economic, and intellectual developments in western Europe in the 1400s led to the Age of Exploration.	European settlement in the Americas led to the founding of the United States.	• Prince Henry • nuclear family • Renaissance • Crusades • hierarchy • Reformation

▲ Prince Henry the Navigator

One European's Story

hmhsocialstudies.com
TAKING NOTES
Use the graphic organizer online to take notes on changes in western Europe in the 1400s.

During the early decades of the 15th century, **Prince Henry** of Portugal, often called "Henry the Navigator," sent Portuguese ships to explore the west coast of Africa. According to his biographer, Prince Henry's driving motivation was the need to know.

★ **A PERSONAL VOICE** GOMES EANES DE ZURARA

" The noble spirit of this Prince . . . was ever urging him both to begin and to carry out very great deeds. For which reason . . . he had also a wish to know the land that lay beyond the isles of Canary and that Cape called Bojador, for that up to his time, neither by writings, nor by the memory of man, was known with any certainty the nature of the land beyond that Cape. . . . it seemed to him that if he or some other lord did not endeavor to gain that knowledge, no mariners or merchants would ever dare to attempt it. . . . "

—The Chronicle of the Discovery and Conquest of Guinea

Prince Henry's curiosity was typical of the "noble spirit" of the **Renaissance,** (rĕn´ĭ-säns´) a period when Europeans began investigating all aspects of the physical world. The term *Renaissance* means "rebirth" of the kind of interest in the physical world that had characterized ancient Greece and Rome. With his burning desire for knowledge, Prince Henry helped launch the era of European expansion.

The European Social Order

In the late 1400s, most Europeans, like most Native Americans and most Africans, lived in small villages, bound to the land and to ancient traditions.

THE SOCIAL HIERARCHY European communities were based on social **hierarchy,** that is, they were organized according to rank. Monarchs and nobles held most of the wealth and power at the top of the hierarchy. At the bottom labored the peasants, who constituted the majority of the people. The nobility offered their peasants land and protection. In return, the peasants supplied the nobles with livestock or crops—and sometimes with military service.

Within the social structure, few individuals moved beyond the position into which they were born. Europeans generally accepted their lot as part of a larger order ordained by God and reflected in the natural world. Writing in the late 1500s, William Shakespeare expressed the fixed nature of this order in one of his plays.

★ **A PERSONAL VOICE** WILLIAM SHAKESPEARE

" **The heavens themselves, the planets, and this center [earth]**
Observe degree, priority, and place . . .
Take but degree away, untune that string,
And hark! what discord follows. . . . "

—*Troilus and Cressida*

One group that did experience social mobility was composed of artisans and merchants, the people who created and traded goods for money. Although this group was relatively small in the 1400s, the profit they earned from trade would eventually make them a valuable source of tax revenue. Monarchs needed them to finance costly overseas exploration and expansion. Ⓐ

THE FAMILY IN SOCIETY While Europeans recognized and respected kinship ties, the extended family was not as important for them as it was for Native American and African societies at this time. Instead, life centered around the **nuclear family,** the household made up of a mother and father and their children. As in other societies, gender largely determined the division of labor. Among peasant families, for example, men generally did most of the field labor and herded livestock. Women did help in the fields, but they also handled child care and household labor, such as preparing and preserving the family's food.

MAIN IDEA

Forming Generalizations

Ⓐ Why did artisans and merchants experience social mobility?

History Through **Art**

JUNE, *FROM* LES TRÈS RICHES HEURES DU DUC DE BERRY

This miniature painting, representing the month of June, is a page from a prayer book calendar made by the Limbourg brothers around the year 1416. The book, made for a younger son of the French king, tells us a great deal about the aristocratic view of the European social order.

In the background, the walls of the city of Paris protect a palace and the royal chapel, buildings that represent the two most powerful institutions in medieval European society: church and aristocracy.

In the foreground, peasants mow the fields in an orderly world of peace and tranquility. However, the image is a fantasy, an idealized vision painted to please the aristocracy. There is no hint of the peasants' grinding poverty or of the violence of the Hundred Years' War that was at that moment devastating northern France.

SKILLBUILDER Interpreting Visual Sources

1. What does the painting tell you about the importance of gender in the division of labor during the 1400s?

2. Why might images of poverty have displeased the aristocracy?

 SEE SKILLBUILDER HANDBOOK, PAGE R23.

Christianity Shapes the European Outlook

The Roman Catholic Church was the dominant religious institution in western Europe. The leader of the church—the pope—and his bishops had great political and spiritual authority. In the spiritual realm, church leaders determined most matters of faith. Parish priests interpreted the scriptures and urged the faithful to endure earthly sufferings in exchange for the promise of eternal life in heaven, or salvation. Priests also administered important rituals called the sacraments—such as baptism and communion—that were thought to ensure salvation.

Hand in hand with the belief in salvation was the call to convert people of other faiths. This missionary call spurred Europe to reach out beyond its borders first to defend, and then to spread, the faith.

CRUSADING CHRISTIANITY By the early 700s, Muslim armies had seized huge areas of Asia and North Africa, along with most of the Iberian Peninsula, where Spain and Portugal sit. To regain this territory, Spanish Christians waged a campaign called the *reconquista*, or reconquest. By 1492, the forces of the combined kingdoms of Queen Isabella of Castile and King Ferdinand of Aragon, who married in 1469, finally drove the Muslims from the peninsula. This victory ended more than seven centuries of religious warfare. A united Spain stood ready to assert itself internationally and to spread Christianity around the globe.

Meanwhile, Christian armies from all over western Europe responded to the church's call to force the Muslims out of the Holy Land around Jerusalem. From 1096 to 1270, Europeans launched the **Crusades,** a series of military expeditions to the Middle East in the name of Christianity.

In the end, these bloody Crusades failed to "rescue" the Holy Land, but they had two consequences that encouraged European exploration and expansion. First, they sparked an increase in trade, as crusaders returned home with a new taste for products from Asia. Second, the Crusades weakened the power of European nobles, many of whom lost their lives or fortunes in the wars. Monarchs were able to take advantage of the nobles' weakened ranks by consolidating their own power. Eventually, monarchs sponsored overseas exploration in order to increase their wealth and power.

DECLINE IN CHURCH AUTHORITY The Crusades had a third long-term consequence: the decline of the power of the pope. The ultimate failure of these campaigns weakened the prestige of the papacy (the office of the pope), which had led the quest. Power struggles in the 1300s and 1400s between the church and European kings further reduced papal authority and tipped the balance of power in favor of the monarchies.

Disagreements over church authority, along with outrage over corrupt practices among the clergy, led to a reform movement in the early 1500s. This movement, known as the **Reformation,** divided Christianity in western Europe between Catholicism and Protestantism. This split deepened the rivalries between European nations during the period of American colonization and sent newly formed Protestant sects across the Atlantic to seek religious freedom. **B**

KEY PLAYER

"KING ISABELLA"
1451–1504

Queen Isabella, who played a central role in European exploration by sponsoring Christopher Columbus's voyages to the Americas, made her mark on the Old World as well. As co-ruler of Spain, Isabella participated in her country's religious and military matters.

The queen often defied the pope to ensure that her candidates were appointed to positions in the Spanish church. In addition, Isabella tasted battle more frequently than most rulers, either male or female. The queen rode among her troops in full armor, personally commanding them in Ferdinand's absence. Whenever Isabella appeared, her troops shouted, "Castile, Castile, for our King Isabella!"

MAIN IDEA

Recognizing Effects
B How did religious changes in Europe affect the European colonization of the Americas?

Limit of Islamic influence
Limit of Roman Catholic influence
Limit of Eastern Orthodox influence

0   250   500 miles
0   250   500 kilometers

ENGLAND

HOLY
ROMAN
EMPIRE

FRANCE

HUNGARY

VENICE

ATLANTIC
OCEAN

PORTUGAL

SPANISH STATES
(Castile, Aragon,
and Granada)

PAPAL STATES

NAPLES

OTTOMAN
EMPIRE

Black Sea

Adriatic Sea

North
Sea

Mediterranean Sea

AFRICA

GEOGRAPHY SKILLBUILDER
1. **Region** What were the most important European powers at this time?
2. **Location** Why were Portugal and Spain particularly well placed for overseas exploration?

Changes Come to Europe

As the 1400s began, European societies were still recovering from a series of disasters during the previous century. From 1314 to 1316, heavy rain and disease wiped out crops and livestock. Thousands of peasants died of starvation. Then, beginning in the 1340s, an epidemic of plagues killed over 25 million people—a fourth of Europe's population. Meanwhile, long wars also raged across the continent, including the Hundred Years' War between England and France.

However, amid this turmoil, modern Europe began to take shape. After the plague, Europe experienced vigorous growth and change. The expansion of Europe pushed Europeans to look to other lands.

THE GROWTH OF COMMERCE AND POPULATION The Crusades opened up Asian trade routes and whetted the European appetite for Eastern luxuries, such as silk, porcelain, tea, and rugs. Merchants in Italian city-states were the first to profit from trade with Asia. They traded with the Muslim merchants who controlled the flow of goods through much of the Middle East. As trade opportunities increased, new markets were established and new trade routes were opened.

By the end of the 1400s, Europe's population had rebounded from the plagues. This increase stimulated commerce and encouraged the growth of towns. The return to urban life (which had been largely neglected after the fall of Rome) brought about far-reaching social and cultural change. The new urban middle class would assume increasing political power, especially in Britain and its colonies. **C**

THE RISE OF NATIONS The Crusades weakened the nobility and strengthened monarchies. Western European monarchs began exerting more control over their lands by collecting new taxes, raising professional armies, and strengthening central governments. Among the new allies of the monarchs were merchants, who willingly accepted taxes on their newfound wealth in exchange for the protection or expansion of trade. By the late 1400s, four major nations were taking shape in western Europe: Portugal, Spain, France, and England.

Only the king or queen of a unified nation had enough power and resources to finance overseas exploration. Monarchs had a powerful motive to encourage

MAIN IDEA

Developing Historical Perspective
C In what ways would the revival of the cities have affected European social and cultural life?

the quest for new lands and trading routes: they needed money to maintain standing armies and large bureaucracies. So, the monarchs of Portugal, Spain, France, and England began looking overseas for wealth.

THE RENAISSANCE "Thank God it has been permitted to us to be born in this new age, so full of hope and promise," exclaimed Matteo Palmieri, a scholar in 15th-century Italy. Palmieri's optimism captured the enthusiastic spirit of the Renaissance. The Renaissance led to a more secular spirit, an interest in worldly pleasures, and a new confidence in human achievement. Starting in Italy, a region stimulated by commercial contact with Asia and Africa, the Renaissance soon spread throughout Europe. Renaissance artists rejected the flat, two-dimensional images of medieval painting in favor of the deep perspectives and fully rounded forms of ancient sculpture and painting. Although their themes were still often religious in nature, Renaissance artists portrayed their subjects more realistically than had medieval artists, using new techniques such as perspective. European scholars reexamined the writings of ancient philosophers, mathematicians, geographers, and scientists. They also studied scholarly Arab works brought home from the Crusades.

The Renaissance encouraged people to regard themselves as individuals, to have confidence in human capabilities, and to look forward to the fame their achievements might bring. This attitude prompted many to seek glory through adventure, discovery, and conquest. **D**

Vocabulary
secular: worldly rather than spiritual

MAIN IDEA

Drawing Conclusions
D How might Renaissance attitudes and ideas have influenced European explorers?

Science & Technology

🔗 hmhsocialstudies.com **INTERACTIVE**

THE CARAVEL
The caravel, the ship used by most early Portuguese and Spanish explorers, had many advantages over earlier vessels. It was lighter, swifter, and more maneuverable than other ships.

The triangular lateen sails, an innovation borrowed from Muslim ships, allowed the caravel to sail against the wind. Rigged with lateens, the ship could tack (sail on a zigzag course) more directly into the wind than could earlier European vessels.

The smaller deck at the stern provided protection from the rain.

The sternpost rudder allowed greater maneuverability.

The large hatch allowed goods to be stored below deck.

The shallow draft (the depth of the ship below the water line) made the ship ideal for coastal exploration.

Europe Enters a New Age of Expansion

Although Marco Polo's journey to China took place in the 1200s, it was not until 1477 that the first printed edition of Polo's account caused renewed interest in the East. Like other European merchants, Polo traveled to Asia by land. The expense and peril of such journeys led Europeans to seek alternative routes. European merchants and explorers listened to the reports of travelers and reexamined the maps drawn by ancient geographers.

SAILING TECHNOLOGY Europeans, however, needed more than maps to guide them through uncharted waters. On the open seas, winds easily blew ships off course. With only the sun, moon, and stars to guide them, few ships ventured beyond the sight of land. To overcome their fears, European ship captains adopted the compass and the astrolabe, navigating tools that helped plot direction. They also took advantage of innovations in sailing technology that allowed ships such as the caravel to sail against the wind. (See "The Caravel" on page 24.)

PORTUGAL TAKES THE LEAD Under Prince Henry the Navigator, Portugal developed and employed these innovations. Although Henry was only an armchair navigator, he earned his nickname by establishing an up-to-date sailing school and by sponsoring the earliest voyages.

For almost 40 years, Prince Henry sent his captains sailing farther and farther south along the west coast of Africa. Portuguese explorations continued after Prince Henry died. Bartolomeu Dias rounded the southern tip of Africa in 1488. Vasco da Gama reached India ten years later. By sailing around Africa to eastern Asia via the Indian Ocean, Portuguese traders were able to cut their costs and increase their profits.

While cartographers redrew their maps to show the route around Africa, an Italian sea captain named Christopher Columbus traveled from nation to nation with his own collection of maps and figures. Columbus believed there was an even shorter route to Asia—one that lay west across the Atlantic.

In Spain an adviser of Queen Isabella pointed out that support of the proposed venture would cost less than a week's entertainment of a foreign official. Isabella was convinced and summoned Columbus to appear before the Spanish court.

SECTION 4 ASSESSMENT

1. TERMS & NAMES For each term or name, write a sentence explaining its significance.
- Prince Henry
- hierarchy
- Crusades
- Reformation
- Renaissance
- nuclear family

MAIN IDEA

2. TAKING NOTES
Re-create the web below on your paper. Fill it in with the changes taking place in western Europe during the 1400s.

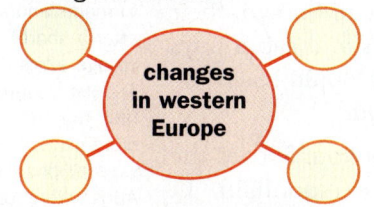

changes in western Europe

How did these changes help lead to the European Age of Exploration?

CRITICAL THINKING

3. ANALYZING ISSUES
Which European event of the late 1400s to early 1500s do you think had the most far-reaching impact on European lives? Explain and support your answer. **Think About:**
- the importance of religion
- the role of adventurers and explorers
- the increase in prosperity

4. SUMMARIZING
How did advances in technology open the way for world exploration?

5. DRAWING CONCLUSIONS
Why do you think other European nations lagged behind Portugal in the race for overseas exploration? Support your reasons with details from the text.

Transatlantic Encounters

MAIN IDEA	WHY IT MATTERS NOW	Terms & Names
Columbus's voyages set off a chain of events that brought together the peoples of Europe, Africa, and the Americas.	The interactions among the people of these three continents laid the foundations for modern multicultural America.	• Christopher Columbus • Taino • colonization • Columbian Exchange • Treaty of Tordesillas

One European's Story

Christopher Columbus, around 1519

hmhsocialstudies.com
TAKING NOTES

Use the graphic organizer online to take notes about Columbus's voyages and their effects.

In January 1492, the Genoese sailor **Christopher Columbus** stood before the Spanish court with a daring plan: he would find a route to Asia by sailing west across the Atlantic Ocean. The plan was accepted, and on August 3, 1492, Columbus embarked on a voyage that changed the course of history. He began his journal by restating the deal he had struck with Spain.

A PERSONAL VOICE CHRISTOPHER COLUMBUS

"Based on the information that I had given Your Highnesses about the land of India and about a Prince who is called the Great Khan [of China], which in our language means 'King of Kings,' Your Highnesses decided to send me . . . to the regions of India, to see . . . the peoples and the lands, and to learn of . . . the measures which could be taken for their conversion to our Holy Faith. . . . Your Highnesses . . . ordered that I shall go to the east, but not by land as is customary. I was to go by way of the west, whence until today we do not know with certainty that anyone has gone. . . . "

—*The Log of Christopher Columbus*

Although Columbus did not find a route to Asia, his voyage set in motion a process that brought together the American, European, and African worlds.

Columbus Crosses the Atlantic

The *Niña, Pinta,* and *Santa Maria* slid quietly out of a Spanish port in the predawn hours of August 3, 1492. Although they were setting out into the unknown, their crews included no soldiers, priests, or ambassadors—only sailors and cabin boys with a taste for the sea. In a matter of months, Columbus's fleet would reach the sandy shores of what was to Europeans an astonishing new world.

FIRST ENCOUNTERS At about 2 A.M. on October 12, 1492, a lookout aboard the *Pinta* caught sight of two white sand dunes sparkling in the moonlight. In between lay a mass of dark rocks. "*Tierra! Tierra!*" he shouted. "Land! Land!"

Background
Columbus had miscalculated the size of the earth and he expected to make landfall after a short voyage across the Atlantic Ocean. In fact, the shortest distance east to west across the Atlantic is about 1,600 miles.

At dawn Columbus went ashore and caught sight of a group of people who called themselves the **Taino** (tī′nō), or "noble ones." He renamed their island San Salvador, or "Holy Savior," and claimed it for Spain.

On the first day of their encounter, the generosity of the Taino startled Columbus. "They are friendly and well-dispositioned people who bear no arms," he wrote in his log. "They traded and gave everything they had with good will." But after only two days, Columbus offered an assessment of the Taino that had dark implications for the future.

A PERSONAL VOICE CHRISTOPHER COLUMBUS

" It would be unnecessary to build . . . [a fort here] because these people are so simple in deeds of arms. . . . If Your Highnesses order either to bring all of them to Castile or to hold them as captivos [slaves] on their own island it could easily be done, because with about fifty men you could control and subjugate them all, making them do whatever you want. "

—quoted in *Columbus: The Great Adventure*

GOLD, LAND, AND RELIGION The search for gold was one of the main reasons for Columbus's journey. On his second day in the Americas, Columbus expressed one of the main reasons he had embarked on his journey. "I have been very attentive," he wrote, "and have tried very hard to find out if there is any gold here." When he did not find gold on San Salvador, he left to look elsewhere. Columbus spent 96 days exploring some small islands in what is now the Bahamas and the coastlines of two other Caribbean islands, known today as Cuba and Hispaniola. All along the way, he bestowed Spanish names on territory he claimed for Spain. "It was my wish to bypass no island without taking possession," he wrote. Columbus also honored his promise to assert Christian domination. "In every place I have entered, islands and lands, I have always planted a cross," he noted on November 16. Less than two weeks later, he predicted, "Your Highnesses will order a city . . . built in these regions [for] these countries will be easily converted." **Ⓐ**

SPANISH FOOTHOLDS In early January 1493, Columbus began his trip back to Spain. Convinced that he had landed on islands off Asia known to Europeans as the Indies, Columbus called the people he met *los indios.* The term translated into "Indian," a word mistakenly applied to all the diverse peoples of the Americas.

Columbus's reports thrilled the Spanish monarchs, who funded three more voyages. When he set sail for the Americas in September 1493, Columbus was no longer an explorer but an empire builder. He commanded a fleet of some 17 ships and several hundred armed soldiers. He also brought five priests and more than 1,000 colonists, including *hidalgos,* or members of the minor nobility.

These European soldiers, priests, and colonists, and the many others that followed, would occupy first the Caribbean and then most of the Americas, and impose their will on the Native Americans who lived there. Their arrival on Hispaniola, the island presently divided between Haiti and the Dominican Republic, signaled the start of a cultural clash that would continue for the next five centuries.

MAIN IDEA

Summarizing
Ⓐ What activities preoccupied Columbus as he explored the Americas?

HISTORICAL SPOTLIGHT

THE VIKINGS

The first Europeans to reach North America were probably Vikings. About 982, the Norwegian Viking Eric the Red crossed the Atlantic in an open boat and set up two colonies on Greenland. Some fifteen years later, his son, Leif, voyaged farther to a place he called Vinland the Good because of its abundant grapes. Historians now believe that present-day Newfoundland is Leif Ericson's Vinland. In 1963, archaeologists discovered there a half-burned timbered house of Norse design that dates to about the year 1000.

According to Norwegian sagas, or tales of great deeds, another Norwegian expedition followed Leif Ericson's and stayed in Newfoundland for three years. Then the Skraelings, as the saga calls the native peoples, drove away the colonists, and the Vikings never returned.

The Impact on Native Americans

The Taino who greeted Columbus in 1492 could not have imagined the colonization and outbreaks of disease that would soon follow. While the Taino resisted Spanish control, there was little they could do against the viruses and diseases that accompanied the new settlers.

METHODS OF COLONIZATION The European system of **colonization**—the establishment of distant settlements controlled by the parent country—was established long before Columbus set sail for Hispaniola. During the Crusades, Italians from Venice had taken over Arab sugar farms in what is now Lebanon. By the late 1400s, the Portuguese had established plantation colonies on islands off the coast of West Africa, and Spain had colonized the Canary Islands.

From this experience, Europeans learned the advantages of using the plantation system. They also realized the economic benefits of using forced labor. Finally, they learned to use European weapons to dominate a people who had less sophisticated weapons. These tactics would be used in full against the peoples that the Europeans called Indians. **B**

RESISTANCE AND CONQUEST The natives of the Caribbean, however, did not succumb to Columbus and the Spaniards without fighting. In November of 1493, Columbus attempted to conquer the present-day island of St. Croix. Instead of surrendering, the inhabitants defended themselves by firing rounds of poisoned arrows. The Spaniards won easily, but the struggle proved that Native Americans would not yield in the easy conquest predicted by Columbus.

Controlling the Taino who inhabited Hispaniola was even more difficult. After several rebellions, the Taino submitted to Columbus for several years but revolted again in 1495. The Spanish response was swift and cruel. A later settler, the missionary Bartolomé de Las Casas, criticized the Spaniards' brutal response.

A PERSONAL VOICE BARTOLOMÉ DE LAS CASAS

"This tactic begun here . . . [will soon] spread throughout these Indies and will end when there is no more land nor people to subjugate and destroy in this part of the world."

—quoted in *Columbus: The Great Adventure*

In this series of drawings from an Aztec codex, or book (c. 1575), a medicine man takes care of an Aztec with smallpox, a deadly disease brought to the Americas by Europeans.

DISEASE RAVAGES THE NATIVE AMERICANS European settlers brought deadly diseases such as measles, mumps, chicken pox, smallpox, and typhus, which devastated Native Americans, who had not developed any natural immunity to these diseases. They died by the thousands. According to one estimate, nearly one-third of Hispaniola's estimated 300,000 inhabitants died during Columbus's time there. By 1508, fewer than 100,000 survivors lived on the island. Sixty years later, only two villages were left. These illnesses would soon spread to the rest of the Americas. More surely than any army, disease conquered region after region. **C**

MAIN IDEA

Summarizing
B Where did Europeans first experiment with the plantation system?

MAIN IDEA

Analyzing Effects
C How did the arrival of European settlers affect Native American societies?

The Slave Trade Begins

With disease reducing the native work force, European settlers turned to Africa for slaves. In the coming years, European slave ships would haul hundreds of thousands of Africans across the Atlantic to toil in the Americas.

A NEW SLAVE LABOR FORCE The enslavement of Native Americans was a controversial issue among the Spaniards. Unfortunately, the Spanish saw the use of Africans as a possible solution to the colonies' labor shortage. Advised Las Casas, "The labor of one . . . [African] . . . [is] more valuable than that of four Indians; every effort should be made to bring many . . . [Africans] from Guinea."

As more natives died of disease, the demand for Africans grew. The price of enslaved Africans rose, and more Europeans joined the slave trade. African slavery was becoming an essential part of the European-American economic system. **D**

AFRICAN LOSSES The Atlantic slave trade would devastate many African societies, which lost many of their fittest members. Before the slave trade ended in the 1800s, it would drain Africa of at least 12 million people.

MAIN IDEA

Forming Generalizations
D Why did European settlers increase their demand for enslaved Africans?

The Impact on Europeans

Columbus's voyages had profound effects on Europe as well. Merchants and monarchs saw an opportunity to increase their wealth and influence. Ordinary people saw a chance to live in a new world, relatively free of social and economic constraints. Within a century, thousands of Europeans began crossing the Atlantic in what became one of the biggest voluntary migrations in history.

THE COLUMBIAN EXCHANGE The voyages of Columbus and others led to the introduction of new plants and animals to Europe, Africa, and the Americas. Ships took plants and animals from the Americas back to Europe and to Africa and brought items from the Eastern Hemisphere to the Western Hemisphere. This global transfer of living things, called the **Columbian Exchange,** began with Columbus's first voyage and continues today.

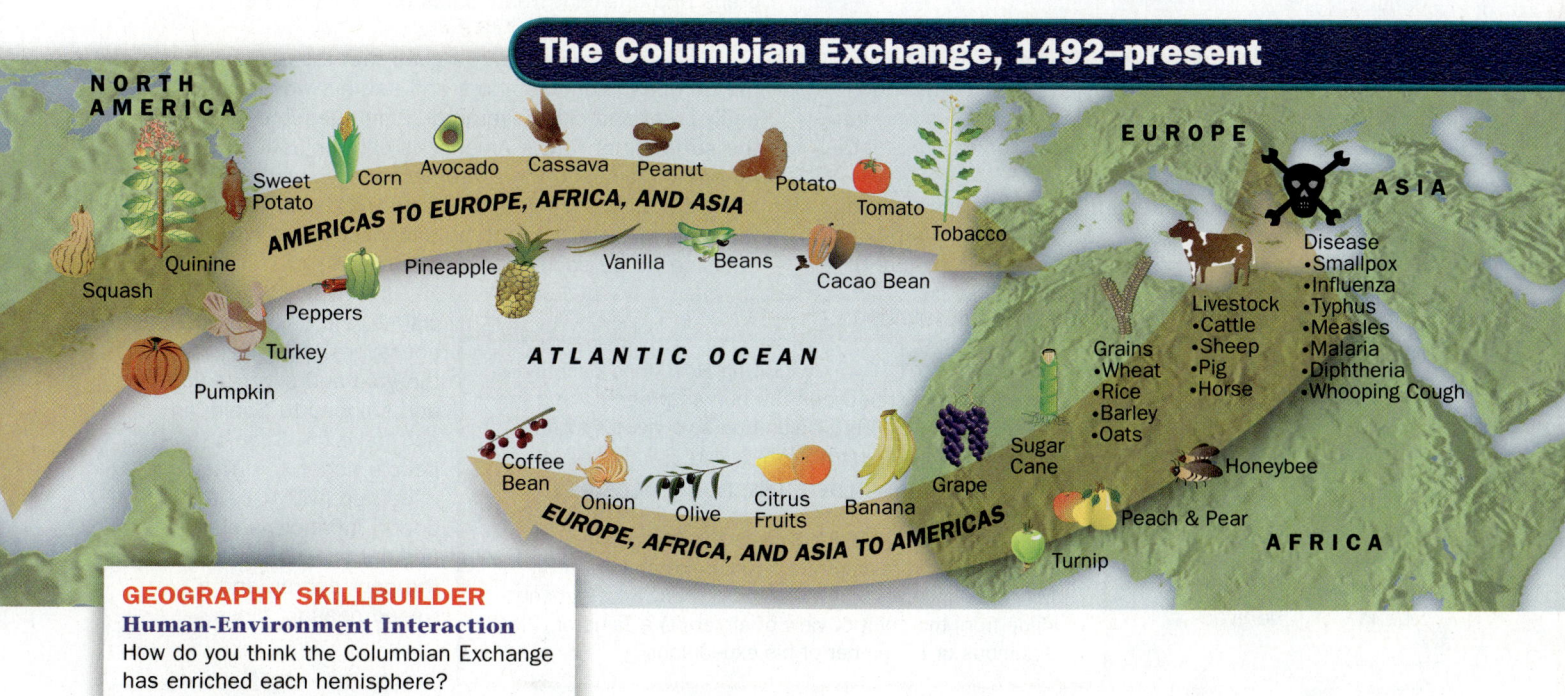

The Columbian Exchange, 1492–present

NORTH AMERICA

EUROPE

ASIA

AMERICAS TO EUROPE, AFRICA, AND ASIA

Sweet Potato · Corn · Avocado · Cassava · Peanut · Potato · Tomato · Tobacco

Quinine · Pineapple · Vanilla · Beans · Cacao Bean

Squash · Peppers · Turkey · Pumpkin

ATLANTIC OCEAN

EUROPE, AFRICA, AND ASIA TO AMERICAS

Coffee Bean · Onion · Olive · Citrus Fruits · Banana · Grape · Sugar Cane · Turnip · Peach & Pear

Grains
•Wheat
•Rice
•Barley
•Oats

Livestock
•Cattle
•Sheep
•Pig
•Horse

Honeybee

Disease
•Smallpox
•Influenza
•Typhus
•Measles
•Malaria
•Diphtheria
•Whooping Cough

AFRICA

GEOGRAPHY SKILLBUILDER
Human-Environment Interaction
How do you think the Columbian Exchange has enriched each hemisphere?

NATIONAL RIVALRIES Overseas expansion inflamed European rivalries. Portugal, the pioneer in navigation and exploration, deeply resented Spain's sudden conquests. In 1493, Pope Alexander VI, a Spaniard, stepped in to avoid war between the two nations. In the **Treaty of Tordesillas** (tôr′də-sē′əs), signed in 1494, Spain and Portugal agreed to divide the Western Hemisphere between them. Lands to the west of an imaginary vertical line drawn in the Atlantic, including most of the Americas, belonged to Spain. Lands to the east of this line, including Brazil, belonged to Portugal.

The plan proved impossible to enforce. Its only long-lasting effect was to give Portugal a colony—Brazil—in a South America that was largely Spanish. Otherwise, the agreement had no effect on the English, Dutch, or French, all of whom began colonizing the Americas during the early 1600s. **E**

HISTORY

VIDEO
Christopher Columbus: Explorer of the New World

hmhsocialstudies.com

A New Society Is Born

Christopher Columbus lived on Hispaniola until 1500. That year, King Ferdinand and Queen Isabella, dissatisfied with the explorer's inability to maintain order on the island, ordered him to leave. After further travels throughout the Caribbean,

MAIN IDEA

Making Inferences
E Why might Spain and Portugal have been willing to go to war over the issue of overseas exploration?

P O I N T

"Columbus's achievements were historic and heroic."

Many historians argue that Columbus's fateful voyages produced many long-term benefits. As the journalist Paul Gray notes, "Columbus's journey was the first step in a long process that eventually produced the United States of America, . . . a symbol and a haven of individual liberty for people throughout the world."

Other historians suggest that respect is due Columbus for the sheer dimension of the change he caused.

"The Columbian discovery was of greater magnitude than any other discovery or invention in human history. . . . both because of the . . . development of the New World and because of the numerous other discoveries that have stemmed from it," asserts the historian Paolo Emilio Taviani.

Some historians contend that, although millions of Native Americans were enslaved or killed by Europeans and the diseases they brought with them, this does not detract from Columbus's achievements. They argue that sacrifice is often necessary for the sake of progress. Further, they claim that, like any historical figure, Columbus was a man of his time and ought not to be condemned for acting according to the values of the age in which he lived.

C O U N T E R P O I N T

"The legacy of Columbus is primarily one of 'genocide, cruelty, and slavery.'"

Some historians have questioned the traditional view of Columbus as a hero. The historian Hans Konig argues that Columbus's legacy should be deplored rather than celebrated: "The year 1492 opened an era of genocide, cruelty, and slavery on a larger scale than had ever been seen before." Speaking to the experience of Native Americans in particular, the activist Suzan Shown Harjo insists that "this half millennium of land grabs and one-cent treaty sales has been no bargain [for Native Americans]."

Historian Howard Zinn argues that the actions of the European conquistadors and settlers were unnecessarily cruel and plainly immoral. Zinn questions whether the suffering of Native Americans can be justified by European gains: "If there *are* necessary sacrifices to be made for human progress, is it not essential to hold to the principle that those to be sacrificed must make the decision [to be sacrificed] themselves?"

In any event, Konig claims, the balance does not favor Columbus: "all the gold and silver stolen and shipped to Spain did not make the Spanish people richer. . . . They ended up [with] . . . a deadly inflation, a starving population, the rich richer, the poor poorer, and a ruined peasant class."

THINKING CRITICALLY

1. **CONNECT TO TODAY** Evaluating How does each side view the tradeoff between the human progress and the violence resulting from Columbus's voyages? With which side do you agree? Why?

    SEE SKILLBUILDER HANDBOOK, PAGE R14.

2. **CONNECT TO HISTORY** Developing Historical Perspective Do research to find out more about the Taino's encounters with Columbus. Then, write a monologue from the point of view of either (1) a Taino or (2) Columbus or a member of his expeditions.

Columbus reluctantly returned to Spain in 1504, where he died two years later. The daring sea captain went to his grave disappointed that he had not reached China.

Neither Columbus nor anyone else could have foreseen the long chain of events that his voyages set in motion. In time, settlers from England would transplant their cultures to colonies in North America. From within these colonies would emerge a new society—and a new nation—based on ideas of representative government and religious tolerance.

The story of the United States of America thus begins with a meeting of North American, African, and European peoples and cultures that radically transformed all three worlds. The upheaval threw unfamiliar peoples and customs together on a grand scale. Although the Europeans tried to impose their ways on Native Americans and Africans, they never completely succeeded. Their need to borrow from the peoples they sought to dominate proved too strong. Furthermore, the Native Americans and Africans resisted giving up their cultural identities. The new nation that emerged would blend elements of these three worlds, as well as others, in a distinctly multicultural society. Throughout the history of the United States, this multiculturalism would be one of its greatest challenges and also one of its greatest assets.

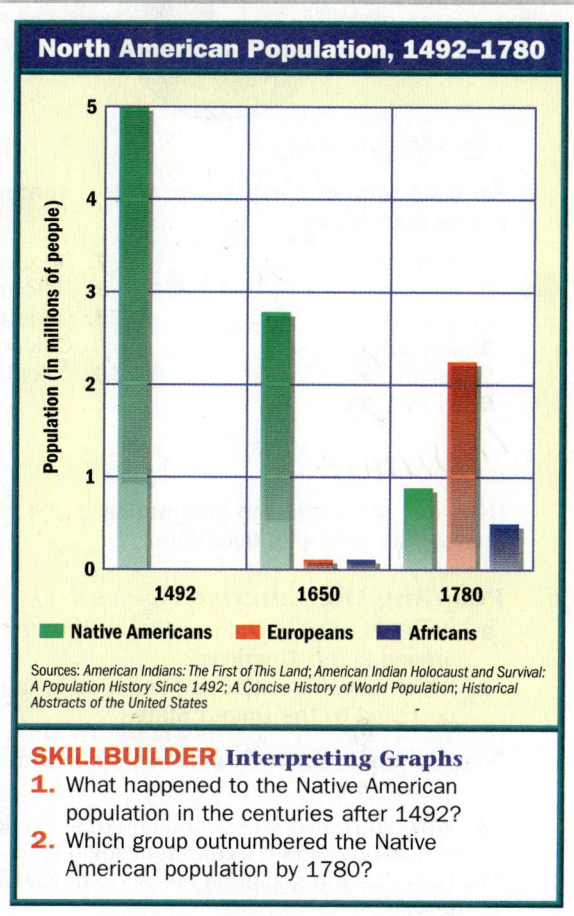

North American Population, 1492–1780

Population (in millions of people)

■ Native Americans   ■ Europeans   ■ Africans

Sources: *American Indians: The First of This Land; American Indian Holocaust and Survival: A Population History Since 1492; A Concise History of World Population; Historical Abstracts of the United States*

SKILLBUILDER Interpreting Graphs
1. What happened to the Native American population in the centuries after 1492?
2. Which group outnumbered the Native American population by 1780?

ASSESSMENT

1. TERMS & NAMES For each term or name, write a sentence explaining its significance.
- Christopher Columbus
- colonization
- Columbian Exchange
- Treaty of Tordesillas
- Taino

MAIN IDEA

2. TAKING NOTES
Create a time line of the major events of Columbus's voyages and interactions with Native Americans. Use the dates already plotted on the time line below as a guide.

How did the Americas change during Columbus's lifetime as a result of his voyages?

CRITICAL THINKING

3. DEVELOPING HISTORICAL PERSPECTIVE
Why did European explorers believe they could simply claim lands for their home countries, even though these lands were already populated?

4. SUMMARIZING
In the centuries before Columbus's voyages, where had Europeans gained experience in colonization?

5. ANALYZING EFFECTS
What do you think were three of the most important long-term consequences of Columbus's encounters in the Americas?
Think About:
- conquering and claiming land
- forced labor of Native Americans and Africans
- the Columbian Exchange

TERMS & NAMES

For each term or name below, write a sentence explaining its significance.

1. nomadic
2. Aztec
3. Iroquois
4. division of labor
5. Islam
6. plantation
7. Renaissance
8. Reformation
9. Christopher Columbus
10. colonization

MAIN IDEAS

Use your notes and the information in the chapter to answer the following questions.

Peopling the Americas *(pages 4–7)*

1. What theories explain when and how the first people arrived in the Americas?
2. Which ancient societies flourished in the region now occupied by the United States?

North American Societies Around 1492
(pages 8–13)

3. Why did Native American societies develop different cultural traditions in different regions?
4. Describe the social organization of Native American groups.

West African Societies Around 1492
(pages 14–19)

5. Why was Timbuktu such an important city?
6. Which religion did traders from North Africa bring with them to West Africa?

European Societies Around 1492
(pages 20–25)

7. How did religion reinforce the social hierarchy of European societies?
8. How did the Reformation deepen rivalries between European nations?

Transatlantic Encounters *(pages 26–31)*

9. What impact did the Columbian Exchange have on people's lives throughout the world?
10. Why did the Spanish want to colonize the Americas?

CRITICAL THINKING

1. **USING YOUR NOTES** In a web like the one shown, describe how trade and commerce affected each region and time period shown.

2. **DEVELOPING HISTORICAL PERSPECTIVE** How do you think the contrasting cultural attitudes to land ownership might have affected the relationship between Europeans and Native Americans?

VISUAL SUMMARY **THREE WORLDS MEET**

c. 20,000 B.C.
Asian peoples began migrating to the Americas.

THE AMERICAS

1400s
In West Africa, sophisticated and ancient societies were flourishing during the 1400s.

1492
The Spanish began exploring and colonizing the southwest and southern regions of North America.

Use the quotation below and your knowledge of U.S. history to answer questions 1 and 2.

> " 'The earth is our mother. The sky is our father.' This concept of nature . . . is at the center of the Native American world view. . . . The Native American's attitudes toward this landscape have been formulated over a long period of time, a span that reaches back to the end of the Ice Age. . . . [T]he Indian has assumed a deep ethical regard for the earth and sky, a reverence for the natural world. . . . It is this ancient ethic of the Native American that must shape our efforts to preserve the earth and the life upon and within it. "
>
> —N. Scott Momaday, "A First American Views His Land," *National Geographic,* July 1976

1 N. Scott Momaday refers to the Ice Age because—

(1) Native Americans' attitudes to the land were formed during the Ice Age.

(2) the landscape of the Americas took its present shape during the last Ice Age.

(3) that was when European immigrants first arrived in the Americas.

(4) he wants to show how long Native Americans have been living in the Americas.

2 In this passage, Momaday describes the "ancient ethic"—Native American reverence for the land—in order to —

(1) contrast it with modern attitudes.

(2) dismiss it as unimportant.

(3) present it as a quaint, old-fashioned idea.

(4) suggest that European Americans will never accept it.

3 Why did the Spanish begin importing enslaved Africans?

(1) The Spanish were weakened by disease and could not work.

(2) There was a labor shortage in the Americas.

(3) They wanted to compete with the British colonies.

(4) The Spanish wanted colonies in Africa.

4 Unlike some West African and Native American societies at the time, European societies in the 1400s had *not* developed —

(1) matrilineal kinship systems.

(2) systems of mathematics and astronomy.

(3) a centralized religious authority.

(4) agriculture.

  hmhsocialstudies.com TEST PRACTICE

For additional test practice, go online for:
- Diagnostic tests
- Tutorials

INTERACT WITH HISTORY

Think about the issues you explored at the beginning of the chapter. Now that you know how Native Americans' way of life was changed by the arrival of the Europeans, form small groups and discuss the following question: Would you have resisted or helped the Europeans if you had been a Native American during the days of European colonization?

FOCUS ON WRITING

Imagine that you are one of the Taino people. You have just seen a landing party from Christopher Columbus's expedition arrive on the shores near your village. Based on what you have read in this chapter, write a paragraph describing your first encounter with the expedition, your reactions to the explorers, and your thoughts about further contact.

COLLABORATIVE LEARNING

Organize into pairs and use library or Internet sources to find excerpts from the journals of early explorers such as Columbus or Cabeza de Vaca. After reading, work together to list the assumptions and conclusions drawn by the writer about the new land and peoples he encountered. Write a paragraph explaining how these assumptions affected the interactions between explorers and native peoples.

THE Maya

The Maya developed one of the most advanced civilizations in the Americas, but their story is shrouded in mystery. Around A.D. 250, the Maya began to build great cities in southern Mexico and Central America. They developed a writing system, practiced astronomy, and built magnificent palaces and pyramids with little more than stone tools. Around A.D. 900, however, the Maya abandoned their cities, leaving their monuments to be reclaimed by the jungle and, for a time, forgotten.

Explore some of the incredible monuments and cultural achievements of the ancient Maya online. You can find a wealth of information, video clips, primary sources, and more at hmhsocialstudies.com .

Destroying the Maya's Past
Watch the video to learn how the actions of one Spanish missionary nearly destroyed the written record of the Maya world.

Finding the City of Palenque
Watch the video to learn about the great Maya city of Palenque and the European discovery of the site in the eighteenth century.

"Thus let it be done! Let the emptiness be filled! Let the water recede and make a void, let the earth appear and become solid; let it be done . . . "Earth!" they said, and instantly it was made."

The Popol Vuh
Read the document to learn how the Maya believed the world was created.

Pakal's Tomb
Watch the video to explore how the discovery of the tomb of a great king helped archaeologists piece together the Maya past.

THE AMERICAN COLONIES EMERGE

Essential Question

What were the reasons for European colonization of the Americas?

 New York Standards

KEY IDEA 1 The study of New York State and United States history requires an analysis of the development of American culture, its diversity and multicultural context, and the ways people are unified by many values, practices, and traditions.

KEY IDEA 3 Study about the major social, political, economic, cultural, and religious developments in New York State and United States history involves learning about the important roles and contributions of individuals and groups.

SECTION 1: Spain's Empire in the Americas

SECTION 2: An English Settlement at Jamestown

SECTION 3: Puritan New England

SECTION 4: Settlement of the Middle Colonies

17th-century English explorers land in North America.

1521 Hernándo Cortés conquers the Aztec Empire.

1540 Coronado explores the American southwest.

1565 Spanish settlers establish Saint Augustine, Florida.

1585 English colonists establish a colony at Roanoke Island.

AMERICAS
WORLD

1500

1550

1517 Martin Luther begins the Protestant Reformation.

1534 Parliament declares Henry VIII head of the English church.

1588 England defeats the Spanish Armada.

INTERACT
WITH HISTORY

It is 1607. You are a colonist about to arrive in the land that England has claimed for itself and named Virginia. Although little is known about this place, you look forward to a life of adventure and prosperity. When you arrive, you are met by Native Americans who ask you why you have come to their land.

Explore the Issues

- As a colonist, how does the presence of another people change your expectations?
- What obligations does a colonist have to natives who already inhabit the land?

1607 John Smith and other colonists establish Jamestown.

1620 English "Pilgrims" found Plymouth Colony.

1630 English Puritans found the Massachusetts Bay Colony.

1664 England takes New Amsterdam from the Dutch.

1681 William Penn receives charter for Pennsylvania.

1650

1700

1618 The Thirty Years War between Catholics and Protestants begins in central Europe.

1649 Oliver Cromwell establishes the Puritan Commonwealth in England.

1660 The English monarchy is restored with the accession of Charles II.

The American Colonies Emerge **35**

PI 3.2

CC Unit 2.I.A.2.a
CC Unit 2.I.A.2.c

Spain's Empire in the Americas

MAIN IDEA

Throughout the 1500s and 1600s, the Spanish conquered Central and portions of North America.

WHY IT MATTERS NOW

Spanish language, religion, and architecture continue to influence the Americas.

Terms & Names

- **Hernándo Cortés**
- **conquistador**
- **New Spain**
- **mestizo**
- *encomienda*
- **Juan Ponce de León**
- **New Mexico**
- **Popé**

One American's Story

hmhsocialstudies.com

TAKING NOTES

Use the graphic organizer online to take notes on how Spain established a profitable empire in the Americas.

In 1519, the native world near Tabasco in southeastern Mexico changed forever. That year, **Hernándo Cortés** led an army into the American mainland, eager to claim new lands for Spain. The peoples of the Tabasco, a province of the mighty Aztec empire, resisted the invaders but were no match for the Spaniards' rifles and cannons.

In surrendering, the natives handed over to the Spaniards 20 women, one of whom came to be called Doña Marina, or Malinche. Malinche easily mastered the Spanish language and soon acted as both translator and guide for Cortés as he fought and negotiated his way through Mexico. She also proved to be a brave and daring warrior. Bernal Díaz del Castillo, one of Cortés's foot soldiers, noted Malinche's courage.

▲ **Malinche** *(center)* **translates for Cortés** *(seated)* **and three Aztec ambassadors.**

★ A PERSONAL VOICE BERNAL DÍAZ DEL CASTILLO

" Doña Marina . . . possessed such manly valor that, although she had heard every day how the Indians were going to kill us and eat our flesh with chili, and had seen us surrounded in the late battles, and knew that all of us were wounded or sick, yet never allowed us to see any sign of fear in her, only . . . courage."

—quoted in *Notable Latin American Women*

Malinche played a key role in the early stages of the Spanish conquest of the Americas. As the first European settlers in the Americas, the Spanish greatly enriched their empire and left a mark on the cultures of North and South America that still exists today.

The Spanish Claim a New Empire

In the wake of Columbus's voyages, Spanish explorers took to the seas to claim new colonies for Spain. Lured by the prospect of vast lands filled with gold and silver, these explorers, known as **conquistadors** (conquerors), pushed first into the Caribbean region—the islands and coast of Central and South America along the Caribbean Sea. Then they swept through Mexico and south to the tip of South America.

CORTÉS SUBDUES THE AZTEC Soon after landing in Mexico, Cortés learned of the vast and wealthy Mexica, or Aztec, empire, located deep in the region's interior. The Aztec, members of the diverse Nahua peoples of central Mexico, dominated the region. Cortés set off to conquer the Aztec with a force of 600 soldiers, 17 horses, numerous dogs, and 10 cannons. As he marched inland, Cortés, a gifted diplomat as well as military leader, convinced those Nahua who had long resented the spread of Aztec power to join his ranks.

After marching for weeks through 200 miles of difficult mountain passes, Cortés and his legions finally looked on the magnificent Aztec capital of Tenochtitlán. The Spaniards marveled at Tenochtitlán, with its towering temples and elaborate engineering works—including a system that brought fresh water into the city. "We were amazed," Bernal Díaz said of his first glimpse of Tenochtitlán. "Some of our soldiers even asked whether the things we saw were not a dream." While the Aztec city astonished the Spaniards, the capital's glittering gold stock seemed to hypnotize them. "They picked up the gold and fingered it like monkeys," one Native American witness recalled. "They hungered like pigs for that gold." **A**

Convinced at first that Cortés was an armor-clad god, the Aztec emperor Montezuma agreed to give the Spanish explorer a share of the empire's existing gold supply. Cortés, who admitted that he and his comrades had "a disease of the heart that only gold can cure," eventually forced the Aztec to mine more gold and silver. In the spring of 1520, the Aztec rebelled against the Spaniards' intrusion. It is believed that, before driving out Cortes's forces, the Aztec stoned Montezuma to death, having come to regard him as a traitor.

While they successfully repelled the Spanish invaders, the natives found they could do little to stop disease. By the time Cortés launched a counterattack in 1521, the Spanish and their native allies overran an Aztec force that was greatly reduced by smallpox and measles. After several months of fighting, the invaders finally sacked and burned Tenochtitlán, and the Aztec surrendered. **B**

A Native American depiction ▶ of Aztec archers battling Cortés's troops

While flames still flickered in the shattered capital, Cortés laid plans for the colony of **New Spain,** whose capital he called Mexico City. Within three years, Spanish churches and homes rose from the foundations of old native temples and palaces in Mexico City. Cathedrals and a university followed.

SPANISH PATTERN OF CONQUEST In building their new American empire, the Spaniards drew from techniques used during the reconquest of Spain from the Moors, a Muslim people from North Africa who had occupied Spain for centuries. When conquering the Moors in the late 1400s, the Spanish lived among them and imposed upon them their Spanish culture.

"You and your people, . . . entering with such speed and fury into my country, . . . as to strike terror into our hearts."

NATIVE AMERICAN CHIEF, TO SPANISH EXPLORER HERNANDO DE SOTO

Spanish settlers in the Americas were mostly men and were known as *peninsulares.* Marriage between peninsulares and native women was common. These marriages created a large **mestizo**— or mixed Spanish and Native American—population. Their descendants live today in Mexico, other Latin American countries, and the United States.

Although the Spanish conquerors lived among and intermarried with the native people, they also oppressed them. In their effort to exploit the land for its precious resources, the Spanish forced the native workers to labor within a system known as *encomienda,* in which the natives farmed, ranched, or mined for Spanish landlords, who had received the rights to their labor from Spanish authorities.

The harsh pattern of labor that emerged under the *encomienda* caused priests such as Antonio de Montesinos to demand its end in a sermon delivered in 1511.

> **A PERSONAL VOICE** FRAY ANTONIO DE MONTESINOS
> "Tell me, by what right or justice do you hold these Indians in such a cruel and horrible servitude? . . . Why do you keep them so oppressed and exhausted, without giving them enough to eat or curing them of the sicknesses they incur from the excessive labor you give them? . . . Are you not bound to love them as you love yourselves? Don't you understand this? Don't you feel this?"
>
> —quoted in *Reflections, Writing for Columbus*

In 1542, the Spanish monarchy, which had tried to encourage fair treatment of native subjects, abolished the *encomienda.* To meet their intense labor needs, the Spaniards instead turned to other labor systems and began to use African slaves. **C**

MAIN IDEA

Analyzing Causes
C Why did the Spanish begin to use African slaves on their plantations in the New World?

The Conquistadors Push North

Dreaming of new conquests and more gold, and afraid that European nations might invade their American empire from the north, Spain undertook a series of expeditions into what would become the southeastern and southwestern United States.

EXPLORING FLORIDA In 1513, on Easter Sunday—a day the Spaniards called *pascua florida,* or "feast of flowers"— explorer **Juan Ponce de León** spied a tree-covered beach. In honor of the holiday, he named the land *La Florida.* For almost five decades, the Spanish probed La Florida and the surrounding areas for gold, battling the local residents, disease, and starvation. In 1562, discouraged by the lack of economic success, Spain abandoned further exploration of Florida.

Within months of Spain's departure, a band of French settlers arrived near what is now Jacksonville. Accompanying the settlers were French pirates, or buccaneers, who quickly took interest in Spain's treasure-filled ships sailing from the Gulf of Mexico. Consequently, Spain reversed its decision to abandon Florida and ordered one of its fiercest warriors, Pedro Menéndez de Avilés, to drive the French out of the area.

VIDEO
Claiming Florida
for Spain

hmhsocialstudies.com

European Exploration of the Americas, 1492–1682

hmhsocialstudies.com **INTERACTIVE MAP**

GREENLAND

ICELAND

Arctic Circle

Hudson 1610–11

Hudson 1609

Cabot 1497

ENGLAND

Cartier 1534–35

EUROPE

FRANCE

Hudson
Bay

NORTH
AMERICA

La Salle
1679–1682

Joliet and Marquette
1672–73

DeSoto
1539–42

PORTUGAL

SPAIN

Azores

ATLANTIC
OCEAN

Coronado
1540–42

Santa Fe

Ponce de Léon
1512–13

Madeira

Cabrillo 1542–43

PACIFIC
OCEAN

Tropic of Cancer

Gulf of
Mexico

Hispaniola

Verrazzano 1524

Canary
Islands

AFRICA

Cortés 1519

CUBA

Columbus 1492

Cabeza de Vaca
1528–36

Veracruz

Santo Domingo

Columbus 1493–96

Tenochtitlán
(Mexico City)

Caribbean Sea

Columbus 1502–03

Vespucci
1499–1500

Balboa
1510–13

Columbus 1498

Pizarro
1530–35

Equator

SOUTH
AMERICA

120°W   100°W   20°W

Juan de la Cosa, pilot-navigator on Columbus's ship *Niña*, drew the known
world on this oxhide map in 1500.

Spanish
Columbus
French
English
Dutch

0   1,000   2,000 miles
0   1,000   2,000 kilometers

GEOGRAPHY SKILLBUILDER
1. **Movement** How many voyages to
   the Americas did Columbus make?
2. **Place** In what years did England
   and France sail to the Americas and
   which regions did they explore?

Spanish Missions in the Southwest

The missions built by the friars who accompanied the conquistadors combined the rich architectural heritage of Spain with symbols and traditions familiar to their Native American converts.

Most missions were a series of buildings grouped around a courtyard, which was used for festivals or services. These courtyards acknowledged the Native American practice of worshipping in the open air.

◀ In Texas and California, bells used to summon people to worship were often hung in *espadañas*, tiered clusters framed by a rounded wall meant to resemble a cloud. To the Native Americans of the Southwest, clouds represented power.

Mission San Miguel, California

Mission San Luis Rey de Francia, California

Menéndez de Avilés not only drove out the French but in 1565 established a lonely outpost, which he called St. Augustine. It has survived to become the oldest European-founded city in the present-day United States.

SETTLING THE SOUTHWEST In 1540, in search of another wealthy empire to conquer, Francisco Vásquez de Coronado led the first Spanish expedition into what is now Arizona, New Mexico, Texas, Oklahoma, and Kansas. After wandering for two years, the only precious metal he carried home was his own battered gold-plated armor.

The Spaniards who followed in Coronado's wake came to the Southwest largely to search for veins of silver ore or to spread the Roman Catholic religion. As the native population dwindled from disease, Spanish priests gathered the surviving natives into large communities, called *congregaciónes*. In the winter of 1609–1610, Pedro de Peralta, governor of Spain's northern holdings, called **New Mexico**, led missionary priests and other settlers to a tributary of the upper Rio Grande. Together they built a capital called Santa Fe, or "Holy Faith." In the next two decades, several Christian missions were built among the Pueblos in the area. The hooves of pack mules wore down a 1,500-mile trail known as *el Camino Real*, or "the Royal Road," as they carried goods back and forth between Santa Fe and Mexico City. **D**

Resistance to the Spanish

The Catholic missionaries who settled north of Mexico not only tried to Christianize the peoples they encountered but also attempted to impose Spanish culture on them. The native inhabitants of New Mexico resisted and eventually rebelled against the Spaniards' attempts to transform their lives and beliefs.

CONFLICT IN NEW MEXICO While Spanish priests converted scores of Native Americans in New Mexico, tension marked the relationship between the priests and their new converts. As they sought to transform the Native Americans' cultures, Spanish priests and soldiers smashed and burned objects held sacred by

Background
The journeys of explorers such as Coronado and Peralta helped the Spanish to appreciate the vastness of the North American continent.

MAIN IDEA

Analyzing Motives
D Why did the Spanish build a road between Santa Fe and Mexico City?

Vocabulary
conversion:
A change in which a person adopts a new belief, opinion, or religion

local communities and suppressed many of their ceremonial dances and rituals.

During the 1670s, priests and soldiers around Santa Fe began forcing Native Americans to help support the missions by paying a tribute, an offering of either goods or services. The tribute was usually a bushel of maize or a deer hide, but the Spanish also forced Native Americans to work for them and sometimes abused them physically. Native Americans who practiced their native religion or refused to pay tribute were beaten.

POPÉ'S REBELLION One unfortunate Native American who felt the sting of a Spanish whip was the Pueblo religious leader **Popé.** The priests punished Popé for his worship practices, which they interpreted as witchcraft. The whipping left the Pueblo leader scarred with hatred and ready for rebellion. In 1680, he led a well-organized uprising against the Spanish that involved some 17,000 people from villages all over New Mexico. The triumphant fighters destroyed Spanish churches, executed priests, and drove the Spaniards back into New Spain. "The heathen," one Spanish officer wrote about the uprising, "have concealed a mortal hatred for our holy faith and enmity for the Spanish nation." For the next 14 years—until Spanish armies regained control of the area—the southwest region of the future United States once again belonged to its original inhabitants. **E**

But Spain would never again have complete control of the Americas. In 1588, England had defeated the Spanish Armada, ending Spain's naval dominance in the Atlantic. In time, England began forging colonies along the eastern shore of North America, thus extending its own empire in the New World.

MAIN IDEA

Analyzing Causes

E Why did the Native Americans of New Mexico revolt against the Spanish settlers?

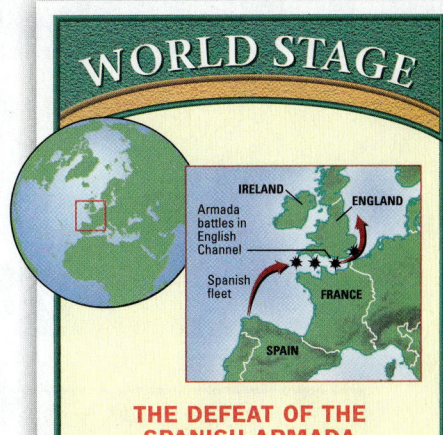

WORLD STAGE

THE DEFEAT OF THE SPANISH ARMADA

To stop English raids on his treasure ships, King Philip II of Spain assembled an armada, or fleet, of about 130 ships, carrying nearly 19,000 soldiers. In the summer of 1588, the Spanish Armada sailed into the English Channel. However, English warships out-maneuvered the vessels, bombarding them with heavy, long-range cannons.

Aiding the English cannons were powerful storms that destroyed much of the Armada. Its defeat dealt a blow to Spain's military power and opened the way for the rest of Europe to venture into the Americas.

SECTION 1 ASSESSMENT

1. TERMS & NAMES For each term or name, write a sentence explaining its significance.
- Hernándo Cortés
- conquistador
- New Spain
- mestizo
- *encomienda*
- Juan Ponce de León
- New Mexico
- Popé

MAIN IDEA

2. TAKING NOTES
Re-create the web below on your paper and fill in events related to the main idea in the center.

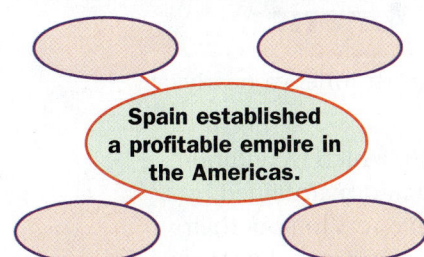

Spain established a profitable empire in the Americas.

CRITICAL THINKING

3. EVALUATING IMPACT
Do you agree or disagree with this statement: The Spanish conquest of the Aztecs, which led to the creation of Mexico, was neither a triumph nor a defeat? Support your opinion with references to the text.

Think About:
- the actions of the conquistadors
- the effects of disease on the native peoples
- the *encomienda* system
- the mestizo population in Mexico today

4. FORMING GENERALIZATIONS
State three main ideas about the Spaniards' exploration and settlement north of Mexico and their interaction with Native Americans there.

5. MAKING INFERENCES
What can you infer from the fact that approximately 17,000 Native Americans from all over New Mexico took part in Popé's rebellion?

An English Settlement at Jamestown

MAIN IDEA	WHY IT MATTERS NOW	Terms & Names
The first permanent English settlement in North America was founded at Jamestown, Virginia, in 1607.	English colonies in Virginia developed into the present states of the southern United States.	• John Smith • joint-stock companies • Jamestown • Powhatan • headright system • indentured servant • royal colony • Nathaniel Bacon

One American's Story

John Smith craved adventure. In 1600, at age 20, Smith trekked across Europe and helped Hungary fight a war against the Turks. For his heroic battle efforts, the Hungarians offered a knighthood to Smith, who inscribed his coat of arms with the phrase *Vincere est vivere*—"to conquer is to live."

In 1606, the daring and often arrogant adventurer approached the members of the Virginia Company, a group of merchants who were interested in founding an English colony in North America. Smith later recalled the opportunities that he saw open to him and other potential colonists.

A PERSONAL VOICE JOHN SMITH

"What man who is poor or who has only his merit to advance his fortunes can desire more contentment than to walk over and plant the land he has obtained by risking his life? . . . Here nature and liberty . . . [give] us freely that which we lack or have to pay dearly for in England. . . . What pleasure can be greater than to grow tired from . . . planting vines, fruits, or vegetables?"

—*The General History of Virginia*

▲ John Smith was a self-proclaimed soldier of fortune, a sea captain, and a poet.

With the help of Smith's leadership and, later, the production of the profitable crop of tobacco, England's small North American settlement survived.

English Settlers Struggle in North America

England's first attempts to carve out a colony of its own in North America nearly collapsed because of disease and starvation.

THE BUSINESS OF COLONIZATION Unlike Spanish colonies, which were funded by Spanish rulers, English colonies were originally funded and maintained by **joint-stock companies.** Stock companies allowed several investors to pool their wealth in support of a colony that would, hopefully, yield a profit. Once they had obtained a charter, or official permit, a stock company accepted responsibility for

hmhsocialstudies.com
TAKING NOTES
Use the graphic organizer online to take notes on the colonization of Virginia.

maintaining the colony, in return for which they would be entitled to receive back most of the profit that the colony might yield.

In 1606, King James I of England granted a charter to the Virginia Company. The company hoped to found a colony along the eastern shores of North America in territory explored earlier by Sir Walter Raleigh. Raleigh had named the territory Virginia after Elizabeth I (1533–1603), "the virgin queen." The Virginia Company had lured financial supporters by asking for a relatively small investment. Stockholders would be entitled to receive four-fifths of all gold and silver found by the colonists. The king would receive the remaining fifth.

The Virginia Company's three ships—*Susan Constant, Discovery,* and *Godspeed*—with nearly 150 passengers and crew members aboard, reached the shores of Virginia in April of 1607. They slipped into a broad coastal river and sailed inland until they reached a small peninsula. There, the colonists claimed the land as theirs. They named the settlement **Jamestown** and the river the James, in honor of their king.

A DISASTROUS START John Smith sensed trouble from the beginning. As he wrote later, "There was no talk, no hope, no work, but dig gold, wash gold, refine gold, load gold." Smith warned of disaster, but few listened to the arrogant captain, who had made few friends on the voyage over.

Disease from contaminated river water struck first. Hunger soon followed. The colonists, many of whom were unaccustomed to a life of labor, had refused to clear fields, plant crops, or even gather shellfish from the river's edge. One settler later described the terrifying predicament.

★ A PERSONAL VOICE

"Thus we lived for the space of five months in this miserable distress . . . our men night and day groaning in every corner of the fort, most pitiful to hear. If there were any conscience in men, it would make their hearts to bleed to hear the pitiful murmurings and outcries of our sick men for relief, every night and day for the space of six weeks: some departing out of the World, many times three or four in a night; in the morning their bodies being trailed out of their cabins like dogs, to be buried."

—A Jamestown colonist quoted in *A New World*

On a cold winter day in 1607, standing among the 38 colonists who remained alive, John Smith took control of the settlement. "You see that power now rests wholly with me," he announced. "You must now obey this law, . . . he that will not work shall not eat." Smith held the colony together by forcing the colonists to farm. He also persuaded the nearby **Powhatan** people to provide food. Unfortunately, later that winter, a stray spark ignited a gunpowder bag Smith was wearing and set him on fire. Badly burned, Smith headed back to England, leaving Jamestown to fend for itself.

In the spring of 1609, about 600 new colonists arrived with hopes of starting a new life in the colony. The Powhatan, by now alarmed at the growing number of settlers, began to kill the colonists' livestock and destroy their farms. By the following winter, conditions in Jamestown had deteriorated to the point of famine. In what became known as the "starving time," the colonists ate roots, rats, snakes, and even boiled shoe leather. Of those 600 new colonists, only about 60 survived. Ⓐ

MAIN IDEA

Summarizing

Ⓐ What factors contributed to the near failure of Jamestown?

Rediscovering Fort James

hmhsocialstudies.com INTERACTIVE

Erosion turned the Jamestown Peninsula into an island and, for many years, the site of the original Fort James was assumed to be under water. However, in 1996, archaeologists from the Association for the Preservation of Virginia Antiquities discovered artifacts on what they concluded was the original site of the fort.

Since then, archaeologists have discovered armor, weapons, even games used by the first colonists. Archaeologists and historians are constantly learning more and more about this long-buried treasure of American history.

16th-century helmet and breastplate. ▶

Site of Jamestown

WASHINGTON, D.C.

MARYLAND

DELAWARE

VIRGINIA

James River

Richmond

Chesapeake Bay

N
W   E
S

75°W

37°N

Jamestown

Norfolk

ATLANTIC OCEAN

| 0 | 15 | 30 miles |
| 0 | 15 | 30 kilometers |

▲ An archaeologist kneels beside holes left from the original palisade fence of Fort James. Note that the palisades were less than one foot in width.

Rounded bulwarks, or watch towers, mounted with cannon were located at each corner of the fort. The range of each cannon was approximately one mile.

The walls of the triangular-shaped fort measured 420 feet on the river side and 300 feet on the other two sides.

A barracks or "bawn" stood along the wall.

Colonists' houses were built about ten feet from the fort's walls. Houses measured sixteen by forty feet and several colonists lived in each.

The main gate, located on the long side, faced the James River.

▲ This illustration re-creates what historians and archaeologists now believe Fort James looked like early in its history.

JAMESTOWN BEGINS TO FLOURISH The surviving colonists decided to abandon the seemingly doomed settlement. However, as they sailed down the James River, they were met by a second English ship whose passengers convinced the fleeing colonists to turn around. Under the watchful eye of new leaders, who did not hesitate to flog or even hang colonists found neglecting their work, Jamestown stabilized and the colony began to expand farther inland along the James River. However, equally important in the colony's growth was the development of a highly profitable crop: tobacco.

"BROWN GOLD" AND INDENTURED SERVANTS Europeans had become aware of tobacco soon after Columbus's first return from the West Indies. In 1612, the Jamestown colonist John Rolfe experimented by cross breeding tobacco from Brazil with a harsh strain of the weed that local Native Americans had grown for years. Rolfe's experiment resulted in a high-quality tobacco strain for which the citizens of England soon clamored. By the late 1620s, colonists exported more than 1.5 million pounds of "brown gold" to England each year. **B**

MAIN IDEA

Analyzing Events
B Why was tobacco so important to the Jamestown colony?

In order to grow tobacco, the Virginia Company needed a key ingredient that was missing from the colony—field laborers. In an effort to lure settlers to Jamestown, the Virginia Company introduced the **headright system** in 1618. Under this system, anyone who paid for their own or another's passage to Virginia received 50 acres of land. Immigration to the colony jumped.

The headright system yielded huge land grants for anyone who was wealthy enough to transport large numbers of people to Virginia. The Company used the term "plantation" for the group of people who settled the land grant, but eventually, the term was used to refer to the land itself. To work their plantations, many owners imported **indentured servants** from England. In exchange for passage to North America, and food and shelter upon arrival, an indentured servant agreed to a limited term of servitude—usually four to seven years. Indentured servants were usually from the lower classes of English society. **C**

MAIN IDEA

Contrasting
C How did the conditions of indentured servitude differ from those of the headright system?

THE FIRST AFRICAN LABORERS Another group of laborers—Africans—first arrived in Virginia aboard a Dutch merchant ship in 1619. Records suggest that the Jamestown colonists treated the group of about 20 Africans as indentured servants. After a few years, most of the Africans received land and freedom. Meanwhile, other Africans continued to arrive in the colony in small numbers, but it would be several decades before the English colonists in North America began the systematic use of Africans as slave labor.

ANOTHER PERSPECTIVE

FANTASIES OF THE "NEW WORLD"

By the early 1600s, many Englishmen, weary of wars and living in overcrowded cities, listened eagerly to early reports about Virginia. Playwrights, poets, and adventurers, most of whom had never seen the "New World," turned those reports into fantasies of a "promised land," a place of fair climate, friendly natives, rich harvests, and bright futures.

A play produced in London in 1605 described Virginia as a place where native children wore rubies and diamonds in their coats and caps. In 1606, the English poet Michael Drayton called Virginia "that delicious land" because of its rich soil and fantastic harvests. By 1607, the Virginia Company officers translated those fantasies into advertisements. During the "starving time," Jamestown colonists must have bitterly recalled the promises made in those advertisements.

▲ This poster, dated 1609, reflects an attempt to attract settlers to the early Virginia colony.

▲ In this 18th-century engraving, a Virginia planter oversees slaves packing tobacco leaves for shipment to England.

One reason for this was economics. In Virginia, where tobacco served as currency in the early 1600s, an indentured servant could be purchased for 1,000 pounds of tobacco, while a slave might cost double or triple that amount. However, by the late 1600s, a decline in the indentured servant population coupled with an increase in the colonies' overall wealth spurred the colonists to begin importing slaves in huge numbers. While the life of indentured servants was difficult, slaves endured far worse conditions. Servants could eventually become full members of society, but slaves were condemned to a life of harsh labor. **D**

MAIN IDEA

Summarizing
D What factors led to the importation of African slaves to Virginia?

The Settlers Clash with Native Americans

As the English settlers expanded their settlement, their uneasy relations with the Native Americans worsened. The colonists' desire for more land led to warfare with the original inhabitants of Virginia.

THE ENGLISH PATTERN OF CONQUEST Unlike the Spanish, whose colonists intermarried with Native Americans, the English followed the pattern used when they conquered the Irish during the 1500s and 1600s. England's Laws of Conquest declared, in part, "Every Irishman shall be forbidden to wear English apparel or weapons upon pain of death." The same law also banned marriages between the English and the Irish.

The English brought this pattern of colonization with them to North America. Viewing the Native Americans as being "like the wild Irish," the English settlers had no desire to live among or intermarry with the Native Americans they defeated.

THE SETTLERS BATTLE NATIVE AMERICANS As the English settlers recovered in the years following the starving time, they never forgot the Powhatan's hostility during the starving time. In retaliation, the leaders of Jamestown demanded tributes of corn and labor from the local native peoples. Soldiers pressed these demands by setting Powhatan villages on fire and kidnapping hostages, especially children. One of the kidnapped children, Chief Powhatan's daughter, Pocahontas, married John Rolfe in 1614. This lay the groundwork for a half-hearted peace. However, the peace would not last, as colonists continued to move further into Native American territory and seize more land to grow tobacco. **E**

MAIN IDEA

Analyzing Causes

E Why were the colonists in conflict with the Powhatan?

By 1622, English settlers had worn out the patience of Chief Opechancanough, Chief Powhatan's brother and successor. In a well-planned attack, Powhatan raiding parties struck at colonial villages up and down the James River, killing more than 340 colonists. The attack forced the Virginia Company to send in more troops and supplies, leaving it nearly bankrupt. In 1624, James I, disgusted by the turmoil in Virginia, revoked the company's charter and made Virginia a **royal colony**—one under direct control of the king. England sent more troops and settlers to strengthen the colony and to conquer the Powhatan. By 1644, nearly 10,000 English men and women lived in Virginia, while the Powhatan population continued to fall.

▲ Pocahontas as she appeared during her visit to England in 1616–1617

Economic Differences Split Virginia

By the 1670s, many of the free white men in Virginia were former indentured servants who, although they had completed their servitude, had little money to buy land. Because they did not own land, they could not vote and therefore enjoyed almost no rights in colonial society. These poor colonists lived mainly on the western outskirts of Virginia, where they constantly fought with Native Americans for land.

Vocabulary
levy: to impose or collect

HOSTILITIES DEVELOP During the 1660s and 1670s, Virginia's poor settlers felt oppressed and frustrated by the policies of the colony's governor, Sir William Berkeley. More and more, Berkeley levied or imposed high taxes, which were paid mostly by the poorer settlers who lived along Virginia's western frontier. Moreover, the money collected by these taxes was used not for the public good but for the personal profit of the "Grandees," or "planters," the wealthy plantation farmers who had settled along the eastern shores of Virginia. Many of these planters occupied positions in the government, positions that they used to protect their own interests. As hostilities began to develop between the settlers along Virginia's western frontier and the Native Americans who lived there, the settlers demanded to know why money collected in taxes and fines was not being used to build forts for their protection.

In 1675, a bloody clash between Virginia's frontier settlers and local natives revealed an underlying tension between the colony's poor whites and its wealthy landowners and sparked a pitched battle between the two classes. In June of 1675, a dispute between the Doeg tribe and a Virginia frontier farmer grew into a bloodbath. A group of frontier settlers who were pursuing Doeg warriors murdered fourteen friendly Susquehannock and then executed five chiefs during a peace conference. Fighting soon broke out between Native Americans and frontier colonists. The colonists pleaded to Governor Berkeley for military support, but the governor, acting on behalf of the wealthy planters, refused to finance a war to benefit the colony's poor frontier settlers.

BACON'S REBELLION Berkeley's refusal did not sit well with a twenty-nine-year-old planter named **Nathaniel Bacon.** Bacon, a tall, dark-haired, hot-tempered son of a wealthy Englishman, detested Native Americans. He called

The House of Burgesses served as the first representative body in colonial America. The House first met in Jamestown on July 30, 1619, and included two citizens, or burgesses, from each of Virginia's eleven districts.

The House claimed the authority to raise taxes and make laws. However, the English governor had the right to veto any legislation the House passed. While the House represented a limited constituency—since only white male landowners could vote—it contributed to the development of representative government in English America. A century and a half after its founding, the House of Burgesses would supply delegates to the Continental Congress—the revolutionary body that orchestrated the break from Great Britain.

them "wolves" who preyed upon "our harmless and innocent lambs." In 1676, Bacon broke from his old friend Berkeley and raised an army to fight Native Americans on the Virginia frontier. **F**

Governor Berkeley quickly declared Bacon's army—one-third of which was made up of landless settlers and debtors—illegal. Hearing this news, Bacon marched on Jamestown in September of 1676 to confront colonial leaders about a number of grievances, including the frontier colonists' lack of representation in the House of Burgesses—Virginia's colonial legislature. Virginia's "rabble," as many planters called the frontier settlers, resented being taxed and governed without their consent. Ironically, 100 years later in 1776, both wealthy and poor colonists would voice this same complaint against Great Britain at the beginning of the American Revolution.

The march turned violent. The rebels set fire to the town as Berkeley and numerous planters fled by ship. However, Bacon had little time to enjoy his victory. He died of illness a month after storming Jamestown. Upon Bacon's death, Berkeley returned to Jamestown and easily subdued the leaderless rebels.

Bacon's Rebellion, as it came to be known, did succeed in drawing King Charles's attention to Berkeley's government, and Charles's commissioners, or investigators, were highly critical of Berkeley's policies. The old governor was recalled to England to explain himself but died before meeting with the king.

Although it spurred the planter class to cling more tightly to power, Bacon's Rebellion exposed the growing power of the colony's former indentured servants. Meanwhile, farther to the north, another group of English colonists, who had journeyed to North America for religious reasons, were steering their own course into the future.

MAIN IDEA

Analyzing Issues

F Why was Nathaniel Bacon frustrated with Governor Berkeley?

SECTION 2 ASSESSMENT

1. **TERMS & NAMES** For each term or name, write a sentence explaining its significance.

- John Smith
- joint-stock companies
- Jamestown
- Powhatan
- headright system
- indentured servant
- royal colony
- Nathaniel Bacon

MAIN IDEA

2. **TAKING NOTES**

Create a time line of the major developments in the colonization of Virginia, using a form such as the one below.

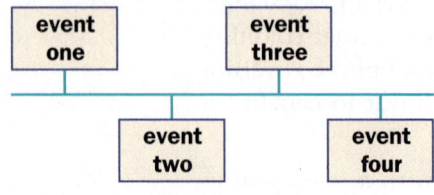

Which event do you think was the most critical turning point? Why?

CRITICAL THINKING

3. **RECOGNIZING EFFECTS**

The success of tobacco farming in Virginia had wide-ranging effects. Describe its impact on each of these groups: the Jamestown colonists, indentured servants, the Powhatan, the planters.

Think About:

- the headright system and indentured servitude
- the colonists' need for more land
- the conflict between rich and poor colonists

4. **ANALYZING PRIMARY SOURCES**

The following lines appear in Michael Drayton's 1606 poem, "To the Virginian Voyage":

" **When as the luscious smell of that delicious land Above the sea that flows The clear wind throws, Your hearts to swell** "

What do these lines tell you about the expectations many colonists had before they arrived in Virginia?

PI 1.2   CC Unit 2.I.A.2.a   CC Unit 2.I.A.2.c
CC Unit 2.I.A.3.a   CC Unit 2.II.B.2.c(1)

Puritan New England

MAIN IDEA	WHY IT MATTERS NOW	Terms & Names
English Puritans came to North America, beginning in 1620.	The United States continues to use an expanded form of representative government begun by the Puritans.	•Puritans •John Winthrop •Separatist •Plymouth Colony •Massachusetts Bay Colony •Roger Williams •Anne Hutchinson •Pequot War •Metacom •King Philip's War

hmhsocialstudies.com
TAKING NOTES

Use the graphic organizer online to take notes on the cause-and-effect relationships discussed in this section.

One American's Story

In 1628, at age 16, a young English woman named Anne Dudley married Simon Bradstreet, who, like herself, was one of a group of **Puritans,** church members who wanted to "purify" or reform the Church of England. Simon, Anne, and her parents left England with other Puritans who hoped to create a "holy" community in New England. There Anne became America's first English-speaking poet, whose poems would provide future generations with a glimpse of Puritan life and values. When her house burned to the ground on a July night in 1666, Anne composed a poem to express her sorrow and her resolve to remain strong.

> ★ **A PERSONAL VOICE** ANNE BRADSTREET
> " Then, coming out, beheld a space
> The flame consume my dwelling place.
> And when I could no longer look,
> I blest His name that gave and took. "
>
> —from "Here Follows Some Verses upon the Burning of Our House (July 10th, 1666)"

Anne Dudley Bradstreet's book of poetry, *The Tenth Muse Lately Sprung Up in America,* is regarded as one of the first important works of American literature.

Puritans Create a "New England"

When Anne Bradstreet and her family boarded the *Arbella,* the flagship of the Puritan expedition to America, the English settlement at Jamestown was still struggling to survive. Unlike the profit-minded colonists at Jamestown, however, the Puritans emigrated in order to create a model new society—what **John Winthrop,** their first governor, called a "City upon a Hill."

▲
This picture of Anne Bradstreet is from a window in St. Botolph's Church, Lincolnshire, England.

ⓧ ANNE BRADSTREET ⓧ

Puritans cherished their Bibles, passing them down as family treasures from one generation to the next. This Bible belonged to Governor William Bradford of the Plymouth Colony.

hmhsocialstudies.com

INTERACTIVE
Explore Plymouth Colony

PURITANS AND PILGRIMS Puritanism had its origins in the English Reformation. After King Henry VIII (1491–1547) broke with Roman Catholicism in the 1530s, his daughter, Elizabeth I (1533–1603) formed the Anglican church, or the Church of England. Although the Anglican church was free of Catholic control, some church members felt that it had kept too much of the Catholic ritual and tradition. These people were called Puritans because they wanted to purify the Anglican church by eliminating all traces of Roman Catholicism. Puritans embraced the idea that every worshipper should experience God directly through faith, prayer, and study of the Bible. Puritans held ministers in respect as a source of religious and moral instruction, but they objected to the authority of Anglican bishops.

Some Puritans felt they should remain in the Church of England and reform it from within. Other Puritans did not think that was possible, so they formed independent congregations with their own ministers. These **Separatists**, known today as the Pilgrims, fled from England to escape persecution, first to Holland and eventually to America. In 1620, this small group of families founded the **Plymouth Colony,** the second permanent English colony in North America. **A**

THE MASSACHUSETTS BAY COMPANY Meanwhile, other English Puritans in the 1620s who were discouraged about Anglican reform also turned their thoughts toward New England. Like the Separatists, they too felt the burden of increasing religious persecution, political repression, and dismal economic conditions. John Winthrop wrote to his wife in 1629, "[the Lord will] provide a shelter and a hiding place for us." Winthrop and others believed that this refuge would be in America.

In 1629, Winthrop and some of his well-connected friends obtained a royal charter for a joint-stock enterprise, the Massachusetts Bay Company. Winthrop and the other colonists transferred both the charter and the company's headquarters to New England. This strategy meant that when the Puritans migrated, they took with them the authority for an independent government. **B**

In September 1630, Winthrop and the other colonists aboard the *Arbella* established the **Massachusetts Bay Colony.** The port town of Boston became their capital. Soon other towns were founded to accommodate the large number of settlers flocking to join the colony. In the first year of the colony's settlement, 17 ships (including the *Arbella*) arrived with about 1,000 English men, women, and children—Puritan and non-Puritan. The migration was greater in size and more thorough in planning than all

HISTORICAL SPOTLIGHT

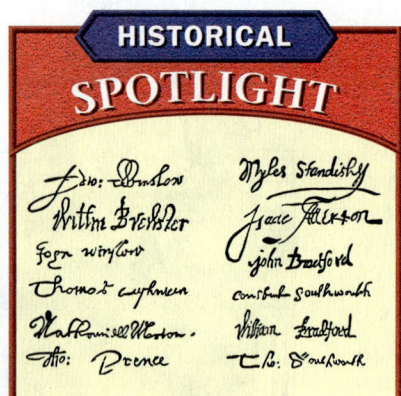

THE MAYFLOWER COMPACT

Although the Pilgrims aimed for Virginia, their ship, the *Mayflower*, strayed far off course to Cape Cod. The Pilgrims knew that New England lay too far north for their colonial charter to be valid. They were also afraid that non-Pilgrim passengers would challenge their authority. Before departing the ship, the Pilgrim men signed a compact, or agreement, in which they created a civil government and pledged loyalty to the king. Some of their signatures are reproduced above.

The Mayflower Compact stated that the purpose of their government in America would be to frame "just and equal laws . . . for the general good of the colony." Laws approved by the majority would be binding on Pilgrims and non-Pilgrims alike. The document became a landmark of American democratic government.

MAIN IDEA

Contrasting
A How were the Separatists different from other Puritans?

MAIN IDEA

Analyzing Motives
B Why did the Puritans leave England?

previous expeditions to North America. Eventually, Plymouth Colony was incorporated into the Massachusetts Bay Colony.

"CITY UPON A HILL" In a sermon delivered before the *Arbella* landed, Winthrop expressed the sense of mission that bound the Puritans together.

> ### ★ A PERSONAL VOICE JOHN WINTHROP
>
> "**We must be knit together in this work; . . . we must uphold [each other] . . . in all meekness, gentleness, patience and liberality [generosity]. We must delight in each other, make others' conditions our own, rejoice together, mourn together, labor and suffer together. . . .**
>
> **So shall we keep the unity of the spirit, in the bond of peace. . . . Ten of us will be able to resist a thousand of our enemies. For we must consider that we [in New England] shall be as a City upon a Hill, the eyes of all people are on us.**"
>
> —"A Model of Christian Charity"

Winthrop's vision, however, did not stem from a belief in either social equality or political democracy. Explained Winthrop in his shipboard sermon, God had decreed that "some must be rich, some poor, some high and eminent in power and dignity, others mean [common] and in subjugation."

Although Puritans made no effort to create a democracy, political power was spread more broadly than in England. The Massachusetts Bay Company extended the right to vote to not only stockholders but to all adult males who belonged to the Puritan church, roughly 40 percent of the colony's men. This was a large electorate by the standards of Europe in the 1630s. These "freemen," as they were called, voted annually for members of a lawmaking body called the General Court, which in turn chose the governor. **C**

CHURCH AND STATE As this system of self-government evolved, so did the close relationship between the government and the Puritan church. Civic officials were members of the Puritan church who believed that they were God's "elect," or chosen, and had a duty to carry out God's will. Puritan laws criminalized

---

MAIN IDEA

Analyzing Issues

C Who could vote in the Massachusetts Bay Colony?

History Through *Art*

PURITAN HEADSTONES

Puritans forbade images in their churches but they permitted them in their cemeteries. The images on a headstone were meant not just to memorialize the dead but to remind both young and old that life was brief and should be lived according to the Puritan virtues of piety and hard work.

▶ Central to virtually every Puritan headstone was the image of the winged skull. The skull itself was meant to symbolize the physical reality of death. The wings represented the soul and the possibility of immortality.

▶ The winged skull motif persisted into the 18th century, when the winged skull was either modified to resemble a cherub or was replaced with a carved portrait of the deceased.

SKILLBUILDER Interpreting Visual Sources
1. What kind of emotions does the image of the winged skull elicit?
2. How do Puritan headstones compare with other memorials you have seen?

 SEE SKILLBUILDER HANDBOOK, PAGE R23.

such sins as drunkenness, swearing, theft, and idleness. "No person . . . shall spend his time idly or unprofitably," decreed the General Court in 1633, "under pain of such punishment as the court shall think meet [appropriate] to inflict."

IMPORTANCE OF THE FAMILY Unlike settlers in Virginia, Puritans generally crossed the Atlantic as families rather than as single men or women. "Without family care," declared one minister, "the labor of Magistrates and Ministers . . . is likely to be in great measure unsuccessful." Puritans kept a watchful eye on the actions of husbands, wives, and children, and the community stepped in when necessary. If parents failed to nip disobedience in the bud, they might find their children placed in more "God-fearing" homes. If a husband and wife quarreled too much, a court might intervene as a form of marriage counseling. If they still bickered, one or both might end up in the stocks or the pillory.

Vocabulary
stocks, pillory: devices in which an offender was shackled and held on public display as a form of punishment

Dissent in the Puritan Community

Division soon threatened Massachusetts Bay. Two dissenters, Roger Williams and Anne Hutchinson, challenged the social order upon which the colony was founded.

THE FOUNDING OF PROVIDENCE "Forced religion stinks in the nostrils of God," declared **Roger Williams** in a sermon to his Salem congregation. Williams, an extreme Separatist, expressed two controversial views. First, he declared that the English settlers had no rightful claim to the land unless they purchased it from Native Americans. He called the royal charter that granted the lands a "National Sinne" and demanded that it be revised to reflect Native American claims. Second, Williams declared that government officials had no business punishing settlers for their religious beliefs. He felt every person should be free to worship according to his or her conscience.

The outraged General Court ordered Williams to be arrested and returned to England. Before this order was carried out, Williams fled Massachusetts. In January 1636, he headed southward to the headwaters of Narragansett Bay. There he negotiated with the local Narragansett tribe for land to set up a new colony, which he called Providence. In Providence, later the capital of Rhode Island, Williams guaranteed separation of church and state and religious freedom. **D**

MAIN IDEA

Contrasting
D What two principles did Providence guarantee that Massachusetts Bay did not?

ANNE HUTCHINSON BANISHED Puritan leaders soon banished another dissenter, **Anne Hutchinson.** To strict Puritans, she posed an even greater threat than Williams. In Bible readings at her home, Hutchinson taught that "the Holy Spirit illumines [enlightens] the heart of every true believer." In other words, worshippers needed neither the church nor its ministers to interpret the Bible for them.

Puritan leaders banished Hutchinson from the colony in 1638. Along with a band of followers, she and her family trudged to Rhode Island. After the death of her husband in 1642, Hutchinson moved with her younger children to the colony of New Netherland (now New York), where the Dutch also practiced religious toleration. The following year, she died in a war fought between the Dutch and Native Americans.

◄ This statue of Anne Hutchinson stands in Boston, Massachusetts. Ironically, she was banished from Massachusetts for leading religious discussions.

Native Americans Resist Colonial Expansion

While Williams and his followers were settling Rhode Island, thousands of other white settlers fanned out to western Massachusetts and to new colonies in New Hampshire and Connecticut. However, as Native Americans saw their lands claimed and cleared for farming, they recognized that the rapid spread of the settlers meant an end to their way of life.

DISPUTES OVER LAND Disputes between the Puritans and Native Americans arose over land use. For every acre a colonial farmer needed to support life, a Native American needed twenty for hunting, fishing, and agriculture. To Native Americans, no one owned the land—it was there for everyone to use. Native Americans saw land treaties with Europeans as agreements in which they received gifts, such as blankets, guns, iron tools, or ornaments, in return for which they agreed to share the land for a limited time. Europeans, however, saw the treaties as a one-time deal in which Native Americans permanently sold their land to new owners. **E**

THE PEQUOT WAR The first major conflict arose in Connecticut in 1637, when the Pequot nation decided to take a stand against the colonists. The colonists formed an alliance with the Narragansett, old enemies of the Pequot. The result of the **Pequot War** was the near destruction of the Pequot nation. The end came in May 1637, when about 90 English colonists and hundreds of their Native American allies surrounded a Pequot fort on the Mystic River. After setting the fort on fire, the colonists shot Pequot men, women, and children as they tried to escape or surrender. The massacre was so awful that the Narragansett pleaded,

> **MAIN IDEA**
>
> **Analyzing Issues**
> **E** How did Native Americans view land treaties?

New England Colonies to 1675

MAINE (Mass.)

Lake Champlain

NEW HAMPSHIRE

Claimed by N.H. and N.Y.

Connecticut River

Merrimack River

Portland (1632)

Portsmouth (1623)

NEW YORK

Hudson River

Deerfield (1669)

Salem (1626)
Boston (1630)
Plymouth (1620)

MASSACHUSETTS

ATLANTIC OCEAN

Cape Cod

Hartford (1635)

Providence (1636)

CONNECTICUT

RHODE ISLAND

New Haven (1638)

Stonington

Long Island

69°W

41°N

73°W

0   25   50 miles
0   25   50 kilometers

The figure of the Indians fort or Palizado in NEW ENGLAND And the maner of the destroying It by Captayne Underhill And Captayne Mason

This British engraving shows the Pequot fort near Stonington, Connecticut. The fort was destroyed in 1637.

GEOGRAPHY SKILLBUILDER
1. **Place** What was the earliest major European settlement in the New England colonies?
2. **Human- Environment Interaction** What characteristics of Boston made it a good place for a settlement?

"This is evil, this is evil, too furious, too many killed." The colonists ignored them, until all but a few out of about 500–600 people in the fort had died. Later, the Narraganset leader Miantonomo declared in a speech to the Montauk tribe,

A PERSONAL VOICE MIANTONOMO

"These English have gotten our land, they with scythes cut down grass, and with axes fell the trees; their cows and horses eat the grass, and their hogs spoil our clam banks, and we shall all be starved. . . .

For so are we all Indians as the English are, and say brother to one another; so must we be one as they are, otherwise we shall be all gone shortly."

—quoted in *Changes in the Land*

KING PHILIP'S WAR Deprived of their land and livelihood, many Native Americans had to toil for the English to earn a living. They also had to obey Puritan laws such as no hunting or fishing on Sunday, the Sabbath day. Wampanoag chief **Metacom,** whom the English called King Philip, bristled under these restrictions. In a last-ditch effort to wipe out the invaders, he organized his tribe and several others into an alliance.

The eruption of **King Philip's War** in the spring of 1675 startled the Puritans with its intensity. Using hit-and-run tactics, Native Americans attacked and burned outlying settlements throughout New England. For over a year, the two sides waged a war of mutual brutality and destruction. Finally, food shortages, disease, and heavy casualties wore down the Native Americans' resistance, and they gradually surrendered or fled.

Wampanoag casualties included Metacom, the victim of a bullet fired by a Native American ally of the English. To commemorate their victory, the Puritans exhibited Metacom's head at Plymouth for 20 years. With his defeat, Native American power in southeastern New England was gone forever.

Still, the English paid a high price for their victory. All told, about one-tenth of the colonial men of military age in New England were killed in King Philip's War, a higher proportion of the total population than would be killed in either the American Revolution or the Civil War of the 1860s.

SECTION 3 ASSESSMENT

1. TERMS & NAMES For each term or name, write a sentence explaining its significance.

- Puritans
- John Winthrop
- Separatist
- Plymouth Colony
- Massachusetts Bay Colony
- Roger Williams
- Anne Hutchinson
- Pequot War
- Metacom
- King Philip's War

MAIN IDEA

2. TAKING NOTES
Identify the effects of each of the causes listed in the chart below.

Cause	Effect
Persecution of Puritans in England	
Puritan belief in hard work	
Roger Williams's dissenting beliefs	
Rapid colonial expansion in New England	
Defeat of King Philip	

CRITICAL THINKING

3. DRAWING CONCLUSIONS
Why do you think Puritan leaders viewed Anne Hutchinson as a threat to their society? Use evidence from the text to support your answer.
Think About:
- Puritan beliefs
- characteristics of Puritan society
- Hutchinson's teachings

4. ANALYZING EFFECTS
What were the immediate effects of King Philip's War for Native Americans and for the settlers?

5. DEVELOPING HISTORICAL PERSPECTIVE
Imagine you have been called upon to negotiate between the New England colonists and Native Americans. What would you tell each side about the other to help them overcome their misunderstandings?
Think About:
- their views on land and religion
- the Pequot War and King Philip's War

SECTION
4

CC Unit 1.I.A.3.f   CC Unit 1.I.A.4.a
CC Unit 2.I.A.2.a   CC Unit 2.I.A.2.c
CC Unit 2.I.A.3.a   CC Unit 2.II.B.2.c(1)

PI 3.1

Settlement of the Middle Colonies

MAIN IDEA	WHY IT MATTERS NOW	Terms & Names
The Dutch settled New Netherland; English Quakers led by William Penn settled Pennsylvania.	The principles of tolerance and equality promoted in the Quaker settlement remain fundamental values in America.	• William Penn • proprietor • New Netherland • Quakers

One American's Story

hmhsocialstudies.com
TAKING NOTES
Use the graphic organizer online to take notes on the similarities and differences between New Netherland and Pennsylvania.

William Penn had frustrated his father, Admiral Sir William Penn. In 1667, at age 22, the younger Penn committed himself to the Society of Friends, or Quakers, a Protestant sect whose religious and social beliefs were radical for the time.

Ironically, his late father would play a key role in helping William Penn realize his dream—establishing a haven for Quakers in America. King Charles II had owed Penn's father money, which the younger Penn asked to be repaid with American land. Charles agreed, and in 1681 he gave Penn a charter for Pennsylvania. Penn had big plans for his colony—a government run on Quaker principles of equality, cooperation, and religious toleration. As he confided to a friend, however, Penn did not reveal the true nature of his plans before receiving the charter.

A PERSONAL VOICE WILLIAM PENN
"For matters of liberty and privilege, I propose that which is extraordinary, and [I intend] to leave myself and successors no power for doing mischief, [in order] that the will of one man may not hinder the good of a whole country; but to publish those things now and here, as matters stand, would not be wise. . . ."

—quoted in *A New World*

▲ This chalk drawing shows William Penn around 1695, at about the age of 50.

While Penn only partially realized his "extraordinary" plans, the tolerant Quaker principles on which he established his colony attracted many settlers of different faiths.

FOCUS ON
In 1625, Peter Minuit bought Manhattan Island from Native Americans for goods worth about $200 in today's money. Minuit named the Dutch settlement that developed on the island *New Amsterdam*.

The Dutch Found New Netherland

While English Puritans were establishing colonies in New England, the Dutch were founding one to the south. As early as 1609, Henry Hudson—an Englishman employed by the Dutch—sailed up what is now known as the Hudson River. In 1621, the Dutch government granted the newly formed Dutch West India Company permission to colonize **New Netherland** and expand the thriving fur trade. New Amsterdam (now New York City), founded in 1625, became the capital of the colony. In 1655, the Dutch extended their claims by taking over New Sweden, a tiny colony of Swedish and Finnish settlers that had established a rival fur trade along the Delaware River.

A DIVERSE COLONY Although the Dutch company profited from its fur trade, New Netherland was slow to attract Dutch colonists. To encourage settlers to come and stay, the colony opened its doors to a variety of people. Gradually, more Dutch as well as Germans, French, Scandinavians, Jews, and other Europeans settled the area. The colony also included many Africans, free as well as enslaved. By the 1660s, one-fifth of New Netherland's population was of African ancestry.

These settlers generally enjoyed friendlier relations with Native Americans than did the English colonists in New England and Virginia. The Dutch were less interested in conquering the Native Americans than in trading with them for furs. The first Dutch traders had the good sense not to anger the powerful and well-organized Iroquois, who controlled a large territory between Dutch traders to the south and French traders to the north. However, the Dutch did engage in fighting with various Native American groups over land claims and trade rivalries. **Ⓐ**

ENGLISH TAKEOVER To the English, New Netherland had become a "Dutch wedge" separating its northern and southern colonies. In 1664, King Charles II granted his brother James, the duke of York (who later became King James II), permission to drive out the Dutch. When the duke's fleet arrived in New Amsterdam's harbor, Peter Stuyvesant, the autocratic and unpopular Dutch governor, raised a call to arms. The call was largely ignored. Severely outmanned, Stuyvesant surrendered to the English without anyone firing a shot. The duke of York, the new **proprietor,** or owner, of the colony, renamed it New York. The duke later gave a portion of this land to two of his friends, naming the territory New Jersey for the British island of Jersey.

MAIN IDEA

Summarizing
Ⓐ What were the important characteristics of the colony of New Netherland?

Middle Colonies to 1700

Lake Ontario

Lake Erie

NEW YORK   Ft. Orange (1624) (Albany)

PENNSYLVANIA

Susquehanna R.

Hudson R.

Delaware R.

41°N

New Amsterdam (1625) (New York)

Philadelphia (1682)   NEW JERSEY

Ft. Christina (1638) (Wilmington)

ATLANTIC OCEAN

39°N

DELAWARE

N W E S

73°W   71°W

GEOGRAPHY SKILLBUILDER
Region What major river partially separated New Netherland from the English middle colonies?

New Netherland (ceded to England in 1664)

0   50   100 miles
0   50   100 kilometers

The Quakers Settle Pennsylvania

The acquisition of New Netherland was an important step in England's quest to extend its American empire after the restoration of the monarchy. The colony that took shape was a marked contrast to England's other North American settlements.

PENN'S "HOLY EXPERIMENT"
William Penn well knew that England in the late 1660s was no place for Quakers. The **Quakers** believed that God's "inner light" burned inside everyone. They held services without formal ministers, allowing any person to speak as the spirit moved him or her. They dressed plainly, refused to defer to persons of rank, and embraced pacifism by opposing war and refusing to serve in the military. For their radical views, they were harassed by Anglicans and Puritans alike. **Ⓑ**

Background
A Commonwealth headed by Oliver Cromwell ruled England from 1649 until 1658. The monarchy was restored under Charles II in 1660.

MAIN IDEA

Comparing
Ⓑ How did Quaker beliefs compare to Puritan beliefs?

History Through Architecture

COLONIAL MEETINGHOUSES

The Puritans of the northeast, the Quakers of Pennsylvania, and the Anglicans of the southern colonies held profound but often different convictions about community, social responsibility, and individual freedom. These convictions were often expressed in the religious services of each group as well as the architecture of the places of worship where these services were held.

MEN'S SEATS

WOMEN'S SEATS

▲
Quaker Meetinghouse

Quaker services, which were called "meetings," relied on the inspiration of the "inner light." Meetings reflected a respect for conscience and freedom of speech.

Men and women entered by separate doors and sat on opposite sides, facing each other. In some meetinghouses, women sat in slightly elevated seats. Both men and women could speak during the meeting.

PULPIT

▲
Puritan Meetinghouse

Puritan services focused on preaching. Sermons, which sometimes lasted for hours, instructed the individual conscience to be mindful of the common good.

The pulpit was the focal point of the meetinghouse. A plain interior reflected a value for austerity and simplicity. Meetinghouses were also used for town meetings.

PULPIT   ALTAR

◄ Anglican Church

The head of the Anglican church was the British monarch. Anglican services valued ritual. Their churches stressed the importance of authority and status.

Anglican churches emphasized the altar through ornamentation and elaborate windows. A screen separated the altar from the congregation. Elaborate pews were reserved for wealthy church members.

SKILLBUILDER Interpreting Visual Sources

1. In what ways do the Puritan and Quaker meetinghouses resemble each other? In what ways are they different?

2. How does the interior of the Anglican church show a respect for hierarchy?

📘 **SEE SKILLBUILDER HANDBOOK, PAGE R23.**

Penn saw his colony as a "holy experiment" in living, a place without a land-owning aristocracy. He guaranteed every adult male settler 50 acres of land and the right to vote. Penn's plan for government called for a representative assembly and freedom of religion. As a lasting symbol of his Quaker beliefs, Penn also helped plan a capital he called the "City of Brotherly Love," or Philadelphia.

Penn's constitution also provided for a separate assembly for the three southern counties along the Delaware Bay. Delaware thereby gained a somewhat separate existence. However, it continued to have the same governor as Pennsylvania.

NATIVE AMERICAN RELATIONS Like most Quakers, Penn believed that people approached in friendship would respond in friendship—sooner or later. So even before setting foot in North America, Penn arranged to have a letter read to the Lenni Lenapi, or Delaware, the tribe that inhabited his settlement area.

Aware that the Delaware had already been ravaged by European diseases and war, Penn wrote,

★ **A PERSONAL VOICE** WILLIAM PENN

"Now I would have you well observe, that I am very sensible of the unkindness and injustice that has been too much exercised towards you by the people of these parts of the world, who have sought . . . to make great advantages by you, . . . sometimes to the shedding of blood. . . . But I am not such a man. . . . I have great love and regard toward you, and I desire to win and gain your love and friendship by a kind, just, and peaceable life."

—quoted in *A New World*

To be sure that his colonists treated the native peoples fairly, Penn regulated trade with them and provided for a court composed of both colonists and Native Americans to settle any differences. The Native Americans respected Penn, and for more than 50 years the Pennsylvania colony had no major conflicts with Native Americans who lived in the colony. **C**

MAIN IDEA

Contrasting
C How did Penn's attitudes and actions toward the Native Americans differ from those of the Puritans?

▶ William Penn's 1682 treaty with the Native Americans is commemorated in this Edward Hicks painting from the 1840s.

A THRIVING COLONY Penn faced the same challenge as the Dutch West India Company; he needed to attract settlers—farmers, builders, and traders—to create a profitable colony. After initially opening the colony to Quakers, he vigorously recruited immigrants from around western Europe. Glowing advertisements for the colony were printed in German, Dutch, and French. In time, settlers came in numbers, including thousands of Germans who brought with them craft skills and farming techniques that helped the colony to thrive.

Penn himself spent only about four years in Pennsylvania. And, despite the colony's success, he never profited financially as proprietor and died in poverty in 1718. Meanwhile, his idealistic vision had faded but not failed. His own Quakers were a minority in a colony thickly populated by people from all over western Europe. Slavery was introduced and, despite Penn's principles, many prominent Quakers in Pennsylvania owned slaves. However, the principles of equality, cooperation, and religious tolerance on which he founded his vision would eventually become fundamental values of the new American nation.

▲ **Quakers offered silver collars like the one above to local Native Americans as a token of peace.**

Courtesy of the Historical Society of Pennsylvania Collection, Atwater Kent Museum of Philadelphia

THIRTEEN COLONIES Throughout the 1600s and 1700s, other British colonies in North America were founded as well, each for very different reasons. In 1632, King Charles I granted a charter for land north of Chesapeake Bay to George Calvert, the first Lord Baltimore. Calvert's son Cecil, the second Lord Baltimore, named the colony Maryland, after Queen Henrietta Maria, Charles's queen. Lord Baltimore, who was a Roman Catholic, obtained a religious toleration law from Maryland's colonial assembly, and the colony became famous for its religious freedom. In 1663, King Charles II awarded a group of key supporters the land between Virginia and Spanish Florida, a territory that soon became North and South Carolina.

In 1732, an English philanthropist named James Ogelthorpe, and several associates received a charter for a colony they hoped could be a haven for those imprisoned for debt. Ogelthorpe named the colony Georgia, after King George II. Few debtors actually came to Georgia, and Ogelthorpe's policies, which prohibited both slavery and the drinking of rum, were reversed when the British crown assumed direct control of the colony in 1752. By that time, there were thirteen British colonies in North America, but a growing desire for independence would soon put a strain on their relationship with England.

SECTION 4 ASSESSMENT

1. **TERMS & NAMES** For each term or name, write a sentence explaining its significance.
   - **William Penn**
   - **New Netherland**
   - **proprietor**
   - **Quakers**

MAIN IDEA

2. **TAKING NOTES**
   Compare the colonies of New Netherland and Pennsylvania, using a Venn diagram such as the one below.

   New Netherland / Both / Pennsylvania

   Write a paragraph comparing and contrasting the two colonies.

CRITICAL THINKING

3. **ANALYZING CAUSES**
   Why was Ogelthorpe's prohibition of slavery reversed?

4. **EVALUATING DECISIONS**
   Both New Netherland and Pennsylvania encouraged settlers to come from all over western Europe. Do you think this was a good decision for these colonies? Why or why not?

5. **DRAWING CONCLUSIONS**
   How did William Penn succeed in achieving his goals for Pennsylvania, and how did he fail? Explain.
   Think About:
   - Penn's actions toward Native Americans
   - Penn's plans for representative government and freedom of religion
   - Quakers who owned slaves

GEOGRAPHY SPOTLIGHT

Surviving in a New World

Early settlers quickly discovered that the "new world" they had chosen to colonize was indeed an extraordinary place, but not in the ways they had expected it to be. Little did colonists know that during the years of colonization, North America was experiencing the worst of what scientists now refer to as the "Little Ice Age." Extremes of cold and heat up and down the eastern seaboard were more severe than they had been in several hundred years. In time, colonists learned about natural resources that were also unknown to them, foods and plants that ultimately saved and sustained their lives.

The Southern Colonies

Jamestown colonists had counted on bartering for food with Native Americans in order to survive, but the Powhatan had little food to spare. The area was being hit with its worst drought in 800 years. The intense heat destroyed crops, and Native Americans were reluctant to trade what little they had.

Average January Temperature: 40–50°F
Average July Temperature: 80–90°F
Rainfall: 20–40 inches per year
Days of Snow Cover: 10–20
Growing Season: 180–210 days
Soil: yellowish and sandy
Crops of Native Peoples: maize (corn), tobacco

The heat created other hardships as well. The swampy Jamestown peninsula bred malaria–bearing mosquitoes, and many colonists died from the disease. Soon, the colonists' drinking water, supplied by the river, became contaminated with salty sea water. Eventually, the colonists' export of tobacco— a crop that Native Americans had been growing for centuries— provided a source of income that attracted more colonists, whose arrival saved the colony.

The New England Colonies

Colonists in New England likewise suffered from extreme weather conditions. The first hurricane recorded in North America occurred in Massachusetts Bay in 1635. Colonists noted in astonishment that it "blew down many hundreds of trees . . . overthrew some houses, drove ships from their anchors." Seasonal temperatures were also extreme. In the summer of 1637 a number of colonists died of sunstroke. Yet, the following winter, three feet of snow covered the ground.

To cope with illnesses brought on by the climate, colonists heeded Native Americans and looked to local plants and herbs as medicines. For instance, colonists learned from Native Americans that the Boneset plant (*Eupatorium perfoliatum*), pictured at left, could be used to break fevers and chills and could treat diseases ranging from colds and influenza to malaria and typhoid.

Average January Temperature: 20–30°F
Average July Temperature: 60–70°F
Rainfall: 20–40 inches per year
Days of Snow Cover: 90–120
Growing Season: 120–150 days
Soil: gray to brown, gravelly, stony
Crops of Native Peoples: maize (corn), beans, squash

The Middle Colonies

The Delaware River Valley would later be a rich farmland, but in the mid-1600s it too was affected by severe weather. Late frosts and wet springs caused poor harvests because conditions were too cold and wet for grains to ripen. Swedish colonists near what is now Wilmington, Delaware, reported in 1657 that onslaughts of frigid temperatures froze the Delaware River in a single day. In time, colonists learned from Native Americans about the crops that grew in the rich soil surrounding the Delaware River.

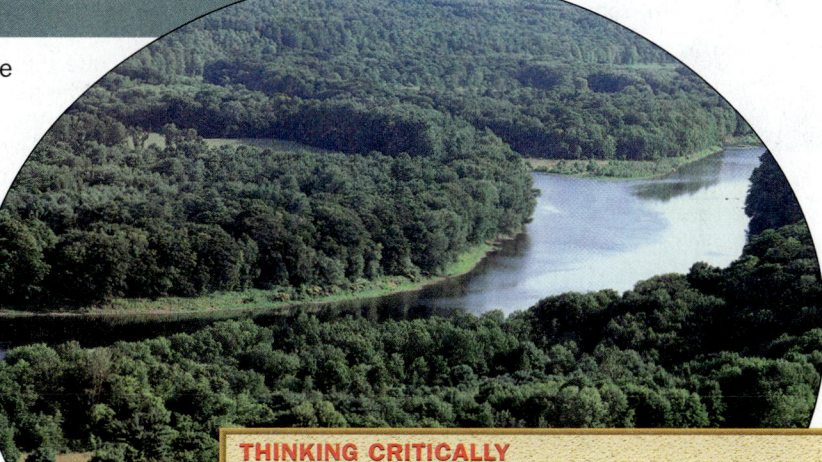

Average January Temperature: 30–40°F
Average July Temperature: 70–80°F
Rainfall: 20–40 inches per year
Days of Snow Cover: 30–40
Growing Season: 150–180 days
Soil: brownish and silty
Crops of Native Peoples: maize (corn), beans, pumpkin

THINKING CRITICALLY

1. **Analyzing Patterns** What seasonal patterns did the colonists in all three regions encounter? How did these patterns affect each colony?

2. **Creating a Diagram** Create an illustrated diagram that explains the interconnections in one of the North American colonies between colonists, Native Americans, and the land itself. Your diagram should include a reference to a particular crisis relating to the land, what the colonists learned from Native Americans, and how this new knowledge helped the colonists to survive.

    SEE SKILLBUILDER HANDBOOK, PAGE R30.

 hmhsocialstudies.com RESEARCH WEB LINKS

VISUAL SUMMARY

THE AMERICAN COLONIES EMERGE: 1513–1681

SPANISH COLONIES

- Hernándo Cortés conquers Mexico (1519–1521)
- Juan Ponce de León establishes Florida (1513)
- Francisco Vasquez de Coronado explores American southwest (1540)
- Pedro de Peralta founds Santa Fe (1609–1610)
- Native Americans led by Popé rebel in southwest (1680)

VIRGINIA

- Virginia Colony is established (1607)
- Colony is saved by export of tobacco (1612)
  - First African slaves are brought to North America (1619)
  - Settlers clash with Powhatan tribe (1622)
  - Settlement burns in Bacon's Rebellion (1676)

NEW ENGLAND

- English Pilgrims establish colony at Plymouth (1620)
- English Puritans establish colony at Boston (1630)
- Roger Williams is banished and founds colony at Providence (1635–1636)
- Anne Hutchinson is banished for heresy (1638)
- Puritans clash with Native Americans in Pequot War (1637) and King Philip's War (1675)

ENGLISH MIDDLE COLONIES

- Dutch found colony of New Netherland (1621)
- English acquire New Netherland and rename it New York (1664)
- William Penn establishes colony of Pennsylvania (1681)
- By the mid-1700s, there are 13 English colonies in North America

Courtesy of the Historical Society of Pennsylvania Collection, Atwater Kent Museum of Philadelphia

TERMS & NAMES

For each term below, write a sentence explaining its connection to the emergence of the American colonies. For each person below, explain his or her role in these colonies.

1. conquistador
2. mestizo
3. Popé
4. John Smith
5. indentured servant
6. John Winthrop
7. Anne Hutchinson
8. Metacom
9. proprietor
10. Quaker

MAIN IDEAS

Use your notes and the information in the chapter to answer the following questions.

Spain's Empire in the Americas *(pages 36–41)*

1. How did Mexican culture develop out of both Spanish and Native American elements?
2. How did Native Americans react to Spanish efforts to establish colonies?

An English Settlement at Jamestown *(pages 42–48)*

3. Explain how John Rolfe transformed the Virginia colony.
4. What conditions caused tension and warfare between settlers and Native Americans in Virginia?
5. What caused Bacon's Rebellion?

Puritan New England *(pages 49–54)*

6. Describe the role of religion in the lives of Puritans living in the Massachusetts Bay Colony.
7. How were the experiences of Roger Williams and Anne Hutchinson similar and different?
8. What caused conflicts between New England colonists and Native Americans?

Settlement of the Middle Colonies *(pages 55–59)*

9. Why did New Netherland gain a reputation for diversity?
10. How did Pennsylvania reflect William Penn's Quaker ideals?

CRITICAL THINKING

1. **USING YOUR NOTES** Using a chart like the one below, summarize the way European settlers and Native Americans interacted in the four listed regions.

Region	Interaction
New Mexico	
Virginia	
New England	
Pennsylvania	

2. **FORMING OPINIONS** John Winthrop dreamed that New England would be "like a City upon a Hill" in which "the eyes of all people are on us." In your opinion, what most impressed you positively and negatively about the founding of each North American colony?

Use the map and your knowledge of U.S. history to answer questions 1 and 2.

1 Which letter on the map shows the first permanent British settlement in North America?

(1) A   **(3)** C
(2) B   **(4)** D

2 Which letter shows an area colonized by Spain?

(1) F   **(3)** H
(2) G   **(4)** J

Use the information in the box and your knowledge of U.S. history to answer question 3.

> · William Penn
> · Roger Williams
> · John Winthrop

3 Of these three colonists, who insisted that Native Americans be paid for land?

(1) William Penn and Roger Williams only
(2) John Winthrop and Roger Williams only
(3) John Winthrop and William Penn only
(4) John Winthrop, William Penn, and Roger Williams

4 Anne Hutchinson was banished from Massachusetts because she taught that —

(1) colonists should remain loyal to the English king.
(2) individuals could interpret the Bible for themselves.
(3) the colonists should not trade with local Native Americans.
(4) the Puritans should break away from the English church.

hmhsocialstudies.com   **TEST PRACTICE**

For additional test practice, go online for:
- Diagnostic tests
- Tutorials

INTERACT WITH HISTORY

Recall the issues that you explored at the beginning of the chapter. Imagine that it is now 1685 and you are a colonist living in one of the English-speaking colonies. Relatives have written to tell you that they are about to emigrate to North America, and they are asking for your thoughts about sharing the land. Write a letter back in which you describe what you think they should know. Include important details from the history of the colonies that you have read about in this chapter.

FOCUS ON WRITING

You have been living in the Massachusetts Bay Colony for nearly a year. You have been asked by leaders of the colony to write an advertisement that will persuade new settlers to come to Massachusetts. Focus your advertisement on the advantages of living in the Massachusetts Bay Colony.

COLLABORATIVE LEARNING

21ST CENTURY

Use the *Electronic Library of Primary Sources* and other reference materials to research a specific law and punishment in 17th-century America. With a group of students, act out a colonial trial. Each student should know the law and perform his or her part carefully. The rest of the class must decide the verdict and punishment. Then have a class discussion about the value of the law and its punishment.

Ponce de Leon

The Spanish conquistador Juan Ponce de Leon was the first European to set foot on land that later became part of the United States. Ponce de Leon first sailed to the Americas with Christopher Columbus on his second voyage in 1493. Once in the Caribbean region, he helped conquer what is now Puerto Rico and was named ruler of the island. In Puerto Rico, Ponce de Leon heard about a nearby island that supposedly held the legendary Fountain of Youth. Its waters were said to make old people young again. In 1513, Ponce de Leon set out to find the island but instead landed in what is now Florida. He named Florida and claimed it for Spain.

Explore important events in the life of Ponce de Leon online. You can find a wealth of information, video clips, primary sources, activities, and more at **hmhsocialstudies.com**.

Caribbean Island Encounters

Watch the video to learn about the first encounters between Spanish explorers and the people of the Caribbean.

Claiming Florida for Spain

Watch the video to learn about Ponce de Leon's first landing on the coast of what is now Florida.

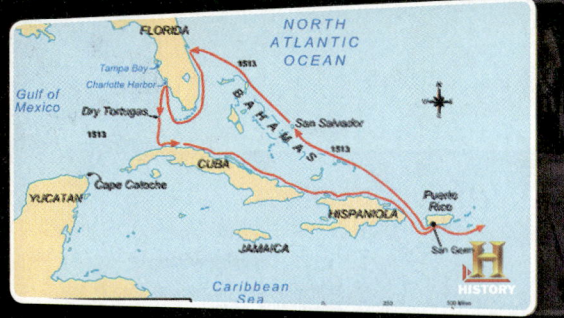

Ponce de Leon's 1513 Route

Study the map to learn about the region of the Americas that Ponce de Leon explored in 1513.

CHAPTER 3
THE COLONIES COME OF AGE

Essential Question

How did the colonies develop economically, socially, and politically?

New York Standards

KEY IDEA 1 The study of New York State and United States history requires an analysis of the development of American culture, its diversity and multicultural context, and the ways people are unified by many values, practices, and traditions.

KEY IDEA 3 Study about the major social, political, economic, cultural, and religious developments in New York State and United States history involves learning about the important roles and contributions of individuals and groups.

SECTION 1: England and Its Colonies

SECTION 2: The Agricultural South

SECTION 3: The Commercial North

SECTION 4: The French and Indian War

View of Boston, around 1764

1651 English Parliament passes first of the Navigation Acts.

1686 James II creates the Dominion of New England.

1693 The College of William and Mary is chartered in Williamsburg, Virginia.

AMERICAS	1650	1660	1670	1680	1690	1700
WORLD						

1652 Dutch settlers establish Cape Town in South Africa.

1660 The English monarchy is restored when Charles II returns from exile.

1688 In England the Glorious Revolution establishes the supremacy of Parliament.

HISTORY

Salem Witch Trials

hmhsocialstudies.com VIDEO

INTERACT
WITH HISTORY

The year is 1750. As a hard-working young colonist, you are proud of the prosperity of your new homeland. However, you are also troubled by the inequalities around you—inequalities between the colonies and Britain, between rich and poor, between men and women, and between free and enslaved.

Explore the Issues

- Can prosperity be achieved without exploiting or enslaving others?
- What does freedom mean, beyond the right to make money without government interference?

1733 Benjamin Franklin publishes *Poor Richard's Almanac.*

1714 Tea is introduced into the colonies.

1754 French and Indian War begins.

1763 Treaty of Paris ends French and Indian War.

| 1710 | 1720 | 1730 | 1740 | 1750 | 1760 |

1707 Act of Union unites England and Wales with Scotland to form Great Britain.

1739 In Japan, 84,000 farmers protest heavy taxation.

1763 Treaty of Paris recognizes British control over much of India.

SECTION
1

CC Unit 2.I.A.1.b   CC Unit 2.I.A.2.c
CC Unit 2.I.A.3.a   CC Unit 2.I.A.3.d
CC Unit 2.I.A.3.e

PI 3.4

England and Its Colonies

MAIN IDEA	WHY IT MATTERS NOW	Terms & Names
England and its largely self-governing colonies prospered under a mutually beneficial trade relationship.	The colonial system of self-governing colonies was the forerunner of our modern system of self-governing states.	• mercantilism • Parliament • Navigation Acts • Dominion of New England • Sir Edmund Andros • Glorious Revolution • salutary neglect

One American's Story

With her father fighting for Britain in the West Indies and her mother ill, 17-year-old Eliza Lucas was left to manage the family's South Carolina plantations. On her own, the enterprising Eliza became the first person in the colonies to grow indigo and developed a way of extracting its deep blue dye. Eliza hoped that her indigo crops would add not only to her family's fortune but to that of the British empire.

A PERSONAL VOICE ELIZA LUCAS PINCKNEY

" We please ourselves with the prospect of exporting in a few years a good quantity from hence, and supplying our mother country [Great Britain] with a manufacture for which she has so great a demand, and which she is now supplied with from the French colonies, and many thousand pounds per annum [year] thereby lost to the nation, when she might as well be supplied here, if the matter were applied to in earnest. "

—quoted in *South Carolina: A Documentary Profile of the Palmetto State*

▲ African slaves working on an indigo plantation in the West Indies; fresh water in a series of leaching basins extracts the dye from the plant.

English settlers like the Lucases exported raw materials such as indigo dye to England, and in return they imported English manufactured goods. This economic relationship benefited both England and its colonies.

England and Its Colonies Prosper

Although many colonists benefited from the trade relationship with the home country, the real purpose of the colonial system was to enrich Britain.

MERCANTILISM The British interest in establishing colonies was influenced by the theory of **mercantilism,** which held that a country's ultimate goal was self-sufficiency and that all countries were in a competition to acquire the most gold and silver.

The Thirteen Colonies to the 1700s

NEW HAMPSHIRE (1623)

MASSACHUSETTS (Plymouth, 1620; Mass. Bay, 1630)

NEW YORK (1624)

RHODE ISLAND (1636)

CONNECTICUT (1633)

NEW JERSEY (1660)

PENNSYLVANIA (1643)

DELAWARE (1638)

MARYLAND (1634)

VIRGINIA (1607)

NORTH CAROLINA (1653)

SOUTH CAROLINA (1670)

GEORGIA (1733)

APPALACHIAN MOUNTAINS

Lake Huron

Lake Ontario

Lake Erie

Hudson River

Connecticut River

Delaware River

Susquehanna River

Potomac River

James River

Roanoke River

Pee Dee River

Savannah River

Santee River

St. Johns River

ATLANTIC OCEAN

40°N

35°N

30°N

25°N

85°W

80°W

75°W

70°W

Economic Activities

New England colonies
Massachusetts . . . . shipbuilding, shipping, fishing, lumber, rum, meat products
New Hampshire . . . . ship masts, lumber, fishing, trade, shipping, livestock, foodstuffs
Connecticut . . . . rum, iron foundries, shipbuilding
Rhode Island . . . . . . snuff, livestock

Middle colonies
New York . . . . furs, wheat, glass, shoes, livestock, shipping, shipbuilding, rum, beer, snuff
Delaware . . . . trade, foodstuffs
New Jersey . . . . . . trade, foodstuffs, copper
Pennsylvania . . . . . flax, shipbuilding

Southern colonies
Virginia . . . . tobacco, wheat, cattle, iron
Maryland . . . . tobacco, wheat, snuff
North Carolina . . . . naval supplies, tobacco, furs
South Carolina . . . . rice, indigo, silk
Georgia . . . . indigo, rice, naval supplies, lumber

GEOGRAPHY SKILLBUILDER
1. **Location** What geographical feature determined the western boundaries of the Southern and Middle colonies?
2. **Region** How did the New England and Middle colonies' economies differ in general from the economy of the South? What may have accounted for this difference?

Legend:
- New England colonies
- Middle colonies
- Southern colonies
- Other British possessions
- French possessions
- Spanish possessions

0   100   200 miles
0   100   200 kilometers

The date provided for each colony indicates the date of the first permanent settlement.

Inspired by mercantilism, nations concentrated on the balance of trade—the amount of goods sold compared to the amount bought—since a favorable balance meant that more gold was coming in than going out. Thus Britain looked to its American colonies as a market for British goods, a source of raw materials that were not native to Britain, and as a producer of goods and materials to be sold to other nations.

THE NAVIGATION ACTS By the mid-1600s, the American colonies were fulfilling their role, at least partially. The colonists exported to England large amounts of raw materials and staples—lumber, furs, fish, and tobacco. In addition, the colonists bought manufactured English goods such as furniture, utensils, books, and china.

However, not all the products the colonists produced for export ended up on English docks. Some of the colonists' lumber and tobacco made its way into the harbors of Spain, France, and Holland. With the nations of Europe clamoring for their goods, many colonial merchants could not resist the opportunity to increase their wealth.

England viewed the colonists' pursuit of foreign markets as an economic threat. According to mercantilist theory, any wealth flowing from the colonies to another nation came at the expense of the home country. As a result, beginning in 1651, England's **Parliament**, the country's legislative body, passed the **Navigation Acts,** a series of laws restricting colonial trade (see chart at left).

The system created by the Navigation Acts benefited England and proved to be good for most colonists as well. Passing all foreign goods through England yielded jobs for English dockworkers and import taxes for the English treasury. Also, by restricting trade to English or colonial ships, the acts spurred a boom in the colonial shipbuilding industry. Ⓐ

The Navigation Acts

- No country could trade with the colonies unless the goods were shipped in either colonial or English ships.

- All vessels had to be operated by crews that were at least three-quarters English or colonial.

- The colonies could export certain products only to England.

- Almost all goods traded between the colonies and Europe first had to pass through an English port.

MAIN IDEA

Analyzing Effects
Ⓐ What effects did the Navigation Acts have on both Britain and its colonies?

Tensions Emerge

The Navigation Acts, however, did not sit well with everyone. A number of colonial merchants resented the trade restrictions, and many continued to smuggle, or trade illegally, goods to and from other countries. For years England did little to stop these violations. Finally, in 1684, King Charles II acted, punishing those colonists whom he believed most resisted English authority: the leaders and merchants of Massachusetts.

CRACKDOWN IN MASSACHUSETTS Charles certainly had evidence to support his belief. The Puritan leaders of Massachusetts had long professed their hostility to royal authority and even suggested that their corporate charter did not require them to obey Parliament.

In 1684, after failing to persuade Massachusetts to obey English laws, England revoked the colony's corporate charter.

◄ Trade between England and her colonies benefited many merchants, such as the wealthy New England trader Moses Marcy.

Massachusetts, the "Puritan utopia," was suddenly a royal colony, under strict control of the crown. **B**

MAIN IDEA

Developing Historical Perspective

B Why did England take action against Massachusetts?

THE DOMINION OF NEW ENGLAND When King James II succeeded his brother Charles in 1685, he immediately aggravated the situation. Seeking to make the colonial governments more obedient, he placed the Northern colonies under a single ruler in Boston. Within three years, the land from southern Maine to New Jersey was united into one vast colony, the **Dominion of New England.**

To rule New England, James picked **Sir Edmund Andros,** a veteran military officer from an aristocratic English family. Andros made his hard-line attitude toward the colonists clear: "You have no more privileges left you, than not to be sold for slaves." Within weeks of arriving in Boston, Andros managed to make thousands of enemies. He angered Puritans by questioning the lawfulness of their religion. He made it clear that the Navigation Acts would be enforced and smugglers prosecuted. Furthermore, he restricted local assemblies and levied taxes without any input from local leaders.

Andros's behavior outraged the Northern colonists. In 1688, the colonists of Massachusetts sent their most prominent minister, Increase Mather, to London to try to get their old charter restored and Andros recalled. However, before Mather could put his diplomatic skills to work, a bloodless revolution in England changed the entire political picture.

THE GLORIOUS REVOLUTION While King James's actions had made him few friends in the colonies, his religious leanings made him even less popular back home. A Roman Catholic who ruled with little respect for Parliament, James had no idea how much his subjects valued their Protestantism and their parliamentary rights. When James fathered a son in 1688, England suddenly faced the possibility of a dynasty of Roman Catholic monarchs.

To head off that possibility, Parliament invited William of Orange, the husband of James's Protestant daughter Mary, to England. William and his army sailed from Holland as James fled the country. In 1689 Parliament voted to offer the throne to William and Mary. In the aftermath of these events, which became known as the **Glorious Revolution,** Parliament passed a series of laws establishing its power over the monarch.

Upon learning of the events in England, the colonists of Massachusetts staged a bloodless rebellion of their own, arresting Andros and his royal councilors. Parliament rapidly restored to their original status the colonies that had been absorbed by the Dominion of New England. In restoring Massachusetts's charter, however, the English government made several changes. The new charter, granted in 1691, called for the king to appoint the governor of Massachusetts and required more religious toleration and non-Puritan representation in the colonial assembly. The Puritans would no longer be able to persecute such groups as the Anglicans—members of the Church of England—and the Quakers.

Background

The first curb on the English monarch's power came in 1215 with Magna Carta, which guaranteed certain civil and political rights to nobles. In time, these rights were extended to all citizens.

Background

Before William and Mary took power they had to accept the English Bill of Rights, which limited the monarchs's power and placed more power in the hands of a representative government.

WORLD STAGE

SCOTLAND

IRELAND (under British rule)

ENGLAND

WALES

ENGLAND BECOMES GREAT BRITAIN

During the period covered in this chapter, England completed the process of absorbing the other kingdoms of the British Isles. This process started when England joined with Wales in 1536. However, to the north of England, Scotland continued to resist English attempts at control.

Weary from constant warfare, the two countries signed the Act of Union in 1707, which joined them as Great Britain.

Today this process of centralization has been reversed. The English Parliament has begun the process of devolution—returning political power to its Celtic neighbors—by reestablishing the Scottish Parliament and creating a Welsh Assembly.

Charles II (1660–1685)

Angered by Massachusetts's refusal to obey English law, he revoked the colony's charter in 1684 and brought Massachusetts under royal control.

James II (1685–1688)

He consolidated the Northern colonies into the Dominion of New England in 1686 and enlisted Sir Edmund Andros to rule the region.

William and Mary (1689–1702)

They succeeded James II after the Glorious Revolution of 1688 and helped establish the supremacy of Parliament. Parliament then dissolved the Dominion of New England and restored the colonies' charters.

England Loosens the Reins

After 1688, England largely turned its attention away from the colonies and toward France, which was competing with England for control of Europe. The home country still expected the colonies to perform their duties of exporting raw materials and importing manufactured goods. As long as they did this, Parliament saw little reason to devote large amounts of money and large numbers of soldiers to aggressively enforcing its colonial laws.

SALUTARY NEGLECT Ironically, England ushered in its new policy of neglect with an attempt to increase its control over the colonies. In the years immediately following the Glorious Revolution, Parliament strengthened the Navigation Acts in two ways. First, it moved smuggling trials from colonial courts—with juries composed of colonists who often found colonial smugglers innocent—to admiralty courts presided over by English judges. Second, it created the Board of Trade, an advisory board with broad powers to monitor colonial trade.

While England appeared to tighten its colonial grip, in reality it loosened its hold. English officials only lightly enforced the new measures as they settled into an overall colonial policy that became known as **salutary neglect.** Salutary—beneficial—neglect meant that England relaxed its enforcement of most regulations in return for the continued economic loyalty of the colonies. As long as raw materials continued flowing into the homeland and the colonists continued to buy English-produced goods, Parliament did not supervise the colonies closely. **C**

THE SEEDS OF SELF-GOVERNMENT This policy of salutary neglect had an important effect on colonial politics as well as economics. In nearly every colony, a governor appointed by the king served as the highest authority. The governor presided over a political structure that included an advisory council, usually appointed by the governor, and a local assembly, elected by eligible colonists (land-owning white males). The governor held a wide range of powers. He had the authority to call and disband the assembly, appoint and dismiss judges, and oversee all aspects of colonial trade.

MAIN IDEA

Synthesizing

C How did both the colonies and Great Britain benefit from the policy of salutary neglect?

FOCUS ON

Even though they were loyal British subjects, the colonists were not beyond criticizing the government. In 1734, a New York printer named John Peter Zenger published several articles critical of the royal governor. Zenger was arrested and charged with libel. At trial, Zenger's lawyer persuaded the jury that the articles could not be considered libel if they were true. Zenger's victory in the trial was an important step toward freedom of the press.

However, just as England's economic policies were stronger in print than in practice, its colonial governors were not as powerful as they might seem. The colonial assembly, not the king, paid the governor's salary. Using their power of the purse liberally, the colonists influenced the governor in a variety of ways, from the approval of laws to the appointment of judges.

Under England's less-than-watchful eye, the colonies were developing a taste for self-government that would eventually create the conditions for rebellion. Nehemiah Grew, a British mercantilist, voiced an early concern about the colonies' growing self-determination. He warned his fellow subjects in 1707.

▲ The sketch above depicts a Puritan meetinghouse built at Plymouth, Massachusetts, in 1683. Meetinghouses served a double purpose, as community halls where people voted on local issues and as religious buildings.

★ A PERSONAL VOICE NEHEMIAH GREW

"**The time may come . . . when the colonies may become populous and with the increase of arts and sciences strong and politic, forgetting their relation to the mother countries, will then confederate and consider nothing further than the means to support their ambition of standing on their [own] legs.**"

—quoted in *The Colonial Period of American History*

However, the policy of salutary neglect that characterized British and colonial relations throughout the first half of the 1700s worked in large part because of the colonists' loyalty to Britain. The men and women of the colonies still considered themselves loyal British subjects, eager to benefit the empire as well as themselves. Aside from a desire for more economic and political breathing room, the colonies had little in common with one another that would unite them against Britain. In particular, the Northern and Southern colonies were developing distinct societies, based on sharply contrasting economic systems.

SECTION 1 ASSESSMENT

1. **TERMS & NAMES** For each term or name, write a sentence explaining its significance.
   - mercantilism
   - Parliament
   - Navigation Acts
   - Dominion of New England
   - Sir Edmund Andros
   - Glorious Revolution
   - salutary neglect

MAIN IDEA

2. **TAKING NOTES**
   Create a problem-solution chart similar to the one below. Fill it in with steps that England took to solve its economic and political problems with the colonists.

Problem	Solutions
Keeping the colonies under economic and political control	1. in 1651
	2. in 1686
	3. after 1688

   Which policy might colonists have resented most and why?

CRITICAL THINKING

3. **ANALYZING ISSUES**
   Reread Grew's warning quoted above. Explain why the British did not want this to happen.
   Think About:
   - the goals of mercantilism
   - what might happen to Great Britain's economy if Grew's prediction came true

4. **SUMMARIZING**
   How did political events in England affect the lives of the colonists? Use evidence from the text to support your response.

5. **PREDICTING EFFECTS**
   Britain established policies to control the American colonies but was inconsistent in its enforcement of those policies. What results might be expected from such inconsistency?

PI 1.1

CC Unit 1.I.A.2.c   CC Unit 1.I.A.2.d
CC Unit 1.I.A.3.g   CC Unit 2.I.A.1.a
CC Unit 2.I.A.2.b   CC Unit 2.I.A.3.c

The Agricultural South

MAIN IDEA	WHY IT MATTERS NOW	Terms & Names
In the Southern colonies, a predominantly agricultural society developed.	The modern South maintains many of its agricultural traditions.	• cash crop • slave • triangular trade • middle passage • Stono Rebellion

One American's Story

hmhsocialstudies.com
TAKING NOTES

Use the graphic organizer online to take notes about Southern society.

In the fall of 1773, Philip Vickers Fithian left his home in Princeton, New Jersey, to tutor the children of Robert Carter III and his wife Frances at their Virginia manor house. Fithian, who kept a journal of his one-year stay there, recalled an evening walk through the plantation.

A PERSONAL VOICE PHILIP VICKERS FITHIAN

" We stroll'd down the Pasture quite to the River, admiring the Pleasantness of the evening, & the delightsome Prospect of the River, Hills, Huts on the Summits, low Bottoms, Trees of various Kinds, and Sizes, Cattle & Sheep feeding some near us, & others at a great distance on the green sides of the Hills. . . . I love to walk on these high Hills . . . where I can have a long View of many Miles & see on the Summits of the Hills Clusters of Savin Trees, through these often a little Farm-House, or Quarter for Negroes. "

—*Journal & Letters of Philip Vickers Fithian*

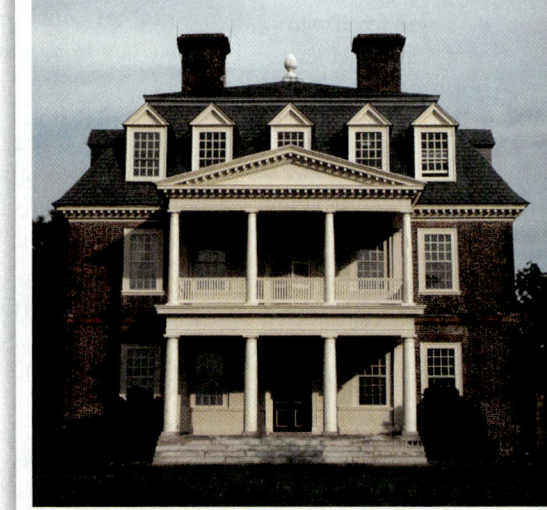

The Shirley plantation house in Virginia is representative of many old Southern mansions. Built in 1723, it was the birthplace of Ann Hill Carter, the mother of Civil War general Robert E. Lee.

Although Fithian's journal goes on to express outrage over the treatment of the slaves, he was fascinated by the plantation system, which had come to dominate the South. The plantation economy led to a largely rural society in which enslaved Africans played an unwilling yet important role.

A Plantation Economy Arises

Since the early days of Jamestown, when the planting of tobacco helped save the settlement, the Southern colonists had staked their livelihood on the fertile soil that stretched from the Chesapeake region to Georgia. Robert Carter, like his father and grandfather before him, specialized in raising a single **cash crop**—one grown primarily for sale rather than for the farmer's own use. In Maryland, Virginia, and North Carolina, farmers grew the broad green leaves of tobacco. In South Carolina and Georgia, rice and later indigo were successful cash crops.

Making Inferences

A How did the geography of the South contribute to the self-sufficiency of Southern plantations?

Throughout the South, plantations developed instead of towns. Because the long and deep rivers allowed access for ocean-going vessels, planters—owners of large profitable plantations—could ship their goods directly to the northern colonies and Europe without the need for city docks and warehouses. Because plantation owners produced most of what they needed on their property, they had little use for shops, bakeries, and markets. There were some cities in the South, including Charles Town (later Charleston), South Carolina, one of the most thriving port cities in the British empire. On the whole, the South developed largely as a rural and self-sufficient society. **A**

Life in Southern Society

As the Southern colonies grew in wealth and population, they also grew in diversity. However, not all groups benefited equally from the South's prosperity.

A DIVERSE AND PROSPEROUS PEOPLE During the 1700s, large numbers of European immigrants traveled to North America in search of a new start. The influx of immigrants helped create a diverse population in both the Northern and Southern colonies. In the South, thousands of Germans settled throughout Maryland and Virginia and as far south as South Carolina. There they raised grain, livestock, and tobacco. A wave of Scots and Scots-Irish also settled in the South, residing mainly along the hills of western North Carolina.

▲ This folk art painting shows an aristocratic Southern mansion perched high on a hill, dominating the warehouses, mill, slave quarters, and other buildings that helped make the plantation self-sufficient. Along the river, a ship carries the plantation's products to the wider world.

Detail from *The Country Housewife*, published in London in 1770. Many settlers brought this guidebook with them when they immigrated to the colonies.

While small farmers formed the majority of the Southern population, the planters controlled much of the South's economy. They also controlled its political and social institutions. The activities at the Carter mansion described by Philip Fithian reflected the luxury of planter life. Fithian recalled attending numerous balls, banquets, dance recitals, and parties that continued for several days.

By the mid-1700s, life was good for many Southern colonists, particularly those in the Chesapeake Bay region. Due to a large growth in the entire colonies' export trade, colonial standards of living rose dramatically in the years from 1700 to 1770. Colonists along the Chesapeake, where tobacco prices had rebounded after tumbling during the late 1600s, saw the greatest economic boom. From 1713 to 1774 tobacco exports there almost tripled, and many Chesapeake farmers and merchants prospered. **B**

THE ROLE OF WOMEN Women in Southern society—and Northern society as well—shared a common trait: second-class citizenship. Women had few legal or social rights; for instance, they could not vote or preach. Even daughters of wealthy Southern planters were usually taught only the basics of reading, writing, and arithmetic. Instead, they were mostly educated in the social graces or in domestic tasks, such as canning and preserving food, sewing, and embroidery.

Throughout the day, the average Southern woman worked over a hot fire baking bread or boiling meat. Her outdoor duties included milking the cows, slaughtering pigs for ham and bacon, and tending the garden. She was also expected to sew, wash clothes, and clean. Women of the planter class escaped most of these tasks, as servants handled the household chores. Regardless of class, however, most

MAIN IDEA

Analyzing Causes

B Explain how colonial standards of living rose so dramatically in the 18th century.

NOW & THEN

TOBACCO AND NORTH CAROLINA'S ECONOMY

Tobacco has long been a key element of the Southern economy. The soil and climate of the South are ideal for growing tobacco, which was first harvested for commercial use in 1612. In recent years, however, tobacco revenues have shrunk as North Carolina lessens its dependence on tobacco and develops a more diversified economy.

The focal point of North Carolina's new economy is the Research Triangle, so called for the cluster of major universities in Raleigh, Durham, and Chapel Hill. These universities cooperate in research and development in many areas, including technology and health care. Other new industries, such as computers and telecommunications, are fueling North Carolina's growth.

NORTH CAROLINA IN THE COLONIAL ERA

- General farming
- Tobacco
- Rice and indigo

NORTH CAROLINA TODAY

- General farming
- Cotton
- Cotton and general farming
- Tobacco and general farming
- Special crops and general farming

Winston-Salem
food products
furniture
machinery
tobacco products

Durham
Chapel Hill
Raleigh

Asheville
the arts
furniture
lumber
paper

Charlotte
banking
chemicals
computers
printing
telecommunications
textiles

Greensboro
finance
heavy equipment
telecommunications

Raleigh, Durham, and Chapel Hill
computers
instruments
medicines
research
telecommunications
textiles

women bowed to their husbands' will. An excerpt from Virginia plantation owner William Byrd's diary hints at Lucia Parke Byrd's subservient position: "My wife and I had another scold about mending my shoes," Byrd wrote, "but it was soon over by her submission." **C**

INDENTURED SERVANTS Also low on Southern society's ladder were indentured servants. Many of these young, mostly white men had traded a life of prison or poverty in Europe for a limited term of servitude in North America. They had few rights while in bondage. Those who lived through their harsh years of labor—and many did not—saw their lives improve only slightly as they struggled to survive on the western outskirts of the Southern colonies.

While historians estimate that indentured servants made up a significant portion of the colonial population in the 1600s—between one-half and two-thirds of all white immigrants after 1630—their numbers declined toward the end of the century. With continuing reports of hardship in the New World, many laborers in Europe decided to stay home. Faced with a depleted labor force and a growing agricultural economy, the Southern colonists turned to another group to meet their labor needs: African slaves.

Slavery Becomes Entrenched

The English colonists gradually turned to the use of African **slaves**—people who were considered the property of others—after efforts to meet their labor needs with enslaved Native Americans and indentured servants failed. During the 1600s and 1700s, plantation owners and other colonists would subject hundreds of thousands of Africans to a life of intense labor and cruelty in North America.

THE EVOLUTION OF SLAVERY In the early days of the colonies, the English, like their Spanish counterparts, had forced Native Americans to work for them. However, the English settlers found it increasingly difficult to enslave Native Americans. Aside from being reluctant to learn English labor techniques, Native Americans could easily escape because they had far better knowledge of the local fields and forests than did the colonists.

As the indentured servant population fell, the price of indentured servants rose. As a result, the English colonists turned to African slaves as an alternative. A slave worked for life and thus brought a much larger return on the investment. In addition, most white colonists convinced themselves that Africans' dark skin was a sign of inferiority, and so had few reservations about subjecting them to a life of servitude. Black Africans were also thought better able to endure the harsh physical demands of plantation labor in hot climates. By 1690, nearly 13,000 black slaves toiled in the Southern colonies. By 1750, that number had increased to almost 200,000. **D**

THE EUROPEAN SLAVE TRADE Before the English began the large-scale importation of African slaves to their colonies on the American mainland, Africans had been laboring as slaves for years in the West Indies. During the late 1600s, English planters in Jamaica and Barbados imported tens of thousands of African slaves to work their sugar plantations. By 1690, the African population on Barbados was about

WORLD STAGE

SERFS, SLAVES, AND SERVANTS

Many forms of servitude existed throughout Europe and the Americas well into the 19th century. Serfs were peasants who were considered part of a lord's property. Unlike slaves, who could be moved to different locations, serfs were obliged to remain on the land that they farmed for the landowner.

While the institution of serfdom declined in the later Middle Ages, it persisted with remarkable strength in the west and south of England. These were the very regions where many Southern landowners and indentured servants originated.

Serfdom was ended in England in the 1600s, but survived in Russia until 1861. Tsar Alexander's Edict of Emancipation freed the Russian serfs just two years before President Lincoln's Emancipation Proclamation began the process of freeing the American slaves.

This plan and section of the British slave ship "Brookes" was published in London around 1790 by a leading British antislavery advocate named Thomas Clarkson. The image effectively conveys the degradation and inhumanity of the slave trade, which reduced human beings to the level of merchandise.

hmhsocialstudies.com

INTERACTIVE MAP

Learn more about the triangular trade.

60,000—three times the white population.

During the 17th century, Africans had become part of a transatlantic trading network described as the **triangular trade.** This term referred to a three-way trading process: merchants carried rum and other goods from New England to Africa; in Africa they traded their merchandise for enslaved people, whom they transported to the West Indies and sold for sugar and molasses; these goods were then shipped to New England to be distilled into rum. The "triangular" trade, in fact, encompassed a network of trade routes criss-crossing the Northern and Southern colonies, the West Indies, England, Europe, and Africa. The network carried an array of traded goods, from furs and fruit to tar and tobacco, as well as African people. **E**

THE MIDDLE PASSAGE The voyage that brought Africans to the West Indies and later to North America was known as the **middle passage,** because it was considered the middle leg of the transatlantic trade triangle. Sickening cruelty characterized this journey. In the bustling ports along West Africa, European traders branded Africans with red-hot irons for identification purposes and packed them into the dark holds of large ships. On board a slave ship, Africans fell victim to whippings and beatings from slavers as well as diseases that swept through the vessel. The smell of blood, sweat, and excrement filled the hold, as the African passengers lived in their own vomit and waste. One African, Olaudah Equiano, recalled the inhumane conditions on his trip from West Africa to the West Indies in 1756 when he was 11 years old.

A PERSONAL VOICE OLAUDAH EQUIANO

"The closeness of the place, and the heat of the climate, added to the number in the ship, which was so crowded that each had scarcely room to turn himself, almost suffocated us. This produced copious perspirations, so that the air soon became unfit for respiration from a variety of loathsome smells, and brought on a sickness among the slaves, of which many died . . . ."

—*The Interesting Narrative of the Life of Olaudah Equiano*

Whether they died from disease or from cruel treatment by merchants, or whether they committed suicide, as many did by plunging into the ocean, up to 20 percent or more of the Africans aboard each slave ship perished during the trip to the New World.

MAIN IDEA

Developing Historical Perspective
E What parts of the world were involved in the triangular trade?

Olaudah Equiano was kidnapped from Africa and sold to a succession of owners before buying his freedom.

SLAVERY IN THE SOUTH Africans who survived their ocean voyage entered an extremely difficult life of bondage in North America. Most slaves—probably 80 to 90 percent—worked in the fields. On large plantations, a white slave owner directed their labor, often through field bosses. On smaller farms, slaves often worked alongside their owner.

The other 10 to 20 percent of slaves worked in the house of their owner or as artisans. Domestic slaves cooked, cleaned, and raised the master's children. While owners did not subject their domestic slaves to the rigors of field labor, they commonly treated them with equal cruelty. Other slaves developed skills as artisans—carpenters, blacksmiths, and bricklayers. Owners often rented these slaves out to work on other plantations.

Whatever their task, slaves led a grueling existence. Full-time work began around age 12 and continued until death. John Ferdinand Smyth, an English traveler, described a typical slave workday.

A PERSONAL VOICE JOHN FERDINAND SMYTH

" He (the slave) is called up in the morning at daybreak, and is seldom allowed time enough to swallow three mouthfuls of hominy, or hoecake, but is driven out immediately to the field to hard labor, at which he continues, without intermission, until noon . . . About noon is the time he eats his dinner, and he is seldom allowed an hour for that purpose . . . They then return to severe labor, which continues in the field until dusk in the evening."

—quoted in *Planters and Pioneers*

MAIN IDEA

Making Inferences

F Why weren't slave owners punished if they killed their slaves?

Slave owners whipped and beat those slaves they thought were disobedient or disrespectful. In Virginia, the courts did not consider slave owners guilty of murder for killing their slaves during punishment. **F**

Africans Cope in Their New World

The Africans who were transported to North America came from a variety of different cultures and spoke varied languages. Forced to labor in a strange new land, these diverse peoples bonded together for support and fought against their plight in numerous ways.

CULTURE AND FAMILY In the midst of the horrors of slavery, Africans developed a way of life based strongly on their cultural heritage. Enslaved people wove baskets and molded pottery as they had done in their homeland. They kept alive their musical traditions and retold the stories of their ancestors. Because slave merchants tore apart many African families, slaves created new families among the people with whom they lived. If a master sold a parent to another plantation, other slaves stepped in to raise the children left behind.

The African influence remained particularly strong among the slaves of South Carolina and Georgia. By the mid-1700s, planters in these colonies had imported large numbers of Africans with rice-growing expertise to help develop rice as the colonies' main cash crop. Many of these slaves came from the same region in West Africa.

Background
Rice was an important crop in West Africa for centuries before the slave trade began.

One of the most important customs that Africans kept alive in North America was their dance. From Maryland to Georgia, slaves continued to practice what became known in the colonies as the ring shout, a circular religious dance. While variations of the dance brought to North America differed throughout the regions in West and Central Africa, the dance paid tribute to the group's ancestors and gods and usually involved loud chants and quick, circular steps. Despite the white colonists' efforts to eradicate it, the ritual endured.

▲ The gourd fiddle and drum, both made by slaves, reflect ways in which enslaved African Americans continued their African traditions.

RESISTANCE AND REVOLT Enslaved Africans also resisted their position of subservience. Throughout the colonies, planters reported slaves faking illness, breaking tools, and staging work slowdowns. One master noted the difficulty in forcing African slaves to accept their lot, commenting that if a slave "must be broke, either from Obstinacy, or, which I am more apt to suppose, from Greatness of Soul, [it] will require . . . hard Discipline. . . . You would really be surpriz'd at their Perseverance . . . they often die before they can be conquer'd."

Some slaves pushed their resistance to open revolt. One such uprising, the **Stono Rebellion,** began on a September Sunday in 1739. That morning, about 20 slaves gathered at the Stono River southwest of Charles Town. Wielding guns and other weapons, they killed several planter families and marched south, beating drums and loudly inviting other slaves to join them in their plan to flee to Spanish-held Florida.

By late Sunday afternoon, a white militia had surrounded the group of escaping slaves. The two sides clashed, and many slaves died in the fighting. Those captured were executed. Despite the rebellion's failure, it sent a chill through many Southern colonists and led to the tightening of harsh slave laws already in place. However, slave rebellions continued into the 1800s.

Despite the severe punishment that escape attempts brought, a number of slaves tried to run away. The runaway notices published in the various newspapers throughout Virginia show that from 1736 to 1801, at least 1,279 enslaved men and women in that state took to flight. Many who succeeded in running away from their masters found refuge with Native American tribes, and marriage between runaway slaves and Native Americans was common.

As the Southern colonies grew, they became ever more dependent on the use of African slavery. This was not the case in the Northern colonies, due mainly to an economy driven by commerce rather than agriculture. This economic distinction spurred the North to develop in ways that differed greatly from the South.

SECTION 2 ASSESSMENT

1. TERMS & NAMES For each term or name, write a sentence explaining its significance.

- cash crop
- slave
- triangular trade
- middle passage
- Stono Rebellion

MAIN IDEA

2. TAKING NOTES
Fill in a chart like the one below to show the social order of Southern society. In the tiers, name and describe the different social classes, ranging from most powerful at the top to least powerful at the bottom.

| 1. planters |
| 2. |
| 3. |
| 4. |
| 5. |

CRITICAL THINKING

3. DRAWING CONCLUSIONS
Why were so many enslaved Africans brought to the Southern colonies? **Think About:**

- why Native Americans were not used instead
- why Europeans were not used instead
- the cash crops of the South
- the triangular trade

4. ANALYZING PRIMARY SOURCES
The ad shown above is from a Virginia newspaper of the 1730s. What does this ad reveal about the brutality of the slave system?

5. ANALYZING CAUSES
Why did fewer cities develop in the South during the 1700s? Use evidence from the text to support your response.

CC Unit 1.I.A.2.d   CC Unit 1.I.A.3.g
CC Unit 2.I.A.2.c   CC Unit 2.I.A.4.b
CC Unit 2.I.A.4.c

PI 1.1

The Commercial North

hmhsocialstudies.com
TAKING NOTES

Use the graphic organizer online to take notes about the Northern colonies.

MAIN IDEA	WHY IT MATTERS NOW	Terms & Names
The Northern colonies developed a predominantly urban society, based on commerce and trade.	The states that were once the Northern colonies remain predominantly urban today.	• Enlightenment • Jonathan Edwards • Benjamin Franklin • Great Awakening

One American's Story

After growing up on a Massachusetts farm, John Adams found city life in Boston distracting. In 1759 he wrote,

A PERSONAL VOICE JOHN ADAMS

"**Who can study in Boston Streets? I am unable to observe the various Objects that I meet, with sufficient Precision. My Eyes are so diverted with Chimney Sweeps, Carriers of Wood, Merchants, Ladies, Priests, Carts, Horses, Oxen, Coaches, Market men and Women, Soldiers, Sailors, and my Ears with the Rattle Gabble of them all that I cant think long enough in the Street upon any one Thing to start and pursue a Thought.**"

—The Diary and Autobiography of John Adams

John Adams

Adams's description illustrates the changes that transformed the New England and Middle colonies during the 18th century. The growth of thriving commercial cities made the North radically different from the agricultural South. In addition, interest in education was on the rise, partially due to intellectual and religious movements. These movements brought about social changes that contributed to the colonies' eventual break with England.

Commerce Grows in the North

The theory of mercantilism held that colonies existed to help the home country amass wealth. However, the American colonies found their own economy prospering more. From 1650 to 1750, the colonies' economy grew twice as fast as Great Britain's economy did. Much of this growth occurred in the New England and middle colonies.

A DIVERSIFIED ECONOMY Unlike farms in the South, those in the New England and middle colonies usually produced several crops instead of a single one. Cold winters and rocky soil restricted New Englanders to small farms. In the more fertile areas of the middle colonies, such as New York and Pennsylvania, farmers raised a variety of crops and livestock, including wheat, corn, cattle, and hogs. They produced so much that they sold their surplus food to the West Indies, where raising sugar cane produced such tremendous profits that planters did not want to waste land growing food for the slaves who worked their fields.

A diverse commercial economy also developed in the New England and Middle colonies. Grinding wheat, harvesting fish, and sawing lumber became thriving industries. Colonists also manufactured impressive numbers of ships and quantities of iron. By 1760, the colonists had built one-third of all British ships and were producing more iron than England was. While at times the North's economy dipped, many colonists prospered. In particular, the number of merchants grew. By the mid-1700s, merchants were one of the most powerful groups in the North. **Ⓐ**

URBAN LIFE The expansion in trade caused port cities to grow. Only one major port, Charles Town, existed in the South. In contrast, the North boasted Boston, New York City, and Philadelphia. In fact, Philadelphia eventually became the second largest city (after London) in the British empire. Philadelphia was the first large city since ancient Roman times to be laid out on a gridlike street plan. For colonists accustomed to the winding medieval streets of European cities, this kind of rational urban planning must have appeared startling and new. Influenced by Sir Christopher Wren's designs for the rebuilding of London after the Great Fire of 1666, Philadelphia included a number of open squares intended for public use. Both the grid plan and the parklike square would become important elements of American urban design in the centuries to come.

With its parks, police patrols, paved streets, and whale-oil lamps to light the sidewalks, Philadelphia was a sophisticated city. However, the high concentration of people without adequate public services caused problems. Firewood and clean water could be hard to come by, whereas garbage was abundant.

Vocabulary
profit: the money left over after costs are subtracted from income

MAIN IDEA

Forming Generalizations
Ⓐ What kinds of industries developed in the North?

Daily Urban Life in Colonial Times

By the mid-18th century, colonial cities were prosperous and growing. Brick rowhouses were replacing the wooden structures of the 17th century, while large mansions and churches, built of brick or stone, were rising everywhere.

English colonists had brought with them a preference for houses (as opposed to apartments, which were the norm in the cities of other European countries). As in Britain, the size of the house indicated the social position of its occupant.

In contemporary Philadelphia, Elfreth's Alley preserves the scale and appearance of a mid-18th-century city street. A neighborhood like this could have commercial and residential uses. Many people lived above the shops where they worked. ▶

◀ The house known as Cliveden, also in Philadelphia, was built in 1767. In contrast to the artisan or lower-middle-class housing of Elfreth's Alley, this large, freestanding mansion shows the kind of building that the rich could afford.

Northern Society Is Diverse

Northern society was composed of diverse groups with sometimes conflicting interests. Groups whose interests clashed with those of the people in power included immigrants, African Americans, and women.

INFLUX OF IMMIGRANTS

Even more so than those in the South, the Northern colonies attracted a variety of immigrants. The Germans and the Scots-Irish were the largest non-English immigrant groups. Germans began arriving in Pennsylvania in the 1680s. Most were fleeing economic distress, but some, such as the Mennonites, came to Pennsylvania because of William Penn's policy of religious freedom and because they shared the Quakers' opposition to war.

The Scots-Irish—descendants of Scottish Protestants who had colonized northern Ireland in the 1600s—entered mostly through Philadelphia.

Colonial Diversity

1700

- African **11%**
- Dutch **4%**
- Scottish **3%**
- Other European **2%**
- English/Welsh **80%**

1755

- African **20%**
- German **7%**
- Scots-Irish **7%**
- Irish **5%**
- Scottish **4%**
- Dutch **3%**
- Other European **2%**
- English/Welsh **52%**

Source: *The Enduring Vision*

SKILLBUILDER Interpreting Graphs
What new ethnic groups had settled in the American colonies by 1755?

SEE SKILLBUILDER HANDBOOK, PAGE R28.

They commonly arrived as families. Many established farms in frontier areas such as western Pennsylvania, where they often clashed with Native Americans.

Other ethnic groups included the Dutch in New York, Scandinavians in Delaware, and Jews in such cities as Newport and Philadelphia. The different groups did not always mix. Benjamin Franklin, echoing the sentiments of many English colonists, made the following complaint in 1751.

★ A PERSONAL VOICE BENJAMIN FRANKLIN

" Why should the [Germans] be suffered to swarm into our Settlements and, by herding together establish their Language and Manners to the Exclusion of ours? Why should Pennsylvania, founded by the English, become a Colony of Aliens, who will shortly be so numerous as to Germanize us instead of our Anglifying them? "

—"Observations Concerning the Increase of Mankind, Peopling of Countries, etc."

MAIN IDEA

Analyzing Effects

B What were the negative and positive effects of the growing ethnic diversity in the colonies?

In spite of this fear of being swamped by non-English speakers, English colonists found ways of getting along with their new neighbors, thus furthering the evolution of a truly diverse American society. **B**

SLAVERY IN THE NORTH

Because raising wheat and corn did not require as much labor as raising tobacco or rice, Northerners had less incentive to turn to slavery than did Southerners. However, slavery did exist in New England and was extensive throughout the Middle colonies, as were racial prejudices against blacks—free or enslaved.

While still considered property, most enslaved persons in New England enjoyed greater legal standing than slaves elsewhere in the colonies. They could sue and be sued, and they had the right of appeal to the highest courts. As in the South, however, enslaved persons in the North led harsh lives and were considered less than human beings. Laws forbade them to gather or to carry weapons, and there were no laws to protect them from cruel treatment. Reacting to the harsh conditions, slaves sometimes rebelled. An uprising occurred in 1712 in New York, leading to the execution of 21 people. In 1741, a series of suspicious fires and robberies led New Yorkers to fear another uprising. They decided to make an example of the suspected ringleaders, burning alive 13 persons and hanging 18.

WOMEN IN NORTHERN SOCIETY As in the South, women in the North had extensive work responsibilities but few legal rights. Most people in the colonies still lived on farms, where women faced unceasing labor. A colonial wife had virtually no legal rights. She could not vote. Most women could not enter into contracts, buy or sell property, or keep their own wages if they worked outside the home. Only single women and widows could run their own businesses.

In New England, religion as well as law served to keep women under their husbands' rule. Puritan clergymen insisted that wives must submit to their husbands, saying, "Wives are part of the House and Family, and ought to be under a Husband's Government: they should Obey their own Husbands."

WITCHCRAFT TRIALS IN SALEM The strict limitations on women's roles, combined with social tensions, the strained relations with the Native Americans, and religious fanaticism, contributed to one of the most bizarre episodes in American history. In February 1692, several Salem girls accused a West Indian slave woman, Tituba, of practicing witchcraft. In this Puritan New England town of Salem, where the constant fear of Native American attacks encouraged a preoccupation with violence and death, the girls' accusations drew a great deal of attention. When the girls accused others of witchcraft, the situation grew out of control, as those who were accused tried to save themselves by naming other "witches."

Hysteria gripped the town as more and more people made false accusations. The accusations highlighted social and religious tensions. Many of the accusers were poor and brought charges against richer residents. In addition, a high proportion of victims were women who might be considered too independent.

The accusations continued until the girls dared to charge such prominent citizens as the governor's wife. Finally realizing that they had been hearing false evidence, officials closed the court. The witchcraft hysteria ended—but not before 19 persons had been hanged and another person killed by being crushed to death. Four or five more "witches" died in jail, and about 150 were imprisoned. **C**

MAIN IDEA

Analyzing Causes

C What were the underlying causes of the Salem witch hunts in 1692?

New Ideas Influence the Colonists

The Salem trials of 1692 caused many people to question the existence of witchcraft. During the 1700s, individuals began to make other changes in the way they viewed the world.

THE ENLIGHTENMENT Since before the Renaissance, philosophers in Europe had been using reason and the scientific method to obtain knowledge. Scientists looked beyond religious doctrine to investigate how the world worked. Influenced by the observations of Nicolaus Copernicus, Galileo Galilei, and Sir Isaac Newton, people determined that the earth revolved around the sun and not vice versa. They also concluded that the world is governed not by chance or miracles but by fixed mathematical laws. These ideas about nature gained prevalence in the 1700s in a movement called the **Enlightenment.**

Enlightenment ideas traveled from Europe to the colonies and spread quickly in numerous books and pamphlets. Literacy was particularly high in New England because the Puritans had long supported public education to ensure that everyone could read the Bible.

One outstanding Enlightenment figure was **Benjamin Franklin.** Franklin embraced the notion of obtaining truth through experimentation and reasoning. For example, his most famous experiment—flying a kite in a thunderstorm— demonstrated that lightning was a form of electrical power.

Background
One Enlightenment thinker who had an impact on American thought was the French writer Voltaire. In his works, Voltaire condemned political corruption, social injustice, and religious intolerance. He also was a vigorous defender of freedom of speech.

The Enlightenment also had a profound effect on political thought in the colonies. Colonial leaders such as Thomas Jefferson used reason to conclude that individuals have natural rights, which governments must respect. Enlightenment principles eventually would lead many colonists to question the authority of the British monarchy. **D**

MAIN IDEA

Forming Generalizations
D Why was the Enlightenment such a revolutionary movement?

THE GREAT AWAKENING By the early 1700s, the Puritan church had lost its grip on society, and church membership was in decline. The new Massachusetts charter of 1691 forced Puritans to allow freedom of worship and banned the practice of permitting only Puritan church members to vote. Furthermore, many people seemed to be doing so well in this world that they paid little attention to the next. As Puritan merchants prospered, they developed a taste for material possessions and sensual pleasures.

Jonathan Edwards, of Northampton, Massachusetts, was one member of the clergy who sought to revive the intensity and commitment of the original Puritan vision. Edwards preached that church attendance was not enough for salvation; people must acknowledge their sinfulness and feel God's love for them. In his most famous sermon, delivered in 1741, Edwards vividly described God's mercy.

★ **A PERSONAL VOICE**
JONATHAN EDWARDS

" **The God that holds you over the pit of hell, much as one holds a spider, or some loathsome insect over the fire, abhors [hates] you, and is dreadfully provoked: His wrath towards you burns like fire; He looks upon you as worthy of nothing else but to be cast into the fire; . . . and yet it is nothing but His hand that holds you from falling into the fire every moment.** "

— "Sinners in the Hands of an Angry God"

Other preachers traveled from village to village, stirring people to rededicate themselves to God. Such traveling preachers attracted thousands, making it necessary for revival meetings to be held outdoors. The resulting religious revival, known as the **Great Awakening,** lasted throughout the 1730s and 1740s.

KEY PLAYERS

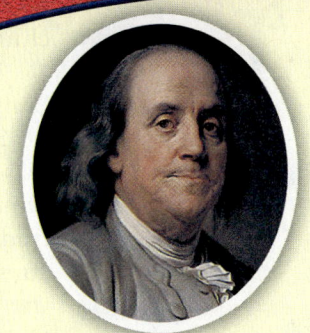

**BENJAMIN FRANKLIN
1706–1790**

Benjamin Franklin was one of the leading champions of Enlightenment ideals in America. Like other scientists and philosophers of the Enlightenment, Franklin believed that human beings could use their intellectual powers to improve their lot.

Franklin's observations and experiments led to a number of inventions, including the lightning rod, bifocals, and a new kind of heating system that became known as the Franklin stove. Inventions like these proved that knowledge derived from scientific experiment could be put to practical use.

Franklin's achievements brought him world renown. In 1756 British scholars elected him to the Royal Society, and in 1772 France honored him with membership in the French Academy of Sciences.

**JONATHAN EDWARDS
1703–1758**

Descended from a long line of Puritan ministers, Jonathan Edwards denied that humans had the power to perfect themselves. He believed that "however you may have reformed your life in many things," as a sinner you were destined for hell unless you had a "great change of heart."

Edwards was a brilliant thinker who entered Yale College when he was only 13. His preaching was one of the driving forces of the Great Awakening. Ironically, when the religious revival died down, Edwards's own congregation rejected him for being too strict about doctrine. Edwards moved to Stockbridge, Massachusetts, in 1751, where he lived most of his remaining years as missionary to a Native American settlement.

The Great Awakening brought many colonists, as well as Native Americans and African Americans, into organized Christian churches for the first time. As the movement gained momentum, it also challenged the authority of established churches. Some colonists abandoned their old Puritan or Anglican congregations. At the same time, independent denominations, such as the Baptists and Methodists, gained new members. The Great Awakening also led to an increased interest in higher education, as several Protestant denominations founded colleges such as Princeton (originally the College of New Jersey), Brown, Columbia (originally King's College), and Dartmouth to train ministers for their rapidly growing churches.

While the Great Awakening and the Enlightenment emphasized opposing aspects of human experience—emotionalism and reason, respectively—they had similar consequences. Both caused people to question traditional authority. Moreover, both stressed the importance of the individual—the Enlightenment by emphasizing human reason, and the Great Awakening by de-emphasizing the role of church authority.

These movements helped lead the colonists to question Britain's authority over their lives. The separation between Britain and the colonies was further hastened by another significant event, a North American war between Great Britain and France, in which the colonists fought on Britain's side.

Vocabulary
denomination: a large group of religious congregations united by shared beliefs

The British minister George Whitefield was a major force behind the Great Awakening. In his seven journeys to the American colonies between 1738 and 1770, Whitefield preached dramatic sermons that brought many listeners to tears.

SECTION 3 ASSESSMENT

1. TERMS & NAMES For each term or name, write a sentence explaining its significance.
• **Enlightenment** • **Benjamin Franklin** • **Jonathan Edwards** • **Great Awakening**

MAIN IDEA

2. TAKING NOTES
Re-create the diagram below on your paper and fill it in with historical examples that illustrate the main idea at the top.

The Diversity of Northern Colonies		
Economy	Population	Religious Groups
examples	examples	examples

Name the advantages and the disadvantages of this kind of society.

CRITICAL THINKING

3. COMPARING
What positive and negative trends that emerged in the Northern colonies during the 1700s do you think still affect the United States today? Support your responses with details from the text. **Think About:**

• the growth of cities
• the influx of immigrants
• the status of women and African Americans
• the effects of the Enlightenment and the Great Awakening

4. MAKING INFERENCES
How do you think a person who believed in the ideas of the Enlightenment might have assessed the Salem witchcraft trials? Support your response with reasons.

5. CONTRASTING
In what ways did the Northern colonies differ from the Southern colonies in the 1700s? Use evidence from the text to support your response.

SECTION
4

PI 1.1
PI 3.4

CC Unit 2.I.A.2.a   CC Unit 2.I.A.2.c
CC Unit 2.I.A.3.e   CC Unit 2.I.A.4.a
CC Unit 2.I.A.4.c

The French and Indian War

MAIN IDEA	WHY IT MATTERS NOW	Terms & Names
British victory over the French in North America enlarged the British empire but led to new conflicts with the colonists.	British victories helped spread the English language throughout North America.	•New France •George Washington •French and Indian War •William Pitt •Pontiac •Proclamation of 1763 •George Grenville •Sugar Act

One American's Story

hmhsocialstudies.com
TAKING NOTES

Use the graphic organizer online to take notes on the major events of the French and Indian War.

Joseph Nichols and other Massachusetts men joined British soldiers in fighting the French near the Hudson River in 1758. Yet even though the colonists and the British had united against a common enemy, the two groups held conflicting ideas about authority. On October 31, 1758, Nichols recorded the following dispute.

A PERSONAL VOICE JOSEPH NICHOLS

"About sunrise, the chief officer of the fort came to our regiment and ordered all our men up to the falls to meet the wagons and teams. Our men seemed to be loath to go before they eat. Those that refused to turn out, he drove out, and some he struck with his staff, which caused a great uproar among us. Our people in general declare in case we are so used tomorrow, blows shall end the dispute."

—quoted in *A People's Army*

▲ The British general Edward Braddock met defeat and death near Fort Duquesne in 1755. In the French and Indian War, the colonists and the British fought side by side for nine years.

This "uproar" demonstrates that the British and the colonists differed in their views about authority and individual freedom. During the war between Great Britain and France, these conflicting viewpoints triggered divisions between Great Britain and its colonies that would never heal.

Rivals for an Empire

In the 1750s, France was Great Britain's biggest rival in the struggle to build a world empire, and one major area of contention between them was the rich Ohio River Valley. The colonists favored Great Britain because they still thought of themselves as British; as well, they were eager to expand the colonies westward from the increasingly crowded Atlantic seaboard.

FRANCE'S NORTH AMERICAN EMPIRE France had begun its North American empire in 1534, when Jacques Cartier explored the St. Lawrence River. In 1608, Samuel de Champlain founded the town of Quebec, the first permanent French settlement in North America.

After establishing Quebec, French priests and traders spread into the heart of the continent. In 1682, Robert Cavelier, Sieur de La Salle, claimed the entire Mississippi Valley for France, naming it Louisiana in honor of King Louis XIV. However, by 1754 the European population of **New France,** the French colony in North America, had grown to only about 70,000 (compared to more than 1,000,000 in the British colonies).

From the start, New France differed from the British colonies. Typical French colonists included fur traders and Catholic priests who wanted to convert Native Americans. Neither had a desire to build towns or raise families.

The French colonists also developed friendlier relations with Native Americans than did the British. They relied on Hurons, Ottawas, Ojibwas, and others to do most of the trapping and then traded with them for the furs, which were in great demand in Europe. This trade relationship led to several military alliances. As early as 1609, for example, the Algonquin and other Native Americans used Champlain's help to defeat their traditional enemies, the Mohawk Iroquois. **Ⓐ**

MAIN IDEA

Contrasting
Ⓐ How was the French colony in North America unlike the British colonies?

Britain Defeats an Old Enemy

As the French empire in North America expanded, it collided with the growing British empire. France and Great Britain had already fought two inconclusive wars during the previous half-century. In 1754, the French-British conflict reignited. In that year, the French built Fort Duquesne at the point where the Allegheny and Monongahela rivers join to form the Ohio—the site of modern Pittsburgh.

However, the British had previously granted 200,000 acres of land in the Ohio country to a group of wealthy planters. The Virginia governor sent militia, a group of ordinary citizens who performed military duties, to evict the French.

The small band, led by an ambitious 22-year-old officer named **George Washington,** established an outpost called Fort Necessity about 40 miles from Fort Duquesne. In May 1754, Washington's militia attacked a small detachment of French soldiers, and the French swiftly counterattacked. In the battle that followed in July, the French forced Washington to surrender. Although neither side realized it, these battles at Fort Necessity were the opening of the **French and Indian War,** the fourth war between Great Britain and France for control of North America.

EARLY FRENCH VICTORIES A year after his defeat, Washington again headed into battle, this time as an aide to the British general Edward Braddock, whose mission was to drive the French out of the Ohio Valley.

Braddock first launched an attack on Fort Duquesne. As Braddock and nearly 1,500 soldiers neared the fort, French soldiers and their Native American allies ambushed them. The British soldiers, accustomed to enemies who marched in orderly rows rather than ones who fought from behind trees, turned and fled.

HISTORICAL SPOTLIGHT

WASHINGTON'S RESIGNATION

George Washington's military career nearly ended shortly after it started. In 1754, as the British prepared to wage war on France in North America, Washington eagerly awaited a position with the regular British army.

The governor of Virginia offered Washington the rank of captain— a demotion from Washington's position as colonel. Washington angrily rejected the offer as well as a later proposal that he retain the rank of colonel but have the authority and pay of a captain.

The young Virginian's patriotism, however, was too strong. He swallowed his pride and relaunched his military career as a volunteer aide to General Braddock in the spring of 1755.

Washington showed incredible courage, while the weakness of the supposedly invincible British army surprised him and many other colonists. They began to question the competence of the British army, which suffered defeat after defeat during 1755 and 1756.

PITT AND THE IROQUOIS TURN THE TIDE Angered by French victories, Britain's King George II selected new leaders to run his government in 1757. One of these was **William Pitt,** an energetic, self-confident politician. Under Pitt, the reinvigorated British army finally began winning battles, which prompted the powerful Iroquois to support them. Now Britain had some Native American allies to balance those of France.

In September 1759, the war took a dramatic and decisive turn on the Plains of Abraham just outside Quebec. Under the cover of night, British troops under General James Wolfe scaled the high cliffs that protected Quebec. Catching the French and their commander, the Marquis de Montcalm, by surprise, they won a short but deadly battle. The British triumph at Quebec led them to victory in the war.

The French and Indian War officially ended in 1763 with the Treaty of Paris. Great Britain claimed all of North America east of the Mississippi River. This included Florida, which Britain acquired from Spain, an ally of France. Spain gained the French lands west of the Mississippi, including the city of New Orleans. France kept control of only a few small islands near Newfoundland and in the West Indies. The other losers in the war were Native Americans, who found the victorious British harder to bargain with than the French had been. **B**

MAIN IDEA

Summarizing
B How did Great Britain's victory change the balance of power in North America?

European Claims in North America

1754 | **1763**

Legend:
- British territory
- French territory
- Spanish territory
- Disputed territory

0   400   800 miles
0   400   800 kilometers

GEOGRAPHY SKILLBUILDER
1. **Region** What do these maps tell you about the British Empire in the mid-18th century?
2. **Place** What happened to France's possessions between 1754 and 1763?

The Colonies Come of Age **87**

VICTORY BRINGS NEW PROBLEMS Claiming ownership of the Ohio River Valley brought Great Britain trouble. Native Americans feared that the growing number of British settlers crossing the Appalachian mountains would soon drive away the game they depended on for survival. In the spring of 1763, the Ottawa leader **Pontiac** recognized that the French loss was a loss for Native Americans.

★ **A PERSONAL VOICE** PONTIAC

" When I go to see the English commander and say to him that some of our comrades are dead, instead of bewailing their death, as our French brothers do, he laughs at me and at you. If I ask for anything for our sick, he refuses with the reply that he has no use for us. From all this you can well see that they are seeking our ruin. Therefore, my brothers, we must all swear their destruction and wait no longer. "

—quoted in *Red and White*

Led by Pontiac, Native Americans captured eight British forts in the Ohio Valley and laid siege to two others. In angry response, British officers presented smallpox-infected blankets to two Delaware chiefs during peace negotiations, and the virus spread rapidly among the Native Americans. Weakened by disease and war, most Native American groups negotiated treaties with the British by the end of 1765.

▲ **Pontiac, the Ottawa chief, depicted in an 18th-century engraving.**

To avoid further conflicts with Native Americans, the British government issued the **Proclamation of 1763,** which banned all settlement west of the Appalachians. This ban established a Proclamation Line, which the colonists were not to cross. (See the map on page 87.) However, the British could not enforce this ban any more effectively than they could enforce the Navigation Acts, and colonists continued to move west onto Native American lands.

FOCUS ON

To mark the 250th anniversary of the French and Indian War, New York hosted a series of events throughout 2010. These events highlighted key turning points in the war.

The Colonies and Britain Grow Apart

Because the Proclamation of 1763 sought to halt expansion, it convinced the colonists that the British government did not care about their needs. A second result of the French and Indian War—Britain's financial crisis—brought about new laws that reinforced the colonists' opinion even more.

BRITISH POLICIES ANGER COLONISTS By 1763, tensions between Britain and one colony, Massachusetts, had already been increasing. During the French and Indian War, the British had cracked down on colonial smuggling. In 1761, the royal governor of Massachusetts authorized the use of the writs of assistance, which allowed British customs officials to search any ship or building. Because many merchants worked out of their residences, the writs enabled officials to search colonial homes. The merchants of Boston were outraged.

PROBLEMS RESULTING FROM THE WAR After the war, the British government stationed 10,000 troops in its territories to control the Native Americans and former French subjects. Although this army was meant to protect the colonies, the colonists viewed it as a standing army that might turn against them. Maintaining troops in North America was an added expense on an already strained British budget. Britain had borrowed so much money during the war that it nearly doubled its national debt. **C**

Hoping to lower the debt, King George III chose a financial expert, **George Grenville,** to serve as prime minister in 1763. Grenville soon angered merchants

MAIN IDEA

Making Inferences
C Why were the colonists so afraid of the troops stationed in Britain's new territories?

"JOIN, OR DIE"

In 1754 Benjamin Franklin drew this image of a severed snake to encourage the British colonies to unite against the threat posed by French and Indian forces. The design was inspired by a superstition that a sliced snake would revive if the pieces of its body were joined before sunset.

The image, the first political cartoon to be published in an American newspaper, was widely circulated in 1754 and later during the American Revolution. A remarkably direct and simple cartoon, it reveals the beginning of a sense of national identity.

SKILLBUILDER Analyzing Political Cartoons
1. Why are there only eight segments of the snake?
2. Why do you think this image was so persuasive to colonists who may never have thought of the separate colonies as parts of a whole?

 SEE SKILLBUILDER HANDBOOK, PAGE R24.

---

throughout the colonies. He began to suspect that the colonists were smuggling goods into the country. In 1764 he prompted Parliament to enact a law known as the **Sugar Act.** The Sugar Act did three things. It halved the duty on foreign-made molasses (in the hopes that colonists would pay a lower tax rather than risk arrest by smuggling). It placed duties on certain imports. Most important, it strengthened the enforcement of the law allowing prosecutors to try smuggling cases in a vice-admiralty court rather than in a more sympathetic colonial court.

By the end of 1764, the colonies and Great Britain were disagreeing more and more about how the colonies should be taxed and governed. These feelings of dissatisfaction soon would swell into outright rebellion.

 SECTION 4 ASSESSMENT

1. **TERMS & NAMES** For each term or name, write a sentence explaining its significance.
   - New France
   - George Washington
   - French and Indian War
   - William Pitt
   - Pontiac
   - Proclamation of 1763
   - George Grenville
   - Sugar Act

MAIN IDEA

2. **TAKING NOTES**
   Create a time line of the major events of the French and Indian War and its aftermath. Use the dates already plotted on the time line below as a guide.

   How long was the war? Why do you think it lasted so long?

CRITICAL THINKING

3. **ANALYZING CAUSES**
   How did the French and Indian War lead to tension between the colonists and the British government?

4. **EVALUATING DECISIONS**
   If you had been a Native American living in the Northeast during the French and Indian War, would you have formed a military alliance with France or with Great Britain? Support your choice with reasons.

5. **HYPOTHESIZING**
   What if the outcome of the French and Indian War had been different and France had won? How might this have affected the 13 colonies?
   Think About:
   - the actual outcome of the Treaty of Paris
   - France's patterns of colonization
   - France's relations with Native Americans

Colonial Courtship

The concept of dating among teenagers was nonexistent in colonial times. Young people were considered either children or adults, and as important as marriage was in the colonies, sweethearts were older than one might suspect. The practices of courtship and marriage varied among the different communities.

▼ FRONTIER OR BACKCOUNTRY PEOPLE

Andrew Jackson, depicted with his wife in the painting below, "stole" his wife (she was willing) from her family. Jackson was following a custom of the backcountry people, who lived along the western edge of the colonies.

These colonists, mostly Scots-Irish, based their marriages on the old custom of "abduction"—stealing the bride—often with her consent. Even regular marriages began with the groom and his friends coming to "steal" the bride. Much drinking and dancing accompanied these wild and hilarious weddings.

PURITANS

For Puritans, marriage was a civil contract, not a religious or sacred union. Although adults strictly supervised a couple's courting, parents allowed two unusual practices. One was the use of a courting stick, a long tube into which the couple could whisper while the family was in another room. The other was the practice of "bundling": a young man spent the night in the same bed as his sweetheart, with a large bundling board (shown below) between them.

Before marrying, the couple had to allow for Puritan leaders to voice any objections to the marriage at the meeting house. Passing that, the couple would marry in a very simple civil ceremony and share a quiet dinner.

THE SOUTH ▲

Many African slaves married in a "jumping the broomstick" ceremony, in which the bride and groom jumped over a broomstick to seal their union. Although there is disagreement among African-American scholars, some suggest that the above painting depicts a slave wedding on a South Carolina plantation in the late 1700s.

◀ QUAKERS

Quaker couples intent on marrying needed the consent not only of the parents but also of the whole Quaker community. Quakers who wanted to marry had to go through a 16-step courtship phase before they could wed. Quaker women, however, were known to reject men at the last minute.

VIRGINIA ▶

In Virginia, marriage was a sacred union. Since the marriage often involved a union of properties, and love was not necessary, parents were heavily involved in the negotiations. In this illustration from a dance manual (right), a young upper-class couple work to improve their social graces by practicing an elaborate dance step.

DATA FILE

WHO MARRIED?

Puritans:
- 98% of males and 94% of females married
- Grooms were usually a few years older than brides
- Discouraged marriages between first cousins

Virginians:
- 25% of males never married; most females married
- Grooms nearly 10 years older than brides
- Allowed first-cousin marriages

Quakers:
- 16% of women single at age 50
- forbade first-cousin marriages

Frontier People:
- Almost all women and most men married
- Ages of bride and groom about the same
- Youngest group to marry

Average Age at Marriage

Group	Males	Females
Puritan	26	23
Virginians	26	19
Quakers		
in Delaware	31	29
in Penn. & N.J.	26	22
Philadelphians	26	23
Frontier People	21	19
Modern Americans	27	25

Who Could Divorce?

Puritans:	Yes
Virginians:	No
Quakers:	No

Source: David Hackett Fischer, Albion's Seed

THINKING CRITICALLY

CONNECT TO HISTORY

1. **Interpreting Data** What was a common characteristic of courtship among Puritans, Quakers, and Virginians?

   SEE SKILLBUILDER HANDBOOK, PAGE R22.

CONNECT TO TODAY

2. **Synthesizing** Research modern courtship practices by interviewing your parents or relatives. Write a brief paper comparing and contrasting modern-day and colonial courtship practices.

hmhsocialstudies.com RESEARCH WEB LINKS

TERMS & NAMES

For each term or name below, write a sentence explaining its significance for the growth of the colonies to the mid-18th century.

1. mercantilism
2. Dominion of New England
3. triangular trade
4. middle passage
5. Stono Rebellion
6. Enlightenment
7. Great Awakening
8. New France
9. Pontiac
10. Proclamation of 1763

MAIN IDEAS

Use your notes and the information in the chapter to answer the following questions.

England and Its Colonies *(pages 66–71)*

1. Why did Parliament pass the Navigation Acts?
2. How did the policy of salutary neglect benefit both England and its colonies?

The Agricultural South *(pages 72–78)*

3. Which ethnic groups besides the English began to settle in the South?
4. Which social class came to control the economy as well as the political and social institutions of the South?

The Commercial North *(pages 79–84)*

5. Why did large, single-crop plantations not develop in the North?
6. What factors contributed to the witchcraft hysteria in late 17th-century Salem?

The French and Indian War *(pages 85–89)*

7. How did the goals of the French colonists differ from those of the English colonists?
8. What problems were brought about for Britain by its victory in the French and Indian War?

CRITICAL THINKING

1. **USING YOUR NOTES** In a chart like the one below, show the differences between the Northern and Southern economies that led to the development of two distinct cultural regions.

Northern Economy	Southern Economy

2. **DEVELOPING HISTORICAL PERSPECTIVE** How did immigration contribute to the ethnic diversity of the American colonies after 1700?

3. **ANALYZING EFFECTS** How did the French and Indian War help inspire a sense of unity and shared identity among the colonists?

VISUAL SUMMARY THE COLONIES COME OF AGE

Trade

The colonies supplied Britain with raw materials and bought Britain's manufactured goods.

Colonies — Britain

Regional Distinctions

Industry developed in the Northern colonies, while the South became predominantly agricultural.

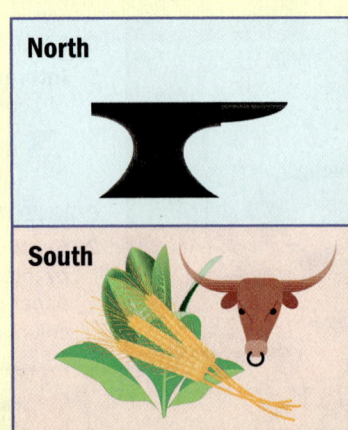

North

South

French and Indian War

The British victory in the French and Indian War brought about both territorial expansion and new tensions with the American colonies.

Tensions

Britain limits westward expansion.

Colonists want to expand westward.

Use the chart and your knowledge of U.S. history to answer questions 1 and 2.

Kings and Queens of England, 1685–1820	
James II	1685–1688
William III & Mary II	1689–1702
Anne	1702–1714
George I	1714–1727
George II	1727–1760
George III	1760–1820

1 Why was the Glorious Revolution of 1688 significant to the colonies?

(1) William and Mary supported capitalism instead of mercantilism.
(2) William and Mary practiced Catholicism instead of Anglicanism.
(3) William and Mary supported the supremacy of Parliament.
(4) William and Mary appointed Sir Edmund Andros to enforce the Navigation Acts.

2 The Treaty of Paris ending the French and Indian War was signed during the reign of —

(1) Queen Anne
(2) King George I
(3) King George II
(4) King George III

3 In the 1700s an intellectual movement known as the Enlightenment developed in Europe and spread to the colonies. Benjamin Franklin and Thomas Jefferson were among those colonists heavily influenced by Enlightenment ideas. In which of the following ways did the Enlightenment affect the colonists?

(1) Enlightenment ideas led people to expand the trade in enslaved persons.
(2) Enlightenment ideas stirred people to rededicate themselves to God.
(3) Enlightenment ideas persuaded people to establish colonies in order to generate a favorable balance of trade.
(4) Enlightenment ideas convinced people of the importance of civil rights.

4 Compared to the Southern colonies, the Northern colonies in 1720 were —

(1) less economically diverse.
(2) less dependent on trade with England.
(3) more dependent on slavery.
(4) more urban.

hmhsocialstudies.com TEST PRACTICE

For additional test practice, go online for:
• Diagnostic tests   • Tutorials

INTERACT WITH HISTORY

Think about the issues you explored at the beginning of the chapter. In a small group, discuss whether or not equality and freedom have been achieved in the United States today. Prepare an oral or visual presentation comparing equality and freedom in the United States today with equality and freedom in the colonies in the early 1700s.

FOCUS ON WRITING

The British Parliament has just enacted the Sugar Act of 1764. As a colonial leader, you need to decide if you are for or against the Sugar Act. Write a pamphlet in which you support or oppose the new tax. Begin by clearly identifying your position and then prepare a clear list of evidence that supports your position. Also, be sure to counter arguments for the opposing viewpoint.

COLLABORATIVE LEARNING

21ST CENTURY

Working in small groups, do library or Internet research to learn more about the history of one of the 13 colonies. Create an exhibit documenting the first 100 years of the colony's development. Find images and write text to highlight key events and important people in the early history of the colony.

CHAPTER 4

THE WAR FOR INDEPENDENCE

New York Standards

KEY IDEA 1 The study of New York State and United States history requires an analysis of the development of American culture, its diversity and multicultural context, and the ways people are unified by many values, practices, and traditions.

KEY IDEA 3 Study about the major social, political, economic, cultural, and religious developments in New York State and United States history involves learning about the important roles and contributions of individuals and groups.

SECTION 1: The Stirrings of Rebellion

SECTION 2: Ideas Help Start a Revolution

SECTION 3: Struggling Toward Saratoga

SECTION 4: Winning the War

The Sons of Liberty pull down a statue of George III on the Bowling Green, New York, July 9, 1776.

1765 The British Parliament passes the Stamp Act.

1767 Parliament passes the Townshend Acts.

1770 Five colonists are killed in the "Boston Massacre."

1773 Colonists stage the Boston Tea Party.

1774 Parliament passes the Intolerable Acts.

1774 First Continental Congress convenes.

USA				
1768	**1770**	**1772**	**1774**	

WORLD

1760 George III becomes king of Great Britain.

1769 Scotland's James Watt patents a steam engine capable of running other machines.

1770 Tukolor Kingdom arises in the former Songhai region of West Africa.

1774 The Reign of Louis XVI begins in France.

INTERACT
WITH HISTORY

It is 1767, and your Boston printing shop may soon be forced to close. British import taxes have all but eliminated your profits. In response to petitions to repeal the tax, the king has instead stationed troops throughout the city. Some of your neighbors favor further petitions, but others urge stronger measures. How do you think the colonists should respond?

Explore the Issues

- Should American colonists obey every law passed in Britain?
- Are colonists entitled to the same rights as all other British subjects?

1776 Thomas Paine publishes *Common Sense*.

1776 The American colonies declare independence.

1777 The colonists' victory at Saratoga marks a turning point in the war.

1781 The British surrender at Yorktown.

1783 Colonists and British sign the Treaty of Paris, ending the war.

1776 **1778** **1780** **1782**

1776 Adam Smith's *The Wealth of Nations* is published.

1779 Spain declares war on Britain.

1782 Spain puts down a Native American rebellion in Peru.

The War for Independence **95**

The Stirrings of Rebellion

MAIN IDEA	WHY IT MATTERS NOW	Terms & Names
Conflict between Great Britain and the American colonies grew over issues of taxation, representation, and liberty.	The events that shaped the American Revolution are a turning point in humanity's fight for freedom.	•Stamp Act •Boston Tea Party •Samuel Adams •King George III •Townshend Acts •Intolerable Acts •Boston Massacre •martial law •committees of •minutemen correspondence

One American's Story

On the cold, clear night of March 5, 1770, a mob gathered outside the Customs House in Boston. They heckled the British sentry on guard, calling him a "lobster-back" to mock his red uniform. More soldiers arrived, and the mob began hurling stones and snowballs at them. At that moment, Crispus Attucks, a sailor of African and Native American ancestry, arrived with a group of angry laborers.

> ### A PERSONAL VOICE JOHN ADAMS
> "This Attucks . . . appears to have undertaken to be the hero of the night; and to lead this army with banners . . . up to King street with their clubs . . . [T]his man with his party cried, 'Do not be afraid of them. . . .' He had hardiness enough to fall in upon them, and with one hand took hold of a bayonet, and with the other knocked the man down."
>
> —quoted in *The Black Presence in the Era of the American Revolution*

▲ **Crispus Attucks**

Attucks's action ignited the troops. Ignoring orders not to shoot, one soldier and then others fired on the crowd. Five people were killed; several were wounded. Crispus Attucks was, according to a newspaper account, the first to die.

The Colonies Organize to Resist Britain

The uprising at the Customs House illustrated the rising tensions between Britain and its American colonies. In order to finance debts from the French and Indian War, as well as from European wars, Parliament had turned hungry eyes on the colonies' resources.

THE STAMP ACT The seeds of increased tension were sown in March 1765 when Parliament, persuaded by Prime Minister George Grenville, passed the **Stamp Act.** The Stamp Act required colonists to purchase special stamped paper for every legal document, license, newspaper, pamphlet, and almanac, and imposed special "stamp duties" on packages of playing cards and dice. The tax reached into every colonial pocket. Colonists who disobeyed the law were to be tried in the vice-admiralty courts, where convictions were probable.

STAMP ACT PROTESTS When word of the Stamp Act reached the colonies in May of 1765, the colonists united in their defiance. Boston shopkeepers, artisans, and laborers organized a secret resistance group called the Sons of Liberty. One of its founders was Harvard-educated **Samuel Adams,** who, although unsuccessful in business and deeply in debt, proved himself to be a powerful and influential political activist.

By the end of the summer, the Sons of Liberty were harassing customs workers, stamp agents, and sometimes royal governors. Facing mob threats and demonstrations, stamp agents all over the colonies resigned. The Stamp Act was to become effective on November 1, 1765, but colonial protest prevented any stamps from being sold.

During 1765 and early 1766, the individual colonial assemblies confronted the Stamp Act measure. Virginia's lower house adopted several resolutions put forth by a 29-year-old lawyer named Patrick Henry. These resolutions stated that Virginians could be taxed only by the Virginia assembly— that is, only by their own representatives. Other assemblies passed similar resolutions.

The colonial assemblies also made a strong collective protest. In October 1765, delegates from nine colonies met in New York City. This Stamp Act Congress issued a Declaration of Rights and Grievances, which stated that Parliament lacked the power to impose taxes on the colonies because the colonists were not represented in Parliament. More than 10 years earlier, the colonies had rejected Benjamin Franklin's Albany Plan of Union, which called for a joint colonial council to address defense issues. Now, for the first time, the separate colonies began to act as one.

Merchants in New York, Boston, and Philadelphia agreed not to import goods manufactured in Britain until the Stamp Act was repealed. They expected that British merchants would force Parliament to repeal the Stamp Act. The widespread boycott worked. In March 1766, Parliament repealed the Stamp Act; but on the same day, to make its power clear, Parliament issued the Declaratory Act. This act asserted Parliament's full right to make laws "to bind the colonies and people of America . . . in all cases whatsoever."

THE TOWNSHEND ACTS Within a year after Parliament repealed the Stamp Act, Charles Townshend, the leading government minister at the time, impetuously decided on a new method of gaining revenue from the American colonies. His proposed revenue laws, passed by Parliament in 1767, became known as the **Townshend Acts.** Unlike the Stamp Act, which was a direct tax, these were indirect taxes, or duties levied on imported materials—glass, lead, paint, and paper— as they came into the colonies from Britain. The acts also imposed a three-penny tax on tea, the most popular drink in the colonies.

The colonists reacted with rage and well-organized resistance. Educated Americans spoke out against the Townshend Acts, protesting "taxation without representation." Boston's Samuel Adams called for another boycott of British goods, and American women of every rank in society became involved in the protest. Writer Mercy Otis Warren of Massachusetts urged women to lay their British "female ornaments aside," foregoing "feathers, furs, rich sattins and . . . capes." Wealthy women stopped buying British luxuries and joined other women in spinning bees. These were public displays of spinning and weaving of colonial-made cloth designed to show colonists' determination to boycott British-made cloth. Housewives also boycotted British tea and exchanged recipes for tea made from birch bark and sage. **Ⓐ**

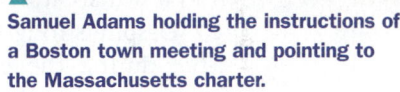

▲ Samuel Adams holding the instructions of a Boston town meeting and pointing to the Massachusetts charter.

Background
A New York branch of the Sons of Liberty was also founded at around the same time as the Boston chapter.

Vocabulary
boycott: a collective refusal to use, buy, or deal with, especially as an act of protest

MAIN IDEA

Comparing
Ⓐ How would you compare reactions to the Townshend Acts with reactions to the Stamp Act?

Conflict intensified in June 1768. British agents in Boston seized the *Liberty*, a ship belonging to local merchant John Hancock. The customs inspector claimed that Hancock had smuggled in a shipment of wine from Madeira and had failed to pay the customs taxes. The seizure triggered riots against customs agents. In response, the British stationed 2,000 "redcoats," or British soldiers—so named for the red jackets they wore—in Boston. **B**

MAIN IDEA

Evaluating
B Do you think that the colonists' reaction to the seizing of the *Liberty* was justified?

Tension Mounts in Massachusetts

The presence of British soldiers in Boston's streets charged the air with hostility. The city soon erupted in clashes between British soldiers and colonists and later in a daring tea protest, all of which pushed the colonists and Britain closer to war.

THE BOSTON MASSACRE One sore point was the competition for jobs between colonists and poorly paid soldiers who looked for extra work in local shipyards during off-duty hours. On the cold afternoon of March 5, 1770, a fist-fight broke out over jobs. That evening a mob gathered in front of the Customs House and taunted the guards. When Crispus Attucks and several dockhands appeared on the scene, an armed clash erupted, killing three men including Attucks, and fatally wounding two more. Instantly, Samuel Adams and other colonial agitators labeled this confrontation the **Boston Massacre,** thus presenting it as a British attack on defenseless citizens.

Despite strong feelings on both sides, the political atmosphere relaxed somewhat during the next two years until 1772, when a group of Rhode Island colonists attacked a British customs schooner that patrolled the coast for smugglers. After the ship accidentally ran aground near Providence, the colonists boarded the vessel and burned it to the waterline. In response, King George named a special commission to seek out the suspects and bring them to England for trial.

History Through Art

THE BOSTON MASSACRE

Paul Revere was not only a patriot, he was a silversmith and an engraver as well. One of the best-known of his engravings, depicting the Boston Massacre, is a masterful piece of anti-British propaganda. Widely circulated, Revere's engraving played a key role in rallying revolutionary fervor.

- The sign above the redcoats reads "Butcher's Hall."
- The British commander, Captain Prescott (standing at the far right of the engraving) appears to be inciting the troops to fire, whereas in fact, he tried to calm the situation.
- At the center foreground is a small dog, a detail that gave credence to the rumor that, following the shootings, dogs licked the blood of the victims from the street.

SKILLBUILDER Interpreting Visual Sources
1. According to the details of the engraving, what advantages do the redcoats have that the colonists do not? What point does the artist make through this contrast?
2. How could this engraving have contributed to the growing support for the Patriots' cause?

SEE SKILLBUILDER HANDBOOK, PAGE R23.

The plan to haul Americans to England for trial ignited widespread alarm. The assemblies of Massachusetts and Virginia set up **committees of correspondence** to communicate with other colonies about this and other threats to American liberties. By 1774, such committees formed a buzzing communication network linking leaders in nearly all the colonies. **C**

THE BOSTON TEA PARTY Early in 1773, Lord Frederick North, the British prime minister, faced a new problem. The British East India Company, which held an official monopoly on tea imports, had been hit hard by the colonial boycotts. With its warehouses bulging with 17 million pounds of tea, the company was nearing bankruptcy. To save it, North devised the Tea Act, which granted the company the right to sell tea to the colonies free of the taxes that colonial tea sellers had to pay. This action would cut colonial merchants out of the tea trade, because the East India Company could sell its tea directly to consumers for less. North hoped the American colonists would simply buy the cheaper tea; instead, they protested violently.

On the moonlit evening of December 16, 1773, a large group of Boston rebels disguised themselves as Native Americans and proceeded to take action against three British tea ships anchored in the harbor. John Andrews, an onlooker, wrote a letter on December 18, 1773, describing what happened.

★ **A PERSONAL VOICE** JOHN ANDREWS

" They muster'd . . . to the number of about two hundred, and proceeded . . . to Griffin's wharf, where [the three ships] lay, each with 114 chests of the *ill fated* article . . . and before *nine* o'clock in the evening, every chest from on board the three vessels was knock'd to pieces and flung over the sides.

They say the actors were *Indians* from *Narragansett*. Whether they were or not, . . . they appear'd as *such*, being cloath'd in Blankets with the heads muffled, and copper color'd countenances, being each arm'd with a hatchet or axe. . . . "

—quoted in *1776: Journals of American Independence*

In this incident, later known as the **Boston Tea Party**, the "Indians" dumped 18,000 pounds of the East India Company's tea into the waters of Boston Harbor.

THE INTOLERABLE ACTS **King George III** was infuriated by this organized destruction of British property, and he pressed Parliament to act. In 1774, Parliament responded by passing a series of measures that colonists called the **Intolerable Acts.** One law shut down Boston Harbor because the colonists had refused to pay for the damaged tea. Another, the Quartering Act, authorized British commanders to house soldiers in vacant private homes and other buildings. In addition to these measures, General Thomas Gage, commander in chief of British forces in North America, was appointed the new governor of Massachusetts. To keep the peace, he placed Boston under **martial law,** or rule imposed by military forces. **D**

The committees of correspondence quickly moved into action and assembled the First Continental Congress. In September 1774, 56 delegates met in Philadelphia and drew up a declaration of colonial rights. They defended the colonies' right to run their own affairs. They supported the protests in Massachusetts and stated that if the British used force against the colonies, the colonies should fight back. They also agreed to reconvene in May 1775 if their demands weren't met.

MAIN IDEA

Analyzing Motives

D What did King George set out to achieve when he disciplined Massachusetts?

NOW & THEN

PROPOSITION 13

A more recent tax revolt occurred in California on June 6, 1978, when residents voted in a tax reform law known as Proposition 13. By the late 1970s, taxes in California were among the highest in the nation. The property tax alone was fifty-two percent above the national norm.

Proposition 13, initiated by ordinary citizens, limited the tax on real property to one percent of its value in 1975–1976. It passed with sixty-five percent of the vote.

Because of the resulting loss of revenue, many state agencies were scaled down or cut. In 1984, California voters approved a state lottery that provides supplemental funds for education. Proposition 13 still remains a topic of heated debate.

1765 STAMP ACT

__British Action__
Britain passes the Stamp Act, a tax law requiring colonists to purchase special stamps to prove payment of tax.

__Colonial Reaction__
Colonists harass stamp distributors, boycott British goods, and prepare a Declaration of Rights and Grievances.

1767 TOWNSHEND ACTS

__British Action__
Britain taxes certain colonial imports and stations troops at major colonial ports to protect customs officers.

__Colonial Reaction__
Colonists protest "taxation without representation" and organize a new boycott of imported goods.

1770 BOSTON MASSACRE

__British Action__
British troops stationed in Boston are taunted by an angry mob. The troops fire into the crowd, killing five colonists.

__Colonial Reaction__
Colonial agitators label the conflict a massacre and publish a dramatic engraving depicting the violence.

▲
This colonial engraving was meant to warn of the effects of the Stamp Act.

Fighting Erupts at Lexington and Concord

After the First Continental Congress, colonists in many eastern New England towns stepped up military preparations. **Minutemen,** or civilian soldiers, began to quietly stockpile firearms and gunpowder. General Gage soon learned about these activities and prepared to strike back.

TO CONCORD, BY THE LEXINGTON ROAD   The spring of 1775 was a cold one in New England. Because of the long winter frosts, food was scarce. General Gage had been forced to put his army on strict rations, and British morale was low. Around the same time, Gage became concerned about reports brought to him concerning large amounts of arms and munitions hidden outside of Boston.

In March, Gage sent agents toward Concord, a town outside of Boston reported to be the site of one of the stockpiles. The agents returned with maps detailing where arms were rumored to be stored in barns, empty buildings, and private homes. The agents also told that John Hancock and Samuel Adams, perhaps the two most prominent leaders of resistance to British authority, were staying in Lexington, a smaller community about five miles east of Concord. As the snows melted and the roads cleared, Gage drew up orders for his men to march along the Lexington Road to Concord, where they would seize and destroy all munitions that they could find.

"THE REGULARS ARE COMING!"   As General Gage began to ready his troops quartered in Boston, minutemen were watching. Rumors were that a strike by British troops against resistance activities would come soon, although no one knew exactly when, nor did they know which towns would be targeted.

With Hancock and Adams in hiding, much of the leadership of resistance activity in Boston fell to a prominent young physician named Joseph Warren. Sometime during the afternoon of April 18, Doctor Warren consulted a confidential source close to the British high command. The source informed him that Gage intended to march on Concord by way of Lexington, seize Adams and Hancock, and destroy all hidden munitions. Warren immediately sent for Paul Revere, a member of the Sons of Liberty, and told him to warn Adams and Hancock as well as the townspeople along the way. Revere began to organize a network of riders who would spread the alarm. **E**

On the night of April 18, Paul Revere, William Dawes, and Samuel Prescott rode out to spread word that 700 British Regulars, or army soldiers, were headed

MAIN IDEA

Summarizing
E What did Warren order Paul Revere to do?

1773 TEA ACT

British Action
Britain gives the East India Company special concessions in the colonial tea business and shuts out colonial tea merchants.

Colonial Reaction
Colonists in Boston rebel, dumping 18,000 pounds of East India Company tea into Boston Harbor.

1774 INTOLERABLE ACTS

British Action
King George III tightens control over Massachusetts by closing Boston Harbor and quartering troops.

Colonial Reaction
Colonial leaders form the First Continental Congress and draw up a declaration of colonial rights.

1775 LEXINGTON AND CONCORD

British Action
General Gage orders troops to march to Concord, Massachusetts, and seize colonial weapons.

Colonial Reaction
Minutemen intercept the British and engage in battle—first at Lexington, and then at Concord.

> **SKILLBUILDER** Interpreting Charts
> In what ways did colonial reaction to British rule intensify between 1765 and 1775?

▲ **This bottle contains tea that colonists threw into Boston Harbor during the Boston Tea Party.**

for Concord. Before long, the darkened countryside rang with church bells and gunshots—prearranged signals to warn the population that the Regulars were coming.

Revere burst into the house where Adams and Hancock were staying and warned them to flee to the backwoods. He continued his ride until he, like Dawes, was detained by British troops. As Revere was being questioned, shots rang out and the British officer realized that the element of surprise had been lost. When more shots rang out, the officer ordered the prisoners released so that he could travel with greater speed to warn the other British troops marching toward Lexington that resistance awaited them there.

▲ The Battle of Lexington, as depicted in a mid-nineteenth-century painting.

◀ *A View of the Town of Concord*, painted by an unknown artist, shows British troops assembling on the village green.

"A GLORIOUS DAY FOR AMERICA" By the morning of April 19, 1775, the king's troops reached Lexington. As they neared the town, they saw 70 minutemen drawn up in lines on the village green. The British commander ordered the minutemen to leave, and the colonists began to move out without laying down their muskets. Then someone fired, and the British soldiers sent a volley of shots into the departing militia. Eight minutemen were killed and ten more were wounded, but only one British soldier was injured. The Battle of Lexington lasted only 15 minutes.

The British marched on to Concord, where they found an empty arsenal. After a brief skirmish with minutemen, the British soldiers lined up to march back to Boston, but the march quickly became a slaughter. Between 3,000 and 4,000 minutemen had assembled by now, and they fired on the marching troops from behind stone walls and trees. British soldiers fell by the dozen. Bloodied and humiliated, the remaining British soldiers made their way back to Boston.

While the battles were going on, Adams and Hancock were fleeing deeper into the New England countryside. At one point, they heard the sound of musketfire in the distance. Adams remarked that it was a fine day and Hancock, assuming that his companion was speaking of the weather said, "Very pleasant." "I mean," Adams corrected Hancock, "this is a glorious day for America."

SECTION 1 ASSESSMENT

1. **TERMS & NAMES** For each term or name, write a sentence explaining its significance.

- Stamp Act
- Samuel Adams
- Townshend Acts
- Boston Massacre
- committees of correspondence
- Boston Tea Party
- King George III
- Intolerable Acts
- martial law
- minutemen

MAIN IDEA

2. **TAKING NOTES**
Create a cluster diagram like the one shown and fill it in with events that demonstrate the conflict between Great Britain and the American colonies.

Conflict grows

Choose one event to further explain in a paragraph.

CRITICAL THINKING

3. **DEVELOPING HISTORICAL PERSPECTIVE**
What opinion might a British soldier have had about the Boston Massacre? Explain and support your response. **Think About:**

- the start of the conflict on March 5, 1770
- the behavior of Crispus Attucks and other colonists
- the use of the event as propaganda

4. **MAKING GENERALIZATIONS**
Explain whether you think the British government acted wisely in its dealings with the colonies between 1765 and 1775. Support your explanation with examples from the text. **Think About:**

- the reasons for British actions
- the reactions of colonists
- the results of British actions

Ideas Help Start a Revolution

MAIN IDEA	WHY IT MATTERS NOW	Terms & Names
Tensions increased throughout the colonies until the Continental Congress declared independence on July 4, 1776.	The Declaration of Independence continues to inspire and challenge people everywhere.	•Second Continental Congress •Olive Branch Petition •*Common Sense* • •Thomas Jefferson •Declaration of Independence •Patriots •Loyalists

One American's Story

Use the graphic organizer online to take notes on the writing and impact of the Declaration of Independence.

William Franklin, son of the famous American writer, scientist, states-man, and diplomat Benjamin Franklin, was royal governor of New Jersey. Despite his father's patriotic sympathies, William remained stubbornly loyal to King George. In a letter written on August 2, 1775, to Lord Dartmouth, he stated his position and that of oth-ers who resisted revolutionary views.

A PERSONAL VOICE WILLIAM FRANKLIN

"**There is indeed a dread in the minds of many here that some of the leaders of the people are aiming to establish a republic. Rather than submit . . . we have thousands who will risk the loss of their lives in defense of the old Constitution. [They] are ready to declare themselves whenever they see a chance of its being of any avail.**"

—quoted in *A Little Revenge: Benjamin Franklin and His Son*

▲
William Franklin

Because of William's stand on colonial issues, communication between him and his father virtually ceased. The break between William Franklin and his father exemplified the chasm that now divided American from American.

The Colonies Hover Between Peace and War

In May of 1775, colonial leaders convened a second Continental Congress in Philadelphia to debate their next move. Beyond their meeting hall, however, events continued moving quickly, as minutemen and British soldiers clashed in a bloody battle outside Boston, and an increasingly furious King George readied his country for war.

THE SECOND CONTINENTAL CONGRESS The loyalties that divided colonists sparked endless debates at the **Second Continental Congress.** John Adams of Massachusetts suggested a sweeping, radical plan—that each colony set up its own government and that the Congress declare the colonies independent.

Furthermore, he argued, the Congress should consider the militiamen besieging Boston to be the Continental Army and name a general to lead them. Moderate John Dickinson of Pennsylvania strongly disagreed with Adams's call for revolt. In private, he confronted Adams.

PERSONAL VOICE JOHN DICKINSON

" What is the reason, Mr. Adams, that you New England men oppose our measures of reconciliation? . . . If you don't concur with us in our pacific system, I and a number of us will break off from you in New England, and we will carry on the opposition by ourselves in our own way. "

—quoted in *Patriots: The Men Who Started the American Revolution*

The debates raged on into June, but one stubborn fact remained: colonial militiamen were still encamped around Boston. The Congress agreed to recognize them as the Continental Army and appointed as its commander a 43-year-old veteran of the French and Indian War, George Washington. The Congress, acting like an independent government, also authorized the printing of paper money to pay the troops and organized a committee to deal with foreign nations. These actions came just in time. **A**

THE BATTLE OF BUNKER HILL Cooped up in Boston, British General Thomas Gage decided to strike at militiamen who had dug in on Breed's Hill, north of the city and near Bunker Hill. On the steamy summer morning of June 17, 1775, Gage sent out nearly 2,400 British troops. The British, sweating in wool uniforms and heavy packs, began marching up Breed's Hill in their customary broad lines. The colonists held their fire until the last minute, then began to shoot down the advancing redcoats. The surviving British troops made a second attack, and then a third. The third assault succeeded, but only because the militiamen ran low on ammunition.

MAIN IDEA

Evaluating Leadership
A Do you think that the Continental Congress was responsible in the actions that it took?

This painting shows "Bunker's Hill" before the battle, as shells from Boston set nearby Charles Town ablaze. At the battle, the British demonstrated a maneuver they used throughout the war: they massed together, were visible for miles, and failed to take advantage of ground cover.

▼

By the time the smoke cleared, the colonists had lost 450 men, while the British had suffered over 1,000 casualties. The misnamed Battle of Bunker Hill would prove to be the deadliest battle of the war.

THE OLIVE BRANCH PETITION By July, the Second Continental Congress was readying the colonies for war while still hoping for peace. Most of the delegates, like most colonists, felt deep loyalty to George III and blamed the bloodshed on the king's ministers. On July 8, 1775, the Congress sent the king the so-called **Olive Branch Petition,** urging a return to "the former harmony" between Britain and the colonies. **B**

King George flatly rejected the petition. Furthermore, he issued a proclamation stating that the colonies were in rebellion and urged Parliament to order a naval blockade of the American coast.

MAIN IDEA

Evaluating

B Do you think that the Olive Branch Petition was too little too late?

The Patriots Declare Independence

In the months after the Olive Branch Petition, a thin document containing the powerful words of an angry citizen began to circulate and change public opinion.

COMMON SENSE In **Common Sense,** an anonymous 50-page pamphlet, the colonist Thomas Paine attacked King George III. Paine explained that his own revolt against the king had begun with Lexington and Concord.

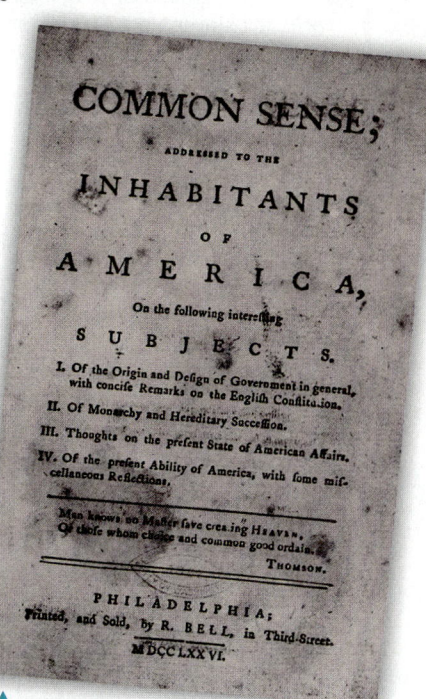

⭐ **A PERSONAL VOICE** THOMAS PAINE

"No man was a warmer wisher for a reconciliation than myself, before the fatal nineteenth of April, 1775, but the moment the event of that day was made known, I rejected the hardened, sullen tempered Pharaoh of England for ever . . . the wretch, that with the pretended title of Father of his people can unfeelingly hear of their slaughter, and composedly sleep with their blood upon his soul."

—*Common Sense*

Paine declared that the time had come for colonists to proclaim an independent republic. He argued that independence, which was the American "destiny," would allow America to trade freely with other nations for guns and ammunition and win foreign aid from British enemies. Finally, Paine stated, independence would give Americans the chance to create a better society—one free from tyranny, with equal social and economic opportunities for all.

Common Sense sold nearly 500,000 copies and was widely applauded. In April 1776, George Washington wrote, "I find *Common Sense* is working a powerful change in the minds of many men." **C**

▲ Thomas Paine's pamphlet *Common Sense* helped to overcome many colonists' doubts about separating from Britain.

MAIN IDEA

Analyzing Issues

C Why do you think that *Common Sense* was so effective?

DECLARING INDEPENDENCE By early summer 1776, events pushed the wavering Continental Congress toward a decision. North Carolina had declared itself independent, and a majority of Virginians told their delegates that they favored independence. At last, the Congress urged each colony to form its own government. On June 7, Virginia delegate Richard Henry Lee moved that "these United Colonies are, and of a right ought to be, free and independent States."

While talks on this fateful motion were under way, the Congress appointed a committee to prepare a formal declaration explaining the reasons for the colonies' actions. Virginia lawyer **Thomas Jefferson,** known for his broad knowledge and skillfully crafted prose, was chosen to express the committee's points.

Jefferson's masterful **Declaration of Independence** drew on the concepts of the English philosopher John Locke, who maintained that people enjoy "natural rights" to life, liberty, and property. Jefferson described these rights as "Life, Liberty and the pursuit of Happiness."

In keeping with Locke's ideas, Jefferson then declared that governments derive "their just powers from the consent of the governed"—that is, from the people. This right of consent gave the people the right "to alter or to abolish" any government that threatened their unalienable rights and to install a government that would uphold these principles. On the basis of this reasoning, the American colonies declared their independence from Britain, listing in the Declaration the numerous ways in which the British king had violated the "unalienable rights" of the Americans. **D**

The Declaration states flatly that "all men are created equal." When this phrase was written, it expressed the common belief that free citizens were political equals. It did not claim that all people had the same abilities or ought to have equal wealth. It was not meant to embrace women, Native Americans, and African-American slaves—a large number of Americans. However, Jefferson's words presented ideals that would later help these groups challenge traditional attitudes.

In his first draft, Jefferson included an eloquent attack on the cruelty and injustice of the slave trade. However, South Carolina and Georgia, the two colonies most dependent on slavery, objected. In order to gain the votes of those two states, Jefferson dropped the offending passage.

On July 2, 1776, the delegates voted unanimously that the American colonies were free, and on July 4, 1776, they adopted the Declaration of Independence. While delegates created a formal copy of the Declaration, the document was read to a crowd in front of the Pennsylvania State House—now called Independence Hall. A rush of pride and anxiety ran through the **Patriots**—the supporters of independence—when they heard the closing vow: "We mutually pledge to each other our Lives, our Fortunes, and our Sacred Honor."

MAIN IDEA

Summarizing
D What reasons did Thomas Jefferson give to justify revolt by the colonies?

Americans Choose Sides

Americans now faced a difficult, bitter choice: revolution or loyalty to the Crown. This issue divided communities, friends, and even families throughout the colonies.

LOYALISTS AND PATRIOTS The exact number of **Loyalists**—those who opposed independence and remained loyal to the Crown—is unknown. Many with Loyalist sympathies changed sides as the war progressed.

Some Loyalists felt a special tie to the king because they had served as judges, councilors, or governors. Most Loyalists, however, were ordinary people of modest means. They included some people who lived far from the cities and knew little of the events that turned other colonists into revolutionaries. Other people remained loyal because they thought that the British were going to win the war and they wanted to avoid being punished as rebels. Still others were Loyalists because they thought that the crown would protect their rights more effectively than the new colonial governments would. **E**

Patriots drew their numbers from people who saw economic opportunity in an independent America. The Patriot cause embraced farmers, artisans, merchants,

MAIN IDEA

Contrasting
E How did the thinking of the Loyalists differ from that of the Patriots?

Colonists Choose Sides

Loyalists and Patriots had much to gain and much to lose in the American colonies' struggle for independence. Fortunes, family ties, and religious obligations as well as personal convictions were at stake. For many, the most important issue was that of national identity. Both sides believed that they were fighting for their country as well as being loyal to what was best for America.

PATRIOTS

LOYALISTS

Nathanael Greene

A pacifist Quaker, Nathanael Greene nonetheless chose to fight against the British.

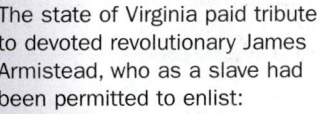

"**I am determined to defend my rights and maintain my freedom or sell my life in the attempt.**"

Charles Inglis

A clergyman of the Church of England, Charles Inglis was loyal to the king and argued against independence:

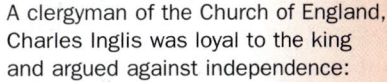

"**By a reconciliation with Britain, [an end] would be put to the present calamitous war, by which many lives have been lost, and so many more must be lost, if it continues.**"

James Armistead

The state of Virginia paid tribute to devoted revolutionary James Armistead, who as a slave had been permitted to enlist:

"**At the peril of his life [Armistead] found means to frequent the British camp, and thereby faithfully executed important commissions entrusted to him by the marquis.**"

Joseph Brant

Mohawk chief Joseph Brant fought for the British during the French and Indian War and remained loyal to the crown during the Revolutionary War.

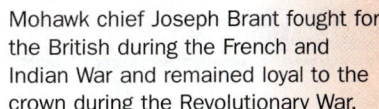

"**If we . . . [do] nothing for the British . . . there will be no peace for us. Our throats will be cut by the Red Coat man or by America. . . . We should go and join the father [Britain] . . . this is the only way for us.**"

Mercy Otis Warren

Patriot Mercy Otis Warren wrote,

"**I see the inhabitants of our plundered cities quitting the elegancies of life, possessing nothing but their freedom, I behold faction & discord tearing up an Island we once held dear and a mighty Empire long the dread of distant nations, tott'ring to the very foundation.**"

Isaac Wilkins

Isaac Wilkins had to leave his home after he opposed sending delegates to the Second Continental Congress.

"**I leave America and every endearing connection because I will not raise my hand against my Sovereign, nor will I draw my sword against my country. When I can conscientiously draw it in her favor, my life shall be cheerfully devoted to her service.**"

Analyzing Political Cartoons

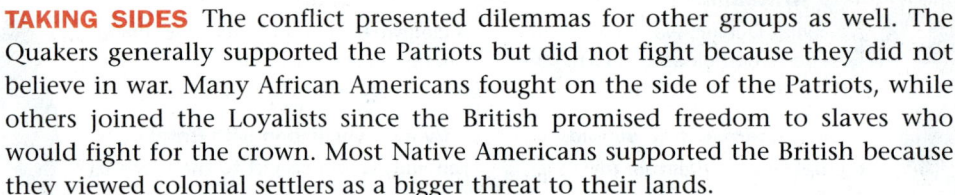

MOB RULE

This British cartoon portrays the events of the Boston Tea Party from the Loyalist perspective. While Patriots are dumping tea, a British tax collector, having been tarred and feathered, is having tea poured down his throat. The "Liberty Tree," where a copy of the Stamp Act has been nailed upside down, has been converted into a gallows, a device used for hanging people.

SKILLBUILDER Analyzing Political Cartoons

 1. How does the cartoonist make the mob look sinister?
2. What kind of comment does the cartoonist make by suspending a hangman's noose from the "Liberty Tree"? Explain.

📁 **SEE SKILLBUILDER HANDBOOK, PAGE R24.**

landowners, and elected officials. German colonists in Pennsylvania, Maryland, and Virginia also joined the fight for independence. While Patriots made up nearly half the population, many Americans remained neutral.

TAKING SIDES The conflict presented dilemmas for other groups as well. The Quakers generally supported the Patriots but did not fight because they did not believe in war. Many African Americans fought on the side of the Patriots, while others joined the Loyalists since the British promised freedom to slaves who would fight for the crown. Most Native Americans supported the British because they viewed colonial settlers as a bigger threat to their lands.

Now the colonies were plunged into two wars—a war for independence and a civil war in which Americans found themselves on opposing sides. The price of choosing sides could be high. In declaring their independence, the Patriots had invited war with the mightiest empire on earth.

ASSESSMENT

SECTION 2

1. **TERMS & NAMES** For each term or name, write a sentence explaining its significance.

- **Second Continental Congress**
- **Olive Branch Petition**
- *Common Sense*
- **Thomas Jefferson**
- **Declaration of Independence**
- **Patriots**
- **Loyalists**

MAIN IDEA

2. **TAKING NOTES**

Re-create the cluster diagram below on your paper. Fill it in with details presenting causes, ideas, and results related to the Declaration of Independence.

The Declaration of Independence

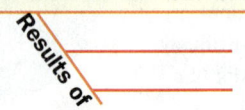

CRITICAL THINKING

3. **HYPOTHESIZING**

Imagine that King George had accepted the Olive Branch Petition and sought a diplomatic resolution with the Congress. Do you think colonists would still have pressed for independence? **Think About:**

- the attitudes of the king and Parliament toward the colonies
- the impact of fighting at Lexington, Concord, and Breed's Hill
- the writings of Thomas Paine

4. **ANALYZING PRIMARY SOURCES**

Thomas Paine wrote in the introduction to *Common Sense*:

> "The cause of America is in a great measure the cause of all mankind."

Evaluate the significance of Paine's statement. **Think About:**

- Locke's ideas about natural rights
- Jefferson's ideas about "unalienable rights"

The Declaration of Independence

Thomas Jefferson's Declaration of Independence is one of the most important and influential legal documents of modern times. Although the text frequently refers to eighteenth-century events, its Enlightenment philosophy and politics have continuing relevance today. For more than 200 years the Declaration of Independence has inspired leaders of other independence movements and has remained a crucial document in the struggle for civil rights and human rights.

In Congress, July 4, 1776.

A Declaration by the Representatives of the United States of America, in General Congress assembled.

When in the Course of human events, it becomes necessary for one people to dissolve the political bands which have connected them with another, and to assume among the powers of the earth, the separate and equal station to which the Laws of Nature and of Nature's God entitle them, a decent respect to the opinions of mankind requires that they should declare the causes which impel them to the separation.

We hold these truths to be self-evident, that all men are created equal, that they are endowed by their Creator with certain unalienable Rights, that among these are Life, Liberty and the pursuit of Happiness; that, to secure these rights, Governments are instituted among Men, deriving their just powers from the consent of the governed; that whenever any Form of Government becomes destructive of these ends, it is the Right of the People to alter or to abolish it, and to institute new Government, laying its foundation on such principles and organizing its powers in such form, as to them shall seem most likely to effect their Safety and Happiness. Prudence, indeed, will dictate that Governments long established should not be changed for light and transient causes; and accordingly all experience hath shewn that mankind are more disposed to suffer, while evils are sufferable, than to right themselves by abolishing the forms to which they are accustomed. But when a long train of abuses and usurpations, pursuing invariably the same Object, evinces a design to reduce them under absolute Despotism, it is their right, it is their duty, to throw off such Government, and to provide new Guards for their future security.

Such has been the patient sufferance of these Colonies; and such is now the necessity which constrains them to alter their former Systems of Government. The history of the present King of Great Britain is a history of repeated injuries and usurpations, all having in direct object the establishment of an absolute Tyranny over these States. To prove this, let facts be submitted to a candid world.

He has refused his Assent to Laws, the most wholesome and necessary for the public good.

He has forbidden his Governors to pass Laws of immediate and pressing importance, unless suspended in their operation till his assent should be obtained; and, when so suspended, he has utterly neglected to attend to them.

He has refused to pass other Laws for the accommodation of large districts of people, unless those people would relinquish the right of Representation in the Legislature, a right inestimable to them, and formidable to tyrants only.

Jefferson begins the Declaration by attempting to legally and philosophically justify the revolution that was already underway. Here Jefferson is saying that, now that the colonists have begun to separate themselves from British rule, it is time to explain why the colonists have taken this course of action.

These passages reveal the influence of the English philosopher John Locke. In *Two Treatises of Government* (1690), Locke argued that if a government does not allow its citizens to enjoy certain rights and freedoms, the people have a right to replace that government.

Here begins the section in which Jefferson condemns the behavior of King George, listing the king's many tyrannical actions that have forced his American subjects to rebel. This section reveals the influence of French philosopher Jean-Jacques Rouseau. In *The Social Contract* (1763), Rousseau argued that the ruler governs only with the consent of the governed. When a ruler abuses the rights of the governed, as King George had, the governed have a right to change the government.

This is a reference to the 10,000 troops that the British government stationed in North America after the French and Indian War. Although the British government saw the troops as protection for the colonists, the colonists themselves viewed the troops as a standing army that threatened their freedom.

Here Jefferson condemns both the king and Parliament for passing the Intolerable Acts. Most of these laws were intended to punish the people of Massachusetts for the Boston Tea Party. For example, the Quartering Act of 1774 forced colonists to provide lodging for British troops. Another act allowed British soldiers accused of murder to be sent back to England for trial. The Boston Port Bill closed the port of Boston, "cutting off our Trade with all parts of the world."

Here Jefferson refers to the Quebec Act, which extended the boundaries of the province. He then refers to another act that changed the charter of Massachusetts and restricted town meetings.

He has called together legislative bodies at places unusual, uncomfortable, and distant from the depository of their public Records, for the sole purpose of fatiguing them into compliance with his measures.

He has dissolved Representative Houses repeatedly, for opposing with manly firmness his invasions on the rights of the people.

He has refused for a long time, after such dissolutions, to cause others to be elected; whereby the Legislative powers, incapable of Annihilation, have returned to the people at large for their exercise; the State remaining in the mean time exposed to all the dangers of invasions from without, and convulsions within.

He has endeavoured to prevent the population of these States; for that purpose obstructing the Laws for Naturalization of Foreigners; refusing to pass others to encourage their migration hither, and raising the conditions of new Appropriations of Lands.

He has obstructed the Administration of Justice, by refusing his Assent to Laws for establishing Judiciary powers.

He has made Judges dependent on his Will alone, for the tenure of their offices, and the amount and payment of their salaries.

He has erected a multitude of New Offices, and sent hither swarms of Officers to harass our people and eat out their substance.

He has kept among us, in times of peace, Standing Armies, without the Consent of our legislatures.

He has affected to render the Military independent of and superior to the Civil power.

He has combined with others to subject us to a jurisdiction foreign to our constitution and unacknowledged by our laws; giving his Assent to their Acts of pretended Legislation:

For quartering large bodies of armed troops among us;

For protecting them, by a mock Trial, from punishment for any Murders which they should commit on the Inhabitants of these States;

For cutting off our Trade with all parts of the world;

For imposing Taxes on us without our Consent;

For depriving us, in many cases, of the benefits of Trial by Jury;

For transporting us beyond Seas to be tried for pretended offenses;

For abolishing the free System of English Laws in a neighboring Province, establishing therein an Arbitrary government, and enlarging its Boundaries so as to render it at once an example and fit instrument for introducing the same absolute rule into these Colonies;

For taking away our Charters, abolishing our most valuable laws, and altering fundamentally the Forms of our Governments;

For suspending our own Legislatures, and declaring themselves invested with power to legislate for us in all cases whatsoever.

He has abdicated Government here, by declaring us out of his Protection and waging War against us.

He has plundered our seas, ravaged our Coasts, burnt our towns, and destroyed the lives of our people.

He is at this time transporting large Armies of foreign Mercenaries to compleat the works of death, desolation, and tyranny, already begun with circumstances of Cruelty & perfidy scarcely paralleled in the most barbarous ages, and totally unworthy the Head of a civilized nation.

He has constrained our fellow Citizens, taken Captive on the high Seas, to bear Arms against their Country, to become the executioners of their friends and Brethren, or to fall themselves by their Hands.

He has excited domestic insurrections amongst us, and has endeavoured to bring on the inhabitants of our frontiers the merciless Indian Savages, whose known rule of warfare is an undistinguished destruction of all ages, sexes and conditions.

In every stage of these Oppressions We have Petitioned for Redress in the most humble terms; Our repeated Petitions have been answered only by repeated injury. A Prince, whose character is thus marked by every act which may define a Tyrant, is unfit to be the ruler of a free people.

Nor have We been wanting in attentions to our British brethren. We have warned them from time to time of attempts by their legislature to extend an unwarrantable jurisdiction over us. We have reminded them of the circumstances of our emigration and settlement here. We have appealed to their native justice and magnanimity, and we have conjured them by the ties of our common kindred, to disavow these usurpations, which would inevitably interrupt our connections and correspondence. They too have been deaf to the voice of justice and of consanguinity. We must, therefore, acquiesce in the necessity, which denounces our Separation, and hold them, as we hold the rest of mankind, Enemies in War, in Peace Friends.

We, therefore, the Representatives of the United States of America, in General Congress, Assembled, appealing to the Supreme Judge of the world for the rectitude of our intentions, do, in the name, and by the Authority of the good People of these Colonies solemnly publish and declare, That these United Colonies are, and of Right ought to be, Free and Independent States; that they are Absolved from all Allegiance to the British Crown, and that all political connection between them and the State of Great Britain is, and ought to be, totally dissolved; and that as Free and Independent States, they have full Power to levy War, conclude Peace, contract Alliances, establish Commerce, and do all other Acts and Things which Independent States may of right do.

Here Jefferson turns his attention away from the king and toward the British people. Calling the British the "common kindred" of the colonists, Jefferson reminds them how often the Americans have appealed to their sense of justice. Reluctantly the colonists are now forced to break their political connections with their British kin.

In this final paragraph, the delegates declare independence.

The Declaration ends with the delegates' pledge, or pact. The delegates at the Second Continental Congress knew that, in declaring their independence from Great Britain, they were committing treason—a crime punishable by death. "We must all hang together," Benjamin Franklin reportedly said, as the delegates prepared to sign the Declaration, "or most assuredly we shall all hang separately."

KEY PLAYER

JOHN HANCOCK
1737–1793

Born in Braintree, Massachusetts, and raised by a wealthy uncle, John Hancock became one of the richest men in the colonies. He traveled around Boston in a luxurious carriage and dressed only in the finest clothing. "He looked every inch an aristocrat," noted one acquaintance, "from his dress and powdered wig to his smart pumps of grained leather."

Beneath Hancock's refined appearance, however, burned the heart of a patriot. He was only too glad to lead the Second Continental Congress. When the time came to sign the Declaration of Independence, Hancock scrawled his name in big, bold letters. "There," he reportedly said, "I guess King George will be able to read that."

And for the support of this Declaration, with a firm reliance on the protection of divine Providence, we mutually pledge to each other our Lives, our Fortunes, and our sacred Honor.

[Signed by]

John Hancock **[President of the Continental Congress]**

[Georgia]
Button Gwinnett
Lyman Hall
George Walton

[Rhode Island]
Stephen Hopkins
William Ellery

[Connecticut]
Roger Sherman
Samuel Huntington
William Williams
Oliver Wolcott

[North Carolina]
William Hooper
Joseph Hewes
John Penn

[South Carolina]
Edward Rutledge
Thomas Heyward, Jr.
Thomas Lynch, Jr.
Arthur Middleton

[Maryland]
Samuel Chase
William Paca
Thomas Stone
Charles Carroll

[Virginia]
George Wythe
Richard Henry Lee
Thomas Jefferson
Benjamin Harrison
Thomas Nelson, Jr.
Francis Lightfoot Lee
Carter Braxton

[Pennsylvania]
Robert Morris
Benjamin Rush
Benjamin Franklin
John Morton
George Clymer
James Smith
George Taylor
James Wilson
George Ross

[Delaware]
Caesar Rodney
George Read
Thomas McKean

[New York]
William Floyd
Philip Livingston
Francis Lewis
Lewis Morris

[New Jersey]
Richard Stockton
John Witherspoon
Francis Hopkinson
John Hart
Abraham Clark

[New Hampshire]
Josiah Bartlett
William Whipple
Matthew Thornton

[Massachusetts]
Samuel Adams
John Adams
Robert Treat Paine
Elbridge Gerry

Struggling Toward Saratoga

MAIN IDEA	WHY IT MATTERS NOW	Terms & Names
After a series of setbacks, American forces won at Saratoga and survived.	Determination, resilience, and unity have become part of the American character.	•Valley Forge •inflation •Trenton •profiteering •Saratoga

One American's Story

hmhsocialstudies.com
TAKING NOTES
Use the graphic organizer online to take notes on the early battles of the American Revolution.

After the colonists had declared independence, few people thought the rebellion would last. A divided colonial population of about two and a half million people faced a nation of 10 million that was backed by a worldwide empire.

Albigense Waldo worked as a surgeon at **Valley Forge** outside Philadelphia, which served as the site of the Continental Army's camp during the winter of 1777–1778. While British troops occupied Philadelphia and found quarters inside warm homes, the underclothed and underfed Patriots huddled in makeshift huts in the freezing, snow-covered Pennsylvania woods. Waldo, who wrote of his stay at Valley Forge, reported on what was a common sight at the camp.

A PERSONAL VOICE ALBIGENSE WALDO

"Here comes a bowl of beef soup full of dead leaves and dirt. There comes a soldier. His bare feet are seen through his worn-out shoes—his legs nearly naked from the tattered remains of an only pair of stockings—his Breeches [trousers] are not sufficient to cover his nakedness—his Shirt hanging in Strings—his hair disheveled—his face meager."

—quoted in *Valley Forge, the Making of an Army*

The ordeal at Valley Forge marked a low point for General Washington's troops, but even as it occurred, the Americans' hopes of winning began to improve.

General Washington's troops march to Valley Forge.
▼

The War Moves to the Middle States

The British had previously retreated from Boston in March 1776, moving the theater of war to the Middle states. As part of a grand plan to stop the rebellion by isolating New England, the British decided to seize New York City.

DEFEAT IN NEW YORK Two brothers, General William Howe and Admiral Richard Howe, joined forces on Staten Island and sailed into New York harbor in the summer of 1776 with the largest British expeditionary force ever assembled—32,000 soldiers, including thousands of German mercenaries, or soldiers who fight solely for money. The Americans called these troops Hessians, because many of them came from the German region of Hesse.

Washington rallied 23,000 men to New York's defense, but he was vastly outnumbered. Most of his troops were untrained recruits with poor equipment. The battle for New York ended in late August with an American retreat following heavy losses. Michael Graham, a Continental Army volunteer, described the chaotic withdrawal on August 27, 1776.

★ A PERSONAL VOICE MICHAEL GRAHAM

" It is impossible for me to describe the confusion and horror of the scene that ensued: the artillery flying . . . over the horses' backs, our men running in almost every direction, . . . [a]nd the enemy huzzahing when they took prisoners. . . . At the time, I could not account for how it was that our troops were so completely surrounded but have since understood there was another road across the ridge several miles above Flatbush that was left unoccupied by our troops. Here the British passed and got betwixt them and Brooklyn unobserved. This accounts for the disaster of that day. "

—quoted in *The Revolution Remembered: Eyewitness Accounts of the War for Independence*

By late fall, the British had pushed Washington's army across the Delaware River into Pennsylvania. The vast majority of Washington's men had either deserted or had been killed or captured. Fewer than 8,000 men remained under Washington's command, and the terms of their enlistment were due to end on December 31. Washington desperately needed some kind of victory for his men to keep them from going home.

THE BATTLE OF TRENTON Washington resolved to risk everything on one bold stroke set for Christmas night, 1776. In the face of a fierce storm, he led 2,400 men in small rowboats across the ice-choked Delaware River.

By 8 o'clock the next morning, the men had marched nine miles through sleet and snow to the objective—**Trenton,** New Jersey, held by a garrison of Hessians. Lulled into confidence by the storm, most of the Hessians had drunk too much rum the night before and were still sleeping it off. In a surprise attack, the Americans killed 30 of the enemy and took 918 captives and six Hessian cannons.

The Americans were rallied by another astonishing victory eight days later against 1,200 British stationed at Princeton. Encouraged by these victories, Washington marched his army into winter camp near Morristown, in northern New Jersey. **A**

THE FIGHT FOR PHILADELPHIA As the muddy fields dried out in the spring of 1777, General Howe began his campaign to seize the American capital at Philadelphia. His troops sailed from New York to the head of Chesapeake Bay, and landed near the capital in late August. The Continental Congress fled the city while Washington's troops unsuccessfully tried to block the redcoats at nearby Brandywine Creek. The British captured Philadelphia, and the pleasure-loving General Howe settled in to enjoy the hospitality of the city's grateful Loyalists.

MAIN IDEA

Analyzing Effects
A Why were the victories at Trenton and Princeton so important to the Continental Army?

VICTORY AT SARATOGA Meanwhile, one of Howe's fellow British generals, General John "Gentleman Johnny" Burgoyne, convinced the London high command to allow him to pursue a complex scheme. Burgoyne's plan was to lead an army down a route of lakes from Canada to Albany, where he would meet Howe's troops as they arrived from New York City. According to Burgoyne's plan, the two generals would then join forces to isolate New England from the rest of the colonies.

Burgoyne set out with 4,000 redcoats, 3,000 mercenaries, and 1,000 Mohawk under his command. His army had to haul 30 wagons containing 138 pieces of artillery along with extra personal items, such as fine clothes and champagne. South of Lake Champlain, swamps and gullies, as well as thick underbrush, bogged down Burgoyne's army. Food supplies ran low.

The Continental Congress had appointed General Horatio Gates to command the Northern Department of the Continental Army. Gates, a popular commander, gathered militiamen and soldiers from all over New York and New England. Burgoyne lost several hundred men every time his forces clashed with the Americans, such as when Ethan Allen and his Green Mountain Boys attacked Burgoyne at Bennington, in what is now Vermont. Even worse, Burgoyne didn't realize that Howe was preoccupied with conquering and occupying Philadelphia and wasn't coming to meet him.

Massed American troops finally surrounded Burgoyne at **Saratoga,** where he surrendered his battered army to General Gates on October 17, 1777. The surrender at Saratoga dramatically changed Britain's war strategy. From that time on, the British generally kept their troops along the coast, close to the big guns and supply bases of the British fleet. **B**

> **MAIN IDEA**
>
> **Summarizing**
> **B** What factors contributed to General Burgoyne's defeat at Saratoga?

HISTORY

VIDEO
Saratoga: Force Surrender

hmhsocialstudies.com

Revolutionary War, 1775–1778

hmhsocialstudies.com **INTERACTIVE MAP**

Map Legend:
- American campaign
- British campaign
- American victory
- British victory

Map labels: CANADA (British), Montréal, Québec, 1775, MAINE (MASS.), Colonel Arnold, St. Lawrence R., Lake Champlain, General Burgoyne, Fort Ticonderoga, 1775, 1777, Saratoga, 1777, N.H., Lexington, 1775, Concord, 1775, Bunker Hill, 1775, General Gates, Albany, Hudson R., MASS., Boston, N.Y., CONN., R.I., General Washington, New York, Admiral Howe, Long Island, 1776, Trenton, 1776, PENN., Valley Forge, Philadelphia, Brandywine, 1777, N.J., MD., DEL., VIRGINIA, NORTH CAROLINA, APPALACHIAN MOUNTAINS, Delaware R., Lake Huron, Lake Ontario, Lake Erie, ATLANTIC OCEAN, 40°N, 35°N, 75°W, 70°W, 65°W

Scale: 0 100 200 miles / 0 100 200 kilometers

Military Strengths and Weaknesses

UNITED STATES

Strengths
- familiarity of home ground
- leadership of George Washington and other officers
- inspiring cause of the independence

Weaknesses
- most soldiers untrained and undisciplined
- shortage of food and ammunition
- inferior navy
- no central government to enforce wartime policies

GREAT BRITAIN

Strengths
- strong, well-trained army and navy
- strong central government with available funds
- support of colonial Loyalists and Native Americans

Weaknesses
- large distance separating Britain from battlefields
- troops unfamiliar with terrain
- weak military leaders
- sympathy of certain British politicans for the American cause

GEOGRAPHY SKILLBUILDER
1. **Location** From which city did General Burgoyne march his troops to Saratoga?
2. **Place** What characteristics did many of the battle sites have in common? Why do you think this was so?

A TURNING POINT Still bitter from their defeat by the British in the French and Indian War, the French had secretly sent weapons to the Patriots since early 1776. The Saratoga victory bolstered French trust in the American army, and France now agreed to support the Revolution. The French recognized American independence and signed an alliance, or treaty of cooperation, with the Americans in February 1778. According to the terms, France agreed not to make peace with Britain unless Britain also recognized American independence. **C**

WINTER AT VALLEY FORGE It would take months for French aid to arrive. In the meantime, the British controlled New York and parts of New England. While British troops wintered comfortably in Philadelphia, Washington and his meager Continental Army struggled to stay alive amidst bitter cold and primitive conditions at winter camp in Valley Forge, Pennsylvania. Soldiers suffered from exposure and frostbite, and surgeons like Albigense Waldo worked constantly but often unsuccessfully to save arms and limbs from amputation. Washington's letters to the Congress and his friends were filled with reports of the suffering and endurance of his men.

MAIN IDEA

Summarizing
C What did France agree to do in its treaty of cooperation with the Americans?

A PERSONAL VOICE GEORGE WASHINGTON

"To see men without Clothes to cover their nakedness, without Blankets to lay on, without Shoes, by which their Marches might be traced by the blood of their feet, and almost as often without Provision . . . is a mark of patience and obedience which in my opinion can scarcely be paralleled."

—quoted in *Ordeal at Valley Forge*

Of the 10,000 soldiers who braved wind, snow, and hunger at Valley Forge that winter, more than 2,000 died. Yet those who survived remained at their posts.

Colonial Life During the Revolution

The Revolutionary War touched the life of every American, not just the men on the battlefield.

FINANCING THE WAR When the Congress ran out of hard currency—silver and gold—it borrowed money by selling bonds to American investors and foreign governments, especially France. It also printed paper money called Continentals. As Congress printed more and more money, its value plunged, causing rising prices, or **inflation.**

The Congress also struggled to equip the beleaguered army. With few munitions factories and the British navy blockading the coast, the Americans had to smuggle arms from Europe. Some government officials engaged in **profiteering,** selling scarce goods for a profit. Corrupt merchants either hoarded goods or sold defective merchandise like spoiled meat, cheap shoes, and defective weapons. **D**

In 1781, the Congress appointed a rich Philadelphia merchant named Robert Morris as superintendent of finance. His associate was Haym Salomon, a Jewish political refugee from Poland. Morris and Salomon begged and borrowed on their personal credit to raise money to provide salaries for the Continental Army. They raised funds from many sources,

MAIN IDEA

Identifying Problems
D What economic problems did the Americans face in financing the war?

KEY PLAYER

GEORGE WASHINGTON
1732–1799

During the Revolutionary War, Commander in Chief George Washington became a national hero. An imposing man, Washington stood six feet two inches tall. He was broad-shouldered, calm, and dignified, and he was an expert horseman. But it was Washington's character that won hearts and, ultimately, the war.

Washington roused dispirited men into a fighting force. At Princeton, he galloped on his white horse into the line of fire, shouting and encouraging his men. At Valley Forge, he bore the same cold and privation as every suffering soldier. Time and again, Washington's tactics saved his smaller, weaker force to fight another day. By the end of the war, the entire nation idolized General Washington, and adoring soldiers crowded near him just to touch his boots when he rode by.

Molly Pitcher was the heroine of the battle of Monmouth, New Jersey, in 1778.

including Philadelphia's Quakers and Jews. Due to the efforts of Morris and Salomon, on September 8, 1781, the troops were finally paid in specie, or gold coin.

CIVILIANS AT WAR

The demands of war also affected civilians. When men marched off to fight, many wives had to manage farms, shops, and businesses as well as households and families. Some women, such as Benjamin Franklin's daughter, Sarah Franklin Bache of Philadelphia, organized volunteers to mend clothing for the soldiers. Many women made ammunition from their household silver. And hundreds of women followed their husbands to the battlefield, where they washed, mended, and cooked for the troops.

Some women risked their lives in combat. At Fort Washington, New York, Margaret Corbin replaced a gunner who was shot and then was shot herself. Mary Ludwig Hays McCauly took her husband's place at a cannon when he was wounded at the Battle of Monmouth. Known for carrying pitchers of water to the soldiers, McCauly won the nickname "Molly Pitcher." Afterward, General Washington made her a noncommissioned officer for her brave deeds. **E**

Thousands of African-American slaves escaped to freedom, some to the cities, where they passed as free people, others to the frontier, where they sometimes joined Native American tribes. About 5,000 African Americans served in the Continental Army, where their courage, loyalty, and talent impressed white Americans. Native Americans remained on the fringes of the Revolution. Some fought for the British but most remained apart from the conflict.

MAIN IDEA

Summarizing
E In what ways did women contribute to the Revolutionary War?

SECTION 3 ASSESSMENT

1. **TERMS & NAMES** For each term or name, write a sentence explaining its significance.
   - Valley Forge
   - Trenton
   - Saratoga
   - inflation
   - profiteering

MAIN IDEA

2. **TAKING NOTES**
   In a chart like the one below, list each early battle of the American Revolution, its outcome, and why it was important.

Battle	Outcome	Importance

CRITICAL THINKING

3. **HYPOTHESIZING**
   Imagine that Burgoyne and the British had captured Saratoga in 1777. How might the course of the war have changed? **Think About:**
   - the military strength of the British
   - the fighting skills of the Americans
   - French support of the colonists

4. **EVALUATING**
   If you were a woman civilian during the beginning of the American Revolution, what problem caused by the war do you think would affect you the most? **Think About:**
   - inflation and the scarcity of goods
   - the separation of families
   - the demands of the war effort

The War for Independence **117**

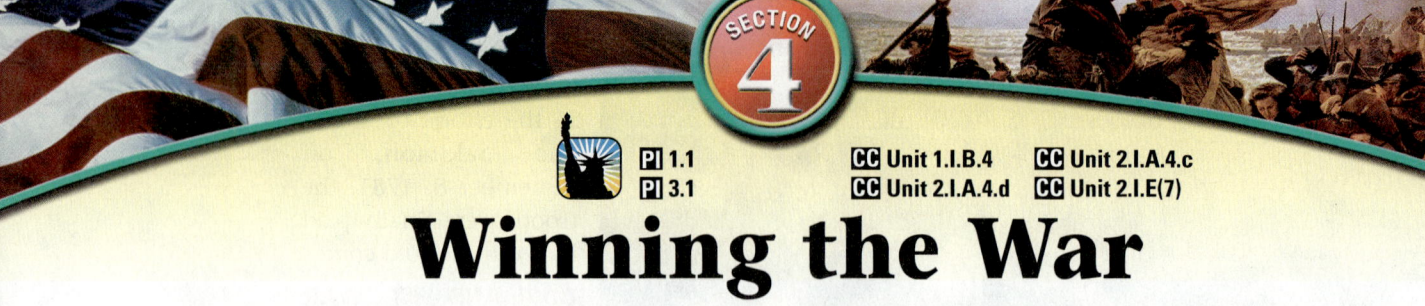

Winning the War

MAIN IDEA	WHY IT MATTERS NOW	Terms & Names
Strategic victories in the South and at Yorktown enabled the Americans to defeat the British.	The American defeat of the British established the United States as an independent Nation.	• Yorktown • Friedrich von Steuben • Marquis de Lafayette • Charles Cornwallis • Treaty of Paris • egalitarianism

One American's Story

Colonel William Fontaine of the Virginia militia stood with the American and French armies lining a road near **Yorktown**, Virginia, on the afternoon of October 19, 1781, to witness the formal British surrender. The French were dressed in bright blue coats and white trousers, while the American troops, standing proudly behind their generals, wore rough hunting shirts and faded Continental uniforms. Colonel Fontaine later described the scene.

> ★ **A PERSONAL VOICE** COLONEL WILLIAM FONTAINE
>
> I had the happiness to see that British army which so lately spread dismay and desolation through all our country, march forth . . . at 3 o'clock through our whole army, drawn up in two lines about 20 yards distance and return disrobed of all their terrors. . . . You could not have heard a whisper or seen the least motion throughout our whole line, but every countenance was erect and expressed a serene cheerfulness.
>
> —quoted in *The Yorktown Campaign and the Surrender of Cornwallis*, 1781

The American Revolution had finally ended, and the Americans had won—a fact that astonished the world. Several years before, in the depths of the Valley Forge winter of 1777–1778, few would have thought such an event possible.

▲ The detail of John Trumbull's painting of the British surrender at Yorktown depicts General Charles O'Hara, who stood in for General Cornwallis at the ceremony.

hmhsocialstudies.com
TAKING NOTES

Use the graphic organizer online to write headlines on the significant events discussed in this section.

European Allies Shift the Balance

In February 1778, in the midst of the frozen winter at Valley Forge, American troops began an amazing transformation. **Friedrich von Steuben** (vŏn stoo′bən), a Prussian captain and talented drillmaster, volunteered his services to General Washington and went to work "to make regular soldiers out of country bumpkins." Von Steuben taught the colonial soldiers to stand at attention, execute field maneuvers, fire and reload quickly, and wield bayonets. With the help of such European military leaders, the raw Continental Army was becoming an effective fighting force.

LAFAYETTE AND THE FRENCH Around the same time, another military leader, the **Marquis de Lafayette** (mär-kē′ də lȧf′ē-ĕt′), a brave, idealistic 20-year-old French aristocrat, offered his assistance. The young Lafayette joined Washington's staff and bore the misery of Valley Forge, lobbied for French reinforcements in France in 1779, and led a command in Virginia in the last years of the war.

The British Move South

After their devastating defeat at Saratoga, the British changed their military strategy; in the summer of 1778 they began to shift their operations to the South. There, the British hoped to rally Loyalist support, reclaim their former colonies in the region, and then slowly fight their way back north.

EARLY BRITISH SUCCESS IN THE SOUTH At the end of 1778, a British expedition easily took Savannah, Georgia, and by the spring of 1779, a royal governor once again commanded Georgia. In 1780, General Henry Clinton, who had replaced Howe in New York, along with the ambitious general **Charles Cornwallis** sailed south with 8,500 men. In their greatest victory of the war, the British captured Charles Town, South Carolina, in May 1780 and marched 5,500 American soldiers off as prisoners of war. Clinton then left for New York, leaving Cornwallis to command the British forces in the South and to conquer South and North Carolina. **A**

For most of 1780, Cornwallis succeeded. As the redcoats advanced, they were joined by thousands of African Americans who had escaped from Patriot slave

MAIN IDEA

Summarizing

A What was the British strategy in the South and how well did it work initially?

Revolutionary War, 1778–1781

hmhsocialstudies.com **INTERACTIVE MAP**

GEOGRAPHY SKILLBUILDER
1. **Place** Where were most of the later Revolutionary War battles fought?
2. **Movement** Why might General Cornwallis's choice of Yorktown as a base have left him at a military disadvantage?

owners to join the British and win their freedom. In August, Cornwallis's army smashed American forces at Camden, South Carolina, and within three months the British had established forts across the state. However, when Cornwallis and his forces advanced into North Carolina, Patriot bands attacked them and cut British communication lines. The continuous harassment forced the redcoats to retreat to South Carolina.

BRITISH LOSSES IN 1781 Washington ordered Nathanael Greene, his ablest general, to march south and harass Cornwallis as he retreated. Greene divided his force into two groups, sending 600 soldiers under the command of General Daniel Morgan to South Carolina. Cornwallis in turn sent Lieutenant Colonel Banastre Tarleton and his troops to pursue Morgan's soldiers.

Morgan and his men led the British on a grueling chase through rough countryside. When the forces met in January 1781 at Cowpens, South Carolina, the British expected the outnumbered Americans to flee; but the Continental Army fought back, and forced the redcoats to surrender.

Angered by the defeat at Cowpens, Cornwallis attacked Greene two months later at Guilford Court House, North Carolina. Cornwallis won the battle, but the victory cost him nearly a fourth of his troops—93 were killed, over 400 were wounded, and 26 were missing. **B**

Greene had weakened the British, but he worried about the fight for the South. On April 3, 1781, he wrote a letter to Lafayette, asking for help.

MAIN IDEA

Summarizing
B How did generals Morgan and Greene work together to defeat British forces?

★ **A PERSONAL VOICE** NATHANAEL GREENE

" [I] wish you to March your force Southward by Alexandria & Fredricksburg to Richmond. . . . It is impossible for the Southern States with all the exertions they can make under the many disadvantages they labour to save themselves. Subsistence is very difficult to be got and therefore it is necessary that the best of troops should be employed. . . . Every exertion should be made for the salvation of the Southern States for on them depend the liberty of the Northern. "

—from *The Papers of General Nathanael Greene*, vol. VIII

Daniel Morgan's colonial forces defeated a crack British regiment under Colonel Tarleton at the battle of Cowpens in 1781. More than 300 British soldiers were killed or wounded, and 600 were taken prisoner. This detail from *The Battle of Cowpens* by William Ranney shows that the Americans included both white and African-American soldiers. ▼

After the exhausting battle in the Carolinas, Cornwallis chose to move the fight to Virginia, where he met up with reinforcements. First he tried to capture the divisions led by Lafayette and von Steuben. When that failed, Cornwallis made a fateful mistake: he led his army of 7,500 onto the peninsula between the James and York rivers and camped at Yorktown, a few miles from the original English settlement of Jamestown (see map, page 119). Cornwallis planned to fortify Yorktown, take Virginia, and then move north to join Clinton's forces.

hmhsocialstudies.com

INTERACTIVE
Explore the Battle of Yorktown

The British Surrender at Yorktown

A combination of good luck and well-timed decisions now favored the American cause. In 1780, a French army of 6,000 had landed in Newport, Rhode Island, after the British left the city to focus on the South. The French had stationed one fleet there and were operating another in the West Indies. When news of Cornwallis's plans reached him, the Marquis de Lafayette suggested that the American and French armies join forces with the two French fleets and attack the British forces at Yorktown.

VICTORY AT YORKTOWN Following Lafayette's plan, the Americans and the French closed in on Cornwallis. A French naval force defeated a British fleet and then blocked the entrance to the Chesapeake Bay, thereby preventing a British rescue by sea. Meanwhile, about 17,000 French and American troops surrounded the British on the Yorktown peninsula and bombarded them day and night. The siege of Yorktown lasted about three weeks. On October 17, 1781, with his troops outnumbered by more than two to one and exhausted from constant shelling, Cornwallis finally raised the white flag of surrender. **C**

On October 19, a triumphant Washington, the French generals, and their troops assembled to accept the British surrender. After General Charles O'Hara, representing Cornwallis, handed over his sword, the British troops laid down their arms. In his diary, Captain Johann Ewald, a German officer, tried to explain this astonishing turn of events.

MAIN IDEA

Analyzing Issues

C How did the French forces contribute to the American victory at Yorktown?

HISTORICAL SPOTLIGHT

BENEDICT ARNOLD

In the early years of the Revolution, Benedict Arnold, a popular Patriot soldier and leader, helped defend New England and then served as the American commandant of Philadelphia. In the later years of the war, however, Arnold and his wife, Peggy Shippen Arnold, lived extravagantly. In 1779, Arnold was court-martialed and found guilty of using government supplies for personal use. Angry with Congress, Arnold, with his wife's support, shifted his allegiance to Great Britain.

In 1780, Arnold decided to hand West Point, a strategic fort north of New York City, on the Hudson River, over to the British. To do so, he requested command of the fort. Despite Arnold's tarnished background, Washington granted his request. Fortunately, the Americans discovered the plot, and Arnold escaped to Britain. He died there, scorned by both sides as a traitor.

★ **A PERSONAL VOICE** CAPTAIN JOHANN EWALD

" With what soldiers in the world could one do what was done by these men, who go about nearly naked and in the greatest privation? Deny the best-disciplined soldiers of Europe what is due them and they will run away in droves, and the general will soon be alone. But from this one can perceive what an enthusiasm—which these poor fellows call 'Liberty'—can do! "

—Diary of the American War

SEEKING PEACE Peace talks began in Paris in 1782. Representatives of four nations—the United States, Great Britain, France, and Spain—joined the negotiations, with each nation looking out for its own interests. Britain hoped to avoid giving America full independence. France supported American independence but feared America's becoming a major power. Spain was interested in acquiring the land between the Appalachian Mountains and the Mississippi River.

Many observers expected the savvy European diplomats to outwit the Americans at the bargaining table. But the Continental Congress chose an able team of negotiators—John Adams, Benjamin Franklin, and John Jay of New York. Together the three demanded that Britain recognize American independence before any other negotiations began. Once Britain agreed to full independence, the talks officially opened.

In September 1783, the delegates signed the **Treaty of Paris,** which confirmed U.S. independence and set the boundaries of the new nation. The United States now stretched from the Atlantic Ocean to the Mississippi River and from Canada to the Florida border.

Some provisions of the treaty promised future trouble. The British made no attempt to protect the land interests of their Native American allies, and the treaty did not specify when the British would evacuate their American forts. On the other side, the Americans agreed that British creditors could collect debts owed them by Americans and promised to allow Loyalists to sue in state courts for recovery of their losses. The state governments, however, later failed to honor this agreement. **D**

MAIN IDEA

Summarizing
D What issues did the Treaty of Paris leave unresolved?

The War Becomes a Symbol of Liberty

With the signing of the Treaty of Paris, all European nations recognized the United States of America. Former British subjects now possessed a new identity as free Americans, loyal to a new ideal. The American Revolution would inspire the world as both a democratic revolution and a war for independence.

THE IMPACT ON AMERICAN SOCIETY Revolutionary ideals set a new course for American society. During the war, class distinctions between rich and poor had begun to blur as the wealthy wore homespun clothing and military leaders showed respect for all of their men. These changes stimulated a rise of **egalitarianism**—a belief in the equality of all people—which fostered a new attitude: the idea that ability, effort, and virtue, not wealth or family, defined one's worth.

The egalitarianism of the 1780s, however, applied only to white males. It did not bring any new political rights to women. A few states made it possible for women to divorce, but common law still dictated that a married woman's property belonged to her husband.

This "A New and Correct Map of the United ► States of North America," of 1784 was one of the first maps produced to show the boundaries of the new nation. Unfortunately, it contained much inaccurate information, such as the incorrect placement of rivers.

Moreover, most African Americans were still enslaved, and even those who were free usually faced discrimination and poverty. However by 1804, many Northern states had taken steps to outlaw slavery.

The Southern states, where slavery was more entrenched, did not outlaw the practice, but most made it easier for slave owners to free their slaves. Planters in the upper South debated the morality of slavery, and some, like George Washington, freed their slaves. In Maryland and Virginia, the number of free blacks increased from about 4,000 to over 20,000 following the war. The slavery debate generally did not reach the Deep South, although some Southern slaveholders did have grave misgivings.

For Native Americans, the Revolution brought uncertainty. During both the French and Indian War and the Revolution, many Native American communities had either been destroyed or displaced, and the Native American population east of the Mississippi had declined by about 50 percent. Postwar developments further threatened Native American interests, as settlers from the United States moved west and began taking tribal lands left unprotected by the Treaty of Paris. **E**

▲ English potter Josiah Wedgwood designed this anti-slavery cameo and sent copies of it to Benjamin Franklin.

MAIN IDEA

Analyzing Issues

E What were the exceptions to the spirit of egalitarianism that arose after the Revolutionary War?

THE CHALLENGE OF CREATING A GOVERNMENT In adopting the Declaration of Independence, Americans had rejected the British system of government, in which kings and nobles held power. In its place, they set out to build a stable republic, a government of the people. The Continental Congress had chosen a motto for the reverse side of the Great Seal of the United States: "a new order of the ages." Creating this new order forced Americans to address complex questions: Who should participate in government? How should the government answer to the people? How could a government be set up so that opposing groups of citizens would all have a voice?

SECTION 4 ASSESSMENT

1. TERMS & NAMES For each term or name, write a sentence explaining its significance.
- Yorktown
- Friedrich von Steuben
- Marquis de Lafayette
- Charles Cornwallis
- Treaty of Paris
- egalitarianism

MAIN IDEA

2. SUMMARIZING
Choose five significant events described in this section. For each, write a newspaper headline that summarizes its significance.

Event	Headline

Choose one of the headlines and write the first paragraph of the article.

CRITICAL THINKING

3. ANALYZING CAUSES
Do you think the colonists could have won independence without aid from foreigners? Explain.
Think About:
- the military needs of the Americans and strengths of the French
- the Americans' belief in their fight for independence
- von Steuben and de Lafayette

4. ANALYZING EFFECTS
What were the effects of the Revolutionary War on the American colonists? **Think About:**
- political effects
- economic effects
- social effects

5. EVALUATING
In your opinion, what was the single biggest challenge facing the new country?

Women and Political Power

In their families and in the workplace, in speeches and in print, countless American women have worked for justice for all citizens. Throughout the history of the United States, women have played whatever roles they felt were necessary to better this country. They also fought to expand their own political power, a power that throughout much of American history has been denied them.

1770s

PROTEST AGAINST BRITAIN ▶

In the tense years leading up to the Revolution, American women found ways to participate in the protests against the British. Homemakers boycotted tea and British-made clothing. In the painting at right, Sarah Morris Mifflin, shown with her husband Thomas, spins her own thread rather than use British thread. Some businesswomen, such as printer Mary Goddard, who produced the official copies of the Declaration of Independence, took more active roles.

1848

A WOMAN'S DECLARATION

ELIZABETH CAD...
the cruel and unjus...
the office of her fa...
child, to find a way...
to the abolitionist...
ly into the curren...
foundation for the...
for woman's right...
inspiring leader. T...
executed the first...
Falls, New York, Ju...

SENECA FALLS ▶

As America grew, women became acutely aware of their unequal status in society, particularly their lack of suffrage, or the right to vote.

In 1848, two women—Elizabeth Cady Stanton, shown above, and Lucretia Mott—launched the first woman suffrage movement in the United States at the Seneca Falls Convention in Seneca Falls, New York. During the convention, Stanton introduced her Declaration of Sentiments, in which she demanded greater rights for women, including the right to vote.

1920

THE RIGHT TO VOTE ▶

More than a half-century after organizing for the right to vote, women finally won their struggle. In 1920, the United States adopted the Nineteenth Amendment, which granted women the right to vote.

Pictured to the right is one of the many suffrage demonstrations of the early 1900s that helped garner public support for the amendment.

1972–1982

THE EQUAL RIGHTS AMENDMENT MOVEMENT ▶

During the mid-1900s, as more women entered the workforce, many women recognized their continuing unequal status, including the lack of equal pay for equal work. By passing an Equal Rights Amendment, some women hoped to obtain the same social and economic rights as men.

Although millions supported the amendment, many men and women feared the measure would prompt unwanted change. The ERA ultimately failed to be ratified for the Constitution.

2010

WOMEN IN CONGRESS ▲

In spite of the failure of the ERA, many women have achieved strong positions for themselves—politically as well as socially and economically.

In the 111th Congress, 73 women served in the House of Representatives and 17 served in the Senate. Shown above is Nancy Pelosi, the first woman to serve as Speaker of the House.

THINKING CRITICALLY

CONNECT TO HISTORY

1. **Synthesizing** How did women's political status change from 1770 to 2010?

   SEE SKILLBUILDER HANDBOOK, PAGE R19.

CONNECT TO TODAY

2. **Researching and Reporting** Think of a woman who has played an important role in your community. What kinds of things did this woman do? What support did she receive in the community? What problems did she run into? Report your findings to the class.

VISUAL SUMMARY

THE WAR FOR INDEPENDENCE

1765 Stamp Acts	**1765**	**1765** Sons of Liberty founded
1767 Townshend Acts	**1767**	
	1770	**1770** Boston Massacre
	1773	**1773** Boston Tea Party
1774 Intolerable Acts	**1774**	
1775 George III rejects Olive Branch Petition	**1775**	**1775** Lexington and Concord; Bunker Hill
1776 British seize New York	**1776**	**1776** DECLARATION OF INDEPENDENCE
1777 British seize Philadelphia	**1777**	**1777** American victory at Saratoga
1778 British seize Savannah, Georgia	**1779**	
1780 British seize Charles Town, South Carolina	**1780**	
1781 British reverses in the South	**1781**	**1781** British surrender at Yorktown
	1783	**1783** Treaty of Paris

TERMS & NAMES

For each term below, write a sentence explaining its connection to the American Revolution. For each person below, explain his role in the event.

1. Stamp Act
2. Boston Massacre
3. committee of correspondence
4. Olive Branch Petition
5. *Common Sense*
6. Thomas Jefferson
7. Saratoga
8. Valley Forge
9. Marquis de Lafayette
10. Yorktown

MAIN IDEAS

The Stirrings of Rebellion (pages 96–102)
11. What methods did colonists use to protest actions by Parliament between 1765 and 1775?
12. Describe the causes and the results of the Boston Tea Party.
13. What were the results of fighting at Lexington and Concord?

Ideas Help Start a Revolution (pages 103–108)
14. What did Jefferson mean, and not mean, by the phrase "all men are created equal"?
15. Why did many colonists not support independence?

Struggling Toward Saratoga (pages 113–117)
16. Why was the Battle of Trenton significant?
17. What British military plan did the colonial victory at Saratoga ruin?
18. Explain how civilians supported the war effort in the colonies.

Winning the War (pages 118–123)
19. How did France help the colonies during the American Revolution?
20. Describe three significant challenges facing the United States when the American Revolution ended.

THINKING CRITICALLY

1. **USING YOUR NOTES** Create a dual-path chart showing how the colonies became independent. On one path, list four or more military events, such as battles and changes in command. On the other, list four or more political events, including protests, publication of documents, and legal actions.

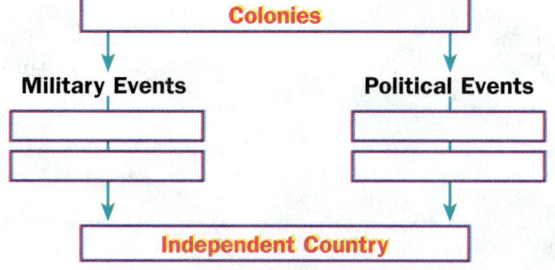

Colonies	
Military Events	**Political Events**
☐	☐
☐	☐
Independent Country	

2. **EVALUATING** Review France's role in helping the colonies rebel against Great Britain. Under what conditions, if any, do you think the United States should help other countries?

Use the cartoon below and your knowledge of U.S. history to answer question 1.

1 This British cartoon was published during the winter of 1775–1776. In it, King George III and his ministers are shown killing the goose that laid the golden egg. The cartoon is criticizing —

(1) the killing of British soldiers at Concord and Bunker Hill.
(2) King George's response to the Olive Branch Petition.
(3) John Locke's theory of natural rights.
(4) Thomas Paine's *Common Sense*.

2 The Battle of Trenton was important to the Americans because —

(1) it prevented the capture of Philadelphia by the British.
(2) it was a badly needed victory that inspired soldiers to reenlist.
(3) it prompted the French to sign an alliance with the Americans.
(4) it ended a series of British victories in the South.

Use the information in the box and your knowledge of U.S. history to answer question 3.

> • Declaration of Independence
> • Battles of Lexington and Concord
> • Second Continental Congress

3 Which of the following lists the events in chronological order from first to last?

(1) Declaration of Independence, Battles of Lexington and Concord, Second Continental Congress
(2) Battles of Lexington and Concord, Second Continental Congress, Declaration of Independence
(3) Second Continental Congress, Battles of Lexington and Concord, Declaration of Independence
(4) Second Continental Congress, Declaration of Independence, Battles of Lexington and Concord

 hmhsocialstudies.com **TEST PRACTICE**

For additional test practice, go online for:
• Diagnostic tests   • Tutorials

INTERACT WITH HISTORY

Recall the issues that you explored at the beginning of the chapter. Imagine that it is 1783, and you have been present at a gathering of your friends who recall the many sacrifices made during the the War for Independence from Great Britain. Write a journal entry in which you try to describe some of those sacrifices. Recall key military events, contributions made by civilians, and key figures who played important roles in the struggle for freedom.

FOCUS ON WRITING

Review the Another Pespective on page 111 and note Abigail Adams's view of the status of women. Write a letter answering her in which you give some ideas about the status of women after the Revolutionary War.

COLLABORATIVE LEARNING

In a small group read and discuss the "One American's Story" at the beginning of Section 2. Then consider the following question: What makes someone a patriot? Using stories and images from the Internet, books, magazines, and newspapers, make a list of people you consider to be patriots. List their names as well as the reasons why you chose them on a chart in your classroom.

THE *American* REVOLUTION

The American Revolution led to the formation of the United States of America in 1776. Beginning in the 1760s, tensions grew between American colonists and their British rulers when Britain started passing a series of new laws and taxes for the colonies. With no representation in the British government, however, colonists had no say in these laws, which led to growing discontent. After fighting broke out in 1775, colonial leaders met to decide what to do. They approved the Declaration of Independence, announcing that the American colonies were free from British rule. In reality, however, freedom would not come until after years of fighting.

Explore some of the people and events of the American Revolution online. You can find a wealth of information, video clips, primary sources, activities, and more at ⬈ **hmhsocialstudies.com**.

> *"I know not what course others may take; but as for me, give me liberty or give me death!"*
>
> – Patrick Henry

📜 **"Give Me Liberty or Give Me Death"**

Read an excerpt from Patrick Henry's famous speech, which urged the colonists to fight against the British.

🎥 **Seeds of Revolution**

Watch the video to learn about colonial discontent in the years before the Revolutionary War.

🎥 **Independence!**

Watch the video to learn about the origins of the Declaration of Independence.

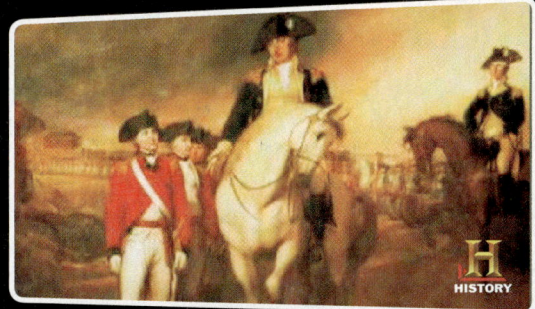

🎥 **Victory!**

Watch the video to learn how the American colonists won the Revolutionary War.

UNIT
2

A New Nation
1781–1850

UNIT PROJECT

Constitution

Work with a small group of class-mates to create a constitution for your class or school. Explain how laws will be passed and changed.

Signing of the Constitution by Howard Chandler Christy

CHAPTER 5

SHAPING A NEW NATION

Washington *(on the far right)* addressing the Constitutional Congress

1785 New York state outlaws slavery.

1781 The Articles of Confederation, which John Dickinson helped write five years earlier, go into effect.

1783 The Treaty of Paris at the end of the Revolutionary War recognizes United States independence.

1784 Russians found colony in Alaska.

1784 Spain closes the Mississippi River to American commerce.

1785 The Treaty of Hopewell concerning Native American lands is signed.

USA

1782

1784

WORLD

1781 Joseph II allows religious toleration in Austria.

1782 Rama I founds a new dynasty in Siam, with Bangkok as the capital.

1783 Russia annexes the Crimean Peninsula.

1783 Ludwig van Beethoven's first works are published.

1785 Jean-Pierre Blanchard and John Jeffries cross the English Channel in a balloon.

INTERACT
WITH HISTORY

The year is 1787. You have recently helped your fellow patriots overthrow decades of oppressive British rule. However, it is easier to destroy an old system of government than to create a new one. In a world of kings and tyrants, your new republic struggles to find its place.

Explore the Issues

- Which should have more power—the states or the national government?
- How can the new nation avoid a return to tyranny?
- How can the rights of all people be protected?

1786 Daniel Shays leads a rebellion of farmers in Massachusetts.

1786 The Annapolis Convention is held.

1786 The Virginia legislature guarantees religious freedom.

1787 The Northwest Ordinance is passed.

1788 The Constitution, which James Madison helped write at the Pennsylvania State House, is ratified.

1786

1788

1786 Charles Cornwallis becomes governor-general of India.

1787 Sierra Leone in Africa becomes a haven for freed American slaves.

1787 War breaks out between Turkey and Russia.

1788 Austria declares war on Turkey.

1788 Bread riots erupt in France.

Experimenting with Confederation

MAIN IDEA	WHY IT MATTERS NOW	Terms & Names
Americans adopted the Articles of Confederation but found the new government too weak to solve the nation's problems.	The reaction to the weak Articles of Confederation led to a stronger central government that has continued to expand its power.	• republic • republicanism • Articles of Confederation • confederation • Land Ordinance of 1785 • Northwest Ordinance of 1787

One American's Story

hmhsocialstudies.com
TAKING NOTES
Use the graphic organizer online to take notes about the Articles of Confederation.

Although John Dickinson had once opposed American independence, he later worked hard to help create a government for the new United States. In 1779 John Dickinson returned to the Continental Congress as a delegate from Delaware. At that time he explained the principles that guided his political decisions.

★ A PERSONAL VOICE JOHN DICKINSON

"Two rules I have laid down for myself throughout this contest . . . first, on all occasions where I am called upon, as a trustee for my countrymen, to deliberate on questions important to their happiness, disdaining all personal advantages to be derived from a suppression of my real sentiments . . . openly to avow [declare] them; and, secondly, . . . whenever the public resolutions are taken, to regard them though opposite to my opinion, as sacred . . . and to join in supporting them as earnestly as if my voice had been given for them."

—quoted in *The Life and Times of John Dickinson, 1732–1808*

Dickinson's two rules became guiding principles for the leaders who faced the formidable task of starting a new nation.

John Dickinson

Americans Debate Republicanism

The task of creating a new government posed a great challenge. Among many other issues, the relationship between the new states and the national government was difficult to define. The debate over the nature of the new government of the United States would consume the political energies of the new nation.

COLONIES BECOME STATES British settlers in North America had founded not one colony but many, each with its own governor, council, and colonial assembly. This system of distinct, self-governing colonies encouraged people to think of the colony as the primary political unit. Because of this, most people's allegiance was to the colony in which they lived. The Revolutionary War gave the colonies a common goal, but as these colonies became states, they remained reluctant to unite under a strong central government. The challenge was to develop a system of government that balanced the interests of the several states with those of the nation. Ⓐ

UNITY THROUGH A REPUBLIC Eighteenth-century Americans believed that a democracy, or government directly by the people, placed too much power in the hands of the uneducated masses. Therefore, they favored a **republic**—a government in which citizens rule through their elected representatives. However, **republicanism,** the idea that governments should be based on the consent of the people (which should not be confused with the Republicanism of the modern-day political party), meant different things to different Americans.

Some, like John Dickinson, believed that a republic required a virtuous people. The new government could only succeed, they argued, if people placed the good of the nation above their personal interests.

Other Americans, influenced by the writings of the philosopher and economist Adam Smith, believed that a republic would benefit from self-interest. They asserted that if a government allowed independent citizens to pursue their own economic and political interests, the whole nation would benefit.

STATE CONSTITUTIONS As the states created their own constitutions, they wrestled with how to put republican ideals into practice. Many state constitutions shared certain similarities. They limited the powers of government leaders. They guaranteed specific rights for citizens, including freedom of speech, religion, and the press. In general, state constitutions emphasized liberty rather than equality and reflected a fear of centralized authority.

At the same time, state constitutions differed widely in granting the right to vote. Although the new states were more democratic than any western nation at this time, it was still only a very limited democracy by modern standards. African Americans were generally not allowed to vote. Some states granted voting rights to all white males. Other states, like Maryland, continued to make property ownership a requirement for voting.

Despite the more active political role that women had played during the Revolution, they were still denied the right to vote in most states. However, New Jersey gave voting rights to all free property owners but neglected to specify males. Consequently, some New Jersey women gained the right to vote—at least until 1807, when this right was revoked.

POLITICAL PRECEDENTS In a world where most nations were still governed by kings, there were few political systems that could serve as models for the new republic. The nation's founders searched history for political precedents for the

MAIN IDEA

Developing Historical Perspective

Ⓐ What relics of the colonial period survived in the new system of government?

Background

In *An Inquiry into the Nature and Causes of the Wealth of Nations*, Adam Smith (1723–1790) argued that social order and progress were the natural result of individualism and self-interest.

HISTORICAL SPOTLIGHT

REPUBLICAN MOTHERHOOD

An important issue in the early years of the nation was the role that women should play in the republic. In the years before and during the Revolutionary War, many women became politically active, organizing boycotts of British goods and helping raise money for the army. This involvement in public affairs was an important departure for women, who had traditionally been confined to the private sphere of family life.

After the Revolution, as the nation readjusted to peace, the new ideal of republican motherhood helped channel women's newfound political awareness and activism back into the home. Women were expected to raise the next generation of patriots by instilling democratic values in their children.

Political Precedents

ATHENS AND ROME

In the 18th century, American leaders revered the political achievements of ancient Athens and Rome. The Greek city of Athens was acknowledged as the birthplace of democracy, while the early Romans were admired for overthrowing monarchy and establishing a republic. However, Greek democracy, like the democracy of the New England town meeting, was workable only at a local level. It was the democracy of a city, not of a huge nation. Neither Greek democracy nor the Roman republic had endured.

▲ Engraving of the ancient Roman Senate

THE ENGLISH COMMONWEALTH

In the mid-17th century the English parliament executed the king and established a republic, which lasted from 1649 to 1660. This republic, called the Commonwealth and Protectorate, was controlled first by Oliver Cromwell and later by his son Richard. The Commonwealth was continually threatened by anarchy and bad leadership and did not long survive Cromwell's death. The failure of the English Commonwealth must have haunted American political leaders as they planned the government of their republic.

◄ The execution of King Charles I

new government. In the previous century, the English had established a short-lived republic after the execution of King Charles I. During the Middle Ages, Italian cities such as Florence, Pisa, Genoa, and Venice had become self-governing city-states. Swiss communities also had resisted royal control, forming alliances that developed into the Swiss Confederation. In ancient times, republics and various democratic systems had existed in Greece and in Rome. However, none of these models could be adapted easily to the political situation of the new United States, with its need to balance the concerns of state and national governments.

The Continental Congress Debates

While the states developed their individual constitutions, the Continental Congress tried to draft one for the states as a whole. However, there was much disagreement over the role of the national government. The delegates had to answer three basic questions.

REPRESENTATION BY POPULATION OR BY STATE? Although the states were equal as political entities, they were unequal in size, wealth, and population. These differences posed a serious dilemma. Should delegates to a new government represent people or states? Should each state elect the same number of representatives regardless of its population? Or should states with large populations have more representatives than states with small populations?

For the time being, the members of the Continental Congress saw themselves as representing independent states. As a result, they made the decision that each state would have one vote regardless of population. **B**

SUPREME POWER: CAN IT BE DIVIDED? Until this time most people assumed that a government could not share supreme power with smaller administrative units, such as provinces or states.

MAIN IDEA

Analyzing Issues

B Why did differences between the states cause problems of representation in the new government?

However, the Congress proposed a new type of government in a set of laws called the **Articles of Confederation**—one in which two levels of government shared fundamental powers. State governments were supreme in some matters, while the national government was supreme in other matters. The delegates called this new form of government a **confederation,** or alliance.

In true Enlightenment fashion, John Dickinson hoped that the new system of government would reflect the order and harmony found in nature.

★ **A Personal Voice** JOHN DICKINSON

"Let our government be like that of the solar system. Let the general government be like the sun and the states the planets, repelled yet attracted, and the whole moving regularly and harmoniously in their several orbits."

—from *The Records of the Federal Convention of 1787*

The Articles of Confederation gave the new national government power to declare war, make peace, and sign treaties. It could borrow money, set standards for coins and for weights and measures, establish a postal service, and deal with Native American peoples. The Articles, however, created no separate executive department to carry out and enforce the acts of Congress and no national court system to interpret the meaning of laws. **C**

MAIN IDEA

Summarizing

C What is a confederation?

WESTERN LANDS: WHO GETS THEM? By 1779, 12 states had agreed to accept the new government, but conflict over western lands delayed final approval for two more years. Some states had claims to lands west of the Appalachian Mountains. Maryland, which had no such claims, feared that states with land claims would expand and overpower smaller states. It refused to approve the Articles until all states turned over their western lands to the United States. Consequently, the landed states gave up their western claims, and with Maryland's approval, the Articles of Confederation went into effect in March 1781.

GOVERNING THE WESTERN LANDS The Confederation Congress then faced the question of how to govern the public lands west of the Appalachians and north of the Ohio River that offered rich land for settlers. Congress passed the **Land Ordinance of 1785,** which established a plan for surveying the land. (See the Geography Spotlight on page 138.) In the **Northwest Ordinance of 1787,** Congress provided a procedure for dividing the land into territories. The Northwest Ordinance also set requirements for the admission of new states, which, however, seemed to overlook Native American land claims. There were three basic stages for becoming a state:

1. Congress would appoint a territorial governor and judges.
2. When a territory had 5,000 voting residents, the settlers could write a temporary constitution and elect their own government.
3. When the total population of a territory reached 60,000 free inhabitants, the settlers could write a state constitution, which had to be approved by Congress before it granted statehood.

The Land Ordinance of 1785 and the Northwest Ordinance of 1787 became the Confederation's greatest achievements. These laws established a blueprint for future growth of the nation. **D**

MAIN IDEA

Contrasting

D What was the basic difference between the Land Ordinance of 1785 and the Northwest Ordinance of 1787?

ANOTHER PERSPECTIVE

JOHN BAPTIST DE COIGNE

John Baptist de Coigne, a Kaskaskia chief, was among a group of Indians from the Northwest Territory who met with leaders of the U.S. government in 1793. He expressed the Native American view of the westward expansion of white settlers during the previous ten years:

"Order your people to be just. They are always trying to get our lands. They come on our lands, they hunt on them; kill our game and kill us. Keep them on one side of the line, and us on the other. Listen, my father, to what we say, and protect the nations of the Wabash and the Mississippi in their lands."

The Confederation Encounters Problems

After its success in dealing with the Northwest Territory, the Confederation encountered overwhelming problems in dealing with more immediate issues. These problems ranged from economic issues, such as taxation and the national debt, to political issues, such as the nature of Congressional representation. In addition to these domestic issues, there were also many foreign-relations problems that the Confederation was powerless to solve.

POLITICAL AND ECONOMIC PROBLEMS The most serious problem was that the country under the Confederation lacked national unity. Each state functioned independently by pursuing its own interests rather than those of the nation as a whole. In addition, the Confederation didn't recognize the differences in population among the states. Each state, regardless of its population, had only one vote in Congress. Thus, the political power of Georgia, with a population of 23,375 in 1770, was equal to that of Massachusetts, with a population of 235,308. Furthermore, the Articles could not be amended without the consent of every state; a single state could stall the amendment process. Therefore, changes in government were difficult to achieve.

The most serious economic problem was the huge debt that the Congress had amassed during the Revolutionary War. The war had cost the nation $190 million—a huge amount of money in those days. The Continental Congress had borrowed from foreign countries and had printed its own paper money. After the war, Continental currency became worthless.

Lacking the power to tax, the Congress requested the states' approval to impose a tariff, or tax on imported goods. It planned to use the revenue to repay foreign loans. However, one state, Rhode Island, rejected the proposed tax, so it was not adopted. Unable to impose taxes, the Confederation Congress also had no control over interstate or foreign trade. **E**

MAIN IDEA

Identifying Problems

E What weakness in the Confederation was highlighted by the actions of Rhode Island?

BORROWERS VERSUS LENDERS Another problem caused by the debt from the Revolution was the struggle between creditors (lenders of money) and debtors (borrowers of money). After the war, wealthy people who had lent money to the states favored high taxes so that the states would be able to pay them back. However, high taxes sent many farmers into debt. When a creditor sued a farmer in court for repayment and won the case, the government seized the farmer's land and animals and sold them at auction.

Debtors and creditors also disagreed over the usefulness of paper money. Debtors wanted to increase the supply of money to lessen its value and enable them to pay off their debts with cheap currency. Creditors, in contrast, wanted to keep the supply of money low so that it would keep its full value. Both groups had much to lose.

▶ Currency, such as this early example from Connecticut, was issued by the colonies and the states.

FOREIGN-RELATIONS PROBLEMS The lack of support from states for national concerns led to foreign-relations problems for the Congress. First, since the United States could not repay its debts to British merchants and would not compensate Loyalists for property losses suffered during the Revolutionary War, Britain refused to evacuate its military forts on the Great Lakes. Furthermore, Spain's presence on the borders of the United States posed another threat to westward expansion. In 1784, Spain closed the Mississippi River to American navigation. This action deprived Western farmers of a means of shipping their crops

Weaknesses of the Articles of Confederation

- Congress could not enact and collect taxes.
- Congress could not regulate interstate or foreign trade.
- Regardless of population, each state had only one vote in Congress.
- Two-thirds majority—9 out of 13 states needed to agree to pass any law.

- Articles could be amended only if all states approved.
- There was no executive branch to enforce the laws of Congress.
- There was no national court system to settle legal disputes.
- There were 13 separate states that lacked national unity.

SKILLBUILDER *Interpreting Charts*
1. How many states' votes were needed to approve changes in the Articles of Confederation?
2. Why did the listed weaknesses lead to an ineffective government?

to Eastern markets through New Orleans. Though Northerners were willing to give up navigation rights on the Mississippi in exchange for more profitable trade concessions, Westerners and Southerners insisted on access to the Mississippi. However, Congress was too weak to resolve either of these challenges by Spain and Britain.

The problems the Congress encountered in dealing with foreign nations revealed the basic weaknesses of the Confederation government. Americans' fear of giving the national government too much power had resulted in a government that lacked sufficient power to deal with the nation's problems. The forthcoming Constitutional Convention would change all of this.

ASSESSMENT

1. **TERMS & NAMES** For each term or name, write a sentence explaining its significance.
   - republic
   - republicanism
   - Articles of Confederation
   - confederation
   - Land Ordinance of 1785
   - Northwest Ordinance of 1787

MAIN IDEA

2. **TAKING NOTES**
   In a diagram like the one below, describe the powers given to the national government by the Articles of Confederation.

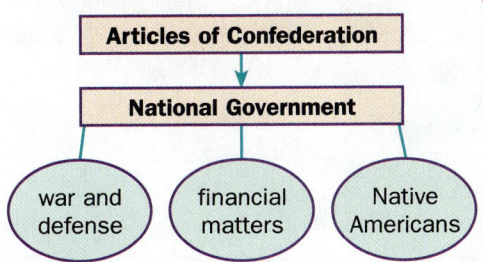

What were the weaknesses of the Articles of Confederation?

CRITICAL THINKING

3. **ANALYZING ISSUES**
   Why were the states afraid of centralized authority and a strong national government?

4. **IDENTIFYING PROBLEMS**
   What was the main problem with the system of representation by state (rather than by population) that was adopted by the Confederation?

5. **HYPOTHESIZING**
   Do you think that the United States would have become a world power if the Articles of Confederation had remained the basis of government? Explain the reasons for your opinion.
   Think About:
   - the power that the Articles gave the states
   - foreign affairs and the Confederation Congress
   - the Confederation Congress's taxation powers

GEOGRAPHY SPOTLIGHT

The Land Ordinance of 1785

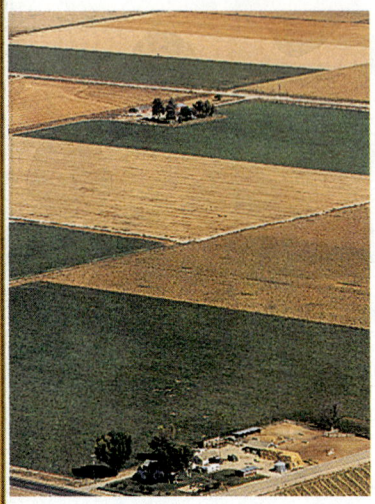

▲ Aerial photograph showing how the Land Ordinance transformed the landscape into a patchwork of farms.

When states ceded, or gave up, their western lands to the United States, the new nation became "land rich" even though it was "money poor." Government leaders searched for a way to use the land to fund such services as public education.

The fastest and easiest way to raise money would have been to sell the land in huge parcels. However, only the rich would have been able to purchase land. The Land Ordinance of 1785 made the parcels small and affordable.

The Land Ordinance established a plan for dividing the land. The government would first survey the land, dividing it into townships of 36 square miles, as shown on the map below. Then each township would be divided into 36 sections of 1 square mile, or about 640 acres, each. An individual or a family could purchase a section and divide it into farms or smaller units. A typical farm of the period was equal to one-quarter section, or 160 acres. The minimum price per acre was one dollar.

Government leaders hoped the buyers would develop farms and establish communities. In this way settlements would spread across the western territories in an orderly way. Government surveyors repeated the process thousands of times, imposing frontier geometry on the land.

In 1787, the Congress further provided for the orderly development of the Northwest Territory by passing the Northwest Ordinance, which established how states would be created out of the territory.

▼ The map below shows how an eastern section of Ohio has been subdivided into townships and sections, according to the Land Ordinance of 1785.

This map shows how a township, now in Meigs County, Ohio, was divided in 1787 into parcels of full square-mile sections and smaller, more affordable plots. The names of the original buyers are written on the full sections. ▶

Ⓐ RELIGION To encourage the growth of religion within the township, the surveyors set aside a full section of land. Most of the land within the section was sold to provide funds for a church and a minister's salary. This practice was dropped after a few years because of concern about the separation of church and state.

Ⓑ EDUCATION The ordinance encouraged public education by setting aside section 16 of every township for school buildings. Local people used the money raised by the sale of land within this section to build a school and hire a teacher. This section was centrally located so that students could reach it without traveling too far.

Ⓒ REVENUE Congress reserved two or three sections of each township for sale at a later date. Congress planned to sell the sections then at a tidy profit. The government soon abandoned this practice because of criticism that it should not be involved in land speculation.

Ⓓ WATER Rivers and streams were very important to early settlers, who used them for transportation. Of most interest, however, was a meandering stream, which indicated flat bottomland that was highly prized for its fertility.

TOWNSHIP N.° VII RANGE N.° XIV   SCALE of forty chains to an inch

THINKING CRITICALLY

1. **Analyzing Distributions** How did the Land Ordinance of 1785 provide for the orderly development of the Northwest Territory? How did it make land affordable?

2. **Creating a Chart** Create a table that organizes and summarizes the information in the map above. To help you organize your thoughts, pose questions that the map suggests and that a table could help answer.

📖 SEE SKILLBUILDER HANDBOOK, PAGE R30.

hmhsocialstudies.com RESEARCH WEB LINKS

SECTION
2

PI 1.2

CC Unit 2.I.A.1.a   CC Unit 2.I.B.1.b
CC Unit 2.I.B.2.a   CC Unit 2.I.B.2.b
CC Unit 2.I.B.2.c   CC Unit 2.I.B.3

Drafting the Constitution

MAIN IDEA	WHY IT MATTERS NOW	Terms & Names
At the Philadelphia convention in 1787, delegates rejected the Articles of Confederation and created a new constitution.	The Constitution remains the basis of our government.	• Shays's Rebellion • James Madison • Roger Sherman • Great Compromise • Three-Fifths Compromise • federalism • legislative branch • executive branch • judicial branch • checks and balances • electoral college

One American's Story

TAKING NOTES
Use the graphic organizer online to take notes about issues debated at the Constitutional Convention.

Daniel Shays was angry. A veteran of the Revolutionary War battles at Bunker Hill and Saratoga, he had returned to his farm in western Massachusetts. Because of the heavy debt that he carried, however, he faced debtors' prison. Shays felt that he was the victim of too much taxation.

During the summer and fall of 1786, farmers like Shays kept demanding that the courts be closed so they would not lose their farms to creditors. Their discontent boiled over into mob action in September of 1786 when Daniel Shays led an army of farmers to close the courts. In 1787, Shays's army, 1,200 strong, marched through the snow toward the arsenal at Springfield.

State officials hurriedly called out the militia. Four of the rebels were killed and the rest were scattered. Clearly, though, if so many farmers were rebelling, there was something seriously wrong.

▲
Shays's Rebellion in 1786–1787 not only resulted in the death of four rebels but also unsettled some of the nation's leaders.

Nationalists Strengthen the Government

Shays's Rebellion, as the farmers' protest came to be called, caused panic and dismay throughout the nation. Every state had debt-ridden farmers. Would rebellion spread from Massachusetts elsewhere? Not only was private property in danger, but so was the new nation's reputation. As George Washington himself exclaimed, "What a triumph for our enemies . . . to find that we are incapable of governing ourselves."

It was clearly time to talk about a stronger national government. In order to prevent abuse of power, the states had placed such severe limits on the government that the government was too weak.

Fearing that the new nation was about to disintegrate, George Washington addressed this issue.

★ A PERSONAL VOICE GEORGE WASHINGTON

"The consequences of . . . [an] inefficient government are too obvious to be dwelt upon. Thirteen sovereignties pulling against each other, and all tugging at the federal head will soon bring ruin on the whole. . . . Let us have [government] by which our lives, liberty, and property will be secured or let us know the worst at once."

CALL FOR CONVENTION One of the nation's biggest problems was trade between the states, which led to quarrels over the taxes that states imposed on one another's goods and disagreements over navigation rights. In September 1786, leaders such as **James Madison** of Virginia and Alexander Hamilton called a meeting of state delegates to discuss issues of interstate trade. Only five states sent representatives to the convention, held in Annapolis, Maryland. Delegates decided to call for another meeting the following year in Philadelphia to deal with trade and other problems.

Meanwhile, the disturbing news of Shays's Rebellion in Massachusetts spread throughout the states. The incident convinced 12 states to send delegates to the Philadelphia convention. **A**

CONVENTION HIGHLIGHTS
In May 1787, delegates from all the states except Rhode Island gathered at the Philadelphia State House—in the same room in which the Declaration of Independence had been signed 11 years earlier. In spite of the sweltering heat, the windows were tightly closed to prevent outsiders from eavesdropping on the discussions.

Most of the 55 delegates were lawyers, merchants, or planters. Most were rich, well-educated men in their thirties or forties. They included some of the most outstanding leaders of the time, such as Benjamin Franklin, Alexander Hamilton, and George Washington. Washington was elected presiding officer by a unanimous vote.

MAIN IDEA

Analyzing Motives

A Why do you think news of Shays's Rebellion made states decide to participate in the Philadelphia convention?

KEY PLAYERS

JAMES MADISON 1751–1836

The oldest of 12 children, James Madison grew up in Virginia. He was a sickly child who suffered all his life from physical ailments. Because of a weak voice, he decided not to become a minister and thus entered politics.

Madison's Virginia Plan resulted from extensive research on political systems that he had done before the convention. He asked Edmund Randolph, a fellow delegate from Virginia, to present the plan because his own voice was too weak to be heard throughout the assembly.

Besides providing brilliant political leadership, Madison kept a record of the debates that took place at the convention. Because of his plan and his leadership, Madison is known as the "Father of the Constitution."

ROGER SHERMAN 1721–1793

Born in Massachusetts, Roger Sherman spoke a New England dialect that some people found laughable. As a young man, he became a successful merchant. Sherman also studied law and became so active in politics that he had to quit his business.

Sherman helped draft the Declaration of Independence. When he returned to Philadelphia in 1787 for the Constitutional Convention, he was 66 years old. He introduced a plan—later called the Great Compromise—that resolved the issue of state representation in the national legislature. Roger Sherman was the only man to sign the Continental Association of 1774, the Declaration of Independence, the Articles of Confederation, and the Constitution.

Conflict Leads to Compromise

Most of the delegates recognized the need to strengthen the central government. Within the first five days of the meeting, they gave up the idea of revising the Articles of Confederation and decided to form a new government.

BIG STATES VERSUS SMALL STATES One big issue the delegates faced was giving fair representation to both large and small states. Madison's Virginia Plan proposed a bicameral, or two-house, legislature, with membership based on each state's population. The voters would elect members of the lower house, who would then elect members of the upper house.

Delegates from the small states vigorously objected to the Virginia Plan because it gave more power to states with large populations. Small states supported William Paterson's New Jersey Plan, which proposed a single-house congress in which each state had an equal vote.

Proponents of the plans became deadlocked. Finally, **Roger Sherman,** a political leader from Connecticut, suggested the **Great Compromise,** which offered a two-house Congress to satisfy both small and big states. Each state would have equal representation in the Senate, or upper house. The size of the population of each state would determine its representation in the House of Representatives, or lower house. Voters of each state would choose members of the House. The state legislatures would choose members of the Senate.

Sherman's plan pleased those who favored government by the people insofar as it allowed voters to choose representatives. It also pleased those who defended states' rights insofar as it preserved the power of state legislatures. **B**

SLAVERY-RELATED ISSUES Representation based on population raised the question of whether slaves should be counted as people. Southern delegates, whose states had many slaves, wanted slaves included in the population count that determined the number of representatives in the House. Northern delegates, whose states had few slaves, disagreed. Not counting Southern slaves would give the Northern states more representatives than the Southern states in the House of Representatives. The delegates eventually agreed to the **Three-Fifths Compromise,** which called for three-fifths of a state's slaves to be counted as population.

The Three-Fifths Compromise settled the political issue but not the economic issue of slavery. Slaveholders, especially in the South, worried that if Congress were given power to regulate foreign trade, it might do away with the

MAIN IDEA

Analyzing Issues

B Why was Sherman's compromise a success?

Key Conflicts in the Constitutional Convention	
STRONG CENTRAL GOVERNMENT vs. STRONG STATES	
• Authority derives from the people. • The central government should be stronger than the states.	• Authority derives from the states. • The states should remain stronger than the central government.
LARGE STATES vs. SMALL STATES	
• Congress should be composed of two houses. • Delegates should be assigned according to population.	• A congress of one house should be preserved. • Each state should have one vote.
NORTH vs. SOUTH	
• Slaves should not be counted when deciding the number of delegates. • Slaves should be counted when levying taxes.	• Slaves should be counted when determining congressional representation. • Slaves should not be counted when levying taxes.

slave trade. To resolve this issue, the convention gave Congress the power to regulate trade but prevented it from interfering with the slave trade for at least 20 years. Although the proposal passed, not all the delegates agreed with it. James Madison predicted, "Twenty years will produce all the mischief that can be apprehended from the liberty to import slaves. So long a term will be more dishonorable to the national character than to say nothing about it in the Constitution."

Creating a New Government

After reaching agreement on questions of slavery and representation, the delegates dealt with other issues. They divided power between the states and the national government and separated the national government's power into three branches.

DIVISION OF POWERS The new system of government was a form of **federalism** that divided power between the national government and the state governments. The powers granted to the national government by the Constitution are known as delegated powers, or enumerated powers. These include such powers as control of foreign affairs, providing national defense, regulating trade between the states, and coining money. Powers kept by the states are called reserved powers. These include powers such as providing and supervising education, establishing marriage laws, and regulating trade within a state. **C**

Both levels of government share such important powers as the right to tax, to borrow money, and to pay debts. They also share the power to establish courts.

SEPARATION OF POWERS The delegates protected the rights of the states, but they also granted some powers exclusively to the national government. At the same time, they limited the authority of the government. First, they created three branches of government—a **legislative branch** to make laws, an **executive branch** to carry out laws, and a **judicial branch** to interpret the law.

Then the delegates established a system of **checks and balances** to prevent one branch from dominating the others. (See the chart below.) For example, the president has considerable power, but the Senate has to approve some of the president's decisions. The president can veto acts of Congress, but Congress can override a veto by a

MAIN IDEA

Summarizing
C Which powers were granted to the national government and to the state governments?

Background
The system of checks and balances among the different branches of government was introduced by Baron de Montesquieu in *The Spirit of the Laws* (1748).

The Checks and Balances of the Federal System

Checks on the Executive Branch
- Congress can override a presidential veto
- Congress approves funding for presidential programs
- Congress can impeach and remove the president or other high officials
- Senate confirms or rejects federal appointments

Checks on the Judicial Branch
- Congress establishes lower federal courts
- Senate confirms or rejects appointments of judges
- Congress can impeach and remove federal judges

LEGISLATIVE BRANCH

EXECUTIVE BRANCH

JUDICIAL BRANCH

Checks on the Legislative Branch
- Can veto bills of Congress
- Can call special sessions of Congress
- Can influence public opinion
- Can propose legislation

Checks on the Judicial Branch
- Appoints federal judges
- Can pardon or reprieve people convicted of federal crimes

Checks on the Executive Branch
- Appointed for life, federal judges are free from presidential control
- Can declare presidential actions unconstitutional

Checks on the Legislative Branch
- Can decide the meaning of laws
- Can declare acts of Congress unconstitutional

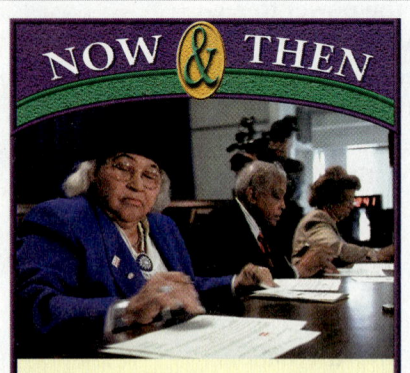

NOW & THEN

THE ELECTORAL COLLEGE

Distrust of popular sovereignty led the framers of the Constitution to devise a complicated system of electing the president. The creation of an electoral college ensured that a college of electors, or representatives, would have the last say in the vote.

In the 2000 presidential election, the electoral college played a decisive role in choosing the president. Even though Al Gore won the popular vote by a margin of almost 540,000, the electors gave George W. Bush 271 electoral votes—one vote more than the 270 votes needed to win the presidency.

two-thirds vote. The Supreme Court assumes the power to interpret the Constitution, but the president appoints the justices, and Congress can bring them to trial for abuses of power.

The procedure for electing the president reflected two main concerns. Because there were no national political parties and because travel and communication were limited, there was a fear that the popular vote would be divided among many regional candidates. Also, many among the upper classes distrusted and feared the lower classes. Some did not trust the common people to vote wisely; others trusted them to vote the upper class out of power. So the delegates came up with a new system of electing the president. Instead of voters choosing the president directly, each state would choose a number of electors equal to the number of senators and representatives the state had in Congress. The group of electors chosen by the states, known as the **electoral college,** would cast ballots for the candidates.

CREATING THE CONSTITUTION Finally, the delegates provided a means of changing the Constitution through the amendment process. After nearly four months of debate and compromise, the delegates succeeded in creating a constitution that was flexible enough to last through the centuries to come. Yet when George Washington adjourned the convention on September 17, 1787, he was somewhat uncertain about the future of the new plan of government. Washington remarked to a fellow delegate, "I do not expect the Constitution to last for more than 20 years."

The convention's work was over, but the new government could not become a reality until the voters agreed. So the Constitution of the United States of America was sent to the Congress, which submitted it to the states for approval.

FOCUS ON

The Framers used the New York State Constitution of 1777 as a model for parts of the United States Constitution. For example, the New York constitution called for a popularly elected executive who could veto laws. New York's first state constitution, then, helped to shape the office of President as we know it today.

SECTION 2 ASSESSMENT

1. TERMS & NAMES For each term or name, write a sentence explaining its significance.

- Shays's Rebellion
- James Madison
- Roger Sherman
- Great Compromise
- Three-Fifths Compromise
- federalism
- legislative branch
- executive branch
- judicial branch
- checks and balances
- electoral college

MAIN IDEA

2. TAKING NOTES
Re-create the web below on your paper, and fill it in with specific issues that were debated.

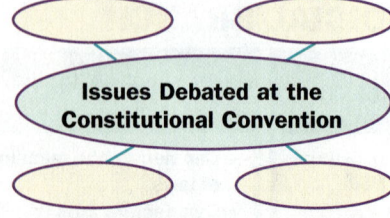

Issues Debated at the Constitutional Convention

Choose one issue and explain how the delegates resolved that issue.

CRITICAL THINKING

3. ANALYZING ISSUES
In what ways did the new system of government fulfill the nation's need for a stronger central government and at the same time allay its fear of a government having too much power?

4. SUMMARIZING
What was the Great Compromise and how did it reconcile the interests of the small states with the interests of the more populous states?

5. EVALUATING DECISIONS
Do you agree or disagree with the creation of a system of checks and balances? Explain your answer.
Think About:
- the main task of each branch
- how the branches function
- the efficiency of governmental operations

PI 1.2

CC Unit 2.I.B.1.a   CC Unit 2.I.B.4.a
CC Unit 2.I.B.4.b   CC Unit 2.I.C
CC Unit 2.I.E(1)   CC Unit 2.I.E(4)

Ratifying the Constitution

MAIN IDEA	WHY IT MATTERS NOW	Terms & Names
During the debate on the Constitution, the Federalists promised to add a bill of rights in order to get the Constitution ratified.	The Bill of Rights continues to protect ordinary citizens.	• ratification • Federalists • Antifederalists • *The Federalist* • Bill of Rights

One American's Story

hmhsocialstudies.com
TAKING NOTES

Use the graphic organizer online to take notes about the Federalists and the Antifederalists.

When John Jay was in college, he refused to reveal the identity of a student who had broken school property. As he was being interrogated, Jay pointed out that the college rules did not require one student to inform on another.

Years later, Jay argued for ratification of the newly written constitution. He warned how other nations would view the United States if it did not unify itself.

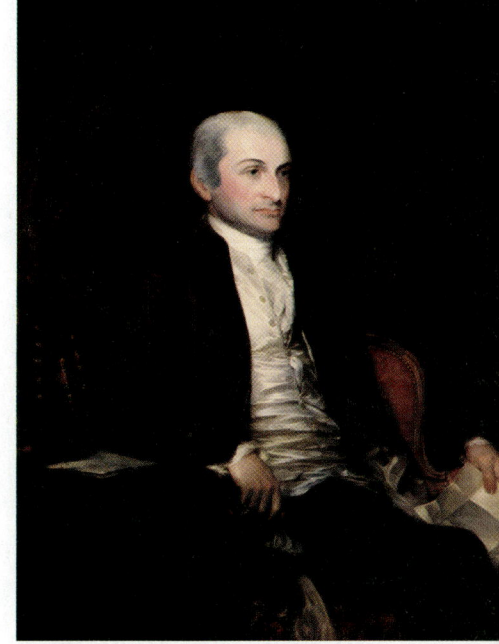

A PERSONAL VOICE JOHN JAY

" What a poor pitiful figure will America make in their eyes! How liable would she become not only to their contempt, but to their outrage; and how soon would dear-bought experience proclaim that when a people or family so divide, it never fails to be against themselves. "
— *The Federalist*, Number 4

Whether Jay was defending his peers or his country's Constitution, his strong principles and commitment to unity gave his arguments tremendous force. Men like John Jay played a key role in ratifying the Constitution.

John Jay

Federalists and Antifederalists

The delegates to the Philadelphia convention had spent four months drafting the Constitution. When newspapers printed the full text of the new Constitution, many Americans were shocked by the radical changes it proposed. They had expected the convention to merely amend the Articles of Confederation. Supporters and opponents battled over controversies that threatened to shatter the framers' hope of uniting the states.

" *They . . . divided the powers, that each [branch of the legislature] might be a check upon the other . . . and I presume that every reasonable man will agree to it.*"

ALEXANDER HAMILTON

" *You are not to inquire how your trade may be increased, nor how you are to become a great and powerful people, but how your liberties can be secured. . . .*"

PATRICK HENRY

CONTROVERSIES OVER THE CONSTITUTION The framers set up a procedure for ratification that called for each state to hold a special convention. The voters would elect the delegates to the convention, who would then vote to accept or reject the Constitution. **Ratification**—official approval—required the agreement of at least nine states. This system largely bypassed the state legislatures, whose members were likely to oppose the Constitution, since it reduced the power of the states. It also gave the framers an opportunity to campaign for delegates in their states who would support ratification.

Supporters of the Constitution called themselves **Federalists,** because they favored the new Constitution's balance of power between the states and the national government. Their opponents became known as **Antifederalists** because they opposed having such a strong central government and thus were against the Constitution.

The Federalists insisted that the division of powers and the system of checks and balances would protect Americans from the tyranny of centralized authority. Antifederalists countered with a long list of possible abuses of power by a strong central government. These included a fear that the government would serve the interests of the privileged minority and ignore the rights of the majority. Antifederalists also raised doubts that a single government could manage the affairs of a large country. Their leading argument, however, centered on the Constitution's lack of protection for individual rights. **A**

THE OPPOSING FORCES Leading Federalists included framers of the Constitution such as George Washington, James Madison, and Alexander Hamilton. They used their experience and powers of persuasion to win support for the document they had drafted. They received heavy support from urban centers, where merchants, skilled workers, and laborers saw the benefit of a national government that could regulate trade. Small states and those with weak economies also favored a strong central government that could protect their interests.

Leading Antifederalists included revolutionary heroes and leaders such as Patrick Henry, Samuel Adams, and Richard Henry Lee. They received support from rural areas, where people feared a strong government that might add to their tax burden. Large states and those with strong economies, such as New York, which had greater freedom under the Articles of Confederation, also were unsupportive of the Constitution at first.

Both sides waged a war of words in the public debate over ratification. *The Federalist,* a series of 85 essays defending the Constitution, appeared in New York newspapers between 1787 and 1788. They were published under the pseudonym *Publius,* but were written by Federalist leaders Alexander Hamilton, James Madison, and John Jay. *The Federalist* provided an analysis and an explanation of Constitutional provisions, such as the separation of powers and the limits on the power of majorities, that remain important today.

Letters from the Federal Farmer, most likely written by Richard Henry Lee, was the most widely read Antifederalist publication. Lee listed the rights the Antifederalists believed should be protected, such as freedom of the press and of religion, guarantees against unreasonable searches of people and their homes, and the right to a trial by jury.

MAIN IDEA

Analyzing Issues
A What were the Antifederalists' major arguments against the Constitution?

The Bill of Rights Leads to Ratification

The proposed U.S. Constitution contained no guarantee that the government would protect the rights of the people or of the states. Some supporters of the Constitution, such as Thomas Jefferson, viewed the Constitution's lack of a bill of rights—a formal summary of citizens' rights and freedoms, as a serious drawback to ratification.

★ **A PERSONAL VOICE** THOMAS JEFFERSON

" I like much the general idea of framing a government, which should go on of itself, peaceably, without needing continual recurrence to the State legislatures. . . . I will now tell you what I do not like. First, the omission of a bill of rights. . . . Let me add, that a bill of rights is what the people are entitled to against every government on earth, general or particular; and what no just government should refuse. . . . "

—letter to James Madison from Paris, December 20, 1787

PEOPLE DEMAND A BILL OF RIGHTS Antifederalists argued that since the Constitution weakened the states, the people needed a national bill of rights. They wanted written guarantees that the people would have freedom of speech, of the press, and of religion. They demanded assurance of the right to trial by jury and the right to bear arms.

Federalists insisted that the Constitution granted only limited powers to the national government so that it could not violate the rights of the states or of the people. They also pointed out that the Constitution gave the people the power to protect their rights through the election of trustworthy leaders. In the end, though, the Federalists yielded to people's overwhelming desire and promised to add a bill of rights if the states would ratify the Constitution. Ⓑ

RATIFICATION OF THE CONSTITUTION Delaware led the country in ratifying the Constitution in December 1787. In June 1788, New Hampshire fulfilled the requirement for ratification by becoming the ninth state to approve the Constitution. Nevertheless, Virginia and New York had not voted, and the new government needed these very large and influential states.

Powerful adversaries squared off in Virginia. Patrick Henry, Richard Henry Lee, and James Monroe led the opposition. Richard Henry Lee, a prominent political

MAIN IDEA

Summarizing

Ⓑ What were the arguments made by Antifederalists and Federalists over adding a bill of rights to the Constitution?

A parade in New York in 1788 celebrates the new Constitution and features the "Ship of State" float. Alexander Hamilton's name emphasizes the key role he played in launching the new government.
▼

figure of his time, claimed that those in favor of the Constitution were voluntarily placing themselves under the power of an absolute ruler.

⭐ **A PERSONAL VOICE** RICHARD HENRY LEE

" 'Tis really astonishing that the same people, who have just emerged from a long and cruel war in defense of liberty, should now agree to fix an elective despotism [absolute power] upon themselves and their posterity."

The struggle for New York pitted John Jay and Alexander Hamilton against a strong Antifederalist majority. Jay, Hamilton, and Madison launched an effective public campaign through *The Federalist*. News of ratification by New Hampshire and Virginia strengthened the Federalists' cause. On July 26, 1788, New York ratified by a vote of 30 to 27. Although Rhode Island did not accept the Constitution until 1790, the new government became a reality in 1789.

SOUTH AFRICA CREATES A BILL OF RIGHTS

On May 8, 1996, South African lawmakers danced in the aisles of South Africa's Parliament. They had just approved a landmark constitution guaranteeing equal rights for blacks and whites in the new South Africa. Included in this constitution was a bill of rights modeled in part on the United States Bill of Rights, though with significant differences.

The South African bill of rights is a much broader and more detailed document than the U.S. Bill of Rights. For example, two pages are devoted to the rights of arrested, detained, and accused persons. One page is devoted to the rights of children. The document forbids discrimination of all kinds and protects the rights of minorities. It also guarantees every citizen the right to freedom of travel within the country, which was often denied blacks under apartheid. In addition, the bill of rights guarantees a range of social and economic rights—including the right to adequate housing, food, water, education, and health care—which were often denied blacks under apartheid.

Nelson Mandela, the first black president of South Africa, greets a crowd celebrating the new constitution May 8, 1996. ▼

People outside the polling station in the black township of Soweto waiting to vote in South Africa's first multiracial election. ▶

ADOPTION OF A BILL OF RIGHTS In several states, ratification had hinged on the Federalists' pledge to add a bill of rights. In September 1789, Congress submitted 12 amendments to the state legislatures for ratification. By December 1791, the required three-fourths of the states had ratified ten of the amendments, which became known as the **Bill of Rights.**

The first eight amendments spell out the personal liberties the states had requested. The Ninth and Tenth Amendments impose general limits on the powers of the federal government.

- The *First Amendment*—guarantees citizens' rights to freedom of religion, speech, the press, and political activity.
- The *Second* and *Third Amendments*—grant citizens the right to bear arms as members of a militia of citizen-soldiers and prevent the government from housing troops in private homes in peacetime.
- The *Fourth* through *Eighth Amendments*—guarantee fair treatment for individuals suspected or accused of crimes.
- The *Ninth Amendment*—makes it clear that people's rights are not restricted to just those specifically mentioned in the Constitution.
- The *Tenth Amendment*—clarifies that the people and the states have all the powers that the Constitution does not specifically give to the national government or deny to the states.

The protection of rights and freedoms did not apply to all Americans at the time the Bill of Rights was adopted. Native Americans and slaves were excluded. Women were not mentioned in the Constitution. Although some northern states permitted free blacks to vote, the Bill of Rights offered them no protection against whites' discrimination and hostility. The expansion of democracy came from later amendments. Nevertheless, the flexibility of the U.S. Constitution made it a model for governments around the world.

FOCUS ON

The New York State Constitution of 1777 did not have a Bill of Rights. However, such rights as freedom of worship and trial by jury were protected under the state constitution.

The Bill of Rights
1. Religious and political freedom
2. Right to bear arms
3. Freedom from quartering troops
4. Freedom against unreasonable search and seizure
5. Rights of accused persons
6. Right to a speedy, public trial
7. Right to a trial by jury
8. Limits on fines and punishments
9. Rights of the people
10. Powers of states and the people

SECTION 3 ASSESSMENT

1. TERMS & NAMES For each term or name, write a sentence explaining its significance.
- ratification
- Federalists
- Antifederalists
- *The Federalist*
- Bill of Rights

MAIN IDEA

2. TAKING NOTES
Use a chart like the one below to show which groups and public figures supported the Federalists and which supported the Antifederalists.

	Public Figures	Groups
Federalists		
Antifederalists		

Which group would you have supported? Explain why.

CRITICAL THINKING

3. EVALUATING
Do you think the Federalists or the Antifederalists had the more valid arguments? Support your opinion with examples from the text.
Think About:
- whom each group represented
- Americans' experience with the Articles of Confederation
- Americans' experience with British rule

4. ANALYZING MOTIVES
Why did the Antifederalists demand the Bill of Rights?

5. HYPOTHESIZING
How might the course of American history have changed if the Bill of Rights had forbidden discrimination of all kinds and had protected the rights of minorities?

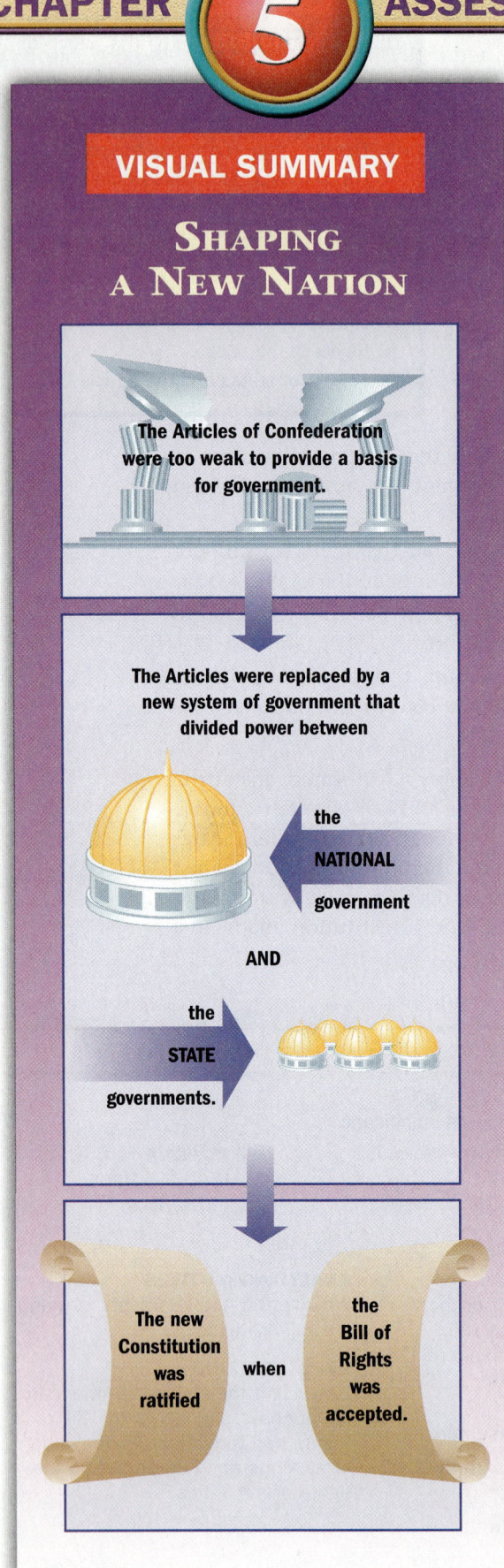

VISUAL SUMMARY

SHAPING A NEW NATION

The Articles of Confederation were too weak to provide a basis for government.

The Articles were replaced by a new system of government that divided power between

the NATIONAL government

AND

the STATE governments.

The new Constitution was ratified when the Bill of Rights was accepted.

TERMS & NAMES

For each term or name below, write a sentence explaining its significance for the United States in the 1780s.

1. republic
2. Articles of Confederation
3. Land Ordinance of 1785
4. Shays's Rebellion
5. James Madison
6. checks and balances
7. electoral college
8. Federalist
9. Antifederalist
10. Bill of Rights

MAIN IDEAS

Use your notes and the information in the chapter to answer the following questions.

Experimenting with Confederation *(pages 132–137)*

1. Why did the new states prefer a republic rather than a democracy for their government?
2. Why did the states fear a strong central government?
3. In what ways was the confederation too weak to handle the nation's problems?

Drafting the Constitution *(pages 140–144)*

4. What issues and events led to the Constitutional Convention?
5. In what ways did compromise play a critical role in the drafting of the Constitution?
6. Why was the slave trade an issue at the Constitutional Convention?
7. Briefly explain the separation of powers established by the Constitution.

Ratifying the Constitution *(pages 145–149)*

8. What were the arguments for and against ratifying the Constitution?
9. What was *The Federalist* and what effect did this publication have on ratification?
10. Why did the states ratify the Constitution once a bill of rights was promised?

CRITICAL THINKING

1. **USING YOUR NOTES** In a chart like the one below, list the beliefs and goals of the Federalists and Antifederalists.

	Federalists	**Antifederalists**
Beliefs		
Goals		

2. **DEVELOPING HISTORICAL PERSPECTIVE** How might the United States have developed if the Articles of Confederation had continued to provide the basis for government?

3. **MAKING INFERENCES** In what ways was the land of the Northwest Territory distributed democratically?

Use the quotation below and your knowledge of United States history to answer questions 1 and 2.

> "Among the numerous advantages promised by a well-constructed Union, none deserves to be more accurately developed than its tendency to break and control the violence of faction. . . . By a faction, I understand a number of citizens, whether amounting to a majority or a minority of the whole, who are united and actuated by some common impulse of passion, or of interest, adverse to the rights of other citizens, or to the permanent and aggregate interests of the community. . . . A landed interest, a manufacturing interest, a mercantile interest, a moneyed interest, with many lesser interests, grow up of necessity in civilized nations, and divide them into different classes, actuated by different sentiments and views."
>
> —James Madison, *The Federalist*, Number 10

1 As used by Madison, the term *faction* means —

(1) any interest group.
(2) a religious cult.
(3) either of the two political parties.
(4) anyone who does not own property.

2 Madison believed that factions were —

(1) necessary to the working of government.
(2) characteristic of British government only.
(3) extremely destructive and divisive.
(4) outdated and insignificant.

3 The Constitution was finally ratified because —

(1) the Federalists agreed to grant additional powers to the states.
(2) the Federalists agreed to add a Bill of Rights.
(3) the electoral college voted for ratification.
(4) the Antifederalists agreed to additional restrictions on the power of the states.

4 Why was it so difficult to devise a system of government for the United States?

(1) The new nation was too big.
(2) No one wanted a national government.
(3) Many feared that a national government would infringe upon the power of the states.
(4) Some states did not want to rejoin Britain.

hmhsocialstudies.com TEST PRACTICE

For additional test practice, go online for:
• Diagnostic tests   • Tutorials

INTERACT WITH HISTORY

Think about the issues you explored at the beginning of the chapter. Imagine you are living in the 1780s. Write an article for either *The Federalist* or *Letters from the Federal Farmer*, arguing either for or against giving the national government more power.

FOCUS ON WRITING

You are a representative of one of the former colonies and you have just returned from the Constitutional Convention. Write a letter explaining how the U.S. Constitution is an improvement upon the Articles of Confederation. Support your explanation with reasoning and examples from the chapter.

COLLABORATIVE LEARNING

21ST CENTURY

Organize into pairs and choose an issue debated at the Constitutional Convention. Read the section of the Constitution that contains the final compromise as well as documents that show the various sides of the issue before a compromise was reached. Then prepare a debate of the issue to present to the class. Each partner should draft a three-minute speech defending one side of the issue. The opposing partner should give a short rebuttal after each point of view is presented. Have the class evaluate the two sides of the argument before you remind your classmates how the issue was resolved.

The Living Constitution

"The Constitution was not made to fit us like a straightjacket. In its elasticity lies its chief greatness."
President Woodrow Wilson

PURPOSES OF THE CONSTITUTION

The official charge to the delegates who met in Philadelphia in 1787 was to amend the Articles of Confederation. They soon made a fateful decision, however, to ignore the Articles and to write an entirely new constitution. These delegates—the "framers"—set themselves five purposes to fulfill in their effort to create an effective constitution.

1. Establish Legitimacy

First, the framers of the Constitution had to establish the new government's legitimacy—its right to rule. The patriots' theory of government was set out in the Declaration of Independence, which explained why British rule over the colonies was illegitimate. Now the framers had to demonstrate that their new government met the standards of legitimacy referred to in the Declaration.

For the framers of the Constitution, legitimacy had to be based on a compact or contract among those who are to be ruled. This is why the Constitution starts with the words "We the people of the United States . . . do ordain and establish this Constitution."

2. Create Appropriate Structures

The framers' second purpose was to create appropriate structures for the new government. The framers were committed to the principles of representative democracy. They also believed that any new government must include an important role for state governments and ensure that the states retained some legitimacy to rule within their borders.

To achieve their goals, the framers created the Congress, the presidency, and the judiciary to share the powers of the national government. They also created a system of division of powers between the national government and the state governments.

The original manuscript of the Constitution is now kept in the National Archives in Washington, D.C. ▶

RESEARCHING A CONSTITUTIONAL QUESTION

As you study the Constitution, think about a constitutional question that interests you. Here are some possible questions:

- How much, if at all, can the federal government or a state government restrict the sale of firearms?

- Under what conditions does the president have the power to order American troops into battle without congressional approval?

- Under what conditions may a police officer conduct a search of the inside of an automobile?

Once you have chosen a constitutional question, research that question in articles and books on the Constitution. Also check the indexes of well-known newspapers, such as the *New York Times*, for articles that are relevant.

3. DESCRIBE AND DISTRIBUTE POWER

The framers had as their third purpose to describe governmental powers and to distribute them among the structures they created. The powers of the legislative branch, which are those of Congress, are listed in Article 1, Section 8, of the Constitution. Many of the executive powers belonging to the president are listed in Article 2, Sections 2 and 3. The courts are given judicial powers in Article 3. The words of Article 4 imply that the states retain authority over many public matters.

4. LIMIT GOVERNMENT POWERS

The fourth purpose of the framers was to limit the powers of the structures they created. Limits on the Congress's powers are found in Article 1, Section 9. Some of the limits on the powers of state governments are found in Article 1, Section 10. There the framers enumerate functions that are delegated to the national government and so cannot be directed by the states.

5. ALLOW FOR CHANGE

The framers' fifth purpose was to include some means for changing the Constitution. Here they faced a dilemma: they wanted to make certain that the government endured by changing with the times, but they did not want to expose the basic rules of government to so many changes that the system would be unstable. So in Article 5 they created a difficult but not impossible means for amending the Constitution.

HOW TO READ THE CONSTITUTION

The Constitution, which appears on pages 154–173, is printed on a beige background, while the explanatory notes next to each article, section, or clause are printed on blue. Each article is divided into sections, and the sections are subdivided into clauses. Headings have been added and the spelling and punctuation modernized for easier reading. Portions of the Constitution no longer in use have been crossed out. The Constitutional Insight questions and answers will help you understand significant issues related to the Constitution.

hmhsocialstudies.com RESEARCH WEB LINKS

The Constitution

PREAMBLE. *Purpose of the Constitution*

We the people of the United States, in order to form a more perfect Union, establish justice, insure domestic tranquility, provide for the common defense, promote the general welfare, and secure the blessings of liberty to ourselves and our posterity, do ordain and establish this Constitution for the United States of America.

ARTICLE 1. *The Legislature*

SECTION 1. CONGRESS All legislative powers herein granted shall be vested in a Congress of the United States, which shall consist of a Senate and House of Representatives.

SECTION 2. THE HOUSE OF REPRESENTATIVES

1. **ELECTIONS** The House of Representatives shall be composed of members chosen every second year by the people of the several states, and the electors in each state shall have the qualifications requisite for electors of the most numerous branch of the state legislature.

2. **QUALIFICATIONS** No person shall be a Representative who shall not have attained to the age of twenty-five years, and been seven years a citizen of the United States, and who shall not, when elected, be an inhabitant of that state in which he shall be chosen.

3. **NUMBER OF REPRESENTATIVES** Representatives ~~and direct taxes~~ shall be apportioned among the several states which may be included within this Union, according to their respective numbers, ~~which shall be determined by adding to the whole number of free persons, including those bound to service for a term of years, and excluding Indians not taxed, three fifths of all other persons.~~ The actual enumeration shall be made within three years after the first meeting of the Congress of the United States, and within every subsequent term of ten years, in such manner as they shall by law direct. The number of Representatives shall not exceed one for every thirty thousand, but each state shall have at least one Representative; ~~and until such enumeration shall be made, the state of New Hampshire shall be entitled to choose three, Massachusetts eight, Rhode Island and Providence Plantations one, Connecticut five, New York six, New Jersey four, Pennsylvania eight, Delaware one, Maryland six, Virginia ten, North Carolina five, South Carolina five, and Georgia three.~~

4. **VACANCIES** When vacancies happen in the representation from any state, the executive authority thereof shall issue writs of election to fill such vacancies.

5. **OFFICERS AND IMPEACHMENT** The House of Representatives shall choose their Speaker and other officers; and shall have the sole power of impeachment.

PREAMBLE

***Constitutional Insight* Preamble**
Why does the Preamble say "We the people of the United States . . . ordain and establish" the new government? The Articles of Confederation was an agreement among the states. But the framers of the Constitution wanted to be sure its legitimacy came from the American people, not from the states, which might decide to withdraw their support at any time. This is a basic principle of the Constitution.

ARTICLE 1

***Constitutional Insight* Section 1**
Why does the first article of the Constitution focus on Congress rather than on the presidency or the courts? The framers were intent on stressing the central role of the legislative branch in the new government because it is the branch that most directly represents the people and is most responsive to them.

Ⓐ CRITICAL THINKING
Do you think Congress is still the branch of the federal government that is most directly responsible to the people? Why or why not?

***Constitutional Insight* Section 2.1**
Why are members of the House of Representatives elected every two years? The House of Representatives was designed to be a truly representative body, with members who reflect the concerns and sentiments of their constituents as closely as possible. The framers achieved this timely representation by establishing two years as a reasonable term for members of the House to serve.

Ⓑ CRITICAL THINKING
Do you think electing members of the House of Representatives every two years is a good idea? Why or why not?

Requirements for Holding Federal Office

POSITION	MINIMUM AGE	RESIDENCY	CITIZENSHIP
Representative	25	state in which elected	7 years
Senator	30	state in which elected	9 years
President	35	14 years in the United States	natural-born
Supreme Court Justice	none	none	none

SECTION 3. THE SENATE

1. **NUMBERS** The Senate of the United States shall be composed of two Senators from each state, ~~chosen by the legislature thereof,~~ for six years; and each Senator shall have one vote.

2. **CLASSIFYING TERMS** Immediately after they shall be assembled in consequence of the first election, they shall be divided as equally as may be into three classes. The seats of the Senators of the first class shall be vacated at the expiration of the second year, of the second class at the expiration of the fourth year, and of the third class at the expiration of the sixth year, so that one third may be chosen every second year; ~~and if vacancies happen by resignation, or otherwise, during the recess of the legislature of any state, the executive thereof may make temporary appointments until the next meeting of the legislature, which shall then fill such vacancies.~~

3. **QUALIFICATIONS** No person shall be a Senator who shall not have attained to the age of thirty years, and been nine years a citizen of the United States, and who shall not, when elected, be an inhabitant of that state for which he shall be chosen.

4. **ROLE OF VICE-PRESIDENT** The Vice-President of the United States shall be President of the Senate, but shall have no vote, unless they be equally divided.

5. **OFFICERS** The Senate shall choose their other officers, and also a President pro tempore, in the absence of the Vice-President, or when he shall exercise the office of President of the United States.

6. **IMPEACHMENT TRIALS** The Senate shall have the sole power to try all impeachments. When sitting for that purpose, they shall be on oath or affirmation. When the President of the United States is tried, the Chief Justice shall preside: and no person shall be convicted without the concurrence of two thirds of the members present.

7. **PUNISHMENT FOR IMPEACHMENT** Judgment in cases of impeachment shall not extend further than to removal from office, and disqualification to hold and enjoy any office of honor, trust or profit under the United States; but the party convicted shall nevertheless be liable and subject to indictment, trial, judgment and punishment, according to law.

SECTION 4. CONGRESSIONAL ELECTIONS

1. **REGULATIONS** The times, places and manner of holding elections for Senators and Representatives shall be prescribed in each state by the legislature thereof; but the Congress may at any time by law make or alter such regulations, except as to the places of choosing Senators.

2. **SESSIONS** The Congress shall assemble at least once in every year, ~~and such meeting shall be on the first Monday in December, unless they shall by law appoint a different day.~~

Constitutional Insight **Section 3.1**
Why are members of the Senate elected every six years? The framers feared the possibility of instability in the government. So they decided that senators should have six-year terms and be elected by the state legislatures rather than directly by the people. The Seventeenth Amendment, as you will see later, changed this. The framers also staggered the terms of the senators so that only one-third of them are replaced at any one time. This stabilizes the Senate still further.

C CRITICAL THINKING
Do you think it is important today for the Senate to have more stability than the House of Representatives? If so, why?

Constitutional Insight **Sections 3.6 and 3.7** *Must an impeached president step down from office?* Not necessarily. An impeachment is a formal accusation of criminal behavior or serious misbehavior. By impeaching the president, the U.S. House of Representatives is officially accusing the nation's chief executive of one or more wrong-doings that warrant possible removal from office. It is then the responsibility of the Senate to conduct a trial to determine whether the president is guilty or not guilty of the charges—and thus whether or not the president must step down. Conviction requires a two-thirds vote of the Senate.

D CRITICAL THINKING
Do you think a president should be put on trial for a crime while he or she is still in office? Explain.

SECTION 5. RULES AND PROCEDURES

1. **QUORUM** Each house shall be the judge of the elections, returns and qualifications of its own members, and a majority of each shall constitute a quorum to do business; but a smaller number may adjourn from day to day, and may be authorized to compel the attendance of absent members, in such manner, and under such penalties, as each house may provide.

2. **RULES AND CONDUCT** Each house may determine the rules of its proceedings, punish its members for disorderly behavior, and, with the concurrence of two thirds, expel a member.

3. **CONGRESSIONAL RECORDS** Each house shall keep a journal of its proceedings, and from time to time publish the same, excepting such parts as may in their judgment require secrecy; and the yeas and nays of the members of either house on any question shall, at the desire of one fifth of those present, be entered on the journal.

4. **ADJOURNMENT** Neither house, during the session of Congress, shall, without the consent of the other, adjourn for more than three days, nor to any other place than that in which the two houses shall be sitting.

SECTION 6. PAYMENT AND PRIVILEGES

1. **SALARY** The Senators and Representatives shall receive a compensation for their services, to be ascertained by law, and paid out of the treasury of the United States. They shall in all cases, except treason, felony and breach of the peace, be privileged from arrest during their attendance at the session of their respective houses, and in going to and returning from the same; and for any speech or debate in either house, they shall not be questioned in any other place.

2. **RESTRICTIONS** No Senator or Representative shall, during the time for which he was elected, be appointed to any civil office under the authority of the United States, which shall have been created, or the emoluments whereof shall have been increased, during such time; and no person holding any office under the United States shall be a member of either house during his continuance in office.

SECTION 7. HOW A BILL BECOMES A LAW

1. **TAX BILLS** All bills for raising revenue shall originate in the House of Representatives; but the Senate may propose or concur with amendments as on other bills.

2. **LAWMAKING PROCESS** Every bill which shall have passed the House of Representatives and the Senate shall, before it become a law, be presented to the President of the United States; if he approves he shall sign it, but if not he shall return it with his objections to that house in which it shall have originated, who shall enter the objections at large on their journal, and proceed to reconsider it. If after such reconsideration two thirds of that house shall agree to pass the bill, it shall be sent, together with the objections, to the other house, by which it shall likewise be reconsidered, and if approved by two thirds of that house, it shall become a law. But in all such

cases the votes of both houses shall be determined by yeas and nays, and the names of the persons voting for and against the bill shall be entered on the journal of each house respectively. If any bill shall not be returned by the President within ten days (Sundays excepted) after it shall have been presented to him, the same shall be a law, in like manner as if he had signed it, unless the Congress by their adjournment prevent its return, in which case it shall not be a law.

3. ROLE OF THE PRESIDENT Every order, resolution, or vote to which the concurrence of the Senate and House of Representatives may be necessary (except on a question of adjournment) shall be presented to the President of the United States; and before the same shall take effect, shall be approved by him, or being disapproved by him, shall be repassed by two thirds of the Senate and House of Representatives, according to the rules and limitations prescribed in the case of a bill.

How a Bill in Congress Becomes a Law

1 A bill is introduced in the House or the Senate and referred to a standing committee for consideration.

2 A bill may be reported out of committee with or without changes—or it may be shelved.

3 Either house of Congress debates the bill and may make revisions. If passed, the bill is sent to the other house.

4 If the House and the Senate pass different versions of a bill, both versions go to a conference committee to work out the differences.

5 The conference committee submits a single version of the bill to the House and the Senate.

6 If both houses accept the compromise version, the bill is sent to the president to be signed.

7 If the president signs the bill, it becomes law.

8 If the president vetoes the bill, the House and the Senate may override the veto by a vote of two thirds of the members present in each house, and then the bill becomes law.

SKILLBUILDER Interpreting Charts
How is the constitutional principle of checks and balances reflected in the process of a bill's becoming a law?

SECTION 8. POWERS GRANTED TO CONGRESS

1. **TAXATION** The Congress shall have power to lay and collect taxes, duties, imposts and excises, to pay the debts and provide for the common defense and general welfare of the United States; but all duties, imposts and excises shall be uniform throughout the United States;

2. **CREDIT** To borrow money on the credit of the United States;

3. **COMMERCE** To regulate commerce with foreign nations, and among the several states, and with the Indian tribes;

4. **NATURALIZATION, BANKRUPTCY** To establish a uniform rule of naturalization, and uniform laws on the subject of bankruptcies throughout the United States;

5. **MONEY** To coin money, regulate the value thereof, and of foreign coin, and fix the standard of weights and measures;

6. **COUNTERFEITING** To provide for the punishment of counterfeiting the securities and current coin of the United States;

7. **POST OFFICE** To establish post offices and post roads;

8. **PATENTS, COPYRIGHTS** To promote the progress of science and useful arts, by securing for limited times to authors and inventors the exclusive right to their respective writings and discoveries;

9. **FEDERAL COURTS** To constitute tribunals inferior to the Supreme Court;

10. **INTERNATIONAL LAW** To define and punish piracies and felonies committed on the high seas, and offenses against the law of nations;

11. **WAR** To declare war, grant letters of marque and reprisal, and make rules concerning captures on land and water;

12. **ARMY** To raise and support armies, but no appropriation of money to that use shall be for a longer term than two years;

13. **NAVY** To provide and maintain a navy;

14. **REGULATION OF ARMED FORCES** To make rules for the government and regulation of the land and naval forces;

15. **MILITIA** To provide for calling forth the militia to execute the laws of the Union, suppress insurrections and repel invasions;

16. **REGULATIONS FOR MILITIA** To provide for organizing, arming, and disciplining the militia, and for governing such part of them as may be employed in the service of the United States, reserving to the states respectively the appointment of the officers, and the authority of training the militia according to the discipline prescribed by Congress;

17. **DISTRICT OF COLUMBIA** To exercise exclusive legislation in all cases whatsoever, over such district (not exceeding ten miles square) as may, by cession of particular states, and the acceptance of Congress, become the seat of the government of the United States, and to exercise like authority over all places purchased by the consent of the legislature of the state in which the same shall be, for the erection of forts, magazines, arsenals, dockyards, and other needful buildings;—and

18. **ELASTIC CLAUSE** To make all laws which shall be necessary and proper for carrying into execution the foregoing powers, and all other powers vested by this Constitution in the government of the United States, or in any department or officer thereof.

SECTION 9. POWERS DENIED CONGRESS

1. ~~**SLAVE TRADE** The migration or importation of such persons as any of the states now existing shall think proper to admit, shall not be prohibited by the Congress prior to the year one thousand eight hundred and eight, but a tax or duty may be imposed on such importation, not exceeding ten dollars for each person.~~

2. **HABEAS CORPUS** The privilege of the writ of habeas corpus shall not be suspended, unless when in cases of rebellion or invasion the public safety may require it.

3. **ILLEGAL PUNISHMENT** No bill of attainder or ex post facto law shall be passed.

4. **DIRECT TAXES** No capitation, ~~or other direct, tax~~ shall be laid, ~~unless in proportion to the census or enumeration herein before directed to be taken.~~

5. **EXPORT TAXES** No tax or duty shall be laid on articles exported from any state.

6. **NO FAVORITES** No preference shall be given by any regulation of commerce or revenue to the ports of one state over those of another: nor shall vessels bound to, or from, one state be obliged to enter, clear, or pay duties in another.

7. **PUBLIC MONEY** No money shall be drawn from the treasury, but in consequence of appropriations made by law; and a regular statement and account of the receipts and expenditures of all public money shall be published from time to time.

8. **TITLES OF NOBILITY** No title of nobility shall be granted by the United States: and no person holding any office of profit or trust under them shall, without the consent of the Congress, accept of any present, emolument, office, or title, of any kind whatever, from any king, prince, or foreign state.

SECTION 10. POWERS DENIED THE STATES

1. **RESTRICTIONS** No state shall enter into any treaty, alliance, or confederation; grant letters of marque and reprisal; coin money; emit bills of credit; make anything but gold and silver coin a tender in payment of debts; pass any bill of attainder, ex post facto law, or law impairing the obligation of contracts, or grant any title of nobility.

2. **IMPORT AND EXPORT TAXES** No state shall, without the consent of the Congress, lay any imposts or duties on imports or exports, except what may be absolutely necessary for executing its inspection laws; and the net produce of all duties and imposts, laid by any state on imports or exports, shall be for the use of the treasury of the United States; and all such laws shall be subject to the revision and control of the Congress.

Constitutional Insight Section 9

Why didn't the framers include a bill of rights in the original Constitution? Actually, they did. Article 1, Section 9, defines limits on the powers of Congress, just as the first ten amendments (which we call the Bill of Rights) do. While some of the provisions focus on such issues as slavery and taxation, there are three explicit prohibitions dealing with citizens' rights:

- *Writ of habeas corpus.* Section 9, Clause 2 says that, except in time of rebellion or invasion, Congress cannot suspend people's right to a writ of habeas corpus. This means that people cannot be held in prison or jail without being formally charged with a crime. Habeas corpus is derived from English common law, and it is one of the strongest guarantees of personal liberty.

- *Bill of attainder.* Clause 3 prohibits the passage of any law that convicts or punishes a person directly and without a trial. Any legislative action that would punish someone without recourse to a court of law is called a bill of attainder.

- *Ex post facto law.* The same clause prohibits ex post facto laws. Such a law would punish a person for an act that was legal when it was performed.

The fact that these particular rights were protected by the original document issued by the framers reflects both the framers' experiences during the Revolution and their fear of excessive government power.

🅗 **CRITICAL THINKING**
Why are American citizens today so intent on having protections against government violations of their rights?

Constitutional Insight Section 1.1
What exactly is "executive power"? We know the president has it, but nowhere is it explicitly defined. It is most often defined as the power to carry out the laws of the land, but of course no one person can handle such a chore alone. A more appropriate definition is found in Section 3 of this article, which empowers the president to "take care that the laws be faithfully executed." In this sense, the president is the chief administrator.

① CRITICAL THINKING
Why is it important to have an executive who is the chief administrator?

3. **PEACETIME AND WAR RESTRAINTS** No state shall, without the consent of Congress, lay any duty of tonnage, keep troops or ships of war in time of peace, enter into any agreement or compact with another state, or with a foreign power, or engage in war, unless actually invaded, or in such imminent danger as will not admit of delay.

ARTICLE 2. *The Executive*

SECTION 1. THE PRESIDENCY

1. **TERMS OF OFFICE** The executive power shall be vested in a President of the United States of America. He shall hold his office during the term of four years and, together with the Vice-President, chosen for the same term, be elected as follows:

2. **ELECTORAL COLLEGE** Each state shall appoint, in such manner as the legislature thereof may direct, a number of electors, equal to the whole number of Senators and Representatives to which the state may be entitled in the Congress; but no Senator or Representative, or person holding an office of trust or profit under the United States, shall be appointed an elector.

3. ~~**FORMER METHOD OF ELECTING PRESIDENT** The electors shall meet in their respective states, and vote by ballot for two persons, of whom one at least shall not be an inhabitant of the same state with themselves. And they shall make a list of all the persons voted for, and of the number of votes for each; which list they shall sign and certify, and transmit sealed to the seat of the government of the United States, directed to the President of the Senate. The President of the Senate shall, in the presence of the Senate and House of Representatives, open all the certificates, and the votes shall then be counted. The person having the greatest number of votes shall be the President, if such number be a majority of the whole number of electors appointed; and if there be more than one who have such majority, and have an equal number of votes, then the House of Representatives shall immediately choose by ballot one of them for President; and if no person have a majority, then from the five highest on the list the said house shall in like manner choose the President. But in choosing the President, the votes shall be taken by states, the representation from each state having one vote; a quorum for this purpose shall consist of a member or members from two thirds of the states, and a majority of all the states shall be necessary to a choice. In every case, after the choice of the President, the person having the greatest number of votes of the electors shall be the Vice-President. But if there should remain two or more who have equal votes, the Senate shall choose from them by ballot the Vice-President.~~

4. **ELECTION DAY** The Congress may determine the time of choosing the electors, and the day on which they shall give their votes; which day shall be the same throughout the United States.

5. QUALIFICATIONS No person except a natural-born citizen, ~~or a citizen of the United States at the time of the adoption of this Constitution,~~ shall be eligible to the office of President; neither shall any person be eligible to that office who shall not have attained to the age of thirty-five years, and been fourteen years a resident within the United States.

6. SUCCESSION In case of the removal of the President from office, or of his death, resignation, or inability to discharge the powers and duties of the said office, the same shall devolve on the Vice-President, and the Congress may by law provide for the case of removal, death, resignation, or inability, both of the President and Vice-President, declaring what officer shall then act as President, and such officer shall act accordingly, until the disability be removed, or a President shall be elected.

7. SALARY The President shall, at stated times, receive for his services a compensation, which shall neither be increased nor diminished during the period for which he shall have been elected, and he shall not receive within that period any other emolument from the United States, or any of them.

8. OATH OF OFFICE Before he enter on the execution of his office, he shall take the following oath or affirmation:—"I do solemnly swear (or affirm) that I will faithfully execute the office of President of the United States, and will to the best of my ability, preserve, protect and defend the Constitution of the United States."

SECTION 2. POWERS OF THE PRESIDENT

1. MILITARY POWERS The President shall be commander in chief of the army and navy of the United States, and of the militia of the several states, when called into the actual service of the United States; he may require the opinion, in writing, of the principal officer in each of the executive departments, upon any subject relating to the duties of their respective offices, and he shall have power to grant reprieves and pardons for offenses against the United States, except in cases of impeachment.

2. TREATIES, APPOINTMENTS He shall have power, by and with the advice and consent of the Senate, to make treaties, provided two thirds of the Senators present concur; and he shall nominate, and by and with the advice and consent of the Senate, shall appoint ambassadors, other public ministers and consuls, judges of the Supreme Court, and all other officers of the United States, whose appointments are not herein otherwise provided for, and which shall be established by law; but the Congress may by law vest the appointment of such inferior officers, as they think proper, in the President alone, in the courts of law, or in the heads of departments.

3. VACANCIES The President shall have power to fill up all vacancies that may happen during the recess of the Senate, by granting commissions which shall expire at the end of their next session.

Is it necessary for the president to deliver a State of the Union address before a joint session of Congress at the start of each legislative year? The Constitution requires only that the president report to Congress on the state of the Union from time to time, and nowhere does it call for an annual address. In 1913, President Woodrow Wilson wanted to influence Congress to take action without delay on some legislation that he thought was important. Wilson revived the tradition—which had been discontinued by Jefferson—of delivering the State of the Union address in person.

Ⓛ CRITICAL THINKING

How does the president use the State of the Union address today?

Constitutional Insight Section 4

Have high-level public officials ever been impeached? In all of American history, the House has impeached two presidents, and neither had to leave office. In 1868, the Senate found President Andrew Johnson not guilty by one vote after the House impeached him, charging him with violating a Congressional Act. In 1999, senators acquitted President Bill Clinton after the House impeached him with charges of lying under oath and obstructing justice in the attempted cover-up of a White House scandal.

The only other president to come close to impeachment was Richard Nixon. In 1974, the House Judiciary Committee, in what is the first step of the impeachment process, recommended three articles of impeachment against Nixon for his role in the infamous Watergate scandal. Before the full House could vote for or against the articles of impeachment, however, Nixon resigned from office.

Ⓜ CRITICAL THINKING

Why do you think the framers of the Constitution created such an elaborate and seemingly difficult procedure for removing a sitting president?

SECTION 3. PRESIDENTIAL DUTIES He shall from time to time give to the Congress information of the state of the Union, and recommend to their consideration such measures as he shall judge necessary and expedient; he may, on extraordinary occasions, convene both houses, or either of them, and in case of disagreement between them, with respect to the time of adjournment, he may adjourn them to such time as he shall think proper; he shall receive ambassadors and other public ministers; he shall take care that the laws be faithfully executed, and shall commission all the officers of the United States.

SECTION 4. IMPEACHMENT The President, Vice-President and all civil officers of the United States shall be removed from office on impeachment for, and conviction of, treason, bribery, or other high crimes and misdemeanors.

(above) Rep. Henry Hyde, chairman of the House Judiciary Committee, swears in Independent Counsel Kenneth Starr during the Committee's hearings on impeachment charges against President Bill Clinton in 1998; *(right)* President Andrew Johnson is handed the articles of impeachment before his trial in 1868.

ARTICLE 3. *The Judiciary*

SECTION 1. FEDERAL COURTS AND JUDGES The judicial power of the United States shall be vested in one Supreme Court, and in such inferior courts as the Congress may from time to time ordain and establish. The judges, both of the Supreme and inferior courts, shall hold their offices during good behavior, and shall, at stated times, receive for their services a compensation, which shall not be diminished during their continuance in office.

Section 2. The Courts' Authority

1. **General Authority** The judicial power shall extend to all cases, in law and equity, arising under this Constitution, the laws of the United States, and treaties made, or which shall be made, under their authority;—to all cases affecting ambassadors, other public ministers and consuls;—to all cases of admiralty and maritime jurisdiction;—to controversies to which the United States shall be a party;—to controversies between two or more states;—~~between a state and citizens of another state;~~—between citizens of different states;—between citizens of the same state claiming lands under grants of different states, ~~and between a state, or the citizens thereof, and foreign states, citizens or subjects.~~

2. **Supreme Court** In all cases affecting ambassadors, other public ministers and consuls, and those in which a state shall be party, the Supreme Court shall have original jurisdiction. In all the other cases before mentioned, the Supreme Court shall have appellate jurisdiction, both as to law and fact, with such exceptions, and under such regulations, as the Congress shall make.

3. **Trial by Jury** The trial of all crimes, except in cases of impeachment, shall be by jury; and such trial shall be held in the state where the said crimes shall have been committed; but when not committed within any state, the trial shall be at such place or places as the Congress may by law have directed.

Section 3. Treason

1. **Definition** Treason against the United States shall consist only in levying war against them, or in adhering to their enemies, giving them aid and comfort. No person shall be convicted of treason unless on the testimony of two witnesses to the same overt act, or on confession in open court.

2. **Punishment** The Congress shall have power to declare the punishment of treason, but no attainder of treason shall work corruption of blood, or forfeiture except during the life of the person attainted.

ARTICLE 3

Constitutional Insight **Section 2.1**
What is judicial review? Is it the same as judicial power? Actually, they are not the same. Judicial power is the authority to hear cases involving disputes over the law or the behavior of people. Judicial review, in contrast, is a court's passing judgment on the constitutionality of a law or government action that is being disputed. Interestingly, nowhere does the Constitution mention judicial review. There are places where it is implied (for example, in Section 2 of Article 6), but the only explicit description of the responsibility of the courts is the reference to judicial power in Section 1 of Article 3. The Supreme Court's power to review laws passed by Congress was explicitly affirmed by the Court itself in *Marbury* v. *Madison.* (See page 206.)

Ⓝ CRITICAL THINKING
Why is judicial review, although not mentioned in the Constitution, an important activity of the Supreme Court?

The Supreme Court of the United States as of August 2010. In the front row (*left to right*) are Associate Justices Clarence Thomas and Antonin Scalia, Chief Justice John Roberts, and Associate Justices Anthony Kennedy and Ruth Bader Ginsburg. In the back row (*left to right*) are Associate Justices Sonia Sotomayor, Stephen Breyer, Samuel Alito, and Elena Kagan. ▼

ARTICLE 4. *Relations Among States*

SECTION 1. STATE ACTS AND RECORDS Full faith and credit shall be given in each state to the public acts, records, and judicial proceedings of every other state. And the Congress may by general laws prescribe the manner in which such acts, records, and proceedings shall be proved, and the effect thereof.

SECTION 2. RIGHTS OF CITIZENS

1. **CITIZENSHIP** The citizens of each state shall be entitled to all privileges and immunities of citizens in the several states.

2. **EXTRADITION** A person charged in any state with treason, felony, or other crime, who shall flee from justice, and be found in another state, shall on demand of the executive authority of the state from which he fled, be delivered up, to be removed to the state having jurisdiction of the crime.

3. ~~**FUGITIVE SLAVES** No person held to service or labor in one state, under the laws thereof, escaping into another, shall, in consequence of any law or regulation therein, be discharged from such service or labor, but shall be delivered up on claim of the party to whom such service or labor may be due.~~

SECTION 3. NEW STATES

1. **ADMISSION** New states may be admitted by the Congress into this Union; but no new state shall be formed or erected within the jurisdiction of any other state; nor any state be formed by the junction of two or more states, or parts of states, without the consent of the legislatures of the states concerned as well as of the Congress.

2. **CONGRESSIONAL AUTHORITY** The Congress shall have power to dispose of and make all needful rules and regulations respecting the territory or other property belonging to the United States; and nothing in this Constitution shall be so construed as to prejudice any claims of the United States, or of any particular state.

SECTION 4. GUARANTEES TO THE STATES The United States shall guarantee to every state in this Union a republican form of government, and shall protect each of them against invasion; and on application of the legislature, or of the executive (when the legislature cannot be convened), against domestic violence.

ARTICLE 5. *Amending the Constitution*

The Congress, whenever two thirds of both houses shall deem it necessary, shall propose amendments to this Constitution, or, on the application of the legislatures of two thirds of the several states, shall call a convention for proposing amendments, which, in either case, shall be valid to all intents and purposes, as part of this Constitution, when ratified by the legislatures of three fourths of the several states, or by conventions in three fourths thereof, as the one or the other mode of ratification may be proposed by the Congress; ~~provided that no amendment which may be made prior to the year one thousand eight hundred and eight shall in any manner affect the first and fourth clauses in the ninth section of the first article;~~ and that no state, without its consent, shall be deprived of its equal suffrage in the Senate.

ARTICLE 6. *Supremacy of the National Government*

SECTION 1. VALID DEBTS All debts contracted and engagements entered into, before the adoption of this Constitution, shall be as valid against the United States under this Constitution, as under the Confederation.

SECTION 2. SUPREME LAW This Constitution, and the laws of the United States which shall be made in pursuance thereof; and all treaties made, or which shall be made, under the authority of the United States, shall be the supreme law of the land; and the judges in every state shall be bound thereby, anything in the constitution or laws of any state to the contrary notwithstanding.

SECTION 3. LOYALTY TO CONSTITUTION The Senators and Representatives before mentioned, and the members of the several state legislatures, and all executive and judicial officers, both of the United States and of the several states, shall be bound by oath or affirmation to support this Constitution; but no religious test shall ever be required as a qualification to any office or public trust under the United States.

ARTICLE 7. *Ratification*

The ratification of the conventions of nine states shall be sufficient for the establishment of this Constitution between the states so ratifying the same. Done in convention by the unanimous consent of the states present, the seventeenth day of September in the year of our Lord one thousand seven hundred and eighty-seven and of the independence of the United States of America the twelfth. In witness whereof we have hereunto subscribed our names.

George Washington—President and deputy from Virginia

Delaware: *George Read, Gunning Bedford, Jr., John Dickinson, Richard Bassett, Jacob Broom*

Maryland: *James McHenry, Dan of St. Thomas Jenifer, Daniel Carroll*

Virginia: *John Blair, James Madison, Jr.*

North Carolina: *William Blount, Richard Dobbs Spaight, Hugh Williamson*

South Carolina: *John Rutledge, Charles Cotesworth Pinckney, Charles Pinckney, Pierce Butler*

Georgia: *William Few, Abraham Baldwin*

New Hampshire: *John Langdon, Nicholas Gilman*

Massachusetts: *Nathaniel Gorham, Rufus King*

Connecticut: *William Samuel Johnson, Roger Sherman*

New York: *Alexander Hamilton*

New Jersey: *William Livingston, David Brearley, William Paterson, Jonathan Dayton*

Pennsylvania: *Benjamin Franklin, Thomas Mifflin, Robert Morris, George Clymer, Thomas FitzSimons, Jared Ingersoll, James Wilson, Gouverneur Morris*

ARTICLE 6

Constitutional Insight Section 2 *Just how "supreme" is the "law of the land"?* The Constitution and all federal laws and treaties are the highest law of the land. (To be supreme, federal laws must be constitutional.) All state constitutions and laws and all local laws rank below national law and cannot be enforced if they contradict national law. For example, if the United States enters into a treaty protecting migratory Canadian birds, the states must change their laws to fit the provisions of that agreement. That was the decision of the Supreme Court in the case of *Missouri* v. *Holland* (1920). The state of Missouri argued that the national government could not interfere with its power to regulate hunting within its borders, but the Supreme Court concluded that the treaty was a valid exercise of national power and therefore took priority over state and local laws. The states had to adjust their rules and regulations accordingly.

Q CRITICAL THINKING
What would happen if the national law were not supreme?

ARTICLE 7

Constitutional Insight *Why was ratification by only 9 states sufficient to put the Constitution into effect?* In taking such a momentous step as replacing one constitution (the Articles of Confederation) with another, the framers might have been expected to require the agreement of all 13 states. But the framers were political realists. They knew that they would have a difficult time winning approval from all 13 states. But they also knew that they had a good chance of getting 9 or 10 of the states "on board" and that once that happened, the rest would follow. Their strategy worked, but just barely. Although they had the approval of 9 states by the end of June 1788, 2 of the most important states—Virginia and New York—had not yet decided to ratify. Without the approval of these influential states, the new government would have had a difficult time surviving. Finally, by the end of July, both had given their blessing to the new constitution, but not without intense debate.

And then there was the last holdout—Rhode Island. Not only had Rhode Island refused to send delegates to the Constitutional Convention in 1787, but it turned down ratification several times before finally giving its approval in 1790 under a cloud of economic and even military threats from neighboring states.

R CRITICAL THINKING
Do you think all 50 states would ratify the Constitution today? Why or why not?

Constitutional Insight Amendment 1

Do Americans have an absolute right to free speech? The right to free speech is not without limits. In the case of *Schenck* v. *United States* (1919), Justice Oliver Wendell Holmes wrote that this right does "not protect a man in falsely shouting fire in a theatre and causing a panic." Thus, there are some forms of speech that are not protected by the First Amendment, and Congress is allowed to make laws regarding certain types of expression. (See *Schenck* v. *United States* on page 602.)

A **CRITICAL THINKING**
Why is there controversy over freedom of speech today?

Constitutional Insight Amendment 4

Can the police search your car without a court-issued search warrant when they stop you for speeding? The answer, according to Supreme Court decisions, depends on whether they have good reasons—called "probable cause"—for doing so. If a state trooper notices bloody clothing on the back seat of a vehicle she stops for a traffic violation, there might be probable cause for her to insist on searching the vehicle. There is probably not sufficient reason for a search if the trooper is merely suspicious of the driver because of the way he is acting. In such cases, the trooper may make a casual request, such as "Do you mind if I look inside your vehicle?" If the answer is no, then according to the Court, the driver has waived his or her constitutional right against unreasonable searches. Amendment 4 also provides a strong guarantee of every individual's property rights.

B **CRITICAL THINKING**
Why do you think the right against unreasonable searches and seizures is highly important to most people?

Constitutional Insight Amendment 5

Can you be tried twice for the same offense? The prohibition against "double jeopardy" protects you from having the same charge twice brought against you for the same offense, but you can be tried on different charges related to that offense.

C **CRITICAL THINKING**
What do you think could happen if a person could be tried twice for the same offense?

The Bill of Rights

and Amendments 11–27

Amendments 1–10

Proposed by Congress September 25, 1789. Ratified December 15, 1791.

AMENDMENT 1. RELIGIOUS AND POLITICAL FREEDOM (1791)
Congress shall make no law respecting an establishment of religion, or prohibiting the free exercise thereof; or abridging the freedom of speech, or of the press; or the right of the people peaceably to assemble, and to petition the government for a redress of grievances.

AMENDMENT 2. RIGHT TO BEAR ARMS (1791) A well-regulated militia being necessary to the security of a free state, the right of the people to keep and bear arms shall not be infringed.

AMENDMENT 3. QUARTERING TROOPS (1791) No soldier shall, in time of peace, be quartered in any house without the consent of the owner, nor in time of war, but in a manner to be prescribed by law.

AMENDMENT 4. SEARCH AND SEIZURE (1791) The right of the people to be secure in their persons, houses, papers, and effects, against unreasonable searches and seizures, shall not be violated, and no warrants shall issue, but upon probable cause, supported by oath or affirmation, and particularly describing the place to be searched, and the persons or things to be seized.

AMENDMENT 5. RIGHTS OF ACCUSED PERSONS (1791) No person shall be held to answer for a capital or otherwise infamous crime, unless on a presentment or indictment of a grand jury, except in cases arising in the land or naval forces, or in the militia, when in actual service in time of war or public danger; nor shall any person be subject for the same offense to be twice put in jeopardy of life or limb; nor shall be compelled in any criminal case to be a witness against himself, nor be deprived of life, liberty, or property, without due process of law; nor shall private property be taken for public use, without just compensation.

Analyzing *Political Cartoons*

"THE FEDERAL EDIFICE"

This 1788 cartoon celebrated the ratification of the Constitution by New York, the 11th state to ratify it. This left only North Carolina and Rhode Island to complete all 13 pillars of the federal structure.

SKILLBUILDER Analyzing Political Cartoons
1. What details in the cartoon convey the unity of the states who have voted for ratification?
2. How does the cartoonist contrast the states who have voted for ratification with those who have not? What message does this convey?

 SEE SKILLBUILDER HANDBOOK, PAGE R24.

AMENDMENT 6. RIGHT TO A SPEEDY, PUBLIC TRIAL (1791) In all criminal prosecutions, the accused shall enjoy the right to a speedy and public trial, by an impartial jury of the state and district wherein the crime shall have been committed, which district shall have been previously ascertained by law, and to be informed of the nature and cause of the accusation; to be confronted with the witnesses against him; to have compulsory process for obtaining witnesses in his favor, and to have the assistance of counsel for his defense.

AMENDMENT 7. TRIAL BY JURY IN CIVIL CASES (1791) In suits at common law, where the value in controversy shall exceed twenty dollars, the right of trial by jury shall be preserved, and no fact tried by a jury shall be otherwise reexamined in any court of the United States, than according to the rules of the common law.

AMENDMENT 8. LIMITS OF FINES AND PUNISHMENTS (1791) Excessive bail shall not be required, nor excessive fines imposed, nor cruel and unusual punishments inflicted.

AMENDMENT 9. RIGHTS OF PEOPLE (1791) The enumeration in the Constitution, of certain rights, shall not be construed to deny or disparage others retained by the people.

AMENDMENT 10. POWERS OF STATES AND PEOPLE (1791) The powers not delegated to the United States by the Constitution, nor prohibited by it to the states, are reserved to the states respectively, or to the people.

The CENTINEL   VOL IX

REDEUNT SATURNIA REGNA.
On the erection of the Eleventh PILLAR of the great National DOME, we beg leave most sincerely to felicitate " OUR DEAR COUNTRY."

Rise it will.

The foundation good—it may yet be SAVED.

The FEDERAL EDIFICE.
ELEVEN STARS, in quick succession rise——
ELEVEN COLUMNS strike our wond'ring eyes,
Soon o'er the *whole*, shall swell the beauteous DOME,
COLUMBIA's boast—and FREEDOM's hallow'd home.
  Here shall the ARTS in glorious splendour shine !
And AGRICULTURE give her stores divine !
COMMERCE refin'd, dispense us more than gold,
And this new world, teach WISDOM to the old—
RELIGION here shall fix her blest abode,
Array'd in *mildness*, like its parent GOD !
JUSTICE and LAW, shall endless PEACE maintain,
And the " SATURNIAN AGE," *return again.*

Constitutional Insight **Amendment 6**
What are the Miranda rights? The term comes from the Supreme Court's decision in *Miranda* v. *Arizona* (1966), in which the justices established basic rules that the police must follow when questioning a suspect. If suspected of a crime, you must be told that you have a right to remain silent and that anything you say "can and will" be used against you. You also need to be informed that you have a right to an attorney and that the attorney may be present during questioning. (See *Miranda* v. *Arizona* on page 900.)

D CRITICAL THINKING
How do the Miranda rights protect you?

Constitutional Insight **Amendment 7**
What are the "rules of the common law"? The common law is the body of legal practices and decrees developed in England and English-speaking America from A.D. 1066 through the present. It includes Magna Carta (1215), which acknowledges versions of rights affirmed in the Fifth, Sixth, and Seventh Amendments, as well as the English Bill of Rights (1689), which codified rights asserted in the First, Second, Seventh, and Eighth Amendments. The common law also includes the decisions and published opinions of state and federal appeals courts, including the U.S. Supreme Court.

Constitutional Insight **Amendment 9**
Do you have a right to privacy? Until 1965, no such right had ever been explicitly stated by the courts. That year, in the case of *Griswold* v. *Connecticut*, the Court said there is an implied right of American citizens to make certain personal choices without interference from the government; this case concerned the right to use birth control. Years later, in *Roe* v. *Wade* (1973), the same logic was used to declare unconstitutional a Texas law restricting a woman's right to an abortion in the first stages of pregnancy. Since that decision, both the right to privacy and abortion rights have become the focus of major political controversies.

E CRITICAL THINKING
How do you define the right to privacy?

Amendments 11–27

AMENDMENT 11. LAWSUITS AGAINST STATES (1795) Passed by Congress March 4, 1794. Ratified February 7, 1795.

Note: Article 3, Section 2, of the Constitution was modified by the Eleventh Amendment.

The Judicial power of the United States shall not be construed to extend to any suit in law or equity, commenced or prosecuted against one of the United States by citizens of another state, or by citizens or subjects of any foreign state.

AMENDMENT 12. ELECTION OF EXECUTIVES (1804) Passed by Congress December 9, 1803. Ratified June 15, 1804.

Note: A portion of Article 2, Section 1, of the Constitution was superseded by the Twelfth Amendment.

The electors shall meet in their respective states and vote by ballot for President and Vice-President, one of whom, at least, shall not be an inhabitant of the same state with themselves; they shall name in their ballots the person voted for as President, and in distinct ballots the person voted for as Vice-President, and they shall make distinct lists of all persons voted for as President, and of all persons voted for as Vice-President, and of the number of votes for each, which lists they shall sign and certify, and transmit sealed to the seat of the government of the United States, directed to the President of the Senate;—the President of the Senate shall, in the presence of the Senate and House of Representatives, open all the certificates and the votes shall then be counted;—the person having the greatest number of votes for President shall be the President, if such number be a majority of the whole number of electors appointed; and if no person have such majority, then from the persons having the highest numbers not exceeding three on the list of those voted for as President, the House of Representatives shall choose immediately, by ballot, the President. But in choosing the President, the votes shall be taken by states, the representation from each state having one vote; a quorum for this purpose shall consist of a member or members from two thirds of the states, and a majority of all the states shall be necessary to a choice. And if the House of Representatives shall not choose a President whenever the right of choice shall devolve upon them, ~~before the fourth day of March next following~~, then the Vice-President shall act as President, as in the case of the death or other constitutional disability of the President. The person having the greatest number of votes as Vice-President shall be the Vice-President, if such number be a majority of the whole number of electors appointed, and if no person have a majority, then from the two highest numbers on the list, the Senate shall choose the Vice-President; a quorum for the purpose shall consist of two thirds of the whole number of Senators, and a majority of the whole number shall be necessary to a choice. But no person constitutionally ineligible to the office of President shall be eligible to that of Vice-President of the United States.

AMENDMENT 13. SLAVERY ABOLISHED (1865) Passed by Congress January 31, 1865. Ratified December 6, 1865.

Note: A portion of Article 4, Section 2, of the Constitution was superseded by the Thirteenth Amendment.

Constitutional Insight Amendment 12

How did the election of 1800 lead to the Twelfth Amendment? The election ended in a tie vote between the Republican running mates. The election was decided in Jefferson's favor on the House's 36th ballot. Almost immediately Alexander Hamilton and others designed an amendment that established that the presidential electors would vote for both a presidential and a vice-presidential candidate. This amendment prevents a repeat of the problem experienced in the 1800 election.

F **CRITICAL THINKING**
Why is the Twelfth Amendment important?

NOW & THEN

ELECTION REFORM

A new wave of electoral reform efforts was triggered by the controversial presidential election of 2000, in which George W. Bush's narrow victory over Al Gore left many Americans questioning the system in which a candidate can lose the popular vote but win the election.

Eliminating or reworking the electoral college has been historically the most frequently proposed constitutional amendment. Other reform proposals have included improving access to polling places by allowing voting on weekend hours or making Election Day a national holiday. Still other proposals would modernize inaccurate polling and counting machines or replace them with computer stations or online voting.

SECTION 1 Neither slavery nor involuntary servitude, except as a punishment for crime whereof the party shall have been duly convicted, shall exist within the United States, or any place subject to their jurisdiction.

SECTION 2 Congress shall have power to enforce this article by appropriate legislation.

AMENDMENT 14. CIVIL RIGHTS (1868) Passed by Congress June 13, 1866. Ratified July 9, 1868.

Note: Article 1, Section 2, of the Constitution was modified by Section 2 of the Fourteenth Amendment.

SECTION 1 All persons born or naturalized in the United States, and subject to the jurisdiction thereof, are citizens of the United States and of the state wherein they reside. No state shall make or enforce any law which shall abridge the privileges or immunities of citizens of the United States; nor shall any state deprive any person of life, liberty, or property, without due process of law; nor deny to any person within its jurisdiction the equal protection of the laws.

SECTION 2 Representatives shall be apportioned among the several states according to their respective numbers, counting the whole number of persons in each state, excluding Indians not taxed. But when the right to vote at any election for the choice of electors for President and Vice-President of the United States, Representatives in Congress, the executive and judicial officers of a state, or the members of the legislature thereof, is denied to any of the male inhabitants of such state, being twenty-one years of age, and citizens of the United States, or in any way abridged, except for participation in rebellion, or other crime, the basis of representation therein shall be reduced in the proportion which the number of such male citizens shall bear to the whole number of male citizens twenty-one years of age in such state.

SECTION 3 No person shall be a Senator or Representative in Congress, or elector of President and Vice-President, or hold any office, civil or military, under the United States, or under any state, who, having previously taken an oath, as a member of Congress, or as an officer of the United States, or as a member of any state legislature, or as an executive or judicial officer of any state, to support the Constitution of the United States, shall have engaged in insurrection or rebellion against the same, or given aid or comfort to the enemies thereof. But Congress may, by a vote of two thirds of each house, remove such disability.

SECTION 4 The validity of the public debt of the United States, authorized by law, including debts incurred for payment of pensions and bounties for services in suppressing insurrection or rebellion, shall not be questioned. But neither the United States nor any state shall assume or pay any debt or obligation incurred in aid of insurrection or rebellion against the United States, or any claim for the loss or emancipation of any slave; but all such debts, obligations and claims shall be held illegal and void.

SECTION 5 The Congress shall have power to enforce, by appropriate legislation, the provisions of this article.

Constitutional Insight **Amendment 14, Section 1** *Which personal status takes priority—that of U.S. citizen or that of state citizen?* The Fourteenth Amendment firmly notes that Americans are citizens of both the nation and the states but that no state can "abridge the privileges or immunities" of U.S. citizens, deprive them "of life, liberty, or property, without due process of law," or deny them "equal protection of the laws."

What does it mean to have "equal protection of the laws"? Equal protection means that the laws are to be applied to all persons in the same way. The legal system may discriminate between persons—treat them differently, or unequally—if there are relevant reasons to do so. For example, a person's income and number of dependents are relevant for how much income tax the person should pay; a person's gender is not. The Supreme Court's 1954 decision in *Brown v. Board of Education of Topeka* (see page 914), which declared segregated public schools unconstitutional, was based on an Equal Protection claim; a child's race is not a relevant reason for the state to assign that child to a particular school.

G **CRITICAL THINKING**
Do you agree or disagree with the Supreme Court's decision that separate educational facilities are unequal? Explain your position.

The lawyers who successfully challenged segregation in the *Brown* v. *Board of Education* case in 1954 included (*left to right*) George E. C. Hayes, Thurgood Marshall, and James M. Nabrit, Jr.

Federal agents enforcing the Eighteenth
Amendment prepare to smash containers of
illegal whiskey.

AMENDMENT 15. RIGHT TO VOTE (1870) Passed by Congress February 26, 1869. Ratified February 3, 1870.

SECTION 1 The right of citizens of the United States to vote shall not be denied or abridged by the United States or by any state on account of race, color, or previous condition of servitude.

SECTION 2 The Congress shall have power to enforce this article by appropriate legislation.

AMENDMENT 16. INCOME TAX (1913) Passed by Congress July 12, 1909. Ratified February 3, 1913.

Note: Article 1, Section 9, of the Constitution was modified by the Sixteenth Amendment.

The Congress shall have power to lay and collect taxes on incomes, from whatever source derived, without apportionment among the several states, and without regard to any census or enumeration.

AMENDMENT 17. DIRECT ELECTION OF SENATORS (1913) Passed by Congress May 13, 1912. Ratified April 8, 1913.

Note: Article 1, Section 3, of the Constitution was modified by the Seventeenth Amendment.

CLAUSE 1 The Senate of the United States shall be composed of two Senators from each state, elected by the people thereof, for six years; and each Senator shall have one vote. The electors in each state shall have the qualifications requisite for electors of the most numerous branch of the state legislatures.

CLAUSE 2 When vacancies happen in the representation of any state in the Senate, the executive authority of such state shall issue writs of election to fill such vacancies: Provided, that the legislature of any state may empower the executive thereof to make temporary appointments until the people fill the vacancies by election as the legislature may direct.

CLAUSE 3 This amendment shall not be so construed as to affect the election or term of any Senator chosen before it becomes valid as part of the Constitution.

AMENDMENT 18. PROHIBITION (1919) Passed by Congress December 18, 1917. Ratified January 16, 1919. Repealed by Amendment 21.

SECTION 1 ~~After one year from the ratification of this article the manufacture, sale, or transportation of intoxicating liquors within, the importation thereof into, or the exportation thereof from the United States and all territory subject to the jurisdiction thereof for beverage purposes is hereby prohibited.~~

SECTION 2 ~~The Congress and the several states shall have concurrent power to enforce this article by appropriate legislation.~~

SECTION 3 ~~This article shall be inoperative unless it shall have been ratified as an amendment to the Constitution by the legislatures of the several states, as provided in the Constitution, within seven years from the date of the submission hereof to the states by the Congress.~~

AMENDMENT 19. WOMAN SUFFRAGE (1920) Passed by Congress June 4, 1919. Ratified August 18, 1920.

CLAUSE 1 The right of citizens of the United States to vote shall not be denied or abridged by the United States or by any state on account of sex.

CLAUSE 2 Congress shall have power to enforce this article by appropriate legislation.

AMENDMENT 20. "LAME DUCK" SESSIONS (1933) Passed by Congress March 2, 1932. Ratified January 23, 1933.

Note: Article 1, Section 4, of the Constitution was modified by Section 2 of this amendment. In addition, a portion of the Twelfth Amendment was superseded by Section 3.

SECTION 1 The terms of the President and Vice-President shall end at noon on the 20th day of January, and the terms of Senators and Representatives at noon on the 3rd day of January, of the years in which such terms would have ended if this article had not been ratified; and the terms of their successors shall then begin.

SECTION 2 The Congress shall assemble at least once in every year, and such meeting shall begin at noon on the 3rd day of January, unless they shall by law appoint a different day.

SECTION 3 If, at the time fixed for the beginning of the term of the President, the President elect shall have died, the Vice-President elect shall become President. If a President shall not have been chosen before the time fixed for the beginning of his term, or if the President elect shall have failed to qualify, then the Vice-President elect shall act as President until a President shall have qualified; and the Congress may by law provide for the case wherein neither a President elect nor a Vice-President elect shall have qualified, declaring who shall then act as President, or the manner in which one who is to act shall be selected, and such person shall act accordingly until a President or Vice-President shall have qualified.

SECTION 4 The Congress may by law provide for the case of the death of any of the persons from whom the House of Representatives may choose a President whenever the right of choice shall have devolved upon them, and for the case of the death of any of the persons from whom the Senate may choose a Vice-President whenever the right of choice shall have devolved upon them.

SECTION 5 Sections 1 and 2 shall take effect on the 15th day of October following the ratification of this article.

SECTION 6 This article shall be inoperative unless it shall have been ratified as an amendment to the Constitution by the legislatures of three fourths of the several states within seven years from the date of its submission.

AMENDMENT 21. REPEAL OF PROHIBITION (1933) Passed by Congress February 20, 1933. Ratified December 5, 1933.

SECTION 1 The eighteenth article of amendment to the Constitution of the United States is hereby repealed.

SECTION 2 The transportation or importation into any state, territory, or possession of the United States for delivery or use therein of intoxicating liquors, in violation of the laws thereof, is hereby prohibited.

Constitutional Insight **Amendment 19**
When did women first get the right to vote in the United States? Women had the right to vote in the state of New Jersey between 1776 and 1807. In the late 19th century, some states and territories began to extend full or limited suffrage to women. Then, in 1920, the Nineteenth Amendment prohibited the United States or any state from denying women the right to vote.

K CRITICAL THINKING
How does the right of women to vote affect politics today?

Constitutional Insight **Amendment 20**
Why is the Twentieth Amendment usually called the "Lame Duck" amendment? A lame duck is a person who continues to hold office after his or her replacement has been elected. Such a person is called a lame duck because he or she no longer has any strong political influence. The Twentieth Amendment reduces the time between the election of a new president and vice-president in November and their assumption of the offices, which it sets at January 20 instead of March 4. It also reduces the time new members of Congress must wait to take their seats from 4 months to about 2 months. They are now seated on January 3 following the November election. As a result, the lame duck period is now quite short.

L CRITICAL THINKING
Why may the framers have specified a longer lame duck period?

Constitutional Insight **Amendment 21**
What is unique about the Twenty-first Amendment? Besides being the only amendment that explicitly repeals another, it was the first, and is so far the only one, to have been ratified by the state convention method outlined in Article 5. Congress, probably fearing that state legislatures would not deal swiftly with the issue of repeal, chose to have each state call a special convention to consider the amendment. The strategy worked well, for the elected delegates to the conventions represented public opinion on the issue and ratified the amendment without delay.

M CRITICAL THINKING
Why is it necessary to pass another amendment to revoke or remove an existing amendment?

Constitutional Insight Amendment 23

Why were residents of the District of Columbia without a vote in presidential elections? First, the district was merely an idea at the time the Constitution was written. Second, no one expected the district to include many residents. Third, the framers designed the electoral college on a state framework. By 1960, however, the fact that nearly 800,000 Americans living in the nation's capital could not vote in presidential elections was an embarrassment. The Twenty-third Amendment gives Washington, D.C., residents the right to vote in presidential elections by assigning them electoral votes.

N CRITICAL THINKING

Do you think the District of Columbia should be made a separate state?

Constitutional Insight Amendment 24

Why was the poll tax an issue important enough to require an amendment? The poll tax was used in some places to prevent African-American voters—at least the many who were too poor to pay the tax—from participating in elections. As the civil rights movement gained momentum, the abuse of the poll tax became a major issue, but the national government found it difficult to change the situation because the constitutional provisions in Article 1, Section 4, leave the qualifications of voters in the hands of the states. The Twenty-fourth Amendment changed this by prohibiting the United States or any state from including payment of any tax as a requirement for voting.

O CRITICAL THINKING

What impact do you think the Twenty-fourth Amendment has had on elections?

SECTION 3 This article shall be inoperative unless it shall have been ratified as an amendment to the Constitution by conventions in the several states, as provided in the Constitution, within seven years from the date of the submission hereof to the states by the Congress.

AMENDMENT 22. LIMIT ON PRESIDENTIAL TERMS (1951) Passed by Congress March 21, 1947. Ratified February 27, 1951.

SECTION 1 No person shall be elected to the office of the President more than twice, and no person who has held the office of President, or acted as President, for more than two years of a term to which some other person was elected President shall be elected to the office of the President more than once. ~~But this article shall not apply to any person holding the office of President when this article was proposed by the Congress, and shall not prevent any person who may be holding the office of President, or acting as President, during the term within which this article becomes operative from holding the office of President or acting as President during the remainder of such term.~~

SECTION 2 This article shall be inoperative unless it shall have been ratified as an amendment to the Constitution by the legislatures of three fourths of the several states within seven years from the date of its submission to the states by the Congress.

AMENDMENT 23. VOTING IN DISTRICT OF COLUMBIA (1961) Passed by Congress June 17, 1960. Ratified March 29, 1961.

SECTION 1 The district constituting the seat of government of the United States shall appoint in such manner as Congress may direct: a number of electors of President and Vice-President equal to the whole number of Senators and Representatives in Congress to which the district would be entitled if it were a state, but in no event more than the least populous state; they shall be in addition to those appointed by the states, but they shall be considered, for the purposes of the election of President and Vice-President, to be electors appointed by a state; and they shall meet in the district and perform such duties as provided by the twelfth article of amendment.

SECTION 2 The Congress shall have power to enforce this article by appropriate legislation.

AMENDMENT 24. ABOLITION OF POLL TAXES (1964) Passed by Congress August 27, 1962. Ratified January 23, 1964.

SECTION 1 The right of citizens of the United States to vote in any primary or other election for President or Vice-President, for electors for President or Vice-President, or for Senator or Representative in Congress, shall not be denied or abridged by the United States or any state by reason of failure to pay any poll tax or other tax.

SECTION 2 The Congress shall have power to enforce this article by appropriate legislation.

AMENDMENT 25. PRESIDENTIAL DISABILITY, SUCCESSION (1967) Passed by Congress July 6, 1965. Ratified February 10, 1967.
Note: Article 2, Section 1, of the Constitution was affected by the Twenty-fifth Amendment.

SECTION 1. In case of the removal of the President from office or of his death or resignation, the Vice-President shall become President.

SECTION 2 Whenever there is a vacancy in the office of the Vice-President, the President shall nominate a Vice-President who shall take office upon confirmation by a majority vote of both houses of Congress.

SECTION 3 Whenever the President transmits to the President pro tempore of the Senate and the Speaker of the House of Representatives his written declaration that he is unable to discharge the powers and duties of his office, and until he transmits to them a written declaration to the contrary, such powers and duties shall be discharged by the Vice-President as Acting President.

SECTION 4 Whenever the Vice-President and a majority of either the principal officers of the executive departments or of such other body as Congress may by law provide, transmit to the President pro tempore of the Senate and the Speaker of the House of Representatives their written declaration that the President is unable to discharge the powers and duties of his office, the Vice-President shall immediately assume the powers and duties of the office as Acting President.

Thereafter, when the President transmits to the President pro tempore of the Senate and the Speaker of the House of Representatives his written declaration that no inability exists, he shall resume the powers and duties of his office unless the Vice-President and a majority of either the principal officers of the executive department[s] or of such other body as Congress may by law provide, transmit within four days to the President pro tempore of the Senate and the Speaker of the House of Representatives their written declaration that the President is unable to discharge the powers and duties of his office. Thereupon Congress shall decide the issue, assembling within forty-eight hours for that purpose if not in session. If the Congress, within twenty-one days after receipt of the latter written declaration, or, if Congress is not in session, within twenty-one days after Congress is required to assemble, determines by two thirds vote of both houses that the President is unable to discharge the powers and duties of his office, the Vice-President shall continue to discharge the same as Acting President; otherwise, the President shall resume the powers and duties of his office.

AMENDMENT 26. 18-YEAR-OLD VOTE (1971) Passed by Congress March 23, 1971. Ratified July 1, 1971.

Note: Amendment 14, Section 2, of the Constitution was modified by Section 1 of the Twenty-sixth Amendment.

SECTION 1 The right of citizens of the United States, who are eighteen years of age or older, to vote shall not be denied or abridged by the United States or by any state on account of age.

SECTION 2 The Congress shall have power to enforce this article by appropriate legislation.

AMENDMENT 27. CONGRESSIONAL PAY (1992) Proposed by Congress September 25, 1789. Ratified May 7, 1992.

No law, varying the compensation for the services of the Senators and Representatives, shall take effect, until an election of Representatives shall have intervened.

Constitutional Insight **Amendment 26**
Why was the Twenty-sixth Amendment passed? Granting 18-year-olds the right to vote became an issue in the 1960s, during the Vietnam War, when people questioned the justice of requiring 18-year-old men to submit to the military draft but refusing them the right to vote. In 1970, Congress passed a voting rights act giving 18-year-olds the right to vote in elections. When the constitutionality of this act was challenged, the Supreme Court decided that states had to honor the 18-year-old vote for congressional and presidential elections but could retain higher age requirements for state and local elections. To avoid confusion at the polls, the Twenty-sixth Amendment was passed. It guarantees 18-year-olds the right to vote in national and state elections.

P CRITICAL THINKING
Do you think 18-year-olds should have the right to vote? Why or why not?

(above) **President Richard M. Nixon signs the Twenty-sixth Amendment to the Constitution, adopted in 1971.**

Constitutional Insight **Amendment 27**
How long did it take to ratify this amendment? Although the Twenty-seventh Amendment was one of the 12 amendments proposed in 1789 as part of the Bill of Rights, it was not ratified until 1992. This amendment, which deals with congressional compensation, allows the members of Congress to increase Congressional pay, but delays the increase until after a new Congress is seated.

Q CRITICAL THINKING
Do you think members of Congress should be able to vote themselves a pay increase? Explain your answer.

Voting Rights

When the American colonists declared their independence from Great Britain in 1776, their struggle to create a representative government was just beginning. The state constitutions that were drafted at that time established voting rights, but only for certain citizens. The Articles of Confederation did not address voting rights; therefore, existing state laws remained intact.

Even the new Constitution that replaced the Articles in 1788 did not extend voting rights to many groups of people living in the new United States. As the Constitution has been amended over the years however, things changed. The right to vote was gradually extended to more and more citizens, enabling them to participate in local and national government.

1789

MALE PROPERTY OWNERS ▶

In the early years of the United States, property qualifications were relaxed in some states (Pennsylvania, Delaware, North Carolina, Georgia, and Vermont) to include all male taxpayers. With few exceptions, women were not allowed to vote. Most state constitutions also required that a voting male be at least 21 years of age.

Those who qualified to vote were generally white, although some states allowed free African Americans to vote.

1870

◀ AFRICAN-AMERICAN MALES

The Fifteenth Amendment to the Constitution attempted to guarantee African-American males the right to vote by stating that the right of U.S. citizens "to vote shall not be denied or abridged [limited] by the United States or by any state on account of race, color, or previous condition of servitude." The picture to the left shows African-American males voting in a state election in 1867. African-American males, however, were often kept from voting through the use of poll taxes, which were finally abolished by the Twenty-fourth Amendment in 1964, and literacy tests, which were suspended by the Voting Rights Act of 1965.

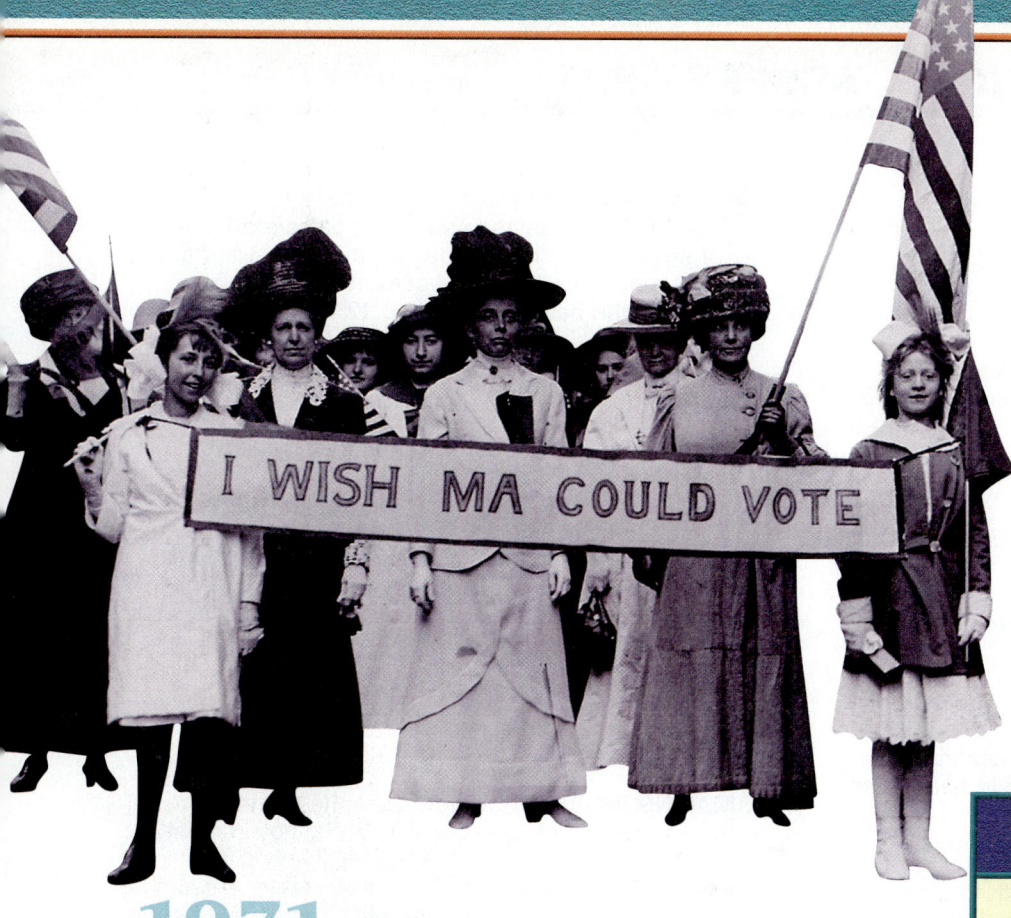

1920

◀ **WOMAN SUFFRAGE**

In 1920, the Nineteenth Amendment, granting voting rights to women, was finally ratified. Elizabeth Cady Stanton, Susan B. Anthony, and many other women, such as those shown at left marching in a woman suffrage parade in 1919, worked tirelessly for women's voting rights.

Four years after ratification of the Nineteenth Amendment, in 1924, citizenship—including the right to vote—was extended to Native Americans.

1971

▼ **EIGHTEEN-YEAR-OLD VOTE**

The Twenty-sixth Amendment, ratified in 1971, granted the right to vote to citizens "eighteen years of age or older." Voting rights for young people had become an issue in the 1960s during the Vietnam War. Many people questioned drafting 18-year-olds to fight but refusing them the right to vote. The picture below shows a young woman exercising her new right to vote.

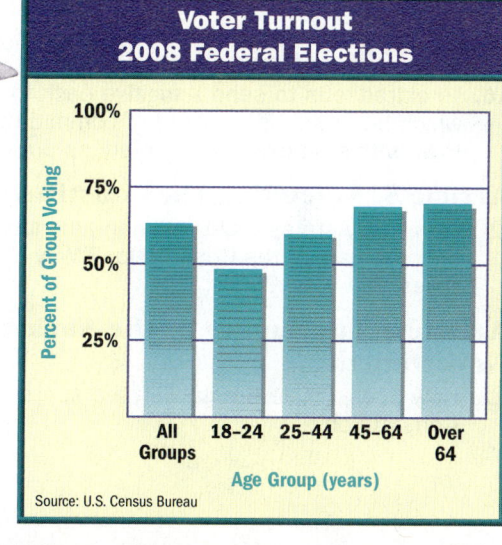

**Voter Turnout
2008 Federal Elections**

Percent of Group Voting vs. Age Group (years): All Groups, 18–24, 25–44, 45–64, Over 64

Source: U.S. Census Bureau

THINKING CRITICALLY

CONNECT TO HISTORY

1. **Forming Generalizations** What does the information on these pages demonstrate about how voting rights in the United States have changed? How did the Constitution help bring about the changes?

 SEE SKILLBUILDER HANDBOOK, PAGE R21.

CONNECT TO TODAY

2. **Interpreting Data** Research voter turnout statistics from a recent election. What age group scored highest? Which scored lowest?

 hmhsocialstudies.com **RESEARCH WEB LINKS**

MAIN IDEAS

Article 1. The Legislature

1. Why does the legislative branch of the government represent the people most directly? What is the principal job of this branch?
2. Why are there more members of the House of Representatives than of the Senate?
3. Name four powers Congress has.
4. What powers are denied to Congress? to the states?

Article 2. The Executive

5. What is the main function of the executive branch?
6. Who officially elects the president of the United States? Explain.
7. How can the president lose his or her job before election time?

Article 3. The Judiciary

8. How are Supreme Court justices appointed?
9. What kinds of cases go before the Supreme Court? Why is the Court's decision whether to hear a case important?

Article 4. Relations Among States

10. To extradite is to send a fugitive back to the state in which he or she is accused of committing a crime. How is this an example of relations among states?

Article 5. Amending the Constitution

11. How many states must ratify an amendment for it to become part of the Constitution? Why do you think it takes that many?

Article 6. Supremacy of the National Government

12. How does Article 6 establish the supremacy of the Constitution?

The Amendments

13. Does the First Amendment allow complete freedom of speech—the right to say anything you want at any time, anywhere? Explain your answer.
14. What is the newest amendment? What protection does that amendment give to the American people?

THINKING CRITICALLY

1. **TAKING NOTES** The powers of the federal government are separated among the three branches. Create a chart like the one below that shows how the Constitution's framers used checks and balances to ensure that no one branch of the government could become too much stronger than the others.

Executive	Legislative	Judicial

2. **MAKING INFERENCES** How does the Constitution reflect the fear of too strong a central government?

3. **EVALUATING** The Bill of Rights guarantees a defendant a speedy, public trial. Do you think it is being observed today? Explain.

4. **ANALYZING MOTIVES** Why did the framers make it so difficult to amend the Constitution? Do you agree or disagree with their philosophy? Explain.

5. **DEVELOPING HISTORICAL PERSPECTIVE** The Fifteenth, Nineteenth, and Twenty-sixth amendments give voting rights to specific groups. Why was it necessary for Congress to spell out these groups' rights in amendments?

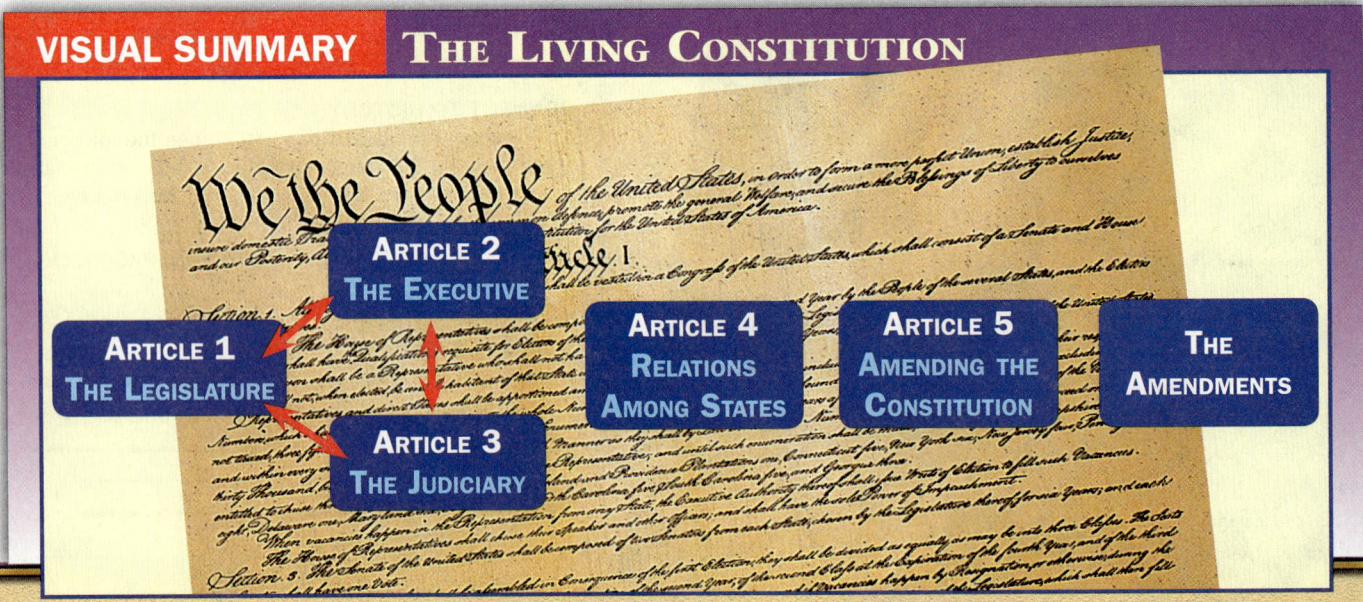

VISUAL SUMMARY   **THE LIVING CONSTITUTION**

ARTICLE 2 THE EXECUTIVE

ARTICLE 1 THE LEGISLATURE

ARTICLE 3 THE JUDICIARY

ARTICLE 4 RELATIONS AMONG STATES

ARTICLE 5 AMENDING THE CONSTITUTION

THE AMENDMENTS

Use the cartoon and your knowledge of U.S. history to answer question 1.

a 1968 Herblock Cartoon, copyright by The Herb Block Foundation

"It's Awful The Way They're Trying To Influence Congress. Why Don't They Serve Cocktails And Make Campaign Contributions Like We Do?"

1 In the Constitutional Convention, the framers adopted certain principles to be embodied in the Constitution. Which of the following Constitutional principles does the cartoon support?

  (1) The federal government's power should be divided into separate branches.

  (2) The federal government should be stronger than the state governments.

  (3) The federal legislature should be responsive to the will of the people.

  (4) The legislature and the president should check each other's power.

Use the quotation and your knowledge of U.S. history to answer question 2.

" [The president] shall have power, by and with the advice and consent of the Senate, to make treaties, provided two thirds of the Senators present concur; and he shall nominate, and by and with the advice and consent of the Senate, shall appoint ambassadors, other public ministers and consuls, judges of the Supreme Court, and all other officers of the United States . . . "

—U.S. Constitution, Art. 2, Sec. 2, part 2

2 The passage describes checks on the power of—

  (1) the president.

  (2) the Senate.

  (3) the judiciary.

  (4) the states.

3 Which of the following must ratify Constitutional amendments?

  (1) Congress

  (2) the people

  (3) the states

  (4) the president

 hmhsocialstudies.com **TEST PRACTICE**

For additional test practice, go online for:

• Diagnostic tests   • Tutorials

FOCUS ON WRITING

Imagine that it is 1787, and you are a citizen of one of the original thirteen states. Your vote is necessary to ratify the new Constitution that has been approved by the convention in Philadelphia. You have studied the seven articles and listened to spirited discussions about how you and your state will be affected. Write a journal entry in which you express your views about this document that is so important for the new United States. Make sure you include references to what you have read and heard about the Constitution.

MULTIMEDIA ACTIVITY

21ST CENTURY

Visit the links for Chapter Assessment to learn more about how bills become law. Because of the process by which bills become laws, problems may occur when the president and a majority of members of Congress are from different political parties. Using the Internet, research bills that were proposed by the president but became stalled in Congress because of party differences. Then divide into groups. Have each group research a different bill. Try to follow the debate and see how party differences affected the discussion. Did the bill pass and become law? Present your findings to the class.

hmhsocialstudies.com

Applying the Constitution

The United States Constitution is admired the world over. But a healthy democracy depends on the continuing participation of its citizens—including you. Here are four projects that will help you learn the rewards and challenges of responsible citizenship.

↗ **hmhsocialstudies.com** **RESEARCH WEB LINKS** Visit the links for the Constitution for more information that will help you with these Projects for Citizenship.

PROJECT 1

BECOMING AN EDUCATED VOTER

ENDORSING A CANDIDATE

Choose a campaign for elective office and learn about the issues and the candidates in the campaign. After doing your research, write an endorsement, or a statement in favor, of one of the candidates.

LEARNING ABOUT THE CANDIDATES

✔ **Examine news media and news services.** During campaigns, some services and publications offer endorsements that explain why particular candidates are worthy of support.

✔ **Get information from political parties.** They provide information on the candidates, but their perspective is biased toward their own candidates. The major parties have Internet sites, as do many local groups and individual candidates.

✔ **Contact interest groups,** such as the Sierra Club and the National Association of Manufacturers. They often list candidates' positions on issues and support candidates who share their beliefs.

✔ **Look at databases and voters' guides** published by nonpartisan organizations such as the League of Women Voters and Project Vote Smart.

As you use each source, try to identify any bias. Think about the following questions.

- What does the author of this source stand to gain from supporting a particular candidate?
- Is the information in the source complete and accurate?
- Does the author use loaded or inflammatory language?

PRESENTING YOUR PROJECT

After you have written your endorsement, you might send it to a media outlet, such as a newspaper or a television station, or post it on the Internet. Or you might send it to your local or school newspaper.

PROJECT 2

EXPRESSING POLITICAL OPINIONS

WRITING A LETTER TO THE EDITOR

Identify an issue that concerns you. Then write a letter or send an e-mail message about that issue to the editor of a newspaper or magazine.

WRITING A PERSUASIVE LETTER

✔ **Find an issue** that has been in the news lately and about which you feel strongly.

✔ **Read recent articles,** editorials, and cartoons in newspapers or magazines. Notice how they have addressed this issue.

✔ **Compose a letter** that clearly and concisely explains your views about the issue you have chosen. Your letter should also include reasons and facts that support your opinion on the issue. It might also advocate some specific action to be taken to address the issue.

✔ **Identify the person** to whom you should send your letter, and note any requirements the newspaper or magazine has for writing letters to the editor.

✔ **Edit your letter carefully.** Be sure to use standard grammar, spelling, sentence structure, and punctuation.

PRESENTING YOUR PROJECT

Present the letter you wrote to the rest of the class. When you do, explain why you chose to write about this issue.

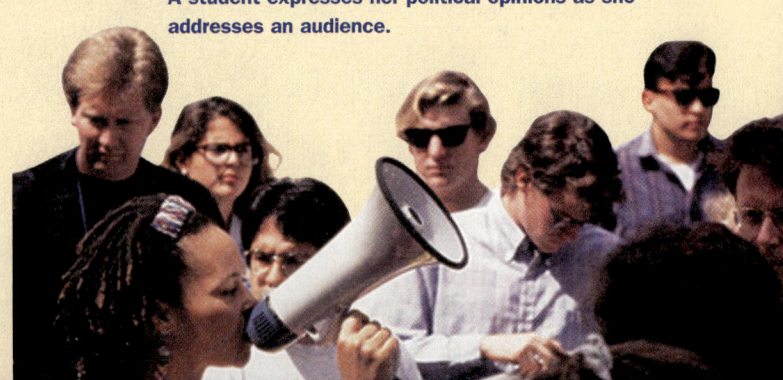

A student expresses her political opinions as she addresses an audience.

PROJECT 3

UNDERSTANDING HOW TO LOBBY

PLANNING A LOBBYING CAMPAIGN

Form a committee with other students to organize a lobbying campaign—a campaign to influence legislation or public policy. Create a plan for the campaign that includes materials to be presented to government officials. In creating your plan, keep the following points in mind.

CREATING A LOBBYING PLAN

✔ **Establish a clear goal** of what you want to achieve. Make sure all members of the group understand and agree with the established goal.

✔ **Identify the appropriate people to lobby**—the people who can best help you to achieve your goal. For example, if your group is planning to lobby to have a bill passed, you would lobby the legislators who will vote on the bill. However, if your group wants to lobby for a local improvement—such as cleaning up an abandoned factory site—you should lobby the local officials who make those decisions.

✔ **Gather statistics** and other information that support your case. Explore a variety of resources, including the library, the Internet, and news services. Conduct interviews with appropriate state or local officials. Use the information you gather to develop a brief written report that can be given to the officials you intend to lobby.

✔ **Organize public opinion** in favor of your case. Gather signatures on petitions or conduct a letter-writing campaign to encourage people who support your goal to contact government officials. You can also create fliers calling attention to your cause.

✔ **Present your case** to government officials firmly but politely. Practice your presentation several times before you actually appear before them.

PRESENTING YOUR PROJECT

Share your lobbying plan with the rest of the class in the form of a written proposal that includes materials, such as petition forms, that you will use in your lobbying effort. If you implement your lobbying plan, describe to the class what response you received from the officials you lobbied.

PROJECT 4

VOLUNTEERING IN YOUR COMMUNITY

MAKING AN ORAL REPORT

Identify a local community organization that you might want to help. Find out what kinds of volunteer activities the organization has, such as answering phones in the office, serving food to the homeless, or cleaning vacant lots. Then volunteer to participate in one of those activities. Prepare an oral report to present to the rest of the class about your experiences as a volunteer. Keep the following points in mind as you choose which organization to help.

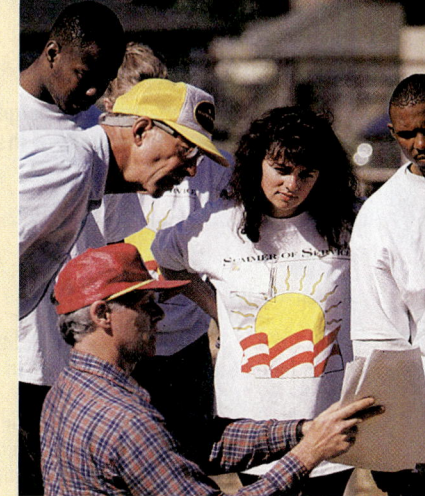

A group of young volunteers in the Summer of Service project discusses plans with carpenters.

SUGGESTIONS FOR VOLUNTEERING

✔ **Decide what kinds of public service projects might interest you.** You might talk to your parents, a teacher, friends, a local church, or a local political organization to learn what kinds of volunteer services are needed in your community.

✔ **Call local community organizations** to find out what kinds of volunteer opportunities they offer and decide whether you would like to volunteer for those projects.

✔ **Decide what cause you want to support** and identify an organization that addresses that cause.

✔ **Decide what type of work you want to do** and work with that organization.

PRESENTING YOUR PROJECT

Deliver an oral report to your class about your experiences as a volunteer. Explain why you chose the specific volunteer activity that you did. Describe the activity you performed. Then explain what effect your volunteering had as well as whether you felt the experience was a good one.

CHAPTER 6

LAUNCHING THE NEW NATION

Essential Question

What major domestic and foreign problems faced the leaders of the new Republic?

 New York Standards

KEY IDEA 1 The study of New York State and United States history requires an analysis of the development of American culture, its diversity and multicultural context, and the ways people are unified by many values, practices, and traditions.

KEY IDEA 3 Study about the major social, political, economic, cultural, and religious developments in New York State and United States history involves learning about the important roles and contributions of individuals and groups.

SECTION 1: Washington Heads the New Government

SECTION 2: Foreign Affairs Trouble the Nation

SECTION 3: Jefferson Alters the Nation's Course

SECTION 4: The War of 1812

Lake George, New York, in 1817

1789 George Washington is elected president.

1792 George Washington is reelected president.

1794 The Whiskey Rebellion breaks out.

1796 John Adams is elected president.

1800 Thomas Jefferson is elected president.

USA
WORLD

1790   **1795**   **1800**

1789 The French Revolution begins.

1791 Slaves revolt in Saint Domingue, now known as Haiti.

1793 French King Louis XVI is executed in the French Revolution.

1799 Napoleon Bonaparte seizes control of the French government.

1801 Act of Union, uniting Great Britain and Ireland, goes into effect.

INTERACT
WITH HISTORY

You are a teacher in a small town on the western frontier in 1789. You ask your students what the new government means to them. A girl whose parents own the general store says that her father worries about taxes. Her brother says that he wants to join the army. A boy from a small farm in the backcountry replies that the government is only for town people.

Explore the Issues

• How can a government win people's trust?

• How can a government build a unified nation out of a people with diverse interests and concerns?

1803 France and the United States sign the Louisiana Purchase.

1804 Thomas Jefferson is reelected president.

1808 James Madison is elected president.

1812 James Madison is reelected.

1814 The Treaty of Ghent ends the War of 1812.

1816 James Monroe is elected president.

1805   **1810**   **1815**

1804 Haiti declares itself independent from France.

1807 Great Britain outlaws the slave trade.

1815 Napoleon is defeated at Waterloo.

Washington Heads the New Government

MAIN IDEA	WHY IT MATTERS NOW	Terms & Names
President Washington transformed the ideas of the Constitution into a real government.	The Cabinet, an institution Washington created, is still a key element of every presidential administration.	• Judiciary Act of 1789 • Alexander Hamilton • Cabinet • Bank of the United States • Democratic-Republicans • two-party system • protective tariff • excise tax

One American's Story

George Washington had no desire to be president after the Constitutional Convention. His dream was to settle down to a quiet life at his Virginia estate, Mount Vernon. The American people had other ideas, though. They wanted a strong national leader of great authority as their first president. As the hero of the Revolution, Washington was the unanimous choice in the first presidential ballot. When the news reached him on April 16, 1789, Washington reluctantly accepted the call to duty. Two days later he set out for New York City to take the oath of office.

George Washington

A PERSONAL VOICE GEORGE WASHINGTON

"About ten o'clock I bade adieu [farewell] to Mount Vernon, to private life, and to domestic felicity [happiness]; and with a mind oppressed with more anxious and painful sensations than I have words to express, set out for New York . . . with the best dispositions [intentions] to render service to my country in obedience to its call, but with less hope of answering its expectations."

—The Diaries of George Washington

When Washington took office as the first president of the United States under the Constitution, he and Congress faced a daunting task—to create an entirely new government. The momentous decisions that these early leaders made have resounded through American history.

The New Government Takes Shape

Washington took charge of a political system that was a bold experiment. Never before had a nation tried to base a government on the Enlightenment ideals of republican rule and individual rights. No one knew if a government based on the will of the people could really work.

Although the Constitution provided a strong foundation, it was not a detailed blueprint for governing. To create a working government, Washington and Congress had to make many practical decisions—such as how to raise revenue and provide for defense—with no precedent, or prior example, for American leaders to follow. Perhaps James Madison put it best: "We are in a wilderness without a single footstep to guide us."

JUDICIARY ACT OF 1789 One of the first tasks Washington and Congress tackled was the creation of a judicial system. The Constitution had authorized Congress to set up a federal court system, headed by a Supreme Court, but it failed to spell out the details. What type of additional courts should there be and how many? What would happen if federal court decisions conflicted with state laws?

The **Judiciary Act of 1789** answered these critical questions, creating a judicial structure that has remained essentially intact. This law provided for a Supreme Court consisting of a chief justice and five associate justices. It also set up 3 federal circuit courts and 13 federal district courts throughout the country. (The numbers of justices and courts increased over time.) Section 25 of the Judiciary Act, one of the most important provisions of the law, allowed state court decisions to be appealed to a federal court when constitutional issues were raised. This section guaranteed that federal laws remained "the supreme Law of the Land," as directed by Article 6 of the Constitution. Ⓐ

WASHINGTON SHAPES THE EXECUTIVE BRANCH At the same time that Congress shaped the judiciary, Washington faced the task of building an executive branch to help him make policies and carry out the laws passed by Congress. In 1789, when Washington took office, the executive branch of government consisted of two officials, the president and the vice-president. To help these leaders govern, Congress created three executive departments: the Department of State, to deal with foreign affairs; the Department of War, to handle military matters; and the Department of the Treasury, to manage finances.

To head these departments, Washington chose capable leaders he knew and trusted. He picked Thomas Jefferson as secretary of state, **Alexander Hamilton** as secretary of the treasury, and Henry Knox, who had served as Washington's general of artillery during the Revolution, as secretary of war. Finally, he chose Edmund Randolph as attorney general, the chief lawyer of the federal government. These department heads soon became the president's chief advisers, or **Cabinet.**

MAIN IDEA

Analyzing Motives

Ⓐ Why did federal law have to be "the supreme Law of the Land" in the new nation?

NOW & THEN

THE CABINET

The Constitution provided the president the right to "require the opinion, in writing, of the principal officer in each of the executive departments." Washington chose to seek those opinions, in person, on a regular basis. In 1793, James Madison called this group the Cabinet, a term used in Britain for advisers to the king.

Since Washington's time the number of departments has increased to 15. In addition to the secretaries of these 15 departments, Cabinet officers include other executive branch officials such as the director of the Central Intelligence Agency, the administrator of the Environmental Protection Agency, and the vice-president. The Cabinet meets at the request of the president and frequency varies from administration to administration.

▶ President Washington *(far right)* meets with his first Cabinet: *(from left to right)* Henry Knox, Thomas Jefferson, Edmund Randolph *(with back turned),* and Alexander Hamilton.

Hamilton and Jefferson Debate

Hamilton and Jefferson were brilliant thinkers, but they had very different political ideas. The differences between the two also caused bitter disagreements, many of which centered on Hamilton's plan for the economy.

HAMILTON AND JEFFERSON IN CONFLICT Political divisions in the new nation were great. No two men embodied these differences more than Hamilton and Jefferson. Hamilton believed in a strong central government led by a prosperous, educated elite of upper-class citizens. Jefferson distrusted a strong central government and the rich. He favored strong state and local governments rooted in popular participation. Hamilton believed that commerce and industry were the keys to a strong nation. Jefferson favored a society of farmer-citizens.

Overall, Hamilton's vision of America was that of a country much like Great Britain, with a strong central government, commerce, and industry. His views found more support in the North, particularly New England, whereas Jefferson's views won endorsement in the South and the West. **B**

MAIN IDEA

Contrasting

B How did Jefferson's and Hamilton's views of government differ?

HAMILTON'S ECONOMIC PLAN As secretary of the treasury, Hamilton's job was to set in order the nation's finances and to put the nation's economy on a firm footing. To do this, he proposed a plan to manage the country's debts and a plan to establish a national banking system.

According to Hamilton's calculations in his *Report on the Public Credit*, the public debt of the United States in 1790 (most of it incurred during the Revolution) was many millions of dollars. The national government was responsible for about two-thirds of this debt, and individual states were responsible for the rest. The new nation owed some of the debt to foreign governments and some to private citizens, including soldiers who had received bonds—certificates that promised payment plus interest—as payment for their service during the war.

Hamilton proposed to pay off the foreign debt and to issue new bonds to cover the old ones. He also proposed that the federal government assume the debts of the states. Although this would increase the federal debt, Hamilton reasoned that assuming state debts would give creditors—the people who

KEY PLAYERS

THOMAS JEFFERSON
1743–1826

The writer of the Declaration of Independence, Thomas Jefferson began his political career at age 26, when he was elected to Virginia's colonial legislature. In 1779 he was elected governor of Virginia, and in 1785 he was appointed minister to France. He served as secretary of state from 1790 to 1793. A Southern planter, Jefferson was also an accomplished scholar, the architect of Monticello (his Virginia house), an inventor (of, among other things, a machine that made copies of letters), and the founder of the University of Virginia in 1819. Despite his elite background and his ownership of slaves, he was a strong ally of the small farmer and average citizen.

ALEXANDER HAMILTON
1755–1804

Born into poverty in the British West Indies, Alexander Hamilton was orphaned at age 13 and went to work as a shipping clerk. He later made his way to New York, where he attended King's College (now Columbia University). He joined the army during the Revolution and became an aide to General Washington. Intensely ambitious, Hamilton quickly moved up in society. Although in his humble origins Hamilton was the opposite of Jefferson, he had little faith in the common citizen and sided with the interests of upper-class Americans. Hamilton said of Jefferson's beloved common people: "Your people, sir, your people is a great beast!"

Contrasting Views of the Federal Government

HAMILTON	JEFFERSON
• Concentrating power in federal government	• Sharing power with state and local governments; limited national government
• Fear of mob rule	• Fear of absolute power or ruler
• Republic led by a well-educated elite	• Democracy of virtuous farmers and tradespeople
• Loose interpretation of the Constitution	• Strict interpretation of the Constitution
• National bank constitutional (loose interpretation)	• National bank unconstitutional (strict interpretation)
• Economy based on shipping and manufacturing	• Economy based on farming
• Payment of national and state debts (favoring creditors)	• Payment of only the national debt (favoring debtors)
• Supporters: merchants, manufacturers, landowners, investors, lawyers, clergy	• Supporters: the "plain people" (farmers, tradespeople)

SKILLBUILDER Interpreting Charts
1. Whose view of the federal government was a wealthy person more likely to favor? Why?
2. How do you think Jefferson differed from Hamilton in his view of people and human nature?

originally loaned the money—an incentive to support the new federal government. If the government failed, these creditors would never get their money back. However, this proposal made many people in the South furious. Some Southern states had already paid off most of their debts. Southerners resented assumption of state debts because they thought that they would be taxed to help pay the debts incurred by the Northern states. **C**

PLAN FOR A NATIONAL BANK Hamilton's line of reasoning also motivated his proposal for a national bank that would be funded by both the federal government and wealthy private investors. Hamilton hoped to tie wealthy investors to the country's welfare. The **Bank of the United States** would issue paper money and handle tax receipts and other government funds.

Hamilton's proposals aroused a storm of controversy. Opponents of a national bank, including James Madison, claimed that the bank would forge an unhealthy alliance between the government and wealthy business interests. Madison also argued that since the Constitution made no provision for a national bank, Congress had no right to authorize it. This argument began the debate between those who favored a "strict" interpretation of the Constitution, one in which the federal government has very limited powers, and a "loose" interpretation, which favors greater federal powers. The latter group appealed to the so-called elastic clause of the Constitution (Article 1, Section 8, Clause 18), which gives Congress the authority to do whatever is "necessary and proper" to carry out its specific enumerated powers, such as regulating commerce. In the end, however, Hamilton convinced Washington and a majority in Congress to accept his views, and the federal government established the Bank of the United States.

THE DISTRICT OF COLUMBIA To win support for his debt plan from Southern states, Hamilton offered a suggestion: What if the nation's capital were moved from New York City to a new city in the South, on the banks of the Potomac River? This idea pleased Southerners, particularly Virginians such as Madison and Jefferson, who believed that a Southern site for the capital would make the government more responsive to their interests. With this incentive, Virginians agreed to back the debt plan. In 1790, the debt bill passed Congress, along with authorization for the construction of a new national capital in the District of Columbia, located between Maryland and Virginia.

MAIN IDEA

Analyzing Issues
C Why did the new nation need to pay off its debts?

Launching the New Nation **185**

Pierre L'Enfant, a French engineer, drew up plans for the new capital. L'Enfant was later fired by George Washington for being obstinate. He was replaced by Andrew Ellicott, who redrew L'Enfant's plan, but kept much of the grand vision. An African-American surveyor, Benjamin Banneker, assisted Ellicott with the surveying work. They made their plan on a grand scale, incorporating boulevards, traffic circles, and monuments reminiscent of European capitals. By 1800, the capital had been moved to its new site on the Potomac.

▲ Pierre L'Enfant proposed a federal capital of spacious, tree-lined boulevards, symbolizing the freedom of the young republic.

The First Political Parties and Rebellion

President Washington tried to remain above the arguments between Hamilton and Jefferson and to encourage them to work together despite their basic differences. These differences were so great, however, that the two men continued to clash over government policy. Their conflict divided the cabinet and fueled a growing division in national politics.

FEDERALISTS AND DEMOCRATIC-REPUBLICANS The split in Washington's cabinet helped give rise to the country's first political parties. The two parties formed around one of the key issues in American history—the power and size of the federal government in relation to state and local governments. Those who shared Hamilton's vision of a strong central government called themselves Federalists. Those who supported Jefferson's vision of strong state governments called themselves Republicans. No relation to today's Republican Party, Jefferson's Republicans—later called **Democratic-Republicans**—were in fact the ancestors of today's Democratic Party. **D**

The very existence of political parties worried many leaders, including Washington, who saw parties as a danger to national unity. At the close of his presidency, Washington criticized what he called "the spirit of party."

> ★ **A PERSONAL VOICE** GEORGE WASHINGTON
>
> **"It serves always to distract the public councils and enfeeble the public administration. It agitates the community with ill-founded jealousies and false alarms; kindles the animosity of one part against another; foments [incites] occasionally riot and insurrection. It opens the door to foreign influence and corruption. . . ."**
>
> —"Farewell Address," 1796

Despite criticism, the two parties continued to develop. The **two-party system** was well established by the time Washington left office.

THE WHISKEY REBELLION During Washington's second term, an incident occurred that reflected the tension between federal and regional interests. In 1789, Congress had passed a **protective tariff,** an import tax on goods produced in Europe. This tax, meant to encourage American production, brought in a great deal of revenue, but Secretary Hamilton wanted more. So he pushed through an **excise tax**—a tax on a product's manufacture, sale, or distribution—to be levied on the manufacture of whiskey.

MAIN IDEA

Contrasting
D How did the Federalists and the Democratic-Republicans differ from each other?

Background
In addition to promoting American goods, the Tariff Act of 1789, as well as tariffs that followed, provided the majority of the federal government's revenue until the 20th century.

A group of rebels taking part in the Whiskey Rebellion tar and feather a tax collector.

Most whiskey producers were small frontier farmers. Their major crop was corn. Corn was too bulky to carry across the Appalachian Mountains and sell in the settled areas along the Atlantic. Therefore, the farmers distilled the corn into whiskey, which could be more easily sent to market on the backs of mules.

Since whiskey was the main source of cash for these frontier farmers, Hamilton knew that the excise tax would make them furious. And it did. In 1794, farmers in western Pennsylvania refused to pay the tax. They beat up federal marshals in Pittsburgh, and they even threatened to secede from the Union.

Hamilton looked upon the Whiskey Rebellion as an opportunity for the federal government to show that it could enforce the law along the western frontier. Accordingly, some 15,000 militiamen were called up. Accompanied by Washington part of the way and by Hamilton all the way, the federal troops hiked over the Alleghenies and scattered the rebels without the loss of a single life.

The Whiskey Rebellion was a milestone in the consolidation of federal power in domestic affairs. At the same time, the new government was also facing critical problems and challenges in foreign affairs—particularly in its relations with Europe and with Native American peoples west of the Appalachians.

SECTION 1 ASSESSMENT

1. TERMS & NAMES For each term or name, write a sentence explaining its significance.
- Judiciary Act of 1789
- Alexander Hamilton
- Cabinet
- Bank of the United States
- Democratic-Republicans
- two-party system
- protective tariff
- excise tax

MAIN IDEA

2. TAKING NOTES

In a chart, list the leaders, beliefs, and goals of the country's first political parties.

Federalists	Democratic-Republicans

If you had lived in that time, which party would you have favored?

CRITICAL THINKING

3. EVALUATING DECISIONS

How would you judge President Washington's decision to put two such opposed thinkers as Hamilton and Jefferson on his Cabinet?

Think About:
- both men's merits
- their philosophies
- the conflicts that developed

4. ANALYZING ISSUES

How was the Whiskey Rebellion an opportunity for the federal government to demonstrate its authority?

5. ANALYZING

Would you have supported Hamilton's economic plan? Explain why or why not. **Think About:**
- the money problems the nation faced
- other problems the nation faced

Young People in the Early Republic

Whether in farms on the frontier or in any of the cities and towns sprouting up throughout the nation, life in the early United States required energy and perseverance. This was especially true for young people, who were expected to shoulder responsibilities that, in our own time, even an adult would find challenging. Children worked alongside adults from the time they could walk and were considered adults at 14. School and leisure-time activities were work oriented and were meant to prepare young people for the challenges that lay ahead.

▲ EDUCATION

Country children attended school only when they weren't needed to do chores at home or in the fields. Schoolhouses were one-room log cabins and supplies were scarce. Younger and older children learned their lessons together by reciting spelling, multiplication tables, and verses from the Bible. Schoolmasters, seldom more learned than their students, punished wrong answers and restless behavior with severe beatings.

Some city children were either tutored at home or attended private schools. Girls studied etiquette, sewing, and music. Boys prepared for professional careers. "Professors" punished poor students by beating their hands. There were no laws requiring a child to attend school until the mid-1800s.

◄ WORK

Country children were expected to work alongside their parents from the time they were about six. Even when children went to school, they were expected to put in many hours performing such chores as chopping wood, watering the horses, gathering vegetables, and spooling yarn.

City boys as young as eight years old—especially poorer ones—went to work as "apprentices" for a tradesman who taught them such trades as printing, or, like the boys pictured here, dying cloth. Other boys worked in shops or went to sea. Girls learned from their mothers how to sew, spin, mend, and cook.

▼ LEISURE

Young people from the country gathered for events that were both entertaining as well as practical, such as the "husking bee" pictured here. Huskers were divided into teams, and the team that stripped the husks off the most ears of corn was the winner. Cheating, though resented, was expected and was usually followed by a fight.

Young people from the city gathered for cultured social events such as the cotillion, or dance, pictured at right. Young men and women were expected to follow the lead of their elders with regard to the strict social codes that determined how one behaved in polite society.

DATA FILE

CHILD MORTALITY

In Puritan America, one out of every two children died before they reached their teens. Child mortality remained high throughout the 18th and 19th centuries. Common causes of death for children were cholera, smallpox, diphtheria, and dysentery.

CHILDREN IN THE MILITARY

From the American Revolution until World War I, boys 14 and younger served in the United States military. Some as young as six were musicians and aides in the army and marines, while others served as deckhands and cartridge carriers in the United States Navy.

CHILDREN AND CAPITAL PUNISHMENT

Colonial law forbade the execution of children under 14, but exceptions were made. In December 1786, in New London, Connecticut, 12-year-old Hannah Ocuish was hanged for killing a six-year-old girl who had accused her of stealing strawberries.

CHILD LABOR

Apprentices who learned a trade could later go into business for themselves, but children who worked in factories had no such future. Virtually every industry in the country depended on child labor. Children worked in mills, mines, factories, and laundries.

Child Labor Data

- **1790:** All of the workers—seven boys and two girls—in the first American textile mill in Pawtucket, Rhode Island, were under the age of 12.
- **1830s:** One third of the labor force in New England was under the age of 16.
- **1842:** For the first time, Massachusetts law limited the workday of children under the age of 12 to ten hours a day.

THINKING CRITICALLY

CONNECT TO HISTORY

1. **Identifying Problems** What types of physical hardships were young people exposed to during this period in history?

   SEE SKILLBUILDER HANDBOOK, PAGE R5.

CONNECT TO TODAY

2. **Researching Jobs** In our own day, young people work at many different kinds of jobs. Some have even started their own businesses and have been very successful. Research some of the businesses that youths run on their own and present a report to the class.

hmhsocialstudies.com RESEARCH WEB LINKS

PI 3.4

CC Unit 2.I.F.2   CC Unit 2.I.F.3.a
CC Unit 2.I.F.3.b   CC Unit 2.I.F.4.a
CC Unit 2.I.F.4.b   CC Unit 2.II.B.2.c(1)

Foreign Affairs Trouble the Nation

MAIN IDEA	**WHY IT MATTERS NOW**	**Terms & Names**
Events in Europe sharply divided American public opinion in the late 18th century.	Foreign policy remains a key element of every presidential administration.	• neutrality • Edmond Genêt • Thomas Pinckney • Little Turtle • John Jay • sectionalism • XYZ Affair • Alien and Sedition Acts • nullification

One American's Story

hmhsocialstudies.com
TAKING NOTES

Use the graphic organizer online to take notes on some of the disputes discussed in this section.

Gouverneur Morris, the man responsible for the final draft of the Constitution, witnessed one of the great events of history—the French Revolution. On July 14, 1789, a mob stormed the Bastille, the infamous Paris prison, releasing the prisoners and killing the prison governor. Not long afterward, while walking on a Paris street, Morris got a close look at revolutionary violence.

A PERSONAL VOICE GOUVERNEUR MORRIS

" [T]he Head and Body of Mr. de Foulon are introduced in Triumph. The Head on a Pike, the Body dragged naked on the Earth. Afterwards this horrible Exhibition is carried thro the different Streets. His crime [was] to have accepted a Place in the Ministry. This mutilated form of an old Man of seventy five is shewn to Bertier, his Son in Law, the Intend't. [another official] of Paris, and afterwards he also is put to Death and cut to Pieces, the Populace carrying about the mangled Fragments with a Savage Joy. "

—quoted from his journal

▲ French revolutionaries storm the Bastille in Paris, France, on July 14, 1789.

Morris was appointed minister to France in 1792. Despite his horror at the violence around him, Morris remained at his post throughout the bloodiest days of the Revolution. Meanwhile, at home, Americans were divided in their views concerning the events underway in France.

U.S. Response to Events in Europe

Most Americans initially supported the French Revolution because, like the American Revolution, it was inspired by the ideal of republican rule. Heartened by the American struggle against royal tyranny, the French set out to create a government based on the will of the people. The alliance between France and the United States, created by the Treaty of 1778, served as an additional bond between the two nations. Whether or not the United States should support the French Revolution was one of the most important foreign policy questions that the young nation faced.

REACTIONS TO THE FRENCH REVOLUTION Despite the bonds between the nations, Americans soon became divided over the Revolution. In early 1793, a radical group called the Jacobins seized power in France. They beheaded the French king, Louis XVI, and launched the Reign of Terror against their opponents, sending moderate reformers and royalists alike to the guillotine. In an excess of revolutionary zeal, the Jacobins also declared war on other monarchies, including Great Britain.

Because of their alliance with the United States, the French expected American help. The American reaction tended to split along party lines. Democratic-Republicans, such as Thomas Jefferson and James Madison, wanted to honor the 1778 treaty and support France. Federalists, such as Alexander Hamilton, wanted to back the British. President Washington took a middle position. On April 22, 1793, he issued a declaration of **neutrality,** a statement that the United States would support neither side in the conflict. Hamilton and Jefferson came to agree; entering a war was not in the new nation's interest. **A**

Earlier in April, the French had sent a young diplomat, **Edmond Genêt,** to win American support. Before following diplomatic procedure and presenting his credentials to the Washington administration, Genêt began to recruit Americans for the war effort against Great Britain. This violation of American neutrality and diplomatic protocol outraged Washington, who demanded that the French recall Genêt. By then, however, Genêt's political backers had fallen from power in Paris. Fearing for his life, the young envoy remained in the United States and became a U.S. citizen. Although Jefferson protested against Genêt's actions, Federalists called Jefferson a radical because he supported France. Frustrated by these attacks and by his ongoing feud with Hamilton, Jefferson resigned from the cabinet in 1793.

MAIN IDEA

Analyzing Motives

A Why did the United States want to maintain its neutrality?

Politics and Style

Events in France not only affected politics in the United States, they influenced styles of clothing as well. Political differences could often be detected by observing different styles of dress and appearance.

DEMOCRATIC-REPUBLICANS favored a more informal style, similar to that found in France after the French Revolution.

loose hair

neckerchief

narrow coattails
"trowsers"

laces

FEDERALISTS tended to be pro-British, which was evident in their more formal dress.

wig or powdered hair to resemble a wig

bow tie

broad coattails
breeches and stockings

buckles

TREATY WITH SPAIN The United States wanted to secure land claims west of the Appalachian mountains and to gain shipping rights on the Mississippi River. To do this, it needed to come to an agreement with Spain, which still held Florida and the Louisiana Territory, a vast area of land west of the Mississippi River.

Negotiations stalled because of the turmoil in Europe. Spain, unlike Britain, signed a treaty with France. Spain then feared British retaliation and suspected that a joint British-American action might be launched against the Louisiana Territory. Suddenly, Spain agreed to meet with U.S. minister to Great Britain **Thomas Pinckney,** and on October 27, 1795, both sides signed a treaty.

Pinckney's Treaty of 1795, also known as the Treaty of San Lorenzo, included virtually every concession that the Americans desired. Spain gave up all claims to land east of the Mississippi (except Florida) and recognized the 31st parallel as the southern boundary of the United States and the northern boundary of Florida. Spain also agreed to open the Mississippi River to traffic by Spanish subjects and U.S. citizens, and to allow American traders to use the port of New Orleans. **B**

MAIN IDEA

Recognizing Effects
B Why did the United States want access to the Mississippi River?

Native Americans Resist White Settlers

Pioneers moving west assumed that the 1783 Treaty of Paris, in which Great Britain had ceded its land rights west of the Appalachians, gave them free rein to settle the area. But the British still maintained forts in the Northwest Territory—an area that included what is now Ohio, Indiana, Illinois, Michigan, and Wisconsin—in direct violation of the treaty. In addition to this continued British presence, the settlers met fierce resistance from the original inhabitants.

British Forts on U.S. Land, 1783–1794

British Territory (Canada)
Montreal
Ft. Point-au-Fer
Ft. Dutchman's Point
Ft. Oswegatchie
VERMONT
Ft. Oswego
Ft. Mackinac
Ft. Niagara
NEW YORK
TERRITORY NORTHWEST OF THE OHIO RIVER
Ft. Detroit
FALLEN TIMBERS Aug. 20, 1794
Ft. Miami
SPANISH TERRITORY (Louisiana)
Ft. Wayne
Maumee River
Ft. Defiance
Ft. Laurens
PENNSYLVANIA
Ft. Recovery
ST. CLAIR'S DEFEAT Nov. 4, 1791
Ft. Greenville
Pittsburgh
ATLANTIC OCEAN
Ft. Hamilton
Ft. Harmar
Ft. Finney
Cincinnati
Vincennes
Ohio River
VIRGINIA
KENTUCKY (1792)
70°W
40°N

Legend:
- British-held fort
- U.S.-held fort
- Battle

0   75   150 miles
0   75   150 kilometers

GEOGRAPHY SKILLBUILDER
1. **Location** What is one common feature of the locations of most of the British forts on this map?
2. **Human–Environment Interaction** Why would this feature be of great importance to an army?

The Miami war chief Little Turtle negotiates with General Anthony Wayne.

MAIN IDEA

Analyzing Issues

C Why did Native Americans demand negotiations with the United States over the Northwest Territory?

FIGHTS IN THE NORTHWEST Having been excluded from the negotiations that led to the Treaty of Paris, Native Americans in the Northwest Territory never accepted the provisions. They continued to claim their tribal lands and demanded direct negotiations with the United States. They also took heart from the presence of British troops, who encouraged their resistance. When white settlers moved into their territory, Native Americans often attacked them. **C**

To gain control over the area that would become Ohio, the federal government sent an army led by General Josiah Harmar. In 1790, Harmar's troops clashed with a confederacy of Native American groups led by a chieftain of the Miami tribe named **Little Turtle.** The Native Americans won that battle. The following year, the Miami Confederacy inflicted an even worse defeat on a federal army led by General Arthur St. Clair.

BATTLE OF FALLEN TIMBERS Finally, in 1792, Washington appointed General Anthony Wayne to lead federal troops against the Native Americans. Known as "Mad Anthony" for his reckless courage, Wayne spent an entire year drilling his men. Greatly impressed, Little Turtle urged his people to seek peace.

A PERSONAL VOICE LITTLE TURTLE

"We have beaten the enemy twice under different commanders. . . . The Americans are now led by a chief who never sleeps. . . . We have never been able to surprise him. . . . It would be prudent to listen to his offers of peace."

—speech to his allies

The other chiefs did not agree with Little Turtle and replaced him with a less able leader. On August 20, 1794, Wayne defeated the Miami Confederacy at the Battle of Fallen Timbers, near present-day Toledo, Ohio. After the battle, Wayne's army marched defiantly past the British Fort Miami, only two miles away, and then built an American post nearby.

This victory ended Native American resistance in Ohio. The following year, the Miami Confederacy signed the Treaty of Greenville, agreeing to give up most of the land in Ohio in exchange for $20,000 worth of goods and an annual payment of nearly $10,000. This settlement continued a pattern in which settlers and the government paid Native Americans much less for their land than it was worth. Meanwhile, in the Northwest Territory, new sources of conflict were developing between Britain and the United States.

JAY'S TREATY At the time of the Battle of Fallen Timbers, **John Jay,** the chief justice of the Supreme Court, was in London to negotiate a treaty with Britain. One of the disputed issues was which nation would control territories west of the Appalachian Mountains. When news of Wayne's victory at Fallen Timbers arrived, the British agreed to evacuate their posts in the Northwest Territory and a treaty was signed on November 19, 1794. The treaty managed to pass the Senate, but many Americans, especially western settlers, were angry at its terms, which allowed the British to continue their fur trade on the American side of the U.S.-Canadian border. **D**

MAIN IDEA

Analyzing Issues
D Why were so many Americans dissatisfied with Jay's treaty with Britain?

Adams Provokes Criticism

The bitter political fight over Jay's Treaty, along with the growing division between Federalists and Democratic-Republicans, convinced Washington not to seek a third term in office. In his "Farewell Address" he urged the United States to "steer clear of permanent alliances" with other nations. Then, in 1797, Washington retired to his home at Mount Vernon.

In the presidential election of 1796, Americans faced a new situation: a contest between opposing parties. The Federalists nominated Vice-President John Adams for president and Thomas Pinckney for vice-president. The Democratic-Republicans nominated Thomas Jefferson for president and Aaron Burr for vice-president.

In the election, Adams received 71 electoral votes, while Jefferson received 68. Because the Constitution stated that the runner-up should become vice-president, the country found itself with a Federalist president and a Democratic-Republican vice-president. What had seemed sensible when the Constitution was written had become a problem because of the unexpected rise of political parties.

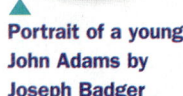
▲ Portrait of a young John Adams by Joseph Badger

The election also underscored the growing danger of **sectionalism—** placing the interests of one region over those of the nation as a whole. Almost all the electors from the southern states voted for Jefferson, while all the electors from the northern states voted for Adams. **E**

MAIN IDEA

Analyzing Issues
E How did political parties affect the results of the election of 1796?

ADAMS TRIES TO AVOID WAR Soon after taking office, President Adams faced his first crisis: a looming war with France. The French government, which regarded the Jay treaty with Britain as a violation of the French-American alliance, refused to receive the new American ambassador and began to seize American ships bound for Britain. Adams sent a three-man delegation consisting of Charles Pinckney, minister to France; future Chief Justice John Marshall; and Elbridge Gerry to Paris to negotiate a solution.

By this time, the Reign of Terror had ceased and the French government consisted of a legislature and a five-man executive branch called the Directory. French power and prestige were at a high point because of the accomplishments of a young general named Napoleon Bonaparte who had conquered most of western Europe. The Directory had little patience with the concerns of the Americans.

The American delegation planned to meet with the French foreign minister, Talleyrand. Instead, the Directory sent three low-level officials, whom Adams in

"THE PARIS MONSTER"

"*Cinque-tetes*, or the Paris Monster," is the title of this political cartoon satirizing the XYZ Affair. On the right, the five members of the French Directory, or ruling executive body, are depicted as a five-headed monster demanding money. The three American representatives, Elbridge Gerry, Charles Pinckney, and John Marshall, are on the left, exclaiming "Cease bawling, monster! We will not give you six-pence!"

SKILLBUILDER Analyzing Political Cartoons

1. How would you contrast the cartoon's depiction of the American representatives with its depiction of the French Directory?

2. What other details in the cartoon show the cartoonist's attitude toward the French?

SEE SKILLBUILDER HANDBOOK, PAGE R24.

his report to Congress called "X, Y, and Z." These officials demanded a $250,000 bribe as payment for seeing Talleyrand. News of this insult, which became known as the **XYZ Affair,** provoked a wave of anti-French feeling at home. "Millions for defense, but not one cent for tribute" became the slogan of the day. The mood was so anti-French that audiences refused to listen to French music.

 In 1798, Congress created a navy department and authorized American ships to seize French vessels. Twelve hundred men marched to the president's residence to volunteer for war. Congress authorized the creation of an army of 50,000 troops and brought George Washington yet again out of retirement to be "Lieutenant General and Commander in Chief of the armies raised or to be raised." While war was never officially declared, for the next two years an undeclared naval war raged between France and the United States.

Vocabulary
alien: belonging to or coming from another country; foreign

Vocabulary
sedition: rebellion against one's country; treason

THE ALIEN AND SEDITION ACTS Anti-French feeling continued to flourish, and many Federalists believed that French agents were everywhere, plotting to overthrow the government. New arrivals from foreign countries were soon held in particular suspicion, especially because many immigrants were active in the Democratic-Republican party. Some of the most vocal critics of the Adams administration were foreign-born. They included French and British radicals as well as recent Irish immigrants who lashed out at anyone who was even faintly pro-British, including the Federalist Adams.

To counter what they saw as a growing threat against the government, the Federalists pushed through Congress in 1798 four measures that became known as the **Alien and Sedition Acts.** Three of these measures, the Alien Acts, raised the residence requirement for American citizenship from five years to 14 years and allowed the president to deport or jail any alien considered undesirable.

The fourth measure, the Sedition Act, set fines and jail terms for anyone trying to hinder the operation of the government or expressing "false, scandalous, and malicious statements" against the government. Under the terms of this act, the federal government prosecuted and jailed a number of Democratic-Republican editors, publishers, and politicians. Outraged Democratic-Republicans called the laws a violation of freedom of speech guaranteed by the First Amendment.

VIRGINIA AND KENTUCKY RESOLUTIONS The two main Democratic-Republican leaders, Jefferson and James Madison, saw the Alien and Sedition Acts as a serious misuse of power on the part of the federal government. They decided to organize opposition to the Alien and Sedition Acts by appealing to the states. Madison drew up resolutions that were adopted by the Virginia legislature, while Jefferson wrote resolutions that were approved in Kentucky. The Kentucky Resolutions in particular asserted the principle of **nullification**—that states had the right to nullify, or consider void, any act of Congress that they deemed unconstitutional. Virginia and Kentucky viewed the Alien and Sedition Acts as unconstitutional violations of First Amendment citizens rights. **F**

The resolutions warned of the dangers that the Alien and Sedition Acts posed to a government of checks and balances guaranteed by the Constitution.

MAIN IDEA

Analyzing Issues

F How did the Kentucky Resolutions challenge the authority of the federal government?

⭐**A PERSONAL VOICE** THOMAS JEFFERSON

" Let the honest advocate of confidence [in government] read the alien and sedition acts, and say if the Constitution has not been wise in fixing limits to the government it created, and whether we should be wise in destroying those limits. "

—8th Resolution, The Virginia and Kentucky Resolutions

Moreover, Virginia and Kentucky claimed the right to declare null and void federal laws going beyond powers granted by the Constitution to the Federal government.

The resolutions also called for other states to adopt similar declarations. No other state did so, however, and the issue died out by the next presidential election. Nevertheless, the resolutions showed that the balance of power between the states and the federal government remained a controversial issue. In fact, the election of 1800 between Federalist John Adams and Republican Thomas Jefferson would center on this critical debate.

THE DEATH OF WASHINGTON Throughout 1799, George Washington remained active, writing letters to recruit possible generals and making plans for the army that might be needed in a possible war against France. However, on December 14, Washington died after catching a severe cold. Washington was buried according to his wishes with a military funeral at Mount Vernon.

Ironically, Washington's death was instrumental in improving relations with France. Napoleon Bonaparte, now first consul of France, hoped to lure American friendship away from the British and back to the French. Napoleon ordered ten days of mourning to be observed in the French armies for the American leader. Soon, Napoleon would offer even greater concessions to the Americans.

SECTION 2 ASSESSMENT

1. TERMS & NAMES For each term or name, write a sentence explaining its significance.

- **neutrality**
- **Edmond Genêt**
- **Thomas Pinckney**
- **Little Turtle**
- **John Jay**
- **sectionalism**
- **XYZ Affair**
- **Alien and Sedition Acts**
- **nullification**

MAIN IDEA

2. TAKING NOTES

List some of the disputes mentioned in this section. Indicate the dispute and each side's arguments.

Dispute	
One side	Other side

Choose one dispute and defend one side's arguments.

CRITICAL THINKING

3. ANALYZING ISSUES

Do you agree with the Democratic-Republicans that the Alien and Sedition Acts were a violation of the First Amendment? Were they necessary? Support your opinion. **Think About:**

- the intent of the First Amendment
- what was happening in Europe
- what was happening in America

4. EVALUATING DECISIONS

Should the United States have officially supported the French revolutionaries against the British? Support your opinion with examples from the text. **Think About:**

- Federalist and Republican attitudes toward France and Great Britain
- the Reign of Terror
- U.S. gratitude to France for its support against Britain

CC Unit 2.I.F.2   CC Unit 2.I.F.3.a
CC Unit 2.II.A.3   CC Unit 2.II.C.1
CC Unit 2.II.C.2

PI 1.1

Jefferson Alters the Nation's Course

MAIN IDEA	WHY IT MATTERS NOW	Terms & Names
The United States expanded its borders during Thomas Jefferson's administration.	Part or all of 15 states now occupy the territory Jefferson acquired in the Louisiana Purchase.	• Lewis and Clark • Aaron Burr • John Marshall • Judiciary Act of 1801 • midnight judges • *Marbury* v. *Madison* • judicial review • Louisiana Purchase • Sacajawea

One American's Story

▲ Patrick Gass

hmhsocialstudies.com
TAKING NOTES

Use the graphic organizer online to take notes on the accomplishments of Jefferson's presidency.

Patrick Gass was born on June 12, 1771 and died on April 2, 1870. During that time, the country grew from the original 13 colonies to 37 states. Gass played a part in that expansion as a participant in the **Lewis and Clark** expedition commissioned by President Jefferson to explore the West. Setting out from St. Louis, Missouri, in 1804, the expedition traveled overland to the Pacific Ocean. Along the way, Gass kept a journal. The following passage is from his journal entry of May 14, 1805.

> **A PERSONAL VOICE** PATRICK GASS
>
> " This forenoon we passed a large creek on the North side and a small river on the South. About 4 in the afternoon we passed another small river on the South side near the mouth of which some of the men discovered a large brown bear, and six of them went out to kill it. They fired at it; but having only wounded it, it made battle and was near seizing some of them, but they all fortunately escaped, and at length succeeded in dispatching it. "
>
> —*A Journal of the Voyages and Travels of a Corps of Discovery*

By charting unexplored territory, the Lewis and Clark expedition helped lay the foundations for western expansion. It was one of the great achievements of the Jefferson presidency.

Jefferson Wins Presidential Election of 1800

The presidential campaign of 1800 was a bitter struggle between Thomas Jefferson, a Democratic-Republican, and his Federalist opponent, President John Adams. Each party hurled wild charges at the other. To Democratic-Republicans, Adams was a tool of the rich who wanted to turn the executive branch into a British-style monarchy. To Federalists, Jefferson was a dangerous supporter of revolutionary France and an atheist bent on destroying organized religion.

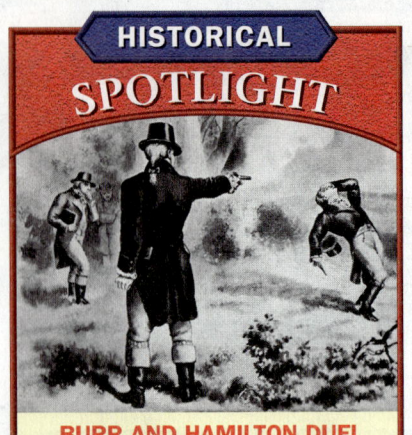
ELECTORAL DEADLOCK In the balloting, Jefferson defeated Adams by eight electoral votes. However, since Jefferson's running mate, **Aaron Burr,** received the same number of votes in the electoral college as Jefferson, the House of Representatives was called upon to choose between the two highest vote getters. For six feverish days, the House took one ballot after another—35 ballots in all. Finally, Alexander Hamilton intervened. Hamilton persuaded enough Federalists to cast blank votes to give Jefferson a majority of two votes. Burr then became vice-president. Although Hamilton opposed Jefferson's philosophy of government, he regarded Jefferson as much more qualified for the presidency than Burr was.

The deadlock revealed a flaw in the electoral process as spelled out in the Constitution. As a result, Congress passed the Twelfth Amendment, which called for electors to cast separate ballots for president and vice-president. This system is still in effect today.

The Jefferson Presidency

In his inaugural address, Jefferson extended the hand of peace to his opponents. "Every difference of opinion is not a difference of principle," he said. "We are all [Democratic-]Republicans; we are all Federalists." Nevertheless, Jefferson planned to wage a "peaceful revolution" to restore what he saw as the republican ideals of 1776 against the strong-government policies of Federalism. Under Washington and Adams, Federalists had filled the vast majority of government positions. Jefferson reversed this pattern by replacing some Federalist officials with Democratic-Republican ones. By 1803, the government bureaucracy was more evenly balanced between Democratic-Republicans and Federalists.

SIMPLIFYING THE PRESIDENCY Jefferson believed that a simple government best suited the needs of a republic. In a symbolic gesture, he walked to his own inauguration instead of riding in a carriage. As president, he took off his powdered wig and sometimes wore work clothes and frayed slippers when receiving visitors.

In accord with his belief in decentralized power, Jefferson also tried to shrink the government and cut costs wherever possible. He reduced the size of the army, halted a planned expansion of the navy, and lowered expenses for government social functions. He also rolled back Hamilton's economic program by eliminating all internal taxes and reducing the influence of the Bank of the United States. Jefferson strongly favored free trade rather than government-controlled trade and tariffs. He believed that free trade would benefit the United States because the raw materials and food that Americans were producing were in short supply in Europe. **A**

SOUTHERN DOMINANCE OF POLITICS Jefferson was the first president to take office in the new federal capital, Washington, D.C. Though in appearance the city was a primitive place of dirt roads and few buildings, its location between Virginia and Maryland reflected the growing importance of the South in national politics. In fact, Jefferson and the two presidents who followed him—James Madison and James Monroe—all were from Virginia.

MAIN IDEA

Drawing Conclusions
A How did Jefferson's actions reflect his philosophy of government?

This pattern of Southern dominance underscored the declining influence of both New England and the Federalists in national political life. The decline of the Federalists was hastened by Jefferson's political moderation. Also, many Federalists refused to participate in political campaigns because they did not want to appeal to the common people for support. Furthermore, national expansion worked against the Federalists because settlers in the new states tended to vote for the Democratic-Republicans, who represented farmers' interests.

JOHN MARSHALL AND THE SUPREME COURT Federalists continued to exert great influence in the judicial branch, however. Adams had appointed **John Marshall,** a staunch Federalist, as chief justice of the Supreme Court. Marshall served on the Court for more than 30 years, handing down decisions that would strengthen the power of the Supreme Court and the federal government.

Some of Adams's other judicial appointments proved to be less effective, however. Just prior to leaving office as president, Adams had pushed through Congress the **Judiciary Act of 1801,** which increased the number of federal judges by 16. In an attempt to control future federal judicial decisions, Adams promptly filled most of these positions with Federalists. These judges were called **midnight judges** because Adams signed their appointments late on the last day of his administration.

Adams's packing of the courts with Federalists angered Jefferson and the Democratic-Republicans. Since the documents authorizing some of the appointments had not been delivered by the time Adams left office, Jefferson argued that these appointments were invalid.

MARBURY v. MADISON This argument led to one of the most important Supreme Court decisions of all time: *Marbury v. Madison* (1803). William Marbury was one of the midnight judges who had never received his official papers. James Madison was Jefferson's Secretary of State, whose duty it was to deliver the papers. The Judiciary Act of 1789 required the Supreme Court to order that the papers be delivered, and Marbury sued to enforce this provision. Chief Justice Marshall decided that this provision of the act was unconstitutional because the Constitution did not empower the Supreme Court to issue such orders. (See *Marbury* v. *Madison* on page 206). The decision was later recognized as significant for affirming the principle of **judicial review**—the ability of the Supreme Court to declare an act of Congress unconstitutional. **B**

MAIN IDEA

Summarizing

B What is judicial review, and why is it important?

The United States Expands West

During Jefferson's presidency, Americans continued their westward migration across the Appalachians. For instance, between 1800 and 1810, the population of Ohio grew from 45,000 to 231,000. Although pioneer life was hard, the pioneers kept coming.

A PERSONAL VOICE F. A. MICHAUX

"The houses that they inhabit are built upon the borders of the river, . . . whence they enjoy the most delightful prospects [views]; still, their mode of building does not correspond with the beauties of the spot, being nothing but miserable log houses, without windows, and so small that two beds occupy the greatest part of them."

—from *Travels to the West of the Allegheny Mountains*

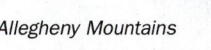
Supplies for the journey west.

Lewis and Clark Expedition, 1804–1806

hmhsocialstudies.com **INTERACTIVE MAP**

This dollar coin honors Sacajawea, a young Shoshone woman, who served as an interpreter and guide for the expedition.

Mandan Village, by Karl Bodmer

5 April 25–26, 1805
In high winds and cold, Lewis searches by land for the Yellowstone River. He rejoins Clark at the junction of the Missouri and Yellowstone rivers.

4 April 7, 1805
A party of 32, including Clark's black servant York, French-Canadian trader Charbonneau, his wife Sacajawea, and their son, depart at 5 P.M. to continue the journey. High northwest wind but otherwise fair weather.

3 November 3, 1804
A hard wind from the northwest sets in as the party makes camp.

December 17, 1804
In minus-45-degree weather, sentries have to be changed every half-hour.

6 December 8, 1805–March 23, 1806
Lack of provisions forces departure from winter camp.

7 July 3, 1806
The party divides. Lewis takes the direct route to the falls of the Missouri. Clark heads toward the Jefferson and Yellowstone rivers.

August 11, 1806
Lewis is accidentally shot by a member of his own party. In pain, he rejoins Clark's party the next day.

2 August 20, 1804
Sergeant Floyd dies, the only fatality of the expedition.

1 May 14, 1804
The party departs camp near Saint Louis about 4 P.M. in heavy rain.

8 September 23, 1806
Taking a shortcut that saves about 580 miles, the party reaches Saint Louis at 12 noon. Total mileage: 7,690.

BRITISH TERRITORY

Fort Clatsop
Traveler's Rest
Three Forks
Fort Mandan

LOUISIANA PURCHASE (1803)

UNITED STATES

NEW SPAIN

St. Louis
New Orleans

Gulf of Mexico

PACIFIC OCEAN

Arkansas R.
Red R.
Missouri R.
Mississippi R.

Page from the journal of Lewis and Clark

Compass of Lewis and Clark

Legend:
- Journey west, 1804–1805
- Journey home, 1806
- Lewis's route home
- Clark's route home
- Fort

0   250   500 miles
0   250   500 kilometers

GEOGRAPHY SKILLBUILDER
1. **Movement** About how many miles did the expedition travel on its route to the Pacific Ocean?
2. **Movement** On average, how many miles per day did they travel from Fort Clatsop to the place where the party split up on July 3, 1806?

Most of the settlers who arrived in Ohio, Kentucky, and Tennessee came through the Cumberland Gap, a natural passage through the Appalachians near where Kentucky, Tennessee, and Virginia meet. A generation earlier, in 1775, Daniel Boone, one of America's great frontier guides, had led the clearing of a road from Virginia, through the Cumberland Gap, into the heart of Kentucky. When it was finished, the Wilderness Road became one of the major routes for westward migration.

THE LOUISIANA PURCHASE In 1800, Napoleon Bonaparte of France persuaded Spain to return the Louisiana Territory, which it had received from France in 1762. When news of the secret transfer leaked out, Americans reacted with alarm. Jefferson feared that a strong French presence in the midcontinent would force the United States into an alliance with Britain. **C**

Jefferson wanted to resolve the problem by buying New Orleans and western Florida from the French. He sent James Monroe to join American ambassador Robert Livingston in Paris. Before Monroe arrived, however, Napoleon had abandoned his hopes for an American empire. He had failed to reconquer France's most important island colony, Saint Domingue (now known as Haiti). By the time that Monroe arrived in Paris in April 1803, Napoleon had decided to sell the entire Louisiana Territory to the United States.

With no time to consult their government, Monroe and Livingston went ahead and closed the deal for $15 million. Jefferson, though, was not certain that the purchase was constitutional. As a strict constructionist, he doubted whether the Constitution gave the government the power to acquire new territory. But, after a delay, he submitted the treaty finalizing the purchase, and the Senate ratified it. With the **Louisiana Purchase,** which included all the land drained by the western tributaries of the Mississippi River, the size of the United States more than doubled.

LEWIS AND CLARK Jefferson was eager to explore the new territory. In 1803, he appointed Meriwether Lewis to lead the expedition he called the Corps of Discovery from St. Louis to the Pacific coast. Jefferson ordered the Corps to collect scientific information about unknown plants and animals en route to the Pacific and to learn as much as possible about the Native American tribes encountered along the way. Lewis chose William Clark to be second in command. Starting off with some 50 soldiers and woodsmen, including Patrick Gass, the expedition later became smaller but added a Native American woman, **Sacajawea,** who served as interpreter and guide. The Lewis and Clark expedition took two years and four months and recorded invaluable information about the western territories.

MAIN IDEA

Analyzing Issues

C Why was the United States concerned about the Louisiana Territory?

Background
Even before the Louisiana Purchase, Jefferson had planned to explore the West. In February 1803, Congress approved Jefferson's request for funds to finance an expedition.

SECTION 3 ASSESSMENT

1. TERMS & NAMES For each term or name, write a sentence explaining its significance.

- Lewis and Clark
- Aaron Burr
- John Marshall
- Judiciary Act of 1801
- midnight judges
- *Marbury* v. *Madison*
- judicial review
- Louisiana Purchase
- Sacajawea

MAIN IDEA

2. TAKING NOTES
Make a chart like the one below listing the major accomplishments of Jefferson's presidency and the significance of each.

Event	Significance

CRITICAL THINKING

3. EVALUATING
How did the Louisiana Purchase and the Lewis and Clark expedition affect the expansion of the United States?

4. ANALYZING ISSUES
Why was *Marbury* v. *Madison* such an important case? **Think About:**

- Judge Marshall's decision
- its effects on the future

5. ANALYZING PRIMARY SOURCES
How does this sketch—from Patrick Gass's journal—of a man treed by a grizzly bear illustrate fanciful ideas about the West?

The War of 1812

MAIN IDEA	WHY IT MATTERS NOW	Terms & Names
War broke out again between the United States and Britain in 1812.	The War of 1812 confirmed American independence and strengthened nationalism.	• blockade • impressment • embargo • William Henry Harrison • Tecumseh • war hawk • Andrew Jackson • Treaty of Ghent • armistice

One American's Story

hmhsocialstudies.com
TAKING NOTES
Use the graphic organizer online to take notes on why the war hawks wanted war with Great Britain.

During the War of 1812, Samuel Wilson became a symbol for the nation. The owner of a meat-packing business in Troy, New York, he began supplying barrels of salted meat to the army, stamping the barrels with the initials "U.S.," for United States. One of Wilson's employees joked that the letters stood for "Uncle Sam," Wilson's nickname. Soon army recruits were calling themselves "Uncle Sam's soldiers." One of Wilson's great-nephews, Lucius Wilson, spoke about his famous relative in 1917.

★ **A PERSONAL VOICE** LUCIUS E. WILSON

"He was the old original Uncle Sam that gave the name to the United States. . . . [He] engaged in many enterprises, employed many hands [workers], had extensive acquaintance, was jolly, genial, generous, and known [as] and called "Uncle Sam" by everyone."

—*Uncle Sam: The Man and the Legend*

The story took on the features of a legend. Uncle Sam came to symbolize American values of honesty and hard work. The war during which the phrase caught on was just around the corner for the United States.

▲
One of the earliest depictions of Uncle Sam

The War Hawks Demand War

Jefferson's popularity soared after the Louisiana Purchase, and he won reelection in 1804. During his second term, renewed fighting between Britain and France threatened American shipping. In 1806, Napoleon decided to exclude British goods from Europe. In turn, Great Britain decided that the best way of attacking Napoleon's Europe was to **blockade** it, or seal up its ports and prevent ships from entering or leaving. By 1807, Britain had seized more than 1,000 American ships and confiscated their cargoes, and France had seized about half that number.

GRIEVANCES AGAINST BRITAIN Although both France and Britain engaged in these acts of aggression, Americans focused their anger on the British. One reason was the British policy of **impressment,** the practice of seizing Americans at sea and "impressing," or drafting, them into the British navy. Another reason was the *Chesapeake* incident. In June 1807, the commander of a British warship demanded the right to board and search the U.S. naval frigate *Chesapeake* for British deserters. When the U.S. captain refused, the British opened fire, killing 3 Americans and wounding 18.

Jefferson convinced Congress to declare an **embargo,** a ban on exporting products to other countries. He believed that the Embargo Act of 1807 would hurt Britain and the other European powers and force them to honor American neutrality. The embargo hurt America more than Britain, and in 1809 Congress lifted the ban on foreign trade—except with France and Britain. **A**

TECUMSEH'S CONFEDERACY Another source of trouble appeared in 1809, when General **William Henry Harrison,** the governor of the Indiana Territory, invited several Native American chiefs to Fort Wayne, Indiana, and persuaded them to sign away three million acres of tribal land to the U.S. government.

Not all chiefs gave in. Like Little Turtle and chiefs from other tribes, the Shawnee chief **Tecumseh** believed that the only way for Native Americans to protect their homeland against intruding white settlers was to form a confederacy, a united Native American nation.

Tecumseh was aided by his younger brother, known as the Prophet. Around 1805, the Prophet had started a reform movement within the Shawnee tribe to cast off all traces of the white "civilization," including Christianity. Both the Prophet and Tecumseh warned that the Great Spirit was angry with all of the tribes who had abandoned their traditional practices and beliefs. The time had come to return to those beliefs, they urged, and to implore the aid of the Great Spirit in driving out the invaders.

More practical than his brother, Tecumseh was a brilliant strategist and a skillful diplomat. While continuing to press Harrison to withdraw from Native American land, Tecumseh began negotiations with the British for assistance in what seemed like an inevitable war with the Americans. Throughout 1810 and 1811, Tecumseh traveled throughout the Midwest and the South, trying to win followers to his confederacy. Unfortunately, many tribes had already accepted payment for their lands. Others were reluctant to give up tribal autonomy by joining the kind of confederacy that Tecumseh proposed.

THE WAR HAWKS In November 1811, while Tecumseh was absent, his brother led the Shawnee in an attack on Harrison and his troops. Harrison struck back. On the banks of the Tippecanoe river, he burned the Shawnee capital known as Prophetstown to the ground. Harrison's victory at what came to be known as the Battle of Tippecanoe made him a national hero, but his troops suffered heavy losses. When it was discovered that the Native American confederacy was using arms from British Canada, a group of young congressmen from the South and the West known as the **war hawks** called for war against Britain. Led by Senator John C. Calhoun of South Carolina and Henry Clay of Kentucky, the Speaker of the House of Representatives, the war hawks rallied behind their motto: "On to Canada!" **B**

"The Great Spirit gave this great land to his red children."
TECUMSEH

MAIN IDEA

Analyzing Issues

A What was Jefferson's reasoning behind the embargo of 1807?

MAIN IDEA

Analyzing Motives

B Why did the war hawks call for the war with Britain?

The War Brings Mixed Results

In the election of 1808, another Virginia Democratic-Republican—James Madison—coasted to victory against a weak Federalist opponent, Charles C. Pinckney. By the spring of 1812, President Madison had decided to go to war against Britain. Madison believed that Britain was trying to strangle American trade and cripple the American economy. Congress approved the war declaration in early June.

THE WAR IN CANADA Declaring war was one thing—but fighting it was another. The American military was unprepared for war. Detroit was captured by the British shortly after war was declared and the Americans suffered numerous setbacks, including a failed attempt to take Montreal. The following year, a fleet commanded by Oliver Hazard Perry defeated a British fleet on Lake Erie, and American soldiers retook Detroit and won several battles. Different Native American groups allied with British or U.S. forces, depending on relationships they had developed before the war. Tecumseh, like many Native Americans, had fought for the British with the hopes of continuing British aid in stopping U.S. expansion. The Shawnee leader was killed at the Battle of the Thames in 1813.

THE WAR AT SEA The war was an opportunity for the relatively young U.S. Navy to test its ability. Badly outnumbered with only 16 ships, the United States was aided by its three 44-gun frigates, or warships, the *President,* the *United States,* and the *Constitution.* Known for their speed and ability to sail close to enemy vessels and open fire, these ships sailed alone. Each scored victories against British vessels.

However, the superior numbers of the British navy began to tell. In November of 1812, the British government ordered a blockade of the Chesapeake and Delaware bays (see the map below). As the war progressed and U.S. frigates scored

VIDEO
War of 1812:
Madison
Declares War

hmhsocialstudies.com

The War of 1812

hmhsocialstudies.com **INTERACTIVE MAP**

BRITISH TERRITORY (Canada)

Lake Champlain, Sept. 11, 1814
U.S. gains control of lake, and British retreat to Canada.

Montreal

FORT MACKINAC July 17, 1812

YORK (TORONTO) April 27, 1813

Boston

FORT ERIE Aug. 2–Sept. 21, 1814

Thames, Oct. 5, 1813
Death of Tecumseh leads to collapse of Native American support for British.

Detroit

New York

40°N

ATLANTIC OCEAN

FORT DEARBORN August 15, 1812

Tippecanoe, Nov. 7, 1811
With British support, Native Americans try to stop U.S. westward expansion but Harrison defeats them.

Baltimore, Sept. 12–14, 1814
British fail to capture city and withdraw from Chesapeake Bay in October.

Delaware Bay

Chesapeake Bay

Put-in-Bay, Sept. 10, 1813
U.S. Naval forces under Oliver Hazard Perry gain control of Lake Erie.

Washington, D.C., Aug. 24–25, 1814
British burn Capitol, White House, and other important buildings.

New Orleans, Jan. 8, 1815
After defeating Native Americans in Mississippi Territory, Andrew Jackson moves to defend this city. Battle is fought two weeks after peace treaty was signed at Ghent, Dec. 24, 1814.

HORSESHOE BEND March 27, 1814

Mississippi River

Pensacola

British Blockade

SPANISH TERRITORY (Florida)

30°N

90°W   **80°W**

Gulf of Mexico

→ U.S. forces
→ British forces
✦ U.S. victory
✦ British victory
▲▲▲ Blockade

| 0 | 150 | 300 miles |
| 0 | 150 | 300 kilometers |

GEOGRAPHY SKILLBUILDER
1. Location Why do you think there were a number of battles on the Great Lakes?
2. Human-Environment Interaction Why do you think the British blockaded the coast from Boston to Georgia?

more victories against British ships, the blockade was extended along the east coast. By the end of 1813, most American ships were bottled up in port.

BRITISH BURN THE WHITE HOUSE By 1814, the British were raiding and burning towns all along the Atlantic coast. The redcoats brushed aside some hastily assembled American troops and entered Washington, D.C. In retaliation for the U.S. victory at the Battle of York, the capital of Upper Canada, in which U.S. forces burned the governor's mansion and the legislative assembly buildings, the British burned the Capitol, the White House, and other public buildings. On August 24, Madison and other federal officials had to flee from their own capital.

THE BATTLE OF NEW ORLEANS At the same time, a general from Tennessee named **Andrew Jackson** was winning a series of battles that gained him national fame. After a six months' campaign involving four battles, Jackson defeated Native Americans of the Creek tribe at the battle of Horseshoe Bend in March of 1814. The Creeks had earlier been victorious at the battle of Fort Mims in which all but 36 of the fort's 553 inhabitants were killed. Jackson's victory at Horseshoe Bend destroyed the military power of Native Americans in the south.

Ironically, Jackson's greatest victory came after the war was over. On January 8, 1815, Jackson's troops defeated a superior British force at the Battle of New Orleans. Hundreds of British troops died, while just a handful of Americans lost their lives.

THE TREATY OF GHENT Unknown to Jackson, British and American diplomats had already signed a peace agreement. The **Treaty of Ghent,** signed on Christmas Eve 1814, declared an **armistice,** or end to the fighting. Although it did not address the issues of impressment or neutral shipping rights, Americans were eager for peace and welcomed the treaty.

Within a few years, the United States and Great Britain were able to reach agreement on many of the issues left open at Ghent. In 1815, a commercial treaty reopened trade between the two countries. In 1817, the Rush-Bagot agreement limited the number of warships on the Great Lakes. In 1818, a British-American commission set the northern boundary of the Louisiana Territory at the 49th parallel as far west as the Rocky Mountains. The two nations then agreed to a ten-year joint occupation of the Oregon Territory. But at home, Americans were unable to resolve differences that had already begun to divide the nation.

SECTION 4 ASSESSMENT

1. TERMS & NAMES For each term or name, write a sentence explaining its significance.
- blockade
- impressment
- embargo
- William Henry Harrison
- Tecumseh
- war hawk
- Andrew Jackson
- Treaty of Ghent
- armistice

MAIN IDEA

2. TAKING NOTES
In the web below, show the reasons why the war hawks wanted war with Great Britain.

CRITICAL THINKING

3. EVALUATING
What was the most important achievement of the U.S. in this period? **Think About:**
- relations between the U.S. and Britain
- the results of the war

4. ANALYZING
Even though it was fought after an armistice had been signed, why was the Battle of New Orleans an important victory for the Americans?

5. EVALUATING
Do you think that Tecumseh's confederacy helped or hurt the cause of Native Americans? **Think About:**
- the loss of Native American lands
- the reluctance of certain tribes to join the confederacy
- Tecumseh's role in the War of 1812

MARBURY v. MADISON (1803)

ORIGINS OF THE CASE A few days before Thomas Jefferson's inauguration, outgoing president John Adams appointed William Marbury to be a justice of the peace. But the commission was not delivered to Marbury. Later, Jefferson's new secretary of state, James Madison, refused to give Marbury the commission. Marbury asked the Supreme Court to force Madison to give him his commission.

THE RULING The Court declared that the law on which Marbury based his claim was unconstitutional, and therefore it refused to order Madison to give Marbury his commission.

LEGAL REASONING

Writing for the Court, Chief Justice John Marshall decided that Marbury had a right to his commission, and he scolded Madison at length for refusing to deliver it.

However, he then considered Marbury's claim that, under the Judiciary Act of 1789, the Supreme Court should order Madison to deliver the commission. As Marshall pointed out, the powers of the Supreme Court are set by the Constitution, and Congress does not have the authority to alter them. The Judiciary Act attempted to do just that.

Marshall reasoned that, since the Constitution is the "supreme law of the land, no law that goes against the Constitution can be valid."

> "If . . . the courts are to regard the constitution, and the constitution is superior to any ordinary act of the legislature, the constitution, and not such ordinary act, must govern the case to which they both apply."

If an act of Congress violates the Constitution, then a judge must uphold the Constitution and declare the act void. In choosing to obey the Constitution, the Supreme Court did declare the Judiciary Act unconstitutional and void, and so refused to grant Marbury's request.

◀ **Chief Justice John Marshall**

LEGAL SOURCES

U.S. CONSTITUTION

U.S. CONSTITUTION, ARTICLE III, SECTION 2 (1789)
"The judicial power shall extend to all cases . . . arising under this Constitution, the laws of the United States, and treaties made . . . under their authority."

U.S. CONSTITUTION, ARTICLE VI, CLAUSE 2 (1789)
"This Constitution, and the laws of the United States which shall be made in pursuance thereof . . . shall be the supreme law of the land; and the judges in every State shall be bound thereby."

RELATED CASES

FLETCHER v. PECK (1810)
The Court ruled a state law unconstitutional for the first time.

COHENS v. VIRGINIA (1821)
The Court overturned a state court decision for the first time.

GIBBONS v. OGDEN (1824)
The Court ruled that the federal Congress—not the states—had the power under the Constitution to regulate interstate commerce.

◀ **William Marbury**

WHY IT MATTERED

In 1803, interest in Marbury's commission was primarily about partisan politics. The fight was just one skirmish in the ongoing battle between Federalists, such as Adams, and Democratic-Republicans, led by Jefferson and Madison, which had intensified in the election of 1800.

When Jefferson won the election, Adams made a final effort to hinder Jefferson's promised reforms. Before leaving office, he tried to fill the government with Federalists, including the "midnight" justices such as Marbury. Madison's refusal to deliver Marbury's appointment was part of Jefferson's subsequent effort to rid his administration of Federalists.

Marshall's opinion in *Marbury* might seem like a victory for Jefferson because it denied Marbury his commission. However, by scolding Madison and extending the principle of judicial review—the power of courts to decide whether or not specific laws are valid—the Court sent a message to Jefferson and to the Congress that the judiciary had the power to affect legislation. The Marshall Court, however, never declared another act of Congress unconstitutional.

HISTORICAL IMPACT

In striking down part of the Judiciary Act, an act of Congress, Marshall gave new force to the principle of judicial review. The legacy of John Marshall and of *Marbury* is that judicial review has become a cornerstone of American government. One scholar has called it "America's novel contribution to political theory and the practice of constitutional government." As Justice Marshall recognized, judicial review is an essential component of democratic government; by ensuring that Congress exercises only those powers granted by the Constitution, the courts protect the sovereignty of the people.

Perhaps more importantly, the principle of judicial review plays a vital role in our federal system of checks and balances. With *Marbury,* the judicial branch secured its place as one of three coequal branches of the federal government. The judiciary has no power to make laws or to carry them out. However, judges have an important role in deciding what the law is and how it is carried out.

In *City of Boerne* v. *Flores* (1997), for instance, the Supreme Court declared void the Religious Freedom Restoration Act of 1993. Members of Congress had passed the act in an attempt to change the way federal courts apply the First Amendment's Free Exercise Clause. The Supreme Court ruled that Congress does not have the authority to decide what the First Amendment means—in effect, to define its own powers. The Court, and not Congress, is the interpreter of the Constitution.

Through the 2007–2008 term, the Court had rendered 162 decisions striking down—in whole or part—acts of Congress. It had also voided or restricted the enforcement of state laws 1,179 times. That the entire country has with few exceptions obeyed these decisions, no matter how strongly they disagreed, proves Americans' faith in the Supreme Court as the protector of the rule of law.

THINKING CRITICALLY

CONNECT TO HISTORY

1. **Comparing** Read encyclopedia articles about another Marshall Court decision, such as *Fletcher* v. *Peck,* *Cohens* v. *Virginia,* or *Gibbons* v. *Ogden.* Compare that decision with *Marbury* and consider what the two cases and opinions have in common. Write a paragraph explaining the major similarities between the cases.

 SEE SKILLBUILDER HANDBOOK, PAGE R8.

CONNECT TO TODAY

2. Visit the links for Historic Decisions of the Supreme Court to research a recent Supreme Court decision involving judicial review of an act of Congress. Write a case summary in which you describe the law's purpose, the Court's ruling, and the potential impact of the decision.

 hmhsocialstudies.com **INTERNET ACTIVITY**

VISUAL SUMMARY

LAUNCHING THE NEW NATION

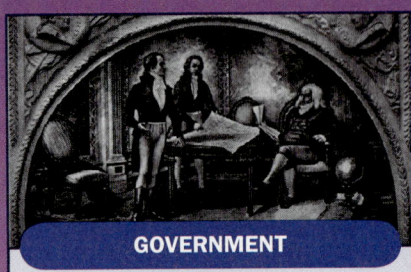

GOVERNMENT

• Washington forms the Cabinet.
• The Judiciary Act of 1789 establishes the Supreme Court.
• Hamilton founds the Bank of the United States.
• National capital is established in the District of Columbia.

CONFLICTS

• The Federalist and Democratic-Republican parties emerge.
• The Whiskey Rebellion protests Hamilton's excise tax.
• The Alien and Sedition Acts restrict protest.
• The Virginia and Kentucky Resolutions assert nullification.

TERRITORIES

• The Louisiana Purchase more than doubles the size of the U.S.
• Lewis and Clark explore the new territory.
• Differences between North and South continue to grow.
• More and more settlers push west.

WAR AND PEACE

• Native Americans, aided by the British, fight loss of their lands.
• War hawks urge war with Britain.
• War of 1812 occurs.
• Treaty of Ghent is signed.

TERMS & NAMES

For each term or name below, write a sentence explaining its connection to the new United States.

1. Alexander Hamilton
2. Cabinet
3. neutrality
4. Alien and Sedition Acts
5. John Marshall
6. Louisiana Purchase
7. Meriwether Lewis
8. embargo
9. Tecumseh
10. Andrew Jackson

MAIN IDEAS

Use your notes and the information in the chapter to answer the following questions.

Washington Heads the New Government
(pages 182–187)

1. What were the first steps taken by the Washington administration in building a new government?
2. Why did President Washington want both Thomas Jefferson and Alexander Hamilton to be among his closest advisers?
3. Why was the Whiskey Rebellion a significant event in the early days of the new government?

Foreign Affairs Trouble the Nation *(pages 190–196)*

4. What were three major international issues at this time, and how did the United States respond to them?
5. How did the United States manage to stay out of war during this period?
6. How did the expanding nation deal with Native Americans?

Jefferson Alters the Nation's Course *(pages 197–201)*

7. What were some of the accomplishments of Jefferson's first administration?
8. How did the Louisiana Purchase change the United States?

The War of 1812 *(pages 202–205)*

9. What events led to the War of 1812?
10. What did the Treaty of Ghent accomplish?

CRITICAL THINKING

1. **CONTRASTING** Create a chart listing some of the more important differences in the beliefs and goals of the Federalists and the Democratic-Republicans. Whose ideas appeal to you more?

Federalists	Democratic-Republicans

2. **HYPOTHESIZING** What if you had been your current age in 1800? What might have been some of the advantages and disadvantages of growing up in this period? Write two paragraphs describing what you like and dislike about the U.S. at that time. Provide examples from the text in your answer.

THE FALL of WASHINGTON ─ or Maddy in full flight.

Use the cartoon and your knowledge of U.S. history to answer the question below.

1 The British cartoon above entitled "The Fall of Washington— or Maddy [Madison] in full flight" was published in 1814. In it, a character exclaims, "The great Washington fought for Liberty, but we are fighting for shadows." The character is contrasting the Revolutionary War and —

(1) Shays's Rebellion.
(2) the XYZ Affair.
(3) the War of 1812.
(4) Washington's declaration of neutrality.

 hmhsocialstudies.com **TEST PRACTICE**

For additional test practice, go online for:

• Diagnostic tests   • Tutorials

INTERACT WITH HISTORY

Recall the issues that you explored at the beginning of the chapter. Imagine that it is now 1814, and one of your former students has written to ask your opinion about how the United States has grown as a nation. Write a response in which you mention events from the chapter that show key challenges and achievements that helped to shape the young republic.

FOCUS ON WRITING

Imagine you are a citizen during the early years of the United States. Select an important issue from that time period. Write a persuasive letter to the federal government in opposition to its decision or policy. In your letter, clearly present why you are opposed to the government's actions and present an alternate plan of action that you feel the government should pursue.

COLLABORATIVE LEARNING

In a small group read and discuss the "One American's Story" at the beginning of Section 3. Then consider the following questions: Who do you think are the explorers of our time? What challenges do they face in their journeys of exploration? Prepare a report and present it to the class.

Lewis and Clark

In 1804 Meriwether Lewis, William Clark, and the 33-man Corps of Discovery began a 8,000-mile journey across uncharted territory. Under orders from President Thomas Jefferson, the expedition mapped a route across the Louisiana Purchase to the Pacific Ocean. From St. Louis, Missouri, they traveled west up the Missouri River, then across the Rocky Mountains, and to the Pacific. They met Native American peoples and cataloged geography, plants, and animals. Not only was their mission one of history's greatest explorations, it also secured an American claim to the Pacific Coast and helped inspire millions to migrate west.

Explore entries from Lewis's journal and other primary sources online. You can find a wealth of information, video clips, activities, and more at ⇗ hmhsocialstudies.com.

"...the Indian woman recognized the point of a high plain to our right which she informed us was not very distant from the summer retreat of her nation on a river beyond the mountains which runs to the west."

— Meriwether Lewis

"Lewis's Journal, Entry 1"

Read an excerpt from Meriwether Lewis's journal that details Sacagawea's assistance during the journey.

Underway on the Missouri

Watch the video to see how the Corps of Discovery sailed up the Missouri River to begin their expedition.

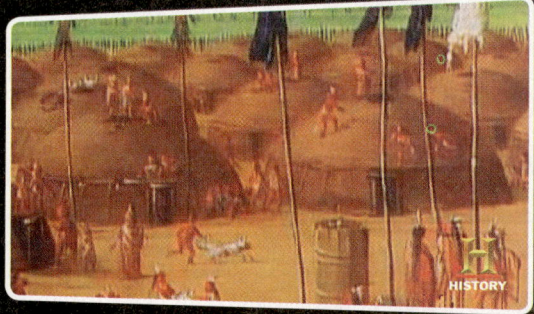

Making Friends Upriver

Watch the video to see which Native American peoples the Corps met and traded with as they made their journey west.

The Shores of the Pacific

Watch the video to see how the Corps tried to adapt to a different climate and the new peoples that they met along the Pacific coast.

CHAPTER 7

BALANCING NATIONALISM AND SECTIONALISM

Essential Question

How did regional differences contribute to the growing conflict over states' rights versus federal power?

New York Standards

KEY IDEA 1 The study of New York State and United States history requires an analysis of the development of American culture, its diversity and multicultural context, and the ways people are unified by many values, practices, and traditions.

KEY IDEA 3 Study about the major social, political, economic, cultural, and religious developments in New York State and United States history involves learning about the important roles and contributions of individuals and groups.

SECTION 1: Regional Economies Create Differences

SECTION 2: Nationalism at Center Stage

SECTION 3: The Age of Jackson

SECTION 4: States' Rights and the National Bank

The port of New Orleans, Louisiana, a major center for the cotton trade

1817 Construction begins on the Erie Canal.

1819 U.S. acquires Florida from Spain.

1820 James Monroe is reelected president.

1820 Congress agrees to the Missouri Compromise.

1824 John Quincy Adams is elected president.

USA	1815	1820	1825	
WORLD				

1815 Napoleon is defeated at Waterloo.

1819 Simón Bolívar becomes president of Colombia.

1822 Freed U.S. slaves found Liberia on the west coast of Africa.

1824 Mexico becomes a republic.

INTERACT
WITH HISTORY

The year is 1828. You are a senator from a Southern state. Congress has just passed a high tax on imported cloth and iron in order to protect Northern industry. The tax will raise the cost of these goods in the South and will cause Britain to buy less cotton. Southern states hope to nullify, or cancel, such federal laws that they consider unfair.

Explore the Issues

- What might happen if some states enforce laws and others don't?
- How can Congress address the needs of different states?
- What does it mean to be a nation?

1828 Andrew Jackson is elected president.

1832 Andrew Jackson is reelected.

1836 Martin Van Buren is elected president.

1838 Removal of the Cherokee along the Trail of Tears begins.

1840 William Henry Harrison is elected president.

1830

1835

1840

1830 France invades Algeria.

1833 British Parliament takes steps to end employment of children under nine years of age.

1837 Victoria becomes queen of England.

1839 Opium War breaks out in China.

SECTION 1
PI 1.1

CC Unit 1.I.A.2.a   CC Unit 1.I.A.2.b
CC Unit 2.II.A.2   CC Unit 2.II.B.1.a
CC Unit 2.II.B.1.d   CC Unit 2.II.B.1.e

Regional Economies Create Differences

MAIN IDEA	WHY IT MATTERS NOW	Terms & Names
The North and the South developed different economic systems that led to political differences between the regions.	Different regions of the country continue to have differing political and economic interests today.	• Eli Whitney • interchangeable parts • mass production • Industrial Revolution • cotton gin • Henry Clay • American System • National Road • Erie Canal • Tariff of 1816

One American's Story

In a dramatic presentation in front of President John Adams in 1801, inventor **Eli Whitney** demonstrated the first musket made of **interchangeable parts,** parts that are exactly alike. He assembled a musket from pieces chosen at random from crates full of parts. Whitney had made his musket parts the old-fashioned way, by hand. Nonetheless, his efforts were the first steps toward developing tools with which unskilled workers could make uniform parts.

A PERSONAL VOICE ELI WHITNEY

" One of my primary objects is to form the tools so the tools themselves shall fashion the work and give to every part its just proportion—which when once accomplished will give expedition, uniformity, and exactness to the whole. . . . In short, the tools which I contemplate are similar to an engraving on copper plate from which may be taken a great number of impressions exactly alike. "

—quoted in *Eli Whitney and the Birth of American Technology*

▲ In 1798, Eli Whitney manufactured 10,000 muskets in just two years. At that time, arms factories could produce only around 300 guns a year.

Better tools sped up the manufacture of goods and improved their reliability. Inventions and ideas such as these would affect different regions of the young nation in different ways.

Another Revolution Affects America

During the 19th century, new approaches to manufacturing, such as Whitney's interchangeable parts, took industry out of American households and artisans' workshops. Factories became the new centers of industry. The factory system (using power-driven machinery and laborers assigned to different tasks) made **mass production**—the production of goods in large quantities—possible. These changes in manufacturing brought about an **Industrial Revolution**—social and economic reorganization that took place as machines replaced hand tools and large-scale factory production developed.

GREAT BRITAIN STARTS A REVOLUTION The Industrial Revolution actually first began in Great Britain. It was in Britain, during the 18th century, that inventors came up with ways to generate power using swiftly flowing streams and bountiful supplies of coal. Inventors then developed power-driven machinery and ways to use this machinery to quickly mass-produce goods such as textiles. British merchants built the first factories. When these factories prospered, their owners had the money to build more factories, invent more labor-saving machines, and industrialize the nation.

THE INDUSTRIAL REVOLUTION IN THE UNITED STATES The primary source of income in America after the War of Independence was international trade, not manufacturing. Farms and plantations produced agricultural products such as grain and tobacco, which were shipped to Great Britain, southern Europe, and the West Indies. However, two events—the passage of President Thomas Jefferson's Embargo Act of 1807 and the War of 1812—turned the attention of Americans toward the development of domestic industries. Jefferson's embargo, which prohibited Americans from shipping goods to Europe, brought to a standstill the once-thriving foreign trade. In fact, by the time Congress repealed the act in 1809, many shipping centers—especially those in New England—had shut down.

Then, just as these seaports recovered, the War of 1812 broke out, and the British navy blockaded much of the coastline. With ships unable to get into or out of U.S. harbors, Americans had to invest their capital in ventures other than overseas shipping. **Ⓐ**

NEW ENGLAND INDUSTRIALIZES Probably nowhere else in the nation was the push to invest in industry as great as in New England. There, citizens had depended heavily upon shipping and foreign trade for income. Agriculture in the region was not highly profitable.

In 1793, a British immigrant named Samuel Slater had established in Pawtucket, Rhode Island, the first successful mechanized textile factory in America. However, Slater's factory and those modeled after it still only mass-produced one part of the textile, or finished cloth: thread.

Then, in 1813, three Bostonians revolutionized the American textile industry by mechanizing all the stages in the manufacture of cloth. Using plans from an English mill, Francis Cabot Lowell, Nathan Appleton, and Patrick Tracy Jackson built a weaving factory in Waltham, Massachusetts, and outfitted it with power machinery. By 1822 Appleton and Jackson had made enough money to build a larger operation. The changes that their factory triggered in the town of Lowell—named for their deceased partner, Francis Cabot Lowell—exemplify the changes wrought by the Industrial Revolution. By the late 1820s, quiet little Lowell had become a booming manufacturing center. Thousands of people—mostly young women who came to Lowell because their families' farms were in decline—journeyed there in search of work. **Ⓑ**

MAIN IDEA

Analyzing Effects

Ⓐ What effects did the Embargo Act of 1807 and the War of 1812 have on Americans involved in shipping and foreign trade?

MAIN IDEA

Summarizing

Ⓑ How did manufacturing develop in New England?

Samuel Slater's cotton mill drew its power from the Blackstone River in Pawtucket, Rhode Island.
▼

hmhsocialstudies.com **INTERACTIVE**

A NEW ENGLAND TEXTILE MILL

In a typical mill, water was channeled to turn the mill wheel, a large wooden cylinder made up of many angled slats. The mill wheel then turned a gear called the main drum. Belts enabled the drum to rotate gears connected to shafts, or heavy iron rods, on each level of the factory. Small gears and belts transferred the power to individual machines.

Fabric woven in 1848

4 Power looms weave the thread into cloth.

3 Spinning machines turn the fibers into thread.

Bobbins with machine-spun thread

1 Moving water turns a wheel, which then turns a system of belts and shafts, which powers the machines.

2 Carding and drawing machines straighten raw cotton fibers and twist them loosely.

▲ Carding machine

Two Economic Systems Develop

Northeasterners, prompted by changing economic conditions, invested their capital in factories and manufacturing operations. Cash crops did not grow well in the Northern soil and climate. Southerners, on the other hand, had begun to reap huge profits from cotton by the mid-1790s. The South had little incentive to industrialize. As a result, the North and the South continued to develop two distinct economies, including very different agricultural systems.

AGRICULTURE IN THE NORTH The North had not eliminated agriculture. However, the type of land and the growth of cities in the North encouraged farmers to cultivate smaller farms than Southerners did, and to grow crops that did not require much labor to flourish.

Farmers in the North usually started out growing only what their families needed. Then farming practices in the Old Northwest—the area north of the Ohio River, encompassing what is now the states of Ohio, Indiana, Illinois, Wisconsin, and Michigan—diverged from farming practices in the Northeast. As cities grew, farmers in the Old Northwest discovered that they could raise one or two types of crops or livestock (corn and cattle, for example), and sell what they produced at city markets. They could then purchase from stores whatever else they needed. Such grain crops as corn did not require much labor to grow, nor were they hugely profitable, so there was little demand for slaves. In the Northeast, farms were even smaller than those in the Northwest, so here too there was little demand for slavery.

By the late 1700s, slavery in the North was dying out. Farmers had little economic motivation to use slaves, and an increasing number of Northerners began to voice their religious and political opposition to slavery. Consequently, by 1804 almost all of the Northern states had voluntarily abolished slavery. **C**

COTTON IS KING IN THE SOUTH Eli Whitney's invention of a **cotton gin** (short for "cotton engine") in 1793 had helped to set the South on a different course of development from the North. Short-staple (or short-fiber) cotton was easier to grow but harder to clean than long-staple cotton. Whitney's gin made it possible for Southern farmers to grow short-staple cotton for a profit. Since cotton was in great demand in Britain and, increasingly, in the North, an efficient machine for cleaning the seeds from short-staple cotton proved a major breakthrough. Armed with the cotton gin, poor, nonslaveholding farmers quickly claimed land in the area between the Appalachians and the Mississippi south of the Ohio to begin cultivating this cash-producing crop. Wealthier planters followed, bought up huge areas of land, and then put an enormous slave labor force to work cultivating it. By 1820, this plantation system of farming had transformed Louisiana, Mississippi, and Alabama into a booming Cotton Kingdom. In this way, the cotton gin accelerated the expansion of slavery. **D**

SLAVERY BECOMES ENTRENCHED Although slave importation had declined during the American Revolution, by the 1820s the demand for slaves had begun

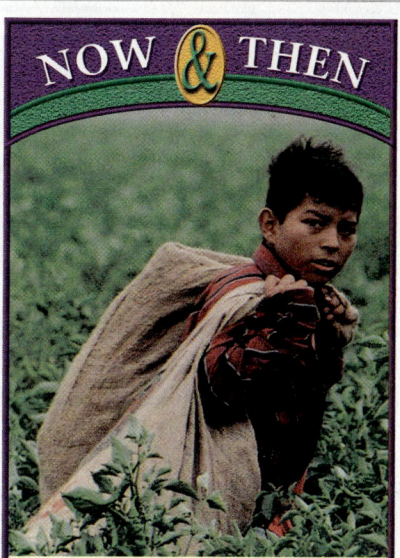

NOW & THEN

AGRICULTURE AND MIGRATION

Changes in agricultural technology often cause large population movements. Today's agricultural technology enables farmers to plant and grow crops with fewer workers than in the past, but many hands are still needed at harvest time. The United States has about half a million migrant agricultural workers. Whole families may move seasonally following the harvest. Children of migrant workers, like this 11-year old boy in Plainview, Texas, often help in the fields at peak harvest times.

In the early 1800s, the cotton gin led to a mass movement of planters and slaves into Alabama, Mississippi, and Louisiana. Mechanical cotton pickers replaced huge communities of field hands in the 1930s. Many laborers were African Americans, who then migrated from rural to urban areas in search of work.

MAIN IDEA

Analyzing Causes
C Why was slavery abolished in the North?

MAIN IDEA

Comparing
D How were the agricultural systems of the North and South different?

THE COTTON GIN

In 1794, Eli Whitney was granted a patent for a "new and useful improvement in the mode of Ginning [cleaning] Cotton." Workers who previously could clean only one pound of cotton per day could now, using the gin, clean as much as fifty pounds per day. Cotton production increased from three thousand bales in 1790 to more than two million bales in 1850. Increased cotton production meant an increase in the number of slaves needed on plantations.

1 Raw cotton is placed in the gin.

2 A hand crank turns a series of rollers.

3 A roller with tight rows of wire teeth removes seeds from the cotton fiber.

4 The teeth pass through a slotted metal grate, pushing the cotton fiber through but not the seeds, which are too large to pass.

5 The cotton seeds fall into a hopper.

6 A second roller, with brushes, removes the cleaned cotton from the roller.

7 A "clearer compartment" catches the cleaned cotton.

African-American Population in the United States, 1790–1860

African-American Population (in millions) vs. years 1790, 1800, 1810, 1820, 1830, 1840, 1850, 1860. Legend: Total, Slave, Free.

Source: U.S. Department of Commerce, U.S. Bureau of the Census, *Negro Population: 1790–1915.*

SKILLBUILDER Interpreting Graphs

1. About how many African-American slaves were in the United States in 1860?
2. How do the number of free African Americans and the number of slaves compare from 1790 to 1860?

to grow. Increases in cotton production and increases in the number of slaves owned paralleled each other. From 1790 to 1810, cotton production surged from 3,000 bales a year to 178,000 bales, while the number of slaves in the South leapt from 700,000 to 1,200,000. By 1808 slave traders had brought 250,000 additional Africans to the United States—as many as had been brought to the mainland American colonies between 1619 and 1776.

Clay Proposes the American System

As the North and South developed different economies, the creation of a plan to unify the nation became increasingly important. In 1815, President Madison presented such a plan to Congress. He hoped his agenda would both unite the different regions of the country and create a strong, stable economy that would make the nation self-sufficient. His plan included three major points:

- developing transportation systems and other internal improvements
- establishing a protective tariff
- resurrecting the national bank (established during Washington's administration under Hamilton's guidance, and then much reduced in influence under Jefferson)

The plan held promise. Recognizing this, even former critics of the president—Henry Clay and John C. Calhoun—rallied behind it. House Speaker **Henry Clay** began to promote it as the **American System.**

As Clay explained it, the American System would unite the nation's economic interests. An increasingly industrial North would produce the manufactured goods that farmers in the South and West would buy. Meanwhile, a predominantly agricultural South and West would produce most of the grain, meat, and cotton needed in the North. A nationally accepted currency and improved transportation network would facilitate the exchange of goods. With each part of the country sustaining the other, Americans would finally be economically independent of Britain and other European nations. **E**

MAIN IDEA

Summarizing
E What was the intention of the American System?

ERIE CANAL AND OTHER INTERNAL IMPROVEMENTS For people in different regions to do business with one another and for the economy to grow, they had to communicate, travel, and transport goods. The first steam locomotive in the United States was built in 1825. Railroads offered several advantages over existing modes of transport; they were fast, able to cross almost any terrain, and possible to operate in severe weather. Most transportation at this time, however, was still accomplished using roads and canals. Eventually, better roads and canals would lower costs. But in the short run, they would cost money.

Many states built turnpikes, which paid for themselves through the collection of tolls paid by users who, literally, turned a pike (or spiked pole) to continue their journey along the road. At the same time the federal government experimented with funding highways, which would connect different regions by land. Construction of the **National Road** began in 1811. By 1838 the new road extended from Cumberland, Maryland, to Vandalia, Illinois.

One of the most impressive projects, the **Erie Canal,** stretched 363 miles. The "Big Ditch," as it was called, took eight years to dig, and by 1825 had linked the Hudson River to Lake Erie—or, in effect, the Atlantic Ocean to the Great Lakes. Just 12 years after it had opened, canal tolls had completely paid for its construction. New York City had become the dominant port in the country. In their rush to make similar profits, other states built over 3,000 miles of canals by 1837.

Major Roads, Canals, and Railroads, 1840

hmhsocialstudies.com INTERACTIVE MAP

Road
Canal
Railroad
National Road

0   150   300 miles
0   150   300 kilometers

GEOGRAPHY SKILLBUILDER
1. **Movement** Were roads or canals a more powerful factor in unifying the United States in the first half of the 1800s?
2. **Region** Which region had the heaviest concentration of roads, canals, and railroads? Why?

Balancing Nationalism and Sectionalism **217**

TARIFFS AND THE NATIONAL BANK Why were the tariffs on imports proposed by Madison and promoted by Clay necessary? Ever since the end of the War of 1812, British goods such as iron and textiles—stockpiled during the war—were sold far below the cost of American-made merchandise. Consequently, few bought the more expensive American products. Placing a tariff on imports would increase the cost of foreign goods and thereby eliminate their price advantage. Moreover, tariff revenues would help pay for internal improvements, such as roads, canals, and lighthouses. For these reasons, President James Madison proposed the **Tariff of 1816.**

Most Northeasterners welcomed protective tariffs with relief. However, people in the South and West, whose livelihoods did not depend on manufacturing, were not as eager to tax European imports. They resented any government intervention that would make goods more expensive. Nevertheless, Clay, who was from the West (Kentucky), and Calhoun, a Southerner from South Carolina, managed to sway congressmen from their regions to approve the Tariff of 1816 in the national interest.

Attitudes toward the proposed Second Bank of the United States (BUS) were less divided. Most leaders agreed that a national bank would benefit all. The Second Bank would make available a currency guaranteed to be accepted nationwide, thus making it easier for people in different regions to do business with one another. In 1816, Congress chartered the Second Bank of the United States for a 20-year period.

People were pleased with the way the country was developing. In 1816, they elected James Monroe of Virginia as president. Soon after his inauguration in 1817, Monroe took a goodwill tour of New England, receiving a warm welcome in Boston. The idea of a Republican from Virginia being welcomed in this northern Federalist stronghold impressed the nation. The Boston *Columbian Centinel* declared that Americans had entered an "Era of Good Feelings."

SECTION 1 ASSESSMENT

1. TERMS & NAMES For each term or name, write a sentence explaining its significance.

- Eli Whitney
- interchangeable parts
- mass production
- Industrial Revolution
- cotton gin
- Henry Clay
- American System
- National Road
- Erie Canal
- Tariff of 1816

MAIN IDEA

2. TAKING NOTES

In a two-column chart like the one shown, describe the economic systems of the North and the South with regard to both agriculture and manufacturing.

Economies	
North	**South**
Agriculture	Agriculture
Manufacturing	Manufacturing

CRITICAL THINKING

3. ANALYZING EFFECTS

What shifts in population might be attributed to advances in technology and changes in regional economies during America's Industrial Revolution? Support your answer with examples from the text.

Think About:

- the industrialization of New England
- agricultural changes in the South
- improvements in internal transportation systems

4. SYNTHESIZING

How was the American System expected to unite the nation's economic interests? Provide several examples.

5. PREDICTING EFFECTS

Do you think the invention of the railroad would hasten or slow the construction of new roads and canals? Why?

PI 1.1

CC Unit 2.I.F.2   CC Unit 2.I.F.4.e
CC Unit 2.II.A.2   CC Unit 2.II.B.3
CC Unit 2.II.C.2   CC Unit 2.II.C.4

Nationalism at Center Stage

MAIN IDEA	WHY IT MATTERS NOW	Terms & Names
Nationalism exerted a strong influence in the courts, foreign affairs, and westward expansion in the early 1800s.	Nationalism continues to affect such decisions as whether or not we should involve the country in foreign conflicts and what limits can be placed on business, communications, and other trade.	• *McCulloch* v. *Maryland* • John Quincy Adams • nationalism • Adams-Onís Treaty • Monroe Doctrine • Missouri Compromise

One American's Story

hmhsocialstudies.com
TAKING NOTES
Use the graphic organizer online to take notes about how nationalism influenced the United States.

In 1807 Robert Fulton's boat, the *Clermont*, propelled by a steam engine, cruised the 150 miles up the Hudson River from New York City to Albany in 32 hours. This successful demonstration marked the beginning of the steamboat era. Another one of Fulton's boats was so luxurious that it had a wood-paneled dining room and private bedrooms. Fulton posted regulations on his opulent steamboats.

Like Fulton's *Clermont*, the *Telegraph* was a 19th-century steamboat.

★ A PERSONAL VOICE ROBERT FULTON

" As the steamboat has been fitted up in an elegant style, order is necessary to keep it so; gentlemen will therefore please to observe cleanliness, and a reasonable attention not to injure the furniture; for this purpose no one must sit on a table under the penalty of half a dollar each time, and every breakage of tables, chairs, sofas, or windows, tearing of curtains, or injury of any kind must be paid for before leaving the boat. "

—quoted in *Steamboats Come True: American Inventors in Action*

Steamboats carried freight as well as passengers, and this new method of transportation spread quickly to the Ohio and Mississippi rivers. For the next 20 years, the steamboat was one factor that helped to unite the economic life of the North and the South. It thus contributed to the growing national spirit.

The Supreme Court Boosts National Power

In 1808, Robert Fulton and Robert Livingston received a charter from the New York legislature that gave them the exclusive right to run steamboats on rivers in that state. They profited from this state charter, which granted them a monopoly (exclusive legal control of a commercial activity), by charging steamboat operators for licenses to operate on various stretches of river.

One of these operators was Aaron Ogden. Ogden was licensed by Fulton and Livingston under the laws of New York State to run his steamship line between New York and New Jersey. Ogden believed that he was the only operator legally entitled to run a steamboat service on that stretch of the Hudson. Then Thomas Gibbons began to run a similar service in the same area, claiming that he was entitled to do so according to federal law. Ogden took Gibbons to court to stop him. However, in 1824 the Supreme Court ruled that interstate commerce could be regulated only by the federal government. In other words, Ogden's "exclusive" right granted by New York was not legal, since the route crossed state lines.

More important, by clarifying that Congress had authority over interstate commerce, the *Gibbons* v. *Ogden* decision helped to ensure that the federal government has the power to regulate just about everything that crosses state lines. In modern life, that authority means everything from air traffic to television and radio waves to interstate cellular communications. In addition, this decision led to future rulings favoring competition over monopolies. In this way, nationalism exerted a strong influence on the legal system.

STRENGTHENING GOVERNMENT ECONOMIC CONTROL

In *McCulloch v. Maryland* (1819), as in *Gibbons* v. *Ogden*, Chief Justice John Marshall had also guided the Supreme Court to a ruling that strengthened the federal government's control over the economy. The Court's ruling also supported the national government over the state governments.

Maryland had levied a heavy tax on the local branch of the Bank of the United States, hoping to make it fail. Marshall declared that if this were allowed, states would in effect be overturning laws passed by Congress. The Chief Justice denied the right of Maryland to tax the Bank, stating that "the power to tax is the power to destroy." He declared the Bank of the United States constitutional.

LIMITING STATE POWERS

Under Chief Justice Marshall, the Supreme Court made several rulings that blocked state interference in business and commerce—even when this meant overturning state law. In *Fletcher* v. *Peck* (1810), for example, the Court nullified a Georgia law that had violated individuals' constitutional right to enter into contracts. In the *Dartmouth College* v. *Woodward* (1819) decision, the Court declared that the state of New Hampshire could not revise the original charter it had granted to the college's trustees in colonial times. A charter was a contract, the Court said, and the Constitution did not permit states to interfere with contracts. Ⓐ

▲
John Marshall was appointed Chief Justice of the Supreme Court in 1801 by Federalist President John Adams.

MAIN IDEA

Summarizing
Ⓐ In what ways did the Supreme Court boost federal power?

Nationalism Shapes Foreign Policy

Chief Justice Marshall guided the Supreme Court to decisions that increased the power of the federal government over the state government. At the same time, Secretary of State **John Quincy Adams** established foreign policy guided by **nationalism**—the belief that national interests should be placed ahead of regional concerns or the interests of other countries.

TERRITORY AND BOUNDARIES

Working under President James Monroe, Adams prioritized the security of the nation and expansion of its territory. To further these interests, Adams worked out a treaty with Great Britain to reduce the Great Lakes fleets of both countries to only a few military vessels. The Rush-Bagot

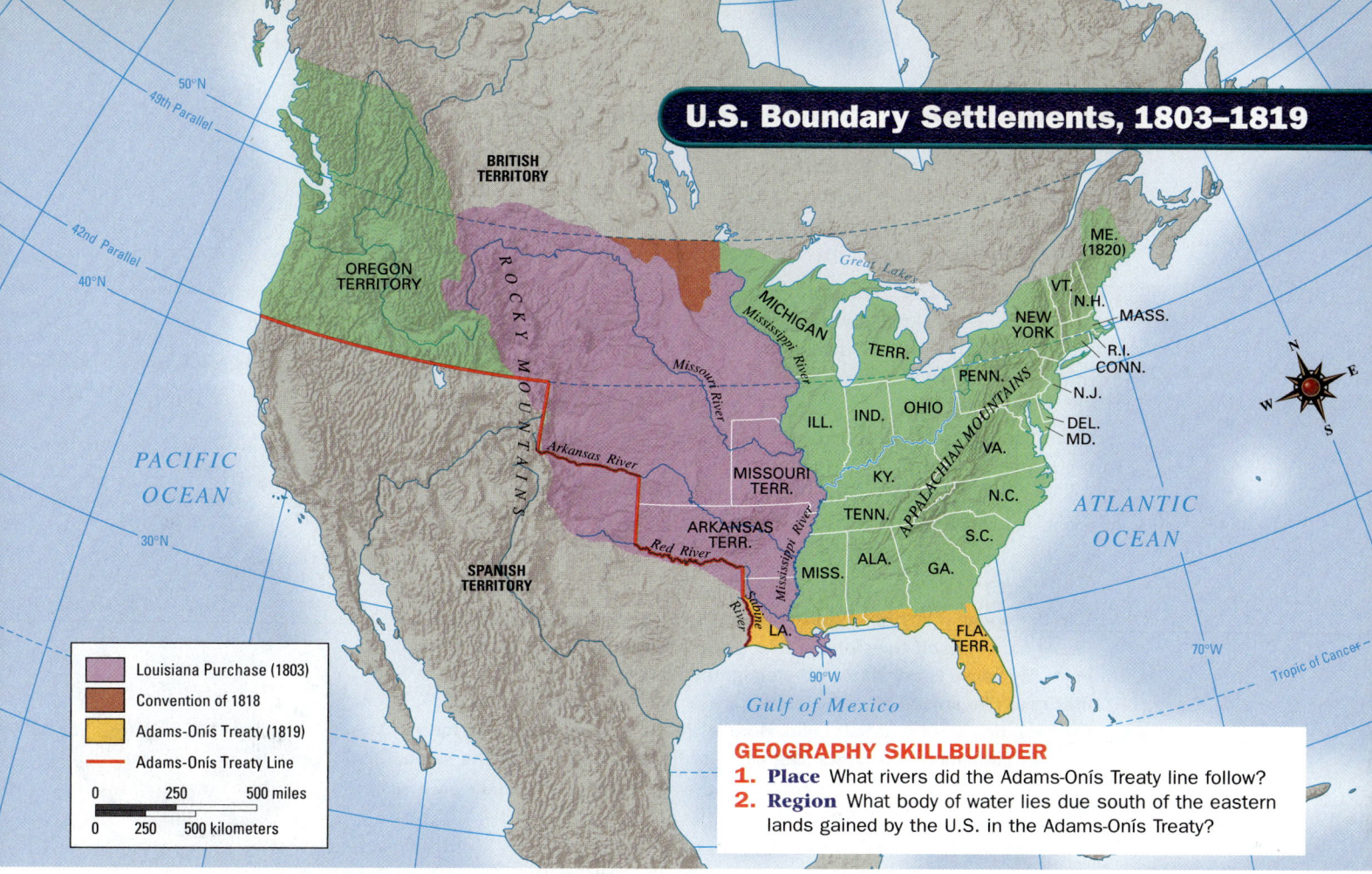

BRITISH TERRITORY

OREGON TERRITORY

ROCKY MOUNTAINS

PACIFIC OCEAN

SPANISH TERRITORY

Arkansas River

Red River

Missouri River

Mississippi River

Sabine River

Great Lakes

MICHIGAN TERR.

ME. (1820)

VT. N.H.

NEW YORK

MASS.

R.I. CONN.

PENN.

N.J.

ILL. IND. OHIO

DEL. MD.

VA.

APPALACHIAN MOUNTAINS

MISSOURI TERR.

KY.

ARKANSAS TERR.

TENN.

N.C.

S.C.

MISS. ALA. GA.

LA.

FLA. TERR.

ATLANTIC OCEAN

Gulf of Mexico

Tropic of Cancer

Louisiana Purchase (1803)
Convention of 1818
Adams-Onís Treaty (1819)
Adams-Onís Treaty Line

0   250   500 miles
0   250   500 kilometers

GEOGRAPHY SKILLBUILDER
1. **Place** What rivers did the Adams-Onís Treaty line follow?
2. **Region** What body of water lies due south of the eastern lands gained by the U.S. in the Adams-Onís Treaty?

Treaty (1817) eventually led the United States and Canada to completely demilitarize their common border. Adams also arranged the Convention of 1818, which fixed the U.S. border at the 49th parallel up to the Rocky Mountains. Finally, he reached a compromise with Britain to jointly occupy the Oregon Territory, the territory west of the Rockies, for ten years.

There remained one outstanding piece of business. Most Americans assumed that Spanish Florida would eventually become part of the United States. In 1819, too weak to police its New World territories, Spain ceded Florida to the United States in the **Adams-Onís Treaty** and gave up its claims to the Oregon Territory.

THE MONROE DOCTRINE After Spain and Portugal defeated Napoleon in 1815, these European powers wanted to reclaim their former colonies in Latin America. Meanwhile, the Russians, who had been in Alaska since 1784, were establishing trading posts in what is now California.

With Spain and Portugal trying to move back into their old colonial areas, and with Russia pushing in from the northwest, the United States knew it had to do something. Many Americans were interested in acquiring northern Mexico and the Spanish colony of Cuba. Moreover, the Russian action posed a threat to American trade with China, which brought huge profits.

MAIN IDEA

Synthesizing

B How did the foreign policies of John Quincy Adams and James Monroe serve national interests?

Hence, in his 1823 message to Congress, President Monroe warned all outside powers not to interfere with affairs in the Western Hemisphere. They should not attempt to create new colonies, he said, or try to overthrow the newly independent republics in the hemisphere. The United States would consider such action "dangerous to our peace and safety." At the same time, the United States would not involve itself in European affairs or interfere with existing colonies in the Western Hemisphere. These principles became known as the **Monroe Doctrine**. **B**

Nationalism Pushes America West

While Presidents Adams and Monroe established policies that expanded U.S. territory, American settlers pushed into the Northwest Territory (present-day Ohio, Indiana, Illinois, Wisconsin, and Michigan), felling forests, turning lush prairies into farms and waterfronts into city centers.

EXPANSION TO THE WEST While some settlers went west to escape debts or even the law, most pushed westward in search of economic gain—for land was not only plentiful and fertile but cheap. There were also social gains to be made. For example, one could change occupations more easily on the frontier. Jim Beckwourth (1798–1867), the son of a white man and an African-American woman, ventured westward with a fur-trading expedition in 1823. He lived among the Crow, who gave him the name "Bloody Arm" because of his skill as a fighter. Later he served as an Army scout. In California in 1850, he decided to settle down and become a rancher, yet this was not the last of his occupations.

★ **A PERSONAL VOICE** JIM BECKWOURTH

"In the spring of 1852 I established myself in Beckwourth Valley, and finally found myself transformed into a hotel-keeper and chief of a trading-post. My house is considered the emigrant's landing-place, as it is the first ranch he arrives at in the golden state, and is the only house between this point and Salt Lake. Here is a valley two hundred and forty miles in circumference, containing some of the choicest land in the world."

—quoted in *The Life and Adventures of James P. Beckwourth*

Jim Beckwourth

THE MISSOURI COMPROMISE When a territory's population reached about 60,000, the people of the territory could petition the Union for admission, draft a state constitution, elect representatives, and become part of the United States, once Congress approved. In 1819, however, when settlers in Missouri requested admission into the Union, conflict arose. In Missouri, the new spirit of nationalism was challenged by an issue that had previously confronted the framers of the Constitution. That issue was the question of slavery.

Until 1818, the United States had consisted of ten free and ten slave states. The government admitted Illinois as the eleventh free state in 1818. Southerners then expected that Missouri would become the eleventh slave state, thereby maintaining the balance between free states and slave states in Congress. However, New York Congressman James Tallmadge amended the Missouri statehood bill to require Missouri to gradually free its slaves, a bill that passed the House. Southerners, perceiving a threat to their power, blocked the bill's passage in the Senate. As arguments raged, Alabama was then admitted to the Union as a slave state. With 11 free to 11 slave states, Missouri's status became crucial to the delicate balance.

The slaveholding states claimed that Northerners were trying to end slavery. Northerners accused Southerners of plotting to extend the institution into new territories. Hostilities became so intense that at times people on both sides even mentioned civil war and the end of the Union. Indeed, the issues that came to light during these debates foreshadowed the war to come. "We have the wolf by the ears," wrote the aging Thomas Jefferson of this crisis, "and we can neither hold him, nor safely let him go."

Under the leadership of Henry Clay, however, Congress managed to temporarily resolve the crisis with a series of agreements collectively called the **Missouri Compromise.** Maine was admitted as a free state and Missouri as a slave state, thus preserving the sectional balance in the Senate. The rest of the Louisiana Territory was split into two spheres of interest, one for slaveholders and one for free settlers. The dividing line was set at 36° 30´ north latitude. South

The Missouri Compromise, 1820–1821

MAINE Free state, 1820

BRITISH TERRITORY

OREGON TERRITORY

UNORGANIZED TERRITORY

MICHIGAN TERRITORY

VT. N.H. MASS. R.I. CONN.

NEW YORK

PENN.

N.J. DEL. MD.

NEW SPAIN (Mexico)

ILL. IND. OHIO

VA.

ATLANTIC OCEAN

PACIFIC OCEAN

Slave state, 1821

MISSOURI

KY.

N.C.

36°30′N Missouri Compromise Line

TENN.

ARKANSAS TERRITORY

S.C.

MISS. ALA. GA.

LA.

FLORIDA TERRITORY

Gulf of Mexico

40°N

120°W

Legend:
- Free states and territories
- Closed to slavery by Missouri Compromise
- Slave states and territories
- Open to slavery by Missouri Compromise
- Disputed by U.S. and Great Britain

0   200   400 miles
0   200   400 kilometers

GEOGRAPHY SKILLBUILDER

1. **Place** Which two slave states bordered the free state of Illinois?
2. **Region** In which two territories was slavery permitted?

of the line, slavery was legal. North of the line—except in Missouri—slavery was banned. Thomas Jefferson was among those who feared for the Union's future after the Missouri Compromise. His words would prove prophetic.

★ A PERSONAL VOICE THOMAS JEFFERSON

"**This momentous question, like a firebell in the night, awakened and filled me with terror. I considered it at once as the knell of the Union. It is hushed, indeed, for the moment. But this is a reprieve only, not a final sentence.**"

—letter to John Holmes, April 22, 1820

President Monroe signed the Missouri Compromise in 1820. For a generation, the problem of slavery in federal territories seemed settled.

SECTION 2 ASSESSMENT

1. **TERMS & NAMES** For each term or name, write a sentence explaining its significance.
   - *McCulloch* v. *Maryland*
   - **John Quincy Adams**
   - **nationalism**
   - **Adams-Onís Treaty**
   - **Monroe Doctrine**
   - **Missouri Compromise**

MAIN IDEA

2. **TAKING NOTES**
   In a diagram like the one shown, write historical examples that illustrate the influence of nationalism.

Influence of Nationalism

Nation's Courts — examples
Foreign Affairs — examples
Westward Expansion — examples

CRITICAL THINKING

3. **HYPOTHESIZING**
   What short- and long-term goals might President Monroe have had in mind when he formulated the Monroe Doctrine in 1823? Support your answer. **Think About:**
   - European nations' presence in the Western Hemisphere
   - the influence of nationalism on foreign policy
   - the nation's westward expansion

4. **SYNTHESIZING**
   What agreements did Congress reach that are regarded collectively as the Missouri Compromise? Why were they important at the time?

5. **EVALUATING**
   From what you know about the Missouri Compromise and the controversy that preceded it, do you think the new spirit of nationalism in the United States was strong or fragile? Support your opinion.

The Age of Jackson

MAIN IDEA	WHY IT MATTERS NOW	Terms & Names
Andrew Jackson's policies spoke for the common people but violated Native American rights.	The effects of land losses and persecution faced by Native Americans in the 1800s continue to be reflected in their legal struggles today.	• Andrew Jackson • Democratic-Republican Party • spoils system • Indian Removal Act • Trail of Tears

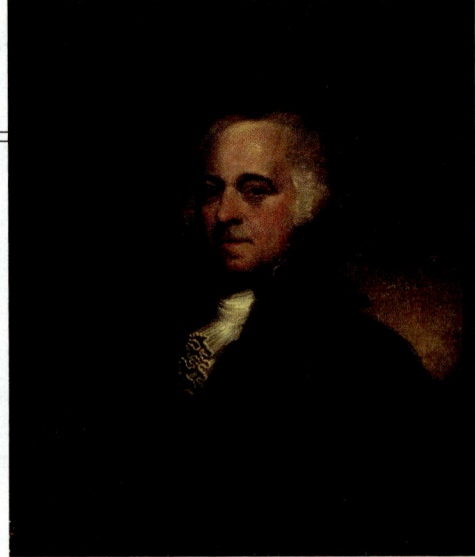

▲
This Gilbert Stuart portrait of John Adams was begun in 1798, when Adams was 63.

One American's Story

hmhsocialstudies.com
TAKING NOTES

Use the graphic organizer online to take notes on key events during the Age of Jackson.

The era of the leaders who had founded the nation passed with Adams's and Jefferson's deaths in 1826. During an extended conversation with John Adams in 1776, Thomas Jefferson had tried to convince him to draft the Declaration of Independence.

A PERSONAL VOICE JOHN ADAMS

" [Adams] said 'I will not.' . . .
'What can be your reasons?'
'Reason first—You are a Virginian, and a Virginian ought to appear at the head of this business. Reason second—I am obnoxious, suspected, and unpopular. You are very much otherwise. Reason third—You can write ten times better than I can.'
'Well,' said Jefferson, 'if you are decided, I will do as well as I can.' "

—quoted in *John Adams: A Biography in His Own Words*

Thus began a mutual regard that would last for 50 years. On July 4, 1826, exactly 50 years after the delegates approved the Declaration of Independence, both men died. Now the presidency belonged to another generation.

Expanding Democracy Changes Politics

When John Adams died, his son John Quincy Adams was in the second year of his single term as president. He had succeeded James Monroe as president but was not effective as the nation's chief executive. The principal reason was **Andrew Jackson,** his chief political opponent.

TENSION BETWEEN ADAMS AND JACKSON In the election of 1824, Andrew Jackson won the popular vote but lacked the majority of electoral votes. The House of Representatives had to decide the outcome, since no candidate had received a majority of the votes of the electoral college.

Because of his power in the House, Henry Clay could swing the election either way. Clay disliked Jackson personally and mistrusted his lack of political experience. "I cannot believe," Clay commented, "that killing twenty-five hundred Englishmen at New Orleans qualifies [him] for the various difficult and complicated duties of [the presidency]." Adams, on the other hand, agreed with Clay's American System. In the end, Adams was elected president by a majority of the states represented in the House.

Jacksonians, or followers of Jackson, accused Adams of stealing the presidency. When Adams appointed Clay secretary of state, the Jacksonians claimed that Adams had struck a corrupt bargain. The Jacksonians left the Republican Party to form the **Democratic-Republican Party** (forerunner of today's Democratic Party) and did whatever they could to sabotage Adams's policies.

DEMOCRACY AND CITIZENSHIP During Adams's presidency, most states eased the voting requirements, thereby enlarging the voting population. Fewer states now had property qualifications for voting. In the presidential election of 1824, approximately 350,000 white males voted. In 1828, over three times that number voted, and their votes helped Andrew Jackson. However, certain groups still lacked political power. Free African Americans and women did not enjoy the political freedoms of white males. **A**

MAIN IDEA

Predicting Effects
A How might reducing property requirements for voting affect political campaigns?

Background
The Battle of New Orleans in 1815 made Jackson a national hero. The British attacked Jackson's forces at New Orleans in January 1815. American riflemen mowed down advancing British forces. American casualties totaled 71, compared to Britain's 2,000.

Jackson's New Presidential Style

The expansion of voting rights meant that candidates had to be able to speak to the concerns of ordinary people. Andrew Jackson had this common touch.

JACKSON'S APPEAL TO THE COMMON CITIZEN During the 1828 campaign, Jackson characterized Adams as an intellectual elitist and, by contrast, portrayed himself as a man of humble origins—though he was actually a wealthy plantation owner. Jackson won the election by a landslide. He was so popular that record numbers of people came to Washington to see "Old Hickory" inaugurated.

President-elect Andrew Jackson on his way to Washington, D.C., to be inaugurated in 1829

Mrs. Samuel Harrison Smith described the scene.

HISTORY

VIDEO
Jackson's
Personality and
Legacy

hmhsocialstudies.com

A PERSONAL VOICE MRS. SAMUEL HARRISON SMITH

" The President, after having been *literally* nearly pressed to death and almost suffocated and torn to pieces by the people in their eagerness to shake hands with Old Hickory [Jackson], had retreated through the back way, or south front, and had escaped to his lodgings at Gadsby's. Cut glass and china to the amount of several thousand dollars had been broken in the struggle to get the refreshments. . . . Ladies fainted, men were seen with bloody noses, and such a scene of confusion took place as is impossible to describe; those who got in could not get out by the door again but had to scramble out of windows. "

—from a letter dated March 1829

JACKSON'S SPOILS SYSTEM If Jackson knew how to inspire loyalty and enthusiasm during a campaign, he also knew how to use the powers of the presidency upon gaining office. He announced that his appointees to federal jobs would serve a maximum of four-year terms. Unless there was a regular turnover of personnel, he declared, officeholders would become inefficient and corrupt.

Jackson's administration practiced the **spoils system**—so called from the saying "To the victor belong the spoils of the enemy"—in which incoming officials throw out former appointees and replace them with their own friends. He fired nearly 10 percent of the federal employees, most of them holdovers from the Adams administration, and gave their jobs to loyal Jacksonians. Jackson's friends also became his primary advisers, dubbed his "kitchen cabinet" because they supposedly slipped into the White House through the kitchen. **B**

KEY PLAYER

ANDREW JACKSON
1767–1845

Andrew Jackson thought of himself as a man of the people. The son of Scots-Irish immigrants, he had been born in poverty in the Carolinas. He was the first president since George Washington without a college education.

At the time of his election at the age of 61, however, Jackson had built a highly successful career. He had worked in law, politics, land speculation, cotton planting, and soldiering. Victory at New Orleans in the War of 1812 had made him a hero. His Tennessee home, the Hermitage, was a mansion. Anyone who owned more than a hundred slaves, as Jackson did, was wealthy.

Underlying Jackson's iron will was a fiery temper. He survived several duels, one of which left a bullet lodged near his heart and another of which left his opponent dead. His ire, however, was most often reserved for special-interest groups and those whose power came from privilege.

MAIN IDEA

Summarizing
B What is the spoils system?

Removal of Native Americans

Since the 1600s, white settlers had held one of two attitudes toward Native Americans. Some whites favored the displacement and dispossession of all Native Americans. Others wished to convert Native Americans to Christianity, turn them into farmers, and absorb them into the white culture.

Since the end of the War of 1812, some Southeastern tribes—the Cherokee, Choctaw, Seminole, Creek, and Chickasaw—had begun to adopt the European culture of their white neighbors. These "five civilized tribes," as they were called by whites, occupied large areas in Georgia, North and South Carolina, Alabama, Mississippi, and Tennessee. Many white planters and miners wanted that land.

INDIAN REMOVAL ACT OF 1830 Jackson thought that assimilation could not work. Another possibility—allowing Native Americans to live in their original areas—would have required too many troops to keep the areas free of white settlers. Jackson believed that the only solution was to move the Native Americans from their lands to areas farther west.

Congress passed the **Indian Removal Act** in 1830. Under this law, the federal government funded negotiation of treaties that would force the Native Americans to move west.

Effects of the Indian Removal Act, 1830s–1840s

↗ hmhsocialstudies.com **INTERACTIVE MAP**

Many Cherokee in the western territory, like the woman pictured here, taught their children at home in order to keep the Cherokee language and customs alive.

Sequoyah, or George Guess, devised the Cherokee alphabet in 1821 to help preserve the culture of the Cherokee Nation against the growing threat of American expansion. ▶

By 1840, about 16,000 Cherokee had been forcibly moved 800 miles west on routes afterward called the Trail of Tears. Because of the suffering they endured from cold, hunger, and diseases such as tuberculosis, smallpox, and cholera, one-fourth died.

Nearly 15,000 Creek, many in manacles and chains, were moved from Alabama and Georgia to the Canadian River in Indian Territory in 1835.

By 1834, about 14,000 Choctaw had relocated along the Red River under the terms of the Indian Removal Act of 1830. About 7,000 remained in Mississippi.

Map labels

WISCONSIN TERRITORY
MICHIGAN
Ottawa
Sauk and Fox
Potawatomi
Miami
INDIANA
ILLINOIS
Mississippi River
Lake Michigan
Lake Huron
Lake Erie
MAINE
VT.
PENNSYLVANIA
NEW JERSEY
DELAWARE
MARYLAND
Delaware
OHIO
Shawnee and Seneca
VIRGINIA
KENTUCKY
Ohio River
MISSOURI
Arkansas River
INDIAN TERRITORY
Canadian River
ARKANSAS
Chickasaw
MISSISSIPPI
Choctaw
Red River
Tennessee River
TENNESSEE
NORTH CAROLINA
SOUTH CAROLINA
Cherokee
GEORGIA
ALABAMA
Creek
REPUBLIC OF TEXAS (after 1836)
LOUISIANA
FLORIDA TERRITORY
Seminole
Gulf of Mexico
ATLANTIC OCEAN
MEXICO
40°N
30°N
90°W
80°W

Legend

Color	Tribe
(red arrows)	Cherokee
(yellow arrows)	Chickasaw
(teal arrows)	Choctaw
(purple arrows)	Creek
(orange arrows)	Seminole
(brown arrows)	Other tribes

0   100   200 miles
0   100   200 kilometers

▲ Detail from "Trail of Tears," a painting by Robert Lindeux

GEOGRAPHY SKILLBUILDER

1. **Place** Where were most of the tribes moved?
2. **Movement** What do you think were the long-term effects of this removal on Native Americans?

About 90 treaties were signed. For Jackson, the removal policy was "not only liberal, but generous," but his arguments were mainly based on the rights of states to govern within their own boundaries. **C**

In 1830, Jackson pressured the Choctaw to sign a treaty that required them to move from Mississippi. In 1831, he ordered U.S. troops to forcibly remove the Sauk and Fox from their lands in Illinois and Missouri. In 1832, he forced the Chickasaw to leave their lands in Alabama and Mississippi.

THE CHEROKEE FIGHT BACK Meanwhile, the Cherokee Nation tried to win just treatment through the U.S. legal system. Chief Justice John Marshall refused to rule on the first case the Cherokee brought against Georgia, though, because in his view the Cherokee Nation had no federal standing; it was neither a foreign nation nor a state, but rather a "domestic dependent nation." Undaunted, the Cherokee teamed up with Samuel Austin Worcester, a missionary who had been jailed for teaching Indians without a state license. The Cherokee knew the Court would have to recognize a citizen's right to be heard.

In *Worcester* v. *Georgia* (1832), the Cherokee Nation finally won recognition as a distinct political community. The Court ruled that Georgia was not entitled to regulate the Cherokee nor to invade their lands. Jackson refused to abide by the Supreme Court decision, saying: "John Marshall has made his decision; now let him enforce it."

Cherokee leader John Ross still tried to fight the state in the courts, but other Cherokee began to promote relocation. In 1835, federal agents declared the

VIDEO
Jackson v. the Cherokee and South Carolina

hmhsocialstudies.com

MAIN IDEA

Analyzing Issues

C Why did Jackson think that Native Americans should be moved west of the Mississippi?

POINT

"The Indian Removal Act of 1830 was a terrible injustice."

John Marshall, chief justice of the Supreme Court, believed that the Cherokee had "an unquestionable right" to their territory "until title should be extinguished by voluntary cession to the United States."

In their protest against the Indian Removal Act, the Cherokee people referred to past treaties with the federal government and stated, "We have a perfect and original right to remain without interruption and molestation." Congressman Edward Everett of Massachusetts described Indian removal as "inflicting the pains of banishment from their native land on seventy or eighty thousand human beings." Rejecting claims that the removal was necessary to protect the Indians against white settlers, Everett demanded, "What other power has the Executive over a treaty or law, but to enforce it?"

In their 1832 protest against the Act, the Creek pointedly asked, "Can [our white brethren] exempt us from intrusion in our promised borders, if they are incompetent to our protection where we are?"

COUNTERPOINT

"The Indian Removal Act of 1830 was unfortunate but necessary."

Blame for the displacement of Native Americans was sometimes placed on the states or on the law, which, it was argued, all people must obey. As Secretary of War John Eaton explained to the Creek of Alabama: "It is not your Great Father who does this; but the laws of the Country, which he and every one of his people is bound to regard."

President Andrew Jackson contended that the Indian Removal Act would put an end to "all possible danger of collision between the authorities of the General and State Governments on account of the Indians."

Jackson also claimed that the Indian Removal Act would protect Native Americans against further removal from their lands. He found support for his point of view from Secretary of War Lewis Cass, who defended "the progress of civilization and improvement." Cass wished "that the aboriginal population had accommodated themselves to the inevitable change of their condition," but asserted that "such a wish is vain."

THINKING CRITICALLY

1. **CONNECT TO HISTORY** **Analyzing Primary Sources**
   On what central issue regarding the Indian Removal Act did Jackson and Native American tribes disagree? Explain your opinion of the Act.

    SEE SKILLBUILDER HANDBOOK, PAGE R22.

2. **CONNECT TO TODAY** **Analyzing Issues** Research how one of the five tribes was affected by the Indian Removal Act. Write a proposal for how the U.S. government might today make reparations to the group for land losses in the 19th century.

minority who favored relocation the true representatives of the Cherokee Nation and promptly had them sign the Treaty of New Echota. This treaty gave the last eight million acres of Cherokee land to the federal government in exchange for approximately $5 million and land "west of the Mississippi." The signing of this treaty marked the beginning of the Cherokee exodus. However, when by 1838 nearly 20,000 Cherokee still remained in the East, President Martin Van Buren (Jackson's successor) ordered their forced removal. U.S. Army troops under the command of General Winfield Scott rounded up the Cherokee and drove them into camps to await the journey. **D**

MAIN IDEA

Analyzing Effects

D How did the Cherokee react to the Indian Removal Act?

THE TRAIL OF TEARS Beginning in October and November of 1838, the Cherokee were sent off in groups of about 1,000 each on the long journey. The 800-mile trip was made partly by steamboat and railroad but mostly on foot. As the winter came on, more and more of the Cherokee died en route.

A PERSONAL VOICE TRAIL OF TEARS SURVIVOR

" Children cry and many men cry, and all look sad like when friends die, but they say nothing and just put heads down and keep on go towards West. Many days pass and people die very much."

—quoted in *From the Heart: Voices of the American Indian*

Along the way, government officials stole the Cherokee's money, while outlaws made off with their livestock. The Cherokee buried more than a quarter of their people along what came to be known as the **Trail of Tears.** When they reached their final destination, they ended up on land far inferior to that which they had been forced to leave.

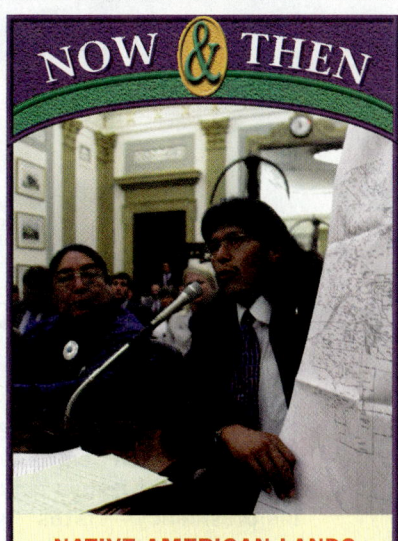

NOW & THEN

NATIVE AMERICAN LANDS

Native Americans continue to struggle for recognition of land rights.

In the 2002 picture above, Native American leaders testify during a Congressional hearing on the protection of sacred sites. Many of these sites are threatened by development, pollution, or vandalism.

Other present-day Native Americans have won recognition of their land claims. Over the past 30 years, the federal government has settled property disputes with several tribes in Connecticut, Maine, and other states and has provided them with funds to purchase ancestral lands.

SECTION 3 ASSESSMENT

1. **TERMS & NAMES** For each term or name, write a sentence explaining its significance.
   - **Andrew Jackson**
   - **Democratic-Republican Party**
   - **spoils system**
   - **Indian Removal Act**
   - **Trail of Tears**

MAIN IDEA

2. **TAKING NOTES**
   Create a time line like the one shown here, listing key events relating to Jackson's political career.

   Do you think Jackson was an effective leader? Why or why not?

CRITICAL THINKING

3. **EVALUATING**
   If you were a U.S. citizen voting in the 1828 presidential election, would you cast your ballot for John Quincy Adams or Andrew Jackson? Support your choice. **Think About:**
   - each candidate's background and political experience
   - each candidate's views of the national bank and tariffs
   - where you might live—the South, the West, or New England

4. **ANALYZING EVENTS**
   In your opinion, what factors set the stage for the Indian Removal Act? Support your answer. **Think About:**
   - the attitude of white settlers toward Native Americans
   - Jackson's justification of the Indian Removal Act
   - why Jackson was able to defy the Supreme Court's ruling in *Worcester* v. *Georgia*

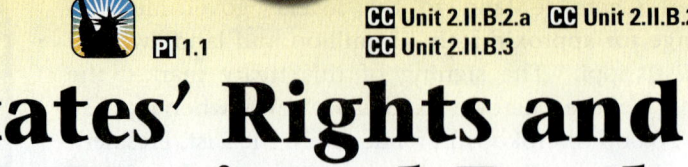

States' Rights and the National Bank

MAIN IDEA	WHY IT MATTERS NOW	Terms & Names
Andrew Jackson confronted two important issues during his presidency—states' rights and a national bank.	The conflict between states' rights and federal government control continues to flare up in such arenas as education, commerce, and law enforcement.	• Daniel Webster • John C. Calhoun • Tariff of Abominations • Bank of the United States • Whig Party • Martin Van Buren • panic of 1837 • William Henry Harrison • John Tyler

One American's Story

On January 26, 1830, Massachusetts senator **Daniel Webster** rose in the Senate and delivered one of the great speeches of American history.

> ★ **A PERSONAL VOICE** DANIEL WEBSTER
>
> "When my eyes shall be turned to behold for the last time the sun in heaven, may I not see him shining on the broken and dishonored fragments of a once glorious Union. . . . Let their last feeble and lingering glance rather behold the gorgeous ensign of the republic . . . bearing for its motto, no such miserable interrogatory as 'What is all this worth?' nor those other words of delusion and folly, 'Liberty first and Union afterwards'; but everywhere, spread all over in characters of living light, . . . that other sentiment, dear to every true American heart—Liberty *and* Union, now and forever, one and inseparable!"
>
> —speech delivered in the Senate on January 26 and 27, 1830

▲ **Daniel Webster defended the federal government's power to make laws that applied to all states in the Union.**

Webster's Reply to Hayne (date unknown), G.P.A. Healy. Courtesy of the Boston Art Commission 2007

hmhsocialstudies.com
TAKING NOTES

Use the graphic organizer online to take notes about key issues during Jackson's presidency.

"Liberty first and Union afterwards" was favored by John C. Calhoun, one of Webster's greatest opponents in the struggle between states' rights and federal authority. The question of how much power the federal—as opposed to the state—government should have came to a head over the issue of tariffs.

A Tariff Raises the States' Rights Issue

When the War of 1812 ended, British manufacturers wanted to destroy their American competitors by flooding the U.S. market with inexpensive goods. In response, Congress in 1816 passed a tariff to protect the infant American industries. The tariff was increased in 1824 and again in 1828.

THE NULLIFICATION THEORY Jackson's vice-president, **John C. Calhoun** of South Carolina, called the 1828 tariff a **Tariff of Abominations,** a "disgusting and loathsome" tariff. As an agricultural region dependent on cotton, the South had to compete in the world market. The high tariff on manufactured goods reduced British exports to the United States and forced the South to buy the more expensive Northern manufactured goods. From the South's point of view, the North was getting rich at the expense of the South. One observer remarked that when Southerners "see the flourishing villages of New England they cry, 'We pay for all this.'"

Calhoun was in an unusual and politically dangerous position. He had long been known as a nationalist spokesman, and he had supported the protective tariff of 1816. Calhoun was building a career as a national statesman, having served under both Adams and Jackson as vice-president. The situation in his home state, however, had made him change his views. South Carolina's economy had failed to recover fully from an economic depression. Cotton prices remained low because planters and their slaves were moving to more fertile lands in Alabama and in the lower Mississippi River valley. Some South Carolinians began to wonder if Calhoun really cared about the needs of his state. He soon showed them that he did.

Calhoun devised a nullification theory, which basically questioned the legality of applying some federal laws in sovereign states. Calhoun's argument was that the United States Constitution was based on a compact among the sovereign states. If the Constitution had been established by 13 sovereign states, he reasoned, then each had the right to nullify, or reject, a federal law that it considered unconstitutional. In 1828 Calhoun wrote down his theory in a document entitled "The South Carolina Exposition," but he did not sign his name to it. Nor did he say what he privately felt. Calhoun believed that if the federal government refused to permit a state to nullify a federal law, the state had the right to withdraw from the Union. **Ⓐ**

KEY PLAYERS

JOHN C. CALHOUN
1782–1850

John Caldwell Calhoun entered national politics in 1811 when he was elected to the House of Representatives. There he was labeled a War Hawk for his support of the War of 1812. As President Monroe's secretary of war starting in 1817, Calhoun improved the army's organization.

This ambitious and handsome man with dark, flashing eyes served as vice-president under two presidents—John Quincy Adams, elected in 1824, and Andrew Jackson, elected in 1828.

Calhoun had a hard and humorless side. He took a tough position on slavery, arguing that it was not only necessary but even good:

"There never has yet existed a wealthy and civilized society in which one portion of the community did not . . . live on the labor of the other."

DANIEL WEBSTER
1782–1852

In New England he was known as the "godlike Daniel." New Hampshire native Daniel Webster actually began his career in favor of states' rights. After moving to Boston, Massachusetts, in 1816, however, his views changed. New England's textile manufacturers needed a strong national government to protect their interests. As a lawyer and a congressman, Webster represented Boston's business interests. He argued several landmark cases before the Supreme Court, including *Gibbons* v. *Ogden*.

Webster was best known for his skill as an orator, but he hungered after the presidency. He ran for the highest office twice, never winning. Late in his career he said:

"I have given my life to law and politics. Law is uncertain and politics is utterly vain."

MAIN IDEA

Summarizing
Ⓐ What was Calhoun's nullification theory?

HAYNE AND WEBSTER DEBATE STATES' RIGHTS The tariff question (and the underlying states' rights issue) was discussed in one of the great debates in American history. In January 1830, visitors to the Senate listened to Senator

Robert Hayne of South Carolina debate Senator Daniel Webster of Massachusetts. Hayne delivered a pointed condemnation of the tariff.

A PERSONAL VOICE SENATOR ROBERT HAYNE

"The measures of the federal government . . . will soon involve the whole South in irretrievable ruin. But even this evil, great as it is, is not the chief ground of our complaints. It is the principle involved in the contest—a principle, which substituting the discretion of Congress for the limitations of the constitution, brings the States and the people to the feet of the federal government, and leaves them nothing they can call their own."

—from a speech to Congress, January 21, 1830

On January 26 Webster replied that he could not conceive of a "middle course, between submission to the laws, when regularly pronounced constitutional, on the one hand, and open resistance, which is revolution, or rebellion, on the other."

Once the debates ended, the people wanted to hear President Jackson's position. On April 13, at a public dinner, he clarified his position in a toast: "Our Union: it must be preserved." Calhoun replied with an equally pointed toast: "The Union, next to our liberty, the most dear; may we all remember that it can only be preserved by respecting the rights of the States and distributing equally the benefit and burden of the Union." The two men would not work together again; in fact, Calhoun resigned the vice-presidency in 1832. Jackson would run for reelection with former secretary of state Martin Van Buren.

South Carolinians wore emblems made from palmetto leaves to show their support for nullification.

SOUTH CAROLINA REBELS The issue of states' rights was finally put to a test in 1832 when Congress passed a tariff law that South Carolina legislators still found unacceptable. They responded by declaring the tariffs of 1828 and 1832 "unauthorized by the Constitution" and "null, void, and no law." Then they threatened to secede, or withdraw, from the Union, if customs officials tried to collect duties.

Jackson was furious. Although himself a Southerner and a slaveholder, he believed that South Carolina's action in declaring a federal law null and void flouted the will of the people as expressed in the U.S. Constitution. He declared South Carolina's actions treasonous and threatened to hang Calhoun and march federal troops into South Carolina to enforce the tariff. To make good on his threats, Jackson next persuaded Congress to pass the Force Bill in 1833. This bill allowed the federal government to use the army and navy against South Carolina if state authorities resisted paying proper duties.

A bloody confrontation seemed inevitable until Henry Clay stepped in. In 1833 the Great Compromiser proposed a tariff bill that would gradually lower duties over a ten-year period. For now, the crisis between states' rights and federal authority was controlled, but the issue would continue to cause conflict in the 1840s and 1850s and would be a major cause of the Civil War. **B**

MAIN IDEA

Contrasting
B What were Jackson's and Calhoun's differing opinions on states' rights versus federal authority?

Jackson Attacks the National Bank

Although Andrew Jackson never did resort to sending troops into South Carolina, he did wage a very personal war on the **Bank of the United States** (BUS). In fact, during the same year he dealt with the South Carolina crisis, 1832, he vetoed the bill to recharter the Bank.

JACKSON OPPOSES THE BANK The Second Bank's 20-year charter was not due to expire until 1836, but Henry Clay and Daniel Webster wanted to introduce the renewal earlier to make it a campaign issue. They thought that Jackson might veto a new charter and, in so doing, lose some of his support. They underestimated, however, both the public's dislike of the BUS and Jackson's political skill.

Jackson and his allies made certain that the general public came to think of the BUS as a privileged institution. Jacksonians did have some powerful facts to support their opinions. Since all federal tax revenues were deposited in the BUS rather than state or private banks, the Second Bank had an unfair advantage over other banks. Furthermore, BUS stockholders, not average American taxpayers, earned the interest from these deposits. A privileged few were making money that should have benefited all the taxpayers. In addition, the bank's president, Nicholas Biddle, often extended loans to congressmen at much lower rates of interest than the bank gave to the average citizen. **C**

PET BANKS In 1832, Jackson told his running mate, Martin Van Buren, that the BUS was a "monster" that corrupted "our statesmen" and wanted "to destroy our republican institution." "The bank, Mr. Van Buren, is trying to kill me, but *I will kill it.*" After Jackson's reelection in 1832, he tried to kill the BUS before its charter ran out in 1836. He appointed a secretary of the treasury who was willing to place all government funds in certain state banks. The banks were called "pet banks" because of their loyalty to the Democratic Party.

In an attempt to save the BUS, Nicholas Biddle decided to have the bank call in—or demand repayment of—loans. He also refused to make new loans. He hoped that these actions would cause a frustrated public to demand the passage of a new bank charter. Businessmen descended on Washington, D.C., to plead

MAIN IDEA

Analyzing Motives

C What were some of Jackson's reasons for opposing the Second Bank of the United States?

HISTORY

VIDEO
Jackson v. the Bank of America

hmhsocialstudies.com

Analyzing *Political Cartoons*

"KING ANDREW THE FIRST"

Andrew Jackson once justified his tendency to place personal prerogative above constitutional law or national policy by stating that "One man with courage makes a majority." His critics replied with accusations of tyranny. The *New York American* condemned Jackson as a "maniac," who would "trample the rights of our people under his feet." The Whig convention of 1834 declared, "your president has become your MONARCH."

Both of those sentiments are reflected in this political cartoon which portrays Jackson as a king. Ancient portraits of kings often depicted them grinding their conquered enemies beneath their heels. Notice that beneath Jackson's feet are the torn pages of the Constitution. Notice, too, that in one hand Jackson is holding a scepter, a symbol of kingly power, while in the other he is holding the veto, a symbol of presidential power.

SKILLBUILDER **Analyzing Political Cartoons**
1. What does this cartoon suggest about Jackson's attitude towards the Constitution?
2. How does this cartoon specifically comment on Jackson's use of presidential power?

 SEE SKILLBUILDER HANDBOOK, PAGE R24.

BORN TO COMMAND.

OF VETO MEMORY.

HAD I BEEN CONSULTED.

KING ANDREW THE FIRST.

with Jackson for help. Jackson firmly told them they were talking to the wrong man. "Go to Nicholas Biddle," he said.

Pressure from financial leaders finally forced Biddle to adopt a more generous loan policy. However, the entire chain of events had by this time cost Biddle much of his backing. In 1836, when its charter expired, the Second Bank of the United States became just another Philadelphia bank. Five years later, it went out of business.

WHIG PARTY FORMS Jackson's tactics and policies had angered many people, including some members of his own Democratic Party. In 1834 the discontented— including Henry Clay, John Quincy Adams, and Daniel Webster—channeled their frustrations into action; they formed a new political party called the **Whig Party.** The Whigs backed the ideals of the American System, as promoted by Henry Clay. Besides a protective tariff, they wanted to use federal money to construct roads and canals to foster the exchange of goods between regions. The Whigs also backed federal control of the banking system and a nationally accepted currency. **D**

MAIN IDEA

Analyzing Causes

D Why was this a good time for the formation of the Whig Party?

Van Buren Deals with Jackson's Legacy

When Jackson announced that he would not run for a third term, the Democrats chose Vice-President **Martin Van Buren** as their candidate. The newly formed Whig Party, which in 1836 was not able to agree on a single candidate, ran three regional candidates against him. With Jackson's support Van Buren won the election easily. Along with the presidency, however, Van Buren inherited the dire consequences of Jackson's bank war and money policies.

JACKSON'S LEGACY Many of Jackson's pet banks—where federal funds had been deposited—were wildcat banks. These banks printed bank notes wildly in excess of the gold and silver they had on deposit, and were doomed to fail when many people attempted to redeem their currency for gold or silver.

Since the notes printed by wildcat banks were nearly worthless, the federal government was left holding the bag when people used them to purchase land from the government. Jackson realized what was happening. He caused the Treasury Department to issue an order that made only gold and silver, called specie, acceptable payment for public land. The order went into effect on August 15, 1836, and sent people rushing to banks to trade paper currency for gold and silver. In turn, many banks, which had limited specie, suspended the redemption of bank notes.

By May 1837, New York banks stopped accepting all paper currency. Other banks soon did the same. In the **panic of 1837,** bank closings and the collapse of the credit system cost many people their savings, bankrupted hundreds of businesses, and put more than a third of the population out of work.

Van Buren tried to help by reducing federal spending, but that caused already declining prices to drop further. Then he tried to set up an independent treasury that would use only gold and silver coin. In 1840 Congress established this treasury, but the demand for gold and silver it created only worsened matters. **E**

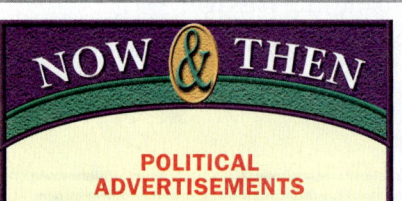

NOW & THEN

POLITICAL ADVERTISEMENTS

In 1840, the campaign slogan "Tippecanoe and Tyler, too" helped William Henry Harrison win the White House. Harrison's party, the Whigs, printed their slogan on ribbons, metal badges, and even dinner plates.

Today, politicians find TV an efficient way to reach a large audience. During the 2000 election cycle, political parties, candidates, and issue advocacy groups spent 77 percent more on TV ads than they had in 1996.

However, critics believe that television ads have a negative impact on the democratic process. Candidates outside the two-party system rarely can afford as many TV ads as the major-party candidates. In 1998, a presidential advisory committee recommended that TV stations voluntarily provide five minutes a day of candidate coverage to help balance this inequality; only seven percent of TV stations participated in 2000.

MAIN IDEA

Analyzing Causes

E How did Jackson's actions hurt the nation's economy?

HARRISON AND TYLER That same year, the Democratic Party candidate Van Buren ran for reelection against Whig Party candidate **William Henry Harrison**—but this time the Whigs had an advantage. They portrayed Harrison, the old war hero, as a man of the people and Van Buren as a pampered, privileged aristocrat. Actually, Van Buren was more of a common man; he was the son of a tavern owner and never earned much money. Harrison, on the other hand, came from a wealthy family and lived in a 16-room mansion.

Harrison won and immediately took steps to enact the Whig program to revitalize the economy, which was still in a severe depression. However, just a month after his inauguration he died of pneumonia.

John Tyler, Harrison's vice-president and successor, opposed many parts of the Whig program for economic recovery. The Whigs had put Tyler on the ballot to pick up Southern votes; they never thought he would play much of a role in government. During the next four years, however, they would see his inclusion on the ticket as a grave mistake—and would begin referring to President Tyler as "His Accidency."

◄ An almanac cover celebrating the election of William Henry Harrison and John Tyler. His campaign symbols, hard cider (an alcoholic beverage) and a log cabin, were meant to show that Harrison was a man of the people.

SECTION 4 ASSESSMENT

1. **TERMS & NAMES** For each term or name, write a sentence explaining its significance.
   - Daniel Webster
   - John C. Calhoun
   - Tariff of Abominations
   - Bank of the United States
   - Whig Party
   - Martin Van Buren
   - panic of 1837
   - William Henry Harrison
   - John Tyler

MAIN IDEA

2. **TAKING NOTES**
In a chart like the one shown, list the key issues that Jackson confronted and the important legacies of his administration.

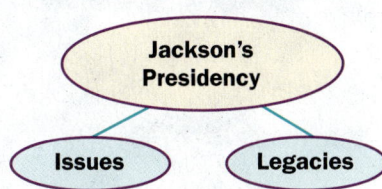

In what ways does one of these legacies continue today?

THINKING CRITICALLY

3. **FORMING GENERALIZATIONS**
In what ways do you think the tariff crises of 1828 and 1832 might be considered important milestones in American history before the Civil War? Use evidence from the text to support your response.
Think About:
- Calhoun's nullification theory
- the Hayne-Webster debate
- why Jackson pushed Congress to pass the Force Bill

4. **ANALYZING ISSUES**
How do you think Jackson might have countered his critics' accusation that he was acting like a king? Support your answer.

5. **COMPARING**
Compare the strategy William Henry Harrison used in the 1840 presidential campaign to strategies used in today's political campaigns. In what ways are they alike? Give examples.

TERMS & NAMES

For each term or name below, write a sentence explaining its significance during the early 19th century.

1. Eli Whitney
2. Industrial Revolution
3. John Quincy Adams
4. nationalism
5. Missouri Compromise
6. Andrew Jackson
7. spoils system
8. Trail of Tears
9. Bank of the United States (BUS)
10. Whig Party

MAIN IDEAS

Use your notes and the information in the chapter to answer the following questions.

Regional Economies Create Differences
(pages 212–218)

1. What key changes in technology and methods of organizing manufacturing spurred the Industrial Revolution?
2. How did people in the Northeast, the South, and the West react to the Tariff of 1816?

Nationalism at Center Stage *(pages 219–223)*

3. Cite two ways in which the *Gibbons* v. *Ogden* decision set the stage for future Supreme Court rulings.
4. Why did conflict arise when Missouri requested admission into the Union?

The Age of Jackson *(pages 224–229)*

5. What changes occurred in the voting population and in voting patterns between the presidential elections of 1824 and 1828?
6. What alternatives did Jackson have in shaping a policy to tackle the problem of Native Americans?

States' Rights and the National Bank
(pages 230–235)

7. What measures was Jackson willing to take in response to South Carolina's threat to secede in 1832?
8. Why did Jackson oppose the Bank of the United States?

CRITICAL THINKING

1. **USING YOUR NOTES** Create a continuum similar to the one below, labeled with *compromise* at one end and *confrontation* at the other. Mark where you think Andrew Jackson, Henry Clay, and John C. Calhoun would fall on the continuum. Support your ratings by citing historical events in which these men played critical roles.

compromise   confrontation

2. **HYPOTHESIZING** What do you think would have happened if the Indian Removal Act of 1830 had not been passed, and Native Americans had remained on their lands? Use evidence to support your answer.

3. **ANALYZING PRIMARY SOURCES** Read the quotation from John C. Calhoun. How does his choice of words reflect issues of the time? Explain your response.

> " I never use the word 'Nation' in speaking of the United States. We are not a Nation, but a Union, a confederacy of equal and sovereign States. "

VISUAL SUMMARY | **BALANCING NATIONALISM AND SECTIONALISM**

FACTORS CONTRIBUTING TO NATIONALISM

- The American System
- U.S. Supreme Court under John Marshall
- John Quincy Adams's foreign policy
- Monroe Doctrine
- Missouri Compromise
- Westward expansion
- Indian Removal Act of 1830

FACTORS CONTRIBUTING TO SECTIONALISM

- Industrial Revolution
- Development of different economic systems in the North and South
- Slavery
- Tariffs of 1828 and 1832

Use the quotation below and your knowledge of U.S. history to answer question 1.

> " Every man is equally entitled to protection by law; but when the laws undertake to add to these natural and just advantages artificial distinctions, to grant . . . exclusive privileges, to make the rich richer and the potent more powerful, the humble members of society—the farmers, mechanics, and laborers—who have neither the time nor the means of securing like favors to themselves, have a right to complain of the injustice of their Government. There are no necessary evils in government. Its evils exist only in its abuses. If it would confine itself to equal protection, and, as Heaven does its rains, shower its favors alike on the high and the low, the rich and the poor, it would be an unqualified blessing. In the act [to recharter the Second Bank of the United States] before me there seems to be a wide and unnecessary departure from these just principles. "
>
> —Andrew Jackson, from *A Compilation of the Messages and Papers of the Presidents, 1789–1902*

1 The excerpt suggests that Jackson's vision of government's role in a democracy is to —

  (1) address the rights and concerns of all citizens.

  (2) increase the power of wealthy citizens.

  (3) provide a national bank for its citizens.

  (4) support only the poor citizens.

2 Which reason best explains why the theory of nullification was widely supported in the South?

  (1) Southerners believed that states had the right to determine whether federal laws were constitutional.

  (2) Southerners wanted to continue buying manufactured goods from Britain.

  (3) Southerners wanted to divide the United States into two separate countries.

  (4) Southerners did not want to pay the high tariffs that Congress passed.

3 Two politicians who each were elected president after campaigning as the candidate of the "common man" were —

  (1) John C. Calhoun and Andrew Jackson.

  (2) William Henry Harrison and John Tyler.

  (3) Andrew Jackson and William Henry Harrison.

  (4) Andrew Jackson and Henry Clay.

hmhsocialstudies.com **TEST PRACTICE**

For additional test practice, go online for:
- Diagnostic tests
- Tutorials

INTERACT WITH HISTORY

Think about the issues you explored at the beginning of the chapter. Now that you know more about nullification and the fight over tariffs and states' rights, form small groups and discuss the following question: Would you have supported the federal or state government?

FOCUS ON WRITING

The clash between supporters of states' rights and the federal government has come to a head. This conflict has divided the nation. Write a persuasive essay arguing for or against states' rights. In your essay, include a clear argument for your position. Use examples to support your point of view.

MULTIMEDIA ACTIVITY

Choose a technological development of the early 1800s and create a Web site to advertise it. Visit the Chapter Assessment links for research leads. Possible inventions include the cotton gin, the steam engine, and the spinning mule. Use vivid language to describe how the invention works, what it accomplishes, what kind of labor it requires, and its effects on how people live or work. Include an image of the invention.

hmhsocialstudies.com

CHAPTER 8

REFORMING AMERICAN SOCIETY

Essential Question

What were the causes and effects of the Second Great Awakening and the various reform movements that swept the nation in the first half of the 19th century?

 New York Standards

KEY IDEA 2 Important ideas, social and cultural values, beliefs, and traditions from New York State and United States history illustrate the connections and interactions of people and events across time and from a variety of perspectives.

KEY IDEA 3 Study about the major social, political, economic, cultural, and religious developments in New York State and United States history involves learning about the important roles and contributions of individuals and groups.

SECTION 1: Religion Sparks Reform

SECTION 2: Slavery and Abolition

SECTION 3: Women and Reform

SECTION 4: The Changing Workplace

This 1834 engraving shows women and children working in a New England textile mill.

1822 Large textile mill opens in Lowell, Massachusetts.

1827 Sojourner Truth is freed from slavery.

1829 David Walker prints *Appeal*, a pamphlet urging slaves to revolt.

1831 Nat Turner leads slave rebellion.

1834 National Trades' Union is formed.

USA
WORLD

1820

1830

1820 Revolts break out in Spain and Portugal.

1832 Britain passes its first Reform Bill.

1833 Britain abolishes slavery in its empire.

INTERACT
WITH HISTORY

The year is 1834. You work in the textile mills in Massachusetts and provide most of the income for your family. The mill owners have gradually increased your workload to 12 hours a day. Now they are going to cut your pay by 15 percent. Coworkers are angry and are discussing what they can do.

Explore the Issues

- What are some conditions you would not tolerate?
- What actions pressure businesses to change?
- What moral arguments would you present?

1838 Frederick Douglass flees to New York City to escape slavery.

1841 Utopian community is established at Brook Farm.

1845 Henry David Thoreau moves to Walden Pond.

1848 Seneca Falls Convention on women's rights is held.

1840

1850

1839 French and British introduce first forms of photography.

1840 World's Anti-Slavery Convention is held in London.

1845 Great Potato Famine begins in Ireland.

1848 Revolutions erupt across Europe, causing many Germans and others to move to America.

SECTION 1

PI 2.3
PI 3.2

CC Unit 1.I.D.1.d
CC Unit 2.II.B.2.d

CC Unit 2.II.B.1.b
CC Unit 7.III.A.3.a(2)

Religion Sparks Reform

MAIN IDEA	WHY IT MATTERS NOW	Terms & Names
A renewal of religious sentiment—known as the Second Great Awakening—inspired a host of reform movements.	Many modern social and political reform movements grew out of the reform movements of 19th-century America.	• Charles Grandison Finney • Second Great Awakening • revival • Ralph Waldo Emerson • transcendentalism • Henry David Thoreau • civil disobedience • utopian community • Dorothea Dix

One American's Story

When **Charles Grandison Finney** preached, his listeners shrieked, moaned, and fainted. The most famous preacher of the era, Finney inspired emotional religious faith, using a speaking style that was as much high drama as prayer or sermon. Converted at the age of 29, Finney traveled by horseback to deliver his message. Finney seated the most likely converts in his audiences on a special "anxious bench," where he could fasten his eyes upon them. He lectured on the depth of the conversion experience.

★ A PERSONAL VOICE CHARLES GRANDISON FINNEY

"I know this is all so much algebra to those who have never felt it. But to those who have experienced the agony of wrestling, prevailing prayer, for the conversion of a soul, you may depend upon it, that soul . . . appears as dear as a child is to the mother who brought it forth with pain."

—*Lectures on Revivals of Religions*

▲ Charles Grandison Finney

The convert's duty was to spread the word about personal salvation to others. This religious activism—or evangelism—was part of an overall era of reform that started in the 1830s. Reforms of the period included women's rights, school reform, and abolition, the movement to outlaw slavery. All of these movements emerged as responses to rapid changes in American society such as early industrial growth, increasing migration and immigration, and new means of communication.

The Second Great Awakening

Much of the impulse toward reform was rooted in the revivals of the broad religious movement that swept the United States after 1790, known as the **Second Great Awakening.** Finney and his contemporaries were participants in the Second Great Awakening. These preachers rejected the 18th-century Calvinistic belief that God predetermined one's salvation or damnation—whether a person went to heaven or hell. Instead, they emphasized individual responsibility for seeking salvation, and they insisted that people could improve themselves and society.

Religious ideas current in the early 19th century promoted individualism and responsibility, similar to the emphasis of Jacksonian democracy on the power of the common citizen. Christian churches split over these ideas, as various denominations competed to proclaim the message of a democratic God, one who extends the possibility of salvation to all people. The forums for their messages were large gatherings, where some preachers could draw audiences of 20,000 or more at outdoor camps.

REVIVALISM Such a gathering was called a **revival,** an emotional meeting designed to awaken religious faith through impassioned preaching and prayer. A revival might last 4 or 5 days. During the day the participants studied the Bible and examined their souls. In the evening they heard emotional preaching that could make them cry out, burst into tears, or tremble with fear.

Revivalism swept across the United States in the early 19th century. Some of the most intense revivals took place in a part of western New York known as the burned-over district because of the religious fires that frequently burned there. Charles Finney fanned these flames, conducting some of his most successful revivals in Rochester, New York. The Rochester revivals earned Finney the reputation of "the father of modern revivalism." Revivalism had a strong impact on the public. According to one estimate, in 1800 just 1 in 15 Americans belonged to a church, but by 1850, 1 in 6 was a member. **A**

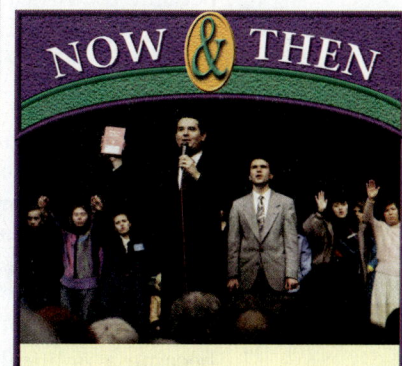

MODERN REVIVALISM

Evangelical Christianity reemerged in several different religious organizations in the late 20th century. One example is the Christian Coalition, a religiously based citizen-action organization with almost 2 million members.

As with the Second Great Awakening, members of these religious organizations often are active in political movements that spring from personal religious beliefs. Indeed, some of the organizations use television much like Finney used the revival meeting to encourage believers to act on their faith.

MAIN IDEA

Analyzing Effects

A How did the Second Great Awakening revolutionize the American religious tradition?

This early-19th-century tray depicts Lemuel Haynes preaching in his Vermont Congregational Church. ▼

THE AFRICAN-AMERICAN CHURCH The Second Great Awakening also brought Christianity on a large scale to enslaved African Americans. There was a strong democratic impulse in the new churches and a belief that all people—black or white—belonged to the same God. Thus, the camp meetings and the new Baptist or Methodist churches were open to both blacks and whites. Slaves in the rural South—though they were segregated in pews of their own—worshiped in the same churches, heard the same sermons, and sang the same hymns as did the slave owners. Enslaved African Americans, however, interpreted the Christian message as a promise of freedom for their people.

In the East, many free African Americans worshiped in separate black churches, like Richard Allen's Bethel African Church in Philadelphia, which by 1816 would become the African Methodist Episcopal Church. Allen inspired his congregation to strengthen its faith as well as to fight against slavery.

A PERSONAL VOICE RICHARD ALLEN

" Our only design is to secure to ourselves, our rights and privileges to regulate our affairs temporal and spiritual, the same as if we were white people, and to guard against any oppression which might possibly arise from the improper prejudices or administration of any individual having the exercise of Discipline over us. "

—quoted in *Segregated Sabbaths*

Membership in the African Methodist Episcopal Church grew rapidly. It became a political, cultural, and social center for African Americans, providing schools and other services that whites denied them.

Eventually the African-American church developed a political voice and organized the first black national convention, held in Philadelphia in September 1830. Richard Allen convened the meeting, in which participants agreed to explore the possible settlement of free African Americans and fugitive slaves in Canada. Allen's convention was the first of what would become an annual convention of free blacks in the North. The African-American church gave its members a deep inner faith, a strong sense of community— and the spiritual support to oppose slavery. **B**

MAIN IDEA

Summarizing
B How did the African-American church support its followers?

Transcendentalism and Reforms

Many reform-minded individuals sought an alternative to traditional religion but found revivalism too public a forum for religious expression.

TRANSCENDENTALISM By the mid-1800s, some Americans were taking new pride in their emerging culture. **Ralph Waldo Emerson,** a New England writer, nurtured this pride. He led a group practicing **transcendentalism**—a philosophical

History Through Art

A VIEW OF THE MOUNTAIN PASS CALLED THE NOTCH OF THE WHITE MOUNTAINS (CRAWFORD NOTCH) (1839)

This painting by Thomas Cole is an example of the Hudson River school. Like the transcendentalists, its painters celebrated the beauty of the American landscape, and the truth found in personal emotion.
What relationship between humans and nature does Cole's painting portray?

and literary movement that emphasized living a simple life and celebrated the truth found in nature and in personal emotion and imagination.

Exalting the dignity of the individual, the transcendentalists spawned a literary movement that stressed American ideas of optimism, freedom, and self-reliance. Emerson's friend **Henry David Thoreau** put the idea of self-reliance into practice. Abandoning community life, he built himself a cabin on the shore of Walden Pond near Concord, Massachusetts, where he lived alone for two years. (See Literature of the Transcendentalists, page 246.) In *Walden* (1854), Thoreau advised readers to follow their inner voices.

> ★ **A PERSONAL VOICE** HENRY DAVID THOREAU
>
> "I learned this, at least, by my experiment; that if one advances confidently in the direction of his dreams, and endeavors to live the life which he has imagined, he will meet with a success unexpected in common hours. . . . If you have built castles in the air, your work need not be lost; that is where they should be. Now put the foundations under them."
>
> —*Walden*

Because Thoreau believed in the importance of individual conscience, he urged people not to obey laws they considered unjust. Instead of protesting with violence, they should peacefully refuse to obey those laws. This form of protest is called **civil disobedience.** For example, Thoreau did not want to support the U.S. government, which allowed slavery and fought the War with Mexico. Instead of paying taxes that helped finance the war, Thoreau went to jail. **C**

UNITARIANISM Rather than appealing to the emotions, Unitarians emphasized reason and appeals to conscience as the paths to perfection. In New England, Unitarians quickly attracted a wealthy and educated following. In place of the dramatic conversions produced by the revivals, Unitarians believed conversion was a gradual process. William Ellery Channing, a prominent Unitarian leader, asserted that the purpose of Christianity was "the perfection of human nature, the elevation of men into nobler beings." Unitarians agreed with revivalists that individual and social reform were both possible and important. **D**

MAIN IDEA

Synthesizing
C In what way did Thoreau's experience at Walden reflect transcendentalist beliefs?

MAIN IDEA

Contrasting
D How did the Unitarians' approach to religious experience differ from the revivalists'?

Americans Form Ideal Communities

Some of the optimism of religious and social reform also inspired the establishment of **utopian communities,** experimental groups who tried to create a "utopia," or perfect place. These communities varied in their philosophies and living arrangements but shared common goals such as self-sufficiency. One of the best-known utopian communities was established in New Harmony, Indiana. Another was Brook Farm, located near Boston.

In 1841 transcendentalist George Ripley established Brook Farm to "prepare a society of liberal, intelligent and cultivated persons, whose relations with each other would permit a more wholesome and simple life than can be led amidst the pressure of our competitive institutions." A fire destroyed the main building at Brook Farm in 1847, and the community immediately disbanded. Most utopias lasted no more than a few years.

> **ANOTHER PERSPECTIVE**
>
> **HAWTHORNE AT BROOK FARM**
>
> New England writer Nathaniel Hawthorne spent about six months at Brook Farm in 1841. He hoped to find solitude in which to write, but instead spent close to ten hours a day working in the barns and fields. He was forced to conclude that life there was "unnatural and unsuitable" for him.
>
> Ten years after he left Brook Farm, Hawthorne, now considered an established author, wrote *The Blithedale Romance* (1852). A fictional account of communal life based on Brook Farm, the book suggests that striving for perfection may yield unexpected results.

The failure of the utopian communities did not lessen the zeal of the religious reformers. Many became active in humanitarian reform movements, such as the abolition of slavery and improved conditions for women.

SHAKER COMMUNITIES Religious belief spurred other ideal communities. The Shakers, who followed the teachings of Ann Lee, set up their first communities in New York, New England, and on the frontier. Shakers shared their goods with each other, believed that men and women are equal, and refused to fight for any reason. When a person became a Shaker, he or she vowed not to marry or have children. Shakers depended on converts and adopting children to keep their communities going. In the 1840s, the Shakers had 6,000 members—their highest number. In 2009, only about three Shakers remained in the entire United States.

Schools and Prisons Undergo Reform

By the mid-19th century, thousands of Americans holding a variety of philosophical positions had joined together to fight the various social ills that troubled the young nation. Some social reformers focused their attention on schools and other institutions.

REFORMING ASYLUMS AND PRISONS In 1831, French writer Alexis de Tocqueville had visited the United States to study its penitentiary system. Observing prisoners who were physically punished or isolated for extended periods, de Tocqueville concluded that "While society in the United States gives the example of the most extended liberty, the prisons of the same country offer the spectacle of the most complete despotism [rigid and severe control]." Reformers quickly took up the cause.

Dorothea Dix was compelled by personal experience to join the movement for social reform. On visiting a Massachusetts house of correction, Dix was horrified to discover that jails often housed mentally ill people.

> ★ **A PERSONAL VOICE** DOROTHEA DIX
>
> "I proceed, gentlemen, briefly to call your attention to the present state of insane persons confined within this Commonwealth. . . . Chained, naked, beaten with rods, and lashed into obedience! . . . Injustice is also done to the convicts: it is certainly very wrong that they should be doomed day after day and night after night to listen to the ravings of madmen and madwomen."
>
> —Report to the Massachusetts Legislature

In 1843 she sent a report of her findings to the Massachusetts legislature, who in turn passed a law aimed at improving conditions. Between 1845 and 1852, Dix persuaded nine Southern states to set up public hospitals for the mentally ill.

Prison reformers—and Dorothea Dix in her efforts on behalf of the mentally ill—emphasized the idea of rehabilitation, treatment that might reform the sick or imprisoned person to a useful position in society. There was, as revivalists suggested, hope for everyone. **E**

IMPROVING EDUCATION Before the mid-1800s, no uniform educational policy existed in the United States. School conditions varied across regions. Massachussetts and Vermont were the only states before the Civil War to pass a compulsory school

These fine oval wooden boxes were made in the Shaker village in Canterbury, New Hampshire. They were used for storing small items.

▲ Dorothea Dix (ca. 1846)

MAIN IDEA

Analyzing Effects
E How did the reformers change the treatment of the mentally ill and prisoners?

attendance law. Classrooms in the early schools were not divided by grade, so younger and older pupils were thrown together. Few children continued in school beyond the age of ten.

In the 1830s, Americans increasingly began to demand tax-supported public schools. For example, in 1834 Pennsylvania established a tax-supported public school system. Although the system was optional, a storm of opposition erupted from well-to-do taxpayers. They saw no reason to support schools that their children, who were mostly enrolled in private schools, would not attend. Opposition also came from some German immigrants who feared that their children would forget the German language and culture. Within three years, however, about 42 percent of the elementary-school-age children in Pennsylvania were attending public schools.

One remarkable leader in the public school reform movement was Horace Mann of Massachusetts. After a childhood spent partly at work and partly in poor schools, Mann declared, "If we do not prepare children to become good citizens, . . . if we do not enrich their minds with knowledge, then our republic must go down to destruction, as others have gone before it." In 1837 he became the first secretary of the Massachusetts Board of Education. In 12 years of service, Mann established teacher-training programs and instituted curriculum reforms. He also doubled the money that the state spent on schools.

MAIN IDEA

Summarizing
Ⓕ What efforts were made to improve education in the 1830s?

Other states soon followed Massachusetts's and Pennsylvania's good example. By the 1850s every state had provided some form of publicly funded elementary schools. In states in the far West and in Southern states, however, it took years before public schools were firmly established. Ⓕ

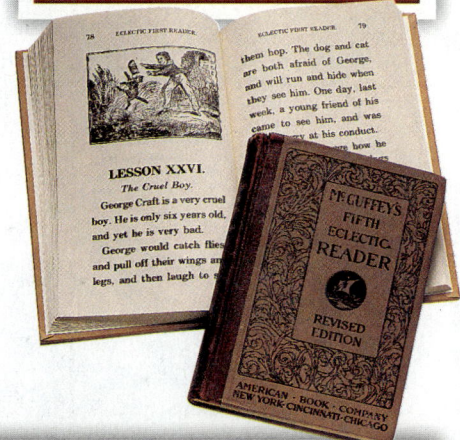

HISTORICAL SPOTLIGHT

MCGUFFEY'S READERS

If you attended school during the mid- to late-1800s, you probably would have used a McGuffey's reader. William H. McGuffey, a teacher and preacher in Ohio, first published his popular grade-school reading books in the 1830s.

The readers, which had sold more than 60 million copies by 1879, taught reading, writing, and arithmetic, as well as the democratic cultural values of hard work, honesty, and love of country. They also contained little moral lessons to live by, such as "Idleness is the nest in which mischief lays its eggs."

SECTION 1 ASSESSMENT

1. TERMS & NAMES For each term or name, write a sentence explaining its significance.
- Charles Grandison Finney
- Second Great Awakening
- revival
- Ralph Waldo Emerson
- transcendentalism
- Henry David Thoreau
- civil disobedience
- utopian community
- Dorothea Dix

MAIN IDEA

2. TAKING NOTES
In a web similar to the one shown, fill in events and ideas that relate to the Second Great Awakening.

Second Great Awakening

individual responsibilities

Why did revivalism catch hold in the early 19th century?

CRITICAL THINKING

3. SYNTHESIZING
Consider the philosophical and religious ideas expressed during the Second Great Awakening and other religious reform movements. What were the key values and beliefs that guided 19th-century reformers' actions? **Think About:**
- concepts of individualism and individual salvation
- attitudes toward social responsibility
- the viewpoints of Finney, Channing, and Emerson

4. ANALYZING ISSUES
How do you think the 19th-century reform movements in schools, prisons, and asylums might have influenced reform movements today?

5. COMPARING
Why might the idea of utopian communities appeal to the transcendentalists?

The Literature of the Transcendentalists

1820–1850 One of the most influential American thinkers of the 19th century was Ralph Waldo Emerson. A poet, essayist, and lecturer, Emerson traveled to England in the early 1830s, where he met writers who were part of the romantic movement. Romanticism embodied a style of art, literature, and thought that stressed the human development of emotional forms of expression. Building on these ideas, Emerson developed transcendentalism—a distinctly American philosophical and literary movement that emphasized living a simple life that is not dictated by any organized system of belief.

Members of the transcendentalist movement included New England writers Bronson Alcott, Margaret Fuller, and Henry David Thoreau. Although the movement was kindled by European romanticism, threads of transcendentalist thinking can be found in New England puritan thought, and some transcendentalists were students of Buddhism and other Asian traditions.

◄ MARGARET FULLER

Margaret Fuller was one of the editors of the transcendentalist journal *The Dial*. In 1845, Fuller published *Woman in the Nineteenth Century*, a work that demanded equality and fulfillment for women.

"Is it not enough," cries the irritated trader, "that you have done all you could to break up the national union, and thus destroy the prosperity of our country, but now you must be trying to break up family union, to take my wife away from the cradle and the kitchen-hearth to vote at polls and preach from a pulpit? Of course, if she does such things, she cannot attend to those of her own sphere. She is happy enough as she is. She has more leisure than I have—every means of improvement, every indulgence."

"Have you asked her whether she was satisfied with these *indulgences?*"

"No, but I know she is. . . . I will never consent to have our peace disturbed by any such discussions."

"Consent—you? It is not consent from you that is in question—it is assent from your wife."

"Am not I the head of my house?"

"You are not the head of your wife. God has given her a mind of her own."

—*Woman in the Nineteenth Century* (1845)

HENRY DAVID THOREAU

Henry David Thoreau believed that people must be free to act by their own idea of right and wrong. His work helped shape many reform movements of his time. In *Walden*, published in 1854, Thoreau wrote about living alone in the woods. Thoreau urged people to reject the greed and materialism that were affecting Americans in their daily lives.

Simplicity, simplicity, simplicity! I say, let your affairs be as two or three, and not a hundred or a thousand; instead of a million count half a dozen, and keep your accounts on your thumb-nail. . . . Simplify, simplify. Instead of three meals a day, if it be necessary eat but one; instead of a hundred dishes, five; and reduce other things in proportion. . . .

If we respected only what is inevitable and has a right to be, music and poetry would resound along the streets. When we are unhurried and wise, we perceive that only great and worthy things have any permanent and absolute existence, that petty fears and petty pleasures are but the shadow of the reality. . . .

Time is but the stream I go a-fishing in. I drink at it; but while I drink I see the sandy bottom and detect how shallow it is. Its thin current slides away, but eternity remains. I would drink deeper; fish in the sky, whose bottom is pebbly with stars. I cannot count one. I know not the first letter of the alphabet. I have always been regretting that I was not as wise as the day I was born. . . .

—*Walden* (published 1854)

RALPH WALDO EMERSON

Emerson's poem "Berrying" expresses his celebration of the truth found in nature and in personal emotion and imagination.

"May be true what I had heard,
Earth's a howling wilderness
Truculent with fraud and force,"
Said I, strolling through the pastures,
And along the riverside.
Caught among the blackberry vines,
Feeding on the Ethiops sweet,
Pleasant fancies overtook me:
I said, "What influence me preferred
Elect to dreams thus beautiful?"
The vines replied, "And didst thou deem
No wisdom to our berries went?"

—"Berrying"
(published 1846)

THINKING CRITICALLY

1. **Comparing and Contrasting** What does each selection reveal about habits and attitudes in 1850s America? Cite details to help explain your answers.

   SEE SKILLBUILDER HANDBOOK, PAGE R8.

2. **INTERNET ACTIVITY**

   Use the links for American Literature to research and create an annotated book of famous transcendentalist quotations. Well-known examples might include: Emerson's "Hitch your wagon to a star," or Thoreau's "The mass of men lead lives of quiet desperation." The quotations you choose for each writer should contain information on the source of the quotation and a short description of how each quotation expresses transcendentalist beliefs.

CC Unit 2.II.B.1.b   CC Unit 2.II.B.1.d
CC Unit 2.II.B.1.e   CC Unit 2.II.B.2.d
CC Unit 2.II.B.3

PI 3.2

Slavery and Abolition

<table>
<tr><td>MAIN IDEA</td><td>WHY IT MATTERS NOW</td><td>Terms & Names</td></tr>
<tr><td>Slavery became an explosive issue, as more Americans joined reformers working to put an end to it.</td><td>The people of the United States continue to be challenged by questions of economic and social inequality.</td><td><ul><li>abolition</li><li>William Lloyd Garrison</li><li>emancipation</li><li>David Walker</li></ul><ul><li>Frederick Douglass</li><li>Nat Turner</li><li>antebellum</li><li>gag rule</li></ul></td></tr>
</table>

One American's Story

hmhsocialstudies.com
TAKING NOTES

Use the graphic organizer online to take notes on antislavery and proslavery activities during the years from 1820 to 1850.

James Forten's great-grandfather had been brought from Africa to the American colonies in chains, but James was born free. In 1781, the 15-year-old James went to sea to fight for American independence. Captured by the British and offered passage to England, the patriotic youth refused, saying, "I am here a prisoner for the liberties of my country. I never, NEVER shall prove a traitor to her interests."

By the 1830s Forten had become a wealthy sailmaker in Philadelphia, with a fortune rumored to exceed $100,000. Though some people argued that free blacks should return to Africa, Forten disagreed and responded with sarcasm.

▲
James Forten, a wealthy leader of Philadelphia's free black community, took an active role in a variety of political causes.

A PERSONAL VOICE JAMES FORTEN

"Here I have dwelt until I am nearly sixty years of age, and have brought up and educated a family. . . . Yet some ingenious gentlemen have recently discovered that I am still an African; that a continent three thousand miles, and more, from the place where I was born, is my native country. And I am advised to go home. . . . Perhaps if I should only be set on the shore of that distant land, I should recognize all I might see there, and run at once to the old hut where my forefathers lived a hundred years ago."

—quoted in *Forging Freedom: The Formation of Philadelphia's Black Community 1720–1840*

Forten's unwavering belief that he was an American led him to oppose the effort to resettle free blacks in Africa and also pushed him fervently to oppose slavery.

Abolitionists Speak Out

By the 1820s more than 100 antislavery societies were advocating for resettlement of blacks in Africa—based on the belief that African Americans were an inferior race that could not coexist with white society. Yet most free blacks considered America their home, and only about 1,400 blacks emigrated to Africa between

1820 and 1830. As one black pastor from New York angrily proclaimed, "We are natives of this country. We only ask that we be treated as well as foreigners."

African Americans increasingly were joined by whites in public criticism of slavery. White support for **abolition,** the call to outlaw slavery, was fueled by preachers like Charles G. Finney, who termed slavery "a great national sin."

WILLIAM LLOYD GARRISON The most radical white abolitionist was an editor named **William Lloyd Garrison.** Active in religious reform movements in Massachusetts, Garrison started his own paper, *The Liberator*, in 1831 to deliver an uncompromising message: immediate **emancipation**—the freeing of slaves, with no payment to slaveholders.

William Lloyd Garrison's newspaper, *The Liberator*, bore the motto: "Our country is the world—Our countrymen are all mankind."

★ A PERSONAL VOICE WILLIAM LLOYD GARRISON

" [I]s there not cause for severity? I *will* be harsh as truth, and as uncompromising as justice. On this subject [immediate emancipation], I do not wish to think or speak or write, with moderation. . . . I am in earnest—I will not equivocate—I will not excuse—I will not retreat a single inch—AND I WILL BE HEARD. "

—*The Liberator*

As white abolitionists began to respond to Garrison's ideas, he founded the New England Anti-Slavery Society in 1832, followed by the national American Anti-Slavery Society a year later. Garrison enjoyed core black support; three out of four early subscribers were African Americans. Whites who opposed abolition, however, hated him. Some whites supported abolition but opposed Garrison when he attacked churches and the government for failing to condemn slavery. Garrison alienated whites even more when he associated with fiery abolitionist David Walker.

FREE BLACKS In his *Appeal to the Colored Citizens of the World*, published in 1829, **David Walker,** a free black, advised blacks to fight for freedom rather than to wait for slave owners to end slavery. He wrote, "The man who would not fight . . . ought to be kept with all of his children or family, in slavery, or in chains, to be butchered by his cruel enemies."

Many free blacks, more willing to compromise than Walker, had joined one of many antislavery societies active by the end of the 1820s. In 1850, most of the 434,000 free blacks in the South worked as day laborers, but some held jobs as artisans. Northern free blacks discovered that only the lowest-paying jobs were open to them. Recalling his youth in Rhode Island in the 1830s, William J. Brown wrote, "To drive carriages, carry a market basket after the boss, and brush his boots . . . was as high as a colored man could rise." Frederick Douglass, however, rose above such limitations. **A**

FREDERICK DOUGLASS Born into slavery in 1817, **Frederick Douglass** had been taught to read and write by the wife of one of his owners. Her husband ordered her to stop teaching Douglass, however, because reading "would forever unfit him to be a slave." When Douglass realized that knowledge could be his "pathway from slavery to freedom," he studied even harder.

HISTORY

VIDEO
Frederick Douglass

hmhsocialstudies.com

Frederick Douglass, 1851

MAIN IDEA

Synthesizing
A What was radical at the time about Garrison's and Walker's ideas on abolition?

By 1838, Douglass held a skilled job as a ship caulker in Baltimore. He earned the top wages in the yard but was not allowed to keep any of his earnings. After a disagreement with his owner, Douglass decided to escape. Borrowing the identity of a free black sailor and carrying official papers, he reached New York and tasted freedom for the first time.

Douglass became an eager reader of *The Liberator*, which, he said, "sent a thrill of joy through my soul, such as I had never felt before." When Garrison heard him speak of his experiences, he was so impressed he sponsored Douglass as a lecturer for the American Anti-Slavery Society. A superb speaker, Douglass thrilled huge audiences. "I appear before the immense assembly this evening as a thief and a robber," he would say. "I stole this head, these limbs, this body from my master and ran off with them." Hoping that abolition could be achieved through political actions, Douglass broke with Garrison in 1847 and began his own antislavery newspaper. He named it *The North Star*, after the star that guided runaway slaves to freedom. **B**

MAIN IDEA

Contrasting
B How did the various antislavery groups differ in approach?

Life Under Slavery

▲ Planters' children—like Charlotte Helen Middleton, shown with her nurse Lydia in 1857—often were tended by slaves who had been forced to give up their own children.

After 1830, Americans hotly debated the issue of slavery, but many African Americans still lived in bondage. In fact, the population of slaves in America had nearly doubled in the years between 1810 and 1830, growing from 1.2 million to roughly 2 million.

The institution of slavery had changed substantially since the 18th century. In those days, most slaves had recently arrived from the Caribbean or Africa and spoke one of several non-English languages. Most of these slaves worked on small farms alongside people with whom they could not easily communicate. By 1830, the majority had been born in America and spoke enough English to be able to communicate with other slaves. The rise of the plantation in the mid-18th century brought further change to the lives of the enslaved.

RURAL SLAVERY On large plantations, men, women, and even children toiled from dawn to dusk in the fields. The whip of the overseer or slave driver compelled them to work faster. Solomon Northup, who was born free and later enslaved, recalled the never-ending labor.

A PERSONAL VOICE SOLOMON NORTHUP

"The hands are required to be in the cotton field as soon as it is light in the morning, and, with the exception of ten or fifteen minutes, which is given them at noon to swallow their allowance of cold bacon, they are not permitted to be a moment idle until it is too dark to see, and when the moon is full, they often times labor till the middle of the night. They do not dare to stop even at dinner time, nor return to the quarters, however late it be, until the order to halt is given by the driver."

—*Twelve Years a Slave*

By 1850 most slaves lived on plantations or large farms that employed ten or more slaves, but many lived on small farms, laboring beside their owners. Others lived and worked in the cities. **C**

URBAN SLAVERY By the 1830s the promise of cotton wealth had lured many Southern whites into farming, thus creating a shortage of white laborers for such

MAIN IDEA

Summarizing
C Describe typical work experiences of rural Southern slaves.

Southern Plantations

Plantations were virtually self-contained, self-sufficient worlds over which owners ruled with absolute authority. Owners established the boundaries that a slave could not cross without punishment or death. But no boundary protected a slave from the owner's demands or cruel treatment.

Slave quarters, from a photograph taken around 1865

African Americans in the South, 1860

Free African Americans (6%)

Slaves owned in groups of 10–99 (61%)

Slaves owned in groups of 1–9 (25%)

Slaves owned in groups of 100 or more (8%)

Sources: 1860 figures from *Eighth Census of the United States;* Lewis C. Gray, *History of Agriculture in the Southern United States.*

SKILLBUILDER Interpreting Graphs
1. According to the pie graph, what was the smallest group of African Americans living in the American South in 1860?
2. Under what conditions did 61% of slaves in the South live? Explain.

industries as mining and lumber. As a result, a demand arose for slaves as workers in mills and on ships. Slaves who had developed specialized skills on plantations were now in demand in Southern cities. For example, slaves filled skilled occupations such as blacksmithing or carpentry, resulting in a new class of skilled black laborers. Most slaves lived rurally—2.8 million in 1850, compared with the 400,000 slaves living in cities. However, enslaved blacks could hire themselves out as artisans in Southern cities, often more easily than free blacks in the North, where racial discrimination prevailed.

Many enslaved women and children worked the same jobs as men in Southern industry. Slave owners "hired out" their slaves to factory owners. In return, the slave owners collected the pay of their slaves without having to supervise their activities. Thus, urban slaves spent more time beyond the watchful eye of their slave owners. Frederick Douglass remarked on differences between rural and urban slavery, noting that "a city slave is almost a freeman, compared with a slave on the plantation. He is much better fed and clothed, and enjoys privileges altogether unknown to the slave on the plantation." Douglass also noted that "a vestige of decency" in the cities limited the acts of "atrocious cruelty" to slaves that were common on plantations.

Still slaves never lost sight of their goal of freedom. For some, it was time to take more drastic and organized action.

NAT TURNER'S REBELLION Nat Turner was born into slavery in 1800 in Southampton County, Virginia. A gifted preacher, Turner believed that he had been chosen to lead his people out of bondage. In August, 1831, Turner judged an eclipse of the sun to be a divine signal for action. With nearly 80 followers, Turner's band attacked four plantations and killed almost 60 white inhabitants before being captured by state and federal troops.

Though Turner himself hid out for several weeks, eventually he was captured, tried, and hanged. In the retaliation that followed, whites killed as many as 200 blacks—many of them innocent of any connection with the uprising. Turner's bloody rebellion strengthened the resolve of Southern whites to defend slavery and to control their slaves.

▲ Artist Felix Darley completed this tinted drawing in 1863 for a history book. Nat Turner is shown (standing) preaching to his followers.

Slave Owners Defend Slavery

In some states, in the aftermath of the Turner rebellion, people argued that the only way to prevent further slave revolts was through emancipation. Others, however, chose to tighten restrictions on all African Americans.

VIRGINIA DEBATE Virginia governor John Floyd wrote of his wish for a "law . . . gradually abolishing slavery in this State." By January 1832 the state legislature was hotly debating that very prospect. "Nothing else could have prompted [the discussions]," reported the *Richmond Enquirer*, "but the bloody massacre [Turner's Rebellion] in the month of August."

The debate over the future of slavery in Virginia resulted in a motion for abolition in the state legislature. The motion lost by a 73 to 58 vote, primarily because the state legislature was balanced toward eastern slaveholders rather than non-slaveholders in the western part of the state. That loss closed the debate on slavery in the **antebellum** (pre-Civil War) South.

BACKLASH FROM REVOLTS In addition to forcing the Virginia debate, whites' fear of future slave revolts had another important effect. Most slave owners believed that education and privilege inspired revolt. Thus, many slave owners pushed their state legislatures to further tighten controls on African Americans. These controls became known as slave codes. **D**

In 1833, for example, Alabama forbade free and enslaved blacks from preaching the gospel unless "respectable" slaveholders were present. Georgia followed suit. In 1835 North Carolina became the last Southern state to deny the vote to free blacks. In some states, free blacks lost the right to own guns, purchase alcohol, assemble in public, and testify in court. In some Southern cities, African Americans could no longer own property, learn to

MAIN IDEA

Analyzing Effects

D How did Turner's revolt harden Southern white attitudes about basic liberties for blacks?

read and write, or work independently as carpenters or blacksmiths.

PROSLAVERY DEFENSES Some proslavery advocates used the Bible to defend slavery, citing passages that counseled servants to obey their masters. Slavery, Southern slave owners argued, actually benefited blacks by making them part of a prosperous and Christian civilization. Even Southern white Christian ministers gradually shifted toward accepting slavery during this period. Some had attacked slavery in the early 1800s, but by the 1830s most white ministers in the South agreed that slavery and Christianity could coexist.

Slave owners invented the myth of the happy slave, a cherished addition to the plantation family. To this image they contrasted that of the Northern wage slave, a wage-earning immigrant or free black who worked for pennies in dark and airless factories. George Fitzhugh, a Virginia slave owner, argued that whereas Northern mill owners fired their workers when they became too old or sick to work, Southerners cared for their slaves for a lifetime.

Abolitionists, however, continued to campaign for emancipation. One maneuver was to swamp Congress with petitions to end slavery in the District of Columbia. Southern representatives countered in 1836 by securing the adoption of a **gag rule,** a rule limiting or preventing debate on an issue—which meant that citizens submitting petitions were deprived of their right to have them heard. The gag rule eventually was repealed in 1844.

Nevertheless, as abolitionists' efforts intensified during the 1850s, some turned to violence. The more clear-sighted began to sound the alarm: this turmoil over slavery would lead to a divided nation.

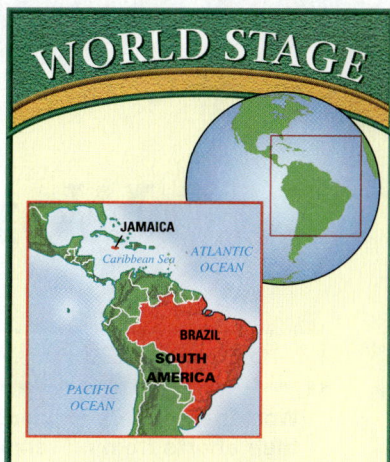

WORLD STAGE

SLAVERY IN THE AMERICAS

Slaves formed a smaller portion of the total population in the American South than in the Caribbean and in Brazil. African slaves formed almost 80 percent of the population of Jamaica, a colony of Great Britain. Because so many slaves in that colony died, slave owners demanded a constant renewal of their supply from Africa, thus maintaining the Atlantic slave trade. Slavery ended in the British empire in 1833.

Brazil also had a large proportion of slaves. During the 1800s slaves made up more than half the colonial population of Brazil and worked primarily on large coffee plantations. Slavery was abolished in Brazil in 1888.

SECTION 2 ASSESSMENT

1. TERMS & NAMES For each term or name, write a sentence explaining its significance.

- **abolition**
- **William Lloyd Garrison**
- **emancipation**
- **David Walker**
- **Frederick Douglass**
- **Nat Turner**
- **antebellum**
- **gag rule**

MAIN IDEA

2. TAKING NOTES

In a two-column chart, list the major antislavery and proslavery actions that occurred from 1820 to 1850.

Antislavery Actions	Proslavery Actions

Which activity do you think was most effective? Explain.

CRITICAL THINKING

3. SYNTHESIZING

Which do you think was a more effective strategy for achieving the abolitionists' goal of eliminating slavery—violence or nonviolence? Why? **Think About:**

- Garrison's and Walker's remarks
- Frederick Douglass's views
- Southerners' reactions to Nat Turner's rebellion

4. SUMMARIZING

What arguments did Southern proslavery whites employ to defend slavery?

5. COMPARING

Compare the similarities and differences between the situations of free blacks in the North and slaves in the South.

PI 2.4   CC Unit 2.II.B.1.b   CC Unit 2.II.B.2.d
PI 3.2   CC Unit 4.I.B.2.b(1)   CC Unit 4.I.B.2.d

Women and Reform

MAIN IDEA	WHY IT MATTERS NOW	Terms & Names
Women reformers expanded their efforts from movements such as abolition and temperance to include women's rights.	The efforts of 19th-century women reformers inspired both woman suffragists in the early-1900s and present-day feminist movements.	• Elizabeth Cady Stanton • Lucretia Mott • cult of domesticity • Sarah Grimké • Angelina Grimké • temperance movement • Seneca Falls Convention • Sojourner Truth

One American's Story

hmhsocialstudies.com
TAKING NOTES
Use the graphic organizer online to take notes on how women approached the question of inequality.

Elizabeth Cady Stanton timed her marriage in 1840 so that she could accompany her husband to London for the World's Anti-Slavery Convention, where her husband was a delegate. At the antislavery convention, Stanton and the other women delegates received an unpleasant surprise.

A PERSONAL VOICE ELIZABETH CADY STANTON

" Though women were members of the National Anti-Slavery society, accustomed to speak and vote in all its conventions, and to take an equally active part with men in the whole antislavery struggle, and were there as delegates from associations of men and women, as well as those distinctively of their own sex, yet all alike were rejected because they were women. "

—quoted in *Elizabeth Cady Stanton*

At the convention, Stanton found a friend in the Quaker abolitionist **Lucretia Mott.** Stanton and Mott vowed "to hold a convention as soon as we returned home, and form a society to advocate the rights of women." They kept their pledge and headed the first women's rights convention, assembled at Seneca Falls, New York, in 1848.

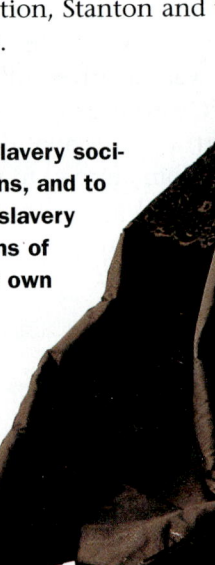

▲
Elizabeth Cady Stanton

Women's Roles in the Mid-1800s

In the early 19th century, women faced limited options. Prevailing customs demanded that women restrict their activities after marriage to the home and family. Housework and child care were considered the only proper activities for married women. Later that tradition became known as the **cult of domesticity.**

By 1850, roughly one in five white women had worked for wages a few years before they were married. About one in ten single white women worked outside

MAIN IDEA

Identifying
Problems

A What were the
main problems
faced by women in
the mid-1800s?

the home, earning about half the pay men received to do the same job. Women could neither vote nor sit on juries in the early 1800s, even if they were taxpayers. Typically, when a woman married, her property and any money she earned became her husband's. In many instances, married women lacked guardianship rights over their children. **A**

Women Mobilize for Reform

Despite such limits, women actively participated in all the important reform movements of the 19th century. Many middle-class white women were inspired by the optimistic message of the Second Great Awakening. Women were often shut out of meetings by disapproving men, and responded by expanding their efforts to seek equal rights for themselves.

WOMEN ABOLITIONISTS **Sarah and Angelina Grimké,** daughters of a South Carolina slaveholder, spoke eloquently for abolition. In 1836 Angelina Grimké published *An Appeal to Christian Women of the South*, in which she called upon women to "overthrow this horrible system of oppression and cruelty." Women abolitionists also raised money, distributed literature, and collected signatures for petitions to Congress.

Some men supported women's efforts. William Lloyd Garrison, for example, joined the determined women who had been denied participation in the World's Anti-Slavery Convention in 1840. Garrison said, "After battling so many long years for the liberties of African slaves, I can take no part in a convention that strikes down the most sacred rights of all women." Other men, however, denounced the female abolitionists. The Massachusetts clergy criticized the Grimké sisters for assuming "the place and tone of man as public reformer."

MAIN IDEA

Summarizing

B In what ways
were women
excluded from the
abolitionist
movement?

Opposition only served to make women reformers more determined. The abolitionist cause became a powerful spur to other reform causes, as well as to the women's rights movement. **B**

WORKING FOR TEMPERANCE The **temperance movement,** the effort to prohibit the drinking of alcohol, was another offshoot of the influence of churches and the women's rights movement. Speaking at a temperance meeting in 1852, Mary C. Vaughan attested to the evils of alcohol.

⭐ **A PERSONAL VOICE** MARY C. VAUGHAN

" There is no reform in which woman can act better or more appropriately than temperance. . . . Its effects fall so crushingly upon her . . . she has so often seen its slow, insidious, but not the less surely fatal advances, gaining upon its victim. . . . Oh! the misery, the utter, hopeless misery of the drunkard's wife! "

—quoted in *Women's America: Refocusing the Past*

In the early 19th century, alcohol flowed freely in America. Liquor helped wash down the salted meat and fish that composed the dominant diet and, until the development of anesthetics in the 1840s, doctors dosed their patients with whiskey or brandy before operating.

Many Americans, however, recognized drunkenness as a serious problem. Lyman Beecher, a prominent Connecticut minister, had begun lecturing against all use of liquor in 1825. A year later, the American Temperance Society was founded. By 1833, some 6,000 local temperance societies dotted the country.

KEY PLAYER

LUCRETIA MOTT
1793–1880

History has it that Lucretia Mott was so talkative as a child that her mother called her Long Tongue. As an adult, she used her considerable public-speaking skills to campaign against slavery.

Mott became interested in women's rights when she learned that her salary as a teacher would be roughly half of what a man might receive. She was a prominent figure at the Seneca Falls Convention, at which she delivered the opening and closing addresses. Mott and her husband later acted on their abolitionist principles by taking in runaway slaves escaping on the Underground Railroad.

▲ This engraving is from a temperance society tract of around 1840. It depicts a family driven to despair by alcohol.

They held rallies, produced pamphlets, and brought about a decline in the consumption of alcohol that would continue into the 1860s.

EDUCATION FOR WOMEN

Until the 1820s, American girls had few educational avenues open to them beyond elementary school. As Sarah Grimké, who ran a school for women with her sister Angelina, complained in *Letters on the Equality of the Sexes and the Condition of Woman* (1838), a woman who knew "chemistry enough to keep the pot boiling, and geography enough to know the location of the different rooms in her house," was considered learned enough.

★ A PERSONAL VOICE SARAH GRIMKÉ

" During the early part of my life, my lot was cast among the butterflies of the fashionable world, I am constrained to say . . . that their education is miserably deficient. . . . Our brethren may reject my doctrine . . . but I believe they would be 'partakers of the benefit' . . . and would find that woman, as their equal, was unspeakably more valuable than woman as their inferior, both as a moral and an intellectual being. "

—*Letters on the Equality of the Sexes and the Condition of Woman*

▲ Sarah Grimké *(above)* and her sister Angelina spoke out against slavery and gender inequality.

In 1821 Emma Willard opened one of the nation's first academically rigorous schools for girls in Troy, New York. The Troy Female Seminary became the model for a new type of women's school. Despite much mockery that "they will be educating cows next," Willard's school prospered.

In 1837 Mary Lyon overcame heated resistance to found another important institution of higher learning for women, Mount Holyoke Female Seminary (later Mount Holyoke College) in South Hadley, Massachusetts. In the same year Ohio's Oberlin College admitted four women to its degree program, thus becoming the nation's first fully coeducational college.

African-American women faced greater obstacles to getting an education. In 1831 white Quaker Prudence Crandall opened a school for girls in Canterbury, Connecticut. Two years later she admitted an African-American girl, but the townspeople protested so vigorously against desegregated education that Crandall decided to admit only African-American students. This aroused even more opposition, and in 1834 Crandall was forced to close the school and leave town. Only after the Civil War would the severely limited educational opportunities for African-American women finally, though slowly, begin to expand. **C**

WOMEN AND HEALTH REFORM In the mid-19th century, educated women also began to work for health reforms. Elizabeth Blackwell, who in 1849 became the first woman to graduate from medical college, later opened the New York Infirmary for Women and Children. In the 1850s, Lyman Beecher's daughter, Catharine, undertook a national survey of women's health. To her dismay, Beecher found three sick women for every healthy one. It was no wonder: women

MAIN IDEA

Summarizing
C What gains did women make in education in the 1820s and 1830s? Did these gains extend to African-American women?

rarely bathed or exercised, and the fashion of the day included corsets so restrictive that breathing sometimes was difficult.

Amelia Bloomer, publisher of a temperance newspaper, rebelled. Bloomer often wore a costume of loose-fitting pants tied at the ankles and covered by a short skirt. Readers besieged her with requests for the sewing pattern. Most women who sewed the "bloomers," however, considered it a daring venture, as many men were outraged by women wearing pants.

▲ Amelia Bloomer adopted the full trousers that became known as bloomers in 1851.

Women's Rights Movement Emerges

The various reform movements of the mid-19th century fed the growth of the women's movement by providing women with increased opportunities to act outside the home.

SENECA FALLS In 1848 Elizabeth Cady Stanton and Lucretia Mott decided to hold a women's rights convention. They announced what would become known as the **Seneca Falls Convention** (for the New York town in which it was held). Stanton and Mott composed an agenda and a detailed statement of grievances. Stanton carefully modeled this "Declaration of Sentiments" on the Declaration of Independence. The second paragraph began with a revision of very familiar words: "We hold these truths to be self-evident: that all men and women are created equal." Some of the resolutions that were also proposed at the convention spoke to the circumstances with which women reformers had struggled.

★ A PERSONAL VOICE

" *Resolved*, That all laws which prevent women from occupying such a station in society as her conscience shall dictate, or which place her in a position inferior to that of man, are contrary to the great precept of nature, and therefore of no force or authority.
Resolved, That woman is man's equal—was intended to be so by the Creator, and the highest good of the race demands that she should be recognized as such. "

—Resolutions adopted at Seneca Falls Convention, 1848

Nearly 300 women and men gathered at the Wesleyan Methodist Church for the convention. The participants approved all parts of the declaration unanimously—including several resolutions to encourage women to participate in all public issues on an equal basis with men—except one. The one exception, which still passed by a narrow majority, was the resolution calling for women "to secure to

◀ In 1888, delegates to the First International Council of Women met to commemorate the 40th anniversary of Seneca Falls. Stanton is seated third from the right.

257

KEY PLAYER

SOJOURNER TRUTH
1797–1883

Sojourner Truth, born Isabella Van Wagener (or Baumfree), became legally free on July 4, 1827, when slavery was abolished in New York. A deeply spiritual woman, Truth became a traveling preacher dedicated to pacifism, abolitionism, and equality. She earned a reputation for tenacity, successfully suing for the return of her youngest son who had been illegally sold into slavery.

Truth was not taught to read or write but dictated her memoirs, published in 1850 as The *Narrative of Sojourner Truth: A Northern Slave.*

After the Emancipation Proclamation, Truth's final cause was to lobby (unsuccessfully) for land distribution for former slaves.

themselves their sacred right to the elective franchise," the right to vote. The vote remained a controversial aim. Some thought suffrage was an extreme solution to a nonexistent problem. As Lucy Stone's sister wrote in 1846, "I can't vote, but what care I for that, I would not if I could." **D**

SOJOURNER TRUTH Women reformers made significant contributions to improving social conditions in the mid-19th century. Yet conditions for slaves worsened. Isabella Baumfree, a slave for the first 30 years of her life, took the name **Sojourner Truth** when she decided to sojourn (travel) throughout the country preaching, and later, arguing for abolition. At a women's rights convention in 1851, the tall, muscular black woman was hissed at in disapproval. Because Truth supported abolition, some participants feared her speaking would make their own cause less popular. But Truth won applause with her speech that urged men to grant women their rights.

A PERSONAL VOICE SOJOURNER TRUTH

" Look at me! Look at my arm! I have ploughed and planted, and gathered into barns, and no man could head me! And ain't I a woman? I could work as much and eat as much as a man—when I could get it—and bear the lash as well! And ain't I a woman? I have borne thirteen children, and seen most all sold off to slavery, and when I cried out with my mother's grief, none but Jesus heard me! And ain't I a woman? "

—quoted in *Narrative of Sojourner Truth: A Northern Slave*

As Truth showed, hard work was a central fact of life for most women. In the mid-19th century, this continued to be the case as women entered the emerging industrial workplace. Once there, they continued the calls for women's rights and other social reforms.

MAIN IDEA

Contrasting
D How did the Seneca Falls Convention differ from the World's Anti-Slavery Convention held in 1840?

ASSESSMENT

1. **TERMS & NAMES** For each term or name, write a sentence explaining its significance.
   - •Elizabeth Cady Stanton
   - •Lucretia Mott
   - •cult of domesticity
   - •Sarah and Angelina Grimké
   - •temperance movement
   - •Seneca Falls Convention
   - •Sojourner Truth

MAIN IDEA

2. TAKING NOTES
In a diagram similar to the one shown, fill in historical events, ideas, or people that relate to the main idea.

CRITICAL THINKING

3. ANALYZING ISSUES
The Seneca Falls "Declaration of Sentiments" asserted that "Woman is man's equal." In what ways would that change the status women held at that time? Cite facts to support your answer. **Think About:**
- women's social, economic, and legal status in the mid-1800s
- married women's domestic roles
- single women's career opportunities and wages

4. EVALUATING
In what ways did the reform movements affect the lives of women—both white and African American? Use details from the section to support your answer.

5. DRAWING CONCLUSIONS
Why do you think that many of the people who fought for abolition also fought for women's rights?

SECTION 4

PI 2.4
PI 3.2

CC Unit 2.II.B.1.a(2)   CC Unit 2.II.B.1.a(3)
CC Unit 2.II.B.1.a(4)   CC Unit 2.II.B.1.a(5)
CC Unit 2.II.B.1.c   CC Unit 3.III.C.2(1)

The Changing Workplace

MAIN IDEA	WHY IT MATTERS NOW	Terms & Names
A growing industrial work force faced problems arising from manufacturing under the factory system.	The National Trades' Union was the forerunner of America's labor unions today.	• cottage industry • apprentice • master • strike • journeyman • National Trades' Union

One American's Story

hmhsocialstudies.com
TAKING NOTES
Use the graphic organizer online to take notes on the changing workplace in the first half of the nineteenth century.

In 1841 a brief narrative appeared in the *Lowell Offering*, the first journal written by and for female mill workers. A young girl who toiled in the mill—identified only by the initials F.G.A.—wrote about the decision of "Susan Miller" to save her family's farm by working in the Lowell, Massachusetts, textile mills.

At first, Susan found the factory work dispiriting, but she made friends, and was proud of the wages she sent home.

A PERSONAL VOICE F.G.A.

"**Every morning the bells pealed forth the same clangor, and every night brought the same feeling of fatigue. But Susan felt. . . that she could bear it for a while. There are few who look upon factory labor as a pursuit for life. It is but a temporary vocation; and most of the girls resolve to quit the Mill when some favorite design is accomplished. Money is their object—not for itself, but for what it can perform.**"

—*Lowell Offering*, 1841

▲ A young worker from the mills in Waltham, or Lowell, 1850.

Just a few decades earlier, work outside the home might not have been an option for girls like Susan. At the same time that women's roles began to expand, changes occurred in the way goods were manufactured.

Industry Changes Work

Before "Susan" and other girls began to leave the farms for New England's textile mills, women had spun and sewn most of their families' clothing from raw fibers. In fact, in the early 19th century almost all clothing manufacturing was produced at home. Moving production from the home to the factory split families, created new communities, and transformed traditional relationships between employers and employees. The textile industry pioneered the new manufacturing techniques that would affect rules and behavior required of most American workers.

▲ Families used spinning wheels to spin yarn, which they wove into cloth on home looms. They sold their cloth to local merchants.

RURAL MANUFACTURING

Until the 1820s, only the first step in the manufacture of clothing—the spinning of cotton into thread—had been mechanized widely in America. People then finished the work in a **cottage industry** system in which manufacturers provided the materials for goods to be produced at home. Though women did most of this work, men and children sometimes helped too. The participants in this cottage industry brought the finished articles to the manufacturer, who paid them by the piece and gave them new materials for the next batch of work.

When entrepreneurs like Patrick Jackson, Nathan Appleton, and Francis Cabot Lowell opened their weaving factories in Waltham and later Lowell, Massachusetts (see Chapter 7, page 213), their power looms replaced the cottage industries. Mechanizing the entire process and housing the tools in the same place slashed the production time, as well as the cost, of textile manufacture. By the 1830s, the company that Lowell and his partners had formed owned eight factories in Massachusetts with over 6,000 employees, at an investment of over $6 million.

EARLY FACTORIES Textiles led the way, but other areas of manufacture also shifted from homes to factories. In the early 19th century, skilled artisans had typically produced items that a family could not make for itself—furniture and tools, for example. As in cottage industries, the artisans usually worked in shops attached to their own homes. The most experienced artisans had titles: a **master** might be assisted by a **journeyman,** a skilled worker employed by a master, and assisted by an **apprentice,** a young worker learning a craft. Master artisans and their assistants traditionally handcrafted their products until the 1820s, when manufacturers began using production processes that depended on the use of interchangeable parts.

The rapid spread of factory production revolutionized industry. The cost of making household items and clothing dramatically dropped. In addition, new machines allowed unskilled workers to perform tasks that once had employed trained artisans. Unskilled artisans shifted from farm work to boring and repetitive factory work and to the tight restrictions imposed by factory managers. Nowhere were these restrictions more rigid than in the factory town of Lowell, Massachusetts. **A**

Farm Worker to Factory Worker

Under the strict control of female supervisors, a work force—consisting almost entirely of unmarried farm girls—clustered in Lowell and the other mill towns that soon dotted New England. At their boarding houses, the "mill girls" lived under strict curfews. The girls' behavior and church attendance was closely monitored, but despite this scrutiny, most mill girls found time to enjoy the company of their coworkers. By 1828 women made up nine-tenths of the work force in the New England mills, and four out of five of the women were not yet 30 years old.

MAIN IDEA

Analyzing Effects
A How did factory production change American manufacturing?

Northern Cities and Industry, 1830–1850

Lake Superior

Lake Huron

Lake Michigan

WISCONSIN

MICHIGAN

Mississippi River

Lake Ontario

Lake Erie

Buffalo

MAINE

VT.

N.H.

NEW YORK

Boston

MASS.

R.I.

CONN.

Detroit

Cleveland

Allegheny River

Hudson River

Newark

New York

Brooklyn

N.J.

Chicago

IOWA

Schuylkill River

Pittsburgh

Philadelphia

Delaware Bay

ILLINOIS

INDIANA

OHIO

PENN.

Baltimore

DEL.

MD.

Washington, D.C.

ATLANTIC OCEAN

Wabash River

Cincinnati

Monongahela River

Missouri River

St. Louis

Ohio River

Louisville

Richmond

VIRGINIA

MISSOURI

KENTUCKY

Chesapeake Bay

0   50   100 miles
0   50   100 kilometers

Legend

- ◉ Cities with over 100,000 population
- F Flour
- 🪡 Textiles
- 👕 Clothing and footwear
- ⛏ Iron and copper ore
- C Coal
- 🪵 Timber
- ⚙ Machinery and equipment
- 🔫 Weaponry
- —— Canal
- —— Railroad

GEOGRAPHY SKILLBUILDER

1. **Region** In areas where the textile industry was strong, what other industry was also prominent?
2. **Place** How did the sites of New York City, Philadelphia, and Cincinnati encourage their growth as industrial towns?

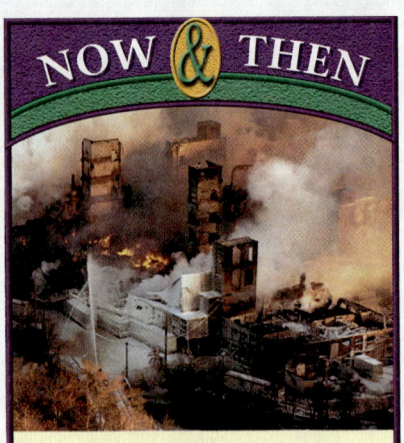

FROM THE ASHES

Malden Mills, the largest employer in Lawrence, Massachusetts (near Lowell) was devasted by fire in December 1995, as shown above.

The mills' owner, septuagenarian Aaron Feuerstein, not only announced that he intended to rebuild but pledged to keep his employees on the payroll during reconstruction.

To much acclaim for his generosity, Mr. Feuerstein said:

"Everything I did after the fire was in keeping with the ethical standards I've tried to maintain my entire life. . . . Whether I deserve it or not, I guess I became a symbol of what the average worker would like corporate America to be in a time when the American dream has been pretty badly injured."

After it was rebuilt, production of Malden Mills' popular synthetic product—Polartec—doubled.

THE LOWELL MILL Mill owners hired females because they could pay them lower wages than men who did similar jobs. To the girls in the mills, though, textile work offered better pay than their only alternatives: teaching, sewing, and domestic work. In an 1846 letter to her father in New Hampshire, 16-year-old Mary Paul expressed her satisfaction with her situation at Lowell.

★ A PERSONAL VOICE MARY PAUL

"I am at work in a spinning room tending four sides of warp which is one girl's work. The overseer tells me that he never had a girl get along better than I do. . . . I have a very good boarding place, have enough to eat. . . . The girls are all kind and obliging. . . . I think that the factory is the best place for me and if any girl wants employment, I advise them to come to Lowell."

—quoted in *Women and the American Experience*

Like Mary Paul, who eventually left factory work to pursue other work, most female workers stayed at Lowell for only a few years. Harriet Hanson Robinson, a mill girl who later became involved in the abolition and women's rights movements, applauded the mill girls' influence in carrying "new fashions, new books, new ideas" back to their homes.

CONDITIONS AT LOWELL The workday at Lowell began at 5 A.M., Mary Paul wrote her father, with a bell ringing "for the folks to get up. At seven they are called to the mill. At half past twelve we have dinner, are called back again at one and stay until half past seven."

These hours probably didn't seem long to farm girls, but heat, darkness, and poor ventilation in the factories contributed to discomfort and illness. Overseers would nail windows shut to seal in the humidity they thought prevented the threads from breaking, so that in the summer the weaving rooms felt like ovens. In the winter, pungent smoke from whale-oil lamps blended with the cotton dust to make breathing difficult.

Mill conditions continued to deteriorate in the 1830s. Managers forced workers to increase their pace. Between 1836 and 1850, Lowell owners tripled the number of spindles and looms but hired only 50 percent more workers to operate them. Factory rules tightened too. After gulping a noon meal, workers now had to rush back to the weaving rooms to avoid fines for lateness. Mill workers began to organize. In 1834, the Lowell mills announced a 15 percent wage cut. Eight hundred mill girls conducted a **strike,** a work stoppage in order to force an employer to respond to demands. **B**

STRIKES AT LOWELL Under the heading "UNION IS POWER," the Lowell Mills strikers of 1834 issued a proclamation declaring that they would not return to work "unless our wages are continued to us as they have been." For its part, the company threatened to recruit local women to fill the strikers' jobs. Criticized by the Lowell press and clergy, most of the strikers agreed to return to work at reduced wages. The mill owners fired the strike leaders.

In 1836, Lowell mill workers struck again, this time over an increase in their board charges that was equivalent to a 12.5 percent pay cut. Twice as many

Background
Living conditions for workers in the growing factory towns and other urban areas were harsh. Most workers lived in tenements—poorly made, crowded apartment buildings. Lacking adequate lighting, ventilation, and sanitation, tenements were unhealthy places to live.

MAIN IDEA

Analyzing Causes
B What factors contributed to the worsening conditions workers endured at Lowell beginning in the 1830s?

▲
Lowell mill
workers often
lived in company-
owned boarding
houses.

women participated as had two years earlier. Only 11 years old at the time of the strike, Harriet Hanson later recalled the protest.

★ A PERSONAL VOICE HARRIET HANSON

"As I looked back at the long line that followed me, I was more proud than I have ever been since at any success I may have achieved, and more proud than I shall ever be again until my own beloved State gives to its women citizens the right of suffrage [voting]."

—quoted in *Women's America: Refocusing the Past*

Again, the company prevailed. It fired the strike leaders and dismissed Harriet Hanson's widowed mother, a boarding-house supervisor. Most of the strikers returned to their spindles and looms.

In the 1840s, the mill girls took their concerns to the political arena. In 1845, Sarah Bagley founded the Lowell Female Labor Reform Association to petition the Massachusetts state legislature for a ten-hour workday. The proposed legislation failed, but the Lowell Association was able to help defeat a local legislator who opposed the bill. **C**

MAIN IDEA

Evaluating Decisions

C Based on the results, do you think the decision to strike at Lowell was a good one? Explain.

Workers Seek Better Conditions

Conditions for all workers deteriorated during the 1830s. Skilled artisans, who had originally formed unions to preserve their own interests, began to ally themselves with unskilled laborers. When Philadelphia coal workers struck for a 10-hour day and a wage increase in 1835, for example, carpenters, printers, and other artisans joined them in what became the first general strike in the United States.

Although only 1 or 2 percent of U.S. workers were organized, the 1830s and 1840s saw dozens of strikes—many for higher wages, but some for a shorter workday. Employers won most of these strikes because they could easily replace unskilled workers with strikebreakers who would toil long hours for low wages. Many strikebreakers were immigrants who had fled even worse poverty in Europe.

"I regard my work people just as I regard my machinery."

TEXTILE MILL MANAGER, 1840s

IMMIGRATION INCREASES European immigration rose dramatically in the United States between 1830 and 1860. In the decade 1845–1854 alone nearly

3 million immigrants were added to the U.S. population that had numbered just over 20 million. The majority of the immigrants were German or Irish.

Most immigrants avoided the South because slavery limited their economic opportunity. What's more, Southerners were generally hostile to European, particularly Catholic, immigrants. German immigrants clustered in the upper Mississippi Valley and in the Ohio Valley. Most German immigrants had been farmers in Europe, but some became professionals, artisans, and shopkeepers in the United States.

A SECOND WAVE Irish immigrants settled in the large cities of the East. Nearly a million Irish immigrants had settled in America between 1815 and 1844. Between 1845 and 1854 Irish immigration soared after a blight destroyed the peasants' staple crop, potatoes, which led to a famine in Ireland. The Great Potato Famine killed as many as 1 million of the Irish people and drove over 1 million more to new homes in America.

Irish immigrants faced bitter prejudice, both because they were Roman Catholic and because they were poor. Frightened by allegations of a Catholic conspiracy to take over the country, Protestant mobs in New York, Philadelphia, and Boston rampaged through Irish neighborhoods. Native-born artisans, whose wages had fallen because of competition from unskilled laborers and factory production, considered Irish immigrants the most unfair competition of all. Their willingness to work for low wages under terrible conditions made the desperate Irish newcomers easy prey for employers who sought to break strikes with cheap labor.

NATIONAL TRADES' UNION In their earliest attempts to organize, journeymen formed trade unions specific to each trade. For example, journeymen shoemakers

Background
The hostility and resentment that Irish immigrants faced, unfortunately, became part of the larger immigrant experience. Later, Jews, eastern and southern Europeans, Mexicans, and the Chinese would suffer the same kind of prejudice and stereotyping.

This 1848 engraving shows immigrants arriving in New York City from Europe.

▼

organized one of the nation's earliest strikes in 1806. During the 1830s, the trade unions in different towns began to join together to establish unions for such trades as carpentry, shoemaking, weaving, printing, and comb making. By means of these unions, the workers sought to standardize wages and conditions throughout each industry.

In a few cities the trade unions united to form federations. In 1834, for example, journeymen's organizations from six industries formed the largest of these unions, the **National Trades' Union,** which lasted until 1837. The trade-union movement faced fierce opposition from bankers and owners, who threatened the unions by forming associations of their own. In addition, workers' efforts to organize were at first hampered by court decisions declaring strikes illegal. **D**

MAIN IDEA

Evaluating

D Why was the national trade union movement important?

COURT BACKS STRIKERS In 1842, however, the Massachusetts Supreme Court supported workers' right to strike in the case of *Commonwealth v. Hunt.* In this case, Chief Justice Lemuel Shaw declared that Boston's journeymen bootmakers could act "in such a manner as best to subserve their own interests." A prominent American court finally had upheld the rights of labor. Although by 1860 barely 5,000 workers were members of what would now be called labor unions, far larger numbers of workers, 20,000 or more, participated in strikes for improved working conditions and wages.

The religious and social reform movements in the nation in the mid-19th century went hand in hand with economic changes that set in place the foundation for the modern American economy. While some Americans poured their efforts into reforming society, others sought new opportunities for economic growth and expansion. As the nation adjusted to the newly emerging market economy, migration west became a popular option.

▲ This trade union banner was made for the glass cutters organization around 1840.

SECTION 4 ASSESSMENT

1. TERMS & NAMES For each term or name, write a sentence explaining its significance.
- cottage industry
- master
- journeyman
- apprentice
- strike
- National Trades' Union

MAIN IDEA

2. TAKING NOTES
In a chart like the one shown, name things that contributed to the changing workplace in the first half of the 19th century.

The Changing Workplace

Which of these are still part of the workplace today?

CRITICAL THINKING

3. ANALYZING ISSUES
Do you think the positive effects of mechanizing the manufacturing process outweighed the negative effects? Why or why not?

Think About:
- changes in job opportunities for artisans, women, and unskilled male laborers
- changes in employer-employee relationships
- working conditions in factories
- the cost of manufactured goods

4. EVALUATING DECISIONS
If you were working in a factory during the mid-1800s, would you be a striker or a strikebreaker? Support your choice with details from the text.

5. IDENTIFYING PROBLEMS
How did the influx of new immigrants from Germany and Ireland affect circumstances in the American workplace?

Working at Mid-Century

In the years before the Civil War, most workers labored from dawn to dusk, six days a week, without benefits. Although many Northerners criticized the South for exploiting slave labor, Southerners criticized the industrial wage system, mostly in the North, for exploiting free workers. Both North and South used children—cheap labor—for full workdays. While 10-year-old slave children worked in the fields like adults, one Northern mill employed 100 children ages four to ten.

◀ COTTON PLANTATION FIELD SLAVES

The field slave's day during cotton harvest began with a bell an hour before dawn, a quick breakfast, and then a march to the fields. Men, women, and children spent the entire day picking cotton, bundling it, and coming back after dark carrying bales of cotton to the gin house. They then made their own suppers and ate quickly before falling asleep on wooden planks. No other antebellum workers had such harsh, brutal treatment imposed on them. For most field slaves, the master's whip was a constant threat.

Length of Day: pre-dawn until after dark
Type of Labor: picking and bundling cotton
Payment: substandard food and shelter

Courtesy George Eastman House

MILL WORKERS ▶

Approximately 80 percent of textile-mill workers were young women between the ages of 15 and 30. The day began with a bell for a quick breakfast in the boarding house, followed by a march to the factory, and the tending of machines all day. Workers put up with heavy dust, the roar of machines, and hot air with windows nailed shut to keep in the humidity. When competitive pressure increased on the owners, workers had to speed up their work for lower wages. Children made $1 a week; older girls and women, $3; men, $6.

Length of Day: 12 hours
Type of Labor: operating machines
Payment: $1 to $6 a week

Haymaking (1864), Winslow Homer. Oil on Canvas, 16" x 11". Museum purchase, Howald Fund/Columbus Museum of Art, Ohio

▲ FARMERS

Because farmers' livelihoods depended on the weather, soil conditions, and the market prices of crops, their earnings were unpredictable—but usually very low. Generally men spent their days clearing land, plowing, planting, and hoeing the fields, while women raised vegetables for family consumption, helped harvest fields, cared for livestock and for the family, and made clothing.

Length of Day: dawn until after dark
Type of Labor: planting, tending crops, caring for livestock
Payment: dependent on crop prices

DATA FILE
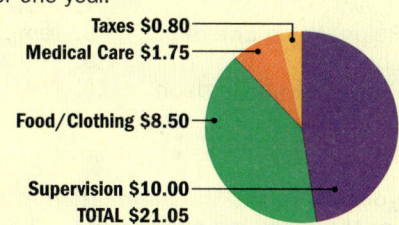

ANNUAL COST OF MAINTAINING A FIELD SLAVE

A typical Southern plantation owner in 1848–1860 would spend the following to take care of a field slave for one year.

Taxes $0.80
Medical Care $1.75
Food/Clothing $8.50
Supervision $10.00
TOTAL $21.05

Source: *Slavery and the Southern Economy*, Harold D. Woodman, editor

WORKERS IN THE MID-19TH CENTURY

Average monthly earnings from 1830 to 1850 for a few common occupations:

Job	Year	Monthly Earnings
Artisan	1830	$ 45
Laborer	1830	$ 26
Teacher, male	1840	$ 15
Teacher, female	1840	$ 7
Northern farmhand	1850	$ 13
Southern farmhand	1850	$ 9

Source: *Historical Statistics of the United States*

WORKERS IN THE EARLY 21ST CENTURY

Average monthly salaries for each profession:

Job	Monthly Salary
Teacher—elementary	$ 4,353
Teacher—high school	$ 4,533
Construction worker	$ 3,529
Service worker	$ 2,423

Source: *Occupational Employment and Statistics*, May 2008. U.S. Department of Labor

THINKING CRITICALLY

CONNECT TO HISTORY

1. **Drawing Conclusions** What attitudes about women and children do you see reflected in work patterns during the mid-19th century?

   📘 **SEE SKILLBUILDER HANDBOOK, PAGE R18.**

CONNECT TO TODAY

2. **Researching Children's Rights** Report on labor laws and societal changes that protected children's rights and prevented child labor in factories.

hmhsocialstudies.com RESEARCH WEB LINKS

TERMS & NAMES

For each term or name, write a sentence explaining its significance during the mid-19th century.

1. Second Great Awakening
2. revival
3. Ralph Waldo Emerson
4. abolition
5. William Lloyd Garrison
6. Frederick Douglass
7. Elizabeth Cady Stanton
8. temperance movement
9. strike
10. National Trades' Union

MAIN IDEAS

Use your notes and the information in the chapter to answer the following questions.

Religion Sparks Reform *(pages 240–245)*

1. What new religious ideas set the stage for the reform movements of the mid-19th century?
2. How did Dorothea Dix contribute to reform?

Slavery and Abolition *(pages 248–253)*

3. How did William Lloyd Garrison, Frederick Douglass, and David Walker each propose ending slavery?
4. What steps did white Southerners take to suppress slave revolts?

Women and Reform *(pages 254–258)*

5. What was the cult of domesticity?
6. What was the purpose of the Seneca Falls Convention?

The Changing Workplace *(pages 259–265)*

7. How did working conditions in the Lowell textile mills present new opportunities and new hazards?
8. Describe the two waves of U.S. immigration in the mid-1800s.

CRITICAL THINKING

1. **USING YOUR NOTES** Use a diagram similar to the one shown below to list the various reform movements that grew out of early-19th-century religious movements.

Religious Movements

2. **EVALUATING** What was the most important reform of this period? Support your answer with references to the text.

3. **INTERPRETING MAPS** Look at the map on page 261. From the pattern of industries shown on the map, what conclusions can you draw about the kinds of industries that were the first to develop in the West? Support your answer with references to the text.

4. **SYNTHESIZING** What means did the abolitionists use to try to convince the public that slavery should be abolished?

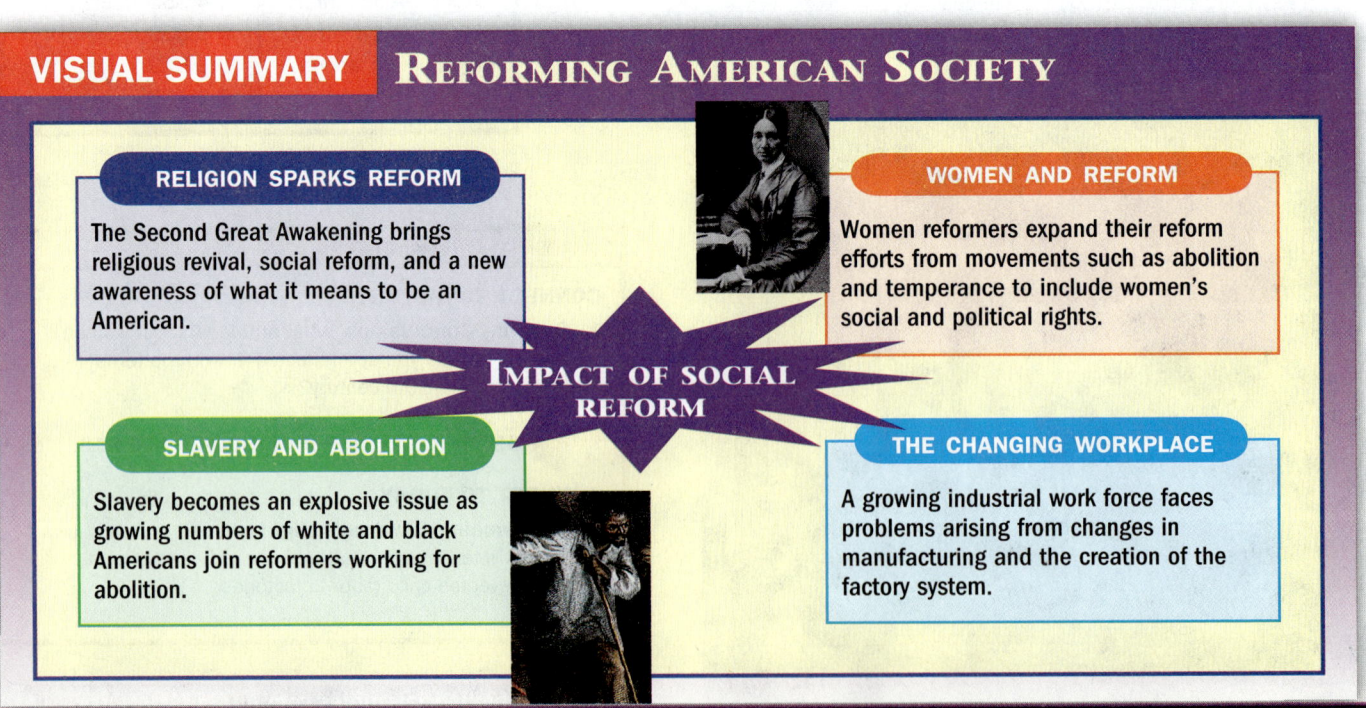

VISUAL SUMMARY REFORMING AMERICAN SOCIETY

RELIGION SPARKS REFORM

The Second Great Awakening brings religious revival, social reform, and a new awareness of what it means to be an American.

WOMEN AND REFORM

Women reformers expand their reform efforts from movements such as abolition and temperance to include women's social and political rights.

IMPACT OF SOCIAL REFORM

SLAVERY AND ABOLITION

Slavery becomes an explosive issue as growing numbers of white and black Americans join reformers working for abolition.

THE CHANGING WORKPLACE

A growing industrial work force faces problems arising from changes in manufacturing and the creation of the factory system.

Use the quotation below and your knowledge of U.S. history to answer question 1.

" We affirm that while women are liable to punishment for acts, which the laws call criminal, or while they are taxed in their labor or property for the support of government, they have a self-evident and indisputable right to a direct voice in the enactment of those laws and the formation of that government. . . . Who are citizens? Why males? Why foreigners? because they pay a poll-tax—the intemperate, the vicious, the ignorant, anybody and everybody who has the wit to elude pauperism and guardianship, if they are only *males*. And yet women are to live under this city charter, obey, be taxed to support, and no pauper establishment or guardianship is thought necessary for them . . . How inconsistent is all this!"

—**Harriot Kezia Hunt,** letter to *"Frederick U. Tracy . . . of the City of Boston, and the Citizens generally, and the Legislature in particular, November 15, 1854."*

1 In this passage, Dr. Harriot Kezia Hunt, an early-19th-century feminist, is asking that —

(1) women be entitled to vote.
(2) women pay their share of taxes.
(3) immigrants be subject to taxation.
(4) only intelligent people be entitled to vote.

2 The National Trades' Union was supported by all of the following groups *except* —

(1) factory workers and farmers.
(2) immigrants.
(3) business owners and bankers.
(4) journeymen and apprentices.

Use the quotation below and your knowledge of U.S. history to answer question 3.

" What is a man born for but to be a Reformer, a Remaker of what man has made; a renouncer of lies; a restorer of truth and good . . . The power, which is at once spring and regulator in all efforts of reform, is the conviction that there is infinite worthiness in man which will appear at the call of worth, and that all particular reforms are the removing of some impediment. . . . I see at once how paltry is all this generation of unbelievers, and what a house of cards their institutions are, and I see what one brave man, what one great thought executed might effect."

—**Ralph Waldo Emerson,** "Man the Reformer"

3 How does Emerson characterize his belief in reform?

(1) All people are capable of positive reform.
(2) Some people are good; others are not.
(3) Most people are too selfish for reform.
(4) Most institutions are ungodly and will fall.

4 The Seneca Falls Convention agenda modeled its resolutions on —

(1) the cult of domesticity.
(2) the Declaration of Independence.
(3) the Fourteenth Amendment.
(4) the temperance movement.

For additional test practice, go online for:
• Diagnostic tests • Tutorials

INTERACT WITH HISTORY

Recall the issues that you explored at the beginning of the chapter. Now that you know more about the changing workplace, address some specific actions to address workers' grievances. Work with a small group to develop a plan of action.

FOCUS ON WRITING

Reread the excerpt from the Declaration of Sentiments on page 257. Then write a paragraph explaining whether or not the resolutions proposed in the document have been achieved.

MULTIMEDIA ACTIVITY

Visit the links for Chapter Assessment to find out more about utopian communities. If you were a utopian reformer, what kind of community would you form? Prepare an oral report that describes your plans for a utopian community.

An Era of Growth and Disunion 1825–1877

UNIT PROJECT

Television News Broadcast

As you read Unit 3, choose an event that you can present in a television news broadcast. Compile a list of information for a script. Make a list of the visual images that you will use to illustrate your report. Present your news report to the class.

The Battle of Fredericksburg, December 13, 1862 by Carl Rochling

270

CHAPTER 9

EXPANDING MARKETS AND MOVING WEST

Essential Question

What were the causes and consequences of westward expansion?

New York Standards

KEY IDEA 2 Important ideas, social and cultural values, beliefs, and traditions from New York State and United States history illustrate the connections and interactions of people and events across time and from a variety of perspectives.

KEY IDEA 3 Important ideas, social and cultural values, beliefs, and traditions from New York State and United States history illustrate the connections and interactions of people and events across time and from a variety of perspectives.

William Ranney's 1853 painting *Advice on the Prairie* is an idealistic image of a family travelling west in the mid-1800s.

1825 The Erie Canal connects the East to the West.

1828 Andrew Jackson is elected president.

1830 Joseph Smith establishes the Mormon Church.

1832 Chief Black Hawk leads Sauk rebellion.

1832 Andrew Jackson is reelected.

1836 Martin Van Buren is elected president.

USA
WORLD

1825   **1830**   **1835**

1828 Uruguay becomes an independent republic.

1830 Revolutions occur in Belgium, France, and Poland.

1833 Santa Anna is elected president of Mexico.

1835 Ferdinand I becomes emperor of Austria.

INTERACT
WITH HISTORY

In the 1820s and 1830s the country was energized by new inventions and new business. Now it is 1840, and an economic downturn dampens the hopes of workers and business owners alike. Newspaper ads urge Americans to pack up and move west. But many people and nations already inhabit the North American West. Mexico owns a large part of the area, and Native Americans have been living there for centuries.

Explore the Issues

• What are some reasons countries expand their borders?

• What might be benefits or drawbacks of expansion?

1837 John Deere invents the steel plow.

1841 John Tyler becomes president when President William Henry Harrison dies.

1844 James K. Polk is elected president.

1848 Gold is discovered in California.

1848 Zachary Taylor is elected president.

1840

1845

1850

1837 Constitutional revolts occur in Lower and Upper Canada.

1840 Benito Juárez begins liberal reform movement in Mexico.

1847 U.S. wins Mexican-American War.

1848 Marx and Engels issue the *Communist Manifesto.*

Expanding Markets and Moving West **273**

CC Unit 1.I.A.2.c   CC Unit 1.I.A.3.b
CC Unit 2.II.A.2   CC Unit 2.II.B.1.a(1)
CC Unit 2.II.B.1.d   CC Unit 3.II.B.4

PI 3.3

The Market Revolution

MAIN IDEA	WHY IT MATTERS NOW	Terms & Names
Technological changes created greater interaction and more economic diversity among the regions of the nation.	The linking of markets continues today, as new technologies are opening the United States to globalized trade.	• Samuel F. B. Morse • specialization • market revolution • capitalism • entrepreneur • telegraph • John Deere • Cyrus McCormick

One American's Story

hmhsocialstudies.com
TAKING NOTES

Use the graphic organizer online to take notes on important inventions in the early 19th century.

In 1837, painter and scientist **Samuel F. B. Morse,** with Leonard Gale, built an electromagnetic telegraph. Morse's first model could send signals ten miles through copper wire. Morse asked Congress to fund an experimental telegraphic communication that would travel for 100 miles.

A PERSONAL VOICE SAMUEL F. B. MORSE

"This mode of instantaneous communication must inevitably become an instrument of immense power, to be wielded for good or for evil. . . . Let the sole right of using the Telegraph belong, in the first place, to the Government, who should grant . . . the right to lay down a communication between any two points for the purpose of transmitting intelligence."
—quoted in *Samuel F. B. Morse: His Letters and Journals*

Congress granted Morse $30,000 to build a 40-mile telegraph line between Baltimore and Washington, D.C. In 1844, Morse tapped out in code the words "What hath God wrought?" The message sped from Washington, D.C., over a metal wire in less than a second. As new communication links began to put people into instant communication with one another, new transportation links carried goods and people across vast regions.

▲ Samuel Morse was a painter before he became famous as an inventor.

U.S. Markets Expand

In the early 19th century, rural American workers produced their own goods or traded with neighbors to meet almost all of their needs. Farm families were self-sufficient—they grew crops and raised animals for food and made their own clothing, candles, and soap. At local markets, farmers sold wood, eggs, or butter for cash, which they used to purchase the coffee, tea, sugar, or horseshoes they couldn't produce themselves.

By midcentury, however, the United States had become more industrialized, especially in the Northeast, where the rise of textile mills and the factory system changed the lives of workers and consumers. Now, workers spent their earnings on goods produced by other workers. Farmers began to shift from self-sufficiency to **specialization,** raising one or two cash crops that they could sell at home or abroad.

These developments led to a **market revolution,** in which people bought and sold goods rather than making them for their own use. The market revolution created a striking change in the U.S. economy and in the daily lives of Americans. In these decades, goods and services multiplied while incomes rose. In fact, in the 1840s, the national economy grew more than it had in the previous 40 years.

THE ENTREPRENEURIAL SPIRIT The quickening pace of U.S. economic growth depended on **capitalism,** the economic system in which private businesses and individuals control the means of production—such as factories, machines, and land—and use them to earn profits. For example, in 1813, Francis Cabot Lowell and other Boston merchants had put up $400,000 to form the Boston Manufacturing Company, which produced textiles. Other businesspeople supplied their own funds to create capital—the money, property, machines, and factories that fueled America's expanding economy.

These investors, called **entrepreneurs** from a French word that means "to undertake," risked their own money in new industries. They risked losing their investment, but they also stood to earn huge profits if they succeeded. Alexander Mackay, a Scottish journalist who lived in Canada and traveled in the United States, applauded the entrepreneurs' competitive spirit. Ⓐ

MAIN IDEA

Analyzing Causes

Ⓐ What led to the rise of capitalism?

A PERSONAL VOICE ALEXANDER MACKAY

" America is a country in which fortunes have yet to be made. . . . All cannot be made wealthy, but all have a chance of securing a prize. This stimulates to the race, and hence the eagerness of the competition. "

—quoted in *The Western World*

NEW INVENTIONS Inventor-entrepreneurs began to develop goods to make life more comfortable for more people. For example, Charles Goodyear developed vulcanized rubber in 1839. Unlike untreated India rubber, the new product didn't freeze in cold weather or melt in hot weather. People first used the product to protect their boots, but, in the early 1900s, it became indispensable in the manufacturing of automobile tires.

A natural place for the growth of industrialization was in producing clothing, a process greatly aided by the invention of the sewing machine. Patented by Elias Howe in 1846, the sewing machine found its first use in shoe factories. Homemakers appreciated I. M. Singer's addition of the foot treadle, which drastically reduced the time it took to sew garments. More importantly,

ECONOMIC BACKGROUND

GOODYEAR AS ENTREPRENEUR

One entrepreneur who developed an industry still vital today was Charles Goodyear (1800–1860). Goodyear took a big risk that paid off for the American public—but left him penniless.

While he was exploring the problem of how to keep rubber elastic and waterproof under extreme temperatures, Goodyear purchased the rights of an inventor who had mixed rubber with sulfur. In 1839, Goodyear discovered that when heated, the mixture toughened into a durable elastic. In 1844, he received a patent for the process, named vulcanization after Vulcan, the mythological god of fire.

Unfortunately, Goodyear earned only scant monetary reward for his discovery, which others stole and used. The inventor was deep in debt when he died in 1860.

I. M. Singer's foot-treadle sewing machine was patented in 1851 and soon dominated the industry.
▼

the foot-treadle sewing machine led to the factory production of clothing. When clothing prices tumbled by more than 75 percent, increasing numbers of working people could afford to buy store-bought clothes.

IMPACT ON HOUSEHOLD ECONOMY While entrepreneurial activity boosted America's industrial output, American agriculture continued to flourish. Workers in industrial cities needed food. To meet this demand, American farmers began to use mechanized farm equipment produced in factories. Farmers, therefore, made significant contributions to the American industrial machine and became important consumers of manufactured items.

Manufactured items grew less expensive as technology advances lowered expenses. For example, a clock that had cost $50 to craft by hand in 1800 could be turned out by machine for half a dollar by midcentury. Falling prices meant that many workers became regular consumers. They purchased new products not only for work, but for comfort as well. **B**

MAIN IDEA

Analyzing Effects
B Describe the impact of the market revolution on potential customers.

The Economic Revolution

NOW & THEN

FROM TELEGRAPH TO INTERNET

What do the telegraph and the Internet have in common? They are both tools for instant communication. The telegraph relied on a network of wires that spanned the country. The Internet—an international network of smaller computer networks—allows any computer user to communicate instantly with any other computer user in the world.

These new inventions, many developed in the United States, contributed immensely to changes in American life. Some inventions simply made life more enjoyable. Other inventions fueled the economic revolution of the midcentury, and transformed manufacturing, transportation and communication.

IMPACT ON COMMUNICATION Improving on a device developed by Joseph Henry, Samuel F. B. Morse, a New England artist, created the **telegraph** in 1837 to carry messages, tapped in code, across copper wire. Within ten years, telegraph lines connected the larger cities on the East Coast.

Businesses used the new communication device to transmit orders and to relay up-to-date information on

MORSE CODE In 1837 Samuel Morse patents the telegraph, the first instant electronic communicator. Morse taps on a key to send bursts of electricity down a wire to the receiver, where an operator "translates" the coded bursts into understandable language within seconds.

TELEPHONE In 1876 Alexander Graham Bell invents the telephone, which relies on a steady stream of electricity, rather than electrical bursts, to transmit sounds. By 1900, there are over one million telephones in the United States.

MARCONI RADIO In 1895, Guglielmo Marconi, an Italian inventor, sends telegraph code through the air as electromagnetic waves. By the early 1900s, "the wireless" makes voice transmissions possible. Commercial radio stations are broadcasting music and entertainment programs by the 1920s.

1837   **1876**   **1895**

prices and sales. The telegraph was a huge success. The new railroads employed the telegraph to keep trains moving regularly and to warn engineers of safety hazards. By 1854, 23,000 miles of telegraph wire crossed the country.

IMPACT ON TRANSPORTATION Better and faster transportation became essential to the expansion of agriculture and industry. Farmers and manufacturers alike sought more direct ways to ship their goods to market. In 1807, Pennsylvanian Robert Fulton had ushered in the steamboat era when his boat, the *Clermont*, made the 150-mile trip up the Hudson River from New York City to Albany, New York, in 32 hours. Ships that had previously only been able to drift southward down the Mississippi with the current could now turn around to make the return trip because they were powered by steam engines. By 1830, 200 steamboats traveled the nation's western rivers, thus slashing freight rates as well as voyage times.

Water transport was particularly important in moving heavy machinery and such raw materials as lead and copper. Where waterways didn't exist, workers excavated them. In 1816, America had a mere 100 miles of canals. Twenty-five years later, the country boasted more than 3,300 miles of canals.

The Erie Canal was the nation's first major canal, and it was used heavily. Shipping charges fell to about a tenth of the cost of sending goods over land. Before the first shovel broke ground on the Erie Canal in 1817, for example, freight charges between Buffalo, New York, and New York City averaged 19 cents a ton per mile. By 1830, that average had fallen to less than 2 cents.

The Erie Canal's success led to dozens of other canal projects. Farmers in Ohio no longer depended on Mississippi River passage to New Orleans. They could now ship their grain via canal and river to New York City, the nation's major port. The canals also opened the heartland of America to world markets by connecting the Northeast to the Midwest.

EMERGENCE OF RAILROADS The heyday of the canals lasted only until the 1860s, due to the rapid emergence of railroads. Although shipping by rail cost significantly more in the 1840s than did shipping by canal, railroads offered the advantage of speed. In addition, trains could operate in the winter, and they brought goods to people who lived inland.

TELEVISION In the late 1800s, scientists begin to experiment with transmitting pictures as well as words through the air. In 1923, Vladimir Zworykin, a Russian-born American scientist, files a patent for the iconoscope, the first television camera tube suitable for broadcasting. In 1924 he files a patent for the kinescope, the picture tube used in receiving television signals. In 1929, Zworykin demonstrated his new television.

1929

COMPUTERS Scientists develop electronically powered computers during the 1940s. In 1951, UNIVAC I (UNIVersal Automatic Computer) becomes the first commercially available computer. In 1964, IBM initiates System/360, a family of mutually compatible computers that allow several terminals to be attached to one computer system.

1964

INTERNET Today, on the Internet, through e-mail (electronic mail) or online conversation, any two people can have instant dialogue. The Internet becomes the modern tool for instant global communication not only of words, but images, too.

By the 1840s, steam engines pulled freight at ten miles an hour—more than four times faster than canal boats traveled. Passengers found such speeds exciting, although early train travel was far from comfortable, as Samuel Breck, a Philadelphia merchant, complained.

A Personal Voice SAMUEL BRECK

" If one could stop when one wanted, and if one were not locked up in a box with 50 or 60 tobacco-chewers; and the engine and fire did not burn holes in one's clothes . . . and the smell of the smoke, of the oil, and of the chimney did not poison one . . . and [one] were not in danger of being blown sky-high or knocked off the rails—it would be the perfection of travelling. "

—quoted in *American Railroads*

Eventually, railroads grew to be both safe and reliable, and the cost of rail freight gradually came down. By 1850, almost 10,000 miles of track had been laid, and by 1859, railroads carried 2 billion tons of freight a year. **C**

New Markets Link Regions

By the 1840s, improved transportation and communication made America's regions interdependent. Arteries like the National Road, whose construction began in 1811, had also opened up western travel. By 1818, the road extended from Cumberland, Maryland, west to Wheeling, Virginia; by 1838, it reached as far west as Springfield, Illinois.

Growing links between America's regions contributed to the development of regional specialties. The South exported its cotton to England as well as to New England. The West's grain and livestock fed hungry factory workers in eastern cities and in Europe. The East manufactured textiles and machinery.

SOUTHERN AGRICULTURE Most of the South remained agricultural and relied on such crops as cotton, tobacco, and rice. Southerners who had seen the North's "filthy, overcrowded, licentious factories" looked with disfavor on industrialization. Even if wealthy Southerners wanted to build factories, they usually lacked the capital to do so because their money was tied up in land and the slaves required to plant and harvest the crops.

Though the new transportation and communication lines were less advanced in the South, these improvements helped keep Americans from every region in touch with one another. Furthermore, they changed the economic relationships between the regions, creating new markets and interdependencies.

NORTHEAST SHIPPING AND MANUFACTURING Heavy investment in canals and railroads transformed the Northeast into the center of American commerce. After the opening of the Erie Canal in 1825, New York City became the central link between American agriculture and European markets. In fact, more cotton was exported through New York City than through any other American city.

The most striking development of the era, however, was the rise in manufacturing. Although most Americans still lived in rural areas and only 14 percent of workers had manufacturing jobs, these workers produced more and better goods at lower prices than had ever been produced before. **D**

WORLD STAGE

BRITAIN'S COTTON IMPORTS

By 1840, the American South, the world's leading producer of cotton, was also the leading supplier of cotton to Great Britain. In all, Great Britain imported four-fifths of its cotton from the South. Cotton directly or indirectly provided work for one in eight people in Britain, then the world's leading industrial power.

For its part, Britain relied so heavily on Southern cotton that some cotton growers incorrectly assumed that the British would actively support the South during the Civil War. "No power on earth dares make war upon [cotton]," a South Carolina senator boldly declared in 1858. "Cotton is king."

MAIN IDEA

Analyzing Effects

C How did new products, communications methods, and transportation methods help the U.S. economy?

MAIN IDEA

Analyzing Causes

D How did the transportation revolution bind U.S. regions to one another and to the rest of the world?

"OUR FIELD IS THE WORLD."

McCormick Harvesting Machine Co., Chicago.
ESTABLISHED 1831.

MIDWEST FARMING

As the Northeast began to industrialize, many people moved to farm the fertile soil of the Midwest. First, however, they had to work very hard to make the land arable, or fit to cultivate. Many wooded areas had to be cleared before fields could be planted. Then two ingenious inventions allowed farmers to develop the farmland more efficiently and cheaply, and made farming more profitable. In 1837, blacksmith **John Deere** invented the first steel plow. It sliced through heavy soil much more easily than existing plows and therefore took less animal power to pull. Deere's steel plow enabled farmers to replace their oxen with horses.

Once harvest time arrived, the mechanical reaper, invented by **Cyrus McCormick,** permitted one farmer to do the work of five hired hands. The reaper was packed in parts and shipped to the farmer, along with a handbook of directions for assembling and operating. Armed with plows and reapers, ambitious farmers could shift from subsistence farming to growing such cash crops as wheat and corn.

Meanwhile, the rapid changes encouraged Southerners as well as Northerners to seek land in the seemingly limitless West.

▲ Cyrus McCormick patented the first successful horse-drawn grain reaper *(above left).* The McCormick company grew into the huge International Harvester Company. Their ads helped persuade farmers to revolutionize farming.

ASSESSMENT

1. TERMS & NAMES For each term or name, write a sentence explaining its significance.
- Samuel F. B. Morse
- specialization
- market revolution
- capitalism
- entrepreneur
- telegraph
- John Deere
- Cyrus McCormick

MAIN IDEA

2. TAKING NOTES

Create a time line like the one below, on which you label and date the important innovations in transportation, communication, and manufacturing during the early 19th century.

1825   1850

Which innovation do you think was most important, and why?

CRITICAL THINKING

3. COMPARING AND CONTRASTING

Compare economies of the different regions of the United States in the mid-1800s. Use details from the section to support your answer.

4. DRAWING CONCLUSIONS

Why were the reaper and the steel plow important?

5. ANALYZING EFFECTS

During the 1830s and 1840s, transportation and communication linked the country more than ever before. How did these advances affect ordinary Americans?

Think About:

- the new kinds of transportation
- specific changes in communications
- the new industries of the time period

Manifest Destiny

MAIN IDEA	WHY IT MATTERS NOW	Terms & Names
Americans moved west, energized by their belief in the rightful expansion of the United States from the Atlantic to the Pacific.	The South and Southwest are now the fastest-growing regions of the United States.	• manifest destiny • Mormons • Treaty of Fort • Joseph Smith Laramie • Brigham Young • Santa Fe Trail • "Fifty-Four Forty • Oregon Trail or Fight!"

One American's Story

Use the graphic organizer online to take notes about the reasons Americans headed west.

Amelia Stewart Knight's diary of her family's five-month journey to Oregon in 1853 described "the beautiful Boise River, with her green timber," which delighted the family. The last entry in the diary describes when she and her family reached their destination, Oregon.

A PERSONAL VOICE AMELIA STEWART KNIGHT

" [M]y eighth child was born. After this we picked up and ferried across the Columbia River, utilizing a skiff, canoes and flatboat. It took three days. Here husband traded two yoke of oxen for a half section of land with one-half acre planted to potatoes and a small log cabin and lean-to with no windows. This is the journey's end. "

—quoted in *Covered Wagon Women*

Knight's situation was by no means unique; probably one in five women who made the trek was pregnant. Her condition, however, did little to lighten her workload. Even young children shouldered important responsibilities on the trail.

▲
Amelia Stewart Knight told of camping by hot springs where she could brew tea without starting a fire.

The Frontier Draws Settlers

Many Americans assumed that the United States would extend its dominion to the Pacific Ocean and create a vast republic that would spread the blessings of democracy and civilization across the continent.

AMERICAN MISSION Thomas Jefferson had dreamed that the United States would become an "empire for liberty" by expanding across the continent "with room enough for our descendants to the thousandth and thousandth generation."

Toward that end, Jefferson's Louisiana Purchase in 1803 had doubled the young nation's size. For a quarter century after the War of 1812, Americans explored this huge territory in limited numbers. Then, in the 1840s, expansion fever gripped the country. Americans began to believe that their movement westward and southward was destined and ordained by God.

The editor of the *United States Magazine and Democratic Review* described the annexation of Texas in 1845 as "the fulfillment of our manifest destiny to over-spread the continent allotted by Providence for the free development of our yearly multiplying millions." Many Americans immediately seized on the phrase **"manifest destiny"** to express their belief that the United States' destiny was to expand to the Pacific Ocean and into Mexican territory. They believed that this destiny was manifest, or obvious. **A**

MAIN IDEA

Summarizing
A Explain the concept of manifest destiny.

ATTITUDES TOWARD THE FRONTIER Most Americans had practical reasons for moving west. Many settlers endured the trek because of personal economic problems. The panic of 1837, for example, had dire consequences and convinced many people that they would be better off attempting a fresh start in the West.

The abundance of land in the West was the greatest attraction. Whether for farming or speculation, land ownership was an important step toward prosperity. As farmers and miners moved west, merchants followed, seeking new markets.

While Americans had always traded with Europe, the transportation revolution increased opportunities for trade with Asia as well. Several harbors in the Oregon Territory helped expand trade with China and Japan and also served as naval stations for a Pacific fleet.

Settlers and Native Americans

The increasing number of U.S. settlers moving west inevitably affected Native American communities. Most Native Americans tried to maintain strong cultural traditions, even if forced to move from ancestral lands. Some began to assimilate—or become part of—the advancing white culture. Still others, although relatively few in number, fought hard to keep whites away from their homes.

THE BLACK HAWK WAR In the early 1830s, white settlers in western Illinois and eastern Iowa placed great pressure on the Native American people there to move west of the Mississippi River. Consequently, representatives from several Native American tribes visited Chief Black Hawk of the Sauk tribe, and one told of a prophet who had a vision of future events involving Black Hawk.

▲
John Wesley Jarvis painted Black Hawk *(left)* and his son, Whirling Thunder *(right)* in 1833.

A Personal Voice
" He said that the Big Black Bird Hawk was the man to lead the [Native American] nations and win back the old homes of the people; that when the fight began . . . the warriors would be without number; that back would come the buffalo . . . and that in a little while the white man would be driven to the eastern ocean and across to the farther shore from whence he came. "

—tribal elder quoted in *Native American Testimony*

MAIN IDEA

Evaluating Leadership
B What motivated Black Hawk to rebel against the United States?

The story convinced Black Hawk to lead a rebellion against the United States. The Black Hawk War started in Illinois and spread to the Wisconsin Territory. It ended in August 1832, when Illinois militia members slaughtered more than 200 Sauk and Fox people. As a result, the Sauk and Fox tribes were forcibly removed to areas west of the Mississippi. **B**

MIDDLE GROUND The place that neither the Native Americans nor the settlers dominated, according to historian Richard White, was the middle ground. As long as settlers needed Native Americans as trading partners and guides, relations between settlers and Native Americans could be beneficial. Amelia Stewart Knight described such an encounter on the middle ground.

By the 1840s, the middle ground was well west of the Mississippi, because the Indian Removal Act of 1830 and other Indian removal treaties had pushed Native Americans off their eastern lands to make room for the settlers.

FORT LARAMIE TREATY As settlers moved west, small numbers of displaced Native Americans occasionally fought them. The U.S. government responded to the settlers' fears of attack by calling a conference near what is now Laramie, Wyoming. The Cheyenne, Arapaho, Sioux, Crow, and others joined U.S. representatives in swearing "to maintain good faith and friendship in all their mutual intercourse, and to make an effective and lasting peace."

The 1851 **Treaty of Fort Laramie** provided various Native American nations control of the Central Plains, land east of the Rocky Mountains that stretched roughly from the Arkansas River north to Canada. In turn, these Native Americans promised not to attack settlers and to allow the construction of government forts and roads. The government pledged to honor the agreed-upon boundaries and to make annual payments to the Native Americans.

Still the movement of settlers increased. Traditional Native American hunting lands were trampled and depleted of buffalo and elk. The U.S. government repeatedly violated the terms of the treaty. Subsequent treaties demanded that Native Americans abandon their lands and move to reservations. **C**

Trails West

While the westward movement of many U.S. settlers had disastrous effects on the Native American communities there, the experience was also somewhat perilous for traders and settlers. Nevertheless, thousands made the trek, using a series of old Native American trails and new routes.

THE SANTA FE TRAIL One of the busiest and most well-known avenues of trade was the **Santa Fe Trail,** which led 780 miles from Independence, Missouri, to Santa Fe, New Mexico.

Each spring between 1821 and the 1860s, Missouri traders loaded their covered wagons with cloth, knives, and guns, and set off toward Santa Fe. For about the first 150 miles—to Council Grove, Kansas—wagons traveled alone. After that, fearing attacks by Kiowa and Comanche, among others, the traders banded into

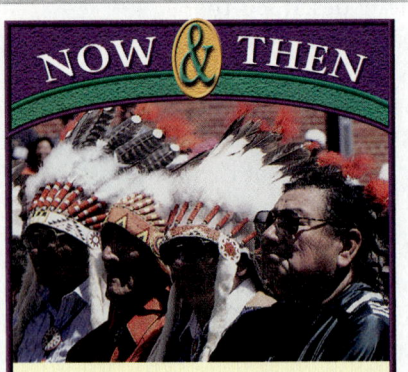

NOW & THEN

THE OGLALA SIOUX

Following the Fort Laramie Treaty, the federal government gradually reclaimed the Sioux's sacred Black Hills, and since 1889 the Oglala Sioux have lived on the Pine Ridge reservation in South Dakota.

In the 1990s, tourism was the largest source of revenue for Pine Ridge, which boasts some of the most beautiful territory in the Northern Plains. Visitors also come for the annual pow-wow, held in August, and the tribe's Prairie Winds casino.

Nevertheless, with only 20 percent of adults employed and a 61 percent poverty rate, the reservation remains one of the poorest areas in the United States.

MAIN IDEA

Analyzing Effects
C What were the effects of the U.S. government policies toward Native Americans in the mid-1800s?

American Trails West, 1860

The interior of a covered wagon may have looked like this on its way west. ▶

Blackfoot

Portland
Columbia R.
Yakima
CASCADE RANGE

Nez Perce

Crow

ROCKY MOUNTAINS

Sioux

Snake River

Fort Hall

Cheyenne

Pawnee

N. Platte River

Missouri River

Mississippi River

Council Bluffs

Nauvoo

Great Salt Lake
Sacramento

Salt Lake City

GREAT PLAINS

St. Louis

San Francisco

SIERRA NEVADA

Ute

Colorado River

Independence

Cimarron Cutoff

Arkansas River

Los Angeles

Navajo

Rio Grande

Santa Fe

Cherokee
Creek
Seminole
Choctaw
Chickasaw

Fort Smith

Mississippi River

PACIFIC OCEAN

El Paso

Red River

120°W

90°W

A Navajo man and woman in photographs taken by Edward S. Curtis

Legend:
— Butterfield Overland Trail
— California Trail
— Mormon Trail
— Old Spanish Trail
— Oregon Trail
— Sante Fe Trail

0   100   200 miles
0   100   200 kilometers

N
W   E
S

GEOGRAPHY SKILLBUILDER
1. **Location** Approximately how long was the trail from St. Louis to El Paso?
2. **Movement** At a wagon train speed of about 15 miles a day, about how long would that trip take?

Expanding Markets and Moving West **283**

Conestoga wagons were usually pulled by six horses. These wagons were capable of hauling loads up to six tons.

organized groups of up to 100 wagons. Scouts rode along the column to check for danger. At night the traders formed the wagons into squares with their wheels interlocked, forming a corral for horses, mules, and oxen.

Teamwork ended when Santa Fe came into view. Traders charged off on their own as each tried to be the first to enter the Mexican province of New Mexico. After a few days of trading, they loaded their wagons with silver, gold, and furs, and headed back to the United States. These traders established the first visible American presence in New Mexico and in the Mexican province of Arizona.

THE OREGON TRAIL In 1836, Marcus and Narcissa Whitman, Methodist missionaries, made their way into Oregon Territory where they set up mission schools to convert Native Americans to Christianity and educate them. By driving their wagon as far as Fort Boise, they proved that wagons could travel on the **Oregon Trail,** which started in Independence, Missouri, and ended in Portland, Oregon, in the Willamette Valley. Their letters east praising the fertile soil and abundant rainfall attracted hundreds of other Americans to the Oregon Trail. The route from Independence to Portland traced some of the same paths that Lewis and Clark had followed several decades earlier.

" Eastward I go only by force, but westward I go free."

HENRY DAVID THOREAU

Following the Whitmans' lead, some of the Oregon pioneers bought wooden-wheeled covered Conestoga wagons. But most walked, pushing handcarts loaded with a few precious possessions. The trip took months. Fever, diarrhea, and cholera killed many travelers, who were then buried alongside the trail.

Caravans provided protection against possible attack by Native Americans. They also helped combat the loneliness of the difficult journey, as Catherine Haun, who migrated from Iowa, explained.

⭐ **A PERSONAL VOICE** CATHERINE HAUN

" We womenfolk visited from wagon to wagon or congenial friends spent an hour walking, ever westward, and talking over our home life back in 'the states'; telling of the loved ones left behind; voicing our hopes for the future . . . and even whispering a little friendly gossip of emigrant life. "

—quoted in *Frontier Women*

By 1844, about 5,000 American settlers had arrived in Oregon and were farming its green and fertile Willamette Valley. **D**

THE MORMON MIGRATION One group that migrated westward along the Oregon Trail consisted of the **Mormons,** a religious community that would play a major role in the settling of the West. Mormon history began in western New York in 1827 when **Joseph Smith** and five associates established the Church of Jesus Christ of Latter-day Saints in Fayette, New York, in 1830.

Smith and a growing band of followers decided to move west. They settled in Nauvoo, Illinois, in 1839. Within five years, the community numbered 20,000. When Smith's angry neighbors printed protests against polygamy, the Mormons'

MAIN IDEA

Analyzing Events

D What difficulties were faced by families like the Whitmans and the Hauns?

practice of having more than one wife, Smith destroyed their printing press. As a result, in 1844 he was jailed for treason. An anti-Mormon mob broke into the jail and murdered Smith and his brother.

Smith's successor, **Brigham Young,** decided to move his followers beyond the boundaries of the United States. Thousands of Mormons travelled by wagon north to Nebraska, across Wyoming to the Rockies, and then southwest. In 1847, the Mormons stopped at the edge of the lonely desert near the Great Salt Lake. **E**

The Mormons awarded plots of land to each family according to its size but held common ownership of two critical resources—water and timberland. Soon they had coaxed settlements and farms from the bleak landscape by irrigating their fields. Salt Lake City blossomed out of the land the Mormons called Deseret.

RESOLVING TERRITORIAL DISPUTES The Oregon Territory was only one point of contention between the United States and Britain. In the early 1840s, Great Britain still claimed areas in parts of what are now Maine and Minnesota. The Webster-Ashburton Treaty of 1842 settled these disputes in the East and the Midwest, but the two nations merely continued "joint occupation" of the Oregon Territory.

In 1844, Democrat James K. Polk's presidential platform called for annexation of the entire Oregon Territory. Reflecting widespread support for Polk's views, newspapers adopted the slogan **"Fifty-Four Forty or Fight!"** The slogan referred to the latitude 54°40', the northern limit of the disputed Oregon Territory. By the mid-1840s, however, the fur trade was in decline, and Britain's interest in the territory waned. On the American side, Polk's advisors deemed the land north of 49° latitude unsuited for agriculture. Consequently, the two countries peaceably agreed in 1846 to extend the mainland boundary with Canada along the forty-ninth parallel westward from the Rocky Mountains to Puget Sound, establishing the current U.S. boundary. Unfortunately, establishing the boundary in the Southwest would not be so easy.

MAIN IDEA

Analyzing Motives

E Why did the Mormons move farther west in their search for a new home?

Americans Headed West to...
• escape religious persecution
• find new markets for commerce
• claim land for farming, ranching, and mining
• locate harbors on the Pacific
• seek employment and avoid creditors after the panic of 1837
• spread the virtues of democracy

---

2 ASSESSMENT

1. TERMS & NAMES For each term or name, write a sentence explaining its significance.
- manifest destiny
- Treaty of Fort Laramie
- Santa Fe Trail
- Oregon Trail
- Mormons
- Joseph Smith
- Brigham Young
- "Fifty-Four Forty or Fight!"

MAIN IDEA

2. TAKING NOTES
Use a chart like this one to compare the motivations of travelers on the Oregon, Santa Fe, and Mormon trails.

Trail	Motivations
Oregon Trail	
Mormon Trail	
Santa Fe Trail	

Which do you think was the most common motive? Explain.

CRITICAL THINKING

3. EVALUATING
What were the benefits and drawbacks of the belief in manifest destiny? Use specific references to the section to support your response. **Think About:**
- the various reasons for the move westward
- the settlers' point of view
- the impact on Native Americans
- the impact on the nation as a whole

4. ANALYZING PRIMARY SOURCES
John L. O'Sullivan, editor of the *United States Magazine and Democratic Review*, described manifest destiny as meaning that American settlers should "possess the whole of the continent which Providence has given us for the development of the great experiment of liberty and . . . self-government." Do you think the same attitudes exist today? Explain.

GEOGRAPHY SPOTLIGHT

Mapping the Oregon Trail

In 1841, Congress appropriated $30,000 for a survey of the Oregon Trail. John C. Frémont was named to head the expeditions. Frémont earned his nickname "the Pathfinder" by leading four expeditions—which included artists, scientists, and cartographers, among them the German-born cartographer Charles Preuss—to explore the American West between 1842 and 1848. When Frémont submitted the report of his second expedition, Congress immediately ordered the printing of 10,000 copies, which were widely distributed.

The "Topographical Map of the Road from Missouri to Oregon," drawn by Preuss, appeared in seven sheets. Though settlers first used this route in 1836, it was not until 1846 that Preuss published his map to guide them. The long, narrow map shown here is called a "strip" map, a map that shows a thin strip of the earth's surface—in this case, the last stretch of the trail before reaching Fort Wallah-Wallah.

⑤ THE WHITMAN MISSION

The explorers came upon the Whitmans' missionary station. They found thriving families living primarily on potatoes of a "remarkably good quality."

⑥ THE NEZ PERCE PRAIRIE

Chief Looking Glass (left, in 1871) and the Nez Perce had "harmless" interactions with Frémont and his expedition.

1 FORT BOISÉE (BOISE)

This post became an important stopping point for settlers along the trail. Though salmon were plentiful in summer, Frémont noted that in the winter Native Americans often were forced to eat "every creeping thing, however loathsome and repulsive," to stay alive.

2 MAP NOTATION

Preuss recorded dates, distances, temperatures, and geographical features as the expedition progressed along the trail.

3 RECORDING NATURAL RESOURCES

On October 13, Frémont traveled through a desolate valley of the Columbia River to a region of "arable mountains," where he observed "nutritious grasses" and good soil that would support future flocks and herds.

4 CROSSING THE MOUNTAINS

Pioneers on the trail cut paths through the Blue Mountains, a wooded range that Frémont believed had been formed by "violent and extensive igneous [volcanic] action."

THINKING CRITICALLY

1. **Analyzing Patterns** Use the map to identify natural obstacles that settlers faced on the Oregon Trail.

2. **Creating a Thematic Map** Do research to find out more about early mapping efforts for other western trails. Then create a settler's map of a small section of one trail. To help you decide what information you should show, pose some questions that a settler might have and that your map will answer. Then, sketch and label your map.

 SEE SKILLBUILDER HANDBOOK, PAGE R32.

hmhsocialstudies.com **RESEARCH WEB LINKS**

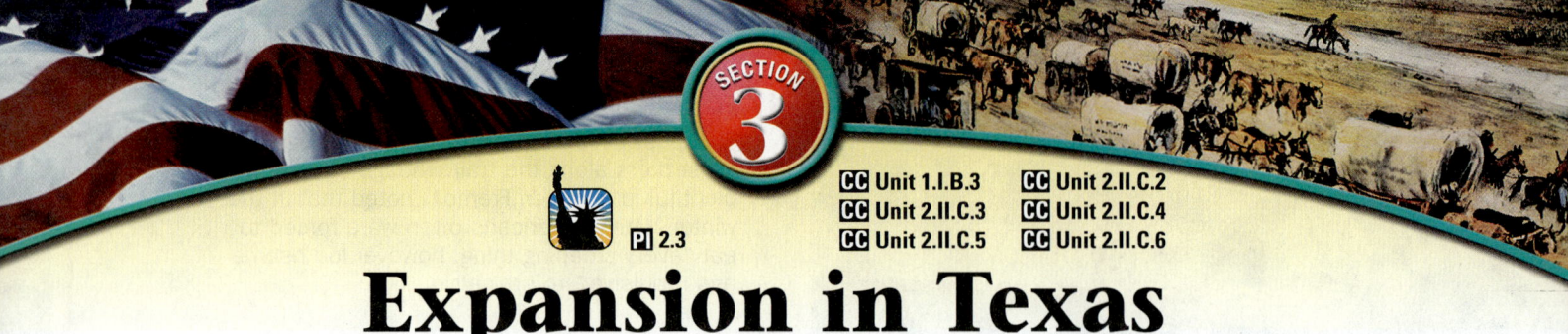

SECTION 3

PI 2.3

CC Unit 1.I.B.3
CC Unit 2.II.C.3
CC Unit 2.II.C.5

CC Unit 2.II.C.2
CC Unit 2.II.C.4
CC Unit 2.II.C.6

Expansion in Texas

MAIN IDEA	WHY IT MATTERS NOW	Terms & Names
Mexico offered land grants to American settlers, but conflict developed over religion and other cultural differences, and the issue of slavery.	Today, the state of Texas shares an important trading partnership with Mexico.	• Stephen F. Austin • land grant • Antonio López de Santa Anna • Texas Revolution • Alamo • Sam Houston • Republic of Texas • annex

One American's Story

hmhsocialstudies.com
TAKING NOTES

Use the graphic organizer online to take notes about American settlements in Texas.

In 1821, **Stephen F. Austin** led the first of several groups of American settlers to a fertile area "as good in every respect as man could wish for, land first rate, plenty of timber, fine water—beautifully rolling" along the Brazos River. However, Austin's plans didn't work out as well as he had hoped; 12 years later, he found himself in a Mexican prison and his new homeland in an uproar. After his release, Austin spoke about the impending crisis between Texas and Mexico.

▲ Stephen Austin established a colony of American settlers in *Tejas,* or Texas, then the northern-most province of the Mexican state of Coahuila.

A PERSONAL VOICE STEPHEN F. AUSTIN

"Texas needs peace, and a local government; its inhabitants are farmers, and they need a calm and quiet life. . . . [But] my efforts to serve Texas involved me in the labyrinth of Mexican politics. I was arrested, and have suffered a long persecution and imprisonment. . . . I fully hoped to have found Texas at peace and in tranquillity, but regret to find it in commotion; all disorganized, all in anarchy, and threatened with immediate hostilities. . . . Can this state of things exist without precipitating the country into a war? I think it cannot."

—quoted in *Texas: An Album of History*

Austin's warning proved to be prophetic. The conflict between Texas and Mexico would soon escalate into a bloody struggle.

Americans Settle in the Southwest

During three centuries of Spanish rule of Mexico, only a few thousand Mexican settlers had migrated to the vast landscape of what is now Texas. Despite the region's rich natural resources and a climate conducive to agriculture, a number of problems scared off many potential Mexican settlers. One was the growing friction between Native American and Mexican inhabitants of the area.

THE MISSION SYSTEM Since the earliest Spanish settlements, the Native American and Mexican populations in the Southwest had come into close contact. Before Mexico won its independence in 1821, Spain's system of Roman

Catholic missions in California, New Mexico, and Texas tried to convert Native Americans to Catholicism and to settle them on mission lands. To protect the missions, Spanish soldiers manned nearby *presidios,* or forts.

The mission system declined during the 1820s and 1830s, after Mexico had won its independence. After wresting the missions from Spanish control, the Mexican government offered the surrounding lands to government officials and ranchers. While some Native Americans were forced to remain as unpaid laborers, many others fled the missions, returning to traditional ways. When Mexicans captured Native Americans for forced labor, groups of hostile Comanche and Apache retaliated by sweeping through Texas, terrorizing Mexican settlements and stealing livestock that supported many American settlers and Mexican settlers, or *Tejanos.* Ⓐ

MAIN IDEA

Analyzing Effects

Ⓐ How did relations between the Mexicans and Native Americans in the Southwest change after 1821?

THE IMPACT OF MEXICAN INDEPENDENCE Trade opportunities between Mexico's northern provinces and the United States multiplied. Tejano livestock, mostly longhorn cattle, provided tallow, hides, and other commercial goods to trade in Santa Fe, New Mexico, north and west of Texas.

Newly free, Mexico sought to improve its economy. Toward that end, the country eased trade restrictions and made trade with the United States more attractive than trade between northern Mexico and other sections of Mexico. Gradually, the ties loosened between Mexico and the northern provinces, which included present-day New Mexico, California, Texas, Arizona, Nevada, and Utah.

Mexico was beginning to discover what Spain had previously learned: owning a vast territory did not necessarily mean controlling it. Mexico City—the seat of Mexican government—lay far from the northern provinces and often seemed indifferent to the problems of settlers in Texas. Native American groups, such as the Apache and the Comanche, continued to threaten the thinly scattered Mexican settlements in New Mexico and Texas. Consequently, the Mexican government began to look for ways to strengthen ties between Mexico City and the northern provinces.

MEXICO INVITES U.S. SETTLERS To prevent border violations by horse thieves and to protect the territory from Native American attacks, the Mexican government encouraged American farmers to settle in Texas. In 1821, and again in 1823 and 1824, Mexico offered enormous **land grants** to agents, who were called *empresarios.* The empresarios, in turn, attracted American settlers, who eagerly bought cheap land in return for a pledge to obey Mexican laws and observe the official religion of Roman Catholicism.

Many Americans as well as Mexicans rushed at the chance. The same restless determination that produced new inventions and manufactured goods fed the American urge to remove any barrier to settlement of the West. The population of Anglo, or English-speaking, settlers from Europe and the United States soon surpassed the population of Tejanos who lived in Texas. Until the 1830s, the Anglo settlers lived as naturalized Mexican citizens. Ⓑ

MAIN IDEA

Analyzing Motives

Ⓑ What did Mexico hope to gain from Anglo settlement in Texas?

AUSTIN IN TEXAS The most successful empresario, Stephen F. Austin, established a colony between the Brazos and Colorado rivers, where "no drunkard, no gambler, no profane swearer, and no idler" would be allowed. By 1825, Austin had issued 297 land grants to the group that later

NOW & THEN

TEJANO CULTURE

The Anglo and Mexican cultures of Texas have shaped one another, especially in terms of music, food, and language.

For example, Tejano music reflects roots in Mexican mariachi as well as American country and western music and is now a $100 million a year industry. As for language, *Tejanos* often speak a mixture of Spanish and English called Spanglish.

As Enrique Madrid, who lives in the border area between Texas and Mexico, says, "We have two very powerful cultures coming to terms with each other every day on the banks of the Rio Grande and creating a new culture."

became known as Texas's Old Three Hundred. Each family received 177 very inexpensive acres of farmland, or 4,428 acres for stock grazing, as well as a 10-year exemption from paying taxes. "I am convinced," Austin said, "that I could take on fifteen hundred families as easily as three hundred."

At the colony's capital in San Felipe, a visiting blacksmith, Noah Smithwick, described an established town, with "weddings and other social gatherings." Smithwick stayed in a simple home but learned that "in the course of time the pole cabin gave place to a handsome brick house and that the rude furnishings were replaced by the best the country boasted." **C**

In 1836, Mary Austin Holley, Stephen Austin's cousin, wrote admiringly about towns such as Galveston on the Gulf Coast and Bastrop.

MAIN IDEA

Evaluating Leadership
C Why was Stephen Austin's colony so successful?

★ **A PERSONAL VOICE** MARY AUSTIN HOLLEY

"Bastrop . . . continues to grow rapidly. It is a favorite spot for new settlers, and is quite the rage at present. . . . It is situated on a bend of the [Colorado], sloping beautifully down to the water, with ranges of timber—first oak, then pine, then cedar, rising in regular succession behind it."

—quoted in *Texas: An Album of History*

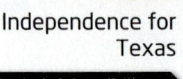

VIDEO
Independence for Texas

hmhsocialstudies.com

Word about Texas spread throughout the United States. Posters boldly stated, "Go To Texas!" Confident that Texas eventually would yield great wealth, Americans increasingly discussed extending the U.S. boundaries to the river they called the Rio Grande (known in Mexico as the Rio Bravo). President John Quincy Adams had previously offered to buy Texas for $1 million; President Andrew Jackson later upped the bid to $5 million. Mexico not only refused to sell Texas but also began to regret its hospitality to Anglo immigrants.

Texas Fights for Independence

As Texas's Anglo population surged, tensions grew with Mexico over cultural differences, as well as slavery. The overwhelmingly Protestant settlers spoke English rather than Spanish. Many of the settlers were Southern cotton or sugar farmers who had brought slaves with them. Mexico, which had abolished slavery in 1824, insisted in vain that the Texans free their slaves.

"COME TO TEXAS" In 1830, Mexico sealed its borders and slapped a heavy tax on the importation of American goods. Mexico, however, lacked sufficient troops to police its borders well. Despite restrictions, the Anglo population of Texas doubled between 1830 and 1834. In 1834, Austin won a repeal of the prohibition on immigration. By 1835, more than 1,000 Anglos each month streamed into Texas, scrawling the initials "G.T.T." on their doors to indicate that they had "Gone to Texas." A year later, Texas's population included only 3,500 Tejanos, 12,000 Native Americans, 45,000 Anglos, and 5,000 African Americans. **D**

Meanwhile, Mexican politics became increasingly unstable. Austin had traveled to Mexico City late in 1833 to present petitions for greater self-government for Texas to Mexican president **Antonio López de Santa Anna.**

KEY PLAYER

SANTA ANNA
1795–1876

Antonio López de Santa Anna began his career fighting for Spain in the war over Mexican independence. Later, he switched sides to fight for Mexico.

Declaring himself the "Napoleon of the West," Santa Anna took control of the government about ten years after Mexico won independence in 1821. He spent the next 34 years alternately serving as president, leading troops into battle, and living in exile. He served as president 11 times. Santa Anna was a complex man with much charm. He sacrificed his considerable wealth to return again and again to the battlefield and died in poverty and almost forgotten.

MAIN IDEA

Contrasting
D List some of the cultural conflicts caused by the influx of Anglo settlers into Texas.

While Austin was on his way home, Santa Anna suspended the 1824 Mexican constitution and had Austin imprisoned for inciting revolution. After Santa Anna revoked local powers in Texas and other Mexican states, several rebellions erupted, including what would eventually be known as the **Texas Revolution.**

"REMEMBER THE ALAMO!" Austin had argued with Santa Anna for self-government for Texas, but without success. Determined to force Texas to obey laws he had established, Santa Anna marched toward San Antonio at the head of a 4,000-member army. At the same time, Austin and his followers issued a call for Texans to arm themselves.

Late in 1835, the Texans attacked. They drove the Mexican forces from the **Alamo,** an abandoned mission and fort. In response, Santa Anna swept northward and stormed and destroyed the small American garrison in the Alamo. All 187 U.S. defenders died, including the famous frontiersmen Jim Bowie, who had designed the razor-sharp Bowie knife, and Davy Crockett, who sported a raccoon cap with a long tail hanging down his back. Hundreds of Mexicans also perished. Only a few women and children were spared. **E**

THE LONE STAR REPUBLIC Later in March of 1836, Santa Anna's troops executed 300 rebels at Goliad. The Alamo and Goliad victories would prove costly for Santa Anna. Six weeks after the defeat of the Alamo, on April 21, the Texans

MAIN IDEA

Comparing
E Compare the reasons for the Texas Revolution with the reasons for the American Revolution.

hmhsocialstudies.com
INTERACTIVE
Witness the action of the Battle of San Jacinto.

War for Texas Independence, 1835–1836

hmhsocialstudies.com   INTERACTIVE MAP

Land disputed by Texas and Mexico

UNITED STATES

REPUBLIC OF TEXAS

Legend:
- Texan forces
- Mexican forces
- Texan victory
- Mexican victory

0   75   150 miles
0   75   150 kilometers

Red River
Sabine River
Trinity River
Neches River
Brazos River
Colorado River
Pecos River
Rio Grande
Nueces River

Nacogdoches
Waterloo (Austin)
Washington-on-the-Brazos
ALAMO, Feb. 23–Mar. 6, 1836
SAN ANTONIO, Dec. 10, 1835
Houston
SAN JACINTO, Apr. 21, 1836
Santa Anna
GOLIAD, Mar. 20, 1836
Galveston
Matagorda
REFUGIO, Mar. 12–15, 1836
Laredo
Corpus Christi
MEXICO
Matamoros

Gulf of Mexico

95°W   91°W

Henry Arthur McArdle conveys the brutality of the fighting in *Dawn at the Alamo*, painted between 1876 and 1883.

GEOGRAPHY SKILLBUILDER
1. **Place** What geographical feature marked the northern border of the Republic of Texas?
2. **Region** What does the map show as a major disagreement left unresolved by the war?

Expanding Markets and Moving West **291**

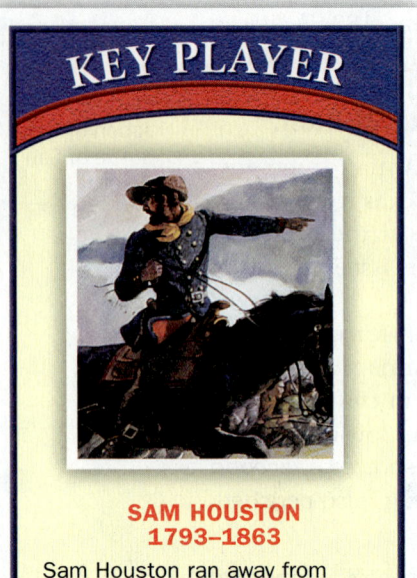

KEY PLAYER

SAM HOUSTON
1793–1863

Sam Houston ran away from home at about age 15 and lived for nearly three years with the Cherokee. He later fought in the U.S. Army, studied law, was elected to Congress, and became governor of Tennessee.

In his memoirs, Houston told of listening in vain for the signal guns indicating that the Alamo still stood.

"I listened with an acuteness of sense which no man can understand whose hearing has not been sharpened by the teachings of the dwellers of the forest."

struck back. Led by **Sam Houston,** they defeated Santa Anna at the Battle of San Jacinto. With shouts of "Remember the Alamo!" the Texans killed 630 of Santa Anna's soldiers in 18 minutes and captured Santa Anna. The victorious Texans set Santa Anna free after he signed the Treaty of Velasco, which granted independence to Texas. In September 1836, Houston became president of the **Republic of Texas.** The new "Lone Star Republic" set up an army and a navy and proudly flew its new silk flag with the lone gold star.

TEXAS JOINS THE UNION On March 2, 1836, as the battle for the Alamo was raging, Texans had declared their independence from Mexico. Believing that Mexico had deprived them of their fundamental rights, the Texas rebels had likened themselves to the American colonists who had chafed under British rule 60 years earlier. On March 16, they ratified a constitution based on that of the United States. In 1838, Sam Houston invited the United States to **annex,** or incorporate, the Texas republic into the United States. Most people within Texas hoped this would happen. U.S. opinion, however, divided along sectional lines. Southerners sought to extend slavery, already established in Texas. Northerners feared that annexation of more slave territory would tip the uneasy balance in the Senate in favor of slave states—and prompt war with Mexico. **F**

Then in 1844, the U.S. presidential election featured a debate on westward expansion. The man who would win the presidency, James K. Polk, a slaveholder, firmly favored annexation of Texas "at the earliest practicable period."

On December 29, 1845, Texas became the 28th state in the Union. A furious Mexican government recalled its ambassador from Washington. Events were moving quickly toward war.

MAIN IDEA

Contrasting
F Explain the differences between the Northern and Southern positions on the annexation of Texas.

SECTION 3 ASSESSMENT

1. TERMS & NAMES For each term or name, write a sentence explaining its significance.
- Stephen F. Austin
- land grant
- Antonio López de Santa Anna
- Texas Revolution
- Alamo
- Sam Houston
- Republic of Texas
- annex

MAIN IDEA

2. TAKING NOTES
Use a diagram similar to this one to analyze the relationship between Mexican authorities and Anglos settling in Texas.

	Mexico	Settlers
Goals		
Actions		
Outcomes		

What other actions might Mexico or the settlers have taken to avoid conflict?

CRITICAL THINKING

3. COMPARING
Compare and contrast Santa Anna and Austin as leaders. Use details from the section to explain your answer. **Think About:**
- Santa Anna's role as president of Mexico
- Santa Anna's qualities as a military leader
- Austin's settlement in Texas
- Austin's abilities as a negotiator

4. SYNTHESIZING
Which group or country gained the most from the entry of Texas into the United States? Who lost the most? Support your opinion with specific references to the section.

SECTION
4

PI 2.5
PI 3.1

CC Unit 1.I.B.3
CC Unit 2.II.C.4
CC Unit 2.II.C.6

CC Unit 2.II.C.3
CC Unit 2.II.C.5

The War with Mexico

MAIN IDEA	WHY IT MATTERS NOW	Terms & Names
Tensions over the U.S. annexation of Texas led to war with Mexico, resulting in huge territorial gains for the United States.	The United States has achieved its goal of expanding across the continent from east to west.	• James K. Polk • Zachary Taylor • Stephen Kearny • Republic of California • Winfield Scott • Treaty of Guadalupe Hidalgo • Gadsden Purchase • forty-niners • gold rush

One American's Story

hmhsocialstudies.com
TAKING NOTES

Use the graphic organizer online to take notes about the war with Mexico and its effect on the U.S. border.

Robert E. Lee was born into a prominent Virginia family in 1807. His father had been a hero of the American Revolution. In 1846, the war with Mexico provided the 39-year-old captain with his first combat experience. Among the soldiers whom Lee directed in battle was his younger brother, Sidney Smith Lee. The elder Lee wrote about the battle.

A PERSONAL VOICE ROBERT E. LEE

" No matter where I turned, my eyes reverted to [my brother], and I stood by his gun whenever I was not wanted elsewhere. Oh, I felt awfully, and am at a loss what I should have done had he been cut down before me. I thank God that he was saved. . . . [The service from the American battery] was terrific, and the shells thrown from our battery were constant and regular discharges, so beautiful in their flight and so destructive in their fall. It was awful! My heart bled for the inhabitants. The soldiers I did not care so much for, but it was terrible to think of the women and children."

—a letter cited in *R. E. Lee* by Douglas Southall Freeman

▲ **Robert E. Lee followed his father into a military career, graduating from the new U.S. Military Academy at West Point.**

In recoiling at the ugliness of the war with Mexico, Lee hardly stood alone. From the start, Americans hotly debated whether the United States should pursue the war.

Polk Urges War

Hostilities between the United States and Mexico, which had flared during the Texas Revolution in 1836, reignited over the American annexation of Texas in 1845. The two countries might have solved these issues peaceably if not for the continuing instability of the Mexican government and the territorial aspirations of the U.S. president, **James K. Polk.**

James Polk, also known as "Polk the Purposeful"

Polk now believed that war with Mexico would bring not only Texas but also New Mexico and California into the Union. The president supported Texas's claims in disputes with Mexico over the Texas-Mexico border. While Texas insisted that its southern border extended to the Rio Grande, Mexico insisted that Texas's border stopped at the Nueces River, 100 miles northeast of the Rio Grande.

SLIDELL'S REJECTION In 1844, Santa Anna was ousted as Mexico's president. The Mexican political situation was confusing and unpredictable. In late 1845, "Polk the Purposeful" sent a Spanish-speaking emissary, John Slidell, to Mexico to purchase California and New Mexico and to gain approval of the Rio Grande as the Texas border. When Slidell arrived, Mexican officials refused to receive him. Hoping for Mexican aggression that would unify Americans behind a war, Polk then issued orders for General **Zachary Taylor** to march to the Rio Grande and blockade the river. Mexicans viewed this action as a violation of their rights.

Many Americans shared Polk's goals for expansion, but public opinion was split over resorting to military action. Slavery would soon emerge as the key issue complicating this debate.

SECTIONAL ATTITUDES TOWARD WAR The idea of war unleashed great public celebrations. Volunteers swarmed recruiting stations, and the advent of daily newspapers, printed on new rotary presses, gave the war a romantic appeal.

Not everyone cheered. The abolitionist James Russell Lowell considered the war a "national crime committed in behoof of slavery, our common sin." Even proslavery spokesman John C. Calhoun saw the perils of expansionism. Mexico, he said, was "the forbidden fruit; the penalty of eating it would be to subject our institutions to political death."

Many Southerners, however, saw the annexation of Texas as an opportunity to extend slavery and increase Southern power in Congress. Furthermore, the Wilmot Proviso, a proposed amendment to a military appropriations bill of 1846, prohibited slavery in lands that might be gained from Mexico. This attack on slavery solidified Southern support for war by transforming the debate on war into a debate on slavery.

Northerners mainly opposed the war. Antislavery Whigs and abolitionists saw the war as a plot to expand slavery and ensure Southern domination of the Union. In a resolution adopted by the Massachusetts legislature, Charles Sumner proclaimed that "the lives of Mexicans are sacrificed in this cause; and a domestic question, which should be reserved for bloodless debate in our own country, is transferred to fields of battle in a foreign land." **A**

MAIN IDEA

Analyzing Efects
A How did the issue of slavery affect the debate over the war with Mexico?

The War Begins

As Taylor positioned his forces at the Rio Grande in 1845–1846, John C. Frémont led an exploration party through Mexico's Alta California province, another violation of Mexico's territorial rights. The Mexican government had had enough.

Mexico responded to Taylor's invasion of the territory it claimed by sending troops across the Rio Grande. In a skirmish near Matamoros, Mexican soldiers killed 9 U.S. soldiers. Polk immediately sent a war message to Congress, declaring that by shedding "American blood upon American soil," Mexico had started the war. Representative Abraham Lincoln questioned the truthfulness of the message, asking "whether our citizens, whose blood was shed, as in his message declared, were or were not, at that time, armed officers and soldiers, sent into that settlement by the military order of the President." Lincoln introduced a "Spot Resolution," asking Polk to certify the spot where the skirmish had occurred.

Truthful or not, Polk's message persuaded the House to recognize a state of war with Mexico by a vote of 174 to 14, and the Senate by a vote of 40 to 2, with numerous abstentions. Some antislavery Whigs had tried to oppose the war but were barely allowed to gain the floor of Congress to speak. Since Polk withheld key facts, the full reality of what had happened on the distant Rio Grande was not known. But the theory and practice of manifest destiny had launched the United States into its first war on foreign territory. **B**

MAIN IDEA

Analyzing Causes

B How did President Polk provoke Mexico to attack U.S. forces?

KEARNY MARCHES WEST In 1846, as part of his plan to seize New Mexico and California, Polk ordered Colonel **Stephen Kearny** to march from Fort Leavenworth, Kansas, across the desert to Santa Fe, New Mexico. Kearny earned the nickname "the Long Marcher" as he and his men crossed 800 miles of barren ground. They were met in Santa Fe by a New Mexican contingent that included upper-class Mexicans who wanted to join the United States. New Mexico fell to the United States without a shot being fired. After dispatching some of his troops south to Mexico, the Long Marcher led the rest on another long trek, this time to southern California. **C**

MAIN IDEA

Analyzing Motives

C How do Kearny's actions support the idea of manifest destiny?

▲ This 19th-century wood engraving shows Colonel Stephen Kearny capturing Santa Fe, New Mexico.

THE REPUBLIC OF CALIFORNIA By the turn of the 19th century, Spanish settlers had set up more than 20 missions along the California coast. After independence, the Mexican government took over these missions, just as it had done in Texas. By the late 1830s, about 12,000 Mexican settlers had migrated to California to set up cattle ranches, where they pressed Native Americans into service as workers. By the mid-1840s, about 500 U.S. settlers also lived in California.

Polk's offer to buy California in 1845 aroused the indignation of the Mexican government. A group of American settlers, led by Frémont, seized the town of Sonoma in June 1846. Hoisting a flag that featured a grizzly bear, the rebels proudly declared their independence from Mexico and proclaimed the nation of the **Republic of California.** Kearny arrived from New Mexico and joined forces with Frémont and a U.S. naval expedition led by Commodore John D. Sloat. The Mexican troops quickly gave way, leaving U.S. forces in control of California.

THE WAR IN MEXICO For American troops in Mexico, one military victory followed another. Though Mexican soldiers gallantly defended their own soil, their army labored under poor leadership. In contrast, U.S. soldiers served under some of the nation's best officers, such as Captain Robert E. Lee and Captain Ulysses S. Grant, both West Point graduates.

Legend

- ✦ U.S. victory
- ✦ Mexican victory
- → U.S. forces
- → Mexican forces
- ▮ Acquired by U.S. in Texas annexation of 1845
- ▮ Acquired by U.S. in Treaty of Guadalupe Hidalgo, 1848
- ▮ Acquired by U.S. in Gadsden Purchase, 1853

0   200   400 miles
0   200   400 kilometers

PACIFIC OCEAN

San Francisco
MONTEREY July 7, 1846
SAN PASQUAL Dec. 6, 1846
Los Angeles
30°N
Santa Fe
Las Vegas
Albuquerque
Fort Leavenworth
Bent's Fort
Kearny
Arkansas R.
Red River
Colorado River
Gila River
Kearny
EL BRAZITO Dec. 25, 1846
El Paso
SACRAMENTO Feb. 28, 1847
Doniphan
Rio Grande
San Antonio
MEXICO
CHIHUAHUA Mar. 1–Apr. 28, 1847
Wool
MONTERREY Sept. 20–24, 1846
Corpus Christi
New Orleans
90°W
Gulf of Mexico
Matamoros
Taylor
Saltillo
Taylor
BUENA VISTA Feb. 22–23, 1847
Santa Anna
Mazatlán
TAMPICO Nov. 14, 1846
Tropic of Cancer
San Luis Potosí
110°W
20°N
MEXICO CITY Sept. 13–14, 1847
CHURUBUSCO Aug. 20, 1847
Scott
VERACRUZ Mar. 9–29, 1847
St. Lawrence R.

UNITED STATES, 1830

BRITISH NORTH AMERICA
OREGON TERRITORY
UNITED STATES
MEXICO

UNITED STATES, 1853

BRITISH NORTH AMERICA
UNITED STATES
MEXICO

GEOGRAPHY SKILLBUILDER

1. **Location** From which locations in Texas did U.S. forces come to Buena Vista?
2. **Region** In which country were most of the battles fought?

HISTORY

VIDEO
The Mexican-American War
↗ hmhsocialstudies.com

The American invasion of Mexico lasted about a year and featured a pair of colorful generals, Zachary Taylor and **Winfield Scott.** Affectionately nicknamed "Old Rough and Ready" because he sported a casual straw hat and plain brown coat, Taylor attacked and captured Monterrey, Mexico, in September 1846, but allowed the Mexican garrison to escape.

Meanwhile, Polk hatched a bizarre scheme with Santa Anna, who had been living in exile in Cuba. If Polk would help him sneak back to Mexico, Santa Anna promised he would end the war and mediate the border dispute. Polk agreed, but when Santa Anna returned to Mexico, he resumed the presidency, took command of the army and, in February 1847, ordered an attack on Taylor's forces at Buena Vista. Though the Mexican army boasted superior numbers, its soldiers suffered from exhaustion. Taylor's more rested troops pushed Santa Anna into Mexico's interior.

Scott's forces took advantage of Santa Anna's failed strategy and captured Veracruz in March. General Scott always wore a full-dress blue uniform with a yellow sash, which won him the nickname "Old Fuss and Feathers." Scott supervised an amphibious landing at Veracruz, in which an army of 10,000 landed on an island off Veracruz in 200 ships and ferried 67 boats in less than 5 hours. Scott's troops then set off for Mexico City, which they captured on September 14, 1847. Covering 260 miles, Scott's army had lost not a single battle.

America Gains the Spoils of War

For Mexico, the war in which it lost at least 25,000 lives and nearly half its land marked an ugly milestone in its relations with the United States. America's victory came at the cost of about 13,000 lives. Of these, nearly 2,000 died in battle or from wounds and more than 11,000 perished from diseases, such as yellow fever. However, the war enlarged U.S. territory by approximately one-third.

THE TREATY OF GUADALUPE HIDALGO On February 2, 1848, the United States and Mexico signed the **Treaty of Guadalupe Hidalgo.** Mexico agreed to the Rio Grande border for Texas and ceded New Mexico and California to the United States. The United States agreed to pay $15 million for the Mexican cession, which included present-day California, Nevada, New Mexico, Utah, most of Arizona, and parts of Colorado and Wyoming. The treaty guaranteed Mexicans living in these territories freedom of religion, protection of property, bilingual elections, and open borders.

Five years later, in 1853, President Franklin Pierce would authorize his emissary James Gadsden to pay Mexico an additional $10 million for another piece of territory south of the Gila River. Along with the settlement of Oregon and the Treaty of Guadalupe Hidalgo, the **Gadsden Purchase** established the current borders of the lower 48 states.

TAYLOR'S ELECTION IN 1848 In 1848 the Democrats nominated Lewis Cass for president and hesitated about the extension of slavery into America's vast new holdings. A small group of antislavery Democrats nominated Martin Van Buren to lead the Free-Soil Party, which supported a congressional prohibition on the extension of slavery into the territories. Van Buren captured 10 percent of the popular vote and no electoral votes. The Whig nominee, war hero Zachary Taylor, easily won the election. Taylor's victory, however, was soon overshadowed by a glittering discovery in one of America's new territories.

The California Gold Rush

In January 1848, James Marshall, an American carpenter working on John Sutter's property in the California Sierra Nevadas, discovered gold at Sutter's Mill. Word of the chance discovery traveled east.

THE RUSH BEGINS Soon after the news reached San Francisco, residents traveled to the Sacramento Valley in droves to pan for gold. Lacking staff and readers, San Francisco's newspaper, the *Californian,* suspended publication. An editorial in the final issue, dated May 29, complained that the whole country "resounds with the sordid cry of gold, GOLD, GOLD! while the field is left half-plowed, the house half-built, and everything neglected but the manufacture of shovels and pickaxes."

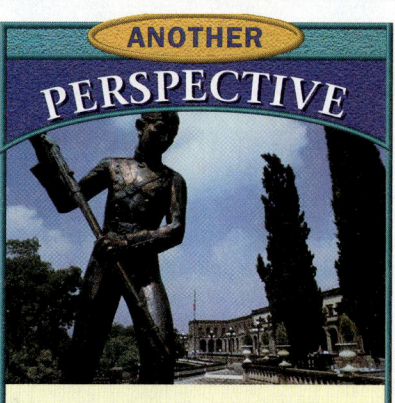

ANOTHER PERSPECTIVE

LOS NIÑOS HÉROES
Though most Americans know little about the war with Mexico, Mexicans view the war as a crucial event in their history.

On September 14, 1847, General Winfield Scott captured Mexico City after the hard-fought Battle of Chapultepec, the site of the Mexican military academy. There, six young cadets leaped from Chapultepec Castle to commit suicide rather than surrender to the U.S. Army. A monument *(shown above)* that honors *los Niños Héroes* (the boy heroes) inspires pilgrimages every September.

MAIN IDEA

Summarizing
D Explain the importance of the Treaty of Guadalupe Hidalgo and the Gadsden Purchase.

"THE WAY THEY GO TO CALIFORNIA"

This cartoon lithograph by Nathaniel Currier (1813–1888) was inspired by the California gold rush. Currier was a founder of the Currier and Ives company, which became famous for detailed lithographs of 19th-century daily life.

Here Currier portrays some of the hordes of prospectors who flocked from all over the world to California in 1849. The mob wields picks and shovels, desperate to find any means of transport to the "Golden West." While some miners dive into the water, weighed down by heavy tools, one clever prospector has invented a new type of airship to speed him to the treasure.

SKILLBUILDER
Analyzing Political Cartoons

1. How has the cartoonist added humor to this portrayal of the gold seekers?
2. What clues tell you that this cartoon is about the California gold rush?

 SEE SKILLBUILDER HANDBOOK, PAGE R24.

VIDEO
Gold Rush: Dangerous Shortcut to the West

 hmhsocialstudies.com

On June 6, 1848, Monterey's Mayor Walter Colton sent a scout to report on what was happening. After the scout returned on June 14, the mayor described the scene that had taken place in the middle of the town's main street.

A PERSONAL VOICE WALTER COLTON

"The blacksmith dropped his hammer, the carpenter his plane, the mason his trowel, the farmer his sickle, the baker his loaf, and the tapster his bottle. All were off for the mines. . . . I have only a community of women left, and a gang of prisoners, with here and there a soldier who will give his captain the slip at first chance. I don't blame the fellow a whit; seven dollars a month, while others are making two or three hundred a day!"

—quoted in *California: A Bicentennial History*

As gold fever traveled eastward, overland migration to California skyrocketed, from 400 in 1848 to 44,000 in 1850. The rest of the world soon caught the fever. Among the so-called **forty-niners,** the prospectors who flocked to California in 1849 in the **gold rush,** were people from Asia, South America, and Europe. **E**

IMPACT OF GOLD FEVER Because of its location as a supply center, San Francisco became "a pandemonium of a city," according to one traveler. Indeed, the city's population exploded from 1,000 in 1848 to 35,000 in 1850. Ferrying people and supplies, ships clogged San Francisco's harbor with a forest of masts.

Louisa Clapp and her husband, Fayette, left the comforts of a middle-class family in New England to join the gold rush for adventure. After living in San Francisco for more than a year, the Clapps settled in a log cabin in the interior

MAIN IDEA

Comparing
E What common dreams did people who sought gold in California share with those who settled in Oregon?

mining town of Rich Bar. While her husband practiced medicine, Louisa tried her hand at mining and found it hardly to her liking.

▲ These miners are prospecting in Spanish Flat, California, in 1852.

★ A PERSONAL VOICE
LOUISA CLAPP

"I have become a mineress; that is, if having washed a pan of dirt with my own hands, and procured therefrom three dollars and twenty-five cents in gold dust . . . will entitle me to the name. I can truly say, with the black-smith's apprentice at the close of his first day's work at the anvil, that 'I am sorry I learned the trade;' for I wet my feet, tore my dress, spoilt a pair of new gloves, nearly froze my fingers, got an awful headache, took cold and lost a valuable breastpin, in this my labor of love."

—quoted in *They Saw the Elephant*

GOLD RUSH BRINGS DIVERSITY By 1849, California's population exceeded 100,000. The Chinese were the largest group to come from overseas. Free blacks also came by the hundreds, and many struck it rich. By 1855, the wealthiest African Americans in the country were living in California. The fast-growing population included large numbers of Mexicans as well. The California demographic mix also included slaves—that is until a constitutional convention in 1849 drew up a state constitution that outlawed slavery.

California's application for statehood provoked fiery protest in Congress and became just one more sore point between irate Northerners and Southerners, each intent on winning the sectional argument over slavery. Nevertheless, California did win statehood in 1850.

SECTION 4 ASSESSMENT

1. **TERMS & NAMES** For each term or name, write a sentence explaining its significance.
   - James K. Polk
   - Zachary Taylor
   - Stephen Kearny
   - Republic of California
   - Winfield Scott
   - Treaty of Guadalupe Hidalgo
   - Gadsden Purchase
   - forty-niners
   - gold rush

MAIN IDEA

2. **TAKING NOTES**
   Draw a chart showing how the boundaries of the contiguous United States were formed.

   Effect: **Present-Day U.S. Borders**

   Causes:

   How did the United States pursue its goal of expanding in the 1840s?

CRITICAL THINKING

3. **EVALUATING**
   How would you evaluate President Polk's attitude and behavior toward Mexico? Use specific references to the chapter to support your response. **Think About:**
   - Polk's position on expansion
   - his actions once in office
   - his relationship with Santa Anna

4. **ANALYZING EFFECTS**
   What were some of the effects of the California gold rush?

5. **EVALUATING DECISIONS**
   Would you have supported the controversial war with Mexico? Why or why not? Explain your answer, including details from the chapter.

VISUAL SUMMARY

EXPANDING MARKETS AND MOVING WEST

UNITED STATES IN 1830

MARKET REVOLUTION
- technological changes
- economic interdependence
- greater economic diversity among the regions of the nation

MANIFEST DESTINY
- the idea of manifest destiny used to justify settling the land
- increasing westward migration

EXPANSION IN TEXAS
- land grants offered by Mexico
- American settlement of Texas
- conflict over cultural differences, and over slavery
- American uprising
- Texas independence
- U.S. annexation of Texas

WAR WITH MEXICO
- tension over annexation of Texas
- war with Mexico
- huge territorial gains for the U.S.
- greater westward movement of settlers

CALIFORNIA GOLD RUSH
- discovery of gold in California
- population and economic boom in California
- California statehood (1850)

UNITED STATES IN 1853

TERMS & NAMES

For each term or name below, write a sentence explaining its connection to the expansion of the U.S. in the mid-19th century.

1. Samuel F. B. Morse
2. manifest destiny
3. Oregon Trail
4. Brigham Young
5. Antonio López de Santa Anna
6. Alamo
7. Sam Houston
8. Republic of Texas
9. James K. Polk
10. Treaty of Guadalupe Hidalgo

MAIN IDEAS

Use your notes and the information in the chapter to answer the following questions.

The Market Revolution (pages 274–279)

1. What inventions and technological advancements changed lives as part of the market revolution?
2. How did the inventions and innovations of the mid-19th century encourage various regions to specialize in certain industries?

Manifest Destiny (pages 280–285)

3. Why was the concept of manifest destiny of particular appeal to Americans in the 1840s?
4. What were the factors that drew settlers west during the first half of the 19th century?

Expansion in Texas (pages 288–292)

5. What made Americans want to settle in Texas?
6. What were the major events that led to Texas joining the Union?

The War with Mexico (pages 293–299)

7. What developments caused the United States to go to war with Mexico?
8. What effect did the gold rush have on the growth of California?

CRITICAL THINKING

1. **USING YOUR NOTES** What were America's goals and ideals during this period of expansion and economic change? Draw a chart in which you list goals from the period, how they were achieved, and in what ways their effects were positive or negative.

Goal	How Achieved	Positive/Negative Effects

2. **INTERPRETING MAPS** Review the map on pages 286–287. In what ways would this map have been helpful to settlers following the Oregon Trail to a new home? Explain your answer.

3. **ANALYZING EFFECTS** What was the impact of the new methods of communication during this period? Use details from the text to support your response.

Use the map and your knowledge of U.S. history to answer questions 1 and 2.

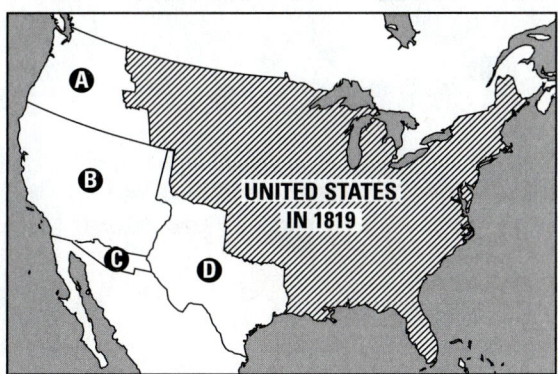

UNITED STATES IN 1819

1 Which area on the map corresponds to the label "Mexican Cession, 1848"?

(1) Area A
(2) Area B
(3) Area C
(4) Area D

2 Which area on the map corresponds to the label "Oregon territory"?

(1) Area A
(2) Area B
(3) Area C
(4) Area D

Use the quotation below and your knowledge of U.S. history to answer question 3.

" [T]he right of our manifest destiny to over spread and to possess the whole of the continent which Providence has given us for the development of the great experiment of liberty and . . . development of self government entrusted to us. It is [a] right such as that of the tree to the space of air and the earth suitable for the full expansion of its principle and destiny of growth. "

—John L. O'Sullivan,
United States Magazine and Democratic Review

3 In this passage, the writer uses the term "manifest destiny" to mean that —

(1) expansion is not only good but bound to happen.
(2) neighboring territories will resent U.S. expansion.
(3) America's growth can be compared to a tree.
(4) self-government leads to expansion.

4 All of the following were outcomes of the California Gold Rush *except* —

(1) increased diversity in the region.
(2) the rapid growth of San Francisco.
(3) an increase in overland migration.
(4) the expansion of slavery in California.

hmhsocialstudies.com **TEST PRACTICE**

For additional test practice, go online for:

• Diagnostic tests   • Tutorials

INTERACT WITH HISTORY

Think about the issues you explored at the beginning of the chapter. Organize into small groups and hold a debate about the way the United States acquired land from Mexico. Use information from the chapter to support your viewpoint.

FOCUS ON WRITING

Imagine you are a member of Congress, and you believe that the Treaty of Guadalupe Hidalgo is flawed. Write a different version of the treaty for Congress to adopt. For each main point in your treaty, compare it to the Treaty of Guadalupe Hidalgo and explain why your version is better.

MULTIMEDIA ACTIVITY

21ST CENTURY

Visit the links for Chapter Assessment to find out more about the revolution in technology and communication in the first half of the 19th century. What invention most appeals to you, and why? Prepare a multimedia presentation that describes the impact that your favorite invention had on society at the time.

hmhsocialstudies.com

The Real West:
Rush for Gold

When gold was discovered in northern California in 1848, it caused a sensation. Gold seekers from the United States and the rest of the world rushed to California to find their fortunes. The conditions of the trip were difficult, as was the labor required to extract the gold from rivers and mines. Although some people became wealthy, many more never found the riches they had expected. So many people arrived so quickly that California became a state within three years of gold being discovered.

Explore some of the history and documents of the California Gold Rush online. You can find a wealth of information, video clips, primary sources, activities, and more at ⏏ **hmhsocialstudies.com**.

CALIFORNIA!
Mutual Protection
Trading & Mining Co.

"If any man has his health & will work, he can make more than ten times as much here as he can in the states in the same length of time. But many, very many, that come here meet with bad success & thousands will leave their bones here."

— S. Shufelt

A Miner's Letter Home
Read the document to learn about one miner's opinion on the possibility of becoming rich in California.

Heading West
Watch the video to learn about the dangers that overland travelers faced when trying to get to California from the eastern United States.

Search for the Mother Lode
Watch the video to see the various methods that forty-niners used to mine the gold in California.

Statehood
Watch the video to discover the political issues surrounding the admission of California as a free state and its implications for the rest of the nation.

CHAPTER 10

THE UNION IN PERIL

Essential Question

How did conflict over slavery and other regional tensions lead to the Civil War?

New York Standards

KEY IDEA 2 Important ideas, social and cultural values, beliefs, and traditions from New York State and United States history illustrate the connections and interactions of people and events across time and from a variety of perspectives.

KEY IDEA 3 Study about the major social, political, economic, cultural, and religious developments in New York State and United States history involves learning about the important roles and contributions of individuals and groups.

SECTION 1: The Divisive Politics of Slavery

SECTION 2: Protest, Resistance, and Violence

SECTION 3: The Birth of the Republican Party

SECTION 4: Slavery and Secession

Soldiers arrest abolitionist John Brown and his followers at the federal arsenal at Harpers Ferry, Virginia (now West Virginia), 1859. Brown had hoped to steal weapons and use them to instigate a nationwide slave rebellion.

1850 Congress passes Compromise of 1850.

1850 California enters the Union.

1852 Franklin Pierce is elected president.

1852 Harriet Beecher Stowe publishes *Uncle Tom's Cabin*.

1854 Congress approves the Kansas-Nebraska Act.

1854 The Republican Party forms.

USA
WORLD

1850   1852   1854

1850 Taiping Rebellion in China begins.

1853 Crimean War begins.

1854 Charles Dickens's *Hard Times* is published.

HISTORY

Abolitionists and the Underground Railroad.

hmhsocialstudies.com VIDEO

INTERACT
WITH HISTORY

The year is 1850. Across the United States a debate is raging, dividing North from South: Is slavery a property right, or is it a violation of liberty and human dignity? The future of the Union depends on compromise—but for many people on both sides, compromise is unacceptable.

Explore the Issues

- Is it possible to compromise on an ethical issue such as slavery?

- What are the obstacles to altering an institution, such as slavery, that is fundamental to a region's economy and way of life?

1856 James Buchanan is elected president.

1857 The Supreme Court rules against Dred Scott.

1859 John Brown attacks the arsenal at Harpers Ferry, Virginia.

1860 Abraham Lincoln is elected president.

1861 The Confederacy is formed.

1856 **1858** **1860**

1858 The 13.5-ton bell, "Big Ben," is cast in Britain.

1859 Charles Darwin's *Origin of Species* is published.

1861 Russian serfs emancipated by Czar Alexander II.

PI 3.3 CC Unit 2.II.B.1.d CC Unit 2.II.B.1.e
CC Unit 2.II.B.3 CC Unit 2.II.D.1.a

The Divisive Politics of Slavery

MAIN IDEA	WHY IT MATTERS NOW	Terms & Names
The issue of slavery dominated U.S. politics in the early 1850s.	U.S. society continues to be challenged by issues of fairness, equality, race, and class.	• Wilmot Proviso • secession • Compromise of 1850 • popular sovereignty • Stephen A. Douglas • Millard Fillmore

One American's Story

hmhsocialstudies.com
TAKING NOTES

Use the graphic organizer online to take notes on the regional differences discussed in the section.

South Carolina senator John C. Calhoun was so sick that he had missed four months of debate over whether California should enter the Union as a free state. On March 4, 1850, Calhoun, explaining that he was too ill to deliver a prepared speech, asked Senator James M. Mason of Virginia to deliver it for him.

★ **A PERSONAL VOICE** JOHN C. CALHOUN

" I have, Senators, believed from the first that the agitation of the subject of slavery would, if not prevented by some timely and effective measure, end in disunion. . . . The agitation has been permitted to proceed . . . until it has reached a period when it can no longer be disguised or denied that the Union is in danger. You have thus had forced upon you the greatest and the gravest question that can ever come under your consideration: How can the Union be preserved?"

—quoted in *The Compromise of 1850*, edited by Edwin C. Rozwenc

Senator Calhoun called on the North to give the South "justice, simple justice." He demanded that slavery be allowed throughout the territories won in the war with Mexico. If it was not, he declared, the South would secede, or withdraw, from the Union. Once again, the issue of slavery had brought about a political crisis, deepening the gulf between the North and the South.

▲
John C. Calhoun was vice-president under John Quincy Adams and Andrew Jackson. His last words were: "The South. The poor South."

Differences Between North and South

Senator Calhoun argued that although the North and the South had been politically equal when the Constitution was adopted, the "perfect equilibrium" between the two sections no longer existed. At any rate, the two sections certainly had developed different ways of life by the 1850s.

INDUSTRY AND IMMIGRATION IN THE NORTH The North industrialized rapidly as factories turned out ever-increasing amounts of products, from textiles and sewing machines to farm equipment and guns. Railroads—with more than 20,000 miles of track laid during the 1850s—carried raw materials eastward and manufactured goods and settlers westward. Small towns like Chicago matured into cities almost overnight, due to the sheer volume of goods and people arriving by railroad. Telegraph wires strung along the railroad tracks provided a network of instant communication for the North.

Immigrants from Europe entered the industrial workplace in growing numbers. Many became voters with a strong opposition to slavery. They feared the expansion of slavery for two main reasons. First, it might bring slave labor into direct competition with free labor, or people who worked for wages. Second, it threatened to reduce the status of white workers who could not successfully compete with slaves.

AGRICULTURE AND SLAVERY IN THE SOUTH Unlike the North, the South remained a predominantly rural society, consisting mostly of plantations and small farms. The Southern economy relied on staple crops such as cotton. Though one-third of the nation's population lived in the South in 1850, the South produced under 10 percent of the nation's manufactured goods. At the same time that Northern railroad lines were expanding, Southerners were mostly using rivers to transport goods. In addition, few immigrants settled in the South, because African Americans, whether enslaved or free, met most of the available need for artisans, mechanics, and laborers. Those immigrants who did settle in the South, however, displayed significant opposition to slavery. For example, German-American newspapers in Texas and in Baltimore, Maryland published editorials in favor of universal voting rights and freedom for African Americans.

The conflict over slavery rattled Southern society. In three Southern states, Mississippi, Louisiana, and South Carolina, African Americans were in the majority. In Alabama and Florida, African Americans composed almost half of the population. While blacks dreamed of an end to slavery, many Southern whites feared that any restriction of slavery would lead to a social and economic revolution. Furthermore, Calhoun warned that such a revolution would condemn blacks as well as whites "to the greatest calamity, and the [South] to poverty, desolation, and wretchedness." **A**

MAIN IDEA

Contrasting
A List three ways in which the North and the South differed in the mid 1800s.

History Through *Architecture*

GREEK REVIVAL ARCHITECTURE

The Greek Revival was an architectural style that spread throughout the United States between 1825 and 1860. Like ancient Greek temples, many buildings in this style had columns on all four sides. This style was applied to all types of buildings in Greek Revival architecture, from small houses to state capitols. The hot, humid climate of the South encouraged the development of a high porch and with columns rising to the full height of a building. These wide porches were unusual in the cooler climate of Europe but well-suited to tropical regions. In the hands of Greek Revival architects in the South, the porches became grand living spaces where families could find shelter from the summer heat.

Oak Alley Plantation, Louisiana ▼

SKILLBUILDER **Interpreting Visual Sources**
1. How would you be able to tell that this home is an example of the Greek Revival style?
2. How did the architecture help cool the house?

SEE SKILLBUILDER HANDBOOK, PAGE R23.

Slavery in the Territories

On August 8, 1846, Pennsylvania Democrat David Wilmot heightened tensions between North and South by introducing an amendment to a military appropriations bill proposing that "neither slavery nor involuntary servitude shall ever exist" in any territory the United States might acquire as a result of the war with Mexico. In strictly practical terms, the **Wilmot Proviso** meant that California, as well as the territories of Utah and New Mexico, would be closed to slavery forever.

THE WILMOT PROVISO The Wilmot Proviso divided Congress along regional lines. Northerners, angry over the refusal of Southern congressmen to vote for internal improvements, such as the building of canals and roads, supported the proviso. They also feared that adding slave territory would give slave states more members in Congress and deny economic opportunity to free workers.

Southerners, as expected, opposed the proviso, which, some argued, raised complex constitutional issues. Slaves were property, Southerners claimed, and property was protected by the Constitution. Laws like the Wilmot Proviso would undermine such constitutional protections.

Many Southerners feared that if the Wilmot Proviso became law, the inevitable addition of new free states to the Union would shift the balance of power permanently to the North. The House of Representatives approved the proviso, but the Senate rejected it. Congressman Alexander H. Stephens of Georgia issued a dire prediction. **B**

Membership in House of Representatives		
Year	Members from Free States	Members from Slave States
1800	77	65
1810	105	81
1820	123	90
1830	142	100
1840	141	91
1850	144	90

Source: *Historical Statistics of the United States*

SKILLBUILDER Interpreting Charts
About what percentage of House members represented free states in 1850?

MAIN IDEA

Analyzing Motives
B Explain why Northerners favored the Wilmot Proviso and why Southerners did not.

A Personal Voice — ALEXANDER H. STEPHENS

" The North is going to stick the Wilmot amendment to every appropriation and then all the South will vote against any measure thus clogged. Finally a tremendous struggle will take place and perhaps [President] Polk in starting one war may find half a dozen on his hands. I tell you the prospect ahead is dark, cloudy, thick and gloomy. "

—quoted in *The Coming of the Civil War*

STATEHOOD FOR CALIFORNIA As a result of the gold rush, California had grown in population so quickly that it skipped the territorial phase of becoming a state. In late 1849, California held a constitutional convention, adopted a state constitution, elected a governor and a legislature, and applied to join the Union.

California's new constitution forbade slavery, a fact that alarmed many Southerners. They had assumed that because most of California lay south of the Missouri Compromise line of 36°30′, the state would be open to slavery. They had hoped that the compromise, struck in 1820, would apply to new territories, including California, which would have become a slave state.

General Zachary Taylor, who succeeded Polk as president in 1849, supported California's admission as a free state. Moreover, he felt that the South could counter abolitionism most effectively by leaving the slavery issue up to individual territories rather than to Congress. Southerners, however, saw this as a move to block slavery in the territories and as an attack on the Southern way of life—and began to question whether the South should remain in the Union. **C**

California's admission to the Union in 1850 increased tensions between North and South. ▼

MAIN IDEA

Analyzing Effects
C Why did California's application for statehood cause an uproar?

The Senate Debates

The 31st Congress opened in December 1849 in an atmosphere of distrust and bitterness. The question of California statehood topped the agenda. Of equal concern was the border dispute in which the slave state of Texas claimed the eastern half of New Mexico Territory, where the issue of slavery had not yet been settled. In the meantime, Northerners demanded the abolition of slavery in the District of Columbia, while Southerners accused the North of failing to enforce the Fugitive Slave Act of 1793. As passions rose, some Southerners threatened **secession,** the formal withdrawal of a state from the Union. Could anything be done to prevent the United States from becoming two nations?

CLAY'S COMPROMISE Henry Clay worked night and day to shape a compromise that both the North and the South could accept. Though ill, he visited his old rival Daniel Webster on January 21, 1850, and obtained Webster's support. Eight days later, Clay presented to the Senate a series of resolutions later called the **Compromise of 1850,** which he hoped would settle "all questions in controversy between the free and slave states, growing out of the subject of Slavery."

TERMS OF THE COMPROMISE Clay's compromise (summarized on the chart shown on page 308) contained provisions to appease Northerners as well as Southerners. To satisfy the North, the compromise provided that California be admitted to the Union as a free state. To satisfy the South, the compromise proposed a new and more effective fugitive slave law.

Other provisions of the compromise had elements that appealed to both regions. For example, a provision that allowed residents of the territories of New Mexico and Utah **popular sovereignty**—the right of residents of a territory to vote for or against slavery—appealed to both North and South. As part of the compromise, the federal government would pay Texas $10 million to surrender its claim to New Mexico. Northerners were pleased because, in effect, it limited slavery in Texas to within its current borders. Southerners were pleased because the money would help defray Texas's expenses and debts from the war with Mexico. **D**

> **MAIN IDEA**
>
> **Comparing**
> **D** What Northern issues and Southern issues were addressed by the Compromise of 1850?

1 Daniel Webster strongly supported Clay's compromise. He left the Senate before Stephen Douglas could engineer passage of all the provisions of the compromise.

2 Henry Clay offered his compromise to the Senate in January 1850. In his efforts to save the Union, Clay earned the name "the Great Compromiser."

3 John C. Calhoun opposed the compromise. He died two months after Clay proposed it.

On February 5, Clay defended his resolutions and begged both the North and the South to consider them thoughtfully. The alternative was disunion—and, in Clay's opinion, quite possibly war.

★ A PERSONAL VOICE HENRY CLAY

" And such a war as it would be, following the dissolution of the Union! Sir, we may search the pages of history, and none so ferocious, so bloody, so implacable, so exterminating . . . would rage with such violence. . . . I implore gentlemen, I adjure them, whether from the South or the North . . . to pause at the edge of the precipice, before the fearful and dangerous leap be taken into the yawning abyss below. "

—quoted in *Voices from the Civil War*

CALHOUN AND WEBSTER RESPOND Clay's speech marked the start of one of the greatest political debates in United States history. Within a month, Calhoun had presented the Southern case for slavery in the territories. He was followed three days later by Daniel Webster, who began his eloquent appeal for national unity by saying, "I wish to speak today, not as a Massachusetts man, nor as a Northern man, but as an American. . . . 'Hear me for my cause.'" He urged Northerners to try to compromise with the South by passing a stricter fugitive slave law, and he warned Southern firebrands to think more cautiously about the danger of secession.

★ A PERSONAL VOICE DANIEL WEBSTER

" I hear with pain, and anguish, and distress, the word *secession,* especially when it falls from the lips of those who are eminently patriotic. . . . Secession! Peaceable secession! . . . There can be no such thing as a peaceable secession. . . . Is the great Constitution under which we live . . . to be thawed and melted away by secession. . . . No, sir! I will not state what might produce the disruption of the states; . . . [What] that disruption must produce . . . [would be] such a war as I will not describe. "

—"Seventh of March" speech, quoted in *The American Spirit*

The Compromise of 1850

Calhoun's Goals	Terms of the Compromise	Webster's Goals
Calhoun believed strongly in states' rights over federal power and held the interests of the slaveholding South as his highest priority. He had long believed that "the agitation of the subject of slavery would . . . end in disunion." He blamed the sectional crisis on Northern abolitionists and argued that the South had "no concession or surrender to make" on the issue of slavery.	• California admitted as a free state • Utah and New Mexico territories decide about slavery • Texas-New Mexico boundary dispute resolved; Texas paid $10 million by federal government. • The sale of slaves banned in the District of Columbia. But slavery itself may continue there. • Fugitive Slave Act required people in the free states to help capture and return escaped slaves.	Webster had argued with Northern Whigs that slavery should not be extended into the territories. Upon hearing Calhoun's threat of secession, he took to the Senate floor and endorsed Clay's compromise "for the preservation of the Union. . . . a great, popular, constitutional government, guarded by legislation, by law, by judicature, and defended by the whole affections of the people."

SKILLBUILDER Interpreting Charts
1. How did Calhoun and Webster disagree over states' rights? **2.** How did the compromise try to satisfy both sides?

Webster's speech became one of the most famous in the history of the Senate. Spectators packed the Senate chamber for the event.

THE COMPROMISE IS ADOPTED The Senate rejected the proposed compromise in July. Discouraged, Clay left Washington. **Stephen A. Douglas** of Illinois picked up the pro-compromise reins.

To avoid another defeat, Douglas developed a shrewd plan. He unbundled the package of resolutions and reintroduced them one at a time, hoping to obtain a majority vote for each measure individually. Thus, any individual congressman could vote for the provisions that he liked and vote against, or abstain from voting on, those that he disliked. It appeared as though Douglas had found the key to passing the entire compromise.

The unexpected death of President Taylor on July 9 aided Douglas's efforts. Taylor's successor, **Millard Fillmore**, made it clear that he supported the compromise. In the meantime, the South was ready to negotiate. Calhoun's death had removed one obstacle to compromise. Southern leaders came out in favor of Clay's individual proposals as being the best the South could secure without radical action. After eight months of effort, the Compromise of 1850 was voted into law. **E**

President Fillmore embraced the compromise as the "final settlement" of the question of slavery and sectional differences. For the moment, the crisis over slavery in the territories had passed. However, the relief was short-lived. Even as crowds in Washington celebrated the passage of the compromise, the next crisis loomed ominously on the horizon—enforcement of the new fugitive slave law.

MAIN IDEA

Analyzing Effects

E What was the result of Douglas's unbundling of Clay's resolutions?

SECTION 1 ASSESSMENT

1. TERMS & NAMES For each term or name, write a sentence explaining its significance.
- **Wilmot Proviso**
- **secession**
- **Compromise of 1850**
- **popular sovereignty**
- **Stephen A. Douglas**
- **Millard Fillmore**

MAIN IDEA

2. TAKING NOTES
Create a chart similar to this one. Complete it by indicating each region's position on an issue or trend covered in this section.

Issue or Trend	North	South
1.		
2.		
3.		
4.		
5.		

How was each region affected by the issue or trend?

CRITICAL THINKING

3. HYPOTHESIZING
Do you think there are any points at which a different action or leader might have resolved the conflict between the North and the South? Support your opinion with references from this section. **Think About:**
- issues raised by the Wilmot Proviso, California statehood, and the Compromise of 1850
- constitutional issues raised by Southerners

4. ANALYZING PRIMARY SOURCES
When California applied for statehood in 1850, Mississippi senator Jefferson Davis warned, "For the first time, we are about permanently to destroy the balance of power between the sections." Why might Davis have felt this way?

5. EVALUATING
Do you think the North or the South won more significant concessions in the Compromise of 1850? Explain your answer.

PI 3.1   CC Unit 2.II.B.1.e   CC Unit 2.II.B.2.d
          CC Unit 2.II.B.3   CC Unit 2.II.D.1.a

Protest, Resistance, and Violence

MAIN IDEA	WHY IT MATTERS NOW	Terms & Names
Proslavery and antislavery factions disagreed over the treatment of fugitive slaves and the spread of slavery to the territories.	The antislavery leaders became role models for leaders of civil rights movements in the 20th century.	• Fugitive Slave Act • personal liberty laws • Underground Railroad • Harriet Tubman • Harriet Beecher Stowe • *Uncle Tom's Cabin* • Kansas-Nebraska Act • John Brown • Bleeding Kansas

One American's Story

Use the graphic organizer online to take notes on the major events in the growing conflict between the North and the South.

On June 2, 1854, thousands lined the streets of Boston. Flags flew at half-mast, and a black coffin bearing the words "The Funeral of Liberty" dangled from a window. Federal soldiers, bayonets ready for action, marched a lone African American, Anthony Burns, toward the harbor. Charlotte Forten, a free black, wrote about the day.

A PERSONAL VOICE CHARLOTTE FORTEN

" Today Massachusetts has again been disgraced. . . . With what scorn must that government be regarded, which cowardly assembles thousands of soldiers to satisfy the demands of slave-holders; to deprive of his freedom a man, created in God's own image, whose sole offense is the color of his skin! . . . A cloud seems hanging over me, over all our persecuted race, which nothing can dispel."

—quoted in *The Underground Railroad*, by Charles L. Blockson

▲ Charlotte Forten was the grand-daughter of James Forten, a Philadelphia abolitionist who fought in the Revolutionary War.

Anthony Burns was being forced back into slavery in Virginia. As a result of his trial, antislavery sentiment in the North soared. "We went to bed one night old-fashioned, conservative, compromise Union Whigs," wrote one Northerner, "and waked up stark mad Abolitionists."

Fugitive Slaves and the Underground Railroad

Burns's return to slavery followed the passage of the **Fugitive Slave Act,** which was a component of the Compromise of 1850. Many people were surprised by the harsh terms of the act. Under the law, alleged fugitives were not entitled to a trial by jury, despite the Sixth Amendment provision calling for a speedy and public jury trial and the right to counsel. Nor could fugitives testify on their own behalf.

A statement by a slave owner was all that was required to have a slave returned. Frederick Douglass bitterly summarized the situation.

★ **A PERSONAL VOICE** FREDERICK DOUGLASS

" The colored men's rights are less than those of a jackass. No man can take away a jackass without submitting the matter to twelve men in any part of this country. A black man may be carried away without any reference to a jury. It is only necessary to claim him, and that some villain should swear to his identity. There is more protection there for a horse, for a donkey, or anything, rather than a colored man. "

—quoted in *Voices from the Civil War*

Federal commissioners charged with enforcing the law were to receive a $10 fee if they returned an alleged fugitive, but only $5 if they freed him or her, an obvious incentive to "return" people to slavery. Finally, anyone convicted of helping an alleged fugitive was subject to a fine of $1,000, imprisonment for six months, or both.

RESISTING THE LAW Infuriated by the Fugitive Slave Act, some Northerners resisted it by organizing vigilance committees to send endangered African Americans to safety in Canada. Others resorted to violence to rescue fugitive slaves. Nine Northern states passed **personal liberty laws,** which forbade the imprisonment of runaway slaves and guaranteed that they would have jury trials. And Northern lawyers dragged these trials out—often for three or four years—in order to increase slave catchers' expenses. Southern slave owners were enraged by Northern resistance to the Fugitive Slave Act, prompting one Harvard law student from Georgia to tell his mother, "Do not be surprised if when I return home you find me a confirmed disunionist." **A**

HARRIET TUBMAN AND THE UNDERGROUND RAILROAD As time went on, free African Americans and white abolitionists developed a secret network of people who would, at great risk to themselves, aid fugitive slaves in their escape. This network became known as the **Underground Railroad.** The "conductors" hid fugitives in secret tunnels and false cupboards, provided them with food and clothing, and escorted or directed them to the next "station," often in disguise.

One of the most famous conductors was **Harriet Tubman,** born a slave in 1820 or 1821. As a young girl, she suffered a severe head injury when a plantation overseer hit her with a lead weight. The blow damaged her brain, causing her to lose consciousness several times a day. To compensate for her disability, Tubman increased her strength until she became strong enough to perform tasks that most men could not do. In 1849, after Tubman's owner died, she decided to make a break for freedom and succeeded in reaching Philadelphia.

Shortly after passage of the Fugitive Slave Act, Tubman became a conductor on the Underground Railroad. In all, she made 19 trips back to the South and is said to have helped 300 slaves—including her own parents—flee to freedom. Neither Tubman nor the slaves she helped were ever captured. Later she became an ardent speaker for abolition.

For slaves, escaping from slavery was indeed a dangerous process. It meant traveling on foot at night without any sense of distance or direction except for the North Star and other natural signs. It meant avoiding patrols of armed men on horseback and struggling through forests and across rivers. Often it meant going

MAIN IDEA

Analyzing Effects

A What effect did the Fugitive Slave Act have on abolitionist feelings in the North?

With a price of $40,000 on her head, Harriet Tubman was called "Moses" by those she helped escape on the Underground Railroad. ▼

The Union in Peril **311**

KEY PLAYER

HARRIET BEECHER STOWE
1811–1896

Harriet Beecher Stowe was born in Connecticut into a prominent reform family. Her father was a Presbyterian minister and temperance advocate, Lyman Beecher. Her brother, Henry, was a clergyman and abolitionist.

Stowe moved with her family to Cincinnati, where the issue of slavery—once rather remote—became painfully familiar. She never forgot standing on the banks of the Ohio River, watching boats fill with slaves from Kentucky to be shipped to slave markets. Her hatred of slavery grew until she resolved to express herself in writing, and *Uncle Tom's Cabin* resulted. The novel made such an impact that when Abraham Lincoln met Stowe a decade later, during the Civil War, he said, "So this is the little lady who made the big war."

without food for days at a time. Harry Grimes, a slave who ran away from North Carolina, described the difficulties of escaping to the North.

★ A PERSONAL VOICE   HARRY GRIMES

" In the woods I lived on nothing. . . . I stayed in the hollow of a big poplar tree for seven months. . . . I suffered mighty bad with the cold and for something to eat. One time a snake come to the tree . . . and I took my axe and chopped him in two. It was . . . the poisonest kind of snake we have. While in the woods all my thoughts was how to get away to a free country. "

—quoted in *The Underground Railroad,* by Charles L. Blockson

Once fugitive slaves reached the North, many elected to remain there and take their chances. (See map on p. 313.) Other fugitives continued their journey all the way to Canada to be completely out of reach of slave catchers. Meanwhile, a new abolitionist voice spoke out and brought slavery to the attention of a great many Americans. **B**

UNCLE TOM'S CABIN In 1852, ardent abolitionist **Harriet Beecher Stowe** published *Uncle Tom's Cabin.* Stirring strong reactions from North and South alike, the novel became an instant bestseller. More than a million copies had sold by the middle of 1853.

The novel's plot was melodramatic and many of its characters were stereotypes, but *Uncle Tom's Cabin* delivered the message that slavery was not just a political contest, but also a great moral struggle. Readers tensed with excitement as the slave Eliza fled across the frozen Ohio River, clutching her infant son in her arms. They wept bitterly when Simon Legree, a wicked Northern slave owner who moved to the South, bought Uncle Tom and had him whipped to death.

In quick response, Northern abolitionists increased their protests against the Fugitive Slave Act, while Southerners criticized the book as an attack on the South as a whole. The furor over *Uncle Tom's Cabin* had barely begun to settle when a new controversy over slavery drew heated debate.

Tension in Kansas and Nebraska

Abolitionist feelings in the North further intensified when the issue of slavery in the territories—supposedly settled by the Compromise of 1850—surfaced once again. Ironically, Senator Stephen Douglas, who had helped to steer the compromise to victory, was the person most responsible for resurrecting the issue.

> **MAIN IDEA**
>
> **Summarizing**
> **B** How did the Underground Railroad operate?

CAUTION!!

COLORED PEOPLE
OF BOSTON, ONE & ALL,
You are hereby respectfully CAUTIONED and advised, to avoid conversing with the
Watchmen and Police Officers
of Boston,
For since the recent ORDER OF THE MAYOR & ALDERMEN, they are empowered to act as
KIDNAPPERS
AND
Slave Catchers,
And they have already been actually employed in
KIDNAPPING, CATCHING, AND KEEPING
SLAVES. Therefore, if you value your LIBERTY,
and the Welfare of the Fugitives among you, Shun
them in every possible manner, as so many HOUNDS
on the track of the most unfortunate of your race.

Keep a Sharp Look Out for
KIDNAPPERS, and have your
TOP EYE open.

APRIL 24, 1851.

◀ An abolitionist poster distributed in 1851

The Underground Railroad, 1850–1860

CANADA
(British)

Montreal

MAINE

Lake Superior

VT.

N.H.

UNORGANIZED
TERRITORY

WISCONSIN

Lake Michigan

Lake Huron

NEW
YORK

Boston

MASS.

MINNESOTA
(Statehood in 1858)

MICHIGAN

Lake Ontario

Niagara Falls

CONN.

R.I.

Detroit

Erie

New York City

40°N

NEBRASKA
TERRITORY

IOWA

Chicago

Sandusky

PENNSYLVANIA

NEW
JERSEY

Lake Erie

Mississippi River

ILLINOIS

INDIANA

OHIO

Baltimore

MD.

Washington, D.C.

DEL.

Cincinnati
Ripley

VIRGINIA

KANSAS
TERRITORY

St. Louis

Evansville

Ohio River

Petersburg

MISSOURI

KENTUCKY

ATLANTIC
OCEAN

Cairo

NORTH
CAROLINA

INDIAN
TERRITORY

ARKANSAS

TENNESSEE

Fort Smith

Mississippi River

SOUTH
CAROLINA

MISSISSIPPI

ALABAMA

30°N

TEXAS

GEORGIA

	Free states
	Slave states
	Areas with slave population of 50% or more in 1860
	Routes of the Underground Railroad
•	Station on Underground Railroad

0   100   200 miles

0   100   200 kilometers

LOUISIANA

New Orleans

FLORIDA

Gulf of Mexico

80°W

90°W

MEXICO

GEOGRAPHY SKILLBUILDER

1. **Movement** What does this map tell you about the routes of the Underground Railroad?
2. **Place** Name three cities that were destinations on the Underground Railroad.
3. **Location** Why do you think these cities were destinations?

POPULAR SOVEREIGNTY As early as 1844, Douglas was pushing to organize the huge territory west of Iowa and Missouri. In 1854, he developed a proposal to divide the area into two territories, Nebraska and Kansas. His motives were complicated. For one thing, Douglas was pushing for the construction of a railroad between Chicago—his hometown, where he also owned real estate—and San Francisco. To get this route, he had to make a deal with Southerners, who wanted the railroad to start in Memphis or New Orleans.

In addition, Douglas was anxious to organize the western territory because he believed that most of the nation's people wished to see the western lands incorporated into the Union. Along with many other Democrats, Douglas was sure that continued expansion would strengthen his party and unify the nation. He also believed that popular sovereignty—that is, the right of residents of a given territory to vote on slavery for themselves—provided the most fair and democratic way to organize the new state governments. But what Douglas failed to fully understand was how strongly opposed to slavery Northerners had become.

To Douglas, popular sovereignty seemed like an excellent way to decide whether slavery would be allowed in the Nebraska Territory. The only difficulty was that Nebraska Territory lay north of the Missouri Compromise line of 36°30′ and therefore was legally closed to slavery. Douglas assumed, though, that the territory of Nebraska would enter the Union as two states, one free and one slave, and thus maintain the balance in the Senate between North and South.

Douglas was convinced that slavery could not exist on the open prairies, since none of the crops relying on slave labor could be grown there. However, to win over the South, Douglas decided to support repeal of the Missouri Compromise—which now would make slavery legal north of the 36°30′ line—though he predicted it would cause "a storm" in Congress. His prediction was right. **C**

THE KANSAS–NEBRASKA ACT
On January 23, 1854, Douglas introduced a bill in Congress to divide the area into two territories: Nebraska in the north and Kansas in the south. If passed, it would repeal the Missouri Compromise and establish popular sovereignty for both territories. Congressional debate over the bill was bitter. Some Northern congressmen saw the bill as part of a plot to turn the territories into slave states; but nearly

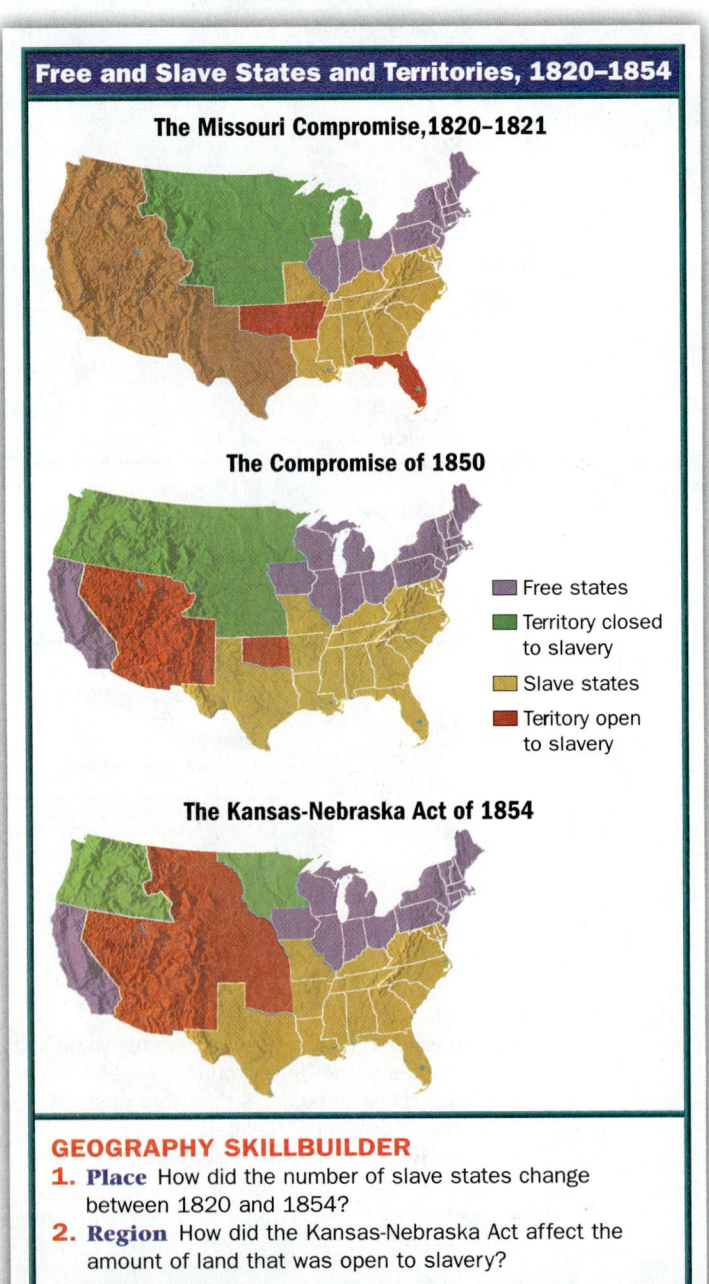

Free and Slave States and Territories, 1820–1854

The Missouri Compromise, 1820–1821

The Compromise of 1850

Legend:
- Free states
- Territory closed to slavery
- Slave states
- Teritory open to slavery

The Kansas–Nebraska Act of 1854

GEOGRAPHY SKILLBUILDER
1. **Place** How did the number of slave states change between 1820 and 1854?
2. **Region** How did the Kansas-Nebraska Act affect the amount of land that was open to slavery?

MAIN IDEA

Analyzing Issues
C Explain why popular sovereignty was so controversial.

90 percent of Southern congressmen voted for the bill. The bitterness spilled over into the general population, which deluged Congress with petitions both for and against the bill.

In the North, Douglas found himself ridiculed for betraying the Missouri Compromise. Yet he did not waver. He believed strongly that popular sovereignty was the democratic way to resolve the slavery issue.

A PERSONAL VOICE STEPHEN A. DOUGLAS

" If the people of Kansas want a slaveholding state, let them have it, and if they want a free state they have a right to it, and it is not for the people of Illinois, or Missouri, or New York, or Kentucky, to complain, whatever the decision of Kansas may be. "

—quoted in *The Civil War*, by Geoffrey C. Ward

With the help of President Franklin Pierce, a Democrat elected in 1852, Douglas steered his proposal through the Senate. After months of struggle and strife, the **Kansas-Nebraska Act** became law in May 1854. All eyes turned westward as the fate of the new territories hung in the balance.

Violence Erupts in "Bleeding Kansas"

The race for the possession of Kansas was on. New York senator William Seward threw down the gauntlet: "Come on, then, gentlemen of the Slave States. . . . We will engage in competition for the virgin soil of Kansas and God give the victory to the side that is stronger in numbers as it is in right."

From both the North and the South, settlers poured into the Kansas Territory. Some were simply farmers in search of new land. Most were sent by emigrant aid societies, groups formed specifically to supply rifles, animals, seed, and farm equipment to antislavery migrants.

This organized party of Kansas-bound armed settlers was one of the groups known as "Free-State batteries." ▶

By March 1855, Kansas had enough settlers to hold an election for a territorial legislature. However, thousands of "border ruffians" from the slave state of Missouri, led by Missouri senator David Atchison, crossed into Kansas with their revolvers cocked and voted illegally. They won a fraudulent majority for the proslavery candidates, who set up a government at Lecompton and promptly issued a series of proslavery acts. Furious over events in Lecompton, abolitionists organized a rival government in Topeka in fall 1855. **D**

"THE SACK OF LAWRENCE" Before long, violence surfaced in the struggle for Kansas. Antislavery settlers had founded a town named Lawrence. A proslavery grand jury condemned Lawrence's inhabitants as traitors and called on the local sheriff to arrest them. On May 21, 1856, a proslavery posse of 800 armed men swept into Lawrence to carry out the grand jury's will. The posse burned down the antislavery headquarters, destroyed two newspapers' printing presses, and looted many houses and stores. Abolitionist newspapers dubbed the event "the sack of Lawrence."

"THE POTTAWATOMIE MASSACRE" The news from Lawrence soon reached **John Brown,** an abolitionist described by one historian as "a man made of the stuff of saints." Brown believed that God had called on him to fight slavery. He also had the mistaken impression that the proslavery posse in Lawrence had killed five men. Brown was set on revenge. On May 24th, he and his followers pulled five men from their beds in the proslavery settlement of Pottawatomie Creek, hacked off their hands, and stabbed them with broadswords. This attack became famous as the "Pottawatomie Massacre" and quickly led to cries for revenge. It became the bloody shirt that proslavery Kansas settlers waved in summoning attacks on Free-Soilers.

The massacre triggered dozens of incidents throughout Kansas. Some 200 people were killed. John Brown fled Kansas but left behind men and women who lived with rifles by their sides. People began calling the territory **Bleeding Kansas,** as it had become a violent battlefield in a civil war.

VIOLENCE IN THE SENATE Violence was not restricted to Kansas, however. On May 19, Massachusetts senator Charles Sumner delivered in the Senate an impassioned speech later called "The Crime Against Kansas." For two days he verbally attacked his colleagues for their support of slavery. Sumner was particularly abusive toward the aged senator Andrew P. Butler of South Carolina, sneering at him for his proslavery beliefs and making fun of his impaired speech.

On May 22, Butler's nephew, Congressman Preston S. Brooks, walked into the Senate chamber and over to Sumner's desk. "I have read your speech twice over, carefully," Brooks said softly. "It is a libel on South Carolina and Mr. Butler, who is a relative of mine." With that, he lifted up his cane and struck Sumner on the head repeatedly before the cane broke. Sumner suffered shock and apparent brain damage and did not return to his Senate seat for over three years.

Southerners applauded and showered Brooks with new canes, including one inscribed with the words, "Hit him again!" Northerners condemned the incident as yet

MAIN IDEA

Analyzing Causes

D Why did Kansas become a center of controversy over the issue of slavery?

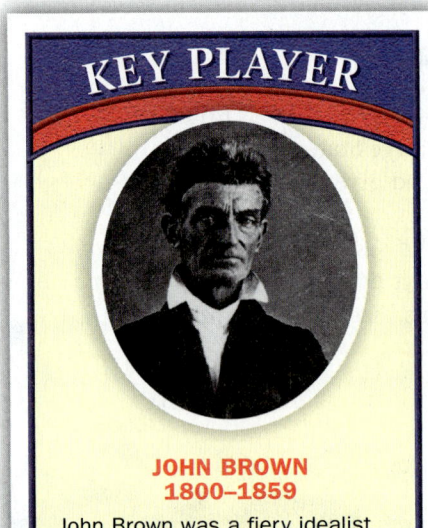

KEY PLAYER

**JOHN BROWN
1800–1859**

John Brown was a fiery idealist who believed that God had called on him to fight slavery. He was raised in a deeply religious antislavery family. Brown was never financially successful although he tried a variety of ventures, from farming to land speculation.

By 1849, Brown was living in the black community of North Elba, New York. He supported many abolitionist causes, such as David Walker's *Appeal* and helped finance farms for fugitive slaves.

Brown became a powerful symbol of the moral issue of slavery in the North and reinforced the worst fears of the South. After a number of raids on proslavery settlers in Kansas and a raid on Harpers Ferry, Virginia, Brown was caught. He was hanged for treason in 1859.

SOUTHERN CHIVALRY — ARGUMENT VERSUS CLUB'S.

another example of Southern brutality and antagonism toward free speech. Northerners and Southerners, it appeared, had met an impasse. **E**

The widening gulf between the North and the South had far-reaching implications for party politics as well. The compromises that had been tried from the time of the Wilmot Proviso until the Kansas-Nebraska Act could not satisfy either the North or the South. The tensions that resulted led to new political alliances as well as to violence. As the two sections grew further apart, the old national parties were torn apart and new political parties emerged.

▲
This 1856 cartoon shows Preston Brooks attacking Charles Sumner in the U.S. Senate chamber.

SECTION 2 ASSESSMENT

1. TERMS & NAMES For each term or name, write a sentence explaining its significance.

- **Fugitive Slave Act**
- **personal liberty laws**
- **Underground Railroad**
- **Harriet Tubman**
- **Harriet Beecher Stowe**
- ***Uncle Tom's Cabin***
- **Kansas-Nebraska Act**
- **John Brown**
- **Bleeding Kansas**

MAIN IDEA

2. TAKING NOTES
Create a time line highlighting the major events in the growing conflict between the North and the South. Use a form similar to the one below.

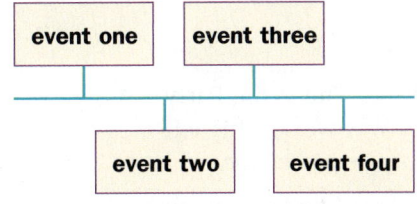

Select one event. Explain how it was representative of North–South conflict.

CRITICAL THINKING

3. ANALYZING EFFECTS
Explain how *Uncle Tom's Cabin* affected the abolitionist cause. Use details from the section to support your answer.

4. ANALYZING ISSUES
Why was the Kansas-Nebraska Act so controversial? Use details from the section to support your answer.

5. SYNTHESIZING
Explain the concept of popular sovereignty and describe Northern and Southern reactions to it as a way of making decisions about slavery in the territories. Use evidence from the text to support your answer. **Think About:**

- Douglas's view on continued expansion
- Douglas and the Missouri Compromise
- the congressional balance of power

The Birth of the Republican Party

MAIN IDEA	WHY IT MATTERS NOW	Terms & Names
In the mid-1850s, the issue of slavery and other factors split political parties and led to the birth of new ones.	The Republican and Democratic parties remain the major political forces in the United States today.	• Franklin Pierce • nativism • Know-Nothing Party • Free-Soil Party • Republican Party • Horace Greeley • John C. Frémont • James Buchanan

One American's Story

hmhsocialstudies.com
TAKING NOTES

Use the graphic organizer online to take notes on the growth of the Republican Party in the 1850s.

As editor of the *New York Tribune*, Horace Greeley always spoke his mind. A staunch abolitionist, Greeley consistently argued in his columns against popular sovereignty and in favor of forcible resistance to slave catchers.

In March 1855, after Greeley became frustrated with the Whig Party's shifting position on slavery, he issued a call to arms for "the friends of freedom" to "be girding up their loins for future contests" and join a new antislavery political party, the Republican Party.

★ **A PERSONAL VOICE** HORACE GREELEY

" [The Republicans have] the heart, the conscience and the understanding of the people with them. . . . All that is noble, all that is true, all that is pure, all that is manly, and estimable in human character, goes to swell the power of the anti-slavery party of the North. That party. . . . now embraces every Northern man who does not want to see the government converted into a huge engine for the spread of slavery over the whole continent, every man . . . opposed to . . . the passage of the Kansas-Nebraska bill. "

—quoted in *The Coming of the Civil War*

Greeley's appeal accurately reflected the changing national political scene. With the continuing tension over slavery, many Americans needed a national political voice. That voice was to be the Republican Party.

▲
Horace Greeley founded the *New York Tribune* in 1841.

New Political Parties Emerge

By the end of 1856, the nation's political landscape had shifted. The Whig Party had split over the issue of slavery, and the Democratic Party was weak. This left the new Republican Party to move within striking distance of the presidency.

SLAVERY DIVIDES WHIGS Divisions in the Whig Party widened in 1852 when General Winfield Scott became the Whig nominee for president. Scott owed his nomination to Northern Whigs who opposed the Fugitive Slave Act and gave only lukewarm support to the Compromise of 1850. Southern Whigs, however, backed the compromise in order to appear both proslavery and pro-Union. Because of Scott's position, the Whig vote in the South fell from 50 percent in 1848, to 35 percent in 1852, handing the election to the Democratic candidate **Franklin Pierce**.

In 1854 the Kansas-Nebraska Act brought about the demise of the Whigs, who once again took opposing positions on legislation that involved the issue of slavery. Unable to agree on a national platform, the Southern faction splintered as its members looked for a proslavery, pro-Union party to join, while Whigs in the North sought a political alternative.

▲ The 1854 campaign banner for the Know-Nothing Party reflects its members' fear and resentment of immigrants.

NATIVISM One alternative was the American Party which had its roots in a secret organization known as the Order of the Star-Spangled Banner. Members of this society believed in **nativism,** the favoring of native-born Americans over immigrants. Using secret handshakes and passwords, members were told to answer questions about their activities by saying, "I know nothing." When nativists formed the American Party in 1854, it soon became better known as the **Know-Nothing Party.**

Primarily middle-class Protestants, nativists were dismayed not only at the total number of new immigrants but also at the number of Catholics among them. To nativists, the Catholic immigrants who had flooded into the country during the 1830s and 1840s were overly influenced by the Pope and could form a conspiracy to overthrow democracy.

While the Democratic Party courted immigrant voters, nativists voted for Know-Nothing candidates. The Know-Nothing Party did surprisingly well at the polls in 1854. However, like the Whig Party, the Know-Nothings split over the issue of slavery in the territories. Southern Know-Nothings looked for another alternative to the Democrats. Meanwhile, Northern Know-Nothings began to edge toward the Republican Party. **A**

MAIN IDEA

Analyzing Causes

A What impact did the slavery issue have on the Democratic and Whig parties?

Antislavery Parties Form

Two forerunners of the Republican Party had emerged during the 1840s. In 1844 the tiny abolitionist Liberty Party—whose purpose was to pursue the cause of abolition by passing new laws—received only a small percentage of votes in the presidential election. Yet the Liberty Party won enough votes to throw the election to Democrat James K. Polk instead of Whig candidate Henry Clay.

In 1848 the **Free-Soil Party,** which opposed the extension of slavery into the territories, nominated former Democratic president Martin Van Buren. Although the Free-Soil Party failed to win any electoral votes in 1848, it received 10 percent of the popular vote, thus sending a clear message: even if some Northerners did not favor abolition, they definitely opposed the extension of slavery into the territories.

THE FREE–SOILERS Many Northerners were Free-Soilers without being abolitionists. A number of Northern Free-Soilers supported laws prohibiting black settlement in their communities and denying blacks the right to vote. Free-Soilers objected to slavery's impact on free white workers in the wage-based labor force, upon which the North depended. Abolitionist William Lloyd Garrison considered the Free-Soil Party "a sign of discontent with things political . . . reaching for something better. . . . It is a party for keeping Free Soil and not for setting men free."

Major Political Parties 1850–1860		
Party	**Established**	**Major Platform**
Free-Soil	1848	• against extension of slavery • pro-labor
Know-Nothing	1854 (as American Party)	• anti-immigration • anti-Catholic
Whig	Organized 1834	• pro-business • divided on slavery
Republican	1854	• opposed expansion of slavery into territories
Democratic	1840 (The Democratic-Republican party adopted "Democratic Party" as official name)	• states' rights • limited government • divided on slavery

SKILLBUILDER Interpreting Charts
What issue is addressed by almost all the parties shown on the chart?

Free-Soilers detected a dangerous pattern in such events as the passage of the Fugitive Slave Act and the repeal of the Missouri Compromise. They were convinced that a conspiracy existed on the part of the "diabolical slave power" to spread slavery throughout the United States. Something or someone, according to the Free-Soilers, had to prevent this spread. **B**

MAIN IDEA

Analyzing Motives
B Why did most Free-Soilers object to slavery?

REPUBLICAN PARTY In February 1854, at a school house in Ripon, Wisconsin, some discontented Northern Whigs held a meeting with antislavery Democrats and Free-Soilers to form a new political party. On July 6, the new **Republican Party** was formally organized in Jackson, Michigan. Among its founders was **Horace Greeley.**

The Republican Party was united in opposing the Kansas-Nebraska Act and in keeping slavery out of the territories. Otherwise, it embraced a wide range of opinions. The conservative faction hoped to resurrect the Missouri Compromise. At the opposite extreme were some radical abolitionists. The Republican Party's ability to draw support from such diverse groups provided the party with the strength to win a political tug of war with the other parties.

The main competition for the Republican Party was the Know-Nothing Party. Both parties targeted the same groups of voters. By 1855 the Republicans had set up party organizations in about half of the Northern states, but they lacked a national organization. Then, in quick succession, came the fraudulent territorial election in Kansas in March 1855, and the sack of Lawrence, the Pottawatomie massacre, and the caning of Sumner in 1856. Between "Bleeding Kansas" and "Bleeding Sumner," the Republicans had the issues they needed in order to challenge the Democrats for the presidency in 1856.

THE 1856 ELECTION The Republicans chose **John C. Frémont,** the famed "Pathfinder" who had mapped the Oregon Trail and led U.S. troops into California during the war with Mexico, as their candidate in 1856. The Know-Nothings split their allegiance, with Northerners endorsing Frémont and Southerners selecting former U.S. president Millard Fillmore. Although Fillmore had once been a Whig, for all practical purposes, the Whigs had now dissolved.

The Free-Soilers' banner features John C. Frémont and calls for an end to the spread of "slave power" in the nation. ▼

The Democrats nominated **James Buchanan** of Pennsylvania. Although he was a Northerner, most of his Washington friends were Southerners. Furthermore, as minister to Great Britain he had been out of the country during the disputes over the Kansas-Nebraska Act in 1854. Thus, he had antagonized neither the North nor the South. Buchanan was the only truly national candidate. To balance support between the North and the South, the Democrats chose John C. Breckinridge of Kentucky as Buchanan's running mate.

If Frémont had won, the South might well have seceded then and there. Judge P. J. Scruggs of Mississippi put it bluntly.

A PERSONAL VOICE P. J. SCRUGGS

" **The election of Frémont would present, at once, to the people of the South, the question whether they would tamely crouch at the feet of their despoilers, or . . . openly defy their enemies, and assert their independence. In my judgment, anything short of immediate, prompt, and unhesitating secession, would be an act of servility that would seal our doom for all time to come.** "

—quoted in *The Coming of the Civil War*

Buchanan, however, carried the day. Although he received only 45 percent of the popular vote, he won the entire South except for Maryland. Frémont, who carried 11 of the 16 free states, came in a strong second with 33 percent, while Fillmore brought up the rear with 22 percent.

MAIN IDEA

Analyzing Effects

C Why was the election of 1856 so important to the growth of the Republican Party?

The meaning was clear. First, the Democrats could win the presidency with a national candidate who could compete in the North without alienating Southerners. Second, the Know-Nothings were in decline. Third, the Republicans were a political force in the North. **C**

The 1856 presidential campaign had been hard-fought. However, the dissension that characterized party politics in the mid-1850s was only a pale preview of the turmoil that would divide the nation before the end of the decade.

---

3 ASSESSMENT

1. TERMS & NAMES For each term or name, write a sentence explaining it significance.
- Franklin Pierce
- nativism
- Know-Nothing Party
- Free-Soil Party
- Republican Party
- Horace Greeley
- John C. Frémont
- James Buchanan

MAIN IDEA

2. TAKING NOTES
Show how various events led to the growth of the Republican Party in the 1850s. Use a chart similar to the one below.

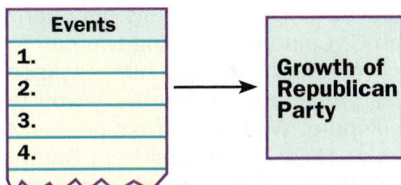

Events
1.
2.
3.
4.

→ Growth of Republican Party

Which event was most important in the rise of the Republican Party?

CRITICAL THINKING

3. CONTRASTING
How did the attitudes toward slavery held by abolitionists, Free-Soilers, and Know-Nothings differ? Explain your answer. **Think About:**
- the ultimate goal of abolitionists
- the reason Free-Soilers objected to slavery
- what caused the split in the Know-Nothing Party

4. SYNTHESIZING
How did the way in which the Republican Party was formed indicate that the party stood a good chance at success?

5. ANALYZING ISSUES
Why might the newly formed Republican Party have chosen John C. Frémont as their first presidential candidate in 1856?

TRACING THEMES

States' Rights

The power struggle between states and the federal government has caused controversy since the country's beginning. At its worst, the conflict resulted in the Civil War. Today, state and federal governments continue to square off on jurisdictional issues.

- In 1996, the Supreme Court ruled that congressional districts in Texas and North Carolina that had been redrawn to increase minority representation were unconstitutional.
- In 2000, the Supreme Court agreed to hear another case in the ongoing—since 1979—dispute between the federal government and the state of Alaska over who has authority to lease offshore land for oil and gas drilling.

Constitutional conflicts between states' rights and federal jurisdiction are pictured here. As you read, see how each issue was resolved.

1787

▼ CONSTITUTIONAL CONVENTION

ISSUE: The Constitution tried to resolve the original debate over states' rights versus federal authority.

At the Constitutional Convention in Philadelphia, delegates wanted to create a federal government that was stronger than the one created by the Articles of Confederation. But delegates disagreed about whether the federal government should have more power than the states. They also disagreed about whether large states should have more power than small states in the national legislature. The convention compromised—the Constitution reserves certain powers for the states, delegates other powers to the federal government, divides some powers between state and federal governments, and tries to balance the differing needs of the states through two houses of Congress.

1832

NULLIFICATION ▲

ISSUE: The state of South Carolina moved to nullify, or declare void, a tariff set by Congress.

In the cartoon above, President Andrew Jackson, right, is playing a game called bragg. One of his opponents, Vice-President John C. Calhoun, is hiding two cards, "Nullification" and "Anti-Tariff," behind him. Jackson is doing poorly in this game, but he eventually won the real nullification dispute. When Congress passed high tariffs on imports in 1832, politicians from South Carolina, led by Calhoun, tried to nullify the tariff law, or declare it void. Jackson threatened to enforce the law with federal troops. Congress reduced the tariff to avoid a confrontation, and Calhoun resigned the vice-presidency.

1860

◀ **SOUTH CAROLINA'S SECESSION**

ISSUE: The conflict over a state's right to secede, or withdraw, from the Union led to the Civil War.

In December 1860, Southern secessionists cheered "secession" enthusiastically in front of the Mills House (left), a hotel in Charleston, South Carolina. South Carolina seceded after the election of Abraham Lincoln, whom the South perceived as anti-states' rights and antislavery. Lincoln took the position that states did not have the right to secede from the Union. In 1861, he ordered that provisions be sent to the federal troops stationed at Fort Sumter in Charleston harbor. South Carolinians fired on the fort—and the Civil War was under way. The Union's victory in the war ended the most serious challenge to federal authority: states did not have the right to secede from the Union.

1957

LITTLE ROCK CENTRAL HIGH SCHOOL ▲

ISSUE: Some Southern governors refused to obey federal desegregation mandates for schools.

In 1957, President Eisenhower mobilized federal troops in Little Rock, Arkansas, to enforce the Supreme Court's 1954 ruling in the case of *Brown* v. *Board of Education of Topeka.* This ruling made segregation in public schools illegal. The Arkansas National Guard escorted nine African-American students into Little Rock Central High School against the wishes of Governor Orval Faubus, who had tried to prevent the students from entering the school. After this incident, Faubus closed the high schools in Little Rock in 1958 and 1959, thereby avoiding desegregation.

THINKING CRITICALLY

CONNECT TO HISTORY

1. **Creating a Chart** For each incident pictured, create a chart that tells who was on each side of the issue, summarizes each position, and explains how the issue was resolved.

CONNECT TO TODAY

2. **Using Primary and Secondary Sources** Research one of the controversies in the bulleted list in the opening paragraph or another states' rights controversy of the 1990s or 2000s. Decide which side you support. Write a paragraph explaining your position on the issue.

    SEE SKILLBUILDER HANDBOOK, PAGE R22.

↗ **hmhsocialstudies.com** **RESEARCH WEB LINKS**

SECTION
4

PI 2.3
PI 3.1

CC Unit 2.II.B.3
CC Unit 2.II.D.1.a
CC Unit 2.II.D.1.b

Slavery and Secession

MAIN IDEA	WHY IT MATTERS NOW	Terms & Names
A series of controversial events heightened the sectional conflict that brought the nation to the brink of war.	Secession created deep divisions in American society that persist to the present time.	• Dred Scott • Harpers Ferry • Roger B. Taney • Confederacy • Abraham Lincoln • Jefferson Davis • Freeport Doctrine

One American's Story

TAKING NOTES

Use the graphic organizer online to take notes on how the major events discussed in this section sharpened the North-South conflict.

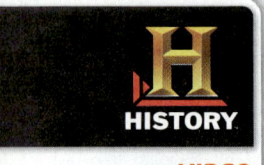

VIDEO
Lincoln's House Divided Speech

hmhsocialstudies.com

On June 16, 1858, the Republican Party of Illinois nominated its state chairman, Abraham Lincoln, to run for the U.S. Senate against Democratic incumbent Stephen A. Douglas. That night Lincoln launched his campaign with a ringing address to the convention. It included a biblical quotation.

A PERSONAL VOICE ABRAHAM LINCOLN

" 'A house divided against itself cannot stand.' I believe this government cannot endure permanently half *slave* and half *free*. I do not expect the Union to be *dissolved* —I do not expect the house to fall—but I do expect it will cease to be divided. It will become *all* one thing or all the other. Either the *opponents* of slavery will arrest the further spread of it . . . or its *advocates* will push it forward, till it shall become alike lawful in *all* the States, *old* as well as *new*, *North* as well as *South*."

—1858 speech

▲ This photograph shows Lincoln in about 1858, before the Civil War took its toll.

Lincoln was correct in that the United States could not survive for long with such a deep gulf between the North and the South—but was he right that the Union would not dissolve? With a weak president in James Buchanan and new legal questions over slavery, the United States faced the future with apprehension. Some suspected that events would lead like a trail of powder to a final explosion.

Slavery Dominates Politics

For strong leaders, slavery was a difficult issue. But it presented even more of a challenge for the indecisive President Buchanan, whose administration was plagued by slavery-related controversies. The first one arose on March 6, 1857.

DRED SCOTT DECISION In 1856 an important legal question came before the Supreme Court. The case concerned **Dred Scott,** a slave from Missouri. Scott's owner had taken him north of the Missouri Compromise line in 1834. For four years they had lived in free territory in Illinois and Wisconsin. Later they returned to Missouri, where Scott's owner died. Scott then began a lawsuit to gain his freedom. He claimed that he had become a free person by living in free territory for several years.

On March 6, 1857, Supreme Court Chief Justice **Roger B. Taney** handed down the decision. (See *Dred Scott* v. *Sandford,* page 332.) The Court ruled that slaves did not have the rights of citizens. Furthermore, said the court, Dred Scott had no claim to freedom, because he had been living in Missouri, a slave state, when he began his suit. Finally, the Court ruled that the Missouri Compromise was unconstitutional. Congress could not forbid slavery in any part of the territories. Doing so would interfere with slaveholders' right to own property, a right protected by the Fifth Amendment.

▲ Dred Scott's lawsuit dragged on for years, and set off even more controversy over slavery.

MAIN IDEA

Analyzing Effects

Ⓐ What was the significance of the *Dred Scott* decision?

Sectional passions exploded immediately. Southerners cheered the Court's decision. Northerners were stunned. By striking down the Missouri Compromise, the Supreme Court had cleared the way for the extension of slavery. Opponents of slavery now pinned their hopes on the Republican Party. If the Republicans became strong enough, they could still keep slavery in check. Ⓐ

THE LECOMPTON CONSTITUTION In fall 1857, the proslavery government at Lecompton, Kansas, wrote a constitution and applied for admission to the Union. Free-Soilers—who by this time outnumbered proslavery settlers in Kansas by nearly ten to one—rejected the proposed constitution because it protected the rights of slaveholders. The legislature called for a referendum in which the people could vote on the proslavery constitution. They voted against it.

At this point President Buchanan made a poor decision: he endorsed the proslavery Lecompton constitution. He owed his presidency to Southern support and believed that since Kansas contained only about 200 slaves, the Free-Soilers were overreacting.

MAIN IDEA

Analyzing Motives

Ⓑ Why did Buchanan support the Lecompton constitution?

Buchanan's endorsement provoked the wrath of Illinois Democrat Stephen A. Douglas, who did not care "whether [slavery] is voted down or voted up." What he cared about was popular sovereignty. Backed by an antislavery coalition of Republicans and Northern Democrats, Douglas persuaded Congress to authorize another referendum on the constitution. In summer 1858, voters rejected the constitution once again. Northerners hailed Douglas as a hero, Southerners scorned him as a traitor, and the two wings of the Democratic Party moved still farther apart. Ⓑ

Lincoln-Douglas Debates

That summer witnessed the start of one of Illinois's greatest political contests: the 1858 race for the U.S. Senate between Democratic incumbent Douglas and Republican challenger **Abraham Lincoln.** To many outsiders, it must have seemed like an uneven match. Douglas was a two-term senator with an outstanding record and a large campaign chest. Who was Lincoln?

A self-educated man with a dry wit, Lincoln was known locally as a successful lawyer and politician. Elected as a Whig to one term in Congress in 1846, he broke with his party after the passage of the Kansas-Nebraska Act in 1854 and became a Republican two years later.

LINCOLN CHALLENGES DOUGLAS As the senatorial campaign progressed, the Republican Party decided that Lincoln needed to counteract the "Little Giant's" well-known name and extensive financial resources. As a result, Lincoln challenged Douglas to a series of seven open-air debates to be held throughout Illinois on the issue of slavery in the territories. Douglas accepted the challenge, and the stage was set for some of the most celebrated debates in U.S. history.

Lincoln and Douglas had very different speaking styles. Douglas exuded self-confidence, pacing back and forth on the stage and dramatically using his fists to pound home his points. Lincoln, on the other hand, delivered his comments solemnly, using direct and plain language.

The Lincoln-Douglas debates created quite a spectacle, partly due to the opponents' difference in height.

POSITIONS AND ARGUMENTS The two men's positions were simple and consistent. Douglas believed deeply in popular sovereignty, in allowing the residents of a territory to vote for or against slavery. Although he did not think that slavery was immoral, he did believe that it was a backward labor system unsuitable to prairie agriculture. The people, Douglas figured, understood this and would vote Kansas and Nebraska free. However, Lincoln, like many Free-Soilers, believed that slavery was immoral—a labor system based on greed.

The crucial difference between the two was that Douglas believed that popular sovereignty would allow slavery to pass away on its own, while Lincoln doubted that slavery would cease to spread without legislation outlawing it in the territories.

In the course of the debates, each candidate tried to distort the views of the other. Lincoln tried to make Douglas look like a defender of slavery and of the *Dred Scott* decision. In turn, Douglas accused Lincoln of being an abolitionist and an advocate of racial equality. Lincoln responded by saying, "I am not, nor ever have been, in favor of bringing about in any way the social and political equality of the white and black races." He did, however, insist that slavery was a moral, social, and political wrong that should not be allowed to spread.

THE FREEPORT DOCTRINE In their second debate, held at Freeport, Lincoln asked his opponent a crucial question. Could the settlers of a territory vote to exclude slavery before the territory became a state? Everyone knew that the *Dred Scott* decision said no—that territories could not exclude slavery. Popular sovereignty, Lincoln implied, was thus an empty phrase.

Douglas's response to Lincoln's question became later known as the **Freeport Doctrine.** Douglas contended, "Slavery cannot exist a day or an hour anywhere, unless it is supported by local police regulations." If the people of a territory were Free-Soilers, he explained, then all they had to do was elect representatives who would not enforce slave property laws. In other words, regardless of theory or the Supreme Court's ruling, people could get around the *Dred Scott* decision.

MAIN IDEA

Comparing
Ⓒ Explain the similarities and differences between Lincoln's position on slavery and that of Douglas.

Douglas won the Senate seat, but his response had worsened the split between the Northern and Southern wings of the Democratic Party. As for Lincoln, his attacks on the "vast moral evil" of slavery drew national attention, and some Republicans began thinking of him as an excellent candidate for the presidency in 1860. Ⓒ

Passions Ignite

If 1858 was a year of talk, then 1859 turned out to be a year of action. Most Americans probably would have welcomed a respite from the issue of slavery. Instead, "God's angry man," John Brown, reemerged on the scene and ended all hopes of a compromise over slavery between the North and the South.

HARPERS FERRY While politicians debated the slavery issue, John Brown was studying the slave uprisings that had occurred in ancient Rome and on the French island of Haiti. He believed that the time was ripe for similar uprisings in the United States. Brown secretly obtained financial backing from several prominent Northern abolitionists. On the night of October 16, 1859, he led a band of 21 men, black and white, into **Harpers Ferry,** Virginia (now West Virginia). His aim was to seize the federal arsenal there, distribute the captured arms to slaves in the area, and start a general slave uprising.

Sixty of the town's prominent citizens were held hostage by Brown who hoped that their slaves would then join the insurrection. No slaves came forward. Instead, local troops killed eight of Brown's men. Then a detachment of U.S. Marines, commanded by Colonel Robert E. Lee, raced to Harpers Ferry, stormed the engine house where Brown and his men had barricaded themselves, killed two more of the raiders, and captured Brown. Brown was then turned over to Virginia to be tried for treason.

Historians have long debated Brown's actions. There is no doubt that he hated slavery with all his heart. However, why did he fail to tell slaves in the area about his plans beforehand? Why didn't he provide his men with enough food to last for even one day? In any case, Brown certainly hoped that his actions would arouse Northern fury and start a war for abolition.

JOHN BROWN'S HANGING On December 2, 1859, Brown was hanged for high treason in the presence of federal troops and a crowd of curious observers. Public reaction was immediate and intense. Although Lincoln and Douglas condemned Brown as a murderer, many other Northerners expressed admiration for him and for his cause. Bells tolled at the news of his execution, guns fired salutes, and huge crowds gathered to hear fiery speakers denounce the South. Some Northerners began to call Brown a martyr for the sacred cause of freedom.

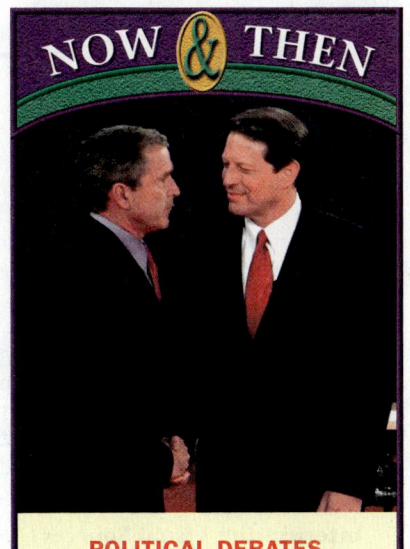

NOW & THEN

POLITICAL DEBATES
In the mid-19th century, people flocked to public grandstands, where the political candidates debated the issues of the day.

When Lincoln debated Douglas, thousands of people came to listen. Each debate lasted for three hours, and listeners stood the entire time, interrupting the speakers with cheers and an occasional heckle. When the debate ended, spectators adjourned to tables of barbecued meat and ice cream. Torchlit parades ended the day.

The first televised presidential debate, in 1960, featured candidates Kennedy and Nixon. Since then, presidential candidates, including Bush and Gore (above), have made televised debating a cornerstone of presidential campaigning.

JOHN BROWN GOING TO HIS HANGING (1942)

This scene, painted by the African-American artist Horace Pippin in 1942, shows John Brown being transported by wagon to his execution. The artist has focused our attention on the cruelty of Brown's fate.

The abolitionist is shown tied with the rope that will be used to hang him, and sitting on the coffin that will receive his body after death. Brown's dark shape is silhouetted by the large white building behind him, a structure that combines the features of both courthouse and prison.

SKILLBUILDER
Interpreting Visual Sources

1. Why do you think the African-American woman in the right-hand corner is looking away from the scene?

2. How has the artist expressed the hopelessness of the situation?

 SEE SKILLBUILDER HANDBOOK, PAGE R23.

John Brown Going to His Hanging (1942), Horace Pippin. Oil on canvas, 24 1/8" x 30 1/4". Courtesy of the Museum of American Art of the Pennsylvania Academy of the Fine Arts, Philadelphia, Pennsylvania. John Lambert Fund [1943.11]

The response was equally extreme in the South, where outraged mobs assaulted whites who were suspected of holding antislavery views. Harpers Ferry terrified Southern slaveholders, who were convinced the North was plotting slave uprisings everywhere. Even longtime supporters of the Union called for secession. As one former Unionist explained, "I am willing to take the chances of . . . disunion, sooner than submit any longer to Northern insolence and Northern outrage." **D**

Lincoln Is Elected President

Despite the tide of hostility that now flowed between North and South, the Republican Party eagerly awaited its presidential convention in May 1860. When the convention began, almost everyone believed that the party's candidate would be Senator William H. Seward of New York. However, events took a dramatic turn.

THE REPUBLICAN CONVENTION The convention took place in Chicago, which had quickly transformed itself into a convention city with more than 50 hotels and an 18,000-square-foot wooden meeting center named the Wigwam. Republicans flooded into the frontier city in such crowds that despite the preparations, many ended up sleeping on pool tables in the hotels.

The convention opened to a surging crowd of delegates, newsmen, and spectators. The 4,500-person delegate floor overflowed within minutes. To gain seating in the galleries, which were reserved for gentlemen who had come with ladies, determined single men even offered schoolgirls a quarter for their company. The first day of the convention was passed in forming committees, listening to prayers, and gossiping about politics. As events came to a close, campaign managers for the candidates retreated to their headquarters and began bargaining for delegates' votes, some working late into the night.

MAIN IDEA

Analyzing Effects

D Why did Harpers Ferry increase tensions between the North and the South?

SEWARD AND LINCOLN Senator William H. Seward appeared to have everything one needed in order to be a successful presidential candidate: the credential of having led anti-slavery forces in Congress, the financial support of New York political organizations—and a desire to be the center of attention. In fact, Seward himself had little doubt that he would be nominated. Well before the voting took place, Seward drafted his senatorial resignation speech, which he planned to deliver when his nomination became official.

Seward's well-known name and his reputation may have worked against him, however. Abraham Lincoln's being relatively unknown probably won him the nomination. Unlike Seward, Lincoln had not had much chance to offend his fellow Republicans. The delegates rejected Seward and his talk of an "irrepressible conflict" between North and South. On the third ballot, they nominated Lincoln, who seemed more moderate in his views. Although Lincoln pledged to halt the further spread of slavery "as with a chain of steel," he also tried to reassure Southerners that a Republican administration would not "directly, or indirectly, interfere with their slaves, or with them, about their slaves." His reassurances fell on deaf ears. In Southern eyes, he was a "black Republican," whose election would be "the greatest evil that has ever befallen this country."

▲ Because Lincoln was virtually unknown in the East, his first name was written incorrectly as "Abram" on this 1860 election flag.

MAIN IDEA

Drawing Conclusions
E) How did slavery affect U.S. political parties in 1860?

THE ELECTION OF 1860 Three major candidates vied for office in addition to Lincoln. The Democratic Party split over the issue of slavery. Northern Democrats backed Stephen Douglas and his doctrine of popular sovereignty. Southern Democrats backed Vice-President John C. Breckinridge of Kentucky. Former Know-Nothings and Whigs from the South, along with some moderate Northerners, organized the Constitutional Union Party, which ignored the issue of slavery altogether. They nominated John Bell of Tennessee. **E)**

Analyzing *Political Cartoons*

"A POLITICAL RACE"

This cartoon depicts the major candidates in the 1860 presidential election. Three of the candidates, Bell, Breckinridge, and Douglas, are in hot pursuit of the front runner—Republican Abraham Lincoln. It was a close race. Lincoln defeated Douglas in the North. Breckinridge carried most of the South. Because the North had a higher population than the South, Lincoln won the election.

SKILLBUILDER
Analyzing Political Cartoons
1. Who, in the opinion of the artist, is the fittest man in the race?
2. How does this cartoon suggest the course of the election of 1860?

 SEE SKILLBUILDER HANDBOOK, PAGE R24.

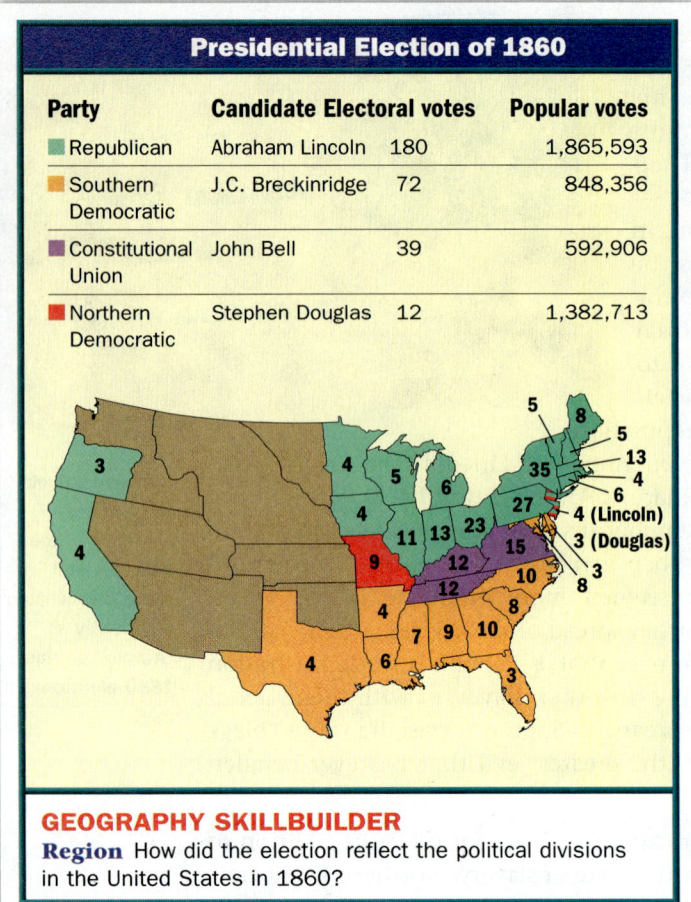

Presidential Election of 1860

Party	Candidate	Electoral votes	Popular votes
Republican	Abraham Lincoln	180	1,865,593
Southern Democratic	J.C. Breckinridge	72	848,356
Constitutional Union	John Bell	39	592,906
Northern Democratic	Stephen Douglas	12	1,382,713

GEOGRAPHY SKILLBUILDER
Region How did the election reflect the political divisions in the United States in 1860?

Lincoln emerged as the winner, but like Buchanan in the previous election, he received less than half the popular vote. In fact, although Lincoln defeated his combined opponents in the electoral vote by 180 to 123, he received no electoral votes from the South. Unlike Buchanan, Lincoln had sectional rather than national support, carrying every free state but not even appearing on the ballot in most of the slave states. The outlook for the Union was grim.

Southern Secession

Lincoln's victory convinced Southerners that they had lost their political voice in the national government. Fearful that Northern Republicans would submit the South to what noted Virginia agriculturist Edmund Ruffin called "the most complete subjection and political bondage," some Southern states decided to act. South Carolina led the way, seceding from the Union on December 20, 1860. Four days later, the news reached William Tecumseh Sherman, superintendent of the Louisiana State Seminary of Learning and Military Academy. In utter dismay, Sherman poured out his fears for the South.

A PERSONAL VOICE WILLIAM TECUMSEH SHERMAN

" This country will be drenched in blood. . . . [T]he people of the North. . . . are not going to let the country be destroyed without a mighty effort to save it. Besides, where are your men and appliances of war to contend against them? . . . You are rushing into war with one of the most powerful, ingeniously mechanical and determined people on earth—right at your doors. . . . Only in spirit and determination are you prepared for war. In all else you are totally unprepared. "

—quoted in *None Died in Vain*

Even Sherman underestimated the depth and intensity of the South's commitment. For many Southern planters, the cry of "States' rights!" meant the complete independence of Southern states from federal government control. Most white Southerners also feared that an end to their entire way of life was at hand. Many were desperate for one last chance to preserve the slave labor system and saw secession as the only way. Mississippi followed South Carolina's lead and seceded on January 9, 1861. Florida seceded the next day. Within a few weeks, Alabama, Georgia, Louisiana, and Texas had also seceded. **F**

THE SHAPING OF THE CONFEDERACY On February 4, 1861, delegates from the secessionist states met in Montgomery, Alabama, where they formed the **Confederacy,** or Confederate States of America. The Confederate constitution closely resembled that of the United States. The most notable difference was that the Confederate constitution "protected and recognized" slavery in new

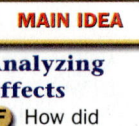

MAIN IDEA

Analyzing Effects
F How did Lincoln's election affect the South?

PRESIDENT DAVIS.

This 1864 playing card bears the portrait of Jefferson Davis, president of the Confederate States of America.

territories. The new constitution also stressed that each state was to be "sovereign and independent," a provision that would hamper efforts to unify the South.

On February 9, delegates to the Confederate constitutional convention unanimously elected former senator **Jefferson Davis** of Mississippi as president and Alexander Stephens of Georgia as vice-president. Davis had made his position clear, noting that to present a show of strength to the North, the South should "offer no doubtful or divided front." At his inauguration, Davis declared, "The time for compromise has now passed." His listeners responded by singing "Farewell to the Star-Spangled Banner" and "Dixie."

THE CALM BEFORE THE STORM As the nation awaited Lincoln's inauguration in March, its citizens were confused. What would happen now? Seven slave states had seceded and formed a new nation. Eight slave states remained within the Union. Would they secede also?

President Buchanan was uncertain. He announced that secession was illegal, but that it also would be illegal for him to do anything about it. He tied his own hands, but in truth there was not much that he could have done.

One problem was that Washington, D.C. was very much a Southern city. There were secessionists in Congress and in all of the departments of the federal government, as well as in the president's cabinet. Consequently, mass resignations took place. To some people it seemed as if the federal government were melting away. One key question remained in everyone's mind: Would the North allow the South to leave the Union without a fight?

HISTORICAL SPOTLIGHT

SECESSION AND THE BORDER STATES

Four slave states—Maryland, Kentucky, Missouri, and Delaware—were undecided about secession. Lincoln believed that these states would be essential to the success of the Union if war broke out. They had thriving industries and good access to important rail and water routes. Also, bordering North and South made the four states crucial to the movement of troops and supplies. Moreover, Maryland almost surrounded Washington, D.C., the seat of government.

As president, Lincoln faced a choice: free the slaves and make abolitionists happy, or ignore slavery for the moment to avoid alienating the border states. He chose the latter, but that did not prevent violent conflicts between secessionists and Unionists in Maryland, Kentucky, and Missouri. With militia intervention, and some political maneuvering, Lincoln kept the four border states in the Union.

SECTION 4 ASSESSMENT

1. **TERMS & NAMES** For each term or name, write a sentence explaining its significance.
   - Dred Scott
   - Roger B. Taney
   - Abraham Lincoln
   - Freeport Doctrine
   - Harpers Ferry
   - Confederacy
   - Jefferson Davis

MAIN IDEA

2. **TAKING NOTES**
   List six major events described in this section and explain how each one sharpened the North-South conflict.

Event	Result
1.	⟶
2.	⟶
3.	⟶

CRITICAL THINKING

3. **CONTRASTING**
   How did Lincoln and Douglas disagree about slavery? Which of their views were facts, and which were opinions?

4. **EVALUATING**
   If you had been voting in the presidential election of 1860, for whom would you have voted, other than Abraham Lincoln? Explain your reasoning by using specific references to the chapter.

5. **ANALYZING PRIMARY SOURCES**
   In *Dred Scott* v. *Sandford* of 1857, the Supreme Court found that:

   " A free negro of the African race, whose ancestors were brought to this country and sold as slaves, is not a "citizen" within the meaning of the Constitution of the United States."

   How did the Supreme Court decision add to the tensions over slavery in the 1850s?

DRED SCOTT v. SANDFORD (1857)

ORIGINS OF THE CASE Dred Scott's slave master had brought him from the slave state of Missouri to live for a time in free territory and in the free state of Illinois. Eventually they returned to Missouri. Scott believed that because he had lived in free territory, he should be free. In 1854 he sued in federal court for his freedom. The court ruled against him, and he appealed to the Supreme Court.

THE RULING The Supreme Court ruled that African Americans were not and could never be citizens. Thus, Dred Scott had no right even to file a lawsuit and remained enslaved.

LEGAL REASONING

The Court's decision, based primarily on Chief Justice Roger Taney's written opinion, made two key findings. First, it held that because Scott was a slave, he was not a citizen and had no right to sue in a United States court.

> "We think they [slaves] . . . are not included, and were not intended to be included, under the word 'citizens' in the Constitution, and can therefore claim none of the rights and privileges which that instrument provides for and secures to citizens of the United States."

This could have been the end of the matter, but Taney went further. He said that by banning slavery, Congress was, in effect, taking away property. Such an action, he wrote, violated the Fifth Amendment, which guarantees the right not to be deprived of property without due process of law (such as a hearing). Thus, all congressional efforts to ban slavery in the territories were prohibited.

Justices John McLean and Benjamin Curtis strongly dissented on both points. They showed that the U.S. Constitution, state constitutions, and other laws had recognized African Americans as citizens. They also pointed to the clause in the Constitution giving Congress the power to "make all needful Rules and Regulations" to govern U.S. territories. In their view, this clause gave Congress the power to prohibit slavery in the territories.

◄ **Chief Justice Roger Taney**

LEGAL SOURCES

U.S. CONSTITUTION

U.S. CONSTITUTION, ARTICLE 4, SECTION 2 (1789)
"No Person held to Service or Labor in one State, . . . escaping into another, shall, in Consequence of any Law or Regulation therein, be discharged from such Service or Labor. . . ."

U.S. CONSTITUTION, ARTICLE 4, SECTION 3 (1789)
"The Congress shall have Power to dispose of and make all needful Rules and Regulations respecting the Territory or other Property belonging to the United States. . . ."

U.S. CONSTITUTION, FIFTH AMENDMENT (1791)
"No person shall be . . . deprived of life, liberty, or property, without due process of law. . . ."

RELATED CASES

ABLEMAN v. BOOTH (1858)
The Court decided that the Fugitive Slave Act was constitutional and that laws passed in Northern states that prohibited the return of fugitive slaves were unconstitutional.

WHY IT MATTERED

Taney's opinion in *Dred Scott* had far-reaching consequences. Legally, the opinion greatly expanded the reach of slavery. Politically, it heightened the sectional tensions that would lead to the Civil War.

Before the Court decided *Dred Scott*, Americans widely accepted the idea that Congress and the states could limit slavery. As the dissenters argued, many previous acts of Congress had limited slavery—for example, the Northwest Ordinance had banned slavery in the Northwest Territory—and no one had claimed that those acts violated property rights.

Taney's opinion in *Dred Scott*, however, was a major change. This expansion of slaveholders' rights cast doubt on whether free states could prevent slave owners from bringing or even selling slaves into free areas.

As a result, *Dred Scott* intensified the slavery debate as no single event had before. In going beyond what was needed to settle the case before him, Taney's ruling became a political act, and threw into question the legitimacy of the Court. Further, Taney's opinion took the extreme proslavery position and installed it as the national law. It not only negated all the compromises made to date by pro- and anti-slavery forces, but it seemed to preclude any possible future compromises.

▲ Contemporary newspaper article describing the *Dred Scott* case.

HISTORICAL IMPACT

It took four years of bitter civil war to find out if Taney's opinion would stand as the law of the land. It would not. Immediately after the Civil War, the federal government moved to abolish slavery with the Thirteenth Amendment (1865) and then to extend state and national citizenship with the Fourteenth Amendment (1868) to "[a]ll persons born or naturalized in the United States." The wording of these amendments was expressly intended to nullify *Dred Scott*.

These amendments meant that *Dred Scott* would no longer be used as a precedent—an earlier ruling that can be used to justify a current one. Instead, it is now pointed to as an important lesson on the limits of the Supreme Court's power, as a key step on the road to the Civil War, and as one of the worst decisions ever made by the Supreme Court.

THINKING CRITICALLY

CONNECT TO HISTORY
1. **Developing Historical Perspective** Use the library to find commentaries on *Dred Scott* written at the time the decision was made. Read two of these commentaries and identify which section—North or South—the writer or speaker came from. Explain how each person's region shaped his or her views.

 SEE SKILLBUILDER HANDBOOK, PAGE R11.

CONNECT TO TODAY
2. Visit the links for Historic Decisions of the Supreme Court to research what it means to be a citizen of the United States and what rights that citizenship extends. Research which constitutional amendments, U.S. laws, and Supreme Court decisions guarantee the rights of citizens. Prepare an oral presentation or annotated display to summarize your findings.

 hmhsocialstudies.com INTERNET ACTIVITY

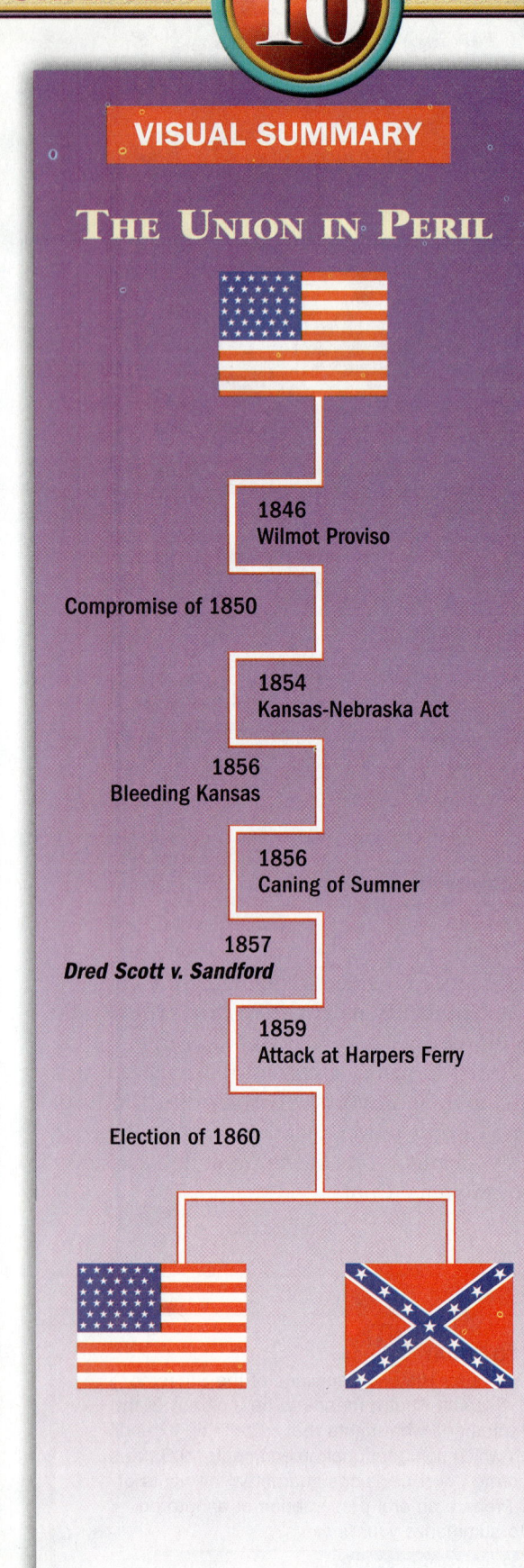

VISUAL SUMMARY

THE UNION IN PERIL

1846
Wilmot Proviso

Compromise of 1850

1854
Kansas-Nebraska Act

1856
Bleeding Kansas

1856
Caning of Sumner

1857
Dred Scott v. Sandford

1859
Attack at Harpers Ferry

Election of 1860

TERMS & NAMES

For each term below, write a sentence explaining its connection to the growing conflict in the 1850s.

1. secession
2. Compromise of 1850
3. popular sovereignty
4. Stephen A. Douglas
5. Fugitive Slave Act
6. Harriet Tubman
7. nativism
8. Horace Greeley
9. John Brown
10. Dred Scott

MAIN IDEAS

Use your notes and the information in the chapter to answer the following questions.

The Divisive Politics of Slavery (pages 304–309)

1. Describe the economic differences between the North and the South in the 1850s.
2. What were the major terms of the Compromise of 1850?

Protest, Resistance, and Violence (pages 310–317)

3. Discuss the impacts Harriet Tubman and Harriet Beecher Stowe had on antislavery attitudes in the North.
4. What were the basic provisions and results of the Kansas-Nebraska Act?

The Birth of the Republican Party (pages 318–321)

5. Why did the Republican Party grow as the Whig and Know-Nothing parties declined in the 1850s?
6. Summarize the results of the election of 1856.

Slavery and Secession (pages 324–331)

7. Compare and contrast Abraham Lincoln's and Stephen A. Douglas's views about slavery in the territories.
8. Why was the South so upset by Lincoln's election?

CRITICAL THINKING

1. **USING YOUR NOTES** In a chart like the one shown, explain how the following key events led to secession.

KEY EVENT	FUEL FOR SECESSION
Wilmot Proviso of 1846	
Compromise of 1850	
Kansas-Nebraska Act of 1854	
Election of 1860	

2. **DRAWING CONCLUSIONS** John Brown, Harriet Tubman, and Harriet Beecher Stowe all opposed slavery. Explain whether you consider any of these people to be heroes. Defend your viewpoint with references from the chapter.

3. **INTERPRETING MAPS** Review the map on page 313. Think about the terrain and bodies of water that an escaping slave would have faced. In what ways might these physical features have helped or hindered a fugitive's progress?

Use the pie charts and your knowledge of U.S. history to answer question 1.

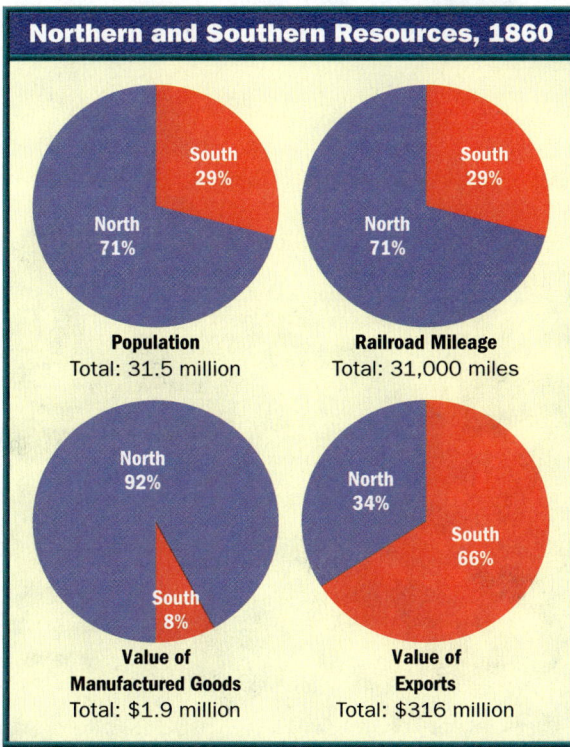

Northern and Southern Resources, 1860

Population
Total: 31.5 million

South 29%
North 71%

Railroad Mileage
Total: 31,000 miles

South 29%
North 71%

Value of Manufactured Goods
Total: $1.9 million

North 92%
South 8%

Value of Exports
Total: $316 million

North 34%
South 66%

1 Which of the following statements is *not* supported by the pie charts?

(1) The South was at a disadvantage in population.
(2) The South had no advantages over the North.
(3) The North held an advantage in the value of manufactured goods.
(4) The North and South had unequal resources.

Use the quotation below and your knowledge of U.S. history to answer question 2.

" The State of Ohio is separated from Kentucky just by one river; on either side of it the soil is equally fertile, and the situation equally favourable, and yet everything is different. Here [on the Ohio side] a population devoured by feverish activity, trying every means to make its fortune. . . . There [on the Kentucky side] is a people which makes others work for it and shows little compassion, a people without energy, mettle or the spirit of enterprise. . . . These differences cannot be attributed to any other cause but slavery. It degrades the black population and enervates [saps the energy of] the white. "

—Alexis de Tocqueville, *Journey to America*

2 Why might an abolitionist in the 1850s have been eager to support de Tocqueville's point of view?

(1) to publicize the virtues of Ohio
(2) to persuade people to settle in Kansas
(3) to argue that slavery was bad for slave and master
(4) to show that immigrants don't understand American traditions

3 The Wilmot Proviso failed to pass in the Senate because —

(1) Northerners controlled the Senate.
(2) Southerners controlled the Senate.
(3) California was against it.
(4) Mexico was in support of it.

 hmhsocialstudies.com **TEST PRACTICE**

For additional test practice, go online for:

• Diagnostic tests   • Tutorials

INTERACT WITH HISTORY

Recall the issues that you explored at the beginning of the chapter. Now that you know more about the road leading to the secession crisis, would you change any of your responses? Write a plan of action in the voice of a presidential adviser.

FOCUS ON WRITING

Imagine it is 1858. You are Abraham Lincoln preparing to debate Stephen Douglas. Write a speech arguing against popular sovereignty. In your speech, use persuasive appeals to convince Illinois voters to oppose popular sovereignty and ultimately to give you their votes in the next election.

MULTIMEDIA ACTIVITY

21ST CENTURY

Visit the links for Chapter Assessment to find out more about John Brown and the raid at Harpers Ferry. Discuss one of the following questions in a short essay.

• How was John Brown regarded by abolitionists?
• Was John Brown's plan destined to fail?

hmhsocialstudies.com

CHAPTER 11 THE CIVIL WAR

Essential Question

What were the strategies, outcomes, and legacies of the Civil War?

 New York Standards

KEY IDEA 1 The study of New York State and United States history requires an analysis of the development of American culture, its diversity and multicultural context, and the ways people are unified by many values, practices, and traditions.

KEY IDEA 3 Study about the major social, political, economic, cultural, and religious developments in New York State and United States history involves learning about the important roles and contributions of individuals and groups.

SECTION 1: The Civil War Begins

SECTION 2: The Politics of War

SECTION 3: Life During Wartime

SECTION 4: The North Takes Charge

SECTION 5: The Legacy of the War

Union soldiers in the trenches at Petersburg, Virginia, in 1865

1861 Inauguration of President Lincoln

1861 Fort Sumter is taken by the Confederates.

1862 North and South clash at Shiloh.

1863 President Lincoln issues the Emancipation Proclamation.

1863 The Union wins at Gettysburg and Vicksburg.

USA
WORLD

| 1861 | 1862 | 1863 |

1861 Victor Emmanuel II proclaims an independent Kingdom of Italy.

1861 Alexander II emancipates the Russian serfs.

1862 Otto von Bismarck is named prime minister of Prussia.

1863 Shir 'Ali Khan becomes emir of Afghanistan.

INTERACT
WITH HISTORY

The year is 1861. Seven Southern states
have seceded from the Union over the issues
of slavery and states' rights. They have
formed their own government, called the
Confederacy, and raised an army. In March,
the Confederate army attacks and seizes Fort
Sumter, a Union stronghold in South Carolina.
President Lincoln responds by issuing a call
for volunteers to serve in the Union army.

Explore the Issues

- Can diplomacy prevent a war between the
  states?

- What makes a civil war different from a
  foreign war?

- How might a civil war affect society and
  the U.S. economy?

1864 The
Confederate vessel
Hunley makes
the first successful
submarine attack in history.

1864
Abraham
Lincoln is
reelected.

1865 Lee surrenders to Grant
at Appomattox.

1865 Andrew Johnson becomes
president after Lincoln's assassination.

1863   1864   1865

1864 Leo Tolstoy
writes *War and
Peace*.

1865 Joseph Lister
pioneers antiseptic
surgery.

The Civil War Begins

MAIN IDEA	WHY IT MATTERS NOW	Terms & Names
The secession of Southern states caused the North and the South to take up arms.	The nation's identity was forged in part by the Civil War.	• Fort Sumter • Anaconda plan • Bull Run • Stonewall Jackson • George McClellan • Ulysses S. Grant	• Shiloh • David G. Farragut • *Monitor* • *Merrimack* • Robert E. Lee • Antietam

One American's Story

hmhsocialstudies.com
TAKING NOTES

Use the graphic organizer online to take notes about early Civil War battles.

On April 18, 1861, the federal supply ship *Baltic* dropped anchor off the coast of New Jersey. Aboard was Major Robert Anderson, a 35-year army veteran on his way from Charleston, South Carolina, to New York City. That day, Anderson wrote out a report to the secretary of war, describing his most recent command.

A PERSONAL VOICE
ROBERT ANDERSON

"**Having defended Fort Sumter for thirty-four hours, until the quarters were entirely burned, the main gates destroyed by fire, . . . the magazine surrounded by flames, . . . four barrels and three cartridges of powder only being available, and no provisions but pork remaining, I accepted terms of evacuation . . . and marched out of the fort . . . with colors flying and drums beating . . . and saluting my flag with fifty guns.**"

—quoted in *Fifty Basic Civil War Documents*

Major Anderson *(far left)* and Fort Sumter's Union troops

The flag that Major Anderson saluted was the Stars and Stripes. After it came down, the Confederates raised their own flag, the Stars and Bars. The confederate attack on Fort Sumter signaled the start of the Civil War.

Confederates Fire on Fort Sumter

The seven southernmost states that had already seceded formed the Confederate States of America on February 4, 1861. Confederate soldiers immediately began taking over federal installations in their states—courthouses, post offices, and especially forts. By the time of Abraham Lincoln's inauguration on March 4, only two Southern forts remained in Union hands. The more important was South Carolina's **Fort Sumter,** on an island in Charleston harbor.

The day after his inauguration, the new president received an urgent dispatch from the fort's commander, Major Anderson. The Confederacy was demanding that he surrender or face an attack, and his supplies of food and ammunition would last six weeks at the most.

LINCOLN'S DILEMMA The news presented Lincoln with a dilemma. If he ordered the navy to shoot its way into Charleston harbor and reinforce Fort Sumter, he would be responsible for starting hostilities, which might prompt the slave states still in the Union to secede. If he ordered the fort evacuated, he would be treating the Confederacy as a legitimate nation. Such an action would anger the Republican Party, weaken his administration, and endanger the Union.

FIRST SHOTS Lincoln executed a clever political maneuver. He would not abandon Fort Sumter, but neither would he reinforce it. He would merely send in "food for hungry men."

Now it was Jefferson Davis who faced a dilemma. If he did nothing, he would damage the image of the Confederacy as a sovereign, independent nation. On the other hand, if he ordered an attack on Fort Sumter, he would turn peaceful secession into war. Davis chose war. At 4:30 A.M. on April 12, Confederate batteries began thundering away. Charleston's citizens watched and cheered as though it were a fireworks display. The South Carolinians bombarded the fort with more than 4,000 rounds before Anderson surrendered. **A**

VIRGINIA SECEDES News of Fort Sumter's fall united the North. When Lincoln called for 75,000 volunteers to serve for three months, the response was overwhelming. In Iowa, 20 times the state's quota rushed to enlist.

Lincoln's call for troops provoked a very different reaction in the states of the upper South. On April 17, Virginia, unwilling to fight against other Southern states, seceded—a terrible loss to the Union. Virginia was the most heavily populated state in the South and the most industrialized (with a crucial ironworks and navy yard). In May, Arkansas, Tennessee, and North Carolina followed Virginia, bringing the number of Confederate states to 11. However, the western counties of Virginia were antislavery, so they seceded from Virginia and were admitted into the Union as West Virginia in 1863. The four remaining slave states—Maryland, Delaware, Kentucky, and Missouri—remained in the Union, although many of the citizens in those states fought for the Confederacy.

MAIN IDEA

Analyzing Causes
A Why did Jefferson Davis choose to go to war?

Most Union troops saw the war as a struggle to preserve the Union. ▼

Most Confederate soldiers fought to protect the South from Northern aggression. ▼

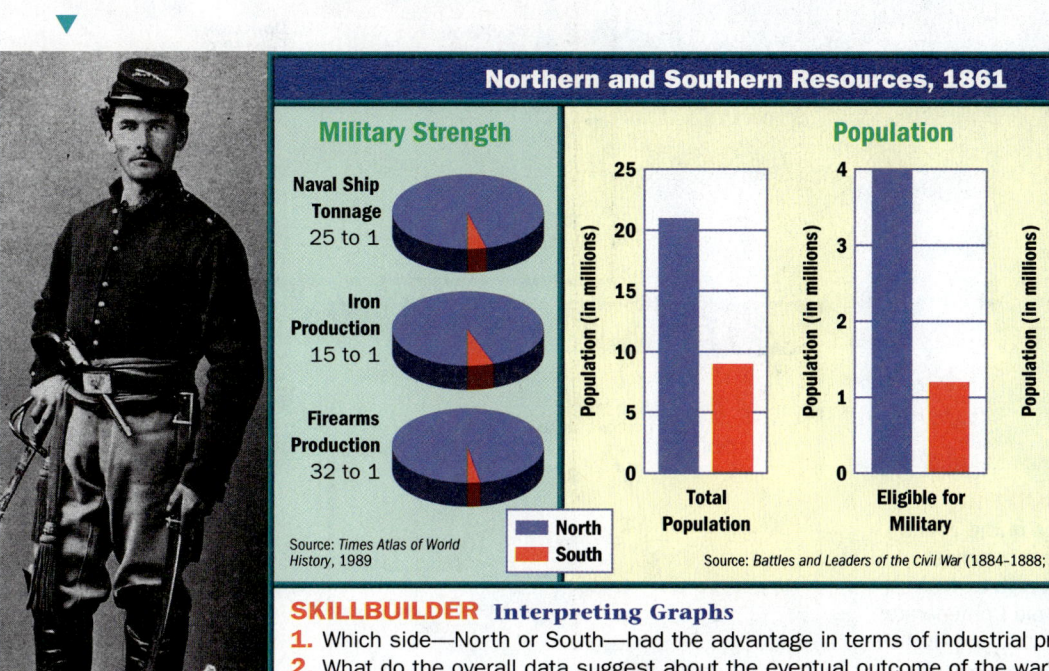

Northern and Southern Resources, 1861

Military Strength

Naval Ship Tonnage
25 to 1

Iron Production
15 to 1

Firearms Production
32 to 1

Source: *Times Atlas of World History*, 1989

■ North
■ South

Population

Total Population

Eligible for Military

Industrial Workers

Source: *Battles and Leaders of the Civil War* (1884–1888; reprinted ed., 1956)

SKILLBUILDER Interpreting Graphs
1. Which side—North or South—had the advantage in terms of industrial production?
2. What do the overall data suggest about the eventual outcome of the war?

The Civil War **339**

Americans Expect a Short War

Northerners and Confederates alike expected a short, glorious war. Soldiers left for the front with bands playing and crowds cheering. Both sides felt that right was on their side.

UNION AND CONFEDERATE STRATEGIES In reality the two sides were unevenly matched. The Union enjoyed enormous advantages in resources over the South—more fighting power, more factories, greater food production, and a more extensive railroad system. In addition, Lincoln proved to be a decisive yet patient leader, skillful at balancing political factions.

The Confederacy likewise enjoyed some advantages, notably "King Cotton" (and the profits it earned on the world market), first-rate generals, a strong military tradition, and soldiers who were highly motivated because they were defending their homeland. However, the South had a tradition of local and limited government, and there was resistance to the centralization of government necessary to run a war. Several Southern governors were so obstinate in their assertion of states' rights that they refused to cooperate with the Confederate government. **B**

The two sides pursued different military strategies. The Union, which had to conquer the South to win, devised a three-part plan: (1) the Union navy would blockade Southern ports, so they could neither export cotton nor import much-needed manufactured goods, (2) Union riverboats and armies would move down the Mississippi River and split the Confederacy in two, and (3) Union armies would capture the Confederate capital at Richmond, Virginia.

> *"The die was cast; war was declared . . . and we were all afraid it would be over and we [would] not be in the fight."*
>
> SAM WATKINS, CONFEDERATE SOLDIER

MAIN IDEA

Contrasting
B Contrast the strengths of the North and the South.

Civil War, 1861–1862

⬀ hmhsocialstudies.com **INTERACTIVE MAP**

- Area controlled by Union
- Area won by Union, 1861–1862
- Area controlled by Confederacy
- Union troop movements
- Confederate troop movements
- Union victory
- Confederate victory
- ■ Fort
- ✪ Capital

0 200 400 miles
0 200 400 kilometers

Battles of the West

ILLINOIS IND. Ohio R.
Mississippi R.
Curtis MISSOURI Grant & Foote KY.
Pope FT. HENRY Feb. 1862
PEA RIDGE Mar. 1862 FT. DONELSON Feb. 1862 Grant Buell TENN.
ARK. SHILOH Apr. 1862 Corinth Johnston
MISS. ALA.

0 50 100 miles
0 50 100 kilometers

Fall of New Orleans

LOUISIANA Vicksburg ALA.
MISS.
Farragut Mississippi R.
NEW ORLEANS April 1862
Gulf of Mexico

0 50 100 miles
0 50 100 kilometers

GEOGRAPHY SKILLBUILDER
1. **Region** In which region of the country did Northern forces have the most success?
2. **Place** In which states did Confederate troops attempt invasions of the North?

Northern newspapers dubbed the strategy the **Anaconda plan,** after a snake that suffocates its victims in its coils. Because the Confederacy's goal was its own survival as a nation, its strategy was mostly defensive. However, Southern leaders encouraged their generals to attack—and even to invade the North—if the opportunity arose.

BULL RUN The first major bloodshed occurred on July 21, about three months after Fort Sumter fell. An army of 30,000 inexperienced Union soldiers on its way toward the Confederate capital at Richmond, only 100 miles from Washington, D.C., came upon an equally inexperienced Confederate army encamped near the little creek of **Bull Run,** just 25 miles from the Union capital. Lincoln commanded General Irvin McDowell to attack, noting, "You are green, it is true, but they are green also."

The battle was a seesaw affair. In the morning the Union army gained the upper hand, but the Confederates held firm, inspired by General Thomas J. Jackson. "There is Jackson standing like a stone wall!" another general shouted, originating the nickname **Stonewall Jackson.** In the afternoon Confederate reinforcements arrived and turned the tide of battle into the first victory for the South. The routed Union troops began a panicky retreat to the capital.

HISTORICAL SPOTLIGHT

PICNIC AT BULL RUN

Before the First Battle of Bull Run, the inexperienced soldiers weren't the only ones who expected the war to be a "picnic." In Washington, ladies and gentlemen put on their best clothes and mounted their carriages. Carrying baskets of food and iced champagne, they rode out to observe the first encounter of the war.

The battle did not turn out to be the entertainment viewers expected. When the Confederates forced the Union to retreat, the Northerners were blocked by the carriages of the panicking civilians. After that disaster, no one in the North predicted that the war would be over after just one skirmish.

A newspaper reporter described the chaos at the scene.

A PERSONAL VOICE

" I saw officers . . . —majors and colonels who had deserted their commands—
pass me galloping as if for dear life. . . . For three miles, hosts of Federal troops . . .
all mingled in one disorderly rout. Wounded men lying along the banks . . .
appealed with raised hands to those who rode horses, begging to be lifted behind,
but few regarded such petitions. "

—correspondent, New York *World*, July 21, 1861

Fortunately for the Union, the Confederates were too exhausted and disorganized to attack Washington. Still, Confederate morale soared. Bull Run "has secured our independence," declared a Georgia secessionist, and many Southern soldiers, confident that the war was over, left the army and went home. **C**

MAIN IDEA

Analyzing Effects
C How did Southerners react to the outcome of Bull Run?

Union Armies in the West

Lincoln responded to the defeat at Bull Run by calling for the enlistment of 500,000 men to serve for three years instead of three months. Three days later, he called for an additional 500,000 men. He also appointed General **George McClellan** to lead this new Union army, encamped near Washington. While McClellan drilled his men—soon to be known as the Army of the Potomac—the Union forces in the West began the fight for control of the Mississippi.

" No terms except unconditional and immediate surrender . . ."
ULYSSES S. GRANT

FORTS HENRY AND DONELSON In February 1862 a Union army invaded western Tennessee. At its head was General **Ulysses S. Grant,** a rumpled West Point graduate who had failed at everything he had tried in civilian life—whether as farmer, bill collector, real estate agent, or store clerk. He was, however, a brave, tough, and decisive military commander.

In just 11 days, Grant's forces captured two Confederate forts that held strategic positions on important rivers, Fort Henry on the Tennessee River and Fort Donelson on the Cumberland River. In the latter victory, Grant informed the Southern commander that "no terms except unconditional and immediate surrender can be accepted." The Confederates surrendered and, from then on, people said that Grant's initials stood for "Unconditional Surrender" Grant.

▲ **Grant, at Shiloh in 1862**

SHILOH One month after the victories at Fort Henry and Fort Donelson, in late March of 1862, Grant gathered his troops near a small Tennessee church named **Shiloh,** which was close to the Mississippi border. On April 6 thousands of yelling Confederate soldiers surprised the Union forces. Many Union troops were shot while making coffee; some died while they were still lying in their blankets. With Union forces on the edge of disaster, Grant reorganized his troops, ordered up reinforcements, and counterattacked at dawn the following day. By midafternoon the Confederate forces were in retreat. The Battle of Shiloh taught both sides a strategic lesson. Generals now realized that they had to send out scouts, dig trenches, and build fortifications. Shiloh also demonstrated how bloody the war might become, as nearly one-fourth of the battle's 100,000 troops were killed, wounded, or captured. Although the battle seemed to be a draw, it had a long-range impact on the war. The Confederate failure to hold on to its Ohio-Kentucky frontier showed that at least part of the Union's three-way strategy, the drive to take the Mississippi and split the Confederacy, might succeed. **D**

MAIN IDEA

Summarizing
D What did the battle of Shiloh show about the future course of the Civil War?

FARRAGUT ON THE LOWER MISSISSIPPI As Grant pushed toward the Mississippi River, a Union fleet of about 40 ships approached the river's mouth in Louisiana. Its commander was sixty-year-old **David G. Farragut;** its assignment, to seize New Orleans, the Confederacy's largest city and busiest port.

On April 24, Farragut ran his fleet past two Confederate forts in spite of booming enemy guns and fire rafts heaped with burning pitch. Five days later, the U.S. flag flew over New Orleans. During the next two months, Farragut took control of Baton Rouge and Natchez. If the Union captured all the major cities along the lower Mississippi, then Texas, Louisiana, Arkansas, and Tennessee would be cut off. Only Port Hudson, Louisiana, and Vicksburg, Mississippi, perched high on a bluff above the river, still stood in the way.

A Revolution in Warfare

Instrumental in the successes of Grant and Farragut in the West was a new type of war machine: the ironclad ship. This and other advances in technology changed military strategy and contributed to the war's high casualty rate.

IRONCLADS The ironclad ship could splinter wooden ships, withstand cannon fire, and resist burning. Grant used four ironclad ships when he captured Forts Henry and Donelson. On March 9, 1862, two ironclads, the North's **Monitor** and the South's **Merrimack** (renamed by the South as the *Virginia*) fought an historic duel.

A Union steam frigate, the *Merrimack*, had sunk off the coast of Virginia in 1861. The Confederates recovered the ship, and Confederate secretary of the navy Stephen R. Mallory put engineers to work plating it with iron. When Union secretary of the navy Gideon Welles heard of this development, he was determined to respond in kind. Naval engineer John Ericsson designed a ship, the *Monitor*, that resembled a "gigantic cheese box" on an "immense shingle," with two guns mounted on a revolving turret. On March 8, 1862, the *Merrimack* attacked three wooden Union warships, sinking the first, burning the second, and driving the third aground. The *Monitor* arrived and, the following day, engaged the Confederate vessel. Although the battle was a draw, the era of wooden fighting ships was over. **E**

MAIN IDEA

Evaluating
E What advantages did ironclad ships have over wooden ships?

NEW WEAPONS Even more deadly than the development of ironclad ships was the invention of the rifle and the minié ball. Rifles were more accurate than old-fashioned muskets, and soldiers could load rifles more quickly and therefore fire more rounds during battle. The minié ball was a soft lead bullet that was more destructive than earlier bullets. Troops in the Civil War also used primitive hand grenades and land mines.

◀ An engagement between the *Monitor* and the *Merrimack*, March, 9, 1862, painted by J. G. Tanner

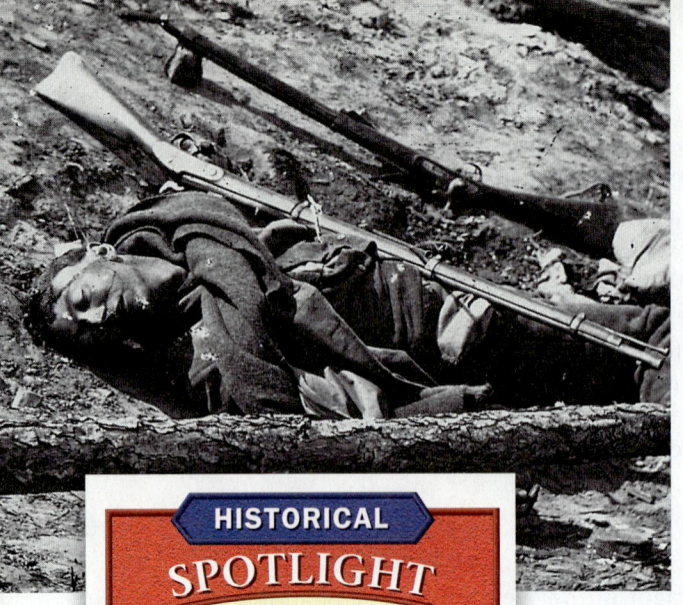

The new technology gradually changed military strategy. Because the rifle and the minié could kill far more people than older weapons, soldiers fighting from inside trenches or behind barricades had a great advantage in mass infantry attacks. **F**

The War for the Capitals

As the campaign in the west progressed and the Union navy tightened its blockade of Southern ports, the third part of the North's three-part strategy—the plan to capture the Confederate capital at Richmond—faltered. One of the problems was General McClellan.

Although he was an excellent administrator and popular with his troops, McClellan was extremely cautious. After five full months of training an army of 120,000 men, he insisted that he could not move against Richmond until he had 270,000 men. He complained that there were only two bridges across the Potomac, not enough for an orderly retreat should the Confederates repulse the Federals. Northern newspapers began to mock his daily bulletins of "All quiet on the Potomac," and even the patient Lincoln commented that he would like to "borrow McClellan's army if the general himself was not going to use it." **G**

"ON TO RICHMOND" After dawdling all winter, McClellan finally got under way in the spring of 1862. He transported the Army of the Potomac slowly toward the Confederate capital. On the way he encountered a Confederate army commanded by General Joseph E. Johnston. After a series of battles, Johnston was wounded, and command of the army passed to **Robert E. Lee.**

Lee was very different from McClellan—modest rather than vain, and willing to go beyond military textbooks in his tactics. He had opposed secession. However, he declined an offer to head the Union army and cast his lot with his beloved state of Virginia.

Determined to save Richmond, Lee moved against McClellan in a series of battles known collectively as the Seven Days' Battles, fought from June 25 to July 1, 1862. Although the Confederates had fewer soldiers and suffered higher casualties, Lee's determination and unorthodox tactics so unnerved McClellan that he backed away from Richmond and headed down the peninsula to the sea.

ANTIETAM Now Lee moved against the enemy's capital. On August 29 and 30, his troops won a resounding victory at the Second Battle of Bull Run. A few days later, they crossed the Potomac into the Union state of Maryland. A resident of one Potomac River town described the starving Confederate troops.

A PERSONAL VOICE MARY BEDINGER MITCHELL

" All day they crowded to the doors of our houses, with always the same drawling complaint: 'I've been a-marchin' and a-fightin' for six weeks stiddy, and I ain't had n-a-r-thin' to eat 'cept green apples an' green cawn, an' I wish you'd please to gimme a bite to eat.' . . . That they could march or fight at all seemed incredible. "

—quoted in *Battle Cry of Freedom*

HISTORICAL SPOTLIGHT

BOYS IN WAR

Both the Union and Confederate armies had soldiers who were under 18 years of age. Union soldier Arthur MacArthur (father of World War II hero Douglas MacArthur) became a colonel when he was only 19.

Examination of some Confederate recruiting lists for 1861–1862 reveals that approximately 5 percent were 17 or younger—with some as young as 13. The percentage of boys in the Union army was lower, perhaps 1.5 percent. These figures, however, do not count the great number of boys who ran away to follow each army without officially enlisting. The young man pictured above was killed at Petersburg, Virginia, shortly before the end of the war.

MAIN IDEA

Analyzing Effects

F How did technology affect military strategy during the Civil War?

MAIN IDEA

Contrasting

G Contrast Grant and McClellan as generals.

At this point McClellan had a tremendous stroke of luck. A Union corporal, exploring a meadow where the Confederates had camped, found a copy of Lee's army orders wrapped around a bunch of cigars! The plan revealed that Lee's and Stonewall Jackson's armies were separated for the moment.

For once McClellan acted aggressively and ordered his men forward after Lee. The two armies fought on September 17 beside a sluggish creek called the **Antietam** (ăn-tē′təm). The clash proved to be the bloodiest single-day battle in American history. Casualties totaled more than 26,000, as many as in the War of 1812 and the war with Mexico combined. Instead of pursuing the battered Confederate army and possibly ending the Civil War, however, McClellan, cautious as always, did nothing. Though the battle itself was a standoff, the South, which had lost a quarter of its men, retreated the next day across the Potomac into Virginia.

On November 7, 1862, Lincoln fired McClellan. This solved one problem by getting rid of the general whom Lincoln characterized as having "the slows." However, the president would soon face a diplomatic conflict with Britain and increased pressure from abolitionists.

 Lincoln and McClellan confer at Antietam in 1862.

ASSESSMENT

1. TERMS & NAMES For each term or name, write a sentence explaining its significance.
- Fort Sumter
- Anaconda plan
- Bull Run
- Stonewall Jackson
- George McClellan
- Ulysses S. Grant
- Shiloh
- David G. Farragut
- *Monitor*
- *Merrimack*
- Robert E. Lee
- Antietam

MAIN IDEA

2. TAKING NOTES
For each month listed below, create a newspaper headline summarizing a key Civil War battle that occurred. Write your headlines in a chart like the one shown.

1861	
Month	**Headline**
• April	
• July	
1862	
Month	**Headline**
• February	
• April	
• September	

CRITICAL THINKING

3. HYPOTHESIZING
What if Virginia had not seceded from the Union in 1861? Speculate on how this might have affected the course of the war. Support your answer with examples. **Think About:**
- Virginia's influence on other Southern states
- Virginia's location and its human and material resources
- how the North's military strategy might have been different

4. DRAWING CONCLUSIONS
What do you think were General McClellan's major tactical errors? Support your response with details from the text.

5. EVALUATING DECISIONS
Do you think Lincoln's decision to fire McClellan was a good one? Why or why not?

PI 3.2   CC Unit 1.I.B.4   CC Unit 2.II.D.2.a
CC Unit 2.II.D.2.c   CC Unit 2.II.D.2.d

The Politics of War

MAIN IDEA	WHY IT MATTERS NOW	Terms & Names
By issuing the Emancipation Proclamation, President Lincoln made slavery the focus of the war.	The Proclamation was a first step toward improving the status of African Americans.	• Emancipation Proclamation • habeas corpus • Copperhead • conscription

▲ William Yancey, 1851

hmhsocialstudies.com
TAKING NOTES
Use the graphic organizer online to take notes about political issues during the Civil War.

One American's Story

Shortly after the Civil War began, William Yancey of Alabama and two other Confederate diplomats asked Britain—a major importer of Southern cotton—to formally recognize the Confederacy as an independent nation. The British Secretary of State for Foreign Affairs met with them twice, but in May 1861, Britain announced its neutrality. Insulted, Yancey returned home and told his fellow Southerners not to hope for British aid.

A PERSONAL VOICE WILLIAM YANCEY

" You have no friends in Europe. . . . The sentiment of Europe is anti-slavery, and that portion of public opinion which forms, and is represented by, the government of Great Britain, is abolition. They will never recognize our independence until our conquering sword hangs dripping over the prostrate heads of the North. . . . It is an error to say that 'Cotton is King.' It is not. It is a great and influential factor in commerce, but not its dictator. "

—quoted in *The Civil War: A Narrative*

In spite of Yancey's words, many Southerners continued to hope that economic necessity would force Britain to come to their aid. Meanwhile, abolitionists waged a public opinion war against slavery, not only in Europe, but in the North.

Britain Remains Neutral

A number of economic factors made Britain no longer dependent on Southern cotton. Not only had Britain accumulated a huge cotton inventory just before the outbreak of war, it also found new sources of cotton in Egypt and India. Moreover, when Europe's wheat crop failed, Northern wheat and corn replaced cotton as an essential import. As one magazine put it, "Old King Cotton's dead and buried." Britain decided that neutrality was the best policy—at least for a while.

THE TRENT AFFAIR In the fall of 1861, an incident occurred to test that neutrality. The Confederate government sent two diplomats, James Mason and John Slidell, in a second attempt to gain support from Britain and France. The two men traveled aboard a British merchant ship, the *Trent*. Captain Charles Wilkes of the American warship *San Jacinto* stopped the *Trent* and arrested the two men. The British threatened war against the Union and dispatched 8,000 troops to Canada. Aware of the need to fight just "one war at a time," Lincoln freed the two prisoners, publicly claiming that Wilkes had acted without orders. Britain was as relieved as the United States was to find a peaceful way out of the crisis.

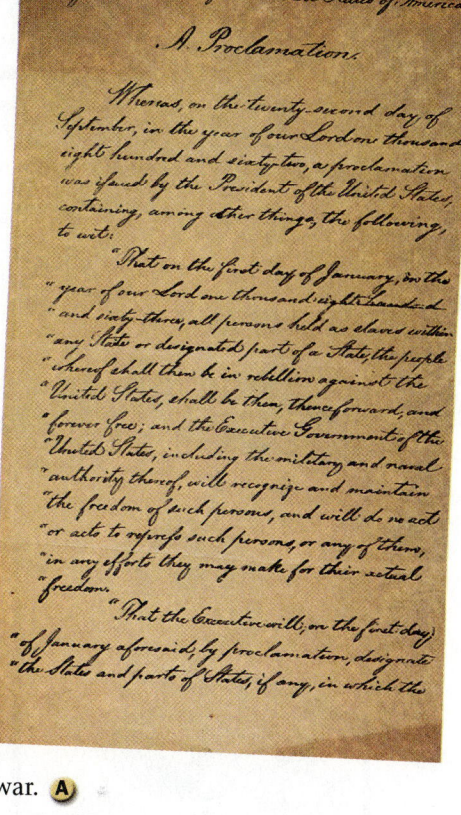

The first page of Lincoln's handwritten copy of the Emancipation Proclamation ▼

Proclaiming Emancipation

As the South struggled in vain to gain foreign recognition, abolitionist feeling grew in the North. Some Northerners believed that just winning the war would not be enough if the issue of slavery was not permanently settled.

LINCOLN'S VIEW OF SLAVERY Although Lincoln disliked slavery, he did not believe that the federal government had the power to abolish it where it already existed. When Horace Greeley urged him in 1862 to transform the war into an abolitionist crusade, Lincoln replied that although it was his personal wish that all men could be free, his official duty was different: "My paramount object in this struggle is to save the Union, and is not either to save or destroy Slavery."

As the war progressed, however, Lincoln did find a way to use his constitutional war powers to end slavery. Slave labor built fortifications and grew food for the Confederacy. As commander in chief, Lincoln decided that, just as he could order the Union army to seize Confederate supplies, he could also authorize the army to emancipate slaves.

Emancipation offered a strategic benefit. The abolitionist movement was strong in Britain, and emancipation would discourage Britain from supporting the Confederacy. Emancipation was not just a moral issue; it became a weapon of war. **A**

MAIN IDEA

Summarizing

A In what way was the Emancipation Proclamation a part of Lincoln's military strategy?

EMANCIPATION PROCLAMATION On January 1, 1863, Lincoln issued his **Emancipation Proclamation**. The following portion captured national attention.

from THE EMANCIPATION PROCLAMATION ABRAHAM LINCOLN

" All persons held as slaves within any State or designated part of a State the people whereof shall then be in rebellion against the United States, shall be then, thenceforward, and forever free. . . . And upon this act, sincerely believed to be an act of justice, warranted by the Constitution upon military necessity, I invoke the considerate judgment of mankind, and the gracious favor of Almighty God. "

Lincoln presents the Emancipation Proclamation to his cabinet, 1862. ▼

The Proclamation did not free any slaves immediately because it applied only to areas behind Confederate lines, outside Union control. Since the Proclamation was a military action aimed at the states in rebellion, it did not apply to Southern territory already occupied by Union troops nor to the slave states that had not seceded.

REACTIONS TO THE PROCLAMATION Although the Proclamation did not have much practical effect, it had immense symbolic importance. For many, the Proclamation gave the war a high moral purpose by turning the struggle into a fight to free the slaves. In Washington, D.C., the Reverend Henry M. Turner, a free-born African American, watched the capital's inhabitants receive the news of emancipation.

★ A PERSONAL VOICE HENRY M. TURNER

" **Men squealed, women fainted, dogs barked, white and colored people shook hands, songs were sung, and by this time cannons began to fire at the navy yard. . . . Great processions of colored and white men marched to and fro and passed in front of the White House. . . . The President came to the window . . . and thousands told him, if he would come out of that palace, they would hug him to death.** "

—quoted in *Voices from the Civil War*

Free blacks also welcomed the section of the Proclamation that allowed them to enlist in the Union army. Even though many had volunteered at the beginning of the war, the regular army had refused to take them. Now they could fight and help put an end to slavery.

Not everyone in the North approved of the Emancipation Proclamation, however. The Democrats claimed that it would only prolong the war by antagonizing the South. Many Union soldiers accepted it grudgingly, saying they had no love for abolitionists or African Americans, but they would support emancipation if that was what it took to reunify the nation.

Confederates reacted to the Proclamation with outrage. Jefferson Davis called it the "most execrable [hateful] measure recorded in the history of guilty man." As Northern Democrats had predicted, the Proclamation had made the Confederacy more determined than ever to fight to preserve its way of life.

After the Emancipation Proclamation, compromise was no longer an option. The Confederacy knew that if it lost, its slave-holding society would perish, and the Union knew that it could win only by completely defeating the Confederacy. From January 1863 on, it was a fight to the death. **B**

KEY PLAYERS

ABRAHAM LINCOLN
1809–1865

Abraham Lincoln was born to illiterate parents, and once said that in his boyhood there was "absolutely nothing to excite ambition for education." Yet he hungered for knowledge.

He educated himself and, after working as rail-splitter, storekeeper, and surveyor, he taught himself law. This led to a career in politics—and eventually to the White House. In Europe at that time, people were more or less fixed in the station into which they had been born. In the United States, Lincoln was free to achieve whatever he could. Small wonder that he fought to preserve the nation he described as "the last best hope of earth."

JEFFERSON DAVIS
1808–1889

Jefferson Davis, who was named after Thomas Jefferson, was born in Kentucky and grew up in Mississippi. After graduating from West Point, he served in the army and then became a planter. He was elected to the U.S. Senate in 1846 and again in 1856, resigning when Mississippi seceded.

His election as president of the Confederacy dismayed him. As his wife Varina wrote, "I thought his genius was military, but as a party manager he would not succeed."

Varina was right. Davis had poor relations with many Confederate leaders, causing them to put their states' welfare above the Confederacy's.

MAIN IDEA

Analyzing Effects
B What effects did the Emancipation Proclamation have on the war?

Both Sides Face Political Problems

Neither side in the Civil War was completely unified. There were Confederate sympathizers in the North, and Union sympathizers in the South. Such divided loyalties created two problems: How should the respective governments handle their critics? How could they ensure a steady supply of fighting men for their armies?

DEALING WITH DISSENT Lincoln dealt forcefully with disloyalty. For example, when a Baltimore crowd attacked a Union regiment a week after Fort Sumter, Lincoln sent federal troops to Maryland. He also suspended in that state the writ of **habeas corpus,** a court order that requires authorities to bring a person held in jail before the court to determine why he or she is being jailed. Lincoln used this same strategy later in the war to deal with dissent in other states. As a result, more than 13,000 suspected Confederate sympathizers in the Union were arrested and held without trial, although most were quickly released. The president also seized telegraph offices to make sure no one used the wires for subversion. When Supreme Court Chief Justice Roger Taney declared that Lincoln had gone beyond his constitutional powers, the president ignored his ruling.

Those arrested included **Copperheads,** or Northern Democrats who advocated peace with the South. Ohio congressman Clement Vallandigham was the most famous Copperhead. Vallandigham was tried and convicted by a military court for urging Union soldiers to desert and for advocating an armistice.

Jefferson Davis at first denounced Lincoln's suspension of civil liberties. Later, however, Davis found it necessary to follow the Union president's example. In 1862, he suspended habeas corpus in the Confederacy.

Lincoln's action in dramatically expanding presidential powers to meet the crises of wartime set a precedent in U.S. history. Since then, some presidents have cited war or "national security" as a reason to expand the powers of the executive branch of government. **C**

MAIN IDEA

Evaluating Leadership

C What actions did Lincoln take to deal with dissent?

CONSCRIPTION Although both armies originally relied on volunteers, it didn't take long before heavy casualties and widespread desertions led to **conscription,** a draft that would force certain members of the population to serve in the army. The Confederacy passed a draft law in 1862, and the Union followed suit in 1863. Both laws ran into trouble.

The Confederate law drafted all able-bodied white men between the ages of 18 and 35. (In 1864, as the Confederacy suffered more losses, the limits changed to 17 and 50.) However, those who could afford to were allowed to hire substitutes to serve in their places. The law also exempted planters who owned 20 or more slaves. Poor Confederates howled that it was a "rich man's war but a poor man's fight." In spite of these protests, almost 90 percent of eligible Southern men served in the Confederate army.

Vocabulary
commutation: the substitution of one kind of payment for another

The Union law drafted white men between 20 and 45 for three years, although it, too, allowed draftees to hire substitutes. It also provided for commutation, or paying a $300 fee to avoid conscription altogether. In the end, only 46,000 draftees actually went into the army. Ninety-two percent of the approximately 2 million soldiers who served in the Union army were volunteers—180,000 of them African-American.

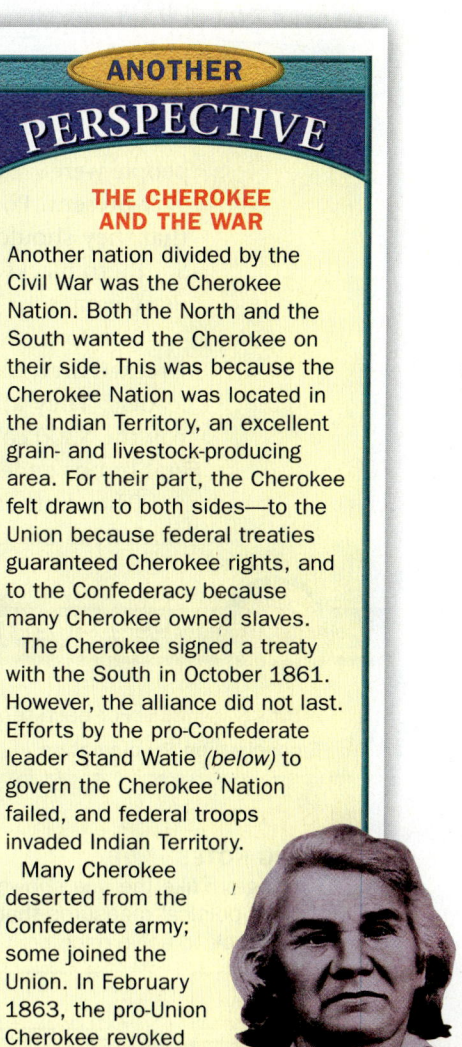

ANOTHER

PERSPECTIVE

THE CHEROKEE AND THE WAR

Another nation divided by the Civil War was the Cherokee Nation. Both the North and the South wanted the Cherokee on their side. This was because the Cherokee Nation was located in the Indian Territory, an excellent grain- and livestock-producing area. For their part, the Cherokee felt drawn to both sides—to the Union because federal treaties guaranteed Cherokee rights, and to the Confederacy because many Cherokee owned slaves.

The Cherokee signed a treaty with the South in October 1861. However, the alliance did not last. Efforts by the pro-Confederate leader Stand Watie (below) to govern the Cherokee Nation failed, and federal troops invaded Indian Territory.

Many Cherokee deserted from the Confederate army; some joined the Union. In February 1863, the pro-Union Cherokee revoked the Confederate treaty.

THE RIOT CONTINUED.

Violence and Pillage.

General Rioting About the City.

The Mob Repulsed by the Police and Military.

LABOR SUSPENDED IN FACTORIES

CITIZENS STONED AND BEATEN.

A Number of the Rioters Supposed to be Killed.

COL. O'BRIEN BEATEN ALMOST TO DEATH.

RAILROAD TRAVEL SUSPENDED.

MAYOR OPDYKE'S HOUSE ATTACKED.

Details of the Riot Throughout the City.

▲ **In New York City in July 1863, draft rioters vented their anger on African-American institutions such as this orphanage.**

DRAFT RIOTS In 1863 New York City was a tinderbox waiting to explode. Poor people were crowded into slums, crime and disease ran rampant, and poverty was ever-present. Poor white workers—especially Irish immigrants—thought it unfair that they should have to fight a war to free slaves. The white workers feared that Southern blacks would come north and compete for jobs. When officials began to draw names for the draft, angry men gathered all over the city to complain.

For four days, July 13–16, mobs rampaged through the city. The rioters wrecked draft offices, Republican newspaper offices, and the homes of antislavery leaders. They attacked well-dressed men on the street (those likely to be able to pay the $300 commutation fee) and attacked African Americans. By the time federal troops ended the melee, more than 100 persons lay dead.

The draft riots were not the only dramatic development away from the battlefield. Society was also experiencing other types of unrest.

 ASSESSMENT

1. TERMS & NAMES For each term or name, write a sentence explaining its significance.
- •Emancipation Proclamation
- •habeas corpus
- •Copperhead
- •conscription

MAIN IDEA

2. TAKING NOTES
In a diagram like the one shown, note the political measures that Lincoln took to solve each problem.

CRITICAL THINKING

3. EVALUATING LEADERSHIP
Do you think that Lincoln's measures to deal with disloyalty and dissent represented an abuse of power? Why or why not? **Think About:**
- conditions of wartime versus peacetime
- Lincoln's primary goal
- Supreme Court Justice Roger Taney's view of Lincoln's powers

4. ANALYZING PRIMARY SOURCES

"**To fight against slaveholders, without fighting against slavery, is but a half-hearted business, and paralyzes the hands engaged in it.**"

—Frederick Douglass, quoted in *Battle Cry of Freedom*

How do you think Lincoln would have replied to Douglass?

PI 3.1

CC Unit 2.II.D.2.a CC Unit 2.II.D.2.b
CC Unit 2.II.D.2.c CC Unit 2.II.D.2.d
CC Unit 3.I.B.1

Life During Wartime

MAIN IDEA	WHY IT MATTERS NOW	Terms & Names
The Civil War brought about dramatic social and economic changes in American society.	The expansion of roles for African Americans and women set the stage for later equalities of opportunity.	• Fort Pillow • Clara Barton • income tax • Andersonville

One American's Story

TAKING NOTES

Use the graphic organizer online to take notes about economic changes during the Civil War and their effects.

Mary Chesnut, a well-born Southerner whose husband served in the Confederate government, kept a diary describing key war events, such as the attack on Fort Sumter. Her diary paints a vivid picture as well of the marriages and flirtations, hospital work, and dinner parties that comprised daily life in the South.

In 1864, Chesnut found that her social standing could no longer protect her from the economic effects of the war.

A PERSONAL VOICE MARY CHESNUT

" September 19th . . . My pink silk dress I have sold for six hundred dollars, to be paid in installments, two hundred a month for three months. And I sell my eggs and butter from home for two hundred dollars a month. Does it not sound well— four hundred dollars a month, regularly? In what? 'In Confederate money.' Hélas! [Alas!] "

—quoted in *Mary Chesnut's Civil War*

The "Confederate money" Chesnut received was almost worthless. Inflation, or a sharp increase in the cost of living, had devalued Confederate currency to such an extent that $400 was worth only a dollar or two compared to prewar currency. Not all the effects of the Civil War were economic—the war also caused profound social changes.

African Americans Fight for Freedom

African Americans played an important role in the struggle to end slavery. Some served as soldiers, while others took action away from the battlefield.

AFRICAN–AMERICAN SOLDIERS When the Civil War started, it was a white man's war. Neither the Union nor the Confederacy officially accepted African Americans as soldiers.

In 1862, Congress passed a law allowing African Americans to serve in the military. It was only after the Emancipation Proclamation was decreed, however,

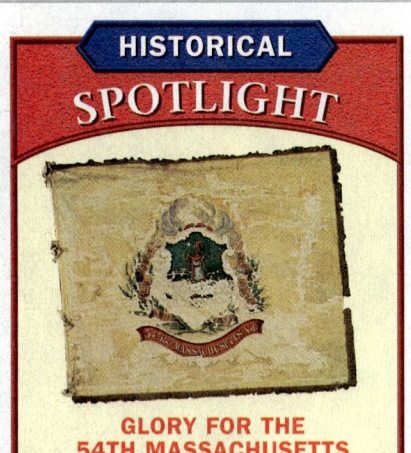

▲
**Battery A of the
2nd United States
Colored Artillery
at gun drill**

that large-scale enlistment occurred. Although African Americans made up only 1 percent of the North's population, by war's end nearly 10 percent of the Union army was African American. The majority were former slaves from Virginia and other slave states, both Confederate and Union.

Although accepted as soldiers, African Americans suffered discrimination. They served in separate regiments commanded by white officers. Usually African Americans could not rise above the rank of captain—although Alexander T. Augustana, a surgeon, did attain the rank of Lieutenant Colonel. White privates earned $13 a month, plus a $3.50 clothing allowance. Black privates earned only $10 a month, with no clothing allowance. Blacks protested, and several regiments served without pay for months rather than accept the lesser amount. Congress finally equalized the pay of white and African-American soldiers in 1864.

The mortality rate for African-American soldiers was higher than that for white soldiers, primarily because many African Americans were assigned to labor duty in the garrisons, where they were likely to catch typhoid, pneumonia, malaria, or some other deadly disease. Then, too, the Confederacy would not treat captured African-American soldiers as prisoners of war. Many were executed on the spot, and those who were not killed were returned to slavery. A particularly gruesome massacre occurred at **Fort Pillow,** Tennessee, in 1864. Confederate troops killed over 200 African-American prisoners and some whites as they begged for their lives.

Even though most Southerners opposed the idea of African-American soldiers, the Confederacy did consider drafting slaves and free blacks in 1863 and again in 1864. One Louisiana planter argued that since slaves "*caused* the fight," they should share in the burden of battle. Georgia general Howell Cobb responded, "If slaves will make good soldiers our whole theory of slavery is wrong."

SLAVE RESISTANCE IN THE CONFEDERACY As Union forces pushed deeper into Confederate territory, thousands of slaves sought freedom behind the lines of the Union army. Those who remained on plantations sometimes engaged in sabotage, breaking plows, destroying fences, and neglecting livestock. When Southern plantation owners fled before approaching Union troops, many slaves refused to be dragged along. They waited to welcome the Yankees, who had the power to liberate them. Ⓐ

For whites on farms and plantations in the South, slave resistance compounded the stresses and privations of the war. Fearful of a general slave uprising, Southerners tightened slave patrols and spread rumors about how Union soldiers abused runaways. No general uprising occurred, but slave resistance gradually weakened the plantation system. By 1864 even many Confederates realized that slavery was doomed.

HISTORICAL

SPOTLIGHT

GLORY FOR THE
54TH MASSACHUSETTS

In July 1863, the African-American 54th Massachusetts Infantry, including two sons of Frederick Douglass, led an assault on Fort Wagner, near Charleston harbor. The attack failed. More than 40 percent of the soldiers were killed. Confederates found the regiment's flag *(above)* under a pile of dead soldiers. Among the dead was the white commander, Colonel Robert G. Shaw. Among the survivors were Douglass's sons and Sergeant William Carney, the first African American to win a Congressional Medal of Honor.

As the New York *Tribune* pointed out, "If this Massachusetts 54th had faltered when its trial came, 200,000 troops for whom it was a pioneer would never have put into the field." Shaw's father declared that his son lay "with his brave, devoted followers. . . . what a bodyguard he has!"

MAIN IDEA

**Drawing
Conclusions**
Ⓐ How did African Americans contribute to the struggle to end slavery?

The War Affects Regional Economies

The decline of the plantation system was not the only economic effect that the Civil War caused. Other effects included inflation and a new type of federal tax. In general, the war expanded the North's economy while shattering that of the South.

SOUTHERN SHORTAGES The Confederacy soon faced a food shortage due to three factors: the drain of manpower into the army, the Union occupation of food-growing areas, and the loss of slaves to work in the fields. Meat became a once-a-week luxury at best, and even such staples as rice and corn were in short supply. Food prices skyrocketed. In 1861 the average family spent $6.65 a month on food. By mid-1863, it was spending $68 a month—if it could find any food to buy. The situation grew so desperate that in 1863 hundreds of women and children—and some men—stormed bakeries and rioted for bread. Mrs. Roger A. Pryor remembered talking to an 18-year-old member of a mob in Richmond on April 2, 1863. **B**

A PERSONAL VOICE MRS. ROGER A. PRYOR

" As she raised her hand to remove her sunbonnet, her loose calico sleeve slipped up, and revealed a mere skeleton of an arm. She perceived my expression as I looked at it, and hastily pulled down her sleeve with a short laugh. 'This is all that's left of me!' she said. 'It seems real funny, don't it? . . . We are going to the bakeries and each of us will take a loaf of bread. That is little enough for the government to give us after it has taken all our men.' "

—quoted in *Battle Cry of Freedom*

The mob broke up only when President Jefferson Davis climbed up on a cart, threw down all the money he had, and ordered the crowd to disperse or be shot. The next day, the Confederate government distributed some of its stocks of rice.

The Union blockade of Southern ports created shortages of other items, too, including salt, sugar, coffee, nails, needles, and medicines. One result was that many Confederates smuggled cotton into the North in exchange for gold, food, and other goods. Deploring this trade with the enemy, one Confederate general raged that cotton had made "more damn rascals on both sides than anything else."

NORTHERN ECONOMIC GROWTH Overall, the war's effect on the economy of the North was much more positive. Although a few industries, such as cotton textiles, declined, most boomed. The army's need for uniforms, shoes, guns, and other supplies supported woolen mills, steel foundries, coal mines, and many other industries. Because the draft reduced the available work force, western wheat farmers bought reapers and other labor-saving machines, which benefited the companies that manufactured those machines. **C**

The economic boom had a dark side, though. Wages did not keep up with prices, and many people's standard of living declined. When white male workers went out on strike, employers hired free blacks, immigrants, women, and boys to replace them for lower pay.

MAIN IDEA

Analyzing Causes

B What caused food shortages in the South?

MAIN IDEA

Analyzing Causes

C Why was the war less damaging to the economy of the North than to that of the South?

ECONOMIC BACKGROUND

CURRENCY AND INFLATION

To raise revenue, both the Union and the Confederacy issued paper money. The Union passed a law declaring that its currency was legal tender, so everyone had to accept it. This national currency succeeded because the public maintained confidence in the Northern economy.

The currency issued by the Confederate treasury (pictured below) was unbacked by gold. Added to this, each state in the Confederacy continued to use its own currency. Because of the war-weakened Southern economy, the public lost faith in Confederate currency—its value plummeted, and prices soared. The Confederacy's war inflation rate reached close to 7,000 percent; prices were 70 times higher at the end of the war than at the beginning. The Union inflation rate was 80 percent.

Northern women—who like many Southern women replaced men on farms and in city jobs—also obtained government jobs for the first time. They worked mostly as clerks, copying ledgers and letters by hand. Although they earned less than men, they remained a regular part of the Washington work force after the war.

Because of the booming economy and rising prices, many businesses in the North made immense profits. This was especially true of those with government contracts, mostly because such contractors often cheated. They supplied uniforms and blankets made of "shoddy"—fibers reclaimed from rags—that came apart in the rain. They passed off spoiled meat as fresh and demanded twice the usual price for guns. This corruption spilled over into the general society. The New York *Herald* commented on the changes in the American character: "The individual who makes the most money—no matter how—and spends the most—no matter for what—is considered the greatest man. . . . The world has seen its iron age, its silver age, its golden age, and its brazen age. This is the age of shoddy."

Congress decided to help pay for the war by tapping its citizens' wealth. In 1863 Congress enacted the tax law that authorized the nation's first **income tax,** a tax that takes a specified percentage of an individual's income.

Soldiers Suffer on Both Sides

Both Union and Confederate soldiers had marched off to war thinking it would prove to be a glorious affair. They were soon disillusioned, not just by heavy casualties but also by poor living conditions, diet, and medical care.

LIVES ON THE LINES Garbage disposal and latrines in army camps were almost unknown. Although army regulations called for washing one's hands and face every day and taking a complete bath once a week, many soldiers failed to do so. As a result, body lice, dysentery, and diarrhea were common.

Army rations were far from appealing. Union troops subsisted on beans, bacon, and hardtack—square biscuits that were supposedly hard enough to stop a bullet. As one Northerner wrote:

> The soldiers' fare is very rough,
> The bread is hard, the beef is tough;
> If they can stand it, it will be,
> Through love of God, a mystery.

Wounded Union troops recuperate after battle near a makeshift field hospital.
▼

BATTLEFIELD MEDICINE

In the Civil War, weapons technology overtook medical technology. Minié balls, soft lead bullets, caused traumatic wounds that could often be treated only by amputation. As the effects of bacteria were not yet known, surgeons never sterilized instruments, making infection one of soldiers' worst enemies.

Field Hospitals ▼

The badly wounded were taken to field hospitals, like this one at Gettysburg. The surgeon is preparing for an amputation; the man behind the patient administers an anesthetic, probably chloroform.

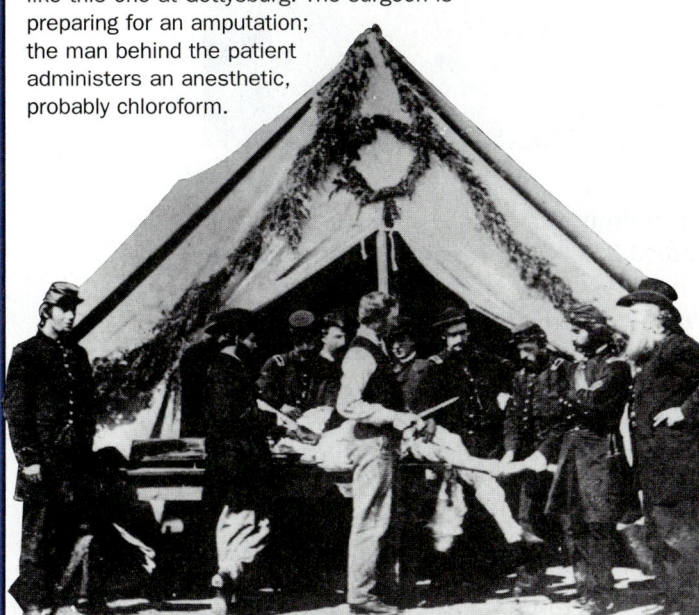

Clara Barton ▶

As a war nurse, Clara Barton collected and distributed supplies and dug bullets out of soldiers' bodies with her penknife. Barton was particularly good at anticipating troop movements and sometimes arrived at the battlefield before the fighting had even begun. Most women, however, served in hospitals rather than at the front lines. On the battlefield soldiers were usually attended by male medics.

Surgeon's Tools ▼

A surgeon's kit might contain cloth for bandages or administering chloroform, opium pills to kill pain, forceps and knives for cleaning wounds, and saws for amputations.

Confederate troops fared equally poorly. A common food was "cush," a stew of small cubes of beef and crumbled cornbread mixed with bacon grease. Fresh vegetables were hardly ever available. Both sides loved coffee, but Southern soldiers had only substitutes brewed from peanuts, dried apples, or corn.

CIVIL WAR MEDICINE Soon after Fort Sumter fell, the federal government set up the United States Sanitary Commission. Its task was twofold: to improve the hygienic conditions of army camps and to recruit and train nurses. The "Sanitary" proved a great success. It sent out agents to teach soldiers such things as how to avoid polluting their water supply. It developed hospital trains and hospital ships to transport wounded men from the battlefield.

At the age of 60, Dorothea Dix became the nation's first superintendent of women nurses. To discourage women looking for romance, Dix insisted applicants be at least 30 and "very plain-looking." Impressed by the work of women nurses he observed, the surgeon general required that at least one-third of Union hospital nurses be women; some 3,000 served. Union nurse **Clara Barton** often cared for the sick and wounded at the front lines. After her courage under fire at Antietam, a surgeon described her as the "angel of the battlefield."

As a result of the Sanitary Commission's work, the death rate among Union wounded, although terrible by 20th-century standards, showed considerable improvement over that of previous wars. **D**

The Confederacy did not have a Sanitary Commission, but thousands of Southern women volunteered as nurses. Sally Tompkins, for example, performed so heroically in her hospital duties that she eventually was commissioned as a captain.

MAIN IDEA

Summarizing
D How did the Sanitary Commission improve medical treatment during the war?

The Confederate prison at Andersonville, Georgia, in 1864 ▶

PRISONS Improvements in hygiene and nursing did not reach the war prisons, where conditions were even worse than in army camps. The worst Confederate prison, at **Andersonville,** Georgia, jammed 33,000 men into 26 acres, or about 34 square feet per man. The prisoners had no shelter from the broiling sun or chilling rain except what they made themselves by rigging primitive tents of blankets and sticks. They drank from the same stream that served as their sewer. About a third of Andersonville's prisoners died. Part of the blame rested with the camp's commander, Henry Wirz (whom the North eventually executed as a war criminal). The South's lack of food and tent canvas also contributed to the appalling conditions. In addition, the prisons were overcrowded because the North had halted prisoner exchanges when the South refused to return African-American soldiers who had been captured in battle.

Prison camps in the North—such as those at Elmira, New York, and at Camp Douglas, Illinois—were only slightly better. Northern prisons provided about five times as much space per man, barracks for sleeping, and adequate food. However, thousands of Confederates, housed in quarters with little or no heat, contracted pneumonia and died. Hundreds of others suffered from dysentery and malnutrition, from which some did not recover. Historians estimate that 15 percent of Union prisoners in Southern prisons died, while 12 percent of Confederate prisoners died in Northern prisons.

A series of battles in the Mississippi Valley and in the East soon sent a fresh wave of prisoners of war flooding into prison camps.

SECTION 3 ASSESSMENT

1. TERMS & NAMES For each term or name, write a sentence explaining its significance.
- Fort Pillow
- income tax
- Clara Barton
- Andersonville

MAIN IDEA

2. TAKING NOTES
In a two-column chart, list the economic changes that occurred in the North and South as a result of the Civil War. Explain how these changes affected the two regions.

ECONOMIC CHANGES

North	South

CRITICAL THINKING

3. ANALYZING EFFECTS
What effects did the Civil War have on women and African Americans?
Think About:
- new opportunities in both the North and the South
- discriminatory practices that persisted for both groups

4. SYNTHESIZING
Imagine you were one of the Northern women and doctors who convinced the government to establish the Sanitary Commission. What reasons would you have offered to justify this commission? Use details from the text to support your response.

The North Takes Charge

MAIN IDEA	WHY IT MATTERS NOW	Terms & Names
Key victories at Vicksburg and Gettysburg helped the Union wear down the Confederacy.	These victories clinched the North's win and led to the preservation of the Union.	•Gettysburg •Chancellorsville •Vicksburg •Gettysburg Address •William Tecumseh Sherman •Appomattox Court House

One American's Story

hmhsocialstudies.com
TAKING NOTES

Use the graphic organizer online to take notes on major events in the last two years of the Civil War.

Shortly after three o'clock on the afternoon of July 3, 1863, from behind a stone wall on a ridge south of the little town of Gettysburg, Pennsylvania, Union troops watched thousands of Confederate soldiers advance toward them across an open field. Union officer Frank Aretas Haskell described the scene.

A PERSONAL VOICE
FRANK ARETAS HASKELL

" More than half a mile their front extends . . . man touching man, rank pressing rank. . . . The red flags wave, their horsemen gallop up and down, the arms of [thirteen] thousand men, barrel and bayonet, gleam in the sun, a sloping forest of flashing steel. Right on they move, as with one soul, in perfect order without impediment of ditch, or wall, or stream, over ridge and slope, through orchard and meadow, and cornfield, magnificent, grim, irresistible. "

—quoted in *The Civil War: An Illustrated History*

▲ A Confederate charge during the battle of Gettysburg

An hour later, half of the Confederate force lay dead or wounded, cut down by crossfire from massed Union guns. Because of the North's heavy weaponry, it had become suicide for unprotected troops to assault a strongly fortified position.

Armies Clash at Gettysburg

The July 3 infantry charge was part of a three-day battle at **Gettysburg,** which many historians consider the turning point of the Civil War. The battle of Gettysburg crippled the South so badly that General Lee would never again possess sufficient forces to invade a Northern state.

Battle of Gettysburg, July 1863

hmhsocialstudies.com **INTERACTIVE MAP**

College

Gettysburg

Seminary

Willoughby Run

SEMINARY RIDGE

Rock Creek

Cemetery Hill

wheat field

CEMETERY RIDGE

peach orchard

Little Round Top

Round Top

N
W   E
S

**Inset map labels:**

PENNSYLVANIA

NEW JERSEY

OHIO

Gettysburg

MARYLAND

DELAWARE

Washington, D.C.

WEST VIRGINIA

VIRGINIA

ATLANTIC OCEAN

KENTUCKY

Richmond

NORTH CAROLINA

SOUTH CAROLINA

Union
Confederate

Map legend:

	July 1	July 2	July 3
Confederate positions			
Union positions			

Roads
Railroad
Confederate assaults

0   .5   1 mile
0   .5   1 kilometer

GEOGRAPHY SKILLBUILDER

1. **Movement** Which side clearly took the offensive in the battle of Gettysburg?
2. **Location** Based on the information in the larger map, what factor may have made it easier for reinforcements to enter the Gettysburg area?

HISTORY

VIDEO
Gettysburg Address

hmhsocialstudies.com

PRELUDE TO GETTYSBURG The year 1863 actually had gone well for the South. During the first four days of May, the South defeated the North at **Chancellorsville,** Virginia. Lee outmaneuvered Union general Joseph Hooker and forced the Union army to retreat. The North's only consolation after Chancellorsville came as the result of an accident. As General Stonewall Jackson returned from a patrol on May 2, Confederate guards mistook him for a Yankee and shot him in the left arm. A surgeon amputated his arm the following day. When Lee heard the news, he exclaimed, "He has lost his left arm, but I have lost my right." But the true loss was still to come; Jackson caught pneumonia and died May 10.

Despite Jackson's tragic death, Lee decided to press his military advantage and invade the North. He needed supplies, he hoped that an invasion would force Lincoln to pull troops away from Vicksburg, and he thought that a major Confederate victory on Northern soil might tip the political balance of power in the Union to pro-Southern Democrats. Accordingly, he crossed the Potomac into Maryland and then pushed on into Pennsylvania. **A**

GETTYSBURG The most decisive battle of the war was fought near Gettysburg, Pennsylvania. The town was an unlikely spot for a bloody battle—and indeed, no one planned to fight there.

Confederate soldiers led by A. P. Hill, many of them barefoot, heard there was a supply of footwear in Gettysburg and went to find it, and also to meet up with forces under General Lee. When Hill's troops marched toward Gettysburg, they ran into a couple of brigades of Union cavalry under the command of John Buford, an experienced officer from Illinois.

MAIN IDEA

Analyzing Motives
A What did Lee hope to gain by invading the North?

Buford ordered his men to take defensive positions on the hills and ridges surrounding the town, from which they engaged Hill's troops. The shooting attracted more troops and each side sent for reinforcements.

The Northern armies, now under the command of General George Meade, that were north and west of Gettysburg began to fall back under a furious rebel assault. The Confederates took control of the town. Lee knew, however, that the battle would not be won unless the Northerners were also forced to yield their positions on Cemetery Ridge, the high ground south of Gettysburg. **B**

THE SECOND DAY On July 2, almost 90,000 Yankees and 75,000 Confederates stood ready to fight for Gettysburg. Lee ordered General James Longstreet to attack Cemetery Ridge, which was held by Union troops. At about 4:00 P.M., Longstreet's troops advanced from Seminary Ridge, through the peach orchard and wheat field that stood between them and the Union position.

The yelling Rebels overran Union troops who had mistakenly left their positions on Little Round Top, a hill that overlooked much of the southern portion of the battlefield. As a brigade of Alabamans approached the hill, however, Union leaders noticed the undefended position. Colonel Joshua L. Chamberlain, who had been a language professor before the war, led his Maine troops to meet the Rebels, and succeeded in repulsing repeated Confederate attacks. When his soldiers ran short of ammunition and more than a third of the brigade had fallen, Chamberlain ordered a bayonet charge at the Confederates.

The Rebels, exhausted by the uphill fighting and the 25-mile march of the previous day, were shocked by the Union assault and surrendered in droves. Chamberlain and his men succeeded in saving the Union lines from certain rebel artillery attacks from Little Round Top. Although the Union troops had given some ground, their lines still held at the close of day.

THE THIRD DAY Lee was optimistic, however. With one more day of determined attack, he felt he could break the Union defenses. Early in the afternoon of July 3, Lee ordered an artillery barrage on the middle of the Union lines. For two hours, the two armies fired at one another in a vicious exchange that could be heard in Pittsburgh. When the Union

MAIN IDEA

Analyzing Effects

B Why was it important that the Union held on to the high ground in Gettysburg?

History Through Art

GETTYSBURG CYCLORAMA (detail) (1884)

Twenty years after the fact, French artist Paul Philippoteaux depicted the battle of Gettysburg in a giant painting. To ensure that the 360-foot-long and 26-foot-high work was realistic, Philippoteaux studied the battle site and interviewed survivors.

What details in the painting contribute to its realism and sense of action?

artillery fell silent, Lee insisted that Longstreet press forward. Longstreet reluctantly ordered his men, including those under the command of General Pickett, to attack the center of the Union lines. Deliberately, they marched across the farmland toward the Union high ground. Suddenly, Northern artillery renewed its barrage. Some of the Confederates had nearly reached the Union lines when Yankee infantry fired on them as well. Devastated, the Confederates staggered back. The Northerners had succeeded in holding the high ground south of Gettysburg.

Lee sent cavalry led by General James E. B. (Jeb) Stuart circling around the right flank of Meade's forces, hoping they would surprise the Union troops from the rear and meet Longstreet's men in the middle. Stuart's campaign stalled, however, when his men clashed with Union forces under David Gregg three miles away.

Not knowing that Gregg had stopped Stuart nor that Lee's army was severely weakened, Union general Meade never ordered a counterattack. After the battle, Lee gave up any hopes of invading the North and led his army in a long, painful retreat back to Virginia through a pelting rain.

The three-day battle produced staggering losses. Total casualties were more than 30 percent. Union losses included 23,000 men killed or wounded. For the Confederacy, approximately 28,000 were killed or wounded. Fly-infested corpses lay everywhere in the July heat; the stench was unbearable. Lee would continue to lead his men brilliantly in the next two years of the war, but neither he nor the Confederacy would ever recover from the loss at Gettysburg or the surrender of Vicksburg, which occurred the very next day. **C**

MAIN IDEA

Analyzing Effects
C Why was the battle of Gettysburg a disaster for the South?

Grant Wins at Vicksburg

While the Army of the Potomac was turning back the Confederates in central Pennsylvania, Union general Ulysses S. Grant continued his campaign in the west. **Vicksburg,** Mississippi, was one of only two Confederate holdouts preventing the Union from taking complete control of the Mississippi River, an important waterway for transporting goods.

U. S. Grant, photographed in August 1864 ▼

VICKSBURG UNDER SIEGE In the spring of 1863, Grant sent a cavalry brigade to destroy rail lines in central Mississippi and draw attention away from the port city. While the Confederate forces were distracted, Grant was able to land infantry south of Vicksburg late on April 30. In 18 days, Union forces whipped several rebel units and sacked Jackson, the capital of the state.

Their confidence growing with every victory, Grant and his troops rushed to Vicksburg. Two frontal assaults on the city failed; so, in the last week of May 1863, Grant settled in for a siege. He set up a steady barrage of artillery, shelling the city from both the river and the land for several hours a day and forcing its residents to take shelter in caves that they dug out of the yellow clay hillsides.

Food supplies ran so low that people ate dogs and mules. At last some of the starving Confederate soldiers defending Vicksburg sent their commander a petition saying, "If you can't feed us, you'd better surrender."

On July 3, 1863, the same day as Pickett's charge, the Confederate commander of Vicksburg asked Grant for terms of surrender. The city fell on July 4. Five days later Port Hudson, Louisiana, the last Confederate holdout on the Mississippi, also fell—and the Confederacy was cut in two.

Vicksburg Campaign, April–July 1863

hmhsocialstudies.com **INTERACTIVE MAP**

Legend:
- Union forces
- Union positions
- Confederate forces
- Confederate positions
- Union victory
- Railroad

0   10   20 miles
0   10   20 kilometers

April 20 Grant moves main body of Union forces south.

April 30 Grant's army crosses Mississippi unopposed.

MISSISSIPPI

Milliken's Bend
Duckport Canal
Yazoo River
Sherman
Johnston
BIG BLACK RIVER, May 17
Bolton Depot
Bridgeport
Clinton
Grant
Williams-Grant Canal
SIEGE OF VICKSBURG begins May 19. City surrenders July 4.
CHAMPION HILL, May 16
Sherman and McPherson
JACKSON, May 14
McClernand and Sherman
RAYMOND, May 12
New Carthage
LOUISIANA
Grant
Hard Times
Big Black River
Rocky Springs
Big Bayou Pierre
Bruinsburg
PORT GIBSON, May 1

GEOGRAPHY SKILLBUILDER
1. **Movement** How many days did it take Union forces to reach Vicksburg after the victory at Jackson?
2. **Location** Which river lies just to the east of Vicksburg?

The Gettysburg Address

In November 1863, a ceremony was held to dedicate a cemetery in Gettysburg. The first speaker was Edward Everett, a noted orator, who gave a flowery two-hour oration. Then Abraham Lincoln spoke for a little more than two minutes. According to the historian Garry Wills, Lincoln's **Gettysburg Address** "remade America." Before the war, people said, "The United States *are*." After Lincoln's speech, they said, "The United States *is*."

THE GETTYSBURG ADDRESS ABRAHAM LINCOLN

" Four score and seven years ago our fathers brought forth on this continent a new nation, conceived in Liberty, and dedicated to the proposition that all men are created equal.

Now we are engaged in a great civil war, testing whether that nation, or any nation so conceived and so dedicated, can long endure. We are met on a great battlefield of that war. We have come to dedicate a portion of that field, as a final resting place for those who here gave their lives that that nation might live. It is altogether fitting and proper that we should do this.

But, in a larger sense, we can not dedicate—we can not consecrate—we can not hallow—this ground. The brave men, living and dead, who struggled here, have consecrated it, far above our poor power to add or detract. The world will little note, nor long remember what we say here, but it can never forget what they did here. It is for us the living, rather, to be dedicated here to the unfinished work which they who fought here have thus far so nobly advanced. It is rather for us to be here dedicated to the great task remaining before us—that from these honored dead we take increased devotion to that cause for which they gave the last full measure of devotion—that we here highly resolve that these dead shall not have died in vain—that this nation, under God, shall have a new birth of freedom—and that government of the people, by the people, for the people, shall not perish from the earth. " **D**

—*The Gettysburg Address*, November 19, 1863

MAIN IDEA

Summarizing
D What beliefs about the United States did Lincoln express in the Gettysburg Address?

The Confederacy Wears Down

The twin defeats at Gettysburg and Vicksburg cost the South much of its limited fighting power. The Confederacy was already low on food, shoes, uniforms, guns, and ammunition. No longer able to attack, it could hope only to hang on long enough to destroy Northern morale and work toward an armistice—a cease-fire agreement based on mutual consent—rather than a surrender. That plan proved increasingly unlikely, however. Southern newspapers, state legislatures, and individuals began to call openly for an end to the hostilities, and President Lincoln finally found not just one but two generals who would fight.

CONFEDERATE MORALE As war progressed, morale on the Confederacy's home front deteriorated. The Confederate Congress passed a weak resolution in 1863 urging planters to grow fewer cash crops like cotton and tobacco and increase production of food. Farmers resented the tax that took part of their produce and livestock, especially since many rich planters continued to cultivate cotton and tobacco—in some cases even selling crops to the North. Many soldiers deserted after receiving letters from home about the lack of food and the shortage of farm labor to work the farms. In every Southern state except South Carolina, there were soldiers who decided to turn and fight for the North—for example, 2,400 Floridians served in the Union army.

Discord in the Confederate government made it impossible for Jefferson Davis to govern effectively. Members of the Confederate Congress squabbled among themselves. In South Carolina, the governor was upset when troops from his state were placed under the command of officers from another state.

In 1863, North Carolinians who wanted peace held more than 100 open meetings in their state. A similar peace movement sprang up in Georgia in early 1864. Although these movements failed, by mid-1864, Assistant Secretary of War John Campbell was forced to acknowledge that active opposition to the war "in the mountain districts of North Carolina, South Carolina, Georgia, and Alabama menaces the existence of the Confederacy as fatally as . . . the armies of the United States." **E**

KEY PLAYERS

ULYSSES S. GRANT
1822–1885

U. S. Grant once said of himself, "A military life had no charms for me." Yet, a military man was what he was destined to be. He fought in the war with Mexico—even though he termed it "wicked"—because he believed his duty was to serve his country. His next post was in the West, where Grant grew so lonely for his family that he resigned.

When the Civil War began, Grant served as colonel of the Illinois volunteers because General McClellan had been too busy to see him!

However, once Grant began fighting in Tennessee, Lincoln recognized his abilities. When newspapers demanded Grant's dismissal after Shiloh, Lincoln replied, "I can't spare this man. He fights."

ROBERT E. LEE
1807–1870

Lee was an aristocrat. His father had been one of George Washington's best generals, and his wife was the great-granddaughter of Martha Washington. As a man who believed slavery was evil, Lee nonetheless fought for the Confederacy out of loyalty to his beloved home state of Virginia. "I did only what my duty demanded. I could have taken no other course without dishonor," he said.

As a general, Lee was brilliant, but he seldom challenged civilian leaders about their failure to provide his army with adequate supplies. His soldiers—who called him Uncle Robert—almost worshiped him because he insisted on sharing their hardships.

MAIN IDEA

Analyzing Effects
E How did discontent among members of the Confederate Congress affect the war?

Map Legend:
- Area controlled by Union
- Area won by Union
- Area controlled by Confederacy
- Union forces
- Confederate forces
- Union victory
- Confederate victory
- Union blockade
- Capital

0 150 300 miles
0 150 300 kilometers

**Main map labels:**

WISC. — MICHIGAN — Lake Michigan — Lake Huron — L. Ontario — Lake Erie — OHIO — PENN. — NEW JERSEY — New York City — Philadelphia — MD. — DELAWARE — Washington, D.C. — VIRGINIA — Richmond — Charleston — KENTUCKY — Ohio R. — ILL. — IND.

NASHVILLE Dec. 15–16, 1864 — CHATTANOOGA– LOOKOUT MOUNTAIN Nov. 25, 1863 — TENN. — N.C. — RALEIGH Apr. 13, 1865 — WILMINGTON Feb. 22, 1865 — S.C. — Sherman

Memphis — Hood — Grant — CHICKAMAUGA Sept. 19–20, 1863 — ATLANTA Sept. 2, 1864 — Sherman — SAVANNAH Dec. 21, 1864 — GA. — ARK. — MISS. — Montgomery — ALA. — VICKSBURG Apr.–July, 1863 — Mississippi R. — LA. — TEXAS — Mobile — Pensacola — PORT HUDSON July 8, 1863 — New Orleans — Farragut — MOBILE BAY Aug. 5, 1864 — FLORIDA — Gulf of Mexico — ATLANTIC OCEAN — 90°W — 80°W — 40°N

Inset map (Virginia):

PENNSYLVANIA — GETTYSBURG, July 1–3, 1863 — MARYLAND — Potomac R. — Washington, D.C. — THE WILDERNESS, May 5–7, 1864 — CHANCELLORSVILLE, May 1–5, 1863 — Rappahannock R. — Chesapeake Bay — SPOTSYLVANIA COURT HOUSE, May 8–19, 1864 — James R. — Lee — Grant — VIRGINIA — Richmond — APPOMATTOX COURT HOUSE, Apr. 9, 1865– Lee surrenders to Grant — COLD HARBOR, June 3, 1864 — PETERSBURG, June 1864– April 1865

GEOGRAPHY SKILLBUILDER
1. **Movement** What route did General Sherman and his troops follow from Chattanooga?
2. **Movement** After what battle did Grant and Lee go to Appomattox?

GRANT APPOINTS SHERMAN In March 1864, President Lincoln appointed Ulysses S. Grant, the hero of the battle at Vicksburg, commander of all Union armies. Grant in turn appointed **William Tecumseh Sherman** as commander of the military division of the Mississippi. These two appointments would change the course of the war.

Old friends and comrades in arms, both men believed in total war. They believed that it was essential to fight not only the South's armies and government but its civilian population as well. They reasoned, first, that civilians produced the weapons, grew the food, and transported the goods on which the armies relied, and, second, that the strength of the people's will kept the war going. If the Union destroyed that will to fight, the Confederacy would collapse.

GRANT AND LEE IN VIRGINIA Grant's overall strategy was to immobilize Lee's army in Virginia while Sherman raided Georgia. Even if Grant's casualties ran twice as high as those of Lee—and they did—the North could afford it. The South could not.

Starting in May 1864, Grant threw his troops into battle after battle, the first in a wooded area, known as the Wilderness, near Fredericksburg, Virginia. The fighting was brutal, made even more so by the fires spreading through the thick trees. The string of battles continued at Spotsylvania, at Cold Harbor (where Grant lost 7,000 men in one hour), and finally at Petersburg, which would remain under Union attack from June 1864 to April 1865.

During the period from May 4 to June 18, 1864, Grant lost nearly 60,000 men—which the North could replace—to Lee's 32,000 men—which the South could not replace. Democrats and Northern newspapers called Grant a butcher. However, Grant kept going because he had promised Lincoln, "Whatever happens, there will be no turning back."

Sherman *(front)* instructed his troops in Atlanta to destroy train tracks by heating and bending the metal rails.

SHERMAN'S MARCH After Sherman's army occupied the transportation center of Atlanta on September 2, 1864, a Confederate army tried to circle around him and cut his railroad supply lines. Sherman decided to fight a different battle. He would abandon his supply lines and march southeast through Georgia, creating a wide path of destruction and living off the land as he went. He would make Southerners "so sick of war that generations would pass away before they would again appeal to it." In mid-November he burned most of Atlanta and set out toward the coast. A Georgia girl described the result.

⭐ **A PERSONAL VOICE** ELIZA FRANCES ANDREWS

" The fields were trampled down and the road was lined with carcasses of horses, hogs, and cattle that the invaders, unable either to consume or to carry away with them, had wantonly shot down, to starve out the people and prevent them from making their crops. . . . The dwellings that were standing all showed signs of pillage . . . while here and there lone chimney stacks, 'Sherman's sentinels,' told of homes laid in ashes. "

—quoted in *Voices from the Civil War*

After taking Savannah just before Christmas, Sherman's troops turned north to help Grant "wipe out Lee." Following behind them now were about 25,000 former slaves eager for freedom. As the army marched through South Carolina in 1865, it inflicted even more destruction than it had in Georgia. As one Union private exclaimed, "Here is where treason began and, by God, here is where it shall end!" The army burned almost every house in its path. In contrast, when Sherman's forces entered North Carolina, which had been the last state to secede, they stopped destroying private homes and—anticipating the end of the war—began handing out food and other supplies. **F**

THE ELECTION OF 1864 As the 1864 presidential election approached, Lincoln faced heavy opposition. Many Democrats, dismayed at the war's length, its high casualty rates, and recent Union losses, joined pro-Southern party members to nominate George McClellan on a platform of an immediate armistice. Still resentful over having been fired by Lincoln, McClellan was delighted to run.

Lincoln's other opponents, the Radical Republicans, favored a harsher proposal than Lincoln's for readmitting the Confederate states. They formed a third political party and nominated John C. Frémont as their candidate. To attract Democrats, Lincoln's supporters dropped the Republican name, retitled themselves the National Union Party, and chose Andrew Johnson, a pro-Union Democrat from Tennessee, as Lincoln's running mate.

Lincoln was pessimistic about his chances. "I am going to be beaten," he said in August, "and unless some great change takes place, badly beaten." However, some great change did take place. On August 5, Admiral David Farragut entered Mobile Bay in Alabama and within three weeks shut down that major Southern port. On September 2, Sherman telegraphed, "Atlanta is ours." By month's end, Frémont had withdrawn from the presidential race. On October 19, General

MAIN IDEA

Analyzing Motives
F What were Sherman's objectives in marching his troops from Atlanta to Savannah?

▶ Thomas Lovell's *Surrender at Appomattox* is a modern rendering of Lee's surrender to Grant.

Philip Sheridan finally chased the Confederates out of the Shenandoah Valley in northern Virginia. The victories buoyed the North, and with the help of absentee ballots cast by Union soldiers, Lincoln won a second term.

THE SURRENDER AT APPOMATTOX By late March 1865, it was clear that the end of the Confederacy was near. Grant and Sheridan were approaching Richmond from the west, while Sherman was approaching from the south. On April 2—in response to news that Lee and his troops had been overcome by Grant's forces at Petersburg—President Davis and his government abandoned their capital, setting it afire to keep the Northerners from taking it. Despite the fire-fighting efforts of Union troops, flames destroyed some 900 buildings and damaged hundreds more.

Lee and Grant met to arrange a Confederate surrender on April 9, 1865, in a Virginia village called **Appomattox** (ăpʹə-mătʹəks) **Court House.** At Lincoln's request, the terms were generous. Grant paroled Lee's soldiers and sent them home with their personal possessions, horses, and three days' rations. Officers were permitted to keep their side arms. Within two months all remaining Confederate resistance collapsed. After four long years, at tremendous human and economic costs, the Civil War was over.

ASSESSMENT

1. **TERMS & NAMES** For each term or name, write a sentence explaining its significance.
   - Gettysburg
   - Chancellorsville
   - Vicksburg
   - Gettysburg Address
   - William Tecumseh Sherman
   - Appomattox Court House

MAIN IDEA

2. **TAKING NOTES**
   Create a time line of the major battles and political events relating to the final two years of the Civil War. Use the dates already plotted on the time line below as a guide.

   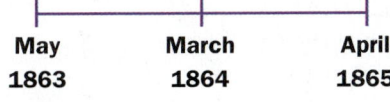

May	March	April
1863	1864	1865

   Which event was the turning point? Why?

CRITICAL THINKING

3. **EVALUATING**
   Do you think that a general's win-loss record on the battlefield is the best gauge of measuring greatness as a military leader? Why or why not? **Think About:**
   - Grant's campaign in Virginia, Sherman's march to Atlanta, and Lee's surrender
   - Democrats' and Northern newspapers' criticism of Grant
   - the criteria you would use to evaluate a military leader

4. **EVALUATING DECISIONS**
   Grant and Sherman presented a logical rationale for using the strategy of total war. Do you think the end—defeating the Confederacy—justified the means—causing harm to civilians? Explain.

5. **ANALYZING MOTIVES**
   Why do you think Lincoln urged generous terms for a Confederate surrender?

The Legacy of the War

MAIN IDEA	WHY IT MATTERS NOW	Terms & Names
The Civil War settled long-standing disputes over states' rights and slavery.	The federal government established supreme authority, and no state has threatened secession since.	• National Bank Act • Thirteenth Amendment • Red Cross • John Wilkes Booth

One American's Story

Garland H. White, a former slave from Virginia, marched with other Yankee soldiers into the Confederate capital of Richmond after it fell. Now chaplain of the 28th United States Colored troops, White was returning to the state where he had once served in bondage. As the soldiers marched along the city streets, thousands of African Americans cheered. A large crowd of soldiers and civilians gathered in the neighborhood where the slave market had been. Garland White remembered the scene.

A PERSONAL VOICE   GARLAND H. WHITE

" I marched at the head of the column, and soon I found myself called upon by the officers and men of my regiment to make a speech, with which, of course, I readily complied. A vast multitude assembled on Broad Street, and I was aroused amid the shouts of 10,000 voices, and proclaimed for the first time in that city freedom to all [humankind]. "

—quoted in *Been in the Storm So Long*

▲ Union troops in the South sometimes came upon slave markets like this one.

Freedom for slaves was not the only legacy of the Civil War. The struggle transformed the nation's economy, its government, the conduct of warfare, and the future careers of many of its participants.

The War Changes the Nation

In 1869 Professor George Ticknor of Harvard commented that since the Civil War, "It does not seem to me as if I were living in the country in which I was born." The Civil War caused tremendous political, economic, technological, and social change in the United States. It also exacted a high price in the cost of human life.

POLITICAL CHANGES Decades before the war, Southern states had threatened secession when federal policies angered them. After the war, the federal government assumed supreme national authority and no state has ever seceded again. The states' rights issue did not go away; it simply led in a different direction from secession. Today, arguments about states' rights versus federal control focus on such issues as whether the state or national government should determine how to use local funds.

In addition to ending the threat of secession, the war greatly increased the federal government's power. Before the Civil War, the federal government had little impact on most people's daily lives. Most citizens dealt only with their county governments. During the war, however, the federal government reached into people's pockets, taxing private incomes. It also required everyone to accept its new paper currency (even those who had previously contracted to be repaid in coins). Most dramatically, the federal government tore reluctant men from their families to fight in the war. After the war, U.S. citizens could no longer assume that the national government in Washington was too far away to bother them. **Ⓐ**

ECONOMIC CHANGES The Civil War had a profound impact on the nation's economy. Between 1861 and 1865, the federal government did much to help business, in part through subsidizing construction of a national railroad system. The government also passed the **National Bank Act** of 1863, which set up a system of federally chartered banks, set requirements for loans, and provided for banks to be inspected. These measures helped make banking safer for investors.

The economy of the Northern states boomed. Northern entrepreneurs had grown rich selling war supplies to the government and thus had money to invest in new businesses after the war. As army recruitment created a labor shortage in the North, the sale of labor-saving agricultural tools such as the reaper increased dramatically. By war's end, large-scale commercial agriculture had taken hold.

The war devastated the South economically. It took away the South's source of cheap labor—slavery—and also wrecked most of the region's industry. It wiped out 40 percent of the livestock, destroyed much of the South's farm machinery and railroads, and left thousands of acres of land uncultivated.

The economic gap between North and South had widened drastically. Before the war, Southern states held 30 percent of the national wealth; in 1870 they held

MAIN IDEA

Analyzing Effects

Ⓐ How did the power of the federal government increase during the war?

Though both Union and Confederate soldiers were lucky to escape the war with their lives, thousands— like this young amputee—faced an uncertain future. ▼

The Costs of the Civil War

Deaths

Deaths (in thousands)

Civil War: Union	~365
Civil War: Confederacy	~260
Other Major U.S. Wars	~645

Source: *Warfare and Armed Conflicts: A Statistical Reference to Casualty and Other Figures, 1500-2000;* U.S. Department of Defense

Economic Costs

· Union war costs totaled $2.3 billion.

· Confederate war costs ran to $1 billion.

· Union war costs increased the national debt from $65 million in 1860 to $2.7 billion in 1865.

· Confederate debt ran over $1.8 billion in 1864.

· Union inflation peaked at 182% in 1864.

· Confederate inflation rose to 7,000%.

SKILLBUILDER Interpreting Data
1. Based on the bar graph, how did the combined Union and Confederate losses compare with those of other wars?
2. Why was inflation worse in the Confederacy than in the Union?

only 12 percent. In 1860, Southerners earned about 70 percent of the Northern average; in 1870, they earned less than 40 percent. This economic disparity between the regions would not diminish until the 20th century.

COSTS OF THE WAR The human costs of the Civil War were staggering. They affected almost every American family. Approximately 360,000 Union soldiers and 260,000 Confederates died, nearly as many as in all other American wars combined. Another 275,000 Union soldiers and 225,000 Confederates were wounded. Veterans with missing limbs became a common sight nationwide. In addition, military service had occupied some 2,400,000 men—nearly 10 percent of the nation's population of approximately 31,000,000—for four long years. It disrupted their education, their careers, and their families.

The Civil War's economic costs were just as extensive. Historians estimate that the Union and the Confederate governments spent a combined total of about $3.3 billion during the four years of war, or more than twice what the government had spent in the previous 80 years! The costs did not stop when the war ended. Twenty years later, interest payments on the war debt plus veterans' pensions still accounted for almost two-thirds of the federal budget.

The War Changes Lives

The war not only impacted the nation's economy and politics, it also changed individual lives. Perhaps the biggest change came for African Americans.

NEW BIRTH OF FREEDOM The Emancipation Proclamation, which Lincoln had issued under his war powers, freed only those slaves who lived in the states that were behind Confederate lines and not yet under Union control. The government had to decide what to do about the border states, where slavery was still legal.

The president believed that the only solution would be a constitutional amendment abolishing slavery. The Republican-controlled Senate approved an amendment in the summer of 1864, but the House, with its large Democratic membership, did not. After Lincoln's reelection, the amendment was reintroduced in the House in January of 1865. This time the administration convinced a few Democrats to vote in its favor with promises of government jobs after they left office. The amendment passed with two votes to spare. Spectators—many of them African Americans who were now allowed to sit in the congressional galleries—burst into cheers, while Republicans on the floor shouted in triumph.

By year's end 27 states, including 8 from the South, had ratified the **Thirteenth Amendment.** The U.S. Constitution now stated that "Neither slavery nor involuntary servitude, except as a punishment for crime whereof the party shall have been duly convicted, shall exist within the United States."

A store in Richmond, Virginia, decorated in celebration of Liberation Day, the anniversary of the Emancipation Proclamation

MATHEW BRADY'S PHOTOGRAPHS

The Civil War marked the first time in United States history that photography, a resource since 1839, played a major role in a military conflict. Hundreds of photographers traveled with the troops, working both privately and for the military. The most famous Civil War photographer was Mathew Brady, who employed about 20 photographers to meet the public demand for pictures from the battlefront. This was the beginning of American news photography, or photojournalism.

Many of Brady's photographs are a mix of realism and artificiality. Due to the primitive level of photographic technology, subjects had to be carefully posed and remain still during the long exposure times.

In this 1864 photograph Brady posed a kneeling soldier, offering a canteen of water, beside a wounded soldier with his arm in a sling. Images like this, showing the wounded or the dead, brought home the harsh reality of war to the civilian population.

▼

▲

"Encampment of the Army of the Potomac" (May 1862). Few photographs of the Civil War are as convincing in their naturalism as this view over a Union encampment. Simply by positioning the camera behind the soldiers, the photographer draws the viewer into the composition. Although we cannot see the soldiers' faces, we are compelled to see through their eyes.

SKILLBUILDER Interpreting Visual Sources

1. What elements in the smaller photograph seem posed or contrived? What elements are more realistic?
2. How do these photographs compare with more heroic imagery of traditional history painting?

📁 **SEE SKILLBUILDER HANDBOOK, PAGE R23.**

NOW & THEN

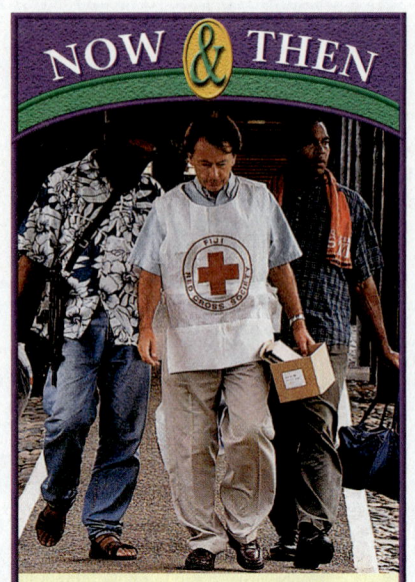

THE RED CROSS

Civil War nurse Clara Barton led the American branch of the Red Cross for 23 years. Today's International Red Cross can be found wherever human suffering occurs, not just in conventional armed conflicts. In Fiji in June 2000, rebels took the country's prime minister and 30 members of parliament hostage. The Red Cross employee above was given safe passage to give hostages medical attention, mattresses, and blankets.

Swiss businessman Henri Dunant first had the idea for the Red Cross when, in 1859, he saw injured soldiers abandoned on the battlefield in Italy. Horrified, he organized local people to provide aid to the wounded. Back in Switzerland, Dunant, and a group of lawyers and doctors, founded an international committee for the relief of wounded soldiers.

CIVILIANS FOLLOW NEW PATHS After the war ended, those who had served—Northerners and Southerners alike—had to find new directions for their lives.

Some war leaders continued their military careers, while others returned to civilian life. William Tecumseh Sherman remained in the army and spent most of his time fighting Native Americans in the West. Robert E. Lee lost Arlington, his plantation, which the Secretary of War of the Union had turned into a cemetery for Union dead. Lee became president of Washington College in Virginia, now known as Washington and Lee University. Lee swore renewed allegiance to the United States, but Congress accidentally neglected to restore his citizenship (until 1975). Still, Lee never spoke bitterly of Northerners or the Union.

Many veterans returned to their small towns and farms after the war. Others, as Grant noted, "found they were not satisfied with the farm, the store, or the workshop of the villages, but wanted larger fields." Many moved to the burgeoning cities or went west in search of opportunity.

Others tried to turn their wartime experience to good. The horrors that Union nurse Clara Barton witnessed during the war inspired her to spend her life helping others. In 1869, Barton went to Europe to rest and recuperate from her work during the war. She became involved in the activities of the International Committee of the Red Cross during the Franco-Prussian War. Returning to the United States, Barton helped found the American **Red Cross** in 1881. **B**

THE ASSASSINATION OF LINCOLN Whatever plans Lincoln had to reunify the nation after the war, he never got to implement them. On April 14, 1865, five days after Lee surrendered to Grant at Appomattox Court House, Lincoln and his wife went to Ford's Theatre in Washington to see a British comedy, *Our American Cousin*. During the play's third act, a man silently opened the unguarded doors to the presidential box. He crept up behind Lincoln, raised a pistol, and fired, hitting the president in the back of the head.

The assassin, **John Wilkes Booth**—a 26-year-old actor and Southern sympathizer—then leaped down to the stage. In doing so, he caught his spur on one of the flags draped across the front of the box. Booth landed hard on his left leg and broke it. He rose and said something that the audience had trouble understanding. Some thought it was the state motto of Virginia, *"Sic semper tyrannis"*—in English "Thus be it ever to tyrants." Others thought he said, "The South is avenged!" Then he limped offstage into the wings.

Despite a broken leg, Booth managed to escape. Twelve days later, Union cavalry trapped him in a Virginia tobacco barn, and set the building on fire. When Booth still refused to surrender, a shot was fired. He may have been shot by cavalry or by himself, but the cavalry dragged him out. Booth is said to have whispered, "Tell my mother I died for my country. I did what I thought was best." His last words were "Useless, useless."

After Lincoln was shot, he remained unconscious through the night. He died at 7:22 A.M. the following morning, April 15. It was the first time a president of the United States had been assassinated. Secretary of the Navy Gideon Welles recorded the public's immediate reactions in his diary.

MAIN IDEA

Summarizing
B What were some effects that the war had on individuals?

A PERSONAL VOICE
GIDEON WELLES

" It was a dark and gloomy morning, and rain set in. . . . On the Avenue in front of the White House were several hundred colored people, mostly women and children, weeping and wailing their loss. This crowd did not appear to diminish through the whole of that cold, wet day; they seemed not to know what was to be their fate since their great benefactor was dead, and their hope-less grief affected me more than almost anything else, though strong and brave men wept when I met them. "

—quoted in *Voices from the Civil War*

▲ Lincoln's body lies in state.

The funeral train that carried Lincoln's body from Washington to his hometown of Springfield, Illinois, took 14 days for its journey. Approximately 7 million Americans, or almost one-third of the entire Union population, turned out to publicly mourn the martyred leader.

The Civil War had ended. Slavery and secession were no more. Now the country faced two different problems: how to restore the Southern states to the Union and how to integrate approximately 4 million newly freed African Americans into national life.

SECTION 5 ASSESSMENT

1. **TERMS & NAMES** For each term or name, write a sentence explaining its significance.

   • **National Bank Act** • **Thirteenth Amendment** • **Red Cross** • **John Wilkes Booth**

MAIN IDEA

2. **TAKING NOTES**

   Copy the multiple-effects chart below on your paper and fill it in with consequences of the Civil War.

   Consequences of the Civil War
   - Political
   - Economic
   - Technological
   - Social

CRITICAL THINKING

3. **HYPOTHESIZING**

   Imagine that you are a member of a group of Southern leaders who must rebuild the South after the war. What would you recommend that the government do to help the South?
   Think About:
   - the economic devastation of the South
   - the human costs of the war
   - the numbers of newly freed slaves

4. **ANALYZING ISSUES**

   What political and social issues from the Civil War era do you think are still issues today? Use details from the text to support your answer.

5. **SYNTHESIZING**

   Write three questions that you have about the lives of African Americans after the Civil War.

VISUAL SUMMARY

THE CIVIL WAR

LONG-TERM CAUSES

- Conflict over slavery in territories
- Economic differences between North and South
- Conflict between states' rights and federal control

IMMEDIATE CAUSES

- Election of Lincoln
- Secession of southern states
- Firing on Fort Sumter

THE CIVIL WAR

IMMEDIATE EFFECTS

- Abolition of slavery
- Widening gap between economies of North and South
- Physical devastation of the South
- Reunification of the country

LONG-TERM EFFECTS

- Reconstruction of the South
- Industrial boom
- Increased federal authority

TERMS & NAMES

For each term or name below, write a sentence explaining its connection to the Civil War.

1. Ulysses S. Grant
2. Robert E. Lee
3. Emancipation Proclamation
4. conscription
5. income tax
6. Andersonville
7. Gettysburg Address
8. Appomattox Court House
9. Thirteenth Amendment
10. John Wilkes Booth

MAIN IDEAS

Use your notes and the information in the chapter to answer the following questions.

The Civil War Begins (pages 338–345)

1. What were the military strategies of the North and South at the outset of the Civil War?
2. What advantages did the North have over the South?

The Politics of War (pages 346–350)

3. How did different groups react to the Emancipation Proclamation? Give examples.

Life During Wartime (pages 351–356)

4. What acts of protest occurred in both the North and South?

The North Takes Charge (pages 357–365)

5. In what ways did the South's morale deteriorate?
6. What was Grant and Sherman's rationale for using the strategy of total war?

The Legacy of the War (pages 366–371)

7. How did the Civil War provide the economic foundation for the United States to become an industrial giant?

CRITICAL THINKING

1. **USING YOUR NOTES** On a continuum like the one shown, mark where Abraham Lincoln's and Jefferson Davis's policies would fall. Support your ratings with evidence from the text.

◄ less federal control | | | more federal control ►

2. **ANALYZING PRIMARY SOURCES** Poet Walt Whitman made the following observation about Lincoln.

" He leaves for America's history and biography, so far, not only its most dramatic reminiscence—he leaves, in my opinion, the greatest . . . personality. . . . By many has *this Union* been . . . help'd; but if one name, one man, must be pick'd out, he, most of all, is the conservator of it, to the future. He was assassinated—but the Union is not assassinated. "

—Walt Whitman, *Specimen Days*

Do you agree or disagree about Lincoln's legacy? Explain why.

3. **INTERPRETING MAPS** Compare the maps on pages 340–341 and 363. What do they tell you about the progress of the Civil War from 1861–1865? Explain your answer.

Use the cartoon and your knowledge of U.S. history to answer question 1.

LINCOLN'S TWO DIFFICULTIES.

Lin. "WHAT? NO MONEY! NO MEN!"

1 According to the cartoon, President Lincoln's "two difficulties" are how to —

(1) pay government salaries and build support in Congress.
(2) reduce taxes and find good generals.
(3) avoid bankruptcy and stop the draft riots.
(4) finance the war and find enough soldiers to fight.

2 What technological advance contributed most to the Civil War's high casualty rate?

(1) the ironclad ship
(2) the minié ball
(3) the land mine
(4) the camera

3 Which pair of events are listed in the order in which they occurred?

(1) Battle of Gettysburg; Battle of Antietam
(2) New York City draft riots; First Battle of Bull Run
(3) Battle of Gettysburg; fall of Atlanta
(4) First Battle of Bull Run; firing on Fort Sumter

4 Which of the following is *not* true of the South after the Civil War?

(1) It held 30 percent of the national wealth.
(2) Most of its industry was destroyed.
(3) Its labor system was dismantled.
(4) As much as 40 percent of its livestock was wiped out.

 hmhsocialstudies.com **TEST PRACTICE**

For additional test practice, go online for:
• Diagnostic tests   • Tutorials

INTERACT WITH HISTORY

Think about the issues you explored at the beginning of the chapter. In light of what you now know about the Civil War, consider whether the use of force can preserve a nation. Write a short editorial for an 1861 newspaper supporting or opposing the war. Discuss what might have happened if the North allowed the South to secede.

FOCUS ON WRITING

Imagine that you are a U.S. citizen living during the Civil War, and the Emancipation Proclamation has just been issued. Decide whether you think the proclamation was effective. Write a letter to President Lincoln expressing your point of view.

COLLABORATIVE LEARNING

21ST CENTURY

Use the Internet to find Mary Chesnut's diary of the Civil War. As a group, read several entries and discuss them. Then create three diary entries that Mary Chesnut might have written. Make sure the entries are in keeping with her personality and writing style. Each entry should refer to significant events, issues, or people of the Civil War. Share your group's entries with the class.

DAYS OF DARKNESS:
THE GETTYSBURG CIVILIANS

Gettysburg, Pennsylvania, was a sleepy agricultural town of about 2,400 residents when the Civil War arrived on its doorstep in the early summer of 1863. Many of the town's men were elsewhere, either fighting in the war or guarding their livestock in the countryside. This left mostly women and children to endure the battle. For three terrifying days they hid in basements or in tightly shuttered houses. Even after the battle finally ended the horrors continued, as the Gettysburg civilians emerged to find a scene of unimaginable death and destruction.

Explore some of the personal stories and recollections of the Gettysburg civilians online. You can find a wealth of information, video clips, primary sources, activities, and more at **hmhsocialstudies.com**.

> "I had scarcely reached the front door, when, on looking up the street, I saw some of the men on horseback . . .
>
> What a horrible sight! . . .
>
> I was fully persuaded that the Rebels had actually come at last. What they would do with us was a fearful question to my young mind . . ."
>
> — Tillie Pierce, age 15

A Young Woman's Account

Read the document to witness the arrival of Confederate troops through the eyes of a Gettysburg teenager.

A Citizen-Soldier

Watch the video to meet John Burns, the man who would come to be called the "Citizen Hero of Gettysburg."

A Family's Story

Watch the video to discover the story of courage and commitment exhibited by one Gettysburg family.

The National Cemetery

Watch the video to learn about the Soldiers' National Cemetery and the speech President Lincoln gave there.

CHAPTER 12

RECONSTRUCTION AND ITS EFFECTS

Essential Question

What were the political struggles, accomplishments, and failures of Reconstruction in the years following the Civil War?

 New York Standards

KEY IDEA 2 Important ideas, social and cultural values, beliefs, and traditions from New York State and United States history illustrate the connections and interactions of people and events across time and from a variety of perspectives.

KEY IDEA 4 The skills of historical analysis include the ability to: explain the significance of historical evidence; weigh the importance, reliability, and validity of evidence; understand the concept of multiple causation; understand the importance of changing and competing interpretations of different historical developments.

SECTION 1: The Politics of Reconstruction

SECTION 2: Reconstructing Society

SECTION 3: The Collapse of Reconstruction

After the Civil War, Charleston, South Carolina, and other Southern cities lay in ruins.

1865 Confederacy surrenders at Appomattox.

1865 Andrew Johnson becomes president after Lincoln's assassination.

1866 President Johnson presses for moderate Reconstruction policies.

1867 U.S. buys Alaska from Russia for $7.2 million.

1868 Congress impeaches President Johnson.

1868 Ulysses S. Grant is elected president.

USA

1864

1868

WORLD

1866 Austro-Prussian War is fought.

1869 Mohandas K. Gandhi is born in India.

President Ulysses S. Grant: Scandal and Legacy

↗ hmhsocialstudies.com **VIDEO**

INTERACT
WITH HISTORY

The year is 1865, and at last the Civil War is over. The South's primary labor system, slavery, has been abolished. About 4.5 million African Americans now have their freedom but lack money, property, education, and opportunity. Southern states are beginning the process of readmission to the Union, but the effects of war continue to be felt throughout the South. Rail lines are unusable. Farms, plantations, and factories lie in ruins.

Explore the Issues

- How can Northern resources help the South?

- In what ways can the South rebuild its economy?

- What can the government do to assist African Americans?

Timeline

1871 U.S. and Great Britain sign Treaty of Washington.

1872 Horace Greeley runs for president as a Liberal Republican.

1872 President Grant is reelected.

1876 Hayes-Tilden presidential election results in deadlock.

1877 Federal troops withdraw from the South.

1877 Rutherford B. Hayes is inaugurated.

1872

1876

1870 Unification of Italy is completed.

1871 Kaiser Wilhelm I unifies Germany.

1874 British declare Gold Coast of Africa a colony.

1875 France's National Assembly votes to continue the Third Republic.

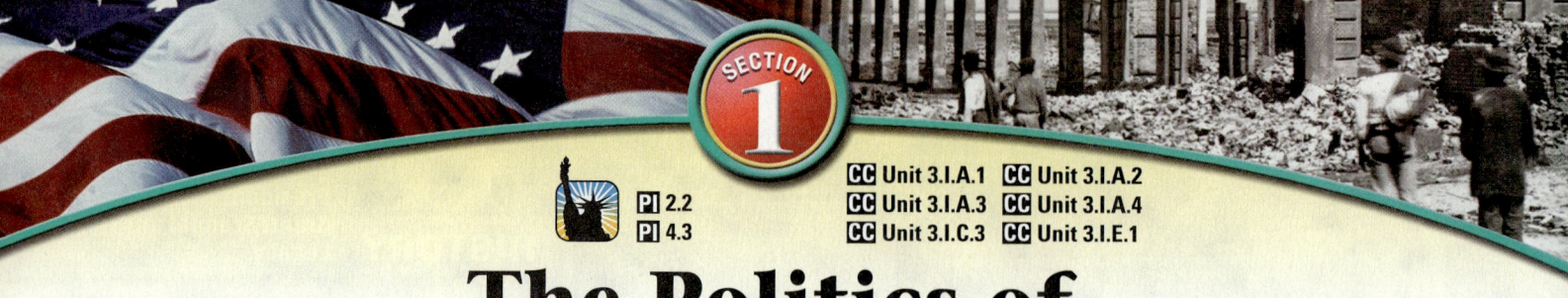

SECTION
1

PI 2.2
PI 4.3

CC Unit 3.I.A.1 CC Unit 3.I.A.2
CC Unit 3.I.A.3 CC Unit 3.I.A.4
CC Unit 3.I.C.3 CC Unit 3.I.E.1

The Politics of Reconstruction

MAIN IDEA	WHY IT MATTERS NOW	Terms & Names
Congress opposed Lincoln's and Johnson's plans for Reconstruction and instead implemented its own plan to rebuild the South.	Reconstruction was an important step in African Americans' struggle for civil rights.	• Andrew Johnson • Reconstruction • Radical Republicans • Thaddeus Stevens • Wade-Davis Bill / • Freedmen's Bureau • black codes • Fourteenth Amendment • impeach • Fifteenth Amendment

One American's Story

hmhsocialstudies.com
TAKING NOTES
Use the graphic organizer online to take notes on presidential Reconstruction and congressional Reconstruction.

As a young man, **Andrew Johnson**—who succeeded Abraham Lincoln as president—entered politics in Tennessee. He won several important offices, including those of congressman, governor, and U.S. senator.

After secession, Johnson was the only senator from a Confederate state to remain loyal to the Union. A former slave-owner, by 1863 Johnson supported abolition. He hated wealthy Southern planters, whom he held responsible for dragging poor whites into the war. Early in 1865, he endorsed harsh punishment for the rebellion's leaders.

A PERSONAL VOICE ANDREW JOHNSON

" **The time has arrived when the American people should understand what crime is, and that it should be punished, and its penalties enforced and inflicted. . . . Treason must be made odious . . . traitors must be punished and impoverished . . . their social power must be destroyed. I say, as to the leaders, punishment. I say leniency, conciliation, and amnesty to the thousands whom they have misled and deceived.** "

—quoted in *Reconstruction: The Ending of the Civil War*

▲
Andrew Johnson, the 17th president of the United States

On becoming president, Johnson faced not only the issue of whether to punish or pardon former Confederates but also a larger problem: how to bring the defeated Confederate states back into the Union.

Lincoln's Plan for Reconstruction

Reconstruction was the period during which the United States began to rebuild after the Civil War, lasting from 1865 to 1877. The term also refers to the process the federal government used to readmit the Confederate states. Complicating the process was the fact that Abraham Lincoln, Andrew Johnson, and Congress had differing ideas on how Reconstruction should be handled.

LINCOLN'S TEN-PERCENT PLAN Lincoln, before his death, had made it clear that he favored a lenient Reconstruction policy. Lincoln believed that secession was constitutionally impossible and therefore that the Confederate states had never left the Union. He contended that it was individuals, not states, who had rebelled and that the Constitution gave the president the power to pardon individuals. Lincoln wished to make the South's return to the Union as quick and easy as possible.

In December 1863, President Lincoln announced his Proclamation of Amnesty and Reconstruction, also known as the Ten-Percent Plan. The government would pardon all Confederates—except high-ranking Confederate officials and those accused of crimes against prisoners of war—who would swear allegiance to the Union. After ten percent of those on the 1860 voting lists took this oath of allegiance, a Confederate state could form a new state government and gain representation in Congress. **A**

MAIN IDEA

Summarizing

A What was President Lincoln's planned approach to Reconstruction?

Under Lincoln's terms, four states—Arkansas, Louisiana, Tennessee, and Virginia—moved toward readmission to the Union. However, Lincoln's moderate Reconstruction plan angered a minority of Republicans in Congress, known as **Radical Republicans.** Led by Senator Charles Sumner of Massachusetts and Representative **Thaddeus Stevens** of Pennsylvania, the Radicals wanted to destroy the political power of former slaveholders. Most of all, they wanted African Americans to be given full citizenship and the right to vote. In 1865, the idea of African-American suffrage was truly radical; no other country that had abolished slavery had given former slaves the vote.

RADICAL REACTION In July 1864, the Radicals responded to the Ten-Percent Plan by passing the **Wade-Davis Bill,** which proposed that Congress, not the president, be responsible for Reconstruction. It also declared that for a state government to be formed, a majority—not just ten percent—of those eligible to vote in 1860 would have to take a solemn oath to support the Constitution.

Lincoln used a pocket veto to kill the Wade-Davis Bill after Congress adjourned. According to the Constitution, a president has ten days to either sign or veto a bill passed by Congress. If the president does neither, the bill will automatically become law. When a bill is passed less than ten days before the end of a congressional session, the president can prevent its becoming law by simply ignoring, or "pocketing," it. The Radicals called Lincoln's pocket veto an outrage and asserted that Congress had supreme authority over Reconstruction. The stage was set for a presidential-congressional showdown.

KEY PLAYER

**THADDEUS STEVENS
1792–1868**

The Radical Republican leader Thaddeus Stevens had a commanding physical presence and was famous for his quick wit and sarcasm. One colleague called him "a rude jouster in political and personal warfare."

Before serving in Congress, he had practiced law in Pennsylvania, where he defended runaway slaves. Stevens hated slavery and in time came to hate white Southerners as well. He declared, "I look upon every man who would permit slavery . . . as a traitor to liberty and disloyal to God."

After Stevens died, at his own request he was buried in an integrated cemetery, because he wanted to show in death "the principles which I advocated throughout a long life: Equality of Man before his Creator."

Johnson's Plan

Lincoln's assassination in April 1865 left his successor, the Democrat Andrew Johnson, to deal with the Reconstruction controversy. A staunch Unionist, Johnson had often expressed his intent to deal harshly with Confederate leaders. Most white Southerners therefore considered Johnson a traitor to his region, while Radicals believed that he was one of them. Both were wrong.

Former Confederate officers George Washington Custis Lee, Robert E. Lee, and Walter Taylor, photographed in 1865

JOHNSON CONTINUES LINCOLN'S POLICIES In May 1865, with Congress in recess, Johnson announced his own plan, Presidential Reconstruction. He declared that each remaining Confederate state—Alabama, Florida, Georgia, Mississippi, North Carolina, South Carolina, and Texas—could be readmitted to the Union if it would meet several conditions. Each state would have to withdraw its secession, swear allegiance to the Union, annul Confederate war debts, and ratify the Thirteenth Amendment, which abolished slavery.

To the dismay of Thaddeus Stevens and the Radicals, Johnson's plan differed little from Lincoln's. The one major difference was that Johnson wished to prevent most high-ranking Confederates and wealthy Southern landowners from taking the oath needed for voting privileges. The Radicals were especially upset that Johnson's plan, like Lincoln's, failed to address the needs of former slaves in three areas: land, voting rights, and protection under the law. **B**

MAIN IDEA

Contrasting
B How did the views of Presidents Lincoln and Johnson on Reconstruction differ from the views of the Radicals?

If Johnson's policies angered Radicals, they relieved most white Southerners. Johnson's support of states' rights instead of a strong central government reassured the Southern states. Although Johnson supported abolition, he was not in favor of former slaves gaining the right to vote—he pardoned more than 13,000 former Confederates because he believed that "white men alone must manage the South."

The remaining Confederate states quickly agreed to Johnson's terms. Within a few months, these states—all except Texas—held conventions to draw up new state constitutions, to set up new state governments, and to elect representatives to Congress. However, some Southern states did not fully comply with the conditions for returning to the Union. For example, Mississippi did not ratify the Thirteenth Amendment.

Despite such instances of noncompliance, in December 1865, the newly elected Southern legislators arrived in Washington to take their seats. Fifty-eight of them had previously sat in the Congress of the Confederacy, six had served in the Confederate cabinet, and four had fought against the United States as Confederate generals. Johnson pardoned them all—a gesture that infuriated the Radicals and made African Americans feel they had been betrayed. In an 1865 editorial, an African-American newspaper publisher responded to Johnson's actions.

A PERSONAL VOICE PHILIP A. BELL

"The war does not appear to us to be ended, nor rebellion suppressed. They have commenced reconstruction on disloyal principles. If rebel soldiers are allowed to mumble through oaths of allegiance, and vote Lee's officers into important offices, and if Legislatures, elected by such voters, are allowed to define the provisions of the Amnesty Proclamation, then were our conquests vain. . . . Already we see the fruits of this failure on the part of Government to mete out full justice to the loyal blacks, and retribution to the disloyal whites."

—quoted in *Witness for Freedom: African American Voices on Race, Slavery, and Emancipation*

PRESIDENTIAL RECONSTRUCTION COMES TO A STANDSTILL When the 39th Congress convened in December 1865, the Radical Republican legislators, led by Thaddeus Stevens, disputed Johnson's claim that Reconstruction was complete. Many of them believed that the Southern states were not much different from the way they had been before the war. As a result, Congress refused to admit the newly elected Southern legislators.

At the same time, moderate Republicans pushed for new laws to remedy weaknesses they saw in Johnson's plan. In February 1866, Congress voted to continue and enlarge the **Freedmen's Bureau.** The bureau, established by Congress in the last month of the war, assisted former slaves and poor whites in the South by distributing clothing and food. In addition, the Freedmen's Bureau set up more than 40 hospitals, approximately 4,000 schools, 61 industrial institutes, and 74 teacher-training centers.

One important project of the Freedmen's Bureau was establishing primary schools, like the one shown here, for the children of former slaves.

CIVIL RIGHTS ACT OF 1866 Two months later, Congress passed the Civil Rights Act of 1866, which gave African Americans citizenship and forbade states from passing discriminatory laws—**black codes**—that severely restricted African Americans' lives. Mississippi and South Carolina had first enacted black codes in 1865, and other Southern states had rapidly followed suit.

Black codes had the effect of restoring many of the restrictions of slavery by prohibiting blacks from carrying weapons, serving on juries, testifying against whites, marrying whites, and traveling without permits. In some states, African Americans were forbidden to own land. Even worse, in many areas resentful whites used violence to keep blacks from improving their position in society. To many members of Congress, the passage of black codes indicated that the South had not given up the idea of keeping African Americans in bondage. **C**

MAIN IDEA

Analyzing Causes

C How did black codes help bring about the passage of the Civil Rights Act of 1866?

Johnson shocked everyone when he vetoed both the Freedmen's Bureau Act and the Civil Rights Act. Congress, Johnson contended, had gone far beyond anything "contemplated by the authors of the Constitution." These vetoes proved to be the opening shots in a battle between the president and Congress. By rejecting the two acts, Johnson alienated the moderate Republicans who were trying to improve his Reconstruction plan. He also angered the Radicals by appearing to support Southerners who denied African Americans their full rights. Johnson had not been in office a year when presidential Reconstruction ground to a halt.

Congressional Reconstruction

Angered by Johnson's actions, radical and moderate Republican factions decided to work together to shift the control of the Reconstruction process from the executive branch to the legislature, beginning a period of "congressional Reconstruction."

MODERATES AND RADICALS JOIN FORCES In mid-1866, moderate Republicans joined with Radicals to override the president's vetoes of the Civil Rights and Freedmen's Bureau acts. The Civil Rights Act of 1866 became the first major legislation ever enacted over a presidential veto. In addition, Congress drafted the **Fourteenth Amendment,** which provided a constitutional basis for the Civil Rights Act.

The Fourteenth Amendment made "all persons born or naturalized in the United States" citizens of the country. All were entitled to equal protection of the law, and no state could deprive any person of life, liberty, or property without due process of law. The amendment did not specifically give African Americans the vote. However, it did specify that if any state prevented a portion of its male citizens from voting, that state would lose a percentage of its congressional seats equal to the percentage of citizens kept from the polls. Another provision barred most Confederate leaders from holding federal or state offices unless they were permitted to do so by a two-thirds-majority vote of Congress. **D**

Congress adopted the Fourteenth Amendment and sent it to the states for approval. If the Southern states had voted to ratify it, most Northern legislators and their constituents would have been satisfied to accept them back into the Union. President Johnson, however, believed that the amendment treated former Confederate leaders too harshly and that it was wrong to force states to accept an amendment that their legislators had no part in drafting. Therefore, he advised the Southern states to reject the amendment. All but Tennessee did reject it, and the amendment was not ratified until 1868.

1866 CONGRESSIONAL ELECTIONS The question of who should control Reconstruction became one of the central issues in the bitter 1866 congressional elections. Johnson, accompanied by General Ulysses S. Grant, went on a speaking tour, urging voters to elect representatives who agreed with his Reconstruction policy. But his train trip from Washington to St. Louis and Chicago and back was a disaster. Johnson offended many voters with his rough language and behavior. His audiences responded by jeering at him and cheering Grant.

In addition, race riots in Memphis, Tennessee, and New Orleans, Louisiana, caused the deaths of at least 80 African Americans. Such violence convinced Northern voters that the federal government must step in to protect former slaves. In the 1866 elections, moderate and Radical Republicans won a landslide victory over Democrats. The Republicans gained a two-thirds majority in Congress, ensuring them the numbers they needed to override presidential vetoes. By March 1867, the 40th Congress was ready to move ahead with its Reconstruction policy. **E**

RECONSTRUCTION ACT OF 1867 Radicals and moderates joined in passing the Reconstruction Act of 1867, which did not recognize state governments formed under the Lincoln and Johnson plans—except for that of Tennessee, which had ratified the Fourteenth Amendment and had been readmitted to the Union. The act divided the other ten former Confederate states into five military districts, each headed by a Union general. The voters in the districts—including African-American men—would elect delegates to conventions in which new state

MAIN IDEA

Summarizing
D What were the main benefits that the Fourteenth Amendment offered African Americans?

MAIN IDEA

Analyzing Effects
E What effect did the election of 1866 have on Republicans' ability to carry out their plan for Reconstruction?

Major Reconstruction Legislation, 1865–1870

Legislation	Provisions
Freedmen's Bureau Acts (1865–1866)	Offered assistance, such as medical aid and education, to freed slaves and war refugees
Civil Rights Act of 1866	Granted citizenship and equal protection under the law to African Americans
Fourteenth Amendment (ratified 1868)	Makes all persons "born or naturalized in the United States" citizens; stipulates that states that prevented male citizens from voting would lose a percentage of their congressional seats; barred most Confederate leaders from holding political offices
Reconstruction Act of 1867	Abolished governments formed in the former Confederate states; divided those states into five military districts; set up requirements for readmission to the Union
Fifteenth Amendment (ratified 1870)	States that no one can be kept from voting because of "race, color, or previous condition of servitude"
Enforcement Act of 1870	Protected the voting rights of African Americans and gave the federal government power to enforce the Fifteenth Amendment

Southern Military Districts, 1867

Legend:
- General John Schofield
- General Daniel Sickles
- General John Pope
- General Edward Ord
- General Philip Sheridan

1868 Date state readmitted to the Union

0 — 150 — 300 miles
0 — 150 — 300 kilometers

VIRGINIA 1870
NORTH CAROLINA 1868
TENNESSEE (not in a military district) 1866
SOUTH CAROLINA 1868
ARKANSAS 1868
MISS. 1870
GEORGIA 1870
ALABAMA 1868
TEXAS 1870
LOUISIANA 1868
FLORIDA 1868

ATLANTIC OCEAN

GEOGRAPHY SKILLBUILDER
1. **Place** Which former Confederate state was not included in any military district?
2. **Place** When were the latest readmissions of former Confederate states? Which states were readmitted in this year?

constitutions would be drafted. In order for a state to reenter the Union, its constitution had to ensure African-American men the vote, and the state had to ratify the Fourteenth Amendment.

Johnson vetoed the Reconstruction Act of 1867 because he believed it was in conflict with the Constitution. Congress promptly overrode the veto.

JOHNSON IMPEACHED Radical leaders felt President Johnson was not carrying out his constitutional obligation to enforce the Reconstruction Act. For instance, Johnson removed military officers who attempted to enforce the act. The Radicals looked for grounds on which to **impeach** the president—that is, to formally charge him with misconduct in office. The House of Representatives has the sole power to impeach federal officials, who are then tried in the Senate.

In March 1867, Congress had passed the Tenure of Office Act, which stated that the president could not remove cabinet officers "during the term of the president by whom they may have been appointed" without the consent of the Senate. One purpose of this act was to protect Secretary of War Edwin Stanton, the Radicals' ally.

Johnson, along with many others, was certain that the Tenure of Office Act was unconstitutional. To force a court test of the act, Johnson fired Secretary of War Stanton. His action provided the Radicals with the opportunity they needed—the House brought 11 charges of impeachment against Johnson, 9 of which were based on his violation of the Tenure of Office Act. Johnson's lawyers disputed these charges by pointing out that President Lincoln, not Johnson, had appointed Secretary Stanton, so the act did not apply.

Johnson's trial before the Senate took place from March to May 1868. On the day the final vote was taken at the trial, tension

The lucky holders of tickets like this one could see Johnson's impeachment proceedings in 1868.

Reconstruction and Its Effects **381**

A campaign poster supporting the Republican ticket in the election of 1868

mounted in the jammed Senate galleries. Would the Radicals get the two-thirds vote needed for conviction? People in the Senate chamber held their breath as one by one the senators gave their verdicts. When the last senator declared "Not guilty," the vote was 35 to 19, one short of the two-thirds majority needed.

ULYSSES S. GRANT ELECTED The Democrats knew that they could not win the 1868 presidential election with Johnson, so they nominated the wartime governor of New York, Horatio Seymour. Seymour's Republican opponent was the Civil War hero Ulysses S. Grant. In November, Grant won the presidency by a wide margin in the electoral college, but the popular vote was less decisive. Out of almost 6 million ballots cast, Grant received a majority of only 306,592 votes. About 500,000 Southern African Americans had voted, most of them for Grant, bringing home the importance of the African-American vote to the Republican Party.

After the election, the Radicals feared that pro-Confederate Southern whites might try to limit black suffrage. Therefore, the Radicals introduced the **Fifteenth Amendment,** which states that no one can be kept from voting because of "race, color, or previous condition of servitude." The amendment would also affect Northern states, many of which at this time barred African Americans from voting.

The Fifteenth Amendment, which was ratified by the states in 1870, was an important victory for the Radicals. Some Southern governments refused to enforce the Fourteenth and Fifteenth Amendments, and some white Southerners used violence to prevent African Americans from voting. In response, Congress passed the Enforcement Act of 1870, giving the federal government more power to punish those who tried to prevent African Americans from exercising their rights.

Such political achievements were not, however, the only changes taking place during Reconstruction. The period was also a time of profound social and economic changes in the South.

SECTION 1 ASSESSMENT

1. TERMS & NAMES For each term or name, write a sentence explaining its significance.
- **Andrew Johnson**
- **Reconstruction**
- **Radical Republicans**
- **Thaddeus Stevens**
- **Wade-Davis Bill**
- **Freedmen's Bureau**
- **black codes**
- **Fourteenth Amendment**
- **impeach**
- **Fifteenth Amendment**

MAIN IDEA

2. TAKING NOTES
Fill in a chart like the one shown with features of presidential Reconstruction and congressional Reconstruction.

Presidential Reconstruction	Congressional Reconstruction

Why did presidential Reconstruction fail?

CRITICAL THINKING

3. HYPOTHESIZING
Describe how Reconstruction might have been different if Abraham Lincoln had lived.

4. INTERPRETING CHARTS
Look again at the chart on page 380. What was the primary focus of the major Reconstruction legislation?

5. EVALUATING DECISIONS
Do you think the Radical Republicans were justified in impeaching President Johnson? Why or why not? **Think About:**
- the controversy over Reconstruction policies
- the meaning of the Tenure of Office Act
- Johnson's vetoes

SECTION
2

PI 2.3
PI 4.1

CC Unit 3.I.A.4   CC Unit 3.I.C.1
CC Unit 3.I.C.2.a   CC Unit 3.I.C.5
CC Unit 3.I.E.2   CC Unit 3.I.E.5

Reconstructing Society

MAIN IDEA	WHY IT MATTERS NOW	Terms & Names
Various groups contributed to the rebuilding of Southern society after the war.	Many African-American institutions, including colleges and churches, were established during Reconstruction.	• scalawag • sharecropping • carpetbagger • tenant farming • Hiram Revels

One American's Story

hmhsocialstudies.com
TAKING NOTES

Use the graphic organizer online to take notes on problems facing the South after the Civil War and solutions that were offered for those problems.

Robert G. Fitzgerald, an African American, was born free in Delaware in 1840. During the Civil War, he served in both the U.S. Army and the U.S. Navy. In 1866, the Freedmen's Bureau sent Fitzgerald to teach in a small Virginia town. His students were former slaves of all ages who were hungry to learn reading, writing, spelling, arithmetic, and geography.

A PERSONAL VOICE ROBERT G. FITZGERALD

" I came to Virginia one year ago on the 22nd of this month. Erected a school, organized and named the Freedman's Chapel School. Now (June 29th) have about 60 who have been for several months engaged in the study of arithmetic, writing, etc. etc. This morning sent in my report accompanied with compositions from about 12 of my advanced writers instructed from the Alphabet up to their [present] condition, their progress has been surprisingly rapid. "

—quoted in *Proud Shoes*

▲
Robert Fitzgerald

Fitzgerald was one of many who labored diligently against the illiteracy and poverty that slavery had forced upon most African Americans. The need to help former slaves, however, was just one of many issues the nation confronted during Reconstruction.

Conditions in the Postwar South

Under the congressional Reconstruction program, state constitutional conventions met and Southern voters elected new, Republican-dominated governments. In 1868, the former Confederate states of Alabama, Arkansas, Florida, Louisiana, North Carolina, and South Carolina reentered the Union (joining Tennessee, which had reentered earlier). The remaining four former Confederate states completed the process by 1870. However, even after all the states were back in the Union, the Republicans did not end the process of Reconstruction because they wanted to make economic changes in the South.

Clearing battlefields of human remains was just one of many tasks facing Reconstruction governments.

PHYSICAL AND ECONOMIC CONDITIONS Because the Civil War was fought mostly on Southern soil, many of the new Southern state governments faced the challenge of physically rebuilding a battle-scarred region. The Union general William T. Sherman estimated that his troops alone had destroyed about $100 million worth of Confederate property in Georgia and South Carolina. Charred buildings, twisted railroad tracks, demolished bridges, neglected roads, and abandoned farms had to be restored or replaced.

The economic effects of the war were devastating for the South. Property values had plummeted. Those who had invested in Confederate bonds had little hope of recovering their money. Many small farms were ruined or in disrepair. As a result of these and other factors, Southerners of every economic class were poorer than they had been at the start of the war. In one county of Alabama, for example, the wealth per capita among whites dropped from $18,000 in 1860 to about $3,000 in 1870.

Not only were many of the South's economic resources destroyed, but the region's population was devastated. More than one-fifth of the adult white men of the Confederacy died in the war. Many of those who did return from battle were maimed for life. Tens of thousands of Southern African-American men also died, either fighting for the Union or working in Confederate labor camps. **A**

PUBLIC WORKS PROGRAMS The Republican governments built roads, bridges, and railroads and established orphanages and institutions for the care of people with mental illnesses and disabilities. They also created the first public school systems that most Southern states had ever had.

These ambitious projects—and the larger state governments that were required to administer them—were expensive. Few financial resources were available, and Northern capitalists were reluctant to invest in the region. To raise money, most Southern state governments increased taxes of all kinds, draining existing resources and slowing the region's recovery.

MAIN IDEA

Identifying Problems
A What were the main postwar problems that Reconstruction governments in the South had to solve?

◀ Southern families like this one lost their homes and most of their possessions because of economic problems after the Civil War.

Politics in the Postwar South

Another difficulty facing the new Republican governments was that different groups within the Republican Party in the South often had conflicting goals.

SCALAWAGS AND CARPETBAGGERS Although the terms *scalawag* and *carpetbagger* were negative labels imposed by political enemies, historians still use the terms when referring to the two groups. Democrats, opposed to the Republicans' plan for Reconstruction, called white Southerners who joined the Republican Party **scalawags.** Some scalawags hoped to gain political offices with the help of the African-American vote and then use those offices to enrich themselves. Southern Democrats unfairly pointed to these unscrupulous individuals as representative of all white Southern Republicans. Some so-called scalawags honestly thought that a Republican government offered the best chances for the South to rebuild and industrialize. The majority were small farmers who wanted to improve their economic and political position and to prevent the former wealthy planters from regaining power.

The Democrats used an equally unflattering name for the Northerners who moved to the South after the war—**carpetbaggers.** The name referred to the belief that Northerners arrived with so few belongings that everything could fit in a carpetbag, a small piece of luggage made of carpeting. Most white Southerners believed that the carpetbaggers wanted to exploit the South's postwar turmoil for their own profit. However, like the scalawags, carpetbaggers had mixed motives. Some were Freedmen's Bureau agents, teachers, and ministers who felt a moral duty to help former slaves. Others wanted to buy land or hoped to start new industries legitimately. Still others truly were the dishonest businesspeople whom the Southerners scorned. **B**

MAIN IDEA

Comparing

B What were some similarities in the goals of scalawags and carpetbaggers? of carpetbaggers and African Americans?

Northerners were thought to carry their belongings in carpetbags such as this one. ▼

Analyzing *Political Cartoons*

UNWELCOME GUEST

Of all the political cartoonists of the 19th century, Thomas Nast (1840–1902) had the greatest and most long-lasting influence. Nast created symbols that have become part of America's visual heritage, symbols that include the Democratic donkey, the Republican elephant, and Santa Claus.

This cartoon from a Southern Democratic newspaper depicts Carl Schurz, a liberal Republican who advocated legal equality for African Americans. Schurz is shown as a carpetbagger trudging down a dusty Southern road as a crowd of people watch his arrival.

SKILLBUILDER Analyzing Political Cartoons
1. Is Schurz shown in a positive or negative light? How can you tell?
2. Why do you think the cartoonist portrays the Southern people standing in a group, far away from Schurz?

 SEE SKILLBUILDER HANDBOOK, PAGE R24.

▲
This woodcut from a newspaper shows freedmen voting in Washington, D.C., June 1867.

AFRICAN AMERICANS AS VOTERS

African Americans—who made up the largest group of Southern Republicans—gained voting rights as a result of the Fifteenth Amendment. During Reconstruction, African-American men registered to vote for the first time; nine out of ten of them supported the Republican Party. Although most former slaves had little experience with politics, and relatively few could read and write, they were eager to exercise their voting rights.

A PERSONAL VOICE
WILLIAM BEVERLY NASH

"We are not prepared for this suffrage. But we can learn. Give a man tools and let him commence to use them and in time he will earn a trade. So it is with voting. We may not understand it at the start, but in time we shall learn to do our duty."

—quoted in *The Trouble They Seen: Black People Tell the Story of Reconstruction*

In many areas of the South, almost 90 percent of the qualified African-American voters voted. Early in 1868, a Northerner in Alabama observed that "in defiance of fatigue, hardship, hunger, and threats of employers," African Americans still flocked to the polls.

POLITICAL DIFFERENCES Conflicting goals among Republican Party members led to disunity in the party's ranks. In particular, few scalawags shared the Republican commitment to civil rights and suffrage for African Americans. Over time, many of them returned to the Democratic Party.

In addition, some Republican governors began to appoint white Democrats to office in an attempt to persuade more white voters to vote Republican. This policy backfired—it convinced very few white Democrats to change parties, and it made blacks feel betrayed.

The new status of African Americans required fundamental changes in the attitudes of most Southern whites. Some whites supported the Republicans during Reconstruction and thought that the end of slavery would ultimately benefit the South. In addition, some Southern farmers and merchants thought that investment by Northerners would help the South recover from the war. Many white Southerners, though, refused to accept blacks' new status and resisted the idea of equal rights. A Freedmen's Bureau agent noted that some "Southern whites are quite indignant if they are not treated with the same deference as they were accustomed to" under the system of slavery.

Moreover, white Southerners had to accept defeat and the day-to-day involvement of Northerners in their lives. Eva B. Jones, the wife of a former Confederate officer, understood how difficult that adjustment was for many. In a letter to her mother-in-law, she expressed emotions that were typical of those felt by many ex-Confederates.

MAIN IDEA

Analyzing Motives

C What do you think the former Confederates who emigrated hoped to accomplish?

★ **A PERSONAL VOICE** EVA B. JONES

" A joyless future of probable ignominy, poverty, and want is all that spreads before us. . . . You see, it is with no resigned spirit that *I* yield to the iron yoke our conqueror forges for his fallen and powerless foe. The degradation of a whole country and a proud people is indeed a mighty, an all-enveloping sorrow. "

—quoted in *The Children of Pride: A True Story of Georgia and the Civil War*

Not all white Southerners were willing to remain in the South. Several thousand planters emigrated to Europe, Mexico, and Brazil after the war. **C**

Former Slaves Face Many Challenges

Amid the turmoil of the South during Reconstruction, African Americans looked forward to new opportunities. Slaves had been forbidden to travel without permission, to marry legally, to attend school, and to live and work as they chose. After the war, the 4 million former slaves gained the chance to take control of their lives.

NEW-WON FREEDOMS At first, many former slaves were cautious about testing the limits of their freedom. One freedman explained, "We was afraid to move. Just like . . . turtles after emancipation. Just stick our heads out to see how the land lay." As the reality of freedom sank in, freed African Americans faced many decisions. Without land, jobs, tools, money, and with few skills besides those of farming, what were they to do? How would they feed and clothe themselves? How and where would they live?

During slavery, slaves were forbidden to travel without a pass. White planters had enforced that rule by patrolling the roads. During Reconstruction, African Americans took advantage of their new freedom to go where they wanted. One former slave from Texas explained the passion for traveling: "They seemed to want to get closer to freedom, so they'd know what it was—like it was a place or a city."

The majority of freed African Americans who moved, however, were not just testing their freedom. Thousands were eager to leave plantations that they associated with oppression and move to Southern towns and cities where they could find jobs. From 1865 to 1870, the African-American population of the ten largest Southern cities doubled.

REUNIFICATION OF FAMILIES Slavery had split many African-American families apart; spouses sometimes lived on different plantations, and children were often separated from their parents. During Reconstruction, many freed African Americans took advantage of their new mobility to search for loved ones. In 1865, for example, one man walked more than 600 miles from Georgia to North Carolina, looking for his wife and children.

Many former slaves bought charts like this one to keep track of their family histories. ▼

▼

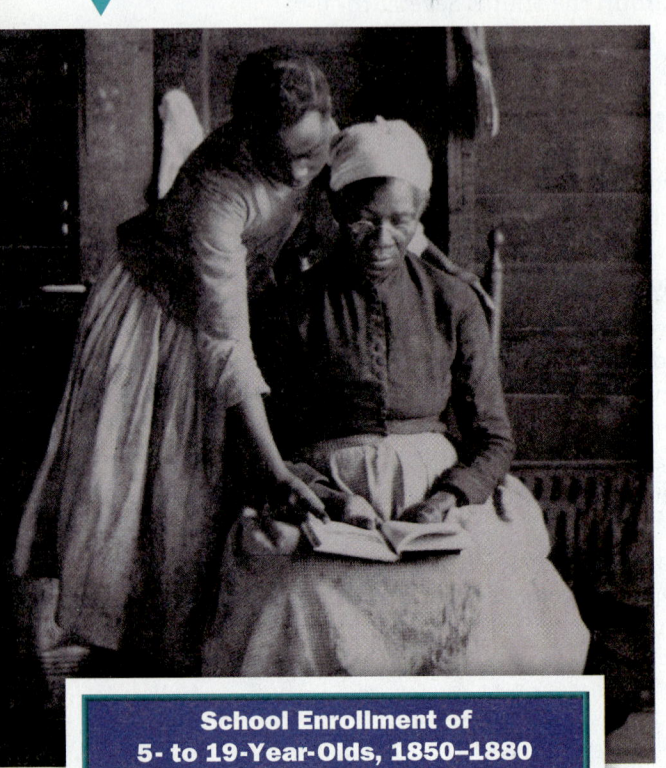

The Freedmen's Bureau worked to reunite families, and African-American newspapers printed poignant "Information Wanted" notices about missing relatives. Tragically, in many cases the lost family members were never found. However, freed persons, who had been denied legal unions under slavery, could now marry legally, and raise children without the fear that someone would sell them. For African Americans, reconstructing their families was an important part of establishing an identity as a free people.

EDUCATION Because slaves had been punished if they tried to learn how to read and write, nearly 80 percent of freed African Americans over the age of 20 were illiterate in 1870. During Reconstruction, however, freed people of all ages—grandparents, parents, and children alike—sought education.

African Americans established educational institutions with assistance from a number of public and private organizations, including the Freedmen's Bureau and African-American churches. One college founded during Reconstruction was Hampton Institute in Hampton, Virginia. By 1870, African Americans had spent more than $1 million on education. Initially, most teachers in black schools were Northern whites, about half of whom were women. However, educated African Americans like Robert G. Fitzgerald also became teachers, and by 1869, black teachers outnumbered whites in these schools.

Some white Southerners, outraged by the idea of educated African Americans, responded violently. In one instance, the former slave Washington Eager was murdered because, as his brother explained, he had become "too big a man . . . he [could] write and read and put it down himself." Despite the threat of violence, freed people were determined to learn. By 1877, more than 600,000 African Americans were enrolled in elementary schools.

CHURCHES AND VOLUNTEER GROUPS During slavery many plantation slaves had attended white churches and camp meetings with their owners. Resenting the preachers who urged them to obey their masters, the slaves had also held their own religious gatherings called "praise meetings."

After the war many African Americans founded their own churches, which were usually Baptist or Methodist, and held services similar to the earlier praise meetings. Because churches were the principal institutions that African Americans fully controlled, African-American ministers emerged as influential community leaders. They often played an important role in the broader political life of the country as well.

School Enrollment of 5- to 19-Year-Olds, 1850–1880

Percent enrolled (y-axis: 0, 10, 20, 30, 40, 50, 60, 70, 80, 90, 100)
(x-axis: 1850, 1860, 1870, 1880)

■ White   ■ Black and other races

Source: *Historical Statistics of the United States, Colonial Times to 1970*

SKILLBUILDER Interpreting Graphs
How might you explain why white school enrollment decreased between 1860 and 1870 while enrollment of others increased?

Besides organizing their own schools and churches, freed African Americans formed thousands of volunteer organizations. They established their own fire companies, trade associations, political organizations, and drama groups, to name just a few. These groups not only fostered independence but also provided financial and emotional support for their members, while offering African Americans opportunities to gain the leadership skills that slavery had often denied them.

POLITICS AND AFRICAN AMERICANS The period from 1865 to 1877 saw growing African-American involvement in politics at all levels. For the first time, African Americans held office in local, state, and federal government. At first, most African Americans in politics were freeborn. Many of these black officeholders were ministers or teachers who had been educated in the North. By 1867, however, former slaves were playing an increasing role in political organizations and were winning a greater number of offices.

Nevertheless, even though there were almost as many black citizens as white citizens in the South, African-American officeholders remained in the minority. Only South Carolina had a black majority in the state legislature. No Southern state elected an African-American governor. Moreover, out of 125 Southerners elected to the U.S. Congress during congressional Reconstruction, only 16 were African Americans. Among these was **Hiram Revels,** the first African-American senator. **D**

LAWS AGAINST SEGREGATION By the end of 1866, most of the Republican Southern state governments had repealed the black codes. African-American legislators took social equality a step further by proposing bills to desegregate public transportation. In 1871, Texas passed a law prohibiting railroads from making distinctions between groups of passengers, and several other states followed suit. However, many antisegregation laws were not enforced. State orphanages, for example, usually had separate facilities for white and black children.

African Americans themselves focused more on building up the black community than on total integration. By establishing separate African-American institutions—such as schools, churches, and political and social organizations—they were able to focus on African-American leadership and escape the interference of the whites who had so long dominated their lives.

> **MAIN IDEA**
>
> **Summarizing**
> **D** How did freed African Americans try to improve their lives?

Changes in the Southern Economy

When asked to explain the idea of freedom, Garrison Frazier, a former slave turned Baptist minister, said that freedom consisted in "placing us where we could reap the fruit of our own labor." To accomplish this, Frazier said, freed African Americans needed "to have land, and turn it and till it." Few former slaves, however, had enough money to buy land, and those who did have cash were frequently frustrated by whites' refusal to sell property to them.

40 ACRES AND A MULE In January 1865, during the Civil War, General Sherman had promised the freed slaves who followed his army 40 acres per family and the use of army mules. Soon afterward, about 40,000 freed persons settled on 400,000 abandoned or forfeited acres in coastal Georgia and South Carolina. The freed African Americans farmed their plots until August 1865, when President Johnson ordered that the original landowners be allowed to reclaim their land and evict the former slaves.

Many freed African Americans asserted that they deserved part of the planters' land. An Alabama black convention declared, "The property which they hold was nearly all earned by the sweat of *our* brows." Some Radical Republicans agreed. Thaddeus Stevens called for the government to confiscate plantations and to redistribute part of the land to former slaves. However, many Republicans considered it wrong to seize citizens' private property. As a result, Congress either rejected land-reform proposals or passed weak legislation. An example was the 1866 Southern Homestead Act. Although it set aside 44 million acres in the South for freed blacks and loyal whites, the land was swampy and unsuitable for farming. Furthermore, few homesteaders had the resources—seed, tools, plows, and horses—to farm successfully. **E**

RESTORATION OF PLANTATIONS Although African Americans and poor whites wanted to own small farms, the planter class wanted to restore the plantation system, in which many acres were devoted to a single profitable cash crop, such as cotton. Some wealthy Northern merchants and owners of textile mills encouraged the planters in their efforts to reestablish plantations and resume widespread cotton production.

Planters claimed that to make the plantation system work, they needed to have almost complete control over their laborers.

Before the abolition of slavery, planters had forced young and old and men and women to work in the fields for extremely long hours. Now the planters feared that they might not be able to make a profit, since they had to pay their laborers and could no longer force field hands to put in such brutally long workdays. In addition, many former slaveholders deeply resented having to negotiate for the services of former slaves.

Planters also faced a labor shortage, caused by a number of factors. The high death toll of the war had reduced the number of able-bodied workers. Many African-American women and children refused to work in the fields after they were freed. Finally, many freed persons felt that raising cotton under the direction of white overseers was too much like slavery.

As an alternative, some former slaves worked in mills or on railroad-construction crews. Others tried subsistence farming—growing just enough food for their own families. To stop this trend, white planters were determined to keep the former slaves from getting land that they could use to support themselves.

MAIN IDEA

Identifying Problems
E What caused land-reform proposals to fail?

SHARECROPPING AND TENANT FARMING Without their own land, freed African Americans could not grow crops to sell or to feed their families. Economic necessity thus forced many former slaves to sign labor contracts with planters. In exchange for wages, housing, and food, freedmen worked in the fields. Although the Freedmen's Bureau promoted this wage-labor system, the arrangement did not satisfy either freedmen or planters. On the one hand, freedmen thought that the wages were too low and that white employers had too much control over them. On the other hand, planters often lacked sufficient cash to pay workers. These conditions led planters and laborers to experiment with two alternative arrangements: sharecropping and tenant farming.

In the system of **sharecropping,** landowners divided their land and gave each worker—either freed African American or poor white—a few acres, along with seed and tools. At harvest time, each worker gave a share of his crop, usually half, to the landowner. This share paid the owner back and ended the arrangement until it was renewed the following year.

In theory, "croppers" who saved a little and bought their own tools could drive a better bargain with landowners. They might even rent land for cash from the planters, and keep all their harvest, in a system known as **tenant farming.** Eventually they might move up the economic ladder to become outright owners of their farms.

A sharecropper works a Georgia cotton field in 1870. ▼

Sharecropping

hmhsocialstudies.com **INTERACTIVE**

A CYCLE OF POVERTY

Sharecroppers were supposed to have a chance to climb the economic ladder, but by the time they had shared their crops and paid their debts, they rarely had any money left. A sharecropper often became tied to one plantation, having no choice but to work until his or her debts were paid.

1. Sharecroppers are given small plots of land and seed by the landowners.

2. Sharecroppers buy food, clothing, and supplies on credit.

3. They plant a crop. (Yields are low, and the same crop year after year depletes the soil.)

4. Sharecroppers must give the landlords a large share of the harvested crops.

5. Sharecroppers sell what crops remain but are at the mercy of low market prices.

6. Sharecroppers pay off accounts. Some landlords and merchants charge unjust fines for late payments.

7. A few sharecroppers with leftover cash might become tenant farmers.

SKILLBUILDER *Interpreting Charts*
How did the sharecropping system make it hard for small farmers to improve their standard of living?
SEE SKILLBUILDER HANDBOOK, PAGE R27.

One successful Southern industry was the manufacture of tobacco products.

The arrangement seldom worked that way in practice, however. Most tenant farmers bought their supplies on credit, often from merchants who charged them inflated prices. Farmers rarely harvested enough crops to pay for both past debts and future supplies. The end result was that very few farmers saved enough cash to buy land.

COTTON NO LONGER KING Another economic change turned Southern agriculture upside down: cotton was no longer king. During the war, demand for Southern cotton had begun to drop as other countries increased their cotton production. As a result, prices plummeted after the war. In 1869, the price of cotton was 16.5 cents per pound. By the late 1870s, the price had fallen to about 8 cents per pound. Instead of diversifying—or varying—their crops, Southern planters tried to make up for the lower prices by growing more cotton—an oversupply that only drove down prices even further.

The South's agricultural problems did lead to attempts to diversify the region's economy. Textile mills sprang up, and a new industry—tobacco-product manufacturing—took hold. Diversification helped raise the average wage in the South, though it was still much lower than that of Northern workers.

At the end of the Civil War, most of the state banks in the South were saddled with Confederate debts—loans made to the Confederate government. The banks awaited repayment that, in most cases, would never come. In the following years, falling cotton prices and mounting planters' debts caused many banks to fail. The only credit that Southerners in rural areas could get was that offered by local merchants. Despite efforts to improve the Southern economy, the devastating economic impact of the Civil War rippled through Southern life into the 20th century. **F**

Many whites, frustrated by their loss of political power and by the South's economic stagnation, took out their anger on African Americans. In the late 1860s and early 1870s, certain white groups embarked on a campaign to terrorize African Americans into giving up their political rights and their efforts at economic improvement.

> **MAIN IDEA**
>
> **Analyzing Causes**
> **F** What factors contributed to the stagnation of the Southern economy?

ASSESSMENT

1. **TERMS & NAMES** For each term or name, write a sentence explaining its significance.
   - •scalawag
   - •carpetbagger
   - •Hiram Revels
   - •sharecropping
   - •tenant farming

MAIN IDEA

2. **TAKING NOTES**
   In a chart like the one shown, list five problems facing the South after the Civil War and at least one attempted solution for each one.

Problem	Attempted Solution

CRITICAL THINKING

3. **FORMING GENERALIZATIONS**
   How did the Civil War weaken the Southern economy? Give examples to support your answer.

4. **ANALYZING ISSUES**
   Thaddeus Stevens believed that giving land to former slaves was more important than giving them the vote. Do you agree or disagree? Why?

5. **EVALUATING**
   Which accomplishment of African Americans during Reconstruction do you consider most significant? Explain your choice. **Think About:**
   - the development of a free African-American community
   - the lingering effects of slavery
   - opportunities for leadership

The Collapse of Reconstruction

MAIN IDEA	WHY IT MATTERS NOW	Terms & Names
Southern opposition to Radical Reconstruction, along with economic problems in the North, ended Reconstruction.	The failure of Congress and the Supreme Court to protect the rights of African Americans during Reconstruction delayed blacks' achievement of full civil rights by over a century.	• Ku Klux Klan (KKK) • panic of 1873 • redemption • Rutherford B. Hayes • Samuel J. Tilden • Compromise of 1877 • home rule

One American's Story

In 1868, white Georgia legislators, who were in the majority in both houses, expelled 27 black members of the state senate and House of Representatives. The new state constitution gave African Americans the right to vote, they argued, but not to hold office. Outraged by this expulsion, Henry M. Turner, an African-American legislator, addressed the Georgia House of Representatives.

A PERSONAL VOICE   HENRY M. TURNER

"Whose Legislature is this? Is it a white man's Legislature or is it a black man's . . . ? . . . It is said that Congress never gave us the right to hold office. I want to know . . . if the Reconstruction measures did not base their action on the ground that no distinction should be made on account of race, color or previous condition! . . . We have built up your country. We have worked in your fields, and garnered your harvests, for two hundred and fifty years! Do we ask you for compensation? . . . We are willing to let the dead past bury its dead; but we ask you, now, for our RIGHTS."

—quoted in *The Trouble They Seen: Black People Tell the Story of Reconstruction*

▲ Henry M. Turner became a leading proponent of African-American emigration to Africa.

The expelled legislators petitioned the U.S. Congress and were eventually reinstated in office. But by the time Congress acted, more than a year later, the terms of Turner and his colleagues were almost at an end.

Opposition to Reconstruction

White Southerners who took direct action against African-American participation in government were in the minority. Most white Southerners swallowed whatever resentment they felt over African Americans' change in status. However, some bitter Southern whites relied on violence to keep African Americans from participating in politics.

KU KLUX KLAN Founded as a social club for Confederate veterans, the **Ku Klux Klan (KKK)** started in Tennessee in 1866. As membership in the group spread rapidly through the South, many of the new chapters turned into violent terrorist organizations. By 1868, the Klan existed in practically every Southern state. Its overarching goal was to restore white supremacy. Its method was to prevent African Americans from exercising their political rights. Between 1868 and 1871, the Klan and other secret groups killed thousands of men, women, and children, and burned schools, churches, and property.

Abram Colby, who organized a branch of Georgia's Equal Rights Association and later served as a Republican member of the Georgia legislature, testified before Congress about Klan atrocities.

▲ Klan members wore costumes to conceal their identities and to appear more menacing. These Klan members were captured in an Alabama riot in 1868.

A PERSONAL VOICE ABRAM COLBY

" [The Klan] broke my door open, took me out of bed, took me to the woods and whipped me three hours or more and left me for dead. They said to me, 'Do you think you will ever vote another damned radical ticket?' . . . I supposed they would kill me anyhow. I said, 'If there was an election tomorrow, I would vote the radical ticket.' They set in and whipped me a thousand licks more, with sticks and straps that had buckles on the ends of them. "

—quoted in *Testimony Taken by the Joint Select Committee to Inquire into the Condition of Affairs in the Late Insurrectionary States*

While the vast majority of the Klan's victims were African-American, whites who tried to help African Americans—whether by educating them, renting land to them, or buying their crops—were also in danger.

Another Klan objective was to turn the Republicans, who had established the Reconstruction governments, out of power. The North Carolina state senator John Stephens, a white Republican, answered warnings that his life was in danger by saying that some 3,000 African-American voters had supported him "at the risk of persecution and starvation" and that he would not abandon them. Stephens was assassinated in 1870.

While Klan members tried to conceal their identities when they struck, Southern Democrats openly used violence to intimidate Republicans before the 1875 state election in Mississippi. Democrats rioted and attacked Republican leaders and prominent African Americans. Their terrorist campaign frightened the African-American majority away from the polls, and white Democratic candidates swept the election. The Democrats used similar tactics to win the 1876 elections in Florida, South Carolina, and Louisiana. **A**

ECONOMIC PRESSURE The Klan and other secret groups tried to prevent African Americans from making economic, as well as political, progress. African Americans who owned their own land or who worked in occupations other than agriculture were subject to attacks and destruction of property.

In fact, economic necessity forced most former slaves—who had little money or training in other occupations—to work for whites as wage laborers or sharecroppers. Some white Southerners refused to hire or do business with African Americans who were revealed by election officials to have voted Republican. The fear of economic reprisals kept many former slaves from voting at all.

> **MAIN IDEA**
>
> **Analyzing Motives**
> **A** What were the goals of the KKK?

LEGISLATIVE RESPONSE To curtail Klan violence and Democratic intimidation, Congress passed a series of Enforcement Acts in 1870 and 1871. One act provided for the federal supervision of elections in Southern states. Another act gave the president the power to use federal troops in areas where the Klan was active. However, President Grant was not aggressive in his use of the power given to him by the Enforcement Acts, and in 1882, the Supreme Court ruled that the 1871 Enforcement Act was unconstitutional.

Although federal enforcement of anti-Klan legislation was limited, it did contribute to a decrease in the Klan's activities in the late 1870s. However, the reason for the reduction in Klan violence was the Klan's own success—by 1880, terrorist groups had managed to restore white supremacy throughout the South. The Klan no longer needed such organized activity to limit the political and civil rights of most African Americans. **B**

MAIN IDEA

Identifying Problems

B Why was the government weak in its ability to confront the Klan?

Vocabulary
amnesty: a pardon granted by a government, especially for political offenses

SHIFTS IN POLITICAL POWER By passing the Enforcement Acts, Congress seemed to shore up Republican power. But shortly after these acts went into effect, Congress passed legislation that severely weakened the Republican Party in the South.

With the Amnesty Act, passed in May 1872, Congress returned the right to vote and the right to hold federal and state offices—revoked by the Fourteenth Amendment—to about 150,000 former Confederates, who would almost certainly vote Democratic. In the same year Congress allowed the Freedmen's Bureau to expire, believing that it had fulfilled its purpose. As a result of these actions, Southern Democrats had an opportunity to shift the balance of political power in their favor.

Scandals and Money Crises Hurt Republicans

As Southern Republicans struggled to maintain their hold on Reconstruction governments, widespread political corruption in the federal government weakened their party. During the early 1870s, scandals plagued the Grant administration. These scandals diverted public attention away from conditions in the South.

FRAUD AND BRIBERY President Grant was considered an honest man. However, he had had no political experience before becoming president and found it difficult to believe that others might use him for their own political advantage. When making political appointments, he often selected friends and acquaintances rather than people of proven ability. Too frequently, Grant's appointees turned out to be dishonest.

Beginning in 1872, a series of long-simmering scandals associated with Grant's administration boiled over. First, a newspaper exposed how the Crédit Mobilier, a construction company working for the Union Pacific Railroad, had skimmed off large profits from the railroad's government contract. Implicated were several top Republicans, including Vice-President Schuyler Colfax.

REPUBLICAN UNITY SHATTERED A group of Republicans, angered by the corruption, called for honest, efficient government. They formed the Liberal Republican Party in 1872, hoping to oust Grant in that year's presidential election.

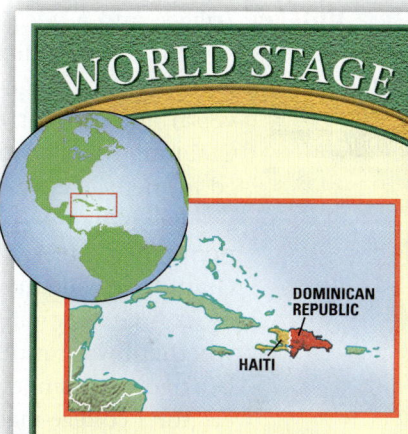

WORLD STAGE

THE DOMINICAN REPUBLIC
Although the United States focused largely on domestic problems during Reconstruction, the nation did have one significant dealing with a foreign power. In 1870, President Grant attempted to annex the Dominican Republic, one of two nations sharing the Caribbean island of Hispaniola (the other being Haiti).

This action aroused a storm of controversy. The plan's supporters believed that annexation would increase Caribbean trade and spread "the blessings of our free institutions." Opponents pointed out that the Dominican Republic was caught up in a civil war and felt that the United States should avoid involvement in the conflict. The Senate rejected the annexation treaty.

Analyzing *Political Cartoons*

SCANDAL IN THE GRANT ADMINISTRATION

Political cartoonists had a field day with Grant's troubles and often criticized the president's refusal to believe that his associates were dishonest. In this cartoon, President Grant pulls packets labeled with the names of various scandals out of a barrel. The caption—"I hope I get to the bottom soon"— suggests that the corruption in Grant's administration runs deep and that there may be more scandals to come.

SKILLBUILDER Analyzing Political Cartoons
1. What political scandals can you identify from the packets lying outside the barrel?
2. Why do you think the cartoonist portrayed Grant as having his head stuck in a barrel?

 SEE SKILLBUILDER HANDBOOK, PAGE R24.

U. S. Grant: "I hope I get to the bottom soon."

VIDEO
President Ulysses
S. Grant: Scandal
and Legacy

 hmhsocialstudies.com

As the 1872 presidential election approached, the Liberal Republicans held a separate convention. They chose Horace Greeley, the editor of the *New York Tribune* and a vocal pre-Civil War abolitionist, as their candidate. He had supported some Radical Republican causes—abolition and the Fourteenth and Fifteenth Amendments. However, he had broken with Radicals by calling for universal amnesty for Confederates and for an end to military rule in the South. Claiming that Reconstruction governments had achieved their purpose, he wanted former slaves to fend for themselves.

Believing that it would take a united effort to oust Grant, the Democrats also nominated Greeley. Nevertheless, Greeley lost the 1872 presidential election to Grant by a wide margin. "I was the worst beaten man that ever ran for that high office," Greeley said, "and I have been assailed so bitterly that I hardly know whether I was running for President or the penitentiary." Physically exhausted by his rigorous campaign, Greeley died a few weeks after the election—before the electoral college made his defeat official.

Although the Liberal Republicans did not win the White House, they did weaken the Radicals' hold over the Republican Party. The breakdown of Republican unity made it even harder for the Radicals to continue to impose their Reconstruction plan on the South.

CONTINUED SCANDAL Despite the rift in the Republican party that resulted from the scandals, corruption in Grant's administration continued. In 1875, the so-called Whiskey Ring was exposed. Internal-revenue collectors and other officials accepted bribes from whiskey distillers who wanted to avoid paying taxes on their product—a conspiracy that defrauded the federal government of millions of dollars. One of the 238 persons indicted in this scandal was Grant's private secretary, General Orville E. Babcock. Grant refused to believe that such a close associate was guilty and helped him escape conviction.

Finally, in 1876, an investigation revealed that Secretary of War William W. Belknap had accepted bribes from merchants who wanted to keep their profitable trading concessions in Indian territory. The House of Representatives impeached Belknap, who promptly resigned. The public also learned that the secretary of the navy had taken bribes from shipbuilders and the secretary of the interior had had shady dealings with land speculators. As the evidence mounted, there was increasing disgust with the blatant corruption in the Grant administration, and Grant did not seek reelection in 1876. **C**

MAIN IDEA

Summarizing
C Give examples of corruption in the Grant administration.

Economic Turmoil

As if political scandals were not enough for the country to deal with, a wave of economic troubles hit the nation in 1873.

THE PANIC OF 1873 The economy had been expanding since the end of the Civil War, and investors became convinced that business profits would continue to increase indefinitely. Eager to take advantage of new business opportunities in the South, Northern and Southern investors borrowed increasing amounts of money and built new facilities as quickly as possible.

Unfortunately, many of those who invested in these new businesses took on more debt than they could afford. A Philadelphia banker named Jay Cooke invested heavily in railroads. Not enough investors bought shares in Cooke's railroad lines to cover his ballooning construction costs, and he could not pay his debts. In September 1873, Cooke's banking firm, the nation's largest dealer in government securities, went bankrupt, setting off a series of financial failures known as the **panic of 1873.** Smaller banks closed, and the stock market temporarily collapsed. Within a year, 89 railroads went broke. By 1875, more than 18,000 companies had folded. The panic triggered a five-year economic depression—a period of reduced business activity and high unemployment—in which 3 million workers lost their jobs. **D**

MAIN IDEA

Predicting Effects

D What effect do you think the panic of 1873 might have had on the Republican Party?

CURRENCY DISPUTE The economic depression following the panic of 1873 also fueled a dispute over currency. This dispute had its roots in the Civil War. During the war, the federal government had begun to issue greenbacks, paper money that was not backed by equal value in gold. When the war ended, many financial experts advocated withdrawing the greenbacks and returning the nation completely to a currency backed by gold. This action would have reduced the number of dollars in circulation.

In contrast, Southern and Western farmers and manufacturers wanted the government to issue even more greenbacks. They believed that "easy money"—a large money supply—would help them pay off their debts.

In 1875, Congress passed the Specie Resumption Act, which promised to put the country back on the gold standard. This act sparked further debate over monetary policies. As the economy improved, beginning in 1878, the controversy died down. However, the passionate debate over the money question in the 1870s was one of many factors that drew the attention of voters and politicians away from Reconstruction.

Judicial and Popular Support Fades

In 1874, a Southern Democratic senator wrote, "*Radicalism* is dissolving—going to pieces." Indeed, political scandals, economic problems, and the restoration of political rights to former Confederate Democrats seriously weakened the Radical Republicans. In addition, the Supreme Court began to undo some of the social and political changes that the Radicals had made.

SUPREME COURT DECISIONS Although Congress had passed important laws to protect the political and civil rights of African Americans, the Supreme Court began to take away those same protections. During the 1870s, the Court issued a series of decisions that undermined both the Fourteenth and Fifteenth Amendments.

In the *Slaughterhouse* cases of 1873, for example, the Court decided that the Fourteenth Amendment protected only the rights people had by virtue of their citizenship in the United States, such as the right of interstate travel and the right to federal protection when traveling on the high seas and abroad. The Court contended that most of Americans' basic civil rights were obtained through their citizenship in a state and that the amendment did not protect those rights.

Another setback for Reconstruction was *U.S. v. Cruikshank* in 1876, in which the Court ruled that the Fourteenth Amendment did not give the federal government the right to punish individual whites who oppressed blacks. The same year, in *U.S. v. Reese,* the Court ruled in favor of officials who had barred African Americans from voting, stating that the Fifteenth Amendment did not "confer the right of suffrage on anyone" but merely listed grounds on which states could not deny suffrage. By the late 1870s, the Supreme Court's restrictive rulings had narrowed the scope of these amendments so much that the federal government no longer had much power to protect the rights of African Americans. Although the Supreme Court would later overturn them, these decisions impeded African Americans' efforts to gain equality for years to come. **E**

MAIN IDEA

Analyzing Effects
E How did the *Slaughterhouse* and *Reese* decisions affect African Americans' pursuit of civil rights?

NORTHERN SUPPORT FADES As the Supreme Court rejected Reconstruction policies in the 1870s, Northern voters grew indifferent to events in the South. Weary of the "Negro question" and sick of "carpetbag government," many Northern voters shifted their attention to such national concerns as the panic of 1873 and the corruption in Grant's administration. In addition, a desire for reconciliation between the regions spread through the North. Although political violence continued in the South and African Americans were denied civil and political rights, the tide of public opinion in the North began to turn against Reconstruction policies.

As both judicial and public support decreased, Republicans began to back away from their commitment to Reconstruction. The impassioned Radicals who had led the fight for congressional Reconstruction, Charles Sumner and Thaddeus Stevens, were dead. Business interests diverted the attention of both moderates and Radicals, and scalawags and carpetbaggers deserted the Republican Party. Moreover, Republicans gradually came to believe that government could not impose the moral and social changes needed for former slaves to make progress in the South. As a result, Republicans slowly retreated from the policies of Reconstruction. **F**

MAIN IDEA

Analyzing Issues
F Why did Northern attitudes toward Reconstruction change?

Civil Rights Setbacks in the Supreme Court		
Date	**Decision(s)**	**Ruling**
1873	*Slaughterhouse* cases	Most civil rights were ruled to be state, rather than federal, rights and therefore unprotected by the Fourteenth Amendment.
1876	*U.S. v. Cruikshank*	The Fourteenth Amendment was ruled not to grant the federal government power to punish whites who oppressed blacks.
1876	*U.S. v. Reese*	The Fifteenth Amendment was determined not to grant voting rights to anyone, but rather to restrict types of voter discrimination.

Democrats "Redeem" the South

Between 1869 and 1875, Democrats recaptured the state governments of Alabama, Arkansas, Georgia, Mississippi, North Carolina, Tennessee, Texas, and Virginia. As a result of **redemption**—as the Democrats called their return to power in the South—and the national election of 1876, congressional Reconstruction came to an end.

ELECTION OF 1876 In 1876, Grant decided not to run for a third term. The Republicans then chose the stodgy governor of Ohio, **Rutherford B. Hayes,** as their candidate. Smelling victory, the Democrats put up one of their ablest leaders, Governor **Samuel J. Tilden** of New York. Tilden had helped clean up the graft that had flourished in New York City under the corrupt Tweed Ring.

As most people had expected, Tilden won the popular vote. However, he fell one short of the number of electoral votes needed to win, and 20 electoral votes were disputed. Congress appointed a commission to deal with the problem. The commission, which had a Republican majority, gave the election to the Republican, Hayes, even though he had received a minority of the popular vote.

For the first time in U.S. history, a candidate who had lost the popular election became president. How did it happen? In the oldest tradition of politics, party leaders made a deal. Although Republicans controlled the electoral commission, Democrats controlled the House of Representatives, which had to approve the election results. Southern Democrats were willing to accept Hayes if they could get something in return.

The price they demanded was, first of all, the withdrawal of federal troops from Louisiana and South Carolina—two of the three Southern states that Republicans still governed. Second, the Democrats wanted federal money to build a railroad from Texas to the West Coast and to improve Southern rivers, harbors, and bridges. Third, they wanted Hayes to appoint a conservative Southerner to the cabinet. In the **Compromise of 1877,** Republican leaders agreed to these demands, and Hayes was peacefully inaugurated. The acceptance of this compromise meant the end of Reconstruction in the South.

HOME RULE IN THE SOUTH After the 1876 election, Republicans and Democrats disputed the results in Louisiana's and South Carolina's elections, and both states ended up with two rival state governments! When Hayes later removed the federal troops in those states, the Democrats took over. Florida also had questionable election returns, but the state supreme court ruled in favor of the Democrats. As a result, Republicans no longer controlled the government of any Southern state.

The Democrats had achieved their long-desired goal of **home rule**—the ability to run state governments without federal intervention. These so-called Redeemers set out to rescue the South from what they viewed as a decade of mismanagement by Northerners, Republicans, and African Americans. They passed laws that restricted the rights of African Americans, wiped out social programs, slashed taxes, and dismantled public schools. **G**

MAIN IDEA

Analyzing Causes
G How did the Compromise of 1877 bring about the end of Reconstruction?

HISTORICAL SPOTLIGHT

THE ELECTORAL COLLEGE AND THE 1876 ELECTION

The nation was in such turmoil over the disputed 1876 election that people talked of another civil war. Of the 20 contested electoral votes, 19 came from Florida, South Carolina, and Louisiana. Republican officials in those states threw out election returns from counties where violence kept Republican voters from the polls. The Democrats refused to accept the altered returns, and each party sent its own set of results to Washington, D.C.

Fortunately for the country, the warlike slogans proved to be just political rhetoric. After a joint session of Congress met to witness the counting of electoral votes, which did not settle the dispute, the parties struck a deal—the Compromise of 1877.

TILDEN.   HAYES.

—

OF THE TWO EVILS
CHOOSE THE LEAST.

▲ An advertisement expresses ambivalence about the two candidates in the 1876 election.

LEGACY OF RECONSTRUCTION Despite the efforts of African Americans and many Radical Republicans, Reconstruction ended without much real progress in the battle against discrimination. Charles Harris, an African-American Union Army veteran and former Alabama legislator, expressed his frustration in an 1877 letter.

★ A PERSONAL VOICE CHARLES HARRIS

"We obey laws; others make them. We support state educational institutions, whose doors are virtually closed against us. We support asylums and hospitals, and our sick, deaf, dumb, or blind are met at the doors by . . . unjust discriminations. . . . From these and many other oppressions . . . our people long to be *free.*"

—quoted in American Colonization Society Papers in the *Congressional Record*

Although Radical Republicans wanted to help the former slaves, they made several serious mistakes. First, they assumed that extending certain civil rights to freed persons would enable them to protect themselves through participation in government, especially in lawmaking. However, Congress did not adequately protect those rights, and the Supreme Court undermined them. Second, the Radicals balked at distributing land to former slaves, which prevented them from becoming

POINT

"Reconstruction was a failure."

Federal and state governments failed to secure the rights guaranteed to former slaves by constitutional amendments.

- State Republican parties could not preserve black-white voter coalitions that would have enabled them to stay in power and continue political reform.
- Radical Republican governments were unable or unwilling to enact land reform or to provide former slaves with the economic resources needed to break the cycle of poverty.
- Racial bias was a national, not a regional, problem. After the Panic of 1873, Northerners were more concerned with economic problems than with the problems of former slaves.
- The Supreme Court undermined the power of the Fourteenth and Fifteenth Amendments.

At the end of Reconstruction, former slaves found themselves once again in a subordinate position in society. The historian Eric Foner concludes, "Whether measured by the dreams inspired by emancipation or the more limited goals of securing blacks' rights as citizens. . . . Reconstruction can only be judged a failure."

COUNTERPOINT

"Reconstruction was a success."

Reconstruction was an attempt to create a social and political revolution despite economic collapse and the opposition of much of the white South. Under these conditions its accomplishments were extraordinary.

- African Americans only a few years removed from slavery participated at all levels of government.
- State governments had some success in solving social problems; for example, they funded public school systems open to all citizens.
- African Americans established institutions that had been denied them during slavery: schools, churches, and families.
- The breakup of the plantation system led to some redistribution of land.
- Congress passed the Fourteenth and Fifteenth Amendments, which helped African Americans to attain full civil rights in the 20th century.

W. E. B. Du Bois summarized the achievements of the period this way: "[I]t was Negro loyalty and the Negro vote alone that restored the South to the Union; established the new democracy, both for white and black."

Despite the loss of ground that followed Reconstruction, African Americans succeeded in carving out a measure of independence within Southern society.

THINKING CRITICALLY

1. **CONNECT TO HISTORY** **Evaluating** What are the two major arguments each side makes as to whether Reconstruction was a success or failure? Which perspective do you agree with, and why?

    SEE SKILLBUILDER HANDBOOK, PAGE R16.

2. **CONNECT TO TODAY** **Analyzing Issues** One historian has referred to Reconstruction as "America's Unfinished Revolution." Is the U.S. still dealing with issues left over from that period? Research Reconstruction's legacy using newspapers, magazines, or other sources. Make a short persuasive presentation in class.

economically independent of the landowning planter class. Finally, the Radicals did not fully realize the extent to which deep-seated racism in society would weaken the changes that Congress had tried to make.

But congressional Reconstruction was not a complete failure. The Thirteenth Amendment permanently abolished slavery in all of the states. Furthermore, Radical Republicans did succeed in passing the Fourteenth and Fifteenth Amendments, and although the Supreme Court narrowed the interpretation of the amendments during the 1870s, they remained part of the Constitution. In the 20th century, the amendments provided the necessary constitutional foundation for important civil rights legislation.

During Reconstruction, African Americans had founded many black colleges and volunteer organizations, and the percentage of literate African Americans had gradually increased. The memory of this time of expanding opportunities lived on in the African-American community and inspired the fight to regain civil rights.

◀ Medical students at Howard University, an African-American institution founded in 1867

ASSESSMENT

SECTION 3

1. **TERMS & NAMES** For each term or name, write a sentence explaining its significance.
   - Ku Klux Klan (KKK)
   - panic of 1873
   - redemption
   - Rutherford B. Hayes
   - Samuel J. Tilden
   - Compromise of 1877
   - home rule

MAIN IDEA

2. **TAKING NOTES**
   Re-create the time line below. Fill in the major events that ended Reconstruction.

   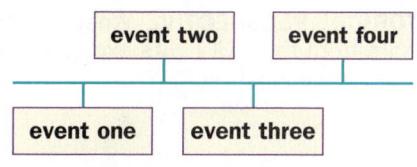

   Which event do you think was most significant and why?

CRITICAL THINKING

3. **ANALYZING EFFECTS**
   What were the positive and negative effects of Reconstruction?

4. **EVALUATING LEADERSHIP**
   During Reconstruction, was the presidency weak or strong? Support your answer with details from the text.

5. **EVALUATING DECISIONS**
   Do you think the political deal to settle the election of 1876 was an appropriate solution? Explain why or why not. **Think About:**
   - the causes of the conflict over the election
   - other possible solutions to the controversy
   - the impact of the settlement

VISUAL SUMMARY

RECONSTRUCTION AND ITS EFFECTS

FOUNDATIONS

- Presidents Lincoln and Johnson propose lenient policies toward the former Confederate states.
- Radical Republicans gain control of Congress and pass the Reconstruction Act of 1867.
- Conflict over approach leads Congress to impeach Johnson.

PROGRESS

- States ratify the Fourteenth and Fifteenth Amendments.
- Republicans control most state governments in the South.
- States start public works programs and public schools.
- Former slaves reunite families, work for wages, and build African-American culture.

COLLAPSE

- War debt and low demand for cotton slow the South's recovery.
- African Americans are terrorized by racist violence.
- Supreme Court decisions undermine Fourteenth and Fifteenth Amendments.
- Republican Party is weakened by internal conflict, scandal, and financial panic.
- Republicans withdraw troops from the South to gain Hayes the presidency in 1876.
- Democrats control governments, weaken civil rights, and eliminate public schools and programs.

TERMS & NAMES

For each term or name below, write a sentence explaining its connection to Reconstruction.

1. Andrew Johnson
2. Radical Republicans
3. Freedmen's Bureau
4. Fourteenth Amendment
5. Fifteenth Amendment
6. carpetbagger
7. Hiram Revels
8. sharecropping
9. Ku Klux Klan (KKK)
10. Rutherford B. Hayes

MAIN IDEAS

Use your notes and the information in the chapter to answer the following questions.

The Politics of Reconstruction *(pages 376–382)*

1. How did Andrew Johnson's plan to reconstruct the Confederate states differ from Lincoln's?
2. How did the Civil Rights Act of 1866 become law?
3. Why did the Radicals want to impeach Andrew Johnson?

Reconstructing Society *(pages 383–392)*

4. What three groups made up the Republican Party in the South during Reconstruction?
5. In what ways did emancipated slaves exercise their freedom?
6. How did white landowners in the South reassert their economic power in the decade following the Civil War?

The Collapse of Reconstruction *(pages 393–401)*

7. How did Southern whites regain political power during Reconstruction?
8. What economic and political developments weakened the Republican Party during Grant's second term?
9. What significance did the victory by Rutherford B. Hayes in the 1876 presidential race have for Reconstruction?

CRITICAL THINKING

1. **USING YOUR NOTES** In a chart like the one below, list the results of the national elections of 1866, 1868, 1870, 1872, and 1876. Then note how each result affected Reconstruction.

Year	Results	Significance

2. **ANALYZING ISSUES** How do you think Reconstruction could have been made more effective in rebuilding the South and ensuring the rights of the freed slaves?

3. **EVALUATING** Do you think the changes in the South during Reconstruction benefited Southerners? Support your opinion.

4. **DEVELOPING HISTORICAL PERSPECTIVE** What might Americans today learn from the civil rights experiences of African Americans during Reconstruction?

Use the quotation below and your knowledge of U.S. history to answer question 1.

> "On the coast of South Carolina, after a year of experimenting on the willingness of the freedmen to work and their ability to support themselves, a plan was begun of cutting up the large estates into twenty and forty acre plots, to be sold to the freedmen at government prices. . . . This plan was eminently fair and just; it was also a radical abolishment of slavery. It made the freedman owner of his own labor, and also an owner of a fair share of the land. . . . At the first sale of these lands, the freedmen came up promptly and bought largely, showing the thrift and shrewdness of men worthy of citizenship."
>
> —**James McCune Smith**, quoted in *Witness for Freedom: African American Voices on Race, Slavery, and Emancipation*

1 According to the point of view expressed in the quotation, the best way to help former slaves was to —

(1) encourage plantation owners to hire former slaves.

(2) allow plantation owners to buy back their land.

(3) assist former slaves in gaining ownership of land.

(4) divide large plantations into smaller plots.

2 In the Reconstruction Act of 1867, Congress set requirements for the readmission of former Confederate states into the Union. Which of the following problems did the act address?

(1) Southern states did not allow African Americans to vote.

(2) Southern states had little money to pay for public works projects.

(3) Former slaves needed education.

(4) Confederate bonds and money were worthless.

3 Which of the following items was responsible for finally ending Reconstruction in the South?

(1) ratification of the Fifteenth Amendment

(2) the Compromise of 1877

(3) President Grant's failure to win reelection

(4) the decisions of the Supreme Court in the 1870s

 hmhsocialstudies.com **TEST PRACTICE**

For additional test practice, go online for:
- Diagnostic tests
- Tutorials

INTERACT WITH HISTORY

Recall the issues that you explored at the beginning of the chapter. Now that you have read more about efforts to reconstruct the South, what is your opinion of how the government handled Reconstruction? Write an opinion statement. Consider the following questions:
- What goals did the government actually set for Reconstruction?
- How could the government have pursued its goals more effectively?
- What additional goals should the government have set? Why?

FOCUS ON WRITING

During Reconstruction, many leaders felt that it was the president's responsibility to restore the Union. Others felt it was the responsibility of Congress. Write a persuasive essay expressing your view on who should oversee Reconstruction in the former Confederacy. Be sure to include evidence that supports your position while also highlighting the negative aspects of the alternative plan for Reconstruction.

COLLABORATIVE LEARNING

In a small group read and discuss the "One American's Story" at the beginning of Section 2. Then create a presentation that Robert Fitzgerald might have used to convince Northerners to support the Freedmen's Bureau and schools for former slaves. What if Fitzgerald had had access to 21st-century technology? Use audio, video, or computer software to make the presentation more effective. Present the final product to your class.

4

Migration and Industrialization 1877–1917

UNIT PROJECT

Oral Report

This unit describes how the United States transformed itself from a rural, agricultural society to an urban, industrial one. Prepare an oral report that summarizes one or more of the factors that caused this change. Create visuals to accompany your report.

Champions of the Mississippi by Currier and Ives

CHAPTER 13

CHANGES ON THE WESTERN FRONTIER

Essential Question

How did westward migration after the Civil War affect the United States?

New York Standards

KEY IDEA 3 Study about the major social, political, economic, cultural, and religious developments in New York State and United States history involves learning about the important roles and contributions of individuals and groups.

KEY IDEA 4 The skills of historical analysis include the ability to: explain the significance of historical evidence; weigh the importance, reliability, and validity of evidence; understand the concept of multiple causation; understand the importance of changing and competing interpretations of different historical developments.

SECTION 1: Cultures Clash on the Prairie

SECTION 2: Settling on the Great Plains

SECTION 3: Farmers and the Populist Movement

Until the 1860s, the migratory Indians of Montana—including the Blackfeet shown here—followed the buffalo herds and traded peacefully with whites in the region.

1870 Red Cloud, chief of the Oglala Sioux, states his people's case in Washington, D.C.

1880 James Garfield is elected president.

1881 Garfield is assassinated. Chester Arthur becomes president.

1884 Grover Cleveland is elected president.

USA	1870	1880
WORLD		

1869 Suez Canal is opened.

1872 Secret ballot is adopted in Britain.

1881 French occupy Tunisia.

INTERACT
WITH HISTORY

It is the late 1890s. The American West is the last frontier. Ranchers, cowboys, and miners have changed forever the lives of the Native Americans who hunted on the Western plains. Now westward fever intensifies as "boomers" rush to grab "free" farm land with the government's blessing.

Explore the Issues

- What might be some ways to make a living on the Western frontier?
- If native peoples already live in your intended home, how will you co-exist?
- How might settlers and Native Americans differ regarding use of the land?

1889 Oklahoma opened for settlement; the land rush begins.

1890 Sioux are massacred at Wounded Knee.

1893 Diminished U.S. gold reserve triggers the panic of 1893.

1896 William McKinley is elected president.

1896 William Jennings Bryan runs for president.

1890

1900

1893 France takes over Indochina.

1899 Berlin Conference divides Africa among European nations.

1900 Boxer Rebellion takes place in China.

Changes on the Western Frontier **407**

SECTION
1

PI 3.1
PI 3.4
PI 4.3

CC Unit 1.I.2.d
CC Unit 3.III.D.1.b
CC Unit 3.III.D.2.b

CC Unit 1.I.3.c
CC Unit 3.III.D.2.a
CC Unit 3.III.D.3

Cultures Clash on the Prairie

MAIN IDEA	WHY IT MATTERS NOW	Terms & Names
The cattle industry boomed in the late 1800s, as the culture of the Plains Indians declined.	Today, ranchers and Plains Indians work to preserve their cultural traditions.	• **Great Plains** • **Treaty of Fort Laramie** • **Sitting Bull** • **George A. Custer** • **assimilation** / • **Dawes Act** • **Battle of Wounded Knee** • **longhorn** • **Chisholm Trail** • **long drive**

One American's Story

Zitkala-Ša was born a Sioux in 1876. As she grew up on the Great Plains, she learned the ways of her people. When Zitkala-Ša was eight years old she was sent to a Quaker school in Indiana. Though her mother warned her of the "white men's lies," Zitkala-Ša was not prepared for the loss of dignity and identity she experienced, which was symbolized by the cutting of her hair.

A PERSONAL VOICE ZITKALA-ŠA

" I cried aloud . . . and heard them gnaw off one of my thick braids. Then I lost my spirit. Since the day I was taken from my mother I had suffered extreme indignities. . . . And now my long hair was shingled like a coward's! In my anguish I moaned for my mother, but no one came. . . . Now I was only one of many little animals driven by a herder. "

—*The School Days of an Indian Girl*

Zitkala-Ša experienced firsthand the clash of two very different cultures that occurred as ever-growing numbers of white settlers moved onto the Great Plains. In the resulting struggle, the Native American way of life was changed forever.

The Culture of the Plains Indians

Zitkala-Ša knew very little about the world east of the Mississippi River. Most Easterners knew equally little about the West, picturing a vast desert occupied by savage tribes. That view could not have been more inaccurate. In fact, distinctive and highly developed Native American ways of life existed on the **Great Plains**, the grassland extending through the west-central portion of the United States. (See map on page 411.)

To the east, near the lower Missouri River, tribes such as the Osage and Iowa had, for more than a century, hunted and planted crops and settled in small villages. Farther west, nomadic tribes such as the Sioux and Cheyenne gathered wild foods and hunted buffalo. Peoples of the Plains, abiding by tribal law, traded and produced beautifully crafted tools and clothing.

THE HORSE AND THE BUFFALO After the Spanish brought horses to New Mexico in 1598, the Native American way of life began to change. As the native peoples acquired horses—and then guns—they were able to travel farther and hunt more efficiently. By the mid-1700s, almost all the tribes on the Great Plains had left their farms to roam the plains and hunt buffalo.

Their increased mobility often led to war when hunters in one tribe trespassed on other tribes' hunting grounds. For the young men of a tribe, taking part in war parties and raids was a way to win prestige. A Plains warrior gained honor by killing his enemies, as well as by "counting coup." This practice involved touching a live enemy with a coup stick and escaping unharmed. And sometimes warring tribes would call a truce so that they could trade goods, share news, or enjoy harvest festivals. Native Americans made tepees from buffalo hides and also used the skins for clothing, shoes, and blankets. Buffalo meat was dried into jerky or mixed with berries and fat to make a staple food called pemmican. While the horse gave Native Americans speed and mobility, the buffalo provided many of their basic needs and was central to life on the Plains. (See chart on page 413.) Ⓐ

FAMILY LIFE Native Americans on the plains usually lived in small extended family groups with ties to other bands that spoke the same language. Young men trained to become hunters and warriors. The women helped butcher the game and prepared the hides that the men brought back to the camp; young women sometimes chose their own husbands.

The Plains Indian tribes believed that powerful spirits controlled events in the natural world. Men or women who showed particular sensitivity to the spirits became medicine men or women, or shamans. Children learned proper behavior and culture through stories and myths, games, and good examples. Despite their communal way of life, however, no individual was allowed to dominate the group. The leaders of a tribe ruled by counsel rather than by force, and land was held in common for the use of the whole tribe.

Settlers Push Westward

The culture of the white settlers differed in many ways from that of the Native Americans on the plains. Unlike Native Americans, who believed that land could not be owned, the settlers believed that owning land, making a mining claim, or starting a business would give them a stake in the country. They argued that the Native Americans had forfeited their rights to the land because they hadn't settled down to "improve" it. Concluding that the plains were "unsettled," migrants streamed westward along railroad and wagon trails to claim the land.

Vocabulary
coup: a feat of bravery performed in battle

MAIN IDEA

Summarizing
Ⓐ How did the horse influence Native American life on the Great Plains?

▲
A portrait of a Sioux man and woman in the late 19th century.

This Yankton Sioux coup stick was used by warriors.
▼

THE LURE OF SILVER AND GOLD The prospect of striking it rich was one powerful attraction of the West. The discovery of gold in Colorado in 1858 drew tens of thousands of miners to the region.

Most mining camps and tiny frontier towns had filthy, ramshackle living quarters. Rows of tents and shacks with dirt "streets" and wooden sidewalks had replaced unspoiled picturesque landscapes. Fortune seekers of every description —including Irish, German, Polish, Chinese, and African-American men—crowded the camps and boomtowns. A few hardy, business-minded women tried their luck too, working as laundresses, freight haulers, or miners. Cities such as Virginia City, Nevada, and Helena, Montana, originated as mining camps on Native American land.

VIDEO
Sitting Bull: Chief of the Lakota Nation

hmhsocialstudies.com

The Government Restricts Native Americans

While allowing more settlers to move westward, the arrival of the railroads also influenced the government's policy toward the Native Americans who lived on the plains. In 1834, the federal government had passed an act that designated the entire Great Plains as one enormous reservation, or land set aside for Native American tribes. In the 1850s, however, the government changed its policy and created treaties that defined specific boundaries for each tribe. Most Native Americans spurned the government treaties and continued to hunt on their traditional lands, clashing with settlers and miners—with tragic results. **B**

MASSACRE AT SAND CREEK One of the most tragic events occurred in 1864. Most of the Cheyenne, assuming they were under the protection of the U.S. government, had peacefully returned to Colorado's Sand Creek Reserve for the winter. Yet General S. R. Curtis, U.S. Army commander in the West, sent a telegram to militia colonel John Chivington that read, "I want no peace till the Indians suffer more." In response, Chivington and his troops descended on the Cheyenne and Arapaho—about 200 warriors and 500 women and children—camped at Sand Creek. The attack at dawn on November 29, 1864 killed over 150 inhabitants, mostly women and children.

DEATH ON THE BOZEMAN TRAIL The Bozeman Trail ran directly through Sioux hunting grounds in the Bighorn Mountains. The Sioux chief, Red Cloud (Mahpiua Luta), had unsuccessfully appealed to the government to end white settlement on the trail. In December 1866, the warrior Crazy Horse ambushed Captain William J. Fetterman and his company at Lodge Trail Ridge. Over 80 soldiers were killed. Native Americans called this fight the Battle of the Hundred Slain. Whites called it the Fetterman Massacre.

Skirmishes continued until the government agreed to close the Bozeman Trail. In return, the **Treaty of Fort Laramie,** in which the Sioux agreed to live on a reservation along the Missouri River, was forced on the leaders of the Sioux in 1868. **Sitting Bull** (Tatanka Iyotanka), leader of the Hunkpapa Sioux, had never signed it. Although the Ogala and Brule Sioux did sign the treaty, they expected to continue using their traditional hunting grounds.

MAIN IDEA

Analyzing Issues
B What was the government's policy toward Native American land?

KEY PLAYER

**SITTING BULL
1831–1890**

As a child, Sitting Bull was known as Hunkesni, or Slow; he earned the name Tatanka Iyotanka (Sitting Bull) after a fight with the Crow, a traditional enemy of the Sioux.

Sitting Bull led his people by the strength of his character and purpose. He was a warrior, spiritual leader, and medicine man, and he was determined that whites should leave Sioux territory. His most famous fight was at the Little Bighorn River. About his opponent, George Armstrong Custer, he said, "They tell me I murdered Custer. It is a lie. . . . He was a fool and rode to his death."

After Sitting Bull's surrender to the federal government in 1881, his dislike of whites did not change. He was killed by Native American police at Standing Rock Reservation in December 1890.

Shrinking Native American Lands, and Battle Sites

1819

1894

Area of main map

2000

PACIFIC
OCEAN

130°W

40°N

NEZ PERCE

BLACKFOOT

SIOUX

CHEYENNE

SHASTA

Snake River

ROCKY

BOZEMAN TRAIL

Little Bighorn, 1876

Fetterman Massacre, 1866

SIOUX

SIOUX

BLACK HILLS

Wounded Knee, 1890

SHOSHONE

ARAPAHO
SHOSHONE

Fort Laramie

Missouri River

UTE

M
O
U
N
T
A
I
N
S

Colorado River

NAVAJO

UTE

Sand Creek Massacre, 1864

HOPI

PAWNEE

APACHE

Rio Grande

ARAPAHO
CHEYENNE

APACHE
COMANCHE
KIOWA

Mississippi River

Legend:
- Great Plains
- Indian reservation
- ★ Battle site

0   100   200 miles
0 100 200 kilometers

GEOGRAPHY SKILLBUILDER

1. Location Which battles took place on Native American land?

2. Movement About what percentage of Native American lands had the government taken over by 1894?

A Sioux encampment near the South Dakota-Nebraska border.

Bloody Battles Continue

The Treaty of Fort Laramie provided only a temporary halt to warfare. The conflict between the two cultures continued as settlers moved westward and Native American nations resisted the restrictions imposed upon them. A Sioux warrior explained why.

★ **A PERSONAL VOICE** GALL, A HUNKPAPA SIOUX

" [We] have been taught to hunt and live on the game. You tell us that we must learn to farm, live in one house, and take on your ways. Suppose the people living beyond the great sea should come and tell you that you must stop farming, and kill your cattle, and take your houses and lands, what would you do? Would you not fight them? "

—quoted in *Bury My Heart at Wounded Knee*

RED RIVER WAR In late 1868, war broke out yet again as the Kiowa and Comanche engaged in six years of raiding that finally led to the Red River War of 1874–1875. The U.S. Army responded by herding the people of friendly tribes onto reservations while opening fire on all others. General Philip Sheridan, a Union Army veteran, gave orders "to destroy their villages and ponies, to kill and hang all warriors, and to bring back all women and children." With such tactics, the army crushed resistance on the southern plains.

GOLD RUSH Within four years of the Treaty of Fort Laramie, miners began searching the Black Hills for gold. The Sioux, Cheyenne, and Arapaho protested the encroachment on their lands to no avail. In 1874, when Colonel **George A. Custer** reported that the Black Hills had gold "from the grass roots down," a gold rush was on. Red Cloud and Spotted Tail, another Sioux chief, vainly appealed again to government officials.

CUSTER'S LAST STAND In early June 1876, the Sioux and Cheyenne held a sun dance, during which Sitting Bull had a vision of soldiers and some Native Americans falling from their horses. When Colonel Custer and his troops reached the Little Bighorn River, the Native Americans were ready for them.

Led by Crazy Horse, Gall, and Sitting Bull, the warriors— with raised spears and rifles—outflanked and crushed Custer's troops. Within an hour, Custer and all of the men of the Seventh Cavalry were dead. By late 1876, however, the Sioux were beaten. Sitting Bull and a few followers took refuge in Canada, where they remained until 1881. Eventually, to prevent his people's starvation, Sitting Bull was forced to surrender. Later, in 1885, he appeared in William F. "Buffalo Bill" Cody's Wild West Show. **C**

Colonel George Armstrong Custer, 1865 ▼

The Winchester '76 rifle used by government troops, and a Sioux war bow. ▼

MAIN IDEA

Analyzing Effects
C What were the results of Custer's last stand?

The Government Supports Assimilation

The Native Americans still had supporters in the United States, and debate over the treatment of Native Americans continued. The well-known writer Helen Hunt Jackson, for example, exposed the government's many broken promises in her 1881 book *A Century of Dishonor*. At the same time many sympathizers supported **assimilation,** a plan under which Native Americans would give up their beliefs and way of life and become part of the white culture.

THE DAWES ACT In 1887, Congress passed the **Dawes Act** aiming to "Americanize" the Native Americans. The act broke up the reservations and gave some of the reservation land to individual Native Americans—160 acres to each head of household and 80 acres to each unmarried adult. The government would sell the remainder of the reservations to settlers, and the resulting income would be used by Native Americans to buy farm implements. By 1932, whites had taken about two-thirds of the territory that had been set aside for Native Americans. In the end, the Native Americans received no money from the sale of these lands.

THE DESTRUCTION OF THE BUFFALO Perhaps the most significant blow to tribal life on the plains was the destruction of the buffalo. Tourists and fur traders shot buffalo for sport. U.S. General Sheridan noted with approval that buffalo hunters were destroying the Plains Indians' main source of food, clothing, shelter, and fuel. In 1800, approximately 65 million buffalo roamed the plains; by 1890, fewer than 1000 remained. In 1900, the United States sheltered, in Yellowstone National Park, a single wild herd of buffalo.

The Battle of Wounded Knee

The Sioux continued to suffer poverty and disease. In desperation, they turned to a Paiute prophet who promised that if the Sioux performed a ritual called the Ghost Dance, Native American lands and way of life would be restored.

The Ghost Dance movement spread rapidly among the 25,000 Sioux on the Dakota reservation. Alarmed military leaders ordered the arrest of Sitting Bull. In December 1890, about 40 Native American police were sent to arrest him. Sitting Bull's friend and bodyguard, Catch-the-Bear, shot one of them. The police then killed Sitting Bull. In the aftermath, Chief Big Foot led the fearful Sioux away.

WOUNDED KNEE On December 28, 1890, the Seventh Cavalry—Custer's old regiment—rounded up about 350 starving and freezing Sioux and took them to a camp at Wounded Knee Creek in South Dakota. The next day, the soldiers demanded that the Native Americans give up all their weapons. A shot was fired; from which side, it was not clear. The soldiers opened fire with deadly cannon.

Importance of the Buffalo

The buffalo provided the Plains Indians with more than just a high-protein food source.

1800 65,000,000

1870 1,000

2000 260,000

THE SKULL of the buffalo was considered sacred and was used in many Native American rituals.

THE HORNS were carved into bowls and spoons.

THE BONES of the buffalo were made into hide scrapers, tool handles, sled runners, and hoe blades. The hoofs were ground up and used as glue.

THE HIDE was by far the most precious part of the buffalo. Native American clothing, tepees, and even arrow shields were made from buffalo hide.

Within minutes, the Seventh Cavalry slaughtered as many as 300 mostly unarmed Native Americans, including several children. The soldiers left the corpses to freeze on the ground. This event, the **Battle of Wounded Knee,** brought the Indian wars—and an entire era—to a bitter end. **D**

MAIN IDEA

Analyzing Causes
D What events led to the Battle of Wounded Knee?

A PERSONAL VOICE   BLACK ELK

"I did not know then how much was ended. When I look back . . . I can still see the butchered women and children lying heaped and scattered all along the crooked gulch. . . . And I can see that something else died there in the bloody mud, and was buried in the blizzard. A people's dream died there. It was a beautiful dream."

—*Black Elk Speaks*

Cattle Becomes Big Business

As the great herds of buffalo disappeared, and Native Americans were forced onto smaller and less desirable reservations, horses and cattle flourished on the plains. As cattle ranchers opened up the Great Plains to big business, ranching from Texas to Kansas became a profitable investment.

VAQUEROS AND COWBOYS American settlers had never managed large herds on the open range, and they learned from their Mexican neighbors how to round up, rope, brand, and care for the animals. The animals themselves, the Texas **longhorns,** were sturdy, short-tempered breeds accustomed to the dry grasslands of southern Spain. Spanish settlers raised longhorns for food and brought horses to use as work animals and for transportation.

As American as the cowboy seems today, his way of life stemmed directly from that of those first Spanish ranchers in Mexico. The cowboy's clothes, food, and vocabulary were heavily influenced by the Mexican *vaquero*, who was the first to wear spurs, which he attached with straps to his bare feet and used to control his horse. His *chaparreras*, or leather overalls, became known as chaps. He ate *charqui*, or "jerky"—dried strips of meat. The Spanish *bronco caballo*, or "rough horse" that ran wild, became known as a bronco or bronc. The strays, or *mesteños*, were the same mustangs that the American cowboy tamed and prized. The Mexican *rancho* became the American ranch. Finally, the English words *corral* and

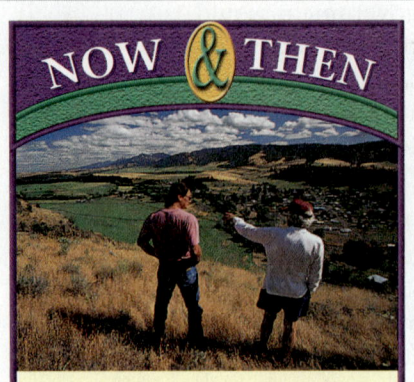

NEZ PERCE IN OREGON

Forced off their tribal lands in Wallowa County, Oregon, in 1877, the Nez Perce are returning almost 120 years later. 1999 figures put the number of Nez Perce in the Oregon area at around 3,000.

In 1997, Wallowa community leaders obtained a grant to develop the Wallowa Band Nez Perce Trail Interpretive Center—a cultural center that hosts powwows and other activities to draw tourists.

"I never thought I'd see the day," said Earl (Taz) Conner, a direct descendant of Chief Joseph, the best known of the Nez Perce. And, in the words of Soy Redthunder, another tribe member, "[We] look at it as homecoming."

This 1877 painting by James Walker shows Mexican vaqueros in a horse corral. ▶

MAIN IDEA

Drawing Conclusions

E What does the American cowboy tradition owe to the Mexican vaquero?

rodeo were borrowed from Spanish. In his skills, dress, and speech, the Mexican vaquero was the true forerunner of the American "buckaroo" or cowboy. **E**

Despite the plentiful herds of Western cattle, cowboys were not in great demand until the railroads reached the Great Plains. Before the Civil War, ranchers for the most part didn't stray far from their homesteads with their cattle. There were, of course, some exceptions. During the California gold rush in 1849, some hardy cattlemen on horseback braved a long trek, or drive, through Apache territory and across the desert to collect $25 to $125 a head for their cattle. In 1854, two ranchers drove their cattle 700 miles to Muncie, Indiana, where they put them on stock cars bound for New York City. When the cattle were unloaded in New York, the stampede that followed caused a panic on Third Avenue. Parts of the country were not ready for the mass transportation of animals.

GROWING DEMAND FOR BEEF After the Civil War, the demand for beef skyrocketed, partly due to the rapidly growing cities. The Chicago Union Stock Yards opened in 1865, and by spring 1866, the railroads were running regularly through Sedalia, Missouri. From Sedalia, Texas ranchers could ship their cattle to Chicago and markets throughout the East. They found, however, that the route to Sedalia presented several obstacles: including thunderstorms and rain-swollen rivers. Also, in 1866, farmers angry about trampled crops blockaded cattle in Baxter Springs, Kansas, preventing them from reaching Sedalia. Some herds then had to be sold at cut-rate prices, others died of starvation. **F**

MAIN IDEA

Summarizing

F What developments led to the rapid growth of the cattle industry?

THE COW TOWN The next year, cattlemen found a more convenient route. Illinois cattle dealer Joseph McCoy approached several Western towns with plans to create a shipping yard where the trails and rail lines came together. The tiny Kansas town of Abilene enthusiastically agreed to the plan. McCoy built cattle pens, a three-story hotel, and helped survey the **Chisholm Trail**—the major cattle route from San Antonio, Texas, through Oklahoma to Kansas. Thirty-five thousand head of cattle were shipped out of the yard in Abilene during its first

VIDEO
Wild West:
Cattle Drive

hmhsocialstudies.com

Cattle Trails and the Railroads, 1870s–1890s

hmhsocialstudies.com **INTERACTIVE MAP**

Legend:
- Range and ranch cattle area
- Railroad
- Major meat packing center
- Range of the Texas longhorn

Scale: 0 — 200 — 400 miles / 0 — 200 — 400 kilometers

GEOGRAPHY SKILLBUILDER
1. **Region** At what towns did the cattle trails and the railroads intersect to form cattle-shipping centers?
2. **Place** Which cities were served by the most railroads?

year in operation. The following year, business more than doubled, to 75,000 head. Soon ranchers were hiring cowboys to drive their cattle to Abilene. Within a few years, the Chisholm Trail had worn wide and deep.

A Day in the Life of a Cowboy

The meeting of the Chisholm Trail and the railroad in Abilene ushered in the heyday of the cowboy. As many as 55,000 worked the plains between 1866 and 1885. Although folklore and postcards depicted the cowboy as Anglo-American, about 25 percent of them were African American, and at least 12 percent were Mexican. The romanticized American cowboy of myth rode the open range, herding cattle and fighting villains. Meanwhile, the real-life cowboy was doing nonstop work.

A DAY'S WORK A cowboy worked 10 to 14 hours a day on a ranch and 14 or more on the trail, alert at all times for dangers that might harm or upset the herds. Some cowboys were as young as 15; most were broken-down by the time they were 40. A cowboy might own his saddle, but his trail horse usually belonged to his boss. He was an expert rider and roper. His gun might be used to protect the herd from wild or diseased animals rather than to hurt or chase outlaws.

ROUNDUP The cowboy's season began with a spring roundup, in which he and other hands from the ranch herded all the longhorns they could find on the open range into a large corral. They kept the herd penned there for several days, until the cattle were so hungry that they preferred grazing to running away. Then the cowboys sorted through the herd, claiming the cattle that were marked with the brand of their ranch and calves that still needed to be branded. After the herd was gathered and branded, the trail boss chose a crew for the long drive.

THE LONG DRIVE This overland transport, or **long drive,** of the animals often lasted about three months. A typical drive included one cowboy for every 250 to 300 head of cattle; a cook who also drove the chuck wagon and set up camp; and a wrangler who cared for the extra horses. A trail boss earned $100 or more a month for supervising the drive and negotiating with settlers and Native Americans.

During the long drive, the cowboy was in the saddle from dawn to dusk. He slept on the ground and bathed in rivers. He risked death and loss every day of the drive, especially at river crossings, where cattle often hesitated and were swept away. Because lightning was a constant danger, cowboys piled their spurs, buckles, and other metal objects at the edge of their camp to avoid attracting lightning bolts. Thunder, or even a sneeze, could cause a stampede. **G**

MAIN IDEA

Comparing

G How did the cowboy's life differ from the myth about it?

LEGENDS OF THE WEST Legendary figures like James Butler "Wild Bill" Hickok and Martha Jane Burke (Calamity Jane) actually never dealt with cows. Hickok served as a scout and a spy during the Civil War and, later, as a marshal in Abilene, Kansas. He was a violent man who was shot and killed while holding a pair of aces and a pair of eights in a poker game, a hand still known as the "dead man's hand." Calamity Jane was an expert sharpshooter who dressed as a man. She may have been a scout for Colonel George Custer.

The End of the Open Range

Almost as quickly as cattle herds multiplied and ranching became big business, the cattle frontier met its end. Overgrazing of the land, extended bad weather, and the invention of barbed wire were largely responsible.

Between 1883 and 1887 alternating patterns of dry summers and harsh winters wiped out whole herds. Most ranchers then turned to smaller herds of high-grade stock that would yield more meat per animal. Ranchers fenced the land with barbed wire, invented by Illinois farmer Joseph F. Glidden. It was cheap and easy to use and helped to turn the open plains into a series of fenced-in ranches. The era of the wide-open West was over.

SECTION 1 ASSESSMENT

1. **TERMS & NAMES** For each term or name, write a sentence explaining its significance.
   - Great Plains
   - Treaty of Fort Laramie
   - Sitting Bull
   - George A. Custer
   - assimilation
   - Dawes Act
   - Battle of Wounded Knee
   - longhorn
   - Chisholm Trail
   - long drive

MAIN IDEA

2. **TAKING NOTES**
   Fill in supporting details about the culture of the Plains Indians.

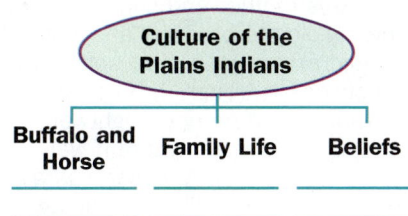

Culture of the Plains Indians

Buffalo and Horse | Family Life | Beliefs

CRITICAL THINKING

3. **MAKING INFERENCES**
   Why do you think the assimilation policy of the Dawes Act failed? Support your opinion with information from the text.
   Think About:
   - the experience of Native Americans such as Zitkala-Ša
   - the attitudes of many white leaders toward Native Americans
   - the merits of owning property
   - the importance of cultural heritage

4. **ANALYZING CAUSES**
   What economic opportunities drew large numbers of people to the Great Plains beginning in the mid-1800s?

5. **DRAWING CONCLUSIONS**
   Identify the reasons for the rise and the decline of the cattle industry.

Gold Mining

GOLD! Some struck it rich—some struck out. Between the Civil War and the turn of the century, deposits of the precious yellow metal were discovered in scattered sites from the Black Hills of South Dakota and Cripple Creek, Colorado, to Nome, Alaska. The dream of riches lured hundreds of thousands of prospectors into territories that were previously inhabited only by native peoples. The fortune seekers came from all walks: grizzled veterans from the California gold rush of 1849, youths seeking adventure, middle-class professionals, and even some families.

PANNING FOR GOLD ▶

At the start of a gold rush, prospectors usually looked for easily available gold—particles eroded from rocks and washed downstream. Panning for it was easy—even children could do it. They scooped up mud and water from the streambed in a flat pan and swirled it. The circular motion of the water caused the sand to wash over the side and the remaining minerals to form layers according to weight. Gold, which is heavier than most other minerals, sank to the bottom.

◀ SLUICES AND ROCKERS

In 1898, prospectors like this mother and son in Fairbanks, Alaska, found sluicing to be more efficient than panning, since it could extract gold from soil. They would shovel soil into a sluice—a trough through which water flowed—and the water would carry off lightweight materials. The gold sank to the bottom, where it was caught in wooden ridges called cleats. A rocker was a portable sluice that combined the mobility of panning with the efficiency of sluicing.

▼ IN THE BOWELS OF THE EARTH

Although surface gold could be extracted by panning and sluicing, most gold was located in veins in underground rock. Mining these deposits involved digging tunnels along the veins of gold and breaking up tons of ore—hard and dangerous work. Tunnels often collapsed, and miners who weren't killed were trapped in utter darkness for days.

Heat was a problem, too. As miners descended into the earth, the temperature inside the mine soared. At a depth of about 2,000 feet, the temperature of the water that invariably flooded the bottom of a mine could be 160°F.

Cave-ins and hot water weren't the only dangers that miners faced. The pressure in the underground rock sometimes became so intense that it caused deadly explosions.

A FAMILY AFFAIR ▲

This early placer, or surface, mine at Cripple Creek attracted many women and children. It grew out of the vision of a young rancher, Bob Womack. He had found gold particles washed down from higher land and was convinced that the Cripple Creek area was literally a gold mine.

Because Womack was generally disliked, the community ignored him. When a German count struck gold there, however, business boomed. Womack died penniless—but the mines produced a $400 million bonanza.

D A T A   F I L E

BOOM TO BUST

Gold-rush towns could blossom out of the wilderness virtually overnight—but they could also die out almost as quickly.

LONG ODDS

These statistics for the Klondike gold rush, from 1896 to 1899, show the incredible odds against striking it rich.

100,000 people set out for the Klondike.

40,000 people make it.

20,000 stake claims.

4,000 prospectors find gold.

200 become rich.

DEADLY DIGGING

An estimated 7,500 people died while digging for gold and silver during the Western gold rushes. That was more than the total number of people who died in the Indian wars.

THINKING CRITICALLY

CONNECT TO HISTORY

1. **Creating Graphs** Use the Data File to create a bar graph that shows the percentage of people who set out for the Klondike who did not get there, got there, staked claims, found gold, and became rich.

    SEE SKILLBUILDER HANDBOOK, PAGE R30.

CONNECT TO TODAY

2. **Researching Ghost Towns** Research the history of a ghost town from boom to bust. Present a short report on life in the town and its attempts to survive beyond the gold rush.

hmhsocialstudies.com RESEARCH WEB LINKS

PI 3.1 CC Unit 1.I.4.c CC Unit 3.III.D.1.a
PI 3.4 CC Unit 3.III.D.1.c CC Unit 3.III.D.2.a
PI 4.1 CC Unit 3.III.D.2.b

Settling on the Great Plains

MAIN IDEA	WHY IT MATTERS NOW	Terms & Names
Settlers on the Great Plains transformed the land despite great hardships.	The Great Plains region remains the breadbasket of the United States.	• Homestead Act • Morrill Act • exoduster • bonanza farm • soddy

One American's Story

When Esther Clark Hill was a girl on the Kansas prairie in the 1800s, her father often left the family to go on hunting or trading expeditions. His trips left Esther's mother, Allena Clark, alone on the farm.

Esther remembered her mother holding on to the reins of a runaway mule team, "her black hair tumbling out of its pins and over her shoulders, her face set and white, while one small girl clung with chattering teeth to the sides of the rocking wagon." The men in the settlement spoke admiringly about "Leny's nerve," and Esther thought that daily life presented a challenge even greater than driving a runaway team.

▲ Plains settlers, like this woman depicted in Harvey Dunn's painting *Pioneer Woman*, had to be strong and self-reliant.

A PERSONAL VOICE ESTHER CLARK HILL

" I think, as much courage as it took to hang onto the reins that day, it took more to live twenty-four hours at a time, month in and out, on the lonely and lovely prairie, without giving up to the loneliness."

—quoted in *Pioneer Women*

As the railroads penetrated the frontier and the days of the free-ranging cowboy ended, hundreds of thousands of families migrated west, lured by vast tracts of cheap, fertile land. In their effort to establish a new life, they endured extreme hardships and loneliness.

Settlers Move Westward to Farm

It took over 250 years—from the first settlement at Jamestown until 1870—to turn 400 million acres of forests and prairies into flourishing farms. Settling the second 400 million acres took only 30 years, from 1870 to 1900. Federal land policy and the completion of transcontinental railroad lines made this rapid settlement possible.

RAILROADS OPEN THE WEST From 1850 to 1871, the federal government made huge land grants to the railroads—170 million acres, worth half a billion dollars—for laying track in the West. In one grant, both the Union Pacific and the Central Pacific received 10 square miles of public land for every mile of track laid in a state and 20 square miles of land for every mile of track laid in a territory.

In the 1860s, the two companies began a race to lay track. The Central Pacific moved eastward from Sacramento, and the Union Pacific moved westward from Omaha. Civil War veterans, Irish and Chinese immigrants, African Americans, and Mexican Americans did most of the grueling labor. In late 1868, workers for the Union Pacific cut their way through the solid rock of the mountains, laying up to eight miles of track a day. Both companies had reached Utah by the spring of 1869. Fifteen years later, the country boasted five transcontinental railroads. The rails to the East and West Coasts were forever linked.

The railroad companies sold some of their land to farmers for two to ten dollars an acre. Some companies successfully sent agents to Europe to recruit buyers. By 1880, 44 percent of the settlers in Nebraska and more than 70 percent of those in Minnesota and Wisconsin were immigrants. **Ⓐ**

GOVERNMENT SUPPORT FOR SETTLEMENT Another powerful attraction of the West was the land itself. In 1862, Congress passed the **Homestead Act**, offering 160 acres of land free to any citizen or intended citizen who was head of the household. From 1862 to 1900, up to 600,000 families took advantage of the government's offer. Several thousand settlers were **exodusters**—African Americans who moved from the post-Reconstruction South to Kansas.

Despite the massive response by homesteaders, or settlers on this free land, private speculators and railroad and state government agents sometimes used the law for their own gain. Cattlemen fenced open lands, while miners and woodcutters claimed national resources. Only about 10 percent of the land was actually settled by the families for whom it was intended. In addition, not all plots of land were of equal value. Although 160 acres could provide a decent living in the fertile soil of Iowa or Minnesota, settlers on drier Western land required larger plots to make farming worthwhile.

Eventually, the government strengthened the Homestead Act and passed more legislation to encourage settlers. In 1889, a major land giveaway in what is now Oklahoma attracted thousands of people. In less than a day, land-hungry settlers claimed 2 million acres in a massive land rush. Some took possession of the land before the government officially declared it open. Because these settlers claimed land sooner than they were supposed to, Oklahoma came to be known as the Sooner State. **Ⓑ**

MAIN IDEA

Analyzing Causes

Ⓐ How did the railroads help open the West?

Vocabulary
speculator: a person who buys or sells something that involves a risk on the chance of making a profit

MAIN IDEA

Analyzing Effects

Ⓑ In what ways did government policies encourage settlement of the West?

Posters like the one shown here drew hundreds of thousands of settlers to the West. Among the settlers were thousands of exodusters—freed slaves who had left the South.

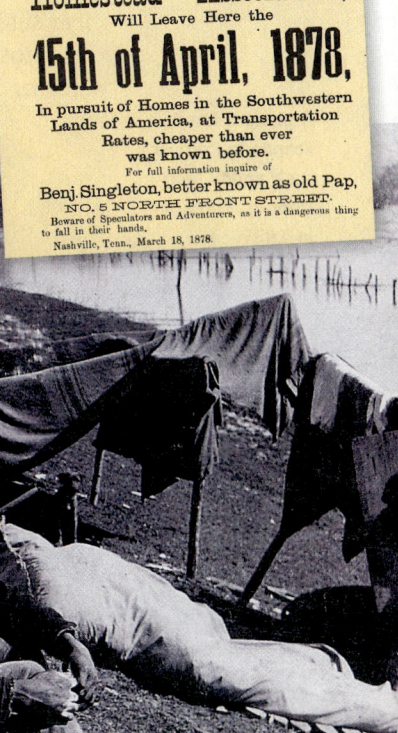

Ho for Kansas!

Brethren, Friends, & Fellow Citizens:
I feel thankful to inform you that the
REAL ESTATE
AND
Homestead Association,
Will Leave Here the
15th of April, 1878,

In pursuit of Homes in the Southwestern Lands of America, at Transportation Rates, cheaper than ever was known before.
For full information inquire of
Benj. Singleton, better known as old Pap,
NO. 5 NORTH FRONT STREET.
Beware of Speculators and Adventurers, as it is a dangerous thing to fall in their hands.
Nashville, Tenn., March 18, 1878.

THE CLOSING OF THE FRONTIER As settlers gobbled up Western land, Henry D. Washburn and fellow explorer Nathaniel P. Langford asked Congress to help protect the wilderness from settlement. In 1870, Washburn, who was surveying land in northwestern Wyoming, described the area's geysers and bubbling springs as: "objects new in experience . . . possessing unlimited grandeur and beauty."

In 1872, the government created Yellowstone National Park. Seven years later, the Department of the Interior forced railroads to give up their claim to Western landholdings that were equal in area to New York, New Jersey, Pennsylvania, Delaware, Maryland, and Virginia combined. Even so, by 1880, individuals had bought more than 19 million acres of government-owned land. Ten years later, the Census Bureau declared that the country no longer had a continuous frontier line—the frontier no longer existed. To many, the frontier was what had made America unique. In an 1893 essay entitled "The Significance of the Frontier in American History," the historian Frederick Jackson Turner agreed.

Background
The U.S. Census Bureau is the permanent collector of timely, relevant data about the people and economy of the United States.

★ **A PERSONAL VOICE** FREDERICK JACKSON TURNER

" American social development has been continually beginning over again on the frontier. This perennial rebirth, this fluidity of American life, this expansion westward with its new opportunities, its continuous touch with the simplicity of primitive society, furnish the forces dominating American character. "

—"The Significance of the Frontier in American History"

Today many historians question Turner's view. They think he gave too much importance to the frontier in the nation's development and in shaping a special American character. **C**

Settlers Meet the Challenges of the Plains

The frontier settlers faced extreme hardships—droughts, floods, fires, blizzards, locust plagues, and occasional raids by outlaws and Native Americans. Yet the number of people living west of the Mississippi River grew from 1 percent of the nation's population in 1850 to almost 30 percent by the turn of the century.

DUGOUTS AND SODDIES Since trees were scarce, most settlers built their homes from the land itself. Many pioneers dug their homes into the sides of ravines or small hills. A stovepipe jutting from the ground was often the only clear sign of such a dugout home.

Those who moved to the broad, flat plains often made freestanding houses by stacking blocks of prairie turf. Like a dugout, a sod home, or **soddy**, was warm in

MAIN IDEA

Summarizing
C What was Turner's view of the role of the American frontier in 1893?

Vocabulary
locust: any of numerous grasshoppers that travel in large swarms, often doing great damage to crops

Background
During much of the 1800s, most people considered the western Great Plains unsuitable for settlement—so much so that this region became known as the Great American Desert. Eventually, people realized that this area was prime farming land because it was located atop a huge natural underground reservoir.

A pioneer family stands in front of their soddy near Coburg, Nebraska, in 1887. ▶

winter and cool in summer. Soddies were small, however, and offered little light or air. They were havens for snakes, insects, and other pests. Although they were fireproof, they leaked continuously when it rained.

WOMEN'S WORK Virtually alone on the flat, endless prairie, homesteaders had to be almost superhumanly self-sufficient. Women often worked beside the men in the fields, plowing the land and planting and harvesting the predominant crop, wheat. They sheared the sheep and carded wool to make clothes for their families. They hauled water from wells that they had helped to dig, and made soap and candles from tallow. At harvest time, they canned fruits and vegetables. They were skilled in doctoring—from snakebites to crushed limbs. Women also sponsored schools and churches in an effort to build strong communities.

TECHNICAL SUPPORT FOR FARMERS Establishing a homestead was challenging. Once accomplished, it was farming the prairie, year in and year out, that became an overwhelming task. In 1837, John Deere had invented a steel plow that could slice through heavy soil. In 1847, Cyrus McCormick began to mass-produce a reaping machine. But a mass market for these devices didn't fully develop until the late 1800s with the migration of farmers onto the plains.

Other new and improved devices made farm work speedier—the spring-tooth harrow to prepare the soil (1869), the grain drill to plant the seed (1841), barbed wire to fence the land (1874), and the corn binder (1878). Then came a reaper that could cut and thresh wheat in one pass. By 1890, there were more than 900 manufacturers of farm equipment. In 1830, producing a bushel of grain took about 183 minutes. By 1900, with the use of these machines, it took only 10 minutes. These inventions made more grain available for a wider market. **D**

MAIN IDEA

Summarizing
D How did new inventions change farming in the West?

AGRICULTURAL EDUCATION The federal government supported farmers by financing agricultural education. The **Morrill Act** of 1862 and 1890 gave federal land to the states to help finance agricultural colleges, and the Hatch Act of 1887 established agricultural experiment stations to inform farmers of new developments. Agricultural researchers developed grains for arid soil and techniques for dry farming, which helped the land to retain moisture. These innovations enabled the dry eastern plains to flourish and become "the breadbasket of the nation."

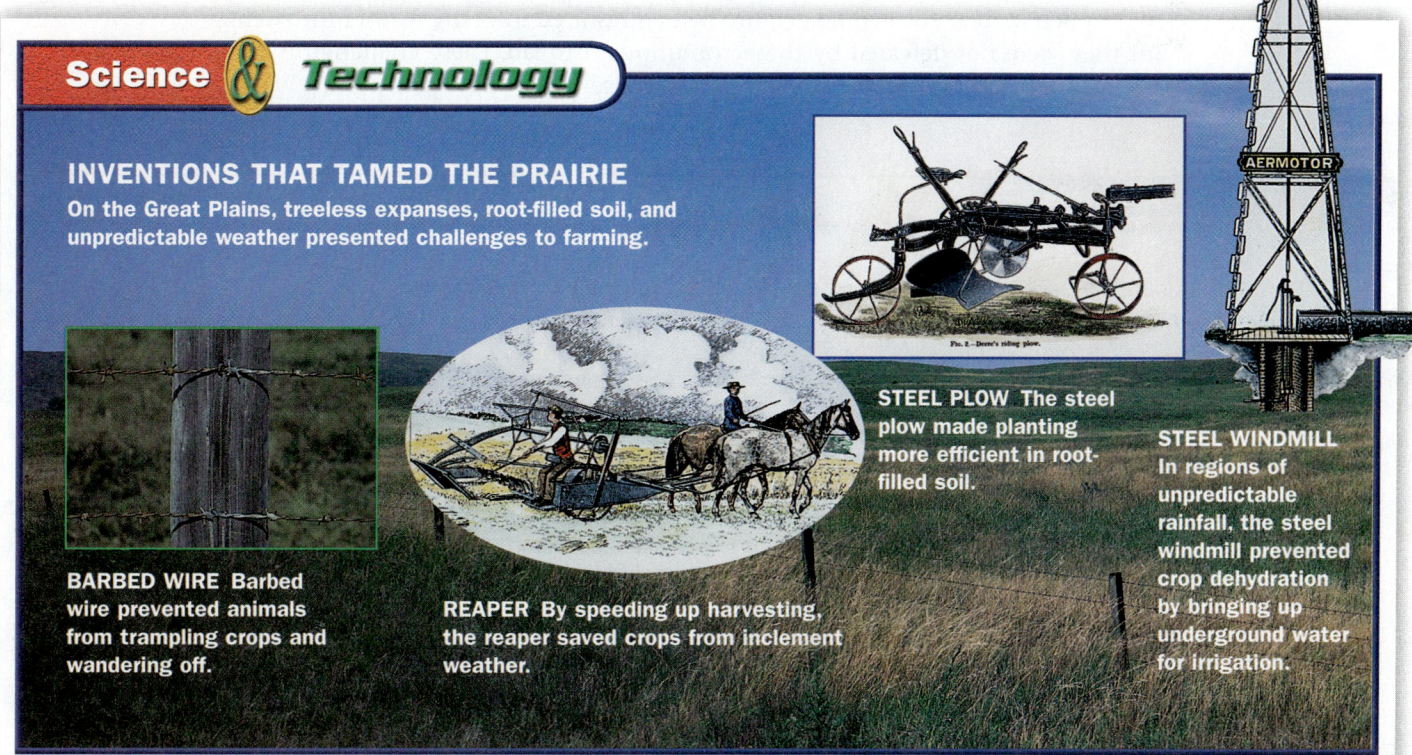

Science & Technology

INVENTIONS THAT TAMED THE PRAIRIE
On the Great Plains, treeless expanses, root-filled soil, and unpredictable weather presented challenges to farming.

BARBED WIRE Barbed wire prevented animals from trampling crops and wandering off.

REAPER By speeding up harvesting, the reaper saved crops from inclement weather.

STEEL PLOW The steel plow made planting more efficient in root-filled soil.

STEEL WINDMILL In regions of unpredictable rainfall, the steel windmill prevented crop dehydration by bringing up underground water for irrigation.

Bonanza farms like this one required the labor of hundreds of farm hands and horses.

FARMERS IN DEBT Elaborate machinery was expensive, and farmers often had to borrow money to buy it. When prices for wheat were higher, farmers could usually repay their loans. When wheat prices fell, however, farmers needed to raise more crops to make ends meet. This situation gave rise to a new type of farming in the late 1870s. Railroad companies and investors created **bonanza farms**, enormous single-crop spreads of 15,000–50,000 acres. The Cass-Cheney-Dalrymple farm near Cassleton, North Dakota, for example, covered 24 square miles. By 1900, the average farmer had nearly 150 acres under cultivation. Some farmers mortgaged their land to buy more property, and as farms grew bigger, so did farmers' debts. Between 1885 and 1890, much of the plains experienced drought, and the large single-crop operations couldn't compete with smaller farms, which could be more flexible in the crops they grew. The bonanza farms slowly folded into bankruptcy.

Farmers also felt pressure from the rising cost of shipping grain. Railroads charged Western farmers a higher fee than they did farmers in the East. Also, the railroads sometimes charged more for short hauls, for which there was no competing transportation, than for long hauls. The railroads claimed that they were merely doing business, but farmers resented being taken advantage of. "No other system of taxation has borne as heavily on the people as those extortions and inequalities of railroad charges" wrote Henry Demarest Lloyd in an article in the March 1881 edition of *Atlantic Monthly*.

Many farmers found themselves growing as much grain as they could grow, on as much land as they could acquire, which resulted in going further into debt. But they were not defeated by these conditions. Instead, these challenging conditions drew farmers together in a common cause.

Vocabulary
mortgage: to legally pledge property to a creditor as security for the payment of a loan or debt

Vocabulary
extortion: illegal use of one's official position or powers to obtain property or funds

---

SECTION 2 ASSESSMENT

1. TERMS & NAMES For each term or name, write a sentence explaining its significance.
- Homestead Act
- exoduster
- soddy
- Morrill Act
- bonanza farm

MAIN IDEA

2. TAKING NOTES
Create a time line of four events that shaped the settling of the Great Plains.

How might history be different if one of these events hadn't happened?

CRITICAL THINKING

3. EVALUATING
How successful were government efforts to promote settlement of the Great Plains? Give examples to support your answer. **Think About:**
- the growth in population on the Great Plains
- the role of railroads in the economy
- the Homestead Act

4. DRAWING CONCLUSIONS
Review the changes in technology that influenced the life of settlers on the Great Plains in the late 1800s. Explain how you think settlement of the plains would have been different without these inventions.

5. IDENTIFYING PROBLEMS
How did the railroads take advantage of farmers?

Farmers and the Populist Movement

MAIN IDEA	WHY IT MATTERS NOW	Terms & Names
Farmers united to address their economic problems, giving rise to the Populist movement.	Many of the Populist reform issues, such as income tax and legally protected rights of workers, are now taken for granted.	• Oliver Hudson Kelley • Grange • Farmers' Alliances • Populism • bimetallism • gold standard • William McKinley • William Jennings Bryan

One American's Story

As a young adult in the early 1870s, Mary Elizabeth Lease left home to teach school on the Kansas plains. After marrying farmer Charles Lease, she joined the growing Farmers' Alliance movement and began speaking on issues of concern to farmers. Lease joked that her tongue was "loose at both ends and hung on a swivel," but her golden voice and deep blue eyes hypnotized her listeners.

A PERSONAL VOICE MARY ELIZABETH LEASE

" What you farmers need to do is to raise less corn and more Hell! We want the accursed foreclosure system wiped out. . . . We will stand by our homes and stay by our firesides by force if necessary, and we will not pay our debts to the loan-shark companies until the Government pays its debts to us. "

—quoted in "The Populist Uprising"

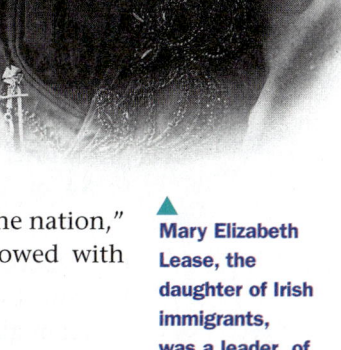

▲ Mary Elizabeth Lease, the daughter of Irish immigrants, was a leader of the Populist Party.

Farmers had endured great hardships in helping to transform the plains from the "Great American Desert" into the "breadbasket of the nation," yet every year they reaped less and less of the bounty they had sowed with their sweat.

Farmers Unite to Address Common Problems

In the late 1800s, many farmers were trapped in a vicious economic cycle. Prices for crops were falling, and farmers often mortgaged their farms so that they could buy more land and produce more crops. Good farming land was becoming scarce, though, and banks were foreclosing on the mortgages of increasing numbers of farmers who couldn't make payments on their loans. Moreover, the railroads were taking advantage of farmers by charging excessive prices for shipping and storage.

THE PLIGHT OF THE FARMERS

Farmers were particularly hard hit in the decades leading to the financial panic of 1893. They regarded big business interests as insurmountable enemies who were bringing them to their knees and leaving them with debts at every turn. This cartoon is a warning of the dangers confronting not only the farmers but the entire nation.

SKILLBUILDER Analyzing Political Cartoons

1. How does this cartoon depict the plight of the farmers?
2. Who does the cartoonist suggest is responsible for the farmers' plight?

 SEE SKILLBUILDER HANDBOOK, PAGE R24.

ECONOMIC DISTRESS The troubles of the farmers were part of a larger economic problem affecting the entire nation. During the Civil War, the United States had issued almost $500 million in paper money, called greenbacks. Greenbacks could not be exchanged for silver or gold money. They were worth less than hard money of the same face value. Hard money included both coins and paper money printed in yellow ink that could be exchanged for gold. After the war, the government began to take the greenbacks out of circulation.

Retiring the greenbacks caused some discontent. It increased the value of the money that stayed in circulation. It meant that farmers who had borrowed money had to pay back their loans in dollars that were worth more than the dollars they had borrowed. At the same time they were receiving less money for their crops. Between 1867 and 1887, for example, the price of a bushel of wheat fell from $2.00 to 68 cents. In effect, farmers lost money at every turn. **A**

Throughout the 1870s, the farmers and other debtors pushed the government to issue more money into circulation. Those tactics failed—although the Bland-Allison Act of 1878 required the government to buy and coin at least $2 million to $4 million worth of silver each month. It wasn't enough to support the increase in the money supply that the farmers wanted.

PROBLEMS WITH THE RAILROADS Meanwhile, farmers paid outrageously high prices to transport grain. Lack of competition among the railroads meant that it might cost more to ship grain from the Dakotas to Minneapolis by rail than from Chicago to England by boat. Also, railroads made secret agreements with middlemen—grain brokers and merchants—that allowed the railroads to control grain storage prices and to influence the market price of crops.

Many farmers mortgaged their farms for credit with which to buy seed and supplies. Suppliers charged high rates of interest, sometimes charging more for items bought on credit than they did for cash purchases. Farmers got caught in a cycle of credit that meant longer hours and more debt every year. It was time for reform. **B**

THE FARMERS' ALLIANCES To push effectively for reforms, however, farmers needed to organize. In 1867, **Oliver Hudson Kelley** started the Patrons of

MAIN IDEA

Analyzing Issues
A Why did farmers think that an increased money supply would help solve their economic problems?

MAIN IDEA

Analyzing Causes
B What were some of the causes of farmers' economic problems?

Husbandry, an organization for farmers that became popularly known as the **Grange**. Its original purpose was to provide a social outlet and an educational forum for isolated farm families. By the 1870s, however, Grange members spent most of their time and energy fighting the railroads. The Grange's battle plan included teaching its members how to organize, how to set up farmers' cooperatives, and how to sponsor state legislation to regulate railroads.

The Grange gave rise to other organizations, such as **Farmers' Alliances.** These groups included many others who sympathized with farmers. Alliances sent lecturers from town to town to educate people about topics such as lower interest rates on loans and government control over railroads and banks. Spellbinding speakers such as Mary Elizabeth Lease helped get the message across.

Membership grew to more than 4 million—mostly in the South and the West. The Southern Alliance, made up of white Southern farmers, was the largest. About 250,000 African Americans belonged to the Colored Farmers' National Alliance. Some alliance members promoted cooperation between black and white alliances, but most members accepted the separation of the organizations.

Vocabulary
regulate: to control or direct according to a rule or law

HISTORICAL SPOTLIGHT

THE COLORED FARMERS' NATIONAL ALLIANCE

A white Baptist missionary, R. M. Humphrey, organized the Colored Farmers' National Alliance in 1886 in Houston, Texas. Like their counterparts in the white alliances, members of the local colored farmers' alliances promoted cooperative buying and selling. Unlike white organizations, however, the black alliances had to work mostly in secret to avoid racially motivated violence at the hands of angry landowners and suppliers.

The Rise and Fall of Populism

Leaders of the alliance movement realized that to make far-reaching changes, they would need to build a base of political power. **Populism**—the movement of the people—was born with the founding of the Populist, or People's, Party, in 1892. On July 2, 1892, a Populist Party convention in Omaha, Nebraska, demanded reforms to lift the burden of debt from farmers and other workers and to give the people a greater voice in their government.

THE POPULIST PARTY PLATFORM The economic reforms proposed by the Populists included an increase in the money supply, which would produce a rise in prices received for goods and services; a graduated income tax; and a federal loan program. The proposed governmental reforms included the election of U.S. senators by popular vote, single terms for the president and the vice-president, and a secret ballot to end vote fraud. Finally, the Populists called for an eight-hour workday and restrictions on immigration.

The proposed changes were so attractive to struggling farmers and desperate laborers that in 1892 the Populist presidential candidate won almost 10 percent of the total vote. In the West, the People's Party elected five senators, three governors, and about 1,500 state legislators. The Populists' programs eventually became the platform of the Democratic Party and kept alive the concept that the government is responsible for reforming social injustices. **C**

MAIN IDEA

Summarizing
C What was the Populist Party platform?

THE PANIC OF 1893 During the 1880s, farmers were overextended with debts and loans. Railroad construction had expanded faster than markets. In February 1893, the Philadelphia and Reading Railroad went bankrupt, followed by the Erie, the Northern Pacific, the Union Pacific, and the Santa Fe. The government's gold supply had worn thin, partly due to its obligation to purchase silver. People panicked and traded paper money for gold. The panic also spread to Wall Street, where the prices of stocks fell rapidly. The price of silver then plunged, causing silver mines to close. By the end of the year, over 15,000 businesses and 500 banks had collapsed.

**WILLIAM JENNINGS BRYAN
1860–1925**

William Jennings Bryan might be considered a patron saint of lost causes, largely because he let beliefs, not politics, guide his actions. He resigned his position as secretary of state (1913–1915) under Woodrow Wilson, for example, to protest the president's movement away from neutrality regarding the war in Europe.

Near the end of his life, he went to Tennessee to assist the prosecution in the Scopes "monkey trial," contesting the teaching of evolution in public schools. He is perhaps best characterized by a quote from his own "Cross of Gold" speech: "The humblest citizen in all the land, when clad in the armor of a righteous cause, is stronger than all the hosts of error."

Investments declined, and consumer purchases, wages, and prices also fell. Panic deepened into depression as 3 million people lost their jobs. By December 1894, a fifth of the work force was unemployed. Many farm families suffered both hunger and unemployment. **D**

SILVER OR GOLD Populists watched as the two major political parties became deeply divided in a struggle between different regions and economic interests. Business owners and bankers of the industrialized Northeast were Republicans; the farmers and laborers of the agrarian South and West were Democrats.

The central issue of the campaign was which metal would be the basis of the nation's monetary system. On one side were the "silverites," who favored **bimetallism**, a monetary system in which the government would give citizens either gold or silver in exchange for paper currency or checks. On the other side were President Cleveland and the "gold bugs," who favored the **gold standard**—backing dollars solely with gold.

The backing of currency was an important campaign issue because people regarded paper money as worthless if it could not be turned in for gold or silver. Because silver was more plentiful than gold, backing currency with both metals, as the silverites advocated, would make more currency (with less value per dollar) available. Supporters of bimetallism hoped that this measure would stimulate the stagnant economy. Retaining the gold standard would provide a more stable, but expensive, currency.

BRYAN AND THE "CROSS OF GOLD" Stepping into the debate, the Populist Party called for bimetallism and free coinage of silver. Yet their strategy was undecided: should they join forces with sympathetic candidates in the major parties and risk losing their political identity, or should they nominate their own candidates and risk losing the election?

As the 1896 campaign progressed, the Republican Party stated its firm commitment to the gold standard and nominated Ohioan **William McKinley** for president. After much debate, the Democratic Party came out in favor of a combined gold and silver standard, including unlimited coinage of silver. At the Democratic convention, former Nebraska congressman **William Jennings Bryan**, editor of the *Omaha World-Herald*, delivered an impassioned address to the assembled

MAIN IDEA

Analyzing Causes

D What caused the panic of 1893?

Gold Bugs and Silverites		
	Gold Bugs	**Silverites**
Who They Were	bankers and businessmen	farmers and laborers
What They Wanted	gold standard less money in circulation	bimetallism more money in circulation
Why	Loans would be repaid in stable money.	Products would be sold at higher prices.
Effects	DEFLATION • Prices fall. • Value of money increases. • Fewer people have money.	INFLATION • Prices rise. • Value of money decreases. • More people have money.

delegates. An excerpt of what has become known as the "Cross of Gold" speech follows.

A PERSONAL VOICE WILLIAM JENNINGS BRYAN

"**Having behind us the producing masses of this nation and the world, supported by the commercial interests, the laboring interests, and the toilers everywhere, we will answer their demand for a gold standard by saying to them: You shall not press down upon the brow of labor this crown of thorns, you shall not crucify mankind upon a cross of gold.**"

—Democratic convention speech, Chicago, July 8, 1896

Bryan won the Democratic nomination. When the Populist convention met two weeks later, the delegates were both pleased and frustrated. They liked Bryan and the Democratic platform, but they detested the Democratic vice-presidential candidate, Maine banker Arthur Sewall. Nor did they like giving up their identity as a party. They compromised by endorsing Bryan, nominating their own candidate, Thomas Watson of Georgia, for vice-president, and keeping their party organization intact. **E**

▲ **William Jennings Bryan's "Cross of Gold" speech inspired many cartoonists.**

MAIN IDEA

Analyzing Issues

E Why was the metal that backed paper currency such an important issue in the 1896 presidential campaign?

THE END OF POPULISM Bryan faced a difficult campaign. His free-silver stand had led gold bug Democrats to nominate their own candidate. It also weakened his support in cities, where consumers feared inflation because it would make goods more expensive. In addition, Bryan's meager funds could not match the millions backing McKinley. Bryan tried to make up for lack of funds by campaigning in 27 states and sometimes making 20 speeches a day. McKinley, on the other hand, campaigned from his front porch, while thousands of well-known people toured the country speaking on his behalf.

McKinley got approximately 7 million votes and Bryan about 6.5 million. As expected, McKinley carried the East, while Bryan carried the South and the farm vote of the Middle West. The voters of the industrial Middle West, with their fear of inflation, brought McKinley into office.

With McKinley's election, Populism collapsed, burying the hopes of the farmers. The movement left two powerful legacies, however: a message that the downtrodden could organize and have political impact, and an agenda of reforms, many of which would be enacted in the 20th century.

SECTION 3 ASSESSMENT

1. TERMS & NAMES For each term or name, write a sentence explaining its significance.
- •Oliver Hudson Kelley
- •Grange
- •Farmers' Alliances
- •Populism
- •bimetallism
- •gold standard
- •William McKinley
- •William Jennings Bryan

MAIN IDEA

2. TAKING NOTES
Identify the causes of the rise of the Populist Party and the effects the party had.

Which effect has the most impact today? Explain.

CRITICAL THINKING

3. EVALUATING
What do you think were the most significant factors in bringing an end to the Populist Party? **Think about:**

- monetary policy
- third-party status
- source of popular support
- popular participation policy

4. MAKING INFERENCES
How did the Grange and the Farmers' Alliances pave the way for the Populist Party?

Literature of the West

1850–1900 After gold was discovered in California, Americans came to view the West as a region of unlimited possibility. Those who could not venture there in person enjoyed reading about the West in colorful tales by writers such as Mark Twain (Samuel Clemens) and Bret Harte. Dime novels, cheaply bound adventure stories that sold for a dime, were also enormously popular in the second half of the 19th century.

Since much of the West was Spanish-dominated for centuries, Western literature includes legends and songs of Hispanic heroes and villains. It also includes the haunting words of Native Americans whose lands were taken and cultures threatened as white pioneers moved west.

▲ **Mark Twain**

THE CELEBRATED JUMPING FROG OF CALAVERAS COUNTY

The American humorist Samuel Clemens—better known as Mark Twain—was a would-be gold and silver miner who penned tales of frontier life. "The Celebrated Jumping Frog of Calaveras County" is set in a California mining camp. Most of the tale is told by Simon Wheeler, an old-timer given to exaggeration.

"Well, Smiley kep' the beast in a little lattice box, and he used to fetch him downtown sometimes and lay for a bet. One day a feller—a stranger in the camp, he was—come acrost him with his box, and says:

"'What might it be that you've got in the box?'

"And Smiley says, sorter indifferent-like, 'It might be a parrot, or it might be a canary, maybe, but it ain't—it's only just a frog.'

"And the feller took it, and looked at it careful, and turned it round this way and that, and says, 'H'm—so 'tis. Well, what's *he* good for?'

"'Well,' Smiley says, easy and careless, 'he's good enough for *one* thing, I should judge—he can outjump any frog in Calaveras County.'

"The feller took the box again, and took another long, particular look, and give it back to Smiley, and says, very deliberate, 'Well,' he says, 'I don't see no p'ints about that frog that's any better'n any other frog.'

"'Maybe you don't,' Smiley says. 'Maybe you understand frogs and maybe you don't understand 'em; maybe you've had experience, and maybe you ain't only a amature, as it were. Anyways, I've got my opinion, and I'll resk forty dollars that he can outjump any frog in Calaveras County.'"

—Mark Twain, "The Celebrated Jumping Frog of Calaveras County"
(1865)

THE BALLAD OF GREGORIO CORTEZ

In the border ballads, or *corridos*, of the American Southwest, few figures are as famous as the Mexican vaquero, Gregorio Cortez. This excerpt from a ballad about Cortez deals with a confrontation between Cortez and a group of Texas lawmen. Although he is hotly pursued, Cortez has an amazingly long run before being captured.

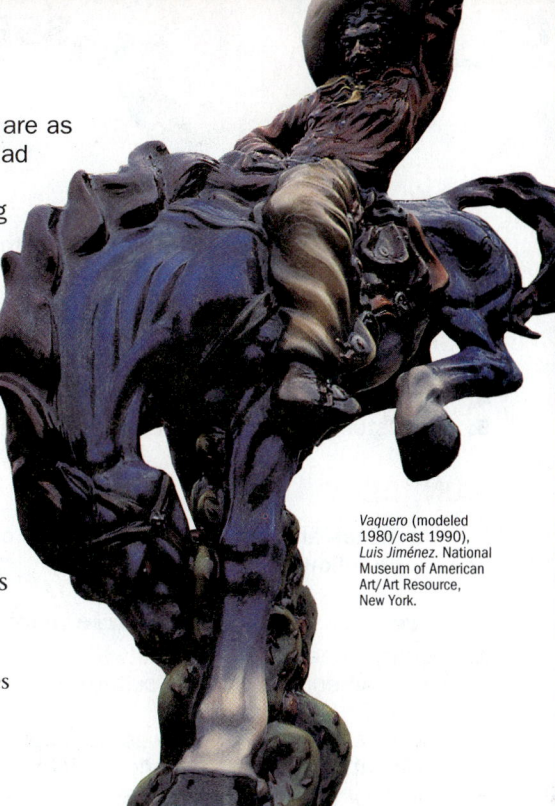

Vaquero (modeled 1980/cast 1990), *Luis Jiménez*. National Museum of American Art/Art Resource, New York.

. . . And in the county of Kiansis
They cornered him after all;
Though they were more than
    three hundred
He leaped out of their corral.

Then the Major Sheriff said,
As if he was going to cry,
"Cortez, hand over your weapons;
We want to take you alive."

Then said Gregorio Cortez,
And his voice was like a bell,
"You will never get my
    weapons
Till you put me in a cell."

Then said Gregorio Cortez,
With his pistol in his hand,
"Ah, so many mounted Rangers
Just to take one Mexican!"

—Anonymous, "The Ballad of Gregorio Cortez," translated by Américo Paredes

▲ **Chief Satanta**

CHIEF SATANTA'S SPEECH AT THE MEDICINE LODGE CREEK COUNCIL

Known as the Orator of the Plains, Chief Satanta represented the Kiowa people in the 1867 Medicine Lodge Creek negotiations with the U.S. government. The speech from which this excerpt is taken was delivered by Satanta in Spanish but was translated into English and widely published in leading newspapers of the day.

All the land south of the Arkansas belongs to the Kiowas and Comanches, and I don't want to give away any of it. I love the land and the buffalo and will not part with it. I want you to understand well what I say. Write it on paper. Let the Great Father [U.S. president] see it, and let me hear what he has to say. I want you to understand also, that the Kiowas and Comanches don't want to fight, and have not been fighting since we made the treaty. I hear a great deal of good talk from the gentlemen whom the Great Father sends us, but they never do what they say. I don't want any of the medicine lodges [schools and churches] within the country. I want the children raised as I was. When I make peace, it is a long and lasting one—there is no end to it. . . . A long time ago this land belonged to our fathers; but when I go up to the river I see camps of soldiers on its banks. These soldiers cut down my timber; they kill my buffalo; and when I see that, my heart feels like bursting; I feel sorry. I have spoken.

—Chief Satanta, speech at the Medicine Lodge Creek Council (1867)

THINKING CRITICALLY

1. **Comparing and Contrasting** Compare and contrast the views these selections give of the American frontier in the second half of the 19th century. Use details from the selections to help explain your answer.

   📘 **SEE SKILLBUILDER HANDBOOK, PAGE R8.**

2. **hmhsocialstudies.com**   **INTERNET ACTIVITY**

   From the gauchos of the Argentine pampas to the workers on Australian sheep stations, many nations have had their own versions of the cowboys of the American West. Use the links for American Literature to research one such nation. Prepare a bulletin-board display that shows the similarities and differences between Western cowboys and their counterparts in that country.

TERMS & NAMES

For each term or name below, write a sentence explaining its connection to changes on the Great Plains.

1. Homestead Act
2. Sitting Bull
3. assimilation
4. Morrill Act
5. exoduster
6. George A. Custer
7. William Jennings Bryan
8. William McKinley
9. Populism
10. Grange

MAIN IDEAS

Use your notes and the information in the chapter to answer the following questions.

Cultures Clash on the Prairie *(pages 408–417)*

1. Identify three differences between the culture of the Native Americans and the culture of the white settlers on the Great Plains.
2. How effective was the Dawes Act in promoting the assimilation of Native Americans into white culture?
3. Why did the cattle industry become a big business in the late 1800s?
4. How did cowboy culture reflect the ethnic diversity of the United States?

Settling on the Great Plains *(pages 420–424)*

5. What measures did the government take to support settlement of the frontier?
6. How did settlers overcome the challenges of living on the Great Plains?

Farmers and the Populist Movement
(pages 425–429)

7. What economic problems confronted American farmers in the 1890s?
8. According to farmers and other supporters of free silver, how would bimetallism help the economy?

CRITICAL THINKING

1. **USING YOUR NOTES** Create a cause/effect diagram identifying the reasons that agricultural output from the Great Plains increased during the late 1800s.

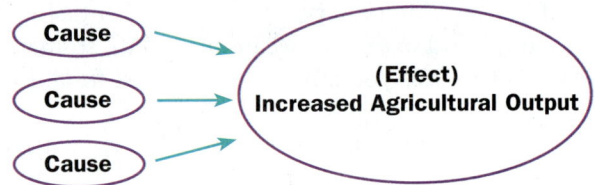

Cause →

Cause → **(Effect)** **Increased Agricultural Output**

Cause →

2. **ANALYZING MOTIVES** In 1877, Nez Perce Chief Joseph said, "My people have always been the friends of white men. Why are you in such a hurry?" Why do you think white people hurried to settle the West, with so little regard for Native Americans? Give evidence from the chapter to support your position.

3. **INTERPRETING CHARTS** Look at the chart of Gold Bugs and Silverites on page 428. What would be the result of the policies favored by the gold bugs? by the silverites?

VISUAL SUMMARY   CHANGES ON THE WESTERN FRONTIER

CLASH OF CULTURES ON THE FRONTIER

NATIVE AMERICANS

Native Americans of the plains hunted, farmed, and traded in traditional ways. Plains peoples relied on the buffalo for a variety of survival needs.

MINERS

Discoveries of gold and other precious metals led to the growth of mining camps and boomtowns in the Rocky Mountains and to the west.

RANCHERS AND COWHANDS

Ranchers and cowboys ushered in the era of the long drive and the roundup. Texas longhorn cattle took the place of the buffalo as the dominant animal on the Great Plains.

HOMESTEADERS

Hundreds of thousands of homesteaders settled on the plains, claiming land grants from the U.S. government.

FARMERS AND THE POPULIST MOVEMENT

New settlement, barbed wire, and bad weather ended the cattle boom. Farmers across the South, Midwest, and West organized to address their common economic problems.

Use the flowchart and your knowledge of U.S. history to answer question 1.

Rise and Fall of the Farm Economy, Late 1800s

New mechanized farm tools lead to increased production.

⬇

Crop output rises steadily from 1870–1900.

⬇

Prices for agricultural products fall.

⬇

?

1 Which effect accurately completes the flowchart?

(1) Farmers have less money to repay loans, and many lose their farms.

(2) Small farmers live off the land, so are not affected by the economy.

(3) Wealthy farmers hoard gold, rather than depend on paper money.

(4) The government subsidizes farmers to help them pay their bills.

Use the quotation and your knowledge of U.S. history to answer question 2.

" [We] have been taught to hunt and live on the game. You tell us that we must learn to farm, live in one house, and take on your ways. Suppose the people living beyond the great sea should come and tell you that you must stop farming, and kill your cattle, and take your houses and lands, what would you do? Would you not fight them? "

—Gall, a Hunkpapa Sioux, quoted in *Bury My Heart at Wounded Knee*

2 What was Gall's view of future relations between the Plains Indians and the settlers?

(1) peaceful coexistence

(2) further conflict

(3) mutual respect

(4) equality before the law

3 How did the invention of barbed wire change the look of the Western frontier?

(1) It endangered wildlife.

(2) It ended the cattle frontier.

(3) It increased cattle stocks.

(4) It enriched the cow towns.

hmhsocialstudies.com TEST PRACTICE

For additional test practice, go online for:
• Diagnostic tests   • Tutorials

INTERACT WITH HISTORY

Think about the issues you explored at the beginning of the chapter. Suppose you are a frontier settler. Write a letter to the family members you left behind describing your journey west and how you are living now. Use information from the chapter to provide some vivid impressions of life on the frontier.

FOCUS ON WRITING

You are a historian studying the development of the American West. Write an essay explaining how Americans settled the West in the late 1800s and how the region changed as a result. Use specific examples to support your main idea.

COLLABORATIVE LEARNING   21ST CENTURY

Work in pairs to research federal policy toward Native Americans between 1830 and 1890. Then work together to create a time line identifying key events that shaped the policy and the relationships between whites and Native Americans during the time period. Begin your time line with the passage of the Indian Removal Act in 1830 and end it with the Battle of Wounded Knee in 1890.

CHAPTER 14

A NEW INDUSTRIAL AGE

Essential Question

What impact did scientific discoveries and manufacturing processes have on the nature of work, the American labor movement, and American businesses?

 New York Standards

KEY IDEA 2 Important ideas, social and cultural values, beliefs, and traditions from New York State and United States history illustrate the connections and interactions of people and events across time and from a variety of perspectives.

KEY IDEA 3 Study about the major social, political, economic, cultural, and religious developments in New York State and United States history involves learning about the important roles and contributions of individuals and groups.

SECTION 1: The Expansion of Industry

SECTION 2: The Age of the Railroads

SECTION 3: Big Business and Labor

Laborers blasted tunnels and constructed bridges to send the railroad through the rugged Sierra Nevada mountains.

1869 Central Pacific and Union Pacific complete the transcontinental railroad.

1876 Alexander Graham Bell invents the telephone.

1877 *Munn v. Illinois* establishes government regulation of railroads.

Mother Jones supports the Great Strike of 1877.

1879 Thomas A. Edison invents a workable light bulb.

1884 Grover Cleveland is elected president.

USA
WORLD

1870

1880

1870 Franco-Prussian War breaks out.

1875 British labor unions win right to strike.

1882 United States restricts Chinese immigration.

1883 Germany becomes the first nation to provide national health insurance.

HISTORY

Great Minds in Business:
Andrew Carnegie

hmhsocialstudies.com VIDEO

INTERACT
WITH HISTORY

The year is 1863 and railroad construction is booming. In six years, the U.S. will be linked by rail from coast to coast. Central Pacific Railroad employs mainly Chinese immigrants to blast tunnels, lay track, and drive spikes, all for low wages. You are a journalist assigned to describe this monumental construction project for your readers.

Explore the Issues

• What dangers do the railroad workers encounter?

• How will businesses and the general public benefit from the transcontinental railroad?

• How might railroad construction affect the environment?

1886 Haymarket riot turns public sentiment against unions.

1890 Congress passes the Sherman Antitrust Act.

1894 President Cleveland sends federal troops to Illinois to end the Pullman strike.

1896 William McKinley is elected president.

1900 William McKinley is reelected.

1890

1900

1890 Colonization of sub-Saharan Africa peaks.

1893 Women in New Zealand gain voting rights.

1896 First modern Olympic Games are held in Athens, Greece.

PI 2.1 CC Unit 3.II.B.2 CC Unit 3.II.B.3
PI 3.1 CC Unit 3.II.B.4 CC Unit 3.III.A.2.b
        CC Unit 3.III.A.3.a CC Unit 3.III.A.3.c

The Expansion of Industry

MAIN IDEA	**WHY IT MATTERS NOW**	**Terms & Names**
At the end of the 19th century, natural resources, creative ideas, and growing markets fueled an industrial boom.	Technological developments of the late 19th century paved the way for the continued growth of American industry.	• Edwin L. Drake • Bessemer process • Thomas Alva Edison • Christopher Sholes • Alexander Graham Bell

One American's Story

hmhsocialstudies.com
TAKING NOTES

Use the graphic organizer online to take notes on the causes of the industrial boom and their impact on industrialization.

One day, Pattillo Higgins noticed bubbles in the springs around Spindletop, a hill near Beaumont in southeastern Texas. This and other signs convinced him that oil was underground. If Higgins found oil, it could serve as a fuel source around which a vibrant industrial city would develop.

Higgins, who had been a mechanic and a lumber merchant, couldn't convince geologists or investors that oil was present, but he didn't give up. A magazine ad seeking investors got one response—from Captain Anthony F. Lucas, an experienced prospector who also believed that there was oil at Spindletop. When other investors were slow to send money, Higgins kept his faith, not only in Spindletop, but in Lucas.

▲ **Pattillo Higgins**

A PERSONAL VOICE PATTILLO HIGGINS

" Captain Lucas, . . . these experts come and tell you this or that can't happen because it has never happened before. You believe there is oil here, . . . and I think you are right. I know there is oil here in greater quantities than man has ever found before."

—quoted in *Spindletop*

In 1900, the two men found investors, and they began to drill that autumn. After months of difficult, frustrating work, on the morning of January 10, 1901, oil gushed from their well. The Texas oil boom had begun.

Natural Resources Fuel Industrialization

After the Civil War, the United States was still largely an agricultural nation. By the 1920s—a mere 60 years later—it had become the leading industrial power in the world. This immense industrial boom was due to several factors, including: a wealth of natural resources, government support for business, and a growing urban population that provided both cheap labor and markets for new products.

BLACK GOLD Though eastern Native American tribes had made fuel and medicine from crude oil long before Europeans arrived on the continent, early American settlers had little use for oil. In the 1840s, Americans began using kerosene to light lamps after the Canadian geologist Abraham Gesner discovered how to distill the fuel from oil or coal.

It wasn't until 1859, however, when **Edwin L. Drake** successfully used a steam engine to drill for oil near Titusville, Pennsylvania, that removing oil from beneath the earth's surface became practical. This breakthrough started an oil boom that spread to Kentucky, Ohio, Illinois, Indiana, and, eventually, Texas. Petroleum-refining industries arose in Cleveland and Pittsburgh as entrepreneurs rushed to transform the oil into kerosene. Gasoline, a byproduct of the refining process, originally was thrown away. But after the automobile became popular, gasoline became the most important form of oil.

BESSEMER STEEL PROCESS Oil was not the only natural resource that was plentiful in the United States. There were also abundant deposits of coal and iron. In 1887, prospectors discovered iron ore deposits more than 100 miles long and up to 3 miles wide in the Mesabi Range of Minnesota. At the same time, coal production skyrocketed—from 33 million tons in 1870 to more than 250 million tons in 1900.

Iron is a dense metal, but it is soft and tends to break and rust. It also usually contains other elements, such as carbon. Removing the carbon from iron produces a lighter, more flexible, and rust-resistant metal—steel. The raw materials needed to make steel were readily available; all that was needed was a cheap and efficient manufacturing process. The **Bessemer process,** developed independently by the British manufacturer Henry Bessemer and American ironmaker William Kelly around 1850, soon became widely used. This technique involved injecting air into molten iron to remove the carbon and other impurities. By 1880, American manufacturers were using the new method to produce more than 90 percent of the nation's steel. In this age of rapid change and innovation, even

Vocabulary
entrepreneur: a person who organizes, operates, and assumes the risk for a business venture

Natural Resources and the Birth of a Steel Town, 1886–1906

Pittsburgh

- ○ Steel mills, 1886
- ● Steel mills, 1906

- ◉ Major industrial city
- • Other cities
- Coal mining
- Iron ore mining
- Oil
- Steel production

0   150   300 miles
0   150   300 kilometers

GEOGRAPHY SKILLBUILDER
1. **Region** Which state had the most steel-producing areas?
2. **Human-Environment Interaction** What connection can you draw between natural resources (including water) and steel production in Pittsburgh?

1826 1831 1837 1846 1860 1867 1873 1877 1895 1903
1876 1879

• Photography
• Reaper
• Telegraph
• Sewing Machine
Internal-Combustion Engine
• Dynamite
• Typewriter
• Light Bulb
• Phonograph
• Telephone
• Electric Motor
• Radio
• Motion Pictures
• X-Ray
• Airplane

the successful Bessemer process was bettered by the 1860s. It was eventually replaced by the open-hearth process, enabling manufacturers to produce quality steel from scrap metal as well as from raw materials. **A**

NEW USES FOR STEEL The railroads, with thousands of miles of track, became the biggest customers for steel, but inventors soon found additional uses for it. Joseph Glidden's barbed wire and McCormick's and Deere's farm machines helped transform the plains into the food producer of the nation.

Steel changed the face of the nation as well, as it made innovative construction possible. One of the most remarkable structures was the Brooklyn Bridge. Completed in 1883, it spanned 1,595 feet of the East River in New York City. Its steel cables were supported by towers higher than any man-made and weight-bearing structure except the pyramids of Egypt. Like those ancient marvels, the completed bridge was called a wonder of the world.

Around this time, setting the stage for a new era of expansion upward as well as outward, William Le Baron Jenney designed the first skyscraper with a steel frame—the Home Insurance Building in Chicago. Before Jenney had his pioneering idea, the weight of large buildings was supported entirely by their walls or by iron frames, which limited the buildings' height. With a steel frame to support the weight, however, architects could build as high as they wanted. As structures soared into the air, not even the sky seemed to limit what Americans could achieve.

Inventions Promote Change

By capitalizing on natural resources and their own ingenuity, inventors changed more than the landscape. Their inventions affected the very way people lived and worked.

THE POWER OF ELECTRICITY In 1876, **Thomas Alva Edison** became a pioneer on the new industrial frontier when he established the world's first research laboratory in Menlo Park, New Jersey. There Edison perfected the incandescent light bulb—patented in 1880—and later invented an entire system for producing and distributing electrical power. Another inventor, George Westinghouse, along with Edison, added innovations that made electricity safer and less expensive.

The harnessing of electricity completely changed the nature of business in America. By 1890, electric power ran numerous machines, from fans to printing presses. This inexpensive, convenient source of energy soon became available in homes and spurred the invention of time-saving appliances. Electric streetcars made urban travel cheap and efficient and also promoted the outward spread of cities.

More important, electricity allowed manufacturers to locate their plants

---

MAIN IDEA

Summarizing
A What natural resources were most important for industrialization?

HISTORICAL SPOTLIGHT

ILLUMINATING THE LIGHT BULB

Shortly after moving into a long wooden shed at Menlo Park, Thomas Alva Edison and his associates set to work to develop the perfect incandescent bulb. Arc lamps already lit some city streets and shops, using an electric current passing between two sticks of carbon, but they were glaring and inefficient.

Edison hoped to create a long-lasting lamp with a soft glow, and began searching for a filament that would burn slowly and stay lit. Edison tried wires, sticks, blades of grass, and even hairs from his assistants' beards. Finally, a piece of carbonized bamboo from Japan did the trick. Edison's company used bamboo filaments until 1911, when it began using tungsten filaments, which are still used today.

Vocabulary
incandescent: giving off visible light as a result of being heated

---

wherever they wanted—not just near sources of power, such as rivers. This enabled industry to grow as never before. Huge operations, such as the Armour and Swift meatpacking plants, and the efficient processes that they used became the models for new consumer industries. **B**

INVENTIONS CHANGE LIFESTYLES Edison's light bulb was only one of several revolutionary inventions. **Christopher Sholes** invented the typewriter in 1867 and changed the world of work. Next to the light bulb, however, perhaps the most dramatic invention was the telephone, unveiled by **Alexander Graham Bell** and Thomas Watson in 1876. It opened the way for a worldwide communications network.

The typewriter and the telephone particularly affected office work and created new jobs for women. Although women made up less than 5 percent of all office workers in 1870, by 1910 they accounted for nearly 40 percent of the clerical work force. New inventions also had a tremendous impact on factory work, as well as on jobs that traditionally had been done at home. For example, women had previously sewn clothing by hand for their families. With industrialization, clothing could be mass-produced in factories, creating a need for garment workers, many of whom were women.

Industrialization freed some factory workers from backbreaking labor and helped improve workers' standard of living. By 1890, the average workweek had been reduced by about ten hours. However, many laborers felt that the mechanization of so many tasks reduced human workers' worth. As consumers, though, workers regained some of their lost power in the marketplace. The country's expanding urban population provided a vast potential market for the new inventions and products of the late 1800s.

▲
The typewriter shown here dates from around 1890.

SECTION 1 ASSESSMENT

1. **TERMS & NAMES** For each term or name, write a sentence explaining its significance.
   - Edwin L. Drake
   - Bessemer process
   - Thomas Alva Edison
   - Christopher Sholes
   - Alexander Graham Bell

MAIN IDEA

2. **TAKING NOTES**
   In a chart like the one below, list resources, ideas, and markets that affected the industrial boom of the 19th century. In the second column, note how each item contributed to industrialization.

Resources, Ideas, Markets	Impact

CRITICAL THINKING

3. **MAKING INFERENCES**
   Do you think that consumers gained power as industry expanded in the late 19th century? Why or why not?

4. **HYPOTHESIZING**
   If the U.S. had been poor in natural resources, how would industrialization have been affected?

5. **ANALYZING EFFECTS**
   Which invention or development described in this section had the greatest impact on society? Justify your choice. **Think About:**
   - the applications of inventions
   - the impact of inventions on people's daily lives
   - the effect of inventions on the workplace

Industry Changes the Environment

By the mid-1870s, new ideas and technology were well on the way to changing almost every aspect of American life. The location of Cleveland, Ohio, on the shores of Lake Erie, gave the city access to raw materials and made it ripe for industrialization. What no one foresaw were the undesirable side effects of rapid development and technological progress.

1 FROM HAYSTACKS TO SMOKESTACKS

In 1874, parts of Cleveland were still rural, with farms like the one pictured dotting the landscape. The smokestacks of the Standard Oil refinery in the distance, however, indicate that industrialization had begun.

2 REFINING THE LANDSCAPE

Industries like the Standard Oil refinery shown in this 1889 photo soon became a source of prosperity for both Cleveland and the entire country. The pollution they belched into the atmosphere, however, was the beginning of an ongoing problem: how to balance industrial production and environmental concerns.

WESTPART OF THE 14th Ward OF CLEVELAND
Scale 400 Feet to an Inch.

③ A RIVER OF FIRE

Industrial pollution would affect not only the air but also the water. Refineries and steel mills discharged so much oil into the Cuyahoga River that major fires broke out on the water in 1936, 1952, and 1969. The 1952 blaze, pictured above, destroyed three tugboats, three buildings, and the ship-repair yards. In the decade following the 1969 fire, changes in the way industrial plants operated, along with the construction of wastewater treatment plants, helped restore the quality of the water.

THINKING CRITICALLY

1. **Analyzing Patterns** Locate the Standard Oil Company on the map of Cleveland. What can you conclude about where industry was located as compared with the location of residential neighborhoods?

2. **Creating a Thematic Map** Pose a historical question about the relationship between industry and areas of the Midwest. For example, what types of industry developed near Chicago and why? Then research and create a map that answers your question.

   SEE SKILLBUILDER HANDBOOK, PAGE R32.

hmhsocialstudies.com RESEARCH WEB LINKS

PI 2.3   CC Unit 3.II.A.1   CC Unit 3.II.A.2.d
PI 3.1   CC Unit 3.II.B.1   CC Unit 3.II.D.1
         CC Unit 3.II.D.2   CC Unit 3.II.D.3

The Age of the Railroads

MAIN IDEA	WHY IT MATTERS NOW	Terms & Names
The growth and consolidation of railroads benefited the nation but also led to corruption and required government regulation.	Railroads made possible the expansion of industry across the United States.	• transcontinental railroad • George M. Pullman • Crédit Mobilier • *Munn* v. *Illinois* • Interstate Commerce Act

One American's Story

hmhsocialstudies.com
TAKING NOTES

Use the graphic organizer online to take notes on the effects of the rapid growth of the railroads.

In October 1884, the economist Richard Ely visited the town of Pullman, Illinois, to write about it for *Harper's* magazine. At first, Ely was impressed with the atmosphere of order, planning, and well-being in the town George M. Pullman had designed for the employees of his railroad-car factory. But after talking at length with a dissatisfied company officer, Ely concluded the town had a fatal flaw: it too greatly restricted its residents. Pullman employees were compelled to obey rules in which they had no say. Ely concluded that "the idea of Pullman is un-American."

▲ The town of Pullman was carefully laid out and strictly controlled.

★ **A PERSONAL VOICE** RICHARD T. ELY

" It is benevolent, well-wishing feudalism [a medieval social system], which desires the happiness of the people, but in such way as shall please the authorities. . . . If free American institutions are to be preserved, we want no race of men reared as underlings. "

—"Pullman: A Social Study"

As the railroads grew, they came to influence many facets of American life, including, as in the town of Pullman, the personal lives of the country's citizens. They caused the standard time and time zones to be set and influenced the growth of towns and communities. However, the unchecked power of railroad companies led to widespread abuses that spurred citizens to demand federal regulation of the industry.

Railroads Span Time and Space

Rails made local transit reliable and westward expansion possible for business as well as for people. Realizing how important railroads were for settling the West and developing the country, the government made huge land grants and loans to the railroad companies.

A NATIONAL NETWORK By 1856, the railroads extended west to the Mississippi River, and three years later, they crossed the Missouri. Just over a decade later, crowds across the United States cheered as the Central Pacific and Union Pacific Railroads met at Promontory, Utah, on May 10, 1869. A golden spike marked the spanning of the nation by the first **transcontinental railroad**. Other transcontinental lines followed, and regional lines multiplied as well. At the start of the Civil War, the nation had had about 30,000 miles of track. By 1890, that figure was nearly six times greater.

ROMANCE AND REALITY The railroads brought the dreams of available land, adventure, and a fresh start within the grasp of many Americans. This romance was made possible, however, only by the harsh lives of railroad workers.

The Central Pacific Railroad employed thousands of Chinese immigrants. The Union Pacific hired Irish immigrants and desperate, out-of-work Civil War veterans to lay track across treacherous terrain while enduring attacks by Native Americans. Accidents and diseases disabled and killed thousands of men each year. In 1888, when the first railroad statistics were published, the casualties totaled more than 2,000 employees killed and 20,000 injured.

RAILROAD TIME In spite of these difficult working conditions, the railroad laborers helped to transform the diverse regions of the country into a united nation. Though linked in space, each community still operated on its own time, with noon when the sun was directly overhead. Noon in Boston, for example, was almost 12 minutes later than noon in New York. Travelers riding from Maine to California might reset their watches 20 times.

In 1869, to remedy this problem, Professor C. F. Dowd proposed that the earth's surface be divided into 24 time zones, one for each hour of the day. Under his plan, the United States would contain four zones: the Eastern, Central, Mountain, and Pacific time zones. The railroad companies endorsed Dowd's plan enthusiastically, and many towns followed suit.

Finally, on November 18, 1883, railroad crews and towns across the country synchronized their watches. In 1884, an international conference set worldwide time zones that incorporated railroad time. The U.S. Congress, however, didn't officially adopt railroad time as the standard for the nation until 1918. As strong a unifying force as the railroads were, however, they also opened the way for abuses that led to social and economic unrest. **A**

Opportunities and Opportunists

The growth of the railroads influenced the industries and businesses in which Americans worked. Iron, coal, steel, lumber, and glass industries grew rapidly as they tried to keep pace with the railroads' demand for materials and parts. The rapid spread of railroad lines also fostered the growth of towns, helped establish new markets, and offered rich opportunities for both visionaries and profiteers.

⬈ hmhsocialstudies.com

INTERACTIVE
Explore the impact of the railroads on Chicago.

Pullman cars brought luxury to the rails, as shown in this advertisement from around 1890. ▼

NEW TOWNS AND MARKETS By linking previously isolated cities, towns, and settlements, the railroads promoted trade and interdependence. As part of a nationwide network of suppliers and markets, individual towns began to specialize in particular products. Chicago soon became known for its stockyards and Minneapolis for its grain industries. These cities prospered by selling large quantities of their products to the entire country. New towns and communities also grew up along the railroad lines. Cities as diverse as Abilene, Kansas; Flagstaff, Arizona; Denver, Colorado; and Seattle, Washington, owed their prosperity, if not their very existence, to the railroads. **B**

PULLMAN The railroads helped cities not only grow up but branch out. In 1880, for example, **George M. Pullman** built a factory for manufacturing sleepers and other railroad cars on the Illinois prairie. The nearby town that Pullman built for his employees followed in part the models of earlier industrial experiments in Europe. Whereas New England textile manufacturers had traditionally provided housing for their workers, the town of Pullman provided for almost all of workers' basic needs. Pullman residents lived in clean, well-constructed brick houses and apartment buildings with at least one window in every room—a luxury for city dwellers. In addition, the town offered services and facilities such as doctors' offices, shops, and an athletic field.

As Richard Ely observed, however, the town of Pullman remained firmly under company control. Residents were not allowed to loiter on their front steps or to drink alcohol. Pullman hoped that his tightly controlled environment would ensure a stable work force. However, Pullman's refusal to lower rents after cutting his employees' pay led to a violent strike in 1894.

CRÉDIT MOBILIER Pullman created his company town out of the desire for control and profit. In some other railroad magnates, or powerful and influential industrialists, these desires turned into self-serving corruption. In one of the most infamous schemes, stockholders in the Union Pacific Railroad formed, in 1864, a construction company called **Crédit Mobilier** (krĕd'ĭt mō-bēl'yər). The stockholders gave this company a contract to lay track at two to three times the actual cost—and pocketed the profits. They donated shares of stock to about 20 representatives in Congress in 1867.

A congressional investigation of the company, spurred by reports in the *New York Sun*, eventually found that the officers of the Union Pacific had taken up to $23 million in stocks, bonds, and cash. Testimony implicated such well-known and respected federal officials as Vice-President Schuyler Colfax and Congressman James Garfield, who later became president. Although these public figures kept their profits and received little more than a slap on the wrist, the reputation of the Republican Party was tarnished. **C**

The Grange and the Railroads

Farmers were especially disturbed by what they viewed as railroad corruption. The Grangers—members of the Grange, a farmers' organization founded in 1867—began demanding governmental control over the railroad industry.

MAIN IDEA

Summarizing
B How did the railroads affect cities?

MAIN IDEA

Summarizing
C How did railroad owners use Crédit Mobilier to make huge, undeserved profits?

Eastern time
Central time
Mountain time
Pacific time
Railroads by 1870
Railroads by 1890

0   150   300 miles
0   150   300 kilometers

GEOGRAPHY SKILLBUILDER
1. **Human-Environment Interaction** What factor led to rapid growth in Chicago, Minneapolis, and Denver?
2. **Movement** Why was rail construction concentrated in the East before 1870 and in the West after 1870?

Background
Price fixing occurs when companies within an industry all agree to charge the same price for a given service, rather than competing to offer the lowest price.

RAILROAD ABUSES Farmers were angry with railroad companies for a host of reasons. They were upset by misuse of government land grants, which the railroads sold to other businesses rather than to settlers, as the government intended. The railroads also entered into formal agreements to fix prices, which helped keep farmers in their debt. In addition, they charged different customers different rates, often demanding more for short hauls—for which there was no alternative carrier—than they did for long hauls.

GRANGER LAWS In response to these abuses by the railroads, the Grangers took political action. They sponsored state and local political candidates, elected legislators, and successfully pressed for laws to protect their interests. In 1871 Illinois authorized a commission "to establish maximum freight and passenger rates and prohibit discrimination." Grangers throughout the West, Midwest, and Southeast convinced state legislators to pass similar laws, called Granger laws.

The railroads fought back, challenging the constitutionality of the regulatory laws. In 1877, however, in the case of **Munn v. Illinois,** the Supreme Court upheld the Granger laws by a vote of seven to two. The states thus won the right to regulate the railroads for the benefit of farmers and consumers. The Grangers also helped establish an important principle—the federal government's right to regulate private industry to serve the public interest. **D**

MAIN IDEA

Analyzing Issues
D How did the Grangers, who were largely poor farmers, do battle with the giant railroad companies?

INTERSTATE COMMERCE ACT The Grangers' triumph was short-lived, however. In 1886, the Supreme Court ruled that a state could not set rates on interstate commerce—railroad traffic that either came from or was going to another state. In response to public outrage, Congress passed the **Interstate Commerce Act** in 1887. This act reestablished the right of the federal government to supervise railroad activities and established a five-member Interstate Commerce Commission (ICC) for that purpose. The ICC had difficulty regulating railroad rates because of a long legal process and resistance from the railroads. The final

"THE MODERN COLOSSUS OF (RAIL) ROADS"

Joseph Keppler drew this cartoon in 1879, featuring the railroad "giants" William Vanderbilt (top), Jay Gould (bottom right), and Cyrus W. Fields (bottom left). The three magnates formed a railroad trust out of their Union Pacific, New York Central, and Lake Shore & Dependence lines.

SKILLBUILDER Analyzing Political Cartoons

1. The title of this cartoon is a pun on the Colossus of Rhodes, a statue erected in 282 B.C. on an island near Greece. According to legend, the 100-foot-tall statue straddled Rhodes's harbor entrance. Do you think the artist means the comparison as a compliment or a criticism? Why?

2. The reins held by the railroad magnates attach not only to the trains but also to the tracks and the railroad station. What does this convey about the magnates' control of the railroads?

 SEE SKILLBUILDER HANDBOOK, PAGE R24.

blow to the commission came in 1897, when the Supreme Court ruled that it could not set maximum railroad rates. Not until 1906, under President Theodore Roosevelt, did the ICC gain the power it needed to be effective.

PANIC AND CONSOLIDATION Although the ICC presented few problems for the railroads, corporate abuses, mismanagement, overbuilding, and competition pushed many railroads to the brink of bankruptcy. Their financial problems played a major role in a nationwide economic collapse. The panic of 1893 was the worst depression up to that time: by the end of 1893, around 600 banks and 15,000 businesses had failed, and by 1895, 4 million people had lost their jobs. By the middle of 1894, a quarter of the nation's railroads had been taken over by financial companies. Large investment firms such as J. P. Morgan & Company reorganized the railroads. As the 20th century dawned, seven powerful companies held sway over two-thirds of the nation's railroad tracks.

Vocabulary
consolidation: the act of uniting or combining

 ASSESSMENT

SECTION 2

1. **TERMS & NAMES** For each term or name, write a sentence explaining its significance.
   - transcontinental railroad
   - George M. Pullman
   - Crédit Mobilier
   - *Munn* v. *Illinois*
   - Interstate Commerce Act

MAIN IDEA

2. **TAKING NOTES**
   In a chart like the one below, fill in effects of the rapid growth of railroads.

   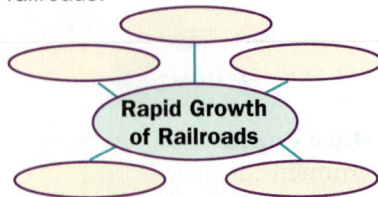

   How did the growth of railroads affect people's everyday lives? How did it affect farmers?

CRITICAL THINKING

3. **MAKING INFERENCES**
   Do you think the government and private citizens could have done more to curb the corruption and power of the railroads? Give examples to support your opinion.
   Think About:
   - why the railroads had power
   - the rights of railroad customers and workers
   - the scope of government regulations

4. **SYNTHESIZING**
   The federal government gave land and made loans to the railroad companies. Why was the government so eager to promote the growth of railroads?

5. **ANALYZING MOTIVES**
   Reread "Another Perspective" on railroads (page 444). Why do you think that some Americans disliked this new means of transportation?

SECTION 3

PI 2.2
PI 3.4

CC Unit 3.II.A.2.a   CC Unit 3.II.A.2.c
CC Unit 3.II.C   CC Unit 3.II.E.1.a
CC Unit 3.II.E.1.d   CC Unit 3.II.E.2

Big Business and Labor

MAIN IDEA	WHY IT MATTERS NOW	Terms & Names
The expansion of industry resulted in the growth of big business and prompted laborers to form unions to better their lives.	Many of the strategies used today in industry and in the labor movement, such as consolidation and the strike, have their origins in the late 19th century.	• Andrew Carnegie • vertical and horizontal integration • Social Darwinism • John D. Rockefeller • Sherman Antitrust Act • Samuel Gompers • American Federation of Labor (AFL) • Eugene V. Debs • Industrial Workers of the World (IWW) • Mary Harris Jones

─── **One American's Story** ───

hmhsocialstudies.com
TAKING NOTES
Use the graphic organizer online to take notes on the achievements and setbacks of the labor movement between 1876 and 1911.

Born in Scotland to penniless parents, **Andrew Carnegie** came to this country in 1848, at age 12. Six years later, he worked his way up to become private secretary to the local superintendent of the Pennsylvania Railroad. One morning, Carnegie single-handedly relayed messages that unsnarled a tangle of freight and passenger trains. His boss, Thomas A. Scott, rewarded Carnegie by giving him a chance to buy stock. Carnegie's mother mortgaged the family home to make the purchase possible. Soon Carnegie received his first dividend.

A PERSONAL VOICE ANDREW CARNEGIE

" One morning a white envelope was lying upon my desk, addressed in a big John Hancock hand, to 'Andrew Carnegie, Esquire.' . . . All it contained was a check for ten dollars upon the Gold Exchange Bank of New York. I shall remember that check as long as I live. . . . It gave me the first penny of revenue from capital—something that I had not worked for with the sweat of my brow. 'Eureka!' I cried. 'Here's the goose that lays the golden eggs.' "

—*Autobiography of Andrew Carnegie*

▲ Nineteenth-century industrialist Andrew Carnegie gave money to build public libraries, hoping to help others write their own rags-to-riches stories.

Andrew Carnegie was one of the first industrial moguls to make his own fortune. His rise from rags to riches, along with his passion for supporting charities, made him a model of the American success story.

Carnegie's Innovations

By 1865, Carnegie was so busy managing the money he had earned in dividends that he happily left his job at the Pennsylvania Railroad. He entered the steel business in 1873 after touring a British steel mill and witnessing the awesome spectacle of the Bessemer process in action. By 1899, the Carnegie Steel Company

Vertical and Horizontal Integration

RESOURCES
Raw materials, fields, forests, and farms

VERTICAL

HORIZONTAL

HORIZONTAL

MANUFACTURING
Production and processing

DISTRIBUTION
Shipping and transportation, delivery to customers

VERTICAL

manufactured more steel than all the factories in Great Britain.

NEW BUSINESS STRATEGIES
Carnegie's success was due in part to management practices that he initiated and that soon became widespread. First, he continually searched for ways to make better products more cheaply. He incorporated new machinery and techniques, such as accounting systems that enabled him to track precise costs. Second, he attracted talented people by offering them stock in the company, and he encouraged competition among his assistants.

In addition to improving his own manufacturing operation, Carnegie attempted to control as much of the steel industry as he could. He did this mainly by **vertical integration,** a process in which he bought out his suppliers—coal fields and iron mines, ore freighters, and railroad lines—in order to control the raw materials and transportation systems. Carnegie also attempted to buy out competing steel producers. In this process, known as **horizontal integration,** companies producing similar products merge. Having gained control over his suppliers and having limited his competition, Carnegie controlled almost the entire steel industry. By the time he sold his business in 1901, Carnegie's companies produced by far the largest portion of the nation's steel. **A**

MAIN IDEA

Summarizing
A What were Andrew Carnegie's management and business strategies?

Social Darwinism and Business

Andrew Carnegie explained his extraordinary success by pointing to his hard work, shrewd investments, and innovative business practices. Late-19th-century social philosophers offered a different explanation for Carnegie's success. They said it could be explained scientifically by a new theory—Social Darwinism.

Popular literature promoted the possibility of rags-to-riches success for anyone who was virtuous and hard-working.

PRINCIPLES OF SOCIAL DARWINISM The philosophy called **Social Darwinism** grew out of the English naturalist Charles Darwin's theory of biological evolution. In his book *On the Origin of Species*, published in 1859, Darwin described his observations that some individuals of a species flourish and pass their traits along to the next generation, while others do not. He explained that a process of "natural selection" weeded out less-suited individuals and enabled the best-adapted to survive.

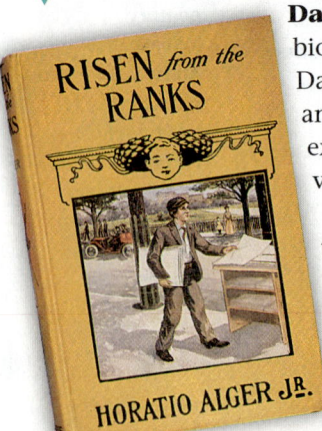

RISEN *from the* RANKS

HORATIO ALGER JR.

The English philosopher Herbert Spencer used Darwin's biological theories to explain the evolution of human society. Soon, economists found in Social Darwinism a way to justify the doctrine of laissez faire (a French term meaning "allow to do"). According to this doctrine, the marketplace should not be regulated. William G. Sumner, a political science professor at Yale University, promoted the theory that success and failure in business were governed by natural law and that no one had the right to intervene.

A NEW DEFINITION OF SUCCESS The premise of the survival and success of the most capable naturally made sense to the 4,000 millionaires who had emerged since the Civil War. Because the theory supported the notion of individual responsibility and blame, it also appealed to the Protestant work ethic of

Background
The work ethic, or the belief that hard work and virtue brings success, was first advanced by Cotton Mather, a New England Puritan minister. In the years after the Civil war, the "rags-to-riches" novels of Horatio Alger brought this idea into popular culture.

many Americans. According to Social Darwinism, riches were a sign of God's favor, and therefore the poor must be lazy or inferior people who deserved their lot in life.

Fewer Control More

Although some business owners endorsed the "natural law" in theory, in practice most entrepreneurs did everything they could to control the competition that threatened the growth of their business empires.

GROWTH AND CONSOLIDATION Many industrialists took the approach "If you can't beat 'em, join 'em." They often pursued horizontal integration in the form of mergers. A merger usually occurred when one corporation bought out the stock of another. A firm that bought out all its competitors could achieve a monopoly, or complete control over its industry's production, wages, and prices.

One way to create a monopoly was to set up a holding company, a corporation that did nothing but buy out the stock of other companies. Headed by banker J. P. Morgan, United States Steel was one of the most successful holding companies. In 1901, when it bought the largest manufacturer, Carnegie Steel, it became the world's largest business.

Corporations such as the Standard Oil Company, established by **John D. Rockefeller,** took a different approach to mergers: they joined with competing companies in trust agreements. Participants in a trust turned their stock over to a group of trustees—people who ran the separate companies as one large corporation. In return, the companies were entitled to dividends on profits earned by the trust. Trusts were not legal mergers, however. Rockefeller used a trust to gain total control of the oil industry in America. **B**

ROCKEFELLER AND THE "ROBBER BARONS" In 1870, Rockefeller's Standard Oil Company of Ohio processed two or three percent of the country's crude oil. Within a decade, it controlled 90 percent of the refining business. Rockefeller reaped huge profits by paying his employees extremely low wages and driving his competitors out of business by selling his oil at a lower price than it cost to produce it. Then, when he controlled the market, he hiked prices far above original levels.

Alarmed at the tactics of industrialists, critics began to call them robber barons. But industrialists were also philanthropists. Although Rockefeller kept most of his assets, he still gave away over $500 million, establishing the Rockefeller Foundation, providing funds to found the University of Chicago, and creating a medical institute that helped find a cure for yellow fever.

MAIN IDEA

Summarizing
B What strategies enabled big businesses to eliminate competition?

KEY PLAYER

**JOHN D. ROCKEFELLER
1839–1937**

At the height of John Davison Rockefeller's power, an associate noted that he "always sees a little farther than the rest of us—and then he sees around the corner."

Rockefeller's father was a flashy peddler of phony cancer cures with a unique approach to raising children. "I cheat my boys every chance I get. . . . I want to make 'em sharp," he boasted.

It seems that this approach succeeded with the oldest son, John D., who was sharp enough to land a job as an assistant bookkeeper at the age of 16. Rockefeller was very proud of his own son, who succeeded him in the family business. At the end of his life, Rockefeller referred not to his millions but to John D., Jr., as "my greatest fortune."

This 1900 cartoon, captioned "What a funny little government!" is a commentary on the power of the Standard Oil empire. John D. Rockefeller holds the White House in his hand.

Andrew Carnegie donated about 90 percent of the wealth he accumulated during his lifetime; his fortune still supports the arts and learning today. "It will be a great mistake for the community to shoot the millionaires," he said, "for they are the bees that make the most honey, and contribute most to the hive even after they have gorged themselves full." **C**

SHERMAN ANTITRUST ACT Despite Carnegie's defense of millionaires, the government was concerned that expanding corporations would stifle free competition. In 1890, the **Sherman Antitrust Act** made it illegal to form a trust that interfered with free trade between states or with other countries.

Prosecuting companies under the Sherman Act was not easy, however, because the act didn't clearly define terms such as *trust*. In addition, if firms such as Standard Oil felt pressure from the government, they simply reorganized into single corporations. The Supreme Court threw out seven of the eight cases the federal government brought against trusts. Eventually, the government stopped trying to enforce the Sherman act, and the consolidation of businesses continued.

BUSINESS BOOM BYPASSES THE SOUTH Industrial growth concentrated in the North, where natural and urban resources were plentiful. The South was still trying to recover from the Civil War, hindered by a lack of capital—money for investment. After the war, people were unwilling to invest in risky ventures. Northern businesses already owned 90 percent of the stock in the most profitable Southern enterprise, the railroads, thereby keeping the South in a stranglehold. The South remained mostly agricultural, with farmers at the mercy of railroad rates. Entrepreneurs suffered not only from excessive transportation costs, but also from high tariffs on raw materials and imported goods, and from a lack of skilled workers. The post-Reconstruction South seemed to have no way out of economic stagnation. However, growth in forestry and mining, and in the tobacco, furniture, and textile industries, offered hope. **D**

MAIN IDEA

Evaluating
C Do you agree with Carnegie's defense of millionaires? Why or why not?

MAIN IDEA

Synthesizing
D How did economic factors limit industrialization in the South?

In this photograph, taken by Lewis Hine in 1912, a young sweatshop laborer in New York City carries piecework home.

▼

Labor Unions Emerge

As business leaders merged and consolidated their forces, it seemed necessary for workers to do the same. Although Northern wages were generally higher than Southern wages, exploitation and unsafe working conditions drew workers together across regions in a nationwide labor movement. Laborers—skilled and unskilled, female and male, black and white—joined together in unions to try to improve their lot.

LONG HOURS AND DANGER One of the largest employers, the steel mills, often demanded a seven-day workweek. Seamstresses, like factory workers in most industries, worked 12 or more hours a day, six days a week. Employees were not entitled to vacation, sick leave, unemployment compensation, or reimbursement for injuries suffered on the job.

Yet injuries were common. In dirty, poorly ventilated factories, workers had to perform repetitive, mind-dulling tasks, sometimes with dangerous or faulty equipment. In 1882, an average of 675 laborers were killed in work-related accidents each week. In addition, wages were so low that most families could not survive unless everyone held a job. Between 1890 and 1910, for example, the number of women working for wages doubled, from 4 million to more than 8 million. Twenty percent of the boys and 10 percent of the girls under age 15—some as young as five years old—also held full-time jobs. With little time or energy left for school, child laborers forfeited their futures to help their families make ends meet.

In sweatshops, or workshops in tenements rather than in factories, workers had little choice but to put up with the conditions. Sweatshop employment, which was tedious and required few skills, was often the only avenue open to women and children. Jacob Riis described the conditions faced by "sweaters."

A PERSONAL VOICE JACOB RIIS

" The bulk of the sweater's work is done in the tenements, which the law that regulates factory labor does not reach. . . . In [them] the child works unchallenged from the day he is old enough to pull a thread. There is no such thing as a dinner hour; men and women eat while they work, and the 'day' is lengthened at both ends far into the night. "

—How the Other Half Lives

Not surprisingly, sweatshop jobs paid the lowest wages—often as little as 27 cents for a child's 14-hour day. In 1899, women earned an average of $267 a year, nearly half of men's average pay of $498. The very next year Andrew Carnegie made $23 million—with no income tax.

EARLY LABOR ORGANIZING Skilled workers had formed small, local unions since the late 1700s. The first large-scale national organization of laborers, the National Labor Union (NLU), was formed in 1866 by ironworker William H. Sylvis. The refusal of some NLU local chapters to admit African Americans led to the creation of the Colored National Labor Union (CNLU). Nevertheless, NLU membership grew to 640,000. In 1868, the NLU persuaded Congress to legalize an eight-hour day for government workers. **E**

NLU organizers concentrated on linking existing local unions. In 1869, Uriah Stephens focused his attention on individual workers and organized the Noble Order of the Knights of Labor. Its motto was "An injury to one is the concern of all." Membership in the Knights of Labor was officially open to all workers, regardless of race, gender, or degree of skill. Like the NLU, the Knights supported an eight-hour workday and advocated "equal pay for equal work" by men and women. They saw strikes, or refusals to work, as a last resort and instead advocated arbitration. At its height in 1886, the Knights of Labor had about 700,000 members. Although the Knights declined after the failure of a series of strikes, other unions continued to organize.

Union Movements Diverge

As labor activism spread, it diversified. Two major types of unions made great gains under forceful leaders.

CRAFT UNIONISM One form of labor organization was craft unionism, which included skilled workers from one or more trades. Jewish immigrant **Samuel Gompers** led the Cigar Makers' International Union to join other craft unions in 1886. The **American Federation of Labor (AFL)**,

MAIN IDEA

Analyzing Issues
E How did industrial working conditions contribute to the growth of the labor movement?

Vocabulary
arbitration: a method of settling disputes in which both sides submit their differences to a mutually approved judge

HISTORICAL
SPOTLIGHT

AFRICAN AMERICANS AND THE LABOR MOVEMENT

Angered by their exclusion from the NLU, African American laborers formed the Colored National Labor Union (CNLU) in 1869. Led by Isaac Meyers, a caulker from Baltimore, the CNLU emphasized cooperation between management and labor and the importance of political reform.

The CNLU disbanded in the early 1870s, but many African-American laborers found a home in the Knights of Labor, the first union to welcome blacks and whites alike. The Great Strike of 1877 brought whites and African Americans together, but the labor movement remained largely divided along racial lines.

Management often hired African Americans as strikebreakers, which intensified white unions' resistance to accepting blacks. African Americans continued to organize on their own, but discrimination and their small numbers relative to white unions hurt black unions' effectiveness.

with Gompers as its president, focused on collective bargaining, or negotiation between representatives of labor and management, to reach written agreements on wages, hours, and working conditions. Unlike the Knights of Labor, the AFL used strikes as a major tactic. Successful strikes helped the AFL win higher wages and shorter workweeks. Between 1890 and 1915, the average weekly wages in unionized industries rose from $17.50 to $24, and the average workweek fell from almost 54.5 hours to just under 49 hours.

INDUSTRIAL UNIONISM Some labor leaders felt that unions should include all laborers—skilled and unskilled—in a specific industry. This concept captured the imagination of **Eugene V. Debs,** who attempted to form such an industrial union—the American Railway Union (ARU). Most of the new union's members were unskilled and semiskilled laborers, but skilled engineers and firemen joined too. In 1894, the new union won a strike for higher wages. Within two months, its membership climbed to 150,000, dwarfing the 90,000 enrolled in the four skilled railroad brotherhoods. Though the ARU, like the Knights of Labor, never recovered after the failure of a major strike, it added to the momentum of union organizing. **F**

" The strike is the weapon of the oppressed. "

EUGENE V. DEBS

SOCIALISM AND THE IWW In an attempt to solve the problems faced by workers, Eugene Debs and some other labor activists eventually turned to socialism, an economic and political system based on government control of business and property and equal distribution of wealth. Socialism, carried to its extreme form—communism, as advocated by the German philosopher Karl Marx—would result in the overthrow of the capitalist system. Most socialists in late-19th-century America drew back from this goal, however, and worked within the labor movement to achieve better conditions for workers. In 1905, a group of radical unionists and socialists in Chicago organized the **Industrial Workers of the World (IWW),** or the Wobblies. Headed by William "Big Bill" Haywood, the Wobblies included miners, lumberers, and cannery and dock workers. Unlike the ARU, the IWW welcomed African Americans, but membership never topped 100,000. Its only major strike victory occurred in 1912. Yet the Wobblies, like other industrial unions, gave dignity and a sense of solidarity to unskilled workers.

OTHER LABOR ACTIVISM IN THE WEST In April 1903, about 1,000 Japanese and Mexican workers organized a successful strike in the sugar-beet fields of Ventura County, California. They formed the Sugar Beet and Farm Laborers' Union of Oxnard. In Wyoming, the State Federation of Labor supported a union of Chinese and Japanese miners who sought the same wages and treatment as other union miners. These small, independent unions increased both the overall strength of the labor movement and the tension between labor and management.

Strikes Turn Violent

Industry and government responded forcefully to union activity, which they saw as a threat to the entire capitalist system.

THE GREAT STRIKE OF 1877 In July 1877, workers for the Baltimore and Ohio Railroad (B&O) struck to protest their second wage cut in two months. The work stoppage spread to other lines. Most freight and even some passenger traffic, covering over 50,000 miles, was stopped for more than a week. After several state governors asked President Rutherford B. Hayes to intervene, saying that the strikers were impeding interstate commerce, federal troops ended the strike.

THE HAYMARKET AFFAIR Encouraged by the impact of the 1877 strike, labor leaders continued to press for change. On the evening of May 4, 1886, 3,000 people gathered at Chicago's Haymarket Square to protest police brutality—a striker had been killed and several had been wounded at the McCormick Harvester plant the day before. Rain began to fall at about 10 o'clock, and the crowd was dispersing when police arrived. Then someone tossed a bomb into the police line. Police fired on the workers; seven police officers and several workers died in the chaos that followed. No one ever learned who threw the bomb, but the three speakers at the demonstration and five other radicals were charged with inciting a riot. All eight were convicted; four were hanged and one committed suicide in prison. After Haymarket, the public began to turn against the labor movement. **G**

THE HOMESTEAD STRIKE Despite the violence and rising public anger, workers continued to strike. The writer Hamlin Garland described conditions at the Carnegie Steel Company's Homestead plant in Pennsylvania.

> ### A PERSONAL VOICE HAMLIN GARLAND
>
> "Everywhere . . . groups of pale, lean men slouched in faded garments, grimy with the soot and grease of the mills. . . . A roar as of a hundred lions, a thunder as of cannons, . . . jarring clang of falling iron. . . !"
>
> —quoted in *McClure's Magazine*

The steelworkers finally called a strike on June 29, 1892, after the company president, Henry Clay Frick, announced his plan to cut wages. Frick hired armed

MAIN IDEA

Analyzing Causes

G How did the 1877 strike and Haymarket cause the public to resent the labor movement?

The Growth of Union Membership, 1878–1904

Members in Thousands

- Total Nationwide Union Membership
- American Federation of Labor
- Knights of Labor
- American Railway Union

Wabash Railroad Strike

Haymarket Riot

Pullman Strike

1878 1880 1882 1884 1886 1888 1890 1892 1894 1896 1898 1900 1902 1904

SKILLBUILDER
Interpreting Graphs
1. Which union's membership increased in 1889–1890?
2. What effect(s) did the Haymarket Riot have on union membership?

guards from the Pinkerton Detective Agency to protect the plant so that he could hire scabs, or strikebreakers, to keep it operating. In a pitched battle that left at least three detectives and nine workers dead, the steelworkers forced out the Pinkertons and kept the plant closed until the Pennsylvania National Guard arrived on July 12. The strike continued until November, but by then the union had lost much of its support and gave in to the company. It would take 45 years for steelworkers to mobilize once again.

THE PULLMAN COMPANY STRIKE Strikes continued in other industries, however. During the panic of 1893 and the economic depression that followed, the Pullman company laid off more than 3,000 of its 5,800 employees and cut the wages of the rest by 25 to 50 percent, without cutting the cost of its employee housing. After paying their rent, many workers took home less than $6 a week. A strike was called in the spring of 1894, when the Pullman company failed to restore wages or decrease rents. Eugene Debs asked for arbitration, but Pullman refused to negotiate with the strikers. So the ARU began boycotting Pullman trains.

After Pullman hired strikebreakers, the strike turned violent, and President Grover Cleveland sent in federal troops. In the bitter aftermath, Debs was jailed. Pullman fired most of the strikers, and the railroads blacklisted many others, so they could never again get railroad jobs.

WOMEN ORGANIZE Although women were barred from many unions, they united behind powerful leaders to demand better working conditions, equal pay for equal work, and an end to child labor. Perhaps the most prominent organizer in the women's labor movement was **Mary Harris Jones.** Jones supported the Great Strike of 1877 and later organized for the United Mine Workers of America (UMW). She endured death threats and jail with the coal miners, who gave her the nickname Mother Jones. In 1903, to expose the cruelties of child labor, she led 80 mill children—many with hideous injuries—on a march to the home of President Theodore Roosevelt. Their crusade influenced the passage of child labor laws.

Other organizers also achieved significant gains for women. In 1909, Pauline Newman, just 16 years old, became the first female organizer of the International Ladies' Garment Workers' Union (ILGWU). A garment worker from the age of eight, Newman also supported

KEY PLAYERS

EUGENE V. DEBS
1855–1926

Born in Indiana, Eugene V. Debs left home at the age of 14 to work for the railroads. In 1875 he helped organize a local lodge of the Brotherhood of Locomotive Firemen, and after attempts to unite the local railroad brotherhoods failed, Debs organized the American Railway Union.

While in prison following the Pullman strike in 1894, Debs read the works of Karl Marx and became increasingly disillusioned with capitalism. He became a spokesperson for the Socialist Party of America and was its candidate for president five times. In 1912, he won about 900,000 votes—an amazing 6 percent of the total.

MOTHER JONES
1830–1930

Mary Harris "Mother" Jones was a native of Ireland who immigrated to North America as a child. She became involved in the American labor movement after receiving assistance from the Knights of Labor. According to a reporter who followed "the mother of the laboring class" on her children's march in 1903, "She fights their battles with a Mother's Love." Jones continued fighting until her death at age 100.

Jones was definitely not the kind of woman admired by industrialists. "God almighty made women," she declared, "and the Rockefeller gang of thieves made ladies."

the "Uprising of the 20,000," a 1909 seamstresses' strike that won labor agreements and improved working conditions for some strikers.

The public could no longer ignore conditions in garment factories after a fire broke out at the Triangle Shirtwaist factory in New York City on March 25, 1911. The fire spread swiftly through the oil-soaked machines and piles of cloth, engulfing the eighth, ninth, and tenth floors. As workers attempted to flee, they discovered that the company had locked all but one of the exit doors to prevent theft. The unlocked door was blocked by fire. The factory had no sprinkler system, and the single fire escape collapsed almost immediately. In all, 146 women died; some were found huddled with their faces raised to a small window. Public outrage flared after a jury acquitted the factory owners of manslaughter. In response, the state of New York set up a task force to study factory working conditions.

▲ The fire department's ladders reached only to the sixth floor, two floors below the burning Triangle Shirtwaist Company.

MAIN IDEA

Summarizing

Ⓗ What factors made the Triangle Shirtwaist fire so lethal?

MANAGEMENT AND GOVERNMENT PRESSURE UNIONS

The more powerful the unions became, the more employers came to fear them. Management refused to recognize unions as representatives of the workers. Many employers forbade union meetings, fired union members, and forced new employees to sign "yellow-dog contracts," swearing that they would not join a union.

Finally, industrial leaders, with the help of the courts, turned the Sherman Antitrust Act against labor. All a company had to do was say that a strike, picket line, or boycott would hurt interstate trade, and the state or federal government would issue an injunction against the labor action. Legal limitations made it more and more difficult for unions to be effective. Despite these pressures, workers—especially those in skilled jobs—continued to view unions as a powerful tool. By 1904, the AFL had about 1,700,000 members in its affiliated unions; by the eve of World War I, AFL membership would climb to over 2 million.

SECTION 3 ASSESSMENT

1. TERMS & NAMES For each term or name, write a sentence explaining its significance.

- Andrew Carnegie
- vertical and horizontal integration
- Social Darwinism
- John D. Rockefeller
- Sherman Antitrust Act
- Samuel Gompers
- American Federation of Labor (AFL)
- Eugene V. Debs
- Industrial Workers of the World (IWW)
- Mary Harris Jones

MAIN IDEA

2. TAKING NOTES
Make a time line of the notable achievements and setbacks of the labor movement between 1876 and 1911.

In what ways did strikes threaten industry?

CRITICAL THINKING

3. EVALUATING LEADERSHIP
Do you think that the tycoons of the late 19th century are best described as ruthless robber barons or as effective captains of industry?
Think About:

- their management tactics and business strategies
- their contributions to the economy
- their attitude toward competition

4. DRAWING CONCLUSIONS
Does the life of Andrew Carnegie support or counter the philosophy of Social Darwinism? Explain.

5. HYPOTHESIZING
If the government had supported unions instead of management in the late 19th century, how might the lives of workers have been different?

VISUAL SUMMARY

A NEW INDUSTRIAL AGE

LONG-TERM CAUSES

- abundant natural resources
- harnessing of early power sources such as water and coal
- invention of the steam engine
- construction of roads, canals, and railroads in early 1800s

IMMEDIATE CAUSES

- expansion of railroads in late 1800s
- cheap labor supply provided by increasing immigration
- burst of technological innovation
- new management techniques and business strategies
- investment capital

BIG BUSINESS BOOMS
1880–1914

IMMEDIATE EFFECTS

- growth of large corporations
- new and plentiful manufactured goods
- poor working conditions in factories and sweatshops
- increased labor activism

LONG-TERM EFFECTS

- regional economies are linked
- labor movement wins shorter workweek

TERMS & NAMES

For each term or name below, write a sentence explaining its connection to the industrialization of the late 19th century.

1. Thomas Alva Edison
2. Alexander Graham Bell
3. George M. Pullman
4. transcontinental railroad
5. Interstate Commerce Act
6. Andrew Carnegie
7. Sherman Antitrust Act
8. Samuel Gompers
9. American Federation of Labor (AFL)
10. Mary Harris Jones

MAIN IDEAS

Use your notes and the information in the chapter to answer the following questions.

The Expansion of Industry (pages 436–439)

1. How did the growth of the steel industry influence the development of other industries?
2. How did inventions and developments in the late 19th century change the way people worked?

The Age of the Railroads (pages 442–446)

3. Why did people, particularly farmers, demand regulation of the railroads in the late 19th century?
4. Why were attempts at railroad regulation often unsuccessful?

Big Business and Labor (pages 447–455)

5. Why were business leaders such as John D. Rockefeller called robber barons?
6. Why did the South industrialize more slowly than the North did?
7. Why did workers form unions in the late 19th century?
8. What factors limited the success of unions?

CRITICAL THINKING

1. **USING YOUR NOTES** In a chart like the one shown, list what you see as the overall costs and benefits of industrialization.

INDUSTRIALIZATION	
Costs	Benefits

2. **RECOGNIZING BIAS** In 1902 George Baehr, head of the Philadelphia and Reading Railway Company, said, "The rights and interests of the labor man will be protected and cared for not by the labor agitators but by the Christian men to whom God in his infinite wisdom has given the control of the property interests of the country." What bias does this statement reveal? How does Baehr's view reflect Social Darwinism?

3. **IDENTIFYING PROBLEMS** Consider the problems that late-19th-century workers faced and the problems that workers face today. How important do you think unions are for present-day workers? Support your answer.

Use the quotation below and your knowledge of U.S. history to answer question 1.

> " No man, however benevolent, liberal, and wise, can use a large fortune so that it will do half as much good in the world as it would if it were divided into moderate sums and in the hands of workmen who had earned it by industry and frugality. "
>
> —Rutherford B. Hayes, from *The Diary and Letters of Rutherford Birchard Hayes*

1 Which of the following people could best be described by Rutherford B. Hayes's words *benevolent*, *liberal*, and *a large fortune*?

- **(1)** Thomas Edison
- **(2)** Eugene V. Debs
- **(3)** Charles Darwin
- **(4)** Andrew Carnegie

2 The American Federation of Labor (AFL) differed from the Knights of Labor in that the Knights of Labor focused on —

- **(1)** collective bargaining and aggressive use of strikes.
- **(2)** organizing only unskilled workers.
- **(3)** arbitration and use of strikes as a last resort.
- **(4)** winning a shorter workweek.

3 How did the railroads both benefit from and contribute to the industrialization of the United States?

- **(1)** The railroads needed government protection, and their development helped government grow.
- **(2)** The railroads used new inventions and brought people to see the inventions.
- **(3)** The railroads used steel and coal and delivered both to new markets.
- **(4)** The railroads needed passengers, and passengers needed to get to new industries.

4 In the 19th century, government attempts to regulate industry in the United States included the Interstate Commerce Act (1887) and the Sherman Antitrust Act (1890). What posed the biggest obstacle to enforcement of these laws?

- **(1)** the business tactics of industrialists
- **(2)** the use of vertical integration
- **(3)** the rulings of the Supreme Court
- **(4)** the theory of Social Darwinism

↗ hmhsocialstudies.com **TEST PRACTICE**

For additional test practice, go online for:
- Diagnostic tests
- Tutorials

INTERACT WITH HISTORY

Recall the issues that you explored at the beginning of the chapter. Consider how your answer might be different based on what you now know about the effects of railroad expansion and business consolidation. Then write a newspaper editorial about the Great Strike of 1877 (see page 453), supporting the position of either the railroad owners or the striking workers.

FOCUS ON WRITING

Imagine you are a union leader in a factory. If your demands for better working conditions are not met, all of the employees will stop work and go on strike. Write a persuasive letter in which you urge your employer to adopt specific reforms to improve working conditions.

COLLABORATIVE LEARNING

21ST CENTURY

In a small group read and discuss the "One American's Story" at the beginning of Section 1. Consider the following question: What qualities did Pattillo Higgins have that made him successful? Then make a poster describing Pattillo Higgins's personal qualities and how they helped him to achieve his dream. What present-day figures share Higgins's traits? Add images of these people, with captions, to the poster and display it in your classroom.

CHAPTER 15

IMMIGRANTS AND URBANIZATION

Essential Question

What were the economic, social, and political effects of immigration?

New York Standards

KEY IDEA 2 Important ideas, social and cultural values, beliefs, and traditions from New York State and United States history illustrate the connections and interactions of people and events across time and from a variety of perspectives.

KEY IDEA 3 Study about the major social, political, economic, cultural, and religious developments in New York State and United States history involves learning about the important roles and contributions of individuals and groups.

SECTION 1: The New Immigrants

SECTION 2: The Challenges of Urbanization

SECTION 3: Politics in the Gilded Age

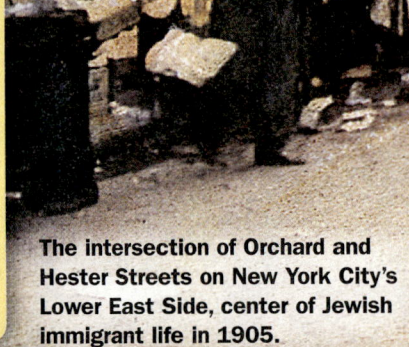

The intersection of Orchard and Hester Streets on New York City's Lower East Side, center of Jewish immigrant life in 1905.

1877 Rutherford B. Hayes is elected president.

1880 James A. Garfield is elected president.

1881 Chester A. Arthur succeeds Garfield after Garfield's assassination.

1884 Grover Cleveland is elected president.

1888 Benjamin Harrison is elected president.

1892 Grover Cleveland is elected to a second term.

USA

1880

1890

WORLD

1876 Porfirio Díaz seizes power in Mexico.

1884 Berlin Conference meets to divide Africa among European nations.

1885 Indian National Congress forms.

1893 France establishes Indochina.

HESTER ST.

HISTORY

Ellis Island:
Arrival

hmhsocialstudies.com VIDEO

THE

INTERACT
WITH HISTORY

The year is 1880. New York City's swelling population has created a housing crisis. Immigrant families crowd into apartments that lack light, ventilation, and sanitary facilities. Children have nowhere to play except in the streets and are often kept out of school to work and help support their families. You are a reformer who wishes to help immigrants improve their lives.

Explore the Issues

- How can immigrants gain access to the services they need?
- What skills do newcomers need?
- How might immigrants respond to help from an outsider?

1896 William McKinley is elected president.

1898 Hawaii is annexed by the United States.

1900 McKinley is reelected.

1903 The Wright Brothers achieve the first successful airplane flight.

1910 The appearance of Halley's comet causes widespread panic.

1912 Woodrow Wilson is elected president.

1900   1910

1901 The Commonwealth of Australia is founded.

1905 Workers revolt in St. Petersburg, Russia.

1908 Oil is discovered in Persia.

1912 Qing dynasty in China is overthrown.

1914 Panama Canal opens.

Immigrants and Urbanization   **459**

PI 2.3   CC Unit 1.I.D.2   CC Unit 1.I.D.4.a
PI 3.1   CC Unit 3.III.A.3.f(1)   CC Unit 3.III.B.1
       CC Unit 3.III.B.4   CC Unit 3.III.C.2

The New Immigrants

MAIN IDEA	WHY IT MATTERS NOW	Terms & Names
Immigration from Europe, Asia, the Caribbean, and Mexico reached a new high in the late 19th and early 20th centuries.	This wave of immigration helped make the United States the diverse society it is today.	•Ellis Island •Angel Island •melting pot •nativism	•Chinese Exclusion Act •Gentlemen's Agreement

One American's Story

hmhsocialstudies.com
TAKING NOTES
Use the graphic organizer online to take notes about immigration to the United States.

In 1871, 14-year-old Fong See came from China to "Gold Mountain"—the United States. Fong See stayed, worked at menial jobs, and saved enough money to buy a business. Despite widespread restrictions against the Chinese, he became a very successful importer and was able to sponsor many other Chinese who wanted to enter the United States. Fong See had achieved the American dream. However, as his great-granddaughter Lisa See recalls, he was not satisfied.

A PERSONAL VOICE LISA SEE

"He had been trying to achieve success ever since he had first set foot on the Gold Mountain. His dream was very 'American.' He wanted to make money, have influence, be respected, have a wife and children who loved him. In 1919, when he traveled to China, he could look at his life and say he had achieved his dream. But once in China, he suddenly saw his life in a different context. In America, was he really rich? Could he live where he wanted? . . . Did *Americans* care what he thought? . . . The answers played in his head—no, no, no."

—*On Gold Mountain*

Despite Fong See's success, he could not, upon his death in 1957, be buried next to his Caucasian wife because California cemeteries were still segregated.

Through the "Golden Door"

Millions of immigrants like Fong See entered the United States in the late 19th and early 20th centuries, lured by the promise of a better life. Some of these immigrants sought to escape difficult conditions—such as famine, land shortages, or religious or political persecution. Others, known as "birds of passage," intended to immigrate temporarily to earn money, and then return to their homelands.

EUROPEANS Between 1870 and 1920, approximately 20 million Europeans arrived in the United States. Before 1890, most immigrants came from countries in western and northern Europe. Beginning in the 1890s, however, increasing numbers came from southern and eastern Europe. In 1907 alone, about a million people arrived from Italy, Austria-Hungary, and Russia.

Why did so many leave their homelands? Many of these new immigrants left to escape religious persecution. Whole villages of Jews were driven out of Russia by pogroms, organized attacks often encouraged by local authorities. Other Europeans left because of rising population. Between 1800 and 1900, the population in Europe doubled to nearly 400 million, resulting in a scarcity of land for farming. Farmers competed with laborers for too few industrial jobs. In the United States, jobs were supposedly plentiful. In addition, a spirit of reform and revolt had spread across Europe in the 19th century. Influenced by political movements at home, many young European men and women sought independent lives in America.

CHINESE AND JAPANESE While waves of Europeans arrived on the shores of the East Coast, Chinese immigrants came to the West Coast in smaller numbers. Between 1851 and 1883, about 300,000 Chinese arrived. Many came to seek their fortunes after the discovery of gold in 1848 sparked the California gold rush. Chinese immigrants helped build the nation's railroads, including the first transcontinental line. When the railroads were completed, they turned to farming, mining, and domestic service. Some, like Fong See, started businesses. However, Chinese immigration was sharply limited by a congressional act in 1882.

In 1884, the Japanese government allowed Hawaiian planters to recruit Japanese workers, and a Japanese emigration boom began. The United States' annexation of Hawaii in 1898 resulted in increased Japanese immigration to the West Coast. Immigration continued to increase as word of comparatively high American wages spread. The wave peaked in 1907, when 30,000 left Japan for the United States. By 1920, more than 200,000 Japanese lived on the West Coast.

Background
From 1815 to 1848, a wave of revolutions—mostly sparked by a desire for constitutional governments—shook Europe. In 1830, for example, the Polish people rose up against their Russian rulers.

HISTORY

VIDEO
Italians in America: Old World, New Land

hmhsocialstudies.com

U.S. Immigration Patterns, as of 1900

hmhsocialstudies.com   **INTERACTIVE MAP**

Pie chart:
- Scandinavia 11%
- England 8%
- Italy 5%
- Russia 4%
- Poland 3.5%
- Mexico, China, Japan — 1.5% total
- Ireland 16%
- Germany 26%
- Other 25%

Settlement figures in thousands

New York: 480, 425, 182, 165, 135, 66, 42, 7
Wisconsin: 242, 61, 30, 23
Illinois: 332, 129, 114, 64, 64, 28, 23
Massachusetts: 249, 82, 32, 28, 26
California: 72, 44, 40, 35, 10, 8
Texas: 72, 48
Ohio: 204, 55, 44
Pennsylvania: 212, 205, 114, 72, 66, 50

GEOGRAPHY SKILLBUILDER
1. **Movement** Where did the greatest number of Italian immigrants settle?
2. **Movement** From which country did the smallest percentage of immigrants come?

SEE SKILLBUILDER HANDBOOK, PAGE R28.

THE WEST INDIES AND MEXICO Between 1880 and 1920, about 260,000 immigrants arrived in the eastern and southeastern United States from the West Indies. They came from Jamaica, Cuba, Puerto Rico, and other islands. Many West Indians left their homelands because jobs were scarce and the industrial boom in the United States seemed to promise work for everyone.

Mexicans, too, immigrated to the United States to find work, as well as to flee political turmoil. The 1902 National Reclamation Act, which encouraged the irrigation of arid land, created new farmland in Western states and drew Mexican farm workers northward. After 1910, political and social upheavals in Mexico prompted even more immigration. About 700,000 people—7 percent of the population of Mexico at the time—came to the U.S. over the next 20 years. Ⓐ

Life in the New Land

No matter what part of the globe immigrants came from, they faced many adjustments to an alien—and often unfriendly—culture.

A DIFFICULT JOURNEY By the 1870s, almost all immigrants traveled by steamship. The trip across the Atlantic Ocean from Europe took approximately one week, while the Pacific crossing from Asia took nearly three weeks.

Many immigrants traveled in steerage, the cheapest accommodations in a ship's cargo holds. Rarely allowed on deck, immigrants were crowded together in the gloom, unable to exercise or catch a breath of fresh air. They often had to sleep in louse-infested bunks and share toilets with many other passengers. Under these conditions, disease spread quickly, and some immigrants died before they reached their destination. For those who survived, the first glimpse of America could be breathtaking.

★ A PERSONAL VOICE ROSA CAVALLERI

" *America!* . . . We were so near it seemed too much to believe. Everyone stood silent—like in prayer. . . . Then we were entering the harbor. The land came so near we could almost reach out and touch it. . . . Everyone was holding their breath. Me too. . . . Some boats had bands playing on their decks and all of them were tooting their horns to us and leaving white trails in the water behind them. "

—quoted in *Rosa: The Life of an Italian Immigrant*

European governments used passports to control the number of professionals and young men of military age who left the country. ▼

ELLIS ISLAND After initial moments of excitement, the immigrants faced the anxiety of not knowing whether they would be admitted to the United States. They had to pass inspection at immigration stations, such as the one at Castle Garden in New York, which was later moved to **Ellis Island** in New York Harbor. About 20 percent of the immigrants at Ellis Island were detained for a day or more before being inspected. However, only about 2 percent of those were denied entry.

The processing of immigrants on Ellis Island was an ordeal that might take five hours or more. First, they had to pass a physical examination by a doctor. Anyone with a serious health problem or a contagious disease, such as tuberculosis, was promptly sent home. Those who passed the medical exam then reported to a government inspector. The inspector checked documents and questioned immigrants

MAIN IDEA

Analyzing Causes

Ⓐ What reasons did people from other parts of the world have for immigrating to the United States?

FOCUS ON

It is estimated that nearly half of all Americans today can trace their origins to at least one immigrant who entered the country at Ellis Island.

Vocabulary

tuberculosis: a bacterial infection, characterized by fever and coughing, that spreads easily

TESTS FOR DETECTION OF DEFECTIVES.

FIG. 4.—Moon Section of "V. C." test. The subject should be able to point out the four moons that are looking to the left in fourteen seconds, if he is directed to begin at the upper right hand corner and proceed systematically along each line, left to right.

A.

B.

C.

D.

E.

FIG. 5.—The Key Section of the "V. C." test. The time element has not been worked out for this section, but it is hardly the less valuable. "A" is shown the subject and he is asked to find the nearest like it in Fig. 1, "B" is shown and he is asked to find it in Fig. 3, "C" is shown and he is asked to find it in Fig. 2, and "E" is shown and he is asked to find it in Fig. 4.

Vocabulary
felony: any one of the most serious crimes under the law, including murder, rape, and burglary

to determine whether they met the legal requirements for entering the United States. The requirements included proving they had never been convicted of a felony, demonstrating that they were able to work, and showing that they had some money (at least $25 after 1909). One inspector, Edward Ferro, an Italian immigrant himself, gave this glimpse of the process.

★ A PERSONAL VOICE EDWARD FERRO

" The language was a problem of course, but it was overcome by the use of interpreters. . . . It would happen sometimes that these interpreters—some of them—were really softhearted people and hated to see people being deported, and they would, at times, help the aliens by interpreting in such a manner as to benefit the alien and not the government. "

—quoted in *I Was Dreaming to Come to America*

From 1892 to 1924, Ellis Island was the chief immigration station in the United States. An estimated 17 million immigrants passed through its noisy, bustling facilities.

ANGEL ISLAND While European immigrants arriving on the East Coast passed through Ellis Island, Asians—primarily Chinese—arriving on the West Coast gained admission at **Angel Island** in San Francisco Bay. Between 1910 and 1940, about 50,000 Chinese immigrants entered the United States through Angel Island. Processing at Angel Island stood in contrast to the procedure at Ellis Island. Immigrants endured harsh questioning and a long detention in filthy, ramshackle buildings while they waited to find out whether they would be admitted or rejected. **B**

COOPERATION FOR SURVIVAL Once admitted to the country, immigrants faced the challenges of finding a place to live, getting a job, and getting along in daily life while trying to understand an unfamiliar language and culture. Many immigrants sought out people who shared their cultural values, practiced their religion,

MAIN IDEA

Identifying Problems
B What difficulties did immigrants face in gaining admission to the United States?

VIDEO
Angel Island: Ellis Island of the West

hmhsocialstudies.com

and spoke their native language. The ethnic communities were life rafts for immigrants. People pooled their money to build churches or synagogues. They formed social clubs and aid societies. They founded orphanages and homes for the elderly, and established cemeteries. They even published newspapers in their own languages.

Committed to their own cultures but also trying hard to grow into their new identities, many immigrants came to think of themselves as "hyphenated" Americans. As hard as they tried to fit in, these new Polish- and Italian- and Chinese-Americans felt increasing friction as they rubbed shoulders with people born and raised in the United States. Native-born people often disliked the immigrants' unfamiliar customs and languages, and viewed them as a threat to the American way of life. **C**

Immigration Restrictions

Many native-born Americans thought of their country as a **melting pot,** a mixture of people of different cultures and races who blended together by abandoning their native languages and customs. Many new immigrants, however, did not wish to give up their cultural identities. As immigration increased, strong anti-immigrant feelings emerged.

THE RISE OF NATIVISM One response to the growth in immigration was **nativism,** or overt favoritism toward native-born Americans. Nativism gave rise to anti-immigrant groups and led to a demand for immigration restrictions.

Many nativists believed that Anglo-Saxons—the Germanic ancestors of the English—were superior to other ethnic groups. These nativists did not object to immigrants from the "right" countries. Prescott F. Hall, a founder in 1894 of the Immigration Restriction League, identified desirable immigrants as "British, German, and Scandinavian stock, historically free, energetic, progressive." Nativists thought that problems were caused by immigrants from the "wrong" countries— "Slav, Latin, and Asiatic races, historically down-trodden . . . and stagnant."

Nativists sometimes objected more to immigrants' religious beliefs than to their ethnic backgrounds. Many native-born Americans were Protestants and thought that Roman Catholic and Jewish immigrants would undermine the democratic institutions established by the country's Protestant founders. The American Protective Association, a nativist group founded in 1887, launched vicious anti-Catholic attacks, and many colleges, businesses, and social clubs refused to admit Jews.

In 1897, Congress—influenced by the Immigration Restriction League—passed a bill requiring a literacy test for immigrants. Those who could not read 40 words in English or their native language would be refused entry. Although President Cleveland vetoed the bill, it was a powerful statement of public sentiment. In 1917, a similar bill would be passed into law in spite of President Woodrow Wilson's veto.

ANTI-ASIAN SENTIMENT Nativism also found a foothold in the labor movement, particularly in the West, where native-born workers feared that jobs would go to Chinese

Chinese immigrants wait outside the hospital on Angel Island in San Francisco Bay, 1910.

immigrants, who would accept lower wages. The depression of 1873 intensified anti-Chinese sentiment in California. Work was scarce, and labor groups exerted political pressure on the government to restrict Asian immigration. The founder of the Workingmen's Party, Denis Kearney, headed the anti-Chinese movement in California. He made hundreds of speeches throughout the state, each ending with the message, "The Chinese must go!"

In 1882, Congress slammed the door on Chinese immigration for ten years by passing the **Chinese Exclusion Act.** This act banned entry to all Chinese except students, teachers, merchants, tourists, and government officials. In 1892, Congress extended the law for another ten years. In 1902, Chinese immigration was restricted indefinitely; the law was not repealed until 1943.

THE GENTLEMEN'S AGREEMENT The fears that had led to anti-Chinese agitation were extended to Japanese and other Asian people in the early 1900s. In 1906, the local board of education in San Francisco segregated Japanese children by putting them in separate schools. When Japan raised an angry protest at this treatment of its emigrants, President Theodore Roosevelt worked out a deal. Under the **Gentlemen's Agreement** of 1907–1908, Japan's government agreed to limit emigration of unskilled workers to the United States in exchange for the repeal of the San Francisco segregation order.

Although doorways for immigrants had been all but closed to Asians on the West Coast, cities in the East and the Midwest teemed with European immigrants—and with urban opportunities and challenges.

▲
Fear and resentment of Chinese immigrants sometimes resulted in mob attacks, like the one shown here.

 SECTION 1

ASSESSMENT

1. TERMS & NAMES For each term or name, write a sentence explaining its significance.
- Ellis Island
- Angel Island
- melting pot
- nativism
- Chinese Exclusion Act
- Gentlemen's Agreement

MAIN IDEA

2. TAKING NOTES
Create a diagram such as the one below. List two or more causes of each effect.

Causes ———▶	Effects
1. 2. 3.	Immigrants leave their home countries.
1. 2. 3.	Immigrants face hardships in the United States.
1. 2. 3.	Some nativists want to restrict immigration.

CRITICAL THINKING

3. IDENTIFYING PROBLEMS
Which group of immigrants do you think faced the greatest challenges in the United States? Why?

4. ANALYZING EFFECTS
What were the effects of the massive influx of immigrants to the U.S. in the late 1800s?

5. EVALUATING
What arguments can you make against nativism and anti-immigrant feeling? **Think About:**
- the personal qualities of immigrants
- the reasons for anti-immigrant feeling
- the contributions of immigrants to the United States

Diversity and the National Identity

Before the first Europeans arrived, a variety of cultural groups—coastal fishing societies, desert farmers, plains and woodland hunters—inhabited North America. With the arrival of Europeans and Africans, the cultural mix grew more complex. Although this diversity has often produced tension, it has also been beneficial. As different groups learned from one another about agriculture, technology, and social customs, American culture became a rich blend of cultures from around the world.

1610s–1870s

◀ SPANISH NORTH AMERICA

Spanish missionaries in the Southwest tried to impose their culture upon Native Americans. However, many Native Americans retained aspects of their original cultures even as they took on Spanish ways. For example, today many Pueblo Indians of New Mexico perform ancient ceremonies, such as the Corn Dance, in addition to celebrating the feast days of Catholic saints. Later, the first cowboys—descendants of the Spanish—would introduce to white Americans cattle-ranching techniques developed in Mexico.

1776

THE DECLARATION OF INDEPENDENCE ▶

The signers of the Declaration of Independence were descendants of immigrants. The founders' ancestors had come to North America in search of economic opportunity and freedom of religious expression. When the Second Continental Congress declared a "United States" in 1776, they acknowledged that the country would contain diverse regions and interests. Thus the founders placed on the presidential seal the motto *"E Pluribus Unum"*—"out of many, one."

1862–1863

THE EMANCIPATION PROCLAMATION ▲

At the midpoint of the Civil War, President Abraham Lincoln issued the Emancipation Proclamation, freeing all slaves in areas of the Union that were in rebellion. Although the Proclamation could not be enforced immediately, it was a strong statement of opposition to slavery, and it paved the way for African Americans' citizenship.

1886

THE STATUE OF LIBERTY ▶

Jewish poet Emma Lazarus wrote the famous lines inscribed at the foot of the Statue of Liberty, "Give me your tired, your poor,/Your huddled masses yearning to breathe free, . . ." The statue's dedication took place during the most extensive wave of immigration the United States has ever known.

Many native-born Americans felt that the newcomers should fully immerse themselves in their new culture. However, most immigrants combined American language and customs with their traditional ways. As immigrants celebrated Independence Day and Thanksgiving, they introduced into American culture new celebrations, such as Chinese New Year and Cinco de Mayo.

2000

◀ 21ST-CENTURY DIVERSITY

In 1998, three countries (Mexico, China, and India) contributed a third of the total number of immigrants to the United States. The rest of 1998's immigrants came from countries as diverse as Vietnam, Sudan, and Bosnia.

American athletes at the 2000 Olympic Games in Sydney, Australia, reflected the increasing diversity of the U.S., pointing toward a future in which there may no longer be a majority racial or ethnic group.

THINKING CRITICALLY

CONNECT TO HISTORY

1. **Analyzing Motives** Why do you think some groups have tried to suppress the culture of others over the course of history? Why have many groups persisted in retaining their cultural heritage?

    SEE SKILLBUILDER HANDBOOK, PAGE R6.

CONNECT TO TODAY

2. **Predicting Effects** Research current U.S. policy on immigration. How might this policy affect cultural diversity? Write a short editorial from one of the following viewpoints:
   • U.S. immigration policy needs to change.
   • U.S. immigration policy should be maintained.

hmhsocialstudies.com RESEARCH WEB LINKS

SECTION 2

PI 2.3
PI 3.1

CC Unit 3.III.A.1.b   CC Unit 3.III.A.1.c
CC Unit 3.III.A.1.d   CC Unit 3.III.A.2.a
CC Unit 3.III.C.3   CC Unit 4.I.B.2.a

The Challenges of Urbanization

MAIN IDEA	WHY IT MATTERS NOW	Terms & Names
The rapid growth of cities forced people to contend with problems of housing, transportation, water, and sanitation.	Consequently, residents of U.S. cities today enjoy vastly improved living conditions.	• urbanization • Social Gospel movement • Americanization movement • settlement house • tenement • Jane Addams • mass transit

One American's Story

hmhsocialstudies.com
TAKING NOTES
Use the graphic organizer online to take notes about urbanization and its problems.

In 1870, at age 21, Jacob Riis left his native Denmark for the United States. Riis found work as a police reporter, a job that took him into some of New York City's worst slums, where he was shocked at the conditions in the overcrowded, airless, filthy tenements. Riis used his talents to expose the hardships of New York City's poor.

A PERSONAL VOICE JACOB RIIS

"Be a little careful, please! The hall is dark and you might stumble over the children pitching pennies back there. Not that it would hurt them; kicks and cuffs are their daily diet. They have little else. . . . Close [stuffy]? Yes! What would you have? All the fresh air that ever enters these stairs comes from the hall-door that is forever slamming. . . . Here is a door. Listen! That short hacking cough, that tiny, helpless wail—what do they mean? . . . The child is dying with measles. With half a chance it might have lived; but it had none. That dark bedroom killed it."

—How the Other Half Lives

▲ As many as 12 people slept in rooms such as this one in New York City, photographed by Jacob Riis around 1889.

Making a living in the late 19th and early 20th centuries was not easy. Natural and economic disasters had hit farmers hard in Europe and in the United States, and the promise of industrial jobs drew millions of people to American cities. The urban population exploded from 10 million to 54 million between 1870 and 1920. This growth revitalized the cities but also created serious problems that, as Riis observed, had a powerful impact on the new urban poor.

Urban Opportunities

The technological boom in the 19th century contributed to the growing industrial strength of the United States. The result was rapid **urbanization,** or growth of cities, mostly in the regions of the Northeast and Midwest.

IMMIGRANTS SETTLE IN CITIES

Most of the immigrants who streamed into the United States in the late 19th century became city dwellers because cities were the cheapest and most convenient places to live. Cities also offered unskilled laborers steady jobs in mills and factories. By 1890, there were twice as many Irish residents in New York City as in Dublin, Ireland. By 1910, immigrant families made up more than half the total population of 18 major American cities.

The **Americanization movement** was designed to assimilate people of wide-ranging cultures into the dominant culture. This social campaign was sponsored by the government and by concerned citizens. Schools and voluntary associations provided programs to teach immigrants skills needed for citizenship, such as English literacy and American history and government. Subjects such as cooking and social etiquette were included in the curriculum to help the newcomers learn the ways of native-born Americans. **A**

Despite these efforts, many immigrants did not wish to abandon their traditions. Ethnic communities provided the social support of other immigrants from the same country. This enabled them to speak their own language and practice their customs and religion. However, these neighborhoods soon became overcrowded, a problem that was intensified by the arrival of new transplants from America's rural areas.

New York City, 1910

Ethnic enclaves of at least 20% of population:
- Austro-Hungarian
- German
- Irish
- Italian
- Russian
- Scandinavian
- Nonresidential
- Boundary between Brooklyn and Queens

BRONX

MANHATTAN

QUEENS

BROOKLYN

GEOGRAPHY SKILLBUILDER
1. **Place** What general pattern of settlement do you notice?
2. **Movement** Which ethnic group settled in the largest area of New York City?

MIGRATION FROM COUNTRY TO CITY Rapid improvements in farming technology during the second half of the 19th century were good news for some farmers but bad news for others. Inventions such as the McCormick reaper and the steel plow made farming more efficient but meant that fewer laborers were needed to work the land. As more and more farms merged, many rural people moved to cities to find whatever work they could.

Many of the Southern farmers who lost their livelihoods were African Americans. Between 1890 and 1910, about 200,000 African Americans moved north and west, to cities such as Chicago and Detroit, in an effort to escape racial violence, economic hardship, and political oppression. Many found conditions only somewhat better than those they had left behind. Segregation and discrimination were often the reality in Northern cities. Competition for jobs, housing, and public services between blacks and white immigrants caused further racial tension.

Urban Problems

As the urban population skyrocketed, city governments faced the problems of how to provide residents with needed services and safe living conditions.

HOUSING When the industrial age began, working-class families in cities had two housing options. They could either buy a house on the outskirts of town, where they would face transportation problems, or rent cramped rooms in a boardinghouse in the central city. As the urban population increased, however, new types of housing were designed. For example, row houses—single-family dwellings that shared side walls with other similar houses—packed many single-family residences onto a single block.

After working-class families left the central city, immigrants often took over their old housing, sometimes with two or three families occupying a one-family residence. As Jacob Riis pointed out, these multifamily urban dwellings, called **tenements,** were overcrowded and unsanitary.

In 1879, to improve such slum conditions, New York City passed a law that set minimum standards for plumbing and ventilation in apartments. Landlords began building tenements with air shafts that provided an outside window for each room. Since garbage was picked up infrequently, people sometimes dumped it into the air shafts, where it attracted vermin. To keep out the stench, residents nailed windows shut. Though established with good intent, these new tenements soon became even worse places to live than the converted single-family residences. **B**

TRANSPORTATION Innovations in **mass transit,** transportation systems designed to move large numbers of people along fixed routes, enabled workers to go to and from jobs more easily. Street cars were introduced in San Francisco in 1873 and electric subways in Boston in 1897. By the early 20th century, mass-transit networks in many urban areas linked city neighborhoods to one another and to outlying communities. Cities struggled to repair old transit systems and to build new ones to meet the demand of expanding populations.

WATER Cities also faced the problem of supplying safe drinking water. As the urban population grew in the 1840s and 1850s, cities such as New York and Cleveland built public waterworks to handle the increasing demand. As late as the 1860s, however, the residents of many cities had grossly inadequate piped water—or none at all. Even in large cities like New York, homes seldom had indoor plumbing, and residents had to collect water in pails from faucets on the street and heat it for bathing. The necessity of improving water quality to control diseases such as cholera and typhoid fever was obvious. To make city water safer, filtration was introduced in the 1870s and chlorination in 1908. However, in the early 20th century, many city dwellers still had no access to safe water.

SANITATION As the cities grew, so did the challenge of keeping them clean. Horse manure piled up on the streets, sewage flowed through open gutters, and factories spewed foul smoke into the air. Without dependable trash collection, people dumped their garbage on the streets. Although private contractors called scavengers were hired to sweep the streets, collect garbage, and clean outhouses, they

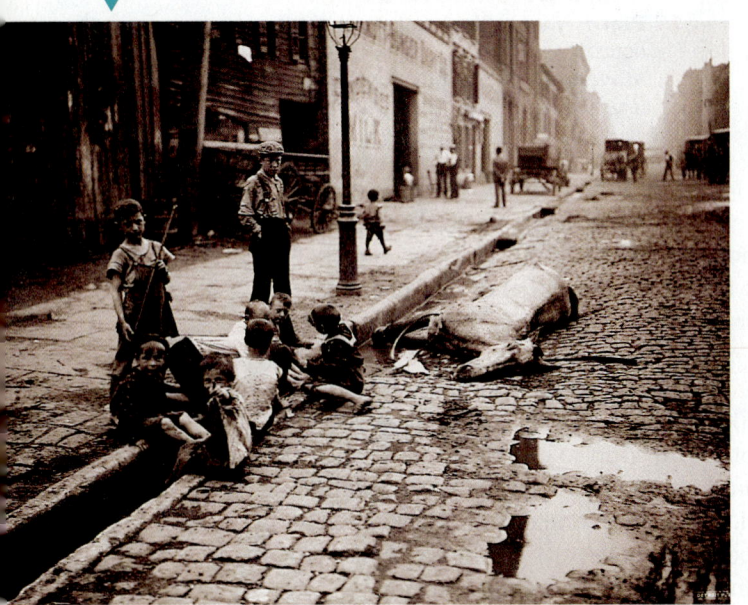

Sanitation problems in big cities were overwhelming. It was not unusual to see a dead horse in the street.

MAIN IDEA

Identifying Problems

B What housing problems did urban working-class families face?

Vocabulary
chlorination: a method of purifying water by mixing it with the chemical chlorine

MAIN IDEA

Analyzing
Effects

C How did
conditions in cities
affect people's
health?

often did not do the jobs properly. By 1900, many cities had developed sewer lines and created sanitation departments. However, the task of providing hygienic living conditions was an ongoing challenge for urban leaders. **C**

CRIME As the populations of cities increased, pickpockets and thieves flourished. Although New York City organized the first full-time, salaried police force in 1844, it and most other city law enforcement units were too small to have much impact on crime.

FIRE The limited water supply in many cities contributed to another menace: the spread of fires. Major fires occurred in almost every large American city during the 1870s and 1880s. In addition to lacking water with which to combat blazes, most cities were packed with wooden dwellings, which were like kindling waiting to be ignited. The use of candles and kerosene heaters also posed a fire hazard. In San Francisco, deadly fires often broke out during earthquakes. Jack London described the fires that raged after the San Francisco earthquake of 1906.

A PERSONAL VOICE JACK LONDON

"On Wednesday morning at a quarter past five came the earthquake. A minute later the flames were leaping upward. In a dozen different quarters south of Market Street, in the working-class ghetto, and in the factories, fires started. There was no opposing the flames. . . . And the great water-mains had burst. All the shrewd contrivances and safeguards of man had been thrown out of gear by thirty seconds' twitching of the earth-crust."

—"The Story of an Eye-witness"

At first, most city firefighters were volunteers and not always available when they were needed. Cincinnati, Ohio, tackled this problem when it established the nation's first paid fire department in 1853. By 1900, most cities had full-time professional fire departments. The introduction of a practical automatic fire sprinkler in 1874 and the replacement of wood as a building material with brick, stone, or concrete also made cities safer.

FIRE: Enemy of the City

The Great Chicago Fire October 8–10, 1871

- The fire burned for over 24 hours.
- An estimated 300 people died.
- 100,000 were left homeless.
- More than 3 square miles of the city center was destroyed.
- Property loss was estimated at $200 million.
- 17,500 buildings were destroyed.

The San Francisco Earthquake April 18, 1906

- The quake lasted 28 seconds; fires burned for 4 days.
- An estimated 1,000 people died.
- Over 200,000 were left homeless.
- Fire swept through 5 square miles of the city.
- Property loss was estimated at $500 million.
- 28,000 buildings were destroyed.

Reformers Mobilize

As problems in cities mounted, concerned Americans worked to find solutions. Social welfare reformers targeted their efforts at relieving urban poverty.

THE SETTLEMENT HOUSE MOVEMENT An early reform program, the **Social Gospel movement,** preached salvation through service to the poor. Inspired by the message of the Social Gospel movement, many 19th-century reformers responded to the call to help the urban poor. In the late 1800s, a few reformers established **settlement houses,** community centers in slum neighborhoods that provided assistance to people in the area, especially immigrants. Many settlement workers lived at the houses so that they could learn firsthand about the problems caused by urbanization and help create solutions.

Run largely by middle-class, college-educated women, settlement houses provided educational, cultural, and social services. They provided classes in such subjects as English, health, and painting, and offered college extension courses. Settlement houses also sent visiting nurses into the homes of the sick and provided whatever aid was needed to secure "support for deserted women, insurance for bewildered widows, damages for injured operators, furniture from the clutches of the installment store."

Settlement houses in the United States were founded by Charles Stover and Stanton Coit in New York City in 1886. **Jane Addams**—one of the most influential members of the movement—and Ellen Gates Starr founded Chicago's Hull House in 1889. In 1890, Janie Porter Barrett founded Locust Street Social Settlement in Hampton, Virginia—the first settlement house for African Americans. By 1910, about 400 settlement houses were operating in cities across the country. The settlement houses helped cultivate social responsibility toward the urban poor.

FOCUS ON

Some religious leaders worked against politicians who they felt were holding back reform. In New York City, Presbyterian minister Charles Parkhurst waged war on Tammany Hall because of its support of illegal bars and gambling.

SECTION 2 ASSESSMENT

1. TERMS & NAMES For each term or name, write a sentence explaining its significance.
- urbanization
- Americanization movement
- tenement
- mass transit
- Social Gospel movement
- settlement house
- Jane Addams

MAIN IDEA

2. TAKING NOTES
Re-create the spider map below on your paper. List urban problems on the vertical lines. Fill in details about attempts that were made to solve each problem.

> **Solutions to Urban Problems**

CRITICAL THINKING

3. ANALYZING MOTIVES
Why did immigrants tend to group together in cities?

4. EVALUATING
Which solution (or attempted solution) to an urban problem discussed in this section do you think had the most impact? Why?

5. ANALYZING EFFECTS
What effects did the migration from rural areas to the cities in the late 19th century have on urban society?
Think About:
- why people moved to cities
- the problems caused by rapid urban growth
- the differences in the experiences of whites and blacks

PI 2.2

CC Unit 3.III.B.6
CC Unit 4.I.C.1.a(2)

Politics in the Gilded Age

MAIN IDEA	WHY IT MATTERS NOW	Terms & Names
Local and national political corruption in the 19th century led to calls for reform.	Political reforms paved the way for a more honest and efficient government in the 20th century and beyond.	• political machine • graft • Boss Tweed • patronage • civil service • Rutherford B. Hayes • James A. Garfield • Chester A. Arthur • Pendleton Civil Service Act • Grover Cleveland • Benjamin Harrison

One American's Story

hmhsocialstudies.com
TAKING NOTES

Use the graphic organizer online to take notes about political corruption in the Gilded Age.

Mark Twain described the excesses of the late 19th century in a satirical novel, *The Gilded Age*, a collaboration with the writer Charles Dudley Warner. The title of the book has since come to represent the period from the 1870s to the 1890s. Twain mocks the greed and self-indulgence of his characters, including Philip Sterling.

A PERSONAL VOICE
MARK TWAIN AND CHARLES DUDLEY WARNER

" There are many young men like him [Philip Sterling] in American society, of his age, opportunities, education and abilities, who have really been educated for nothing and have let themselves drift, in the hope that they will find somehow, and by some sudden turn of good luck, the golden road to fortune. . . . He saw people, all around him, poor yesterday, rich to-day, who had come into sudden opulence by some means which they could not have classified among any of the regular occupations of life. "

—*The Gilded Age*

▲ A luxurious apartment building rises behind a New York City shanty-town in 1889.

Twain's characters find that getting rich quick is more difficult than they had thought it would be. Investments turn out to be worthless; politicians' bribes eat up their savings. The glittering exterior of the age turns out to hide a corrupt political core and a growing gap between the few rich and the many poor.

The Emergence of Political Machines

In the late 19th century, cities experienced rapid growth under inefficient government. In a climate influenced by dog-eat-dog Social Darwinism, cities were receptive to a new power structure, the political machine, and a new politician, the city boss.

THE POLITICAL MACHINE An organized group that controlled the activities of a political party in a city, the **political machine** also offered services to voters and businesses in exchange for political or financial support. In the decades after the Civil War, political machines gained control of local government in Baltimore, New York, San Francisco, and other major cities.

The machine was organized like a pyramid. At the pyramid's base were local precinct workers and captains, who tried to gain voters' support on a city block or in a neighborhood and who reported to a ward boss. At election time, the ward boss worked to secure the vote in all the precincts in the ward, or electoral district. Ward bosses helped the poor and gained their votes by doing favors or providing services. As Martin Lomasney, elected ward boss of Boston's West End in 1885, explained, "There's got to be in every ward somebody that any bloke can come to . . . and get help. Help, you understand; none of your law and your justice, but help." At the top of the pyramid was the city boss, who controlled the activities of the political party throughout the city. Precinct captains, ward bosses, and the city boss worked together to elect their candidates and guarantee the success of the machine. **A**

THE ROLE OF THE POLITICAL BOSS Whether or not the boss officially served as mayor, he controlled access to municipal jobs and business licenses, and influenced the courts and other municipal agencies. Bosses like Roscoe Conkling in New York used their power to build parks, sewer systems, and waterworks, and gave money to schools, hospitals, and orphanages. Bosses could also provide government support for new businesses, a service for which they were often paid extremely well.

It was not only money that motivated city bosses. By solving urban problems, bosses could reinforce voters' loyalty, win additional political support, and extend their influence.

IMMIGRANTS AND THE MACHINE Many precinct captains and political bosses were first-generation or second-generation immigrants. Few were educated beyond grammar school. They entered politics early and worked their way up from the bottom. They could speak to immigrants in their own language and understood the challenges that newcomers faced. More important, the bosses were able to provide solutions. The machines helped immigrants with naturalization (attaining full citizenship), housing, and jobs—the newcomers' most pressing needs. In return, the immigrants provided what the political bosses needed—votes. **B**

"Big Jim" Pendergast, an Irish-American saloonkeeper, worked his way up from precinct captain to Democratic city boss in Kansas City by aiding Italian, African-American, and Irish voters in his ward. By 1900, he controlled Missouri state politics as well.

▲ A corrupt 19th-century boss robs the city treasury by easily cutting government red tape, or bureaucracy.

MAIN IDEA

Summarizing
A In what way did the structure of the political machine resemble a pyramid?

MAIN IDEA

Analyzing Motives
B Why did immigrants support political machines?

★ **A PERSONAL VOICE** JAMES PENDERGAST

" I've been called a boss. All there is to it is having friends, doing things for people, and then later on they'll do things for you. . . . You can't coerce people into doing things for you—you can't make them vote for you. I never coerced anybody in my life. Wherever you see a man bulldozing anybody he don't last long. "

—quoted in *The Pendergast Machine*

Municipal Graft and Scandal

While the well-oiled political machines provided city dwellers with services, many political bosses fell victim to corruption as their influence grew.

ELECTION FRAUD AND GRAFT When the loyalty of voters was not enough to carry an election, some political machines turned to fraud. Using fake names, party faithfuls cast as many votes as were needed to win.

Once a political machine got its candidates into office, it could take advantage of numerous opportunities for **graft,** the illegal use of political influence for personal gain. For example, by helping a person find work on a construction project for the city, a political machine could ask the worker to bill the city for more than the actual cost of materials and labor. The worker then "kicked back" a portion of the earnings to the machine. Taking these kickbacks, or illegal payments for their services, enriched the political machines—and individual politicians.

Political machines also granted favors to businesses in return for cash and accepted bribes to allow illegal activities, such as gambling, to flourish. Politicians were able to get away with shady dealings because the police rarely interfered. Until about 1890, police forces were hired and fired by political bosses.

THE TWEED RING SCANDAL William M. Tweed, known as **Boss Tweed,** became head of Tammany Hall, New York City's powerful Democratic political machine, in 1868. Between 1869 and 1871, Boss Tweed led the Tweed Ring, a group of corrupt politicians, in defrauding the city.

One scheme, the construction of the New York County Courthouse, involved extravagant graft. The project cost taxpayers $13 million, while the actual construction cost was $3 million. The difference went into the pockets of Tweed and his followers.

Vocabulary
extortion: illegal use of one's official position to obtain property or funds

Thomas Nast, a political cartoonist, helped arouse public outrage against Tammany Hall's graft, and the Tweed Ring was finally broken in 1871. Tweed was indicted on 120 counts of fraud and extortion and was sentenced to 12 years in jail. His sentence was reduced to one year, but after leaving jail, Tweed was quickly arrested on another charge. While serving a second sentence, Tweed escaped. He was captured in Spain when officials identified him from a Thomas Nast cartoon. By that time, political corruption had become a national issue.

▲
Boss Tweed, head of Tammany Hall.

Analyzing Political Cartoons

"THE TAMMANY TIGER LOOSE"

Political cartoonist Thomas Nast ridiculed Boss Tweed and his machine in the pages of *Harper's Weekly.* Nast's work threatened Tweed, who reportedly said, "I don't care so much what the papers write about me—my constituents can't read; but . . . they can see pictures!"

SKILLBUILDER Analyzing Political Cartoons
1. Under the Tammany tiger's victim is a torn paper that reads "LAW." What is its significance?
2. Boss Tweed and his cronies, portrayed as noblemen, watch from the stands on the left. The cartoon's caption reads "What are you going to do about it?" What effect do you think Nast wanted to have on his audience?

 SEE SKILLBUILDER HANDBOOK, PAGE R24.

RUTHERFORD B. HAYES (1877–1881)

" Nobody ever left the presidency with less regret . . . than I do."

JAMES A. GARFIELD (1881)

" Assassination can be no more guarded against than death by lightning."

CHESTER A. ARTHUR (1881–1885)

" There doesn't seem to be anything else for an ex-president to do but . . . raise big pumpkins."

Civil Service Replaces Patronage

The desire for power and money that made local politics corrupt in the industrial age also infected national politics.

PATRONAGE SPURS REFORM Since the beginning of the 19th century, presidents had complained about the problem of **patronage,** or the giving of government jobs to people who had helped a candidate get elected. In Andrew Jackson's administration, this policy was known as the spoils system. People from cabinet members to workers who scrubbed the steps of the Capitol owed their jobs to political connections. As might be expected, some government employees were not qualified for the positions they filled. Moreover, political appointees, whether qualified or not, sometimes used their positions for personal gain.

Reformers began to press for the elimination of patronage and the adoption of a merit system of hiring. Jobs in **civil service**—government administration—should go to the most qualified persons, reformers believed. It should not matter what political views they held or who recommended them. **C**

REFORM UNDER HAYES, GARFIELD, AND ARTHUR Civil service reform made gradual progress under Presidents Hayes, Garfield, and Arthur. Republican president **Rutherford B. Hayes,** elected in 1876, could not convince Congress to support reform, so he used other means. Hayes named independents to his cabinet. He also set up a commission to investigate the nation's customhouses, which were notorious centers of patronage. On the basis of the commission's report, Hayes fired two of the top officials of New York City's customhouse, where jobs were controlled by the Republican Party. These firings enraged the Republican New York senator and political boss Roscoe Conkling and his supporters, the Stalwarts.

When Hayes decided not to run for reelection in 1880, a free-for-all broke out at the Republican convention, between the Stalwarts—who opposed changes in the spoils system—and reformers. Since neither Stalwarts nor reformers could win a majority of delegates, the convention settled on an independent presidential candidate, Ohio congressman **James A. Garfield.** To balance out Garfield's ties to reformers, the Republicans nominated for vice-president **Chester A. Arthur,** one of Conkling's supporters. Despite Arthur's inclusion on the ticket, Garfield angered the Stalwarts by giving reformers most of his patronage jobs once he was elected.

On July 2, 1881, as President Garfield walked through the Washington, D.C., train station, he was shot two times by a mentally unbalanced lawyer named Charles Guiteau, whom Garfield had turned down for a job. The would-be assassin announced, "I did it and I will go to jail for it. I am a Stalwart and Arthur is now president." Garfield finally died from his wounds on September 19. Despite his ties to the Stalwarts, Chester Arthur turned reformer when he became president. His first message to Congress urged legislators to pass a civil service law.

The resulting **Pendleton Civil Service Act** of 1883 authorized a bipartisan civil service commission to make

> **MAIN IDEA**
>
> **Analyzing Causes**
> **C** How did patronage contribute to government incompetence and fraud?

appointments to federal jobs through a merit system based on candidates' performance on an examination. By 1901, more than 40 percent of all federal jobs had been classified as civil service positions, but the Pendleton Act had mixed consequences. On the one hand, public administration became more honest and efficient. On the other hand, because officials could no longer pressure employees for campaign contributions, politicians turned to other sources for donations.

Business Buys Influence

MAIN IDEA

Analyzing Effects

D What were the positive and the negative effects of the Pendleton Civil Service Act?

With employees no longer a source of campaign contributions, politicians turned to wealthy business owners. Therefore, the alliance between government and big business became stronger than ever. **D**

HARRISON, CLEVELAND, AND HIGH TARIFFS Big business hoped the government would preserve, or even raise, the tariffs that protected domestic industries from foreign competition. The Democratic Party, however, opposed high tariffs because they increased prices. In 1884, the Democratic Party won a presidential election for the first time in 28 years with candidate **Grover Cleveland.** As president, Cleveland tried to lower tariff rates, but Congress refused to support him.

In 1888, Cleveland ran for reelection on a low-tariff platform against the former Indiana senator **Benjamin Harrison,** the grandson of President William Henry Harrison. Harrison's campaign was financed by large contributions from companies that wanted tariffs even higher than they were. Although Cleveland won about 100,000 more popular votes than Harrison, Harrison took a majority of the electoral votes and the presidency. He signed the McKinley Tariff Act of 1890, which raised tariffs on manufactured goods to their highest level yet.

In 1892, Cleveland was elected again—the only president to serve two nonconsecutive terms. He supported a bill for lowering the McKinley Tariff but refused to sign it because it also provided for a federal income tax. The Wilson-Gorman Tariff became law in 1894 without the president's signature. In 1897, William McKinley was inaugurated president and raised tariffs once again.

The attempt to reduce the tariff had failed, but the spirit of reform was not dead. New developments in areas ranging from technology to mass culture would help redefine American society as the United States moved into the 20th century.

SECTION 3 ASSESSMENT

1. TERMS & NAMES For each term or name, write a sentence explaining its significance.
- political machine
- graft
- Boss Tweed
- patronage
- civil service
- Rutherford B. Hayes
- James A. Garfield
- Chester A. Arthur
- Pendleton Civil Service Act
- Grover Cleveland
- Benjamin Harrison

MAIN IDEA

2. TAKING NOTES
In a chart like the one shown, list examples of corruption in 19th-century politics.

Corruption

CRITICAL THINKING

3. EVALUATING LEADERSHIP
Reread the quotation from James Pendergast on page 474. Explain whether you agree or disagree that machine politicians did not coerce people.

4. ANALYZING CAUSES
Why do you think tariff reform failed? Support your response with evidence from the chapter.

5. HYPOTHESIZING
How do you think politics in the United States would have been different if the Pendleton Civil Service Act had not been passed?

THINK ABOUT:
- the act's impact on federal workers
- the act's impact on political fundraising
- Republican Party conflicts

TERMS & NAMES

For each term or name below, write a sentence explaining its connection to immigration and urbanization.

1. Ellis Island
2. Gentlemen's Agreement
3. Americanization movement
4. Jane Addams
5. political machine
6. graft
7. Boss Tweed
8. patronage
9. Rutherford B. Hayes
10. Pendleton Civil Service Act

MAIN IDEAS

Use your notes and the information in the chapter to answer the following questions.

The New Immigrants (pages 460–465)

1. What trends or events in other countries prompted people to move to the United States in the late 19th and early 20th centuries?
2. What difficulties did many of these new immigrants face?

The Challenges of Urbanization
(pages 468–472)

3. Why did cities in the United States grow rapidly in the decades following the Civil War?
4. What problems did this rapid growth pose for cities?
5. What solutions to urban problems did the settlement-house movement propose?

Politics in the Gilded Age (pages 473–477)

6. Why did machine politics become common in big cities in the late 19th century?
7. What government problems arose as a result of patronage?
8. Summarize the views of Grover Cleveland and Benjamin Harrison on tariffs.

CRITICAL THINKING

1. **USING YOUR NOTES** In a diagram like the one below, show one result of and one reaction against (a) the increase in immigration and (b) the increase in machine politics.

	Result	Reaction
Increased Immigration →	_____ →	_____
Increased Machine Politics →	_____ →	_____

2. **EVALUATING** In the 1860s, Horace Greeley—editor of the *New York Tribune*—remarked, "We cannot all live in the cities, yet nearly all seem determined to do so." Why do you think this was true at the end of the 19th century? Do you think it is still true? Why or why not?

3. **COMPARING** How were politicians like Boss Tweed similar to industrial magnates like Carnegie and Rockefeller?

VISUAL SUMMARY IMMIGRANTS AND URBANIZATION

URBANIZATION

- The influx of immigrants and migrants causes a population boom in cities.
- City services, such as housing, transportation, water, and sanitation, are stretched to the limit.
- Reformers try to fix urban problems through education, training, charity, and political action.

IMMIGRATION AND MIGRATION

- Poverty and persecution cause millions of people to leave Europe, China, Japan, the Caribbean, and Mexico for the United States.
- Immigrants are forced to adapt to a new language and culture.
- Changes in agriculture cause people to migrate from the rural U.S. to the cities in search of work.
- Many immigrants and migrants face discrimination in their efforts to find jobs and housing.

POLITICS

- Political machines develop to take advantage of the needs of immigrants and the urban poor.
- City politicians use fraud and graft to maintain political power.
- Corruption in national politics results in the call for civil service jobs to be awarded on the basis of merit.
- Big business's growing influence on politics defeats tariff reform that would aid wage-earners.

Use the quotation and your knowledge of U.S. history to answer question 1.

> "The Chinese . . . ask for fair treatment. . . . Since the first restriction law was passed the United States has received as immigrants more than two million Austro-Hungarians, two million Italians and a million and a half Russians and Finns. Each of these totals is from five to seven times the whole amount of Chinese immigration of all classes during thirty years of free immigration. . . . The question is not now of the admission of laborers, but whether other Chinese who are entitled to come under both law and treaty shall receive the same courtesies as people of other nations, and shall be relieved from many harassing regulations. They must no longer be detained, photographed and examined as if they were suspected of crime."

—Ng Poon Chew, from *The Treatment of the Exempt Classes of Chinese in the United States*

1 The information in the passage supports which *one* of the following points of view?

(1) European immigration should be restricted.

(2) Chinese laborers should be allowed to immigrate.

(3) All immigrants are treated like criminals.

(4) Chinese immigrants and European immigrants should be treated the same.

Use the cartoon and your knowledge of U.S. history to answer question 2.

WHO STOLE THE PEOPLE'S MONEY? — DO TELL . N.Y.TIMES.   'TWAS HIM

2 The cartoon suggests that Boss Tweed (the large figure at left) —

(1) was solely responsible for stealing the people's money.

(2) did not steal the people's money.

(3) had help from his associates in stealing the people's money.

(4) was loyal to his associates.

hmhsocialstudies.com **TEST PRACTICE**

For additional test practice, go online for:
• Diagnostic tests   • Tutorials

INTERACT WITH HISTORY

Think about the issues you explored at the beginning of the chapter. With what you have learned about the challenges faced by immigrants in the 19th century, consider the following question: What were the best solutions attempted by government and reformers in the 1800s? Create a pamphlet promoting the reform, improvement, or government solution you chose.

FOCUS ON WRITING

Imagine you are a senator and the Senate is about to vote on the Chinese Exclusion Act. Prepare a persuasive speech arguing against the new law. For the first part of your speech, explain why this law is unjust and unfair to the Chinese. For the second part, address the concerns of those in favor of the act and provide an alternate solution for the issues prompting the Chinese Exclusion Act.

COLLABORATIVE LEARNING

21ST CENTURY

Organize into small groups and discuss stories of immigration or the experiences of recent immigrants to the U.S. that you have heard or read about. With the group, create a multimedia presentation of these stories. Use pictures, text, and sound to represent the stories.

Ellis Island

For most European immigrants, Ellis Island was the first stop. Between 1892 and 1954, the immigration station processed over 12 million immigrants. These immigrants went through an inspection before they were allowed to enter the United States. Those with serious health problems were sent home, as were those who did not meet various legal requirements. Others were sent home because they exceeded immigration quotas. However, if immigrants could clear these hurdles, they were free to enter the United States and begin their new lives.

Go online to explore some of the personal stories and recollections of immigrants who made the journey to America and passed through Ellis Island. You can find a wealth of information, video clips, primary sources, activities, and more at **hmhsocialstudies.com**.

1. Doctors examined immigrants as they headed upstairs to the Great Hall.
2. Lines were long, but the inspection often lasted only a few minutes.
3. Immigrants who passed the inspection could exchange money, send mail or telegrams, or buy train tickets.
4. Immigrants then met relatives or loved ones.
5. Immigrants who had to stay overnight were assigned to dormitories.

🎥 The Golden Door
Watch the video to see how and why immigrants traveled to the United States.

🎥 Examination
Watch the video to see the physical examination that immigrants experienced at Ellis Island.

🎥 Quotas
Watch the video to see how immigration quotas affected immigrants trying to come to the United States.

CHAPTER 16

LIFE AT THE TURN OF THE 20TH CENTURY

Essential Question

What were the significant trends in areas such as technology, education, race relations, and mass culture at the turn of the 20th century?

New York Standards

KEY IDEA 2 Important ideas, social and cultural values, beliefs, and traditions from New York State and United States history illustrate the connections and interactions of people and events across time and from a variety of perspectives.

KEY IDEA 4 The skills of historical analysis include the ability to: explain the significance of historical evidence; weigh the importance, reliability, and validity of evidence; understand the concept of multiple causation; understand the importance of changing and competing interpretations of different historical developments.

SECTION 1: Science and Urban Life

SECTION 2: Expanding Public Education

SECTION 3: Segregation and Discrimination

SECTION 4: The Dawn of Mass Culture

The World's Columbian Exposition, commemorating the 400th anniversary of Columbus sailing to the Americas.

1883 Construction of the Brooklyn Bridge is completed.

1888 Electric trolleys are first introduced.

1892 Ida B. Wells crusades against lynching.

1896 Supreme Court establishes "separate-but-equal" doctrine in *Plessy* v. *Ferguson.*

USA
WORLD
1880   **1885**   **1890**   **1895**

1878 Bicycle touring club is founded in Europe.

1884 Fifteen-nation conference on the division of Africa convenes in Berlin.

1889 Barnum & Bailey Circus opens in London.

INTERACT
WITH HISTORY

It is the summer of 1893. In Chicago, the World's Columbian Exposition is in full swing. Besides Thomas Edison's kinetograph—a camera that records motion—attractions include a towering "Ferris wheel" that lifts trolley cars into the sky and the first hamburgers in America. More than 21 million people will attend the exposition. You will be one of them.

Explore the Issues

- How can technology contribute to new forms of recreation?
- What types of inventions transform communications?
- Why would mass media emerge at this time?

1901 McKinley is assassinated.

1900 William McKinley is reelected.

1901 Theodore Roosevelt becomes president.

1904 Theodore Roosevelt is elected president.

1908 Henry Ford introduces the Model T.

1908 William H. Taft is elected president.

1912 Woodrow Wilson is elected president.

1916 Woodrow Wilson is reelected.

1900   **1905**   **1910**   **1915**

1899 Austrian psychoanalyst Sigmund Freud publishes *The Interpretation of Dreams.*

1910 Mexican Revolution begins.

1914 World War I begins in Europe.

Life at the Turn of the 20th Century   **481**

SECTION
1

PI 2.2
PI 4.1

CC Unit 3.II.B.1
CC Unit 3.II.B.2
CC Unit 3.III.A.1.c

Science and Urban Life

MAIN IDEA	WHY IT MATTERS NOW	Terms & Names
Advances in science and technology helped solve urban problems, including overcrowding.	American cities continue to depend on the results of scientific and technological research.	• Louis Sullivan • Daniel Burnham • Frederick Law Olmsted • Orville and Wilbur Wright • George Eastman

hmhsocialstudies.com
TAKING NOTES

Use the graphic organizer online to take notes on important changes in city design, communications, and transportation.

One American's Story

The Brooklyn Bridge, connecting Brooklyn to the island of Manhattan in New York City, opened in 1883. It took 14 years to build. Each day, laborers descended to work in a caisson, or watertight chamber, that took them deep beneath the East River. E. F. Farrington, a mechanic who worked on the bridge, described the working conditions.

A PERSONAL VOICE E. F. FARRINGTON

"Inside the caisson everything wore an unreal, weird appearance. There was a confused sensation in the head . . . What with the flaming lights, the deep shadows, the confusing noise of hammers, drills, and chains, the half-naked forms flitting about . . . one might, if of a poetic temperament, get a realizing sense of Dante's Inferno."
—quoted in *The Great Bridge*

Four years later, trains ran across the bridge 24 hours a day and carried more than 30 million travelers each year.

▲ In 1883, New Yorkers celebrated the opening of the world's longest suspension bridge, the 1,595-foot-long Brooklyn Bridge.

Technology and City Life

Engineering innovations, such as the Brooklyn Bridge, laid the groundwork for modern American life. Cities in every industrial area of the country expanded both outward and upward. In 1870, only 25 American cities had populations of 50,000 or more; by 1890, 58 cities could make that claim. By the turn of the 20th century, due to the increasing number of industrial jobs, four out of ten Americans made their homes in cities.

In response to these changes, technological advances began to meet the nation's needs for communication, transportation, and space. One remedy for more urban space was to build toward the sky.

SKYSCRAPERS Architects were able to design taller buildings because of two factors: the invention of elevators and the development of internal steel skeletons to bear the weight of buildings. In 1890–1891, architect **Louis Sullivan** designed the ten-story Wainwright Building in St. Louis. He called the new breed of sky-scraper a "proud and soaring thing." The tall building's appearance was graceful because its steel framework supported both floors and walls.

The skyscraper became America's greatest contribution to architecture, "a new thing under the sun," according to the architect Frank Lloyd Wright, who studied under Sullivan. Skyscrapers solved the practical problem of how to make the best use of limited and expensive space. The unusual form of another sky-scraper, the Flatiron Building, seemed perfect for its location at one of New York's busiest intersections. **Daniel Burnham** designed this slender 285-foot tower in 1902. The Flatiron Building and other new buildings served as symbols of a rich and optimistic society. **A**

ELECTRIC TRANSIT As skyscrapers expanded upward, changes in transportation allowed cities to spread outward. Before the Civil War, horses had drawn the earliest streetcars over iron rails embedded in city streets. In some cities during the 1870s and 1880s, underground moving cables powered streetcar lines. Electricity, however, transformed urban transportation.

In 1888 Richmond, Virginia, became the first American city to electrify its urban transit. Other cities followed. By the turn of the twentieth century, intricate networks of electric streetcars—also called trolley cars—ran from outlying neighborhoods to downtown offices and department stores.

New railroad lines also fed the growth of suburbs, allowing residents to commute to downtown jobs. New York's northern suburbs alone supplied 100,000 commuters each day to the central business district.

A few large cities moved their streetcars far above street level, creating elevated or "el" trains. Other cities, like New York, built subways by moving their rail lines underground. These streetcars, elevated trains, and subways enabled cities to annex suburban developments that mushroomed along the advancing transportation routes. **B**

ENGINEERING AND URBAN PLANNING Steel-cable suspension bridges, like the Brooklyn Bridge, also brought cities' sections closer together. Sometimes these bridges provided recreational opportunities. In his design for the Brooklyn Bridge, for example, John Augustus Roebling provided an elevated promenade whose "principal use will be to allow people of leisure, and old and young invalids, to promenade over the bridge on fine days." This need for open spaces in the midst of crowded commercial cities inspired the emerging science of urban planning.

City planners sought to restore a measure of serenity to the environment by designing recreational areas. Landscape architect **Frederick Law Olmsted** spearheaded the movement for planned urban parks.

In 1857 Olmsted, along with English-born architect Calvert Vaux, helped draw up a plan for "Greensward," which was selected to become Central Park, in New York City. Olmsted envisioned the park as a rustic haven in the center of the busy city. The finished park featured boating and

MAIN IDEA

Analyzing Causes

A How did new technologies make the building of skyscrapers practical?

MAIN IDEA

Summarizing

B How did electric transit impact urban life?

Vocabulary

promenade: a public place for walking

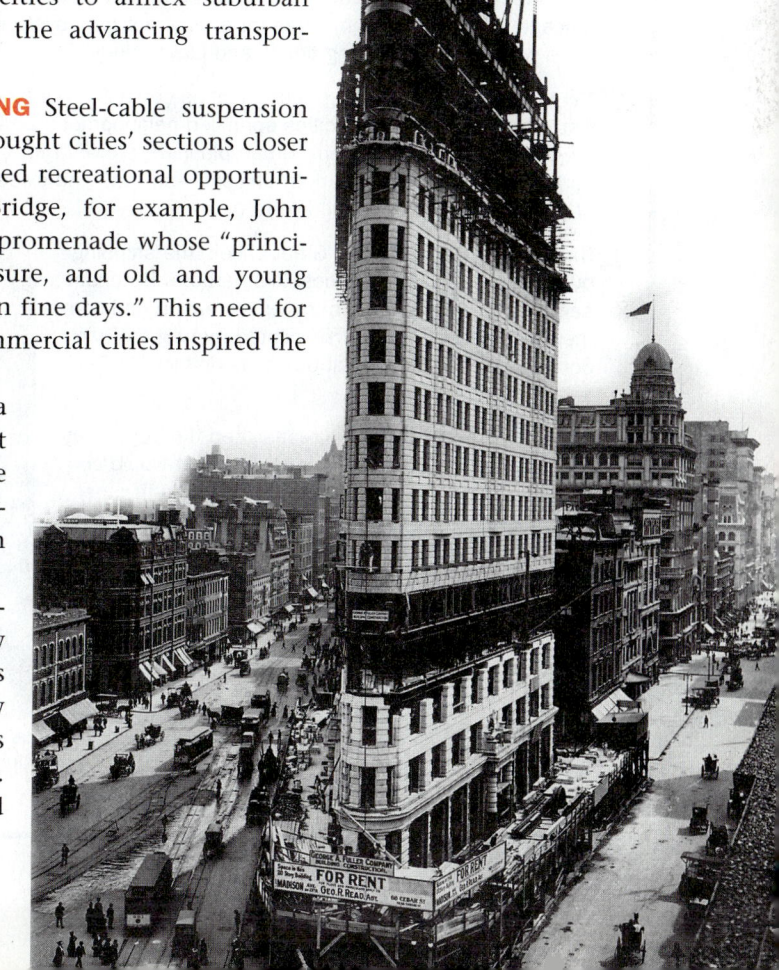

The Flatiron Building, shown here under construction, stands at the intersection of Fifth Avenue and 23rd Street in New York City.

tennis facilities, a zoo, and bicycle paths. Olmsted hoped that the park's beauty would soothe the city's inhabitants and let them enjoy a "natural" setting.

A PERSONAL VOICE FREDERICK LAW OLMSTED

"The main object and justification [of the park] is simply to produce a certain influence in the minds of people and through this to make life in the city healthier and happier. The character of this influence . . . is to be produced by means of scenes, through observation of which the mind may be more or less lifted out of moods and habits."

—quoted in *Frederick Law Olmsted's New York*

In the 1870s, Olmsted planned landscaping for Washington, D.C., and St. Louis. He also drew the initial designs for "the Emerald Necklace," Boston's parks system. Boston's Back Bay area, originally a 450-acre swamp, was drained and developed by urban planners into an area of elegant streets and cultural attractions, including Olmsted's parks.

CITY PLANNING By contrast, Chicago, with its explosive growth from 30,000 people in 1850 to 300,000 in 1870, represented a nightmare of unregulated expansion. Fortunately for the city, a local architect, Daniel Burnham, was intrigued

---

History Through *Architecture*

THE CHICAGO PLAN

This map from Daniel Burnham's original plan of Chicago looks deceptively like an ordinary map today. But at the time, it was almost revolutionary in its vision, and it inspired city planners all over the country.

1 Chicago's Lakefront First, Burnham designed the "White City" to host the 1893 World's Columbian Exposition. His greatest legacy to Chicago may have been his idea for a lakefront park system, complete with beaches, playing fields, and playgrounds.

2 Neighborhood Parks Though not all cities could claim a lakefront vista for recreation, most cities sprinkled neighborhood parks where their residents needed them. Urban planners provided for local parks—such as Lincoln Park in Chicago—so that "the sweet breath of plant life" would be available to everyone.

3 Harbors For Cities On the Great Lakes, the shipping business depended on accessible harbors. Burnham saw the advantage of harbors for recreation and commercial purposes, but he advocated moving the harbors away from the central business districts to free space for public use.

4 The Civic Center Burnham redesigned the street pattern to create a group of long streets that would converge on a grand plaza, a practice reflected in other American cities. The convergence of major thoroughfares at a city's center helped create a unified city from a host of neighborhoods.

SKILLBUILDER Interpreting Visual Sources
1. Why did Chicago's location make it a good choice for urban planning?
2. How was Chicago's importance as a shipping center maintained?

 SEE SKILLBUILDER HANDBOOK, PAGE R23.

▲ Unity was the goal of the architect of Chicago's city center.

by the prospect of remaking the city. His motto was "Make no little plans. They have no magic to stir men's blood." He oversaw the transformation of a swampy area near Lake Michigan into a glistening White City for Chicago's 1893 World's Columbian Exposition. Majestic exhibition halls, statues, the first Ferris wheel, and a lagoon greeted more than 21 million visitors who came to the city.

Many urban planners saw in Burnham's White City glorious visions of future cities. Burnham, however, left Chicago an even more important legacy: an overall plan for the city, crowned by elegant parks strung along Lake Michigan. As a result, Chicago's lakefront today features curving banks of grass and sandy beaches instead of a jumbled mass of piers and warehouses. **C**

MAIN IDEA

Summarizing
C List three major changes in cities near the turn of the century. What effect did each have?

New Technologies

New developments in communication brought the nation closer together. In addition to a railroad network that now spanned the nation, advances in printing, aviation, and photography helped to speed the transfer of information.

A REVOLUTION IN PRINTING By 1890, the literacy rate in the United States had risen to nearly 90 percent. Publishers turned out ever-increasing numbers of books, magazines, and newspapers to meet the growing demand of the reading public. A series of technological advances in printing aided their efforts.

American mills began to produce huge quantities of cheap paper from wood pulp. The new paper proved durable enough to withstand high-speed presses. The electrically powered web-perfecting press, for example, printed on both sides of a continuous paper roll, rather than on just one side. It then cut, folded, and counted the pages as they came down the line. Faster production and lower costs made newspapers and magazines more affordable. People could now buy newspapers for a penny a copy.

AIRPLANES In the early 20th century, brothers **Orville** and **Wilbur Wright**, bicycle manufacturers from Dayton, Ohio, experimented with new engines powerful enough to keep "heavier-than-air" craft aloft. First the Wright brothers built a glider. Then they commissioned a four-cylinder internal combustion engine, chose a propeller, and designed a biplane with a 40'4" wingspan. Their first successful flight—on December 17, 1903, at Kitty Hawk, North Carolina—covered 120 feet and lasted 12 seconds. Orville later described the take-off.

Vocabulary
internal combustion engine: an engine in which fuel is burned within the engine rather than in an external furnace

★ A PERSONAL VOICE ORVILLE WRIGHT

" After running the motor a few minutes to heat it up, I released the wire that held the machine to the track, and the machine started forward into the wind. Wilbur ran at the side of the machine . . . to balance it. . . . Unlike the start on the 14th, made in a calm, the machine, facing a 27-mile wind, started very slowly. . . . One of the life-saving men snapped the camera for us, taking a picture just as the machine had reached the end of the track and had risen to a height of about two feet. "

—quoted in *Smithsonian Frontiers of Flight*

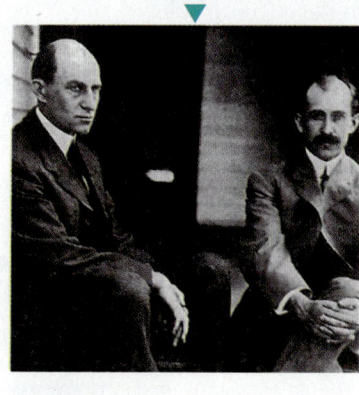

Orville (*right*) and Wilbur Wright at home in Dayton, Ohio, in 1909.
▼

AVIATION PIONEERS

In 1892, Orville and Wilbur Wright opened a bicycle shop in Dayton, Ohio. They used the profits to fund experiments in aeronautics, the construction of aircraft. In 1903, the Wright brothers took a gasoline-powered airplane that they had designed to a sandy hill outside Kitty Hawk, North Carolina.

▶ The airplane was powered by a 4-cylinder 12-horse-power piston engine, designed and constructed by the bicycle shop's mechanic, Charles Taylor. The piston—a solid cylinder fit snugly into a hollow cylinder that moves back and forth under pressure—was standard until jet-propelled aircraft came into service in the 1940s.

▶ The engine is the heaviest component in airplane construction. The design of lighter engines was the most important development in early aviation history.

HISTORY

VIDEO
The Wright Brothers Controversy

hmhsocialstudies.com

Early Airplane Engines and Their Weights

Date	Name of Engine	Approximate Weight per Unit of Horsepower
1880s	Otto	440 lbs (200 kg)
1903	Wright	13 lbs (6 kg)
1910	Gnome	3.3 lbs (1.5 kg)
1918	V-12 Liberty	2 lbs (1 kg)
1944	Wright Cyclone	1.1 lbs (0.5 kg)

Source: *The History of Invention,* Trevor I. Williams

◀ On December 17, Orville Wright made the first successful flight of a powered aircraft in history. The public paid little attention. But within two years, the brothers were making 30-minute flights. By 1908, the pioneer aviators had signed a contract for production of the Wright airplane with the U.S. Army.

▲ By 1918, the Postal Service began airmail service, as shown in this preliminary sketch of a DH4-Mail. Convinced of the great potential of flight, the government established the first transcontinental airmail service in 1920.

Within two years, the Wright brothers had increased their flights to 24 miles. By 1920, convinced of the great potential of flight, the U.S. government had established the first transcontinental airmail service.

PHOTOGRAPHY EXPLOSION Before the 1880s, photography was a professional activity. Because of the time required to take a picture and the weight of the equipment, a photographer could not shoot a moving object. In addition, photographers had to develop their shots immediately.

New techniques eliminated the need to develop pictures right away. **George Eastman** developed a series of more convenient alternatives to the heavy glass plates previously used. Now, instead of carrying their darkrooms around with them, photographers could use flexible film, coated with gelatin emulsions, and could send their film to a studio for processing. When professional photographers were slow to begin using the new film, Eastman decided to aim his product at the masses.

In 1888, Eastman introduced his Kodak camera. The purchase price of $25 included a 100-picture roll of film. After taking the pictures, the photographer would send the camera back to Eastman's Rochester, New York, factory. For $10, the pictures were developed and returned with the camera reloaded. Easily held and operated, the Kodak prompted millions of Americans to become amateur photographers. The camera also helped to create the field of photojournalism. Reporters could now photograph events as they occurred. When the Wright brothers first flew their simple airplane at Kitty Hawk, an amateur photographer captured the first successful flight on film.

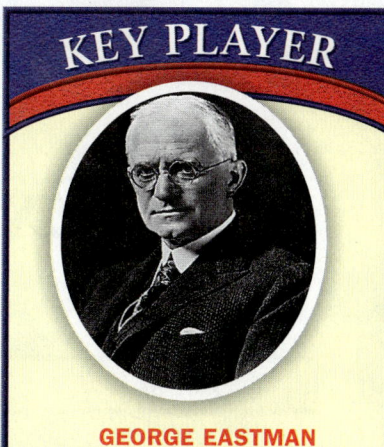

KEY PLAYER

GEORGE EASTMAN
1854–1932

In 1877, when George Eastman took up photography as a hobby, he had to lug more than 100 pounds of equipment for one day's outing. To lighten his load, he replaced heavy glass plates with film that could be rolled onto a spool.

In 1888, Eastman sold his first roll-film camera. Eastman called his new camera (shown at left) the Kodak, because the made-up name was short and memorable. It was popularized by the slogan "You Press the Button, We Do the Rest."

SECTION 1 ASSESSMENT

1. TERMS & NAMES For each term or name, write a sentence explaining its significance.
- Louis Sullivan
- Daniel Burnham
- Frederick Law Olmsted
- Orville and Wilbur Wright
- George Eastman

MAIN IDEA

2. TAKING NOTES
Using a three-column chart, such as the one below, list three important changes in city design, communication, and transportation.

City Design	Communication	Transportation
1.	1.	1.
2.	2.	2.
3.	3.	3.

Which change had the greatest impact on urban life? Why?

CRITICAL THINKING

3. HYPOTHESIZING
If you had been an urban planner at the turn of the century, what new ideas would you have included in your plan for the ideal city?
Think About:
- Olmsted's plans for Central Park
- Burnham's ideas for Chicago
- the concept of the garden city

4. EVALUATING
Which scientific or technological development described in this section had the greatest impact on American culture? Use details from the text to justify your choice.

5. SUMMARIZING
How did bridge building contribute to the growth of cities?

SECTION 2

PI 2.2
PI 2.3
PI 4.1

CC Unit 3.I.C.2.b
CC Unit 3.I.C.5
CC Unit 3.III.A.1.a

Expanding Public Education

MAIN IDEA	WHY IT MATTERS NOW	Terms & Names
Reforms in public education led to a rise in national literacy and the promotion of public education.	The public education system is the foundation of the democratic ideals of American society.	• Booker T. Washington • Tuskegee Normal and Industrial Institute • W. E. B. Du Bois • Niagara Movement

One American's Story

hmhsocialstudies.com
TAKING NOTES

Use the graphic organizer online to take notes on developments in education at the turn of the 20th century.

William Torrey Harris was an educational reformer who saw the public schools as a great instrument "to lift all classes of people into . . . civilized life." As U.S. commissioner of education from 1889 to 1906, Harris promoted the ideas of great educators like Horace Mann and John Dewey—particularly the belief that schools exist for the children and not the teachers. Schools, according to Harris, should properly prepare students for full participation in community life.

A PERSONAL VOICE WILLIAM TORREY HARRIS

" Every [educational] method must . . . be looked at from two points of view: first, its capacity to secure the development of rationality or of the true adjustment of the individual to the social whole; and, second, its capacity to strengthen the individuality of the pupil and avoid the danger of obliterating the personality of the child by securing blind obedience in place of intelligent cooperation, and by mechanical memorizing in place of rational insight. "

—quoted in *Public Schools and Moral Education*

▲ Compulsory attendance laws, though slow to be enforced, helped fill classrooms at the turn of the 20th century.

Many other middle-class reformers agreed with Harris and viewed the public schools as training grounds for employment and citizenship. People believed that economic development depended on scientific and technological knowledge. As a result, they viewed education as a key to greater security and social status. Others saw the public schools as the best opportunity to assimilate the millions of immigrants entering American society. Most people also believed that public education was necessary for a stable and prosperous democratic nation.

Expanding Public Education

Although most states had established public schools by the Civil War, many school-age children still received no formal schooling. The majority of students who went to school left within four years, and few went to high school.

SCHOOLS FOR CHILDREN Between 1865 and 1895, states passed laws requiring 12 to 16 weeks annually of school attendance by students between the ages of 8 and 14. The curriculum emphasized reading, writing, and arithmetic. However, the emphasis on rote memorization and the uneven quality of teachers drew criticism. Strict rules and physical punishment made many students miserable.

One 13-year-old boy explained to a Chicago school inspector why he hid in a warehouse basement instead of going to school.

★ **A PERSONAL VOICE**

"**They hits ye if yer don't learn, and they hits ye if ye whisper, and they hits ye if ye have string in yer pocket, and they hits ye if yer seat squeaks, and they hits ye if ye don't stan' up in time, and they hits ye if yer late, and they hits ye if ye ferget the page.**"

—anonymous schoolboy quoted in *The One Best System*

In spite of such problems, children began attending school at a younger age. Kindergartens, which had been created outside the public school system to offer childcare for employed mothers, became increasingly popular. The number of kindergartens surged from 200 in 1880 to 3,000 in 1900, and, under the guidance of William Torrey Harris, public school systems began to add kindergartens to their programs. **Ⓐ**

Although the pattern in public education in this era was one of growth, opportunities differed sharply for white and black students. In 1880, about 62 percent of white children attended elementary school, compared to about 34 percent of African-American children. Not until the 1940s would public school education become available to the majority of black children living in the South.

THE GROWTH OF HIGH SCHOOLS In the new industrial age, the economy demanded advanced technical and managerial skills. Moreover, business leaders like Andrew Carnegie pointed out that keeping workers loyal to capitalism required society to "provide ladders upon which the aspiring can rise."

By early 1900, more than half a million students attended high school. The curriculum expanded to include courses in science, civics, and social studies. And new vocational courses prepared male graduates for industrial jobs in drafting, carpentry, and mechanics, and female graduates for office work.

MAIN IDEA

Drawing Conclusions

Ⓐ Why did American children begin attending school at a younger age?

Expanding Education/Increasing Literacy

Year	Students Enrolled	Literacy in English (% of Population age 10 and over)
1871	7.6 million	80%
1880	9.9 million	83%
1890	12.7 million	87%
1900	15.5 million	89%
1910	17.8 million	92%
1920	21.6 million	94%

† = 1,000,000 students

Sources: *Statistical Abstract of the United States, 1921; Historical Statistics of the United States.*

SKILLBUILDER
Interpreting Graphs
1. By how much did the illiteracy rate drop from 1871 to 1920?
2. Does the number of immigrants during this period make the reduction more or less impressive? Why?

Life at the Turn of the 20th Century **489**

RACIAL DISCRIMINATION African Americans were mostly excluded from public secondary education. In 1890, fewer than 1 percent of black teenagers attended high school. More than two-thirds of these students went to private schools, which received no government financial support. By 1910, about 3 percent of African Americans between the ages of 15 and 19 attended high school, but a majority of these students still attended private schools.

EDUCATION FOR IMMIGRANTS Unlike African Americans, immigrants were encouraged to go to school. Of the nearly 10 million European immigrants settled in the United States between 1860 and 1890, many were Jewish people fleeing poverty and systematic oppression in eastern Europe. Most immigrants sent their children to America's free public schools, where they quickly became "Americanized." Years after she became a citizen, the Russian Jewish immigrant Mary Antin recalled the large numbers of non-English-speaking immigrant children. By the end of the school year, they could recite "patriotic verses in honor of George Washington and Abraham Lincoln . . . with plenty of enthusiasm."

Some people resented the suppression of their native languages in favor of English. Catholics were especially concerned because many public school systems had mandatory readings from the (Protestant) King James Version of the Bible. Catholic communities often set up parochial schools to give their children a Catholic education.

Thousands of adult immigrants attended night school to learn English and to qualify for American citizenship. Employers often offered daytime programs to Americanize their workers. At his Model T plant in Highland Park, Michigan, Henry Ford established a "Sociology Department," because "men of many nations must be taught American ways, the English language, and the right way to live." Ford's ideas were not universally accepted. Labor activists often protested that Ford's educational goals were aimed at weakening the trade union movement by teaching workers not to confront management. **B**

Vocabulary
parochial school:
a school supported by a church parish

MAIN IDEA

Summarizing
B What institutions encouraged European immigrants to become assimilated?

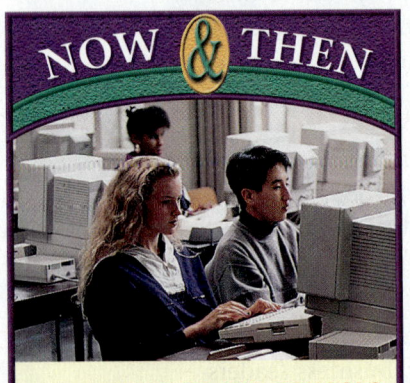

TECHNOLOGY AND SCHOOLS

In 1922, Thomas Edison predicted that motion pictures would eventually replace textbooks. More recently, it has been predicted that computers will replace traditional classrooms and texts. Computers are used for video course sharing, in which students in many locations participate in the same class. Teachers are using electronic interactive whiteboards to help them lead and record presentations and discussions. Students are also using computers to access and share scientific data and to communicate with peers around the world.

Expanding Higher Education

Although the number of students attending high school had increased by the turn of the century, only a minority of Americans had high school diplomas. At the same time, an even smaller minority—only 2.3 percent—of America's young people attended colleges and universities.

CHANGES IN UNIVERSITIES Between 1880 and 1920, college enrollments more than quadrupled. And colleges instituted major changes in curricula and admission policies. Industrial development changed the nation's educational needs. The research university emerged—offering courses in modern languages, the physical sciences, and the new disciplines of psychology and sociology. Professional schools in law and medicine were established. Private colleges and universities required entrance exams, but some state universities began to admit students by using the high school diploma as the entrance requirement.

HIGHER EDUCATION FOR AFRICAN AMERICANS After the Civil War, thousands of freed African Americans pursued higher education, despite their exclusion from white institutions. With the help of the Freedmen's Bureau and other groups, blacks founded Howard, Atlanta, and Fisk Universities, all of which opened between 1865 and 1868. Private donors could not, however, financially support or educate a sufficient number of black college graduates to meet the needs of the segregated communities. By 1900, out of about 9 million African Americans, only 3,880 were in attendance at colleges or professional schools. **C**

MAIN IDEA

Synthesizing
C Describe the state of higher education for African Americans at the turn of the century.

The prominent African American educator, **Booker T. Washington,** believed that racism would end once blacks acquired useful labor skills and proved their economic value to society. Washington, who was born enslaved, graduated from Virginia's Hampton Institute. By 1881, he headed the **Tuskegee Normal and Industrial Institute,** now called Tuskegee University, in Alabama. Tuskegee aimed to equip African Americans with teaching diplomas and useful skills in agricultural, domestic, or mechanical work."No race," Washington said, "can prosper till it learns that there is as much dignity in tilling a field as in writing a poem."

By contrast, **W. E. B. Du Bois,** the first African American to receive a doctorate from Harvard (in 1895), strongly disagreed with Washington's gradual approach. In 1905, Du Bois founded the **Niagara Movement,** which insisted that blacks should seek a liberal arts education so that the African-American community would have well-educated leaders.

Du Bois proposed that a group of educated blacks, the most "talented tenth" of the community, attempt to achieve immediate inclusion into mainstream American life. "We are Americans, not only by birth and by citizenship," Du Bois argued, "but by our political ideals. . . . And the greatest of those ideals is that ALL MEN ARE CREATED EQUAL."

By the turn of the 20th century, millions of people received the education they needed to cope with a rapidly changing world. At the same time, however, racial discrimination remained a thorn in the flesh of American society.

▲
Medical students and their professors work in the operating theater of the Moorland-Spingarn Research Center at Howard University.

SECTION 2 ASSESSMENT

1. TERMS & NAMES For each term or name, write a sentence explaining its significance.
- • Booker T. Washington
- • Tuskegee Normal and Industrial Institute
- • W. E. B. Du Bois
- • Niagara Movement

MAIN IDEA

2. TAKING NOTES
In a chart like the one below, list at least three developments in education at the turn of the 20th century and their major results.

Development	Result
1.	
2.	
3.	

Which educational development do you think was most important? Explain your choice.

CRITICAL THINKING

3. HYPOTHESIZING
How might the economy and culture of the United States have been different without the expansion of public schools? **Think About:**
- • the goals of public schools and whether those goals have been met
- • why people supported expanding public education
- • the impact of public schools on the development of private schools

4. COMPARING
Compare and contrast the views of Booker T. Washington and W. E. B. Du Bois on the subject of the education of African Americans.

Segregation and Discrimination

MAIN IDEA	WHY IT MATTERS NOW	Terms & Names
African Americans led the fight against voting restrictions and Jim Crow laws.	Today, African Americans have the legacy of a century-long battle for civil rights.	• Ida B. Wells • poll tax • grandfather clause • segregation • Jim Crow laws • *Plessy* v. *Ferguson* • debt peonage

One American's Story

Born into slavery shortly before emancipation, **Ida B. Wells** moved to Memphis in the early 1880s to work as a teacher. She later became an editor of a local paper. Racial justice was a persistent theme in Wells's reporting. The events of March 9, 1892 turned that theme into a crusade. Three African-American businessmen, friends of Wells, were lynched—illegally executed without trial. Wells saw lynching for what it was.

A PERSONAL VOICE   IDA B. WELLS

"Thomas Moss, Calvin McDowell, and Lee Stewart had been lynched in Memphis . . . [where] no lynching had taken place before. . . . This is what opened my eyes to what lynching really was. An excuse to get rid of Negroes who were acquiring wealth and property and thus keep the race terrorized."

—quoted in *Crusade for Justice*

▲ Ida B. Wells moved north to continue her fight against lynching by writing, lecturing, and organizing for civil rights.

African Americans were not the only group to experience violence and racial discrimination. Native Americans, Mexican residents, and Chinese immigrants also encountered bitter forms of oppression, particularly in the American West.

African Americans Fight Legal Discrimination

As African Americans exercised their newly won political and social rights during Reconstruction, they faced hostile and often violent opposition from whites. African Americans eventually fell victim to laws restricting their civil rights but never stopped fighting for equality. For at least ten years after the end of Reconstruction in 1877, African Americans in the South continued to vote and occasionally to hold political office. By the turn of the 20th century, however, Southern states had adopted a broad system of legal policies of racial discrimination and devised methods to weaken African-American political power.

VOTING RESTRICTIONS All Southern states imposed new voting restrictions and denied legal equality to African Americans. Some states, for example, limited the vote to people who could read, and required registration officials to administer a literacy test to test reading. Blacks trying to vote were often asked more difficult questions than whites, or given a test in a foreign language. Officials could pass or fail applicants as they wished.

Another requirement was the **poll tax**, an annual tax that had to be paid before qualifying to vote. Black as well as white sharecroppers were often too poor to pay the poll tax. To reinstate white voters who may have failed the literacy test or could not pay the poll tax, several Southern states added the **grandfather clause** to their constitutions. The clause stated that even if a man failed the literacy test or could not afford the poll tax, he was still entitled to vote if he, his father, or his grandfather had been eligible to vote before January 1, 1867. The date is important because before that time, freed slaves did not have the right to vote. The grandfather clause therefore did not allow them to vote.

This theater in Leland, Mississippi, was segregated under the Jim Crow laws.

JIM CROW LAWS During the 1870s and 1880s, the Supreme Court failed to overturn the poll tax or the grandfather clause, even though the laws undermined all federal protections for African Americans' civil rights. At the same time that blacks lost voting rights, Southern states passed racial **segregation** laws to separate white and black people in public and private facilities. These laws came to be known as **Jim Crow laws** after a popular old minstrel song that ended in the words "Jump, Jim Crow." Racial segregation was put into effect in schools, hospitals, parks, and transportation systems throughout the South.

PLESSY v. FERGUSON Eventually a legal case reached the U.S. Supreme Court to test the constitutionality of segregation. In 1896, in **Plessy v. Ferguson**, the Supreme Court ruled that the separation of races in public accommodations was legal and did not violate the Fourteenth Amendment. The decision established the doctrine of "separate but equal," which allowed states to maintain segregated facilities for blacks and whites as long as they provided equal service. The decision permitted legalized racial segregation for almost 60 years. (See *Plessy v. Ferguson*, page 496.) **A**

Vocabulary
minstrel: one of a troupe of entertainers in blackface presenting a comic variety show

MAIN IDEA

Analyzing Effects
A How did the *Plessy* v. *Ferguson* ruling affect the civil rights of African Americans?

Turn-of-the-Century Race Relations

African Americans faced not only formal discrimination but also informal rules and customs, called racial etiquette, that regulated relationships between whites and blacks. Usually, these customs belittled and humiliated African Americans, enforcing their second-class status. For example, blacks and whites never shook hands, since shaking hands would have implied equality. Blacks also had to yield the sidewalk to white pedestrians, and black men always had to remove their hats for whites.

HISTORICAL SPOTLIGHT

WASHINGTON *VS.* DU BOIS

Booker T. Washington argued for a gradual approach to racial equality—suggesting that "it is at the bottom of life we must begin, and not at the top."

Ten years later, W. E. B. Du Bois denounced this view of gradual equality. Du Bois demanded full social and economic equality for African Americans, declaring that "persistent manly agitation is the way to liberty."

In 1909 the Niagara Movement, founded by Du Bois in 1905, became the National Association for the Advancement of Colored People (NAACP), with Du Bois as the editor of its journal, *The Crisis.* He wrote, "We refuse to surrender . . . leadership . . . to cowards and trucklers. We are men; we will be treated as men." The NAACP continues the fight for racial equality today.

Some moderate reformers, like Booker T. Washington, earned support from whites. Washington suggested that whites and blacks work together for social progress.

★ A PERSONAL VOICE BOOKER T. WASHINGTON

"To those of the white race . . . I would repeat what I say to my own race. . . . Cast down your bucket among these people who have, without strikes and labour wars, tilled your fields, cleared your forests, builded your railroads and cities, and brought forth treasures from the bowels of the earth. . . . In all things that are purely social we can be as separate as the fingers, yet one as the hand in all things essential to mutual progress."

—Atlanta Exposition address, 1895

Washington hoped that improving the economic skills of African Americans would pave the way for long-term gains. People like Ida B. Wells and W. E. B. Du Bois, however, thought that the problems of inequality were too urgent to postpone. **B**

VIOLENCE African Americans and others who did not follow the racial etiquette could face severe punishment or death. All too often, blacks who were accused of violating the etiquette were lynched. Between 1882 and 1892, more than 1,400 African-American men and women were shot, burned, or hanged without trial in the South. Lynching peaked in the 1880s and 1890s but continued well into the 20th century.

DISCRIMINATION IN THE NORTH Most African Americans lived in the segregated South, but by 1900, a number of blacks had moved to Northern cities. Many blacks migrated to Northern cities in search of better-paying jobs and social equality. But after their arrival, African Americans found that there was racial discrimination in the North as well. African Americans found themselves forced into segregated neighborhoods. They also faced discrimination in the workplace. Labor unions often discouraged black membership, and employers hired African-American labor only as a last resort and fired blacks before white employees.

Sometimes the competition between African Americans and working-class whites became violent, as in the New York City race riot of 1900. Violence erupted after a young black man, believing that his wife was being mistreated by a white policeman, killed the policeman. Word of the killing spread, and whites retaliated by attacking blacks. Northern blacks, however, were not alone in facing discrimination. Non-whites in the West also faced oppression. **C**

Discrimination in the West

Western communities were home to people of many backgrounds working and living side by side. Native Americans still lived in the Western territories claimed by the United States. Asian immigrants went to America's Pacific Coast in search of wealth and work. Mexicans continued to inhabit the American Southwest. African Americans were also present, especially in former slave-holding areas, such as Texas. Still, racial tensions often made life difficult.

MEXICAN WORKERS In the late 1800s, the railroads hired more Mexicans than members of any other ethnic group to construct rail lines in the Southwest.

MAIN IDEA

Summarizing

B What were Booker T. Washington's views about establishing racial equality?

MAIN IDEA

Contrasting

C How did conditions for African Americans in the North differ from their circumstances in the South?

Mexicans were accustomed to the region's hot, dry climate. But the work was grueling, and the railroads made them work for less money than other ethnic groups.

Mexicans were also vital to the development of mining and agriculture in the Southwest. When the 1902 National Reclamation Act gave government assistance for irrigation projects, many southwest desert areas bloomed. Mexican workers became the major labor force in the agricultural industries of the region.

Some Mexicans, however, as well as African Americans in the Southwest, were forced into **debt peonage,** a system that bound laborers into slavery in order to work off a debt to the employer. Not until 1911 did the Supreme Court declare involuntary peonage a violation of the Thirteenth Amendment.

Vocabulary
peon: a worker bound in servitude to a landlord creditor

EXCLUDING THE CHINESE By 1880, more than 100,000 Chinese immigrants lived in the United States. White people's fear of job competition with the Chinese immigrants often pushed the Chinese into segregated schools and neighborhoods. Strong opposition to Chinese immigration developed, and not only in the West. (See Chinese Exclusion Act, page 465.)

Racial discrimination posed terrible legal and economic problems for non-whites throughout the United States at the turn of the century. More people, however, whites in particular, had leisure time for new recreational activities, as well as money to spend on a growing arrray of consumer products.

ASSESSMENT

1. TERMS & NAMES For each term or name, write a sentence explaining its significance.
- Ida B. Wells
- poll tax
- grandfather clause
- segregation
- Jim Crow laws
- *Plessy* v. *Ferguson*
- debt peonage

MAIN IDEA

2. TAKING NOTES
Review the section, and find five key events to place on a time line as shown.

```
1890      Event       Event      1900
  |_____|_____|_____|
       Event      Event      Event
```

Which of these events do you think was most important? Why?

CRITICAL THINKING

3. IDENTIFYING PROBLEMS
How did segregation and discrimination affect the lives of African Americans at the turn of the 20th century?

4. COMPARING
What did some African-American leaders do to fight discrimination?

5. CONTRASTING
How did the challenges and opportunities for Mexicans in the United States differ from those for African Americans? **Think About:**
- the types of work available to each group
- the effects of government policies on each group
- the effect of the legal system on each group

HISTORIC DECISIONS OF THE SUPREME COURT

PLESSY v. FERGUSON (1896)

ORIGINS OF THE CASE In 1892, Homer Plessy took a seat in the "Whites Only" car of a train and refused to move. He was arrested, tried, and convicted in the District Court of New Orleans for breaking Louisiana's segregation law. Plessy appealed, claiming that he had been denied equal protection under the law. The Supreme Court handed down its decision on May 18, 1896.

THE RULING The Court ruled that separate-but-equal facilities for blacks and whites did not violate the Constitution.

LEGAL REASONING

Plessy claimed that segregation violated his right to equal protection under the law. Moreover he claimed that, being "of mixed descent," he was entitled to "every recognition, right, privilege and immunity secured to the citizens of the United States of the white race."

Justice Henry B. Brown, writing for the majority, ruled:

> " **The object of the [Fourteenth] amendment was . . . undoubtedly to enforce the absolute equality of the two races before the law, but . . . it could not have been intended to abolish distinctions based upon color, or to enforce social, as distinguished from political equality, or a commingling of the two races upon terms unsatisfactory to either. Laws permitting, and even requiring, their separation in places where they are liable to be brought into contact do not necessarily imply the inferiority of either race to the other.** "

In truth, segregation laws did perpetrate an unequal and inferior status for African Americans. Justice John Marshall Harlan understood this fact and dissented from the majority opinion. He wrote, "In respect of civil rights, all citizens are equal before the law." He condemned the majority for letting "the seeds of race hate . . . be planted under the sanction of law." He also warned that "The thin disguise of 'equal' accommodations . . . will not mislead any one, nor atone for the wrong this day done."

Justice John Marshall Harlan

LEGAL SOURCES

LEGISLATION

U.S. CONSTITUTION, FOURTEENTH AMENDMENT (1868)
"No state shall . . . deny to any person within its jurisdiction the equal protection of the laws."

LOUISIANA ACTS 1890, NO. 111
". . . that all railway companies carrying passengers in their coaches in this State, shall provide equal but separate accommodations for the white, and colored races."

RELATED CASES

CIVIL RIGHTS CASES (1883)
The Court ruled that the Fourteenth Amendment could not be used to prevent private citizens from discriminating against others on the basis of race.

WILLIAMS v. MISSISSIPPI (1898)
The Court upheld a state literacy requirement for voting that, in effect, kept African Americans from the polls.

CUMMING v. BOARD OF EDUCATION OF RICHMOND COUNTY (1899)
The Court ruled that the federal government cannot prevent segregation in local school facilities because education is a local, not federal, issue.

One result of Jim Crow laws was separate drinking fountains for whites and African Americans.

WHY IT MATTERED

In the decades following the Civil War [1861–1865], Southern state legislatures passed laws that aimed to limit civil rights for African Americans. The Black Codes of the 1860s, and later Jim Crow laws, were intended to deprive African Americans of their newly won political and social rights granted during Reconstruction.

Plessy was one of several Supreme Court cases brought by African Americans to protect their rights against segregation. In these cases, the Court regularly ignored the Fourteenth Amendment and upheld state laws that denied blacks their rights. *Plessy* was the most important of these cases because the Court used it to establish the separate-but-equal doctrine.

As a result, city and state governments across the South—and in some other states—maintained their segregation laws for more than half of the 20th century. These laws limited African Americans' access to most public facilities, including restaurants, schools, and hospitals. Without exception, the facilities reserved for whites were superior to those reserved for nonwhites. Signs reading "Colored Only" and "Whites Only" served as constant reminders that facilities in segregated societies were separate but not equal.

HISTORICAL IMPACT

It took many decades to abolish legal segregation. During the first half of the 20th century, the National Association for the Advancement of Colored People (NAACP) led the legal fight to overturn *Plessy*. Although they won a few cases over the years, it was not until 1954 in *Brown* v. *Board of Education* that the Court overturned any part of *Plessy*. In that case, the Supreme Court said that separate-but-equal was unconstitutional in public education, but it did not completely overturn the separate-but-equal doctrine.

In later years, the Court did overturn the separate-but-equal doctrine, and it used the *Brown* decision to do so. For example, in 1955, Rosa Parks was convicted for violating a Montgomery, Alabama, law for segregated seating on buses. A federal court overturned the conviction, finding such segregation unconstitutional. The case was appealed to the Supreme Court, which upheld without comment the lower court's decision. In doing so in this and similar cases, the Court signaled that the reasoning behind *Plessy* no longer applied.

As secretary of the Montgomery chapter of the NAACP, Rosa Parks had protested segregation through everyday acts long before Sepember 1955.

THINKING CRITICALLY

CONNECT TO TODAY

1. **Analyzing Primary Sources** Read the part of the Fourteenth Amendment reprinted in this feature. Write a paragraph explaining what you think "equal protection of the laws" means. Use evidence to support your ideas.

 SEE SKILLBUILDER HANDBOOK, PAGE R22.

CONNECT TO HISTORY

2. Visit the links for Historic Decisions of the Supreme Court to research and read Justice Harlan's entire dissent in *Plessy* v. *Ferguson*. Based on his position, what view might Harlan have taken toward laws that denied African Americans the right to vote? Write a paragraph or two expressing what Harlan would say about those laws.

 hmhsocialstudies.com **INTERNET ACTIVITY**

SECTION
4

PI 1.1
PI 4.1

CC Unit 3.II.A.2.e
CC Unit 3.III.A.4
CC Unit 3.II.A.5

The Dawn of Mass Culture

MAIN IDEA	WHY IT MATTERS NOW	Terms & Names
As Americans had more time for leisure activities, a modern mass culture emerged.	Today, the United States has a worldwide impact on mass culture.	• Joseph Pulitzer • Mark Twain • William Randolph Hearst • rural free delivery (RFD) • Ashcan school

One American's Story

Along the Brooklyn seashore, on a narrow sandbar just nine miles from busy Manhattan, rose the most famous urban amusement center, Coney Island. In 1886, its main developer, George Tilyou, bragged, "If Paris is France, then Coney Island . . . is the world." Indeed, tens of thousands of visitors mobbed Coney Island after work each evening and on Sundays and holidays. When Luna Park, a spectacular amusement park on Coney Island, opened in May 1903, a reporter described the scene.

A PERSONAL VOICE BRUCE BLEN

" [Inside the park was] an enchanted, storybook land of trellises, columns, domes, minarets, lagoons, and lofty aerial flights. And everywhere was life—a pageant of happy people; and everywhere was color—a wide harmony of orange and white and gold. . . . It was a world removed—shut away from the sordid clatter and turmoil of the streets. "

—quoted in *Amusing the Million*

Coney Island offered Americans a few hours of escape from the hard work week. A schoolteacher who walked fully dressed into the ocean explained her unusual behavior by saying, "It has been a hard year at school, and when I saw the big crowd here, everyone with the brakes off, the spirit of the place got the better of me." The end of the 19th century saw the rise of a "mass culture" in the United States.

▲
The sprawling amusement center at Coney Island became a model for urban amusement parks.

American Leisure

Middle-class Americans from all over the country shared experiences as new leisure activities, nationwide advertising campaigns, and the rise of a consumer culture began to level regional differences. As the 19th century drew to a close, many Americans fought off city congestion and dull industrial work by enjoying amusement parks, bicycling, new forms of theater, and spectator sports.

AMUSEMENT PARKS To meet the recreational needs of city dwellers, Chicago, New York City, and other cities began setting aside precious green space for outdoor enjoyment. Many cities built small playgrounds and playing fields throughout their neighborhoods for their citizens' enjoyment.

Some amusement parks were constructed on the outskirts of cities. Often built by trolley-car companies that sought more passengers, these parks boasted picnic grounds and a variety of rides. The roller coaster drew daredevil customers to Coney Island in 1884, and the first Ferris wheel drew enthusiastic crowds to the World's Columbian Exposition in Chicago in 1893. Clearly, many Americans were ready for new and innovative forms of entertainment—and a whole panorama of recreational activities soon became available.

"Eight hours for work, eight hours for rest, eight hours for what we will"

THE CARPENTERS' UNION, WORCESTER, MASSACHUSETTS

BICYCLING AND TENNIS With their huge front wheels and solid rubber tires, the first American bicycles challenged their riders. Because a bump might toss the cyclist over the handlebars, bicycling began as a male-only sport. However, the 1885 manufacture of the first commercially successful "safety bicycle," with its smaller wheels and air-filled tires, made the activity more popular. And the Victor safety bicycle, with a dropped frame and no crossbar, held special appeal to women.

Abandoning their tight corsets, women bicyclists donned shirtwaists (tailored blouses) and "split" skirts in order to cycle more comfortably. This attire soon became popular for daily wear. The bicycle also freed women from the scrutiny of the ever-present chaperone. The suffragist Susan B. Anthony declared, "I think [bicycling] has done more to emancipate women than anything else in the world. . . . It gives women a feeling of freedom and self-reliance." Fifty thousand men and women had taken to cycles by 1888. Two years later 312 American firms turned out 10 million bikes in one year. **Ⓐ**

Americans took up the sport of tennis as enthusiastically as they had taken up cycling. The modern version of this sport originated in North Wales in 1873. A year later, the United States saw its first tennis match. The socialite Florence Harriman recalled that in the 1880s her father returned from England with one of New York's first tennis sets. At first, neighbors thought the elder Harriman had installed the nets to catch birds.

Hungry or thirsty after tennis or cycling? Turn-of-the-century enthusiasts turned to new snacks with recognizable brand names. They could munch on a Hershey chocolate bar, first sold in 1900, and wash down the chocolate with a Coca-Cola®. An Atlanta pharmacist originally formulated the drink as a cure for headaches in 1886. The ingredients included extracts from Peruvian coca leaves as well as African cola nuts.

MAIN IDEA

Making Inferences

Ⓐ How did the mass production of bicycles change women's lives?

Bicycling and other new sports became fads in the late 1800s.
▼

SPECTATOR SPORTS Americans not only participated in new sports, but became avid fans of spectator sports, especially boxing and baseball. Though these two sports had begun as popular informal activities, by the turn of the 20th century they had become profitable businesses. Fans who couldn't attend an important boxing match jammed barbershops and hotel lobbies to listen to telegraphed transmissions of the contest's highlights.

BASEBALL New rules transformed baseball into a professional sport. In 1845, Alexander J. Cartwright, an amateur player, organized a club in New York City and set down regulations that used aspects of an English sport called rounders. Five years later, 50 baseball clubs had sprung up in the United States, and New York alone boasted 12 clubs in the mid-1860s.

In 1869, a professional team named the Cincinnati Red Stockings toured the country. Other clubs soon took to the road, which led to the formation of the National League in 1876 and the American League in 1900. In the first World Series, held in 1903, the Boston Pilgrims beat the Pittsburgh Pirates. African-American baseball players, who were excluded from both leagues because of racial discrimination, formed their own clubs and two leagues—the Negro National League and the Negro American League.

The novelist Mark Twain called baseball "the very symbol . . . and visible expression of the drive and push and rush and struggle of the raging, tearing, booming nineteenth century." By the 1890s, baseball had a published game schedule, official rules, and a standard-sized diamond. **B**

The Spread of Mass Culture

As increasing numbers of Americans attended school and learned to read, the cultural vistas of ordinary Americans expanded. Art galleries, libraries, books, and museums brought new cultural opportunities to more people. Other advances fostered mass entertainment. New media technology led to the release of hundreds of motion pictures. Mass-production printing techniques gave birth to thousands of books, magazines, and newspapers.

MASS CIRCULATION NEWSPAPERS Looking for ways to captivate readers' attention, American newspapers began using sensational headlines. For example, to introduce its story about the horrors of the Johnstown, Pennsylvania flood of 1889, in which more than 2,000 people died, one newspaper used the headline "THE VALLEY OF DEATH."

Joseph Pulitzer, a Hungarian immigrant who had bought the *New York World* in 1883, pioneered popular innovations, such as a large Sunday edition,

MAIN IDEA

Drawing Conclusions

B Why do you think sports were so popular among Americans at the turn of the century?

comics, sports coverage, and women's news. Pulitzer's paper emphasized "sin, sex, and sensation" in an attempt to surpass his main competitor, the wealthy **William Randolph Hearst**, who had purchased the New York *Morning Journal* in 1895. Hearst, who already owned the San Francisco *Examiner*, sought to outdo Pulitzer by filling the *Journal* with exaggerated tales of personal scandals, cruelty, hypnotism, and even an imaginary conquest of Mars. **C**

MAIN IDEA

Drawing Conclusions

C How did the *World* and the *Journal* attract readers?

The escalation of their circulation war drove both papers to even more sensational news coverage. By 1898, the circulation of each paper had reached more than one million copies a day.

PROMOTING FINE ARTS By 1900, at least one art gallery graced every large city. Some American artists, including Philadelphian Thomas Eakins, began to embrace realism, an artistic school that attempted to portray life as it is really lived. Eakins had studied anatomy with medical students and used painstaking geometric perspective in his work. By the 1880s, Eakins was also using photography to make realistic studies of people and animals.

In the early 20th century, the **Ashcan school** of American art, led by Eakins's student Robert Henri, painted urban life and working people with gritty realism and no frills. Both Eakins and the Ashcan school, however, soon were challenged by the European development known as abstract art, a direction that most people found difficult to understand.

In many cities, inhabitants could walk from a new art gallery to a new public library, sometimes called "the poor man's university." By 1900, free circulating libraries in America numbered in the thousands.

History Through Art

THE CHAMPION SINGLE SCULLS (MAX SCHMITT IN A SINGLE SCULL) (1871)

This painting by Thomas Eakins is an example of the realist movement—an artistic school that aimed at portraying people and environments as they really are.

What realistic details do you see portrayed in this painting?

Highly popular dime novels often featured adventure stories.

POPULAR FICTION As literacy rates rose, scholars debated the role of literature in society. Some felt that literature should uplift America's literary tastes, which tended toward crime tales and Western adventures.

Most people preferred to read light fiction. Such books sold for a mere ten cents, hence their name, "dime novels." Dime novels typically told glorified adventure tales of the West and featured heroes like Edward Wheeler's *Deadwood Dick*. Wheeler published his first Deadwood Dick novel in 1877 and in less than a decade produced over 30 more. **D**

Some readers wanted a more realistic portrayal of American life. Successful writers of the era included Sarah Orne Jewett, Theodore Dreiser, Stephen Crane, Jack London, and Willa Cather. Most portrayed characters less polished than the upper-class men and women of Henry James's and Edith Wharton's novels. Samuel Langhorne Clemens, the novelist and humorist better known as **Mark Twain,** inspired a host of other young authors when he declared his independence of "literature and all that bosh." Yet, some of his books have become classics of American literature. *The Adventures of Huckleberry Finn*, for example, remains famed for its rendering of life along the Mississippi River.

Although art galleries and libraries attempted to raise cultural standards, many Americans had scant interest in high culture—and others did not have access to it. African Americans, for example, were excluded from visiting many museums and other white-controlled cultural institutions.

New Ways to Sell Goods

Along with enjoying new leisure activities, Americans also changed the way they shopped. Americans at the turn of the 20th century witnessed the beginnings of the shopping center, the development of department and chain stores, and the birth of modern advertising.

URBAN SHOPPING Growing city populations made promising targets for enterprising merchants. The nation's earliest form of a shopping center opened in Cleveland, Ohio, in 1890. The glass-topped arcade contained four levels of jewelry, leather goods, and stationery shops. The arcade also provided band music on Sundays so that Cleveland residents could spend their Sunday afternoons strolling through the elegant environment and gazing at the window displays.

Retail shopping districts formed where public transportation could easily bring shoppers from outlying areas. To anchor these retail shopping districts, ambitious merchants started something quite new, the modern department store.

THE DEPARTMENT STORE Marshall Field of Chicago first brought the department store concept to America. While working as a store clerk, Field found that paying close attention to women customers could increase sales considerably. In 1865, Field opened his own store, featuring several floors of specialized departments. Field's motto was "Give the lady what she wants." Field also pioneered the bargain basement, selling bargain goods that were "less expensive but reliable."

THE CHAIN STORE Department stores prided themselves on offering a variety of personal services. New chain stores—retail stores offering the same merchandise under the same ownership—sold goods for less by buying in quantity and limiting personal service. In the 1870s, F. W. Woolworth found that if he offered an item at a very low price, "the consumer would purchase it on the spur of the

MAIN IDEA

Analyzing Causes

D What factors contributed to the popularity of dime novels?

Vocabulary
consumer: a person who purchases goods or services for direct use or ownership

moment" because "it was only a nickel." By 1911, the Woolworth chain boasted 596 stores and sold more than a million dollars in goods a week.

ADVERTISING An explosion in advertising also heralded modern consumerism. Expenditures for advertising were under $10 million a year in 1865 but increased tenfold, to $95 million, by 1900. Patent medicines grabbed the largest number of advertising lines, followed by soaps and baking powders. In addition to newspapers and magazines, advertisers used ingenious methods to push products. Passengers riding the train between New York and Philadelphia in the 1870s might see signs for Dr. Drake's Plantation Bitters on barns, houses, billboards, and even rocks.

CATALOGS AND RFD Montgomery Ward and Sears Roebuck brought retail merchandise to small towns. Ward's catalog, launched in 1872, grew from a single sheet the first year to a booklet with ordering instructions in ten languages. Richard Sears started his company in 1886. Early Sears catalogs stated that the company received "hundreds of orders every day from young and old who never [before] sent away for goods." By 1910, about 10 million Americans shopped by mail. The United States Post Office boosted mail-order businesses. In 1896 the Post Office introduced a **rural free delivery (RFD)** system that brought packages directly to every home.

The turn of the 20th century saw prosperity that caused big changes in Americans' daily lives. At the same time, the nation's growing industrial sector faced problems that called for reform.

NOW & THEN

CATALOG SHOPPING

Catalogs were a novelty when Sears and Montgomery Ward arrived on the scene. However, by the mid-1990s, more than 13 billion catalogs filled the mailboxes of Americans.

Today, the world of mail-order business is changing. After over 100 years of operation, Montgomery Ward filed for bankruptcy on December 28, 2000.

Online shopping is challenging mail-order commerce today. Online retail sales grew from $500 million in 1998 to nearly $89 billion in 2007. What do online shoppers order? Computer equipment, computer software, and electronic appliances make up about 25 percent of online spending.

SECTION 4 ASSESSMENT

1. TERMS & NAMES For each term or name, write a sentence explaining its significance.
- Joseph Pulitzer
- William Randolph Hearst
- Ashcan school
- Mark Twain
- rural free delivery (RFD)

MAIN IDEA

2. TAKING NOTES
Re-create the spider diagram below. Add examples to each category.

Leisure

Modern Mass Culture Emerges

Culture

Why is mass culture often described as a democratic phenomenon?

CRITICAL THINKING

3. SUMMARIZING
How did American methods of selling goods change at the turn of the 20th century?
Think About:
- how city people did their shopping
- how rural residents bought goods
- how merchants advertised their products

4. ANALYZING VISUAL SOURCES
This cartoon shows the masters of the "new journalism." According to the cartoonist, where were Pulitzer and Hearst leading American journalism?

Life at the Turn of the 20th Century **503**

Going to the Show

As Americans moved from rural areas to cities, they looked for new ways to spend their weekend and evening leisure time. Live theatrical performances brought pleasure to cities and small towns alike. Stars, popular performers who could attract large audiences, compensated for the less-talented supporting actors. Audiences could choose from a wide range of music, drama, circus, and the latest in entertainment—moving pictures.

◄ VAUDEVILLE THEATER

Performances that included song, dance, juggling, slapstick comedy, and sometimes chorus lines of female performers were characteristic of vaudeville. Promoters sought large audiences with varied backgrounds. Writing in *Scribner's Magazine* in October 1899, actor Edwin Milton Royle hailed vaudeville theater as "an American invention" that offered something to attract nearly everyone.

Until the 1890s, African-American performers filled roles mainly in minstrel shows that featured exaggerated imitations of African-American music and dance and reinforced racist stereotypes of blacks. By the turn of the century, however, minstrel shows had largely been replaced by more sophisticated musicals, and many black performers entertained in vaudeville.

Bill "Bojangles" Robinson was a popular tap dancer.

▲ THE CIRCUS

The biggest spectacle of all was often the annual visit of the Barnum & Bailey Circus, which its founders, P. T. Barnum and Anthony Bailey, touted as "The Greatest Show on Earth." Established in 1871, the circus arrived by railroad and staged a parade through town to advertise the show.

▲ THE SILVER SCREEN

The first films, one-reel, ten-minute sequences, consisted mostly of vaudeville skits or faked newsreels. In 1903, the first modern film—an eight-minute silent feature called *The Great Train Robbery*—debuted in five-cent theaters called nickelodeons. By showing a film as often as 16 times a day, entrepreneurs could generate greater profits than by a costly stage production. By 1907, an estimated 3,000 nickelodeons dotted the country.

◄ RAGTIME MUSIC

A blend of African-American spirituals and European musical forms, ragtime originated in the 1880s in the saloons of the South. African-American pianist and composer Scott Joplin's ragtime compositions made him famous in the first decade of the 1900s. Ragtime led later to jazz, rhythm and blues, and rock 'n' roll. These forms of popular American culture spread worldwide, creating new dances and fashions that emulated the image of "loud, loose, American rebel."

DATA FILE

A LOOK AT THE FACTS

A shorter workweek allowed many Americans more time for leisure activities, and they certainly took advantage of it.

- In 1890, an average of 60,000 fans attended professional baseball games daily.

- In 1893, a crowd of 50,000 attended the Princeton-Yale football game.

- *A Trip to Chinatown,* one of the popular new musical comedies, ran for an amazing 650 performances in the 1890s.

- In 1900, 3 million phonograph records of Broadway-produced musical comedies were sold.

- The love of the popular musicals contributed to the sale of $42 million worth of musical instruments in 1900.

- By 1900, almost 500 men's social clubs existed. Nine hundred college fraternity and sorority chapters had over 150,000 members.

Changes in the U.S. Workweek

Year	Hours per week
1860	66
1890	60
1920	51

Source: *Historical Statistics of the United States*

THINKING CRITICALLY

CONNECT TO HISTORY

1. **Interpreting Data** Study the statistics in the Data File. What summary statements about the culture and attitudes of this time period can you make? Is this a time in history when you would like to have lived? Why or why not?

   📖 SEE SKILLBUILDER HANDBOOK, PAGE R27.

CONNECT TO TODAY

2. **Chronological Order** Trace the development and impact on the rest of the world of one area—music, theater, or film—of popular American culture. Use a time line from the turn of the 20th to the 21st century with "United States developments" on one side and "world impacts" on the other.

hmhsocialstudies.com RESEARCH WEB LINKS

TERMS & NAMES

For each term or name, write a sentence explaining its connection to late 19th-century American life.

1. Louis Sullivan
2. Orville and Wilbur Wright
3. Booker T. Washington
4. W. E. B. Du Bois
5. Niagara Movement
6. Ida B. Wells
7. Jim Crow laws
8. *Plessy* v. *Ferguson*
9. debt peonage
10. rural free delivery

MAIN IDEAS

Use your notes and the information in the chapter to answer the following questions.

Science and Urban Life (pages 482–487)

1. How did new technology promote urban growth around the turn of the century?
2. In what ways did methods of communication improve in the late 19th and early 20th centuries?

Expanding Public Education
(pages 488–491)

3. How did late 19th century public schools change?
4. Why did some immigrants oppose sending their children to public schools?

Segregation and Discrimination
(pages 492–495)

5. In what ways was racial discrimination reinforced by the federal government's actions and policies?
6. How did Mexicans help make the Southwest prosperous in the late 19th century?

Dawn of Mass Culture (pages 498–503)

7. What leisure activities flourished at the turn of the 20th century?
8. What innovations in retail methods changed the way Americans shopped during this time period?

CRITICAL THINKING

1. **USING YOUR NOTES** Create a table similar to the one shown, listing at least six important trends at the turn of the century, along with a major impact of each.

Trend	Impact
1.	
2.	
3.	
4.	
5.	
6.	

2. **DRAWING CONCLUSIONS** How had changes in technology affected urban life by the turn of the 20th century?

3. **INTERPRETING GRAPHS** Look at the graph of Expanding Education/Increasing Literacy on page 489. Which year reported the greatest gain in the literacy rate? What do you think were the implications on society of a more literate population?

VISUAL SUMMARY LIFE AT THE TURN OF THE 20TH CENTURY

SCIENCE AND URBAN LIFE

Improvements in transportation and communications transform growing cities.

SEGREGATION AND DISCRIMINATION

African Americans and other minorities continue to confront legal and social discrimination.

AMERICAN LIFE AROUND 1900

EXPANDING PUBLIC EDUCATION

Millions of immigrants are assimilated into the growing public school system.

DAWN OF MASS CULTURE

Rapid growth and technological improvements make daily life and work easier—providing leisure time and extra income for consumer goods.

Use the quotation below and your knowledge of U.S. history to answer question 1.

> "We boast of the freedom enjoyed by our people above all other peoples. But it is difficult to reconcile that boast with a state of the law which, practically, puts the brand of servitude and degradation upon a large class of our fellow-citizens, our equals before the law."
>
> —Justice John Marshall Harlan in the dissenting opinion in *Plessy* v. *Ferguson*

1 Justice Harlan used this reasoning for what purpose?

(1) to celebrate American democracy

(2) to justify segregation

(3) to denounce the "separate-but-equal" argument

(4) to demonstrate that equality before the law is not practical

2 Which of the following was *not* an outcome of expanding public education in the early 20th century?

(1) the establishment of public high schools and colleges

(2) the growth of equal education for all

(3) a rise in the literacy rate

(4) the founding of kindergartens

3 The turn of the 20th century brought shorter work hours and more leisure time to many urban Americans. Which of the following bar graphs correctly reflects these factors?

(1)

(2)

(3)

(4)

hmhsocialstudies.com TEST PRACTICE

For additional test practice, go online for:

• Diagnostic tests   • Tutorials

INTERACT WITH HISTORY

Recall the issues that you explored at the beginning of the chapter. Now that you know more about the role of technology in people's lives, would you change any of your responses? Discuss your ideas with a small group. Then make a cause-and-effect chart about one technological innovation of the era and its lasting impact on society.

FOCUS ON WRITING

Imagine you are a newspaper editor in 1896. Write an editorial explaining what you think of the Supreme Court ruling in *Plessy* v. *Ferguson*. Be sure to address the "separate but equal" argument.

MULTIMEDIA ACTIVITY

Visit the links for Chapter Assessment to find out more about the World's Columbian Exposition held in Chicago in 1893. In a small group, make a list of the "famous firsts," such as the first elevated railway, introduced at the exposition. Illustrate your list, adding pictures and informative captions, on a colorful poster for display in the classroom.

hmhsocialstudies.com

Modern America Emerges 1890–1920

UNIT PROJECT

News Story

As you read Unit 5, identify a
person, issue, or event that
interests you. Plan and write an
illustrated news story about the
subject you have chosen. Use
your text as well as information
that you research in the library
and on the Internet.

The Statue of Liberty by Francis
Hopkinson Smith

CHAPTER 17

THE PROGRESSIVE ERA

A 1916 suffrage parade.

Essential Question

How did the progressive movement try to bring about social change?

 New York Standards

KEY IDEA 1 The study of New York State and United States history requires an analysis of the development of American culture, its diversity and multicultural context, and the ways people are unified by many values, practices, and traditions.

KEY IDEA 3 Study about the major social, political, economic, cultural, and religious developments in New York State and United States history involves learning about the important roles and contributions of individuals and groups.

1896 William McKinley is elected president.

1900 William McKinley is reelected.

1901 McKinley is assassinated; Theodore Roosevelt becomes president.

1904 Theodore Roosevelt is elected president.

USA

WORLD

1890

1900

1889 Eiffel Tower opens for visitors.

1898 Marie Curie discovers radium.

1899 Boer War in South Africa begins.

1901 Commonwealth of Australia is created.

INTERACT
WITH HISTORY

It is the dawn of the 20th century, and the reform movement is growing. Moral reformers are trying to ban alcoholic beverages. Political reformers work toward fair government and business practices. Women fight for equal wages and the right to vote. Throughout society, social and economic issues take center stage.

Explore the Issues

- What types of actions might pressure big business to change?
- How can individuals bring about change in their government?
- How might reformers recruit others?

1908 William H. Taft is elected president.

1909 W. E. B. Du Bois helps found the National Association for the Advancement of Colored People (NAACP).

1912 Woodrow Wilson is elected president.

1916 Woodrow Wilson is reelected.

1919 Eighteenth Amendment outlaws alcoholic beverages.

1920 Nineteenth Amendment grants women the right to vote.

1910

1920

1910 Mexican revolution begins.

1912 China's Qin dynasty topples.

1914 World War I begins in Europe.

1919 Mohandas Gandhi becomes leader of the independence movement in India.

VOTES FOR WOMEN

The Progressive Era **511**

PI 1.1 CC Unit 4.I.A.1   CC Unit 4.I.C.1.a(1)
        CC Unit 4.I.C.1.a(2)   CC Unit 4.I.C.1.b

The Origins of Progressivism

MAIN IDEA	WHY IT MATTERS NOW	Terms & Names
Political, economic, and social change in late 19th century America led to broad progressive reforms.	Progressive reforms in areas such as labor and voting rights reinforced democratic principles that continue to exist today.	•progressive movement •Robert M. La Follette •Florence Kelley •initiative •prohibition •referendum •muckraker •recall •scientific management •Seventeenth Amendment

One American's Story

hmhsocialstudies.com
TAKING NOTES
Use the graphic organizer online to take notes about progressive reform organizations.

Camella Teoli was just 12 years old when she began working in a Lawrence, Massachusetts, textile mill to help support her family. Soon after she started, a machine used for twisting cotton into thread tore off part of her scalp. The young Italian immigrant spent seven months in the hospital and was scarred for life.

Three years later, when 20,000 Lawrence mill workers went on strike for higher wages, Camella was selected to testify before a congressional committee investigating labor conditions such as workplace safety and underage workers. When asked why she had gone on strike, Camella answered simply, "Because I didn't get enough to eat at home." She explained how she had gone to work before reaching the legal age of 14.

★ A PERSONAL VOICE CAMELLA TEOLI

"I used to go to school, and then a man came up to my house and asked my father why I didn't go to work, so my father says I don't know whether she is 13 or 14 years old. So, the man say You give me $4 and I will make the papers come from the old country [Italy] saying [that] you are 14. So, my father gave him the $4, and in one month came the papers that I was 14. I went to work, and about two weeks [later] got hurt in my head."

—at congressional hearings, March 1912

▲ Mill workers on strike in 1912 in Lawrence, Massachusetts

After nine weeks of striking, the mill workers won the sympathy of the nation as well as five to ten percent pay raises. Stories like Camella's set off a national investigation of labor conditions, and reformers across the country organized to address the problems of industrialization.

Four Goals of Progressivism

At the dawn of the new century, middle-class reformers addressed many of the problems that had contributed to the social upheavals of the 1890s. Journalists and writers exposed the unsafe conditions often faced by factory workers, including women and children. Intellectuals questioned the dominant role of large corporations in American society. Political reformers struggled to make government more responsive to the people. Together, these reform efforts formed the **progressive movement,** which aimed to restore economic opportunities and correct injustices in American life.

Even though reformers never completely agreed on the problems or the solutions, each of their progressive efforts shared at least one of the following goals:

- protecting social welfare
- promoting moral improvement
- creating economic reform
- fostering efficiency

PROTECTING SOCIAL WELFARE Many social welfare reformers worked to soften some of the harsh conditions of industrialization. The Social Gospel and settlement house movements of the late 1800s, which aimed to help the poor through community centers, churches, and social services, continued during the Progressive Era and inspired even more reform activities.

The Young Men's Christian Association (YMCA), for example, opened libraries, sponsored classes, and built swimming pools and handball courts. The Salvation Army fed poor people in soup kitchens, cared for children in nurseries, and sent "slum brigades" to instruct poor immigrants in middle-class values of hard work and temperance.

In addition, many women were inspired by the settlement houses to take action. **Florence Kelley** became an advocate for improving the lives of women and children. She was appointed chief inspector of factories for Illinois after she had helped to win passage of the Illinois Factory Act in 1893. The act, which prohibited child labor and limited women's working hours, soon became a model for other states.

KEY PLAYER

**FLORENCE KELLEY
1859–1932**

The daughter of an antislavery Republican congressman from Pennsylvania, Florence Kelley became a social reformer whose sympathies lay with the powerless, especially working women and children. During a long career, Kelley pushed the government to solve America's social problems.

In 1899, Kelley became general secretary of the National Consumers' League, where she lobbied to improve factory conditions. "Why," Kelley pointedly asked while campaigning for a federal child-labor law, "are seals, bears, reindeer, fish, wild game in the national parks, buffalo, [and] migratory birds all found suitable for federal protection, but not children?"

PROMOTING MORAL IMPROVEMENT Other reformers felt that morality, not the workplace, held the key to improving the lives of poor people. These reformers wanted immigrants and poor city dwellers to uplift themselves by improving their personal behavior. **Prohibition,** the banning of alcoholic beverages, was one such program.

Prohibitionist groups feared that alcohol was undermining American morals. Founded in Cleveland in 1874, the Woman's Christian Temperance Union (WCTU) spearheaded the crusade for prohibition. Members advanced their cause by entering saloons, singing, praying, and urging saloonkeepers to stop selling alcohol. As momentum grew, the Union was transformed by Frances Willard from a small midwestern religious group in 1879 to a national organization. Boasting 245,000 members by 1911, the WCTU became the largest women's group in the nation's history. **A**

WCTU members followed Willard's "do everything" slogan and began opening kindergartens for immigrants, visiting

MAIN IDEA

Analyzing Motives
A Why did the prohibition movement appeal to so many women?

◄ In the 1890s, Carry Nation worked for prohibition by walking into saloons, scolding the customers, and using her hatchet to destroy bottles of liquor.

513

ANTI–SALOON LEAGUE

Quietly founded by progressive women in 1895, the Anti-Saloon League called itself "the Church in action against the saloon." Whereas early temperance efforts had asked individuals to change their ways, the Anti-Saloon League worked to pass laws to force people to change and to punish those who drank.

The Anti-Saloon League endorsed politicians who opposed "Demon Rum," no matter which party they belonged to or where they stood on other issues. It also organized statewide referendums to ban alcohol. Between 1900 and 1917, voters in nearly half of the states—mostly in the South and the West—prohibited the sale, production, and use of alcohol. Individual towns, city wards, and rural areas also voted themselves "dry."

inmates in prisons and asylums, and working for suffrage. The WCTU reform activities, like those of the settlement-house movement, provided women with expanded public roles, which they used to justify giving women voting rights.

Sometimes efforts at prohibition led to trouble with immigrant groups. Such was the case with the Anti-Saloon League, founded in 1895. As members sought to close saloons to cure society's problems, tension arose between them and many immigrants, whose customs often included the consumption of alcohol. Additionally, saloons filled a number of roles within the immigrant community such as cashing paychecks and serving meals.

CREATING ECONOMIC REFORM As moral reformers sought to change individual behavior, a severe economic panic in 1893 prompted some Americans to question the capitalist economic system. As a result, some Americans, especially workers, embraced socialism. Labor leader Eugene V. Debs, who helped organize the American Socialist Party in 1901, commented on the uneven balance among big business, government, and ordinary people under the free-market system of capitalism.

A PERSONAL VOICE EUGENE V. DEBS

"Competition was natural enough at one time, but do you think you are competing today? Many of you think you are competing. Against whom? Against [oil magnate John D.] Rockefeller? About as I would if I had a wheelbarrow and competed with the Santa Fe [railroad] from here to Kansas City."

—*Debs: His Life, Writings and Speeches*

Though most progressives distanced themselves from socialism, they saw the truth of many of Debs's criticisms. Big business often received favorable treatment from government officials and politicians and could use its economic power to limit competition.

Journalists who wrote about the corrupt side of business and public life in mass circulation magazines during the early 20th century became known as **muckrakers** (mŭk′rāk′r). (The term refers to John Bunyan's "Pilgrim's Progress," in which a character is so busy using a rake to clean up the muck of this world that he does not raise his eyes to heaven.) In her "History of the Standard Oil Company," a monthly serial in *McClure's Magazine*, the writer Ida M. Tarbell described the company's cutthroat methods of eliminating competition. "Mr. Rockefeller has systematically played with loaded dice," Tarbell charged, "and it is doubtful if there has been a time since 1872 when he has run a race with a competitor and started fair." **B**

FOSTERING EFFICIENCY Many progressive leaders put their faith in experts and scientific principles to make society and the workplace more efficient. In defending an Oregon law that limited women factory and laundry workers to a ten-hour day, lawyer Louis D. Brandeis paid little attention to legal argument. Instead, he focused on data produced by social scientists documenting the high costs of long working hours for both the individual and society. This type of argument—the "Brandeis brief"—would become a model for later reform litigation.

Within industry, Frederick Winslow Taylor began using time and motion studies to improve efficiency by breaking manufacturing tasks into simpler parts. "Taylorism" became a management fad, as industry reformers applied these **scientific management** studies to see just how quickly each task could be performed.

MAIN IDEA

Evaluating
B What contribution did muckrakers make to the reform movement?

◀ Workers at the Ford flywheel factory cope with the demanding pace of the assembly line to earn five dollars a day—a good wage in 1914.

However, not all workers could work at the same rate, and although the introduction of the assembly lines did speed up production, the system required people to work like machines. This caused a high worker turnover, often due to injuries suffered by fatigued workers. To keep automobile workers happy and to prevent strikes, Henry Ford reduced the workday to eight hours and paid workers five dollars a day. This incentive attracted thousands of workers, but they exhausted themselves. As one homemaker complained in a letter to Henry Ford in 1914, "That $5 is a blessing—a bigger one than you know but oh they earn it."

Such efforts at improving efficiency, an important part of progressivism, targeted not only industry, but government as well. **C**

MAIN IDEA

Contrasting
C Contrast the goals of scientific management with other progressive reforms.

" Everybody will be able to afford [a car], and about everyone will have one."
HENRY FORD, 1909

Cleaning Up Local Government

Cities faced some of the most obvious social problems of the new industrial age. In many large cities, political bosses rewarded their supporters with jobs and kickbacks and openly bought votes with favors and bribes. Efforts to reform city politics stemmed in part from the desire to make government more efficient and more responsive to its constituents. But those efforts also grew from distrust of immigrants' participation in politics.

REFORMING LOCAL GOVERNMENT Natural disasters sometimes played an important role in prompting reform of city governments. In 1900, a hurricane and tidal wave almost demolished Galveston, Texas. The politicians on the city council botched the huge relief and rebuilding job so badly that the Texas legislature appointed a five-member commission of experts to take over. Each expert took charge of a different city department, and soon Galveston was rebuilt. This success prompted the city to adopt the commission idea as a form of government, and by 1917, 500 cities had followed Galveston's example.

Another natural disaster—a flood in Dayton, Ohio, in 1913—led to the widespread adoption of the council-manager form of government. Staunton, Virginia, had already pioneered this system, in which people elected a city council to make laws. The council in turn appointed a manager, typically a person with training and experience in public administration, to run the city's departments. By 1925, managers were administering nearly 250 cities.

REFORM MAYORS In some cities, mayors such as Hazen Pingree of Detroit, Michigan (1890–1897), and Tom Johnson of Cleveland, Ohio (1901–1909), introduced progressive reforms without changing how government was organized.

Concentrating on economics, Pingree instituted a fairer tax structure, lowered fares for public transportation, rooted out corruption, and set up a system of work relief for the unemployed. Detroit city workers built schools, parks, and a municipal lighting plant.

Johnson was only one of 19 socialist mayors who worked to institute progressive reforms in America's cities. In general, these mayors focused on dismissing corrupt and greedy private owners of utilities—such as gasworks, waterworks, and transit lines—and converting the utilities to publicly owned enterprises. Johnson believed that citizens should play a more active role in city government. He held meetings in a large circus tent and invited them to question officials about how the city was managed. **D**

MAIN IDEA

Summarizing
D How did city government change during the Progressive Era?

Reform at the State Level

Local reforms coincided with progressive efforts at the state level. Spurred by progressive governors, many states passed laws to regulate railroads, mines, mills, telephone companies, and other large businesses.

HISTORICAL SPOTLIGHT

JAMES S. HOGG, TEXAS GOVERNOR (1891–1895)

Among the most colorful of the reform governors was James S. Hogg of Texas. Hogg helped to drive illegal insurance companies from the state and championed antitrust legislation. His chief interest, however, was in regulating the railroads. He pointed out abuses in rates—noting, for example, that it cost more to ship lumber from East Texas to Dallas than to ship it all the way to Nebraska. A railroad commission, established largely as a result of his efforts, helped increase milling and manufacturing in Texas by lowering freight rates.

REFORM GOVERNORS Under the progressive Republican leadership of **Robert M. La Follette,** Wisconsin led the way in regulating big business. "Fighting Bob" La Follette served three terms as governor before he entered the U.S. Senate in 1906. He explained that, as governor, he did not mean to "smash corporations, but merely to drive them out of politics, and then to treat them exactly the same as other people are treated."

La Follette's major target was the railroad industry. He taxed railroad property at the same rate as other business property, set up a commission to regulate rates, and forbade railroads to issue free passes to state officials. Other reform governors who attacked big business interests included Charles B. Aycock of North Carolina and James S. Hogg of Texas.

PROTECTING WORKING CHILDREN As the number of child workers rose dramatically, reformers worked to protect workers and to end child labor. Businesses hired children because they performed unskilled jobs for lower wages and because children's small hands made them more adept at handling small parts and tools. Immigrants and rural migrants often sent their children to work because they viewed their children as part of the family economy. Often wages were so low for adults that every family member needed to work to pull the family out of poverty.

In industrial settings, however, children were more prone to accidents caused by fatigue. Many developed serious health problems and suffered from stunted growth. **E**

Formed in 1904, the National Child Labor Committee sent investigators to gather evidence of children working in harsh conditions. They then organized exhibitions with photographs and statistics to dramatize the children's plight. They were joined by labor union members who argued that child labor lowered wages for all workers. These groups pressured

MAIN IDEA

Analyzing Causes
E Why did reformers seek to end child labor?

IMAGES OF CHILD LABOR

In 1908, Lewis Hine quit his teaching job to document child labor practices. Hine's photographs and descriptions of young laborers—some only three years old—were widely distributed and displayed in exhibits. His compelling images of exploitation helped to convince the public of the need for child labor regulations.

Hine devised a host of clever tactics to gain access to his subjects, such as learning shop managers' schedules and arriving during their lunch breaks. While talking casually with the children, he secretly scribbled notes on paper hidden in his pocket.

Because of their small size, spindle boys and girls *(top)* were forced to climb atop moving machinery to replace parts. For four-year-old Mary *(left)*, shucking two pots of oysters was a typical day's work.

SKILLBUILDER Interpreting Visual Sources
1. Lewis Hine believed in the power of photography to move people to action. What elements of these photographs do you find most striking?
2. Why do you think Hine was a successful photographer?

SEE SKILLBUILDER HANDBOOK, PAGE R23.

---

national politicians to pass the Keating-Owen Act in 1916. The act prohibited the transportation across state lines of goods produced with child labor.

Two years later the Supreme Court declared the act unconstitutional due to interference with states' rights to regulate labor. Reformers did, however, succeed in nearly every state by effecting legislation that banned child labor and set maximum hours.

FOCUS ON

In *Lochner* v. *New York* (1905), the Supreme Court refused to uphold a New York state law limiting bakers to a 10-hour workday on the grounds that the law interfered with the workers' right to negotiate contracts with their employers.

EFFORTS TO LIMIT WORKING HOURS The Supreme Court sometimes took a more sympathetic view of the plight of workers. In the 1908 case of *Muller* v. *Oregon*, Louis D. Brandeis—assisted by Florence Kelley and Josephine Goldmark—persuasively argued that poor working women were much more economically insecure than large corporations. Asserting that women required the state's protection against powerful employers, Brandeis convinced the Court to uphold an Oregon law limiting women to a ten-hour workday. Other states responded by enacting or strengthening laws to reduce women's hours of work. A similar Brandeis brief in *Bunting* v. *Oregon* in 1917 persuaded the Court to uphold a ten-hour workday for men.

Progressives also succeeded in winning workers' compensation to aid the families of workers who were hurt or killed on the job. Beginning with Maryland in 1902, one state after another passed legislation requiring employers to pay benefits in death cases.

REFORMING ELECTIONS In some cases, ordinary citizens won state reforms. William S. U'Ren prompted his state of Oregon to adopt the secret ballot (also called the Australian ballot), the initiative, the referendum, and the recall. The initiative and referendum gave citizens the power to create laws. Citizens could petition to place an **initiative**—a bill originated by the people rather than lawmakers—on the ballot. Then voters, instead of the legislature, accepted or rejected the initiative by **referendum,** a vote on the initiative. The **recall** enabled voters to remove public officials from elected positions by forcing them to face another election before the end of their term if enough voters asked for it. By 1920, 20 states had adopted at least one of these procedures.

In 1899, Minnesota passed the first mandatory statewide primary system. This enabled voters, instead of political machines, to choose candidates for public office through a special popular election. About two-thirds of the states had adopted some form of direct primary by 1915.

DIRECT ELECTION OF SENATORS It was the success of the direct primary that paved the way for the **Seventeenth Amendment** to the Constitution. Before 1913, each state's legislature had chosen its own United States senators, which put even more power in the hands of party bosses and wealthy corporation heads. To force senators to be more responsive to the public, progressives pushed for the popular election of senators. At first, the Senate refused to go along with the idea, but gradually more and more states began allowing voters to nominate senatorial candidates in direct primaries. As a result, Congress approved the Seventeenth Amendment in 1912. Its ratification in 1913 made direct election of senators the law of the land. **F**

Government reform—including efforts to give Americans more of a voice in electing their legislators and creating laws—drew increased numbers of women into public life. It also focused renewed attention on the issue of woman suffrage.

> **MAIN IDEA**
>
> **Summarizing**
> **F** Summarize the impact of the direct election of senators.

  ASSESSMENT

1. TERMS & NAMES For each term or name, write a sentence explaining its significance.
- •**progressive movement**
- •**Florence Kelley**
- •**prohibition**
- •**muckraker**
- •**scientific management**
- •**Robert M. La Follette**
- •**initiative**
- •**referendum**
- •**recall**
- •**Seventeenth Amendment**

MAIN IDEA

2. TAKING NOTES
Copy the web below on your paper. Fill it in with examples of organizations that worked for reform in the areas named.

Which group was most successful and why?

CRITICAL THINKING

3. FORMING GENERALIZATIONS
In what ways might Illinois, Wisconsin, and Oregon all be considered trailblazers in progressive reform? Support your answers. **Think About:**
- legislative and electoral reforms at the state level
- the leadership of William U'Ren and Robert La Follette
- Florence Kelley's appointment as chief inspector of factories for Illinois

4. INTERPRETING VISUAL SOURCES
This cartoon shows Carry Nation inside a saloon that she has attacked. Do you think the cartoonist had a favorable or unfavorable opinion of this prohibitionist? Explain.

SECTION
2

PI 1.1   CC Unit 3.III.A.3.a   CC Unit 3.III.A.3.b
PI 3.1   CC Unit 3.III.A.3.c   CC Unit 3.III.A.3.d
          CC Unit 4.I.B.2.b(1)   CC Unit 4.I.B.2.b(1)

Women in Public Life

MAIN IDEA	WHY IT MATTERS NOW	Terms & Names
As a result of social and economic change, many women entered public life as workers and reformers.	Women won new opportunities in labor and education that are enjoyed today.	• NACW • Susan B. Anthony • suffrage • NAWSA

One American's Story

hmhsocialstudies.com
TAKING NOTES

Use the graphic organizer online to take notes about women and work in the late 1800s.

In 1879, Susette La Flesche, a young Omaha woman, traveled east to translate into English the sad words of Chief Standing Bear, whose Ponca people had been forcibly removed from their homeland in Nebraska. Later, she was invited with Chief Standing Bear to go on a lecture tour to draw attention to the Ponca's situation.

A PERSONAL VOICE SUSETTE LA FLESCHE

" We are thinking men and women. . . . We have a right to be heard in whatever concerns us. Your government has driven us hither and thither like cattle. . . . Your government has no right to say to us, Go here, or Go there, and if we show any reluctance, to force us to do its will at the point of the bayonet. . . . Do you wonder that the Indian feels outraged by such treatment and retaliates, although it will end in death to himself? "

—quoted in *Bright Eyes*

▲ Susette La Flesche

La Flesche testified before congressional committees and helped win passage of the Dawes Act of 1887, which allowed individual Native Americans to claim reservation land and citizenship rights. Her activism was an example of a new role for American women, who were expanding their participation in public life.

Women in the Work Force

Before the Civil War, married middle-class women were generally expected to devote their time to the care of their homes and families. By the late 19th century, however, only middle-class and upper-class women could afford to do so. Poorer women usually had no choice but to work for wages outside the home.

FARM WOMEN On farms in the South and the Midwest, women's roles had not changed substantially since the previous century. In addition to household tasks such as cooking, making clothes, and laundering, farm women handled a host of other chores such as raising livestock. Often the women had to help plow and plant the fields and harvest the crops.

WOMEN IN INDUSTRY As better-paying opportunities became available in towns, and especially cities, women had new options for finding jobs, even though men's labor unions excluded them from membership. At the turn of the century,

◀ Telephone operators manually connect phone calls in 1915.

one out of five American women held jobs; 25 percent of them worked in manufacturing.

The garment trade claimed about half of all women industrial workers. They typically held the least skilled positions, however, and received only about half as much money as their male counterparts or less. Many of these women were single and were assumed to be supporting only themselves, while men were assumed to be supporting families.

Women also began to fill new jobs in offices, stores, and classrooms. These jobs required a high school education, and by 1890, women high school graduates outnumbered men. Moreover, new business schools were preparing bookkeepers and stenographers, as well as training female typists to operate the new machines. **A**

DOMESTIC WORKERS Many women without formal education or industrial skills contributed to the economic survival of their families by doing domestic work, such as cleaning for other families. After almost 2 million African-American women were freed from slavery, poverty quickly drove nearly half of them into the work force. They worked on farms and as domestic workers, and migrated by the thousands to big cities for jobs as cooks, laundresses, scrubwomen, and maids. Altogether, roughly 70 percent of women employed in 1870 were servants.

Unmarried immigrant women also did domestic labor, especially when they first arrived in the United States. Many married immigrant women contributed to the family income by taking in piecework or caring for boarders at home.

Women Lead Reform

Dangerous conditions, low wages, and long hours led many female industrial workers to push for reforms. Their ranks grew after 146 workers, mostly Jewish and Italian immigrant girls, died in a 1911 fire in the Triangle Shirtwaist Factory in New York City. Middle- and upper-class women also entered the public sphere. By 1910, women's clubs, at which these women discussed art or literature, were nearly half a million strong. These clubs sometimes grew into reform groups that addressed issues such as temperance or child labor.

WOMEN IN HIGHER EDUCATION Many of the women who became active in public life in the late 19th century had attended the new women's colleges. Vassar

---

MAIN IDEA

Analyzing Causes

A What kinds of job opportunities prompted more women to complete high school?

FOCUS ON

Working in the slums of New York City helped shape the ideas of Margaret Sanger. In 1921, Sanger founded the Birth Control League, which was the forerunner of today's Planned Parenthood.

College—with a faculty of 8 men and 22 women—accepted its first students in 1865. Smith and Wellesley Colleges followed in 1875. Though Columbia, Brown, and Harvard Colleges refused to admit women, each university established a separate college for women.

Although women were still expected to fulfill traditional domestic roles, women's colleges sought to grant women an excellent education. In her will, Smith College's founder, Sophia Smith, made her goals clear.

★ A PERSONAL VOICE SOPHIA SMITH

" [It is my desire] to furnish for my own sex means and facilities for education equal to those which are afforded now in our College to young men. . . . It is not my design to render my sex any the less feminine, but to develop as fully as may be the powers of womanhood & furnish women with means of usefulness, happiness, & honor now withheld from them. "

—quoted in *Alma Mater*

MAIN IDEA

Analyzing Effects

B What social and economic effects did higher education have on women?

By the late 19th century, marriage was no longer a woman's only alternative. Many women entered the work force or sought higher education. In fact, almost half of college-educated women in the late 19th century never married, retaining their own independence. Many of these educated women began to apply their skills to needed social reforms. **B**

WOMEN AND REFORM Uneducated laborers started efforts to reform workplace health and safety. The participation of educated women often strengthened existing reform groups and provided leadership for new ones. Because women were not allowed to vote or run for office, women reformers strove to improve conditions at work and home. Their "social housekeeping" targeted workplace reform, housing reform, educational improvement, and food and drug laws.

In 1896, African-American women founded the National Association of Colored Women, or **NACW,** by merging two earlier organizations. Josephine Ruffin identified the mission of the African-American women's club movement as "the moral education of the race with which we are identified." The NACW managed nurseries, reading rooms, and kindergartens.

After the Seneca Falls convention of 1848, women split over the Fourteenth and Fifteenth Amendments, which granted equal rights including the right to vote to African American men, but excluded women. **Susan B. Anthony,** a leading proponent of woman **suffrage,** the right to vote, said "[I] would sooner cut off my right hand than ask the ballot for the black man and not for women." In 1869 Anthony and Elizabeth Cady Stanton had founded the National Women Suffrage Association (NWSA), which united with another group in 1890 to

Suffragists recruit supporters for a march.

KEY PLAYER

SUSAN B. ANTHONY
1820–1906

Born to a strict Quaker family, Susan B. Anthony was not allowed to enjoy typical childhood entertainment such as music, games, and toys. Her father insisted on self-discipline, education, and a strong belief system for all of his eight children. At an early age, Anthony developed a positive view of womanhood from a teacher named Mary Perkins who educated the children in their home.

After voting illegally in the presidential election of 1872, Anthony was fined $100 at her trial. "Not a penny shall go to this unjust claim," she defiantly declared. She never paid the fine.

become the National American Woman Suffrage Association, or **NAWSA.** Other prominent leaders included Lucy Stone and Julia Ward Howe, the author of "The Battle Hymn of the Republic."

Woman suffrage faced constant opposition. The liquor industry feared that women would vote in support of prohibition, while the textile industry worried that women would vote for restrictions on child labor. Many men simply feared the changing role of women in society.

A THREE–PART STRATEGY FOR SUFFRAGE Suffragist leaders tried three approaches to achieve their objective. First, they tried to convince state legislatures to grant women the right to vote. They achieved a victory in the territory of Wyoming in 1869, and by the 1890s Utah, Colorado, and Idaho had also granted voting rights to women. After 1896, efforts in other states failed.

Second, women pursued court cases to test the Fourteenth Amendment, which declared that states denying their male citizens the right to vote would lose congressional representation. Weren't women citizens, too? In 1871 and 1872, Susan B. Anthony and other women tested that question by attempting to vote at least 150 times in ten states and the District of Columbia. The Supreme Court ruled in 1875 that women were indeed citizens—but then denied that citizenship automatically conferred the right to vote.

Third, women pushed for a national constitutional amendment to grant women the vote. Stanton succeeded in having the amendment introduced in California, but it was killed later. For the next 41 years, women lobbied to have it reintroduced, only to see it continually voted down. **C**

Before the turn of the century, the campaign for suffrage achieved only modest success. Later, however, women's reform efforts paid off in improvements in the treatment of workers and in safer food and drug products—all of which President Theodore Roosevelt supported, along with his own plans for reforming business, labor, and the environment.

> **MAIN IDEA**
>
> **Making Inferences**
> **C** Why did suffragist leaders employ a three-part strategy for gaining the right to vote?

ASSESSMENT

1. TERMS & NAMES For each term or name, write a sentence explaining its significance.
- NACW
- suffrage
- Susan B. Anthony
- NAWSA

MAIN IDEA

2. TAKING NOTES
In a chart like the one below, fill in details about working women in the late 1800s.

What generalizations can you make about women workers at this time?

CRITICAL THINKING

3. SYNTHESIZING
What women and movements during the Progressive Era helped dispel the stereotype that women were submissive and nonpolitical?

4. MAKING INFERENCES
Why do you think some colleges refused to accept women in the late 19th century?

5. ANALYZING ISSUES
Imagine you are a woman during the Progressive Era. Explain how you might recruit other women to support the following causes: improving education, housing reform, food and drug laws, the right to vote. **Think About:**
- the problems that each movement was trying to remedy
- how women benefited from each cause

CC Unit 4.I.B.1.a   CC Unit 4.I.B.1.c
CC Unit 4.I.B.c(1)   CC Unit 4.I.B.2.e
CC Unit 4.I.C.2   CC Unit 4.I.C.3

PI 3.1

Teddy Roosevelt's Square Deal

MAIN IDEA	WHY IT MATTERS NOW	Terms & Names
As president, Theodore Roosevelt worked to give citizens a Square Deal through progressive reforms.	As part of his Square Deal, Roosevelt's conservation efforts made a permanent impact on environmental resources.	•Upton Sinclair •*The Jungle* •Theodore Roosevelt •Square Deal •Meat Inspection Act •Pure Food and Drug Act •conservation •NAACP

One American's Story

hmhsocialstudies.com
TAKING NOTES

Use the graphic organizer online to take notes about Theodore Roosevelt's presidency.

When muckraking journalist **Upton Sinclair** began research for a novel in 1904, his focus was the human condition in the stockyards of Chicago. Sinclair intended his novel to reveal "the breaking of human hearts by a system [that] exploits the labor of men and women for profits." What most shocked readers in Sinclair's book ***The Jungle*** (1906), however, was the sickening conditions of the meatpacking industry.

A PERSONAL VOICE UPTON SINCLAIR

" There would be meat that had tumbled out on the floor, in the dirt and sawdust, where the workers had tramped and spit uncounted billions of consumption [tuberculosis] germs. There would be meat stored in great piles in rooms; . . . and thousands of rats would race about on it. . . . A man could run his hand over these piles of meat and sweep off handfuls of the dried dung of rats. These rats were nuisances, and the packers would put poisoned bread out for them; they would die, and then rats, bread, and meat would go into the hoppers together. "

—The Jungle

Upton Sinclair poses with his son at the time of the writing of *The Jungle.*

President **Theodore Roosevelt,** like many other readers, was nauseated by Sinclair's account. The president invited the author to visit him at the White House, where Roosevelt promised that "the specific evils you point out shall, if their existence be proved, and if I have the power, be eradicated."

A Rough-Riding President

Theodore Roosevelt was not supposed to be president. In 1900, the young governor from New York was urged to run as McKinley's vice-president by the state's political bosses, who found Roosevelt impossible to control. The plot to nominate Roosevelt worked, taking him out of state office. However, as vice-president,

When the president spared a bear cub on a hunting expedition, a toymaker marketed a popular new product, the teddy bear.

Roosevelt stood a heartbeat away from becoming president. Indeed, President McKinley had served barely six months of his second term before he was assassinated, making Roosevelt the most powerful person in the government.

ROOSEVELT'S RISE Theodore Roosevelt was born into a wealthy New York family in 1858. An asthma sufferer during his childhood, young Teddy drove himself to accomplish demanding physical feats. As a teenager, he mastered marksmanship and horseback riding. At Harvard College, Roosevelt boxed and wrestled.

At an early age, the ambitious Roosevelt became a leader in New York politics. After serving three terms in the New York State Assembly, he became New York City's police commissioner and then assistant secretary of the U.S. Navy. The aspiring politician grabbed national attention, advocating war against Spain in 1898. His volunteer cavalry brigade, the Rough Riders, won public acclaim for its role in the battle at San Juan Hill in Cuba. Roosevelt returned a hero and was soon elected governor of New York and then later won the vice-presidency.

THE MODERN PRESIDENCY When Roosevelt was thrust into the presidency in 1901, he became the youngest president ever at 42 years old. Unlike previous presidents, Roosevelt soon dominated the news with his many exploits. While in office, Roosevelt enjoyed boxing, although one of his opponents blinded him in the left eye. On another day, he galloped 100 miles on horseback, merely to prove the feat possible.

In politics, as in sports, Roosevelt acted boldly, using his personality and popularity to advance his programs. His leadership and publicity campaigns helped create the modern presidency, making him a model by which all future presidents would be measured. Citing federal responsibility for the national welfare, Roosevelt thought the government should assume control whenever states proved incapable of dealing with problems. He explained, "It is the duty of the president to act upon the theory that he is the steward of the people, and . . . to assume that he has the legal right to do whatever the needs of the people demand, unless the Constitution or the laws explicitly forbid him to do it."

Teddy Roosevelt enjoyed an active lifestyle, as this 1902 photo reveals. ▶

MAIN IDEA

Synthesizing

A What actions and characteristics of Teddy Roosevelt contributed to his reputation as the first modern president?

Roosevelt saw the presidency as a "bully pulpit," from which he could influence the news media and shape legislation. If big business victimized workers, then President Roosevelt would see to it that the common people received what he called a **Square Deal.** This term was used to describe the various progressive reforms sponsored by the Roosevelt administration. **A**

Using Federal Power

Roosevelt's study of history—he published the first of his 44 books at the age of 24—convinced him that modern America required a powerful federal government. "A simple and poor society can exist as a democracy on the basis of sheer individualism," Roosevelt declared, "but a rich and complex industrial society cannot so exist." The young president soon met several challenges to his assertion of federal power.

TRUSTBUSTING By 1900, trusts—legal bodies created to hold stock in many companies—controlled about four-fifths of the industries in the United States. Some trusts, like Standard Oil, had earned poor reputations with the public by the use of unfair business practices. Many trusts lowered their prices to drive competitors out of the market and then took advantage of the lack of competition to jack prices up even higher. Although Congress had passed the Sherman Antitrust Act in 1890, the act's vague language made enforcement difficult. As a result, nearly all the suits filed against the trusts under the Sherman Act were ineffective.

President Roosevelt did not believe that all trusts were harmful, but he sought to curb the actions of those that hurt the public interest. The president concentrated his efforts on filing suits under the Sherman Antitrust Act. In 1902, Roosevelt made newspaper headlines as a trustbuster when he ordered the Justice Department to sue the Northern Securities Company, which had established a monopoly over northwestern railroads. In 1904, the Supreme Court dissolved the company. Although the Roosevelt administration filed 44 antitrust suits, winning a number of them and breaking up some of the trusts, it was unable to slow the merger movement in business.

VIDEO

Teddy Roosevelt vs. Corporate America

hmhsocialstudies.com

THE LION-TAMER

Analyzing *Political Cartoons*

"THE LION-TAMER"

As part of his Square Deal, President Roosevelt aggressively used the Sherman Antitrust Act of 1890 to attack big businesses engaging in unfair practices. His victory over his first target, the Northern Securities Company, earned him a reputation as a hard-hitting trustbuster committed to protecting the public interest. This cartoon shows Roosevelt trying to tame the wild lions that symbolize the great and powerful companies of 1904.

SKILLBUILDER Analyzing Political Cartoons
1. What do the lions stand for?
2. Why are all the lions coming out of a door labeled "Wall St."?
3. What do you think the cartoonist thinks about trustbusting? Cite details from the cartoon that support your interpretation.

📖 SEE SKILLBUILDER HANDBOOK, PAGE R24.

1902 COAL STRIKE When 140,000 coal miners in Pennsylvania went on strike and demanded a 20 percent raise, a nine-hour workday, and the right to organize a union, the mine operators refused to bargain. Five months into the strike, coal reserves ran low. Roosevelt, seeing the need to intervene, called both sides to the White House to talk, and eventually settled the strike. Irked by the "extraordinary stupidity and bad temper" of the mine operators, he later confessed that only the dignity of the presidency had kept him from taking one owner "by the seat of the breeches" and tossing him out of the window.

Faced with Roosevelt's threat to take over the mines, the opposing sides finally agreed to submit their differences to an arbitration commission—a third party that would work with both sides to mediate the dispute. In 1903, the commission issued its compromise settlement. The miners won a 10 percent pay hike and a shorter, nine-hour workday. With this, however, they had to give up their demand for a closed shop—in which all workers must belong to the union—and their right to strike during the next three years.

> *"In life, as in a football game, the principle . . . is: Hit the line hard."*
> **THEODORE ROOSEVELT**

President Roosevelt's actions had demonstrated a new principle. From then on, when a strike threatened the public welfare, the federal government was expected to intervene. In addition, Roosevelt's actions reflected the progressive belief that disputes could be settled in an orderly way with the help of experts, such as those on the arbitration commission. **B**

MAIN IDEA

Analyzing Effects
B What was significant about the way the 1902 coal strike was settled?

Vocabulary
collude: to act together secretly to achieve an illegal or deceitful purpose

RAILROAD REGULATION Roosevelt's real goal was federal regulation. In 1887, Congress had passed the Interstate Commerce Act, which prohibited wealthy railroad owners from colluding to fix high prices by dividing the business in a given area. The Interstate Commerce Commission (ICC) was set up to enforce the new law but had little power. With Roosevelt's urging, Congress passed the Elkins Act in 1903, which made it illegal for railroad officials to give, and shippers to receive, rebates for using particular railroads. The act also specified that railroads could not change set rates without notifying the public.

The Hepburn Act of 1906 strictly limited the distribution of free railroad passes, a common form of bribery. It also gave the ICC power to set maximum railroad rates. Although Roosevelt had to compromise with conservative senators who opposed the act, its passage boosted the government's power to regulate the railroads.

Health and the Environment

President Roosevelt's enthusiasm and his considerable skill at compromise led to laws and policies that benefited both public health and the environment. He wrote, "We recognize and are bound to war against the evils of today. The remedies are partly economic and partly spiritual, partly to be obtained by laws, and in greater part to be obtained by individual and associated effort."

REGULATING FOODS AND DRUGS After reading *The Jungle* by Upton Sinclair, Roosevelt responded to the public's clamor for action. He appointed a commission of experts to investigate the meatpacking industry. The commission issued a scathing report backing up Sinclair's account of the disgusting conditions in the industry. True to his word, in 1906 Roosevelt pushed for passage of the **Meat Inspection Act,**

NOW & THEN

MEAT INSPECTION

During the Progressive Era, people worried about the kinds of things that might fall—or walk—into a batch of meat being processed. Today, Americans worry more about contamination by unseen dangers, such as E. coli bacteria, mad cow disease, and antibiotics or other chemicals that may pose long-range health risks to people.

In July 1996, Congress passed the most extensive changes in standards for meat inspection since the Meat Inspection Act of 1906. The costs of the new, more scientific inspections amount to about a tenth of a penny per pound of meat. The FDA has also adopted restrictions on importation of feed and livestock from other countries to prevent the spread of disease.

Coal Mining in the Early 1900s

hmhsocialstudies.com INTERACTIVE

Coal played a key role in America's industrial boom around the turn of the century, providing the United States with about 90 percent of its energy. Miners often had to dig for coal hundreds of feet below the earth's surface. The work in these mines was among the hardest and most dangerous in the world. Progressive Era reforms helped improve conditions for miners, as many won wage increases and shorter work hours.

The coal mines employed thousands of children, like this boy pictured in 1909. In 1916, progressives helped secure passage of a child labor law that forbade interstate commerce of goods produced by children under the age of 14. ▶

Most underground mines had two shafts—an elevator shaft (shown here) for transporting workers and coal, and an air shaft for ventilation.

◀ Like these men working in 1908, miners typically spent their days in dark, cramped spaces underground.

pillars   air shaft   room   elevator shaft

room

The miners' main tool was the pick. Many also used drilling machines.

Donkeys or mules pulled the coal cars to the elevators, which transported the coal to the surface.

Most mines used a room-and-pillar method for extracting coal. This entailed digging out "rooms" of coal off a series of tunnels, leaving enough coal behind to form a pillar that prevented the room from collapsing.

Government workers inspect meat as it moves through the packinghouse. ▶

which dictated strict cleanliness requirements for meatpackers and created the program of federal meat inspection that was in use until it was replaced by more sophisticated techniques in the 1990s.

The compromise that won the act's passage, however, left the government paying for the inspections and did not require companies to label their canned goods with date-of-processing information. The compromise also granted meatpackers the right to appeal negative decisions in court.

PURE FOOD AND DRUG ACT Before any federal regulations were established for advertising food and drugs, manufacturers had claimed that their products accomplished everything from curing cancer to growing hair. In addition, popular children's medicines often contained opium, cocaine, or alcohol. In a series of lectures across the country, Dr. Harvey Washington Wiley, chief chemist at the Department of Agriculture, criticized manufacturers for adding harmful preservatives to food and brought needed attention to this issue.

In 1906, Congress passed the **Pure Food and Drug Act,** which halted the sale of contaminated foods and medicines and called for truth in labeling. Although this act did not ban harmful products outright, its requirement of truthful labels reflected the progressive belief that given accurate information, people would act wisely. **C**

A typical late-19th-century product advertisement. ▼

HALL'S HAIR RENEWER
VEGETABLE SICILIAN
THICKENS THE GROWTH OF THE HAIR, PREVENTS BALDNESS, CURES DANDRUFF, AND RESTORES GRAY HAIR TO ITS ORIGINAL COLOR AND BEAUTY.
R.P HALL & Co PROPRIETORS, NASHUA, N.H.

CONSERVATION AND NATURAL RESOURCES Before Roosevelt's presidency, the federal government had paid very little attention to the nation's natural resources. Despite the establishment of the U.S. Forest Bureau in 1887 and the subsequent withdrawal from public sale of 45 million acres of timberlands for a national forest reserve, the government stood by while private interests gobbled up the shrinking wilderness.

> **MAIN IDEA**
>
> **Comparing**
> **C** What similarities did the Meat Inspection Act and Pure Food and Drug Act share?

In the late 19th century Americans had shortsightedly exploited their natural environment. Pioneer farmers leveled the forests and plowed up the prairies. Ranchers allowed their cattle to overgraze the Great Plains. Coal companies cluttered the land with refuse from mines. Lumber companies ignored the effect of their logging operations on flood control and neglected to plant trees to replace those they had cut down. Cities dumped untreated sewage and industrial wastes into rivers, poisoning the streams and creating health hazards.

CONSERVATION MEASURES Roosevelt condemned the view that America's resources were endless and made conservation a primary concern. John Muir, a naturalist and writer with whom Roosevelt camped in California's Yosemite National Park in 1903, persuaded the president to set aside 148 million acres of forest reserves. Roosevelt also set aside 1.5 million acres of water-power sites and another 80 million acres of land that experts from the U.S. Geological Survey would explore for mineral and water resources. Roosevelt also established more than 50 wildlife sanctuaries and several national parks.

True to the Progressive belief in using experts, in 1905 the president named Gifford Pinchot as head of the U.S. Forest Service. A professional conservationist, Pinchot had administrative skill as well as the latest scientific and technical information. He advised Roosevelt to conserve forest and grazing lands by keeping large tracts of federal land exempt from private sale.

Conservationists like Roosevelt and Pinchot, however, did not share the views of Muir, who advocated complete preservation of the wilderness. Instead, **conservation** to them meant that some wilderness areas would be preserved while others would be developed for the common good. Indeed, Roosevelt's federal water projects transformed some dry wilderness areas to make agriculture possible. Under the National Reclamation Act of 1902, known as the Newlands

Federal Conservation Lands

Federal Conservation Lands
- Created 1909–1996
- Created 1901–1908
- Created 1872–1900

0   200   400 miles
0   200   400 kilometers

GEOGRAPHY SKILLBUILDER
1. **Region** Prior to 1901, which regions had the greatest amount of conservation lands?
2. **Human Environment Interaction** Describe the effects of Roosevelt's conservation efforts and the impact he had on the environment.

Act, money from the sale of public lands in the West funded large-scale irrigation projects, such as the Roosevelt Dam in Arizona and the Shoshone Dam in Wyoming. The Newlands Act established the precedent that the federal government would manage the precious water resources of the West. **D**

Roosevelt and Civil Rights

Roosevelt's concern for the land and its inhabitants was not matched in the area of civil rights. Though Roosevelt's father had supported the North, his mother, Martha, may well have been the model for the Southern belle Scarlett O'Hara in Margaret Mitchell's famous novel, *Gone with the Wind*. In almost two terms as president, Roosevelt—like most other progressives—failed to support civil rights for African Americans. He did, however, support a few individual African Americans.

Despite opposition from whites, Roosevelt appointed an African American as head of the Charleston, South Carolina, customhouse. In another instance, when some whites in Mississippi refused to accept the black postmistress he had appointed, he chose to close the station rather than give in. In 1906, however, Roosevelt angered many African Americans when he dismissed without question an entire regiment of African-American soldiers accused of conspiracy in protecting others charged with murder in Brownsville, Texas.

As a symbolic gesture, Roosevelt invited Booker T. Washington to dinner at the White House. Washington—head of the Tuskegee Normal and Industrial Institute, an all-black training school—was then the African-American leader most respected by powerful whites. Washington faced opposition, however, from other African

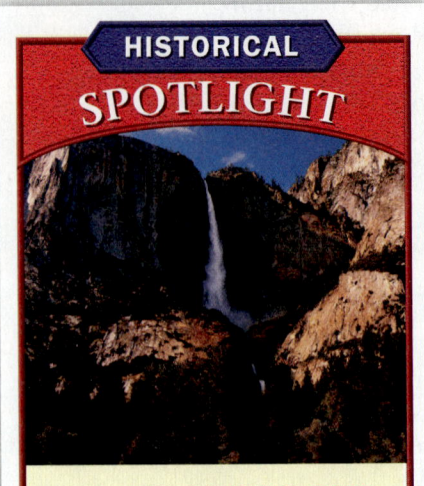

YOSEMITE NATIONAL PARK

The naturalist John Muir visited the Yosemite region of central California in 1868 and made it his home base for a period of six years while he traveled throughout the West.

Muir was the first to suggest that Yosemite's spectacular land formations had been shaped by glaciers. Today the park's impressive cliffs, waterfalls, lakes, and meadows draw sports enthusiasts and tourists in all seasons.

Civil rights leaders gather at the 1905 Niagara Falls conference. ▶

Americans, such as W. E. B. Du Bois, for his accommodation of segregationists and for blaming black poverty on blacks and urging them to accept discrimination.

Persistent in his criticism of Washington's ideas, Du Bois renewed his demands for immediate social and economic equality for African Americans. In his 1903 book *The Souls of Black Folk*, Du Bois wrote of his opposition to Washington's position.

★ A PERSONAL VOICE W. E. B. DU BOIS

" So far as Mr. Washington preaches Thrift, Patience, and Industrial Training for the masses, we must hold up his hands and strive with him. . . . But so far as Mr. Washington apologizes for injustice, North or South, does not rightly value the privilege and duty of voting, belittles the emasculating effects of caste distinctions, and opposes the higher training and ambition of our brighter minds,—so far as he, the South, or the Nation, does this,—we must unceasingly and firmly oppose them. "

—*The Souls of Black Folk*

Du Bois and other advocates of equality for African Americans were deeply upset by the apparent progressive indifference to racial injustice. In 1905 they held a civil rights conference in Niagara Falls, and in 1909 a number of African Americans joined with prominent white reformers in New York to found the **NAACP**—the National Association for the Advancement of Colored People. The NAACP, which had over 6,000 members by 1914, aimed for nothing less than full equality among the races. That goal, however, found little support in the Progressive Movement, which focused on the needs of middle-class whites. The two presidents who followed Roosevelt also did little to advance the goal of racial equality.

Background
In 1913, the Jewish organization B'nai B'rith set up the Anti-Defamation League (ADL) to fight anti-semitism, or hostility toward Jews.

KEY PLAYER

W. E. B. DU BOIS
1868–1963

In 1909, W. E. B. Du Bois helped to establish the NAACP and entered into the forefront of the early U.S. civil rights movement. However, in the 1920s, he faced a power struggle with the NAACP's executive secretary, Walter White.

Ironically, Du Bois had retreated to a position others saw as dangerously close to that of Booker T. Washington. Arguing for a separate economy for African Americans, Du Bois made a distinction, which White rejected, between enforced and voluntary segregation. By mid-century, Du Bois was outside the mainstream of the civil rights movement. His work remained largely ignored until after his death in 1963.

SECTION 3 ASSESSMENT

1. TERMS & NAMES For each term or name, write a sentence explaining its significance.
- Upton Sinclair
- *The Jungle*
- Theodore Roosevelt
- Square Deal
- Meat Inspection Act
- Pure Food and Drug Act
- conservation
- NAACP

MAIN IDEA

2. TAKING NOTES
Create five problem-solution diagrams like the one below to show how the following problems were addressed during Roosevelt's presidency:
(a) 1902 coal strike, (b) Northern Securities Company monopoly, (c) unsafe meat processing, (d) exploitation of the environment, and (e) racial injustice.

| Problems | → | Solutions |

Write headlines announcing the solutions.

CRITICAL THINKING

3. FORMING GENERALIZATIONS
In what ways do you think the progressive belief in using experts played a role in shaping Roosevelt's reforms? Refer to details from the text. **Think About:**
- Roosevelt's use of experts to help him tackle political, economic, and environmental problems
- how experts' findings affected legislative actions

4. EVALUATING
Research the coal strike of 1902. Do you think Roosevelt's intervention was in favor of the strikers or of the mine operators? Why?

5. ANALYZING ISSUES
Why did W. E. B. Du Bois oppose Booker T. Washington's views on racial discrimination?

The Muckrakers

AMERICAN LITERATURE

1902–1917 The tradition of the investigative reporter uncovering corruption was established early in the 20th century by the writers known as muckrakers. Coined by President Theodore Roosevelt, the term *muckraker* alludes to the English author John Bunyan's famous 17th-century religious allegory *The Pilgrim's Progress*, which features a character too busy raking up the muck to see a heavenly crown held over him. The originally negative term soon was applied to many writers whose reform efforts Roosevelt himself supported. The muckraking movement spilled over from journalism as writers such as Upton Sinclair made use of the greater dramatic effects of fiction.

◀ IDA M. TARBELL

Ida M. Tarbell's "The History of the Standard Oil Company" exposed the ruthlessness with which John D. Rockefeller had turned his oil business into an all-powerful monopoly. Her writing added force to the trustbusting reforms of the early 20th century. Here Tarbell describes how Standard Oil used lower transportation rates to drive out smaller refineries, such as Hanna, Baslington and Company.

Mr. Hanna had been refining since July, 1869. . . . Some time in February, 1872, the Standard Oil Company asked [for] an interview with him and his associates. They wanted to buy his works, they said. "But we don't want to sell," objected Mr. Hanna. "You can never make any more money, in my judgment," said Mr. Rockefeller. "You can't compete with the Standard. We have all the large refineries now. If you refuse to sell, it will end in your being crushed." Hanna and Baslington were not satisfied. They went to see . . . General Devereux, manager of the Lake Shore road. They were told that the Standard had special rates; that it was useless to try to compete with them. General Devereux explained to the gentlemen that the privileges granted the Standard were the legitimate and necessary advantage of the larger shipper over the smaller. . . . General Devereux says they "recognised the propriety" of his excuse. They certainly recognised its authority. They say that they were satisfied they could no longer get rates to and from Cleveland which would enable them to live, and "reluctantly" sold out. It must have been reluctantly, for they had paid $75,000 for their works, and had made thirty per cent. a year on an average on their investment, and the Standard appraiser allowed them $45,000.

—Ida M. Tarbell, "The History of the Standard Oil Company" (1904)

LINCOLN STEFFENS ▶

Lincoln Steffens is usually named as a leading figure of the muckraking movement. He published exposés of business and government corruption in *McClure's Magazine* and other magazines. These articles were then collected in two books: *The Shame of the Cities* and *The Struggle for Self-Government*. Below is a section from an article Steffens wrote to expose voter fraud in Philadelphia.

> The police are forbidden by law to stand within thirty feet of the polls, but they are at the box and they are there to see that the [Republican political] machine's orders are obeyed and that repeaters whom they help to furnish are permitted to vote without "intimidation" on the names they, the police, have supplied. The editor of an anti-machine paper who was looking about for himself once told me that a ward leader who knew him well asked him into a polling place. "I'll show you how it's done," he said, and he had the repeaters go round and round voting again and again on the names handed them on slips. . . . The business proceeds with very few hitches; there is more jesting than fighting. Violence in the past has had its effect; and is not often necessary nowadays, but if it is needed the police are there to apply it.

—Lincoln Steffens, *The Shame of the Cities* (1904)

UPTON SINCLAIR

Upton Sinclair's chief aim in writing *The Jungle* was to expose the shocking conditions that immigrant workers endured. The public, however, reacted even more strongly to the novel's revelations of unsanitary conditions in the meatpacking industry. Serialized in 1905 and published in book form one year later, *The Jungle* prompted a federal investigation that resulted in passage of the Meat Inspection Act in 1906.

> Jonas had told them how the meat that was taken out of pickle would often be found sour, and how they would rub it up with [baking] soda to take away the smell, and sell it to be eaten on free-lunch counters; also of all the miracles of chemistry which they performed, giving to any sort of meat, fresh or salted, whole or chopped, any color and any flavor and any odor they chose. . . .
>
> It was only when the whole ham was spoiled that it came into the department of Elzbieta. Cut up by the two-thousand-revolutions-a-minute flyers, and mixed with half a ton of other meat, no odor that ever was in a ham could make any difference. There was never the least attention paid to what was cut up for sausage; there would come all the way back from Europe old sausage that had been rejected, and that was moldy and white—it would be dosed with borax and glycerine, and dumped into the hoppers, and made over again for home consumption.

—Upton Sinclair, *The Jungle* (1906)

THINKING CRITICALLY

1. **Comparing and Contrasting** State the main idea of each of these selections. What role do details play in making the passages convincing?

    SEE SKILLBUILDER HANDBOOK, PAGE R8.

2. hmhsocialstudies.com **INTERNET ACTIVITY** 🌐 **21ST CENTURY**

   Visit the links for American Literature: The Muckrakers to learn more about the muckrakers. What topics did they investigate? How did they affect public opinion? What legal changes did they help to bring about? Write a summary of the muckrakers' impact on society.

PI 1.1
CC Unit 4.I.C.3.c
CC Unit 4.I.C.4.a

Progressivism Under Taft

MAIN IDEA	WHY IT MATTERS NOW	Terms & Names
Taft's ambivalent approach to progressive reform led to a split in the Republican Party and the loss of the presidency to the Democrats.	Third-party candidates continue to wrestle with how to become viable candidates.	• Gifford Pinchot • William Howard Taft • Payne-Aldrich Tariff • Bull Moose Party • Woodrow Wilson

One American's Story

hmhsocialstudies.com
TAKING NOTES
Use the graphic organizer online to take notes about difficulties during Taft's presidency.

Early in the 20th century, Americans' interest in the preservation of the country's wilderness areas intensified. Writers proclaimed the beauty of the landscape, and new groups like the Girl Scouts gave city children the chance to experience a different environment. The desire for preservation clashed with business interests that favored unrestricted development. **Gifford Pinchot** (pĭn′shō′), head of the U.S. Forest Service under President Roosevelt, took a middle ground. He believed that wilderness areas could be scientifically managed to yield public enjoyment while allowing private development.

A PERSONAL VOICE GIFFORD PINCHOT

" The American people have evidently made up their minds that our natural resources must be conserved. That is good. But it settles only half the question. For whose benefit shall they be conserved— for the benefit of the many, or for the use and profit of the few? . . . There is no other question before us that begins to be so important, or that will be so difficult to straddle, as the great question between special interest and equal opportunity, between the privileges of the few and the rights of the many, between government by men for human welfare and government by money for profit. "

—The Fight for Conservation

▲ Gifford Pinchot

President Roosevelt, a fellow conservationist, favored Pinchot's multi-use land program. However, when he left office in 1909, this approach came under increasing pressure from business people who favored unrestricted commercial development.

Taft Becomes President

After winning the election in 1904, Roosevelt pledged not to run for reelection in 1908. He handpicked his secretary of war, **William Howard Taft,** to run against William Jennings Bryan, who had been nominated by the Democrats for the third time. Under the slogan "Vote for Taft this time, You can vote for Bryan any time," Taft and the Republicans won an easy victory.

TAFT STUMBLES As president, Taft pursued a cautiously progressive agenda, seeking to consolidate rather than to expand Roosevelt's reforms. He received little credit for his accomplishments, however. His legal victories, such as busting 90 trusts in a four-year term, did not bolster his popularity. Indeed, the new president confessed in a letter to Roosevelt that he never felt like the president. "When I am addressed as 'Mr. President,'" Taft wrote, "I turn to see whether you are not at my elbow."

The cautious Taft hesitated to use the presidential bully pulpit to arouse public opinion. Nor could he subdue troublesome members of his own party. Tariffs and conservation posed his first problems.

THE PAYNE–ALDRICH TARIFF Taft had campaigned on a platform of lowering tariffs, a staple of the progressive agenda. When the House passed the Payne Bill, which lowered rates on imported manufactured goods, the Senate proposed an alternative bill, the Aldrich Bill, which made fewer cuts and increased many rates. Amid cries of betrayal from the progressive wing of his party, Taft signed the **Payne-Aldrich Tariff,** a compromise that only moderated the high rates of the Aldrich Bill. This angered progressives who believed Taft had abandoned progressivism. The president made his difficulties worse by clumsily attempting to defend the tariff, calling it "the best [tariff] bill the Republican party ever passed."

DISPUTING PUBLIC LANDS Next, Taft angered conservationists by appointing as his secretary of the interior Richard A. Ballinger, a wealthy lawyer from Seattle. Ballinger, who disapproved of conservationist controls on western lands, removed 1 million acres of forest and mining lands from the reserved list and returned it to the public domain.

When a Department of the Interior official was fired for protesting Ballinger's actions, the fired worker published a muckraking article against Ballinger in *Collier's Weekly* magazine. Pinchot added his voice. In congressional testimony he accused Ballinger of letting commercial interests exploit the natural resources that rightfully belonged to the public. President Taft sided with Ballinger and fired Pinchot from the U.S. Forest Service. Ⓐ

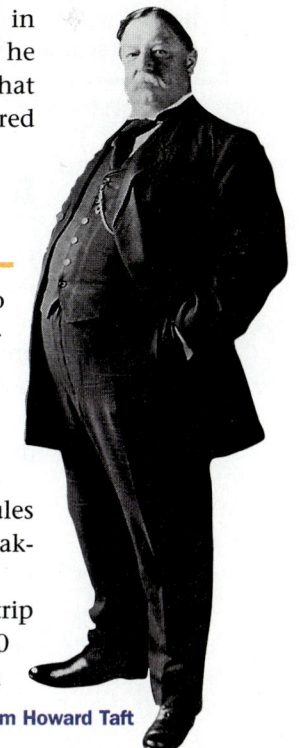

William Howard Taft

The Republican Party Splits

Taft's cautious nature made it impossible for him to hold together the two wings of the Republican Party: progressives who sought change and conservatives who did not. The Republican Party began to fragment.

PROBLEMS WITHIN THE PARTY Republican conservatives and progressives split over Taft's support of the political boss Joseph Cannon, House Speaker from Illinois. A rough-talking, tobacco-chewing politician, "Uncle Joe" often disregarded seniority in filling committee slots. As chairman of the House Rules Committee, which decides what bills Congress considers, Cannon often weakened or ignored progressive bills.

Reform-minded Republicans decided that their only alternative was to strip Cannon of his power. With the help of Democrats, they succeeded in March 1910 with a resolution that called for the entire House to elect the Committee on Rules and excluded the Speaker from membership in the committee.

MAIN IDEA

Analyzing Issues

Ⓐ How did Taft's appointee Richard Ballinger anger conservationists?

DIFFICULT DECISIONS

CONTROLLING RESOURCES

Historically, conservationists such as Gifford Pinchot have stood for the balanced use of natural resources, preserving some and using others for private industry. Free-market advocates like Richard Ballinger pressed for the private development of wilderness areas. Preservationists such as John Muir advocated preserving all remaining wilderness.

1. Examine the pros and cons of each position. With which do you agree? What factors do you think should influence decisions about America's wilderness areas?

2. If you'd been asked in 1902 to decide whether to develop or preserve America's wilderness areas, what would you have decided? Why?

KEY PLAYER

WILLIAM HOWARD TAFT
1857–1930

William Howard Taft never wanted to be president. After serving one term, Taft left the White House, which he called "the lonesomest place in the world," and taught constitutional law at Yale for eight years.

In 1921, President Harding named Taft chief justice of the Supreme Court. The man whose family had nicknamed him "Big Lub" called this appointment the highest honor he had ever received. As chief justice, Taft wrote that "in my present life I don't remember that I ever was President."

However, Americans remember Taft for, among many other things, initiating in 1910 the popular presidential custom of throwing out the first ball of the major league baseball season.

By the midterm elections of 1910, however, the Republican Party was in shambles, with the progressives on one side and the "old guard" on the other. Voters voiced concern over the rising cost of living, which they blamed on the Payne-Aldrich Tariff. They also believed Taft to be against conservation. When the Republicans lost the election, the Democrats gained control of the House of Representatives for the first time in 18 years.

THE BULL MOOSE PARTY After leaving office, Roosevelt headed to Africa to shoot big game. He returned in 1910 to a hero's welcome, and responded with a rousing speech proposing a "New Nationalism," under which the federal government would exert its power for "the welfare of the people."

By 1912, Roosevelt had decided to run for a third term as president. The primary elections showed that Republicans wanted Roosevelt, but Taft had the advantage of being the incumbent—that is, the holder of the office. At the Republican convention in June 1912, Taft supporters maneuvered to replace Roosevelt delegates with Taft delegates in a number of delegations. Republican progressives refused to vote and formed a new third party, the Progressive Party. They nominated Roosevelt for president.

The Progressive Party became known as the **Bull Moose Party**, after Roosevelt's boast that he was "as strong as a bull moose." The party's platform called for the direct election of senators and the adoption in all states of the initiative, referendum, and recall. It also advocated woman suffrage, workmen's compensation, an eight-hour workday, a minimum wage for women, a federal law against child labor, and a federal trade commission to regulate business. **B**

The split in the Republican ranks handed the Democrats their first real chance at the White House since the election of Grover Cleveland in 1892. In the 1912 presidential election, they put forward as their candidate a reform governor of New Jersey named **Woodrow Wilson**.

Vocabulary
"old guard": conservative members of a group

MAIN IDEA

Contrasting
B What were the differences between Taft's and Roosevelt's campaign platforms?

Democrats Win in 1912

Under Governor Woodrow Wilson's leadership, the previously conservative New Jersey legislature had passed a host of reform measures. Now, as the Democratic presidential nominee, Wilson endorsed a progressive platform called the New Freedom. It demanded even stronger antitrust legislation, banking reform, and reduced tariffs.

The split between Taft and Roosevelt, former Republican allies, turned nasty during the fall campaign. Taft labeled Roosevelt a "dangerous egotist," while Roosevelt branded Taft a "fathead" with the brain of a "guinea pig." Wilson distanced himself, quietly gloating, "Don't interfere when your enemy is destroying himself."

The election offered voters several choices: Wilson's New Freedom, Taft's conservatism, Roosevelt's progressivism, or the Socialist Party policies of Eugene V. Debs. Both Roosevelt and Wilson supported a stronger government role in economic affairs but differed over strategies. Roosevelt supported government action to supervise big business but did not oppose all business monopolies, while Debs called for an end to capitalism. Wilson supported small business and free-market competition and characterized all business monopolies as evil. In a speech, Wilson explained why he felt that all business monopolies were a threat.

A PERSONAL VOICE
WOODROW WILSON

" If the government is to tell big business men how to run their business, then don't you see that big business men have to get closer to the government even than they are now? Don't you see that they must capture the government, in order not to be restrained too much by it? . . . I don't care how benevolent the master is going to be, I will not live under a master. That is not what America was created for. America was created in order that every man should have the same chance as every other man to exercise mastery over his own fortunes."

—quoted in *The New Freedom*

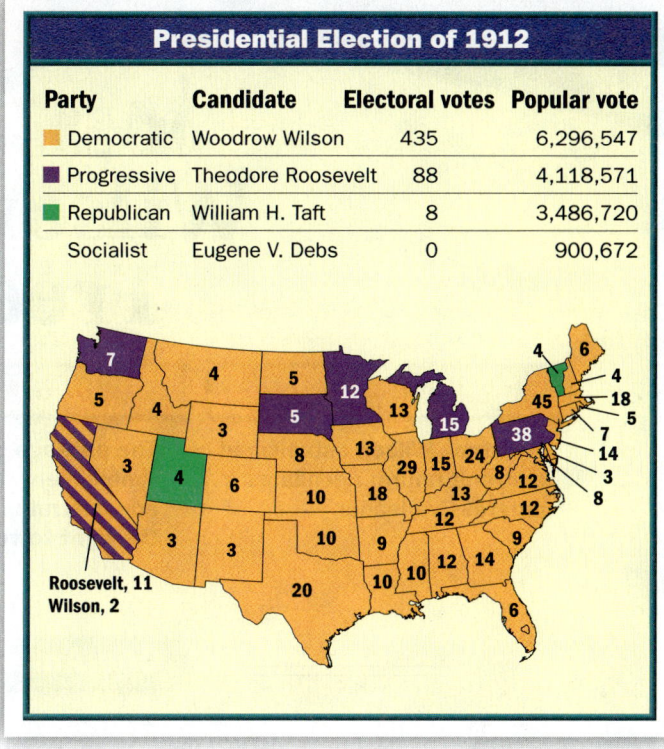

Presidential Election of 1912

Party	Candidate	Electoral votes	Popular vote
Democratic	Woodrow Wilson	435	6,296,547
Progressive	Theodore Roosevelt	88	4,118,571
Republican	William H. Taft	8	3,486,720
Socialist	Eugene V. Debs	0	900,672

Roosevelt, 11
Wilson, 2

MAIN IDEA

Predicting Effects

C What might be one of Wilson's first issues to address as president?

Although Wilson captured only 42 percent of the popular vote, he won an overwhelming electoral victory and a Democratic majority in Congress. As a third-party candidate, Roosevelt defeated Taft in both popular and electoral votes. But reform claimed the real victory, with more than 75 percent of the vote going to the reform candidates—Wilson, Roosevelt, and Debs. In victory, Wilson could claim a mandate to break up trusts and to expand the government's role in social reform. **C**

SECTION 4 ASSESSMENT

1. TERMS & NAMES For each term or name, write a sentence explaining its significance.
- **Gifford Pinchot**
- **William Howard Taft**
- **Payne-Aldrich Tariff**
- **Bull Moose Party**
- **Woodrow Wilson**

MAIN IDEA

2. TAKING NOTES
Re-create the chart below on your paper. Then fill in the causes Taft supported that made people question his leadership.

Which causes do you think would upset most people today? Explain.

CRITICAL THINKING

3. HYPOTHESIZING
What if Roosevelt had won another term in office in 1912? Speculate on how this might have affected the future of progressive reforms. Support your answer. **Think About:**
- Roosevelt's policies that Taft did not support
- the power struggles within the Republican Party
- Roosevelt's perception of what is required of a president

4. EVALUATING
Both Roosevelt and Taft resorted to mudslinging during the 1912 presidential campaign. Do you approve or disapprove of negative campaign tactics? Support your opinion.

SECTION
5

PI 1.1
PI 3.4

CC Unit 4.I.B.2.b(1)   CC Unit 4.I.C.4.b
CC Unit 4.I.C.4.c   CC Unit 4.I.C.4.d
CC Unit 4.I.C.4.e

Wilson's New Freedom

MAIN IDEA	WHY IT MATTERS NOW	Terms & Names
Woodrow Wilson established a strong reform agenda as a progressive leader.	The passage of the Nineteenth Amendment during Wilson's administration granted women the right to vote.	• Carrie Chapman Catt • Clayton Antitrust Act • Federal Trade Commission (FTC) • Federal Reserve System • Nineteenth Amendment

One American's Story

hmhsocialstudies.com
TAKING NOTES
Use the graphic organizer online to take notes about progressivism during Wilson's first term.

On March 3, 1913, the day of Woodrow Wilson's inauguration, 5,000 woman suffragists marched through hostile crowds in Washington, D.C. Alice Paul and Lucy Burns, the parade's organizers, were members of the National American Woman Suffrage Association (NAWSA). As police failed to restrain the rowdy gathering and congressmen demanded an investigation, Paul and Burns could see the momentum building for suffrage.

By the time Wilson began his campaign for a second term in 1916, the NAWSA's president, **Carrie Chapman Catt**, saw victory on the horizon. Catt expressed her optimism in a letter to her friend Maud Wood Park.

A PERSONAL VOICE CARRIE CHAPMAN CATT

" I do feel keenly that the turn of the road has come. . . . I really believe that we might pull off a campaign which would mean the vote within the next six years if we could secure a Board of officers who would have sufficient momentum, confidence and working power in them. . . . Come! My dear Mrs. Park, gird on your armor once more. "

—letter to Maud Wood Park

Carrie Chapman Catt

Catt called an emergency suffrage convention in September 1916, and invited President Wilson, who cautiously supported suffrage. He told the convention, "There has been a force behind you that will . . . be triumphant and for which you can afford. . . . to wait." They did have to wait, but within four years, the passage of the suffrage amendment became the capstone of the progressive movement.

Wilson Wins Financial Reforms

Like Theodore Roosevelt, Woodrow Wilson claimed progressive ideals, but he had a different idea for the federal government. He believed in attacking large concentrations of power to give greater freedom to average citizens. The prejudices of his Southern background, however, prevented him from using federal power to fight off attacks directed at the civil rights of African Americans.

WILSON'S BACKGROUND Wilson spent his youth in the South during the Civil War and Reconstruction. The son, grandson, and nephew of Presbyterian ministers, he received a strict upbringing. Before entering politics, Wilson worked as a lawyer, a history professor, and later as president of Princeton University. In 1910, Wilson became the governor of New Jersey. As governor, he supported progressive legislation programs such as a direct primary, worker's compensation, and the regulation of public utilities and railroads.

As America's newly elected president, Wilson moved to enact his program, the "New Freedom," and planned his attack on what he called the triple wall of privilege: the trusts, tariffs, and high finance.

TWO KEY ANTITRUST MEASURES "Without the watchful . . . resolute interference of the government," Wilson said, "there can be no fair play between individuals and such powerful institutions as the trusts. Freedom today is something more than being let alone." During Wilson's administration, Congress enacted two key antitrust measures. The first, the **Clayton Antitrust Act** of 1914, sought to strengthen the Sherman Antitrust Act of 1890. The Clayton Act prohibited corporations from acquiring the stock of another if doing so would create a monopoly; if a company violated the law, its officers could be prosecuted.

The Clayton Act also specified that labor unions and farm organizations not only had a right to exist but also would no longer be subject to antitrust laws. Therefore, strikes, peaceful picketing, boycotts, and the collection of strike benefits became legal. In addition, injunctions against strikers were prohibited unless the strikers threatened damage that could not be remedied. Samuel Gompers, president of the American Federation of Labor (AFL), saw great value to workers in the Clayton Act. He called it a Magna Carta for labor, referring to the English document, signed in 1215, in which the English king recognized that he was bound by the law and that the law granted rights to his subjects.

The second major antitrust measure, the Federal Trade Commission Act of 1914, set up the **Federal Trade Commission (FTC).** This "watchdog" agency was given the power to investigate possible violations of regulatory statutes, to require periodic reports from corporations, and to put an end to a number of unfair business practices. Under Wilson, the FTC administered almost 400 cease-and-desist orders to companies engaged in illegal activity.

MAIN IDEA

Summarizing
A What was the impact of the two antitrust measures?

A NEW TAX SYSTEM In an effort to curb the power of big business, Wilson worked to lower tariff rates, knowing that supporters of big business hadn't allowed such a reduction under Taft.

Wilson lobbied hard in 1913 for the Underwood Act, which would substantially reduce tariff rates for the first time since the Civil War. He summoned Congress to a special session to plead his case, and established a precedent of delivering the State of the Union message in person. Businesses lobbied too, looking to block tariff reductions. When manufacturing lobbyists—people hired by manufacturers to present their case to government officials—descended on the capital to urge senators to vote no, passage seemed unlikely. Wilson denounced the lobbyists and urged voters to monitor their senators' votes. Because of the new president's use of the bully pulpit, the Senate voted to cut tariff rates even more deeply than the House had done.

NOW & THEN

DEREGULATION

In recent years the railroad, airline, and telecommunications industries have all been deregulated, or permitted to compete without government control. It is hoped that this will improve their efficiency and lower prices.

During the Progressive Era, reformers viewed regulation as a necessary role of government to ensure safety and fairness for consumers as well as industrial competitors. Opponents of regulation, however, believed that government regulation caused inefficiency and high prices.

Modern critics of deregulation argue that deregulated businesses may skimp on safety. They may also neglect hard-to-serve populations, such as elderly, poor, or disabled people, while competing for more profitable customers.

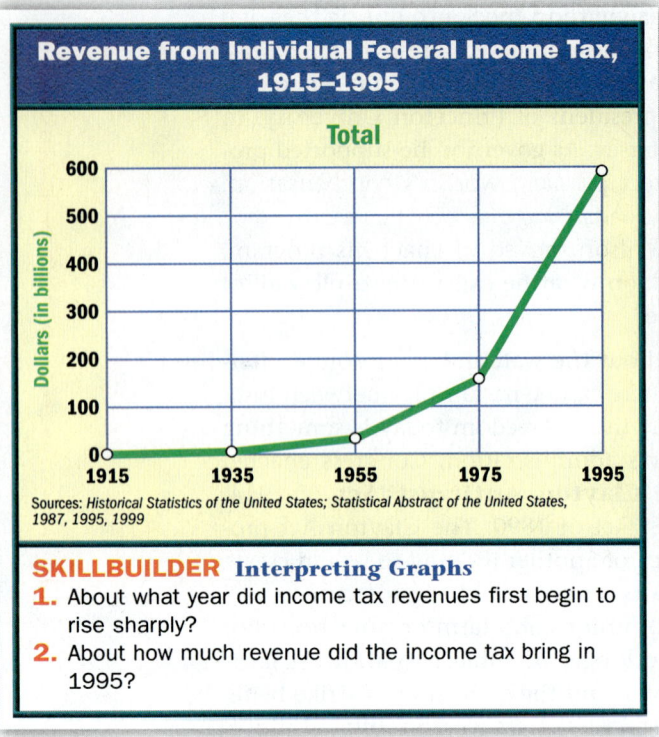

Revenue from Individual Federal Income Tax, 1915–1995

Total

Dollars (in billions)

600
500
400
300
200
100
0

1915 1935 1955 1975 1995

Sources: *Historical Statistics of the United States; Statistical Abstract of the United States, 1987, 1995, 1999*

SKILLBUILDER Interpreting Graphs
1. About what year did income tax revenues first begin to rise sharply?
2. About how much revenue did the income tax bring in 1995?

FEDERAL INCOME TAX With lower tariff rates, the federal government had to replace the revenue that tariffs had previously supplied. Ratified in 1913, the Sixteenth Amendment legalized a federal income tax, which provided revenue by taxing individual earnings and corporate profits.

Under this graduated tax, larger incomes were taxed at higher rates than smaller incomes. The tax began with a modest tax on family incomes over $4,000, and ranged from 1 percent to a maximum of 6 percent on incomes over $500,000. Initially, few congressmen realized the potential of the income tax, but by 1917, the government was receiving more money on the income tax than it had ever gained from tariffs. Today, income taxes on corporations and individuals represent the federal government's main source of revenue.

FEDERAL RESERVE SYSTEM Next, Wilson turned his attention to financial reform. The nation needed a way to strengthen the ways in which banks were run, as well as a way to quickly adjust the amount of money in circulation. Both credit availability and money supply had to keep pace with the economy.

Wilson's solution was to establish a decentralized private banking system under federal control. The Federal Reserve Act of 1913 divided the nation into 12 districts and established a regional central bank in each district. These "banker's banks" then served the other banks within the district.

The federal reserve banks could issue new paper currency in emergency situations, and member banks could use the new currency to make loans to their customers. Federal reserve banks could transfer funds to member banks in trouble, saving the banks from closing and protecting customers' savings. By 1923, roughly 70 percent of the nation's banking resources were part of the **Federal Reserve System**. One of Wilson's most enduring achievements, this system still serves as the basis of the nation's banking system. **B**

MAIN IDEA

Evaluating
B Why were tariff reform and the Federal Reserve System important?

Women Win Suffrage

While Wilson pushed hard for reform of trusts, tariffs, and banking, determined women intensified their push for the vote. The educated, native-born, middle-class women who had been active in progressive movements had grown increasingly impatient about not being allowed to vote. As of 1910, women had federal voting rights only in Wyoming, Utah, Colorado, Washington, and Idaho.

Determined suffragists pushed on, however. They finally saw success come within reach as a result of three developments: the increased activism of local groups, the use of bold new strategies to build enthusiasm for the movement, and the rebirth of the national movement under Carrie Chapman Catt.

LOCAL SUFFRAGE BATTLES The suffrage movement was given new strength by growing numbers of college-educated women. Two Massachusetts organizations, the Boston Equal Suffrage Association for Good Government and the College Equal Suffrage League, used door-to-door campaigns to reach potential supporters. Founded by Radcliffe graduate Maud Wood Park, the Boston group spread the message of suffrage to poor and working-class women. Members also took trolley tours where, at each stop, crowds would gather to watch the unusual sight of a woman speaking in public.

Many wealthy young women who visited Europe as part of their education became involved in the suffrage movement in Britain. Led by Emmeline Pankhurst, British suffragists used increasingly bold tactics, such as heckling government officials, to advance their cause. Inspired by their activism, American women returned to the United States armed with similar approaches in their own campaigns for suffrage.

CATT AND THE NATIONAL MOVEMENT Susan B. Anthony's successor as president of NAWSA was Carrie Chapman Catt, who served from 1900 to 1904 and resumed the presidency in 1915. When Catt returned to NAWSA after organizing New York's Women Suffrage Party, she concentrated on five tactics: (1) painstaking organization; (2) close ties between local, state, and national workers; (3) establishing a wide base of support; (4) cautious lobbying; and (5) gracious, ladylike behavior.

Although suffragists saw victories, the greater number of failures led some suffragists to try more radical tactics. Lucy Burns and Alice Paul formed their own more radical organization, the Congressional Union, and its successor, the National Woman's Party. They pressured the federal government to pass a suffrage amendment, and by 1917 Paul had organized her followers to mount a round-the-clock picket line around the White House. Some of the picketers were arrested, jailed, and even force-fed when they attempted a hunger strike.

These efforts, and America's involvement in World War I, finally made suffrage inevitable. Patriotic American women who headed committees, knitted socks for soldiers, and sold liberty bonds now claimed their overdue reward for supporting the war effort. In 1919, Congress passed the **Nineteenth Amendment,** granting women the right to vote. The amendment won final ratification in August 1920—72 years after women had first convened and demanded the vote at the Seneca Falls convention in 1848. **C**

WORLD STAGE

EMMELINE PANKHURST

American women struggling for suffrage received valuable tutoring from their English counterparts, whose bold maneuvers had captured media coverage.

The noted British suffragist Emmeline Pankhurst, who helped found the National Women's Social and Political Union, often engaged in radical tactics. Pankhurst and other suffragists staged parades, organized protest meetings, endured hunger strikes, heckled candidates for Parliament, and spat on policemen who tried to quiet them. They were often imprisoned for their activities, before Parliament granted them the right to vote in 1928.

The Limits of Progressivism

Despite Wilson's economic and political reforms, he disappointed Progressives who favored social reform. In particular, on racial matters Wilson appeased conservative Southern Democratic voters but disappointed his Northern white and black supporters. He placed segregationists in charge of federal agencies, thereby expanding racial segregation in the federal government, the military, and Washington, D.C.

WILSON AND CIVIL RIGHTS Like Roosevelt and Taft, Wilson retreated on civil rights once in office. During the presidential campaign of 1912, he won the support of the NAACP's black intellectuals and white liberals by promising to treat blacks equally and to speak out against lynching.

FROM SPLENDOR TO SIMPLICITY

The progressive movement, which influenced numerous aspects of society, also impacted the world of American architecture. One of the most prominent architects of the time was Frank Lloyd Wright, who studied under the renowned designer Louis Sullivan. In the spirit of progressivism, Wright sought to design buildings that were orderly, efficient, and in harmony with the world around them.

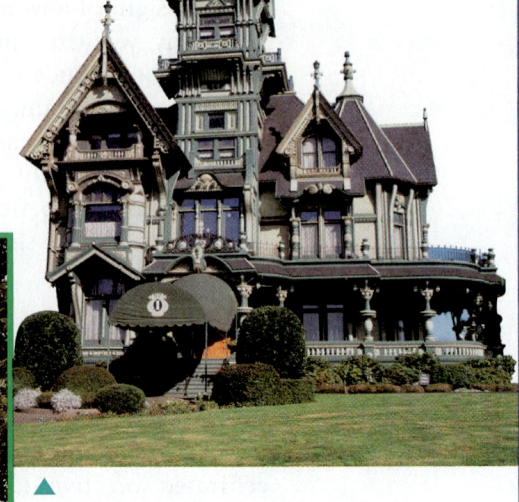

▲ Architecture of the Gilded Age featured ornate decoration and detail, as seen here in this Victorian-style house built between 1884 and 1886. Wright rejected these showy and decorative styles in favor of more simplistic designs.

▲ Wright's "prairie style" design features a low, horizontal, and well-defined structure made predominantly of wood, concrete, brick, and other simple materials. Shown here is the Robie House (1909), one of Wright's most famous prairie-style structures, which incorporates these architectural qualities.

SKILLBUILDER Interpreting Visual Sources
1. What are the most striking differences between the two houses? Cite examples that contrast the two buildings.
2. How does Wright's style reflect the progressive spirit?

 SEE SKILLBUILDER HANDBOOK, PAGE R23.

As president, however, Wilson opposed federal antilynching legislation, arguing that these crimes fell under state jurisdiction. In addition, the Capitol and the federal offices in Washington, D.C., which had been desegregated during Reconstruction, resumed the practice of segregation shortly after Wilson's election.

Wilson appointed to his cabinet fellow white Southerners who extended segregation. Secretary of the Navy Josephus Daniels, for example, proposed at a cabinet meeting to do away with common drinking fountains and towels in his department. According to an entry in Daniel's diary, President Wilson agreed because he had "made no promises in particular to negroes, except to do them justice." Segregated facilities, in the president's mind, were just.

African Americans and their liberal white supporters in the NAACP felt betrayed. Oswald Garrison Villard, a grandson of the abolitionist William Lloyd Garrison, wrote to Wilson in dismay, "The colored men who voted and worked for you in the belief that their status as American citizens was safe in your hands are deeply cast down." Wilson's response—that he had acted "in the interest of the negroes" and "with the approval of some of the most influential negroes I know"— only widened the rift between the president and some of his former supporters.

On November 12, 1914, the president's reception of an African-American delegation brought the confrontation to a bitter climax. William Monroe Trotter, editor-in-chief of the *Guardian*, an African-American Boston newspaper, led the delegation. Trotter complained that African Americans from 38 states had asked the president to reverse the segregation of government employees, but that segregation had since increased. Trotter then commented on Wilson's inaction.

★ **A PERSONAL VOICE** WILLIAM MONROE TROTTER

" Only two years ago you were heralded as perhaps the second Lincoln, and now the Afro-American leaders who supported you are hounded as false leaders and traitors to their race. . . . As equal citizens and by virtue of your public promises we are entitled at your hands to freedom from discrimination, restriction, imputation, and insult in government employ. Have you a 'new freedom' for white Americans and a new slavery for your 'Afro-American fellow citizens'? God forbid! "

—address to President Wilson, November 12, 1914

MAIN IDEA

Analyzing Effects

D What actions of Wilson disappointed civil rights advocates?

Wilson found Trotter's tone infuriating. After an angry Trotter shook his finger at the president to emphasize a point, the furious Wilson demanded that the delegation leave. Wilson's refusal to extend civil rights to African Americans pointed to the limits of progressivism under his administration. America's involvement in the war raging in Europe would soon reveal other weaknesses. **D**

THE TWILIGHT OF PROGRESSIVISM After taking office in 1913, Wilson had said, "There's no chance of progress and reform in an administration in which war plays the principal part." Yet he found that the outbreak of World War I in Europe in 1914 demanded America's involvement. Meanwhile, distracted Americans and their legislators allowed reform efforts to stall. As the pacifist and reformer Jane Addams mournfully reflected, "The spirit of fighting burns away all those impulses . . . which foster the will to justice."

International conflict was destined to be part of Wilson's presidency. During the early years of his administration, Wilson had dealt with issues of imperialism that had roots in the late 19th century. However, World War I dominated most of his second term as president. The Progressive Era had come to an end.

SECTION 5 ASSESSMENT

1. TERMS & NAMES For each term or name, write a sentence explaining its significance.
- Carrie Chapman Catt
- Clayton Antitrust Act
- Federal Trade Commission (FTC)
- Federal Reserve System
- Nineteenth Amendment

MAIN IDEA

2. TAKING NOTES
Create a time line of key events relating to Progressivism during Wilson's first term. Use the dates already plotted on the time line below as a guide.

1913   1914   1915   1916

Write a paragraph explaining which event you think best demonstrates progressive reform.

CRITICAL THINKING

3. ANALYZING PRIMARY SOURCES
Wilson said, "Without the watchful . . . resolute interference of the government, there can be no fair play between individuals and . . . the trusts." How does this statement reflect Wilson's approach to reform? Support your answer. **Think About:**
- the government's responsibility to the public
- the passage of two key antitrust measures

4. ANALYZING MOTIVES
Why do you think Wilson failed to push for equality for African Americans, despite his progressive reforms? **Think About:**
- progressive presidents before Wilson
- Wilson's background
- the primary group of people progressive reforms targeted

TERMS & NAMES

For each term or name below, write a sentence explaining its connection to the Progressive Era.

1. progressive movement
2. muckraker
3. suffrage
4. Susan B. Anthony
5. Theodore Roosevelt
6. NAACP
7. Gifford Pinchot
8. Woodrow Wilson
9. Clayton Antitrust Act
10. Federal Reserve System

MAIN IDEAS

Use your notes and the information in the chapter to answer the following questions.

The Origins of Progressivism *(pages 512–518)*

1. What were the four goals that various progressive reform movements struggled to achieve?
2. What kind of state labor laws resulted from progressives' lobbying to protect workers?
3. How did government change during the Progressive Era? How were these changes important?

Women in Public Life *(pages 519–522)*

4. In the late 1890s, what job opportunities were available to uneducated women without industrial skills?
5. Give two examples of national women's organizations committed to social activism. Briefly describe their progressive missions.

Teddy Roosevelt's Square Deal *(pages 523–531)*

6. What scandalous practices did Upton Sinclair expose in his novel *The Jungle*? How did the American public, Roosevelt, and Congress respond?
7. How did Roosevelt earn his reputation as a trust-buster?

Progressivism Under Taft *(pages 534–537)*

8. As a progressive, how did Taft compare with Roosevelt?
9. Why did the Republican Party split during Taft's administration?

Wilson's New Freedom *(pages 538–543)*

10. How did the Clayton Antitrust Act benefit labor?
11. Cite two examples of social welfare legislation that Wilson opposed during his presidency and the arguments he used to defend his position.

CRITICAL THINKING

1. **USING YOUR NOTES** Create a Venn diagram to show some of the similarities and differences between Roosevelt's Square Deal and Wilson's New Freedom.

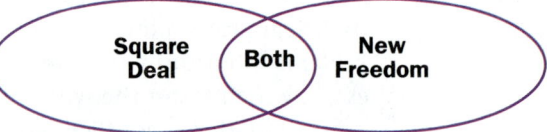

Square Deal — Both — New Freedom

2. **DEVELOPING HISTORICAL PERSPECTIVE** What social, political, and economic trends in American life do you think caused the reform impulse during the Progressive Era? Support your answer with details from the text.

VISUAL SUMMARY — THE PROGRESSIVE ERA

ECONOMIC
- Roosevelt establishes a Square Deal
- new tax system is instituted
- Roosevelt breaks up trusts

POLITICAL
- elections are reformed
- citizens given greater voice in government: recall, initiative, referendum

SOCIAL & MORAL
- women fight for the right to vote
- Eighteenth Amendment bans alcoholic beverages
- Social services for women, children, and the poor

INDUSTRY
- National Child Labor Committee organizes to end child labor
- reformers improve workplace conditions and set maximum working hours

PROGRESSIVISM

HEALTH & ENVIRONMENT
- conservationists establish wilderness conservation areas and preserve natural resources
- Pure Food and Drug Act protects consumers

Use the quotation and your knowledge of U.S. history to answer question 1.

> "Labor began to organize itself in Trade Unions and to confront the industrialists with a stiff bargaining power. These developments were to lead to a period of protest and reform in the early twentieth century. The gains conferred by large-scale industry were great and lasting, but the wrongs that had accompanied their making were only gradually righted."
>
> —Winston Churchill, *The Great Republic: A History of America*

1 In the passage, Winston Churchill attempts to explain what prompted Progressive Era reformers. The passage explains the actions of which of the following labor reform leaders?

(1) Maria Mitchell
(2) Carry Nation
(3) Susan B. Anthony
(4) Florence Kelley

2 The muckrakers served Progressivism by —

(1) informing people about abuses so that they could protest.
(2) enacting legislation to prevent political corruption.
(3) cleaning up unhealthy meat processing plants.
(4) filing and prosecuting antitrust lawsuits.

3 In the presidential election of 1912, three candidates attempted to win the liberal, progressive vote. Which candidate for president in 1912 ran on a conservative platform?

(1) Woodrow Wilson
(2) William Taft
(3) Theodore Roosevelt
(4) Eugene V. Debs

hmhsocialstudies.com **TEST PRACTICE**

For additional test practice, go online for:
• Diagnostic tests   • Tutorials

INTERACT WITH HISTORY

Think about the issues you explored at the beginning of the chapter. As a class, discuss what progressive reformers did to bring about changes in government and society. Consider what else they might have done to be more effective. Rank their efforts in order of effectiveness and offer suggestions for improvement.

FOCUS ON WRITING

Conservation of natural resources became a focus of federal attention in the early 1900s. Write an explanation of the two different perspectives on conservation advocated by Gifford Pinchot and John Muir. Then decide which position you agree with and explain why.

COLLABORATIVE LEARNING

21ST CENTURY

Imagine you are a reporter covering a 1912 congressional hearing investigating labor conditions in a textile mill. Work with a partner to write two newspaper articles—one that shows bias in favor of the mill workers, and one that shows bias in favor of the mill. Share the articles with the class and analyze how language can affect the reporting of information.

CHAPTER 18

AMERICA CLAIMS AN EMPIRE

Essential Question

Which individuals and events moved the United States into the role of a world power?

New York Standards

KEY IDEA 3 Study about the major social, political, economic, cultural, and religious developments in New York State and United States history involves learning about the important roles and contributions of individuals and groups.

KEY IDEA 4 The skills of historical analysis include the ability to: explain the significance of historical evidence; weigh the importance, reliability, and validity of evidence; understand the concept of multiple causation; understand the importance of changing and competing interpretations of different historical developments.

This lithograph of Roosevelt leading the Rough Riders at San Juan Hill shows the men on horseback, although they actually fought on foot.

1893 Business groups, aided by U.S. marines, overthrow Hawaii's Queen Liliuokalani.

1898 *U.S.S. Maine* explodes and sinks. The Spanish-American War begins.

1901 Theodore Roosevelt becomes president after McKinley is assassinated.

USA

1890

1900

WORLD

1895 Guglielmo Marconi develops the technology that led to the modern radio.

1898 Marie Curie discovers radium.

1900 In China, the Boxers rebel.

1903 Panama declares its independence from Colombia.

INTERACT
WITH HISTORY

In the late 1890s, American newspapers are running sensational stories about Spain's harsh rule of Cuba. Such articles anger Americans. Among those willing to fight for Cuba's freedom are a group of volunteers, the Rough Riders. Led by future president Theodore Roosevelt, the Rough Riders become a model for others to follow.

Explore the Issues

- When should the U.S. intervene in the affairs of another country?

- In what ways do dramatic headlines influence American opinion?

1908 William Howard Taft is elected president.

1912 Woodrow Wilson is elected president.

1914 The Panama Canal opens.

1917 Puerto Ricans become U.S. citizens.

1917 The United States enters World War I.

1910

1920

1910 The Mexican Revolution begins.

1914 World War I begins in Europe.

1917 Mexico revises and adopts its constitution.

WAKE UP, AMERICA!

CIVILIZATION CALLS
EVERY MAN WOMAN AND CHILD!

America Claims an Empire **547**

PI 3.4

CC Unit 1.I.B.3   CC Unit 3.II.A.2.d
CC Unit 4.II.A.1.a(2)   CC Unit 4.II.A.2.b

Imperialism and America

MAIN IDEA	WHY IT MATTERS NOW	Terms & Names
Beginning in 1867 and continuing through the century, global competition caused the United States to expand.	During this time period, the United States acquired Hawaii and Alaska, both of which became states in 1959.	• Queen Liliuokalani • imperialism • Alfred T. Mahan • William Seward • Pearl Harbor • Sanford B. Dole

One American's Story

hmhsocialstudies.com
TAKING NOTES

Use the graphic organizer online to take notes on events and concepts that illustrate the roots of imperialism.

In 1893 **Queen Liliuokalani** (lə-lē′ə-ō-kə-lä′nē) realized that her reign in Hawaii had come to an end. More than 160 U.S. sailors and marines stood ready to aid the *haoles* (white foreigners) who planned to overthrow the Hawaiian monarchy. In an eloquent statement of protest, the proud monarch surrendered to the superior force of the United States.

★ **A PERSONAL VOICE** QUEEN LILIUOKALANI

" I, Liliuokalani, . . . do hereby solemnly protest against any and all acts done against myself and the constitutional government of the Hawaiian Kingdom. . . . Now, to avoid any collision of armed forces and perhaps the loss of life, I do under this protest . . . yield my authority until such time as the Government of the United States shall . . . undo the action of its representatives and reinstate me in the authority which I claim as the constitutional sovereign of the Hawaiian Islands. "

—quoted in *Those Kings and Queens of Old Hawaii*

▲ Hawaii's "Queen Lil" announced that if restored to power, she would behead those who had conspired to depose her.

U.S. ambassador to Hawaii John L. Stevens informed the State Department, "The Hawaiian pear is now fully ripe, and this is the golden hour for the United States to pluck it." The annexation of Hawaii was only one of the goals of America's empire builders in the late 19th century.

American Expansionism

Americans had always sought to expand the size of their nation, and throughout the 19th century they extended their control toward the Pacific Ocean. However, by the 1880s, many American leaders had become convinced that the United States should join the imperialist powers of Europe and establish colonies overseas. **Imperialism**—the policy in which stronger nations extend their economic, political, or military control over weaker territories—was already a trend around the world.

GLOBAL COMPETITION European nations had been establishing colonies for centuries. In the late 19th century Africa had emerged as a prime target of European expansionism. By the early 20th century, only two countries in all of Africa—Ethiopia and Liberia—remained independent. **Ⓐ**

Imperialists also competed for territory in Asia, especially in China. In its late-19th-century reform era, Japan replaced its old feudal order with a strong central government. Hoping that military strength would bolster industrialization, Japan joined European nations in competition for China in the 1890s.

Most Americans gradually warmed to the idea of expansion overseas. With a belief in manifest destiny, they already had pushed the U.S. border to the Pacific Ocean. Three factors fueled the new American imperialism:

- desire for military strength
- thirst for new markets
- belief in cultural superiority

DESIRE FOR MILITARY STRENGTH Seeing that other nations were establishing a global military presence, American leaders advised that the United States build up its own military strength. One such leader was Admiral **Alfred T. Mahan** of the U.S. Navy. Mahan urged government officials to build up American naval power in order to compete with other powerful nations. As a result of the urging of Mahan and others, the United States built nine steel-hulled cruisers between 1883 and 1890. The construction of modern battleships such as the *Maine* and the *Oregon* transformed the country into the world's third largest naval power.

THIRST FOR NEW MARKETS In the late 19th century, advances in technology enabled American farms and factories to produce far more than American citizens could consume. Now the United States needed raw materials for its factories and new markets for its agricultural and manufactured goods. Imperialists viewed foreign trade as the solution to American overproduction and the related problems of unemployment and economic depression.

KEY PLAYER

**ADMIRAL ALFRED T. MAHAN
1840–1914**

Alfred T. Mahan joined the U.S. Navy in the late 1850s and served for nearly forty years. In 1886, he became president of the newly established Naval War College in Newport, Rhode Island.

Throughout his lifetime, Mahan was one of the most outspoken advocates of American military expansion. In his book *The Influence of Sea Power upon History, 1660–1783* (published in 1890), Mahan called for the United States to develop a modern fleet capable of protecting American business and shipping interests around the world. He also urged the United States to establish naval bases in the Caribbean, to construct a canal across the Isthmus of Panama, and to acquire Hawaii and other Pacific islands.

In the early 1900s, the Navy's Great White Fleet, so named because its ships were painted white, was a sign of America's growing military power. ▶

BELIEF IN CULTURAL SUPERIORITY Cultural factors also were used to justify imperialism. Some Americans combined the philosophy of Social Darwinism—a belief that free-market competition would lead to the survival of the fittest—with a belief in the racial superiority of Anglo-Saxons. They argued that the United States had a responsibility to spread Christianity and "civilization" to the world's "inferior peoples." This viewpoint narrowly defined "civilization" according to the standards of only one culture.

The United States Acquires Alaska

An early supporter of American expansion was **William Seward,** Secretary of State under presidents Abraham Lincoln and Andrew Johnson. In 1867, Seward arranged for the U.S. to buy Alaska from the Russians for $7.2 million. Seward had some trouble persuading the House of Representatives to approve funding for the purchase. Some people thought it was silly to buy what they called "Seward's Icebox" or "Seward's folly." Time showed how wrong they were. In 1959, Alaska became a state. For about two cents an acre, the United States had acquired a land rich in timber, minerals, and, as it turned out, oil. **B**

MAIN IDEA

Developing Historical Perspective
B How did time prove that the purchase of Alaska was not an act of folly?

The United States Takes Hawaii

In 1867, the same year in which Alaska was purchased, the United States took over the Midway Islands, which lie in the Pacific Ocean about 1300 miles north of Hawaii. No one lived on the islands, so the event did not attract much attention.

Hawaii was another question. The Hawaiian Islands had been economically important to the United States for nearly a century. Since the 1790s, American merchants had stopped there on their way to China and East India. In the 1820s, Yankee missionaries founded Christian schools and churches on the islands. Their children and grandchildren became sugar planters who sold most of their crop to the United States.

THE CRY FOR ANNEXATION In the mid-19th century, American-owned sugar plantations accounted for about three-quarters of the islands' wealth. Plantation owners imported thousands of laborers from Japan, Portugal, and China. By 1900, foreigners and immigrant laborers outnumbered native Hawaiians about three to one.

White planters profited from close ties with the United States. In 1875, the United States agreed to import Hawaiian sugar duty-free. Over the next 15 years, Hawaiian sugar production increased nine times. Then the McKinley Tariff of 1890 provoked a crisis by eliminating the duty-free status of Hawaiian sugar. As a result, Hawaiian sugar growers faced competition in the American market. American planters in Hawaii called for the United States to annex the islands so they wouldn't have to pay the duty.

U.S. military and economic leaders already understood the value of the islands. In 1887, they pressured Hawaii to allow the United States to build a naval base at **Pearl Harbor,** the kingdom's best port. The base became a refueling station for American ships.

Vocabulary
annex: to incorporate territory into an existing country or state

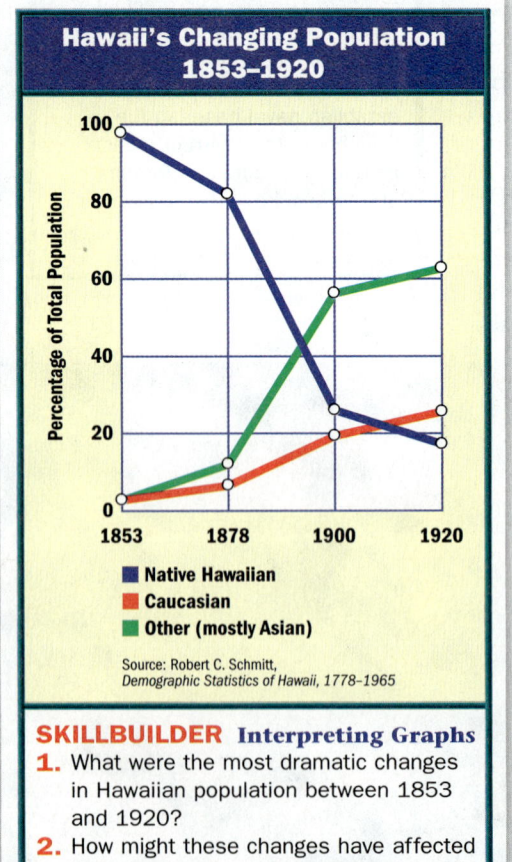

Hawaii's Changing Population 1853–1920

Percentage of Total Population

1853   1878   1900   1920

■ Native Hawaiian
■ Caucasian
■ Other (mostly Asian)

Source: Robert C. Schmitt, *Demographic Statistics of Hawaii, 1778–1965*

SKILLBUILDER Interpreting Graphs
1. What were the most dramatic changes in Hawaiian population between 1853 and 1920?
2. How might these changes have affected the political climate there?

THE END OF A MONARCHY Also in that year, Hawaii's King Kalakaua had been strong-armed by white business leaders. They forced him to amend Hawaii's constitution, effectively limiting voting rights to only wealthy land-owners. But when Kalakaua died in 1891, his sister Queen Liliuokalani came to power with a "Hawaii for Hawaiians" agenda. She proposed removing the property-owning qualifications for voting. To prevent this from happening, business groups—encouraged by Ambassador John L. Stevens—organized a revolution. With the help of marines, they overthrew the queen and set up a government headed by **Sanford B. Dole.**

President Cleveland directed that the queen be restored to her throne. When Dole refused to surrender power, Cleveland formally recognized the Republic of Hawaii. But he refused to consider annexation unless a majority of Hawaiians favored it.

In 1897, William McKinley, who favored annexation, succeeded Cleveland as president. On August 12, 1898, Congress proclaimed Hawaii an American territory, although Hawaiians had never had the chance to vote. In 1959, Hawaii became the 50th state of the United States. **C**

MAIN IDEA

Analyzing Events

C What factors led to the annexation of Hawaii in 1898?

Alaska, 1867, and Hawaii, 1898

United States and its possessions

0   800   1,600 miles
0   800   1,600 kilometers

GEOGRAPHY SKILLBUILDER

1. **Location** Where do the Hawaiian Islands lie in relation to the United States?
2. **Human-Environment Interaction** Given their geographic location, why were Hawaii and Alaska of value to the United States?

SECTION 1 ASSESSMENT

1. TERMS & NAMES For each term or name, write a sentence explaining its significance.

- Queen Liliuokalani
- imperialism
- Alfred T. Mahan
- William Seward
- Pearl Harbor
- Sanford B. Dole

MAIN IDEA

2. TAKING NOTES
Copy this web on your paper and fill it in with events and concepts that illustrate the roots of imperialism.

Political

Roots of U.S. Imperialism

Economic   Cultural

Choose one event to explain further in a paragraph.

CRITICAL THINKING

3. DRAWING CONCLUSIONS
Manifest destiny greatly influenced American policy during the first half of the 19th century. How do you think manifest destiny set the stage for American imperialism at the end of the century?

4. EVALUATING
In your opinion, did Sanford B. Dole and other American planters have the right to stage a revolt in Hawaii in 1893? **Think About:**

- American business interests in Hawaii
- the rights of native Hawaiians

5. ANALYZING PRIMARY SOURCES
In the following passage, how does Indiana Senator Albert J. Beveridge explain the need for the U.S. to acquire new territories?

"**Fate has written our policy for us; the trade of the world must and shall be ours. . . . We will establish trading posts throughout the world as distributing points for American products. . . Great colonies govern-ing themselves, flying our flag and trading with us, will grow about our posts of trade.**"

—quoted in *Beveridge and the Progressive Era*

CC Unit 1.I.B.4   CC Unit 4.II.A.1.a(2)
CC Unit 4.II.A.3.a   CC Unit 4.II.A.3.b(1)
PI 4.1   CC Unit 4.II.A.3.b(2)

The Spanish-American War

MAIN IDEA	WHY IT MATTERS NOW	Terms & Names
In 1898, the United States went to war to help Cuba win its independence from Spain.	U.S. involvement in Latin America and Asia increased greatly as a result of the war and continues today.	• José Martí • George Dewey • Valeriano Weyler • Rough Riders • yellow journalism • San Juan Hill • *U.S.S. Maine* • Treaty of Paris

One American's Story

hmhsocialstudies.com
TAKING NOTES

Use the graphic organizer online to take notes on the pros and cons of annexing the Philippines.

Early in 1896, James Creelman traveled to Cuba as a *New York World* reporter, covering the second Cuban war for independence from Spain. While in Havana, he wrote columns about his observations of the war. His descriptions of Spanish atrocities aroused American sympathy for Cubans.

★ **A PERSONAL VOICE** JAMES CREELMAN

" No man's life, no man's property is safe [in Cuba]. American citizens are imprisoned or slain without cause. American property is destroyed on all sides. . . . Wounded soldiers can be found begging in the streets of Havana. . . . The horrors of a barbarous struggle for the extermination of the native population are witnessed in all parts of the country. Blood on the roadsides, blood in the fields, blood on the doorsteps, blood, blood, blood! . . . Is there no nation wise enough, brave enough to aid this blood-smitten land? "

—*New York World*, May 17, 1896

Newspapers during that period often exaggerated stories like Creelman's to boost their sales as well as to provoke American intervention in Cuba.

▲ Cuban rebels burn the town of Jaruco in March 1896.

Cubans Rebel Against Spain

By the end of the 19th century, Spain—once the most powerful colonial nation on earth—had lost most of its colonies. It retained only the Philippines and the island of Guam in the Pacific, a few outposts in Africa, and the Caribbean islands of Cuba and Puerto Rico in the Americas.

AMERICAN INTEREST IN CUBA The United States had long held an interest in Cuba, which lies only 90 miles south of Florida. In 1854, diplomats recommended to President Franklin Pierce that the United States buy Cuba from Spain. The Spanish responded by saying that they would rather see Cuba sunk in the ocean.

But American interest in Cuba continued. When the Cubans rebelled against Spain between 1868 and 1878, American sympathies went out to the Cuban people.

The Cuban revolt against Spain was not successful, but in 1886 the Cuban people did force Spain to abolish slavery. After the emancipation of Cuba's slaves, American capitalists began investing millions of dollars in large sugar cane plantations on the island.

THE SECOND WAR FOR INDEPENDENCE Anti-Spanish sentiment in Cuba soon erupted into a second war for independence. **José Martí,** a Cuban poet and journalist in exile in New York, launched a revolution in 1895. Martí organized Cuban resistance against Spain, using an active guerrilla campaign and deliberately destroying property, especially American-owned sugar mills and plantations. Martí counted on provoking U.S. intervention to help the rebels achieve *Cuba Libre!*—a free Cuba.

Public opinion in the United States was split. Many business people wanted the government to support Spain in order to protect their investments. Other Americans, however, were enthusiastic about the rebel cause. The cry "Cuba Libre!" was, after all, similar in sentiment to Patrick Henry's "Give me liberty or give me death!" **(A)**

War Fever Escalates

In 1896, Spain responded to the Cuban revolt by sending General **Valeriano Weyler** to Cuba to restore order. Weyler tried to crush the rebellion by herding the entire rural population of central and western Cuba into barbed-wire concentration camps. Here civilians could not give aid to rebels. An estimated 300,000 Cubans filled these camps, where thousands died from hunger and disease.

HEADLINE WARS Weyler's actions fueled a war over newspaper circulation that had developed between the American newspaper tycoons William Randolph Hearst and Joseph Pulitzer. To lure readers, Hearst's *New York Journal* and Pulitzer's *New York World* printed exaggerated accounts—by reporters such as James Creelman—of "Butcher" Weyler's brutality. Stories of poisoned wells and of children being thrown to the sharks deepened American sympathy for the rebels. This sensational style of writing, which exaggerates the news to lure and enrage readers, became known as **yellow journalism.**

Hearst and Pulitzer fanned war fever. When Hearst sent the gifted artist Frederic Remington to Cuba to draw sketches of reporters' stories, Remington informed the publisher that a war between the United States and Spain seemed very unlikely. Hearst reportedly replied, "You furnish the pictures and I'll furnish the war."

THE DE LÔME LETTER American sympathy for "Cuba Libre!" grew with each day's headlines. When President William McKinley took office in 1897, demands for American intervention in Cuba were on the rise. Preferring to avoid war with Spain, McKinley tried diplomatic means to resolve the crisis. At first, his efforts appeared to succeed. Spain recalled General Weyler, modified the policy regarding concentration camps, and offered Cuba limited self-government.

Vocabulary
guerrilla: a member of a military force that harasses the enemy

MAIN IDEA

Analyzing Motives

(A) Why did José Martí encourage Cuban rebels to destroy sugar mills and plantations?

KEY PLAYER

JOSÉ MARTÍ
1853–1895

The Cuban political activist José Martí dedicated his life to achieving independence for Cuba. Expelled from Cuba at the age of 16 because of his revolutionary activities, Martí earned a master's degree and a law degree. He eventually settled in the United States.

Wary of the U.S. role in the Cuban struggle against the Spanish, Martí warned, "I know the Monster, because I have lived in its lair." His fears of U.S. imperialism turned out to have been well-founded. U.S. troops occupied Cuba on and off from 1906 until 1922.

Martí died fighting for Cuban independence in 1895. He is revered today in Cuba as a hero and martyr.

In February 1898, however, the *New York Journal* published a private letter written by Enrique Dupuy de Lôme, the Spanish minister to the United States. A Cuban rebel had stolen the letter from a Havana post office and leaked it to the newspaper, which was thirsty for scandal. The de Lôme letter criticized President McKinley, calling him "weak" and "a bidder for the admiration of the crowd." The embarrassed Spanish government apologized, and the minister resigned. Still, Americans were angry over the insult to their president.

THE *U.S.S. MAINE* EXPLODES Only a few days after the publication of the de Lôme letter, American resentment toward Spain turned to outrage. Early in 1898, President McKinley had ordered the ***U.S.S. Maine*** to Cuba to bring home American citizens in danger from the fighting and to protect American property. On February 15, 1898, the ship blew up in the harbor of Havana. More than 260 men were killed.

At the time, no one really knew why the ship exploded; however, American newspapers claimed that the Spanish had blown up the ship. The *Journal*'s headline read "The warship *Maine* was split in two by an enemy's secret infernal machine." Hearst's paper offered a reward of $50,000 for the capture of the Spaniards who supposedly had committed the outrage. **B**

MAIN IDEA

Summarizing
B What events increased the tension between the United States and Spain?

War with Spain Erupts

Now there was no holding back the forces that wanted war. "Remember the *Maine!*" became the rallying cry for U.S. intervention in Cuba. It made no difference that the Spanish government agreed, on April 9, to almost everything the United States demanded, including a six-month cease-fire.

▲ When the *U.S.S. Maine* exploded in the harbor of Havana, newspapers like the *New York Journal* were quick to place the blame on Spain.

The Spanish-American War, 1898

War in the Caribbean

FLORIDA
Tampa
ATLANTIC OCEAN
BAHAMAS (Br.)
Shafter June 22–July 1, 1898
Tropic of Cancer
Havana
CUBA
Schley
Santiago
Sampson
HAITI
DOMINICAN REPUBLIC
JAMAICA (Br.)
Cervera May, 1898
Miles July 25–Aug. 13, 1898
PUERTO RICO
Caribbean Sea
15°N

U.S. Forces
U.S. Naval Blockade
Spanish Forces
Battle

0   100   300 miles
0   100   300 kilometers

War in the Philippines

Hong Kong
20°N
Dewey Apr 25–May 1, 1898
PACIFIC OCEAN
Luzon
Manila
Philippine Islands
Mindoro
Samar
South China Sea
10°N
Panay
Negros
Palawan
Mindanao

U.S. Forces
Battle

0   100   200 miles
0   100   200 kilometers

GEOGRAPHY SKILLBUILDER
1. Location Where does Cuba lie in relation to the United States?
2. Location Look at the location of the Philippines. How does the map help explain why Spain was surprised by the American attack in the Philippines?

MAIN IDEA

Analyzing Events

C How did the Spanish try to avoid war with the United States?

Despite the Spanish concessions, public opinion favored war. On April 11, McKinley asked Congress for authority to use force against Spain. After a week of debate, Congress agreed, and on April 20 the United States declared war. **C**

THE WAR IN THE PHILIPPINES The Spanish thought the Americans would invade Cuba. But the first battle of the war took place in a Spanish colony on the other side of the world—the Philippine Islands.

On April 30, the American fleet in the Pacific steamed to the Philippines. The next morning, Commodore **George Dewey** gave the command to open fire on the Spanish fleet at Manila, the Philippine capital. Within hours, Dewey's men had destroyed every Spanish ship there. Dewey's victory allowed U.S. troops to land in the Philippines.

Dewey had the support of the Filipinos who, like the Cubans, also wanted freedom from Spain. Over the next two months, 11,000 Americans joined forces with Filipino rebels led by Emilio Aguinaldo. In August, Spanish troops in Manila surrendered to the United States.

THE WAR IN THE CARIBBEAN In the Caribbean, hostilities began with a naval blockade of Cuba. Admiral William T. Sampson effectively sealed up the Spanish fleet in the harbor of Santiago de Cuba.

Dewey's victory at Manila had demonstrated the superiority of United States naval forces. In contrast, the army maintained only a small professional force, supplemented by a larger inexperienced and ill-prepared volunteer force. About

125,000 Americans had volunteered to fight. The new soldiers were sent to training camps that lacked adequate supplies and effective leaders. Moreover, there were not enough modern guns to go around, and the troops were outfitted with heavy woolen uniforms unsuitable for Cuba's tropical climate. In addition, the officers—most of whom were Civil War veterans—had a tendency to spend their time recalling their war experiences rather than training the volunteers.

ROUGH RIDERS Despite these handicaps, American forces landed in Cuba in June 1898 and began to converge on the port city of Santiago. The army of 17,000 included four African-American regiments of the regular army and the **Rough Riders,** a volunteer cavalry under the command of Leonard Wood and Theodore Roosevelt. Roosevelt, a New Yorker, had given up his job as Assistant Secretary of the Navy to lead the group of volunteers. He would later become president of the United States.

Background
The Rough Riders trained as cavalry but fought on foot because their horses didn't reach Cuba in time.

The most famous land battle in Cuba took place near Santiago on July 1. The first part of the battle, on nearby Kettle Hill, featured a dramatic uphill charge by the Rough Riders and two African-American regiments, the Ninth and Tenth Cavalries. Their victory cleared the way for an infantry attack on the strategically important **San Juan Hill.** Although Roosevelt and his units played only a minor role in the second victory, U.S. newspapers declared him the hero of San Juan Hill.

Two days later, the Spanish fleet tried to escape the American blockade of the harbor at Santiago. The naval battle that followed, along the Cuban coast, ended in the destruction of the Spanish fleet. On the heels of this victory, American troops invaded Puerto Rico on July 25.

TREATY OF PARIS The United States and Spain signed an armistice, a cease-fire agreement, on August 12, ending what Secretary of State John Hay called "a splendid little war." The actual fighting in the war had lasted only 15 weeks.

On December 10, 1898, the United States and Spain met in Paris to agree on a treaty. At the peace talks, Spain freed Cuba and turned over the islands of Guam in the Pacific and Puerto Rico in the West Indies to the United States. Spain also sold the Philippines to the United States for $20 million. **D**

▲ These African-American troops prepare for battle during the Spanish-American War.

DEBATE OVER THE TREATY The **Treaty of Paris** touched off a great debate in the United States. Arguments centered on whether or not the United States had the right to annex the Philippines, but imperialism was the real issue. President McKinley told a group of Methodist ministers that he had prayed for guidance on Philippine annexation and had concluded "that there was nothing left for us to do but to take them all [the Philippine Islands], and to educate the Filipinos, and uplift and Christianize them." McKinley's need to justify imperialism may

MAIN IDEA

Summarizing
D What were the terms of the Treaty of Paris?

have clouded his memory—most Filipinos had been Christian for centuries.

Other prominent Americans presented a variety of arguments—political, moral, and economic—against annexation. Some felt that the treaty violated the Declaration of Independence by denying self-government to the newly acquired territories. The African-American educator Booker T. Washington argued that the United States should settle race-related issues at home before taking on social problems elsewhere. The labor leader Samuel Gompers feared that Filipino immigrants would compete for American jobs.

On February 6, 1899, the annexation question was settled with the Senate's approval of the Treaty of Paris. The United States now had an empire that included Guam, Puerto Rico, and the Philippines. The next question Americans faced was how and when the United States would add to its dominion.

COASTING.

▲ This lithograph criticizes American foreign policy in 1898. In the cartoon, Uncle Sam is riding a bicycle with wheels labeled "western hemisphere" and "eastern hemisphere." He has abandoned his horse, on whose saddle appears "Monroe Doctrine," because the horse is too slow.

SECTION 2 ASSESSMENT

1. TERMS & NAMES For each term or name, write a sentence explaining its significance.

- José Martí
- Valeriano Weyler
- yellow journalism
- *U.S.S. Maine*
- George Dewey
- Rough Riders
- San Juan Hill
- Treaty of Paris

MAIN IDEA

2. TAKING NOTES
In 1898, a debate raged in the United States over whether the U.S. had the right to annex the Philippines. Use a graphic organizer like the one below to summarize the pros and cons of this debate.

```
      The Annexation of
      the Philippines
        /         \
Reasons in Favor   Reasons Against
of Annexation       Annexation
```

Which side do you support? Why?

CRITICAL THINKING

3. MAKING INFERENCES
What do you think were the unstated editorial policies of yellow journalism? Support your answer with evidence from the text.

Think About:
- James Creelman's account of Spanish atrocities against Cubans (page 552)
- Hearst's remark to Remington
- the *Journal* headline about the explosion of the battleship *Maine*

4. ANALYZING EFFECTS
Many anti-imperialists worried that imperialism might threaten the American democratic system. How might this happen?

5. DRAWING CONCLUSIONS
In 1898 Theodore Roosevelt resigned his post as Assistant Secretary of the Navy to organize the Rough Riders. Why do you think Roosevelt was willing to take this risk? How do you think this decision affected his political career?

SECTION
3

PI 3.4
PI 4.3

CC Unit 4.II.A.1.a(2)   CC Unit 4.II.A.1.b
CC Unit 4.II.A.2.a   CC Unit 4.II.A.2.b
CC Unit 4.II.A.2.d   CC Unit 4.II.A.3.b(3)

Acquiring New Lands

MAIN IDEA	WHY IT MATTERS NOW	Terms & Names
In the early 1900s, the United States engaged in conflicts in Puerto Rico, Cuba, and the Philippines.	Today, the United States maintains a strong military and political presence in strategic worldwide locations.	• Foraker Act • John Hay • Platt Amendment • Open Door notes • protectorate • Boxer Rebellion • Emilio Aguinaldo

One American's Story

hmhsocialstudies.com
TAKING NOTES
Use the graphic organizer online to take notes on key events relating to U.S. relations with Cuba, Puerto Rico, and the Philippines.

When Puerto Rico became part of the United States after the Spanish-American War, many Puerto Ricans feared that the United States would not give them the measure of self-rule that they had gained under the Spanish. Puerto Rican statesman and publisher Luis Muñoz Rivera was one of the most vocal advocates of Puerto Rican self-rule. Between 1900 and 1916, he lived primarily in the United States and continually worked for the independence of his homeland. Finally, in 1916, the U.S. Congress, facing possible war in Europe and wishing to settle the issue of Puerto Rico, invited Muñoz Rivera to speak. On May 5, 1916, Muñoz Rivera stood before the U.S. House of Representatives to discuss the future of Puerto Rico.

▲ **Luis Muñoz Rivera**

A PERSONAL VOICE LUIS MUÑOZ RIVERA

" You, citizens of a free fatherland, with its own laws, its own institutions, and its own flag, can appreciate the unhappiness of the small and solitary people that must await its laws from your authority. . . . when you acquire the certainty that you can found in Puerto Rico a republic like that founded in Cuba and Panama . . . give us our independence and you will stand before humanity as . . . a great creator of new nationalities and a great liberator of oppressed peoples. "

—quoted in *The Puerto Ricans*

Muñoz Rivera returned to Puerto Rico where he died in November 1916. Three months later, the United States made Puerto Ricans U.S. citizens.

Ruling Puerto Rico

Not all Puerto Ricans wanted independence, as Muñoz Rivera did. Some wanted statehood, while still others hoped for some measure of local self-government as an American territory. As a result, the United States gave Puerto Ricans no promises regarding independence after the Spanish-American War.

MILITARY RULE During the Spanish-American War, United States forces, under General Nelson A. Miles, occupied the island. As his soldiers took control, General Miles issued a statement assuring Puerto Ricans that the Americans were there to "bring you protection, not only to yourselves but to your property, to promote your prosperity, and to bestow upon you the immunities and blessings of the liberal institutions of our government." For the time being, Puerto Rico would be controlled by the military until Congress decided otherwise.

RETURN TO CIVIL GOVERNMENT Although many Puerto Ricans had dreams of independence or statehood, the United States had different plans for the island's future. Puerto Rico was strategically important to the United States, both for maintaining a U.S. presence in the Caribbean and for protecting a future canal that American leaders wanted to build across the Isthmus of Panama. In 1900, Congress passed the **Foraker Act,** which ended military rule and set up a civil government. The act gave the president of the United States the power to appoint Puerto Rico's governor and members of the upper house of its legislature. Puerto Ricans could elect only the members of the legislature's lower house. **A**

In 1901, in the Insular Cases, the U.S. Supreme Court ruled that the Constitution did not automatically apply to people in acquired territories. Congress, however, retained the right to extend U.S. citizenship, and it granted that right to Puerto Ricans in 1917. It also gave them the right to elect both houses of their legislature.

MAIN IDEA

Analyzing Issues

A Why was Puerto Rico important to the United States?

NOW & THEN

PUERTO RICO

Ever since their transfer under the Treaty of Paris from Spain to the United States, Puerto Ricans have debated their status, as shown above. In 1967, 1993, and 1998, Puerto Ricans rejected both statehood and independence in favor of commonwealth, a status given the island in 1952.

As members of a commonwealth, Puerto Ricans are U.S. citizens. They can move freely between the island and the mainland and are subjected to the military draft but cannot vote in U.S. presidential elections. A majority of Puerto Ricans have rejected statehood because they fear it would mean giving up their Latino culture.

Cuba and the United States

When the United States declared war against Spain in 1898, it recognized Cuba's independence from Spain. It also passed the Teller Amendment, which stated that the United States had no intention of taking over any part of Cuba. The Treaty of Paris, which ended the war, further guaranteed Cuba the independence that its nationalist leaders had been demanding for years.

AMERICAN SOLDIERS Though officially independent, Cuba was occupied by American troops when the war ended. José Martí, the Cuban patriot who had led the movement for independence from Spain, had feared that the United States would merely replace Spain and dominate Cuban politics. In some ways, Martí's prediction came true. Under American occupation, the same officials who had served Spain remained in office. Cubans who protested this policy were imprisoned or exiled.

On the other hand, the American military government provided food and clothing for thousands of families, helped farmers put land back into cultivation, and organized elementary schools. Through improvement of sanitation and medical research, the military government helped eliminate yellow fever, a disease that had killed hundreds of Cubans each year.

Background

Yellow fever damages many body parts, especially the liver. Dr. Carlos Finlay discovered that the disease is carried by mosquitoes. Clearing out the mosquitos' breeding places helped eliminate the disease in Cuba.

PLATT AMENDMENT In 1900 the newly formed Cuban government wrote a constitution for an independent Cuba. The constitution, however, did not specify the relationship between Cuba and the United States. Consequently, in 1901, the United States insisted that Cuba add to its constitution several provisions, known as the **Platt Amendment,** stating that

- Cuba could not make treaties that might limit its independence or permit a foreign power to control any part of its territory
- the United States reserved the right to intervene in Cuba
- Cuba was not to go into debt that its government could not repay
- the United States could buy or lease land on the island for naval stations and refueling stations

The United States made it clear that its army would not withdraw until Cuba adopted the Platt Amendment. In response, a torchlight procession marched on the residence of Governor-General Leonard Wood in protest. Some protestors even called for a return to arms to defend their national honor against this American insult. The U.S. government stood firm, though, and Cubans reluctantly ratified the new constitution. In 1903, the Platt Amendment became part of a treaty between the two nations, and it remained in effect for 31 years. Under the terms of the treaty, Cuba became a U.S. **protectorate,** a country whose affairs are partially controlled by a stronger power.

Vocabulary
ratify: to make valid by approving

PROTECTING AMERICAN BUSINESS INTERESTS The most important reason for the United States to maintain a strong political presence in Cuba was to protect American businesses that had invested in the island's sugar, tobacco, and mining industries, as well as in its railroads and public utilities.

Analyzing *Political Cartoons*

"WELL, I HARDLY KNOW WHICH TO TAKE FIRST!"

Throughout the early 1900s, the United States intervened in the affairs of its Latin American neighbors several times. American troops withdrew from Cuba in 1902 but later returned three times to quell popular uprisings against conservative leaders. The U.S. also intervened in Nicaragua and Haiti. Not surprisingly, few Latin Americans welcomed United States intervention. As the cartoon shows, the United States had a different point of view.

SKILLBUILDER
Analyzing Political Cartoons
1. What is on the bill of fare, or menu, in this restaurant?
2. Which president does the waiter portray?
3. What seems to be Uncle Sam's attitude toward the offerings on the menu?

 SEE SKILLBUILDER HANDBOOK, PAGE R24.

WELL, I HARDLY KNOW WHICH TO TAKE FIRST!

Although many businesspeople were convinced that annexing and imposing colonial rule on new territories was necessary to protect American business interests, some were concerned about colonial entanglements. The industrialist Andrew Carnegie argued against the taking of nations as colonies.

A PERSONAL VOICE ANDREW CARNEGIE

"The exports of the United States this year [1898] are greater than those of any other nation in the world. Even Britain's exports are less, yet Britain 'possesses' . . . a hundred 'colonies' . . . scattered all over the world. The fact that the United States has none does not prevent her products and manufactures from invading . . . all parts of the world in competition with those of Britain."

—quoted in *Distant Possessions*

Despite such concerns, the U.S. state department continued to push for control of its Latin American neighbors. In the years to come, the United States would intervene time and again in the affairs of other nations in the Western Hemisphere.

Filipinos Rebel

In the Philippines, Filipinos reacted with outrage to the Treaty of Paris, which called for American annexation of the Philippines. The rebel leader **Emilio Aguinaldo** (ĕ-mēl′yō ä′gē-näl′dō) believed that the United States had promised independence. When he and his followers learned the terms of the treaty, they vowed to fight for freedom.

PHILIPPINE–AMERICAN WAR In February 1899, the Filipinos, led by Aguinaldo, rose in revolt. The United States assumed almost the same role that Spain had played, imposing its authority on a colony that was fighting for freedom. When Aguinaldo turned to guerrilla tactics, the United States forced Filipinos to live in designated zones, where poor sanitation, starvation, and disease killed thousands. This was the very same practice that Americans had condemned Spain for using in Cuba.

During the occupation, white American soldiers looked on the Filipinos as inferiors. However, many of the 70,000 U.S. troops sent to the Philippines were African Americans. When African-American newspapers questioned why blacks were helping to spread racial prejudice to the Philippines, some African-American soldiers deserted to the Filipino side and developed bonds of friendship with the Filipinos.

It took the Americans nearly three years to put down the rebellion. About 20,000 Filipino rebels died fighting for independence. The war claimed 4,000 American lives and cost $400 million—20 times the price the United States had paid to purchase the islands. **B**

AFTERMATH OF THE WAR After suppressing the rebellion, the United States set up a government similar to the one it had established for Puerto Rico. The U.S. president would appoint a governor, who would then appoint the upper house of the legislature. Filipinos would elect the lower house. Under American rule, the Philippines moved gradually toward independence and finally became an independent republic on July 4, 1946.

▲ U.S. military action in the Philippines resulted in suffering for Filipino civilians. About 200,000 people died as a result of malnutrition, disease, and such guerrilla tactics as the burning of villages.

MAIN IDEA

Contrasting

B What were the aims of the Filipinos? of the Americans?

U.S. Imperialism, 1867–1906

hmhsocialstudies.com **INTERACTIVE MAP**

Bering Sea, 1893 International tribunal denies U.S. claims to exclusive rights to waters of Bering Sea.

Alaskan Boundary Crisis, 1902–1903 After gold is discovered in Klondike, Canadians want to redraw boundary to Alaskan Panhandle. A tribunal settles in favor of U.S.

Algeciras Conference, 1906 Roosevelt offers U.S. "good offices" to settle Franco-German differences over Morocco.

Open Door Policy, 1899 U.S. aims to prevent foreign powers in China from shutting out the United States from Chinese markets.

Big Stick Diplomacy, 1904 Roosevelt sends warships to Morocco when local authorities detain a Greek citizen with disputed U.S. citizenship.

Pearl Harbor, 1887 Hawaii gives U.S. exclusive rights to build a naval base.

Samoa, 1889–1899 Hurricane destroys U.S., British, and German ships, preventing armed clash over control of Samoa. Ten years later, the U.S. splits islands with Germany.

Congo Conference, 1885 U.S. persuades European powers to agree to freedom of trade and abolition of slave trade in central Africa.

Alaska 1867
Midway Island 1867
Wake Island 1899
Guam 1898
Philippine Islands 1898
Hawaiian Islands 1898
Puerto Rico 1898
Panama Canal Zone 1903

ASIA · CHINA · NORTH AMERICA · UNITED STATES · EUROPE · MOROCCO · AFRICA · PACIFIC OCEAN · ATLANTIC OCEAN · SOUTH AMERICA · CONGO · AUSTRALIA

Territory and date of acquisition

0   1,500   3,000 miles
0   1,500   3,000 kilometers

GEOGRAPHY SKILLBUILDER
1. **Location** On what islands does Pearl Harbor lie?
2. **Human-Environment Interaction** What events show the United States acting as a mediator in international disputes? What does this role indicate about the status of the U.S. in the world?

Foreign Influence in China

U.S. imperialists saw the Philippines as a gateway to the rest of Asia, particularly to China. China was seen as a vast potential market for American products. It also presented American investors with new opportunities for large-scale railroad construction.

Weakened by war and foreign intervention, China had become known as the "sick man of Asia." France, Germany, Britain, Japan, and Russia had established prosperous settlements along the coast of China. They also had carved out spheres of influence, areas where each nation claimed special rights and economic privileges.

JOHN HAY'S OPEN DOOR NOTES The United States began to fear that China would be carved into colonies and American traders would be shut out. To protect American interests, U.S. Secretary of State **John Hay** issued, in 1899, a series of policy statements called the **Open Door notes.** The notes were letters addressed to the leaders of imperialist nations proposing that the nations share their trading rights with the United States, thus creating an open door. This meant that no single nation would have a monopoly on trade with any part of China. The other imperialist powers reluctantly accepted this policy. **C**

MAIN IDEA

Analyzing Causes

C Why did Secretary of State John Hay issue the policy statements known as the Open Door notes?

▲ During the Boxer Rebellion, shown here in this Chinese print, Chinese patriots demanded that all foreigners be expelled from the country. The Boxers surrounded the European section of Beijing and kept it under siege for several months.

THE BOXER REBELLION IN CHINA

Although China kept its freedom, Europeans dominated most of China's large cities. Resentment simmered beneath the surface as some Chinese formed secret societies pledged to rid the country of "foreign devils." The most famous of these secret groups were the Boxers, so named by Westerners because members practiced martial arts.

The Boxers killed hundreds of missionaries and other foreigners, as well as Chinese converts to Christianity. In August 1900, troops from Britain, France, Germany, and Japan joined about 2,500 American soldiers and marched on the Chinese capital. Within two months, the international forces put down the **Boxer Rebellion.** Thousands of Chinese people died during the fighting.

PROTECTING AMERICAN RIGHTS

After the Boxer Rebellion, the United States feared that European nations would use their victory to take even greater control of China. To prevent this, John Hay issued a second series of Open Door notes, announcing that the United States would "safeguard for the world the principle of equal and impartial trade with all parts of the Chinese Empire." This policy paved the way for greater American influence in Asia.

The Open Door policy reflected three deeply held American beliefs about the United States industrial capitalist economy. First, Americans believed that the growth of the U.S. economy depended on exports. Second, they felt the United States had a right to intervene abroad to keep foreign markets open. Third, they feared that the closing of an area to American products, citizens, or ideas threatened U.S. survival. These beliefs became the bedrock of American foreign policy.

Vocabulary
martial arts: combat or self-defense arts that originated in East Asia, such as judo or karate

Background
American imperial ambitions in Asia were established nearly 50 years before the United States' venture in China. In 1854, U.S. Navy Commodore Matthew Perry, using a combination of force and negotiation, persuaded the leaders of the long-isolated country of Japan to open their ports to American traders.

WORLD STAGE

THE BOXER PROTOCOL

On September 7, 1901, China and 11 other nations signed the Boxer Protocol—a final settlement of the Boxer Rebellion.

The Qing government agreed to execute some Chinese officials, to punish others, and to pay about $332 million in damages. The United States was awarded a settlement of $24.5 million. It used about $4 million to pay American citizens for actual losses incurred during the rebellion. In 1908, the U.S. government returned the rest of the money to China to be used for the purpose of educating Chinese students in their own country and in the United States.

The Impact of U.S. Territorial Gains

In 1900, Republican William McKinley, a reluctant but confirmed imperialist, was elected to a second term against Democrat William Jennings Bryan, who staunchly opposed imperialism. McKinley's reelection confirmed that a majority of Americans favored his policies. Under McKinley, the United States had gained an empire.

Yet even before McKinley was reelected, an Anti-Imperialist League had sprung into being. The league included some of the most prominent people in America, such as former president Grover Cleveland, industrial leader Andrew Carnegie, the social worker Jane Addams, and many leading writers. Anti-imperialists had different and sometimes conflicting reasons for their opposition, but all agreed that it was wrong for the United States to rule other people without their consent. The novelist Mark Twain questioned the motives for imperialism in a satirical piece written in 1901.

 A PERSONAL VOICE MARK TWAIN

"**Shall we go on conferring our Civilization upon the peoples that sit in darkness, or shall we give those poor things a rest? . . . Extending the Blessings of Civilization to our Brother who Sits in Darkness has been a good trade and has paid well, on the whole; and there is money in it yet . . . but not enough, in my judgment, to make any considerable risk advisable.**"

—quoted in *To the Person Sitting in Darkness*

As a novelist, Twain had great influence on American culture but little influence on foreign policy. In the early 20th century, the United States under President Theodore Roosevelt and President Woodrow Wilson would continue to exert its power around the globe.

▲ **Mark Twain**

SECTION 3 ASSESSMENT

1. TERMS & NAMES For each term or name, write a sentence explaining its significance.
- Foraker Act
- Platt Amendment
- protectorate
- Emilio Aguinaldo
- John Hay
- Open Door notes
- Boxer Rebellion

MAIN IDEA

2. TAKING NOTES
Create a time line of key events relating to U.S. relations with Cuba, Puerto Rico, and the Philippines. Use the dates already plotted on the time line below as a guide.

Which event do you think was most significant? Why?

CRITICAL THINKING

3. EVALUATING
How did American rule of Puerto Rico harm Puerto Ricans? How did it help Puerto Ricans? Do you think the benefits outweighed the harmful effects? Why or why not?

4. COMPARING
How was U.S. policy toward China different from U.S. policy toward the Philippines? To what can you attribute the difference?

5. ANALYZING ISSUES
How did U.S. foreign policy at the turn of the century affect actions taken by the United States toward China? **Think About:**
- why the United States wanted access to China's markets
- the purpose of the Open Door notes
- the U.S. response to the Boxer Rebellion

SECTION
4

PI 4.1
PI 4.2

CC Unit 4.II.A.1.a(2)   CC Unit 4.II.A.4.a
CC Unit 4.II.A.4.b   CC Unit 4.II.A.4.c
CC Unit 4.II.A.4.d

America as a World Power

MAIN IDEA	WHY IT MATTERS NOW	Terms & Names
The Russo-Japanese War, the Panama Canal, and the Mexican Revolution added to America's military and economic power.	American involvement in conflicts around 1900 led to involvement in World War I and later to a peacekeeper role in today's world.	• Panama Canal • Francisco "Pancho" Villa • Roosevelt Corollary • Emiliano Zapata • dollar diplomacy • John J. Pershing

One American's Story

hmhsocialstudies.com
TAKING NOTES

Use the graphic organizer online to take notes on how Teddy Roosevelt and Woodrow Wilson used American power around the world.

Joseph Bucklin Bishop, a policy adviser to the canal's chief engineer, played an important role in the building of the Panama Canal. As editor of the *Canal Record*, a weekly newspaper that provided Americans with updates on the project, Bishop described a frustrating problem that the workers encountered.

A PERSONAL VOICE JOSEPH BUCKLIN BISHOP

" The Canal Zone was a land of the fantastic and the unexpected. No one could say when the sun went down what the condition of the Cut would be when [the sun] rose. For the work of months or even years might be blotted out by an avalanche of earth or the toppling over of a mountain of rock. It was a task to try men's souls; but it was also one to kindle in them a joy of combat . . . and a faith in ultimate victory which no disaster could shake. "

—quoted in *The Impossible Dream: The Building of the Panama Canal*

▲ Workers digging the Panama Canal faced hazardous landslides and death from disease.

The building of the Panama Canal reflected America's new role as a world power. As a technological accomplishment, the canal represented a confident nation's refusal to let any physical obstacle stand in its way.

Teddy Roosevelt and the World

The assassination of William McKinley in 1901 thrust Vice-President Theodore Roosevelt into the role of a world leader. Roosevelt was unwilling to allow the imperial powers of Europe to control the world's political and economic destiny. In 1905, building on the Open Door notes to increase American influence in East Asia, Roosevelt mediated a settlement in a war between Russia and Japan.

ROOSEVELT THE PEACEMAKER In 1904, Russia and Japan, Russia's neighbor in East Asia, were both imperialist powers, and they were competing for control of Korea. The Japanese took the first action in what would become the Russo-Japanese War with a sudden attack on the Russian Pacific fleet. To everyone's surprise, Japan destroyed it. Japan then proceeded to destroy a second fleet sent as reinforcement. Japan also won a series of land battles, securing Korea and Manchuria.

As a result of these battles, Japan began to run out of men and money, a fact that it did not want to reveal to Russia. Instead, Japanese officials approached President Roosevelt in secret and asked him to mediate peace negotiations. Roosevelt agreed, and in 1905, Russian and Japanese delegates convened in Portsmouth, New Hampshire.

The first meeting took place on the presidential yacht. Roosevelt had a charming way of greeting people with a grasp of the hand, a broad grin, and a hearty "Dee-lighted." Soon the opposing delegates began to relax and cordially shook hands.

The Japanese wanted Sakhalin Island, off the coast of Siberia, and a large sum of money from Russia. Russia refused. Roosevelt persuaded Japan to accept half the island and forgo the cash payment. In exchange, Russia agreed to let Japan take over Russian interests in Manchuria and Korea. The successful efforts in negotiating the Treaty of Portsmouth won Roosevelt the 1906 Nobel Peace Prize.

As U.S. and Japanese interests expanded in East Asia, the two nations continued diplomatic talks. In later agreements, they pledged to respect each other's possessions and interests in East Asia and the Pacific. **Ⓐ**

PANAMA CANAL By the time Roosevelt became president, many Americans, including Roosevelt, felt that the United States needed a canal cutting across Central America. Such a canal would greatly reduce travel time for commercial and military ships by providing a shortcut between the Atlantic and Pacific oceans. (See Geography Spotlight, page 572.) As early as 1850, the United States and Britain had agreed to share the rights to such a canal. In the Hay-Pauncefote Treaty of 1901, however, Britain gave the United States exclusive rights to build and control a canal through Central America.

Engineers identified two possible routes for the proposed canal. One, through Nicaragua, posed fewer obstacles because much of it crossed a large lake. The other route crossed through Panama (then a province of Colombia) and was shorter and filled with mountains and swamps. In the late 1800s, a French company had tried to build a canal in Panama. After ten years, the company gave up. It sent an agent, Philippe Bunau-Varilla, to Washington to convince the United States to buy its claim. In 1903, the president and Congress decided to use the Panama route and agreed to buy the French company's route for $40 million.

Before beginning work on the **Panama Canal,** the United States had to get permission from Colombia, which then ruled Panama. When these negotiations broke down, Bunau-Varilla helped organize a Panamanian rebellion against Colombia. On November 3, 1903, nearly a dozen U.S. warships were present as Panama declared its independence. Fifteen days later, Panama and the United

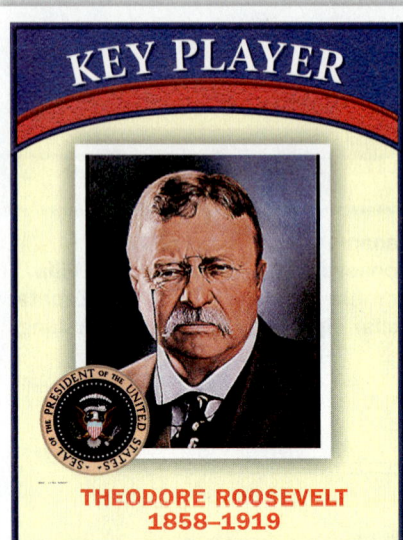

KEY PLAYER

THEODORE ROOSEVELT
1858–1919

Rimless glasses, a bushy mustache, and prominent teeth made Roosevelt easy for cartoonists to caricature. His great enthusiasm for physical activity—boxing, tennis, swimming, horseback riding, and hunting—provided cartoonists with additional material. Some cartoons portrayed Roosevelt with the toy teddy bear that he inspired.

Roosevelt had six children, who became notorious for their rowdy antics. Their father once sent a message through the War Department, ordering them to call off their "attack" on the White House. Roosevelt thrived on the challenges of the presidency. He wrote, "I do not believe that anyone else has ever enjoyed the White House as much as I have."

MAIN IDEA

Analyzing Effects
Ⓐ What were the results of Roosevelt's negotiations with the Japanese and Russians?

↗ hmhsocialstudies.com **INTERACTIVE**

THE PANAMA CANAL

Locks are used to raise and lower ships a total of 170 feet during the 51-mile trip through the Panama Canal. For example, ships from the Atlantic Ocean are lifted by the Gatún Locks to the level of Gatún Lake. The ships cross the human-made lake, then move through another waterway, the Gaillard Cut. The Pedro Miguel and Miraflores locks then lower the ships to the level of the Pacific Ocean.

Gold Hill

Gaillard Cut
85 feet above sea level

Continental Divide

Pacific Ocean

Gatún Lake

Atlantic Ocean

Miraflores
Locks

Pedro Miguel
Locks

Gatún Locks

1 A ship enters a lock when the lower gates are open.

2 When all gates are shut, water is let into the lock through a sluice (small gate).

3 When the water has risen, the upper gates are opened, and the ship passes through the lock to the next level.

▲ This photo shows a ship that has entered the canal from the Pacific Ocean side and is heading north through the Miraflores Locks. Ships and boats can also enter the canal through the Atlantic Ocean side and head south through the Gatún Locks.

HISTORY

VIDEO
Panama Canal: Locks
↗ hmhsocialstudies.com

States signed a treaty in which the United States agreed to pay Panama $10 million plus an annual rent of $250,000 for an area of land across Panama, called the Canal Zone. The payments were to begin in 1913.

CONSTRUCTING THE CANAL Construction of the Panama Canal ranks as one of the world's greatest engineering feats. Builders fought diseases, such as yellow fever and malaria, and soft volcanic soil that proved difficult to remove from where it lay. Work began in 1904 with the clearing of brush and draining of swamps. By 1913, the height of the construction, more than 43,400 workers were employed. Some had come from Italy and Spain; three-quarters were blacks from the British West Indies. More than 5,600 workers on the canal died from accidents or disease. The total cost to the United States was about $380 million. **B**

On August 15, 1914, the canal opened for business, and more than 1,000 merchant ships passed through during its first year. U.S.-Latin American relations, however, had been damaged by American support of the rebellion in Panama. The resulting ill will lasted for decades, despite Congress's paying Colombia $25 million in 1921 to compensate the country for its lost territory.

MAIN IDEA

Identifying Problems

B What problems did canal workers encounter in constructing the canal?

"THE WORLD'S CONSTABLE"

This cartoon, drawn by Louis Dalrymple in 1905, shows Teddy Roosevelt implementing his new world diplomacy. The cartoon implies that Roosevelt has the right to execute police power to keep the countries of Europe (shown on the right) out of the affairs of Latin American countries (shown on the left).

SKILLBUILDER
Analyzing Political Cartoons
1. How does the cartoonist portray President Roosevelt?
2. Why is "The World's Constable" a good title for this cartoon?

 SEE SKILLBUILDER HANDBOOK, PAGE R24.

THE ROOSEVELT COROLLARY Financial factors drew the United States further into Latin American affairs. In the late 19th century, many Latin American nations had borrowed huge sums from European banks to build railroads and develop industries. Roosevelt feared that if these nations defaulted on their loans, Europeans might intervene. He was determined to make the United States the predominant power in the Caribbean and Central America.

Roosevelt reminded European powers of the Monroe Doctrine, which had been issued in 1823 by President James Monroe. The Monroe Doctrine demanded that European countries stay out of the affairs of Latin American nations. Roosevelt based his Latin America policy on a West African proverb that said, "Speak softly and carry a big stick." In his December 1904 message to Congress, Roosevelt added the **Roosevelt Corollary** to the Monroe Doctrine. He warned that disorder in Latin America might "force the United States . . . to the exercise of an international police power." In effect, the corollary said that the United States would now use force to protect its economic interests in Latin America.

> *"Speak softly and carry a big stick; you will go far."*
> **THEODORE ROOSEVELT**

Vocabulary
corollary: an additional statement that follows logically from the first one

DOLLAR DIPLOMACY During the next decade, the United States exercised its police power on several occasions. For example, when a 1911 rebellion in Nicaragua left the nation near bankruptcy, President William H. Taft, Roosevelt's successor, arranged for American bankers to loan Nicaragua enough money to pay its debts. In return, the bankers were given the right to recover their money by collecting Nicaragua's customs duties. The U.S. bankers also gained control of Nicaragua's state-owned railroad system and its national bank. When Nicaraguan citizens heard about this deal, they revolted against President Adolfo Díaz. To prop up

Díaz's government, some 2,000 marines were sent to Nicaragua. The revolt was put down, but some marine detachments remained in the country until 1933.

The Taft administration followed the policy of using the U.S. government to guarantee loans made to foreign countries by American businesspeople. This policy was called **dollar diplomacy** by its critics and was often used to justify keeping European powers out of the Caribbean.

Woodrow Wilson's Missionary Diplomacy

The Monroe Doctrine, issued by President James Monroe in 1823, had warned other nations against expanding their influence in Latin America. The Roosevelt Corollary asserted, in 1904, that the United States had a right to exercise international police power in the Western Hemisphere. In 1913, President Woodrow Wilson gave the Monroe Doctrine a moral tone.

According to Wilson's "missionary diplomacy," the United States had a moral responsibility to deny recognition to any Latin American government it viewed as oppressive, undemocratic, or hostile to U.S. interests. Prior to this policy, the United States recognized any government that controlled a nation, regardless of that nation's policies or how it had come to power. Wilson's policy pressured nations in the Western Hemisphere to establish democratic governments. Almost immediately, the Mexican Revolution put Wilson's policy to the test.

THE MEXICAN REVOLUTION Mexico had been ruled for more than three decades by a military dictator, Porfirio Díaz. A friend of the United States, Díaz had long encouraged foreign investments in his country. As a result, foreigners, mostly Americans, owned a large share of Mexican oil wells, mines, railroads, and ranches. While foreign investors and some Mexican landowners and politicians had grown rich, the common people of the country were desperately poor.

In 1911, Mexican peasants and workers led by Francisco Madero overthrew Díaz. Madero promised democratic reforms, but he proved unable to satisfy the conflicting demands of landowners, peasants, factory workers, and the urban middle class. After two years, General Victoriano Huerta took over the government. Within days Madero was murdered. Wilson refused to recognize the government that Huerta formed. He called it "a government of butchers." **C**

INTERVENTION IN MEXICO Wilson adopted a plan of "watchful waiting," looking for an opportunity to act against Huerta. The opportunity came in April 1914, when one of Huerta's officers arrested a small group of American sailors in Tampico, on Mexico's eastern shore. The Mexicans quickly released them and apologized, but Wilson used the incident as an excuse to intervene in Mexico and ordered U.S. Marines to occupy Veracruz, an important Mexican port. Eighteen Americans and at least 200 Mexicans died during the invasion.

The incident brought the United States and Mexico close to war. Argentina, Brazil, and Chile stepped in to mediate the conflict. They proposed that Huerta step down and that U.S. troops withdraw without paying Mexico for damages. Mexico rejected the plan, and Wilson refused to recognize a government that had come to power as a result of violence. The Huerta regime soon collapsed, however, and Venustiano Carranza, a nationalist leader, became president in 1915. Wilson withdrew the troops and formally recognized the Carranza government.

VIDEO
The Peasant Revolution
hmhsocialstudies.com

MAIN IDEA

Analyzing Motives
C Why did President Wilson refuse to recognize Huerta's government?

ANOTHER PERSPECTIVE

INTERVENTION IN MEXICO

Most U.S. citizens supported American intervention in Mexico. Edith O'Shaughnessy, wife of an American diplomat in Mexico City, had another perspective. After touring Veracruz, O'Shaughnessy wrote to her mother:

"I think we have done a great wrong to these people; instead of cutting out the sores with a clean, strong knife of war . . . and occupation, . . . we have only put our fingers in each festering wound and inflamed it further."

ZAPATISTAS (1931)

José Orozco, one of Mexico's foremost artists, painted these Zapatistas (followers of Zapata), to honor the peasant men and women who fought in the Mexican revolution. Orozco did many paintings in support of the revolution.
What aspects of the image does the artist use to convey strength and unity?

REBELLION IN MEXICO Carranza was in charge, but like others before him, he did not have the support of all Mexicans. Rebels under the leadership of **Francisco "Pancho" Villa** (vē′ə) and **Emiliano Zapata** (ĕ-mēl-yä′nō zə-pä′tə) opposed Carranza's provisional government. Zapata—son of a mestizo peasant—was dedicated to land reform. "It is better to die on your feet than live on your knees," Zapata told the peasants who joined him. Villa, a fierce nationalist, had frequently courted the support and aid of the United States.

★ **A PERSONAL VOICE** PANCHO VILLA

" [A]s long as I have anything to do with the affairs in Mexico there will be no further friction between my country and my friends of the North . . . To President Wilson, the greatest American, I stand pledged to do what I can to keep the faith he has in my people, and if there is anything he may wish I will gladly do it, for I know it will be for the good of my country. "

—*New York Times*, January 11, 1915

Despite Villa's talk of friendship, when President Wilson recognized Carranza's government, Villa threatened reprisals against the United States. In January 1916, Carranza invited American engineers to operate mines in northern Mexico. Before they reached the mines, however, Villa's men took the Americans off a train and shot them. Two months later, some of Villa's followers raided Columbus, New Mexico, and killed 17 Americans. Americans held Villa responsible.

CHASING VILLA With the American public demanding revenge, President Wilson ordered Brigadier General **John J. Pershing** and an expeditionary force of about 15,000 soldiers into Mexico to capture Villa dead or alive. For almost a year, Villa eluded Pershing's forces. Wilson then called out 150,000 National Guardsmen and stationed them along the Mexican border. In the meantime,

Mexicans grew angrier over the U.S. invasion of their land. In June 1916, U.S. troops clashed with Carranza's army, resulting in deaths on both sides.

Carranza demanded the withdrawal of U.S. troops, but Wilson refused. War seemed imminent. However, in the end, both sides backed down. The United States, facing war in Europe, needed peace on its southern border. In February 1917, Wilson ordered Pershing to return home. Later that year, Mexico adopted a constitution that gave the government control of the nation's oil and mineral resources and placed strict regulations on foreign investors.

▲ Pancho Villa directs a column of his troops through northern Mexico in 1914.

Although Carranza had called for the constitution of 1917, he failed to carry out its measures. Instead, he ruled oppressively until 1920 when a moderate named Alvaro Obregón came to power. Obregón's presidency marked the end of civil war and the beginning of reform.

U.S. intervention in Mexican affairs provided a clear model of American imperialist attitudes in the early years of the 20th century. Americans believed in the superiority of free-enterprise democracy, and the American government attempted to extend the reach of this economic and political system, even through armed intervention.

The United States pursued and achieved several foreign policy goals in the early 20th century. First, it expanded its access to foreign markets in order to ensure the continued growth of the domestic economy. Second, the United States built a modern navy to protect its interests abroad. Third, the United States exercised its international police power to ensure dominance in Latin America.

SECTION 4 ASSESSMENT

1. TERMS & NAMES For each term or name below, write a sentence explaining its significance.
- Panama Canal
- dollar diplomacy
- Emiliano Zapata
- Roosevelt Corollary
- Francisco "Pancho" Villa
- John J. Pershing

SUMMARIZING

2. TAKING NOTES
In a two-column chart, list ways Teddy Roosevelt and Woodrow Wilson used American power around the world during their presidencies.

Using American Power	
Roosevelt	Wilson

Choose one example and discuss its impact with your classmates.

CRITICAL THINKING

3. COMPARING AND CONTRASTING
What do you think were the similarities and differences between Roosevelt's Big Stick policy and Wilson's missionary diplomacy? Use evidence from the text to support your response. **Think About:**
- the goal of each of these foreign policies
- how the policies defined the role of U.S. intervention in international affairs
- how the policies were applied

4. EVALUATING DECISIONS
In your opinion, should the United States have become involved in the affairs of Colombia, Nicaragua, and Mexico during the early 1900s? Support your answer with details. **Think About:**
- the effect of the Roosevelt Corollary
- the results of dollar diplomacy
- the implication of Wilson's missionary diplomacy

The Panama Canal: Funnel for Trade

By the late 19th century, the U.S. position in global trade was firmly established. A glance at a world map during that time revealed the trade advantages of cutting through the world's great landmasses at two strategic points. The first cut, through the Isthmus of Suez in Egypt, was completed in 1869 and was a spectacular success. A second cut, this one through Panama, in Central America, would be especially advantageous to the United States. Such a cut, or canal, would substantially reduce the sailing time between the nation's Atlantic and Pacific ports.

It took the United States ten years, from 1904 to 1914, to build the Panama Canal. By 1999, more than 700,000 vessels, flying the flags of about 70 nations, had passed through its locks. On December 31, 1999, Panama assumed full control of the canal.

INTERCOASTAL TRADE ▲

The first boat through the canal heralded the arrival of increased trade between the Atlantic and Pacific ports of the United States.

NUMBERS TELL THE STORY ▶

A ship sailing from New York to San Francisco by going around South America travels 13,000 miles; the canal shortens the journey to 5,200 miles.

San Francisco

New York

■ 13,000 mi.
■ 5,200 mi.

to Asia

San Francisco

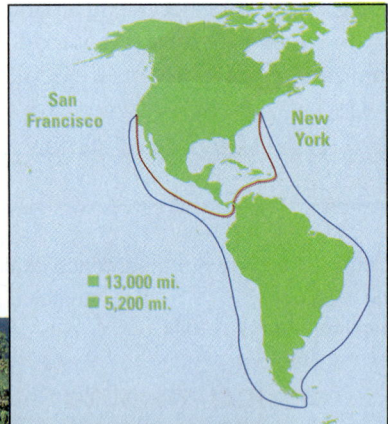

◀ **OCEANGOING VESSELS**

Ships, like this one, must be of a certain dimension in order to fit through the canal's locks. These container ships must be no more than 106 feet across and 965 feet in length, with a draft (the depth of the vessel below the water line when fully loaded) of no more than 39.5 feet. Each ship pays a toll based on its size, its cargo, and the number of passengers it carries.

◀ **NEW YORK CITY**

New York City and other U.S. Atlantic ports accounted for about 60 percent of the traffic using the Panama Canal in the early decades of its existence.

NEW ORLEANS ▲

Since its founding in 1718, New Orleans has served as a major port for the products of the areas along the Mississippi River. In 1914, the Panama Canal brought Pacific markets into its orbit.

New York

to Europe

to Africa

New Orleans

Panama Canal

to South America

Panama is a narrow stretch of land—or isthmus —that connects North and South America. In building the canal, engineers took advantage of natural waterways. Moving ships through the mountains of the Continental Divide required the use of massive locks. Locks allow a section of the canal to be closed off so that the water level can be raised or lowered.

THINKING CRITICALLY

1. **Analyzing Patterns** On a world map, identify the route that ships took to get from New York City to San Francisco before the Panama Canal opened. How did this route change after the opening of the canal?

2. **Creating a Model** Use clay to shape a model of a cross-section of the Panama Canal as shown in the Science and Technology feature on page 567. For the locks, use foam blocks or pieces of wood that you have glued together. Paint the model, and then label each part of the canal.

   SEE SKILLBUILDER HANDBOOK, PAGE R31.

hmhsocialstudies.com **RESEARCH WEB LINKS**

VISUAL SUMMARY

AMERICA CLAIMS AN EMPIRE

CAUSES

- Economic competition among industrial nations

- Political and military competition, including the creation of a strong naval force

- A belief in Anglo-Saxon superiority

AMERICAN IMPERIALISM

EFFECTS

- The U.S. purchased Alaska in 1867.
- The U.S. annexed Hawaii in 1898.

- In 1898, the U.S. helped Cuba win independence from Spain.
- In the Treaty of Paris, the U.S. gained Puerto Rico, Guam, and the Philippine Islands.

- Following the Spanish-American War, the U.S.
  - —reorganized the government of Puerto Rico
  - —established a protectorate over Cuba
  - —crushed a revolt in Philippines
- In 1899, the Open Door policy established U.S. trading rights in China.

- In the early 1900s, President Roosevelt initiated plans for the Panama Canal and asserted the right of the U.S. to exercise police power in the Western Hemisphere.
- President Wilson pressured Mexico and other countries in the Western Hemisphere to establish democratic governments.

TERMS & NAMES

For each term or name below, write a sentence explaining its significance to U.S. foreign policy between 1890 and 1920.

1. Queen Liliuokalani
2. imperialism
3. José Martí
4. yellow journalism
5. *U.S.S. Maine*
6. protectorate
7. Open Door notes
8. Boxer Rebellion
9. Panama Canal
10. Roosevelt Corollary

MAIN IDEAS

Use your notes and the information in the chapter to answer the following questions.

Imperialism and America (pages 548–551)

1. What three factors spurred American imperialism?
2. How did Queen Liliuokalani's main goal conflict with American imperialists' goals?

The Spanish-American War (pages 552–557)

3. Why was American opinion about Cuban independence divided?
4. Briefly describe the terms of the Treaty of Paris of 1898.

Acquiring New Lands (pages 558–564)

5. Why was the U.S. interested in events in Puerto Rico?
6. What sparked the Boxer Rebellion in 1900, and how was it crushed?
7. What three key beliefs about America's industrial capitalist economy were reflected in the Open Door policy?

America as a World Power (pages 565–571)

8. What conflict triggered the war between Russia and Japan?
9. Why is the construction of the Panama Canal considered one of the world's greatest engineering feats?
10. Explain the key difference between Woodrow Wilson's moral diplomacy and Teddy Roosevelt's "big stick" diplomacy.

CRITICAL THINKING

1. **USING YOUR NOTES** Create a Venn diagram like the one below to show the similarities and differences between José Martí of Cuba and Emilio Aguinaldo of the Philippines.

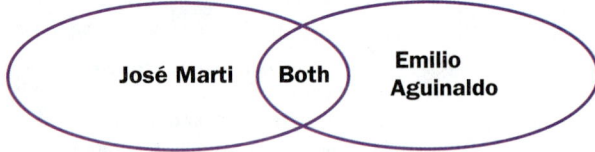

José Marti   Both   Emilio Aguinaldo

2. **HYPOTHESIZING** Would Cuba have won its independence in the late 19th century if the United States had not intervened there? Support your opinion with details from the text.

3. **INTERPRETING MAPS** Look carefully at the Caribbean map on page 555 and the world map on page 562. Why do you think American naval bases in the Caribbean and the Pacific were beneficial to the United States?

Use the cartoon and your knowledge of U.S. history to answer question 1.

1   What is the cartoonist's point of view concerning the relationship between the United States and Cuba?

(1) The United States wishes to be friends with Cuba.
(2) The United States will devour Cuba.
(3) The United States is wasting its time fighting over such a small area.
(4) The United States has no interest in Cuba.

Use the map and your knowledge of U.S. history to answer question 2.

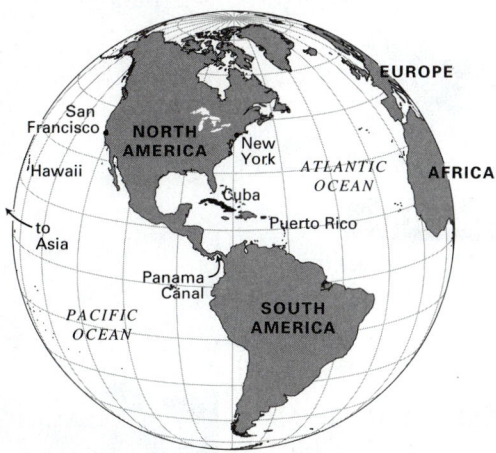

2   How did the building of the Panama Canal support United States efforts to become a world power?

(1) It gave the United States a colony in Central America.
(2) It prevented Japan and China from attacking Hawaii.
(3) It opened up a new avenue for trade with China.
(4) By providing a shortcut between the Atlantic Ocean and Pacific Ocean, it opened up new trading opportunities.

hmhsocialstudies.com   **TEST PRACTICE**

For additional test practice, go online for:
• Diagnostic tests   • Tutorials

INTERACT WITH HISTORY

Recall the issues that you explored at the beginning of the chapter. Suppose you are a journalist at the end of the Spanish-American War. You work for William Randolph Hearst's *New York Journal*. Write a newspaper editorial that presents your point of view about whether or not the Senate should ratify the Treaty of Paris, thus annexing the Philippines.

FOCUS ON WRITING

Imagine you are a worker helping to build the Panama Canal. Write a diary entry giving details about the work you are doing, the hardships you face, and why you think the project is worthwhile.

MULTIMEDIA ACTIVITY

21ST CENTURY

Use the *Electronic Library of Primary Sources* and Internet resources to research opinions on imperialism between 1895 and 1920.

• Choose a document, incident, or piece of writing about imperialism. Decide if you support it or disagree with it.
• Write a speech that presents your point of view. Decide how you will make your arguments clear and convincing while also addressing opposing concerns.
• Practice your speech aloud and then present it to the class.

hmhsocialstudies.com

CHAPTER 19

THE FIRST WORLD WAR

Essential Question

How did World War I affect the United States and Europe?

New York Standards

KEY IDEA 2 Important ideas, social and cultural values, beliefs, and traditions from New York State and United States history illustrate the connections and interactions of people and events across time and from a variety of perspectives.

KEY IDEA 4 The skills of historical analysis include the ability to: explain the significance of historical evidence; weigh the importance, reliability, and validity of evidence; understand the concept of multiple causation; understand the importance of changing and competing interpretations of different historical developments.

Battle scene on the western front during World War I.

1914 Hollywood, California, becomes the center of movie production in the U.S.

1915 German U-boats sink the *Lusitania*, and 1,198 people die.

1915 Alexander Graham Bell makes first transcontinental telephone call.

1916 Woodrow Wilson is reelected president.

USA

WORLD

1914   1915   1916

1914 Archduke Franz Ferdinand and his wife are assassinated.

1914 Germany declares war on Russia and France. Great Britain declares war on Germany and Austria-Hungary.

1915 Albert Einstein proposes his general theory of relativity.

1916 The battles of Verdun and the Somme claim millions of lives.

Dear Home: Letters from World War I

hmhsocialstudies.com ▸ VIDEO

INTERACT
WITH HISTORY

The year is 1917. A bitter war is raging in Europe—a war that has been called a threat to civilization. At home many people are urging America to wake up and get involved, while others are calling for the country to isolate itself and avoid the fight.

Explore the Issues

• Is it right for America to intervene in foreign conflicts?

• When American lives are threatened, how should the government respond?

• Should America go to war to make the world "safe for democracy"?

1917 The Selective Service Act sets up the draft.

1917 The United States declares war on Germany.

1918 Congress passes the Sedition Act.

1918 President Wilson proposes the League of Nations.

1919 Congress approves the Nineteenth Amendment, granting women the vote.

1917   1918   1919

1917 Russia withdraws from the war.

1918 The Bolsheviks establish a Communist regime in Russia.

1918 The First World War ends.

1919 A worldwide influenza epidemic kills over 30 million.

INFLUENZA
FREQUENTLY COMPLICATED WITH
PNEUMONIA
IS PREVALENT AT THIS TIME THROUGHOUT AMERICA.
THIS THEATRE IS CO-OPERATING WITH THE DEPARTMENT OF HEALTH.
YOU MUST DO THE SAME
IF YOU HAVE A COLD AND ARE COUGHING AND
SNEEZING DO NOT ENTER THIS THEATRE
GO HOME AND GO TO BED UNTIL YOU ARE WELL
Coughing, Sneezing or Spitting Will Not be
Permitted In the Theatre. In case you
must cough or Sneeze, do so in your own
handkerchief, and if the Cough or Sneeze
is repeated, leave the Theatre At Once.
This Theatre has Agreed to cooperate with
the Department of Health In disseminating
the truth about Influenza, and thus serve
a great educational purpose.
**HELP US TO KEEP CHICAGO THE
HEALTHIEST CITY IN THE WORLD**
JOHN DILL ROBERTSON
COMMISSIONER OF HEALTH

World War I Begins

MAIN IDEA	WHY IT MATTERS NOW	Terms & Names
As World War I intensified, the United States was forced to abandon its neutrality.	The United States remains involved in European and world affairs.	• nationalism • militarism • Allies • Central Powers • Archduke Franz Ferdinand • no man's land • trench warfare • *Lusitania* • Zimmermann note

One American's Story

hmhsocialstudies.com
TAKING NOTES
Use the graphic organizer online to take notes on the causes of World War I.

It was about 1:00 A.M. on April 6, 1917, and the members of the U.S. House of Representatives were tired. For the past 15 hours they had been debating President Wilson's request for a declaration of war against Germany. There was a breathless hush as Jeannette Rankin of Montana, the first woman elected to Congress, stood up. Rankin declared, "I want to stand by my country but I cannot vote for war. I vote no." Later she reflected on her action.

A PERSONAL VOICE JEANNETTE RANKIN

"I believe that the first vote I cast was the most significant vote and a most significant act on the part of women, because women are going to have to stop war. I felt at the time that the first woman [in Congress] should take the first stand, that the first time the first woman had a chance to say no to war she should say it."

—quoted in *Jeannette Rankin: First Lady in Congress*

▲ **Jeannette Rankin was the only member of the House to vote against the U.S. entering both World War I and World War II.**

After much debate as to whether the United States should join the fight, Congress voted in favor of U.S. entry into World War I. With this decision, the government abandoned the neutrality that America had maintained for three years. What made the United States change its policy in 1917?

Causes of World War I

Although many Americans wanted to stay out of the war, several factors made American neutrality difficult to maintain. As an industrial and imperial power, the United States felt many of the same pressures that had led the nations of Europe into devastating warfare. Historians generally cite four long-term causes of the First World War: nationalism, imperialism, militarism, and the formation of a system of alliances.

NATIONALISM Throughout the 19th century, politics in the Western world were deeply influenced by the concept of **nationalism**—a devotion to the interests and culture of one's nation. Often, nationalism led to competitive and antagonistic rivalries among nations. In this atmosphere of competition, many feared Germany's growing power in Europe.

In addition, various ethnic groups resented domination by others and longed for their nations to become independent. Many ethnic groups looked to larger nations for protection. Russia regarded itself as the protector of Europe's Slavic peoples, no matter which government they lived under. Among these Slavic peoples were the Serbs. Serbia, located in the Balkans, was an independent nation, but millions of ethnic Serbs lived under the rule of Austria-Hungary. As a result, Russia and Austria-Hungary were rivals for influence over Serbia.

MAIN IDEA

Analyzing Causes

A How did nationalism and imperialism lead to conflict in Europe?

IMPERIALISM For many centuries, European nations had been building empires, slowly extending their economic and political control over various peoples of the world. Colonies supplied the European imperial powers with raw materials and provided markets for manufactured goods. As Germany industrialized, it competed with France and Britain in the contest for colonies. **A**

MILITARISM Empires were expensive to build and to defend. The growth of nationalism and imperialism led to increased military spending. Because each nation wanted stronger armed forces than those of any potential enemy, the imperial powers followed a policy of **militarism**—the development of armed forces and their use as a tool of diplomacy.

By 1890 the strongest nation on the European continent was Germany, which had set up an army reserve system that drafted and trained young men. Britain was not initially alarmed by Germany's military expansion. As an island nation, Britain had always relied on its navy for defense and protection of its shipping routes— and the British navy was the strongest in the world. However, in 1897, Wilhelm II, Germany's kaiser, or emperor, decided that his nation should also become a major sea power in order to compete more successfully against the British. Soon British and German shipyards competed to build the largest battleships and destroyers. France, Italy, Japan, and the United States quickly joined the naval arms race.

Vocabulary
alliance: a formal agreement or union between nations

ALLIANCE SYSTEM By 1907 there were two major defense alliances in Europe. The Triple Entente, later known as the **Allies,** consisted of France, Britain, and Russia. The Triple Alliance consisted of Germany, Austria-Hungary, and Italy.

German Emperor Wilhelm II *(center)* marches with two of his generals, Hindenburg *(left)* and Ludendorff, during World War I.

Germany and Austria-Hungary, together with the Ottoman Empire—an empire of mostly Middle Eastern lands controlled by the Turks—were later known as the **Central Powers.** The alliances provided a measure of international security because nations were reluctant to disturb the balance of power. As it turned out, a spark set off a major conflict.

An Assassination Leads to War

That spark flared in the Balkan Peninsula, which was known as "the powder keg of Europe." In addition to the ethnic rivalries among the Balkan peoples, Europe's leading powers had interests there. Russia wanted access to the Mediterranean Sea. Germany wanted a rail link to the Ottoman Empire. Austria-Hungary, which had taken control of Bosnia in 1878, accused Serbia of subverting its rule over Bosnia. The "powder keg" was ready to explode.

In June 1914, **Archduke Franz Ferdinand,** heir to the Austrian throne, visited the Bosnian capital Sarajevo. As the royal entourage drove through the city, Serbian nationalist Gavrilo Princip stepped from the crowd and shot the Archduke and his wife Sophie. Princip was a member of the Black Hand, an organization promoting Serbian nationalism. The assassinations touched off a diplomatic crisis. On July 28, Austria-Hungary declared what was expected to be a short war against Serbia.

The alliance system pulled one nation after another into the conflict. On August 1, Germany, obligated by treaty to support Austria-Hungary, declared war on Russia. On August 3, Germany declared war on Russia's ally France. After Germany invaded Belgium, Britain declared war on Germany and Austria-Hungary. The Great War had begun. **B**

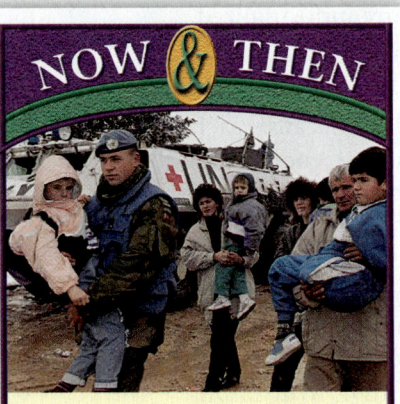

CRISIS IN THE BALKANS

After World War I, Bosnia became part of a country that eventually became known as Yugoslavia. Although Yugoslavia included various religious and ethnic groups, the government was dominated by Serbs.

In 1991, Yugoslavia broke apart, and Bosnia declared independence in 1992. However, Serbs wanted Bosnia to remain part of Serbian-controlled Yugoslavia.

A bloody civil war broke out. This war became notorious for the mass murder and deportation of Bosnian Muslims, a process known as "ethnic cleansing." In 1995, the United States helped negotiate a cease-fire.

But peace in the Balkans did not last. In the late 1990s, Albanians in the province of Kosovo also tried to break away from Serbia. Serbia's violent response, which included the "ethnic cleansing" of Albanians, prompted NATO to intervene. Kosovo declared its independence in 2008, despite Serbia's opposition.

> **MAIN IDEA**
>
> **Analyzing Effects**
> **B** Why were so many European nations pulled into the conflict?

The Fighting Starts

On August 3, 1914, Germany invaded Belgium, following a strategy known as the Schlieffen Plan. This plan called for a holding action against Russia, combined with a quick drive through Belgium to Paris; after France had fallen, the two German armies would defeat Russia. As German troops swept across Belgium, thousands of civilians fled in terror. In Brussels, the Belgian capital, an American war correspondent described the first major refugee crisis of the 20th century.

> **Vocabulary**
> **refugee:** a person who flees in search of protection or shelter, as in times of war or religious persecution

A PERSONAL VOICE RICHARD HARDING DAVIS

"[We] found the side streets blocked with their carts. Into these they had thrown mattresses, or bundles of grain, and heaped upon them were families of three generations. Old men in blue smocks, white-haired and bent, old women in caps, the daughters dressed in their one best frock and hat, and clasping in their hands all that was left to them, all that they could stuff into a pillow-case or flour-sack. . . . Heart-broken, weary, hungry, they passed in an unending caravan."

—from *Hooray for Peace, Hurrah for War*

Europe at the Start of World War I

hmhsocialstudies.com **INTERACTIVE MAP**

Tannenberg, Aug. 1914
Germans stop Russian advance.

British Blockade

May 1915
Lusitania sunk.

NORWAY

SWEDEN

Petrograd (St. Petersburg)

Moscow

R U S S I A

ATLANTIC

IRELAND (Br.)

North Sea

DENMARK

Baltic Sea

Tannenberg

Eastern Front Oct. 1917

OCEAN

50°N

GREAT BRITAIN

NETHERLANDS

London

Berlin

GERMANY

Brussels

BELGIUM

Paris

LUXEMBOURG

Vienna

Bay of Biscay

SWITZERLAND

AUSTRIA-HUNGARY

PORTUGAL

40°N

FRANCE

ROMANIA

Black Sea

SPAIN

ITALY

Adriatic Sea

Sarajevo

SERBIA

BULGARIA

MONTENEGRO

B A L K A N

Sarajevo, June 1914
Archduke Franz Ferdinand is assassinated.

Rome

ALBANIA

P E N I N S U L A

Constantinople (Istanbul)

10°W

GREECE

Aegean Sea

GALLIPOLI

O T T O M A N E M P I R E

Mediterranean Sea

0°

Gallipoli, April 1915–Jan. 1916
Allied forces defeated in bid to establish a supply route to Russia.

The Western Front 1914–1916

English Channel

NETHERLANDS

Brussels

B BELGIUM

Meuse

Somme

D

Oise

Aisne

Front on July 1, 1916

LUXEMBOURG

A

Seine

C

Marne

Metz

Paris

Meuse

Rhine

Farthest German advance, Sept. 5, 1914

Lunéville

G E R M A N Y

Moselle

N

W E

S

F R A N C E

SWITZERLAND

A **MARNE, 1st battle, Sept. 1914**
Allies stop German advance on Paris.

B **YPRES, 2nd battle, May 1915**
Germans use chemical weapons for the first time.

C **VERDUN, Feb.–July 1916**
French hold the line in longest battle of the war.

D **SOMME, 1st battle, July–Nov. 1916**
Disastrous British offensive.

→ German troop movement
→ Allied troop movement

| | 0 | 50 | 100 miles |
| 0 | 50 | 100 kilometers |

| Allied Powers, 1916 |
| Central Powers, 1916 |
| Neutral countries |
| German submarine activity |
| Battle |

| 0 | 250 | 500 miles |
| 0 | 250 | 500 kilometers |

GEOGRAPHY SKILLBUILDER

1. **Location** About how many miles separated the city of Paris from German forces at the point of their closest approach?

2. **Place** Consider the geographical location of the Allies in relation to the Central Powers. What advantage might the Allies have had?

Unable to save Belgium, the Allies retreated to the Marne River in France, where they halted the German advance in September 1914. After struggling to outflank each other's armies, both sides dug in for a long siege. By the spring of 1915, two parallel systems of deep, rat-infested trenches crossed France from the Belgian coast to the Swiss Alps. German soldiers occupied one set of trenches, Allied soldiers the other. There were three main kinds of trenches—front line, support, and reserve. Soldiers spent a period of time in each kind of trench. Dugouts, or underground rooms, were used as officers' quarters and command posts. Between the trench complexes lay **"no man's land"**—a barren expanse of mud pockmarked with shell craters and filled with barbed wire. Periodically, the soldiers charged enemy lines, only to be mowed down by machine gun fire. **C**

The scale of slaughter was horrific. During the First Battle of the Somme—which began on July 1, 1916, and lasted until mid-November—the British suffered 60,000 casualties the first day alone. Final casualties totaled about 1.2 million, yet only about seven miles of ground changed hands. This bloody **trench warfare,** in which armies fought for mere yards of ground, continued for over three years. Elsewhere, the fighting was just as devastating and inconclusive.

MAIN IDEA

Drawing Conclusions
C Why do you think soldiers were rotated in the trenches?

HISTORY

VIDEO
Trench Warfare

↗ hmhsocialstudies.com

Trench Warfare

↗ hmhsocialstudies.com **INTERACTIVE**

A Front line trench
B Support trench
C Reserve trench
D Enemy trench

Artillery fire "softened up" resistance before an infantry attack.

Communication trenches connected the three kinds of trenches.

Barbed wire entanglements

"No Man's Land" (from 25 yards to a mile wide)

Dugout

Saps were shallower trenches in "no man's land," allowing access to machine-gun nests, grenade-throwing positions, and observation posts.

Americans Question Neutrality

In 1914, most Americans saw no reason to join a struggle 3,000 miles away. The war did not threaten American lives or property. This does not mean, however, that individual Americans were indifferent to who would win the war. Public opinion was strong—but divided.

DIVIDED LOYALTIES Socialists criticized the war as a capitalist and imperialist struggle between Germany and England to control markets and colonies in China, Africa, and the Middle East. Pacifists, such as lawyer and politician William Jennings Bryan, believed that war was evil and that the United States should set an example of peace to the world.

Many Americans simply did not want their sons to experience the horrors of warfare, as a hit song of 1915 conveyed.

> "I didn't raise my boy to be a soldier,
> I brought him up to be my pride and joy.
> Who dares to place a musket on his shoulder,
> To shoot some other mother's darling boy?"

Vocabulary
emigrate: to leave one's country or region to settle in another; to move

Millions of naturalized U.S. citizens followed the war closely because they still had ties to the nations from which they had emigrated. For example, many Americans of German descent sympathized with Germany. Americans of Irish descent remembered the centuries of British oppression in Ireland and saw the war as a chance for Ireland to gain its independence.

On the other hand, many Americans felt close to Britain because of a common ancestry and language as well as similar democratic institutions and legal systems. Germany's aggressive sweep through Belgium increased American sympathy for the Allies. The Germans attacked civilians, destroying villages, cathedrals, libraries, and even hospitals. Some atrocity stories—spread by British propaganda—later proved to be false, but enough proved true that one American magazine referred to Germany as "the bully of Europe."

More important, America's economic ties with the Allies were far stronger than its ties with the Central Powers. Before the war, American trade with Britain and France was more than double its trade with Germany. During the first two years of the war, America's transatlantic trade became even more lopsided, as the Allies flooded American manufacturers with orders for all sorts of war supplies, including dynamite, cannon powder, submarines, copper wire and tubing, and armored cars. The United States shipped millions of dollars of war supplies to the Allies, but requests kept coming. By 1915, the United States was experiencing a labor shortage. **D**

MAIN IDEA

Analyzing Motives
D Why did the United States begin to favor Britain and France?

ECONOMIC BACKGROUND

TRADE ALLIANCES

Maintaining neutrality proved difficult for American businesses. Trade with Germany became increasingly risky. Shipments were often stopped by the British blockade. In addition, President Wilson and others spoke out against German atrocities and warned of the threat that the German Empire posed to democracy.

From 1912 to 1917, U.S. trade relationships with European countries shifted dramatically. From 1914 on, trade with the Allies quadrupled, while trade with Germany fell to near zero.

Also, by 1917, American banks had loaned $2.3 billion to the Allies, but only $27 million to the Central Powers. Many U.S. leaders, including Treasury Secretary William McAdoo, felt that American prosperity depended upon an Allied victory.

U.S. Exports to Europe, 1912–1917

Legend:
- Great Britain
- France
- Germany
- All Other European Countries

SKILLBUILDER Interpreting Graphs
1. By how much did total U.S. exports to Europe rise or fall between 1914 and 1917?
2. What trends does the graph show before the start of the war, and during the war?

This image of a U-boat crew machine-gunning helpless survivors of the *Lusitania* was clearly meant as propaganda. In fact, U-boats seldom lingered after an attack.

The War Hits Home

Although the majority of Americans favored victory for the Allies rather than the Central Powers, they did not want to join the Allies' fight. By 1917, however, America had mobilized for war against the Central Powers for two reasons: to ensure Allied repayment of debts to the United States and to prevent the Germans from threatening U.S. shipping.

THE BRITISH BLOCKADE As fighting on land continued, Britain began to make more use of its naval strength. It blockaded the German coast to prevent weapons and other military supplies from getting through. However, the British expanded the definition of contraband to include food. They also extended the blockade to neutral ports and mined the entire North Sea.

The results were twofold. First, American ships carrying goods for Germany refused to challenge the blockade and seldom reached their destination. Second, Germany found it increasingly difficult to import foodstuffs and fertilizers for crops. By 1917, famine stalked the country. An estimated 750,000 Germans starved to death as a result of the British blockade.

Americans had been angry at Britain's blockade, which threatened freedom of the seas and prevented American goods from reaching German ports. However, Germany's response to the blockade soon outraged American public opinion.

GERMAN U–BOAT RESPONSE Germany responded to the British blockade with a counterblockade by U-boats (from *Unterseeboot*, the German word for a submarine). Any British or Allied ship found in the waters around Britain would be sunk—and it would not always be possible to warn crews and passengers of an attack.

One of the worst disasters occurred on May 7, 1915, when a U-boat sank the British liner **Lusitania** (lōō′sĭ-tā′nē-ə) off the southern coast of Ireland. Of the 1,198 persons lost, 128 were Americans. The Germans defended their action on the grounds that the liner carried ammunition. Despite Germany's explanation, Americans became outraged with Germany because of the loss of life. American public opinion turned against Germany and the Central Powers.

A newspaper ad for the *Lusitania* included a warning from the German Embassy.

Despite this provocation, President Wilson ruled out a military response in favor of a sharp protest to Germany. Three months later, in August 1915, a U-boat sank another British liner, the *Arabic*, drowning two Americans. Again the United States protested, and this time Germany agreed not to sink any more passenger ships. But in March 1916 Germany broke its promise and torpedoed an unarmed French passenger steamer, the *Sussex*. The *Sussex* sank, and about 80 passengers, including Americans, were killed or injured. Once again the United States warned that it would break off diplomatic relations unless Germany changed its tactics. Again Germany agreed, but there was a condition: if the United States could not persuade Britain to lift its blockade against food and fertilizers, Germany would consider renewing unrestricted submarine warfare. **E**

THE 1916 ELECTION In November 1916 came the U.S. presidential election. The Democrats renominated Wilson, and the Republicans nominated Supreme Court Justice Charles Evans Hughes. Wilson campaigned on the slogan "He Kept Us Out of War." Hughes pledged to uphold America's right to freedom of the seas but also promised not to be too severe on Germany.

The election returns shifted from hour to hour. In fact, Hughes went to bed believing he had been elected. When a reporter tried to reach him with the news of Wilson's victory, an aide said, "The president can't be disturbed." "Well," replied the reporter, "when he wakes up, tell him he's no longer president."

▲ Wilson campaign button

The United States Declares War

After the election, Wilson tried to mediate between the warring alliances. The attempt failed. In a speech before the Senate in January 1917, the president called for "a peace without victory. . . . a peace between equals," in which neither side would impose harsh terms on the other. Wilson hoped that all nations would join in a "league for peace" that would work to extend democracy, maintain freedom of the seas, and reduce armaments.

GERMAN PROVOCATION The Germans ignored Wilson's calls for peace. Germany's leaders hoped to defeat Britain by resuming unrestricted submarine warfare. On January 31 the kaiser announced that U-boats would sink all ships in British waters—hostile or neutral—on sight. Wilson was stunned. The German decision meant that the United States would have to go to war. However, the president held back, saying that he would wait for "actual overt acts" before declaring war.

The overt acts came. First was the **Zimmermann note,** a telegram from the German foreign minister to the German ambassador in Mexico that was intercepted by British agents. The telegram proposed an alliance between Mexico and Germany and promised that if war with the United States broke out, Germany would support Mexico in recovering "lost territory in Texas, New Mexico, and Arizona." Next came the sinking of four unarmed American merchant ships, with a loss of 36 lives. **F**

Finally, events in Russia removed the last significant obstacle to direct U.S. involvement in the war. In March, the oppressive Russian monarchy was

MAIN IDEA

Analyzing Effects

E How did the German U-boat campaign affect U.S. public opinion?

MAIN IDEA

Making Inferences

F Why did the Zimmermann note alarm the U.S. government?

Alliances During WWI		
Allies		**Central Powers**
Australia	India	Austria-Hungary
Belgium	Italy	Bulgaria
British Colonies	Japan	Germany
Canada &	Montenegro	Ottoman Empire
Newfoundland	New Zealand	
France	Portugal	
French North	Romania	
Africa & French	Russia	
Colonies	Serbia	
Great Britain	South Africa	
Greece	United States	

Although not all of the countries listed above sent troops into the war, they all joined the war on the Allied side at various times.

REVOLUTION IN RUSSIA

At first, the Russians surprised the Germans by mobilizing rapidly. Russian troops advanced quickly into German territory but were turned back at the Battle of Tannenberg in August 1914.

Throughout 1915, the Russians endured defeats and continued to retreat. By the end of 1915 they had suffered about 2.5 million casualties. The war also caused massive bread shortages in Russia.

Revolutionaries ousted the czar in March 1917 and established a provisional government. In November, the Bolsheviks, led by Lenin and Trotsky, overthrew the provisional government. They set up a Communist state and sought peace with the Central Powers.

replaced with a representative government. Now supporters of American entry into the war could claim that this was a war of democracies against brutal monarchies.

AMERICA ACTS A light drizzle fell on Washington on April 2, 1917, as senators, representatives, ambassadors, members of the Supreme Court, and other guests crowded into the Capitol building to hear President Wilson deliver his war resolution.

A PERSONAL VOICE WOODROW WILSON

"Property can be paid for; the lives of peaceful and innocent people cannot be. The present German submarine warfare against commerce is a warfare against mankind. . . . We are glad . . . to fight . . . for the ultimate peace of the world and for the liberation of its peoples. . . . The world must be made safe for democracy. . . . We have no selfish ends to serve. We desire no conquest, no dominion. We seek no indemnities. . . . It is a fearful thing to lead this great peaceful people into war. . . . But the right is more precious than peace."

—quoted in *American Voices*

Congress passed the resolution a few days later. With the hope of neutrality finally shattered, U.S. troops would follow the stream of American money and munitions that had been heading to the Allies throughout the war. But Wilson's plea to make the world "safe for democracy" wasn't just political posturing. Indeed, Wilson and many Americans truly believed that the United States had to join the war to pave the way for a future order of peace and freedom. A resolved but anxious nation held its breath as the United States prepared for war.

ASSESSMENT

1. TERMS & NAMES For each term or name, write a sentence explaining its significance.

- nationalism
- militarism
- Allies
- Central Powers
- Archduke Franz Ferdinand
- no man's land
- trench warfare
- *Lusitania*
- Zimmermann note

MAIN IDEA

2. TAKING NOTES
In a chart like the one shown, list the causes for the outbreak of World War I.

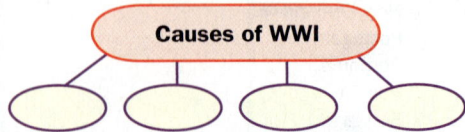

Which was the most significant cause? Explain your answer.

CRITICAL THINKING

3. SYNTHESIZING
Describe some ways in which World War I threatened the lives of civilians on both sides of the Atlantic.

4. SUMMARIZING
Why were America's ties with the Allies stronger than its ties with the Central Powers?

5. ANALYZING ISSUES
Why do you think Germany escalated its U-boat attacks in 1917? **Think About:**

- Germany's military buildup
- the effects of the British blockade
- Germany's reason for using submarine warfare

SECTION
2

PI 2.3
PI 4.1
CC Unit 1.I.B.4
CC Unit 4.II.B.2.c
CC Unit 4.II.C.1

American Power Tips the Balance

MAIN IDEA	WHY IT MATTERS NOW	Terms & Names
The United States mobilized a large army and navy to help the Allies achieve victory.	During World War I, the United States military evolved into the powerful fighting force that it remains today.	• Eddie Rickenbacker • Selective Service Act • convoy system • American Expeditionary Force • General John J. Pershing • Alvin York • conscientious objector • armistice

One American's Story

Eddie Rickenbacker, famous fighter pilot of World War I, was well known as a racecar driver before the war. He went to France as a driver but transferred to the aviation division. He learned to fly on his own time and eventually joined the U.S. Army Air Service. Rickenbacker repeatedly fought the dreaded Flying Circus—a German air squadron led by the "Red Baron," Manfred von Richthofen.

A PERSONAL VOICE EDDIE RICKENBACKER

" I put in six or seven hours of flying time each day. . . . My narrowest escape came at a time when I was fretting over the lack of action. . . . Guns began barking behind me, and sizzling tracers zipped by my head. . . . At least two planes were on my tail. . . .

They would expect me to dive. Instead I twisted upward in a corkscrew path called a 'chandelle.' I guessed right. As I went up, my two attackers came down, near enough for me to see their faces. I also saw the red noses on those Fokkers [German planes]. I was up against the Flying Circus again."

—*Rickenbacker: An Autobiography*

▲
World War I flying ace
Eddie Rickenbacker

After engaging in 134 air battles and downing 26 enemy aircraft, Rickenbacker won fame as the Allied pilot with the most victories—"American ace of aces."

America Mobilizes

The United States was not prepared for war. Only 200,000 men were in service when war was declared, and few officers had combat experience. Drastic measures were needed to build an army large and modern enough to make an impact in Europe.

Drafted men line up for service at Camp Travis in San Antonio, Texas, around 1917.

James Montgomery Flagg's portrayal of Uncle Sam became the most famous recruiting poster in American history.

RAISING AN ARMY To meet the government's need for more fighting power, Congress passed the **Selective Service Act** in May 1917. The act required men to register with the government in order to be randomly selected for military service. By the end of 1918, 24 million men had registered under the act. Of this number, almost 3 million were called up. About 2 million troops reached Europe before the truce was signed, and three-fourths of them saw actual combat. Most of the inductees had not attended high school, and about one in five was foreign-born.

About 400,000 African Americans served in the armed forces. More than half of them served in France. African American soldiers served in segregated units and were excluded from the navy and marines. Most African Americans were assigned to noncombat duties, although there were exceptions. The all-black 369th Infantry Regiment saw more continuous duty on the front lines than any other American regiment. Two soldiers of the 369th, Henry Johnson and Needham Roberts, were the first Americans to receive France's highest military honor, the Croix de Guerre—the "cross of war."

The eight-month training period took place partly in the United States and partly in Europe. During this time the men put in 17-hour days on target practice, bayonet drill, kitchen duty, and cleaning up the grounds. Since real weapons were in short supply, soldiers often drilled with fake weapons—rocks instead of hand grenades, or wooden poles instead of rifles.

Although women were not allowed to enlist, the army reluctantly accepted women in the Army Corps of Nurses, but denied them army rank, pay, and benefits. Meanwhile, some 13,000 women accepted noncombat positions in the navy and marines, where they served as nurses, secretaries, and telephone operators, with full military rank. **A**

MASS PRODUCTION In addition to the vast army that had to be created and trained, the United States had to find a way to transport men, food, and equipment over thousands of miles of ocean. It was an immense task, made more difficult by German submarine activity, which by early 1917 had sunk twice as much ship tonnage as the Allies had built. In order to expand its fleet, the U.S. government took four crucial steps.

Vocabulary
segregated: separated or isolated from others

MAIN IDEA

Summarizing
A How did the United States raise an army for the war?

First, the government exempted many shipyard workers from the draft and gave others a "deferred" classification, delaying their participation in the draft. Second, the U.S. Chamber of Commerce joined in a public relations campaign to emphasize the importance of shipyard work. They distributed service flags to families of shipyard workers, just like the flags given to families of soldiers and sailors. They also urged automobile owners to give shipyard employees rides to and from work, since streetcars were so crowded. Third, shipyards used prefabrication techniques. Instead of building an entire ship in the yard, standardized parts were built elsewhere and then assembled at the yard. This method reduced construction time substantially. As a result, on just one day—July 4, 1918—the United States launched 95 ships. Fourth, the government took over commercial and private ships and converted them for transatlantic war use. **B**

MAIN IDEA

Summarizing
B How did the United States expand its navy so quickly?

America Turns the Tide

German U-boat attacks on merchant ships in the Atlantic were a serious threat to the Allied war effort. American Vice Admiral William S. Sims convinced the British to try the **convoy system,** in which a heavy guard of destroyers escorted merchant ships back and forth across the Atlantic in groups. By fall of 1917, shipping losses had been cut in half.

The U.S. Navy also helped lay a 230-mile barrier of mines across the North Sea from Scotland to Norway. The barrier was designed to bottle up the U-boats that sailed from German ports and keep them out of the Atlantic Ocean.

By early 1918 the Germans found it increasingly difficult to replace their losses and to staff their fleet with trained submariners. Of the almost 2 million Americans who sailed to Europe during the war, only 637 were lost to U-boat attacks.

World War I Convoy System

cruiser · safe zone · merchant ships · defensive boundary · destroyer · enemy submarine

FIGHTING IN EUROPE After two and a half years of fighting, the Allied forces were exhausted and demoralized. One of the main contributions that American troops made to the Allied war effort, apart from their numbers, was their freshness and enthusiasm. They were determined to hit the Germans hard. Twenty-two-year-old Joseph Douglas Lawrence, a U.S. Army lieutenant, remarked on the importance of American enthusiasm when he described his first impression of the trenches.

★ **A PERSONAL VOICE** JOSEPH DOUGLAS LAWRENCE

" I have never seen or heard of such an elaborate, complete line of defense as the British had built at this point. There was a trench with dugouts every three hundred yards from the front line in Ypres back four miles to and including Dirty Bucket. Everything was fronted with barbed wire and other entanglements. Artillery was concealed everywhere. Railroad tracks, narrow and standard gauge, reached from the trenches back into the zone of supply. Nothing had been neglected to hold this line, save only one important thing, enthusiasm among the troops, and that was the purpose of our presence."

—*Fighting Soldier: The AEF in 1918*

Lieutenant Joseph D. Lawrence

Fighting "Over There"

The **American Expeditionary Force** (AEF), led by **General John J. Pershing,** included men from widely separated parts of the country. American infantrymen were nicknamed doughboys, possibly because of the white belts they wore, which they cleaned with pipe clay, or "dough." Most doughboys had never ventured far from the farms or small towns where they lived, and the sophisticated sights and sounds of Paris made a vivid impression. However, doughboys were also shocked by the unexpected horrors of the battlefield and astonished by the new weapons and tactics of modern warfare.

NEW WEAPONS The battlefields of World War I saw the first large-scale use of weapons that would become standard in modern war. Although some of these weapons were new, others, like the machine gun, had been so refined that they changed the nature of warfare. The two most innovative weapons were the tank and the airplane. Together, they heralded mechanized warfare, or warfare that relies on machines powered by gasoline and diesel engines. **Ⓒ**

Tanks ran on caterpillar treads and were built of steel so that bullets bounced off. The British first used tanks during the 1916 Battle of the Somme, but not very effectively. By 1917, the British had learned how to drive large numbers of tanks through barbed wire defenses, clearing a path for the infantry.

The early airplanes were so flimsy that at first both sides limited their use to scouting. After a while, the two sides used tanks to fire at enemy planes that were gathering information. Early dogfights, or individual air combats, like the one described by Eddie Rickenbacker, resembled duels. Pilots sat in their open cockpits and shot at each other with pistols. Because it was hard to fly a plane and shoot a pistol at the same time, planes began carrying mounted machine guns. But the planes' propeller blades kept getting in the way of the bullets. Then the Germans introduced an interrupter gear that permitted the stream of bullets to avoid the whirring blades.

MAIN IDEA

Forming Generalizations
Ⓒ How did World War I change the nature of warfare?

Background
When the U.S. entered the war, its air power was weak. Then, in July 1917, Congress appropriated a hefty $675 million to build an air force.

Science & Technology

TECHNOLOGY AT WAR

Both sides in World War I used new technology to attack more soldiers from greater distances than ever before. Aircraft and long-range guns were even used to fire on civilian targets—libraries, cathedrals, and city districts. The biggest guns could shell a city from 75 miles.

Machine Guns
Firepower increased to 600 rounds per minute.

Airships and Airplanes
One of the most famous WWI planes, the British Sopwith Camel, had a front-mounted machine gun for "dogfights." Planes were also loaded with bombs, as were the floating gas-filled "airships" called zeppelins.

Meanwhile, airplanes were built to travel faster and carry heavy bomb loads. By 1918 the British had built up a strategic bomber force of 22,000 planes with which to attack German weapons factories and army bases.

Observation balloons were used extensively by both sides in the war in Europe. Balloons were so important strategically that they were often protected by aircraft flying close by, and they became prime targets for Rickenbacker and other ace pilots.

The War Introduces New Hazards

The new weapons and tactics of World War I led to horrific injuries and hazards. The fighting men were surrounded by filth, lice, rats, and polluted water that caused dysentery. They inhaled poison gas and smelled the stench of decaying bodies. They suffered from lack of sleep. Constant bombardments and other experiences often led to battle fatigue and "shell shock," a term coined during World War I to describe a complete emotional collapse from which many never recovered.

Physical problems included a disease called trench foot, caused by standing in cold wet trenches for long periods of time without changing into dry socks or boots. First the toes would turn red or blue, then they would become numb, and finally they would start to rot. The only solution was to amputate the toes, and in some cases the entire foot. A painful infection of the gums and throat, called trench mouth, was also common among the soldiers. **D**

Red Cross ambulances, often staffed by American volunteers, carried the wounded from the battlefield to the hospital. An American nurse named Florence Bullard recounted her experience in a hospital near the front in 1918.

★ A PERSONAL VOICE FLORENCE BULLARD

"The Army is only twelve miles away from us and only the wounded that are too severely injured to live to be carried a little farther are brought here. . . . Side by side I have Americans, English, Scotch, Irish, and French, and apart in the corners are Boche [Germans]. They have to watch each other die side by side. I am sent for everywhere—in the . . . operating-room, the dressing-room, and back again to the rows of men. . . . The cannon goes day and night and the shells are breaking over and around us. . . . I have had to write many sad letters to American mothers. I wonder if it will ever end."

—quoted in *Over There: The Story of America's First Great Overseas Crusade*

In fact, the end was near, as German forces mounted a final offensive.

Antiaircraft Gun

Poison Gas
A yellow-green chlorine fog sickened, suffocated, burned, and blinded its victims. Gas masks became standard issue.

Tanks
Tanks, like this French light tank, were used to "mow down" barbed wire and soldiers.

Allied Victories, 1917–1918

hmhsocialstudies.com **INTERACTIVE MAP**

Legend:
- Allied Powers (green)
- Central Powers (orange)
- Neutral countries (purple)
- German offensive, Mar.–July 1918
- Armistice line, Nov. 11, 1918
- Battle

0   50   100 miles
0   50   100 kilometers

Map labels: GREAT BRITAIN, North Sea, Channel, English, NETHERLANDS, Brussels, Lille, BELGIUM, Cologne, Rhine, Arras, Somme, GERMANY, Compiègne, Laon, Sedan, Mosel, LUXEMBOURG, Seine, Oise, Aisne, Metz, AUSTRIA–HUNGARY, Paris, Marne, FRANCE, ARGONNE FOREST, Meuse, Lunéville, SWITZERLAND

Ypres, 3rd battle, July–Nov. 1917 Allied victory costs over half a million casualties.

Cantigny, May 1918 U.S. troops fill gaps between French and British lines during German offensive.

Château-Thierry, June 1918 U.S. troops help stop the German advance on Paris.

Meuse-Argonne, Sept.–Nov. 1918 American advance helps end the war.

St. Mihiel, Sept. 1918 Pershing leads American army to victory.

Marne, 2nd battle, July–Aug. 1918 The turning point of the war. Allies advance steadily after defeating the Germans.

GEOGRAPHY SKILLBUILDER
1. **Location** Did the Germans achieve their goal of capturing Paris in their March 1918 offensive? Why or why not?
2. **Place** What geographical feature of northern France made it particularly well suited to trench warfare?

American Troops Go on the Offensive

When Russia pulled out of the war in 1917, the Germans shifted their armies from the eastern front to the western front in France. By May they were within 50 miles of Paris. The Americans arrived just in time to help stop the German advance at Cantigny in France. Several weeks later, U.S. troops played a major role in throwing back German attacks at Château-Thierry and Belleau Wood. In July and August, they helped win the Second Battle of the Marne. The tide had turned against the Central Powers. In September, U.S. soldiers began to mount offensives against the Germans at Saint-Mihiel and in the Meuse-Argonne area. **E**

"Bullets were cracking just over my head."

SERGEANT YORK

AMERICAN WAR HERO During the fighting in the Meuse-Argonne area, one of America's greatest war heroes, **Alvin York,** became famous. A redheaded mountaineer and blacksmith from Tennessee, York sought exemption as a **conscientious objector,** a person who opposes warfare on moral grounds, pointing out that the Bible says, "Thou shalt not kill."

York eventually decided that it was morally acceptable to fight if the cause was just. On October 8, 1918, armed only with a rifle and a revolver, York killed 25 Germans and—with six other doughboys—captured 132 prisoners. General Pershing called him the outstanding soldier of the AEF, while Marshal Foch, the commander of Allied forces in Europe, described his feat as "the greatest thing accomplished by any private soldier of all the armies of Europe." For his heroic acts, York was promoted to sergeant and became a celebrity when he returned to the United States.

THE COLLAPSE OF GERMANY On November 3, 1918, Austria-Hungary surrendered to the Allies. That same day, German sailors mutinied against government authority. The mutiny spread quickly. Everywhere in Germany, groups of soldiers and workers organized revolutionary councils. On November 9, socialist leaders in the capital, Berlin, established a German republic. The kaiser gave up the throne.

MAIN IDEA

Drawing Conclusions
E How did American forces help the Allies win the war?

Although there were no Allied soldiers on German territory and no truly decisive battle had been fought, the Germans were too exhausted to continue fighting. So at the eleventh hour, on the eleventh day, in the eleventh month of 1918, Germany agreed to a cease-fire and signed the **armistice,** or truce, that ended the war.

THE FINAL TOLL World War I was the bloodiest war in history up to that time. Deaths numbered about 22 million, more than half of them civilians. In addition, 20 million people were wounded, and 10 million more became refugees. The direct economic costs of the war may have been about $338 billion. The United States lost 48,000 men in battle, with another 62,000 dying of disease. More than 200,000 Americans were wounded.

For the Allies, news of the armistice brought great relief. Private John Barkley described the reaction to the news.

★ A PERSONAL VOICE JOHN L. BARKLEY

" About 9 o'clock in the evening we heard wild commotion in the little town. The French people, old and young, were running through the streets. Old men and women we'd seen sitting around their houses too feeble to move, were out in the streets yelling, 'Vive la France! Vive la France! Vive l'America!'. . . .

Down the street came a soldier. He was telling everybody the armistice had been signed. I said, 'What's an armistice?' It sounded like some kind of machine to me. The other boys around there didn't know what it meant either.

When the official word came through that it meant peace, we couldn't believe it. Finally Jesse said, 'Well kid, I guess it really does mean the war is over.' I said, 'I just can't believe it's true.' But it was."

—*No Hard Feelings*

Across the Atlantic, Americans also rejoiced at the news. Many now expected life to return to normal. However, people found their lives at home changed almost as much as the lives of those who had fought in Europe.

SECTION 2 ASSESSMENT

1. TERMS & NAMES For each term or name, write a sentence explaining its significance.
- Eddie Rickenbacker
- Selective Service Act
- convoy system
- American Expeditionary Force
- General John J. Pershing
- Alvin York
- conscientious objector
- armistice

MAIN IDEA

2. TAKING NOTES
Fill in a web like the one below to show how Americans responded to the war.

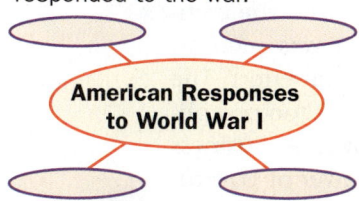

American Responses to World War I

Why was the entire population affected by America's entry into World War I?

CRITICAL THINKING

3. DRAWING CONCLUSIONS
In what ways did WWI represent a frightening new kind of warfare? **Think About:**
- the casualty figures
- new military technology
- shell shock

4. ANALYZING VISUAL SOURCES
This World War I poster shows the role of non-combatants overseas. What is the message in this propaganda poster?

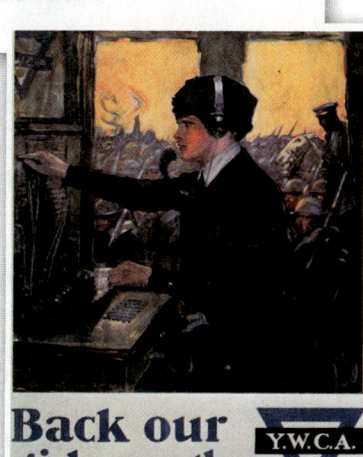

Back our girls over there
United War Work Campaign
Y.W.C.A.

PI 2.3
PI 4.1

CC Unit 3.III.A.2.e   CC Unit 4.II.C.1
CC Unit 4.II.C.2   CC Unit 4.II.C.3
CC Unit 5.I.A.1   CC Unit 5.I.A.3

The War at Home

MAIN IDEA	WHY IT MATTERS NOW	Terms & Names
World War I spurred social, political, and economic change in the United States.	Such changes increased government powers and expanded economic opportunities.	• War Industries Board • Bernard M. Baruch • propaganda • George Creel • Espionage and Sedition Acts • Great Migration

One American's Story

hmhsocialstudies.com
TAKING NOTES

Use the graphic organizer online to take notes on how World War I changed American life.

The suffragist Harriot Stanton Blatch visited a munitions plant in New Jersey during World War I and proudly described women at work.

A PERSONAL VOICE HARRIOT STANTON BLATCH

" The day I visited the place, in one of the largest shops women had only just been put on the work, but it was expected that in less than a month they would be found handling all of the twelve hundred machines under that one roof alone. The skill of the women staggers one. After a week or two they master the operations on the 'turret,' gauging and routing machines. The best worker on the 'facing' machine is a woman. She is a piece worker, as many of the women are. . . . This woman earned, the day I saw her, five dollars and forty cents. She tossed about the fuse parts, and played with that machine, as I would with a baby. "

—quoted in *We, the American Women*

▲ **Harriot Stanton Blatch followed in the footsteps of her famous mother, Elizabeth Cady Stanton.**

Before World War I, women had been excluded from many jobs. However, the wartime need for labor brought over a million more women into the work force. For women, as for the rest of society, World War I brought about far-reaching changes.

Congress Gives Power to Wilson

Winning the war was not a job for American soldiers alone. As Secretary of War Newton Baker said, "War is no longer Samson with his shield and spear and sword, and David with his sling. It is the conflict of smokestacks now, the combat of the driving wheel and the engine." Because World War I was such an immense conflict, the entire economy had to be refocused on the war effort. The shift from producing consumer goods to producing war supplies was too complicated and important a job for private industry to handle on its own, so business and government collaborated in the effort. In the process, the power of government was greatly expanded. Congress gave President Wilson direct control over much of the economy, including the power to fix prices and to regulate—even to nationalize—certain war-related industries.

WAR INDUSTRIES BOARD The main regulatory body was the **War Industries Board** (WIB). It was established in 1917 and reorganized in 1918 under the leadership of **Bernard M. Baruch** (bə-rōōk'), a prosperous businessman. The board encouraged companies to use mass-production techniques to increase efficiency. It also urged them to eliminate waste by standardizing products—for instance, by making only 5 colors of typewriter ribbons instead of 150. The WIB set production quotas and allocated raw materials.

Under the WIB, industrial production in the United States increased by about 20 percent. However, the WIB applied price controls only at the wholesale level. As a result, retail prices soared, and in 1918 they were almost double what they had been before the war. Corporate profits soared as well, especially in such industries as chemicals, meatpacking, oil, and steel.

The WIB was not the only federal agency to regulate the economy during the war. The Railroad Administration controlled the railroads, and the Fuel Administration monitored coal supplies and rationed gasoline and heating oil. In addition, many people adopted "gasless Sundays" and "lightless nights" to conserve fuel. In March 1918, the Fuel Administration introduced another conservation measure: daylight-saving time, which had first been proposed by Benjamin Franklin in the 1770s as a way to take advantage of the longer days of summer.

WAR ECONOMY Wages in most industries rose during the war years. Hourly wages for blue-collar workers—those in the metal trades, shipbuilding, and meatpacking, for example—rose by about 20 percent. A household's income, however, was largely undercut by rising food prices and housing costs.

By contrast, stockholders in large corporations saw enormous profits. One industrial manufacturer, the DuPont Company, saw its stock multiply in value 1,600 percent between 1914 and 1918. By that time the company was earning a $68-million yearly profit. As a result of the uneven pay between labor and management, increasing work hours, child labor, and dangerously "sped-up" conditions, unions boomed. Union membership climbed from about 2.5 million in 1916 to more than 4 million in 1919. More than 6,000 strikes broke out during the war months.

To deal with disputes between management and labor, President Wilson established the National War Labor Board in 1918. Workers who refused to obey board decisions could lose their draft exemptions. "Work or fight," the board told them. However, the board also worked to improve factory conditions. It pushed for an eight-hour workday, promoted safety inspections, and enforced the child labor ban. Ⓐ

FOOD ADMINISTRATION To help produce and conserve food, Wilson set up the Food Administration under Herbert Hoover. Instead of rationing food, he called on people to follow the "gospel of the clean plate." He declared one day a week "meatless," another "sweetless," two days "wheatless," and two other days "porkless." Restaurants removed sugar bowls from the table and served bread only after the first course.

Background
In 1913 Henry Ford speeded up factory production with a constantly moving assembly line. Wartime production spread this technique throughout the country.

MAIN IDEA

Making Inferences
Ⓐ Why would labor disputes affect the war effort?

The War Economy, 1914–1920

Average Annual Income

Year	Income
1914	$627
1915	$633
1916	$708
1917	$830
1918	$1,047
1919	$1,201
1920	$1,407

Source: *Historical Statistics of the United States*

Consumer Price Index*

*A measure of changes in the prices of goods and services commonly bought by consumers

SKILLBUILDER Interpreting Graphs
1. How did the rise in average annual income compare with the rise in prices from 1914 to 1920?
2. How might the combined change in wages and prices affect a working family?

Food is Ammunition— *Don't waste it.*

Homeowners planted "victory gardens" in their yards. Schoolchildren spent their after-school hours growing tomatoes and cucumbers in public parks. As a result of these and similar efforts, American food shipments to the Allies tripled. Hoover also set a high government price on wheat and other staples. Farmers responded by putting an additional 40 million acres into production. In the process, they increased their income by almost 30 percent.

Selling the War

Once the government had extended its control over the economy, it was faced with two major tasks: raising money and convincing the public to support the war.

WAR FINANCING The United States spent about $35.5 billion on the war effort. The government raised about one-third of this amount through taxes, including a progressive income tax (which taxed high incomes at a higher rate than low incomes), a war-profits tax, and higher excise taxes on tobacco, liquor, and luxury goods. It raised the rest through public borrowing by selling "Liberty Loan" and "Victory Loan" bonds.

The government sold bonds through tens of thousands of volunteers. Movie stars spoke at rallies in factories, in schools, and on street corners. As Treasury Secretary William G. McAdoo put it, only "a friend of Germany" would refuse to buy war bonds. **B**

COMMITTEE ON PUBLIC INFORMATION To popularize the war, the government set up the nation's first **propaganda** agency, the Committee on Public Information (CPI). Propaganda is a kind of biased communication designed to influence people's thoughts and actions. The head of the CPI was a former muck-raking journalist named **George Creel.**

Creel persuaded the nation's artists and advertising agencies to create thousands of paintings, posters, cartoons, and sculptures promoting the war. He recruited some 75,000 men to serve as "Four-Minute Men," who spoke about everything relating to the war: the draft, rationing, bond drives, victory gardens, and topics such as "Why We Are Fighting" and "The Meaning of America."

Nor did Creel neglect the written word. He ordered a printing of almost 25 million copies of "How the War Came to America"—which included Wilson's war message—in English and other languages. He distributed some 75 million pamphlets, booklets, and leaflets, many with the enthusiastic help of the Boy

MAIN IDEA

Summarizing
B How did the government raise money for the war effort?

Scouts. Creel's propaganda campaign was highly effective. However, while the campaign promoted patriotism, it also inflamed hatred and violations of the civil liberties of certain ethnic groups and opponents of the war.

Attacks on Civil Liberties Increase

Early in 1917, President Wilson expressed his fears about the consequences of war hysteria.

A PERSONAL VOICE WOODROW WILSON

" Once lead this people into war and they'll forget there ever was such a thing as tolerance. To fight you must be brutal and ruthless, and the spirit of ruthless brutality will enter into the very fiber of our national life, infecting Congress, the courts, the policeman on the beat, the man in the street. Conformity would be the only virtue, and every man who refused to conform would have to pay the penalty."

—quoted in *Cobb of "The World"*

The president's prediction came true. As soon as war was declared, conformity indeed became the order of the day. Attacks on civil liberties, both unofficial and official, erupted.

ANTI-IMMIGRANT HYSTERIA The main targets of these attacks were Americans who had emigrated from other nations, especially those from Germany and Austria-Hungary. The most bitter attacks were directed against the nearly 2 million Americans who had been born in Germany, but other foreign-born persons and Americans of German descent suffered as well. **C**

Many Americans with German names lost their jobs. Orchestras refused to play the music of Mozart, Bach, Beethoven, and Brahms. Some towns with German names changed them. Schools stopped teaching the German language, and librarians removed books by German authors from the shelves. People even resorted to violence against German Americans, flogging them or smearing them

---

MAIN IDEA

Developing Historical Perspective
 What effect did the war have on the lives of recent immigrants?

Analyzing *Political Cartoons*

THE ENEMY WITHIN

After the United States entered the war, government propaganda helped inflame prejudice against recent immigrants. In the suspicious atmosphere of the time, conspiracy theories flourished, and foreign spies were believed to be everywhere. This cartoon reveals the hysteria that gripped the country in 1917.

SKILLBUILDER Analyzing Political Cartoons
1. What is happening in this cartoon?
2. What does the cartoonist suggest will happen to "enemy aliens"?

SEE SKILLBUILDER HANDBOOK, PAGE R24.

Stripped! By J. H. Cassel

with tar and feathers. A mob in Collinsville, Illinois, wrapped a German flag around a German-born miner named Robert Prager and lynched him. A jury cleared the mob's leader.

Finally, in a burst of anti-German fervor, Americans changed the name of German measles to "liberty measles." Hamburger—named after the German city of Hamburg—became "Salisbury steak" or "liberty sandwich," depending on whether you were buying it in a store or eating it in a restaurant. Sauerkraut was renamed "liberty cabbage," and dachshunds turned into "liberty pups."

ESPIONAGE AND SEDITION ACTS In June 1917 Congress passed the Espionage Act, and in May 1918 it passed the Sedition Act. Under the **Espionage and Sedition Acts** a person could be fined up to $10,000 and sentenced to 20 years in jail for interfering with the war effort or for saying anything disloyal, profane, or abusive about the government or the war effort.

Vocabulary
sedition: rebellion against one's government; treason

Like the Alien and Sedition Acts of 1798, these laws clearly violated the spirit of the First Amendment. Their passage led to over 2,000 prosecutions for loosely defined antiwar activities; of these, over half resulted in convictions. Newspapers and magazines that opposed the war or criticized any of the Allies lost their mailing privileges. The House of Representatives refused to seat Victor Berger, a socialist congressman from Wisconsin, because of his antiwar views. Columbia University fired a distinguished psychologist because he opposed the war. A colleague who supported the war thereupon resigned in protest, saying, "If we have to suppress everything we don't like to hear, this country is resting on a pretty wobbly basis."

▲ This Industrial Workers of the World (IWW) sticker encourages workers to join the union.

The Espionage and Sedition Acts targeted socialists and labor leaders. Eugene V. Debs was handed a ten-year prison sentence for speaking out against the war and the draft. The anarchist Emma Goldman received a two-year prison sentence and a $10,000 fine for organizing the No Conscription League. When she left jail, the authorities deported her to Russia. "Big Bill" Haywood and other leaders of the Industrial Workers of the World (IWW) were accused of sabotaging the war effort because they urged workers to strike for better conditions and higher pay. Haywood was sentenced to a long prison term. (He later skipped bail and fled to Russia.) Under such federal pressure, the IWW faded away. **D**

MAIN IDEA

Analyzing Effects
D What impact did the Espionage and Sedition Acts have on free speech?

The War Encourages Social Change

Wars often unleash powerful social forces. The period of World War I was no exception; important changes transformed the lives of African Americans and women.

AFRICAN AMERICANS AND THE WAR Black public opinion about the war was divided. On one side were people like W. E. B. Du Bois, who believed that blacks should support the war effort.

A PERSONAL VOICE W. E. B. DU BOIS

"That which the German power represents today spells death to the aspirations of Negroes and all darker races for equality, freedom and democracy. . . . Let us, while this war lasts, forget our special grievances and close our ranks shoulder to shoulder with our own white fellow citizens and the allied nations that are fighting for democracy."

—"Close Ranks"

W. E. B. Du Bois ▶

Du Bois believed that African-American support for the war would strengthen calls for racial justice. In contrast, William Monroe Trotter, founder of the *Boston Guardian*, believed that victims of racism should not support a racist government. Trotter condemned Du Bois's accommodationist approach and favored protest instead. Nevertheless, despite grievances over continued racial inequality in the United States, most African Americans backed the war.

THE GREAT MIGRATION In concrete terms, the greatest effect of the First World War on African Americans' lives was that it accelerated the **Great Migration,** the large-scale movement of hundreds of thousands of Southern blacks to cities in the North. This great population shift had already begun before the war in the late 19th century, when African Americans trickled northward to escape the Jim Crow South—but after the turn of the century, the trickle became a tidal wave.

Several factors contributed to the tremendous increase in black migration. First, many African Americans sought to escape racial discrimination in the South, which made it hard to make a living and often threatened their lives. Also, a boll weevil infestation, aided by floods and droughts, had ruined much of the South's cotton fields. In the North, there were more job opportunities. For example, Henry Ford opened his automobile assembly line to black workers in 1914. The outbreak of World War I and the drop in European immigration increased job opportunities for African Americans in steel mills, munitions plants, and stockyards. Northern manufacturers sent recruiting agents to distribute free railroad passes through the South. In addition, the publisher of the black-owned newspaper *Chicago Defender* bombarded Southern blacks with articles contrasting Dixieland lynchings with the prosperity of African Americans in the North. **E**

> **MAIN IDEA**
>
> **Making Inferences**
>
> **E** How did the war open opportunities for African Americans?

History Through *Art*

THE MIGRATION OF THE NEGRO, PANEL NO. 1 (1940–41)

This painting by Jacob Lawrence shows three of the most common destinations for African Americans leaving the South. **Why do you think the artist has not shown any individual facial features?**

HISTORICAL SPOTLIGHT

RACE RIOTS

Racial prejudice against African Americans in the North sometimes took violent forms. In July 1917, a race riot exploded in East St. Louis, Illinois. White workers, furious over the hiring of African Americans as strikebreakers at a munitions plant, rampaged through the streets. Forty blacks and nine whites died.

Another riot erupted in July 1919 in Chicago when a 17-year-old African American swam from the water off a "black beach" to the water off a "white beach." There, white bathers threw rocks at him until he drowned.

African Americans retaliated, and several riots broke out in the city. Order was restored after several days of violence that involved about 10,000 people.

However, racial prejudice against African Americans also existed in the North. The press of new migrants to Northern cities caused overcrowding and intensified racial tensions.

Nevertheless, between 1910 and 1930, hundreds of thousands of African Americans migrated to such cities as Chicago, New York, and Philadelphia. Author Richard Wright described the great exodus.

A PERSONAL VOICE RICHARD WRIGHT

"We are bitter no more; we are leaving! We are leaving our homes, pulling up stakes to move on. We look up at the high southern sky and remember all the sunshine and all the rain and we feel a sense of loss, but we are leaving. We look out at the wide green fields which our eyes saw when we first came into the world and we feel full of regret, but we are leaving. We scan the kind black faces we have looked upon since we first saw the light of day, and, though pain is in our hearts, we are leaving. We take one last furtive look over our shoulders to the Big House—high upon a hill beyond the railroad tracks—where the Lord of the Land lives, and we feel glad, for we are leaving."

—quoted in *12 Million Black Voices*

WOMEN IN THE WAR While African Americans began new lives, women moved into jobs that had been held exclusively by men. They became railroad workers, cooks, dockworkers, and bricklayers. They mined coal and took part in shipbuilding. At the same time, women continued to fill more traditional jobs as nurses, clerks, and teachers. Many women worked as volunteers, serving at Red Cross facilities and encouraging the sale of bonds and the planting of victory gardens. Other women, such as Jane Addams, were active in the peace movement. Addams helped found the Women's Peace Party in 1915 and remained a pacifist even after the United States entered the war. **F**

President Wilson acknowledged, "The services of women during the supreme crisis have been of the most signal usefulness and distinction; it is high time that part of our debt should be acknowledged." While acknowledgment of that debt did not include equal pay for equal work, it did help bolster public support for woman suffrage. In 1919, Congress finally passed the Nineteenth Amendment, granting women the right to vote. In 1920 the amendment was ratified by the states.

MAIN IDEA

Analyzing Effects
F What effect did the war have on women's lives?

Women worked in a variety of jobs during the war. Here, women assemble an aircraft wing.

THE FLU EPIDEMIC In the fall of 1918, the United States suffered a home-front crisis when an international flu epidemic affected about one-quarter of the U.S. population. The effect of the epidemic on the economy was devastating. Mines shut down, telephone service was cut in half, and factories and offices staggered working hours to avoid contagion. Cities ran short of coffins, and the corpses of poor people lay unburied for as long as a week. The mysterious illness seemed to strike people who were otherwise in the best of health, and death could come in a matter of days. Doctors did not know what to do, other than to recommend cleanliness and quarantine. One epidemic survivor recalled that "so many people died from the flu they just rang the bells; they didn't dare take [corpses] into the church."

New York City street cleaners wore masks to avoid catching influenza.

In the army, where living conditions allowed contagious illnesses to spread rapidly, more than a quarter of the soldiers caught the disease. In some AEF units, one-third of the troops died. Germans fell victim in even larger numbers than the Allies. Possibly spread around the world by soldiers, the epidemic killed about 500,000 Americans before it disappeared in 1919. Historians believe that the influenza virus killed as many as 30 million people worldwide. **G**

World War I brought death and disease to millions but, like the flu epidemic, the war also came to a sudden end. After four years of slaughter and destruction, the time had come to forge a peace settlement. Americans hoped that this "war to end all wars" would do just that. Leaders of the victorious nations gathered at Versailles outside Paris to work out the terms of peace, and President Wilson traveled to Europe to ensure it.

MAIN IDEA

Making Inferences
G How did wartime conditions help spread the flu?

SECTION 3 ASSESSMENT

1. TERMS & NAMES For each term or name, write a sentence explaining its significance.

- War Industries Board
- Bernard M. Baruch
- propaganda
- George Creel
- Espionage and Sedition Acts
- Great Migration

MAIN IDEA

2. TAKING NOTES
In a chart like the one shown, list some of the changes that the war brought about for each group.

Changes Brought About by the War	
African Americans	
Women	
Immigrants	

Explain how each group benefited from or was disadvantaged by these changes.

CRITICAL THINKING

3. DRAWING CONCLUSIONS
How did the war affect government power? **Think About:**

- how private business worked with government
- how much control the president gained over the economy
- the Espionage and Sedition Acts

4. MAKING INFERENCES
Why do you think the flu spread so quickly among the troops?

5. EVALUATING
Do you think that the war had a positive or a negative effect on American society? **Think About:**

- how the propaganda campaign influenced people's behavior
- the new job opportunities for African Americans and women
- how the government controlled industry

SCHENCK v. UNITED STATES (1919)

ORIGINS OF THE CASE Charles Schenck, an official of the U.S. Socialist Party, distributed leaflets that called the draft a "deed against humanity" and compared conscription to slavery, urging conscripts to "assert your rights." Schenck was convicted of sedition and sentenced to prison, but he argued that the conviction, punishment, and even the law itself violated his right to free speech. The Supreme Court agreed to hear his appeal.

THE RULING A unanimous court upheld Schenck's conviction, stating that under wartime conditions, the words in the leaflets were not protected by the right to free speech.

LEGAL REASONING

The Supreme Court's opinion in the *Schenck* case, written by Justice Oliver Wendell Holmes, Jr., has become famous as a guide for how the First Amendment defines the right of free speech. Holmes wrote:

> "The question in every case is whether the words used are used in such circumstances and are of such a nature as to create a clear and present danger that they will bring about the substantive evils that Congress has a right to prevent."

Justice Holmes noted that "in ordinary times" the First Amendment might have protected Schenck, but "[w]hen a nation is at war many things that might be said in time of peace . . . will not be endured."

The analogy that Holmes used to explain why Schenck could be punished for his words has become probably the best-known observation ever made about free speech:

> "Protection of free speech would not protect a man in falsely shouting 'Fire!' in a theatre and causing a panic."

Writing for the Court, Holmes implied that during wartime, Schenck's leaflet was just that dangerous.

Oliver Wendell Holmes, Jr., Supreme Court Justice 1902–1932 ▶

LEGAL SOURCES

LEGISLATION

U.S. CONSTITUTION, FIRST AMENDMENT (1791)
"Congress shall make no law . . . abridging the freedom of speech, or of the press."

THE SEDITION ACT (1918)
"(W)hoever . . . shall willfully utter, print, write or publish any disloyal, profane, scurrilous, or abusive language about the form of government, . . . Constitution, . . . military or naval forces, . . . flag, . . . or the uniform of the Army or Navy of the United States . . . shall be punished by a fine of not more than $10,000 or imprisonment for not more than twenty years, or both."

RELATED CASES

DEBS v. UNITED STATES (MARCH, 1919)
The conviction against Eugene Debs for speaking against the war and the draft is upheld.

FROHWERK v. UNITED STATES (MARCH, 1919)
The publisher of a newspaper that had criticized the war is sentenced with a fine and ten years in prison.

ABRAMS v. UNITED STATES (NOV., 1919)
Leaflets criticizing the U.S. expeditionary force in Russia are found to be unprotected by the First Amendment. Holmes writes a dissenting opinion calling for the "free trade of ideas."

WHY IT MATTERED

During the course of World War I, the federal government brought approximately 2,000 prosecutions for violations of the Espionage Act of 1917 or the Sedition Act of 1918, the same laws under which it convicted Schenck, Debs, and Frohwerk.

By the fall of 1919, however, Holmes had changed his mind. The case of *Abrams* v. *United States* concerned leaflets that criticized President Wilson's "capitalistic" government for sending troops to put down the Russian Revolution. Justice Holmes, joined by Justice Louis Brandeis, dissented from the majority of the Court, which upheld the conviction. In his dissent, Holmes emphasized the importance of a free exchange of ideas so that truth will win out in the intellectual marketplace. His reasoning won him acclaim as a protector of free speech.

The belief that truth will eventually win out in the marketplace of ideas has become important legal justification for promoting freedom of speech.

HISTORICAL IMPACT

Disagreements about what kinds of speech are "free" under the First Amendment continue. During the 1950s, when people were jailed for supporting Communism, and during the Vietnam War, when war protestors supported draft resistance, these issues again reached the Supreme Court.

The Court has also been asked to decide if young people in schools have the same First Amendment rights as adults. In *Tinker* v. *Des Moines School District* (1969), the Court ordered a school to readmit students who had been suspended for wearing black arm bands in protest of the war in Vietnam.

This so-called symbolic speech, such as wearing an armband or burning a draft card or a flag to express an opinion, has sparked heated debate. In *Texas* v. *Johnson* (1989), the Court, by a narrow five to four vote, invalidated a law under which a man who burned an American flag to protest Reagan administration policies had been convicted. The decision so outraged some people that members of Congress considered amending the Constitution to prohibit any "physical desecration" of the flag. The amendment did not pass. Our freedoms of expression continue to depend upon the words in the first article of the Bill of Rights, written more than 200 years ago.

Eugene Debs was arrested for antiwar speeches like the one he gave at this 1916 presidential campaign stop.

In 1965 Mary Beth Tinker and her brother, John, were suspended from school for wearing armbands that symbolically criticized the Vietnam War.

THINKING CRITICALLY

CONNECT TO HISTORY

1. **Analyzing Primary Sources** Read Justice Holmes's dissent in *Abrams* v. *United States*. Compare it with the opinion he wrote in *Schenck* v. *United States*. Explain the major difference or similarity in the two opinions.

   SEE SKILLBUILDER HANDBOOK, PAGE R22.

CONNECT TO TODAY

2. Visit the links for Historic Decisions of the Supreme Court to research articles about free speech issues. Select several of these issues—such as whether hate groups have a right to march—to discuss with other students in your class. Choose one issue and, as a group, write down as many arguments as you can on both sides of the issue. Then present a debate to the class.

   hmhsocialstudies.com INTERNET ACTIVITY

Wilson Fights for Peace

MAIN IDEA	WHY IT MATTERS NOW	Terms & Names
European leaders opposed most of Wilson's peace plan, and the U.S. Senate failed to ratify the peace treaty.	Many of the nationalist issues left unresolved after World War I continue to trouble the world today.	• Fourteen Points • League of Nations • Georges Clemenceau • David Lloyd George • Treaty of Versailles • reparations • war-guilt clause • Henry Cabot Lodge

hmhsocialstudies.com
TAKING NOTES

Use the graphic organizer online to take notes on the Treaty of Versailles.

One American's Story

In January 1918, at the magnificent Palace of Versailles outside Paris, President Wilson tried to persuade the Allies to construct a just and lasting peace and to establish a League of Nations. Colonel E. M. House, a native of Texas and a member of the American delegation to Versailles, later wrote about the conference.

A PERSONAL VOICE COLONEL E. M. HOUSE

" How splendid it would have been had we blazed a new and better trail! . . . It may be that Wilson might have had the power and influence if he had remained in Washington and kept clear of the Conference. When he stepped from his lofty pedestal and wrangled with representatives of other states, upon equal terms, he became as common clay. . . . To those who are saying that the Treaty is bad and should never have been made and that it will involve Europe in infinite difficulties in its enforcement, I feel like admitting it. But I would also say in reply that empires cannot be shattered and new states raised upon their ruins without disturbance. "

—quoted in *Hooray for Peace, Hurrah for War*

House saw what happened when Wilson's idealism ran up against practical politics. The Allied victors, vengeful toward Germany after four years of warfare, rejected most of Wilson's peace program.

▲ Colonel Edward M. House was a friend and advisor to President Woodrow Wilson.

Wilson Presents His Plan

Rejection was probably the last thing Wilson expected when he arrived in Europe. Everywhere he went, people gave him a hero's welcome. Italians displayed his picture in their windows; Parisians strewed the street with flowers. Representatives of one group after another, including Armenians, Jews, Ukrainians, and Poles, appealed to him for help in setting up independent nations for themselves.

FOURTEEN POINTS Even before the war was over, Wilson presented his plan for world peace. On January 18, 1918, he delivered his now famous **Fourteen Points** speech before Congress. The points were divided into three groups. The first five points were issues that Wilson believed had to be addressed to prevent another war:

1. There should be no secret treaties among nations.
2. Freedom of the seas should be maintained for all.
3. Tariffs and other economic barriers among nations should be lowered or abolished in order to foster free trade.
4. Arms should be reduced "to the lowest point consistent with domestic safety, thus lessening the possibility of military responses" during diplomatic crises.
5. Colonial policies should consider the interests of the colonial peoples as well as the interests of the imperialist powers.

Vocabulary
free trade: the buying and selling of goods without tariffs, or fees

The next eight points dealt with boundary changes. Wilson based these provisions on the principle of self-determination "along historically established lines of nationality." In other words, groups that claimed distinct ethnic identities were to form their own nation-states or decide for themselves to what nations they would belong.

The fourteenth point called for the creation of an international organization to address diplomatic crises like those that had sparked the war. This **League of Nations** would provide a forum for nations to discuss and settle their grievances without having to resort to war.

THE ALLIES REJECT WILSON'S PLAN Wilson's naiveté about the political aspects of securing a peace treaty showed itself in his failure to grasp the anger felt by the Allied leaders. The French premier, **Georges Clemenceau** (klĕm′ən-sō′), had lived through two German invasions of France and was determined to prevent future invasions. **David Lloyd George,** the British prime minister, had just won reelection on the slogan "Make Germany Pay." The Italian prime minister, Vittorio Orlando, wanted control of Austrian-held territory. **A**

MAIN IDEA

Developing Historical Perspective
A Why did the Allies reject Wilson's plan?

Contrary to custom, the peace conference did not include the defeated Central Powers. Nor did it include Russia, which was now under the control of a Communist government, or the smaller Allied nations. Instead, the "Big Four"— Wilson, Clemenceau, Lloyd George, and Orlando—worked out the treaty's details among themselves. Wilson conceded on most of his Fourteen Points in return for the establishment of the League of Nations.

KEY PLAYER

WOODROW WILSON
1856–1924
At the end of the war, President Wilson wanted the United States to become more involved in international affairs. He believed the nation had a moral obligation to help maintain peace in the world. Wilson's sense of moral purpose had a lasting influence on American foreign policy.

(left to right) David Lloyd George, Georges Clemenceau, ▶ and Woodrow Wilson in Paris in 1919.

Europe and the Middle East, 1915

hmhsocialstudies.com INTERACTIVE MAP

Legend:
- Allied Powers
- Central Powers
- Neutral countries

0   250   500 miles
0   250 500 kilometers

Europe and the Middle East, 1923

0   250   500 miles
0   250 500 kilometers

Legend:
- New nations
- Allied-occupied zones
- French Mandate
- British Mandate

GEOGRAPHY SKILLBUILDER
1. **Region** What had happened to German territory in the east by 1923?
2. **Location** Which new nation absorbed Serbia and Montenegro by 1923?

Debating the Treaty of Versailles

On June 28, 1919, the Big Four and the leaders of the defeated nations gathered in the Hall of Mirrors of the Palace of Versailles to sign the peace treaty. After four years of devastating warfare, everyone hoped that the treaty would create stability for a rebuilt Europe. Instead, anger held sway.

PROVISIONS OF THE TREATY The **Treaty of Versailles** (vər-sī′) established nine new nations—including Poland, Czechoslovakia, and Yugoslavia—and shifted the boundaries of other nations. It carved five areas out of the Ottoman Empire and gave them to France and Great Britain as mandates, or temporary colonies. Those two Allies were to administer their respective mandates until the areas were ready for self-rule and then independence.

The treaty barred Germany from maintaining an army. It also required Germany to return the region of Alsace-Lorraine to France and to pay **reparations,** or war damages, amounting to $33 billion to the Allies.

THE TREATY'S WEAKNESSES This treatment of Germany weakened the ability of the Treaty of Versailles to provide a lasting peace in Europe. Several basic flaws in the treaty sowed the seeds of postwar international problems that eventually would lead to the Second World War.

First, the treaty humiliated Germany. It contained a **war-guilt clause** forcing Germany to admit sole responsibility for starting World War I. Although German militarism had played a major role in igniting the war, other European nations had been guilty of provoking diplomatic crises before the war. Furthermore, there was no way Germany could pay the huge financial reparations. Germany was stripped of its colonial possessions in the Pacific, which might have helped it pay its reparations bill. **B**

VIDEO
The Treaty of Versailles
hmhsocialstudies.com

MAIN IDEA

Summarizing
B How did the Treaty of Versailles affect Germany?

In addition, for three years the Russians had fought on the side of the Allies, suffering higher casualties than any other nation. However, because Russia was excluded from the peace conference, it lost more territory than Germany did. The Union of Soviet Socialist Republics (or Soviet Union), as Russia was officially called after 1922, became determined to regain its former territory.

Finally, the treaty ignored claims of colonized people for self-determination, as in the case of Southeast Asia, where the Vietnamese people were beginning to demand the same political rights enjoyed by people in Western nations.

OPPOSITION TO THE TREATY When Wilson returned to the United States, he faced strong opposition to the treaty. Some people, including Herbert Hoover, believed it was too harsh. Hoover noted, "The economic consequences alone will pull down all Europe and thus injure the United States." Others considered the treaty a sell-out to imperialism because it simply exchanged one set of colonial rulers for another. Some ethnic groups objected to the treaty because the new national boundaries it established did not satisfy their particular demands for self-determination. For example, before the war many Poles had been under German rule. Now many Germans were under Polish rule.

Background
In 1920, the League of Nations set up the Permanent Court of International Justice, or World Court. The Court was designed to settle international disagreements between member nations.

DEBATE OVER THE LEAGUE OF NATIONS The main domestic opposition, however, centered on the issue of the League of Nations. A few opponents believed that the League threatened the U.S. foreign policy of isolationism. Conservative senators, headed by **Henry Cabot Lodge,** were suspicious of the provision for joint economic and military action against aggression, even though it was voluntary. They wanted the constitutional right of Congress to declare war included in the treaty.

POINT

"The League of Nations was the world's best hope for lasting peace."

President Wilson campaigned for the League of Nations as "necessary to meet the differing and unexpected contingencies" that could threaten world peace. Wilson believed that the League would create a forum where nations could talk through their disagreements. He also hoped it would provide collective security, in which nations would "respect and preserve as against external aggression the territorial integrity and existing political independence of all members of the League," and thereby prevent devastating warfare.

Critics complained that membership in the League would limit American independence in international affairs. However, Wilson argued that League membership included "a moral, not a legal, obligation" that would leave Congress free to decide its own course of action. Wilson tried to assure Congress as well as the general public that the League was "not a straitjacket, but a vehicle of life." It was also "a definite guaranty . . . against the things that have just come near bringing the whole structure of civilization into ruin."

COUNTERPOINT

"The League of Nations posed a threat to U.S. self-determination."

Senator William Borah was one of the foremost critics of the Treaty of Versailles because he objected to U.S. membership in the League of Nations. Borah feared that membership in the League "would draw America away from her isolation and into the internal affairs and concerns of Europe" and involve the United States in foreign wars. "Once having surrendered and become a part of the European concerns," Borah wondered, "where, my friends, are you going to stop?"

Many opponents also feared that the League would nullify the Monroe Doctrine by limiting "the right of our people to govern themselves free from all restraint, legal or moral, of foreign powers."

Although Wilson argued that the League of Nations would have no such power of restraint, Borah was unconvinced. He responded to Wilson's argument by asking, "What will your League amount to if it does not contain powers that no one dreams of giving it?"

THINKING CRITICALLY

1. **CONNECT TO HISTORY** **Summarizing** Both supporters and opponents of the League hoped to preserve peace. How did each group propose to secure peace for the United States?

    SEE SKILLBUILDER HANDBOOK, PAGE R4.

2. **CONNECT TO TODAY** **Identifying Problems** What are some contemporary arguments against United States participation in international organizations such as the United Nations or the World Court?

History Through `Film`

ECHOES OF THE GREAT WAR

In the 1920s and 1930s, a number of Hollywood horror films were influenced by memories of the Great War. *The Hunchback of Notre Dame* and *The Phantom of the Opera* featured men who, like many veterans, were forced to live with shameful disfigurements.

Other films recalled the war's bleak landscapes. For example, parts of the movie *Frankenstein* were filmed on the same sets as *All Quiet on the Western Front*, the famous war film. James Whale, who directed *Frankenstein*, was a veteran of the war. Like many of his generation, he remained profoundly disturbed by the horrors the war had unleashed.

◀ **Lon Chaney in** **The Phantom of the Opera** **(1925)**

Chaney in *The Hunchback* *of Notre Dame* **(1923)** ▲

(top) *All Quiet on the Western Front* **(1930)** ▲
(bottom) *Frankenstein* **(1931)**

SKILLBUILDER Interpreting Visual Sources

1. Why might the theme of human disfigurement be especially powerful to the generation that lived through World War I?

2. How do horror films of your time reflect specific fears and anxieties of the current generation?

📖 **SEE SKILLBUILDER HANDBOOK, PAGE R23.**

WILSON REFUSES TO COMPROMISE Wilson unwisely ignored the Republican majority in the Senate when he chose the members of the American delegation. If he had been more willing to accept a compromise on the League, it would have been more likely that the Senate would have approved the treaty. Wilson, however, was exhausted from his efforts at Versailles.

Despite ill health, Wilson set out in September 1919 on an 8,000-mile tour. He delivered 34 speeches in about 3 weeks, explaining why the United States should join the League of Nations. On October 2, Wilson suffered a stroke (a ruptured blood vessel to the brain) and lay partially paralyzed for more than two months, unable to even meet with his cabinet. His once-powerful voice was no more than a thick whisper.

When the treaty came up for a vote in the Senate in November 1919, Senator Lodge introduced a number of amendments, the most important of which qualified the terms under which the United States would enter the League of Nations. It was feared that U.S. membership in the League would force the United States to form its foreign policy in accord with the League. Although the Senate rejected the amendments, it also failed to ratify the treaty.

Wilson refused to compromise. "I will not play for position," he proclaimed. "This is not a time for tactics. It is a time to stand square. I can stand defeat; I cannot stand retreat from conscientious duty." The treaty again came up for a vote in March 1920. The Senate again rejected the Lodge amendments—and again failed to muster enough votes for ratification.

The United States finally signed a separate treaty with Germany in 1921, after Wilson was no longer president. The United States never joined the League of Nations, but it maintained an unofficial observer at League meetings. **C**

MAIN IDEA

Making Inferences
C Why were some people afraid of the treaty's influence over American foreign policy?

The Legacy of the War

When World War I ended, many Americans looked forward to a return of what Warren G. Harding called "normalcy." However, both the United States and the rest of the world had been utterly transformed by the war. At home, World War I had strengthened both the U.S. military and the power of government. It had also accelerated social change, especially for African Americans and women. In addition, the propaganda campaign had provoked powerful fears and antagonisms that were left unchanneled when the war finally came to an end.

In Europe the destruction and massive loss of life severely damaged social and political systems. In many countries the war created political instability and violence that persisted for decades. During the war years, the first Communist state was established in Russia, while after the war, militant fascist organizations seized control in Italy, Spain, and Germany.

Appalled by the scale of destruction, Americans began to call World War I "the war to end all wars," in the hope that humanity would never again be willing to fight such a war. However, unresolved issues in Europe would eventually drag America into an even wider war. The Treaty of Versailles had settled nothing. In fact, some Europeans longed to resume the fight. The ominous shape of things to come emerged in the writings of an Austrian named Adolf Hitler, an angry veteran of World War I: "It cannot be that two million [Germans] should have fallen in vain. . . . No, we do not pardon, we demand—vengeance!" Two decades after the end of the Great War, Adolf Hitler's desire for vengeance would plunge the world into an even greater war, in which the United States would play a leading role.

Vocabulary
fascist: characteristic of or relating to fascism, a system of totalitarian government

Domestic Consequences of World War I

- accelerated America's emergence as the world's greatest industrial power

- contributed to the movement of African Americans to Northern cities

- intensified anti-immigrant and anti-radical sentiments among mainstream Americans

- brought over one million women into the work force

SECTION 4 ASSESSMENT

1. TERMS & NAMES For each term or name, write a sentence explaining its significance.
- Fourteen Points
- League of Nations
- Georges Clemenceau
- David Lloyd George
- Treaty of Versailles
- reparations
- war-guilt clause
- Henry Cabot Lodge

MAIN IDEA

2. TAKING NOTES
Re-create the spider diagram shown below. Fill in the web with information about the provisions and weaknesses of the Treaty of Versailles and opposition to it.

Do you think Congress should have rejected the treaty?

CRITICAL THINKING

3. DEVELOPING HISTORICAL PERSPECTIVE
Why didn't the Treaty of Versailles lay the foundations for a lasting peace?

4. SUMMARIZING
Why did so many Americans oppose the Treaty of Versailles?

5. HYPOTHESIZING
Predict Germany's reaction to the Treaty of Versailles. Give reasons for your predictions.
Think About:
- what Germans thought of the war-guilt clause
- German reaction to reparations
- how Germans felt about the loss of territory

America in World Affairs

The United States has not always been as involved in world affairs as it is today. Throughout its history, the nation's foreign policy has swung back and forth between a commitment to involvement with the world and the desire for isolation. "Steer clear of permanent alliances," George Washington cautioned Americans in his Farewell Address of 1796. Washington's warning to the young nation became a theme of government policy for the next hundred years, as domestic issues dominated Americans' attention.

In the late 1800s, however, Americans began to look outward to the larger world. The country had reached the limits of its continental expansion and stretched from ocean to ocean. As its economic power grew stronger, the United States became more involved in the affairs of its neighbors in the Western Hemisphere.

1823–1898

THE UNITED STATES AND LATIN AMERICA ▶

Throughout the 19th century, the United States expanded its influence in the Western Hemisphere. The Monroe Doctrine was intended to diminish European interference. After the Civil War, American trade with Latin America, including the Spanish colony of Cuba, grew. In fact, the United States traded more heavily with Cuba than Spain did.

When the Cubans rebelled against Spain, Americans sympathized with the rebels. After the battleship U.S.S. *Maine* sank in the Cuban harbor of Havana, Americans blamed the Spanish, and Congress declared war. After defeating the Spanish, the United States extended its influence in territories such as Puerto Rico, Panama, and Mexico. A new expansionist era had begun.

1917–1939

◀ INVOLVEMENT AND ISOLATIONISM

Before World War I, the United States had generally limited its military involvement to the Western Hemisphere. As the war in Europe progressed, this position became impossible to maintain, as German U-boats increasingly threatened American lives. In spite of fierce opposition from isolationists, the United States joined World War I in 1917. U.S. involvement in the conflict greatly strengthened its armed forces and revealed the nation's military potential.

After the war, the United States returned to a policy of isolationism. A decade later, as European dictators began menacing other European countries, American public opinion was sharply divided. Many argued that the best way to preserve American democracy was to stay out of war in Europe. It took Japan's attack on Pearl Harbor, Hawaii, in 1941 to force the United States into World War II.

U.S. forces in Vietnam in 1968

This statue of Lenin, the leader of the 1917 Russian Revolution, was toppled by Latvian citizens in 1991.

1945–1991

▲ THE COLD WAR

After World War II, tensions between the United States and Communist countries like the Soviet Union and China developed into a nonmilitary conflict known as the Cold War. During the Cold War, which lasted for nearly 50 years, the United States and the Soviet Union competed to extend their political and economic influence. In some parts of the world, such as Korea and Vietnam, the Cold War led to prolonged military warfare.

The great costs of these conflicts—both in money and in lives—led to renewed calls for isolationism. Nevertheless, the U.S. remained actively involved in the Cold War throughout the 1980s.

1939–1945

INVOLVEMENT IN EUROPE ▼

When the fascist threat to democracy became too great to ignore, the United States joined the Allies in fighting the Axis Powers during World War II. The United States and the Soviet Union emerged from the war as the two strongest military powers in the world. It was now impossible for the nation to return to isolationism. The United States took an active role in rebuilding Europe through programs like the Marshall Plan and was instrumental in establishing the United Nations. The United States also stayed involved with Europe militarily during the Cold War as a member of the North Atlantic Treaty Organization (NATO).

THINKING CRITICALLY

CONNECT TO TODAY

1. **Analyzing Motives** What were America's motives for getting involved in each of the wars described on these two pages? Do you think these motives would be valid today?

   📖 SEE SKILLBUILDER HANDBOOK, PAGE R6.

CONNECT TO HISTORY

2. **Writing About Wartime Experience** Imagine that you are a reporter writing at the time about one of the wars in the 20th century. Interview someone you know—or look for information in the library or on the Internet—to find out how a soldier, nurse, cook, sailor, or pilot spent each day as part of the war effort. Write a feature article for a local newspaper, quoting that person.

🗨 hmhsocialstudies.com RESEARCH WEB LINKS

VISUAL SUMMARY

THE FIRST WORLD WAR

LONG-TERM CAUSES

- Nationalist tensions in Europe
- Competition for colonies
- Arms races and militarism
- Formation of defense alliances

IMMEDIATE CAUSES

- Assassination of Franz Ferdinand
- Austria-Hungary's retaliation against Serbia
- Declarations of war between rival alliances
- Germany's invasion of Belgium

WORLD WAR I

IMMEDIATE EFFECTS

- Destruction and immense loss of life
- Revolution in Russia
- Social change in United States
- Allied victory over Central Powers
- Treaty of Versailles
- Formation of mandates (temporary colonies)
- League of Nations

LONG-TERM EFFECTS

- Breakup of empires
- U.S. policy of isolationism
- United States' emergence as global economic giant
- Rise of militant extremist parties in Europe
- Eruption of World War II

TERMS & NAMES

For each term or name below, write a sentence explaining its connection to World War I.

1. nationalism
2. trench warfare
3. Zimmermann note
4. Selective Service Act
5. General John J. Pershing
6. armistice
7. Espionage and Sedition Acts
8. Great Migration
9. Fourteen Points
10. Treaty of Versailles

MAIN IDEAS

Use your notes and the information in the chapter to answer the following questions.

World War I Begins *(pages 578–586)*

1. What were the main reasons for U.S. involvement in the war?
2. Where did Germany begin its war offensive, and what happened there?

American Power Tips the Balance *(pages 587–593)*

3. How did the United States mobilize a strong military during World War I?
4. What new weapons made fighting in World War I deadlier than fighting in previous wars?

The War at Home *(pages 594–601)*

5. What methods did the U.S. government use to sell the war to the nation?
6. What events during the war undermined civil liberties?

Wilson Fights for Peace *(pages 604–609)*

7. What were the major effects of the Treaty of Versailles?
8. How did Wilson's support for the League of Nations stand in the way of Senate support for the Treaty of Versailles?

CRITICAL THINKING

1. **USING YOUR NOTES** In a chart like the one shown, provide causes for the listed effects of World War I.

Causes	Effects
	U.S. enters World War I
	Germany collapses
	U.S. economy becomes more productive

2. **DEVELOPING HISTORICAL PERSPECTIVE** Between 1914 and 1920, Americans debated the role their country should have in world affairs. From the events of World War I, what might Americans have learned about intervention in the affairs of other nations?

3. **INTERPRETING MAPS** Look at the maps of Europe before and after World War I (page 606). Describe the changes in national boundaries after the Versailles peace settlement.

Use the map and your knowledge of United States history to answer question 1.

1 Which country was an ally of the United States during World War I?

(1) country A
(2) country B
(3) country C
(4) country D

Use the graph and your knowledge of United States history to answer question 2.

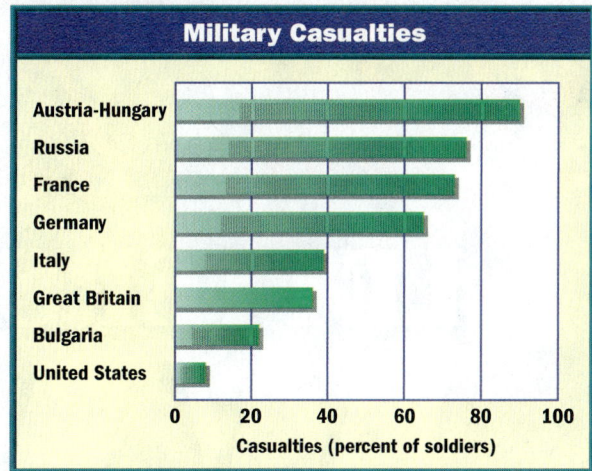

2 The countries with the greatest percentage of military casualties were all —

(1) members of the Allied Powers.
(2) members of the Central Powers.
(3) located far from the battlefront.
(4) bordering one of the war's two fronts.

For additional test practice, go online for:

• Diagnostic tests   • Tutorials

INTERACT WITH HISTORY

Think about the issues you explored at the beginning of the chapter. Write a speech, arguing for or against American involvement in World War I. Use information from the chapter to support your argument. Give your speech to the class.

FOCUS ON WRITING

Imagine you are a diplomat participating in the peace talks at the end of World War I. Decide whether you support or oppose the provisions of the Treaty of Versailles. Then write an essay convincing the other participants to adopt your point of view. If you support the treaty, explain why. If you oppose it, offer an alternate version. Use persuasive language and clear examples.

COLLABORATIVE LEARNING

Organize into small groups and review the story of Eddie Rickenbacker, the famous World War I fighter pilot. Rickenbacker's bravery and aviation skills made him a hero. What qualities make people heroes? Using stories and images from magazines and newspapers, make a list of current heroes on a chart for display in your classroom. Identify why each individual on the list is considered heroic.

Dear home: LETTERS FROM WWI

When U.S. troops arrived in Europe in 1917 to fight in World War I, the war had been dragging on for nearly three years. The American soldiers suddenly found themselves in the midst of chaos. Each day, they faced the threats of machine gun fire, poison gas, and aerial attacks. Still, the arrival of American reinforcements had sparked a new zeal among the Allies, who believed the new forces could finally turn the tide in their favor. The letters soldiers wrote to their families back home reveal the many emotions they felt on the battlefield: confusion about their surroundings, fear for their own safety, concern for friends and loved ones, and hope that the war would soon be over.

Explore World War I online through the eyes of the soldiers who fought in it. You can find a wealth of information, video clips, primary sources, activities, and more at ↗ hmhsocialstudies.com.

"I have been on every front in France. You cant imagine how torn up this country really is. Every where there are wire entanglements and trenches and dugouts. Even out of the war zone there are entanglements and dugouts to protect the civilians from air raids."

–Corp. Albert Smith, U.S. soldier

Letter from France
Read the document to learn about one soldier's observations of wartime life.

Over There
Watch the video to learn about the experiences of American soldiers on the way to Europe and upon their arrival.

War on the Western Front
Watch the video to hear one soldier's vivid account of battle and its aftermath.

Surrender!
Watch the video to experience soldiers' reactions to the news that the war was finally over.

The 1920s and the Great Depression 1920–1940

UNIT PROJECT

Multimedia Presentation
Create a multimedia presentation that reflects popular culture in the 1920s. Gather a wide variety of sources including excerpts from vintage radio broadcasts and selections of literature. Use sound, visuals, and text in your presentation.

Street Scene by Joe Jones

CHAPTER 20

POLITICS OF THE ROARING TWENTIES

Essential Question

What political and social changes took place after World War I and through the 1920s?

 New York Standards

KEY IDEA 3 Study about the major social, political, economic, cultural, and religious developments in New York State and United States history involves learning about the important roles and contributions of individuals and groups.

KEY IDEA 4 The skills of historical analysis include the ability to: explain the significance of historical evidence; weigh the importance, reliability, and validity of evidence; understand the concept of multiple causation; understand the importance of changing and competing interpretations of different historical developments.

SECTION 1: Americans Struggle with Postwar Issues

SECTION 2: The Harding Presidency

SECTION 3: The Business of America

Angry mill workers riot after walking off the job during a strike of Tennessee textile plants.

1919–1920 Palmer Raids

1920 Warren G. Harding is elected president.

1921 Sacco and Vanzetti are convicted.

1921 Federal-Aid Road Act funds a national highway system.

1923 President Harding dies and Calvin Coolidge becomes president.

USA
WORLD

1919   1921   1923

1921 Chinese Communist Party is founded in Shanghai.

1922 Benito Mussolini is appointed prime minister of Italy.

1923 German economic crisis.

INTERACT
WITH HISTORY

World War I has ended. As Americans struggle to rebuild broken lives, the voices of angry
workers can be silenced no longer. Despite
public criticism, many risk losing their jobs to
strike and join unions. The streets become a
battleground for fair pay and better working
conditions.

Explore the Issues

- Do city workers have a responsibility not
  to go on strike?

- Should the government intervene in disputes between labor and business?

- Does the success of a strike depend on
  you?

1924 Calvin Coolidge is elected president.

1925 A. Philip Randolph organizes the Brotherhood of Sleeping Car Porters.

1927 Henry Ford introduces the Model A.

1928 Herbert Hoover is elected president.

1925   1927   1929

1924 Vladimir Ilich Lenin, founder of the Soviet Union, dies.

1926 British laborers declare a general strike.

1926 Hirohito becomes emperor of Japan.

1928 Joseph Stalin launches the first of his Five-Year-Plans in the USSR.

1929 National Revolutionary Party is organized in Mexico.

Politics of the Roaring Twenties   **617**

SECTION 1

PI 3.2
PI 4.1

CC Unit 3.III.C.2   CC Unit 4.II.B.1.d
CC Unit 4.II.C.4   CC Unit 5.I.A.3
CC Unit 5.I.C.2.a   CC Unit 5.I.C.2.d

Americans Struggle with Postwar Issues

MAIN IDEA	WHY IT MATTERS NOW	Terms & Names
A desire for normality after the war and a fear of communism and "foreigners" led to postwar isolationism.	Americans today continue to debate political isolationism and immigration policy.	• nativism • Sacco and Vanzetti • isolationism • quota system • communism • John L. Lewis • anarchists

One American's Story

TAKING NOTES

Use the graphic organizer online to take notes on the aftereffects of World War I.

During the 1920s and 1930s, Irving Fajans, a department store sales clerk in New York City, tried to persuade fellow workers to join the Department Store Employees Union. He described some of the techniques union organizers used.

★ A PERSONAL VOICE IRVING FAJANS

" If you were caught distributing . . . union literature around the job you were instantly fired. We thought up ways of passing leaflets without the boss being able to pin anybody down. . . . We . . . swiped the key to the toilet paper dispensers in the washroom, took out the paper and substituted printed slips of just the right size! We got a lot of new members that way—It appealed to their sense of humor. "

—quoted in *The Jewish Americans*

▲ **Irving Fajans organized department store workers in their efforts to gain better pay and working conditions during the 1920s.**

During the war, workers' rights had been suppressed. In 1919, workers began to cry out for fair pay and better working conditions. Tensions arose between labor and management, and a rash of labor strikes broke out across the country. The public, however, was not supportive of striking workers. Many citizens longed to get back to normal, peaceful living—they felt resentful of anyone who caused unrest.

Postwar Trends

World War I had left much of the American public exhausted. The debate over the League of Nations had deeply divided America. Further, the Progressive Era had caused numerous wrenching changes in American life. The economy, too, was in a difficult state of adjustment. Returning soldiers faced unemployment or took their old jobs away from women and minorities. Also, the cost of living had doubled. Farmers and factory workers suffered as wartime orders diminished.

Many Americans responded to the stressful conditions by becoming fearful of outsiders. A wave of **nativism**, or prejudice against foreign-born people, swept the nation. So, too, did a belief in **isolationism**, a policy of pulling away from involvement in world affairs.

Fear of Communism

One perceived threat to American life was the spread of **communism**, an economic and political system based on a single-party government ruled by a dictatorship. In order to equalize wealth and power, Communists would put an end to private property, substituting government ownership of factories, railroads, and other businesses.

THE RED SCARE The panic in the United States began in 1919, after revolutionaries in Russia overthrew the czarist regime. Vladimir I. Lenin and his followers, or Bolsheviks ("the majority"), established a new Communist state. Waving their symbolic red flag, Communists, or "Reds," cried out for a worldwide revolution that would abolish capitalism everywhere.

A Communist Party formed in the United States. Seventy-thousand radicals joined, including some from the Industrial Workers of the World (IWW). When several dozen bombs were mailed to government and business leaders, the public grew fearful that the Communists were taking over. U.S. Attorney General A. Mitchell Palmer took action to combat this "Red Scare."

A PERSONAL VOICE A. MITCHELL PALMER

"The blaze of revolution was sweeping over every American institution of law and order . . . . eating its way into the homes of the American workman, its sharp tongues of revolutionary heat . . . licking the altars of the churches, leaping into the belfry of the school bell, crawling into the sacred corners of American homes, . . . burning up the foundations of society."

—"The Case Against the Reds"

ECONOMIC BACKGROUND

ROOTS OF COMMUNISM

The first Communist government in Russia was based on the teachings of Karl Marx and Friedrich Engels. In 1848, these two had published *The Communist Manifesto*, which outlined a theory of class struggle. It said that a class that had economic power also had social and political power.

It also said that two classes, the "haves" and the "have-nots," have struggled for control throughout history. During the Industrial Revolution, Communists believed, the struggle was between the capitalists, who owned capital—land, money, and machinery— and workers, who owned only their labor. Marx and Engels urged workers to seize political power and the means of production. Ultimately, they believed, laborers would overthrow capitalism in all industrialized nations.

THE PALMER RAIDS In August 1919, Palmer appointed J. Edgar Hoover as his special assistant. Palmer, Hoover, and their agents hunted down suspected Communists, socialists, and **anarchists**—people who opposed any form of government. They trampled people's civil rights, invading private homes and offices and jailing suspects without allowing them legal counsel. Hundreds of foreign-born radicals were deported without trials.

But Palmer's raids failed to turn up evidence of a revolutionary conspiracy— or even explosives. Many thought Palmer was just looking for a campaign issue to gain support for his presidential aspirations. Soon, the public decided that Palmer didn't know what he was talking about. Ⓐ

SACCO AND VANZETTI Although short-lived, the Red Scare fed people's suspicions of foreigners and immigrants. This nativist attitude led to ruined reputations and wrecked lives. The two most famous victims of this attitude were Nicola Sacco and Bartolomeo Vanzetti, a shoemaker and a fish peddler. Both were Italian immigrants and anarchists; both had evaded the draft during World War I.

In May 1920, **Sacco and Vanzetti** were arrested and charged with the robbery and murder of a factory paymaster and his guard in South Braintree, Massachusetts. Witnesses had said the criminals appeared to be Italians. The accused asserted their innocence and provided alibis; the evidence against them was circumstantial; and the presiding judge made prejudicial remarks. Nevertheless, the jury still found them guilty and sentenced them to death.

MAIN IDEA

Analyzing Motives

Ⓐ Why did Attorney General A. Mitchell Palmer launch a series of raids against suspected Communists?

Protests rang out in the United States, Europe, and Latin America. Many people thought Sacco and Vanzetti were mistreated because of their radical beliefs; others asserted it was because they were immigrants. The poet Edna St. Vincent Millay donated proceeds from her poem "Justice Denied in Massachusetts" to their defense. She personally appealed to Governor Fuller of Massachusetts for their lives. However, after reviewing the case and interviewing Vanzetti, the governor decided to let the executions go forward. The two men died in the electric chair on August 23, 1927. Before he was executed, Vanzetti made a statement.

A PERSONAL VOICE BARTOLOMEO VANZETTI

" In all my life I have never stole, never killed, never spilled blood. . . . We were tried during a time . . . when there was hysteria of resentment and hate against the people of our principles, against the foreigner. . . . I am suffering because I am a radical and indeed I am a radical; I have suffered because I was an Italian and indeed I am an Italian. . . . If you could execute me two times, and if I could be reborn two other times, I would live again to do what I have done already." **B**

—quoted in *The National Experience*

In 1961, new ballistics tests showed that the pistol found on Sacco was in fact the one used to murder the guard. However, there was no proof that Sacco had actually pulled the trigger.

Limiting Immigration

During the wave of nativist sentiment, "Keep America for Americans" became the prevailing attitude. Anti-immigrant attitudes had been growing in the United States ever since the 1880s, when new immigrants began arriving from southern and eastern Europe. Many of these immigrants were willing to work for low wages in industries such as coal mining, steel production, and textiles. But after World War I, the need for unskilled labor in the United States decreased. Nativists believed that because the United States now had fewer unskilled jobs available, fewer immigrants should be let into the country. Nativist feelings were fueled by

MAIN IDEA

Analyzing Events

B According to Vanzetti, what were the reasons for his imprisonment?

Background

On August 23, 1977, exactly 50 years after the executions, Massachusetts governor Michael Dukakis declared that Sacco and Vanzetti had not been given a fair trial.

the fact that some of the people involved in postwar labor disputes were immigrant anarchists and socialists, who many Americans believed were actually Communists. Racist ideas like those expressed by Madison Grant, an anthropologist at the American Museum of Natural History in New York City, fed people's attitudes.

★ A PERSONAL VOICE MADISON GRANT

" The result of unlimited immigration is showing plainly in the rapid decline in the birth rate of native Americans . . . [who] will not bring children into the world to compete in the labor market with the Slovak, the Italian, the Syrian and the Jew. The native American is too proud to mix socially with them. "

—quoted in *United States History: Ideas in Conflict*

Vocabulary
bigot: a person who is intolerant of any creed, race, religion, or political belief that differs from his own

THE KLAN RISES AGAIN As a result of the Red Scare and anti-immigrant feelings, different groups of bigots used anti-communism as an excuse to harass any group unlike themselves. One such group was the Ku Klux Klan (KKK). The KKK was devoted to "100 percent Americanism." By 1924, KKK membership reached 4.5 million "white male persons, native-born gentile citizens." The Klan also believed in keeping blacks "in their place," destroying saloons, opposing unions, and driving Roman Catholics, Jews, and foreign-born people out of the country. KKK members were paid to recruit new members into their world of secret rituals and racial violence. Though the Klan dominated state politics in many states, by the end of the decade its criminal activity led to a decrease in power. **C**

MAIN IDEA

Analyzing Issues
C What were the main goals of the Ku Klux Klan at this time?

▲
In 1925, nearly 60,000 Ku Klux Klan members marched along Pennsylvania Avenue in Washington, D.C.

THE QUOTA SYSTEM From 1919 to 1921, the number of immigrants had grown almost 600 percent—from 141,000 to 805,000 people. Congress, in response to nativist pressure, decided to limit immigration from certain countries, namely those in southern and eastern Europe.

The Emergency Quota Act of 1921 set up a **quota system**. This system established the maximum number of people who could enter the United States from each foreign country. The goal of the quota system was to cut sharply European immigration to the United States. As the charts on page 622 show, the system achieved that goal.

As amended in 1924, the law limited immigration from each European nation to 2 percent of the number of its nationals living in the United States in 1890. This provision discriminated against people from eastern and southern Europe—mostly Roman Catholics and Jews—who had not started coming to the United States in large numbers until after 1890. Later, the base year was shifted to 1920. In 1927, the law reduced the total number of persons to be admitted in any one year to 150,000.

In addition, the law prohibited Japanese immigration, causing much ill will between the two nations. Japan—which had faithfully kept the Gentlemen's Agreement to limit immigration to the United States, negotiated by Theodore Roosevelt in 1907—expressed anger over the insult.

U.S. Patterns of Immigration, 1921–1929

The map and graph below show the change in immigration patterns resulting from the Emergency Quota Act, among other factors. Hundreds of thousands of people were affected. For example, while the number of immigrants from Mexico rose from 30,758 in 1921 to 40,154 in 1929, the number of Italian immigrants dropped drastically from 222,260 in 1921 to 18,008 in 1929.

Ellis Island in Upper New York Harbor was the port of entry for most European immigrants.

CANADA

PACIFIC OCEAN

EUROPE

UNITED STATES

MEXICO

ATLANTIC OCEAN

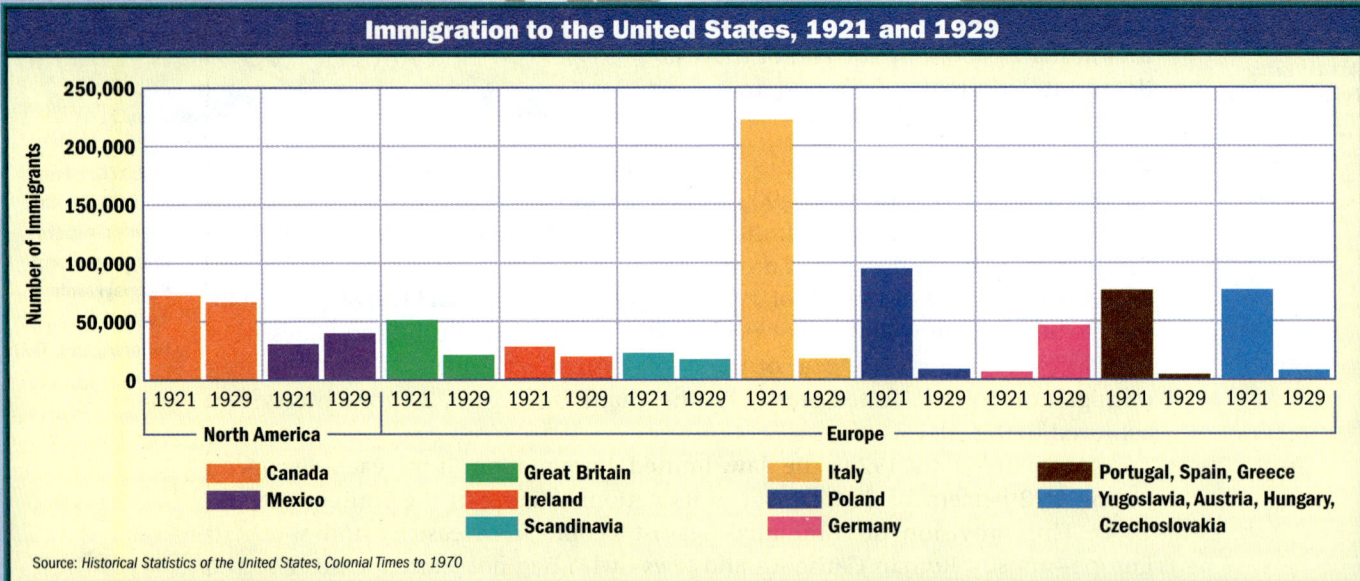

Immigration to the United States, 1921 and 1929

Number of Immigrants

1921 1929 | 1921 1929 | 1921 1929 | 1921 1929 | 1921 1929 | 1921 1929 | 1921 1929 | 1921 1929 | 1921 1929 | 1921 1929

North America — Europe

- Canada
- Mexico
- Scandinavia
- Great Britain
- Ireland
- Germany
- Italy
- Poland
- Portugal, Spain, Greece
- Yugoslavia, Austria, Hungary, Czechoslovakia

Source: *Historical Statistics of the United States, Colonial Times to 1970*

SKILLBUILDER Interpreting Graphs

1. Which geographical areas show the sharpest decline in immigration to the U.S. between 1921 and 1929? What are the only areas to register an increase in immigration to the U.S.?

2. How did the quota system affect where immigrants came from?

 SEE SKILLBUILDER HANDBOOK, PAGE R28.

The national origins quota system did not apply to immigrants from the Western Hemisphere, however. During the 1920s, about a million Canadians and almost 500,000 Mexicans crossed the nation's borders. **D**

A Time of Labor Unrest

Another severe postwar conflict formed between labor and management. During the war, the government wouldn't allow workers to strike because nothing could interfere with the war effort. The American Federation of Labor (AFL) pledged to avoid strikes.

However, 1919 saw more than 3,000 strikes during which some 4 million workers walked off the job. Employers didn't want to give raises, nor did they want employees to join unions. Some employers, either out of a sincere belief or because they saw a way to keep wages down, attempted to show that union members were planning a revolution. Employers labeled striking workers as Communists. Newspapers screamed, "Plots to Establish Communism." Three strikes in particular grabbed public attention.

▲ Strikers included working women tailors who fought for improved working conditions.

THE BOSTON POLICE STRIKE The Boston police had not been given a raise since the beginning of World War I. Among their many grievances was that they had been denied the right to unionize. When representatives asked for a raise and were fired, the remaining policemen decided to strike. Massachusetts governor Calvin Coolidge called out the National Guard. He said, "There is no right to strike against the public safety by anybody, anywhere, any time." The strike ended but members weren't allowed to return to work; new policemen were hired instead. People praised Coolidge for saving Boston, if not the nation, from communism and anarchy. In the 1920 election he became Warren G. Harding's vice-presidential running mate.

THE STEEL MILL STRIKE Workers in the steel mills wanted the right to negotiate for shorter working hours and a living wage. They also wanted union recognition and collective bargaining rights. In September 1919, the U.S. Steel Corporation refused to meet with union representatives. In response, over 300,000 workers walked off their jobs. Steel companies hired strikebreakers—employees who agreed to work during the strike—and used force. Striking workers were beaten by police, federal troops, and state militias. Then the companies instituted a propaganda campaign, linking the strikers to Communists. In October 1919, negotiations between labor and management produced a deadlock. President Woodrow Wilson made a written plea to the combative "negotiators."

A PERSONAL VOICE WOODROW WILSON

" At a time when the nations of the world are endeavoring to find a way of avoiding international war, are we to confess that there is no method to be found for carrying on industry except . . . the very method of war? . . . Are our industrial leaders and our industrial workers to live together without faith in each other? "

—quoted in *Labor in Crisis*

The steel strike ended in January 1920. In 1923, a report on the harsh working conditions in steel mills shocked the public. The steel companies agreed to an eight-hour day, but the steelworkers remained without a union. **E**

MAIN IDEA

Developing Historical Perspective

D Why did Congress make changes in immigration laws during the 1920s?

MAIN IDEA

Comparing

E Compare the results of the Boston police strike and the steel strike.

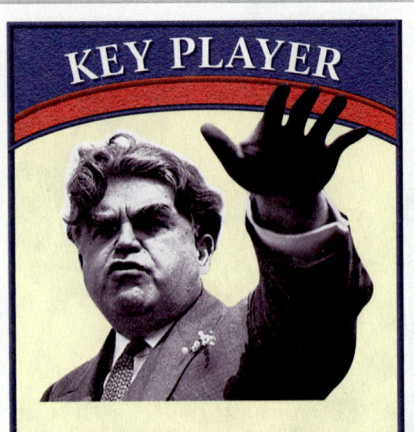

**JOHN LLEWELLYN LEWIS
1880–1969**

John L. Lewis was born in the little mining town of Lucas, Iowa. His family had traditionally been concerned with labor rights and benefits.

Lewis grew up with a fierce determination to fight for what he believed companies owed their employees: decent working conditions and a fair salary. As he said years later,

"I have pleaded your case not in the tones of a feeble mendicant [beggar] asking alms but in the thundering voice of the captain of a mighty host, demanding the rights to which free men are entitled."

THE COAL MINERS' STRIKE Unionism was more successful in America's coalfields. In 1919, the United Mine Workers of America, organized since 1890, got a new leader—**John L. Lewis**. In protest of low wages and long workdays, Lewis called his union's members out on strike on November 1, 1919. Attorney General Palmer obtained a court order sending the miners back to work. Lewis then declared it over, but he quietly gave the word for it to continue. In defiance of the court order, the mines stayed closed another month. Then President Wilson appointed an arbitrator, or judge, to put an end to the dispute. The coal miners received a 27 percent wage increase, and John L. Lewis became a national hero. The miners, however, did not achieve a shorter workday and a five-day workweek until the 1930s.

LABOR MOVEMENT LOSES APPEAL In spite of limited gains, the 1920s hurt the labor movement badly. Over the decade, union membership dropped from more than 5 million to around 3.5 million. Membership declined for several reasons:

- much of the work force consisted of immigrants willing to work in poor conditions,
- since immigrants spoke a multitude of languages, unions had difficulty organizing them,
- farmers who had migrated to cities to find factory jobs were used to relying on themselves, and
- most unions excluded African Americans.

By 1929, about 82,000 African Americans—or less than 1 percent of their population—held union memberships. By contrast, just over 3 percent of all whites were union members. However, African Americans joined some unions like the mine workers', longshoremen's, and railroad porters' unions. In 1925, A. Philip Randolph founded the Brotherhood of Sleeping Car Porters to help African Americans gain a fair wage.

While America's attitude toward unions was changing, so, too, was its faith in the presidency.

 SECTION 1 ASSESSMENT

1. TERMS & NAMES For each term or name, write a sentence explaining its significance.

- nativism
- isolationism
- communism
- anarchists
- Sacco and Vanzetti
- quota system
- John L. Lewis

MAIN IDEA

2. TAKING NOTES
In a cause-and-effect chart like the one shown, list examples of the aftereffects of World War I.

Event	Result
1.	→
2.	→

What event do you think was the most significant? Explain your choice.

CRITICAL THINKING

3. EVALUATING
Do you think Americans were justified in their fear of radicals and foreigners in the decade following World War I? Explain your answer.

Think About:
- the goals of the leaders of the Russian Revolution
- the challenges facing the United States

4. ANALYZING ISSUES
In the various fights between management and union members, what did each side believe?

5. DRAWING CONCLUSIONS
What do you think the Sacco and Vanzetti case shows about America in the 1920s?

PI 4.1

CC Unit 4.II.D.5   CC Unit 4.II.D.6
CC Unit 5.I.A.3   CC Unit 5.I.B.2

The Harding Presidency

MAIN IDEA	WHY IT MATTERS NOW	Terms & Names
The Harding administration appealed to America's desire for calm and peace after the war, but resulted in scandal.	The government must guard against scandal and corruption to merit public trust.	• Warren G. Harding • Charles Evans Hughes • Fordney-McCumber Tariff • Ohio gang • Teapot Dome scandal • Albert B. Fall

One American's Story

hmhsocialstudies.com
TAKING NOTES

Use the graphic organizer online to take notes on the causes and effects of the major events discussed in the section.

Warren G. Harding was described as a good-natured man who "looked like a president ought to look." When the silver-haired Ohio senator assumed the presidency in 1921, the public yearned for what Harding described as "normalcy," or the simpler days before the Progressive Era and the Great War. His words of peace and calm comforted the healing nation.

★ **A PERSONAL VOICE** WARREN G. HARDING

" America's present need is not heroics, but healing; not nostrums, but normalcy; not revolution, but restoration; not agitation, but adjustment; not surgery, but serenity; not the dramatic, but the dispassionate; . . . not submergence in internationality, but sustainment in triumphant nationality."

—quoted in *The Rise of Warren Gamaliel Harding*

Despite Harding's soothing speeches, his judgment turned out to be poor. The discord among the major world powers and the conduct within his own cabinet would test his politics and his character.

▲
Warren G. Harding, shown here in 1923, looked presidential, but he is considered one of the least successful presidents.

Harding Struggles for Peace

After World War I, problems surfaced relating to arms control, war debts, and the reconstruction of war-torn countries. In 1921, President Harding invited several major powers to the Washington Naval Conference. Russia was left out because of its Communist government. At the conference, Secretary of State **Charles Evans Hughes** urged that no more warships be built for ten years. He suggested that the five major naval powers—the United States, Great Britain, Japan, France, and Italy—scrap many of their battleships, cruisers, and aircraft carriers.

Conference delegates cheered, wept, and threw their hats into the air. For the first time in history, powerful nations agreed to disarm. Later, in 1928, fifteen countries signed the Kellogg-Briand Pact, which renounced war as a national policy. However, the pact was futile, as it provided no means of enforcement.

HIGH TARIFFS AND REPARATIONS New conflicts arose when it came time for Britain and France to pay back the $10 billion they had borrowed from America. They could do this in two ways: by selling goods to the United States or by collecting reparations from Germany. However, in 1922, America adopted the **Fordney-McCumber Tariff,** which raised taxes on some U.S. imports to 60 percent—the highest level ever. The tax protected U.S. businesses—especially in the chemical and metals industries—from foreign competition, but made it impossible for Britain and France to sell enough goods in the U.S. to repay debts. **A**

The two countries looked to Germany, which was experiencing terrible inflation. When Germany defaulted on (failed to make) payment, French troops marched in. To avoid another war, American banker Charles G. Dawes was sent to negotiate loans. Through what came to be known as the Dawes Plan, American investors loaned Germany $2.5 billion to pay back Britain and France with annual payments on a fixed scale. Those countries then paid the United States. Thus, the United States arranged to be repaid with its own money.

The solution caused resentment all around. Britain and France considered the United States a miser for not paying a fair share of the costs of World War I. Further, the U.S. had benefited from the defeat of Germany, while Europeans had paid for the victory with millions of lives. At the same time, the United States considered Britain and France financially irresponsible.

▲
In 1923, a German man papers his walls with money made nearly worthless by high inflation following World War I.

Vocabulary
reparations: payments demanded from a defeated enemy

MAIN IDEA

Summarizing
A What were the reasons European countries were not paying their war debts?

Scandal Hits Harding's Administration

On domestic issues, Harding favored a limited role for government in business affairs and in social reform. Still, he did set up the Bureau of the Budget to help run the government more efficiently, and he urged U.S. Steel to abandon the 12-hour day.

HARDING'S CABINET Harding appointed Charles Evans Hughes as secretary of state. Hughes later went on to become chief justice of the Supreme Court. The president made Herbert Hoover the secretary of commerce. Hoover had done a masterful job of handling food distribution and refugee problems during World War I. Andrew Mellon, one of the country's wealthiest men, became secretary of the treasury and set about drastically cutting taxes and reducing the national debt. However, the cabinet also included the so-called **Ohio gang,** the president's poker-playing cronies, who would soon cause a great deal of embarrassment. **B**

SCANDAL PLAGUES HARDING The president's main problem was that he didn't understand many of the issues. He admitted as much to a secretary.

MAIN IDEA

Evaluating Leadership
B What do Harding's appointments indicate about his judgment?

★ **A PERSONAL VOICE** WARREN G. HARDING

"John, I can't make a . . . thing out of this tax problem. I listen to one side and they seem right, and then . . . I talk to the other side and they seem just as right. . . . I know somewhere there is an economist who knows the truth, but I don't know where to find him and haven't the sense to know him and trust him when I find him. . . . What a job!"

—quoted in *Only Yesterday*

Harding's administration began to unravel as his corrupt friends used their offices to become wealthy through graft. Charles R. Forbes, the head of the Veterans Bureau, was caught illegally selling government and hospital supplies to private companies. Colonel Thomas W. Miller, the head of the Office of Alien Property, was caught taking a bribe.

THE TEAPOT DOME SCANDAL The most spectacular example of corruption was the **Teapot Dome scandal**. The government had set aside oil-rich public lands at Teapot Dome, Wyoming, and Elk Hills, California, for use by the U.S. Navy. Secretary of the Interior **Albert B. Fall,** a close friend of various oil executives, managed to get the oil reserves transferred from the navy to the Interior Department. Then, Fall secretly leased the land to two private oil companies, including Henry Sinclair's Mammoth Oil Company at Teapot Dome. Although Fall claimed that these contracts were in the government's interest, he suddenly received more than $400,000 in "loans, bonds, and cash." He was later found guilty of bribery and became the first American to be convicted of a felony while holding a cabinet post. **C**

In the summer of 1923, Harding declared, "I have no trouble with my enemies. . . . But my . . . friends, they're the ones that keep me walking the floor nights!" Shortly thereafter, on August 2, 1923, he died suddenly, probably from a heart attack or stroke.

Americans sincerely mourned their good-natured president. The crimes of the Harding administration were coming to light just as Vice-President Calvin Coolidge assumed the presidency. Coolidge, a respected man of integrity, helped to restore people's faith in their government and in the Republican Party. The next year, Coolidge was elected president.

MAIN IDEA

Making Inferences

C How did the scandals of the Harding administration hurt the country economically?

▲ The elephant, shaped like a teapot here, is the symbol of the Republican Party (Grand Old Party). The cartoonist implies that Republicans were responsible for the Teapot Dome scandal.

SECTION 2 ASSESSMENT

1. TERMS & NAMES For each term or name, write a sentence explaining its significance.

- Warren G. Harding
- Charles Evans Hughes
- Fordney-McCumber Tariff
- Ohio gang
- Teapot Dome scandal
- Albert B. Fall

MAIN IDEA

2. TAKING NOTES

List five significant events from this section and their effects, using a table like the one shown.

Event	Effects
1.	
2.	

Which event benefited the country the most? Why?

CRITICAL THINKING

3. MAKING INFERENCES

How do you think the Harding administration viewed the role of America in world affairs? Support your response with examples from the text.

4. EVALUATING

How successful was Harding in fulfilling his campaign pledge of returning the country to "normalcy"? Support your opinion with specific examples.

5. ANALYZING EFFECTS

How do you think the postwar feelings in America influenced the election of 1920? **Think About:**

- the desire for normalcy
- Harding's image
- the issues Americans wanted to focus on

SECTION
3

PI 3.4
PI 4.3

CC Unit 5.I.B.1   CC Unit 5.I.B.3
CC Unit 5.I.B.4.a CC Unit 5.I.C.1.a
CC Unit 5.I.C.1.b CC Unit 5.I.C.1.c

The Business of America

MAIN IDEA	WHY IT MATTERS NOW	Terms & Names
Consumer goods fueled the business boom of the 1920s as America's standard of living soared.	Business, technological, and social developments of the 1920s launched the era of modern consumerism.	•Calvin Coolidge •installment plan •urban sprawl

One American's Story

In 1927, the last Model T Ford—number 15,077,033—rolled off the assembly line. On December 2, some 1 million New Yorkers mobbed show rooms to view the new Model A. One striking difference between the two models was that customers could order the Model A in such colors as "Arabian Sand" and "Niagara Blue"; the old Model T had come only in black. A Ford spokesman explained some additional advantages of the new automobile.

▲ The Model A was a more luxurious car than the Model T. It was introduced at $495. Model T's were selling for $290.

A PERSONAL VOICE

"Good-looking as that car is, its performance is better than its appearance. We don't brag about it, but it has done seventy-one miles an hour. It will ride along a railroad track without bouncing. . . . It's the smoothest thing you ever rode in."
—a Ford salesman quoted in *Flappers, Bootleggers, "Typhoid Mary," and the Bomb*

The automobile became the backbone of the American economy in the 1920s (and remained such until the 1970s). It profoundly altered the American landscape and American society, but it was only one of several factors in the country's business boom of the 1920s.

American Industries Flourish

hmhsocialstudies.com
TAKING NOTES

Use the graphic organizer online to take notes on technology and business changes in the 1920s.

The new president, **Calvin Coolidge**, fit into the pro-business spirit of the 1920s very well. It was he who said, "the chief business of the American people is business. . . . The man who builds a factory builds a temple—the man who works there worships there." Both Coolidge and his Republican successor, Herbert Hoover, favored government policies that would keep taxes down and business profits up, and give businesses more available credit in order to expand. Their goal was to keep government interference in business to a minimum and to allow private enterprise to flourish. For most of the 1920s, this approach seemed to work. Coolidge's administration continued to place high tariffs on foreign imports, which helped American manufacturers. Reducing income taxes meant that people had more money in their pockets. Wages were rising because of new technology and so was productivity.

THE IMPACT OF THE AUTOMOBILE The automobile literally changed the American landscape. Its most visible effect was the construction of paved roads suitable for driving in all weather. One such road was the legendary Route 66, which provided a route for people trekking west from Chicago to California. Many, however, settled in towns along the route. In addition to the changing landscape, architectural styles also changed, as new houses typically came equipped with a garage or carport and a driveway—and a smaller lawn as a result. The automobile also launched the rapid construction of gasoline stations, repair shops, public garages, motels, tourist camps, and shopping centers. The first automatic traffic signals began blinking in Detroit in the early 1920s. The Holland Tunnel, the first underwater tunnel designed specifically for motor vehicles, opened in 1927 to connect New York City and Jersey City, New Jersey. The Woodbridge Cloverleaf, the first cloverleaf intersection, was built in New Jersey in 1929. **A**

The automobile liberated the isolated rural family, who could now travel to the city for shopping and entertainment. It also gave families the opportunity to vacation in new and faraway places. It allowed both women and young people to become more independent through increased mobility. It allowed workers to live

> **MAIN IDEA**
>
> **Analyzing Effects**
>
> **A** What was the impact of the automobile?

Gas for cars was cheap and plentiful. Gas stations sprung up on Route 66 charging 25¢ per gallon. ▼

Roadside stands offering food, drink, and other items appeared in increasing numbers.

Route 66

🔗 hmhsocialstudies.com **INTERACTIVE MAP**

Commissioned on the cusp of the Depression, Route 66 symbolized the road to opportunity. Also known as "the Mother Road," it became the subject of countless songs, films, books, and legends.

1916 Federal-Aid Road Act sets up highway program with the federal government paying half the cost of states' highway construction.

1921 Highway construction in 11 western states begins under administration of Bureau of Public Roads.

1926 U.S. Highway 66, which would run 2,448 miles from Chicago to Los Angeles, California, is established.

The "Auto Camp" developed as towns-people roped off spaces alongside the road where travelers could sleep at night.

Route 66 linked hundreds of rural communities in Illinois, Missouri, and Kansas to Chicago, enabling farmers to transport produce.

PACIFIC OCEAN

CALIFORNIA · WYOMING · IOWA · Chicago · OHIO · INDIANA · ILLINOIS · Springfield · UTAH · ROCKY MOUNTAINS · Colorado River · COLORADO · KANSAS · Missouri River · MISSOURI · St. Louis · KENTUCKY · Arkansas River · *MOJAVE DESERT* · Barstow · *PAINTED DESERT* · Los Angeles · Winslow · Holbrook · Albuquerque · Tucumcari · Galena · Springfield · Tulsa · Claremore · TENNESSEE · ARIZONA · Santa Rosa · Amarillo · OKLAHOMA · ARKANSAS · NEW MEXICO · Red River · TEXAS · 120°W

0 100 200 miles
0 100 200 kilometers

Routing of highway through 392 miles of Oklahoma gave the state more miles, more jobs, and more income than other states on Route 66.

GEOGRAPHY SKILLBUILDER

1. **Place** What do you think were some of the reasons government officials decided to build Route 66 through the Southwest rather than straight west from Chicago?

2. **Movement** How do you think the increase in traffic affected the cities along this route?

Politics of the Roaring Twenties **629**

**CALVIN COOLIDGE
1872–1933**

Stepping into office in 1923, the tightlipped Vermonter was respected for his solemnity and wisdom. Coolidge supported American business and favored what he called "a constructive economy."

Known for his strength of character, Coolidge forced the resignation of Attorney General Daugherty and other high officials who had created scandal in office.

Shortly after Coolidge was elected, his son died of blood poisoning. Coolidge later wrote, "The power and the glory of the presidency went with him." When he decided not to seek reelection in 1928, Coolidge stumped the nation. Keeping in character, he said, "Goodby, I have had a very enjoyable time in Washington."

miles from their jobs, resulting in **urban sprawl** as cities spread in all directions. The automobile industry also provided an economic base for such cities as Akron in Ohio, and Detroit, Dearborn, Flint, and Pontiac in Michigan. The industry drew people to such oil-producing states as California and Texas. The automobile even became a status symbol—both for individual families and to the rest of the world. In their work *Middletown*, the social scientists Robert and Helen Lynd noted one woman's comment: "I'll go without food before I'll see us give up the car."

The auto industry symbolized the success of the free enterprise system and the Coolidge era. Nowhere else in the world could people with little money own their own automobile. By the late 1920s, around 80 percent of all registered motor vehicles in the world were in the United States—about one automobile for every five people. The humorist Will Rogers remarked to Henry Ford, "It will take a hundred years to tell whether you helped us or hurt us, but you certainly didn't leave us where you found us." **B**

THE YOUNG AIRPLANE INDUSTRY Automobiles weren't the only form of transportation taking off. The airplane industry began as a mail carrying service for the U.S. Post Office. Although the first flight in 1918 was a disaster, a number of successful flights soon established the airplane as a peacetime means of transportation. With the development of weather forecasting, planes began carrying radios and navigational instruments. Henry Ford made a trimotor airplane in 1926. Transatlantic flights by Charles Lindbergh and Amelia Earhart helped to promote cargo and commercial airlines. In 1927, the Lockheed Company produced a single-engine plane, the Vega. It was one of the most popular transport airplanes of the late 1920s. Founded in 1927, Pan American Airways inaugurated the first transatlantic passenger flights.

**Vocabulary
status symbol:** a possession believed to enhance the owner's social standing

MAIN IDEA

Analyzing Effects
B How did the widespread use of the automobile affect the environment and the lives of Americans?

Flight attendants train for an early United Airlines flight. When commercial airline flights began, all flight attendants were female and white. ▶

America's Standard of Living Soars

The years from 1920 to 1929 were prosperous ones for the United States. Americans owned around 40 percent of the world's wealth, and that wealth changed the way most Americans lived. The average annual income rose more than 35 percent during the period—from $522 to $705. People found it easy to spend all that extra income and then some.

ELECTRICAL CONVENIENCES Gasoline powered much of the economic boom of the 1920s, but the use of electricity also transformed the nation. American factories used electricity to run their machines. Also, the development of an alternating electrical current made it possible to distribute electric power efficiently over longer distances. Now electricity was no longer restricted to central cities but could be transmitted to suburbs. The number of electrified households grew, although most farms still lacked power.

By the end of the 1920s, more and more homes had electric irons, while well-to-do families used electric refrigerators, cooking ranges, and toasters. Eunice Fuller Barnard listed prices for electrical appliances in a 1928 magazine article:

▲ American consumers in the 1920s could purchase the latest household electrical appliances, such as a refrigerator, for as little as a dollar down and a dollar a week.

Goods and Prices, 1900 and 1928			
1900		**1928**	
wringer and washboard	$ 5	washing machine	$150
brushes and brooms	$ 5	vacuum cleaner	$ 50
sewing machine (mechanical)	$25	sewing machine (electric)	$ 60

MAIN IDEA

Forming Generalizations
C How did the use of electricity affect Americans' lifestyle?

These electrical appliances made the lives of housewives easier, freed them for other community and leisure activities, and coincided with a growing trend of women working outside the home. **C**

THE DAWN OF MODERN ADVERTISING With new goods flooding the market, advertising agencies no longer just informed the public about products and prices. Now they hired psychologists to study how to appeal to people's desire for youthfulness, beauty, health, and wealth. Results were impressive. The slogan "Say it with flowers" doubled florists' business between 1912 and 1924. "Reach for a Lucky instead of a sweet" lured weight-conscious Americans to cigarettes and away from candy. Brand names became familiar from coast to coast, and luxury items now seemed like necessities.

One of those "necessities" was mouthwash. A 1923 Listerine advertisement aimed to convince readers that without Listerine a person ran the risk of having halitosis—bad breath—and that the results could be a disaster.

A PERSONAL VOICE

"She was a beautiful girl and talented too. She had the advantages of education and better clothes than most girls of her set. She possessed that culture and poise that travel brings. Yet in the one pursuit that stands foremost in the mind of every girl and woman—marriage—she was a failure."

—Listerine Advertisement

Businesspeople applied the power of advertising to other areas of American life. Across the land, they met for lunch with fellow members of such service organizations as Rotary, Kiwanis, and the Lions. As one observer noted, they sang songs, raised money for charities, and boosted the image of the businessman "as a builder, a doer of great things, yes, and a dreamer whose imagination was ever seeking out new ways of serving humanity." Many Americans idolized business during these prosperous times.

A Superficial Prosperity

During the 1920s, most Americans believed prosperity would go on forever—the average factory worker was producing 50 percent more at the end of the decade than at its start. Hadn't national income grown from $64 billion in 1921 to $87 billion in 1929? Weren't most major corporations making fortunes? Wasn't the stock market reaching new heights?

PRODUCING GREAT QUANTITIES OF GOODS As productivity increased, businesses expanded. There were numerous mergers of companies that manufactured automobiles, steel, and electrical equipment, as well as mergers of companies that provided public utilities. Chain stores sprouted, selling groceries, drugs, shoes, and clothes. Five-and-dime stores like Woolworth's also spread rapidly. Congress passed a law that allowed national banks to branch within cities of their main office. But as the number of businesses grew, so did the income gap between workers and managers. There were a number of other clouds in the blue sky of prosperity. The iron and railroad industries, among others, weren't very prosperous, and farms nationwide suffered losses—with new machinery, they were producing more food than was needed and this drove down food prices.

BUYING GOODS ON CREDIT In addition to advertising, industry provided another solution to the problem of luring consumers to purchase the mountain of goods produced each year: easy credit, or "a dollar down and a dollar forever." The **installment plan**, as it was then called, enabled people to buy goods over

Background
In the years immediately after World War I, demand for American goods fell, and the economy went into recession. Unemployment rose rapidly, and many businesses failed. However, the economy began to recover in 1922.

Analyzing *Political Cartoons*

"YES, SIR, HE'S MY BABY"

This cartoon depicts Calvin Coolidge playing a saxophone labeled "Praise" while a woman representing "Big Business" dances up a storm.

SKILLBUILDER Analyzing Political Cartoons
1. The dancing woman is a 1920s "flapper"—independent, confident, and assertive. In what ways was big business in the 1920s comparable to the flappers?
2. What do you think the cartoonist suggests about Coolidge's relationship with big business?

 SEE SKILLBUILDER HANDBOOK, PAGE R24.

an extended period, without having to put down much money at the time of purchase. Banks provided the money at low interest rates. Advertisers pushed the "installment plan" idea with such slogans as "You furnish the girl, we'll furnish the home" and "Enjoy while you pay."

Some economists and business owners worried that installment buying might be getting out of hand and that it was really a sign of fundamental weaknesses behind a superficial economic prosperity. One business owner even wrote to President Coolidge and related a conversation he had overheard on a train. **D**

★ A PERSONAL VOICE

"Have you an automobile yet?"
"No, I talked it over with John and he felt we could not afford one."
"Mr. Budge who lives in your town has one and they are not as well off as you are."
"Yes, I know. Their second installment came due, and they had no money to pay it."
"What did they do? Lose the car?"
"No, they got the money and paid the installment."
"How did they get the money?"
"They sold the cook-stove."
"How could they get along without a cook-stove?"
"They didn't. They bought another on the installment plan."

—a business owner quoted in *In the Time of Silent Cal*

Still, most Americans focused their attention on the present, with little concern for the future. What could possibly go wrong with the nation's economy? The decade of the 1920s had brought about many technological and economic changes. And yet the Coolidge era was built on paradox—the president stood for economy and a frugal way of life, but he was favored by a public who had thrown all care to the wind. Life definitely seemed easier and more enjoyable for hundreds of thousands of Americans. From the look of things, there was little warning of what was to come. **E**

MAIN IDEA

Analyzing Issues

D What were the main advantage and disadvantage of buying on credit?

MAIN IDEA

Predicting Effects

E How do you think the changes in spending will affect the economy?

Automobile Registration 1910–1930

Source: *Historical Statistics of the United States.*

SECTION 3 ASSESSMENT

1. TERMS & NAMES For each term or name, write a sentence explaining its significance.
• Calvin Coolidge
• urban sprawl
• installment plan

MAIN IDEA

2. TAKING NOTES
Re-create the web below on your paper and fill it in with events that illustrate the central idea.

Choose one event from the web and explain its significance in the 1920s.

CRITICAL THINKING

3. EVALUATING
Do you agree with President Coolidge's statement "The man who builds a factory builds a temple—the man who works there worships there"? Explain your answer. **Think About:**

• the goals of business and of religion
• the American idolization of business
• the difference between workers and management

4. INTERPRETING GRAPHS
What trend does the graph show between 1920 and 1930? What were some of the reasons for this trend?

Economic Opportunity

The courage to take risks, the confidence to rely on one's self, the strength to stand in the face of despair, and the resourcefulness to make the most of opportunity— these are all qualities often considered distinctly American. Freedom requires individuals to discover or create opportunities for themselves. However, the government has also played a key role in distributing and creating economic opportunities.

CARAVAN OF EMIGRANTS FOR CALIFORNIA.
(Crossing the Great American Desert in Nebraska.)

1830s–1860s

◀ HOMESTEADING

Even before 1763, Americans looked toward the untamed west in search of greater wealth and freedom. In the 1830s, the Mormons went west to escape religious as well as economic persecution. The government helped to expand economic opportunities for whites by first clearing the land of its native inhabitants, relocating them to reservations or killing them.

As the nation claimed ownership of the land, it also gave it away. The Homestead Act of 1862 provided free of charge 160 acres of public land to anyone 21 years of age or older or the head of a family who had inhabited the land for five years and had improved it. This provided Americans a chance to be independent and self-sufficient if they would work hard. From 1862 until 1900, between 400,000 and 600,000 families were provided homesteads.

1900s

IMMIGRATION ▶

While many people have come to the U.S. seeking political and religious freedom, economic opportunity has also been a key reason for immigration. In 1905, for instance, almost half a million people from southern and eastern Europe migrated to the United States in search of economic freedom and opportunity, as well as to escape religious persecution. Many found work at menial jobs for low pay but still were able to save enough money to eventually open their own businesses.

1960s–1970s

EQUALITY OF OPPORTUNITY AND AFFIRMATIVE ACTION ▶

In the 1960s and 1970s, groups pressed for changes in the law to remove barriers to economic opportunity. Laws such as the Civil Rights Act of 1964 were passed to prevent discrimination against women and racial and ethnic minorities in order to provide equity in educational and business opportunities.

As well, affirmative action policies were designed to remedy effects of past discrimination. The term affirmative action—first used by Lyndon B. Johnson in 1965—includes efforts to give work and educational opportunities to members of historically disadvantaged groups. Some have labeled affirmative action "reverse discrimination," while others view it as a means to counterbalance continued discrimination that the law has been unable to prevent.

2000s

▼ COMPUTERS AND INTERNET STARTUPS

In recent years, many of the brightest college students have chosen to study computer science in hopes of landing a high-paying job. Alternatively, independent-minded computer experts might become entrepreneurs—people who start and run their own businesses. For an initial period of several months to several years, an entrepreneur may work upwards of 70 or 80 hours each week, yet the business will have no income.

Since the late 1990s, both groups have increasingly looked to the Internet for opportunities. Entrepreneurs seek money-making opportunities as they develop ways to expand the capabilities of this developing technology. In turn, the growth of Internet-based businesses creates jobs for people who have specialized computer skills.

THINKING CRITICALLY

CONNECT TO HISTORY

1. **Identifying Problems** What were some obstacles to achieving equal opportunity in each of the cases described on these two pages? Choose one of the time periods discussed and write a paragraph describing how these obstacles were overcome.

   SEE SKILLBUILDER HANDBOOK, PAGE R5.

CONNECT TO TODAY

2. **Evaluating a Business Opportunity** What economic opportunities available to you seem most promising? Discuss with your family and teachers or guidance counselor what jobs and business opportunities they think you might be suited for, then choose one and investigate it. Summarize your research by making a chart listing the pros and cons of the opportunity.

 hmhsocialstudies.com **RESEARCH WEB LINKS**

TERMS & NAMES

For each term or name below, write a sentence explaining its connection to the decade following World War I.

1. communism
2. Sacco and Vanzetti
3. Calvin Coolidge
4. John L. Lewis
5. Warren G. Harding
6. Fordney-McCumber Tariff
7. isolationism
8. quota system
9. Teapot Dome scandal
10. installment plan

MAIN IDEAS

Use your notes and the information in the chapter to answer the following questions.

Americans Struggle with Postwar Issues

(pages 618–624)

1. Explain how the Red Scare, the Sacco and Vanzetti case, and the rise of the Ku Klux Klan reflected concerns held by many Americans.
2. Describe the primary goal of the immigration quota system established in 1921.

The Harding Presidency *(pages 625–627)*

3. What did Harding want to do to return America to "normalcy"?
4. Summarize the Teapot Dome scandal.

The Business of America *(pages 628–633)*

5. How did changes in technology in the 1920s influence American life?
6. What evidence suggests that the prosperity of the 1920s was not on a firm foundation?

CRITICAL THINKING

1. **USING YOUR NOTES** Create a cause-and-effect web, similar to the one shown, in which you give several causes for the declining power of labor unions in the 1920s and give examples of the unions' decline.

2. **HISTORICAL PERSPECTIVE** Calvin Coolidge said, "After all, the chief business of the American people is business." What events and trends of the 1920s support Coolidge's statement?

3. **INTERPRETING MAPS** Look at the path of Route 66 in the map on page 629. What factors may have influenced where and why the highway was built? Explain your answer.

VISUAL SUMMARY   POLITICS OF THE ROARING TWENTIES

LIFE IN POSTWAR AMERICA

ECONOMIC
- a superficial prosperity ensued
- increased production of consumer goods
- buying on credit
- increased standard of living and consumer spending

GOVERNMENTAL
- election of pro-business presidents Harding and Coolidge
- isolationist philosophy
- immigration quotas
- tariffs on imports to discourage foreign business competition
- corruption in Harding's administration

SOCIETAL/SOCIAL
- a perceived threat of communism
- fear and distrust of immigrants
- fear of the labor movement and faith in business
- strikes and worker unrest

TECHNOLOGY/INDUSTRY
- growth of automobile industry
- introduction of airlines as transportation
- widespread use of electricity
- advertising gains popularity

Use the cartoon and your knowledge of United States history to answer question 1.

WHAT A FRIEND WE HAVE IN COOLIDGE!

THE CASH REGISTER CHORUS.

1 The cartoon criticizes President Coolidge by suggesting that —

(1) Coolidge's policies benefited wealthy business owners.

(2) Coolidge was known as "Silent Cal" because he had no economic policy.

(3) Coolidge provided cash assistance to struggling industries.

(4) Coolidge had supported the Immigration Act.

2 After World War I ended, workers in many industries went on strike for wage increases and better working conditions. But in the decade that followed, public support of labor unions declined, as did union membership. Which of the following helps to explain this decline in labor union popularity?

(1) Wages and working conditions in most industries had already improved before the mid-1920s.

(2) Most labor unions actively opposed isolationist policies.

(3) Most labor unions had large immigrant memberships.

(4) Few labor unions would allow unskilled veterans returning from the war to join.

3 Which of the following beliefs did not result from America's desire for "normalcy" after World War I?

(1) isolationism

(2) conservatism

(3) nativism

(4) anarchism

 hmhsocialstudies.com **TEST PRACTICE**

For additional test practice, go online for:
• Diagnostic tests   • Tutorials

INTERACT WITH HISTORY

Recall the issues that you explored at the beginning of the chapter. Suppose you are a reporter covering the Boston police strike. Write a column for your newspaper that explains why people acted as they did. Also describe the mood and tension created by the strike. Invent realistic quotations from workers, union members, strikebreakers, and management.

FOCUS ON WRITING

Imagine it is the 1920s. Write a persuasive letter to your member of Congress in support of or in opposition to a quota system for controlling immigration. In the first part of your letter, present the evidence that supports your position on immigration. In the second half of your letter, provide a counterargument to address the concerns of the opposing viewpoint.

MULTIMEDIA ACTIVITY

21ST CENTURY

Visit the links for Chapter Assessment to research incomes, prices, employment levels, divorce rates, or other statistics that show how people were affected by the events of the 1920s. Use your findings to create a graph.

• Decide the main purpose of your graph. What statistics will you show?

• Choose the type of graph that would best show your data. Consider using a line graph, bar graph, or circle graph.

• Clearly label the parts of the graph.

• Share your graph with the class.

hmhsocialstudies.com **INTERNET ACTIVITY**

Henry Ford

Henry Ford was a brilliant inventor and industrialist and founder of the Ford Motor Company. He helped bring about a time of rapid growth and progress that forever changed how people worked and lived. Henry Ford grew up on his family's farm near Dearborn, Michigan. As a child, he disliked life on the farm. He found the clicks and whirs of machinery much more exciting. When Ford was 16, he went to nearby Detroit to work in a machine shop. From there, he turned his ideas for how to make affordable and well-built cars into one of the world's largest automobile companies.

Explore the amazing life and career of Henry Ford online. You can find a wealth of information, video clips, primary sources, activities, and more at ⏎ hmhsocialstudies.com.

"My 'gasoline buggy' was the first and for a long time the only automobile in Detroit. It was considered . . . a nuisance, for it made a racket and it scared horses."

— Henry Ford

 My Life and Work
Read the document to learn more about Henry Ford's life and career in his own words.

Big Plans
Watch the video to learn more about Henry Ford's early career.

Taking the Low Road
Watch the video to explore Henry Ford's vision for his car company.

The Assembly Line
Watch the video to see how Henry Ford used the assembly line to produce cars more efficiently and cheaply.

CHAPTER 21

THE ROARING LIFE OF THE 1920s

Essential Question

How did newfound prosperity change American life in the 1920s?

 New York Standards

KEY IDEA 2 Important ideas, social and cultural values, beliefs, and traditions from New York State and United States history illustrate the connections and interactions of people and events across time and from a variety of perspectives.

KEY IDEA 4 The skills of historical analysis include the ability to: explain the significance of historical evidence; weigh the importance, reliability, and validity of evidence; understand the concept of multiple causation; understand the importance of changing and competing interpretations of different historical developments.

SECTION 1: Changing Ways of Life

SECTION 2: The Twenties Woman

SECTION 3: Education and Popular Culture

SECTION 4: The Harlem Renaissance

Blues singer Gertrude "Ma" Rainey performs with her Georgia Jazz Band in Chicago, Illinois, 1923.

1920 Nineteenth Amendment gives women the right to vote.

1922 Louis Armstrong plays for King Oliver's Creole Jazz Band in Chicago.

1923 *Time* magazine begins publication.

1924 Calvin Coolidge is elected president.

USA
WORLD

1920 **1922** **1924**

1921 China's Communist Party is founded.

1922 King Tut's tomb is discovered in Egypt.

1923 Mustafa Kemal becomes first president of new Republic of Turkey.

INTERACT
WITH HISTORY

The year is 1920. The World War has just ended. Boosted by the growth of the wartime industry, the U.S. economy is flourishing. Americans live life to the fullest as new social and cutural trends sweep the nation.

Explore the Issues

- As Americans leave farms and small towns to take jobs in the cities, how might their lives change?
- How will economic prosperity affect married and unmarried women?
- How might rural and urban areas change as more and more families acquire automobiles?

1925 The Scopes trial takes place in Tennessee.

1927 Charles Lindbergh makes the first nonstop solo transatlantic flight.

1928 Herbert Hoover is elected president.

1926 **1928** **1930**

1926 Hirohito becomes emperor of Japan.

1928 President Álvaro Obregón of Mexico is assassinated.

PI 2.3
PI 4.3
CC Unit 4.I.B.2.d
CC Unit 5.I.C.2.b
CC Unit 5.I.C.2.c

Changing Ways of Life

MAIN IDEA	WHY IT MATTERS NOW	Terms & Names
Americans experienced cultural conflicts as customs and values changed in the 1920s.	The way in which different groups react to change continues to cause conflict today.	• Prohibition • speakeasy • bootlegger • fundamentalism • Clarence Darrow • Scopes trial

One American's Story

hmhsocialstudies.com
TAKING NOTES

Use the graphic organizer online to take notes on government efforts to address social concerns in the 1920s.

As the 1920s dawned, social reformers who hoped to ban alcohol—and the evils associated with it—rejoiced. The Eighteenth Amendment to the Constitution, banning the manufacture, sale, and transportation of alcohol, took effect in January of 1920. Billy Sunday, an evangelist who preached against the evils of drinking, predicted a new age of virtue and religion.

> **A PERSONAL VOICE** BILLY SUNDAY
>
> " The reign of tears is over! The slums will soon be only a memory. We will turn our prisons into factories and our jails into storehouses and corncribs. Men will walk upright now, women will smile and the children will laugh. Hell will be forever for rent! "
>
> —quoted in *How Dry We Were: Prohibition Revisited*

Sunday's dream was not to be realized in the 1920s, as the law proved unenforceable. The failure of Prohibition was a sign of cultural conflicts most evident in the nation's cities. Lured by jobs and by the challenge and freedom that the city represented, millions of people rode excitedly out of America's rural past and into its urban future.

▲
1920s evangelist Billy Sunday

Rural and Urban Differences

America changed dramatically in the years before 1920, as was revealed in the 1920 census. According to figures that year, 51.2 percent of Americans lived in communities with populations of 2,500 to more than 1 million. Between 1922 and 1929, migration to the cities accelerated, with nearly 2 million people leaving farms and towns each year. "Cities were the place to be, not to get away from," said one historian. The agricultural world that millions of Americans left behind was largely unchanged from the 19th century—that world was one of small towns and farms bound together by conservative moral values and close social relationships. Yet small-town attitudes began to lose their hold on the American mind as the city rose to prominence.

THE NEW URBAN SCENE At the beginning of the 1920s, New York, with a population of 5.6 million people, topped the list of big cities. Next came Chicago, with nearly 3 million, and Philadelphia, with nearly 2 million. Another 65 cities claimed populations of 100,000 or more, and they grew more crowded by the day. Life in these booming cities was far different from the slow-paced, intimate life in America's small towns. Chicago, for instance, was an industrial powerhouse, home to native-born whites and African Americans, immigrant Poles, Irish, Russians, Italians, Swedes, Arabs, French, and Chinese. Each day, an estimated 300,000 workers, 150,000 cars and buses, and 20,000 trolleys filled the pulsing downtown. At night people crowded into ornate movie theaters and vaudeville houses offering live variety shows.

"How ya gonna keep 'em down on the farm, after they've seen Paree?"

POPULAR SONG OF THE 1920s

For small-town migrants, adapting to the urban environment demanded changes in thinking as well as in everyday living. The city was a world of competition and change. City dwellers read and argued about current scientific and social ideas. They judged one another by accomplishment more often than by background. City dwellers also tolerated drinking, gambling, and casual dating—worldly behaviors considered shocking and sinful in small towns. **A**

For all its color and challenge, though, the city could be impersonal and frightening. Streets were filled with strangers, not friends and neighbors. Life was fast-paced, not leisurely. The city demanded endurance, as a foreign visitor to Chicago observed.

MAIN IDEA

Contrasting
A How did small-town life and city life differ?

★ **A PERSONAL VOICE** WALTER L. GEORGE

" It is not for nothing that the predominating color of Chicago is orange. It is as if the city, in its taxicabs, in its shop fronts, in the wrappings of its parcels, chose the color of flame that goes with the smoky black of its factories. It is not for nothing that it has repelled the geometric street arrangement of New York and substituted . . . great ways with names that a stranger must learn if he can. . . . He is in a [crowded] city, and if he has business there, he tells himself, 'If I weaken I shan't last long.' "

—*Hail Columbia!*

History Through *Art*

SONG OF THE TOWERS

This mural by Aaron Douglas is part of a series he painted inside the 135th Street Branch of the New York Public Library to symbolize different aspects of African-American life during the 1920s. In this panel, *Song of the Towers*, he depicts figures before a city backdrop. As seen here, much of Douglas's style was influenced by jazz music and geometric shapes.

SKILLBUILDER **Analyzing Visual Sources**
1. What is the focal point of this panel?
2. What parts of this painting might be symbolic of African Americans' move north?
3. How does Douglas represent new freedoms in this mural? Support your answer with examples.

 SEE SKILLBUILDER HANDBOOK, PAGE R23.

In the city, lonely migrants from the country often ached for home. Throughout the 1920s, Americans found them-selves caught between rural and urban cultures—a tug that pitted what seemed to be a safe, small-town world of close ties, hard work, and strict morals against a big-city world of anonymous crowds, moneymakers, and pleasure seekers.

THE PROHIBITION EXPERIMENT One vigorous clash between small-town and big-city Americans began in earnest in January 1920, when the Eighteenth Amendment went into effect. This amendment launched the era known as **Prohibition,** during which the manufacture, sale, and transportation of alcoholic beverages were legally prohibited.

Reformers had long considered liquor a prime cause of corruption. They thought that too much drinking led to crime, wife and child abuse, accidents on the job, and other serious social problems. Support for Prohibition came largely from the rural South and West, areas with large populations of native-born Protestants. The church-affiliated Anti-Saloon League had led the drive to pass the Prohibition amendment. The Woman's Christian Temperance Union, which consid-ered drinking a sin, had helped push the measure through.

At first, saloons closed their doors, and arrests for drunkenness declined. But in the aftermath of World War I, many Americans were tired of making sacrifices; they want-ed to enjoy life. Most immigrant groups did not consider drinking a sin but a natural part of socializing, and they resented government meddling.

Eventually, Prohibition's fate was sealed by the government, which failed to budget enough money to enforce the law. The Volstead Act established a Prohibition Bureau in the Treasury Department in 1919, but the agency was underfunded. The job of enforcement involved patrolling 18,700 miles of coastline as well as inland borders, tracking down illegal stills (equip-ment for distilling liquor), monitoring highways for truckloads of illegal alcohol, and overseeing all the industries that legally used alcohol to be sure none was siphoned off for illegal purposes. The task fell to approximately 1,500 poorly paid federal agents and local police—clearly an impossible job.

SPEAKEASIES AND BOOTLEGGERS To obtain liquor ille-gally, drinkers went underground to hidden saloons and nightclubs known as **speakeasies**—so called because when inside, one spoke quietly, or "easily," to avoid detection. Speakeasies could be found everywhere—in penthouses, cel-lars, office buildings, rooming houses, tenements, hardware stores, and tearooms. To be admitted to a speakeasy, one had to present a card or use a password. Inside, one would find a mix of fashionable middle-class and upper-middle-class men and women.

Before long, people grew bolder in getting around the law. They learned to distill alcohol and built their own stills. Since alco-hol was allowed for medicinal and religious purposes, prescriptions

◀ A young woman demonstrates one of the means used to conceal alcohol—hiding it in containers strapped to one's legs. ▶

for alcohol and sales of sacramental wine (intended for church services) skyrocketed. People also bought liquor from **bootleggers** (named for a smuggler's practice of carrying liquor in the legs of boots), who smuggled it in from Canada, Cuba, and the West Indies. "The business of evading [the law] and making a mock of it has ceased to wear any aspects of crime and has become a sort of national sport," wrote the journalist H. L. Mencken. **B**

ORGANIZED CRIME Prohibition not only generated disrespect for the law, it also contributed to organized crime in nearly every major city. Chicago became notorious as the home of Al Capone, a gangster whose bootlegging empire netted over $60 million a year. Capone took control of the Chicago liquor business by killing off his competition. During the 1920s, headlines reported 522 bloody gang killings and made the image of flashy Al Capone part of the folklore of the period. In 1940, the writer Herbert Asbury recalled the Capone era in Chicago.

A PERSONAL VOICE HERBERT ASBURY

" The famous seven-ton armored car, with the pudgy gangster lolling on silken cushions in its darkened recesses, a big cigar in his fat face, and a $50,000 diamond ring blazing from his left hand, was one of the sights of the city; the average tourist felt that his trip to Chicago was a failure unless it included a view of Capone out for a spin. The mere whisper: 'Here comes Al,' was sufficient to stop traffic and to set thousands of curious citizens craning their necks along the curbing. "

—*Gem of the Prairie*

By the mid-1920s, only 19 percent of Americans supported Prohibition. The rest, who wanted the amendment changed or repealed, believed that Prohibition caused worse effects than the initial problem. Rural Protestant Americans, however, defended a law that they felt strengthened moral values. The Eighteenth Amendment remained in force until 1933, when it was repealed by the Twenty-first Amendment. **C**

MAIN IDEA

Developing Historical Perspective
B Why do you think the Eighteenth Amendment failed to eliminate alcohol consumption?

MAIN IDEA

Analyzing Effects
C How did criminals take advantage of Prohibition?

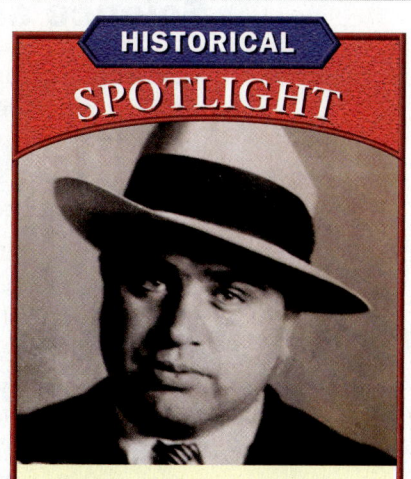

HISTORICAL SPOTLIGHT

AL CAPONE
By age 26, Al Capone headed a criminal empire in Chicago, which he controlled through the use of bribes and violence. From 1925 to 1931, Capone bootlegged whiskey from Canada, operated illegal breweries in Chicago, and ran a network of 10,000 speakeasies. In 1927, the "Big Fellow," as he liked to be called, was worth an estimated $100 million.

The end came quickly for Capone, though. In 1931, the gangster chief was arrested for tax evasion and went to jail. That was the only crime of which the authorities were ever able to convict him. Capone was later released from jail, but he died several years later at age 48.

Prohibition, 1920–1933	
Causes	**Effects**
• Various religious groups thought drinking alcohol was sinful. • Reformers believed that the government should protect the public's health. • Reformers believed that alcohol led to crime, wife and child abuse, and accidents on the job. • During World War I, native-born Americans developed a hostility to German-American brewers and toward other immigrant groups that used alcohol.	• Consumption of alcohol declined. • Disrespect for the law developed. • An increase in lawlessness, such as smuggling and bootlegging, was evident. • Criminals found a new source of income. • Organized crime grew.

Science and Religion Clash

Another bitter controversy highlighted the growing rift between traditional and modern ideas during the 1920s. This battle raged between fundamentalist religious groups and secular thinkers over the validity of certain scientific discoveries.

AMERICAN FUNDAMENTALISM The Protestant Christian movement grounded in a literal, or nonsymbolic, interpretation of the Bible was known as **fundamentalism**. Fundamentalists were skeptical of some scientific discoveries and theories; they argued that all important knowledge could be found in the Bible. They believed that the Bible was inspired by God, and that therefore its stories in all their details were true.

Their beliefs led fundamentalists to reject the theory of evolution advanced by Charles Darwin in the 19th century—a theory stating that plant and animal species had developed and changed over millions of years. The claim they found most unbelievable was that humans had evolved from apes. They pointed instead to the Bible's account of creation, in which God made the world and all its life forms, including humans, in six days.

Fundamentalism expressed itself in several ways. In the South and West, preachers led religious revivals based on the authority of the Scriptures. One of the most powerful revivalists was Billy Sunday, a baseball player turned preacher who staged emotional meetings across the South. In Los Angeles, Aimee Semple McPherson used Hollywood showmanship to preach the word to homesick Midwestern migrants and devoted followers of her radio broadcasts. In the 1920s, fundamentalism gained followers who began to call for laws prohibiting the teaching of evolution. **D**

▲ The evangelist Aimee Semple McPherson in 1922

MAIN IDEA

Summarizing
D Summarize the beliefs of fundamentalism.

THE SCOPES TRIAL In March 1925, Tennessee passed the nation's first law that made it a crime to teach evolution. Immediately, the American Civil Liberties Union (ACLU) promised to defend any teacher who would challenge the law. John T. Scopes, a young biology teacher in Dayton, Tennessee, accepted the challenge. In his biology class, Scopes read this passage from *Civic Biology:* "We have now learned that animal forms may be arranged so as to begin with the simple one-celled forms and culminate with a group which includes man himself." Scopes was promptly arrested, and his trial was set for July.

The ACLU hired **Clarence Darrow,** the most famous trial lawyer of the day, to defend Scopes. William Jennings Bryan, three-time Democratic candidate for president and a devout fundamentalist, served as a special prosecutor. There was no real question of guilt or innocence: Scopes was honest about his action. The **Scopes trial** was a fight over evolution and the role of science and religion in public schools and in American society.

The trial opened on July 10, 1925, and almost overnight became a national sensation. Darrow called Bryan as an expert on the Bible—the contest that everyone had been waiting for. To handle the throngs of Bryan supporters, Judge Raulston moved the court outside, to a platform built under the maple trees. There, before a crowd of several

Vocabulary
culminate:
to come to completion; end

NOW & THEN

EVOLUTION, CREATIONISM, AND EDUCATION

There is still great controversy today over the teaching of evolution in the public schools. Some people believe evolution should be taught as the only theory of the origin of life. Some believe the theories of creationism or intelligent design should also be taught. Others want to focus on the debate surrounding evolution.

The issue of what should be taught about the origin of life—and who should decide this issue—continues to stir up debate. Some have suggested that science and religion are not necessarily incompatible. They believe that a theory of the origin of life can accommodate both the scientific theory of evolution and religious beliefs.

thousand, Darrow relentlessly questioned Bryan about his beliefs. Bryan stood firm, a smile on his face.

⭐ A PERSONAL VOICE
CLARENCE DARROW AND WILLIAM JENNINGS BRYAN

Mr. Darrow—"You claim that everything in the Bible should be literally interpreted?"
Mr. Bryan—"I believe everything in the Bible should be accepted as it is given there. Some of the Bible is given illustratively. For instance: 'Ye are the salt of the earth.' I would not insist that man was actually salt, or that he had flesh of salt, but it is used in the sense of salt as saving God's people."

—quoted in *Bryan and Darrow at Dayton*

"When Shall We Three Meet Again?"

Darrow asked Bryan if he agreed with Bishop James Ussher's calculation that, according to the Bible, Creation happened in 4004 B.C. Had every living thing on earth appeared since that time? Did Bryan know that ancient civilizations had thrived before 4004 B.C.? Did he know the age of the earth? Bryan grew edgy but stuck to his guns. Finally, Darrow asked Bryan, "Do you think the earth was made in six days?" Bryan answered, "Not six days of 24 hours." People sitting on the lawn gasped. **E**

With this answer, Bryan admitted that the Bible might be interpreted in different ways. But in spite of this admission, Scopes was found guilty and fined $100. The Tennessee Supreme Court later changed the verdict on a technicality, but the law outlawing the teaching of evolution remained in effect.

This clash over evolution, the Prohibition experiment, and the emerging urban scene all were evidence of the changes and conflicts occurring during the 1920s. During that period, women also experienced conflict as they redefined their roles and pursued new lifestyles.

MAIN IDEA

Analyzing Issues
E What was the conflict between fundamentalists and those who accepted evolution?

▲ A 1925 newspaper cartoon portrays Bryan (*left*) and Darrow (*right*) at the close of the Scopes "monkey" trial on the teaching of evolution, so-called because of a theory of evolution that humans evolved from apes.

ASSESSMENT

1. **TERMS & NAMES** For each term or name, write a sentence explaining its significance.
   - Prohibition
   - speakeasy
   - bootlegger
   - fundamentalism
   - Clarence Darrow
   - Scopes trial

MAIN IDEA

2. **TAKING NOTES**
   Create two diagrams like the one below. Show how government attempted to deal with (a) problems thought to stem from alcohol use and (b) the teaching of evolution.

Issue
↓
Legislation
↓
Outcome

   Was the legislation effective? Explain.

CRITICAL THINKING

3. **ANALYZING ISSUES**
   How might the overall atmosphere of the 1920s have contributed to the failure of Prohibition?

4. **ANALYZING CAUSES**
   Why do you think organized crime spread so quickly through the cities during the 1920s? Explain your answer.

5. **EVALUATING**
   Do you think the passage of the Volstead Act and the ruling in the Scopes trial represented genuine triumphs for traditional values?
   Think About:
   - changes in urban life in the 1920s
   - the effects of Prohibition
   - the legacy of the Scopes trial

SECTION
2

PI 4.1

CC Unit 3.III.A.3.c   CC Unit 5.I.C.3.a
CC Unit 5.I.C.3.b(1)   CC Unit 5.I.C.3.b(3)
CC Unit 5.I.C.3.b(4)   CC Unit 5.I.C.3.b(5)

The Twenties Woman

MAIN IDEA	WHY IT MATTERS NOW	Terms & Names
American women pursued new lifestyles and assumed new jobs and different roles in society during the 1920s.	Workplace opportunities and trends in family life are still major issues for women today.	•flapper •double standard

hmhsocialstudies.com
TAKING NOTES

Use the graphic organizer online to take notes on how women's lives changed in the 1920s.

One American's Story

When Zelda Sayre broke off her engagement with would-be writer F. Scott Fitzgerald in 1925, she told him that he would have to become successful on his own. Later, she wrote about how a woman can achieve greatness.

★ **A PERSONAL VOICE** ZELDA SAYRE FITZGERALD

" Rouge means that women want to choose their man—not take what lives in the next house. . . . Look back over the pages of history and see how the loveliness of women has always stirred men—and nations—on to great achievement! There have been women who were not pretty, who have swayed hearts and empires, but these women . . . did not disdain that thing for which paint and powder stands. They wanted to choose their destinies—to be successful competitors in the great game of life. "

—"Paint and Powder," *The Smart Set*, May 1929

Zelda Sayre Fitzgerald

Zelda Sayre and F. Scott Fitzgerald married one week after Scott published his first novel, and Zelda continued to be the model for Scott's independent, unconventional, ambitious female characters. He even copied from her letters and other writings. Ironically, Zelda's devotion to her marriage and to motherhood stifled her career ambitions. Nevertheless, she became a model for a generation of young American women who wanted to break away from traditions and forget the hardships of the war years.

Young Women Change the Rules

By the 1920s, the experiences of World War I, the pull of cities, and changing attitudes had opened up a new world for many young Americans. These "wild young people," wrote John F. Carter, Jr., in a 1920 issue of *Atlantic Monthly*, were experiencing a world unknown to their parents: "We have seen man at his lowest, woman at her lightest, in the terrible moral chaos of Europe. We have been forced to question, and in many cases to discard, the religion of our fathers. . . .We have been forced to live in an atmosphere of 'tomorrow we die,' and so, naturally, we drank and were merry." In the rebellious, pleasure-loving atmosphere of the twenties, many women began to assert their independence, reject the values of the 19th century, and demand the same freedoms as men.

Flappers compete in a Charleston dance competition in 1926.

THE FLAPPER During the twenties, a new ideal emerged for some women: the **flapper,** an emancipated young woman who embraced the new fashions and urban attitudes of the day. Close-fitting felt hats, bright waistless dresses an inch above the knees, skin-toned silk stockings, sleek pumps, and strings of beads replaced the dark and prim ankle-length dresses, whalebone corsets, and petticoats of Victorian days. Young women clipped their long hair into boyish bobs and dyed it jet black.

Many young women became more assertive. In their bid for equal status with men, some began smoking cigarettes, drinking in public, and talking openly about sex—actions that would have ruined their reputations not many years before. They danced the fox trot, camel walk, tango, Charleston, and shimmy with abandon.

Attitudes toward marriage changed as well. Many middle-class men and women began to view marriage as more of an equal partnership, although both agreed that housework and child-rearing remained a woman's job. **A**

THE DOUBLE STANDARD Magazines, newspapers, and advertisements promoted the image of the flapper, and young people openly discussed courtship and relationships in ways that scandalized their elders. Although many young women donned the new outfits and flouted tradition, the flapper was more an image of rebellious youth than a widespread reality; it did not reflect the attitudes and values of many young people. During the 1920s, morals loosened only so far. Traditionalists in churches and schools protested the new casual dances and women's acceptance of smoking and drinking.

In the years before World War I, when men "courted" women, they pursued only women they intended to marry. In the 1920s, however, casual dating became increasingly accepted. Even so, a **double standard**—a set of principles granting greater sexual freedom to men than to women—required women to observe stricter standards of behavior than men did. As a result, many women were pulled back and forth between the old standards and the new.

Women Shed Old Roles at Home and at Work

The fast-changing world of the 1920s produced new roles for women in the workplace and new trends in family life. A booming industrial economy opened new work opportunities for women in offices, factories, stores, and professions. The same economy churned out time-saving appliances and products that reshaped the roles of housewives and mothers.

MAIN IDEA

Evaluating
A How was the flapper like and unlike women of today?

A young woman works as a typesetter in a publishing house in 1920.

NEW WORK OPPORTUNITIES Although women had worked successfully during the war, afterwards employers who believed that men had the responsibility to support their families financially often replaced female workers with men. Women continued to seek paid employment, but their opportunities changed. Many female college graduates turned to "women's professions" and became teachers, nurses, and librarians. Big businesses required extensive correspondence and record keeping, creating a huge demand for clerical workers such as typists, filing clerks, secretaries, stenographers, and office-machine operators. Others became clerks in stores or held jobs on assembly lines. A handful of women broke the old stereotypes by doing work once reserved for men, such as flying airplanes, driving taxis, and drilling oil wells. **B**

By 1930, 10 million women were earning wages; however, few rose to managerial jobs, and wherever they worked, women earned less than men. Fearing competition for jobs, men argued that women were just temporary workers whose real job was at home. Between 1900 and 1930, the patterns of discrimination and inequality for women in the business world were established.

THE CHANGING FAMILY Widespread social and economic changes reshaped the family. The birthrate had been declining for several decades, and it dropped at a slightly faster rate in the 1920s. This decline was due in part to the wider availability of birth-control information. Margaret Sanger, who had opened the first birth-control clinic in the United States in 1916, founded the American Birth Control League in 1921 and fought for the legal rights of physicians to give birth-control information to their patients.

At the same time, social and technological innovations simplified household labor and family life. Stores overflowed with ready-made clothes, sliced bread, and canned foods. Public agencies provided services for the elderly, public health clinics served the sick, and workers' compensation assisted those who could no longer work. These innovations and institutions had the effect of freeing homemakers from some of their traditional family responsibilities. Many middle-class housewives, the main shoppers and money managers, focused their attention on their homes, husbands, children, and pastimes. "I consider time for reading clubs and my children more important than . . . careful housework and I just don't do it," said an Indiana woman in the 1920s.

MAIN IDEA

Analyzing Effects
B How did the growth of business and industry affect women?

Women's Changing Employment, 1910–1930

1910
- Domestic[1] 31.3%
- Manufacturing & Mechanical 22.6%
- Professional 9.1%
- Transportation & Communication 1.3%
- Trade[2] 5.9%
- Clerical 7.3%
- Agriculture[3] 22.4%

1920
- Domestic[1] 25.6%
- Manufacturing & Mechanical 22.6%
- Professional 11.9%
- Transportation & Communication 2.6%
- Trade[2] 7.9%
- Clerical 16.6%
- Agriculture[3] 12.7%

1930
- Domestic[1] 29.6%
- Manufacturing & Mechanical 17.5%
- Professional 14.2%
- Transportation & Communication 2.6%
- Trade[2] 9.0%
- Clerical 18.5%
- Agriculture[3] 8.5%

[1] Includes restaurant workers and beauticians.   [2] Includes sales clerks.   [3] Includes forestry and fishing.   Source: Grace Hutchins, *Women Who Work*

As their spheres of activity and influence expanded, women experienced greater equality in marriage. Marriages were based increasingly on romantic love and companionship. Children, no longer thrown together with adults in factory work, farm labor, and apprenticeships, spent most of their days at school and in organized activities with others their own age. At the same time, parents began to rely more heavily on manuals of child care and the advice of experts.

Working-class and college-educated women quickly discovered the pressure of juggling work and family, but the strain on working-class women was more severe. Helen Wright, who worked for the Women's Bureau in Chicago, recorded the struggle of an Irish mother of two.

★ A PERSONAL VOICE HELEN WRIGHT

"She worked in one of the meat-packing companies, pasting labels from 7 a.m. to 3:30 p.m. She had entered the eldest child at school but sent her to the nursery for lunch and after school. The youngest was in the nursery all day. She kept her house 'immaculately clean and in perfect order,' but to do so worked until eleven o'clock every night in the week and on Saturday night she worked until five o'clock in the morning. She described her schedule as follows: on Tuesday, Wednesday, Thursday, and Friday she cleaned one room each night; Saturday afternoon she finished the cleaning and put the house in order; Saturday night she washed; Sunday she baked; Monday night she ironed."

—quoted in *Wage-Earning Women*

As women adjusted to changing roles, some also struggled with rebellious adolescents, who put an unprecedented strain on families. Teens in the 1920s studied and socialized with other teens and spent less time with their families. As peer pressure intensified, some adolescents resisted parental control, much as the flappers resisted societal control. **C**

This theme of adolescent rebelliousness can be seen in much of the popular culture of the 1920s. Education and entertainment reflected the conflict between traditional attitudes and modern ways of thinking.

MAIN IDEA

Summarizing
C What changes affected families in the 1920s?

SECTION 2 ASSESSMENT

1. TERMS & NAMES For each term or name, write a sentence explaining its significance.
- flapper
- double standard

MAIN IDEA

2. TAKING NOTES
Copy the concept web shown below and add to it examples that illustrate how women's lives changed in the 1920s.

lifestyles

Changes: Women in the 1920s

families   jobs

Write a paragraph explaining how you think women's lives changed most dramatically in the 1920s.

CRITICAL THINKING

3. EVALUATING
During the 1920s, a double standard required women to observe stricter codes of behavior than men. Do you think that some women of this decade made real progress towards equality? Support your answer with examples. **Think About:**
- the flapper's style and image
- changing views of marriage

4. ANALYZING PRIMARY SOURCES
In 1920, veteran suffragist Anna Howard Shaw stated that equality in the workplace would be harder for women to achieve than the vote.

"You younger women will have a harder task than ours. You will want equality in business, and it will be even harder to get than the vote."

—Anna Howard Shaw

Why do you think Shaw held this belief? Support your answer with evidence from the text.

Youth in the Roaring Twenties

The decade known as the Roaring Twenties was a celebration of youth and its culture. Crazy and frenetic dances, silly songs, and radically new styles of clothing captured the public's fancy.

During this period of relative prosperity, many people questioned the values of the past and were willing to experiment with new values and behavior as well as with new fashions. This was an especially liberating period for women, who received the right to vote in 1920. Many women also opted for a liberating change of fashion—short skirts and short hair—as well as the freedom to smoke and drink in public.

▼ FLAGPOLE SITTING

One of the more bizarre fads of the 1920s began in 1924 as a publicity stunt to attract viewers to movie theaters. The most famous flagpole sitter was "Shipwreck" Kelly (right, waving from high above a movie theater in Union City, New Jersey). In 1929, for a total of 145 days, Kelly took up residence atop various flagpoles throughout the country. Imitators, of course, followed. At one point that year, Baltimore had at least 17 boys and 3 girls sitting atop 18-foot hickory poles, with their friends and families cheering them on.

BESSIE SMITH ▶

Bessie Smith was "Empress of the Blues." In 1923, she sold a million recordings of "Down Hearted Blues."

◀ BOBBED HAIR

In keeping with the liberating influence of their new clothing, women bobbed their hair—that is, they had it cut much shorter—freeing themselves of the long tresses that had been fashionable for years. The woman shown is having her hair cut at a barber shop.

◀ DANCE FADS

The Charleston was the dance craze of the 1920s. An energetic dance that involved wild, flailing movements of the arms and legs, it demanded an appropriate costume for the woman dancer—a short, straight dress without a waistline.

Another craze was the dance marathon, a contest in which couples would dance continuously for days—taking a 15-minute break every hour—with each alternately holding up the other as he or she slept. Needless to say, dancers dropped from exhaustion.

▼ GENTLEMEN'S FASHIONS

Gentlemen enjoyed some outrageous fashions of their own. This young man, with the aid of two flappers, displays the latest fashion in trousers, sometimes called Oxford bags. He also sports "patent-leather hair," parted on the side or in the middle and slicked down close to the head.

THINKING CRITICALLY

CONNECT TO TODAY

1. **Comparing** With a small group, listen to several of the songs listed above or to others from the period. Discuss their lyrics and melodies, and compare them with those of popular songs today. What commonalities can you find? How does the music from each period reflect its times? Report your findings to the class.

   📁 **SEE SKILLBUILDER HANDBOOK, PAGE R8.**

CONNECT TO HISTORY

2. **Researching Clothing Styles** Find out more about the clothing styles just before the flapper era. How severe were the changes in fashion in the 1920s? How do you think parents of flappers reacted to these changes? If you had lived at this time, would you have chosen to wear the new styles? Why or why not?

↗ **hmhsocialstudies.com** RESEARCH WEB LINKS

Education and Popular Culture

MAIN IDEA	WHY IT MATTERS NOW	Terms & Names
The mass media, movies, and spectator sports played important roles in creating the popular culture of the 1920s—a culture that many artists and writers criticized.	Much of today's popular culture can trace its roots to the popular culture of the 1920s.	• Charles A. Lindbergh • George Gershwin • Georgia O'Keeffe • Sinclair Lewis • F. Scott Fitzgerald • Edna St. Vincent Millay • Ernest Hemingway

One American's Story

On September 22, 1927, approximately 50 million Americans sat listening to their radios as Graham McNamee, radio's most popular announcer, breathlessly called the boxing match between the former heavyweight champ Jack Dempsey and the current title-holder, Gene Tunney.

▲ Gene Tunney, down for the "long count," went on to defeat Jack Dempsey in their epic 1927 battle.

A PERSONAL VOICE GRAHAM MCNAMEE

" Good evening, Ladies & Gentlemen of the Radio Audience. This is a big night. Three million dollars' worth of boxing bugs are gathering around a ring at Soldiers' Field, Chicago. . . .

Here comes Jack Dempsey, climbing through the ropes . . . white flannels, long bathrobe. . . . Here comes Tunney. . . . The announcer shouting in the ring . . . trying to quiet 150,000 people. . . . Robes are off. "

—*Time* magazine, October 3, 1927

After punches flew for ten rounds, Tunney defeated the legendary Dempsey. So suspenseful was the brutal match that a number of radio listeners died of heart failure. The "fight of the century" was just one of a host of spectacles and events that transformed American popular culture in the 1920s.

Schools and the Mass Media Shape Culture

During the 1920s, developments in education and mass media had a powerful impact on the nation.

SCHOOL ENROLLMENTS In 1914, approximately 1 million American students attended high school. By 1926, that number had risen to nearly 4 million, an increase sparked by prosperous times and higher educational standards for industry jobs.

Prior to the 1920s, high schools had catered to college-bound students. In contrast, high schools of the 1920s began offering a broad range of courses such as vocational training for those interested in industrial jobs.

The public schools met another challenge in the 1920s—teaching the children of new immigrant families. The years before World War I had seen the largest stream of immigrants in the nation's history—close to 1 million a year. Unlike the earlier English and Irish immigrants, many of the new immigrants spoke no English. By the 1920s their children filled city classrooms. Determined teachers met the challenge and created a large pool of literate Americans. **A**

Taxes to finance the schools increased as well. School costs doubled between 1913 and 1920, then doubled again by 1926. The total cost of American education in the mid-1920s amounted to $2.7 billion a year.

MAIN IDEA

Summarizing

A How did schools change during the 1920s?

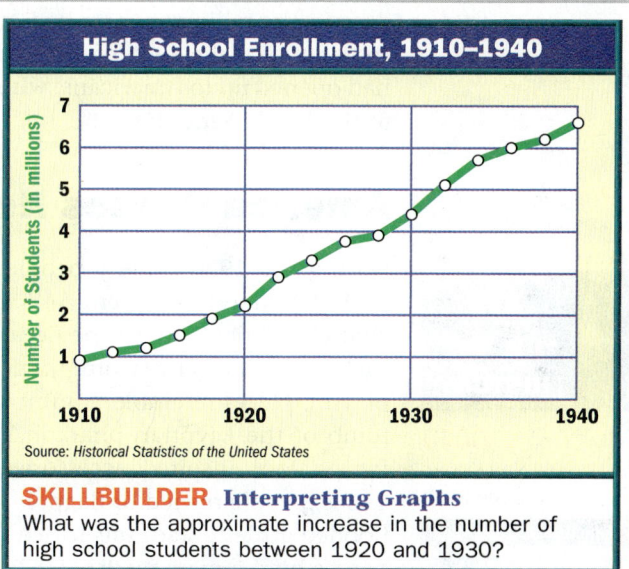

High School Enrollment, 1910–1940

Number of Students (in millions)

Source: *Historical Statistics of the United States*

SKILLBUILDER Interpreting Graphs
What was the approximate increase in the number of high school students between 1920 and 1930?

EXPANDING NEWS COVERAGE Widespread education increased literacy in America, but it was the growing mass media that shaped a mass culture. Newspaper circulation rose as writers and editors learned how to hook readers by imitating the sensational stories in the tabloids. By 1914, about 600 local papers had shut down and 230 had been swallowed up by huge national chains, giving readers more expansive coverage from the big cities. Mass-circulation magazines also flourished during the 1920s. Many of these magazines summarized the week's news, both foreign and domestic. By the end of the 1920s, ten American magazines—including *Reader's Digest* (founded in 1922) and *Time* (founded in 1923)—boasted a circulation of over 2 million each.

RADIO COMES OF AGE Although major magazines and newspapers reached big audiences, radio was the most powerful communications medium to emerge in the 1920s. Americans added terms such as "airwaves," "radio audience," and "tune in" to their everyday speech. By the end of the

Radio Broadcasts of the 1920s

Prior to the 1920s, radio broadcasts were used primarily for transmitting important messages and speeches regarding World War I. After the first commercial radio station—KDKA Pittsburgh—made its debut on the airwaves in 1920, the radio industry changed forever. Listeners tuned in for news, entertainment, and advertisements.

By 1930, 40 percent of U.S. households had radios, like this 1927 Cosser three-valve Melody Maker.

In the 1920s, radio was a formal affair. Announcers and musicians dressed in their finest attire, even without a live audience.

Radio dance parties were common in the 1920s.

decade, the radio networks had created something new in the United States—the shared national experience of hearing the news as it happened. The wider world had opened up to Americans, who could hear the voice of their president or listen to the World Series live. **B**

MAIN IDEA

Analyzing Effects
B Why did radio become so popular?

America Chases New Heroes and Old Dreams

During the 1920s, many people had money and the leisure time to enjoy it. In 1929, Americans spent $4.5 billion on entertainment, much of it on ever-changing fads. Early in the decade, Americans engaged in new leisure pastimes such as working crossword puzzles and playing mahjong, a Chinese game whose playing pieces resemble dominoes. In 1922, after explorers opened the dazzling tomb of the Egyptian pharaoh Tutankhamen, consumers mobbed stores for pharaoh-inspired accessories, jewelry, and furniture. In the mid-1920s, people turned to flagpole sitting and dance marathons. They also flooded athletic stadiums to see sports stars, who were glorified as super-heroes by the mass media.

HISTORY

VIDEO
Did You Know: Babe Ruth

hmhsocialstudies.com

Sports Heroes of the 1920s

Although the media glorified sports heroes, the Golden Age of Sports reflected common aspirations. Athletes set new records, inspiring ordinary Americans. When poor, unknown athletes rose to national fame and fortune, they restored Americans' belief in the power of the individual to improve his or her life.

Gertude Ederle ▶

In 1926, at the age of 19, Gertrude Ederle became the first woman to swim the English Channel. Here, an assistant applies heavy grease to help ward off the effects of the cold Channel waters.

Babe Ruth ▲

New York Yankees slugger Babe Ruth smashed home run after home run during the 1920s. When this legendary star hit a record 60 home runs in 1927, Americans went wild.

◀ **Andrew "Rube" Foster**

A celebrated pitcher and team manager, Andrew "Rube" Foster made his greatest contribution to black baseball in 1920 when he founded the Negro National League. Although previous attempts to establish a league for black players had failed, Foster led the league to success, earning him the title "The Father of Black Baseball."

Helen Wills ▶

Helen Wills dominated women's tennis, winning the singles title at the U.S. Open seven times and the Wimbledon title eight times. Her nickname was "Little Miss Poker Face."

May 20–21, 1932 Amelia Earhart is the first woman to fly solo across the Atlantic, in a record time of about 15 hours from Newfoundland to Ireland.

March 14, 1927 Pan American Airways is founded to handle airmail deliveries. First route is between Key West, Florida, and Havana.

1920 First transcontinental airmail service in the U.S.

May 20–21, 1927 Charles Lindbergh establishes a record of 33 hours 29 minutes in his 3,614–mile nonstop solo flight across the Atlantic.

NORTH AMERICA

Hudson Bay

San Francisco

CANADA

NEWFOUNDLAND

Chicago

Cleveland

UNITED STATES

New York

Harbour Grace

Gulf of Mexico

Key West

Havana **CUBA**

ATLANTIC OCEAN

North Sea

Londonderry

IRELAND

Paris

FRANCE

EUROPE

AFRICA

LINDBERGH'S FLIGHT America's most beloved hero of the time wasn't an athlete but a small-town pilot named **Charles A. Lindbergh,** who made the first nonstop solo flight across the Atlantic. A handsome, modest Minnesotan, Lindbergh decided to go after a $25,000 prize offered for the first nonstop solo transatlantic flight. On May 20, 1927, he took off near New York City in the *Spirit of St. Louis*, flew up the coast to Newfoundland, and headed over the Atlantic. The weather was so bad, Lindbergh recalled, that "the average altitude for the whole . . . second 1,000 miles of the [Atlantic] flight was less than 100 feet." After 33 hours and 29 minutes, Lindbergh set down at Le Bourget airfield outside of Paris, France, amid beacons, searchlights, and mobs of enthusiastic people.

Paris threw a huge party. On his return to the U.S., New York showered Lindbergh with ticker tape, the president received him at the White House, and America made him its idol. In an age of sensationalism, excess, and crime, Lindbergh stood for the honesty and bravery the nation seemed to have lost. The novelist F. Scott Fitzgerald, a fellow Minnesotan, caught the essence of Lindbergh's fame.

★ A PERSONAL VOICE F. SCOTT FITZGERALD

" In the spring of 1927, something bright and alien flashed across the sky. A young Minnesotan who seemed to have nothing to do with his generation did a heroic thing, and for a moment people set down their glasses in country clubs and speakeasies and thought of their old best dreams. "

—quoted in *The Lawless Decade*

Lindbergh's accomplishment paved the way for others. In the next decade, Amelia Earhart was to undertake many brave aerial exploits, inspired by Lindbergh's example.

▲
Edward Hopper's
Night Windows
(1928).

ENTERTAINMENT AND THE ARTS

Despite the feats of real-life heroes, America's thirst for entertainment in the arts and on the screen and stage seemed unquenchable in the 1920s.

Even before the introduction of sound, movies became a national pastime, offering viewers a means of escape through romance and comedy. The first major movie with sound, *The Jazz Singer*, was released in 1927. Walt Disney's *Steamboat Willie,* the first animated film with sound, was released in 1928. By 1930, the new "talkies" had doubled movie attendance, with millions of Americans going to the movies every week. **C**

Both playwrights and composers of music broke away from the European traditions of the 1920s. Eugene O'Neill's plays, such as *The Hairy Ape*, forced Americans to reflect upon modern isolation, confusion, and family conflict. Fame was given to Jewish composer **George Gershwin** when he merged popular concert music with American jazz, thus creating a new sound that was identifiably American.

Painters appealed to Americans by recording an America of realities and dreams. Edward Hopper caught the loneliness of American life in his canvases of empty streets and solitary people, while **Georgia O'Keeffe** produced intensely colored canvases that captured the grandeur of New York.

WRITERS OF THE 1920s

The 1920s also brought an outpouring of fresh and insightful writing, making it one of the richest eras in the country's literary history.

Sinclair Lewis, the first American to win a Nobel Prize in literature, was among the era's most outspoken critics. In his novel *Babbitt*, Lewis used the main character of George F. Babbitt to ridicule Americans for their conformity and materialism.

★ **A PERSONAL VOICE** SINCLAIR LEWIS

"**A sensational event was changing from the brown suit to the gray the contents of his pockets. He was earnest about these objects. They were of eternal importance, like baseball or the Republican Party. They included a fountain pen and a silver pencil . . . which belonged in the righthand upper vest pocket. Without them he would have felt naked. On his watch-chain were a gold penknife, silver cigar-cutter, seven keys . . . and incidentally a good watch. . . . Last, he stuck in his lapel the Boosters' Club button. With the conciseness of great art the button displayed two words: 'Boosters—Pep!'**"

—*Babbitt*

It was **F. Scott Fitzgerald** who coined the term "Jazz Age" to describe the 1920s. In *This Side of Paradise* and *The Great Gatsby*, he revealed the negative side of the period's gaiety and freedom, portraying wealthy and attractive people leading imperiled lives in gilded surroundings. In New York City, a brilliant group of writers routinely lunched together at the Algonquin Hotel's "Round Table." Among the best known of them was Dorothy Parker, a short story writer, poet, and essayist. Parker was famous for her wisecracking wit, expressed in such lines as "I was the toast of two continents—Greenland and Australia."

MAIN IDEA

Making Inferences
C Why were Americans so delighted by movies in the 1920s?

Many writers also met important issues head on. In *The Age of Innocence*, Edith Wharton dramatized the clash between traditional and modern values that had undermined high society 50 years earlier. Willa Cather celebrated the simple, dignified lives of people such as the immigrant farmers of Nebraska in *My Ántonia*, while **Edna St. Vincent Millay** wrote poems celebrating youth and a life of independence and freedom from traditional constraints.

Some writers such as Fitzgerald, Ernest Hemingway, and John Dos Passos were so soured by American culture that they chose to settle in Europe, mainly in Paris. Socializing in the city's cafes, they formed a group that the writer Gertrude Stein called the Lost Generation. They joined other American writers already in Europe such as the poets Ezra Pound and T. S. Eliot, whose poem *The Waste Land* presented an agonized view of a society that seemed stripped of humanity. **D**

Several writers saw action in World War I, and their early books denounced war. Dos Passos's novel *Three Soldiers* attacked war as a machine designed to crush human freedom. Later, he turned to social and political themes, using modern techniques to capture the mood of city life and the losses that came with success. **Ernest Hemingway,** wounded in World War I, became the best-known expatriate author. In his novels *The Sun Also Rises* and *A Farewell to Arms*, he criticized the glorification of war. He also introduced a tough, simplified style of writing that set a new literary standard, using sentences a *Time* reporter compared to "round stones polished by rain and wind."

During this rich literary era, vital developments were also taking place in African-American society. Black Americans of the 1920s began to voice pride in their heritage, and black artists and writers revealed the richness of African-American culture.

MAIN IDEA

Analyzing Causes

D Why did some writers reject American culture and values?

Vocabulary

expatriate: a person who has taken up residence in a foreign country

---

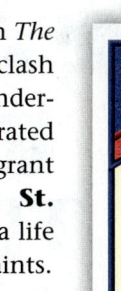

KEY PLAYER

F. SCOTT FITZGERALD
1900–1940

F. Scott Fitzgerald married vivacious Zelda Sayre in 1920 after his novel *This Side of Paradise* became an instant hit. He said of this time in his life:

"Riding in a taxi one afternoon
between very tall buildings under
a mauve and rosy sky,
I began to bawl because I had
everything I wanted and knew I
would never be so happy again."

Flush with money, the couple plunged into a wild social whirl and outspent their incomes. The years following were difficult. Zelda suffered from repeated mental breakdowns, and Scott's battle with alcoholism took its toll.

SECTION 3 **ASSESSMENT**

1. TERMS & NAMES For each of the following names, write a sentence explaining his or her significance.
- Charles A. Lindbergh
- George Gershwin
- Georgia O'Keeffe
- Sinclair Lewis
- F. Scott Fitzgerald
- Edna St. Vincent Millay
- Ernest Hemingway

MAIN IDEA

2. TAKING NOTES
Create a time line of key events relating to 1920s popular culture. Use the dates below as a guide.

1920 **1926** **1928**

1923 **1927**

In a sentence or two, explain which of these events interests you the most and why.

CRITICAL THINKING

3. SYNTHESIZING
In what ways do you think the mass media and mass culture helped Americans create a sense of national community in the 1920s? Support your answer with details from the text. **Think About:**

- the content and readership of newspapers and magazines
- attendance at sports events and movie theaters
- the scope of radio broadcasts

4. EVALUATING
Do you think the popular heroes of the 1920s were heroes in a real sense? Why or why not?

5. SUMMARIZING
In two or three sentences, summarize the effects of education and mass media on society in the 1920s.

SECTION
4

PI 2.3
PI 4.1

CC Unit 4.I.B.2.c(3)
CC Unit 5.I.C.3.c(2)
CC Unit 5.II.B.7.b

The Harlem Renaissance

MAIN IDEA	WHY IT MATTERS NOW	Terms & Names
African-American ideas, politics, art, literature, and music flourished in Harlem and elsewhere in the United States.	The Harlem Renaissance provided a foundation of African-American intellectualism to which African-American writers, artists, and musicians contribute today.	• Zora Neale Hurston • Claude McKay • James Weldon Johnson • Langston Hughes • Marcus Garvey • Paul Robeson • Harlem Renaissance • Louis Armstrong • Duke Ellington • Bessie Smith

One American's Story

hmhsocialstudies.com
TAKING NOTES
Use the graphic organizer online to take notes on the achievements of the Harlem Renaissance.

When the spirited **Zora Neale Hurston** was a girl in Eatonville, Florida, in the early 1900s, she loved to read adventure stories and myths. The powerful tales struck a chord with the young, talented Hurston and made her yearn for a wider world.

A PERSONAL VOICE ZORA NEALE HURSTON

" My soul was with the gods and my body in the village. People just would not act like gods. . . . Raking back yards and carrying out chamber-pots, were not the tasks of Thor. I wanted to be away from drabness and to stretch my limbs in some mighty struggle. "

—quoted in *The African American Encyclopedia*

▲ Zora Neale Hurston

After spending time with a traveling theater company and attending Howard University, Hurston ended up in New York where she struggled to the top of African-American literary society by hard work, flamboyance, and, above all, grit. "I have seen that the world is to the strong regardless of a little pigmentation more or less," Hurston wrote later. "I do not weep at [being Negro]—I am too busy sharpening my oyster knife." Hurston was on the move, like millions of others. And, like them, she went after the pearl in the oyster—the good life in America.

African-American Voices in the 1920s

During the 1920s, African Americans set new goals for themselves as they moved north to the nation's cities. Their migration was an expression of their changing attitude toward themselves—an attitude perhaps best captured in a phrase first used around this time, "Black is beautiful."

THE MOVE NORTH Between 1910 and 1920, in a movement known as the Great Migration, hundreds of thousands of African Americans had uprooted themselves from their homes in the South and moved north to the big cities in search of jobs. By the end of the decade, 5.2 million of the nation's 12 million African Americans—over 40 percent—lived in cities. Zora Neale Hurston documented the departure of some of these African Americans.

A PERSONAL VOICE ZORA NEALE HURSTON

"Some said goodbye cheerfully . . . others fearfully, with terrors of unknown dangers in their mouths . . . others in their eagerness for distance said nothing. The daybreak found them gone. The wind said North."

—quoted in *Sorrow's Kitchen: The Life and Folklore of Zora Neale Hurston*

MAIN IDEA

Analyzing Effects

A How did the influx of African Americans change Northern cities?

However, Northern cities in general had not welcomed the massive influx of African Americans. Tensions had escalated in the years prior to 1920, culminating, in the summer of 1919, in approximately 25 urban race riots. **A**

AFRICAN-AMERICAN GOALS Founded in 1909, The National Association for the Advancement of Colored People (NAACP) urged African Americans to protest racial violence. W. E. B. Du Bois, a founding member of the NAACP, led a parade of 10,000 African-American men in New York to protest such violence. Du Bois also used the NAACP's magazine, *The Crisis*, as a platform for leading a struggle for civil rights.

Under the leadership of **James Weldon Johnson**— poet, lawyer, and NAACP executive secretary—the organization fought for legislation to protect African-American rights. It made antilynching laws one of its main priorities. In 1919, three antilynching bills were introduced in Congress, although none was passed. The NAACP continued its campaign through antilynching organizations that had been established in 1892 by Ida B. Wells. Gradually, the number of lynchings dropped. The NAACP represented the new, more militant voice of African Americans.

MARCUS GARVEY AND THE UNIA Although many African Americans found their voice in the NAACP, they still faced daily threats and discrimination. **Marcus Garvey,** an immigrant from Jamaica, believed that African Americans should build a separate society. His different, more radical message of black pride aroused the hopes of many.

In 1914, Garvey founded the Universal Negro Improvement Association (UNIA). In 1918, he moved the UNIA to New York City and opened offices in urban ghettos in order to recruit followers. By the mid-1920s, Garvey claimed he had a million followers. He appealed to African Americans with a combination of spellbinding oratory, mass meetings, parades, and a message of pride.

Vocabulary
oratory: the art of public speaking

A PERSONAL VOICE MARCUS GARVEY

"In view of the fact that the black man of Africa has contributed as much to the world as the white man of Europe, and the brown man and yellow man of Asia, we of the Universal Negro Improvement Association demand that the white, yellow, and brown races give to the black man his place in the civilization of the world. We ask for nothing more than the rights of 400 million Negroes."

—speech at Liberty Hall, New York City, 1922

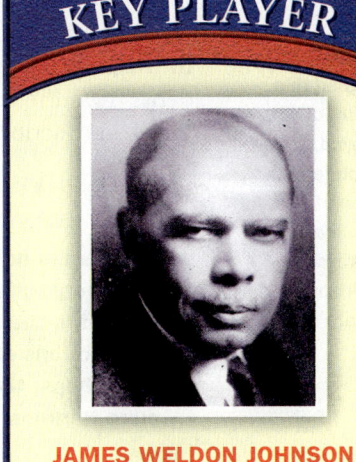

KEY PLAYER

JAMES WELDON JOHNSON
1871–1938

James Weldon Johnson worked as a school principal, newspaper editor, and lawyer in Florida. In 1900, he wrote the lyrics for "Lift Every Voice and Sing," the song that became known as the black national anthem. The first stanza begins as follows:

"Lift every voice and sing
Till earth and heaven ring,
Ring with the harmonies of
  Liberty;
Let our rejoicing rise
High as the listening skies,
Let it resound loud as the
  rolling sea."

In the 1920s, Johnson straddled the worlds of politics and art. He served as executive secretary of the NAACP, spearheading the fight against lynching. In addition, he wrote well-known works, such as *God's Trombones*, a series of sermon-like poems, and *Black Manhattan*, a look at black cultural life in New York during the Roaring Twenties.

The Roaring Life of the 1920s **659**

Garvey also lured followers with practical plans, especially his program to promote African-American businesses. Further, Garvey encouraged his followers to return to Africa, help native people there throw off white colonial oppressors, and build a mighty nation. His idea struck a chord in many African Americans, as well as in blacks in the Caribbean and Africa. Despite the appeal of Garvey's movement, support for it declined in the mid-1920s, when he was convicted of mail fraud and jailed. Although the movement dwindled, Garvey left behind a powerful legacy of newly awakened black pride, economic independence, and reverence for Africa. **B**

MAIN IDEA

Summarizing
B What approach to race relations did Marcus Garvey promote?

▲
Marcus Garvey designed this uniform of purple and gold, complete with feathered hat, for his role as "Provisional President of Africa."

The Harlem Renaissance Flowers in New York

Many African Americans who migrated north moved to Harlem, a neighborhood on the Upper West Side of New York's Manhattan Island. In the 1920s, Harlem became the world's largest black urban community, with residents from the South, the West Indies, Cuba, Puerto Rico, and Haiti. James Weldon Johnson described Harlem as the capital of black America.

★ **A PERSONAL VOICE** JAMES WELDON JOHNSON

"Harlem is not merely a Negro colony or community, it is a city within a city, the greatest Negro city in the world. It is not a slum or a fringe, it is located in the heart of Manhattan and occupies one of the most beautiful . . . sections of the city. . . . It has its own churches, social and civic centers, shops, theaters, and other places of amusement. And it contains more Negroes to the square mile than any other spot on earth."

—"Harlem: The Culture Capital"

Like many other urban neighborhoods, Harlem suffered from overcrowding, unemployment, and poverty. But its problems in the 1920s were eclipsed by a flowering of creativity called the **Harlem Renaissance,** a literary and artistic movement celebrating African-American culture.

AFRICAN–AMERICAN WRITERS Above all, the Harlem Renaissance was a literary movement led by well-educated, middle-class African Americans who expressed a new pride in the African-American experience. They celebrated their heritage and wrote with defiance and poignancy about the trials of being black in a white world. W. E. B. Du Bois and James Weldon Johnson helped these young talents along, as did the Harvard-educated former Rhodes scholar Alain Locke. In 1925, Locke published *The New Negro*, a landmark collection of literary works by many promising young African-American writers.

Claude McKay, a novelist, poet, and Jamaican immigrant, was a major figure whose militant verses urged African Americans to resist prejudice and discrimination. His poems also expressed the pain of life in the black ghettos and the strain of being black in a world dominated by whites. Another gifted writer of the time was Jean Toomer. His experimental book *Cane*—a mix of poems and sketches about blacks in the North and the South—was among the first full-length literary publications of the Harlem Renaissance.

Missouri-born **Langston Hughes** was the movement's best-known poet. Many of Hughes's 1920s poems described the difficult lives of working-class African Americans. Some of his poems moved to the tempo of jazz and the blues. (See Literature in the Jazz Age on page 664.)

The Fletcher Henderson Orchestra became one of the most influential jazz bands during the Harlem Renaissance. Here, Henderson, the band's founder, sits at the drums, with Louis Armstrong on trumpet (third from left).

Harlem in the 1920s

At the turn of the century, New York's Harlem neighborhood was overbuilt with new apartment houses. Enterprising African-American realtors began buying and leasing property to other African Americans who were eager to move into the prosperous neighborhood. As the number of blacks in Harlem increased, many whites began moving out. Harlem quickly grew to become the center of black America and the birthplace of the political, social, and cultural movement known as the Harlem Renaissance.

North

Harlem River

145th St.

Cotton Club

140th St.

Savoy Ballroom

James Weldon Johnson home

135th St.

Fifth Ave.

Madison Ave.

Park Ave.

Library

Lafayette Theatre

130th St.

Eighth Ave.

Seventh Ave.

Marcus Garvey home

Lenox Ave.

125th St.

Apollo Theatre

In the mid 1920s, the Cotton Club was one of a number of fashionable entertainment clubs in Harlem. Although many venues like the Cotton Club were segregated, white audiences packed the clubs to hear the new music styles of black performers such as Duke Ellington and Bessie Smith.

New York City

NEW JERSEY

Harlem River

The Bronx

Harlem

Hudson River

Central Park

Manhattan

East River

Queens

Brooklyn

predominantly black neighborhoods

| 0 | 1 mile |
| 0 | 1 kilometer |

In 1927, Harlem was a bustling neighborhood.

In many of her novels, short stories, poems, and books of folklore, Zora Neale Hurston portrayed the lives of poor, unschooled Southern blacks—in her words, "the greatest cultural wealth of the continent." Much of her work celebrated what she called the common person's art form—the simple folkways and values of people who had survived slavery through their ingenuity and strength. **C**

AFRICAN–AMERICAN PERFORMERS The spirit and talent of the Harlem Renaissance reached far beyond the world of African-American writers and intellectuals. Some observers, including Langston Hughes, thought the movement was launched with *Shuffle Along*, a black musical comedy popular in 1921. "It gave just the proper push . . . to that Negro vogue of the '20s," he wrote. Several songs in *Shuffle Along*, including "Love Will Find a Way," won popularity among white audiences. The show also spotlighted the talents of several black performers, including the singers Florence Mills, Josephine Baker, and Mabel Mercer.

During the 1920s, African Americans in the performing arts won large followings. The tenor Roland Hayes rose to stardom as a concert singer, and the singer and actress Ethel Waters debuted on Broadway in the musical *Africana*. **Paul Robeson,** the son of a one-time slave, became a major dramatic actor. His performance in Shakespeare's *Othello*, first in London and later in New York City, was widely acclaimed. Subsequently, Robeson struggled with the racism he experienced in the United States and the indignities inflicted upon him because of his support of the Soviet Union and the Communist Party. He took up residence abroad, living for a time in England and the Soviet Union.

MAIN IDEA

Synthesizing

C In what ways did writers of the Harlem Renaissance celebrate a "rebirth"?

Background
See Historical Spotlight on page 823.

The Hot Five included (*from left*) Louis Armstrong, Johnny St. Cyr, Johnny Dodds, Kid Ory, and Lil Hardin Armstrong.

AFRICAN AMERICANS AND JAZZ Jazz was born in the early 20th century in New Orleans, where musicians blended instrumental ragtime and vocal blues into an exuberant new sound. In 1918, Joe "King" Oliver and his Creole Jazz Band traveled north to Chicago, carrying jazz with them. In 1922, a young trumpet player named **Louis Armstrong** joined Oliver's group, which became known as the Creole Jazz Band. His talent rocketed him to stardom in the jazz world.

Famous for his astounding sense of rhythm and his ability to improvise, Armstrong made personal expression a key part of jazz. After two years in Chicago, in 1924 he joined Fletcher Henderson's band, then the most important big jazz band in New York City. Armstrong went on to become perhaps the most important and influential musician in the history of jazz. He often talked about his anticipated funeral.

★ **A PERSONAL VOICE** LOUIS ARMSTRONG

"They're going to blow over me. Cats will be coming from everywhere to play. I had a beautiful life. When I get to the Pearly Gates I'll play a duet with Gabriel. We'll play 'Sleepy Time Down South.' He wants to be remembered for his music just like I do."

—quoted in *The Negro Almanac*

Jazz quickly spread to such cities as Kansas City, Memphis, and New York City, and it became the most popular music for dancing. During the 1920s, Harlem pulsed to the sounds of jazz, which lured throngs of whites to the showy, exotic nightclubs there, including the famed Cotton Club. In the late 1920s, **Edward Kennedy "Duke" Ellington,** a jazz pianist and composer, led his ten-piece orchestra at the Cotton Club. In a 1925 essay titled "The Negro Spirituals," Alain Locke seemed almost to predict the career of the talented Ellington.

A PERSONAL VOICE ALAIN LOCKE

" Up to the present, the resources of Negro music have been tentatively exploited in only one direction at a time—melodically here, rhythmically there, harmonically in a third direction. A genius that would organize its distinctive elements in a formal way would be the musical giant of his age. "

—quoted in *Afro-American Writing: An Anthology of Prose and Poetry*

Through the 1920s and 1930s, Ellington won renown as one of America's greatest composers, with pieces such as "Mood Indigo" and "Sophisticated Lady."

Cab Calloway, a talented drummer, saxophonist, and singer, formed another important jazz orchestra, which played at Harlem's Savoy Ballroom and the Cotton Club, alternating with Duke Ellington. Along with Louis Armstrong, Calloway popularized "scat," or improvised jazz singing using sounds instead of words.

Bessie Smith, a female blues singer, was perhaps the outstanding vocalist of the decade. She recorded on black-oriented labels produced by the major record companies. She achieved enormous popularity and in 1927 became the highest-paid black artist in the world. **D**

The Harlem Renaissance represented a portion of the great social and cultural changes that swept America in the 1920s. The period was characterized by economic prosperity, new ideas, changing values, and personal freedom, as well as important developments in art, literature, and music. Most of the social changes were lasting. The economic boom, however, was short-lived.

MAIN IDEA

Summarizing
D Besides literary accomplishments, in what areas did African Americans achieve remarkable results?

SECTION 4 ASSESSMENT

1. **TERMS & NAMES** For each term or name, write a sentence explaining its significance.
   - Zora Neale Hurston
   - James Weldon Johnson
   - Marcus Garvey
   - Harlem Renaissance
   - Claude McKay
   - Langston Hughes
   - Paul Robeson
   - Louis Armstrong
   - Duke Ellington
   - Bessie Smith

MAIN IDEA

2. **TAKING NOTES**
   In a tree diagram, identify three areas of artistic achievement in the Harlem Renaissance. For each, name two outstanding African Americans.

Harlem Renaissance: Areas of Achievement
1.
2.
| 1.
| 2.
| 1.
| 2.

   Write a paragraph explaining the impact of these achievements.

CRITICAL THINKING

3. **ANALYZING CAUSES**
   Speculate on why an African-American renaissance flowered during the 1920s. Support your answer. **Think About:**
   - racial discrimination in the South
   - campaigns for equality in the North
   - Harlem's diverse cultures
   - the changing culture of all Americans

4. **FORMING GENERALIZATIONS**
   How did popular culture in America change as a result of the Great Migration?

5. **DRAWING CONCLUSIONS**
   What did the Harlem Renaissance contribute to both black and general American history?

Literature in the Jazz Age

1920–1929 After World War I, American literature—like American jazz—moved to the vanguard of the international artistic scene. Many American writers remained in Europe after the war, some settling in London but many more joining the expatriate community on the Left Bank of the Seine River in Paris, where they could live cheaply.

Back in the United States, such cities as Chicago and New York were magnets for America's young artistic talents. New York City gave birth to the Harlem Renaissance, a blossoming of African-American culture named for the New York City neighborhood where many African-American writers and artists settled. Further downtown, the artistic community of Greenwich Village drew literary talents such as the poets Edna St. Vincent Millay and E. E. Cummings and the playwright Eugene O'Neill.

F. SCOTT FITZGERALD

The foremost chronicler of the Jazz Age was the Minnesota-born writer F. Scott Fitzgerald, who in Paris, New York, and later Hollywood rubbed elbows with other leading American writers of the day. In the following passage from Fitzgerald's novel *The Great Gatsby*, the narrator describes a fashionable 1920s party thrown by the title character at his Long Island estate.

By seven o'clock the orchestra has arrived, no thin five-piece affair, but a whole pitful of oboes and trombones and saxophones and viols and cornets and piccolos, and low and high drums. The last swimmers have come in from the beach now and are dressing up-stairs; the cars from New York are parked five deep in the drive, and already the halls and salons and verandas are gaudy with primary colors, and hair shorn in strange new ways, and shawls beyond the dreams of Castile. The bar is in full swing, and floating rounds of cocktails permeate the garden outside, until the air is alive with chatter and laughter, and casual innuendo and introductions forgotten on the spot, and enthusiastic meetings between women who never knew each other's names.

The lights grow brighter as the earth lurches away from the sun, and now the orchestra is playing yellow cocktail music, and the opera of voices pitches a key higher. Laughter is easier minute by minute, spilled with prodigality, tipped out at a cheerful word. The groups change more swiftly, swell with new arrivals, dissolve and form in the same breath; already there are wanderers, confident girls who weave here and there among the stouter and more stable, become for a sharp, joyous moment the center of a group, and then, excited with triumph, glide on through the sea-change of faces and voices and color under the constantly changing light.

Suddenly one of these gypsies, in trembling opal, seizes a cocktail out of the air, dumps it down for courage and, moving her hands like Frisco, dances out alone on the canvas platform. A momentary hush; the orchestra leader varies his rhythm obligingly for her, and there is a burst of chatter as the erroneous news goes around that she is Gilda Gray's understudy from the Follies. The party has begun.

—F. Scott Fitzgerald, *The Great Gatsby* (1925)

EDNA ST. VINCENT MILLAY

In the 1920s, Edna St. Vincent Millay was the quintessential modern young woman, a celebrated poet living a bohemian life in New York's Greenwich Village. The following quatrain memorably proclaims the exuberant philosophy of the young and fashionable in the Roaring Twenties.

> My candle burns at both ends;
>   It will not last the night;
> But ah, my foes, and oh, my friends—
>   It gives a lovely light!

—Edna St. Vincent Millay, "First Fig,"
from *A Few Figs from Thistles* (1920)

LANGSTON HUGHES ▶

A towering figure of the Harlem Renaissance, Langston Hughes often imbued his poetry with the rhythms of jazz and blues. In the poem "Dream Variations," for example, the two stanzas resemble improvised passages played and varied by a jazz musician. The dream of freedom and equality is a recurring symbol in Hughes's verse and has appeared frequently in African-American literature since the 1920s, when Hughes penned this famous poem.

> To fling my arms wide
> In some place of the sun,
> To whirl and to dance
> Till the white day is done.
> Then rest at cool evening
> Beneath a tall tree
> While night comes on gently,
>   Dark like me—
> That is my dream!
>
> To fling my arms wide
> In the face of the sun,
> Dance! Whirl! Whirl!
> Till the quick day is done.
> Rest at pale evening . . .
> A tall, slim tree . . .
> Night coming tenderly
>   Black like me.

—Langston Hughes, "Dream Variations,"
from *The Weary Blues* (1926)

THINKING CRITICALLY

1. **Comparing** What connections can you make between the literary and music scenes during the Jazz Age?

    SEE SKILLBUILDER HANDBOOK, PAGE R8.

2.   INTERNET ACTIVITY

   Visit the links for American Literature to research writers of the Jazz Age. Then, create a short report on one writer's life. Include titles of published works and an example of his or her writing style.

VISUAL SUMMARY

THE ROARING LIFE OF THE 1920s

NEW FORMS OF ENTERTAINMENT

- Movies become a national pastime.
- Radio is a prime source of news and entertainment.
- Americans celebrate sports heroes.

NEW MOVEMENTS IN THE ARTS

- Composers create distinctly American music.
- Writers explore new topics.
- Artists depict life in the 1920s.
- Harlem Renaissance flourishes.

PROBLEMS OF URBANIZATION

- Industrialization leads to growth of big cities.
- African Americans continue to move North.
- Cities struggle with prohibition and organized crime.

NEW ATTITUDES AND FASHION

- Changing attitudes toward women allow them greater freedoms.
- Americans adopt radical new fashions and style.
- Traditional and modern ideals collide.

TERMS & NAMES

For each term or name below, write a sentence explaining its historical significance or contribution to the 1920s.

1. bootlegger
2. fundamentalism
3. flapper
4. double standard
5. Charles A. Lindbergh
6. George Gershwin
7. F. Scott Fitzgerald
8. Zora Neale Hurston
9. Harlem Renaissance
10. Paul Robeson

MAIN IDEAS

Use your notes and the information in the chapter to answer the following questions.

Changing Ways of Life (pages 640–645)

1. Why was heavy funding needed to enforce the Volstead Act?
2. Explain the circumstances and outcome of the trial of the biology teacher John Scopes.

The Twenties Woman (pages 646–649)

3. In what ways did flappers rebel against the earlier styles and attitudes of the Victorian age?
4. What key social, economic, and technological changes of the 1920s affected women's marriages and family life?

Education and Popular Culture (pages 652–657)

5. How did high schools change in the 1920s?
6. Cite examples of the flaws of American society that some famous 1920s authors attacked in their writing.

The Harlem Renaissance (pages 658–663)

7. What do the Great Migration and the growth of the NAACP and UNIA reveal about the African-American experience in this period?
8. What were some of the important themes treated by African-American writers in the Harlem Renaissance?

CRITICAL THINKING

1. **USING YOUR NOTES** Create a concept web like the one below, and fill it in with trends in popular culture that emerged in the 1920s and continue to influence American society today.

Enduring Cultural Trends of the Roaring Twenties

2. **EVALUATING** In "Literature in the Jazz Age," on pages 664–665, you read excerpts from works written in the 1920s by F. Scott Fitzgerald, Edna St. Vincent Millay, and Langston Hughes. How might a phrase current at the time—"flaming youth"—be an appropriate and accurate phrase to describe the young people and voices in these excerpts?

Use the visual below and your knowledge of United States history to answer question 1.

1 The woman shown on this magazine cover represents a lifestyle championed by which of the following 1920s figures?

(1) Zelda Sayre Fitzgerald
(2) Edna St. Vincent Millay
(3) Anna Howard Shaw
(4) Aimee Semple McPherson

2 The great flowering of African-American artistic activity in the 1920s is known as —

(1) the Jazz Age
(2) the speakeasy
(3) the Harlem Renaissance
(4) American fundamentalism

Use the quotation and your knowledge of U.S. history to answer question 3.

" No more fear, no more cringing, no more sycophantic begging and pleading; but the Negro must strike straight from the shoulder for manhood rights and for full liberty. Africa calls now more than ever. "

3 The quotation supports the "Back to Africa" movement. One important leader of this movement in the 1920s was —

(1) Marcus Garvey
(2) James Weldon Johnson
(3) Zora Neale Hurston
(4) Paul Robeson

↗ hmhsocialstudies.com **TEST PRACTICE**

For additional test practice, go online for:
• Diagnostic tests   • Tutorials

INTERACT WITH HISTORY

Think about the issues you explored at the beginning of the chapter. Now that you have read about life in the 1920s, what do you think was the most significant cultural development during this time? Write a paragraph describing how this change affected society and how it evolved. Share your paragraph with your class.

FOCUS ON WRITING

Imagine that you live in a small town in the year 1920. Prepare a persuasive speech that you will deliver at a town hall meeting in favor of or in opposition to Prohibition. Be sure to support your position with evidence and specific details. Use words and phrases that engage your audience. Additionally, you may want to anticipate the arguments of the opposing viewpoint and respond to them.

MULTIMEDIA ACTIVITY

21ST CENTURY

Organize into small groups. Use the Internet and other sources to research the changes in American films during the 1920s that contributed to their growing popularity. Then create a multimedia presentation that describes these changes, including references to important films, actors, and directors.

CHAPTER 22

THE GREAT DEPRESSION BEGINS

Essential Question

What were the causes and consequences of the Great Depression?

 New York Standards

KEY IDEA 4 The skills of historical analysis include the ability to: explain the significance of historical evidence; weigh the importance, reliability, and validity of evidence; understand the concept of multiple causation; understand the importance of changing and competing interpretations of different historical developments.

SECTION 1: The Nation's Sick Economy

SECTION 2: Hardship and Suffering During the Depression

SECTION 3: Hoover Struggles with the Depression

1929 The first Academy Awards are presented.

1929 The stock market crashes.

1930-1933 More than 40% of the nation's banks fail.

1931 Jane Addams shares the Nobel Peace Prize.

1931 8.02 million Americans are unemployed.

USA
WORLD

1929

1930

1931

1930 Army officers led by José Uriburu seize control of the government of Argentina.

1931 Japan invades Manchuria.

The year is 1929. The U.S. economy has collapsed. Farms, businesses, and banks nationwide are failing, causing massive unemployment and poverty. You are out of work with little prospect of finding a job.

Explore the Issues

- What groups of people will be most hurt by the economic crash?

- What can you do to find a paying job?

- What can unemployed and impoverished people do to help each other?

Women serve soup and slices of bread to unemployed men in an outdoor breadline in Los Angeles, California, during the Great Depression.

1933 "Century of Progress Exposition" begins.

1932 The Bonus Army arrives in Washington, D.C.

1932 Franklin Delano Roosevelt is elected president.

1933 The Twenty-first Amendment ends Prohibition.

1933 More than 13 million Americans are unemployed.

1932　1933　1934

1932 Ibn Sa'ud becomes king of newly-united Saudi Arabia.

1932 From prison, Mohandas K. Gandhi leads a protest against British policies in India.

1933 Adolf Hitler takes power in Germany.

1933 Japan withdraws from the League of Nations.

The Great Depression Begins **669**

SECTION 1

CC Unit 5.I.B.5   CC Unit 5.II.A.1.a
CC Unit 5.II.A.1.b   CC Unit 5.II.A.2.a
CC Unit 5.II.A.2.b   CC Unit 5.II.A.2.c

PI 4.1

The Nation's Sick Economy

MAIN IDEA	WHY IT MATTERS NOW	Terms & Names
As the prosperity of the 1920s ended, severe economic problems gripped the nation.	The Great Depression has had lasting effects on how Americans view themselves and their government.	• price support • credit • Alfred E. Smith • Dow Jones Industrial Average • speculation • buying on margin • Black Tuesday • Great Depression • Hawley-Smoot Tariff Act

One American's Story

hmhsocialstudies.com
TAKING NOTES
Use the graphic organizer online to take notes on the causes of the 1929 stock market crash.

Gordon Parks, the well-known photographer, author, and film-maker, was a 16-year-old high school student in the fall of 1929. He supported himself as a busboy at the exclusive Minnesota Club, where prosperous club members spoke confidently about the economy. Parks, too, looked forward to a bright future. Then came the stock market crash of October 1929. In his autobiography, Parks recalled his feelings at the time.

A PERSONAL VOICE GORDON PARKS

" I couldn't imagine such financial disaster touching my small world; it surely concerned only the rich. But by the first week of November . . . I was without a job. All that next week I searched for any kind of work that would prevent my leaving school. Again it was, 'We're firing, not hiring.'. . . I went to school and cleaned out my locker, knowing it was impossible to stay on. A piercing chill was in the air as I walked back to the rooming house. "

—*A Choice of Weapons*

▲ Gordon Parks, shown here in 1968 discussing the movie version of his autobiographical novel, *The Learning Tree.*

The crash of 1929, and the depression that followed, dealt a crushing blow to the hopes and dreams of millions of Americans. The high-flying prosperity of the 1920s was over. Hard times had begun.

Economic Troubles on the Horizon

As the 1920s advanced, serious problems threatened economic prosperity. Though some Americans became wealthy, many more could not earn a decent living. Important industries struggled, and farmers grew more crops and raised more livestock than they could sell at a profit. Both consumers and farmers were steadily going deeper into debt. As the decade drew to a close, these slippages in the economy signaled the end of an era.

INDUSTRIES IN TROUBLE The superficial prosperity of the late 1920s shrouded weaknesses that would signal the onset of the Great Depression. Key basic industries, such as railroads, textiles, and steel had barely made a profit. Railroads lost business to new forms of transportation (trucks, buses, and private automobiles, for instance).

Mining and lumbering, which had expanded during wartime, were no longer in high demand. Coal mining was especially hard-hit, in part due to stiff competition from new forms of energy, including hydroelectric power, fuel oil, and natural gas. By the early 1930s, these sources supplied more than half the energy that had once come from coal. Even the boom industries of the 1920s—automobiles, construction, and consumer goods—weakened. One important economic indicator that declined during this time was housing starts—the number of new dwellings being built. When housing starts fall, so do jobs in many related industries, such as furniture manufacturing and lumbering. **Ⓐ**

MAIN IDEA

Identifying Problems
Ⓐ What industrial weakness signaled a declining economy in the 1920s?

FARMERS NEED A LIFT Perhaps agriculture suffered the most. During World War I, prices rose and international demand for crops such as wheat and corn soared. Farmers had planted more and taken out loans for land and equipment. However, demand fell after the war, and crop prices declined by 40 percent or more.

Farmers boosted production in the hopes of selling more crops, but this only depressed prices further. Between 1919 and 1921 annual farm income declined from $10 billion to just over $4 billion. Farmers who had gone into debt had difficulty in paying off their loans. Many lost their farms when banks foreclosed and seized the property as payment for the debt. As farmers began to default on their loans, many rural banks began to fail. Auctions were held to recoup some of the banks' losses.

Congress tried to help out farmers with a piece of legislation called the McNary-Haugen bill. This called for federal **price supports** for key products such as wheat, corn, cotton, and tobacco. The government would buy surplus crops at guaranteed prices and sell them on the world market.

President Coolidge vetoed the bill twice. He commented, "Farmers have never made money. I don't believe we can do much about it."

CONSUMERS HAVE LESS MONEY TO SPEND As farmers' incomes fell, they bought fewer goods and services, but the problem was larger. By the late 1920s,

Farm equipment is auctioned off in Hastings, Nebraska.
▼

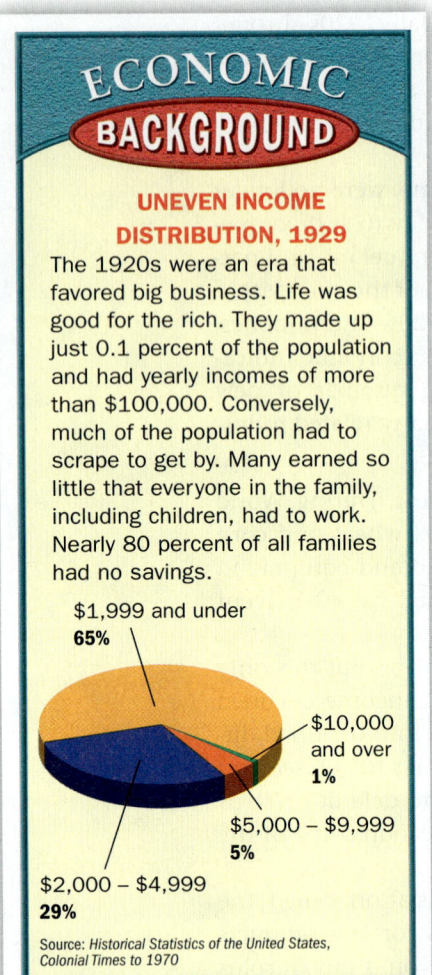

Americans were buying less—mainly because of rising prices, stagnant wages, unbalanced distribution of income, and overbuying on credit in the preceding years. Production had also expanded much faster than wages, resulting in an ever-widening gap between the rich and the poor.

LIVING ON CREDIT Although many Americans appeared to be prosperous during the 1920s, in fact they were living beyond their means. They often bought goods on **credit**— an arrangement in which consumers agreed to buy now and pay later for purchases. This was often in the form of an installment plan (usually in monthly payments) that included interest charges.

By making credit easily available, businesses encouraged Americans to pile up a large consumer debt. Many people then had trouble paying off their growing debts. Faced with debt, consumers cut back on spending.

UNEVEN DISTRIBUTION OF INCOME During the 1920s, the rich got richer, and the poor got poorer. Between 1920 and 1929, the income of the wealthiest 1 percent of the population rose by 75 percent, compared with a 9 percent increase for Americans as a whole.

More than 70 percent of the nation's families earned less than $2,500 per year, then considered the minimum amount needed for a decent standard of living. Even families earning twice that much could not afford many of the household products that manufacturers produced. Economists estimate that the average man or woman bought a new outfit of clothes only once a year. Scarcely half the homes in many cities had electric lights or a furnace for heat. Only one city home in ten had an electric refrigerator.

This unequal distribution of income meant that most Americans could not participate fully in the economic advances of the 1920s. Many people did not have the money to purchase the flood of goods that factories produced. The prosperity of the era rested on a fragile foundation. **B**

> **MAIN IDEA**
>
> **Forming Generalizations**
> **B** What did the experience of farmers and consumers at this time suggest about the health of the economy?

Hoover Takes the Nation

Although economic disaster was around the corner, the election of 1928 took place in a mood of apparent national prosperity. This election pitted Republican candidate Herbert Hoover against Democrat **Alfred E. Smith.**

THE ELECTION OF 1928 Hoover, the secretary of commerce under Harding and Coolidge, was a mining engineer from Iowa who had never run for public office. Smith was a career politician who had served four terms as governor of New York. He was personable and enjoyed being in the limelight, unlike the quiet and reserved Hoover. Still, Hoover had one major advantage: he could point to years of prosperity under Republican administrations since 1920. Many Americans believed him when he declared, "We in America are nearer to the final triumph over poverty than ever before."

It was an overwhelming victory for Hoover. The message was clear: most Americans were happy with Republican leadership.

DREAMS OF RICHES IN THE STOCK MARKET By 1929, some economists had warned of weaknesses in the economy, but most Americans

" We in America are nearer to the final triumph over poverty than ever before."

HERBERT HOOVER

maintained the utmost confidence in the nation's economic health. In increasing numbers, those who could afford to invested in the stock market. The stock market had become the most visible symbol of a prosperous American economy. Then, as now, the **Dow Jones Industrial Average** was the most widely used barometer of the stock market's health. The Dow is a measure based on the stock prices of 30 representative large firms trading on the New York Stock Exchange.

Through most of the 1920s, stock prices rose steadily. The Dow had reached a high of 381 points, nearly 300 points higher than it had been five years earlier. Eager to take advantage of this "bull market"—a period of rising stock prices— Americans rushed to buy stocks and bonds. One observer wrote, "It seemed as if all economic law had been suspended and a new era opened up in which success and prosperity could be had without knowledge or industry." By 1929, about 4 million Americans—or 3 percent of the nation's population—owned stocks. Many of these investors were already wealthy, but others were average Americans who hoped to strike it rich.

However, the seeds of trouble were taking root. People were engaging in **speculation**—that is, they bought stocks and bonds on the chance of a quick profit, while ignoring the risks. Many began **buying on margin**—paying a small percentage of a stock's price as a down payment and borrowing the rest. With easy money available to investors, the unrestrained buying and selling fueled the market's upward spiral. The government did little to discourage such buying or to regulate the market. In reality, these rising prices did not reflect companies' worth. Worse, if the value of stocks declined, people who had bought on margin had no way to pay off the loans. **C**

MAIN IDEA

Analyzing Events
C How did speculation and margin buying cause stock prices to rise?

The Stock Market Crashes

In early September 1929, stock prices peaked and then fell. Confidence in the market started to waver, and some investors quickly sold their stocks and pulled out. On October 24, the market took a plunge. Panicked investors unloaded their shares. But the worst was yet to come.

Analyzing *Political Cartoons*

DAY OF WRATH

After the apparent prosperity of the 1920s, virtually few were prepared for the devastating effects of the stock market crash. This cartoon by James N. Rosenberg, which shows Wall Street crumbling on October 29, 1929, is titled *Dies Irae*, Latin for "day of wrath."

SKILLBUILDER Analyzing Political Cartoons
1. What does the cartoonist suggest will happen to individuals because of the crash?
2. How does the cartoonist convey the sense of fear and shock?
3. What do the looks on people's faces indicate about the impact of the crash?

 SEE SKILLBUILDER HANDBOOK, PAGE R24.

BLACK TUESDAY On October 29—now known as **Black Tuesday**—the bottom fell out of the market and the nation's confidence. Shareholders frantically tried to sell before prices plunged even lower. The number of shares dumped that day was a record 16.4 million. Additional millions of shares could not find buyers. People who had bought stocks on credit were stuck with huge debts as the prices plummeted, while others lost most of their savings.

NOW & THEN

NEW YORK STOCK EXCHANGE

In the twenty-first century, the New York Stock Exchange (NYSE) remains at its core what it has been since it opened its doors in 1792: the nation's premier marketplace for the buying and selling of stocks. There, stockbrokers known as "members" take orders from their customers to buy and sell shares of stock in any one of more than 3,000 companies.

To execute their customers' orders, the members offer and receive bids in what resembles a loud and fast-paced auction. In general, customers submit two types of orders. A limit order tells the broker to buy or sell only if the stock reaches a certain price. A market order tells the broker to execute a transaction immediately, no matter what the price.

Despite remaining close to its roots, the NYSE is today undergoing perhaps the most significant changes in its long history, in large part due to the use of computers and the Internet.

A Pen and Paper Operation

In the 1920s, orders to buy or sell a stock arrived at brokers' telephone booths located around the edge of the trading floor. They were then carried by hand or sent by pneumatic tube to the trading post where that stock would be traded.

NYSE employees called reporters had to record every transaction. For each new sale, they wrote out a slip of paper containing the stock's abbreviation, the number of shares, and the price, and then transmitted it to the ticker room. Market information was typed into a keyboard that converted the keystrokes into electrical impulses that drove the clattering print wheels in ticker machines along the network. People would read the current display at the trading posts.

The trading floor in 1914. ▲

Technological Changes

With the introduction of computer technology, the activities of the exchange are less and less centered on human interaction. For example, some 99 percent of trades on the NYSE now go through an electronic database known as the Super Display Book system. With this system, a trade can be completed in milliseconds. Further, electronic communications networks now allow individuals to buy and sell stocks themselves over the Internet at a fraction of what it would cost to use a specialist.

Such innovation has prompted some to insist that all future trading will be done via computers, thus eliminating the need for physical exchanges such as the NYSE.

SKILLBUILDER

1. **Hypothesizing** What scenarios can you imagine that might prompt someone to submit a market order on a certain stock?
2. **Comparing** How has technology on the trading floor changed since the 1920s?

The trading floor in 2000. ▼

By mid-November, investors had lost about $30 billion, an amount equal to how much America spent in World War I. The stock market bubble had finally burst. One eyewitness to these events, Frederick Lewis Allen, described the resulting situation.

★ **A PERSONAL VOICE** FREDERICK LEWIS ALLEN

"**The Big Bull Market was dead. Billions of dollars' worth of profits—and paper profits—had disappeared. The grocer, the window cleaner, and the seamstress had lost their capital [savings]. In every town there were families which had suddenly dropped from showy affluence into debt. . . . With the Big Bull Market gone and prosperity going, Americans were soon to find themselves living in an altered world which called for new adjustments, new ideas, new habits of thought, and a new order of values.**"

—*Only Yesterday*

Financial Collapse

The stock market crash signaled the beginning of the **Great Depression**—the period from 1929 to 1940 in which the economy plummeted and unemployment skyrocketed. The crash alone did not cause the Great Depression, but it hastened the collapse of the economy and made the depression more severe.

BANK AND BUSINESS FAILURES After the crash, many people panicked and withdrew their money from banks. But some couldn't get their money because the banks had invested it in the stock market. In 1929, 600 banks closed. By 1933, 11,000 of the nation's 25,000 banks had failed. Because the government did not protect or insure bank accounts, millions of people lost their savings accounts.

The Great Depression hit other businesses, too. Between 1929 and 1932, the gross national product—the nation's total output of goods and services—was cut nearly in half, from $104 billion to $59 billion. Approximately 90,000 businesses went bankrupt. Among these failed enterprises were once-prosperous automobile and railroad companies.

As the economy plunged into a tailspin, millions of workers lost their jobs. Unemployment leaped from 3 percent (1.6 million workers) in 1929 to 25 percent (13 million workers) in 1933. One out of every four workers was out of a job. Those who kept their jobs faced pay cuts and reduced hours.

Not everyone fared so badly, of course. Before the crash, some speculators had sold off their stocks and made money. Joseph P. Kennedy, the father of future president John F. Kennedy, was one who did. Most, however, were not so lucky or shrewd. **D**

WORLDWIDE SHOCK WAVES The United States was not the only country gripped by the Great Depression. Much of Europe, for example, had suffered throughout the 1920s. European countries trying to recover from the ravages of World War I faced high war debts. In addition, Germany had to pay war reparations—payments to compensate the Allies for the damages Germany had caused. The Great Depression compounded these problems by limiting America's ability to import European goods. This made it difficult to sell American farm products and manufactured goods abroad.

MAIN IDEA

Analyzing Effects
D What happened to ordinary workers during the Great Depression?

This British ▲ election poster shows that the Great Depression was a global event.

Depression Indicators

Economic indicators are measures that signal trends in a nation's economy. During the Great Depression several trends were apparent. Those indicated at the right are linked—the conditions of one can affect another. For instance, when banks fail **1**, some businesses may have to close down **2**, which can cause unemployment to rise **3**. Thus, people have less money and spending declines **4**.

SKILLBUILDER Interpreting Graphs

1. In what year did the biggest jump in bank failures occur?

2. What measure on the graphs seems to indicate an improvement in the U.S. economy during the Depression? What might explain this?

1

2

3

4
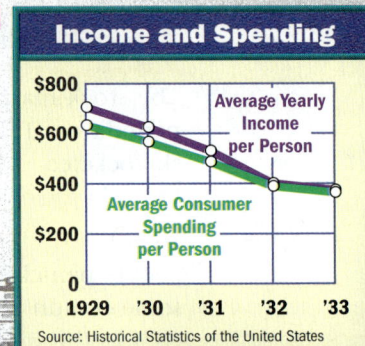

Source: Historical Statistics of the United States

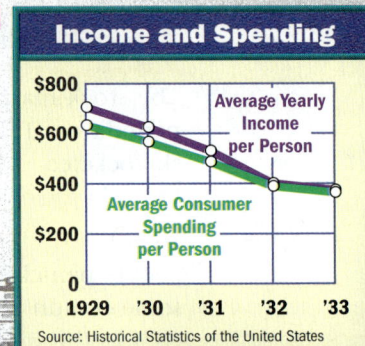
Distraught men try to withdraw their savings from a failing bank.

In 1930, Congress passed the **Hawley-Smoot Tariff Act,** which established the highest protective tariff in United States history. It was designed to protect American farmers and manufacturers from foreign competition. Yet it had the opposite effect. By reducing the flow of goods into the United States, the tariff prevented other countries from earning American currency to buy American goods. The tariff made unemployment worse in industries that could no longer export goods to Europe. Many countries retaliated by raising their own tariffs. Within a few years, world trade had fallen more than 40 percent. **E**

MAIN IDEA

Summarizing

E How did the Great Depression affect the world economy?

CAUSES OF THE GREAT DEPRESSION Although historians and economists differ on the main causes of the Great Depression, most cite a common set of factors, among them:

- tariffs and war debt policies that cut down the foreign market for American goods
- a crisis in the farm sector
- the availability of easy credit
- an unequal distribution of income

These factors led to falling demand for consumer goods, even as newly mechanized factories produced more products. The federal government contributed to the crisis by keeping interest rates low, thereby allowing companies and individuals to borrow easily and build up large debts. Some of this borrowed money was used to buy the stocks that later led to the crash.

At first people found it hard to believe that economic disaster had struck. In November 1929, President Hoover encouraged Americans to remain confident about the economy. Yet, the most severe depression in American history was well on its way.

WORLD STAGE

GLOBAL EFFECTS OF THE DEPRESSION

As the American economy collapsed, so too did Europe's. The world's nations had become interdependent; international trade was important to most countries. However, when the U.S. economy failed, American investors withdrew their money from European markets.

To keep U.S. dollars in America, the government raised tariffs on goods imported from other countries. World trade dropped. Unemployment rates around the world soared. Germany and Austria were particularly hard hit. In 1931 Austria's largest bank failed. In Asia, both farmers and urban workers suffered as the value of exports fell by half between 1929 and 1931. The crash was felt in Latin America as well. As U.S. and European demand for Latin American products like sugar, beef, and copper dropped, prices collapsed.

SECTION 1 ASSESSMENT

1. TERMS & NAMES For each term or name, write a sentence explaining its significance.

- price support
- credit
- Alfred E. Smith
- Dow Jones Industrial Average
- speculation
- buying on margin
- Black Tuesday
- Great Depression
- Hawley-Smoot Tariff Act

MAIN IDEA

2. TAKING NOTES

In a diagram like this, record the causes of the 1929 stock market crash.

Which do you see as the biggest cause? Why?

CRITICAL THINKING

3. MAKING INFERENCES

How did the economic trends of the 1920s help cause the Great Depression? **Think About:**

- what happened in industry
- what happened in agriculture
- what happened with consumers

4. DRAWING CONCLUSIONS

Judging from the events of the late 1920s and early 1930s, how important do you think public confidence is to the health of the economy? Explain. **Think About:**

- what happened when overconfidence in the stock market led people to speculate and buy on margin
- how confidence affects consumer borrowing

SECTION
2

PI 4.1
PI 4.2

CC Unit 1.I.D.3
CC Unit 5.II.A.4
CC Unit 5.II.B.6.c

Hardship and Suffering During the Depression

MAIN IDEA	WHY IT MATTERS NOW	Terms & Names
During the Great Depression Americans did what they had to do to survive.	Since the Great Depression, many Americans have been more cautious about saving, investing, and borrowing.	• shantytown • Dust Bowl • soup kitchen • direct relief • bread line

One American's Story

hmhsocialstudies.com
TAKING NOTES

Use the graphic organizer online to take notes on the impact of the Great Depression on farmers and city dwellers.

Ann Marie Low lived on her parents' North Dakota farm when the stock market crashed in 1929 and the Great Depression hit. Hard times were familiar to Ann's family. But the worst was yet to come. In the early 1930s, a ravenous drought hit the Great Plains, destroying crops and leaving the earth dry and cracked. Then came the deadly dust storms. On April 25, 1934, Ann wrote an account in her diary.

★ **A PERSONAL VOICE** ANN MARIE LOW

" [T]he air is just full of dirt coming, literally, for hundreds of miles. It sifts into everything. After we wash the dishes and put them away, so much dust sifts into the cupboards we must wash them again before the next meal. . . . Newspapers say the deaths of many babies and old people are attributed to breathing in so much dirt. "

—*Dust Bowl Diary*

▲
Ann Marie Low

The drought and winds lasted for more than seven years. The dust storms in Kansas, Colorado, New Mexico, Nebraska, the Dakotas, Oklahoma, and Texas were a great hardship—but only one of many—that Americans faced during the Great Depression.

The Depression Devastates People's Lives

Statistics such as the unemployment rate tell only part of the story of the Great Depression. More important was the impact that it had on people's lives: the Depression brought hardship, homelessness, and hunger to millions.

THE DEPRESSION IN THE CITIES In cities across the country, people lost their jobs, were evicted from their homes and ended up in the streets. Some slept in parks or sewer pipes, wrapping themselves in newspapers to fend off the cold.

Others built makeshift shacks out of scrap materials. Before long, numerous **shantytowns**—little towns consisting of shacks—sprang up. An observer recalled one such settlement in Oklahoma City: "Here were all these people living in old, rusted-out car bodies. . . . There were people living in shacks made of orange crates. One family with a whole lot of kids were living in a piano box. . . . People were living in whatever they could junk together."

Every day the poor dug through garbage cans or begged. **Soup kitchens** offering free or low-cost food and **bread lines,** or lines of people waiting to receive food provided by charitable organizations or public agencies, became a common sight. One man described a bread line in New York City.

▲ Unemployed people built shacks in a shantytown in New York City in 1932.

★ **A PERSONAL VOICE** HERMAN SHUMLIN

"Two or three blocks along Times Square, you'd see these men, silent, shuffling along in a line. Getting this handout of coffee and doughnuts, dealt out from great trucks. . . . I'd see that flat, opaque, expressionless look which spelled, for me, human disaster. Men . . . who had responsible positions. Who had lost their jobs, lost their homes, lost their families . . . They were destroyed men."

—quoted in *Hard Times*

Conditions for African Americans and Latinos were especially difficult. Their unemployment rates were higher, and they were the lowest paid. They also dealt with increasing racial violence from unemployed whites competing for the same jobs. Twenty-four African Americans died by lynching in 1933.

Latinos—mainly Mexicans and Mexican Americans living in the Southwest—were also targets. Whites demanded that Latinos be deported, or expelled from the country, even though many had been born in America. By the late 1930s, hundreds of thousands of people of Mexican descent relocated to Mexico. Some left voluntarily; others were deported by the federal government. Ⓐ

THE DEPRESSION IN RURAL AREAS Life in rural areas was hard, but it did have one advantage over city life: most farmers could grow food for their families. With falling prices and rising debt, though, thousands of farmers lost their land. Between 1929 and 1932, about 400,000 farms were lost through foreclosure—the process by which a mortgage holder takes back property if an occupant has not made payments. Many farmers turned to tenant farming and barely scraped out a living.

ANOTHER
PERSPECTIVE

AN AFRICAN-AMERICAN VIEW OF THE DEPRESSION

Although the suffering of the 1930s was severe for many people, it was especially grim for African Americans. Hard times were already a fact of life for many blacks, as one African-American man noted:

"The Negro was born in depression. It didn't mean too much to him, The Great American Depression. . . . The best he could be is a janitor or a porter or shoeshine boy. It only became official when it hit the white man."

Nonetheless, the African-American community was very hard hit by the Great Depression. In 1932, the unemployment rate among African Americans stood at over 50 percent, while the overall unemployment rate was approximately 25 percent.

The Dust Bowl, 1933–1936

hmhsocialstudies.com **INTERACTIVE MAP**

Nebraska, 1935–1937
Over two years, federal workers help soil conservation by planting 360,000 trees and completing 62 dams, 517 ponds, and 500 acres of terracing.

Chicago, Nov. 1933
Crowds at Chicago Exposition world's fair are caught in 50 mph gale of dust.

Boston, May 1934
Midwestern dust is found on airplanes landing in Boston; it collected on the planes at altitudes of up to 20,000 ft.

Beaver, Okla., March 24, 1936
Grain-elevator operators estimate that 20% of wheat crop has been blown away by dust storms.

New York City, May 12, 1934
Dust lowers humidity from normal 57% to 34%. Dust is reported on ships 500 miles out to sea.

Tucumcari, N. Mex. March 30, 1936
Clouds of dust blown by 50-mph winds cause complete darkness.

Area of Dust Bowl
Area of damage
Area covered by May 1934 dust storm

0   150   300 miles
0   150   300 kilometers

GEOGRAPHY SKILLBUILDER
1. **Region** Which states were in the region known as the Dust Bowl?
2. **Movement** Why might most of the migrants who left the Dust Bowl have traveled west?

THE DUST BOWL The drought that began in the early 1930s wreaked havoc on the Great Plains. During the previous decade, farmers from Texas to North Dakota had used tractors to break up the grasslands and plant millions of acres of new farmland. Plowing had removed the thick protective layer of prairie grasses. Farmers had then exhausted the land through overproduction of crops, and the grasslands became unsuitable for farming. When the drought and winds began in the early 1930s, little grass and few trees were left to hold the soil down. Wind scattered the topsoil, exposing sand and grit underneath. The dust traveled hundreds of miles. One windstorm in 1934 picked up millions of tons of dust from the plains and carried it to East Coast cities.

The region that was the hardest hit, including parts of Kansas, Oklahoma, Texas, New Mexico, and Colorado, came to be known as the **Dust Bowl.** Plagued by dust storms and evictions, thousands of farmers and sharecroppers left their land behind. They packed up their families and few belongings and headed west, following Route 66 to California. Some of these migrants—known as Okies (a term that originally referred to Oklahomans but came to be used negatively for all migrants)—found work as farmhands. But others continued to wander in search of work. By the end of the 1930s, hundreds of thousands of farm families had migrated to California and other Pacific Coast states.

▲
A farmer and his sons brave a dust storm in 1936.

Background
The most severe storms were called "black blizzards." They were said to have darkened the sky in New York City and Washington, D.C.

Effects on the American Family

In the face of the suffering caused by the Great Depression, the family stood as a source of strength for most Americans. Although some people feared that hard times would undermine moral values, those concerns were largely unfounded. In general, Americans believed in traditional values and emphasized the importance of family unity. At a time when money was tight, many families entertained themselves by staying at home and playing board games, such as Monopoly (invented in 1933), and listening to the radio. Nevertheless, the economic difficulties of the Great Depression put severe pressure on family life. Making ends meet was a daily struggle, and, in some cases, families broke apart under the strain.

MEN IN THE STREETS Many men had difficulty coping with unemployment because they were accustomed to working and supporting their families. Every day, they would set out to walk the streets in search of jobs. As Frederick Lewis Allen noted in *Since Yesterday*, "Men who have been sturdy and self-respecting workers can take unemployment without flinching for a few weeks, a few months, even if they have to see their families suffer; but it is different after a year . . . two years . . . three years." Some men became so discouraged that they simply stopped trying. Some even abandoned their families.

During the Great Depression, as many as 300,000 transients—or "hoboes" as they were called—wandered the country, hitching rides on railroad boxcars and sleeping under bridges. These hoboes of the 1930s, mainly men, would occasionally turn up at homeless shelters in big cities. The novelist Thomas Wolfe described a group of these men in New York City. **B**

HISTORICAL

SPOTLIGHT

HOBO SYMBOLS

Hoboes shared a hidden language that helped them meet the challenges of the road. Over time a set of symbols developed for hoboes to alert each other as to where they could get food or work or a place to sleep, and what houses to avoid. They often marked the symbols, such as those shown below, on the sides of houses and fences near railroad yards.

Sit down meal

Only bread given here

Good place for a handout

Sleep in barn

Good water

Danger

MAIN IDEA

Analyzing Causes

B Why did so many men leave their homes during the Depression?

★ A PERSONAL VOICE THOMAS WOLFE

"These were the wanderers from town to town, the riders of freight trains, the thumbers of rides on highways, the uprooted, unwanted male population of America. They . . . gathered in the big cities when winter came, hungry, defeated, empty, hopeless, restless . . . always on the move, looking everywhere for work, for the bare crumbs to support their miserable lives, and finding neither work nor crumbs."

—*You Can't Go Home Again*

During the early years of the Great Depression, there was no federal system of **direct relief**—cash payments or food provided by the government to the poor. Some cities and charity services did offer relief to those who needed it, but the benefits were meager. In New York City, for example, the weekly payment was just $2.39 per family. This was the most generous relief offered by any city, but it was still well below the amount needed to feed a family.

WOMEN STRUGGLE TO SURVIVE Women worked hard to help their families survive adversity during the Great Depression. Many women canned food and sewed clothes. They also carefully managed household budgets. Jeane Westin, the author of *Making Do: How Women Survived the '30s*, recalled, "Those days you did everything to save a penny. . . . My next door neighbor and I used to shop together. You could get two pounds of hamburger for a quarter, so we'd buy two pounds and split it—then one week she'd pay the extra penny and the next week I'd pay."

Many women also worked outside the home, though they usually received less money than men did. As the Depression wore on, however, working women became the targets of enormous resentment. Many people believed that women, especially married women, had no right to work when there were men who were unemployed.

In the early 1930s, some cities refused to hire married women as schoolteachers.

Many Americans assumed that women were having an easier time than men during the Great Depression because few were seen begging or standing in bread lines. As a matter of fact, many women were starving to death in cold attics and rooming houses. As one writer pointed out, women were often too ashamed to reveal their hardship.

★ A PERSONAL VOICE MERIDEL LE SEUER

" I've lived in cities for many months, broke, without help, too timid to get in bread lines. I've known many women to live like this until they simply faint in the street. . . . A woman will shut herself up in a room until it is taken away from her, and eat a cracker a day and be as quiet as a mouse. . . . [She] will go for weeks verging on starvation, . . . going through the streets ashamed, sitting in libraries, parks, going for days without speaking to a living soul, shut up in the terror of her own misery. "

—*America in the Twenties*

CHILDREN SUFFER HARDSHIPS Children also suffered during the 1930s. Poor diets and a lack of money for health care led to serious health problems. Milk consumption declined across the country, and clinics and hospitals reported a dramatic rise in malnutrition and diet-related diseases, such as rickets. At the same time, child-welfare programs were slashed as cities and states cut their budgets in the face of dwindling resources.

Falling tax revenues also caused school boards to shorten the school year and even close schools. By 1933, some 2,600 schools across the nation had shut down, leaving more than 300,000 students out of school. Thousands of children went to work instead; they often labored in sweatshops under horrendous conditions. **C**

Many teenagers looked for a way out of the suffering. Hundreds of thousands of teenage boys and some girls hopped aboard America's freight trains to zigzag the country in search of work, adventure, and an escape from poverty. These "wild boys" came from every section of the United States, from every corner of society. They were the sons of poor farmers, and out-of-work miners, and wealthy parents who had lost everything. "Hoover tourists," as they were called, were eager to tour America for free.

From the age of eleven until seventeen, George Phillips rode the rails, first catching local freights out of his home town of Princeton, Missouri.

"There is no feeling in the world like sitting in a side-door Pullman and watching the world go by, listening to the clickety-clack of the wheels, hearing that old steam whistle blowing for crossings and towns."

While exciting, the road could also be deadly. Many riders were beaten or jailed by "bulls"—armed freight yard patrolmen. Often riders had to sleep standing up in a constant deafening rumble. Some were accidentally locked in ice cars for days on end. Others fell prey to murderous criminals. From 1929 to 1939, 24,647 trespassers were killed and 27,171 injured on railroad property.

" If I leave my mother, it will mean one less mouth to feed."

EUGENE WILLIAMS, AGE 13

▼ Two young boys, ages 15 and 16, walk beside freight cars in the San Joaquin Valley.

Background
Rickets is caused by a vitamin D deficiency and results in defective bone growth.

MAIN IDEA

Analyzing Effects
C How did the Great Depression affect women and children?

SOCIAL AND PSYCHOLOGICAL EFFECTS The hardships of the Great Depression had a tremendous social and psychological impact. Some people were so demoralized by hard times that they lost their will to survive. Between 1928 and 1932, the suicide rate rose more than 30 percent. Three times as many people were admitted to state mental hospitals as in normal times.

The economic problems forced many Americans to accept compromises and make sacrifices that affected them for the rest of their lives. Adults stopped going to the doctor or dentist because they couldn't afford it. Young people gave up their dreams of going to college. Others put off getting married, raising large families, or having children at all.

▲ This Ozark sharecropper family was photographed in Arkansas during the 1930s by the artist Ben Shahn.

Vocabulary
stigma: a mark or indication of disgrace

For many people, the stigma of poverty and of having to scrimp and save never disappeared completely. For some, achieving financial security became the primary focus in life. As one woman recalled, "Ever since I was twelve years old there was one major goal in my life . . . one thing . . . and that was to never be poor again."

During the Great Depression many people showed great kindness to strangers who were down on their luck. People often gave food, clothing, and a place to stay to the needy. Families helped other families and shared resources and strengthened the bonds within their communities. In addition, many people developed habits of saving and thriftiness—habits they would need to see themselves through the dark days ahead as the nation and President Hoover struggled with the Great Depression. These habits shaped a whole generation of Americans.

SECTION 2 ASSESSMENT

1. TERMS & NAMES For each term or name, write a sentence explaining its significance.
- shantytown
- soup kitchen
- bread line
- Dust Bowl
- direct relief

MAIN IDEA

2. TAKING NOTES
In a Venn diagram, list the effects that the Great Depression had on farmers and city dwellers. Find the differences and the similarities.

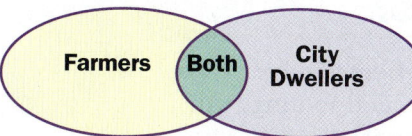

Which group do you think suffered less?

CRITICAL THINKING

3. CONTRASTING
How was what happened to men during the Great Depression different from what happened to women? children? **Think About:**

- each group's role in their families
- the changes each group had to make
- what help was available to them

4. ANALYZING EFFECTS
How did Dust Bowl conditions in the Great Plains affect the entire country?

5. DRAWING CONCLUSIONS
In what ways did the Great Depression affect people's outlook?

PI 4.1
PI 4.3

CC Unit 5.II.A.2.d   CC Unit 5.II.A.3.a
CC Unit 5.II.A.3.b   CC Unit 5.II.A.4

Hoover Struggles with the Depression

MAIN IDEA	WHY IT MATTERS NOW	Terms & Names
President Hoover's conservative response to the Great Depression drew criticism from many Americans.	Worsening conditions in the country caused the government to become more involved in the health and wealth of the people.	• Herbert Hoover • Boulder Dam • Federal Home Loan Bank Act • Reconstruction Finance Corporation • Bonus Army

One American's Story

hmhsocialstudies.com
TAKING NOTES

Use the graphic organizer online to take notes on President Hoover's response to the Great Depression.

Oscar Ameringer was a newspaper editor in Oklahoma City during the Great Depression. In 1932, he traveled around the country collecting information on economic and social conditions. Testifying in unemployment hearings that same year, Ameringer described desperate people who were losing patience with the government. "Unless something is done for them and done soon you will have a revolution on hand." Ameringer told the following story.

▲ A Depression-era family from Arkansas walks through Texas, looking for work in the cotton fields along the Rio Grande.

A PERSONAL VOICE OSCAR AMERINGER

" The roads of the West and Southwest teem with hungry hitchhikers. . . . Between Clarksville and Russellville, Ark., I picked up a family. The woman was hugging a dead chicken under a ragged coat. When I asked her where she had procured the fowl, first she told me she had found it dead in the road, and then added in grim humor, 'They promised me a chicken in the pot, and now I got mine.' "

—quoted in *The American Spirit*

The woman was recalling President Hoover's empty 1928 campaign pledge: "A chicken in every pot and a car in every garage." Now many Americans were disillusioned. They demanded that the government help them.

Hoover Tries to Reassure the Nation

After the stock market crash of October 1929, President **Herbert Hoover** tried to reassure Americans that the nation's economy was on a sound footing. "Any lack of confidence in the economic future . . . is foolish," he declared. In his view, the important thing was for Americans to remain optimistic and to go about their business as usual. Americans believed depressions were a normal part of the business cycle. According to this theory, periods of rapid economic growth were naturally followed by periods of depression. The best course in a slump, many experts believed, was to do nothing and let the economy fix itself. Hoover took a slightly different position. He felt that government could play a limited role in helping to solve problems.

HOOVER'S PHILOSOPHY Herbert Hoover had been an engineer, and he put great faith in the power of reason. He was also a humanitarian, as he made clear in one of his last speeches as president.

> ★ **A PERSONAL VOICE** HERBERT HOOVER
>
> "Our first objective must be to provide security from poverty and want. . . . We want to see a nation built of home owners and farm owners. We want to see their savings protected. We want to see them in steady jobs. We want to see more and more of them insured against death and accident, unemployment and old age. We want them all secure."
>
> —"Challenge to Liberty," October 1936

Like many Americans of the time, Hoover believed that one of government's chief functions was to foster cooperation between competing groups and interests in society. If business and labor were in a conflict, for example, government should step in and help them find a solution that served their mutual interests. This cooperation must be voluntary rather than forced, he said. Government's role was to encourage and facilitate cooperation, not to control it.

On the other hand, Americans also valued "rugged individualism"—the idea that people should succeed through their own efforts. They should take care of themselves and their families, rather than depend on the government to bail them out. Thus, Hoover opposed any form of federal welfare, or direct relief to the needy. He believed that handouts would weaken people's self-respect and "moral fiber." His answer to the needy was that individuals, charities, and local organizations should pitch in to help care for the less fortunate. The federal government should direct relief measures, but not through a vast federal bureaucracy. Such a bureaucracy, he said, would be too expensive and would stifle individual liberties. **A**

MAIN IDEA

Summarizing
A What were some of Hoover's key convictions about government?

However, when the Depression took hold, moral fiber wasn't what people were worried about. Hoover's response shocked and frustrated suffering Americans.

HOOVER TAKES CAUTIOUS STEPS Hoover's political philosophy caused him to take a cautious approach to the depression. Soon after the stock market crash, he called together key leaders in the fields of business, banking, and labor. He urged them to work together to find solutions to the nation's economic woes and to act in ways that would not make a bad situation worse. For example, he asked employers not to cut wages or lay off workers, and he asked labor leaders not to demand higher wages or go on strike. He also created a special organization to help private charities generate contributions for the poor.

None of these steps made much of a difference. A year after the crash, the economy was still shrinking, and unemployment was still rising. More companies went out of business, soup kitchens became a common sight, and general misery continued to grow. Shantytowns arose in every city, and hoboes continued to roam.

KEY PLAYER

HERBERT HOOVER
1874–1964

Born to a Quaker family in Iowa, Herbert Hoover was orphaned at an early age. His life was a rags-to-riches story. He worked his way through Stanford University and later made a fortune as a mining engineer and consultant in China, Australia, Europe, and Africa. During and after World War I, he coordinated U.S. relief efforts in Europe, earning a reputation for efficiency and humanitarian ideals.

As president, Hoover asserted, "Every time we find solutions outside of government, we have not only strengthened character, but we have preserved our sense of real government."

LOOKING DOWNSTREAM, COLORADO RIVER

OAKES PHOTO

SHOWING THE IMMENSE CONCRETE FORMS OF BOULDER DAM

▲
This 1930s postcard, displaying a hand-colored photograph, shows the mammoth scale of Boulder Canyon and Boulder Dam.

BOULDER DAM One project that Hoover approved did make a difference. Years earlier, when Hoover served as secretary of commerce, one of his earliest proposed initiatives was the construction of a dam on the Colorado River. Aiming to minimize federal intervention, Hoover proposed to finance the dam's construction by using profits from sales of the electric power that the dam would generate. He also helped to arrange an agreement on water rights among the seven states of the Colorado River basin—Arizona, California, Colorado, Nevada, New Mexico, Utah, and Wyoming.

By the time the massive project won congressional approval in 1928, as part of a $700 million public works program, Hoover had been elected to the White House. In the fall of 1929, nearly one year into his presidency, Hoover was finally able to authorize construction of **Boulder Dam** (later called Hoover Dam). At 726 ft. high and 1,244 ft. long it would be the world's tallest dam and the second largest. In addition to providing electricity and flood control, the dam also provided a regular water supply, which enabled the growth of California's massive agricultural economy. Today, the dam also helps to provide water for cities such as Los Angeles and Las Vegas.

DEMOCRATS WIN IN 1930 CONGRESSIONAL ELECTIONS As the country's economic difficulties increased, the political tide turned against Hoover and the Republicans. In the 1930 congressional elections, the Democrats took advantage of anti-Hoover sentiments to win more seats in Congress. As a result of that election, the Republicans lost control of the House of Representatives and saw their majority in the Senate dwindle to one vote.

As Americans grew more and more frustrated by the Depression, they expressed their anger in a number of ways. Farmers stung by low crop prices burned their corn and wheat and dumped their milk on highways rather than sell it at a loss. Some farmers even declared a "farm holiday" and refused to work their fields. A number blocked roads to prevent food from getting to market, hoping that food shortages would raise prices. Some farmers also used force to prevent authorities from foreclosing on farms.

By 1930, people were calling the shantytowns in American cities "Hoovervilles"—a direct slap at the president's policies. Homeless people called the newspapers they wrapped themselves in "Hoover blankets." Empty pockets turned inside out were "Hoover flags." Many Americans who had hailed Hoover as a great humanitarian a few years earlier now saw him as a cold and heartless leader.

MAIN IDEA

Making Inferences

B Why do you think people blamed Hoover for the nation's difficulties?

Despite public criticism, Hoover continued to hold firm to his principles. He refused to support direct relief or other forms of federal welfare. Some Americans were going hungry, and many blamed Hoover for their plight. Criticism of the president and his policies continued to grow. An anonymous ditty of the time was widely repeated. **B**

" Mellon pulled the whistle
Hoover rang the bell
Wall Street gave the signal
And the country went to hell. "

Hoover Takes Action

As time went on and the depression deepened, President Hoover gradually softened his position on government intervention in the economy and took a more activist approach to the nation's economic troubles.

HOOVER BACKS COOPERATIVES In Hoover's view, Boulder Dam was a model of how the federal government could encourage cooperation. His attempts to relieve the depression involved negotiating agreements among private entities, again reflecting his belief in small government. For example, he backed the creation of the Federal Farm Board, an organization of farm cooperatives. The Farm Board was intended to raise crop prices by helping members to buy crops and keep them off the market temporarily until prices rose.

In addition, Hoover tried to prop up the banking system by persuading the nation's largest banks to establish the National Credit Corporation. This organization loaned money to smaller banks, which helped them stave off bankruptcy.

DIRECT INTERVENTION By late 1931, however, many people could see that these measures had failed to turn the economy around. With a presidential election looming, Hoover appealed to Congress to pass a series of measures to reform banking, provide mortgage relief, and funnel more federal money into business investment. In 1932, Hoover signed into law the **Federal Home Loan Bank Act,** which lowered mortgage rates for homeowners and allowed farmers to refinance their farm loans and avoid foreclosure. It was not until Hoover's time in office was over that Congress passed the Glass-Steagall Banking Act, which separated investment from commercial banking and would, Congress hoped, prevent another crash.

Hoover's most ambitious economic measure, however, was the **Reconstruction Finance Corporation** (RFC), approved by Congress in January 1932. It authorized up to $2 billion for emergency financing for banks, life insurance companies, railroads, and other large businesses. Hoover believed that the money would trickle down to the average citizen through job growth and higher wages. Many critics questioned this approach; they argued that the program would benefit only corporations and that the poor still needed direct relief. Hungry people could not wait for the benefits to trickle down to their tables.

In its first five months of operation, the RFC loaned more than $805 million to large corporations, but business failures continued. The RFC was an unprecedented example of federal involvement in a peacetime economy, but in the end it was too little, too late. **C**

Vocabulary
refinance: to provide new financing; to discharge a mortgage with a new mortgage obtained at a lower interest rate

MAIN IDEA

Evaluating Decisions

C What were some of the projects proposed by Hoover, and how effective were they?

▲ This cartoon's caption plays on the two different meanings of the word *credit* to suggest that farmers and the president should help each other.

Gassing the Bonus Army

In 1932, an incident further damaged Hoover's image and public morale. That spring, between 10,000 and 20,000 World War I veterans and their families arrived in Washington, D.C., from various parts of the country. They called themselves the Bonus Expeditionary Force, or the **Bonus Army**.

THE PATMAN BILL DENIED Led by Walter Waters, an unemployed cannery worker from Oregon, the Bonus Army came to the nation's capital to support a bill under debate in Congress. The Patman Bill authorized the government to pay a bonus to World War I veterans who had not been compensated adequately for their wartime service. This bonus, which Congress had approved in 1924, was supposed to be paid out in 1945 in the form of cash and a life insurance policy, but Congressman Wright Patman believed that the money—an average of $500 per soldier—should be paid immediately.

Hoover thought that the Bonus Marchers were "communists and persons with criminal records" rather than veterans. He opposed the legislation, but he respected the marchers' right to peaceful assembly. He even provided food and supplies so that they could erect a shantytown within sight of the Capitol. On June 17, however, the Senate voted down the Patman Bill. Hoover then called on

In 1932, these veterans from Muncie, Indiana, decided to remain in the capital until their bonus was paid to them.

the Bonus Army marchers to leave. Most did, but approximately 2,000, still hoping to meet with the president, refused to budge. **D**

HOOVER DISBANDS THE BONUS ARMY Nervous that the angry group could become violent, President Hoover decided that the Bonus Army should be disbanded. On July 28, a force of 1,000 soldiers under the command of General Douglas MacArthur and his aide, Major Dwight D. Eisenhower, came to roust the veterans. A government official watching from a nearby office recalled what happened next.

⭐ **A PERSONAL VOICE** A. EVERETTE MCINTYRE

" The 12th infantry was in full battle dress. Each had a gas mask and his belt was full of tear gas bombs. . . . At orders, they brought their bayonets at thrust and moved in. The bayonets were used to jab people, to make them move. Soon, almost everybody disappeared from view, because tear gas bombs exploded. The entire block was covered by tear gas. Flames were coming up, where the soldiers had set fire to the buildings to drive these people out. . . . Through the whole afternoon, they took one camp after another. "

—quoted in *Hard Times*

In the course of the operation, the infantry gassed more than 1,000 people, including an 11-month-old baby, who died, and an 8-year-old boy, who was partially blinded. Two people were shot and many were injured. Most Americans were stunned and outraged at the government's treatment of the veterans.

Once again, President Hoover's image suffered, and now an election was nearing. In November, Hoover would face a formidable opponent, the Democratic candidate Franklin Delano Roosevelt. When Roosevelt heard about the attack on the Bonus Army, he said to his friend Felix Frankfurter, "Well, Felix, this will elect me." The downturn in the economy and Hoover's inability to deal effectively with the Depression had sealed his political fate.

SECTION 3 ASSESSMENT

1. TERMS & NAMES For each term or name, write a sentence explaining its significance.

- Herbert Hoover
- Boulder Dam
- Federal Home Loan Bank Act
- Reconstruction Finance Corporation
- Bonus Army

MAIN IDEA

2. TAKING NOTES
In a cluster diagram, record what Hoover said and did in response to the Great Depression.

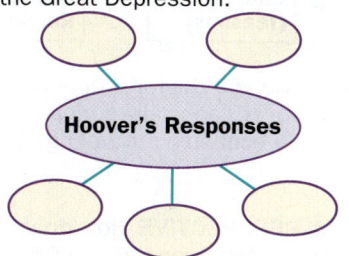

Which response was most helpful? Explain your choice.

CRITICAL THINKING

3. ANALYZING ISSUES
How did Hoover's belief in "rugged individualism" shape his policies during the Great Depression?
Think About:

- what his belief implies about his view of people
- how that translates into the role of government
- Hoover's policies

4. DRAWING CONCLUSIONS
When Franklin Delano Roosevelt heard about the attack on the Bonus Army, why was he so certain that he would defeat Hoover?
Think About:

- the American public's impression of Hoover
- Hoover's actions to alleviate the Great Depression
- how people judged Hoover after the attack

VISUAL SUMMARY

THE GREAT DEPRESSION BEGINS

CAUSES

- stock-based economy; superficial prosperity
- unequal distribution of income
- problems in industry and the farm sector
- increasing consumer debt
- stock market speculation and crash

THE GREAT DEPRESSION

EFFECTS

- people out of work
- rise of shantytowns
- banks fail and schools close
- world economy suffers
- Hoover employs more active governmental involvement

TERMS & NAMES

For each term below, write a sentence explaining its connection to the period 1929–1933. For the person below, explain his role in the events of the period.

1. credit
2. speculation
3. buying on margin
4. Black Tuesday
5. Dow Jones Industrial Average
6. Great Depression
7. Dust Bowl
8. direct relief
9. Herbert Hoover
10. Bonus Army

MAIN IDEAS

Use your notes and the information in the chapter to answer the following questions.

The Nation's Sick Economy *(pages 670–677)*

1. How did what happened to farmers during the 1920s foreshadow events of the Great Depression?
2. What were some of the effects of the stock market crash in October 1929?

Hardship and Suffering During the Depression *(pages 678–683)*

3. How were shantytowns, soup kitchens, and bread lines a response to the Depression?
4. Why did minorities often experience an increase in discrimination during the Great Depression?
5. What pressures did the American family experience during the Depression?

Hoover Struggles with the Depression *(pages 684–689)*

6. How did Hoover's treatment of the Bonus Army affect his standing with the public?
7. In what ways did Hoover try to use the government to relieve the Depression?

CRITICAL THINKING

1. **USING YOUR NOTES** In a chart like the one shown below, show Hoover's responses to the Great Depression. Indicate how his philosophy changed and the reasons for that change.

   Herbert Hoover's Philosophy

   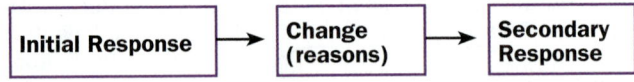

   | Initial Response | → | Change (reasons) | → | Secondary Response |

2. **ECONOMIC OPPORTUNITY** Do you think it would have been difficult for individuals to recover financially during the Depression without the entire economy recovering? Why or why not?

3. **DEVELOPING HISTORICAL PERSPECTIVE** How do you think the Great Depression changed Americans' view of themselves? Consider the roles of men, women, and children in society and in the family.

Use the cartoon and your knowledge of U.S. history to answer question 1.

1 The cartoon illustrates which event leading to the Great Depression?

(1) bank failures
(2) Black Tuesday
(3) Bonus March
(4) the election of Herbert Hoover

2 In the 1930s, some areas of the country suffered from especially harsh environmental conditions. Thousands of farmers and sharecroppers were forced to abandon their land and look for other work. In which of the following areas were these conditions worst?

(1) parts of Idaho, Wyoming, and Oregon
(2) parts of Missouri, Illinois, and Iowa
(3) parts of Florida, Alabama, and Georgia
(4) parts of Kansas, Texas, and Oklahoma

3 How did World War I contribute to causing the Great Depression?

(1) Soldiers returning from the war were unskilled and so had difficulty finding employment.
(2) Foreign countries had borrowed heavily to pay for the war and so could not afford to buy American goods.
(3) Americans had spent their money on war bonds and so had little savings.
(4) American industry was geared for producing weapons and could not retool to produce consumer goods.

↗ hmhsocialstudies.com **TEST PRACTICE**

For additional test practice, go online for:
• Diagnostic tests   • Tutorials

INTERACT WITH HISTORY

Recall the issues that you explored at the beginning of the chapter. Suppose the year is 1930 and you are the head of your household. Write a letter to a relative overseas in which you describe your family's situation and how you handled the crisis. Discuss the challenges created by the Great Depression and what you've learned as a result of enduring such hardships.

FOCUS ON WRITING

Imagine you are President Hoover's head speech-writer in the year 1931. The president is scheduled to give a radio address and needs a persuasive speech. Write a speech in which you present Hoover's proposed economic policies to help end the Great Depression.

COLLABORATIVE LEARNING

21ST CENTURY

In a small group read and discuss the "One American's Story" at the beginning of Section 2. Then use the Internet and library resources to research accounts of the Dust Bowl. Use your findings to create an illustrated magazine article about the impact of the Dust Bowl on the lives of Americans in rural areas.

The Great Depression

The Great Depression, which lasted from 1929 to 1939, was the most severe economic downturn in the history of the United States. The boom times of the 1920s concealed severe weaknesses in the American economy. The stock market crash of 1929 exposed the economy's shaky foundations and plunged the country into a deep economic depression. To stimulate the economy, President Franklin Delano Roosevelt introduced a host of government programs. This New Deal alleviated the worst aspects of the Great Depression. However, it would take a world war to bring the country to full economic recovery.

Explore the impact of the Great Depression online. You can find a wealth of information, video clips, primary sources, activities, and more at hmhsocialstudies.com.

A Picture Worth 1,000 Words
Watch the video to learn about the work of photographer Dorothea Lange, who chronicled the Great Depression.

A New Deal
Watch the video to see how President Roosevelt intended to fight the Great Depression.

Public Works
Watch the video to see examples of the New Deal programs introduced by President Roosevelt.

From Depression to War
Watch the video to see how the American economy finally recovered from the Great Depression.

CHAPTER 23

THE NEW DEAL

Essential Question

How did the government's reaction to the Great Depression affect the United States?

 New York Standards

KEY IDEA 1 The study of New York State and United States history requires an analysis of the development of American culture, its diversity and multicultural context, and the ways people are unified by many values, practices, and traditions.

KEY IDEA 2 Important ideas, social and cultural values, beliefs, and traditions from New York State and United States history illustrate the connections and interactions of people and events across time and from a variety of perspectives.

SECTION 1: A New Deal Fights the Depression

SECTION 2: The Second New Deal Takes Hold

SECTION 3: The New Deal Affects Many Groups

SECTION 4: Culture in the 1930s

SECTION 5: The Impact of the New Deal

The Civil Works Administration provided millions of jobs during the Great Depression.

 1933 Franklin Delano Roosevelt is inaugurated.

 1934 Congress creates the SEC to regulate the stock market.

1934 Indian Reorganization Act is passed.

 1935 Congress passes the Social Security Act.

1936 President Roosevelt is reelected.

USA **1933**   **1934**   **1935**   **1936**
WORLD

1933 Hitler and the Nazi party come to power in Germany.

 1935 Mussolini leads Italian invasion of Ethiopia.

1935 British Parliament passes the Government of India Act.

1936 Civil war begins in Spain.

HISTORY® **FDR's New Deal**

↗ hmhsocialstudies.com **VIDEO**

INTERACT
WITH HISTORY

It is 1933, the height of the Great Depression. Thousands of banks and businesses have failed, and a quarter of the adult population is out of work. Now a new president takes office, promising to bring relief to the ailing economy.

Explore the Issues

- How can the government help failing industries?

- What can be done to ease unemployment?

- What would you do to restore public confidence and economic security?

- How would you get money to pay for your proposed recovery programs?

1937 Labor unions begin using sit-down strikes.

1938 Route 66 is completed, linking Chicago, Illinois, to Los Angeles, California.

1939 *The Wizard of Oz* is released in movie theaters.

1940 President Roosevelt is elected a third time.

1937   **1938**   **1939**   **1940**

1937 Japan invades Northern China.

1937 *Hindenburg* disaster

1939 Germany invades Poland.

A New Deal Fights the Depression

MAIN IDEA	WHY IT MATTERS NOW	Terms & Names
After becoming president, Franklin Delano Roosevelt used government programs to combat the Depression.	Americans still benefit from programs begun in the New Deal, such as bank and stock market regulations and the Tennessee Valley Authority.	• Franklin Delano Roosevelt • New Deal • Glass-Steagall Act • Federal Securities Act • Agricultural Adjustment Act (AAA) • Civilian Conservation Corps (CCC) • National Industrial Recovery Act (NIRA) • deficit spending • Huey Long

One American's Story

hmhsocialstudies.com
TAKING NOTES

Use the graphic organizer online to take notes on Roosevelt's proposed solutions to the problems of the Great Depression.

Hank Oettinger was working as a printing press operator in a small town in Wisconsin when the Great Depression began. He lost his job in 1931 and was unemployed for the next two years. In 1933, however, President Roosevelt began creating work programs. Through one of these programs, the Civil Works Administration (CWA), Oettinger went back to work in 1933. As he later recalled, the CWA was cause for great celebration in his town.

A PERSONAL VOICE HANK OETTINGER

" I can remember the first week of the CWA checks. It was on a Friday. That night everybody had gotten his check. The first check a lot of them had in three years. . . . I never saw such a change of attitude. Instead of walking around feeling dreary and looking sorrowful, everybody was joyous. Like a feast day. They were toasting each other. They had money in their pockets for the first time. "

—quoted in *Hard Times*

▲ The Civil Works Administration enabled these men to get jobs repairing typewriters and sewing machines.

Programs like the CWA raised the hopes of the American people and sparked great enthusiasm for the new president. To many Americans, it appeared as if the country had turned a corner and was beginning to emerge from the nightmare of the Great Depression.

Americans Get a New Deal

The 1932 presidential election showed that Americans were clearly ready for a change. Because of the depression, people were suffering from a lack of work, food, and hope.

ELECTING FRANKLIN DELANO ROOSEVELT Although the Republicans renominated President Hoover as their candidate, they recognized he had little chance of winning. Too many Americans blamed Hoover for doing too little about the depression and wanted a new president. The Democrats pinned their hopes on **Franklin Delano Roosevelt,** known popularly as FDR, the two-term governor of New York and a distant cousin of former president Theodore Roosevelt.

As governor, FDR had proved to be an effective, reform-minded leader, working to combat the problems of unemployment and poverty. Unlike Hoover, Roosevelt possessed a "can-do" attitude and projected an air of friendliness and confidence that attracted voters.

Indeed, Roosevelt won an overwhelming victory, capturing nearly 23 million votes to Hoover's nearly 16 million. In the Senate, Democrats claimed a nearly two-thirds majority. In the House, they won almost three-fourths of the seats, their greatest victory since before the Civil War.

WAITING FOR ROOSEVELT TO TAKE OVER Four months would elapse between Roosevelt's victory in the November election and his inauguration as president in March 1933. The 20th Amendment, which moved presidential inaugurations to January, was not ratified until February 1933 and did not apply to the 1932 election.

FDR was not idle during this waiting period, however. He worked with his team of carefully picked advisers—a select group of professors, lawyers, and journalists that came to be known as the "Brain Trust." Roosevelt began to formulate a set of policies for his new administration. This program, designed to alleviate the problems of the Great Depression, became known as the **New Deal,** a phrase taken from a campaign speech in which Roosevelt had promised "a new deal for the American people." New Deal policies focused on three general goals: relief for the needy, economic recovery, and financial reform. **Ⓐ**

MAIN IDEA

Summarizing

Ⓐ What plans did Roosevelt make in the four months while he waited to take office?

THE HUNDRED DAYS On taking office, the Roosevelt administration launched a period of intense activity known as the Hundred Days, lasting from March 9 to June 16, 1933. During this period, Congress passed more than 15 major pieces of New Deal legislation. These laws, and others that followed, significantly expanded the federal government's role in the nation's economy.

KEY PLAYERS

FRANKLIN D. ROOSEVELT
1882–1945

Born into an old, wealthy New York family, Franklin Delano Roosevelt entered politics as a state senator in 1910 and later became assistant secretary of the navy. In 1921, he was stricken with polio and became partially paralyzed from the waist down. He struggled to regain the use of his legs, and he eventually learned to stand with the help of leg braces.

Roosevelt became governor of New York in 1928, and because he "would not allow bodily disability to defeat his will," he went on to the White House in 1933. Always interested in people, Roosevelt gained greater compassion for others as a result of his own physical disability.

ELEANOR ROOSEVELT
1884–1962

A niece of Theodore Roosevelt and a distant cousin of her husband, Franklin, Eleanor Roosevelt lost her parents at an early age. She was raised by a strict grandmother.

As first lady, she often urged the president to take stands on controversial issues. A popular public speaker, Eleanor was particularly interested in child welfare, housing reform, and equal rights for women and minorities. In presenting a booklet on human rights to the United Nations in 1958, she said, "Where, after all, do human rights begin? . . . [In] the world of the individual person: the neighborhood . . . the school . . . the factory, farm or office where he works."

Roosevelt's first step as president was to carry out reforms in banking and finance. By 1933, widespread bank failures had caused most Americans to lose faith in the banking system. On March 5, one day after taking office, Roosevelt declared a bank holiday and closed all banks to prevent further withdrawals. He persuaded Congress to pass the Emergency Banking Relief Act, which authorized the Treasury Department to inspect the country's banks. Those that were sound could reopen at once; those that were insolvent—unable to pay their debts—would remain closed. Those that needed help could receive loans. This measure revived public confidence in banks, since customers now had greater faith that the open banks were in good financial shape.

AN IMPORTANT FIRESIDE CHAT On March 12, the day before the first banks were to reopen, President Roosevelt gave the first of his many fireside chats—radio talks about issues of public concern, explaining in clear, simple language his New Deal measures. These informal talks made Americans feel as if the president were talking directly to them. In his first chat, President Roosevelt explained why the nation's welfare depended on public support of the government and the banking system. "We have provided the machinery to restore our financial system," he said, "and it is up to you to support and make it work." He explained the banking system to listeners.

> *"The only thing we have to fear is fear itself."*
>
> **FRANKLIN DELANO ROOSEVELT**

A PERSONAL VOICE FRANKLIN DELANO ROOSEVELT

" When you deposit money in a bank the bank does not put the money into a safe deposit vault. It invests your money. . . . A comparatively small part of the money that you put into the bank is kept in currency—an amount which in normal times is wholly sufficient to cover the cash needs of the average citizen."

The president then explained that when too many people demanded their savings in cash, banks would fail. This was not because banks were weak but because even strong banks could not meet such heavy demands. Over the next few weeks, many Americans returned their savings to banks. **B**

REGULATING BANKING AND FINANCE Congress took another step to reorganize the banking system by passing the **Glass-Steagall Act** of 1933, which established the Federal Deposit Insurance Corporation (FDIC). The FDIC provided federal insurance for individual bank accounts of up to $5,000, reassuring millions of bank customers that their money was safe. It also required banks to act cautiously with their customers' money.

Congress and the president also worked to regulate the stock market, in which people had lost faith because of the crash of 1929. The **Federal Securities Act,** passed in May 1933, required corporations to provide complete information on all stock offerings and made them liable for any misrepresentations. In June of 1934, Congress created the Securities and Exchange Commission (SEC) to regulate the stock market. One goal of this commission was to prevent people with inside information about companies from "rigging" the stock market for their own profit.

In addition, Roosevelt persuaded Congress to approve a bill allowing the manufacture and sale of some alcoholic beverages. The bill's main purpose was to raise government revenues by taxing alcohol. By the end of 1933, the passage of the 21st Amendment had repealed prohibition altogether.

MAIN IDEA

Evaluating Leadership
B How successful was FDR's fireside chat?

Franklin D. Roosevelt holds his dog Fala and talks to a young family friend.

Helping the American People

While working on banking and financial matters, the Roosevelt administration also implemented programs to provide relief to farmers, perhaps the hardest hit by the depression. It also aided other workers and attempted to stimulate economic recovery.

RURAL ASSISTANCE The **Agricultural Adjustment Act (AAA)** sought to raise crop prices by lowering production, which the government achieved by paying farmers to leave a certain amount of every acre of land unseeded. The theory was that reduced supply would boost prices. In some cases, crops were too far advanced for the acreage reduction to take effect. As a result, the government paid cotton growers $200 million to plow under 10 million acres of their crop. It also paid hog farmers to slaughter 6 million pigs. This policy upset many Americans, who protested the destruction of food when many people were going hungry. It did, however, help raise farm prices and put more money in farmers' pockets.

An especially ambitious program of regional development was the Tennessee Valley Authority (TVA), established on May 18, 1933. (See Geography Spotlight on page 726.) Focusing on the badly depressed Tennessee River Valley, the TVA renovated five existing dams and constructed 20 new ones, created thousands of jobs, and provided flood control, hydroelectric power, and other benefits to an impoverished region.

PROVIDING WORK PROJECTS The administration also established programs to provide relief through work projects and cash payments. One important program, the **Civilian Conservation Corps (CCC),** put young men aged 18 to 25 to work building roads, developing parks, planting trees, and helping in soil-erosion and flood-control projects. By the time the program ended in 1942, almost 3 million young men had passed through the CCC. The CCC paid a small wage, $30 a month, of which $25 was automatically sent home to the worker's family. It also supplied free food and uniforms and lodging in work camps. Many of the camps were located on the Great Plains, where, within a period of eight years, the men of the CCC planted more than 200 million trees. This tremendous reforestation program was aimed at preventing another Dust Bowl.

The Public Works Administration (PWA), created in June 1933 as part of the **National Industrial Recovery Act (NIRA),** provided money to states to create jobs chiefly in the construction of schools and other community buildings. When these programs failed to make a sufficient dent in unemployment, President Roosevelt established the Civil Works Administration in November 1933. It provided 4 million immediate jobs during the winter of 1933–1934. Although some critics of the CWA claimed that the programs were "make-work" projects and a waste of money, the CWA built 40,000 schools and paid the salaries of more than 50,000 schoolteachers in America's rural areas. It also built more than half a million miles of roads. **C**

> **MAIN IDEA**
>
> **Analyzing Effects**
> **C** How did New Deal programs affect various regions of the United States?

Civilian Conservation Corps

- The CCC provided almost 3 million men aged 18–25 with work and wages between 1933 and 1942.

- The men lived in work camps under a strict regime. The majority of the camps were racially segregated.

- By 1938, the CCC had an 11 percent African-American enrollment.

- Accomplishments of the CCC include planting over 3 billion trees, developing over 800 state parks, and building more than 46,000 bridges.

The New Deal **697**

PROMOTING FAIR PRACTICES The NIRA also sought to promote industrial growth by establishing codes of fair practice for individual industries. It created the National Recovery Administration (NRA), which set prices of many products and established standards. The aim of the NRA was to promote recovery by interrupting the trend of wage cuts, falling prices, and layoffs. The economist Gardiner C. Means attempted to justify the NRA by stating the goal of industrial planning.

★ **A PERSONAL VOICE** GARDINER C. MEANS

"**The National Recovery Administration [was] created in response to an overwhelming demand from many quarters that certain elements in the making of industrial policy . . . should no longer be left to the market place and the price mechanism but should be placed in the hands of administrative bodies.**"

—*The Making of Industrial Policy*

The codes of fair practice had been drafted in joint meetings of businesses and representatives of workers and consumers. These codes both limited production and established prices. Because businesses were given new concessions, workers made demands. Congress met their demands by passing a section of the NIRA guaranteeing workers' right to unionize and to bargain collectively. **D**

Many businesses and politicians were critical of the NRA. Charges arose that the codes served large business interests. There were also charges of increasing code violations.

FOOD, CLOTHING, AND SHELTER A number of New Deal programs concerned housing and home mortgage problems. The Home Owners Loan Corporation (HOLC) provided government loans to homeowners who faced foreclosure because they couldn't meet their loan payments. In addition, the 1934 National Housing Act created the Federal Housing Administration (FHA). This agency continues to furnish loans for home mortgages and repairs today.

Another program, the Federal Emergency Relief Administration (FERA), was funded with $500 million to provide direct relief for the needy. Half of the money was given to the states as direct grants-in-aid to help furnish food and clothing to the unemployed, the aged, and the ill. The rest was distributed to states to support work relief programs—for every $3 within the state program, FERA donated $1. Harry Hopkins, who headed this program, believed that, whereas money helped people buy food, it was meaningful work that enabled them to gain confidence and self-respect.

The New Deal Comes Under Attack

By the end of the Hundred Days, millions of Americans had benefited from the New Deal programs. As well, the public's confidence in the nation's future had rebounded. Although President Roosevelt agreed to a policy of **deficit spending**— spending more money than the government receives in revenue—he did so with great reluctance. He regarded deficit spending as a necessary evil to be used only at a time of great economic crisis. Nevertheless, the New Deal did not end the depression, and opposition grew among some parts of the population.

ECONOMIC BACKGROUND

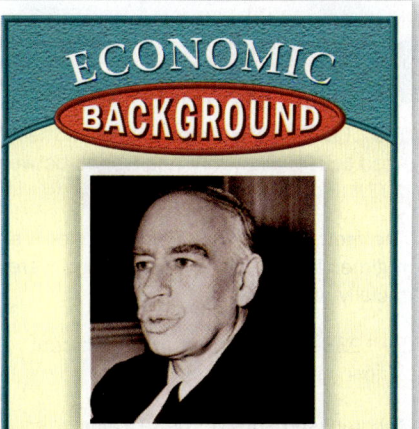

DEFICIT SPENDING
John Maynard Keynes, an influential British economist, promoted the idea of deficit spending to stimulate economic recovery. In his view, a country should spend its way out of a depression by putting money into the hands of consumers. This would make it possible for them to buy goods and services and thus fuel economic growth. Therefore, even if a government has to go deeply into debt, it should spend great amounts of money to help get the economy growing again. When the Great Depression began, many considered Keynes's ideas to be revolutionary.

CHANGING COURSE

With hopes of lessening opposition to his programs, Roosevelt proposed a court reform bill that would essentially have allowed him to "pack" the Court with judges supportive of the New Deal. This cartoon shows Roosevelt as a sea captain ordering a shocked Congress to change course.

SKILLBUILDER Analyzing Political Cartoons

1. What "compass" did Roosevelt want to change? Explain.
2. How does the cartoonist portray FDR's attitude regarding his power as president?

 SEE SKILLBUILDER HANDBOOK, PAGE R24.

THAT COMPASS DOESN'T POINT THE WAY I WANT TO GO. CHANGE IT. NOW!

MAIN IDEA

Contrasting

Ⓔ How did liberal and conservative critics differ in their opposition to the New Deal?

Liberal critics argued that the New Deal did not go far enough to help the poor and to reform the nation's economic system. Conservative critics argued that Roosevelt spent too much on direct relief and used New Deal policies to control business and socialize the economy. Conservatives were particularly angered by laws such as the Agricultural Adjustment Act and the National Industrial Recovery Act, which they believed gave the federal government too much control over agriculture and industry. Many critics believed the New Deal interfered with the workings of a free-market economy. Ⓔ

THE SUPREME COURT REACTS By the mid-1930s, conservative opposition to the New Deal had received a boost from two Supreme Court decisions. In *Schechter Poultry Corporation* v. *United States* (1935), the Court struck down the NIRA as unconstitutional. It declared that the law gave legislative powers to the executive branch and that the enforcement of industry codes within states went beyond the federal government's constitutional powers to regulate interstate commerce. The next year, the Supreme Court struck down the AAA on the grounds that agriculture is a local matter and should be regulated by the states, not the federal government.

Fearing that further Court decisions might dismantle the New Deal, President Roosevelt proposed in February 1937 that Congress enact a court-reform bill to reorganize the federal judiciary and allow him to appoint six new Supreme Court justices. This "Court-packing bill" aroused a storm of protest in Congress and the press. Many people believed that the president was violating principles of judicial independence and the separation of powers. As it turned out, the president got his way without reorganizing the judiciary. In 1937, an elderly justice retired, and Roosevelt appointed the liberal Hugo S. Black, shifting the balance of the Court. Rulings of the Court began to favor the New Deal. (See *NLRB* v. *Jones and Laughlin Steel Corp.* on page 708.) Over the next four years, because of further resignations, Roosevelt was able to appoint seven new justices.

THREE FIERY CRITICS In 1934, some of the strongest conservative opponents of the New Deal banded together to form an organization called the American Liberty League. The American Liberty League opposed New Deal measures that it believed violated respect for the rights of individuals and property. Three of the toughest critics the president faced, however, were three men who expressed views that appealed to poor Americans: Charles Coughlin, Dr. Francis Townsend, and Huey Long.

Father Charles Coughlin speaks to a radio audience in 1935. ▼

Every Sunday, Father Charles Coughlin, a Roman Catholic priest from a suburb of Detroit, broadcast radio sermons that combined economic, political, and religious ideas. Initially a supporter of the New Deal, Coughlin soon turned against Roosevelt. He favored a guaranteed annual income and the nationalization of banks. At the height of his popularity, Father Coughlin claimed a radio audience of as many as 40–45 million people, but his increasingly anti-Semitic (anti-Jewish) views eventually cost him support.

Vocabulary
nationalization: conversion from private to governmental ownership

Another critic of New Deal policies was Dr. Francis Townsend, a physician and health officer in Long Beach, California. He believed that Roosevelt wasn't doing enough to help the poor and elderly, so he devised a pension plan that would provide monthly benefits to the aged. The plan found strong backing among the elderly, thus undermining their support for Roosevelt.

Perhaps the most serious challenge to the New Deal came from Senator **Huey Long** of Louisiana. Like Coughlin, Long was an early supporter of the New Deal, but he, too, turned against Roosevelt. Eager to win the presidency for himself, Long proposed a nationwide social program called Share-Our-Wealth. Under the banner "Every Man a King," he promised something for everyone.

Huey Long

★ A PERSONAL VOICE HUEY LONG

"We owe debts in America today, public and private, amounting to $252 billion. That means that every child is born with a $2,000 debt tied around his neck. . . . We propose that children shall be born in a land of opportunity, guaranteed a home, food, clothes, and the other things that make for living, including the right to education."

—*Record*, 74 Congress, Session 1

Long's program was so popular that by 1935 he boasted of having perhaps as many as 27,000 Share-Our-Wealth clubs and 7.5 million members. That same year, however, at the height of his popularity, Long was assassinated by a lone gunman.

As the initial impetus of the New Deal began to wane, President Roosevelt started to look ahead. He knew that much more needed to be done to help the people and to solve the nation's economic problems.

ASSESSMENT

1. **TERMS & NAMES** For each of the terms and names below, write a sentence explaining its significance.

- Franklin Delano Roosevelt
- New Deal
- Glass-Steagall Act
- Federal Securities Act
- Agricultural Adjustment Act (AAA)
- Civilian Conservation Corps (CCC)
- National Industrial Recovery Act (NIRA)
- deficit spending
- Huey Long

MAIN IDEA

2. **TAKING NOTES**
In a two-column chart, list problems that President Roosevelt confronted and how he tried to solve them.

Problems		Solutions

Write a paragraph telling which solution had the greatest impact, and why.

CRITICAL THINKING

3. **EVALUATING**
Of the New Deal programs discussed in this section, which do you consider the most important? Explain your choice. **Think About:**
- the type of assistance offered by each program
- the scope of each program
- the impact of each program

4. **EVALUATING LEADERSHIP**
Do you think Roosevelt was wrong to try to "pack" the Supreme Court with those in favor of the New Deal? Explain your answer.

5. **DEVELOPING HISTORICAL PERSPECTIVE**
The New Deal has often been referred to as a turning point in American history. Cite examples to explain why.

PI 1.2
PI 2.4

CC Unit 5.II.B.1.c   CC Unit 5.II.B.2.c
CC Unit 5.II.B.3.c   CC Unit 5.II.B.3.d(1)
CC Unit 5.II.B.5.b   CC Unit 5.II.B.6.b

The Second New Deal Takes Hold

MAIN IDEA	WHY IT MATTERS NOW	Terms & Names
The Second New Deal included new programs to extend federal aid and stimulate the nation's economy.	Second New Deal programs continue to assist homebuyers, farmers, workers, and the elderly in the 2000s.	• Eleanor Roosevelt • Works Progress Administration (WPA) • National Youth Administration • Wagner Act • Social Security Act

One American's Story

hmhsocialstudies.com
TAKING NOTES

Use the graphic organizer online to take notes on groups helped by the Second New Deal.

Dorothea Lange was a photographer who documented American life during the Great Depression and the era of the New Deal. Lange spent considerable time getting to know her subjects—destitute migrant workers—before she and her assistant set up their cameras.

A PERSONAL VOICE DOROTHEA LANGE

" So often it's just sticking around and remaining there, not swooping in and swooping out in a cloud of dust. . . . We found our way in . . . not too far away from the people we were working with. . . . The people who are garrulous and wear their heart on their sleeve and tell you everything, that's one kind of person. But the fellow who's hiding behind a tree and hoping you don't see him, is the fellow that you'd better find out why. "

—quoted in *Restless Spirit: The Life and Work of Dorothea Lange*

▲ Dorothea Lange taking photographs on the Texas plains in 1934.

Lange also believed that her distinct limp, the result of a childhood case of polio, worked to her advantage. Seeing that Lange, too, had suffered, people were kind to her and more at ease.

Much of Lange's work was funded by federal agencies, such as the Farm Security Administration, which was established to alleviate rural poverty. Her photographs of migrant workers helped draw attention to the desperate conditions in rural America and helped to underscore the need for direct relief.

The Second Hundred Days

By 1935, the Roosevelt administration was seeking ways to build on the programs established during the Hundred Days. Although the economy had improved during FDR's first two years in office, the gains were not as great as he had expected. Unemployment remained high despite government work programs, and production still lagged behind the levels of the 1920s.

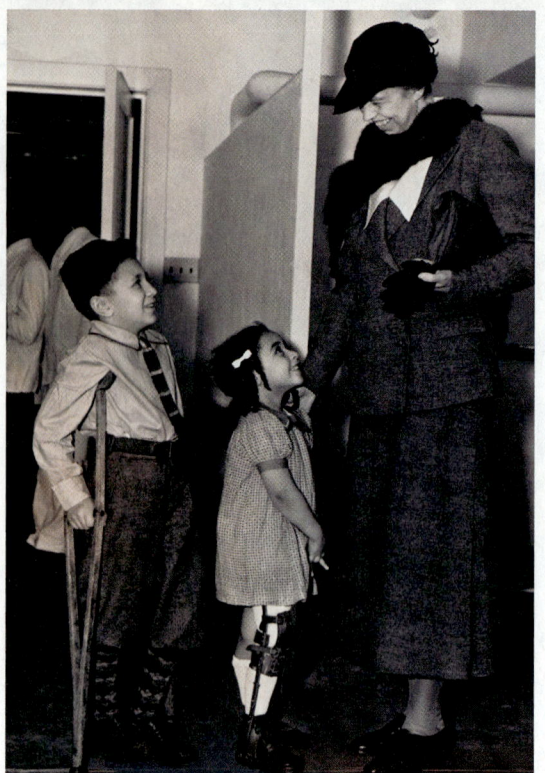

Eleanor Roosevelt visits a children's hospital in 1937.

Nevertheless, the New Deal enjoyed widespread popularity, and President Roosevelt launched a second burst of activity, often called the Second New Deal or the Second Hundred Days. During this phase, the president called on Congress to provide more extensive relief for both farmers and workers.

The president was prodded in this direction by his wife, **Eleanor Roosevelt,** a social reformer who combined her deep humanitarian impulses with great political skills. Eleanor Roosevelt traveled the country, observing social conditions and reminding the president about the suffering of the nation's people. She also urged him to appoint women to government positions. Ⓐ

REELECTING FDR The Second New Deal was under way by the time of the 1936 presidential election. The Republicans nominated Alfred Landon, the governor of Kansas, while the Democrats, of course, nominated President Roosevelt for a second term. The election resulted in an overwhelming victory for the Democrats, who won the presidency and large majorities in both houses. The election marked the first time that most African Americans had voted Democratic rather than Republican, and the first time that labor unions gave united support to a presidential candidate. The 1936 election was a vote of confidence in FDR and the New Deal.

MAIN IDEA

Summarizing
Ⓐ Why did Roosevelt launch the Second Hundred Days?

Helping Farmers

In the mid-1930s, two of every five farms in the United States were mortgaged, and thousands of small farmers lost their farms. The novelist John Steinbeck described the experience of one tenant farmer and his family.

A poster promotes the movie adaption of John Steinbeck's novel *The Grapes of Wrath.*

A PERSONAL VOICE JOHN STEINBECK

" Across the dooryard the tractor cut, and the hard, foot-beaten ground was seeded field, and the tractor cut through again; the uncut space was ten feet wide. And back he came. The iron guard bit into the house-corner, crumbled the wall, and wrenched the little house from its foundation so that it fell sideways, crushed like a bug. . . . The tractor cut a straight line on, and the air and the ground vibrated with its thunder. The tenant man stared after it, his rifle in his hand. His wife was beside him, and the quiet children behind. And all of them stared after the tractor. "

—*The Grapes of Wrath*

FOCUSING ON FARMS When the Supreme Court struck down the AAA early in 1936, Congress passed another law to replace it: the Soil Conservation and Domestic Allotment Act. This act paid farmers for cutting production of soil-depleting crops and rewarded farmers for practicing good soil conservation methods. Two years later, in 1938, Congress approved a second Agricultural Adjustment Act that brought back many features of the first AAA. The second AAA did not include a processing tax to pay for farm subsidies, a provision of the first AAA that the Supreme Court had declared unconstitutional.

"MIGRANT MOTHER" (1936), DOROTHEA LANGE

In February 1936, Dorothea Lange visited a camp in Nipomo, California, where some 2,500 destitute pea pickers lived in tents or, like this mother of seven children, in lean-tos. Lange talked briefly to the woman and then took five pictures, successively moving closer to her subjects and directing more emphasis on the mother. The last photo, "Migrant Mother" (at right), was published in the *San Francisco News* March 10, 1936.

▶ "Migrant Mother" became one of the most recognizable symbols of the Depression and perhaps the strongest argument in support of New Deal relief programs. Roy Stryker, who hired Lange to document the harsh living conditions of the time, described the mother: "She has all the suffering of mankind in her, but all the perseverance too. A restraint and a strange courage."

◀ Lange reflected upon her assignment. "I saw and approached the hungry and desperate mother, as if drawn by a magnet. . . . She said that they had been living on frozen vegetables from the surrounding fields, and birds that the children killed. She had just sold the tires from her car to buy food."

SKILLBUILDER Interpreting Visual Sources
1. What might the woman be thinking about? Why do you think so?
2. Why do you think "Migrant Mother" was effective in persuading people to support FDR's relief programs?

 SEE SKILLBUILDER HANDBOOK, PAGE R23.

The Second New Deal also attempted to help sharecroppers, migrant workers, and many other poor farmers. The Resettlement Administration, created by executive order in 1935, provided monetary loans to small farmers to buy land. In 1937, the agency was replaced by the Farm Security Administration (FSA), which loaned more than $1 billion to help tenant farmers become landholders and established camps for migrant farm workers, who had traditionally lived in squalid housing.

The FSA hired photographers such as Dorothea Lange, Ben Shahn, Walker Evans, Arthur Rothstein, and Carl Mydans to take many pictures of rural towns and farms and their inhabitants. The agency used their photographs to create a pictorial record of the difficult situation in rural America.

Roosevelt Extends Relief

As part of the Second New Deal, the Roosevelt administration and Congress set up a series of programs to help youths, professionals, and other workers. One of the largest was the **Works Progress Administration (WPA),** headed by Harry Hopkins, the former chief of the Federal Emergency Relief Administration.

The WPA set out to create as many jobs as possible as quickly as possible. Between 1935 and 1943, it spent $11 billion to give jobs to more than 8 million workers, most of them unskilled. These workers built 850 airports throughout the country, constructed or repaired 651,000 miles of roads and streets, and put up more than 125,000 public buildings. Women workers in sewing groups made 300 million garments for the needy. Although criticized by some as a make-work project, the WPA produced public works of lasting value to the nation and gave working people a sense of hope and purpose. As one man recalled, "It was really great. You worked, you got a paycheck and you had some dignity. Even when a man raked leaves, he got paid, he had some dignity."

In addition, the WPA employed many professionals who wrote guides to cities, collected historical slave narratives, painted murals on the walls of schools

This photograph by Margaret Bourke-White shows people waiting for food in a Kentucky bread line in 1937.

WORLD'S HIGHEST STANDARD OF LIVING

There's no way like the American Way

and other public buildings, and performed in theater troupes around the country. At the urging of Eleanor Roosevelt, the WPA made special efforts to help women, minorities, and young people. **B**

Another program, the **National Youth Administration** (NYA), was created specifically to provide education, jobs, counseling, and recreation for young people. The NYA provided student aid to high school, college, and graduate students. In exchange, students worked in part-time positions at their schools. One participant later described her experience.

MAIN IDEA

Evaluating
B Do you think work programs like the WPA were a valid use of federal money? Why or why not?

★ **A PERSONAL VOICE** HELEN FARMER

" I lugged . . . drafts and reams of paper home, night after night. . . . Sometimes I typed almost all night and had to deliver it to school the next morning. . . . This was a good program. It got necessary work done. It gave teenagers a chance to work for pay. Mine bought me clothes and shoes, school supplies, some movies and mad money. Candy bars, and big pickles out of a barrel. It gave my mother relief from my necessary demands for money. "

—quoted in *The Great Depression*

The NYA helped young people, such as this dental assistant (*third from left*), receive training and job opportunities.

For graduates unable to find jobs, or youth who had dropped out of school, the NYA provided part-time jobs, such as working on highways, parks, and the grounds of public buildings.

Improving Labor and Other Reforms

In a speech to Congress in January 1935, the president declared, "When a man is convalescing from an illness, wisdom dictates not only cure of the symptoms but also removal of their cause." During the Second New Deal, Roosevelt, with the help of Congress, brought about important reforms in the areas of labor relations and economic security for retired workers. (See the chart on page 706.)

IMPROVING LABOR CONDITIONS In 1935, the Supreme Court declared the NIRA unconstitutional, citing that the federal government had violated legislative authority reserved for individual states. One of the first reforms of the Second New Deal was passage of the National Labor Relations Act. More commonly called the **Wagner Act,** after its sponsor, Senator Robert F. Wagner of New York, the act reestablished the NIRA provision of collective bargaining. The federal government again protected the right of workers to join unions and engage in collective bargaining with employers.

The Wagner Act also prohibited unfair labor practices such as threatening workers, firing union members, and interfering with union organizing. The act set up the National Labor Relations Board (NLRB) to hear testimony about unfair practices and to hold elections to find out if workers wanted union representation. **C**

In 1938, Congress passed the Fair Labor Standards Act, which set maximum hours at 44 hours per week, decreasing to 40 hours after two years. It also set minimum wages at 25 cents an hour, increasing to 40 cents an hour by 1945. In addition, the act set rules for the employment of workers under 16 and banned hazardous work for those under 18.

MAIN IDEA

Analyzing Issues
C Why was the Wagner Act significant?

New Deal Programs

EMPLOYMENT PROJECTS

		PURPOSE
1933	Civilian Conservation Corps (CCC)	Provided jobs for single males on conservation projects.
1933	Federal Emergency Relief Administration (FERA)	Helped states to provide aid for the unemployed.
1933	Public Works Administration (PWA)	Created jobs on government projects.
1933	Civil Works Administration (CWA)	Provided work in federal jobs.
1935	Works Progress Administration (WPA)	Quickly created as many jobs as possible—from construction jobs to positions in symphony orchestras.
1935	National Youth Administration (NYA)	Provided job training for unemployed young people and part-time jobs for needy students.

BUSINESS ASSISTANCE AND REFORM

1933	Emergency Banking Relief Act (EBRA)	Banks were inspected by Treasury Department and those stable could reopen.
1933	Federal Deposit Insurance Corporation (FDIC)	Protected bank deposits up to $5,000. (Today, accounts are protected up to $250,000.)
1933	National Recovery Administration (NRA)	Established codes of fair competition.
1934	Securities and Exchange Commission (SEC)	Supervised the stock market and eliminated dishonest practices.
1935	Banking Act of 1935	Created seven-member board to regulate the nation's money supply and the interest rates on loans.
1938	Food, Drug and Cosmetic Act (FDC)	Required manufacturers to list ingredients in foods, drugs, and cosmetic products.

FARM RELIEF AND RURAL DEVELOPMENT

1933	Agricultural Adjustment Administration (AAA)	Aided farmers and regulated crop production.
1933	Tennessee Valley Authority (TVA)	Developed the resources of the Tennessee Valley.
1935	Rural Electrification Administration (REA)	Provided affordable electricity for isolated rural areas.

HOUSING

1933	Home Owners Loan Corporation (HOLC)	Loaned money at low interest to homeowners who could not meet mortgage payments.
1934	Federal Housing Administration (FHA)	Insured loans for building and repairing homes.
1937	United States Housing Authority (USHA)	Provided federal loans for low-cost public housing.

LABOR RELATIONS

1935	National Labor Relations Board (Wagner Act)	Defined unfair labor practices and established the National Labor Relations Board (NLRB) to settle disputes between employers and employees.
1938	Fair Labor Standards Act	Established a minimum hourly wage and a maximum number of hours in the workweek for the entire country. Set rules for the employment of workers under 16 and banned hazardous factory work for those under 18.

RETIREMENT

1935	Social Security Administration	Provided a pension for retired workers and their spouses and aided people with disabilities.

THE SOCIAL SECURITY ACT One of the most important achievements of the New Deal was creating the Social Security system. The **Social Security Act,** passed in 1935, was created by a committee chaired by Secretary of Labor Frances Perkins. The act had three major parts:

- *Old-age insurance for retirees 65 or older and their spouses.* The insurance was a supplemental retirement plan. Half of the funds came from the worker and half from the employer. Although some groups were excluded from the system, it helped to make retirement comfortable for millions of people.

- *Unemployment compensation system.* The unemployment system was funded by a federal tax on employers. It was administered at the state level. The initial payments ranged from $15 to $18 per week.

- *Aid to families with dependent children and people with disabilities.* The aid was paid for by federal funds made available to the states.

MAIN IDEA

Drawing Conclusions

D Whom did Social Security help?

Although the Social Security Act was not a total pension system or a complete welfare system, it did provide substantial benefits to millions of Americans. **D**

EXPANDING AND REGULATING UTILITIES The Second New Deal also included laws to promote rural electrification and to regulate public utilities. In 1935, only 12.6 percent of American farms had electricity. Roosevelt established under executive order the Rural Electrification Administration (REA), which financed and worked with electrical cooperatives to bring electricity to isolated areas. By 1945, 48 percent of America's farms and rural homes had electricity. That figure rose to 90 percent by 1949.

The Public Utility Holding Company Act of 1935 took aim at financial corruption in the public utility industry. It outlawed the ownership of utilities by multiple holding companies—a practice known as the pyramiding of holding companies. Lobbyists for the holding companies fought the law fiercely, and it proved extremely difficult to enforce.

As the New Deal struggled to help farmers and other workers overcome the Great Depression, it assisted many different groups in the nation, including women, African Americans, and Native Americans.

SECTION 2 ASSESSMENT

1. TERMS & NAMES For each term or name, write a sentence explaining its significance.

- **Eleanor Roosevelt**
- **Works Progress Administration (WPA)**
- **National Youth Administration**
- **Wagner Act**
- **Social Security Act**

MAIN IDEA

2. TAKING NOTES
Create a chart similar to the one below to show how groups such as farmers, the unemployed, youth, and retirees were helped by Second New Deal programs.

Second New Deal	
Group	How Helped

Which group do you think benefited the most from the Second New Deal? Explain.

CRITICAL THINKING

3. EVALUATING DECISIONS
Why might the Social Security Act be considered the most important achievement of the New Deal?
Think About:
- the types of relief needed in the 1930s
- alternatives to government assistance to the elderly, the unemployed, and people with disabilities
- the scope of the act

4. INTERPRETING VISUAL SOURCES
Many WPA posters were created to promote New Deal programs—in this case the Rural Electrification Administration. How does this poster's simplistic design convey the program's goal?

NLRB v. JONES AND LAUGHLIN STEEL CORP. (1937)

ORIGINS OF THE CASE In 1936, the Jones and Laughlin Steel Corporation was charged with intimidating union organizers and firing several union members. The National Labor Relations Board (NLRB) found the company guilty of "unfair labor practices" and ordered it to rehire the workers with back pay.

THE RULING The Supreme Court ruled that Congress had the power to regulate labor relations and confirmed the authority of the NLRB.

LEGAL REASONING

In the 1935 National Labor Relations Act, or Wagner Act, Congress claimed that its authority to regulate labor relations came from the commerce clause of the Constitution. Jones and Laughlin Steel argued that its manufacturing business did not involve interstate commerce—it operated a plant and hired people locally.

The Court disagreed. Although production itself may occur within one state, it said, production is a part of the interstate "flow of commerce." If labor unrest at a steel mill would create "burdens and obstructions" to interstate commerce, then Congress has the power to prevent labor unrest at the steel mill.

The Court also explained that the act went "no further than to safeguard the right of employees to self-organization and to select representatives . . . for collective bargaining." Departing from earlier decisions, the Court affirmed that these are "fundamental" rights.

"**Long ago we . . . said . . . that a single employee was helpless in dealing with an employer; that he was dependent . . . on his daily wage for the maintenance of himself and family; that, if the employer refused to pay him the wages that he thought fair, he was . . . unable to leave the employ and resist arbitrary and unfair treatment; that union was essential to give laborers opportunity to deal on an equality with their employer.**"

As a result, the Wagner Act was allowed to stand.

Chief Justice Charles ▶ Evans Hughes

LEGAL SOURCES

LEGISLATION

U.S. CONSTITUTION, ARTICLE 1, SECTION 8 (COMMERCE CLAUSE)
"The Congress shall have Power . . . To regulate Commerce with foreign Nations and among the several States."

NATIONAL LABOR RELATIONS ACT (1935)
"The term 'affecting commerce' means . . . tending to lead to a labor dispute burdening or obstructing commerce or the free flow of commerce."

"It shall be an unfair labor practice for an employer . . . to interfere with, restrain, or coerce employees in the exercise of the rights [to organize unions]."

RELATED CASES

SCHECHTER POULTRY CORP. v. UNITED STATES (1935)
The Court struck down the National Industrial Recovery Act, a key piece of New Deal legislation.

◄ Choosing to work despite the strike, a storekeeper at the Jones and Laughlin Steel Corporation tries to pass through picket lines.

WHY IT MATTERED

The 1935 Wagner Act was one of the most important pieces of New Deal legislation. Conservative justices on the Supreme Court, however, thought New Deal legislation increased the power of the federal government beyond what the Constitution allowed. By the time the Jones and Laughlin case reached the Court in 1937, the Court had already struck down numerous New Deal laws. It appeared to many as if the Wagner Act was doomed.

In February 1937, Roosevelt announced a plan to appoint enough justices to build a Court majority in favor of the New Deal. Critics immediately accused Roosevelt of trying to pack the Supreme Court, thus crippling the Constitution's system of checks and balances.

Two months later, the Court delivered its opinion in *Jones and Laughlin* and at about the same time upheld other New Deal legislation as well. Most historians agree that the Court's switch was not a response to Roosevelt's "Court-packing" plan, which already seemed destined for failure. Nevertheless, the decision resolved a potential crisis.

HISTORICAL IMPACT

The protection that labor unions gained by the Wagner Act helped them to grow quickly. Union membership among non-farm workers grew from around 12 percent in 1930 to around 31 percent by 1950. This increase helped improve the economic standing of many working-class Americans in the years following World War II.

Most significantly, *Jones and Laughlin* greatly broadened Congress's power. Previously, neither the federal nor the state governments were thought to have sufficient power to control the large corporations and holding companies doing business in many states. Now, far beyond the power to regulate interstate commerce, Congress had the power to regulate anything "essential or appropriate" to that function. For example, federal laws barring discrimination in hotels and restaurants rest on the Court's allowing Congress to decide what is an "essential or appropriate" subject of regulation.

More recently, the Court has placed tighter limits on Congress's power to regulate interstate commerce. In *United States* v. *Lopez* (1995), the Court struck down a law that banned people from having handguns near a school. The Court said Congress was not justified in basing this law on its power to regulate interstate commerce.

THINKING CRITICALLY

CONNECT TO HISTORY

1. **Developing Historical Perspective** Lawyers for Jones and Laughlin said that the Wagner Act violated the Tenth Amendment. Chief Justice Hughes said that since the act fell within the scope of the commerce clause, the Tenth Amendment did not apply. Read the Tenth Amendment and then write a paragraph defending Hughes's position.

 SEE SKILLBUILDER HANDBOOK, PAGE R11.

CONNECT TO TODAY

2. Visit the links for Historic Decisions of the Supreme Court and read the opening sections of *United States* v. *Lopez*. There, Chief Justice Rehnquist offers a summary of the Court's interpretation of the commerce clause over the years. Summarize in your own words Rehnquist's description of the current meaning of the commerce clause.

 hmhsocialstudies.com   INTERNET ACTIVITY

The New Deal Affects Many Groups

MAIN IDEA	WHY IT MATTERS NOW	Terms & Names
New Deal policies and actions affected various social and ethnic groups.	The New Deal made a lasting impact on increasing the government's role in the struggle for equal rights.	• Frances Perkins • Mary McLeod Bethune • John Collier • New Deal coalition ・Congress of Industrial Organizations (CIO)

One American's Story

Pedro J. González came to this country from Mexico in the early 1920s and later became a United States citizen. As the first Spanish-language disc jockey in Los Angeles, González used his radio program to condemn discrimination against Mexicans and Mexican Americans, who were often made scapegoats for social and economic problems during the Depression. For his efforts, González was arrested, jailed, and deported on trumped-up charges. Later in life, he reflected on his experiences.

★ A PERSONAL VOICE PEDRO J. GONZÁLEZ

" Seeing how badly they treated Mexicans back in the days of my youth I could have started a rebellion. But now there could be a cultural understanding so that without firing one bullet, we might understand each other. We [Mexicans] were here before they [Anglos] were, and we are not, as they still say, 'undesirables' or 'wetbacks.' They say we come to this land and it's not our home. Actually, it's the other way around. "

—quoted in the *Los Angeles Times*, December 9, 1984

Pedro J. González became a hero to many Mexican Americans and a symbol of Mexican cultural pride. His life reflected some of the difficulties faced by Mexicans and other minority groups in the United States during the New Deal era.

The New Deal Brings New Opportunities

In some ways, the New Deal represented an important opportunity for minorities and women, but what these groups gained was limited. Long-standing patterns of prejudice and discrimination continued to plague them and to prevent their full and equal participation in national life.

WOMEN MAKE THEIR MARK One of the most notable changes during the New Deal was the naming of several women to important government positions. **Frances Perkins** became America's first female cabinet member. As secretary of labor, she played a major role in creating the Social Security system and supervised labor legislation. President Roosevelt, encouraged by his wife Eleanor and seeking the support of women voters, also appointed two female diplomats and a female federal judge.

However, women continued to face discrimination in the workplace from male workers who believed that working women took jobs away from men. A Gallup poll taken in 1936 reported that 82 percent of Americans said that a wife should not work if her husband had a job.

Additionally, New Deal laws yielded mixed results. The National Recovery Administration, for example, set wage codes, some of which set lower minimum wages for women. The Federal Emergency Relief Administration and the Civil Works Administration hired far fewer women than men, and the Civilian Conservation Corps hired only men.

In spite of these barriers, women continued their movement into the workplace. Although the overall percentage of women working for wages increased only slightly during the 1930s, the percentage of married women in the workplace grew from 11.7 percent in 1930 to 15.6 percent in 1940. In short, widespread criticism of working women did not halt the long-term trend of women working outside the home.

African-American Activism

The 1930s witnessed a growth of activism by African Americans. One notable figure was A. Philip Randolph, who organized the country's first all-black trade union, the Brotherhood of Sleeping Car Porters. His work and that of others laid the groundwork for what would become the civil rights movement.

AFRICAN AMERICANS TAKE LEADERSHIP ROLES During the New Deal, Roosevelt appointed more than 100 African Americans to key positions in the government. **Mary McLeod Bethune**—an educator who dedicated herself to promoting opportunities for young African Americans—was one such appointee. Hired by the president to head the Division of Negro Affairs of the National Youth Administration, Bethune worked to ensure that the NYA hired African-American administrators and provided job training and other benefits to minority students.

Bethune also helped organize a "Black Cabinet" of influential African Americans to advise the Roosevelt administration on racial issues. Among these figures were William H. Hastie and Robert C. Weaver, both appointees to Roosevelt's Department of Interior. Never before had so many African Americans had a voice in the White House. **Ⓐ**

Eleanor Roosevelt played a key role in opening doors for African Americans in government. She was also instrumental in bringing about one of the most dramatic cultural events of the

◀ Mary McLeod Bethune, a close friend of Eleanor Roosevelt, was a strong supporter of the New Deal.

period: a performance by the African-American singer Marian Anderson in 1939. When the Daughters of the American Revolution chose not to allow Anderson to perform in their concert hall in Washington, D.C., because of her race, Eleanor Roosevelt resigned from the organization. She then arranged for Anderson to perform at the Lincoln Memorial on Easter Sunday. At the concert, Walter White, an official of the NAACP, noticed one girl in the crowd.

★ A PERSONAL VOICE WALTER WHITE

"Her hands were particularly noticeable as she thrust them forward and upward, trying desperately . . . to touch the singer. They were hands which despite their youth had known only the dreary work of manual labor. Tears streamed down the girl's dark face. Her hat was askew, but in her eyes flamed hope bordering on ecstasy. . . . If Marian Anderson could do it, the girl's eyes seemed to say, then I can, too."

—*A Man Called White*

▲ Marian Anderson sang from the steps of the Lincoln Memorial on April 9, 1939.

THE PRESIDENT FAILS TO SUPPORT CIVIL RIGHTS Despite efforts to promote racial equality, Roosevelt was never committed to full civil rights for African Americans. He was afraid of upsetting white Democratic voters in the South, an important segment of his supporters. He refused to approve a federal antilynching law and an end to the poll tax, two key goals of the civil rights movement. Further, a number of New Deal agencies clearly discriminated against African Americans, including the NRA, the CCC, and the TVA. These programs gave lower wages to African Americans and favored whites.

African Americans recognized the need to fight for their rights and to improve conditions in areas that the New Deal ignored. In 1934, they helped organize the Southern Tenant Farmers Union, which sought to protect the rights of tenant farmers and sharecroppers, both white and black. In the North, the union created tenants' groups and launched campaigns to increase job opportunities.

In general, however, African Americans supported the Roosevelt administration and the New Deal, generally seeing them as their best hope for the future. As one man recalled, "Roosevelt touched the temper of the black community. You did not look upon him as being white, black, blue or green. He was President Roosevelt." **B**

Mexican-American Fortunes

Mexican Americans also tended to support the New Deal, even though they received even fewer benefits than African Americans did. Large numbers of Mexican Americans had come to the United States during the 1920s, settling mainly in the Southwest. Most found work laboring on farms, an occupation that was essentially unprotected by state and federal laws. During the Depression, farm wages fell to as little as nine cents an hour. Farm workers who tried to unionize

MAIN IDEA

Evaluating
B Evaluate the actions and policies of the Roosevelt administration on civil rights.

MAIN IDEA

Identifying Problems

C Why was life difficult for farm laborers during the Depression?

often met with violence from employers and government authorities. Although the CCC and WPA helped some Mexican Americans, these agencies also discriminated against them by disqualifying from their programs migrant workers who had no permanent address. **C**

Native Americans Gain Support

Native Americans received strong government support from the New Deal. In 1924, Native Americans had received full citizenship by law. In 1933, President Roosevelt appointed **John Collier** as commissioner of Indian affairs. Collier helped create the Indian Reorganization Act of 1934. This act was an extreme change in government policy. It moved away from assimilation and toward Native American autonomy. It also helped to restore some reservation lands to tribal ownership. The act mandated changes in three areas:

- *economic*—Native American lands would belong to an entire tribe. This provision strengthened Native American land claims by prohibiting the government from taking over unclaimed reservation lands and selling them to people other than Native Americans.
- *cultural*—The number of boarding schools for Native American children was reduced, and children could attend school on the reservations.
- *political*—Tribes were given permission to elect tribal councils to govern their reservations.

MAIN IDEA

Summarizing

D What changes occurred for Native Americans as a result of the New Deal?

Some Native Americans who valued their tribal traditions hailed the act as an important step forward. Others who had become more "Americanized" as individual landowners under the previous Dawes Act objected, because they were tired of white people telling them what was good for them. **D**

▲ John Collier talks with Chief Richard, one of several Native American chiefs attending the Four Nation Celebration held at Niagara Falls, New York, in September 1934.

FDR Creates the New Deal Coalition

Although New Deal policies had mixed results for minorities, these groups generally backed President Roosevelt. In fact, one of FDR's great achievements was to create the **New Deal coalition**—an alignment of diverse groups dedicated to supporting the Democratic Party. The coalition included Southern whites, various urban groups, African Americans, and unionized industrial workers. As a result, Democrats dominated national politics throughout the 1930s and 1940s.

LABOR UNIONS FLOURISH As a result of the Wagner Act and other prolabor legislation passed during the New Deal, union members enjoyed better working conditions and increased bargaining power. In their eyes, President Roosevelt was a "friend of labor." Labor unions donated money to Roosevelt's reelection campaigns, and union workers pledged their votes to him.

Between 1933 and 1941, union membership grew from less than 3 million to more than 10 million. Unionization especially affected coal miners and workers in mass-production industries, such as the automobile, rubber, and electrical industries. It was in these industries, too, that a struggle for dominance within the labor movement began to develop.

The Growing Labor Movement, 1933–1940

Robert F. Wagner

A Democratic senator from New York (1927–1949), Robert F. Wagner was especially interested in workers' welfare. Wagner introduced the National Labor Relations Act in Congress in 1935.

The Growth of Union Membership, 1930–1940

Union Members (in millions)

9, 8, 7, 6, 5, 4, 3, 2, 1, 0

1930 1932 1934 1936 1938 1940

Source: *Historical Statistics of the United States*

Sit-down strikes ▶

Union workers—such as these CIO strikers at the Fisher automobile plant in Flint, Michigan, in 1937—found the sit-down strike an extremely effective method for getting their demands met.

ORGANIZE?

WITH 1250000 WORKERS BACKING US

OF COURSE WE WILL **ORGANIZE**

◀ **Union membership soars**

A Ben Shahn poster from the late 1930s boasted of the rise in union membership.

The American Federation of Labor (AFL) had traditionally been restricted to the craft unions, such as carpenters and electricians. Most of the AFL leaders opposed industrywide unions that represented all the workers in a given industry, such as automobile manufacturing. **E**

Frustrated by this position, several key labor leaders, including John L. Lewis of the United Mine Workers of America and David Dubinsky of the International Ladies Garment Workers, formed the Committee for Industrial Organization to organize industrial unions. The committee rapidly signed up unskilled and semi-skilled workers, and within two years it succeeded in gaining union recognition in the steel and automobile industries. In 1938, the Committee for Industrial Organization was expelled from the AFL and changed its name to the **Congress of Industrial Organizations (CIO).** This split lasted until 1955.

LABOR DISPUTES One of the main bargaining tactics of the labor movement in the 1930s was the sit-down strike. Instead of walking off their jobs, workers remained inside their plants, but they did not work. This prevented the factory owners from carrying on production with strikebreakers, or scabs. Some Americans disapproved of the sit-down strike, calling it a violation of private property. Nonetheless, it proved to be an effective bargaining tool.

Not all labor disputes in the 1930s were peaceful. Perhaps the most dramatic incident was the clash at the Republic Steel plant in Chicago on Memorial Day, 1937. Police attacked striking steelworkers outside the plant. One striker, an African-American man, recalled the experience.

> ### A PERSONAL VOICE JESSE REESE
>
> "I began to see people drop. There was a Mexican on my side, and he fell; and there was a black man on my side and he fell. Down I went. I crawled around in the grass and saw that people were getting beat. I'd never seen police beat women, not white women. I'd seen them beat black women, but this was the first time in my life I'd seen them beat white women—with sticks."
>
> —quoted in *The Great Depression*

MAIN IDEA

Analyzing Effects

E How did New Deal policies affect organized labor?

Ten people were killed and 84 wounded in this incident, which became known as the Memorial Day Massacre. Shortly afterward, the National Labor Relations Board stepped in and required the head of Republic Steel, Tom Girdler, to negotiate with the union. This and other actions helped labor gain strength during the 1930s.

FDR WINS IN 1936 Urban voters were another important component of the New Deal coalition. Support for the Democratic Party surged, especially in large Northern cities, such as New York, Boston, Philadelphia, and Chicago. These and other cities had powerful city political organizations that provided services, such as jobs, in exchange for votes. In the 1936 election, President Roosevelt carried the nation's 12 largest cities.

Support for President Roosevelt came from various religious and ethnic groups—Roman Catholics, Jews, Italians, Irish, and Polish and other Slavic peoples—as well as from African Americans. His appeal to these groups was based on New Deal labor laws and work-relief programs, which aided the urban poor. The president also made direct and persuasive appeals to urban voters at election time. To reinforce his support, he also appointed many officials of urban-immigrant backgrounds, particularly Roman Catholics and Jews, to important government positions.

Women, African Americans, Mexican Americans, Native Americans, and workers from all walks of life were greatly affected by the New Deal. It also had a tremendous influence on American society and culture.

▲ Chicago police attack strikers at what would become known as the Memorial Day Massacre (1937).

ASSESSMENT

1. **TERMS & NAMES** For each of the following terms and names, write a sentence explaining its significance.
   - Frances Perkins
   - Mary McLeod Bethune
   - John Collier
   - New Deal coalition
   - Congress of Industrial Organizations (CIO)

MAIN IDEA

2. **TAKING NOTES**
   Using a web diagram like the partial one shown here, note the effects of New Deal policies on American women, African Americans, Mexican Americans, Native Americans, unionized workers, and urban Americans.

   Write a paragraph explaining the effects of the New Deal on one of the groups.

CRITICAL THINKING

3. **SUMMARIZING**
   What steps did women take toward equality during the 1930s?
   Think About:
   - the role of women in government
   - hiring practices in federal programs
   - women's opportunities in business and industry

4. **EVALUATING**
   In your opinion, did organized labor become too powerful in the 1930s? Explain your answer. **Think About:**
   - why workers joined unions
   - how unions organized workers
   - the role of unions in politics

5. **ANALYZING MOTIVES**
   Why did urban voters support President Roosevelt?

PI 1.1   CC Unit 5.II.B.7.a   CC Unit 5.II.B.7.b
PI 2.2   CC Unit 5.II.B.7.c

Culture in the 1930s

MAIN IDEA	WHY IT MATTERS NOW	Terms & Names
Motion pictures, radio, art, and literature blossomed during the New Deal.	The films, music, art, and literature of the 1930s still captivate today's public.	• *Gone With the Wind* • Orson Welles • Grant Wood • Richard Wright • *The Grapes of Wrath*

One American's Story

Don Congdon, editor of the book *The Thirties: A Time to Remember*, was a high school student when the New Deal began. While many writers and artists in the 1930s produced works that reflected the important issues of the day, it was the movies and radio that most clearly captured the public imagination. Congdon remembers the role movies played at the time.

★ **A PERSONAL VOICE**   DON CONGDON

" Lots of us enjoyed our leisure at the movies. The experience of going was like an insidious [tempting] candy we could never get quite enough of; the visit to the dark theater was an escape from the drab realities of Depression living, and we were entranced by the never-ending variety of stories. Hollywood, like Scheherazade [the storyteller] in *The Thousand and One Nights*, supplied more the next night, and the next night after that. "

—*The Thirties: A Time to Remember*

▲ People line up to get into a movie theater during the Great Depression.

During the Great Depression, movies provided a window on a different, more exciting world. Despite economic hardship, many people gladly paid the 25 cents it cost to go to the movies. Along with radio, motion pictures became an increasingly dominant feature of American life.

The Lure of Motion Pictures and Radio

Although the 1930s were a difficult time for many Americans, it was a profitable and golden age for the motion-picture and radio industries. By late in the decade, approximately 65 percent of the population was attending the movies once a week. The nation boasted over 15,000 movie theaters, more than the number of banks and double the number of hotels. Sales of radios also greatly increased during the 1930s, from just over 13 million in 1930 to 28 million by 1940. Nearly 90 percent of American households owned a radio. Clearly, movies and radio had taken the country by storm.

AMERICAN GOTHIC (1930)

Grant Wood's 1930 painting, *American Gothic,* became one of the most famous portrayals of life in the Midwest during the Great Depression. Painted in the style known as Regionalism, Wood painted familiar subjects in realistic ways. The house in the background was discovered by Wood in Eldon, Iowa, while he was looking for subjects to paint. He returned home with a sketch and a photograph, and used his sister and his dentist as models for the farmer and daughter in the painting's foreground.

SKILLBUILDER Interpreting Visual Sources

1. What is the message Wood portrays in this painting? Explain your answer.
2. Do you think this painting is representative of the Great Depression? Why or why not?

📖 **SEE SKILLBUILDER HANDBOOK, PAGE R23.**

American Gothic (1930), Grant Wood. Oil on beaver board, 30 11/16" x 25 11/16" (78 cm x 65.3 cm) unframed. The Art Institute of Chicago, Friends of American Art Collection [1930.934]. Photography © The Art Institute of Chicago/All rights reserved by the Estate of Nan Wood Graham/ Licensed by VAGA, New York, NY

Mexican muralists such as Diego Rivera, typically portrayed the dignity of ordinary Americans at work. One artist, Robert Gwathmey, recalled these efforts.

★ A PERSONAL VOICE ROBERT GWATHMEY

" The director of the Federal Arts Project was Edward Bruce. He was a friend of the Roosevelts—from a polite family—who was a painter. He was a man of real broad vision. He insisted there be no restrictions. You were a painter: Do your work. You were a sculptor: Do your work. . . . That was a very free and happy period."

—quoted in *Hard Times*

During the New Deal era, outstanding works of art were produced by a number of American painters, such as Edward Hopper, Thomas Hart Benton, and Iowa's **Grant Wood,** whose work includes the famous painting *American Gothic.*

The WPA's Federal Theater Project hired actors to perform plays and artists to provide stage sets and props for theater productions that played around the country. It subsidized the work of important American playwrights, including Clifford Odets, whose play *Waiting for Lefty* (1935) dramatized the labor struggles of the 1930s. **C**

MAIN IDEA

Summarizing
C In what ways did the New Deal deliver art to the public?

WOODY GUTHRIE SINGS OF AMERICA Experiencing firsthand the tragedies of the Depression, singer and songwriter Woody Guthrie used music to capture the hardships of America. Along with tens of thousands of people from the Great Plains region, Guthrie was forced by the Dust Bowl to seek a better life elsewhere. He took the road west in search of brighter opportunities and wrote about his experiences in his songs. These "Dust Bowl Ballads" told of the devastation brought by the dust storms, the trials of the journey west, and the challenges that migrant farm workers faced.

A likable and easy-going performer, Guthrie had his own radio show—first in Los Angeles and later in New York City. However, disagreements with management and Guthrie's desire to be on the move meant that he rarely stayed at a job very long. When he was traveling, Guthrie wrote, often at the pace of a song a day. The hundreds of simple but honest songs Guthrie wrote about hard times and hope became popular around the country. Most notably, his song "This Land is Your Land" would become a classic American folk song. Woody Guthrie had a major influence on the course of American folk music.

Woody Guthrie

Walker Evans took this photograph of a sharecropper for the influential book *Let Us Now Praise Famous Men.*
▼

DIVERSE WRITERS DEPICT AMERICAN LIFE Many writers received support through yet another WPA program, the Federal Writers' Project. This project gave the future Pulitzer and Nobel Prize winner Saul Bellow his first writing job. It also helped **Richard Wright,** an African-American author, complete his acclaimed novel *Native Son* (1940), about a young man trying to survive in a racist world. Zora Neale Hurston wrote a stirring novel with FWP assistance—*Their Eyes Were Watching God* (1937), about a young woman growing up in rural Florida.

John Steinbeck, one of this country's most famous authors, received assistance from the Federal Writers' Project. He was able to publish his epic novel **The Grapes of Wrath** (1939), which reveals the lives of Oklahomans who left the Dust Bowl and ended up in California, where their hardships continued. Before his success, however, Steinbeck had endured the difficulties of the Depression like most other writers. **D**

Other books and authors examined the difficulties of life during the 1930s. James T. Farrell's *Studs Lonigan* trilogy (1932–1935) provides a bleak picture of working-class life in an Irish neighborhood of Chicago, while Jack Conroy's novel *The Disinherited* (1933) portrays the violence and poverty of the Missouri coalfields, where Conroy's own father and brother died in a mine disaster.

Nevertheless, other writers found hope in the positive values of American culture. The writer James Agee and the photographer Walker Evans collaborated on a book about Alabama sharecroppers, *Let Us Now Praise Famous Men* (1941). Though it deals with the difficult lives of poor farmers, it portrays the dignity and strength of character in the people it presents. Thornton Wilder's play *Our Town* (1938) captures the beauty of small-town life in New England.

Although artists and writers recognized America's flaws, they contributed positively to the New Deal legacy. These intellectuals praised the virtues of American life and took pride in the country's traditions and accomplishments.

SECTION 4 ASSESSMENT

1. TERMS & NAMES For each term or name below, write a sentence explaining its significance.

- *Gone With the Wind*
- Grant Wood
- Richard Wright
- *The Grapes of Wrath*
- Orson Welles

MAIN IDEA

2. TAKING NOTES
Create a web like the one below, filling in the names of those who contributed to each aspect of American culture in the 1930s.

Cultural Figures of the 1930s

What contribution did each group make?

CRITICAL THINKING

3. HYPOTHESIZING
What type of movies do you think might have been produced if the government had supported moviemaking as part of the New Deal? Use evidence from the chapter to support your response.

4. ANALYZING EFFECTS
How did the entertainment industry affect the economy?

5. DRAWING CONCLUSIONS
In your opinion, what were the main benefits of government support for art and literature in the 1930s? Support your response with details from the text. **Think About:**

- the experiences of Americans in the Great Depression
- the writers who got their start through the FWP
- the subject matter of WPA murals and other New Deal-sponsored art

SECTION
5

CC Unit 5.II.B.1.c   CC Unit 5.II.B.3.a
CC Unit 5.II.B.3.b   CC Unit 5.II.B.3.c
CC Unit 5.II.B.3.d   CC Unit 5.II.B.5.a(3)

PI 4.2

The Impact of the New Deal

MAIN IDEA	WHY IT MATTERS NOW	Terms & Names
The New Deal affected American society not only in the 1930s but also in the decades that followed.	Americans still debate over how large a role government should play in American life.	• **Federal Deposit Insurance Corporation (FDIC)** • **Securities and Exchange Commission (SEC)** • **National Labor Relations Board (NLRB)** • **parity** • **Tennessee Valley Authority (TVA)**

One American's Story

hmhsocialstudies.com
TAKING NOTES
Use the graphic organizer online to take notes on the long-term effects of the New Deal.

George Dobbin, a 67-year-old cotton-mill worker, staunchly supported Franklin Delano Roosevelt and his New Deal policies. In an interview for a book entitled *These Are Our Lives,* compiled by the Federal Writers' Project, Dobbin explained his feelings about the president.

A PERSONAL VOICE GEORGE DOBBIN

"I do think that Roosevelt is the biggest-hearted man we ever had in the White House. . . . It's the first time in my recollection that a President ever got up and said, 'I'm interested in and aim to do somethin' for the workin' man.' Just knowin' that for once . . . [there] was a man to stand up and speak for him, a man that could make what he felt so plain nobody could doubt he meant it, has made a lot of us feel a sight [lot] better even when [there] wasn't much to eat in our homes."

—quoted in *These Are Our Lives*

▲ A coal miner, Zeno Santinello, shakes hands with Franklin D. Roosevelt as he campaigns in Elm Grove, West Virginia, in 1932.

FDR was extremely popular among working-class Americans. Far more important than his personal popularity, however, was the impact of the policies he initiated. Even today, reforms begun under the New Deal continue to influence American politics and society.

New Deal Reforms Endure

During his second term in office, President Roosevelt hinted at plans to launch a Third New Deal. In his inaugural address, the president exclaimed, "I see millions of families trying to live on incomes so meager that the pall of family disaster hangs over them day by day. . . . I see one third of a nation ill-housed, ill-clad, ill-nourished."

However, FDR did not favor deficit spending. More importantly, by 1937 the economy had improved enough to convince many Americans that the Depression was finally ending. Although economic troubles still plagued the nation, President

Roosevelt faced rising pressure from Congress to scale back New Deal programs, which he did. As a result, industrial production dropped again, and the number of unemployed increased from 7.7 million in 1937 to 10.4 million in 1938. By 1939, the New Deal was effectively over, and Roosevelt was increasingly concerned with events in Europe, particularly Hitler's rise to power in Germany. **Ⓐ**

SUPPORTERS AND CRITICS OF THE NEW DEAL Over time, opinions about the New Deal have ranged from harsh criticism to high praise. Most conservatives think President Roosevelt's policies made the federal government too large and too powerful. They believe that the government stifled free enterprise and individual initiative. Liberal critics, in contrast, argue that President Roosevelt didn't do enough to socialize the economy and to eliminate social and economic inequalities. Supporters of the New Deal contend, however, that the president struck a reasonable balance between two extremes—unregulated capitalism and overregulated socialism—and helped the country recover from its economic difficulties. One of Roosevelt's top advisers made this assessment of the president's goals.

MAIN IDEA

Analyzing Issues

Ⓐ Why did industrial production drop and unemployment go up again in 1938?

★ **A PERSONAL VOICE** REXFORD TUGWELL

"He had in mind a comprehensive welfare concept, infused with a stiff tincture of morality. . . . He wanted all Americans to grow up healthy and vigorous and to be practically educated. He wanted business men to work within a set of understood rules. Beyond this he wanted people free to vote, to worship, to behave as they wished so long as a moral code was respected; and he wanted officials to behave as though office were a public trust."

—quoted in *Redeeming the Time*

POINT

"The New Deal transformed the way American government works."

Supporters of the New Deal believe that it was successful. Many historians and journalists make this judgment by using the economic criterion of creating jobs. *The New Republic*, for example, argued that the shortcomings of the WPA "are insignificant beside the gigantic fact that it has given jobs and sustenance to a minimum of 1,400,000 and a maximum of 3,300,000 persons for five years."

Some historians stress that the New Deal was more than a temporary solution to a crisis. Professor A. A. Berle stated that, "human beings cannot indefinitely be sacrificed by millions to the operation of economic forces."

According to the historian William E. Luechtenburg, "It is hard to think of another period in the whole history of the republic that was so fruitful or of a crisis that was met with as much imagination."

To Pulitzer Prize-winning historian Allan Nevins, the New Deal was a turning point in which the U.S. government assumed a greater responsibility for the economic welfare of its citizens.

COUNTERPOINT

"Many more problems have been created than solved by the New Deal."

Critics of the New Deal believe that it failed to reach its goals. The historian Barton J. Bernstein accepted the goals of the New Deal but declared that they were never met. To him, the New Deal "failed to raise the impoverished, it failed to redistribute income, [and] it failed to extend equality."

In Senator Robert A. Taft's opinion, "many more problems have been created than solved" by the New Deal. He maintained, "Whatever else has resulted from the great increase in government activity . . . it has certainly had the effect of checking private enterprise completely. This country was built up by the constant establishment of new business and the expansion of old businesses. . . . In the last six years this process has come to an end because of government regulation and the development of a tax system which penalizes hard work and success." Senator Taft claimed that "The government should gradually withdraw from the business of lending money and leave that function to private capital under proper regulation."

THINKING CRITICALLY

CONNECT TO HISTORY

1. **Comparing and Contrasting** How did the New Deal succeed? How did it fail? Write a paragraph that summarizes the main points.

    SEE SKILLBUILDER HANDBOOK, PAGE R8.

CONNECT TO TODAY

2. **Draft a Proposal** Research the programs of the WPA and draft a proposal for a WPA-type program that would benefit your community.

EXPANDING GOVERNMENT'S ROLE IN THE ECONOMY The Roosevelt administration expanded the power of the federal government, giving it—and particularly the president—a more active role in shaping the economy. It did this by infusing the nation's economy with millions of dollars, by creating federal jobs, by attempting to regulate supply and demand, and by increasing the government's active participation in settling labor and management disputes. The federal government also established agencies, such as the **Federal Deposit Insurance Corporation (FDIC)** and the **Securities and Exchange Commission (SEC),** to regulate banking and investment activities. Although the New Deal did not end the Great Depression, it did help reduce the suffering of thousands of men, women, and children by providing them with jobs, food, and money. It also gave people hope and helped them to regain a sense of dignity.

Unemployed workers sit on a street in a 1936 photograph by Dorothea Lange.

The federal government had to go deeply into debt to provide jobs and aid to the American people. The federal deficit increased to $2.9 billion in fiscal year 1934. As a result of the cutbacks in federal spending made in 1937–1938, the deficit dropped to $100 million. But the next year it rose again, to $2.9 billion. What really ended the Depression, however, was the massive amount of spending by the federal government for guns, tanks, ships, airplanes, and all the other equipment and supplies the country needed for the World War II effort. During the war, the deficit reached a high of about $54.5 billion in 1943.

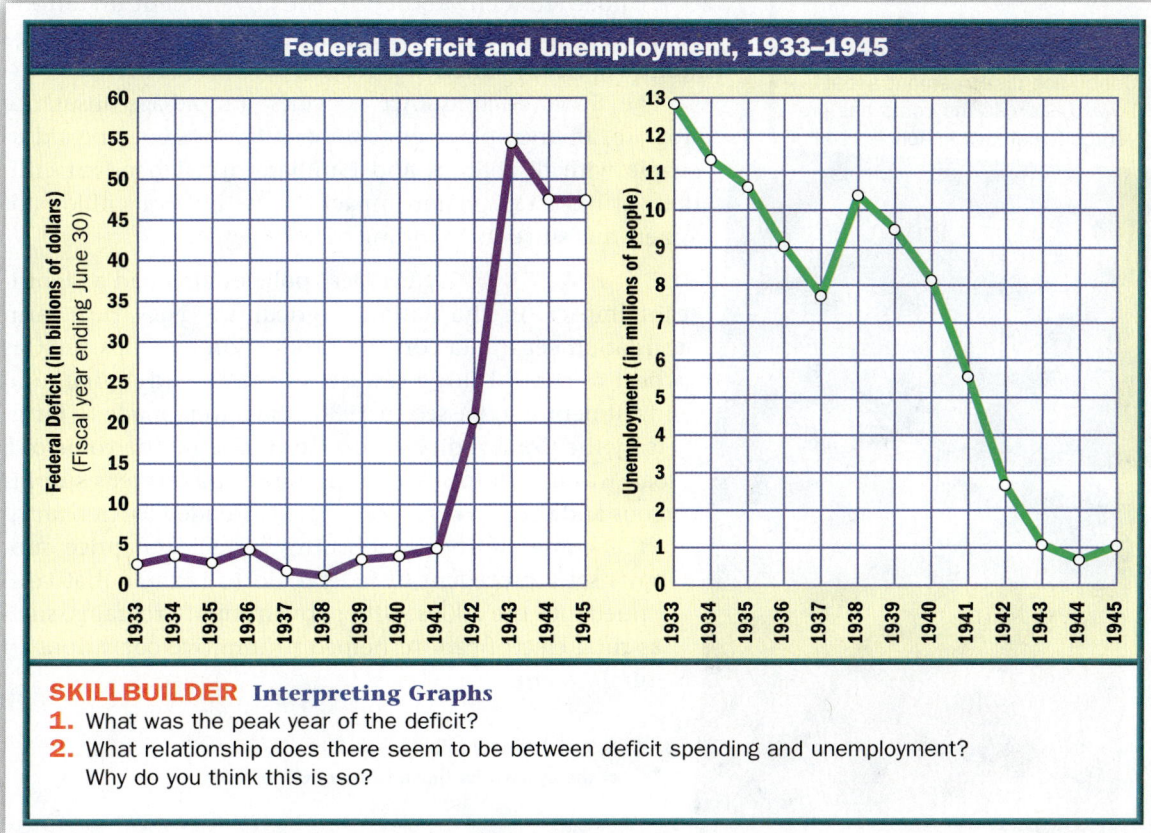

SKILLBUILDER Interpreting Graphs
1. What was the peak year of the deficit?
2. What relationship does there seem to be between deficit spending and unemployment? Why do you think this is so?

PROTECTING WORKERS' RIGHTS One of the areas in which New Deal policies have had a lasting effect is the protection of workers' rights. New Deal legislation, such as the Wagner Act and the Fair Labor Standards Act, set standards for wages and hours, banned child labor, and ensured the right of workers to organize and to bargain collectively with employers. Today, the **National Labor Relations Board (NLRB),** created under the Wagner Act, continues to act as a mediator in labor disputes between unions and employers.

BANKING AND FINANCE New Deal programs established new policies in the area of banking and finance. The Securities and Exchange Commission (SEC), created in 1934, continues to monitor the stock market and enforce laws regarding the sale of stocks and bonds. The Federal Deposit Insurance Corporation (FDIC), created by the Glass-Steagall Act of 1933, has shored up the banking system by reassuring individual depositors that their savings are protected against loss in the event of a bank failure. Today, individual accounts in United States federal banks are insured by the Federal Deposit Insurance Corporation for up to $250,000.

NOW & THEN

SOCIAL SECURITY

Today the Social Security system continues to rely on mandatory contributions paid by workers—through payroll deductions—and by employers. The money is invested in a trust fund, from which retirement benefits are later paid. However, several problems have surfaced. For example, benefits have expanded, and Americans live longer than they did in 1935. Also, the ratio of workers to retirees is shrinking: fewer people are contributing to the system relative to the number who are eligible to receive benefits.

The long-range payment of benefits may be in jeopardy because of the large number of recipients. Continuing disagreement about how to address the costs has prevented legislative action.

Social and Environmental Effects

New Deal economic and financial reforms, including the creation of the FDIC, the SEC, and Social Security, have helped to stabilize the nation's finances and economy. Although the nation still experiences economic downturns, known as recessions, people's savings are insured, and they can receive unemployment compensation if they lose their jobs.

SOCIAL SECURITY One of the most important legacies of the New Deal has been that the federal government has assumed some responsibility for the social welfare of its citizens. Under President Roosevelt, the government undertook the creation of a Social Security system that would help a large number of needy Americans receive some assistance.

The Social Security Act provides an old-age insurance program, an unemployment compensation system, and aid to people with disabilities and families with dependent children. It has had a major impact on the lives of millions of Americans since its founding in 1935. **B**

THE RURAL SCENE New Deal policies also had a significant impact on the nation's agriculture. New Deal farm legislation set quotas on the production of crops such as wheat to control surpluses. Under the second Agricultural Adjustment Act, passed in 1938, loans were made to farmers by the Commodity Credit Corporation. The value of a loan was determined by the amount of a farmer's surplus crops and the **parity** price, a price intended to keep farmers' income steady. Establishing agricultural price supports set a precedent of federal aid to farmers that continued into the 2000s. Other government programs, such as rural electrification, helped to improve conditions in rural America.

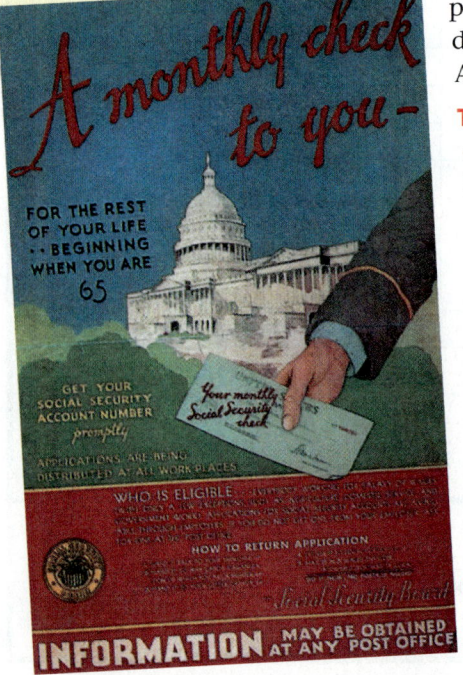

◄ A Social Security poster proclaims the benefits of the system for those who are 65 or older.

THE ENVIRONMENT Americans also continue to benefit from New Deal efforts to protect the environment. President Roosevelt was highly committed to conservation and promoted policies designed to protect the nation's natural resources. The Civilian Conservation Corps planted trees, created hiking trails, and built fire lookout towers. The Soil Conservation Service taught farmers how to conserve the soil through contour plowing, terracing, and crop rotation. Congress also passed the Taylor Grazing Act in 1934 to help reduce grazing on public lands. Such grazing had contributed to the erosion that brought about the dust storms of the 1930s.

The **Tennessee Valley Authority** (**TVA**) harnessed water power to generate electricity and to help prevent disastrous floods in the Tennessee Valley. The government also added to the national park system in the 1930s, established new wildlife refuges and set aside large wilderness areas. On the other hand, government-sponsored stripmining and coal burning caused air, land, and water pollution. **C**

The New Deal legacy has many dimensions. It brought hope and gratitude from some people for the benefits and protections they received. It also brought anger and criticism from those who believed that it took more of their money in taxes and curtailed their freedom through increased government regulations. The deficit spending necessary to fund New Deal programs grew immensely as the nation entered World War II.

> ▲
> This 1933 cartoon depicts Roosevelt spurring on a slow-moving Congress with his many reform policies.

MAIN IDEA

Analyzing Effects
 C How did New Deal programs benefit and harm the environment?

SECTION 5 ASSESSMENT

1. TERMS & NAMES For each term or name, write a sentence explaining its significance.
- Federal Deposit Insurance Corporation (FDIC)
- Securities and Exchange Commission (SEC)
- National Labor Relations Board (NLRB)
- parity
- Tennessee Valley Authority (TVA)

MAIN IDEA

2. TAKING NOTES
In a cluster diagram like the one below, show long-term effects of the New Deal.

```
        (   )     (   )
           \       /
          New Deal's
         Long-Term Effects
           /       \
        (   )     (   )
              (   )
```

Which long-term benefit do you think has had the most impact? Why?

CRITICAL THINKING

3. MAKING GENERALIZATIONS
Some critics have charged that the New Deal was antibusiness and anti–free enterprise. Explain why you agree or disagree with this charge.
Think About:
- the expanded power of the federal government
- the New Deal's effect on the economy
- the New Deal's effect on the American people

4. EVALUATING LEADERSHIP
How successful do you think Franklin Roosevelt was as a president? Support your answer with details from the text.

5. INTERPRETING VISUAL SOURCES
Look at the political cartoon above. What does it suggest about Roosevelt's leadership and the role of Congress? Explain.

The Tennessee Valley Authority

The Tennessee Valley Authority (TVA) is a federal agency that was established in 1933 to construct dams and power plants along the Tennessee River and its tributaries. The Tennessee River basin is one of the largest river basins in the United States, and people who live in this area have a number of common concerns. The TVA has helped the region in various ways: through flood and navigation control, the conservation of natural resources, and the generation of electric power, as well as through agricultural and industrial development.

The Tennessee Valley covers parts of seven states. Thus, the TVA became an enormous undertaking, eventually comprising dozens of major dams, each with associated power plants, recreational facilities, and navigation aids.

MISSOURI

ARKANSAS

HYDROELECTRIC DAM

A hydroelectric dam uses water power to create electricity. The deeper the reservoir, the greater is the force pushing water through the dam.

A The water is forced through the intake and into the penstock.

D The generator produces electricity and transmits it through the power lines.

C The turbine drives the generator.

E Once it passes through the turbine, the water reenters the river.

B The water force spins the blades of the turbine.

1 KENTUCKY DAM

Over a mile and a half long and 206 feet high, the Kentucky Dam created the 184-mile-long Kentucky Lake, a paradise for fishing.

2 THE CUMBERLAND RIVER

A similar series of dams, operated by the Corps of Engineers, is found on the Cumberland River. This system cooperates with the TVA.

3 NORRIS DAM ▲

Located on the Clinch River, a tributary of the Tennessee River, the Norris Dam is named after Senator George W. Norris of Nebraska. Norris was a progressive leader who called for government involvement in the development of the power potential of the Tennessee River.

Map legend:
- Tennessee River watershed
- Region served by TVA power
- TVA Dam

0   50   100 miles
0   50   100 kilometers

▲ Before 1930, most homes in the area had no electricity. Women wash clothes outside this homestead near Andersonville, Tennessee, in 1933. Their estate was submerged when the Norris Dam filled.

THINKING CRITICALLY

1. **Analyzing Distributions** Locate the dams on this map. Why do you think they might have been placed in these particular areas?

2. **Creating a Model** Create a 3-D model of a dam. Before you begin, pose a historical question your model will answer. Think about environmental changes caused by the construction of a dam.

   SEE SKILLBUILDER HANDBOOK, PAGE R31.

 hmhsocialstudies.com   RESEARCH WEB LINKS

VISUAL SUMMARY

THE NEW DEAL

PROBLEMS

- Industries and farms failed.
- U.S. stock market crashed and banks closed.
- Bankrupt businesses
- Unemployment
- Homelessness

SOLUTIONS

- Work projects help the unemployed.
- Money given to farmers, sharecroppers, and migrant workers.
- New opportunities for women and minorities.
- Social Security Act allocates money to people who are elderly, unemployed, or disabled.
- NLRB protects workers' rights.
- SEC monitors stock market.
- FDIC protects individuals' deposits in banks.
- Fireside chats increase public confidence.

CONTINUING EFFECTS

- Banking and finance are reformed.
- Government takes a more active role in the economy.
- Workers benefit from labor standards.
- Social Security system continues to provide for the needy.
- Conservation efforts continue to preserve the environment.

TERMS & NAMES

For each term or name below, write a sentence explaining its historical significance or contribution to the New Deal.

1. Franklin Delano Roosevelt
2. New Deal
3. Eleanor Roosevelt
4. Works Progress Administration (WPA)
5. Social Security Act
6. Mary McLeod Bethune
7. Congress of Industrial Organizations (CIO)
8. Orson Welles
9. Richard Wright
10. Tennessee Valley Authority (TVA)

MAIN IDEAS

Use your notes and the information in the chapter to answer the following questions.

A New Deal Fights the Depression *(pages 694–700)*

1. How did Franklin Roosevelt change the role of the federal government during his first Hundred Days?
2. Summarize the reasons why some people opposed the New Deal.

The Second New Deal Takes Hold *(pages 701–707)*

3. In what ways did the New Deal programs extend federal aid?
4. How did the Wagner Act help working people?

The New Deal Affects Many Groups *(pages 710–715)*

5. Summarize the impact the New Deal had on various ethnic groups.
6. Why did many urban voters support Roosevelt and the Democratic party?

Culture in the 1930s *(pages 716–720)*

7. What purpose did movies and radio serve during the Great Depression?
8. Explain how the New Deal programs supported artists and writers in the 1930s.

The Impact of the New Deal *(pages 721–725)*

9. List five New Deal agencies that are still in place today.
10. What benefits did the Tennessee Valley Authority provide? What negative impact did it have?

THINKING CRITICALLY

1. **USING YOUR NOTES** Copy the web below and fill it in with actions that Americans took to end the economic crisis of the 1930s.

American Actions to End Economic Crisis

2. **DEVELOPING HISTORICAL PERSPECTIVE** What federal programs instituted in the 1930s and later discontinued might be of use to the nation today? Explain and support your opinion in a paragraph or two.

Use the information on the time line and your knowledge of U.S. history to answer question 1.

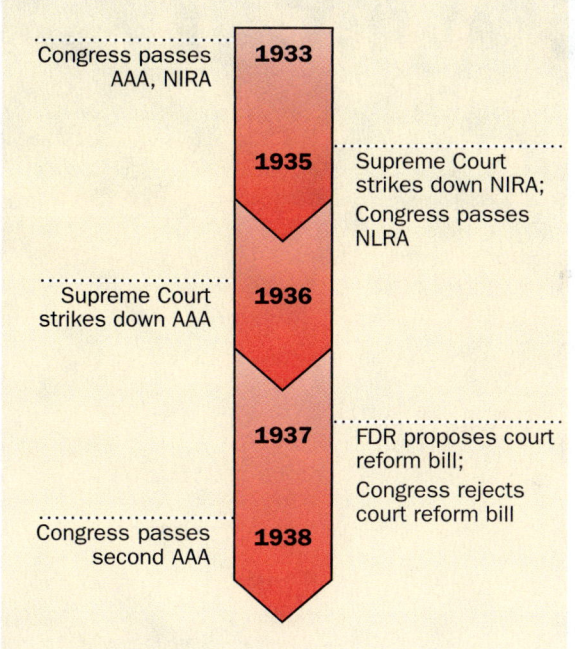

Congress passes AAA, NIRA	**1933**
	1935 — Supreme Court strikes down NIRA; Congress passes NLRA
Supreme Court strikes down AAA	**1936**
	1937 — FDR proposes court reform bill; Congress rejects court reform bill
Congress passes second AAA	**1938**

1 The Supreme Court killed several New Deal programs by declaring them unconstitutional. Which of the following resulted from those decisions?

(1) FDR packed the Court with New Deal supporters.

(2) Congress created replacement programs.

(3) The New Deal lost popular support.

(4) The power of the federal government was expanded.

2 What was the purpose of the Glass-Steagall Act?

(1) to combat unemployment

(2) to provide home mortgage loans

(3) to assist farmers

(4) to regulate the banking system

Use the quotation and your knowledge of United States history to answer question 3.

> "Little by little the American federation is transforming itself into a union, marked by the growth in importance of the role of the federal capital. In the beginning, the United States had only a small federal bureaucracy. Today the central administration is powerful and rich."
>
> —André Maurois, *This Was America*

3 Author André Maurois traveled through the United States in the 1930s and observed a growing unity in the American people. How did the New Deal help to bring Americans closer together?

(1) The New Deal involved the federal government trying to fix a national problem.

(2) New Deal jobs and public works programs gave people something to agree upon.

(3) President Roosevelt, who designed the New Deal, was elected four times.

(4) The New Deal encouraged the spread of popular culture through radio and the movies.

↗ hmhsocialstudies.com **TEST PRACTICE**

For additional test practice, go online for:
- Diagnostic tests
- Tutorials

INTERACT WITH HISTORY

Think about the issues you explored at the beginning of the chapter. Now that you have read the chapter, do you think President Roosevelt adequately addressed the needs of the ailing economy? Do you think his New Deal policies extended far enough to restore public confidence? Support your opinions with examples.

FOCUS ON WRITING

Imagine that you are a journalist during the Great Depression. You are writing a feature about the New Deal, and your editor has asked you to write a sidebar focused on just one program to accompany your piece. Select one New Deal program. Explain who the program is meant to help and how it is supposed to work. Then analyze its effectiveness.

MULTIMEDIA ACTIVITY

21ST CENTURY

Organize into small groups. Use the Internet and other sources to research how photographer Dorothea Lange used her camera to tell stories of life during the Great Depression. Then create a Web site that describes Lange's life and analyzes how her work depicts the Great Depression. Include some of Lange's images, and make sure to credit them properly.

UNIT PROJECT

Debate

As you read Unit 7, pay attention to arguments on either side of a political issue. Work with a group to stage a debate. Write a proposition, such as "Resolved: The U.S. has a responsibility to end its isolationism and enter World War II." Choose teams to argue either for or against the resolution.

Dawn Patrol Launching by Paul Sample

World War II and Its Aftermath
1931–1960

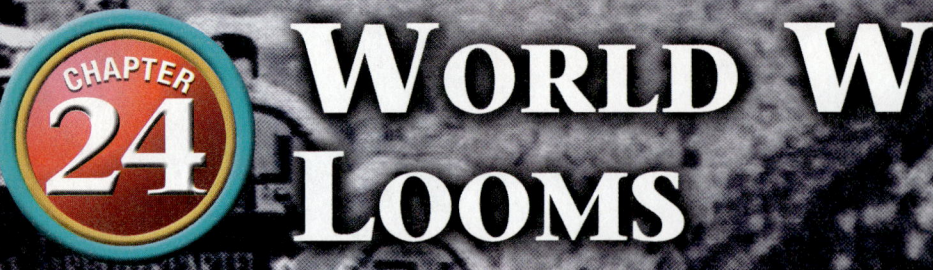

WORLD WAR LOOMS

Essential Question

How did the rise of dictators contribute to the outbreak of World War II?

 New York Standards

KEY IDEA 3 Study about the major social, political, economic, cultural, and religious developments in New York State and United States history involves learning about the important roles and contributions of individuals and groups.

KEY IDEA 4 The skills of historical analysis include the ability to: explain the significance of historical evidence; weigh the importance, reliability, and validity of evidence; understand the concept of multiple causation; understand the importance of changing and competing interpretations of different historical developments.

SECTION 1: Dictators Threaten World Peace

SECTION 2: War in Europe

SECTION 3: The Holocaust

SECTION 4: America Moves Toward War

Flanked by storm troopers, Adolf Hitler arrives at a Nazi rally in September 1934.

1931 The Empire State Building opens in New York City.

1932 Franklin Delano Roosevelt is elected president.

1933 Prohibition ends.

1936 Jesse Owens wins four gold medals at Olympics in Berlin, Germany.

1936 Roosevelt is reelected.

USA | **1931** | **1933** | **1935**
WORLD

1931 Japan conquers Manchuria, in northern China.

1933 Adolf Hitler is appointed German chancellor and sets up Dachau concentration camp.

1934 Stalin begins great purge in USSR.

1934 Chinese communists flee in the Long March.

1936 Ethiopia's Haile Selassie asks League of Nations for help against Italian invasion.

1936 General Francisco Franco leads a fascist rebellion in Spain.

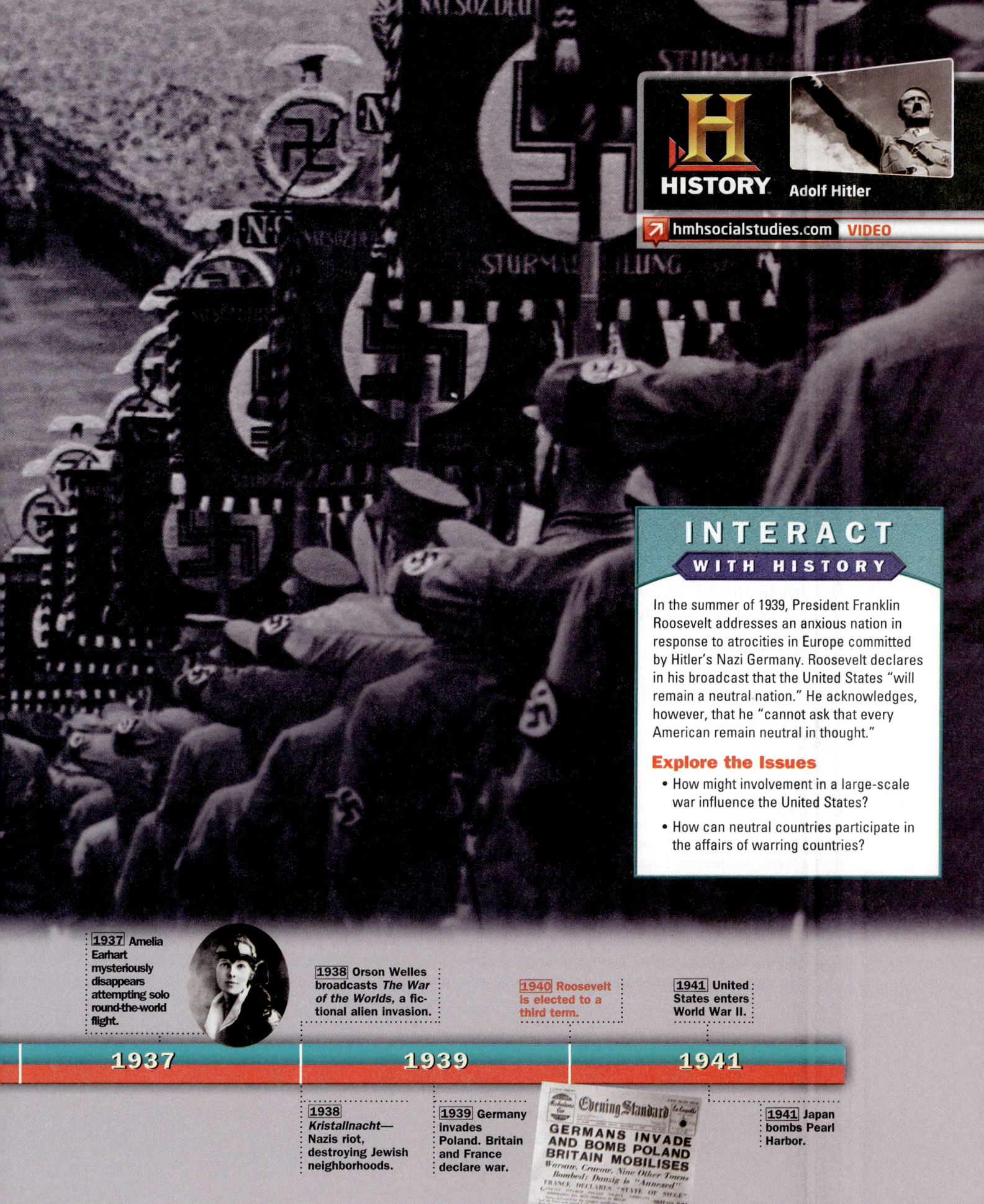

INTERACT
WITH HISTORY

In the summer of 1939, President Franklin Roosevelt addresses an anxious nation in response to atrocities in Europe committed by Hitler's Nazi Germany. Roosevelt declares in his broadcast that the United States "will remain a neutral nation." He acknowledges, however, that he "cannot ask that every American remain neutral in thought."

Explore the Issues

- How might involvement in a large-scale war influence the United States?
- How can neutral countries participate in the affairs of warring countries?

1937 Amelia Earhart mysteriously disappears attempting solo round-the-world flight.

1938 Orson Welles broadcasts *The War of the Worlds*, a fictional alien invasion.

1940 Roosevelt is elected to a third term.

1941 United States enters World War II.

1937

1939

1941

1938 *Kristallnacht*— Nazis riot, destroying Jewish neighborhoods.

1939 Germany invades Poland. Britain and France declare war.

1941 Japan bombs Pearl Harbor.

Evening Standard

GERMANS INVADE AND BOMB POLAND BRITAIN MOBILISES

Warsaw, Cracow, Nine Other Towns Bombed; Danzig is "Annexed"

FRANCE DECLARES "STATE OF SIEGE"

Dictators Threaten World Peace

MAIN IDEA	WHY IT MATTERS NOW	Terms & Names
The rise of rulers with total power in Europe and Asia led to World War II.	Dictators of the 1930s and 1940s changed the course of history, making world leaders especially watchful for the actions of dictators today.	• Joseph Stalin • Adolf Hitler • totalitarian • Nazism • Benito Mussolini • Francisco Franco • fascism • Neutrality Acts

One American's Story

hmhsocialstudies.com
TAKING NOTES

Use the graphic organizer online to take notes on the ambitions of the dictators of the 1930s.

Martha Gellhorn arrived in Madrid in 1937 to cover the brutal civil war that had broken out in Spain the year before. Hired as a special correspondent for *Collier's Weekly*, she had come with very little money and no special protection. On assignment there, she met the writer Ernest Hemingway, whom she later married. To Gellhorn, a young American writer, the Spanish Civil War was a deadly struggle between tyranny and democracy. For the people of Madrid, it was also a daily struggle for survival.

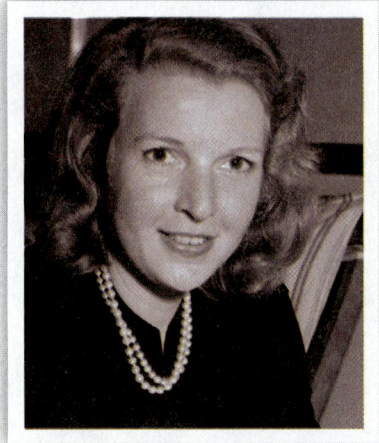

A PERSONAL VOICE MARTHA GELLHORN

" You would be walking down a street, hearing only the city noises of streetcars and automobiles and people calling to one another, and suddenly, crushing it all out, would be the huge stony deep booming of a falling shell, at the corner. There was no place to run, because how did you know that the next shell would not be behind you, or ahead, or to the left or right? "

—*The Face of War*

▲ Martha Gellhorn, one of the first women war correspondents, began her career during the Spanish Civil War.

Less than two decades after the end of World War I—"the war to end all wars"—fighting erupted again in Europe and in Asia. As Americans read about distant battles, they hoped the conflicts would remain on the other side of the world.

Nationalism Grips Europe and Asia

The seeds of new conflicts had been sown in World War I. For many nations, peace had brought not prosperity but revolution fueled by economic depression and struggle. The postwar years also brought the rise of powerful dictators driven by the belief in nationalism—loyalty to one's country above all else—and dreams of territorial expansion.

◀ Germany was expected to pay off huge debts while dealing with widespread poverty. By 1923, an inflating economy made a five-million German mark worth less than a penny. Here children build blocks with stacks of useless German marks.

FAILURES OF THE WORLD WAR I PEACE SETTLEMENT Instead of securing a "just and secure peace," the Treaty of Versailles caused anger and resentment. Germans saw nothing fair in a treaty that blamed them for starting the war. Nor did they find security in a settlement that stripped them of their overseas colonies and border territories. These problems overwhelmed the Weimar Republic, the democratic government set up in Germany after World War I. Similarly, the Soviets resented the carving up of parts of Russia. (See map, Chapter 19, p. 606.)

The peace settlement had not fulfilled President Wilson's hope of a world "safe for democracy." New democratic governments that emerged in Europe after the war floundered. Without a democratic tradition, people turned to authoritarian leaders to solve their economic and social problems. The new democracies collapsed, and dictators were able to seize power. Some had great ambitions. **Ⓐ**

MAIN IDEA

Identifying Problems
Ⓐ Why did the new democracies set up after World War I fail?

JOSEPH STALIN TRANSFORMS THE SOVIET UNION In Russia, hopes for democracy gave way to civil war, resulting in the establishment of a communist state, officially called the Soviet Union, in 1922. After V. I. Lenin died in 1924, **Joseph Stalin,** whose last name means "man of steel," took control of the country. Stalin focused on creating a model communist state. In so doing, he made both agricultural and industrial growth the prime economic goals of the Soviet Union. Stalin abolished all privately owned farms and replaced them with collectives—large government-owned farms, each worked by hundreds of families.

Stalin moved to transform the Soviet Union from a backward rural nation into a great industrial power. In 1928, the Soviet dictator outlined the first of several "five-year plans," to direct the industrialization. All economic activity was placed under state management. By 1937, the Soviet Union had become the world's second-largest industrial power, surpassed in overall production only by the United States. The human costs of this transformation, however, were enormous.

In his drive to purge, or eliminate, anyone who threatened his power, Stalin did not spare even his most faithful supporters. While the final toll will never be known, historians estimate that Stalin was responsible for the deaths of 8 million to 13 million people. Millions more died in famines caused by the restructuring of Soviet society.

MAIN IDEA

Summarizing
Ⓑ What are the characteristics of a totalitarian state?

By 1939, Stalin had firmly established a **totalitarian** government that tried to exert complete control over its citizens. In a totalitarian state, individuals have no rights, and the government suppresses all opposition. **Ⓑ**

The Rise of Nationalism, 1922–1941

Adolf Hitler offers economic stability to unemployed Germans during the Great Depression and becomes chancellor in 1933.

Joseph Stalin grabs control of the Soviet Union in 1924 and squelches all opposition after V. I. Lenin, founder of the communist regime, dies.

Fascist dictatorship
Communist dictatorship
Imperialist military regime

0   750   1,500 miles
0   750   1,500 kilometers

Benito Mussolini rises to power in 1922 and attempts to restore Italy to its former position as a world power.

Francisco Franco leads the rebel Nationalist army to victory in Spain and gains complete control of the country in 1939.

Hideki Tojo, the force behind Japanese strategy, becomes Japan's prime minister in 1941. Emperor Hirohito becomes a powerless figurehead.

SOVIET UNION
Moscow
GREAT BRITAIN
London
Berlin
GERMANY
Paris
FRANCE
ITALY
Rome
SPAIN
Madrid
Mediterranean Sea
CHINA
JAPAN
Tokyo
PACIFIC OCEAN
ATLANTIC OCEAN
Arctic Circle
Tropic of Cancer

GEOGRAPHY SKILLBUILDER
1. **Region** In which countries did authoritarian leaders come to power? Who were the leaders?
2. **Location** What geographic features might have led Japan to expand?

THE RISE OF FASCISM IN ITALY While Stalin was consolidating his power in the Soviet Union, **Benito Mussolini** was establishing a totalitarian regime in Italy, where unemployment and inflation produced bitter strikes, some of which were communist led. Alarmed by these threats, the middle and upper classes demanded stronger leadership. Mussolini took advantage of this situation. A powerful speaker, Mussolini knew how to appeal to Italy's wounded national pride. He played on the fears of economic collapse and communism. In this way, he won the support of many discontented Italians.

> " *Italy wants peace, work, and calm. I will give these things with love if possible, with force if necessary.* "
> **BENITO MUSSOLINI**

By 1921, Mussolini had established the Fascist Party. **Fascism** (făsh′ĭz′əm) stressed nationalism and placed the interests of the state above those of individuals. To strengthen the nation, Fascists argued, power must rest with a single strong leader and a small group of devoted party members. (The Latin *fasces*—a bundle of rods tied around an ax handle—had been a symbol of unity and authority in ancient Rome.)

In October 1922, Mussolini marched on Rome with thousands of his followers, whose black uniforms gave them the name "Black Shirts." When important government officials, the army, and the police sided with the Fascists, the Italian king appointed Mussolini head of the government.

Calling himself *Il Duce*, or "the leader," Mussolini gradually extended Fascist control to every aspect of Italian life. Tourists marveled that *Il Duce* had even "made the trains run on time." Mussolini achieved this efficiency, however, by crushing all opposition and by making Italy a totalitarian state. **C**

MAIN IDEA

Analyzing Causes
C What factors led to the rise of Fascism in Italy?

The Faces of Totalitarianism

Fascist Italy	Nazi Germany	Communist Soviet Union
• Extreme nationalism • Militaristic expansionism • Charismatic leader • Private property with strong government controls • Anticommunist	• Extreme nationalism and racism • Militaristic expansionism • Forceful leader • Private property with strong government controls • Anticommunist	• Create a sound communist state and wait for world revolution • Revolution by workers • Eventual rule by working class • State ownership of property

▲ Left to right: Benito Mussolini, Adolf Hitler, Joseph Stalin

THE NAZIS TAKE OVER GERMANY In Germany, **Adolf Hitler** had followed a path to power similar to Mussolini's. At the end of World War I, Hitler had been a jobless soldier drifting around Germany. In 1919, he joined a struggling group called the National Socialist German Workers' Party, better known as the Nazi Party. Despite its name, this party had no ties to socialism.

Hitler proved to be such a powerful public speaker and organizer that he quickly became the party's leader. Calling himself *Der Führer*—"the Leader"—he promised to bring Germany out of chaos.

In his book *Mein Kampf* [My Struggle], Hitler set forth the basic beliefs of Nazism that became the plan of action for the Nazi Party. **Nazism** (nät′sĭz′əm), the German brand of fascism, was based on extreme nationalism. Hitler, who had been born in Austria, dreamed of uniting all German-speaking people in a great German empire.

Hitler also wanted to enforce racial "purification" at home. In his view, Germans—especially blue-eyed, blond-haired "Aryans"—formed a "master race" that was destined to rule the world. "Inferior races," such as Jews, Slavs, and all nonwhites, were deemed fit only to serve the Aryans.

A third element of Nazism was national expansion. Hitler believed that for Germany to thrive, it needed more *lebensraum*, or living space. One of the Nazis' aims, as Hitler wrote in *Mein Kampf*, was "to secure for the German people the land and soil to which they are entitled on this earth," even if this could be accomplished only by "the might of a victorious sword." **D**

The Great Depression helped the Nazis come to power. Because of war debts and dependence on American loans and investments, Germany's economy was hit hard. By 1932, some 6 million Germans were unemployed. Many men who were out of work joined Hitler's private army, the *storm troopers* (or *Brown Shirts*). The German people were desperate and turned to Hitler as their last hope.

By mid 1932, the Nazis had become the strongest political party in Germany. In January 1933, Hitler was appointed chancellor (prime minister). Once in power, Hitler quickly dismantled Germany's democratic Weimar Republic. In its place he established the *Third Reich*, or Third German Empire. According to Hitler, the Third Reich would be a "Thousand-Year Reich"—it would last for a thousand years.

MAIN IDEA

Summarizing
D What were the key ideas and goals that Hitler presented in *Mein Kampf*?

Background
According to Hitler there were three German empires: the Holy Roman Empire; The German Empire of 1871–1918; and The Third Reich.

Japan Invades Manchuria, 1931

SOVIET UNION

Japan took control of the southern half of Sakhalin Island in 1905.

MONGOLIA

MANCHURIA
(Province of China)

Mukden

CHINA

KOREA

Sea of Japan
(East Sea)

JAPAN

Tokyo

In 1910, Korea was annexed by Japan.

Yellow Sea

East China Sea

PACIFIC OCEAN

135°E

Tropic of Cancer

0   200   400 miles
0   200   400 kilometers

Italy Invades Ethiopia, 1935–1936

ITALY

Rome

Mediterranean Sea

Red Sea

15°N

ETHIOPIA

Addis Ababa

0°

Equator

INDIAN OCEAN

0°

15°S

Tropic of Capricorn

0   400   800 miles
0   400   800 kilometers

GEOGRAPHY SKILLBUILDER

1. Location What countries were aggressors during this period?

2. Movement Notice the size and location of Italy and of Japan with respect to the country each invaded. What similarities do you see?

MILITARISTS GAIN CONTROL IN JAPAN Halfway around the world, nationalistic military leaders were trying to take control of the imperial government of Japan. These leaders shared in common with Hitler a belief in the need for more living space for a growing population. Ignoring the protests of more moderate Japanese officials, the militarists launched a surprise attack and seized control of the Chinese province of Manchuria in 1931. Within several months, Japanese troops controlled the entire province, a large region about twice the size of Texas, that was rich in natural resources. **E**

The watchful League of Nations had been established after World War I to prevent just such aggressive acts. In this greatest test of the League's power, representatives were sent to Manchuria to investigate the situation. Their report condemned Japan, who in turn simply quit the League. Meanwhile, the success of the Manchurian invasion put the militarists firmly in control of Japan's government.

AGGRESSION IN EUROPE AND AFRICA The failure of the League of Nations to take action against Japan did not escape the notice of Europe's dictators. In 1933, Hitler pulled Germany out of the League. In 1935, he began a military buildup in violation of the Treaty of Versailles. A year later, he sent troops into the Rhineland, a German region bordering France and Belgium that was demilitarized as a result of the Treaty of Versailles. The League did nothing to stop Hitler.

MAIN IDEA

Analyzing Motives

E Why did Japan invade Manchuria?

Background

Military government had centuries-old roots in Japan. The shogun lords of the Middle Ages had been military leaders.

Meanwhile, Mussolini began building his new Roman Empire. His first target was Ethiopia, one of Africa's few remaining independent countries. By the fall of 1935, tens of thousands of Italian soldiers stood ready to advance on Ethiopia. The League of Nations reacted with brave talk of "collective resistance to all acts of unprovoked aggression."

When the invasion began, however, the League's response was an ineffective economic boycott—little more than a slap on Italy's wrist. By May 1936, Ethiopia had fallen. In desperation, Haile Selassie, the ousted Ethiopian emperor, appealed to the League for assistance. Nothing was done. "It is us today," he told them. "It will be you tomorrow."

CIVIL WAR BREAKS OUT IN SPAIN In 1936, a group of Spanish army officers led by General **Francisco Franco**, rebelled against the Spanish republic. Revolts broke out all over Spain, and the Spanish Civil War began. The war aroused passions not only in Spain but throughout the world. About 3,000 Americans formed the Abraham Lincoln Battalion and traveled to Spain to fight against Franco. "We knew, we just knew," recalled Martha Gellhorn, "that Spain was the place to stop fascism." Among the volunteers were African Americans still bitter about Mussolini's invasion of Ethiopia the year before.

Such limited aid was not sufficient to stop the spread of fascism, however. The Western democracies remained neutral. Although the Soviet Union sent equipment and advisers, Hitler and Mussolini backed Franco's forces with troops, weapons, tanks, and fighter planes. The war forged a close relationship between the German and Italian dictators, who signed a formal alliance known as the Rome-Berlin Axis. After a loss of almost 500,000 lives, Franco's victory in 1939 established him as Spain's fascist dictator. Once again a totalitarian government ruled in Europe. **F**

MAIN IDEA

Summarizing
F What foreign countries were involved in the Spanish Civil War?

HISTORICAL SPOTLIGHT

AFRICAN AMERICANS STAND BY ETHIOPIANS

When Mussolini invaded Ethiopia, many Europeans and Americans—especially African Americans—were outraged. Almost overnight, African Americans organized to raise money for medical supplies, and a few went to fight in Ethiopia. Years later, the Ethiopian emperor Haile Selassie (shown above) said of these efforts,

"We can never forget the help Ethiopia received from Negro Americans during the terrible crisis. . . . It moved me to know that Americans of African descent did not abandon their embattled brothers, but stood by us."

◀ A French journalist escapes from Spain to France with a child he rescued from a street battle. Fighting would soon engulf not only France but the rest of Europe and parts of Asia.

The United States Responds Cautiously

Most Americans were alarmed by the international conflicts of the mid-1930s but believed that the United States should not get involved. In 1928, the United States had signed the Kellogg-Briand Pact. The treaty was signed by 62 countries and declared that war would not be used "as an instrument of national policy." Yet it did not include a plan to deal with countries that broke their pledge. The Pact was, therefore, only a small step toward peace.

AMERICANS CLING TO ISOLATIONISM In the early 1930s, a flood of books argued that the United States had been dragged into World War I by greedy bankers and arms dealers. Public outrage led to the creation of a congressional committee, chaired by North Dakota Senator Gerald Nye, that held hearings on these charges. The Nye committee fueled the controversy by documenting the large profits that banks and manufacturers made during the war. As the furor grew over these "merchants of death," Americans became more determined than ever to avoid war. Antiwar feeling was so strong that the Girl Scouts of America changed the color of its uniforms from khaki to green to appear less militaristic. **G**

Americans' growing isolationism eventually had an impact on President Roosevelt's foreign policy. When he had first taken office in 1933, Roosevelt felt comfortable reaching out to the world in several ways. He officially recognized the Soviet Union in 1933 and agreed to exchange ambassadors with Moscow. He continued the policy of nonintervention in Latin America—begun by Presidents Coolidge and Hoover—with his Good Neighbor Policy and withdrew armed forces stationed there. In 1934, Roosevelt pushed the Reciprocal Trade Agreement Act through Congress. This act lowered trade barriers by giving the president the power to make trade agreements with other nations and was aimed at reducing

MAIN IDEA

Analyzing Causes

G What factors contributed to Americans' growing isolationism?

Analyzing Political Cartoons

"THE ONLY WAY WE CAN SAVE HER"

During the late 1930s, Americans watched events in Europe with growing alarm. Dictators were destroying democratic systems of government throughout Europe and dragging the continent into war. These political events overseas divided American public opinion. Some Americans felt that the United States should help European democracies. However, isolationists—people who believed that the United States should not interfere in other nations' affairs—strictly opposed getting involved in the disputes of "war-mad Europe."

SKILLBUILDER
Analyzing Political Cartoons

1. Why is America labeled "The last refuge of democracy"?
2. What does the kneeling figure fear will happen to America if Uncle Sam gets involved?
3. What U.S. policy does the cartoon support?

 SEE SKILLBUILDER HANDBOOK, PAGE R24.

tariffs by as much as 50 percent. In an effort to keep the United States out of future wars, beginning in 1935, Congress passed a series of **Neutrality Acts**. The first two acts outlawed arms sales or loans to nations at war. The third act was passed in response to the fighting in Spain. This act extended the ban on arms sales and loans to nations engaged in civil wars.

NEUTRALITY BREAKS DOWN Despite congressional efforts to legislate neutrality, Roosevelt found it impossible to remain neutral. When Japan launched a new attack on China in July 1937, Roosevelt found a way around the Neutrality Acts. Because Japan had not formally declared war against China, the president claimed there was no need to enforce the Neutrality Acts. The United States continued sending arms and supplies to China. A few months later, Roosevelt spoke out strongly against isolationism in a speech delivered in Chicago. He called on peace-loving nations to "quarantine," or isolate, aggressor nations in order to stop the spread of war.

A PERSONAL VOICE FRANLKIN DELANO ROOSEVELT

" The peace, the freedom, and the security of 90 percent of the population of the world is being jeopardized by the remaining 10 percent who are threatening a breakdown of all international order and law. Surely the 90 percent who want to live in peace under law and in accordance with moral standards that have received almost universal acceptance through the centuries, can and must find some way . . . to preserve peace. "

—"Quarantine Speech," October 5, 1937

At last Roosevelt seemed ready to take a stand against aggression—that is, until isolationist newspapers exploded in protest, accusing the president of leading the nation into war. Roosevelt backed off in the face of criticism, but his speech did begin to shift the debate. For the moment the conflicts remained "over there."

ASSESSMENT

1. TERMS & NAMES For each term or name, write a sentence explaining its significance.
- Joseph Stalin
- totalitarian
- Benito Mussolini
- fascism
- Adolf Hitler
- Nazism
- Francisco Franco
- Neutrality Acts

MAIN IDEA

2. TAKING NOTES
Using a web diagram like the one below, fill it in with the main ambition of each dictator.

What ambitions did the dictators have in common?

CRITICAL THINKING

3. ANALYZING CAUSES
How did the Treaty of Versailles sow the seeds of instability in Europe?
Think About:
- effects of the treaty on Germany and the Soviet Union
- effects of the treaty on national pride
- the economic legacy of the war

4. DRAWING CONCLUSIONS
Why do you think Hitler found widespread support among the German people? Support your answer with details from the text.

5. FORMING GENERALIZATIONS
Would powerful nations or weak nations be more likely to follow an isolationist policy? Explain.

PI 3.4   CC Unit 1.I.B.4   CC Unit 6.I.B.1
PI 4.3   CC Unit 6.I.B.2   CC Unit 6.I.B.3

War in Europe

MAIN IDEA	WHY IT MATTERS NOW	Terms & Names
Using the sudden mass attack called *blitzkrieg*, Germany invaded and quickly conquered many European countries.	Hitler's actions started World War II and still serve as a warning to be vigilant about totalitarian government.	• Neville Chamberlain • Winston Churchill • appeasement • nonaggression pact • *blitzkrieg* • Charles de Gaulle

One American's Story

hmhsocialstudies.com
TAKING NOTES

Use the graphic organizer online to take notes on major events in German expansion from 1937 to 1940.

In 1940, CBS correspondent William Shirer stood in the forest near Compiègne, where 22 years earlier defeated German generals had signed the armistice ending World War I. Shirer was now waiting for Adolf Hitler to deliver his armistice terms to a defeated France. He watched as Hitler walked up to the monument and slowly read the inscription: "Here on the eleventh of November 1918 succumbed the criminal pride of the German empire . . . vanquished by the free peoples which it tried to enslave." Later that day, Shirer wrote a diary entry describing the führer's reaction.

A PERSONAL VOICE WILLIAM SHIRER

" I have seen that face many times at the great moments of his life. But today! It is afire with scorn, anger, hate, revenge, triumph. He steps off the monument and contrives to make even this gesture a masterpiece of contempt. . . . He glances slowly around the clearing, and now, as his eyes meet ours, you grasp the depth of his hatred. But there is triumph there too—revengeful, triumphant hate. "

—*Berlin Diary: The Journal of a Foreign Correspondent, 1934–1941*

▲
William Shirer, a journalist and historian, became well known for his radio broadcasts from Berlin at the beginning of World War II.

Again and again Shirer had heard Hitler proclaim that "Germany needs peace. . . . Germany wants peace." The hatred and vengefulness that drove the dictator's every action, however, drew Germany ever closer to war.

Austria and Czechoslovakia Fall

On November 5, 1937, Hitler met secretly with his top military advisers. He boldly declared that to grow and prosper Germany needed the land of its neighbors. His plan was to absorb Austria and Czechoslovakia into the Third Reich. When one of his advisers protested that annexing those countries could provoke war, Hitler replied, "'The German Question' can be solved only by means of force, and this is never without risk."

UNION WITH AUSTRIA Austria was Hitler's first target. The Paris Peace Conference following World War I had created the relatively small nation of Austria out of what was left of the Austro-Hungarian Empire. The majority of Austria's 6 million people were Germans who favored unification with Germany. On March 12, 1938, German troops marched into Austria unopposed. A day later, Germany announced that its *Anschluss*, or "union," with Austria was complete. The United States and the rest of the world did nothing.

BARGAINING FOR THE SUDETENLAND Hitler then turned to Czechoslovakia. About 3 million German-speaking people lived in the western border regions of Czechoslovakia called the Sudetenland. The mountainous region formed Czechoslovakia's main defense against German attack. (See map, p. 744.) Hitler wanted to annex Czechoslovakia in order to provide more living space for Germany as well as to control its important natural resources.

Hitler charged that the Czechs were abusing the Sudeten Germans, and he began massing troops on the Czech border. The U.S. correspondent William Shirer, then stationed in Berlin, wrote in his diary: "The Nazi press [is] full of hysterical headlines. All lies. Some examples: 'Women and Children Mowed Down by Czech Armored Cars,' or 'Bloody Regime—New Czech Murders of Germans.'"

Early in the crisis, both France and Great Britain promised to protect Czechoslovakia. Then, just when war seemed inevitable, Hitler invited French premier Édouard Daladier and British prime minister **Neville Chamberlain** to meet with him in Munich. When they arrived, the führer declared that the annexation of the Sudetenland would be his "last territorial demand." In their eagerness to avoid war, Daladier and Chamberlain chose to believe him. On September 30, 1938, they signed the Munich Agreement, which turned the Sudetenland over to Germany without a single shot being fired. **Ⓐ**

Chamberlain returned home and proclaimed: "My friends, there has come back from Germany peace with honor. I believe it is peace in our time."

KEY PLAYER

ADOLF HITLER
1889–1945

"All great world-shaking events have been brought about not by written matter, but by the spoken word!" declared Adolf Hitler. A shy and awkward speaker at first, Hitler rehearsed carefully. He even had photographs (shown above) taken of his favorite gestures so he could study them and make changes to produce exactly the desired effect.

Hitler's extraordinary power as a speaker, wrote Otto Strasser, stemmed from an intuitive ability to sense "the vibration of the human heart . . . telling it what it most wants to hear."

MAIN IDEA

Summarizing
Ⓐ What moves did Germany make in its quest for *lebensraum*?

German Advances, 1938–1941

hmhsocialstudies.com INTERACTIVE MAP

Legend:
- Axis powers
- Axis-controlled by Dec. 1941
- Allied territory, Dec. 1941
- Neutral countries
- German troop movements
- Maginot Line

0   200   400 miles
0   200   400 kilometers

GEOGRAPHY SKILLBUILDER
1. **Region** Which European countries did Germany invade?
2. **Location** How was Germany's geographic location an advantage?

Chamberlain's satisfaction was not shared by **Winston Churchill,** Chamberlain's political rival in Great Britain. In Churchill's view, by signing the Munich Agreement, Daladier and Chamberlain had adopted a shameful policy of **appeasement**—or giving up principles to pacify an aggressor. As Churchill bluntly put it, "Britain and France had to choose between war and dishonor. They chose dishonor. They will have war." Nonetheless, the House of Commons approved Chamberlain's policy toward Germany and Churchill responded with a warning.

★ **A PERSONAL VOICE** WINSTON CHURCHILL

" [W]e have passed an awful milestone in our history. . . . And do not suppose that this is the end. . . . This is only the first sip, the first foretaste of a bitter cup which will be proffered to us year by year unless, by a supreme recovery of moral health and martial vigor, we arise again and take our stand for freedom as in the olden time." **B**

—speech to the House of Commons, quoted in *The Gathering Storm*

MAIN IDEA

Analyzing Motives
B What was appeasement, and why did Churchill oppose it so strongly?

The German Offensive Begins

As Churchill had warned, Hitler was not finished expanding the Third Reich. As dawn broke on March 15, 1939, German troops poured into what remained of Czechoslovakia. At nightfall Hitler gloated, "Czechoslovakia has ceased to exist." After that, the German dictator turned his land-hungry gaze toward Germany's eastern neighbor, Poland.

THE SOVIET UNION DECLARES NEUTRALITY Like Czechoslovakia, Poland had a sizable German-speaking population. In the spring of 1939, Hitler began his familiar routine, charging that Germans in Poland were mistreated by the Poles and needed his protection. Some people thought that this time Hitler must be bluffing. After all, an attack on Poland might bring Germany into conflict with the Soviet Union, Poland's eastern neighbor. At the same time, such an attack would most likely provoke a declaration of war from France and Britain—both of whom had promised military aid to Poland. The result would be a two-front war. Fighting on two fronts had exhausted Germany in World War I. Surely, many thought, Hitler would not be foolish enough to repeat that mistake.

As tensions rose over Poland, Stalin surprised everyone by signing a **nonaggression pact** with Hitler. Once bitter enemies, on August 23, 1939 fascist Germany and communist Russia now committed never to attack each other. Germany and the Soviet Union also signed a second, secret pact, agreeing to divide Poland between them. With the danger of a two-front war eliminated, the fate of Poland was sealed.

BLITZKRIEG IN POLAND As day broke on September 1, 1939, the German _Luftwaffe_, or German air force, roared over Poland, raining bombs on military bases, airfields, railroads, and cities. At the same time, German tanks raced across the Polish countryside, spreading terror and confusion. This invasion was the first test of Germany's newest military strategy, the **_blitzkrieg_**, or lightning war. Blitzkrieg made use of advances in military technology—such as fast tanks and more powerful aircraft—to take the enemy by surprise and then quickly crush all opposition with overwhelming force. On September 3, two days following the terror in Poland, Britain and France declared war on Germany. **C**

The blitzkrieg tactics worked perfectly. Major fighting was over in three weeks, long before France, Britain, and their allies could mount a defense. In the last week of fighting, the Soviet Union attacked Poland from the east, grabbing some of its territory. The portion Germany annexed in western Poland contained almost two-thirds of Poland's population. By the end of the month, Poland had ceased to exist—and World War II had begun.

Background
Luftwaffe in German means "air weapon."

MAIN IDEA

Evaluating
C How did German blitzkrieg tactics rely on new military technology?

▲ German Junkers JU-87 dive-bombers, commonly known as Stukas, were a mainstay of Germany's blitzkrieg style of attack.

◄ A German tank unit in Western Poland in 1939.

THE PHONY WAR For the next several months after the fall of Poland, French and British troops on the Maginot Line, a system of fortifications built along France's eastern border (see map on p. 744), sat staring into Germany, waiting for something to happen. On the Siegfried Line a few miles away German troops stared back. The blitzkrieg had given way to what the Germans called the *sitzkrieg* ("sitting war"), and what some newspapers referred to as the phony war.

After occupying eastern Poland, Stalin began annexing the Baltic states of Estonia, Latvia, and Lithuania. Late in 1939, Stalin sent his Soviet army into Finland. After three months of fighting, the outnumbered Finns surrendered.

Suddenly, on April 9, 1940, Hitler launched a surprise invasion of Denmark and Norway in order "to protect [those countries'] freedom and independence." But in truth, Hitler planned to build bases along the coasts to strike at Great Britain. Next, Hitler turned against the Netherlands, Belgium, and Luxembourg, which were overrun by the end of May. The phony war had ended. **D**

▲
For months there was nothing much to defend against, as the war turned into a *sitzkrieg* endured by soldiers such as this French one on the Maginot Line.

MAIN IDEA

Analyzing Motives
D How did Hitler rationalize the German invasion of Denmark and Norway?

France and Britain Fight On

France's Maginot Line proved to be ineffective; the German army threatened to bypass the line during its invasion of Belgium. Hitler's generals sent their tanks through the Ardennes, a region of wooded ravines in northeast France, thereby avoiding British and French troops who thought the Ardennes were impassable. The Germans continued to march toward Paris.

THE FALL OF FRANCE The German offensive trapped almost 400,000 British and French soldiers as they fled to the beaches of Dunkirk on the French side of the English Channel. In less than a week, a makeshift fleet of fishing trawlers, tugboats, river barges, pleasure craft—more than 800 vessels in all—ferried about 330,000 British, French, and Belgian troops to safety across the Channel.

A few days later, Italy entered the war on the side of Germany and invaded France from the south as the Germans closed in on Paris from the north. On June 22, 1940, at Compiègne, as William Shirer and the rest of the world watched, Hitler handed French officers his terms of surrender. Germans would occupy the northern part of France, and a Nazi-controlled puppet government, headed by Marshal Philippe Pétain, would be set up at Vichy, in southern France.

After France fell, a French general named **Charles de Gaulle** fled to England, where he set up a government-in-exile. De Gaulle proclaimed defiantly, "France has lost a battle, but France has not lost the war."

THE BATTLE OF BRITAIN In the summer of 1940, the Germans began to assemble an invasion fleet along the French coast. Because its naval power could not compete with that of Britain, Germany also launched an air war at the same time. The Luftwaffe began making bombing

Background
Hitler demanded that the surrender take place in the same railroad car where the French had dictated terms to the Germans in World War I.

◀ Children watch with wonder and fear as the battling British and German air forces set the skies of London aflame.

runs over Britain. Its goal was to gain total control of the skies by destroying Britain's Royal Air Force (RAF). Hitler had 2,600 planes at his disposal. On a single day—August 15—approximately 2,000 German planes ranged over Britain. Every night for two solid months, bombers pounded London.

The Battle of Britain raged on through the summer and fall. Night after night, German planes pounded British targets. At first the Luftwaffe concentrated on airfields and aircraft. Next it targeted cities. Londoner Len Jones was just 18 years old when bombs fell on his East End neighborhood.

★ A PERSONAL VOICE LEN JONES

" After an explosion of a nearby bomb, you could actually feel your eyeballs being sucked out. I was holding my eyes to try and stop them going. And the suction was so vast, it ripped my shirt away, and ripped my trousers. Then I couldn't get my breath, the smoke was like acid and everything round me was black and yellow. "

—quoted in *London at War*

The RAF fought back brilliantly. With the help of a new technological device called radar, British pilots accurately plotted the flight paths of German planes, even in darkness. On September 15, 1940 the RAF shot down over 185 German planes; at the same time, they lost only 26 aircraft. Six weeks later, Hitler called off the invasion of Britain indefinitely. "Never in the field of human conflict," said Churchill in praise of the RAF pilots, "was so much owed by so many to so few."

Still, German bombers continued to pound Britain's cities trying to disrupt production and break civilian morale. British pilots also bombed German cities. Civilians in both countries unrelentingly carried on.

KEY PLAYER

WINSTON CHURCHILL 1874–1965

Churchill was possibly Britain's greatest weapon as that nation faced the Nazis. A born fighter, Churchill became prime minister in May 1940 and used his gift as a speaker to arouse Britons and unite them:

"[W]e shall defend our island, whatever the cost may be, we shall fight on the beaches, we shall fight on the landing-grounds, we shall fight in the fields and in the streets, we shall fight in the hills; we shall never surrender."

VIDEO
Winston Churchill
hmhsocialstudies.com

 ASSESSMENT

1. TERMS & NAMES For each term or name, write a sentence explaining its significance.

- Neville Chamberlain
- Winston Churchill
- appeasement
- nonaggression pact
- *blitzkrieg*
- Charles de Gaulle

MAIN IDEA

2. TAKING NOTES
Trace the movement of German expansion from 1937 to the end of 1940 by supplying events to follow the dates shown on the time line.

What event was the most significant? Why?

CRITICAL THINKING

3. ANALYZING MOTIVES
To what extent do you think lies and deception played a role in Hitler's tactics? Support your answer with examples. **Think About:**

- William Shirer's diary entry about headlines in the Nazi newspapers
- Soviet-German relations
- Hitler's justifications for military aggression

4. EVALUATING DECISIONS
If you had been a member of the British House of Commons in 1938, would you have voted for or against the Munich Agreement? Support your decision.

5. DRAWING CONCLUSIONS
Review Germany's aggressive actions between 1938 and 1945. At what point do you think Hitler concluded that he could take any territory without being stopped? Why?

PI 3.4
PI 4.2
CC Unit 6.I.C.5.c

The Holocaust

MAIN IDEA	**WHY IT MATTERS NOW**	**Terms & Names**

During the Holocaust, the Nazis systematically executed 6 million Jews and 5 million other "non-Aryans."

After the atrocities of the Holocaust, agencies formed to publicize human rights. These agencies have remained a force in today's world.

- Holocaust
- *Kristallnacht*
- genocide
- ghetto
- concentration camp

One American's Story

hmhsocialstudies.com
TAKING NOTES

Use the graphic organizer online to take notes on events that led to the Holocaust.

Gerda Weissmann was a carefree girl of 15 when, in September 1939, invading German troops shattered her world. Because the Weissmanns were Jews, they were forced to give up their home to a German family. In 1942, Gerda, her parents, and most of Poland's 3,000,000 Jews were sent to labor camps. Gerda recalls when members of Hitler's elite *Schutzstaffel*, or "security squadron" (SS), came to round up the Jews.

A PERSONAL VOICE GERDA WEISSMANN KLEIN

"We had to form a line and an SS man stood there with a little stick. I was holding hands with my mother and . . . he looked at me and said, 'How old?' And I said, 'eighteen,' and he sort of pushed me to one side and my mother to the other side. . . . And shortly thereafter, some trucks arrived . . . and we were loaded onto the trucks. I heard my mother's voice from very far off ask, 'Where to?' and I shouted back, 'I don't know.'"

—quoted in the film *One Survivor Remembers*

▲ Gerda Weissmann Klein in her mid-teens

When the American lieutenant Kurt Klein, who would later become Gerda's husband, liberated her from the Nazis in 1945—just one day before her 21st birthday—she weighed 68 pounds and her hair had turned white. Even so, of all her family and friends, she alone had survived the Nazis' campaign to exterminate Europe's Jews.

The Persecution Begins

On April 7, 1933, shortly after Hitler took power in Germany, he ordered all "non-Aryans" to be removed from government jobs. This order was one of the first moves in a campaign for racial purity that eventually led to the **Holocaust**—the systematic murder of 6 million Jews across Europe. The Nazis also murdered 5 million other people.

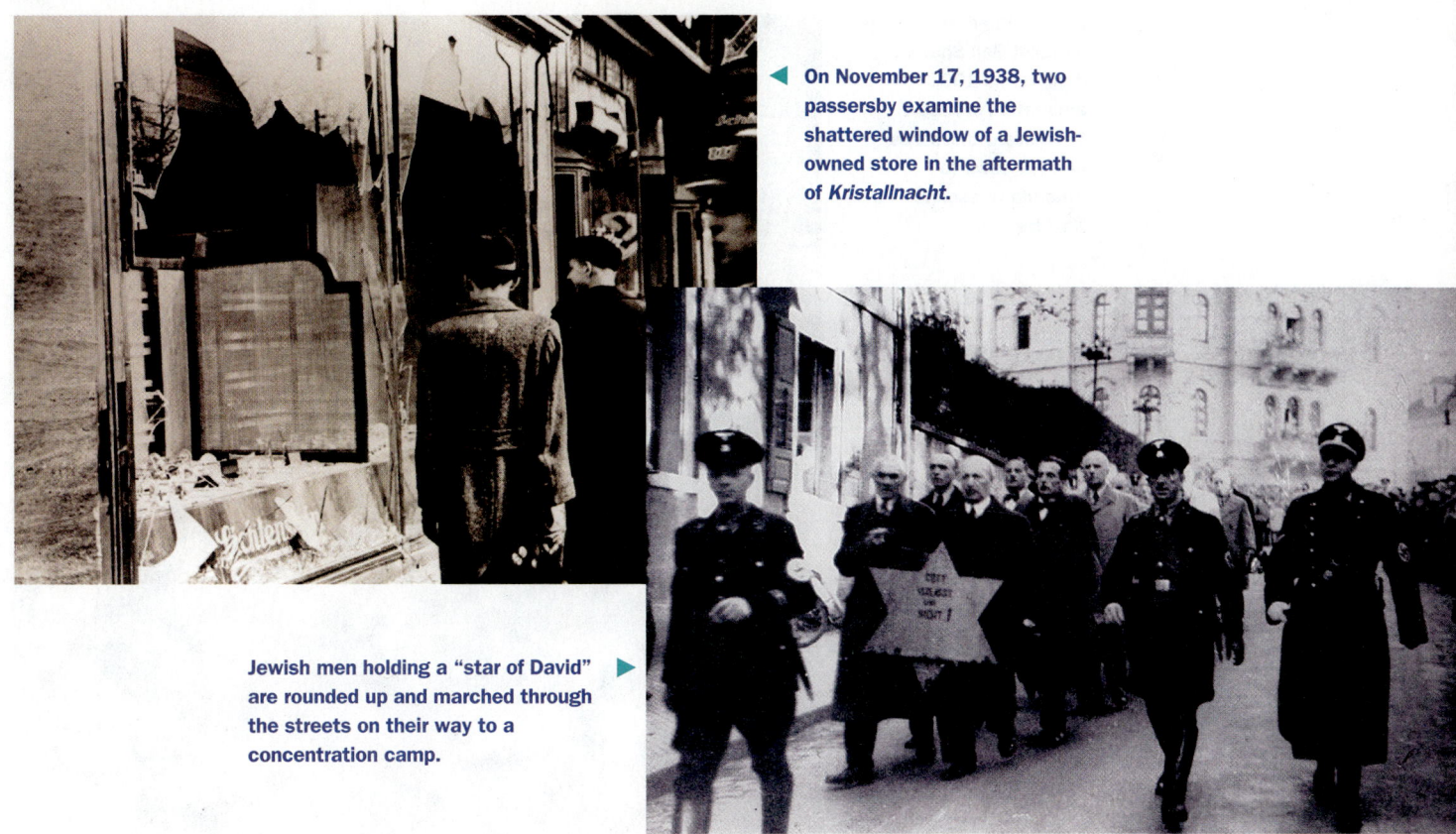

On November 17, 1938, two passersby examine the shattered window of a Jewish-owned store in the aftermath of *Kristallnacht*.

Jewish men holding a "star of David" are rounded up and marched through the streets on their way to a concentration camp.

JEWS TARGETED Although Jews were not the only victims of the Holocaust, they were the center of the Nazis' targets. Anti-Semitism, or hatred of the Jews, had a long history in many European countries. For decades many Germans looking for a scapegoat had blamed the Jews as the cause of their failures. Hitler found that a majority of Germans were willing to support his belief that Jews were responsible for Germany's economic problems and defeat in World War I.

As the Nazis tightened their hold on Germany, their persecution of the Jews increased. In 1935, the Nuremberg Laws stripped Jews of their German citizenship, jobs, and property. To make it easier for the Nazis to identify them, Jews had to wear a bright yellow Star of David attached to their clothing. Worse was yet to come.

KRISTALLNACHT November 9–10, 1938, became known as ***Kristallnacht*** (krĭs′täl′nächt′), or "Night of Broken Glass." Nazi storm troopers attacked Jewish homes, businesses, and synagogues across Germany and Austria. An American who witnessed the violence wrote, "Jewish shop windows by the hundreds were systematically and wantonly smashed. . . . The main streets of the city were a positive litter of shattered plate glass." Around 100 Jews were killed, and hundreds more were injured. Some 30,000 Jews were arrested and hundreds of synagogues were burned. Afterward, the Nazis blamed the Jews for the destruction. Ⓐ

A FLOOD OF JEWISH REFUGEES Kristallnacht marked a step-up in the Nazi policy of Jewish persecution. Nazis tried to speed Jewish emigration but encountered difficulty. Jews fleeing Germany had trouble finding nations that would accept them. France already had 40,000 Jewish refugees and did not want more. The British worried about fueling anti-Semitism and refused to admit more than 80,000 Jewish refugees. They also controlled the Palestine Mandate (part of which later became Israel) and allowed 30,000 refugees to settle there. Late in 1938, Germany's foreign minister, Joachim von Ribbentrop, observed, "We all want to get rid of our Jews. The difficulty is that no country wishes to receive them."

Vocabulary
scapegoat: someone who is made to bear the blame of others

MAIN IDEA

Analyzing Issues
Ⓐ What problems did German Jews face in Nazi Germany from 1935 to 1938?

▶ Jewish American muralist Ben Shahn depicts the 1933 emigration of Albert Einstein and thousands of other Jews to America to escape Nazi terrorism.

Although the average Jew had little chance of reaching the United States, "persons of exceptional merit," including physicist Albert Einstein, author Thomas Mann, architect Walter Gropius, and theologian Paul Tillich were among 100,000 refugees the United States accepted. Many Americans wanted the door closed. Americans were concerned that letting in more refugees during the Great Depression would deny U.S. citizens jobs and threaten economic recovery. Among Americans, there was widespread anti-Semitism and fear that "enemy agents" would be allowed to enter the country. President Roosevelt said that while he sympathized with the Jews, he would not "do anything which would conceivably hurt the future of present American citizens." **B**

THE PLIGHT OF THE *ST. LOUIS* Official indifference to the plight of Germany's Jews was in evidence in the case of the ship *St. Louis*. This German ocean liner passed Miami in 1939. Although 740 of the liner's 943 passengers had U.S. immigration papers, the Coast Guard followed the ship to prevent anyone from disembarking in America. The ship was forced to return to Europe. "The cruise of the St. Louis," wrote the New York Times, "cries to high heaven of man's inhumanity to man." Passenger Liane Reif-Lehrer recalls her childhood experiences.

A PERSONAL VOICE LIANE REIF-LEHRER

" My mother and brother and I were among the passengers who survived. . . . We were sent back to Europe and given haven in France, only to find the Nazis on our doorstep again a few months later. "

—Liane Reif-Lehrer

MAIN IDEA

Analyzing Effects
B How did the United States respond to Jewish refugees?

More than half of the passengers were later murdered in the Holocaust.

Hitler's "Final Solution"

By 1939 only about a quarter million Jews remained in Germany. But other nations that Hitler occupied had millions more. Obsessed with a desire to rid Europe of its Jews, Hitler imposed what he called the "Final Solution"—a policy of **genocide,** the deliberate and systematic murder of an entire population.

HISTORY

VIDEO
The Holocaust
hmhsocialstudies.com

THE CONDEMNED Hitler's Final Solution rested on the belief that Aryans were a superior people and that the strength and purity of this "master race" must be preserved. To accomplish this, the Nazis condemned to slavery and death not only the Jews but other groups that they viewed as inferior or unworthy or as "enemies of the state."

After taking power in 1933, the Nazis had concentrated on silencing their political opponents—communists, socialists, liberals, and anyone else who spoke out against the government. Once the Nazis had eliminated these enemies, they turned against other groups in Germany. In addition to Jews, these groups included the following:

- *Gypsies*—whom the Nazis believed to be an "inferior race"
- *Freemasons*—whom the Nazis charged as supporters of the "Jewish conspiracy" to rule the world
- *Jehovah's Witnesses*—who refused to join the army or salute Hitler

The Nazis also targeted other Germans whom they found unfit to be part of the "master race." Such victims included homosexuals, the mentally deficient, the mentally ill, the physically disabled, and the incurably ill.

Hitler began implementing his Final Solution in Poland with special Nazi death squads. Hitler's elite Nazi "security squadrons" (or SS), rounded up Jews—men, women, children, and babies— and shot them on the spot.

FORCED RELOCATION Jews also were ordered into dismal, overcrowded **ghettos,** segregated Jewish areas in certain Polish cities. The Nazis sealed off the ghettos with barbed wire and stone walls.

Life inside the ghetto was miserable. The bodies of victims piled up in the streets faster than they could be removed. Factories were built alongside ghettos where people were forced to work for German industry. In spite of the impossible living conditions, the Jews hung on. While some formed resistance movements inside the ghettos, others resisted by other means. They published and distributed underground newspapers. Secret schools were set up to educate Jewish children. Even theater and music groups continued to operate.

ANOTHER PERSPECTIVE

DENMARK'S RESISTANCE

King Christian X led the Danish resistance in World War II. In 1942, he rejected the Nazis' demand to enforce the Nuremberg Laws against the Jews in occupied Denmark. In August 1943, the king spoke out against the German occupying forces, an act that led to his imprisonment for the remainder of the war. Virtually all Danish Jews were rescued by being taken to Sweden in boats.

Estimated Jewish Losses

	Pre-Holocaust Population	Number Murdered	
		Low Estimate	High Estimate
Austria	191,000	50,000	65,500
Belgium	60,000	25,000	29,000
Bohemia/Moravia	92,000	77,000	78,300
Denmark	8,000	60	116
Estonia	4,600	1,500	2,000
France	260,000	75,000	77,000
Germany	566,000	135,000	142,000
Greece	73,000	59,000	67,000
Hungary	725,000	502,000	569,000
Italy	48,000	6,500	9,000
Latvia	95,000	70,000	72,000
Lithuania	155,000	130,000	143,000
Luxembourg	3,500	1,000	2,000
Netherlands	112,000	100,000	105,000
Norway	1,700	800	800
Poland	3,250,000	2,700,000	3,000,000
Romania	441,000	121,000	287,000
Slovakia	89,000	60,000	71,000
USSR	2,825,000	700,000	1,100,000
Yugoslavia	68,000	56,000	65,000
TOTALS	9,067,800	4,869,860	5,894,716

Source: Columbia Guide to the Holocaust

SKILLBUILDER Interpreting Charts
Approximately what percentage of the total Jewish population in Europe was murdered during the Holocaust?

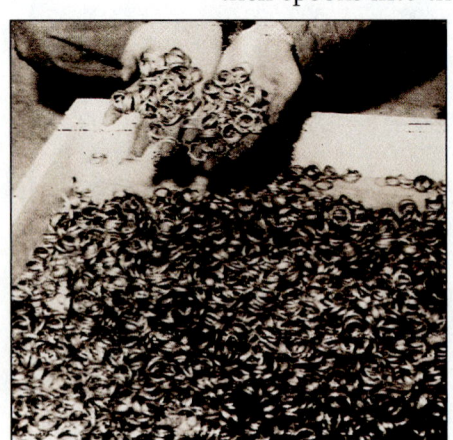

On May 9, 1945, inmates at the Ebensee concentration camp in Austria were liberated by U.S. soldiers.

CONCENTRATION CAMPS Finally, Jews in communities not reached by the killing squads were dragged from their homes and herded onto trains or trucks for shipment to **concentration camps,** or labor camps. Families were often separated, sometimes—like the Weissmanns—forever.

Nazi concentration camps were originally set up to imprison political opponents and protesters. The camps were later turned over to the SS, who expanded the concentration camp and used it to warehouse other "undesirables." Life in the camps was a cycle of hunger, humiliation, and work that almost always ended in death.

The prisoners were crammed into crude wooden barracks that held up to a thousand people each. They shared their crowded quarters, as well as their meager meals, with hordes of rats and fleas. Hunger was so intense, recalled one survivor, "that if a bit of soup spilled over, prisoners would converge on the spot, dig their spoons into the mud and stuff the mess into their mouths."

Inmates in the camps worked from dawn to dusk, seven days a week, until they collapsed. Those too weak to work were killed. Some, like Rudolf Reder, endured. He was one of only two Jews to survive the camp at Belzec, Poland.

After stripping their victims of life and dignity, the Nazis hoarded whatever articles of value the victims had possessed, such as wedding rings and gold fillings from teeth.

A PERSONAL VOICE RUDOLF REDER

"The brute Schmidt was our guard; he beat and kicked us if he thought we were not working fast enough. He ordered his victims to lie down and gave them 25 lashes with a whip, ordering them to count out loud. If the victim made a mistake, he was given 50 lashes. . . . Thirty or 40 of us were shot every day. A doctor usually prepared a daily list of the weakest men. During the lunch break they were taken to a nearby grave and shot. They were replaced the following morning by new arrivals from the transport of the day. . . . It was a miracle if anyone survived for five or six months in Belzec."

—quoted in *The Holocaust*

The Final Stage

The Final Solution reached its final stage in early 1942. At a meeting held in Wannsee, a lakeside suburb near Berlin, Hitler's top officials agreed to begin a new phase of the mass murder of Jews. To mass slaughter and starvation they would add a third method of killing—murder by poison gas. **C**

MASS EXTERMINATIONS As deadly as overwork, starvation, beatings, and bullets were, they did not kill fast enough to satisfy the Nazis. The Germans built six death camps in Poland. The first, Chelmno, began operating in 1941—before the meeting at Wannsee. Each camp had several huge gas chambers in which as many as 12,000 people could be killed a day.

When prisoners arrived at Auschwitz, the largest of the death camps, they had to parade by several SS doctors. With a wave of the hand, the doctors separated those strong enough to work from those who would die that day. Both groups were told to leave all their belongings behind, with a promise that they would be returned later. Those destined to die were then led into a room outside the gas chamber and were told to undress for a shower. To complete the deception, the prisoners were even

MAIN IDEA

Summarizing
C What was the goal of the Nazis' Final Solution, and how was that goal nearly achieved?

Prisoners were required to wear color-coded triangles on their uniforms. The categories of prisoners include communists, socialists, criminals, emigrants, Jehovah's Witnesses, homosexuals, Germans "shy of work," and other nationalities "shy of work." The vertical categories show a variation. One for repeat offenders, one for prisoners assigned to punish other prisoners, and double triangles for Jews. Letters on top of a patch indicate nationality.

Children taken from Eastern Europe and imprisoned in Auschwitz look out from behind the barbed-wire fence in July 1944.

given pieces of soap. Finally, they were led into the chamber and poisoned with cyanide gas that spewed from vents in the walls. This orderly mass extermination was sometimes carried out to the accompaniment of cheerful music played by an orchestra of camp inmates who had temporarily been spared execution.

At first the bodies were buried in huge pits. At Belzec, Rudolf Reder was part of a 500-man death brigade that labored all day, he said, "either at grave digging or emptying the gas chambers." But the decaying corpses gave off a stench that could be smelled for miles around. Worse yet, mass graves left evidence of the mass murder. Lilli Kopecky recalls her arrival at Auschwitz.

★ A PERSONAL VOICE LILLI KOPECKY

"When we came to Auschwitz, we smelt the sweet smell. They said to us: 'There the people are gassed, three kilometers over there.' We didn't believe it."

—quoted in *Never Again*

At some camps, to try to cover up the evidence of their slaughter, the Nazis installed huge crematoriums, or ovens, in which to burn the dead. At other camps, the bodies were simply thrown into a pit and set on fire.

Gassing was not the only method of extermination used in the camps. Prisoners were also shot, hanged, or injected with poison.

Still others died as a result of horrible medical experiments carried out by camp doctors. Some of these victims were injected with deadly germs in order to study the effect of disease on different groups of people. Many more were used to test methods of sterilization, a subject of great interest to some Nazi doctors in their search for ways to improve the "master race."

THE SURVIVORS An estimated six million Jews died in the death camps and in the Nazi massacres. But some miraculously escaped the worst of the Holocaust. Many had help from ordinary people who were appalled by the Nazis' treatment of Jews. Some Jews even survived the horrors of the concentration camps.

In Gerda Weissmann Klein's view, survival depended as much on one's spirit as on getting enough to eat. "I do believe that if you were blessed with imagination, you could work through it," she wrote. "If, unfortunately, you were a person that faced reality, I think you didn't have much of a chance." Those who did come out of the camps alive were forever changed by what they had witnessed. For survivor Elie Wiesel, who entered Auschwitz in 1944 at the age of 14, the sun had set forever.

" Survival is both an exalted privilege and a painful burden."
GERDA WEISSMANN KLEIN

★ A PERSONAL VOICE ELIE WIESEL

" Never shall I forget that night, the first night in camp, that turned my life into one long night seven times sealed. Never shall I forget that smoke. Never shall I forget the small faces of the children whose bodies I saw transformed into smoke under a silent sky. Never shall I forget those flames that consumed my faith forever. Never shall I forget the nocturnal silence that deprived me of all eternity of the desire to live. Never shall I forget those moments that murdered my God and my soul and turned my dreams to ashes. Never shall I forget those things, even were I condemned to live as long as God Himself. Never. "

—*Night*

▲
Elie Wiesel, 1986

ASSESSMENT

1. TERMS & NAMES For each term or name, write a sentence explaining its significance.
- Holocaust
- *Kristallnacht*
- genocide
- ghetto
- concentration camp

MAIN IDEA

2. TAKING NOTES
List at least four events that led to the Holocaust.

Cause	Effect
→	The Holocaust

Write a paragraph summarizing one of the events that you listed.

CRITICAL THINKING

3. EVALUATING DECISIONS
Do you think that the United States was justified in not allowing more Jewish refugees to immigrate? Why or why not? **Think About:**
- the views of isolationists in the United States
- some Americans' prejudices and fears
- the incident on the German luxury liner *St. Louis*

4. DEVELOPING HISTORICAL PERSPECTIVE
Why do you think the Nazi system of systematic genocide was so brutally effective? Support your answer with details from the text.

5. ANALYZING MOTIVES
How might concentration camp doctors and guards have justified to themselves the death and suffering they caused other human beings?

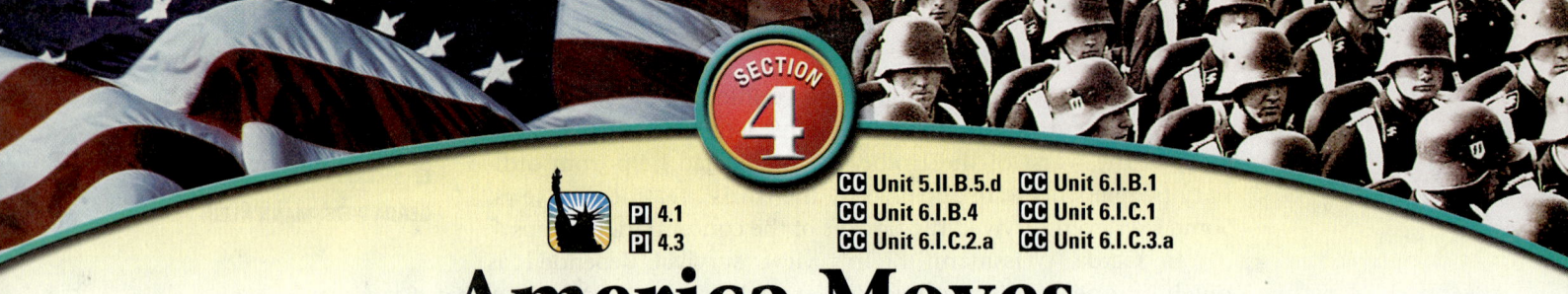

CC Unit 5.II.B.5.d **CC** Unit 6.I.B.1
CC Unit 6.I.B.4 **CC** Unit 6.I.C.1
CC Unit 6.I.C.2.a **CC** Unit 6.I.C.3.a

PI 4.1
PI 4.3

America Moves Toward War

MAIN IDEA	WHY IT MATTERS NOW	Terms & Names
In response to the fighting in Europe, the United States provided economic and military aid to help the Allies achieve victory.	The military capability of the U. S. became a deciding factor in World War II and in world affairs ever since.	• Axis powers • Allies • Lend-Lease Act • Hideki Tojo • Atlantic Charter

One American's Story

TAKING NOTES

Use the graphic organizer online to take notes on the key events leading to the entry of the United States into World War II.

Two days after Hitler invaded Poland, President Roosevelt spoke reassuringly to Americans about the outbreak of war in Europe.

> ★ **A PERSONAL VOICE** FRANKLIN DELANO ROOSEVELT
>
> " This nation will remain a neutral nation, but I cannot ask that every American remain neutral in thought as well. . . . Even a neutral cannot be asked to close his mind or his conscience. . . . I have said not once, but many times, that I have seen war and I hate war. . . . As long as it is my power to prevent, there will be no blackout of peace in the U.S. "
>
> —radio speech, September 3, 1939

Although Roosevelt knew that Americans were still deeply committed to staying out of war, he also believed that there could be no peace in a world controlled by dictators.

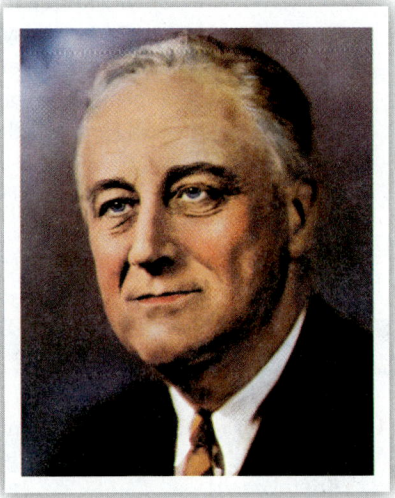
▲
Franklin D. Roosevelt

The United States Musters Its Forces

As German tanks thundered across Poland, Roosevelt revised the Neutrality Act of 1935. At the same time, he began to prepare the nation for the struggle he feared lay just ahead.

MOVING CAUTIOUSLY AWAY FROM NEUTRALITY In September of 1939, Roosevelt persuaded Congress to pass a "cash-and-carry" provision that allowed warring nations to buy U.S. arms as long as they paid cash and transported them in their own ships. Providing the arms, Roosevelt argued, would help France and Britain defeat Hitler and keep the United States out of the war. Isolationists attacked Roosevelt for his actions. However, after six weeks of heated debate, Congress passed the Neutrality Act of 1939, and a cash-and-carry policy went into effect.

CARVING IT UP

The three Axis nations—Germany, Italy, and Japan—were a threat to the entire world. They believed they were superior and more powerful than other nations, especially democracies. By signing a mutual defense pact, the Axis powers believed the United States would never risk involvement in a two-ocean war. This cartoon shows the Axis powers' obsession with global domination.

SKILLBUILDER Analyzing Political Cartoons
1. What are the Axis leaders—Hitler, Mussolini, and Tojo—greedily carving up?
2. What do you think the artist means by showing Hitler doing the carving?

 SEE SKILLBUILDER HANDBOOK, PAGE R24.

THE AXIS THREAT The United States cash-and-carry policy began to look like too little, too late. By summer 1940, France had fallen and Britain was under siege. Roosevelt scrambled to provide the British with "all aid short of war." By June he had sent Britain 500,000 rifles and 80,000 machine guns, and in early September the United States traded 50 old destroyers for leases on British military bases in the Caribbean and Newfoundland. British prime minister Winston Churchill would later recall this move with affection as "a decidedly unneutral act."

On September 27 Americans were jolted by the news that Germany, Italy, and Japan had signed a mutual defense treaty, the Tripartite Pact. The three nations became known as the **Axis powers.**

The Tripartite Pact was aimed at keeping the United States out of the war. Under the treaty, each Axis nation agreed to come to the defense of the others in case of attack. This meant that if the United States were to declare war on any one of the Axis powers, it would face its worst military nightmare—a two-ocean war, with fighting in both the Atlantic and the Pacific.

BUILDING U.S. DEFENSES Meanwhile, Roosevelt asked Congress to increase spending for national defense. Despite years of U.S. isolationism, Nazi victories in 1940 changed U.S. thinking, and Congress boosted defense spending. Congress also passed the nation's first peacetime military draft—the Selective Training and Service Act. Under this law 16 million men between the ages of 21 and 35 were registered. Of these, 1 million were to be drafted for one year but were only allowed to serve in the Western Hemisphere. Roosevelt himself drew the first draft numbers as he told a national radio audience, "This is a most solemn ceremony." **A**

MAIN IDEA

Analyzing Effects

A What impact did the outbreak of war in Europe have on U.S. foreign and defense policy?

ROOSEVELT RUNS FOR A THIRD TERM That same year, Roosevelt decided to break the tradition of a two-term presidency, begun by George Washington, and run for reelection. To the great disappointment of isolationists, Roosevelt's Republican opponent, a public utilities executive named Wendell Willkie, supported Roosevelt's policy of aiding Britain. At the same time, both Willkie and Roosevelt promised to keep the nation out of war. Because there was so little difference between the candidates, the majority of voters chose the one they knew better. Roosevelt was reelected with nearly 55 percent of the votes cast.

"The Great Arsenal of Democracy"

Not long after the election, President Roosevelt told his radio audience during a fireside chat that it would be impossible to negotiate a peace with Hitler. "No man can tame a tiger into a kitten by stroking it." He warned that if Britain fell, the Axis powers would be left unchallenged to conquer the world, at which point, he said, "all of us in all the Americas would be living at the point of a gun." To prevent such a situation, the United States had to help defeat the Axis threat by turning itself into what Roosevelt called "the great arsenal of democracy."

THE LEND-LEASE PLAN By late 1940, however, Britain had no more cash to spend in the arsenal of democracy. Roosevelt tried to help by suggesting a new plan that he called a lend-lease policy. Under this plan, the president would lend or lease arms and other supplies to "any country whose defense was vital to the United States."

Roosevelt compared his plan to lending a garden hose to a neighbor whose house was on fire. He asserted that this was the only sensible thing to do to prevent the fire from spreading to your own property. Isolationists argued bitterly against the plan, but most Americans favored it, and Congress passed the **Lend-Lease Act** in March 1941.

Vocabulary
lease: to grant use or occupation of under the terms of a contract

---

POINT

"The United States should not become involved in European wars."

Still recovering from World War I and struggling with the Great Depression, many Americans believed their country should remain strictly neutral in the war in Europe.

Representative James F. O'Connor voiced the country's reservations when he asked, "Dare we set America up and commit her as the financial and military blood bank of the rest of the world?" O'Connor maintained that the United States could not "right every wrong" or "police [the] world."

The aviator Charles Lindbergh stated his hope that "the future of America . . . not be tied to these eternal wars in Europe." Lindbergh asserted that "Americans [should] fight anybody and everybody who attempts to interfere with our hemisphere." However, he went on to say, "Our safety does not lie in fighting European wars. It lies in our own internal strength, in the character of the American people and American institutions." Like many isolationists, Lindbergh believed that democracy would not be saved "by the forceful imposition of our ideals abroad, but by example of their successful operation at home."

COUNTERPOINT

"The United States must protect democracies throughout the world."

As the conflict in Europe deepened, interventionists embraced President Franklin D. Roosevelt's declaration that "when peace has been broken anywhere, peace of all countries everywhere is in danger." Roosevelt emphasized the global character of 20th-century commerce and communication by noting, "Every word that comes through the air, every ship that sails the sea, every battle that is fought does affect the American future."

Roosevelt and other political leaders also appealed to the nation's conscience. Secretary of State Cordell Hull noted that the world was "face to face . . . with an organized, ruthless, and implacable movement of steadily expanding conquest." In the same vein, Undersecretary of State Sumner Welles called Hitler "a sinister and pitiless conqueror [who] has reduced more than half of Europe to abject serfdom."

After the war expanded into the Atlantic, Roosevelt declared, "It is time for all Americans . . . to stop being deluded by the romantic notion that the Americas can go on living happily and peacefully in a Nazi-dominated world." He added, "Let us not ask ourselves whether the Americas should begin to defend themselves after the first attack . . . or the twentieth attack. The time for active defense is now."

THINKING CRITICALLY

1. **CONNECT TO TODAY** Making Inferences After World War I, many Americans became isolationists. Do you recommend that the United States practice isolationism today? Why or why not?

2. **CONNECT TO HISTORY** Researching and Reporting Do research to find out more about Charles Lindbergh's antiwar activities. Present your findings in an editorial.

 SEE SKILLBUILDER HANDBOOK, PAGE R34.

MAIN IDEA

Drawing Conclusions

B Why did Roosevelt take one "unneutral" step after another to assist Britain and the Soviet Union in 1941?

SUPPORTING STALIN Britain was not the only nation to receive lend-lease aid. In June 1941, Hitler broke the agreement he had made in 1939 with Stalin not to go to war and invaded the Soviet Union. Acting on the principle that "the enemy of my enemy is my friend," Roosevelt began sending lend-lease supplies to the Soviet Union. Some Americans opposed providing aid to Stalin; Roosevelt, however, agreed with Winston Churchill, who had said "if Hitler invaded Hell," the British would be prepared to work with the devil himself. **B**

GERMAN WOLF PACKS Providing lend-lease aid was one thing, but to ensure the safe delivery of goods to Britain and to the Soviet Union, supply lines had to be kept open across the Atlantic Ocean. To prevent delivery of lend-lease shipments, Hitler deployed hundreds of German submarines—U-boats—to attack supply ships.

From the spring through the fall of 1941, individual surface attacks by individual U-boats gave way to what became known as the wolf pack attack. At night groups of up to 40 submarines patrolled areas in the North Atlantic where convoys could be expected. Wolf packs were successful in sinking as much as 350,000 tons of shipments in a single month. In June 1941, President Roosevelt granted the navy permission for U.S. warships to attack German U-boats in self-defense. By late 1943, the submarine menace was contained by electronic detection techniques (especially radar), and by airborne antisubmarine patrols operating from small escort aircraft carriers.

Science & Technology

hmhsocialstudies.com **INTERACTIVE**

GERMAN WOLF PACKS

On October 17, 1940, near Rockall, west of Ireland, a British Convoy, SC-7 (shown below), was attacked by a German wolf pack. The convoy was outlined clearly against a moonlit sky, making the merchant ships easy prey.

At the start of the war, the British had too few warships to escort the convoys.

A tanker burns and sinks in the Atlantic Ocean after being torpedoed by a German U-boat.

German aircraft could patrol 1,000 miles out to sea to scout for convoys.

The Germans used radios to summon U-boats into a fighting wolf pack.

U-boats used hydrophonic equipment to pick up the sound of convoy propellers up to 100 miles away.

Convoys pinned their hopes on finding U-boats using ASDIC—sonar apparatus that could detect submerged submarines.

FDR Plans for War

Although Roosevelt was popular, his foreign policy was under constant attack. American forces were seriously underarmed. Roosevelt's August 1941 proposal to extend the term of draftees passed in the House of Representatives by only one vote. With the army provided for, Roosevelt began planning for the war he was certain would come.

THE ATLANTIC CHARTER While Congress voted on the extension of the draft, Roosevelt and Churchill met secretly at a summit aboard the battleship USS *Augusta*. Although Churchill hoped for a military commitment, he settled for a joint declaration of war aims, called the **Atlantic Charter.** Both countries pledged the following: collective security, disarmament, self-determination, economic cooperation, and freedom of the seas. Roosevelt disclosed to Churchill that he couldn't ask Congress for a declaration of war against Germany, but "he would wage war" and do "everything" to "force an incident."

The Atlantic Charter became the basis of a new document called "A Declaration of the United Nations." The term *United Nations* was suggested by Roosevelt to express the common purpose of the **Allies**, those nations that had fought the Axis powers. The declaration was signed by 26 nations, "four-fifths of the human race" observed Churchill. **C**

MAIN IDEA

Summarizing
C Why was the Atlantic Charter important?

SHOOT ON SIGHT After a German submarine fired on the U.S. destroyer *Greer* in the Atlantic on September 4, 1941, Roosevelt ordered navy commanders to respond. "When you see a rattlesnake poised to strike," the president explained, "you crush him." Roosevelt ordered the navy to shoot the German submarines on sight.

Two weeks later, the *Pink Star*, an American merchant ship, was sunk off Greenland. In mid-October, a U-boat torpedoed the U.S. destroyer *Kearny*, and 11 lives were lost.

Days later, German U-boats sank the U.S. destroyer *Reuben James*, killing more than 100 sailors. "America has been attacked," Roosevelt announced grimly. "The shooting has started. And history has recorded who fired the first shot." As the death toll mounted, the Senate finally repealed the ban against arming merchant ships. A formal declaration of a full-scale war seemed inevitable. **D**

MAIN IDEA

Analyzing Causes
D Why did the United States enter into an undeclared shooting war with Germany in fall 1941?

Japan Attacks the United States

The United States was now involved in an undeclared naval war with Hitler. However, the attack that brought the United States into the war came from Japan.

JAPAN'S AMBITIONS IN THE PACIFIC Germany's European victories created new opportunities for Japanese expansionists. Japan was already in control of Manchuria. In July 1937, **Hideki Tojo** (hē′d-kē tō′jō′), chief of staff of Japan's Kwantung Army, launched the invasion into China. As French, Dutch, and British colonies lay unprotected in Asia, Japanese leaders leaped at the opportunity to unite East Asia under Japanese control by seizing the colonial lands. By 1941, the British were too busy fighting Hitler to block Japanese expansion. Only the U.S. and its Pacific islands remained in Japan's way.

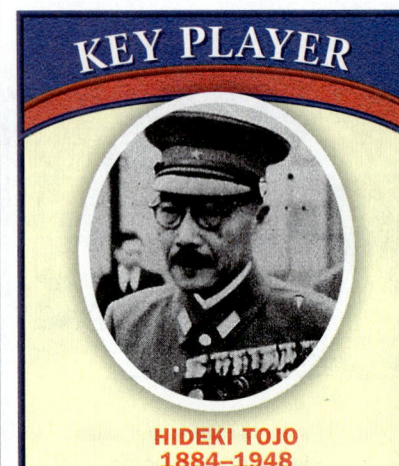

KEY PLAYER

HIDEKI TOJO
1884–1948

U.S. newspapers described Hideki Tojo as "smart, hard-boiled, resourceful, [and] contemptuous of theories, sentiments, and negotiations."

The Nazi press in Germany praised Tojo as "a man charged with energy, thinking clearly and with a single purpose." To a British paper, Tojo was "the son of Satan" whose single purpose was "unleashing all hell on the Far East." In Japan, however, Tojo was looked up to as a man whose "decisive leadership was a signal for the nation to rise and administer a great shock to the anti-Axis powers."

The Japanese began their southward push in July 1941 by taking over French military bases in Indochina (now Vietnam, Cambodia, and Laos). The United States protested this new act of aggression by cutting off trade with Japan. The embargoed goods included one Japan could not live without—oil to fuel its war machine. Japanese military leaders warned that without oil, Japan could be defeated without its enemies ever striking a blow. The leaders declared that Japan must either persuade the United States to end its oil embargo or seize the oil fields in the Dutch East Indies. This would mean war. **E**

MAIN IDEA

Analyzing Issues

E How was oil a source of conflict between Japan and the United States?

PEACE TALKS ARE QUESTIONED Shortly after becoming the prime minister of Japan, Hideki Tojo met with emperor Hirohito. Tojo promised the emperor that the Japanese government would attempt to preserve peace with the Americans. But on November 5, 1941, Tojo ordered the Japanese navy to prepare for an attack on the United States.

The U.S. military had broken Japan's secret communication codes and learned that Japan was preparing for a strike. What it didn't know was where the attack would come. Late in November, Roosevelt sent out a "war warning" to military commanders in Hawaii, Guam, and the Philippines. If war could not be avoided, the warning said, "the United States desires that Japan commit the first overt act." And the nation waited.

The peace talks went on for a month. Then on December 6, 1941, Roosevelt received a decoded message that instructed Japan's peace envoy to reject all American peace proposals. "This means war," Roosevelt declared.

THE ATTACK ON PEARL HARBOR Early the next morning, a Japanese dive-bomber swooped low over Pearl Harbor—the largest U.S. naval base in the Pacific. The bomber was followed by more than 180 Japanese warplanes launched from six aircraft carriers. As the first Japanese bombs found their targets, a radio operator flashed this message: "Air raid on Pearl Harbor. This is not a drill."

For an hour and a half, the Japanese planes were barely disturbed by U.S. antiaircraft guns and blasted target after target. By the time the last plane soared off around 9:30 A.M., the devastation was appalling. John Garcia, a pipe fitter's apprentice, was there.

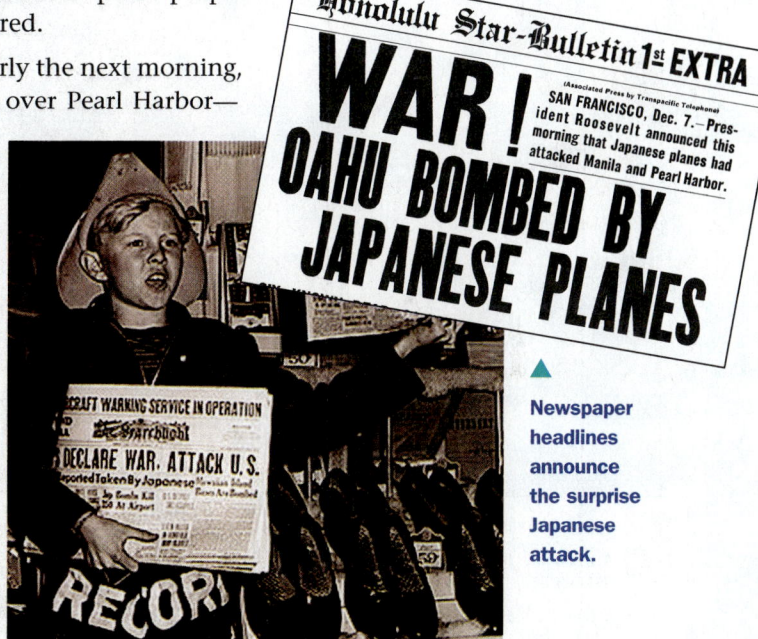

▲ Newspaper headlines announce the surprise Japanese attack.

A PERSONAL VOICE JOHN GARCIA

"It was a mess. I was working on the U.S.S. *Shaw*. It was on a floating dry dock. It was in flames. I started to go down into the pipe fitter's shop to get my toolbox when another wave of Japanese came in. I got under a set of concrete steps at the dry dock where the battleship *Pennsylvania* was. An officer came by and asked me to go into the *Pennsylvania* and try to get the fires out. A bomb had penetrated the marine deck, and . . . three decks below. Under that was the magazines: ammunition, powder, shells. I said "There ain't no way I'm gonna go down there." It could blow up any minute. I was young and 16, not stupid."

—quoted in *The Good War*

Japanese Aggression, 1931–1941

hmhsocialstudies.com **INTERACTIVE MAP**

MONGOLIA

SOVIET UNION

MANCHURIA (Province of China)

Peking

Yellow R.

CHINA

KOREA

JAPAN

Shanghai

Yangtze R.

BURMA

Hong Kong

Formosa

THAILAND

FRENCH INDOCHINA

PHILIPPINES

MALAYA

Singapore

DUTCH EAST INDIES

Ryukyu Islands

Tropic of Cancer

150°E 165°E

Kamchatka

Sakhalin

Kurile Islands

PACIFIC OCEAN

Midway Islands

Mariana Islands

Wake Island

Guam

Caroline Islands

Marshall Islands

New Guinea

Solomon Islands

INDIAN OCEAN

150°E 165°E

AUSTRALIA

Pearl Harbor Invasion, Dec. 7, 1941

Hawaiian Islands (U.S.)

Pearl Harbor Invasion

First Attack, 7:55 A.M

Second Attack, 8:55 A.M

PACIFIC OCEAN

Fighters

Oahu

Fighters

Wheeler Air Force Base

Torpedo bombers

Dive bombers

Horizontal bombers

2130'N

Dive bombers

Horizontal bombers

Kaneohe Naval Air Station

Pearl Harbor Naval Base

Honolulu

Pearl Harbor

158°W

0 — 8 — 16 miles
0 — 8 — 16 kilometers

U.S. Ships at Pearl Harbor

Detroit

Raleigh

Utah

Tangier

Curtiss

Solace

Phoenix

Ford Island

Arizona

Nevada

Vestal

West Virginia

Tennessee

Maryland

Neosho

Oklahoma

California

Oglala

Helena

Shaw

Pennsylvania

Cassin

Downes

U.S. NAVAL STATION

Harbor

New Orleans

San Francisco

Honolulu

St. Louis

Pearl

- ● Ships undamaged
- ● Ships damaged
- ● Ships sunk

0 — .25 — .5 miles
0 — .25 — .5 kilometers

Legend

- ■ Japanese Empire in 1931
- ■ Areas under Japanese control, 1941
- — Extent of Japanese control, 1941

0 — 600 — 1,200 miles
0 — 600 — 1,200 kilometers

GEOGRAPHY SKILLBUILDER
1. **Region** Which countries had Japan invaded by 1941?
2. **Movement** Notice the placement of the U.S. ships in Pearl Harbor— on the lower inset map. What might the navy have done differently to minimize damage from a surprise attack?

At Pearl Harbor, American sailors are rescued by motorboat after their battleships, the USS *West Virginia* and the USS *Tennessee*, were bombed.

In less than two hours, the Japanese had killed 2,403 Americans and wounded 1,178 more. The surprise raid had sunk or damaged 21 ships, including 8 battleships—nearly the whole U.S. Pacific fleet. More than 300 aircraft were severely damaged or destroyed. These losses constituted greater damage than the U.S. Navy had suffered in all of World War I. By chance, three aircraft carriers at sea escaped the disaster. Their survival would prove crucial to the war's outcome.

REACTION TO PEARL HARBOR In Washington, the mood ranged from outrage to panic. At the White House, Eleanor Roosevelt watched closely as her husband absorbed the news from Hawaii, "each report more terrible than the last." Beneath the president's calm, Eleanor could see how worried he was. "I never wanted to have to fight this war on two fronts," Roosevelt told his wife. "We haven't the Navy to fight in both the Atlantic and the Pacific . . . so we will have to build up the Navy and the Air Force and that will mean that we will have to take a good many defeats before we can have a victory."

Vocabulary
infamy: evil fame or reputation

The next day, President Roosevelt addressed Congress. "Yesterday, December 7, 1941, a date which will live in infamy," he said, "[the Japanese launched] an unprovoked and dastardly attack." Congress quickly approved Roosevelt's request for a declaration of war against Japan. Three days later, Germany and Italy declared war on the United States.

For all the damage done at Pearl Harbor, perhaps the greatest was to the cause of isolationism. Many who had been former isolationists now supported an all-out American effort. After the surprise attack, isolationist senator Burton Wheeler proclaimed, "The only thing now to do is to lick the hell out of them."

ECONOMIC BACKGROUND

WAR AND THE DEPRESSION

The approach of war did what all the programs of the New Deal could not do—end the Great Depression. As defense spending skyrocketed in 1940, long-idle factories came back to life as they converted from making consumer goods to producing war supplies. A merry-go-round company began producing gun mounts; a stove factory made lifeboats; a famous New York toy maker made compasses; a pinball-machine company made armor-piercing shells.

With factories hiring again, the nation's unemployment rolls began shrinking rapidly—by 400,000 in August 1940 and by another 500,000 in September. By the time the Japanese attacked Pearl Harbor, America was heading back to work.

SECTION 4 ASSESSMENT

1. TERMS & NAMES For each term or name, write a sentence explaining its significance.
- Axis powers
- Lend-Lease Act
- Atlantic Charter
- Allies
- Hideki Tojo

MAIN IDEA

2. TAKING NOTES
Create a time line of key events leading to America's entry into World War II. Use the dates below as a guide.

March 1941   August 1941

September 1940   June 1941   December 1941

Which of the events that you listed was most influential in bringing the United States into the war? Why?

CRITICAL THINKING

3. EVALUATING DECISIONS
Do you think that the United States should have waited to be attacked before declaring war? **Think About:**
- the reputation of the United States
- the influence of isolationists
- the events at Pearl Harbor

4. PREDICTING EFFECTS
What problem would the Japanese attack on Pearl Harbor solve for Roosevelt? What new problems would it create?

5. ANALYZING PRIMARY SOURCES
Although the U.S. Congress was still unwilling to declare war early in 1941, Churchill told his war cabinet,

" We must have patience and trust to the tide which is flowing our way, and to events. "

What do you think Churchill meant by this remark? Support your answer.

VISUAL SUMMARY

WORLD WAR LOOMS

1931
Japan invades Manchuria.

1932
Nazi Party becomes the most powerful in Germany.

Mar. 1933
First concentration camp opens at Oranienburg. Adolf Hitler becomes dictator of Germany.

Sept. 1935
Nuremberg Laws instituted against Jews in Germany.

Oct. 1935
Italian troops invade Ethiopia.

Mar. 1936
Germany occupies Rhineland.
Jul. 1936
Spanish Civil War begins.
Oct. 1936
Germany and Italy form Axis.

1937
Japan invades China.

Nov. 1938
Kristallnacht, Night of Broken Glass, Nazis destroy property and arrest over 20,000 Jews.

Mar. 1939
Germany seizes all of Czechoslovakia.
Sept. 1939
Germany invades Poland. Britain and France declare war on Germany and World War II begins.

June 1940
France surrenders.
Sept. 1940
Japan signs tripartite pact with Germany and Italy.

Mar. 1941
Roosevelt signs the Lend-Lease Act.
Jun. 1941
Nazis begin mass murder of the Jews.
Dec. 1941
Pearl Harbor is bombed. U.S. declares war.

TERMS & NAMES

For each term or name below, write a sentence explaining its significance in U.S. foreign affairs between 1931 and 1941.

1. fascism
2. Adolf Hitler
3. Nazism
4. Winston Churchill
5. appeasement
6. Charles de Gaulle
7. Holocaust
8. genocide
9. Axis powers
10. Allies

MAIN IDEAS

Use your notes and the information in the chapter to answer the following questions about the early years of World War II.

Dictators Threaten World Peace (*pages 734–741*)

1. What were Stalin's goals and what steps did he take to achieve them?
2. How did Germany's and Italy's involvement affect the outcome of the Spanish Civil War?

War in Europe (*pages 742–747*)

3. Why was the blitzkrieg effective?
4. What terms of surrender did Hitler demand of the French after the fall of France in 1940? What was General Charles de Gaulle's reaction?

The Holocaust (*pages 748–755*)

5. What groups did Nazis deem unfit to belong to the Aryan "master race"?
6. How did some Europeans show their resistance to Nazi persecution of the Jews?

America Moves Toward War (*pages 756–763*)

7. What congressional measures paved the way for the U.S. entry into World War II?
8. Why did the United States enter World War II?

CRITICAL THINKING

1. **USING YOUR NOTES** In a chart like the one shown, identify the effects of each of these early events of World War II.

Cause	Effect
First blitzkrieg	
Allies stranded at Dunkirk	
British radar detects German aircraft	
Lend-Lease Act	

2. **COMPARING** Compare the ways in which Hitler, Churchill, and Roosevelt used their powers as gifted speakers to accomplish their political aims during World War II. Use details from the chapter text.

3. **INTERPRETING MAPS** Look at the map of German advances on page 744. How might Poland's location have influenced the secret pact that Germany and the Soviet Union signed on August 23, 1939?

Use the cartoon and your knowledge of U.S. history to answer questions 1 and 2.

I HOPE YOU HAVE BETTER LUCK THAN I DID

WILSON

U.S. NEUTRALI

F.D.R.

1 All of the following are true of F.D.R.'s neutrality policy *except* —

(1) Roosevelt found it hard to keep the United States neutral.

(2) Roosevelt did not always enforce the Neutrality Acts.

(3) Roosevelt promoted the Neutrality Policy of the United States throughout the war.

(4) Roosevelt spoke out against isolationism.

2 President Wilson's image rises above President Roosevelt to wish him luck for —

(1) helping to pass the bill he is signing.

(2) keeping the United States out of a war.

(3) winning the next presidential election.

(4) gaining greater revenues from Europe.

Use the quotation and your knowledge of U.S. history to answer question 3.

> " In the future days, which we seek to make secure, we look forward to a world founded upon four essential human freedoms. The first is freedom of speech and expression. —everywhere in the world. The second is freedom of every person to worship God in his own way. —everywhere in the world. The third is freedom from want. . . . The fourth is freedom from fear."
>
> —Franklin Roosevelt, Address to Congress, 1941

3 The "four freedoms" speech helped gain widespread support in the United States for —

(1) increasing aid to the Allies.

(2) decreasing immigration.

(3) a military and arms buildup.

(4) a presidential election.

↗ hmhsocialstudies.com **TEST PRACTICE**

For additional test practice, go online for:

• Diagnostic tests   • Tutorials

INTERACT WITH HISTORY

Recall the issues that you explored at the beginning of the chapter. Imagine that you are a political cartoonist whose work is seen by millions of Americans. Draw a political cartoon that supports or opposes the policy of neutrality.

FOCUS ON WRITING

The preparations for World War II brought many changes to life in the United States. Imagine that you are an American citizen at this time. Write a journal entry that describes the changes going on around you.

COLLABORATIVE LEARNING

21ST CENTURY

In a small group read and discuss The "One American's Story" at the beginning of Section 3. Collect quotations and historical data about the Holocaust. Then write a book introduction about the Holocaust that incorporates quotations and the importance of the first-person accounts of survivors, such as Gerda Weissmann Klein.

CHAPTER 25

THE UNITED STATES IN WORLD WAR II

Essential Question

How did the United States use its resources to win World War II?

 New York Standards

KEY IDEA 3 Study about the major social, political, economic, cultural, and religious developments in New York State and United States history involves learning about the important roles and contributions of individuals and groups.

SECTION 1: Mobilizing for Defense

SECTION 2: The War for Europe and North Africa

SECTION 3: The War in the Pacific

SECTION 4: The Home Front

The raid on Pearl Harbor disabled the bulk of the U.S. fleet, including the *Tennessee (left)* and the *Arizona (right)*.

1941 The Japanese bomb Pearl Harbor.

1941 A. Philip Randolph demands that war industries hire African Americans.

1942 Roosevelt creates the War Production Board to coordinate mobilization.

1942 Japanese Americans are sent to relocation centers.

ARE YOU HELPING? WITH SALVAGE

USA
WORLD

1941   **1942**

1941 Hitler invades the Soviet Union.

1942 In the Pacific, the Battle of Midway turns the tide in favor of the Allies.

1942 Nazis develop the "final solution" for exterminating Jews.

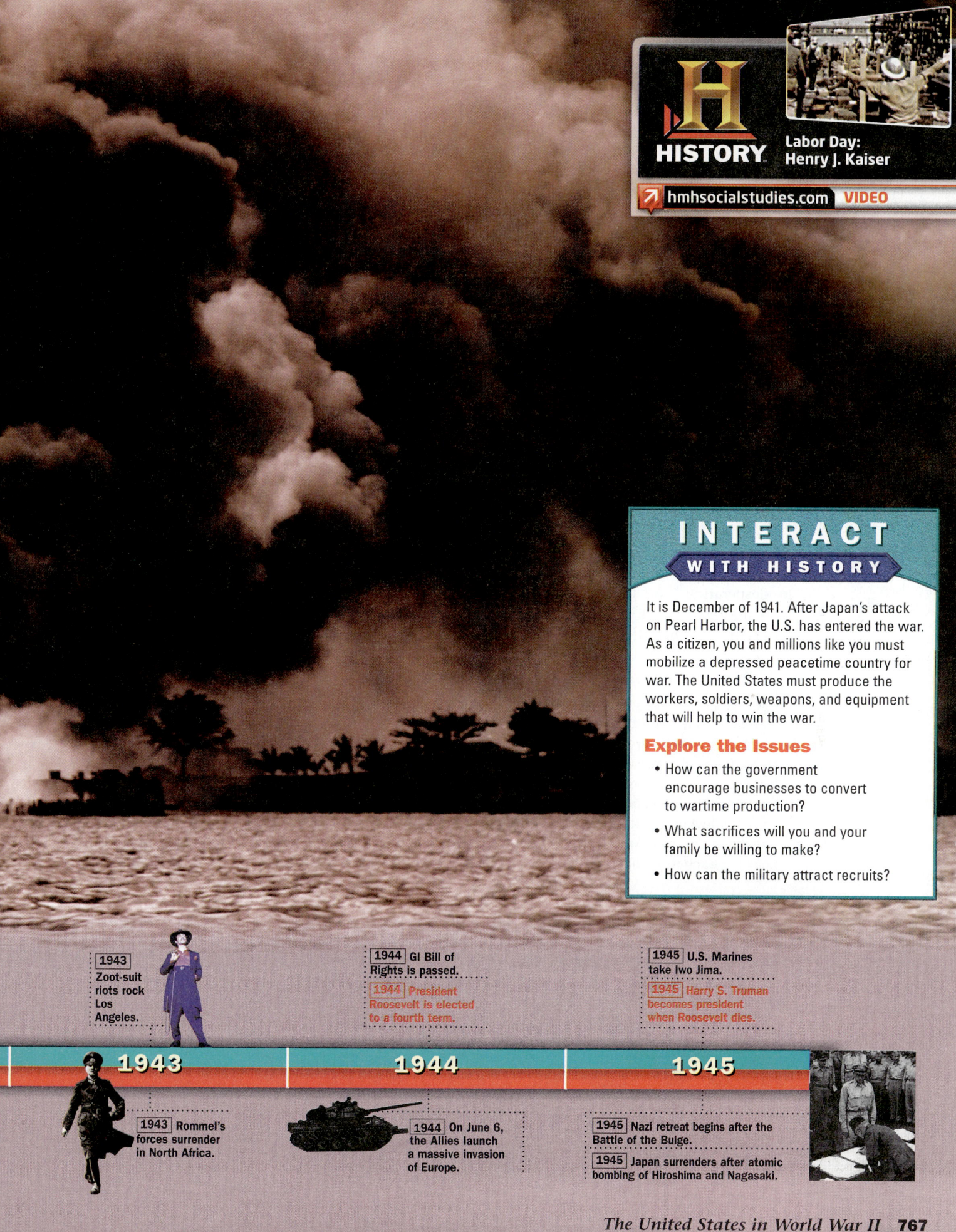

INTERACT
WITH HISTORY

It is December of 1941. After Japan's attack on Pearl Harbor, the U.S. has entered the war. As a citizen, you and millions like you must mobilize a depressed peacetime country for war. The United States must produce the workers, soldiers, weapons, and equipment that will help to win the war.

Explore the Issues

- How can the government encourage businesses to convert to wartime production?

- What sacrifices will you and your family be willing to make?

- How can the military attract recruits?

1943
Zoot-suit riots rock Los Angeles.

1944 GI Bill of Rights is passed.

1944 President Roosevelt is elected to a fourth term.

1945 U.S. Marines take Iwo Jima.

1945 Harry S. Truman becomes president when Roosevelt dies.

1943

1944

1945

1943 Rommel's forces surrender in North Africa.

1944 On June 6, the Allies launch a massive invasion of Europe.

1945 Nazi retreat begins after the Battle of the Bulge.

1945 Japan surrenders after atomic bombing of Hiroshima and Nagasaki.

SECTION 1

CC Unit 6.I.C.2.a   CC Unit 6.I.C.2.b
CC Unit 6.I.C.2.c   CC Unit 6.I.C.2.d
CC Unit 6.I.C.2.e   CC Unit 6.I.C.4.a

PI 3.1

Mobilizing for Defense

MAIN IDEA	WHY IT MATTERS NOW	Terms & Names
Following the attack on Pearl Harbor, the United States mobilized for war.	Military industries in the United States today are a major part of the American economy.	• George Marshall • Women's Auxiliary Army Corps (WAAC) • A. Philip Randolph • Manhattan Project • Office of Price Administration (OPA) • War Production Board (WPB) • rationing

One American's Story

hmhsocialstudies.com
TAKING NOTES
Use the graphic organizer online to take notes about how the United States prepared for war.

Charles Swanson looked all over his army base for a tape recorder on which to play the tape his wife had sent him for Christmas. "In desperation," he later recalled, "I had it played over the public-address system. It was a little embarrassing to have the whole company hear it, but it made everyone long for home."

A PERSONAL VOICE MRS. CHARLES SWANSON

" Merry Christmas, honey. Surprised? I'm so glad I have a chance to say hello to you this way on our first Christmas apart. . . . About our little girl. . . . She is just big enough to fill my heart and strong enough to help Mommy bear this ache of loneliness. . . . Her dearest treasure is her daddy's picture. It's all marked with tiny handprints, and the glass is always cloudy from so much loving and kissing. I'm hoping you'll be listening to this on Christmas Eve, somewhere over there, your heart full of hope, faith and courage, knowing each day will bring that next Christmas together one day nearer. "

—quoted in *We Pulled Together . . . and Won!*

▲ Mrs. Charles Swanson and her daughter, Lynne, with a picture of her husband.

As the United States began to mobilize for war, the Swansons, like most Americans, had few illusions as to what lay ahead. It would be a time filled with hard work, hope, sacrifice, and sorrow.

Americans Join the War Effort

The Japanese had attacked Pearl Harbor with the expectation that once Americans had experienced Japan's power, they would shrink from further conflict. The day after the raid, the *Japan Times* boasted that the United States, now reduced to a third-rate power, was "trembling in her shoes." But if Americans were trembling, it was with rage, not fear. Uniting under the battle cry "Remember Pearl Harbor!" they set out to prove Japan wrong.

SELECTIVE SERVICE AND THE GI

After Pearl Harbor, eager young Americans jammed recruiting offices. "I wanted to be a hero, let's face it," admitted Roger Tuttrup. "I was havin' trouble in school. . . . The war'd been goin' on for two years. I didn't wanna miss it. . . . I was an American. I was seventeen."

Even the 5 million who volunteered for military service, however, were not enough to face the challenge of an all-out war on two global fronts—Europe and the Pacific. The Selective Service System expanded the draft and eventually provided another 10 million soldiers to meet the armed forces' needs.

The volunteers and draftees reported to military bases around the country for eight weeks of basic training. In this short period, seasoned sergeants did their best to turn raw recruits into disciplined, battle-ready GIs.

According to Sergeant Debs Myers, however, there was more to basic training than teaching a recruit how to stand at attention, march in step, handle a rifle, and follow orders.

▲ In March 1941, a group of African-American men in New York City enlisted in the United States Army Air Corps. This was the first time the Army Air Corps opened its enlistment to African Americans.

A PERSONAL VOICE SERGEANT DEBS MYERS

"The civilian went before the Army doctors, took off his clothes, feeling silly; jigged, stooped, squatted, wet into a bottle; became a soldier. He learned how to sleep in the mud, tie a knot, kill a man. He learned the ache of loneliness, the ache of exhaustion, the kinship of misery. He learned that men make the same queasy noises in the morning, feel the same longings at night; that every man is alike and that each man is different."

—quoted in *The GI War: 1941–1945*

EXPANDING THE MILITARY The military's work force needs were so great that Army Chief of Staff General **George Marshall** pushed for the formation of a **Women's Auxiliary Army Corps (WAAC).** "There are innumerable duties now being performed by soldiers that can be done better by women," Marshall said in support of a bill to establish the Women's Auxiliary Army Corps. Under this bill, women volunteers would serve in noncombat positions.

Despite opposition from some members of Congress who scorned the bill as "the silliest piece of legislation" they had ever seen, the bill establishing the WAAC became law on May 15, 1942. The law gave the WAACs an official status and salary but few of the benefits granted to male soldiers. In July 1943, after thousands of women had enlisted, the U.S. Army dropped the "auxiliary" status, and granted WACs full U.S. Army benefits. WACs worked as nurses, ambulance drivers, radio operators, electricians, and pilots—nearly every duty not involving direct combat.

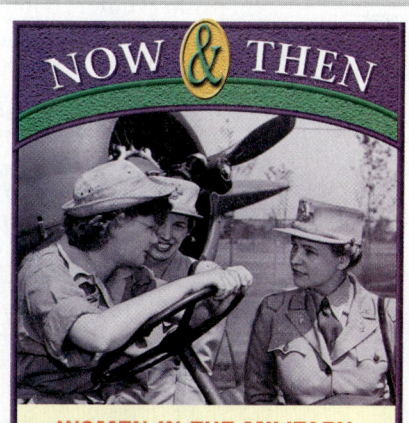

NOW & THEN

WOMEN IN THE MILITARY

A few weeks after the bill to establish the Women's Auxiliary Army Corps (WAAC) had become law, Oveta Culp Hobby *(shown, far right)*, a Texas newspaper executive and the first director of the WAAC, put out a call for recruits. More than 13,000 women applied on the first day. In all, some 350,000 women served in this and other auxiliary branches during the war.

The WAC remained a separate unit of the army until 1978 when male and female forces were integrated. In 2006, more than 200,000 women served in the United States armed forces.

RECRUITING AND DISCRIMINATION For many minority groups—especially African Americans, Native Americans, Mexican Americans, and Asian Americans—the war created new dilemmas. Restricted to racially segregated neighborhoods and reservations and denied basic citizenship rights, some members of these groups questioned whether this was their war to fight. "Why die for democracy for some foreign country when we don't even have it here?" asked an editorial in an African-American newspaper. On receiving his draft notice, an African American responded unhappily, "Just carve on my tombstone, 'Here lies a black man killed fighting a yellow man for the protection of a white man.'"

DRAMATIC CONTRIBUTIONS Despite discrimination in the military, more than 300,000 Mexican Americans joined the armed forces. While Mexican Americans in Los Angeles made up only a tenth of the city's population, they suffered a fifth of the city's wartime casualties.

About one million African Americans also served in the military. African-American soldiers lived and worked in segregated units and were limited mostly to noncombat roles. After much protest, African Americans did finally see combat beginning in April 1943.

Asian Americans took part in the struggle as well. More than 13,000 Chinese Americans, or about one of every five adult males, joined the armed forces. In addition, 33,000 Japanese Americans put on uniforms. Of these, several thousand volunteered to serve as spies and interpreters in the Pacific war. "During battles," wrote an admiring officer, "they crawled up close enough to be able to hear [Japanese] officers' commands and to make verbal translations to our soldiers."

Some 25,000 Native Americans enlisted in the armed services, too, including 800 women. Their willingness to serve led *The Saturday Evening Post* to comment, "We would not need the Selective Service if all volunteered like Indians." Ⓐ

MAIN IDEA

Contrasting
Ⓐ How did the American response to the Japanese raid on Pearl Harbor differ from Japanese expectations?

A Production Miracle

Early in February 1942, American newspapers reported the end of automobile production for private use. The last car to roll off an automaker's assembly line was a gray sedan with "victory trim,"—that is, without chrome-plated parts. This was just one more sign that the war would affect almost every aspect of life.

THE INDUSTRIAL RESPONSE Within weeks of the shutdown in production, the nation's automobile plants had been retooled to produce tanks, planes, boats, and

The Production Miracle

Aircraft and Ship Production, 1940–45

U.S. Budget Expenditure, 1941–45

Source: *The Times Atlas of the Second World War*

SKILLBUILDER Interpreting Graphs
1. Study the first graph. In what year did aircraft and ship production reach their highest production levels?
2. How does the second graph help explain how this production miracle was possible?

command cars. They were not alone. Across the nation, factories were quickly converted to war production. A maker of mechanical pencils turned out bomb parts. A bedspread manufacturer made mosquito netting. A soft-drink company converted from filling bottles with liquid to filling shells with explosives.

Meanwhile, shipyards and defense plants expanded with dizzying speed. By the end of 1942, industrialist Henry J. Kaiser had built seven massive new shipyards that turned out Liberty ships (cargo carriers), tankers, troop transports, and "baby" aircraft carriers at an astonishing rate. Late that year, Kaiser invited reporters to Way One in his Richmond, California, shipyard to watch as his workers assembled *Hull 440*, a Liberty ship, in a record-breaking four days. Writer Alyce Mano Kramer described the first day and night of construction.

★ A PERSONAL VOICE ALYCE MANO KRAMER

" At the stroke of 12, Way One exploded into life. Crews of workers, like a champion football team, swarmed into their places in the line. Within 60 seconds, the keel was swinging into position. . . . *Hull 440* was going up. The speed of [production] was unbelievable. At midnight, Saturday, an empty way—at midnight Sunday, a full-grown hull met the eyes of graveyard workers as they came on shift. "

—quoted in *Home Front, U.S.A.*

Before the fourth day was up, 25,000 amazed spectators watched as *Hull 440* slid into the water. How could such a ship be built so fast? Kaiser used prefabricated, or factory-made, parts that could be quickly assembled at his shipyards. Equally important were his workers, who worked at record speeds.

LABOR'S CONTRIBUTION When the war began, defense contractors warned the Selective Service System that the nation did not have enough workers to meet both its military and its industrial needs. They were wrong. By 1944, despite the draft, nearly 18 million workers were laboring in war industries, three times as many as in 1941.

More than 6 million of these new workers were women. At first, war industries feared that most women lacked the necessary stamina for factory work and were reluctant to hire them. But once women proved they could operate welding torches or riveting guns as well as men, employers could not hire enough of them—especially since women earned only about 60 percent as much as men doing the same jobs.

Defense plants also hired more than 2 million minority workers during the war years. Like women, minorities faced strong prejudice at first. Before the war, 75 percent of defense contractors simply refused to hire African Americans, while another 15 percent employed them only in menial jobs. "Negroes will be considered only as janitors," declared the general manager of North American Aviation. "It is the company policy not to employ them as mechanics and aircraft workers." **B**

▲
During the war, women took many jobs previously held by men. In this 1943 photo, a young woman is seen operating a hand drill in Nashville, Tennessee.

MAIN IDEA

Forming Generalizations
B What difficulties did women and minorities face in the wartime work force?

To protest such discrimination both in the military and in industry, **A. Philip Randolph,** president and founder of the Brotherhood of Sleeping Car Porters and the nation's most respected African-American labor leader, organized a march on Washington. Randolph called on African Americans everywhere to come to the capital on July 1, 1941, and to march under the banner "We Loyal Colored Americans Demand the Right to Work and Fight for Our Country."

Fearing that the march might provoke white resentment or violence, President Roosevelt called Randolph to the White House and asked him to back down. "I'm sorry Mr. President," the labor leader said, "the march cannot be called off." Roosevelt then asked, "How many people do you plan to bring?" Randolph replied, "One hundred thousand, Mr. President." Roosevelt was stunned. Even half that number of African-American protesters would be far more than Washington—still a very segregated city—could feed, house, and transport.

In the end it was Roosevelt, not Randolph, who backed down. In return for Randolph's promise to cancel the march, the president issued an executive order calling on employers and labor unions "to provide for the full and equitable participation of all workers in defense industries, without discrimination because of race, creed, color, or national origin."

▲ **A. Philip Randolph in 1942.**

History Through Film

HOLLYWOOD HELPS MOBILIZATION

In the aftermath of Pearl Harbor, Hollywood churned out war-oriented propaganda films. Heroic movies like *Mission to Moscow* and *Song of Russia* glorified America's new wartime ally, the Soviet Union. On the other hand, "hiss-and-boo" films stirred up hatred against the Nazis. In this way, movies energized people to join the war effort.

As the war dragged on, people grew tired of propaganda and war themes. Hollywood responded with musicals, romances, and other escapist fare designed to take filmgoers away from the grim realities of war, if only for an hour or two.

▲ ***Hitler, Beast of Berlin***, produced in 1939, was one of the most popular hiss-and-boo films. Viewing audiences watched in rage as the Nazis conducted one horrible act after another.

▲ Moviemakers also turned out informational films. The most important of these films—the *Why We Fight* series—were made by the great director Frank Capra. Capra is shown (*right*) consulting with Colonel Hugh Stewart (commander of the British Army film unit) in a joint effort in the making of *Tunisian Victory*, the first official film record of the campaign that expelled Germany from North Africa.

SKILLBUILDER Interpeting Visual Sources
1. How does the image from *Hitler, Beast of Berlin* portray the Nazis?
2. How might audiences have responded to propaganda films?

 SEE SKILLBUILDER HANDBOOK, PAGE R23.

MOBILIZATION OF SCIENTISTS That same year, in 1941, Roosevelt created the Office of Scientific Research and Development (OSRD) to bring scientists into the war effort. The OSRD spurred improvements in radar and sonar, new technologies for locating submarines underwater. It encouraged the use of pesticides like DDT to fight insects. As a result, U.S. soldiers were probably the first in history to be relatively free from body lice. The OSRD also pushed the development of "miracle drugs," such as penicillin, that saved countless lives on and off the battlefield.

The most significant achievement of the OSRD, however, was the secret development of a new weapon, the atomic bomb. Interest in such a weapon began in 1939, after German scientists succeeded in splitting uranium atoms, releasing an enormous amount of energy. This news prompted physicist and German refugee Albert Einstein to write a letter to President Roosevelt, warning that the Germans could use their discovery to construct a weapon of enormous destructive power.

Roosevelt responded by creating an Advisory Committee on Uranium to study the new discovery. In 1941, the committee reported that it would take from three to five years to build an atomic bomb. Hoping to shorten that time, the OSRD set up an intensive program in 1942 to develop a bomb as quickly as possible. Because much of the early research was performed at Columbia University in Manhattan, the **Manhattan Project** became the code name for research work that extended across the country. **C**

MAIN IDEA

Summarizing
C Why did President Roosevelt create the OSRD, and what did it do?

The Federal Government Takes Control

As war production increased, there were fewer consumer products available for purchase. Much factory production was earmarked for the war. With demand increasing and supplies dropping, prices seemed likely to shoot upwards.

ECONOMIC CONTROLS Roosevelt responded to this threat by creating the **Office of Price Administration (OPA).** The OPA fought inflation by freezing prices on most goods. Congress also raised income tax rates and extended the tax to millions of people who had never paid it before. The higher taxes reduced consumer demand on scarce goods by leaving workers with less to spend. In addition,

The Government Takes Control of the Economy, 1942–1945	
Agencies and Laws	**What the Regulations Did**
Office of Price Administration (OPA)	• Fought inflation by freezing wages, prices, and rents • Rationed foods, such as meat, butter, cheese, vegetables, sugar, and coffee
National War Labor Board (NWLB)	• Limited wage increases • Allowed negotiated benefits, such as paid vacation, pensions, and medical insurance • Kept unions stable by forbidding workers to change unions
War Production Board (WPB)	• Rationed fuel and materials vital to the war effort, such as gasoline, heating oil, metals, rubber, and plastics
Department of the Treasury	• Issued war bonds to raise money for the war effort and to fight inflation
Revenue Act of 1942	• Raised the top personal-income tax rate to 88% • Added lower- and middle-income Americans to the income-tax rolls
Smith-Connally Anti-Strike Act (1943)	• Limited the right to strike in industries crucial to the war effort • Gave the president power to take over striking plants

▲ Children of all ages helped with wartime recycling. This 5-year-old boy pounded the pavement in New York City collecting aluminum.

the government encouraged Americans to use their extra cash to buy war bonds. As a result of these measures, inflation remained below 30 percent—about half that of World War I—for the entire period of World War II.

Besides controlling inflation, the government needed to ensure that the armed forces and war industries received the resources they needed to win the war. The **War Production Board (WPB)** assumed that responsibility. The WPB decided which companies would convert from peacetime to wartime production and allocated raw materials to key industries. The WPB also organized drives to collect scrap iron, tin cans, paper, rags, and cooking fat for recycling into war goods. Across America, children scoured attics, cellars, garages, vacant lots, and back alleys, looking for useful junk. During one five-month-long paper drive in Chicago, schoolchildren collected 36 million pounds of old paper—about 65 pounds per child. **D**

RATIONING In addition, the OPA set up a system for **rationing,** or establishing fixed allotments of goods deemed essential for the military. Under this system, households received ration books with coupons to be used for buying such scarce goods as meat, shoes, sugar, coffee, and gasoline. Gas rationing was particularly hard on those who lived in western regions, where driving was the only way to get around. First Lady Eleanor Roosevelt sympathized with their complaints. "To tell the people in the West not to use their cars," she observed, "means that these people may never see another soul for weeks and weeks nor have a way of getting a sick person to a doctor."

Most Americans accepted rationing as a personal contribution to the war effort. Workers carpooled or rode bicycles. Families coped with shortages of everything from tires to toys. Inevitably, some cheated by hoarding scarce goods or by purchasing them through the "black market," where rationed items could be bought illegally without coupons at inflated prices.

While people tightened their belts at home, millions of other Americans put their lives on the line in air, sea, and land battles on the other side of the world.

FOCUS ON

New York outpaced all other states in production of wartime goods, manufacturing 12 percent of the nation's military weapons, ammunition, and vehicles.

MAIN IDEA

Identifying Problems

D What basic problems were the OPA and WPB created to solve?

SECTION 1

ASSESSMENT

1. **TERMS & NAMES** For each term or name, write a sentence explaining its significance.
   - George Marshall
   - Women's Auxiliary Army Corps (WAAC)
   - A. Philip Randolph
   - Manhattan Project
   - Office of Price Administration (OPA)
   - War Production Board (WPB)
   - rationing

MAIN IDEA

2. **TAKING NOTES**
   Re-create the web below on your paper, and fill in ways that America prepared for war.

Preparation for War, 1941–1942

CRITICAL THINKING

3. **ANALYZING EVENTS**
   How did government regulations impact the lives of civilians?

4. **ANALYZING VISUAL SOURCES**
   What is the message of the World War II poster to the right? Why was this message important?

When you ride ALONE you ride with Hitler!

Join a Car-Sharing Club TODAY!

CC Unit 6.I.C.2.f   CC Unit 6.I.C.3.b
CC Unit 6.I.C.3.c   CC Unit 6.I.C.5.b
PI 3.1   CC Unit 6.I.C.5.c

The War for Europe and North Africa

MAIN IDEA	WHY IT MATTERS NOW	Terms & Names
Allied forces, led by the United States and Great Britain, battled Axis powers for control of Europe and North Africa.	During World War II, the United States assumed a leading role in world affairs that continues today.	• Dwight D. Eisenhower • D-Day • Omar Bradley • George Patton • Battle of the Bulge • V-E Day • Harry S. Truman

One American's Story

It was 1951, and John Patrick McGrath was just finishing his second year in drama school. For an acting class, his final exam was to be a performance of a death scene. McGrath knew his lines perfectly. But as he began the final farewell, he broke out in a sweat and bolted off the stage. Suddenly he had a flashback to a frozen meadow in Belgium during the Battle of the Bulge in 1945. Three German tanks were spraying his platoon with machine-gun fire.

A PERSONAL VOICE JOHN PATRICK MCGRATH

" Only a few feet away, one of the men in my platoon falls. . . . He calls out to me. 'Don't leave me. Don't. . . .' The tanks advance, one straight for me. I grab my buddy by the wrist and pull him across the snow. . . . The tank nearest to us is on a track to run us down. . . . When the German tank is but 15 yards away, I grab my buddy by the wrist and feign a lurch to my right. The tank follows the move. Then I lurch back to my left. The German tank clamors by, only inches away. . . . In their wake the meadow is strewn with casualties. I turn to tend my fallen comrade. He is dead. "

—A Cue for Passion

Private John P. McGrath carried this bullet-riddled letter in a pack that saved his life. In 1990, he visited Anzio, where members of his company were buried.

Like countless other soldiers, McGrath would never forget both the heroism and the horrors he witnessed while fighting to free Europe.

The United States and Britain Join Forces

"Now that we are, as you say, 'in the same boat,'" British Prime Minister Winston Churchill wired President Roosevelt two days after the Pearl Harbor attack, "would it not be wise for us to have another conference . . . . and the sooner the better." Roosevelt responded with an invitation for Churchill to come at once. So began a remarkable alliance between the two nations.

WAR PLANS Prime Minister Churchill arrived at the White House on December 22, 1941, and spent the next three weeks working out war plans with President Roosevelt and his advisors. Believing that Germany and Italy posed a greater threat than Japan, Churchill convinced Roosevelt to strike first against Hitler. Once the Allies had gained an upper hand in Europe, they could pour more resources into the Pacific War.

By the end of their meeting, Roosevelt and Churchill had formed, in Churchill's words, "a very strong affection, which grew with our years of comradeship." When Churchill reached London, he found a message from the president waiting for him. "It is fun," Roosevelt wrote in the message, "to be in the same decade with you."

THE BATTLE OF THE ATLANTIC After the attack on Pearl Harbor, Hitler ordered submarine raids against ships along America's east coast. The German aim in the Battle of the Atlantic was to prevent food and war materials from reaching Great Britain and the Soviet Union. Britain depended on supplies from the sea. The 3,000-mile-long shipping lanes from North America were her lifeline. Hitler knew that if he cut that lifeline, Britain would be starved into submission.

For a long time, it looked as though Hitler might succeed in his mission. Unprotected American ships proved to be easy targets for the Germans. In the first four months of 1942, the Germans sank 87 ships off the Atlantic shore. Seven months into the year, German wolf packs had destroyed a total of 681 Allied ships in the Atlantic. Something had to be done or the war at sea would be lost.

▲
A convoy of British and American ships ride at anchor in the harbor of Hvalfjord, Iceland.

The Allies responded by organizing their cargo ships into convoys. Convoys were groups of ships traveling together for mutual protection, as they had done in the First World War. The convoys were escorted across the Atlantic by destroyers equipped with sonar for detecting submarines underwater. They were also accompanied by airplanes that used radar to spot U-boats on the ocean's surface. With this improved tracking, the Allies were able to find and destroy German U-boats faster than the Germans could build them. In late spring of 1943, Admiral Karl Doenitz, the commander of the German U-boat offensive, reported that his losses had "reached an unbearable height."

At the same time, the United States launched a crash shipbuilding program. By early 1943, 140 Liberty ships were produced each month. Launchings of Allied ships began to outnumber sinkings.

By mid-1943, the tide of the Battle of the Atlantic had turned. A happy Churchill reported to the House of Commons that June "was the best month [at sea] from every point of view we have ever known in the whole 46 months of the war." **Ⓐ**

MAIN IDEA

Analyzing Causes
Ⓐ Why had the tide turned in the Battle of the Atlantic by mid-1943?

The Eastern Front and the Mediterranean

By the winter of 1943, the Allies began to see victories on land as well as sea. The first great turning point came in the Battle of Stalingrad.

THE BATTLE OF STALINGRAD The Germans had been fighting in the Soviet Union since June 1941. In November 1941, the bitter cold had stopped them in their tracks outside the Soviet cities of Moscow and Leningrad. When spring came, the German tanks were ready to roll.

In the summer of 1942, the Germans took the offensive in the southern Soviet Union. Hitler hoped to capture Soviet oil fields in the Caucasus Mountains. He also wanted to wipe out Stalingrad, a major industrial center on the Volga River. (See map, page 778.)

The German army confidently approached Stalingrad in August 1942. "To reach the Volga and take Stalingrad is not so difficult for us," one German soldier wrote home. "Victory is not far away." The Luftwaffe—the German air force—prepared the way with nightly bombing raids over the city. Nearly every wooden building in Stalingrad was set ablaze. The situation looked so desperate that Soviet officers in Stalingrad recommended blowing up the city's factories and abandoning the city. A furious Stalin ordered them to defend his namesake city no matter what the cost.

For weeks the Germans pressed in on Stalingrad, conquering it house by house in brutal hand-to-hand combat. By the end of September, they controlled nine-tenths of the city—or what was left of it. Then another winter set in. The Soviets saw the cold as an opportunity to roll fresh tanks across the frozen landscape and begin a massive counterattack. The Soviet army closed around Stalingrad, trapping the Germans in and around the city and cutting off their supplies. The Germans' situation was hopeless, but Hitler's orders came: "Stay and fight! I won't go back from the Volga."

The fighting continued as winter turned Stalingrad into a frozen wasteland. "We just lay in our holes and froze, knowing that 24 hours later and 48 hours later we should be shivering precisely as we were now," wrote a German soldier, Benno Zieser. "But there was now no hope whatsoever of relief, and that was the worst thing of all." The German commander surrendered on January 31, 1943. Two days later, his starving troops also surrendered.

In defending Stalingrad, the Soviets lost a total of 1,100,000 soldiers—more than all American deaths during the entire war. Despite the staggering death toll, the Soviet victory marked a turning point in the war. From that point on, the Soviet army began to move westward toward Germany. **B**

VIDEO
Battle of Stalingrad

hmhsocialstudies.com

MAIN IDEA

Synthesizing
B What two key decisions determined the final outcome at Stalingrad?

Dazed, starved, and freezing, these German soldiers were taken prisoner after months of struggle. But they were the lucky ones. More than 230,000 of their comrades died in the Battle of Stalingrad.

THE NORTH AFRICAN FRONT While the Battle of Stalingrad raged, Stalin pressured Britain and America to open a "second front" in Western Europe. He argued that an invasion across the English Channel would force Hitler to divert troops from the Soviet front. Churchill and Roosevelt didn't think the Allies had enough troops to attempt an invasion on European soil. Instead, they launched Operation Torch, an invasion of Axis-controlled North Africa, commanded by American General **Dwight D. Eisenhower.**

In November 1942, some 107,000 Allied troops, the great majority of them Americans, landed in Casablanca, Oran, and Algiers in North Africa. From there they sped eastward, chasing the Afrika Korps led by General Erwin Rommel, the legendary Desert Fox. After months of heavy fighting, the last of the Afrika Korps surrendered in May 1943. British general Harold Alexander sent a message to Churchill, reporting that "All enemy resistance has ceased. We are masters of the North African shores." American war correspondent Ernie Pyle caught the mood of the victorious troops. **C**

American journalist Ernie Pyle, shown here in 1944, was one of the most famous war correspondents of World War II.

MAIN IDEA

Summarizing
C What was the outcome of the North African campaign?

A PERSONAL VOICE ERNIE PYLE

" This colossal German surrender has done more for American morale here than anything that could possibly have happened. Winning in battle is like winning at poker or catching lots of fish. . . . As a result, the hundreds of thousands of Americans in North Africa now are happy men. "

—*Ernie's War: The Best of Ernie Pyle's World War II Dispatches*

World War II: Europe and Africa, 1942–1944

hmhsocialstudies.com **INTERACTIVE MAP**

Legend:
- Axis and Axis controlled
- Allies
- Neutral countries
- Axis forces
- Allied forces
- Soviet forces
- Major battles

0   200   400 miles
0   200 400 kilometers

FINLAND
SOVIET UNION
NORWAY   SWEDEN
Leningrad **1944**
North Sea
DENMARK
Moscow
Baltic Sea
GREAT BRITAIN
London
NETH.   Berlin
EAST PRUSSIA
Warsaw
BELG.   GERMANY
POLAND
CZECHOSLOVAKIA
SOVIET UNION
1943
Paris
EUROPE
FRANCE   SWITZ.   AUSTRIA   HUNGARY
ROMANIA
1942   Stalingrad
Volga R.
1942
ATLANTIC OCEAN
YUGOSLAVIA
ITALY
Adriatic Sea
BULGARIA
Black Sea
Caspian Sea
ASIA
Rome
Anzio
ALBANIA
GREECE
TURKEY
Lisbon
Madrid
PORTUGAL   SPAIN
Algiers
Oran   TUNISIA
1943
Mediterranean Sea
Casablanca
MOROCCO   ALGERIA
Tobruk **1942**
El Alamein
AFRICA   LIBYA   EGYPT   SAUDI ARABIA
Persian Gulf

November 8, 1942
Operation Torch

November 1942
Farthest Axis advance

May 13, 1943
Axis surrender of North Africa

GEOGRAPHY SKILLBUILDER
1. **Place** Which countries were neutral in 1942?
2. **Movement** What was the name of the invasion that the Allies launched in North Africa?

60°N
30°N
15°W

THE ITALIAN CAMPAIGN Even before the battle in North Africa was won, Roosevelt, Churchill, and their commanders met in Casablanca. At this meeting, the two leaders agreed to accept only the unconditional surrender of the Axis powers. That is, enemy nations would have to accept whatever terms of peace the Allies dictated. The two leaders also discussed where to strike next. The Americans argued that the best approach to victory was to assemble a massive invasion fleet in Britain and to launch it across the English Channel, through France, and into the heart of Germany. Churchill, however, thought it would be safer to first attack Italy.

The Italian campaign got off to a good start with the capture of Sicily in the summer of 1943. Stunned by their army's collapse in Sicily, the Italian government forced dictator Benito Mussolini to resign. On July 25, 1943, King Victor Emmanuel III summoned *Il Duce* (Italian for "the leader") to his palace, stripped him of power, and had him arrested. "At this moment," the king told Mussolini, "you are the most hated man in Italy." Italians began celebrating the end of the war.

Their cheers were premature. Hitler was determined to stop the Allies in Italy rather than fight on German soil. One of the hardest battles the Allies encountered in Europe was fought less than 40 miles from Rome. This battle, "Bloody Anzio," lasted four months—until the end of May 1944—and left about 25,000 Allied and 30,000 Axis casualties. During the year after Anzio, German armies continued to put up strong resistance. The effort to free Italy did not succeed until 1945, when Germany itself was close to collapse. **D**

MAIN IDEA

Analyzing Effects

D What were the results of the Italian campaign?

HEROES IN COMBAT Among the brave men who fought in Italy were pilots of the all-black 99th Pursuit Squadron—the Tuskegee Airmen. In Sicily, the squadron registered its first victory against an enemy aircraft and went on to more impressive strategic strikes against the German forces throughout Italy. The Tuskegee Airmen won two Distinguished Unit Citations (the military's highest commendation) for their outstanding aerial combat against the German Luftwaffe.

Another African-American unit to distinguish itself was the famous 92nd Infantry Division, nicknamed the Buffaloes. In just six months of fighting in Europe, the Buffaloes won 7 Legion of Merit awards, 65 Silver Stars, and 162 Bronze Stars for courage under fire.

Like African Americans, most Mexican Americans served in segregated units. Seventeen Mexican-American soldiers were awarded the Congressional Medal of Honor. An all-Chicano unit—Company E of the 141st Regiment, 36th Division became one of the most decorated of the war.

Japanese Americans also served in Italy and North Africa. At the urging of General Delos Emmons, the army created the 100th Battalion, which consisted of 1,300 Hawaiian Nisei. (The word *Nisei* refers to American citizens whose parents had emigrated from Japan.) The 100th saw brutal combat and became known as the Purple Heart Battalion. Later the 100th was merged into the all-Nisei 442nd Regimental Combat Team. It became the most decorated unit in U.S. history.

On May 31, 1943, the 99th Pursuit Squadron, the first group of African-American pilots trained at the Tuskegee Institute, arrived in North Africa. Below is their regimental insignia.

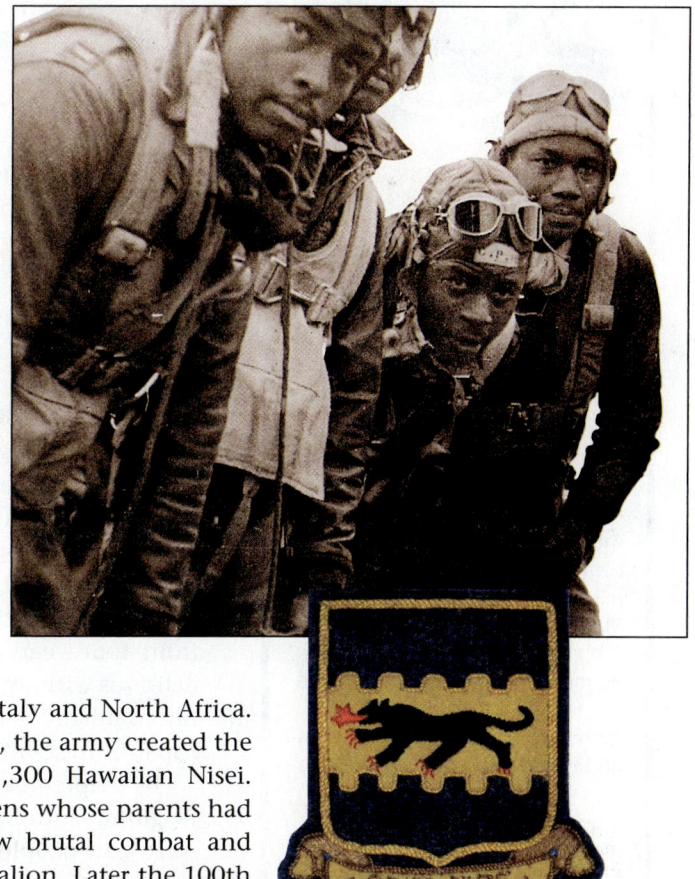

The Allies Liberate Europe

Even as the Allies were battling for Italy in 1943, they had begun work on a dramatic plan to invade France and free Western Europe from the Nazis. The task of commanding Operation Overlord, as it was called, fell to American General Dwight D. ("Ike") Eisenhower.

hmhsocialstudies.com
INTERACTIVE
Explore the action of D-Day.

D-DAY Under Eisenhower's direction in England, the Allies gathered a force of nearly 3 million British, American, and Canadian troops, together with mountains of military equipment and supplies. Eisenhower planned to attack Normandy in northern France. To keep their plans secret, the Allies set up a huge phantom army with its own headquarters and equipment. In radio messages they knew the Germans could read, Allied commanders sent orders to this make-believe army to attack the French port of Calais—150 miles away—where the English Channel is narrowest. As a result, Hitler ordered his generals to keep a large army at Calais.

The Allied invasion, code-named Operation Overlord, was originally set for June 5, but bad weather forced a delay. Banking on a forecast for clearing skies, Eisenhower gave the go-ahead for **D-Day**—June 6, 1944, the first day of the invasion. Shortly after midnight, three divisions parachuted down behind German lines. They were followed in the early morning hours by thousands upon thousands of seaborne soldiers—the largest land-sea-air operation in army history.

Despite the massive air and sea bombardment by the Allies, German retaliation was brutal, particularly at Omaha Beach. "People were yelling, screaming, dying, running on the beach, equipment was flying everywhere, men were bleeding to death, crawling, lying everywhere, firing coming from all directions," soldier Felix Branham wrote of the scene there. "We dropped down behind anything that was the size of a golf ball."

THE ALLIES GAIN GROUND Despite heavy casualties, the Allies held the beachheads. After seven days of fighting, the Allies held an 80-mile strip of France. Within a month, they had landed a million troops, 567,000 tons of supplies, and 170,000 vehicles in France. On July 25, General **Omar Bradley** unleashed massive air and land bombardment against the enemy at St. Lô, providing a gap in the German line of defense through which General **George Patton** and his Third Army could advance. On August 23, Patton and the Third Army reached the Seine River south of Paris. Two days later, French resistance forces and American troops liberated the French capital from four years of German occupation. Parisians were delirious with joy. Patton announced this joyous event to his commander in a message that read, "Dear Ike: Today I spat in the Seine."

By September 1944, the Allies had freed France, Belgium, and Luxembourg. This good news—and the American people's desire not to "change horses in midstream"—helped elect Franklin Roosevelt to an unprecedented fourth term in November, along with his running mate, Senator Harry S. Truman. **E**

KEY PLAYER

DWIGHT D. "IKE" EISENHOWER 1890–1969

When Army Chief of Staff General George Marshall chose modest Lieutenant General Dwight David Eisenhower to become the Supreme Commander of U.S. forces in Europe, he knew what he was doing. Ike was a superb planner and possessed a keen mind for military tactics.

More important, Eisenhower had an uncommon ability to work with all kinds of people, even competitive and temperamental allies. After V-E Day, a grateful Marshall wrote to Ike, saying, "You have been selfless in your actions, always sound and tolerant in your judgments and altogether admirable in the courage and wisdom of your military decisions. You have made history, great history for the good of mankind." In 1953, Dwight D. Eisenhower became president of the United States.

Background
American paratroopers on D-Day carried a simple signaling device to help them find one another in the dark. Each had a metal toy cricket to click. No German radio operators could intercept these messages.

MAIN IDEA

Evaluating
E Was the Allied invasion of Europe successful? Explain your answer.

On D-Day morning, a platoon of American infantry wade ashore to Omaha Beach.

D-Day, June 6, 1944

hmhsocialstudies.com **INTERACTIVE MAP**

GREAT BRITAIN

London
Dover
Portsmouth
Torquay
Portland
Calais
Strait of Dover
50°N
English Channel
Cherbourg
FRANCE

English Channel

21st ARMY GROUP
COMMANDER OF GROUND FORCES
Montgomery

U.S. 1st ARMY
Bradley

BRITISH 2nd ARMY
Dempsey

UTAH BEACH

OMAHA BEACH
GOLD BEACH
JUNO BEACH
SWORD BEACH

Ste-Mère-Eglise
La Madeleine
Vierville-sur-Mer
Colleville
Arromanches
Courseulles
Lion
Carentan
Isigny
Trévières
Bayeux
Caen

FRANCE

Mulberry Harbor
In order to accommodate the vast number of invading ships, the Allies built two enormous concrete ports and towed them to Gold Beach on the French coast on D-Day. They sank 70 old ships to create a breakwater for the artificial harbor.

Legend
- Allied forces
- Flooded area
- Glider landing area
- Planned drop zone
- Canal

0   3   6 miles
0   3   6 kilometers

to St. Lô

Prefabricated barriers
Prefabricated barriers
Sunken ships
Mulberry Harbor
Stores Pier
Floating Jetties
LST Pier
Barge Pier
Arromanches

GEOGRAPHY SKILLBUILDER
1. **Place** How does the inset map at the top of the page help explain why Hitler was expecting the invasion to cross from Dover to Calais over the Strait of Dover?
2. **Human-Environment Interaction** Was D-Day a simple or complex operation? How can you tell?

The United States in World War II **781**

AUDIE MURPHY

Near the end of the Second World War, Audie Murphy became famous as the most decorated American soldier of the war. He received 24 medals from the United States—including the Congressional Medal of Honor. He was also awarded three medals by France and one more by Belgium.

Born in Kingston, Texas, Murphy enlisted in the army in 1942. He served in North Africa and Europe, and in 1944 he rose to the rank of second lieutenant. His most impressive act of bravery occurred in January 1945 near Colmar, France, when in the midst of a furious German attack, he jumped onto a burning tank destroyer and killed about 50 Axis troops with his machine gun. Although wounded in the leg, he rallied his troops to retake the ground the Germans had gained earlier in the day.

THE BATTLE OF THE BULGE In October 1944, Americans captured their first German town, Aachen. Hitler responded with a desperate last-gasp offensive. He ordered his troops to break through the Allied lines and to recapture the Belgian port of Antwerp. This bold move, the Führer hoped, would disrupt the enemy's supply lines and demoralize the Allies.

On December 16, under cover of dense fog, eight German tank divisions broke through weak American defenses along an 80-mile front. Hitler hoped that a victory would split American and British forces and break up Allied supply lines. Tanks drove 60 miles into Allied territory, creating a bulge in the lines that gave this desperate last-ditch offensive its name, the **Battle of the Bulge.** As the Germans swept westward, they captured 120 American GIs near Malmédy. Elite German troops—the SS troopers—herded the prisoners into a large field and mowed them down with machine guns and pistols.

The battle raged for a month. When it was over, the Germans had been pushed back, and little seemed to have changed. But, in fact, events had taken a decisive turn. The Germans had lost 120,000 troops, 600 tanks and assault guns, and 1,600 planes in the Battle of the Bulge—soldiers and weapons they could not replace. From that point on, the Nazis could do little but retreat. **F**

LIBERATION OF THE DEATH CAMPS Meanwhile, Allied troops pressed eastward into the German heartland, and the Soviet army pushed westward across Poland toward Berlin. Soviet troops were the first to come upon one of the Nazi death camps, in July 1944. As the Soviets drew near a camp called Majdanek in Poland, SS guards worked feverishly to bury and burn all evidence of their hideous crimes. But they ran out of time. When the Soviets entered Majdanek, they found a thousand starving prisoners barely alive, the world's largest crematorium, and a storehouse containing 800,000 shoes. "This is not a concentration camp," reported a stunned Soviet war correspondent, "it is a gigantic murder plant." The Americans who later liberated Nazi death camps in Germany were equally horrified.

Vocabulary
elite: a small and privileged group

MAIN IDEA

Analyzing Effects
F Why was the Battle of the Bulge important?

★ **A PERSONAL VOICE** ROBERT T. JOHNSON

"We started smelling a terrible odor and suddenly we were at the concentration camp at Landsberg. Forced the gate and faced hundreds of starving prisoners. . . . We saw emaciated men whose thighs were smaller than wrists, many had bones sticking out thru their skin. . . . Also we saw hundreds of burned and naked bodies. . . . That evening I wrote my wife that 'For the first time I truly realized the evil of Hitler and why this war had to be waged.'"

—quoted in *Voices: Letters from World War II*

UNCONDITIONAL SURRENDER By April 25, 1945, the Soviet army had stormed Berlin. As Soviet shells burst overhead, the city panicked. "Hordes of soldiers stationed in Berlin deserted and were shot on the spot or hanged from the nearest tree," wrote Claus Fuhrmann, a Berlin clerk. "On their chests they had placards reading, 'We betrayed the Führer.'"

In his underground headquarters in Berlin, Hitler prepared for the end. On April 29, he married Eva Braun, his longtime companion. The same day, he wrote out his last address to the German people. In it he blamed the Jews for starting the war and his generals for losing it. "I die with a happy heart aware of the immeasurable deeds of our soldiers at the front. I myself and my wife choose to die in order to escape the disgrace of . . . capitulation," he said. The next day Hitler shot himself while his new wife swallowed poison. In accordance with Hitler's orders, the two bodies were carried outside, soaked with gasoline, and burned.

Vocabulary
capitulation:
surrender

A week later, General Eisenhower accepted the unconditional surrender of the Third Reich. On May 8, 1945, the Allies celebrated **V-E Day**—Victory in Europe Day. The war in Europe was finally over.

ROOSEVELT'S DEATH President Roosevelt did not live to see V-E Day. On April 12, 1945, while posing for a portrait in Warm Springs, Georgia, the president had a stroke and died. That night, Vice President **Harry S. Truman** became the nation's 33rd president.

▲
New Yorkers celebrate V-E Day with a massive party that began in Times Square and went on for days at sites throughout the city.

SECTION 2

ASSESSMENT

1. **TERMS & NAMES** For each term or name, write a sentence explaining its significance.
   - Dwight D. Eisenhower
   - D-Day
   - Omar Bradley
   - George Patton
   - Battle of the Bulge
   - V-E Day
   - Harry S. Truman

MAIN IDEA

2. **TAKING NOTES**
   Create a time line of the major events influencing the fighting in Europe and North Africa.

   event two   event four

   event one   event three

   Write a paragraph indicating how any two of these events are related.

CRITICAL THINKING

3. **EVALUATING DECISIONS**
   Do you agree with the decision made by Roosevelt and Churchill to require unconditional surrender by the Axis powers? Why or why not?
   Think About:
   - the advantages of defeating a foe decisively
   - the advantages of ending a war quickly
   - how other conflicts, such as the Civil War and World War I, ended

4. **ANALYZING PRIMARY SOURCES**
   When President Roosevelt's body was brought by train to Washington, Betty Conrad was among the servicewomen who escorted his casket.

   " The body in the casket was not only our leader but the bodies of all the men and women who had given their lives for freedom. They must not and will not have died in vain. "

   What did Roosevelt's body symbolize to Betty Conrad?

SECTION 3

CC Unit 6.I.C.4.b   CC Unit 6.I.C.4.c
CC Unit 6.I.C.4.d   CC Unit 6.I.C.5.d
PI 3.2   CC Unit 6.II.B.1   CC Unit 6.II.C.1.a

The War in the Pacific

MAIN IDEA	WHY IT MATTERS NOW	Terms & Names
In order to defeat Japan and end the war in the Pacific, the United States unleashed a terrible new weapon, the atomic bomb.	Countries of the modern world struggle to find ways to prevent the use of nuclear weapons.	•Douglas MacArthur •J. Robert Oppenheimer •Chester Nimitz •Hiroshima •Battle of Midway •Nagasaki •kamikaze •Nuremberg trials

One American's Story

hmhsocialstudies.com
TAKING NOTES

Use the graphic organizer online to take notes on the war in the Pacific.

The writer William Manchester left college after Pearl Harbor to join the marines. Manchester says that, as a child, his "horror of violence had been so deep-seated that I had been unable to trade punches with other boys." On a Pacific island, he would have to confront that horror the first time he killed a man in face-to-face combat. Manchester's target was a Japanese sniper firing on Manchester's buddies from a fisherman's shack.

★ **A PERSONAL VOICE** WILLIAM MANCHESTER

" My mouth was dry, my legs quaking, and my eyes out of focus. Then my vision cleared. I . . . kicked the door with my right foot, and leapt inside. . . .
I . . . saw him as a blur to my right. . . . My first shot missed him, embedding itself in the straw wall, but the second caught him dead-on . . . . A wave of blood gushed from the wound. . . . He dipped a hand in it and listlessly smeared his cheek red. . . . Almost immediately a fly landed on his left eyeball. . . . A feeling of disgust and self-hatred clotted darkly in my throat, gagging me. "
—from *Goodbye Darkness: A Memoir of the Pacific War*

▲ American soldiers on Leyte in the Philippine Islands in late 1944.

The Pacific War was a savage conflict fought with raw courage. Few who took part in that fearsome struggle would return home unchanged.

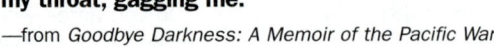

The Allies Stem the Japanese Tide

While the Allies agreed that the defeat of the Nazis was their first priority, the United States did not wait until V-E Day to move against Japan. Fortunately, the Japanese attack on Pearl Harbor in 1941 had missed the Pacific Fleet's submarines. Even more importantly, the attack had missed the fleet's aircraft carriers, which were out at sea at the time.

JAPANESE ADVANCES In the first six months after Pearl Harbor, the Japanese conquered an empire that dwarfed Hitler's Third Reich. On the Asian mainland, Japanese troops overran Hong Kong, French Indochina, Malaya, Burma, Thailand, and much of China. They also swept south and east across the Pacific, conquering the Dutch East Indies, Guam, Wake Island, the Solomon Islands, and countless other outposts in the ocean, including two islands in the Aleutian chain, which were part of Alaska.

In the Philippines, 80,000 American and Filipino troops battled the Japanese for control. At the time of the Japanese invasion in December 1941, General **Douglas MacArthur** was in command of Allied forces on the islands. When American and Filipino forces found themselves with their backs to the wall on Bataan, President Roosevelt ordered MacArthur to leave. On March 11, 1942, MacArthur left the Philippines with his wife, his son, and his staff. As he left, he pledged to the many thousands of men who did not make it out, "I shall return."

DOOLITTLE'S RAID In the spring of 1942, the Allies began to turn the tide against the Japanese. The push began on April 18 with a daring raid on Tokyo and other Japanese cities. Lieutenant Colonel James Doolittle led 16 bombers in the attack. The next day, Americans awoke to headlines that read "Tokyo Bombed! Doolittle Do'od It." Pulling off a Pearl Harbor–style air raid over Japan lifted America's sunken spirits. At the same time, it dampened spirits in Japan.

BATTLE OF THE CORAL SEA The main Allied forces in the Pacific were Americans and Australians. In May 1942 they succeeded in stopping the Japanese drive toward Australia in the five-day Battle of the Coral Sea. During this battle, the fighting was done by airplanes that took off from enormous aircraft carriers. Not a single shot was fired by surface ships. For the first time since Pearl Harbor, a Japanese invasion had been stopped and turned back.

THE BATTLE OF MIDWAY Japan's next thrust was toward Midway, a strategic island which lies northwest of Hawaii. Here again the Allies succeeded in stopping the Japanese. Americans had broken the Japanese code and knew that Midway was to be their next target.

Admiral **Chester Nimitz,** the commander of American naval forces in the Pacific, moved to defend the island. On June 3, 1942, his scout planes found the Japanese fleet. The Americans sent torpedo planes and dive bombers to the attack. The Japanese were caught with their planes still on the decks of their carriers. The results were devastating. By the end of the Battle of Midway, the Japanese had lost four aircraft carriers, a cruiser, and 250 planes. In the words of a Japanese official, at Midway the Americans had "avenged Pearl Harbor." Ⓐ

The **Battle of Midway** was a turning point in the Pacific War. Soon the Allies began "island hopping." Island by island they won territory back from the Japanese. With each island, Allied forces moved closer to Japan.

Background
Allied forces held out against 200,000 invading Japanese troops for four months on the Bataan Peninsula. Hunger, disease, and bombardments killed 14,000 Allied troops and wounded 48,000.

MAIN IDEA

Comparing
Ⓐ In what ways were the American victory at Midway and the Japanese triumph at Pearl Harbor alike?

HISTORICAL SPOTLIGHT

NAVAJO CODE TALKERS

On each of the Pacific islands that American troops stormed in World War II, the Japanese heard a "strange language gurgling" in their radio headsets. The code seemed to have Asian overtones, but it baffled everyone who heard it. In fact, the language was Navajo, which was spoken only in the American Southwest and traditionally had no alphabet or other written symbols. Its "hiddenness" made it a perfect candidate for a code language.

Though the Navajo had no words for combat terms, they developed terms such as *chicken hawk* for *divebomber* and *war chief* for *commanding general.* Throughout the Pacific campaign—from Midway to Iwo Jima—the code talkers were considered indispensable to the war effort. They finally received national recognition in 1969.

▲
Four hundred Navajo were recruited into the Marine Corps as code talkers. Their primary duty was transmitting telephone and radio messages.

War in the Pacific and in Europe

PACIFIC

- U.S. surrenders Bataan in the Philippines.
- Allies turn back Japanese fleet in Battle of the Coral Sea.
- U.S. declares war on Japan.
- Allies defeat Japan in Battle of Midway.
- U.S. marines land on Guadalcanal.

1941 Apr Jun Dec 1942 Apr May Jun Aug Nov 1943 Feb May

EUROPE

- Germany invades the Soviet Union.
- Germany invades Greece and Yugoslavia.
- Germany and Italy declare war on the United States.
- Hitler orders attack on Stalingrad.
- Allies land in North Africa.
- German troops surrender at Stalingrad.
- Axis forces surrender in North Africa.

World War II: The War in the Pacific, 1942–1945

hmhsocialstudies.com **INTERACTIVE MAP**

ALASKA (U.S.)

Bering Sea

SOVIET UNION

MONGOLIA

MANCHURIA (Province of China)

Sakhalin

Kurile Islands

Aleutian Islands

Attu I.

Beijing

CHINA

KOREA

JAPAN

Doolittle Raid, April 1942

PACIFIC OCEAN

BATTLE OF MIDWAY, June 1942

NAGASAKI, Aug. 9, 1945

Allied air supply route to China

Chongqing

Tokyo

HIROSHIMA, Aug. 6, 1945

Shanghai

Kohima Ledo Road

Imphal Kunming

INDIA Burma Road

BURMA

Rangoon

OKINAWA, April–June 1945

IWO JIMA, Feb.–Mar. 1945

Tropic of Cancer

Wake I.

Pearl Harbor

Hawaiian Is. (U.S.)

Formosa

Hong Kong

THAILAND

Luzon

PHILIPPINES

Manila

Mariana Islands

PHILIPPINE SEA, June 1944

Tinian I.

SAIPAN, June–July 1944

INDOCHINA Mindoro

South China Sea

GUAM, July–Aug. 1944

ENEWETAK, Feb. 1944

Marshall Is.

KWAJALEIN, Jan.–Feb. 1944

BRUNEI

Palau I.

LEYTE GULF, Oct. 1944

PELELIU, Sept.–Nov. 1944

Caroline Is.

MALAYA Singapore

Borneo

TARAWA, Nov. 1943 Gilbert Is.

Equator

Sumatra

Hollandia

New Guinea Rabaul

BOUGAINVILLE, Mar. 1944

DUTCH EAST INDIES

PAPUA

Solomon Is.

Java

CORAL SEA, May 1942

GUADALCANAL, Aug. 1942–Feb. 1943

INDIAN OCEAN

Fiji Is.

Coral Sea

AUSTRALIA

Legend:
- Japanese Empire and conquest
- Major Allied campaign
- Limit of Japanese advance
- Atomic bombing
- Major battle

0 800 1,600 miles
0 800 1,600 kilometers

GEOGRAPHY SKILLBUILDER

1. Movement Which island served as a jumping-off point for several Pacific battles?

2. Human-Environment Interaction How do you think the distances between the Pacific islands affected U.S. naval strategy?

Allies capture Okinawa.

U.S. drops atomic bombs on
Hiroshima and Nagasaki.

Allies win Battle of
the Philippine Sea.

Allies win Battle
of Leyte Gulf.

Allies capture
Iwo Jima.

Japan surrenders.

| Jul | Sep | **1944** May | Jun Jul Aug | Oct | Dec | **1945** | Mar Apr May Jun | Aug Sep | **1946** |

Allies
invade
Sicily.

Italy secretly
surrenders
to Allies.

Allies liberate Paris.

Soviets first liberate death camps.

Allies invade Europe on D-Day.

"Bloody Anzio" ends.

Germans attack Allies
in Battle of the Bulge.

V-E Day ends war in Europe.

Italians execute Mussolini.

Hitler commits suicide.

The Allies Go on the Offensive

The first Allied offensive began in August 1942 when 19,000 troops stormed Guadalcanal in the Solomon Islands. By the time the Japanese abandoned Guadalcanal six months later, they called it the Island of Death. To war correspondent Ralph Martin and the troops who fought there, it was simply "hell."

A PERSONAL VOICE RALPH G. MARTIN

" Hell was red furry spiders as big as your fist, giant lizards as long as your leg, leeches falling from trees to suck blood, armies of white ants with a bite of fire, scurrying scorpions inflaming any flesh they touched, enormous rats and bats everywhere, and rivers with waiting crocodiles. Hell was the sour, foul smell of the squishy jungle, humidity that rotted a body within hours, . . . stinking wet heat of dripping rain forests that sapped the strength of any man. "

—*The GI War*

Guadalcanal marked Japan's first defeat on land, but not its last. The Americans continued leapfrogging across the Pacific toward Japan, and in October 1944, some 178,000 Allied troops and 738 ships converged on Leyte Island in the Philippines. General MacArthur, who had left the Philippines two years earlier, waded ashore and announced, "People of the Philippines: I have returned."

THE JAPANESE DEFENSE The Japanese threw their entire fleet into the Battle of Leyte Gulf. They also tested a new tactic, the **kamikaze** (kä´mǐkä´zē), or suicide-plane, attack in which Japanese pilots crashed their bomb-laden planes into Allied ships. (*Kamikaze* means "divine wind" and refers to a legendary typhoon that saved Japan in 1281 by destroying a Mongol invasion.) In the Philippines, 424 kamikaze pilots embarked on suicide missions, sinking 16 ships and damaging another 80.

Americans watched these terrifying attacks with "a strange mixture of respect and pity" according to Vice Admiral Charles Brown. "You have to admire the devotion to country demonstrated by those pilots," recalled Seaman George Marse. "Yet, when they were shot down, rescued and brought aboard our ship, we were surprised to find the pilots looked like ordinary, scared young men, not the wide-eyed fanatical 'devils' we imagined them to be."

Despite the damage done by the kamikazes, the Battle of Leyte Gulf was a disaster for Japan. In three days of battle, it lost 3 battleships, 4 aircraft carriers, 13 cruisers, and almost 500 planes. From then on, the Imperial Navy played only a minor role in the defense of Japan. **B**

Japanese kamikaze pilots pose—smiling—just before taking off on the mission that would be their last. ▼

MAIN IDEA

Drawing Conclusions
B Why was the Battle of Leyte Gulf so crucial to the Allies?

RAISING THE FLAG ON IWO JIMA

On February 19, 1945, the war in Europe was nearing its end, but in the Pacific one of the fiercest battles of World War II was about to erupt. On that day, 70,000 marines converged on the tiny, Japanese-controlled island of Iwo Jima. Four days later, they had captured Mount Suribachi, the island's highest point, but the battle for Iwo Jima would rage on for four more weeks.

Photographer Lou Lowery documented the men of "Easy Company" hoisting an American flag on a makeshift pole atop Mount Suribachi. But the original flag was soon taken down to be kept as a souvenir by the commanding officer. ▶

▲
Six marines were sent to replace the flag with an even larger one. Joe Rosenthal, a wire-service photographer, saw the second flag raising, grabbed his camera, and clicked off a frame without even looking through his viewfinder. Rosenthal's photo appeared the next morning on the front pages of American newspapers. In the minds of Americans, it immediately replaced the gloomy, blurred images of Pearl Harbor going up in flames.

SKILLBUILDER Interpeting Visual Sources
1. One of the Mount Suribachi images became one of the most recognized, most reproduced images of World War II. Study the details and point of view in each photo. Explain why you think Rosenthal's image, rather than Lowery's, became important.
2. What human qualities or events do you think Rosenthal's photograph symbolizes?

 SEE SKILLBUILDER HANDBOOK, PAGE R23.

IWO JIMA After retaking much of the Philippines and liberating the American prisoners of war there, the Allies turned to Iwo Jima, an island that writer William Manchester later described as "an ugly, smelly glob of cold lava squatting in a surly ocean." Iwo Jima (which means "sulfur island" in Japanese) was critical to the United States as a base from which heavily loaded bombers might reach Japan. It was also perhaps the most heavily defended spot on earth, with 20,700 Japanese troops entrenched in tunnels and caves. More than 6,000 marines died taking this desolate island, the greatest number in any battle in the Pacific to that point. Only 200 Japanese survived. Just one obstacle now stood between the Allies and a final assault on Japan—the island of Okinawa.

THE BATTLE FOR OKINAWA In April 1945, U.S. Marines invaded Okinawa. The Japanese unleashed more than 1,900 kamikaze attacks on the Allies during the Okinawa campaign, sinking 30 ships, damaging more than 300 more, and killing almost 5,000 seamen.

Once ashore, the Allies faced even fiercer opposition than on Iwo Jima. By the time the fighting ended on June 21, 1945, more than 7,600 Americans had died. But the Japanese paid an even ghastlier price—110,000 lives—in defending Okinawa. This total included two generals who chose ritual suicide over the shame of surrender. A witness to this ceremony described their end: "A simultaneous shout and a flash of the sword . . . and both generals had nobly accomplished their last duty to their Emperor."

The Battle for Okinawa was a chilling foretaste of what the Allies imagined the invasion of Japan's home islands would be. Churchill predicted the cost would be a million American lives and half that number of British lives. **C**

KEY PLAYER

DOUGLAS MACARTHUR
1880–1964
Douglas MacArthur was too arrogant and prickly to be considered a "regular guy" by his troops. But he was arguably the most brilliant Allied strategist of World War II. For every American soldier killed in his campaigns, the Japanese lost ten.

He was considered a real hero of the war, both by the military and by the prisoners on the Philippines, whom he freed. "MacArthur took more territory with less loss of life," observed journalist John Gunther, "than any military commander since Darius the Great [king of Persia, 522–486 B.C.]."

MAIN IDEA

Drawing Conclusions
C Why was Okinawa a significant island in the war in the Pacific?

The Atomic Bomb Ends the War

The taking of Iwo Jima and Okinawa opened the way for an invasion of Japan. However, Allied leaders knew that such an invasion would become a desperate struggle. Japan still had a huge army that would defend every inch of homeland. President Truman saw only one way to avoid an invasion of Japan. He decided to use a powerful new weapon that had been developed by scientists working on the Manhattan Project—the atomic bomb.

THE MANHATTAN PROJECT Led by General Leslie Groves with research directed by Jewish American scientist **J. Robert Oppenheimer,** the development of the atomic bomb was not only the most ambitious scientific enterprise in history, it was also the best-kept secret of the war. At its peak, more than 600,000 Americans were involved in the project, although few knew its ultimate purpose. Even Truman did not learn about it until he became president.

The first test of the new bomb took place on the morning of July 16, 1945, in an empty expanse of desert near Alamogordo, New Mexico. A blinding flash, which was visible 180 miles away, was followed by a deafening roar as a tremendous shock wave rolled across the trembling desert. Otto Frisch, a scientist on the project, described the huge mushroom cloud that rose over the desert as "a redhot elephant standing balanced on its trunk." The bomb worked!

President Truman now faced a difficult decision. Should the Allies use the bomb to bring an end to the war? Truman did not hesitate. On July 25, 1945, he ordered the military to make final plans for dropping two atomic bombs on Japanese targets. A day later, the United States warned Japan that it faced "prompt and utter destruction" unless it surrendered at once. Japan refused. Truman later wrote, "The final decision of where and when to use the atomic bomb was up to me. Let there be no mistake about it. I regarded the bomb as a military weapon and never had any doubt that it should be used."

HIROSHIMA AND NAGASAKI On August 6, a B-29 bomber named *Enola Gay* released an atomic bomb, code-named Little Boy, over **Hiroshima,** an important Japanese military center. Forty-three seconds later, almost every building in the city collapsed into dust from the force of the blast. Hiroshima had ceased to exist. Still, Japan's leaders hesitated to surrender. Three days later, a second bomb, code-named Fat Man, was dropped on **Nagasaki,** leveling half the city. By the end of the year, an estimated 200,000 people had died as a result of injuries and radiation poisoning caused by the atomic blasts. Yamaoka Michiko was 15 years old and living near the center of Hiroshima when the first bomb hit.

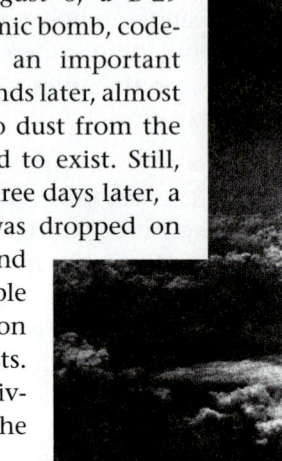

A PERSONAL VOICE YAMAOKA MICHIKO

" They say temperatures of 7,000 degrees centigrade hit me. . . . Nobody there looked like human beings. . . . Humans had lost the ability to speak. People couldn't scream, 'It hurts!' even when they were on fire. . . . People with their legs wrenched off. Without heads. Or with faces burned and swollen out of shape. The scene I saw was a living hell."

—quoted in *Japan at War: An Oral History*

Emperor Hirohito was horrified by the destruction wrought by the bomb. "I cannot bear to see my innocent people suffer any longer," he told Japan's leaders tearfully. Then he ordered them to draw up papers "to end the war." On September 2, formal surrender ceremonies took place on the U.S. battleship *Missouri* in Tokyo Bay. "Today the guns are silent," said General MacArthur in a speech marking this historic moment. "The skies no longer rain death—the seas bear only commerce—men everywhere walk upright in the sunlight. The entire world is quietly at peace."

Hiroshima in ruins following the atomic bomb blast on August 6, 1945 ▶

POINT

"The only way to end the war against Japan was to bomb the Japanese mainland."

Many advisors to President Truman, including Secretary of War Henry Stimson, had this point of view. They felt the bomb would end the war and save American lives. Stimson said, "The face of war is the face of death."

Some scientists working on the bomb agreed— even more so as the casualty figures from Iwo Jima and Okinawa sank in. "Are we to go on shedding American blood when we have available a means to a steady victory?" they petitioned. "No! If we can save even a handful of American lives, then let us use this weapon—now!"

Two other concerns pushed Americans to use the bomb. Some people feared that if the bomb were not dropped, the project might be viewed as a gigantic waste of money.

The second consideration involved the Soviet Union. Tension and distrust were already developing between the Western Allies and the Soviets. Some American officials believed that a successful use of the atomic bomb would give the United States a powerful advantage over the Soviets in shaping the postwar world.

COUNTERPOINT

"Japan's staggering losses were enough to force Japan's surrender."

Many of the scientists who had worked on the bomb, as well as military leaders and civilian policymakers, had doubts about using it. Dr. Leo Szilard, a Jewish Hungarian-born physicist who had helped President Roosevelt launch the project and who had a major role in developing the bomb, was a key figure opposing its use.

A petition drawn up by Szilard and signed by 70 other scientists argued that it would be immoral to drop an atomic bomb on Japan without fair warning. Many supported staging a demonstration of the bomb for Japanese leaders, perhaps by exploding one on a deserted island near Japan, to convince the Japanese to surrender.

Supreme Allied Commander General Dwight D. Eisenhower agreed. He maintained that "dropping the bomb was completely unnecessary" to save American lives and that Japan was already defeated. Ike told Secretary of War Henry Stimson, "I was against it [the bomb] on two counts. First the Japanese were ready to surrender and it wasn't necessary to hit them with that awful thing. Second, I hated to see our country be the first to use such a weapon."

THINKING CRITICALLY

1. **CONNECT TO HISTORY** **Summarizing** What were the main arguments for and against dropping the atomic bomb on Japan?

   SEE SKILLBUILDER HANDBOOK, PAGE R4.

2. **CONNECT TO TODAY** **Evaluating Decisions** Do you think the United States was justified in using the bomb against the Japanese? In a paragraph, explain why or why not.

Rebuilding Begins

With Japan's surrender, the Allies turned to the challenge of rebuilding war-torn nations. Even before the last guns fell silent, they began thinking about principles that would govern the postwar world.

THE YALTA CONFERENCE In February 1945, as the Allies pushed toward victory in Europe, an ailing Roosevelt had met with Churchill and Stalin at the Black Sea resort city of Yalta in the Soviet Union. Stalin graciously welcomed the president and the prime minister, and the Big Three, as they were called, toasted the defeat of Germany that now seemed certain.

For eight grueling days, the three leaders discussed the fate of Germany and the postwar world. Stalin, his country devastated by German forces, favored a harsh approach. He wanted to keep Germany divided into occupation zones—areas controlled by Allied military forces—so that Germany would never again threaten the Soviet Union.

When Churchill strongly disagreed, Roosevelt acted as a mediator. He was prepared to make concessions to Stalin for two reasons. First, he hoped that the Soviet Union would stand by its commitments to join the war against Japan that was still waging in the Pacific. (The first test of the atom bomb was still five months away.) Second, Roosevelt wanted Stalin's support for a new world peace-keeping organization, to be named the United Nations.

MAIN IDEA

Analyzing Motives

D Why was Roosevelt anxious to make concessions to Stalin concerning the fate of postwar Germany?

The historic meeting at Yalta produced a series of compromises. To pacify Stalin, Roosevelt convinced Churchill to agree to a temporary division of Germany into four zones, one each for the Americans, the British, the Soviets, and the French. Churchill and Roosevelt assumed that, in time, all the zones would be brought together in a reunited Germany. For his part, Stalin promised "free and unfettered elections" in Poland and other Soviet-occupied Eastern European countries.

Stalin also agreed to join in the war against Japan. That struggle was expected to continue for another year or more. In addition, he agreed to participate in an international conference to take place in April in San Francisco. There, Roosevelt's dream of a United Nations (UN) would become a reality. **E**

THE NUREMBERG WAR TRIALS Besides geographic division, Germany had another price to pay for its part in the war. The discovery of Hitler's death camps led the Allies to put 24 surviving Nazi leaders on trial for crimes against humanity, crimes against the peace, and war crimes. The trials were held in the southern German town of Nuremberg.

At the **Nuremberg trials,** the defendants included Hitler's most trusted party officials, government ministers, military leaders, and powerful industrialists. As the trial began, U.S. Supreme Court Justice Robert Jackson explained the significance of the event.

MAIN IDEA

Summarizing
E What decisions did Roosevelt, Churchill, and Stalin make at the Yalta Conference?

★ **A PERSONAL VOICE** JUSTICE ROBERT JACKSON

" The wrongs which we seek to condemn and punish have been so calculated, so malignant and so devastating, that civilization cannot tolerate their being ignored because it cannot survive their being repeated. . . . It is hard now to perceive in these miserable men . . . the power by which as Nazi leaders they once dominated much of the world and terrified most of it. Merely as individuals, their fate is of little consequence to the world. What makes this inquest significant is that these prisoners represent sinister influences that will lurk in the world long after their bodies have returned to dust. They are living symbols of racial hatreds, of terrorism and violence, and of the arrogance and cruelty of power. . . . Civilization can afford no compromise with the social forces which would gain renewed strength if we deal ambiguously or indecisively with the men in whom those forces now precariously survive. "

—quoted in opening address to the Nuremberg War Crimes Trial

War Criminals on Trial, 1945–1949

Each defendant at the Nuremberg trials was accused of one or more of the following crimes:

- **Crimes Against the Peace**—planning and waging an aggressive war

- **War Crimes**—acts against the customs of warfare, such as the killing of hostages and prisoners, the plundering of private property, and the destruction of towns and cities

- **Crimes Against Humanity**—the murder, extermination, deportation, or enslavement of civilians

In the end, 12 of the 24 defendants were sentenced to death, and most of the remaining were sent to prison. In later trials of lesser leaders, nearly 200 more Nazis were found guilty of war crimes. Still, many people have argued that the trials did not go far enough in seeking out and punishing war criminals. Many Nazis who took part in the Holocaust did indeed go free.

Yet no matter how imperfect the trials might have been, they did establish an important principle—the idea that individuals are responsible for their own actions, even in times of war. Nazi executioners could not escape punishment by claiming that they were merely "following orders." The principle of individual responsibility was now firmly entrenched in international law.

"I was only following orders."

DEFENDANTS AT THE NUREMBERG TRIALS

Background
In the years after World War II, Communists took control of several Asian countries. As a result, the U.S. wanted to maintain its military presence in Japan. The 1951 peace treaty signed by the two countries returned Japan to independence but also allowed the American military to remain.

THE OCCUPATION OF JAPAN Japan was occupied by U.S. forces under the command of General Douglas MacArthur. In the early years of the occupation, more than 1,100 Japanese, from former Prime Minister Hideki Tojo to lowly prison guards, were arrested and put on trial. Seven, including Tojo, were sentenced to death. In the Philippines, in China, and in other Asian battlegrounds, additional Japanese officials were tried for atrocities against civilians or prisoners of war.

During the seven-year American occupation, MacArthur reshaped Japan's economy by introducing free-market practices that led to a remarkable economic recovery. MacArthur also worked to transform Japan's government. He called for a new constitution that would provide for woman suffrage and guarantee basic freedoms. In the United States, Americans followed these changes with interest. The *New York Times* reported that "General MacArthur . . . has swept away an autocratic regime by a warrior god and installed in its place a democratic government presided over by a very human emperor and based on the will of the people as expressed in free elections." The Japanese apparently agreed. To this day, their constitution is known as the MacArthur Constitution.

SECTION 3 ASSESSMENT

1. TERMS & NAMES For each term or name, write a sentence explaining its significance.

- Douglas MacArthur
- Chester Nimitz
- Battle of Midway
- kamikaze
- J. Robert Oppenheimer
- Hiroshima
- Nagasaki
- Nuremberg trials

MAIN IDEA

2. TAKING NOTES
Using a chart such as the one below, describe the significance of key military actions in the Pacific during World War II.

Military Action	Significance
1.	
2.	
3.	
4.	
5.	

Which military action was a turning point for the Allies?

CRITICAL THINKING

3. DEVELOPING HISTORICAL PERSPECTIVE
At the trials, many Nazis defended themselves by saying they were only following orders. What does this rationale tell you about the German military? Why was it important to negate this justification?

4. DRAWING CONCLUSIONS
Explain how the United States was able to defeat the Japanese in the Pacific.

5. EVALUATING DECISIONS
Is it legitimate to hold people accountable for crimes committed during wartime? Why or why not?
Think About:

- the laws that govern society
- the likelihood of conducting a fair trial
- the behavior of soldiers, politicians, and civilians during war

Science and Technology

Radar, guided missiles, nuclear submarines, reconnaissance satellites, atomic bombs—the inventions of the 20th century seem intended mainly for war, with the usual dreaded results. But these technological developments have also had far-reaching applications in peacetime. Because the innovations were originally intended for the battlefield, they were developed quickly and with a narrow purpose. However, their applications during peacetime have led to life-enhancing benefits that will extend far into the 21st century.

1914–1918 WORLD WAR I

FIGHTER PLANES TO COMMUTER FLIGHTS ▼

Airplanes were first used to gather military information but were soon put to work as fighters and bombers. The *Sopwith Camel* (*shown at right*), was one of the most successful British fighter planes, bringing down almost 1,300 enemy aircraft during World War I. The development of flight technology eventually led to sophisticated supersonic aircraft. Today, non-military aircraft are primarily used for travel and cargo transport. Jumbo jets carry hundreds of passengers with each takeoff.

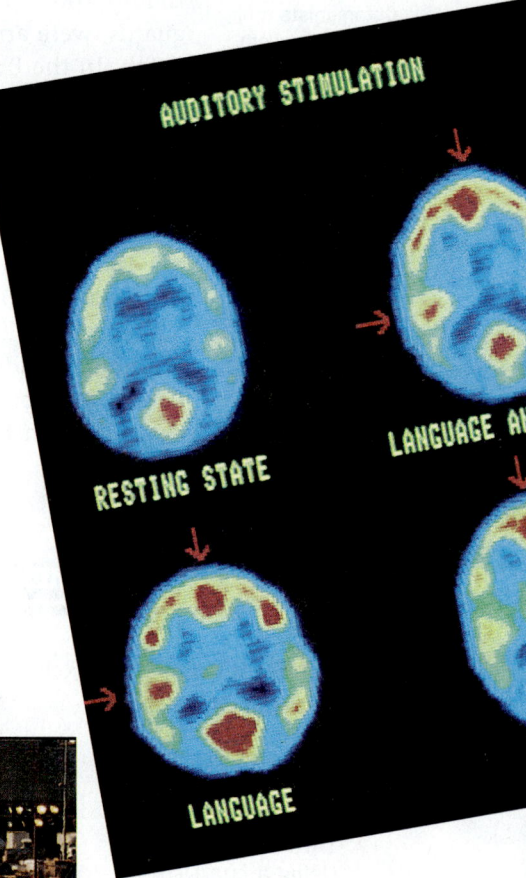

AUDITORY STIMULATION

RESTING STATE

LANGUAGE AN

LANGUAGE

1939–1945 WORLD WAR II

▼ ATOM BOMBS TO BRAIN SCANS

Faced with alarming rumors of work on a German atomic bomb, America mobilized some of the finest scientific minds in the world to create its own atomic bomb. The energy released by its nuclear reaction was enough to kill hundreds of thousands of people, as evidenced by the destruction of Hiroshima and Nagasaki. But the resulting ability to harness the atom's energy also led to new technologies for diagnosing and treating human diseases. Techniques such as positron emission tomography (PET) now reveal the inner workings of the human brain itself.

Applications of World War II Technology

TECHNOLOGY	MILITARY USE	PEACETIME USE
Semiconductors	Navigation	Transistors, radios, electronics
Computers	Code breaking	Software programs, video games
Freeze-dried food	Soldiers' rations	TV dinners, space-shuttle rations
Synthetic materials	Parachutes, weapons parts, tires	Telephones, automobile fenders, pacemakers
Radar	Tracking and surveillance	Weather tracking, air traffic control, archaeological digs

1945–1991 THE COLD WAR

▼ SATELLITES TO CELLULAR PHONES

The Soviet Union launched *Sputnik*, the first successful artificial space satellite, in 1957. As the United States raced to catch up with the Soviets in space, both countries eventually produced satellites that have improved life for people around the world. Satellites not only track weather patterns and control air traffic but also link the continents in a vast communications network.

THINKING CRITICALLY

CONNECT TO HISTORY

1. **Hypothesizing** Do you think that peacetime technologies would have been developed without the stimulus provided by war? Support your answer.

    SEE SKILLBUILDER HANDBOOK, PAGE R13.

CONNECT TO TODAY

2. **Evaluating Technological Impact** What invention or technological breakthrough do you think has had the greatest impact on American society? Write a paragraph to explain your answer. Stage a debate with your classmates in which you defend your choice.

 hmhsocialstudies.com **RESEARCH WEB LINKS**

The Home Front

MAIN IDEA	WHY IT MATTERS NOW	Terms & Names
After World War II, Americans adjusted to new economic opportunities and harsh social tensions.	Economic opportunities afforded by World War II led to a more diverse middle class in the United States.	•GI Bill of Rights •James Farmer •Congress of Racial Equality (CORE) •internment •Japanese American Citizens League (JACL)

One American's Story

hmhsocialstudies.com
TAKING NOTES
Use the graphic organizer online to take notes on the war's effects on the home front.

The writer and poet Maya Angelou was a teenager living in San Francisco when the United States got involved in World War II. The first change she noticed was the disappearance of the city's Japanese population. The second change was an influx of workers, including many African Americans, from the South. San Franciscans, she noted, maintained that there was no racism in their city by the bay. But Angelou knew differently.

A PERSONAL VOICE MAYA ANGELOU

" A story went the rounds about a San Franciscan white matron who refused to sit beside a Negro civilian on the streetcar, even after he made room for her on the seat. Her explanation was that she would not sit beside a draft dodger who was a Negro as well. She added that the least he could do was fight for his country the way her son was fighting on Iwo Jima. The story said that the man pulled his body away from the window to show an armless sleeve. He said quietly and with great dignity, 'Then ask your son to look around for my arm, which I left over there.' "

—*I Know Why the Caged Bird Sings*

TWICE A PATRIOT

EX-PRIVATE OBIE BARTLETT LOST LEFT ARM—PEARL HARBOR
RELEASED: DEC., 1941—NOW AT WORK WELDING
IN A WEST COAST SHIPYARD...

▲
Like many minority veterans, Obie Bartlett was twice a patriot— and was still regarded as a second-class citizen.

At the end of the war, returning veterans—even those who weren't disabled—had to begin dealing with the very real issues of reentry and adjustment to a society that offered many opportunities but still had many unsolved problems.

Opportunity and Adjustment

In contrast to the Great Depression, World War II was a time of opportunity for millions of Americans. Jobs abounded, and despite rationing and shortages, people had money to spend. At the end of World War II, the nation emerged as the world's dominant economic and military power.

ECONOMIC GAINS The war years were good ones for working people. As defense industries boomed, unemployment fell to a low of 1.2 percent in 1944. Even with price and wage controls, average weekly pay (adjusted for inflation) rose 10 percent during the war. And although workers still protested long hours, overtime, and night shifts, they were able to save money for the future. Some workers invested up to half their paychecks in war bonds.

Farmers also prospered during the war. Unlike the depression years, when farmers had battled dust storms and floods, the early 1940s had good weather for growing crops. Farmers benefited from improvements in farm machinery and fertilizers and reaped the profits from rising crop prices. As a result, crop production increased by 50 percent, and farm income tripled. Before the war ended, many farmers could pay off their mortgages.

Women also enjoyed employment gains during the war, although many lost their jobs when the war ended. Over 6 million women had entered the work force for the first time, boosting the percentage of women in the total work force to 35 percent. A third of those jobs were in defense plants, which offered women more challenging work and better pay than jobs traditionally associated with women, such as as waitressing, clerking, and domestic service. With men away at war, many women also took advantage of openings in journalism and other professions. "The war really created opportunities for women," said Winona Espinosa, a wife and mother who became a riveter and bus driver during the war. "It was the first time we got a chance to show that we could do a lot of things that only men had done before."

"THE GIRL HE LEFT BEHIND" IS STILL BEHIND HIM
She's a **WOW**
WOMAN ORDNANCE WORKER

▲ The war gave women the chance to prove they could be just as productive as men. But their pay usually did not reflect their productivity.

POPULATION SHIFTS

In addition to revamping the economy, the war triggered one of the greatest mass migrations in American history. Americans whose families had lived for decades in one place suddenly uprooted themselves to seek work elsewhere. More than a million newcomers poured into California between 1941 and 1944. Towns with defense industries saw their populations double and even triple, sometimes almost overnight. As shown in the map to the right, African Americans left the South for cities in the North in record numbers. **Ⓐ**

Vocabulary
migration: the act of moving from one country or region to another

MAIN IDEA

Analyzing Causes
Ⓐ How did World War II cause the U.S. population to shift?

African-American Migration, 1940–1950

West Coast

Mountain and Plains States

Midwest

New England

Middle Atlantic

+26,300

+523,200

+386,800

+24,900

South −1,244,800

+283,600

GEOGRAPHY SKILLBUILDER
1. **Movement** To which geographic region did the greatest number of African Americans migrate?
2. **Movement** How did the wartime economy contribute to this mass migration?

SOCIAL ADJUSTMENTS Families adjusted to the changes brought on by war as best they could. With millions of fathers in the armed forces, mothers struggled to rear their children alone. Many young children got used to being left with neighbors or relatives or in child-care centers as more and more mothers went to work. Teenagers left at home without parents sometimes drifted into juvenile delinquency. And when fathers finally did come home, there was often a painful period of readjustment as family members got to know one another again.

The war helped create new families, too. Longtime sweethearts—as well as couples who barely knew each other—rushed to marry before the soldier or sailor was shipped overseas. In booming towns like Seattle, the number of marriage licenses issued went up by as much as 300 percent early in the war. A New Yorker observed in 1943, "On Fridays and Saturdays, the City Hall area is blurred with running soldiers, sailors, and girls hunting the license bureau, floral shops, ministers, blood-testing laboratories, and the Legal Aid Society."

In 1944, to help ease the transition of returning servicemen to civilian life, Congress passed the Servicemen's Readjustment Act, better known as the **GI Bill of Rights.** This bill provided education and training for veterans, paid for by the federal government. Just over half the returning soldiers, or about 7.8 million veterans, attended colleges and technical schools under the GI Bill. The act also provided federal loan guarantees to veterans buying homes or farms or starting new businesses. **B**

Discrimination and Reaction

Despite the opportunities that opened up for women and minorities during the war, old prejudices and policies persisted, both in the military and at home.

CIVIL RIGHTS PROTESTS African Americans made some progress on the home front. During the war, thousands of African Americans left the South. The majority moved to the Midwest, where better jobs could be found. Between 1940 and 1944, the percentage of African Americans working in skilled or semiskilled jobs rose from 16 to 30 percent.

Wherever African Americans moved, however, discrimination presented tough hurdles. In 1942, civil rights leader **James Farmer** founded an interracial organization called the **Congress of Racial Equality (CORE)** to confront urban segregation in the North. That same year, CORE staged its first sit-in at a segregated Chicago restaurant.

As African-American migrants moved into already overcrowded cities, tensions rose. In 1943, a tidal wave of racial violence swept across the country. The worst conflict erupted in Detroit on a hot Sunday afternoon in June. What started as a tussle between blacks and whites at a beach on the Detroit River mushroomed into a riot when white sailors stationed nearby joined the fray. The fighting raged for three days, fueled by false rumors that whites had murdered a black woman and her child and that black rioters had killed 17 whites. By the time President Roosevelt sent federal troops to restore order, 9 whites and 25 blacks lay dead or dying.

The violence of 1943 revealed to many Americans—black and white alike—just how serious racial tensions had become in the United States. By 1945, more than 400 committees had been established by American communities to improve race relations. Progress was slow, but African Americans were determined not to give up the gains they had made. **C**

MAIN IDEA

Analyzing Causes

C What caused the race riots in the 1940s?

TENSION IN LOS ANGELES Mexican Americans also experienced prejudice during the war years. In the violent summer of 1943, Los Angeles exploded in anti-Mexican "zoot-suit" riots. The zoot suit was a style of dress adopted by Mexican-American youths as a symbol of their rebellion against tradition. It consisted of a long jacket and pleated pants. Broad-brimmed hats were often worn with the suits.

The riots began when 11 sailors in Los Angeles reported that they had been attacked by zoot-suit-wearing Mexican Americans. This charge triggered violence involving thousands of servicemen and civilians. Mobs poured into Mexican neighborhoods and grabbed any zoot-suiters they could find. The attackers ripped off their victims' clothes and beat them senseless. The riots lasted almost a week and resulted in the beating of hundreds of Mexican-American youth and other minorities.

Despite such unhappy experiences with racism, many Mexican Americans believed that their sacrifices during wartime would lead to a better future.

▲ These Mexican Americans, involved in the 1943 Los Angeles riots, are seen here leaving jail to make court appearances.

★ **A PERSONAL VOICE** MANUEL DE LA RAZA

" This war . . . is doing what we in our Mexican-American movement had planned to do in one generation. . . . It has shown those 'across the tracks' that we all share the same problems. It has shown them what the Mexican American will do, what responsibility he will take and what leadership qualities he will demonstrate. After this struggle, the status of the Mexican Americans will be different."

—quoted in *A Different Mirror: A History of Multicultural America*

Japanese Relocation Camps, 1942

IDAHO
Minidoka

Heart Mountain

WYOMING

Tule Lake

UTAH

CALIFORNIA

COLORADO
Granada (Amache)

Topaz

Manzanar

ARIZONA

Poston

Gila River

ARKANSAS
Rohwer
Jerome

GEOGRAPHY SKILLBUILDER
1. **Location** How many Japanese internment camps existed in 1942?
2. **Place** Why do you think the majority of these camps were located in the West?

▲
On March 3, 1942, a Japanese-American mother carries her sleeping daughter during their relocation to an internment camp.

Internment of Japanese Americans

While Mexican Americans and African Americans struggled with racial tension, the war produced tragic results for Japanese Americans. When the war began, 120,000 Japanese Americans lived in the United States. Most of them were citizens living on the West Coast.

The surprise Japanese attack on Pearl Harbor in Hawaii had stunned the nation. After the bombing, panic-stricken citizens feared that the Japanese would soon attack the United States. Frightened people believed false rumors that Japanese Americans were committing sabotage by mining coastal harbors and poisoning vegetables.

This sense of fear and uncertainty caused a wave of prejudice against Japanese Americans. Early in 1942, the War Department called for the mass evacuation of all Japanese Americans from Hawaii. General Delos Emmons, the military governor of Hawaii, resisted the order because 37 percent of the people in Hawaii were Japanese Americans. To remove them would have destroyed the islands' economy and hindered U.S. military operations there. However, he was eventually forced to order the **internment,** or confinement, of 1,444 Japanese Americans, 1 percent of Hawaii's Japanese-American population.

On the West Coast, however, panic and prejudice ruled the day. In California, only 1 percent of the people were Japanese, but they constituted a minority large enough to stimulate the prejudice of many whites, without being large enough to effectively resist internment. Newspapers whipped up anti-Japanese sentiment by running ugly stories attacking Japanese Americans.

On February 19, 1942, President Roosevelt signed an order requiring the removal of people of Japanese ancestry from California and parts of Washington, Oregon, and Arizona. Based on strong recommendations from the military, he justified this step as necessary for national security. In the following weeks, the army rounded up some 110,000 Japanese Americans and shipped them to ten hastily constructed remote "relocation centers," euphemisms for prison camps.

MAIN IDEA

Analyzing Motives

D Why did President Roosevelt order the internment of Japanese Americans?

About two-thirds were Nisei, or Japanese people born in this country of parents who emigrated from Japan. Thousands of Nisei had already joined the armed forces, and to Ted Nakashima, an architectural draftsman from Seattle, the evacuation seemed utterly senseless. **D**

A PERSONAL VOICE TED NAKASHIMA

" **[There are] electricians, plumbers, draftsmen, mechanics, carpenters, painters, farmers—every trade—men who are able and willing to do all they can to lick the Axis. . . . We're on this side and we want to help. Why won't America let us?** "

—from *New Republic* magazine, June 15, 1942

No specific charges were ever filed against Japanese Americans, and no evidence of subversion was ever found. Faced with expulsion, terrified families were forced to sell their homes, businesses, and all their belongings for less than their true value.

Japanese Americans fought for justice, both in the courts and in Congress. The initial results were discouraging. In 1944, the Supreme Court decided, in *Korematsu* v. *United States*, that the government's policy of evacuating Japanese Americans to camps was justified on the basis of "military necessity." (See pages 802–803.) After the war, however, the **Japanese American Citizens League (JACL)** pushed the government to compensate those sent to the camps for their lost property. In 1965, Congress authorized the spending of $38 million for that purpose—less than a tenth of Japanese Americans' actual losses.

The JACL did not give up its quest for justice. In 1978, it called for the payment of reparations, or restitution, to each individual that suffered internment. A decade later, Congress passed, and President Ronald Reagan signed, a bill that promised $20,000 to every Japanese American sent to a relocation camp. When the checks were sent in 1990, a letter from President George Bush accompanied them, in which he stated, "We can never fully right the wrongs of the past. But we can take a clear stand for justice and recognize that serious injustices were done to Japanese Americans during World War II."

SECTION 4 ASSESSMENT

1. TERMS & NAMES For each term or name, write a sentence explaining its significance.
- **GI Bill of Rights**
- **James Farmer**
- **Congress of Racial Equality (CORE)**
- **internment**
- **Japanese American Citizens League (JACL)**

MAIN IDEA

2. TAKING NOTES

List the advances and problems in the economy and in civil rights during World War II.

	Advances	Problems
Economy		
Civil Rights		

Which of these advances and problems do you think had the most far-reaching effect? Explain your answer.

CRITICAL THINKING

3. COMPARING

How were the experiences of African Americans, Mexican Americans, and Japanese Americans similar during World War II? How were they different?

4. DEVELOPING HISTORICAL PERSPECTIVE

Do you think that the government's policy of evacuating Japanese Americans to camps was justified on the basis of "military necessity"? Explain your answer.

5. ANALYZING EFFECTS

What effect did World War II have on American families? **Think About:**

- the role of women in families and the economy
- the relationship between the races
- the impact of the federal government on society

KOREMATSU v. UNITED STATES (1944)

ORIGINS OF THE CASE Following the Japanese attack on Pearl Harbor on December 7, 1941, U.S. military officials argued that Japanese Americans posed a threat to the nation's security. Based on recommendations from the military, President Franklin Roosevelt issued Executive Order 9066, which gave military officials the power to limit the civil rights of Japanese Americans. Military authorities began by setting a curfew for Japanese Americans. Later, they forced Japanese Americans from their homes and moved them into detention camps. Fred Korematsu was convicted of defying the military order to leave his home. At the urging of the American Civil Liberties Union (ACLU), Korematsu appealed that conviction.

THE RULING The Court upheld Korematsu's conviction and argued that military necessity made internment constitutional.

LEGAL REASONING

Executive Order 9066 was clearly aimed at one group of people—Japanese Americans. Korematsu argued that this order was unconstitutional because it was based on race. Writing for the Court majority, Justice Hugo Black agreed "that all legal restrictions which curtail the civil rights of a single racial group are immediately suspect." However, in this case, he said, the restrictions were based on "a military imperative" and not "group punishment based on antagonism to those of Japanese origin." As such, Justice Black stated that the restrictions were constitutional.

> "Compulsory exclusion of large groups, . . . except under circumstances of direct emergency and peril, is inconsistent with our basic governmental institutions. But when under conditions of modern warfare our shores are threatened by hostile forces, the power to protect must be commensurate with the threatened danger."

Justice Frank Murphy, however, dissented—he opposed the majority. He believed that military necessity was merely an excuse that could not conceal the racism at the heart of the restrictions.

> "This exclusion . . . ought not to be approved. Such exclusion goes over 'the very brink of constitutional power' and falls into the ugly abyss of racism."

Two other justices also dissented, but Korematsu's conviction stood.

LEGAL SOURCES

LEGISLATION

U.S. CONSTITUTION, FIFTH AMENDMENT (1791)
"No person shall . . . be deprived of life, liberty, or property, without due process of law."

EXECUTIVE ORDER 9066 (1942)
"I hereby authorize and direct the Secretary of War . . . to prescribe military areas in such places and of such extent as he . . . may determine, from which any or all persons may be excluded."

RELATED CASES

HIRABAYASHI v. UNITED STATES (JUNE 1943)
The Court upheld the conviction of a Japanese-American man for breaking curfew. The Court argued that the curfew was within congressional and presidential authority.

EX PARTE ENDO (DECEMBER 1944)
The Court ruled that a Japanese-American girl, whose loyalty had been clearly established, could not be held in an internment camp.

WHY IT MATTERED

About 110,000 Japanese Americans were forced into internment camps, as shown above, during World War II. Many had to sell their businesses and homes at great loss. Thousands were forced to give up their possessions. In the internment camps, Japanese Americans lived in a prison-like setting under constant guard.

The Court ruled that these government actions did not violate people's rights because the restrictions were based on military necessity rather than on race. But the government treated German Americans and Italian Americans much differently. In those instances, the government identified potentially disloyal people but did not harass the people it believed to be loyal. By contrast, the government refused to make distinctions between loyal and potentially disloyal Japanese Americans.

HISTORICAL IMPACT

In the end, the internment of Japanese Americans became a national embarrassment. In 1976, President Gerald R. Ford repealed Executive Order 9066.

▲ President Clinton presents Fred Korematsu with a Presidential Medal of Freedom during a ceremony at the White House on January 15, 1998.

Similarly, the Court's decision in *Korematsu* became an embarrassing example of court-sanctioned racism often compared to the decisions on *Dred Scott* (1857) and *Plessy* v. *Ferguson* (1896). In the early 1980s, a scholar conducting research obtained copies of government documents related to the *Hirabayashi* and *Korematsu* cases. The documents showed that the army had lied to the Court in the 1940s. Japanese Americans had not posed any security threat. Korematsu's conviction was overturned in 1984. Hirabayashi's conviction was overturned in 1986. In 1988, Congress passed a law ordering reparations payments to surviving Japanese Americans who had been detained in the camps.

THINKING CRITICALLY

CONNECT TO HISTORY

1. **Hypothesizing** The internment of Japanese Americans during World War II disrupted lives and ripped apart families. What do you think can be done today to address this terrible mistake? How can the government make amends?

    SEE SKILLBUILDER HANDBOOK, PAGE R13.

CONNECT TO TODAY 21ST CENTURY

2. Visit the links for Historic Decisions of the Supreme Court to locate the three dissenting opinions in *Korematsu* written by Justices Frank Murphy, Robert Jackson, and Owen Roberts. Read one of these opinions, and then write a summary that states its main idea. What constitutional principle, if any, does the opinion use?

   hmhsocialstudies.com **INTERNET ACTIVITY**

VISUAL SUMMARY

THE UNITED STATES IN WORLD WAR II

LONG-TERM CAUSES

- Discontent about Treaty of Versailles
- Economic instability in Europe
- Rise of totalitarian governments

IMMEDIATE CAUSES

- Expansion of Germany, Italy, and Japan
- Failure of appeasement
- German invasion of Poland
- Japanese attack on Pearl Harbor

WORLD WAR II

IMMEDIATE EFFECTS

- Defeat of Axis powers
- Destruction and immense loss of life
- Recognition of Holocaust
- Founding of United Nations

LONG-TERM EFFECTS

- Rise of United States and Soviet Union as superpowers
- Cold War
- Soviet control of Eastern Europe
- Divided Germany
- Development of nuclear capability

TERMS & NAMES

For each term or name below, write a sentence explaining its connection to World War II.

1. A. Philip Randolph
2. Manhattan Project
3. rationing
4. Dwight D. Eisenhower
5. D-Day
6. V-E Day
7. Douglas MacArthur
8. Hiroshima
9. GI Bill of Rights
10. Congress of Racial Equality (CORE)

MAIN IDEAS

Use your notes and the information in the chapter to answer the following questions.

Mobilizing for Defense (pages 768–774)

1. How did the U.S. military reflect the diversity of American society during World War II?
2. How did the federal government's actions influence civilian life during World War II?
3. What role did the media play in helping the country mobilize?

The War for Europe and North Africa (pages 775–783)

4. How did the Allies win control of the Atlantic Ocean between 1941 and 1943?
5. What was the significance of the Battle of Stalingrad?
6. How did the Battle of the Bulge signal the beginning of the end of World War II in Europe?

The War in the Pacific (pages 784–793)

7. Briefly describe the island war in the Pacific.
8. Why did President Truman decide to use atomic weapons?

The Home Front (pages 796–801)

9. How did the U.S. economy change during World War II?
10. What events show the persistence of racial tensions?

CRITICAL THINKING

1. **USING YOUR NOTES** In a chart like the one shown, provide causes for the listed effects of World War II.

Causes		Effects
	→	The U.S. enters the war.
	→	Congress creates the Office of Price Administration.
	→	Japanese Americans are sent to relocation centers.
	→	Top Nazi officials are put on trial at Nuremberg.

2. **ANALYZING ISSUES** Would you support the use of nuclear weapons today, and if so, under what circumstances?

3. **INTERPRETING MAPS** Judging from the map on page 778, why was a victory in North Africa essential to an invasion of southern Europe?

Use the map and your knowledge of U.S. history to answer question 1.

MANCHURIA (Province of China)

45°N

135°E

150°E

JAPAN

KOREA

Tokyo

★

PACIFIC OCEAN

CHINA

30°N

Okinawa

Iwo Jima

Formosa

120°E

0   500   1000 miles

PHILIPPINES

0   500   1000 kilometers

1 Why was it critical for the Allies to take the Japanese-held islands of Iwo Jima and Okinawa?

(1) The islands were highly populated areas with little military protection.

(2) The islands were critical as bases from which Allied bombers could reach Japan.

(3) The islands were centers for Japanese development of a nuclear bomb.

(4) The Allies intended to drop atomic bombs on the islands.

2 How did World War II lead to one of the largest population shifts in U.S. history?

(1) Service men and women were forced to leave their homes for Europe.

(2) The loss of loved ones led people to move in with their families.

(3) People moved to states with military bases and factories for better jobs.

(4) People moved to the middle of the country to escape wars on both coasts.

3 How did natural geography contribute to Germany's defeat in World War II?

(1) Large bodies of water stood between Germany and its enemies.

(2) Germany had to fight a war on three fronts: North Africa, Western Europe, and Eastern Europe and the Soviet Union.

(3) There were too few rivers to be used for German supplies.

(4) Switzerland pledged to remain neutral throughout the war.

↗ hmhsocialstudies.com   **TEST PRACTICE**

For additional test practice, go online for:

• Diagnostic tests   • Tutorials

INTERACT WITH HISTORY

Think about the issues you explored at the beginning of the chapter. Write a newspaper article in which you describe the ways in which the United States used its resources during World War II. Include information about rationing and about the various offices that the federal government established to monitor inflation and convert a peacetime economy into a wartime economy.

FOCUS ON WRITING

Imagine that you work for the U.S. military. Your job is to recruit new soldiers. Write a persuasive essay to be published in newspapers across the nation. In your essay, use vivid details and figurative language to describe the significance of the attack on Pearl Harbor and to explain why the military needs Americans to enlist.

MULTIMEDIA ACTIVITY

21ST CENTURY

Visit the Chapter Assessment links to find out more about A. Philip Randolph. Create a Web site dedicated to his lifelong contributions as a labor leader. Include a biography with details about his life and his work.

↗ hmhsocialstudies.com

Memories of
WORLD WAR II

A global conflict, World War II shaped the history of both the United States and the world. Americans contributed to the war effort in numerous ways. Many enlisted in the military and served in Africa, Europe, and the Pacific. Others contributed by working in factories to produce the massive amounts of ships, planes, guns, and other supplies necessary to win the war. In the process, these Americans left behind firsthand accounts of their experiences during the war, both at home and abroad.

Explore some of the personal stories and recollections of World War II online. You can find a wealth of information, video clips, primary sources, activities, and more at **hmhsocialstudies.com**.

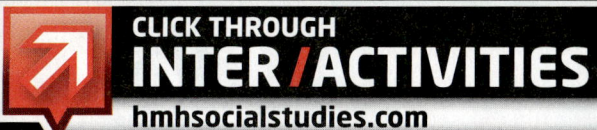

> "I am allowed to write of my own personal combat experiences and I can say that I have been fortunate so far. War is like something you cannot imagine. I had no idea what it was about and still don't."
>
> — Erwin Blonder, U.S. soldier

V ···— MAIL

A Soldier's Letter Home

Read the document to learn about one soldier's wartime experiences in southern France.

America Mobilizes for War

Watch the video to see how the United States mobilized its citizens for war and how society changed as a result.

Air War Over Germany

Watch the video to see how the P-51 Mustang helped the Allies win the air war over Germany.

The Pacific Islands

Watch the video to hear veterans describe their experiences fighting in the Pacific theater.

CHAPTER 26

COLD WAR CONFLICTS

Essential Question

What international and domestic tensions resulted from the Cold War?

New York Standards

KEY IDEA 2 Important ideas, social and cultural values, beliefs, and traditions from New York State and United States history illustrate the connections and interactions of people and events across time and from a variety of perspectives.

SECTION 1: Orgins of the Cold War

SECTION 2: The Cold War Heats Up

SECTION 3: The Cold War at Home

SECTION 4: Two Nations Live on the Edge

Senator Joseph McCarthy, shown here, charged that Communists had infiltrated many areas of American life.

1952 U.S. explodes first hydrogen bomb.

1948 Harry S. Truman is elected president.

1949 United States joins NATO.

1950 U.S. sends troops to Korea.

1952 Dwight D. Eisenhower is elected president.

USA
WORLD

1945

1950

1945 United Nations is established.

1946 Churchill gives his "Iron Curtain" speech.

1948 Berlin airlift begins.

1948 State of Israel is created.

1949 China becomes communist under Mao Zedong.

1950 Korean War begins.

HISTORY

Korea: The Forgotten War

hmhsocialstudies.com VIDEO

INTERACT
WITH HISTORY

At the end of World War II, Americans begin to be haunted by a new fear. The Soviets have embraced a tightly controlled political system called communism. Many believe it threatens the American way of life. Throughout the nation, suspected communists are called before a House subcommittee for questioning. Anyone accused of un-American activity faces public humiliation and professional ruin.

Explore the issues

- Do Americans with communist beliefs pose a threat to the nation?

- What can individual citizens do to protect the rights of all people?

- Should citizens speak out to preserve the rights of others?

1953 Julius and Ethel Rosenberg are executed as spies.

1954 Senator Joseph McCarthy alleges Communist involvement in U.S. Army.

1960 Francis Gary Powers's U-2 spy plane is shot down by the Soviets.

1960 John F. Kennedy is elected president.

1955

1960

1953 Participants in Korean War agree on cease-fire.

1954 French are defeated in Vietnam.

1957 Soviets launch *Sputnik*.

1959 Fidel Castro comes to power in Cuba.

PI 2.5
PI 2.6

CC Unit 6.II.A.1   CC Unit 6.II.A.3
CC Unit 6.II.B.1   CC Unit 6.II.B.2
CC Unit 6.II.B.3

Origins of the Cold War

MAIN IDEA	WHY IT MATTERS NOW	Terms & Names
The United States and the Soviet Union emerged from World War II as two "superpowers" with vastly different political and economic systems.	After World War II, differences between the United States and the Soviet Union led to a Cold War that lasted almost to the 21st century.	•United Nations (UN) •satellite nation •containment •iron curtain •Cold War •Truman Doctrine •Marshall Plan •Berlin airlift •North Atlantic Treaty Organization (NATO)

One American's Story

hmhsocialstudies.com
TAKING NOTES
Use the graphic organizer online to take notes on the actions of the United States and the Soviet Union that contributed most to the Cold War.

Seventy miles south of Berlin, Joseph Polowsky and a patrol of American soldiers were scouting for signs of the Soviet army advancing from the east. As the soldiers neared the Elbe River, they saw lilacs in bloom. Polowsky later said the sight of the flowers filled them with joy.

Across the Elbe, the Americans spotted Soviet soldiers, who signaled for them to cross over. When the Americans reached the opposite bank, their joy turned to shock. They saw to their horror that the bank was covered with dead civilians, victims of bombing raids.

★ **A PERSONAL VOICE** JOSEPH POLOWSKY

" Here we are, tremendously exhilarated, and there's a sea of dead. . . . [The platoon leader] was much moved. . . . He said, 'Joe, let's make a resolution with these Russians here and also the ones on the bank: this would be an important day in the lives of the two countries.' . . . It was a solemn moment. There were tears in the eyes of most of us. . . . We embraced. We swore never to forget."

—quoted in *The Good War*

32 USA

U.S. and Soviets link up at Elbe River, April 1945

American and Soviet soldiers meet *(top)* at the Elbe River in Germany near the end of World War II. A 1996 postage stamp *(above)* commemorates the historic meeting.

The Soviet and U.S. soldiers believed that their encounter would serve as a symbol of peace. Unfortunately, such hopes were soon dashed. After World War II, the United States and the Soviet Union emerged as rival superpowers, each strong enough to greatly influence world events.

Former Allies Clash

The United States and the Soviet Union had very different ambitions for the future. These differences created a climate of icy tension that plunged the two countries into a bitter rivalry.

Under Soviet communism, the state controlled all property and economic activity, while in the capitalistic American system, private citizens controlled almost all economic activity. In the American system, voting by the people elected a president and a congress from competing political parties; in the Soviet Union, the Communist Party established a totalitarian government with no opposing parties.

The United States was furious that Joseph Stalin—the leader of the Soviet Union—had been an ally of Hitler for a time. Stalin had supported the Allies only after Hitler invaded the Soviet Union in June 1941. In some ways, the Americans and Soviets became more suspicious of each other during the war. Stalin resented the Western Allies' delay in attacking the Germans in Europe. Such an attack, he thought, would draw part of the German army away from the Soviet Union. Relations worsened after Stalin learned that the United States had kept its development of the atomic bomb secret. **Ⓐ**

MAIN IDEA

Analyzing Causes

Ⓐ What caused the tension between the Soviet Union and the United States after the war?

THE UNITED NATIONS In spite of these problems, hopes for world peace were high at the end of the war. The most visible symbol of these hopes was the **United Nations (UN).** On April 25, 1945, the representatives of 50 nations met in San Francisco to establish this new peacekeeping body. After two months of debate, on June 26, 1945, the delegates signed the charter establishing the UN.

Ironically, even though the UN was intended to promote peace, it soon became an arena in which the two superpowers competed. Both the United States and the Soviet Union used the UN as a forum to spread their influence over others.

TRUMAN BECOMES PRESIDENT For the United States, the key figure in the early years of conflict with the Soviets was President Harry S. Truman. On April 12, 1945, Truman had suddenly become president when Franklin Roosevelt died. This former Missouri senator had been picked as Roosevelt's running mate in 1944. He had served as vice-president for just a few months before Roosevelt's death. During his term as vice-president, Truman had not been included in top policy decisions. He had not even known that the United States was developing an atomic bomb. Many Americans doubted Truman's ability to serve as president. But Truman was honest and had a willingness to make tough decisions—qualities that he would need desperately during his presidency.

KEY PLAYERS

**HARRY S. TRUMAN
1884–1972**

Harry S. Truman, the son of a Missouri livestock trader, did not seem destined for greatness. When he graduated from high school in 1901, he drifted from job to job. After World War I, he invested in a men's clothing store, but the business failed.

Discouraged by his business failure, Truman sought a career in politics. As a politician, his blunt and outspoken style won both loyal friends and bitter enemies. As president, his decisiveness and willingness to accept responsibility for his decisions ("The Buck Stops Here" read a sign on his desk) earned him respect that has grown over the years.

**JOSEPH STALIN
1879–1953**

As a young revolutionary, Iosif Vissarionovich Dzhugashvili took the name *Stalin*, which means "man of steel" in Russian.

His father was a failed shoemaker and an alcoholic. His mother helped support the family as a washerwoman.

Stalin is credited with turning the Soviet Union into a world power but at a terrible cost to its citizens. He ruled with terror and brutality and saw "enemies" everywhere, even among friends and supporters. He subdued the population with the use of secret police and labor camps, and he is believed to have been responsible for the murder of millions of Soviets.

THE POTSDAM CONFERENCE Truman's test as a diplomat came in July 1945 when the Big Three—the United States, Great Britain, and the Soviet Union—met at the final wartime conference at Potsdam near Berlin. The countries that participated were the same ones that had been present at Yalta in February 1945. Stalin still represented the Soviet Union. Clement Attlee replaced Churchill as Britain's representative mid-conference, because Churchill's party lost a general election. And Harry Truman took Roosevelt's place.

At Yalta, Stalin had promised Roosevelt that he would allow free elections—that is, a vote by secret ballot in a multiparty system—in Poland and other parts of Eastern Europe that the Soviets occupied at the end of the war. By July 1945, however, it was clear that Stalin would not keep this promise. The Soviets prevented free elections in Poland and banned democratic parties. **Ⓑ**

MAIN IDEA

Analyzing Causes
Ⓑ What did Stalin do to make President Truman distrust him?

Tension Mounts

Stalin's refusal to allow free elections in Poland convinced Truman that U.S. and Soviet aims were deeply at odds. Truman's goal in demanding free elections was to spread democracy to nations that had been under Nazi rule. He wanted to create a new world order in which all nations had the right of self-determination.

BARGAINING AT POTSDAM At the Yalta conference, the Soviets had wanted to take reparations from Germany to help repay Soviet wartime losses. Now, at Potsdam, Truman objected to that. After hard bargaining, it was agreed that the Soviets, British, Americans, and French would take reparations mainly from their own occupation zones within Germany.

Truman also felt that the United States had a large economic stake in spreading democracy and free trade across the globe. U.S. industry boomed during the war, making the United States the economic leader of the world. To continue growing, American businesses wanted access to raw materials in Eastern Europe, and they wanted to be able to sell goods to Eastern European countries.

SOVIETS TIGHTEN THEIR GRIP ON EASTERN EUROPE The Soviet Union had also emerged from the war as a nation of enormous economic and military strength. However, unlike the United States, the Soviet Union had suffered heavy devastation on its own soil. Soviet deaths from the war have been estimated at 20 million, half of whom were civilians. As a result, the Soviets felt justified in their claim to Eastern Europe. By dominating this region, the Soviets felt they could stop future invasions from the west.

U.S. Aims Versus Soviet Aims in Europe	
The United States wanted to . . .	**The Soviets wanted to . . .**
• Create a new world order in which all nations had the right of self-determination • Gain access to raw materials and markets for its industries • Rebuild European governments to ensure stability and to create new markets for American goods • Reunite Germany, believing that Europe would be more secure if Germany were productive	• Encourage communism in other countries as part of the worldwide struggle between workers and the wealthy • Rebuild its war-ravaged economy using Eastern Europe's industrial equipment and raw materials • Control Eastern Europe to balance U.S. influence in Western Europe • Keep Germany divided and weak so that it would never again threaten the Soviet Union

SKILLBUILDER Interpreting Charts
1. Which aims involved economic growth of the United States?
2. Which Soviet aims involved self-protection?

Postwar Germany, 1949

North Sea

British Zone · Berlin
WEST GERMANY · EAST GERMANY
French Zone · American Zone
French Zone

French Zone
British Zone · East Berlin
West Berlin
American Zone
Havel R. · Spree R.

0   6   12 miles
0   6   12 kilometers

0   150   300 miles
0   150   300 kilometers

NORWAY   SWEDEN   FINLAND
North Sea   *Baltic Sea*
DEN.   SOVIET UNION
IRELAND   GREAT BRITAIN   NETH.   POLAND
EAST GERMANY   The "Iron Curtain"
BELG.   WEST GERMANY   CZECH.
LUX.
ATLANTIC OCEAN   FRANCE   SWITZ.   AUSTRIA   HUNGARY
ROMANIA
ITALY   *Adriatic Sea*   YUGOSLAVIA
BULGARIA
PORTUGAL   SPAIN   ALBANIA
GREECE   TURKEY

Communist nations
0   250   500 miles
0   250   500 kilometers

GEOGRAPHY SKILLBUILDER
1. **Location** Which communist nations were located between the Soviet Union and the iron curtain?
2. **Human-Environment Interaction** Why did the Soviet Union want to control these nations?

Stalin installed communist governments in Albania, Bulgaria, Czechoslovakia, Hungary, Romania, and Poland. These countries became known as **satellite nations,** countries dominated by the Soviet Union. In early 1946, Stalin gave a speech announcing that communism and capitalism were incompatible—and that another war was inevitable.

UNITED STATES ESTABLISHES A POLICY OF CONTAINMENT Faced with the Soviet threat, American officials decided it was time, in Truman's words, to stop "babying the Soviets." In February 1946, George F. Kennan, an American diplomat in Moscow, proposed a policy of **containment.** By containment he meant taking measures to prevent any extension of communist rule to other countries. This policy began to guide the Truman administration's foreign policy. **C**

Europe was now divided into two political regions, a mostly democratic Western Europe and a communist Eastern Europe. In March 1946, Winston Churchill traveled to the United States and gave a speech that described the situation in Europe.

MAIN IDEA

Analyzing Motives
C What were Truman's goals in establishing the policy of containment?

A PERSONAL VOICE WINSTON CHURCHILL

"A shadow has fallen upon the scenes so lately lighted by the Allied victory. . . . From Stettin in the Baltic to Trieste in the Adriatic, an iron curtain has descended across the Continent. Behind that line lie all the capitals of the ancient states of Central and Eastern Europe. . . . All these famous cities and the populations around them lie in . . . the Soviet sphere, and all are subject in one form or another, not only to Soviet influence but to a very high and . . . increasing measure of control from Moscow."
—"Iron Curtain" speech in Fulton, Missouri

Winston Churchill, Prime Minister of Great Britain

The phrase **"iron curtain"** came to stand for the division of Europe. When Stalin heard about the speech, he declared in no uncertain terms that Churchill's words were a "call to war."

Cold War in Europe

The conflicting U.S. and Soviet aims in Eastern Europe led to the **Cold War,** a conflict between the United States and the Soviet Union in which neither nation directly confronted the other on the battlefield. The Cold War would dominate global affairs—and U.S. foreign policy—from 1945 until the breakup of the Soviet Union in 1991.

THE TRUMAN DOCTRINE The United States first tried to contain Soviet influence in Greece and Turkey. Britain was financially supporting both nations' resistance to growing communist influence in the region. However, Britain's economy had been badly hurt by the war, and the formerly wealthy nation could no longer afford to give aid. It asked the United States to take over the responsibility.

President Truman accepted the challenge. On March 12, 1947, Truman asked Congress for $400 million in economic and military aid for Greece and Turkey. In a statement that became known as the **Truman Doctrine,** he declared that "it must be the policy of the United States to support free peoples who are resisting attempted subjugation by armed minorities or by outside pressures." Congress agreed with Truman and decided that the doctrine was essential to keeping Soviet influence from spreading. Between 1947 and 1950, the United States sent $400 million in aid to Turkey and Greece, greatly reducing the danger of communist takeover in those nations.

Vocabulary
subjugation: bringing under control

THE MARSHALL PLAN Like post-war Greece, Western Europe was in chaos. Most of its factories had been bombed or looted. Millions of people were living in refugee camps while European governments tried to figure out where to resettle them. To make matters worse, the winter of 1946–1947 was the bitterest in several centuries. The weather severely damaged crops and froze rivers, cutting off water transportation and causing a fuel shortage.

Background
In 1946, the UN set up the International Refugee Organization (IRO) to oversee the resettlement of refugees. Over the next few years, the IRO resettled more than 1 million displaced people.

In June 1947, Secretary of State George Marshall proposed that the United States provide aid to all European nations that needed it, saying that this move was directed "not against any country or doctrine but against hunger, poverty, desperation, and chaos."

The **Marshall Plan** revived European hopes. Over the next four years, 16 countries received some $13 billion in aid. By 1952, Western Europe was flourishing, and the Communist party had lost much of its appeal to voters.

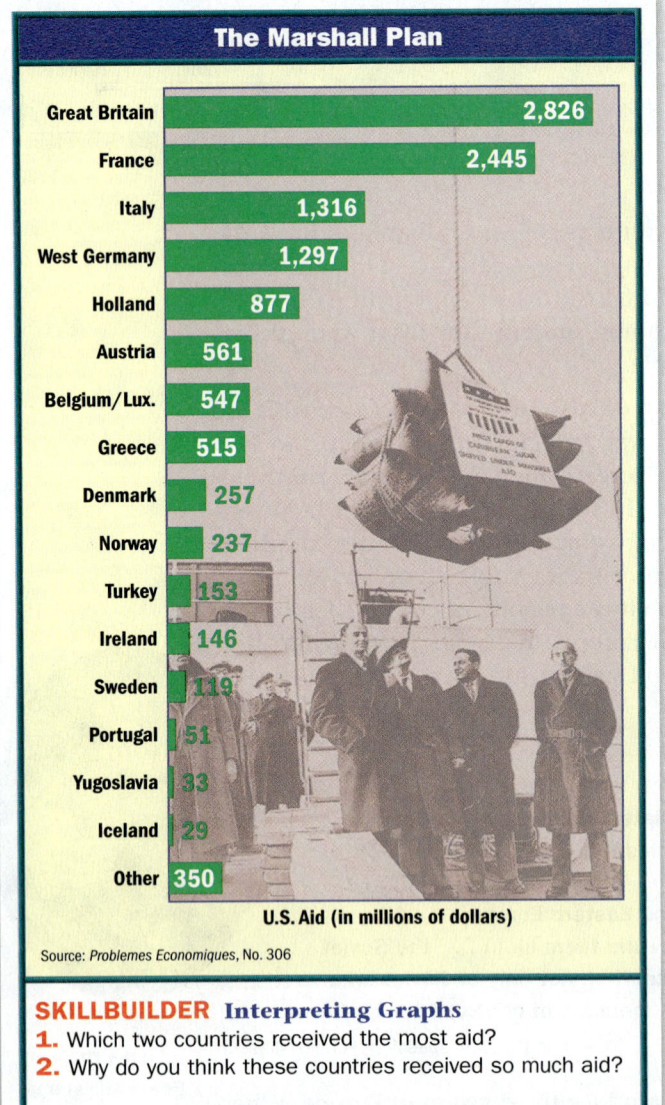

The Marshall Plan

Country	U.S. Aid (in millions of dollars)
Great Britain	2,826
France	2,445
Italy	1,316
West Germany	1,297
Holland	877
Austria	561
Belgium/Lux.	547
Greece	515
Denmark	257
Norway	237
Turkey	153
Ireland	146
Sweden	119
Portugal	51
Yugoslavia	33
Iceland	29
Other	350

U.S. Aid (in millions of dollars)

Source: *Problemes Economiques*, No. 306

SKILLBUILDER Interpreting Graphs
1. Which two countries received the most aid?
2. Why do you think these countries received so much aid?

Superpowers Struggle over Germany

As Europe began to get back on its feet, the United States and its allies clashed with the Soviet Union over the issue of German reunification. At the end of World War II, Germany was divided into four zones occupied by the United States, Great Britain, and France in the west and the Soviet Union in the east. In 1948, Britain, France, and the United States decided to combine their three zones into one nation. The western part of Berlin, which had been occupied by the French, British, and Americans, was surrounded by Soviet-occupied territory. (See map, page 811.)

Although the three nations had a legal right to unify their zones, they had no written agreement with the Soviets guaranteeing free access to Berlin by road or rail. Stalin saw this loophole as an opportunity. If he moved quickly, he might be able to take over the part of Berlin held by the three Western powers. In June 1948, Stalin closed all highway and rail routes into West Berlin. As a result, no food or fuel could reach that part of the city. The 2.1 million residents of the city had only enough food to last for approximately five weeks.

THE BERLIN AIRLIFT The resulting situation was dire. In an attempt to break the blockade, American and British officials started the **Berlin airlift** to fly food and supplies into West Berlin. For 327 days, planes took off and landed every few minutes, around the clock. In 277,000 flights, they brought in 2.3 million tons of supplies—everything from food, fuel, and medicine to Christmas presents that the planes' crews bought with their own money.

West Berlin survived because of the airlift. In addition, the mission to aid Berlin boosted American prestige around the world. By May 1949, the Soviet Union realized it was beaten and lifted the blockade. **D**

MAIN IDEA

Analyzing Effects

D What were the effects of the Berlin airlift?

Beginning in June 1948, planes bringing tons of food and other supplies to West Berlin landed every few minutes.

▼

In the same month, the western part of Germany officially became a new nation, the Federal Republic of Germany, also called West Germany. It included West Berlin. A few months later, from its occupation zone, the Soviet Union created the German Democratic Republic, called East Germany. It included East Berlin.

 This cartoon depicts the nations that signed the North Atlantic Pact, which created NATO in 1949. The nations, shown as hats, are arranged in a pyramid to show the bigger countries on the bottom supporting the smaller, weaker nations on top.

THE NATO ALLIANCE The Berlin blockade increased Western European fear of Soviet aggression. As a result, ten Western European nations—Belgium, Denmark, France, Great Britain, Iceland, Italy, Luxembourg, the Netherlands, Norway, and Portugal—joined with the United States and Canada on April 4, 1949, to form a defensive military alliance called the **North Atlantic Treaty Organization (NATO).** (See map, page 830.) The 12 members of NATO pledged military support to one another in case any member was attacked. For the first time in its history, the United States had entered into a military alliance with other nations during peacetime. The Cold War had ended any hope of a return to U.S. isolationism. Greece and Turkey joined NATO in 1952, and West Germany joined in 1955. By then, NATO kept a standing military force of more than 500,000 troops as well as thousands of planes, tanks, and other equipment.

SECTION 1 ASSESSMENT

1. TERMS & NAMES For each term or name, write a sentence explaining its significance.

- United Nations (UN)
- satellite nation
- containment
- iron curtain
- Cold War
- Truman Doctrine
- Marshall Plan
- Berlin airlift
- North Atlantic Treaty Organization (NATO)

MAIN IDEA

2. TAKING NOTES

Use a graphic organizer like the one below to describe the U.S. actions and the Soviet actions that contributed most to the Cold War.

U.S. Actions	Soviet Actions

Write a paragraph explaining which country was more responsible and why you think so.

CRITICAL THINKING

3. EVALUATING LEADERSHIP

People who had served as aides to President Franklin Roosevelt worried that Truman was not qualified to handle world leadership. Considering what you learned in this section, evaluate Truman as a world leader.

Think About:

- his behavior toward Stalin
- his economic support of European nations
- his support of West Berlin

4. MAKING INFERENCES

Which of the two superpowers do you think was more successful in achieving its aims during the period 1945–1949? Support your answer by referring to historical events.

5. ANALYZING MOTIVES

What were Stalin's motives in supporting Communist governments in Eastern Europe?

SECTION
2

CC Unit 6.II.C.2.a CC Unit 6.II.C.2.b
CC Unit 6.II.C.4.a CC Unit 6.II.C.4.b
CC Unit 6.II.C.4.c CC Unit 6.II.C.5

PI 2.6

The Cold War Heats Up

MAIN IDEA	**WHY IT MATTERS NOW**	**Terms & Names**
After World War II, China became a communist nation and Korea was split into a communist north and a democratic south.	Ongoing tensions with China and North Korea continue to involve the United States.	• Chiang Kai-shek • 38th parallel • Mao Zedong • Korean War • Taiwan

One American's Story

First Lieutenant Philip Day, Jr., vividly remembers his first taste of battle in Korea. On the morning of July 5, 1950, Philip Day spotted a column of eight enemy tanks moving toward his company.

A PERSONAL VOICE PHILIP DAY, JR.

" I was with a 75-mm recoilless-rifle team. 'Let's see,' I shouted, 'if we can get one of those tanks.' We picked up the gun and moved it to where we could get a clean shot. I don't know if we were poorly trained, . . . but we set the gun on the forward slope of the hill. When we fired, the recoilless blast blew a hole in the hill which instantly covered us in mud and dirt. . . . When we were ready again, we moved the gun to a better position and began banging away. I swear we had some hits, but the tanks never slowed down. . . . In a little less than two hours, 30 North Korean tanks rolled through the position we were supposed to block as if we hadn't been there. "

—quoted in *The Korean War: Pusan to Chosin*

▲ **American soldiers in Korea, November 1950.**

Only five years after World War II ended, the United States became embroiled in a war in Korea. The policy of containment had led the United States into battle to halt communist expansion. In this conflict, however, the enemy was not the Soviet Union, but North Korea and China.

China Becomes a Communist Country

For two decades, Chinese Communists had struggled against the nationalist government of **Chiang Kai-shek** (chăng′ kī′shĕk′). The United States supported Chiang. Between 1945 and 1949, the American government sent the Nationalists approximately $3 billion in aid.

Nationalists Versus Communists, 1945

Nationalists Leader: Chiang Kai-shek	Communists Leader: Mao Zedong
• Ruled in southern and eastern China • Relied heavily on aid from United States • Struggled with inflation and a failing economy • Suffered from weak leadership and poor morale	• Ruled in northern China • Relied heavily on financial aid from Soviet Union • Attracted peasants with promises of land reform • Benefited from experienced guerrilla army and a highly motivated leadership

Many Americans were impressed by Chiang Kai-shek and admired the courage and determination that the Chinese Nationalists showed in resisting the Japanese during the war. However, U.S. officials who dealt with Chiang held a different view. They found his government inefficient and hopelessly corrupt.

Furthermore, the policies of Chiang's government undermined Nationalist support. For example, the Nationalists collected a grain tax from farmers even during the famine of 1944. When city dwellers demonstrated against a 10,000 percent increase in the price of rice, Chiang's secret police opened fire on them.

In contrast, the Communists, led by **Mao Zedong** (mou'dzŭ'dŏng'), gained strength throughout the country. In the areas they controlled, Communists worked to win peasant support. They encouraged peasants to learn to read, and they helped to improve food production. As a result, more and more recruits flocked to the Communists' Red Army. By 1945, much of northern China was under communist control.

RENEWED CIVIL WAR As soon as the defeated Japanese left China at the end of World War II, cooperation between the Nationalists and the Communists ceased. Civil war erupted again between the two groups. In spite of the problems in the Nationalist regime, American policy favored the Nationalists because they opposed communism.

From 1944 to 1947, the United States played peacemaker between the two groups while still supporting the Nationalists. However, U.S. officials repeatedly failed to negotiate peace. Truman refused to commit American soldiers to back up the nationalists, although the United States did send $2 billion worth of military equipment and supplies.

The aid wasn't enough to save the Nationalists, whose weak military leadership and corrupt, abusive practices drove the peasants to the Communist side. In May 1949, Chiang and the remnants of his demoralized government fled to the island of **Taiwan,** which Westerners called Formosa. After more than 20 years of struggle, the Communists ruled all of mainland China. They established a new government, the People's Republic of China, which the United States refused to accept as China's true government. **A**

MAIN IDEA

Analyzing Causes

A What factors led to the Communist takeover in China?

Background
President Truman felt that one way to halt the spread of communism was to make the poor nations of Africa, Asia, and Latin America more prosperous. Since this was the fourth point in Truman's plan to combat communism, the program to assist developing nations was called Point Four Aid.

AMERICA REACTS TO COMMUNIST TAKEOVER The American public was stunned that China had become Communist. Containment had failed! In Congress, conservative Republicans and Democrats attacked the Truman administration for supplying only limited aid to Chiang. If containing communism was important in Europe, they asked, why was it not equally important in Asia?

The State Department replied by saying that what had happened in China was a result of internal forces. The United States had failed in its attempts to influence these forces, such as Chiang's inability to retain the support of his people. Trying to do more would only have started a war in Asia—a war that the United States wasn't prepared to fight.

Some conservatives in Congress rejected this argument as a lame excuse. They claimed that the American government was riddled with Communist agents. Like wildfire, American fear of communism began to burn out of control, and the flames were fanned even further by events in Korea the following year.

The Korean War

Japan had taken over Korea in 1910 and ruled it until August 1945. As World War II ended, Japanese troops north of the **38th parallel** (38° North latitude) surrendered to the Soviets. Japanese troops south of the parallel surrendered to the Americans. As in Germany, two nations developed, one communist and one democratic.

In 1948, the Republic of Korea, usually called South Korea, was established in the zone that had been occupied by the United States. Its government, headed by Syngman Rhee, was based in Seoul, Korea's traditional capital. Simultaneously, the Communists formed the Democratic People's Republic of Korea in the north. Kim Il Sung led its government, which was based in Pyongyang. (See map, page 819.) **B**

MAIN IDEA

Analyzing Events

B How did Korea become a divided nation after World War II?

Soon after World War II, the United States had cut back its armed forces in South Korea. As a result, by June of 1949 there were only 500 American troops there. The Soviets concluded that the United States would not fight to defend South Korea. They prepared to back North Korea with tanks, airplanes, and money in an attempt to take over the entire peninsula.

NORTH KOREA ATTACKS SOUTH KOREA On June 25, 1950, North Korean forces swept across the 38th parallel in a surprise attack on South Korea. The conflict that followed became known as the **Korean War.**

Within a few days, North Korean troops had penetrated deep into South Korea. South Korea called on the United Nations to stop the North Korean invasion. When the matter came to a vote in the UN Security Council, the Soviet Union was not there. The Soviets were boycotting the council in protest over the presence of Nationalist China (Taiwan). Thus, the Soviets could not veto the UN's plan of military action. The vote passed.

On June 27, in a show of military strength, President Truman ordered troops stationed in Japan to support the South Koreans. He also sent an American fleet into the waters between Taiwan and China.

WORLD STAGE

TAIWAN

In 1949, Chiang Kai-shek and other Nationalist leaders retreated to the island of Taiwan, which lies about 100 miles off the southeast coast of the Chinese mainland. There the United States helped set up a Nationalist government— the Republic of China. From 1949 through the 1960s, the United States poured millions of dollars of aid into the Taiwanese economy.

During the 1970s, a number of nations, including the United States, decided to end diplomatic relations with Taiwan and established ties with Communist China. With the collapse of Soviet communism in the early 1990s, relations between Taiwan and the United States improved. During the early 2000s, the United States sold weapons to Taiwan to bolster the nation's defense system.

In all, 16 nations sent some 520,000 troops to aid South Korea. Over 90 percent of these troops were American. South Korean troops numbered an additional 590,000. The combined forces were placed under the command of General Douglas MacArthur, former World War II hero in the Pacific.

The United States Fights in Korea

At first, North Korea seemed unstoppable. Driving steadily south, its troops captured Seoul. After a month of bitter combat, the North Koreans had forced UN and South Korean troops into a small defensive zone around Pusan in the southeastern corner of the peninsula.

MACARTHUR'S COUNTERATTACK MacArthur launched a counterattack with tanks, heavy artillery, and fresh troops from the United States. On September 15, 1950, his troops made a surprise amphibious landing behind enemy lines at Inchon, on Korea's west coast. Other troops moved north from Pusan. Trapped between the two attacking forces, about half of the North Korean troops surrendered; the rest fled back across the 38th parallel. MacArthur's plan had saved his army from almost certain defeat.

The UN army chased the retreating North Korean troops across the 38th parallel into North Korea. In late November, UN troops approached the Yalu River, the border between North Korea and China. It seemed as if Korea was about to become a single country again.

THE CHINESE FIGHT BACK The Chinese, however, had other ideas. Communist China's foreign minister, Zhou En-lai, warned that his country would not stand idly by and "let the Americans come to the border"—meaning the Yalu River. In late November 1950, 300,000 Chinese troops joined the war on the side of North Korea. The Chinese wanted North Korea as a Communist buffer state to protect their northeastern provinces that made up Manchuria. They also felt threatened by the American fleet that lay off their coast. The fight between North Korea and South Korea had escalated into a war in which the main opponents were the Chinese communists and the Americans.

By sheer force of numbers, the Chinese drove the UN troops southward. At some points along the battlefront, the Chinese outnumbered UN forces ten to one. By early January 1951, all UN and South Korean troops had been pushed out of North Korea. The Chinese advanced to the south, capturing the South Korean capital, Seoul. "We face an entirely new war," declared MacArthur. **C**

For two years, the two sides fought bitterly to obtain strategic positions in the Korean hills, but neither side was able to make important advances. One officer remembered the standoff.

Vocabulary
amphibious: capable of traveling both on land and on water

MAIN IDEA

Analyzing Causes

C How did the involvement of communist China affect the Korean War?

Beverly Scott

A PERSONAL VOICE BEVERLY SCOTT

"Our trenches . . . were only about 20 meters in front of theirs. We were eyeball to eyeball. . . . We couldn't move at all in the daytime without getting shot at. Machine-gun fire would come in, grenades, small-arms fire, all from within spitting distance. It was like World War I. We lived in a maze of bunkers and deep trenches. . . . There were bodies strewn all over the place. Hundreds of bodies frozen in the snow."

—quoted in *No Bugles, No Drums: An Oral History of the Korean War*

The Korean War, 1950–1953

hmhsocialstudies.com **INTERACTIVE MAP**

American paratroopers comb through a village in North Korea on October 20, 1950, during the Korean War.

SOVIET UNION

CHINA

Sea of Japan

(East Sea)

NORTH KOREA

Truce Line, 1953 (present-day boundary)

Yalu River

Pyongyang

Panmunjom

38th Parallel

Inchon

Seoul

Yellow Sea

SOUTH KOREA

Pusan

PACIFIC OCEAN

42°N

128°E

30°N

N W E S

0 100 200 miles
0 100 200 kilometers

June 1950
North Korean troops invade South Korea and capture the capital, Seoul.

September 1950
North Koreans push South Koreans and UN troops south to the perimeter of Pusan.

September to October 1950
UN troops under MacArthur land at Inchon and move north from Pusan. This two-pronged attack drives the North Koreans out of South Korea. UN troops then continue into North Korea, take Pyongyang, and advance to the Yalu River.

November 1950 to January 1951
The Chinese intervene and force UN troops to retreat across the 38th parallel.

GEOGRAPHY SKILLBUILDER
1. **Movement** How far south did North Korean troops push the UN forces?
2. **Place** Why do you think MacArthur chose Inchon as his landing place?

Cold War Conflicts 819

INDIA'S VIEWPOINT

Nonaligned nations such as India were on neither side of the Cold War and had their own perspectives. In 1951, the prime minister of India, Jawaharlal Nehru *(shown above)*, had this to say about the Korean War:

"This great struggle between the United States and Soviet Russia is hardly the proper role in this world for those great powers. . . . Their role should be to function in their own territories and not be a threat to others."

General Douglas MacArthur *(left)* and President Truman *(right)* strongly disagreed about how best to proceed in the Korean War.

▼

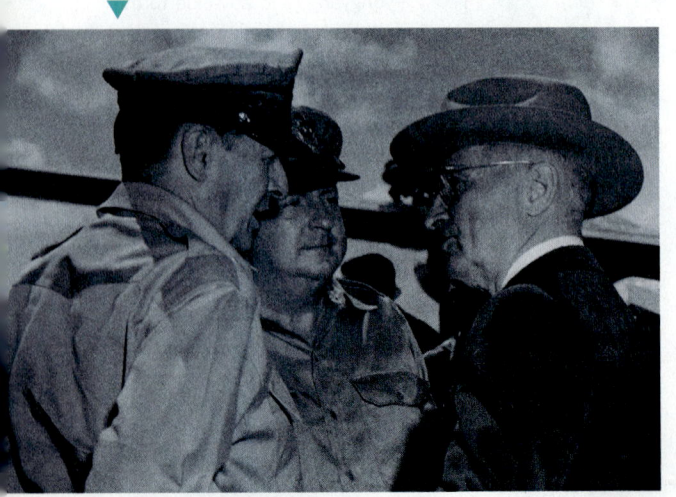

MACARTHUR RECOMMENDS ATTACKING CHINA To halt the bloody stalemate, in early 1951, MacArthur called for an extension of the war into China. Convinced that Korea was the place "where the Communist conspirators have elected to make their play for global conquest," MacArthur called for the use of nuclear weapons against Chinese cities.

Truman rejected MacArthur's request. The Soviet Union had a mutual-assistance pact with China. Attacking China could set off World War III. As General Omar N. Bradley, chairman of the Joint Chiefs of Staff, said, an all-out conflict with China would be "the wrong war, at the wrong place, at the wrong time, and with the wrong enemy."

Instead of attacking China, the UN and South Korean forces began to advance once more, using the U.S. Eighth Army, led by Matthew B. Ridgway, as a spearhead. By April 1951, Ridgway had retaken Seoul and had moved back up to the 38th parallel. The situation was just what it had been before the fighting began.

MACARTHUR VERSUS TRUMAN Not satisfied with the recapture of South Korea, MacArthur continued to urge the waging of a full-scale war against China. Certain that his views were correct, MacArthur tried to go over the president's head. He spoke and wrote privately to newspaper and magazine publishers and, especially, to Republican leaders.

MacArthur's superiors informed him that he had no authority to make decisions of policy. Despite repeated warnings to follow orders, MacArthur continued to criticize the president. President Truman, who as president was commander-in-chief of the armed forces and thus MacArthur's boss, was just as stubborn as MacArthur. Truman refused to stand for this kind of behavior. He wanted to put together a settlement of the war and could no longer tolerate a military commander who was trying to sabotage his policy. On April 11, 1951, Truman made the shocking announcement that he had fired MacArthur. **D**

Many Americans were outraged over their hero's downfall. A public opinion poll showed that 69 percent of the American public backed General MacArthur. When MacArthur returned to the United States, he gave an address to Congress, an honor usually awarded only to heads of government. New York City honored him with a ticker-tape parade. In his closing remarks to Congress, MacArthur said, "Old soldiers never die, they just fade away."

Throughout the fuss, Truman stayed in the background. After MacArthur's moment of public glory passed, the Truman administration began to make its case. Before a congressional committee investigating MacArthur's dismissal, a parade of witnesses argued the case for limiting the war. The committee agreed with them. As a result, public opinion swung around to the view that Truman had done the right thing. As a political figure, MacArthur did indeed fade away.

Vocabulary
conspirator: a person who takes part in secretly planning something unlawful

MAIN IDEA

Comparing
D How did Truman and MacArthur differ over strategy in the Korean War?

SETTLING FOR STALEMATE As the MacArthur controversy died down, the Soviet Union unexpectedly suggested a cease-fire on June 23, 1951. Truce talks began in July 1951. The opposing sides reached agreement on two points: the location of the cease-fire line at the existing battle line and the establishment of a demilitarized zone between the opposing sides. Negotiators spent another year wrangling over the exchange of prisoners. Finally, in July 1953, the two sides signed an armistice ending the war.

At best, the agreement was a stalemate. On the one hand, the North Korean invaders had been pushed back, and communism had been contained without the use of atomic weapons. On the other hand, Korea was still two nations rather than one.

On the home front, the war had affected the lives of ordinary Americans in many ways. It had cost 54,000 American lives and $67 billion in expenditures. The high cost of this unsuccessful war was one of many factors leading Americans to reject the Democratic Party in 1952 and to elect a Republican administration under World War II hero Dwight D. Eisenhower. In addition, the Korean War increased fear of communist aggression and prompted a hunt for Americans who might be blamed for the communist gains.

Vocabulary
demilitarize: to ban military forces in an area or region

Background
In 1954, partly in response to the Korean War, the United States organized the Southeast Asia Treaty Organization (SEATO), an alliance of nations pledged to protect one another from Communist aggression in Asia.

NOW & THEN

THE TWO KOREAS

Korea is still split into North Korea and South Korea, even after more than 50 years. South Korea is booming economically, while North Korea, still communist, struggles with severe shortages of food and energy.

Periodically, discussions about reuniting the two countries resume. In 2000, South Korean President Kim Dae-jung won the Nobel Peace Prize for his efforts to improve ties with North Korea. The two nations met in North Korea for the first time since the nations were established in 1948. Although economic and political differences continue to keep the two countries apart, there is hope that one day Korea will become a united nation.

◀ South Korean President Kim Dae-jung waves to cheering North Koreans on June 13, 2000.

SECTION 2 ASSESSMENT

1. TERMS & NAMES For each term or name, write a sentence explaining its significance.
- Chiang Kai-shek
- Mao Zedong
- Taiwan
- 38th parallel
- Korean War

MAIN IDEA

2. TAKING NOTES
On a time line such as the one shown below, list the major events of the Korean War.

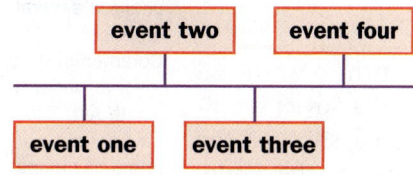

Choose two events and explain how one event led to the other.

CRITICAL THINKING

3. HYPOTHESIZING
What might have happened if MacArthur had convinced Truman to expand the fighting into China? How might today's world be different?

4. ANALYZING EVENTS
Many Americans have questioned whether fighting the Korean War was worthwhile. What is your opinion? Why? **Think About:**
- the loss of American lives
- the fear of communism that enveloped the country at the time
- the stalemate that ended the war

5. EVALUATING DECISIONS
At the end of China's civil war, the United States refused to accept the communist People's Republic of China as China's true government. What were the advantages of such a policy? What were the disadvantages? Do you agree with this decision? Why or why not?

The Cold War at Home

MAIN IDEA	WHY IT MATTERS NOW	Terms & Names
During the late 1940s and early 1950s, fear of communism led to reckless charges against innocent citizens.	Americans today remain vigilant about unfounded accusations.	• HUAC • Hollywood Ten • blacklist • Alger Hiss • Ethel and Julius Rosenberg • Joseph McCarthy • McCarthyism

One American's Story

Tony Kahn

hmhsocialstudies.com
TAKING NOTES

Use the graphic organizer online to take notes on how anticommunist fear gripped the United States.

Tony Kahn made the neighbors uncomfortable because they thought his father, Gordon Kahn, was a Communist. In 1947, Gordon Kahn was a successful screenwriter. However, when a congressional committee began to investigate Communists in Hollywood, Kahn was blacklisted—named as unfit to hire. Later, in 1951, he was scheduled to testify before the committee himself.

To save himself, Gordon Kahn simply had to name others as Communists, but he refused. Rather than face the congressional committee, he fled to Mexico. Tony Kahn remembers how the Cold War hurt him and his family.

A PERSONAL VOICE TONY KAHN

" The first time I was called a Communist, I was four years old. . . . I'll never forget the look in our neighbors' eyes when I walked by. I thought it was hate. I was too young to realize it was fear. "

—from *The Cold War Comes Home*

The members of the Kahn family were among thousands of victims of the anti-Communist hysteria that gripped this country in the late 1940s and early 1950s. By the end of the period, no one was immune from accusations.

Fear of Communist Influence

In the early years of the Cold War, many Americans believed that there was good reason to be concerned about the security of the United States. The Soviet domination of Eastern Europe and the Communist takeover of China shocked the American public, fueling a fear that communism would spread around the world. In addition, at the height of World War II, about 80,000 Americans claimed membership in the Communist Party. Some people feared that the first loyalty of these American Communists was to the Soviet Union.

Background
In 1949, the government charged several American Communist Party leaders under the Smith Act. This law made it a crime to belong to an organization that called for the overthrow of the U.S. government.

LOYALTY REVIEW BOARD Strongly anti-Communist Republicans began to accuse Truman of being soft on communism. Consequently, in March 1947, President Truman issued an executive order setting up the Federal Employee Loyalty Program, which included the Loyalty Review Board. Its purpose was to investigate government employees and to dismiss those who were found to be disloyal to the U.S. government. The U.S. attorney general drew up a list of 91 "subversive" organizations; membership in any of these groups was grounds for suspicion.

From 1947 to 1951, government loyalty boards investigated 3.2 million employees and dismissed 212 as security risks. Another 2,900 resigned because they did not want to be investigated or felt that the investigation violated their constitutional rights. Individuals under investigation were not allowed to see the evidence against them. **A**

THE HOUSE UN-AMERICAN ACTIVITIES COMMITTEE

Other agencies investigated possible Communist influence, both inside and outside the U.S. government. The most famous of these was the **House Un-American Activities Committee (HUAC).** HUAC first made headlines in 1947, when it began to investigate Communist influence in the movie industry. The committee believed that Communists were sneaking propaganda into films. The committee pointed to the pro-Soviet films made during World War II when the Soviet Union had been a United States ally.

HUAC subpoenaed 43 witnesses from the Hollywood film industry in September 1947. Many of the witnesses were "friendly," supporting the accusation that Communists had infiltrated the film industry. For example, the movie star Gary Cooper said he had "turned down quite a few scripts because I thought they were tinged with Communistic ideas." However, when asked which scripts he meant, Cooper couldn't remember their titles.

Ten "unfriendly" witnesses were called to testify but refused. These men, known as the **Hollywood Ten,** decided not to cooperate because they believed that the hearings were unconstitutional. Because the Hollywood Ten refused to answer questions, they were sent to prison.

MAIN IDEA

Drawing Conclusions
A How did the Loyalty Review Board pose a threat to civil liberties?

Background
In *Watkins* v. *United States* (1957), the Supreme Court limited the inquiry powers of Congress. The decision held that Congress did not have the right to invade people's privacy.

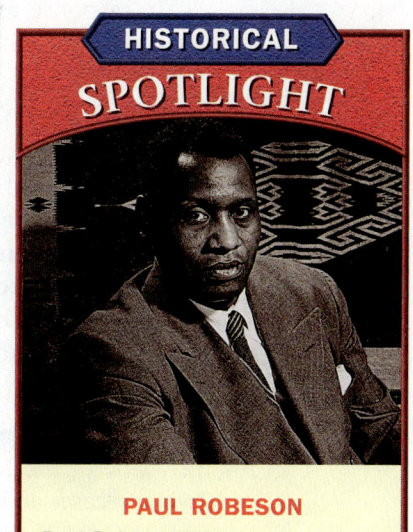

HISTORICAL SPOTLIGHT

PAUL ROBESON

Paul Robeson was an all-American football player and Phi Beta Kappa member at Rutgers University. After earning a law degree in 1923, he began a distinguished international career as a singer and actor. He was a vocal civil rights activist, and he was sympathetic to the Soviet culture and political philosophy.

In 1950, when he refused to sign an affidavit indicating whether he had ever been a member of the Communist Party, the State Department revoked his passport for eight years. During that time, he was unable to perform abroad and was blacklisted at home. His income fell from $150,000 a year to $3,000 a year.

Protesters demonstrate in support of the Hollywood Ten. ▼

In response to the hearings, Hollywood executives instituted a **blacklist**, a list of people whom they condemned for having a Communist background. People who were blacklisted—approximately 500 actors, writers, producers, and directors—had their careers ruined because they could no longer work. **B**

THE McCARRAN ACT As Hollywood tried to rid itself of Communists, Congress decided that Truman's Loyalty Review Board did not go far enough. In 1950, Congress passed the McCarran Internal Security Act. This made it unlawful to plan any action that might lead to the establishment of a totalitarian dictatorship in the United States. Truman vetoed the bill, saying, "In a free country, we punish men for the crimes they commit, but never for the opinions they have." But Congress enacted the law over Truman's veto.

MAIN IDEA

Analyzing Causes
B Why was Hollywood a target of anti-Communist investigations by Congress?

Spy Cases Stun the Nation

Two spy cases added to fear that was spreading like an epidemic across the country. One case involved a former State Department official named Alger Hiss.

ALGER HISS In 1948, a former Communist spy named Whittaker Chambers accused **Alger Hiss** of spying for the Soviet Union. To support his charges, Chambers produced microfilm of government documents that he claimed had been typed on Hiss's typewriter. Too many years had passed for government prosecutors to charge Hiss with espionage, but a jury convicted him of perjury—for lying about passing the documents—and sent him to jail. A young conservative Republican congressman named Richard Nixon gained fame for pursuing the charges against Hiss. Within four years of the highly publicized case, Nixon was elected vice president of the United States.

Hiss claimed that he was innocent and that Chambers had forged the documents used against him. However, in the 1990s, Soviet cables released by the National Security Agency seemed to prove Hiss's guilt.

NOW & THEN

TELEVISION: MAKING NEWS

Historians of popular culture believe that the early 1950s were the best years of television. Most programs were filmed live and had a fresh, unrehearsed look. Along with variety shows, early television presented some of the best serious drama of the age.

Since the 1950s, television has also become a major vehicle for reporting the news. Not only does television report the news, it also has increasingly helped to shape it.

1954 In 1954, the Communist-hunting senator Joseph McCarthy, in U.S. Senate hearings that were televised live, accused the U.S. Army of "coddling Communists." As many as 20 million Americans watched the combative senator malign people who had no chance to defend themselves.

1960 In the 1960 presidential election, a major factor in John Kennedy's victory over Richard Nixon was a series of four televised debates, the first televised presidential debates in history. An estimated 85 million to 120 million Americans watched one or more of the debates, which turned the tide in favor of Kennedy.

THE ROSENBERGS Another spy case rocked the nation even more than the Hiss case, partially because of international events occurring about the same time. On September 3, 1949, Americans learned that the Soviet Union had exploded an atomic bomb. Most American experts had predicted that it would take the Soviets three to five more years to make the bomb. People began to wonder if Communist supporters in the United States had leaked the secret of the bomb.

This second spy case seemed to confirm that suspicion. In 1950, the German-born physicist Klaus Fuchs admitted giving the Soviet Union information about America's atomic bomb. The information probably enabled Soviet scientists to develop their own atomic bomb years earlier than they would have otherwise. Implicated in the Fuchs case were **Ethel and Julius Rosenberg,** minor activists in the American Communist Party.

MAIN IDEA

Analyzing Causes

C Why did the cases of Alger Hiss and the Rosenbergs heighten the anti-Communist mood of Americans?

When asked if they were Communists, the Rosenbergs denied the charges against them and pleaded the Fifth Amendment, choosing not to incriminate themselves. They claimed they were being persecuted both for being Jewish and for holding radical beliefs. The Rosenbergs were found guilty of espionage and sentenced to death. In pronouncing their sentence, Judge Irving Kaufman declared their crime "worse than murder." To him, they were directly responsible for one of the deadliest clashes of the Cold War. **C**

▲ **Ethel and Julius Rosenberg were executed in June 1953 despite numerous pleas to spare their lives.**

★ **A PERSONAL VOICE** IRVING KAUFMAN

"I believe your conduct in putting into the hands of the Russians the A-bomb years before our best scientists predicted Russia would perfect the bomb has already caused, in my opinion, the Communist aggression in Korea. . . ."

—quoted in *The Unquiet Death of Julius and Ethel Rosenberg*

1967 By 1967, American support for the Vietnam War had plummeted as millions of TV viewers witnessed the horrors of war on the nightly news.

1974 The Watergate scandal that toppled Richard Nixon's presidency in 1974 played to a rapt TV audience. During the Senate hearings in 1973, the televised testimony of John Dean, the president's counsel, had convinced two out of three Americans that the president had committed a crime.

2000 During the 2000 presidential election, the TV networks first projected that Al Gore would win Florida. Later, George W. Bush was declared the winner of Florida, a declaration that led Al Gore to concede. Then, when the Florida vote became too close to call, Gore retracted his concession. That "election muddle" blurred even further the already indistinct line between reporting the news and making it.

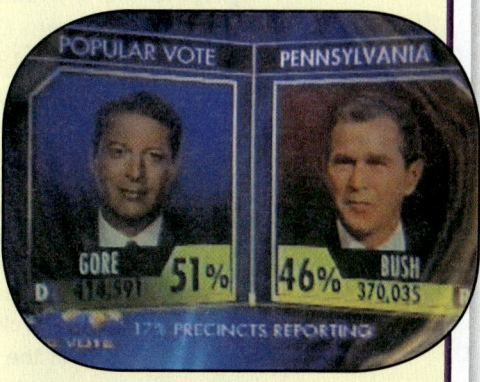

"IT'S OK—WE'RE HUNTING COMMUNISTS"

The fear of Communist subversion affected the entire society. People were so suspicious that almost any unusual opinion might be labeled "un-American." The climate of suspicion was most severe in the years 1947–1954, but it lasted throughout the 1950s.

SKILLBUILDER Analyzing Political Cartoons

1. What organization does the car represent?
2. What does the cartoon imply about the methods of this organization?

 SEE SKILLBUILDER HANDBOOK, PAGE R24.

a 1947 Herblock Cartoon, copyright by the Herb Block Foundation

People from all over the world appealed for clemency for the Rosenbergs. Many considered the evidence and the testimony too weak to warrant the death sentence. The case was appealed to the U.S. Supreme Court, but the Court refused to overturn the conviction. Julius and Ethel Rosenberg died in the electric chair in June 1953, leaving behind two sons. They became the first U.S. civilians executed for espionage.

McCarthy Launches His "Witch Hunt"

The most famous anti-Communist activist was Senator **Joseph McCarthy,** a Republican from Wisconsin. During his first three years in the Senate, he had acquired a reputation for being an ineffective legislator. By January 1950, he realized that he was going to need a winning issue in order to be reelected in 1952. Looking for such an issue, McCarthy charged that Communists were taking over the government.

MCCARTHY'S TACTICS Taking advantage of people's concerns about communism, McCarthy made one unsupported accusation after another. These attacks on suspected Communists in the early 1950s became known as **McCarthyism.** Since that time, McCarthyism has referred to the unfair tactic of accusing people of disloyalty without providing evidence. At various times McCarthy claimed to have in his hands the names of 57, 81, and 205 Communists in the State Department. (He never actually produced a single name.) He also charged that the Democratic Party was guilty of "20 years of treason" for allowing Communist infiltration into the government. He was always careful to do his name-calling only in the Senate, where he had legal immunity that protected him from being sued for slander.

The Republicans did little to stop McCarthy's attacks because they believed they would win the 1952 presidential election if the public saw them purging the nation of Communists. But one small group of six senators, led by Senator Margaret Chase Smith of Maine, did speak out.

Vocabulary
infiltration: the act of penetrating a group or organization without being noticed for purposes such as spying

★ **A PERSONAL VOICE** MARGARET CHASE SMITH

" I speak as a Republican. I speak as a woman. I speak as a United States senator. I speak as an American. . . . I am not proud of the way in which the Senate has been made a publicity platform for irresponsible sensationalism. I am not proud of the reckless abandon in which unproved charges have been hurled from this side of the aisle."

—Declaration of Conscience

MCCARTHY'S DOWNFALL Finally, in 1954, McCarthy made accusations against the U.S. Army, which resulted in a nationally televised Senate investigation. McCarthy's bullying of witnesses alienated the audience and cost him public support. The Senate condemned him for improper conduct that "tended to bring the Senate into dishonor and disrepute." Three years later, Joseph McCarthy, suffering from alcoholism, died a broken man.

OTHER ANTI-COMMUNIST MEASURES
Others besides Joseph McCarthy made it their mission to root communism out of American society. By 1953, 39 states had passed laws making it illegal to advocate the violent overthrow of the government, even though such laws clearly violated the constitutional right of free speech. Across the nation, cities and towns passed similar laws.

At times, the fear of communism seemed to have no limits. In Indiana, professional wrestlers had to take a loyalty oath. In experiments run by newspapers, pedestrians on the street refused to sign petitions that quoted the Declaration of Independence because they were afraid the ideas were communist. The government investigated union leaders, librarians, newspaper reporters, and scientists. It seemed that no profession was safe from the hunt for Communists.

Causes and Effects of McCarthyism
Causes
• Soviets successfully establish Communist regimes in Eastern Europe after World War II.
• Soviets develop the atomic bomb more quickly than expected.
• Korean War ends in a stalemate.
• Republicans gain politically by accusing Truman and Democrats of being soft on communism.
Effects
• Millions of Americans are forced to take loyalty oaths and undergo loyalty investigations.
• Activism by labor unions goes into decline.
• Many people are afraid to speak out on public issues.
• Anti-communism continues to drive U.S. foreign policy.

SKILLBUILDER Interpreting Charts
1. How did world events help lead to McCarthyism?
2. How did McCarthyism affect the behavior of individual Americans?

"I Can't Do This To Me!" a 1954 Herblock Cartoon, copyright by the Herb Block Foundation

---

SECTION 3 ASSESSMENT

1. **TERMS & NAMES** For each term or name, write a sentence explaining its significance.
   - HUAC
   - Hollywood Ten
   - blacklist
   - Alger Hiss
   - Ethel and Julius Rosenberg
   - Joseph McCarthy
   - McCarthyism

MAIN IDEA

2. **TAKING NOTES**
   Re-create the web below on your paper and fill in events that illustrate the main idea in the center.

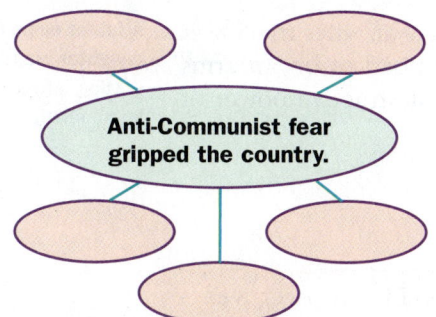

Anti-Communist fear gripped the country.

   Which event had the greatest impact on the country?

CRITICAL THINKING

3. **HYPOTHESIZING**
   If you had lived in this period and had been accused of being a Communist, what would you have done? **Think About:**
   - the Hollywood Ten, who refused to answer questions
   - the Rosenbergs, who pleaded the Fifth Amendment

4. **ANALYZING MOTIVES**
   Choose one of the following roles: Harry Truman, a member of HUAC, Judge Irving Kaufman, or Joseph McCarthy. As the person you have chosen, explain your motivation for opposing communism.

5. **ANALYZING VISUAL SOURCES**
   What does this cartoon suggest about McCarthy's downfall?

PI 2.2   CC Unit 6.II.C.3   CC Unit 6.II.D.2
PI 2.6   CC Unit 7.II.A.1   CC Unit 6.II.D.2
         CC Unit 7.II.B.4   CC Unit 7.II.B.8

Two Nations Live on the Edge

MAIN IDEA	WHY IT MATTERS NOW	Terms & Names
During the 1950s, the United States and the Soviet Union came to the brink of nuclear war.	The Cold War continued into the following decades, affecting U.S. policies in Cuba, Central America, Southeast Asia, and the Middle East.	• H-bomb • Dwight D. Eisenhower • John Foster Dulles • brinkmanship • Central Intelligence Agency (CIA)	• Warsaw Pact • Eisenhower Doctrine • Nikita Khrushchev • Francis Gary Powers • U-2 incident

One American's Story

TAKING NOTES

Use the graphic organizer online to take notes on Cold War trouble spots around the world.

Writer Annie Dillard was one of thousands of children who grew up in the 1950s with the chilling knowledge that nuclear war could obliterate their world in an instant. Dillard recalls practicing what to do in case of a nuclear attack.

A PERSONAL VOICE ANNIE DILLARD

"At school we had air-raid drills. We took the drills seriously; surely Pittsburgh, which had the nation's steel, coke, and aluminum, would be the enemy's first target. . . . When the air-raid siren sounded, our teachers stopped talking and led us to the school basement. There the gym teachers lined us up against the cement walls and steel lockers, and showed us how to lean in and fold our arms over our heads. . . . The teachers stood in the middle of the room, not talking to each other. We tucked against the walls and lockers. . . . We folded our skinny arms over our heads, and raised to the enemy a clatter of gold scarab bracelets and gold bangle bracelets."

—*An American Childhood*

▲ A father helps his daughter practice getting into a bomb shelter.

The fear of nuclear attack was a direct result of the Cold War. After the Soviet Union developed its atomic bomb, the two superpowers embarked on an arms race that enormously increased both the number and the destructive power of weapons.

Brinkmanship Rules U.S. Policy

Although air-raid drills were not common until the Eisenhower years (1953–1961), the nuclear arms race began during Truman's presidency. When the Soviet Union exploded its first atomic bomb in 1949, President Truman had to make a terrible decision—whether to develop an even more horrifying weapon.

RACE FOR THE H-BOMB The scientists who developed the atomic bomb had suspected since 1942 that it was possible to create an even more destructive thermonuclear weapon—the hydrogen bomb, or **H-bomb.** They estimated that such a bomb would have the force of 1 million tons of TNT (67 times the power of the bomb dropped on Hiroshima). But they argued vehemently about the morality of creating such a destructive weapon.

Despite such concerns, the United States entered into a deadly race with the Soviet Union to see which country would be the first to produce an H-bomb. On November 1, 1952, the United States won the race when it exploded the first H-bomb. However, the American advantage lasted less than a year. In August 1953, the Soviets exploded their own thermonuclear weapon. **(A)**

THE POLICY OF BRINKMANSHIP By the time both countries had the H-bomb, **Dwight D. Eisenhower** was president. His secretary of state, **John Foster Dulles,** was staunchly anti-Communist. For Dulles, the Cold War was a moral crusade against communism. Dulles proposed that the United States could prevent the spread of communism by promising to use all of its force, including nuclear weapons, against any aggressor nation. The willingness of the United States, under President Eisenhower, to go to the edge of all-out war became known as **brinkmanship.** Under this policy, the United States trimmed its army and navy and expanded its air force (which would deliver the bombs) and its buildup of nuclear weapons. The Soviet Union followed suit.

The threat of nuclear attack was unlike any the American people had ever faced. Even if only a few bombs reached their targets, millions of civilians would die. Schoolchildren like Annie Dillard practiced air-raid procedures, and some families built underground fallout shelters in their back yards. Fear of nuclear war became a constant in American life for the next 30 years.

MAIN IDEA

Analyzing Causes
A How did the U.S. and the Soviet Union start the arms race?

A dramatic civil defense poster shows the fear of nuclear attack.

The Cold War Spreads Around the World

As the nation shifted to a dependence on nuclear arms, the Eisenhower administration began to rely heavily on the recently formed **Central Intelligence Agency (CIA)** for information. The CIA used spies to gather information abroad. The CIA also began to carry out covert, or secret, operations to weaken or overthrow governments unfriendly to the United States.

COVERT ACTIONS IN THE MIDDLE EAST AND LATIN AMERICA One of the CIA's first covert actions took place in the Middle East. In 1951, Iran's prime minister, Mohammed Mossadegh, nationalized Iran's oil fields; that is, he placed the formerly private industries (owned mostly by Great Britain) under Iranian control. To protest, the British stopped buying Iranian oil. As the Iranian economy

The Warsaw Pact and NATO, 1955

Warsaw Pact countries
European NATO members
Nonaligned nations

0   300   600 miles
0   300   600 kilometers

ICELAND

NORWAY

SWEDEN

FINLAND

SOVIET UNION

IRELAND

UNITED KINGDOM

North Sea

DENMARK

Baltic Sea

Gulf of Finland

NETHERLANDS

BELGIUM

EAST GERMANY

POLAND

ATLANTIC OCEAN

LUXEMBOURG

WEST GERMANY

CZECHOSLOVAKIA

SWITZERLAND

AUSTRIA

HUNGARY

FRANCE

ROMANIA

Black Sea

PORTUGAL

SPAIN

YUGOSLAVIA

BULGARIA

ITALY

ALBANIA

TURKEY

Mediterranean Sea

GREECE

GEOGRAPHY SKILLBUILDER

1. **Region** Which nations shown on the map belonged to NATO, and which to the Warsaw Pact?

2. **Region** Which nations shown on the map did not belong to either defense alliance?

faltered, the United States feared that Mossadegh might turn to the Soviets for help. In 1953, the CIA gave several million dollars to anti-Mossadegh supporters. The CIA wanted the pro-American Shah of Iran, who had recently been forced to flee, to return to power. The plan worked. The Shah returned to power and turned over control of Iranian oil fields to Western companies.

In 1954, the CIA also took covert actions in Guatemala, a Central American country just south of Mexico. Eisenhower believed that Guatemala's government had Communist sympathies because it had given more than 200,000 acres of American-owned land to peasants. In response, the CIA trained an army, which invaded Guatemala. The Guatemalan army refused to defend the president, and he resigned. The army's leader then became dictator of the country. **B**

THE WARSAW PACT In spite of the growing tension between the superpowers, U.S.-Soviet relations seemed to thaw following the death of Joseph Stalin in 1953. The Soviets recognized West Germany and concluded peace treaties with Austria and Japan. However, in 1955, when West Germany was allowed to rearm and join NATO, the Soviet Union grew fearful. It formed its own military alliance, known as the **Warsaw Pact.** The Warsaw Pact linked the Soviet Union with seven Eastern European countries.

A SUMMIT IN GENEVA In July 1955, Eisenhower traveled to Geneva, Switzerland, to meet with Soviet leaders. There Eisenhower put forth an "open skies" proposal. The United States and the Soviet Union would allow flights over each other's territory to guard against surprise nuclear attacks. Although the Soviet Union rejected this proposal, the world hailed the "spirit of Geneva" as a step toward peace.

MAIN IDEA

Summarizing
B What was the role of the CIA in the Cold War?

THE SUEZ WAR In 1955, the same year in which the Geneva Summit took place, Great Britain and the United States agreed to help Egypt finance construction of a dam at Aswan on the Nile River. However, Gamal Abdel-Nasser, Egypt's head of government, tried to play the Soviets and the Americans against each other, by improving relations with each one in order to get more aid. In 1956, after learning that Nasser was making deals with the Soviets, Dulles withdrew his offer of a loan. Angered, Nasser responded by nationalizing the Suez Canal, the Egyptian waterway that was owned by France and Great Britain. The French and the British were outraged.

Egyptian control of the canal also affected Israel. Nasser refused to let ships bound for Israel pass through the canal, even though the canal was supposed to be open to all nations. Great Britain, France, and Israel responded by sending troops. The three countries seized the Mediterranean end of the canal. The UN quickly stepped in to stop the fighting. It persuaded Great Britain, France, and Israel to withdraw. However, it allowed Egypt to keep control of the canal. **C**

MAIN IDEA

Analyzing Effects

C What were the results of the Suez War?

THE EISENHOWER DOCTRINE The Soviet Union's prestige in the Middle East rose because of its support for Egypt. To counterbalance this development, President Eisenhower issued a warning in January 1957. This warning, known as the **Eisenhower Doctrine,** said that the United States would defend the Middle East against an attack by any communist country. In March, Congress officially approved the doctrine.

THE HUNGARIAN UPRISING Even as fighting was raging in the Middle East, a revolt began in Hungary. Dominated by the Soviet Union since the end of World War II, the Hungarian people rose in revolt in 1956. They called for a democratic government.

Imre Nagy, the most popular and liberal Hungarian Communist leader, formed a new government. He promised free elections, denounced the Warsaw Pact, and demanded that all Soviet troops leave Hungary.

Background
Earlier in 1956, Polish workers held demonstrations demanding better working conditions. The protest was violently put down by the Polish military.

The Soviet response was swift and brutal. In November 1956, Soviet tanks rolled into Hungary and killed approximately 30,000 Hungarians. Armed with only pistols and bottles, thousands of Hungarian freedom fighters threw up barricades in the streets and fought the invaders to no avail. The Soviets overthrew the Nagy government and replaced it with pro-Soviet leaders. Nagy himself was executed. Some 200,000 Hungarians fled to the west.

Although the Truman Doctrine had promised to support free peoples who resisted communism, the United States did nothing to help Hungary break free of Soviet control. Many

---

WORLD STAGE

ISRAEL

On May 14, 1948, the United Nations created the nation of Israel by partitioning the Palestine Mandate into two states, one Jewish and one Arab. Thousands of Jews had immigrated to the Palestine Mandate from Europe before and during World War II. Modern Israel became like the "promised land" of biblical times. The creation of Israel was one of the few issues upon which the United States and the Soviet Union agreed, as the world reacted uniformly to the horror that had befallen the Jews in the Holocaust.

Crowds surround a captured Russian tank during the anti-Communist revolution in Hungary.

Hungarians were bitterly disappointed. The American policy of containment did not extend to driving the Soviet Union out of its satellites.

No help came to Hungary from the United Nations either. Although the UN passed one resolution after another condemning the Soviet Union, the Soviet veto in the Security Council stopped the UN from taking any action.

The Cold War Takes to the Skies

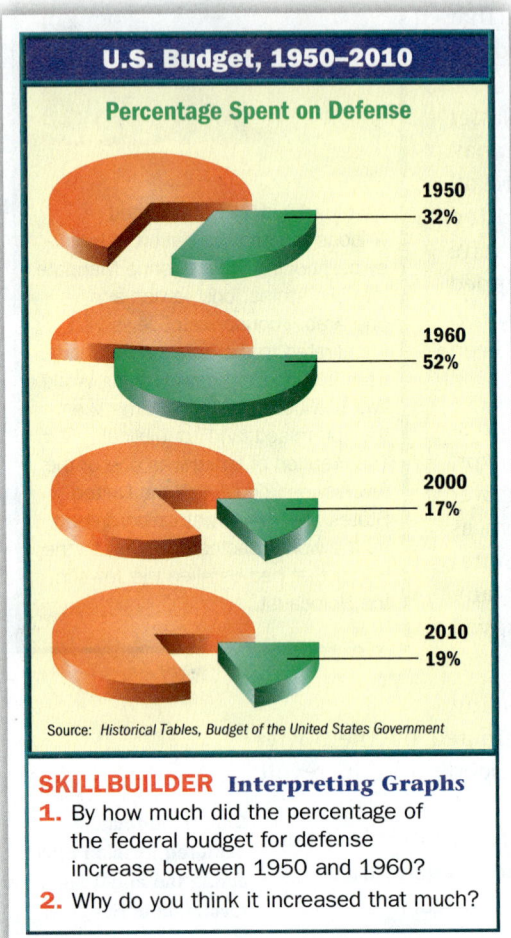

U.S. Budget, 1950–2010

Percentage Spent on Defense

1950
32%

1960
52%

2000
17%

2010
19%

Source: *Historical Tables, Budget of the United States Government*

SKILLBUILDER Interpreting Graphs
1. By how much did the percentage of the federal budget for defense increase between 1950 and 1960?
2. Why do you think it increased that much?

After Stalin's death in 1953, the Soviet Union had no well-defined way for one leader to succeed another. For the first few years, a group of leaders shared power. As time went by, however, one man did gain power. That man was **Nikita Khrushchev** (krŏŏsh'chĕf). Like Stalin, Khrushchev believed that communism would take over the world, but Khrushchev thought it could triumph peacefully. He favored a policy of peaceful coexistence in which two powers would compete economically and scientifically. **D**

THE SPACE RACE In the competition for international prestige, the Soviets leaped to an early lead in what came to be known as the space race. On October 4, 1957, they launched *Sputnik*, the world's first artificial satellite. *Sputnik* traveled around the earth at 18,000 miles per hour, circling the globe every 96 minutes. Its launch was a triumph of Soviet technology.

Americans were shocked at being beaten and promptly poured money into their own space program. U.S. scientists worked frantically to catch up to the Soviets. The first attempt at an American satellite launch was a humiliating failure, with the rocket toppling to the ground. However, on January 31, 1958, the United States successfully launched its first satellite.

A U-2 IS SHOT DOWN Following the rejection of Eisenhower's "open skies" proposal at the 1955 Geneva summit conference, the CIA began making secret high-altitude flights over Soviet territory. The plane used for these missions was the U-2, which could fly at high altitudes without detection. As a U-2 passed over the Soviet Union, its infrared cameras took detailed photographs of troop movement and missile sites.

By 1960, however, many U.S. officials were nervous about the U-2 program for two reasons. First, the existence and purpose of the U-2 was an open secret among some members of the American press. Second, the Soviets had been aware of the flights since 1958, as **Francis Gary Powers,** a U-2 pilot, explained.

MAIN IDEA

Comparing
D Compare Joseph Stalin with Nikita Khrushchev. How were they alike? How were they different?

A PERSONAL VOICE FRANCIS GARY POWERS

" We . . . knew that the Russians were radar-tracking at least some of our flights. . . . We also knew that SAMs [surface-to-air missiles] were being fired at us, that some were uncomfortably close to our altitude. But we knew too that the Russians had a control problem in their guidance system. . . . We were concerned, but not greatly. "

—*Operation Overflight: The U-2 Spy Pilot Tells His Story for the First Time*

HISTORY

VIDEO
U-2 Spy Plane
Shot Down

hmhsocialstudies.com

Finally, Eisenhower himself wanted the flights discontinued. He and Khrushchev were going to hold another summit conference on the arms race on May 15, 1960. "If one of these aircraft were lost when we were engaged in apparently sincere deliberations, it could . . . ruin my effectiveness," he told an aide. However, Dulles persuaded him to authorize one last flight.

That flight took place on May 1, and the pilot was Francis Gary Powers. Four hours after Powers entered Soviet airspace, a Soviet pilot shot down his plane, and Powers was forced to parachute into Soviet-controlled territory. The Soviets sentenced Powers to ten years in prison.

◀ Francis Gary Powers's military identification card

Francis Gary Powers at a Senate committee hearing following his release by the Soviets ▼

Background
After 18 months, Francis Gary Powers was released from the Soviet Union in exchange for Soviet agent Rudolf Abel, who had been convicted of spying in the United States.

RENEWED CONFRONTATION At first, Eisenhower denied that the U-2 had been spying. The Soviets had evidence, however, and Eisenhower finally had to admit it. Khrushchev demanded an apology for the flights and a promise to halt them. Eisenhower agreed to stop the U-2 flights, but he would not apologize.

Khrushchev angrily called off the summit. He also withdrew his invitation to Eisenhower to visit the Soviet Union. Because of the **U-2 incident,** the 1960s opened with tension between the two superpowers as great as ever.

SECTION 4 ASSESSMENT

1. **TERMS & NAMES** For each term or name, write a sentence explaining its significance.
   - H-bomb
   - Dwight D. Eisenhower
   - John Foster Dulles
   - brinkmanship
   - Central Intelligence Agency (CIA)
   - Warsaw Pact
   - Eisenhower Doctrine
   - Nikita Khrushchev
   - Francis Gary Powers
   - U-2 incident

MAIN IDEA

2. **TAKING NOTES**
   List Cold War trouble spots in Iran, Guatemala, Egypt, and Hungary. For each, write a newspaper headline that summarizes the U.S. role and the outcome of the situation.

Trouble Spot	Headline

   Choose one headline and write a paragraph about that trouble spot.

CRITICAL THINKING

3. **HYPOTHESIZING**
   How might the Cold War have progressed if the U-2 incident had never occurred? **Think About:**
   - the mutual distrust between the Soviet Union and the United States
   - the outcome of the incident

4. **EVALUATING**
   Which of the two superpowers do you think contributed more to Cold War tensions during the 1950s?

5. **FORMING GENERALIZATIONS**
   Should one nation have the right to remove another nation's head of government from power? If so, when? If not, why?

Science Fiction Reflects Cold War Fears

1950–1959 Many writers of science fiction draw on the scientific and social trends of the present to describe future societies that might arise if those trends were to continue. Nuclear proliferation, the space race, early computer technology, and the pervasive fear of known and unknown dangers during the Cold War were the realities that prompted a boom in science fiction during the 1950s and 1960s.

THE BODY SNATCHERS

Published in 1955 at the height of the Great Fear, Jack Finney's *The Body Snatchers* (on which the movie *Invasion of the Body Snatchers* was based) tells of giant seed pods from outer space that descend on the inhabitants of a California town. The pods create perfect physical duplicates of the townspeople and lack only one thing—human souls.

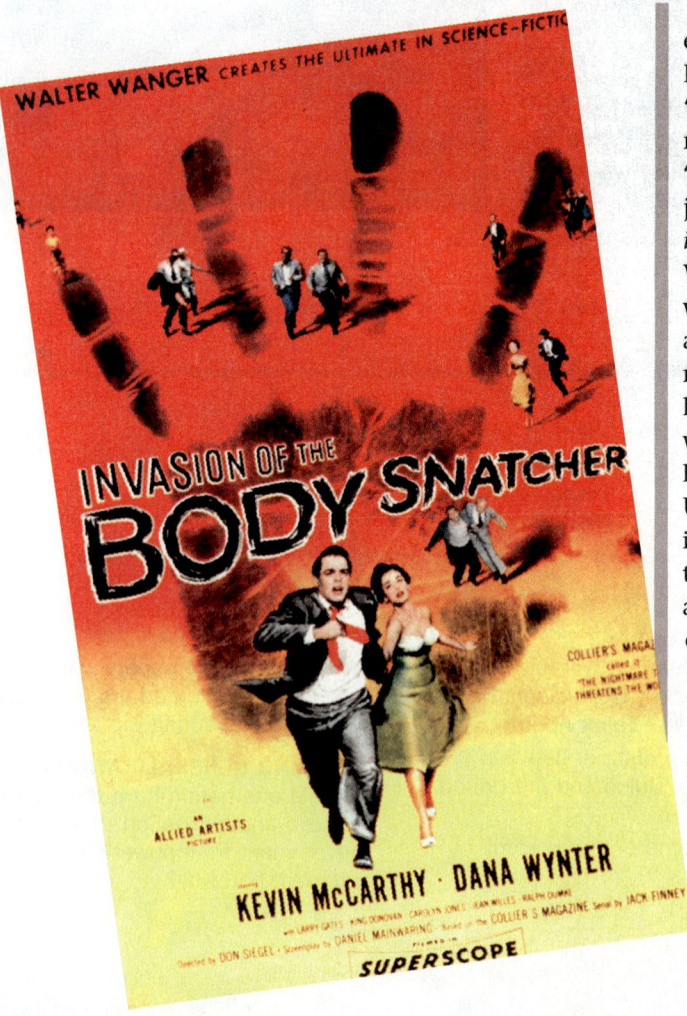

"Miles, he looks, sounds, acts, and remembers exactly like Ira. On the outside. But *inside* he's different. His responses"—she stopped, hunting for the word—"aren't *emotionally* right, if I can explain that. He remembers the past, in detail, and he'll smile and say 'You were sure a cute youngster, Willy. Bright one, too,' just the way Uncle Ira did. But there's something *missing,* and the same thing is true of Aunt Aleda, lately." Wilma stopped, staring at nothing again, face intent, wrapped up in this, then she continued. "Uncle Ira was a father to me, from infancy, and when he talked about my childhood, Miles, there was—always—a special look in his eyes that meant he was remembering the wonderful quality of those days for him. Miles, that look, 'way in back of the eyes, is gone. With this—*this* Uncle Ira, or whoever or whatever he is, I have the feeling, the absolutely certain *knowledge,* Miles, that he's talking by rote. That the facts of Uncle Ira's memories are all in his mind in every last detail, ready to recall. But the emotions are not. There *is* no emotion—none—only the pretense of it. The words, the gestures, the tones of voice, everything else—but not the feeling."

Her voice was suddenly firm and commanding: "Miles, memories or not, appearances or not, possible or impossible, that is not my Uncle Ira."

—Jack Finney, *The Body Snatchers* (1955)

THE MARTIAN CHRONICLES

In *The Martian Chronicles*, Ray Bradbury describes how earthlings who have colonized Mars watch helplessly as their former planet is destroyed by nuclear warfare.

They all came out and looked at the sky that night. They left their suppers or their washing up or their dressing for the show and they came out upon their now-not-quite-as-new porches and watched the green star of Earth there. It was a move without conscious effort; they all did it, to help them understand the news they had heard on the radio a moment before. There was Earth and there the coming war, and there hundreds of thousands of mothers or grandmothers or fathers or brothers or aunts or uncles or cousins. They stood on the porches and tried to believe in the existence of Earth, much as they had once tried to believe in the existence of Mars; it was a problem reversed. To all intents and purposes, Earth now was dead; they had been away from it for three or four years. Space was an anesthetic; seventy million miles of space numbed you, put memory to sleep, depopulated Earth, erased the past, and allowed these people here to go on with their work. But now, tonight, the dead were risen, Earth was reinhabited, memory awoke, a million names were spoken: What was so-and-so doing tonight on Earth? What about this one and that one? The people on the porches glanced sidewise at each other's faces.

At nine o'clock Earth seemed to explode, catch fire, and burn.

The people on the porches put up their hands as if to beat the fire out.

They waited.

—Ray Bradbury, *The Martian Chronicles* (1950)

▼ Ray Bradbury in 1965.

A CANTICLE FOR LEIBOWITZ

In *A Canticle for Leibowitz*, Walter M. Miller, Jr., portrays the centuries after a nuclear holocaust as a new "Dark Age" for humanity on earth.

He had been wandering for a long time. The search seemed endless, but there was always the promise of finding what he sought across the next rise or beyond the bend in the trail. When he had finished fanning himself, he clapped the hat back on his head and scratched at his bushy beard while blinking around at the landscape. There was a patch of unburned forest on the hillside just ahead. It offered welcome shade, but still the wanderer sat there in the sunlight and watched the curious buzzards. . . .

Pickings were good for a while in the region of the Red River; but then out of the carnage, a city-state arose. For rising city-states, the buzzards had no fondness, although they approved of their eventual fall. They shied away from Texarkana and ranged far over the plain to the west. After the manner of all living things, they replenished the Earth many times with their kind.

Eventually it was the Year of Our Lord 3174.

There were rumors of war.

—Walter M. Miller, Jr., *A Canticle for Leibowitz* (1959)

THINKING CRITICALLY

1. **Comparing** What themes, or general messages about life or humanity, do you think these three books convey? How might readers' interpretations of these messages today differ from readers' interpretations during the Cold War?

   SEE SKILLBUILDER HANDBOOK, PAGE R8.

2. hmhsocialstudies.com **INTERNET ACTIVITY**

   Visit the links for American Literature to learn more about Ray Bradbury and *The Martian Chronicles*. When was *The Martian Chronicles* published? How does it reflect Cold War fears? What does the writing tell you about Ray Bradbury's view of American society at the time?

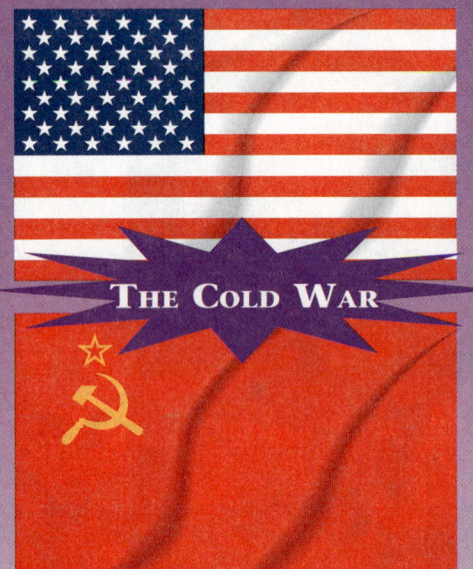

VISUAL SUMMARY

COLD WAR CONFLICTS

CAUSES

- Soviet domination of Eastern Europe
- Communist victory in China
- Mutual suspicion between United States and Soviet Union

THE COLD WAR

IMMEDIATE EFFECTS

- Truman Doctrine and Marshall Plan
- East-West tensions over Berlin
- Establishment of NATO and Warsaw Pact
- McCarthyism

LONG-TERM EFFECTS

- Arms race between superpowers
- Superpower rivalry for world power

TERMS & NAMES

For each term or name below, write a sentence explaining its significance to the Cold War.

1. containment
2. North Atlantic Treaty Organization (NATO)
3. Mao Zedong
4. Korean War
5. McCarthyism
6. John Foster Dulles
7. brinkmanship
8. Central Intelligence Agency (CIA)
9. Nikita Khrushchev
10. U-2 incident

MAIN IDEAS

Use your notes and the information in the chapter to answer the following questions.

Origins of the Cold War *(pages 808–814)*

1. What were the goals of U.S. foreign policy in the Cold War?
2. Describe the Truman Doctrine and how America reacted to it.
3. What was the purpose of the NATO alliance?

The Cold War Heats Up *(pages 815–821)*

4. What global events led to U.S. involvement in Korea?
5. What issue between General Douglas MacArthur and President Truman eventually cost MacArthur his job?

The Cold War at Home *(pages 822–827)*

6. What actions of Joseph McCarthy worsened the national hysteria about communism?
7. How did the Rosenberg case fuel anti-communist feeling?

Two Nations Live on the Edge *(pages 828–833)*

8. How did the U.S., including the CIA, wage the Cold War in the 1950s?

CRITICAL THINKING

1. **USING YOUR NOTES** Create a cause-and-effect diagram like the one shown for each of these events: (a) the United States' adoption of a policy of containment, and (b) the beginning of the nuclear arms race between the United States and the Soviet Union.

2. **ANALYZING EVENTS** What government actions during the Communist scare conflicted with the Bill of Rights? Explain.

3. **INTERPRETING MAPS** Look carefully at the map on page 811. How did the absence of a natural barrier on the western border of the Soviet Union affect post-World War II Soviet foreign policy? Explain your answer.

Use the quotation below and your knowledge of U.S. history to answer question 1.

> "In 1945 I had ordered the A Bomb dropped on Japan at two places devoted almost exclusively to war production. We were at war. We were trying to end it in order to save the lives of our soldiers and sailors. . . . We stopped the war and saved thousands of casualties on both sides.
>
> In Korea we were fighting a police action with sixteen allied nations to support the World Organization which had set up the Republic of Korea. We had held the Chinese after defeating the North Koreans and whipping the Russian Air Force. I just could not make the order for a Third World War. I know I was *right.*"
>
> —*Off the Record: The Private Papers of Harry S. Truman*

1 According to President Truman, what was the main difference between using the atomic bomb on Japan in 1945 and the possibility of using it on China in 1951?

(1) Japan was more of a military power in 1945 than China was in 1951.

(2) In 1945 we had many allies, but in 1951 we had only two.

(3) In 1945 the bomb ended a world war, but in 1951 it would have started one.

(4) The Japanese were much fiercer fighters than the Chinese were.

Use the cartoon below and your knowledge of U.S. history to answer question 2.

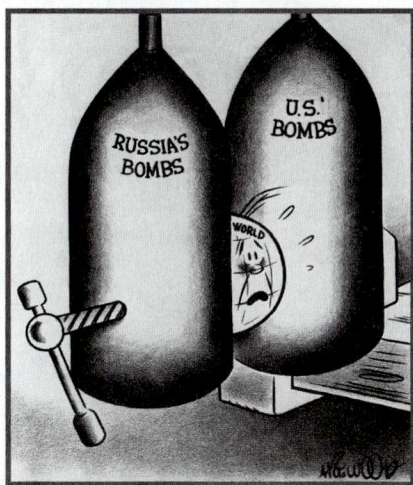

2 What point of view about the arms race does this 1950 cartoon *best* support?

(1) The arms race between "Russia" and the United States is as dangerous as a war.

(2) Communism uncontained will spread.

(3) The bombs of the United States only threaten countries other than the United States.

(4) The United States needs to build up its arsenal in order to compete with "Russia."

hmhsocialstudies.com **TEST PRACTICE**

For additional test practice, go online for:

• Diagnostic tests   • Tutorials

INTERACT WITH HISTORY

Recall the issues that you explored at the beginning of the chapter. Suppose your best friend has been accused of being a Communist. You have been called to serve as a character witness for him or her. Write a speech that you will present to the House Un-American Activities Committee (HUAC). In your speech explain why you feel that your friend's constitutional rights are being violated.

FOCUS ON WRITING

Write a five-paragraph essay that explains how the United States became involved in the Korean War.

COLLABORATIVE LEARNING

21ST CENTURY

In a small group read and discuss the "One American's Story" at the begining of Section 4. Then use the Internet and library resources to research the steps Americans took to protect themselves from nuclear attack. Use your findings to create a brief illustrated report.

CHAPTER 27

THE POSTWAR BOOM

New York Standards

KEY IDEA 2 Important ideas, social and cultural values, beliefs, and traditions from New York State and United States history illustrate the connections and interactions of people and events across time and from a variety of perspectives.

KEY IDEA 4 The skills of historical analysis include the ability to: explain the significance of historical evidence; weigh the importance, reliability, and validity of evidence; understand the concept of multiple causation; understand the importance of changing and competing interpretations of different historical developments.

SECTION 1: Postwar America

SECTION 2: The American Dream in the Fifties

SECTION 3: Popular Culture

SECTION 4: The Other America

In the 1950s, the backyard was the perfect place for suburban homeowners to relax.

1946 Baby boom begins.

1947 Jackie Robinson integrates major league baseball.

1948 Harry S. Truman is elected president.

1950's Disc jockey Alan Freed is the first to use the term "rock 'n' roll" on the air.

1952 Dwight D. Eisenhower is elected president.

| USA | 1946 | 1948 | 1950 | 1952 |
| WORLD | | | | |

1949 Mao Zedong's Communist forces gain control of China.

1950 Korean War begins.

INTERACT
WITH HISTORY

You have returned home from serving in World War II to find that your country is changing. The cities have swelled. Outlying suburbs are being built up with almost identical homes. America produces more and cheaper goods. In a booming economy, couples marry and start families in record numbers. As you watch clever ads on TV for the newest labor-saving gadgets, you feel nostalgia for a simpler time.

Explore the Issues

- How does pressure to conform affect the American dream?
- Who might be excluded from the new prosperity?
- How does advertising promote certain lifestyles and ideals?

1953 Korean War cease-fire is signed.

1954 *Brown* v. *Board of Education of Topeka* outlaws school segregation.

1956 Eisenhower is reelected.

1958 NASA— the National Aeronautics and Space Administration— is established.

1959 Alaska and Hawaii become the 49th and 50th states.

1960 John F. Kennedy is elected president.

1954   **1956**   **1958**   **1960**

1954 USSR opens the first small nuclear power plant.

1956 Soviets crush uprising in Hungary.

1957 Soviets launch *Sputnik I*.

1959 Fidel Castro comes to power in Cuba.

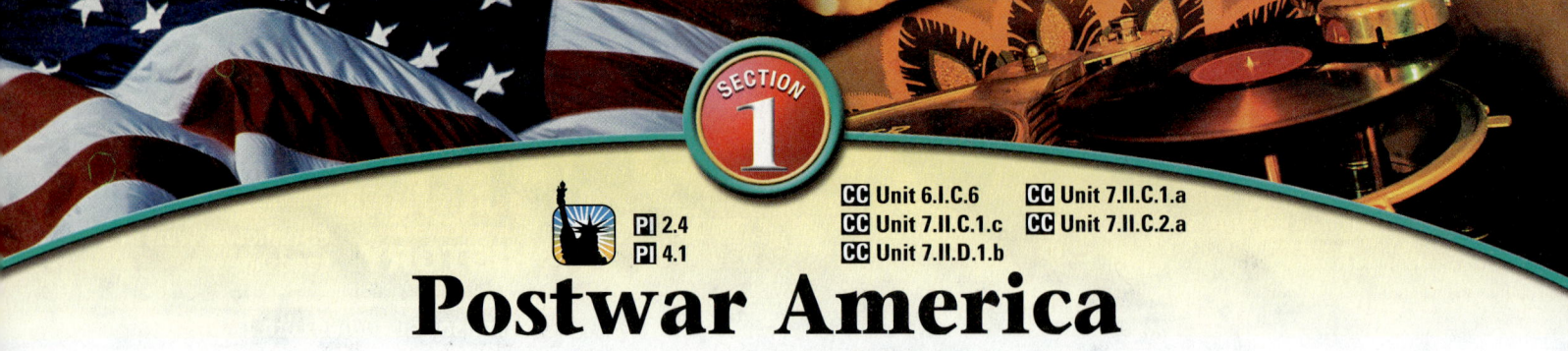

SECTION 1

PI 2.4
PI 4.1

CC Unit 6.I.C.6   CC Unit 7.II.C.1.a
CC Unit 7.II.C.1.c   CC Unit 7.II.C.2.a
CC Unit 7.II.D.1.b

Postwar America

MAIN IDEA	WHY IT MATTERS NOW	Terms & Names
The Truman and Eisenhower administrations led the nation to make social, economic, and political adjustments following World War II.	In the years after World War II, the United States became the economic and military power that it still is today.	• GI Bill of Rights • Dixiecrat • suburb • Fair Deal • Harry S. Truman

One American's Story

Sam Gordon had been married less than a year when he was shipped overseas in July 1943. As a sergeant in the United States Army, he fought in Belgium and France during World War II. Arriving back home in November 1945, Sam nervously anticipated a reunion with his family. A friend, Donald Katz, described Sam's reactions.

A PERSONAL VOICE DONALD KATZ

" Sam bulled through the crowd and hailed a taxi. The cab motored north through the warm autumn day as he groped for feelings appropriate to being back home alive from a terrible war. . . . [He was] nearly panting under the weight of fear. . . . *Back home alive . . . married to a girl I haven't seen since 1943 . . . father of a child I've never seen at all.* "

— *Home Fires*

▲ GIs returned home to their families after World War II with new hope, but also with new problems.

Sam Gordon met his daughter, Susan, for the first time the day he returned home from the war, and he went to work the next morning. Like many other young couples, the Gordons began to put the nightmare of the war behind them and to return to normality.

Readjustment and Recovery

By the summer of 1946, about 10 million men and women had been released from the armed forces. Veterans like Sam Gordon—along with the rest of American society—settled down to rebuild their lives.

THE IMPACT OF THE GI BILL To help ease veterans' return to civilian life, Congress passed the Servicemen's Readjustment Act, or the **GI Bill of Rights,** in 1944. In addition to encouraging veterans to get an education by paying part of their tuition, the GI Bill guaranteed them a year's worth of unemployment benefits while job hunting. It also offered low-interest, federally guaranteed loans. Millions of young families used these benefits to buy homes and farms or to establish businesses.

HOUSING CRISIS In 1945 and 1946, returning veterans faced a severe housing shortage. Many families lived in cramped apartments or moved in with relatives. In response to this housing crisis, developers like William Levitt and Henry Kaiser used efficient, assembly-line methods to mass-produce houses. Levitt, who bragged that his company could build a house in 16 minutes, offered homes in small residential communities surrounding cities, called **suburbs,** for less than $7,000.

▲ The suburbs were a mass phenomenon, even on moving day.

Levitt's first postwar development—rows of standardized homes built on treeless lots—was located on New York's Long Island and named Levittown. These homes looked exactly alike, and certain zoning laws ensured that they would stay the same. Despite their rigid conformity, Americans loved the openness and small-town feel to the planned suburbs. With the help of the GI Bill, many veterans and their families moved in and cultivated a new lifestyle.

REDEFINING THE FAMILY Tension created by changes in men's and women's roles after the war contributed to a rising divorce rate. Traditionally, men were the breadwinners and heads of households, while women were expected to stay home and care for the family. During the war, however, about 8 million women, 75 percent of whom were married, entered the paid work force. These women supported their families and made important household decisions. Many were reluctant to give up their newfound independence when their husbands returned. Although most women did leave their jobs, by 1950, more than a million war marriages had ended in divorce.

ECONOMIC READJUSTMENT After World War II, the United States converted from a wartime to a peacetime economy. The U.S. government immediately canceled war contracts totaling $35 billion. Within ten days of Japan's surrender, more than a million defense workers were laid off. Unemployment increased as veterans joined laid-off defense workers in the search for jobs. At the peak of postwar unemployment, in March 1946, nearly 3 million people were seeking work.

Rising unemployment was not the nation's only postwar economic problem, however. During the war, the Office of Price Administration (OPA) had halted inflation by imposing maximum prices on goods. When these controls ended on June 30, 1946, prices skyrocketed. In the next two weeks, the cost of consumer products soared 25 percent, double the increase of the previous three years. In some cities, consumers stood in long lines, hoping to buy scarce items, such as sugar, coffee, and beans. Prices continued to rise for the next two years until the supply of goods caught up with the demand.

MAIN IDEA

Identifying Problems
Ⓐ What problems did Americans face after World War II?

While prices spiraled upward, many American workers also earned less than they had earned during the war. To halt runaway inflation and to help the nation convert to a peacetime economy, Congress eventually reestablished controls similar to the wartime controls on prices, wages, and rents. Ⓐ

REMARKABLE RECOVERY Most economists who had forecast a postwar depression were proved wrong because they had failed to consider consumers' pent-up accumulation of needs and wants. People had gone without many goods for so long that by the late 1940s, with more than $135 billion in savings from defense work, service pay, and investments in war bonds, Americans suddenly had money to spend. They snatched up everything from automobiles to houses. After a brief period of postwar economic readjustment, the American economy boomed. The demand for goods and services outstripped the supply and increased production, which created new jobs. Judging from the graphs (shown left), many Americans prospered in the 1950s in what the economist John Kenneth Galbraith called "the affluent society."

The Cold War also contributed to economic growth. Concern over Soviet expansion kept American defense spending high and people employed. Foreign-aid programs, such as the Marshall Plan, provided another boost to the American economy. By helping nations in Western Europe recover from the war, the United States helped itself by creating strong foreign markets for its exports. **Ⓑ**

MAIN IDEA

Analyzing Causes
Ⓑ What factors contributed to the American postwar economic boom?

A Dynamic Economy

Home Ownership

Millions of Homeowners / 1950 1952 1954 1956 1958 1960

Automobile Registrations

Millions of Registrations / 1950 1952 1954 1956 1958 1960

Median Family Income

Income in Dollars / 1950 1952 1954 1956 1958 1960

Savings Accounts

Billions of Dollars / 1950 1952 1954 1956 1958 1960 1962

Source: Historical Statistics of the United States, Colonial times to 1970

SKILLBUILDER
Interpreting Graphs
1. From 1950 to 1960, by what percentage did each of the economic indicators shown above increase?
2. Which years show the biggest increases for each of the graphs above?

Meeting Economic Challenges

Despite an impressive recovery, Americans faced a number of economic problems. Their lives had been in turmoil throughout the war, and a desire for stability made the country more conservative.

PRESIDENT TRUMAN'S INHERITANCE When **Harry S. Truman** suddenly became president after Franklin D. Roosevelt's death in 1945, he asked Roosevelt's widow, Eleanor, whether there was anything he could do for her. She replied, "Is there anything we can do for you? For you are the one in trouble now." In many ways, President Truman was in trouble.

★ **A PERSONAL VOICE** HARRY S. TRUMAN

" I don't know whether you fellows ever had a load of hay fall on you, but when they told me yesterday what had happened [Roosevelt's death], I felt like the moon, the stars, and all the planets had fallen on me. "

—excerpt from a speech, April 13, 1945

Despite his lack of preparation for the job, Truman was widely viewed as honorable, down-to-earth, and self-confident. Most important of all, he had the ability to make difficult decisions and to accept full responsibility for their consequences. As the plaque on his White House desk read, "The Buck Stops Here." Truman faced two huge challenges: dealing with the rising threat of communism, as discussed in Chapter 26, and restoring the American economy to a strong footing after the war's end.

TRUMAN FACES STRIKES One economic problem that Truman had to address was strikes. Facing higher prices and lower wages, 4.5 million discontented workers, including steelworkers, coal miners, and railroad workers, went on strike in 1946. Although he generally supported organized labor, Truman refused to let strikes cripple the nation. He threatened to draft the striking workers and to order them as soldiers to stay on the job. He authorized the federal government to seize the mines, and he threatened to take control of the railroads as well. Truman appeared before Congress and asked for the authority to draft the striking railroad workers into the army. Before he could finish his speech, the unions gave in. **C**

"HAD ENOUGH?" Disgusted by shortages of goods, rising inflation, and labor strikes, Americans were ready for a change. The Republicans asked the public, "Had enough?" Voters gave their answer at the polls: in the 1946 congressional elections, the Republican Party won control of both the Senate and the House of Representatives for the first time since 1928. The new 80th Congress ignored Truman's domestic proposals. In 1947, Congress passed the Taft-Hartley Act over Truman's veto. This bill overturned many rights won by the unions under the New Deal.

Social Unrest Persists

Problems arose not only in the economy but in the very fabric of society. After World War II, a wave of racial violence erupted in the South. Many African Americans, particularly those who had served in the armed forces during the war, demanded their rights as citizens.

TRUMAN SUPPORTS CIVIL RIGHTS Truman put his presidency on the line for civil rights. "I am asking for equality of opportunity for all human beings," he said, ". . . and if that ends up in my failure to be reelected, that failure will be in a good cause." In 1946, Truman created a President's Commission on Civil Rights. Following the group's recommendations, Truman asked Congress for several measures including a federal antilynching law, a ban on the poll tax as a voting requirement, and a permanent civil rights commission.

Congress refused to pass these measures, or a measure to integrate the armed forces. As a result, Truman himself took action. In July 1948, he issued an executive order for integration of the armed forces, calling for "equality of treatment and opportunity in the armed forces without regard to race, color, religion, or national origin." In addition, he ordered an end to discrimination in the hiring of government employees. The Supreme Court also ruled that the lower courts could not bar

MAIN IDEA

Summarizing
C What actions did President Truman take to avert labor strikes?

Background
The drive for civil rights in the United States coincided with the debate over the UN's Universal Declaration of Human Rights. Many Southern senators were opposed to a human rights treaty because they did not want the UN to support African Americans in their struggle for rights.

Vocabulary
discrimination: treatment based on class or category rather than individual merit

HISTORICAL SPOTLIGHT

JACKIE ROBINSON
Jackie Robinson took a brave step when he turned the Brooklyn Dodgers into an integrated baseball team in 1947. But he—and the country—had a long way to go.

Unhappy fans hurled insults at Robinson from the stands. Some players on opposing teams tried to hit him with pitches or to injure him with the spikes on their shoes. He even received death threats. But he endured this with poise and restraint, saying,

"Plenty of times, I wanted to haul off when somebody insulted me for the color of my skin but I had to hold to myself. I knew I was kind of an experiment."

In 1949, Robinson was voted the National League's most valuable player. He later became the first African American to be inducted into the Baseball Hall of Fame.

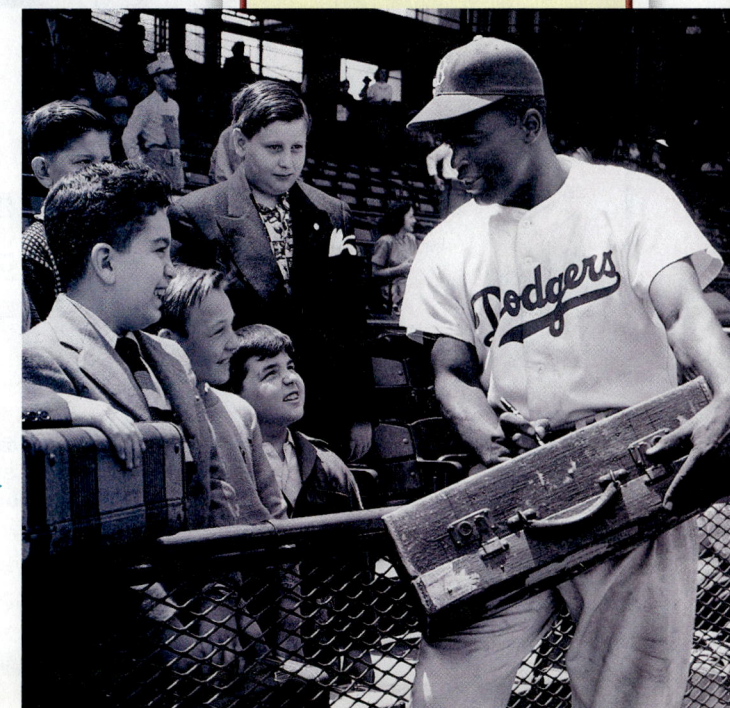

In 1947, Jackie Robinson joined the ▶ Brooklyn Dodgers, angering some fans but winning the hearts, and respect, of many others.

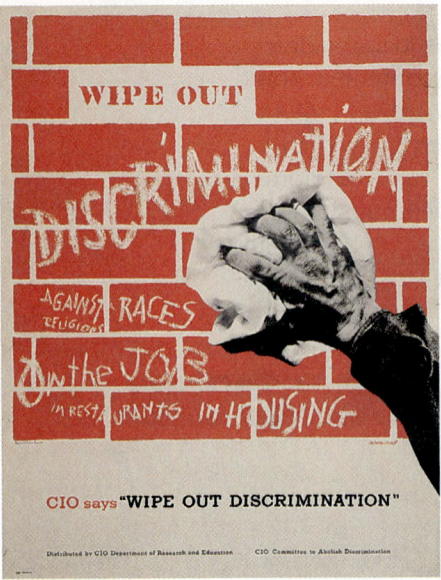

Wipe Out Discrimination (1949), a poster by Milton Ackoff, depicts the civil rights consciousness that angered the Dixiecrats.

African Americans from residential neighborhoods. These actions represented the beginnings of a federal commitment to dealing with racial issues. **D**

THE 1948 ELECTION Although many Americans blamed Truman for the nation's inflation and labor unrest, the Democrats nominated him for president in 1948. To protest Truman's emphasis on civil rights, a number of Southern Democrats—who became known as **Dixiecrats**—formed the States' Rights Democratic Party, and nominated their own presidential candidate, Governor J. Strom Thurmond of South Carolina. Discontent reigned at the far left of the Democratic spectrum as well. The former vice-president Henry A. Wallace led his supporters out of mainstream Democratic ranks to form a more liberal Progressive Party.

As the election approached, opinion polls gave the Republican candidate, New York Governor Thomas E. Dewey, a comfortable lead. Refusing to believe the polls, Truman poured his energy into the campaign. First, he called the Republican-dominated Congress into a special session. He challenged it to pass laws supporting such elements of the Democratic Party platform as public housing, federal aid to education, a higher minimum wage, and extended Social Security coverage. Not one of these laws was passed. He took his campaign to the people. He traveled from one end of the country to the other by train, speaking from the rear platform in a sweeping "whistlestop campaign." Day after day, people heard the president denounce the "do-nothing, 80th Congress."

STUNNING UPSET Truman's "Give 'em hell, Harry" campaign worked. He won the election in a close political upset. The Democrats gained control of Congress as well, even though they suffered losses in the South, which had been solidly Democratic since Reconstruction.

MAIN IDEA

Summarizing

D How did Truman use his executive power to advance civil rights?

Presidential Election of 1948

Truman surprised the newspapers by winning the 1948 election. ▶

Party	Candidate	Electoral Votes	Popular Votes
Democratic	Harry S. Truman	303	24,179,000
Republican	Thomas E. Dewey	189	21,991,000
States' Rights	J. Strom Thurmond	39	1,176,000
Progressive	Henry A. Wallace	—	1,157,000

Map electoral votes: 8, 6, 4, 3, 4, 4, 3, 25, 4, 4, 6, 4, 4, 23, 11, 3, 6, 8, 10, 9, 10, 12*, 9, 11, 12, 8, 12, 19, 10, 28, 13, 25, 15, 11, 8, 11, 14, 8, 35, 8, 16, 3, 47, 16, 4, 4, 3, 5

*Tennessee—11 electoral votes for Truman, 1 electoral vote for Thurmond

GEOGRAPHY SKILLBUILDER

1. **Region** In which regions of the country did Truman carry states? Dewey? Thurmond?
2. **Region** In which regions was support for Truman the weakest?

THE FAIR DEAL After his victory, Truman continued proposing an ambitious economic program. Truman's **Fair Deal,** an extension of Roosevelt's New Deal, included proposals for a nationwide system of compulsory health insurance and a crop-subsidy system to provide a steady income for farmers. In Congress, some Northern Democrats joined Dixiecrats and Republicans in defeating both measures.

In other instances, however, Truman's ideas prevailed. Congress raised the hourly minimum wage from 40 cents to 75 cents, extended Social Security coverage to about 10 million more people, and initiated flood control and irrigation projects. Congress also provided financial support for cities to clear out slums and build 810,000 housing units for low-income families. **E**

MAIN IDEA

Evaluating Leadership
E What were some of Truman's achievements as president?

Republicans Take the Middle Road

Despite these social and economic victories, Truman's approval rating sank to an all-time low of 23 percent in 1951. The stalemate in the Korean War and the rising tide of McCarthyism, which cast doubt on the loyalty of some federal employees, became overwhelming issues. Truman decided not to run for reelection. The Democrats nominated the intellectual and articulate governor Adlai Stevenson of Illinois to run against the Republican candidate, General Dwight D. Eisenhower, known popularly as "Ike."

I LIKE IKE! During the campaign, the Republicans accused the Democrats of "plunder at home and blunder abroad." To fan the anti-Communist hysteria that was sweeping over the country, Republicans raised the specter of the rise of communism in China and Eastern Europe. They also criticized the growing power of the federal government and the alleged bribery and corruption among Truman's political allies.

Eisenhower's campaign hit a snag, however, when newspapers accused his running mate, California Senator Richard M. Nixon, of profiting from a secret slush fund set up by wealthy supporters. Nixon decided to reply to the charges. In an emotional speech to an audience of 58 million, now known as the "Checkers speech," he exhibited masterful use of a new medium—television. Nixon denied any wrongdoing, but he did admit to accepting one gift from a political supporter.

► Campaign accessories expressed Ike's popularity and projected an upbeat political mood.

Tee up with "IKE"

SEE THAT YOUR CANDIDATE WINS! Only WEAR A PAIR AND SHOW YOUR FRIENDS

I LIKE IKE

Vocabulary
slush fund: a fund often designated for corrupt practices, such as bribery

▶ **A PERSONAL VOICE** RICHARD M. NIXON

" You know what it was? It was a little cocker spaniel dog in a crate, that he'd [the political supporter] sent all the way from Texas. Black and white spotted. And our little girl—Tricia, the six-year-old—named it Checkers. And you know the kids, like all kids, love the dog and I just want to say this right now, that regardless of what they say about it, we're going to keep it. "

—"Checkers speech," September 23, 1952

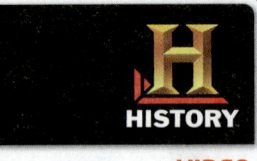

▲
Countering slush fund charges, Richard Nixon speaks to TV viewers about his daughters and their dog, Checkers.

VIDEO
Nixon's
Checkers Speech

hmhsocialstudies.com

Nixon's speech saved his place on the Republican ticket. In November 1952, Eisenhower won 55 percent of the popular vote and a majority of the electoral college votes, while the Republicans narrowly captured Congress.

WALKING THE MIDDLE OF THE ROAD
President Eisenhower's style of governing differed from that of the Democrats. His approach, which he called "dynamic conservatism," was also known as "Modern Republicanism." He called for government to be "conservative when it comes to money and liberal when it comes to human beings."

Eisenhower followed a middle-of-the-road course and avoided many controversial issues, but he could not completely sidestep a persistent domestic issue—civil rights—that gained national attention due to court rulings and acts of civil disobedience in the mid-1950s. The most significant judicial action occurred in 1954, when the Supreme Court ruled in *Brown* v. *Board of Education of Topeka* that public schools must be racially integrated. (See page 914.) In a landmark act of civil disobedience a year later, a black seamstress named Rosa Parks refused to give up her seat on a bus to a white man. Her arrest sparked a boycott of the entire Montgomery, Alabama, bus system. The civil rights movement had entered a new era.

Although Eisenhower did not assume leadership on civil rights issues, he accomplished much on the domestic scene. Shortly after becoming president, Eisenhower pressed hard for programs that would bring around a balanced budget and a cut in taxes. During his two terms, Ike's administration raised the minimum wage, extended Social Security and unemployment benefits, increased funding for public housing, and backed the creation of interstate highways and the Department of Health, Education, and Welfare. His popularity soared, and he won reelection in 1956.

SECTION 1 ASSESSMENT

1. **TERMS & NAMES** For each term or name, write a sentence explaining its significance.
   - •GI Bill of Rights
   - •Harry S. Truman
   - •Dixiecrat
   - •Fair Deal
   - •suburb

MAIN IDEA

2. **TAKING NOTES**
   Create a time line of key events relating to postwar America. Use the dates below as a guide.

   1946 1947 1948 1949   1952

   Write a paragraph describing the effects of one of these events.

CRITICAL THINKING

3. **DRAWING CONCLUSIONS**
   Do you think Eisenhower's actions reflected his philosophy of dynamic conservatism? Why or why not?
   Think About:
   - the definition of dynamic conservatism
   - Eisenhower's actions on civil rights policies
   - Eisenhower's accomplishments on other domestic issues

4. **EVALUATING LEADERSHIP**
   Why do you think most Americans went along with Eisenhower's conservative approach to domestic policy?

5. **CONTRASTING**
   How did Presidents Truman and Eisenhower differ regarding civil rights?

CC Unit 1.I.D.5.b   CC Unit 7.I.A.2
CC Unit 7.I.A.5   CC Unit 7.II.D.1.a
PI 4.1   CC Unit 7.II.D.1.c   CC Unit 7.II.D.2.a

The American Dream in the Fifties

MAIN IDEA	WHY IT MATTERS NOW	Terms & Names
During the 1950s, the economy boomed, and many Americans enjoyed material comfort.	The "American dream," a notion that was largely shaped by the 1950s, is still pursued today.	• conglomerate • consumerism • franchise • planned • baby boom obsolescence • Dr. Jonas Salk

One American's Story

hmhsocialstudies.com
TAKING NOTES
Use the graphic organizer online to take notes on the American dream in the 1950s.

Settled into her brand new house near San Diego, California, Carol Freeman felt very fortunate. Her husband Mark had his own law practice, and when their first baby was born, she became a full-time homemaker. She was living the American dream, yet Carol felt dissatisfied—as if there were "something wrong" with her because she was not happy.

A PERSONAL VOICE CAROL FREEMAN

" As dissatisfied as I was, and as restless, I remember so well this feeling [we] had at the time that the world was going to be your oyster. You were going to make money, your kids were going to go to good schools, everything was possible if you just did what you were supposed to do. The future was rosy. There was a tremendous feeling of optimism. . . . Much as I say it was hateful, it was also hopeful. It was an innocent time. "

—quoted in *The Fifties: A Women's Oral History*

After World War II ended, Americans turned their attention to their families and jobs. The economy prospered. New technologies and business ideas created fresh opportunities for many, and by the end of the decade Americans were enjoying the highest standard of living in the world. The American dream of a happy and successful life seemed within the reach of many people.

▲ The dream woman of the 1950s was depicted in advertising and on TV as doing constant housework, but always with a smile.

The Organization and the Organization Man

During the 1950s, businesses expanded rapidly. By 1956, the majority of Americans no longer held blue-collar, or industrial, jobs. Instead, more people worked in higher-paid, white-collar positions—clerical, managerial, or professional occupations. Unlike blue-collar workers, who manufactured goods for sale, white-collar workers tended to perform services in fields like sales, advertising, insurance, and communications.

CONGLOMERATES Many white-collar workers performed their services in large corporations or government agencies. Some of these corporations continued expanding by forming **conglomerates**. (A conglomerate is a major corporation that includes a number of smaller companies in unrelated industries.) For example, one conglomerate, International Telephone and Telegraph (ITT), whose original business was communications, bought car-rental companies, insurance companies, and hotel and motel chains. Through this diversification, or investment in various areas of the economy, ITT tried to protect itself from declines in individual industries. Other huge parent companies included American Telephone and Telegraph, Xerox, and General Electric.

FRANCHISES In addition to diversifying, another strategy for business expansion—franchising—developed at this time. A **franchise** is a company that offers similar products or services in many locations. (*Franchise* is also used to refer to the right, sold to an individual, to do business using the parent company's name and the system that the parent company developed.) **A**

Fast-food restaurants developed some of the first and most successful franchises. McDonald's, for example, had its start when the McDonald brothers developed unusually efficient service, based on assembly-line methods, at their small drive-in restaurant in San Bernardino, California. They simplified the menu, featured 15-cent hamburgers, and mechanized their kitchen.

Salesman Ray Kroc paid the McDonalds $2.7 million for the franchise rights to their hamburger drive-in. In April 1955, he opened his first McDonald's restaurant in Des Plaines, Illinois, where he further improved the assembly-line process and introduced the trademark arches that are now familiar all over the world.

MAIN IDEA

Comparing
A How were conglomerates and franchises alike and how were they different?

NOW & THEN

FRANCHISES

In the decades since Ray Kroc opened his first McDonald's restaurant (shown below), franchising has become all but a way of life in the United States. Today, nearly 3,000 franchised companies operate over 500,000 businesses throughout the country. Officials estimate that franchises account for nearly one-third of all U.S. retail sales. American franchises today provide a wide array of goods and services, from car maintenance, to tax services, to hair care.

In an attempt to tap into the international market, hundreds of U.S. companies have established overseas franchises. The franchise with perhaps the greatest global reach is the one that started it all. In addition to its more than 13,000 U.S. franchises, McDonald's now operates over 18,600 franchises in dozens of countries around the world.

A PERSONAL VOICE RAY KROC

" It requires a certain kind of mind to see the beauty in a hamburger bun. Yet is it any more unusual to find grace in the texture and softly curved silhouette of a bun than to reflect lovingly on the . . . arrangements and textures and colors in a butterfly's wings? . . . Not if you view the bun as an essential material in the art of serving a great many meals fast. "

—quoted in *The Fifties*

SOCIAL CONFORMITY While franchises like McDonald's helped standardize what people ate, some American workers found themselves becoming standardized as well. Employees who were well paid and held secure jobs in thriving companies sometimes paid a price for economic advancement: a loss of their individuality. In general, businesses did not want creative thinkers, rebels, or anyone who would rock the corporate boat.

In *The Organization Man*, a book based on a classic 1956 study of suburban Park Forest, Illinois, and other communities, William H. Whyte described how the new, large organizations created "company people." Companies would give personality tests to people applying for jobs to make sure they would "fit in" the corporate culture. Companies rewarded employees for teamwork, cooperation, and loyalty and so contributed to the growth of conformity, which Whyte called "belongingness." Despite their success, a number of workers questioned whether pursuing the American dream exacted too high a price, as conformity replaced individuality. **B**

MAIN IDEA

Analyzing Effects

B What effects did the climate in many corporations have on some workers?

The Suburban Lifestyle

Though achieving job security did take a psychological toll on some Americans who resented having to repress their own personalities, it also enabled people to provide their families with the so-called good things in life. Most Americans worked in cities, but fewer and fewer of them lived there. New highways and the availability and affordability of automobiles and gasoline made commuting possible. By the early 1960s, every large city in the United States was surrounded by suburbs. Of the 13 million new homes built in the 1950s, 85 percent were built in the suburbs. For many people, the suburbs embodied the American dream of an affordable single-family house, good schools, a safe, healthy environment for children, and congenial neighbors just like themselves.

The "organization man" had to step lively to keep up with the Joneses.

THE BABY BOOM As soldiers returned from World War II and settled into family life, they contributed to an unprecedented population explosion known as the **baby boom.** During the late 1940s and through the early 1960s, the birthrate (number of live births per 1,000 people) in the United States soared. At the height of the baby boom, in 1957, one American infant was born every seven seconds—a total of 4,308,000 that year. The result was the largest generation in the nation's history.

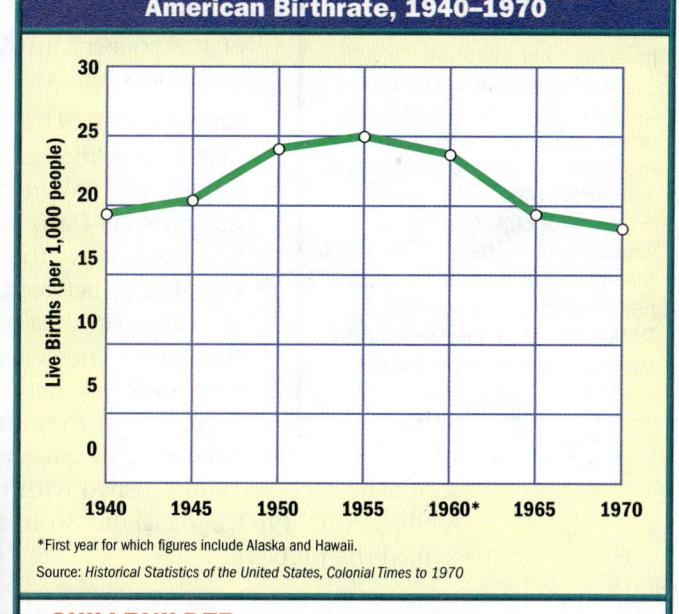

American Birthrate, 1940–1970

Live Births (per 1,000 people)

*First year for which figures include Alaska and Hawaii.

Source: *Historical Statistics of the United States, Colonial Times to 1970*

SKILLBUILDER Interpreting Graphs
1. What was the overall trend in the birthrate at the start of World War II, and after the war ended?
2. What was the difference in the birthrate between 1960 and 1970?

◀ Some of the 40 million new Americans who were born during the baby boom.

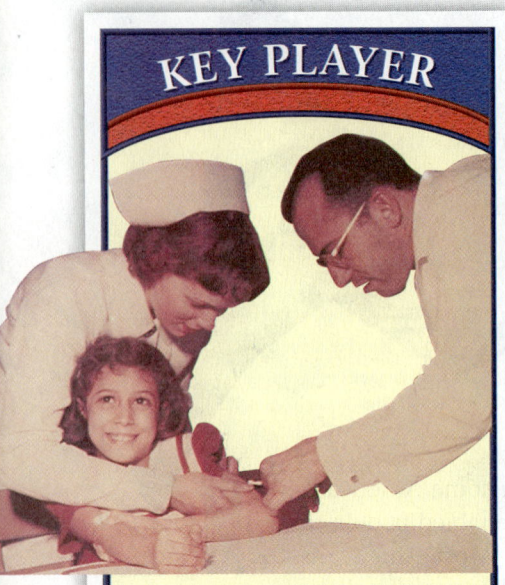
Contributing to the size of the baby-boom generation were many factors, including: reunion of husbands and wives after the war, decreasing marriage age, desirability of large families, confidence in continued economic prosperity, and advances in medicine.

ADVANCES IN MEDICINE AND CHILDCARE Among the medical advances that saved hundreds of thousands of children's lives was the discovery of drugs to fight and prevent childhood diseases, such as typhoid fever. Another breakthrough came when **Dr. Jonas Salk** developed a vaccine for the crippling disease poliomyelitis—polio.

Many parents raised their children according to guidelines devised by the author and pediatrician Dr. Benjamin Spock. His *Common Sense Book of Baby and Child Care*, published in 1946, sold nearly 10 million copies during the 1950s. In it, he advised parents not to spank or scold their children. He also encouraged families to hold meetings in which children could express themselves. He considered it so important for mothers to be at home with their children that he proposed having the government pay mothers to stay home.

The baby boom had a tremendous impact not only on child care but on the American economy and the educational system as well. In 1958, toy sales alone reached $1.25 billion. During the decade, 10 million new students entered the elementary schools. The sharp increase in enrollment caused overcrowding and teacher shortages in many parts of the country. In California, a new school opened every seven days. **C**

WOMEN'S ROLES During the 1950s, the role of homemaker and mother was glorified in popular magazines, movies, and TV programs such as *Father Knows Best* and *The Adventures of Ozzie and Harriet*. *Time* magazine described the homemaker as "the key figure in all suburbia, the thread that weaves between family and community—the keeper of the suburban dream." In contrast to the ideal portrayed in the media, however, some women, like Carol Freeman, who spoke of her discontentment, were not happy with their roles; they felt isolated, bored, and unfulfilled. According to one survey in the 1950s, more than one-fifth of suburban wives were dissatisfied with their lives. Betty Friedan, author of the groundbreaking 1963 book about women and society, *The Feminine Mystique*, described the problem.

MAIN IDEA

Analyzing Effects
C How did the baby boom affect American life in the 1950s?

Background
The percentage of women college students in the 1950s was smaller than in the 1920s.

A PERSONAL VOICE BETTY FRIEDAN

"For the first time in their history, women are becoming aware of an identity crisis in their own lives, a crisis which . . . has grown worse with each succeeding generation. . . . I think this is the crisis of women growing up—a turning point from an immaturity that has been called femininity to full human identity."

—*The Feminine Mystique*

The number of women working outside the home rose steadily during the decade. By 1960, almost 40 percent of mothers with children between ages 6 and 17 held paying jobs.

But having a job didn't necessarily contribute to a woman's happiness. A woman's career opportunities tended to be limited to fields such as nursing, teaching, and office support, which paid less than other professional and business positions did. Women also earned less than men for comparable work. Although increasing numbers of women attended four-year colleges, they generally received little financial, academic, or psychological encouragement to pursue their goals. **D**

MAIN IDEA

Contrasting

D How did women's roles and opportunities in the 1950s differ from women's roles today?

LEISURE IN THE FIFTIES Most Americans of the 1950s had more leisure time than ever before. Employees worked a 40-hour week and earned several weeks' vacation per year. People owned more labor-saving devices, such as washing machines, clothes dryers, dishwashers, and power lawn mowers, which allowed more time for leisure activities. *Fortune* magazine reported that, in 1953, Americans spent more than $30 billion on leisure goods and activities.

Americans also enjoyed a wide variety of recreational pursuits—both active and passive. Millions of people participated in such sports as fishing, bowling, hunting, boating, and golf. More fans than ever attended baseball, basketball, and football games; others watched professional sports on television.

Americans also became avid readers. They devoured books about cooking, religion, do-it-yourself projects, and homemaking. They also read mysteries, romance novels, and fiction by popular writers such as Ernest Hemingway, John Steinbeck, Daphne du Maurier, and J. D. Salinger. Book sales doubled, due in part to a thriving paperback market. The circulation of popular magazines like *Reader's Digest* and *Sports Illustrated* steadily rose, from about 148 million to more than 190 million readers. Sales of comic books also reached a peak in the mid-1950s.

History Through *Art*

AFTER THE PROM (1957)

The artist, Norman Rockwell, chose an innocent junior-high couple to illustrate the easy emotions and the ordinary events of postwar America. **What does this painting convey about life in the 1950s?**

▶ 3-D comics and 3-D movies were two of the many fads that mesmerized the nation in the 1950s.

The Automobile Culture

During World War II, the U.S. government had rationed gasoline to curb inflation and conserve supplies. After the war, however, an abundance of both imported and domestically produced petroleum—the raw material from which gasoline is made—led to inexpensive, plentiful fuel for consumers. Easy credit terms and extensive advertising persuaded Americans to buy cars in record numbers. In response, new car sales rose from 6.7 million in 1950 to 7.9 million in 1955. The total number of private cars on the road jumped from 40 million in 1950 to over 60 million in 1960.

AUTOMANIA Suburban living made owning a car a necessity. Most of the new suburbs, built in formerly rural areas, did not offer public transportation, and people had to drive to their jobs in the cities. In addition, many of the schools, stores, synagogues, churches, and doctors' and dentists' offices were not within walking distance of suburban homes. **E**

THE INTERSTATE HIGHWAY SYSTEM The more cars there were, the more roads were needed. "Automania" spurred local and state governments to construct roads linking the major cities while connecting schools, shopping centers, and workplaces to residential suburbs. The Interstate Highway Act, which President Eisenhower signed in 1956, authorized the building of a nationwide highway network—41,000 miles of expressways. The new roads, in turn, encouraged the development of new suburbs farther from the cities.

Interstate highways also made high-speed, long-haul trucking possible, which contributed to a decline in the commercial use of railroads. Towns along the new highways prospered, while towns along the older, smaller roads experienced hard times. The system of highways also helped unify and homogenize the nation. As John Keats observed in his 1958 book, *The Insolent Chariots,* "Our new roads, with their ancillaries, the motels, filling stations, and restaurants advertising Eats, have made it possible for you to drive from Brooklyn to Los Angeles without a change of diet, scenery, or culture." With access to cars, affordable gas, and new highways, more and more Americans hit the road. They flocked to mountains, lakes, national parks, historic sites, and amusement parks for family vacations. Disneyland, which opened in California in July 1955, attracted 3 million visitors the next year.

MOBILITY TAKES ITS TOLL As the automobile industry boomed, it stimulated production and provided jobs in other areas, such as drive-in movies, restaurants, and shopping malls. Yet cars also created new problems for both society and the environment. Noise and exhaust polluted the air. Automobile accidents claimed more lives every year. Traffic jams raised people's stress levels, and heavy use damaged the roads. Because cars made it possible for Americans to live in suburbs, many upper-class and middle-class whites left the crowded cities. Jobs and businesses eventually followed them to the suburbs. Public transportation declined, and poor people in the inner cities were often left without jobs and vital services. As a result, the economic gulf between suburban and urban dwellers and between the middle class and the poor widened. **F**

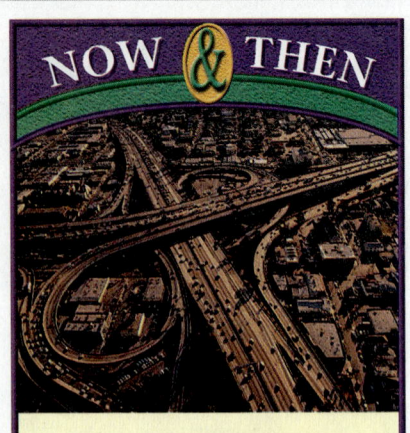

NOW & THEN

SOUTHERN CALIFORNIA AND THE AUTOMOBILE

No state has exemplified automania in the U.S. more than California. By the late 1990s, Californians owned more cars, held more driver's licenses, and traveled more miles on their roads than the people of any other state. The center of this automobile culture is the metropolitan area of Los Angeles.

Contributing to the importance of the automobile is Southern California's suburban lifestyle. This dependence on cars has contributed to problems of air pollution and traffic jams. But, California is addressing these problems by reviving public transportation systems and promoting the use of electric cars that produce no pollution.

MAIN IDEA

Analyzing Causes
E Why did auto sales surge in the 1950s?

Vocabulary
homogenize: to make the same or similar

MAIN IDEA

Analyzing Effects
F What positive and negative effects did the mass availability of the automobile have on American life in the 1950s?

Americans Hit the Road

In the 1950s Americans loved their cars—big, powerful, and flashy. Some car owners spent their leisure time maintaining their automobiles for the daily commute to work or for the annual family vacation on any one of the nation's 22 new interstate highways.

▲ The Drive-Thru

Fast-food restaurants catered to the car culture by offering drive-up service. Waitresses wearing fancy uniforms or roller skates added to the fun of front-seat dining.

▲ The Drive-In

Young suburban families piled into their cars to see a movie at one of the country's 5,000 or so drive-in theaters.

Car Ads ▶

Not just for transport, cars were marketed for fashion and fun. Car ads used words like "fresh" and "frisky."

◀ Cruising Teens

Often teenagers drove around familiar neighborhoods ending up at popular teen meeting places to see and be seen.

Consumerism Unbound

By the mid-1950s, nearly 60 percent of Americans were members of the middle class, about twice as many as before World War II. They wanted, and had the money to buy, increasing numbers of products. **Consumerism,** buying material goods, came to be equated with success.

NEW PRODUCTS One new product after another appeared in the marketplace, as various industries responded to consumer demand. *Newsweek* magazine reported in 1956 that "hundreds of brand-new goods have become commonplace overnight." Consumers purchased electric household appliances—such as washing machines, dryers, blenders, freezers, and dishwashers—in record numbers.

With more and more leisure time to fill, people invested in recreational items. They bought televisions, tape recorders, and the new hi-fi (high-fidelity) record players. They bought casual clothing to suit their suburban lifestyles and power lawn mowers, barbecue grills, swimming pools, and lawn decorations for their suburban homes.

PLANNED OBSOLESCENCE In addition to creating new products, manufacturers began using a marketing strategy called **planned obsolescence.** In order to encourage consumers to purchase more goods, manufacturers purposely designed products to become obsolete—that is, to wear out or become outdated—in a short period of time. Carmakers brought out new models every year, urging consumers to stay up-to-date. Because of planned obsolescence, Americans came to expect new and better products, and they began to discard items that were sometimes barely used. Some observers commented that American culture was on its way to becoming a "throwaway society." **G**

BUY NOW, PAY LATER Many consumers made their purchases on credit and therefore did not have to pay for them right away. The Diner's Club issued the first credit card in 1950, and the American Express card was introduced in 1958. In addition, people bought large items on the installment plan and made regular payments over a fixed time. Home mortgages (loans for buying a house) and automobile loans worked the same way. During the decade, the total private debt grew from $73 billion to $179 billion. Instead of saving money, Americans were spending it, confident that prosperity would continue.

THE ADVERTISING AGE The advertising industry capitalized on this runaway consumerism by encouraging even more spending. Ads were everywhere—in newspapers and magazines, on radio and television, and on billboards along the

Now! In a full console at only $299.95*, Zenith's revolutionary
Top Tuning

How does your kitchen rate on the electrical living scale?

LIVE BETTER ...Electrically

In the 1950s, advertisers made "keeping up with the Joneses" a way of life for consumers.

MAIN IDEA

Analyzing Causes
G How did manufacturers influence Americans to become a "throwaway society"?

highways—prompting people to buy goods that ranged from cars to cereals to cigarettes. Advertisers spent about $6 billion in 1950; by 1955, the figure was up to $9 billion. Since most Americans had satisfied their basic needs, advertisers tried to convince them to buy things they really didn't need.

★ **A PERSONAL VOICE** VANCE PACKARD

" On May 18, 1956, *The New York Times* printed a remarkable interview with a young man named Gerald Stahl, executive vice-president of the Package Designers Council. He stated: 'Psychiatrists say that people have so much to choose from that they want help—they will like the package that hypnotizes them into picking it.' He urged food packers to put more hypnosis into their package designing, so that the housewife will stick out her hand for it rather than one of many rivals.

Mr. Stahl has found that it takes the average woman exactly twenty seconds to cover an aisle in a supermarket if she doesn't tarry; so a good package design should hypnotize the woman like a flashlight waved in front of her eyes. "

—*The Hidden Persuaders*

More and more, ad executives and designers turned to psychology to create new strategies for selling. Advertisers appealed to people's desire for status and "belongingness" and strived to associate their products with those values.

Television became a powerful new advertising tool. The first one-minute TV commercial was produced in 1941 at a cost of $9. In 1960, advertisers spent a total of $1.6 billion for television ads. By 2001, a 30-second commercial during the Superbowl cost an advertiser $2.2 million. Television had become not only the medium for mass transmission of cultural values, but a symbol of popular culture itself.

SECTION 2 ASSESSMENT

1. **TERMS & NAMES** For each term or name, write a sentence explaining its significance.
   - conglomerate
   - franchise
   - baby boom
   - Dr. Jonas Salk
   - consumerism
   - planned obsolescence

MAIN IDEA

2. **TAKING NOTES**
   In a graphic organizer like the one below, list examples of specific goals that characterized the American dream for suburbanites in the 1950s.

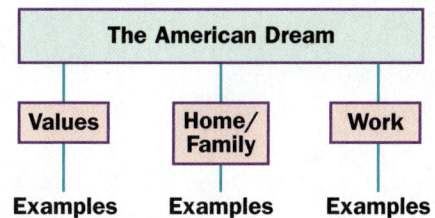

The American Dream

Values | Home/Family | Work

Examples | Examples | Examples

What do you think the most important goal was?

CRITICAL THINKING

3. **ANALYZING EFFECTS**
   In what ways do you think current environmental consciousness is related to the "throwaway society" of the 1950s? Support your answer.
   Think About:
   - the purchasing habits of 1950s consumers
   - the effects of planned obsolescence
   - today's emphasis on recycling

4. **EVALUATING**
   Do you think that the life of a typical suburban homemaker during the 1950s was fulfilling or not? Support your answer.

THE FINAL FROST BARRIER!

5. **INTERPRETING VISUAL SOURCES**
   This ad is typical of how the advertising industry portrayed housewives in the 1950s. What message about women is conveyed by this ad?

The Road to Suburbia

"Come out to Park Forest where small-town friendships grow—and you still live so close to a big city." Advertisements like this one for a scientifically planned Chicago suburb captured the lure of the suburbs for thousands of growing families in the 1950s. The publicity promised affordable housing, congenial neighbors, fresh air and open spaces, good schools, and easy access to urban jobs and culture. Good transportation was the lifeline of suburban growth a half century ago, and it continues to spur expansion today.

PROPOSED PLAN ... VILLAGE OF PARK FOREST, ILLINOIS

Chicagoland's **COMPLETELY PLANNED** *Suburb*

SHARED PRIVACY ▶

By 1952, development in Park Forest, Illinois had expanded to include both low-cost rental units and single-family homes. All the streets were curved to slow traffic, present a pleasing sweep of space, and give residents maximum privacy and space for yards.

1 WHERE THE 'BURBS ARE

Park Forest was planned from its conception in 1945 to be a "complete community for middle-income families with children." The setting was rural—amidst cornfields and forest preserves about 30 miles south of Chicago. But it was convenient to commuter lines, like the Illinois Central (IC) Railroad, and to major roads, such as Western Avenue.

2 THE COMMUTER CRUSH

Men commuted to work on the IC railroad, while their wives usually stayed home to take care of the children, who thrived in Park Forest's safe, wholesome family environment.

3 SHOPPING CENTERS

Consumerism became a driving force in the 1950s, and Park Forest kept up with the trend. The central shopping center served the community well until the late 1960s. When Interstate 57 was built, a mammoth mall, built just off the highway, caused the original shopping area to decline. Park Forest is still struggling to revive its central shopping area.

THINKING CRITICALLY

1. **Analyzing Patterns** How did the availability of transportation influence the creation and ongoing development of Park Forest?

2. **Creating a Database** Pose a historical question about a suburb near you. Collect statistics about changes in population, living patterns, income, and economic development in that suburb. Use those statistics to create a database that will help answer your questions.

SEE SKILLBUILDER HANDBOOK, PAGE R33.

  hmhsocialstudies.com RESEARCH WEB LINKS

PI 2.3
PI 4.1   CC Unit 7.II.D.1.a

Popular Culture

MAIN IDEA	WHY IT MATTERS NOW	Terms & Names
Mainstream Americans, as well as the nation's subcultures, embraced new forms of entertainment during the 1950s.	Television and rock 'n' roll, integral parts of the nation's culture today, emerged during the postwar era.	• mass media • Federal Communications Commission (FCC) • beat movement • rock 'n' roll • jazz

One American's Story

H. B. Barnum, a 14-year-old saxophone player who later became a music producer, was one of many teenagers in the 1950s drawn to a new style of music that featured hard-driving African-American rhythm and blues. Barnum described the first time he saw the rhythm-and-blues performer Richard Wayne Penniman, better known as Little Richard.

A PERSONAL VOICE H. B. BARNUM

" He'd just burst onto the stage from anywhere, and you wouldn't be able to hear anything but the roar of the audience. . . . He'd be on the stage, he'd be off the stage, he'd be jumping and yelling, screaming, whipping the audience on. . . . Then when he finally did hit the piano and just went into di-di-di-di-di-di-di, you know, well nobody can do that as fast as Richard. It just took everybody by surprise. "

—quoted in *The Rise and Fall of Popular Music*

Born poor, Little Richard wore flashy clothes on stage, curled his hair, and shouted the lyrics to his songs. As one writer observed, "In two minutes [he] used as much energy as an all-night party." The music he and others performed became a prominent part of the American culture in the 1950s, a time when both mainstream America and those outside it embraced new and innovative forms of entertainment.

▲ **Little Richard helped change rhythm and blues into a new musical genre—rock 'n' roll.**

New Era of the Mass Media

Compared with other **mass media**—means of communication that reach large audiences—television developed with lightning speed. First widely available in 1948, television had reached 9 percent of American homes by 1950 and 55 percent of homes by 1954. In 1960, almost 90 percent—45 million—of American homes had television sets. Clearly, TV was the entertainment and information marvel of the postwar years.

THE RISE OF TELEVISION Early television sets were small boxes with round screens. Programming was meager, and broadcasts were in black and white. The first regular broadcasts, beginning in 1949, reached only a small part of the East Coast and offered only two hours of programs per week. Post–World War II innovations such as microwave relays, which could transmit television waves over long distances, sent the television industry soaring. By 1956, the **Federal Communications Commission (FCC)**—the government agency that regulates and licenses television, telephone, telegraph, radio, and other communications industries—had allowed 500 new stations to broadcast.

This period of rapid expansion was the "golden age" of television entertainment—and entertainment in the 1950s often meant comedy. Milton Berle attracted huge audiences with *The Texaco Star Theater,* and Lucille Ball and Desi Arnaz's early situation comedy, *I Love Lucy*, began its enormously popular run in 1951.

At the same time, veteran radio broadcaster Edward R. Murrow introduced two innovations: on-the-scene news reporting, with his program, *See It Now* (1951–1958), and interviewing, with *Person to Person* (1953–1960). Westerns, sports events, and original dramas shown on *Playhouse 90* and *Studio One* offered entertainment variety. Children's programs, such as *The Mickey Mouse Club* and *The Howdy Doody Show*, attracted loyal young fans.

American businesses took advantage of the opportunities offered by the new television industry. Advertising expenditures on TV, which were $170 million in 1950, reached nearly $2 billion in 1960.

Sales of *TV Guide*, introduced in 1953, quickly outpaced sales of other magazines. In 1954, the food industry introduced a new convenience item, the frozen TV dinner. Complete, ready-to-heat individual meals on disposable aluminum trays, TV dinners made it easy for people to eat without missing their favorite shows. **Ⓐ**

MAIN IDEA

Analyzing Effects

Ⓐ How did the emergence of television affect American culture in the 1950s?

HISTORICAL SPOTLIGHT

TV QUIZ SHOWS

Beginning with *The $64,000 Question* in 1955, television created hit quiz shows by adopting a popular format from radio and adding big cash prizes.

The quiz show *Twenty-One* made a star of a shy English professor named Charles Van Doren. He rode a wave of fame and fortune until 1958, when a former contestant revealed that, to heighten the dramatic impact, producers had been giving some of the contestants the right answers.

A scandal followed when a congressional subcommittee confirmed the charges. Most of the quiz shows soon left the air.

Glued to the Set

Households with TV Sets, 1950–2000

Source: Nielsen Media Research, 2000

Average Daily Hours of TV Viewing, 1950–2000

Source: Nielsen Media Research, 2007

SKILLBUILDER Interpreting Graphs
1. During which decade did the number of households with TV sets increase the most?
2. During what period did TV viewing decline?

STEREOTYPES AND GUNSLINGERS Not everyone was thrilled with television, though. Critics objected to its effects on children and its stereotypical portrayal of women and minorities. Women did, in fact, appear in stereotypical roles, such as the ideal mothers of *Father Knows Best* and *The Adventures of Ozzie and Harriet*. Male characters outnumbered women characters three to one. African Americans and Latinos rarely appeared in television programs at all.

Television in the 1950s portrayed an idealized white America. For the most part, it omitted references to poverty, diversity, and contemporary conflicts, such as the struggle of the civil rights movement against racial discrimination. Instead, it glorified the historical conflicts of the Western frontier in hit shows such as *Gunsmoke* and *Have Gun Will Travel*. The level of violence in these popular shows led to ongoing concerns about the effect of television on children. In 1961, Federal Communications Commission chairman Newton Minow voiced this concern to the leaders of the television industry.

▲
Lucille Ball had to fight to have her real-life husband, Cuban-born Desi Arnaz, cast in the popular TV series *I Love Lucy.*

A PERSONAL VOICE NEWTON MINOW

" When television is bad, nothing is worse. I invite you to sit down in front of your television set when your station goes on the air . . . and keep your eyes glued to that set until the station signs off. I can assure you that you will observe a vast wasteland. " **B**

—speech to the National Association of Broadcasters, Washington, D.C., May 9, 1961

RADIO AND MOVIES Although TV turned out to be wildly popular, radio and movies survived. But instead of competing with television's mass market for drama and variety shows, radio stations turned to local programming of news, weather, music, and community issues. The strategy paid off. During the decade, radio advertising rose by 35 percent, and the number of radio stations increased by 50 percent.

From the beginning, television cut into the profitable movie market. In 1948, 18,500 movie theaters had drawn nearly 90 million paid admissions per week. As more people stayed home to watch TV, the number of moviegoers decreased by nearly half. As early as 1951, producer David Selznick worried about Hollywood: "It'll never come back. It'll just keep on crumbling until finally the wind blows the last studio prop across the sands."

But Hollywood did not crumble and blow away. Instead, it capitalized on the advantages that movies still held over television—size, color, and stereophonic sound. Stereophonic sound, which surrounded the viewer, was introduced in 1952. By 1954, more than 50 percent of movies were in color. By contrast, color television, which became available that year, did not become widespread until the

James Dean, seen here in the movie *Giant*, had a self-confident indifference that made him the idol of teenagers. He died in a car accident at age 24.
▼

MAIN IDEA

Summarizing

C How did radio and movies maintain their appeal in the 1950s?

next decade. In 1953, 20th Century Fox introduced CinemaScope, which projected a wide-angle image on a broad screen. The industry also tried novelty features: Smell-O-Vision and Aroma-Rama piped smells into the theaters to coincide with events shown on the screen. Three-dimensional images, viewed through special glasses supplied by the theaters, appeared to leap into the audience. **C**

A Subculture Emerges

Although the mass media found a wide audience for their portrayals of mostly white popular culture, dissenting voices rang out throughout the 1950s. The messages of the beat movement in literature, and of rock 'n' roll in music, clashed with the tidy suburban view of life and set the stage for the counterculture that would burst forth in the late 1960s.

THE BEAT MOVEMENT Centered in San Francisco, Los Angeles, and New York City's Greenwich Village, the **beat movement** expressed the social and literary nonconformity of artists, poets, and writers. The word *beat* originally meant "weary" but came to refer as well to a musical beat.

Followers of this movement, called beats or beatniks, lived nonconformist lives. They tended to shun regular work and sought a higher consciousness through Zen Buddhism, music, and, sometimes, drugs.

Many beat poets and writers believed in imposing as little structure as possible on their artistic works, which often had a free, open form. They read their poetry aloud in coffeehouses and other gathering places. Works that capture the essence of this era include Allen Ginsberg's long, free-verse poem, *Howl*, published in 1956, and Jack Kerouac's novel of the movement, *On the Road*, published in 1957. This novel describes a nomadic search across America for authentic experiences, people, and values.

★ **A PERSONAL VOICE** JACK KEROUAC

" [T]he only people for me are the mad ones, the ones who are mad to live, mad to talk, mad to be saved . . . the ones who never yawn or say a commonplace thing, but burn, burn, burn like fabulous yellow roman candles exploding like spiders across the stars. "

—*On the Road*

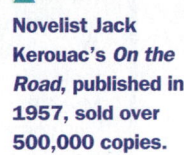

▲
Novelist Jack Kerouac's *On the Road*, published in 1957, sold over 500,000 copies.

MAIN IDEA

Analyzing Causes

D Why do you think many young Americans were attracted to the beat movement?

Many mainstream Americans found this lifestyle less enchanting. *Look* magazine proclaimed, "There's nothing really new about the beat philosophy. It consists merely of the average American's value scale—turned inside out. The goals of the Beat are *not* watching TV, *not* wearing gray flannel, *not* owning a home in the suburbs, and especially—*not* working." Nonetheless, the beatnik attitudes, way of life, and literature attracted the attention of the media and fired the imaginations of many college students. **D**

African Americans and Rock 'n' Roll

While beats expressed themselves in unstructured literature, musicians in the 1950s added electronic instruments to traditional blues music, creating rhythm and blues. In 1951, a Cleveland, Ohio, radio disc jockey named Alan Freed was among the first to play the music. This audience was mostly white but the music usually was produced by African-American musicians. Freed's listeners responded enthusiastically, and Freed began promoting the new music that grew out of rhythm and blues and country and pop. He called the music **rock 'n' roll**, a name that has come to mean music that's both black and white—music that is American.

▲ Chuck Berry is as much known for his "duck walk" as for his electric guitar-playing heard on hit records including "Johnny B. Goode" and "Maybellene."

ROCK 'N' ROLL In the early and mid-1950s, Richard Penniman, Chuck Berry, Bill Haley and His Comets, and especially Elvis Presley brought rock 'n' roll to a frantic pitch of popularity among the newly affluent teens who bought their records. The music's heavy rhythm, simple melodies, and lyrics—featuring love, cars, and the problems of being young—captivated teenagers across the country.

Elvis Presley, the unofficial "King of Rock 'n' Roll," first developed his musical style by singing in church and listening to gospel, country, and blues music on the radio in Memphis, Tennessee. When he was a young boy, his mother gave him a guitar, and years later he paid four dollars of his own money to record two songs in 1953. Sam Phillips, a rhythm-and-blues producer, discovered Presley and produced his first records. In 1955, Phillips sold Presley's contract to RCA for $35,000.

Presley's live appearances were immensely popular, and 45 of his records sold over a million copies, including "Heartbreak Hotel," "Hound Dog," "All Shook Up," "Don't Be Cruel," and "Burning Love." Although *Look* magazine dismissed him as "a wild troubadour who wails rock 'n' roll tunes, flails erratically at a guitar, and wriggles like a peep-show dancer," Presley's rebellious style captivated young audiences. Girls screamed and fainted when he performed, and boys tried to imitate him. **E**

Not surprisingly, many adults condemned rock 'n' roll. They believed that the new music would lead to teenage delinquency and immorality. In a few cities, rock 'n' roll concerts were banned. But despite this controversy, television and radio exposure helped bring rock 'n' roll into the mainstream, and it became more acceptable by the end of the decade. Record sales, which were 189 million in 1950, grew with the popularity of rock 'n' roll, reaching 600 million in 1960.

MAIN IDEA

Making Inferences
E Based on Elvis Presley's song titles, what do you think were teenagers' concerns in the 1950s?

History Through Music

"HOUND DOG"— A ROCK 'N' ROLL CROSSOVER

Few examples highlight the influence African Americans had on rock 'n' roll—and the lack of credit and compensation they received for their efforts—more than the story of Willie Mae "Big Mama" Thornton.

In 1953, she recorded and released the song "Hound Dog" to little fanfare. She received a mere $500 in royalties. Only three years later, Elvis Presley recorded a version of the tune, which sold millions of records. Despite her contributions, Thornton reaped few rewards and struggled her entire career to make ends meet.

SKILLBUILDER
Developing Historical Perspective
1. Why might black musicians have been commercially less successful than white musicians in the 1950s? Explain.
2. What concerns of the current generation are reflected in today's popular music?

 SEE SKILLBUILDER HANDBOOK, PAGE R11.

▲ Willie Mae "Big Mama" Thornton is remembered as the first artist to record "Hound Dog."

Elvis Presley recorded "Hound Dog" in 1956— making it a popular hit. ▶

THE RACIAL GAP African-American music had inspired the birth of rock 'n' roll, and many of the genre's greatest performers were—like Berry and Penniman—African Americans. In other musical genres, singers Nat "King" Cole and Lena Horne, singer and actor Harry Belafonte, and many others paved the way for minority representation in the entertainment fields. Musicians like Miles Davis, Sonny Rollins, Charlie Parker, Dizzy Gillespie, and Thelonius Monk played a style of music characterized by the use of improvisation, called **jazz.** These artists entertained audiences of all races.

But throughout the 1950s, African-American shows were mostly broadcast on separate stations. By 1954, there were 250 radio stations nationwide aimed specifically at African-American listeners. African-American stations were part of radio's attempt to counter the mass popularity of television by targeting specific audiences. These stations also served advertisers who wanted to reach a large African-American audience. But it was the black listeners—who had fewer television sets than whites and did not find themselves reflected in mainstream programming—who appreciated the stations most. Thulani Davis, a poet, journalist, and playwright, expressed the feelings of one listener about African-American radio (or "race radio" as the character called it) in her novel *1959*.

▲ Innovative American jazz trumpeter and composer Miles Davis, shown during a recording session in 1959, continued to blaze musical trails throughout his career.

A PERSONAL VOICE THULANI DAVIS

" Billie Holiday died and I turned twelve on the same hot July day. The saddest singing in the world was coming out of the radio, race radio that is, the radio of the race. The white stations were on the usual relentless rounds of Pat Boone, Teresa Brewer, and anybody else who couldn't sing but liked to cover songs that were once colored. . . . White radio was at least honest—they knew anybody in the South could tell Negro voices from white ones, and so they didn't play our stuff. "
—*1959*

At the end of the 1950s, African Americans were still largely segregated from the dominant culture. This ongoing segregation—and the racial tensions it fed—would become a powerful force for change in the turbulent 1960s.

SECTION 3 ASSESSMENT

1. TERMS & NAMES For each term, write a sentence explaining its significance.

- mass media
- Federal Communications Commission (FCC)
- beat movement
- rock 'n' roll
- jazz

MAIN IDEA

2. SUMMARIZING
Create a "Who's Who" chart of popular culture idols of the 1950s. Identify the art form and major achievements associated with each person.

Person	Art Form	Achievements

Why do you think they appealed to the young people of the 1950s?

CRITICAL THINKING

3. EVALUATING
Do you agree with Newton Minow's statement, on page 860, that TV was "a vast wasteland"? Support your answer with details from the text.

4. ANALYZING EFFECTS
How did radio, TV, and the movies contribute to the success of rock 'n' roll?

5. COMPARING AND CONTRASTING
In what ways were the rock 'n' roll musicians and the beat poets of the 1950s similar and different? Support your answer with details from the text. **Think About:**

- the values the musicians and poets believed in
- people's reactions to the musicians, poets, and writers

The Emergence of the Teenager

Life after World War II brought changes in the family. For the first time, the teenage years were recognized as an important and unique developmental stage between childhood and adulthood. The booming postwar economy made it possible for teenagers to stay in school instead of working to help support their families, and allowed their parents to give them generous allowances. American business, particularly the music and movie industries, rushed to court this new consumer group.

▲ **TEENS AS CONSUMERS**
Comic books, pimple creams, and soft drinks were just a few of the products aimed at teenagers with money to spend.

THE TEEN MOVIE SCENE ▲

Teenagers with money in their pockets often found themselves at the movies. Hollywood responded by producing films especially for teens. *Rebel Without a Cause* (1955) told the story of a troubled youth driven by anger and fear. It starred teen heart-throbs James Dean and Natalie Wood.

◄ ROCKING TO A NEW BEAT

Teenagers seeking a collective identity found it in rock 'n' roll, a fresh form of music that delighted teenagers and enraged their parents. Dick Clark's *American Bandstand* (shown at left) showcased young performers playing music ranging from doo-wop (shown above) to hard-driving rhythm and blues. The songs they sang underscored themes of alienation and heartbreak.

DATA FILE

TEENAGE TIDBITS

- A *Life* magazine survey showed that, during the 1950s, teens spent $20 million on lipstick alone.
- In 1956, a total of 42,000 drive-in movie theaters—heavily frequented by teenagers—took in one-quarter of the year's total box-office receipts.
- College enrollments more than doubled between 1946 and 1960.
- A weekly credit payment for a record player was $1.

U.S. School Enrollments, 1950–1990

Thousands of Teenagers

— Elementary — High School — College

Source: *Statistical Abstract of the United States, 1995*

Teenagers and Employment, 1950–1990

Millions of Teenagers

— Males 16–19 years — Females 16–19 years

Source: *Statistical Abstract of the United States, 1995*

THINKING CRITICALLY

CONNECT TO HISTORY

1. **Interpreting Data** What were some causes of the booming teenage market in the 1950s? To answer the question, review the entire feature, including the Data File.

 SEE SKILLBUILDER HANDBOOK, PAGE R28.

CONNECT TO TODAY

2. **Analyzing Movies Today** What types of movies do American studios make for the teenage market today? How do these movies differ from those of the 1950s?

 hmhsocialstudies.com **RESEARCH WEB LINKS**

The Other America

MAIN IDEA	WHY IT MATTERS NOW	Terms & Names
Amidst the prosperity of the 1950s, millions of Americans lived in poverty.	America today continues to experience a marked income gap between affluent and nonaffluent people.	• urban renewal • bracero • termination policy

One American's Story

James Baldwin was born in New York City, the eldest of nine children, and grew up in the poverty of the Harlem ghetto. As a novelist, essayist, and playwright, he eloquently portrayed the struggles of African Americans against racial injustice and discrimination. He wrote a letter to his young nephew to mark the 100th anniversary of emancipation, although, in his words, "the country is celebrating one hundred years of freedom one hundred years too soon."

A PERSONAL VOICE JAMES BALDWIN

" [T]hese innocent and well-meaning people, your countrymen, have caused you to be born under conditions not very far removed from those described for us by Charles Dickens in the London of more than a hundred years ago. . . . This innocent country set you down in a ghetto in which, in fact, it intended that you should perish. . . . You were born where you were born and faced the future that you faced because you were black and *for no other reason*. "

—*The Fire Next Time*

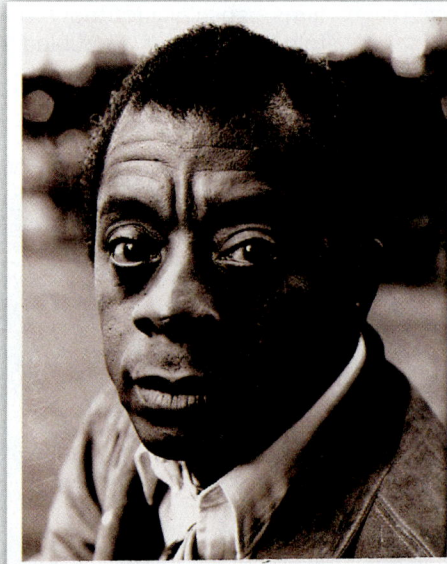

▲ **James Baldwin**

For many Americans, the 1950s were a time of unprecedented prosperity. But not everyone experienced this financial well-being. In the "other" America, about 40 million people lived in poverty, untouched by the economic boom.

The Urban Poor

Despite the portrait painted by popular culture, life in postwar America did not live up to the "American dream." In 1962, nearly one out of every four Americans was living below the poverty level. Many of these poor were elderly people, single women and their children, or members of minority groups, including African Americans, Latinos, and Native Americans.

WHITE FLIGHT In the 1950s, millions of middle-class white Americans left the cities for the suburbs, taking with them precious economic resources and isolating themselves from other races and classes. At the same time, the rural poor migrated to the inner cities. Between the end of World War II and 1960, nearly 5 million African Americans moved from the rural South to urban areas.

The urban crisis prompted by the "white flight" had a direct impact on poor whites and nonwhites. The cities lost not only people and businesses but also the property they owned and income taxes they had paid. City governments could no longer afford to properly maintain or improve schools, public transportation, and police and fire departments—and the urban poor suffered.

THE INNER CITIES While poverty grew rapidly in the decaying inner cities, many suburban Americans remained unaware of it. Some even refused to believe that poverty could exist in the richest, most powerful nation on earth. Each year, the federal government calculates the minimum amount of income needed to survive—the poverty line. In 1959, the poverty line for a family of four was $2,973. In 2000, it was $17,601. **A**

After living among the nation's poor across America, Michael Harrington published a shocking account that starkly illuminated the issue of poverty. In *The Other America: Poverty in the United States* (1962), he not only confirmed that widespread poverty existed but also exposed its brutal reality.

MAIN IDEA

Analyzing Effects

A What effect did white flight have on America's cities?

> **A PERSONAL VOICE** MICHAEL HARRINGTON
>
> "The poor get sick more than anyone else in the society. . . . When they become sick, they are sick longer than any other group in the society. Because they are sick more often and longer than anyone else, they lose wages and work, and find it difficult to hold a steady job. And because of this, they cannot pay for good housing, for a nutritious diet, for doctors."
>
> —*The Other America*

URBAN RENEWAL Most African Americans, Native Americans, and Latinos in the cities had to live in dirty, crowded slums. One proposed solution to the housing problem in inner cities was **urban renewal.** The National Housing Act of 1949 was passed to provide "a decent home and a suitable living environment for every American family." This act called for tearing down rundown neighborhoods and constructing low-income housing. Later, the nation's leaders would create a new cabinet position, Housing and Urban Development (HUD), to aid in improving conditions in the inner city.

Although dilapidated areas were razed, parking lots, shopping centers, highways, parks, and factories were constructed on some of the cleared land, and there was seldom enough new housing built to accommodate all the displaced people. For example, a *barrio* in Los Angeles was torn down to make way for Dodger Stadium, and poor people who were displaced from their homes simply moved from one ghetto to another. Some critics of urban renewal claimed that it had merely become urban *removal.* **B**

MAIN IDEA

Analyzing Effects

B Why were attempts at urban renewal viewed as less than successful?

Income Gap in America
(Ratio of Black Male Earnings to White Male Earnings*)

Black Earnings as Percentage of White Earnings

*Figures are for year-round, full-time employment.
Source: *The First Measured Century,* Theodore Caplow, 2001

SKILLBUILDER Interpreting Graphs
1. What trend does the graph show from 1940–1980?
2. What factors affecting people's lives might contribute to the income gap?

Poverty Leads to Activism

Despite ongoing poverty, during the 1950s, African Americans began to make significant strides toward the reduction of racial discrimination and segregation. Inspired by the African-American civil rights movement, other minorities also began to develop a deeper political awareness and a voice. Mexican-American activism gathered steam after veterans returned from World War II, and a major change in government policy under Eisenhower's administration fueled Native American protest.

▲ In 1942, Mexican farm workers on their way to California bid farewell to their families.

MEXICANS SEEK EMPLOYMENT Many Mexicans had become U.S. citizens during the 19th century, when the United States had annexed the Southwest after the War with Mexico. Large numbers of Mexicans had also crossed the border to work in the United States during and after World War I.

When the United States entered World War II, the shortage of agricultural laborers spurred the federal government to initiate, in 1942, a program in which Mexican *braceros* (brə-sâr′ōs), or hired hands, were allowed into the United States to harvest crops. Hundreds of thousands of braceros entered the United States on a short-term basis between 1942 and 1947. When their employment was ended, the braceros were expected to return to Mexico. However, many remained in the United States illegally. In addition, hundreds of thousands of Mexicans entered the country illegally to escape poor economic conditions in Mexico.

Background
In 1954, the U.S. launched a program designed to find and return undocumented immigrants to Mexico. Between 1953 and 1955, the U.S. deported more than 2 million illegal Mexican immigrants.

THE LONGORIA INCIDENT One of the more notorious instances of prejudice against Mexican Americans involved the burial of Felix Longoria. Longoria was a Mexican-American World War II hero who had been killed in the Philippines. The only undertaker in his hometown in Texas refused to provide Longoria's family with funeral services.

In the wake of the Longoria incident, outraged Mexican Americans stepped up their efforts to stamp out discrimination. In 1948, Mexican-American veterans organized the G.I. Forum. Meanwhile, activist Ignacio Lopez founded the Unity League of California to register Mexican-American voters and to promote candidates who would represent their interests. **C**

NATIVE AMERICANS CONTINUE THEIR STRUGGLE Native Americans also continued to fight for their rights and identity. From the passage of the Dawes Act, in 1887, until 1934, the policy of the federal government toward Native Americans had been one of "Americanization" and assimilation. In 1924, the Snyder Act granted citizenship to all Native Americans, but they remained second-class citizens.

In 1934, the Indian Reorganization Act moved official policy away from assimilation and toward Native American autonomy. Its passage signaled a change in federal policy. In addition, because the government was reeling from

MAIN IDEA

Analyzing Issues
C How did the Longoria incident motivate Mexican Americans to increase their political and social activism?

the Great Depression, it wanted to stop subsidizing the Native Americans. Native Americans also took the initiative to improve their lives. In 1944, they established the National Congress of American Indians. The congress had two main goals: (1) to ensure for Native Americans the same civil rights that white Americans had, and (2) to enable Native Americans on reservations to retain their own customs.

During World War II, over 65,000 Native Americans left their reservations for military service and war work. As a result, they became very aware of discrimination. When the war ended, Native Americans stopped receiving family allotments and wages. Outsiders also grabbed control of tribal lands, primarily to exploit their deposits of minerals, oil, and timber.

THE TERMINATION POLICY In 1953, the federal government announced that it would give up its responsibility for Native American tribes. This new approach, known as the **termination policy,** eliminated federal economic support, discontinued the reservation system, and distributed tribal lands among individual Native Americans. In response to the termination policy, the Bureau of Indian Affairs began a voluntary relocation program to help Native Americans resettle in cities.

The termination policy was a dismal failure, however. Although the Bureau of Indian Affairs helped relocate 35,000 Native Americans to urban areas during the 1950s, they were often unable to find jobs in their new locations because of poor training and racial prejudice. They were also left without access to medical care when federal programs were abolished. In 1963, the termination policy was abandoned.

▲
Native Americans like the man above received job training from the Bureau of Indian Affairs to help them settle in urban areas.

SECTION 4 ASSESSMENT

1. **TERMS & NAMES** For each term, write a sentence explaining its significance.
   • urban renewal   • bracero   • termination policy

MAIN IDEA

2. TAKING NOTES
In overlapping circles like the ones below, fill in the common problems that African Americans, Mexican Americans, and Native Americans faced during the 1950s.

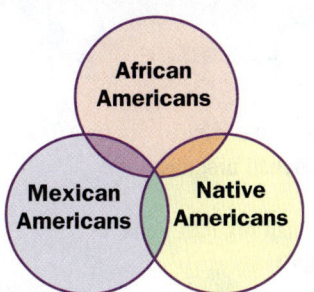

What do these problems illustrate about life in the 1950s?

CRITICAL THINKING

3. EVALUATING
Do you think that urban renewal was an effective approach to the housing problem in inner cities? Why or why not? **Think About:**

- the goals of the National Housing Act of 1949
- the claims made by some critics of urban renewal
- the residents' best interest

4. ANALYZING ISSUES
How did Native Americans work to increase their participation in the U.S. political process?

5. DRAWING CONCLUSIONS
Which major population shift— "white flight," migration from Mexico, or relocation of Native Americans—do you think had the greatest impact on U.S. society? Why? **Think About:**

- the impact of "white flight"
- the influx of "braceros"
- the effects of the termination policy

The Postwar Boom **869**

TERMS & NAMES

For each item below, write a sentence explaining its historical significance in the 1950s.

1. suburb
2. Dixiecrat
3. Fair Deal
4. conglomerate
5. baby boom
6. mass media
7. beat movement
8. rock 'n' roll
9. urban renewal
10. *bracero*

MAIN IDEAS

Use your notes and the information in the chapter to answer the following questions.

Postwar America *(pages 840–846)*

1. How did the GI Bill of Rights help World War II veterans?
2. What domestic and foreign issues concerned voters during the 1952 presidential election?

The American Dream in the Fifties

(pages 847–855)

3. What shift in employment trends had occurred by the mid-1950s?
4. How did life in the suburbs provide the model for the American dream?

Popular Culture *(pages 858–863)*

5. What strategies did radio stations use to counteract the mass popularity of television?

6. How did African-American performers influence American popular culture in the 1950s?

The Other America *(pages 866–869)*

7. How did many major cities change in the 1950s?
8. What obstacles to improving their lives did Native Americans face in the 1950s?

CRITICAL THINKING

1. **USING YOUR NOTES** In a web like the one below, show the postwar technological advances you consider most influential.

Breakthroughs

2. **HYPOTHESIZING** During America's first two centuries, the national character was marked by individualism. Why do you think conformity became the norm in the 1950s?

3. **ANALYZING PRIMARY SOURCES** Do you agree or disagree with the following quotation from *Life* magazine on American culture in 1954: "Never before so much for so few"? Support your answer with evidence.

VISUAL SUMMARY THE POSTWAR BOOM

SUBURBAN GROWTH

- Baby boom causes population growth.
- Demand for goods exceeds supply.
- Highways and affordable homes make suburban living desirable.

POLITICS

- Eisenhower's presidency brings prosperity and political conservatism.
- Equal rights remains a problem.
- The Cold War creates fear and anxiety.

LIFE IN POSTWAR AMERICA 1945–1960

POPULAR CULTURE

- Rock 'n' roll and jazz pave the way for minority representation.
- The beat movement rejects conformity.
- Recreation and consumerism flourish.
- Television portrays an idealized white America.

UNEQUAL OPPORTUNITIES

- Urban areas fall into decay.
- Minorities experience prejudice and discrimination.
- Minorities establish organizations to improve civil rights.

Use the chart and your knowledge of U.S. history to answer questions 1 and 2.

Geographic Distribution of U.S. Population, 1930–1970

Year	Central Cities	Suburbs	Rural Areas and Small Towns
1930	31.8%	18.0%	50.2%
1940	31.6%	19.5%	48.9%
1950	32.3%	23.8%	43.9%
1960	32.6%	30.7%	36.7%
1970	31.4%	37.6%	31.0%

Source: Adapted from U.S. Bureau of the Census, *Decennial Censuses, 1930–1970*

1 Which of the following statements supports the information in the chart?

(1) From 1940–1960, more people lived in cities than in rural areas.

(2) In 1960, twice as many people lived in cities as in suburbs.

(3) By 1960, suburbs had surpassed cities in total population.

(4) From 1930–1970, the percentage of U.S. population in rural areas decreased every decade.

2 From 1940–1970 the distribution doubled —

(1) in cities and suburbs.

(2) only in suburbs.

(3) only in cities.

(4) only in rural areas.

Use the song lyric below and your knowledge of U.S. history to answer question 3.

"Little Boxes"
Little boxes on the hillside,
Little boxes made of ticky-tacky,
Little boxes on the hillside,
Little boxes all the same.
There's a pink one and a green one
And a blue one and a yellow one,
And they're all made out of ticky-tacky
And they all look just the same.

—Malvina Reynolds

3 This popular song of the era describes —

(1) planned obsolescence.

(2) urban renewal.

(3) suburban communities.

(4) beatnik life style.

 hmhsocialstudies.com **TEST PRACTICE**

For additional test practice, go online for:
• Diagnostic tests   • Tutorials

INTERACT WITH HISTORY

Think about the issues you explored at the beginning of the chapter. Suppose you are a beat poet and have been asked to write an original poem entitled *A Postwar American Dream*. Use information from Chapter 27 and your knowledge of American history to support your poem. Remember to include a wide range of lifestyles in your poem.

FOCUS ON WRITING

In 1956, President Eisenhower signed the Interstate Highway Act that led to the construction of a nationwide highway network. Write a persuasive essay supporting the law. In the first part of your essay, clearly outline the benefits created by the law. In the second part of your essay, address the concerns of those who oppose the law.

MULTIMEDIA ACTIVITY

21st CENTURY

Visit the links for Chapter Assessment to plan and prepare a Web page about one aspect of popular culture—music, television, fashion, or the movies—from the 1950s. Include particular events and personalities of that period.

 hmhsocialstudies.com

UNIT 8

UNIT PROJECT

Lobbying Campaign

This unit covers years of great social and political turmoil. Imagine that you have decided to lobby for—convince government officials to support—a cause or issue that is important to you. Create a plan for lobbying in which you encourage others to support your point of view.

Civil Rights March, 1965 **by James Karales**

Living with Great Turmoil
1954–1975

CHAPTER 28

THE NEW FRONTIER AND THE GREAT SOCIETY

New York Standards

KEY IDEA 2 Important ideas, social and cultural values, beliefs, and traditions from New York State and United States history illustrate the connections and interactions of people and events across time and from a variety of perspectives.

KEY IDEA 4 The skills of historical analysis include the ability to: explain the significance of historical evidence; weigh the importance, reliability, and validity of evidence; understand the concept of multiple causation; understand the importance of changing and competing interpretations of different historical developments.

SECTION 1: Kennedy and the Cold War

SECTION 2: The New Frontier

SECTION 3: The Great Society

Scientific and technological advances in the early 1960s made possible the first American spacewalk during the *Gemini 4* mission on June 3, 1965.

1962 John Glenn becomes the first American to orbit the earth.

1960 John F. Kennedy is elected president.

1961 U.S. launches the Bay of Pigs invasion.

1962 U.S. and USSR face off in the Cuban missile crisis.

1963 President Kennedy is assassinated; Lyndon B. Johnson becomes president.

USA
WORLD

1960   1961   1962   1963

1960 Seventeen African countries gain independence.

1961 Soviet cosmonaut Yuri Gagarin becomes the first human in outer space.

1962 The drug thalidomide is pulled from the market after it is found responsible for thousands of birth defects in Europe.

JFK Sets Goal for
Man on Moon

↗ hmhsocialstudies.com | VIDEO

1964 Lyndon B. Johnson is elected president.

1964 Congress passes the Economic Opportunity Act and Civil Rights Act.

1965 U.S. troops enter Vietnam.

1967 Thurgood Marshall becomes the first African-American justice of the Supreme Court.

1968 Richard M. Nixon is elected president.

1964　　1965　　1966　　1967

1965 Ferdinand Marcos becomes president of the Philippines.

1966 Indira Gandhi becomes prime minister of India.

1967 Israel wins Arab territories in the Six Day War.

1968 Warsaw Pact troops invade Czechoslovakia.

The New Frontier and the Great Society **875**

SECTION
1

PI 2.5
PI 4.3
CC Unit 7.III.A.1.a(2)
CC Unit 7.III.A.2.b
CC Unit 7.III.A.2.h
CC Unit 7.III.A.2.a
CC Unit 7.III.A.2.c

Kennedy and the Cold War

MAIN IDEA	WHY IT MATTERS NOW	Terms & Names
The Kennedy administration faced some of the most dangerous Soviet confrontations in American history.	America's response to Soviet threats developed the United States as a military superpower.	•John F. Kennedy •flexible response •Fidel Castro •Berlin Wall •hot line •Limited Test Ban Treaty

One American's Story

John F. Kennedy became the 35th president of the United States on a crisp and sparkling day in January 1961. Appearing without a coat in freezing weather, he issued a challenge to the American people. He said that the world was in "its hour of maximum danger," as Cold War tensions ran high. Rather than shrinking from the danger, the United States should confront the "iron tyranny" of communism.

A PERSONAL VOICE JOHN F. KENNEDY

"Let the word go forth from this time and place, to friend and foe alike, that the torch has been passed to a new generation of Americans, born in this century, tempered by war, disciplined by a hard and bitter peace, proud of our ancient heritage, and unwilling to witness or permit the slow undoing of those human rights to which this nation has always been committed. . . .

Let every nation know, whether it wishes us well or ill, that we shall pay any price, bear any burden, meet any hardship, support any friend, oppose any . . . foe, in order to assure . . . the survival and the success of liberty."

—Inaugural Address, January 20, 1961

The young president won praise for his well-crafted speech. However, his words were put to the test when several Cold War crises tried his leadership.

hmhsocialstudies.com
TAKING NOTES

Use the graphic organizer online to take notes on the outcomes of events discussed in this section.

▲ John F. Kennedy delivers his inaugural address on January 20, 1961.

The Election of 1960

In 1960, as President Eisenhower's second term drew to a close, a mood of restlessness arose among voters. The economy was in a recession. The USSR's launch of *Sputnik I* in 1957 and its development of long-range missiles had sparked fears that the American military was falling behind that of the Soviets. Further setbacks including the U-2 incident and the alignment of Cuba with the Soviet Union had Americans questioning whether the United States was losing the Cold War.

John F. Kennedy (*right*) appeared confident and at ease during a televised debate with his opponent Richard M. Nixon.

The Democratic nominee for president, Massachusetts senator John Kennedy, promised active leadership "to get America moving again." His Republican opponent, Vice President Richard M. Nixon, hoped to win by riding on the coattails of Eisenhower's popularity. Both candidates had similar positions on policy issues. Two factors helped put Kennedy over the top: television and the civil rights issue.

THE TELEVISED DEBATE AFFECTS VOTES Kennedy had a well-organized campaign and the backing of his wealthy family, and was handsome and charismatic. Yet many felt that, at 43, he was too inexperienced. If elected, he would be the second-youngest president in the nation's history.

Americans also worried that having a Roman Catholic in the White House would lead either to influence of the pope on American policies or to closer ties between church and state. Kennedy was able to allay worries by discussing the issue openly.

One event in the fall determined the course of the election. Kennedy and Nixon took part in the first televised debate between presidential candidates. On September 26, 1960, 70 million TV viewers watched the two articulate and knowledgeable candidates debating issues. Nixon, an expert on foreign policy, had agreed to the forum in hopes of exposing Kennedy's inexperience. However, Kennedy had been coached by television producers, and he looked and spoke better than Nixon. **A**

> *" That night, image replaced the printed word as the natural language of politics."*
>
> **RUSSELL BAKER**

Kennedy's success in the debate launched a new era in American politics: the television age. As journalist Russell Baker, who covered the Nixon campaign, said, "That night, image replaced the printed word as the natural language of politics."

KENNEDY AND CIVIL RIGHTS A second major event of the campaign took place in October. Police in Atlanta, Georgia, arrested the Reverend Martin Luther King, Jr., and 33 other African-American demonstrators for sitting at a segregated lunch counter. Although the other demonstrators were released, King was sentenced to months of hard labor—officially for a minor traffic violation. The Eisenhower administration refused to intervene, and Nixon took no public position.

When Kennedy heard of the arrest and sentencing, he telephoned King's wife, Coretta Scott King, to express his sympathy. Meanwhile, Robert Kennedy, his brother and campaign manager, persuaded the judge who had sentenced King to release the civil rights leader on bail, pending appeal. News of the incident captured the immediate attention of the African-American community, whose votes would help Kennedy carry key states in the Midwest and South.

The Camelot Years

President and Mrs. Kennedy enjoy time with their children, Caroline and John, Jr., while vacationing in Hyannis Port, Massachusetts. ▼

The election in November 1960 was the closest since 1884; Kennedy won by fewer than 119,000 votes. His inauguration set the tone for a new era at the White House: one of grace, elegance, and wit. On the podium sat over 100 writers, artists, and scientists that the Kennedys had invited, including opera singer Marian Anderson, who had once been barred from singing at Constitution Hall because she was African American. Kennedy's inspiring speech called for hope, commitment, and sacrifice. "And so, my fellow Americans," he proclaimed, "ask not what your country can do for you—ask what you can do for your country."

During his term, the president and his beautiful young wife, Jacqueline, invited many artists and celebrities to the White House. In addition, Kennedy often appeared on television. The press loved his charm and wit and helped to bolster his image.

THE KENNEDY MYSTIQUE Critics of Kennedy's presidency argued that his smooth style lacked substance. But the new first family fascinated the public. For example, after learning that JFK could read 1,600 words a minute, thousands of people enrolled in speed-reading courses. The first lady, too, captivated the nation with her eye for fashion and culture. It seemed the nation could not get enough of the first family. Newspapers and magazines filled their pages with pictures and stories about the president's young daughter Caroline and his infant son John.

With JFK's youthful glamour and his talented advisers, the Kennedy White House reminded many of a modern-day Camelot, the mythical court of King Arthur. Coincidentally, the musical *Camelot* had opened on Broadway in 1960. Years later, Jackie recalled her husband and the vision of Camelot.

★ **A PERSONAL VOICE** JACQUELINE KENNEDY

"At night, before we'd go to sleep, Jack liked to play some records and the song he loved most came at the very end of [the *Camelot*] record. The lines he loved to hear were: 'Don't let it be forgot, that once there was a spot, for one brief shining moment that was known as Camelot.' There'll be great presidents again . . . but there'll never be another Camelot again." **B**

—quoted in *Life magazine, John F. Kennedy Memorial Edition*

THE BEST AND THE BRIGHTEST Kennedy surrounded himself with a team of advisers that one journalist called "the best and the brightest." They included McGeorge Bundy, a Harvard University dean, as national security adviser; Robert McNamara, president of Ford Motor Company, as secretary of defense; and Dean Rusk, president of the Rockefeller Foundation, as secretary of state. Of all the advisers who filled Kennedy's inner circle, he relied most heavily on his 35-year-old brother Robert, whom he appointed attorney general.

Background
The fictional King Arthur was based on a real fifth- or sixth-century Celt. In literature, Arthur's romantic world is marked by chivalry and magic.

MAIN IDEA

Developing Historical Perspective

B What factors help explain the public's fascination with the Kennedys?

A New Military Policy

Vocabulary
third world:
during the Cold War, the developing nations not allied with either the United States or the Soviet Union

From the beginning, Kennedy focused on the Cold War. He thought the Eisenhower administration had not done enough about the Soviet threat. The Soviets, he concluded, were gaining loyalties in the economically less-developed third-world countries of Asia, Africa, and Latin America. He blasted the Republicans for allowing communism to develop in Cuba, at America's doorstep.

DEFINING A MILITARY STRATEGY Kennedy believed his most urgent task was to redefine the nation's nuclear strategy. The Eisenhower administration had relied on the policy of massive retaliation to deter Soviet aggression and imperialism. However, threatening to use nuclear arms over a minor conflict was not a risk Kennedy wished to take. Instead, his team developed a policy of **flexible response.** Kennedy's secretary of defense, Robert McNamara, explained the policy.

A PERSONAL VOICE ROBERT S. MCNAMARA

"**The Kennedy administration worried that [the] reliance on nuclear weapons gave us no way to respond to large non-nuclear attacks without committing suicide. . . . We decided to broaden the range of options by strengthening and modernizing the military's ability to fight a nonnuclear war.**"

—*In Retrospect*

MAIN IDEA

Summarizing

C What was the goal of the doctrine of flexible response?

Kennedy increased defense spending in order to boost conventional military forces—nonnuclear forces such as troops, ships, and artillery—and to create an elite branch of the army called the Special Forces, or Green Berets. He also tripled the overall nuclear capabilities of the United States. These changes enabled the United States to fight limited wars around the world while maintaining a balance of nuclear power with the Soviet Union. However, even as Kennedy hoped to reduce the risk of nuclear war, the world came perilously close to nuclear war under his command as a crisis arose over the island of Cuba. **C**

Crises over Cuba

The first test of Kennedy's foreign policy came in Cuba, just 90 miles off the coast of Florida. About two weeks before Kennedy took office, on January 3, 1961, President Eisenhower had cut off diplomatic relations with Cuba because of a revolutionary leader named **Fidel Castro.** Castro openly declared himself a communist and welcomed aid from the Soviet Union.

THE CUBAN DILEMMA Castro gained power with the promise of democracy. From 1956 to 1959, he led a guerrilla movement to topple dictator Fulgencio Batista. He won control in 1959 and later told reporters, "Revolutionaries are not born, they are made by poverty, inequality, and dictatorship." He then promised to eliminate these conditions from Cuba.

Vocabulary
guerrilla: a soldier who travels in a small group, harassing and undermining the enemy

The United States was suspicious of Castro's intentions but nevertheless recognized the new government. However, when Castro seized three American and British oil refineries, relations between the United States and Cuba worsened. Castro also broke up commercial farms into communes that would be worked by formerly landless peasants. American sugar companies,

---

ANOTHER PERSPECTIVE

EISENHOWER'S WARNING

The increase in defense spending in the 1960s continued the trend in which Defense Department suppliers were becoming more dominant in the American economy. Before leaving office, President Eisenhower warned against the dangers of what he called the "military-industrial complex." He included in his parting speech the following comments:

"This conjunction of an immense military establishment and a large arms industry is new in the American experience. The total influence—economic, political, even spiritual—is felt in every city, every statehouse, every office of the federal government. We recognize the imperative need for this development. Yet we must not fail to comprehend its grave implications. . . . The potential for the disastrous rise of misplaced power exists and will persist."

---

which controlled 75 percent of the crop land in Cuba, appealed to the U.S. government for help. In response, Congress erected trade barriers against Cuban sugar.

Castro relied increasingly on Soviet aid—and on the political repression of those who did not agree with him. While some Cubans were taken by his charisma and his willingness to stand up to the United States, others saw Castro as a tyrant who had replaced one dictatorship with another. About 10 percent of Cuba's population went into exile, mostly to the United States. Within the large exile community of Miami, Florida, a counterrevolutionary movement took shape.

THE BAY OF PIGS In March 1960, President Eisenhower gave the CIA permission to secretly train Cuban exiles for an invasion of Cuba. The CIA and the exiles hoped it would trigger a mass uprising that would overthrow Castro. Kennedy learned of the plan only nine days after his election. Although he had doubts, he approved it.

On the night of April 17, 1961, some 1,300 to 1,500 Cuban exiles supported by the U.S. military landed on the island's southern coast at Bahia de Cochinos, the Bay of Pigs. Nothing went as planned. An air strike had failed to knock out the Cuban air force, although the CIA reported that it had succeeded. A small advance group sent to distract Castro's forces never reached shore. When the main unit landed, it lacked American air support as it faced 25,000 Cuban troops backed up by Soviet tanks and jets. Some of the invading exiles were killed, others imprisoned.

The Cuban media sensationalized the defeat of "North American mercenaries." One United States commentator observed that Americans "look like fools to our friends, rascals to our enemies, and incompetents to the rest." The disaster left Kennedy embarrassed. Publicly, he accepted blame for the fiasco. Privately, he asked, "How could that crowd at the CIA and the Pentagon be this wrong." **D**

Kennedy negotiated with Castro for the release of surviving commandos and paid a ransom of $53 million in food and medical supplies. In a speech in Miami, he promised exiles that they would one day return to a "free Havana." Although Kennedy warned that he would resist further Communist expansion in the Western Hemisphere, Castro defiantly welcomed further Soviet aid.

THE CUBAN MISSILE CRISIS Castro had a powerful ally in Moscow: Soviet Premier Nikita Khrushchev, who promised to defend Cuba with Soviet arms. During the summer of 1962, the flow to Cuba of Soviet weapons—including nuclear missiles—increased greatly. President Kennedy responded with a warning that America would not tolerate offensive nuclear weapons in Cuba. Then, on October 14, photographs taken by American planes revealed Soviet missile bases in Cuba—and some contained missiles ready to launch. They could reach U.S. cities in minutes.

On October 22, Kennedy informed an anxious nation of the existence of Soviet missile sites in Cuba and of his plans to remove them. He made it clear that any missile attack from Cuba would trigger an all-out attack on the Soviet Union.

▲
(top) Castro celebrates after gaining power in Cuba.
(above) The Bay of Pigs mission was said to have blown up in Kennedy's face.

Vocabulary
political repression: government intimidation of those with different political views

MAIN IDEA

Analyzing Effects

D What were the consequences of the failed invasion for the United States?

Cuban Missile Crisis, October 1962

hmhsocialstudies.com **INTERACTIVE MAP**

Legend:
- Missile complex
- Possible missile path *
- Range of quarantine
- U.S. military installation

0 200 400 miles
0 200 400 kilometers

PACIFIC OCEAN

UNITED STATES

2,000 MILES (17 MINUTES)
1,500 MILES (15 MINUTES)
1,898 MILES
1,000 MILES (12 MINUTES)
1,554 MILES
1,259 MILES
1,432 MILES
837 MILES
1,020 MILES

Denver
Chicago
New York
Washington, D.C.
Atlanta
Houston

ATLANTIC OCEAN

Gulf of Mexico

Tropic of Cancer

CUBA
Havana
Guantanamo

Caribbean Sea

MISSILE EQUIPMENT
MARIEL PORT FACILITY
4 NOVEMBER 1962

4 MISSILE TRANSPORTERS
OXIDIZER TRAILERS
OXIDIZER TRAILERS
FUEL TRAILERS

U.S. spy planes reveal nuclear missile sites in Cuba.

Kennedy tells the nation of his intention to halt the missile buildup.

Khrushchev announces plan to remove missiles from Cuba.

| OCT. 14 | OCT. 22 | OCT. 24 | OCT. 25 | OCT. 28 |

*Missile path times and distances are approximate.

Kennedy implements a naval "quarantine" of Cuba, blocking Soviet ships from reaching the island. (*below*) A U.S. patrol plane flies over a Soviet freighter.

Soviet ships approaching Cuba come to a halt.

GEOGRAPHY SKILLBUILDER
1. **Movement** About how long would it have taken for a missile launched from Cuba to reach New York?
2. **Human-Environment Interaction** Why do you think it may have been important for Soviet missiles to reach the U.S. cities shown above?

The New Frontier and the Great Society **881**

KEY PLAYERS

JOHN F. KENNEDY
1917–1963

John F. "Jack" Kennedy grew up in a politically powerful family that helped make his dreams possible. His parents instilled in him the drive to accomplish great things.

During World War II he enlisted in the navy and was decorated for heroism. In 1946, he won his first seat in Congress from a Boston district where he had never lived. While a senator, he won a Pulitzer Prize for his book *Profiles in Courage*.

Although he radiated self-confidence, Kennedy suffered many ailments, including Addison's disease—a debilitating condition that he treated with daily injections of cortisone. "At least one half of the days that he spent on this earth were days of intense physical pain," recalled his brother Robert.

NIKITA KHRUSHCHEV
1894–1971

"No matter how humble a man's beginnings," boasted Nikita Khrushchev, "he achieves the stature of the office to which he is elected." Khrushchev, the son of a miner, became a Communist Party organizer in the 1920s. Within four years of Stalin's death in 1953, Khrushchev had consolidated his power in the Soviet Union.

During his regime, which ended in 1964, Khrushchev kept American nerves on edge with alternately conciliatory and aggressive behavior. During a 1959 trip to the United States, he met for friendly talks with President Eisenhower. The next year, in front of the UN General Assembly, he took off his shoe and angrily pounded it on a desk to protest the U-2 incident.

For the next six days, the world faced the terrifying possibility of nuclear war. In the Atlantic Ocean, Soviet ships—presumably carrying more missiles—headed toward Cuba, while the U.S. Navy prepared to quarantine Cuba and prevent the ships from coming within 500 miles of it. In Florida, 100,000 troops waited—the largest invasion force ever assembled in the United States. C. Douglas Dillon, Kennedy's secretary of the treasury and a veteran of nuclear diplomacy, recalled those tension-filled days of October.

★ A PERSONAL VOICE
C. DOUGLAS DILLON

"The only time I felt a fear of nuclear war or a use of nuclear weapons was on the very first day, when we'd decided that we had to do whatever was necessary to get the missiles out. There was always some background fear of what would eventually happen, and I think this is what was expressed when people said they feared they would never see another Saturday."

—quoted in *On the Brink*

The first break in the crisis occurred when the Soviet ships stopped suddenly to avoid a confrontation at sea. Secretary of State Dean Rusk said, "We are eyeball to eyeball, and the other fellow just blinked." A few days later, Khrushchev offered to remove the missiles in return for an American pledge not to invade Cuba. The United States also secretly agreed to remove missiles from Turkey. The leaders agreed, and the crisis ended. "For a moment, the world had stood still," Robert Kennedy wrote years later, "and now it was going around again."

KENNEDY AND KHRUSHCHEV TAKE THE HEAT The crisis severely damaged Khrushchev's prestige in the Soviet Union and the world. Kennedy did not escape criticism either. Some people criticized Kennedy for practicing brinkmanship when private talks might have resolved the crisis without the threat of nuclear war. Others believed he had passed up an ideal chance to invade Cuba and oust Castro. (It was learned in the 1990s that the CIA had underestimated the numbers of Soviet troops and nuclear weapons on the island.)

The effects of the crisis lasted long after the missiles had been removed. Many Cuban exiles blamed the Democrats for "losing Cuba" (a charge that Kennedy had earlier leveled at the Republicans) and switched their allegiance to the GOP.

MAIN IDEA

Analyzing Effects

E What were the results of the Cuban missile crisis?

Meanwhile, Castro closed Cuba's doors to the exiles in November 1962 by banning all flights to and from Miami. Three years later, hundreds of thousands of people took advantage of an agreement that allowed Cubans to join relatives in the United States. By the time Castro sharply cut down on exit permits in 1973, the Cuban population in Miami had increased to about 300,000. **E**

Crisis over Berlin

One goal that had guided Kennedy through the Cuban missile crisis was that of proving to Khrushchev his determination to contain communism. All the while, Kennedy was thinking of their recent confrontation over Berlin, which had led to the construction of the **Berlin Wall,** a concrete wall topped with barbed wire that severed the city in two.

THE BERLIN CRISIS In 1961, Berlin was a city in great turmoil. In the 11 years since the Berlin Airlift, almost 3 million East Germans—20 percent of that country's population—had fled into West Berlin because it was free from Communist rule. These refugees advertised the failure of East Germany's Communist government. Their departure also dangerously weakened that country's economy.

hmhsocialstudies.com

INTERACTIVE
Explore the Berlin Wall.

The "death strip" stretched like a barren moat around West Berlin, with patrols, floodlights, electric fences, and vehicle traps between the inner and outer walls.

Walls and other barriers 10–15 feet high surrounded West Berlin. The length of the barriers around the city totaled about 110 miles.

Guard dogs and machine guns dissuaded most people from crossing over illegally, yet some still dared.

The Berlin Wall was first made of brick and barbed wire, but was later erected in cement and steel.

WORLD STAGE

THE BERLIN WALL, 1961

In 1961, Nikita Khrushchev, the Soviet premier, ordered the Berlin Wall built to stop the flow of refugees from East to West Berlin. Most were seeking freedom from Communist rule.

The wall isolated West Berlin from a hostile German Democratic Republic (GDR). Passing from East to West was almost impossible without the Communist government's permission.

During the 28 years the wall was standing, approximately 5,000 people succeeded in fleeing. Almost 200 people died in the attempt; most were shot by the GDR border guards. In 1989, East Germany opened the Berlin Wall to cheering crowds. Today the few remnants of the wall are a reminder of Cold War tensions between East and West.

> *"I want peace. But, if you want war, that is your problem."*
>
> **SOVIET PREMIER NIKITA KHRUSHCHEV**

Khrushchev realized that this problem had to be solved. At a summit meeting in Vienna, Austria, in June 1961, he threatened to sign a treaty with East Germany that would enable that country to close all the access roads to West Berlin. When Kennedy refused to give up U.S. access to West Berlin, Khrushchev furiously declared, "I want peace. But, if you want war, that is your problem."

After returning home, Kennedy told the nation in a televised address that Berlin was "the great testing place of Western courage and will." He pledged "[W]e cannot and will not permit the Communists to drive us out of Berlin."

Kennedy's determination and America's superior nuclear striking power prevented Khrushchev from closing the air and land routes between West Berlin and West Germany. Instead, the Soviet premier surprised the world with a shocking decision. Just after midnight on August 13, 1961, East German troops began to unload concrete posts and rolls of barbed wire along the border. Within days, the Berlin Wall was erected, separating East Germany from West Germany.

The construction of the Berlin Wall ended the Berlin crisis but further aggravated Cold War tensions. The wall and its armed guards successfully reduced the flow of East German refugees to a tiny trickle, thus solving Khrushchev's main problem. At the same time, however, the wall became an ugly symbol of Communist oppression. **F**

SEARCHING FOR WAYS TO EASE TENSIONS Showdowns between Kennedy and Khrushchev made both leaders aware of the gravity of split-second decisions that separated Cold War peace from nuclear disaster. Kennedy, in particular, searched for ways to tone down his hard-line stance. In 1963, he announced that the two nations had established a **hot line** between the White House and the Kremlin. This dedicated phone enabled the leaders of the two countries to communicate at once should another crisis arise. Later that year, the United States and Soviet Union also agreed to a **Limited Test Ban Treaty** that barred nuclear testing in the atmosphere.

▲ Reading from this note card during a speech in West Berlin, Kennedy proclaimed "Ich bin ein Berliner" ("I am a Berliner").

MAIN IDEA

Analyzing Motives

F What led Khrushchev to erect the Berlin Wall?

 ASSESSMENT

1. **TERMS & NAMES** For each term or name, write a sentence explaining its significance.

   • John F. Kennedy
   • flexible response
   • Fidel Castro
   • Berlin Wall
   • hot line
   • Limited Test Ban Treaty

MAIN IDEA

2. **TAKING NOTES**
Using diagrams such as the one below, list two outcomes for each of these events: first Kennedy-Nixon debate, Bay of Pigs invasion, Cuban missile crisis, and construction of the Berlin Wall.

Event → Outcome / Outcome

Which of these outcomes led directly to other events listed here or described in this section?

CRITICAL THINKING

3. **EVALUATING DECISIONS**
How well do you think President Kennedy handled the Cuban missile crisis? Justify your opinion with specific examples from the text.
   Think About:
   • Kennedy's decision to impose a naval "quarantine" of Cuba
   • the nuclear showdown between the superpowers
   • Kennedy's decision not to invade Cuba

4. **ANALYZING VISUAL SOURCES**
Examine the cartoon above of Kennedy (*left*) facing off with Khrushchev and Castro. What do you think the cartoonist was trying to convey?

5. **DRAWING CONCLUSIONS**
What kind of political statement was made by the United States' support of West Berlin?

KENNEDY ASKS ...
TO ACCELERATE SPACE EXPLORATION,
FOREIGN AID, BOLSTER DEFENSE
SCHOOL-AID BILL
ON DALLAS STRE
...OTE OF 49.34 JOHNSON BECOMES PRESIDE
JOHNSON S
NEDY SLA

PI 2.1
PI 4.3
CC Unit 1.I.D.3
CC Unit 7.III.A.2.f
CC Unit 7.III.A.4
CC Unit 7.III.A.2.e
CC Unit 7.III.A.2.g

The New Frontier

MAIN IDEA	WHY IT MATTERS NOW	Terms & Names
While Kennedy had trouble getting his ideas for a New Frontier passed, several goals were achieved.	Kennedy's space program continues to generate scientific and engineering advances that benefit Americans.	• New Frontier • mandate • Peace Corps • Alliance for Progress • Warren Commission

One American's Story

hmhsocialstudies.com
TAKING NOTES
Use the graphic organizer online to take notes on the programs of the New Frontier.

On May 5, 1961, American astronaut Alan Shepard climbed into *Freedom 7*, a tiny capsule on top of a huge rocket booster. The capsule left the earth's atmosphere in a ball of fire and returned the same way, and Shepard became the first American to travel into space. Years later, he recalled his emotions when a naval crew fished him out of the Atlantic.

A PERSONAL VOICE ALAN SHEPARD

" Until the moment I stepped out of the flight deck . . . I hadn't realized the intensity of the emotions and feelings that so many people had for me, for the other astronauts, and for the whole manned space program. . . . I was very close to tears as I thought, it's no longer just our fight to get 'out there.' The struggle belongs to everyone in America. . . . From now on there was no turning back. "

—*Moon Shot: The Inside Story of America's Race to the Moon*

The entire trip—which took only 15 minutes from liftoff to splashdown—reaffirmed the belief in American ingenuity. John F. Kennedy inspired many Americans with the same kind of belief.

▲ Astronaut Alan Shepard (*inset*) prepares to enter the space capsule for his *Mercury* flight.

The Promise of Progress

Background
One area where President Kennedy wanted progress was the status of women. In 1961, he set up a commission to explore issues relating to women, particularly employment and education.

Kennedy set out to transform his broad vision of progress into what he called the **New Frontier.** "We stand today on the edge of a New Frontier," Kennedy had announced upon accepting the nomination for president. He called on Americans to be "new pioneers" and explore "uncharted areas of science and space, . . . unconquered pockets of ignorance and prejudice, unanswered questions of poverty and surplus."

Kennedy had difficulty turning his vision into reality, however. He offered Congress proposals to provide medical care for the aged, rebuild blighted urban areas, and aid education, but he couldn't gather enough votes. Kennedy faced the same conservative coalition that had blocked President Truman's Fair Deal.

In his efforts to push his domestic reform measures through Congress, Kennedy showed little skill. Since he had been elected by the slimmest of margins, he lacked a popular **mandate**—a clear indication that voters approved of his plans. As a result, he often tried to play it safe politically. Nevertheless, Kennedy did persuade Congress to enact measures to boost the economy, build the national defense, provide international aid, and fund a massive space program. **A**

STIMULATING THE ECONOMY One domestic problem the Kennedy team tackled was the economy. By 1960 America was in a recession. Unemployment hovered around 6 percent, one of the highest levels since World War II. During the campaign, Kennedy had criticized the Eisenhower administration for failing to stimulate growth. The American economy, he said, was lagging behind those of other Western democracies and the Soviet Union.

Kennedy's advisers pushed for the use of deficit spending, which had been the basis for Roosevelt's New Deal. They said that stimulating economic growth depended on increased government spending and lower taxes, even if it meant that the government spent more than it took in.

Accordingly, the proposals Kennedy sent to Congress in 1961 called for increased spending. The Department of Defense received a nearly 20 percent budget increase for new nuclear missiles, nuclear submarines, and an expansion of the armed services. Congress also approved a package that increased the minimum wage to $1.25 an hour, extended unemployment insurance, and provided assistance to cities with high unemployment.

ADDRESSING POVERTY ABROAD One of the first campaign promises Kennedy fulfilled was the creation of the **Peace Corps,** a program of volunteer assistance to the developing nations of Asia, Africa, and Latin America. Critics in the United States called the program "Kennedy's Kiddie Korps" because many volunteers were just out of college. Some foreign observers questioned whether Americans could understand other cultures.

Despite these reservations, the Peace Corps became a huge success. People of all ages and backgrounds signed up to work as agricultural advisers, teachers, or health aides or to do whatever work the host country needed. By 1968, more than 35,000 volunteers had served in 60 nations around the world.

A second foreign aid program, the **Alliance for Progress,** offered economic and technical assistance to Latin American countries. Between 1961 and 1969, the United States invested almost

MAIN IDEA

Identifying Problems

A Why did Kennedy have difficulty achieving many of his New Frontier goals?

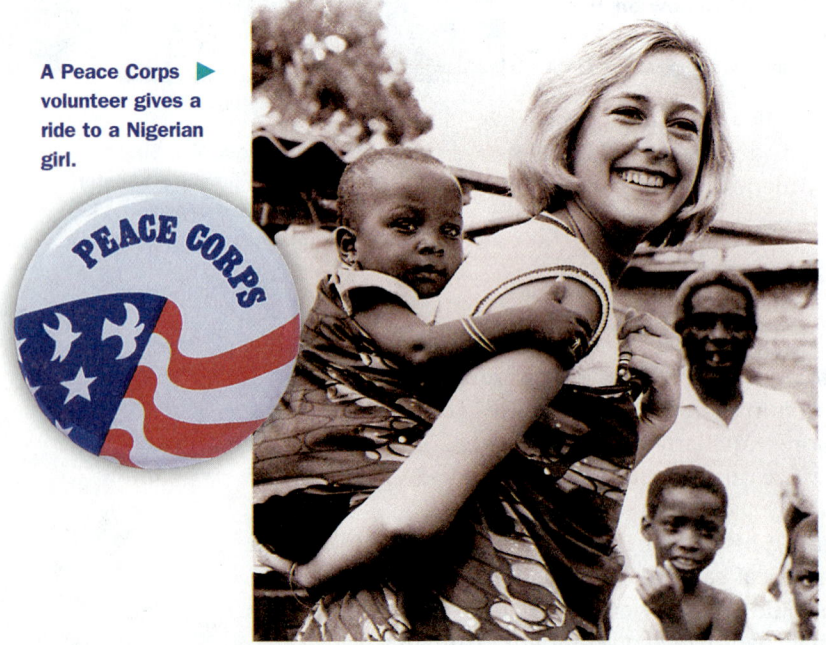

A Peace Corps ▶ volunteer gives a ride to a Nigerian girl.

MAIN IDEA

Analyzing
Motives

B Why did
Kennedy want to
invest in foreign
aid?

$12 billion in Latin America, in part to deter these countries from picking up Fidel Castro's revolutionary ideas. While the money brought some development to the region, it didn't bring fundamental reforms. **B**

RACE TO THE MOON On April 12, 1961, Soviet cosmonaut Yuri A. Gagarin became the first human in space. Kennedy saw this as a challenge and decided that America would surpass the Soviets by sending a man to the moon.

In less than a month the United States had duplicated the Soviet feat. Later that year, a communications satellite called Telstar relayed live television pictures across the Atlantic Ocean from Maine to Europe. Meanwhile, America's National Aeronautics and Space Administration (NASA) had begun to construct new launch facilities at Cape Canaveral, Florida, and a mission control center in Houston, Texas. America's pride and prestige were restored. Speaking before a crowd at Houston's Rice University, Kennedy expressed the spirit of "the space race."

★ **A PERSONAL VOICE** PRESIDENT JOHN F. KENNEDY

" We choose to go to the moon in this decade and do the other things, not because they are easy, but because they are hard, because that goal will serve to organize and measure the best of our energies and skills, because that challenge is one that we are willing to accept, one we are unwilling to post-pone, and one which we intend to win, and the others, too. "

—Address on the Nation's Space Effort, September 12, 1962

Seven years later, on July 20, 1969, the U.S. would achieve its goal. An excited nation watched with bated breath as U.S. astronaut Neil Armstrong took his first steps on the moon.

MAIN IDEA

Analyzing
Effects

C What effect
did the space
program have on
other areas of
American life?

As a result of the space program, universities expanded their science pro-grams. The huge federal funding for research and development gave rise to new industries and new technologies, many of which could be used in business and industry and also in new consumer goods. Space- and defense-related industries sprang up in the Southern and Western states, which grew rapidly. **C**

HISTORICAL
SPOTLIGHT

JOHNSON AND MISSION CONTROL

President Kennedy appointed Vice President Johnson as chair-man of the National Aeronautics and Space Council shortly after they assumed office in 1961. The chairman's duties were vague, but Johnson spelled them out: "He is to advise the presi-dent of what this nation's space policy ought to be." And Johnson's advice was to land a man on the moon.

A new home for the moon pro-gram's Manned Spacecraft Center was created. Some NASA administrators had wanted to consolidate the center and the launch site in Florida. However, when Johnson's friends at Humble Oil donated land to Rice University, which sold 600 acres to NASA and donated the rest, the debate was over. Houston became the center of the new space program.

U.S. Space Race Expenditures, 1959–1975

Government Expenditures for Space Activities

Spending (in billions of dollars): 8, 7, 6, 5, 4, 3, 2, 1, 0

'59 '61 '63 '65 '67 '69 '71 '73 '75

Geographical Distribution of NASA Contracts (1961–1975)

California 39% $15.4 billion
Texas 6% $2.5 billion
Other States 39% $15.6 billion
New York 9% $3.4 billion
Florida 7% $2.8 billion

Source: NASA

SKILLBUILDER Interpreting Graphs and Charts
1. In which year did the federal government spend the most money on the space race?
2. What state benefited the most?

ADDRESSING DOMESTIC PROBLEMS While progress was being made on the new frontiers of space exploration and international aid, many Americans suffered at home. In 1962, the problem of poverty in America was brought to national attention in Michael Harrington's book *The Other America*. Harrington profiled the 50 million people in America who scraped by each year on less than $1,000 per person. The number of poor shocked many Americans.

While Harrington awakened the nation to the nightmare of poverty, the fight against segregation took hold. Throughout the South, demonstrators raised their voices in what would become some of the most controversial civil rights battles of the 1960s. (See Chapter 29.) Kennedy had not pushed aggressively for legislation on the issues of poverty and civil rights, although he effected changes by executive action. However, now he felt that it was time to live up to a campaign promise.

In 1963, Kennedy began to focus more closely on the issues at home. He called for a "national assault on the causes of poverty." He also ordered Robert Kennedy's Justice Department to investigate racial injustices in the South. Finally, he presented Congress with a sweeping civil rights bill and a proposal to cut taxes by over $10 billion. **D**

MAIN IDEA

Making Inferences

D In what directions did President Kennedy seem to be taking his administration in 1963?

Tragedy in Dallas

In the fall of 1963, public opinion polls showed that Kennedy was losing popularity because of his advocacy of civil rights. Yet most still supported their beloved president. No one could foresee the terrible national tragedy just ahead.

FOUR DAYS IN NOVEMBER On the sunny morning of November 22, 1963, *Air Force One*, the presidential aircraft, landed in Dallas, Texas. President and Mrs. Kennedy had come to Texas to mend political fences with members of the state's Democratic Party. Kennedy had expected a cool reception from the conservative state, but he basked instead in warm waves of applause from crowds that lined the streets of downtown Dallas.

Jacqueline and her husband sat in the back seat of an open-air limousine. In front of them sat Texas Governor John Connally and his wife, Nellie. As the car approached a state building known as the Texas School Book Depository, Nellie Connally turned to Kennedy and said, "You can't say that Dallas isn't friendly to you today." A few seconds later, rifle shots rang out, and Kennedy was shot in the head. His car raced to a nearby hospital, where doctors frantically tried to revive him, but it was too late. President Kennedy was dead.

As the tragic news spread through America's schools, offices, and homes, people reacted with disbelief. Questions were on everyone's lips: Who had killed the president, and why? What would happen next?

John Kennedy, Jr., salutes his father's casket as it is ▶ prepared for the trip to Arlington National Cemetery. His uncles, Edward Kennedy and Attorney General Robert Kennedy; his mother; and his sister look on.

During the next four days, television became "the window of the world." A photograph of a somber Lyndon Johnson taking the oath of office aboard the presidential airplane was broadcast. Soon, audiences watched as Dallas police charged Lee Harvey Oswald with the murder. His palm print had been found on the rifle used to kill John F. Kennedy.

The 24-year-old ex-Marine had a suspicious past. After receiving a dishonorable discharge, Oswald had briefly lived in the Soviet Union, and he supported Castro. On Sunday, November 24, as millions watched live television coverage of Oswald being transferred between jails, a nightclub owner named Jack Ruby broke through the crowd and shot and killed Oswald.

The next day, all work stopped for Kennedy's funeral as America mourned its fallen leader. The assassination and televised funeral became a historic event. Americans who were alive then can still recall what they were doing when they first heard about the shooting of their president.

Vocabulary
conspiracy: an agreement by two or more persons to take illegal political action

UNANSWERED QUESTIONS The bizarre chain of events made some people wonder if Oswald was part of a conspiracy. In 1963, the **Warren Commission** investigated and concluded that Oswald had shot the president while acting on his own. Later, in 1979, a reinvestigation concluded that Oswald was part of a conspiracy. Investigators also said that two persons may have fired at the president. Numerous other people have made investigations. Their explanations have ranged from a plot by anti-Castro Cubans, to a Communist-sponsored attack, to a conspiracy by the CIA. **E**

MAIN IDEA

Contrasting

E How did the Warren Commission's findings differ from other theories?

What Americans did learn from the Kennedy assassination was that their system of government is remarkably sturdy. A crisis that would have crippled a dictatorship did not prevent a smooth transition to the presidency of Lyndon Johnson. In a speech to Congress, Johnson expressed his hope that "from the brutal loss of our leader we will derive not weakness but strength." Not long after, Johnson drove through Congress the most ambitious domestic legislative package since the New Deal.

NOW & THEN

KENNEDY'S ASSASSINATION

From the beginning, people have questioned the Warren Commission report. Amateur investigators have led to increasing public pressure on the government to tell all it knows about the assassination.

In response, Congress passed the JFK Records Act in 1992, which created a panel to review government and private files and decide which should be part of the public record.

Since the law was enacted, newly declassified information has added some weight to a body of evidence that JFK was shot from the front (the Warren Commission had concluded that a single bullet struck the president from behind) and that Oswald, thus, could not have acted alone. While such evidence challenges the Warren Commission's report, no information has yet surfaced that conclusively disproves its findings.

SECTION 2 **ASSESSMENT**

1. TERMS & NAMES For each term or name, write a sentence explaining its significance.

- New Frontier
- mandate
- Peace Corps
- Alliance for Progress
- Warren Commission

MAIN IDEA

2. TAKING NOTES
Re-create the web shown and fill it in with programs of the New Frontier.

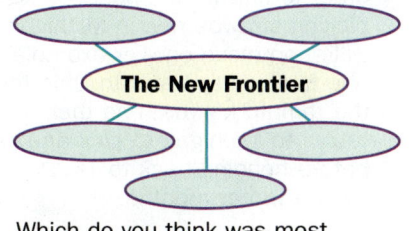

The New Frontier

Which do you think was most successful? Why?

CRITICAL THINKING

3. ANALYZING MOTIVES
Why do you think Congress was so enthusiastic about allocating funds for the space program but rejected spending in education, social services, and other pressing needs?

4. MAKING INFERENCES
Why do you think Kennedy lost popularity for supporting civil rights?

5. EVALUATING LEADERSHIP
Do you think President Kennedy was a successful leader? Explain your viewpoint. **Think About:**

- the reasons for his popularity
- the goals he expressed
- his foreign policy
- his legislative record

The Movement of Migrant Workers

The nation's 2 million farm workers are responsible for harvesting much of the fruit and vegetables that families eat each day. Most field workers on United States farms remain in one place most of the year. Others are migrant workers, who move with their entire family from one region to the next as the growing seasons change. Nationally, migrant workers make up some 50 percent of hired farm workers, depending on the season and other factors.

As the map shows, there were three major streams of migrant worker movements in the 1960s: the Pacific Coast, the Midwest, and the Atlantic Coast. While these paths may have changed slightly since then, the movement of migrant workers into nearly every region of the nation continues today.

▼ THE PACIFIC COAST

The Pacific Coast region's moderate climate allows for year-round harvesting. Most of California's migrant farm workers work on large fruit farms for much of the year. About 65,000 workers make their way up to Washington each year to pick cherries, apples, and other crops.

▲ THE MIDWEST

Workers along the Midwest and East Coast streams, where crops are smaller, must keep moving in order to find work. These workers picking strawberries in Michigan will soon move on. For example, one family may travel to Ohio for the tomato harvest and then return to Michigan to pick apples before heading back to Texas for the winter months.

The map above shows the three major streams of migrant worker movements in the 1960s.

Legend:
- Pacific Coast paths
- Midwest paths
- Atlantic Coast paths
- Year-round work
- Migrant base areas

0   250   500 miles
0   250   500 kilometers

▲ THE ATLANTIC COAST

While some workers along the Atlantic Coast stream remain in Florida, others travel as far north as New Hampshire and New York, like the workers shown here harvesting onions. There, they work from March through September. Due to the winters, migrant workers in most of the Midwest and Atlantic regions can find work for only six months out of the year.

THINKING CRITICALLY

CONNECT TO HISTORY
1. **Analyzing Patterns** Retrace the movement of migrant workers in the three regions. Why do you think migrant workers have to keep moving?

CONNECT TO TODAY
2. **Creating a Database** Pose a historical question about the relationship between crops and planting seasons. For example, what types of crops are harvested in Michigan during the fall? Then research and create a database that answers this and other such questions.

SEE SKILLBUILDER HANDBOOK, PAGE R33

hmhsocialstudies.com   RESEARCH WEB LINKS

SECTION 3

PI 2.3
PI 4.2

CC Unit 7.III.B.1.a   CC Unit 7.III.B.1.b
CC Unit 7.III.B.1.c   CC Unit 7.III.B.1.d
CC Unit 7.V.C.5.a

The Great Society

MAIN IDEA	WHY IT MATTERS NOW	Terms & Names
The demand for reform helped create a new awareness of social problems, especially on matters of civil rights and the effects of poverty.	Reforms made in the 1960s have had a lasting effect on the American justice system by increasing the rights of minorities.	• Lyndon Baines Johnson • Economic Opportunity Act • Great Society • Medicare and Medicaid • Immigration Act of 1965 • Warren Court • reapportionment

One American's Story

In 1966, family finances forced Larry Alfred to drop out of high school in Mobile, Alabama. He turned to the Job Corps, a federal program that trained young people from poor backgrounds. He learned to operate construction equipment, but his dream was to help people. On the advice of his Job Corps counselor, he joined VISTA—Volunteers in Service to America—often called the "domestic Peace Corps."

Both the Job Corps and VISTA sprang into being in 1964, when President Lyndon B. Johnson signed the Economic Opportunity Act. This law was the main offensive of Johnson's "war on poverty" and a cornerstone of the Great Society.

VISTA assigned Alfred to work with a community of poor farm laborers in Robstown, Texas, near the Mexican border. There he found a number of children with mental and physical disabilities who had no special assistance, education, or training. So he established the Robstown Association for Retarded People, started a parents education program, sought state funds, and created a rehabilitation center. At age 20, Larry Alfred was a high school dropout, Job Corps graduate, VISTA volunteer, and in Robstown, an authority on people with disabilities. Alfred embodied Johnson's Great Society in two ways: its programs helped him turn his life around, and he made a difference in people's lives.

▲ VISTA volunteers worked in a variety of capacities. This woman is teaching art to young pupils.

LBJ's Path to Power

By the time **Lyndon Baines Johnson,** or LBJ, as he was called, succeeded to the presidency, his ambition and drive had become legendary. In explaining his frenetic energy, Johnson once remarked, "That's the way I've been all my life. My daddy used to wake me up at dawn and shake my leg and say, 'Lyndon, every boy in town's got an hour's head start on you.'"

FROM THE TEXAS HILLS TO CAPITOL HILL A fourth-generation Texan, Johnson grew up in the dry Texas hill country of Blanco County. The Johnsons never knew great wealth, but they also never missed a meal.

LBJ entered politics in 1937 when he won a special election to fill a vacant seat in the U.S. House of Representatives. Johnson styled himself as a "New Dealer" and spokesperson for the small ranchers and struggling farmers of his district. He caught the eye of President Franklin Roosevelt, who took Johnson under his wing. Roosevelt helped him secure key committee assignments in Congress and steer much-needed electrification and water projects to his Texas district. Johnson, in turn, idolized FDR and imitated his leadership style.

Once in the House, Johnson eagerly eyed a seat in the Senate. In 1948, after an exhausting, bitterly fought campaign, he won the Democratic primary election for the Senate by a margin of only 87 votes out of 988,000.

A MASTER POLITICIAN Johnson proved himself a master of party politics and behind-the-scenes maneuvering, and he rose to the position of Senate majority leader in 1955. People called his legendary ability to persuade senators to support his bills the "LBJ treatment." As a reporter for the *Saturday Evening Post* explained, Johnson also used this treatment to win over reporters.

★ A PERSONAL VOICE STEWART ALSOP

"**The Majority Leader [Johnson] was, it seemed, in a relaxed, friendly, reminiscent mood. But by gradual stages this mood gave way to something rather like a human hurricane. Johnson was up, striding about his office, talking without pause, occasionally leaning over, his nose almost touching the reporter's, to shake the reporter's shoulder or grab his knee. . . . Appeals were made, to the Almighty, to the shades of the departed great, to the reporter's finer instincts and better nature, while the reporter, unable to get a word in edgewise, sat collapsed upon a leather sofa, eyes glazed, mouth half open.**"

—"The New President," *Saturday Evening Post*, December 14, 1963

Johnson's deft handling of Congress led to the passage of the Civil Rights Act of 1957, a voting rights measure that was the first civil rights legislation since Reconstruction. Johnson's knack for achieving legislative results had captured John F. Kennedy's attention, too, during Kennedy's run for the White House. To Kennedy, Johnson's congressional connections and his Southern Protestant background compensated for his own drawbacks as a candidate, so he asked Johnson to be his running mate. Johnson's presence on the ticket helped Kennedy win key states in the South, especially Texas, which went Democratic by just a few thousand votes. **A**

KEY PLAYER

LYNDON B. JOHNSON
1908–1973

LBJ received his teaching degree from Southwest Texas State Teachers College in 1930. To finance his own education, Johnson took a year off from college to work at a Mexican-American school in Cotulla, Texas. He later taught public speaking and debate at the Sam Houston High School in Houston. At age 26, he became the state director of the National Youth Administration, a New Deal agency.

As president, Johnson pushed hard for the passage of the Elementary and Secondary Education Act. In 1965, he signed the act at the one-room schoolhouse near Stonewall, Texas, where his own education had begun. Johnson later wrote,

"My education had begun with what I learned in that schoolroom. Now what I had learned and experienced since that time had brought me back to fulfill a dream."

MAIN IDEA

Analyzing Motives

 A Why did Kennedy choose Johnson to be his running mate?

VIDEO
LBJ's Management Style

hmhsocialstudies.com

Johnson's Domestic Agenda

In the wake of Kennedy's assassination, President Johnson addressed a joint session of Congress. It was the fifth day of his administration. "All I have I would have given gladly not to be standing here today," he began. Kennedy had inspired Americans to begin to solve national and world problems. Johnson urged Congress to pass the civil rights and tax-cut bills that Kennedy had sent to Capitol Hill.

WORLD STAGE

THE WAR IN VIETNAM

As LBJ pushed through his domestic programs, the U.S. grew more interested in halting the spread of communism around the world. In Vietnam, anti-Communist nationalists controlled South Vietnam while Communist leader Ho Chi Minh had taken over North Vietnam. The Geneva Accords had temporarily provided peace, dividing Vietnam along the 17th parallel into two distinct political regions. Despite this treaty, the North was supporting Communist rebels who were trying to take over the South.

Though Presidents Eisenhower and Kennedy had provided economic and military aid to South Vietnam, soon the U.S. would be directly involved in fighting the war.

In February 1964 Congress passed a tax reduction of over $10 billion into law. As the Democrats had hoped, the tax cut spurred economic growth. People spent more, which meant profits for businesses, which increased tax revenues and lowered the federal budget deficit from $6 billion in 1964 to $4 billion in 1966.

Then in July, Johnson pushed the Civil Rights Act of 1964 through Congress, persuading Southern senators to stop blocking its passage. It prohibited discrimination based on race, religion, national origin, and sex and granted the federal government new powers to enforce its provisions.

THE WAR ON POVERTY Following these successes, LBJ pressed on with his own agenda—to alleviate poverty. Early in 1964, he had declared "unconditional war on poverty in America" and proposed sweeping legislation designed to help Americans "on the outskirts of hope."

In August 1964, Congress enacted the **Economic Opportunity Act** (EOA), approving nearly $1 billion for youth programs, antipoverty measures, small-business loans, and job training. The EOA legislation created:

- the Job Corps Youth Training Program
- VISTA (Volunteers in Service to America)
- Project Head Start, an education program for underprivileged preschoolers
- the Community Action Program, which encouraged poor people to participate in public-works programs. **B**

THE 1964 ELECTION In 1964, the Republicans nominated conservative senator Barry Goldwater of Arizona to oppose Johnson. Goldwater believed the federal government had no business trying to right social and economic wrongs such as poverty, discrimination, and lack of opportunity. He attacked such long-established federal programs as Social Security, which he wanted to make voluntary, and the Tennessee Valley Authority, which he wanted to sell.

In 1964, most American people were in tune with Johnson—they believed that government could and should help solve the nation's problems. Moreover, Goldwater had frightened many Americans by suggesting that he might use nuclear weapons on Cuba and North Vietnam. Johnson's campaign capitalized on this fear. It produced a chilling television commercial in which a picture of a little girl counting the petals on a daisy dissolved into a mushroom cloud created by an atomic bomb. Where Goldwater advocated intervention in Vietnam, Johnson assured the American people that sending U.S. troops there "would offer no solution at all to the real problem of Vietnam."

LBJ won the election by a landslide, winning 61 percent of the popular vote and 486 electoral votes, while Senator Goldwater won only 52. The Democrats also increased their majority in Congress. For the first time since 1938, a Democratic president did not need the votes of conservative Southern Democrats in order to get laws passed. Now Johnson could launch his reform program in earnest.

Campaign ▶ buttons like this one capitalized on the nation's growing liberal democratic sentiments.

I USED TO BE A REPUBLICAN
vote **LBJ**

MAIN IDEA

Identifying Problems

B What problems in American society did the Economic Opportunity Act seek to address?

Building the Great Society

In May 1964, Johnson had summed up his vision for America in a phrase: the **Great Society.** In a speech at the University of Michigan, Johnson outlined a legislative program that would end poverty and racial injustice. But, he told an enthusiastic crowd, that was "just the beginning." Johnson envisioned a legislative program that would create not only a higher standard of living and equal opportunity, but also promote a richer quality of life for all.

★ A PERSONAL VOICE LYNDON B. JOHNSON

" The Great Society is a place where every child can find knowledge to enrich his mind and to enlarge his talents. It is a place where leisure is a welcome chance to build and reflect, not a feared cause of boredom and restlessness. It is a place where the city of man serves not only the needs of the body and the demands of commerce but the desire for beauty and the hunger for community. It is a place where man can renew contact with nature. It is a place which honors creation for its own sake and for what it adds to the understanding of the race. "

—"The Great Society," May 22, 1964

Like his idol FDR, LBJ wanted to change America. By the time Johnson left the White House in 1969, Congress had passed 206 of his measures. The president personally led the battle to get most of them passed.

EDUCATION During 1965 and 1966, the LBJ administration introduced a flurry of bills to Congress. Johnson considered education "the key which can unlock the door to the Great Society." The Elementary and Secondary Education Act of 1965 provided more than $1 billion in federal aid to help public and parochial schools purchase textbooks and new library materials. This was the first major federal aid package for education in the nation's history.

Great Society Programs, 1964–1967

POVERTY

1964 Tax Reduction Act cut corporate and individual taxes to stimulate growth.

1964 Economic Opportunity Act created Job Corps, VISTA, Project Head Start, and other programs to fight the "war on poverty."

1965 Medicare Act established Medicare and Medicaid programs.

1965 Appalachian Regional Development Act targeted aid for highways, health centers, and resource development in that economically depressed area.

CITIES

1965 Omnibus Housing Act provided money for low-income housing.

1965 Department of Housing and Urban Development was formed to administer federal housing programs.

1966 Demonstration Cities and Metropolitan Area Redevelopment Act funded slum rebuilding, mass transit, and other improvements for selected "model cities."

EDUCATION

1965 Elementary and Secondary Education Act directed money to schools for textbooks, library materials, and special education.

1965 Higher Education Act funded scholarships and low-interest loans for college students.

1965 National Foundation on the Arts and the Humanities was created to financially assist painters, musicians, actors, and other artists.

1967 Corporation for Public Broadcasting was formed to fund educational TV and radio broadcasting.

DISCRIMINATION

1964 Civil Rights Act outlawed discrimination in public accommodations, housing, and jobs; increased federal power to prosecute civil rights abuses.

1964 Twenty-Fourth Amendment abolished the poll tax in federal elections.

1965 Voting Rights Act ended the practice of requiring voters to pass literacy tests and permitted the federal government to monitor voter registration.

1965 Immigration Act ended national-origins quotas established in 1924.

ENVIRONMENT

1965 Wilderness Preservation Act set aside over 9 million acres for national forest lands.

1965 Water Quality Act required states to clean up their rivers.

1965 Clean Air Act Amendment directed the federal government to establish emission standards for new motor vehicles.

1967 Air Quality Act set federal air pollution guidelines and extended federal enforcement power.

CONSUMER ADVOCACY

1966 Truth in Packaging Act set standards for labeling consumer products.

1966 National Traffic and Motor Vehicle Safety Act set federal safety standards for the auto and tire industries.

1966 Highway Safety Act required states to set up highway safety programs.

1966 Department of Transportation was created to deal with national air, rail, and highway transportation.

SKILLBUILDER Interpreting Charts
What did the Great Society programs indicate about the federal government's changing role?

HEALTHCARE LBJ and Congress changed Social Security by establishing Medicare and Medicaid. **Medicare** provided hospital insurance and low-cost medical insurance for almost every American age 65 or older. **Medicaid** extended health insurance to welfare recipients. **C**

HOUSING Congress also made several important decisions that shifted the nation's political power from rural to urban areas. These decisions included appropriating money to build some 240,000 units of low-rent public housing and help low- and moderate-income families pay for better private housing; establishing the Department of Housing and Urban Development (HUD); and appointing Robert Weaver, the first African-American cabinet member in American history, as Secretary of HUD.

MAIN IDEA

Comparing

C How are Medicare and Medicaid similar?

IMMIGRATION The Great Society also brought profound changes to the nation's immigration laws. The Immigration Act of 1924 and the National Origins Act of 1924 had established immigration quotas that discriminated strongly against people from outside Western Europe. The Act set a quota of about 150,000 people annually. It discriminated against southern and eastern Europeans and barred Asians completely. The **Immigration Act of 1965** opened the door for many non-European immigrants to settle in the United States by ending quotas based on nationality. **D**

MAIN IDEA

Analyzing Effects

D How did the Immigration Act of 1965 change the nation's immigration system?

THE ENVIRONMENT In 1962, *Silent Spring*, a book by Rachel Carson, had exposed a hidden danger: the effects of pesticides on the environment. Carson's book and the public's outcry resulted in the Water Quality Act of 1965, which required states to clean up rivers. Johnson also ordered the government to search out the worst chemical polluters. "There is no excuse . . . for chemical companies and oil refineries using our major rivers as pipelines for toxic wastes." Such words and actions helped trigger the environmental movement in the United States. (See Chapter 32.)

CONSUMER PROTECTION Consumer advocates also made headway. They convinced Congress to pass major safety laws, including a truth-in-packaging law that set standards for labeling consumer goods. Ralph Nader, a young lawyer, wrote a book, *Unsafe at Any Speed,* that sharply criticized the U.S. automobile industry for ignoring safety concerns. His testimony helped persuade Congress to establish safety standards for automobiles and tires. Precautions extended to food, too. Congress passed the Wholesome Meat Act of 1967. "Americans can feel a little safer now in their homes, on the road, at the supermarket, and in the department store," said Johnson.

NOW & THEN

MEDICARE ON THE LINE

When President Johnson signed the Medicare bill in 1965, only half of the nation's elderly had health insurance. Today, thanks largely to Medicare, nearly all persons 65 years or older have medical coverage.

Over the years, federal spending on Medicare has steadily increased and today accounts for about 12 percent of all federal outlays. Experts have debated whether Medicare can be sustained as people live longer, health care costs increase, and the baby boomer generation reaches retirement age. Though most Americans are not in favor of cutbacks to Medicare, efforts have been made in the last few years to cut the growth in spending.

Reforms of the Warren Court

Background

In *Engel* v. *Vitale* (1962), the Warren Court banned formal prayers in public schools. Such prayers, the Court said, violated the First Amendment's guarantee that government should not establish an "official" religion.

The wave of liberal reform that characterized the Great Society also swept through the Supreme Court of the 1960s. Beginning with the 1954 landmark decision *Brown* v. *Board of Education*, which ruled school segregation unconstitutional, the Court under Chief Justice Earl Warren took an activist stance on the leading issues of the day.

Several major court decisions in the 1960s affected American society. The **Warren Court** banned prayer in public schools and declared state-required loyalty oaths unconstitutional. It limited the power of communities to censor books and films and said that free speech included the wearing of black armbands to school by antiwar students. Furthermore, the Court brought about change in federal and state reapportionment and the criminal justice system.

CONGRESSIONAL REAPPORTIONMENT In a key series of decisions, the Warren Court addressed the issue of **reapportionment,** or the way in which states redraw election districts based on the changing number of people in them. By 1960, about 80 percent of Americans lived in cities and suburbs. However, many states had failed to change their congressional districts to reflect this development; instead, rural districts might have fewer than 200,000 people, while some urban districts had more than 600,000. Thus the voters in rural areas had more representation—and also more power—than those in urban areas.

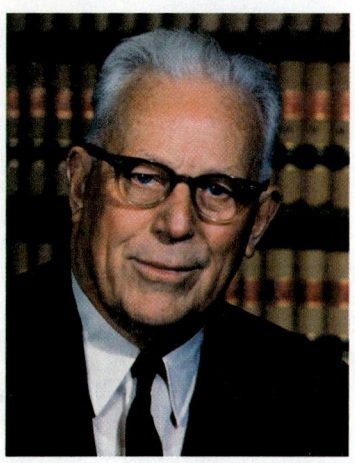

Chief Justice Earl Warren

Baker v. *Carr* (1962) was the first of several decisions that established the principle of "one person, one vote." The Court asserted that the federal courts had the right to tell states to reapportion—redivide—their districts for more equal representation. In later decisions, the Court ruled that congressional district boundaries should be redrawn so that districts would be equal in population, and in *Reynolds* v. *Sims* (1964), it extended the principle of "one person, one vote" to state legislative districts. (See *Reynolds* v. *Sims,* page 980.) These decisions led to a shift of political power throughout the nation from rural to urban areas.

RIGHTS OF THE ACCUSED Other Warren Court decisions greatly expanded the rights of people accused of crimes. In *Mapp* v. *Ohio* (1961), the Court ruled that evidence seized illegally could not be used in state courts. This is called the exclusionary rule. In *Gideon* v. *Wainwright* (1963), the justices required criminal courts to provide free legal counsel to those who could not afford it. In *Escobedo* v. *Illinois* (1964), the justices ruled that an accused person has a right to have a lawyer present during police questioning. In 1966, the Court went one step further in *Miranda* v. *Arizona*, where it ruled that all suspects must be read their rights before questioning. (See *Miranda* v. *Arizona,* page 900.)

These rulings greatly divided public opinion. Liberals praised the decisions, arguing that they placed necessary limits on police power and protected the right of all citizens to a fair trial. Conservatives, however, bitterly criticized the Court. They claimed that *Mapp* and *Miranda* benefited criminal suspects and severely limited the power of the police to investigate crimes. During the late 1960s and 1970s, Republican candidates for office seized on the "crime issue," portraying liberals and Democrats as being soft on crime and citing the decisions of the Warren Court as major obstacles to fighting crime. **E**

MAIN IDEA

Contrasting

E What were the differing reactions to the Warren Court decisions on the rights of the accused?

P O I N T

"The Great Society succeeded in prompting far-reaching social change."

Defenders of the Great Society contend that it bettered the lives of millions of Americans. Historian John Morton Blum notes, "The Great Society initiated policies that by 1985 had had profound consequences: Blacks now voted at about the same rate as whites, and nearly 6,000 blacks held public offices; almost every elderly citizen had medical insurance, and the aged were no poorer than Americans as a whole; a large majority of small children attended preschool programs."

Attorney Margaret Burnham argues that the civil rights gains alone justify the Great Society: "For tens of thousands of human beings . . . giving promise of a better life was significant . . . . What the Great Society affirmed was the responsibility of the federal government to take measures necessary to bring into the social and economic mainstream any segment of the people [who had been] historically excluded."

C O U N T E R P O I N T

"Failures of the Great Society prove that government-sponsored programs do not work."

The major attack on the Great Society is that it created "big government": an oversized bureaucracy, too many regulations, waste and fraud, and rising budget deficits. As journalist David Alpern writes, this comes from the notion that government could solve all the nation's problems: "The Great Society created unwieldy new mechanisms like the Office of Economic Opportunity and began 'throwing dollars at problems . . . .' Spawned in the process were vast new constituencies of government bureaucrats and beneficiaries whose political clout made it difficult to kill programs off."

Conservatives say the Great Society's social welfare programs created a culture of dependency. Economist Paul Craig Roberts argues that "The Great Society . . . reflected our lack of confidence in the institutions of a free society. We came to the view that it is government spending and not business innovation that creates jobs and that it is society's fault if anyone is poor."

THINKING CRITICALLY

CONNECT TO HISTORY
1. **Evaluating** Do you think the Great Society was a success or a failure? Explain.

 SEE SKILLBUILDER HANDBOOK, PAGE R17.

CONNECT TO TODAY
2. **Analyzing Social Problems** Research the most pressing problems in your own neighborhood or precinct. Then propose a social program you think would address at least one of those problems while avoiding the pitfalls of the Great Society programs.

Impact of the Great Society

The Great Society and the Warren Court changed the United States. People disagree on whether these changes left the nation better or worse, but most agree on one point: no president in the post–World War II era extended the power and reach of the federal government more than Lyndon Johnson. The optimism of the Johnson presidency fueled an activist era in all three branches of government, for at least the first few years.

The "war on poverty" did help. The number of poor people fell from 21 percent of the population in 1962 to 11 percent in 1973. However, many of Johnson's proposals, though well intended, were hastily conceived and proved difficult to accomplish.

Johnson's massive tax cut spurred the economy. But funding the Great Society contributed to a growing budget deficit—a problem that continued for decades. Questions about government finances, as well as debates over the effectiveness of these programs and the role of the federal government, left a number of people disillusioned. A conservative backlash began to take shape as a new group of Republican leaders rose to power. In 1966, for example, a conservative Hollywood actor named Ronald Reagan swept to victory in the race for governor of California over the Democratic incumbent.

Thousands of miles away, the increase of Communist forces in Vietnam also began to overshadow the goals of the Great Society. The fear of communism was deeply rooted in the minds of Americans from the Cold War era. Four years after initiating the Great Society, Johnson, a peace candidate in 1964, would be labeled a "hawk"—a supporter of one of the most divisive wars in recent U.S. history. **F**

MAIN IDEA

Identifying Problems

F What events and problems may have affected the success of the Great Society?

"SUNRISE....ALL THE FOREIGN TROUBLE MAKERS GOIN' TO SLEEP AN' ALL THE DOMESTIC ONES WAKIN' UP"

As this cartoon points out, President Johnson had much to deal with at home and abroad. This autographed copy was presented to President Johnson by the cartoonist.

SECTION 3 ASSESSMENT

1. TERMS & NAMES For each term or name, write a sentence explaining its significance.
- Lyndon Baines Johnson
- Economic Opportunity Act
- Great Society
- Medicare and Medicaid
- Immigration Act of 1965
- Warren Court
- reapportionment

MAIN IDEA

2. TAKING NOTES
List four or more Great Society programs and Warren Court rulings.

Great Society Programs	Warren Court Rulings
1.	1.
2.	2.
3.	3.
4.	4.

Choose one item and describe its lasting effects.

CRITICAL THINKING

3. EVALUATING LEADERSHIP
Explain how Lyndon Johnson's personal and political experiences might have influenced his actions as president. **Think About:**
- his family's background and education
- his relationship with Franklin Roosevelt
- his powers of persuasion

4. ANALYZING VISUAL SOURCES
Look at the political cartoon above. What do you think the artist was trying to convey about the Johnson administration?

MIRANDA v. ARIZONA (1966)

ORIGINS OF THE CASE In 1963, Ernesto Miranda was arrested at his home in Phoenix, Arizona, on charges of kidnapping and rape. After two hours of questioning by police, he signed a confession and was later convicted, largely based on the confession. Miranda appealed. He claimed that his confession was invalid because it was coerced and because the police never advised him of his right to an attorney or his right to avoid self-incrimination.

THE RULING The Court overturned Miranda's conviction, holding that the police must inform criminal suspects of their legal rights at the time of arrest and may not interrogate suspects who invoke their rights.

LEGAL REASONING

Chief Justice Earl Warren wrote the majority opinion in *Miranda v. Arizona.* He based his argument on the Fifth Amendment, which guarantees that an accused person cannot be forced "to be a witness against himself" or herself. Warren stressed that when suspects are interrogated in police custody, the situation is "inherently intimidating." Such a situation, he argued, undermines any evidence it produces because "no statement obtained from the defendant [while in custody] can truly be the product of his free choice."

For this reason, the Court majority found that Miranda's confession could not be used as evidence. In the opinion, Chief Justice Warren responded to the argument that police officials might find this requirement difficult to meet.

> " Not only does the use of the third degree [harassment or torture used to obtain a confession] involve a flagrant violation of law by the officers of the law, but it involves also the dangers of false confessions, and it tends to make police and prosecutors less zealous in the search for objective evidence. "

LEGAL SOURCES

U.S. CONSTITUTION

U.S. CONSTITUTION, FIFTH AMENDMENT (1791)
"No person . . . shall be compelled in any criminal case to be a witness against himself, nor be deprived of life, liberty, or property, without due process of law."

RELATED CASES

MAPP v. OHIO (1961)
The Court ruled that prosecutors may not use evidence obtained in illegal searches (exclusionary rule).

GIDEON v. WAINWRIGHT (1963)
The Court said that a defendant accused of a felony has the right to an attorney, which the government must supply if the defendant cannot afford one.

ESCOBEDO v. ILLINOIS (1964)
The Court held that a suspect has the right to an attorney when being questioned by police.

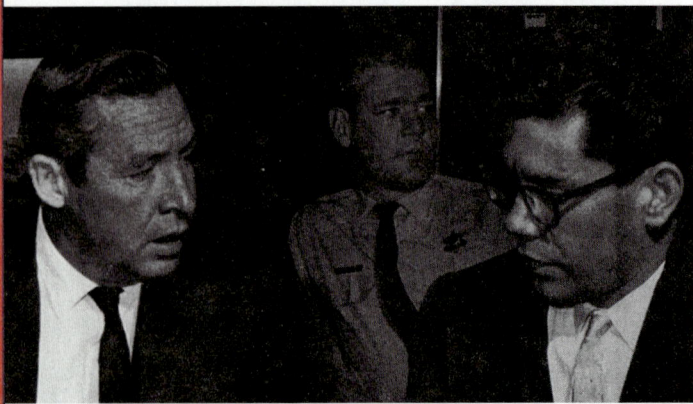

▲ Ernesto Miranda (*at right*) converses with attorney John J. Flynn in February 1967.

WHY IT MATTERED

Miranda was one of four key criminal justice cases decided by the Warren Court (see Related Cases). In each case, the decision reflected the chief justice's strong belief that all persons deserve to be treated with respect by their government. In *Miranda,* the Court directed police to inform every suspect of his or her rights at the time of arrest and even gave the police detailed instructions about what to say.

The rights of accused people need to be protected in order to ensure that innocent people are not punished. These protections also ensure that federal, state, or local authorities will not harass people for political reasons—as often happened to civil rights activists in the South in the 1950s and 1960s, for example.

Critics of the Warren Court claimed that *Miranda* would lead to more crime because it would become more difficult to convict criminals. Police departments, however, adapted to the decision. They placed the list of suspects' rights mentioned in *Miranda* on cards for police officers to read to suspects. The statement of these rights became known as the *Miranda* warning and quickly became familiar to anyone who watched a police show on television.

As for the defendant, Ernesto Miranda, he was retried and convicted on the basis of other evidence.

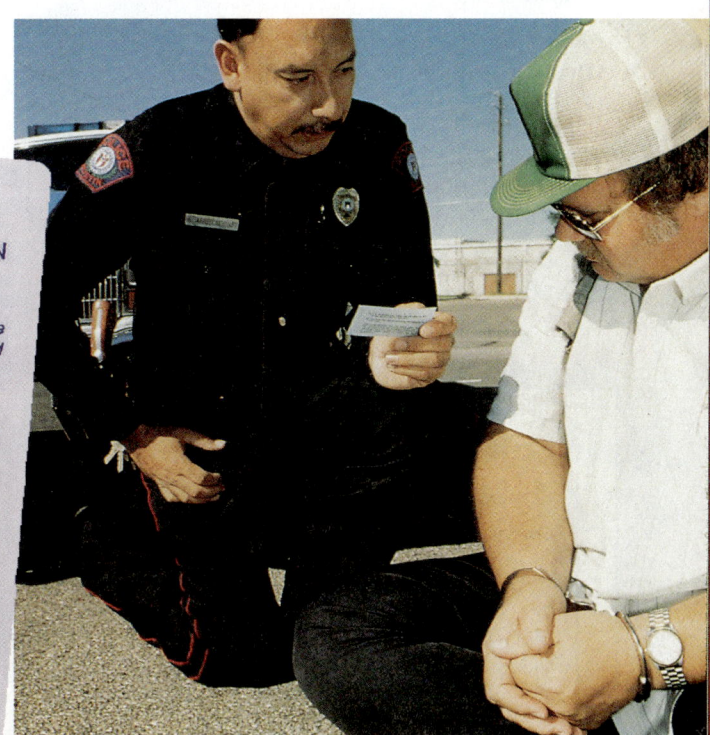

MIRANDA WARNING
CUSTODIAL INTERROGATION
JUVENILE & ADULT

The officer must determine whether the suspect understands the warning and waives his rights.

1. You have the right to remain silent.
2. Anything you say can be used as evidence against you.
3. You have a right to consult with an attorney before questioning and to have him with you during questioning.
4. If you can not afford an attorney, one will be appointed to represent you free of charge.
5. Knowing these rights, do you want to talk to me without having a lawyer present? You may stop talking to me at any time and you may also demand a lawyer at any time.

(right) This card is carried by police officers in order to read suspects their rights. **(far right)** An officer reads a suspect his rights.

HISTORICAL IMPACT

The *Miranda* decision was highly controversial. Critics complained that the opinion would protect the rights of criminals at the expense of public safety.

Since *Miranda,* the Court has continued to try to strike a balance between public safety and the rights of the accused. Several cases in the 1970s and 1980s softened the *Miranda* ruling and gave law enforcement officers more power to gather evidence without informing suspects of their rights. Even so, conservatives still hoped to overturn the *Miranda* decision.

In 2000, however, the Supreme Court affirmed *Miranda* by a 7-to-2 majority in *Dickerson* v. *United States.* Writing for the majority, Chief Justice William Rehnquist argued, "There is no such justification here for overruling *Miranda. Miranda* has become embedded in routine police practice to the point where warnings have become part of our national culture."

THINKING CRITICALLY

CONNECT TO HISTORY

1. **Drawing Conclusions** Critics charged that *Miranda* incorrectly used the Fifth Amendment. The right to avoid self-incrimination, they said, should only apply to trials, not to police questioning. Do you agree or disagree? Why?

 SEE SKILLBUILDER HANDBOOK, PAGE R18.

CONNECT TO TODAY

2. Visit the links for Historic Decisions of the Supreme Court to research laws and other court decisions related to *Mapp* and *Miranda.* Then, prepare a debate on whether courts should or should not set a guilty person free if the government broke the law in establishing that person's guilt.

 hmhsocialstudies.com **INTERNET ACTIVITY**

TERMS & NAMES

For each term or name below, write a sentence explaining its connection to the Kennedy and Johnson administrations.

1. John F. Kennedy
2. Fidel Castro
3. Berlin Wall
4. hot line
5. New Frontier
6. Peace Corps
7. Warren Commission
8. Great Society
9. Medicare and Medicaid
10. Warren Court

MAIN IDEAS

Use your notes and the information in the chapter to answer the following questions.

Kennedy and the Cold War (pages 876–884)

1. Explain the factors that led to Kennedy's victory over Nixon in the 1960 presidential campaign.
2. What were the most significant results of the Cuban missile crisis?

The New Frontier (pages 885–889)

3. What was Kennedy's New Frontier? Why did he have trouble getting his New Frontier legislation through Congress?
4. What two international aid programs were launched during the Kennedy administration?
5. How did Kennedy's assassination affect the public?

The Great Society (pages 892–899)

6. Describe ways that Great Society programs addressed the problem of poverty.
7. How did the courts increase the political power of people in urban areas and those accused of crimes?

CRITICAL THINKING

1. **USING YOUR NOTES** Use a Venn diagram to show the major legislative programs of the New Frontier and the Great Society.

NEW FRONTIER — GREAT SOCIETY

Passed under JFK | Proposed by JFK, passed under LBJ | Passed under LBJ

2. **MAKING GENERALIZATIONS** John F. Kennedy said, "[M]y fellow Americans, ask not what your country can do for you—ask what you can do for your country." Do you agree with his view about the relationship between individuals and the country? Explain your opinion.

3. **EVALUATING** Do you think the Great Society helped people achieve their hopes of making life better for themselves and their children? Explain.

VISUAL SUMMARY THE NEW FRONTIER AND THE GREAT SOCIETY

JFK

- Peace Corps
- new "flexible response" strategy for Cold War
- Cuban missile crisis
- Bay of Pigs
- race to the moon
- boosted the economy by increasing government spending
- increased minimum wage to $1.25
- extended unemployment insurance
- provided assistance to cities with high unemployment
- supported civil rights

LBJ

- Great Society reform legislation and federal assistance programs
- war on poverty
- increased protection of individual rights
- pushed civil rights bill through Congress
- EOA, VISTA, Project Head Start
- established Medicare and Medicaid
- changed immigration laws to open doors for many non-European immigrants
- furthered environmental movement
- cut taxes but increased budget deficit

Use the quotation and your knowledge of United States history to answer questions 1 and 2.

> "It is our purpose to win the Cold War, not merely wage it in the hope of attaining a standoff. . . . [I]t is really astounding that our government has never stated its purpose to be that of complete victory over the tyrannical forces of international communism. . . . We need a declaration that our intention is victory. . . . And we need an official act, such as the resumption of nuclear testing, to show our own peoples and the other freedom-loving peoples of the world that we mean business."
>
> —Senator Barry Goldwater,
> address to the U.S. Senate, July 14, 1961

1 Based on the quotation, it is reasonable to infer that Senator Goldwater probably opposed —

(1) the space race.
(2) the Bay of Pigs invasion.
(3) the Tax Reduction Act.
(4) the Limited Test Ban Treaty.

2 Lyndon Johnson helped to bring about all of the following except —

(1) the Voting Rights Act.
(2) Head Start.
(3) Social Security.
(4) Medicare.

Use the graph as well as your knowledge of United States history to answer question 3.

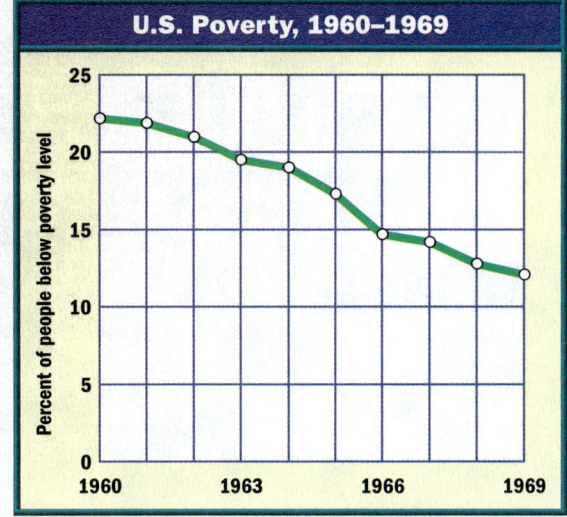

U.S. Poverty, 1960–1969

3 Which of the following is true about the graph?

(1) Johnson's war on poverty failed.
(2) Poverty began to rise again after 1969.
(3) Poverty decreased throughout the 1960s.
(4) In 1960, the poverty level was about 12%.

hmhsocialstudies.com **TEST PRACTICE**

For additional test practice, go online for:
• Diagnostic tests
• Tutorials

INTERACT WITH HISTORY

Recall the issues that you explored at the beginning of the chapter. Then write a job description for "U.S. President." Include sections on "Responsibilities" and "Requirements" that list necessary traits and experience.

Think About:

• Kennedy's and Johnson's (and Nixon's) background and style
• the role of the media
• the challenges each leader faced and how he dealt with them
• the American public's tastes and preferences

FOCUS ON WRITING

Imagine that the year is 1964. President Johnson has introduced a series of programs as a part of his vision for a Great Society. Write a persuasive letter to your congressional representative telling him or her to either support or oppose the new programs.

COLLABORATIVE LEARNING

21ST CENTURY

It is June 1963, and President Kennedy announces his intention to negotiate with the Soviets to limit or halt nuclear testing. What is your reaction to this plan—do you approve or disapprove? Working with a partner, design and create a poster that supports or criticizes President Kennedy's proposal.

OCTOBER FURY:
THE CUBAN MISSILE CRISIS

The Cuban missile crisis was perhaps the most dangerous event of the Cold War period. For several days in October 1962, the United States and the Soviet Union stood on the brink of nuclear war. The crisis began when the Soviet Union sent weapons, including nuclear missiles, to Cuba. It deepened when the United States blockaded Cuba to prevent the Soviets from delivering more missiles. With Soviet ships sailing toward the blockade, a confrontation seemed inevitable. However, at the last moment, the Soviet ships turned back and war was averted.

Explore the development and resolution of the Cuban missile crisis online. You can find a wealth of information, video clips, primary sources, activities, and more at **hmhsocialstudies.com**.

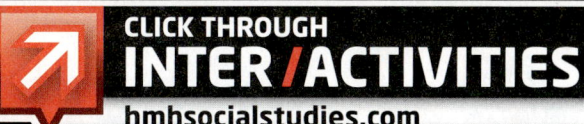
Prelude to Crisis

Watch the video to learn about the buildup to the Cuban missile crisis.

UNITED KINGDOM

UNITED STATES

Getting Ready for War

Watch the video to see how the missiles in Cuba created tension between the United States and the Soviet Union.

FALLOUT SHELTER IN BASEMENT

Crisis Averted?

Watch the video to see how the Cuban missile crisis brought the United States and the Soviet Union to the brink of nuclear war.

Lessons Learned

Watch the video to learn about the impact of the Cuban missile crisis.

CIVIL RIGHTS

Essential Question

In what ways did African Americans fight discrimination during the civil rights era?

New York Standards

KEY IDEA 2 Important ideas, social and cultural values, beliefs, and traditions from New York State and United States history illustrate the connections and interactions of people and events across time and from a variety of perspectives.

KEY IDEA 3 Study about the major social, political, economic, cultural, and religious developments in New York State and United States history involves learning about the important roles and contributions of individuals and groups.

SECTION 1: Taking on Segregation

SECTION 2: The Triumphs of a Crusade

SECTION 3: Challenges and Changes in the Movement

Civil Rights activists lead the 1965 voting rights march from Selma to Montgomery, Alabama.

THIS DOOR
WHITE ONLY
COLORED IN REAR

1954 *Brown* v. *Board of Education* decision orders the desegregation of public schools.

1955 Montgomery bus boycott begins.

1956 Dwight D. Eisenhower is reelected.

1957 School desegregation crisis occurs in Little Rock, Arkansas.

1960 John F. Kennedy is elected president.

USA
WORLD

1955

1960

1956 Suez Canal crisis occurs in Egypt.

1957 African nation of Ghana wins independence.

1959 Fidel Castro assumes power in Cuba.

HISTORY Civil Rights Bill

hmhsocialstudies.com **VIDEO**

INTERACT
WITH HISTORY

The year is 1960, and segregation divides the nation's people. African Americans are denied access to jobs and housing and are refused service at restaurants and stores. But the voices of the oppressed rise up in the churches and in the streets, demanding civil rights for all Americans.

Explore the Issues

- Are all Americans entitled to the same civil rights?
- What are the risks of demanding rights?
- Why might some people fight against equal rights?

1963 Lyndon B. Johnson becomes president upon John F. Kennedy's assassination.

1964 Lyndon B. Johnson is elected president.

1964 Congress passes the Civil Rights Act.

1967 Race riots occur in major U.S. cities.

1968 Richard M. Nixon is elected president.

1968 Martin Luther King, Jr., is assassinated.

1969 U.S. astronauts walk on the moon.

1965

1970

1962 South African civil rights leader Nelson Mandela is imprisoned.

1966 Cultural Revolution begins in China.

1968 Tet offensive begins in Vietnam.

1970 President Nasser of Egypt dies.

SECTION
1

PI 2.6
PI 3.4

CC Unit 7.II.C.2.b   CC Unit 7.II.C.2.c
CC Unit 7.III.A.1.a(2)   CC Unit 7.III.B.3.a(1)
CC Unit 7.III.B.3.b(1)   CC Unit 7.III.B.3.b(4)

Taking on Segregation

MAIN IDEA	WHY IT MATTERS NOW	Terms & Names
Activism and a series of Supreme Court decisions advanced equal rights for African Americans in the 1950s and 1960s.	Landmark Supreme Court decisions beginning in 1954 have guaranteed civil rights for Americans today.	•Thurgood Marshall •*Brown* v. *Board of Education of Topeka* •Rosa Parks •Martin Luther King, Jr. •Southern Christian Leadership Conference (SCLC) •Student Nonviolent Coordinating Committee (SNCC) •sit-in

One American's Story

hmhsocialstudies.com
TAKING NOTES
Use the graphic organizer online to take notes on the civil rights movement's efforts.

Jo Ann Gibson Robinson drew back in self-defense as the white bus driver raised his hand as if to strike her. "Get up from there!" he shouted. Robinson, laden with Christmas packages, had forgotten the rules and sat down in the front of the bus, which was reserved for whites.

Humiliating incidents were not new to the African Americans who rode the segregated buses of Montgomery, Alabama, in the mid-1950s. The bus company required them to pay at the front and then exit and reboard at the rear. "I felt like a dog," Robinson later said. A professor at the all-black Alabama State College, Robinson was also president of the Women's Political Council, a group of professional African-American women determined to increase black political power.

★ **A PERSONAL VOICE** JO ANN GIBSON ROBINSON

"We had members in every elementary, junior high, and senior high school, and in federal, state, and local jobs. Wherever there were more than ten blacks employed, we had a member there. We were prepared to the point that we knew that in a matter of hours, we could corral the whole city."

—quoted in *Voices of Freedom: An Oral History of the Civil Rights Movement*

Jo Ann Gibson Robinson

On December 1, 1955, police arrested an African-American woman for refusing to give up her seat on a bus. Robinson promptly sent out a call for all African Americans to boycott Montgomery buses.

The Segregation System

Segregated buses might never have rolled through the streets of Montgomery if the Civil Rights Act of 1875 had remained in force. This act outlawed segregation in public facilities by decreeing that "all persons . . . shall be entitled to the full and equal enjoyment of the accommodations . . . of inns, public conveyances on land or water, theaters, and other places of public amusement." In 1883, however, the all-white Supreme Court declared the act unconstitutional.

PLESSY V. FERGUSON During the 1890s, a number of other court decisions and state laws severely limited African-American rights. In 1890, Louisiana passed a law requiring railroads to provide "equal but separate accommodations for the white and colored races." In the *Plessy* v. *Ferguson* case of 1896, the Supreme Court ruled that this "separate but equal" law did not violate the Fourteenth Amendment, which guarantees all Americans equal treatment under the law.

Armed with the *Plessy* decision, states throughout the nation, but especially in the South, passed what were known as Jim Crow laws, aimed at separating the races. These laws forbade marriage between blacks and whites and established many other restrictions on social and religious contact between the races. There were separate schools as well as separate streetcars, waiting rooms, railroad coaches, elevators, witness stands, and public restrooms. The facilities provided for blacks were always inferior to those for whites. Nearly every day, African Americans faced humiliating signs that read: "Colored Water"; "No Blacks Allowed"; "Whites Only!" **A**

SEGREGATION CONTINUES INTO THE 20TH CENTURY

After the Civil War, some African Americans tried to escape Southern racism by moving north. This migration of Southern African Americans speeded up greatly during World War I, as many African-American sharecroppers abandoned farms for the promise of industrial jobs in Northern cities. However, they discovered racial prejudice and segregation there, too. Most could find housing only in all-black neighborhoods. Many white workers also resented the competition for jobs. This sometimes led to violence.

Background
See *Plessy* v. *Ferguson* on page 496.

MAIN IDEA

Analyzing Effects

A What were the effects of the Supreme Court decision *Plessy* v. *Ferguson*?

WORLD STAGE

APARTHEID—SEGREGATION IN SOUTH AFRICA

In 1948, the white government of South Africa passed laws to ensure that whites would stay in control of the country. Those laws established a system called apartheid, which means "apartness." The system divided South Africans into four segregated racial groups—whites, blacks, coloreds of mixed race, and Asians. It restricted what jobs nonwhites could hold, where they could live, and what rights they could exercise. Because of apartheid, the black African majority were denied the right to vote.

In response to worldwide criticism, the South African government gradually repealed the apartheid laws, starting in the late 1970s. In 1994, South Africa held its first all-race election and elected as president Nelson Mandela, a black anti-apartheid leader whom the white government had imprisoned for nearly 30 years.

U.S. School Segregation, 1952

Legend:
- Segregation required
- Segregation permitted
- Segregation prohibited
- No specific legislation, or local option

These photos of the public schools for white children *(top)* and for black children *(above)* in a Southern town in the 1930s show that separate facilities were often unequal in the segregation era.

GEOGRAPHY SKILLBUILDER
Region In which regions were schools segregated by law? In which were segregation expressly prohibited?

A DEVELOPING CIVIL RIGHTS MOVEMENT In many ways, the events of World War II set the stage for the civil rights movement. First, the demand for soldiers in the early 1940s created a shortage of white male laborers. That labor shortage opened up new job opportunities for African Americans, Latinos, and white women.

Second, nearly one million African Americans served in the armed forces, which needed so many fighting men that they had to end their discriminatory policies. Such policies had previously kept African Americans from serving in fighting units. Many African-American soldiers returned from the war determined to fight for their own freedom now that they had helped defeat fascist regimes overseas.

Third, during the war, civil rights organizations actively campaigned for African-American voting rights and challenged Jim Crow laws. In response to protests, President Roosevelt issued a presidential directive prohibiting racial discrimination by federal agencies and all companies that were engaged in war work. The groundwork was laid for more organized campaigns to end segregation throughout the United States. **B**

MAIN IDEA

Developing Historical Perspective

B How did events during World War II lay the groundwork for African Americans to fight for civil rights in the 1950s?

Challenging Segregation in Court

The desegregation campaign was led largely by the NAACP, which had fought since 1909 to end segregation. One influential figure in this campaign was Charles Hamilton Houston, a brilliant Howard University law professor who also served as chief legal counsel for the NAACP from 1934 to 1938.

THE NAACP LEGAL STRATEGY In deciding the NAACP's legal strategy, Houston focused on the inequality between the separate schools that many states provided. At that time, the nation spent ten times as much money educating a white child as an African-American child. Thus, Houston focused the organization's limited resources on challenging the most glaring inequalities of segregated public education.

In 1938, he placed a team of his best law students under the direction of **Thurgood Marshall.** Over the next 23 years, Marshall and his NAACP lawyers would win 29 out of 32 cases argued before the Supreme Court.

Several of the cases became legal milestones, each chipping away at the segregation platform of *Plessy* v. *Ferguson*. In the 1946 case *Morgan* v. *Virginia*, the Supreme Court declared unconstitutional those state laws mandating segregated seating on interstate buses. In 1950, the high court ruled in *Sweatt* v. *Painter* that state law schools must admit black applicants, even if separate black schools exist.

BROWN V. BOARD OF EDUCATION Marshall's most stunning victory came on May 17, 1954, in the case known as **Brown v. Board of Education of Topeka.** (See page 914.) In this case, the father of eight-year-old Linda Brown had charged the board of education of Topeka, Kansas, with violating Linda's rights by denying her admission to an all-white elementary school four blocks from her house. The nearest all-black elementary school was 21 blocks away.

In a landmark verdict, the Supreme Court unanimously struck down segregation in schooling as an unconstitutional violation of the Fourteenth Amendment's Equal Protection

KEY PLAYER

THURGOOD MARSHALL 1908–1993

Thurgood Marshall dedicated his life to fighting racism. His father had labored as a steward at an all-white country club, his mother as a teacher at an all-black school. Marshall himself was denied admission to the University of Maryland Law School because of his race.

In 1961, President John F. Kennedy nominated Marshall to the U.S. Court of Appeals. Lyndon Johnson picked Marshall for U.S. solicitor general in 1965 and two years later named him as the first African-American Supreme Court justice. In that role, he remained a strong advocate of civil rights until he retired in 1991.

After Marshall died in 1993, a copy of the *Brown* v. *Board of Education* decision was placed beside his casket. On it, an admirer wrote: "You shall always be remembered."

Clause. Chief Justice Earl Warren wrote that, "[I]n the field of public education, the doctrine of separate but equal has no place." The *Brown* decision was relevant for some 12 million schoolchildren in 21 states.

MAIN IDEA

Making Inferences

C How did the *Brown* decision affect schools outside of Topeka?

Reaction to the *Brown* Decision

Official reaction to the ruling was mixed. In Kansas and Oklahoma, state officials said they expected segregation to end with little trouble. In Texas the governor warned that plans might "take years" to work out. He actively prevented desegregation by calling in the Texas Rangers. In Mississippi and Georgia, officials vowed total resistance. Governor Herman Talmadge of Georgia said "The people of Georgia will not comply with the decision of the court. . . . We're going to do whatever is necessary in Georgia to keep white children in white schools and colored children in colored schools."

RESISTANCE TO SCHOOL DESEGREGATION Within a year, more than 500 school districts had desegregated their classrooms. In Baltimore, St. Louis, and Washington, D.C., black and white students sat side by side for the first time in history. However, in many areas where African Americans were a majority, whites resisted desegregation. In some places, the Ku Klux Klan reappeared and White Citizens Councils boycotted businesses that supported desegregation.

To speed things up, in 1955 the Supreme Court handed down a second ruling, known as *Brown II,* that ordered school desegregation implemented "with all deliberate speed." Initially President Eisenhower refused to enforce compliance. "The fellow who tries to tell me that you can do these things by force is just plain nuts," he said. Events in Little Rock, Arkansas, would soon force Eisenhower to go against his personal beliefs.

CRISIS IN LITTLE ROCK In 1948, Arkansas had become the first Southern state to admit African Americans to state universities without being required by a court order. By the 1950s, some scout troops and labor unions in Arkansas had quietly ended their Jim Crow practices. Little Rock citizens had elected two men to the school board who publicly backed desegregation—and the school superintendent, Virgil Blossom, began planning for desegregation soon after *Brown.*

However, Governor Orval Faubus publicly showed support for segregation. In September 1957, he ordered the National Guard to turn away the "Little Rock Nine"—nine African-American students who had volunteered to integrate Little Rock's Central High School as the first step in Blossom's plan. A federal judge ordered Faubus to let the students into school.

NAACP members called eight of the students and arranged to drive them to school. They could not reach the ninth student, Elizabeth Eckford, who did not have a phone, and she set out alone. Outside Central High, Eckford faced an abusive crowd. Terrified, the 15-year-old made it to a bus stop where two friendly whites stayed with her.

As white students jeer her and Arkansas National Guards look on, Elizabeth Eckford enters Little Rock Central High School in 1957.

▼

MAIN IDEA

Analyzing Causes

D Why weren't schools in all regions desegregated immediately after the *Brown II* decision?

The crisis in Little Rock forced Eisenhower to act. He placed the Arkansas National Guard under federal control and ordered a thousand paratroopers into Little Rock. The nation watched the televised coverage of the event. Under the watch of soldiers, the nine African-American teenagers attended class.

But even these soldiers could not protect the students from troublemakers who confronted them in stairways, in the halls, and in the cafeteria. Throughout the year African-American students were regularly harassed by other students. At the end of the year, Faubus shut down Central High rather than let integration continue.

On September 9, 1957, Congress passed the Civil Rights Act of 1957, the first civil rights law since Reconstruction. Shepherded by Senator Lyndon B. Johnson of Texas, the law gave the attorney general greater power over school desegregation. It also gave the federal government jurisdiction—or authority—over violations of African-American voting rights. **E**

The Montgomery Bus Boycott

The face-to-face confrontation at Central High School was not the only showdown over segregation in the mid-1950s. Impatient with the slow pace of change in the courts, African-American activists had begun taking direct action to win the rights promised to them by the Fourteenth and Fifteenth Amendments to the Constitution. Among those on the frontline of change was Jo Ann Robinson.

BOYCOTTING SEGREGATION Four days after the *Brown* decision in May 1954, Robinson wrote a letter to the mayor of Montgomery, Alabama, asking that bus drivers no longer be allowed to force riders in the "colored" section to yield their seats to whites. The mayor refused. Little did he know that in less than a year another African-American woman from Alabama would be at the center of this controversy, and that her name and her words would far outlast segregation.

On December 1, 1955, **Rosa Parks,** a seamstress and an NAACP officer, took a seat in the front row of the "colored" section of a Montgomery bus. As the bus filled up, the driver ordered Parks and three other African-American passengers to empty the row they were occupying so that a white man could sit down without having to sit next to any African Americans. "It was time for someone to stand up—or in my case, sit down," recalled Parks. "I refused to move."

As Parks stared out the window, the bus driver said, "If you don't stand up, I'm going to call the police and have you arrested." The soft-spoken Parks replied, "You may do that."

News of Parks's arrest spread rapidly. Jo Ann Robinson and NAACP leader E. D. Nixon suggested a bus boycott. The leaders of the African-American community, including many ministers, formed the Montgomery Improvement Association to organize the boycott. They elected the pastor of the Dexter Avenue Baptist Church, 26-year-old **Martin Luther King, Jr.,** to lead the group. An ordained minister since 1948, King had just earned a Ph.D. degree in theology from Boston University. "Well, I'm not sure I'm the best person for the position," King confided to Nixon, "but if no one else is going to serve, I'd be glad to try."

During the bus boycott, Montgomery's black citizens relied on an efficient car pool system that ferried people between more than forty pickup stations like the one shown.

WALKING FOR JUSTICE On the night of December 5, 1955, Dr. King made the following declaration to an estimated crowd of between 5,000 and 15,000 people.

A PERSONAL VOICE MARTIN LUTHER KING, JR.

" There comes a time when people get tired of being trampled over by the iron feet of oppression. . . . I want it to be known—that we're going to work with grim and bold determination—to gain justice on buses in this city. And we are not wrong. . . . If we are wrong—the Supreme Court of this nation is wrong. If we are wrong—God Almighty is wrong. . . . If we are wrong—justice is a lie. "

—quoted in *Parting the Waters: America in the King Years, 1954–63*

King's passionate and eloquent speech brought people to their feet and filled the audience with a sense of mission. African Americans filed a lawsuit and for 381 days refused to ride the buses in Montgomery. In most cases they had to find other means of transportation by organizing car pools or walking long distances. Support came from within the black community—workers donated one-fifth of their weekly salaries—as well as from outside groups like the NAACP, the United Auto Workers, Montgomery's Jewish community, and sympathetic white southerners. The boycotters remained nonviolent even after a bomb ripped apart King's home (no one was injured). Finally, in 1956, the Supreme Court outlawed bus segregation. **F**

MAIN IDEA

Synthesizing

F Why was Rosa Parks's action on December 1, 1955, significant?

Martin Luther King and the SCLC

The Montgomery bus boycott proved to the world that the African-American community could unite and organize a successful protest movement. It also proved the power of nonviolent resistance, the peaceful refusal to obey unjust laws. Despite threats to his life and family, King urged his followers, "Don't ever let anyone pull you so low as to hate them."

CHANGING THE WORLD WITH SOUL FORCE King called his brand of nonviolent resistance "soul force." He based his ideas on the teachings of several people. From the teachings of Jesus, he learned to love one's enemies. From writer Henry David Thoreau he took the concept of civil disobedience—the refusal to obey an unjust law. From labor organizer A. Philip Randolph he learned to organize massive demonstrations. From Mohandas Gandhi, the leader who helped India throw off British rule, he learned to resist oppression without violence. **G**

"We will not hate you," King said to white racists, "but we cannot . . . obey your unjust laws. . . . We will soon wear you down by our capacity to suffer. And in winning our freedom, we will so appeal to your heart and conscience that we will win you in the process."

MAIN IDEA

Summarizing

G What were the central points of Dr. King's philosophy?

King held steadfast to his philosophy, even when a wave of racial violence swept through the South after the *Brown* decision. The violence included the 1955 murder of Emmett Till—a 14-year-old African-American boy who had allegedly flirted with a white woman. There were also shootings and beatings, some fatal, of civil rights workers.

FROM THE GRASSROOTS UP After the bus boycott ended, King joined with ministers and civil rights leaders in 1957 to found the **Southern Christian Leadership Conference (SCLC).** Its purpose was "to carry on nonviolent crusades against the evils of second-class citizenship." Using African-American churches as a base, the SCLC planned to stage protests and demonstrations throughout the South. The leaders hoped to build a movement from the grassroots up and to win the support of ordinary African Americans of all ages. King, president of the SCLC, used the power of his voice and ideas to fuel the movement's momentum.

The nuts and bolts of organizing the SCLC was handled by its first director, Ella Baker, the granddaughter of slaves. While with the NAACP, Baker had served as national field secretary, traveling over 16,000 miles throughout the South. From 1957 to 1960, Baker used her contacts to set up branches of the SCLC in Southern cities. In April 1960, Baker helped students at Shaw University, an African-American university in Raleigh, North Carolina, to organize a national protest group, the **Student Nonviolent Coordinating Committee,** or **SNCC,** pronounced "snick" for short.

It had been six years since the *Brown* decision, and many college students viewed the pace of change as too slow. Although these students risked a great deal—losing college scholarships, being expelled from college, being physically harmed—they were determined to challenge the system. SNCC hoped to harness the energy of these student protesters; it would soon create one of the most important student activist movements in the nation's history. **H**

MAIN IDEA

Evaluating
H What was the role of the SCLC?

The Movement Spreads

Although SNCC adopted King's ideas in part, its members had ideas of their own. Many people called for a more confrontational strategy and set out to reshape the civil rights movement.

DEMONSTRATING FOR FREEDOM The founders of SNCC had models to build on. In 1942 in Chicago, the Congress of Racial Equality (CORE) had staged the first **sit-ins,** in which African-American protesters sat down at segregated lunch counters and refused to leave until they were served. In February 1960, African-American students from North Carolina's Agricultural and Technical College staged a sit-in at a whites-only lunch counter at a Woolworth's store in Greensboro. This time, television crews brought coverage of the protest into homes throughout the United States. There was no denying the ugly face of racism. Day after day, news reporters captured the scenes of whites beating, jeering at, and pouring food over students who refused to strike back. The coverage sparked many other sit-ins across the South. Store managers called

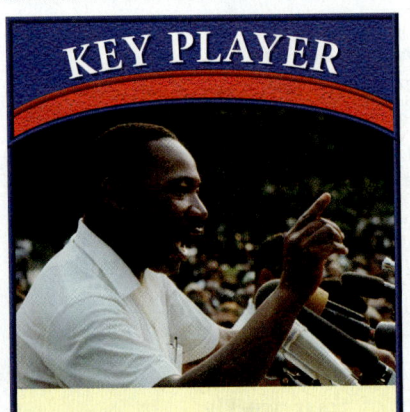

KEY PLAYER

MARTIN LUTHER KING, JR.
1929–1968

Born Michael Luther King, Jr., King had to adjust to a new name in 1934. In that year, his father—Rev. Michael King, Sr.—returned home from a trip to Europe, where he had toured the site where Martin Luther had begun the Protestant Reformation. Upon his return home, the elder King changed his and his son's names to Martin.

Like Luther, the younger King became a reformer. In 1964, he won the Nobel Peace Prize. Yet there was a side of King unknown to most people—his inner battle to overcome his hatred of the white bigots. As a youth, he had once vowed "to hate all white people." As leader of the civil rights movement, King said all Americans had to be freed: "Negroes from the bonds of segregation and shame, whites from the bonds of bigotry and fear."

© Fred Blackwell

in the police, raised the price of food, and removed counter seats. But the movement continued and spread to the North. There, students formed picket lines around national chain stores that maintained segregated lunch counters in the South.

By late 1960, students had descended on and desegregated lunch counters in some 48 cities in 11 states. They endured arrests, beatings, suspension from college, and tear gas and fire hoses, but the army of nonviolent students refused to back down. "My mother has always told me that I'm equal to other people," said Ezell Blair, Jr., one of the students who led the first SNCC sit-in in 1960. For the rest of the 1960s, many Americans worked to convince the rest of the country that blacks and whites deserved equal treatment.

SECTION 1 ASSESSMENT

1. TERMS & NAMES For each term or name, write a sentence explaining its significance.

- Thurgood Marshall
- *Brown* v. *Board of Education of Topeka*
- Rosa Parks
- Martin Luther King, Jr.
- Southern Christian Leadership Conference (SCLC)
- Student Nonviolent Coordinating Committee (SNCC)
- sit-in

MAIN IDEA

2. TAKING NOTES

Fill in a spider diagram like the one below with examples of tactics, organizations, leaders, and Supreme Court decisions of the civil rights movement up to 1960.

CRITICAL THINKING

3. EVALUATING

Do you think the nonviolence used by civil rights activists was a good tactic? Explain. **Think About:**

- the Montgomery bus boycott
- television coverage of events
- sit-ins

4. CONTRASTING

How did the tactics of the student protesters from SNCC differ from those of the boycotters in Montgomery?

5. DRAWING CONCLUSIONS

After the *Brown* v. *Board of Education of Topeka* ruling, what do you think was the most significant event of the civil rights movement prior to 1960? Why? **Think About:**

- the role of civil rights leaders
- the results of confrontations and boycotts
- the role of grassroots organizations

Civil Rights **913**

HISTORIC DECISIONS OF THE SUPREME COURT

BROWN v. BOARD OF EDUCATION OF TOPEKA (1954)

ORIGINS OF THE CASE In the early 1950s, the school system of Topeka, Kansas, like all Southern elementary school systems, operated separate schools for "the two races"—blacks and whites. Reverend Oliver Brown protested that this was unfair to his eight-year-old daughter Linda. Although the Browns lived near a "white" school, Linda was forced to take a long bus ride to her "black" school across town.

THE RULING The Court ruled that segregated public schools were "inherently" unequal and therefore unconstitutional.

Linda Brown's name headed a list of five school desegregation cases heard by the Supreme Court. ▶

LEGAL REASONING

While the correctness of the *Brown* ruling seems obvious today, some justices had difficulty agreeing to it. One reason was the force of legal precedent. Normally, judges follow a policy of *stare decisis,* "let the decision stand." The *Plessy* v. *Ferguson* decision endorsing segregation (see page 496) had stood for over 50 years. It clearly stated that "separate but equal" facilities did not violate the Fourteenth Amendment.

Thurgood Marshall, the NAACP lawyer who argued *Brown,* spent years laying the groundwork to chip away at Jim Crow—the local laws that required segregated facilities. Marshall had recently won two Supreme Court decisions in 1950 (*McLaurin* and *Sweatt;* see Legal Sources at right) that challenged segregation at graduate schools. Then in 1952, the Supreme Court agreed to hear the Browns' case. The Court deliberated for two years deciding how to interpret the Fourteenth Amendment.

In the end, Chief Justice Earl Warren carefully sidestepped *Plessy,* claiming that segregated schools were not and never could be equal. On Monday, May 17, 1954, Warren read the unanimous decision:

> " **Does segregation of children in public schools . . . deprive children of . . . equal opportunities? We believe it does. . . . To separate them . . . solely because of their race generates a feeling of inferiority . . . that may affect their hearts and minds in a way unlikely ever to be undone.** "
>
> —*Brown v. Board of Education of Topeka*

LEGAL SOURCES

U.S. CONSTITUTION

FOURTEENTH AMENDMENT, EQUAL PROTECTION CLAUSE (1868)
"No state shall . . . deny to any person within its jurisdiction the equal protection of the laws."

RELATED CASES

PLESSY v. FERGUSON (1896)
- Upheld Louisiana's laws requiring that train passengers be segregated by race.
- Established the doctrine of "separate but equal."

MCLAURIN v. OKLAHOMA STATE (1950)
Ruled that Oklahoma State University violated the Constitution by keeping its one "Negro" student in the back of the class and the cafeteria.

SWEATT v. PAINTER (1950)
Required the University of Texas to admit an African-American student to its previously all-white law school.

WHY IT MATTERED

The Court's decision in *Brown* had an immediate impact on pending rulings. In a series of cases after *Brown,* the Supreme Court prohibited segregation in housing, at public beaches, at recreation facilities, and in restaurants. Later decisions extended equal access to other groups, including women and resident aliens.

The decision encountered fierce resistance, however. It awakened the old battle cry of states' rights. Directly following *Brown,* some Congress members circulated the "Southern Manifesto," claiming the right of the states to ignore the ruling. In taking a stand on a social issue, they said, the Court had taken a step away from simply interpreting legal precedents. Critics charged that the Warren Court had acted as legislators and even as sociologists.

The *Brown* case strengthened the Civil Rights movement, however, and paved the way for the end of Jim Crow. The NAACP had fought and won the legal battle and had gained prestige and momentum. Americans got the strong message that the federal government now took civil rights seriously.

HISTORICAL IMPACT

Three of the parties involved in *Brown*—Delaware, Kansas, and the District of Columbia—began to integrate schools in 1954. Topeka County informed the Court that 123 black students were already attending formerly all-white schools. Even so, the Supreme Court was well aware that its decision would be difficult to enforce. In a follow-up ruling, *Brown II* (1955), the Court required that integration take place with "all deliberate speed." To some this meant quickly. Others interpreted *deliberate* to mean slowly.

Only two Southern states even began to integrate classrooms in 1954: Texas and Arkansas opened one and two districts, respectively. By 1960, less than one percent of the South's students attended integrated schools. Many school districts were ordered to use aggressive means to achieve racial balance. Courts spent decades supervising forced busing, a practice that often pitted community against community.

Still, despite the resistance and the practical difficulties of implementation, *Brown* stands today as a watershed, the single point at which breaking the "color barrier" officially became a federal priority.

Thurgood Marshall was appointed the first African-American Supreme Court justice by President Johnson in 1967.

PI 2.4
PI 3.1

CC Unit 7.III.A.1.a(1)   CC Unit 7.III.A.1.a(2)
CC Unit 7.III.A.1.a(3)   CC Unit 7.III.A.3.a(4)
CC Unit 7.III.B.3.b(3)   CC Unit 7.III.B.3.c

The Triumphs of a Crusade

MAIN IDEA	WHY IT MATTERS NOW	Terms & Names
Civil rights activists broke through racial barriers. Their activism prompted landmark legislation.	Activism pushed the federal government to end segregation and ensure voting rights for African Americans.	• freedom riders • James Meredith • Civil Rights Act of 1964 • Freedom Summer • Fannie Lou Hamer • Voting Rights Act of 1965

One American's Story

hmhsocialstudies.com
TAKING NOTES

Use the graphic organizer online to take notes on the steps taken to challenge segregation from 1962 to 1965.

In 1961, James Peck, a white civil rights activist, joined other CORE members on a historic bus trip across the South. The two-bus trip would test the Supreme Court decisions banning segregated seating on interstate bus routes and segregated facilities in bus terminals. Peck and other **freedom riders** expected a violent reaction. They hoped that this would convince the Kennedy administration to enforce the law. The violence was not long in coming.

At the Alabama state line, white racists got on Bus One carrying chains, brass knuckles, and pistols. They brutally beat African-American riders and white activists who tried to intervene. Still the riders managed to go on. Then on May 4, 1961—Mother's Day—the bus pulled into the Birmingham bus terminal. James Peck saw a hostile mob waiting, some holding iron bars.

A PERSONAL VOICE JAMES PECK

"I looked at them and then I looked at Charles Person, who had been designated as my team mate. . . . When I looked at him, he responded by saying simply, 'Let's go.' As we entered the white waiting room, . . . we were grabbed bodily and pushed toward the alleyway . . . and out of sight of onlookers in the waiting room, six of them started swinging at me with fists and pipes. Five others attacked Person a few feet ahead."

—*Freedom Ride*

▲ Three days after being beaten unconscious in Birmingham, freedom rider James Peck demonstrates in New York City to pressure national bus companies to support desegregation.

The ride of Bus One had ended, but Bus Two continued southward on a journey that would shock the Kennedy administration into action.

Riding for Freedom

In Anniston, Alabama, about 200 angry whites attacked Bus Two. The mob followed the activists out of town. When one of the tires blew, they smashed a window and tossed in a fire bomb. The freedom riders spilled out just before the bus exploded.

NEW VOLUNTEERS The bus companies refused to carry the CORE freedom riders any farther. Even though the determined volunteers did not want to give up, they ended their ride. However, CORE director James Farmer announced that a group of SNCC volunteers in Nashville were ready to pick up where the others had left off.

When a new band of freedom riders rode into Birmingham, policemen pulled them from the bus, beat them, and drove them into Tennessee. Defiantly, they returned to the Birmingham bus terminal. Their bus driver, however, feared for his life and refused to transport them. In protest, they occupied the whites-only waiting room at the terminal for eighteen hours until a solution was reached. After an angry phone call from U.S. Attorney General Robert Kennedy, bus company officials convinced the driver to proceed. The riders set out for Montgomery on May 20.

ARRIVAL OF FEDERAL MARSHALS Although Alabama officials had promised Kennedy that the riders would be protected, a mob of whites—many carrying bats and lead pipes—fell upon the riders when they arrived in Montgomery. John Doer, a Justice Department official on the scene, called the attorney general to report what was happening. "A bunch of men led by a guy with a bleeding face are beating [the passengers]. There are no cops. It's terrible. There's not a cop in sight. People are yelling. 'Get 'em, get 'em.' It's awful."

The violence provoked exactly the response the freedom riders wanted. Newspapers throughout the nation and abroad denounced the beatings.

President Kennedy arranged to give the freedom riders direct support. The Justice Department sent 400 U.S. marshals to protect the riders on the last part of their journey to Jackson, Mississippi. In addition, the attorney general and the Interstate Commerce Commission banned segregation in all interstate travel facilities, including waiting rooms, restrooms, and lunch counters. **A**

> ▲ In May 1961, a mob firebombed this bus of freedom riders outside Anniston, Alabama, and attacked passengers as they tried to escape.

> *"We will continue our journey one way or another. . . . We are prepared to die."*
> **JIM ZWERG, FREEDOM RIDER**

MAIN IDEA

Analyzing Issues

A What did the freedom riders hope to achieve?

Standing Firm

With the integration of interstate travel facilities under way, some civil rights workers turned their attention to integrating some Southern schools and pushing the movement into additional Southern towns. At each turn they encountered opposition and often violence.

INTEGRATING OLE MISS In September 1962, Air Force veteran **James Meredith** won a federal court case that allowed him to enroll in the all-white University of Mississippi, nicknamed Ole Miss. But when Meredith arrived on campus, he faced Governor Ross Barnett, who refused to let him register as a student.

President Kennedy ordered federal marshals to escort Meredith to the registrar's office. Barnett responded with a heated radio appeal: "I call on every Mississippian to keep his faith and courage. We will never surrender." The broadcast turned out white demonstrators by the thousands.

On the night of September 30, riots broke out on campus, resulting in two deaths. It took thousands of soldiers, 200 arrests, and 15 hours to stop the rioters. In the months that followed, federal officials accompanied Meredith to class and protected his parents from nightriders who shot up their house.

News photos and television coverage of police dogs in Birmingham attacking African Americans shocked the nation. ▶

HEADING INTO BIRMINGHAM The trouble continued in Alabama. Birmingham, a city known for its strict enforcement of total segregation in public life, also had a reputation for racial violence, including 18 bombings from 1957 to 1963.

Reverend Fred Shuttlesworth, head of the Alabama Christian Movement for Human Rights and secretary of the SCLC, decided something had to be done about Birmingham and that it would be the ideal place to test the power of nonviolence. He invited Martin Luther King, Jr., and the SCLC to help desegregate the city. On April 3, 1963, King flew into Birmingham to hold a planning meeting with members of the African-American community. "This is the most segregated city in America," he said. "We have to stick together if we ever want to change its ways."

After days of demonstrations led by Shuttlesworth and others, King and a small band of marchers were finally arrested during a demonstration on Good Friday, April 12th. While in jail, King wrote an open letter to white religious leaders who felt he was pushing too fast.

A PERSONAL VOICE MARTIN LUTHER KING, JR.

"I guess it is easy for those who have never felt the stinging darts of segregation to say, 'Wait.' But when you have seen vicious mobs lynch your mothers and fathers at whim; when you have seen hate-filled policemen curse, kick, brutalize and even kill your black brothers and sisters; . . . when you see the vast majority of your twenty million Negro brothers smothering in the air-tight cage of poverty; . . . when you have to concoct an answer for a five-year-old son asking: . . . 'Daddy, why do white people treat colored people so mean?' . . . then you will understand why we find it difficult to wait."

—"Letter from a Birmingham Jail"

On April 20, King posted bail and began planning more demonstrations. On May 2, more than a thousand African-American children marched in Birmingham. Police commissioner Eugene "Bull" Connor's men arrested 959 of them. On May 3, a second "children's crusade" came face to face with a helmeted police force. Police swept the marchers off their feet with high-pressure fire hoses, set attack dogs on them, and clubbed those who fell. TV cameras captured all of it, and millions of viewers heard the children screaming.

Continued protests, an economic boycott, and negative media coverage finally convinced Birmingham officials to end segregation. This stunning civil rights victory inspired African Americans across the nation. It also convinced President Kennedy that only a new civil rights act could end racial violence and satisfy the demands of African Americans—and many whites—for racial justice. **B**

MAIN IDEA

Chronological Order
B What events led to desegregation in Birmingham?

ERNEST WITHERS

Born in Memphis in 1922, photographer Ernest Withers believed that if the struggle for equality could be shown to people, things would change. Armed with only a camera, he braved violent crowds to capture the heated racism during the Montgomery bus boycott, the desegregation of Central High in Little Rock, and the 1968 Memphis sanitation workers strike (below) led by Martin Luther King, Jr. The night before the Memphis march, Withers had helped make some of the signs he photographed.

> "G. C. Brown printed those 'I AM A MAN' signs right over there. . . . I had a car and it was snowing, so we went and rented the saw and came back that night and cut the sticks."

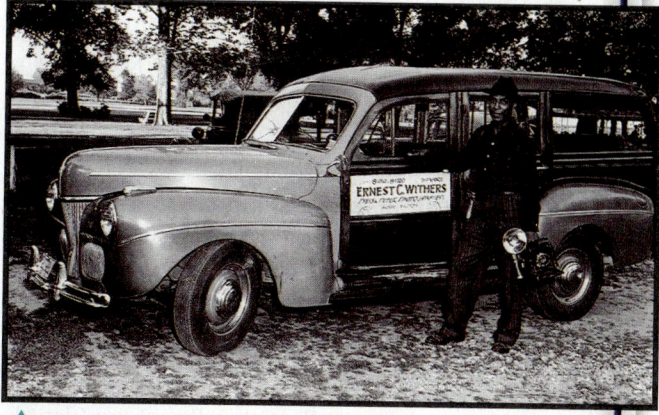

▲ Withers in 1950

Withers had to be careful about his involvement in groups like the NAACP and COME (Community On the Move for Equality), for he had a wife and children to support. He went to several meetings a night, sometimes taking pictures, other times offering a suggestion. "I always had FBI agents looking over my shoulder and wanting to question me. I never tried to learn any high-powered secrets."

◀ Withers in 1992

SKILLBUILDER Interpreting Visual Sources

1. What do the signs tell you about African Americans' struggle for civil rights?

2. What kind of treatment do you suppose these men had experienced? Why do you think so?

📖 SEE SKILLBUILDER HANDBOOK, PAGE R23.

KENNEDY TAKES A STAND On June 11, 1963, the president sent troops to force Governor George Wallace to honor a court order desegregating the University of Alabama. That evening, Kennedy asked the nation: "Are we to say to the world—and much more importantly, to each other—that this is the land of the free, except for the Negroes?" He demanded that Congress pass a civil rights bill.

A tragic event just hours after Kennedy's speech highlighted the racial tension in much of the South. Shortly after midnight, a sniper murdered Medgar Evers, NAACP field secretary and World War II veteran. Police soon arrested a white supremacist, Byron de la Beckwith, but he was released after two trials resulted in hung juries. His release brought a new militancy to African Americans. Many demanded, "Freedom now!"

Background
Beckwith was finally convicted in 1994, after the case was reopened based on new evidence.

Marching to Washington

The civil rights bill that President Kennedy sent to Congress guaranteed equal access to all public accommodations and gave the U.S. attorney general the power to file school desegregation suits. To persuade Congress to pass the bill, two veteran organizers—labor leader A. Philip Randolph and Bayard Rustin of the SCLC—summoned Americans to a march on Washington, D.C.

THE DREAM OF EQUALITY On August 28, 1963, more than 250,000 people—including about 75,000 whites—converged on the nation's capital. They assembled on the grassy lawn of the Washington Monument and marched to the Lincoln Memorial. There, people listened to speakers demand the immediate passage of the civil rights bill. **C**

When Dr. Martin Luther King, Jr., appeared, the crowd exploded in applause. In his now famous speech, "I Have a Dream," he appealed for peace and racial harmony.

MAIN IDEA

Analyzing Events
C Why did civil rights organizers ask their supporters to march on Washington?

A PERSONAL VOICE MARTIN LUTHER KING, JR.

"I have a dream that one day this nation will rise up and live out the true meaning of its creed: 'We hold these truths to be self-evident; that all men are created equal.' . . . I have a dream that my four little children will one day live in a nation where they will not be judged by the color of their skin but by the content of their character. . . . I have a dream that one day the state of Alabama . . . will be transformed into a situation where little black boys and black girls will be able to join hands with little white boys and white girls and walk together as sisters and brothers."

—"I Have a Dream"

MORE VIOLENCE Two weeks after King's historic speech, four young Birmingham girls were killed when a rider in a car hurled a bomb through their church window. Two more African Americans died in the unrest that followed.

Two months later, an assassin shot and killed John F. Kennedy. His successor, President Lyndon B. Johnson, pledged to carry on Kennedy's work. On July 2, 1964, Johnson signed the **Civil Rights Act of 1964,** which prohibited discrimination because of race, religion, national origin, and gender. It gave all citizens the right to enter libraries, parks, washrooms, restaurants, theaters, and other public accommodations.

Background
The Supreme Court upheld the 1964 Civil Rights Act in *Heart of Atlanta Motel* v. *United States* (1964). The Court found that the law was a valid exercise of the commerce clause.

Civil Rights Acts of the 1950s and 1960s

CIVIL RIGHTS ACT OF 1957
- Established federal Commission on Civil Rights
- Established a Civil Rights Division in the Justice Department to enforce civil rights laws
- Enlarged federal power to protect voting rights

CIVIL RIGHTS ACT OF 1964
- Banned most discrimination in employment and in public accommodations
- Enlarged federal power to protect voting rights and speed up school desegregation
- Established Equal Employment Opportunity Commission to ensure fair treatment in employment

VOTING RIGHTS ACT OF 1965
- Eliminated voter literacy tests
- Enabled federal examiners to register voters

CIVIL RIGHTS ACT OF 1968
- Prohibited discrimination in the sale or rental of most housing
- Strengthened antilynching laws
- Made it a crime to harm civil rights workers

SKILLBUILDER
Interpreting Charts
Which law do you think benefited the most people? Explain your choice.

Fighting for Voting Rights

Meanwhile, the right of all African Americans to vote remained elusive. In 1964, CORE and SNCC workers in the South began registering as many African Americans as they could to vote. They hoped their campaign would receive national publicity, which would in turn influence Congress to pass a voting rights act. Focused in Mississippi, the project became known as **Freedom Summer.**

FREEDOM SUMMER To fortify the project, civil rights groups recruited college students and trained them in nonviolent resistance. Thousands of student volunteers—mostly white, about one-third female—went into Mississippi to help register voters. For some, the job proved deadly. In June of 1964, three civil rights workers disappeared in Neshoba County, Mississippi. Investigators later learned that Klansmen and local police had murdered the men, two of whom were white. Through the summer, the racial beatings and murders continued, along with the burning of businesses, homes, and churches. **D**

A NEW POLITICAL PARTY African Americans needed a voice in the political arena if sweeping change was to occur. In order to gain a seat in Mississippi's all-white Democratic Party, SNCC organized the Mississippi Freedom Democratic Party (MFDP). **Fannie Lou Hamer,** the daughter of Mississippi sharecroppers, would be their voice at the 1964 Democratic National Convention. In a televised speech that shocked the convention and viewers nationwide, Hamer described how she was jailed for registering to vote in 1962, and how police forced other prisoners to beat her.

> ★ **A PERSONAL VOICE** FANNIE LOU HAMER
>
> " The first [prisoner] began to beat [me], and I was beat by the first until he was exhausted. . . . The second [prisoner] began to beat. . . . I began to scream and one white man got up and began to beat me in my head and tell me to 'hush.' . . . All of this on account we want to register, to become first-class citizens, and if the Freedom Democratic Party is not seated now, I question America. "
>
> —quoted in *The Civil Rights Movement: An Eyewitness History*

In response to Hamer's speech, telegrams and telephone calls poured in to the convention in support of seating the MFDP delegates. President Johnson feared losing the Southern white vote if the Democrats sided with the MFDP, so his administration pressured civil rights leaders to convince the MFDP to accept a compromise. The Democrats would give 2 of Mississippi's 68 seats to the MFDP, with a promise to ban discrimination at the 1968 convention.

When Hamer learned of the compromise, she said, "We didn't come all this way for no two seats." The MFDP and supporters in SNCC felt that the leaders had betrayed them. **E**

MAIN IDEA

Analyzing Motives
D Why did civil rights groups organize Freedom Summer?

MAIN IDEA

Developing Historical Perspective
E Why did young people in SNCC and the MFDP feel betrayed by some civil rights leaders?

THE SELMA CAMPAIGN At the start of 1965, the SCLC conducted a major voting rights campaign in Selma, Alabama, where SNCC had been working for two years to register voters. By the end of 1965, more than 2,000 African Americans had been arrested in SCLC demonstrations. After a demonstrator named Jimmy Lee Jackson was shot and killed, King responded by announcing a 50-mile protest march from Selma to Montgomery, the state capital. On March 7, 1965, about 600 protesters set out for Montgomery.

That night, mayhem broke out. Television cameras captured the scene. The rest of the nation watched in horror as police swung whips and clubs, and clouds of tear gas swirled around fallen marchers. Demonstrators poured into Selma by the hundreds. Ten days later, President Johnson presented Congress with a new voting rights act and asked for its swift passage. **F**

On March 21, 3,000 marchers again set out for Montgomery, this time with federal protection. Soon the number grew to an army of 25,000.

VOTING RIGHTS ACT OF 1965 That summer, Congress finally passed Johnson's **Voting Rights Act of 1965.** The act eliminated the so-called literacy tests that had disqualified many voters. It also stated that federal examiners could enroll voters who had been denied suffrage by local officials. In Selma, the proportion of African Americans registered to vote rose from 10 percent in 1964 to 60 percent in 1968. Overall the percentage of registered African-American voters in the South tripled.

Although the Voting Rights Act marked a major civil rights victory, some felt that the law did not go far enough. Centuries of discrimination had produced social and economic inequalities. Anger over these inequalities led to a series of violent disturbances in the cities of the North.

MAIN IDEA

Comparing
F In what ways was the civil rights campaign in Selma similar to the one in Birmingham?

---

2 ASSESSMENT

1. TERMS & NAMES For each term or name, write a sentence explaining its significance.
- freedom riders
- James Meredith
- Civil Rights Act of 1964
- Freedom Summer
- Fannie Lou Hamer
- Voting Rights Act of 1965

MAIN IDEA

2. TAKING NOTES
In a graphic like the one shown, list the steps that African Americans took to desegregate buses and schools from 1962 to 1965.

1965
1964
1963
1962

CRITICAL THINKING

3. ANALYZING ISSUES
What assumptions and beliefs do you think guided the fierce opposition to the civil rights movement in the South? Support your answer with evidence from the text. **Think About:**
- the social and political structure of the South
- Mississippi governor Ross Barnett's comment during his radio address
- the actions of police and some white Southerners

4. ANALYZING PRIMARY SOURCES
Just after the Civil Rights Act of 1964 was passed, white Alabama governor George Wallace said,

" It is ironical that this event occurs as we approach the celebration of Independence Day. On that day we won our freedom. On this day we have largely lost it. "

What do you think Wallace meant by his statement?

SECTION
3

P|| 2.3
P|| 3.1

CC Unit 7.III.A.3   CC Unit 7.III.B.1.b(1)
CC Unit 7.III.B.3.b(5)   CC Unit 7.III.B.3.b(6)
CC Unit 7.III.B.3.c(5)   CC Unit 7.IV.A.6.b

Challenges and Changes in the Movement

MAIN IDEA	WHY IT MATTERS NOW	Terms & Names
Disagreements among civil rights groups and the rise of black nationalism created a violent period in the fight for civil rights.	From the fight for equality came a resurgence of racial pride for African Americans, a legacy that influences today's generations.	• de facto segregation • de jure segregation • Malcolm X • Nation of Islam • Stokely Carmichael • Black Power • Black Panthers • Kerner Commission • Civil Rights Act of 1968 • affirmative action

One American's Story

hmhsocialstudies.com
TAKING NOTES

Use the graphic organizer online to take notes on key events of the civil rights movement.

Alice Walker, the prize-winning novelist, became aware of the civil rights movement in 1960, when she was 16. Her mother had recently scraped together enough money to purchase a television.

A PERSONAL VOICE ALICE WALKER

" Like a good omen for the future, the face of Dr. Martin Luther King, Jr., was the first black face I saw on our new television screen. And, as in a fairy tale, my soul was stirred by the meaning for me of his mission—at the time he was being rather ignominiously dumped into a police van for having led a protest march in Alabama—and I fell in love with the sober and determined face of the Movement. "

—In Search of Our Mothers' Gardens

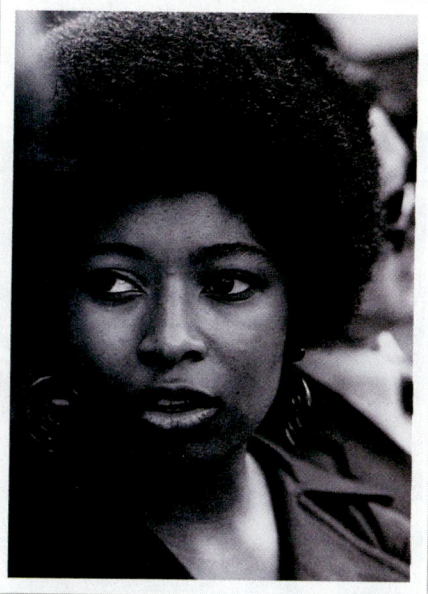

▲
Alice Walker during an interview in New York's Central Park in August 1970

The next year, Walker attended the all-black Spelman College. In 1963, Walker took part in the March on Washington and then traveled to Africa to discover her spiritual roots. After returning home in 1964, she worked on voter registration, taught African American history and writing, and wrote poetry and fiction.

Walker's interest in her heritage was part of a growing trend among African Americans in the mid-1960s. But millions of African Americans were still living in poverty. Angry and frustrated over the difficulty in finding jobs and decent housing, some participated in riots that broke out between 1964 and 1966.

African Americans Seek Greater Equality

What civil rights groups had in common in the early 1960s were their calls for a newfound pride in black identity and a commitment to change the social and economic structures that kept people in a life of poverty. However, by 1965, the leading civil rights groups began to drift apart. New leaders emerged as the movement turned its attention to the North, where African Americans faced not legal segregation but deeply entrenched and oppressive racial prejudice.

NORTHERN SEGREGATION The problem facing African Americans in the North was **de facto segregation**—segregation that exists by practice and custom. De facto segregation can be harder to fight than **de jure** (dē jŏŏr′ē) **segregation,** or segregation by law, because eliminating it requires changing people's attitudes rather than repealing laws. Activists in the mid-1960s would find it much more difficult to convince whites to share economic and social power with African Americans than to convince them to share lunch counters and bus seats. **Ⓐ**

De facto segregation intensified after African Americans migrated to Northern cities during and after World War II. This began a "white flight," in which great numbers of whites moved out of the cities to the nearby suburbs. By the mid-1960s, most urban African Americans lived in decaying slums, paying rent to landlords who didn't comply with housing and health ordinances. The schools for African-American children deteriorated along with their neighborhoods. Unemployment rates were more than twice as high as those among whites.

In addition, many blacks were angry at the sometimes brutal treatment they received from the mostly white police forces in their communities. In 1966, King spearheaded a campaign in Chicago to end de facto segregation there and create an "open city." On July 10, he led about 30,000 African Americans in a march on City Hall.

In late July, when King led demonstrators through a Chicago neighborhood, angry whites threw rocks and bottles. On August 5, hostile whites stoned King as he led 600 marchers. King left Chicago without accomplishing what he wanted, yet pledging to return.

URBAN VIOLENCE ERUPTS In the mid 1960s, clashes between white authority and black civilians spread like wildfire. In New York City in July 1964, an encounter between white police and African-American teenagers ended in the death of a 15-year-old student. This sparked a race riot in central Harlem. On August 11, 1965, only five days after President Johnson signed the Voting

MAIN IDEA

Comparing

Ⓐ How were civil rights problems in Northern cities similar to those in the South?

Between 1964 and 1968, more than 100 race riots erupted in major American cities. The worst included Watts in Los Angeles in 1965 *(top)* and Detroit in 1967 *(right).* In Detroit, 43 people were killed and property damage topped $40 million.

Rights Act into law, one of the worst race riots in the nation's history raged through the streets of Watts, a predominantly African-American neighborhood in Los Angeles. Thirty-four people were killed, and hundreds of millions of dollars worth of property was destroyed. The next year, 1966, saw even more racial disturbances, and in 1967 alone, riots and violent clashes took place in more than 100 cities.

The African-American rage baffled many whites. "Why would blacks turn to violence after winning so many victories in the South?" they wondered. Some realized that what African Americans wanted and needed was economic equality of opportunity in jobs, housing, and education. **B**

Even before the riots in 1964, President Johnson had announced his War on Poverty, a program to help impoverished Americans. But the flow of money needed to fund Johnson's Great Society was soon redirected to fund the war in Vietnam. In 1967, Dr. King proclaimed, "The Great Society has been shot down on the battlefields of Vietnam."

New Leaders Voice Discontent

The anger that sent rioters into the streets stemmed in part from African-American leaders who urged their followers to take complete control of their communities, livelihoods, and culture. One such leader, **Malcolm X,** declared to a Harlem audience, "If you think we are here to tell you to love the white man, you have come to the wrong place."

AFRICAN-AMERICAN SOLIDARITY Malcolm X, born Malcolm Little, went to jail at age 20 for burglary. While in prison, he studied the teachings of Elijah Muhammad, the head of the **Nation of Islam**, or the Black Muslims. Malcolm changed his name to Malcolm X (dropping what he called his "slave name") and, after his release from prison in 1952, became an Islamic minister. As he gained a following, the brilliant thinker and engaging speaker openly preached Elijah Muhammad's views that whites were the cause of the black condition and that blacks should separate from white society.

Malcolm's message appealed to many African Americans and their growing racial pride. At a New York press conference in March 1964, he also advocated armed self-defense.

A PERSONAL VOICE MALCOLM X

" Concerning nonviolence: it is criminal to teach a man not to defend himself when he is the constant victim of brutal attacks. It is legal and lawful to own a shotgun or a rifle. We believe in obeying the law. . . . [T]he time has come for the American Negro to fight back in self-defense whenever and wherever he is being unjustly and unlawfully attacked. "

—quoted in *Eyewitness: The Negro in American History*

The press gave a great deal of publicity to Malcolm X because his controversial statements made dramatic news stories. This had two effects. First, his call for armed self-defense frightened most whites and many moderate African Americans. Second, reports of the attention Malcolm received awakened resentment in some other members of the Nation of Islam. **C**

MAIN IDEA

Analyzing Causes

B What were some of the causes of urban rioting in the 1960s?

Background
See "Islam" on page 15.

MAIN IDEA

Synthesizing

C Why did some Americans find Malcolm X's views alarming?

KEY PLAYER

**MALCOLM X
1925–1965**

Malcolm X's early life left him alienated from white society. His father was allegedly killed by white racists, and his mother had an emotional collapse, leaving Malcolm and his siblings in the care of the state. At the end of eighth grade, Malcolm quit school and was later jailed for criminal behavior. In 1946, while in prison, Malcolm joined the Nation of Islam. He developed a philosophy of black superiority and separatism from whites.

In the later years of his life, he urged African Americans to identify with Africa and to work with world organizations and even progressive whites to attain equality. Although silenced by gunmen, Malcolm X is a continuing inspiration for many Americans.

BALLOTS OR BULLETS? In March 1964, Malcolm broke with Elijah Muhammad over differences in strategy and doctrine and formed another Muslim organization. One month later, he embarked on a pilgrimage to Mecca, in Saudi Arabia, a trip required of followers of orthodox Islam. In Mecca, he learned that orthodox Islam preached racial equality, and he worshiped alongside people from many countries. Wrote Malcolm, "I have [prayed] . . . with fellow Muslims whose eyes were the bluest of blue, whose hair was the blondest of blond, and whose skin was the whitest of white." When he returned to the United States, his attitude toward whites had changed radically. He explained his new slogan, "Ballots or bullets," to a follower: "Well, if you and I don't use the ballot, we're going to be forced to use the bullet. So let us try the ballot."

Because of his split with the Black Muslims, Malcolm believed his life might be in danger. "No one can get out without trouble," he confided. On February 21, 1965, while giving a speech in Harlem, the 39-year-old Malcolm X was shot and killed.

BLACK POWER In early June of 1966, tensions that had been building between SNCC and the other civil rights groups finally erupted in Mississippi. Here, James Meredith, the man who had integrated the University of Mississippi, set out on a 225-mile "walk against fear." Meredith planned to walk all the way from the Tennessee border to Jackson, but he was shot by a white racist and was too injured to continue.

Martin Luther King, Jr., of the SCLC, Floyd McKissick of CORE, and **Stokely Carmichael** of SNCC decided to lead their followers in a march to finish what Meredith had started. But it soon became apparent that SNCC and CORE members were quite militant, as they began to shout slogans similar to those of the black separatists who had followed Malcolm X. When King tried to rally the marchers with the refrain of "We Shall Overcome," many SNCC workers—bitter over the violence they'd suffered during Freedom Summer—began singing, "We shall overrun."

Police in Greenwood, Mississippi, arrested Carmichael for setting up a tent on the grounds of an all-black high school. When Carmichael showed up at a rally later, his face swollen from a beating, he electrified the crowd.

Stokely Carmichael (1968). The slogan "Black Power" became the battle-cry of militant civil rights activists. ▼

A PERSONAL VOICE STOKELY CARMICHAEL

"This is the twenty-seventh time I have been arrested—and I ain't going to jail no more! . . . We been saying freedom for six years—and we ain't got nothin'. What we're gonna start saying now is BLACK POWER."

—quoted in *The Civil Rights Movement: An Eyewitness History*

Black Power, Carmichael said, was a "call for black people to begin to define their own goals . . . [and] to lead their own organizations." King urged him to stop using the phrase because he believed it would provoke African Americans to violence and antagonize whites. Carmichael refused and urged SNCC to stop recruiting whites and to focus on developing African-American pride. **D**

BLACK PANTHERS Later that year, another development demonstrated the growing radicalism of some segments of the African-American community. In Oakland, California, in October 1966, Huey Newton and Bobby Seale founded a political party known as the **Black Panthers** to fight police brutality in the ghetto. The party advocated self-sufficiency for African-American communities, as well as full employment and decent housing. Members maintained that African Americans should be exempt from military service because an unfair number of black youths had been drafted to serve in Vietnam.

MAIN IDEA

Analyzing Motives

D Why did some leaders of SCLC disagree with SNCC tactics?

Dressed in black leather jackets, black berets, and sunglasses, the Panthers preached self-defense and sold copies of the writings of Mao Zedong, leader of the Chinese Communist revolution. Several police shootouts occurred between the Panthers and police, and the FBI conducted numerous investigations of group members (sometimes using illegal tactics). Even so, many of the Panthers' activities—the establishment of daycare centers, free breakfast programs, free medical clinics, assistance to the homeless, and other services—won support in the ghettos. **E**

1968—A Turning Point in Civil Rights

Martin Luther King, Jr., objected to the Black Power movement. He believed that preaching violence could only end in grief. King was planning to lead a Poor People's March on Washington, D.C. However, this time the people would have to march without him.

KING'S DEATH Dr. King seemed to sense that death was near. On April 3, 1968, he addressed a crowd in Memphis, where he had gone to support the city's striking garbage workers. "I may not get there with you but . . . we as a people will get to the Promised Land." He added, "I'm not fearing any man. Mine eyes have seen the glory of the coming of the Lord." The next day as King stood on his hotel balcony, James Earl Ray thrust a high-powered rifle out of a window and squeezed the trigger. King crumpled to the floor.

REACTIONS TO KING'S DEATH The night King died, Robert F. Kennedy was campaigning for the Democratic presidential nomination. Fearful that King's death would spark riots, Kennedy's advisers told him to cancel his appearance in an African-American neighborhood in Indianapolis. However, Kennedy attended anyway, making an impassioned plea for nonviolence.

(above) Coretta Scott King mourns her husband at his funeral service.
(below) Robert F. Kennedy

★ A PERSONAL VOICE ROBERT F. KENNEDY

"For those of you who are black—considering the evidence . . . that there were white people who were responsible—you can be filled with bitterness, with hatred, and a desire for revenge. We can move in that direction as a country, in great polarization—black people amongst black, white people amongst white, filled with hatred toward one another.

Or we can make an effort, as Martin Luther King did, to understand and comprehend, and to replace that violence, that stain of bloodshed that has spread across our land, with an effort to understand [with] compassion and love."

—"A Eulogy for Dr. Martin Luther King, Jr."

Despite Kennedy's plea, rage over King's death led to the worst urban rioting in United States history. Over 100 cities exploded in flames. The hardest-hit cities included Baltimore, Chicago, Kansas City, and Washington, D.C. Then in June 1968, Robert Kennedy himself was assassinated by a Jordanian immigrant who was angry over Kennedy's support of Israel.

Legacy of the Civil Rights Movement

On March 1, 1968, the **Kerner Commission,** which President Johnson had appointed to study the causes of urban violence, issued its 200,000-word report. In it, the panel named one main cause: white racism. Said the report: "This is our basic conclusion: Our nation is moving toward two societies, one black, one white—separate and unequal." The report called for the nation to create new jobs, construct new housing, and end de facto segregation in order to wipe out the destructive ghetto environment. However, the Johnson administration ignored many of the recommendations because of white opposition to such sweeping changes. So what had the civil rights movement accomplished?

Background
The Civil Rights Act of 1968 is more commonly known as the Fair Housing Act.

CIVIL RIGHTS GAINS The civil rights movement ended de jure segregation by bringing about legal protection for the civil rights of all Americans. Congress passed the most important civil rights legislation since Reconstruction, including the **Civil Rights Act of 1968,** which ended discrimination in housing. After school segregation ended, the numbers of African Americans who finished high school and who went to college increased significantly. This in turn led to better jobs and business opportunities.

Another accomplishment of the civil rights movement was to give African Americans greater pride in their racial identity. Many African Americans adopted African-influenced styles and proudly displayed symbols of African history and culture. College students demanded new Black Studies programs so they could study African-American history and literature. In the entertainment world, the "color bar" was lowered as African Americans began to appear more frequently in movies and on television shows and commercials.

In addition, African Americans made substantial political gains. By 1970, an estimated two-thirds of eligible African Americans were registered to vote, and a significant increase in African-American elected officials resulted. The number of African Americans holding elected office grew from fewer than 100 in 1965 to more than 7,000 in 1992. Many civil rights activists went on to become political leaders, among them Reverend Jesse Jackson, who sought the Democratic nomination for president in 1984 and 1988; Vernon Jordan, who led voter-registration drives that enrolled about 2 million African Americans; and Andrew Young, who has served as UN ambassador and Atlanta's mayor. **F**

UNFINISHED WORK The civil rights movement was successful in changing many discriminatory laws. Yet as the 1960s turned to the 1970s, the challenges for the movement changed. The issues it confronted—housing and job discrimination, educational inequality, poverty, and racism—involved the difficult task of changing people's attitudes and behavior. Some of the proposed solutions, such as more tax monies spent in the inner cities and the forced busing of schoolchildren, angered some whites, who resisted further changes. Public support for the civil rights movement declined because some whites were frightened by the urban riots and the Black Panthers.

By 1990, the trend of whites fleeing the cities for the suburbs had reversed much of the progress toward school

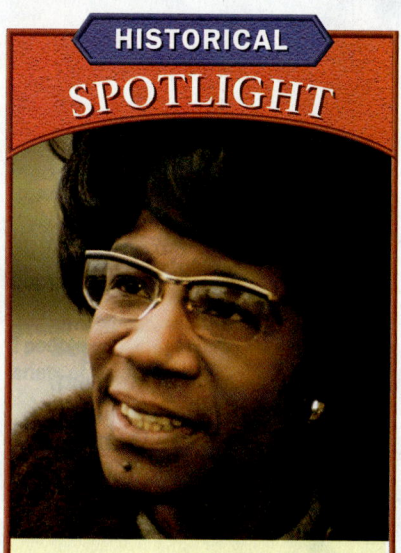

HISTORICAL SPOTLIGHT

SHIRLEY CHISHOLM

African-American women such as Shirley Chisholm exemplified the advances won in the civil rights movement. In 1968, Chisholm became the first African-American woman in the United States House of Representatives.

In the mid-1960s, Chisholm served in the New York state assembly, representing a district in New York City. While there, she supported programs to establish public day-care centers and provide unemployment insurance to domestic workers.

In 1972, Chisholm gained national prominence by running for the Democratic presidential nomination. Despite the fact that she never won more than 10% of the vote in the primaries, she controlled 152 delegates at the Democratic convention in Miami.

MAIN IDEA

Evaluating
F What were some accomplishments of the civil rights movement?

integration. In 1996–1997, 28 percent of blacks in the South and 50 percent of blacks in the Northeast were attending schools with fewer than 10 percent whites. Lack of jobs also remained a serious problem for African Americans, who had a poverty rate three times that of whites.

To help equalize education and job opportunities, the government in the 1960s began to promote **affirmative action.** Affirmative-action programs involve making special efforts to hire or enroll groups that have suffered discrimination. Many colleges and almost all companies that do business with the federal government adopted such programs. But in the late 1970s, some people began to criticize affirmative-action programs as "reverse discrimination" that set minority hiring or enrollment quotas and deprived whites of opportunities. In the 1980s, Republican administrations eased affirmative-action requirements for some government contractors. The fate of affirmative action is still to be decided.

Today, African Americans and whites interact in ways that could have only been imagined before the civil rights movement. In many respects, Dr. King's dream has been realized—yet much remains to be done.

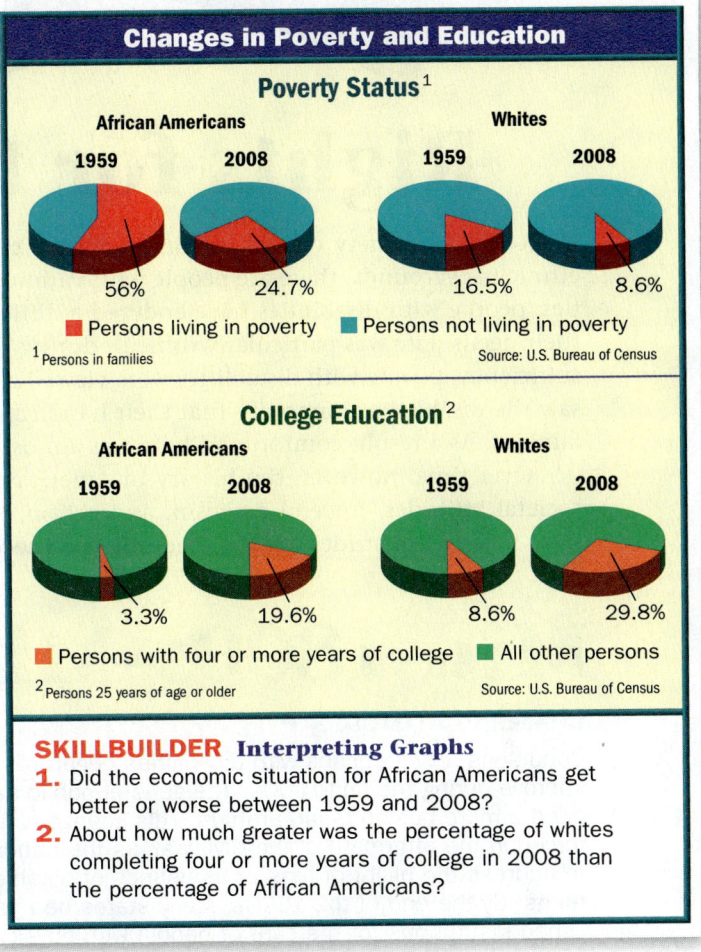

Changes in Poverty and Education

Poverty Status[1]

African Americans

1959 — 56%
2008 — 24.7%

Whites

1959 — 16.5%
2008 — 8.6%

■ Persons living in poverty   ■ Persons not living in poverty

[1] Persons in families   Source: U.S. Bureau of Census

College Education[2]

African Americans

1959 — 3.3%
2008 — 19.6%

Whites

1959 — 8.6%
2008 — 29.8%

■ Persons with four or more years of college   ■ All other persons

[2] Persons 25 years of age or older   Source: U.S. Bureau of Census

SKILLBUILDER Interpreting Graphs
1. Did the economic situation for African Americans get better or worse between 1959 and 2008?
2. About how much greater was the percentage of whites completing four or more years of college in 2008 than the percentage of African Americans?

SECTION 3 ASSESSMENT

1. **TERMS & NAMES** For each term or name, write a sentence explaining its significance.
   - de facto segregation
   - de jure segregation
   - Malcolm X
   - Nation of Islam
   - Stokely Carmichael
   - Black Power
   - Black Panthers
   - Kerner Commission
   - Civil Rights Act of 1968
   - affirmative action

MAIN IDEA

2. **TAKING NOTES**
   Create a timeline of key events of the civil rights movement.

   In your opinion, which event was most significant? Why?

CRITICAL THINKING

3. **ANALYZING ISSUES**
   What factors contributed to the outbreak of violence in the fight for civil rights? **Think About:**
   - different leaders' approach to civil rights issues
   - living conditions in urban areas
   - de facto and de jure segregation

4. **COMPARING AND CONTRASTING**
   Compare and contrast the civil rights strategies of Malcolm X and Martin Luther King, Jr. Whose strategies do you think were more effective? Explain and support your response.

Rights for the Disabled

United States society consists of many diverse groups. In addition to people of different racial and ethnic backgrounds, there are people with various physical and mental disabilities. Like other minorities, people with disabilities have endured a difficult history marked by prejudice and indifference to their needs. Life was particularly difficult during the nation's early years. In a society that valued self-sufficiency, people with disabilities were viewed as a burden on the community. Further, some people saw the disabled as immoral—that their handicaps were the result of their own sins or those of their families. As a result, comfort and help was almost nonexistent.

Over time, however, the history of Americans with disabilities has changed. Through changing societal attitudes, forceful activism, and action by the federal government, people with disabilities have made great strides toward shedding their second-class status and attaining full and equal rights.

Mid-1800s–Mid-1900s

CHANGING ATTITUDES ▶

Conditions for Americans with disabilities began to improve during the mid-1800s. The general public developed a more humanitarian attitude. This change was reinforced in the aftermath of the Civil War, as the nation tried to address the plight of tens of thousands of disabled veterans. By the end of the 1800s, many states had established institutions for the care of people with physical and mental disabilities.

During the early 1900s, attitudes shifted again, as society grew to see the disabled as more than just patients in need of care. "The really new element," declared a social worker, "is in the general acceptance of the idea that [the disabled can] lead a productive life and be . . . contributing member[s] of society."

1960s

◀ **THE KENNEDY ADMINISTRATION**

During John F. Kennedy's presidency the status of people with disabilities improved markedly. In 1961, Kennedy established the President's Panel on Mental Retardation to increase awareness of mental disability. He also sought to improve the system of care for those with mental disabilities.

Kennedy's efforts to raise awareness of mental disability, in part, led to the establishment of the Special Olympics. This sporting event for people with mental disabilities is now held in the same year as the Olympic Games. Athletes with physical disabilities take part in the Paralympic Games, which also are held in the same years as the Olympics.

MAJOR LEGISLATION GUARANTEEING RIGHTS FOR THE DISABLED		
LEGISLATION	**YEAR**	**DESCRIPTION**
Amendments to Elementary and Secondary Education Act	1966	Authorized funds for creating and improving education programs for handicapped students
Rehabilitation Act	1973	Prohibited federal agencies and institutions from discriminating against people with disabilities
Education for All Handicapped Children Act	1975	Prohibited public schools from excluding students with disabilities; required school districts to establish special education programs
Americans with Disabilities Act	1990	Guaranteed the disabled equal opportunity in employment; required that disabled have equal access to public transportation and public facilities

1970s–2000

NORMALIZATION ▶

In the mid-1900s, when other minority groups began to fight for greater civil rights, people with disabilities also demanded equal rights. The legislative measures that were passed in response dramatically expanded their rights. New approaches to care also gave some disabled people greater freedom. Perhaps the most significant new approach was deinstitutionalization, which called for people with disabilities to be treated in home or community settings rather than in institutions. Questions have been raised about the success of deinstitutionalization, but its supporters insist that helping people with disabilities to lead a normal existence is a worthy and valid goal.

The Present

ONGOING ISSUES

Mainstreaming—the practice of teaching children with handicaps in a regular classroom setting—is another approach that has caused controversy. Proponents of mainstreaming feel that students with handicaps learn better when taught in a regular classroom than in a special education class. Others suggest that the regular classroom is not equipped, and teachers do not have the unique skills needed, to deal with students with special needs.

The early years of the 21st century have been marked not only by controversy, but also by renewed activism—particularly by veterans. For example, many soldiers returning from active service in Iraq and Afghanistan have pushed for funding to treat disabilities caused by traumatic head injury.

THINKING CRITICALLY

CONNECT TO HISTORY

1. **Comparing** Compare how American society viewed people with disabilities in the 19th century, the early 20th century, and the late 20th century. Why do you think attitudes changed over time?

 SEE SKILLBUILDER HANDBOOK, PAGE R8.

CONNECT TO TODAY

2. **Writing About Issues** What issues affect the lives of Americans with disabilities today? Use the Internet and library resources to research a current-day disability issue. Write an account of this issue and share it with your class.

↗ **hmhsocialstudies.com** | **RESEARCH WEB LINKS**

VISUAL SUMMARY

CIVIL RIGHTS

1954
Brown v. Board of Education of Topeka

1954

1955

1955
Montgomery bus boycott

1956

1957

1957
School desegregation crisis in Arkansas

1958

1957
Southern Christian Leadership Conference (SCLC) is formed to "carry on nonviolent crusades."

1959

1960

1961
Freedom riders begin a bus ride through the South to protest segregation.

1961

1962

1963

1963
More than 250,000 people march on Washington to demand immediate passage of the civil rights bill.

1964
Congress passes the Civil Rights Act.

1964

1965

1965
Malcolm X is assassinated.

1966

1965
March from Selma to Montgomery to fight for voting rights

1967
Rioting in Detroit and more than 100 other cities.

1967

1965
Congress passes the Voting Rights Act.

1968
Martin Luther King, Jr., is assassinated.

1968

TERMS & NAMES

For each term or name below, write a sentence explaining its connection to the civil rights movement.

1. *Brown v. Board of Education of Topeka*
2. Rosa Parks
3. Martin Luther King, Jr.
4. Student Nonviolent Coordinating Committee
5. freedom rider
6. Civil Rights Act of 1964
7. Fannie Lou Hamer
8. de facto segregation
9. Malcolm X
10. Black Power

MAIN IDEAS

Use your notes and the information in the chapter to answer the following questions.

Taking on Segregation (pages 906–913)

1. What were Jim Crow laws and how were they applied?
2. What were the roots of Martin Luther King, Jr.'s beliefs in nonviolent resistance?

The Triumphs of a Crusade (pages 916–922)

3. What was the significance of the federal court case won by James Meredith in 1962?
4. Cite three examples of violence committed between 1962 and 1964 against African Americans and civil rights activists.

Challenges and Changes in the Movement
(pages 923–929)

5. What were some of the key beliefs advocated by Malcolm X?
6. Why did some civil rights leaders urge Stokely Carmichael to stop using the slogan "Black Power"?

THINKING CRITICALLY

1. **USING YOUR NOTES** On your own paper, draw a cluster diagram like the one shown below. Then, fill it in with four events from the civil rights movement that were broadcast on nationwide television and that you find the most compelling.

example: example:

TV Coverage of Civil Rights Movement

example: example:

2. **HISTORICAL PERSPECTIVE** Overall, would you characterize the civil rights struggle as a unified or disunified movement? Explain.

3. **INTERPRETING MAPS** Look carefully at the map of U.S. school segregation on page 907. What regional differences do you think spurred civil rights activists to target the South before the North?

Use the diagram and your knowledge of United States history to answer question 1.

Civil Rights Strategies and Actions, 1954-1968

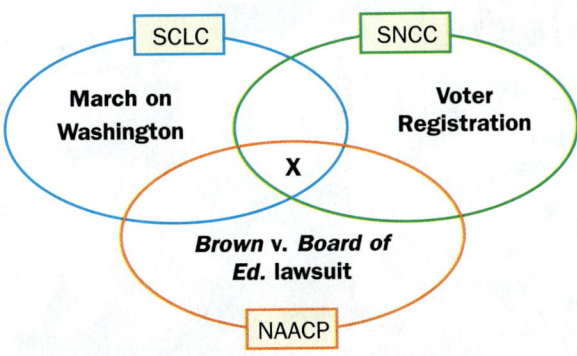

SCLC

SNCC

March on Washington

Voter Registration

X

Brown v. *Board of Ed.* lawsuit

NAACP

1 The Venn diagram is partially filled in with the strategies of various civil rights groups in the 1960s. Which of the following could be added to the area of the diagram labeled **X**?

(1) provide social services to the needy

(2) boycotts

(3) nonviolent demonstrations

(4) armed self-defense

Use the quotation as well as your knowledge of United States history to answer question 2.

> "An illegal attack, an unjust attack, and an immoral attack can be made against you by any one. Just because a person has on a [police] uniform does not give him the right to come and shoot up your neighborhood. No, this is not right, and my suggestion would be that as long as the police department doesn't use those methods in white neighborhoods, they shouldn't come . . . and use them in our neighborhood. . . ."
>
> —MALCOLM X, *"Prospects for Freedom in 1965"*

2 Which of the following events justifies Malcolm X's concerns about police brutality?

(1) the Rosa Parks incident in 1955

(2) the 1963 Birmingham demonstrations

(3) the desegregation of Little Rock's Central High in 1957

(4) the first sit-ins in 1942

⬈ hmhsocialstudies.com **TEST PRACTICE**

For additional test practice, go online for:

• Diagnostic tests   • Tutorials

INTERACT WITH HISTORY

Think about the issues you explored at the beginning of the chapter. Choose one participant in the civil rights movement. Write a speech from that person's perspective in which you evaluate your role in the movement. Consider what civil rights you worked for, why those rights are important, how sucessful you were, and the costs of your struggle.

FOCUS ON WRITING

Imagine you are a leader of the civil rights movement. Write a persuasive speech urging citizens to support the movement, explaining why civil rights for all people are necessary. Support your argument by listing the benefits that civil rights provide for all citizens. Use vivid details and descriptive language.

COLLABORATIVE LEARNING

21ST CENTURY

Working with a partner, use library or Internet sources to learn more about the Montgomery bus boycott. Then work together to create a pamphlet designed to teach others about the boycott and to encourage them to become involved. Consider what information you should include and how you should organize it to maximize your pamphlet's effectiveness.

THE VIETNAM WAR YEARS

What were the military and political events of the Vietnam War and how did this conflict impact life in the United States?

New York Standards

KEY IDEA 2 Important ideas, social and cultural values, beliefs, and traditions from New York State and United States history illustrate the connections and interactions of people and events across time and from a variety of perspectives.

KEY IDEA 3 Study about the major social, political, economic, cultural, and religious developments in New York State and United States history involves learning about the important roles and contributions of individuals and groups.

SECTION 1: Moving Toward Conflict

SECTION 2: U.S. Involvement and Escalation

SECTION 3: A Nation Divided

SECTION 4: 1968: A Tumultuous Year

SECTION 5: The End of the War and Its Legacy

U.S. troops on patrol with helicopter support in Vietnam, 1965.

1960 John F. Kennedy is elected president.

1963 Kennedy is assassinated; Lyndon B. Johnson becomes president.

1964 Lyndon B. Johnson is elected president.

1965 First major U.S. combat units arrive in Vietnam.

USA
WORLD

1960

1965

1960 The National Liberation Front forms in South Vietnam.

1962 The African nation of Uganda becomes independent.

1966 Mao Zedong begins the Cultural Revolution in China.

1967 Israel captures Gaza Strip and West Bank in Six-Day War.

hmhsocialstudies.com **VIDEO**

H HISTORY

LBJ and Vietnam: In the Eye of the Storm

INTERACT
WITH HISTORY

In 1965, America's fight against communism has spread to Southeast Asia, where the United States is becoming increasingly involved in another country's civil war. Unable to claim victory, U.S. generals call for an increase in the number of combat troops. Facing a shortage of volunteers, the president implements a draft.

Explore the Issues

- Should people who believe the war is wrong be forced to fight?
- Should people with special skills be exempt?
- How can a draft be made fair?

1968 Martin Luther King, Jr., and Robert Kennedy are assassinated.

1968 Richard M. Nixon is elected president.

1969 U.S. troops begin their withdrawal from Vietnam.

1970 Ohio National Guard kills four students at Kent State University.

1972 Richard M. Nixon is reelected.

1973 United States signs cease-fire with North Vietnam and Vietcong.

1974 Gerald R. Ford becomes president after Richard M. Nixon resigns.

1970

1975

1972 Ferdinand Marcos declares martial law in the Philippines.

1975 Communists capture Saigon; South Vietnam surrenders.

Moving Toward Conflict

MAIN IDEA	WHY IT MATTERS NOW	Terms & Names
To stop the spread of communism in Southeast Asia, the United States used its military to support South Vietnam.	The United States' support role in Vietnam began what would become America's longest and most controversial war in its history.	•Ho Chi Minh •Ngo Dinh Diem •Vietminh •Vietcong •domino theory •Ho Chi Minh Trail •Dien Bien Phu •Tonkin Gulf •Geneva Accords Resolution

One American's Story

hmhsocialstudies.com
TAKING NOTES

Use the graphic organizer online to take notes on the Vietnam policies of Presidents Truman, Eisenhower, Kennedy, and Johnson.

On the morning of September 26, 1945, Lieutenant Colonel A. Peter Dewey was on his way to the Saigon airport in Vietnam. Only 28, Dewey served in the Office of Strategic Services, the chief intelligence-gathering body of the U.S. military and forerunner of the Central Intelligence Agency. Dewey was sent to assess what was becoming an explosive situation in Vietnam, a Southeast Asian country that had recently been freed from Japanese rule as a result of the allied victory in World War II. (See map on page 939.)

Before the war, France had ruled Vietnam and the surrounding countries; now it sought—with British aid—to regain control of the region. The Vietnamese had resisted Japanese occupation; now they were preparing to fight the French. Dewey saw nothing but disaster in France's plan. "Cochinchina [southern Vietnam] is burning," he reported, "the French and British are finished here, and we [the United States] ought to clear out of Southeast Asia."

On his way to the airport, Dewey encountered a roadblock staffed by Vietnamese soldiers and shouted at them in French. Presumably mistaking him for a French soldier, the guards shot him in the head. Thus, A. Peter Dewey, whose body was never recovered, was the first American to die in Vietnam.

▲
Lieutenant Colonel A. Peter Dewey

Unfortunately, Dewey would not be the last. As Vietnam's independence effort came under communist influence, the United States grew increasingly concerned about the small country's future. Eventually, America would fight a war to halt the spread of communism in Vietnam. The war would claim the lives of almost 60,000 Americans and more than 2 million Vietnamese. It also would divide the American nation as no other event since the Civil War.

America Supports France in Vietnam

America's involvement in Vietnam began in 1950, during the French Indochina War, the name given to France's attempt to reestablish its rule in Vietnam after World War II. Seeking to strengthen its ties with France and to help fight the spread of communism, the United States provided the French with massive economic and military support.

FRENCH RULE IN VIETNAM From the late 1800s until World War II, France ruled most of Indochina, including Vietnam, Laos, and Cambodia. French colonists, who built plantations on peasant land and extracted rice and rubber for their own profit, encountered growing unrest among the Vietnamese peasants. French rulers reacted harshly by restricting freedom of speech and assembly and by jailing many Vietnamese nationalists. These measures failed to curb all dissent, and opposition continued to grow.

The Indochinese Communist Party, founded in 1930, staged a number of revolts under the leadership of **Ho Chi Minh.** Although the French condemned Ho Chi Minh to death for his rebellious activity, he fled Vietnam and orchestrated Vietnam's growing independence movement from exile in the Soviet Union and later from China.

In 1940 the Japanese took control of Vietnam. The next year, Ho Chi Minh returned home and helped form the **Vietminh,** an organization whose goal it was to win Vietnam's independence from foreign rule. When the Allied defeat of Japan in August 1945 forced the Japanese to leave Vietnam, that goal suddenly seemed a reality. On September 2, 1945, Ho Chi Minh stood in the middle of a huge crowd in the northern city of Hanoi and declared Vietnam an independent nation.

FRANCE BATTLES THE VIETMINH France, however, had no intention of relinquishing its former colony. French troops moved back into Vietnam by the end of 1945, eventually regaining control of the cities and the country's southern half. Ho Chi Minh vowed to fight from the North to liberate the South from French control. "If ever the tiger pauses," Ho had said, referring to the Vietminh, "the elephant [France] will impale him on his mighty tusks. But the tiger will not pause, and the elephant will die of exhaustion and loss of blood."

In 1950, the United States entered the Vietnam struggle—despite A. Peter Dewey's warnings. That year, President Truman sent nearly $15 million in economic aid to France. Over the next four years, the United States paid for much of France's war, pumping nearly $1 billion into the effort to defeat a man America had once supported. Ironically, during World War II, the United States had forged an alliance with Ho Chi Minh, supplying him with aid to resist the Japanese. But by 1950, the United States had come to view its one-time ally as a communist aggressor. Ⓐ

THE VIETMINH DRIVE OUT THE FRENCH Upon entering the White House in 1953, President Eisenhower continued the policy of supplying aid to the French war effort. By this time, the United States had settled for a stalemate with the communists in Korea, which only stiffened America's resolve to halt the spread of communism elsewhere. During a news conference in 1954, Eisenhower explained the **domino theory,** in which he likened the countries on the brink of communism to a row of dominoes waiting to fall one after the other. "You have a row of dominoes set up," the president said. "You knock over the first one, and what will happen to the last one is the certainty that it will go over very quickly."

Despite massive U.S. aid, however, the French could not retake Vietnam. They were forced to surrender in May of 1954, when the Vietminh overran the French outpost at **Dien Bien Phu,** in northwestern Vietnam.

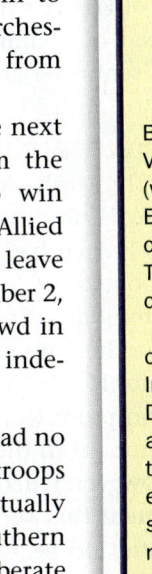

KEY PLAYER

**HO CHI MINH
1890–1969**

Born Nguyen Tat Thanh to a poor Vietnamese family, Ho Chi Minh (which means "He Who Enlightens") found work as a cook on a French steamship. This allowed him to visit such cities as Boston and New York.

Ho Chi Minh based the phrasing of the Vietnamese Declaration of Independence on the U.S. Declaration of Independence. His admiration for the United States turned to disappointment, however, after the government chose to support France rather than his nationalist movement.

The Communist ruler's name lived on after his death in 1969. In 1975, the North Vietnamese Army conquered South Vietnam and changed the name of the South's capital from Saigon to Ho Chi Minh City.

From May through July 1954, the countries of France, Great Britain, the Soviet Union, the United States, China, Laos, and Cambodia met in Geneva, Switzerland, with the Vietminh and with South Vietnam's anti-Communist nationalists to hammer out a peace agreement. The **Geneva Accords** temporarily divided Vietnam along the 17th parallel. The Communists and their leader, Ho Chi Minh, controlled North Vietnam from the capital of Hanoi. The anti-Communist nationalists controlled South Vietnam from the capital and southern port city of Saigon. An election to unify the country was called for in 1956.

The United States Steps In

In the wake of France's retreat, the United States took a more active role in halting the spread of communism in Vietnam. Wading deeper into the country's affairs, the Eisenhower and the Kennedy administrations provided economic and military aid to South Vietnam's non-Communist regime.

DIEM CANCELS ELECTIONS Although he directed a brutal and repressive regime, Ho Chi Minh won popular support in the North by breaking up large estates and redistributing land to peasants. Moreover, his years of fighting the Japanese and French had made him a national hero. Recognizing Ho Chi Minh's widespread popularity, South Vietnam's president, **Ngo Dinh Diem** (ngō′ dĭn′ dē-ĕm′), a strong anti-Communist, refused to take part in the countrywide election of 1956. The United States also sensed that a countrywide election might spell victory for Ho Chi Minh and supported canceling elections. The Eisenhower administration promised military aid and training to Diem in return for a stable reform government in the South. **B**

Diem, however, failed to hold up his end of the bargain. He ushered in a corrupt government that suppressed opposition of any kind and offered little or no land distribution to peasants. In addition, Diem, a devout Catholic, angered the country's majority Buddhist population by restricting Buddhist practices.

By 1957, a Communist opposition group in the South, known as the **Vietcong,** had begun attacks on the Diem government, assassinating thousands of South Vietnamese government officials. Although the political arm of the group would later be called the National Liberation Front (NLF), the United States continued to refer to the fighters as the Vietcong.

Ho Chi Minh supported the group, and in 1959 began supplying arms to the Vietcong via a network of paths along the borders of Vietnam, Laos, and Cambodia that became known as the **Ho Chi Minh Trail.** (See map on page 939.) As the fighters stepped up their surprise attacks, or guerrilla tactics, South Vietnam grew more unstable. The Eisenhower administration took little action, however, deciding to "sink or swim with Ngo Dinh Diem."

KENNEDY AND VIETNAM The Kennedy administration, which entered the White House in 1961, also chose initially to "swim" with Diem. Wary of accusations that Democrats were "soft" on communism, President Kennedy increased financial aid to Diem's teetering regime and sent thousands of military advisers to help train South Vietnamese troops. By the end of 1963, 16,000 U.S. military personnel were in South Vietnam.

Meanwhile, Diem's popularity plummeted because of ongoing corruption and his failure to respond to calls for land reform. To combat the growing Vietcong presence in the South's countryside, the Diem administration initiated the strategic hamlet program, which meant moving all villagers to protected areas.

The Vietcong saw the United States and South Vietnam as oppressors. This propaganda poster reads, "Vietnam will surely be victorious and America will surely be defeated."

MAIN IDEA

Analyzing Motives
B Why did the United States support canceling elections?

Background
The Buddhist religion is based on the teachings of Siddhartha Gautama, also known as Shakyamuni, an Indian mystic who believed that spiritual enlightenment could be obtained through right conduct, meditation, and wisdom.

Indochina, 1959

C H I N A

Red River

NORTH VIETNAM

Dien Bien Phu • Hanoi ✪

• Haiphong

LAOS

Gulf of Tonkin

BURMA

Vientiane ✪

Mekong River

THAILAND

17th Parallel

• Hue

• Da Nang

15°N

• My Lai

Bangkok ✪

CAMBODIA

Ho Chi Minh Trail

SOUTH VIETNAM

Phnom Penh ✪

• Cam Ranh Bay

Saigon ✪

Gulf of Thailand

South China Sea

0   300   300 miles
0   300   300 kilometers

After parachuting into the mountains north of Dien Bien Phu, South Vietnamese troops await orders from French officers in 1953.

105°E

Equator

Rivers serve as places to work, bathe, and wash clothing.

The swampy terrain of South Vietnam made for difficult and dangerous fighting. This 1961 photograph shows South Vietnamese Army troops in combat operations against Vietcong.

GEOGRAPHY SKILLBUILDER
1. **Movement** Through which countries did the Ho Chi Minh Trail pass?
2. **Location** How might North Vietnam's location have enabled it to get aid from its ally, China?

A Buddhist monk sets himself on fire in a busy Saigon intersection in 1963 as a protest against the Diem regime. ▶

Many Vietnamese deeply resented being moved from their home villages where they had lived for generations and where ancestors were buried.

Diem also intensified his attack on Buddhism. Fed up with continuing Buddhist demonstrations, the South Vietnamese ruler imprisoned and killed hundreds of Buddhist clerics and destroyed their temples. To protest, several Buddhist monks and nuns publicly burned themselves to death. Horrified, American officials urged Diem to stop the persecutions, but Diem refused. **C**

It had become clear that for South Vietnam to remain stable, Diem would have to go. On November 1, 1963, a U.S.-supported military coup toppled Diem's regime. Against Kennedy's wishes, Diem was assassinated. A few weeks later, Kennedy, too, fell to an assassin's bullet. The United States presidency—along with the growing crisis in Vietnam—now belonged to Lyndon B. Johnson.

MAIN IDEA

Forming Generalizations
C Why was the Diem regime unpopular?

Vocabulary
coup: a sudden appropriation of leadership; a takeover

President Johnson Expands the Conflict

Shortly before his death, Kennedy had announced his intent to withdraw U.S. forces from South Vietnam. "In the final analysis, it's their war," he declared. Whether Kennedy would have withdrawn from Vietnam remains a matter of debate. However, Lyndon Johnson escalated the nation's role in Vietnam and eventually began what would become America's longest war.

THE SOUTH GROWS MORE UNSTABLE Diem's death brought more chaos to South Vietnam. A string of military leaders attempted to lead the country, but each regime was more unstable and inefficient than Diem's had been. Meanwhile, the Vietcong's influence in the countryside steadily grew.

President Johnson believed that a communist takeover of South Vietnam would be disastrous. Johnson, like Kennedy, was particularly sensitive to being perceived as "soft" on communism. "If I . . . let the communists take over South Vietnam," Johnson said, "then . . . my nation would be seen as an appeaser and we would . . . find it impossible to accomplish anything . . . anywhere on the entire globe."

THE TONKIN GULF RESOLUTION On August 2, 1964, a North Vietnamese patrol boat fired a torpedo at an American destroyer, the USS *Maddox*, which was patrolling in the Gulf of Tonkin off the North Vietnamese coast. The torpedo missed its target, but the *Maddox* returned fire and inflicted heavy damage on the patrol boat.

▲ The Navy destroyer
U.S.S. *Maddox*.

Two days later, the *Maddox* and another destroyer were again off the North Vietnamese coast. In spite of bad weather that could affect visibility, the crew reported enemy torpedoes, and the American destroyers began firing. The crew of the *Maddox* later declared, however, that they had neither seen nor heard hostile gunfire.

The alleged attack on the U.S. ships prompted President Johnson to launch bombing strikes on North Vietnam. He asked Congress for powers to take "all necessary measures to repel any armed attack against the forces of the United States and to prevent further aggression." Congress approved Johnson's request, with only two senators voting against it, and adopted the **Tonkin Gulf Resolution** on August 7. While not a declaration of war, it granted Johnson broad military powers in Vietnam.

Johnson did not tell Congress or the American people that the United States had been leading secret raids against North Vietnam. The *Maddox* had been in the Gulf of Tonkin to collect information for these raids. Furthermore, Johnson had prepared the resolution months beforehand and was only waiting for the chance to push it through Congress.

In February of 1965, President Johnson used his newly granted powers. In response to a Vietcong attack that killed eight Americans, Johnson unleashed "Operation Rolling Thunder," the first sustained bombing of North Vietnam. In March of that year the first American combat troops began arriving in South Vietnam. By June, more than 50,000 U.S. soldiers were battling the Vietcong. The Vietnam War had become Americanized. **D**

MAIN IDEA

Developing Historical Perspective

D How did the Tonkin Gulf Resolution lead to greater U.S. involvement in the Vietnam War?

SECTION 1 ASSESSMENT

1. TERMS & NAMES For each term or name, write a sentence explaining its significance.
- Ho Chi Minh
- Vietminh
- domino theory
- Dien Bien Phu
- Geneva Accords
- Ngo Dinh Diem
- Vietcong
- Ho Chi Minh Trail
- Tonkin Gulf Resolution

MAIN IDEA

2. TAKING NOTES
In a chart like the one below, cite the Vietnam policy for each of the following presidents: Truman, Eisenhower, Kennedy, and Johnson.

President	Vietnam Policy

Choose one of the four presidents and explain his goals in Vietnam.

CRITICAL THINKING

3. MAKING INFERENCES
How did the United States become more involved in the war? Explain your answer in a short paragraph.

4. SYNTHESIZING
In what ways was America's support of the Diem government a conflict of interests? Cite examples to support your answer.

5. EVALUATING
Do you think Congress was justified in passing the Tonkin Gulf Resolution? Use details from the text to support your response.

Think About:
- the questionable report of torpedo attacks on two U.S. destroyers
- the powers that the resolution would give the president
- the fact that the resolution was not a declaration of war

CC Unit 7.IV.A.2 CC Unit 7.IV.A.3
CC Unit 7.IV.A.4.a CC Unit 7.IV.A.4.b
PI 2.5

SECTION 2

U.S. Involvement and Escalation

MAIN IDEA	WHY IT MATTERS NOW	Terms & Names
The United States sent troops to fight in Vietnam, but the war quickly turned into a stalemate.	Since Vietnam, Americans are more aware of the positive and negative effects of using U.S. troops in foreign conflicts.	• Robert McNamara • Dean Rusk • William Westmoreland • Army of the Republic of Vietnam (ARVN) • napalm • Agent Orange • search-and-destroy mission • credibility gap

One American's Story

Tim O'Brien is a novelist who has written several books about his experience in Vietnam and its lasting effects. Drafted at the age of 21, O'Brien was sent to Vietnam in August 1968. He spent the first seven months of his nearly two-year duty patrolling the fields outside of Chu Lai, a seacoast city in South Vietnam. O'Brien described one of the more nerve-racking experiences of the war: walking through the fields and jungles, many of which were filled with land mines and booby traps.

▲ Vietnam's terrain was often treacherous, such as the thick jungles and rivers these U.S. soldiers encountered in 1966.

A PERSONAL VOICE TIM O'BRIEN

" You do some thinking. You hallucinate. You look ahead a few paces and wonder what your legs will resemble if there is more to the earth in that spot than silicates and nitrogen. Will the pain be unbearable? Will you scream and fall silent? Will you be afraid to look at your own body, afraid of the sight of your own red flesh and white bone? . . .

It is not easy to fight this sort of self-defeating fear, but you try. You decide to be ultra-careful—the hard-nosed realistic approach. You try to second-guess the mine. Should you put your foot to that flat rock or the clump of weeds to its rear? Paddy dike or water? You wish you were Tarzan, able to swing on the vines. You trace the footprints of the men to your front. You give up when he curses you for following too closely; better one man dead than two. "

—quoted in *A Life in a Year: The American Infantryman in Vietnam 1965–1972*

Deadly traps were just some of the obstacles that U.S. troops faced. As the infiltration of American ground troops into Vietnam failed to score a quick victory, a mostly supportive U.S. population began to question its government's war policy.

Johnson Increases U.S. Involvement

Much of the nation supported Lyndon Johnson's determination to contain communism in Vietnam. In the years following 1965, President Johnson began sending large numbers of American troops to fight alongside the South Vietnamese.

STRONG SUPPORT FOR CONTAINMENT Even after Congress had approved the Tonkin Gulf Resolution, President Johnson opposed sending U.S. ground troops to Vietnam. Johnson's victory in the 1964 presidential election was due in part to charges that his Republican opponent, Barry Goldwater, was an anti-Communist who might push the United States into war with the Soviet Union. In contrast to Goldwater's heated, warlike language, Johnson's speeches were more moderate, yet he spoke determinedly about containing communism. He declared he was "not about to send American boys 9 or 10,000 miles away from home to do what Asian boys ought to be doing for themselves."

However, in March of 1965, that is precisely what the president did. Working closely with his foreign-policy advisers, particularly Secretary of Defense **Robert McNamara** and Secretary of State **Dean Rusk,** President Johnson began dispatching tens of thousands of U.S. soldiers to fight in Vietnam. Some Americans viewed Johnson's decision as contradictory to his position during the presidential campaign. However, most saw the president as following an established and popular policy of confronting communism anywhere in the world. Congress, as well as the American public, strongly supported Johnson's strategy. A 1965 poll showed that 61 percent of Americans supported the U.S. policy in Vietnam, while only 24 percent opposed.

There were dissenters within the Johnson administration, too. In October of 1964, Undersecretary of State George Ball had argued against escalation, warning that "once on the tiger's back, we cannot be sure of picking the place to dismount." However, the president's closest advisers strongly urged escalation, believing the defeat of communism in Vietnam to be of vital importance to the future of America and the world. Dean Rusk stressed this view in a 1965 memo to President Johnson. **A**

MAIN IDEA

Contrasting

A What differing opinions did Johnson's advisers have about Vietnam?

★ **A PERSONAL VOICE** DEAN RUSK

" The integrity of the U.S. commitment is the principal pillar of peace throughout the world. If that commitment becomes unreliable, the communist world would draw conclusions that would lead to our ruin and *almost certainly to a catastrophic war.* So long as the South Vietnamese are prepared to fight for themselves, we cannot abandon them without disaster to peace and to our interests throughout the world."

—quoted in *In Retrospect*

THE TROOP BUILDUP ACCELERATES By the end of 1965, the U.S. government had sent more than 180,000 Americans to Vietnam. The American commander in South Vietnam, General **William Westmoreland,** continued to request more troops. Westmoreland, a West Point graduate who had served in World War II and Korea, was less than impressed with the fighting ability of the South Vietnamese Army, or the **Army of the Republic of Vietnam (ARVN).** The ARVN "cannot stand up to this pressure without substantial U.S. combat support on the ground," the general reported. "The only possible response is the aggressive deployment of U.S. troops." Throughout the early years of the war, the Johnson administration complied with Westmoreland's requests; by 1967, the number of U.S. troops in Vietnam had climbed to about 500,000.

KEY PLAYER

GENERAL WILLIAM WESTMORELAND (1914–2005)

General Westmoreland retired from the military in 1972, but even in retirement, he could not escape the Vietnam War.

In 1982, CBS-TV aired a documentary entitled *The Uncounted Enemy: A Vietnam Deception.* The report, viewed by millions, asserted that Westmoreland and the Pentagon had deceived the U.S. government about the enemy's size and strength during 1967 and 1968 to make it appear that U.S. forces were winning the war.

Westmoreland, claiming he was the victim of "distorted, false, and specious information . . . derived by sinister deception," filed a $120 million libel suit against CBS. The suit was eventually settled, with both parties issuing statements pledging mutual respect. CBS, however, stood by its story.

Fighting in the Jungle

The United States entered the war in Vietnam believing that its superior weaponry would lead it to victory over the Vietcong. However, the jungle terrain and the enemy's guerrilla tactics soon turned the war into a frustrating stalemate.

AN ELUSIVE ENEMY Because the Vietcong lacked the high-powered weaponry of the American forces, they used hit-and-run and ambush tactics, as well as a keen knowledge of the jungle terrain, to their advantage. Moving secretly in and out of the general population, the Vietcong destroyed the notion of a traditional front line by attacking U.S. troops in both the cities and the countryside. Because some of the enemy lived amidst the civilian population, it was difficult for U.S. troops to discern friend from foe. A woman selling soft drinks to U.S. soldiers might be a Vietcong spy. A boy standing on the corner might be ready to throw a grenade.

Adding to the Vietcong's elusiveness was a network of elaborate tunnels that allowed them to withstand airstrikes and to launch surprise attacks and then disappear quickly. Connecting villages throughout the countryside, the tunnels became home to many guerrilla fighters. "The more the Americans tried to drive us away from our land, the more we burrowed into it," recalled Nguyen Quoc, a major in the Vietcong army.

In addition, the terrain was laced with countless booby traps and land mines. Because the exact location of the Vietcong was often unknown, U.S. troops laid land mines throughout the jungle. The Vietcong also laid their own traps, and disassembled and reused U.S. mines. American soldiers marching through South

Tunnels of the Vietcong

hmhsocialstudies.com **INTERACTIVE**

Remote smoke outlets

Submerged entrance

Kitchen

Ventilation shaft

Punji stake pit

Firing post

Conference chamber

Sleeping chamber

Conical air raid shelter that also amplified sound of approaching aircraft

Blast, gas, and waterproof trap doors

False tunnel

Booby trap grenade

Storage cache for weapons, explosives, and rice

First-aid station powered by bicycle

Well

Vietnam's jungles and rice paddies not only dealt with swelter- ing heat and leeches but also had to be cautious of every step. In a 1969 letter to his sister, Specialist Fourth Class Salvador Gonzalez described the tragic result from an unexploded U.S. bomb that the North Vietnamese Army had rigged. **B**

MAIN IDEA

Drawing Conclusions

B Why did the U.S. forces have difficulty fighting the Vietcong?

★ **A PERSONAL VOICE** SALVADOR GONZALEZ

" Two days ago 4 guys got killed and about 15 wounded from the first platoon. Our platoon was 200 yards away on top of a hill. One guy was from Floral Park [in New York City]. He had five days left to go [before being sent home]. He was standing on a 250-lb. bomb that a plane had dropped and didn't explode. So the NVA [North Vietnamese Army] wired it up. Well, all they found was a piece of his wallet. "

—quoted in *Dear America: Letters Home from Vietnam*

A FRUSTRATING WAR OF ATTRITION Westmoreland's strat- egy for defeating the Vietcong was to destroy their morale through a war of attrition, or the gradual wearing down of the enemy by continuous harassment. Introducing the concept of the body count, or the tracking of Vietcong killed in battle, the general believed that as the number of Vietcong dead rose, the guerrillas would inevitably surrender.

However, the Vietcong had no intention of quitting their fight. Despite the growing number of casualties and the relentless pounding from U.S. bombers, the Vietcong—who received supplies from China and the Soviet Union— remained defiant. Defense Secretary McNamara confessed his frustration to a reporter in 1966: "If I had thought they would take this punish- ment and fight this well, . . . I would have thought differently at the start."

General Westmoreland would say later that the United States never lost a bat- tle in Vietnam. Whether or not the general's words were true, they underscored the degree to which America misunderstood its foe. The United States viewed the war strictly as a military struggle; the Vietcong saw it as a battle for their very exis- tence, and they were ready to pay any price for victory. **C**

MAIN IDEA

Making Inferences

C In what way did the United States under- estimate the Vietcong?

THE BATTLE FOR "HEARTS AND MINDS" Another key part of the American strategy was to keep the Vietcong from winning the support of South Vietnam's rural population. Edward G. Lansdale, who helped found the fighting unit known as the U.S. Army Special Forces, or Green Berets, stressed the plan's importance. "Just remember this. Communist guerrillas hide among the people. If you win the people over to your side, the communist guerrillas have no place to hide."

The campaign to win the "hearts and minds" of the South Vietnamese villagers proved more difficult than imagined. For instance, in their attempt to expose Vietcong tunnels and hideouts, U.S. planes dropped **napalm,** a gasoline-based bomb that set fire to the jungle. They also sprayed **Agent Orange,** a leaf-killing toxic chemical. The saturation use of these weapons often wounded civilians and left villages and their surroundings in ruins. Years later, many would blame Agent Orange for cancers suffered by Vietnamese civilians and American veterans.

U.S. soldiers conducted **search-and-destroy missions,** uprooting civilians with suspected ties to the Vietcong, killing their livestock, and burning villages. Many villagers fled into the cities or refugee camps, creating by 1967 more than 3 million refugees in the South. The irony of the strategy was summed up in February 1968 by a U.S. major whose forces had just leveled the town of Ben Tre: "We had to destroy the town in order to save it."

NOW & THEN

LAND MINES

Perhaps 3 million armed mines remain in Vietnam, and they are still claiming lives. Between 1999 and 2008, 589 Vietnamese have been killed and another 956 have been injured by these remnants of the Vietnam War.

The 1997 Mine Ban Treaty bans production and use of antiperson- nel mines worldwide. As of 2010, 156 nations had agreed to the treaty, with the notable exceptions of the United States, Russia, and China. In 1998, President Clinton declared that the United States would sign the treaty by 2006, if "suitable alternatives" to land mines had been developed, and asked the military to begin work- ing toward this goal. In 2004, however, President George W. Bush said he would not sign the treaty. The Obama administration, too, decided to leave U.S. policy on mines unchanged.

▲
This U.S. soldier in Vietnam wears symbols of both war and peace on his chest.

SINKING MORALE The frustrations of guerrilla warfare, the brutal jungle conditions, and the failure to make substantial headway against the enemy took their toll on the U.S. troops' morale. Philip Caputo, a marine lieutenant in Vietnam who later wrote several books about the war, summarized the soldiers' growing disillusionment: "When we marched into the rice paddies . . . we carried, along with our packs and rifles, the implicit convictions that the Vietcong could be quickly beaten. We kept the packs and rifles; the convictions, we lost."

As the war continued, American morale dropped steadily. Many soldiers, required by law to fight a war they did not support, turned to alcohol, marijuana, and other drugs. Low morale even led a few soldiers to murder their officers. Morale worsened during the later years of the war when soldiers realized they were fighting even as their government was negotiating a withdrawal. **D**

Another obstacle was the continuing corruption and instability of the South Vietnamese government. Nguyen Cao Ky, a flamboyant air marshal, led the government from 1965 to 1967. Ky ignored U.S. pleas to retire in favor of an elected civilian government. Mass demonstrations began, and by May of 1966, Buddhist monks and nuns were once again burning themselves in protest against the South Vietnamese government. South Vietnam was fighting a civil war within a civil war, leaving U.S. officials confused and angry.

FULFILLING A DUTY Most American soldiers, however, firmly believed in their cause—to halt the spread of communism. They took patriotic pride in fulfilling their duty, just as their fathers had done in World War II.

Most American soldiers fought courageously. Particularly heroic were the thousands of soldiers who endured years of torture and confinement as prisoners of war. In 1966, navy pilot Gerald Coffee's plane was shot down over North Vietnam. Coffee spent the next seven years—until he was released in 1973 as part of a cease-fire agreement—struggling to stay alive in an enemy prison camp.

> ◢ **A PERSONAL VOICE** GERALD COFFEE
>
> " My clothes were filthy and ragged. . . . With no boots, my socks—which I'd been able to salvage—were barely recognizable. . . . Only a few threads around my toes kept them spread over my feet; some protection, at least, as I shivered through the cold nights curled up tightly on my morguelike slab. . . . My conditions and predicament were so foreign to me, so stifling, so overwhelming. I'd never been so hungry, so grimy, and in such pain. "
>
> —*Beyond Survival*

The Early War at Home

The Johnson administration thought the war would end quickly. As it dragged on, support began to waver, and Johnson's domestic programs began to unravel.

MAIN IDEA

Analyzing Causes

D What factors led to the low morale of U.S. troops?

THE GREAT SOCIETY SUFFERS As the number of U.S. troops in Vietnam continued to mount, the war grew more costly, and the nation's economy began to suffer. The inflation rate, which was less than 2 percent through most of the early 1960s, more than tripled to 5.5 percent by 1969. In August of 1967, President Johnson asked for a tax increase to help fund the war and to keep inflation in check. Congressional conservatives agreed, but only after demanding and receiving a $6 billion reduction in funding for Great Society programs. Vietnam was slowly claiming an early casualty: Johnson's grand vision of domestic reform.

THE LIVING-ROOM WAR Through the media, specifically television, Vietnam became America's first "living-room war." The combat footage that appeared nightly on the news in millions of homes showed stark pictures that seemed to contradict the administration's optimistic war scenario.

Quoting body-count statistics that showed large numbers of communists dying in battle, General Westmoreland continually reported that a Vietcong surrender was imminent. Defense Secretary McNamara backed up the general, saying that he could see "the light at the end of the tunnel."

The repeated television images of Americans in body bags told a different story, though. While communists may have been dying, so too were Americans—over 16,000 between 1961 and 1967. Critics charged that a **credibility gap** was growing between what the Johnson administration reported and what was really happening.

One critic was Senator J. William Fulbright, chairman of the powerful Senate Foreign Relations Committee. Fulbright, a former Johnson ally, charged the president with a "lack of candor" in portraying the war effort. In early 1966, the senator conducted a series of televised committee hearings in which he asked members of the Johnson administration to defend their Vietnam policies. The Fulbright hearings delivered few major revelations, but they did contribute to the growing doubts about the war. One woman appeared to capture the mood of Middle America when she told an interviewer, "I want to get out, but I don't want to give in." **E**

By 1967, Americans were evenly split over supporting and opposing the war. However, a small force outside of mainstream America, mainly from the ranks of the nation's youth, already had begun actively protesting the war. Their voices would grow louder and capture the attention of the entire nation.

MAIN IDEA

Analyzing Effects
E What led to the growing concern in America about the Vietnam War?

First used in World War I, dog tags were stamped with personal identification information and worn by U.S. military personnel.

SECTION 2 ASSESSMENT

1. **TERMS & NAMES** For each term or name, write a sentence explaining its significance.
   - Robert McNamara
   - Dean Rusk
   - William Westmoreland
   - Army of the Republic of Vietnam (ARVN)
   - napalm
   - Agent Orange
   - search-and-destroy mission
   - credibility gap

MAIN IDEA

2. **TAKING NOTES**
   Re-create the chart below. Then, show key military tactics and weapons of the Vietcong and Americans.

	Vietcong	U.S.
Tactics		
Weapons		

   Which weapons and tactics do you think were most successful? Explain.

CRITICAL THINKING

3. **DRAWING CONCLUSIONS**
   Why did Americans fail to win the "hearts and minds" of the Vietnamese?

4. **CONTRASTING**
   In a paragraph, contrast the morale of the U.S. troops with that of the Vietcong. Use evidence from the text to support your response.

5. **FORMING GENERALIZATIONS**
   What were the effects of the nightly TV coverage of the Vietnam War? Support your answer with examples from the text. **Think About:**
   - television images of Americans in body bags
   - the Johnson administration's credibility gap

PI 2.3
PI 3.2

CC Unit 7.IV.A.5.a
CC Unit 7.IV.A.5.b
CC Unit 7.IV.A.6.d

A Nation Divided

MAIN IDEA	WHY IT MATTERS NOW	Terms & Names
An antiwar movement in the U.S. pitted supporters of the government's war policy against those who opposed it.	The painful process of healing a divided nation continues today.	• draft • New Left • Students for a Democratic Society (SDS)	• Free Speech Movement • dove • hawk

One American's Story

hmhsocialstudies.com
TAKING NOTES

Use the graphic organizer online to take notes on the antiwar movement.

In 1969, Stephan Gubar was told to report for possible military service in Vietnam. Gubar, 22, a participant in the civil rights movement, had filed as a conscientious objector (CO), or someone who opposed war on the basis of religious or moral beliefs. He was granted 1-A-O status, which meant that while he would not be forced to carry a weapon, he still qualified for noncombatant military duty. That year, Gubar was drafted—called for military service.

As did many other conscientious objectors, Gubar received special training as a medic. He described the memorable day his training ended.

A PERSONAL VOICE STEPHAN GUBAR

"The thing that stands out most was . . . being really scared, being in formation and listening to the names and assignments being called. The majority of COs I knew had orders cut for Vietnam. And even though I could hear that happening, even though I could hear that every time a CO's name came up, the orders were cut for Vietnam, I still thought there was a possibility I might not go. Then, when they called my name and said 'Vietnam,'. . . I went to a phone and I called my wife. It was a tremendous shock."

—quoted in *Days of Decision*

Stephan Gubar

While many young Americans proudly went off to war, some found ways to avoid the draft, and others simply refused to go. The growing protest movement sharply divided the country between supporters and opponents of the government's policy in Vietnam.

The Working Class Goes to War

The idea of fighting a war in a faraway place for what they believed was a questionable cause prompted a number of young Americans to resist going to Vietnam.

A "MANIPULATABLE" DRAFT Most soldiers who fought in Vietnam were called into combat under the country's Selective Service System, or **draft,** which had been established during World War I. Under this system, all males had to register with their local draft boards when they turned 18. All registrants were screened, and unless they were excluded—such as for medical reasons—in the event of war, men between the ages of 18 and 26 would be called into military service.

As Americans' doubts about the war grew, thousands of men attempted to find ways around the draft, which one man characterized as a "very manipulatable system." Some men sought out sympathetic doctors to grant medical exemptions, while others changed residences in order to stand before a more lenient draft board. Some Americans even joined the National Guard or Coast Guard, which often secured a deferment from service in Vietnam.

One of the most common ways to avoid the draft was to receive a college deferment, by which a young man enrolled in a university could put off his military service. Because university students during the 1960s tended to be white and financially well-off, many of the men who fought in Vietnam were lower-class whites or minorities who were less privileged economically. With almost 80 percent of American soldiers coming from lower economic levels, Vietnam was a working-class war.

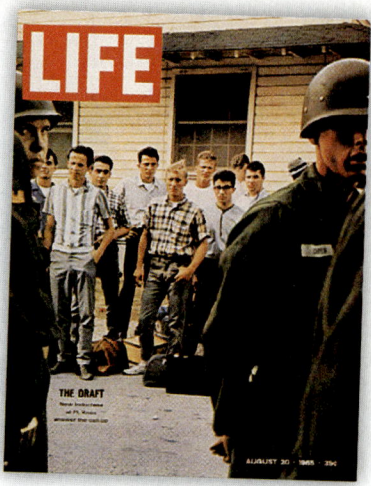

▲ A *Life* magazine cover shows new draft inductees arriving for training at Fort Knox, Kentucky.

AFRICAN AMERICANS IN VIETNAM African Americans served in disproportionate numbers as ground combat troops. During the first several years of the war, blacks accounted for more than 20 percent of American combat deaths despite representing only about 10 percent of the U.S. population. The Defense Department took steps to correct that imbalance by instituting a draft lottery system in 1969.

Martin Luther King, Jr., had refrained from speaking out against the war for fear that it would divert attention from the civil rights movement. But he could not maintain that stance for long. In 1967 he lashed out against what he called the "cruel irony" of American blacks dying for a country that still treated them as second-class citizens.

A PERSONAL VOICE DR. MARTIN LUTHER KING, JR.

"We were taking the young black men who had been crippled by our society and sending them eight thousand miles away to guarantee liberties in Southeast Asia which they had not found in Southwest Georgia and East Harlem. . . . We have been repeatedly faced with the cruel irony of watching Negro and white boys on TV screens as they kill and die together for a nation that has been unable to seat them together in the same schools."

—quoted in *America's Vietnam War: A Narrative History*

Racial tension ran high in many platoons, and in some cases, the hostility led to violence. The racism that gripped many military units was yet another factor that led to low troop morale in Vietnam. Ⓐ

Despite racial tensions, black and white soldiers fought side by side in Vietnam.
▼

U.S. Military Personnel in Vietnam*

536,000

Troops (in thousands)

600
500
400
300
200
100
0

1963 1964 1965 1966 1967 1968 1969 1970 1971 1972

Source: *Statistical Abstract of the United States, 1985; Encyclopedia Americana*   *Year-end figures

SKILLBUILDER Interpreting Graphs
What years signaled a rapid increase in the deployment of U.S. troops?

Two U.S. nurses rest at Cam Ranh Bay, the major entry point in South Vietnam for American supplies and troops.

WOMEN JOIN THE RANKS While the U.S. military in the 1960s did not allow females to serve in combat, 10,000 women served in Vietnam—most of them as military nurses. Thousands more volunteered their services in Vietnam to the American Red Cross and the United Services Organization (USO), which delivered hospitality and entertainment to the troops.

As the military marched off to Vietnam to fight against communist guerrillas, some of the men at home, as well as many women, waged a battle of their own. Tensions flared across the country as many of the nation's youths began to voice their opposition to the war.

The Roots of Opposition

Even before 1965, students were becoming more active socially and politically. Some participated in the civil rights struggle, while others pursued public service. As America became more involved in the war in Vietnam, college students across the country became a powerful and vocal group of protesters.

THE NEW LEFT The growing youth movement of the 1960s became known as the **New Left.** The movement was "new" in relation to the "old left" of the 1930s, which had generally tried to move the nation toward socialism, and, in some cases, communism. While the New Left movement did not preach socialism, its followers demanded sweeping changes in American society.

Voicing these demands was one of the better-known New Left organizations, **Students for a Democratic Society (SDS),** founded in 1960 by Tom Hayden and Al Haber. The group charged that corporations and large government institutions had taken over America. The SDS called for a restoration of "participatory democracy" and greater individual freedom.

In 1964, the **Free Speech Movement** (FSM) gained prominence at the University of California at Berkeley. The FSM grew out of a clash between students and administrators over free speech on campus. Led by Mario Savio, a philosophy student, the FSM focused its criticism on what it called the American "machine," the nation's faceless and powerful business and government institutions. **B**

CAMPUS ACTIVISM Across the country the ideas of the FSM and SDS quickly spread to college campuses. Students addressed mostly campus issues, such as dress codes, curfews, dormitory regulations, and mandatory Reserved Officer

MAIN IDEA

Making Inferences

B What concerns about American democratic society did the New Left voice?

Training Corps (ROTC) programs. At Fairleigh Dickinson University in New Jersey, students marched merely as "an expression of general student discontent."

With the onset of the Vietnam War, students across the country found a galvanizing issue and joined together in protest. By the mid-sixties, many youths believed the nation to be in need of fundamental change.

The Protest Movement Emerges

Throughout the spring of 1965, groups at a number of colleges began to host "teach-ins" to protest the war. At the University of Michigan, where only a year before President Johnson had announced his sweeping Great Society Program, teachers and students now assailed his war policy. "This is no longer a casual form of campus spring fever," journalist James Reston noted about the growing demonstrations. As the war continued, the protests grew and divided the country.

THE MOVEMENT GROWS In April of 1965, SDS helped organize a march on Washington, D.C., by some 20,000 protesters. By November of that year, a protest rally in Washington drew more than 30,000. Then, in February of 1966, the Johnson administration changed deferments for college students, requiring students to be in good academic standing in order to be granted a deferment. Campuses around the country erupted in protest. SDS called for civil disobedience at Selective Service Centers and openly counseled students to flee to Canada or Sweden. By the end of 1969, SDS had chapters on nearly 400 campuses.

Youths opposing the war did so for several reasons. The most common was the belief that the conflict in Vietnam was basically a civil war and that the U.S. military had no business there. Some said that the oppressive South Vietnamese regime was no better than the Communist regime it was fighting. Others argued that the United States could not police the entire globe and that war was draining American strength in other important parts of the world. Still others saw war simply as morally unjust. **C**

MAIN IDEA

Summarizing

C For what reasons did the protesters oppose the Vietnam War?

The antiwar movement grew beyond college campuses. Small numbers of returning veterans began to protest the war. Folk singers such as Pete Seeger, Joan Baez, Phil Ochs, and the trio Peter, Paul, and Mary used music as a popular protest vehicle. The number one song in September 1965 was "Eve of Destruction," in which singer Barry McGuire stressed the ironic fact that young men could be drafted at age 18 but had to be 21 to vote. Perhaps the most popular antiwar song of the time was "I-Feel-Like-I'm-Fixin'-to-Die Rag" by Country Joe and the Fish. Written by bandleader Joe McDonald, a Vietnam veteran, this song sarcastically encouraged young men, politicians, businesses, and even parents to give their whole-hearted support to the war.

FROM PROTEST TO RESISTANCE By 1967, the antiwar movement had intensified, with no sign of slowing down. "We were having no effect on U.S. policy," recalled one protest leader, "so we thought we had to up the ante." In the spring of 1967, nearly half a million protesters of all ages gathered in New York's Central Park. Shouting "Burn cards, not people!" and "Hell, no, we won't go!" hundreds tossed their draft cards into a bonfire. A woman from New Jersey told a reporter, "So many of us are frustrated. We want to criticize this war because we think it's wrong, but we want to do it in the framework of loyalty."

HISTORICAL SPOTLIGHT

"THE BALLAD OF THE GREEN BERETS"

Not every Vietnam-era pop song about war was an antiwar song. At the top of the charts for five weeks in 1966 was "The Ballad of the Green Berets" by Staff Sergeant Barry Sadler of the U.S. Army Special Forces, known as the Green Berets:

Fighting soldiers from the sky,
Fearless men who jump and die,
Men who mean just what they say,
The brave men of the Green Beret.

The recording sold over a million copies in its first two weeks of release and was *Billboard* magazine's song of the year.

As the fighting in Vietnam intensified, young men of draft age who opposed the war found themselves considering one of two options: register with the draft board and risk heading off to war, or find a way to avoid military service. Ways to avoid service included medical and educational deferments. But a great many men did not qualify for these. The choices that remained, such as fleeing the country, going to jail, or giving in and joining the ranks, came with a high price. Once a decision was made, there was no turning back.

1. Imagine you oppose the war and are called to serve in Vietnam. What decision would you make? Would you feel guilty if you avoided the draft? If you chose to serve, how would you view those who did not serve your country?

2. Do you think more young men would have been willing to serve had this been a different war? Explain.

Others were more radical in their view. David Harris, who would spend 20 months in jail for refusing to serve in Vietnam, explained his motives.

A PERSONAL VOICE DAVID HARRIS

"Theoretically, I can accept the notion that there are circumstances in which you have to kill people. I could not accept the notion that Vietnam was one of those circumstances. And to me that left the option of either sitting by and watching what was an enormous injustice . . . or [finding] some way to commit myself against it. And the position that I felt comfortable with in committing myself against it was total noncooperation—I was not going to be part of the machine."

—quoted in *The War Within*

Draft resistance continued from 1967 until President Nixon phased out the draft in the early 1970s. During these years, the U.S. government accused more than 200,000 men of draft offenses and imprisoned nearly 4,000 draft resisters. (Although some were imprisoned for four or five years, most won parole after 6 to 12 months.) Throughout these years, about 10,000 Americans fled, many to Canada. **D**

In October of 1967, a demonstration at Washington's Lincoln Memorial drew about 75,000 protesters. After listening to speeches, approximately 30,000 demonstrators locked arms for a march on the Pentagon in order "to disrupt the center of the American war machine," as one organizer explained. As hundreds of protesters broke past the military police and mounted the Pentagon steps, they were met by tear gas and clubs. About 1,500 demonstrators were injured and at least 700 arrested.

WAR DIVIDES THE NATION By 1967, Americans increasingly found themselves divided into two camps regarding the war. Those who strongly opposed the war and believed the United States should withdraw were known as **doves.** Feeling just as strongly that America should unleash much of its greater military force to win the war were the **hawks.**

Despite the visibility of the antiwar protesters, a majority of American citizens in 1967 still remained committed to the war. Others, while less certain about the proper U.S. role in Vietnam, were shocked to see protesters publicly criticize a war in which their fellow Americans were fighting and dying. A poll taken in December of 1967 showed that 70 percent of Americans believed the war protests were "acts of disloyalty." A firefighter who lost his son in Vietnam articulated the bitter feelings a number of Americans felt toward the antiwar movement.

A PERSONAL VOICE

"I'm bitter. . . . It's people like us who give up our sons for the country. . . . The college types, the professors, they go to Washington and tell the government what to do. . . . But their sons, they don't end up in the swamps over there, in Vietnam. No sir. They're deferred, because they're in school. Or they get sent to safe places. . . . What bothers me about the peace crowd is that you can tell from their attitude, the way they look and what they say, that they don't really love this country."

—a firefighter quoted in *Working-Class War*

This sign reflects the view of many Americans that the antiwar protests undermined the war effort in Vietnam. ▶

MAIN IDEA

Evaluating
D Do you think it was right for the government to imprison draft resisters? Explain.

Responding to antiwar posters, Americans who supported the government's Vietnam policy developed their own slogans: "Support our men in Vietnam" and "America—love it or leave it." **E**

JOHNSON REMAINS DETERMINED Throughout the turmoil and division that engulfed the country during the early years of the war, President Johnson remained firm. Attacked by doves for not withdrawing and by hawks for not increasing military power rapidly enough, Johnson was dismissive of both groups and their motives. He continued his policy of slow escalation.

★ **A PERSONAL VOICE** LYNDON B. JOHNSON

" **There has always been confusion, frustration, and difference of opinion in this country when there is a war going on. . . . You know what President Roosevelt went through, and President Wilson in World War I. He had some senators from certain areas . . . that gave him serious problems until victory was assured. . . . We are going to have these differences. No one likes war. All people love peace. But you can't have freedom without defending it.** "

—quoted in *No Hail, No Farewell*

However, by the end of 1967, Johnson's policy—and the continuing stalemate—had begun to create turmoil within his own administration. In November, Defense Secretary Robert McNamara, a key architect of U.S. escalation in Vietnam, quietly announced he was resigning to become head of the World Bank. "It didn't add up," McNamara recalled later. "What I was trying to find out was how . . . the war went on year after year when we stopped the infiltration [from North Vietnam] or shrunk it and when we had a very high body count and so on. It just didn't make sense."

As it happened, McNamara's resignation came on the threshold of the most tumultuous year of the sixties. In 1968 the war—and Johnson's presidency—would take a drastic turn for the worse.

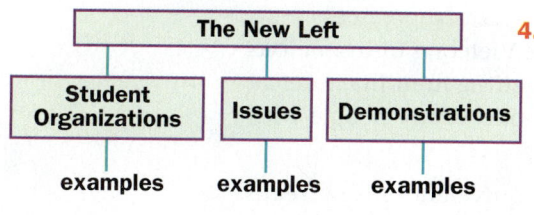

I WANT OUT

SECTION 3 ASSESSMENT

1. **TERMS & NAMES** For each of the following, write a sentence explaining its significance.

- draft
- New Left
- Students for a Democratic Society (SDS)
- Free Speech Movement
- dove
- hawk

MAIN IDEA

2. **TAKING NOTES**
Re-create the tree diagram below on your paper. Then fill it in with examples of student organizations, issues, and demonstrations of the New Left.

The New Left
- Student Organizations
- Issues
- Demonstrations

examples   examples   examples

CRITICAL THINKING

3. **DEVELOPING HISTORICAL PERSPECTIVE**
Imagine it is 1967. Do you think you would ally yourself with the hawks or the doves? Give reasons that support your position.

4. **EVALUATING**
Do you agree that antiwar protests were "acts of disloyalty"? Why or why not?

5. **ANALYZING VISUAL SOURCES**
This antiwar poster is a parody of the World War I Uncle Sam poster (shown on page 588), which states, "I want you for the U.S. Army." Why might the artist have chosen this American character to express the antiwar message?

SECTION
4

PI 2.3   CC Unit 7.IV.A.4.b   CC Unit 7.IV.A.5.b
PI 3.2   CC Unit 7.IV.A.6.a   CC Unit 7.IV.A.6.b
      CC Unit 7.IV.A.6.c   CC Unit 7.IV.A.6.d

1968:
A Tumultuous Year

MAIN IDEA	WHY IT MATTERS NOW	Terms & Names
An enemy attack in Vietnam, two assassinations, and a chaotic political convention made 1968 an explosive year.	Disturbing events in 1968 accentuated the nation's divisions, which are still healing in the 21st century.	• Tet offensive • Clark Clifford • Robert Kennedy • Eugene McCarthy • Hubert Humphrey • George Wallace

One American's Story

hmhsocialstudies.com
TAKING NOTES

Use the graphic organizer online to take notes on the major events of 1968.

On June 5, 1968, John Lewis, the first chairman of the Student Nonviolent Coordinating Committee, fell to the floor and wept. Robert F. Kennedy, a leading Democratic candidate for president, had just been fatally shot. Two months earlier, when Martin Luther King, Jr., had fallen victim to an assassin's bullet, Lewis had told himself he still had Kennedy. And now they both were gone. Lewis, who later became a congressman from Georgia, recalled the lasting impact of these assassinations.

A PERSONAL VOICE JOHN LEWIS

"There are people today who are afraid, in a sense, to hope or to have hope again, because of what happened in . . . 1968. Something was taken from us. The type of leadership that we had in a sense invested in, that we had helped to make and to nourish, was taken from us. . . . Something died in all of us with those assassinations."

—quoted in *From Camelot to Kent State*

John Lewis

These violent deaths were but two of the traumatic events that rocked the nation in 1968. From a shocking setback in Vietnam to a chaotic Democratic National Convention in Chicago, the events of 1968 made it the most tumultuous year of a turbulent decade.

The Tet Offensive Turns the War

The year 1968 began with a daring surprise attack by the Vietcong on numerous cities in South Vietnam. The simultaneous strikes, while ending in military defeat for the Communist guerrillas, stunned the American public. Many people with moderate views began to turn against the war.

A SURPRISE ATTACK January 30 was the Vietnamese equivalent of New Year's Eve, the beginning of the lunar new year festivities known in Vietnam as Tet.

Throughout that day in 1968, villagers—taking advantage of a week-long truce proclaimed for Tet—streamed into cities across South Vietnam to celebrate their new year. At the same time, many funerals were being held for war victims. Accompanying the funerals were the traditional firecrackers, flutes, and, of course, coffins.

The coffins, however, contained weapons, and many of the villagers were Vietcong agents. That night the Vietcong launched an overwhelming attack on over 100 towns and cities in South Vietnam, as well as 12 U.S. air bases. The fighting was especially fierce in Saigon and the former capital of Hue. The Vietcong even attacked the U.S. embassy in Saigon, killing five Americans. The **Tet offensive** continued for about a month before U.S. and South Vietnamese forces re-gained control of the cities.

General Westmoreland declared the attacks an overwhelming defeat for the Vietcong, whose "well-laid plans went afoul." From a purely military standpoint, Westmoreland was right. The Vietcong lost about 32,000 soldiers during the month-long battle, while the American and ARVN forces lost little more than 3,000.

Tet Offensive, Jan. 30–Feb. 24, 1968

hmhsocialstudies.com **INTERACTIVE MAP**

GEOGRAPHY SKILLBUILDER

Location What were the geographical destinations of the Tet offensive attacks? What does this suggest about the Vietcong forces?

TET CHANGES PUBLIC OPINION From a psychological—and political—standpoint, Westmoreland's claim could not have been more wrong. The Tet offensive greatly shook the American public, which had been told repeatedly and had come to believe that the enemy was close to defeat. Now the Pentagon's continued reports of favorable body counts—or massive Vietcong casualties—rang hollow. Daily, Americans saw the shocking images of attacks by an enemy that seemed to be everywhere.

In a matter of weeks, the Tet offensive changed millions of minds about the war. Despite the years of antiwar protest, a poll taken just before Tet showed that only 28 percent of Americans called themselves doves, while 56 percent claimed to be hawks. After Tet, both sides tallied 40 percent. The mainstream media, which had reported the war in a skeptical but generally balanced way, now openly criticized the war. One of the nation's most respected journalists, Walter Cronkite, told his viewers that it now seemed "more certain than ever that the bloody experience of Vietnam is to end in a stalemate." **A**

Minds were also changing at the White House. To fill the defense secretary position left vacant by Robert McNamara's resignation, Johnson picked **Clark Clifford,** a friend and supporter of the president's Vietnam policy. However, after settling in and studying the situation, Clifford concluded that the war was unwinnable. "We seem to have a sinkhole," Clifford said. "We put in more—they match it. I see more and more fighting with more and more casualties on the U.S. side and no end in sight to the action."

VIDEO
Command Decisions: Tet Refugees

hmhsocialstudies.com

MAIN IDEA

Analyzing Issues

A Why did American support for the war change after the Tet offensive?

Following the Tet offensive, Johnson's popularity plummeted. In public opinion polls taken at the end of February 1968, nearly 60 percent of Americans disapproved of his handling of the war. Nearly half of the country now felt it had been a mistake to send American troops to Vietnam.

"If I've lost Walter [Cronkite], then it's over. I've lost Mr. Average Citizen."
LYNDON B. JOHNSON

War weariness eventually set in, and 1968 was the watershed year. Johnson recognized the change, too. Upon learning of Cronkite's pessimistic analysis of the war, the president lamented, "If I've lost Walter, then it's over. I've lost Mr. Average Citizen."

Days of Loss and Rage

The growing division over Vietnam led to a shocking political development in the spring of 1968, a season in which Americans also endured two assassinations, a series of urban riots, and a surge in college campus protests.

▲ The Vietnam War and the divisiveness it caused took its toll on President Johnson.

JOHNSON WITHDRAWS Well before the Tet offensive, an antiwar coalition within the Democratic Party had sought a Democratic candidate to challenge Johnson in the 1968 primary elections. **Robert Kennedy,** John F. Kennedy's brother and a senator from New York, decided not to run, citing party loyalty. However, in November of 1967, Minnesota senator **Eugene McCarthy** answered the group's call, declaring that he would run against Johnson on a platform to end the war in Vietnam.

McCarthy's early campaign attracted little notice, but in the weeks following Tet it picked up steam. In the New Hampshire Democratic primary in March 1968, the little-known senator captured 42 percent of the vote. While Johnson won the primary with 48 percent of the vote, the slim margin of victory was viewed as a defeat for the president. Influenced by Johnson's perceived weakness at the polls, Robert Kennedy declared his candidacy for president. The Democratic Party had become a house divided.

In a televised address on March 31, 1968, Johnson announced a dramatic change in his Vietnam policy—the United States would seek negotiations to end the war. In the meantime, the policy of U.S. escalation would end, the bombing would eventually cease, and steps would be taken to ensure that the South Vietnamese played a larger role in the war.

The president paused and then ended his speech with a statement that shocked the nation. Declaring that he did not want the presidency to become "involved in the partisan divisions that are developing in this political year," Lyndon Johnson announced, "Accordingly, I shall not seek, and I will not accept, the nomination of my party for another term as your president." The president was stepping down from national politics, his grand plan for domestic reform done in by a costly and divisive war. "That . . . war," Johnson later admitted, "killed the lady I really loved—the Great Society." **B**

VIOLENCE AND PROTEST GRIP THE NATION The Democrats—as well as the nation—were in for more shock in 1968. On April 4, America was rocked by the assassination of Martin Luther King, Jr. Violence ripped through more than 100 U.S. cities as enraged followers of the slain civil rights leader burned buildings and destroyed neighborhoods.

Just two months later, a bullet cut down yet another popular national figure. Robert Kennedy had become a strong candidate in the Democratic primary, drawing support from minorities and urban Democratic voters. On June 4, Kennedy won the crucial California primary. Just after midnight of June 5, he gave a victory

MAIN IDEA

Analyzing Motives
B Why did President Johnson decide not to run again?

speech at a Los Angeles hotel. On his way out he passed through the hotel's kitchen, where a young Palestinian immigrant, Sirhan Sirhan, was hiding with a gun. Sirhan, who later said he was angered by Kennedy's support of Israel, fatally shot the senator.

Jack Newfield, a speechwriter for Kennedy, described the anguish he and many Americans felt over the loss of two of the nation's leaders.

★ A PERSONAL VOICE JACK NEWFIELD

"Things were not really getting better . . . we shall not overcome. . . . We had already glimpsed the most compassionate leaders our nation could produce, and they had all been assassinated. And from this time forward, things would get worse: Our best political leaders were part of memory now, not hope."

—quoted in *Nineteen Sixty-Eight*

▲ Hotel busboy Juan Romero was the first person to reach Robert Kennedy after he was shot June 5, 1968. Kennedy had just won the California Democratic primary.

Meanwhile, the nation's college campuses continued to protest. During the first six months of 1968, almost 40,000 students on more than 100 campuses took part in more than 200 major demonstrations. While many of the demonstrations continued to target U.S. involvement in the Vietnam War, students also clashed with university officials over campus and social issues. A massive student protest at Columbia University in New York City held the nation's attention for a week in April. There, students protesting the university's community policies took over several buildings. Police eventually restored order and arrested nearly 900 protesters.

Recalling the violence and turmoil that plagued the nation in 1968, the journalist and historian Garry Wills wrote, "There was a sense everywhere . . . that things were giving way. That [people] had not only lost control of [their] history, but might never regain it." **C**

MAIN IDEA

Analyzing Issues

C Why was 1968 characterized as a year of "lost control" in America?

A Turbulent Race for President

The chaos and violence of 1968 climaxed in August, when thousands of antiwar demonstrators converged on the city of Chicago to protest at the Democratic National Convention. The convention, which featured a bloody riot between protesters and police, fractured the Democratic Party and thus helped a nearly forgotten Republican win the White House.

TURMOIL IN CHICAGO With Lyndon Johnson stepping down and Robert Kennedy gone, the 1968 Democratic presidential primary race pitted Eugene McCarthy against **Hubert Humphrey,** Johnson's vice-president. McCarthy, while still popular with the nation's antiwar segment, had little chance of defeating Humphrey, a loyal party man who had President Johnson's support. During the last week of August, the Democrats met at their convention in Chicago, supposedly to choose a candidate. In reality, Humphrey's nomination had already been determined, a decision that upset many antiwar activists.

As the delegates arrived in Chicago, so, too, did nearly 10,000 protesters. Led by men such as SDS veteran Tom Hayden, many demonstrators sought to pressure the Democrats into adopting an antiwar platform. Others came to voice their

Vocabulary

platform: a formal declaration of the principles on which a political party makes its appeal to the public

Chicago police attempt to disperse antiwar demonstrators at the 1968 Democratic convention. Protesters shouted, "The whole world is watching!" ▶

displeasure with Humphrey's nomination. Still others, known as Yippies (members of the Youth International Party), had come hoping to provoke violence that might discredit the Democratic Party. Chicago's mayor, Richard J. Daley, was determined to keep the protesters under control. With memories of the nation-wide riots after King's death still fresh, Daley mobilized 12,000 Chicago police officers and over 5,000 National Guard. "As long as I am mayor," Daley vowed, "there will be law and order."

Order, however, soon collapsed. On August 28, as delegates cast votes for Humphrey, protesters were gathering in a downtown park to march on the convention. With television cameras focused on them, police moved into the crowd, sprayed the protesters with Mace, and beat them with nightsticks. Many protesters tried to flee, while others retaliated, pelting the riot-helmeted police with rocks and bottles. "The whole world is watching!" protesters shouted, as police attacked demonstrators and bystanders alike. **D**

The rioting soon spilled out of the park and into the downtown streets. One nearby hotel, observed a *New York Times* reporter, became a makeshift aid station.

★ A PERSONAL VOICE J. ANTHONY LUKAS

" Demonstrators, reporters, McCarthy workers, doctors, all began to stagger into the [hotel] lobby, blood streaming from face and head wounds. The lobby smelled from tear gas, and stink bombs dropped by the Yippies. A few people began to direct the wounded to a makeshift hospital on the fifteenth floor, the McCarthy staff headquarters. "

—quoted in *Decade of Shocks*

Disorder of a different kind reigned inside the convention hall, where delegates bitterly debated an antiwar plank in the party platform. When word of the riot filtered into the hall, delegates angrily shouted at Mayor Daley, who was present as a delegate himself. Daley returned their shouts with equal vigor. The whole world indeed was watching—on their televisions. The images of the Democrats—both inside and outside the convention hall—as a party of disorder became etched in the minds of millions of Americans.

MAIN IDEA

Summarizing
D What were the reasons protesters demonstrated in Chicago?

NIXON TRIUMPHS One beneficiary of this turmoil was Republican presidential candidate Richard M. Nixon, who by 1968 had achieved one of the greatest political comebacks in American politics. After his loss to Kennedy in the presidential race of 1960, Nixon tasted defeat again in 1962 when he ran for governor of California. His political career all but dead, Nixon joined a New York law firm, but he never strayed far from politics. In 1966, Nixon campaigned for Republican candidates in congressional elections, helping them to win back 47 House seats and 3 Senate seats from Democrats. In 1968, Nixon announced his candidacy for president and won the party's nomination.

During the presidential race, Nixon campaigned on a promise to restore law and order, which appealed to many middle-class Americans tired of years of riots and protests. He also promised, in vague but appealing terms, to end the war in Vietnam. Nixon's candidacy was helped by the entry of former Alabama governor **George Wallace** into the race as a third-party candidate. Wallace, a Democrat running on the American Independent Party ticket, was a longtime champion of school segregation and states' rights. Labeled the "white backlash" candidate, Wallace captured five Southern states. In addition, he attracted a surprisingly high number of Northern white working-class voters disgusted with inner-city riots and antiwar protests.

In the end, Nixon defeated Humphrey and inherited the quagmire in Vietnam. He eventually would end America's involvement in Vietnam, but not before his war policies created even more protest and uproar within the country.

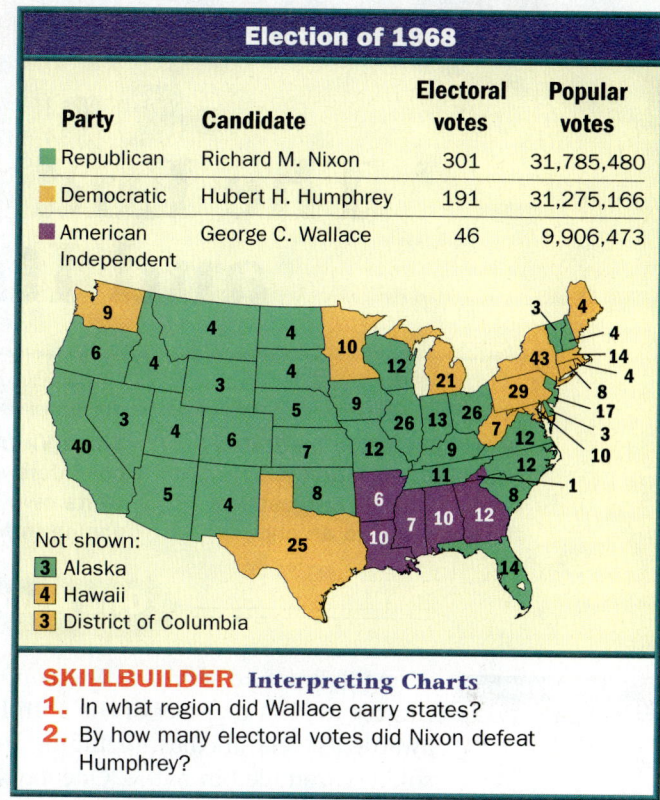

Election of 1968

Party	Candidate	Electoral votes	Popular votes
Republican	Richard M. Nixon	301	31,785,480
Democratic	Hubert H. Humphrey	191	31,275,166
American Independent	George C. Wallace	46	9,906,473

Not shown:
3 Alaska
4 Hawaii
3 District of Columbia

SKILLBUILDER Interpreting Charts
1. In what region did Wallace carry states?
2. By how many electoral votes did Nixon defeat Humphrey?

SECTION 4 ASSESSMENT

1. TERMS & NAMES For each term or name, write a sentence explaining its significance.
- Tet offensive
- Clark Clifford
- Robert Kennedy
- Eugene McCarthy
- Hubert Humphrey
- George Wallace

MAIN IDEA

2. TAKING NOTES
Create a time line of major events that occurred in 1968. Use the months already plotted on the time line below as a guide.

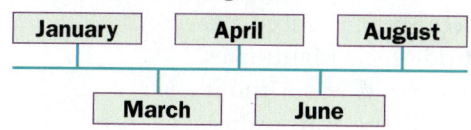

January   April   August

March   June

Which event do you think was most significant? Explain.

CRITICAL THINKING

3. ANALYZING EVENTS
Why do you think the Tet offensive turned so many Americans against the war? Support your answer with reasons.

4. MAKING INFERENCES
Refer to President Johnson's quote on page 956. What do you think he meant when he said "If I've lost Walter [Cronkite], then it's over. I've lost Mr. Average Citizen"? Explain.

5. MAKING INFERENCES
Do you think there might have been a relationship between the violence of the Vietnam War and the growing climate of violence in the United States during 1968? Why or why not?

PI 2.3   CC Unit 7.IV.A.5.b   CC Unit 7.IV.A.6.d
PI 3.4   CC Unit 7.V.A.2.a(1)   CC Unit 7.IV.A.2.a(2)

The End of the War and Its Legacy

MAIN IDEA	WHY IT MATTERS NOW	Terms & Names
President Nixon instituted his Vietnamization policy, and America's longest war finally came to an end.	Since Vietnam, the United States considers more carefully the risks to its own interests before intervening in foreign affairs.	• Richard Nixon • Kent State University • Henry Kissinger • Pentagon Papers • Vietnamization • War Powers Act • silent majority • My Lai

One American's Story

Alfred S. Bradford served in Vietnam from September 1968 to August 1969. A member of the 25th Infantry Division, he was awarded several medals, including the Purple Heart, given to soldiers wounded in battle. One day, Bradford's eight-year-old daughter, Elizabeth, inquired about his experience in Vietnam. "Daddy, why did you do it?" she asked. Bradford recalled what he had told himself.

A PERSONAL VOICE ALFRED S. BRADFORD

"Vietnam was my generation's adventure. I wanted to be part of that adventure and I believed that it was my duty as an American, both to serve my country and particularly not to stand by while someone else risked his life in my place. I do not regret my decision to go, but I learned in Vietnam not to confuse America with the politicians elected to administer America, even when they claim they are speaking for America, and I learned that I have a duty to myself and to my country to exercise my own judgment based upon my own conscience."
—quoted in *Some Even Volunteered*

▲ A U.S. soldier sits near Quang Tri, Vietnam, during a break in the fighting.

The legacy of the war was profound; it dramatically affected the way Americans viewed their government and the world. Richard Nixon had promised in 1968 to end the war, but it would take nearly five more years—and over 20,000 more American deaths—to end the nation's involvement in Vietnam.

President Nixon and Vietnamization

In the summer of 1969, newly elected president **Richard Nixon** announced the first U.S. troop withdrawals from Vietnam. "We have to get rid of the nightmares we inherited," Nixon later told reporters. "One of the nightmares is war without end." However, as Nixon pulled out the troops, he continued the war against North Vietnam, a policy that some critics would charge prolonged the "war without end" for several more bloody years.

THE PULLOUT BEGINS As President Nixon settled into the White House in January of 1969, negotiations to end the war in Vietnam were going nowhere. The United States and South Vietnam insisted that all North Vietnamese forces withdraw from the South and that the government of Nguyen Van Thieu, then South Vietnam's ruler, remain in power. The North Vietnamese and Vietcong demanded that U.S. troops withdraw from South Vietnam and that the Thieu government step aside for a coalition government that would include the Vietcong.

In the midst of the stalled negotiations, Nixon conferred with National Security Adviser **Henry Kissinger** on a plan to end America's involvement in Vietnam. Kissinger, a German emigrant who had earned three degrees from Harvard, was an expert on international relations. Their plan, known as **Vietnamization,** called for the gradual withdrawal of U.S. troops in order for the South Vietnamese to take on a more active combat role in the war. By August of 1969, the first 25,000 U.S. troops had returned home from Vietnam. Over the next three years, the number of American troops in Vietnam dropped from more than 500,000 to less than 25,000. **A**

MAIN IDEA

Synthesizing
A What was the impact of Vietnamization on the United States?

"PEACE WITH HONOR" Part of Nixon and Kissinger's Vietnamization policy was aimed at establishing what the president called a "peace with honor." Nixon intended to maintain U.S. dignity in the face of its withdrawal from war. A further goal was to preserve U.S. clout at the negotiation table, as Nixon still demanded that the South Vietnamese government remain intact. With this objective—and even as the pullout had begun—Nixon secretly ordered a massive bombing campaign against supply routes and bases in North Vietnam. The president also ordered that bombs be dropped on the neighboring countries of Laos and Cambodia, which held a number of Vietcong sanctuaries. Nixon told his aide H. R. Haldeman that he wanted the enemy to believe he was capable of anything.

★ **A PERSONAL VOICE** RICHARD M. NIXON

"I call it the madman theory, Bob. . . . I want the North Vietnamese to believe I've reached the point where I might do anything to stop the war. We'll just slip the word to them that 'for God's sake, you know Nixon is obsessed about Communists. We can't restrain him when he's angry—and he has his hand on the nuclear button' —and Ho Chi Minh himself will be in Paris in two days begging for peace."

—quoted in *The Price of Power*

Total U.S. Bomb Tonnage

World War II and Korean War — 2.6 million tons

Vietnam War — 8 million tons

Source: *Vietnam War Almanac*

U.S. Aerial Bomb Tonnage, 1965–1971

Tons (in thousands)

Source: *The Air War in Indochina*

SKILLBUILDER Interpreting Graphs

1. Examine the graph. How did the Vietnam conflict change over time?

2. Based on the chart, what type of war would you say was fought in Vietnam?

Trouble Continues on the Home Front

Seeking to win support for his war policies, Richard Nixon appealed to what he called the **silent majority**—moderate, mainstream Americans who quietly supported the U.S. efforts in Vietnam. While many average Americans did support the president, the events of the war continued to divide the country.

THE MY LAI MASSACRE In November of 1969, Americans learned of a shocking event. That month, *New York Times* correspondent Seymour Hersh reported that on March 16, 1968, a U.S. platoon under the command of Lieutenant William Calley, Jr., had massacred innocent civilians in the small village of **My Lai** (mē' lī') in northern South Vietnam. Calley was searching for Vietcong rebels. Finding no sign of the enemy, the troops rounded up the villagers and shot more than 200 innocent Vietnamese—mostly women, children, and elderly men. "We all huddled them up," recalled 22-year-old Private Paul Meadlo. "I poured about four clips into the group. . . . The mothers was hugging their children. . . . Well, we kept right on firing."

The troops insisted that they were not responsible for the shootings because they were only following Lieutenant Calley's orders. When asked what his directive had been, one soldier answered, "Kill anything that breathed." Twenty-five army officers were charged with some degree of responsibility, but only Calley was convicted and imprisoned.

THE INVASION OF CAMBODIA Despite the shock over My Lai, the country's mood by 1970 seemed to be less explosive. American troops were on their way home, and it appeared that the war was finally winding down.

On April 30, 1970, President Nixon announced that U.S. troops had invaded Cambodia to clear out North Vietnamese and Vietcong supply centers. The president defended his action: "If when the chips are down, the world's most powerful nation acts like a pitiful, helpless giant, the forces of totalitarianism and anarchy will threaten free nations . . . throughout the world."

Upon hearing of the invasion, college students across the country burst out in protest. In what became the first general student strike in the nation's history, more than 1.5 million students closed down some 1,200 campuses. The president of Columbia University called the month that followed the Cambodian invasion "the most disastrous month of May in the history of . . . higher education."

▲
President Nixon points to a map of Cambodia during a televised speech on April 30, 1970.

VIOLENCE ON CAMPUS Disaster struck hardest at **Kent State University** in Ohio, where a massive student protest led to the burning of the ROTC building. In response to the growing unrest, the local mayor called in the National Guard. On May 4, 1970, the Guards fired live ammunition into a crowd of campus protesters who were hurling rocks at them. The gunfire wounded nine people and killed four, including two who had not even participated in the rally.

Ten days later, similar violence rocked the mostly all-black college of Jackson State in Mississippi. National Guardsmen there confronted a group of antiwar demonstrators and fired on the crowd after several bottles were thrown. In the hail of bullets, 12 students were wounded and 2 were killed, both innocent bystanders.

In a sign that America still remained sharply divided about the war, the country hotly debated the campus shootings. Polls indicated that many Americans supported the National Guard; respondents claimed that the students "got what

Background
Calley was imprisoned only a short time before President Nixon granted him house arrest. Calley was paroled in 1974, having served three years.

History Through *Photojournalism*

KENT STATE

Photographer John Filo was a senior at Kent State University when anti-war demonstrations rocked the campus. When the National Guard began firing at student protesters, Filo began shooting pictures, narrowly escaping a bullet himself.

As he continued to document the horrific scene, a girl running to the side of a fallen student caught his eye. Just as she dropped to her knees and screamed, Filo snapped a photograph that would later win the Pulitzer Prize and become one of the most memorable images of the decade.

Mary Ann Vecchio grieves over the body of Jeffrey Glenn Miller, a student shot by National Guard troops at Kent State. In the original photograph, a fence post appeared behind the woman's head. It is believed that someone manipulated the image in the early 1970s to make it more visually appealing.

SKILLBUILDER **Analyzing Visual Sources**
1. Why do you think this photograph remains a symbol of the Vietnam War era today? Explain your answer with specific details of the photograph.
2. What do you think is the most striking element of this photograph? Why?

SEE SKILLBUILDER HANDBOOK, PAGE R23.

MAIN IDEA

Analyzing Issues

B How did the campus shootings demonstrate the continued divisions within the country?

they were asking for." The weeks following the campus turmoil brought new attention to a group known as "hardhats," construction workers and other blue-collar Americans who supported the U.S. government's war policies. In May of 1970, nearly 100,000 members of the Building and Construction Trades Council of New York held a rally outside city hall to support the government. **B**

THE PENTAGON PAPERS Nixon and Kissinger's Cambodia policy, however, cost Nixon significant political support. By first bombing and then invading Cambodia without even notifying Congress, the president stirred anger on Capitol Hill. On December 31, 1970, Congress repealed the Tonkin Gulf Resolution, which had given the president near independence in conducting policy in Vietnam.

Support for the war eroded even further when in June of 1971 former Defense Department worker Daniel Ellsberg leaked what became known as the **Pentagon Papers.** The 7,000-page document, written for Defense Secretary Robert McNamara in 1967–1968, revealed among other things that the government had drawn up plans for entering the war even as President Lyndon Johnson promised that he would not send American troops to Vietnam. Furthermore, the papers showed that there was never any plan to end the war as long as the North Vietnamese persisted.

Background
In *New York Times v. U.S.* (1971), the Supreme Court barred the government from stopping the publication of the Pentagon Papers.

For many Americans, the Pentagon Papers confirmed their belief that the government had not been honest about its war intentions. The document, while not particularly damaging to the Nixon administration, supported what opponents of the war had been saying.

America's Longest War Ends

In March of 1972, the North Vietnamese launched their largest attack on South Vietnam since the Tet offensive in 1968. President Nixon responded by ordering a massive bombing campaign against North Vietnamese cities. He also ordered that mines be laid in Haiphong harbor, the North's largest harbor, into which Soviet and Chinese ships brought supplies. The Communists "have never been bombed like they are going to be bombed this time," Nixon vowed. The bombings halted the North Vietnamese attack, but the grueling stalemate continued. It was after this that the Nixon administration took steps to finally end America's involvement in Vietnam.

"PEACE IS AT HAND" By the middle of 1972, the country's growing social division and the looming presidential election prompted the Nixon administration to change its negotiating policy. Polls showed that more than 60 percent of Americans in 1971 thought that the United States should withdraw all troops from Vietnam by the end of the year.

Henry Kissinger, the president's adviser for national security affairs, served as Nixon's top negotiator in Vietnam. Since 1969, Kissinger had been meeting privately with North Vietnam's chief negotiator, Le Duc Tho. Eventually, Kissinger dropped his insistence that North Vietnam withdraw all its troops from the South before the complete withdrawal of American troops. On October 26, 1972, days before the presidential election, Kissinger announced, "Peace is at hand."

THE FINAL PUSH President Nixon won reelection, but the promised peace proved to be elusive. The Thieu regime, alarmed at the prospect of North Vietnamese troops stationed in South Vietnam, rejected Kissinger's plan. Talks broke off on December 16. Two days later, the president unleashed a ferocious bombing campaign against Hanoi and Haiphong, the two largest cities in North Vietnam. In what became known as the "Christmas bombings," U.S. planes dropped 100,000 bombs over the course of eleven straight days, pausing only on Christmas Day.

At this point, calls to end the war resounded from the halls of Congress as well as from Beijing and Moscow. Everyone, it seemed, had finally grown weary of the war. The warring parties returned to the peace table, and on January 27, 1973, the United States signed an "Agreement on Ending the War and Restoring Peace in Vietnam." Under the agreement, North Vietnamese troops would remain in South Vietnam. However, Nixon promised to respond "with full force" to any violation of the peace agreement. On March 29, 1973, the last U.S. combat troops left for home. For America, the Vietnam War had ended. **C**

THE FALL OF SAIGON The war itself, however, raged on. Within months of the United States' departure, the cease-fire agreement between North and South Vietnam collapsed. In March of 1975, after several years of fighting, the North Vietnamese launched a full-scale invasion against the South. Thieu appealed to the United States for help. America provided economic aid but refused to send troops. Soon thereafter, President Gerald Ford—who assumed the presidency after the Watergate scandal forced President Nixon to resign—gave a speech in which he captured the nation's attitude toward the war:

MAIN IDEA

Chronological Order
C Summarize what led to the agreement to end the war in Vietnam.

KEY PLAYER

**HENRY KISSINGER
1923–**

Henry Kissinger, who helped negotiate America's withdrawal from Vietnam and who later would help forge historic new relations with China and the Soviet Union, held a deep interest in the concept of power. "You know," he once noted, "most of these world leaders, you wouldn't want to know socially. Mostly they are intellectual mediocrities. The thing that is interesting about them is . . . their power."

At first, Kissinger seemed an unlikely candidate to work for Richard Nixon. Kissinger declared, "That man Nixon is not fit to be president." However, the two became trusted colleagues.

MAIN IDEA

Evaluating Decisions

Ⓓ Why might the United States have refused to reenter the war?

"America can regain its sense of pride that existed before Vietnam. But it cannot be achieved by refighting a war that is finished as far as America is concerned." On April 30, 1975, North Vietnamese tanks rolled into Saigon and captured the city. Soon after, South Vietnam surrendered to North Vietnam. Ⓓ

The War Leaves a Painful Legacy

The Vietnam War exacted a terrible price from its participants. In all, 58,000 Americans were killed and some 303,000 were wounded. North and South Vietnamese deaths topped 2 million. In addition, the war left Southeast Asia highly unstable, which led to further war in Cambodia. In America, a divided nation attempted to come to grips with an unsuccessful war. In the end, the conflict in Vietnam left many Americans with a more cautious outlook on foreign affairs and a more cynical attitude toward their government.

AMERICAN VETERANS COPE BACK HOME While families welcomed home their sons and daughters, the nation as a whole extended a cold hand to its returning Vietnam veterans. There were no brass bands, no victory parades, no cheering crowds. Instead, many veterans faced indifference or even hostility from an America still torn and bitter about the war. Lily Jean Lee Adams, who served as an army nurse in Vietnam, recalled arriving in America in 1970 while still in uniform.

A PERSONAL VOICE LILY JEAN LEE ADAMS

" In the bus terminal, people were staring at me and giving me dirty looks. I expected the people to smile, like, 'Wow, she was in Vietnam, doing something for her country—wonderful.' I felt like I had walked into another country, not my country. So I went into the ladies' room and changed. "

—quoted in *A Piece of My Heart*

Many Vietnam veterans readjusted successfully to civilian life. However, about 15 percent of the 3.3 million soldiers who served developed post-traumatic stress disorder. Some had recurring nightmares about their war experiences, while many suffered from severe headaches and memory lapses. Other veterans became

◄ Lieutenant Colonel Robert Stirm, a returning POW, receives a warm welcome from his family in 1973. The longest-held Vietnam POW was Lieutenant Everett Alvarez, Jr., of California. He was imprisoned for more than eight years.

▲ Each year, over two million people visit the Vietnam Veterans Memorial. Many leave remembrances that are collected nightly by park rangers and stored in a museum. Inscribed on the memorial are over 58,000 names of Americans who died in the war or were then still listed as missing in action.

highly apathetic or began abusing drugs or alcohol. Several thousand even committed suicide.

In an effort to honor the men and women who served in Vietnam, the U.S. government unveiled the Vietnam Veterans Memorial in Washington, D.C., in 1982. Many Vietnam veterans, as well as their loved ones, have found visiting the memorial a deeply moving, even healing, experience.

FURTHER TURMOIL IN SOUTHEAST ASIA The end of the Vietnam War ushered in a new period of violence and chaos in Southeast Asia. In unifying Vietnam, the victorious Communists initially held out a conciliatory hand to the South Vietnamese. "You have nothing to fear," declared Colonel Bui Tin of the North Vietnamese Army.

However, the Communists soon imprisoned more than 400,000 South Vietnamese in harsh "reeducation," or labor, camps. As the Communists imposed their rule throughout the land, nearly 1.5 million people fled Vietnam. They included citizens who had supported the U.S. war effort, as well as business owners, whom the Communists expelled when they began nationalizing the country's business sector.

Also fleeing the country was a large group of poor Vietnamese, known as boat people because they left on anything from freighters to barges to rowboats. Their efforts to reach safety across the South China Sea often met with tragedy; nearly 50,000 perished on the high seas due to exposure, drowning, illness, or piracy.

The people of Cambodia also suffered greatly after the war. The U.S. invasion of Cambodia had unleashed a brutal civil war in which a communist group known as the Khmer Rouge, led by Pol Pot, seized power in 1975. In an effort to transform the country into a peasant society, the Khmer Rouge executed professionals and anyone with an education or foreign ties. During its reign of terror, the Khmer Rouge is believed to have killed at least 1 million Cambodians.

THE LEGACY OF VIETNAM Even after it ended, the Vietnam War remained a subject of great controversy for Americans. Many hawks continued to insist that the war could have been won if the United States had employed more military power. They also blamed the antiwar movement at home for destroying American morale. Doves countered that the North Vietnamese had displayed incredible resiliency and that an increase in U.S. military force would have resulted only in a continuing stalemate. In addition, doves argued that an unrestrained war against North Vietnam might have prompted a military reaction from China or the Soviet Union. **E**

The war resulted in several major U.S. policy changes. First, the government abolished the draft, which had stirred so much antiwar sentiment. The country also took steps to curb the president's war-making powers. In November 1973, Congress passed the **War Powers Act**, which stipulated that a president must inform Congress within 48 hours of sending forces into a hostile area without a declaration of war. In addition, the troops may remain there no longer than 90 days unless Congress approves the president's actions or declares war.

In a broader sense, the Vietnam War significantly altered America's views on foreign policy. In what has been labeled the Vietnam syndrome, Americans now pause and consider possible risks to their own interests before deciding whether to intervene in the affairs of other nations.

Finally, the war contributed to an overall cynicism among Americans about their government and political leaders that persists today. Americans grew suspicious of a government that could provide as much misleading information or conceal as many activities as the Johnson and Nixon administrations had done. Coupled with the Watergate scandal of the mid-1970s, the war diminished the optimism and faith in government that Americans felt during the Eisenhower and Kennedy years.

MAIN IDEA

Contrasting
E Contrast the two viewpoints regarding the legacy of the Vietnam War.

U.S. RECOGNITION OF VIETNAM

In July of 1995, more than 20 years after the Vietnam War ended, the United States extended full diplomatic relations to Vietnam. In announcing the resumption of ties with Vietnam, President Bill Clinton declared, "Let this moment . . . be a time to heal and a time to build." Demonstrating how the war still divides Americans, the president's decision drew both praise and criticism from members of Congress and veterans' groups.

In an ironic twist, Clinton nominated as ambassador to Vietnam a former prisoner of war from the Vietnam War, Douglas Peterson, a congress member from Florida. Peterson, a former air force pilot, was shot down over North Vietnam in 1966 and spent six and a half years in a Hanoi prison.

SECTION 5 **ASSESSMENT**

1. TERMS & NAMES For each term or name, write a sentence explaining its significance.
- Richard Nixon
- Henry Kissinger
- Vietnamization
- silent majority
- My Lai
- Kent State University
- Pentagon Papers
- War Powers Act

MAIN IDEA

2. TAKING NOTES
In a web like the one shown, list the effects of the Vietnam War on America.

Vietnam War's Effect on America

Choose one effect to further explain in a paragraph.

CRITICAL THINKING

3. ANALYZING EFFECTS
In your opinion, what was the main effect of the U.S. government's deception about its policies and military conduct in Vietnam? Support your answer with evidence from the text. **Think About:**

- the contents of the Pentagon Papers
- Nixon's secrecy in authorizing military maneuvers

4. MAKING INFERENCES
How would you account for the cold homecoming American soldiers received when they returned from Vietnam? Support your answer with reasons.

5. SYNTHESIZING
In the end, do you think the United States' withdrawal from Vietnam was a victory for the United States or a defeat? Explain your answer.

Literature of the Vietnam War

Throughout history, soldiers as well as citizens have written about the traumatic and moving experiences of war. The Vietnam War, which left a deep impression on America's soldiers and citizens alike, has produced its share of literature. From the surreal fantasy of *Going After Cacciato* to the grim realism of *A Rumor of War,* much of this literature reflects the nation's lingering disillusionment with its involvement in the Vietnam War.

GOING AFTER CACCIATO

In *Going After Cacciato*, Vietnam veteran Tim O'Brien tells the story of Paul Berlin, a newcomer to Vietnam who fantasizes that his squad goes all the way to Paris, France, in pursuit of an AWOL soldier.

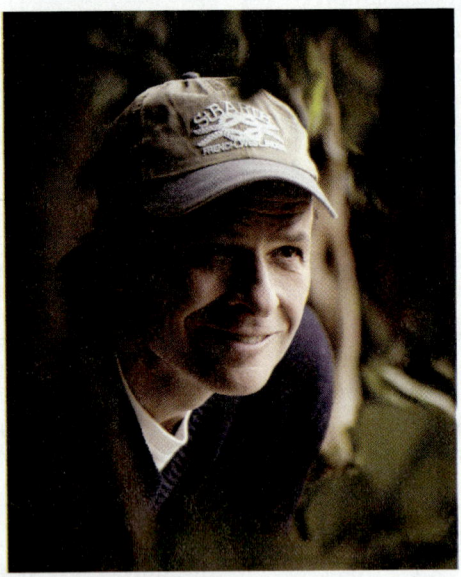

▲ Tim O'Brien in 2002

"How many days you been at the war?" asked Alpha's [Alpha Company's] mail clerk, and Paul Berlin answered that he'd been at the war seven days now.

The clerk laughed. "Wrong," he said. "Tomorrow, man, that's your first day at the war."

And in the morning PFC [Private First Class] Paul Berlin boarded a resupply chopper that took him fast over charred pocked mangled country, hopeless country, green skies and speed and tangled grasslands and paddies and places he might die, a million possibilities. He couldn't watch. He watched his hands. He made fists of them, opening and closing the fists. His hands, he thought, not quite believing. *His* hands.

Very quickly, the helicopter banked and turned and went down.

"How long you been at the war?" asked the first man he saw, a wiry soldier with ringworm in his hair.

PFC Paul Berlin smiled. "This is it," he said. "My first day."

—Tim O'Brien, *Going After Cacciato* (1978)

A RUMOR OF WAR

In *A Rumor of War*, considered to be among the best nonfiction accounts of the war, former marine Philip Caputo reflects on his years as a soldier in Vietnam.

> At the age of twenty-four, I was more prepared for death than I was for life. . . . I knew how to face death and how to cause it, with everything on the evolutionary scale of weapons from the knife to the 3.5-inch rocket launcher. The simplest repairs on an automobile engine were beyond me, but I was able to field-strip and assemble an M-14 rifle blindfolded. I could call in artillery, set up an ambush, rig a booby trap, lead a night raid.
>
> Simply by speaking a few words into a two-way radio, I had performed magical feats of destruction. Summoned by my voice, jet fighters appeared in the sky to loose their lethal droppings on villages and men. High-explosive bombs blasted houses to fragments, napalm sucked air from lungs and turned human flesh to ashes. All this just by saying a few words into a radio transmitter. Like magic.

—Philip Caputo,
A Rumor of War (1977)

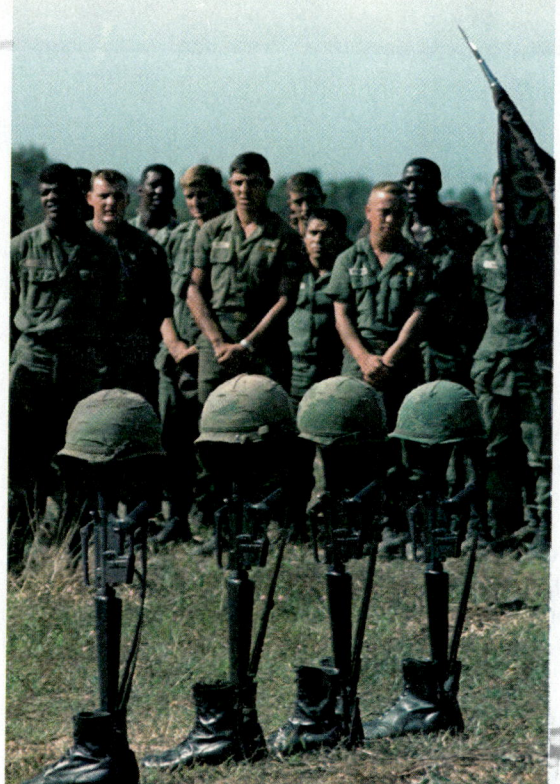

U.S. 101st Airborne Brigade memorial service—
Lai Khe, Vietnam, 1965

FALLEN ANGELS

Richie Perry, a 17-year-old Harlem youth, describes his harrowing tour of duty in Vietnam in Walter Dean Myers's novel *Fallen Angels*.

> The war was about us killing people and about people killing us, and I couldn't see much more to it. Maybe there were times when it was right. I had thought that this war was right, but it was only right from a distance. Maybe when we all got back to the World and everybody thought we were heroes for winning it, then it would seem right from there. . . . But when the killing started, there was no right or wrong except in the way you did your job, except in the way that you were part of the killing.
>
> What you thought about, what filled you up more than anything, was the being scared and hearing your heart thumping in your temples and all the noises, the terrible noises, the screeches and the booms and the guys crying for their mothers or for their wives.

—Walter Dean Myers,
Fallen Angels (1988)

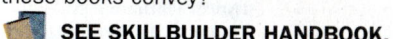

"It is a tale that is as thought-provoking as it is entertaining . . ."
—*The New York Times*

FALLEN ANGELS

Walter Dean Myers

THINKING CRITICALLY

1. **Comparing** What similar views about war do you think these books convey?

   SEE SKILLBUILDER HANDBOOK, PAGE R8.

2. hmhsocialstudies.com INTERNET ACTIVITY 21ST CENTURY

   Visit the links for American Literature to research personal accounts of the Vietnam War, such as interviews, letters, and essays. Copy several excerpts you find particularly interesting or moving and assemble them in a book. Write an introduction to your collection explaining why you chose them. Share your book with the class.

VISUAL SUMMARY

THE VIETNAM WAR YEARS

1964
Congress passes the Tonkin Gulf Resolution, giving the president broad military powers in Vietnam.

1964

1965

1965
First major U.S. combat troops arrive in Vietnam to fight the Vietcong and North Vietnamese Army.

1966

1967
Antiwar protests in the United States intensify.

1967

1968

1968
Vietcong launch massive Tet offensive on numerous South Vietnamese cities.

1969
Paris peace talks begin in earnest; President Nixon announces Vietnamization of war—gradual withdrawal of U.S. troops.

1969

1970

1970
President Nixon orders invasion of Cambodia to destroy enemy supply bases; American college campuses erupt in protest.

1971

1972
Nixon unleashes "Christmas bombings" on North Vietnamese cities after peace talks break off.

1972

I WANT OUT

1973

1973
United States and North Vietnam sign a truce; the U.S. withdraws the last of its troops from Vietnam.

1974

1975

TERMS AND NAMES

For each term or name below, write a sentence explaining its connection to the Vietnam War years.

1. Ho Chi Minh
2. Ngo Dinh Diem
3. Vietcong
4. William Westmoreland
5. napalm
6. Tet offensive
7. Robert Kennedy
8. Henry Kissinger
9. Vietnamization
10. Pentagon Papers

MAIN IDEAS

Use your notes and the information in the chapter to answer the following questions.

Moving Toward Conflict (pages 936–941)

1. How did the Tonkin Gulf Resolution lead to greater U.S. involvement in Vietnam?
2. What was President Eisenhower's explanation of the domino theory?

U.S. Involvement and Escalation (pages 942–947)

3. Why did so much of the American public and many in the Johnson administration support U.S. escalation in Vietnam?
4. Why did the war begin to lose support at home? What contributed to the sinking morale of the U.S. troops?

A Nation Divided (pages 948–953)

5. What race-related problems existed for African-American soldiers who served in the Vietnam War?
6. Summarize the ways in which the United States was sharply divided between hawks and doves.

1968: A Tumultuous Year (pages 954–959)

7. What circumstances set the stage for President Johnson's public announcement that he would not seek another term as president?
8. What acts of violence occurred in the United States during 1968 that dramatically altered the mood of the country?

The End of the War and Its Legacy (pages 960–967)

9. Briefly describe the military conflict in Vietnam soon after the last U.S. combat troops departed in 1973.
10. List the immediate effects and the more lasting legacies of America's involvement in the Vietnam War.

CRITICAL THINKING

1. **USING YOUR NOTES** Create a cause-and-effect diagram like the one below for each of these congressional measures: **a.** Tonkin Gulf Resolution (1964), **b.** repeal of the Tonkin Gulf Resolution (1970), **c.** War Powers Act (1973).

cause → Congressional Measure → effect

2. **DEVELOPING HISTORICAL PERSPECTIVE** Why do you think so many young Americans became so vocal in their condemnation of the Vietnam War?

Use the cartoon and your knowledge of U.S. history to answer question 1.

a 1972 Herblock Cartoon, copyright by The Herb Block Foundation

20,000 AMERICAN DEAD SINCE 1968

SECRET ELECTION-YEAR "PLANS TO END THE WAR"

©1972 HERBLOCK

1 In which of the following ways did the Vietnam War affect Americans' attitudes towards their government?

(1) Americans tried to change their government from representative democracy to Communism.

(2) Americans lost confidence that those in government would tell the truth.

(3) Americans took new pride in their country's reputation abroad.

(4) Americans worried that the United States would start another world war.

Use the quotation and your knowledge of U.S. history to answer question 2.

" Perhaps the place to start looking for a credibility gap is not in the offices of the government in Washington, but in the studios of the networks in New York. "

—Spiro T. Agnew

2 During the Vietnam War, the term "credibility gap" referred to the American people's lack of trust in —

(1) Presidents Johnson and Nixon.

(2) television news reporters.

(3) antiwar protesters.

(4) Ho Chi Minh.

3 What happened to Vietnam after the U.S. pullout in 1973?

(1) The North and South remained divided and at peace.

(2) The North and South remained enemies, separated by a United Nations-controlled demilitarized zone.

(3) The North became a Chinese puppet state; the South experienced continual violent rebellions.

(4) The North defeated the South and incorporated it under a communist government.

 hmhsocialstudies.com **TEST PRACTICE**

For additional test practice, go online for:

• Diagnostic tests   • Tutorials

INTERACT WITH HISTORY

Recall the issues that you explored at the beginning of the chapter. What lessons do you think can be learned from the ways in which Americans reacted to the draft? Write a paragraph expressing and giving reasons for your judgments. **Think About:**

• how the draft affected Americans' views on the Vietnam War

• how the draft affected Americans' participation in the Vietnam War

• how draft protests affected other Americans.

FOCUS ON WRITING

Imagine you are a television news journalist. Write a script for a brief news report on the events of the Tet Offensive or the Democratic National Convention.

COLLABORATIVE LEARNING

21ST CENTURY

Organize two teams for debate. One team should argue for the side of the hawks, and the other team should argue on behalf of the doves. Research the arguments put forth by both sides and debate the issue before the class.

CHAPTER 31

AN ERA OF SOCIAL CHANGE

Essential Question

Why did social protests and calls for change sweep across the United States in the 1960s?

New York Standards

KEY IDEA 2 Important ideas, social and cultural values, beliefs, and traditions from New York State and United States history illustrate the connections and interactions of people and events across time and from a variety of perspectives.

KEY IDEA 3 Study about the major social, political, economic, cultural, and religious developments in New York State and United States history involves learning about the important roles and contributions of individuals and groups.

SECTION 1: Latinos and Native Americans Seek Equality

SECTION 2: Women Fight for Equality

SECTION 3: Culture and Counterculture

Hippies gather in El Rito, New Mexico, at a Fourth of July parade in 1969.

1962 César Chávez and Dolores Huerta found the National Farm Workers Association.

1964 Lyndon B. Johnson is elected president.

1966 National Organization for Women (NOW) is formed.

USA

WORLD

1960   **1962**   **1964**   **1966**

1962 Chinese forces invade India.

1963 Civil war breaks out between Greeks and Turks on Cyprus.

1967 Six-Day War between Israel and Arab nations.

INTERACT
WITH HISTORY

In the late 1960s, a new breed of youth known as the counterculture rejects the fashions, traditions, and morals of American society. Minority groups assert their equal rights, demanding changes to long-standing practices and prejudices. Women protest forms of oppression and male privileges that have "always," it seems, been taken for granted. Many Americans begin to feel as if the whole nation has been turned on its side.

Explore the Issues

- Does every individual have a responsibility to follow the unwritten rules of society?

- What are the positive and negative aspects of change?

1968 Richard M. Nixon is elected president.

1970 Political party La Raza Unida is formed.

1970 Grape boycott forces growers to sign contracts with United Farm Workers.

BOYCOTT NON-UFW GRAPES

1972 Richard M. Nixon is reelected.

1973 Native Americans stage protest at Wounded Knee, South Dakota.

1968

1970

1972

1974

1969 President Charles de Gaulle of France resigns.

1970 Anwar el-Sadat becomes president of Egypt.

1972 Earthquake kills 10,000 in Nicaragua.

Latinos and Native Americans Seek Equality

MAIN IDEA	WHY IT MATTERS NOW	Terms & Names
Latinos and Native Americans confronted injustices in the 1960s.	Campaigns for civil rights and economic justice won better representation and opportunity for Latinos and Native Americans.	• César Chávez • United Farm Workers Organizing Committee • La Raza Unida • American Indian Movement (AIM)

One American's Story

Jessie Lopez de la Cruz's life changed one night in 1962, when **César Chávez** came to her home. Chávez, a Mexican-American farm worker, was trying to organize a union for California's mostly Spanish-speaking farm workers. Chávez said, "The women have to be involved. They're the ones working out in the fields with their husbands." Soon Jessie was in the fields, talking to farm workers about the union.

A PERSONAL VOICE JESSIE LOPEZ DE LA CRUZ

"Wherever I went to speak . . . I told them about . . . how we had no benefits, no minimum wage, nothing out in the fields—no restrooms, nothing. . . . I said, 'Well! Do you think we should be putting up with this in this modern age? . . . We can stand up! We can talk back! . . . This country is very rich, and we want a share of the money those growers make [off] our sweat and our work by exploiting us and our children!'"

—quoted in *Moving the Mountain: Women Working for Social Change*

The efforts of Jessie Lopez de la Cruz were just part of a larger rights movement during the turbulent and revolutionary 1960s. As African Americans were fighting for civil rights, Latinos and Native Americans rose up to assert their own rights and improve their lives.

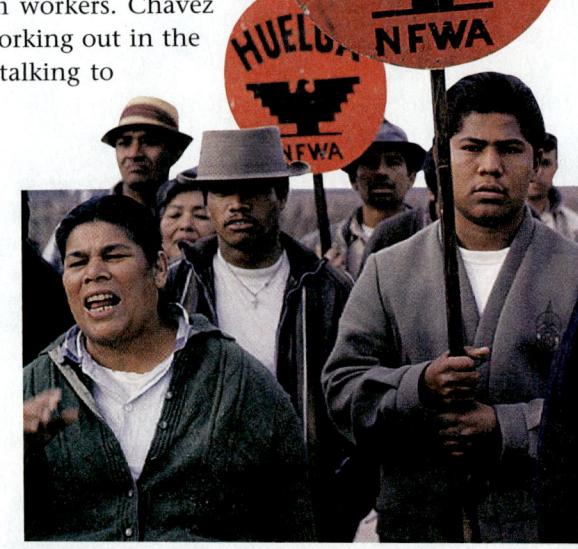

▲ Carrying signs that say "Strike" (*huelga*), Mexican-American farm workers protest poor working conditions.

The Latino Presence Grows

Latinos, or Americans of Latin American descent, are a large and diverse group. During the 1960s, the Latino population in the United States grew from 3 million to more than 9 million. Today the Latino population includes people from several different areas, primarily Mexico, Puerto Rico, Cuba, the Dominican Republic, Central America, and South America. Each of these groups has its own history, its

In the 1920s, thousands of Mexican people came to the U.S. and settled in *barrios*. Shown here, Hispanic men gather in a park in California.

own pattern of settlement in the United States, and its own set of economic, social, cultural, and political concerns.

LATINOS OF VARIED ORIGINS Mexican Americans, the largest Latino group, have lived mostly in the Southwest and California. This group includes descendants of the nearly 100,000 Mexicans who had lived in territories ceded by Mexico to the United States in 1848. Another million or so Mexicans came to the United States in the 1910s, following Mexico's revolution. Still others came as *braceros*, or temporary laborers, during the 1940s and 1950s. In the 1960s close to half a million Mexicans immigrated, most in search of better paying jobs.

Puerto Ricans began immigrating to the United States after the U.S. occupation of Puerto Rico in 1898. As of 1960, almost 900,000 Puerto Ricans were living in the continental United States, including almost half a million on New York City's West Side.

Large Cuban communities also formed in New York City and in Miami and New Jersey. This is because hundreds of thousands of Cubans, many of whom were academics and professionals, fled to the United States in 1959 to escape Fidel Castro's Communist rule. In addition, tens of thousands of Salvadorans, Guatemalans, Nicaraguans, and Colombians immigrated to the United States after the 1960s to escape civil war and chronic poverty.

Wherever they had settled, during the 1960s many Latinos encountered ethnic prejudice and discrimination in jobs and housing. Most lived in segregated *barrios*, or Spanish-speaking neighborhoods. The Latino jobless rate was nearly 50 percent higher than that of whites, as was the percentage of Latino families living in poverty. **A**

Latinos Fight for Change

As the presence of Latinos in the United States grew, so too did their demand for greater representation and better treatment. During the 1960s, Latinos demanded not only equal opportunity, but also a respect for their culture and heritage.

MAIN IDEA

Identifying Problems

A What problems did different groups of Latino immigrants share?

HISTORICAL SPOTLIGHT

DESPERATE JOURNEYS

In the 1960s and 1970s, thousands of poor Mexicans illegally crossed the 2,000-mile border between the United States and Mexico each year. The journey these illegal aliens undertook was often made more difficult by "coyotes," guides who charged large amounts of money to help them cross the border, but who often didn't deliver on their promises.

Illegal immigrants' problems didn't end when they entered the United States, where they were denied many social services, including unemployment insurance and food stamps. In addition, the Immigration and Naturalization Service urged businesses to refrain from hiring them. As a result, some owners stopped employing people with Latino names, including legal immigrants.

THE FARM WORKER MOVEMENT As Jessie Lopez de la Cruz explained, thousands working on California's fruit and vegetable farms did backbreaking work for little pay and few benefits. César Chávez believed that farm workers had to unionize, that their strength would come from bargaining as a group. In 1962, Chávez and Dolores Huerta established the National Farm Workers Association. Four years later, this group merged with a Filipino agricultural union (also founded by Huerta) to form the **United Farm Workers Organizing Committee** (UFWOC).

" To us, the boycott of grapes was the most near-perfect of nonviolent struggles."
CÉSAR CHÁVEZ

Chávez and his fellow organizers insisted that California's large fruit and vegetable companies accept their union as the bargaining agent for the farm workers. In 1965, when California's grape growers refused to recognize the union, Chávez launched a nationwide boycott of the companies' grapes. Chávez, like Martin Luther King, Jr., believed in using nonviolence to reach his goal. The union sent farm workers across the country to convince supermarkets and shoppers not to buy California grapes. Chávez then went on a three-week fast in which he lost 35 pounds. He ended his fast by attending Mass with Senator Robert F. Kennedy. The efforts of the farm workers eventually paid off. In 1970, Huerta negotiated a contract between the grape growers and the UFWOC. Union workers would finally be guaranteed higher wages and other benefits long denied them. **B**

CULTURAL PRIDE The activities of the California farm workers helped to inspire other Latino "brown power" movements across the country. In New York, members of the Puerto Rican population began to demand that schools offer Spanish-speaking children classes taught in their own language as well as programs about their culture. In 1968, Congress enacted the Bilingual Education Act, which provided funds for schools to develop bilingual and cultural heritage programs for non-English-speaking children.

Young Mexican Americans started to call themselves Chicanos or Chicanas—a shortened version of "Mexicanos" that expressed pride in their ethnic heritage. A Chicano community action group called the Brown Berets formed under the leadership of David Sanchez. In 1968, the Brown Berets organized walkouts in East Los Angeles high schools. About 15,000 Chicano students walked out of class demanding smaller classes, more Chicano teachers and administrators, and programs designed to reduce the high Latino dropout rate. Militant Mexican-American students also won the establishment of Chicano studies programs at colleges and universities.

POLITICAL POWER Latinos also began organizing politically during the 1960s. Some worked within the two-party system. For example, the Mexican American Political Association (MAPA) helped elect Los Angeles politician Edward Roybal to the House of Representatives. During the 1960s, eight Hispanic Americans served in the House, and one Hispanic senator was elected—Joseph Montoya of New Mexico.

Others, like Texan José Angel Gutiérrez, sought to create an independent Latino political movement. In 1970, he established **La Raza Unida** (The People United). In the 1970s, La Raza Unida ran Latino candidates in five states and won races for mayor, as well as other local positions on school boards and city councils.

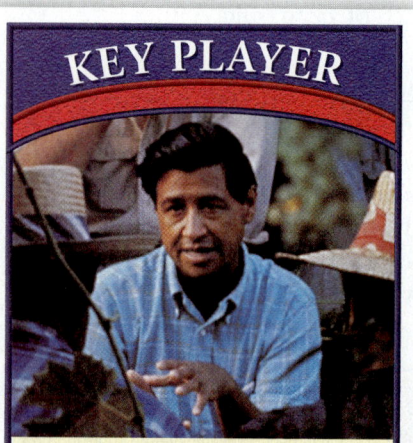

KEY PLAYER

CÉSAR CHÁVEZ
1927–1993

César Chávez spoke from experience when he said, "Many things in farm labor are terrible."

As a teenager, Chávez moved with his family from farm to farm, picking such crops as grapes, apricots, and olives. "The worst crop was the olives," Chávez recalled. "The olives are so small you can never fill the bucket."

The seeds of protest grew early in Chávez. As a teenager, he once went to see a movie, only to find that the theater was segregated—whites on one side of the aisle and Mexicans on the other side. "I really hadn't thought much about what I was going to do, but I had to do something," Chávez recalled. The future union leader sat down in the whites-only section and stayed there until the police arrived and arrested him.

MAIN IDEA

Analyzing Effects
B What impact did the grape boycott have?

Background
Prior to 1960, 32 Hispanics had been elected to Congress, beginning with Joseph Hernandez in 1822.

Still other Latinos took on a more confrontational tone. In 1963, one-time evangelical preacher Reies Tijerina founded the Alianza Federal de Mercedes (Federal Alliance of Land Grants) to help reclaim U.S. land taken from Mexican landholders in the 19th century. He and his followers raided the Rio Arriba County Courthouse in Tierra Amarilla, New Mexico, in order to force authorities to recognize the plight of New Mexican small farmers. They were later arrested.

Native Americans Struggle for Equality

As are Latinos, Native Americans are sometimes viewed as a single homogeneous group, despite the hundreds of distinct Native American tribes and nations in the United States. One thing that these diverse tribes and nations have shared is a mostly bleak existence in the United States and a lack of autonomy, or ability to control and govern their own lives. Through the years, many Native Americans have clung to their heritage, refusing to assimilate, or blend, into mainstream society. Native American nationalist Vine Deloria, Jr., expressed the view that mainstream society was nothing more than "ice cream bars and heart trouble and . . . getting up at six o'clock in the morning to mow your lawn in the suburbs."

NATIVE AMERICANS SEEK GREATER AUTONOMY

Despite their cultural diversity, Native Americans as a group have been the poorest of Americans and have suffered from the highest unemployment rate. They have also been more likely than any other group to suffer from tuberculosis and alcoholism. Although the Native American population rose during the 1960s, the death rate among Native American infants was nearly twice the national average, while life expectancy was several years less than for other Americans.

In 1954, the Eisenhower administration enacted a "termination" policy to deal with these problems, but it did not respect Native American culture. Native Americans were relocated from isolated reservations into mainstream urban American life. The plan failed miserably. Most who moved to the cities remained desperately poor.

In 1961, representatives from 61 Native American groups met in Chicago and drafted the Declaration of Indian Purpose, which stressed the determination of Native Americans to "choose our own way of life." The declaration called for an end to the termination program in favor of new policies designed to create economic opportunities for Native Americans on their reservations. In 1968, President Lyndon Johnson established the National Council on Indian Opportunity to "ensure that programs reflect the needs and desires of the Indian people." **C**

VOICES OF PROTEST

Many young Native Americans were dissatisfied with the slow pace of reform. Their discontent fueled the growth of the **American Indian Movement (AIM),** an often militant Native American rights organization. While AIM began in 1968 largely as a self-defense group against police brutality, it soon branched out to include protecting the rights of large Native American populations in northern and western states.

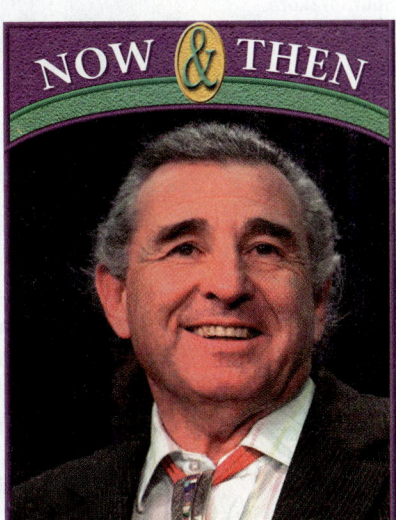

NOW & THEN

BEN NIGHTHORSE CAMPBELL

Whereas many Native Americans rejected assimilation, Ben Nighthorse Campbell chose to work within the system to improve the lives of Native Americans. Campbell's father was a North Cheyenne, and his great-grandfather, Black Horse, fought in the 1876 Battle of the Little Bighorn—in which the Cheyenne and the Sioux defeated Lieutenant Colonel George Custer.

In 1992, Campbell was elected to the U.S. Senate from Colorado, marking the first time since 1929 that a Native American had been elected to the Senate. Campbell stated that while he served the entire nation, the needs of Native Americans would always remain a priority. He retired from the Senate in 2004.

AIM leader Dennis Banks speaks at the foot of Mount Rushmore, in South Dakota, during a 1970s rally.

For some, this new activism meant demanding that Native American lands, burial grounds, and fishing and timber rights be restored. Others wanted a new respect for their culture. Mary Crow Dog, a Lakota Sioux, described AIM's impact.

★ A PERSONAL VOICE MARY CROW DOG

"My first encounter with AIM was at a pow-wow held in 1971. . . . One man, a Chippewa, stood up and made a speech. I had never heard anybody talk like that. He spoke about genocide and sovereignty, about tribal leaders selling out. . . . He had himself wrapped up in an upside-down American flag, telling us that every star in this flag represented a state stolen from the Indians. . . . Some people wept. An old man turned to me and said, 'These are the words I always wanted to speak, but had kept shut up within me.'"

—*Lakota Women*

CONFRONTING THE GOVERNMENT In its early years, AIM, as well as other groups, actively—and sometimes violently—confronted the government. In 1972, AIM leader Russell Means organized the "Trail of Broken Treaties" march in Washington, D.C., to protest the U.S. government's treaty violations throughout history. Native Americans from across the country joined the march. They sought the restoration of 110 million acres of land. They also pushed for the abolition of the Bureau of Indian Affairs (BIA), which many believed was corrupt. The marchers temporarily occupied the BIA building, destroyed records, and caused $2 million in property damage.

> *"If the government doesn't start living up to its obligations, armed resistance . . . will have to become a regular thing."*
> **CHIPPEWA PROTESTER**

A year later, AIM led nearly 200 Sioux to the tiny village of Wounded Knee, South Dakota, where the U.S. cavalry had massacred a Sioux village in 1890. In protest against both tribal leadership and federal policies, the Sioux seized the town, taking hostages. After tense negotiations with the FBI and a shootout that left two Native Americans dead and others wounded, the confrontation ended with a government promise to reexamine Native American treaty rights. **D**

NATIVE AMERICAN VICTORIES Congress and the federal courts did make some reforms on behalf of Native Americans. In 1972, Congress passed the Indian Education Act. In 1975, it passed the Indian Self-Determination and Education

MAIN IDEA

Summarizing
D What tactics did AIM use in its attempts to gain reforms?

1970
Taos of New Mexico regain possession of Blue Lake as well as surrounding forestland.

1971
Alaska Native Claims Settlement Act gives Alaskan natives 44 million acres and more than $962 million.

1979
Maine Implementing Act provides $81.5 million for native tribes, including Penobscot and Passamaquoddy, to buy back land.

1980
U.S. awards Sioux $106 million for illegally taken land in South Dakota.

1988
U.S. awards Puyallup tribe $162 million for land claims in Washington.

Assistance Act. These laws gave tribes greater control over their own affairs and over their children's education.

Armed with copies of old land treaties that the U.S. government had broken, Native Americans went to federal court and regained some of their rights to land. In 1970, the Taos of New Mexico regained possession of their sacred Blue Lake, as well as a portion of its surrounding forestland. Land claims by natives of Alaska resulted in the Alaska Native Claims Settlement Act of 1971. This act gave more than 40 million acres to native peoples and paid out more than $962 million in cash. Throughout the 1970s and 1980s, Native Americans won settlements that provided legal recognition of their tribal lands as well as financial compensation.

While the 1960s and the early 1970s saw a wave of activism from the nation's minority groups, another group of Americans also pushed for changes. Women, while not a minority group, were in many ways treated like second-class citizens, and many joined together to demand equal treatment in society.

ASSESSMENT

1. **TERMS & NAMES** For each term or name, write a sentence explaining its significance.
   - César Chávez
   - United Farm Workers Organizing Committee
   - La Raza Unida
   - American Indian Movement (AIM)

MAIN IDEA

2. **TAKING NOTES**
Create a Venn diagram like the one below to show the broad similarities between the issues faced by Latinos and Native Americans during the 1960s, as well as the unique concerns of the two groups.

Issues Faced by Latinos and Native Americans

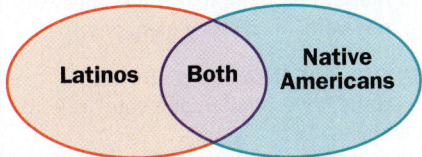

Which group do you think had more to gain by fighting for what they wanted?

CRITICAL THINKING

3. **EVALUATING**
How would you judge whether an activist organization was effective? List criteria you would use, and justify your criteria. **Think About:**
   - UFWOC, MAPA, and La Raza Unida
   - AIM
   - the leaders and activities of these organizations

4. **ANALYZING EFFECTS**
In what ways did the Latino campaign for economic and social equality affect non-Latino Americans?

5. **ANALYZING PRIMARY SOURCES**
Vine Deloria, Jr., said,

"When you get far enough away from the reservation, you can see it's the urban man who has no identity."

What do you think he meant by this?

HISTORIC DECISIONS OF THE SUPREME COURT

REYNOLDS v. SIMS (1964)

ORIGINS OF THE CASE In 1901, seats in the Alabama state legislature were apportioned, or assigned to districts, based on population. By the early 1960s, each Alabama county still had the same number of representatives as it did in 1901, even though the populations of the counties had changed. A group of voters sued to make representation proportional to the changed populations. When the suit succeeded, state legislators who were threatened with losing their seats appealed to the Supreme Court.

THE RULING The Supreme Court upheld the principle of "one person, one vote" and ruled that the equal protection clause required representation in state legislatures to be based on population.

LEGAL REASONING

Prior to *Reynolds*, the Court had already applied the "one person, one vote" principle to federal congressional elections (see Legal Sources). In *Reynolds*, Chief Justice Earl Warren extended this principle to state legislatures. He argued that when representation does not reflect population, some people's votes are worth more than others'.

> " The fundamental principle of representative government in this country is one of equal representation for equal numbers of people, without regard to . . . place of residence within a State. . . . Legislators represent people, not trees or acres. Legislators are elected by voters, not farms or cities or economic interests."

Warren concluded that Alabama's apportionment scheme discriminated against people because of where they live.

For these reasons, the Court ruled that any acceptable apportionment plan must provide an equal number of legislative seats for equally populated areas. A plan that does not is unconstitutional because it denies some voters the equal protection of the laws.

LEGAL SOURCES

U.S. CONSTITUTION

U.S. CONSTITUTION, FOURTEENTH AMENDMENT (1868)
"No state shall . . . deprive any person of life, liberty, or property, without due process of law; nor deny to any person within its jurisdiction the equal protection of the laws."

RELATED CASES

BAKER v. CARR (1962)
The Court decided that federal courts could settle issues of apportionment. Previously, federal courts had refused to address such issues on the grounds that they were political issues.

GRAY v. SANDERS (1963)
The Court ruled that states must follow the principle of "one person, one vote" in primary elections.

WESBERRY v. SANDERS (1964)
The Court applied the "one person, one vote" rule to congressional districts.

◄ Chief Justice Warren *(front, center)* and members of the 1964 Supreme Court.

WHY IT MATTERED

The voters who initiated the suit against Alabama's apportionment were part of America's tremendous urban growth in the 20th century. During and after World War II, tens of thousands of Americans—including large numbers of African Americans—moved from rural areas to cities and suburbs. Voters in Alabama's more urban areas found that they were underrepresented. Likewise, before *Reynolds*, urban residents as a whole paid far more in taxes than they received in benefits. A great deal was at stake.

The "one person, one vote" principle increased the influence of urban residents by forcing legislatures to create new election districts in the cities to reflect their large populations. As more legislators representing urban and suburban needs were elected, they were able to change funding formulas, funneling more money into their districts. In addition, minorities, immigrants, and professionals, who tend to make up a large proportion of urban populations, gained better representation.

On the other hand, the power of farmers was eroded as election districts in rural areas were combined and incumbents had to campaign against each other for a single seat.

HISTORICAL IMPACT

The Warren Court's reapportionment decisions in *Baker* v. *Carr*, *Gray* v. *Sanders*, *Wesberry* v. *Sanders*, and *Reynolds* were a revolution in U.S. politics. The lawsuit that culminated in the *Reynolds* decision was also part of a broader movement in the 1960s to protect voting rights. Largely because of the Voting Rights Act of 1965, voter registration among African Americans in Mississippi, for instance, climbed from 6.7 percent to 59.8 percent. Viewed together, the combination of increased protection of voting rights and acceptance of the "one person, one vote" principle brought the United States several steps closer to fulfilling its democratic ideals.

In the 1990s, the Court revisited reapportionment. A 1982 act of Congress had required states to create districts with "minority majorities" in order to increase the number of nonwhite representatives. As a result, following the 1990 census, a record number of African Americans were elected to Congress. But opponents contended that defining districts by race violated equal protection and "one person, one vote." In a series of decisions, the Court agreed and abolished minority districting.

These two apportionment maps show Alabama's 35 state senatorial districts in 1901 *(left)* and 1973 *(right)*. The 1973 map shows how the districts were redrawn after the *Reynolds* decision, based on the 1970 census. Notice how the 1973 map reflects the growth of Alabama cities.

ALABAMA 1901

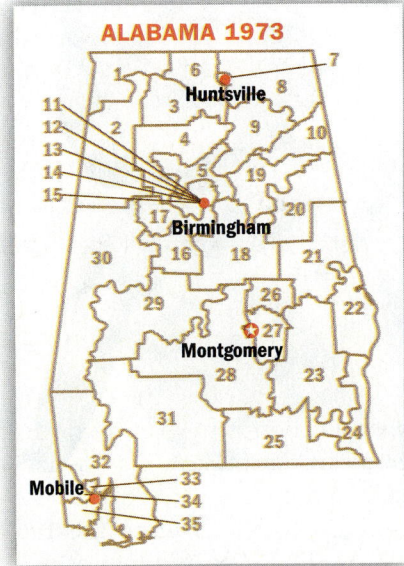

ALABAMA 1973

THINKING CRITICALLY

CONNECT TO TODAY

1. Analyzing Maps Obtain a map of the state legislative districts in your state. Then compare the map created following the 2000 census with the map based on the 1990 census. Study the differences in the size and location of the districts. Write a paragraph explaining which regions of the state gained representatives and which lost representatives.

 SEE SKILLBUILDER HANDBOOK, PAGE R25.

CONNECT TO HISTORY

2. Visit the links for Historic Decisions of the Supreme Court to research minority redistricting decisions such as *Shaw* v. *Hunt* (1996). Write a summary of the rulings and how they have affected elections.

 hmhsocialstudies.com INTERNET ACTIVITY

SECTION
2

PI 2.4
PI 3.2

CC Unit 7.III.B.4.a(2)   CC Unit 7.III.B.4.b(1)
CC Unit 7.III.B.4.b(2)   CC Unit 7.III.B.4.b(3)
CC Unit 7.III.B.4.b(4)   CC Unit 7.V.A.1.f

Women Fight for Equality

MAIN IDEA	WHY IT MATTERS NOW	Terms & Names
Through protests and marches, women confronted social and economic barriers in American society.	The rise of the women's movement during the 1960s advanced women's place in the work force and in society.	•Betty Friedan •feminism •National Organization for Women (NOW) •Gloria Steinem •Equal Rights Amendment (ERA) •Phyllis Schlafly

One American's Story

hmhsocialstudies.com
TAKING NOTES
Use the graphic organizer online to take notes on key events of the women's movement.

During the 1950s, writer **Betty Friedan** seemed to be living the American dream. She had a loving husband, healthy children, and a house in the suburbs. According to the experts—doctors, psychologists, and women's magazines—that was all a woman needed to be fulfilled. Why, then, wasn't she happy? In 1957, after conducting a survey of her Smith College classmates 15 years after graduation, she found she was not alone. Friedan eventually wrote a book, *The Feminine Mystique*, in which she addressed this "problem that has no name."

A PERSONAL VOICE BETTY FRIEDAN

"The problem lay buried, unspoken. . . . It was a strange stirring, a sense of dissatisfaction, a yearning that women suffered in the middle of the twentieth century in the United States. Each suburban wife struggled with it alone. As she made the beds, shopped for groceries, matched slipcover material, ate peanut butter sandwiches with her children, chauffeured Cub Scouts and Brownies, lay beside her husband at night—she was afraid to ask even of herself the silent question—'Is this all?' "

—*The Feminine Mystique*

▲
Betty Friedan, November 1967

During the 1960s, women answered Friedan's question with a resounding "no." In increasing numbers they joined the nation's African Americans, Latinos, and Native Americans in the fight for greater civil rights and equality in society.

A New Women's Movement Arises

The theory behind the women's movement of the 1960s was **feminism,** the belief that women should have economic, political, and social equality with men. Feminist beliefs had gained momentum during the mid-1800s and in 1920 won women the right to vote. While the women's movement declined after this achievement, it reawakened during the 1960s, spurred by the political activism of the times.

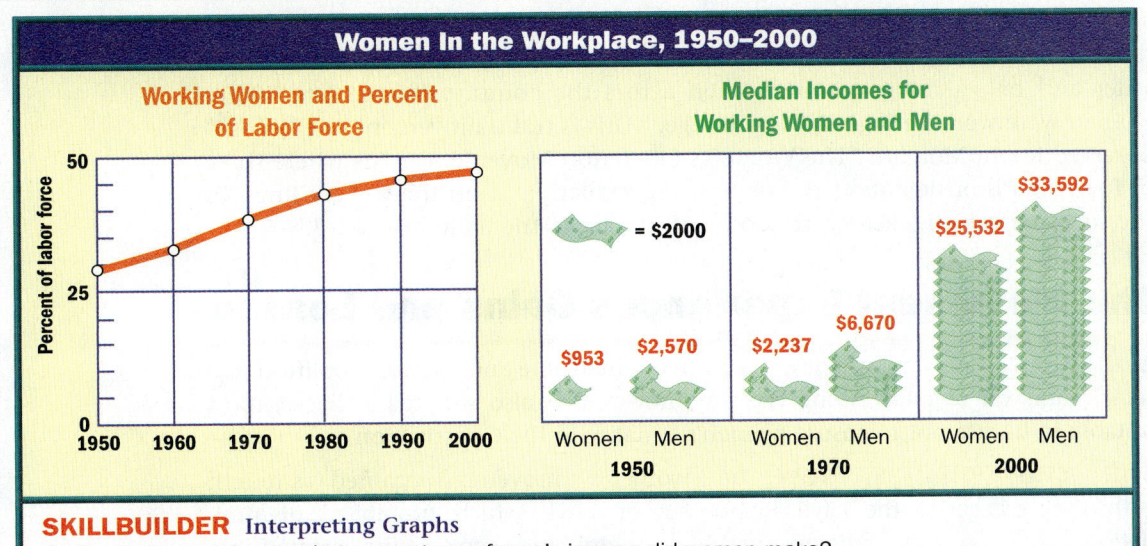

Women In the Workplace, 1950–2000

Working Women and Percent of Labor Force

Percent of labor force: 50, 25, 0
1950 1960 1970 1980 1990 2000

Median Incomes for Working Women and Men

= $2000

	1950	1970	2000
Women	$953	$2,237	$25,532
Men	$2,570	$6,670	$33,592

SKILLBUILDER Interpreting Graphs
1. For each year shown, what percentage of men's income did women make?
2. About how many more women were working in 1990 than in 1960?

SEE SKILLBUILDER HANDBOOK, PAGE R28.

This 1960s pin displays a slogan used by Betty Friedan at the National Women's Political Caucus. ▼

WOMEN MAKE POLICY NOT COFFEE

WOMEN IN THE WORKPLACE In 1950, only one out of three women worked for wages. By 1960, that number had increased to about 40 percent. Still, during this time, certain jobs were considered "men's work" and women were shut out. The jobs available to women—mostly clerical work, domestic service, retail sales, social work, teaching, and nursing—paid poorly.

The country largely ignored this discrimination until President Kennedy appointed the Presidential Commission on the Status of Women in 1961. In 1963, the commission reported that women were paid far less than men, even when doing the same jobs. Furthermore, women were seldom promoted to management positions, regardless of their education, experience, and ability. These newly publicized facts awakened many women to their unequal status in society.

WOMEN AND ACTIVISM Ironically, many women felt the sting of discrimination when they became involved in the civil rights and antiwar movements—movements that toted the ideological banner of protecting people's rights. Within some of these organizations, such as SNCC and SDS, men led most of the activities, while women were assigned lesser roles. When women protested this arrangement, the men usually brushed them aside.

"Move on little girl; we have more important issues to talk about here than women's liberation."

A MALE ANTIWAR ACTIVIST

Vocabulary
ideological: concerned with a certain set of ideas

MAIN IDEA

Analyzing Effects
Ⓐ What effects did the civil rights and the antiwar movements have on many women?

Such experiences led some women to organize small groups to discuss their concerns. During these discussions, or "consciousness-raising" sessions, women shared their lives with each other and discovered that their experiences were not unique. Rather, they reflected a much larger pattern of sexism, or discrimination based on gender. Author Robin Morgan delineated this pattern. Ⓐ

★ **A PERSONAL VOICE** ROBIN MORGAN

" It makes you very sensitive—raw, even, this consciousness. Everything, from the verbal assault on the street, to a 'well-meant' sexist joke your husband tells, to the lower pay you get at work (for doing the same job a man would be paid more for), to television commercials, to rock-song lyrics, to the pink or blue blanket they put on your infant in the hospital nursery, to speeches by male 'revolutionaries' that reek of male supremacy—everything seems to barrage your aching brain. . . . You begin to see how all-pervasive a thing is sexism. "

—quoted in *Sisterhood Is Powerful: An Anthology of Writings from the Women's Liberation Movement*

THE WOMEN'S MOVEMENT EMERGES *The Feminine Mystique,* which captured the very discontent that many women were feeling, quickly became a best-seller and helped to galvanize women across the country. By the late 1960s, women were working together for change. "This is not a movement one 'joins,'" observed Robin Morgan. "The Women's Liberation Movement exists where three or four friends or neighbors decide to meet regularly . . . on the welfare lines, in the supermarket, the factory, the convent, the farm, the maternity ward."

The Movement Experiences Gains and Losses

As the women's movement grew, it achieved remarkable and enduring political and social gains for women. Along the way, however, it also suffered setbacks, most notably in its attempt to ensure women's equality in the Constitution.

THE CREATION OF NOW The women's movement gained strength with the passage of the Civil Rights Act of 1964, which prohibited discrimination based on race, religion, national origin, and gender and created the Equal Employment Opportunity Commission (EEOC) to handle discrimination claims. By 1966, however, some women argued that the EEOC didn't adequately address women's grievances. That year, 28 women, including Betty Friedan, created the **National Organization for Women (NOW)** to pursue women's goals. "The time has come," the founders of NOW declared, "to confront with concrete action the conditions which now prevent women from enjoying the equality of opportunity . . . which is their right as individual Americans and as human beings." **B**

NOW members pushed for the creation of child-care facilities that would enable mothers to pursue jobs and education. NOW also pressured the EEOC to enforce more vigorously the ban on gender discrimination in hiring. NOW's efforts prompted the EEOC to declare sex-segregated job ads illegal and to issue guidelines to employers, stating that they could no longer refuse to hire women for traditionally male jobs.

A DIVERSE MOVEMENT In its first three years, NOW's ranks swelled to 175,000 members. A number of other women's groups sprang up around the country, too. In 1968, a militant group known as the New York Radical Women staged a well-publicized demonstration at the annual Miss America Pageant. The women threw bras, girdles, wigs, and other "women's garbage" into a "Freedom Trash Can." They then crowned a sheep "Miss America." Around this time, **Gloria Steinem,** a journalist, political activist, and ardent supporter of the women's liberation movement, made her voice heard on the subjects of feminism and equality. Steinem's grandmother had served as president of the Ohio Woman's Suffrage Association from 1908 to 1911; Steinem had inherited her passion and conviction. In 1971, Steinem helped found the National Women's Political Caucus, a moderate group that encouraged women to seek political office. In 1972, she and other women created a new women's magazine, *Ms.,* designed to treat contemporary issues from a feminist perspective.

LEGAL AND SOCIAL GAINS As the women's movement progressed, women began to question all sorts of gender-based distinctions. People protested that a woman's physical

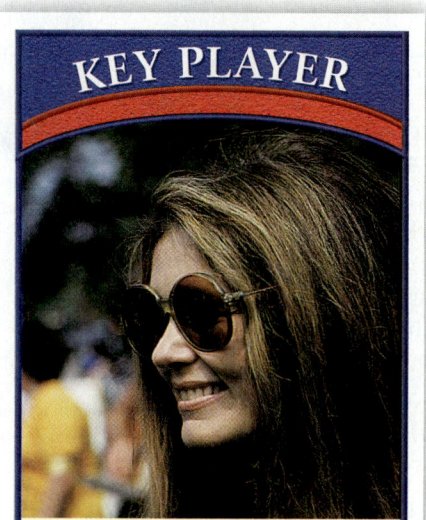

KEY PLAYER

**GLORIA STEINEM
1934–**

Gloria Steinem became one of the more prominent figures of the women's movement after she and several other women founded *Ms.* magazine in 1972. The magazine soon became a major voice of the women's movement.

Steinem said that she decided to start the feminist magazine after editors in the mainstream media continually rejected her stories about the women's movement:

"Editors who had assumed I had some valuable biological insight into food, male movie stars, and textured stockings now questioned whether I or other women writers were biologically capable of writing objectively about feminism. That was the beginning."

MAIN IDEA

Analyzing Causes
B What prompted women to establish NOW?

appearance was often considered a job qualification. Girls' exclusion from sports such as baseball and football came into question. Some women began using the title Ms., instead of the standard Miss or Mrs., and refused to adopt their husband's last name upon marriage.

These changes in attitude were paralleled by numerous legal changes. In 1972, Congress passed a ban on gender discrimination in "any education program or activity receiving federal financial assistance," as part of the Higher Education Act. As a result, several all-male colleges opened their doors to women. That same year, Congress expanded the powers of the EEOC and gave working parents a tax break for child-care expenses. **C**

ROE v. WADE One of the more controversial positions that NOW and other feminist groups supported was a woman's right to have an abortion. In 1973, the Supreme Court ruled in *Roe* v. *Wade* that women do have the right to choose an abortion during the first three months of pregnancy. Some thought the ruling might "bring to an end the emotional and divisive public argument. . . ." However, the issue still divides Americans today.

THE EQUAL RIGHTS AMENDMENT (ERA) In what seemed at first to be another triumph for the women's movement, Congress passed the **Equal Rights Amendment (ERA)** in 1972. The amendment then needed ratification by 38 states to become part of the Constitution. First introduced to Congress in 1923, the ERA would guarantee that both men and women would enjoy the same rights and protections under the law. It was, many supporters said, a matter of "simple justice."

The amendment scared many people, and a Stop-ERA campaign was launched in 1972. Conservative **Phyllis Schlafly,** along with conservative religious groups, political organizations, and many anti-feminists, felt that the ERA would lead to "a parade of horribles," such as the drafting of women, the end of laws protecting homemakers, the end of a husband's responsibility to provide for his family, and same-sex marriages. Schlafly said that radical feminists "hate men, marriage, and children" and were oppressed "only in their distorted minds."

A PERSONAL VOICE PHYLLIS SCHLAFLY

"The U.S. Constitution is not the place for symbols or slogans, it is not the proper device to alleviate psychological problems of personal inferiority. Symbols and slogans belong on bumper strips—not in the Constitution. It would be a tragic mistake for our nation to succumb to the tirades and demands of a few women who are seeking a constitutional cure for their personal problems."

— quoted in *The Equal Rights Amendment: The History and the Movement*

THE NEW RIGHT EMERGES In order to combat the ERA and the pro-abortion supporters, conservatives built what they called a new "pro-family" movement. In the 1970s, this coalition—which focused on social, cultural, and moral problems—came to be known as the New Right. The New Right and the women's movement debated family-centered issues such as whether the government should pay for daycare, which the New Right opposed. Throughout the 1970s, the New Right built grassroots support for social conservatism. It would later play a key role in the election of Ronald Reagan to the presidency in 1980. **D**

Phyllis Schlafly in 1977.

MAIN IDEA

Making Generalizations
C What sort of gains did the women's movement make by the early 1970s?

MAIN IDEA

Analyzing Motives
D What concerns motivated those who opposed the ERA?

The Movement's Legacy

The New Right and the women's movement clashed most dramatically over the ERA. By 1977 it had won approval from 35 of the 38 states needed for ratification, but the New Right gained strength. By June of 1982—the deadline for ratification—not enough states had approved the amendment. The ERA went down in defeat.

Despite ERA's defeat, the women's movement altered society in countless ways, such as by transforming women's conventional roles and their attitudes toward career and family. Interviews with women graduates at Stanford University reflect the change. Of graduates in 1965, 70 percent planned not to work at all when their children were of preschool age. When the class of 1972 was surveyed, only 7 percent said they would stop working to raise children.

The women's movement also succeeded in expanding career opportunities for women. For instance, as of 1970, 8 percent of all medical school graduates and 5 percent of all law school graduates were women. By 1998, those proportions had risen to 42 and 44 percent, respectively. Yet many women ran into a "glass ceiling"—an invisible, but very real, resistance to promoting women into top positions.

By 1983 women held 13.5 percent of elected state offices as well as 24 seats in the U.S. Congress. More importantly, as historian Sara Evans has noted, by 1980 "feminist concerns were firmly on the national political agenda and clearly there to stay." Most of all, the women's movement helped countless women open their lives to new possibilities. "For we have lived the second American revolution," wrote Betty Friedan in 1976, "and our very anger said a 'new YES' to life."

As this poster shows, women have made significant political strides by being elected to the U.S. Congress. ▼

SECTION 2 ASSESSMENT

1. TERMS & NAMES
For each term or name, write a sentence explaining its significance.

- Betty Friedan
- feminism
- National Organization for Women (NOW)
- Gloria Steinem
- Equal Rights Amendment (ERA)
- Phyllis Schlafly

MAIN IDEA

2. TAKING NOTES
Create a time line of key events relating to the women's movement.

1964		1973

1966	1971	1972

Explain which event you think best demonstrates progressive reform.

CRITICAL THINKING

3. HYPOTHESIZING
What if the Equal Rights Amendment had been ratified? Speculate on how women's lives might have been different. Use reasons to support your answer.

Think About:

- rights addressed by the amendment
- legal support that the amendment might have provided
- possible reactions from groups opposing the amendment

4. ANALYZING VISUAL SOURCES
Examine the drawing on this 1972 cover of *Ms.* The woman shown has eight arms and is holding a different object in each hand. What do you think these objects symbolize in terms of women's roles? What do you think this drawing says about women in the 1960s? Explain.

PI 2.4
PI 3.2

CC Unit 7.IV.A.5.c

Culture and Counterculture

MAIN IDEA	WHY IT MATTERS NOW	Terms & Names
The ideals and lifestyle of the counterculture challenged the traditional views of Americans.	The music, art, and politics of the counterculture have left enduring marks on American society.	• counterculture • the Beatles • Haight-Ashbury • Woodstock

One American's Story

hmhsocialstudies.com
TAKING NOTES
Use the graphic organizer online to take notes on the counterculture of the 1960s.

In 1966, Alex Forman left his conventional life in mainstream America and headed to San Francisco. Arriving there with little else but a guitar, he joined thousands of others who were determined to live in a more peaceful and carefree environment. He recalled his early days in San Francisco's Haight-Ashbury district, the hub of hippie life.

▲ **A PERSONAL VOICE** ALEX FORMAN

" It was like paradise there. Everybody was in love with life and in love with their fellow human beings to the point where they were just sharing in incredible ways with everybody. Taking people in off the street and letting them stay in their homes. . . . You could walk down almost any street in Haight-Ashbury where I was living, and someone would smile at you and just go, 'Hey, it's beautiful, isn't it?'. . . It was a very special time. "
—quoted in *From Camelot to Kent State*

▲ Members of the counterculture relax in a California park.

Forman was part of the **counterculture**—a movement made up mostly of white, middle-class college youths who had grown disillusioned with the war in Vietnam and injustices in America during the 1960s. Instead of challenging the system, they turned their backs on traditional America and tried to establish a whole new society based on peace and love. Although their heyday was short-lived, their legacy remains.

The Counterculture

In the late 1960s, the historian Theodore Roszak deemed these idealistic youths the counterculture. It was a culture, he said, so different from the mainstream "that it scarcely looks to many as a culture at all, but takes on the alarming appearance of a barbarian intrusion."

"TUNE IN, TURN ON, DROP OUT" Members of the counterculture, known as hippies, shared some of the beliefs of the New Left movement. Specifically, they felt that American society—and its materialism, technology, and war—had grown hollow. Influenced by the nonconformist beat movement of the 1950s, hippies embraced the credo of Harvard psychology professor and counterculture philosopher Timothy Leary: "Tune in, turn on, drop out." Throughout the mid- and late 1960s, tens of thousands of idealistic youths left school, work, or home to create what they hoped would be an idyllic community of peace, love, and harmony.

> *" How does it feel to be without a home . . . like a rolling stone?"*
> **BOB DYLAN**

HIPPIE CULTURE The hippie era, sometimes known as the Age of Aquarius, was marked by rock 'n' roll music, outrageous clothing, sexual license, and illegal drugs—in particular, marijuana and a new hallucinogenic drug called LSD, or acid. Timothy Leary, an early experimenter with the drug, promoted the use of LSD as a "mind-expanding" aid for self-awareness. Hippies also turned to Eastern religions such as Zen Buddhism, which professed that one could attain enlightenment through meditation rather than the reading of scriptures.

Hippies donned ragged jeans, tie-dyed T-shirts, military garments, love beads, and Native American ornaments. Thousands grew their hair out, despite the fact that their more conservative elders saw this as an act of disrespect. Signs across the country said, "Make America beautiful—give a hippie a haircut."

Hippies also rejected conventional home life. Many joined communes, in which the members renounced private property to live communally. By the mid-sixties, **Haight-Ashbury** in San Francisco was known as the hippie capital, mainly because California did not outlaw hallucinogenic drugs until 1966.

DECLINE OF THE MOVEMENT After only a few years, the counterculture's peace and harmony gave way to violence and disillusionment. The urban communes eventually turned seedy and dangerous. Alex Forman recalled, "There were ripoffs, violence . . . people living on the street with no place to stay." Having dispensed with society's conventions and rules, the hippies had to rely on each other. Many discovered that the philosophy of "do your own thing" did not provide enough guidance for how to live. "We were together at the level of peace and love," said one disillusioned hippie. "We fell apart over who would cook and wash dishes and pay the bills." By 1970, many had fallen victim to the drugs they used, experiencing drug addiction and mental breakdowns. The rock singer Janis Joplin and the legendary guitarist Jimi Hendrix both died of drug overdoses in 1970.

As the mystique of the 1960s wore off, thousands of hippies lined up at government offices to collect welfare and food stamps—dependent on the very society they had once rejected. **Ⓐ**

MAIN IDEA

Analyzing Causes
Ⓐ What events and other factors hastened the decline of the counterculture movement?

A prominent symbol of the counterculture movement was bright colors. ▶

A Changing Culture

Although short-lived, some aspects of the counterculture—namely, its fine arts and social attitudes—left a more lasting imprint on the world.

ART The counterculture's rebellious style left its mark on the art world. The 1960s saw the rise of pop art (popular art). Pop artists, led by Andy Warhol, attempted to bring art into the mainstream. Pop art was characterized by bright, simple, commercial-looking images often depicting everyday life. For instance, Warhol became famous for his bright silk-screen portraits of soup cans, Marilyn Monroe, and other icons of mass culture. These images were repeated to look mass-produced and impersonal, a criticism of the times implying that individual freedoms had been lost to a more conventional, "cookie-cutter" lifestyle.

MAIN IDEA

Making Inferences
Ⓑ What did rock 'n' roll symbolize for American youth?

ROCK MUSIC During the 1960s, the counterculture movement embraced rock 'n' roll as its loud and biting anthem of protest. The music was an offshoot of African-American rhythm and blues music that had captivated so many teenagers during the 1950s. Ⓑ

▲ The Beatles, shown here in 1967, influenced fashion with their long hair and psychedelic clothing.

The band that, perhaps more than any other, helped propel rock music into mainstream America was **the Beatles.** The British band, made up of four youths from working-class Liverpool, England, arrived in America in 1964 and immediately took the country by storm. By the time the Beatles broke up in 1970, the four "lads" had inspired a countless number of other bands and had won over millions of Americans to rock 'n' roll.

One example of rock 'n' roll's popularity occurred in August 1969 on a farm in upstate New York. More than 400,000 showed up for a music festival called "**Woodstock** Music and Art Fair." This festival represented, as one songwriter put it, "the '60s movement of peace and love and some higher cultural cause." For three days, the most popular bands and musicians performed, including Jimi Hendrix, Janis Joplin, Joe Cocker, Joan Baez, the Grateful Dead, and Jefferson Airplane. Despite the huge crowd, Woodstock was peaceful and well organized. However, Tom Mathews, a writer who attended the Woodstock festival, recalled his experience there as less than blissful.

★ A PERSONAL VOICE TOM MATHEWS

" The last night of the concert I was standing in a narrow pit at the foot of the stage. I made the mistake of looking over the board fence separating the pit from Max Yasgur's hillside. When I peered up I saw 400,000 . . . people wrapped in wet, dirty ponchos, sleeping bags and assorted, tie-dyed mufti slowly slipping toward the stage. It looked like a human mud slide. . . . After that night I couldn't get out of there fast enough. "

—"The Sixties Complex," *Newsweek,* Sept. 5, 1988

CHANGING ATTITUDES While the counterculture movement faded, its casual "do your own thing" philosophy left its mark. American attitudes toward sexual behavior became more casual and permissive, leading to what became known as the sexual revolution. During the 1960s and 1970s, mass culture—including TV, books,

History Through *Music*

PROTEST SONGS OF THE SIXTIES

During the turbulent climate of the sixties, hippies and other activists used music as a vehicle for political expression. In bus terminals, in the streets, and on the White House lawn, thousands united in song, expressing their rejection of mainstream society, their demand for civil rights, and their outrage over the Vietnam War. Musicians like Bob Dylan stirred up antiwar sentiment in songs like "The Times They Are A-Changin'," while Joan Baez and Pete Seeger popularized the great African-American spiritual "We Shall Overcome," which became the anthem of the Civil Rights Movement.

> **We Shall Overcome**
> **(African-American Spiritual)**
>
> We shall overcome,
> We shall overcome,
> We shall overcome some day.
> (*Chorus*) Oh, deep in my heart
> I do believe:
> We shall overcome some day.
>
> We'll walk hand in hand. . . .
> We shall all be free. . . .
> We are not afraid. . . .
> We are not alone. . . .
> The whole wide world around. . . .
> We shall overcome. . . .

▲ Joan Baez, 1965

▲ Joined in harmony, African-American students in Selma, Alabama, gather on the steps of the Tabernacle Baptist Church to sing "We Shall Overcome." (1963)

Bob Dylan, 1966 ▶

> *from* **The Times They Are A-Changin'** (Bob Dylan, 1962)
>
> Come senators, congressmen
> Please heed the call
> Don't stand in the doorway
> Don't block up the hall
> For he that gets hurt
> Will be he who has stalled
> There's a battle outside
> And it is ragin'.
> It'll soon shake your windows
> And rattle your walls
> For the times they are a-changin'.
>
> Come mothers and fathers
> Throughout the land
> And don't criticize
> What you can't understand
> Your sons and your daughters
> Are beyond your command
> Your old road is
> Rapidly agin'.
> Please get out of the new one
> If you can't lend your hand
> For the times they are a-changin'.

magazines, music, and movies—began to address subjects that had once been prohibited, particularly sexual behavior and explicit violence.

While some hailed the increasing permissiveness as liberating, others attacked it as a sign of moral decay. For millions of Americans, the new tolerance was merely an uncivilized lack of respect for established social norms. Eventually, the counterculture movement would lead a great many Americans to more liberal attitudes about dress and appearance, lifestyle, and social behavior; yet in the short run, it produced largely the opposite effect.

The Conservative Response

In the late 1960s, many believed that the country was losing its sense of right and wrong. Increasingly, conservative voices began to express people's anger. At the 1968 Republican convention in Miami, candidate Richard M. Nixon expressed that anger.

> ★ **A PERSONAL VOICE** RICHARD NIXON
>
> " As we look at America we see cities enveloped in smoke and flame. We hear sirens in the night. . . . We see Americans hating each other . . . at home. . . . Did we come all this way for this? . . . die in Normandy and Korea and in Valley Forge for this? "
>
> —Speech at Republican convention, 1968

CONSERVATIVES ATTACK THE COUNTERCULTURE Nixon was not the only conservative voice expressing alarm. FBI Director J. Edgar Hoover issued a warning that "revolutionary terrorism" was a threat on campuses and in cities. Other conservative critics warned that campus rebels posed a danger to traditional values and threatened to plunge American society into anarchy. Conservatives also attacked the counterculture for what they saw as its decadent values. In the view of psychiatrist Bruno Bettelheim, student rebels and members of the counterculture had been pampered in childhood; as young adults, they did not have the ability for delayed gratification. According to some conservative commentators, the counterculture had abandoned rational thought in favor of the senses and uninhibited self-expression. **C**

The angry response of mainstream Americans caused a profound change in the political landscape of the United States. By the end of the 1960s, conservatives were presenting their own solutions on such issues as lawlessness and crime, the size of the federal government, and welfare. This growing conservative movement would propel Nixon into the White House—and set the nation on a more conservative course.

MAIN IDEA

Forming Generalizations
C Why were conservatives angry about the counterculture?

▲ In contrast to the 1968 Democratic convention in Chicago, the Republican convention was orderly and united—particularly in the delegates' opposition to the counterculture.

SECTION 3 ASSESSMENT

1. TERMS & NAMES For each term or name, write a sentence explaining its significance.
- counterculture
- Haight-Ashbury
- the Beatles
- Woodstock

MAIN IDEA

2. TAKING NOTES
Re-create the tree diagram below on your paper. Then fill in examples that illustrate the topics in the second row of boxes.

Which example do you think had the biggest impact on society? Why?

CRITICAL THINKING

3. DEVELOPING HISTORICAL PERSPECTIVE
A stereotype is a generalization made about a group. What stereotype do you think hippies might have formed about mainstream Americans? What stereotype do you think mainstream Americans might have formed about hippies? Why? **Think About:**
- Alex Forman's comments in "A Personal Voice" (page 987)
- hippies' values and lifestyle
- mainstream Americans' values and lifestyle

4. MAKING INFERENCES
In your opinion, why didn't the hippies succeed?

5. ANALYZING ISSUES
What role did the counterculture and antiwar movement play in helping Richard Nixon win the presidency?

Signs of the Sixties

The wave of social change that swept across America during the 1960s affected everyone, but especially the nation's teenagers. Abandoning the conservative and "clean-cut" look of the 1950s, many teens experimented with new and different appearances. In a declaration of their individuality and desire for more freedom, they also embraced a variety of new music and films during the 1960s.

FASHION: A NEW LOOK ▶

During the 1960s, many youths wore a wide range of unconventional clothing. While most Americans did not adopt the outlandish look of hippies, many came out of the sixties wearing longer hair and blue jeans, which became a staple in nearly every wardrobe. Bright colors and psychedelic patterns also became wildly popular.

◀ THE RISE OF SOUL MUSIC

African-American soul artists, whose music had inspired the more popular white rock 'n' roll performers of the 1950s, grew widely popular themselves during the 1960s. During this decade, Detroit's Motown label produced the most popular and successful African-American artists, including Marvin Gaye, Stevie Wonder, and the Supremes (left).

A DIVERSE MUSIC SCENE ▶

Scores of teenagers also tuned to surf music, a harmonic, light sound made popular by a California band, the Beach Boys. Other teens listened to the poetic and socially conscious lyrics of folk rock. Heavy, or psychedelic, rock, sung by bands such as the Doors (whose 1967 concert advertisement appears to the right), also found its way into many album collections. In the later part of the decade, musicians like Jimi Hendrix (far right) took rock 'n' roll in a new direction.

GOING TO THE SHOW ▲

As the nation's movie industry grew, more and more teenagers flocked to the cinema. Teens took in such diverse films as the counterculture classic *Easy Rider* and the science fiction classic *2001: A Space Odyssey* (above), which tells the story of HAL, a spaceship computer that develops a mind of its own.

POP ART ▲

Andy Warhol created this image of movie actress and popular icon Marilyn Monroe. A leader of the pop art movement, Warhol attempted to criticize the conventional lifestyle of the mass culture through commercial-looking images that depicted the loss of individuality.

D A T A
F I L E

POPULAR SONGS

- "Blowin' in the Wind" (1962)
- "Surfin' USA" (1963)
- "Where Did Our Love Go?" (1964)
- "California Dreamin'" (1966)
- "Light My Fire" (1967)
- "Mrs. Robinson" (1967)
- "Aquarius/Let the Sunshine In" (1968)
- "Come Together" (1969)
- "Everyday People" (1968)

POPULAR TV SHOWS

- *The Dick Van Dyke Show* (1962–1966)
- *The Beverly Hillbillies* (1962–1971)
- *Green Acres* (1965–1971)
- *The Addams Family* (1964–1966)
- *The Man from U.N.C.L.E.* (1964–1968)
- *Mission: Impossible* (1966–1973)
- *Laugh-In* (1968–1973)
- *Bonanza* (1959–1973)

1960: Alfred Hitchcock's *Psycho* terrifies movie audiences across the nation.

1960

1962

1962: Wilt Chamberlain scores 100 points in a basketball game.

1963: The movie *Cleopatra*, produced for $37 million, is the most expensive film to date.

1963

1963: Graphic Artist Harvey Ball invents the smiley face for an ad campaign aimed at boosting workers' morale.

1964: The Beatles arrive in America.

1964

1965

1965: The miniskirt is introduced.

1966: The National Association of Broadcasters instructs disc jockeys to screen records for obscene or hidden meanings.

1966

1967

1967: The Green Bay Packers defeat the Kansas City Chiefs in the first Super Bowl.

1968: The government mandates that all new cars must be equipped with seat belts.

1968

1969

1969: Pantsuits become acceptable for everyday wear by women.

THINKING CRITICALLY

CONNECT TO HISTORY

1. **Drawing Conclusions** What conclusions can you draw about teenagers in the 1960s from the images and information in this feature?

   SEE SKILLBUILDER HANDBOOK, PAGE R18.

CONNECT TO TODAY

2. **The Role of Culture** Do the arts merely *reflect* social change, or can art, music, fashion, etc. help to *bring about* social change? Think about how music and fashions affect your actions and opinions. Discuss your thoughts with a small group of classmates.

 hmhsocialstudies.com | **RESEARCH WEB LINKS**

TERMS & NAMES

For each term or name below, write a sentence explaining its connection to the 1960s.

1. César Chávez
2. La Raza Unida
3. American Indian Movement (AIM)
4. feminism
5. Betty Friedan
6. Equal Rights Amendment (ERA)
7. Phyllis Schlafly
8. counterculture
9. Haight-Ashbury
10. Woodstock

MAIN IDEAS

Use your notes and the information in the chapter to answer the following questions.

Latinos and Native Americans Seek Equality
(pages 974–979)

1. What strategies did both César Chávez and the UFWOC use to achieve their goals? How did they successfully apply these tactics?
2. What were the demands of the American Indian Movement (AIM) organizers who staged "The Trail of Broken Treaties" march on Washington in 1972?

Women Fight for Equality (pages 982–986)

3. Name three changes that members of the National Organization of Women (NOW) advocated.
4. What was the Supreme Court's decision in the *Roe* v. *Wade* case?

Culture and Counterculture (pages 987–991)

5. Briefly explain the role Timothy Leary played in the counterculture movement.
6. What unintended impact did the counterculture have on many mainstream Americans?

CRITICAL THINKING

1. **USING YOUR NOTES** Re-create the diagram shown below. Then fill in the appropriate areas with key individual and shared achievements of Latinos, Native Americans, and feminists.

2. **DEVELOPING HISTORICAL PERSPECTIVE** Consider the organizations that Latinos, Native Americans, and women formed during the 1960s. Which do you think was the most influential? Why?

3. **ANALYZING PRIMARY SOURCES** Reread the song lyrics of Bob Dylan's "The Times They Are A-Changin'" on page 990. How do you think this song captured the main message of the counterculture movement?

VISUAL SUMMARY AN ERA OF SOCIAL CHANGE

CHANGES BROUGHT ABOUT BY THE COUNTERCULTURE

POLITICAL
- protests against Vietnam War
- NOW fuels feminism
- the New Right emerges
- ERA defeated
- *Roe* v. *Wade*
- more women in the work force
- AIM wins reforms and land rights
- La Raza Unida and MAPA fight for more rights for Latinos
- bilingual education
- Latino farm workers unionize

SOCIAL
- hippies reject mainstream society
- more communal living
- new fashion trends reflect freedom of expression
- traditional forms of worship rejected in favor of Eastern religious teachings
- more drug use
- women and minorities seek equality
- more permissive sexual behavior
- books, magazines, and movies show explicit violence

MUSIC
- music as political expression
- Motown label produces African-American artists
- rock music; the Beatles; Woodstock festival

ART AND FASHION
- pop art movement
- long hair as rebellion
- hippies popularize bright, colorful clothing, beads, and blue jeans

Use the flowchart and your knowledge of U.S. history to answer question 1.

1. UFWOC organizes a boycott of grapes.

⬇

2. Growers lose money.

⬇

3. UFWOC signs new contracts with growers.

⬇

4.

1 Which event accurately completes the cause-and-effect chain?

(1) EEOC rules that unhealthful working conditions amount to illegal discrimination.

(2) UFWOC disbands.

(3) Grape boycott is extended to apricots and olives.

(4) Working conditions for migrant farm workers are improved.

2 In the 1960s, women fought in Congress, in the courts, and in their everyday lives for treatment as political and social equals. Today, job discrimination against women is illegal because of —

(1) the Fourteenth Amendment.

(2) the ERA.

(3) the Civil Rights Act of 1964.

(4) the *Roe* v. *Wade* decision.

3 Which of the following statements is a fact?

(1) Hippies believed that everyone should love each other.

(2) Hippies spoiled the Woodstock festival.

(3) The hippie movement failed because the hippies' beliefs were too radical.

(4) Hippies invented rock music in Liverpool, England.

4 The women's rights movement largely grew out of—

(1) the counterculture movement.

(2) the civil rights movement.

(3) the movement to organize farm workers.

(4) reaction to the Warren Court decisions.

↗ hmhsocialstudies.com TEST PRACTICE

For additional test practice, go online for:

• Diagnostic tests   • Tutorials

INTERACT WITH HISTORY

Think about the issues you explored at the beginning of the chapter. Write a script in which five characters—a Latino activist, a Native American activist, a member of the women's movement, a member of the counterculture, and a conservative politician who wants to preserve the status quo—debate the following question: How much can a society change?

FOCUS ON WRITING

César Chávez received the Presidential Medal of Honor in 1994. Imagine that you have been asked to introduce Chávez at the presentation ceremony. Write a short speech highlighting his achievements as a labor organizer and Latino activist. You may wish to do additional research to help you.

MULTIMEDIA ACTIVITY

21ST CENTURY

Visit the Chapter Assessment links to find examples of 1960s culture, such as songs, paintings, posters, clothing, cars, and so on. Prepare an electronic museum exhibit of several artifacts that display a trend or theme discussed in the chapter. Write captions for the artifacts explaining their historical context and relating them to your chosen theme.

↗ hmhsocialstudies.com

UNIT

9

CHAPTER 32

An Age of Limits
1968–1980

CHAPTER 33

The Conservative Tide
1980–1992

CHAPTER 34

The United States in Today's World
1992–Present

EPILOGUE

Issues for the 21st Century

UNIT PROJECT

Campaign Scrapbook

As you read this unit, choose a candidate for political office whom you would like to support. Create a scrapbook that recounts your experiences on the campaign trail.

Exhibit at the Ellis Island Immigration Museum, design by MetaForm; portraits in flag by Pablo Delano
Photograph © Norman McGrath

Passage to a New Century
1968–Present

CHAPTER 32

AN AGE OF LIMITS

Essential Question

What were the political, social, and economic events of the 1970s?

New York Standards

KEY IDEA 2 Important ideas, social and cultural values, beliefs, and traditions from New York State and United States history illustrate the connections and interactions of people and events across time and from a variety of perspectives.

KEY IDEA 3 Study about the major social, political, economic, cultural, and religious developments in New York State and United States history involves learning about the important roles and contributions of individuals and groups.

SECTION 1: The Nixon Administration

SECTION 2: Watergate: Nixon's Downfall

SECTION 3: The Ford and Carter Years

SECTION 4: Environmental Activism

Richard Nixon leaves the White House after resigning as president on Friday, August 9, 1974.

1968 Richard M. Nixon is elected president.

1969 Astronaut Neil Armstrong becomes the first person to walk on the moon.

EARTH DAY
APRIL 22

1970 America celebrates the first Earth Day.

1972 Nixon visits China and the Soviet Union.

1972 Nixon is reelected.

1973 Energy crisis begins, and gasoline prices soar.

USA 1968 1969 1970 1971 1972 1973
WORLD

1972 China gives the U.S. two pandas.

1972 Terrorists kill eleven Israeli athletes at the XX Olympiad in Munich.

1973 War breaks out in the Middle East when seven Arab states attack Israel on Yom Kippur.

HISTORY

Nixon and Watergate

hmhsocialstudies.com VIDEO

INTERACT
WITH HISTORY

The date is August 9, 1974. You are serving your country as an honor guard at the White House. As a member of the military, you've always felt patriotic pride in your government. Now the highest officer of that government, President Richard M. Nixon, is stepping down in disgrace. The trust you once placed in your leaders has been broken.

Explore the Issues

- What are some powers granted to the president?
- What systems exist to protect against abuse of power?
- How can a president lose or restore the nation's trust?

1974 Vice President Gerald R. Ford becomes president after the Watergate scandal forces President Nixon to resign.

1976 President Jimmy Carter is elected president.

1976 Americans celebrate the nation's bicentennial.

1977 The movie *Saturday Night Fever* inspires disco fashion.

1979 A nuclear power accident occurs at Three Mile Island in Pennsylvania.

| 1974 | 1975 | 1976 | 1977 | 1978 | 1979 |

1978 Egyptian and Israeli leaders meet and sign the Camp David Accords with President Carter.

1979 Ayatollah Khomeini seizes power in Iran.

An Age of Limits **999**

PI 2.5   CC Unit 7.V.A.1.a   CC Unit 7.V.A.1.b
PI 3.4   CC Unit 7.V.A.2.a(2)   CC Unit 7.V.A.2.a(3)
         CC Unit 7.V.A.2.a(4)

The Nixon Administration

MAIN IDEA	WHY IT MATTERS NOW	Terms & Names
President Richard M. Nixon tried to steer the country in a conservative direction and away from federal control.	American leaders of the early 1970s laid the foundations for the broad conservative base that exists today.	• Richard M. Nixon • New Federalism • revenue sharing • Family Assistance Plan (FAP) • Southern strategy • stagflation • OPEC (Organization of Petroleum Exporting Countries) • realpolitik • détente • SALT I Treaty

One American's Story

hmhsocialstudies.com
TAKING NOTES
Use the graphic organizer online to take notes on Richard's Nixon's policies and whether they promoted or slowed change.

In November of 1968, **Richard M. Nixon** had just been elected president of the United States. He chose Henry Kissinger to be his special adviser on foreign affairs. During Nixon's second term in 1972, as the United States struggled to achieve an acceptable peace in Vietnam, Kissinger reflected on his relationship with Nixon.

A PERSONAL VOICE HENRY KISSINGER

"I . . . am not at all so sure I could have done what I've done with him with another president. . . . I don't know many leaders who would entrust to their aide the task of negotiating with the North Vietnamese, informing only a tiny group of people of the initiative."

—quoted in *The New Republic*, December 16, 1972

▲ President Nixon *(right)* confers with Henry Kissinger.

Nixon and Kissinger ended America's involvement in Vietnam, but as the war wound down, the nation seemed to enter an era of limits. The economic prosperity that had followed World War II was ending. President Nixon wanted to limit the federal government to reduce its power and to reverse some of Johnson's liberal policies. At the same time, he would seek to restore America's prestige and influence on the world stage—prestige that had been hit hard by the Vietnam experience.

Nixon's New Conservatism

President Richard M. Nixon entered office in 1969 determined to turn America in a more conservative direction. Toward that end, he tried to instill a sense of order into a nation still divided over the continuing Vietnam War.

"DOMESTIC LIFE"

Pulitzer Prize–winning cartoonist Paul Szep frequently used Nixon as the subject of his cartoons. Although President Nixon focused his domestic policy on dismantling a number of Great Society social programs, his chief interest was foreign policy.

SKILLBUILDER
Analyzing Political Cartoons

1. What does the cartoonist suggest about Nixon by showing him leaving with his bags packed?

2. Whom do the children represent in this cartoon?

 SEE SKILLBUILDER HANDBOOK, PAGE R24.

NEW FEDERALISM One of the main items on President Nixon's agenda was to decrease the size and influence of the federal government. Nixon believed that Lyndon Johnson's Great Society programs, by promoting greater federal involvement with social problems, had given the federal government too much responsibility. Nixon's plan, known as **New Federalism,** was to distribute a portion of federal power to state and local governments. **A**

To implement this program, Nixon proposed a plan to give more financial freedom to local governments. Normally, the federal government told state and local governments how to spend their federal money. Under **revenue sharing,** state and local governments could spend their federal dollars however they saw fit within certain limitations. In 1972, the revenue-sharing bill, known as the State and Local Fiscal Assistance Act, became law.

WELFARE REFORM Nixon was not as successful, however, in his attempt to overhaul welfare, which he believed had grown cumbersome and inefficient. In 1969, the president advocated the so-called **Family Assistance Plan (FAP).** Under the FAP, every family of four with no outside income would receive a basic federal payment of $1,600 a year, with a provision to earn up to $4,000 a year in supplemental income. Unemployed participants, excluding mothers of preschool children, would have to take job training and accept any reasonable work offered them.

Nixon presented the plan in conservative terms—as a program that would reduce the supervisory role of the federal government and make welfare recipients responsible for their own lives. The House approved the plan in 1970. However, when the bill reached the Senate, lawmakers from both parties attacked it. Liberal legislators considered the minimum payments too low and the work requirement too stiff, while conservatives objected to the notion of guaranteed income. The bill went down in defeat.

NEW FEDERALISM WEARS TWO FACES In the end, Nixon's New Federalism enhanced several key federal programs as it dismantled others. To win backing for his New Federalism program from a Democrat-controlled Congress, Nixon supported a number of congressional measures to increase federal spending for some social programs. Without fanfare, the Nixon administration increased Social

MAIN IDEA

Summarizing
A What was the goal of Nixon's New Federalism?

AMERICANS WALK ON THE MOON

Not all was political war during the Nixon administration. On July 20, 1969, one of America's long-held dreams became a reality.

Nearly ten years after John F. Kennedy challenged America to put a person on the moon, astronaut Neil Armstrong climbed down the ladder of his lunar module and stepped onto the surface of the moon. "That's one small step for man," Armstrong said, "one giant leap for mankind."

Americans swelled with pride and accomplishment as they watched the historic moon landing on their televisions. Speaking to the astronauts from the White House, President Nixon said, "For every American, this has to be the proudest day of our lives."

▲ Neil Armstrong's photograph of Buzz Aldrin on the moon

hmhsocialstudies.com

INTERACTIVE
Explore the first moon landing.

Security, Medicare, and Medicaid payments and made food stamps more accessible.

However, the president also worked to dismantle some of the nation's social programs. Throughout his term, Nixon tried unsuccessfully to eliminate the Job Corps program that provided job training for the unemployed and in 1970 he vetoed a bill to provide additional funding for Housing and Urban Development. Confronted by laws that he opposed, Nixon also turned to a little-used presidential practice called impoundment. Nixon impounded, or withheld, necessary funds for programs, thus holding up their implementation. By 1973, it was believed that Nixon had impounded almost $15 billion, affecting more than 100 federal programs, including those for health, housing, and education.

The federal courts eventually ordered the release of the impounded funds. They ruled that presidential impoundment was unconstitutional and that only Congress had the authority to decide how federal funds should be spent. Nixon did use his presidential authority to abolish the Office of Economic Opportunity, a cornerstone of Johnson's antipoverty program. **B**

LAW AND ORDER POLITICS As President Nixon fought with both houses of Congress, he also battled the more liberal elements of society, including the antiwar movement. Nixon had been elected in 1968 on a dual promise to end the war in Vietnam and mend the divisiveness within America that the war had created. Throughout his first term, Nixon aggressively moved to fulfill both pledges. The president de-escalated America's involvement in Vietnam and oversaw peace negotiations with North Vietnam. At the same time, he began the "law and order" policies that he had promised his "silent majority"—those middle-class Americans who wanted order restored to a country beset by urban riots and antiwar demonstrations.

To accomplish this, Nixon used the full resources of his office—sometimes illegally. Nixon and members of his staff ordered wiretaps of many left-wing individuals and the Democratic Party offices at the Watergate office building in Washington, D.C. The CIA also investigated and compiled documents on thousands of American dissidents—people who objected to the government's policies. The administration even used the Internal Revenue Service to audit the tax returns of antiwar and civil rights activists. Nixon began building a personal "enemies list" of prominent Americans whom the administration would harass.

Nixon also enlisted the help of his combative vice-president, Spiro T. Agnew, to denounce the opposition. The vice-president confronted the antiwar protesters and then turned his scorn on those who controlled the media, whom he viewed as liberal cheerleaders for the antiwar movement. Known for his colorful quotes, Agnew lashed out at the media and liberals as "an effete [weak] corps of impudent snobs" and "nattering nabobs of negativism."

Nixon's Southern Strategy

Even as President Nixon worked to steer the country along a more conservative course, he had his eyes on the 1972 presidential election. Nixon had won a slim majority in 1968—less than one percent of the popular vote. As president, he began

MAIN IDEA

Analyzing Issues
B In what ways did Nixon both strengthen and weaken federal programs?

working to forge a new conservative coalition to build on his support. In one approach, known as the **Southern strategy,** Nixon tried to attract Southern conservative Democrats by appealing to their unhappiness with federal desegregation policies and a liberal Supreme Court. He also promised to name a Southerner to the Supreme Court.

A NEW SOUTH Since Reconstruction, the South had been a Democratic stronghold. But by 1968 many white Southern Democrats had grown disillusioned with their party. In their eyes, the party—champion of the Great Society and civil rights—had grown too liberal. This conservative backlash first surfaced in the 1968 election, when thousands of Southern Democrats helped former Alabama governor George Wallace, a conservative segregationist running as an independent, carry five Southern states and capture 13 percent of the popular vote.

Nixon wanted these voters. By winning over the Wallace voters and other discontented Democrats, the president and his fellow Republicans hoped not only to keep the White House but also to recapture a majority in Congress. **C**

NIXON SLOWS INTEGRATION To attract white voters in the South, President Nixon decided on a policy of slowing the country's desegregation efforts. In September of 1969, less than a year after being elected president, Nixon made clear his views on civil rights. "There are those who want instant integration and those who want segregation forever. I believe we need to have a middle course between those two extremes," he said.

Throughout his first term, President Nixon worked to reverse several civil rights policies. In 1969, he ordered the Department of Health, Education, and Welfare (HEW) to delay desegregation plans for school districts in South Carolina and Mississippi. Nixon's actions violated the Supreme Court's second *Brown* v. *Board of Education* ruling—which called for the desegregation of schools "with all deliberate speed." In response to an NAACP suit, the high court ordered Nixon to abide by the second Brown ruling. The president did so reluctantly, and by 1972, nearly 90 percent of children in the South attended desegregated schools—up from about 20 percent in 1969.

In a further attempt to chip away at civil rights advances, Nixon opposed the extension of the Voting Rights Act of 1965. The act had added nearly one million African Americans to the voting rolls. Despite the president's opposition, Congress voted to extend the act. **D**

CONTROVERSY OVER BUSING President Nixon then attempted to stop yet another civil rights initiative—the integration of schools through busing. In 1971, the Supreme Court ruled in *Swann* v. *Charlotte-Mecklenburg Board of Education* that school districts may bus students to other schools to end the pattern of all-black or all-white educational institutions. White students and parents in cities such as Boston and Detroit angrily protested busing. One South Boston mother spoke for other white Northerners, many of whom still struggled with the integration process.

★ A PERSONAL VOICE

"I'm not against any individual child. I am not a racist, no matter what those high-and-mighty suburban liberals with their picket signs say. I just won't have my children bused to some . . . slum school, and I don't want children from God knows where coming over here."

—A South Boston mother quoted in *The School Busing Controversy, 1970–75*

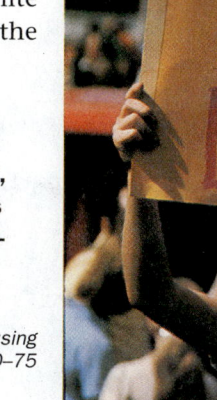

A demonstrator in Boston protests court-ordered school busing during the early 1970s. ▼

Nixon also opposed integration through busing and went on national television to urge Congress to halt the practice. While busing continued in some cities, Nixon had made his position clear to the country—and to the South.

A BATTLE OVER THE SUPREME COURT During the 1968 campaign, Nixon had criticized the Warren Court for being too liberal. Once in the White House, Nixon suddenly found himself with an opportunity to change the direction of the court. During Nixon's first term, four justices, including chief justice Earl Warren, left the bench through retirement. President Nixon quickly moved to put a more conservative face on the Court. In 1969, the Senate approved Nixon's chief justice appointee, U.S. Court of Appeals judge Warren Burger.

Eventually, Nixon placed on the bench three more justices, who tilted the Court in a more conservative direction. However, the newly shaped Court did not always take the conservative route—for example, it handed down the 1971 ruling in favor of racially integrating schools through busing. **E**

MAIN IDEA

Summarizing
E What was Nixon's Southern strategy and how did he implement it?

Confronting a Stagnant Economy

One of the more pressing issues facing Richard Nixon was a troubled economy. Between 1967 and 1973, the United States faced high inflation and high unemployment—a situation economists called **stagflation.**

THE CAUSES OF STAGFLATION The economic problems of the late 1960s and early 1970s had several causes. Chief among them was high inflation—a result of Lyndon Johnson's policy to fund the war and social programs through deficit spending. Also, increased competition in international trade, and a flood of new workers, including women and baby boomers, led to stagflation. Another cause of the nation's economic woes was its heavy dependency on foreign oil. During the 1960s, America received much of its petroleum from the oil-producing countries of the

Dependent on foreign oil, Americans in 1979 wait in line for gas during the oil embargo.

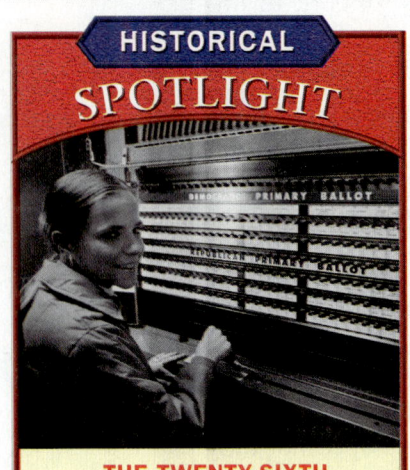

HISTORICAL SPOTLIGHT

THE TWENTY-SIXTH AMENDMENT

During President Nixon's first term, the Twenty-sixth Amendment was ratified in 1971, extending voting rights to Americans 18 years or older. The amendment was one example of efforts in the 1960s and 1970s to expand opportunities to participate in government.

At the time, liberals supported the amendment because they believed that young people were more likely to be liberal. Conservatives opposed it because they didn't want to extend the vote to more liberals.

Opponents also argued that the amendment would be too expensive for states to administer and that 18-year-olds were not mature enough for the responsibility. Many Americans, however, considered it unfair to be asked to fight and die for their country in Vietnam without being allowed to vote.

Middle East. Many of these countries belonged to a cartel called **OPEC (Organization of Petroleum Exporting Countries).** During the 1960s, OPEC gradually raised oil prices. Then in 1973, Egypt and Syria started the Yom Kippur War against Israel. When the United States sent massive military aid to Israel, its longtime ally, Arab oil-producing nations responded by cutting off all oil sales to the United States. When they resumed selling oil to the United States in 1974, the price had quadrupled. This sharp rise in oil prices only worsened the problem of inflation.

NIXON BATTLES STAGFLATION President Nixon took several steps to combat stagflation, but none met with much success. To reverse deficit spending, Nixon attempted to raise taxes and cut the budget. Congress, however, refused to go along with this plan. In another effort to slow inflation, Nixon tried to reduce the amount of money in circulation by urging that interest rates be raised. This measure did little except drive the country into a mild recession, or an overall slowdown of the economy. **F**

In August 1971, the president turned to price and wage controls to stop inflation. He froze workers' wages as well as businesses' prices and fees for 90 days. Inflation eased for a short time, but the recession continued.

MAIN IDEA

Analyzing Causes

F What factors brought on the country's economic problems in the late 1960s and early 1970s?

Nixon's Foreign Policy Triumphs

Richard Nixon admittedly preferred world affairs to domestic policy. "I've always thought this country could run itself domestically without a president," he said in 1968. Throughout his presidency, Nixon's top priority was gaining an honorable peace in Vietnam. At the same time, he also made significant advances in America's relationships with China and the Soviet Union.

KISSINGER AND REALPOLITIK The architect of Nixon's foreign policy was his adviser for national security affairs, Henry Kissinger. Kissinger, who would later become Nixon's secretary of state, promoted a philosophy known as **realpolitik,** from a German term meaning "political realism." According to realpolitik, foreign policy should be based solely on consideration of power, not ideals or moral principles. Kissinger believed in evaluating a nation's power, not its philosophy or beliefs. If a country was weak, Kissinger argued, it was often more practical to ignore that country, even if it was Communist.

Realpolitik marked a departure from the former confrontational policy of containment, which refused to recognize the major Communist countries. On the other hand, Kissinger's philosophy called for the United States to fully confront the powerful nations of the globe. In the world of realpolitik, however, confrontation largely meant negotiation as well as military engagement.

Nixon shared Kissinger's belief in realpolitik, and together the two men adopted a more flexible approach in dealing with Communist nations. They called their policy **détente**—a policy aimed at easing Cold War tensions. One of the most startling applications of détente came in early 1972 when President Nixon—who had risen in politics as a strong anti-Communist—visited Communist China. **G**

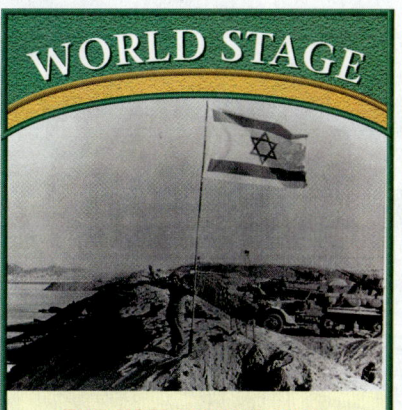

WORLD STAGE

THE YOM KIPPUR WAR

On October 6, 1973, Syria and Egypt invaded Israel on Yom Kippur, the most sacred Jewish holiday. The war—the climax of years of intense border disputes—was short but brutal. Even though fighting lasted only three weeks, as many as 7,700 Egyptians, 7,700 Syrians, and 4,500 Israelis were killed or wounded.

Although the United States supplied massive amounts of military aid to Israel, U.S. officials also worked to broker a cease-fire between the warring nations. In what became known as "shuttle diplomacy," Secretary of State Henry Kissinger traveled back and forth between Middle Eastern countries in an attempt to forge a peace agreement. Kissinger's diplomatic efforts finally paid off. Israel signed a cease-fire with Egypt in January 1974. Four months later in May, Israel signed a cease-fire with Syria.

► President Nixon tours the Great Wall as part of his visit to China in 1972.

NIXON VISITS CHINA Since the takeover of mainland China by the Communists in 1949, the United States had not formally recognized the Chinese Communist government. In late 1971, Nixon reversed that policy by announcing to the nation that he would visit China "to seek the normalization of relations between the two countries."

By going to China, Nixon was trying, in part, to take advantage of the decade-long rift between China and the Soviet Union. China had long criticized the Soviet Union as being too "soft" in its policies against the West. The two Communist superpowers officially broke ties in 1960. Nixon had thought about exploiting the fractured relationship for several years. "We want to have the Chinese with us when we sit down and negotiate with the Russians," he told a reporter in 1968. Upon his arrival at the Beijing Airport in February, 1972, Nixon recalls his meeting with Chinese premier Zhou En-lai.

★ **A PERSONAL VOICE** RICHARD M. NIXON

"I knew that Zhou had been deeply insulted by Foster Dulles's refusal to shake hands with him at the Geneva Conference in 1954. When I reached the bottom step, therefore, I made a point of extending my hand as I walked toward him. When our hands met, one era ended and another began."

—*The Memoirs of Richard Nixon*

Besides its enormous symbolic value, Nixon's visit also was a huge success with the American public. Observers noted that it opened up diplomatic and economic relations with the Chinese and resulted in important agreements between China and the United States. The two nations agreed that neither would try to dominate the Pacific and that both would cooperate in settling disputes peacefully. They also agreed to participate in scientific and cultural exchanges as well as to eventually reunite Taiwan with the mainland. **H**

NIXON TRAVELS TO MOSCOW In May 1972, three months after visiting Beijing, President Nixon headed to Moscow—the first U.S. president ever to visit the

MAIN IDEA

Analyzing Effects
H How did Nixon's trip change the United States' relationship with China?

The Soviet Union regularly displayed its military strength in parades. Shown here is an ICBM in a 1965 parade through Moscow's Red Square.

Soviet Union. Like his visit to China, Nixon's trip to the Soviet Union received wide acclaim. After a series of meetings called the Strategic Arms Limitation Talks (SALT), Nixon and Soviet premier Leonid Brezhnev signed the **SALT I Treaty.** This five-year agreement limited the number of intercontinental ballistic missiles (ICBMs) and submarine-launched missiles to 1972 levels.

The foreign policy triumphs with China and the Soviet Union and the administration's announcement that peace "is at hand" in Vietnam helped reelect Nixon as president in 1972.

But peace in Vietnam proved elusive. The Nixon administration grappled with the war for nearly six more months before withdrawing troops and ending America's involvement in Vietnam. By that time, another issue was about to dominate the Nixon administration—one that would eventually lead to the downfall of the president.

ASSESSMENT

1. TERMS & NAMES For each term or name, write a sentence explaining its significance.

- Richard M. Nixon
- New Federalism
- revenue sharing
- Family Assistance Plan
- Southern strategy
- stagflation
- OPEC (Organization of Petroleum Exporting Countries)
- realpolitik
- détente
- SALT I Treaty

MAIN IDEA

2. TAKING NOTES
In a two-column chart similar to the one shown, list the policies of Richard Nixon that promoted change and those that slowed it down.

Promoted Change	Slowed Change
Policies:	Policies:

In what ways do you think Nixon was most conservative? In what ways was he least conservative? Explain.

CRITICAL THINKING

3. ANALYZING EFFECTS
What were the effects of the Arab OPEC oil embargo on the United States?

4. DRAWING CONCLUSIONS
Why was the timing of Nixon's foreign policy achievements particularly important? Relate his achievements to other events.

5. EVALUATING DECISIONS
In your opinion, did Nixon's policy of détente help solve the country's major foreign policy problems? Support your answer with evidence from the text. **Think About:**

- the definition and origin of détente
- the effect of détente on U.S. dealings with Communist countries
- the effect of détente on the American public

PI 3.2

CC Unit 7.V.A.3.a   CC Unit 7.V.A.3.b
CC Unit 7.V.A.3.c   CC Unit 7.V.A.3.d

Watergate: Nixon's Downfall

MAIN IDEA	WHY IT MATTERS NOW	Terms & Names
President Richard Nixon's involvement in the Watergate scandal forced him to resign from office.	The Watergate scandal raised questions of public trust that still affect how the public and media skeptically view politicians.	• impeachment • Watergate • H. R. Haldeman • John Ehrlichman • John Mitchell • Committee to Reelect the President • John Sirica • Saturday Night Massacre

One American's Story

On July 25, 1974, Representative Barbara Jordan of Texas, a member of the House Judiciary Committee, along with the other committee members, considered whether to recommend that President Nixon be impeached for "high crimes and misdemeanors." Addressing the room, Jordan cited the Constitution in urging her fellow committee members to investigate whether impeachment was appropriate.

★ A PERSONAL VOICE BARBARA JORDAN

" 'We the people'—it is a very eloquent beginning. But when the Constitution of the United States was completed . . . I was not included in that 'We the people'. . . . But through the process of amendment, interpretation, and court decision, I have finally been included in 'We the people'. . . . Today . . . [my] faith in the Constitution is whole. It is complete. It is total. I am not going to sit here and be an idle spectator in the diminution, the subversion, the destruction of the Constitution. . . . Has the President committed offenses . . . which the Constitution will not tolerate? "

—quoted in *Notable Black American Women*

▲ U.S. Representative Barbara Jordan, 1974.

The committee eventually voted to recommend the **impeachment** of Richard Nixon for his role in the Watergate scandal. However, before Congress could take further action against him, the president resigned. Nixon's resignation, the first by a U.S. president, was the climax of a scandal that led to the imprisonment of 25 government officials and caused the most serious constitutional crisis in the United States since the impeachment of Andrew Johnson in 1868.

President Nixon and His White House

The **Watergate** scandal centered on the Nixon administration's attempt to cover up a burglary of the Democratic National Committee (DNC) headquarters at the Watergate office and apartment complex in Washington, D.C. However, the

Watergate story began long before the actual burglary. Many historians believe that Watergate truly began with the personalities of Richard Nixon and those of his advisers, as well as with the changing role of the presidency.

AN IMPERIAL PRESIDENCY When Richard Nixon took office, the executive branch—as a result of the Great Depression, World War II, and the Cold War—had become the most powerful branch of government. In his book *The Imperial Presidency*, the historian Arthur Schlesinger, Jr., argued that by the time Richard Nixon became president, the executive branch had taken on an air of imperial, or supreme, authority.

President Nixon settled into this imperial role with ease. Nixon believed, as he told a reporter in 1980, that "a president must not be one of the crowd. . . . People . . . don't want him to be down there saying, 'Look, I'm the same as you.'" Nixon expanded the power of the presidency with little thought to constitutional checks, as when he impounded funds for federal programs that he opposed, or when he ordered troops to invade Cambodia without congressional approval. **A**

MAIN IDEA

Summarizing
A What is meant by "imperial presidency"?

THE PRESIDENT'S MEN As he distanced himself from Congress, Nixon confided in a small and fiercely loyal group of advisers. They included **H. R. Haldeman,** White House chief of staff; **John Ehrlichman,** chief domestic adviser; and **John Mitchell,** Nixon's former attorney general. These men had played key roles in Nixon's 1968 election victory and now helped the president direct White House policy.

These men also shared President Nixon's desire for secrecy and the consolidation of power. Critics charged that these men, through their personalities and their attitude toward the presidency, developed a sense that they were somehow above the law. This sense would, in turn, prompt President Nixon and his advisers to cover up their role in Watergate, and fuel the coming scandal.

The Inner Circle

H.R. Haldeman
Chief of Staff

John Ehrlichman
Chief Domestic Adviser

John N. Mitchell
Attorney General

John W. Dean III
Presidential Counsel

The Drive Toward Reelection

Throughout his political career, Richard Nixon lived with the overwhelming fear of losing elections. By the end of the 1972 reelection campaign, Nixon's campaign team sought advantages by any means possible, including an attempt to steal information from the DNC headquarters.

MAIN IDEA

Analyzing Motives
B Why would the Nixon campaign team take such a risky action as breaking into the opposition's headquarters?

A BUNGLED BURGLARY At 2:30 A.M., June 17, 1972, a guard at the Watergate complex in Washington, D.C., caught five men breaking into the campaign headquarters of the DNC. The burglars planned to photograph documents outlining Democratic Party strategy and to place wiretaps, or "bugs," on the office telephones. The press soon discovered that the group's leader, James McCord, was a former CIA agent. He was also a security coordinator for a group known as the **Committee to Reelect the President** (CRP). John Mitchell, who had resigned as attorney general to run Nixon's reelection campaign, was the CRP's director. **B**

VIDEO
John Dean on Nixon's Secrets

🔗 hmhsocialstudies.com

Just three days after the burglary, H. R. Haldeman noted in his diary Nixon's near obsession with how to respond to the break-in.

★ **A PERSONAL VOICE** H. R. HALDEMAN

"The P[resident] was concerned about what our counterattack is. . . . He raised it again several times during the day, and it obviously is bothering him. . . . He called at home tonight, saying that he wanted to change the plan for his press conference and have it on Thursday instead of tomorrow, so that it won't look like he's reacting to the Democratic break-in thing."

—*The Haldeman Diaries*

The cover-up quickly began. Workers shredded all incriminating documents in Haldeman's office. The White House, with President Nixon's consent, asked the CIA to urge the FBI to stop its investigations into the burglary on the grounds of national security. In addition, the CRP passed out nearly $450,000 to the Watergate burglars to buy their silence after they were indicted in September of 1972. **C**

Throughout the 1972 campaign, the Watergate burglary generated little interest among the American public and media. Only the *Washington Post* and two of its reporters, Bob Woodward and Carl Bernstein, kept on the story. In a series of articles, the reporters uncovered information that linked numerous members of the administration to the burglary. The White House denied each new *Post* allegation. Upon learning of an upcoming story that tied him to the burglars, John Mitchell told Bernstein, "That's the most sickening thing I ever heard."

The firm White House response to the charges, and its promises of imminent peace in Vietnam, proved effective in the short term. In November, Nixon was reelected by a landslide over liberal Democrat George S. McGovern. But Nixon's popular support was soon to unravel.

The Cover-Up Unravels

In January 1973, the trial of the Watergate burglars began. The trial's presiding judge, **John Sirica,** made clear his belief that the men had not acted alone. On March 20, a few days before the burglars were scheduled to be sentenced, James McCord sent a letter to Sirica, in which he indicated that he had lied under oath. He also hinted that powerful members of the Nixon administration had been involved in the break-in.

THE SENATE INVESTIGATES WATERGATE McCord's revelation of possible White House involvement in the burglary aroused public interest in Watergate. President Nixon moved quickly to stem the growing concern. On April 30, 1973, Nixon dismissed White House counsel John Dean and announced the resignations of Haldeman, Ehrlichman, and Attorney General Richard Kleindienst, who had recently replaced John Mitchell following Mitchell's resignation. The president then went on television and denied any attempt at a cover-up. He announced that he was

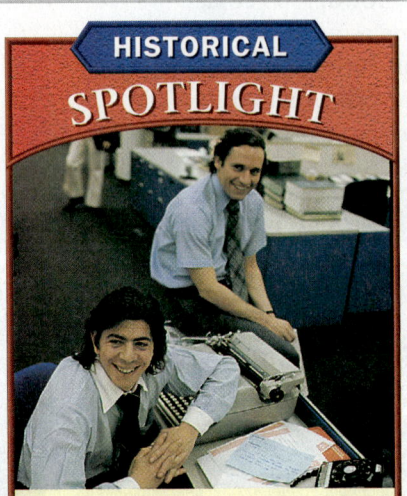

HISTORICAL SPOTLIGHT

WOODWARD AND BERNSTEIN

Bob Woodward and Carl Bernstein of the *Washington Post* seemed an unlikely team. Woodward, 29 (at right in the photo above), had graduated from Yale, while the 28-year-old Bernstein was a college dropout.

As the two men dug deeper into the Watergate break-in, a mysterious inside source helped them to uncover the scandal. For more than 30 years the reporters refused to identify their source. Then in June 2005, W. Mark Felt, the No. 2 man at the FBI at the time of Watergate, stepped forward and identified himself as the inside source of the reporters' information.

While people lauded the two reporters for their dogged determination, some Nixon officials remain bitter toward them.

Woodward defended the reporters' work, saying, "We tried to do our job and, in fact, if you look at it, our coverage was pretty conservative."

MAIN IDEA

Chronological Order

C What steps did the White House take to cover up its involvement in the Watergate break-in?

appointing a new attorney general, Elliot Richardson, and was authorizing him to appoint a special prosecutor to investigate Watergate. "There can be no whitewash at the White House," Nixon said.

The president's reassurances, however, came too late. In May 1973, the Senate began its own investigation of Watergate. A special committee, chaired by Senator Samuel James Ervin of North Carolina, began to call administration officials to give testimony. Throughout the summer millions of Americans sat by their televisions as the "president's men" testified one after another.

STARTLING TESTIMONY John Dean delivered the first bomb. In late June, during more than 30 hours of testimony, Dean provided a startling answer to Senator Howard Baker's repeated question, "What did the president know and when did he know it?" The former White House counsel declared that President Nixon had been deeply involved in the cover-up. Dean referred to one meeting in which he and the president, along with several advisers, discussed strategies for continuing the deceit.

The White House strongly denied Dean's charges. The hearings had suddenly reached an impasse as the committee attempted to sort out who was telling the truth. The answer came in July from an unlikely source: presidential aide Alexander Butterfield. Butterfield stunned the committee when he revealed that Nixon had taped virtually all of his presidential conversations. Butterfield later claimed that the taping system was installed "to help Nixon write his memoirs." However, for the Senate committee, the tapes were the key to revealing what Nixon knew and when he knew it. **D**

> "*Divine right went out with the American Revolution and doesn't belong to White House aides.*"
>
> SENATOR SAM ERVIN

MAIN IDEA

Drawing Conclusions
D What was significant about the revelation that Nixon taped his conversations?

THE SATURDAY NIGHT MASSACRE
A year-long battle for the "Nixon tapes" followed. Archibald Cox, the special prosecutor whom Elliot Richardson had appointed to investigate the case, took the president to court in October 1973 to obtain the tapes. Nixon refused and ordered Attorney General Richardson to fire Cox. In what became known as the **Saturday Night Massacre,** Richardson refused the order and resigned. The deputy attorney general also refused the order, and he was fired. Solicitor General Robert Bork finally fired Cox. However, Cox's replacement, Leon Jaworski, proved equally determined to get the tapes. Several months after the "massacre," the House Judiciary Committee began examining the possibility of an impeachment hearing. **E**

The entire White House appeared to be under siege. Just days before the Saturday Night Massacre, Vice President Spiro Agnew had resigned after it was revealed that he had accepted bribes from engineering firms while governor of Maryland. Agnew pleaded *nolo contendere* (no contest) to the charge. Acting under the Twenty-fifth

MAIN IDEA

Summarizing
E What events led to the Saturday Night Massacre?

▲ The Watergate hearings were chaired by Senator Sam Ervin, shown *(top left)* with Sam Dash, chief counsel to the Senate Watergate Committee. John Dean's testimony *(above)* stunned the nation.

Amendment, Nixon nominated the House minority leader, Gerald R. Ford, as his new vice-president. Congress quickly confirmed the nomination.

The Fall of a President

In March 1974, a grand jury indicted seven presidential aides on charges of conspiracy, obstruction of justice, and perjury. The investigation was closing in on the president of the United States.

▲
The original Nixon White House tape recorder and tape from the 1970s.

NIXON RELEASES THE TAPES In the spring of 1974, President Nixon told a television audience that he was releasing 1,254 pages of edited transcripts of White House conversations about Watergate. Nixon's offering failed to satisfy investigators, who demanded the unedited tapes. Nixon refused, and the case went before the Supreme Court. On July 24, 1974, the high court ruled unanimously that the president must surrender the tapes. The Court rejected Nixon's argument that doing so would violate national security. Evidence involving possible criminal activity could not be withheld, even by a president. President Nixon maintained that he had done nothing wrong. At a press conference in November 1973, he proclaimed defiantly, "I am not a crook."

Background
President Nixon claimed executive privilege—the right to withhold information to protect confidentiality or the public good. In *United States* v. *Nixon* (1974), the Supreme Court found that the President had not made a case for executive privilege.

THE PRESIDENT RESIGNS Even without holding the original tapes, the House Judiciary Committee determined that there was enough evidence to impeach Richard Nixon. On July 27, the committee approved three articles of impeachment, charging the president with obstruction of justice, abuse of power, and contempt of Congress for refusing to obey a congressional subpoena to release the tapes.

Analyzing *Political Cartoons*

THE WHITE HOUSE TAPES

During the Watergate hearings a bombshell exploded when it was revealed that President Nixon secretly tape-recorded all conversations in the Oval Office. Although Nixon hoped the tapes would one day help historians document the triumphs of his presidency, they were used to confirm his guilt.

SKILLBUILDER
Analyzing Political Cartoons
1. What does this cartoon imply about privacy during President Nixon's term in office?
2. What building has been transformed into a giant tape recorder?

 SEE SKILLBUILDER HANDBOOK, PAGE R24.

AUTH copyright © Philadelphia Inquirer. Reprinted with permission of Universal Press Syndicate. All rights reserved.

On August 5, Nixon released the tapes. They contained many gaps, and one tape revealed a disturbing 18½-minute gap. According to the White House, Rose Mary Woods, President Nixon's secretary, accidentally erased part of a conversation between H. R. Haldeman and Nixon. More importantly, a tape dated June 23, 1972—six days after the Watergate break-in— that contained a conversation between Nixon and Haldeman, disclosed the evidence investigators needed. Not only had the president known about the role of members of his administration in the burglary, he had agreed to the plan to obstruct the FBI's investigation.

The evidence now seemed overwhelming. On August 8, 1974, before the full House vote on the articles of impeachment began, President Nixon announced his resignation from office. Defiant as always, Nixon admitted no guilt. He merely said that some of his judgments "were wrong." The next day, Nixon and his wife, Pat, returned home to California. A short time later, Gerald Ford was sworn in as the 38th president of the United States.

THE EFFECTS OF WATERGATE The effects of Watergate have endured long after Nixon's resignation. Eventually, 25 members of the Nixon Administration were convicted and served prison terms for crimes connected to Watergate. Along with the divisive war in Vietnam, Watergate produced a deep disillusionment with the "imperial" presidency. In the years following Vietnam and Watergate, the American public and the media developed a general cynicism about public officials that still exists today. Watergate remains the scandal and investigative story against which all others are measured.

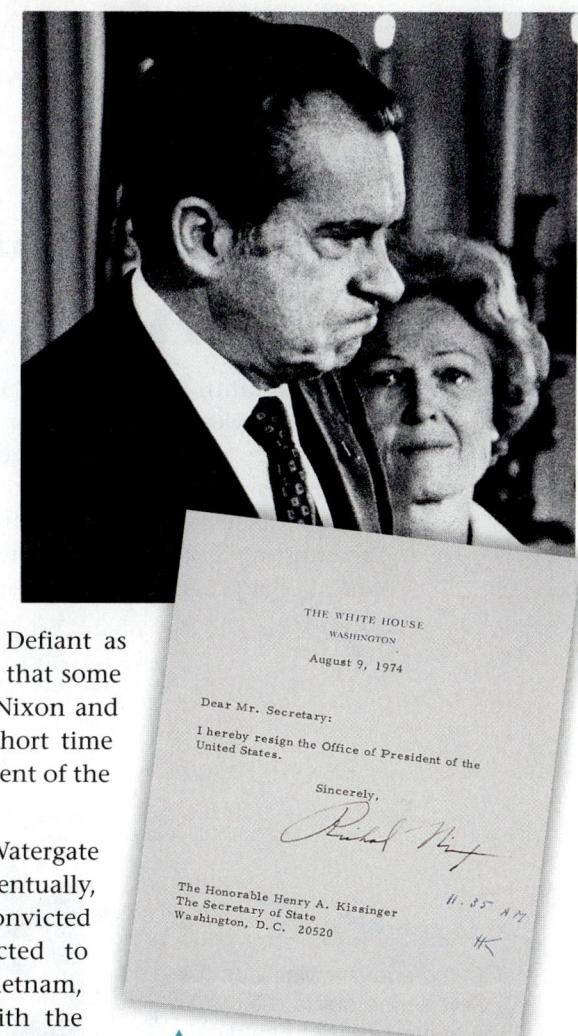

▲ With wife Pat looking on, Richard Nixon bids farewell to his staff on his final day as president. Nixon's resignation letter is shown above.

ASSESSMENT

1. **TERMS & NAMES** For each term or name, write a sentence explaining its significance.
   - impeachment
   - Watergate
   - H. R. Haldeman
   - John Ehrlichman
   - John Mitchell
   - Committee to Reelect the President
   - John Sirica
   - Saturday Night Massacre

MAIN IDEA

2. **TAKING NOTES**
   Use a time line like the one below to trace the events of the Watergate scandal.

   Which event made Nixon's downfall certain?

CRITICAL THINKING

3. **HYPOTHESIZING**
   If Nixon had admitted to and apologized for the Watergate break-in, how might subsequent events have been different? Explain.
   Think About:
   - the extent of the cover-up
   - the impact of the cover-up
   - Nixon's public image

4. **ANALYZING EVENTS**
   How did the Watergate scandal create a constitutional crisis?

5. **EVALUATING**
   Do you think that Nixon would have been forced to resign if the tapes had not existed? Explain your answer.

Television Reflects American Life

From May until November 1973, the Senate Watergate hearings were the biggest daytime TV viewing event of the year. Meanwhile, television programming began to more closely reflect the realities of American life. Shows more often addressed relevant issues, more African-American characters appeared, and working women as well as homemakers were portrayed. In addition, the newly established Public Broadcasting System began showing many issue-oriented programs and expanded educational programming for children.

DIVERSITY ▶

Chico and the Man was the first series set in a Mexican-American barrio, East Los Angeles. The program centered on the relationship between Ed Brown, a cranky garage owner, and Chico Rodriguez, an optimistic young mechanic Brown reluctantly hired.

◀ SOCIAL VALUES

All in the Family was the most popular series of the 1970s. It told the story of a working-class family, headed by the bigoted Archie Bunker and his long-suffering wife, Edith. Through the barbs Bunker traded with his son-in-law and his African-American neighbor, George Jefferson, the show dealt openly with the divisions in American society.

◀ **INDEPENDENT WOMEN**

The Mary Tyler Moore Show depicted Mary Richards, a single woman living in Minneapolis and working as an assistant manager in a local TV news department. Mary symbolized the young career woman of the 1970s.

▼ **CULTURAL IDENTITY**

The miniseries *Roots*, based on a book by Alex Haley, told the saga of several generations of an African-American family. The eight-part story began with Kunta Kinte, who was captured outside his West African village and taken to America as a slave. It ended with his great-grandson's setting off for a new life as a free man. The groundbreaking series, broadcast in January 1977, was one of the most-watched television events in history.

TV EVENTS OF THE 1970s

- A congressional ban on TV cigarette commercials took effect in 1971.

- ABC negotiated an $8-million-a-year contract to televise *Monday Night Football*, first broadcast in September 1970.

- In 1972, President Nixon, accompanied by TV cameras and reporters from the major networks, made a groundbreaking visit to China.

- *Saturday Night Live*—a show that would launch the careers of Dan Aykroyd, Jane Curtin, Eddie Murphy, and many other comic actors—premiered in October 1975.

- WTCG-TV (later WTBS) in Atlanta, owned by Ted Turner, became the basis of the first true satellite-delivered "superstation" in 1976.

- In November 1979, ABC began broadcasting late-night updates on the hostage crisis in Iran. These reports evolved into the program *Nightline* with Ted Koppel.

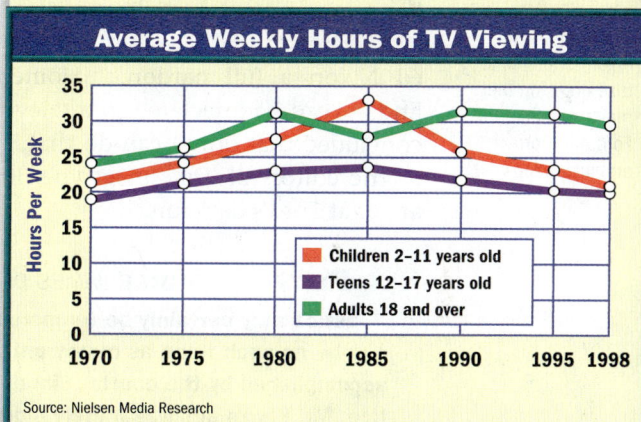

Average Weekly Hours of TV Viewing

Hours Per Week (y-axis: 0, 5, 10, 15, 20, 25, 30, 35)

x-axis: 1970, 1975, 1980, 1985, 1990, 1995, 1998

- Children 2–11 years old
- Teens 12–17 years old
- Adults 18 and over

Source: Nielsen Media Research

THINKING CRITICALLY

CONNECT TO HISTORY

1. **Analyzing Causes** In what ways did television change to reflect American society in the 1970s? What factors might have influenced these changes?

 SEE SKILLBUILDER HANDBOOK, PAGE R7.

CONNECT TO TODAY

2. **Creating a Graph** Use the Internet or an almanac to find data on the number of televisions owned in the United States and the number of hours of TV watched every day. Make a graph that displays the data.

hmhsocialstudies.com **RESEARCH WEB LINKS**

The Ford and Carter Years

MAIN IDEA	WHY IT MATTERS NOW	Terms & Names

<table>
<tr>
<td>The Ford and Carter administrations attempted to remedy the nation's worst economic crisis in decades.</td>
<td>Maintaining a stable national economy has remained a top priority for every president since Ford and Carter.</td>
<td>
• Gerald R. Ford
• Jimmy Carter
• National Energy Act
• human rights
• Camp David Accords
• Ayatollah Ruhollah Khomeini
</td>
</tr>
</table>

One American's Story

hmhsocialstudies.com
TAKING NOTES

Use the graphic organizer online to take notes on the major events of the Ford and Carter administrations.

James D. Denney couldn't believe what he was hearing. Barely a month after Richard Nixon had resigned amid the Watergate scandal, President **Gerald R. Ford** had granted Nixon a full pardon. "[S]omeone must write, 'The End,'" Ford had declared in a televised statement. "I have concluded that only I can do that." Denney wrote a letter to the editors of *Time* magazine, in which he voiced his anger at Ford's decision.

A PERSONAL VOICE JAMES D. DENNEY

" Justice may certainly be tempered by mercy, but there can be no such thing as mercy until justice has been accomplished by the courts. Since it circumvented justice, Mr. Ford's act was merely indulgent favoritism, a bland and unworthy substitute for mercy. "

—*Time*, September 23, 1974

James Denney's feelings were typical of the anger and the disillusionment with the presidency that many Americans felt in the aftermath of the Watergate scandal. During the 1970s, Presidents Gerald Ford and Jimmy Carter sought to restore America's faith in its leaders. At the same time, both men had to focus much of their attention on battling the nation's worsening economic situation.

▲ Two women protest President Ford's pardon of Richard Nixon.

Ford Travels a Rough Road

Upon taking office, Gerald R. Ford urged Americans to put the Watergate scandal behind them. "Our long national nightmare is over," he declared. The nation's nightmarish economy persisted, however, and Ford's policies offered little relief.

Ford appointed Nelson Rockefeller, a former governor of New York, as vice president. Both Ford and Rockefeller became vice president through the Twenty-fifth Amendment, which states that if the office is vacant the president may appoint someone to fill the position.

MAIN IDEA

Making Inferences

Ⓐ Why was Ford's call for voluntary actions to help the economy unsuccessful?

"A FORD, NOT A LINCOLN" Gerald Ford seemed to many to be a likable and honest man. Upon becoming vice president after Spiro Agnew's resignation, Ford candidly admitted his limitations. "I'm a Ford, not a Lincoln," he remarked. On September 8, 1974, President Ford pardoned Richard Nixon in an attempt to move the country beyond Watergate. The move cost Ford a good deal of public support.

FORD TRIES TO "WHIP" INFLATION By the time Ford took office, America's economy had gone from bad to worse. Both inflation and unemployment continued to rise. After the massive OPEC oil-price increases in 1973, gasoline and heating oil costs had soared, pushing inflation from 6 percent to over 10 percent by the end of 1974. Ford responded with a program of massive citizen action, called "Whip Inflation Now" or WIN. The president called on Americans to cut back on their use of oil and gas and to take other energy-saving measures.

In the absence of incentives, though, the plan fell flat. Ford then tried to curb inflation through a "tight money" policy. He cut government spending and encouraged the Federal Reserve Board to restrict credit through higher interest rates. These actions triggered the worst economic recession in 40 years. As Ford implemented his economic programs, he continually battled a Democratic Congress intent on pushing its own economic agenda. During his two years as president, Ford vetoed more than 50 pieces of legislation. Ⓐ

Ford's Foreign Policy

Ford fared slightly better in the international arena. He relied heavily on Henry Kissinger, who continued to hold the key position of secretary of state.

CARRYING OUT NIXON'S FOREIGN POLICIES Following Kissinger's advice, Ford pushed ahead with Nixon's policy of negotiation with China and the Soviet Union. In November 1974, he met with Soviet premier Leonid Brezhnev. Less than a year later, he traveled to Helsinki, Finland, where 35 nations, including the Soviet Union, signed the Helsinki Accords—a series of agreements that promised greater cooperation between the nations of Eastern and Western Europe. The Helsinki Accords would be Ford's greatest presidential accomplishment.

ONGOING TURMOIL IN SOUTHEAST ASIA Like presidents before him, Ford encountered trouble in Southeast Asia. The 1973 cease-fire in Vietnam had broken down. Heavy fighting resumed and Ford asked Congress for over $722 million to help South Vietnam. Congress refused. Without American financial help, South Vietnam surrendered to the North in 1975. In the same year, the Communist government of Cambodia seized the U.S. merchant ship *Mayagüez* in the Gulf of Siam. President Ford responded with a massive show of military force to rescue 39 crew members aboard the ship. The operation cost the lives of 41 U.S. troops. Critics argued that the mission had cost more lives than it had saved.

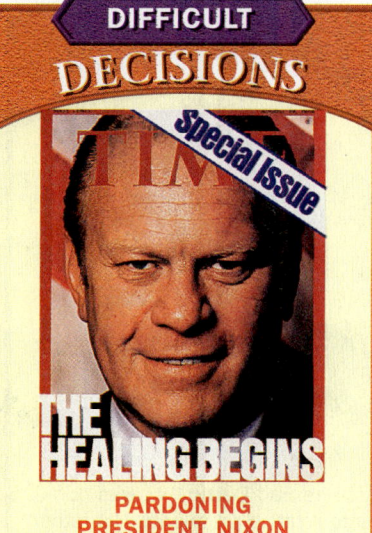

DIFFICULT DECISIONS

THE HEALING BEGINS

PARDONING PRESIDENT NIXON

President Ford's pardon of Richard Nixon outraged many Americans. But President Ford argued that the pardon of Richard Nixon was in the country's best interest. In the event of a Watergate trial, Ford argued, "ugly passions would again be aroused. . . . And the credibility of our free institutions . . . would again be challenged at home and abroad." Ford called the pardon decision "the most difficult of my life, by far."

In 2001, after more than 25 years, Ford received the John F. Kennedy Profiles in Courage Award for his courageous decision in the face of public opposition.

1. How might the country have been affected if a former United States president had gone on trial for possible criminal wrongdoing?

2. If you had been in President Ford's position, would you have pardoned Richard Nixon? Why or why not?

Carter Enters the White House

Gerald Ford won the Republican nomination for president in 1976 after fending off a powerful conservative challenge from former California governor Ronald Reagan. Because the Republicans seemed divided over Ford's leadership, the Democrats confidently eyed the White House. "We could run an aardvark this year and win," predicted one Democratic leader. The Democratic nominee was indeed a surprise: a nationally unknown peanut farmer and former governor of Georgia, **Jimmy Carter.**

MR. CARTER GOES TO WASHINGTON During the post-Watergate era, cynicism toward the Washington establishment ran high. The soft-spoken, personable man from Plains, Georgia, promised to restore integrity to the nation's highest office, "I will never tell a lie to the American people."

Throughout the presidential campaign, Carter and Ford squared off over the key issues of inflation, energy, and unemployment. On Election Day, Jimmy Carter won by a narrow margin, claiming 40.8 million popular votes to Ford's 39.1 million. **B**

From the very beginning, the new first family brought a down-to-earth style to Washington. After settling into office, Carter stayed in touch with the people by holding Roosevelt-like "fireside chats" on radio and television.

Carter failed to reach out to Congress in a similar way, refusing to play the "insider" game of deal making. Relying mainly on a team of advisers from Georgia, Carter even alienated congressional Democrats. Both parties on Capitol Hill often joined to sink the president's budget proposals, as well as his major policy reforms of tax and welfare programs.

Carter's Domestic Agenda

Like Gerald Ford, President Carter focused much of his attention on battling the country's energy and economic crises but was unable to bring the United States out of its economic slump.

CONFRONTING THE ENERGY CRISIS Carter considered the energy crisis the most important issue facing the nation. A large part of the problem, the president believed, was America's reliance on imported oil. On April 18, 1977, during a fireside chat, Carter urged his fellow Americans to cut their consumption of oil and gas.

This 1976 ▶ campaign toy exaggerates Jimmy Carter's well-known smile and parodies his occupation as a peanut farmer.

A PERSONAL VOICE JIMMY CARTER

"The energy crisis . . . is a problem . . . likely to get progressively worse through the rest of this century. . . . Our decision about energy will test the character of the American people. . . . This difficult effort will be the 'moral equivalent of war,' except that we will be uniting our efforts to build and not to destroy."

—quoted in *Keeping Faith*

In addition, Carter presented Congress with more than 100 proposals on energy conservation and development. Representatives from oil- and gas-producing states fiercely resisted some of the proposals. Automobile manufacturers also lobbied against gas-rationing provisions. "It was impossible for me to imagine the bloody legislative battles we would have to win," Carter later wrote.

Out of the battle came the **National Energy Act.** The act placed a tax on gas-guzzling cars, removed price controls on oil and natural gas produced in the United States, and extended tax credits for the development of alternative energy. With the help of the act, as well as voluntary conservation measures, U.S. dependence on foreign oil had eased slightly by 1979. **C**

THE ECONOMIC CRISIS WORSENS Unfortunately, these energy-saving measures could do little to combat a sudden new economic crisis. In the summer of 1979, renewed violence in the Middle East produced a second major fuel shortage in the United States. To make matters worse, OPEC announced another major price hike. In 1979 inflation soared from 7.6 percent to 11.3 percent.

Faced with increasing pressure to act, Carter attempted an array of measures, none of which worked. Carter's scattershot approach convinced many people that he had no economic policy at all. Carter fueled this feeling of uncertainty by delivering his now-famous "malaise" speech, in which he complained of a "crisis of spirit" that had struck "at the very heart and soul of our national will." Carter's address made many Americans feel that their president had given up.

By 1980, inflation had climbed to nearly 14 percent, the highest rate since 1947. The standard of living in the United States slipped from first place to fifth place in the world. Carter's popularity slipped along with it. This economic downswing—and Carter's inability to solve it during an election year—was one key factor in sending Ronald Reagan to the White House.

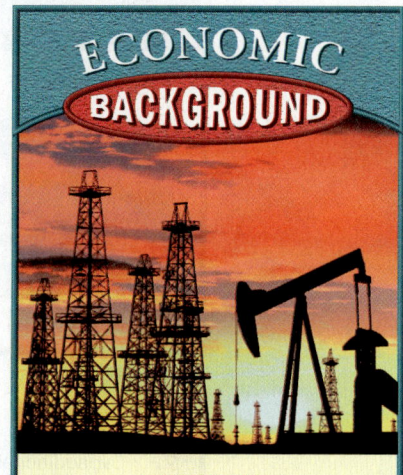

ECONOMIC BACKGROUND

THE 1980s TEXAS OIL BOOM

The economic crisis that gripped the country in the late 1970s was, in large part, caused by the increased cost of oil. Members of the OPEC cartel raised the price of oil by agreeing to restrict oil production. The resulting decrease in the supply of oil in the market caused the price to go up.

Most Americans were hurt by the high energy prices. However, in areas that produced oil, such as Texas, the rise in prices led to a booming economy in the early 1980's. For example, real-estate values—for land on which to drill for oil, as well as for office space in cities like Houston and Dallas—increased markedly.

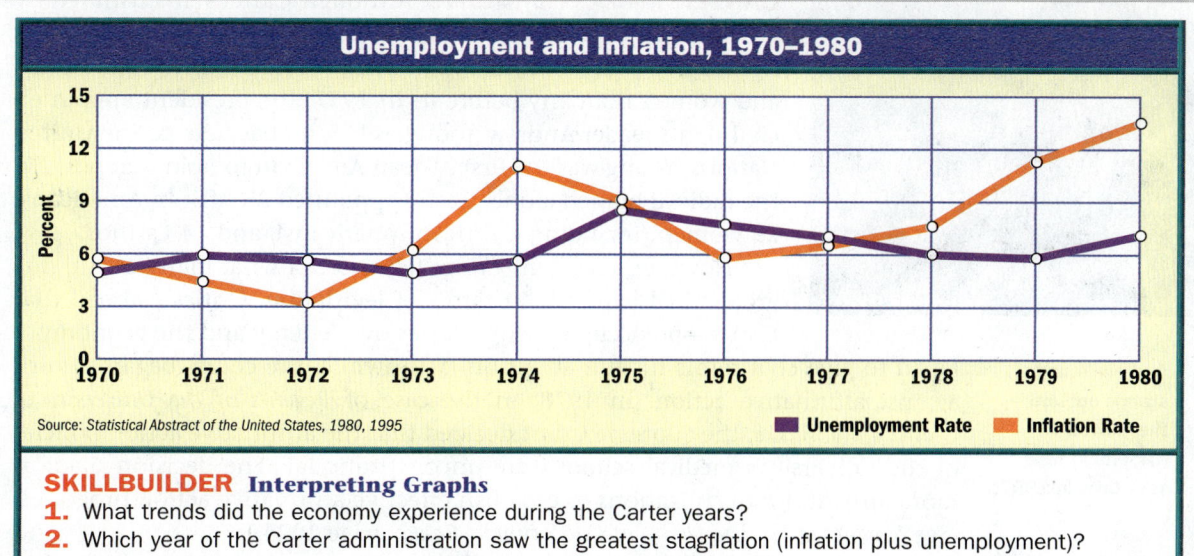

Unemployment and Inflation, 1970–1980

Source: *Statistical Abstract of the United States, 1980, 1995*

■ Unemployment Rate   ■ Inflation Rate

SKILLBUILDER Interpreting Graphs
1. What trends did the economy experience during the Carter years?
2. Which year of the Carter administration saw the greatest stagflation (inflation plus unemployment)?

Nonfarm Employment by Sector, 1950–2000

1950
Services 59%
Goods 41%

1980
Services 72%
Goods 28%

2000
Services 80%
Goods 20%

Sources: *Statistical Abstract of the United States, 2000*; U.S. Bureau of Labor Statistics; *Historical Statistics of the United States*

SKILLBUILDER Interpreting Graphs
1. How much greater was the percentage of employment in service industries in 1980 than in 1950?
2. What additional change is shown by 2000? Has this trend continued into the 2000s?

A CHANGING ECONOMY Many of the economic problems Jimmy Carter struggled with resulted from long-term trends in the economy. Since the 1950s, the rise of automation and foreign competition had reduced the number of manufacturing jobs. At the same time, the service sector of the economy expanded rapidly. This sector includes industries such as communications, transportation, and retail trade.

The rise of the service sector and the decline of manufacturing jobs meant big changes for some American workers. Workers left out of manufacturing jobs faced an increasingly complex job market. Many of the higher-paying service jobs required more education or specialized skills than did manufacturing jobs. The lower-skilled service jobs usually did not pay well.

Growing overseas competition during the 1970s caused further change in America's economy. The booming economies of West Germany and countries on the Pacific Rim (such as Japan, Taiwan, and Korea) cut into many U.S. markets. Many of the nation's primary industries—iron and steel, rubber, clothing, automobiles—had to cut back production, lay off workers, and even close plants. Especially hard-hit were the automotive industries of the Northeast. There, high energy costs, foreign competition, and computerized production led companies to eliminate tens of thousands of jobs. **D**

MAIN IDEA

Analyzing Causes
D What factors played a role in America's economic stagnation?

CARTER AND CIVIL RIGHTS Although Carter felt frustrated by the country's economic woes, he took special pride in his civil rights record. His administration included more African Americans and women than any before it. In 1977, the president appointed civil rights leader Andrew Young as U.S. ambassador to the United Nations. Young was the first African American to hold that post. To the judicial branch alone, Carter appointed 28 African Americans, 29 women (including 6 African Americans), and 14 Latinos.

However, President Carter fell short of what many civil rights groups had expected in terms of legislation. Critics claimed that Carter—preoccupied with battles over energy and the economy—failed to give civil rights his full attention. Meanwhile, the courts began to turn against affirmative action. In 1978, in the case of *Regents of the University of California* v. *Bakke*, the Supreme Court decided that the affirmative action policies of the university's medical school were unconstitutional. The decision made it more difficult for organizations to establish effective affirmative action programs. (See *Regents of the University of California* v. *Bakke*, page 1024.)

▲
Andrew Young stands outside the United Nations in New York City, in 1997.

A Human Rights Foreign Policy

Background

Carter used many diplomatic tools in his foreign policy. For example, when the Soviet Union invaded Afghanistan in 1979, Carter blocked grain shipments to the Soviet Union and announced that the United States would not take part in the 1980 Summer Olympics to be held in Moscow.

Jimmy Carter rejected the philosophy of realpolitik—the pragmatic policy of negotiating with powerful nations despite their behavior—and strived for a foreign policy committed to human rights.

ADVANCING HUMAN RIGHTS Jimmy Carter, like Woodrow Wilson, sought to use moral principles as a guide for U.S. foreign policy. He believed that the United States needed to commit itself to promoting **human rights**—such as the freedoms and liberties listed in the Declaration of Independence and the Bill of Rights—throughout the world.

Putting his principles into practice, President Carter cut off military aid to Argentina and Brazil, countries that had good relations with the United States but had imprisoned or tortured thousands of their own citizens. Carter followed up this action by establishing a Bureau of Human Rights in the State Department.

Carter's philosophy was not without its critics. Supporters of the containment policy felt that the president's policy undercut allies such as Nicaragua, a dictatorial but anti-Communist country. Others argued that by supporting dictators in South Korea and the Philippines, Carter was acting inconsistently. In 1977, Carter's policies drew further criticism when his administration announced that it planned to give up ownership of the Panama Canal. **E**

YIELDING THE PANAMA CANAL Since 1914, when the United States obtained full ownership over the Panama Canal, Panamanians had resented having their nation split in half by a foreign power. In 1977, the two nations agreed to two treaties, one of which turned over control of the Panama Canal to Panama on December 31, 1999.

In 1978, the U.S. Senate, which had to ratify each treaty, approved the agreements by a vote of 68 to 32—one more vote than the required two-thirds. Public opinion was also divided. In the end, the treaties did improve relationships between the United States and Latin America.

THE COLLAPSE OF DÉTENTE When Jimmy Carter took office, détente—the relaxation of tensions between the world's superpowers—had reached a high point. Beginning with President Nixon and continuing with President Ford, U.S. officials had worked to ease relations with the Communist superpowers of China and the Soviet Union.

However, Carter's firm insistence on human rights led to a breakdown in relations with the Soviet Union. President Carter's dismay over the Soviet Union's treatment of dissidents, or opponents of the government's policies, delayed a second round of SALT negotiations. President Carter and Soviet premier Leonid Brezhnev finally met in June of 1979 in Vienna, Austria, where they signed an agreement known as SALT II. Although the agreement did not reduce armaments, it did provide for limits on the number of strategic weapons and nuclear-missile launchers that each side could produce.

The SALT II agreement, however, met sharp opposition in the Senate. Critics argued that it would put the United States at a military disadvantage. Then, in December 1979, the Soviets invaded the neighboring country of Afghanistan. Angered over the invasion, President Carter refused to fight for the SALT II agreement, and the treaty died. **F**

MAIN IDEA

Identifying Problems

E What problems did critics have with Carter's foreign-policy philosophy?

MAIN IDEA

Analyzing Causes

F What led to the collapse of détente with the Soviet Union?

WORLD STAGE

SOVIET–AFGHANISTAN WAR

Afghanistan, an Islamic country along the southern border of the Soviet Union, had been run by a Communist, pro-Soviet government for a number of years. However, a strong Muslim rebel group known as the *mujahideen* was intent on overthrowing the Afghan government. Fearing a rebel victory in Afghanistan, the Soviet Union sent troops to Afghanistan in late 1979.

While the Soviets had superior weaponry, the rebels fought the Soviets to a stalemate by using guerrilla tactics and intimate knowledge of the country's mountainous terrain.

After suffering thousands of casualties, the last Soviet troops pulled out of Afghanistan in February 1989. Fighting between rival factions continued for years. By 2000, the Taliban, a radical Muslim faction, controlled 90 percent of Afghanistan.

Map labels (main map): Black Sea, Caspian Sea, Istanbul, Ankara, TURKEY, Aegean Sea, Algiers, Tunis, CYPRUS, SYRIA, Beirut, LEBANON, Tehran, AFGHANISTAN, Baghdad, Esfahan, TUNISIA, Tripoli, Mediterranean Sea, ISRAEL, Damascus, Amman, IRAQ, IRAN, KUWAIT, Alexandria, Cairo, JORDAN, SAUDI ARABIA, Neutral Zone, Kuwait, Strait of Hormuz, ALGERIA, LIBYA, BAHRAIN, Gulf of Oman, Medina, Riyadh, QATAR, Abu Dhabi, Muscat, EGYPT, Nile River, Red Sea, Mecca, UNITED ARAB EMIRATES, OMAN, Khartoum, Sana, P.D.R. YEMEN, SUDAN, YEMEN, Aden, Gulf of Aden, Arabian Sea, DJIBOUTI, ETHIOPIA, SOMALIA

Inset map labels: LEBANON, SYRIA, GOLAN HEIGHTS, Haifa, Mediterranean Sea, Sea of Galilee, Tel Aviv, Jordan R., WEST BANK, Jerusalem, GAZA STRIP, Dead Sea, ISRAEL, EGYPT, Suez Canal, Cairo, SINAI PENINSULA, JORDAN, Gulf of Suez, Gulf of Aqaba, SAUDI ARABIA, Red Sea

Legend:
- Israel
- Israeli controlled
- Palestinian areas
- Israeli conquests returned to Egypt, 1979–1982
- OPEC Member

GEOGRAPHY SKILLBUILDER
1. Location What OPEC countries are shown on the map?
2. Human-Environment Interaction How does Israel's location contribute to its conflicts?

Triumph and Crisis in the Middle East

Through long gasoline lines and high energy costs, Americans became all too aware of the troubles in the Middle East. In that area of ethnic, religious, and economic conflict, Jimmy Carter achieved one of his greatest diplomatic triumphs—and suffered his most tragic defeat.

THE CAMP DAVID ACCORDS Through negotiation and arm-twisting, Carter helped forge peace between long-time enemies Israel and Egypt. In 1977, Egyptian president Anwar el-Sadat and Israeli prime minister Menachem Begin met in Jerusalem to discuss an overall peace between the two nations. In the summer of 1978, Carter seized on the peace initiative. When the peace talks stalled, he invited Sadat and Begin to Camp David, the presidential retreat in Maryland.

After 12 days of intense negotiations, the three leaders reached an agreement that became known as the **Camp David Accords.** Under this first signed peace agreement with an Arab country, Israel agreed to withdraw from the Sinai Peninsula, which it had captured from Egypt during the Six-Day War in 1967. (See inset map above.) Egypt, in turn, formally recognized Israel's right to exist. **G**

President Carter, President Anwar el-Sadat, and Prime Minister Menachem Begin reach a peace agreement in 1978.
▼

MAIN IDEA

Summarizing
G What was the significance of the Camp David Accords?

Joking at the hard work ahead, Carter wrote playfully in his diary, "I resolved to do everything possible to get out of the negotiating business!" Little did the president know that his next Middle East negotiation would be his most painful.

THE IRAN HOSTAGE CRISIS By 1979, the shah of Iran, an ally of the United States, was in deep trouble. Many Iranians resented his regime's widespread corruption and dictatorial tactics.

In January 1979, revolution broke out. The Muslim religious leader **Ayatollah Ruhollah Khomeini** (ī′yə-tō′lə rōō-hō′lə kō-mā′nē) led the rebels in overthrowing the shah and establishing a religious state based on strict obedience to the Qur'an, the sacred book of Islam. Carter had supported the shah until the very end. In October 1979, the president allowed the shah to enter the United States for cancer treatment, though he had already fled Iran in January 1979.

The act infuriated the revolutionaries of Iran. On November 4, 1979, armed students seized the U.S. embassy in Tehran and took 52 Americans hostage. The militants demanded that the United States send the shah back to Iran in return for the release of the hostages.

Carter refused, and a painful year-long standoff followed, in which the United States continued quiet but intense efforts to free the hostages. The captives were finally released on January 20, 1981, shortly after the new president, Ronald Reagan, was sworn in. Despite the hostages' release after 444 days in captivity, the crisis in Iran seemed to underscore the limits that Americans faced during the 1970s. Americans also realized that there were limits to the nation's environmental resources. This realization prompted both citizens and the government to actively address environmental concerns.

▲ **U.S. hostages were blindfolded and paraded through the streets of Tehran.**

 ASSESSMENT

1. TERMS & NAMES For each term or name, write a sentence explaining its significance.
- •Gerald R. Ford
- •Jimmy Carter
- •National Energy Act
- •human rights
- •Camp David Accords
- •Ayatollah Ruhollah Khomeini

MAIN IDEA

2. TAKING NOTES
Create a time line of the major events of the Ford and Carter administrations, using a form such as the one below.

Which two events do you think were the most important? Why?

CRITICAL THINKING

3. EVALUATING DECISIONS
Do you think that Ford made a good decision in pardoning Nixon? Explain why or why not.

4. COMPARING
How were the actions taken by Presidents Ford and Carter to address the country's economic downturn similar? How did they differ?

5. ANALYZING ISSUES
Do you agree with President Carter that human rights concerns should steer U.S. foreign policy? Why or why not? **Think About:**
- the responsibility of promoting human rights
- the loss of good relations with certain countries
- the collapse of détente with the Soviet Union

An Age of Limits **1023**

REGENTS OF THE UNIVERSITY OF CALIFORNIA v. BAKKE (1978)

ORIGINS OF THE CASE In 1973, Allan Bakke applied to the University of California at Davis medical school. The school had a quota-based affirmative-action plan that reserved 16 out of 100 spots for racial minorities. Bakke, a white male, was not admitted to the school despite his competitive test scores and grades. Bakke sued for admission, arguing that he had been discriminated against on the basis of race. The California Supreme Court agreed with Bakke, but the school appealed the case.

THE RULING The Court ruled that racial quotas were unconstitutional, but that schools could still consider race as a factor in admissions.

LEGAL REASONING

The Court was closely divided on whether affirmative-action plans were constitutional. Two different sets of justices formed 5-to-4 majorities on two different issues in *Bakke*.

Five justices agreed the quota was unfair to Bakke. They based their argument on the equal protection clause of the Fourteenth Amendment. Justice Lewis Powell, writing for the majority, explained their reasoning.

> "The guarantee of equal protection cannot mean one thing when applied to one individual and something else when applied to a person of another color. If both are not accorded the same protection, then it is not equal."

▲ **Allan Bakke receives his degree in medicine from the medical school at U.C. Davis on June 4, 1982.**

The four justices that joined Powell in this part of the decision said race should *never* play a part in admissions decisions. Powell and the other four justices disagreed. These five justices formed a separate majority, arguing that "the attainment of a diverse student body . . . is a constitutionally permissible goal for an institution of higher education." In other words, schools could have affirmative-action plans that consider race as *one* factor in admission decisions in order to achieve a diverse student body.

LEGAL SOURCES

LEGISLATION

U.S. CONSTITUTION, FOURTEENTH AMENDMENT (1868)

"No state shall . . . deprive any person of life, liberty, or property, without due process of law; nor deny to any person within its jurisdiction the equal protection of the laws."

RELATED CASES

UNITED STEELWORKERS OF AMERICA v. WEBER (1979)
The Court said a business could have a short-term program for training minority workers as a way of fixing the results of past discrimination.

ADARAND CONSTRUCTORS v. PENA (1995)
The Court struck a federal law to set aside 10 percent of highway construction funds for minority-owned businesses. The Court also said that affirmative-action programs must be focused to achieve a compelling government interest.

▲ On October 8, 1977, protestors march in suppport of affirmative action at a park in Oakland, California.

WHY IT MATTERED

Many people have faced discrimination in America. The struggle of African Americans for civil rights in the 1950s and 1960s succeeded in overturning Jim Crow segregation. Even so, social inequality persisted for African Americans, as well as women and other minority groups. In 1965, President Lyndon Johnson explained why more proactive measures needed to be taken to end inequality.

> " You do not take a person who for years has been hobbled by chains and . . . bring him up to the starting line of a race and then say, 'you are free to compete with all the others' and still justly believe that you have been completely fair. "

As a result, Johnson urged companies to begin to take "affirmative action" to hire and promote African Americans, helping them to overcome generations of inequality. Critics quickly opposed affirmative action plans as unfair to white people and merely a replacement of one form of racial discrimination with another.

University admissions policies became a focus of the debate over affirmative action. The Court's ruling in *Bakke* allowed race to be used as one factor in admissions decisions. Schools could consider a prospective student's race, but they could not use quotas or use race as the *only* factor for admission.

HISTORICAL IMPACT

Since *Bakke*, the Court has ruled on affirmative action several times, usually limiting affirmative-action plans. For example, in *Adarand Constructors* v. *Pena* (1995), the Court struck a federal law to set aside "not less than 10 percent" of highway construction funds for businesses owned by "socially and economically disadvantaged individuals." The Court said that affirmative-action programs must be narrowly focused to achieve a "compelling government interest."

On cases regarding school affirmative-action plans, the courts have not created clear guidelines. The Supreme Court refused to hear an appeal of a 1996 lower court ruling that outlawed any consideration of race for admission to the University of Texas law school. Yet in the 2003 decision in *Grutter* v. *Bollinger*, the Court protected a University of Michigan law school admissions policy that required the admissions committee to consider the diversity of its student body. The Court reaffirmed the *Bakke* view that "student body diversity is a compelling state interest."

Since the *Grutter* decision, several states have passed laws or constitutional amendments requiring race-blind admissions—effectively barring affirmative action. These laws were passed by ballot initiative, reflecting a popular view that sees affirmative action as "reverse discrimination."

THINKING CRITICALLY

CONNECT TO HISTORY

1. **Evaluating** Research articles about *Bakke* in the library or on the Internet. Read the articles and write a paragraph for each one explaining the writer's point of view on the case. Conclude by telling which article gives the best discussion of the case. Cite examples to support your choice.

    SEE SKILLBUILDER HANDBOOK, PAGE R16.

CONNECT TO TODAY

2. Visit the links for Historic Decisions of the Supreme Court to research and read about Proposition 209, California's 1996 law banning affirmative action at state universities. Prepare arguments for an in-class debate about whether the law will have a positive or negative long-term effect.

    hmhsocialstudies.com INTERNET ACTIVITY

PI 2.5
PI 3.4

CC Unit 1.I.C.2
CC Unit 7.III.B.1.d
CC Unit 7.V.B.2.c(1)

CC Unit 7.I.A.6
CC Unit 7.V.A.1.c
CC Unit 7.V.B.2.c(3)

Environmental Activism

MAIN IDEA	**WHY IT MATTERS NOW**	**Terms & Names**
During the 1970s, Americans strengthened their efforts to address the nation's environmental problems.	The nation today continues to struggle to balance environmental concerns with industrial growth.	• Rachel Carson • Earth Day • environmentalist • Environmental Protection Agency (EPA) • Three Mile Island

One American's Story

hmhsocialstudies.com
TAKING NOTES

Use the graphic organizer online to take notes on how concern for the environment grew in the United States.

In 1972, Lois Gibbs and her family moved to Niagara Falls, New York. Underneath this quiet town, however, was a disaster in the making. In the 1890s, the Love Canal had been built to provide hydroelectric power for the Niagara Falls area. Chemical companies were dumping hazardous waste into the canal. In 1953, bulldozers filled in the canal. Shortly thereafter, a school and rows of homes were built nearby.

In 1977, when Lois Gibbs's son fell sick, she decided to investigate. She eventually uncovered the existence of the toxic waste and mobilized the community to demand government action. In 1980, President Carter authorized funds for many Niagara Falls families to move to safety. Years later, Lois Gibbs wrote a book detailing her efforts.

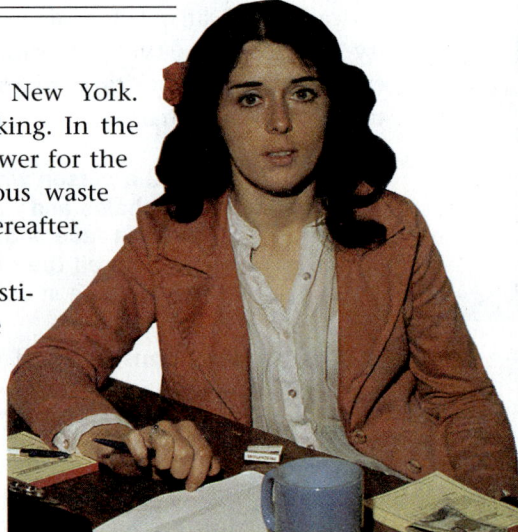

▲
Lois Gibbs

★ A PERSONAL VOICE LOIS GIBBS

" I want to tell you our story—my story—because I believe that ordinary citizens—using the tools of dignity, self-respect, common sense, and perseverance—can influence solutions to important problems in our society. . . . In solving any difficult problem, you have to be prepared to fight long and hard, sometimes at great personal cost; but it can be done. It must be done if we are to survive . . . at all. "

—*Love Canal: My Story*

Lois Gibbs's concerns about environmental hazards were shared by many Americans in the 1970s. Through the energy crisis, Americans learned that their natural resources were limited; they could no longer take the environment for granted. Americans—from grassroots organizations to the government—began to focus on conservation of the environment and new forms of energy.

The Roots of Environmentalism

The widespread realization that pollution and overconsumption were damaging the environment began in the 1960s. One book in particular had awakened

America's concerns about the environment and helped lay the groundwork for the activism of the early seventies.

RACHEL CARSON AND SILENT SPRING In 1962, **Rachel Carson**, a marine biologist, published a book entitled *Silent Spring*. In it, she warned against the growing use of pesticides—chemicals used to kill insects and rodents. Carson argued that pesticides poisoned the very food they were intended to protect and as a result killed many birds and fish.

Carson cautioned that America faced a "silent spring," in which birds killed off by pesticides would no longer fill the air with song. She added that of all the weapons used in "man's war against nature," pesticides were some of the most harmful.

⭐ **A PERSONAL VOICE** RACHEL CARSON

" These sprays, dusts, and aerosols . . . have the power to kill every insect, the 'good' and the 'bad,' to still the song of birds and the leaping of fish in the streams, to coat the leaves with a deadly film, and to linger on in soil—all this though the intended target may be only a few weeds or insects. Can anyone believe it is possible to lay down such a barrage of poisons on the surface of the earth without making it unfit for all life? "

—*Silent Spring*

Within six months of its publication, *Silent Spring* sold nearly half a million copies. Many chemical companies called the book inaccurate and threatened legal action. However, for a majority of Americans, Carson's book was an early warning about the danger that human activity posed to the environment. Shortly after the book's publication, President Kennedy established an advisory committee to investigate the situation.

With Rachel Carson's prodding, the nation slowly began to focus more on environmental issues. Although Carson would not live to see the U.S. government outlaw DDT in 1972, her work helped many Americans realize that their everyday behavior, as well as the nation's industrial growth, had a damaging effect on the environment. **Ⓐ**

KEY PLAYER

**RACHEL CARSON
1907–1964**

The marine biologist Rachel Carson was born far from the sea, in the small town of Springdale, Pennsylvania.

Carson was a sickly child who often had to remain at home, where her mother tutored her. Throughout her youth and into her college years, Carson was a studious, but quiet and aloof, person.

Carson entered college intent on becoming a writer. During her sophomore year, she took a biology class to fulfill her science requirement and quickly fell in love with the study of nature. By the next year Carson switched her major from English to zoology—the study of animals.

MAIN IDEA

Analyzing Effects

Ⓐ What effects did Rachel Carson's book have on the nation as a whole?

A flag celebrating the first Earth Day in 1970. ▼

Environmental Concerns in the 1970s

During the 1970s, the administrations of Richard Nixon and Jimmy Carter confronted such environmental issues as conservation, pollution, and the growth of nuclear energy.

THE FIRST EARTH DAY The United States ushered in the 1970s—a decade in which it would actively address its environmental issues—fittingly enough with the first **Earth Day** celebration. On that day, April 22, 1970, nearly every community in the nation and more than 10,000 schools and 2,000 colleges hosted some type of environmental-awareness activity and spotlighted such problems as pollution, the growth of toxic waste, and the earth's dwindling resources. The Earth Day celebration continues today. Each year on April 22, millions of people around the world gather to heighten public awareness of environmental problems.

THE GOVERNMENT TAKES ACTION Although President Nixon was not considered an **environmentalist,** or someone who takes an active role in the protection of the environment, he recognized the nation's growing concern about the environment. In an effort to "make our peace with nature," President Nixon set out on a course that led to the passage of several landmark measures. In 1970, he consolidated 15 existing federal pollution programs into the **Environmental Protection Agency (EPA).** The new agency was given the power to set and enforce pollution standards, to conduct environmental research, and to assist state and local governments in pollution control. Today, the EPA remains the federal government's main instrument for dealing with environmental issues.

In 1970 Nixon signed a new Clean Air Act that added several amendments to the Clean Air Act of 1963. The new act gave the government the authority to set air standards. Following the 1970 Clean Air Act, Congress also passed the Endangered Species Act, in addition to laws that limited pesticide use and curbed strip mining—the practice of mining for ore and coal by digging gaping holes in the land. Some 35 environmental laws took effect during the decade, addressing every aspect of conservation and clean-up, from protecting endangered animals to regulating auto emissions. **Ⓑ**

BALANCING PROGRESS AND CONSERVATION IN ALASKA During the 1970s, the federal government took steps to ensure the continued well-being of Alaska, the largest state in the nation and one of its most ecologically sensitive.

The discovery of oil there in 1968, and the subsequent construction of a massive pipeline to transport it, created many new jobs and greatly increased state revenues. However, the influx of new development also raised concerns about Alaska's wildlife, as well as the rights of its native peoples. In 1971, Nixon signed the Alaska Native Claims Settlement Act, which turned over millions of acres of land to the state's native tribes for conservation and tribal use. In 1978, President Carter enhanced this conservation effort by setting aside an additional 56 million acres in Alaska as national monuments. In 1980, Congress added another 104 million acres as protected areas.

THE DEBATE OVER NUCLEAR ENERGY As the 1970s came to a close, Americans became acutely aware of the dangers that nuclear power plants posed to both humans and the environment. During the 1970s, as America realized the drawbacks to its heavy dependence on foreign oil for energy, nuclear power seemed to many to be an attractive alternative.

Opponents of nuclear energy warned the public against the industry's growth. They contended that nuclear plants, and the wastes they produced, were potentially dangerous to humans and their environment.

THREE MILE ISLAND In the early hours of March 28, 1979, the concerns of nuclear energy opponents were validated. That morning, one of the nuclear reactors at a plant on **Three Mile Island** near Harrisburg, Pennsylvania, malfunctioned. The reactor overheated after its cooling system failed, and fear quickly arose that radiation might escape and spread over the region. Two days later,

Vocabulary
toxic: capable of causing injury or death, especially by chemical means; poisonous

MAIN IDEA

Summarizing
Ⓑ What were the environmental actions taken during the Nixon administration?

The Trans-Alaska Pipeline, stretching across hundreds of miles of tundra, was completed in 1977.

THE ACCIDENT AT THREE MILE ISLAND

A series of human and mechanical errors that caused the partial meltdown of the reactor core brought the Three Mile Island nuclear power plant to the brink of disaster. The accident at Three Mile Island caused widespread concern about nuclear power throughout the American public.

REACTOR MELTDOWN

1 The radioactive reactor core generates heat as its atoms split during a controlled chain reaction.

2 An inoperative valve releases thousands of gallons of coolant from the reactor core.

3 Half of the 36,816 exposed fuel rods melt in temperatures above five thousand degrees.

4 The melted material burns through the lining of the reactor chamber and spills to the floor of the containment structure.

More than 30 years after the accident, clean-up at Three Mile Island continues. The final 'clean-up bill' could soar to more than $3 billion. The TMI-2 reactor was dangerously contaminated and could not be entered for two years. All the materials in the containment structure, along with anything used in the clean-up, had to be decontaminated. Because the reactor will never be completely free of radioactivity, it will one day be entombed in cement.

low-level radiation actually did escape from the crippled reactor. Officials evacuated some residents, while others fled on their own. One homemaker who lived near the plant recalled her desperate attempt to find safety.

★ A PERSONAL VOICE

" On Friday, a very frightening thing occurred in our area. A state policeman went door-to-door telling residents to stay indoors, close all windows, and turn all air conditioners off. I was alone, as were many other homemakers, and my thoughts were focused on how long I would remain a prisoner in my own home. . . . Suddenly, I was scared, real scared. I decided to get out of there, while I could. I ran to the car not knowing if I should breathe the air or not, and I threw the suitcases in the trunk and was on my way within one hour. If anything dreadful happened, I thought that I'd at least be with my girls. Although it was very hot in the car, I didn't trust myself to turn the air conditioner on. It felt good as my tense muscles relaxed the farther I drove. "

—an anonymous homemaker quoted in *Accident at Three Mile Island: The Human Dimensions*

In all, more than 100,000 residents were evacuated from the surrounding area. On April 9, the Nuclear Regulatory Commission, the federal agency that monitors the nuclear power industry, announced that the immediate danger was over.

The events at Three Mile Island rekindled the debate over nuclear power. Supporters of nuclear power pointed out that no one had been killed or seriously injured. Opponents countered by saying that chance alone had averted a tragedy.

Background

In 2010, President Obama established a commission to develop a long-term plan for the management of used nuclear fuel. This plan, he said, would include not only ideas on disposal, but also ways to reprocess and recycle this waste.

History Through *Film*

HOLLYWOOD AND NUCLEAR FEARS

At the end of the 1970s and in the early 1980s, Hollywood responded to Americans' concerns over nuclear power by making pointed social-awareness films exposing dangers in the nuclear industry. These films alerted the public to the importance of regulations in the relatively new field of atomic energy.

In 1979, *The China Syndrome,* starring Jane Fonda and Jack Lemmon, became the movie everyone was talking about. Only 12 days after the film's release, a serious accident similar to the one portrayed in the movie occurred at the Three Mile Island nuclear power plant. ▶

◀ In 1974, on her way to meet with a reporter from the *New York Times,* Karen Silkwood, a worker at a nuclear power facility, was hit and died in a car crash. In the film dramatization, *Silkwood* (1983), Meryl Streep played Karen, and Kurt Russell and Cher, her co-workers.

SKILLBUILDER Interpreting Visual Sources

1. Why do you think movies based on real events are popular with the general public?
2. How do you think these films influenced present-day nuclear energy policy?

📁 SEE SKILLBUILDER HANDBOOK, PAGE R23.

They demanded that the government call a halt to the construction of new power plants and gradually shut down existing nuclear facilities.

While the government did not do away with nuclear power, federal officials did recognize nuclear energy's potential danger to both humans and the environment. As a result of the accident at Three Mile Island, the Nuclear Regulatory Commission strengthened its safety standards and improved its inspection procedures. **C**

A Continuing Movement

Although the environmental movement of the 1970s gained popular support, opponents of the movement also made their voices heard. In Tennessee, for example, where a federal dam project was halted because it threatened a species of fish, local developers took out ads asking residents to "tell the government that the size of your wallet is more important than some two-inch-long minnow." When confronted with environmental concerns, one unemployed steelworker spoke for others when he remarked, "Why worry about the long run, when you're out of work right now."

The environmental movement that blossomed in the 1970s became in the 1980s and 1990s a struggle to balance environmental concerns with jobs and progress. In the years since the first Earth Day, however, environmental issues have gained increasing attention and support.

MAIN IDEA

Analyzing Effects

C How did the Three Mile Island incident affect the use of nuclear power in America?

SPOTLIGHT

PRIVATE CONSERVATION GROUPS

As concerns about pollution and the depletion of nonrenewable resources grew, so did membership in private, nonprofit organizations dedicated to the preservation of wilderness and endangered species. Many of these groups lobbied government for protective legislation. Some filed lawsuits to block projects such as road or dam construction or logging that would threaten habitats. The Environmental Defense Fund (today Environmental Defense) brought lawsuits that led to the bans on DDT and on leaded gasoline.

Radical groups also emerged. Members of Greenpeace risked their lives at sea to escort whales and protect them from commercial hunters.

SECTION 4 ASSESSMENT

1. TERMS & NAMES For each term or name, write a sentence explaining its significance.

- Rachel Carson
- Earth Day
- environmentalist
- Environmental Protection Agency (EPA)
- Three Mile Island

MAIN IDEA

2. TAKING NOTES
Re-create the web below on your paper and fill in events that illustrate the main idea in the center.

Concern for the environment grew in the United States.

CRITICAL THINKING

3. ANALYZING CAUSES
How much should the United States rely on nuclear power as a source of energy? Explain your view.
Think About:
- the safety of nuclear power
- the alternatives to nuclear power
- U.S. energy demands

4. ANALYZING VISUAL SOURCES
What message does this 1969 poster from the Environmental Protection Agency give about the government's role in pollution?

Clean air is a product of the United States Environmental Protection Agency.

An Age of Limits **1031**

TERMS & NAMES

For each term or name below, write a sentence explaining its significance to the Nixon, Ford, or Carter administrations.

1. Richard M. Nixon
2. stagflation
3. OPEC (Organization of Petroleum Exporting Countries)
4. SALT I Treaty
5. Watergate
6. Saturday Night Massacre
7. Camp David Accords
8. Ayatollah Ruhollah Khomeini
9. Rachel Carson
10. Environmental Protection Agency (EPA)

MAIN IDEAS

Use your notes and the information in the chapter to answer the following questions.

The Nixon Administration *(pages 1000–1007)*

1. In what ways did President Nixon attempt to reform the federal government?
2. How did Nixon try to combat stagflation?

Watergate: Nixon's Downfall *(pages 1008–1013)*

3. In what ways did the participants in Watergate attempt to cover up the scandal?
4. What were the results of the Watergate scandal?

The Ford and Carter Years *(pages 1016–1023)*

5. What were Gerald Ford's greatest successes as president?
6. How did President Carter attempt to solve the energy crisis?

Environmental Activism *(pages 1026–1031)*

7. What factors increased Americans' concerns about environmental issues during the 1960s and 1970s?
8. What was the impact of the Three Mile Island incident?

CRITICAL THINKING

1. **USING YOUR NOTES** In a chart like the one shown, identify one major development for each issue listed that occurred between 1968 and 1980. Indicate whether you think the impact of the development was positive (+) or negative (–).

Issue	Development	Impact
Economic conditions		
Democratic government		
Efficient energy use		
Environmental protection		

2. **ANALYZING EVENTS** Between 1972 and 1974, Americans were absorbed by the fall of President Nixon in the Watergate scandal. What might Americans have learned about the role of the executive office? Explain.

3. **INTERPRETING GRAPHS** Study the graph on page 1019. Describe the changes in unemployment as compared to inflation from 1970 to 1980.

VISUAL SUMMARY **AN AGE OF LIMITS**

THE NIXON ADMINISTRATION
- Revenue sharing
- Law-and-order politics
- Integration delays
- Inflation, recession, and unemployment
- Opening to China
- Détente with the Soviet Union
- Watergate scandal
- Nixon resignation

THE FORD ADMINISTRATION
- Unelected president
- Nixon pardon
- Whip Inflation Now program
- Economic recession
- Mayagüez incident
- Helsinki Accords

THE CARTER ADMINISTRATION
- Energy crisis
- Worsening inflation
- Panama Canal Treaties
- Camp David Accords
- Nuclear power
- Iran hostage crisis

TIME Special Issue — THE HEALING BEGINS

Use the two graphs below and your knowledge of U.S. history to answer question 1.

U.S. Oil Consumption, 1965–1979

Barrels per Day (in millions)

Source: Annual Energy Review, 1999

U.S. Oil Production, 1965–1979

Barrels per Day (in millions)

Source: Annual Energy Review, 1999

1 The OPEC oil embargo hit the United States so hard in 1973 because —

(1) domestic oil consumption decreased as production decreased.

(2) domestic oil consumption remained steady as production decreased.

(3) domestic oil consumption increased while production decreased slightly.

(4) domestic oil consumption increased, although consumption increased faster.

2 How did Watergate affect the presidents who followed after Richard Nixon?

(1) It caused them to be less trusted and less powerful.

(2) It made them reluctant to oppose Congress.

(3) It made them more popular with the media.

(4) It caused them to rely less on the counsel of cabinet members.

3 Which of the following is a contribution made by Rachel Carson to the American environmental movement?

(1) Carson researched "cleaner" sources of energy.

(2) Carson lobbied for the passage of the National Energy Act.

(3) Carson lobbied for making April 22, 1970, the first Earth Day.

(4) Carson published a book on the hazards of pesticide use.

hmhsocialstudies.com **TEST PRACTICE**

For additional test practice, go online for:

• Diagnostic tests   • Tutorials

INTERACT WITH HISTORY

Recall the issues that you explored at the beginning of the chapter. Now that you've learned how your country's highest office holder, President Nixon, lost the nation's trust after the Watergate scandal, would you change your response? Discuss your suggestions with a small group. Then create a list, ranking the misuses from least to most severe.

FOCUS ON WRITING

Based on what you have read in this chapter, write a paragraph that describes the American public's reaction to President Ford's pardon of Richard Nixon.

COLLABORATIVE LEARNING

21ST CENTURY

In a small group, discuss possible environmental problems in each group member's neighborhood, listing them on a sheet of paper. Compare lists with other groups to determine the most common problems. List possible solutions for each problem.

CHAPTER 33

THE CONSERVATIVE TIDE

Essential Question

What were the key political and social events of the 1980s and early 1990s?

 New York Standards

KEY IDEA 2 Important ideas, social and cultural values, beliefs, and traditions from New York State and United States history illustrate the connections and interactions of people and events across time and from a variety of perspectives.

KEY IDEA 3 Study about the major social, political, economic, cultural, and religious developments in New York State and United States history involves learning about the important roles and contributions of individuals and groups.

SECTION 1: A Conservative Movement Emerges

SECTION 2: Conservative Policies Under Reagan and Bush

SECTION 3: Social Concerns in the 1980s

SECTION 4: Foreign Policy After the Cold War

Ronald Reagan addresses the 1980 Republican convention.

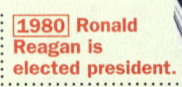

1980 Ronald Reagan is elected president.

1981 Sandra Day O'Connor becomes the first woman appointed to the Supreme Court.

1982 Equal Rights Amendment fails to win ratification.

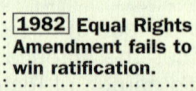

1984 President Reagan is reelected.

USA
WORLD

1980

1982

1984

1980 Zimbabwe claims independence.

1982 Great Britain and Argentina go to war over the Falkland Islands.

1984 South African Bishop Desmond Tutu receives the Nobel Peace Prize.

INTERACT
WITH HISTORY

It is the autumn of 1980. You are a campaign manager for Republican presidential candidate Ronald Reagan, former film star and past governor of California. Reagan must defeat President Jimmy Carter, who has lost support. Carter has failed to bring home the hostages in Iran and to revive the economy. Reagan, an optimist, pledges to do both. He also plans to cut taxes and cut back on government programs.

Explore the Issues

- What qualities in your candidate will win support?
- What issues are important?
- How can you present Reagan as a winner?

1988 George Bush is elected president.

1987 President Reagan and Soviet leader Mikhail Gorbachev sign the Intermediate-Range Nuclear Forces Treaty.

1988 Reverend Jesse Jackson runs for the Democratic presidential nomination.

1986 Iran arms deal is revealed.

1991 Persian Gulf War breaks out.

1986   **1988**   **1990**

1986 The Soviet Union suffers a disastrous accident at the Chernobyl nuclear power plant.

1989 The Chinese government kills student protesters in Tiananmen Square.

1989 Germans dismantle the Berlin Wall.

1991 Soviet Union breaks apart.

The Conservative Tide **1035**

PI 1.1   CC Unit 1.I.D.1.d

A Conservative Movement Emerges

MAIN IDEA	WHY IT MATTERS NOW	Terms & Names
Conservatism reached a high point with the election in 1980 of President Ronald Reagan and Vice-President George Bush.	In the early 21st century, conservative views strongly influenced both major political parties.	• **entitlement program** • **conservative coalition** • **New Right** • **Moral Majority** • **affirmative action** • **Ronald Reagan** • **reverse discrimination**

One American's Story

hmhsocialstudies.com
TAKING NOTES
Use the graphic organizer online to take notes on conservative issues.

Peggy Noonan grew up with a strong sense of social and political justice. As a child, she idolized the liberal Kennedys; as a teenager, she devoured articles on social and political issues. After college, Noonan went to work for CBS.

Over the years, Noonan's political views became increasingly conservative. She eventually won a job as a speechwriter for Ronald Reagan, whose commitment to his conservative values moved her deeply. Noonan recalled that her response to Reagan was not unusual.

> ▲ **A PERSONAL VOICE** PEGGY NOONAN
> "The young people who came to Washington for the Reagan revolution came to make things better. . . . They looked at where freedom was and . . . where freedom wasn't and what that did, and they wanted to help the guerrilla fighters who were trying to overthrow the Communist regimes that had been imposed on them. . . . The thing the young conservatives were always talking about, . . . was freedom, freedom:
> *we'll free up more of your money,*
> *we'll free up more of the world,*
> *freedom freedom freedom—*
> It was the drumbeat that held a disparate group together, the rhythm that kept a fractious, not-made-in-heaven alliance in one piece."
> —*What I Saw at the Revolution: A Political Life in the Reagan Era*

Peggy Noonan

Like millions of other Reagan supporters, Noonan agreed with the slogan that was the heart of Reagan's political creed: "Government is not the solution to our problem. Government is the problem."

The Conservative Movement Builds

Ever since Senator Barry Goldwater of Arizona had run for president in 1964, conservatives had argued that state governments, businesses, and individuals needed more freedom from the heavy hand of Washington, D.C. By 1980, government spending on **entitlement programs**—programs that provide guaranteed benefits to particular groups—was nearly $300 billion annually. The costs together with stories of fraudulently-obtained benefits caused resentment among many taxpayers.

In addition, some people had become frustrated with the government's civil rights policies. Congress had passed the Civil Rights Act of 1964 in an effort to eliminate racial discrimination. Over the years, however, judicial decisions and government regulations had broadened the reach of the act. A growing number of Americans viewed with skepticism what had begun as a movement toward equal opportunity. Although many people had rejected separate schools for blacks and whites as unfair and unequal, few wanted to bus their children long distances to achieve a fixed ratio of black and white students.

THE NEW RIGHT As the 1970s progressed, right-wing grass-roots groups across the country emerged to support and promote single issues that reflected their key interests. These people became known as the **New Right.** The New Right focused its energy on controversial social issues, such as opposing abortion, blocking the Equal Rights Amendment, and evading court-ordered busing. It also called for a return to school prayer, which had been outlawed by the Supreme Court in 1962.

Many in the New Right criticized the policy of **affirmative action.** Affirmative action required employers and educational institutions to give special consideration to women, African Americans, and other minority groups, even though these people were not necessarily better qualified. Many conservatives saw affirmative action as a form of **reverse discrimination,** favoring one group over another on the basis of race or gender. To members of the New Right, liberal positions on affirmative action and other issues represented an assault on traditional values. **A**

▲ **Several high school students in New York hold a prayer meeting in 1973.**

MAIN IDEA

Analyzing Issues

A What was the agenda of the New Right?

THE CONSERVATIVE COALITION Beginning in the mid-1960s, the conservative movement in the United States grew in strength. Eventually conservative groups formed the **conservative coalition**—an alliance of business leaders, middle-class voters, disaffected Democrats, and fundamentalist Christian groups.

Conservative intellectuals argued the cause of the conservative coalition in newspapers such as *The Wall Street Journal* and magazines such as the *National Review*, founded in 1955 by conservative William F. Buckley, Jr. Conservative think tanks, such as the American Enterprise Institute and The Heritage Foundation, were founded to develop conservative policies and principles that would appeal to the majority of voters.

THE MORAL MAJORITY Religion, especially evangelical Christianity, played a key role in the growing strength of the conservative coalition. The 1970s had brought a huge religious revival, especially among fundamentalist sects. Each week, millions of Americans watched evangelist preachers on television or listened to them on the radio. Two of the most influential televangelists were Jerry Falwell and Pat Robertson. Falwell formed an organization called the **Moral Majority.** The Moral Majority consisted mostly of evangelical and fundamentalist Christians who interpreted

Goals of the Conservative Movement

- Shrink the size of the federal government and reduce spending
- Promote family values and patriotic ideals
- Stimulate business by reducing government regulations and lowering taxes
- Strengthen the national defense

the Bible literally and believed in absolute standards of right and wrong. They condemned liberal attitudes and behaviors and argued for a restoration of traditional moral values. They worked toward their political goals by using direct-mail campaigns and by raising money to support candidates. Jerry Falwell became the spokesperson for the Moral Majority. **B**

MAIN IDEA

Summarizing
B What were the main concerns of the Moral Majority?

★ **A PERSONAL VOICE** REVEREND JERRY FALWELL

"**Our nation's internal problems are the direct result of her spiritual condition. . . . Right living must be reestablished as an American way of life. . . . Now is the time to begin calling America back to God, back to the Bible, back to morality.**"

As individual conservative groups formed networks, they created a movement dedicated to bringing back what they saw as traditional "family values." They hoped their ideas would help to reduce the nation's high divorce rate, lower the number of out-of-wedlock births, encourage individual responsibility, and generally revive bygone prosperity and patriotic times.

KEY PLAYER

RONALD REAGAN
1911–2004

Ronald Wilson Reagan was born in 1911 in Tampico, Illinois. He grew up in Dixon, Illinois, graduated from nearby Eureka College, and then worked as a sports announcer in Iowa. In 1937, Reagan moved to Hollywood and became a movie actor, eventually making more than 50 films. As president of the Screen Actors Guild, he worked actively to remove alleged Communist influences from the movie industry.

Reagan had the ability to express his ideas in simple and clear language that the average voter could understand. When he proposed a 10 percent cut in government spending on social programs, he stated, "We can lecture our children about extravagance until we run out of voice and breath. Or we can cure their extravagance by simply reducing their allowance."

Conservatives Win Political Power

In 1976, **Ronald Reagan** lost the Republican nomination to the incumbent, Gerald Ford, in a very closely contested race. Four years later in a series of hard-fought primaries, Reagan won the 1980 nomination and chose George H. W. Bush as his running mate. Reagan and Bush ran against the incumbent president and vice-president, Jimmy Carter and Walter Mondale, who were nominated again by the Democrats despite their low standing in the polls.

REAGAN'S QUALIFICATIONS Originally a New Deal Democrat, Ronald Reagan had become a conservative Republican during the 1950s. He claimed that he had not left the Democratic Party but rather that the party had left him. As a spokesman for General Electric, he toured the country making speeches in favor of free enterprise and against big government. In 1964, he campaigned hard for Barry Goldwater, the Republican candidate for president. His speech supporting Goldwater in October 1964 made Reagan a serious candidate for public office. In 1966, Reagan was elected governor of California, and in 1970, he was reelected.

THE 1980 PRESIDENTIAL ELECTION In 1980, Reagan ran on a number of key issues. Supreme Court decisions on abortion, pornography, the teaching of evolution, and prayer in public schools all concerned conservative voters, and they rallied to Reagan. The prolonged Iranian hostage crisis and the weak economy under Carter, particularly the high rate of inflation, also helped Reagan.

Thanks in part to his acting career and his long experience in the public eye, Reagan was an extremely effective candidate. In contrast to Carter, who often seemed stiff and nervous, Reagan was relaxed, charming, and affable. He loved making quips: "A recession is when your neighbor loses his job. A depression is when you lose yours. And recovery is when Jimmy Carter loses his." Reagan's long-standing skill at simplifying issues and presenting clear-cut answers led his supporters to call him the Great Communicator. Also, his commitment to military and economic strength appealed to many Americans.

Only 52.6 percent of American voters went to the polls in 1980. Reagan won the election by a narrow majority; he got 44 million votes, or 51 percent of the total. His support, however, was spread throughout the country, so that he carried 44 states and won 489 electoral votes. Republicans also gained control of the Senate for the first time since 1954. As Reagan assumed the presidency, many people were buoyed by his genial smile and his assertion that it was "morning again in America." **C**

Now, conservatives had elected one of their own—a true believer in less government, lower taxes, and traditional values. Once elected, Reagan worked to translate the conservative agenda into public policy.

MAIN IDEA

Analyzing Causes

C What factors led to Reagan's victory in 1980?

Presidential Election of 1980

Party	Candidate	Electoral Votes	Popular Votes
Republican	Ronald Reagan	489	43,904,153
Democratic	Jimmy Carter	49	35,483,883
Independent	John Anderson		5,720,060

Not shown:
- **3** Alaska
- **4** Hawaii
- **3** District of Columbia

GEOGRAPHY SKILLBUILDER
1. **Location** Which states and/or district voted for Jimmy Carter in 1980?
2. **Region** Which region of the country—North, South, East, or West—voted exclusively for Ronald Reagan?

ASSESSMENT — SECTION 1

1. TERMS & NAMES For each term or name below, write a sentence explaining its significance.
- entitlement program
- affirmative action
- conservative coalition
- Ronald Reagan
- New Right
- reverse discrimination
- Moral Majority

MAIN IDEA

2. TAKING NOTES
Use a cluster diagram to record the issues that conservatives strongly endorsed.

Choose one issue and explain in a paragraph the conservative position on that issue.

CRITICAL THINKING

3. ANALYZING MOTIVES
How did the leaders of the conservative movement of the 1980s want to change government?
Think About:
- the difference between the conservative view of government and the liberal view
- the groups that made up the conservative coalition
- conservatives' attitudes toward existing government programs

4. ANALYZING EFFECTS
What role did the Moral Majority play in the conservative movement of the 1970s and early 1980s?

5. EVALUATING LEADERSHIP
What personal qualities in Ronald Reagan helped him to win election as president in 1980?

CC Unit 7.V.C.1   CC Unit 7.V.C.2
CC Unit 7.V.C.3   CC Unit 7.VI.A.1
PI 2.4   CC Unit 7.VI.A.2.b   CC Unit 7.VI.A.2.d

Conservative Policies Under Reagan and Bush

MAIN IDEA	WHY IT MATTERS NOW	Terms & Names
Presidents Reagan and Bush pursued a conservative agenda that included tax cuts, budget cuts, and increased defense spending.	The conservative views of Reagan and Bush created policies and priorities that affect government spending and budgeting today.	• **Reaganomics** • **supply-side economics** • **Strategic Defense Initiative** • **Sandra Day O'Connor** • **deregulation** • **Environmental Protection Agency (EPA)** • **Geraldine Ferraro** • **George Bush**

One American's Story

hmhsocialstudies.com
TAKING NOTES

Use the graphic organizer online to take notes on the effects of Reagan's economic policies.

Throughout the 1980 presidential campaign and in the early days of his administration, President Reagan emphasized the perilous state of the economy during the Carter administration. In a speech to the nation on February 5, 1981—his first televised speech from the White House—Reagan announced his new economic program. He called for a reduction in income tax rates for individuals and a big reduction in government spending.

President Ronald Reagan

A PERSONAL VOICE RONALD REAGAN

" I'm speaking to you tonight to give you a report on the state of our nation's economy. I regret to say that we're in the worst economic mess since the Great Depression. . . .
It's time to recognize that we've come to a turning point. We're threatened with an economic calamity of tremendous proportions, and the old business-as-usual treatment can't save us. Together, we must chart a different course. "

—televised speech to the nation, February 5, 1981

President Reagan would deal with these problems by consistently stressing a sweeping package of new economic policies. These economic policies, dubbed "**Reaganomics**," consisted of three parts: (1) budget cuts, (2) tax cuts, and (3) increased defense spending.

"Reaganomics" Takes Over

As soon as Reagan took office, he worked to reduce the size and influence of the federal government, which, he thought, would encourage private investment. Because people were anxious about the economy in 1980, their concern opened the door for new approaches to taxes and the federal budget.

BUDGET CUTS Reagan's strategy for downsizing the federal government included deep cuts in government spending on social programs. Yet his cuts did not affect all segments of the population equally. Entitlement programs that benefited the middle class, such as Social Security, Medicare, and veterans' pensions, remained intact. On the other hand, Congress slashed by 10 percent the budget for programs that benefited other groups: urban mass transit, food stamps, welfare benefits, job training, Medicaid, school lunches, and student loans.

TAX CUTS "Reaganomics" rested heavily upon **supply-side economics.** This theory held that if people paid fewer taxes, they would save more money. Banks could then loan that money to businesses, which could invest the money in resources to improve productivity. The supply of goods then would increase, driving down prices. At Reagan's urging, Congress lowered income taxes by about 25 percent over a three-year period. Reagan based his ideas for supply-side economics on the work of economists such as George Gilder and Arthur Laffer. **A**

> ### A PERSONAL VOICE ARTHUR LAFFER
>
> " The most debilitating act a government can perpetrate on its citizens is to adopt policies that destroy the economy's production base, for it is the production base that generates any prosperity to be found in the society. U.S. tax policies over the last decade have had the effect of damaging this base by removing many of the incentives to economic advancement. It is necessary to restore those incentives if we are to cure our economic palsy. "
>
> —*The Economics of the Tax Revolt: A Reader*

INCREASED DEFENSE SPENDING At the same time, Reagan authorized increases in military spending that more than offset cuts in social programs. Between 1981 and 1984, the Defense Department budget almost doubled. Indeed, the president revived two controversial weapons systems—the MX missile and the B-1 bomber. In 1983, Reagan asked the country's scientists to develop a defense system that would keep Americans safe from enemy missiles. Officially called the **Strategic Defense Initiative,** or SDI, the system quickly became known as Star Wars, after the title of a popular movie. The Defense Department estimated that the system would cost trillions of dollars.

RECESSION AND RECOVERY While Reagan was charting a new course for the American economy, the economy itself was sinking into recession. Lasting from July 1981 until November 1982, it was the most severe recession since the Great Depression. However, early in 1983, an economic upturn began as consumers went on a spending spree. Their confidence in the economy was bolstered by tax cuts, a decline in interest rates, and lower inflation. The stock market surged, unemployment declined, and the gross national product went up by almost 10 percent. The stock market boom lasted until 1987, when the market crashed, losing 508 points in one day. This fall was due in large part to automated and computerized buying and selling systems. However, the market recovered and then continued its upward climb.

THE NATIONAL DEBT CLIMBS Beneath the surface of recovery lay problems that continued to plague the economy. Tax cuts had helped the rich, while social welfare cuts had hurt the poor. Despite large reductions in parts of the

MAIN IDEA

Summarizing

A What are the main ideas of supply-side economics?

Background

President Reagan took a different approach to agricultural policy. He cut farm subsidies and called for lower farm prices to increase exports. Bad weather and poor harvests, however, contributed to the failure of this approach.

ECONOMIC BACKGROUND

THE "TRICKLE-DOWN" THEORY

Ronald Reagan's budget director, David Stockman, used supply-side economics to draft the Economic Recovery Tax Act of 1981. His tax package cut income taxes and business taxes by an average of 25 percent; the largest tax cuts went to those with the highest incomes. Administration officials defended the plan by claiming that as prosperity returned, the profits at the top would trickle down to the middle class and even the poor.

Despite Reagan's "trickle-down" theory, the wealthy gained the most from these tax cuts. In the 1980s, the rich got richer as poverty deepened for many others.

"THE INFLATION STAGECOACH"

During Reagan's first term, federal spending far outstripped federal revenue and created a huge budget deficit. In this cartoon, Reagan (with budget director David Stockman sitting beside him on the inflation stagecoach) sees something that "shouldn't be there."

SKILLBUILDER
Analyzing Political Cartoons
1. What is the meaning of the wheel flying off the stagecoach?
2. Whom do the passengers inside the stagecoach represent?

 SEE SKILLBUILDER HANDBOOK, PAGE R24.

budget, federal spending still outstripped federal revenue. Budget deficits were growing. Even though Reagan backed away from supply-side economics in 1982 and imposed new taxes, they were not enough to balance the budget. By the end of his first term, the national debt had almost doubled. **B**

Judicial Power Shifts to the Right

Anita Hill and Clarence Thomas testify before the Senate Judiciary Committee in October 1991.

One of the most important ways in which Reagan accomplished his conservative goals was through his appointments to the Supreme Court. Reagan nominated **Sandra Day O'Connor,** Antonin Scalia, and Anthony M. Kennedy to fill seats left by retiring judges. O'Connor was the first woman to be appointed to the Court. He also nominated Justice William Rehnquist, the most conservative justice on the court at the time, to the position of chief justice.

President Bush later made the Court even more conservative when David H. Souter replaced retiring justice William Brennan. Bush also nominated Clarence Thomas to take the place of Thurgood Marshall. However, controversy exploded when law professor Anita Hill testified that Thomas had sexually harassed her when she worked for him in the 1980s. During several days of televised Senate hearings, committee members questioned Thomas, Hill, and witnesses for each side. Thomas eventually won approval by a final vote of 52 to 48.

The Reagan and Bush appointments to the Supreme Court ended the liberal control over the Court that had begun under Franklin Roosevelt. These appointments became increasingly significant as the Court revisited constitutional issues related to such topics as discrimination, abortion, and affirmative action. In 1989, the Court, in a series of rulings, restricted a woman's right to an abortion. The Court also imposed new restrictions on civil rights laws that had been designed to protect the rights of women and minorities. During the 1990–1991 session, the Court narrowed the rights of arrested persons.

MAIN IDEA

Analyzing Effects
B What were some of the effects of "Reaganomics"?

Background

In *Cruzan v. Missouri Department of Health* (1990), the Supreme Court began to establish legislative and judicial guidelines on the "right to die" issue. In *Planned Parenthood of Southeastern PA v. Casey* (1992), the Court upheld *Roe v. Wade,* but allowed the restrictions of notification and consent on minors seeking abortions.

Deregulating the Economy

Background
During the 1980s housing boom, deregulated savings and loan institutions loaned out too much of their reserves. When the boom went bust, borrowers could not repay their loans and many S&Ls went bankrupt. The federal government had to step in to save the S&L industry at a cost of about $152 billion.

Reagan achieved one of his most important objectives—reducing the size and power of the federal government—in part by cutting federal entitlement programs but also through **deregulation,** the cutting back of federal regulation of industry. As part of his campaign for smaller government, he removed price controls on oil and eliminated federal health and safety inspections for nursing homes. He deregulated the airline industry (allowing airlines to abandon unprofitable air routes) and the savings and loan industry. One of the positive results of this deregulation was that it increased competition and often resulted in lower prices for consumers.

In a further effort at deregulation, President Reagan cut the budget of the **Environmental Protection Agency (EPA),** which had been established in 1970 to fight pollution and conserve natural resources. He ignored pleas from Canada to reduce acid rain and appointed opponents of the regulations to enforce them. For example, James Watt, Reagan's secretary of the interior, sold millions of acres of public land to private developers—often at bargain prices. He opened the continental shelf to oil and gas drilling, which many people thought posed environmental risks. Watt also encouraged timber cutting in national forests and eased restrictions on coal mining.

Conservative Victories in 1984 and 1988

It was clear by 1984 that Reagan had forged a large coalition of conservative voters who highly approved of his policies. These voters included the following:

- *businesspeople*—who wanted to deregulate the economy
- *Southerners*—who welcomed the limits on federal power
- *Westerners*—who resented federal controls on mining and grazing
- *Reagan Democrats*—who agreed with Reagan on limiting federal government and thought that the Democratic Party had drifted too far to the left

THE 1984 PRESIDENTIAL ELECTION In 1984, Reagan and Bush won the Republican nominations for reelection without challenge. Walter Mondale, who had been vice-president under President Carter, won the Democratic Party's nomination and chose Representative **Geraldine Ferraro** of New York as his running mate. Ferraro became the first woman on a major party's presidential ticket.

In 1984 the economy was strong. Reagan and Bush won by a landslide, carrying every state but Mondale's home state of Minnesota and the District of Columbia.

VIDEO
President Reagan Shot

hmhsocialstudies.com

HISTORICAL SPOTLIGHT

AN ASSASSINATION ATTEMPT
On March 30, 1981, President Reagan and other members of his staff were shot by a mentally unbalanced man named John Hinckley, Jr. While being wheeled into surgery to have a bullet removed, the president said to his wife, "Honey, I forgot to duck" (a line first used by boxer Jack Dempsey in the 1920s, after losing his heavyweight title). In the operating room, Reagan said to the team of surgeons, "I hope you fellas are Republicans." Reagan recovered speedily and his popularity grew.

▲ President Reagan is pushed into a presidential limousine after being shot by a deranged man.

George Bush announces his presidential candidacy at a rally in 1987.

THE 1988 PRESIDENTIAL ELECTION

In 1988, a majority of Americans were economically comfortable, and they attributed their comfort to Reagan and Bush. When Michael Dukakis, the Democratic governor of Massachusetts, ran for the presidency in 1988 against **George Bush**, Reagan's vice-president, most voters saw little reason for change.

George Bush simply built on President Reagan's legacy by promising, "Read my lips: no new taxes" in his acceptance speech at the Republican Convention. He

> *"Read my lips: no new taxes."*
> GEORGE BUSH

stressed his commitment to the conservative ideas of the Moral Majority. Though Bush asserted that he wanted a "kinder, gentler nation," his campaign sponsored a number of negative "attack ads" aimed at his opponents. He told audiences that Dukakis was an ultraliberal whose views were outside the mainstream of American values. In particular, Bush suggested that Dukakis was soft on crime and unpatriotic.

Some commentators believed that the negative ads contributed to the lowest voter turnout in 64 years. Only half of the eligible voters went to the polls in 1988. Fifty-three percent voted for George Bush, who won 426 electoral votes. Bush's electoral victory was viewed, as Reagan's had been, as a mandate for conservative social and political policies. **C**

MAIN IDEA

Analyzing Causes
C What factors contributed to Reagan's victory in 1984 and Bush's victory in 1988?

SECTION 2 ASSESSMENT

1. TERMS & NAMES For each term or name below, write a sentence explaining its significance.

- Reaganomics
- supply-side economics
- Strategic Defense Initiative
- Sandra Day O'Connor
- deregulation
- Environmental Protection Agency (EPA)
- Geraldine Ferraro
- George Bush

MAIN IDEA

2. TAKING NOTES
Use a diagram like the one below to explore the effects of "Reaganomics."

```
DEFINITION OF REAGANOMICS
          ↓
    Short-Term Effects
          ↓
    Long-Term Effects
```

Explain in a paragraph whether you think "Reaganomics" was good or bad for the economy.

CRITICAL THINKING

3. ANALYZING MOTIVES
Why did President Reagan and President Bush think it was important to appoint conservative justices to the Supreme Court?

4. EVALUATING
In your opinion, was Reagan's first term a success? **Think About:**
- how his tax cuts impacted the rich and the poor
- the economy
- the federal budget

5. ANALYZING PRIMARY SOURCES
Read the following excerpt from Ronald Reagan's speech at the 1992 Republican Convention.

> We mustn't forget . . . the very different America that existed just 12 years ago; an America with 21 percent interest rates and . . . double-digit inflation; an America where mortgage payments doubled, paychecks plunged, and motorists sat in gas lines; an America whose leaders told us . . . that what we really needed was another good dose of government control and higher taxes.

What picture did Reagan paint of the Carter administration?

PI 2.3
PI 3.1

CC Unit 7.III.B.4.b(4)   CC Unit 7.V.C.5.c
CC Unit 7.V.C.5.d   CC Unit 7.VI.D.2
CC Unit 7.V.D.3

Social Concerns in the 1980s

MAIN IDEA	WHY IT MATTERS NOW	Terms & Names
Beneath the surge of prosperity that marked the conservative era of the 1980s lay serious social problems.	Issues involving health care, education, civil rights, and equal rights for women continue to challenge American society.	• AIDS (acquired immune deficiency syndrome) • pay equity • L. Douglas Wilder • Jesse Jackson • Lauro Cavazos • Antonia Coello Novello

One American's Story

hmhsocialstudies.com
TAKING NOTES

Use the graphic organizer online to take notes on social problems and government responses during the Reagan and Bush years.

Trevor Ferrell lived an ordinary life in Gladwyne, an affluent suburb 12 miles from downtown Philadelphia. Trevor had brothers and sisters, his own room, a favorite pillow, a fondness for video games, and a bike. In short, he seemed like a typical 11-year-old boy until he watched a television news report about homeless people.

Trevor was astonished. "Do people really live like that?" he asked his parents. "I thought they lived like that in India, but not here, I mean in America." Trevor convinced his parents to drive downtown that night, where he gave a pillow and a blanket to the first homeless man he saw. Soon he and his family were collecting food and clothes to give to the homeless.

A PERSONAL VOICE TREVOR FERRELL

" They have to live on the streets, and right after you see one of them, you see somebody in a limousine pull up to a huge, empty mansion. It's such a difference. Some people can get anything they want, and these other people couldn't get a penny if they needed one. "

—quoted in *Trevor's Place*

Trevor Ferrell offers clothes to a homeless person in Philadelphia, 1983.

As Trevor saw, the restored American economy of the 1980s did not mean renewed prosperity for everyone. As Presidents Reagan and Bush pursued conservative domestic policies, people disagreed about the impact of these policies.

Health, Education, and Cities in Crisis

In the 1980s, both in the cities and in rural and suburban areas, local governments strove to deal with crises in health, education, and safety. Americans directed their attention to issues such as AIDS, drug abuse, abortion, and education.

▲ The AIDS quilt was displayed on the National Mall in Washington, D.C., in 1987. Each panel honors a person who died of AIDS.

HEALTH ISSUES One of the most troubling issues that concerned Americans in the 1980s was **AIDS (acquired immune deficiency syndrome).** Possibly beginning as early as the 1960s, AIDS spread rapidly throughout the world. Caused by a virus that destroys the immune system, AIDS weakens the body so that it is prone to infections and normally rare cancers.

AIDS is transmitted through bodily fluids, and most of the early victims of the disease were either homosexual men or intravenous drug users who shared needles. However, many people also contracted AIDS through contaminated blood transfusions, and children acquired it by being born to infected mothers. As the 1980s progressed, increasing numbers of heterosexuals began contracting AIDS. As the epidemic grew, so did concern over prevention and cure.

ABORTION Many Americans were concerned about abortion in the 1980s. Abortion had been legal in the United States since 1973, when the Supreme Court ruled in *Roe* v. *Wade* that first-trimester abortions were protected by a woman's right to privacy. Opponents of legalized abortion quickly organized under the pro-life banner. They argued that human life begins at conception and that no woman has the right to terminate a human life by her individual decision. Proponents of legalized abortion described themselves as pro-choice. They argued that reproductive choices were personal health-care matters and noted that many women had died from abortions performed by unskilled people in unsterile settings before the procedure was legalized.

In July 1989, the Supreme Court ruled in *Webster* v. *Reproductive Health Care Services* that states had the right to impose new restrictions on abortion. As a result, abortion restrictions varied from state to state. Ⓐ

MAIN IDEA

Contrasting
Ⓐ What are the two viewpoints on legalized abortion?

DRUG ABUSE Battles over abortion rights sometimes competed for public attention with concerns about rising drug abuse. A few people argued that drugs should be legalized to reduce the power of gangs who made a living selling illegal drugs. Others called for treatment facilities to treat addictions. The Reagan administration launched a war on drugs and supported moves to prosecute users as well as dealers. First Lady Nancy Reagan toured the country with an antidrug campaign that admonished students to "Just say no!" to drugs.

> *"Just say no!"*
> NANCY REAGAN, SLOGAN
> IN THE WAR ON DRUGS

EDUCATION Education became another issue that stirred people's concerns. In 1983, a federal commission issued a report on education titled *A Nation at Risk*. The report revealed that American students lagged behind students in most other industrialized nations. In addition, the report stated that 23 million Americans were unable to follow an instruction manual or fill out a job application form.

The commission's findings touched off a debate about the quality of education. The commission recommended more homework, longer school days, and an extended school year. It also promoted increased pay and merit raises for teachers, as well as a greater emphasis on basic subjects such as English, math, science, social studies, and computer science.

In April 1991, President Bush announced an education initiative, "America 2000." He argued that choice was the salvation of American schools and recommended allowing parents to use public funds to send their children to schools of their choice—public, private, or religious. First Lady Barbara Bush toured the country to promote reading and writing skills. **B**

MAIN IDEA

Identifying Problems
B What problems in education emerged during the 1980s?

THE URBAN CRISIS The crisis in education was closely connected to the crisis in the cities. Many undereducated students lived in cities such as Baltimore, Chicago, Detroit, Philadelphia, and Washington, D.C. During the 1970s, the United States had become increasingly suburbanized as more and more white families responded to the lure of new homes, big lawns, shopping malls, and well-equipped schools outside the cities. Businesses moved, too, taking jobs and tax revenue with them.

Poor people and racial minorities were often left in cities burdened by high unemployment rates, crumbling infrastructures, inadequate funds for sanitation and health services, deteriorating schools, and growing social problems. By 1992, thousands of people were homeless, including many families with children. Cities were increasingly divided into wealthy neighborhoods and poverty-stricken areas.

One poverty-stricken area, south-central Los Angeles (which had erupted in violence in 1965 and 1968) erupted again in 1992. Four white police officers had been videotaped beating an African-American man named Rodney King, who had been fleeing from the officers in a speeding car. An all-white jury found the officers not guilty on charges of brutality. This verdict resulted in riots that lasted five days and caused the deaths of 53 people.

DIFFICULT DECISIONS

SENDING MONEY INTO SPACE

Under the Reagan administration, the government shifted the emphasis of the space program from scientific to military and commercial applications.

Beginning in 1981, NASA directed a series of space shuttle flights. The agency hoped to establish a space station and have the shuttle ferry workers and materials to it.

The explosion of the space shuttle *Challenger* in 1986 in which the crew was killed *(crew shown above)* caused a reexamination of ventures into space. Many people thought the money spent on space should be spent on social needs.

1. Should the federal government spend money on space exploration when so many American citizens require basic assistance?

2. If you were a legislator being asked to vote in favor of funding space exploration today, how would you vote? Why?

The Equal Rights Struggle

Within this environment of dwindling resources and social struggle, women worked to achieve economic and social gains.

POLITICAL LOSSES AND GAINS During the early 1980s, women's rights activists worked to obtain ratification of the Equal Rights Amendment (ERA). Although Congress had passed the amendment in 1972, it had not yet been ratified, or approved, by three-fourths of the states. Supporters of the amendment had until June 30, 1982, to gain ratification from 38 states. They obtained only 35 of the 38 ratifications they needed, and the ERA did not become law. With the failure of the Equal Rights Amendment, women's organizations began to concentrate on electing women to public office. More women candidates began to run for office, and in 1984 the Democrats chose Geraldine Ferraro as their vice-presidential candidate. She had spoken of the necessity for women to continue working for equal opportunities in American society.

Geraldine Ferraro speaks at the 1984 Democratic Convention.

A PERSONAL VOICE GERALDINE FERRARO

" It is not just those of us who have reached the top who are fighting this daily battle. It is a fight in which all of us—rich and poor, career and home oriented, young and old—participate, simply because we are women. "

—quoted in *Vital Speeches of the Day*

In the November 1992 election, the number of women in the House of Representatives increased from 23 to 47, and the number of women senators tripled—from two to six. President Reagan also had earlier named two women to his cabinet: In 1983, Elizabeth Dole became secretary of transportation, and Margaret Heckler became secretary of health and human services. Nevertheless, women remained underrepresented in political affairs. **C**

INEQUALITY Several factors contributed to what some called the "feminization of poverty." By 1992, 57.8 percent of the nation's women were part of the work force, and a growing percentage of women worked as professionals and managers. However, in that year women earned only about 75 cents for every dollar men earned. Female college graduates earned only slightly more than male high-school graduates. Also, about 31 percent of female heads of households lived in poverty, and among African-American women, the poverty rate was even higher. New trends in divorce settlements aggravated the situation. Because of no-fault divorce, fewer women won alimony payments, and the courts rarely enforced the meager child support payments they awarded.

To close the income gap that left so many women poor, women's organizations and unions proposed a system of **pay equity.** Jobs would

Women's and Men's Average Yearly Earnings in Selected Careers, 1982		
Career	Women	Men
Accountant	$19,916	$25,272
Advertising Manager	19,396	32,292
Computer Operator	13,728	17,992
Cook	8,476	9,880
Engineer	26,052	31,460
Financial Manager	19,136	30,004
High School Teacher	18,980	21,424
Insurance Salesperson	15,236	22,152
Lawyer	30,264	34,008
Personnel Specialist	17,836	26,832
Physician	21,944	26,884
Police/ Detective	15,548	20,072
Real Estate Salesperson	16,432	24,076
Registered Nurse	20,592	20,696
Retail Sales Worker	8,736	13,728
Social Worker	15,600	20,436
University Professor	20,748	26,832

Source: Bureau of Labor Statistics, Current Population Survey, 1983–1989.

SKILLBUILDER Interpreting Charts
1. Name one career that paid men and women almost equally.
2. What conclusion can you draw from this chart?

be rated on the basis of the amount of education they required, the amount of physical strength needed to perform them, and the number of people that an employee supervised. Instead of relying on traditional pay scales, employers would establish pay rates that reflected each job's requirements. By 1989, 20 states had begun adjusting government jobs to offer pay equity for jobs of comparable worth.

Women also fought for improvements in the workplace. Since many working women headed single-parent households or had children under the age of six, they pressed for family benefits. Government and corporate benefit packages began to include maternity leaves, flexible hours and workweeks, job sharing, and work-at-home arrangements. Some of these changes were launched by individual firms, while others required government intervention. Yet the Reagan administration sharply cut the budget for daycare and other similar programs. **D**

MAIN IDEA

Analyzing Issues

D What gains did women make during the 1980s and early 1990s?

The Fight for Rights Continues

Cuts in government programs and the backlash against civil rights initiatives, such as affirmative action, affected other groups as well.

AFRICAN AMERICANS African Americans made striking political gains during the 1980s, even though their economic progress suffered. By the mid-1980s, African-American mayors governed many cities, including Los Angeles, Detroit, Chicago, Atlanta, New Orleans, Philadelphia, and Washington, D.C. Hundreds of communities in both the North and the South had elected African Americans to serve as sheriffs, school board members, state legislators, and members of Congress. In 1990, **L. Douglas Wilder** of Virginia became the nation's first African-American governor. The Reverend **Jesse Jackson** ran for the Democratic presidential nomination in 1984 and 1988.

Middle-class African Americans often held professional and managerial positions. But the poor faced an uncertain future of diminishing opportunities. In 1989, the newly conservative Supreme Court handed down a series of decisions that continued to change the nation's course on civil rights. In the case of *Richmond* v. *J. A. Croson Company*, for example, the Court further limited the scope of affirmative action, policies that were designed to correct the effects of discrimination in the employment or education of minority groups or women. Other decisions by the Court outlawed contracts set aside for minority businesses. Sylvester Monroe, an African-American correspondent for *Newsweek* magazine, commented on the way in which some African Americans saw the backlash against affirmative action. **E**

MAIN IDEA

Analyzing Issues

E What political gains did African Americans make during the 1980s?

▲ Jesse Jackson campaigns for the Democratic presidential nomination in 1984.

★ **A PERSONAL VOICE** SYLVESTER MONROE

"There's a finite pie and everybody wants his piece. Everybody is afraid of losing his piece of the pie. That's what the fight against affirmative action is all about. People feel threatened. As for blacks, they're passé. They're not in any more. Nobody wants to talk about race."

—quoted in *The Great Divide*

▲ Dr. Antonia Coello Novello served as surgeon general under President George Bush.

GAINS FOR LATINOS Latinos became the fastest growing minority during the 1980s. By 1990, they constituted almost nine percent of the population, and demographers estimated that Latinos would soon outnumber African Americans as the nation's largest minority group. About two out of three Latinos were Mexican Americans, who lived mostly in the Southwest. A Puerto Rican community thrived in the Northeast, and a Cuban population was concentrated in Florida. Like African Americans, Latinos gained political power during the 1980s. Toney Anaya became governor of New Mexico, while Robert Martinez became governor of Florida. In August 1988, President Reagan appointed **Lauro Cavazos** as secretary of education. In 1990, President Bush named Dr. **Antonia Coello Novello** to the post of surgeon general.

Many Latinos supported bilingual education. They feared that abandoning Spanish would weaken their distinctive culture. In the words of Daniel Villanueva, a television executive, "We want to be here, but without losing our language and our culture. They are a richness, a treasure that we don't care to lose." The Bilingual Education Act of 1968 and the 1975 amendent to the Voting Rights Act enabled Spanish speakers to attend school and vote in their own language, but by the mid-1980s opposition to bilingualism was rising. Critics argued that it slowed the rate at which Spanish-speaking people entered mainstream American life. They also feared that the nation would become split between English speakers and Spanish speakers.

NATIVE AMERICANS SPEAK OUT Native Americans also became more self-conscious of their dignity and more demanding of their rights. In the 1970s, they organized schools to teach young Native Americans about their past. They also began to fight for the return of ancestral lands wrongfully taken from them.

During the 1980s, the Reagan administration slashed aid to Native Americans for health, education, and other services. Driven to find new sources of revenue, Native Americans campaigned for gambling casinos on their land as a way to bring in money. After the Supreme Court ruled in favor of Native Americans, many tribes opened Las Vegas-style casinos, which provided additional funding for the tribes that operated them. Nonetheless, the long-term problems faced by Native Americans have not been solved by gambling casinos, although the new wealth has helped to some extent. **F**

AN EXPANDING ASIAN-AMERICAN POPULATION Asian Americans were the second fastest growing minority in the United States during the 1980s. By 1982, the U.S. population included about 8.3 million Asian Americans and Pacific Islanders. Asian Americans constituted 3.25 percent of the population.

Some have cited Asian Americans as an example of how minorities can succeed in the U.S. Yet while Asian Americans have low crime rates, low school dropout rates, and low divorce rates, Asian-American unemployment and poverty have been higher than the national figures.

Vocabulary

demographer: a person who studies the characteristics of human population, such as growth, density, and distribution

NOW & THEN

AFFIRMATIVE ACTION

Affirmative action refers to the effort to provide education and employment opportunities for historically disadvantaged groups, such as women and racial and ethnic minorities. The federal government first instituted affirmative action policies under the Civil Rights Act of 1964.

Presidents Reagan and Bush actively opposed affirmative action and racial quotas. Today the future of affirmative action is uncertain. In 2001, President Bush expressed support for equal opportunity, but his first attorney general, John Ashcroft, was denounced by civil rights groups, in part because of his anti-affirmative action record. In 2003 the Supreme Court protected the University of Michigan's race-conscious admissions policy. But in 2007, initiative campaigns to prohibit affirmative action were active in several states.

MAIN IDEA

Identifying Problems

F What problems did Native Americans face in the 1980s?

A gay rights march in Washington, D.C., October 1987

THE GAY RIGHTS MOVEMENT ADVANCES During the 1970s and 1980s, gay men and lesbians began to fight openly for civil rights. While the gay rights movement suffered a setback during the early 1980s in the face of conservative opposition and the AIDS crisis, by the late 1980s and early 1990s a new surge of gay activism was under way in the country. Direct action groups sprang up throughout the country, calling for an end to anti-gay discrimination. Although several speakers at the 1992 Republican National Convention condemned gay activism, these speakers were unable to slow the pace of change. By the year 1993, seven states and 110 communities had outlawed such discrimination.

SECTION 3 ASSESSMENT

1. TERMS & NAMES For each term or name below, write a sentence explaining its significance.

- AIDS (acquired immune deficiency syndrome)
- pay equity
- L. Douglas Wilder
- Jesse Jackson
- Lauro Cavazos
- Antonia Coello Novello

MAIN IDEA

2. TAKING NOTES
Use a chart like the one below to list some of the social problems of the Reagan and Bush years and how the government responded to them.

Social Problems	Government Responses

Choose one issue and write other responses the government might have made.

CRITICAL THINKING

3. PREDICTING EFFECTS
How might improvements in the educational system help solve other social problems? **Think About:**

- the impact education might have on health-related problems
- the impact that education might have on urban problems
- the impact that education might have on unemployment

4. COMPARING
Compare the political gains and losses experienced by various groups during the Reagan and Bush administrations.

5. FORMING GENERALIZATIONS
Why might a widening gap between the richest and poorest citizens of a country be a cause for concern about that country's future?

Sunbelt, Rustbelt, Ecotopia

In the 1970s, people on the move created new names for areas to which they moved. The West was sometimes called **Ecotopia** because of its varied scenery and ecological attractions. The South and Southwest were called the **Sunbelt** because of their warm climate. The North Central and Northeast regions were called the **Rustbelt** because many of their aging factories had been closed.

As a geographical term, *region* is used to designate an area with common features or characteristics that set it apart from its surroundings. For example, the Mississippi Valley is a large physical region; Warren Woods is a small physical region. The term is often used for groups of states that share an area and certain characteristics.

As people move from state to state, and from region to region, they gradually transform the balance of political and economic power in the nation. Each census in recent times has recorded how certain states have gained population and others have lost population. If the gains or losses are large enough, a state's representation in the U.S. House of Representatives will increase or decrease commensurately.

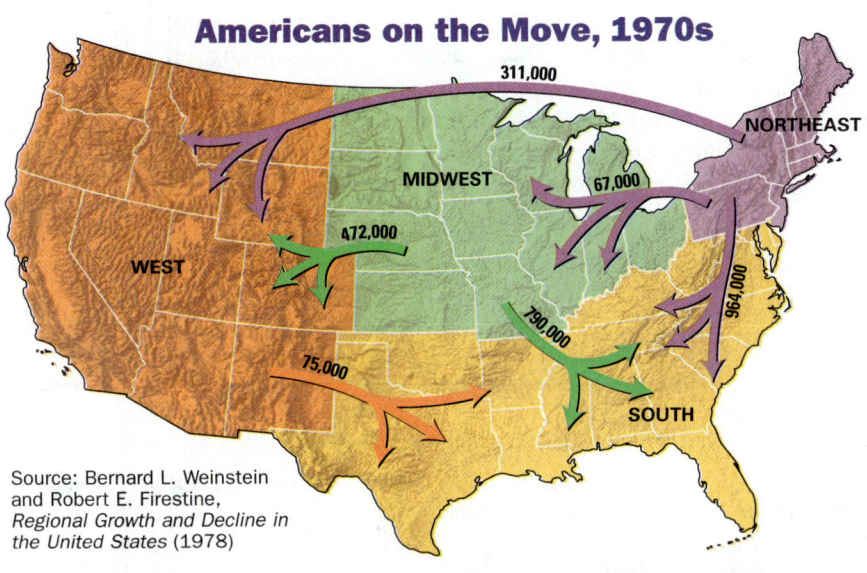

Americans on the Move, 1970s

311,000
NORTHEAST
MIDWEST
67,000
472,000
WEST
964,000
790,000
75,000
SOUTH

Source: Bernard L. Weinstein and Robert E. Firestine, *Regional Growth and Decline in the United States* (1978)

REGIONAL EXCHANGES

Between 1970 and 1975, the population center of the United States, which had generally moved westward for 17 decades, suddenly moved southward as well. The arrows show the net number of Americans who migrated and their patterns of migration in the early 1970s. The West gained 311,000 from the Northeast plus 472,000 from the North Central region, for a total of 783,000 people. However, it also lost 75,000 people to the South. During the 1980s and 1990s the southward and westward shift continued.

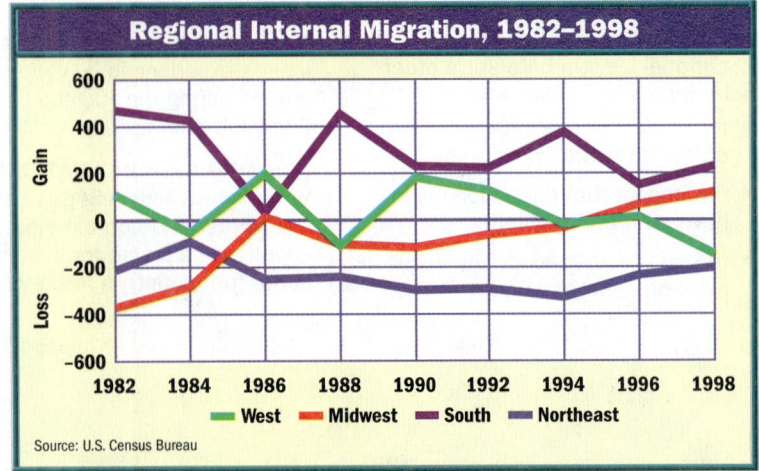

Regional Internal Migration, 1982–1998

Gain / Loss

600
400
200
0
-200
-400
-600

1982 1984 1986 1988 1990 1992 1994 1996 1998

West   Midwest   South   Northeast

Source: U.S. Census Bureau

Americans on the Move, 1990–2000

Between 1990 and 2000, our country's population grew by a record 32.7 million people to 281.4 million. For the first time in the 20th century, all 50 states gained people between census years. But because of internal migration (see graph on page 1052) and other factors, 10 states lost and 8 states gained seats in the 2000 Congressional apportionment.

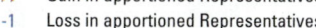

▨	Population increase > 1 million
▨	Population increase < 100,000
5,615	Net gain/loss from domestic migration
+1	Gain in apportioned Representatives
-1	Loss in apportioned Representatives

Source: U.S. Census Bureau

WASH. 381,552
OREGON 270,903
MONTANA 47,875
IDAHO 136,339
N. DAK. -37,387
MINN. 86,847
WYOMING -3,676
S. DAK. -2,881
WIS. 90,224 -1
NEVADA 433,219 -1
UTAH 73,016
NEBRASKA -3,693
IOWA -15,542
MICH. -199,465 -1
CALIFORNIA -2,170,790 +1
COLORADO 402,832 +1
KANSAS -16,224
ILL. -560,003 -1
IND. 82,674 -1
OHIO -166,200 -1
ARIZONA 577,038 +2
NEW MEXICO 42,339
OKLAHOMA 42,688 -1
MO. 101,020
ARK. 110,878
KY. 97,187
W. VA. 2,082
VA. 96,562
N.C. 554,268 +1
TEXAS 569,957 +2
TENN. 356,907
S.C. 143,213
MISS. 44,639 -1
ALA. 112,163
GA. 665,418 +2
LA. -139,704
FLA. 1,108,514 +2
N.H. 29,607
VT. 5,615
MAINE -7,347
MASS. -244,494
N.Y. -1,888,936 -2
R.I. -63,250
CONN.
N.J. -226,370 -1
-378,495
PENN. -250,958 -2
DEL. 35,058
MD. -55,060

CALIFORNIA Despite a net loss through migration to other states of 2 million people in the 1990s, international immigrants and in-state births gave California the greatest net increase in population among the 50 states.

NEVADA There has been such a large influx of people since 1945 that building houses for newcomers has become a major industry in Nevada.

TEXAS During the 1990s, Texas eclipsed New York to become the nation's second-most populous state behind California. Sixty percent of the Texas increase has been driven by Hispanic growth.

WASHINGTON, D.C. While all 50 states gained in population during the decade, the population of Washington, D.C., decreased by nearly 6 percent.

FLORIDA During the 1990s, Florida's population increased 23.5 percent, making it the nation's fourth-largest. With so many new residents, Florida gained two additional House seats, bringing its congressional delegation to 25.

(below) Housing development near Danville, California, 1990

THINKING CRITICALLY

1. **Analyzing Distributions** Which states lost the most people between 1990 and 2000? Which states gained the most people?

2. **Creating a Graph** Choose one of the most populous states and then pose a historical question about population in that state. Create a graph or graphs that show various aspects of population for the state you have chosen. Be sure that the graph(s) help to answer the question you posed. Then display the graph(s) and the question in the classroom.

 SEE SKILLBUILDER HANDBOOK, PAGE R30.

↗ hmhsocialstudies.com **RESEARCH WEB LINKS**

PI 2.3 CC Unit 7.V.E.1 CC Unit 7.V.E.2
PI 3.1 CC Unit 7.V.G CC Unit 7.VI.A.3

Foreign Policy After the Cold War

MAIN IDEA	WHY IT MATTERS NOW	Terms & Names
The end of the Cold War, marked by the breakup of the Soviet Union in 1991, led to a redirection of many U.S. goals and policies.	After the Cold War, the United States provided and continues to provide substantial economic support to the new capitalistic and democratic nations.	• **Mikhail Gorbachev** • *glasnost* • *perestroika* • **INF Treaty** • **Tiananmen Square** • *Sandinistas* • *Contras* • **Operation Desert Storm**

One American's Story

TAKING NOTES

Use the graphic organizer online to take notes on U.S. foreign policy.

Colin Powell did not start out in life with any special privileges. He was born in Harlem and raised in the Bronx, where he enjoyed street games and tolerated school. Then, while attending the City College of New York, he joined the Reserve Officer Training Corps (ROTC). He got straight A's in ROTC, and so he decided to make the army his career.

Powell served first in Vietnam and then in Korea and West Germany. He rose in rank to become a general; then President Reagan made him national security adviser. In this post, Powell noted that the Soviet Union was a factor in all the administration's foreign policy decisions.

> **A PERSONAL VOICE** COLIN POWELL
>
> " Our choosing sides in conflicts around the world was almost always decided on the basis of East-West competition. The new Soviet leader, Mikhail Gorbachev, however, was turning the old Cold War formulas on their head. . . . Ronald Reagan . . . had the vision and flexibility, lacking in many knee-jerk Cold Warriors [participants in the Cold War between the U.S. and the USSR], to recognize that Gorbachev was a new man in a new age offering new opportunities for peace. "
>
> —*My American Journey*

General
Colin Powell

Though U.S. foreign policy in the early 1980s was marked by intense hostility toward the Soviet Union, drastic economic problems in the Soviet Union destroyed its ability to continue the Cold War standoff.

The Cold War Ends

In March of 1985, **Mikhail Gorbachev** became the general secretary of the Communist Party in the Soviet Union. His rise to power marked the beginning of a new era in the Soviet Union.

GORBACHEV INITIATES REFORM Gorbachev had inherited a host of problems in the Soviet Union. Many of them revolved around the Soviet economy, which was under a great amount of stress. Reagan added pressure by increasing U.S. defense spending. When the Soviets attempted to keep up, their economy was pushed to the brink of collapse.

A skilled diplomat and political leader, Gorbachev advocated a policy known as *glasnost* (Russian for "openness"). He allowed open criticism of the Soviet government and took steps toward freedom of the press. In 1985, he outlined his plans for *perestroika,* a restructuring of Soviet society. He called for less government control of the economy, the introduction of some private enterprise, and steps toward establishing a democratic government.

Gorbachev recognized that better relations with the United States would allow the Soviets to reduce their military spending and reform their economy. As a result, he initiated a series of arms-control meetings that led to the **INF Treaty (Intermediate-Range Nuclear Forces Treaty)** signed on December 8, 1987. The treaty eliminated two classes of weapons systems in Europe and allowed each nation to make on-site inspections of the other's military installations. **A**

THE SOVIET UNION DECLINES Gorbachev's introduction of democratic ideals led to a dramatic increase in nationalism on the part of the Soviet Union's non-Russian republics. In December 1991, 14 non-Russian republics declared their independence from the Soviet Union. Muscled aside by Russian reformers who thought he was working too slowly toward democracy, Gorbachev resigned as Soviet president. After 74 years, the Soviet Union dissolved.

A loose federation known as the Commonwealth of Independent States (CIS) took the place of the Soviet Union. In February 1992, President George Bush and Russian president Boris Yeltsin issued a formal statement declaring an end to the Cold War that had plagued the two nations and divided the world since 1945. In January 1993, Yeltsin and Bush signed the START II pact, designed to cut both nations' nuclear arsenals by two-thirds.

THE COLLAPSE OF COMMUNIST REGIMES Before his resignation, Gorbachev had encouraged the people of East Germany and Eastern Europe to go their own ways. In 1988, when the Soviet Union was still intact, he reduced the number of Soviet troops in Eastern Europe and allowed non-Communist parties to organize in satellite nations, such as East Germany and Poland. He encouraged the satellite nations to move toward democracy.

During a speech given at the Berlin Wall in 1987, President Reagan challenged Gorbachev to back up his reforms with decisive action.

WORLD STAGE

DEMOCRATIC ELECTIONS IN RUSSIA

After the Soviet Union dissolved in 1991, Boris Yeltsin continued as president of Russia. Yeltsin ended price controls and increased private business ownership. The Russian parliament opposed Yeltsin's policies, even though a majority of voters supported them.

In December 1993, Russian voters installed a new parliament and approved a new constitution, parts of which resembled the U.S. Constitution. In 1996, Yeltsin won reelection as president of Russia. He was succeeded in 2000 by Vladimir Putin.

★ **A PERSONAL VOICE** RONALD REAGAN

"**General Secretary Gorbachev, if you seek peace, if you seek prosperity for the Soviet Union and Eastern Europe, if you seek liberalization: Come here to this gate! Mr. Gorbachev, open this gate! Mr. Gorbachev, tear down this wall!**"

—speech, June 12, 1987

In October 1989, East Germans startled the world by repudiating their Communist government. On November 9, 1989, East Germany opened the Berlin Wall, allowing free passage between the two parts of the city for the first time in 28 years. East German border guards stood by and watched as Berliners pounded away with hammers and other tools at the despised wall. In early 1990, East Germany held its first free elections, and on October 3 of that year, the two German nations were united. **B**

Other European nations also adopted democratic reforms. Czechoslovakia withdrew from the Soviet bloc. The Baltic states of Latvia, Estonia, and Lithuania declared their independence from the Soviet Union. Hungary, Bulgaria, and Romania made successful transitions from communism.

Yugoslavia, however, collapsed. Four of its six republics seceded. Ethnic rivalries deteriorated into a brutal war among Muslims, Orthodox Serbs, and Roman Catholic Croats, who were dividing Yugoslavia, each claiming parts of it. Serbia backed Serb minorities that were stirring up civil unrest in Croatia and Bosnia.

COMMUNISM CONTINUES IN CHINA Even before perestroika unfolded in the Soviet Union, economic reform had begun in China. Early in the 1980s, the Chinese Communist government loosened its grip on business and eliminated some price controls. Students in China began to demand freedom of speech and a greater voice in government.

In April 1989, university students in China held marches that quickly grew into large demonstrations in Beijing's **Tiananmen** (tyän'än'měn') **Square** and on the streets of other cities. In Tiananmen Square, Chinese students constructed a version of the Statue of Liberty to symbolize their struggle for democracy.

China's premier, Li Peng, eventually ordered the military to crush the protesters. China's armed forces stormed into Tiananmen Square, slaughtering unarmed students. The world's democratic countries watched these events in horror on television. The collapse of the pro-democracy movement left the future in China uncertain. As one student leader said, "The government has won the battle here today. But they have lost the people's hearts."

▲ A demonstrator pounds away on the Berlin Wall as East German border guards look on from above at the Brandenberg Gate, on November 11, 1989.

MAIN IDEA

Analyzing Events

B What signs signaled that the Cold War had come to an end?

HISTORY

VIDEO
Tiananmen Square

↗ hmhsocialstudies.com

A Chinese protester defies the tanks in Tiananmen Square in 1989. ▶

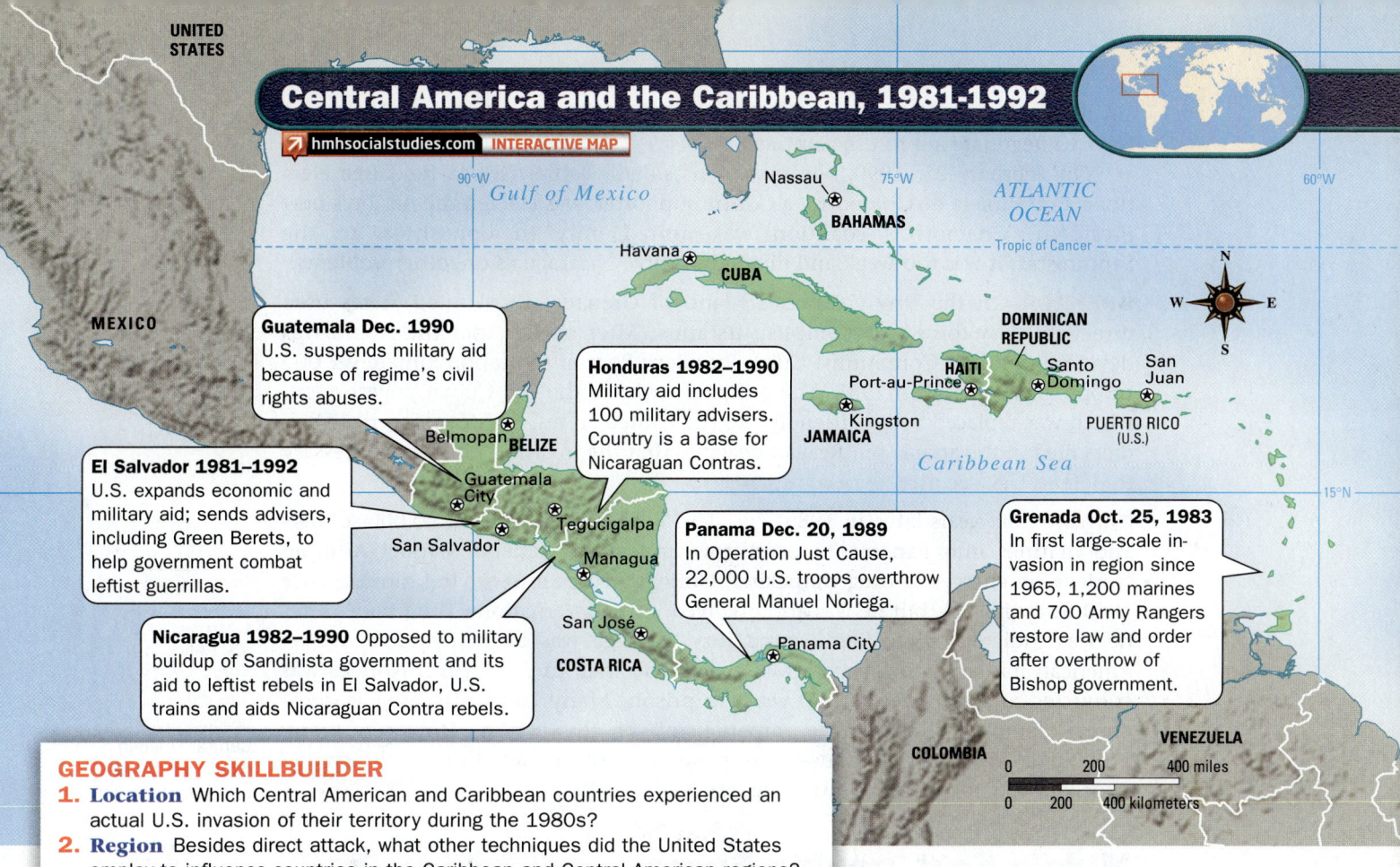

Central America and the Caribbean, 1981–1992

hmhsocialstudies.com **INTERACTIVE MAP**

Guatemala Dec. 1990
U.S. suspends military aid because of regime's civil rights abuses.

El Salvador 1981–1992
U.S. expands economic and military aid; sends advisers, including Green Berets, to help government combat leftist guerrillas.

Nicaragua 1982–1990 Opposed to military buildup of Sandinista government and its aid to leftist rebels in El Salvador, U.S. trains and aids Nicaraguan Contra rebels.

Honduras 1982–1990
Military aid includes 100 military advisers. Country is a base for Nicaraguan Contras.

Panama Dec. 20, 1989
In Operation Just Cause, 22,000 U.S. troops overthrow General Manuel Noriega.

Grenada Oct. 25, 1983
In first large-scale invasion in region since 1965, 1,200 marines and 700 Army Rangers restore law and order after overthrow of Bishop government.

GEOGRAPHY SKILLBUILDER
1. **Location** Which Central American and Caribbean countries experienced an actual U.S. invasion of their territory during the 1980s?
2. **Region** Besides direct attack, what other techniques did the United States employ to influence countries in the Caribbean and Central American regions?

Central American and Caribbean Policy

Cold War considerations during the Reagan and Bush administrations continued to influence affairs in Central America and the Caribbean. In these places, the United States still opposed left-leaning and socialist governments in favor of governments friendly to the United States.

NICARAGUA The United States had had a presence in Nicaragua ever since 1912, when President Taft sent U.S. Marines to protect American investments there. The marines left in 1933, but only after helping the dictator Anastasio Somoza come to power.

The Somoza family ruled Nicaragua for 42 years. To keep control of its business empire, the family rigged elections and assassinated political rivals. Many people believed that only a revolution would end the Somoza dictatorship.

Between 1977 and 1979, Nicaragua was engulfed in a civil war between Somoza's national guard and the **Sandinistas,** rebels who took their name from a rebel leader named Sandino who had been killed in 1934. When Sandinista rebels toppled the dictatorship of Somoza's son in 1979, President Carter recognized the new regime and sent it $83 million in economic aid. The Soviet Union and Cuba sent aid as well.

In 1981, however, President Reagan charged that Nicaragua was a Soviet outpost that was exporting revolution to other Central American countries. Reagan cut all aid to the Sandinista government and threw his support to guerrilla forces known as the **Contras** because they were against the Sandinistas. By 1983, the Contra army had grown to nearly 10,000 men, and American officials from the CIA had stationed themselves to direct operations—without congressional approval. In response, Congress passed the Boland Amendment, banning military aid to the Contras for two years. However, Reagan's administration still found ways to negotiate aid to the Contras.

On February 25, 1990, Nicaraguan president Daniel Ortega held free elections, and Violeta de Chamorro, a Contra supporter, was elected the nation's new president. Chamorro's coalition was united only in opposition to the Sandinistas; it was too weak and divided to solve Nicaragua's ongoing problems.

GRENADA On the tiny Caribbean island of Grenada, the United States used direct military force to accomplish its aims. After noting that the island was developing ties to Communist Cuba, President Reagan sent approximately 2,000 troops to the island in 1983. There they overthrew the pro-Cuban government, which was replaced by one friendlier to the United States. Eighteen American soldiers died in the attack, but Reagan declared that the invasion had been necessary to defend U.S. security.

PANAMA Six years later, in 1989, President Bush sent more than 20,000 soldiers and marines into Panama to overthrow and arrest General Manuel Antonio Noriega on charges of drug trafficking. Noriega had been receiving money since 1960 from the CIA, but he was also involved in the international drug trade. After he was indicted by a Miami grand jury, Noriega was taken by force by the American military and flown to Miami to stand trial. In April 1992, Noriega was convicted and sentenced to 40 years in prison. Many Latin American governments deplored the "Yankee imperialism" of the action. However, many Americans—and Panamanians—were pleased by the removal of a military dictator who supported drug smuggling. **C**

MAIN IDEA

Comparing
C Between 1980 and 1992, how did U.S. policies regarding Central America differ from those regarding Europe?

Middle East Trouble Spots

Results favorable to U.S. interests were more difficult to obtain in the Middle East. Negotiating conflicts between ever-shifting governments drew the United States into scandal and its first major war since Vietnam.

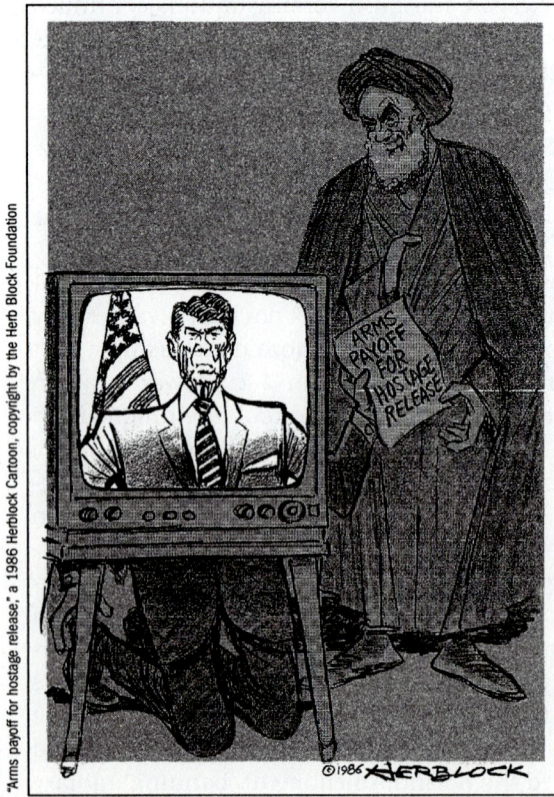

"Arms payoff for hostage release," a 1986 Herblock Cartoon, copyright by the Herb Block Foundation

THE IRAN-CONTRA SCANDAL
In 1983, terrorist groups loyal to Iran took a number of Americans hostage in Lebanon. Reagan denounced Iran and urged U.S. allies not to sell arms to Iran for its war against Iraq. In 1985, he declared that "America will never make concessions to terrorists." Therefore, Americans were shocked to learn in 1986 that President Reagan had approved the sale of arms to Iran. In exchange for those sales, Iran promised to win the release of seven American hostages held in Lebanon by pro-Iranian terrorists. What's more, members of Reagan's staff sent part of

◀ **President Reagan's message to television audiences about selling arms to Iran differed greatly from what was going on behind the scenes.**

the profits from those illegal arms sales to the Contras in Nicaragua—in direct violation of the Boland Amendment. President Reagan held a press conference to explain what had happened.

A PERSONAL VOICE RONALD REAGAN

"I am deeply troubled that the implementation of a policy aimed at resolving a truly tragic situation in the Middle East has resulted in such controversy. As I've stated previously, I believe our policy goals toward Iran were well founded."

—presidential press conference, November 25, 1986

In the summer of 1987, special committees of both houses of Congress conducted a dramatic inquiry into the Iran-Contra affair during a month of joint televised hearings. Among those testifying was Lieutenant Colonel Oliver North, a member of the National Security Council staff who played a key role in providing aid to the Contras. North appeared in military uniform adorned with service ribbons and badges. In defending his actions, North talked about patriotism and love of country. He asserted that he thought he was carrying out the president's wishes and that the end of helping the Contras justified almost any means.

After a congressional investigation, Special Prosecutor Lawrence E. Walsh, early in 1988, indicted various members of the Reagan administration who were involved in the scandal. Oliver North was found guilty of aiding the cover-up. He was fined and sentenced to perform community service. (His conviction was later overturned because he testified under a grant of limited immunity.). On Christmas Eve of 1992, President Bush pardoned a number of Reagan officials.

THE PERSIAN GULF WAR Regardless of the scandal surrounding the Iran-Contra affair, conflict with Iraq (which was Iran's long-standing enemy) and its leader, Saddam Hussein, soon eclipsed U.S. problems with Iran. During the 1980s, Iran and Iraq had fought a prolonged war, and Hussein found himself with enormous war debts to pay. Several times, Hussein had claimed that the oil-rich nation of Kuwait was really part of Iraq. On August 2, 1990, Iraqi troops invaded Kuwait. The Iraqi invaders looted Kuwait; then they headed toward Saudi Arabia and

POINT

COUNTERPOINT

"The United States must occasionally intervene militarily in regional conflicts."

Proponents of U.S. military intervention abroad agreed with General Norman Schwarzkopf that "as the only remaining superpower, we have an awesome responsibility . . . to the rest of the world."

"The United States must take the lead in promoting democracy," urged Morton H. Halperin, former director of the ACLU (American Civil Liberties Union). "To say 'Let the UN do it' is a cop-out," stated adviser Robert G. Neumann.

Political scientist Jane Sharp expressed a similar sentiment. She asked, "Can any nation that has taken no action [in Bosnia] to stop the Serbian practice of ethnic cleansing continue to call itself civilized?"

"The United States should not intervene militarily in regional conflicts."

A foreign-policy analyst at the Cato Institute, Barbara Conry, stated that "intervention in regional wars is a distraction and a drain on resources." What's more, she argued, "it does not work." Recalling the presence of American troops in Lebanon, Conry argued that intervention not only jeopardized American soldiers, it often obstructed what it sought to achieve.

"The internal freedom of a political community can be achieved only by members of that community," agreed Professor Stephen R. Shalom. He added that "using [military action] encourages quick fix solutions that ignore the underlying sources of conflict."

THINKING CRITICALLY

1. **CONNECT TO TODAY** Comparing and Contrasting What do you think are the strongest arguments for and against military intervention in regional conflicts?

    SEE SKILLBUILDER HANDBOOK, PAGE R8.

2. **CONNECT TO HISTORY** Hypothesizing With at least one partner, research the events leading up to U.S. involvement in one of these countries: Lebanon, Grenada, Panama, or Kuwait. Then negotiate to resolve the conflict.

Caspian Sea

Legend:
- Major Iraqi missile target
- Iraqi forces
- UN coalition forces
- US/UN major air strike
- US/UN naval forces

0   100   200 miles
0 100 200 kilometers

TURKEY

CYPRUS

LEBANON

Mediterranean Sea

Beirut

Damascus

SYRIA

Euphrates River

Tigris River

Haifa

ISRAEL

Tel Aviv

Jerusalem

Amman

JORDAN

IRAQ

Baghdad

IRAN

Jan. 16, 1991
US/UN air attacks begin against Iraq.

Aug. 2, 1990
Iraq invades Kuwait.

Basra

KUWAIT

Feb. 23, 1991
UN coalition launches ground war.

Kuwait City

Khafji

EGYPT

Tabuk

Hafar al Batin

King Khalid Military City

Al Jubayl

Manamah

Dhahran

BAHRAIN

Doha

QATAR

SAUDI ARABIA

Nile River

Red Sea

Persian Gulf

Tropic of Cancer

Riyadh

Women served along with men in the military during the Gulf War *(right)*. Massive oil fires started by the Iraqis burned in Kuwait *(below)*.

GEOGRAPHY SKILLBUILDER
1. **Region** What did UN coalition forces probably hope to achieve by moving forces into southern Iraq?
2. **Movement** How did the movements of coalition ground forces show that the intention of the coalition in the Gulf War was ultimately defensive, not offensive?

its oil fields. If Iraq conquered Saudi Arabia as well as Kuwait, it would control one-half of the world's known oil reserves, which would severely threaten U.S. oil supplies. **D**

For several months, President Bush and Secretary of State James Baker organized an international coalition against Iraqi aggression. With the support of Congress and the UN, President Bush launched **Operation Desert Storm** to liberate Kuwait from Iraqi control. On January 16, 1991, the United States and its allies staged a massive air assault against Iraq. On February 23, they launched a successful ground offensive from Saudi Arabia. On February 28, 1991, President Bush announced a cease-fire. Operation Desert Storm was over. Kuwait was liberated.

Millions of Americans turned out for the victory parades that greeted returning soldiers. After the debacle in Vietnam, they were thrilled the war was over, with fewer than 400 casualties among UN coalition forces. (However, there were subsequent reports that Gulf veterans were suffering from disabilities caused by chemicals used in the war.) By contrast, Iraq had suffered an estimated 100,000 military and civilian deaths. During the embargo that followed, many Iraqi children died from outbreaks of cholera, typhoid, enteritis, and other diseases.

BUSH'S DOMESTIC POLICIES Despite his great achievement in the Persian Gulf War, President Bush was not as successful on the domestic front. He was hurt by rising deficits and a recession that began in 1990 and lasted through most of 1992. Bush was forced to raise taxes despite his campaign pledge. His approval rating had dropped to 49 percent by 1992. The weak economy and the tax hike doomed Bush's reelection campaign, and 12 years of Republican leadership came to an end.

KEY PLAYER

H. NORMAN SCHWARZKOPF 1934–

In 1988, Norman Schwarzkopf, shown above, became commander in chief of forces in Asia and Africa. During the Persian Gulf War, more than 540,000 men and women served under the command of "Stormin' Norman." Schwarzkopf said of Saddam Hussein that he was "neither a strategist, nor is he schooled in the operational art, nor is he a tactician, nor is he a general, nor is he a soldier. Other than that, he is a great military man."

SECTION 4

ASSESSMENT

1. TERMS & NAMES For each term or name, write a sentence explaining its meaning.
- **Mikhail Gorbachev**
- *glasnost*
- *perestroika*
- **INF Treaty**
- **Tiananmen Square**
- *Sandinistas*
- *Contras*
- **Operation Desert Storm**

MAIN IDEA

2. TAKING NOTES
Use a chart like the one below to explain U.S. foreign policy toward world regions.

U.S. Foreign Policy
Europe
Central America and Caribbean
Middle East

Now write a paragraph in which you describe a trouble spot in one of these regions.

CRITICAL THINKING

3. ANALYZING CAUSES
What factors caused the end of the Cold War? **Think About:**
- events in the Soviet Union
- events in Germany and Eastern Europe
- how U.S. leaders responded to those events

4. FORMING GENERALIZATIONS
What factors do you think determined whether or not the United States intervened militarily in other nations?

5. HYPOTHESIZING
Is it possible for an authoritarian government to make economic reforms without also making political reforms? Support your answer with details from the text.

TERMS & NAMES

For each term or name below, write a sentence explaining its significance.

1. entitlement program
2. affirmative action
3. Moral Majority
4. Ronald Reagan
5. supply-side economics
6. Geraldine Ferraro
7. AIDS
8. Mikhail Gorbachev
9. *Contras*
10. Operation Desert Storm

MAIN IDEAS

Use your notes and the information in the chapter to answer the following questions.

A Conservative Movement Emerges
(pages 1036–1039)

1. What caused the conservative revolution of the early 1980s?
2. What factors led to Ronald Reagan's victory in 1980?

Conservative Policies Under Reagan and Bush *(pages 1040–1044)*

3. What principles formed the basis of "Reaganomics"?
4. What is deregulation, and how did it affect certain industries in the 1980s?

Social Concerns in the 1980s *(pages 1045–1051)*

5. What progress and obstacles did different minority groups experience in the 1980s?
6. What were some gains that women achieved in the 1980s?

Foreign Policy After the Cold War
(pages 1054–1061)

7. What caused the downfall of the Soviet Union and the founding of the Commonwealth of Independent States?
8. Summarize the U.S. response to Iraq's invasion of Kuwait.

CRITICAL THINKING

1. **USING YOUR NOTES** Choose two events from each of the sections of the chapter and place them in chronological order on a timeline like the one below.

2. **EVALUATING** Review the goals of the conservative movement and the actions of the government under Reagan and Bush. Evaluate how well the goals had been achieved by the end of Bush's term.

3. **INTERPRETING MAPS** Look at the map on page 1057. Between 1982 and 1992, the United States intervened in Latin America many times. How might the presence of a Communist government on the island of Cuba have influenced U.S. actions?

VISUAL SUMMARY — **THE CONSERVATIVE TIDE**

CAUSES

- Dissatisfaction with liberal policies
- Revival of Evangelical Christianity
- Reagan as a spearhead of conservatism
- Inflation and unemployment
- Emergence of the New Right and conservative coalition

EFFECTS

- Republican control of the presidency
- Cuts in taxes and government spending
- Dramatic increase in national debt
- More conservative Supreme Court
- Increased defense spending
- Deregulation

Use the passage and your knowledge of U.S. history to answer question 1.

> "That system [of republican government] has never failed us, but, for a time, we failed the system. We asked things of government that government was not equipped to give. We yielded authority to the national government that properly belonged to states or to local governments or to the people themselves. We allowed taxes and inflation to rob us of our earnings and savings and watched the great industrial machine that had made us the most productive people on Earth slow down and the number of unemployed increase."
>
> —Ronald Reagan, Second Inaugural Address, 1985

1 The passage suggests that President Ronald Reagan supported which point of view?

(1) There should be an end to all social welfare programs.
(2) The role of the federal government should be reduced.
(3) The role of the federal government should be increased.
(4) The federal government should raise taxes.

2 Which of the following events signaled the end of the Cold War?

(1) Operation Desert Storm
(2) Iran-Contra Scandal
(3) collapse of the Soviet Union
(4) protests at Tiananmen Square

Use the graph and your knowledge of U.S. history to answer question 3.

Gross Federal Debt

Source: U.S. Dept. of the Treasury

3 The graph shows that the gross federal debt —

(1) stayed the same during the Reagan and Bush years.
(2) greatly increased during the Reagan and Bush years.
(3) greatly decreased during the Reagan and Bush years.
(4) did not exist during the Reagan and Bush years.

4 Which of the following was *not* a goal of the conservative movement of the 1980s?

(1) strengthen the national defense
(2) reduce government regulations
(3) promote family values and patriotic ideals
(4) increase taxes

hmhsocialstudies.com **TEST PRACTICE**

For additional test practice, go online for:
· Diagnostic tests   · Tutorials

INTERACT WITH HISTORY

Think about the issues you explored at the beginning of the chapter. Imagine that you are working as a speechwriter for Ronald Reagan in 1980. Develop a campaign slogan, and then write a speech that contains your slogan and explains why Americans should vote for Reagan. Present your speech to the class.

FOCUS ON WRITING

Imagine that you are a journalist in the 1980s. Choose the social concern of the period that you believe to be the most significant domestic issue facing the United States. Write a newspaper editorial in which you persuade others that your issue is the most important and outline your approach for solving it. Use descriptive examples and vivid language to convince your audience to support your perspective.

MULTIMEDIA ACTIVITY

21ST CENTURY

Visit the Chapter Assessment links to find out more about Saddam Hussein's rise to power in Iraq. Write and record a short podcast describing the tactics that Hussein used to become dictator and how his policies affected the people of Iraq.

hmhsocialstudies.com

CHAPTER 34

THE UNITED STATES IN TODAY'S WORLD

Essential Question

What are the most important issues that affect the United States and the world today?

New York Standards

KEY IDEA 2 Important ideas, social and cultural values, beliefs, and traditions from New York State and United States history illustrate the connections and interactions of people and events across time and from a variety of perspectives.

KEY IDEA 3 Study about the major social, political, economic, cultural, and religious developments in New York State and United States history involves learning about the important roles and contributions of individuals and groups.

SECTION 1: The 1990s and the New Millennium

SECTION 2: The New Global Economy

SECTION 3: Technology and Modern Life

SECTION 4: The Changing Face of America

Participants at the Walk For Hunger, held annually in Massachusetts, help to support local and emergency food programs.

1992 Twenty-seventh Amendment prohibits midterm congressional pay raises.

1992 William Jefferson Clinton is elected president.

1994 Republicans gain control of both houses of Congress.

1995 "Million Man March" held in Washington, D.C.

1996 President Clinton is reelected.

USA
WORLD

1992 **1994** **1996**

1993 Russia and United States sign START-II treaty reducing warheads and ICBMs.

1994 In South Africa's first all-race election, Nelson Mandela is elected president.

1995 Israeli prime minister Yitzhak Rabin is assassinated.

HUNGER!

INTERACT
WITH HISTORY

You are a high school senior who is active in student government and community service. You have been chosen from among thousands of students nationwide to address an international youth symposium on global issues and reforms. As a U.S. delegate to the event, you address the crowd, confident that young people will be able to change the future.

Explore the Issues

- What makes nations increasingly dependent on one another?
- How does technology affect society worldwide?
- What are the ways to foster cooperation among nations?

1997 Madeleine Albright is the first woman to become secretary of state.

1998 President Clinton is impeached.

2001 On September 11, terrorists attack New York's World Trade Center and the Pentagon with hijacked jets.

2008 Barack Obama is elected 44th president.

1998

2000

Present

1997 Scottish scientist clones "Dolly" the sheep.

1998 Northern Ireland, the Irish Republic, and the United Kingdom sign peace agreements.

2000 George W. Bush is elected 43rd president.

2001 Serbian president Slobodan Milosevic is brought before the UN war crimes tribunal.

2003 U.S. forces invade Iraq.

The United States in Today's World **1065**

SECTION
1

PI 2.5
PI 2.6
PI 3.4

CC Unit 7.VI.A.1.b
CC Unit 7.VI.B.1.a(3)
CC Unit 7.VI.B.1.d

CC Unit 7.VI.B.1.a(1)
CC Unit 7.VI.B.1.c(1)
CC Unit 7.VI.B.2

The 1990s and the New Millennium

MAIN IDEA	WHY IT MATTERS NOW	Terms & Names
The nation became divided as the Democrats gained control of the White House in the 1990s, and the Republicans came to power at the beginning of the new millennium.	Democrats and Republicans need to find a way to work together and unite a divided nation.	•William Jefferson Clinton •H. Ross Perot •Hillary Rodham Clinton •NAFTA / •Newt Gingrich •Contract with America •Al Gore •George W. Bush •Barack Obama

One American's Story

hmhsocialstudies.com
TAKING NOTES

Use the graphic organizer online to take notes on major actions taken by President Clinton during his two terms in office.

On January 20, 1993, poet Maya Angelou was honored as the first woman and the first African American to read her work at a presidential inauguration. Bill Clinton asked Angelou to compose and deliver a poem. Angelou expressed the optimism of the day, recalling the dream of Martin Luther King, Jr., as she recited her poem "On the Pulse of Morning."

★ **A PERSONAL VOICE** MAYA ANGELOU

" Lift up your faces, you have a piercing need
For this bright morning dawning for you.
History, despite its wrenching pain,
Cannot be unlived, but if faced
With courage, need not be lived again.

Lift up your eyes
Upon this day breaking for you.
Give birth again
To the dream. "

—"On the Pulse of Morning"

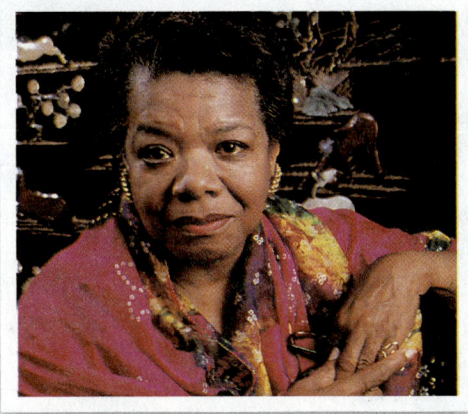

Maya Angelou

Moments later, William Jefferson Clinton was inaugurated as the 42nd president of the United States. Clinton entered the presidency at a time when America was at a turning point. A severe economic recession had made many Americans uneasy about the future. They looked to Clinton to lead a government that would be more responsive to the people.

Clinton Wins the Presidency

Governor **William Jefferson Clinton** of Arkansas became the first member of the baby-boom generation to win the presidency. He captured the White House, at the age of 46, by vowing to strengthen the nation's weak economy and to lead the Democratic Party in a more moderate direction.

THE ELECTION OF 1992 After the U.S. victory in the Persian Gulf War in 1991, Republican president George Bush's popularity had climbed to an 89 percent approval rating. Shortly after the war ended, however, the nation found itself in the grips of a recession. In early 1992, Bush's approval rating nose-dived to 40 percent. In his run for reelection, President Bush could not convince the public that he had a clear strategy for ending the recession and creating jobs. **Ⓐ**

Throughout the presidential race, Bill Clinton campaigned as the candidate who would lead the nation out of its economic crisis. So did a third-party candidate—Texas billionaire **H. Ross Perot.** Perot targeted the soaring federal budget deficit as the nation's number one problem. A budget deficit occurs when the federal government borrows money to meet all its spending commitments. "It's time," Perot declared in his usual blunt style, "to take out the trash and clean up the barn."

Election Day results, however, demonstrated that Clinton's center-of-the-road strategy had the widest appeal. Though Clinton won, he captured only 43 percent of the popular vote. Bush received 38 percent, while Perot managed an impressive 19 percent.

A "NEW" DEMOCRAT Bill Clinton won the presidency in part by promising to move away from traditional Democratic policies. He also emphasized the need to move people off welfare and called for growth in private business as a means to economic progress.

In office, Clinton worked to move the Democratic Party toward the political center by embracing both liberal and conservative programs. According to an ally, Clinton hoped "to modernize liberalism so it could sell again." By doing so, he sought to create a "new" and more inclusive Democratic Party.

Moderate Reform and Economic Boom

President Clinton demonstated his willingness to pursue both liberal and conservative policies on health care, the budget deficit, crime, and welfare.

HEALTH CARE REFORM Clinton had pledged to create a plan to guarantee affordable health care for all Americans, especially for the millions of Americans who lacked medical insurance. Once in office, Clinton appointed First Lady **Hillary Rodham Clinton,** a skilled lawyer and child-welfare advocate, to head the team creating the plan. The president presented the health care reform bill to Congress in September 1993.

Congress debated the plan for a year. Intense lobbying and Republican attacks on the plan for promoting "big government" sealed its doom. In the end, Congress never even voted on the bill. **Ⓑ**

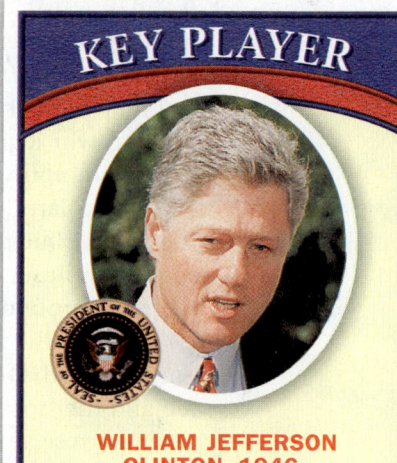

KEY PLAYER

WILLIAM JEFFERSON CLINTON, 1946–

Born in Hope, Arkansas, at the beginning of the baby boom, Bill Clinton had wanted to be president most of his life. As a college student in the 1960s, he had opposed the Vietnam War and pulled strings to avoid being drafted.

After studying in England as a Rhodes scholar and graduating from Yale law school, Clinton returned to Arkansas. He taught at the University of Arkansas School of Law and dived into politics, becoming governor in 1979 at the age of 32.

Hillary Rodham Clinton explains the health care reform plan to a Senate subcommittee.

BALANCED BUDGET AND AN ECONOMIC BOOM President Clinton was more successful in his efforts to reduce the federal budget deficit. Clinton and the Republican-controlled Congress agreed in 1997 on legislation to balance the federal budget by the year 2002. The bill cut spending by billions of dollars, lowered taxes to win Republican support, and included programs aimed at helping children and improving health care.

A year later, Clinton announced that—for the first time in nearly 30 years—the federal budget had a surplus. That is, the government took in more than it spent. Surpluses were used, in part, to pay down the nation's debt, which had soared to around $5.5 trillion.

Perhaps the most effective tool in generating a surplus was the booming economy. About the time Clinton took office, the economy rebounded. Unemployment fell and the stock market soared to new heights. As a result, the government's tax revenues rose, and fewer people received public aid. These factors helped slash the federal debt.

REFORMING WELFARE Clinton and the congressional Republicans cooperated to reform the welfare system. In 1996, a bill was proposed to place limits on how long people could receive benefits. It also put an end to a 61-year federal guarantee of welfare, and instead gave states "block grants"—set amounts of federal money they could spend on welfare or for other social concerns.

Although liberal Democrats feared the effects of eliminating the federal safety net for the poor, the president backed the bill. Over the next few years, states moved millions of people from welfare to jobs. Because of the strong economy, the transition was more successful than some had been predicting.

Crime and Terrorism

Injured victims after the April 1995 bombing of the Alfred P. Murrah Federal Building in Oklahoma City, Oklahoma.

The improved economy—along with enlargement of police forces—combined to lower crime rates in the 1990s. However, fears were raised among Americans by acts of violence and terrorism around the country.

A shocking crime occurred April 1999 when two students at Columbine High School, in Colorado, killed 12 students and a teacher and wounded 23 others, and then shot themselves. Americans were appalled at copycat crimes that began to occur. Some called for tougher gun control, while others argued that exposure to violent imagery should be curtailed. Violence had pervaded television news throughout the decade.

In 1993, terrorists had exploded bombs in the World Trade Center in New York City. This was closely followed by a 1995 blast that destroyed a nine-story federal office building in Oklahoma City, killing 168 children, women, and men. Timothy McVeigh, an American veteran of the Gulf War, was found guilty in the Oklahoma bombing. He was executed in 2001, the first use of the federal death penalty in 38 years. Although American embassies and military targets abroad were subject to sporadic and deadly terrorist attacks during the decade, the U.S. was in no way prepared for a devastating attack that took place on its own soil on the morning of September 11, 2001. **C**

MAIN IDEA

Summarizing
C What acts of terrorism targeted Americans in the decade preceding 2001?

In a coordinated effort, two hijacked commercial jets struck the twin towers of the World Trade Center in New York City, one crashing just minutes after the other. The jets exploded on impact and subsequently leveled the tallest buildings of New York's skyline, the symbolic center of American finance. About an hour later, a third plane tore into the Pentagon building, the U.S. military headquarters outside Washington, D.C. Air travel ceased almost immediately; across the nation planes in the air were ordered to land. During the evacuation of the White House and the New York financial district, a fourth hijacked plane crashed near Pittsburgh, Pennsylvania.

About 3,000 people were killed in the attacks. These included all the passengers on all four planes, workers and visitors in the World Trade Center and the Pentagon, and hundreds of rescue workers. (See the first issue in "Issues for the 21st Century," on page 1100.)

▲ A view across the Brooklyn Bridge shows the devastating impact of two jets used by terrorists as missiles to destroy the World Trade Center.

New Foreign Policy Challenges

Vocabulary
globalization: to make worldwide in scope or application

Conflicts and confused alliances grew in the wake of the Cold War. The question of U.S. intervention overseas, and the globalization of the economy presented the United States with a host of new challenges.

RELATIONS WITH FORMER COLD WAR FOES Maintaining strong relations with Russia and China became major goals for the Clinton administration. Throughout the 1990s, the U.S. and Russia cooperated on economic and arms-control issues. Still, Russia criticized U.S. intervention in Yugoslavia, where a bloody civil war raged. Meanwhile, U.S. officials protested against Russian attacks on rebels in the Russian region of Chechnya.

U.S. relations with China were strained as well. Clinton had stressed that he would lean on China to grant its citizens more democratic rights. As president, however, he put greater emphasis on increasing trade with China. Despite concerns that Chinese spies had stolen U.S. defense secrets, Clinton supported a bill—passed in 2000—granting China permanent trade rights.

Background
In 1993, President Clinton helped broker a peace agreement between Israel and the Palestinians. Known as the Oslo Accords, this agreement was signed by Israeli prime minister Yitzhak Rabin and Palestinian leader Yasser Arafat. Israel agreed to allow Palestinian self-rule in some areas, while the Palestinians recognized Israel's right to exist.

TROOPS ABROAD With the Cold War over, the United States turned more of its attention to regional conflicts. President Clinton proved willing to use troops to end conflicts overseas. In 1991, military leaders in Haiti forced the elected president from office. Thousands of refugees fled the military leaders' harsh rule. In 1994, President Clinton dispatched American troops to Haiti, and the military rulers were forced to step down.

Other interventions occurred in Yugoslavia. In 1991, Yugoslavia broke apart into five nations. In Bosnia, one of the new states, some Serb militias under Slobodan Milosevic began "ethnic cleansing," killing or expelling from their homes people of certain ethnic groups. In 1995, the United States helped negotiate a peace agreement in Bosnia. Clinton sent U.S. troops to join NATO troops to help ensure the deal. About three years later, Serb forces attacked ethnic Albanians in the Serb province of Kosovo. The U.S. and its NATO allies launched air strikes against Serbian targets in 1999, forcing the Serbs to back down. American troops followed up by participating in an international peace-keeping force.

▲ **American workers protest against the North American Free Trade Agreement (NAFTA).**

In both Bosnia and Kosovo, the administration promised early withdrawal. However, the U.S. troops stayed longer than had been intended, drawing criticism of Clinton's policies. **D**

TRADE AND THE GLOBAL ECONOMY Seeing flourishing trade as essential to U.S. prosperity and to world economic and political stability, President Clinton championed the **North American Free Trade Agreement (NAFTA).** This legislation would bring Mexico into the free-trade zone that the United States and Canada already had formed. Supporters said NAFTA would strengthen all three economies and create more American jobs. Opponents insisted that NAFTA would transfer American jobs to Mexico, where wages were lower, and harm the environment because of Mexico's weaker antipollution laws. Congress rejected these arguments, and the treaty was ratified by all three countries' legislatures in 1993. Once the treaty took effect, on January 1, 1994, trade with Mexico increased.

Critics of free trade and the global economy remained vocal, however. In late 1999, the World Trade Organization (WTO), an organization that promotes trade and economic development, met in Seattle. Demonstrators protested that the WTO made decisions with little public input and that these decisions harmed poorer countries, the environment, and American manufacturing workers.

Subsequent anti-globalization protests have been held worldwide. Demonstrations at Summit of the Americas meetings in Quebec City, Canada, in 2001, Miami in 2003, and Mar del Plata, Argentina, in 2005 ended violently. Such protests helped to halt plans to launch the Free Trade Area of the Americas (FTAA)—an enlarged version of NAFTA covering the 34 countries in the Western Hemisphere.

Partisan Politics and Impeachment

While Clinton and Congress worked together on deficit reduction and NAFTA, relations in Washington became increasingly partisan. In the midst of political wrangling, a scandal rocked the White House, and Bill Clinton became the second president in U.S. history to be impeached.

REPUBLICANS TAKE CONTROL OF CONGRESS In mid-1994, after the failure of President Clinton's health care plan and recurring questions regarding his leadership, Republican congressman **Newt Gingrich** began to turn voters' dissatisfaction with Clinton into support for Republicans. He drafted a document called the **Contract with America**—ten items Republicans promised to enact if they won control of Congress. They included congressional term limits, a balanced-budget amendment, tax cuts, tougher crime laws, and welfare reform. **E**

In the November 1994 election, the Republicans handed the Democrats a humiliating defeat. Voters gave Republicans control of both houses of Congress for the first time since 1954. Chosen as the new Speaker of the House, Newt Gingrich was jubilant.

★ **A PERSONAL VOICE** NEWT GINGRICH

" I will never forget mounting the rostrum . . . for the first time. . . . The whole scene gave me a wonderful sense of the romance of America and the magic by which Americans share power and accept changes in government. "

—*To Renew America*

MAIN IDEA

Analyzing Causes
D Why did the United States send troops to Yugoslavia and Kosovo?

Vocabulary
partisan: devoted to or biased in support of a party, group, or cause

MAIN IDEA

Summarizing
E What were some of the provisions of the Contract with America?

President Clinton and the Republican-controlled Congress clashed. Clinton opposed Republican budgets that slowed spending on entitlements such as Social Security and Medicaid. Clinton and Congress refused to compromise, and no budget was passed. As a result, the federal government shut down for almost a week in November 1995, and again for several weeks in the next two months. The President and Congress did eventually work together to pass welfare reform.

THE 1996 REELECTION The budget standoff helped Clinton, as did the strong economy and passage of the welfare reform law of 1996, which suggested an improved working relationship with Congress. As a result, voters reelected Clinton in November 1996. With 49 percent of the popular vote, he outpolled the Republican nominee, U.S. Senator Bob Dole, and the Reform Party candidate, H. Ross Perot. Still, the Republicans maintained control of the House and Senate. Both President Clinton and Republican leaders pledged to work more cooperatively. Soon however, the president faced his most severe problems yet. **F**

MAIN IDEA

Analyzing Causes

F What factors contributed most to Clinton's reelection?

CLINTON IMPEACHED President Clinton was accused of improperly using money from a land deal with the Whitewater Development Company to fund his 1984 gubernatorial reelection campaign. In addition, Clinton allegedly had lied under oath about having an improper relationship with a young White House intern. In 1998, Clinton admitted that he had had an improper relationship with the young woman, but he denied lying about the incident under oath or attempting to obstruct the investigation.

In December 1998, the House of Representatives approved two articles of impeachment, charging the president with perjury and obstruction of justice. Clinton became only the second president—and the first in 130 years—to face a trial in the Senate. At the trial a month later, the Senate fell short of the 67 votes—a two-thirds majority—required to convict him. Clinton remained in office and apologized for his actions.

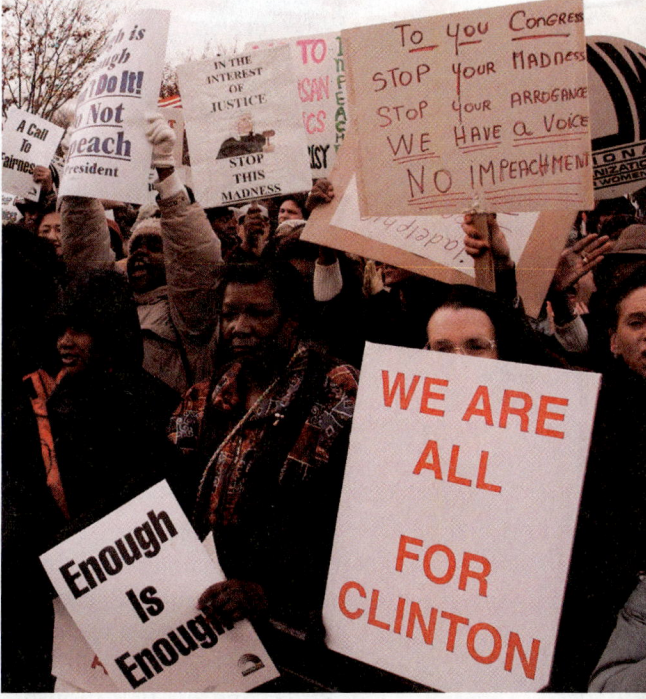

These Americans protested the impeachment. Many Democrats claimed that prosecuting President Clinton was "pure partisanship."

▼

The Race for the White House

In the 2000 presidential race, the Democrats chose Vice President **Al Gore** to succeed Bill Clinton. The Republicans nominated **George W. Bush,** governor of Texas and the son of the former president. Ralph Nader, a long-time consumer advocate, ran for the Green Party, which championed environmental causes and promoted an overall liberal agenda. On the eve of the election, polls showed that the race would be tight. In fact, the election proved one of the closest in U.S. history. Determining a winner would take over a month.

ELECTION NIGHT CONFUSION As election night unfolded, Al Gore appeared to take the lead. The television networks projected that he would win Florida, Pennsylvania, and Michigan—states rich in electoral votes that would ultimately decide the winner of the race. Then, in a stunning turn of events, the TV networks recanted their original projection about Gore's victory in Florida and proclaimed the state "too close to call."

hmhsocialstudies.com

INTERACTIVE

Explore the election of 2000.

As midnight passed, it became clear that whoever won Florida would gain the 270 electoral votes needed to win the election. About 2 A.M., the networks predicted Bush the winner of Florida—and thus the presidency. However, as the final votes in Florida rolled in, Bush's lead shrank considerably and the state again became too close to call. By the next day, Al Gore had won the popular vote by more than 500,000 votes out of 105 million cast across the nation. Meanwhile, George Bush's razor-thin victory in Florida triggered an automatic recount.

DISPUTE RAGES IN FLORIDA In the weeks following the election, lawyers and spokespersons went to Florida to try to secure victory. The recount of the state's ballots gave Bush a win by just over 500 votes—but the battle for the presidency did not end there. The Gore campaign requested manual recounts in four mostly Democratic counties. Bush representatives opposed the manual recounts. James A. Baker III, former secretary of state and leader of the Bush team in Florida, argued that such recounts would raise the possibility of political mischief.

► More than a month after the votes were cast, Al Gore concedes the 2000 presidential election.

THE BATTLE MOVES TO THE COURTS As the manual recounting began on November 12, the Republicans sued to stop the recounts; a month-long court fight followed. The battle ultimately reached the Supreme Court. On December 12, the court voted 5 to 4 to stop the recounts, thus awarding the Florida electoral votes and the presidency to Bush. The justices argued that manual recounts lacked uniform standards and, therefore, violated equal protection for voters. **G**

MAIN IDEA

Analyzing Issues

G How did the election of 2000 highlight both the weaknesses and the strengths of America's election process?

The Bush Administration

After the protests and legal actions subsided, George W. Bush was inaugurated as the 43rd president of the United States on January 20, 2001. Bush inherited several challenges, including a weakening national economy and an energy problem in California.

During his first months as president, Bush began to advance his political agenda. He declared plans to reform the federal role in education and to privatize Social Security. Bush also proposed a $1.35 trillion tax cut, which became law in June 2001.

ANTITERRORIST MEASURES The political landscape changed dramatically after the September 11 terrorist attacks. The Bush administration, now with the overwhelming support of Congress and the American people, shifted its energy and attention to combating terrorism.

In October 2001, Bush signed an antiterrorism bill into law. The law allowed the government to detain foreigners suspected of terrorism for seven days without charging them with a crime. By the following month, Bush had created the Department of Homeland Security, a government body set up to coordinate national efforts to combat terrorism. In addition, the federal government increased its involvement in aviation security.

KEY PLAYER

GEORGE W. BUSH, 1946–

George W. Bush was born into a family steeped in politics. His father, George H. W. Bush, was the 41st president of the United States (1989–1993). However, George W. Bush did not immediately follow in his father's political footsteps. In 1975, he started an oil company in Midland, Texas. For a time, he also was part owner of the Texas Rangers baseball team.

Eventually, Bush was elected governor of Texas in 1994. Six years later, he became the 43rd president of the United States. He won reelection in 2004.

The Bush Administration also began waging a war against terrorism. In October 2001, coalition forces led by the United States began bombing Afghanistan. The Afghan government was harboring Osama bin Laden and his al-Qaeda terrorist network believed responsible for the September 11 attacks. In 2002, the coalition successfully broke up the al-Qaeda network in Afghanistan. Osama bin Laden, however, remained at large. Nonetheless, the Bush administration gained widespread public approval for the decisive steps taken. **H**

MAIN IDEA

Evaluating Leadership

H How do you think the American people responded to Bush's antiterrorist measures?

Bush also scored a major success when direct elections were held for the first time in Afghanistan in October 2004. The Afghan people elected interim president Hamid Karzai as their first democratically elected president. Although Afghanistan still faced many problems, the elections were considered a positive move toward resolving them.

▲ Hamid Karzai is victorious in Afghanistan's first direct presidential election.

WAR AGAINST IRAQ In 2003, Bush expanded the war on terrorism to Iraq. Following the Persian Gulf War, Iraq had agreed to UN demands to stop the production of biological, chemical, and nuclear weapons. However, throughout the 1990s, the leader of Iraq, Saddam Hussein, cooperated only partly with UN arms inspectors and eventually barred them from entering his country.

After the September 11 attacks, Bush alleged that Hussein was supporting terrorists and might supply them with weapons of mass destruction (WMD). Bush called for renewed arms inspections in Iraq. The inspectors determined that Iraq had not resumed its WMD programs; but Hussein had again not cooperated fully with the inspection process. The United States and Great Britain then ended diplomacy with Iraq and invaded in March 2003. Within a month, Iraq's forces were defeated. U.S. forces then began an intensive search for WMD in Iraq. No traces of WMD were found. U.S. forces captured the former dictator in December 2003, and Hussein was later tried and executed by the Iraqi government.

DOMESTIC AGENDA Meanwhile, on the home front, President Bush concentrated on education and the economy. He signed into law an education reform plan entitled No Child Left Behind. This plan called for more accountability by states for students' success, mandatory achievement testing, and more school options available for parents.

The economy posed a greater challenge, as corporate scandals, such as those related to the companies Enron and WorldCom, rocked the nation. The scandals had a negative impact on the U.S. economy. Congress responded by passing the Sarbanes-Oxley Act. This act established a regulatory board to oversee the accounting industry and its involvement with corporations.

In 2003, Congress passed and Bush signed into law a $350 billion tax cut, which Bush claimed would help the sagging economy and create jobs. Democrats in Congress opposed the tax cut, saying it would mostly benefit the rich. The Democrats were overruled, however, because the Republican Party had regained control of the Senate in the 2002 midterm elections.

BUSH REELECTED IN 2004 Although the Bush administration received much initial support for the war on terrorism, many Americans came to question the decision to invade Iraq. They were dismayed by the failure to find WMD there. In 2004, President Bush was reelected, despite deep divisions among the American people.

During Bush's second term, discontent about the war grew. At the same time, controversies arose over warrantless spying on American citizens and allegations that the administration allowed torture of terrorist suspects. The Bush administration was also criticized over its response to Hurricane Katrina. In the 2006 mid-term elections, Democrats regained control of both the House and the Senate.

The Obama Administration

The continuing war in Iraq and a deteriorating economy contributed to President Bush's unpopularity. The collapse of the financial markets in the fall of 2008 did little to improve the situation. More than two-thirds of Americans disapproved of his handling of the presidency. As a result, in the 2008 presidential election, Americans voted for a change in direction by electing Democrat **Barack Obama**, U.S. senator from Illinois. In defeating Republican Senator John McCain of Arizona, Obama made history as the first African American to be elected president of the United States.

On taking office, Obama pushed through an economic stimulus package to combat the recession brought on by the crash of the financial markets. In addition, he fulfilled a campaign promise by passing a sweeping health care reform bill. However, aspects of health care reform drew criticism from some people. And many Americans expressed their unhappiness with continued high levels of unemployment. This discontent allowed Republicans to gain a majority of seats in the U.S. House of Representatives during the 2010 midterm elections.

In foreign policy, Obama drew up plans to end combat operations in Iraq and in Afghanistan. He also continued to combat terrorism. In 2011, the United States struck a blow against al-Qaeda, when special forces tracked down and killed Osama bin Laden in Pakistan.

▲ Barack Obama, his wife, Michelle, and daughters, Sasha and Malia, celebrate his victory at Grant Park in Chicago on November 4, 2008.

ASSESSMENT

1. TERMS & NAMES For each term or name, write a sentence explaining its significance.

- William Jefferson Clinton
- H. Ross Perot
- Hillary Rodham Clinton
- North American Free Trade Agreement (NAFTA)
- Newt Gingrich
- Contract with America
- Al Gore
- George W. Bush
- Barack Obama

MAIN IDEA

2. TAKING NOTES

Create a time line of President Clinton's major actions during his two terms. Use a form such as the one below.

Explain whether each action was a success or a failure for Clinton.

CRITICAL THINKING

3. EVALUATING

What event or trend during the Clinton administration do you think will have the most lasting impact on the United States? Why?

4. ANALYZING MOTIVES

Why did the Gore campaign support manual recounts in Florida and the Bush campaign oppose them?

5. EVALUATING DECISIONS

Do you think President Bush's decision to invade Iraq was justified? Explain why or why not.

Think About:

- arms inspections in Iraq
- fear created by the September 11 attacks
- the search for WMD

SECTION
2

PI 3.4

CC Unit 7.I.A.5   CC Unit 7.VI.B.1.b(4)
CC Unit 7.VI.B.2.b(1) CC Unit 7.VI.B.2.b(2)
CC Unit 7.VI.B.2.b(4)

The New Global Economy

MAIN IDEA	WHY IT MATTERS NOW	Terms & Names
Because of technological advances and new trade laws, the U.S. economy underwent a boom during the late 20th century.	New types of business have meant new work environments and new challenges for American workers.	•service sector •downsize •Bill Gates •NASDAQ •dotcom •General Agreement on Tariffs and Trade (GATT)

One American's Story

hmhsocialstudies.com
TAKING NOTES

Use the graphic organizer online to take notes on the major changes in the U.S. economy during the 1990s and early 2000s.

As Bill Clinton took office in 1993, some regions of the nation, particularly the Northeast, were still in an economic recession. Near Kennebunkport, Maine, the John Roberts clothing factory faced bankruptcy. With help from their union, the factory workers were able to turn their factory into an employee-owned company.

Ethel Beaudoin, who worked for the company for more than 30 years, was relieved that the plant would not be closing.

▲ Workers at the John Roberts clothing factory

A PERSONAL VOICE ETHEL BEAUDOIN

"It's a nice feeling to be part of the process . . . of deciding what this company buys for machinery and to know the customers more intimately. They're our customers, and it's a nicer feeling when the customers know that the coat that we put out is made by owners."

—quoted in *Divided We Fall*

Beaudoin's experience offered one example of the economic possibilities in America. A new global economy—brought about by new technologies, increased international competition, and the end of the Cold War—changed the nation's economic prospects.

The Shifting Economy

Americans heard a great deal of good news about the economy. Millions of new jobs were created between 1993 and 1999. By the fall of 2000, the unemployment rate had fallen to the lowest it had been since 1970.

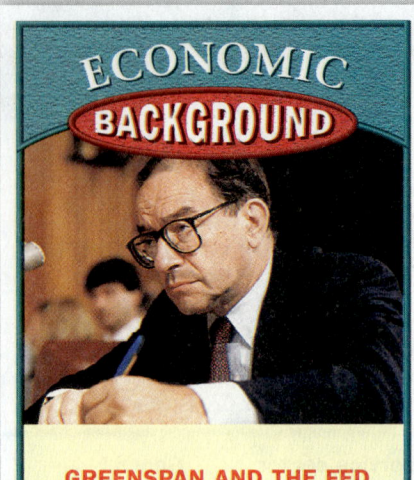
But there was alarming news as well. Wage inequality between upper- and lower-income Americans—the income gap—widened. Median household income began to drop. Although economists disagreed about the reasons for the economy's instability, most everyone agreed it was undergoing significant changes.

MORE SERVICE, LESS SECURITY Chief among the far-reaching changes in the workplace of the 1990s was the explosive growth of jobs in the **service sector,** the part of the economy that provides services to consumers. By 2008, nearly 80 percent of American workers were teachers, medical professionals, lawyers, engineers, store clerks, waitstaff, and other service workers.

Low-paying jobs, such as sales and fast-food, grew fastest. These positions, often part-time or temporary, offered limited benefits. Many corporations, rather than invest in salaries and benefits for full-time staff, hired temporary workers, or temps, and began to **downsize**—trim payrolls to streamline operations and increase profits. Manpower, Inc., a temporary services agency, became the largest U.S. employer, earning $2 billion in 1993 when 640,000 Americans cashed its paychecks. In 2008, about one-fifth of the nation's labor force worked in temporary or part-time positions. **A**

Of those cut in downsizing, younger workers suffered higher rates of unemployment. In 2008, about 14 percent of workers aged 16 to 24 were unemployed—more than double the national rate. And many young Americans are living at home longer and are less financially secure than American youth in the past.

FARMS AND FACTORIES The nation's shift to a service economy came at the expense of America's traditional workplaces. Manufacturing, which surpassed farming mid-century as the largest job sector, experienced a sharp decline in the 1980s and 1990s. In 1992, for example, 140,000 steelworkers did the same work that 240,000 had accomplished ten years earlier. Larry Pugh talked about the downsizing of a farm equipment factory in his hometown of Waterloo, Iowa.

A PERSONAL VOICE LARRY PUGH

"There used to be 17,500 people working here. . . . Now there are 6000. Those people spent their money. They bought the cars. They bought the houses. They were replaced by people that are at the minimum wage—seven or eight dollars an hour, not 15 or 20 dollars an hour. These people can hardly eke out a living."

—quoted in *Divided We Fall*

The decline in industrial jobs contributed to a drop in union membership. In 1945, 35 percent of American workers belonged to unions; by 2008, only 12 percent were union members. In the 1990s and early 2000s, unions had trouble organizing. High-tech and professional workers felt no need for unions, while low-wage service employees feared losing their jobs in a strike. Some workers saw their incomes decline. The increased use of computer-driven robots to make manufactured goods eliminated many jobs, but it also spurred a vibrant high-tech economy. Those with advanced training and specialized technical skills or a sense of entrepreneurial risk-taking saw their salaries rise and their economic security expand. **B**

MAIN IDEA

Summarizing
A How did the change from an industrial economy to a service economy affect Americans' economic security?

MAIN IDEA

Analyzing Effects
B How did downsizing affect people?

Persons Employed in Three Economic Sectors*			
Year	Farming	Manufacturing	Service Producing
1900	11,050	7,252	6,832
1950	6,001	18,475	20,721
2008	2,168	13,431	115,646

*numbers in thousands

Sources: *Historical Statistics of the United States, Colonial Times to 1970; Statistical Abstracts of the United States, 1953, 1954, 2010 (online)*

SKILLBUILDER Interpreting Charts

1. What sector of the U.S. economy has seen the greatest decline in workers over the past century?

2. In terms of employee participation, by roughly how many times did the service sector grow between 1950 and 2008?

HIGH-TECH INDUSTRIES In the late 1990s, entrepreneurs turned innovative ideas about computer technology into huge personal fortunes, hoping to follow in the footsteps of **Bill Gates,** the decade's most celebrated entrepreneur. Gates founded the software company Microsoft. By 2008, it had made him the second wealthiest individual in the world, with assets estimated at about $53 billion.

A rapid outcropping of new businesses accompanied the explosive growth of the Internet late in the decade. The **NASDAQ** (National Association of Securities Dealers Automated Quotation System), a technology-dominated stock index on Wall Street, rose dramatically as enthusiasm grew for high-tech businesses. These businesses were known as **dotcoms,** a nickname derived from their identities, or addresses, on the World Wide Web, which often ended in ".com." The dotcoms expanded rapidly and attracted young talent and at times excessive investment funding for such untested fledgling companies.

Thousands of smaller businesses were quick to anticipate the changes that the Internet would bring. Suddenly companies could work directly with consumers or with other companies. Many predicted that the price of doing business would fall markedly and that overall worldwide productivity would jump dramatically. The boom of new business was termed "The New Economy."

However, the positive economic outlook fueled by "The New Economy" was short lived. In 2000, only 38 percent of online retailing made a profit. As a result, many dotcoms went out of business. This decline had many causes. Entrepreneurs often provided inadequate advertising for their e-companies. Also, many dotcoms had hard-to-use Web sites that confused customers. The unsuccessful dotcoms caused many investors to stop putting money in Internet businesses.

In 2002, the U.S. economy was also hard hit by corporate scandals, when Enron was charged with using illegal accounting practices and WorldCom filed what was then the largest bankruptcy claim in U.S. history. Investors began to lose faith in corporations. In addition, the continued threat of terrorism had a negative effect on the economy. All of these factors caused the NASDAQ to decline. After the NYSE and NASDAQ rose again to record highs in 2007, they both were rocked by the global financial crisis of 2008 and 2009.

At 18 years old, Shawn Fanning started a free music downloading service on the Internet called Napster. He became a multimillionaire after forming an alliance with a German media company.

▼

Map Labels

Arctic Circle

CANADA G8

40°N

UNITED STATES G8

ATLANTIC OCEAN

Tropic of Cancer

PACIFIC OCEAN

0° Equator

JAMAICA

MEXICO

GUATEMALA
EL SALVADOR
NICARAGUA
COSTA RICA
HONDURAS
PANAMA
COLOMBIA
VENEZUELA
GUYANA
SURINAME

ECUADOR

PERU
BOLIVIA
BRAZIL
PARAGUAY
CHILE
URUGUAY
ARGENTINA

UNITED KINGDOM G8
IRELAND
FRANCE G8
GERMANY G8
UKRAINE
SPAIN
ITALY G8
SYRIA
IRAQ
IRAN
KUWAIT
QATAR
EGYPT
SAUDI ARABIA
UNITED ARAB EMIRATES
YEMEN

RUSSIA G8
KAZAKHSTAN
MONGOLIA
SOUTH KOREA
JAPAN G8
CHINA
TAIWAN

MAURITANIA
ALGERIA
LIBYA
CHAD
SUDAN
NIGERIA
CAMEROON
GABON
DEM. REP. OF THE CONGO
ANGOLA
NAMIBIA
BOTSWANA
SOUTH AFRICA
LESOTHO
SWAZILAND
ZAMBIA
ZIMBABWE
MOZAMBIQUE
MALAWI
TANZANIA
SOMALIA
SEYCHELLES
MAURITIUS

INDIA
THAILAND
VIETNAM
MALAYSIA
SINGAPORE
BRUNEI
PHILIPPINES
PAPUA NEW GUINEA
INDONESIA

PACIFIC OCEAN

INDIAN OCEAN

AUSTRALIA

NEW ZEALAND

3,000 Miles
5,000 Kilometers

Legend

- Andean Community (CAN)
- Asia-Pacific Economic Cooperation (APEC)
- Association of Southeast Asian Nations (ASEAN)
- Central American Common Market (CACM)
- Caribbean Community and Common Market (CARICOM)
- Commonwealth of Independent States (CIS)
- Council of Arab Economic Unity (CAEU)
- European Free Trade Association (EFTA)
- European Union (EU)
- G8 Group of Eight (G8)
- Economic and Monetary Community of Central Africa (CEMAC)
- North American Free Trade Agreement (NAFTA)
- Organization of the Petroleum Exporting Countries (OPEC)
- Southern Common Market (MERCOSUR)
- Southern African Development Community (SADC)

GEOGRAPHY SKILLBUILDER
1. **Location** What is the only G-8 country located outside Europe and North America?
2. **Location** To which world trade organizations does the United States belong?

Change and the Global Economy

In 1900, airplanes hadn't yet flown and telephone service was barely 20 years old. U.S. trade with the rest of the world was worth about $2.2 billion (roughly 12 percent of the economy). Over a century later, New Yorkers could hop a jet and arrive in London in a few hours, information traveled instantly by computer, and U.S. trade with other countries exceeded $4 trillion (about 30 percent of the economy). As American companies competed for international and domestic markets, American workers felt the sting of competing with workers in other countries.

INTERNATIONAL TRADE The expansion of U.S. trade abroad was an important goal of President Clinton's foreign policy, as his support of NAFTA had shown. In 1994, in response to increasing international economic competition among trading blocs, the United States joined many other nations in adopting a new version of the **General Agreement on Tariffs and Trade (GATT)**. The new treaty lowered trade barriers, such as tariffs, and established the World Trade Organization (WTO) to resolve trade disputes. As President Clinton announced at the 1994 meeting of the Group of Seven, (the world's seven leading economic powers, which later became the Group of Eight when Russia joined in 1996), "[T]rade as much as troops will increasingly define the ties that bind nations in the twenty-first century."

MAIN IDEA

Analyzing Effects

C What were some of the effects of NAFTA and GATT?

INTERNATIONAL COMPETITION International trade agreements caused some American workers to worry about massive job flight to countries that produced the same goods as the United States but at a lower cost.

In the 1990s, U.S. businesses frequently moved their operations to less economically advanced countries, such as Mexico, where wages were lower. After the passage of NAFTA, more than 100,000 low-wage jobs were lost in U.S. manufacturing industries such as apparel, auto parts, and electronics. Also, competition with foreign companies helped U.S. companies to maintain low wages and decrease benefits. **C**

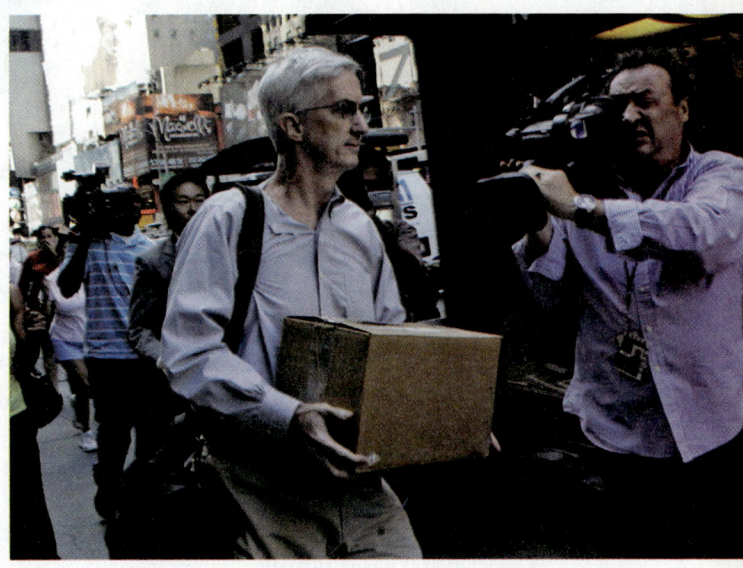

▲ A Lehman Brothers worker is surrounded by photographers on the day that the investment bank declared bankruptcy.

INTERNATIONAL SLOWDOWN Around the turn of the 21st century, the global economy began to slow down. Between 1997 and 2002, the gross domestic product in Japan declined by 6 percent. In 2001, the economies of more than a dozen countries were in recession, and many other countries reported lower growth rates than they had the previous year.

The flow of foreign direct investment (FDI) to developing countries declined dramatically. As a result, the economies of these countries were particularly hard hit. For example, the overall growth of Africa's economies slowed to 2.7 percent in 2002.

The U.S. economy also suffered. As it happened, both the U.S. and world economies began to reverse the downward trend by 2004. But in 2008, a global financial crisis, brought on by the collapse of several major banking firms, left growth in the world's economies sluggish at best.

SECTION 2 ASSESSMENT

1. TERMS & NAMES For each term or name, write a sentence explaining its significance.
- service sector
- downsize
- Bill Gates
- NASDAQ
- dotcom
- General Agreement on Tariffs and Trade (GATT)

MAIN IDEA

2. TAKING NOTES
In a cluster diagram like the one below, record the major changes that occurred in the U.S. economy during the 1990s.

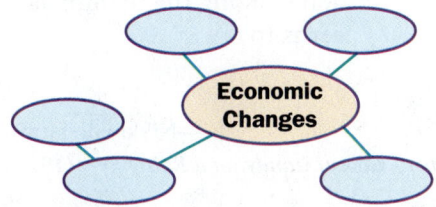

Economic Changes

Which change has affected you the most? Explain.

CRITICAL THINKING

3. ANALYZING EFFECTS
Explain who was negatively affected by the changes in the economy and what negative effects they suffered.
Think About:
- who had the highest unemployment rates
- what types of jobs were eliminated
- what other negative effects there were

4. ANALYZING ISSUES
How do you explain some Americans' fears over the international trade agreements?

5. DRAWING CONCLUSIONS
Considering the economic changes described in this section, how do you think workers can best prepare themselves for the future?

Women Writers Reflect American Diversity

1978–2000 The broadening of opportunities for American women that began in the 1970s is as evident in literature as it is in other fields. Toni Morrison, Mary Oliver, Nikki Giovanni, Amy Tan, Anne Tyler, Alice Walker, Marge Piercy, Sandra Cisneros—these are just a few of the talented women novelists and poets who reflect the multicultural nature of the American identity. These women's writing shares a common characteristic—that of conveying the American experience through the exploration of personal memories, nature, childhood, and family.

◀ NIKKI GIOVANNI

In the late 1960s, Nikki Giovanni won instant attention as an African American poet writing about the Black Power movement. Since then her poetry has often focused on childhood, family ties, and other personal concerns. In the following poem, Giovanni deals with individual empowerment—even under less than ideal circumstances.

Choices

if i can't do
what i want to do
then my job is to not
do what i don't want
to do

it's not the same thing
but it's the best i can
do

if i can't have
what i want then
my job is to want
what i've got
and be satisfied
that at least there
is something more
to want

since i can't go
where i need
to go then i must go
where the signs point
though always understanding
parallel movement
isn't lateral

when i can't express
what i really feel
i practice feeling
what i can express
and none of it is equal
i know
but that's why mankind
alone among the mammals
learns to cry

—Nikki Giovanni,
"Choices," from *Cotton Candy on a Rainy Day* (1978)

AMY TAN

A native of Oakland, California, Amy Tan draws on personal experiences in *The Joy Luck Club*, a series of interconnected stories about four Chinese-American daughters and their immigrant mothers. The four mothers establish a club for socializing and playing the game of mahjong.

My mother started the San Francisco version of the Joy Luck Club in 1949, two years before I was born. This was the year my mother and father left China with one stiff leather trunk filled only with fancy silk dresses. There was no time to pack anything else, my mother had explained to my father after they boarded the boat. Still his hands swam frantically between the slippery silks, looking for his cotton shirts and wool pants.

When they arrived in San Francisco, my father made her hide those shiny clothes. She wore the same brown-checked Chinese dress until the Refugee Welcome Society gave her two hand-me-down dresses, all too large in sizes for American women. The society was composed of a group of white-haired American missionary ladies from the First Chinese Baptist Church. And because of their gifts, my parents could not refuse their invitation to join the church. Nor could they ignore the old ladies' practical advice to improve their English through Bible study class on Wednesday nights and, later, through choir practice on Saturday mornings. This was how my parents met the Hsus, the Jongs, and the St. Clairs. My mother could sense that the women of these families also had unspeakable tragedies they had left behind in China and hopes they couldn't begin to express in their fragile English. Or at least, my mother recognized the numbness in these women's faces. And she saw how quickly their eyes moved when she told them her idea for the Joy Luck Club.

—Amy Tan, *The Joy Luck Club* (1989)

SANDRA CISNEROS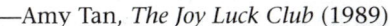

Sandra Cisneros is one of many Chicana writers to win fame in recent years. In *The House on Mango Street*, she traces the experiences of a poor Hispanic girl named Esperanza (Spanish for *hope*) and her warm-hearted family. Nenny is her sister.

Four Skinny Trees

They are the only ones who understand me. I am the only one who understands them. Four skinny trees with skinny necks and pointy elbows like mine. Four who do not belong here but are here. Four raggedy excuses planted by the city. From our room we can hear them, but Nenny just sleeps and doesn't appreciate these things.

Their strength is secret. They send ferocious roots beneath the ground. They grow up and they grow down and grab the earth between their hairy toes and bite the sky with violent teeth and never quit their anger. This is how they keep.

Let one forget his reason for being, they'd all droop like tulips in a glass, each with their arms around the other. Keep, keep, keep, trees say when I sleep. They teach.

When I am too sad and too skinny to keep keeping, when I am a tiny thing against so many bricks, then it is I look at trees. When there is nothing left to look at on this street. Four who grew despite concrete. Four who reach and do not forget to reach. Four whose only reason is to be and be.

—Sandra Cisneros
The House on Mango Street (1989)

THINKING CRITICALLY

1. **Comparing** From these selections, what can you infer about women's experiences in American life today? Cite passages to support your response.

    SEE SKILLBUILDER HANDBOOK, PAGE R8.

2. hmhsocialstudies.com **INTERNET ACTIVITY**

   Visit the links for American Literature to find and choose selections for an anthology of writing by three contemporary American women. Write a "capsule biography" summarizing each writer's background and achievements.

SECTION 3

PI 1.1
PI 3.4
CC Unit 7.I.A.3
CC Unit 7.VI.B.1.b(1)
CC Unit 7.I.A.6

Technology and Modern Life

MAIN IDEA	WHY IT MATTERS NOW	Terms & Names
Advances in technology have increased not only the pace but also the comfort of many Americans' daily lives.	Providing access to the new technology and regulating its use are two current challenges facing 21st-century America.	• information superhighway • Internet • telecommute • Telecommunications Act Of 1996 • genetic engineering

One American's Story

The crowds stand four-deep cheering for 12-year-old Rudy Garcia-Tolson as he captures a new national record for his age group at the San Diego half-marathon. Despite the loss of his legs, Rudy competes in sports and won a gold medal in swimming at the 2004 paralympics.

For years, Rudy was confined to a wheelchair. After undergoing a double amputation he was fitted with carbon fiber prostheses—artificial replacements for missing body parts. These lightweight, strong, and durable new legs now make many things possible for Rudy.

A PERSONAL VOICE RUDY GARCIA-TOLSON

"I told them to cut my legs off. I saw pictures of people running with prosthetic legs. I didn't want to stay in a wheelchair. . . . My legs won't stop me. Nothing stops me. . . . I like to show kids that there's no limitations—kids or challenged people or adults, there's no limitations to what a person can do. . . . My motto is, if you have a brave heart, that's a powerful weapon."

—quoted in *Press-Enterprise*, January 1, 2000

Rudy Garcia-Tolson, 2001

Advances in medical technology have permitted Rudy to live a more fully active life. Throughout the 20th century and into the 21st, technological developments helped Americans become more active in many ways.

The Communications Revolution

The computer industry transformed the 1980s. Instead of giant mainframes and minicomputers, desktop workstations now ruled business. Home computers became widely available, and many thousands of people joined online subscription services that provided electronic mail and magazine-style information.

"VACATION, 2000"

By the end of the 20th century, millions of Americans owned any number of personal communication devices. People were able to speak to or correspond with each other instantaneously almost anytime, almost anywhere. The cartoon suggests that Americans are dependent on their communication devices, and that the once relaxing and peaceful family vacation has given way to the hustle and bustle of constant access.

SKILLBUILDER

Analyzing Political Cartoons

1. What modern-day communication devices are being used in this cartoon?
2. In what ways do the characters in this cartoon seem trapped by modern-day communications technology?

 SEE SKILLBUILDER HANDBOOK, PAGE R24.

VACATION, 2000

ENTERING THE INFORMATION AGE The **information superhighway**—a network of communication devices linking people and institutions across the nation and the world—promised to advance the revolution that had begun with the personal computer. In 1994, Vice President Al Gore began to oversee the government's participation in developing this superhighway. Even though private industries would build the superhighway, the government would keep access democratic, ensure affordable service for everyone, protect privacy and property rights, and develop incentives for investors.

The 1990s enjoyed explosive growth of the **Internet,** an international network linking computers and allowing almost instant transmittal of text, images, and sound. Originally developed in the late 1960s by the U.S. Department of Defense for defense research, the Internet drew early popularity at universities. By the mid-1990s *Internet* became a household word. Use of the network was further popularized by the World Wide Web, which provided a simple visual interface for words and pictures to be seen by an unlimited audience. As businesses, schools, and organizations began to use the Web as a primary form of communication, new forms of social interaction emerged. Users developed online communities, such as MySpace and Facebook, to "meet" and communicate with one another.

NEW TOOLS, NEW MEDIA Through an electronic connection, such as a TV cable or phone line, users accessed an array of media, from streaming video to research archives, from on-line shopping catalogs to customized news broadcasts. Users could interact with each other across the world. By 2009, nearly 228 million Americans used the Internet regularly to send e-mail, to network, to share music, or to browse or search through pages on the Web. During the 1990s, classrooms across the nation increasingly used computer networking. By 2009, 97 percent of public-school classrooms offered Internet access. Long-distance video and audio transmissions also linked American students. Some content was delivered not on networks but stored via CD-ROM (Compact Disc Read-Only Memory). CD-ROMs also carry digital code for pictures, text, and animation to be played on a computer.

Vocabulary
interface: the point of communication between a computer and any other entity, such as a printer or human operator

The late-20th-century advances in computers and communications have had an impact on American society and business comparable to the industrial developments of the late 1800s. Americans now have more entertainment options, as cable service has multiplied the number of television channels available and greater bandwidth has made high-definition television possible. Because of cellular phones, fax machines, the Internet, wireless connectivity, and overnight shipping, people can more readily **telecommute**, or work from a location of their choice instead of going to an office every day. **(A)**

LEGISLATING TECHNOLOGY In the 1980s, the government was slow to recognize the implications of the new communications technology. In 1994, however, the Federal Communications Commission (FCC) began to auction the valuable rights to airwaves and collected over $9 billion. Then, with the rapid growth in the communications industry, the federal government took several steps to ensure that consumers received the best service. Congress passed the **Telecommunications Act of 1996,** removing barriers that had previously prevented one type of communications company from starting up or buying another related one. While it increased competition in the industry, the law also paved the way for major media mergers. When Capital Cities/ABC Inc. joined the Walt Disney Company, industry watchdogs noted that this reflected the trend toward concentrating media influence in the hands of a few powerful conglomerates.

The passage of the Telecommunications Act won applause from the communications industry but only mixed reviews from the public. Consumer activists worried that the law would fail to ensure equal access to new technologies for rural residents and poor people. Civil rights advocates contended that the Communications Decency Act (part of the Telecommunications Act) restricted free speech because it barred the transmission of "indecent" materials to minors via the Internet. Since the early 2000s, the issue of network neutrality has created considerable controversy. Supporters of network neutrality want regulations established that would prevent service providers or the government from restricting access to, or content delivered on, the Internet. **(B)**

MAIN IDEA

Summarizing
(A) Explain the revolutionary nature of communicating via the Internet.

MAIN IDEA

Analyzing Effects
(B) How might the Telecommunications Act affect consumers?

Scientific Advances Enrich Lives

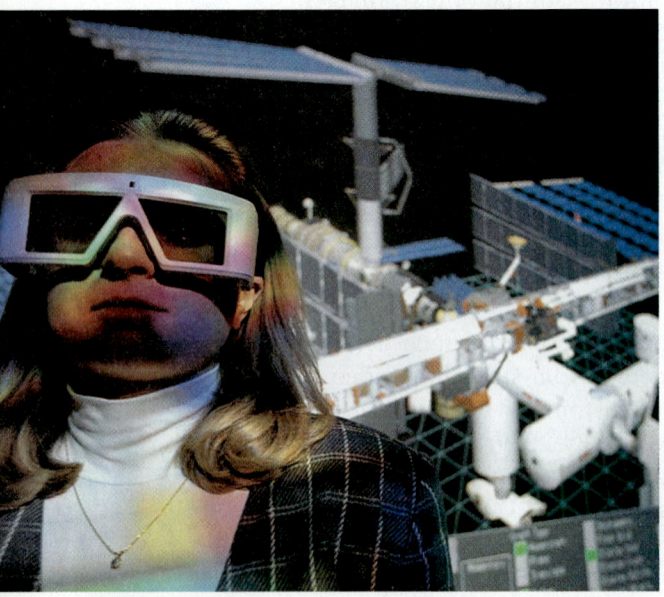

▲
At NASA Langley Research Center in Virginia, an aerospace engineer wearing stereo glasses sees a 3-D view of a space station simulation, as shown in the background.

The exciting growth in the telecommunications industry in the 1990s and early 2000s was matched by developments that revolutionized robotics, space exploration, and medicine. The world witnessed marvels that for many of the baby boom generation echoed science fiction.

SIMULATION, ROBOTICS, AND MACHINE INTELLIGENCE Visual imaging and artificial intelligence (a computer's ability to perform activities that require intelligence) were combined to provide applications in industry, medicine, and education. For example, virtual reality began with the flight simulators used to train military and commercial pilots. Today, with a headset that holds tiny video screens and earphones, and with a data glove that translates hand movements to a computer screen, a user can navigate a "virtual landscape." Doctors have used virtual reality to take a computerized tour of a patient's throat and lungs to check for medical problems. Surgeons have performed long-distance surgery through telepresence systems—gloves, computers, and robotic elements specially wired so that a doctor can operate on a patient hundreds of miles away. Architects and engineers have used virtual reality to create visual, rather than physical, models of their buildings, cars, and other designs. Modeling also affected the nightly newscast. Using supercomputers and improved satellite data, meteorologists could offer extended weather forecasts that reached the accuracy of one-day forecasts of 1980.

As technology became more sophisticated, computers increased in capability. IBM's Deep Blue defeated chess champion Garry Kasparov in 1997. Computational linguists steadily improved natural language understanding in computers, thus fine-tuning the accuracy of voice recognition systems.

Robots grew more humanlike as engineers equipped them with high-capacity chips simulating brain function. By the early 2000s, robots had the ability to walk on two legs, interact with people, learn taught behaviors, and express artificial feelings with facial gestures.

SPACE EXPLORATION In the 1990s, astronomy expanded our view of the universe. In 1997, NASA's *Pathfinder* and its rover *Sojourner* transmitted live pictures of the surface of Mars to millions of Internet users.

Shuttle missions, meanwhile, concentrated on scientific research and assembly, transport, and repair of orbiting objects, paving the way to possible human missions to Mars and other space travel in the coming century. NASA concentrated on working with other nations to build the *International Space Station (ISS)*. The *ISS* promised to offer scientists a zero-gravity laboratory for research in medicine, space mechanics and architecture, and long-term living in space. Ellen Ochoa, part of the first shuttle crew to dock to the *ISS*, hoped to inspire young students:

Dr. Ellen Ochoa

Background
The *International Space Station* was established by joining and expanding upon the Russian station, *Mir*, and the American *Spacelab*.

A PERSONAL VOICE ELLEN OCHOA

"I'm not trying to make everyone an astronaut, but I want students to think about a career and the preparation they'll need. . . . I tell students that the opportunities I had were a result of having a good educational background. Education is what allows you to stand out."

—quoted in *Stanford University School of Engineering Annual Report*, 1997-98.

A shuttle crew in 1993 aboard the *Endeavor* repaired the Hubble Space Telescope, which returns dazzling intergalactic views. In late 1995, astronomers using observatories discovered the first planet outside our own solar system. Since then dozens more have been detected. On July 21, 2011, the *Atlantis* crew completed the final mission of NASA's 30-year shuttle program. However, U.S. space exploration goes on. In August 2011, NASA launched the probe *Juno*, which is expected to reach Jupiter in 2016. Also, American astronauts will continue to spend time on the *ISS*, but they will rely on Russian spacecraft to transport them.

BIOTECHNOLOGY The most profound insight into the book of life came from the field of biotechnology. The Human Genome Project, an international effort to map the genes of the human body, and Celera, a private company in molecular biology, simultaneously announced in 2000 that they had sequenced nearly all of the human genome only a decade after the research began. Cooperation via the Internet and access to computerized databases by multiple research groups vastly accelerated the scientists' ability to identify and order over three billion chemical

▲ Researchers work at the Beijing Genomics Institute at Shenzhen in southern China.

"letters" of the genetic code of DNA. Molecular biologists hoped that this genetic map would offer the key to treating many inherited diseases and diagnosing congenital disabilities, and that drug makers could one day design pharmaceuticals for each patient's particular profile.

DNA had been in the spotlight before the breakthrough announcement. In well-publicized legal proceedings, prosecutors relied on DNA evidence to help prove the guilt of defendants who may have left behind a single hair at a crime scene. Others, wrongly imprisoned, were released when genetic analysis proved their innocence.

But different opinions arose over some of the new "biotechnology." Some speculated that technological progress outpaced social evolution and society's ability to grapple with the consequences. In 1997, Scottish researchers cloned Dolly the sheep from one cell of an adult sheep. Shortly thereafter, two Rhesus monkeys were cloned in Oregon, and many wondered whether human cloning was next. Firms sought to patent genes used for medical and research applications, using the principle of invention and property. Advances such as these, as well as gene therapy, artificial human chromosomes, and testing embryos for genetic defects all sparked heated debates among scientists, ethicists, religious leaders, and politicians.

The use of **genetic engineering**—the artificial changing of the molecular biology of organisms' cells to alter an organism—also aroused public concern. However, the Federal Department of Agriculture (FDA) holds that genetically engineered foods are safe and that they require no extra labeling. Scientists in the late 1990s modified corn and rice to provide resistance to pests and increase nutritional value. In 1996, the European Union limited the importation of such products in response to consumer pressure, allowing only those clearly labeled as having been genetically modified.

MEDICAL PROGRESS People suffering from some diseases benefited from advances in medicine in the 1990s and early 2000s. Cancer survival rates improved drastically as clinicians explored the use of gene therapy, genetically engineered antibodies, and immune system modulation. Improvements in tracking the spread of HIV—the virus that causes AIDS (acquired immune deficiency syndrome)—through the body made researchers better prepared to find a cure. AIDS patients were treated with combination therapies, and public health officials advocated abstinence and "safer sex" practices to control the spread of HIV.

Improved technology for making medical diagnoses offered new hope as well. Magnetic resonance imaging (MRI), for example, was used to produce cross-sectional images of any part of the body. Advances that will make the MRI procedure ten times faster will also make MRI more widely available and cheaper to use. Medical researchers look ahead to using fleets of tiny "nanosensors" one-thousandth the width of a human hair to find tumors and to deploying "nanobots" to repair tissues and even genes. **C**

Background
In 2007, about 14,100 Americans died from AIDS, roughly one-third the 1992 number.

MAIN IDEA

Summarizing
C Describe how technology affected health care.

ALTERNATIVE CARS

In an effort to reduce the nation's dependence on fossil fuels, researchers have been working to develop a "cleaner" car, or one that runs on something other than gasoline. Such alternative models include an electric car, which uses a rechargable battery and gas power, and a vehicle that runs on compressed natural gas.

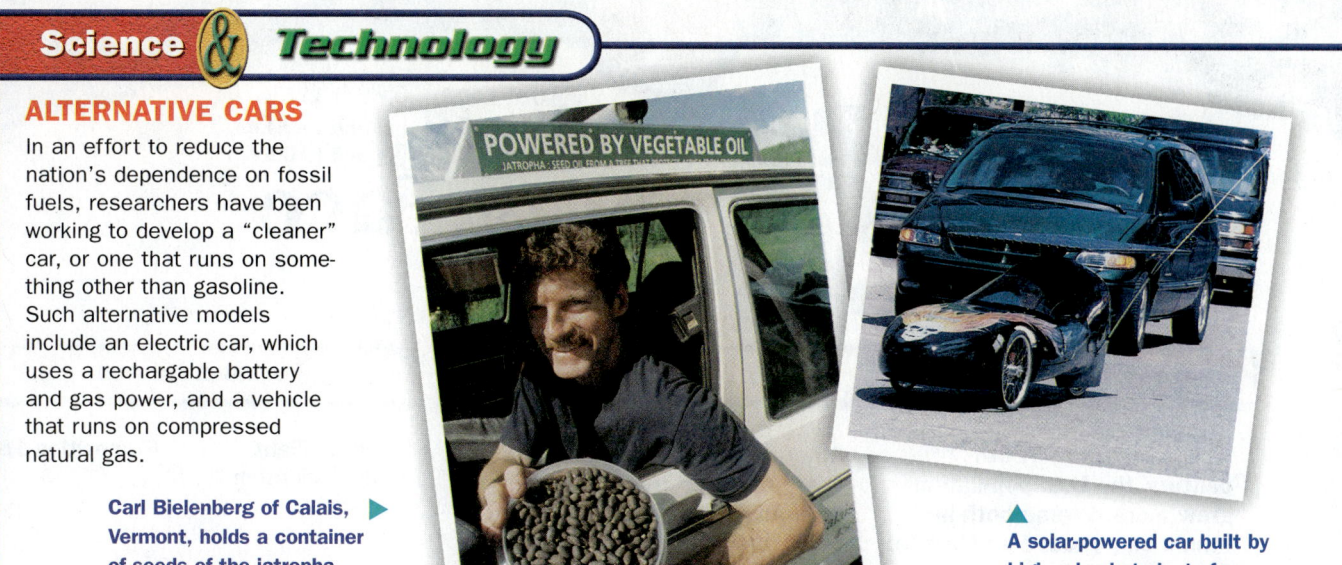

POWERED BY VEGETABLE OIL
JATROPHA · SEED OIL FROM A TREE THAT GROWS

▶ Carl Bielenberg of Calais, Vermont, holds a container of seeds of the jatropha plant. He runs his compact car on vegetable oil that is made from the seed.

▲ A solar-powered car built by high school students from Saginaw, Michigan, makes its way through busy traffic.

ENVIRONMENTAL MEASURES With the spreading use of technology came greater concern about the impact of human activities on the natural environment. Scientists have continued examining ways to reduce American dependence on pollution-producing fossil fuels. Fossil fuels such as oil provided 84 percent of the energy in the United States in 2009 but also contributed to poor air quality, acid rain, and global warming. Many individuals have tried to help by reducing consumption of raw materials. The recycling of glass bottles and jars, plastic bottles, newspapers, cardboard, and aluminum cans and other materials is now commonplace. In 2007, recycling saved the energy equivalent of nearly 11 billion gallons of gasoline.

SECTION 3 ASSESSMENT

1. TERMS & NAMES For each term or name, write a sentence explaining its significance.
- information superhighway
- Internet
- telecommute
- Telecommunications Act of 1996
- genetic engineering

MAIN IDEA

2. TAKING NOTES
On a chart like the one shown, list four of the technological changes described in this section and explain how each change has affected your life.

Technological Change	Effect on Me
1.	
2.	
3.	
4.	

CRITICAL THINKING

3. MAKING INFERENCES
Explain how government, business, and individuals are important to the existence of the information superhighway. **Think About:**
- the costs of developing the superhighway
- the equipment and personnel needed to maintain it
- who uses the superhighway and why they use it

4. ANALYZING ISSUES
Why is genetic engineering a source of controversy?

5. EVALUATING
Which area of technological change described in this section do you think was the most important one for the country? Explain.

SECTION
4

PI 2.3
PI 3.2

CC Unit 1.I.C.3   CC Unit 1.I.C.5
CC Unit 1.I.D.1.c   CC Unit 1.I.D.1.e
CC Unit 1.I.D.5.a   CC Unit 1.I.D.5.c

The Changing Face of America

MAIN IDEA	WHY IT MATTERS NOW	Terms & Names
At the end of the 20th century, the U.S. population grew more diverse both in ethnic background and in age.	Americans of all backgrounds share common goals: the desire for equal rights and economic opportunity.	•urban flight •gentrification •Proposition 187

One American's Story

Every ten years the United States conducts a census, or head count of its population. The results of the census determine, among other things, how billions of federal dollars are spent for housing, health care, and education over the coming decade. The Census Bureau estimates that the 1990 census undercounted Latinos by more than five percent. This undercount resulted in a loss of millions of dollars of aid to municipalities with large Latino populations, as well as denying Latinos political representation in all levels of government.

During the census conducted in 2000, Antonia Hernandez, President and General Counsel of the Mexican American Legal Defense and Education Fund (MALDEF), spearheaded the national *¡Hágase Contar!* Make Yourself Count! campaign. MALDEF workers canvassed neighborhoods urging residents to complete the census. They stressed that all information was confidential and discussed the high stakes of being counted.

★ A PERSONAL VOICE ANTONIA HERNANDEZ

"The census not only measures our growth and marks our place in the community, but it is the first and indispensable step toward fair political representation, equal distribution of resources, and enforcement of our civil rights."

—Public statement for *¡Hágase Contar!* campaign, 2000

Antonia Hernandez, MALDEF's president 1985–2003

Data from the 2000 census revealed that the Hispanic population had grown by close to 58 percent since 1990, reaching 35.3 million. In the next seven years, it grew by nearly 30 percent to 45.5 million.

Urban Flight

One of the most significant socio-cultural changes in American history has been the movement of Americans from the cities to the suburbs. The years after World War II through the 1980s saw a widespread pattern of **urban flight,** the process in which Americans left the cities and moved to the suburbs. At mid-century, the population of cities exceeded that of suburbs. By 1970, the ratio became even.

By the early 2000s, after decades of decline, some major cities across the country had increased their populations while others slowed or halted declines. The transformation of the United States into a nation of suburbs had intensified the problems of the cities.

CAUSES OF URBAN CHANGE Several factors contributed to the movement of Americans out of the cities. Because of the continued movement of job-seeking Americans into urban areas in the 1950s and 1960s, many urban American neighborhoods became overcrowded. Overcrowding in turn contributed to such urban problems as increasing crime rates and decaying housing.

During the 1970s and early 1980s, city dwellers who could afford to do so moved to the suburbs for more space, privacy, and security. Often, families left the cities because suburbs offered newer, less crowded schools. As many middle-class Americans left cities for the suburbs, the economic base of many urban neighborhoods declined, and suburbs grew wealthy. Following the well-educated labor force, more industries relocated to suburban areas in the 1990s. The economic base that provided tax money and supported city services in large cities such as New York, Detroit, and Philadelphia continued to shrink as people and jobs moved outward.

In addition, many downtown districts fell into disrepair as suburban shoppers abandoned city stores for suburban shopping malls. According to the 1990 census, the 31 most impoverished communities in the United States were in cities. **A**

By the mid-1990s, however, as the property values in the nation's inner cities declined, many people returned to live there. In a process known as **gentrification,** they purchased and rehabilitated deteriorating urban property, oftentimes displacing lower income people. Old industrial sites and neighborhoods in locations convenient to downtown became popular, especially among young, single adults who preferred the excitement of city life and the uniqueness of urban neighborhoods to the often more uniform environment of the suburbs.

MAIN IDEA

Analyzing Causes

A List the factors that influenced middle-class residents to leave cities for suburbs.

History Through *Architecture*

REBUILDING THE RIVERFRONTS

As part of the effort to revitalize cities, a number of architects, landscape architects, and urban planners have focused on enhancing what for many urban centers had become a neglected eyesore—their waterfronts. In Pittsburgh, landscape architects turned a dreary strip of concrete and parking lot into Allegheny Riverfront Park, an inviting stretch of natural walkways and recreation areas.

SKILLBUILDER
Interpreting Visual Sources
1. Why might landscape architects consider improving riverfronts to be a key part of revitalizing cities?
2. In what other ways could architects and urban designers make city living more attractive?

   SEE SKILLBUILDER HANDBOOK, PAGE R23.

▲ Allegheny Riverfront Park in 1999

◀ The Allegheny River waterfront in 1984

SUBURBAN LIVING While many suburbanites continued to commute to city jobs during the 1990s and early 2000s, increasing numbers of workers began to telecommute, or use new communications technology, such as computers, modems, and fax machines, to work from their homes. Another notable trend was the movement of minority populations to the suburbs. Nationwide, by the early 2000s, more Latinos, Asians, and African Americans lived in the suburbs than lived in the core cities.

Suburban growth led to intense competition between suburbs and cities, and among the suburbs themselves, for business and industry. Since low-rise suburban homes yielded low tax revenues, tax-hungry suburbs offered tax incentives for companies to locate within their borders. These incentives resulted in lower tax revenues for local governments—meaning that less funds were available for schools, libraries, and police departments. Consequently, taxes were often increased to fund these community services as well as to build the additional roads and other infrastructure necessary to support the new businesses.

The shift of populations from cities to suburbs was not the only significant change in American life in the 1990s and early 2000s. The American public was also growing older, and its aging raised complex issues for policymakers.

Vocabulary
infrastructure: the basic facilities, services, and installations needed for the functioning of a community or society

The Graying of America, 1990–2030

Year	Number of Americans 65 and older*	Percent of U.S. population
1990	31,081	12.4
2000	34,837	12.7
2010	40,229**	13.0**
2020	54,804**	16.1**
2030	72,092**	19.3**

*numbers in thousands
**projected totals

Source: *2010 Statistical Abstract of the United States* (online)

SKILLBUILDER Interpreting Charts
1. Between what years is America's elderly population expected to grow the most?
2. By roughly what percentage is America's elderly population expected to increase between 1990 and 2030?

The Aging of America

The U.S. Census Bureau documents that in 2008 Americans were older than ever before, with a median age of 36.8—four years older than in 1990. Increased longevity and the aging of the baby boom generation were the primary reasons for the rising median age.

Behind the rising median age lie several broad trends. The country's birthrate has slowed slightly, and the number of seniors has increased as Americans live longer because of advances in medical care and living healthier lifestyles. The number of people over 85 has increased at a faster rate than any other segment of the population, to 5.7 million in the year 2008.

The graying of America has placed new demands on the country's programs that provide care for the elderly. These programs accounted for only 6 percent of the national budget in 1955. By 2010, these programs consumed about one-third of the national budget.

The major programs that provide care for elderly and disabled people are Medicare and Social Security. Medicare, which pays medical expenses for senior citizens, began in 1965, when most Americans had lower life expectancies. By 2010, the costs of this program exceeded $465 billion.

◄ Senior athletes compete at the first U.S. National Senior Olympics held in St. Louis, Missouri, in 2000.

Social Security, which pays benefits to retired Americans, was designed to rely on continued funding from a vast number of younger workers who would contribute taxes to support a small number of retired workers. That system worked well when younger workers far outnumbered retirees and when most workers didn't live long after retirement.

In 1996, it took Social Security contributions from three workers to support every retiree. By 2030, however, with an increase in the number of elderly persons and an expected decline in the birthrate, there will be only two workers' contributions available to support each senior citizen. Few issues loomed as large in the recent presidential elections as what to do about Social Security. If the government does not restructure the system, Social Security will eventually pay out more money than it will take in. Some people suggest that the system be reformed by raising deductions for workers, taxing the benefits paid to wealthier Americans, and raising the age at which retirees can collect benefits. **B**

MAIN IDEA

Predicting Effects

B What are the factors that will force an eventual restructuring of Social Security?

The Shifting Population

In addition to becoming increasingly suburban and elderly, the population of the United States has also been transformed by immigration. Between 1970 and 2010, the country's population swelled from 204 million to more than 309 million. Immigration accounted for much of that growth. As the nation's newest residents yearned for U.S. citizenship, however, other Americans debated the effects of immigration on American life.

A CHANGING IMMIGRANT POPULATION The most recent immigrants to the United States differ from immigrants of earlier years. The large numbers of immigrants who entered the country before and just after 1900 came from Europe.

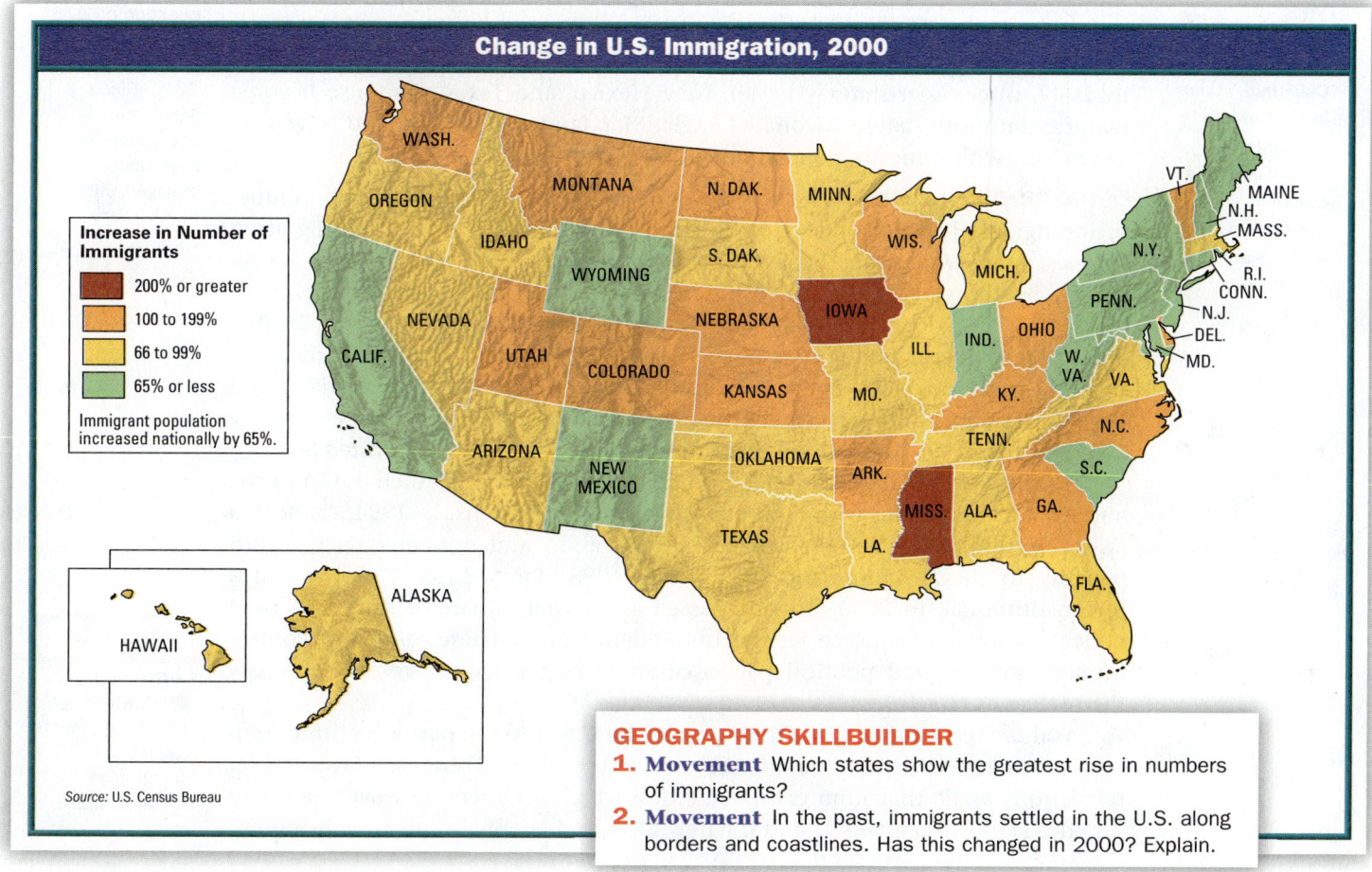

Change in U.S. Immigration, 2000

Increase in Number of Immigrants
- 200% or greater
- 100 to 199%
- 66 to 99%
- 65% or less

Immigrant population increased nationally by 65%.

Source: U.S. Census Bureau

GEOGRAPHY SKILLBUILDER
1. **Movement** Which states show the greatest rise in numbers of immigrants?
2. **Movement** In the past, immigrants settled in the U.S. along borders and coastlines. Has this changed in 2000? Explain.

▲
Lowe Shee Miu, of Oakland, California, stands in front of a monument commemorating Chinese immigrants at Angel Island—the Ellis Island of the West.

In contrast, more than 30 percent of immigrants since the 1960s have come from Asia and about 50 percent from the Western Hemisphere, primarily Mexico.

In Mexico, for example, during three months in 1994–1995, the Mexican peso was devalued by 73 percent. The devaluation made the Mexican economy decline. As a result, almost a million Mexicans lost their jobs. Many of the unemployed headed north in search of jobs in the United States.

This search for a better opportunity continued throughout the 1990s as thousands of legal and illegal immigrants arrived each day—the vast majority from Mexico. To help those persons seeking more opportunity in America, a temporary guest worker program for those immigrants residing illegally in the United States was proposed several times in the early 2000s. By 2010, however, this guest worker program had not been enacted into law.

Census Bureau data indicated that patterns of immigration are changing the country's ethnic and racial makeup. By 2001, for example, California had become a "majority-minority" state, with Asian Americans, Latinos, African Americans, and Native Americans making up more than half its population. By 2009, three other states—Hawaii, New Mexico, and Texas—had also become majority-minority states. Arizona, Georgia, Maryland, Mississippi, and New York were close, with minority populations of 40 percent.

DEBATES OVER IMMIGRATION POLICY The presence of such a large number of immigrants has also added to the continuing debate over U.S. immigration policies. Many Americans believe that their country can't absorb more immigrants. By the early 1990s, an estimated 3.2 million illegal immigrants from Mexico, El Salvador, Guatemala, and Haiti had made their way to the United States. Many illegal immigrants also arrived from Canada, Poland, China, and Ireland. They took jobs many Americans turned down, as farm workers and domestic servants—often receiving the minimum wage or less and no benefits. By 2009, an estimated 10.8 million illegal immigrants resided in the United States.

Hostility toward illegal immigration has increased in states such as California and Arizona, two states with high percentages of immigrants. In 1994, California passed **Proposition 187,** which cut all education and nonemergency health benefits to illegal immigrants. By March 1998, Proposition 187 was ruled unconstitutional. In 2010, Arizona passed a law that enhanced state and local police authority to enforce federal immigration laws. These efforts to control immigration inspired political participation among Hispanic voters, who saw themselves as targets.

As more immigrants make their way to the U.S. and the nation's ethnic composition changes, debates about immigration will continue. Those who favor tighter restrictions argue that immigrants take desired jobs. Others, however, point to America's historical diversity and the new ideas and energy immigrants bring. **C**

Background
The U.S. Census has asked a race question on every census since the first survey in 1790. Since 1890, the categories and definitions have changed with nearly every census.

MAIN IDEA

Comparing
C How are current arguments against immigration similar to those used in the past?

NATIVE AMERICANS CONTINUE LEGAL BATTLES As the nation debated its immigrant policies, the ancestors of America's original inhabitants continued to struggle. The end of the 20th century found most members of this minority enduring extremely difficult lives. In 2007, about 25 percent of Native Americans lived below the poverty line, more than two times the poverty rate for white Americans. Furthermore, Native Americans endured suicide rates and alcoholism rates that were considerably higher than that of the general population.

In the face of such hardships, Native Americans strived to improve their lives. Throughout the 1990s, dozens of tribes attained greater economic independence by establishing thriving gaming resorts. Although controversial for promoting gambling, reservation gaming—$27 billion a year industry by 2008—provided Native Americans with much-needed money for jobs, education, social services, and infrastructure. Over the past decades, Native Americans have used the courts to attain greater recognition of their tribal ancestry and land rights. In 1999, for example, the U.S. Supreme Court ruled that the Chippewa Indians of Minnesota retained fishing and hunting rights on some 13 million acres of land that were guaranteed to them in an 1837 treaty. Across the nation, a number of other tribes have had similar land rights affirmed.

America in a New Millennium

As the 21st century begins, Americans face both new problems and old ones. Environmental concerns have become a global issue and have moved to center stage. Furthermore, poverty remains a problem for many Americans in the late 20th century, as does the increasing threat that terrorist acts pose to Americans at home and abroad.

It is clear that the new century America faces will bring changes, but those changes need not deepen divisions among Americans. With effort and cooperation, the change could foster growth and tolerance. The 20th century brought new ways of both destroying and enriching lives. What will the 21st bring? Much will depend on you—the dreamers, the decision makers, and the voters of the future.

SECTION 4 ASSESSMENT

1. TERMS & NAMES For each term or name, write a sentence explaining its significance.
- urban flight
- gentrification
- Proposition 187

MAIN IDEA

2. TAKING NOTES

Demography is the study of statistics about human populations. Use a table like the one below to summarize the demographic changes occurring in the United States.

Demographic Changes	
Urban distribution	
Age	
Ethnic and racial makeup	

CRITICAL THINKING

3. HYPOTHESIZING

As urban problems become more common in the suburbs, how might the residents of suburbs respond? Base your answer on existing behavior patterns. **Think About:**
- the spread of suburbs farther and farther from the city
- the new ability to telecommute
- the tax problems that suburbs face

4. COMPARING AND CONTRASTING

How was the immigration that occurred in the 1990s and early 2000s similar to and different from earlier waves of immigration?

5. DRAWING CONCLUSIONS

How do disagreements over immigration policy reflect the benefits and challenges of a diverse population?

Immigration and Migration

Immigrants to the United States have been part of a worldwide movement pushing people away from traditional means of support and pulling them toward better opportunities. Most immigrants have left their homelands because of economic problems, though some have fled oppressive governments or political turmoil.

War has often been the deciding factor for people to immigrate to the United States or to migrate within the country. Others have migrated to escape poverty, religious persecution, and racial violence. But the chief lure in coming to the United States or migrating within its borders continues to be the opportunity to earn a living.

1840s

MIGRATING TO THE WEST ▶

Throughout the 19th century, Americans continued their movement westward to the Pacific Ocean. Victory in the War with Mexico in 1848 greatly increased the amount of land under American control, and thousands of Americans moved out West to take advantage of it.

Two important consequences emerged from this movement. First, following the discovery of gold in California, hundreds of thousands of people from around the world rushed in to strike it rich. Within a year, there were enough residents in California to qualify it for statehood. Second, Americans disagreed over whether the new lands should be open to slavery. That disagreement fueled the fires that led to the Civil War.

1910–1920

◀ ADAPTING TO AMERICAN WAYS

With hope and apprehension, millions of foreign immigrants poured into America's pulsing cities during the early 20th century. Bringing with them values, habits, and attire from the Old World, they faced a multitude of new experiences, expectations, and products in the New World.

Many native-born Americans feared that the new immigrants posed a threat to American culture. Instead of the immigrants being allowed to negotiate their existence by combining the old with the new, they were pressured to forget their old cultures, languages, and customs for more "American" ways.

1940s

MIGRATING FOR JOBS ▶

Throughout the 20th century, African Americans migrated across the United States. In the Great Migration of the early 20th century, they left their homes in the rural South. Of the millions of African Americans who left, most moved to cities, usually in the North.

The Second Migration, sparked by World War II, allowed African Americans to take industrial jobs—many formerly held by whites—to support the war effort. This migration had lasting consequences for the civil rights movement. Many African Americans who remained in the South moved to cities, where they developed organizations that helped them fight segregation.

1970–Present

▼ IN SEARCH OF A NEW LIFE

In 1964, 603 Vietnamese lived in the United States. A decade later, as the Vietnam War ended, hundreds of thousands of Vietnamese refugees fled their homeland for other nations, including the United States. Vietnamese immigration to America continued, and by 1998 there were nearly 1 million Vietnamese-born persons living in the United States.

The men and women who made this long and arduous journey from Vietnam are part of the changing face of U.S. immigration. Beginning in the 1970s, Asians and Latin Americans replaced Europeans as the two largest immigrant groups in the United States. Between 1970 and 1990, about 1.5 million Europeans journeyed to America's shores. During that same period, roughly 5.6 million Latin Americans and 3.5 million Asians arrived. This trend has continued. In 2008, the largest immigrant groups in the United States hailed from Mexico, the Philippines, India, and China and Hong Kong respectively. These most recent arrivals to the United States have come for largely the same reasons—greater freedom and economic opportunity and the chance to begin a new life.

THINKING CRITICALLY

CONNECT TO HISTORY

1. **Forming Generalizations** Based on what you have read about immigration, what generalizations can you make about the causes that led to a rise in the number of immigrants to the United States? How have wars affected the flow of immigration? How does this affect economic change?

     SEE SKILLBUILDER HANDBOOK, PAGE R21.

CONNECT TO TODAY

2. **Research** Interview family members and people in your community to find out how immigration and migration have shaped your current surroundings. Try to record specific stories and events that compare a recent immigration with one in the more distant past.

🡥 **hmhsocialstudies.com** **RESEARCH WEB LINKS**

TERMS & NAMES

For each term or name below, write a sentence explaining its significance.

1. William Jefferson Clinton
2. NAFTA
3. Contract with America
4. George W. Bush
5. service sector
6. General Agreement on Tariffs and Trade (GATT)
7. Telecommunications Act of 1996
8. genetic engineering
9. urban flight
10. Proposition 187

MAIN IDEAS

Use your notes and the information in the chapter to answer the following questions.

The 1990s and The New Millennium
(pages 1066–1074)

1. What happened following the investigation of President Clinton?
2. What factors led George W. Bush to victory in 2000?

The New Global Economy *(pages 1075–1079)*

3. Summarize which parts of the economy grew during the 1990s and which declined.
4. Why was the World Trade Organization founded?

Technology and Modern Life *(pages 1082–1087)*

5. What resources did the Internet make available?
6. What were the positive and negative influences that technology had on American lives in the 1990s?

The Changing Face of America
(pages 1088–1093)

7. How has urban flight changed both cities and suburbs?
8. What challenges do experts think the United States will face in the future?

CRITICAL THINKING

1. **USING YOUR NOTES** Create a time line of important events from the 2000 election, using a form like the one below.

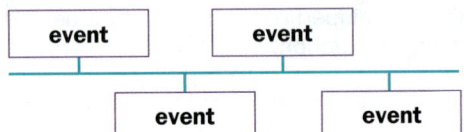

Which event do you think was the turning point? Explain.

2. **PREDICTING EFFECTS** Compile a list of technological innovations of the late 20th century described in the chapter. Then predict what kinds of technological advancements might change American life during the 21st century.

3. **INTERPRETING MAPS** Look carefully at the map on page 1091. What might account for the high percentage change in numbers of immigrants in Iowa and Mississippi, compared with more traditional destinations—such as California and New York?

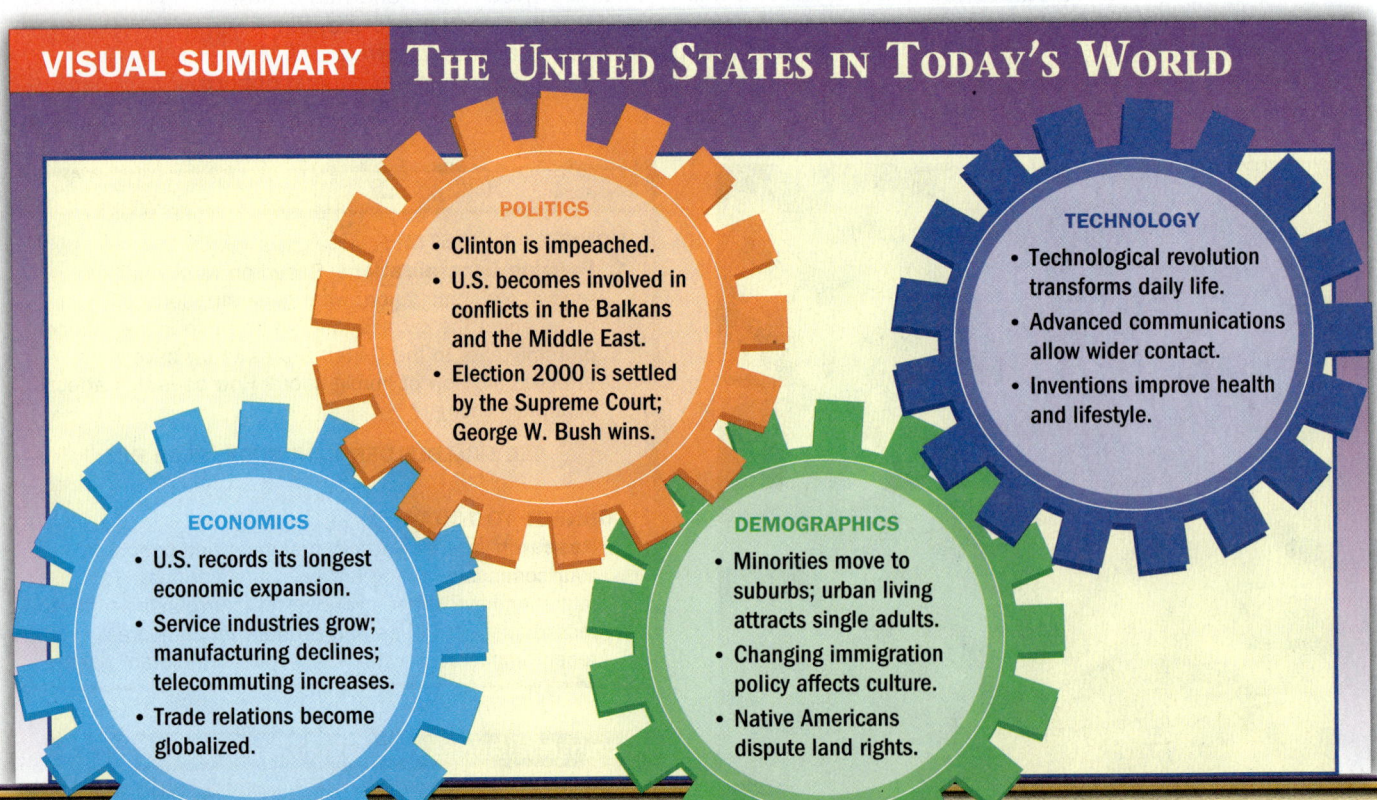

VISUAL SUMMARY THE UNITED STATES IN TODAY'S WORLD

POLITICS
- Clinton is impeached.
- U.S. becomes involved in conflicts in the Balkans and the Middle East.
- Election 2000 is settled by the Supreme Court; George W. Bush wins.

TECHNOLOGY
- Technological revolution transforms daily life.
- Advanced communications allow wider contact.
- Inventions improve health and lifestyle.

ECONOMICS
- U.S. records its longest economic expansion.
- Service industries grow; manufacturing declines; telecommuting increases.
- Trade relations become globalized.

DEMOGRAPHICS
- Minorities move to suburbs; urban living attracts single adults.
- Changing immigration policy affects culture.
- Native Americans dispute land rights.

Use the graphs below and your knowledge of U.S. history to answer questions 1 and 2.

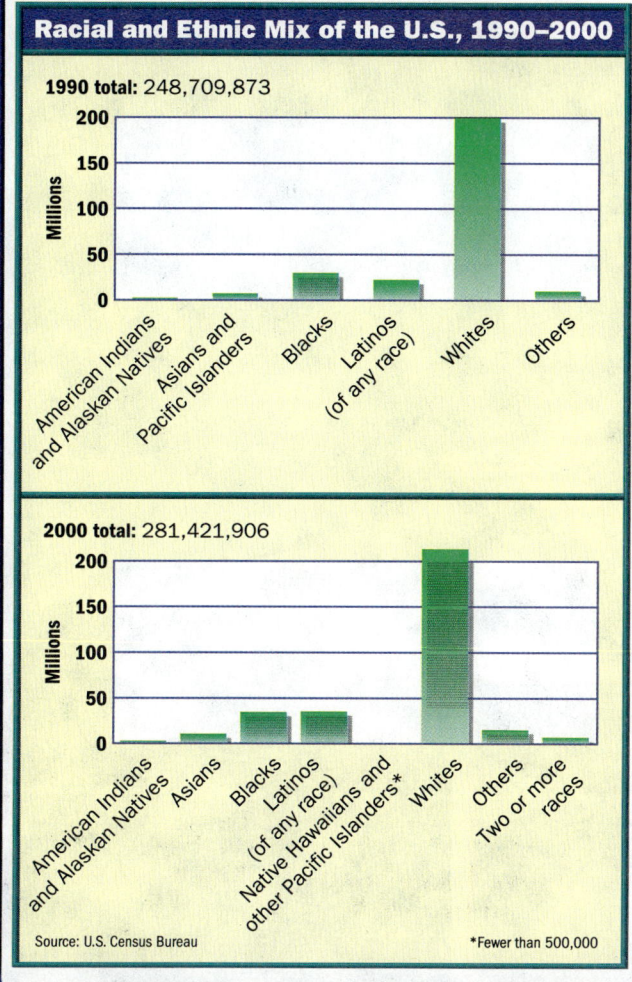

Racial and Ethnic Mix of the U.S., 1990–2000

1990 total: 248,709,873

Millions

200
150
100
50
0

American Indians and Alaskan Natives · Asians and Pacific Islanders · Blacks · Latinos (of any race) · Whites · Others

2000 total: 281,421,906

Millions

200
150
100
50
0

American Indians and Alaskan Natives · Asians · Blacks · Latinos (of any race) · Native Hawaiians and other Pacific Islanders* · Whites · Others · Two or more races

Source: U.S. Census Bureau   *Fewer than 500,000

1 Which U.S. population increased the most between 1990 and 2000?

(1) Latinos
(2) Native Americans
(3) whites
(4) blacks

2 What conclusion can be drawn from the 2000 census data, compared with the data from 1990?

(1) There were more immigrants in the Midwest.
(2) The population of non-Latino whites declined.
(3) The 2000 census reflects a broader range of categories.
(4) Immigration has slowed in the 1990s.

3 Which country was not a member of the G8 in 2000?

(1) China
(2) Japan
(3) Italy
(4) United States

hmhsocialstudies.com   TEST PRACTICE

For additional test practice, go online for:
• Diagnostic tests   • Tutorials

INTERACT WITH HISTORY

Recall the issues that you explored at the beginning of the chapter. As a "think tank" director who researches and analyzes future issues, you are asked to write a concise summary of the five most important issues facing Americans in the 21st century. Present and distribute your summary to the class.

FOCUS ON WRITING

Based on what you have read in this chapter, write a paragraph that describes how the United States will change over the next 20 years.

COLLABORATIVE LEARNING

21ST CENTURY

Working in a small group, use the Internet and library resources to find recent population statistics for the United States.
Consider the following:

• What significant changes have taken place in the United States in recent years?
• How has your state changed?

Present your findings in a poster.

EPILOGUE

KEY IDEA 2 Important ideas, social and cultural values, beliefs, and traditions from New York State and United States history illustrate the connections and interactions of people and events across time and from a variety of perspectives.

ISSUES FOR THE 21ST CENTURY

The War on Terrorism

How can the United States combat terrorism?

On the morning of September 11, 2001, two airliners crashed into the twin towers of the World Trade Center in New York City and a third smashed into a section of the Pentagon, across the river from Washington, D.C. A fourth airliner crashed in a field in the Pennsylvania countryside. Nineteen Arab terrorists had hijacked the four planes and used them as missiles in an attempt to destroy predetermined targets. The first three planes hit their intended targets. In the fourth plane, passengers fought the hijackers and the plane went down short of its target.

Explosions and raging fire severely weakened the twin towers. Within two hours after the attacks, both skyscrapers had crumbled to the ground. One wing of the Pentagon was extensively damaged. About 3,000 people were killed in the attacks—the most destructive acts of terrorism in modern history.

HISTORICAL PERSPECTIVE

Terrorism is the use of violence against people or property to extort changes in societies or governments. Throughout history, individuals and groups have used terror tactics to achieve political or social goals. In recent decades, however, terrorist groups have carried out more and increasingly destructive attacks. The U.S. National Counterterrorism Center recorded over 14,000 terrorist incidents worldwide in 2006 alone.

Modern international terrorism gained world attention during the 1972 Summer Olympic Games in Munich, Germany. Members of a

The twin towers of the World Trade Center in New York burn after the September 11 attacks.

Palestinian group killed two Israeli athletes and took nine others hostage, later killing them. Palestinian terrorists also used airplane hijackings and suicide bombers.

Since then, terrorist activities have occurred across the globe. The Irish Republican Army (IRA) used terrorist tactics for decades to oppose British control of Northern Ireland. The IRA officially renounced violence in 2005. In South America, a group known as the Shining Path terrorized the residents of Peru throughout the late 20th century. The group sought to overthrow the government and establish a Communist state. In 2004, Islamic radicals killed and injured nearly

2000 people with a series of bombs exploded on the Madrid subways.

Groups belonging to the al-Qaeda terrorist organization operate in many countries. Officials have linked several major attacks against U.S. facilities in Africa to al-Qaeda, including bombings at the U.S. embassies in Kenya and Tanzania. Jemaah Islamiah, an Islamic revolutionary group linked to al-Qaeda, has organized numerous attacks throughout Southeast Asia.

TACTICS AND MOTIVES

Most terrorists target high-profile events or crowded places such as subway stations, restaurants, or shopping malls. Terrorists choose these spots carefully to gain the most attention and to achieve the highest level of intimidation.

Terrorists use bullets and bombs as their main weapons. In recent years, however, some terrorist groups have used biological and chemical agents in their attacks. These actions involve the release of bacteria or poisonous gas into the air. Gas was the weapon of choice for a radical Japanese religious cult, Aum Shinrikyo. In 1995, cult members released sarin, a deadly nerve gas, in subway stations in Tokyo. Twelve people were killed and more than 5,700 injured. The possibility of this type of terrorism is particularly worrying, because biochemical agents are relatively easy to acquire.

The reasons for terrorist attacks vary. Traditional motives include gaining independence, expelling foreigners, or changing society. These objectives frequently give rise to domestic terrorism—violence used by people to change the policies of their own government or to overthrow their government.

In the late 20th century, another type of terrorism began to emerge. Terrorists wanted to achieve political ends or destroy what they considered to be forces of evil. They attacked targets not just in their own country, but anywhere in the world. These terrorists were even willing to commit suicide to ensure the success of their attacks.

RESCUE AND REBUILDING

On September 11, the weapons the terrorists used were planes loaded with fuel. The planes became destructive missiles when they crashed into their targets.

Amidst the brutal destruction at the World Trade Center, the courage, selflessness, and noble actions of New York City's firefighters, police officers, and rescue workers stood as a testament. Many of the first firefighters at the scene disappeared into

> # The attacks of September 11 dramatically altered the way Americans looked at life.

the burning buildings to help those inside and never came out again. Entire squads were lost.

Firefighters worked around the clock trying to find survivors in the wreckage. They had to contend with shifting rubble and smoky, ash-filled air. Medical workers from the area rushed to staff the city's trauma centers. But after the first wave of injured were rescued, there were few survivors to treat.

A flood of volunteers assisted rescue workers. From around the country, people sent generous donations of blood, food, and money to New York City.

After the first few days, the work at "ground zero," the World Trade Center disaster site, shifted to recovering bodies and removing the massive amount of debris. The destroyed twin towers accounted for an estimated 2 billion pounds of rubble.

Once the area was cleared, plans to rebuild the site were proposed. In February 2003, a development committee chose a design for a new building complex comprised of several buildings—including Freedom Tower, intended to be the tallest building in New York City—and a memorial park with reflecting pools. Construction of the new design began in 2006.

IMPACT OF 9/11

The attacks of September 11 dramatically altered the way Americans looked at life. For the first time, many Americans became afraid that terrorism could happen in their own country at any time.

This sense of vulnerability intensified when another wave of attacks hit the United States a few days after September 11. Letters containing anthrax spores were sent to people in the news media

A flag flies over the rubble of the World Trade Center while firefighters and rescue workers search for survivors.

and to members of Congress in Washington, D.C. When inhaled, these spores could damage the lungs and cause death. Five people died after inhaling the spores in tainted letters. Two were postal workers.

Some investigators believed that the letters were sent by a lone terrorist and not by a terrorist group. No link between the letters and the September 11 attacks was ever found. The anthrax letters increased Americans' fear of terrorism.

THE UNITED STATES RESPONDS

After conducting a massive investigation, the U.S. government determined that Osama bin Laden, a Saudi Arabian millionaire, had directed the terrorists responsible for the September 11 attacks. The terrorists were part of the al-Qaeda network. The home base for al-Qaeda was Afghanistan, ruled by a strict Islamic regime called the Taliban. The Taliban supported the terrorist group. In return, bin Laden provided fighters to the Taliban.

The United States, led by President George W. Bush, built an international coalition, or alliance, to fight terrorism and the al-Qaeda network. Great Britain played a prominent role in this coalition. After the Taliban refused to turn over bin Laden, coalition forces led by the United States began military action in Afghanistan.

In October 2001, the United States launched Operation Enduring Freedom. The military began bombing Taliban air defenses, airfields, and command centers, as well as al-Qaeda training camps. Within two months, U.S. special forces and marines and fighters from the Northern Alliance, a coalition of anti-Taliban Afghan troops, drove

the Taliban from power. However, the fight to destroy al-Qaeda continued. Bin Laden was not captured, and his fate remained unknown. Meanwhile, the United Nations worked with the Northern Alliance and other Afghan groups to establish an interim government to replace the Taliban. Later, in 2003, Afghan leaders adopted a constitution, and in 2004, Hamid Karzai was elected president of Afghanistan. Peace, however, was elusive. Since 2005, insurgent attacks by Taliban and al-Qaeda militants have posed a continuing threat.

In 2002, President Bush called for a commission to investigate whether the September attacks could have been prevented and how to prevent future attacks. In 2004, the 9/11 Commission issued a report that stressed the need for greater cooperation and coordination within the government. It also recommended the creation of a new

Cabinet post—that of national intelligence director. On April 21, 2005, the U.S. Senate confirmed John Negroponte's appointment to that position.

USA PATRIOT ACT

To give the government the power to conduct search and surveillance of suspected terrorists, the USA PATRIOT Act was signed into law on October 26, 2001. This law allowed the government to:

- detain foreigners suspected of terrorism for seven days without charging them with a crime. In some cases, prisoners were held indefinitely.
- tap all phones used by suspects and monitor their e-mail and Internet use.
- make search warrants valid across states.
- order U.S. banks to investigate sources of large foreign accounts.
- prosecute terrorist crimes without any time restrictions or limitations.

Tom Ridge, the first to hold the position of Secretary of Department of Homeland Security, introduces the color-coded threat advisory system.

History of Terrorist Attacks Against the United States

1978	1983	1988	1993	1995
Theodore Kaczynski, the Unabomber, uses mail bombs to kill 3 people over 17 years.	Shi'ites explode a truck near U.S. military barracks in Beirut, Lebanon, killing 241 Marines.	Libyan terrorists explode a bomb in an airplane, causing it to crash in Lockerbie, Scotland, killing 270 people.	Suspected al-Qaeda terrorists explode bombs in the World Trade Center in New York City, killing 6 and injuring at least 1,040.	Timothy McVeigh uses a truck to destroy the Murrah Federal Building in Oklahoma City, Oklahoma, killing 168 people. (page 1068)

People who opposed the law claimed that it violated the First, Fourth, Fifth, Sixth, and Seventh Amendments. In 2005 it was revealed that President Bush had ordered the National Security Agency (NSA) to spy on American citizens' international telephone calls and e-mails without obtaining warrants.

ANTITERRORIST ACTIONS

To combat terrorism on the home front, the Bush administration created the Department of Homeland Security in 2002, initially headed by former Pennsylvania governor Tom Ridge. This executive department was designed to analyze threats, guard the nation's borders, seaports, and airports, and coordinate the country's response to attacks. To help share information about the risk of terrorist attacks with the American people, the department created the Homeland Security Advisory System. This system used a set of "Threat Conditions" to advise the public about the level of terrorist threats and provided guidelines for response during a period of heightened alert.

The Department of Homeland Security also searched for terrorists in the United States. The government soon discovered that the al-Qaeda network had used "sleepers" to carry out its terrorist attacks. Sleepers are agents who enter a country, blend into a community, and when called upon, secretly prepare for and commit terrorist acts. An intensive search began for any al-Qaeda terrorists, including sleepers, that remained in the United States. U.S. officials detained and questioned Arabs and other Muslims who behaved suspiciously or violated immigration regulations.

An airport security official inspects a traveler's shoe at a security checkpoint.

Many suspects captured in Afghanistan were held in a prison camp at Guantanamo Bay, Cuba. The United States faced criticism at home and abroad regarding its treatment of detainees. Critics claimed that detaining people without charging them and without access to attorneys violated their civil rights. The government argued that limiting civil liberties in wartime to protect national security was not unusual. U.S. officials used the same argument to try some terrorist suspects in military tribunals rather than in criminal courts.

AVIATION SECURITY

The federal government's role in aviation security also increased. National Guard troops began patrolling airports, and sky marshals were assigned to airplanes. In addition, the Federal Aviation Administration (FAA) had bars installed on cockpit doors to prevent hijackers from entering cockpits.

In November 2001, President Bush signed into law the Aviation and Transportation Security Act, which made airport security the responsibility of the federal government. Previously, individual airports had been responsible for their own security. Because of this new law, an agency called the Transportation Security Administration (TSA) was created to inspect airline passengers, baggage, and cargo, as well as noncitizens training to be pilots. The TSA is also responsible for safety on railroads, buses, and mass transit systems. Security operations at airports created several major concerns, including long delays and possible invasion of passengers' privacy. As the United States fights terrorism and tries to balance national security with civil rights, the public debate over security measures continues.

PREDICTING EFFECTS

How effective do you think the antiterrorist measures taken by the Bush administration will be in preventing or dealing with future terrorist attacks?

hmhsocialstudies.com **RESEARCH WEB LINKS**

Visit the links for the Epilogue to find out more about War on Terrorism.

1998

Al-Qaeda explodes bombs near two U.S. embassies in Nairobi, Kenya, and Dar es Salaam, Tanzania, killing 224.

2000

The bombing of the USS *Cole* in Aden, Yemen, is linked to Osama bin Laden and kills 17 American sailors.

2001

Arab terrorists crash planes into the World Trade Center, the Pentagon, and a Pennsylvania field, killing about 3,000.

2011

Osama bin Laden is killed in Pakistan by U.S. special forces.

Iraq: Confronting a Dictatorship

How should the United States deal with dangerous dictators?

Since 1979, Saddam Hussein's regime in Iraq had brutally repressed opposition. The Iraqi dictator had ruled without regard for the welfare of his people or for world opinion. During his State of the Union address in January 2003, President George W. Bush declared Hussein too great a threat to ignore in an age of increased terrorism. He promised to do everything possible to prevent Iraq from launching a terrorist attack on the United States.

HISTORICAL PERSPECTIVE

In August 1990, the Iraqi army had invaded Kuwait, a small country that shares Iraq's southwestern border. Saddam Hussein wanted Kuwait's huge oil reserves. The United Nations (UN) condemned the occupation and approved the use of force to end it.

On January 16, 1991, the Persian Gulf War began. Coalition forces led by the United States drove Iraq's army out of Kuwait within six weeks. A cease-fire agreement with the UN prohibited Iraq from producing chemical, biological, and nuclear weapons.

The United Nations periodically sent arms inspectors to Iraq to make sure Hussein was complying with the cease-fire agreement. However, the Iraqi dictator refused to cooperate fully with the inspectors.

> ## "By seeking weapons of mass destruction, these regimes pose a grave and growing danger."
>
> **PRESIDENT GEORGE W. BUSH**

Because of this, the United States and Great Britain declared in 1998 that they supported the removal of Hussein from his office and the ending of his regime. In response, Hussein barred arms inspectors from entering his country.

STEPS TOWARD WAR

After the attacks on September 11, 2001, the United States called for a renewal of the arms inspections in Iraq. In November 2002, the UN Security Council passed a resolution designed to force Iraq to give up all weapons of mass destruction (WMD). Arms inspections resumed, but Hussein again refused to cooperate fully. Soon, the United States

and Great Britain cut off diplomatic relations with Iraq.

In early February 2003, U.S. Secretary of State Colin Powell gave a presentation to the UN Security Council, maintaining that Iraq was hiding WMD. Soon thereafter, the United States and Great Britain pressed the UN to pass a resolution that authorized the use of military force against Iraq. As an alternative, France, Germany, and Russia presented a plan that called for intensifying the inspections.

The United States and Great Britain countered by claiming that a new UN resolution was not necessary since Iraq was in violation of the old agreement. They also claimed that Iraq's violation justified the use of military force to overturn Hussein's regime.

Meanwhile, protests against a possible war in Iraq increased at home and abroad. Antiwar protesters participated in more than 600 rallies around the globe on a single day in February. An estimated 750,000 protesters turned out in London—the largest demonstration ever in the British capital. Most demonstrations were peaceful.

WAR IN IRAQ

In March 2003, the United States and Great Britain launched Operation Iraqi Freedom. The war began with massive air raids; sec-

History of Saddam Hussein's Regime

1979	1980	1988	1990	1991
Saddam Hussein seizes power in Iraq.	Iraq invades Iran's oil fields, triggering the Iran-Iraq War, which continues until 1988.	The Iraqi Air Force releases poisonous gases over the Kurdish town of Halabja, Iraq, killing about 5,000 people.	Iraq invades Kuwait in an attempt to seize that nation's oil revenues.	The Persian Gulf War begins in January and ends six weeks later. The UN prohibits Iraq from producing WMD.

In Baghdad, Iraqis pull down a statue of Saddam Hussein after the dictator's regime is overthrown.

tions of Baghdad were the primary targets. U.S. ground troops then raced toward the Iraqi capital. By April 2, U.S. forces had reached the outskirts of the city. Within a week, Baghdad had fallen to the U.S. military. Meanwhile, British troops seized the city of Basra. Coalition troops had taken control of most of Iraq by April 14. Hussein survived the attack and was finally captured on December 13, 2003. He was convicted of crimes against humanity and hanged in 2006. In 2004, reports about U.S. treatment of detainees in Iraq's Abu Ghraib prison generated widespread criticism.

SEARCH FOR WMD

The case for going to war against Iraq was based on assertions by the U.S. and British governments that Saddam Hussein had WMD. Once major combat ended on May 1, U.S. forces began an extensive search for these weapons. Movable biological laboratories containing sophisticat-

ed equipment were located, but by mid-2005, no WMD had been found. This led many in the United States and Great Britain to question the necessity for the war. Bush and British Prime Minister Tony Blair responded by claiming that they had based their decision on intelligence later proved to have been faulty. In May 2005, a top-secret memo known as the Downing Street memo became public. It suggested that the Bush administration had planned to invade Iraq as early as July 2002.

IRAQ AFTER HUSSEIN

After the fall of Hussein's regime, the United States led in the establishment of the Coalition Provisional Authority (CPA) to temporarily govern Iraq and oversee its reconstruction. On June 28, 2004, the CPA was replaced by a temporary government made up of Iraqis. And on January 30, 2005, Shiite Muslim parties won a majority of seats

in Iraq's election for a transitional National Assembly that would draft Iraq's constitution. Shiites eventually agreed to allow members of the Sunni Muslim minority to participate in shaping the country's constitution.

On October 15, 2005, Iraqi voters narrowly accepted a new constitution. In December, Iraq held elections to choose a permanent parliament. The Shiites captured a majority of seats, but not enough to control the government. Sunni and Kurdish legislators rejected the Shiites' first candidate for prime minister. In April 2006, the National Assembly approved a compromise candidate, Nuri al-Maliki, as the new prime minister.

Despite this progress, violence between Sunnis and Shiites continued to plague Iraq. Insurgents, or rebels, engaged in acts of violence that killed thousands. Militants also attacked U.S. troops. In response, President Bush announced a plan in January 2007 to send 20,000 more U.S. troops to Iraq. Many Americans opposed the troop surge, but it went into effect later that year. In February 2009, President Obama unveiled a plan to remove all U.S. troops from Iraq by the end of 2011.

Another parliamentary election was held in March 2010. The secular Shiite party of Ayad Allawi, who had served as interim prime minister in 2004, won 91 seats in Iraq's parliament, a narrow margin over the 89 seats claimed by incumbent prime minister Nuri al-Maliki's party.

PREDICTING EFFECTS
How do you think the removal of all U.S. troops from Iraq would affect the Iraqi people?

hmhsocialstudies.com **RESEARCH WEB LINKS**

Visit the links for the Epilogue to find out more about Iraq: Confronting a Dictatorship.

1998	2003	2006
Iraq's refusal to cooperate with UN arms inspectors leads to a four-day air strike by the United States and Great Britain.	In March, the United States and Great Britain launch Operation Iraqi Freedom. Major combat ends in May, and Hussein is overthrown.	Saddam Hussein is convicted of crimes against humanity and executed.

The Debate over Immigration

Should new laws restrict or expand immigration?

For hundreds of years, immigrants working for their dreams have shaped the United States. Latino ranchers developed many of the tools and skills of the American cowboy. Chinese laborers laid the tracks of the transcontinental railroad. African Americans, though not voluntary immigrants, labored to develop the agriculture of the South and the industry of the North. Farmers and workers of every origin built the nation we know today.

HISTORICAL PERSPECTIVE

But immigration has been argued throughout American history. In the 1700s, Benjamin Franklin worried about the number of Germans immigrating to Pennsylvania. Sharp anti-immigration sentiment spurred the nativist movement that developed in the 1830s and the "America First" campaign of the 1920s.

Americans today are divided on the issue. Some agree with former New York City mayor Rudolph Giuliani that immigrants "challenge us with new ideas and new perspectives." Others side with Dan Stein of the Federation for American Immigration Reform, who has said that "large-scale immigration is not serving the needs and interests of the country."

RISING NUMBERS

From 1900 into the 1940s, economic troubles and rapid population

> "America's immigration system is . . . unsuited to the needs of our economy and the values of our country."
>
> **PRESIDENT GEORGE W. BUSH**

growth spurred more than 16 million Europeans to move to the United States. The same pressures have recently hit Asia and Latin America, with the same effect on the United States. Between 1989 and 2009, more than 21 million new immigrants came to the United States.

ILLEGAL ENTRY

Complicating the debate has been the issue of illegal immigrants. By 2009, the number of illegal immigrants living in the United States was estimated at close to 11 million. A 2004 report by the Center for Immigration Studies suggested that

households headed by illegal immigrants each used about $2,700 more in federal government services than they paid in taxes.

Congress had addressed such issues in the 1990s, passing laws that toughened measures to bar illegal entry and that limited benefits to illegal immigrants. In February 2005, President George W. Bush proposed a new approach. Stating that "America's immigration system is . . . unsuited to the needs of our economy and the values of our country," he endorsed a guest worker program. This would have allowed foreigners to work in the United States for a set period of time. However, as of 2010, a guest worker program had not been enacted into law.

In the meantime, some states took action on illegal immigration. For example, in 2010 Arizona passed a law that enhanced state and local police authority to enforce federal immigration laws.

ECONOMIC DEBATE

Those who favor limits claim that immigrants take jobs from Americans. However, data suggest that immigration has not hurt the economy and may have helped fuel its growth. At the same time that millions of immigrant workers—including some undocumented workers—were joining the work

History of Immigration in the United States

1751	1854	1882	1896	1921
Benjamin Franklin denounces German immigrants.	Nativists form Know-Nothing Party to protest increase in immigration (page 319).	Chinese Exclusion Act severely restricts immigration from China (page 465).	President Cleveland vetoes bill requiring immigrants to pass literacy test.	Emergency Quota Act begins era of limits on immigration (page 621).

Members of the Latin American community in Los Angeles raise their hands to bless fruit baskets as a sign of immigrants' daily work in California's fields. The sign reads "This fruit is the product of immigrants' labor."

force, the overall trend in unemployment was downward. However, in 2009, when unemployment rose above 9 percent, the number of illegal immigrants in the United States fell.

Another argument focuses on wages. Economists agree that immigrants tend to work for lower wages than native-born workers. Harvard University economists estimated that one-third of the gap between low-paid and high-paid workers results from higher numbers of immigrants. But they also reported that other factors—foreign trade, declining union membership, and new technology—play a greater role in lowering wages.

Immigrants fill skilled, high-paying jobs as well. Current law limits the number of immigrants who may enter the United States within specific employment categories, or preferences. The 2009 limit was set at about 140,000.

However, there were more applicants than places in 2009.

CITIZENSHIP RESPONSIBILITY
Some people are concerned that certain immigrants never become citizens and so fail to completely participate in U.S. life. Statistics show that legal immigrants are becoming citizens in ever higher numbers. Even so, many immigrants eligible for citizenship have have not applied to become citizens. Experts attribute this to a variety of factors, including the rising cost for filing for citizenship, a backlog of applications, and a presumed lack of interest among some immigrants. The oath of U.S. citizenship carries with it such responsibilities as voting, serving on juries, and, in some cases, military service.

CULTURAL CONCERNS
The diversity of the U.S. population has raised concerns that America has no common culture. Some say

that at 12.6 percent of the population, the foreign-born are too numerous in America. Historian David Kennedy points out that in 1910 the percentage was even higher—14.7 percent.

Those who favor limits claim that new immigrants do not mix with other groups, forming ethnic neighborhoods that divide society. Others believe that immigrants enrich American cultural life.

MORAL ISSUES
The issue of asylum—providing a safe place for people fleeing oppression—has been the toughest of all. While immigration is allowed for political asylum, those who flee famine or poverty are turned away. Are such choices fair?

Some rules allow relatives of immigrants to enter the country. Representative Lamar Smith of Texas believes that these rules admit immigrants who "have no marketable skills and end up on welfare." Yet, social scientist Nathan Glazer says that concern about the number of immigrants conflicts with sympathy for those "trying to bring in wives, children, parents, brothers, and sisters."

Some observers believe that there are simply too many immigrants. Slow immigration for a time, they suggest. In polls taken in mid-2010, about a third of the population seemed to agree with this idea, expressing the opinion that the level of legal immigration should be decreased.

PREDICTING EFFECTS
How might the measures restricting illegal immigrants affect future laws that regulate legal immigration?

hmhsocialstudies.com RESEARCH WEB LINKS

Visit the links for the Epilogue to find out more about The Debate over Immigration.

1965
Immigration Act loosens restrictions in place since 1924 (page 897).

1994
California passes Proposition 187, excluding benefits to illegal immigrants (page 1092).

1996
Congress passes laws that limit benefits to illegal immigrants.

2010
President Obama proposes an overhaul of the immigration system.

Crime and Public Safety

Will tougher gun control laws reduce the incidence of crime?

On an early March day in 2001, Alicia Zimmer, a student at Santana High School outside San Diego, found herself in the middle of gunfire in the hallways. A 15-year-old boy had brought a gun to school and had begun firing at his fellow students. "I was probably about 10 feet away from some of the victims," Zimmer said, adding that she saw "a boy laying on the floor with his face down," and a girl with "blood all over her arm." Before the shooter was apprehended, two people were killed and 13 were injured. School shootings have become more common in the United States and are just one reason why, despite an overall decrease in crime during the 1990s and into the 21st century, Americans continue to express concerns over public safety.

School students at John Bartram High School in Philadelphia go through metal detectors as they enter the school one day after a school shooting.

HISTORICAL PERSPECTIVE

In 1968, opinion polls reported that for the first time, Americans called crime the nation's single worst problem. Since then, crime has remained high on the list of national problems.

Crime rates generally increased during the 1970s, due in part to rising unemployment and inflation, increased drug use, civil unrest, and protests against the Vietnam War. But in the 1980s, the spread of crack cocaine abuse fueled a major jump in crime. From 1986 to the early 1990s, the rates of violent crimes and car thefts increased by more than 20 percent.

Beginning in 1992, however, these rates began to drop and continued declining throughout the decade. The FBI announced that in 2003 violent crime had dipped to a 20-year low and was a third lower than in 1994. In 2000 the murder rate also reached a 20-year low and was relatively stable for the next 6 years.

RECENT SUCCESS

Experts have identified a few causes for falling crime rates:

- There are fewer males aged 15 to 29, the group most likely to commit crimes.
- The trade in crack cocaine slowed.
- The unemployment rate gradually decreased throughout the 1990s. Generally, when more people have jobs, crime rates fall.

Perhaps the biggest factor has been new policing efforts. Police departments have taken officers out of patrol cars and put them back on the streets. Police have also taken a more active role in their neighborhoods. Crime prevention methods now focus on an intense effort to

History of Crime and Public Safety in the United States

1791	1844	1920s	1966	1980s	1993
Second Amendment, protecting right to bear arms, is ratified (page 149).	New York City organizes first full-time, salaried police force (page 471).	Organized crime thrives during Prohibition (page 643).	*Miranda* v. *Arizona*: police must inform suspects of their legal rights (pages 898, 900).	Increased drug abuse contributes to rising crime.	Brady Act aims to reduce the spread of handguns.

intervene with troubled youth before they commit a crime.

CONTINUING EFFORTS

Despite what appears to be a safer nation, however, many Americans continue to worry about crime. For one thing, gun violence is extremely high. According to the FBI, guns were used in 68 percent of all homicides in 2007. In addition, some social scientists contend that with a slumping economy a new crime wave is just over the horizon. Even though the overall murder rate has declined since 1990, crime continues to command public attention. Experts are split over two issues related to reducing crime further: gun control and tougher sentencing.

GUN CONTROL

In 1993, President Bill Clinton signed the Brady Act, which called for states to place a five-day waiting period on the sale of handguns. During that period, police check the potential buyer's background. If they find a criminal record, a gun permit is denied. However, four years later, in June 1997, the Brady Act was substantially weakened when the Supreme Court ruled that the federal government could not force state or local officials to run background checks on potential buyers of handguns.

At the center of the gun-control issue lies a long-standing constitutional debate. The Second Amendment to the Constitution states this: "A well-regulated militia, being necessary to the security of a free state, the right of the people to keep and bear arms shall not be infringed." The National Rifle Association

As the 21st century begins, Americans find themselves grappling with new forms of violent crime.

(NRA), which is opposed to tougher gun-control laws, argues that gun-control laws violate this right to bear arms. Others contend that the amendment was not intended to guarantee a right to personal weapons. Rather, its purpose is to protect the state's right to maintain military units.

TOUGHER SENTENCES

In addition to looking at hand gun laws, Americans have sought to battle crime by putting more people in prison. The federal government and many states recently passed "three strikes" laws. Under these laws, any person found guilty of two previous crimes receives a stiff sentence of twenty to thirty years after conviction for a third.

While many applaud this get-tough policy, others claim that it suffers from a serious problem: racial bias. Blacks represent just 12 percent of the U.S. population and about 13 percent of those who reported using illegal drugs on a monthly basis. Yet three-quarters of all prison sentences for possession of drugs involve African Americans. Many civil rights groups say that such differential treatment must end.

NEW CHALLENGES

As the 21st century begins, Americans face a number of new challenges. Deadly school shootings have brought attention to the issue of youth violence, and violent crime in America's cities remains a national concern. But the greatest challenge to public safety may be the renewed threat of terrorism. During the mid-1990s, a series of bombings signaled a disturbing new era of terrorism in America. The bombing of the World Trade Center in 1993, the 1995 Oklahoma City bombing, and the bombing at Atlanta's Centennial Park in 1996 all contributed to a growing sense of public vulnerability.

Following the events of September 11, 2001, in October President Bush signed into law new anti-terrorism measures. These laws greatly increased the authority of local, state, and federal law enforcement agencies to obtain and to share information about anyone living in the United States, but drew severe criticism for intruding on personal privacy.

It now appears that Americans will be struggling to balance the need for domestic security against its costs—in terms of privacy, convenience, and dollars—well into the 21st century.

PREDICTING EFFECTS

What methods do you think the nation will employ to more effectively prevent terrorist attacks?

🡭 hmhsocialstudies.com **RESEARCH WEB LINKS**

Visit the links for the Epilogue to find out more about Crime and Public Safety.

1994
Republicans include tougher crime laws in their Contract with America (page 1070).

1997
Supreme Court rules that certain provisions of the Brady Act are unconstitutional.

1999
2 students kill 13 and then themselves at Columbine High School in Colorado (page 1068).

2001
On September 11, terrorist attacks in New York and at the Pentagon kill thousands.

Issues in Education

How can a country guarantee equal education for all?

In the winter of 2001, Paul Vallas, former head of the Chicago public school system, received some discouraging news. A three-year study found "little significant change" in the city's ailing public high schools—despite six years of intense reform efforts. "The issue is that the problem is tougher than we thought it was," the study reported, "and we have to find more intense ways of improving what we've been doing." In response to the study, Vallas echoed those sentiments. "We still have a long way to go," he said. The plight of Chicago's public schools highlights the nation's ongoing struggle to improve education.

HISTORICAL PERSPECTIVE

From the earliest days of the nation, American leaders have stressed the importance of education. In the 19th century, reformers helped establish a system of government-supported public schools. By 1900, almost three-quarters of all eight- to fourteen-year-olds attended school. Even with these advances, some groups suffered. Public secondary education failed to reach most African Americans in the early 20th century. Not until 1954, with the Supreme Court decision *Brown* v. *Board of Education of Topeka*, did federal court decisions call for an end to separate—and usually inferior—schools for African Americans.

By the 1960s, the nation's schools wrestled with the problem of a rising discrepancy between suburban schools and inner-city schools. Many students in inner cities attended schools that were housed in decaying buildings and that had dated instructional materials. On the other hand, students in the suburbs enjoyed new facilities and equipment. In both the inner city and the suburbs, violence and drugs have raised issues of safety.

KEY ISSUES

The debate over public education has focused on three key issues. First is the question of how to change schools to improve the

> **From the earliest days of the nation, American leaders have stressed the importance of education.**

quality of education. Second is the issue of school financing. Should different school systems in a state receive equal funding? The third issue has to do with affirmative action—programs intended to remedy past discrimination.

IMPROVING QUALITY

People have offered many ideas on how to improve schools. Some critics say that lack of discipline is a major problem. Others point to the disparity in technology between wealthy and poor schools. During his presidency, Bill Clinton called for all schools in the country to be connected to the Internet and its vast supply of information.

Another reform receiving support is the creation of charter schools. In this plan, certain schools receive a charter, or contract, from a local school district, a state education department, or a university. Charter schools promise innovations in education. In return for freedom to operate as they choose, charter schools promise to increase students' achievement levels. By April 2005, about 3,400 such schools were in place in approximately 40 states.

Some school reformers favor the voucher system, in which states issue a certificate to parents, who then use it to pay for their child's education at a school of their choice. The school exchanges the voucher for payment from the government. Supporters of the voucher system believe that parents will seek schools that provide higher-quality education. Public schools will then be forced to compete with private and parochial schools, and with one another. The competition should increase the overall quality of education, supporters argue.

History of Education in the United States

1821	1837	1865	1954	1965
Emma Willard opens Troy Female Seminary, an academic school for girls (page 256).	Horace Mann begins the push to spread public education (page 245).	African Americans who had been slaves begin to create and attend schools (pages 388, 490–491).	*Brown* v. *Board of Education* finds segregated schools unconstitutional (pages 914–915).	Federal government begins providing aid to public schools (page 895).

During his run for office in 2000, President George W. Bush voiced support for vouchers. "I don't know whether or not the voucher system is a panacea," he said, "but I'm willing to give it a shot to determine whether it makes sense."

FINANCING EDUCATION

In most states, school funding relies on local property taxes—taxes paid on the value of real estate in a town or city. When schools are funded primarily by property taxes, however, schools in poorer areas receive less money than those in wealthier communities. According to the magazine *Washington Monthly*, one New Jersey town spends $13,394 per pupil on schooling. Another town just five miles away spends only $7,889. Court cases have raised legal challenges to unequal school funding in more than 20 states.

In 1993, Michigan voters approved a plan that abandoned reliance on local property taxes as the basis of school funding. Now schools get their money from a smaller state-controlled property tax, an increased sales tax on consumer purchases, and increased taxes on purchases of such items as cigarettes and alcohol. Because the state sets property tax rates and monitors its school systems' budgets, it can even out inequalities.

Jessica Riley, a hearing-impaired volunteer teacher, helps a hearing-impaired second grader with his reading.

AFFIRMATIVE ACTION

Many Americans support the idea of programs that give women and minorities greater opportunities. At the same time, a large majority disapprove of quotas, the setting aside of a certain number of jobs or college admissions for members of these groups.

This point became the focus of a court case challenging affirmative action. The Supreme Court, in *Regents of the University of California* v. *Bakke* (1978), ruled that institutions could use race as one factor among others in determining admission. (See pp. 1024–1025 for more information.) In 2001, in *Hopwood* v. *Texas*, a lower federal court expanded upon the *Bakke* decision by ruling that a university could not have separate admissions tracks for white and minority candidates.

CURRENT CHALLENGES

On January 8, 2002, President Bush signed into law his education program, No Child Left Behind. A cornerstone of the program is accountability for student performance with national annual reading and math assessments in grades 3 through 8. The law required states to report how many students performed at each of four levels: failure, basic, proficient, and advanced. Schools that failed to show enough progress could lose students to other schools, be forced to change staff, or even be closed down.

In 2006, the Center for Education Policy reported that achievement on state tests was rising. Critics claimed that schools were neglecting other subjects. In March 2010, President Obama proposed an education plan to replace No Child Left Behind. The plan focuses on rewarding schools for progress rather than punishing them for failure. Clearly, debate over education reform will continue.

PREDICTING EFFECTS

What do you think will be the most important education issue the country will face in the coming years? Why?

hmhsocialstudies.com RESEARCH WEB LINKS

Visit the links for the Epilogue to find out more about Issues in Education.

1983	1989	1996	2005
A federal commission report *A Nation at Risk* severely criticizes public education (page 1047).	Education summit issues Goals 2000.	California voters ban affirmative action in education and other areas.	Number of charter schools in America reaches roughly 3,400.

The Communications Revolution

Can information on the Internet be both reliable and accessible?

On a spring day in 1997, 12-year-old Sean Redden had just logged onto the Internet in his home in Denton, Texas, when he encountered a startling message: "Would someone help me?" The plea turned out to be a distress call from an Internet user nearly 7,000 miles away in Finland. The person had suffered an asthmatic attack that left her barely able to breathe. After obtaining more information from the woman, Redden contacted his local police. They in turn alerted Finnish authorities, who located the woman and rushed her to medical care at a nearby hospital. This digital rescue is just one example of the power and reach of the Internet, which has dramatically changed American society like nothing else in recent history.

HISTORICAL PERSPECTIVE

In the 1940s, when computers first came into use, they took up huge rooms and required fans or elaborate air-conditioning systems to cool the parts that provided them with power. In the years since, the parts that power computers have become miniaturized and have been made much more powerful. Today, not only can personal computers perform more operations more quickly than the first giant computers did, but they are also affordable for many people. The development

> **Many observers credit computer technology with driving the nation's astonishing economic growth during the 1990s.**

of inexpensive personal computers has made it possible for ordinary families to use the latest technology.

THE INTERNET

A very important component of computer use today is the Internet, a worldwide computer network. In the 1960s, the Department of Defense began to network its computers in order to protect its ability to launch nuclear missiles following a feared Soviet attack. Then in the late 1980s, the National Science Foundation created its own network, NSFNET, and allowed anyone to access it. However, only a small group of

computer-science graduates and professors used the system.

At about this time a digital revolution arose as thousands of industries across the country began using computers to run their businesses, and millions of Americans bought personal computers for their homes. With so many computers suddenly in use, NSFNET steadily grew into the large and crowded Internet, which includes the World Wide Web.

THE COMPUTER REVOLUTION

The numbers alone demonstrate the influence of computer technology on modern life. By 2007, nearly 70 percent of Americans were logging onto the Internet either at home or at work, and close to 66 percent of U.S. households owned at least one personal computer. What's more, nearly every business in the nation, from hospitals to accounting firms and airports, has implemented computer systems to handle many of its daily operations.

Many observers credit computer technology with driving the nation's astonishing economic growth during the 1990s. With computers allowing employees in nearly every field to perform their jobs more quickly and easily, worker productivity and output increased—a major reason for the decade-long boom.

History of the Communications Revolution

1969	1991	1994	1996
U.S. Department of Defense creates ARPANET.	First browser, or software for accessing the World Wide Web, developed.	Three million people worldwide use the Internet.	Congress passes Telecommunications Act, allowing companies to engage in a variety of communications endeavors (page 1084).

EVERYDAY USES

Computer technology not only has improved how Americans work, but also has dramatically altered how they live. Millions of citizens now buy everything from flowers to books to stock online. In 2005, the nation spent over $93 billion in electronic transactions, also known as e-commerce.

While Americans once communicated strictly by phone or letter, they now talk to each other more and more through their computers. Many teenagers spend several hours a day on "social networking" Web sites. Computers have also affected the way Americans learn. In 2002, 92 percent of public school classrooms had Internet access, up 15 percent from 2000. A growing number of universities offer classes and even complete degree programs wholly over the Internet.

HIGH-TECH CHALLENGES

For all the benefits and opportunities it has brought, computer technology also has created its own set of challenges. There are few laws and regulations governing the Internet. Thus, while it is a treasure trove of useful information, the World Wide Web also has become a center for the dissemination of pornographic and hate material.

The growth of computers also has led to the growth of "cybercrime." Computer vandals, known commonly as hackers, engage in everything from the theft of social security numbers and other vital personal information to the disabling of entire computer systems. The Federal Bureau of Investigation estimates that cybercrime costs Americans more than $10 billion a

College senior Demetress Roberts uses a computer program to teach Latino Outreach student Angel Leonardo about fractions.

year. What concerns officials even more is the growing possibility of "cyberterrorism"—hackers stealing or altering vital military information such as nuclear missile codes.

Meanwhile, a large number of Americans worry about the growing "digital divide," the notion that computer technology remains out of reach for many of the nation's poor. According to recent statistics, nearly 92 percent of households earning $75,000 or more owned a computer, compared with only about 42 percent of households earning between $15,000 and $25,000. Many fear that poor families unable to purchase computers are falling even further behind in a country where computer skills are fast becoming a necessity.

CLOSING THE GAP

Actually, the nation is working to close the gap. In San Jose, California, for example, officials were able to invest $90,000 in a program to teach computer skills to welfare recipients and homeless people. Meanwhile, libraries, schools, and senior centers across the country provide free Internet access. A number of proposals to provide people with greater access to computers and training are working their way through the federal and various state governments.

THE FUTURE

As the 21st century begins, the computer revolution shows no sign of slowing. The digital technology that has so transformed the nation continues to improve. Mobile devices and wireless Internet access allow many Americans to get online from almost anywhere in the nation. As the computer age rolls on, Americans and the rest of the world most likely will face exciting new opportunities.

PREDICTING EFFECTS

What do you think will be a new breakthrough and a new challenge for Americans in the next decade of the Computer Age?

hmhsocialstudies.com **RESEARCH WEB LINKS**

Visit the links for the Epilogue to find out more about The Communications Revolution.

1999
First full-service Internet-only bank opens

2001
Over 200 million people around the world use the Internet.

2006
Number of Internet domains surpasses 400 million.

CC Unit 1.I.D.1.b CC Unit 1.I.D.5 CC Unit 7.III.B.1.b
PI 2.1
CC Unit 7.VI.B.1.a(1) CC Unit 7.VI.B.1.b(2)

Curing the Health Care System

How should medical coverage for the uninsured be funded?

To pay for the medicine she needs, 79-year-old Winifred Skinner walks the streets of Des Moines every day collecting cans. "I don't want to ask for handouts. I want to earn it," she insists. The soaring cost of prescription drugs—especially among the elderly—is just one of the key issues facing American health care today.

HISTORICAL PERSPECTIVE

National health insurance for Americans was first proposed by President Harry S. Truman in 1949, but Congress failed to approve it. It took the legislative skill of President Lyndon B. Johnson to enact Medicare in 1965. The program covered most of the cost of medical care for people age 65 and above.

By the 1990s, Medicare was taking an increasing share of federal spending. In hopes of controlling costs and providing universal coverage, President Clinton proposed a complex plan. However, lobbying by doctors and private insurers and the public's mistrust of big government caused Congress to defeat Clinton's plan in 1994.

Meanwhile, many Americans were afraid they would be denied health insurance because of preexisting conditions—medical conditions that are present when a person applies for coverage. The Health Insurance Portability and Account-

Irene Holmes holds her son while technician Roberta Montoya takes a blood sample at the Sandia Health Center.

ability Act, passed in 1996, partly removed that concern. It limited the situations under which insurers could exclude from coverage those with preexisting conditions.

HEALTH CARE REFORM

Health care continued to be a hot topic during the 2000 presidential campaign and beyond. One of the issues up for debate was the need for prescription-drug coverage for the elderly, a reform many thought should be addressed as part of an overhaul of the Medicare system. Also high on the agenda were the

need to protect patients' rights and the need to expand health coverage to the ranks of the uninsured.

SOARING DRUG COSTS

When Medicare began in 1965, the cost of prescription drugs was small compared with that of hospital stays and doctors' visits. But with the development of new medicines and treatments for heart disease, arthritis, and other chronic conditions, drugs became the fastest-growing component of health-care spending. About 40 percent of people on Medicare were without

History of Health Care in the United States

1949	1953	1965	1970s	1981
Truman introduces a bill for national health insurance that is ultimately rejected by Congress (page 845).	Department of Health, Education, and Welfare is established.	President Johnson and Congress enact Medicare and Medicaid into law (page 896).	President Nixon increases funding for Medicare and Medicaid (pages 1001–1002).	AIDS (Acquired Immune Deficiency Syndrome) is first identified (page 1046).

prescription-drug coverage. Many elderly citizens were paying well over $1,000 a year out of pocket for medicine—or else did without.

President George W. Bush took steps to address this issue in 2003 with the Medicare Prescription Drug, Improvement, and Modernization Act (MMA). This law provided access to drug coverage for elderly and disabled people on Medicare, beginning in 2006.

Critics noted that the act allowed for a "doughnut hole" in coverage. That is, there was an initial coverage limit. Once that had been reached, people were responsible for 100 percent of their drug costs. Medicare picked up coverage again later. The Patient Protection and Affordable Care Act, passed in 2010, provided rebates and discounts to those in the "doughnut hole." It also proposed to completely close this coverage gap by 2020.

THE FATE OF MEDICARE

One issue facing policymakers in the early 21st century was how to reform Medicare. Estimates made in 2009 suggested that if nothing changed, Medicare's hospital insurance fund would run out of money by 2017. The reasons are rising costs and demographic changes. Americans are living longer now than they were in 1965—about eight years longer on average. As a result, seniors form a greater proportion of the population than before. While rising numbers of elderly drive up the cost of Medicare, the revenues targeted to pay for it are not keeping pace. As the population ages, fewer people will work and pay the taxes that fund Medicare. Additionally, elderly persons as a group tend to have higher medical costs.

Today, more than three workers pay taxes for every person who

> ## "Health care is too important for any modern society to permit many of its citizens to go without it."
>
> **HENRY J. AARON, FORMER DIRECTOR, BROOKINGS ECONOMIC STUDIES PROGRAM**

receives Medicare, while by 2030, this ratio will stand at 2.4 to 1. Workers' taxes almost certainly will have to go up—especially if health costs rise. Meanwhile, according to one estimate, Medicare pays less than half of its beneficiaries' medical expenses.

What is to be done? Among the approaches that have been proposed are placing more restrictions on Medicare benefits, raising the age of eligibility, or increasing the share to be paid by the elderly. The 2010 Patient Protection and Affordable Care Act offered some different answers. It planned to raise the Medicare tax on people making more than $200,000 and set up a committee to find ways of controlling the rise in Medicare spending. It also introduced procedures to more aggressively root out Medicare fraud and waste.

THE UNINSURED

Another worrying issue for policymakers in the early 2000s was the number of people without health insurance. This problem was extensive—some 17.4 percent of nonelderly Americans were uninsured in 2008. About 8 million of the uninsured were children.

In 1997, the federal government began to address the issue of uninsured young people with the State Children's Health Insurance Program (SCHIP). SCHIP provided funding to states so that they could offer health coverage to children of low-income families who earn too much to qualify for Medicaid (which covers the cost of medical care for the poor). By 2008, more than 7 million children were benefiting from the program.

The Patient Protection and Affordable Care Act extended SCHIP. It also tackled the issue of uninsured adults. It extended private insurance coverage through individual mandates—that is, requiring individuals to get some level of health coverage. Insurance reforms, subsidies to help people pay premiums, and tax credits for small businesses offering employees insurance also aimed to expand private coverage. For the poorest individuals, the act expanded the Medicaid program. Previously, Medicaid covered primarily children and women of childbearing age.

Under these changes, over time some 32 million people would be added to the ranks with health insurance. However, it is unlikely that the Patient Protection and Affordable Care Act will end the debate on health care.

1996

Congress passes Health Insurance Portability and Accountability Act (HIPAA).

1997

The State Children's Health Insurance Program (SCHIP) is enacted.

2010

Congress passes Patient Protection and Affordable Care Act.

PREDICTING EFFECTS

What impact do you think the Patient Protection and Affordable Care Act will have on the health care system? Explain your answer.

hmhsocialstudies.com RESEARCH WEB LINKS

Visit the links for the Epilogue to find out more about Curing the Health Care System.

Breaking the Cycle of Poverty

Who has the responsibility for helping the poor?

Jim, a 55-year-old painter by trade, retreats each night to a Boston homeless shelter. He spends his days engaging in any work he can find—but it's never enough to provide him with a roof over his head. Too many of the jobs available, he says, "pay only the minimum wage or a bit higher, and they cannot cover the rent and other bills." Jim, who says his dream is to "get a steady job, find an apartment, and settle down," insists that he never imagined he would find himself homeless. "I never thought it could happen to me," he says. Jim is just one of almost 40 million citizens considered poor in a nation that continues to cope with the challenge of eradicating poverty.

HISTORICAL PERSPECTIVE

Some part of the American population has faced poverty since the "starving time" at Jamestown during the winter of 1609–1610. In the 20th century, poverty was most widespread during the Great Depression of the 1930s. That economic disaster led to several new government programs such as the 1935 Social Security Act, which created a pension fund for retired people over age 65 and offered government aid to poor people for the first time.

Though the Depression ended with World War II, postwar prosper-

> **Many of those Americans who live in poverty are employed.**

ity did not last. In the 1960s, President Lyndon B. Johnson declared "unconditional war on poverty" as his administration expanded education, training, and financial aid for the poor. The proportion of people living below the poverty level—the minimum income necessary to provide basic living standards—fell from 20 percent in 1962 to only 11 percent in 1973. However, economic hard times reappeared in the early 1980s and the poverty rate began to rise. In 2008, about 39.8 million Americans lived below the poverty line—which that year was marked by an annual income of $21,834 for a family of four.

AMERICANS IN POVERTY

Many Americans who live in poverty are employed. Known as the working poor, they hold low-wage jobs with few benefits and almost never any health insurance. Children also account for a major

share of the poor, and their numbers are growing rapidly for many ethnic groups. The poverty rate among children in the United States is higher than that in any other Western industrialized nation.

Like Jim in Boston, many of the poor are homeless. During the 1980s, cuts in welfare and food stamp benefits brought the problem of homelessness to national attention. According to the National Alliance to End Homelessness (NAEH), about 750,000 Americans are without shelter on any given night.

Many experts on the homeless believe that the lack of housing is simply a symptom of larger problems. These include unemployment, low-wage jobs, and high housing costs, and in some cases, personal problems such as substance abuse or mental illness.

SOME CAUSES OF POVERTY

Experts agree that there are numerous causes of poverty. Lack of skills keeps many welfare recipients from finding or keeping jobs. They need more than job training, many observers insist, they also need training in work habits.

Another factor that holds back increased employment is limited access to child care. Economist David Gordon related the results of a study of mothers who received

History of the Cycle of Poverty in the United States

1894	1935	1962	1964
High unemployment in the wake of the panic of 1893 leaves thousands homeless (pages 427–428).	Social Security Act is passed; government gives aid to poor for first time (pages 698, 707).	Michael Harrington's *The Other America* shocks the nation by revealing extent of poverty (page 888).	President Johnson announces War on Poverty (page 894).

welfare. They could eke out a living, he found, by combining paid work and some outside support with welfare payments and food stamps. But, Gordon asked, suppose one of these mothers left welfare and took a full-time minimum-wage job. "[If] she cannot find free child care and has to pay the going rate, her standard of living . . . would decline by 20 percent." To help meet the need for child care, a 1996 federal welfare law included $3.5 billion in funding for day care.

For millions of Americans, the U.S. public education system has failed to provide the tools necessary for climbing out of poverty. Anne Lewis, an education writer, points out that "three-fourths of all welfare/food stamp recipients perform at the lowest levels of literacy." In turn, she notes, low levels of literacy generally lead to low employment rates and lower wages.

Another factor contributing to poverty has been discrimination against racial minorities. Current statistics highlight how much more prevalent poverty is among minorities. In 2008, the poverty rate among whites was 8.6 percent, while among Hispanics and African Americans it was 23.2 percent and 24.7 percent, respectively.

FEDERAL WELFARE REFORM

As the nation continued to struggle with poverty and homelessness, the cry for welfare reform grew louder. Critics of the system argued that providing financial aid to the poor gave them little incentive to better their lives and thus helped to create a culture of poverty. In 1996, the Republican Congress and President Clinton signed a bill—the Personal Responsibility and Work Opportunity Reconciliation Act—that cut more than $55 billion in welfare spending over six years and put a

five-year limit on how long people could receive welfare payments. In addition, the bill cut benefits to recipients who had not found a job within two years.

Supporters cheered the reforms, claiming that they transformed a system from one that fosters dependence to one that encourages self-reliance. Opponents of the law accused the federal government of turning its back on the poor—especially children.

Both proponents and critics of the bill agreed on one thing: the law's success depended on putting welfare recipients to work. The federal government offered three incentives to encourage businesses to hire people from the welfare rolls: tax credits for employers who hire welfare recipients, wage subsidies, and establishment of enterprise zones, which provide tax breaks to companies that locate in economically depressed areas.

In February 2006, Congress reauthorized the Temporary Assistance for Needy Families (TANF) program created by the 1996 bill. Between August 1996—when the bill creating TANF passed—and March 2006, the number of people on welfare declined to its lowest percentage since 1969. However, with millions of Americans still living below the poverty line, efforts to break the cycle of poverty continue.

PREDICTING EFFECTS

What can be done to provide affordable child care to help the working poor?

hmhsocialstudies.com RESEARCH WEB LINKS

Visit the links for the Epilogue to find out more about Breaking the Cycle of Poverty.

1970

Nixon's welfare reform bill—the Family Assistance Plan—dies in the Senate (page 1001).

1980s

Welfare benefits and food stamps are cut under President Reagan (page 1041).

1996

Congress passes Personal Responsibility and Work Opportunity Reconciliation Act.

2006

The Deficit Reduction Act of 2005 is passed, reauthorizing the TANF program.

Tough Choices About Social Security

How can Social Security be reformed so that it will have enough money to pay retirees?

Economist Lester Thurow gives new meaning to the term *generation gap*. "In the years ahead, class warfare is apt to be redefined as the young against the old, rather than the poor against the rich," he warns. Economics may become a major issue dividing generations, as young workers shoulder the costs of Social Security, Medicare, and Medicaid—the three major entitlement programs funded by the federal government.

HISTORICAL PERSPECTIVE

In the 1935 Social Security Act, or FICA, the government promised to pay a pension to older Americans, funded by a tax on workers and employers. At that time, President Franklin D. Roosevelt said that Social Security was not intended to provide all of an individual's retirement income, but it was a base on which workers would be able to build with private pension funds.

In 1965, new laws extended Social Security support. In addition, the government assumed most health care costs for the elderly through the Medicare program and for the poor through Medicaid. These programs are called entitlements because the recipients are entitled by law to the benefits.

Social Security, Medicare, and Medicaid have received a lot of attention because the United States

Citizens in favor of protecting Social Security rally on the U.S. Capitol grounds.

population is aging. This aging population will put a severe financial strain on these programs.

SOCIAL SECURITY FUNDING

Social Security's problem can be attributed to a few important factors. First, when the baby boomers (those born between 1946 and 1964) retire, their huge numbers—about 70 million by the year 2020—may overburden the entitlement programs. Second, Americans now live longer, so an individual's share of benefits from the program is greater

than in the past. Third, the number of workers paying into Social Security per beneficiary will drop when the boomers start retiring.

Currently, Social Security collects more in taxes than it pays in benefits. The extra goes into a "trust fund" that is invested. Around the year 2016 the program will begin paying out more to beneficiaries than it takes in from the payroll tax. The program will begin to rely on the Social Security Trust Fund to pay retirees. If that trend continues, after 2037, Social Security will be able

History of Entitlements in the United States

1935	1961	1965	1970s	1975
President Roosevelt signs Social Security Act (page 707).	Changes to Social Security allow reduced benefits at early retirement—age 62.	President Johnson signs Medicare and Medicaid into law (page 896).	President Nixon increases Social Security payments (pages 1001–1002).	Congress includes cost-of-living adjustments for Social Security benefits.

to cover only about 75 percent of scheduled benefits.

Most experts recommend reform, and Americans have listened. One poll found that 81 percent of Americans under 40 believe that the Social Security program needs to be changed to guarantee its financial stability.

OPTIONS FOR CHANGE

A number of plans for reforming Social Security have been proposed. These different views have become the main options being debated in Congress and around the country.

- **Raise Social Security Taxes** Some people have suggested small tax hikes, arguing that since people's incomes are expected to rise, they will be able to afford an increase. As of 2010, only the first $106,800 of any individual's income is subject to FICA tax. Some people have suggested that those with higher incomes are not paying their fair share.
- **Cut Benefits** Some argue that benefits should be reduced by ending automatic cost-of-living adjustments or lowering payments made to retirees who earn over a certain amount of money each year. These wealthier people, they say, do not need to receive higher payments.
- **Raise the Retirement Age** Because people can now work productively later in life than they used to, some propose raising the retirement age. That will reduce the payments made and increase tax receipts. Retirement age is set according to date of birth. At present, it is 67 for people born in 1960 or later.

Social Security, Medicare, and Medicaid have received much attention because the U.S. population is aging.

- **Invest Funds in the Stock Market** Some people suggest that the government should invest some of Social Security money in the stock market. They assume that stocks will rise, making the system healthier.
- **Allow Individual Investing** Others agree with allowing the funds to be invested but want individuals to control where their own funds are invested.

THE FUTURE OF THE FUNDS

During the 2000 presidential election, exit polls found that some 57 percent of Americans supported the "privatization" approach outlined by President Bush during his campaign: allow workers to divert a portion of their Social Security taxes into individual stock-market accounts. During the 2004 election campaign and following the election, President Bush continued his attempts to persuade Americans to support his privatization plan.

Meanwhile, the proposal drew its share of critics. Among them were advocates for disabled workers and their families—a group that in 2008 made up 18 percent of all Social Security beneficiaries. According to a report from the General Accounting Office, under President Bush's plan a worker who became disabled and retired at the age of 45, for example, would receive 4 percent to 18 percent less in benefits.

Some women's groups also opposed privatization. They said that it would jeopardize the guarantee of lifetime, inflation-adjusted benefits that the current Social Security system provides. Because women earn less than men, they would have less to invest, and their returns would be lower.

Still others were concerned about the risk involved in relying on a volatile stock market. They questioned whether the funds in which people would invest their Social Security taxes would be secure. In the end, Bush could not garner enough support for his plan.

Not surprisingly, Social Security reform was an issue in the 2008 presidential election. Republican candidate John McCain favored a partial privatization plan. Democrat Barack Obama called for raising the cap on the amount of income subject to the FICA tax. Since the presidential election, little progress has been made on the issue of Social Security. As a result, the funding problem remains unsolved.

PREDICTING EFFECTS
How would the economy be both helped and hurt if Social Security benefits were cut?

hmhsocialstudies.com RESEARCH WEB LINKS
Visit the links for the Epilogue to find out more about Tough Choices About Social Security.

1983
Social Security is reformed to provide financial stability for many years.

1994
President Clinton appoints Advisory Council on Social Security to report on system's financial health.

2008
Social Security reform is an important issue in the presidential election.

Women in the Work Force

Will the American workplace grant men and women equal opportunities?

Thirty-two years after entering a management training program at Boston's Federal Reserve Bank, Cathy Minehan became the bank's president and one of a select group of female executives who held 3.3 percent of the nation's highest-paying jobs. "A critical element in making it to the top is being in the pipeline to do so, . . ." says Minehan. "Aside from . . . [that,] they have to believe they can make it. . . . It is hard for women or minorities to believe they can progress if they cannot look up and see faces like their own at the top."

HISTORICAL PERSPECTIVE

In 1961, President John F. Kennedy named a commission to study the status of women in the workplace. Its report revealed that employers paid women less than men for equal work. The report also said that women were rarely promoted to top positions in their fields.

Almost 40 years later, the U.S. Census Bureau found that more women than ever before worked outside the home—about 60 percent. Women made up 47 percent of the American work force. Yet in 2005 they held only 16.4 percent of the most senior jobs according to a sampling of the Fortune 500, the nation's 500 largest companies.

> **Women are still making less than their male counterparts— averaging only 77 cents for every dollar.**

Some women who pursue careers in business, government, or other organizations feel that a glass ceiling limits their progress. It is said to be glass because it is an invisible barrier that keeps women and minorities from attaining promotion above a certain level. Its invisibility makes it difficult to combat.

POSITIVE TRENDS

Women have made great strides in recent decades. In 2002, they filled half of all jobs in managerial and professional specialty areas. Women have also been entering new fields, including construction work and equipment repair.

In the academic world, women are better represented than ever before. In 2006–2007, women received a record number—50 percent—of all doctorate degrees issued by universities. Women earned an even higher percentage—57—of all bachelor's degrees.

For many women, job success involved getting the right credentials and targeting a growth industry. A 2000 survey by the women's advocacy group Catalyst found that 91 percent of women with MBA degrees working in information technology reported high satisfaction with their current jobs, compared with only 82 percent of their male counterparts. "This translates into opportunity for women in this growing industry," said Sheila Wellington, president of Catalyst.

MONEY AND UPWARD MOBILITY

Despite these positive signs, the key issues of unequal pay and unequal representation remain. Women are still making less than their male counterparts—averaging only 77 cents for every dollar earned by men. According to the National Committee on Pay Equity, there are a variety of reasons for this discrepancy: women are often socialized to aim toward lower-paying jobs, often have limited expectations about

History of Women at Work in the United States

1834	1860	1899	1900	1920s
Women working in Lowell, Massachusetts, textile mills strike (page 262).	1 out of 10 single white women works outside the home, earning half the pay of men.	Average pay for women workers is $267 a year, compared with $498 for men (page 451).	One out of five women works outside the home (pages 519–520).	Women enter new professions but battle unequal wages (page 648).

U.S. Appeals Court judge Rosemary Barkett (*center*) delivers the keynote address during a special session of Florida's high court honoring the state's first 150 female lawyers on June 15, 2000, in Tallahassee, Florida.

their leadership potential, and may have conflicts between the demands of work and family life.

In the nation's most top-level jobs, men continue to vastly outnumber women. As of 2006, women headed only ten Fortune 500 companies. Very few women who became corporate officers held line positions, jobs with profit-and-loss responsibility. In 2005, women held only 10.6 percent of line positions, while in contrast, men held 89.4 percent of them.

Why are women underrepresented in the top jobs? In one Catalyst poll of women executives, blame was placed on three factors: male stereotyping and preconceptions of women, women's exclusion from informal networks of commu-nication, and women's lack of significant management experience.

On the other hand, the respondents suggested some approaches that had helped them succeed in the corporate world: consistently exceed expectations, develop a style with which managers are comfortable, seek out difficult assignments, and have an influential mentor.

STRIKING OUT ON THEIR OWN

Many women who are frustrated by the corporate environment at their existing companies are choosing to start their own business. According to the center for Women's Business Research, in 2004 10.6 million firms were at least 50 percent owned by women—and constituted the fastest-growing sector of all U.S.

firms. Notes Dixie Junk, owner of Junk Architects in Kansas City, "It's more than having a business—you get to create the culture you want."

IT PAYS TO BE FLEXIBLE

Another area of change affecting women in the work force has been an increasing number of options for flexible work arrangements, such as part-time work and telecommuting opportunities. In 2004, 71 percent of companies surveyed had formal policies or guidelines for some type of flexible work arrangement.

A Catalyst study of 24 women who first used flexible work arrangements more than a decade ago found that all of them now held mid- and senior-level positions, and more than half had been promoted in the last 10 years. Says Marcia Brumit Kropf, vice-president of research and information services, "Findings from this report suggest that even though working mothers may reduce career involvement for a period of time—with the support of the right company—career advancement does not have to get sidelined."

In general, women still have the primary responsibility for child care in U.S. society. Women without flexible work arrangements must find others to care for their children at least part of the day. About 65 percent of mothers with children under the age of 6 and 80 percent of mothers with children between the ages of 6 and 13 work. Many people believe that the government should subsidize child-care costs.

PREDICTING EFFECTS
What can be done to afford women the same opportunities as men?

↗ hmhsocialstudies.com **RESEARCH WEB LINKS**

Visit the links for the Epilogue to find out more about Women in the Work Force.

1961	1989	1998	2005
Presidential Commission on the Status of Women reports: women are paid less than men (page 983).	20 states begin adjusting pay scales to equalize pay (page 1049).	Women earn 76 cents for every dollar a man earns.	Women-owned businesses are the fastest-growing sector of the U.S. economy.

The Conservation Controversy

Can the nation balance conservation with economic progress?

In 1990, Oregon logger Bill Haire hung a new ornament on the mirror of his truck: a tiny owl with an arrow through its head. The trinket represented the spotted owl as well as Haire's feelings about the federal government's decision to declare millions of acres of forest off limits to the logging industry in order to protect this endangered species of bird.

"If it comes down to my family or that bird," said Haire, "that bird's going to suffer." The battle between loggers and environmentalists over the fate of the spotted owl is just one example of the nation's on-going struggle to balance conservation with industrial progress.

HISTORICAL PERSPECTIVE

Conservation, the management and protection of the earth's resources, began as a national movement in the United States during the early 1900s. In the wake of the country's industrial revolution, the federal government enacted numerous measures to protect the nation's natural surroundings. President Theodore Roosevelt expressed a particular interest in preserving America's forestlands. "Like other men who had thought about the national future at all," he once remarked, "I had been growing more and more concerned over

Hikers on the Highline Trail in Glacier National Park, northwest Montana

the destruction of the forests." Roosevelt established the first wildlife refuge in Florida and added more than 150 million acres to the nation's forest preserves.

The 1960s and 1970s witnessed a resurgence of the conservation movement. In 1962, marine biologist Rachel Carson published *Silent Spring*, which warned of the destructive effects of pesticides. The book awakened Americans to the damage

they were inflicting on the environment. In the two decades that followed, Congress created the Environmental Protection Agency (EPA) and enacted such measures as the Clean Air Act, the Clean Water Act, and the Endangered Species Act—all in an effort to restore the health of the country's natural resources. And, since 1970, the country nearly tripled the size of its national park space.

History of Conservation in the United States

1903	1933	1962	1970	1973
President Theodore Roosevelt establishes the first federal wildlife refuge (page 529).	President Franklin Roosevelt creates the Civilian Conservation Corps (page 697).	Rachel Carson publishes *Silent Spring* (page 897).	Congress establishes the Environmental Protection Agency; Congress passes Clean Air Act (page 1028).	Congress passes the Endangered Species Act (page 1028).

THE MOVEMENT CONTINUES

By the early 2000s, Americans had done much to improve the environment. Between 1970 and 2008, for example, the nation's yearly production of carbon monoxide emissions into the air dropped from 204 million tons to about 78 million tons.

A number of states have made independent efforts. California, for instance, has some of the nation's strictest air-pollution control laws, and these have helped to provide the Golden State with much cleaner air. Other states are playing their part as well in the nation's ongoing conservation effort.

However, there is still much to be done, especially about water pollution. One indicator is data collected by the Environmental Protection Agency for the first decade of the 2000s, which showed that beach closings—mostly due to unsafe levels of water pollution—were at historically high levels.

Not all action has been through government. Private groups such as the Nature Conservancy and local land trusts have raised money to purchase forest and watershed lands and keep them pristine. In Texas several entrepreneurs created the Fossil Rim Wildlife Center, a 1,700-acre wildlife sanctuary for more than 50 animal species.

ONGOING DEBATES

Despite the strides Americans have made in protecting their natural resources over the past half century, environmental problems still exist, and the nation still struggles to strike a balance between conservation and economic growth. Such a struggle is clearly visible in the greenhouse effect. The greenhouse effect is the rise in temperature that

> **As the 21st century begins, the nation faces the challenge of balancing energy needs with environmental concerns.**

Earth experiences because certain gases in the atmosphere trap energy from the sun. Without these gases, heat would escape back into space and Earth's average temperature would be about 60°F colder.

Some greenhouse gases, such as carbon dioxide, methane, and nitrous oxide, occur naturally in the air. But the burning of fossil fuels and other human activities add to the levels of these gases, amplifying the greenhouse effect and causing an increase in global warming. Global warming could prompt a range of environmental calamities, from severe flooding in some parts of the world to drought in others.

In 2005, a treaty called the Kyoto Protocol took effect. It aims to reduce greenhouse gases overall by requiring developed countries to lower their emissions. The United States—the world's largest producer of greenhouse gases—signed the treaty but did not ratify it. President George W. Bush expressed doubt about global warming for several years. He also claimed that the protocol was unfair because developing countries such as China were exempt. As of 2010, the Obama administration had not pushed for ratification.

Another issue of great concern to Americans today—and one that also is stirring debate between environmentalists and industrialists—is the nation's growing appetite for energy. The United States consumes 21 percent of the world's energy, nearly all of it in the form of fossil fuels such as oil, coal, and natural gas. Much of the fuel America uses comes from overseas—in places such as the oil-rich Middle East. The reliance on foreign sources has left the United States vulnerable to price increases and fuel shortages.

In 2005, President Bush outlined a plan to lessen U.S. dependence on oil imports. He proposed using more nuclear power, giving tax credits to buyers of energy-efficient cars and appliances, building new refineries, and drilling for more oil at home. Five years later, President Obama presented a similar plan. However, he also pushed for heavier use of renewable energy sources and for taxes on businesses that produce high levels of carbon pollution.

Fluctuating gasoline prices in 2007 and 2008 and a massive oil spill in the Gulf of Mexico in 2010 caused new energy worries. Balancing energy needs with environmental concerns is an issue that Americans will grapple with for years.

PREDICTING EFFECTS

Do you think the United States eventually will engage in greater domestic exploration of its natural resources to solve its growing energy needs? Why or why not?

hmhsocialstudies.com RESEARCH WEB LINKS

Visit the links for the Epilogue to find out more about The Conservation Controversy.

1977
- Congress passes Clean Water Act.

1990
- Congress amends Clean Air Act to address new environmental problems, including acid rain and ozone depletion.

2005
- The Kyoto Protocol, which commits countries to reduce greenhouse gas emissions, takes effect.

RAND McNALLY
World Atlas

CONTENTS

Complete Legend for Physical and Political Maps

Symbols

Lake

Salt Lake

Seasonal Lake

River

\ Waterfall

— Canal

△ Mountain Peak

▲ Highest Mountain Peak

Cities

■ Los Angeles — City over 1,000,000 population

▣ Calgary — City of 250,000 to 1,000,000 population

• Haifa — City under 250,000 population

✪ Paris — National Capital

★ Vancouver — Secondary Capital (State, Province, or Territory)

Type Styles Used to Name Features

CHINA — Country

ONTARIO — State, Province, or Territory

PUERTO RICO (U.S.) — Possession

ATLANTIC OCEAN — Ocean or Sea

Alps — Physical Feature

Borneo — Island

Boundaries

International Boundary

Secondary Boundary

Land Elevation and Water Depths

Land Elevation

Meters	Feet
3,000 and over	9,840 and over
2,000 - 3,000	6,560 - 9,840
500 - 2,000	1,640 - 6,560
200 - 500	656 - 1,640
0 - 200	0 - 656

Water Depth

Less than 200	Less than 656
200 - 2,000	656 - 6,560
Over 2,000	Over 6,560

ARCTIC OCEAN

ATLANTIC OCEAN

Gagarino
Kiev

St. Acheul
Chelles
Solutré
Le Moustier
Aurignac
Altamira
Pyrenees
Alps
Hallstadt
La Tène
Villanova

Black Sea
Caucasus
Caspian Sea

Troy
Anau

MEDITERRANEAN
Mersin
Tell Halaf
Hassuna
Jarmo
Hissar

Cnossus
Judeidah
Sialk

SEA
Mt. Carmel
Susa

Jericho
Al-Ubaid
Eridu
Bakun

Gafsa
Merimde
Kulli

Atlas Mountains

SAHARA DESERT
Badari
Naqada
Kharga Oasis

ARABIAN DESERT

N

La Tène European Iron Age Sites

Judeidah Early Agricultural Communities

Le Moustier Palaeolithic Sites

Civilized areas in Third Millennium B.C.

Civilized areas in Second Millennium B.C.

Civilization 1000 B.C. - 200 A.D.

0   200   400   600   800 Miles
0   300   600   900   1200 Kilometers
Copyright by Rand McNally & Co.
Goodes Projection

Irkutsk

Tien *Shan* *Altai* *Mts.* GOBI DESERT

Silk Route First Millennium B.C.

Choukoutien

Ordos

Anyang Lung-Shan

Chi-Chia

Yang-Shao

Quetta

THAR DESERT

Amri

Himalayas

Nyangu Hoa-Binh

PACIFIC OCEAN

Sea Routes
First Millennium B.C.

INDIAN
OCEAN

Kota-Tampan

40°

20°

0°

80° 80°   100°   120°

ARCTIC OCEAN

GREENLAND (Den.)

Arctic Circle

ICELAND

FAROE IS. (Den.)

RUSSIA

ALASKA

Yukon (U.S.)

Baffin Bay

UNITED KINGDOM

IRELAND

London

Anchorage

C A N A D A

Hudson Bay

Aleutian Islands

Newfoundland

FRANCE

Vancouver

Montréal

Ottawa

PORTUGAL

Azores (Port.)

Madrid

SPAIN

Missouri

Chicago

UNITED STATES

New York

Washington, D.C.

Casablanca

MOROCCO

Los Angeles

Colorado

Houston

ATLANTIC

Canary Islands (Sp.)

MIDWAY IS. (U.S.)

MEXICO

Gulf of Mexico

BAHAMAS

W. SAHARA

Tropic of Cancer

Hawaiian Islands (U.S.)

Mexico City

CUBA

HAITI

DOM. REP.

PUERTO RICO (U.S.)

CAPE VERDE

MAURITANIA

MALI

BELIZE

HOND.

JAMAICA

Caribbean Sea

SENEGAL

Niger

PACIFIC

GUAT.

EL SAL.

NIC.

Caracas

TRINIDAD AND TOBAGO

GAMBIA

GUINEA-BISSAU

GUINEA

BURK. FASO

COSTA RICA

PANAMA

VENEZUELA

GUYANA

SURINAME

FRENCH GUIANA

SIERRA LEONE

GHANA

CÔTE D'IVOIRE

COLOMBIA

LIBERIA

KIRIBATI

Equator

Galapagos Islands (Ecuador)

ECUADOR

Amazon

PERU

BRAZIL

O C E A N

SAMOA

AMERICAN SAMOA

COOK ISLANDS (N.Z.)

Lima

ST. HELENA (U.K.)

TONGA

O C E A N

BOLIVIA

FRENCH POLYNESIA

PARAGUAY

Rio de Janeiro

Tropic of Capricorn

Easter Island (Chile)

ARGENTINA

URUGUAY

N

Santiago

Buenos Aires

CHILE

0   1000   2000 Miles

0   1000   2000   3000 Kilometers

Copyright by Rand McNally & Co.
Robinson Projection
M-101519-2

FALKLAND IS. (U.K.)

South Georgia (U.K.)

South Orkney Is. (U.K.)

Antarctic Circle

South Shetland Is. (U.K.)

Weddell Sea

ARCTIC OCEAN

Spitsbergen
(Nor.)

Franz Josef
Land

Novaya
Zemlya

NORWAY
FINLAND
SWEDEN
DEN.
EST.
LAT.
LITH.
North
Sea
GERMANY
POLAND
BELARUS
NETH.
UKRAINE

Moscow

Volga

Ob'

Yenisey

Lena

R U S S I A

Novosibirsk

Bering
Sea

Sea of Okhotsk

60°

45°

30°

15°

0°

KAZAKHSTAN

M O N G O L I A

Beijing

NORTH
KOREA
SOUTH
KOREA

Sea of Japan
(East Sea)

JAPAN
Tokyo

Rome
ITALY
SWITZ.
AUS.
HUNG.
ROM.
BUL.
ALB.
GREECE

UZBEKISTAN
TURKMENISTAN
GEO.
ARM.
AZER.

KYRG.
TAJ.

C H I N A

Shanghai

Black Sea
Caspian Sea

TURKEY
CYPRUS
LEB.
SYRIA
ISRAEL
JORDAN
IRAQ
IRAN
AFGHANISTAN

Chang Jiang
(Yangtze)
Dong

Guangzhou

TAIWAN

PACIFIC

Tropic of Cancer

TUNISIA
Mediterranean Sea
Crete

Cairo

KUWAIT
PAKISTAN

Ganges

Kolkata
(Calcutta)

MYANMAR
LAOS

NORTHERN
MARIANA ISLANDS
(U.S.)

WAKE ISLAND
(U.S.)

ALGERIA
LIBYA
EGYPT

SAUDI
ARABIA

QATAR
U.A.E.
OMAN

Mumbai
(Bombay)

I N D I A

Arabian
Sea

Bay of
Bengal

Bangkok
THAILAND
VIETNAM
CAMBODIA

South China
Sea

PHILIPPINES

GUAM (U.S.)

O C E A N

15°

NIGER
CHAD
SUDAN

Red Sea

ERITREA
YEMEN

DJIBOUTI

SRI LANKA

PALAU

FED. STATES OF
MICRONESIA

MARSHALL
ISLANDS

NIGERIA
Lagos
BENIN
CAMEROON
CENTRAL
AFRICAN
REPUBLIC
SOUTH
SUDAN
Addis
Ababa
ETHIOPIA
SOMALIA

MALDIVES

BRUNEI
MALAYSIA

EQUATORIAL
GUINEA
GABON
REP. OF
CONGO
DEM. REP.
OF CONGO
RWANDA
BURUNDI
UGANDA
KENYA
TANZANIA

Congo

SEYCHELLES

SINGAPORE
Borneo
Sumatra

New Guinea

PAPUA
NEW GUINEA

SOLOMON
ISLANDS

Equator
0°

I N D I A N

Jakarta
Java
INDONESIA
TIMOR-LESTE

ANGOLA
ZAMBIA
MALAWI
ZIMBABWE
MOZAMBIQUE
NAMIBIA
BOTSWANA

COMOROS

MADAGASCAR
MAURITIUS

REUNION
(Fr.)

O C E A N

Darwin

Coral Sea

VANUATU

NEW CALEDONIA
(Fr.)

FIJI

15°

Tropic of Capricorn

SOUTH
AFRICA
SWAZILAND
LESOTHO

A U S T R A L I A

Darling

Perth
Sydney
Melbourne

30°

Cape Town

Kerguelen
Islands
(Fr.)

Tasmania

NEW ZEALAND
Wellington

45°

S O U T H E R N   O C E A N

60°

Antarctic Circle

75°

A N T A R C T I C A

15° 30° 45° 60° 75° 90° 105° 120° 135° 150° 165° 180°

⊛ National Capital

• Major Cities

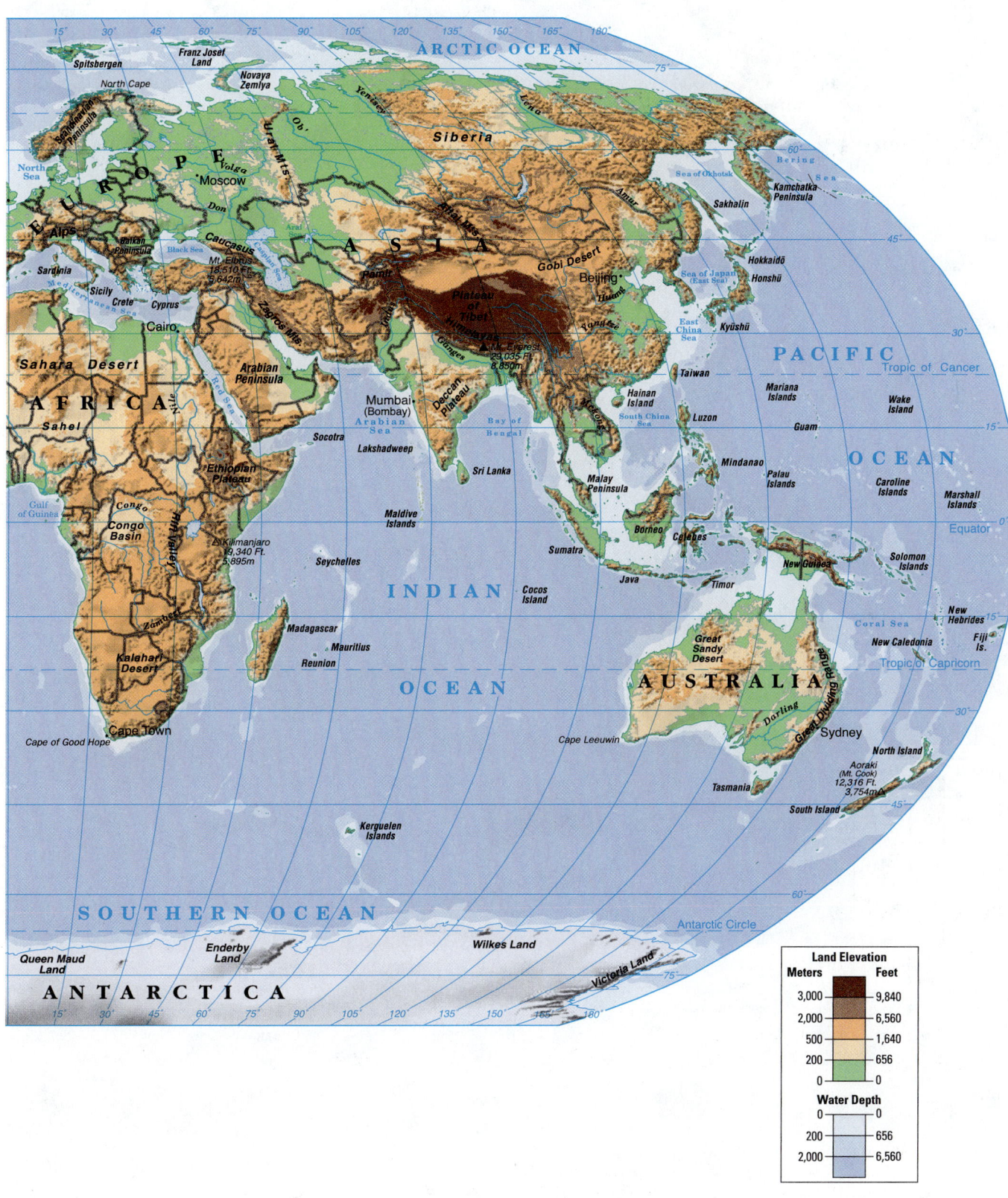

ARCTIC OCEAN

Spitsbergen
Franz Josef Land
North Cape
Novaya Zemlya
Scandinavian Peninsula
North Sea
EUROPE
Moscow
Volga
Don
Alps
Balkan Peninsula
Black Sea
Caucasus
Mt. Elbrus 18,510 Ft. 5,642m
Sardinia
Sicily
Crete
Cyprus
Mediterranean Sea
Cairo
Nile
Sahara Desert
AFRICA
Sahel
Gulf of Guinea
Congo
Congo Basin
Kilimanjaro 19,340 Ft. 5,895m
Zambezi
Kalahari Desert
Cape Town
Cape of Good Hope

Ural Mts.
Ob'
Yenisey
Siberia
Lena
ASIA
Aral
Caspian Sea
Pamir
Zagros Mts.
Tien Shan
Gobi Desert
Plateau of Tibet
Himalayas
Mt. Everest 29,035 Ft. 8,850m
Ganges
Indus
Arabian Peninsula
Red Sea
Ethiopian Plateau
Socotra
Mumbai (Bombay)
Arabian Sea
Deccan Plateau
Lakshadweep
Maldive Islands
Seychelles
Sri Lanka
Bay of Bengal
Mekong
Malay Peninsula
Sumatra
Java
Borneo
Celebes
Madagascar
Mauritius
Reunion
Cocos Island

Beijing
Huang
Yangtze
Amur
Sea of Okhotsk
Sakhalin
Kamchatka Peninsula
Bering Sea
Hokkaidō
Honshū
Sea of Japan (East Sea)
Kyūshū
East China Sea
Taiwan
Hainan Island
South China Sea
Luzon
Mindanao
Palau Islands
New Guinea
Timor
Solomon Islands
Mariana Islands
Guam
Caroline Islands
Wake Island
Marshall Islands

PACIFIC
OCEAN
Tropic of Cancer
Equator

New Hebrides
New Caledonia
Fiji Is.
Coral Sea
Tropic of Capricorn

INDIAN
OCEAN

Great Sandy Desert
AUSTRALIA
Cape Leeuwin
Darling
Great Dividing Range
Sydney
Aoraki (Mt. Cook) 12,316 Ft. 3,754m
North Island
Tasmania
South Island

Kerguelen Islands

SOUTHERN OCEAN
Antarctic Circle

Queen Maud Land
Enderby Land
Wilkes Land
Victoria Land
ANTARCTICA

Land Elevation	
Meters	Feet
3,000	9,840
2,000	6,560
500	1,640
200	656
0	0

Water Depth	
0	0
200	656
2,000	6,560

RAND MCNALLY

A7

Land Elevation

Meters		Feet
3,000		9,840
2,000		6,560
500		1,640
200		656
0		0

Water Depth

0		0
200		656
2,000		6,560

0 200 400 600 800 1000 Miles

0 300 600 900 1200 1500 Kilometers

Copyright by Rand McNally & Co.
Lambert Azimuthal Equal Area Projection

GULF OF MEXICO
NORTH AMERICA
CUBA
Greater Antilles
HAITI
DOMINICAN REPUBLIC
JAMAICA
BELIZE
GUATEMALA
HONDURAS
Gulf of Honduras
EL SALVADOR
NICARAGUA
COSTA RICA
PANAMA
Gulf of Panama
PUERTO RICO (U.S.)
Lesser Antilles
CARIBBEAN SEA
TRINIDAD AND TOBAGO

ATLANTIC OCEAN

Cristóbal Colón Peak 18,948 Ft. 5,775m
Caracas
Llanos
VENEZUELA
Orinoco
GUYANA
SURINAME
FRENCH GUIANA
Cape Orange

Galapagos Islands (Ec.)
ECUADOR
Chimborazo 20,703 Ft. 6,310m
Bogotá
COLOMBIA
Putumayo
Japurá
Amazon
Negro
Manaus
Amazon
Ilha de Marajó
Belém
Equator

Amazon Basin
Selvas
Juruá
Madeira
Tapajós
BRAZIL

PERU
Mt. Huascarán 22,133 Ft. 6,746m
Lima
Ucayali
Andes
Recife

Lake Titicaca
Mt. Illampu 21,066 Ft. 6,421m
BOLIVIA
Mato Grosso Plateau
Brasília
São Francisco
Serra do Espinhaço

Mt. Sajama 21,463 Ft. 6,542m
Cordillera
Atacama Desert
Gran Chaco
PARAGUAY
Paraná
São Paulo
Rio de Janeiro
Tropic of Capricorn

Isla San Ambrosio (Chile)
Isla San Felix (Chile)
Archipiélago Juan Fernández (Chile)
Mt. Ojos del Salado 22,615 Ft. 6,893m
A R G E N T I N A
Paraná
URUGUAY

PACIFIC OCEAN

Mt. Aconcagua 22,831 Ft. 6,959m
Santiago
CHILE
Buenos Aires
Pampas
Río de la Plata

San Matías Gulf
Península Valdés
Chiloé
Patagonia
San Jorge Gulf
Point Medanoso

ATLANTIC OCEAN

N

Grand Bay
FALKLAND ISLANDS (U.K.)
West Falkland
East Falkland
Strait of Magellan
Tierra del Fuego
Cape Horn
South Georgia (U.K.)
South Sandwich Islands (U.K.)

Drake Passage
South Shetland Islands (U.K.)
South Orkney Islands (U.K.)

Land Elevation

Meters		Feet
3,000		9,840
2,000		6,560
500		1,640
200		656
0		0

Water Depth

0		0
200		656
2,000		6,560

0   200   400   600   800   1000 Miles
0   300   600   900   1200   1500 Kilometers
Copyright by Rand McNally & Co.
Lambert Azimuthal Equal Area Projection

RAND MCNALLY

A9

ATLANTIC OCEAN

EUROPE

PORTUGAL
Azores (Port.)
SPAIN
Strait of Gibraltar
Madeira Islands (Port.)
MOROCCO
Canary Islands (Spain)
Atlas Mountains
Algiers
Tropic of Cancer
WESTERN SAHARA (MOROCCO)
Ijafene
Great Western Desert
ALGERIA
Great Eastern Desert
LIBYA
Tahat 9,541 Ft. 2,908m
Ahaggar Mts.
Tibesti Massif
Mt. Koussi 11,204 Ft. 3,415m
Ennedi

MALTA
Mediterranean Sea
Gulf of Sidra
Libyan Desert
EGYPT
Qattara Depression
Cairo
Lake Nasser
Red Sea
Nubian Desert

ITALY
AUS. HUNG. ROMANIA UKRAINE RUSSIA
BOS. SERB. BUL.
ALB. GREECE TURKEY
CYPRUS SYRIA
LEBANON ISRAEL
IRAQ
JORDAN
KUWAIT
SAUDI ARABIA
QATAR
U.A.E.
OMAN
YEMEN

Black Sea
GEORGIA
ARM. AZER.
Caspian Sea
Aral Sea
KAZ.
UZBEKISTAN
TURKMENISTAN
IRAN
ASIA
Persian Gulf

CAPE VERDE
MAURITANIA
Senegal
Cape Verde
Dakar
SENEGAL
GAMBIA
GUINEA-BISSAU
GUINEA
SIERRA LEONE
LIBERIA
COTE D'IVOIRE
MALI
Niger
BURKINA FASO
GHANA
Lake Volta
BENIN
Sahel
Aïr (Mts.)
NIGER
N. Niger
NIGERIA
Jos Plateau
Lagos
Benue
CAMEROON
Mt. Cameroon 13,451 Ft. 4,100m
Bioko
Gulf of Guinea
EQUATORIAL GUINEA
SAO TOME AND PRINCIPE
GABON
REP. OF CONGO
Kinshasa

Sahara Desert
Lake Chad
CHAD
Khartoum
SUDAN
White Nile
Blue Nile
ERITREA
DJIBOUTI
Gulf of Aden
Socotra (Yem.)
Cape Gwardafuy
SOMALIA
Ethiopian Plateau
Lake Tana
ETHIOPIA
Great Rift Valley
As Sudd
SOUTH SUDAN
CENTRAL AFRICAN REPUBLIC
Ubangi
Mountain Nile
Uele
UGANDA
KENYA
Lake Turkana
Mt. Kenya 17,058 Ft. 5,199m
Nairobi
Congo
Congo Basin
DEM. REP. OF CONGO
RWANDA
BURUNDI
Lake Victoria
Serengeti Plain
Kilimanjaro 19,340 Ft. 5,895m
Masai Steppe
Lake Tanganyika
TANZANIA
Zanzibar

Equator

INDIAN OCEAN
SEYCHELLES
Cape Ambre

ATLANTIC OCEAN

Ascension (St. Helena)
St. Helena (U.K.)

Kasai
Kwango
Cuanza
Cunene
ANGOLA
Okavango
Namib Desert
NAMIBIA
Kalahari Desert
BOTSWANA
Orange
Vaal
SOUTH AFRICA
Cape of Good Hope
Cape Agulhas
LESOTHO
Drakensberg
Johannesburg
SWAZILAND
Limpopo
ZIMBABWE
Lake Kariba
Victoria Falls
Zambezi
ZAMBIA
MALAWI
Lake Nyasa
MOZAMBIQUE
Mozambique Channel
Barra Point

COMOROS
Mayotte (Fr.)
Reunion (Fr.)
MAURITIUS
MADAGASCAR
Cape Sainte-Marie

Tropic of Capricorn

Tristan da Cunha Group (St. Helena)

Prince Edward Islands (S. Af.)
Crozet Islands (Fr.)

Land Elevation

Meters		Feet
3,000		9,840
2,000		6,560
500		1,640
200		656
0		0

Water Depth

0		0
200		656
2,000		6,560

0 200 400 600 800 1000 Miles
0 300 600 900 1200 1500 Kilometers

Copyright by Rand McNally
Lambert Azimuthal Equal Area Projection
M-101526-3

PACIFIC OCEAN

Tropic of Cancer

Hawaiian Islands

Hawaii

PITCAIRN
(U.K.)

Marquesas
Is.

FRENCH
POLYNESIA

Tuamotu Archipelago

Equator

Tropic of Capricorn

Tahiti

Kiritimati

Line Islands

P O L Y N E S I A

Society Islands

Austral Is.

Northern Cook
Islands

COOK ISLANDS
(N.Z.)

Southern Cook
Islands

International Date Line

TOKELAU (N.Z.)

AMERICAN
SAMOA

NIUE
(N.Z.)

KIRIBATI

SAMOA

TONGA

WALLIS AND
FUTUNA
(FR.)

Koro Sea

Kermadec Islands
(N.Z.)

Chatham Islands

TUVALU

FIJI

MARSHALL
ISLANDS

M I C R O N E S I A

NAURU

M E L A N E S I A

SOLOMON
ISLANDS

Solomon Sea

VANUATU

NEW
CALEDONIA
(FR.)

New
Caledonia

Coral Sea

NORFOLK
ISLAND
(Aust.)

Auckland
North Island

Wellington

NEW
ZEALAND

Tasman
Sea

South Island

Mt. Cook
3,754m

Cook Strait

NORTHERN
MARIANA
ISLANDS
(U.S.)

FEDERATED STATES
OF MICRONESIA

GUAM
(U.S.)

Bismarck Sea

New Britain

PAPUA
NEW GUINEA

Mount Wilhelm
4,509m

Port Moresby

Torres Strait

Cape York
Peninsula

Great Barrier Reef

Gulf of
Carpentaria

GREAT DIVIDING RANGE

Brisbane

Sydney
Canberra

Mount Kosciuszko
2,229m

Melbourne

Bass Strait

Tasmania

PALAU

TIMOR-LESTE

Timor
Sea

Arafura Sea

Kimberley
Plateau

Great Sandy Desert

AUSTRALIA

Gibson Desert

GREAT VICTORIA
DESERT

Great Australian Bight

Murray

Darling

TAIWAN

Taipei

CHINA

PHILIPPINES

Manila

Luzon

Philippine
Sea

Mindanao

South
China
Sea

Sulu
Sea

Celebes
Sea

Celebes

INDONESIA

0 200 400 600 800 1000 Kilometers
0 200 400 600 800 Miles

Land Elevation
Meters	Feet
3,000	9,840
2,000	6,560
500	1,640
200	656
0	0

Water Depth
0	656
200	2,000
6,560	

⊛ National Capital
■ City over 1,000,000 population
▣ City of 250,000 to 1,000,000 population
• City under 250,000 population

Land Elevation

Meters		Feet
3,000		9,840
2,000		6,560
500		1,640
200		656
0		0

Water Depth

0		0
200		656
2,000		6,560

0   100   200   300   400 Miles
0   200   400   600 Kilometers

Copyright by Rand McNally
Lambert Conformal Conic Projection
M-101522-2

ICELAND
Horn
Fontur
Surtsey

ATLANTIC OCEAN

NORWEGIAN SEA

Arctic Circle

Lofoten Islands

Kebnekaise
6,926 Ft.
2,111m.

Lap

FAROE ISLANDS (Den.)

Scandinavian Peninsula

NORWAY   SWEDEN

Galdhøpiggen
8,100 Ft.
2,469m.

Klarälven
Dalälven

Gulf of Bothnia

Hebrides

Orkney Islands

Grampian Mts.

UNITED KINGDOM

Cheviot Hills

Stockholm

Vänern
Vättern

Öland

BALTIC SEA

IRELAND

Irish Sea

Great Britain

Thames

London

NORTH SEA

DENMARK

Skagerrak

Bornholm (Den.)

LI

RUSSIA

St. George's Channel

NETHERLANDS

Elbe

Berlin

Northern Euro

POLAND

English Channel

Strait of Dover

BELGIUM

Rhine

GERMANY

Oder

Wisła

LUX.

Paris
Paris Basin

Loire

Seine

Bohemian Forest

CZECH REPUBLIC

SLOVAKIA

Bay of Biscay

FRANCE

Saône

Black Forest

Jura

SWITZERLAND   LIECH.

Danube

AUSTRIA

HUNGARY

Great Hungarian Plain

Cantabrian Mts.

Duero

Pyrenees

Massif Central

Mt. Blanc
15,771 Ft.
4,808m

Po

SLOVENIA

Drava

CROATIA

Duero

Iberian Mts.

Ebro

ANDORRA

MONACO

Apennines

SAN MARINO

Dinaric Alps

BOSNIA AND HERZEGOVINA

SERBIA

Balkan

Iberian Peninsula

Tagus

SPAIN

Corsica (Fr.)

ADRIATIC SEA

MONTE-NEGRO

KOSOVO

Lisbon

PORTUGAL

Sierra Morena

Balearic Islands

Minorca

Ibiza   Majorca

Rome

ITALY

Sardinia (It.)

Vesuvius
4,190 Ft.
1,277m.

ALBANIA

MACE-DONIA

Pindus Mts.

Strait of Gibraltar

GIBRALTAR (U.K.)

TYRRHENIAN SEA

IONIAN SEA

Algiers

Mt. Etna
10,902 Ft.
3,323m.

Sicily

MEDITERRAN

MOROCCO   AFRICA   ALGERIA   TUNISIA   MALTA

Murmansk

Kola
Peninsula
Ponoy

WHITE SEA

Timan Ridge

Pechora

Ob'

Irtysh

FINLAND

Onega

Mezen

Northern Dvina

Ural Mountains

ASIA

Lake
Onega

Sukhona

Northern Uvals
(Uplands)

Kama

Lake
Ladoga

Helsinki

Gulf of Finland

Rybinsk
Res.

RUSSIA

50

ESTONIA

Lake
Peipus

Oka

LATVIA

Valdai
Hills

Moscow

Khopër

Ural

UANIA

Plain

Don

KAZAKHSTAN

Aral Sea

Syr Darya

ea-n

Neman

Central
Russian
Upland

Caspian Depression

UZBEKISTAN

BELARUS

Pripyat

Dnieper

Amu Darya

Kiev

Dnieper Lowland

Donets Basin

Volga

UKRAINE

Dnieper

Dniester

MOLDOVA

CASPIAN SEA

TURKMENISTAN

ROMANIA

Sea of Azov

Transylvanian Alps

Crimean
Peninsula

Caucasus

Baku

Danube

Mt. Elbrus
18,510 Ft.
5,642m

GEORGIA

Peninsula

BLACK SEA

ARMENIA

AZERBAIJAN

BULGARIA

AZER.

Istanbul

Mt. Olympus
9,570 Ft.
2,917m

TURKEY

Tehran

IRAN

GREECE

AEGEAN SEA

IRAQ

Rhodes

SEA

SYRIA

Euphrates

Crete

CYPRUS

LEBANON

Tigris

ATLANTIC OCEAN

ARCTIC OCEAN

ICELAND

FAROE ISLANDS (Den.)

IRELAND

London

UNITED KINGDOM

DENMARK

NORWAY

SWEDEN

FINLAND

Barents Sea

Kara Sea

Novaya Zemlya

Severnaya Zemlya

Yamal Pen.

North Sea

Arctic Circle

PORTUGAL

SPAIN

GIBRALTAR (U.K.)

ANDORRA

MONACO

FRANCE

NETH.

BEL.

LUX.

GERMANY

SWITZ.

CZECH REP.

AUSTRIA

SLOVAKIA

HUNGARY

POLAND

BELARUS

LITH.

LATVIA

ESTONIA

UKRAINE

Moscow

Volga

Ural Mountains

Ob

West Siberian Lowland

Irtysh

Yenisey

Novosibirsk

Ob

MOROCCO

ALGERIA

TUNISIA

ITALY

SLOVENIA

CROATIA

BOS.

MONT.

ALBANIA

MACEDONIA

SERB.

ROMANIA

BULGARIA

GREECE

Black Sea

Mediterranean Sea

Caucasus

Caspian Depression

Caspian Sea

Aral Sea

KAZAKHSTAN

Astana

Syr Darya

Lake Balkhash

Tian Shan

KYRGYZSTAN

Ust-Urt Plateau

UZBEKISTAN

Amu Darya

LIBYA

CYPRUS

LEBANON

ISRAEL

TURKEY

Mount Ararat 16,940 ft. 5,165 m

GEORGIA

ARM.

AZER.

Ararat

SYRIA

JORDAN

IRAQ

Euphrates

Tigris

Tehran

Dasht-e Kavir

IRAN

Zagros Mts.

TURKMENISTAN

Kara Kum (Desert)

TAJIKISTAN

Pamirs

Hindu Kush

Tarim Basin

K2 (Qogir Feng) 28,250 Ft. 8,611m

Altun Shan

Kunlun Mts.

EGYPT

Cairo

Nile

Sinai Pen.

An-Nafud

SAUDI ARABIA

Arabian Peninsula

KUWAIT

Persian Gulf

BAHRAIN

QATAR

U.A.E.

Gulf of Oman

AFGHANISTAN

PAKISTAN

Indus

Great Indian Desert

New Delhi

Ganges

NEPAL

HIMALAYA MTS.

Mt. Everest 29,035 Ft. 8,850m

CHAD

SUDAN

Red Sea

ERITREA

DJIBOUTI

ETHIOPIA

YEMEN

Rub Al-Khali

OMAN

Gulf of Aden

Socotra (Yem.)

Arabian Sea

Mumbai (Bombay)

Godavari

Deccan Plateau

Western Ghats

Eastern Ghats

INDIA

Bay of Bengal

SOUTH SUDAN

DEM. REP. OF THE CONGO

UGANDA

RWANDA

BURUNDI

KENYA

SOMALIA

TANZANIA

ZAMBIA

MALAWI

MOZAMBIQUE

Lakshadweep (India)

SRI LANKA

MALDIVES

INDIAN OCEAN

N

0   200   400   600   800 Miles

0   200 400 600 800 1000 Kilometers

Copyright by Rand McNally
Lambert Azimuthal Equal Area Projection
M-101524-3

Land Elevation

Meters	Feet
3,000	9,840
2,000	6,560
500	1,640
200	656
0	0

Water Depth

0	0
200	656
2,000	6,560

Taymyr Peninsula
Laptev Sea
New Siberian Islands
East Siberian Sea
East Siberian Sea
Indigirka
Kolyma
Bering Sea
Aleutian Islands (U.S.)

Central Siberian Uplands
Verkhoyansk Mts.
Sea of Okhotsk
Kamchatka Peninsula

RUSSIA
S i b e r i a
Angara
Lena
Stanovoy Range
Amur
Sakhalin
Kuril Islands

Lake Baikal
Sayan Mountains
Tatar Strait
Hokkaido

Altai Mts.
MONGOLIA
Gobi Desert
Sea of Japan (East Sea)
Honshu
Tokyo
PACIFIC OCEAN
Tropic of Cancer

Qilian Shan
Beijing
NORTH KOREA
SOUTH KOREA
Mt. Fuji 12,388 ft 3,776m
Shikoku
JAPAN
Kyushu

Yellow Sea
Huang
CHINA
Qinling Shandi
Shanghai
East China Sea

NORTHERN MARIANA ISLANDS (U.S.)

Chang (Yangtze)
TAIWAN
GUAM (U.S.)
FEDERATED STATES OF MICRONESIA

BHUTAN
Brahmaputra
Xi
Luzon Strait
Luzon
Philippine Sea

BNGL.
MYANMAR
LAOS
Hainan Island
PHILIPPINES
PALAU

THAILAND
Mekong
VIETNAM
South China Sea
Manila
Mindanao

Bangkok
CAMBODIA
Sulu Sea
Equator

Andaman Islands (India)
Andaman Sea
Gulf of Thailand
Celebes Sea
Moluccas
New Guinea
PAPUA NEW GUINEA

Nicobar Islands (India)
MALAY PENINSULA
BRUNEI
MALAYSIA
Celebes
Ceram

Str. of Malacca
MALAYSIA
Borneo
Banda Sea
Arafura Sea
Gulf of Carpentaria
Coral Sea

Singapore
Greater Sunda Islands
INDONESIA
TIMOR-LESTE
Timor

Sumatra
Java Sea
Timor Sea
AUSTRALIA

Jakarta
Java

National Capital

★ Secondary Capital
(State, Province, or Territory)

■ City over 1,000,000 population

▣ City of 250,000 to 1,000,000 population

• City under 250,000 population

0   100   200   300   400 Miles

0   200   400   600 Kilometers
Copyright by Rand McNally & Co.
Lambert Conformal Conic Projection

N

PACIFIC OCEAN

GULF OF MEXICO

MEXICO

UNITED STATES

CALIFORNIA
Los Angeles
ARIZONA
NEW MEXICO
OKLAHOMA
MISSOURI
KENTUCKY
TENNESSEE
ARKANSAS
MISSISSIPPI
ALABAMA
TEXAS
LOUISIANA
Houston
New Orleans
El Paso

Tijuana Mexicali
Nogales
Ciudad Juárez
BAJA CALIFORNIA
SONORA
CHIHUAHUA
Hermosillo
Ciudad Obregón
Chihuahua
Isla Cedros
BAJA CALIFORNIA SUR
COAHUILA
Nuevo Laredo
NUEVO LEÓN
Los Mochis
DURANGO
Torreón
Saltillo
Reynosa
Monterrey
Matamoros
La Paz
Tropic of Cancer
Culiacán
SINALOA
Durango
ZACATECAS
Ciudad Victoria
TAMAULIPAS
Mazatlán
Islas Marías
Zacatecas
San Luis Potosí
NAYARIT
Tepic
Aguascalientes
SAN LUIS POTOSÍ
Tampico
Puerto Vallarta
León
Guadalajara
Irapuato
Querétaro
JALISCO
GTO.
PRO.
HGO.
Pachuca
COLIMA
Morelia
Toluca
MÉX.
Xalapa
Gulf of Campeche
Mérida
YUCATÁN
Cancún
MEXICO City
TLAX.
Puebla
Veracruz
Campeche
Isla Cozumel
Islas Revillagigedo
Isla San Benedicto
Isla Roca Partida
Isla Socorro
MICHOACAN
MOR.
PUEBLA
VERACRUZ
QUINTANA ROO
Chetumal
GUERRERO
Chilpancingo
Coatzacoalcos
TABASCO
CAMPECHE
Acapulco
Oaxaca
OAXACA
Villahermosa
Belmopan
BELIZE
Tuxtla Gutiérrez
CHIAPAS
Gulf of Honduras
Golfo de Tehuantepec
San Pedro Sula
HONDURAS
Tapachula
GUATEMALA
Guatemala City
Tegucigalpa
San Salvador
EL SALVADOR
León
Managua
Lago de Nicaragua
COSTA

Gulf of California

Rio Grande

Canal de Yucatán

Isla del Mapelo (Col.)

110°   100°   90°
30°
20°
10°

ATLANTIC OCEAN

VIRGINIA

NORTH CAROLINA

SOUTH CAROLINA

GEORGIA

FLORIDA

Lake Okeechobee

Miami

Straits of Florida

Freeport

Abaco

BAHAMAS

Nassau

Eleuthera

Cat Island

Andros

BERMUDA
(U.K.)

Tropic of Cancer

Havana

Santa Clara

CUBA

Isla de la
Juventud

Camagüey

Holguín

Guantánamo

Great
Inagua

TURKS AND CAICOS ISLANDS
(U.K.)

W e s t

CAYMAN ISLANDS
(U.K.)

Santiago
de Cuba

Montego Bay

JAMAICA

Kingston

Santiago

Port-au-
Prince

HAITI

Santo
Domingo

DOMINICAN
REPUBLIC

I n d i e s

San
Juan

PUERTO RICO
(U.S.)

VIRGIN
ISLANDS
(U.S.)

BRITISH
VIRGIN
ISLANDS

ANGUILLA
(U.K.)

Basseterre

SAINT KITTS
AND NEVIS

MONTSERRAT
(U.K.)

ANTIGUA
AND
BARBUDA

Saint John's

GUADELOUPE
(Fr.)

DOMINICA

Roseau

MARTINIQUE
(Fr.)

Castries

SAINT LUCIA

SAINT VINCENT
AND THE
GRENADINES

Kingstown

Bridgetown

BARBADOS

CARIBBEAN SEA

NICARAGUA

Isla de
San Andrés
(Col.)

ARUBA
(Neth.)

Curaçao

Bonaire

NETHERLANDS
ANTILLES

Saint
George's

GRENADA

Port of Spain

TRINIDAD AND TOBAGO

Maracaibo

Caracas

San José

RICA

Panama
Canal

Panama
City

PANAMA

Golfo
de
Panamá

Isla de Coiba

Lago de
Maracaibo

Orinoco

VENEZUELA

Georgetown

GUYANA

SURINAME

COLOMBIA

Bogotá

Orinoco

BRAZIL

80°

70°

60°

30°

20°

10°

80°

70°

60°

PACIFIC OCEAN

Caribbean Sea

WEST INDIES
(British)

Águmud
(Jamaica)

ANÁHUAC
(Aztec Empire, 1519)

Zapotec

Mazatlán
Zacalec Niho
Naco Jicaque
Tenampua
Utatlán
Lenca Tawahka
Nicarao Rama
Boruca
Guayni

Isthmus of Panama

Aruaca Carib
Camanagota
Guamontey
Wayúu
(Guajiro)
Tairona
Sinú
Quimbaya
Chibcha
Chocó

Magdalena

Caquetió
Guahibo
Achagua
Cubeo

ANDES

Quito

Huiloto
Jivaro
Chimú
Jauja
1300s
Pachacamac
Machu Picchu
Andahuaylas

CHIMOR
(Chimú Empire, to 1475)

Chan Chan Huánuco

Cuzco
INCAS 1200s–1300s
Island of the Sun
Tiahuanaco Chiquiabo

TAHUANTINSUYU
(Inca Empire, to 1525)

Lake Titicaca

Copiapó

Santiago

Mapuche
(Araucanians)

PATAGONIA

Tehuelche

Ona
Tierra del Fuego

Caribbean Sea
Carib

Negro
Baraúana
Yuri
Bora
Shipibo
Ucayali
Yanomamo
Otomac

Amazon
Tikuna
Idurimá
Amahuaca
Mashco
Tacana
Guató

Caeté
Tupinambá
Tembé
Timbira
Camacán
Botocudo
São Francisco

Tecuntins
Araguáia
Kayapó
Xingú
Mundurucú
Maué
Apacai
Oyampi
Wayana
Waiwai
Wapishana

Nambicuara
Bororo
Chiquito
Chulupí
Mataco
Toba
Guaraní
Aché
Kaingang
Charrúa

Paraguá
Paraná
Rio de la Plata

Pueiche
Huarpe

Puelche

ANDES

N

Growth of empires, 1470–1525

Areas in decline, 1300–1500

Major migrations, 1200–1500

△ Major religious center

Puelche Major ethnic group

⊛ National capital

0   200   400   600   800   1000 Miles
0   300   600   900   1200   1500 Kilometers

Copyright by Rand McNally & Co.
Robinson Projection

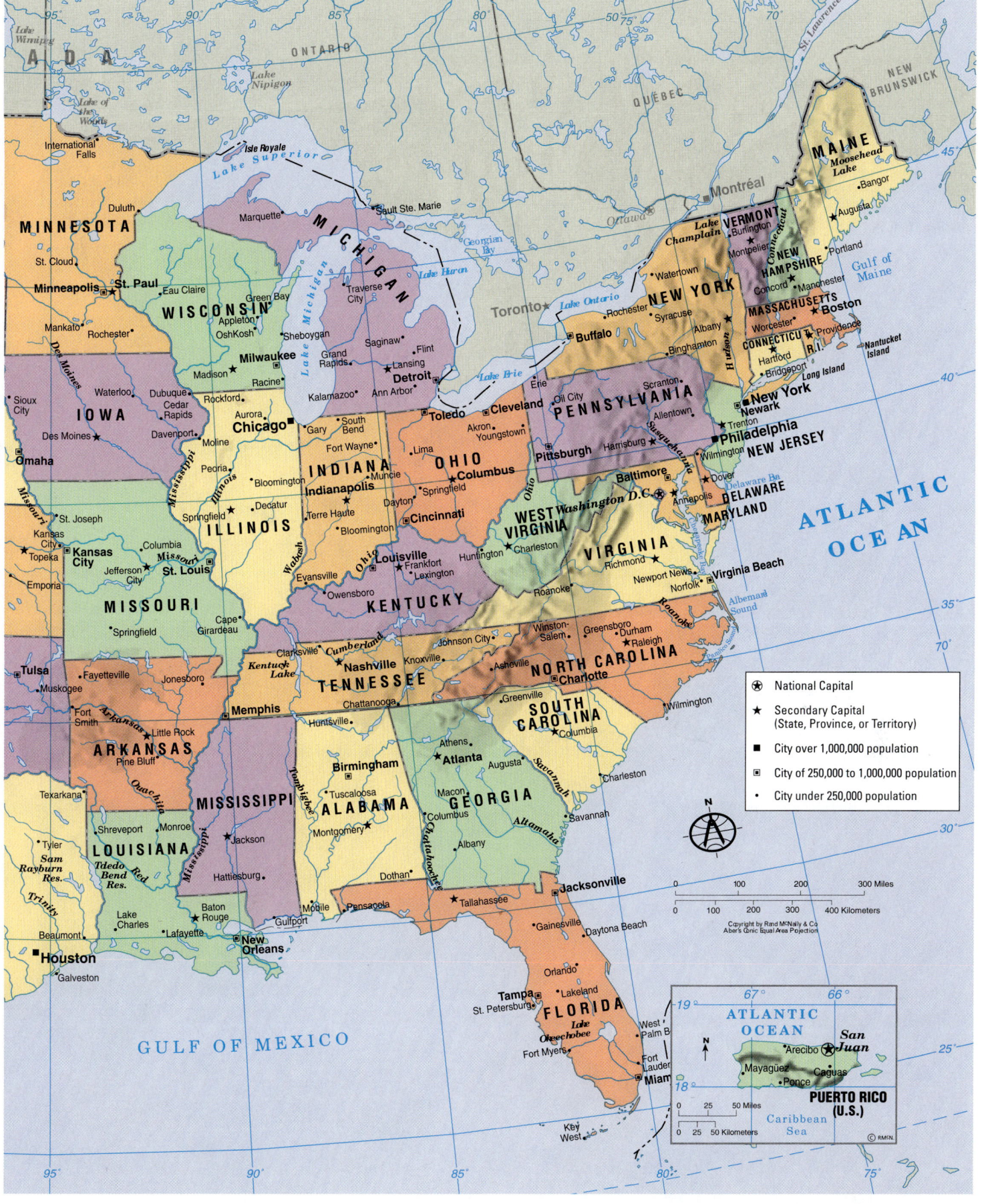

Map Legend

⬢ National Capital

★ Secondary Capital
(State, Province, or Territory)

■ City over 1,000,000 population

▣ City of 250,000 to 1,000,000 population

• City under 250,000 population

Copyright by Rand McNally & Co
Alber's Conic Equal Area Projection

| | 100 | 200 | 300 Miles |
| 0 | 100 | 200 | 300 | 400 Kilometers |

Selected Labels

MINNESOTA · International Falls · Duluth · St. Cloud · Minneapolis · St. Paul · Mankato · Rochester · Eau Claire

WISCONSIN · Green Bay · Appleton · OshKosh · Sheboygan · Madison · Milwaukee · Racine

MICHIGAN · Marquette · Sault Ste. Marie · Traverse City · Grand Rapids · Saginaw · Flint · Lansing · Kalamazoo · Ann Arbor · Detroit

IOWA · Sioux City · Waterloo · Dubuque · Cedar Rapids · Davenport · Des Moines

Omaha · St. Joseph · Kansas City · Topeka · Jefferson City · Emporia

MISSOURI · Columbia · St. Louis · Springfield · Cape Girardeau

ILLINOIS · Rockford · Aurora · Moline · Peoria · Bloomington · Springfield · Decatur · Chicago · Gary

INDIANA · South Bend · Fort Wayne · Muncie · Indianapolis · Terre Haute · Bloomington

OHIO · Toledo · Lima · Columbus · Springfield · Dayton · Cincinnati · Akron · Youngstown · Cleveland

KENTUCKY · Louisville · Frankfort · Lexington · Owensboro · Evansville

TENNESSEE · Nashville · Knoxville · Chattanooga · Memphis · Clarksville · Johnson City

Huntsville · Tupelo

ARKANSAS · Fort Smith · Fayetteville · Jonesboro · Little Rock · Pine Bluff · Texarkana

Tulsa · Muskogee

LOUISIANA · Shreveport · Monroe · Jackson · Hattiesburg · Baton Rouge · New Orleans · Lafayette · Lake Charles

MISSISSIPPI · Birmingham · Tuscaloosa · Montgomery

ALABAMA · Columbus · Dothan · Mobile · Pensacola · Gulfport

Texarkana · Tyler · Beaumont · Houston · Galveston

GEORGIA · Atlanta · Athens · Augusta · Macon · Columbus · Albany · Savannah

SOUTH CAROLINA · Greenville · Columbia · Charleston

NORTH CAROLINA · Winston-Salem · Greensboro · Durham · Raleigh · Asheville · Charlotte · Wilmington

VIRGINIA · Charleston · Roanoke · Richmond · Newport News · Norfolk · Virginia Beach

WEST VIRGINIA · Huntington · Washington D.C.

PENNSYLVANIA · Pittsburgh · Harrisburg · Scranton · Allentown · Oil City

NEW YORK · Buffalo · Rochester · Syracuse · Watertown · Albany · Binghamton · New York · Newark

NEW JERSEY · Trenton · Philadelphia · Wilmington · Dover

DELAWARE · MARYLAND · Baltimore · Annapolis

VERMONT · Burlington · Montpelier

NEW HAMPSHIRE · Concord · Manchester

MASSACHUSETTS · Worcester · Boston · Providence · R.I.

CONNECTICUT · Hartford · Bridgeport · New Haven

MAINE · Moosehead Lake · Bangor · Augusta · Portland

FLORIDA · Jacksonville · Gainesville · Daytona Beach · Orlando · Lakeland · Tampa · St. Petersburg · Fort Myers · West Palm B. · Fort Lauderdale · Miami · Key West · Lake Okeechobee · Tallahassee

GULF OF MEXICO

ATLANTIC OCEAN

Puerto Rico Inset

ATLANTIC OCEAN

San Juan · Arecibo · Mayagüez · Caguas · Ponce

PUERTO RICO (U.S.)

Caribbean Sea

| 0 | 25 | 50 Miles |
| 0 | 25 | 50 Kilometers |

A D A

Lake Winnipeg

Lake of the Woods

ONTARIO

QUÉBEC

Lake Nipigon

Isle Royale

Lake Superior

Keweenaw Peninsula

Whitefish Point

Great Lakes

St. Lawrence

NEW BRUNSWICK

Mt. Katahdin 5,268 Ft. 1,606m

MAINE

Moosehead Lake

MINNESOTA

Upper Peninsula

MICHIGAN

Bruce Peninsula

Georgian Bay

Lake Huron

Montréal

VERMONT

White Mts.

Mt. Washington 6,288 Ft. 1,917m

NEW HAMPSHIRE

Gulf of Maine

Minneapolis

WISCONSIN

Green Bay

Lake Michigan

Saginaw Bay

Lower Peninsula

Grand

Toronto

Lake Ontario

Niagara Falls

Adirondack Mountains

NEW YORK

Lake Champlain

Kennebec

Green Mts.

Connecticut

MASS. ★ Boston

Cape Cod

Minnesota

Lake Winnebago

Muskegon

Detroit

Lake Erie

Allegheny Plateau

Catskill Mts.

CONNECTICUT R.I.

Nantucket Island

IOWA

Iowa

Des Moines

Chicago

INDIANA

Maumee

OHIO

Pennsylvania Mountains

Hudson

Long Island

New York

40°

Mississippi

Illinois

Ohio

Scioto

Susquehanna

Philadelphia

NEW JERSEY

ATLANTIC

OCEAN

Kansas

S T A T E S

ILLINOIS

Wabash

White

Green

WEST VIRGINIA

Allegheny Mountains

Washington D.C.

DELAWARE

MARYLAND

Delaware Bay

Lake of the Ozarks

Missouri

St. Louis

MISSOURI

KENTUCKY

Ohio

VIRGINIA

James

Chesapeake Bay

Flint Hills

Neosho

Ozark Plateau

Lake Cumberland

Cumberland

Cumberland Plateau

Appalachian Mountains

Blue Ridge Mountains

Roanoke

Albemarle Sound

Cape Hatteras

35°

Boston Mts.

White

Kentucky Lake

TENNESSEE

Mt. Mitchell 6,684 Ft. 2,037m

Piedmont

NORTH CAROLINA

Pamlico Sound

Arkansas

Ouachita Mts.

Tennessee

Clarks Hill Lake

SOUTH CAROLINA

Cape Lookout

Land Elevation

Meters | Feet

3,000 | 9,840

2,000 | 6,560

500 | 1,640

200 | 656

0 | 0

ARKANSAS

Ouachita

Yazoo

Atlanta

Pee Dee

Santee

Cape Fear

Cape Fear

Water Depth

0 | 0

200 | 656

2,000 | 6,560

Sabine

MISSISSIPPI

ALABAMA

Tombigbee

GEORGIA

Savannah

Sea Islands

Coastal Plain

N

Sam Rayburn Res.

Toledo Bend Res.

Red

Pearl

Alabama

Chattahoochee

Flint

Altamaha

Sea Islands

30°

Trinity

LOUISIANA

Cape San Blas

Apalachee Bay

Suwannee

Cape Canaveral

0 | 100 | 200 | 300 Miles

0 | 100 | 200 | 300 | 400 Kilometers

Copyright by Rand McNally & Co.
Albers Conic Equal Area Projection

Houston

New Orleans

Atchafalaya Bay

Mississippi Delta

Tampa Bay

FLORIDA

Lake Okeechobee

67°

66°

19°

ATLANTIC OCEAN

San Juan

GULF OF MEXICO

The Everglades

Mia

Arecibo

Mayagüez

Caguas

N

25°

Cape Sable

Ponce

PUERTO RICO (U.S.)

18°

Florida Keys

0 | 25 | 50 Miles

0 | 25 | 50 Kilometers

Caribbean Sea

95°

90°

85°

80°

75°

RAND McNALLY

Guam

Philippine Sea

144° 45'   145°

13° 30'

Agana   •Tamuning

GUAM
(U.S.)

PACIFIC
OCEAN

0 2 4 6 8 10 Miles
0   5   10   15 Kilometers
Copyright by Rand McNally & Co.
Lambert Conformal Conic Projection

144° 45'   145°

13° 15'

Samoa

171°   170°

0 5 10 15 20 25 Miles
0   10   20   30   40 Kilometers
Copyright by Rand McNally & Co
Lambert Conformal Conic Projection

PACIFIC
OCEAN

AMERICAN
SAMOA

14°

Ofu ▸ Olosega
Pago Pago
Aunuu   Tau

Tutuila   Manua Islands

Pacific Islands

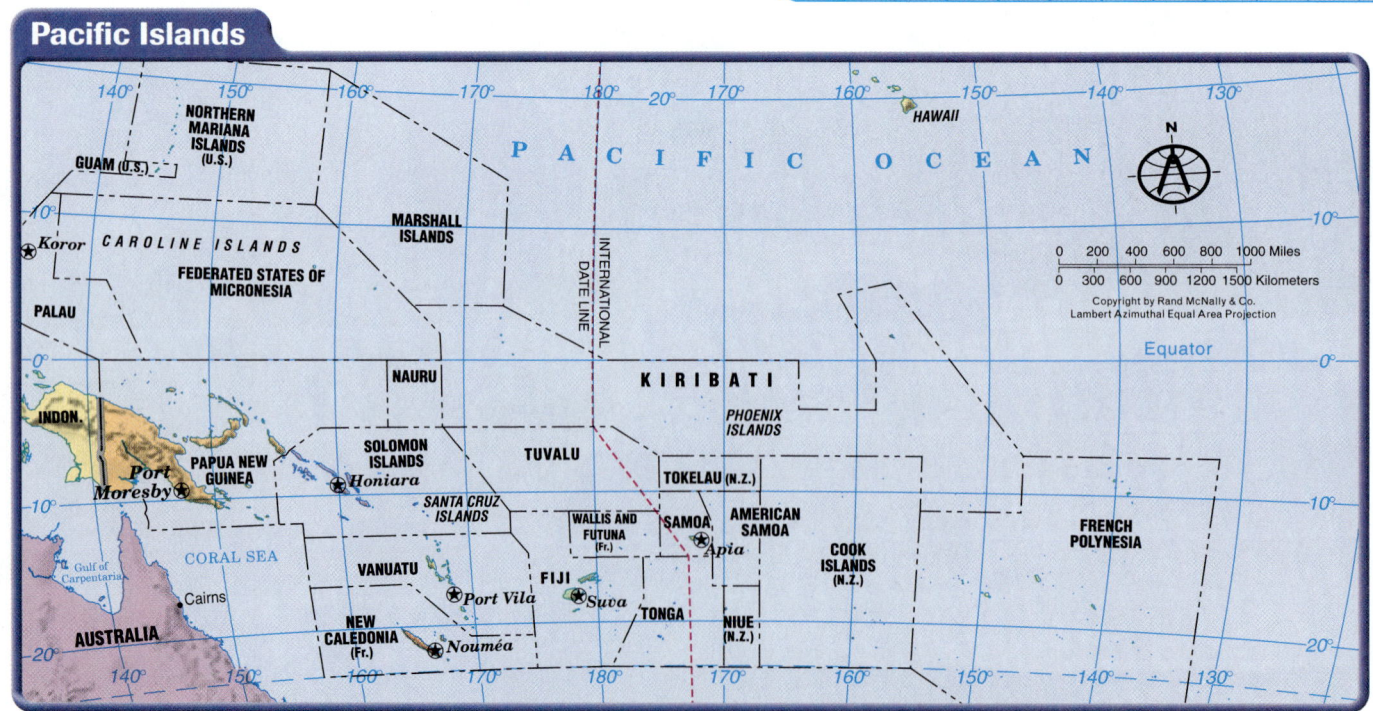

Map (Western Hemisphere)

ARCTIC OCEAN

165° 180° 165° 150° 135° 120° 105° 90° 75° 60° 45°

GREENLAND (Den.) 75°

ALASKA (U.S.)
Anchorage
Arctic Circle
60°

Aleutian Islands

C A N A D A

Vancouver
Seattle

Newfoundland

San Francisco

UNITED STATES

ATLANTIC
45°

Los Angeles

BERMUDA (U.K.)

30°

O C E A N

MIDWAY ISLANDS (U.S.)

Tropic of Cancer

MEXICO

BAHAMAS

CUBA

WAKE ISLAND (U.S.)

Hawai'ian Islands (U.S.)

Mexico City

HAITI DOM. REP.
PUERTO RICO (U.S.)

15°

Johnston Atoll (U.S.)

BELIZE
GUAT. HOND.
EL SAL. NIC.

JAMAICA

MARSHALL ISLANDS

P A C I F I C

COSTA RICA
PANAMA

TRINIDAD AND TOBAGO

FED. STATES OF MICRONESIA

Micronesia

Palmyra (U.S.)

Equator

VENEZUELA

GUYANA SURINAME
FRENCH GUIANA

0°

NAURU KIRIBATI

Phoenix Islands (Kiri.)

Line Islands

O C E A N

COLOMBIA

Galapagos Islands (Ecua.)

ECUADOR

SOLOMON ISLANDS

Polynesia

TUVALU

TOKELAU (N.Z.)

Marquesas Islands (Fr.)

PERU

BRAZIL

Melanesia

SAMOA
AMERICAN SAMOA

Society Islands

Tahiti

Tuamotu Islands (Fr.)

Lima

15°

VANUATU

FIJI

NIUE (N.Z.)

COOK ISLANDS (N.Z.)

FRENCH POLYNESIA

BOLIVIA

NEW CALEDONIA (Fr.)

TONGA

Tropic of Capricorn

PARAGUAY

NORFOLK ISLAND (Austl.)

Easter Island (Chile)

ARGENTINA

URUGUAY

30°

Sydney

Santiago

CHILE

NEW ZEALAND

Wellington

45°

Auckland Islands (N.Z.)

⊛ National Capital

• Major Cities

Macquaire Island (Austl.)

FALKLAND ISLANDS (U.K.)

60°

Antarctic Circle

75°

165° 180° 165° 150° 135° 120° 105° 90° 75° 60° 45°

Puerto Rico and the U.S. Virgin Islands

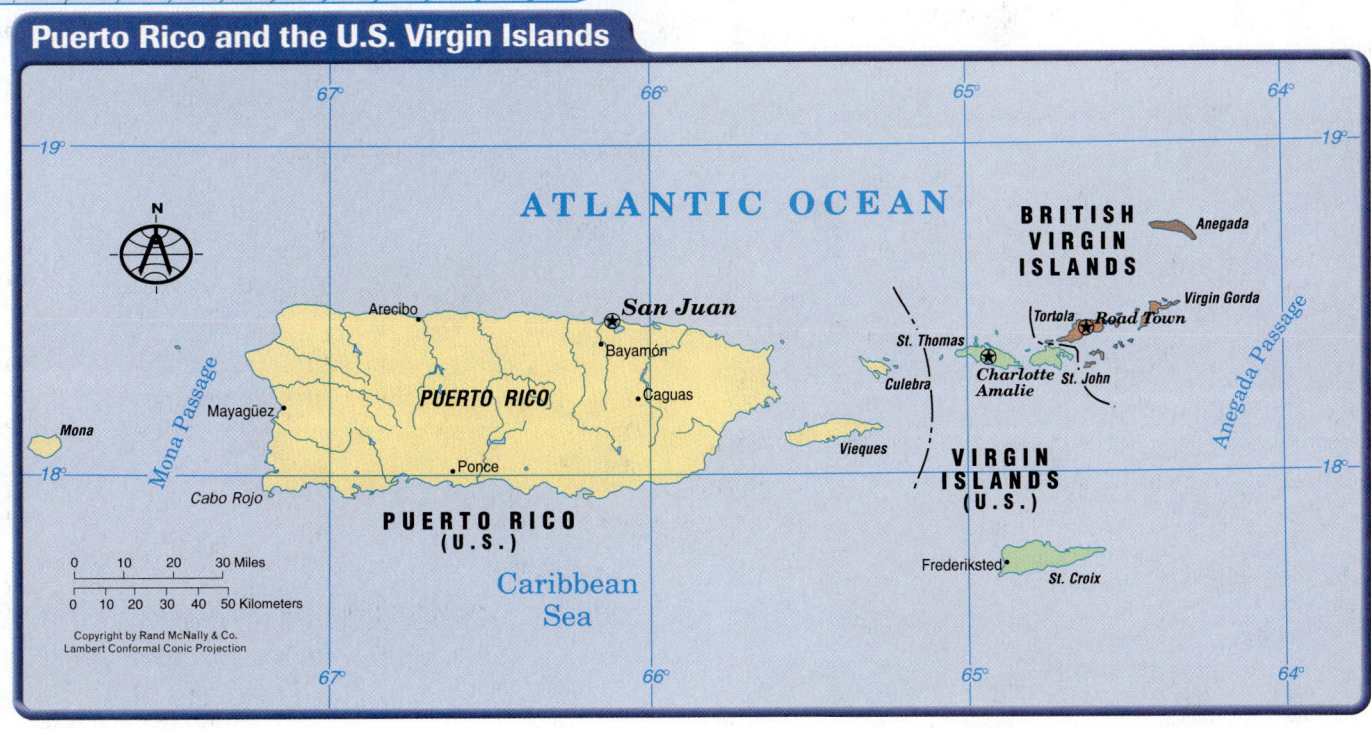

67° 66° 65° 64°

19° 19°

ATLANTIC OCEAN

BRITISH VIRGIN ISLANDS

Anegada

Arecibo

San Juan

Tortola
Virgin Gorda
Road Town

Bayamón

St. Thomas

PUERTO RICO

Caguas

Culebra

Anegada Passage

Mona

Mayagüez

Charlotte Amalie
St. John

Mona Passage

Ponce

Vieques

VIRGIN ISLANDS (U.S.)

18°

Cabo Rojo

PUERTO RICO (U.S.)

0 10 20 30 Miles
0 10 20 30 40 50 Kilometers

Caribbean Sea

Frederiksted
St. Croix

Copyright by Rand McNally & Co.
Lambert Conformal Conic Projection

67° 66° 65° 64°

RAND McNALLY

ATLANTIC OCEAN

Tropic of Cancer

GUADELOUPE (FR.)

MARTINIQUE (FR.)

TOBAGO (BR.)

DOMINICA (BR.)

ST. VINCENT (BR.)

GRENADA (BR.)

PUERTO RICO (SP.)

CARIBBEAN SEA

NEWFOUNDLAND (BR.)

ST. PIERRE (FR.)

MIQUELON (FR.)

CAPE BRETON ISLAND (BR.)

HISPANIOLA

Santo Domingo

HAITI (FR.)

St. Lawrence (in dispute)

JAMAICA (BR.)

Lake Ontario

Lake Erie

UNITED STATES

E. FLORIDA

Lake Huron

CUBA (SP.)

Lake Superior

Lake Michigan

(in dispute)

W. FLORIDA

GULF OF MEXICO

Mississippi

BRITISH

Rio Grande

SPANISH

PACIFIC OCEAN

UNEXPLORED

RAND McNALLY

A26

Copyright by Rand McNally & Co.
Lambert Azimuthal, Equal Area Projection

400 Miles
600 Kilometers

| U.S. | Spanish | British | French | Other | Disputed |

United States 1775-1799 map

HUDSON'S BAY COMPANY

Lake of the Woods
U.S. Claims in this area uncertain

L. Nipigon

QUEBEC

St. Lawrence

NEW BRUNSWICK

Quebec

Montreal

Boundary by Treaty of Paris 1783

Area Disputed by Great Britain

DISTRICT OF MAINE (MASS.)

NOVA SCOTIA

Ft. Oswegatchie

L. Champlain

Lake Superior

VT. 1791

N.H.

Boundary by Treaty of Paris 1783

NORTHWEST TERRITORY

Ft. Mackinac

Lake Michigan

Lake Huron

Area Disputed by Great Britain

Ft. Ontario

Ft. Niagara

NEW YORK

MASS.

Boston

CONN. R.I. Providence Newport

Mississippi

Detroit

Lake Erie

Fallen Timbers 1794

Clark 1778

PENNSYLVANIA

Pittsburgh

New York

N.J.

Philadelphia

Hudson

LOUISIANA

Missouri

St. Louis 1764

Wabash

Hamilton Br. 1778

Vincennes

Clark 1778

Ohio

Cincinnati 1788

Marietta 1788

Frankfort 1786

Louisville 1778

Lexington 1779

KENTUCKY 1792

Willing 1778

MD.

DEL.

Baltimore

Potomac

VIRGINIA

Richmond

APPALACHIAN MOUNTAINS

TENNESSEE 1796

Nashville 1780

TERRITORY SOUTH OF THE OHIO

CUMBERLAND MTS.

NORTH CAROLINA

Organized 1790

Willing 1778

Area Disputed by Spain

Added to Mississippi Territory 1804

Savannah

SOUTH CAROLINA

Charleston

GEORGIA

Savannah

Ft. Nogales

Ft. Confederación

MISSISSIPPI TERRITORY
Organized 1798

Boundary of Treaty of Paris 1783

ATLANTIC OCEAN

1779

Baton Rouge

WEST

Mobile

FLORIDA

Gálvez 1779

Pensacola

New Orleans

Gálvez 1780

EAST FLORIDA

St. Augustine

GULF OF MEXICO

Gálvez from Havana 1781

Lake Moyaco

BAHAMA IS. (Br.)

0   100   200   300 Miles
0   100   200   300   400 Kilometers

Copyright by Rand McNally & Co.
Lambert Azimuthal Equal Area Projection

Gálvez 1782

Nassau

	Thirteen original states
	Territories and additional states
	British possessions after 1783
	Spanish possessions after 1783
	Disputed territory
⊞	Posts retained by the British 1783-96
—	Revolutionary War Routes
	Areas colored as of 1783

RAND McNALLY

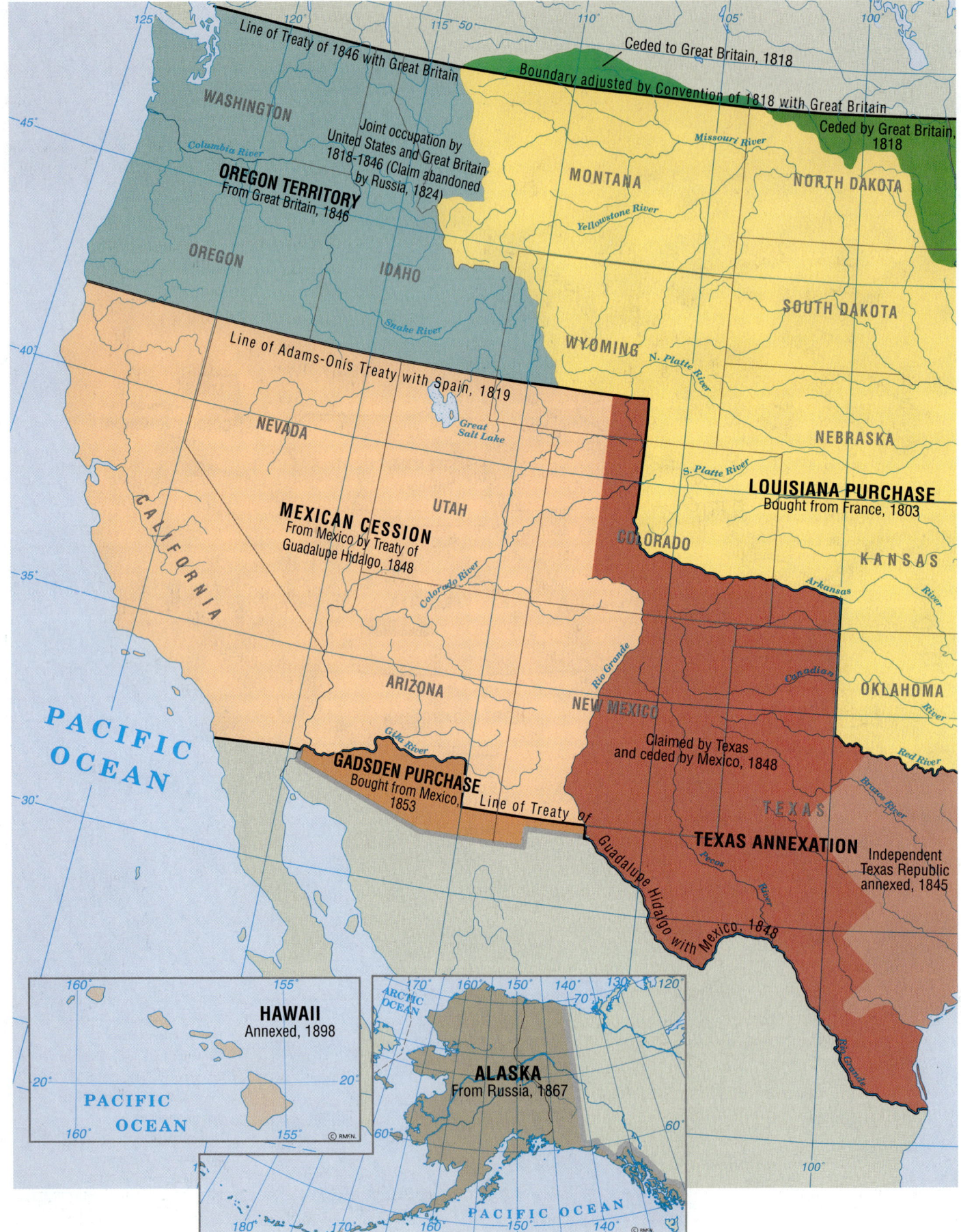

U.S. Territorial Expansion

Line of Treaty of 1846 with Great Britain

Ceded to Great Britain, 1818

Boundary adjusted by Convention of 1818 with Great Britain

Ceded by Great Britain, 1818

WASHINGTON

Columbia River

OREGON TERRITORY
From Great Britain, 1846

Joint occupation by United States and Great Britain 1818–1846 (Claim abandoned by Russia, 1824)

OREGON

IDAHO

Snake River

MONTANA

Missouri River

Yellowstone River

NORTH DAKOTA

SOUTH DAKOTA

WYOMING

N. Platte River

NEBRASKA

Line of Adams-Onis Treaty with Spain, 1819

NEVADA

Great Salt Lake

UTAH

MEXICAN CESSION
From Mexico by Treaty of Guadalupe Hidalgo, 1848

Colorado River

COLORADO

LOUISIANA PURCHASE
Bought from France, 1803

S. Platte River

K A N S A S

Arkansas River

CALIFORNIA

ARIZONA

Gila River

GADSDEN PURCHASE
Bought from Mexico, 1853

Line of Treaty of

Rio Grande

NEW MEXICO

Claimed by Texas and ceded by Mexico, 1848

OKLAHOMA

Canadian River

Red River

PACIFIC OCEAN

Guadalupe Hidalgo with Mexico, 1848

Pecos River

T E X A S

Brazos River

TEXAS ANNEXATION
Independent Texas Republic annexed, 1845

Rio Grande

HAWAII
Annexed, 1898

PACIFIC OCEAN

© RMcN.

ALASKA
From Russia, 1867

ARCTIC OCEAN

PACIFIC OCEAN

© RMcN.

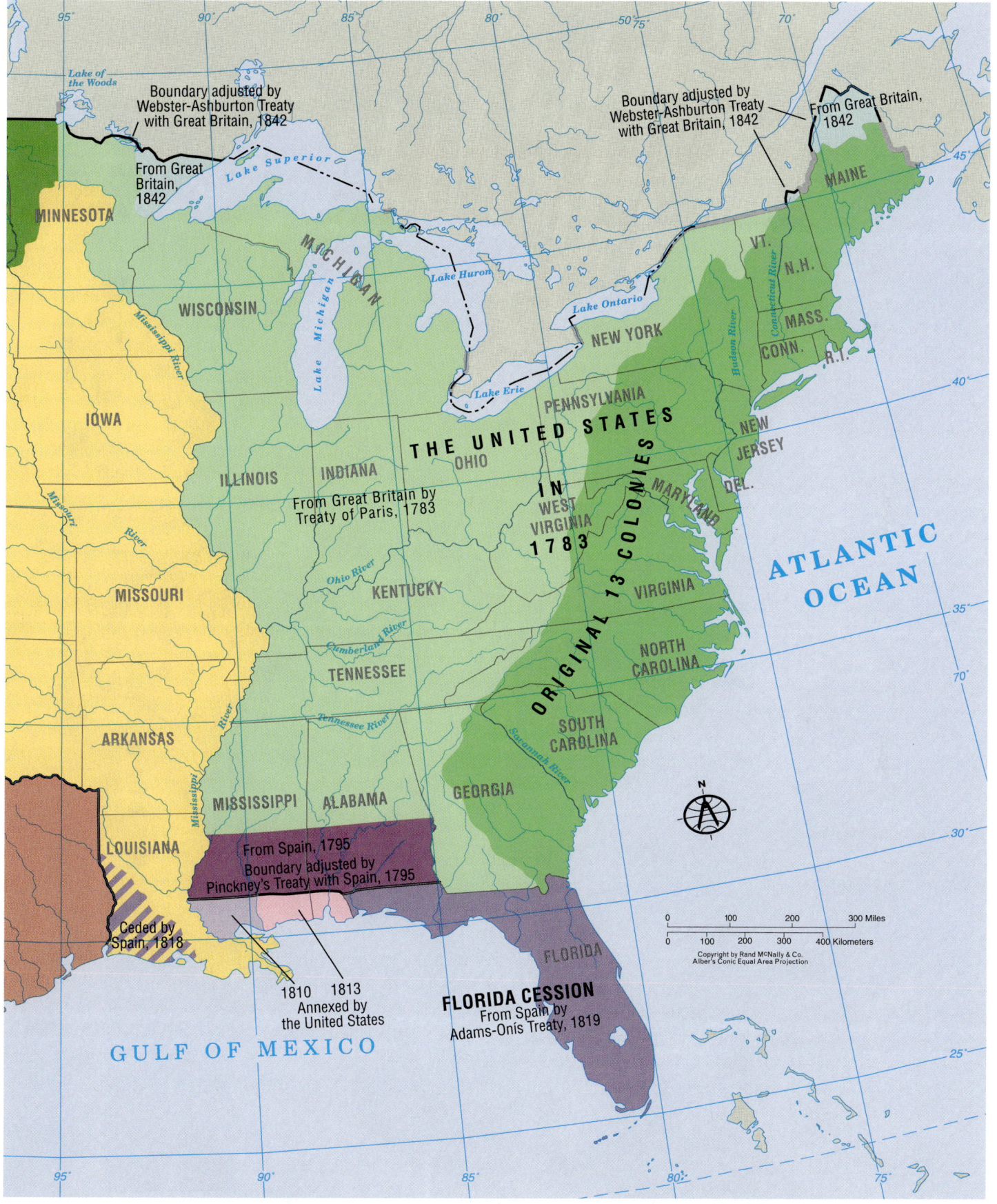

Boundary adjusted by Webster-Ashburton Treaty with Great Britain, 1842

From Great Britain, 1842

Boundary adjusted by Webster-Ashburton Treaty with Great Britain, 1842

From Great Britain, 1842

MINNESOTA

Lake of the Woods

Lake Superior

MICHIGAN

Lake Michigan

Lake Huron

MAINE

VT.

N.H.

MASS.

Connecticut River

Hudson River

CONN.

R.I.

WISCONSIN

Mississippi River

IOWA

Lake Ontario

NEW YORK

Lake Erie

PENNSYLVANIA

ILLINOIS

INDIANA

OHIO

THE UNITED STATES

NEW JERSEY

DEL.

Missouri River

MISSOURI

From Great Britain by Treaty of Paris, 1783

Ohio River

IN

WEST VIRGINIA

1783

MARYLAND

ORIGINAL 13 COLONIES

VIRGINIA

KENTUCKY

Cumberland River

TENNESSEE

Tennessee River

ATLANTIC OCEAN

NORTH CAROLINA

ARKANSAS

River

SOUTH CAROLINA

Savannah River

LOUISIANA

MISSISSIPPI

ALABAMA

GEORGIA

Mississippi River

Ceded by Spain, 1818

From Spain, 1795
Boundary adjusted by Pinckney's Treaty with Spain, 1795

1810   1813
Annexed by the United States

FLORIDA CESSION
From Spain by Adams-Onís Treaty, 1819

FLORIDA

N

0   100   200   300 Miles
0   100   200   300   400 Kilometers
Copyright by Rand McNally & Co.
Alber's Conic Equal Area Projection

GULF OF MEXICO

ATLANTIC OCEAN

PACIFIC OCEAN

GULF OF MEXICO

CANADA

MEXICO

MAINE
V.T.
N.H.
MASS.
CONN.
NEW YORK
NEW JERSEY
PENNSYLVANIA
DEL.
MARYLAND
VIRGINIA
OHIO
INDIANA
ILLINOIS
MICHIGAN
WISCONSIN
MINNESOTA
IOWA
MISSOURI
ARKANSAS
KENTUCKY
TENNESSEE
NORTH CAROLINA
SOUTH CAROLINA
GEORGIA
ALABAMA
MISSISSIPPI
LOUISIANA
FLORIDA
TEXAS

WASHINGTON TERRITORY
Free by Oregon Act 1848
Open to Slavery by Dred Scott Decision 1857
Olympia

OREGON
Free by Oregon Act 1848
Salem

CALIFORNIA
Sacramento
San Francisco
Los Angeles

(UNORGANIZED)
Free by Missouri Compromise 1820
Open to Slavery by Dred Scott Decision 1857

NEBRASKA TERRITORY
Free by Missouri Compromise 1820
Open to Slavery by Kansas-Nebraska Act 1854

KANSAS TERRITORY
Free by Missouri Compromise 1820
Open to Slavery by Kansas-Nebraska Act 1854

UTAH TERRITORY
Open to Slavery by Compromise of 1850

NEW MEXICO TERRITORY
Open to Slavery by Compromise of 1850

INDIAN TERRITORY

Missouri Compromise line 1820 36° 30'

Portland
Boston
Albany
Buffalo
New York
Philadelphia
Baltimore
Washington
Richmond
Norfolk
Wilmington
Charleston
Savannah
St. Augustine
Pittsburgh
Cleveland
Cincinnati
Detroit
Chicago
Milwaukee
Indianapolis
Louisville
Lexington
Nashville
Atlanta
Mobile
New Orleans
Memphis
Little Rock
Shreveport
St. Louis
Jefferson City
Des Moines
St. Paul
Yankton
Omaha
Topeka
Denver City
Santa Fe
Salt Lake City
Carson City
Tucson
San Antonio

Lake Superior
Lake Michigan
Lake Huron
Lake Erie
Lake Ontario
Ohio
Mississippi
Missouri
Snake
Columbia

Legend:
- 50% and over Slaves
- 1% to 50% Slaves
- Open to Slavery
- Free States
- Railroad
- Tobacco (△)
- Cotton
- Sugar (✦)
- Rice (□)
- Abolitionist Incidents (●)
- Slave Revolts (✺)

Copyright by Rand McNally & Co.
Alber's Conic Equal Area Projection

0 100 200 300 400 Miles
0 100 200 300 400 500 600 Kilometers

Legend

Free States
Free Territories
Loyal Slave States
Seceded before April 14, 1861
Seceded after April 14, 1861
Territories adhering to C.S.A.

Boundary line between Union and Confederate territories in 1861
◆ Forts held by Loyal Forces

Seized by Seceding Forces
✦ Forts
△ Arsenals
□ Navy Yards
◉ Branch Mints

RAND McNALLY

RAND McNALLY

Copyright by Rand McNally & Co.
Albers Conic Equal Area Projection

Legend

Settled by 1890

Indian reservations 1880

Railroads

Trails west

Extent of buffalo range 1870

Cattle trails

Mining

Indian battle

Incident of violence

300 Miles
400 Kilometers

ATLANTIC OCEAN

GULF OF MEXICO

BAHAMA ISLANDS

SOUTHERN PORTS BLOCKADED BY U.S. NAVY

GULF PORT BLOCKADED BY U.S. NAVY

CANADA

MEXICO

MAINE

VT. N.H.
MASS.
CONN. R.I.

★ Boston

NEW YORK
★ Albany
★ Buffalo

Lake Ontario

Lake Erie

Lake Huron

Lake Michigan

New York
Philadelphia
★ Harrisburg
Pittsburgh
PENNSYLVANIA
NEW JERSEY
DELAWARE

MICHIGAN
★ Lansing
Detroit

WISCONSIN
Milwaukee
★ Chicago

MINNESOTA

IOWA
★ Des Moines

ILLINOIS
★ Springfield

INDIANA
★ Indianapolis

OHIO
★ Columbus
Cleveland
Cincinnati
Wheeling

KENTUCKY
★ Frankfort
Louisville
Perryville 1862

Cincinnati

WEST VIRGINIA

VIRGINIA (Seceded April 16, 1861)
Richmond
Petersburg
Norfolk
Roanoke I. 1862
New Bern 1862

Washington MARYLAND
Baltimore
Antietam 1862
Gettysburg 1863
Bull Run 1861
Fredericksburg
Chancellorsville 1863
Wilderness 1864
Seven Days Battle
Cold Harbor
Appomattox 1865
Mine Run

NORTH CAROLINA (Seceded May 20, 1861)
Raleigh
Charlotte
Bentonville 1865

SOUTH CAROLINA (Seceded Dec. 20, 1860)
Columbia 1865
Charleston 1863
Ft. Sumter 1861
Ft. Wagner 1863
Port Royal 1861
Ft. Pulaski 1862

GEORGIA (Seceded Jan. 19, 1861)
Atlanta 1864
Milledgeville
Andersonville
Savannah 1864

TENNESSEE (Seceded May 7, 1861)
Knoxville
Nashville
Chattanooga
Chickamauga 1863
Murfreesboro 1862
Shiloh 1862
Ft. Donelson 1862
Ft. Henry 1862
Memphis 1862
Corinth 1862

ALABAMA (Seceded Jan. 11, 1861)
Montgomery
Mobile 1864
Pensacola 1862

MISSISSIPPI (Seceded Jan. 9, 1861)
Jackson 1863
Holly Springs
Vicksburg 1863
Chickasaw Bluffs 1862
Natchez
Port Gibson 1863

LOUISIANA (Seceded Jan. 26, 1861)
Baton Rouge 1862
New Orleans 1862
Shreveport
Ship I. 1861

ARKANSAS (Seceded May 6, 1861)
Little Rock

MISSOURI
Jefferson City
St. Louis
Kansas City

KANSAS
★ Topeka

INDIAN TERRITORY

TEXAS (Seceded Feb. 1, 1861)
★ Austin
Dallas
Houston
San Antonio

FLORIDA (Seceded Jan. 10, 1861)
Tallahassee
Fernandina 1862
St. Augustine 1862

Savannah

Chattahoochee

Tombigbee

Pearl

Red

Sabine

Trinity

Brazos

Colorado

Rio Grande

Cimarron

Arkansas

Ohio

Mississippi

Hudson

Legend:
- Northern limit of Confederate control, 1861
- Coastal point occupied by Union Forces
- Area gained by the Union, 1862
- Area gained by the Union, 1863
- Area gained by the Union, 1864
- Area gained by the Union, 1865
- Confederate victories
- Battle Site
- Union free states
- Union slave states
- Confederate states

0 100 200 300 Miles
0 100 200 300 400 Kilometers

Copyright by Rand McNally & Co.
Albers Conic Equal Area Projection

RAND McNALLY

A33

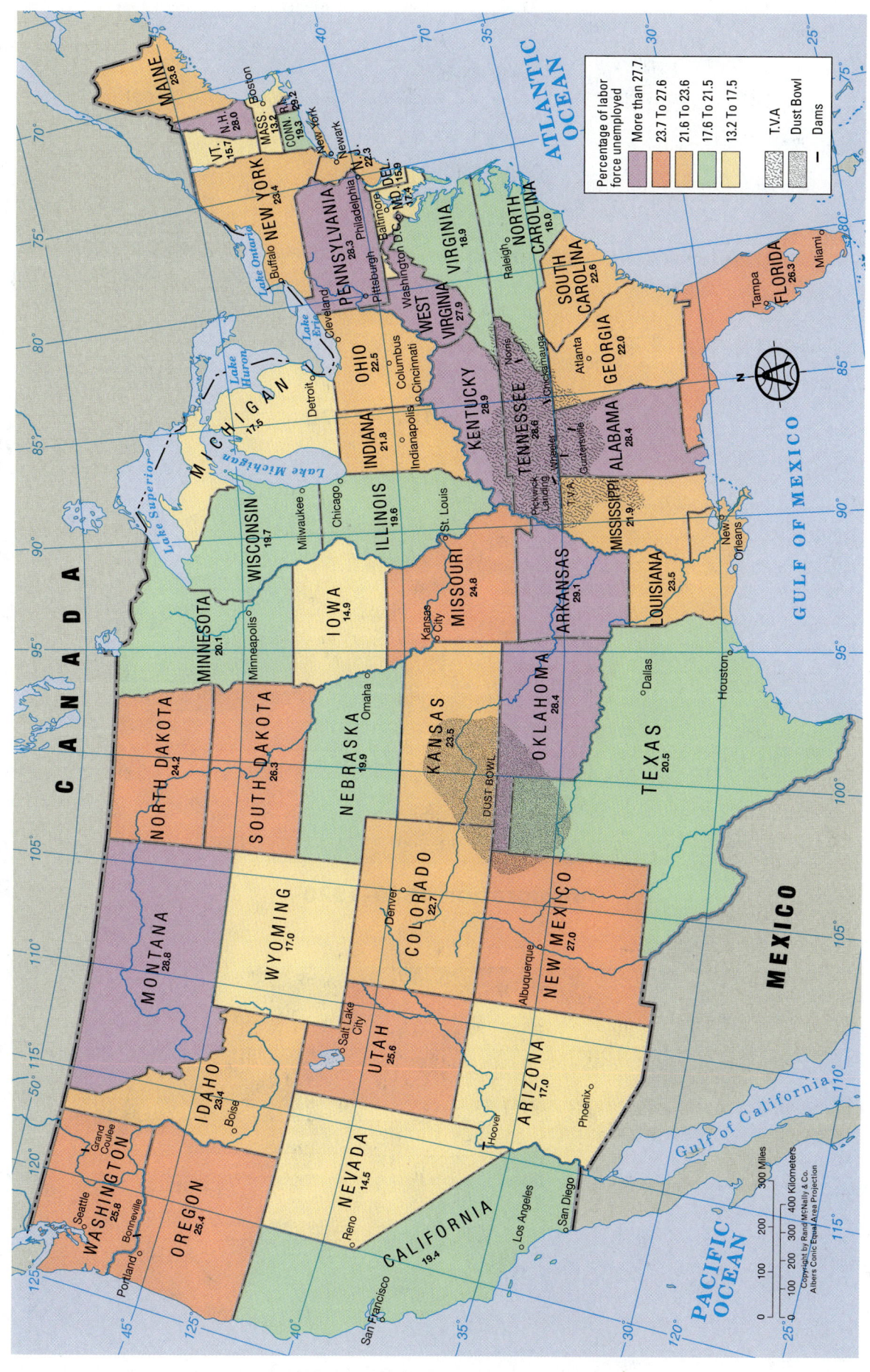

Percentage of labor force unemployed

	More than 27.7
	23.7 To 27.6
	21.6 To 23.6
	17.6 To 21.5
	13.2 To 17.5

T.V.A
Dust Bowl
Dams

ATLANTIC OCEAN

GULF OF MEXICO

PACIFIC OCEAN

Gulf of California

MEXICO

CANADA

MAINE 23.6
VT. 15.7
N.H. 28.0
MASS. 13.2
CONN. 19.3
R.I. 29.2
New York
Newark
N.J. 22.3
DEL. 15.9
MD. 17.4
NEW YORK 23.4
Buffalo
Boston
PENNSYLVANIA 28.3
Philadelphia
Pittsburgh
Washington D.C.
WEST VIRGINIA 27.9
VIRGINIA 18.9
Raleigh
NORTH CAROLINA 18.0
SOUTH CAROLINA 22.6
FLORIDA 26.3
Miami
Tampa
OHIO 22.5
Columbus
Cincinnati
Cleveland
Detroit
MICHIGAN 17.5
KENTUCKY 28.9
Norris
Chickamauga
Atlanta
GEORGIA 22.0
Wheeler
ALABAMA 28.4
Guntersville
TENNESSEE 28.6
Pickwick Landing
T.V.A.
INDIANA 21.8
Indianapolis
ILLINOIS 19.6
Chicago
Milwaukee
WISCONSIN 19.7
St. Louis
MISSISSIPPI 21.9
New Orleans
LOUISIANA 23.5
ARKANSAS 29.1
MISSOURI 24.8
Kansas City
IOWA 14.9
MINNESOTA 20.1
Minneapolis
NORTH DAKOTA 24.2
SOUTH DAKOTA 26.3
NEBRASKA 19.9
Omaha
KANSAS 23.5
DUST BOWL
OKLAHOMA 28.4
TEXAS 20.5
Dallas
Houston
MONTANA 28.8
WYOMING 17.0
COLORADO 22.7
Denver
NEW MEXICO 27.0
Albuquerque
IDAHO 23.4
Boise
UTAH 25.6
Salt Lake City
ARIZONA 17.0
Phoenix
NEVADA 14.5
Reno
Hoover
WASHINGTON 25.8
Seattle
Grand Coulee
Bonneville
OREGON 25.4
Portland
CALIFORNIA 19.4
San Francisco
Los Angeles
San Diego

Lake Superior
Lake Michigan
Lake Huron
Lake Ontario
Lake Erie

N

300 Miles
100   200   300   400 Kilometers
0   100   200   300

Copyright by Rand McNally & Co.
Albers Conic Equal Area Projection

RAND McNALLY

Immigration 1820–1870

Immigration 1880–1920

Immigration 1960s–1990s

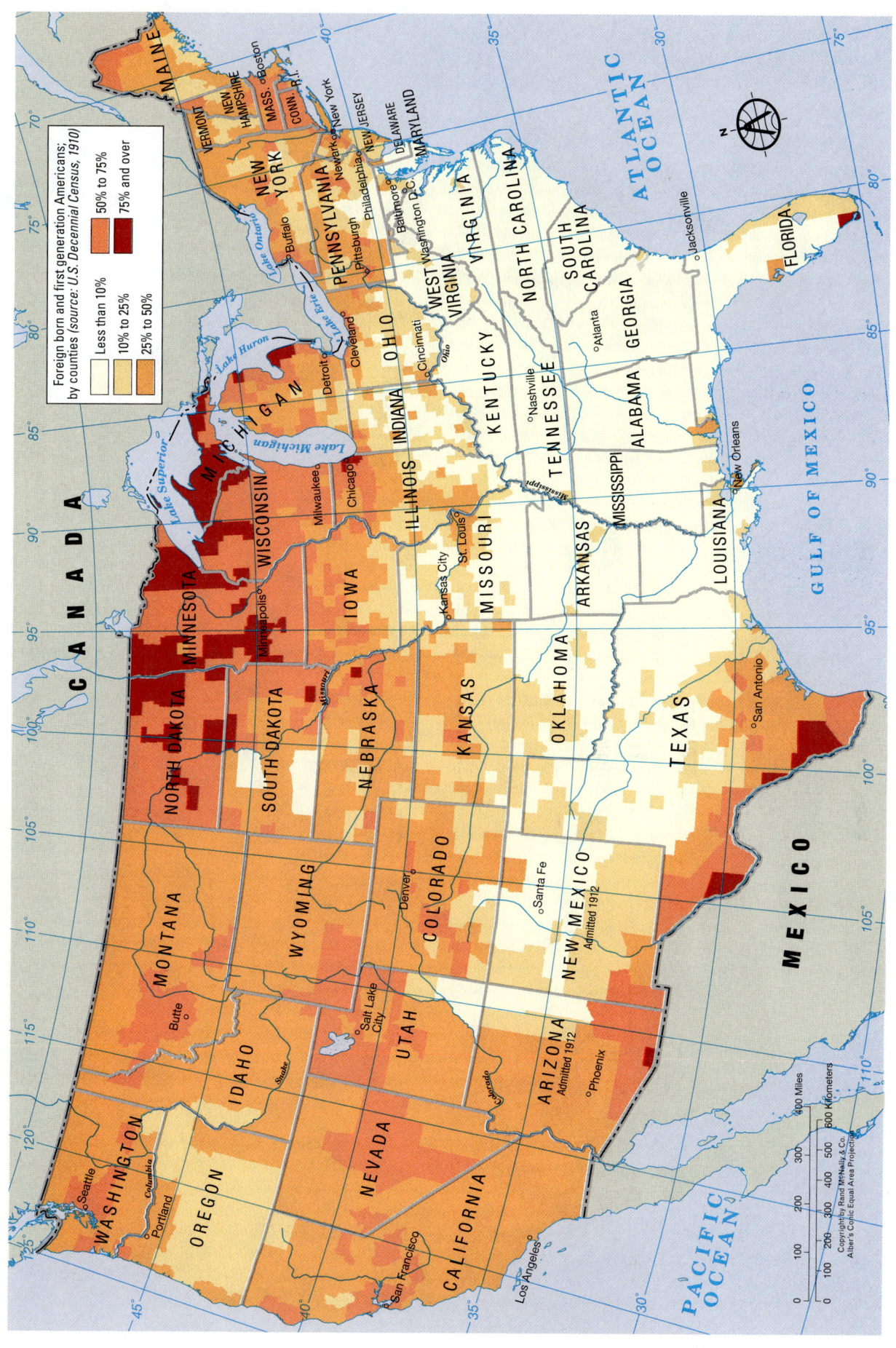

Foreign born and first generation Americans; by counties *(source: U.S. Decennial Census, 1910)*

- Less than 10%
- 10% to 25%
- 25% to 50%
- 50% to 75%
- 75% and over

Copyright by Rand McNally & Co.
Alber's Conic Equal Area Projection

RAND McNALLY

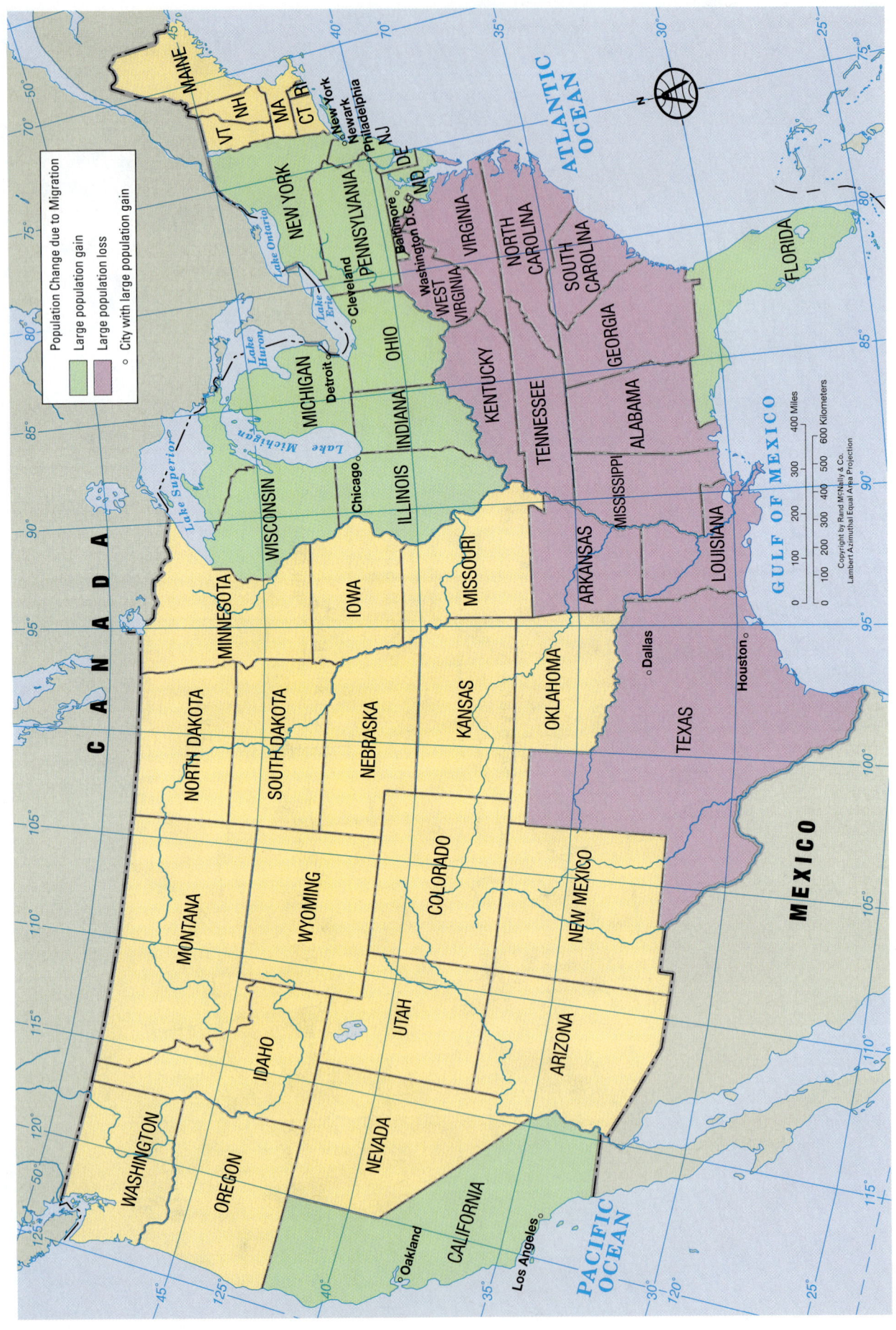

Population Change due to Migration
- Large population gain
- Large population loss
- City with large population gain

Per square mile
(per square kilometer)

Under 2 *(Under 1)*
2-6 *(1-2)*
6-18 *(2-7)*
18-45 *(7-17)*
45-90 *(17-35)*
Over 90 *(Over 35)*
Urban Centers

ATLANTIC OCEAN

Boston
New York
Washington D.C.

Miami

Atlanta

Detroit

Chicago

Minneapolis

St. Louis

Kansas City

Dallas

Houston

GULF OF MEXICO

Denver

Seattle

San Francisco

Los Angeles

PACIFIC OCEAN

300 Miles
100   200   300   400 Kilometers
0   100   200
Copyright by Rand McNally & Co.
Lambert Azimuthal Equal Area Projection

Honolulu

PACIFIC OCEAN

Anchorage

PACIFIC OCEAN

Arctic Circle

REFERENCE SECTION

SKILLBUILDER HANDBOOK

1.1 Finding Main Ideas

DEFINING THE SKILL

Finding main ideas means identifying words that sum up the single most important thought in an entire paragraph or section. To find the main idea of a passage, identify the topic. Then, as you read, ask, What central idea do the many details explain or support?

APPLYING THE SKILL

This excerpt from President Richard M. Nixon's memoirs is about wiretapping, or bugging—planting a concealed microphone to get information. The diagram that follows identifies and organizes information in the passage.

HOW TO FIND MAIN IDEAS

Strategy **1** Identify the topic by looking at the title, or by looking for key words. This passage repeats the words *bugged*, *bugging*, *tapped*, and *wiretap*.

Strategy **2** Look for a topic sentence. Ask whether any one sentence sums up the point of the whole passage. In this passage, the second sentence states Nixon's attitude toward bugging.

Strategy **3** Look for details or examples. The many examples support the attitude that wiretapping was a common practice.

> **NIXON ON WIRETAPPING** **1**
>
> I had been in politics too long, and seen everything from dirty tricks to vote fraud. **2** I could not muster much moral outrage over a political **1** bugging.
>
> Larry O'Brien [director of the Democratic National Committee] might affect astonishment and horror, but he knew as well as I did that political bugging had been around nearly since the invention of the wiretap. **3** As recently as 1970 a former member of Adlai Stevenson's [Democratic candidate for president in 1952 and 1956] campaign staff had publicly stated that he had tapped the [John F.] Kennedy organization's phone lines at the 1960 Democratic convention. **3** Lyndon Johnson felt that the Kennedys had had him tapped; **3** Barry Goldwater said that his 1964 campaign had been bugged; **3** and Edgar Hoover [director of the FBI, 1924–1972] told me that in 1968 Johnson had ordered my campaign plane bugged.
>
> Source: Richard Nixon, *The Memoirs of Richard Nixon* (New York: Grosset & Dunlap, 1978), pp. 628–629.

Make a Diagram

State the topic and list the supporting details in a chart. Use the information you record to help you state the main idea.

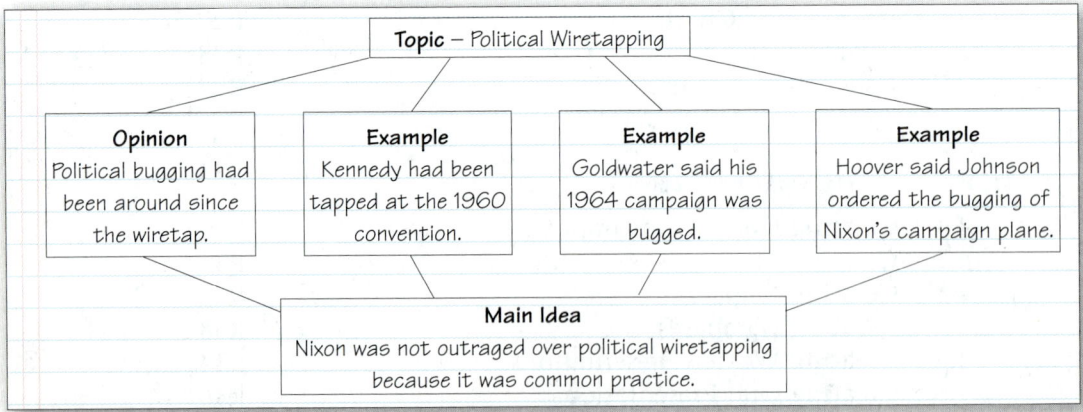

PRACTICING THE SKILL

Turn to Chapter 34, Section 3, p. 1085 and read the passage headed "Space Exploration." Make a diagram, like the one above, to identify the topic, the most important details, and the main idea of the passage.

1.2 Following Chronological Order

DEFINING THE SKILL

Chronological order is "time order"—the sequence of events in time. Chronology may be either relative or absolute. Relative chronology relates one event to another. This helps historians to see causes, effects, and other relationships between events. Absolute chronology ties events to an exact time or date, pinpointing dates in one universal framework—the passage of time.

APPLYING THE SKILL

The following paragraph is about several events leading up to the Watergate scandal that brought down the Nixon administration. The time line that follows puts the events of the passage in chronological order.

HOW TO FOLLOW CHRONOLOGICAL ORDER

Strategy 1 Look for clue words about time. These are words like *initial*, *first*, *next*, *then*, *before*, *after*, *finally*, and *by that time*.

Strategy 2 Use specific dates provided in the text.

Strategy 3 Watch for references to previous historical events that are included in the background. Usually a change in verb tense will indicate a previous event.

The Pentagon Papers

The **1** initial event that many historians believe led to Watergate took place on **2** June 13, 1971, when the *New York Times* began publishing articles called the Pentagon Papers, which divulged government secrets about the U.S. involvement in Vietnam. The information had been leaked by a former Defense Department official, Daniel Ellsberg. The Justice Department asked the courts to suppress publication of the articles, but on **2** July 30, 1971, the Supreme Court ruled that the information could be published. **1** Two months later, in September, a group of special White House agents known as the plumbers burglarized the office of Ellsberg's psychiatrist in a vain attempt to find evidence against Ellsberg. President Nixon **3** had authorized the creation of the plumbers in 1971, after the Pentagon Papers were published, to keep government secrets from leaking to the media and to help ensure his reelection in November 1972.

Make a Time Line

If the events in a passage are numerous and complex, make a time line to represent them. The time line here lists the events from the passage above in time order.

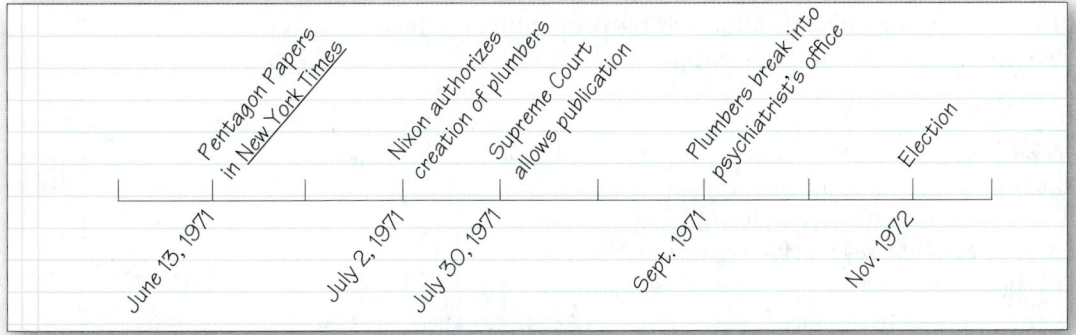

PRACTICING THE SKILL

Skim Chapter 29, Section 2, p. 916 "The Triumphs of a Crusade," to find out how the civil rights movement helped end segregation in the South. Make a list of the important dates you find, starting with the freedom ride in May 1961 and ending with the passage of the Voting Rights Act of 1965. Use the model above to help you create your own time line, showing what happened on each date.

1.3 Clarifying; Summarizing

DEFINING THE SKILL

Clarifying means checking to be sure you clearly understand what you have read. One way to do this is by asking yourself questions. In your answers, you might restate in your own words what you have read.

When you **summarize,** you condense what you have read into fewer words, stating only the main idea and the most important supporting details. It is important to use your own words in a summary.

APPLYING THE SKILL

The excerpt below describes a major oil spill. Following the excerpt is a summary that condenses the key information in the passage into a few sentences.

HOW TO SUMMARIZE

Strategy ❶ Look for topic sentences stating the main ideas. These are often at the beginning of a section or paragraph. In a summary, rewrite the main ideas in your own words.

Strategy ❷ Include only the most important facts and statistics. Pay attention to numbers, dates, quantities, and other data.

Strategy ❸ Clarify understanding by asking questions. Also, look up any words you do not recognize.

> **THE *EXXON VALDEZ* OIL SPILL**
>
> ❶ In March 1989, the oil tanker *Exxon Valdez* ran aground in Prince William Sound along the coast of Alaska, dumping about ❷ 11 million gallons of crude oil into the sea. Within days, 1,800 miles of coastline were fouled with thick black oil that coated rocks and beaches. At least 10 percent of the area's birds, sea otters, and other animals were killed, and commercial fisheries estimated that they would lose at least 50 percent of the season's catch.
>
> The captain of the *Exxon Valdez* was found guilty of ❸ negligence, and attempts were made to clean up the spill. ❷ Ten years later, however, scientists found that pools of oil buried in coves were still poisoning shellfish, otters, and ducks, while several bird species failed to reproduce.
>
> ❷ Between 1989 and 1994, Exxon spent about $2.1 billion in efforts to clean up Prince William Sound. In the meantime, some 34,000 commercial fishers and other Alaskans sued the company for damages, claiming that the oil spill had ruined their livelihoods.

Write a Summary

You can write your summary in a paragraph. The paragraph below summarizes the passage about the *Exxon Valdez* oil spill. After writing your summary, review it to see that you have included only the most important details.

> In 1989, the *Exxon Valdez* ran aground off the Alaskan coast, spilling 11 million gallons of oil. The water and coastline for hundreds of miles were badly polluted, and many animals died. Alaskans sued the oil company for lost income. Exxon spent $2.1 billion for a cleanup effort and was subject to litigation from people who lost their livelihoods because of the spill.

PRACTICING THE SKILLS

Turn to Chapter 22, Section 1, p. 670 and read the passage headed "Economic Troubles on the Horizon." Make notes of the main ideas. Look up any words you don't recognize. Then write a summary of the passage, using the model above as your guide.

1.4 Identifying Problems

DEFINING THE SKILL

Identifying problems means recognizing and understanding difficulties faced by particular people or groups at particular times. Being able to focus on specific problems helps historians understand the motives for actions and the forces underlying historical events.

APPLYING THE SKILL

The following passage tells about the experience of newcomers to Northern cities, like Boston and Philadelphia, in the late 1800s. Below the passage is a chart that organizes the information the passage contains.

HOW TO IDENTIFY PROBLEMS

Strategy 1 Look for problems that are implied but not stated. Problems are sometimes stated indirectly. This sentence implies that many immigrants settled in the cities because of limited opportunities elsewhere.

Strategy 2 Look for difficulties people faced.

Strategy 3 Evaluate solutions to problems.

Strategy 4 Recognize that sometimes the solution to one problem may cause another problem.

IMMIGRANT LIFE IN THE CITIES

1 The lure that drew many immigrants to America and its cities often was the same one that had attracted settlers to the West—opportunity. In the nation's industrialized centers people saw a chance to **2** escape poverty, find work, and carve out a better life.

Cities offered unskilled laborers steady jobs in mills and factories and provided the social support of neighborhoods of people with the same ethnic background. **3** Living among people who shared their background enabled the newcomers to speak their own language while learning about their new home. **4** Overcrowding soon became a problem, however—one that was intensified by the migration of people from America's rural areas.

Make a Chart

The chart below summarizes the problems and solutions in the passage. The chart details what the problems were, what steps people took to solve the problems, and how those solutions affected them.

Problems	Solutions	Outcomes
poverty	coming to U.S. cities	jobs available
lack of opportunity	coming to U.S. cities	jobs, housing, communities
lack of work skills	factory and mill jobs requiring low level of training	enough jobs for the time being
unfamiliarity with language	living in ethnic communities	community but overcrowding

PRACTICING THE SKILL

Turn to Chapter 31, Section 2, p. 982 and read the passage headed "Women Fight for Equality." Note the social and economic problems many women faced in the 1960s and 1970s. Then make a chart, like the one above, in which you summarize the information you found in the passage. Be sure to read to the end of the section so that you can evaluate the solutions attempted and their outcomes.

1.5 Analyzing Motives

DEFINING THE SKILL

Analyzing motives in history means examining the reasons why a person, group, or government took a particular action. These reasons often go back to the needs, emotions, and prior experiences of the person or group, as well as their plans, circumstances, and objectives.

APPLYING THE SKILL

The following paragraphs tell how the early Mormons were treated and why they moved west in the mid-1800s. The diagram below the passage summarizes the Mormons' motives for that journey.

HOW TO ANALYZE MOTIVES

Strategy 1 Look for different kinds of motives. Some motives are negative, and others are positive.

Strategy 2 Look for the influence of important individuals or leaders in motivating others.

Strategy 3 Look for basic needs and human emotions as powerful motivators. Such needs and emotions include food and shelter, greed, ambition, compassion, and fear.

The Mormon Migration

Some of the Mormons' beliefs alarmed and angered other Americans. **1** Plagued by persecution and violence and seeking to convert Native Americans, Mormon church founder Joseph Smith led his followers west to a small community in Illinois. Conflict soon developed again when Smith allowed male members to have more than one wife. This idea infuriated many of Smith's neighbors, and he was eventually murdered by a mob.

2 The Mormons rallied around a new leader, Brigham Young, who urged them to move farther west. There they encountered a desert area near a salt lake, just beyond the mountains of what was then part of Mexico. The salty water was useless for crops and animals. Because the land was not desirable to others, **3** Young realized that his people might be safe there. The Mormons began to build Salt Lake City.

Make a Diagram

In the center of the diagram, list the important actions from the passage. Around it, list motives in different categories.

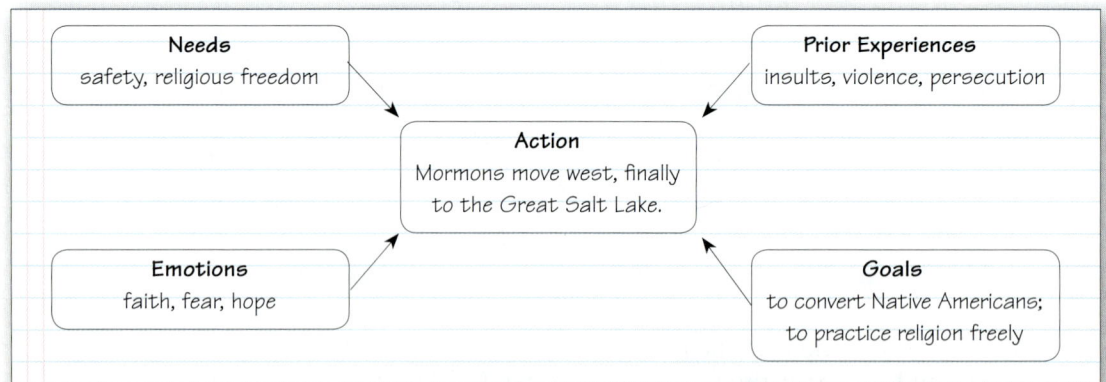

Needs
safety, religious freedom

Prior Experiences
insults, violence, persecution

Action
Mormons move west, finally to the Great Salt Lake.

Emotions
faith, fear, hope

Goals
to convert Native Americans; to practice religion freely

PRACTICING THE SKILL

Turn to Chapter 25, Section 3, p. 789 and read the passage headed "The Atomic Bomb Ends the War." Take notes about President Truman's motives in dropping atomic bombs on Japan. Then create a diagram similar to the one shown here.

1.6 Analyzing Causes and Effects

DEFINING THE SKILL

A **cause** is an action in history that prompts something to happen. An **effect** is a historical event or condition that is the result of the cause. A single event may have several causes. It is also possible for one cause to result in several effects. Historians identify cause-and-effect relationships to help them understand why historical events took place.

APPLYING THE SKILL

The following paragraphs describe the early events leading to the Battle of Little Bighorn. The diagram that follows the passage summarizes the chain of causes and effects.

HOW TO IDENTIFY CAUSES AND EFFECTS

Strategy ❶ Look for reasons behind the events. Here the discovery of gold motivated white Americans to move into Sioux territory.

Strategy ❷ Look for clue words indicating cause. These include *because, due to, since,* and *therefore.*

Strategy ❸ Look for clue words indicating consequences. These include *brought about, led to, as a result, thus, consequently,* and *responded.* Remember that a cause may have several effects.

Broken Treaties

The Treaty of Fort Laramie (1868) had promised the Sioux that they could live forever in Paha Sapa, the Black Hills area of what is now South Dakota and Wyoming. The area was sacred to the Sioux. It was the center of their land and the place where warriors went to await visions from their guardian spirits.

Unfortunately for the Sioux, the Black Hills contained large deposits of gold. ❶ As soon as white Americans learned that gold had been discovered, they poured into the Native Americans' territory and began staking claims.

❷ Because the Sioux valued their land so highly, they appealed to the government to enforce the treaty terms and remove the miners. The government ❸ responded by offering to purchase the land from the Sioux. When the Sioux refused, the government sent in the Seventh Cavalry to remove the Native Americans.

Make a Cause-and-Effect Diagram

Starting with the first cause in a series, fill in the boxes until you reach the end result.

Cause	Effect/Cause	Effect/Cause
Gold was discovered in the Black Hills.	White prospectors flocked to the area.	The Sioux asked the government to enforce the treaty.

Effect/Cause	Effect/Cause	Effect
The government sent a commission to buy lands.	The Sioux refused the commission's offer.	The government sent in the cavalry.

PRACTICING THE SKILL

Turn to Chapter 19, Section 3, p. 598 and read the passage headed "African Americans and the War." Take notes about the causes and effects of African-American migration. Make a diagram, like the one shown above, to organize the information you find.

1.7 Comparing; Contrasting

DEFINING THE SKILL

Comparing involves looking at the similarities and differences between two or more things. **Contrasting** means examining only the differences between them. Historians might compare and contrast events, personalities, beliefs, institutions, works of art, or many other types of things in order to give them a context for the period of history they are studying.

APPLYING THE SKILL

The following passage describes life in colonial America during the last half of the 1600s. The Venn diagram below shows the similarities and differences between the Northern and Southern colonies.

HOW TO COMPARE AND CONTRAST

Strategy ① Look for clue words that show how two things differ. Clue words include *different, differ, unlike, by contrast, however,* and *on the other hand.*

Strategy ② Look for clue words indicating that two things are alike. Clue words include *both, all, like, as, likewise,* and *similarly.*

Strategy ③ Look for features that two things have in common.

> **Life in the Early American Colonies**
>
> Not long after the English colonies were established, it became apparent that two very ① different ways of life were developing in the Northern and Southern colonies. In the South, both ② rich plantation owners and poorer frontier farmers sought land. Virginia and Maryland became known as the tobacco colonies. ③ Large farms, but few towns, appeared there.
>
> Slavery existed in ③ all the colonies, but it became a vital source of labor in the South. ① By contrast, the New England and middle colonies did not rely on slave labor or single staple crops, such as tobacco or rice. Most people were farmers, but they grew a wide variety of crops. The New England colonies traded actively with the islands of the West Indies. In addition to foods, they exported all kinds of other items, ranging from barrels to horses. In return, they imported sugar and molasses. ③ All this trade resulted in the growth of small towns and larger port cities.

Make a Venn Diagram

Use the two ovals to contrast the Northern and Southern colonies and the overlapping area to show what the two regions have in common.

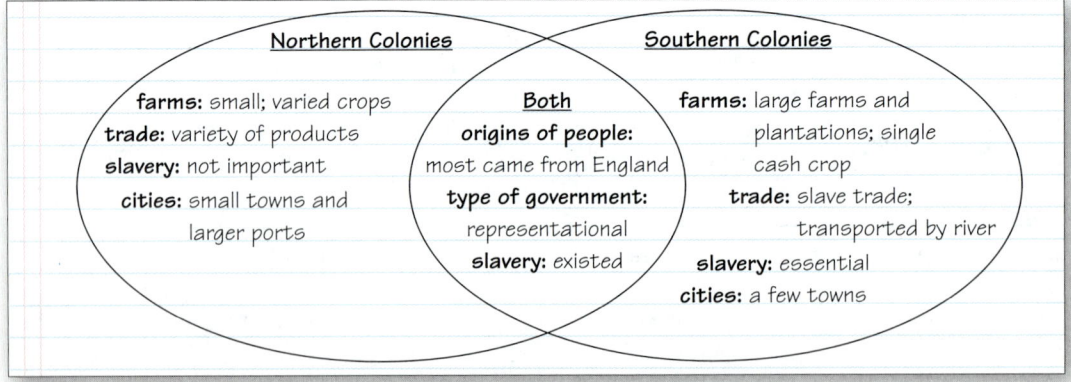

Northern Colonies

farms: small; varied crops
trade: variety of products
slavery: not important
cities: small towns and
  larger ports

Both
origins of people:
most came from England
type of government:
representational
slavery: existed

Southern Colonies

farms: large farms and
  plantations; single
  cash crop
trade: slave trade;
  transported by river
slavery: essential
cities: a few towns

PRACTICING THE SKILL

Turn to Chapter 13, Section 1, pp. 408–409 and read the passages headed "The Culture of the Plains Indians" and "Settlers Push Westward." Pay special attention to descriptions of the American settlers and Native Americans on the Great Plains. Make a Venn diagram showing what the two groups had in common and what made them different.

1.8 Distinguishing Fact from Opinion

DEFINING THE SKILL

Facts are dates, statistics, and accounts of events, or they are statements that are generally known to be true. Facts can be checked for accuracy.
Opinions are the judgments, beliefs, and feelings of a writer or speaker.

APPLYING THE SKILL

The following excerpt describes the 1886 Haymarket affair in Chicago. The chart summarizes the facts and opinions.

HOW TO DISTINGUISH FACT FROM OPINION

Strategy **1** Look for specific events, dates, and statistics that can be verified.

Strategy **2** Look for assertions, claims, hypotheses, and judgments. Here a speaker at the event is expressing an opinion.

Strategy **3** Look for judgments the historian makes about events. Here the writer states the opinion that the event was a disaster and then backs up this opinion by explaining the negative consequences of the event.

The Haymarket Affair

1 At ten o'clock another speaker stepped forward, the main burden of his address being that **2** there was no hope of improving the condition of workingmen through legislation; it must be through their own efforts. . . .

The speaker hurried to a conclusion, but at that point 180 police officers entered the square and headed for the wagon that had served as a speakers' platform. The captain in charge called on the meeting to disperse. . . .

1 At that moment someone threw a bomb into the ranks of the policemen gathered about the speakers. After the initial shock and horror, the police opened fire on the 300 or 400 people who remained. One policeman had been killed by the bomb, and more than 60 injured. One member of the crowd was killed by police fire, and at least 12 were wounded. . . .

3 In almost every . . . way Haymarket was a disaster. It vastly augmented [increased] the already considerable paranoia of most Americans in regard to anarchists, socialists, communists, and radicals in general. It increased hostility toward . . . foreigners. . . . It caused a serious impairment of freedom of speech in every part of the country.

Source: Page Smith, *The Rise of Industrial America* (New York: Penguin, 1990), pp. 244–256.

Make a Chart

List the facts you learn in a passage as well as the opinions that are expressed.

Facts	Opinions
Just after 10:00, as a speaker was finishing up, someone threw a bomb into the group of 180 policemen surrounding the speakers. More than 60 police were injured, and about 13 civilians were injured or killed when police fired into the crowd.	speaker: Workers must improve their own situations since legislation can't do it for them. historian: Nothing good came of the Haymarket affair; and in fact it had many negative consequences: • increased paranoia about radicals • increased hostility toward foreigners • impaired freedom of speech

PRACTICING THE SKILL

Read Chapter 15, Section 3, p. 473, "The Emergence of Political Machines."
Make a chart in which you list some facts about political machines and some opinions on graft expressed in the passage.

1.9 Making Inferences

DEFINING THE SKILL

Making inferences from a piece of historical writing means drawing conclusions based on facts, examples, opinions, and the author's use of language. To make inferences, use clues in the text and your own personal experience, historical knowledge, and common sense.

APPLYING THE SKILL

The following passage is from a speech by President Ronald Reagan promoting his economic program. The chart below lists some inferences that can be drawn from the first paragraph.

HOW TO MAKE INFERENCES

Strategy **1** From the facts in the text and historical knowledge, you can infer that Reagan is blaming the Democrats for the poor economy.

Strategy **2** Look for clues about the writer's opinion. From Reagan's language and the goals of his program, you can infer that he sees government spending and taxation as a major cause of the economic crisis.

Strategy **3** Note opinionated language. You can infer from words such as *exaggerated* and *inaccurate* that Reagan disagrees with criticism of his plan.

On the Program for Economic Recovery

1 All of us are aware of the punishing inflation which has for the first time in 60 years held to double-digit figures for 2 years in a row. Interest rates have reached absurd levels of more than 20 percent and over 15 percent for those who would borrow to buy a home. . . . Almost 8 million Americans are out of work. . . .

2 I am proposing a comprehensive four-point program . . . aimed at reducing the growth in government spending and taxing, reforming and eliminating regulations which are unnecessary and unproductive or counterproductive, and encouraging a consistent monetary policy aimed at maintaining the value of the currency.

Now, I know that **3** exaggerated and inaccurate stories about these cuts have disturbed many people. . . . Those who, through no fault of their own, must depend on the rest of us—the poverty stricken, the disabled, the elderly, all those with true need—can rest assured that the social safety net of programs they depend on are exempt from any cuts.

Make a Chart

Record clues in the text as well as what you know about the topic on the basis of your own experience, knowledge, and common sense.

Clues in the Text: Facts, Examples, Language	Personal Experience, Historical Knowledge, Common Sense	Inference
• inflation in double digits • Interest rates over 20% • 8 milion unemployed • Inflation is "punishing" • Interest rates "absurd"	• Reagan defeated Democratic incumbent Jimmy Carter in the 1980 election.	Reagan blames the Democrats for the current economic problems.

PRACTICING THE SKILL

Turn to Chapter 18, Section 3, p. 564 and read the passage headed "The Impact of U.S. Territorial Gains." Create a chart like the one above, making inferences based on clues in the text and on your own personal experience, historical knowledge, and common sense.

2.1 Developing Historical Perspective

DEFINING THE SKILL

Historical perspective is an understanding of events and people in the context of their times. Using historical perspective can help you avoid judging the past solely in terms of present-day norms and values.

APPLYING THE SKILL

The following passage is the opening portion of an address by President Theodore Roosevelt. Below it is a chart that summarizes the information from a historical perspective.

HOW TO DEVELOP HISTORICAL PERSPECTIVE

Strategy ❶ Identify any historical figures, occasions, events, and dates.

Strategy ❷ Notice words, phrases, and settings that reflect the period. Here the language used by the president reflects the optimism of the Progressive Era.

Strategy ❸ Explain how people's actions and words reflect attitudes, values, and passions of the era. Here Roosevelt equates a strong nation with "manly virtues."

Write a Summary

In a chart, list key words, phrases, and details from the passage, and then write a short paragraph summarizing the basic values and attitudes it conveys.

❶ **INAUGURAL ADDRESS, 1905**
President Theodore Roosevelt

My fellow-citizens, no people on earth have more cause to be thankful than ours, and this is said . . . with gratitude to the Giver of Good who has blessed us with the conditions which have enabled us to achieve so large a measure of well-being and happiness. To us as a people it has been granted to lay the foundations of our national life in a ❷ new continent. We are the ❷ heirs of the ages, and yet we have had to pay few of the penalties which in old countries are exacted by the dead hand of a bygone civilization. We have not been obliged to fight for our existence against any alien race; and yet our life has called for the ❸ vigor and effort without which the manlier and hardier virtues wither away. . . . [The] success which we confidently believe the future will bring, should cause in us no feeling of vainglory, but rather a deep and abiding realization of all which life has offered us; a full acknowledgment of the responsibility which is ours; and a fixed determination to show that under a free government a mighty people can thrive best, alike as regards the things of the body and the things of the soul.

Key Phrases	Attitudes	Roosevelt's Inaugural Address
• Giver of Good • blessed us • heirs of the ages • bygone civilization • manlier and hardier virtues • mighty people • things of the body and things of the soul	• belief in God • optimistic about the future • grateful for the past	Theodore Roosevelt reveals a strong and resilient optimism about the American nation. His confidence is grounded in deep religious faith in God (the "Giver of Good") and God's plan for the nation. Roosevelt clearly believes in the ability of the American people to solve whatever problems they face as they move into a bright future. Roosevelt's faith and appeal to the manly virtues reflects typical attitudes and values of the 19th- and early 20th-century Americans.

PRACTICING THE SKILL

Turn to Chapter 16, Section 2, p. 488 and read the One American's Story feature, which discusses ideas about educational reform in the late 19th century. Use historical perspective to summarize those ideas in a chart like the one above.

2.2 Formulating Historical Questions

DEFINING THE SKILL

Formulating historical questions entails asking questions about events and trends—what caused them, what made them important, and so forth. The ability to formulate historical questions is an important step in doing research. Formulating questions will help you to guide and focus your research as well as to understand maps, graphs, and other historical sources.

APPLYING THE SKILL

At a women's rights convention in the mid-1800s, the delegates adopted a "Declaration of Sentiments" that set forth a number of grievances. The following passage is a description of that event. Below is a web diagram that organizes historical questions about the event.

HOW TO FORMULATE HISTORICAL QUESTIONS

Strategy ❶ Ask about the basic facts of the event. Who were the leaders? What did they do? Where and when did the event take place?

Strategy ❷ Ask about the cause of an event. Why did an event take place?

Strategy ❸ Ask about historical influences on a speaker or event. What other historical events was it similar to? How was it different?

Strategy ❹ Ask about the results produced by various causes. What were the results of the event?

Seneca Falls, 1848

❶ Elizabeth Cady Stanton and Lucretia Mott decided to act on their resolution to hold a women's rights convention. In 1848, more than 300 women and men convened at Seneca Falls, New York, the small town that gave the convention its name. Before the convention, Stanton and Mott spent a day composing an agenda and a ❷ detailed statement of grievances. Stanton carefully modeled this "Declaration of Sentiments" on the ❸ Declaration of Independence. ❹ The participants approved all measures unanimously, except for one: women's right to vote. This measure passed by a narow margin due to Stanton's insistence. The franchise for women, though it passed, remained a controversial topic.

Make a Web Diagram

Using a web diagram, ask a broad question about the event described above. Then ask specific questions to help you explore the first.

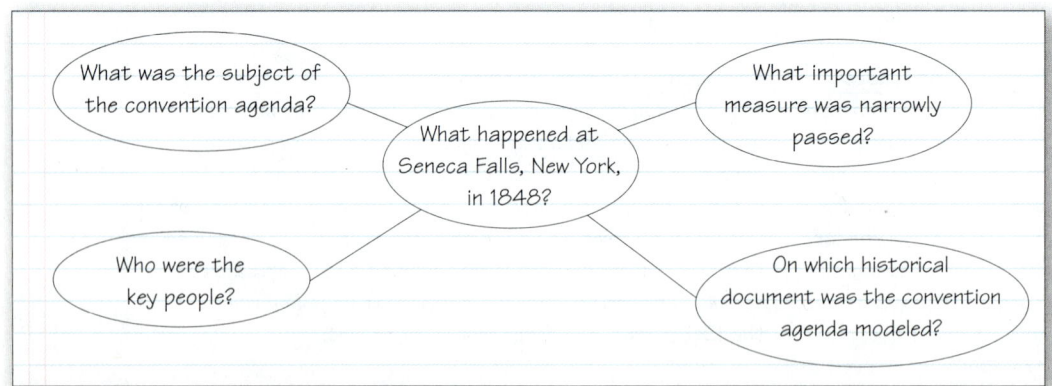

PRACTICING THE SKILL

Turn to Chapter 30, Section 1, p. 940 and read the passage headed "The Tonkin Gulf Resolution." Use a web diagram to write a historical question about the passage, as well as more specific questions that could guide your research into the topic.

2.3 Hypothesizing

DEFINING THE SKILL

Hypothesizing means developing a possible explanation for historical events. A hypothesis is a tentative assumption about what happened in the past or what might happen in the future. A hypothesis takes available information, links it to previous experience and knowledge, and comes up with a possible explanation, conclusion, or prediction.

APPLYING THE SKILL

As the Cold War came to an end, people offered various hypotheses to explain why the Soviet Union broke up and to predict what would replace it. Read this passage and form your own hypothesis. Below the passage is a chart that presents a hypothesis and the facts used to support it.

HOW TO FORM A HYPOTHESIS

Strategy 1 Identify the events, pattern, or trend you want to explain. Develop a hypothesis that might explain the event. You might hypothesize that Gorbachev's new policies would deeply affect politics in the Soviet Union and Eastern Europe.

Strategy 2 Determine what facts you have about the situation. These facts support various hypotheses about how Gorbachev's policies affected politics both inside and outside the Soviet Union.

The Cold War Ends

In March 1985, Mikhail Gorbachev became the general secretary of the Communist Party in the Soviet Union. **1** He initiated a new policy of openness and reform within the USSR, putting an end to the collective ownership of resources, most government censorship, and controlled elections. **2** A dramatic increase in nationalism on the part of the non-Russian republics followed the open elections, and in December 1991, all republics except Russia declared independence. **2** The USSR was replaced by a loose federation of 12 republics called the Commonwealth of Independent States. **2** Gorbachev's new policies led to massive changes in Eastern Europe, as the satellite states, with his encouragement, moved toward democracy.

Make a Chart

Use a chart to summarize your hypothesis about Gorbachev's reforms and the facts that support it. Then you can see what additional information you need to help prove or disprove it.

Hypothesis	Facts that support the hypothesis	Additional information needed
Gorbachev's new policies would help lead to Western victory in the Cold War.	• increase in nationalism in non-Russian republics • USSR replaced by a loose federation • Satellite states moved towards democracy	• Were democratic reforms put into effect? • Did free elections result in greater stability? • Did the end of collective ownership advance private enterprise?

PRACTICING THE SKILL

Turn to Chapter 32, Section 2, p. 1009 and read the passage headed "A Bungled Burglary." Make a chart in which you hypothesize about the consequences of the burglary at the Democratic National Committee headquarters. Then list facts and indicate whether they support your hypothesis.

2.4 Analyzing Issues

DEFINING THE SKILL

Analyzing issues in history means taking apart complicated issues to identify the different points of view in economic, social, political, or moral debates.

APPLYING THE SKILL

The following passage describes working conditions in U.S. factories in the late 1800s and early 1900s. Notice how the cluster diagram below it helps you to analyze the issue of child labor.

HOW TO ANALYZE ISSUES

Strategy **1** Identify the central point of view and how it is defended.

Strategy **2** Look for facts and statistics. The numbers supplied by facts and statistics can help you decide on a position.

Strategy **3** Look for the other side to an issue. You need to look at all sides of an issue before deciding what you think.

Children at Work

1 Wages for most factory workers were so low that many families could not survive unless all their members, including children, worked. **2** Between 1890 and 1910, 20 percent of boys and 10 percent of girls under age 15—some as young as five years old—held full-time jobs. **2** A typical work week was 12 hours a day, six days a week. Many of these children worked from dawn to dusk, wasted by hunger and exhaustion that made them prone to crippling accidents. With little time or energy left for school, child laborers gave up their futures to help their families make ends meet.

3 Nonetheless, factory owners and some parents praised child labor for keeping children out of mischief. They believed that idleness for children was bad and that work provided healthy occupation. Meanwhile, the reformer Jacob Riis and others worked for decent conditions, better wages, and laws that restricted child labor.

Make a Cluster Diagram

In order to better analyze an issue, make a diagram and distinguish the facts as well as the different points of view.

Issue: Should children under 15 have been allowed to work?

Facts:
- Children as young as 5 years old worked.
- 20 percent of boys and 10 percent of girls under 15 held jobs.
- Workers typically put in 72 hours per week.
- Working conditions in many industries were strenuous, exhausting, and dangerous.

In favor of children working:

Who: business owners, some parents

Reasons: Idleness was bad. Working was good for children, and families needed income.

Against children working:

Who: Jacob Riis and other reformers

Reasons: Working meant giving up school. Conditions were inhumane.

PRACTICING THE SKILL

Read the passages headed "The Equal Rights Amendment (ERA)" and "The New Right Emerges" in Chapter 31, Section 2, p. 985. Make a cluster diagram to analyze the central issue and the positions of the people involved.

2.5 Analyzing Assumptions and Biases

DEFINING THE SKILL

An **assumption** is a belief or an idea that is taken for granted. Some assumptions are based on evidence; some are based on feelings. A **bias** is a prejudiced point of view. Historical accounts that are biased reflect the personal prejudices of the author or historian and tend to be one-sided.

APPLYING THE SKILL

The following passage is from *The Americans at Home* by the Scottish minister David Macrae, who wrote the book after visiting the United States in the 1860s. The chart below the excerpt helps to summarize information about the writer's assumptions and biases.

HOW TO ANALYZE ASSUMPTIONS AND BIASES

Strategy 1 Identify the author and information about him or her. Does the author belong to a special-interest group, religious organization, political party, or social movement that might promote a one-sided or slanted viewpoint on the subject?

Strategy 2 Examine the evidence. Is what the author relates consistent with other accounts or supported by factual data?

Strategy 3 Look for words, phrases, statements, or images that might convey a positive or negative slant, and thus reveal the author's bias.

The Americans at Home
1 by David Macrae
[T]he American girls are very delightful. **2** And in one point they fairly surpass the majority of English girls—they are all educated and well informed. . . . The admirable educational system . . . covering the whole area of society, has given them education whether they are rich or poor, has furnished them with a great deal of information, and has quickened their desire for more. . . . **3** Their tendency is perhaps to talk too much, and . . . it seemed to me sometimes to make no perceptible difference whether they knew anything of the subject they talked about or not. But they usually know a little of everything; and their general intelligence and vivacity make them very delightful companions.

Make a Chart
For each of the heads listed on the left-hand side of the chart, summarize what information you can find in the passage.

David Macrae's Impression of American Girls	
speaker	David Macrae
date	1860s
occasion	Macrae's visit to the United States
tone	humorous, light-hearted
assumptions	The author assumes that girls are to be measured by companionship abilities.
bias	The author seems to have a prejudice that girls are inferior to boys or men.

PRACTICING THE SKILL

Look at the opinions expressed by A. Mitchell Palmer in the feature A Personal Voice in Chapter 20, Section 1, p. 619. Summarize his underlying assumptions and biases in a chart like the one shown above.

2.6 Evaluating Decisions and Courses of Action

DEFINING THE SKILL

Evaluating decisions means making judgments about the decisions that historical figures made. Historians evaluate decisions on the basis of their moral implications and their costs and benefits from different points of view. **Evaluating alternative courses** of action means carefully judging the choices that historical figures had in order to better understand why they made the decisions they did.

APPLYING THE SKILL

The following passage describes the decisions President John F. Kennedy had to make when he learned of Soviet missile bases in Cuba. Below the passage is a chart in which one possible alternative decision is analyzed.

HOW TO EVALUATE DECISIONS

Strategy ❶ Look at decisions made by individuals or by groups. Notice the decisions Kennedy made in response to Soviet actions.

Strategy ❷ Look at the outcome of the decisions.

Strategy ❸ Analyze a decision in terms of the alternatives that were possible. Both Kennedy and Khrushchev faced the alternatives of either escalating or defusing the crisis.

Make a Chart

Make a chart evaluating an alternative course of action regarding the Cuban missile crisis based on its possible pros and cons.

The Cuban Missile Crisis

During the summer of 1962, the flow of Soviet weapons into Cuba—including nuclear missiles—greatly increased. ❶ President Kennedy responded cautiously at first, issuing a warning that the United States would not tolerate the presence of offensive nuclear weapons in Cuba.

❶ On the evening of October 22, after the president learned that the Soviets were building missile bases in Cuba, he delivered a public ultimatum: any missile attack from Cuba would trigger an all-out attack on the Soviet Union. Soviet ships continued to head toward the island, while the U.S. military prepared to invade Cuba. To avoid confrontation, ❷ the Soviet premier, Khrushchev, offered to remove the missiles from Cuba in exchange for a pledge not to invade the island. Kennedy agreed, and the crisis ended.

❸ Some people criticized Kennedy for practicing brinkmanship when private talks might have resolved the crisis without the threat of nuclear war. Others believed he had been too soft and had passed up an ideal chance to invade Cuba and to oust its communist leader, Fidel Castro.

---

alternative	pros	cons	evaluation
Negotiate a settlement quietly without threatening nuclear war.	1. Avoid the threat of nuclear war 2. Avoid frightening U.S. citizens	1. The U.S. would not look like a strong world leader. 2. The government would lose favor with Cuban exiles living in the U.S.	your answer: Would this have been a good choice? Why or why not?

PRACTICING THE SKILL

Turn to Chapter 25, Section 3, p. 789 and read the passage headed "The Atomic Bomb Ends the War." Evaluate the U.S. decision to drop the bomb. Make a chart like the one shown to summarize the pros and cons of an alternative decision, and then write an evaluation of that decision.

2.7 Forming Opinions (Evaluating)

DEFINING THE SKILL

Forming opinions, or evaluating, means deciding what your own thoughts or feelings are and making judgments about events and people in history. Opinions should be supported with facts and examples.

APPLYING THE SKILL

The following passage includes comments on the French Revolution by Gouverneur Morris, one of the participants in the Constitutional Convention, and by Thomas Jefferson.

HOW TO FORM AN OPINION AND SUPPORT IT WITH FACTS

Strategy 1 Decide what you think about a subject after reading all the information available to you. After reading this description, you might decide that political causes either do or do not sometimes justify violence.

Strategy 2 Support your opinion with facts, quotations, and examples, including references to similar events in other historical eras.

Strategy 3 Look for the opinions of historians and other experts. Consider their opinions when forming your own.

A Scene of Mob Violence

Gouverneur Morris was a visitor to Paris during the early days of the French Revolution. In the following journal entry he describes a scene of revolutionary mob violence: **1** "The head and body of Mr. de Foulon are introduced in triumph. . . . His crime [was] to have accepted a place in the Ministry. This mutilated form of an old man of seventy-five is shown to Bertier, his son-in-law, the intend't. [another official] of Paris, and afterwards **2** he also is put to death and cut to pieces. . . ." Such violence was common during the French Revolution and shocked a good many Americans. **3** However, Thomas Jefferson was a supporter of the Revolution, saying, "The liberty of the whole earth was depending on the issue of the contest, and . . . rather than it should have failed, I would have seen half the earth desolated."

Make a Chart

Summarize your opinion and supporting information in a chart. List facts, quotations, and examples.

Opinion: The French Revolution was especially violent and cruel.

facts:	quotations:	examples:
• Violence escalated.	"he also is put to death and cut to pieces"	Jacobins beheaded Louis XVI
• Jacobins launched Reign of Terror.		
• Moderates sent to guillotine.		
• Jacobins declared war on other countries.		

PRACTICING THE SKILL

Read the Point/Counterpoint feature in Chapter 23, Section 5, p. 722. Form your own opinion about the success or failure of the New Deal. Record your opinion in a chart like the one shown, and provide supporting information to back it up.

2.8 Drawing Conclusions

DEFINING THE SKILL

Drawing conclusions involves considering the implications of what you have read and forming a final statement about its meaning or consequences. To draw conclusions, you need to look closely at facts and then use your own experience and common sense to decide what those facts mean.

APPLYING THE SKILL

The following passage tells about employment trends in the 1990s. The highlighted text indicates information from which conclusions can be drawn. In the diagram below, the information and conclusions are organized in a clear way.

HOW TO DRAW CONCLUSIONS

Strategy ① Use the facts to draw a conclusion. Conclusion: In general, the economy was good in the mid-1990s.

Strategy ② Read carefully to understand all the facts. Conclusion: Income expectations were lower.

Strategy ③ Ask questions of the material. How did the use of temporary workers affect job security? (It reduced it.) What did employment statistics for young people indicate? (Jobs were harder for young people to find.)

Make a Diagram

Summarize the data and your conclusion about the above passage in a diagram.

Job Outlook in the Mid-1990s

Several trends emerged in the workplace of the 1990s. ① Inflation was at its lowest level since the 1960s, and 10 million new jobs created between 1993 and 1996 helped lower the unemployment rate to 5.1 percent in 1996. ② Median household income adjusted for inflation, however, declined from $33,585 to $31,241, even though there were many households in which both parents worked.

In addition, ③ many jobs once done by permanent employees of a company were done by temporary workers, who were paid only for the time they were needed and who typically received no benefits. Three out of four young Americans thought they would earn less in their lifetimes than their parents did. Unemployment in their age group continued at the same rate, while the unemployment rate for other adults had fallen. ③ In 1993, about one in seven workers between the ages of 16 and 25 was out of work, double the national average.

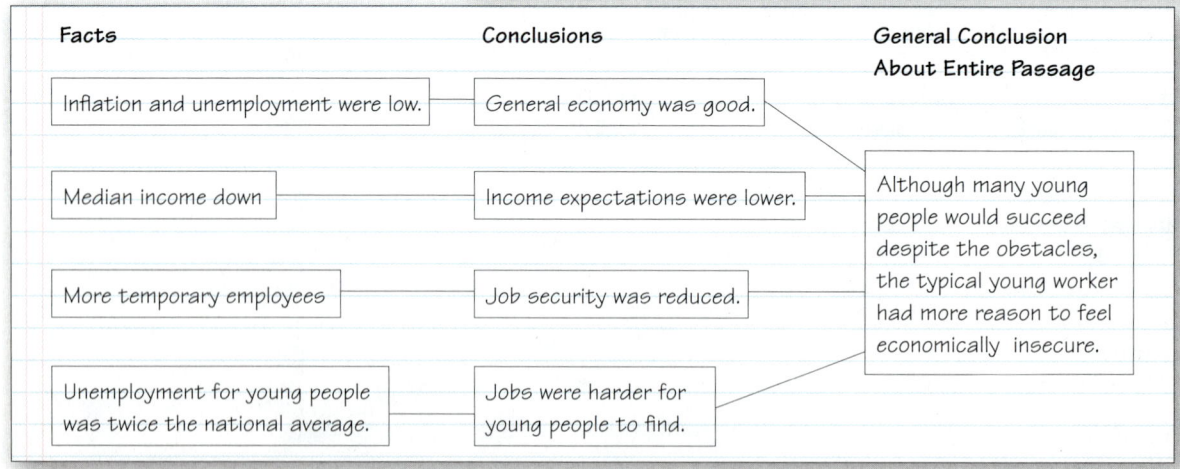

Facts	Conclusions	General Conclusion About Entire Passage
Inflation and unemployment were low.	General economy was good.	Although many young people would succeed despite the obstacles, the typical young worker had more reason to feel economically insecure.
Median income down	Income expectations were lower.	
More temporary employees	Job security was reduced.	
Unemployment for young people was twice the national average.	Jobs were harder for young people to find.	

PRACTICING THE SKILL

Turn to Chapter 34, Section 4, p. 1090 and read the passage headed "The Aging of America." Draw conclusions based on the facts in the passage. Using the model as a guide, create your own diagram, showing the facts and conclusions you have used to arrive at a general conclusion.

2.9 Synthesizing

DEFINING THE SKILL

Synthesizing is the skill historians use in developing interpretations of the past. Like detective work, synthesizing involves putting together clues, information, and ideas to form an overall picture of a historical event.

APPLYING THE SKILL

The following passage describes the earliest inhabitants of the Americas. The high-lighted text indicates how some information leads toward a synthesis—an overall picture.

HOW TO SYNTHESIZE

Strategy ❶ Read carefully to understand the facts.

Strategy ❷ Look for explanations that link the facts together. This assertion is based on the evidence provided in the next couple of sentences.

Strategy ❸ Consider what you already know in order to accept statements as reasonable.

Strategy ❹ Bring together the information you have gathered to arrive at a new understanding of the subject.

The First Americans

From the ❶ discovery of chiseled arrowheads and charred bones at ancient sites, it appears that the earliest Americans lived as big-game hunters. ❷ People gradually shifted to hunting smaller game and gathering available plants. They collected nuts and wild rice. They invented snares, as well as bows and arrows, to hunt small animals, and they wove nets to catch fish.

Between 10,000 and 15,000 years ago, a revolution took place in what is now central Mexico. ❸ People began to raise plants as food. Maize may have been the first domesticated plant. Agriculture eventually spread to other regions.

The rise of agriculture brought tremendous changes to the Americas. Agriculture made it possible for people to remain in one place. It also enabled them to accumulate and store surplus food. As their surplus increased, people had the time to develop skills and more complex ideas about the world. ❹ From this agricultural base rose larger, more stable, and increasingly complex societies.

Make a Cluster Diagram

Use a cluster diagram to organize the facts, opinions, examples, and interpretations that you have brought together to form a synthesis.

Earliest Americans were big-game hunters.

Agriculture allowed people to settle and to develop new skills and ideas.

Synthesis: The shift from hunting and gathering to agriculture allowed for the development of more complex societies in the Americas.

shifted to hunting/gathering

Agriculture began in Mexico.

Agriculture spread to other regions.

PRACTICING THE SKILL

Turn to Chapter 21, Section 2, p. 647 and read "Women Shed Old Roles at Home and at Work." Look for information to support a synthesis about the fundamental changes in the family brought about by women's new opportunities.

2.10 Making Predictions

DEFINING THE SKILL

Making predictions entails identifying situations that leaders or groups face or have faced in the past, and then suggesting what course of action they might take as well as what might happen as a result of that action. Making predictions about the effects of past events helps you to understand how events in the past shape the future. Making predictions about the effects of proposed actions, such as proposed legislation, helps you to evaluate possible courses of action.

APPLYING THE SKILL

The following passage discusses the central weaknesses of the Treaty of Versailles, which ended World War I. Below the passage is a chart that lists decisions made by those who framed the treaty, along with alternative decisions and predictions of possible outcomes.

HOW TO MAKE PREDICTIONS

Strategy **1** Identify the decisions.

Strategy **2** Decide what other decisions might have been made.

Strategy **3** Predict the outcomes of the alternative decisions.

Make a Chart

Record decisions made as well as alternative decisions and possible outcomes.

Weaknesses of the Treaty of Versailles

1 First, the treaty humiliated Germany. The war-guilt clause, which forced Germany to accept blame for the war and pay financial reparations, caused Germans of all political viewpoints to detest the treaty.

2 Second, Russia, which had fought with the Allies, was excluded from the peace conference. Russia had suffered almost the same number of casualties as Germany—the two countries had by far the highest casualty rates of the war. Russia lost more territory than Germany did. The Union of Soviet Socialist Republics, as Russia was called after 1922, grew determined to regain its lost territory.

3 Third, the treaty ignored the claims of colonized people for self-determination. For example, the Allies dismissed the claims of the Vietnamese, who wanted freedom from French colonial rule.

Decision: The treaty included a war-guilt clause.	**Decision:** Russia was excluded from the peace conference.	**Decision:** Treaty ignored the claims of colonized peoples.
Alternative decision: The treaty had no war-guilt clause.	**Alternative decision:** Russia was included in the peace negotiations.	**Alternative decision:** The treaty respected the claims of colonized peoples.
Possible outcome: Germany rebuilds. World War II does not occur.	**Possible outcome:** Tension between the Soviet Union and the West decreases.	**Possible outcome:** Tensions are reduced worldwide; Vietnam War is averted.

PRACTICING THE SKILL

Turn to Chapter 34, Section 1, p. 1068 and read the passage "Reforming Welfare." Make a chart like the one above in which you identify provisions of the welfare reform law, alternative provisions that might have been included, and their possible outcomes. Consider how the effects of each law might change depending on the health of the nation's economy.

2.11 Forming Generalizations

DEFINING THE SKILL

Forming generalizations means making broad judgments based on the information in texts. When you form generalizations, you need to be sure they are valid. They must be based on sufficient evidence, and they must be consistent with the information given.

APPLYING THE SKILL

The following three excerpts deal with Herbert Hoover and his relation to the Great Depression. Notice how the information in the web diagram below supports the generalization drawn.

HOW TO FORM GENERALIZATIONS

Strategy **1** Determine what information the sources have in common. All the sources suggest that people blamed Hoover for the Great Depression.

Strategy **2** State your generalization in sentence form. A generalization often needs a qualifying word, such as *most*, *many*, or *some*, to make it valid.

On President Hoover and the Great Depression

1 "By 1930, people were calling the shantytowns in American cities Hoovervilles. . . . Homeless people called the newspapers in which they wrapped themselves 'Hoover blankets.' Empty pockets turned inside out were 'Hoover flags.'"

—*The Americans*

"[My aunt] told me . . . . **1** People were starving because of Herbert Hoover. My mother was out of work because of Herbert Hoover. Men were killing themselves because of Herbert Hoover."

—Russell Baker

1 "If someone bit an apple and found a worm in it, Hoover would get the blame."

—Will Rogers

Make a Web Diagram

Use a web diagram to record relevant information and make a valid generalization.

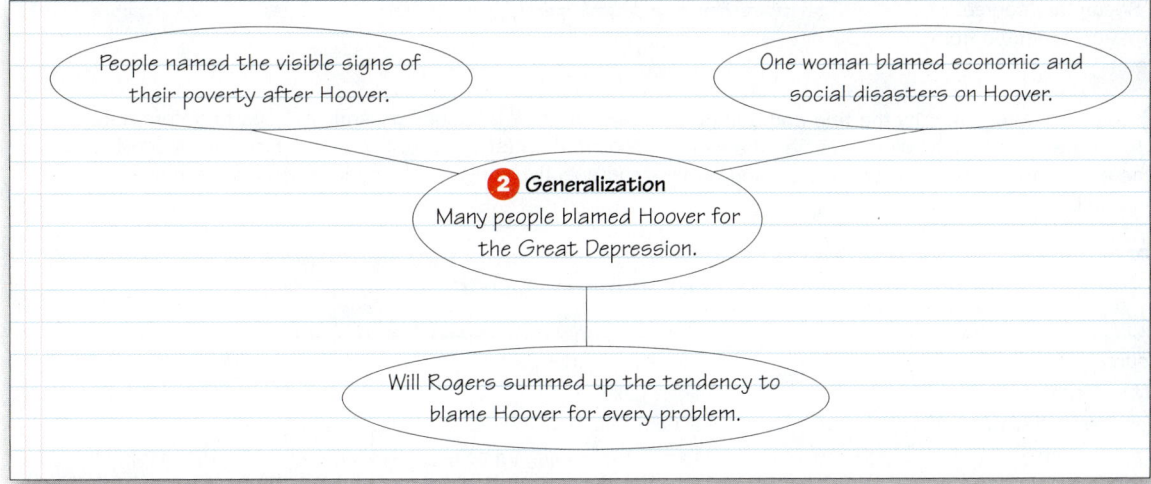

People named the visible signs of their poverty after Hoover.

One woman blamed economic and social disasters on Hoover.

2 Generalization
Many people blamed Hoover for the Great Depression.

Will Rogers summed up the tendency to blame Hoover for every problem.

PRACTICING THE SKILL

Study the Daily Life feature "Signs of the Sixties" in Chapter 31, p. 992. Create a diagram like the one above to make a generalization about teenagers during the 1960s. Use information from textual and visual sources to support your generalization.

3.1 Primary and Secondary Sources

DEFINING THE SKILL

Primary sources are accounts written or created by people who were present at historical events, either as participants or as observers. These include letters, diaries, journals, speeches, some news articles, eyewitness accounts, government data, statutes, court opinions, and autobiographies.

Secondary sources are based on primary sources and are produced by people who were not present at the original events. They often combine information from a number of different accounts. Secondary sources include history books, historical essays, some news articles, and biographies.

APPLYING THE SKILL

The following passage describes the explosion of the first atomic bomb in 1945. It is mainly a secondary source, but it quotes an eyewitness account that is a primary source.

HOW TO LOCATE AND IDENTIFY PRIMARY AND SECONDARY SOURCES

Strategy ❶ Locating sources: The catalog in your school library or a local public library lists resources alphabetically by subject, title, and author. Most of these are secondary sources but may contain copies or excerpts of primary sources. Articles in a general encyclopedia such as *World Book* or *Encyclopedia Americana* can give you an overview of a topic and usually provide references to additional sources.

Strategy ❷ Secondary source: Look for information collected from several sources.

Strategy ❸ Primary source: Identify the title and author and evaluate his or her credentials. What qualifies the writer to report on the event? Here the writer actually worked on developing the bomb.

❶ **The First Atomic Bomb**

As the time to test the bomb drew near, the air around Los Alamos crackled with rumors and fears. ❷ At one end of the scale were fears that the bomb wouldn't work at all. At the other end was the prediction that the explosion would set fire to the atmosphere, which would mean the end of the earth.

On July 16, 1945, the first atomic bomb was detonated in the desert near Alamogordo, New Mexico. ❸ In his book *What Little I Remember*, Otto Frisch, a Manhattan Project scientist, described what happened next:

"[T]hat object on the horizon which looked like a small sun was still too bright to look at. . . . After another ten seconds or so it had grown and . . . was slowly rising into the sky from the ground, with which it remained connected by a lengthening grey stem of swirling dust. . . ."

❹ That blinding flash was followed by a deafening roar as a tremendous shock wave rolled across the trembling desert. The bomb not only worked, but it was more powerful than most had dared hope.

Strategy ❹ Secondary source: Look for information collected after the event. A secondary source provides a perspective that is missing in a primary source.

Make a Chart

Summarize information from primary and secondary sources in a chart.

Primary Source	Secondary Source
Author: Otto Frisch	Author: unknown
Qualifications: scientist working on Manhattan Project	Qualifications: had access to multiple accounts of the time leading up to and following event
Information: detailed description, sensory observations, feeling of awe	Information: description of range of points of view and of information available only after event

PRACTICING THE SKILLS

Turn to Chapter 33, Section 1, p. 1036, and read the One American's Story feature, which includes a quotation. Use a chart like the one above to summarize information from the primary and secondary sources.

3.2 Visual, Audio, Multimedia Sources

DEFINING THE SKILL

Visual sources can be paintings, illustrations, photographs, political cartoons, and advertisements. **Audio sources** include recorded speeches, interviews, press conferences, and radio programs. Movies, CD-ROMs, television, and computer software are the newest kind of historical sources, called **multimedia sources.** These sources are rich with historical details and sometimes convey the feelings and points of view of an era better than words do.

APPLYING THE SKILL

The following photograph shows a group of college students and civil rights activists joined in song as they protest unfair voting laws in 1964.

1 In the summer of 1964, college students volunteered to go to Mississippi to help register that state's African-American voters.

HOW TO INTERPRET VISUAL SOURCES

Strategy ❶ Identify the subject and the source. A title or caption often gives a description of a photo or other visual source. This photograph shows volunteers who worked in the 1964 voting rights drive in Mississippi.

Strategy ❷ Identify important visual details. In this photograph, white and black college students are holding hands and singing. Behind them is a bus.

Strategy ❸ Make inferences from the visual details. Holding hands and singing together suggest fellowship and unity—the students are showing solidarity in the fight for civil rights.

Make a Chart

Summarize your interpretation of the photograph in a simple chart.

PRACTICING THE SKILL

Turn to the photograph in Chapter 29, Section 2, p. 918, showing police dogs in Birmingham, Alabama, attacking African Americans. Use a chart like the one at the right to analyze and interpret the photograph.

Subject	A diverse group of college students.
Details	Bus, joined hands, white and black Americans side by side, singing
Inferences	The subjects share a belief in racial equality, freedom, and solidarity. Some or all of the group may have traveled to Mississippi together on the bus.

3.3 Analyzing Political Cartoons

DEFINING THE SKILL

Political cartoons use humor to make a serious point. Political cartoons often express a point of view on an issue better than words do. Understanding signs and symbols will help you to interpret political cartoons.

Like many text sources that express a point of view, cartoons are often **biased,** or unfairly weighted toward one point of view. To identify a cartoon's bias, look for exaggerations and caricature. Try to restate the message of the cartoon in words, then identify overgeneralizations and opinions stated as facts.

APPLYING THE SKILL

The following political cartoon shows President Calvin Coolidge playing the saxophone while big business dances. The chart below it summarizes historical information gained from interpreting the visual source.

HOW TO INTERPRET VISUAL SOURCES

Strategy ① Identify the subject. This cartoon deals with President Calvin Coolidge's relationship with big business.

Strategy ② Identify important symbols and details. Big business is shown as a carefree flapper of the 1920s. The president's saxophone is labeled "Praise," suggesting his positive attitude toward the fun-loving flapper.

Strategy ③ Interpret the message. The image implies that serving big business interests is important to the president.

Strategy ④ Analyze the point of view. The cartoonist suggests that the relationship between the president and big business is too cozy.

Strategy ⑤ Identify bias. The president is caricatured by being depicted engaging in frivolity and at the service of big business. The cartoon charges that the president does not take his responsibilities seriously.

Make a Chart

Summarize your interpretation of the cartoon in a simple chart.

Subject: Coolidge's Relationship with big business		
Point of View	Symbols/Details	Message
Satirical of the Coolidge administration and of big business	Flapper: big business, carefree and overgrown	Big business and the president are too close.
	President: playing a tune for business	Business is having too good a time—with the president's help.

PRACTICING THE SKILL

Turn to the political cartoon on p. 699, which presents an opinion about Franklin D. Roosevelt's New Deal programs. Use a chart like the one above to analyze and interpret the cartoon.

3.4 Interpreting Maps

DEFINING THE SKILL

Maps are representations of features on the earth's surface. Historians use maps to locate historical events, to demonstrate how geography has influenced history, and to illustrate patterns and distributions of human activity and its environmental effects.

Political maps show political units, from countries, states, and provinces to counties, districts, and towns. **Physical maps** show mountains, hills, plains, rivers, lakes, and oceans. They may include elevations of land and depths of water. **Historical maps** illustrate such things as economic activity, political alliances, migrations, battles, and population density. While reading maps, historians pose questions and use the following features to find answers:

A **compass rose** indicates the map's orientation on the globe. It may show all four cardinal directions (N, S, E, W) or just one, north.

Lines indicate boundaries between political areas, roads and highways, routes of exploration or migration, and rivers and other waterways. Lines may vary in width and color.

Symbols or icons represent real objects or events. Cities, towns, and villages often appear as dots. A capital city is often shown as a star within a circle. An area's products or resources may be indicated by symbols. Battles are often shown by starbursts, troop movements by arrows.

Labels designate key places, such as cities, states, bodies of water, and events.

Lines of longitude and latitude appear on maps to indicate the absolute location of the area shown. Lines of latitude show distance north or south of the equator, measured in degrees. Lines of longitude show distance in degrees east or west of the prime meridian, which runs through Greenwich, England.

A **legend or key** is a small table in which the symbols, types of lines, and special colors that appear in the map are listed and explained.

Sometimes **colors** are used to indicate areas under different political or cultural influence. Colors and **shading** are also used to show distributions, patterns, and such features as altitudes.

A **map's scale** shows the ratio between a unit of length on the map and a unit of distance on the earth. A typical scale shows a one-inch segment and indicates the number of miles that length represents on the map. A map on which an inch represents 500 miles has a scale of 1:31,680,000.

Continued on page R26.

Revolutionary War, 1775–1778

Distributions on a map are where certain symbols, such as those for cities, fall. Sometimes distributions show patterns, such as a cluster, a line, or a wide circle. On this map, for example, the battle symbols show a pattern of being fought near rivers or ports.

APPLYING THE SKILL

The historical maps below show land claims in Europe in 1915 and 1923.
Together they show the political effects of World War I.

HOW TO INTERPRET A HISTORICAL MAP

Strategy ❶ Look at the map's title to learn the subject and purpose of the map. Here the maps show Europe before and after World War I. Pose a historical question about the subject of the map, such as "How were old empires divided and new countries formed?"

Strategy ❷ Use the legend to interpret the map in order to answer your historical question. The legend tells you what the symbols and colors on the map mean.

Strategy ❸ Look at the scale and compass rose. The scale shows you what distances are represented. On these maps, 1.4 cm represents 500 miles. The compass rose shows you which direction on the map is north.

Strategy ❹ Find where the map area is located on the earth. These maps span a large area from the Arctic Circle to below latitude 30° N, and from 10° W to 40° E.

Make a Chart

Relate the map to the five geographic themes by making a chart. The five themes
are described on p. xv. In your chart, also analyze distributions and find patterns.

Location:	Place:	Region:	Movement:	Human-Environment Interaction:
Europe and the Middle East; from the Arctic Circle to below 30° North and from 10° West to 40° East	A continent that is a peninsula surrounded by the Mediterranean Sea, the Atlantic Ocean, the North Sea, as well as western-most Asia	The old empires of the Central Powers are distributed within Central Europe and the Middle East. The new nations and mandates are in Eastern Europe and the Middle East.	Political boundaries shifted after the war. New nations and mandates were established.	The new boundaries fall along rivers, bodies of water, and mountain ranges. There is a pattern. The pattern shows that the new countries form a narrow strip from North to South.

PRACTICING THE SKILL

Study the maps titled "D-Day, June 6, 1944" on p. 781. Make a chart like the
one shown above, in which you summarize what the maps show.

3.5 Interpreting Charts

DEFINING THE SKILL

Charts are visual presentations of material. Historians use charts to organize, simplify, and summarize information in a way that makes it more meaningful or memorable.

Simple charts are used to consolidate or compare information. **Tables** are used to organize numbers, percentages, or other information into columns and rows for easy reference. Diagrams provide visual clues to the meaning of the information they contain. Illustrated diagrams are sometimes called **infographics.**

APPLYING THE SKILL

The following diagram gives a visual representation of how the economy functions. The paragraph below summarizes the information contained in the diagram.

HOW TO INTERPRET CHARTS

Strategy ① Identify the symbols. Here the symbols represent individuals, producers, government, and the product market.

Strategy ② Look for the main idea. The arrows show the cycle of supply and demand in a free enterprise system of economy. Here individuals are at the top of the chart, indicating that they begin the cycle by creating a demand for goods and services.

Strategy ③ Follow the arrows to study the chart. Read the description of each image in the diagram. Together, the images show the flow of economic activity from producers to individuals and back. The government affects the cycle by regulating and stabilizing economic activity.

The Economy

- Create demand
- Offer labor

Individuals

Supplies goods

Demand goods

Product Market

Producers

- Sells goods and services
- Hires labor

- Create goods
- Hire labor

Send goods to market

Government

- Collects taxes
- Offers services
- Regulates economy
- Equalizes distribution of wealth

Write a Summary

Write a paragraph to summarize what you learned from the diagram.

> Individuals want or need products or services. Producers try to fulfill that demand by hiring workers (labor) to produce the good or service. Producers then make the goods and services available for sale on the market. During this process, the government regulates economic activity and equalizes the distribution of wealth, among other functions. Once goods are sent to stores or other distribution centers, people must be hired (labor) to sell the goods.

PRACTICING THE SKILL

Turn to Chapter 14, Section 3, p. 448, and study the chart titled "Vertical and Horizontal Integration." Write a paragraph in which you summarize what you learned from the chart. Tell how the process of vertical integration works, and describe how it is different from horizontal integration.

3.6 Interpreting Graphs

DEFINING THE SKILL

Graphs show statistical information in a visual manner. Historians use graphs to visualize and compare amounts, ratios, economic trends, and changes over time.

Line graphs typically show quantities on the vertical axis (up the left side) and time in various units on the horizontal axis (across the bottom). **Pie graphs** are useful for showing relative proportions. The circle represents the whole and the slices represent the parts belonging to various subgroups. **Bar graphs** are commonly used to display information about quantities.

PRACTICING THE SKILL

The image below shows a double line graph. The lines show the rate of inflation as compared with the rate of unemployment from 1970 to 1980.

HOW TO INTERPRET A GRAPH

Strategy ❶ Read the title to identify the main idea of the graph. When two subjects are shown, such as unemployment and inflation, the graph will probably show a relationship between them.

Strategy ❷ Read the vertical and horizontal axes of the graph. The horizontal axis shows years, and the vertical axis gives percents.

Strategy ❸ Look at the legend. Find out what each symbol in the graph represents. In this graph the gold line represents the inflation rate and the purple line represents the unemployment rate.

Strategy ❹ Summarize the information shown in each part of the graph. What trends do you see in the line graph over certain years? When did unemployment rise and fall? What about inflation? What can you infer from the patterns?

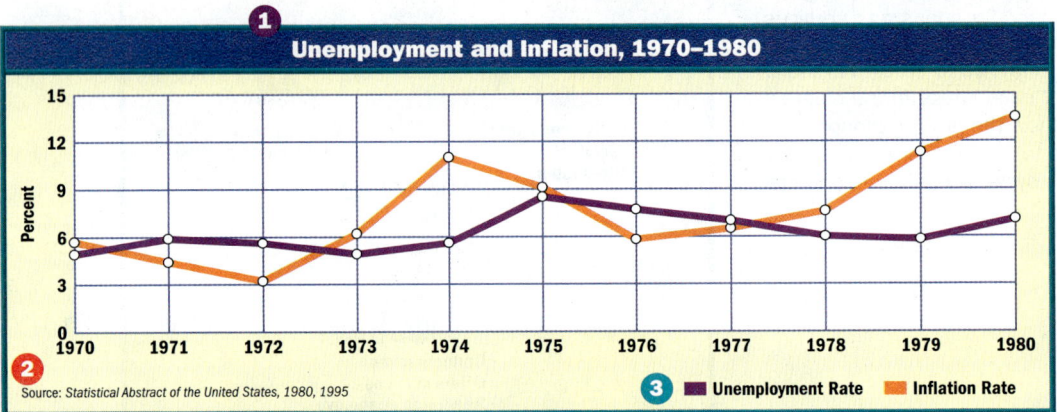

Write a Summary

Write a paragraph to summarize what you learned from the graph.

> Unemployment declined between 1976 and 1979 but rose between 1974 and 1975, while inflation declined between 1975 and 1976 and rose in the periods 1973–1974 and 1977–1980. From the graph it appears that unemployment rises or falls following inflation rate changes, but less dramatically.

PRACTICING THE SKILL

Turn to Chapter 27, Section 3, p. 859, and look at the two graphs titled "Glued to the Set." Study the graphs and write a paragraph in which you summarize what you learned from them. Explain how the two line graphs work together.

3.7 Using the Internet

DEFINING THE SKILL

The **Internet** is a network of computers associated with universities, libraries, news organizations, government agencies, businesses, and private individuals worldwide. Every page of information on the Internet has its own address, or **URL.**

The international collection of sites known as the **World Wide Web** is a source of information about current events as well as research on historical subjects. This textbook contains many suggestions for using the World Wide Web. You can begin by entering the URL for Holt McDougal's site: hmhsocialstudies.com.

APPLYING THE SKILL

The computer screen below shows the home page of the Library of Congress.

HOW TO USE THE INTERNET

Strategy ❶ Go directly to a Web page. If you know the address of a particular Web page, type the address in the strip at the top of the screen and press RETURN. After a few seconds, that page will appear on your screen.

If you want to research the Web for information on a topic, visit a general search site such as www.google.com or www.yahoo.com. The following sites have information that may be useful in your research:

Library of Congress—www.loc.gov

National Archives and Records Administration—www.nara.gov

Smithsonian Institution—www.si.org

PBS—www.pbs.org

National Geographic—www.nationalgeographic.com

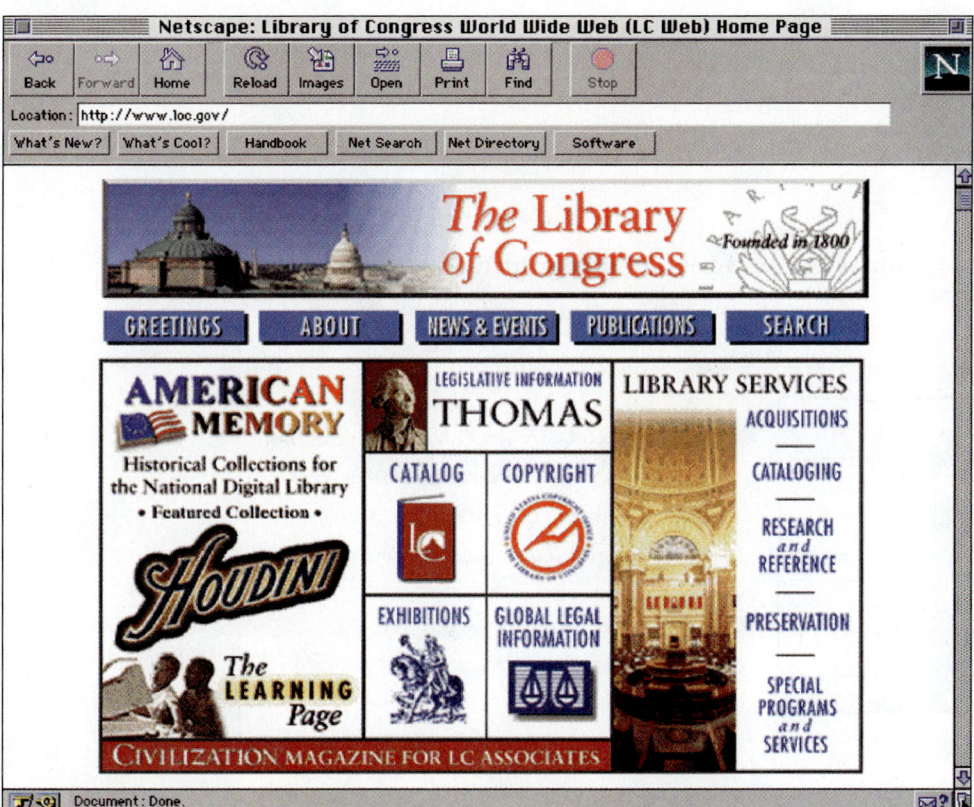

Strategy ❷ Learn about the page. Click on one of the topics across the top of the page to learn more about the Library of Congress and how to use its Web site.

Strategy ❸ Explore the features of the page. Click on any one of the images or topics to find out more about a specific subject.

PRACTICING THE SKILL

Turn to Chapter 29, Section 2, p. 916, "The Triumphs of a Crusade." Read the section, making a list of topics you would like to research. If you have a computer with Internet access, go to the Holt McDougal site, hmhsocialstudies.com. There you will be able to search the Chapter 29 Research Links and other features to explore a variety of historical topics.

4.1 Creating Charts and Graphs

DEFINING THE SKILL

Charts and **graphs** are visual representations of information. (See Skillbuilders 3.5 and 3.6.) Three types of graphs are **bar graphs, line graphs,** and **pie graphs.** Use a bar graph to display information about quantities and to compare related quantities. Use a line graph to show a change in a single quantity over time. Use a pie graph to show relative proportions among parts of a single thing. Charts can be used to condense and organize written information or lists.

APPLYING THE SKILL

The following passage includes data about American commuting choices between 1960 and 1990. The bar graph below shows how the information in the passage might be represented.

HOW TO CREATE A BAR GRAPH

Strategy ① Use a title that sums up the information; include a time span.

Strategy ② Note dates and the percentages. Dates will form the horizontal axis of your graph; percentages will form the vertical axis.

Strategy ③ Organize the data. Group numbers that provide information about the same year.

Strategy ④ Decide how best to represent the information. Sketch a graph and a legend, denoting the meanings of any colors and symbols.

> **American Commuting Choices, 1960–1990**
>
> In 1960, 64% of the population traveled to work by car, truck, or van; 12% took public transportation; 7% worked at home; and 17% got to work by other means. In 1990, 87% traveled to work by car, truck, or van; 5% took public transportation; 3% worked at home; and 5% went to work by other means.

Create a Bar Graph

Clearly label vertical and horizontal axes. Draw bars accurately. Include a legend.

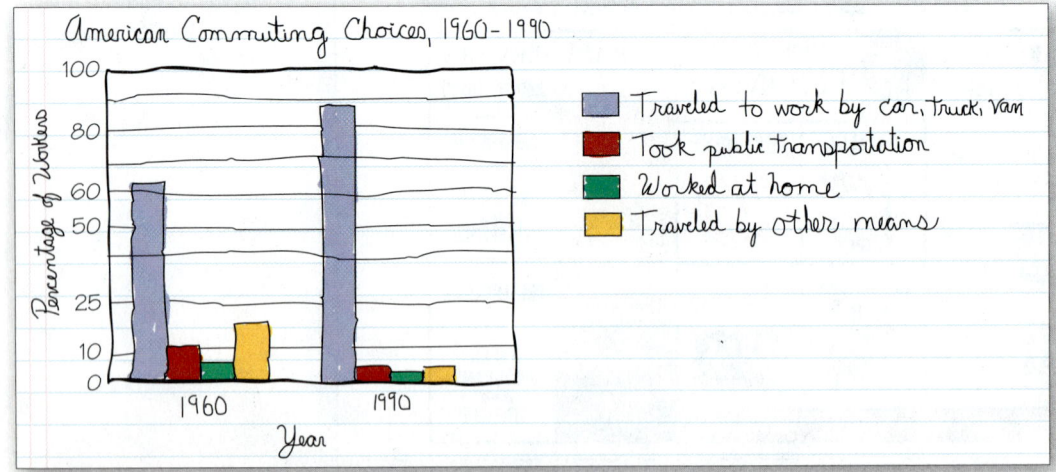

PRACTICING THE SKILL

Turn to Chapter 34, Section 4, p. 1091, and read the passage headed "A Changing Immigrant Population." Use a pie graph to show percentages of ethnic distribution of the American population in 1990.

4.2 Creating Models

DEFINING THE SKILL

Models, like maps, are visual representations of information. Historians make models of geographical areas, villages, cities, inventions, buildings, and other physical objects of historical importance. A model can be a two-dimensional representation, such as a poster or a diagram that explains how something happened. It also can be a three-dimensional representation or even a computer-created image.

APPLYING THE SKILL

The following image is a two-dimensional model of the tunnel system used by the Vietcong during the Vietnam War. Examine the strategies used in making this model to learn how to create your own.

HOW TO CREATE A MODEL

Strategy 1 Gather the information you need to understand the situation or event. Here the creator has gathered information about the tunnel system from various reference sources.

Strategy 2 Think about symbols you may want to use. Since the model should give information in a visual way, think about ways you can use color, pictures, or other visuals to tell the story.

Strategy 3 Gather the supplies you will need to create the model. For this model, the creator might have used computer software or colored markers or pencils.

Strategy 4 Visualize and sketch an idea for your model. Once you have created a picture in your mind from either written text or other images, make an actual sketch to plan how your model might look.

Tunnels of the Vietcong

Remote smoke outlets · Submerged entrance · Kitchen · Punji stake pit · Ventilation shaft · Firing post · Conference chamber · False tunnel · Sleeping chamber · Blast, gas, and waterproof trap doors · Booby trap grenade · Conical air raid shelter that also amplified sound of approaching aircraft · First-aid station powered by bicycle · Well · Storage cache for weapons, explosives, and rice

PRACTICING THE SKILL

Turn to Chapter 14, Section 3, p. 450, and read the text under the heading "Labor Unions Emerge." Use the information to create a model of a "sweatshop" factory during the turn of the century. Use the process described above as a guide.

4.3 Creating Maps

DEFINING THE SKILL

Maps are scale representations, usually of land surfaces. (See Skillbuilder 3.4.) Creating a map involves representing geographical data visually. When you draw a map, it is easiest to use an existing map as a guide. You can include data on climate and population and on patterns or distributions of human activity.

APPLYING THE SKILL

The following chart shows the numbers of 1995 immigrants who planned to settle in the southwestern states of the United States. The map below depicts the data given in the chart.

Immigrants, by State of Intended Residence, 1995					
Arizona	7,700	Nevada	4,306	Texas	49,963
California	166,482	New Mexico	2,758	Utah	2,831
Colorado	7,713				

HOW TO CREATE A MAP

Strategy 1 Determine what map you should use as a guide. Find a map of the Southwest that you can re-create.

Strategy 2 Decide how best to show the data. These data can be grouped in three broad categories of numbers: more than 100,000; 10,000 to 100,000; and less than 10,000.

Strategy 3 Select a title that identifies the geographical area and the map's purpose. Include a date or time span.

Strategy 4 Draw and label the lines of latitude and longitude. Use the guide map's scale and a ruler to help you correctly space the lines of latitude and longitude.

Strategy 5 Draw the subject of your map, following your guide map carefully. Color or mark the map to show its purpose. Use each color or symbol to represent similar information.

Strategy 6 Include a key or legend explaining colors, symbols, or shading. Reproduce the scale and compass rose from the map you used as a guide.

PRACTICING THE SKILL

Turn to p. 812 and study the graph titled "The Marshall Plan." Use the process described above to draw a map that depicts the data. (You can use the map on p. 811 as a guide.) After drawing the map, pose some historical questions about the Marshall Plan. How might your map convey answers to your questions? Write one of the questions and its answer below your map.

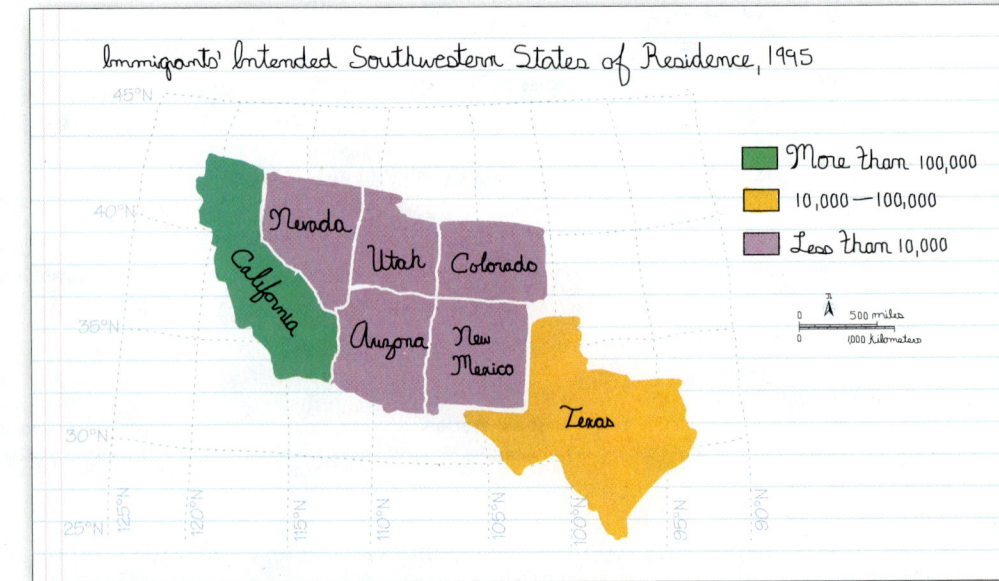

Immigrants' Intended Southwestern States of Residence, 1995

More than 100,000
10,000 — 100,000
Less than 10,000

4.4 Creating Databases

DEFINING THE SKILL

A **database** is a collection of data, or information, that is organized so that you can find and retrieve information on a specific topic quickly and easily. Once a computerized database is set up, you can search it to find specific information without going through the entire database. The database will provide a list of all stored information related to your topic. Learning how to use a database will help you learn how to create one.

APPLYING THE SKILL

The chart below is a database for some of the significant legislation passed during President Johnson's Great Society program.

① Significant Great Society Legislation		
② Legislation	Date	Significance
③ Economic Opportunity Act	1964	④ created Job Corps and other programs to help the poor
Civil Rights Act	1964	outlawed discrimination in public accommodations
Medical Care Act	1965	④ established Medicare and Medicaid programs to help the elderly and the poor
Higher Education Act	1965	provided low-interest loans for college students
Truth in Packaging Act	1966	set standards for labeling consumer products
Highway Safety Act	1966	required states to set up highway safety programs
Demonstration Cities and Metropolitan Area Redevelopment Act	1966	④ provided funds to rebuild poor neighborhoods
Air Quality Act	1967	set federal air pollution guidelines

HOW TO CREATE A DATABASE

Strategy ① Identify the topic of the database. The keywords, or most important words, in the title are "Great Society" and "Legislation." These words were used to begin the research for this database.

Strategy ② Identify the kind of data you need to enter in your database. These will be the column headings—or categories—of your database. The keywords "Legislation," "Date," and "Significance," were chosen to categorize this research.

Strategy ③ Once you find the data you want to include, identify the entries under each heading.

Strategy ④ Use the database to help you find the information quickly. For example, in this database you could search by the word "poor" for programs related to anti-poverty measures.

PRACTICING THE SKILL

Turn to Chapter 19, "The First World War," and create a database of key battles of World War I. Use a format like the one above for your database and include the following column headings: "Battle," "Date," "Location," and "Signficance." You can create your database using computer software or by setting up a 4-column chart on paper.

4.5 Creating Written Presentations

DEFINING THE SKILL
Written presentations are in-depth reports on a topic in history. Often, written presentations take a stand on an issue or try to support a specific conclusion. To successfully report on an event or make a point, your writing needs to be clear, concise, and supported by factual details.

APPLYING THE SKILL
The following is a written presentation about the main goals of progressivism. Use the strategies listed below to help you learn to create a written presentation.

HOW TO CREATE A WRITTEN PRESENTATION

Strategy ❶ Identify a topic that you wish to research, focusing on one or more questions that you hope to answer about the topic. Then research the topic using library resources and the Internet.

Strategy ❷ Formulate a hypothesis. This will serve as the main idea, or thesis, of your presentation. Analyze the information in your sources and develop a hypothesis that answers your questions about the topic.

Strategy ❸ Organize the facts and supporting details around your main idea. These facts and examples should be presented in a way that helps you build a logical case to prove your point.

Strategy ❹ To express your ideas clearly, use standard grammar, spelling, sentence structure, and punctuation. Proofread your work to make sure it is well-organized and grammatically correct.

For more on how to create a historical research paper and other written presentations, see the *Writing for Social Studies* handbook.

Make an Outline
Creating an outline like the one shown here will help you organize your ideas and produce an effective written presentation.

> **❶ The Goals of Progressivism**
> I. **❷** All progressive reforms had one of four goals.
>   A. Protecting Social Welfare
>   **❸** 1. Social Gospel movement sought to help the poor.
>   2. Settlement houses provided aid to poor city dwellers.
>   B. Promoting Moral Improvement
>   1. Reformers sought to improve Americans' personal behavior.
>   2. WCTU worked for prohibition.
>   C. Creating Economic Reform
>   1. Writers criticized capitalism.
>   2. American Socialist Party formed.
>   3. Muckrakers exposed corruption in business and government.
>   D. Fostering Efficiency
>   1. Emergence of scientific management in the workplace
>   2. Development of the assembly line

The Goals of Progressivism

As America approached the 20th century a number of citizens tried to reform society. Their efforts formed what became known as the progressive movement. Progressive reformers had the following four goals social welfare, moral improvement, economic reform, and efficiency.

> Use punctuation marks for their correct purposes. A colon precedes a list.

Many reformers sought to promote social welfare—especially in the crowded, run-down, and unhealthy areas of the cities. The Social Gospel movement inspired followers to erect churches in poor communities. It also persuaded business leaders to treat workers more fair. Other reformers established settlement house in slum neighborhoods which provided educational, cultural, and social services to people—especially to immigrants.

> Use the correct parts of speech. An adverb modifies a verb.
>
> Check for common agreement errors. Subjects and verbs must agree in person and number.

Another group of reformers felt that the lives of poor people could be improved through moral instruction. These reformers offer programs to improve personal behavior. The Women's Christian Temperance Union, for instance, promoted prohibition. It believed that alcohol was the root of many of society's problems.

> Use consistent verb tense. Use past tense for events in the past.
>
> Check spelling with both an electronic spell checker and a dictionary.

Other progressives, such as Henry George and Edward Bellamy, blamed the competitive nature of capitalism for creating a large underclass. Some Americans, especially workers, embraced socialism. In 1898, Eugene Debs helped organize the american socialist party. This organization Advocated communal living and a classless society. During the early 20th century, journalists exposed the corrupt side of business and politics known as muckrakers.

> Capitalize all proper nouns, including names of political parties.
>
> Use correct sentence structure. Every sentence needs a subject and a verb.
>
> Be sure sentence structure leads clearly from one phrase to the next. Correct misplaced modifiers.

Meanwhile, some tried to make American society more efficient. Frederick Winslow Taylor popularized scientific management, the effort to improve efficiency in the workplace by applying scientific principles. Out of this concept emerged the assembly line, which required workers to perform the same task over and over, and thus sped up production.

Through their hard work, the progressives reformed many levels of society and helped Americans live better lives.

PRACTICING THE SKILL

Create a two-page written presentation on a topic of historical importance that interests you. Use the strategies and sample outline and draft to help you create your presentation.

4.6 Creating Oral Presentations

DEFINING THE SKILL

An **oral presentation** is a speech or talk given before an audience. Oral presentations can be given to inform an audience about a certain topic or persuade an audience to think or act in a certain way. You can learn how to give effective oral presentations by examining some of the more famous ones in history.

APPLYING THE SKILL

The following is an excerpt from a student's speech supporting Southern secession. Use the strategies listed below to help you learn to create an oral presentation.

HOW TO CREATE AN ORAL PRESENTATION

Strategy ❶ Choose one central idea or theme and organize your presentation to support it. Here, the writer calls for the United States government to allow the Southern states to secede.

Strategy ❷ Use words or images to persuade your audience. In this speech, the writer has used a metaphor of family conflict to express the antagonism between North and South.

Strategy ❸ Make sure your arguments support your central idea or theme. In this speech, the writer's arguments all support the main theme.

> ❶ The Southern states should be allowed to secede. ❸ Since it was the states that helped create the national government, surely the states have the right to declare their independence from that government.
>
> The industrial North will never understand the needs of the farmers and plantation owners of the South. ❷ The South and the North are like two brothers whose lives and attitudes have become so different that they can no longer live under the same roof. Why should they be forced to remain together?

Giving an Oral Presentation

When you give an oral presentation, make sure to
- maintain eye contact with your audience.
- use gestures and body language to emphasize your main points and to help express your ideas.
- pace yourself. Do not rush to finish your presentation.
- vary your tone of voice to help bring out the meaning of your words.

PRACTICING THE SKILL

Turn to Chapter 24, Section 4, p. 758, and study the Point/Counterpoint feature about U.S. involvement in WWII. Choose a side and create an outline for a speech that supports that side. Use the strategies to help you make an oral presentation.

4.7 Creating Visual Presentations

DEFINING THE SKILL

A **visual presentation** of history uses visual sources to explain a particular historical event. Such sources could include paintings, maps, charts and graphs, costume drawings, photographs, political cartoons, and advertisements. Movies, CD-ROMs, television, and computer software are among the visual sources called multimedia sources because they also include sound. (See Skillbuilder 3.2.) Visual sources can provide much insight into various eras and events of the past. Creating a visual presentation will help you to become more familiar with the many different sources of historical information available.

APPLYING THE SKILL

The image below shows a student using a computer to create a visual presentation. Use the strategies listed below to help you plan out the steps needed to compile a clear, engaging, and informative presentation.

HOW TO CREATE A VISUAL PRESENTATION

Strategy ① Identify the topic of your presentation and decide which types of visuals will most effectively convey your information. For example, you might want to use slides and posters along with a map. If you want to include multimedia sources, you could use documentary film or television footage of an event.

Strategy ② Conduct research to determine what visual sources are available. Some topics, such as wars, may have more visual source material than others. You can create your own visual sources, such as a graph or chart, to accompany what you find.

Strategy ③ Write a script for the presentation. A narration of events to accompany the visuals will tie the various sources together and aid you in telling the story.

Strategy ④ Record the presentation. A video recording will preserve the presentation for future viewing and allow you to show it to different groups of people.

PRACTICING THE SKILL

Turn to Chapter 13, Section 1, p. 416, and read "A Day in the Life of a Cowboy," or choose another section in the chapter. Use the strategies above to create a visual presentation of the topic.

Facts About the States

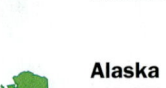

Alabama
4,779,736 people
52,237 sq. mi.
Rank in area: 30
Entered Union in 1819

Alaska
710,231 people
615,230 sq. mi.
Rank in area: 1
Entered Union in 1959

Arizona
6,392,017 people
114,006 sq. mi.
Rank in area: 6
Entered Union in 1912

Arkansas
2,915,918 people
53,182 sq. mi.
Rank in area: 28
Entered Union in 1836

California
37,253,956 people
158,869 sq. mi.
Rank in area: 3
Entered Union in 1850

Colorado
5,029,196 people
104,100 sq. mi.
Rank in area: 8
Entered Union in 1876

Connecticut
3,574,097 people
5,544 sq. mi.
Rank in area: 48
Entered Union in 1788

Delaware
897,934 people
2,396 sq. mi.
Rank in area: 49
Entered Union in 1787

District of Columbia
601,723 people
68 sq. mi.

Florida
18,801,310 people
59,928 sq. mi.
Rank in area: 23
Entered Union in 1845

Georgia
9,687,653 people
58,977 sq. mi.
Rank in area: 24
Entered Union in 1788

Hawaii
1,360,301 people
6,459 sq. mi.
Rank in area: 47
Entered Union in 1959

Idaho
1,567,582 people
83,574 sq. mi.
Rank in area: 14
Entered Union in 1890

Illinois
12,830,632 people
57,918 sq. mi.
Rank in area: 25
Entered Union in 1818

Indiana
6,483,802 people
36,420 sq. mi.
Rank in area: 38
Entered Union in 1816

Iowa
3,046,355 people
56,276 sq. mi.
Rank in area: 26
Entered Union in 1846

Kansas
2,853,118 people
82,282 sq. mi.
Rank in area: 15
Entered Union in 1861

Kentucky
4,339,367 people
40,411 sq. mi.
Rank in area: 37
Entered Union in 1792

Louisiana
4,533,372 people
49,651 sq. mi.
Rank in area: 31
Entered Union in 1812

Maine
1,328,361 people
33,741 sq. mi.
Rank in area: 39
Entered Union in 1820

Maryland
5,773,552 people
12,297 sq. mi.
Rank in area: 42
Entered Union in 1788

Massachusetts
6,547,629 people
9,241 sq. mi.
Rank in area: 45
Entered Union in 1788

Michigan
9,883,640 people
96,705 sq. mi.
Rank in area: 11
Entered Union in 1837

Minnesota
5,303,925 people
86,943 sq. mi.
Rank in area: 12
Entered Union in 1858

Mississippi
2,967,297 people
48,286 sq. mi.
Rank in area: 32
Entered Union in 1817

Missouri
5,988,927 people
69,709 sq. mi.
Rank in area: 21
Entered Union in 1821

Montana
989,415 people
147,046 sq. mi.
Rank in area: 4
Entered Union in 1889

Population figures are according to the Census 2000.

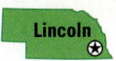
Nebraska
1,826,341 people
77,538 sq. mi.
Rank in area: 16
Entered Union in 1867

Nevada
2,700,551 people
110,567 sq. mi.
Rank in area: 7
Entered Union in 1864

New Hampshire
1,316,470 people
9,283 sq. mi.
Rank in area: 44
Entered Union in 1788

New Jersey
8,791,894 people
8,215 sq. mi.
Rank in area: 46
Entered Union in 1787

New Mexico
2,059,179 people
121,598 sq. mi.
Rank in area: 5
Entered Union in 1912

New York
19,378,102 people
53,989 sq. mi.
Rank in area: 27
Entered Union in 1788

North Carolina
9,535,483 people
52,672 sq. mi.
Rank in area: 29
Entered Union in 1789

North Dakota
672,591 people
70,704 sq. mi.
Rank in area: 18
Entered Union in 1889

Ohio
11,536,504 people
44,828 sq. mi.
Rank in area: 34
Entered Union in 1803

Oklahoma
3,751,351 people
69,903 sq. mi.
Rank in area: 20
Entered Union in 1907

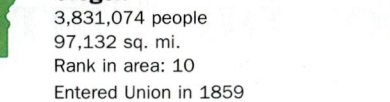
Oregon
3,831,074 people
97,132 sq. mi.
Rank in area: 10
Entered Union in 1859

Pennsylvania
12,702,379 people
46,058 sq. mi.
Rank in area: 33
Entered Union in 1787

Rhode Island
1,052,567 people
1,231 sq. mi.
Rank in area: 50
Entered Union in 1790

South Carolina
4,625,364 people
31,189 sq. mi.
Rank in area: 40
Entered Union in 1788

South Dakota
814,180 people
77,121 sq. mi.
Rank in area: 17
Entered Union in 1889

Tennessee
6,346,105 people
42,146 sq. mi.
Rank in area: 36
Entered Union in 1796

Texas
25,145,561 people
267,277 sq. mi.
Rank in area: 2
Entered Union in 1845

Utah
2,763,885 people
84,904 sq. mi.
Rank in area: 13
Entered Union in 1896

Vermont
625,741 people
9,615 sq. mi.
Rank in area: 43
Entered Union in 1791

Virginia
8,001,024 people
42,326 sq. mi.
Rank in area: 35
Entered Union in 1788

Washington
6,724,540 people
70,637 sq. mi.
Rank in area: 19
Entered Union in 1889

West Virginia
1,852,994 people
24,231 sq. mi.
Rank in area: 41
Entered Union in 1863

Wisconsin
5,686,986 people
64,599 sq. mi.
Rank in area: 22
Entered Union in 1848

Wyoming
563,626 people
97,818 sq. mi.
Rank in area: 9
Entered Union in 1890

United States: Major Dependencies

American Samoa 68,200 people (2007 est.)

Guam 178,000 people (2009 est.)

Commonwealth of Puerto Rico 3,725,789 people (2010)

Virgin Islands of the United States 109,750 people (2010)

PRESIDENTS OF THE UNITED STATES

Dates given are for term in office.

Here are some little-known facts about the presidents of the United States:

- First president born in the new United States: **Martin Van Buren** (8th president)
- Only president who was a bachelor: **James Buchanan**
- First left-handed president: **James A. Garfield**
- Largest president: **William Howard Taft** (6 feet, 2 inches; 332 pounds)
- Youngest president: **Theodore Roosevelt** (42 years old)
- Oldest president: **Ronald Reagan** (77 years old when he left office in 1989)
- First president born west of the Mississippi River: **Herbert Hoover** (born in West Branch, Iowa)
- First president born in the 20th century: **John F. Kennedy** (born May 29, 1917)

1 George Washington
1789–1797
No Political Party
Birthplace: Virginia
Born: February 22, 1732
Died: December 14, 1799

2 John Adams
1797–1801
Federalist
Birthplace: Massachusetts
Born: October 30, 1735
Died: July 4, 1826

3 Thomas Jefferson
1801–1809
Democratic-Republican
Birthplace: Virginia
Born: April 13, 1743
Died: July 4, 1826

4 James Madison
1809–1817
Democratic-Republican
Birthplace: Virginia
Born: March 16, 1751
Died: June 28, 1836

5 James Monroe
1817–1825
Democratic-Republican
Birthplace: Virginia
Born: April 28, 1758
Died: July 4, 1831

6 John Quincy Adams
1825–1829
Republican
Birthplace: Massachusetts
Born: July 11, 1767
Died: February 23, 1848

7 Andrew Jackson
1829–1837
Democrat
Birthplace: South Carolina
Born: March 15, 1767
Died: June 8, 1845

8 Martin Van Buren
1837–1841
Democrat
Birthplace: New York
Born: December 5, 1782
Died: July 24, 1862

9 William H. Harrison
1841
Whig
Birthplace: Virginia
Born: February 9, 1773
Died: April 4, 1841

10 John Tyler
1841–1845
Whig
Birthplace: Virginia
Born: March 29, 1790
Died: January 18, 1862

11 James K. Polk
1845–1849
Democrat
Birthplace: North Carolina
Born: November 2, 1795
Died: June 15, 1849

12 Zachary Taylor
1849–1850
Whig
Birthplace: Virginia
Born: November 24, 1784
Died: July 9, 1850

13 Millard Fillmore
1850–1853
Whig
Birthplace: New York
Born: January 7, 1800
Died: March 8, 1874

14 Franklin Pierce
1853–1857
Democrat
Birthplace: New Hampshire
Born: November 23, 1804
Died: October 8, 1869

15 James Buchanan
1857–1861
Democrat
Birthplace: Pennsylvania
Born: April 23, 1791
Died: June 1, 1868

16 Abraham Lincoln
1861–1865
Republican
Birthplace: Kentucky
Born: February 12, 1809
Died: April 15, 1865

17 Andrew Johnson
1865–1869
Democrat
Birthplace: North Carolina
Born: December 29, 1808
Died: July 31, 1875

18 Ulysses S. Grant
1869–1877
Republican
Birthplace: Ohio
Born: April 27, 1822
Died: July 23, 1885

19 Rutherford B. Hayes
1877–1881
Republican
Birthplace: Ohio
Born: October 4, 1822
Died: January 17, 1893

20 James A. Garfield
1881
Republican
Birthplace: Ohio
Born: November 19, 1831
Died: September 19, 1881

21 Chester A. Arthur
1881–1885
Republican
Birthplace: Vermont
Born: October 5, 1829
Died: November 18, 1886

22 24 Grover Cleveland
1885–1889, 1893–1897
Democrat
Birthplace: New Jersey
Born: March 18, 1837
Died: June 24, 1908

23 Benjamin Harrison
1889–1893
Republican
Birthplace: Ohio
Born: August 20, 1833
Died: March 13, 1901

25 William McKinley
1897–1901
Republican
Birthplace: Ohio
Born: January 29, 1843
Died: September 14, 1901

26 Theodore Roosevelt
1901–1909
Republican
Birthplace: New York
Born: October 27, 1858
Died: January 6, 1919

27 William H. Taft
1909–1913
Republican
Birthplace: Ohio
Born: September 15, 1857
Died: March 8, 1930

28 Woodrow Wilson
1913–1921
Democrat
Birthplace: Virginia
Born: December 29, 1856
Died: February 3, 1924

29 Warren G. Harding
1921–1923
Republican
Birthplace: Ohio
Born: November 2, 1865
Died: August 2, 1923

30 Calvin Coolidge
1923–1929
Republican
Birthplace: Vermont
Born: July 4, 1872
Died: January 5, 1933

31 Herbert C. Hoover
1929–1933
Republican
Birthplace: Iowa
Born: August 10, 1874
Died: October 20, 1964

32 Franklin D. Roosevelt
1933–1945
Democrat
Birthplace: New York
Born: January 30, 1882
Died: April 12, 1945

33 Harry S. Truman
1945–1953
Democrat
Birthplace: Missouri
Born: May 8, 1884
Died: December 26, 1972

34 Dwight D. Eisenhower
1953–1961
Republican
Birthplace: Texas
Born: October 14, 1890
Died: March 28, 1969

35 John F. Kennedy
1961–1963
Democrat
Birthplace: Massachusetts
Born: May 29, 1917
Died: November 22, 1963

36 Lyndon B. Johnson
1963–1969
Democrat
Birthplace: Texas
Born: August 27, 1908
Died: January 22, 1973

37 Richard M. Nixon
1969–1974
Republican
Birthplace: California
Born: January 9, 1913
Died: April 22, 1994

38 Gerald R. Ford
1974–1977
Republican
Birthplace: Nebraska
Born: July 14, 1913
Died: December 26, 2006

39 James E. Carter, Jr.
1977–1981
Democrat
Birthplace: Georgia
Born: October 1, 1924

40 Ronald W. Reagan
1981–1989
Republican
Birthplace: Illinois
Born: February 6, 1911
Died: June 4, 2004

41 George H. W. Bush
1989–1993
Republican
Birthplace: Massachusetts
Born: June 12, 1924

42 William J. Clinton
1993–2001
Democrat
Birthplace: Arkansas
Born: August 19, 1946

43 George W. Bush
2001–2009
Republican
Birthplace: Connecticut
Born: July 6, 1946

44 Barack H. Obama
2009–
Democrat
Birthplace: Hawaii
Born: August 4, 1961

GLOSSARY

The Glossary is an alphabetical listing of many of the key terms from the chapters, along with their meanings. The definitions listed in the Glossary are the ones that apply to the way the words are used in this textbook. The Glossary gives the part of speech of each word. The following abbreviations are used:

adj. = adjective   *n.* = noun   *v.* = verb

PRONUNCIATION KEY

Symbol	Examples	Symbol	Examples	Symbol	Examples
ă	at, gas	m	man, seem	v	van, save
ā	ape, day	n	night, mitten	w	web, twice
ä	father, barn	ng	sing, anger	y	yard, lawyer
âr	fair, dare	ŏ	odd, not	z	zoo, reason
b	bell, table	ō	open, road, grow	zh	treasure, garage
ch	chin, lunch	ô	awful, bought, horse	ə	awake, even, pencil,
d	dig, bored	oi	coin, boy		pilot, focus
ĕ	egg, ten	ŏŏ	look, full	ər	perform, letter
ē	evil, see, meal	ōō	root, glue, through		
f	fall, laugh, phrase	ou	out, cow	**Sounds in Foreign Words**	
g	gold, big	p	pig, cap	KH	*German* ich, auch;
h	hit, inhale	r	rose, star		*Scottish* loch
hw	white, everywhere	s	sit, face	N	*French* entre, bon, fin
ĭ	inch, fit	sh	she, mash	œ	*French* feu, coeur;
ī	idle, my, tried	t	tap, hopped		*German* schön
îr	dear, here	th	thing, with	ü	*French* utile, rue;
j	jar, gem, badge	*th*	then, other		*German* grün
k	keep, cat, luck	ŭ	up, nut		
l	load, rattle	ûr	fur, earn, bird, worm		

STRESS MARKS

ʹ   This mark indicates that the preceding syllable receives the primary stress. For example, in the word *lineage,* the first syllable is stressed: [lĭnʹē-ĭj].

ʹ   This mark is used only in words in which more than one syllable is stressed. It indicates that the preceding syllable is stressed, but somewhat more weakly than the syllable receiving the primary stress. In the word *consumerism,* for example, the second syllable receives the primary stress, and the fourth syllable receives a weaker stress: [kən-sōōʹmə-rĭzʹəm].

Adapted from *The American Heritage Dictionary of the English Language, Fourth Edition;* Copyright © 2000 by Houghton Mifflin Company. Used with the permission of Houghton Mifflin Company.

A

abolition *n.* movement to end slavery. (p. 249)

Adams-Onís [ădʹəmz-ō-nēsʹ] **Treaty** *n.* an 1819 agreement in which Spain gave over control of the territory of Florida to the United States. (p. 221)

Adena [ə-dēʹnə] *n.* a Mound Builder society that was centered in the Ohio River valley and flourished from about 700 B.C. to A.D. 100. (p. 7)

affirmative [ə-fûrʹmə-tĭv] **action** *n.* a policy that seeks to correct the effects of past discrimination by favoring the groups who were previously disadvantaged. (pp. 929, 1037)

Agent Orange *n.* a toxic leaf-killing chemical sprayed by U.S. planes in Vietnam to expose Vietcong hideouts. (p. 945)

Agricultural Adjustment Act (AAA) *n.* a law enacted in 1933 to raise crop prices by paying farmers to leave a certain amount of their land unplanted, thus lowering production. (p. 697)

AIDS [ādz] **(acquired immune deficiency syndrome)** *n.* a disease caused by a virus that weakens the immune system, making the body prone to infections and otherwise rare forms of cancer. (p. 1046)

Alamo, the [ăl'ə-mō'] *n.* a mission and fort in San Antonio, Texas, where Mexican forces massacred rebellious Texans in 1836. (p. 291)

Alien and Sedition [ā'lē-ən] [sĭ-dĭsh'ən] **Acts** *n.* a series of four laws enacted in 1798 to reduce the political power of recent immigrants to the United States. (p. 195)

Alliance [ə-lī'əns] **for Progress** *n.* a U.S. foreign-aid program of the 1960s, providing economic and technical assistance to Latin American countries. (p. 886)

Allies [ăl'īz] *n.* **1.** in World War I, the group of nations—originally consisting of Great Britain, France, and Russia and later joined by the United States, Italy, and others—that opposed the Central Powers. (p. 579). **2.** in World War II, the group of nations—including Great Britain, the Soviet Union, and the United States—that opposed the Axis powers. (p. 760)

American Expeditionary [ĕk'spĭ-dĭsh'ə-nĕr'ē] **Force (AEF)** *n.* the U.S. forces, led by General John Pershing, who fought with the Allies in Europe during World War I. (p. 590)

American Federation of Labor (AFL) *n.* an alliance of trade and craft unions, formed in 1886. (p. 451)

American Indian Movement (AIM) *n.* a frequently militant organization that was formed in 1968 to work for Native American rights. (p. 977)

Americanization [ə-mĕr'ĭ-kə-nĭ-zā'shən] **movement** *n.* education program designed to help immigrants assimilate to American culture. (p. 469)

American System *n.* a pre-Civil War set of measures designed to unify the nation and strengthen its economy by means of protective tariffs, a national bank, and such internal improvements as the development of a transportation system. (p. 216)

Anaconda [ăn'ə-kŏn'də] **plan** *n.* a three-part strategy by which the Union proposed to defeat the Confederacy in the Civil War. (p. 341)

anarchist [ăn'ər-kĭst] *n.* a person who opposes all forms of government. (p. 619)

Anasazi [ä'nə-sä'zē] *n.* a Native American group that lived on the mesa tops, cliff sides, and canyon bottoms of the Four Corners region (where the present-day states of Arizona, New Mexico, Colorado, and Utah meet) from about A.D. 100 to 1300. (p. 7)

annex [ə-nĕks'] *v.* to incorporate a territory into an existing political unit, such as a state or a nation. (p. 292)

antebellum [ăn'tē-bĕl'əm] *adj.* belonging to the period before the Civil War. (p. 252)

Antifederalist [ăn'tē-fĕd'ər-ə-lĭst] *n.* an opponent of a strong central government. (p. 146)

appeasement [ə-pēz'mənt] *n.* the granting of concessions to a hostile power in order to keep the peace. (p. 744)

Appomattox [ăp'ə-măt'əks] **Court House** *n.* town near Appomattox, Virginia, where Lee surrendered to Grant on April 9, 1865, thus ending the Civil War. (37°N 79°W) (p. 365)

apprentice [ə-prĕn'tĭs] *n.* a worker learning a trade or craft, usually under the supervision of a master. (p. 260)

arbitration *n.* a method of settling disputes in which both sides submit their differences to a mutually approved judge. (p. 451)

armistice [är'mĭ-stĭs] *n.* a truce, or agreement to end an armed conflict. (pp. 205, 593)

Army of the Republic of Vietnam (ARVN) *n.* the southern Vietnamese soldiers with whom U.S. troops fought against communism and forces in the North during the Vietnam War. (p. 943)

Articles of Confederation [kən-fĕd'ə-rā'shən] *n.* a document, adopted by the Second Continental Congress in 1777 and finally approved by the states in 1781, that outlined the form of government of the new United States. (p. 135)

Ashcan school *n.* a group of early 20th-century American artists who often painted realistic pictures of city life—such as tenements and homeless people—thus earning them their name. (p. 501)

assimilation [ə-sĭm'ə-lā'shən] *n.* a minority group's adoption of the beliefs and way of life of the dominant culture. (p. 412)

Atlantic Charter *n.* a 1941 declaration of principles in which the United States and Great Britain set forth their goals in opposing the Axis powers. (p. 760)

Axis [ăk'sĭs] **powers** *n.* the group of nations—including Germany, Italy, and Japan—that opposed the Allies in World War II. (p. 757)

Aztec [ăz'tĕk'] *n.* a Native American people that settled in the Valley of Mexico in the 1200s A.D. and later developed a powerful empire. (p. 6)

B

baby boom *n.* the sharp increase in the U.S. birthrate following World War II. (p. 849)

Bank of the United States *n.* either of the two national banks, funded by the federal government and private investors, established by Congress, the first in 1791 and the second in 1816. (pp. 185, 232)

Battle of the Bulge *n.* a month-long battle of World War II, in which the Allies succeeded in turning back the last major German offensive of the war. (p. 782)

Battle of Midway *n.* a World War II battle that took place in early June 1942. The Allies decimated the Japanese fleet at Midway, an island lying northwest of Hawaii. The Allies then took the offensive in the Pacific and began to move closer to Japan. (p. 785)

Battle of Wounded Knee [wo͞on'dĭd nē'] *n.* the massacre by U.S. soldiers of 300 unarmed Native Americans at Wounded Knee Creek, South Dakota, in 1890. (p. 414)

Beatles, the [bēt'lz] *n.* a British band that had an enormous influence on popular music in the 1960s. (p. 989)

beat movement *n.* a social and artistic movement of the 1950s, stressing unrestrained literary self-expression and nonconformity with the mainstream culture. (p. 861)

Benin [bə-nĭn'] *n.* a West African kingdom that flourished in the Niger Delta region (in what is now Nigeria) from the 14th to the 17th century. (p. 17)

Berlin airlift [bûr-lĭn' âr'lĭft'] *n.* a 327-day operation in which U.S. and British planes flew food and supplies into West Berlin after the Soviets blockaded the city in 1948. (p. 813)

Berlin Wall *n.* a concrete wall that separated East Berlin and West Berlin from 1961 to 1989, built by the Communist East German government to prevent its citizens from fleeing to the West. (p. 883)

Bessemer [bĕs'ə-mər] **process** *n.* a cheap and efficient process for making steel, developed around 1850. (p. 437)

Bill of Rights *n.* the first ten amendments to the U.S. Constitution, added in 1791 and consisting of a formal list of citizens' rights and freedoms. (p. 149)

bimetallism [bī-mĕt′l-ĭz′əm] *n.* the use of both gold and silver as a basis for a national monetary system. (p. 428)

black codes *n.* the discriminatory laws passed throughout the post-Civil-War South which severely restricted African Americans' lives, prohibiting such activities as traveling without permits, carrying weapons, serving on juries, testifying against whites, and marrying whites. (p. 379)

blacklist [blăk′lĭst′] *n.* a list of about 500 actors, writers, producers, and directors who were not allowed to work on Hollywood films because of their alleged Communist connections. (p. 824)

Black Panthers *n.* a militant African-American political organization formed in 1966 by Huey Newton and Bobby Seale to fight police brutality and to provide services in the ghetto. (p. 926)

Black Power *n.* a slogan used by Stokely Carmichael in the 1960s that encouraged African-American pride and political and social leadership. (p. 926)

Black Tuesday *n.* a name given to October 29, 1929, when stock prices fell sharply. (p. 674)

Bleeding Kansas *n.* a name applied to the Kansas Territory in the years before the Civil War, when the territory was a battleground between proslavery and antislavery forces. (p. 316)

blitzkrieg [blĭts′krēg′] *n.* from the German word meaning "lightning war," a sudden, massive attack with combined air and ground forces, intended to achieve a quick victory. (p. 745)

blockade [blŏ-kād′] *n.* the use of ships or troops to prevent movement into and out of a port or region controlled by a hostile nation. (p. 202)

bonanza [bə-năn′zə] **farm** *n.* an enormous farm on which a single crop is grown. (p. 424)

Bonus [bō′nəs] **Army** *n.* a group of World War I veterans and their families who marched on Washington, D.C., in 1932 to demand the immediate payment of a bonus they had been promised for military service. (p. 688)

bootlegger [boot′lĕg′ər] *n.* a person who smuggled alcoholic beverages into the United States during Prohibition. (p. 643)

Boston Massacre [bô′stən măs′ə-kər] *n.* a clash between British soldiers and Boston colonists in 1770, in which five of the colonists were killed. (p. 98)

Boston Tea Party *n.* the dumping of 18,000 pounds of tea into Boston Harbor by colonists in 1773 to protest the Tea Act. (p. 99)

Boulder [bōl′dər] **Dam** *n.* a dam on the Colorado River—now called Hoover Dam—that was built during the Great Depression as part of a public-works program intended to stimulate business and provide jobs. (p. 686)

Boxer Rebellion *n.* a 1900 rebellion in which members of a Chinese secret society sought to free their country from Western influence. (p. 563)

bracero [brə-sâr′ō] *n.* a Mexican laborer allowed to enter the United States to work for a limited period of time during World War II. (p. 868)

bread line *n.* a line of people waiting for free food. (p. 679)

brinkmanship [brĭngk′mən-shĭp′] *n.* the practice of threatening an enemy with massive military retaliation for any aggression. (p. 829)

Brown* v. *Board of Education of Topeka *n.* a 1954 case in which the Supreme Court ruled that "separate but equal" education for black and white students was unconstitutional. (p. 908)

Bull Moose Party *n.* a name given to the Progressive Party, formed to support Theodore Roosevelt's candidacy for the presidency in 1912. (p. 536)

buying on margin [mär′jĭn] *n.* the purchasing of stocks by paying only a small percentage of the price and borrowing the rest. (p. 673)

C

cabinet [kăb′ə-nĭt] *n.* the group of department heads who serve as the president's chief advisers. (p. 183)

Camp David Accords [ə-kôrdz′] *n.* historic agreements between Israel and Egypt, reached in negotiations at Camp David in 1978. (p. 1022)

capitalism [kăp′ĭ-tl-ĭz′əm] *n.* an economic system in which private individuals and corporations control the means of production and use them to earn profits. (p. 275)

carpetbagger [kär′pĭt-băg′ər] *n.* a Northerner who moved to the South after the Civil War. (p. 385)

cash crop *n.* a crop grown by a farmer for sale rather than for personal use. (p. 72)

Central Powers *n.* the group of nations—led by Germany, Austria-Hungary, and the Ottoman Empire—that opposed the Allies in World War I. (p. 580)

checks and balances *n.* the provisions in the U.S. Constitution that prevent any branch of the U.S. government from dominating the other two branches. (p. 143)

Chinese Exclusion Act *n.* a law, enacted in 1882, that prohibited all Chinese except students, teachers, merchants, tourists, and government officials from entering the United States. (p. 465)

Chisholm [chĭz′əm] **Trail** *n.* the major cattle route from San Antonio, Texas, through Oklahoma to Kansas. (p. 415)

chlorination *n.* a method of purifying water by mixing it with chemical chlorine. (p. 470)

CIA *n.* the Central Intelligence Agency—a U.S. agency created to gather secret information about foreign governments. (p. 829)

Civilian Conservation Corps [kôr] **(CCC)** *n.* an agency, established as part of the New Deal, that put young unemployed men to work building roads, developing parks, planting trees, and helping in erosion-control and flood-control projects. (p. 697)

civil disobedience [dĭs′ə-bē′dē-əns] *n.* the refusal to obey those laws which are seen as unjust in an effort to bring about a change in governmental policy. Henry David Thoreau wrote about civil disobedience in the 19th century, and the tactic was promoted by Martin Luther King, Jr., during the Civil Rights Era. (p. 243)

Civil Rights Act of 1964 *n.* a law that banned discrimination on the basis of race, sex, national origin, or religion in public places and most workplaces. (p. 920)

Civil Rights Act of 1968 *n.* a law that banned discrimination in housing. (p. 928)

civil service *n.* the nonmilitary branches of government administration. (p. 476)

Clayton Antitrust [klāt'n ăn'tē-trŭst'] **Act** *n.* a law, enacted in 1914, that made certain monopolistic business practices illegal and protected the rights of labor unions and farm organizations. (p. 539)

Cold War *n.* the state of hostility, without direct military conflict, that developed between the United States and the Soviet Union after World War II. (p. 812)

colonization [kŏl'ə-nĭ-zā'shən] *n.* the establishment of outlying settlements by a parent country. (p. 28)

Columbian Exchange [kə-lŭm'bē-ən ĭks-chānj'] *n.* the transfer—beginning with Columbus's first voyage—of plants, animals, and diseases between the Western Hemisphere and the Eastern Hemisphere. (p. 29)

committees of correspondence [kôr'ĭ-spŏn'dəns] *n.* one of the groups set up by American colonists to exchange information about British threats to their liberties. (p. 99)

Committee to Reelect the President *n.* an organization formed to run President Nixon's 1972 reelection campaign, which was linked to the break-in at the Democratic National Committee headquarters that set off the Watergate scandal. (p. 1009)

Common Sense *n.* a pamphlet by Thomas Paine, published in 1776, that called for separation of the colonies from Britain. (p. 105)

communism [kŏm'yə-nĭz'əm] *n.* an economic and political system based on one-party government and state ownership of property. (p. 619)

Compromise [kŏm'prə-mīz'] **of 1850** *n.* a series of congressional measures intended to settle the major disagreements between free states and slave states. (p. 307)

Compromise of 1877 *n.* a series of congressional measures under which the Democrats agreed to accept the Republican candidate Rutherford B. Hayes as president, even though he had lost the popular vote. The measures included the withdrawal of federal troops from Southern states, federal money for improving Southern infrastructure, and the appointment of a conservative Southern cabinet member. (p. 399)

concentration [kŏn'sən-trā'shən] **camp** *n.* a prison camp operated by Nazi Germany in which Jews and other groups considered to be enemies of Adolf Hitler were starved while doing slave labor or were murdered. (p. 752)

Confederacy [kən-fĕd'ər-ə-sē] *n.* the Confederate States of America, a confederation formed in 1861 by the Southern states after their secession from the Union. (p. 330)

confederation [kən-fĕd'ə-rā'shən] *n.* an alliance permitting states or nations to act together on matters of mutual concern. (p. 135)

conglomerate [kən-glŏm'ər-ĭt] *n.* a major corporation that owns a number of smaller companies in unrelated businesses. (p. 848)

Congress of Industrial Organizations (CIO) *n.* a labor organization composed of industrial unions founded in 1938, it merged with the AFL in 1955. (p. 714)

Congress of Racial Equality [rā'shəl ĭ-kwŏl'ĭ-tē] **(CORE)** *n.* an interracial group founded in 1942 by James Farmer to work against segregation in Northern cities. (p. 799)

conquistador [kŏng-kē'stə-dôr'] *n.* one of the Spaniards who traveled to the Americas as an explorer and conqueror in the 16th century. (p. 36)

conscientious objector [kŏn'shē-ĕn'shəs ŏb-jĕk'tər] *n.* a person who refuses, on moral grounds, to participate in warfare. (p. 592)

conscription [kən-skrĭp'shən] *n.* the drafting of citizens for military service. (p. 349)

conservation [kŏn'sûr-vā'shən] *n.* the planned management of natural resources, involving the protection of some wilderness areas and the development of others for the common good. (p. 529)

conservative coalition [kən-sûr'və-tĭv kō'ə-lĭsh'ən] *n.* an alliance formed in the mid-1960s of right-wing groups opposed to big government. (p. 1037)

consolidation [kən-sŏl'ĭ-dā'shən] *n.* the act of uniting or combining. (p. 446)

consumerism [kən-sōō'mə-rĭz'əm] *n.* a preoccupation with the purchasing of material goods. (p. 854)

containment [kən-tān'mənt] *n.* the blocking of another nation's attempts to spread its influence—especially the efforts of the United States to block the spread of Soviet influence during the late 1940s and early 1950s. (p. 811)

Contract [kŏn'trăkt'] **with America** *n.* a document that was drafted by Representative Newt Gingrich and signed by more than 300 Republican candidates in 1994, setting forth the Republicans' conservative legislative agenda. (p. 1070)

Contras [kŏn'trəz] *n.* Nicaraguan rebels who received assistance from the Reagan administration in their efforts to overthrow the Sandinista government in the 1980s. (p. 1057)

convoy [kŏn'voi'] **system** *n.* the protection of merchant ships from U-boat—German submarine—attacks by having the ships travel in large groups escorted by warships. (p. 589)

Copperhead [kŏp'ər-hĕd'] *n.* a Northern Democrat who advocated making peace with the Confederacy during the Civil War. (p. 349)

cottage industry *n.* a system of production in which manufacturers provide the materials for goods to be produced in the home. (p. 260)

cotton gin *n.* a machine for cleaning the seeds from cotton fibers, invented by Eli Whitney in 1793. (p. 215)

counterculture [koun'tər-kŭl'chər] *n.* the culture of the young people who rejected mainstream American society in the 1960s, seeking to create an alternative society based on peace, love, and individual freedom. (p. 987)

credibility [krĕd'ə-bĭl'ĭ-tē] **gap** *n.* a public distrust of statements made by the government. (p. 947)

credit [krĕd'ĭt] *n.* an arrangement in which a buyer pays later for a purchase, often on an installment plan with interest charges. (p. 672)

Crédit Mobilier [krĕd'ĭt mō-bēl'yər] *n.* a construction company formed in 1864 by owners of the Union Pacific Railroad, who used it to fraudulently skim off railroad profits for themselves. (p. 444)

Crusades [krōō-sādz'] *n.* a series of Christian military expeditions to the Middle East between A.D. 1096 and 1270, intended to drive the Muslims from the Holy Land. (p. 22)

cult of domesticity [dō'mĕ-stĭs'ĭ-tē] *n.* a belief that married women should restrict their activities to their home and family. (p. 254)

D

Dawes [dôz] **Act** *n.* a law, enacted in 1887, that was intended to "Americanize" Native Americans by distributing reservation land to individual owners. (p. 412)

D-Day *n.* a name given to June 6, 1944—the day on which the Allies launched an invasion of the European mainland during World War II. (p. 780)

debt peonage [dĕt′ pē′ə-nĭj] *n.* a system in which workers are bound in servitude until their debts are paid. (p. 495)

Declaration [dĕk′lə-rā′shən] **of Independence** *n.* the document, written by Thomas Jefferson in 1776, in which the delegates of the Continental Congress declared the colonies' independence from Britain. (p. 106)

de facto segregation [dĭ făk′tō sĕg′rĭ-gā′shən] *n.* racial separation established by practice and custom, not by law. (p. 924)

deficit [dĕf′ĭ-sĭt] **spending** *n.* a government's spending of more money than it receives in revenue. (p. 698)

de jure segregation [dē joŏr′ē sĕg′rĭ-gā′shən] *n.* racial separation established by law. (p. 924)

Democratic-Republican *n.* political party known for its support of strong state governments, founded by Thomas Jefferson in 1792 in opposition to the Federalist Party. (pp. 186, 225)

deregulation *n.* the cutting back of federal regulation of industry. (p. 1043)

détente [dā-tänt′] *n.* the flexible policy, involving a willingness to negotiate and an easing of tensions, that was adopted by President Richard Nixon and his adviser Henry Kissinger in their dealings with communist nations. (p. 1005)

direct relief [rĭ-lēf′] *n.* the giving of money or food by the government directly to needy people. (p. 681)

division of labor *n.* the assignment of different tasks and responsibilities to different groups or individuals. (p. 13)

Dixiecrat [dĭk′sē-krăt′] *n.* one of the Southern delegates who, to protest President Truman's civil rights policy, walked out of the 1948 Democratic National Convention and formed the States' Rights Democratic Party. (p. 844)

dollar diplomacy [dĭ-plō′mə-sē] *n.* the U.S. policy of using the nation's economic power to exert influence over other countries. (p. 569)

domino theory [dŏm′ə-nō′ thē′ə-rē] *n.* the idea that if a nation falls under communist control, nearby nations will also fall under communist control. (p. 937)

dotcom *n.* a business related to or conducted on the Internet. (p. 1077)

double standard *n.* a set of principles granting greater sexual freedom to men than to women. (p. 647)

dove [dŭv] *n.* a person who opposed the Vietnam War and believed that the United States should withdraw from it. (p. 952)

Dow Jones [dou′ jōnz′] **Industrial Average** *n.* a measure based on the prices of the stocks of 30 large companies, widely used as a barometer of the stock market's health. (p. 673)

downsize [doun′sīz′] *v.* to dismiss numbers of permanent employees in an attempt to make operations more efficient and save money. (p. 1076)

draft *n.* required enrollment in the armed services. (p. 948)

Dust Bowl *n.* the region, including Texas, Oklahoma, Kansas, Colorado, and New Mexico, that was made worthless for farming by drought and dust storms during the 1930s. (p. 680)

E

Earth Day *n.* a day set aside for environmental education, celebrated annually on April 22. (p. 1027)

Economic Opportunity Act *n.* a law, enacted in 1964, that provided funds for youth programs, antipoverty measures, small-business loans, and job training. (p. 894)

egalitarianism [ĭ-găl′ĭ-târ′ē-ə-nĭz′əm] *n.* the belief that all people should have equal political, economic, social, and civil rights. (p. 122)

Eisenhower Doctrine [ī′zən-hou′ər dŏk′trĭn] *n.* a U.S. commitment to defend the Middle East against attack by any communist country, announced by President Dwight D. Eisenhower in 1957. (p. 831)

electoral [ĭ-lĕk′tər-əl] **college** *n.* a group selected by the states to elect the president and the vice-president, in which each state's number of electors is equal to the number of its senators and representatives in Congress. (p. 144)

emancipation *n.* the freeing of slaves. (p. 249)

Emancipation Proclamation [prŏk′lə-mā′shən] *n.* an executive order issued by Abraham Lincoln on January 1, 1863, freeing the slaves in all regions behind Confederate lines. (p. 347)

embargo [ĕm-bär′gō] *n.* a government ban on trade with one or more other nations. (p. 203)

encomienda [ĕng-kô-myĕn′dä] *n.* a system in which Spanish authorities granted colonial landlords the service of Native Americans as forced laborers. (p. 38)

Enlightenment [ĕn-līt′n-mənt] *n.* an 18th-century intellectual movement that emphasized the use of reason and the scientific method as means of obtaining knowledge. (p. 82)

entitlement [ĕn-tīt′l-mənt] **program** *n.* a government program—such as Social Security, Medicare, or Medicaid—that guarantees and provides benefits to a specific group. (p. 1037)

entrepreneur [ŏn′trə-prə-nûr′] *n.* a person who organizes, operates, and assumes the risk for a business venture. (p. 275)

environmentalist [ĕn-vī′rən-mĕn′tl-ĭst] *n.* a person who works to protect the environment from destruction and pollution. (p. 1028)

Environmental Protection Agency (EPA) *n.* a federal agency established in 1970 for the regulation of water and air pollution, toxic waste, pesticides, and radiation. (pp. 1028, 1043)

Equal Rights Amendment (ERA) *n.* a proposed and failed amendment to the U.S. Constitution that would have prohibited any government discrimination on the basis of sex. (p. 985)

Erie Canal [ĭr′ē kə-năl′] *n.* a 363-mile-long artificial waterway connecting the Hudson River with Lake Erie, built between 1817 and 1825. (p. 217)

Espionage and Sedition [ĕs′pē-ə-näzh′ ənd sĭ-dĭsh′ən] **Acts** *n.* two laws, enacted in 1917 and 1918, that imposed harsh penalties on anyone interfering with or speaking against U.S. participation in World War I. (p. 598)

excise [ĕk′sīz′] **tax** *n.* a tax on the production, sale, or consumption of goods produced within a country. (p. 186)

executive [ĭg-zĕk′yə-tĭv] **branch** *n.* the branch of government that administers and enforces the laws. (p. 143)

exoduster [ĕk′sə-dŭs′tər] *n.* an African American who migrated from the South to Kansas in the post-Reconstruction years. (p. 421)

extortion *n.* illegal use of one's official position to obtain property or funds. (p. 475)

F

Fair Deal *n.* President Harry S. Truman's economic program—an extension of Franklin Roosevelt's New Deal—which included measures to increase the minimum wage, to extend social security coverage, and to provide housing for low-income families. (p. 845)

Family Assistance Plan *n.* a welfare-reform proposal, approved by the House of Representatives in 1970 but defeated in the Senate, that would have guaranteed an income to welfare recipients who agreed to undergo job training and to accept work. (p. 1001)

Farmers' Alliances *n.* groups of farmers, or those in sympathy with farming issues, who sent lecturers from town to town to educate people about agricultural and rural issues. (p. 427)

fascism [făsh′ĭz′əm] *n.* a political philosophy that advocates a strong, centralized, nationalistic government headed by a powerful dictator. (p. 736)

Federal Communications Commission (FCC) *n.* an agency that regulates U.S. communications industries, including radio and television broadcasting. (p. 859)

Federal Deposit Insurance Corporation (FDIC) *n.* an agency created in 1933 to insure individuals' bank accounts, protecting people against losses due to bank failures. (p. 723)

Federal Home Loan Bank Act *n.* a law, enacted in 1931, that lowered home mortgage rates and allowed farmers to refinance their loans and avoid foreclosure. (p. 687)

federalism *n.* a political system in which a national government and constituent units, such as state governments, share power. (p. 143)

Federalists [fĕd′ər-ə-lĭst] *n.* supporters of the Constitution and of a strong national government. (p. 146)

Federalist, The *n.* a series of essays defending and explaining the Constitution, written by Alexander Hamilton, James Madison, and John Jay. (p. 146)

Federal Reserve System *n.* a national banking system, established in 1913, that controls the U.S. money supply and the availability of credit in the country. (p. 540)

Federal Securities [sĭ-kyoŏr′ĭ-tēz] **Act** *n.* a law, enacted in 1933, that required corporations to provide complete, accurate information on all stock offerings. (p. 696)

Federal Trade Commission (FTC) *n.* a federal agency established in 1914 to investigate and stop unfair business practices. (p. 539)

feminism [fĕm′ə-nĭz′əm] *n.* the belief that women should have economic, political, and social equality with men. (p. 982)

Fifteenth Amendment *n.* an amendment to the U.S. Constitution, adopted in 1870, that prohibits the denial of voting rights to people because of their race or color or because they have previously been slaves. (p. 382)

"Fifty-Four Forty or Fight!" *n.* a slogan used in the 1844 presidential campaign as a call for the U.S. annexation of the entire Oregon Territory. (p. 285)

flapper *n.* one of the free-thinking young women who embraced the new fashions and urban attitudes of the 1920s. (p. 647)

flexible response [flĕk′sə-bəl rĭ-spŏns′] *n.* a policy, developed during the Kennedy administration, that involved preparing for a variety of military responses to international crises rather than focusing on the use of nuclear weapons. (p. 879)

Foraker [fôr′ə-kər] **Act** *n.* legislation passed by Congress in 1900, in which the U.S. ended military rule in Puerto Rico and set up a civil government. (p. 559)

Fordney-McCumber Tariff [fôrd′nē mə-kŭm′bər tăr′ĭf] *n.* a set of regulations, enacted by Congress in 1922, that raised taxes on imports to record levels in order to protect American businesses against foreign competition. (p. 626)

forty-niner *n.* one of the people who migrated to California in search of riches after gold was discovered there in 1848. (p. 298)

Fourteen Points *n.* the principles making up President Woodrow Wilson's plan for world peace following World War I. (p. 605)

Fourteenth Amendment *n.* an amendment to the U.S. Constitution, adopted in 1868, that makes all persons born or naturalized in the United States—including former slaves—citizens of the country and guarantees equal protection of the laws. (p. 379)

franchise [frăn′chīz′] *n.* a business that has bought the right to use a parent company's name and methods, thus becoming one of a number of similar businesses in various locations. (p. 848)

Freedmen's Bureau [frēd-mĕnz byoŏr′ō] *n.* a federal agency set up to help former slaves after the Civil War. (p. 379)

freedom rider *n.* one of the civil rights activists who rode buses through the South in the early 1960s to challenge segregation. (p. 916)

Freedom Summer *n.* a 1964 project to register African-American voters in Mississippi. (p. 921)

Freeport Doctrine [frē′pôrt′ dŏk′trĭn] *n.* the idea, expressed by Stephen Douglas in 1858, that any territory could exclude slavery by simply refusing to pass laws supporting it. (p. 326)

Free-Soil Party *n.* a political party formed in 1848 to oppose the extension of slavery into U.S. territories. (p. 319)

Free Speech Movement *n.* an antiestablishment New Left organization that originated in a 1964 clash between students and administrators at the University of California at Berkeley. (p. 950)

French and Indian War *n.* a conflict in North America, lasting from 1754 to 1763, that was a part of a worldwide struggle between France and Britain and that ended with the defeat of France and the transfer of French Canada to Britain. (p. 86)

Fugitive [fyoō′jĭ-tĭv] **Slave Act** *n.* a law enacted as part of the Compromise of 1850, designed to ensure that escaped slaves would be returned into bondage. (p. 310)

Fundamentalism [fŭn′də-mĕn′tl-ĭz′əm] *n.* a Protestant religious movement grounded in the belief that all the stories and details in the Bible are literally true. (p. 644)

G

Gadsden [gădz′dən] **Purchase** *n.* an 1853 purchase by the United States of land from Mexico, establishing the present U.S.-Mexico boundary. (p. 297)

gag rule *n.* a rule limiting or preventing debate on an issue. (p. 253)

General Agreement on Tariffs and Trade (GATT) [găt] *n.* an international agreement first signed in 1947. In 1994, the U.S. and other countries adopted a new version of GATT. This treaty lowered trade barriers, such as tariffs, and created the World Trade Organization, which resolves trade disputes. (p. 1078)

genetic engineering [jə-nĕt′ĭk ĕn′jə-nîr′ĭng] *n.* the alteration of the molecular biology of organisms' cells in order to create new varieties of bacteria, plants, and animals. (p. 1086)

Geneva Accords [jə-nē′və ə-kôrdz′] *n.* a 1954 peace agreement that divided Vietnam into Communist-controlled North Vietnam and non-Communist South Vietnam until unification elections could be held in 1956. (p. 938)

genocide [jĕn′ə-sīd′] *n.* the deliberate and systematic extermination of a particular racial, national, or religious group. (p. 750)

Gentlemen's Agreement *n.* A 1907–1908 agreement between the U.S. and Japanese governments to limit Japanese immigration to the United States. (p. 465)

gentrification [jĕn′trə-fĭ-kā′shən] *n.* the process of restoring deteriorated urban property by middle-class people, which often results in the displacement of lower-income residents. (p. 1089)

Gettysburg Address [gĕt′ēz-bûrg′ ə-drĕs′] *n.* a famous speech delivered by Abraham Lincoln in November 1863, at the dedication of a national cemetery on the site of the Battle of Gettysburg. (p. 361)

ghetto [gĕt′ō] *n.* a city neighborhood in which a certain minority group is pressured or forced to live. (p. 751)

GI Bill of Rights *n.* a name given to the Servicemen's Readjustment Act, a 1944 law that provided financial and educational benefits for World War II veterans. (pp. 798, 841)

glasnost [gläs′nəst] *n.* the open discussion of social problems that was permitted in the Soviet Union in the 1980s. (p. 1055)

Glass-Steagall [glăs′ stē′gəl] **Act** *n.* the 1933 law that established the Federal Deposit Insurance Corporation to protect individuals' bank accounts. (p. 696)

Glorious Revolution *n.* the transfer of the British monarchy from James II to William and Mary in 1688–1689. (p. 69)

gold rush *n.* a movement of many people to a region in which gold has been discovered. (p. 298)

gold standard *n.* a monetary system in which the basic unit of currency is defined in terms of a set amount of gold. (p. 428)

Gone with the Wind *n.* a 1939 movie dealing with the life of Southern plantation owners during the Civil War—one of the most popular films of all time. (p. 717)

graft *n.* the illegal use of political influence for personal gain. (p. 475)

grandfather clause *n.* a provision that exempts certain people from a law on the basis of previously existing circumstances—especially a clause formerly in some Southern states' constitutions that exempted whites from the strict voting requirements used to keep African Americans from the polls. (p. 493)

Grange [grānj] *n.* the Patrons of Husbandry—a social and educational organization through which farmers attempted to combat the power of the railroads in the late 19th century. (p. 427)

Grapes of Wrath, The *n.* a novel by John Steinbeck, published in 1939, that deals with a family of Oklahomans who leave the Dust Bowl for California. (p. 720)

Great Awakening *n.* a revival of religious feeling in the American colonies during the 1730s and 1750s. (p. 83)

Great Compromise [kŏm′prə-mīz′] *n.* the Constitutional Convention's agreement to establish a two-house national legislature, with all states having equal representation in one house and each state having representation based on its population in the other house. (p. 142)

Great Depression *n.* a period, lasting from 1929 to 1940, in which the U.S. economy was in severe decline and millions of Americans were unemployed. (p. 675)

Great Migration [mĭ-grā′shən] *n.* the large-scale movement of African Americans from the South to Northern cities in the early 20th century. (p. 599)

Great Plains *n.* the vast grassland that extends through the central portion of North America, from Texas northward to Canada, east of the Rocky Mountains. (p. 408)

Great Society *n.* President Lyndon B. Johnson's program to reduce poverty and racial injustice and to promote a better quality of life in the United States. (p. 895)

H

habeas corpus [hā′bē-əs kôr′pəs] *n.* a court order requiring authorities to bring a prisoner before the court so that the court can determine whether the prisoner is being held legally. (p. 349)

Haight-Ashbury [hāt′ ăsh′bĕr-ē] *n.* a San Francisco district that became the "capital" of the hippie counterculture during the 1960s. (p. 988)

Harlem Renaissance [här′ləm rĕn′ĭ-säns′] *n.* a flowering of African-American artistic creativity during the 1920s, centered in the Harlem community of New York City. (p. 660)

hawk *n.* a person who supported U.S. involvement in the Vietnam War and believed that the United States should use increased military force to win it. (p. 952)

Hawley-Smoot Tariff [hô′lē smōōt′ tăr′ĭf] **Act** *n.* a law, enacted in 1930, that established the highest protective tariff in U.S. history, worsening the depression in America and abroad. (p. 677)

H-bomb *n.* the hydrogen bomb—a thermonuclear weapon much more powerful than the atomic bomb. (p. 829)

headright [hĕd′rīt′] **system** *n.* the Virginia Company's policy of granting 50 acres of land to each settler and to each family member who accompanied him. (p. 45)

hierarchy [hī′ə-rär′kē] *n.* a social ordering by rank or class. (p. 20)

Ho Chi Minh [hō′ chē′ mĭn′] **Trail** *n.* a network of paths used by North Vietnam to transport supplies to the Vietcong in South Vietnam. (p. 938)

Hohokam [hə-hō′kəm] *n.* a Native American group that lived in the valleys of the Salt and Gila rivers (in what is now Arizona) from about 300 B.C. to A.D. 1400. (p. 7)

Hollywood Ten *n.* ten witnesses from the film industry who refused to cooperate with the HUAC's investigation of Communist influence in Hollywood. (p. 823)

Holocaust [hŏl′ə-kôst′] *n.* the systematic murder—or genocide—of Jews and other groups in Europe by the Nazis before and during World War II. (p. 748)

home rule *n.* a state's powers of governing its citizens without federal government involvement. (p. 399)

Homestead [hōm′stěd′] **Act** *n.* a U.S. law enacted in 1862, that provided 160 acres in the West to any citizen or intended citizen who was head of household and would cultivate the land for five years; a law whose passage led to record numbers of U.S. settlers claiming private property which previously had been reserved by treaty and by tradition for Native American nomadic dwelling and use; the same law strengthened in 1889 to encourage individuals to exercise their private property rights and develop homesteads out of the vast government lands. (p. 421)

Hopewell [hōp′wĕl′] *n.* a Mound Builder society that was centered in the Ohio River valley and flourished from about 200 B.C. to A.D. 400. (p. 7)

horizontal integration [hôr′ĭ-zŏn′tl ĭn′tĭ-grā′shən] *n.* the merging of companies that make similar products. (p. 448)

hot line *n.* a communication link established in 1963 to allow the leaders of the United States and the Soviet Union to contact each other in times of crisis. (p. 884)

House Un-American Activities Committee (HUAC) [hyoo̅′ăk′] *n.* a congressional committee that investigated Communist influence inside and outside the U.S. government in the years following World War II. (p. 823)

human rights *n.* the rights and freedoms, such as those named in the Declaration of Independence and the Bill of Rights, to which all people are entitled. (p. 1021)

Immigration Act of 1965 *n.* a law that increased the number of immigrants allowed to settle in the United States. (p. 897)

impeach *v.* to formally charge an official with misconduct in office. The House of Representatives has the sole power to impeach federal officials. (p. 381)

impeachment *n.* the process of accusing a public official of wrongdoing. (p. 1008)

imperialism [ĭm-pîr′ē-ə-lĭz′əm] *n.* the policy of extending a nation's authority over other countries by economic, political, or military means. (p. 548)

impressment [ĭm-prĕs′mənt] *n.* the forcible seizure of men for military service. (p. 202)

Inca [ĭng′kə] *n.* a Native American people that around A.D. 1400 created an empire reaching nearly 2,500 miles along the west coast of South America. (p. 6)

incandescent [ĭn′kən-dĕs′ənt] *adj.* giving off visible light as a result of being heated. (p. 438)

income tax *n.* a tax on earnings. (p. 354)

indentured [ĭn-dĕn′chərd] **servant** *n.* a person who has contracted to work for another for a limited period, often in return for travel expenses, shelter, and sustenance. (p. 45)

Indian Removal Act *n.* a law, enacted in 1830, that forced Native American peoples east of the Mississippi to move to lands in the West. (p. 226)

Industrial Revolution *n.* the change in social and economic organization that resulted from the replacement of hand tools with machines and from the development of large-scale industrial production. (p. 212)

Industrial Workers of the World (IWW) *n.* a labor organization for unskilled workers, formed by a group of radical unionists and socialists in 1905. (p. 452)

inflation [ĭn-flā′shən] *n.* an increase in prices or decline in purchasing power caused by an increase in the supply of money. (p. 116)

information superhighway [soo̅′pər-hī′wā] *n.* a computer communications network linking people and institutions throughout the world, providing individuals with services such as libraries, shopping, movies, and news. (p. 1083)

INF Treaty *n.* the Intermediate-Range Nuclear Forces Treaty—a 1987 agreement between the United States and the Soviet Union that eliminated some weapons systems and allowed for on-site inspection of military installations. (p. 1055)

initiative [ĭ-nĭsh′ə-tĭv] *n.* a procedure by which a legislative measure can be originated by the people rather than by lawmakers. (p. 518)

installment [ĭn-stôl′mənt] **plan** *n.* an arrangement in which a purchaser pays over an extended time, without having to put down much money at the time of purchase. (p. 632)

interchangeable [ĭn′tər-chān′jə-bəl] **parts** *n.* standardized parts that can be used in place of one another. (p. 212)

Internet [ĭn′tər-nĕt′] *n.* a worldwide network, originally developed by the U.S. Department of Defense, that links computers and allows almost immediate communication of texts, pictures, and sounds. (p. 1083)

internment *n.* confinement or a restriction in movement, especially under wartime conditions. (p. 800)

Interstate [ĭn′tər-stāt′] **Commerce Act** *n.* a law, enacted in 1887, that reestablished the federal government's right to supervise railroad activities and created a five-member Interstate Commerce Commission to do so. (p. 445)

Intolerable [ĭn-tŏl′ər-ə-bəl] **Acts** *n.* a series of laws enacted by Parliament in 1774 to punish Massachusetts colonists for the Boston Tea Party. (p. 99)

iron curtain [ī′ərn kûr′tn] *n.* a phrase used by Winston Churchill in 1946 to describe an imaginary line that separated Communist countries in the Soviet bloc of Eastern Europe from countries in Western Europe. (p. 811)

Iroquois [ĭr′ə-kwoi′] *n.* a group of Native American peoples inhabiting the woodlands of the Northeast. (p. 10)

Islam [ĭs-läm′] *n.* a religion founded in Arabia in A.D. 622 by the prophet Muhammad; its believers are called Muslims. (p. 15)

isolationism [ī′sə-lā′shə-nĭzm] *n.* opposition to political and economic entanglements with other countries. (p. 618)

Japanese American Citizens League (JACL) *n.* an organization that pushed the U.S. government to compensate Japanese Americans for property they had lost when they were interned during World War II. (p. 801)

jazz *n.* a style of music characterized by the use of improvisation. (p. 863)

Jim Crow laws *n.* laws enacted by Southern state and local governments to separate white and black people in public and private facilities. (p. 493)

joint-stock companies *n.* businesses in which investors pool their wealth for a common purpose. (p. 42)

journeyman [jûr′nē-mən] *n.* in the apprentice system, a skilled worker employed by a master. (p. 260)

judicial [jōō-dĭsh′əl] **branch** *n.* the branch of government that interprets the laws and the Constitution. (p. 143)

judicial review *n.* the Supreme Court's power to declare an act of Congress unconstitutional. (p. 199)

Judiciary [jōō-dĭsh′ē-ĕr′ē] **Act of 1789** *n.* a law that established the federal court system and the number of Supreme Court justices and that provided for the appeal of certain state court decisions to the federal courts. (p. 183)

Judiciary [jōō-dĭsh′ē-ĕr′ē] **Act of 1801** *n.* a law that increased the number of federal judges, allowing President John Adams to fill most of the new posts with Federalists. (p. 199)

Jungle, The *n.* a novel by Upton Sinclair, published in 1906, that portrays the dangerous and unhealthy conditions prevalent in the meatpacking industry at that time. (p. 523)

K

kamikaze [kä′mĭ-kä′zē] *adj.* involving or engaging in the deliberate crashing of a bomb-filled airplane into a military target. (p. 787)

Kansas-Nebraska Act *n.* a law, enacted in 1854, that established the territories of Kansas and Nebraska and gave their residents the right to decide whether to allow slavery. (p. 315)

Kashaya Pomo [kə-shä′yə pō′mō] *n.* a Native American people that formerly inhabited the coastal marshlands of what is now California. (p. 8)

Kent State University *n.* an Ohio university where National Guardsmen opened fire on students protesting the Vietnam War on May 4, 1970, wounding nine and killing four. (p. 962)

Kerner [kûr′nər] **Commission** *n.* a group that was appointed by President Johnson to study the causes of urban violence and that recommended the elimination of de facto segregation in American society. (p. 928)

King Philip's War *n.* a conflict, in the years 1675–1676, between New England colonists and Native American groups allied under the leadership of the Wampanoag chief Metacom. (p. 54)

kinship [kĭn′shĭp′] *n.* the ties between members of a family. (p. 13)

Know-Nothing Party *n.* a name given to the American Party, formed in the 1850s to curtail the political influence of immigrants. (p. 319)

Kongo [kŏng′gō] *n.* a group of small kingdoms along the Zaire River in West-Central Africa, united under a single leader in the late 1400s. (p. 17)

Korean [kə-rē′ən] **War** *n.* a conflict between North Korea and South Korea, lasting from 1950 to 1953, in which the United States, along with other UN countries, fought on the side of the South Koreans and China fought on the side of the North Koreans. (p. 817)

Kristallnacht [krĭ-stäl′näКНt′] *n.* "night of broken glass," a name given to the night of November 9, 1938, when gangs of Nazi storm troopers attacked Jewish homes, businesses, and synagogues in Germany. (p. 749)

Ku Klux Klan [kōō′ klŭks klăn′] **(KKK)** *n.* a secret organization that used terrorist tactics in an attempt to restore white supremacy in Southern states after the Civil War. (p. 394)

Kwakiutl [kwä′kē-ōōt′l] *n.* a Native American people that formerly inhabited the northwestern coastal region of North America. (p. 9)

L

land grant *n.* a gift of public land to an individual or organization. (p. 289)

Land Ordinance [ôr′dn-əns] **of 1785** *n.* a law that established a plan for surveying and selling the federally owned lands west of the Appalachian Mountains. (p. 135)

La Raza Unida [lä rä′sä ōō-nē′dä] *n.* a Latino political organization founded in 1970 by José Angel Gutiérrez. (p. 976)

League of Nations *n.* an association of nations established in 1920 to promote international cooperation and peace. (p. 605)

legislative [lĕj′ĭ-slā′tĭv] **branch** *n.* the branch of government that makes laws. (p. 143)

Lend-Lease Act *n.* a law, passed in 1941, that allowed the United States to ship arms and other supplies, without immediate payment, to nations fighting the Axis powers. (p. 758)

Limited Test Ban Treaty *n.* the 1963 treaty in which the United States and the Soviet Union agreed not to conduct nuclear-weapons tests in the atmosphere. (p. 884)

lineage [lĭn′ē-ĭj] *n.* a group of people descended from a common ancestor. (p. 18)

long drive *n.* the moving of cattle over trails to a shipping center. (p. 416)

longhorn [lông′hôrn′] *n.* a breed of sturdy, long-horned cattle brought by the Spanish to Mexico and suited to the dry conditions of the Southwest. (p. 414)

Louisiana Purchase *n.* the 1803 purchase by the United States of France's Louisiana Territory—extending from the Mississippi River to the Rocky Mountains—for $15 million. (p. 201)

Loyalists [loi′ə-lĭst] *n.* colonists who supported the British government during the American Revolution. (p. 106)

Lusitania [lōō′sĭ-tā′nē-ə] *n.* a British passenger ship that was sunk by a German U-boat in 1915. (p. 584)

M

mandate [măn′dāt′] *n.* the authority to act that an elected official receives from the voters who elected him or her. (p. 886)

Manhattan Project [măn-hăt′n prŏj′ĕkt′] *n.* the U.S. program to develop an atomic bomb for use in World War II. (p. 773)

manifest destiny [măn′ə-fĕst′ dĕs′tə-nē] *n.* the 19th-century belief that the United States would inevitably expand westward to the Pacific Ocean and into Mexican territory. (p. 281)

Marbury* v. *Madison [mär′bûr-ē vûr′səs măd′ĭ-sən] *n.* an 1803 case in which the Supreme Court ruled that it had the power to abolish legislative acts by declaring them unconstitutional; this power came to be known as judicial review. (p. 199)

market revolution *n.* the major change in the U.S. economy produced by people's beginning to buy and sell goods rather than make them for themselves. (p. 275)

Marshall [mär′shəl] **Plan** *n.* the program, proposed by Secretary of State George Marshall in 1947, under which the United States supplied economic aid to European nations to help them rebuild after World War II. (p. 812)

martial [mär′shəl] **law** *n.* temporary rule by military rather than civilian authority. (p. 99)

mass media [mē′dē-ə] *n.* the means of communication—such as television, newspapers, and radio—that reach large audiences. (p. 858)

mass production *n.* the production of goods in large quantities, made possible by the use of machinery and the division of labor. (p. 212)

mass transit *n.* transportation systems designed to move large numbers of people along fixed routes. (p. 470)

master *n.* a skilled artisan, usually one owning a business and employing others. (p. 260)

Maya [mä′yə] *n.* a Native American people whose civilization flourished in Guatemala and the Yucatán Peninsula between about A.D. 250 and 900. (p. 6)

McCarthyism [mə-kär′thē-ĭz′əm] *n.* the attacks, often unsubstantiated, by Senator Joseph McCarthy and others on people suspected of being Communists in the early 1950s. (p. 826)

McCulloch v. Maryland *n.* an 1819 case in which the Supreme Court ruled that Maryland had no right to tax the Bank of the United States, thereby strengthening the power of the federal government's control over the economy. (p. 220)

Meat Inspection Act *n.* a law, enacted in 1906, that established strict cleanliness requirements for meatpackers and created a federal meat-inspection program. (p. 526)

Medicaid [mĕd′ĭ-kād′] *n.* a program, established in 1965, that provides health insurance for people on welfare. (p. 896)

Medicare [mĕd′ĭ-kâr′] *n.* a federal program, established in 1965, that provides hospital insurance and low-cost medical insurance to Americans aged 65 and over. (p. 896)

melting pot *n.* a mixture of people from different cultures and races who blend together by abandoning their native languages and cultures. (p. 464)

mercantilism [mûr′kən-tē-lĭz′əm] *n.* an economic system in which nations seek to increase their wealth and power by obtaining large amounts of gold and silver and by establishing a favorable balance of trade. (p. 66)

Merrimack [mĕr′ə-măk′] *n.* an ironclad ship used by the South in the Civil War. (p. 343)

mestizo [mĕs-tē′zō] *adj.* of mixed Spanish and Native American ancestry. (p. 38)

middle passage *n.* the voyage that brought enslaved Africans to the West Indies and later to North America. (p. 76)

midnight judge *n.* one of the judges appointed by John Adams in the last hours of his administration. (p. 199)

militarism [mĭl′ĭ-tə-rĭz′əm] *n.* the policy of building up armed forces in aggressive preparedness for war and their use as a tool of diplomacy. (p. 579)

minutemen [mĭn′ĭt-mĕn′] *n.* Patriot civilian soldiers just before and during the Revolutionary War, pledged to be ready to fight at a minute's notice. (p. 100)

Mississippian [mĭs′ĭ-sĭp′ē-ən] *n.* the last and most complex of the Mound Builder societies, inhabiting the Ohio and Mississippi valleys from about A.D. 700 into the 1500s. (p. 7)

Missouri Compromise [kŏm′prə-mīz′] *n.* a series of agreements passed by Congress in 1820–1821 to maintain the balance of power between slave states and free states. (p. 222)

Monitor [mŏn′ĭ-tər] *n.* an ironclad ship used by the North in the Civil War. (p. 343)

Monroe Doctrine [mən-rō′ dŏk′trĭn] *n.* a policy of U.S. opposition to any European interference in the affairs of the Western Hemisphere, announced by President Monroe in 1823. (p. 221)

Moral Majority [môr′əl mə-jôr′ĭ-tē] *n.* a political alliance of religious groups, consisting mainly of evangelical and fundamentalist Christians, that was active in the 1970s and 1980s, condemning liberal attitudes and behavior and raising money for conservative candidates. (p. 1037)

Mormons [môr′mən] *n.* members of a church founded by Joseph Smith and his associates in 1830. (p. 284)

Morrill Acts [môr′əl] *n.* laws enacted in 1862 and 1890 to help create agricultural colleges by giving federal land to states. (p. 423)

muckraker [mŭk′rā′kər] *n.* one of the magazine journalists who exposed the corrupt side of business and public life in the early 1900s. (p. 514)

Munn v. Illinois [mŭn′ vûr′səs ĭl′ə-noi′] *n.* an 1877 case in which the Supreme Court upheld states' regulation of railroads for the benefit of farmers and consumers, thus establishing the right of government to regulate private industry to serve the public interest. (p. 445)

My Lai [mē′ lī′] *n.* a village in northern South Vietnam where more than 200 unarmed civilians, including women and children, were massacred by U.S. troops in May 1968. (p. 962)

N

NAACP [ĕn′ dŭb′əl ā′ sē′ pē′] *n.* the National Association for the Advancement of Colored People—an organization founded in 1909 to promote full racial equality. (p. 531)

NACW *n.* the National Association of Colored Women—a social service organization founded in 1896. (p. 521)

NAFTA [năf′tə] *n.* the North American Free Trade Agreement—a 1993 treaty that lowered tariffs and brought Mexico into the free-trade zone established by the United States and Canada. (p. 1070)

napalm [nā′päm′] *n.* a gasoline-based substance used in bombs that U.S. planes dropped in Vietnam in order to burn away jungle and expose Vietcong hideouts. (p. 945)

NASDAQ [năz′dăk′] *n.* the National Association of Securities Dealers Automated Quotation System—a stock exchange for over-the-counter sales, comprised largely of technology companies. (p. 1077)

National Bank Act *n.* legislation passed in 1863 to make banking safer for investors. Its provisions included a system of federally chartered banks, new requirements for loans, and a system for the inspection of banks. (p. 367)

National Energy Act *n.* a law, enacted during the Carter administration, that established a tax on "gas-guzzling" automobiles, removed price controls on U.S. oil and natural gas, and provided tax credits for the development of alternative energy sources. (p. 1019)

National Industrial Recovery Act (NIRA) *n.* a law enacted in 1933 to establish codes of fair practice for industries and to promote industrial growth. (p. 697)

nationalism *n.* a devotion to the interests and culture of one's nation. (pp. 220, 579)

National Labor Relations Board (NLRB) *n.* an agency created in 1935 to prevent unfair labor practices and to mediate disputes between workers and management. (p. 724)

National Organization for Women (NOW) *n.* an organization founded in 1966 to pursue feminist goals, such as better child-care facilities, improved educational opportunities, and an end to job discrimination. (p. 984)

National Road *n.* a federally funded road begun in 1811 and by 1838 extending from Cumberland, Maryland to Vandalia, Illinois. (p. 217)

National Trades' Union *n.* the first national association of trade unions, formed in 1834. (p. 265)

National Youth Administration *n.* an agency that provided young Americans with aid and employment during the Great Depression. (p. 705)

Nation of Islam [ĭs-läm´] *n.* a religious group, popularly known as the Black Muslims, founded by Elijah Muhammad to promote black separatism and the Islamic religion. (p. 925)

nativism [nā´tĭ-vĭz´əm] *n.* favoring the interests of native-born people over foreign-born people. (pp. 319, 618)

Navigation [năv´ĭ-gā´shən] **Acts** *n.* a series of laws enacted by Parliament, beginning in 1651, to tighten England's control of trade in its American colonies. (p. 68)

NAWSA *n.* the National American Woman Suffrage Association—an organization founded in 1890 to gain voting rights for women. (p. 522)

Nazism [nät´sĭz´əm] *n.* the political philosophy—based on extreme nationalism, racism, and militaristic expansionism—that Adolf Hitler put into practice in Germany from 1933 to 1945. (p. 737)

neutrality *n.* a refusal to take part in a war between other nations. (p. 191)

Neutrality Acts *n.* a series of laws enacted in 1935 and 1936 to prevent U.S. arms sales and loans to nations at war. (p. 741)

New Deal *n.* President Franklin Roosevelt's program to alleviate the problems of the Great Depression, focusing on relief for the needy, economic recovery, and financial reform. (p. 695)

New Deal Coalition [kō´ə-lĭsh´ən] *n.* an alliance of diverse groups—including Southern whites, African Americans, and unionized workers—who supported the policies of the Democratic Party in the 1930s and 1940s. (p. 713)

New Federalism [fĕd´ər-ə-lĭz´əm] *n.* President Richard Nixon's program to turn over part of the federal government's power to state and local governments. (p. 1001)

New Frontier *n.* President John F. Kennedy's legislative program, which included proposals to provide medical care for the elderly, to rebuild blighted urban areas, to aid education, to bolster the national defense, to increase international aid, and to expand the space program. (p. 885)

New Left *n.* a youth-dominated political movement of the 1960s, embodied in such organizations as Students for a Democratic Society and the Free Speech Movement. (p. 950)

New Right *n.* a late-20th-century alliance of conservative special-interest groups concerned with cultural, social, and moral issues. (p. 1037)

Niagara Movement *n.* founded by W. E. B. Du Bois in 1905 to promote the education of African Americans in the liberal arts. (p. 491)

Nineteenth Amendment *n.* an amendment to the U.S. Constitution, adopted in 1920, that gives women the right to vote. (p. 541)

nomadic *adj.* having no fixed home, moving from place to place according to seasons and availability of food and water. (p. 5)

"no man's land" *n.* an unoccupied region between opposing armies. (p. 582)

nonaggression [nŏn´ə-grĕsh´ən] **pact** *n.* an agreement in which two nations promise not to go to war with each other. (p. 745)

North Atlantic Treaty Organization (NATO) *n.* a defensive military alliance formed in 1949 by ten Western European countries, the United States, and Canada. (p. 814)

Northwest Ordinance [ôr´dn-əns] **of 1787** *n.* a law that established a procedure for the admission of new states to the Union. (p. 135)

nuclear [nōō´klē-ər] **family** *n.* a household made up of a mother, a father, and their children. (p. 21)

nullification [nŭl´ə-fĭ-kā´shən] *n.* a state's refusal to recognize an act of Congress that it considers unconstitutional. (p. 196)

Nuremberg [nŏŏr´əm-bûrg´] **trials** *n.* the court proceedings held in Nuremberg, Germany, after World War II, in which Nazi leaders were tried for war crimes. (p. 792)

O

Office of Price Administration (OPA) *n.* an agency established by Congress to control inflation during World War II. (p. 773)

Ohio gang *n.* a group of close friends and political supporters whom President Warren G. Harding appointed to his cabinet. (p. 626)

Olive Branch Petition [pə-tĭsh´ən] *n.* a document sent by the Second Continental Congress to King George III, proposing a reconciliation between the colonies and Britain. (p. 105)

Olmec [ŏl´mĕk] *n.* a Native American people whose civilization flourished in what is now southern Mexico in the period 1200–400 B.C. (p. 6)

OPEC [ō´pĕk´] *n.* the Organization of Petroleum Exporting Countries—an economic association of oil-producing nations that is able to set oil prices. (p. 1005)

Open Door notes *n.* messages sent by Secretary of State John Hay in 1899 to Germany, Russia, Great Britain, France, Italy, and Japan, asking the countries not to interfere with U.S. trading rights in China. (p. 562)

Operation Desert Storm [dĕz´ərt stôrm´] *n.* a 1991 military operation in which UN forces, led by the United States, drove Iraqi invaders from Kuwait. (p. 1061)

Oregon Trail *n.* a route from Independence, Missouri, to Oregon City, Oregon, used by pioneers traveling to the Oregon Territory. (p. 284)

P

Panama Canal [păn´ə-mä´ kə-năl´] *n.* an artificial waterway cut through the Isthmus of Panama to provide a shortcut between the Atlantic and Pacific oceans, opened in 1914. (p. 566)

panic of 1837 *n.* a U.S. financial crisis in which banks closed and the credit system collapsed, resulting in many bankruptcies and high unemployment. (p. 234)

panic of 1873 *n.* a series of financial failures that triggered a five-year depression in the United States. (p. 397)

parity [păr′ĭ-tē] *n.* a government-supported level for the prices of agricultural products, intended to keep farmers' incomes steady. (p. 724)

Parliament [pär′lə-mənt] *n.* the legislative body of England. (p. 68)

Patriots [pā′trē-ət] *n.* colonists who supported American independence from Britain. (p. 106)

patronage [pā′trə-nĭj] *n.* an officeholder's power to appoint people—usually those who have helped him or her get elected—to positions in government. (p. 476)

pay equity [ĕk′wĭ-tē] *n.* the basing of an employee's salary on the requirements of his or her job rather than on the traditional pay scales that have frequently provided women with smaller incomes than men. (p. 1048)

Payne-Aldrich Tariff [pān′ ôl′drĭch tăr′ĭf] *n.* a set of tax regulations, enacted by Congress in 1909, that failed to significantly reduce tariffs on manufactured goods. (p. 535)

Peace Corps *n.* an agency established in 1961 to provide volunteer assistance to developing nations in Asia, Africa, and Latin America. (p. 886)

Pendleton [pĕn′dl-tən] **Civil Service Act** *n.* a law, enacted in 1883, that established a bipartisan civil service commission to make appointments to government jobs by means of the merit system. (p. 476)

Pentagon [pĕn′tə-gŏn′] **Papers** *n.* a 7,000-page document—leaked to the press in 1971 by the former Defense Department worker Daniel Ellsberg—revealing that the U.S. government had not been honest about its intentions in the Vietnam War. (p. 963)

Pequot [pē′kwŏt′] **War** *n.* a 1637 conflict in which the Pequot nation battled Connecticut colonists and their Narragansett allies. (p. 53)

perestroika [pĕr′ĭ-stroi′kə] *n.* the restructuring of the economy and the government instituted in the Soviet Union in the 1980s. (p. 1055)

personal liberty laws *n.* statutes, passed in nine Northern states in the 1850s, that forbade the imprisonment of runaway slaves and guaranteed jury trials for fugitive slaves. (p. 311)

planned obsolescence [ŏb′sə-lĕs′əns] *n.* the designing of products to wear out or to become outdated quickly, so that people will feel a need to replace their possessions frequently. (p. 854)

plantation [plăn-tā′shən] *n.* a large farm on which the labor of slaves or other workers is used to grow a single crop, such as sugar cane or cotton. (p. 16)

Platt [plăt] **Amendment** *n.* a series of provisions that, in 1901, the United States insisted Cuba add to its new constitution, commanding Cuba to stay out of debt and giving the United States the right to intervene in the country and the right to buy or lease Cuban land for naval and fueling stations. (p. 560)

Plessy v. *Ferguson* [plĕs′ē vûr′səs fûr′gə-sən] *n.* an 1896 case in which the Supreme Court ruled that separation of the races in public accommodations was legal, thus establishing the "separate but equal" doctrine. (p. 493)

political machine *n.* an organized group that controls a political party in a city and offers services to voters and businesses in exchange for political and financial support. (p. 474)

poll [pōl] **tax** *n.* an annual tax that formerly had to be paid in some Southern states by anyone wishing to vote. (p. 493)

popular sovereignty [sŏv′ər-ĭn-tē] *n.* a system in which the residents vote to decide an issue. (p. 307)

Populism [pŏp′yə-lĭz′əm] *n.* a late-19th-century political movement demanding that people have a greater voice in government and seeking to advance the interests of farmers and laborers. (p. 427)

Powhatan [pou′ə-tăn′] *n.* a group of Native American peoples that lived in eastern Virginia at the time of the first English settlements there. (p. 43)

price support *n.* the maintenance of a price at a certain level through government intervention. (p. 671)

Proclamation [prŏk′lə-mā′shən] **of 1763** *n.* an order in which Britain prohibited its American colonists from settling west of the Appalachian Mountains. (p. 88)

profiteering [prŏf′ĭ-tîr′ĭng] *n.* the selling of goods in short supply at inflated prices. (p. 116)

progressive [prə-grĕs′ĭv] **movement** *n.* an early-20th-century reform movement seeking to return control of the government to the people, to restore economic opportunities, and to correct injustices in American life. (p. 513)

prohibition [prō′ə-bĭsh′ən] *n.* the banning of the manufacture, sale, and possession of alcoholic beverages. (p. 513)

Prohibition [prō′ə-bĭsh′ən] *n.* the period from 1920–1933 during which the Eighteenth Amendment forbidding the manufacture and sale of alcohol was in force in the United States. (p. 642)

propaganda [prŏp′ə-găn′də] *n.* a kind of biased communication designed to influence people's thoughts and actions. (p. 596)

Proposition 187 *n.* a bill passed in California in 1994 that ended all education and nonemergency health benefits to illegal immigrants. (p. 1092)

proprietor [prə-prī′ĭ-tər] *n.* an owner—particularly one of those granted ownership of, and full governing rights over, certain of the English colonies in North America. (p. 56)

protective tariff [prə-tĕk′tĭv tăr′ĭf] *n.* a tax on imported goods that is intended to protect a nation's businesses from foreign competition. (p. 186)

protectorate [prə-tĕk′tə-rĭt] *n.* a country whose affairs are partially controlled by a stronger power. (p. 560)

Pueblo [pwĕb′lō] *n.* a group of Native American peoples—descendants of the Anasazi—inhabiting the deserts of the Southwest. (p. 9)

Pure Food and Drug Act *n.* a law enacted in 1906 to halt the sale of contaminated foods and drugs and to ensure truth in labeling. (p. 528)

Puritans [pyŏŏr′ĭ-tnz] *n.* members of a group that wanted to eliminate all traces of Roman Catholic ritual and traditions in the Church of England. (p. 49)

Q

Quakers [kwā′kərz] *n.* members of the Society of Friends, a religious group persecuted for its beliefs in 17th-century England. (p. 56)

quota [kwō′tə] **system** *n.* a system that sets limits on how many immigrants from various countries a nation will admit each year. (p. 621)

R

Radical Republican [răd′ĭ-kəl rĭ-pŭb′lĭ-kən] *n.* one of the congressional Republicans who, after the Civil War, wanted to destroy the political power of former slaveholders and to give African Americans full citizenship and the right to vote. (p. 377)

ratification [răt′ə-fĭ-kā′shən] *n.* the official approval of the Constitution, or of an amendment, by the states. (p. 146)

rationing [răsh′ə-nĭng] *n.* a restriction of people's right to buy unlimited amounts of particular foods and other goods, often implemented during wartime to ensure adequate supplies for the military. (p. 774)

Reaganomics [rā′gə-nŏm′ĭks] *n.* the economic policies of President Ronald Reagan, which were focused on budget cuts and the granting of large tax cuts in order to increase private investment. (p. 1040)

realpolitik [rā-äl′pō′lĭ-tēk′] *n.* a foreign policy advocated by Henry Kissinger in the Nixon administration, based on consideration of a nation's power rather than its ideals or moral principles. (p. 1005)

reapportionment [rē′ə-pôr′shən-mənt] *n.* the redrawing of election districts to reflect changes in population. (p. 897)

recall [rĭ-kôl′] *n.* a procedure for removing a public official from office by a vote of the people. (p. 518)

Reconstruction [rē′kən-strŭk′shən] *n.* the period of rebuilding that followed the Civil War, during which the defeated Confederate states were readmitted to the Union. (p. 376)

Reconstruction Finance [fə-năns′] **Corporation (RFC)** *n.* an agency established in 1932 to provide emergency financing to banks, life-insurance companies, railroads, and other large businesses. (p. 687)

Red Cross *n.* an international organization that provides relief to people in times of war or natural disaster. Clara Barton founded the American branch in 1881. (p. 370)

redemption [rĭ-dĕmp′shən] *n.* the Southern Democrats' term for their return to power in the South in the 1870s. (p. 399)

referendum [rĕf′ə-rĕn′dəm] *n.* a procedure by which a proposed legislative measure can be submitted to a vote of the people. (p. 518)

Reformation [rĕf′ər-mā′shən] *n.* a religious movement in 16th-century Europe, growing out of a desire for reform in the Roman Catholic Church and leading to the establishment of various Protestant churches. (p. 22)

Renaissance [rĕn′ĭ-säns′] *n.* a period of European history, lasting from about 1400 to 1600, during which renewed interest in classical culture led to far-reaching changes in art, learning, and views of the world. (p. 20)

reparations [rĕp′ə-rā′shənz] *n.* the compensation paid by a defeated nation for the damage or injury it inflicted during a war. (p. 606)

republic [rĭ-pŭb′lĭk] *n.* a government in which the citizens rule through elected representatives. (p. 133)

Republican Party *n.* the modern political party that was formed in 1854 by opponents of slavery in the territories. (p. 320)

republicanism [rĭ-pŭb′lĭ-kə-nĭz′əm] *n.* the belief that government should be based on the consent of the people. (p. 133)

Republic of California *n.* the nation proclaimed by American settlers in California when they declared their independence from Mexico in 1846. (p. 295)

Republic of Texas *n.* the nation established in 1836 when American settlers in the Mexican province of Texas declared and fought for their independence, also commonly known at that time as the "Lone Star Republic." (p. 292)

revenue [rĕv′ə-nōō] **sharing** *n.* the distribution of federal money to state and local governments with few or no restrictions on how it is spent. (p. 1001)

reverse discrimination [dĭ-skrĭm′ə-nā′shən] *n.* an unfair treatment of members of a majority group—for example, white men—resulting from efforts to correct discrimination against members of other groups. (p. 1037)

revival [rĭ-vī′vəl] *n.* a religious gathering designed to reawaken faith through impassioned preaching. (p. 241)

rock 'n' roll [rŏk′ən-rōl′] *n.* a form of American popular music that evolved in the 1950s out of rhythm and blues, country, jazz, gospel, and pop; the American musical form characterized by heavy rhythms and simple melodies which has spread worldwide having significant impacts on social dancing, clothing fashions, and expressions of protest. (p. 861)

Roosevelt Corollary [rō′zə-vĕlt′ kôr′ə-lĕr-ē] *n.* an extension of the Monroe Doctrine, announced by President Theodore Roosevelt in 1904, under which the United States claimed the right to protect its economic interests by means of military intervention in the affairs of Western Hemisphere nations. (p. 568)

Rough Riders *n.* a volunteer cavalry regiment, commanded by Leonard Wood and Theodore Roosevelt, that served in the Spanish-American War. (p. 556)

royal colony *n.* a colony under the direct control of the English monarch. (p. 47)

rural free delivery (RFD) *n.* the free government delivery of mail and packages to homes in rural areas, begun in 1896. (p. 503)

S

SALT I [sôlt′ wŭn′] **Treaty** *n.* a five-year agreement between the United States and the Soviet Union, signed in 1972, that limited the nations' numbers of intercontinental ballistic missiles and submarine-launched missiles. (p. 1007)

salutary neglect [săl′yə-tĕr′ē nĭ-glĕkt′] *n.* an English policy of relaxing the enforcement of regulations in its colonies in return for the colonies' continued economic loyalty. (p. 70)

Sandinista [săn′dĭ-nēs′tə] *n.* a member of a leftist rebel group that overthrew the Nicaraguan government in 1979. (p. 1057)

Santa Fe [săn′tə fā′] **Trail** *n.* a route from Independence, Missouri, to Santa Fe, New Mexico, used by traders in the early and mid-1800s. (p. 282)

satellite [săt′l-īt′] **nation** *n.* a country that is dominated politically and economically by another nation. (p. 811)

Saturday Night Massacre [măs′ə-kər] *n.* a name given to the resignation of the U.S. attorney general and the firing of his deputy in October 1973, after they refused to carry out President Nixon's order to fire the special prosecutor investigating the Watergate affair. (p. 1011)

savanna [sə-văn′ə] *n.* a dry grassland dotted with trees and bushes, found in sub-Saharan Africa and other tropical or subtropical regions. (p. 17)

scalawag [skăl′ə-wăg′] *n.* a white Southerner who joined the Republican Party after the Civil War. (p. 385)

scientific management *n.* the application of scientific principles to increase efficiency in the workplace. (p. 514)

Scopes [skōps] **trial** *n.* a sensational 1925 court case in which the biology teacher John T. Scopes was tried for challenging a Tennessee law that outlawed the teaching of evolution. (p. 644)

search-and-destroy mission [sûrch′ ənd′ dĭ-stroi′ mĭsh′ən] *n.* a U.S. military raid on a South Vietnamese village, intended to root out villagers with ties to the Vietcong but often resulting in the destruction of the village and the displacement of its inhabitants. (p. 945)

secession [sĭ-sĕsh′ən] *n.* the formal withdrawal of a state from the Union. (p. 307)

Second Continental Congress *n.* the Continental Congress that convened in May 1775, approved the Declaration of Independence, and served as the only agency of national government during the Revolutionary War. (p. 103)

Second Great Awakening *n.* a 19th-century religious movement in which individual responsibility for seeking salvation was emphasized, along with the need for personal and social improvement. (p. 240)

sectionalism [sĕk′shə-nə-lĭz′əm] *n.* the placing of the interests of one's own region ahead of the interests of the nation as a whole. (p. 194)

Securities and Exchange [sĭ-kyŏŏr′ĭ-tez ənd ĭks-chānj′] **Commission (SEC)** *n.* an agency, created in 1934, that monitors the stock market and enforces laws regulating the sale of stocks and bonds. (p. 723)

segregation [sĕg′rĭ-gā′shən] *n.* the separation of people on the basis of race. (p. 493)

Selective [sĭ-lĕk′tĭv] **Service Act** *n.* a law, enacted in 1917, that required men to register for military service. (p. 588)

Seneca Falls [sĕn′ĭ-kə fôlz′] **Convention** *n.* a women's rights convention held in Seneca Falls, New York, in 1848. (p. 257)

Separatist [sĕp′ər-ə-tĭst] *n.* a member of one of the Puritan groups that, denying the possibility of reform within the Church of England, established their own independent congregations. (p. 50)

service sector [sĕk′tər] *n.* the part of the economy that provides consumers with services rather than goods. (p. 1076)

settlement house *n.* a community center providing assistance to residents—particularly immigrants—in a slum neighborhood. (p. 472)

Seventeenth Amendment *n.* an amendment to the U.S. Constitution, adopted in 1913, that provides for the election of U.S. senators by the people rather than by state legislatures. (p. 518)

shantytown [shăn′tē-toun′] *n.* a neighborhood in which people live in makeshift shacks. (p. 679)

sharecropping [shâr′krŏp′ĭng] *n.* a system in which landowners give farm workers land, seed, and tools in return for a part of the crops they raise. (p. 391)

Shays's [shā′zəz] **Rebellion** *n.* an uprising of debt-ridden Massachusetts farmers protesting increased state taxes in 1787. (p. 140)

Sherman Antitrust [shûr′mən ăn′tē-trŭst′] **Act** *n.* a law, enacted in 1890, that was intended to prevent the creation of monopolies by making it illegal to establish trusts that interfered with free trade. (p. 450)

silent majority [mə-jôr′ĭ-tē] *n.* a name given by President Richard Nixon to the moderate, mainstream Americans who quietly supported his Vietnam War policies. (p. 962)

sit-in *n.* a form of demonstration used by African Americans to protest discrimination, in which the protesters sit down in a segregated business and refuse to leave until they are served. (p. 912)

slave *n.* a person who becomes the property of others. (p. 75)

Social Darwinism [sō′shəl där′wĭ-nĭz′əm] *n.* an economic and social philosophy—supposedly based on the biologist Charles Darwin's theory of evolution by natural selection—holding that a system of unrestrained competition will ensure the survival of the fittest. (p. 448)

Social Gospel [gŏs′pəl] **movement** *n.* a 19th-century reform movement based on the belief that Christians have a responsibility to help improve working conditions and alleviate poverty. (p. 472)

Social Security Act *n.* a law enacted in 1935 to provide aid to retirees, the unemployed, people with disabilities, and families with dependent children. (p. 707)

soddy [sŏd′ē] *n.* a home built of blocks of turf. (p. 422)

Songhai [sông′hī′] *n.* an empire that, at the height of its power in the 1500s, controlled much of West Africa. (p. 16)

soup kitchen *n.* a place where free or low cost food is served to the needy. (p. 679)

Southern Christian Leadership Conference (SCLC) *n.* an organization formed in 1957 by Dr. Martin Luther King, Jr., and other leaders to work for civil rights through nonviolent means. (p. 912)

Southern strategy *n.* President Nixon's attempt to attract the support of Southern conservative Democrats who were unhappy with federal desegregation policies and the liberal Supreme Court. (p. 1003)

speakeasy [spēk′ē′zē] *n.* a place where alcoholic drinks were sold and consumed illegally during Prohibition. (p. 642)

specialization [spĕsh′ə-lĭ-zā′shən] *n.* in farming, the raising of one or two crops for sale rather than a variety of foods for personal use. (p. 275)

speculation [spĕk′yə-lā′shən] *n.* an involvement in risky business transactions in an effort to make a quick or large profit. (p. 673)

spoils system *n.* the practice of winning candidates' rewarding their supporters with government jobs. (p. 226)

Square Deal *n.* President Theodore Roosevelt's program of progressive reforms designed to protect the common people against big business. (p. 525)

stagflation [stăg-flā′shən] *n.* an economic condition marked by both inflation and high unemployment. (p. 1004)

Stamp Act *n.* a 1765 law in which Parliament established the first direct taxation of goods and services within the British colonies in North America. (p. 96)

Stono [stō′nō] **Rebellion** *n.* a 1739 uprising of slaves in South Carolina, leading to the tightening of already harsh slave laws. (p. 78)

Strategic Defense Initiative [strə-tē′jĭk dĭ-fĕns′ ĭ-nĭsh′ə-tĭv] **(SDI)** *n.* a proposed defense system—popularly known as Star Wars—intended to protect the United States against missile attacks. (p. 1041)

strike *n.* a work stoppage intended to force an employer to respond to demands. (p. 262)

Student Nonviolent Coordinating [nŏn-vī′ə-lənt kō-ôr′dn-ā′t-ĭng] **Committee (SNCC)** [snĭk] *n.* an organization formed in 1960 to coordinate sit-ins and other protests and to give young blacks a larger role in the civil rights movement. (p. 912)

Students for a Democratic Society (SDS) *n.* an antiestablishment New Left group, founded in 1960, that called for greater individual freedom and responsibility. (p. 950)

suburb [sŭb′ûrb′] *n.* a residential town or community near a city. (p. 841)

suffrage [sŭf′rĭj] *n.* the right to vote. (p. 521)

Sugar Act *n.* a trade law enacted by Parliament in 1764 in an attempt to reduce smuggling in the British colonies in North America. (p. 89)

supply-side economics *n.* the idea that a reduction of tax rates will lead to increases in jobs, savings, and investments, and therefore to an increase in government revenue. (p. 1041)

T

Taino [tī′nō] *n.* a Native American people of the Caribbean islands—the first group encountered by Columbus and his men when they reached the Americas. (p. 27)

Tariff of Abominations [ə-bŏm′ə-nā′shənz] *n.* John C. Calhoun's name for an 1828 tariff increase that seemed to Southerners to be enriching the North at their expense. (p. 230)

Tariff of 1816 *n.* a protective tariff designed to aid American industries. (p. 218)

Teapot Dome scandal [skăn′dl] *n.* Secretary of the Interior Albert B. Fall's secret leasing of oil-rich public land to private companies in return for money and land. (p. 627)

Telecommunications [tĕl′ĭ-kə-myōō′nĭ-kā′shənz] **Act of 1996** *n.* a law enacted in 1996 to remove barriers that had previously prevented communications companies from engaging in more than one type of communications business. (p. 1084)

telecommute [tĕl′ĭ-kə-myōōt′] *v.* to work at home for a company located elsewhere, by using such communications technologies as computers, the Internet, and fax machines. (p. 1084)

telegraph [tĕl′ĭ-grăf′] *n.* a device for the electrical transmission of coded messages over wires. (p. 276)

temperance [tĕm′pər-əns] **movement** *n.* an organized effort to prevent the drinking of alcoholic beverages. (p. 255)

tenant [tĕn′ənt] **farming** *n.* a system in which farm workers supply their own tools and rent farmland for cash. (p. 391)

tenement [tĕn′ə-mənt] *n.* a multifamily urban dwelling, usually overcrowded and unsanitary. (p. 470)

Tennessee Valley Authority (TVA) *n.* a federal corporation established in 1933 to construct dams and power plants in the Tennessee Valley region to generate electricity as well as to prevent floods. (p. 725)

termination [tûr′mə-nā′shən] **policy** *n.* the U.S. government's plan, announced in 1953, to give up responsibility for Native American tribes by eliminating federal economic support, discontinuing the reservation system, and redistributing tribal lands. (p. 869)

Tet offensive [tĕt′ ə-fĕn′sĭv] *n.* a massive surprise attack by the Vietcong on South Vietnamese towns and cities early in 1968. (p. 955)

Texas Revolution *n.* the 1836 rebellion in which Texas gained its independence from Mexico. (p. 291)

Thirteenth Amendment *n.* an amendment to the U.S. Constitution, adopted in 1865, that has abolished slavery and involuntary servitude. (p. 368)

Three-Fifths Compromise [kŏm′prə-mīz′] *n.* the Constitutional Convention's agreement to count three-fifths of a state's slaves as population for purposes of representation and taxation. (p. 142)

Tiananmen [tyän′än′mĕn′] **Square** *n.* the site of 1989 demonstrations in Beijing, China, in which Chinese students demanded freedom of speech and a greater voice in government. (p. 1056)

Tonkin Gulf [tŏn′kĭn′ gŭlf′] **Resolution** *n.* a resolution adopted by Congress in 1964, giving the president broad powers to wage war in Vietnam. (p. 941)

totalitarian [tō-tăl′ĭ-târ′ē-ən] *adj.* characteristic of a political system in which the government exercises complete control over its citizens' lives. (p. 735)

Townshend [toun′zənd] **Acts** *n.* a series of laws enacted by Parliament in 1767, establishing indirect taxes on goods imported from Britain by the British colonies in North America. (p. 97)

Trail of Tears [tîrz] *n.* the marches in which the Cherokee people were forcibly removed from Georgia to the Indian Territory in 1838–1840, with thousands of the Cherokee dying on the way. (p. 229)

transcendentalism [trăn′sĕn-dĕn′tl-ĭz′əm] *n.* a philosophical and literary movement of the 1800s that emphasized living a simple life and celebrated the truth found in nature and in personal emotion and imagination. (p. 242)

transcontinental [trăns′kŏn-tə-nĕn′tl] **railroad** *n.* a railroad line linking the Atlantic and Pacific coasts of the United States, completed in 1869. (p. 443)

Treaty of Fort Laramie *n.* the treaty requiring the Sioux to live on a reservation along the Missouri River. (pp. 282, 410)

Treaty of Ghent [gĕnt] *n.* the 1814 treaty that ended the War of 1812. (p. 205)

Treaty of Guadalupe Hidalgo [gwäd′l-ōōp′ hĭ-däl′gō] *n.* the 1848 treaty ending the U.S. war with Mexico, in which Mexico ceded California and New Mexico to the United States. (p. 297)

Treaty of Paris (1783) *n.* the treaty that ended the Revolutionary War, confirming the independence of the United States and setting the boundaries of the new nation. (p. 122)

Treaty of Paris (1898) *n.* the treaty ending the Spanish-American War, in which Spain freed Cuba, turned over the islands of Guam and Puerto Rico to the United States, and sold the Philippines to the United States for $20 million. (p. 556)

Treaty of Tordesillas [tôr′də-sē′əs] *n.* the 1494 treaty in which Spain and Portugal agreed to divide the lands of the Western Hemisphere between them. (p. 30)

Treaty of Versailles [vər-sī′] *n.* the 1919 peace treaty at the end of World War I which established new nations, borders, and war reparations. (p. 606)

trench warfare *n.* military operations in which the opposing forces attack and counterattack from systems of fortified ditches rather than on an open battlefield. (p. 582)

triangular [trī-ăng′gyə-lər] **trade** *n.* the transatlantic system of trade in which goods and people, including slaves, were exchanged between Africa, England, Europe, the West Indies, and the colonies in North America. (p. 76)

Truman Doctrine [trōō′mən dŏk′trĭn] *n.* a U.S. policy, announced by President Harry S. Truman in 1947, of providing economic and military aid to free nations threatened by internal or external opponents. (p. 812)

Tuskegee [tŭs-kē′gē] **Normal and Industrial Institute** *n.* founded in 1881, and led by Booker T. Washington, to equip African Americans with teaching diplomas and useful skills in the trades and agriculture. (p. 491)

two-party system *n.* a political system dominated by two major parties. (p. 186)

U

Uncle Tom's Cabin *n.* a best-selling novel by Harriet Beecher Stowe, published in 1852, that portrayed slavery as a great moral evil. (p. 312)

Underground Railroad *n.* a system of routes along which runaway slaves were helped to escape to Canada or to safe areas in the free states. (p. 311)

United Farm Workers Organizing Committee (UFWOC) *n.* a labor union formed in 1966 to seek higher wages and better working conditions for Mexican-American farm workers in California. (p. 976)

United Nations (UN) *n.* an international peacekeeping organization to which most nations in the world belong, founded in 1945 to promote world peace, security, and economic development. (p. 809)

urban [ûr′bən] **flight** *n.* a migration of people from cities to the surrounding suburbs. (p. 1088)

urbanization [ûr′bə-nĭ-zā′shən] *n.* the growth of cities. (p. 468)

urban renewal [rĭ-nōō′əl] *n.* the tearing down and replacing of buildings in rundown inner-city neighborhoods. (p. 867)

urban sprawl [sprôl′] *n.* the unplanned and uncontrolled spreading of cities into surrounding regions. (p. 630)

USS *Maine* *n.* a U.S. warship that mysteriously exploded and sank in the harbor of Havana, Cuba, on February 15, 1898. (p. 554)

U-2 incident *n.* the downing of a U.S. spy plane and capture of its pilot by the Soviet Union in 1960. (p. 833)

utopian [yōō-tō′pē-ən] **community** *n.* an experimental community designed to be a perfect society, in which its members could live together in harmony. (p. 243)

V

V-E Day *n.* a name given to May 8, 1945, "Victory in Europe Day" on which General Eisenhower's acceptance of the unconditional surrender of Nazi Germany marked the end of World War II in Europe. (p. 783)

vertical integration [vûr′tĭ-kəl ĭn′tĭ-grā′shən] *n.* a company's taking over its suppliers and distributors and transportation systems to gain total control over the quality and cost of its product. (p. 448)

Vietcong [vē-ĕt′kŏng′] *n.* the South Vietnamese Communists who, with North Vietnamese support, fought against the government of South Vietnam in the Vietnam War. (p. 938)

Vietminh [vē-ĕt′mĭn′] *n.* an organization of Vietnamese Communists and other nationalist groups that between 1946 and 1954 fought for Vietnamese independence from the French. (p. 937)

Vietnamization [vē-ĕt′nə-mī-zā′shən] *n.* President Nixon's strategy for ending U.S. involvement in the Vietnam War, involving the gradual withdrawal of U.S. troops and their replacement with South Vietnamese forces. (p. 961)

Voting Rights Act of 1965 *n.* a law that made it easier for African Americans to register to vote by eliminating discriminatory literacy tests and authorizing federal examiners to enroll voters denied at the local level. (p. 922)

W

Wade-Davis [wād′ dā′vəs] **Bill** *n.* a bill, passed in 1864 and vetoed by President Lincoln, that would have given Congress control of Reconstruction. (p. 377)

Wagner [wăg′nər] **Act** *n.* a law—also known as the National Labor Relations Act—enacted in 1935 to protect workers' rights after the Supreme Court declared the National Industrial Recovery Act unconstitutional. (p. 705)

war-guilt [wôr′ gĭlt′] **clause** *n.* a provision in the Treaty of Versailles by which Germany acknowledged that it alone was responsible for World War I. (p. 606)

war hawk *n.* one of the members of Congress who favored war with Britain in the early years of the 19th century. (p. 203)

War Industries Board (WIB) *n.* an agency established during World War I to increase efficiency and discourage waste in war-related industries. (p. 595)

War Powers Act (WPA) *n.* a law enacted in 1973, limiting a president's right to send troops into battle without consulting Congress. (p. 967)

War Production Board (WPB) *n.* an agency established during World War II to coordinate the production of military supplies by U.S. industries. (p. 774)

Warren [wôr′ən] **Commission** *n.* a group, headed by Chief Justice Earl Warren, that investigated the assassination of President Kennedy and concluded that Lee Harvey Oswald alone was responsible for it. (p. 889)

Warren Court *n.* the Supreme Court during the period when Earl Warren was chief justice, noted for its activism in the areas of civil rights and free speech. (p. 897)

Warsaw [wôr′sô′] **Pact** *n.* a military alliance formed in 1955 by the Soviet Union and its Eastern European satellites. (p. 830)

Watergate [wô′tər-gāt′] *n.* a scandal arising from the Nixon administration's attempt to cover up its involvement in the 1972 break-in at the Democratic National Committee headquarters in the Watergate apartment complex. (p. 1008)

Whig [hwĭg] **Party** *n.* the political party formed in 1834 to oppose the policies of Andrew Jackson. (p. 234)

Wilmot Proviso [wĭl′mət prə-vī′zō] *n.* an amendment to an 1846 military appropriations bill, proposing that none of the territory acquired in the war with Mexico would be open to slavery. (p. 306)

Women's Auxiliary [ôg-zĭl′yə-rē] **Army Corps (WAAC)** *n*. U.S. army unit created during World War II to enable women to serve in noncombat positions. (p. 769)

Woodstock [wŏŏd′stŏk′] *n*. a free music festival that attracted more than 400,000 young people to a farm in upstate New York in August 1969. (p. 989)

Works Progress Administration (WPA) *n*. an agency, established as part of the Second New Deal, that provided the unemployed with jobs in construction, garment making, teaching, the arts, and other fields. (p. 704)

X

XYZ Affair *n*. a 1797 incident in which French officials demanded a bribe from U.S. diplomats. (p. 195)

Y

yellow journalism [jûr′nə-lĭz′əm] *n*. the use of sensationalized and exaggerated reporting by newspapers or magazines to attract readers. (p. 553)

Z

Zimmermann [zĭm′ər-mən] **note** *n*. a message sent in 1917 by the German foreign minister to the German ambassador in Mexico, proposing a German-Mexican alliance and promising to help Mexico regain Texas, New Mexico, and Arizona if the United States entered World War I. (p. 585)

Spanish Glossary

A

abolition [abolición] *s.* movimiento para acabar con la esclavitud. (p. 249)

Adams-Onís Treaty [Tratado de Adams-Onís] *s.* acuerdo de 1819 por el cual España le entregó el control del territorio de Florida a Estados Unidos (p. 221)

Adena *s.* sociedad constructora de túmulos asentada en el valle del río Ohio entre los años 700 a.C. y 100 d.C., aproximadamente; se conoce por sus grandes tumbas cónicas. (p. 7)

affirmative action [acción afirmativa] *s.* medidas para corregir los efectos de la discriminación anterior; favorecen a grupos que estaban en desventaja. (p. 929, 1037)

Agent Orange [Agente Naranja] *s.* químico tóxico exfoliante que fumigaron las tropas estadounidenses en Vietnam para poner al descubierto refugios del Vietcong. (p. 945)

Agricultural Adjustment Act [Ley de Ajustes Agrícolas] *s.* ley de 1933 que elevó el precio de las cosechas al pagarle a los granjeros para que no cultivaran cierta porción de sus tierras, reduciendo así la producción. (p. 697)

AIDS (acquired immune deficiency syndrome) [SIDA, síndrome de inmunodeficiencia adquirida] *s.* enfermedad causada por un virus que debilita el sistema inmunológico y hace que el cuerpo sea vulnerable a infecciones y formas poco comunes de cáncer. (p. 1046)

Alamo, the [El Álamo] *s.* misión y fuerte situado en San Antonio, Texas, en donde fuerzas mexicanas masacraron a rebeldes texanos en 1836. (p. 291)

Alien and Sedition Acts [Leyes de Extranjeros y de Sedición] *s.* cuatro leyes aprobadas en 1798 para reducir el poder político de los nuevos inmigrantes a EE.UU. (p. 195)

Alliance for Progress [Alianza para el Progreso] *s.* programa de los sesenta para ofrecer ayuda económica a los países latinoamericanos. (p. 886)

Allies [Aliados] *s.* 1. en la I Guerra Mundial, naciones aliadas en un tratado contra Alemania y las otras Potencias Centrales; originalmente Gran Bretaña, Francia y Rusia; más adelante se unieron Estados Unidos, Japón, Italia y otros. (p. 579) 2. en la II Guerra Mundial, naciones asociadas contra el Eje, en particular Gran Bretaña, la Unión Soviética y Estados Unidos. (p. 760)

American Expeditionary Force (AEF) [Fuerza Americana de Expediciones] *s.* fuerzas dirigidas por el general John Pershing, quien luchó con los Aliados en Europa durante la Primera Guerra Mundial. (p. 590)

American Federation of Labor (AFL) [Federación Norteamericana del Trabajo] *s.* sindicato de trabajadores calificados creado en 1886 y dirigido por Samuel Gompers. (p. 451)

American Indian Movement (AIM) [Movimiento Indígena Americano] *s.* organización con frecuencia militante creada en 1968 con el fin de luchar por los derechos de los amerindios. (p. 977)

Americanization movement [movimiento de americanización] *s.* programa educativo ideado para facilitar la asimilación de los inmigrantes a la cultura estadounidense. (p. 469)

American System [Sistema Americano] *s.* programa económico previo a la Guerra Civil diseñado para fortalecer y unificar a Estados Unidos por medio de aranceles proteccionistas, un banco nacional y un sistema de transporte eficiente. (p. 216)

Anaconda plan [plan Anaconda] *s.* estrategia de tres pasos durante la Guerra Civil, mediante la cual la Unión propuso derrotar a la Confederación; su nombre viene de una serpiente que aprieta a sus víctimas. (p. 341)

anarchist [anarquista] *s.* persona que se opone a toda forma de gobierno. (p. 619)

Anasazi *s.* grupo amerindio que vivió cerca de la región de Four Corners —donde Arizona, New Mexico, Colorado y Utah se unen— de los años 100 a 1400 d.C., aproximadamente. (p. 7)

annex [anexar] *v.* incorporar un territorio a una unidad política existente tal como un estado o país. (p. 292)

antebellum *adj.* previo a la Guerra Civil. (p. 252)

Antifederalist [antifederalista] *s.* oponente de la Constitución y de un gobierno central fuerte. (p. 146)

appeasement [apaciguamiento] *s.* política de ceder a las demandas de una potencia hostil con el fin de mantener la paz. (p. 744)

Appomattox Court House *s.* pueblo cerca de Appomattox, Virginia, donde Lee se rindió a Grant el 9 de abril de 1865. (37°N 79°O) (p. 365)

apprentice [aprendiz] *s.* trabajador que aprende un oficio, por lo general supervisado por un maestro. (p. 260)

arbitration [arbitraje] *s.* método de resolver disputas en el cual ambos lados someten sus diferencias a un juez elegido por las dos partes. (p. 451)

armistice [armisticio] *s.* tregua o acuerdo para terminar un conflicto armado. (p. 205, 593)

Army of the Republic of Vietnam (ARVN) [Ejército de la República de Vietnam] *s.* soldados del sur de Vietnam que lucharon junto a soldados estadounidenses contra el comunismo y las fuerzas del norte de Vietnam durante la Guerra de Vietnam. (p. 943)

Articles of Confederation [Artículos de la Confederación] *s.* documento aprobado por el Segundo Congreso Continental en 1777 y ratificado por los estados finalmente en 1781. Detallaba la forma del gobierno de los nuevos Estados Unidos. (p. 135)

Ashcan School *s.* grupo de artistas estadounidenses de principios del siglo XX que a menudo pintaban escenas realistas de la vida urbana —como arrabales y gente sin hogar— ganándose así el nombre de la escuela del basurero. (p. 501)

assimilation [asimilación] *s.* adopción, por parte de un grupo minoritario, de las creencias y estilo de vida de la cultura dominante. (p. 412)

Atlantic Charter [Carta del Atlántico] *s.* declaración de principios de 1941 en que Estados Unidos y Gran Bretaña establecieron sus objetivos contra las Potencias del Eje. (p. 760)

Axis powers [Potencias del Eje] *s.* países unidos contra los Aliados en la II Guerra Mundial, que incluyeron a Alemania, Italia y Japón. (p. 757)

Aztec [azteca] *s.* pueblo amerindio que colonizó el Valle de México en 1200 d.C. y desarrolló un gran imperio. (p. 6)

B

baby boom *s.* marcado aumento en el índice de natalidad en Estados Unidos después de la II Guerra Mundial. (p. 849)

Bank of the United States (BUS) [Banco de Estados Unidos] *s.* cualquiera de los dos bancos nacionales establecidos por el Congreso, el primero en 1791 y el segundo en 1816. (p. 185, 232)

Battle of the Bulge [Batalla del Bolsón] *s.* batalla de un mes de duración en la II Guerra Mundial durante la cual los Aliados rompieron la última gran ofensiva alemana de la guerra. (p. 782)

Battle of Midway [Batalla de Midway] *s.* batalla de la Segunda Guerra Mundial que ocurrió a principios de junio en 1942. Los Aliados redujeron la flotilla japonesa en Midway, una isla al noreste de Hawai. A partir de esta batalla los Aliados tomaron la ofensiva y comenzaron a moverse a Japón. (p. 785)

Battle of Wounded Knee [Batalla de Wounded Knee] *s.* masacre de 300 indígenas desarmados en Wounded Knee Creek, South Dakota, en 1890. (p. 414)

Beatles, the *s.* conjunto inglés que tuvo gran influencia en la música popular en los años 60. (p. 989)

beat movement [movimiento beat] *s.* movimiento social y literario de los años 50 que enfatizó la expresión literaria sin reglas y la disconformidad. (p. 861)

Benin *s.* reino de África occidental que existió en la actual Nigeria; floreció en los bosques del delta del Níger del siglo 14 al 17. (p. 17)

Berlin airlift [puente aéreo de Berlín] *s.* operación de 327 días de duración, en la que aviones estadounidenses y británicos llevaron alimentos y provisiones a Berlín Occidental después de que la Unión Soviética bloqueó la ciudad en 1948. (p. 813)

Berlin Wall [Muro de Berlín] *s.* muro de concreto que separó Berlín Oriental y Occidental de 1961 a 1989; construido por Alemania Oriental para impedir que sus ciudadanos se escaparan al occidente. (p. 883)

Bessemer process [método Bessemer] *s.* técnica más eficiente y barata de fabricar acero, desarrollada hacia 1850. (p. 437)

Bill of Rights [Carta de Derechos] *s.* primeras diez enmiendas a la Constitución que identifican los derechos de los ciudadanos; se adoptaron en 1791. (p. 149)

bimetallism [bimetalismo] *s.* sistema monetario nacional que utiliza el oro y la plata para respaldar la moneda. (p. 428)

Black Codes [códigos negros] *s.* leyes discriminatorias aprobadas en el Sur después de la Guerra Civil, las cuales restringían severamente la vida de los afroamericanos, prohibiéndoles actividades como viajar sin permiso, llevar armas, participar como jurado, testificar contra los blancos y casarse con blancos. (p. 379)

blacklist [lista negra] *s.* lista de unos 500 actores, escritores, productores y directores a quienes no se permitía trabajar en películas de Hollywood debido a sus supuestos vínculos comunistas. (p. 824)

Black Panthers [Panteras Negras] *s.* organización política afroamericana militante formada por Huey Newton y Bobby Seale en 1966 para luchar contra la violencia de la policía y suministrar servicios en el ghetto. (p. 926)

Black Power [Poder Negro] *s.* consigna usada por Stokely Carmichael en los años 60, que pedía poder político y social para los afroamericanos. (p. 926)

Black Tuesday [Martes Negro] *s.* octubre 29 de 1929, día en que los precios de las acciones bajaron drásticamente. (p. 674)

Bleeding Kansas [Kansas sangrante] *s.* nombre dado al Territorio de Kansas en los años previos a la Guerra Civil, cuando era un campo de batalla entre las fuerzas en pro y en contra de la esclavitud. (p. 316)

blitzkrieg *s.* proveniente de la palabra alemana que significa "guerra relámpago". Repentina ofensiva de fuerzas aéreas y terrestres a gran escala con el fin de obtener una victoria rápida. (p. 745)

blockade [bloqueo] *s.* acto de sellar un puerto o región para prevenir la entrada o salida durante tiempos de guerra. (p. 202)

bonanza farm [granja de bonanza] *s.* extensa granja dedicada a un solo cultivo. (p. 424)

Bonus Army *s.* grupo de veteranos de la I Guerra Mundial que marcharon en Washington, D.C., en 1932 para exigir bonos prometidos a cambio de su servicio militar. (p. 688)

bootlegger *s.* persona que contrabandeaba bebidas alcohólicas durante la época de Prohibición. (p. 643)

Boston Massacre [Masacre de Boston] *s.* choque entre soldados británicos y colonos en Boston en 1770, durante el cual cinco colonos fueron asesinados. (p. 98)

Boston Tea Party [Motín del Té de Boston] *s.* protesta en 1773 contra el impuesto británico sobre el té; los colonos arrojaron 18,000 libras de té al puerto de Boston. (p. 99)

Boulder Dam [Presa de Boulder] *s.* presa del río Colorado construida durante la Depresión con fondos federales para estimular la economía; ahora llamada Presa Hoover. (p. 686)

Boxer Rebellion [Rebelión de los Boxer] *s.* rebelión encabezada en 1900 por los Boxer, sociedad secreta de China, para detener la difusión de la influencia occidental. (p. 563)

bracero *s.* trabajador mexicano que laboró temporalmente en Estados Unidos durante la Segunda Guerra Mundial. (p. 868)

bread line [cola para comer] *s.* fila de personas que esperan comida gratis. (p. 679)

brinkmanship *s.* práctica de amenazar al enemigo con represalias militares extremas ante cualquier agresión. (p. 829)

Brown v. Board of Education of Topeka *s.* decisión de la Suprema Corte en 1954 que declaró que la segregación de estudiantes negros y blancos era inconstitucional. (p. 908)

Bull Moose Party [Partido Bull Moose] *s.* apodo del Partido Progresista, bajo el que Theodore Roosevelt aspiró, sin éxito, a la presidencia en 1912. (p. 536)

buying on margin [compra con margen] *s.* compra de acciones en la que se paga sólo una porción del valor de la acción al vendedor o corredor de bolsa, y se presta el resto. (p. 673)

C

cabinet [gabinete] *s.* jefes de departamentos que son asesores directos del presidente. (p. 183)

Camp David Accords [Acuerdos de Camp David] *s.* acuerdos de paz históricos entre Israel y Egipto, negociados en Camp David, Maryland, en 1978. (p. 1022)

capitalism [capitalismo] *s.* sistema económico en el que individuos y corporaciones privadas controlan los medios de producción para obtener ganancias. (p. 275)

carpetbagger *s.* norteños que se trasladaron al Sur después de la Guerra Civil. (p. 385)

cash crop [cosecha comercial] *s.* cosecha que se cultiva para su venta más que para uso del granjero. (p. 72)

Central Powers [Potencias Centrales] *s.* en la I Guerra Mundial, el grupo de naciones —Alemania, Austro-Hungría y el imperio otomano— que se opuso a los Aliados. (p. 580)

checks and balances [control y compensación de poderes] *s.* sistema en el cual cada rama del gobierno controla o restringe a las demás ramas. (p. 143)

Chinese Exclusion Act [Ley de Exclusión de Chinos] *s.* ley de 1882 que prohibía la inmigración de ciudadanos chinos, con la excepción de estudiantes, maestros, comerciantes, turistas y funcionarios gubernamentales. (p. 465)

Chisholm Trail [Sendero Chisholm] *s.* la ruta principal de ganado que iba desde San Antonio, Texas, por Oklahoma hasta Kansas. (p. 416)

chlorination [cloración] *s.* purificación del agua al mezclarla químicamente con cloro. (p. 470)

CIA *s.* Central Intelligence Agency (Agencia Central de Inteligencia), agencia gubernamental establecida para espiar y realizar operaciones secretas en países extranjeros. (p. 829)

Civilian Conservation Corps (CCC) [Cuerpo Civil de Conservación] *s.* agencia establecida como parte del New Deal con el fin de ocupar a jóvenes desempleados en trabajos como la construcción de carreteras y el cuidado de parques nacionales y ayudar en situaciones de emergencia. (p. 697)

civil disobedience [desobediencia civil] *s.* rechazo a cumplir leyes que parecían injustas, con el objeto de lograr un cambio en la política de gobierno. En el siglo 19, Henry David Thoreau escribió sobre la desobediencia civil, y dicha táctica fue promovida por Martin Luther King, Jr. durante la era de los Derechos civiles. (p. 243)

Civil Rights Act of 1964 [Ley de Derechos Civiles de 1964] *s.* ley que prohíbe la discriminación en lugares públicos, en la educación y en los empleos por cuestión de raza, color, sexo, nacionalidad o religión. (p. 920)

Civil Rights Act of 1968 [Ley de Derechos Civiles de 1968] *s.* ley que prohíbe la discriminación en la vivienda. (p. 928)

civil service [servicio civil] *s.* cualquier servicio gubernamental en el que se obtiene un cargo mediante exámenes públicos. (p. 476)

Clayton Antitrust Act [Ley Antitrust Clayton] *s.* ley de 1914 que declaraba ilegales ciertas prácticas empresariales injustas y protegía el derecho de los sindicatos y organizaciones agrícolas. (p. 539)

Cold War [Guerra Fría] *s.* estado de hostilidad, sin llegar a conflictos armados, entre Estados Unidos y la Unión Soviética tras la II Guerra Mundial. (p. 812)

colonization [colonización] *s.* establecimiento de asentamientos remotos controlados por otro país. (p. 28)

Columbian Exchange [Transferencia Colombina] *s.* transferencia —iniciada con el primer viaje de Colón a las Américas— de plantas, alimentos, animales y enfermedades entre el Hemisferio Occidental y el Hemisferio Oriental. (p. 29)

committees of correspondence [comités de correspondencia] *s.* red de comunicación escrita entre colonos para mantenerse al tanto de las actividades británicas. (p. 99)

Committee to Reelect the President [Comité de Reelección del Presidente] *s.* grupo que dirigió la campaña para la reelección del presidente Nixon en 1972, cuya conexión con el allanamiento de la Sede Nacional del Partido Demócrata hizo estallar el escándalo Watergate. (p. 1009)

Common Sense [Sentido común] *s.* folleto escrito en 1776 por Thomas Paine que exhortaba la separación de las colonias británicas. (p. 105)

communism [comunismo] *s.* sistema económico y político basado en un gobierno de un solo partido y en la propiedad estatal. (p. 619)

Compromise of 1850 [Compromiso de 1850] *s.* serie de medidas del Congreso para resolver los desacuerdos que surgieron a raíz de la esclavitud entre los estados libres y esclavistas. (p. 307)

Compromise of 1877 [Compromiso de 1877] *s.* serie de medidas tomadas por el Congreso por medio de las cuales los demócratas acordaban aceptar al candidato republicano Rutherford B. Hayes como presidente, aunque éste hubiera perdido el voto popular. Las medidas incluían el retiro de tropas federales de los estados del Sur, el uso de dinero federal para mejorar la infraestructura en el Sur y la designación de un miembro de gabinete que sea sureño y conservador. (p. 399)

concentration camp [campo de concentración] *s.* campamento de presos operado por la Alemania nazi para judíos y otros grupos que consideraba enemigos de Adolfo Hitler; a los presos los mataban o los hacían morir de hambre y a causa de trabajos forzados. (p. 752)

Confederacy [Estados Confederados de América] *s.* confederación formada en 1861 por los estados del Sur después de que se separaron de la unión. (p. 330)

confederation [confederación] *s.* grupo de estados o naciones unidos para actuar en torno a asuntos de interés mutuo. (p. 135)

conglomerate [conglomerado] *s.* corporación grande que posee compañías más pequeñas dedicadas a negocios diversos. (p. 848)

Congress of Industrial Organizations [Congreso de Organizaciones Industriales] *s.* organización sindical expulsada de la Federación Norteamericana del Trabajo en 1938. (p. 714)

Congress of Racial Equality (CORE) [Congreso de Igualdad Racial] *s.* grupo interracial, fundado por James Farmer en 1942, que luchaba contra la segregación en ciudades del Norte. (p. 799)

conquistador *s.* explorador y colonizador español de las Américas en el siglo 16. (p. 36)

conscientious objector [objetor de conciencia] *s.* persona que se opone a toda guerra por principio de conciencia. (p. 592)

conscription [conscripción] *s.* servicio militar obligatorio de ciertos miembros de la población. (p. 349)

conservation [conservación] *s.* práctica de preservar algunas zonas naturales y desarrollar otras por el bien común. (p. 529)

conservative coalition [coalición conservadora] *s.* alianza de grupos de ultraderecha opuestos a la ingerencia del gobierno formada a mediados de los años sesenta. (p. 1037)

consolidation [consolidación] *s.* acto de unir o combinar. (p. 446)

consumerism [consumismo] *s.* gran interés en la compra de bienes materiales. (p. 854)

containment [contención] *s.* política estadounidense de formar alianzas con países más pequeños y débiles con el fin de bloquear la expansión de la infuencia soviética tras la II Guerra Mundial. (p. 811)

Contract with America [Contrato con América] *s.* documento elaborado por el representante Newt Gingrich y firmado por 300 candidatos republicanos el 27 de septiembre de 1994, que presentaba sus planes legislativos conservadores. (p. 1070)

Contras [la contra] *s.* fuerzas anticomunistas nicaragüenses que recibieron asistencia de la administración Reagan para derrocar al gobierno sandinista de Nicaragua. (p. 1057)

convoy system [flotilla de escolta] *s.* medio de proteger los buques mercantes del ataque de submarinos alemanes al hacer que viajaran con una escorta de destructores. (p. 589)

Copperhead *s.* nombre de una serpiente venenosa aplicado a los norteños que simpatizaban con el Sur durante la Guerra Civil. (p. 349)

Cottage industry [industria doméstica] *s.* sistema de producción en el cual los fabricantes proveen materiales para ser producidos en las casas. (p. 260)

cotton gin [desmotadora] *s.* máquina para quitar las semillas de las fibras del algodón, inventada por Eli Whitney en 1793. (p. 215)

counterculture [contracultura] *s.* cultura de la juventud de los años 60 que rechazaba la sociedad tradicional y buscaba paz, amor y libertad individual. (p. 987)

credibility gap [falta de credibilidad] *s.* desconfianza del público en las declaraciones oficiales del gobierno. (p. 947)

credit [crédito] *s.* acuerdo en el que se compran artículos en el presente para ser pagados en el futuro mediante un plan de cuotas con intereses. (p. 672)

Crédit Mobilier *s.* compañía constructora formada en 1864 por los dueños de la Union Pacific Railroad; quienes la usaron ilegalmente para obtener ganancias. (p. 444)

Crusades [Cruzadas] *s.* serie de expediciones militares cristianas al Oriente Medio entre los años 1096 y 1270 d.C., con el fin de rescatar del dominio islámico la "Tierra Santa" alrededor de Jerusalén. (p. 22)

cult of domesticity [culto a la domesticidad] *s.* creencia de que la mujer casada debe restringir sus actividades al hogar y la familia. (p. 254)

D

Dawes Act [Ley Dawes] *s.* ley aprobada por el Congreso en 1887 para "americanizar" a los indígenas distribuyendo a individuos la tierra de las reservaciones. (p. 412)

D-Day [Día D] *s.* junio 6 de 1944, día en que los Aliados emprendieron una invasión por tierra, mar y aire contra el Eje. (p. 780)

debt peonage [deuda por peonaje] *s.* sistema de servidumbre en el que una persona es obligada a trabajar para pagar una deuda. (p. 495)

Declaration of Independence [Declaración de Independencia] *s.* documento escrito por Thomas Jefferson en 1776 en el cual los delegados del Congreso Continental declaron la independencia de las colonias de Gran Bretaña. (p. 106)

de facto segregation [segregación *de facto*] *s.* segregación racial impuesta por la práctica y la costumbre más que por las leyes. (p. 924)

deficit spending [gasto deficitario] *s.* práctica por parte de un gobierno de gastar más de lo que recibe por concepto de rentas públicas. (p. 698)

de jure segregation [segregación *de jure*] *s.* segregación racial impuesta por la ley. (p. 924)

Democratic-Republican [Demócrata-Republicano] *s.* partido político conocido por su apoyo a un fuerte gobierno estatal. Fue fundado por Thomas Jefferson en 1792 en oposición al Federalist Party [Partido Federalista]. (p. 186, 225)

deregulation [liberalización] *s.* acción de limitar el alcance de la regulación federal sobre la industria. (p. 1043)

détente [distensión] *s.* política flexible con la intención de negociar y disminuir tensiones; fue adoptada por Richard Nixon y su consejero Henry Kissinger para tratar con países comunistas. (p. 1005)

direct relief [ayuda directa] *s.* alimentos o dinero que el gobierno da directamente a los necesitados. (p. 681)

division of labor [división del trabajo] *s.* práctica cultural de asignar diferentes tareas y responsabilidades a diferentes grupos o individuos. (p. 13)

Dixiecrat *s.* delegado sureño que se retiró de la convención del Partido Demócrata en 1948 para protestar la plataforma del presidente Truman sobre derechos civiles y formó un grupo denominado States' Rights Democratic Party. (p. 844)

dollar diplomacy [diplomacia del dólar] *s.* política de usar el poder económico o la influencia económica de Estados Unidos para alcanzar sus objetivos de política exterior en otros países. (p. 569)

domino theory [teoría del dominó] *s.* teoría que supone que si una nación se vuelve comunista, las naciones vecinas inevitablemente se volverán comunistas también. (p. 937)

dotcom [puntocom] *s.* negocio relacionado con el Internet o conducido a través de éste. (p. 1077)

double standard [doble moral] *s.* conjunto de principios que permite mayor libertad sexual al hombre que a la mujer. (p. 647)

dove [paloma] *s.* persona que se oponía a la Guerra de Vietnam y creía que Estados Unidos debía retirarse. (p. 952)

Dow Jones Industrial Average [Promedio Industrial Dow Jones] *s.* medida que computa el valor de las acciones de 30 compañías grandes; se usa como barómetro de los mercados bursátiles. (p. 673)

downsize [recortar] *v.* despedir trabajadores de una organización con el fin de hacer las operaciones más eficientes y ahorrar dinero. (p. 1076)

draft [reclutamiento] *s.* requisito de matrícula en las fuerzas armadas. (p. 948)

Dust Bowl *s.* región que incluye Texas, Oklahoma, Kansas, Colorado y New Mexico que quedó inservible para la agricultura debido a la sequía y a las tormentas de arena durante los años 30. (p. 680)

E

Earth Day [Día de la Tierra] *s.* día dedicado a la educación ambiental que desde 1970 se celebra el 22 de abril de cada año. (p. 1027)

Economic Opportunity Act [Ley de Oportunidades Económicas] *s.* ley promulgada en 1964, que adjudicó fondos a programas para la juventud, medidas para combatir la pobreza, préstamos para pequeños negocios y capacitación laboral. (p. 894)

egalitarianism [igualitarismo] *s.* creencia de que todas las personas deben tener igualdad de derechos políticos, económicos, sociales y civiles. (p. 122)

Eisenhower Doctrine [Doctrina Eisenhower] *s.* advertencia del presidente Eisenhower en 1957 de que Estados Unidos defendería el Oriente Medio contra el ataque de cualquier país comunista. (p. 831)

electoral college [colegio electoral] *s.* asamblea elegida por votantes para elegir formalmente al presidente y vicepresidente. Cada estado tiene un número de electores equivalente a los miembros de sus senadores y representantes en el Congreso. (p. 144)

emancipation [emancipación] *s.* proceso de liberarse de la esclavitud. (p. 249)

Emancipation Proclamation [Proclama de Emancipación] *s.* orden ejecutiva de Abraham Lincoln el 1º de enero de 1863 que abolía la esclavitud en los estados confederados. (p. 347)

embargo *s.* orden gubernamental que prohíbe el comercio con otra nación. (p. 203)

encomienda *s.* institución colonial de España en las Américas que repartía indígenas a los conquistadores para hacer trabajos forzados. (p. 38)

Enlightenment [Ilustración] *s.* movimiento intelectual del siglo 18 que enfatizaba la razón y los métodos científicos para obtener conocimientos. (p. 82)

entitlement program [programa de subvención] *s.* programa gubernamental, como Social Security, Medicare y Medicaid, que brinda beneficios a grupos específicos. (p. 1037)

entrepreneur [empresario] *s.* persona que organiza, opera y asume todo el riesgo de una ventura de negocios. (p. 275)

environmentalist [ambientalista] *s.* persona que procura proteger el medio ambiente de la destrucción y de la contaminación. (p. 1028)

Environmental Protection Agency (EPA) [Agencia de Protección Ambiental] *s.* agencia federal establecida en 1970 para la regulación de la contaminación del agua y el aire, los desperdicios tóxicos, los pesticidas y la radiación. (pp. 1028, 1043)

Equal Rights Amendment (ERA) [Enmienda de Igualdad de Derechos] *s.* enmienda propuesta pero rechazada que hubiese prohibido la discriminación del gobierno en razón del sexo de una persona. (p. 985)

Erie Canal [canal del Erie] *s.* vía acuática artificial de 363 millas en New York, construida entre 1817 y 1825 para conectar el río Hudson y el lago Erie. (p. 217)

Espionage and Sedition Acts [Leyes de Espionaje y Sedición] *s.* dos leyes aprobadas en 1917 y 1918, que castigaban fuertemente a quienes criticaran o bloquearan la participación de Estados Unidos en la I Guerra Mundial. (p. 598)

excise tax [impuesto al consumo] *s.* impuesto a la producción, venta o consumo de artículos producidos en el país. (p. 186)

executive branch [rama ejecutiva] *s.* rama gubernamental cuya función es administrar y aplicar las leyes (presidente o gobernador). (p. 143)

exoduster *s.* afroamericano que emigró del Sur a Kansas después de la Reconstrucción. (p. 421)

extortion [extorsión] *s.* uso ilegal de un cargo público para obtener dinero o propiedad. (p. 475)

F

Fair Deal *s.* plan económico del presidente Truman que expandió el New Deal de Roosevelt; aumentó el salario mínimo, amplió el seguro social y le dio vivienda a familias de bajos recursos, entre otras medidas. (p. 845)

Family Assistance Plan [Plan de Asistencia Familiar] *s.* propuesta de reforma a los programas de beneficencia, aprobada por la Cámara de Representantes en 1970 pero rechazada por el Senado, que garantizaba un ingreso a los beneficiarios de ayuda pública que aceptaran capacitarse y emplearse en un oficio. (p. 1001)

Farmers' Alliances [Alianzas de granjeros] *s.* grupos de granjeros o simpatizantes de éstos, que enviaban a oradores a viajar de pueblo a pueblo para educar a la gente sobre cuestiones agrarias y rurales. (p. 427)

fascism [fascismo] *s.* filosofía política que propone un gobierno fuerte, centralizado, nacionalista, caracterizado por una rígida dictadura unipartidista. (p. 736)

Federal Communications Commission (FCC) [Comisión Federal de Comunicaciones] *s.* agencia del gobierno que regula la industria de comunicaciones en EE.UU., incluso la transmisión de radio y televisión. (p. 859)

Federal Deposit Insurance Corporation (FDIC) [Corporación Federal de Seguros de Depósitos] *s.* agencia creada en 1933 para garantizar depósitos bancarios individuales cuando un banco quiebra. (p. 723)

Federal Home Loan Bank Act [Ley Federal para Préstamos de Vivienda] *s.* ley aprobada en 1931 que redujo las cuotas hipotecarias y permitió a los agricultores refinanciar sus préstamos para prevenir juicios hipotecarios. (p. 687)

federalism [federalismo] *s.* sistema político gubernamental en el cual el poder se comparte entre un gobierno nacional y las entidades que lo constituyen, como los gobiernos estatales. (p. 143)

Federalists [federalistas] *s.* partidarios de la Constitución y de un gobierno nacional fuerte. (p. 146)

Federalist, The [El Federalista] *s.* ensayos escritos por Madison, Hamilton y Jay que apoyan y explican la Constitución. (p. 146)

Federal Reserve System [Sistema de la Reserva Federal] *s.* sistema bancario nacional establecido por Woodrow Wilson en 1913 que controla el dinero circulante del país. (p. 540)

Federal Securities Act [Ley Federal de Valores] *s.* ley de 1933 que obliga a las corporaciones a suministrar información completa y fidedigna sobre sus ofertas de acciones. (p. 696)

Federal Trade Commission (FTC) [Comisión Federal de Comercio] *s.* agencia federal establecida en 1914 para investigar y parar prácticas empresariales injustas. (p. 539)

feminism [feminismo] *s.* creencia de que la mujer debe tener igualdad económica, política y social con respecto al hombre. (p. 982)

Fifteenth Amendment [Enmienda 15] *s.* enmienda a la Constitución, adoptada en 1870, que establece que a nadie puede negársele el derecho al voto por motivos de raza, color o por haber sido esclavo. (p. 382)

"Fifty-Four Forty or Fight!" *s.* consigna de la campaña presidencial de 1844 en pro de la anexión del Territorio de Oregon; se refería a la latitud del límite norte del territorio. (p. 285)

flapper *s.* jovencita típica de los años 20 que actuaba y se vestía de manera atrevida y nada convencional. (p. 647)

flexible response [respuesta flexible] *s.* doctrina, desarrollada durante la administración Kennedy, de prepararse para una variedad de respuestas militares, en vez de concentrarse en las armas nucleares. (p. 879)

Foraker Act [Ley Foraker] *s.* legislación que el Congreso aprobó en 1900 para acabar con el gobierno militar en Puerto Rico y autorizar un gobierno civil. (p. 559)

Fordney-McCumber Tariff [Arancel Fordney-McCumber] *s.* serie de reglas, aprobada por el Congreso en 1922, que elevó a niveles sin precedentes los impuestos a las importaciones en 1922 para proteger las compañías estadounidenses de la competencia extranjera. (p. 626)

forty-niner [viajero del 49] *s.* buscador de oro que llegó a California después de 1848 atraído por el oro. (p. 298)

Fourteen Points [los catorce puntos] *s.* plan del presidente Wilson en pro de la paz mundial tras la I Guerra Mundial. (p. 605)

Fourteenth Amendment [Enmienda 14] *s.* enmienda a la constitución adoptada en 1868 que hace ciudadano a toda persona nacida o naturalizada en Estados Unidos, incluso a antiguos esclavos, y garantiza igualdad de protección bajo la ley. (p. 379)

franchise [franquicia] *s.* forma de negocio en la que individuos compran el derecho a usar el nombre y los métodos de una compañía matriz, con lo que la compañía se multiplica. (p. 848)

Freedmen's Bureau [Oficina de libertos] *s.* agencia federal formada después de la Guerra Civil para ayudar a personas que habían sido esclavos antes. (p. 379)

freedom rider *s.* activista de derechos civiles que viajó en autobús a través del Sur a comienzos de los años 60 para protestar contra la segregación. (p. 916)

Freedom Summer *s.* campaña de registro de votantes afroamericanos en el verano de 1964 en Mississippi. (p. 921)

Freeport Doctrine [Doctrina Freeport] *s.* posición que tomó en 1858 Stephen Douglas de que cualquier territorio podría excluir la esclavitud con sólo negarse a promulgar leyes en su favor. (p. 326)

Free-Soil Party [Partido de las Tierras Libres] *s.* partido político formado en 1848 que se oponía a la extensión de la esclavitud a los territorios. (p. 319)

Free Speech Movement [Movimiento de Libre Expresión] *s.* movimiento activista de los años 60 que surgió a raíz de un enfrentamiento entre los estudiantes y la administración de la Universidad de California en Berkeley en 1964. (p. 950)

French and Indian War [Guerra contra Franceses e Indígenas] *s.* guerra librada en Norteamérica (1757-1763) como parte de un conflicto mundial entre Francia y Gran Bretaña; finalizó con la derrota de Francia y el traspaso del Canadá francés a Gran Bretaña. (p. 86)

Fugitive Slave Act [Ley de los Esclavos Fugitivos] *s.* ley aprobada como parte del Compromiso de 1850 que imponía duras sanciones a quien ayudara a escapar de la esclavitud. (p. 310)

Fundamentalism [fundamentalismo] *s.* movimiento religioso protestante basado en la interpretación textual, o palabra por palabra, de las escrituras. (p. 644)

G

Gadsden Purchase [Compra de Gadsden] *s.* compra de tierras de México en 1853 por parte de Estados Unidos que estableció la frontera actual entre los dos países. (p. 297)

gag rule [ley de la mordaza] *s.* orden que limita o previene el debate sobre un determinado asunto. (p. 253)

General Agreement on Tariffs and Trade (GATT) [Acuerdo General de Aranceles y Comercio] *s.* acuerdo internacional firmado inicialmente en 1947. En 1994, EE.UU. y otros países del mundo adoptaron una nueva versión de GATT. Este tratado redujo las barreras de comercio y los aranceles, como las tarifas, y creó la Organización Mundial de Comercio. (p. 1078)

genetic engineering [ingeniería genética] *s.* alteración de la biología molecular de las células de un organismo para crear nuevas variedades de bacterias, plantas o animales. (p. 1086)

Geneva Accords [Acuerdos de Ginebra] *s.* plan de paz de Indochina en 1954 en el que Vietnam fue dividido temporalmente en Vietnam del Norte y Vietnam del Sur, mientras se celebraban las elecciones de 1956. (p. 938)

genocide [genocidio] *s.* exterminio deliberado y sistemático de un grupo de personas por su raza, nacionalidad o religión. (p. 750)

Gentlemen's Agreement [Acuerdo de Caballeros] *s.* acuerdo concertado durante 1907 y 1908, mediante el cual el gobierno de Japón limitaron la inmigración a Estados Unidos. (p. 465)

gentrification [aburguesamiento] *s.* restauración de propiedades urbanas por personas de la clase media que a menudo resulta en la pérdida de vivienda para personas de medios escasos. (p. 1089)

Gettysburg Address [Discurso de Gettysburg] *s.* famoso discurso de Abraham Lincoln durante la Guerra Civil al inaugurar un cementerio nacional en el campo de batalla de Gettysburg, Pennsylvania, el 19 de noviembre de 1863. (p. 361)

ghetto *s.* tipo de vecindario urbano donde cierto grupo minoritario es obligado o forzado a vivir. (p. 751)

GI Bill of Rights [Carta de Derechos de los Veteranos] *s.* nombre dado a la Ley de Reajuste de Militares de 1944, que ofrecía beneficios financieros y educativos a los veteranos de la II Guerra Mundial. (p. 798, 841)

glasnost *s.* la discusión abierta de problemas sociales que se dio en la Unión Soviética durante los años 80. (p. 1055)

Glass-Steagall Banking Act [Ley Bancaria Glass-Steagall] *s.* ley de 1933 que aseguró los depósitos bancarios mediante la Corporación Federal de Seguros de Depósitos. (p. 1055)

Glorious Revolution [Revolución Gloriosa] *s.* revolución incruenta en 1688-89 en la que William y Mary le quitaron el trono de Inglaterra a James II. (p. 69)

gold rush [fiebre del oro] *s.* llegada de gente a una región donde se ha descubierto oro. (p. 298)

gold standard [patrón de oro] *s.* sistema monetario en el cual la unidad básica de moneda se define en relación a una cantidad fija de oro. (p. 428)

Gone with the Wind [Lo que el viento se llevó] *s.* película de 1939 sobre la vida de los dueños de plantaciones del Sur durante la Guerra Civil; una de las más populares de todos los tiempos. (p. 717)

graft [corrupción] *s.* uso ilegal de un cargo político con el fin de ganancia personal. (p. 475)

grandfather clause [cláusula del abuelo] *s.* estipulación que exime de cumplir una ley a ciertas personas por circunstancias previas; específicamente, cláusula de la constitución de algunos estados sureños que eximía a los blancos de los estrictos requisitos que impedían que los afroamericanos votaran. (p. 493)

Grange [la Granja] *s. The Patrons of Husbandry*—organización de granjeros que intentaron, a partir de la década de 1870, combatir el poder de los ferrocarriles. (p. 427)

Grapes of Wrath, The [Las uvas de la ira] *s.* novela de John Steinbeck, publicada en 1939, sobre una familia de Oklahoma que se va de la región del Dust Bowl a California. (p. 720)

Great Awakening [Gran Despertar] *s.* serie de grandes asambleas religiosas en las décadas de 1730 y 1750. (p. 83)

Great Compromise [Gran Compromiso] *s.* plan constitucional para una legislatura de dos cámaras: una que da igual representación a todos los estados y una que basa la representación en la población. (p. 142)

Great Depression [Gran Depresión] *s.* período de 1929 a 1940 en el que la economía estadounidense quebró y millones quedaron sin empleo. (p. 675)

Great Migration [Gran Migración] *s.* movimiento de cientos de miles de afroamericanos sureños a ciudades del Norte a principios del siglo 20. (p. 599)

Great Plains [Grandes Praderas] *s.* vasta pradera que se extiende a través de Norteamérica, de Texas a Canadá en dirección norte y hacia el este de las Montañas Rocosas. (p. 408)

Great Society [Gran Sociedad] *s.* ambicioso programa legislativo del presidente Lyndon B. Johnson para reducir la pobreza y la injusticia racial, y mejorar el nivel de vida. (p. 895)

H

habeas corpus *s.* orden judicial que manda comparecer a las autoridades ante un juez u otro funcionario de un tribunal para explicar que un preso está detenido legalmente. (p. 349)

Haight-Ashbury *s.* distrito de San Francisco, "capital" de la contracultura hippie durante los años 60. (p. 988)

Harlem Renaissance [Renacimiento de Harlem] *s.* período de sobresaliente creatividad afroamericana durante los años 20 y 30, en la zona de Harlem en New York City. (p. 660)

hawk [halcón] *s.* persona que respaldaba la Guerra de Vietnam y creía que Estados Unidos debía incrementar su fuerza militar para ganarla. (p. 952)

Hawley–Smoot Tariff Act [Ley de Aranceles Hawley-Smoot] *s.* ley de 1930 que estableció los más altos aranceles proteccionistas en la historia estadounidense, afectando negativamente el comercio internacional y empeorando le depresión mundial y doméstica. (p. 677)

H-bomb [bomba de hidrógeno] *s.* bomba de hidrógeno, o termonuclear, mucho más poderosa que la bomba atómica. (p. 829)

headright system [sistema de reparto de tierras por cabeza] *s.* sistema empleado en Virginia que otorgaba cincuenta acres de tierra a cada colono y otro tanto por cada acompañante. (p. 45)

hierarchy [jerarquía] *s.* orden social determinado por rango o clase. (p. 20)

Ho Chi Minh Trail [Sendero de Ho Chi Minh] *s.* red de caminos por la que Vietnam del Norte abastecía al Vietcong en Vietnam del Sur. (p. 938)

Hohokam *s.* grupo amerindio que vivió en los valles de los ríos Salt y Gila (hoy Arizona) entre los años 300 a.C. y 1400 d.C., aproximadamente. (p. 7)

Hollywood Ten [los Diez de Hollywood] *s.* diez testigos de la industria cinematográfica que se negaron a cooperar con la investigación de influencia comunista en Hollywood. (p. 823)

Holocaust [Holocausto] *s.* asesinato sistemático o genocidio de judíos y de otros grupos en Europa por los nazis antes y durante la II Guerra Mundial. (p. 748)

home rule [gobierno local] *s.* poder de los estados de gobernar a sus ciudadanos sin intervención federal. (p. 399)

Homestead Act [Ley de la Heredad] *s.* ley aprobada en 1862 que otorgaba 160 acres de tierra en el Oeste a cualquier ciudadano or ciudadano futuro que fuera cabeza de familia y que cultivara la tierra por cinco años; ley cuya aprobación llevó a un gran número de colonos estadounidenses a reclamar como propiedad privada tierra que había sido reservada por tratados y tradiciones para la vivienda de indígenas americanos; la misma ley, reforzada en 1889, dio incentivas para que los individuos ejercieran su derecho de propiedad privada y desarrollaran viviendas. (p. 421)

Hopewell *s.* sociedad constructora de túmulos asentada en el valle del río Ohio entre los años 200 a.C. y 400 d.C., aproximadamente; se conoce por sus grandes tumbas cónicas. (p. 7)

horizontal integration [integración horizontal] *s.* proceso mediante el cual compañías que fabrican productos similares se unen y reducen la competencia. (p. 448)

hot line [línea de emergencia] *s.* línea directa de comunicación establecida en 1963 para que los líderes de Estados Unidos y la Unión Soviética pudieran hablarse durante una crisis. (p. 884)

House Un-American Activities Committee (HUAC) [Comité de la Cámara de Representantes sobre Actividades Antiamericanas] *s.* comité del Congreso creado en 1938 que investigó la influencia comunista dentro y fuera del gobierno durante los años que siguieron la II Guerra Mundial. (p. 823)

human rights [derechos humanos] *s.* derechos y libertades considerados básicos, como los que establece la Declaración de Independencia y la Carta de Derechos. (p. 1021)

Immigration Act of 1965 [Ley de Inmigración de 1965] *s.* ley que abrió las puertas a más inmigrantes. (p. 897)

impeach [acusar] *v.* culpar oficialmente a un funcionario por su conducta inapropiada como tal. La Cámara de Representantes tiene el poder exclusivo de acusar a funcionarios federales. (p. 381)

impeachment [acusación] *s.* proceso por el cual se acusa a un funcionario público de delitos. (p. 1008)

imperialism [imperialismo] *s.* política de controlar países por medios económicos, políticos o militares. (p. 548)

impressment [leva] *s.* práctica de reclutar hombres a la fuerza para prestar servicio militar. (p. 202)

Inca *s.* pueblo amerindio creador de un imperio que abarcó casi 2,500 millas a lo largo de la costa occidental de Suramérica, a partir del año 1400 d.C., aproximadamente. (p. 6)

incandescent [incandescente] *adj.* que emite luz visible como resultado de haber sido calentado (p. 438)

income tax [impuesto sobre la renta] *s.* impuesto que retiene un porcentaje específico de ingresos. (p. 354)

indentured servant [sirviente por contrato] *s.* inmigrante que, a cambio de un pasaje para las Américas, era contratado a trabajar por un periodo límite. (p. 45)

Indian Removal Act [Ley de Traslado de los Indígenas] *s.* ley aprobada por el Congreso en 1830 que ordenaba el traslado obligatorio de todas las tribus indígenas del este del Mississippi a tierras del oeste. (p. 226)

Industrial Revolution [Revolución Industrial] *s.* cambios en la organización social y económica como resultado del remplazo del trabajo manual por máquinas y el desarrollo de fábricas de producción a gran escala. (p. 212)

Industrial Workers of the World (IWW) *s.* sindicato de trabajadores de mano de obra no calificada creado en 1905. (p. 452)

inflation [inflación] *s.* fenómeno económico en el que hay un aumento constante en los precios por el incremento del dinero circulante; reduce el poder adquisitivo. (p. 116)

information superhighway [supercarretera de información] *s.* red de comunicación por computadoras para unir a personas e instituciones por todo el mundo y suministrar a individuos servicios de bibliotecas, compras, cines y noticias. (p. 1083)

INF Treaty [Tratado sobre Fuerzas Nucleares Intermedias] *s.* tratado entre Estados Unidos y la Unión Soviética firmado en 1987, que eliminó algunas armas y permitió la inspección directa de emplazamientos de misiles. (p. 1055)

initiative [iniciativa] *s.* reforma gubernamental que permite a los ciudadanos presentar proyectos de ley en el Congreso o en cuerpos legislativos estatales. (p. 518)

installment plan [pago a plazos] *s.* práctica de comprar a crédito mediante pagos regulares durante determinado período de tiempo. (p. 632)

interchangeable parts [piezas uniformes] *s.* piezas que se pueden usar de manera intercambiable y que se producen en masa. (p. 212)

Internet *s.* red mundial, originalmente diseñada por el Departamento de Defensa, que une computadores y permite una comunicación casi instantánea de textos, ilustraciones y sonidos. (p. 1083)

internment [confinamiento] *s.* restricción de movimiento, en especial durante condiciones de guerra. (p. 800)

Interstate Commerce Act [Ley de Comercio Interestatal] *s.* ley de 1887 que restablecía el derecho del gobierno federal a supervisar los ferrocarriles; creó una Comisión de Comercio Interestatal de cinco miembros. (p. 445)

Intolerable Acts [Leyes Intolerables] *s.* cuatro leyes aprobadas por el Parlamento en 1774 con el fin de castigar a Boston por el Motín del Té de Boston. (p. 99)

iron curtain [cortina de hierro] *s.* frase usada por Winston Churchill en 1946 para describir una línea imaginaria que separaba los países comunistas que estaban en la parte soviética al este de Europa de los países en Europa occidental. (p. 811)

Iroquois [iroqueses] *s.* grupo de pueblos amerindios que vivían en los bosques del Noreste. (p. 10)

Islam [islamismo] *s.* religión fundada en Arabia por el profeta Mahoma en el año 622; a sus seguidores se les llama musulmanes. (p. 15)

isolationism [aislacionismo] *s.* política que se opone a participar en conflictos políticos y económicos con otros países. (p. 618)

J

Japanese Americans Citizens League (JACL) [Sociedad de Ciudadanos Americano-Japoneses] *s.* organización que presionó al gobierno a compensar a los estadounidenses de origen japonés por las propiedades que perdieron al ser internados durante la II Guerra Mundial. (p. 801)

jazz *s.* estilo de música caracterizado por la improvisación. (p. 863)

Jim Crow laws [leyes Jim Crow] *s.* leyes impuestas por los gobiernos estatales y municipales del Sur con el fin de separar a blancos y afroamericanos en instalaciones públicas y privadas. (p. 493)

joint-stock company [sociedad de capitales] *s.* institución empresarial tipo corporación en la que inversionistas unen riquezas con un fin común; se usaron para financiar la exploración de las Américas. (p. 42)

journeyman [oficial] *s.* artesano que trabaja al servicio de un maestro. (p. 260)

judicial branch [rama judicial] *s.* rama gubernamental cuya función es interpretar las leyes y la Constitución (Suprema Corte). (p. 143)

judicial review [revisión judicial] *s.* poder de la Suprema Corte de declarar inconstitucional una ley del Congreso. (p. 199)

Judiciary Act of 1789 [Ley Judicial de 1789] *s.* ley que estableció el sistema de tribunales federales y la Suprema Corte que permitió la apelación a cortes federales de ciertas decisiones tomadas por cortes estatales. (p. 183)

Judiciary Act of 1801 [Ley Judicial de 1801] *s.* ley aprobada con el fin de incrementar el número de jueces federalistas. (p. 199)

Jungle, The [La jungla] *s.* novela publicada en 1906 por el periodista Upton Sinclair que denunciaba la insalubridad de la industria de carne en aquella época; llevó a reformas nacionales. (p. 523)

K

kamikaze *adj.* que estrellaba deliberadamente un avión bombardero contra un blanco militar. (p. 787)

Kansas-Nebraska Act [Ley Kansas y Nebraska] *s.* ley aprobada en 1854 que buscaba un acuerdo sobre la extensión de la esclavitud a los territorios de Kansas y Nebraska. (p. 315)

Kashaya Pomo *s.* pueblo amerindio que floreció hace 500 años en lo que hoy es California; vivía en las tierras pantanosas de la costa. (p. 8)

Kent State University [Universidad Estatal de Kent] *s.* universidad de Ohio donde guardias militares abrieron fuego contra estudiantes durante una protesta contra la Guerra de Vietnam el 4 de mayo de 1970, hiriendo a nueve de ellos y matando a cuatro. (p. 962)

Kerner Commission [Comisión Kerner] *s.* grupo designado por el presidente Lyndon B. Johnson para estudiar las causas de la violencia urbana; recomendó eliminar la segregación de facto en la sociedad estadounidense. (p. 928)

King Philip's War [Guerra del Rey Felipe] *s.* conflicto, en los años 1675 y 1676, entre los colonos de Nueva Inglaterra y grupos amerindios aliados bajo la dirección del cacique Metacom de los wampanoagas. (p. 54)

kinship [parentesco] *s.* lazos indisolubles entre los miembros de una misma familia o tribu. (p. 13)

Know-Nothing Party *s.* nombre dado en la década de 1850 al Partido Americano, un grupo que quería reducir la influencia política de los inmigrantes. (p. 319)

Kongo *s.* serie de pequeños reinos unidos bajo un líder a finales del siglo 15 en las selvas tropicales a lo largo del río Zaire (Congo) en África Central-Occidental. (p. 17)

Korean War [Guerra de Corea] *s.* guerra de 1950 a 1953 entre Corea del Norte y Corea del Sur; China respaldó a Corea del Norte y las tropas de las Naciones Unidas, integradas en su mayoría por soldados estadounidenses, apoyaron a Corea del Sur. (p. 817)

Kristallnacht *s.* "noche del cristal quebrado", noviembre 9 de 1938, noche en que milicianos nazis atacaron viviendas, negocios y sinagogas judías en Alemania. (p. 749)

Ku Klux Klan *s.* sociedad secreta de hombres blancos en los estados sureños después de la Guerra Civil que desató terror para restaurar la supremacía blanca. (p. 394)

Kwakiutl *s.* pueblo amerindio que vivía en la región costera del Noroeste. (p. 9)

L

land grant [concesión de tierras] *s.* lote grande de tierras dado por el gobierno a un agente para su reventa, por lo general con el fin de estimular el desarrollo. (p. 289)

Land Ordinance of 1785 [Ordenanza de Tierras de 1785] *s.* ley que estableció un plan para la agrimensura y venta de las tierras públicas al oeste de los montes Apalaches. (p. 135)

La Raza Unida *s.* organización política latina establecida en 1969 por José Ángel Gutiérrez. (p. 976)

League of Nations [Liga de las Naciones] *s.* organización internacional establecida en 1920 para promover la cooperación y la paz internacional. (p. 605)

legislative branch [rama legislativa] *s.* rama gubernamental compuesta por representantes elegidos que promulgan leyes (Congreso). (p. 143)

Lend-Lease Act [Ley de Préstamo y Alquiler] *s.* ley aprobada en 1941, que autorizó al gobierno a mandar armas y otros productos, sin pago inmediato, a las naciones que luchaban contra el Eje. (p. 758)

Limited Test Ban Treaty [Tratado de Limitación de Pruebas Nucleares] *s.* tratado de 1963 en que Estados Unidos y la Unión Soviética acordaron no realizar pruebas de armas nucleares en la atmósfera. (p. 884)

lineage [linaje] *s.* línea de descendencia de una generación a otra —de abuelo, a hija, a nieto, por ejemplo— con un antepasado común. (p. 18)

long drive [arreo de ganado] *s.* proceso mediante el cual los vaqueros llevaban por tierra ganado hacia el mercado. (p. 416)

longhorn *s.* resistente raza de ganado vacuno de cuernos largos llevada por los españoles a México, muy apta para las condiciones de esa región. (p. 414)

Louisiana Purchase [Compra de Louisiana] *s.* compra de terrenos a Francia por 15 millones de dólares en 1803 de las tierras desde el río Mississippi hasta las montañas Rocosas. (p. 201)

Loyalists [realistas] *s.* colonos que apoyaban al gobierno británico durante la Revolución Norteamericana. (p. 106)

Lusitania *s.* barco británico de pasajeros que se hundió cerca de costas irlandesas el 7 de mayo de 1915, tras ser atacado por un submarino alemán. (p. 584)

M

mandate [mandato] *s.* conquista de una porción suficientemente grande del voto, que indica que un líder elegido tiene apoyo popular para sus programas. (p. 886)

Manhattan Project [Proyecto Manhattan] *s.* programa estadounidense que se inició en 1942 con el fin de diseñar una bomba atómica para la II Guerra Mundial. La primera detonación atómica completa ocurrió en Alamogordo, New Mexico, el 16 de julio de 1945. (p. 773)

manifest destiny [destino manifiesto] *s.* término usado en la década de 1840 para describir la creencia de que Estados Unidos estaba inexorablemente destinado a adquirir más territorio, especialmente mediante su expansión hacia el oeste. (p. 281)

Marbury v. *Madison* *s.* caso de 1803 en que la Suprema Corte decidió que tenía el poder de abolir decretos legislativos declarándolos inconstitucionales; ese poder se conoce como revisión judicial. (p. 199)

market revolution [revolución mercantil] *s.* gran cambio económico que llevó a comprar y vender productos en lugar de hacerlos en el hogar. (p. 275)

Marshall Plan [Plan Marshall] *s.* plan formulado por el Secretario de Estado George Marshall en 1947, mediante el que se ofreció ayuda a países europeos con el fin de reparar los daños de la II Guerra Mundial. (p. 812)

martial law [ley marcial] *s.* gobierno impuesto por fuerzas militares. (p. 99)

mass media [medios informativos] *s.* medios de comunicación —tales como televisión, prensa y radio— que llegan a grandes audiencias. (p. 858)

mass production [producción en masa] *s.* producción de artículos en grandes cantidades, con máquinas y división del trabajo. (p. 212)

mass transit [transporte público] *s.* sistemas de transporte diseñados para llevar grandes números de personas por rutas fijas. (p. 470)

master [maestro] *s.* experto artesano; por lo general era dueño de un negocio y empleaba a otros. (p. 260)

Maya *s.* pueblo amerindio que desarrolló una rica cultura en Guatemala y la península de Yucatán entre los años 250 y 900 d.C. (p. 6)

McCarthyism [macartismo] *s.* ataques, a menudo sin respaldo, del senador Joseph McCarthy y otros contra presuntos comunistas en los años 50. (p. 826)

McCulloch v. *Maryland* [McCulloch vs. Maryland] *s.* caso realizado en 1819, en el cual la Corte Suprema de Justicia estableció que Maryland no tenía derecho a cobrarle impuestos al Banco de los Estados Unidos, y consecuentemente fortaleció el poder de control que tenía el gobierno federal sobre la economía. (p. 220)

Meat Inspection Act [Ley de Inspección de la Carne] *s.* ley de 1906 que establecía estrictos requisitos sanitarios en las empacadoras de carne, así como un programa federal de inspección de carnes. (p. 526)

Medicaid *s.* programa federal que se inició en 1965 para brindar atención médica a las personas que reciben ayuda pública. (p. 896)

Medicare *s.* programa federal que se inició en 1965 para brindar seguros médicos y de hospitalización a bajo costo a los mayores de 65 años. (p. 896)

melting pot [crisol de culturas] *s.* mezcla de personas de diferentes culturas y razas que se amalgaman y abandonan su idioma y cultura natal. (p. 464)

mercantilism [mercantilismo] *s.* sistema económico en que un país aumenta su riqueza y poder al incrementar su posesión de oro y plata, y al exportar más productos de los que importa. (p. 66)

Merrimack *s.* buque blindado que usó el Sur durante la Guerra Civil. (p. 343)

mestizo *adj.* con mezcla de español e indígena. (p. 38)

middle passage [travesía intermedia] *s.* tramo de África a las Antillas; parte del triángulo comercial de esclavos. (p. 76)

midnight judge [juez de media noche] *s.* uno de los jueces designados por John Adams en las últimas horas de su gobierno. (p. 199)

militarism [militarismo] *s.* política de mantener una sólida organización militar como preparación agresiva para la guerra y su empleo como herramienta diplomática. (p. 579)

minutemen [civil armado] *s.* soldados civiles patriotas que lucharon justo antes y durante la Revolución, quienes prometían estar listos para luchar al primer llamado. (p. 100)

Mississippian [misisipiense] *s.* última sociedad constructora de túmulos, que se extendió al este del río Mississippi del siglo 8 al 16. (p. 7)

Missouri Compromise [Acuerdo de Missouri] *s.* serie de acuerdos aprobados por el Congreso en 1820–1821 para mantener un equilibrio seccional entre los estados esclavistas y los estados libres. (p. 222)

Monitor *s.* buque blindado que usó el Norte durante la Guerra Civil. (p. 343)

Monroe Doctrine [Doctrina Monroe] *s.* declaración del presidente Monroe en 1823 que establecía que Estados Unidos no permitiría la interferencia europea en los asuntos del Hemisferio Occidental. (p. 221)

Moral Majority [Mayoría Moral] *s.* coalición política de organizaciones religiosas conservadoras en los años 70 y 80 que recaudó dinero para respaldar agendas y candidatos conservadores, y condenó actitudes y comportamientos liberales. (p. 1037)

Mormons [mormones] *s.* miembros de una comunidad religiosa fundada por Joseph Smith, que terminó estableciéndose en Utah. (p. 284)

Morrill Acts [Leyes Morrill] *s.* leyes aprobadas en 1862 y 1890 que otorgaban tierras federales a los estados para financiar universidades agrícolas. (p. 423)

muckraker *s.* uno de los reporteros de revistas que desenmascaraban el lado corrupto de las empresas y de la vida pública a principios del siglo 20. (p. 514)

Munn v. Illinois *s.* caso de la Suprema Corte en 1877; estableció el derecho del gobierno federal a regular la industria privada en beneficio del interés público. (p. 445)

My Lai *s.* pueblo del norte de Vietnam del Sur, donde más de 200 civiles desarmados, incluso mujeres y niños, fueron masacrados por las tropas de EE.UU. en mayo de 1968. (p. 962)

N

NAACP *s.* National Association for the Advancement of Colored People (Asociación Nacional para el Avance de la Gente de Color), organización fundada en 1909 y dedicada a la igualdad racial. (p. 531)

NACW *s.* National Association of Colored Women (Asociación Nacional de Mujeres de Color), organización de servicio social fundada en 1896. (p. 521)

NAFTA *s.* North American Free Trade Agreement (Tratado de Libre Comercio, TLC), tratado de 1993 que redujo aranceles e incorporó a México en la zona de libre comercio ya vigente entre Estados Unidos y Canadá. (p. 1070)

napalm *s.* sustancia incendiaria de gasolina que lanzaban los aviones estadounidenses en Vietnam, con el fin de incendiar la selva y revelar los escondites del Vietcong. (p. 945)

NASDAQ *s.* sigla de National Association of Securities Dealers Automated Quotation System, una bolsa de valores de venta directa dominada por compañías tecnológicas. (p. 1077)

National Bank Act [Ley del Banco Nacional] *s.* ley aprobada en 1863 para garantizarles a los inversionistas la seguridad de las actividades bancarias. Entre sus medidas establecía un sistema de bancos federales, nuevos requisitos para préstamos y un sistema de inspección de bancos. (p. 367)

National Energy Act [Ley Nacional de Energía] *s.* ley promulgada durante la administración Carter para aliviar la crisis energética; aplicó impuestos a los autos que usan gasolina de manera ineficiente y suspendió el control de precios del petróleo y el gas natural estadounidenses. (p. 1019)

National Industrial Recovery Act (NIRA) [Ley Nacional de Recuperación Industrial] *s.* ley aprobada en 1933 que establecía agencias para supervisar industrias y suministrar empleos. (p. 697)

nationalism [nacionalismo] *s.* devoción a los intereses y la cultura de la nación propia. (p. 220, 579)

National Labor Relations Board (NLRB) [Junta Nacional de Relaciones Laborales] *s.* agencia creada en 1935 con el fin de prevenir prácticas laborales injustas y mediar en disputas laborales. (p. 574)

National Organization for Women (NOW) [Organización Nacional de la Mujer] *s.* organización fundada en 1966 con el fin de impulsar metas feministas, tales como mejores guarderías, mayores oportunidades educativas y el fin de la discriminación laboral. (p. 984)

National Road [Carretera Nacional] *s.* carretera financiada por el gobierno cuya construcción se inició en 1811; iba desde Cumberland, Maryland, hasta Vandalia, Illinois. (p. 217)

National Trades' Union [Unión Nacional de Sindicatos] *s.* primera asociación nacional de sindicatos, creada en 1834. (p. 265)

National Youth Administration [Administración Nacional de Recursos para la Juventud] *s.* programa que suministraba ayuda y empleos a jóvenes durante la Depresión. (p. 705)

Nation of Islam [Nación del Islam] *s.* grupo religioso, popularmente conocido como musulmanes negros, fundado por Elijah Muhammad para promover el separatismo negro y la religión islámica. (p. 925)

nativism [patriotería] *s.* favoritismo de los intereses de las personas nacidas en un lugar sobre los de las personas extranjeras. (p. 319, 618)

Navigation Acts [Leyes de Navegación] *s.* serie de leyes aprobadas a partir de 1651 que imponían un control más rígido del comercio en las colonias inglesas. (p. 68)

NAWSA *s.* National American Woman Suffrage Association (Asociación Nacional Americana del Sufragio Femenino), creada en 1890 para obtener derechos electorales para la mujer. (p. 522)

Nazism [nazismo] *s.* movimiento político basado en un extremo nacionalismo, racismo y expansionismo militar; instituido en Alemania como sistema de gobierno por Adolfo Hitler en 1933. (p. 737)

neutrality [neutralidad] *s.* política de una nación de no participar directa ni indirectamente en una guerra entre otras naciones. (p. 191)

Neutrality Acts [Leyes de Neutralidad] *s.* serie de leyes aprobadas por el Congreso en 1935 y 1936 que prohibieron la venta y el alquiler de armas a naciones en guerra. (p. 741)

New Deal *s.* medidas económicas y políticas adoptadas por el presidente Franklin Roosevelt en los años 30 para promover recuperación económica, ayuda a los necesitados y reforma financiera. (p. 695)

New Deal Coalition [Coalición del New Deal] *s.* alianza temporal de distintos grupos, tales como blancos sureños, afroamericanos y sindicalistas, que apoyaban al Partido Demócrata en los años 30 y 40. (p. 713)

New Federalism [Nuevo Federalismo] *s.* programa del presidente Richard Nixon para distribuir una porción del poder del gobierno federal a gobiernos estatales y locales. (p. 1001)

New Frontier [Nueva Frontera] *s.* agenda legislativa del presidente John F. Kennedy; tenía medidas de atención médica para ancianos, renovación urbana y apoyo a la educación, que fueron rechazadas por el Congreso, así como medidas que sí se aprobaron de defensa nacional, ayuda internacional y programas espaciales. (p. 885)

New Left [Nueva Izquierda] *s.* movimiento político juvenil de los años 60 con organizaciones como Students for a Democratic Society (Estudiantes por una Sociedad Democrática) y el Free Speech Movement (Movimiento de Libre Expresión). (p. 950)

New Right [Nueva Derecha] *s.* alianza política de grupos conservadores de fines del siglo 20, con énfasis en asuntos culturales, sociales y morales. (p. 1037)

Niagara Movement [Movimiento Niágara] *s.* fundado en 1905 por W. E. B. Du Bois para promover la enseñanza de humanidades entre los afroamericanos. (p. 491)

Nineteenth Amendment [Enmienda 19] *s.* enmienda a la Constitución adoptada en 1920 que le otorga a la mujer el derecho de votar. (p. 541)

"no man's land" [tierra de nadie] *s.* en la I Guerra Mundial, extensión baldía de tierra entre trincheras de ejércitos enemigos. (p. 582)

nomadic [nómade] *adj.* que no tiene hogar fijo, que se muda de un lugar a otro según las estaciones y la disponibilidad de comida y agua. (p. 5)

nonaggression pact [pacto de no agresión] *s.* acuerdo entre dos naciones de no luchar entre sí. (p. 745)

North Atlantic Treaty Organization (NATO) [Organización del Tratado del Atlántico Norte] *s.* alianza militar defensiva formada en 1949 por diez países de Europa del oeste, Estados Unidos y Canadá. (p. 814)

Northwest Ordinance of 1787 [Ordenanza del Noroeste de 1787] *s.* procedimiento para la admisión de nuevos estados a la Unión. (p. 135)

nuclear family [familia nuclear] *s.* unidad formada por padre, madre e hijos. (p. 21)

nullification [anulación] *s.* rechazo de un estado a reconocer cualquier ley del Congreso que considere inconstitucional. (p. 196)

Nuremberg trials [juicios de Nuremberg] *s.* juicios llevados a cabo en Nuremberg, Alemania, inmediatamente después de la II Guerra Mundial, a líderes nazis por sus crímenes de guerra. (p. 792)

O

Office of Price Administration (OPA) [Oficina de Administración de Precios] *s.* agencia establecida por el Congreso durante la II Guerra Mundial con facultad para combatir la inflación al congelar los precios de la mayoría de los artículos. (p. 773)

Ohio gang [pandilla de Ohio] *s.* amigos y partidarios políticos del presidente Warren G. Harding, a quienes éste nombró a su gabinete. (p. 626)

Olive Branch Petition [Petición del Ramo de Olivo] *s.* documento enviado por el Segundo Congreso Continental al rey George III; proponía una reconciliación entre las colonias y Gran Bretaña. (p. 105)

Olmec [olmeca] *s.* pueblo amerindio que creó una próspera civilización a lo largo de la costa del golfo de México, entre los años 1200 y 400 a.C. (p. 6)

OPEC *s.* Organization of Petroleum Exporting Countries (Organización de Países Exportadores de Petróleo, OPEP), alianza económica para ejercer influencia sobre los precios del petróleo. (p. 1005)

Open Door notes [notas de Puertas Abiertas] *s.* notas que el Secretario de Estado John Hay envió a Gran Bretaña, Francia, Alemania, Italia, Japón y Rusia, instándolos a no interponerse entre el comercio de Estados Unidos y China. (p. 562)

Operation Desert Storm [Operación Tormenta del Desierto] *s.* operación militar en la que fuerzas de las Naciones Unidas, encabezadas por Estados Unidos, liberaron a Kuwait y derrotaron al ejército iraquí. (p. 1061)

Oregon Trail [Sendero de Oregon] *s.* camino que va de Independence, Missouri, a la ciudad de Oregon, Oregon. (p. 284)

P

Panama Canal [canal de Panamá] *s.* canal artificial construido a través del istmo de Panamá para abrir paso entre los océanos Atlántico y Pacífico; se abrió en 1914. (p. 566)

panic of 1837 [pánico de 1837] *s.* serie de clausuras de bancos y colapso del sistema crediticio; causó muchas quiebras y desempleo. (p. 234)

panic of 1873 [pánico de 1873] *s.* serie de fracasos económicos que provocaron una depresión de cinco años en Estados Unidos. (p. 397)

parity [paridad] *s.* regulación de precios de ciertos productos agrícolas, apoyada por el gobierno, con el fin de mantener estables los ingresos agrícolas. (p. 724)

Parliament [Parlamento] *s.* cuerpo legislativo de Inglaterra. (p. 68)

Patriots [patriotas] *s.* colonos que apoyaban la independencia norteamericana de Gran Bretaña. (p. 106)

patronage [clientelismo] *s.* sistema de otorgar empleos a personas que ayudan a la elección de un candidato. (p. 476)

pay equity [equidad salarial] *s.* sistema que basa el salario de un empleado en los requisitos del trabajo y no en escalas salariales tradicionales, que normalmente pagan menos a la mujer. (p. 1048)

Payne-Aldrich Tariff [Arancel Payne-Aldrich] *s.* serie de reglamentos de impuestos, aprobados por el Congreso en 1909, que no logró reducir mucho los aranceles de productos manufacturados. (p. 535)

Peace Corps [Cuerpo de Paz] *s.* programa fundado en 1965 bajo iniciativa del presidente Kennedy, que envía voluntarios a las naciones en desarrollo de Asia, África y Latinoamérica para ayudar en escuelas, clínicas y otros proyectos. (p. 886)

Pendleton Civil Service Act [Ley Pendleton] *s.* ley de 1883 que autorizaba nombrar empleados del servicio civil por mérito. (p. 476)

Pentagon Papers [Documentos del Pentágono] *s.* documento de 7,000 páginas que dejó filtrar a la prensa en 1971 el antiguo funcionario del Departamento de Defensa Daniel Ellsberg, donde se revela que el gobierno mintió sobre sus planes en la Guerra de Vietnam. (p. 963)

Pequot War [Guerra de los Pequot] *s.* conflicto librado en 1637 entre la tribu pequot y colonos asentados en Connecticut, que se aliaron con la tribu narrangansett. (p. 53)

perestroika *s.* palabra rusa para designar la reestructuración económica y burocrática de la Unión Soviética que ocurrió en los años 80. (p. 1055)

personal liberty laws [leyes de libertad personal] *s.* estatutos aprobados en los estados del Norte que prohibían encarcelar a esclavos fugitivos y les permitían ser juzgados por un jurado. (p. 311)

planned obsolescence [obsolencia planeada] *s.* diseño de artículos que se desgastan o pasan de moda muy pronto, para crear la necesidad de remplazarlos con frecuencia. (p. 854)

plantation [plantación] *s.* finca grande en la que se cultiva una sola cosecha, como caña de azúcar o algodón, usando esclavos u otros trabajadores. (p. 16)

Platt Amendment [Enmienda Platt] *s.* serie de medidas implantadas por Estados Unidos en 1901, las cuales debieron ser incluidas por Cuba en su nueva constitución para quedar libre de su deuda y por las que Estados Unidos obtenía el derecho a intervenir en el país y a comprar o alquilar el territorio cubano para establecer estaciones navales y de combustible. (p. 560)

Plessy v. Ferguson *s.* caso de 1896 en que la Suprema Corte declaró legal la separación de razas en instalaciones públicas y estableció la doctrina de "separados aunque iguales". (p. 493)

political machine [maquinaria política] *s.* grupo organizado que controla un partido político en una ciudad y ofrece servicios a los votantes y negocios a cambio de apoyo político y financiero. (p. 474)

poll tax [impuesto para votar] *s.* impuesto anual que los ciudadanos debían pagar en algunos estados sureños para poder votar. (p. 493)

popular sovereignty [soberanía popular] *s.* sistema en el cual los ciudadanos votan para decidir sobre un tema. (p. 307)

Populism [populismo] *s.* movimiento político de finales del siglo 19 que exigía la voz popular en el gobierno y que representaba los intereses de los granjeros y promovía una reforma del sistema monetario. (p. 427)

Powhatan *s.* grupo de pueblos amerindios que vivía en el este de Virginia cuando se establecieron las primeras colonias inglesas. (p. 43)

price support [apoyo de precios] *s.* apoyo de los precios de ciertos artículos al valor del mercado o por encima, algunas veces mediante la compra de excedentes por parte del gobierno. (p. 671)

Proclamation of 1763 [Proclama de 1763] *s.* decreto británico que prohibía que los colonos se instalaran al oeste de los montes Apalaches. (p. 88)

profiteering [acaparamiento] *s.* retención de un producto para provocar su escasez y venderlo más caro. (p. 116)

progressive [progresista] *s.* que favorece el avance hacia mejores condiciones o nuevas ideas. (p. 513)

progressive movement [movimiento progresista] *s.* movimiento reformista de comienzos del siglo 20 cuyos objetivos eran mejorar el bienestar social, promover la moralidad, incrementar la justicia económica y devolver a la ciudadanía el control del gobierno. (p. 513)

prohibition [prohibición] *s.* prohibición de bebidas alcohólicas. (p. 513)

Prohibition [Ley Seca] *s.* período entre 1920 y 1933 durante el cual, por medio de la decimoctava enmienda, se prohibió la producción y la venta de alcohol en Estados Unidos. (p. 642)

propaganda *s.* comunicación prejuiciada diseñada para influir los pensamientos y actos de la gente. (p. 596)

Proposition 187 [Propuesta 187] *s.* proyecto de ley aprobado en California en 1994, el cual canceló todos los beneficios educativos y de salud que no fueran emergencias a los inmigrantes ilegales. (p. 1092)

proprietor [propietario] *s.* dueño y gobernante de una colonia. (p. 56)

protective tariff [arancel proteccionista] *s.* impuesto aplicado a productos importados para proteger las empresas nacionales de la competencia extranjera. (p. 186)

protectorate [protectorado] *s.* nación cuyo gobierno y asuntos son controlados por una potencia más fuerte. (p. 560)

Pueblo *s.* amerindios descendientes de los anasazi; viven en los desiertos del Suroeste. (p. 9)

Pure Food and Drug Act [Ley de Pureza de Alimentos y Drogas] *s.* ley de 1906 que paró la venta de alimentos y drogas contaminadas y demandó etiquetas fidedignas. (p. 528)

Puritans [puritanos] *s.* miembros de la Iglesia Anglicana que deseaban eliminar las tradiciones católicas y simplificar los servicios religiosos. (p. 49)

Q

Quakers [cuáqueros] *s.* miembros de una secta religiosa considerada radical en el siglo 17, también conocida como Sociedad de Amigos. (p. 56)

quota system [sistema de cuotas] *s.* sistema que limita el número de inmigrantes de varios países que pueden ser admitidos a Estados Unidos cada año. (p. 621)

R

Radical Republican [republicano radical] *s.* uno de los republicanos del Congreso después de la Guerra Civil que querían destruir el poder político de los antiguos dueños de esclavos y darles a los afroamericanos total ciudadanía y derecho a votar. (p. 377)

ratification [ratificación] *s.* aprobación oficial de la Constitución, o de una enmienda, por parte de los estados. (p. 146)

rationing [racionamiento] *s.* medida tomada durante tiempos de guerra para limitar la cantidad de ciertos alimentos y otros productos que cada persona puede comprar. (p. 774)

Reaganomics [reaganomía] *s.* nombre dado a la política económica del presidente Reagan, que abogaba por recortes presupuestarios y por una gran reducción en los impuestos con el fin de incrementar la inversión privada y por consiguiente expandir el suministro de productos y servicios. (p. 1040)

realpolitik s. enfoque de política exterior, identificado con Henry Kissinger y Richard Nixon, que propone hacer lo que resulte realista y práctico en lugar de seguir una política al pie de la letra. (p. 1005)

reapportionment [nueva repartición] *s.* redistribución de distritos electorales cuando cambia el número de personas en un distrito. (p. 897)

recall [destitución] *s.* reforma gubernamental que permite a los votantes deponer a funcionarios públicos elegidos. (p. 518)

Reconstruction [Reconstrucción] *s.* período de reconstrucción después de la Guerra Civil y readmisión a la Unión de los estados de la Confederación que habían sido derrotados; de 1865 a 1877. (p. 376)

Reconstruction Finance Corporation (RFC) [Corporación Financiera de la Reconstrucción] *s.* organización establecida en 1932 para dar financiación de emergencia a bancos, aseguradoras de vida, compañías ferroviarias y otras empresas grandes. (p. 687)

Red Cross [Cruz Roja] *s.* organización internacional que provee ayuda a la gente en tiempos de guerra o de desastres naturales. En 1881, Clara Barton fundó la sede estadounidense. (p. 370)

redemption [redención] *s.* término usado por los demócratas sureños para referirse a su recuperación del poder en el Sur en la década de 1870. (p. 399)

referendum [referendo] *s.* procedimiento que permite someter al voto popular propuestas legislativas. (p. 518)

Reformation [Reforma] *s.* movimiento religioso en la Europa de comienzos del siglo 16, encaminado a reformar la Iglesia Católica Romana; condujo a la formación del protestantismo. (p. 22)

Renaissance [Renacimiento] *s.* período de la historia europea, que se extendió aproximadamente desde 1400 a 1600, durante el cual un renovado interés en la cultura clásica originó cambios trascendentales en las artes, el aprendizaje y la visión del mundo. (p. 20)

reparations [reparación] *s.* compensación que paga una nación derrotada en una guerra por las pérdidas económicas del vencedor o por crímenes cometidos contra individuos. (p. 606)

republic [república] *s.* gobierno en el que los ciudadanos mandan por medio de sus representantes elegidos. (p. 133)

republicanism [republicanismo] *s.* creencia de que los gobiernos deben basarse en el consentimiento del pueblo. (p. 133)

Republican Party [Partido Republicano] *s.* partido actual, formado en 1854 por oponentes de la esclavitud en los territorios. (p. 320)

Republic of California [República de California] *s.* nación proclamada por los colonos estadounidenses en California, al declarar éstos su independencia de México en 1846. (p. 295)

Republic of Texas [república de Texas] *s.* nación fundada en 1836, cuando los colonos estadounidenses de la provincia mexicana de Tejas lucharon y declararon su independencia. En esa época se la conocía también como la "República de la Estrella Solitaria". (p. 292)

revenue sharing [distribución de rentas] *s.* plan puesto en práctica en 1972 que faculta a los gobiernos estatales y locales a invertir el dinero federal a su conveniencia. (p. 1001)

reverse discrimination [discriminación a la inversa] *s.* tratamiento injusto de los miembros de un grupo mayoritario, típicamente hombres blancos, como resultado de los esfuerzos por remediar la discriminación contra otros grupos. (p. 1037)

revival [renovación religiosa] *s.* emotivas reuniones religiosas para revivir la fe, con apasionados sermones. (p. 241)

rock 'n' roll *s.* forma de música popular estadounidense que evolucionó a finales de los 40 y durante los 50, a partir del rhythm and blues, el country, el jazz, el gospel y el pop; forma musical estadounidense caracterizada por ritmos fuertes y melodías simples, la cual se ha expandido por todo el mundo y ha tenido impactos significantes en el baile social, la moda de la vestimenta y las expresiones de protesta. (p. 861)

Roosevelt Corollary [Corolario de Roosevelt] *s.* declaración de 1904 del presidente Theodore Roosevelt en que advertía que Estados Unidos intervendría militarmente en los asuntos de cualquier nación del Hemisferio Occidental para proteger sus intereses económicos si fuera necesario. (p. 568)

Rough Riders *s.* regimiento de caballería voluntario comandado por Leonard Wood y Theodore Roosevelt en la Guerra Española-Norteamericana-Cubana. (p. 556)

royal colony [colonia real] *s.* colonia sujeta al control directo de la corona británica. (p. 47)

rural free delivery (RFD) [correo rural gratuito] *s.* entrega gubernamental gratis de correo y paquetes a zonas rurales; se inició en 1896. (p. 503)

S

SALT I Treaty [Tratado Salt I] *s.* acuerdo de cinco años entre Estados Unidos y la Unión Soviética que surgió de las Conversaciones sobre Limitación de Armas Estratégicas de 1972; limitó el número de misiles balísticos intercontinentales y de misiles de submarinos. (p. 1007)

salutary neglect [indiferencia saludable] *s.* aplicación poco estricta de las leyes comerciales por parte del gobierno británico a cambio de lealtad comercial de las colonias. (p. 70)

Sandinista *s.* un miembro de un grupo rebelde izquierdista que derrocaron al gobierno nicaragüense en 1979; el presidente Reagan, quien respaldaba a la contra anticomunista, se les opuso. (p. 1057)

Santa Fe Trail [Sendero de Santa Fe] *s.* camino que va de Independence, Missouri, a Santa Fe, New Mexico. (p. 282)

satellite nation [nación satélite] *s.* país dominado política y económicamente por otro. (p. 811)

Saturday Night Massacre [Masacre de Sábado en la Noche] *s.* nombre dado a la renuncia del procurador general y al despido de su comisionado el 20 de octubre de 1973, después de haberse negado a acatar la orden del presidente Nixon de despedir al fiscal especial en el caso Watergate. (p. 1011)

savanna [sabana] *s.* pastizal plano y seco con árboles y arbustos espaciados; común en África central y otras regiones tropicales y subtropicales. (p. 17)

scalawag *s.* término despectivo para referirse a los sureños blancos que se unieron al Partido Republicano y apoyaron la Reconstrucción después de la Guerra Civil. (p. 385)

scientific management [administración científica] *s.* aplicación de principios científicos para simplificar y facilitar las tareas laborales. (p. 514)

Scopes trial [juicio de Scopes] *s.* sensacional juicio de 1925 en el que el maestro de biología John T. Scopes fue juzgado por desafiar una ley de Tennessee que prohibía la enseñanza de la evolución. (p. 644)

search-and-destroy mission [misión de búsqueda y destrucción] *s.* ataque militar estadounidense a aldeas de Vietnam del Sur con el fin de erradicar al Vietcong, que solía resultar en la destrucción de la aldea y el desplazamiento de sus habitantes. (p. 945)

secession [secesión] *s.* retiro formal de un estado de la Unión federal. (p. 307)

Second Continental Congress [Segundo Congreso Continental] *s.* nueva convocatoria del Congreso Continental que se inició en 1775 y redactó la Declaración de Independencia. (p. 103)

Second Great Awakening [Segundo Gran Despertar] *s.* movimiento religioso del siglo 19 que ponía énfasis en la responsabilidad individual para lograr la salvación y la superación personal y social. (p. 240)

sectionalism [regionalismo] *s.* preocupación por los intereses de una región por encima de los de la nación como un todo. (p. 194)

Securities and Exchange Commission (SEC) [Comisión de Valores y Cambios] *s.* agencia creada en 1934 para controlar el mercado bursátil y hacer cumplir las leyes que rigen la venta de acciones y bonos. (p. 723)

segregation [segregación] *s.* separación de la gente según su raza. (p. 493)

Selective Service Act [Ley de Servicio Selectivo] *s.* ley aprobada por el Congreso en mayo de 1917 que ordena que todos los hombres se inscriban para el servicio militar obligatorio. (p. 588)

Seneca Falls Convention [convención de Seneca Falls] *s.* convención de derechos femeninos celebrada en 1848 en Seneca Falls, New York. (p. 257)

Separatist [separatista] *s.* miembro de la Iglesia Anglicana que rechazó su reforma y formó una congregación independiente. (p. 50)

service sector [sector de servicios] *s.* renglón de la economía que ofrece servicios en vez de productos. (p. 1076)

settlement house [casa de beneficencia] *s.* centro comunitario en un barrio pobre que ayudaba a los residentes, particularmente a los inmigrantes. (p. 472)

Seventeenth Amendment [Enmienda 17] *s.* enmienda a la Constitución adoptada en 1913; dispone que los senadores federales sean elegidos por los votantes y no por cuerpos legislativos estatales. (p. 518)

shantytown [tugurio] *s.* vecindario en donde la gente vivía en chozas temporales. (p. 679)

sharecropping [aparcería] *s.* sistema en el cual se da a los agricultores tierra, semillas, herramientas y alimentos para vivir, así como una parte de la cosecha, por cultivar la tierra. (p. 391)

Shays's Rebellion [Rebelión de Shays] *s.* sublevación de granjeros endeudados de Massachusetts en 1787, en protesta por los impuestos estatales. (p. 140)

Sherman Antitrust Act [Ley Antitrust Sherman] *s.* ley contra los monopolios de 1890 que declaró ilegal la formación de consorcios que obstruyeran el libre comercio. (p. 450)

silent majority [mayoría silenciosa] *s.* nombre dado por el presidente Richard Nixon a los estadounidenses moderados que apoyaban silenciosamente su involucramiento en la Guerra de Vietnam. (p. 962)

sit-in *s.* forma de protesta —iniciada por el Congreso de Igualdad Racial en los años 40 y empleada con frecuencia en los años 60— en la que afroamericanos ingresaban a un lugar segregado, tal como el mostrador de un restaurante, y se negaban a salir hasta que se les sirviera. (p. 912)

slave [esclavo] *s.* persona que se convierte en propiedad de otra. (p. 75)

Social Darwinism [darvinismo social] *s.* conjunto de creencias políticas y económicas basadas en la teoría del biólogo Charles Darwin sobre la selección natural o supervivencia del más apto; favorecía una competencia libre, no regulada, y creía que los individuos o grupos triunfaban porque eran genéticamente superiores. (p. 448)

Social Gospel movement [movimiento del Evangelio Social] *s.* movimiento de reforma del siglo 19 basado en la noción de que los cristianos tenían la responsabilidad social de mejorar las condiciones laborales y aliviar la pobreza urbana. (p. 472)

Social Security Act [Ley de Seguro Social] *s.* ley aprobada en 1935 para ayudar a los jubilados, desempleados, incapacitados y familias con niños dependientes. (p. 707)

soddy [choza de tepe] *s.* casa provisional hecha de césped, muy común en las llanuras, donde la madera era escasa. (p. 422)

Songhai *s.* imperio que, en la cúspide de su poderío durante el siglo 16, controlaba gran parte de África occidental. (p. 16)

soup kitchen [comedor de beneficencia] *s.* lugar donde se sirven alimentos gratis o a bajo costo a los necesitados, muy común durante la Depresión. (p. 679)

Southern Christian Leadership Conference (SCLC) [Conferencia de Líderes Cristianos del Sur] *s.* organización formada en 1957 por el doctor Martin Luther King, Jr., y otros líderes para promover los derechos civiles sin violencia. (p. 912)

Southern strategy [estrategia sureña] *s.* estrategia del presidente Nixon de apelar a los demócratas conservadores sureños que estaban descontentos con la integración y con una Suprema Corte liberal. (p. 1003)

speakeasy *s.* lugar donde se vendían bebidas alcohólicas ilegalmente, como ocurrió durante la Prohibición. (p. 642)

specialization [especialización] *s.* producción de un número limitado de productos agrícolas para venta nacional o internacional. (p. 275)

speculation [especulación] *s.* transacciones de alto riesgo con el fin de obtener ganancias rápidas o grandes. (p. 673)

spoils system [sistema de prebendas] *s.* práctica de los candidatos ganadores de dar empleos u otras recompensas a sus simpatizantes. (p. 226)

Square Deal *s.* programa de reformas progresistas del presidente Theodore Roosevelt para proteger a la gente común y corriente de las grandes empresas. (p. 525)

stagflation [estanflación] *s.* situación económica en la que hay niveles altos de inflación y desempleo simultáneamente. (p. 1004)

Stamp Act [Ley del Timbre] *s.* primer impuesto directo aplicado en 1765 por Gran Bretaña a una variedad de artículos y servicios, tales como documentos legales y periódicos. (p. 96)

Stono Rebellion [Rebelión de Stono] *s.* rebelión de esclavos en la colonia de South Carolina en 1739; en consecuencia se hicieron más estrictas las leyes pertinentes a los esclavos. (p. 78)

Strategic Defense Initiative (SDI) [Iniciativa para la Defensa Estratégica] *s.* sistema de defensa propuesto en los años 80, popularmente conocido como la Guerra de las Galaxias, cuyo fin era proteger a Estados Unidos de ataques de misiles. (p. 1041)

strike [huelga] *s.* interrupción del trabajo para presionar a un patrono a responder a ciertas demandas. (p. 262)

Student Nonviolent Coordinating Committee (SNCC) [Comité Coordinador de Estudiantes no Violentos] *s.* organización fundada en 1961, conocida como SNCC, para coordinar sit-ins y otras protestas, y para darles a los jóvenes negros mayor participación en el movimiento de derechos civiles. (p. 912)

Students for a Democratic Society (SDS) [Estudiantes por una Sociedad Democrática] *s.* grupo activista de los años 60, conocido como SDS, que urgía una mayor libertad y responsabilidad individual. (p. 950)

suburb [suburbio] *s.* pueblo o comunidad residencial cerca de una ciudad. (p. 841)

suffrage [sufragio] *s.* derecho a votar. (p. 521)

Sugar Act [Ley del Azúcar] *s.* ley británica de 1764 que aplicó un impuesto comercial a la melaza, el azúcar y otras importaciones para reducir el contrabando en las colonias. (p. 89)

supply-side economics [economía de oferta] *s.* teoría económica, practicada por el presidente Ronald Reagan, que sostiene que recortar los impuestos de los ricos beneficia a todos pues aumenta empleos, ahorros e inversiones. (p. 1041)

T

Taino [taíno] *s.* pueblo amerindio que Colón y su tripulación vieron al arribar a la isla hoy conocida como San Salvador, el 12 de octubre de 1492. (p. 27)

Tariff of Abominations [Arancel Abominable] *s.* nombre que le dio Henry Clay a un aumento de aranceles estipulado en 1828, debido al cual los sureños creían que el norte se estaba enriqueciendo a sus expensas. (p. 230)

Tariff of 1816 [Arancel de 1816] *s.* arancel proteccionista para proteger las jóvenes industrias estadounidenses. (p. 218)

Teapot Dome scandal [escándalo de Teapot Dome] *s.* escándalo generado cuando Albert Fall, Secretario del Interior del presidente Warren G. Harding, concedió en secreto valiosas reservas de petróleo en Wyoming y California a compañías privadas a cambio de dinero y tierras. (p. 627)

Telecommunications Act of 1996 [Ley de Telecomunicaciones] *s.* ley de 1996 que retiró las barreras que impedían que un tipo de compañía de comunicaciones ingresara a otro tipo de negocio en el mismo campo. (p. 1084)

telecommute *v.* trabajar desde la casa para una compañía ubicada en otra parte, mediante la nueva tecnología de comunicaciones, como computadoras, Internet y máquinas de fax. (p. 1084)

telegraph [telégrafo] *s.* aparato que convierte un mensaje codificado en impulsos eléctricos que viajan por un hilo metálico. (p. 276)

temperance movement [movimiento de templanza] *s.* campaña para prohibir el consumo y la venta de alcohol. (p. 255)

tenant farming [agricultura de arrendatarios] *s.* sistema en el que los agricultores, llamados arrendatarios, ponen sus propias herramientas y animales, y pagan dinero por el arriendo de tierra para cultivar. (p. 391)

tenement [casa de pisos] *s.* vivienda urbana de varias familias, usualmente sobrepoblada y poco sanitaria. (p. 470)

Tennessee Valley Authority (TVA) [Autoridad del Valle de Tennessee] *s.* corporación federal creada en 1933 para construir presas y centrales eléctricas en la región del valle de Tennessee con el objeto de generar electricidad así como prevenir inundaciones. (p. 725)

termination policy [política de terminación] *s.* programa del gobierno federal en 1953 de cesar su responsabilidad hacia las naciones amerindias y eliminar el apoyo económico federal, suspender el sistema de reservaciones y redistribuir las tierras tribales. (p. 869)

Tet offensive [ofensiva de Tet] *s.* sorpresivo ataque masivo del Vietcong a pueblos y ciudades de Vietnam del Sur a comienzos de 1968; la batalla, de un mes de duración, convenció a muchos estadounidenses de que no era posible ganar la guerra. (p. 955)

Texas Revolution [Revolución de Texas] *s.* rebelión de 1836 con la que Texas se independizó de México. (p. 291)

Thirteenth Amendment [Enmienda 13] *s.* enmienda a la Constitución, ratificada en 1865, que ha abolido la esclavitud y la servidumbre involuntaria. (p. 368)

Three-Fifths Compromise [Acuerdo de los Tres Quintos] *s.* acuerdo constitucional de considerar como población las tres quintas partes de los esclavos de un estado para efectos de representación y cobro de impuestos. (p. 142)

Tiananmen Square [plaza Tianamen] *s.* lugar de protestas estudiantiles en 1989 en Beijing, China, por la falta de libertades democráticas, donde el gobierno atacó a los estudiantes. (p. 1056)

Tonkin Gulf Resolution [Resolución del Golfo de Tonkin] *s.* resolución aprobada por el Congreso en 1964 que le otorgaba al presidente Johnson amplios poderes para la Guerra de Vietnam. (p. 941)

totalitarian [totalitario] *adj.* característico de un sistema político en que el gobierno ejerce completo control sobre la vida de los ciudadanos. (p. 735)

Townshend Acts [Leyes Townshend] *s.* serie de leyes promulgadas por el Parlamento en 1767 que establecían impuestos indirectos a los artículos de Gran Bretaña importados a las colonias. (p. 97)

Trail of Tears [Sendero de las Lágrimas] *s.* marcha obligada del pueblo cherokee desde Georgia hasta el Territorio Indio entre 1838 y 1840, durante la cual murieron miles de ellos. (p. 229)

transcendentalism [trascendentalismo] *s.* movimiento filosófico y literario que proponía llevar una vida sencilla y celebrar la verdad implícita de la naturaleza, la emoción personal y la imaginación. (p. 242)

transcontinental railroad [ferrocarril transcontinental] *s.* línea férrea finalizada en 1869 que unía la costa Atlántica y la costa Pacífica. (p. 443)

Treaty of Fort Laramie [Tratado del Fuerte Laramie] *s.* tratado que requería que los sioux vivieran en una reservación a lo largo del río Missouri. (p. 282, 410)

Treaty of Ghent [Tratado de Gante] *s.* tratado firmado en 1814 que puso fin a la Guerra de 1812. (p. 205)

Treaty of Guadalupe Hidalgo [Tratado de Guadalupe Hidalgo] *s.* tratado de 1848 que puso fin a la guerra entre Estados Unidos y México, mediante el cual Estados Unidos obtuvo enormes tierras en el Oeste y el Suroeste. (p. 297)

Treaty of Paris (1783) [Tratado de París] *s.* tratado que puso fin a la Guerra Revolucionaria Norteamericana y estableció las fronteras de la nueva nación. (p. 122)

Treaty of Paris (1898) [Tratado de París] *s.* tratado el cual puso fin a la guerra entre España y Estados Unidos. Por medio de este tratado España liberó a Cuba, cedió las islas de Guam y Puerto Rico a Estados Unidos y vendió las Filipinas a este país por 20 millones de dólares. (p. 556)

Treaty of Tordesillas [Tratado de Tordesillas] *s.* tratado de 1494 que dividió las Américas entre España y Portugal mediante una línea vertical imaginaria en el Atlántico; cada país tenía poder sobre un lado de la línea. (p. 30)

Treaty of Versailles [Tratado de Versalles] *s.* tratado de paz firmado en 1919 al finalizar la I Guerra Mundial, el cual establecía nuevas naciones, fronteras y reparaciones de guerra. (p. 606)

trench warfare [guerra de trincheras] *s.* guerra en que los combatientes atacan desde un sistema de zanjas fortificadas y no en un campo abierto de batalla. (p. 582)

triangular trade [triángulo comercial de esclavos] *s.* sistema transatlántico de comercio en el cual la mercancía, incluidos los esclavos, se intercambiaba entre África, Inglaterra, Europa, las Indias Occidentales y las colonias de Norteamérica. (p. 76)

Truman Doctrine [Doctrina Truman] *s.* declaración del presidente Truman en 1947, que establecía que Estados Unidos debía dar apoyo económico y militar para liberar a naciones amenazadas por fuerzas internas o externas. (p. 812)

Tuskegee Normal and Industrial Institute [Instituto Normal e Industrial Tuskegee] *s.* fundado en 1881 y dirigido por Booker T. Washington para otorgar diplomas de magisterio y enseñar destrezas comerciales y agrícolas a los afroamericanos. (p. 491)

two-party system [bipartidismo] *s.* sistema político dominado por dos partidos. (p. 186)

U

Uncle Tom's Cabin [La cabaña del tío Tom] *s.* novela famosa (1852) escrita por Harriet Beecher Stowe, que causó intenso furor al retratar la esclavitud como una gran perversión moral. (p. 312)

Underground Railroad [Ferrocarril Subterráneo] *s.* red secreta de personas que ayudaban a los esclavos fugitivos a escapar a lo largo de diversas rutas hacia Canadá o hacia zonas seguras en los estados libres. (p. 311)

United Farm Workers Organizing Committee (UFWOC) [Comité Organizador de Trabajadores Agrícolas Unidos] *s.* sindicato establecido en 1966 por César Chávez para mejorar los salarios y las condiciones laborales de los trabajadores agrícolas. (p. 976)

United Nations (UN) [Naciones Unidas] *s.* organización internacional promotora de la paz a la que pertenecen la mayoría de naciones, fundada en 1945 para fomentar la paz, la seguridad y el desarrollo económico del mundo. (p. 809)

urban flight [huida urbana] *s.* migración de las ciudades a los suburbios aledaños. (p. 1088)

urbanization [urbanización] *s.* movimiento de personas a una ciudad. (p. 468)

urban renewal [renovación urbana] *s.* práctica que se inició con la Ley Nacional de Vivienda de 1949, de remplazar vecindarios urbanos decaídos por viviendas nuevas para gente de bajos recursos. (p. 867)

urban sprawl [explosión urbana] *s.* expansión desordenada y desmedida de las ciudades a las áreas contiguas. (p. 630)

U.S.S. *Maine* *s.* buque de guerra estadounidense que explotó y naufragó misteriosamente el 15 de febrero de 1898 en el puerto de La Habana, Cuba. (p. 554)

U-2 incident [incidente del U-2] *s.* derribo en 1960 de un avión espía estadounidense U-2 en suelo soviético; complicó las conversaciones de paz entre Estados Unidos y la Unión Soviética. (p. 833)

utopian community [comunidad utópica] *s.* comunidad formada por un grupo experimental que vivía unido y buscaba crear un lugar perfecto. (p. 243)

V

V-E Day [Día V-E] *s.* mayo 8 de 1945, día de la victoria europea, cuando el general Eisenhower aceptó la rendición incondicional de Alemania; puso fin a la II Guerra Mundial en Europa. (p. 783)

vertical integration [integración vertical] *s.* proceso mediante el cual una compañía se adueña de sus proveedores y distribuidores así como de los sistemas de transporte, con lo que obtiene control total sobre la calidad y el costo de su producción. (p. 448)

Vietcong *s.* rebeldes comunistas de Vietnam del Sur apoyados por Vietnam del Norte a partir de 1959. (p. 938)

Vietminh [Vietmin] *s.* organización de comunistas vietnamitas y otros grupos nacionalistas que luchó contra los franceses por la independencia de Vietnam de 1946 a 1954. (p. 937)

Vietnamization [vietnamización] *s.* plan del presidente Nixon de retiro gradual de las tropas estadounidenses de Vietnam y su remplazo por el ejército vietnamita. (p. 961)

Voting Rights Act of 1965 [Ley de Derechos Electorales de 1965] *s.* ley para facilitarles a los afroamericanos inscribirse para votar; eliminó las pruebas discriminatorias de lectura y escritura, y autorizó a los examinadores federales inscribir votantes rechazados a nivel local. (p. 922)

W

Wade-Davis Bill [proyecto de ley Wade-Davis] *s.* proyecto de ley, aprobado en 1864 y vetado por el presidente Lincoln, que daba al Congreso control de la Reconstrucción. (p. 377)

Wagner Act [Ley Wagner] *s.* ley —también conocida como Ley Nacional de Relaciones Laborales— promulgada en 1935 para proteger los derechos de los trabajadores después de que la Corte Suprema consideró que la Ley Nacional de Recuperación Industrial (NIRA) era inconstitucional. (p. 705)

war-guilt clause [cláusula de culpabilidad] *s.* cláusula del Tratado de Versalles que obligaba a Alemania a reconocer que había sido totalmente responsable por la I Guerra Mundial. (p. 606)

war hawk [halcón de guerra] *s.* uno de los miembros del Congreso que apoyó la guerra con Gran Bretaña a comienzos del siglo 19. (p. 203)

War Industries Board (WIB) [Junta de Industrias Bélicas] *s.* junta establecida en 1917 que animaba a las compañías a usar técnicas de producción en masa para mejorar la eficiencia durante la I Guerra Mundial. (p. 595)

War Powers Act (WPA) [Ley de Poderes de Guerra] *s.* ley aprobada en 1973 tras la Guerra de Vietnam que limitaba el derecho de un presidente a enviar tropas a combatir sin consultar con el Congreso. (p. 967)

War Production Board (WPB) [Junta de Producción Bélica] *s.* agencia establecida durante la II Guerra Mundial para coordinar la producción de suministros militares por la industria nacional. (p. 774)

Warren Commission [Comisión Warren] *s.* grupo encabezado por Earl Warren, presidente de la Suprema Corte, que realizó la investigación oficial del asesinato del presidente Kennedy y concluyó que Lee Harvey Oswald había actuado por su cuenta. (p. 889)

Warren Court [la Corte Warren] *s.* la Suprema Corte de la que fue presidente Earl Warren, que se destacó por sus actividades en torno a los derechos civiles y la libre expresión. (p. 897)

Warsaw Pact [Pacto de Varsovia] *s.* alianza militar formada en 1955 por la Unión Soviética y las naciones satélite de Europa del este. (p. 830)

Watergate *s.* serie de escándalos en que el presidente Nixon trató de encubrir la participación de su comité de reelección en el allanamiento de la sede del Partido Demócrata en los apartamentos Watergate en 1972. (p. 1008)

Whig Party [Partido Liberal] *s.* miembro de un partido político establecido en 1834 en oposición a Andrew Jackson. (p. 234)

Wilmot Proviso [Cláusula Wilmot] *s.* enmienda a un proyecto de ley de fondos militares de 1846; proponía que ninguna porción del territorio adquirido en la guerra con México debía abrirse a la esclavitud. (p. 306)

Women's Auxiliary Army Corps (WAAC) [Unidad Auxiliar de Mujeres (WAAC)] *s.* unidad del Ejército de EE.UU. creada durante la Segunda Guerra Mundial para permitir que las mujeres colaboraran en puestos que no fueran de combate. (p. 769)

Woodstock *s.* festival gratuito de música que atrajo a más de 400,000 jóvenes a una granja del estado de New York en agosto de 1969. (p. 989)

Works Progress Administration (WPA) [Administración para el Progreso de Obras] *s.* agencia gubernamental del New Deal que empleó a personal desocupado en construcción de escuelas y hospitales, reparación de carreteras, enseñanza, escritura y artes. (p. 704)

X

XYZ Affair [Asunto XYZ] *s.* incidente diplomático de 1797 en el que funcionarios franceses trataron de sobornar a funcionarios estadounidenses para entrevistarse con un alto ministro francés. (p. 195)

Y

yellow journalism [prensa amarillista] *s.* uso de métodos sensacionalistas en periódicos o revistas para atraer o influenciar lectores. (p. 553)

Z

Zimmermann note [nota Zimmermann] *s.* mensaje enviado por el canciller alemán en 1917 al canciller mexicano en el que prometía a México los estados de Texas, New Mexico y Arizona si se aliaba a Alemania en contra de Estados Unidos en la I Guerra Mundial. (p. 585)

INDEX

An *i* in italics preceding a page number refers to an illustration on the page. An *m* or a *c* in italics preceding a page number refers to a map or chart on the page.

A

Allen, Gracie, 717, *i* 718
Allen, Richard, 241–242
Alliance for Progress, 886–887
Allies
in World War I, 579–580, 582, 583, 584, *i* 592
in World War II, 760
al-Qaeda, 1073, 1100–1101, 1102
Amendments to Constitution. *See specific number.*
American Anti-Slavery Society, 249
American Civil Liberties Union (ACLU), 644
American Expeditionary Force (AEF), 590
American Federation of Labor (AFL), 451–452, 539, 623, 714
American Gothic (Wood), 719, *i* 719
American Independent Party, 959
American Indian Movement (AIM), 977–978
American Indians. *See* Native Americans.
Americanization movement, 469
American Liberty League, 699
American Party, 319
American Protective Association, 464
American Railway Union (ARU), 452, 454
American Revolution. *See* Revolutionary War.
American Socialist Party, 515
American System, 216–217
American Temperance Society, 255
Ameringer, Oscar, 684
Amnesty Act, 395
amusement parks, 498–499
Anaconda plan, 341
analyzing causes, 19, 38, 40, 41, 47, 59, 74, 75, 78, 82, 89, 123, 215, 234, 235, 262, 275, 278, 295, 316, 339, 353, 379, 392, 414, 417, 421, 426, 428, 453, 462, 476, 477, 483, 502, 516, 520, 562, 579, 645, 657, 663, 681, 718, 736, 740, 741, 760, 776, 797, 799, 809, 810, 816, 818, 824, 825, 829, 842, 852, 854, 861, 909, 921, 922, 925, 946, 984, 1005, 1015, 1018, 1020, 1021, 1031, 1039, 1044, 1061, 1067, 1070, 1071, 1089, R7
analyzing distributions, 727, 1053, R25, R32
analyzing effects, 5, 7, 19, 28, 31, 54, 80, 92, 93, 114, 123, 218, 241, 252, 260, 276, 278, 279, 282, 289, 294, 300, 306, 309, 311, 317, 321, 325, 328, 330, 342, 348, 356, 359, 360, 362, 367, 380, 398, 401, 412, 421, 439, 443, 465, 471, 472, 477, 493, 521, 526, 543, 549, 557, 566, 580, 585, 591, 598, 600, 627, 629, 630, 643, 648, 654, 659, 675, 682, 683, 697, 714, 720, 725, 750, 757, 779, 782, 798, 801, 813, 831, 849, 850, 852, 855, 859, 863, 867, 880, 883, 887, 897, 899, 907, 947, 967, 976, 983, 1006, 1007, 1027, 1031, 1039, 1042, 1068, 1072, 1076, 1079, 1084, R7

analyzing events, 45, 48, 68, 229, 284, 317, 321, 365, 401, 541, 551, 555, 620, 673, 774, 817, 821, 827, 836, 908, 920, 929, 959, 1013, 1023, 1032, 1056, R13
analyzing issues, 25, 48, 51, 53, 71, 105, 121, 123, 134, 137, 142, 144, 146, 185, 187, 193, 194, 196, 201, 203, 228, 235, 245, 258, 265, 314, 317, 321, 365, 371, 392, 398, 400, 402, 410, 426, 429, 445, 451, 522, 531, 535, 559, 564, 586, 621, 624, 633, 645, 689, 705, 720, 749, 761, 804, 868, 869, 898, 909, 910, 917, 929, 931, 955, 957, 963, 1002, 1023, 1037, 1049, 1073, 1079, 1087, R14
analyzing motives, 37, 50, 99, 141, 149, 176, 183, 191, 203, 233, 285, 289, 295, 306, 320, 325, 358, 364, 365, 387, 394, 432, 446, 467, 469, 472, 474, 513, 543, 553, 569, 583, 611, 619, 738, 744, 746, 747, 755, 791, 801, 811, 814, 827, 884, 889, 893, 926, 938, 956, 977, 985, 1003, 1009, 1039, 1044, 1073, R6
analyzing patterns, 287, 441, 573, 622, *c* 622, 857, 891, R25, R32
analyzing political cartoons, 89, 108, 127, 167, 177, 195, 209, 233, 298, 329, 373, 385, 396, 426, 429, 446, 449, 475, 479, 518, 525, 557, 560, 568, 575, 597, 627, 632, 637, 645, 673, 687, 699, 725, 740, 757, 765, 814, 826, 827, 837, 884, 899, 971, 1001, 1012, 1042, 1083, R24
analyzing primary sources. *See* primary sources, analyzing.
analyzing relationships, 292, 441, *m* 555, *m* 562, 564, 632, *c* 723, 891, 902, 959, 1006, 1063, R28
analyzing visual sources. *See* visual sources, analyzing.
anarchists, 598, 619, 621
Anasazi people, *m* 6, 7, 9
Anaya, Toney, 1050
Anderson, Marian, 712, *i* 712, 878
Anderson, Robert, 338
Andersonville prison, 356, *i* 356
Andrews, Eliza Frances, 364
Andrews, John, 99
Andros, Sir Edmund, 69
Angel Island, 463, *i* 464, *i* 1092
Angelou, Maya, 796, 1066, *i* 1066
Anglican Church. *See* Church of England.
Anthony, Susan B., 521, 522, *i* 522, 541
anthrax, *i* 1102
effects of, 1102
September 11 terrorist attack and, 1102
Antietam, Battle of, 344–345
Antifederalists, 145–148
Anti-Imperialist League, 564
Anti-Saloon League, 514, 642
antislavery movement, 241–242, 305–306, 347
free blacks and, 249
John Brown and, 327
leaders of, 248–249

opposition to, 249, 252–253
political parties and, 319–320
women and, 254, 255–256
antiterrorism bill, 1072
antiterrorism coalition, 1073, 1102
Great Britain and, 1102, 1105
apartheid, 148, 907
Appalachian Mountains, 88, 201
Appeal to Christian Women of the South, An (Angelina Grimké), 255
Appeal to the Colored Citizens of the World (Walker), 249
Appomattox Court House, Virginia, 365, *i* 365, 370
Arapaho people, 282, 412
Arbella, 49, 50
archaeologists, 4
architecture, 57, *i* 57, 484, *i* 484, 542, *i* 542, 1089, *i* 1089
Greek Revival style of, 305, *i* 305
Arizona, 40, 297, 894, 1053
facts about, R38
as Mexican province, 284
Native Americans in, 7
Arkansas, 339, 377, 909, 915, 922, 1066, 1067
facts about, R38
Armistead, James, 107
armistice, 205, 593
Armstrong, Louis, *i* 661, 662, *i* 662, 663
Armstrong, Neil, 1002
Army of the Republic of Vietnam (ARVN), 943
Arnold, Benedict, 121
art, 21, *i* 21, 51, *i* 51, 98, *i* 98, 242, *i* 242, 328, *i* 328, 359, *i* 359, 416, *i* 416, 501, *i* 501, 570, *i* 570, 599, *i* 599, 620, *i* 620, 641, *i* 641, 656, 718–719, *i* 719, 851, *i* 851. *See also specific works, artists, and movements.*
Arthur, Chester A., 476, *i* 476
Articles of Confederation, 135, *c* 137
artificial intelligence, 1084–1085
ARU. *See* American Railway Union.
Asante (Ashanti) people, 19
Asbury, Herbert, 643
Ashcan School of American art, 501
Asia, 4, 25, 26, 27
Asian Americans, 1050, 1090, 1092, 1095. *See also* Chinese immigrants; Japanese Americans; Japanese immigrants.
in World War II, 770
Askia Muhammad, 14, 15, 17
assembly line, 515, *i* 515
assimilation, 411, 412–413, 490, 868–869, 977
assumptions and biases, analyzing, R15
Athens
as birthplace of democracy, 134
Atlanta, Georgia, 1049
in Civil War, 363–364
Atlantic, Battle of the, 776
Atlantic Charter (1941), 760
Atlee, Clement, 810
atomic bomb, 773, 789–790, 791, 795, *i* 795, 828. *See also* nuclear weapons.

Bryan, William Jennings, 428, *i* 428, 534, 564, 583, 644–645, *i* 645
Buchanan, James, 321
    presidency of, 324, 325, 330
Buckley, William F., Jr., 1037
Buddhism, 938
Budget, Bureau of the, 626
buffalo, *i* 413, 414
    Native Americans and, 409, 413
    whites' hunting of, 413
Buford, John, 358–359
Bulge, Battle of the, 782, R54
Bullard, Florence, 591
Bull Moose Party, 536
Bull Run
    First Battle of, 341–342
    Second Battle of, 344
Bunau-Varilla, Philippe, 566
Bunker Hill, Battle of, 104–105, *i* 104
Bunting v. *Oregon*, 517
Burger, Warren, 1004
Burgoyne, John, 115
Burnham, Daniel H., 483, 484–485
Burns, George, 717, *i* 718
Burns, Lucy, 538, 541
Burr, Aaron, 194, 198
BUS. *See* Second Bank of the United States.
Bush, George H. W., 801, 1038, 1043, 1044, *i* 1044, 1050, 1061, 1067
    education and, 1047
    end of Cold War and, 1055
    Iran-Contra scandal and, 1059
    Supreme Court and, 1042
Bush, George W., 144, 825, 1065, 1071–1074, 1115, 1123, *i* 1072
    antiterrorism bill and, 1072
    economy and, 1073
    education and, 1073, 1111
    immigration and, 1106
    social security and, 1119
    Supreme Court and, 1072
    tax cuts and, 1072, 1073
    terrorism and, 1072–1073, 1102–1103, 1104, 1105
    welfare reform and, 1113
business. *See also* corporations; economy; entrepreneurs; free enterprise; industry; trade.
    Andrew Carnegie and, 447–448
    conglomerates, 848
    consolidation of, 449–450
    Cuba and, 560–561
    downsizing and, 1076
    franchises and, *i* 848, 849
    Great Depression and, 675, *c* 676, 698
    growth of, in 1920s, 628–629
    horizontal integration and, 448, *c* 448
    layoffs in, 1043
    on the Internet, 1077
    regulation of, 445–446, 450
    scientific management and, 514
    Social Darwinism and, 448–449
    in South, 450
    temporary workers in, 1076
    vertical integration and, 448, *c* 448
business cycle,
    Cold War and, 810, 812, 817

busing, 929, 1003–1004, *i* 1003, 1037
Butler, Andrew P., 316
Butterfield, Alexander, 1011
Byrd, William, 75

C

Cabinet, 183, R55
    Bush's (George H. W.), 1050, 1051
    FDR's, 711
    Harding's, 626–627
    Kennedy's, 878
    Nixon's, 1009
    Reagan's, 1042, 1043
    Washington's, 183, *i* 183, 186
Cabrillo, Juan Rodriguez, *m* 39
Cagney, James, 717
Cahokia, Illinois, *i* 6, *m* 6, 7
Calamity Jane. *See* Cannary, Martha Jane.
Calhoun, John C., 203, 216, 218, 230, 231–232, *i* 231, 294, 304, *i* 304, 305, *i* 307, 308–309, *i* 308, 322, *i* 322
California, 99, 221, 294, 630
    admission to Union of, 304, 306, *i* 306, 307
    air pollution in, 1030
    facts about, R38
    farm workers in, 976
    gold rush in, 297–299, 306, 415, 430, 461
    immigration and migration and, 298, 299, 464–465, 680, 1053, *c* 1053, 1092, 1094
    Native Americans in, 8, 9, *m* 11, 295
    Republic of, 295
    settlement of, 295
    Spanish missions in, 40, *i* 40, 295
    statehood, 306, 307
    in War with Mexico, 295–296
Calloway, Cab, 663
Cambodia, 962, 963, 966, 1017
Camino Real, 40
Campbell, Ben Nighthorse, 977, *i* 977
Camp David Accords, 1022–1023
Canada, 115, 122, 311, 1070
    British claims in, 87
    United States and, 220–221, 285
    War of 1812 and, 205
canals, 217, *m* 217, 277
Canary Islands, 28
Canby, Thomas, 4
Cane (Toomer), 660
Cannary, Martha Jane (Calamity Jane), 417, *i* 417
Cannon, Joseph, 535
Canticle for Leibowitz, A (Miller), 835
Cape Cod, 50
capitalism, 275, 489. *See also* free enterprise.
Capitol, 205
Capone, Al, 643, *i* 643
Capra, Frank, 717
Caputo, Philip, 969
caravel, *i* 24
Caribbean region, 27, 28, 30, 37, 250, 1057–1058, *m* 1057. *See also* Cuba; Dominican Republic; Puerto Rico; West Indies.

Carmichael, Stokely, 926, *i* 926
Carnegie, Andrew, 447–448, *i* 447, 450, 489, 561, 564
    philanthropy of, 450
Carnegie Steel Company, 447–448, 449, 453
carpetbagger, 385, *i* 385
Carranza, Venustiano, 569, 570–571
Carson, Rachel, 897, 1027
Carter, Jimmy, 1018, *i* 1018, 1038–1039, 1057
    Camp David Accords and, 1022–1023
    civil rights and, 1020
    domestic agenda of, 1018–1019
    early life, 1018
    energy crisis and, 1018–1019
    human rights and, 931, 1021
    inflation under, 1019, *c* 1019
    Iran hostage crisis and, 1023, 1038
    unemployment under, *c* 1019
Carter, Robert, III, 72
Carter, Rosalyn, 931
Cartier, Jacques, *m* 39, 86
Casablanca conference, 779
cash crop, 72, 77, 215
Cass, Lewis, 297
Castro, Fidel, 879–880, *i* 880, 883, 889, 975
categorizing, R6
Cather, Willa, 502, 657
Catholic Church. *See* Roman Catholicism and Roman Catholics.
Catt, Carrie Chapman, 538, *i* 538, 540–541
cattle drive, 415–417, *m* 415
cattle ranching, 414–417, 529
cattle trails, 624–625, *m* 624, 626
causes, analyzing. *See* analyzing causes.
Cavazos, Lauro, 1050
Cayuse people, 12
CCC. *See* Civilian Conservation Corps.
CD-ROMs, 1083
"Celebrated Jumping Frog of Calaveras County, The" (Twain), 224
Celera
    human genome research and, 1085
Cemetery Ridge, 359
census, 1088
Central America, 566, 1057–1058, *m* 851. *See also* Guatemala; Nicaragua; Panama; Panama Canal.
    Spanish and, 37
Central Intelligence Agency (CIA), 829–830, 832, 880, 1002, 1009, 1010
Central Pacific Railroad, 421, 443
Central Park, 483–484
Central Powers, 580, 583, 584, 592
Century of Dishonor, A (Jackson), 412
chain stores, 502–503
Challenger, 1047
Chamberlain, Joshua, 359
Chamberlain, Neville, 743
Chambers, Whittaker, 824
Chamorro, Violeta de, 1058
Champlain, Samuel de, 86
Champlain Lake, 115
Chancellorsville, Battle of, 358

642–643, 685, 687–688, 695, 702, 704–705, 707, 712, 843–846, 877, 886, 887, 888, 899, 918, 920–922, 1002–1005, 1017, 1018–1020, 1040–1042, 1043, 1047, 1067–1068, 1047 *See also* antislavery movement; civil rights; crime; economy; education; environment, protection of; health care; housing; inflation; poverty; Prohibition; unemployment.

corruption under, 395–396, *i* 396

in election of 1868, 382

presidency of, 395–396

Grapes of Wrath (Steinbeck), *i* 702, 720

graphs

bar, 339, 367, 388, 507, 613, 622, 812, 1097, R28, R30

circle, 251, 339, 461, 648, 672, 832, 887, 929, 1020, R28, R30

creating, 419, 637, 993, 1015, 1053, R30

interpreting, 31, 216, 251, 339, 367, 388, 453, 489, 506, 507, 537, 540, 550, 583, 595, 622, 633, 676, 723, 770, 812, 832, 842, 849, 859, 865, 867, 887, 903, 929, 949, 961, 983, 1015, 1019, 1020, 1032, R28

line, 216, 453, 540, 550, 583, 595, 633, 676, 714, 723, 770, 842, 849, 859, 865, 867, 887, 903, 949, 1015, 1019, 1033, 1052, 1063, R28, R30

using, 461, 613, 648, 672, 714, 903, 1015, 1033, 1052, 1063, 1097, R30

Gray, Elizabeth, 264

Gray v. *Sanders*, 980–981

Great Awakening, 83–84

Great Britain. *See also* Declaration of Independence; England; Revolutionary War.

American colonies' relations with, 66, 68–71, 88–89, 96–102, *c* 100–101, 103–104

antiterrorism coalition and, 1102, 1105

Civil War and, 346–347

Emancipation Proclamation and, 347

England becomes, 69

French relations with, 70, 85, 86, 116, 121, 191, 194, 320, 579

Industrial Revolution and, 213

mercantilism and, 66–67

North American claims of, *m* 87, 285

U.S. relations with, 191, 192, 285, 346

Rush-Bagot Treaty and, 220–221

war debts and, 625, 626, 675

War of 1812 and, 202–205

in World War I, 579, 580, 583, 584–585, 589, 590

in World War II, 743, 744, 745, 746, 756, 757–760, 776, 779, 780

Great Compromise, 141, 142

Great Depression, *i* 668–669, 670, *c* 676, *i* 684, 1009, 1112, R40, R41, R59. *See also* New Deal; stock market.

bread line and, 679

causes of, 677

cities and, 678–679, *i* 679

Dust Bowl and, 680

end of, 723

families and, 680–683

as global event, 675, *i* 675, 677

Nazis and, 737

New Deal and, 694–700

psychological impact of, 683

in rural areas, 679, 680, *i* 683, 684

shantytowns in, 679

social impact of, 683

soup kitchens in, 679

stock market crash and, 673, *i* 673, 674–675

women and, 681–682

work projects and, 697–698

worldwide trade and, 677

Great Gatsby, The (Fitzgerald), 656, 664

Great Lakes, 10, 217

Great Migration (of African Americans), 599–600, *i* 599, 658–659, 1095

Great Plains, 408, *m* 408, 415, 529. *See also* cattle ranching.

Dust Bowl in, 681

farming on, 423

Native Americans of, 408–409, 410, 412–413

white settlers on, 409–410, 412, 413, 420

Great Potato Famine, 264

Great Salt Lake, 285

Great Society, 895–897, *c* 896, 925, 947, 1001

impact of, 899

Great Strike of 1877, 453, 454

"Great White Fleet" (U.S. Navy), *i* 549

Greeley, Horace, 318, *i* 318, 320, 347, 396

Greene, Nathanael, 107, *i* 107, 120

Greenspan, Alan, 1076, *i* 1076

Greenville, Treaty of, 194

Gregg, David, 360

Grenada, 1058

Grenville, George, 88–89, 96

Grew, Nehemiah, 71

Grimes, Harry, 312

Grimké, Angelina, 255

Grimké, Sarah, 255, *i* 256

"ground zero," 1101, *i* 1101. *See also* September 11 terrorist attack; war on terrorism.

group, working with a. *See* working with a group.

Guadalcanal, Battle of, 787

Guadalupe Hidalgo, Treaty of, *m* 296, 297

Guam, 552, 556

facts about, R38

Guatemala, 6, 830

Gubar, Stephan, 948, *i* 948

guerrilla warfare

in Vietnam, 944–945

Guilford Court House, North Carolina, 120

Guiteau, Charles, 476

Gulf of Mexico, 6, 7, 38

oil spill in, 1123

Gulf of Tonkin Resolution. *See* Tonkin Gulf Resolution.

Gulf War. *See* Persian Gulf War.

gun control, 1109

Gwathmey, Robert, 719

H

habeas corpus, writ of, 349

Haber, Al, 950

Haida people, 9

Haight-Ashbury, 988

Haile Selassie, 739, *i* 739

Haiti, 27, 201

U.S. troops in, 1069

Haldeman, H. R., 1009, *i* 1009, 1010, 1013

Hamer, Fanny Lou, 921–922

Hamilton, Alexander, 141, 146, *i* 146, 148, 183, *i* 183, 184, *i* 184, 191

Constitutional Convention and, 141

duel with Burr, 198

economic plan of, 184–185, 198

and election of 1800, 198

The Federalist and, 146

views of federal government, *c* 185

Hancock, John, 98, 100

Harding, Warren G., 623, 625, *i* 625, R51

death of, 627

foreign policy of, 625–626

scandals and, 626–627

Harlan, John Marshall, 496, *i* 496

Harlem Renaissance, 660, 661, *i* 661, 662, 664, 665

Harmar, Josiah, 193

Harpers Ferry, Virginia, *i* 302–303

John Brown's raid on, 327–328

Harrington, Michael, 888

Harris, William Torrey, 488, 489

Harrison, Benjamin, 477

Harrison, William Henry, 203, 234, 235, *i* 235, 477

Harte, Bret, 430

Harvard College, 97

Haskell, Frank Aretas, 357

Hastie, William H., 711

Hatch Act (1887), 423

Hawaii, 461, 548, *c* 550, 551–552

1898, *m* 551

facts about, R38

Hawaiian Islands. *See* Hawaii.

hawks, 952, R59

Hawley-Smoot Tariff Act (1930), 677

Hawthorne, Nathaniel, 243

Hay, John, 556, 562, 563

Hayden, Tom, 950, 957

Hayes, Roland, 662

Hayes, Rutherford B., 399, *i* 399, 453, 476, *i* 476

in election of 1876, 399

Haymarket affair, 453

Hayne, Robert, 231–232

Haynes, Lemuel, *i* 241

Hay-Pauncefote Treaty, 566

Hays, Mary Ludwig (Molly Pitcher), 117, *i* 117

Haywood, William "Big Bill," 452, 598

H-bomb, 829

headright system, 45

health care, *c* 1114–1115. *See also* diseases.

in Civil War, 354–355, *i* 355

Medicare and Medicaid and, 896, 1002, 1071, 1090, 1114–1115, 1118

reform of, 1067, 1114

vaccinations, 850

women and, 256–257

in World War I, 591

Health, Education, and Welfare, Department of (HEW), 1003

Health Insurance Portability and Accountability Act, 1114

health maintenance organization (HMO), 1115

Ethiopia and, *m* 738, 739
fascism in, 736
World War I and, 579
World War II and, 757, 779
Iwo Jima, 788, *i* 788, 789
IWW. *See* Industrial Workers of the World.

J

Jackson, Andrew, *i* 226, 232, 233, *i* 233, 290
appeal of, to common citizen, 225, *i* 225
election of 1824 and, 224–225
Native Americans and, 226, 228
spoils system and, 226
states' rights and, 232
in War of 1812, 205
Jackson, Helen Hunt, 412
Jackson, Jesse, 928, 1049, *i* 1049
Jackson, Robert, 792
Jackson State University, 962
Jackson, Thomas J. "Stonewall," 341, 345, 358
Jacksonians, 225
JACL. *See* Japanese American Citizens League.
Jacksonville, Florida, 38
Jamaica, 75, 462
James I (king of England), 43, 47
James II (king of England), 56, 69, *i* 70
James, Henry, 502
James River, 45, 121
Jamestown, Virginia, 43, *i* 44, *m* 44, 45, 49
Japan, 549, 738, 1020
in Russo-Japanese War, 565–566
trade with U.S., 281
in World War II, 757, 760–763, 768, 776, 784, 785, *m* 786, 787, 788, 789–792, 793
Japanese American Citizens League (JACL), 801
Japanese Americans, 452
internment of, during World War II, 800–801, *i* 800, *i* 801, *m* 801, 802–803
as soldiers in World War II, 770, 779, 801
Japanese immigrants, 461, *c* 461, 465, 621
Jaworski, Leon, 1011
Jay, John, 122, 145, *i* 145, 146, 147, 148
Jay's Treaty (1794), 194
jazz, 662–663, 664, 863, *i* 863
Jazz Singer, The, 656
Jefferson, Thomas, 109–111, 183–185, *i* 183, 184, *i* 184, 186, 191, 194–196, 197–199, 222, *i* 224
Alien and Sedition Acts and, 195
as author of Declaration, 105–106, 224
Constitution and, 147
in election of 1796, 194
in election of 1800, 198
embargo and, 203
Enlightenment thought and, 83
Hamilton and, 184
Lewis and Clark expedition and, 201

presidency of, 198–199, 202
views of federal government, *c* 185
Jeffords, Jim, 1074
Jenney, William LeBaron, 437
Jewett, Sarah Orne, 502
Jews, 117, 715, 737
in American colonies, 81
in Holocaust, 748, 749, 750–755, *c* 751, *i* 754
as immigrants, 461, 464, 490
in pre–World War II Germany, 748–750, *i* 749, *i* 750
Jim Crow laws, 493, 497, 907, 914–915
Job Corps, 894, 1002
Johnson, Andrew, 364, 376, *i* 376, 380
impeachment of, 162, *i* 162, 381
Reconstruction and, 376, 377–379, 380, 381
Johnson, Henry, 588
Johnson, James Weldon, 659, *i* 659, 660
Johnson, Lyndon B., 887, 889
affirmative action and, 635, 1025
civil rights and, 893–894, 920, 921, 922
containment policy and, 943
Great Society, 895–899, 925
tax reduction and, 893–894
Tet offensive and, 956
Tonkin Gulf Resolution and, 941
Vietnam and, 940–941, 942–943, 946–947, 951, 953
War on Poverty of, 894, 899, 925
Johnson, Tom, 516
Johnston, Joseph E., 344
joint-stock company, 42–43
Jones, Eva B., 386–387
Jones, Len, 747
Jones, Mary Harris "Mother," 454, *i* 454
Jordan, Barbara, 1008, *i* 1008
Jordan, Vernon, 928
journalism. *See* magazines; newspapers; photography.
Joy Luck Club, The (Tan), 1081
Judaism, 15
judicial branch, 143, 199, R61. *See also* court system; Supreme Court; Supreme Court cases.
authority of, 163
in Constitution, 143, 163, 183
federal courts, 162
treason and, 163
judicial review, 199
Judiciary Act of 1789, 183
Judiciary Act of 1801, 199
Jungle, The (Sinclair), 523, 526, 533

K

Kahn, Gordon, 822
Kahn, Tony, 822, *i* 822
Kaiser, Henry J., 771
Kalakaua (king of Hawaii), 551
kamikaze pilots, 787, *i* 787
Kansas, 40, 312, 313–316, 414, 421, 914–915
conflict over slavery in, 314–316, 325
facts about, R38

Kansas City, Missouri, 474
Kansas-Nebraska Act, 314–315, *m* 314, 317, 319, 320, 321
Karzai, Hamid, 1073, *i* 1073
Katrina, *i* 1074
Kashaya Pomo people, 8, 9
Kearney, Denis, 465
Kearny, Stephen, 295, *i* 295
Keating, Charles, 1013
Keating-Owen Act (1916), 517
Kelley, Florence, 513, *i* 513, 517
Kelley, Oliver Hudson, 426–427
Kellogg-Briand Pact, 625–626, 740
Kelly, William, 437
Kennan, George F., 811
Kennedy, Anthony M., *i* 163, 1042
Kennedy, Jacqueline, 878, *i* 878, *i* 888
Kennedy, John F., 675, 876–877, *i* 876, 880, 882–884, 983, 1120
Alliance for Progress and, 886–887
arms race and, 879
assassination of, 888–889, *i* 888, 920
Bay of Pigs invasion and, 880
Berlin crisis and, 883–884
civil rights and, 877, 888, 917, 918, 920, 930
Cuban missile crisis and, 880, 882
economy and, 886
election of, 876–877
environment and, 1027
New Frontier program of, 885–886
Peace Corps and, 886
space exploration and, 887
Kennedy, Joseph P., 675
Kennedy, Robert F., 878, 888, 917, 927, *i* 927, 928, 956–957, *i* 957, 976
kente cloth, 19, *i* 19
Kent State University, 962–963, *i* 963
Kentucky, 195–196, 201, 331, 339, 437
facts about, R38
Kentucky Resolutions, 195–196
Kerner Commission, 928, R61
kerosene, 437
Kerouac, Jack, 861, *i* 861
Kerry, John, 1074
Keynes, John Maynard, 698, *i* 698
Khmer Rouge, 966
Khomeini, Ayatollah Ruhollah, 1023, *i* 1023
Khrushchev, Nikita, 880, 882, *i* 882
Kim Il Sung, 817
Kim Jong Il, 1105
King, Martin Luther, Jr., 877, *i* 904–905, 911–912, *i* 912, 918, 920, 922, 925, 926, 927, 928, 949, 956
King, Rodney, 1047
King Cotton, 340, 346
King Philip. *See* Metacom.
King Philip's War, 54
Kiowa people, 412, 431
Kissinger, Henry, 964, *i* 964, 1000, *i* 1000, 1005, 1017
Klein, Gerda Weissmann, 748, *i* 748, 755
Knight, Amelia Stewart, 280, *i* 280, 282
Knights of Labor, 451, 452
Know-Nothing Party, 319, *i* 319, 320, *c* 320
Knox, Henry, 183, *i* 183
Kodak camera, 487, *i* 487

under New Deal, 698
under Nixon, 1005
price supports, 671
primary sources, analyzing, 12, 48, 78,
201, 228, 236, 285, 309, 331, 350,
372, 497, 543, 551, 593, 603,
649, 763, 783, 870, 899, 915, 922,
979, 986, 994, 1044, R21. *See also*
sources, primary.
Princip, Gavrilo, 580
printing, 485
prisons, reform of, 244
private property, 140, 174
problems, identifying, 116, 136, 137, 189,
255, 384, 390, 395, 424, 456, 463,
465, 470, 495, 567, 607, 635, 671,
713, 735, 774, 841, 886, 894, 899,
975, 1021, 1047, 1050, R5
problem solving, 265, 392, 531, 700, 763
Proclamation of Amnesty and
Reconstruction, 377
Proclamation of 1763, 88
profiteering, 116
progressive movement *or* progressivism,
512–518, 541–543, 625.
See also Roosevelt, Theodore;
Taft, William Howard; Wilson,
Woodrow.
women and, 520–522
Progressive Party, 536
Prohibition, 513–514, 642–643
Project Head Start, 894
Promontory, Utah, 443
propaganda, 583, *i* 584, 596–597, *i* 597
in motion pictures, 772, *i* 772
property
private, 140, 174
Proposition Thirteen, 99
Proposition 187, 1092, 1106
prosperity, economic
in 1920s, 631–633, 670–671
in 1950s, 847, 849, 850, 851,
854
Prosser, Gabriel, 252
protective tariff. *See* tariffs.
protectorate, 560
Providence, settlement of, 52
Pryor, Mrs. Roger A., 353
Public Utilities Holding Company Act,
707
Public Works Administration (PWA), 697,
c 706
pueblo (housing), *i* 6, *i* 11
Pueblo people, 9, 41
Puerto Ricans, 975, 1050
Puerto Rico, 462, 552, 556, 558, 559,
660, 974, 975
facts about, R39
Pulitzer, Joseph, 500–501, 553
Pullman, George M., 442, 444
Pullman, Illinois, 442, *i* 442, 444
Pullman cars, *i* 444
Pullman strike, 444, 454
Pure Food and Drug Act, 528
Puritans, 49, 56, 82, 83, R64
dissent among, 52
settlement by, 49–52, 57
PWA. *See* Public Works Administration.

Pyle, Ernie, 778, *i* 778
pyramids, 7

Q

Quakers, 55, 56, 58–59
Revolutionary War and, 108, 116–117
Quartering Act, 99, 110
Quebec, 86, 87
Quebec Act, 110
questions
formulating, R4, R12
posing, 287, 441, 857, 891, 1053
quotas, immigration, 621
Qur'an, *i* 14, 15, 1023

R

race riots, 494, 600, 659, 824–825, 1047
racial groups. *See* specific groups.
Radical Republicans, 364, 377, 378–379,
380, 396, 397, 398, 400–401
radicals, 619
radio, 276, *i* 276, 653–654, *i* 653, 717–
718, 860
ragtime, 505, *i* 505
railroads, 217, *m* 217, 304–305, 397, 437,
m 445, 450, 671
cattle ranching and, 415, *m* 415
consolidation of, 446, *i* 446
emergence of, 277–278
farmers and, 424, 425, 426, 444–446
industry and, 443–444
land grants to, 420–421, 422
regulation of, 445–446, 516, 526
time zones and, 443
transcontinental, 443
in West, 415, 420–421
workers on, 421, *i* 434–435, *i* 443,
i 495
urban growth and, 443–444
Rainey, Gertrude "Ma," *i* 638–639
Raleigh, Sir Walter, 43
Randolph, A. Philip, 624, 772, *i* 772, 911,
920
Randolph, Edmund, 183, *i* 183
Rankin, Jeannette, 578, *i* 578
ratification, 146–149
rationing, 774
Ray, James Earl, 927
REA. *See* Rural Electrification
Administration.
Reagan, Nancy, 1047
Reagan, Ronald, 801, 1018, *i* 1034–1035,
1038–1039, *i* 1038, 1040, 1041,
i 1042, 1048, 1050, 1054, 1055,
1057–1058
assassination attempt on, 1043, *i* 1043
deregulation and, 1043
drug abuse and, 1047
economic policy and, 1040–1042,
1043
Grenada and, 1058
Iran-Contra affair and, 1058–1059
national debt and, 1041–1042
Panama and, 1058
space exploration, 1047
Strategic Defense Initiative and, 1041
Supreme Court and, 1042

Reaganomics, 1040–1041
realpolitik, 1005
reaper, 279, *i* 279, 423, *c* 423, 469
reapportionment, 691–692, 980–981
recall, 518
recession, 886
Reciprocal Trade Agreement Act, 740
recognizing effects. *See* effects,
recognizing.
Reconstruction, 492
African Americans and, 377, 378,
379–381, 382, 383, 386, 387–392
assessment of, 400
black codes and, 379
congressional, 379–380
Freedmen's Bureau and, 379, 383,
388, 391
Johnson's Plan, 377–379
legacy of, 400
legislation for, *c* 380
Lincoln's plan, 376–377
military districts and, *m* 381
opposition to, 393–395, 398
presidential, 376–379
public works programs and, 384
Radical Republicans and, 377
Reconstruction Act of 1867, *c* 380,
380–381
Reconstruction Finance Corporation (RFC),
687–688
Red Cloud (Mahpiua Luta), 410, 412
Red Cross, 370, 591, 600, 950
redemption, 399
Reder, Rudolph, 752, 754
Red River War, 412
Red Scare, 619
referendum, 518
Reformation, 22
reform movements, 240–245, 512–518,
520–522
***Regents of the University of California* v.**
Bakke, 1024, 1111
region, xv, 6, 11, 23, 56, 67, 86, 217, 221,
223, 261, 291, 296, 314, 340, 415,
437, 529, 606, 680, 736, 744, 762,
830, 844, 907, 1039, 1057, 1060
Rehnquist, William H., *i* 163, 1042
relationships, analyzing. *See* analyzing
relationships.
religion. *See* Christianity; Great
Awakening; Islam; Judaism;
Native Americans; Second Great
Awakening; West Africa; *specific*
denominations.
Remington, Frederic, 553
Renaissance, 20, 24, 82
reparations, 606
***Report on the Public Credit* (Hamilton),**
184
republicanism, 132–133
Republican Party, 318, 321, 324, 328,
428, 444, 535–536, 686, 1068,
1070–1071, 1073–1074. *See*
also election, presidential.
election of 1866 and, 380
election of 1872 and, 396
forerunners of, 319–320
organization of, in 1850s, 320, *c* 320

Reconstruction and, 377, 378–379, 380

scandals and, 395–396

in the South, 383, 385, 386, 396

researching, 3, 30, 35, 63, 65, 93, 95, 131, 153, 177, 181, 189, 211, 228, 237, 239, 247, 267, 273, 287, 303, 323, 333, 337, 375, 400, 431, 435, 441, 459, 467, 481, 497, 505, 508, 511, 531, 547, 575, 577, 603, 611, 617, 635, 637, 639, 651, 665, 669, 693, 722, 733, 758, 767, 803, 805, 807, 839, 871, 875, 891, 901, 905, 915, 931, 935, 969, 971, 973, 981, 993, 999, 1025, 1035, 1059, 1065, 1095, 1097, 1103, 1105, 1107, 1109, 1111, 1113, 1115, 1117, 1119, 1121, 1123, R12, R29, R34. *See also* Internet, using for research; primary sources; sources, secondary.

Reserve Officer Training Corps (ROTC), 950–951

Resettlement Administration, 704

Revels, Hiram, 389, *i* 389

revenue sharing, 1001

Revere, Paul, 98, 100–101

reverse discrimination, 1037. *See also* affirmative action.

revivalism, 241

Revolutionary War, 96–102

battles of, 102, 104–105, 114–115, *m* 115, 119–120

British Surrender at Yorktown, *i* 118, 121

continental currency and, 116

debt from, 136

financing for, 116–117

French support in, 116, 118, 121

impact of, on American society, 122–123

Loyalists in, 106, 107, *i* 107, 108, 114, 122

military strengths and weaknesses in, *c* 115

Patriots in, 106, 107, *i* 107, 108

peace treaty after, 121–122

women and, 117, 122

Reynolds **v.** *Sims,* 898, 980–981

RFC. *See* Reconstruction Finance Corporation.

RFD. *See* rural free delivery.

Rhee, Syngman, 817

Rhode Island, 52

colonial, *c* 67, *m* 67, 98

facts about, R39

Richardson, Elliot, 1011

Richmond, Virginia, 366, 483

in Civil War, 340, 344, 365

Richmond **v.** *J. A. Croson Company,* 1049

Richthofen, Manfred von, 587

Rickenbacker, Eddie, 587, *i* 587, 590

Riis, Jacob, 451, 468, 470

Rio Grande, 40, 294, 290, 295

Rivera, Diego, 718

roads

in 1800s, *m* 217

Roanoke Island, 43

Roaring Twenties, 650–651, *i* 650–651

robber barons, 449–450

Roberts, Needham, 588

Robertson, Pat, 1037

Robeson, Paul, 662, 823

Robinson, Bill "Bojangles," *i* 504

Robinson, Jackie, 843, *i* 843

Robinson, Jo Ann Gibson, 906, *i* 906

robotics, 1084–1085

Rockefeller, John D., 449, *i* 449, 514, 532

Rockefeller, Nelson, 1017

Rockefeller Foundation, 449

rock 'n' roll, 861–862, *i* 862, 992, R65

Roe **v.** *Wade,* 985, 1046

Rogers, Will, 630

Rolfe, John, 45, 47

Roman Catholicism and Roman Catholics, 22, *m* 23, 40, 50, 490

Crusades and, 22

missions of, 288–89

in New Spain, 40–41

opposition to, 319

prejudice against, 264, 464

Spain and, 22

romanticism, 246

Rome-Berlin Axis Pact, 739

Rommel, Erwin, 778

Roosevelt, Eleanor, 695, *i* 695, 702, *i* 702, 711–712, 763, 774, 842

Roosevelt, Franklin Delano, 689, 694–696, *i* 695, *i* 696, 702, 721–722, 756, *i* 756, 799

Atlantic Charter and, 760

"Day of Infamy" speech of, 763

death of, 783, 842

fireside chats of, 696, 717, 758

Good Neighbor policy of, 740

lend-lease and, 758, 759

New Deal and, 694–700, 701–707, 711–715, 721–722, 802

physical problems of, 695, 850

Supreme Court and, 699

wartime conferences and, 775–776, 791–792

World War II and, 756–761, 763, 772, 773, 775, 776, 779, 792–792

Roosevelt, Theodore, 446, 454, 522, 523–524, *i* 524, 532, 534, 536–537, 564, 566, *i* 566, *i* 568

civil rights and, 530–531

coal strike of 1902 and, 526

conservation and, 528–530

Gentleman's Agreement and, 465, 621

health protection and, 526, 528

Japan and, 566

Latin America and, 568

Panama Canal and, 566–567

railroads and, 526

Rough Riders and, 524, 556

Treaty of Portsmouth and, 566

trusts and, 525

Roosevelt Corollary, 568, 569

Roots, *i* 809, 1015

Rosenberg, Ethel and Julius, 825–826, *i* 825

Ross, John, 228

ROTC. *See* Reserve Officer Training Corps.

Rough Riders, 524, 556

Route 66, 629, *m* 629, 680

row house, 470

royal colony, 47, R65

rubber, 275

Ruffin, Edmund, 330

Rumor of War, A **(Caputo),** 969

Rural Electrification Administration (REA), *c* 706, 707

rural free delivery (RFD), 503

Rush-Bagot agreement, 205

Rusk, Dean, 878, 882, 943

Russia, 461, 607, 1055, 1069. *See also* Soviet Union.

Alaska and, 221

revolution in, 586, 619

war with Japan, 565–566

World War I and, 579, 580, 592

Russo-Japanese War, 565–566

Rustbelt, 1052

Ruth, Babe, 654, *i* 654

S

Sacajawea, *i* 200, *m* 200, 201

Sacco and Vanzetti, 619–620, *i* 620

Sacco, Nicola, 619–620, *i* 620

Sacramento, California, 421

Sadat, Anwar, 1022, *i* 1022

Sahara, 15, 16

sailing technology, 25

St. Augustine, Florida, 40

St. Clair, Arthur, 193

St. Croix, 28

St. Lawrence River, 86

St. Louis, Missouri, 484

Sakhalin Island, 566

Salem, witchcraft in, 82

Salk, Jonas, 850, *i* 850

Salomon, Haym, 116–117

Salt Lake City, Utah, 285

SALT. *See* Strategic Arms Limitation Talks.

salutary neglect, 70

Salvation Army, 513

Sampson, William T., 555

San Antonio, Texas, 291, 415

Sand Creek Massacre, *m* 408, 410

Sandinistas (Nicaragua), 1057, 1058

San Francisco, California, xv, 297, 298, 463, 465, 470, 474

earthquake in, 471, *c* 471, *i* 471

Sanger, Margaret, 520

San Jacinto, Battle of, 292

San Juan Hill, Battle of, 524, 556

San Salvador, 27

Santa Anna, Antonio López de, 290–292, *i* 290, 296

Santa Fe, New Mexico, 40, 282, 284, 289

Santa Fe Railroad, 427

Santa Fe Trail, 282, *m* 282

Santa María, 26

Sarajevo, 580, *m* 581

Saratoga, Battle of, 113–115, *m* 115

Sarbanes-Oxley Act, 1073

Satanta, Chief, 431, *i* 431

Saturday Night Massacre, 1011–1012

Saudi Arabia, 1059, 1061

Sauk and Fox people, 228, 281

savanna, 17

Savannah, Georgia, 119

savings and loan industry, 1043

ACKNOWLEDGMENTS

 Unless otherwise indicated below, all video reference screens are © 2010 A&E Television Networks, LLC. All rights reserved.

TEXT ACKNOWLEDGMENTS

CHAPTER 13, page 431: Excerpt from "El Corrido de Gregorio Cortez," from *With His Pistol in His Hands: A Border Ballad and Its Hero* by Américo Paredes. Copyright © 1958, renewed 1986. Reprinted by permission of the author and the University of Texas Press.

CHAPTER 15, page 463: Excerpt from "The Reminiscences of Edward Ferro," from *I Was Dreaming to Come to America: Memories from the Ellis Island Oral History Project*, page 24. Selected and illustrated by Veronica Lawlor; forward by Rudolph W. Giuliani. Copyright © 1995 by Viking.

CHAPTER 21, page 665: "First Fig," from *Collected Poems* by Edna St. Vincent Millay, published by HarperCollins. Copyright © 1922, 1950 by Edna St. Vincent Millay. Reprinted by permission of Elizabeth Barnett, literary executor.

"Dream Variations," from *The Collected Poems of Langston Hughes* by Langston Hughes. Copyright © 1994 by the Estate of Langston Hughes. Used by permission of Alfred A. Knopf, a division of Random House, Inc.

CHAPTER 22, pages 679, 689: Excerpts from "A. Everette McIntyre" and "Herman Shumlin," from *Hard Times* by Studs Terkel. Copyright © 1970. Reprinted by permission of Donadio & Olson, Inc.

CHAPTER 24, page 748: Excerpt from Gerda Weissmann Klein's interview in the film *One Survivor Remembers*, a production of Home Box Office and the United States Holocaust Museum. By permission of Gary Greenberg for Gerda Weissmann Klein.

page 755: Excerpt from *Night* by Elie Wiesel, translated by Marion Wiesel. Translation copyright © 2006 by Marion Wiesel. Reproduced by permission of Hill and Wang, a division of Farrar, Straus and Giroux, LLC and electronic format by permission of Georges Borchardt, Inc., for Les Editions de Minuit.

CHAPTER 25, page 768: Excerpts from "Wife's Recorded Message Made Many Long for Home," from *We Pulled Together . . . and Won!* by Charles Swanson. Reprinted by permission of Helen Swanson.

CHAPTER 26, page 834: Excerpt from *The Body Snatchers* by Jack Finney. Copyright © 1955 by Jack Finney. Copyright © renewed 1983 by Jack Finney. Reprinted by permission of Don Congdon Associates.

page 835: Excerpt from *The Martian Chronicles* by Ray Bradbury. Text copyright © 1950, renewed 1977 by Ray Bradbury. Reprinted by permission of Don Congdon Associates, Inc.

CHAPTER 30, page 945: Excerpt from *Dear America: Letters Home from Vietnam*, edited by Bernard Edelman for the New York Vietnam Veterans Memorial Commission. Published in 1985 by W. W. Norton & Company. Copyright © 1985 by the New York Vietnam Veterans Memorial Commission. Reprinted by permission of Bernard Edelman.

Page 951: Excerpt from "Ballad of the Green Berets" by Barry Sadler. Reprinted by permission of Estaboga Music.

Page 968: Excerpt from *Going After Cacciato* by Tim O'Brien. Copyright © 1978 by Tim O'Brien. Reprinted by permission of Dell Publishing, a division of Random House, Inc.

Page 969: Excerpt from *A Rumor of War* by Philip Caputo. Text Copyright © 1977 by Philip Caputo. Reprinted by permission of The Aaron M. Priest Literary Agency, on behalf of the author.

Excerpt from *Fallen Angels* by Walter Dean Myers. Copyright © 1988 by Walter Dean Myers. Used by permission of Scholastic. Hardcover, a trademark of Scholastic, Inc.

CHAPTER 33, page 1052: "Migration Patterns: Where Americans Are Going," from *Regional Growth and Decline in the United States*. Copyright © 1985 by Bernard L. Weinstein, Harold T. Gross, and John Rees. Reprinted by permission of Bernard L. Weinstein, University of North Texas, Denton, Texas.

CHAPTER 34, page 1066: Excerpt from "On the Pulse of the Morning" by Maya Angelou. Copyright © 1993 by Maya Angelou. Used by permission of Random House, Inc.

page 1080: "Choices," from *Cotton Candy on a Rainy Day* by Nikki Giovanni. Copyright © 1978 by Nikki Giovanni. Used by permission of HarperCollins Publishers, Inc.

page 1081: Excerpt from *The Joy Luck Club* by Amy Tan. Text copyright © 1989 by Amy Tan. Reprinted by permission of G. P. Putnam's Sons, a division of Penguin Group (USA) Inc.; Sandra Dijkstra Literary Agency, on behalf of the author; and Phoenix Books, Ltd.

"Four Skinny Trees," from *The House on Mango Street* by Sandra Cisneros. Text copyright © 1984 by Sandra Cisneros. Published by Vintage Books, a division of Random House, Inc., and in hardcover by Alfred A. Knopf. Reprinted by permission of Susan Bergholz Literary Services, New York, NY and Lamy, NM.

McDougal Littell Inc. has made every effort to locate the copyright holders for selections used in this book and to make full acknowledgment for their use. Omissions brought to our attention will be corrected in a subsequent edition.

ART CREDITS

COVER, BACK COVER, AND FRONTISPIECE
Abigail Adams: © Bettmann/Corbis
American Flag: © Izzy Schwartz/PhotoDisc/Getty Images
Dwight D. Eisenhower: © STF/AP Images
Pedro Gonzáles: Espinosa Productions
Thomas Jefferson: *Thomas Jefferson* (1791), Charles Wilson Peale. Oil on canvas, 248 x 208 (61 x 50.8 cm). Independence National Historical Park, Philadelphia. © Bettmann/Corbis

Martin Luther King, Jr.: © Howard Sochurek/Time & Life Pictures/Getty Images
Maya Lin: © 1993 Richard Howard/Black Star
Abraham Lincoln: Ambrotype (1858), Abraham Byers. © Bettmann/Corbis
migrant mother: Migrant Mother, Nipomo, California (1936), Dorothea Lange/Library of Congress Prints & Photographs Division [LC-USZ62-95653]
Luis Muñoz Rivera: Puerto Rican Cultural Institute/Library of Congress Prints and Photographs Division
Eleanor Roosevelt: © MPI/Hulton Archive/Getty Images
Zitkala Ša: Courtesy of Harold Lee Library, Brigham Young University
Statue of Liberty: © David Buffington/PhotoDisc/Getty Images
Harriet Tubman: © National Geographic Image Collection
George Washington: © Christie's Images/Corbis

Maps
Atlas maps by Rand McNally A2–A39
Unless otherwise indicated below, all other maps, locators, and globe locators by GeoNova LLC.

Master Elements
American flag photo used in Section Opener banners throughout book © Izzy Schwartz/PhotoDisc/Getty Images.

Supreme Court Facade used in "Historic Decisions of the Supreme Court" feature © PhotoDisc/Getty Images.

The presidential seal is used throughout by permission of The Office of the Counsel to the President, The White House, Washington, D.C. Unless otherwise indicated, photograph provided by The Granger Collection, New York.

TABLE OF CONTENTS
vi *top, Nova Britannia* (1609), Robert Johnson, London, title page (*KC 1609). Rare Books and Manuscripts Division, The New York Public Library, Astor, Lenox and Tilden Foundations; *center, William Franklin* (date unknown) attributed to Mather Brown. Collection of Mrs. Jackson C. Boswell, Arlington, Virginia. Courtesy of the Frick Art Reference Library; *bottom, Molly Pitcher at the Battle of Monmouth* (1854), Dennis Malone Carter. Oil on canvas, 42" x 56". Gift of Herbert P. Whitlock, 1913. Courtesy of Fraunces Tavern® Museum, New York City; **vii** *top* The Granger Collection, New York; *center* © Christie's Images/Corbis; *bottom* Tray depicting Reverend Lemuel Haynes in the pulpit (ca. 1835-1840), English. Oil on molded papier mache, 25-11/16" x 20-15/16". Museum of Art, Rhode Island School of Design, bequest of Lucy Truman Aldrich; **viii** *top* The Granger Collection, New York; *center, Abraham Lincoln* (ca. 1858), Fetter's Picture Gallery Photograph. Ambrotype, Copy Plate, 21/2" x 2" (6.3 x 5.1 cm). National Portrait Gallery, Smithsonian Institution/Art Resource, New York; *bottom* Photograph by Rudolph Eickmeyer/Photographic History Collection, National Museum of American History, Smithsonian Institution (86-11374); **ix** *top, Portrait of Sioux Man and Woman* (date unknown), Gertrude Käsebier. Photographic History Collection, National Museum of American History, Smithsonian Institution (86-2205); *center* National Museum of American History, Smithsonian Institution, Electrical Collections (79-1641); *bottom* Culver Pictures; **x** *top* © Bettmann/Corbis; *center* © Bettmann/Corbis; *bottom* © Bettmann/Corbis; **xi** *top* Culver Pictures; *center* Brown Brothers; *bottom* Franklin D. Roosevelt Library, Hyde Park, New York; **xii** *top* Courtesy of Gerda Weissman Klein; *center* © Bettmann/Corbis; *bottom* © Allied Artists/The Kobal Collection; **xiii** *top* © Blank Archives/Hulton Archive/Getty Images; *center* Courtesy of Arthur L. Freeman; *bottom* © Paul Fusco/Magnum Photos; **xiv** *top* AUTH © 1973 The Philadelphia Inquirer. Reprinted with permission of UNIVERSAL PRESS SYNDICATE. All rights reserved; *bottom* © Scott Nelson/Getty Images; **xv** © Thinkstock/Corbis; **xvi** *top* National Aeronautics and Space Administraton (NASA); *bottom* © Brooks Craft/Corbis; **xvii** *top* The Granger Collection, New York; *center* © Robertstock.com; *bottom* © Howard Sochrek/Time & Life Pictures/Getty Images.

Chapter 1
S34–1 *The Landing of the Pilgrims* (1825), Bartoll, Samuel (1765-1835) oil on panel /© Peabody Essex Museum, Salem, Massachusetts, USA, / The Bridgeman Art Library; **2–3** The Granger Collection, New York; **2** *bottom left* Anthropology Museum, Veracruz University, Jalapa, Mexico/Art Resource, New York; *bottom right* © Richard A. Cooke/Corbis; **3** *bottom right, Portrait of a Man, said to be Christopher Columbus* (born about 1446, died 1506) (1519), Sebastiano del Piombo. Oil on canvas, 42" x 34 3/4". The Metropolitan Museum of Art, gift of J. Pierpont Morgan, 1900 (00.18.2). Photograph copyright © 1979 The Metropolitan Museum of Art; *bottom left* © Leonard de Selva/Corbis; **4** *top right* © Corbis; *center* © Roy Andersen/National Geographic Image Collection; **5** *top* © Warren Morgan/Corbis; **6** *top left* © Macduff Everton/Corbis; *top center* © T. Linck/SuperStock, Inc.; *top right* Michael Hampshire/Courtesy of Cahokia Mounds State Historic Site; *bottom left* © Charles & Josette Lenars/Corbis; *bottom center* Anthropology Museum, Veracruz University, Jalapa, Mexico/Art Resource, New York; *bottom right* © Danny Lehman/Corbis; **8** *center* Courtesy of the Phoebe Apperson Hearst Museum of Anthropology and the Regents of the University of California [Catalog number 15-25500]; *top right* © Corbis; **9** *all* Forensic reconstruction by Sharon A. Long, Wyoming, artist/anthropologist. Photography by Terri Brayton, New York. Courtesy of the Monacan Indian Nation; **10** KC Publications, Inc. Copyright © Southwestern Indian Arts and Crafts; **11** *center* Edward S. Curtis, from Volume XII of The North American Indian,1922 © Corbis; *top* © Henry Guttmann/Hulton Archive/Getty Images; *right* © Nathan Benn/Corbis; **12** The Granger Collection, New York; **13** © Mike Zens/Corbis; **14** *center* © The Trustees of the British Museum; *top right* © Corbis; **16** Stock Montage; **17** *Head of an Oni* (11-15th Century), unknown Yoruba artist. Zinc and brass, height 31 cm. Museum of Ife Antiquities, Ife, Nigeria, Photo © Held Collection/The Bridgeman Art Library; **18** © 1993 Chester Higgins, Jr.; **19** © Peter Turnley/Corbis; **20** *center* The Granger Collection, New York; *top right* © Corbis; **21** *June, Haymaking*. Calendar miniature from Très Riches Heures du Duc de Berry (1416). Musée Condé, Chantilly, France [Ms.65, f.6v]. Photograph by R.G. Ojeda/Réunion des Musées Nationaux / Art Resource, New York; **22** The Granger Collection, New York; **24** Matthew Pippin/McDougal Littell/Houghton Mifflin Co.; **26** *center, Portrait of a Man, said to be Christopher Columbus* (born about 1446, died 1506) (1519), Sebastiano del Piombo. Oil on canvas, 42" x 34 3/4". The Metropolitan Museum of Art, gift of J. Pierpont Morgan, 1900 (00.18.2). Photograph © 1979 The Metropolitan Museum of Art; *top right* © Corbis; **28** The Granger Collection, New York; **32** *background* © Charles & Josette Lenars/Corbis; *bottom center, Portrait of a Man, said to be Christopher Columbus* (born about 1446, died 1506) (1519), Sebastiano del Piombo. Oil on canvas, 42" x 34 3/4". The Metropolitan Museum of Art, gift of J. Pierpont Morgan, 1900 (00.18.2). Photograph copyright © 1979 The Metropolitan Museum of Art; **33** MC1–MC2 © imagebroker/Alamy.

Chapter 2
34 *bottom left, Mask, Quetzalcoatl or Tonatiuh, the Sun God* (early 16th century), Aztec. Turquoise and pearl shell. British Museum, London/Photograph © Werner Forman/Art Resource, New York; *bottom right* © Gianni Dagli Orti/Corbis; **34–35** © MPI/Hulton Archive/Getty Images; **35** *bottom right* The Granger Collection, New York; *bottom left* © Bettmann/Corbis; **36** *center* © Bettmann/Corbis; *top right* Musée de la Marine Paris /Gianni Dagli Orti/The Art Archive; **37** *top* The Granger Collection, New York; *bottom* Courtesy of the Department of Library Services, American Museum of Natural History, New York; **39** *inset* The New York Public Library; **40** *left* © Ted Streshinsky/Corbis; *right* Illustration by Lawrence Ormsby. Reprinted by permission from Spanish Colonial Missions by Gloria Giffords. Published by Western National Parks Association. © 1988; **42** *center* The Granger Collection, New York; *top right* Musée de la Marine Paris/Gianni Dagli Orti/The Art Archive; **43** The Granger Collection, New York; **44** *bottom* © MPI/Hulton Archive/Getty Images; *top right, top center* Courtesy of the Association for the Preservation of Virginia Antiquities; **45** *Nova Britannia* (1609), Robert Johnson, London, title page (*KC 1609). Rare Books and Manuscripts Division, The New York Public Library, Astor, Lenox and Tilden Foundations; **46** The Granger Collection, New York; **47** © Bettmann/Corbis; **49** *center* By kind permission of the Vicar and Churchwardens of St. Botolph's Church, Boston, Lincolnshire, England; *top right* Musée de la Marine

Paris/Gianni Dagli Orti/The Art Archive; **50** *top* Pilgrim Society, Plymouth, Massachusetts; *center left* © Three Lions/Hulton Archive/Getty Images; **51** *bottom right* Sho W. Negami; *left* © Ann Parker & Avon Neal; **52** © 2008 Kindra Clineff; **53** *inset, center* The Granger Collection, New York; **55** *top right* Musée de la Marine Paris/Gianni Dagli Orti/The Art Archive; *center* The Granger Collection, New York; **57** *all* Matthew Pippin/McDougal Littell/Houghton Mifflin Co.; **58** *William Penn's Treaty with the Indians* (ca. 1840), Edwards Hicks. Bridgeman-Giraudon/Art Resource, New York; **59** Courtesy of the Historical Society of Pennsylvania Collection, Atwater Kent Museum of Philadelphia; **60** © Ira Block/National Geographic Image Collection; **61** *top* © Nick Caloyianis/National Geographic Image Collection; *bottom* © Michael P. Gadomski/ Superstock; *top inset* © Hal Horwitz/Corbis; **62** *bottom left* Courtesy of the Historical Society of Pennsylvania Collection, Atwater Kent Museum of Philadelphia; *center left* The Granger Collection, New York; *center right* Pilgrim Society, Plymouth, Massachusetts; *top left, Mask, Quetzalcoatl or Tonatiuh, the Sun God* (early 16th century), Aztec. Turquoise and pearl shell. British Museum, London/Photograph © Werner Forman/Art Resource, New York; **63 MC1–MC2** © Cummer Museum of Art & Gardens/SuperStock.

Chapter 3

64 *bottom right* Courtesy of the Special Collections Research Center, Earl Gregg Swem Library, The College of William and Mary; *bottom center* © Bettmann/Corbis; **64–65** *View of the Long Wharf and the Harbor of Boston* (1764), J. Byron. © Burstein Collection/Corbis; **65** *bottom left* The Granger Collection, New York; *bottom right* © Bettmann/Corbis; **66** *center* The Granger Collection, New York; *top right, SE Prospect of the City of Philadelphia* (Detail) (1720), Peter Cooper, The Library Company of Philadelphia; **68** Overmantle (mid 18th century), unknown artist. Oil on wood panel from the Moses Marcy House, Old Sturbridge Village, Southbridge MA, www.osv.org. [Accession no. 20.19.1]. Photo by Henry E. Peach; **70** *left, Charles II* (mid-17th century), Pieter Nason. Oil on canvas. Private collection, © Philip Mould Ltd, London/The Bridgeman Art Library; *center left* The Granger Collection, New York; *center right, Portrait of King William III* (date unknown), Sir Godfrey Kneller. Oil on canvas. The Crown Estate/The Bridgeman Art Library, New York; *right Mary II* (mid-17th Century), William Wissing. Oil on canvas. Scottish National Portrait Gallery, Edinburgh, Scotland/The Bridgeman Art Library; **71** *The Meetinghouse Drawing*, Courtesy of the Pilgrim Society, Plymouth, Massachusetts; **72** *center* © Lee Snider/Photo Images/Corbis; *top right, SE Prospect of the City of Philadelphia* (Detail) (1720), Peter Cooper, The Library Company of Philadelphia; **73** The Granger Collection, New York; **74** © MPI/Hulton Archive/Getty Images; **76** *bottom* The Granger Collection, New York; *top* Library of Congress Prints and Photographs Division [LC-USZ62-44000]; **77** *top* Collection of the Blue Ridge Institute and Museums/Blue Ridge Heritage Archive of Ferrum College, Ferrum, Virginia; *bottom* © The Trustees of the British Museum; **78** Tom Costa, University of Virginia's College at Wise; **79** *center* The Granger Collection, New York; *top right, SE Prospect of the City of Philadelphia* (Detail) (1720), Peter Cooper, The Library Company of Philadelphia; **80** *right* © Lee Snider/Photo Images/Corbis; *left* Photo by John Chew/Courtesy of Cliveden of the National Trust; **83** *left Benjamin Franklin* (1783), Joseph Siffred Duplessis. Pastel on paper. The Granger Collection, New York; *right* The Granger Collection, New York; **84** The Granger Collection, New York; **85** *center* The Granger Collection, New York; *top right, SE Prospect of the City of Philadelphia* (Detail) (1720), Peter Cooper, The Library Company of Philadelphia; **88** The Granger Collection, New York; **89** Benjamin Franklin, 1774. Library of Congress/Corbis; **90** *bottom left, Celebrating Couple: General Jackson and His Lady* (about 1831), Reverend H. Young, American, active 1823-1831. Pen and Watercolor on brown paper, Karolik cat. 1341, fig. 360 (Folk artists),10 3/16" x 7 9/16". Museum of Fine Arts, Boston, gift of Maxim Karolik for the M. and M. Karolik Collection of American Watercolors and Drawings, 1800-1875 (56.751); **90–91** *Landscape with Figures* (1790), Isaac Heston. Oil on wood panel. Abby Aldrich Rockefeller Folk Art Museum, The Colonial Williamsburg Foundation, Williamsburg, Virginia (1939.101.1); **91** *top, The Old Plantation* (ca. 1795), artist unknown. Watercolor on laid paper. Abby Aldrich Rockefeller Folk Art Museum, The Colonial Williamsburg Foundation, Williamsburg, Virginia (1935.301.3); *bottom* Library of Congress Prints and Photographs Division [LC-USZ62-33939].

Chapter 4

94 *bottom right* © Getty Images; *bottom left* Rare Books and Manuscripts Division of the New York Public Library. Astor, Lenox, and Tilden Foundations; **94–95** The Granger Collection, New York; **95** *bottom left* © Leif Skoogfors/Corbis; *bottom right* The Granger Collection, New York; *bottom center* © Time & Life Pictures/Getty Images; **96** *top right, Washington Crossing The Delaware* (Detail) (1851), Emanuel Gottlieb Leutze. Photograph © Bettmann/Corbis; *center right* Patrick Faricy/McDougal Littell/Houghton Mifflin Co.; **97** © Bettmann/Corbis; **98** The Granger Collection, New York; **100** Rare Books and Manuscript Division of the New York Public Library. Astor, Lenox, and Tilden Foundations; **101** *top* American Antiquarian Society; *bottom, Battle of Lexington* (ca. 1850), Alonzo Chappel. Photograph © Bettmann/Corbis; **102** *top left* The Granger Collection, New York; **103** *center right, William Franklin* (date unknown) attributed to Mather Brown. Collection of Mrs. Jackson C. Boswell, Arlington, Virginia. Courtesy of the Frick Art Reference Library; *top right, Washington Crossing The Delaware* (Detail) (1851), Emanuel Gottlieb Leutze. Photograph © Bettmann/Corbis; **104** The Granger Collection, New York; **105** Library of Congress Prints and Photographs Division [LC-USZ62-106S8]; **107** *top right, top left* Culver Pictures; *center right, center left, bottom left,* U.S. flag The Granger Collection, New York; *British flag* © Ken Biggs/Stone/Getty Images; *bottom right* Westchester County Historical Society; **108** The Granger Collection, New York; **109** The Granger Collection, New York; *signature* National Archives and Records Administration (NARA); **111** *top* Photo by Sharon Hoogstraten/McDougal Littell/Houghton Mifflin Co.; *bottom* © Bettmann/Corbis; **112** *all* National Archives and Records Administration (NARA); **113** *bottom, March to Valley Forge* (1883), William B. Trego. Courtesy of the Valley Forge Historical Society; *top right, Washington Crossing The Delaware* (Detail) (1851), Emanuel Gottlieb Leutze. Photograph © Bettmann/Corbis; **115** *center right* © David Kamerman; *bottom right* © David Kamerman; **116** The Granger Collection, New York; **117** *Molly Pitcher at the Battle of Monmouth* (1854), Dennis Malone Carter. Oil on canvas, 42" x 56". Gift of Herbert P. Whitlock, 1913. Courtesy of Fraunces Tavern® Museum, New York City; **118** *center left* The Granger Collection, New York; *top right, Washington Crossing The Delaware* (Detail) (1851), Emanuel Gottlieb Leutze. Photograph © Bettmann/Corbis; **120** *Battle of Cowpens* (about 1855), William Ranney. Oil on canvas. From the Collection of the State of South Carolina; **122** *A New and Correct Map of the United States* (1783), Abel Buel. From the Collections of the New Jersey Historical Society, Newark; **123** Image by courtesy of the Trustees of the Wedgwood Museum, Barlaston, Staffordshire, England; **124** *top right, Portrait of Mr. and Mrs. Thomas Mifflin* (Sarah Morris) (1773), John Singleton Copley. Oil on ticking, 61" x 48" (156.5 x 121.9 cm). Philadelphia Museum of Art; *center left* Courtesy of the Seneca Falls (New York) Historical Society; **124–125** The Granger Collection, New York; **125** *top* Photo by Sharon Hoogstraten/McDougal Littell/Houghton Mifflin Co.; *top right* © Brooks Craft/Corbis; **126** *bottom* The Granger Collection, New York; *top* © Ken Biggs/Stone/Getty Images; **127** Library of Congress Prints and Photographs Division [LC-USZ62-9487]; **127 MC1–MC2** © Ted Spiegel/Corbis.

Chapter 5

128–129 *Signing of the Constitution*, Howard Chandler Christy. Private collection/Art Resource, New York; **130–131** *Washington as Statesman at the Constitutional Convention* (1856), Junius Brutus Stearns. Oil on canvas, 37 1/2" H x 54" W. Virginia Museum of Fine Arts, Richmond, Virginia; gift of Edgar William and Bernice Chrysler Garbisch. Photograph by Ron Jennings; **130** *bottom center* © Kevin R. Morris/Corbis; *bottom right* © Time & Life Pictures/Getty Images; *center left* © Corbis; **131** *bottom* The Granger Collection, New York; **132** *center right, John Dickinson* (Detail) (about 1835), James Barton Longacre, after Charles Wilson Peale. Sepia watercolor on artist board, 11 5/8" x 8 7/8" (29.5 x 20 cm). National Portrait Gallery, Smithsonian Institution/Art Resource, New York; *top right* © Bettmann/Corbis; **133** *Republican Motherhood* (Detail), date and artist unknown. Silk embroidery. National Museum of American History, Smithsonian Institution (81-5200); **134** *right* Mary Evans Picture Library; *left* © Dutch School/The Bridgeman Art Library/Getty Images; **136** The Granger Collection, New York; **138** *top* © David R. Frazier/ Stone/Getty Images; **139** Township VII, Range XIV, Ohio Company (1787), Rufus Putnam. Clements Library, University of Michigan; **140**

top right © Bettmann/Corbis; center © Hulton Archive/Getty Images; **141** left The Granger Collection, New York; right, Roger Sherman (Detail) (ca.1777), anonymous artist, after Ralph Earl. Oil on canvas, 26 3/8″ x 22 3/16″ (67 x 56.3 cm). National Portrait Gallery, Smithsonian Institution. Gift of Mr. Bradley B. Gilman/Art Resource, New York; **144** top left © Reuters/Corbis; **145** center right, John Jay (Detail) (ca. 1785), begun by Gilbert Stuart and completed by John Trumbull. Oil on canvas, 128.5 x 101.5 cm. National Portrait Gallery, Smithsonian Institution/Art Resource; top right © Bettmann/Corbis; **146** bottom, Patrick Henry (Detail) (ca. 1835), James Barton Longacre, after Lawrence Sully. Watercolor. National Portrait Gallery, Smithsonian Institution/Art Resource, New York; top Alexander Hamilton (Detail) (1806), John Trumbull. Oil on canvas, 76.2 cm x 61 cm (30″ x 24″). National Portrait Gallery, Smithsonian Institution. Gift of Henry Cabot Lodge/Art Resource, New York; **147** The Granger Collection, New York; **148** top © Sasa Krajl/NewsCom/Agence France Presse; bottom © Denis Farrell/AP Images; **152** The Granger Collection, New York; **153** © Bettmann/Corbis; **158** Manuel Balce Cenata; **162** bottom The Granger Collection, New York; top © APTN/AP Images; **163** JIM LO SCALZO/epa/Corbis; **167** The Federal Edifice: On the Erection of the Eleventh Pillar (August 2, 1788). Caricature from The Massachusetts Centinel. Collection of The New-York Historical Society. [Negative no. 33959]; **169** © AP Images; **170** © Bettmann/Corbis; **173** © Bettmann/Corbis; **174** left © Bettmann/Corbis; right, Daniel Boardman (Detail) (1789), Ralph Earl. Oil on canvas, 81 5/8″ x 55 1/4″. © 1996, Board of Trustees, National Gallery of Art, Washington, DC. Gift of Mrs. W. Murray Crane; **175** top © Hulton Archive/Getty Images; bottom © AP Images; **176** The Granger Collection, New York; **177** A 1968 Herblock Cartoon, copyright by The Herb Block Foundation; **178** bottom © David Young-Wolff/PhotoEdit; top Photo by Sharon Hoogstraten/McDougal Littell/Houghton Mifflin Co.; **179** © Mark Richards/PhotoEdit.

Chapter 6

180 bottom left © Corbis; bottom right © Paul Almasy/Corbis; **180–181** Carter's Tavern at the Head of Lake George (1817-18), Francis Guy. Oil on canvas, 101cm x 168cm. The Detroit Institute of Arts, Founders' Society Purchase, R.H. Tannahill Foundation Fund/The Bridgeman Art Library; **181** bottom left © Bettmann/Corbis; bottom right Library of Congress Prints and Photographs Division [LC-USZ62-116232]; **182** center The Granger Collection, New York; top right, Pioneers Travelling in a Flatboat (ca. 1842-1888), Felix Octavius Carr Darley. Colored woodcut. © Bettmann/Corbis; **183** © Time & Life Pictures/Getty Images; **184** right, Alexander Hamilton (ca.1796), James Sharples, the Elder. Pastel on paper, 13 x 12.4 cm. National Portrait Gallery, Smithsonian Institution/Art Resource, New York; left, Thomas Jefferson (1791), Charles Wilson Peale. Oil on canvas, 248 x 208 (61 x 50.8 cm). Independence National Historical Park, Philadelphia. © Bettmann/Corbis; **186** The Granger Collection, New York; **187** Stock Montage; **188** The Granger Collection, New York; **189** center The Granger Collection, New York; top The Granger Collection, New York; bottom inset, Cotillion Dance (1771), James Caldwell after John Collet. Abby Aldrich Rockefeller Folk Art Museum, The Colonial Williamsburg Foundation, Williamsburg, Virginia (1954-484); **190** center, The Taking of the Bastille, July 14, 1789 (late 1700s), Anonymous. Chateaux de Versailles et deTrianon, Versailles, France. Photograph © Erich Lessing/Art Resource, New York; top right, Pioneers Travelling in a Flatboat (ca. 1842-1888), Felix Octavius Carr Darley. Colored woodcut. © Bettmann/Corbis; **191** © 1969 by Edwin Tunis. First appeared in Young United States, published by Thomas Y. Crowell. Reprinted by permission of Curtis Brown, Ltd.; **193** Treaty of Greenville (1795) artist unknown. Chicago History Museum (Negative number P&S-1914.0001); **194** © Bettmann/Corbis; **195** The Granger Collection, New York; **197** center file photo; top right, Pioneers Travelling in a Flatboat (ca. 1842-1888), Felix Octavius Carr Darley. Colored woodcut. © Bettmann/Corbis; **198** © Bettmann/Corbis; **199** barrell Courtesy of the Jefferson National Expansion Memorial/National Park Service; **200** bottom left The Granger Collection, New York; top right, Mih-Tutta-Hangkusch, a Mandan Village after a Painting by Karl Bodmer © Philip de Bay/Historical Picture Archive/Corbis; bottom right National Museum of American History, Smithsonian Institution (75-2348); top left © US Mint/AP Images; **201** Bear Pursuing his Assailant (1810), Mathew Carey. Wood

engraving added to the 1812 publication of the journal of Sergeant Patrick Gass, A Journal of the Voyages and Travels of a Corps of Discovery/Library of Congress, Rare Book and Special Collections Division (72A); **202** center The Granger Collection, New York; top right, Pioneers Travelling in a Flatboat (ca. 1842-1888), Felix Octavius Carr Darley. Colored woodcut. © Bettmann/Corbis; **203** © Bettmann/Corbis; **206** bottom, Portrait of Chief Justice John Marshall, Rembrandt Peale (1835). Collection of the Supreme Court of the United States; **207** Portrait of William Marbury, attributed to Rembrandt Peale (ca. 1820-1830). Collection of the Supreme Court of the United States; **208** © Bettmann/Corbis; **209** Library of Congress Prints and Photographs Division (LC-USZC4-3115); **209** MC1–MC2 Charles Rex Arbogast/AP Photo; **209** MC2 top left © Tetra Images/Corbis.

Chapter 7

210 bottom The Granger Collection, New York; **210–211** Library of Congress Department of Prints and Photographs [LC-USZC4-994]; **211** bottom left, Andrew Jackson (Detail) (1845), Thomas Sully. Oil on canvas, 20 3/8″ x 17 1/4″. © 1996 Board of Trustees, National Gallery of Art, Washington DC, Andrew W. Mellon Foundation; bottom right, The Trail of Tears, Troy Anderson/Marilyn Angel Wynn/Nativestock.com; bottom center The Granger Collection, New York; **212** center, Eli Whitney (Detail) (1822), Samuel F.B. Morse. Oil on canvas. 35 7/8″ x 27 3/4 x 1″ (91.1 x 70.5 x 2.5 cm). Yale University Art Gallery. Gift of George Hoadley, BA 1801. Accession # 1827.1/Art Resource, New York; top right, Erie Canal at Little Falls, New York (1884), William Rickaby Miller. Oil on canvas, 24 1/8″ x 36″. Collection of The New-York Historical Society. [Negative no. 575c]; **213** The first cotton mill in America, established by Samuel Slater on the Blackstone River at Pawtucket, Rhode Island (ca.1790), American School. Oil on canvas. Smithsonian Institution, Washington DC/The Bridgeman Art Library; **214** background Steven N. Patricia/McDougal Littell/Houghton Mifflin Co.; top right, bottom right American Textile History Museum, Lowell, MA; center right North Wind Picture Archives; **215** © Pat Sullivan/AP Images; **216** National Museum of American History, Smithsonian Institution (73-11287); **219** center, The Telegraph (1837) James Bard. Watercolor. The Mariners' Museum, Newport News, VA; top right, Erie Canal at Little Falls, New York (1884), William Rickaby Miller. Oil on canvas, 24 1/8″ x 36″. Collection of The New-York Historical Society. [Negative no. 575c]; **220** John Marshall, Chief Justice of the United States (Detail) (ca.1832), William James Hubard. Oil on canvas, 24 1/4″ x 15 1/8″ (61.6 x 38.9 cm). National Portrait Gallery, Smithsonian Institution/Art Resource, New York; **222** The Granger Collection, New York; **224** center, John Adams, Second President of the United States (1798 and1828), begun by Gilbert Stuart and completed by Jane Stuart. Oil on canvas. National Portrait Gallery, Smithsonian Institution/Art Resource, New York; top right Erie Canal at Little Falls, New York (1884), William Rickaby Miller. Oil on canvas, 24 1/8″ x 36″. Collection of The New-York Historical Society. [Negative no. 575c]; **225** The Granger Collection, New York; **226** Andrew Jackson, 1767-1845, Seventh President of the United States (Detail) (1820), James Barton Longacre. Hand-colored stipple engraving after Thomas Sully, 37.2 cm x 30 cm. National Portrait Gallery, Smithsonian Institution/Art Resource, New York; **227** top right, bottom The Granger Collection, New York; top left National Anthropological Archives, Smithsonian Institution (NAA-1025); **229** © Kamenko Pajic/AP Images; **230** center, Webster's Reply to Hayne (date unknown), G.P.A. Healy. Courtesy of the Boston Art Commission 2007; top right, Erie Canal at Little Falls, New York (1884), William Rickaby Miller. Oil on canvas, 24 1/8″ x 36″. Collection of The New-York Historical Society. [Negative no. 575c]; **231** left, John Caldwell Calhoun (ca. 1820), Charles Bird King. Oil on canvas, 76.2 x 63.5 cm. National Portrait Gallery, Smithsonian Institution/Art Resource, New York; right, Daniel Webster (1782-1852), Statesman (ca. 1828), Chester Harding. National Portrait Gallery, Smithsonian Institution/Art Resource, New York; **232** The Granger Collection, New York; bottom inset The Museum of the Confederacy, Richmond, Virginia; **233** Library of Congress Department of Prints and Photographs [LC-USZ62-1562]; **235** The Granger Collection, New York; **236** © Joseph Sohm/Visions of America/Corbis.

Chapter 8

238 bottom Courtesy of the Lowell Historical Society; **238–239** The Granger Collection, New York; **239** camera © Paul Almasy/Corbis;

potato famine The Granger Collection, New York; *Douglass* © Hulton Archive/Getty Images; *Walden* The Granger Collection, New York; **240** *center right, top right* The Granger Collection, New York; **241** *bottom, Tray depicting Reverend Lemuel Haynes in the pulpit* (ca. 1835-1840), English. Oil on molded papier mache, 25-11/16″ x 20-15/16″. Museum of Art, Rhode Island School of Design, bequest of Lucy Truman Aldrich; *top* © Steve Rayman/Corbis; **242** *A View of the Mountain Pass called The Notch of the White Mountains* (Crawford Notch), (1839), Thomas Cole. Oil on canvas, 102 x 155.8 cm (40 3/16″x 61 5/16″). Andrew W. Mellon Fund. © 1996 Board of Trustees, National Gallery of Art, Washington DC; **244** *right, Dorothea Lynde Dix, American Reformer* (ca.1849), anonymous photographer. Daguerreotype, 5 1/2″ x 4 1/4″ (14.0 x 10.8 cm). National Portrait Gallery, Smithsonian Institution, Washington, DC/Art Resource, New York; *left* Suzanne Courcier/Robert W. Wilkins; **245** Picture Research Consultants & Archives; **246** The Granger Collection, New York; **247** *both* The Granger Collection, New York; **248** *center* Historical Society of Pennsylvania, Leon Gardiner Collection; *top right* The Granger Collection, New York; **249** *top* North Wind Picture Archives; *bottom* The Granger Collection, New York; **250** *Charlotte Helen Middleton and Her Nurse Lydia* (1857), George Cook. Ambrotype. Gibbes Museum of Art/Carolina Art Association Collection, Charleston South Carolina; **251** *background* Matthew Pippin/McDougal Littell/Houghton Mifflin Co.; *inset, Negro Quarters on an Old South Carolina Plantation* (ca. 1865), G.N. Barnard. Collection of The New-York Historical Society, Bagoe Collection. [Negative number 48169]; **252** The Granger Collection, New York; **254** *both* The Granger Collection, New York; **255** The Granger Collection, New York; **256** *top* Culver Pictures; *center* The Granger Collection, New York; **257** *top* Courtesy of the Seneca Falls (New York) Historical Society; *bottom* Library of Congress Prints and Photographs Division; **258** The Granger Collection, New York; **259** *center* Jack Naylor Collection/Picture Research Consultants & Archives; *top right* The Granger Collection, New York; **260** American Textile History Museum, Lowell, MA; **261** *bottom* The Granger Collection, New York; **262** © Matt York/AP Images; **263** National Park Service, Lowell National Historical Park; **264** The Granger Collection, New York; **265** National Museum of American History, Smithsonian Institution (88-10631); **266** *left* Library of Congress Prints and Photographs Division; **266–267** GEH NEG 14250/Courtesy George Eastman House; **267** *top, Haymaking* (1864), Winslow Homer. Oil on canvas, 16″ x11″. Columbus Museum of Art, Ohio. Museum purchase, Howald Fund (1942.083); **268** *bottom* The Granger Collection, New York; *center, Dorothea Lynde Dix, American Reformer* (ca.1849), anonymous photographer. Daguerreotype, 5 1/2″ x 4 1/4″ (14.0 x 10.8 cm). National Portrait Gallery, Smithsonian Institution, Washington, DC/Art Resource, New York.

Chapter 9

270–271 *The Battle of Fredericksburg, December 13, 1862* (Detail) (19th century), Carl Röchling. Oil on canvas, 32 1/8 ″ x 59″ (81.6 x 149.9 cm). Gift of the estate of C.H.T. Collis, 1929, Philadelphia Museum of Art; **272** *bottom right* The Granger Collection, New York; **272–273** *Advice on the Prairie* (1853), William Tylee Ranney. Oil on canvas, 38 3/4″ x 55 1/4″. Private collection/The Bridgeman Art Library; **273** *all others* The Granger Collection, New York; **274** *both* The Granger Collection, New York; **275** Courtesy of the Singer Sewing Machine Co.; **276** *left* National Museum of American History, Smithsonian Institution, Electrical Collections (74-2491); *right* © Bettmann/Corbis; *center* © Robertstock.com; **277** *left* © Bettmann/Corbis; *center* © Charles E. Rotkin/Corbis; *bottom center* School Division, Houghton Mifflin Co.; **279** *both* The Granger Collection, New York; **280** *center* Oregon Historical Society, #OrHi 59564; *top right* The Granger Collection, New York; **281** *Black Hawk and His Son, Whirling Thunder* (1833) John Wesley Jarvis. Oil on canvas. The Granger Collection, New York; **282** © Kevin Lamarque/Reuters/Corbis; **283** *top* National Archives and Records Administration (NARA); *bottom right, bottom left* Edward S. Curtis (ca. 1904). Library of Congress Prints and Photographs Division [LC-USZ62-103498]; **284** © Bettmann/Corbis; **286** *bottom left* National Anthropological Archives, Smithsonian Institution (2953-A); **286–287** National Archives and Records Administration (NARA); **287** *top* Idaho State Historical Society Photo number 1254-D-1; *bottom* © Ric Ergenbright Photography; **288** *both* The Granger Collection, New York; **289** © Gary Conner/PhotoEdit;

290 The Granger Collection, New York; **291** *inset* The Granger Collection, New York; **292** © Bettmann/Corbis; **293** *center* Washington/Custis/Lee Collection, Washington and Lee University, Lexington, Virginia; *top right* The Granger Collection, New York; **294** *James K. Polk* (1846), George Peter Alexander Healy. © Corcoran Gallery of Art/Corbis; **295** The Granger Collection, New York; **297** © Macduff Everton/Corbis; **298** The Granger Collection, New York; **299** Courtesy of the California History Room, California State Library. Sacramento, California; **301** MC1–MC2 The Granger Collection, New York.

Chapter 10

302 *flag* Society of California Pioneers; *ship* © Hulton Archive/Getty Images; *book* Private Collection/Picture Research Consultants & Archives; **302–303** © Corbis; **303** *Lincoln* © Stock Montage/Hulton Archive/Getty Images; *Big Ben* © Corbis; **304** *center* Daguerrotype (1848–1849), Mathew Brady Studio. The Granger Collection, New York; **top right** The Granger Collection, New York; **305** Courtesy of Oak Alley Plantation; **306** © Richard Cummins/Corbis; **307** The Granger Collection, New York; **308** *both* file photo; **309** The Granger Collection, New York; **310** *center* Moorland-Spingarn Research Center, Howard University; *top right* The Granger Collection, New York; **311** Brown Brothers; **312** *bottom* The Granger Collection, New York; *top* The Granger Collection, New York; **315** Kansas State Historical Society; **316** The Granger Collection New York; **317** The Granger Collection, New York; **318** *center* Daguerrotype (ca. 1850), Mathew Brady Studio. The Granger Collection, New York; *top right* The Granger Collection, New York; **319** Courtesy of the Milwaukee Historical Society; **320** Ontario County (New York) Historical Society; **322** *center right* Edward Williams Clay (1831). The Library Company of Philadelphia; *bottom left* The Granger Collection, New York; **323** *center* © Burt Glinn/Magnum Photos; *top* © Bettmann/Corbis; **324** *center, Abraham Lincoln* (ca. 1858), Fetter's Picture Gallery Photograph. Ambrotype, Copy Plate, 21/2″ x 2″ (6.3 x 5.1 cm). National Portrait Gallery, Smithsonian Institution/Art Resource, New York; *top right* The Granger Collection, New York; **325** The Granger Collection, New York; **326** *left, Stephen Douglas* (ca. 1860), Mathew Brady Studio. Photograph, albumen silver print, 3 1/8″ x 2 1/8″ (8.6 x 5.4 cm). National Portrait Gallery, Smithsonian Institution/Art Resource, New York; *right* Unknown photographer (ca. 1860), Springfield, Illinois. The Granger Collection, New York; **327** © Jeff Mitchell/Reuters; **328** *John Brown Going to His Hanging* (1942), Horace Pippin. Oil on canvas, 24 1/8″ x 30 1/4″. Courtesy of the Museum of American Art of the Pennsylvania Academy of the Fine Arts, Philadelphia, Pennsylvania. John Lambert Fund [1943.11]; **329** *top* The Granger Collection, New York; *bottom* Courtesy of Lloyd Ostendorf Collection; **331** © Jefferson Davis Playing Card Printed by W.A. Walker,1864. MPI/Hulton Archive/Getty Images; **332** *bottom* © Bettmann/Corbis; **333** Library of Congress Prints and Photographs Division [US-0989-46].

Chapter 11

336 *Lincoln* The Granger Collection, New York; *cannon* © Heeb Christian/age fotostock; **336–337** Library of Congress Prints and Photographs Division [LC-USZC6-48]; **337** *Hunley* The Museum of the Confederacy, Richmond, Virginia. Photography by Katherine Wetzel; *Lister* © Bettmann/Corbis; *Tolstoy* © Archivo Iconografico, S.A./Corbis; **338** *center* Beverley R. Robinson Collection, U.S. Naval Academy Museum; *top right* © Battle of Gettysburg, color illustration, 1884. Stock Montage/Hulton Archive/Getty Images; **339** *left* GEH NEG 36748/Courtesy George Eastman House; *right* Library of Congress Prints and Photographs Division [LC-B8184-10374]; **342** United States Army Military History Institute; **343** The Granger Collection, New York; **344** The Granger Collection, New York; **345** Alexander Gardner/The Granger Collection, New York; **346** *center* Alabama Department of Archives and History, Montgomery, Alabama; *top right* © Stock Montage/Hulton Archive/Getty Images; **347** *both* The Granger Collection, New York; **348** *left, Abraham Lincoln, Sixteenth President of the United States* (Detail) (1864), William Willard. Oil on canvas, 24″ x 17 15/16″ (61 x 45.5 cm). National Portrait Gallery, Smithsonian Institution/Art Resource, New York; *right* © Bettmann/Corbis; **349** © Oklahoma Historical Society/Marilyn Angel Wynn/Nativestock.com; **350** *right* The Granger Collection, New York; *left* file photo; **351** *center right, Mary Boykin Chesnut* (1856), Samuel S.

Osgood. Oil on canvas adhered to masonite, 48" x 30". Private collection/Art Resource, New York; *top right* © Stock Montage/Hulton Archive/Getty Images; **352** *top* Chicago History Museum (Negative number CHi-07774); *center* Courtesy of the Commonwealth of Massachusetts, Art Commission; **353** The Granger Collection, New York; **354** The Granger Collection, New York; **355** *top right* The Granger Collection, New York; *bottom right* © Tria Giovan/Corbis; *left* © MPI/Hulton Archive/Getty Images; **356** © Corbis; **357** *center* © MPI/Hulton Archive/Getty Images; *top right* © Stock Montage/Hulton Archive/Getty Images; **359** © MPI/Hulton Archive/Getty Images; **360** © Corbis; **362** *left* Library of Congress Prints and Photographs Division [LC-USZ62-115549]; *right* Library of Congress Prints and Photographs Division [LC U5260-20244]; **364** *top* Chicago History Museum (Negative number CHi-22146); *top* © MPI/Hulton Archive/Getty Images; **365** © Tom Lovell/National Geographic Image Collection; **366** *center* © Medford Historical Society Collection/Corbis; *top right* © Stock Montage/Hulton Archive/Getty Images; **367** *left* The Granger Collection, New York; **368** Cook Collection/Valentine Richmond History Center; **369** *top* © Mathew Brady/Hulton Archive/Getty Images; *bottom* Mathew Brady Studio (1862). Library of Congress Prints and Photographs Division [LC-B8171-1214]; **370** © David Gray/Reuters/Corbis; **371** Abraham Lincoln Presidential Library; **372** *left* GEH NEG 36748/Courtesy George Eastman House; *right* Library of Congress Prints and Photographs Division [LC-B8184-10374]; **373** *right* John Tenniel/Library of Congress Prints and Photographs Division; **373** MC1–MC2 © Bettmann/Corbis.

Chapter 12

374 *bottom right, bottom left* The Granger Collection, New York; **374–375** © Mathew B. Brady/Corbis; **375** *Greeley* © Corbis; *Wilhelm* © Hulton Archive/Getty Images; **376** *center* Culver Pictures; *top right* © MPI/Hulton Archive/Getty Images; **377** Culver Pictures; **378** © Mathew B. Brady/Medford Historical Society Collection/Corbis; **379** William Gladstone Collection/Library of Congress Prints and Photographs Division; **381** *bottom* The Granger Collection, New York; **382** © MPI/Hulton Archive/Getty Images; **383** *center* Copyright © 1956, 1978 by Pauli Murray. Reprinted by permission of Frances Collin, literary agent; *top right* © MPI/Hulton Archive/Getty Images; **384** *top, A Burial Party, Civil War, Cold Harbor, Virginia* (1865), Alexander Gardner. Chicago History Museum (Negative number CHi-07868); *bottom* © Bettmann/Corbis; **385** *bottom* The Granger Collection, New York; *top* © 2006 The Children's Museum of Indianapolis, Inc. Photograph by Wendy Kaveney; **386** The Granger Collection, New York; **387** Library of Congress Prints and Photographs Division [LC-USZC4-1733]; **388** Photograph by Rudolph Eickmeyer/Photographic History Collection, National Museum of American History, Smithsonian Institution (86-11374); **389** The Granger Collection, New York; **390** © Dennis Cook/AP Images; **391** © MPI/Hulton Archive/Getty Images; **392** Library of Congress Prints and Photographs Division; **393** *center* © Time & Life Pictures/Getty Images; *top right* © MPI/Hulton Archive/Getty Images; **394** The Granger Collection, New York; **396** Culver Pictures; **397** The Granger Collection, New York; **399** file photo; **401** © Corbis; **402** © Mathew B. Brady/Corbis.

Chapter 13

404–405 *Champions of the Mississippi* (1866), Currier & Ives. Lithograph. Museum of the City of New York/Scala/Art Resource, New York; **406** *Red Cloud* The Granger Collection, New York; *Canal* © Hulton-Deutsch Collection/Corbis; *bottom right* © MPI/Hulton Archive/Getty Images; **406–407** National Anthropological Archives, Smithsonian Institution (4703); **407** *Cleveland* © Bettmann/Corbis; *bottom right* © Blank Archives/Hulton Archive/Getty Images; **408** *center* Courtesy of Harold Lee Library, Brigham Young University; *top right, And So, Unemotionally, There Began One of the Wildest and Strangest Journeys Ever Made in any Land* (date unknown), William Henry David Koerner. Oil on Canvas, 22 1/4 " x 72 1/4". Buffalo Bill Historical Center, Cody, Wyoming (7.69); **409** *top, Portrait of Sioux Man and Woman* (date unknown), Gertrude Käsebier. Photographic History Collection, National Museum of American History, Smithsonian Institution (86-2205); *bottom* The Detroit Institute of Arts. Founders Society Purchase with funds from Flint Ink Corporation; **410** The Granger Collection, New York; **411** *bottom* The Granger Collection, New York; **412** *top right* Gift of Olin Corporation, Winchester Arms Collection. Buffalo Bill Historical Center, Cody Wyoming (1988.8.1310); *left* The Granger Collection, New York; **412** *center right* American Museum of Natural History, New York. Photo by Lee Boltin; **413** *skull* © Steven Fuller/Animals Animals; *hide, bones, horns* © Marilyn Angel Wynn/Nativestock.com; *buffalo* © T. Ulrich/Robertstock.com; **414** *top* © Marilyn Angel Wynn/Nativestock.com; *bottom, Vaqueros in a Horse Corral* (1887), James Walker. Oil on canvas, 24-1/4" x 40". From the collection of the Gilcrease Museum, Tulsa, Oklahoma; **416** *The Stampede* (1908), Frederic Remington. Oil on canvas, 27" x 40." From the collection of the Gilcrease Museum, Tulsa, Oklahoma; **417** The Granger Collection, New York; **418** *left* University of Washington Libraries, Special Collections [Hegg 1312]; *right* The Granger Collection, New York; **419** *bottom* Photo by J.G Wilson. Denver Public Library, Western History Department Collection, call # F8607.; *center, Miners Underground* (1897), unknown photographer. Glass plate negative. Colorado Historical Society, Mazzulla Collection.; *top right* © Pierre Perrin/Zoko/Sygma/Corbis; **420** *center, Pioneer Woman* (1909), Harvey Dunn. Oil on canvas, 24-1/4" h x 30-1/4" w. Hazel L. Meyer Memorial Library, De Smet, South Dakota; *top right, And So, Unemotionally, There Began One of the Wildest and Strangest Journeys Ever Made in any Land* (date unknown), William Henry David Koerner. Oil on Canvas, 22 1/4 " x 72 1/4" . Buffalo Bill Historical Center, Cody, Wyoming (7.69); **421** *right inset* The Granger Collection, New York; *bottom* Library of Congress Prints and Photographs Division; **422** The Granger Collection, New York; **423** *barbed wire, plow* The Granger Collection, New York; *reaper, windmill* North Wind Pictures; *background* © James Schwabel/Panoramic Images; **424** State Historical Society of North Dakota (0355-09); **425** *center* © Corbis; *top right, And So, Unemotionally, There Began One of the Wildest and Strangest Journeys Ever Made in any Land* (date unknown), William Henry David Koerner. Oil on Canvas, 22 1/4 " x 72 1/4". Buffalo Bill Historical Center, Cody, Wyoming (7.69); **426** Culver Pictures; **428** © Corbis; **429** The Granger Collection, New York; **430** The Granger Collection, New York; **431** *left* Photograph by William Stinson Soule, Archives & Manuscripts Division of the Oklahoma Historical Society. Courtesy of Oklahoma Historical Society [Negative no. 3969]; *right Vaquero* (modeled 1980, cast 1990), Luis Jimenez. Acrylic urethane, fiberglass, steel armature, 199" x 114" x 67" (505.5 x 289.6 x 170.2 cm). Gift of Judith and Wilbur L. Ross, Jr., Anne and Ronald Abramson, Thelma and Melvin Lenkin, Smithsonian American Art Museum, Washington DC/Art Resource, New York/Artists Rights Society (ARS), New York. Multimedia product associated with this text program and its contents are protected under copyright law. Any theatrical, televised, or public display or performance, including transmission of any image over a network, excepting a local area network, is prohibited by law, as is the preparation of any derivative work, including the extraction in whole or in part, of any Images without the permission of ARS. Reproduction, including downloading of artist works is prohibited by copyright laws and international conventions without the express written permission of Artists Rights Society (ARS), New York; **432** *top left* American Museum of Natural History, New York. Photo by Lee Boltin; *top right, bottom center* The Granger Collection, New York; *bottom left* © Steven Fuller/Animals Animals; *bottom right* North Wind Pictures.

Chapter 14

434 *bottom right* National Museum of American History, Smithsonian Institution, Electrical Collections (79-1641); *bottom left* Underwood Photo Archives; **434–435** Courtesy California State Railroad Museum; **435** *both* The Granger Collection, New York; **436** *center* Reproduced from *Prospectus: The True History of the Beaumont Oil Fields* by Pattillo Higgins. 1902 Pattillo Higgins. Courtesy of the estate of Pattillo Higgins; *top right* The Granger Collection, New York; **438** The Granger Collection, New York; **439** © Bettmann/Corbis; **440** *top* From *The Atlas of Cuyahoga County, Ohio*, Titus, Simmons and Titus, The Western Reserve Historical Society, Cleveland, Ohio; *bottom* The Western Reserve Historical Society, Cleveland, Ohio; **440–441** From *The Atlas of Cuyahoga County, Ohio*, Titus, Simmons and Titus, The Western Reserve Historical Society, Cleveland, Ohio; **441** *top right* © Bettmann/Corbis; **442** *center* Historic Pullman Foundation Archives,

Chicago; *top right* The Granger Collection, New York; **443** The Granger Collection, New York; **444** The Granger Collection, New York; **446** The Granger Collection, New York; **447** *both* The Granger Collection, New York; **448** *bottom* The Granger Collection, New York; **449** *top* © Bettmann/Corbis; *bottom* Horace Taylor, January 22, 1900 edition of Verdict/Library of Congress Prints and Photographs Division [LC-USZ62-61409]; **450** *Boy Carrying Homework from NY Sweatshop* (1912) Lewis Wickes Hine. Gelatin silver print ,16.7 x 11.7 cm. Gift of the Photo League, New York. GEH NEG 3748/ Courtesy of George Eastman House; **452** © Bettmann/Corbis; **454** *left* Eugene Debs Collection/Tamiment Institute Library, New York University; *right* The Granger Collection, New York; **455** © Underwood & Underwood/Corbis; **456** The Western Reserve Historical Society, Cleveland, Ohio.

Chapter 15

458 *Hayes* © Bettmann/Corbis; **458** *Díaz, Africa* The Granger Collection, New York; **458–459** The Granger Collection, New York; **459** *bottom* The Granger Collection, New York; **460** *both* © Corbis; **462** Courtesy of Ellis Island Immigration Museum; **463** *left* Culver Pictures; *right* New York Academy of Medicine Library; **464** The Granger Collection, New York; **465** © Bettmann/Corbis; **466** *left, Mission Francisco Solano de Sonoma 1877-1884.* Oriana Weatherbee Day (American), (1838-1886). Oil on canvas, 20" x 30". Fine Arts Museum of San Francisco (California), gift of Mrs. Eleanor Martin, 37573; *center* Culver Pictures; *right* Library of Congress Prints and Photographs Division; **467** *left* © Reuters/Corbis; *right* The Granger Collection, New York; **468** *center* Jacob Riis (ca. 1890). The Granger Collection, New York; *top right* © Corbis; **470** Library of Congress Prints and Photographs Division [LC-D4-13645]; **471** *left* The Granger Collection, New York; *right* © Bettmann/Corbis; **472** University of Illinois at Chicago Library, The Jane Addams Memorial Collection (JAMC494); **473** *center* The Granger Collection, New York; *top right* © Corbis; **474** © Bettmann/Corbis; **475** *both* The Granger Collection, New York; **476** *top* The Granger Collection, New York; *center* The Granger Collection, New York; *bottom* The Granger Collection, New York; **479** Harper's Weekly, August 19, 1871/Library of Congress Prints and Photographs Division [LC-USZC4-13085]; **479 MC1–MC2** Illustration by Nick Rotundo/Bizzy Productions, Inc.

Chapter 16

480 *bottom left, bottom right* The Granger Collection, New York; **480–481** Stock Montage; **481** *bottom left* © Bettmann/Corbis; *bottom right* © Three Lions/Hulton Archive/Getty Images; *bottom center* © Charles & Josette Lenars/Corbis; **482** *center* Library of Congress Prints and Photographs Division; *top right* The Granger Collection, New York; **483** Library of Congress Prints and Photographs Division [LC-D401-14278]; **484** *top, Plan of Chicago* (1909), Daniel Hudson Burnham and Edward Herbert Bennett. On permanent loan to The Art Institute of Chicago from the City of Chicago, 1-30.148.1966, The Art Institute of Chicago. Photography © The Art Institute of Chicago.; *bottom* The Granger Collection, New York; **485** © Bettmann/Corbis; **486** *center* Brown Brothers; *top* John Batchelor/Print Solutions; *bottom* National Archives and Records Administration (NARA); **487** *right* © Bettmann/Corbis; *left* Copyright © Eastman Kodak Company; **488** *center* Culver Pictures; *top right* The Granger Collection, New York; **490** © Stephen Frisch/Stock Boston; **491** Moorland-Spingarn Research Center, Howard University; **492** *both* The Granger Collection, New York; **493** © Marion Post Wolcott/Library of Congress/Getty Images; **495** Sacramento Archives and Museum Collection Center; **496** *bottom* The Granger Collection, New York; **497** *top* © Elliott Erwitt/Magnum Photos; *bottom* © Reuters/Corbis; **498** *center* Culver Pictures; *top right* The Granger Collection, New York; **499** file photo; **500** National Baseball Hall of Fame Library, Cooperstown, New York; **501** *The Champion Single Sculls (Max Schmitt in a Single Scull)*, (1871), Thomas Eakins. Oil on canvas, 32-1/4" x 46-1/4 ". The Metropolitan Museum of Art, Purchase, The Alfred N. Punnett Endowment Fund and George D. Pratt Gift, 1934 (34.92). Photograph © 1974 The Metropolitan Museum of Art; **502** The Granger Collection, New York; **503** *top* Courtesy of Sears Roebuck and Company; *bottom* file photo; **504** *left* © Underwood & Underwood/Corbis; *right* The Granger Collection, New York; **505** *top left* © American Stock/Hulton Archive/Getty Images; *bottom* The Granger Collection, New York; *top right* © Photodisc/Getty Images; **506** The Granger Collection, New York.

Chapter 17

508–509 The Statue of Liberty (date unknown), Francis Hopkinson Smith. Oil on canvas, 11" x 15" (27.9 cm x 38.1 cm). Christie's Images Ltd.; **510** *bottom center* © Bettmann/Corbis; *bottom left* © Michael Maslin Historic Photographs/Corbis; **510–511** © Bettmann/Corbis; **511** *bottom right* The Granger Collection, New York; *bottom left* © Bettmann/Corbis; *bottom center* © Peter Ruhe/Gandhiserve Foundation; **512** *both* © Bettmann/Corbis; **513** *top* © Bettmann/Corbis; *bottom* © American Stock/Hulton Archive/Getty Images; **515** © Bettmann/Corbis; **516** Texas State Library & Archives Commission; **517** *left* © Lewis Hine/Corbis; *right* © Lewis Hine/Corbis; **518** © American Stock/Hulton Archive/Getty Images; **519** *center* The Granger Collection, New York; *top right* © Bettmann/Corbis; **520** © Bettmann/Corbis; **521** © Corbis; **522** © Bettmann/Corbis; **523** *both* © Bettmann/Corbis; **524** *top* National Museum of American History, Smithsonian Institution (93-7206); *bottom* © Underwood & Underwood/Corbis; © Bettmann/Corbis; **527** *background, inset illustration* Matthew Pippin/McDougal Littell/Houghton Mifflin Co.; *top right* © Lewis W. Hine/George Eastman House/Getty Images; *center* © James G. Welgos/Hulton Archive/Getty Images; **528** *top* © Bettmann/Corbis; *bottom* The Granger Collection, New York; **530** *top* © Bill Ross/Corbis; *bottom* The Granger Collection, New York; **531** © C. M. Battey/Hulton Archive/Getty Images; **532** The Granger Collection, New York; **533** *top* The Granger Collection, New York; *bottom, The Butchers* (1917), Joesph Pennell. Chicago History Museum (Negative number CHi-4109); **534** *center* The Granger Collection, New York; *top right* © Bettmann/Corbis; **535** © Bettmann/Corbis; **536** The Granger Collection, New York; **538** *both* © Bettmann/Corbis; **541** © Bettmann/Corbis; **542** *left* © Ezra Stoller © Esto/Artists Rights Society (ARS), New York. Multimedia product associated with this text program and its contents are protected under copyright law. Any theatrical, televised, or public display or performance, including transmission of any image over a network, excepting a local area network, is prohibited by law, as is the preparation of any derivative work, including the extraction in whole or in part, of any Images without the permission of ARS. Reproduction, including downloading of artist works is prohibited by copyright laws and international conventions without the express written permission of Artists Rights Society (ARS), New York; *right* © Michael T. Sedam/Corbis.

Chapter 18

546 *bottom left* © Bettmann/Corbis; *bottom right* © Hulton Archive/Getty Images; **546–547** © Corbis; **547** *Canal* © Underwood & Underwood/Corbis; *Poster* © Corbis; **548** *center* © Bettmann/Corbis; *top right* Library of Congress Prints and Photographs Division [LC-USZC4-5232]; **549** *bottom* The Granger Collection, New York; *top* Culver Pictures; **552** *center* © Bettmann/Corbis; *top right* Library of Congress Prints and Photographs Division [LC-USZC4-5232]; **553** The Granger Collection, New York; **554** © Bettmann/Corbis; **556** © Strohmeyer and Wyman/Corbis; **557** © Bettmann/Corbis; **558** *center* Puerto Rican Cultural Institute/Library of Congress Prints and Photographs Division; *top right* Library of Congress Prints and Photographs Division [LC-USZC4-5232]; **559** © AFP/Getty Images; **560** The Granger Collection, New York; **561** Keystone-Mast Collection, UCR/California Museum of Photography, University of California, Riverside (24039); **563** © The Trustees of the British Museum; **564** © Bettmann/Corbis; **565** *center* © Bettmann/Corbis; *top right* Library of Congress Prints and Photographs Division [LC-USZC4-5232]; **566** The Granger Collection, New York; **567** *inset* © Corbis; **568** *top* The Granger Collection, New York; *bottom* Theodore Roosevelt Collection, Harvard College Library; **570** *Zapatistas Marching - Led by Emiliano Zapata and Pancho Villa during the Mexican Revolution of 1911* (1931), Jose Clemente Orozco. Oil on canvas, 45" x 55" (114.3 x 139.7 cm). Private Collection/SOMAAP, Mexico/The Bridgeman Art Library/Artists Rights Society (ARS), New York. Multimedia product associated with this text program and its contents are protected under copyright law. Any theatrical, televised, or public display or performance, including transmission of any image over a network, excepting a local area network, is prohibited by law, as is the preparation of any derivative work, including the extraction in whole or in part, of any Images without the permission of ARS. Reproduction, including downloading of artist works is prohibited by copyright laws and international conventions without the express written permission of Artists Rights Society (ARS), New York; **571** The

Granger Collection, New York; **572** *top* © Underwood & Underwood/Corbis; *bottom left* © Will & Deni McIntyre/Stone/Getty Images; **573** *left* © The Mariners' Museum/Corbis; *right* Courtesy of The Historic New Orleans Collection, accession number 1979.325.3533; **574** © Corbis; **575** *right* Michelle Hlubinka/McDougal Littell/Houghton Mifflin Co.; *left* Culver Pictures.

Chapter 19
576 *camera* © Bettmann/Corbis; *phone* © Dorling Kindersley; *Einstein* © Underwood & Underwood/Corbis; **576–577** © Bettmann/Corbis; **577** *flu sign* San Francisco Chronicle; *statuette* The Granger Collection, New York; **578** *center* © Corbis; *top right* Ian Bellinger/Fotolibra; **579** © Corbis; **580** © Rikard Larma/AP Images; **582** *inset* © Corbis; *background illustration* Chris Costello/McDougal Littell/Houghton Mifflin Co.; **584** *top* © Three Lions Hulton Archive/Getty Images; *center* The Granger Collection, New York; **585** Culver Pictures; **587** *center* © Bettmann/Corbis; *top right* Ian Bellinger/Fotolibra; **588** *top* © Corbis; *center* The Granger Collection, New York; **589** *bottom* file photo; **590** *top* The Granger Collection, New York; *bottom center* Air Team Images; **590–591** © General Photographic Agency/Hulton Archive/Getty Images; **591** *bottom center* © Dorling Kindersley; *bottom right* © Three Lions Hulton Archive/Getty Images; **592** © Bettmann/Corbis; **593** Library of Congress Prints and Photographs Division [LC-USZC4-7709]; **594** *center* Brown Brothers; *top right* Ian Bellinger/Fotolibra; **596** *right* © Bettmann/Corbis; *left* The Granger Collection, New York; **597** © Corbis; **598** *center* Courtesy of The Industrial Workers of the World; www.iww.org; *bottom* © Bettmann/Corbis; **599** *bottom, During the World War There Was a Great Migration North by Southern Negroes (Panel no. 1 from The Migration of the Negro mural series)* (1940–1941), Jacob Lawrence. Casein tempera on hardboard, 12" x 18". The Phillips Collection; acquired 1942/© Estate of Gwendolyn Knight Lawrence / Artists Rights Society (ARS), New York. Multimedia product associated with this text program and its contents are protected under copyright law. Any theatrical, televised, or public display or performance, including transmission of any image over a network, excepting a local area network, is prohibited by law, as is the preparation of any derivative work, including the extraction in whole or in part, of any images without the permission of ARS. Reproduction, including downloading of artist works is prohibited by copyright laws and international conventions without the express written permission of Artists Rights Society (ARS), New York; **600** © Bettmann/Corbis; **601** © Bettmann/Corbis; **602** © Bettmann/Corbis; **603** *both* © Bettmann/Corbis; **604** *left* © Topical Press Agency/Hulton Archive/Getty Images; *top right* Ian Bellinger/Fotolibra; **605** *top, Woodrow Wilson* (detail), F. Graham Cootes. White House Historical Association (White House Collection) (63); *bottom* © Bettmann/Corbis; **608** *top right* © Universal Pictures/Photofest; *left, center* Photofest; *bottom right* © from *Frankenstein* (1931), Universal Pictures/The Kobal Collection; **610** *both* The Granger Collection, New York; **611** *top right* © Philip Jones Griffiths/Magnum Photos; *top left* © Reuters/Bettmann/Corbis; *bottom* © George Rodger/Time & Life Pictures/Getty Images; **613** Michelle Hlubinka/McDougal Littell/Houghton Mifflin Co.; **613** MC1–MC2 © Bettmann/Corbis.

Chapter 20
614–615 *Street Scene* (1933), Joe Jones. Oil on Canvas, 25 1/8" x 36 1/8" (63.7 x 91.1 cm). Smithsonian American Art Museum, Washington DC/Art Resource, New York; **616** *flag* Photograph by Martin Plomer, © Dorling Kindersley; *button* © David J. & Janice L. Frent Collection/Corbis; **616–617** © Bettmann/Corbis; **617** *Randolph, Stalin* © Bettmann/Corbis; *bottom left* © P. Otsup/Hulton Archive/Getty Images; **618** *center* file photo; *top right* © Bettmann/Corbis; **620** *Sacco and Vanzetti* (1932), Ben Shahn. Tempera on canvas 21" x 48". Private Collection. Photograph courtesy of Kennedy Galleries, New York. Copyright © Estate of Ben Shahn/Licensed by VAGA, New York, NY; **621** © Bettmann/Corbis; **622** Underwood and Underwood/Library of Congress Prints and Photographs Division [LC-USZC4-5584]; **623** Library of Congress Prints and Photographs Division [LC-B2-956-14]; **624** © Bettmann/Corbis; **625** *center, Warren Gamaliel Harding* (Detail) (ca.1923), Margaret Lindsay William. Oil on canvas, 135.9 x 99.7 cm. National Portrait Gallery, Smithsonian Institution/Art Resource, New York; *top right* © Bettmann/Corbis; **626** © Hulton Archive/Getty Images; **627** Stock Montage; **628** *center* © Robertstock.com; *top right* ©

Bettmann/Corbis; **629** *both* Brown Brothers; **630** *top left, Calvin Coolidge* (detail), Charles S. Hopkins. White House Historical Association (White House Collection) (8); *bottom* Courtesy of United Airlines; **631** © Camerique/Robertstock.com; **632** Culver Pictures; **634** *center* Library of Congress Prints and Photographs Division [LC-USZC4-2635]; *bottom* Library of Congress Prints and Photographs Division [LC-B2-3982]; **635** *bottom* © Stephen Simpson/Taxi/Getty Images; *top* © Harold M. Lambert/Hulton Archive/Getty Images; **636** *bottom* © Dan McCoy/Rainbow; *center* © American Stock/Hulton Archive/Getty Images; **637** Daniel Fitzpatrick, courtesy of the State Historical Society of Missouri, Columbia, Missouri; **637** MC1–MC2 © Underwood & Underwood/Corbis.

Chapter 21
638 *Tut* © Bettmann/Corbis; *Time* Time Life Pictures/Time Magazine, © Time Inc./Time Life Pictures/Getty Images; *Armstrong* © Hulton Archive/Getty Images; **638–639** © Frank Driggs/Hulton Archive/Getty Images; **639** *Lindbergh, Hirohito* © Bettmann/Corbis; **640** *both* © Bettmann/Corbis; **641** *Aspects of Negro Life: Song of the Towers* (1934), Aaron Douglas. Oil on canvas, 9' x 9'. Schomburg Center for Research in Black Culture, Art & Artifacts Division, the New York Public Library, Astor, Lenox and Tilden Foundations; **642** *both* © Underwood & Underwood/Corbis; **643** © Underwood & Underwood/Corbis; **644** © Bettmann/Corbis; **645** The Granger Collection, New York; **646** *center* © Hulton Archive/GettyImages; *top right* © Bettmann/Corbis; **647** © Hulton Archive/Getty Images; **648** Lewis Wickes Hine (1920) GEH NEG 16682/Courtesy George Eastman House; **650** *bottom left* Brown Brothers; *bottom right* © Frank Driggs Collection/Hulton Archive/Getty Images; **650–651** © Minnesota Historical Society/Corbis; **651** *top* file photo; *bottom* © Bettmann/Corbis; **652** *both* © Bettmann/Corbis; **653** *center, left* © Underwood & Underwood/Corbis; *right* © Hulton-Deutsch Collection/Corbis; **654** *top right* © New York Times Co./Hulton Archive/Getty Images; *center* © Bettmann/Corbis; *bottom left* National Baseball Hall of Fame Library, Cooperstown, New York; *bottom right* © Central Press/Hulton Archive/Getty Images; **655** *top, bottom left* © Bettmann/Corbis; *bottom right* © Corbis; **656** *Night Windows* (1928), Edward Hopper. Oil on canvas, 29" x 34". Museum of Modern Art, New York. Gift of John Hay Whitney [248.1940]. Digital Image © The Museum of Modern Art/Licensed by SCALA/Art Resource, New York; **657** © Hulton Archive/GettyImages; **658** *center* Brown Brothers; *top right* © Bettmann/Corbis; **659** Fisk University, Nashville, Tennessee; **660** © Bettmann/Corbis; **661** *top right* © Hulton-Deutsch Collection/Corbis; *top left* © Redferns/Redferns; *bottom* © Frank Driggs Collection/Hulton Archive/Getty Images; *background illustration* Karen Minot/McDougal Littell/Houghton Mifflin; **662** © Frank Driggs Collection/Hulton Archive/Getty Images; **663** © Frank Driggs Collection/Hulton Archive/Getty Images; **664** © Bettmann/Corbis; **665** *right, Langston Hughes* (ca.1920), Winold Reiss. Pastel on artist board, 76.3 x 54.9 cm. Gift of W. Tjark Reiss in memory of his father, Winold Reiss. National Portrait Gallery, Smithsonian Institution, Washington, DC/Art Resource, New York; *left, Edna St. Vincent Millay, American Writer* (1930), anonymous photographer. National Portrait Gallery, Smithsonian Institution/Art Resource; **666** *Chaplin* Photofest; *fashion* © Bettmann/Corbis; *band* © Frank Driggs Collection/Hulton Archive/Getty Images; *Capone* © Underwood & Underwood/Corbis; **667** Culver Pictures.

Chapter 22
668 *apple seller, Manchuria* © Bettmann/Corbis; *Vanity Fair* © 1933 Condé Nast Publications; **668–669** © American Stock/Hulton Archive/Getty Images; **669** *World's Fair* Chicago History Museum (Negative number CHi-39026); *Gandhi* © Bettmann/Corbis; **670** *center right* © AP Images; *top right* © Photo Collection Alexander Alland, Sr./Corbis; **671** © Arthur Rothstein/Corbis; **672** © Blank Archives/Hulton Archive/Getty Images; **673** *Dies Irae (October 29, 1929)*, James Naumburg Rosenberg. Lithograph on paper, 13 5/8" x 10 1/2". National Museum of American Art, Washington, DC/Art Resource, New York; **674** *top* © Bettmann/Corbis; *bottom* © Reuters/Corbis; **675** Conservative Party Archives, Bodleian Library, University of Oxford; **676** *background* Library of Congress, Prints and Photographs Division [LC-USF34-028362-D]; *right inset* Franklin D. Roosevelt Library, Hyde Park, New York; *left inset* Underwood Photo Archives; **678** *center* Reproduced from *Dust Bowl Diary* by Ann Marie Low, by permission of the University of Nebraska Press. Copyright ©

1984 by the University of Nebraska Press; *top right* © Photo Collection Alexander Alland, Sr./Corbis; **679** © Franklin D. Roosevelt Library/Bettmann/Corbis; **680** Library of Congress Prints and Photographs Division [LC-USZC4-4840]; **682** National Archives and Records Administration (NARA); **683** Farm Security Administration/Library of Congress Prints and Photographs Division [LC-USF33-006068-M5]; **684** *center* Library of Congress Prints and Photographs Division [LC-DIG-ppmsc-00241]; *top right* © Photo Collection Alexander Alland, Sr./Corbis; **685** *Herbert Clark Hoover* (Detail) (1931), Douglas Chandor. Oil on Canvas. National Portrait Gallery, Smithsonian Institution/Art Resource, New York; **686** © Lake County Museum/Corbis; **687** "Ding" Darling Wildlife Society; **688** © Bettmann/Corbis; **691** file photo; **691 MC1–MC2** © Bettmann/Corbis; **691 MC2** *top left* Library of Congress, Prints and Photographs Division, Farm Security Administration/Office of War Information Photograph Collection.

Chapter 23
692 *bottom right* © 1934 Condé Nast Publications; *bottom left* © Corbis; *bottom center* © Bettmann/Corbis; **692–693** Franklin D. Roosevelt Library, Hyde Park, New York; **693** *bottom left* The Granger Collection, New York; *bottom right* © MGM/The Kobal Collection; **694** *center* University of Washington Libraries, Special Collections [UW20896z]; *top right* © Thomas D. McAvoy/Time & Life Pictures/Getty Images; **695** *left, Franklin Delano Roosevelt* (Detail) (1935), Henry Salem Hubbell. Oil on masonite panel, 121.9 x 116.2 cm. National Portrait Gallery, Smithsonian Institution/Art Resource, New York; *right* White House Historical Association (White House Collection); **696** Franklin D. Roosevelt at Hilltop Cottage with Ruthie Bie and Fala (1941), Margaret Suckley. Photograph, Franklin D. Roosevelt Library; **697** National Archives and Records Administration (NARA); **698** © AP Images; **699** *top* Jay N. "Ding" Darling. © 1937 by the Des Moines Register and Tribune Company. Reprinted with permission/Stock Montage; *bottom* © Bettmann/Corbis; **700** © Bettmann/Corbis; **701** *center, Dorothea Lange at Work, Texas* (Detail) (1934), Paul Taylor. © The Dorothea Lange Collection, Oakland Museum of California, City of Oakland. Gift of Paul S. Taylor; *top right* © Thomas D. McAvoy/Time & Life Pictures/Getty Images; **702** *bottom right* Photofest; *top* © Underwood & Underwood/Corbis; **703** *top, Migrant Mother, Nipomo, California* (1936), Dorothea Lange/Library of Congress [Prints & Photographs Division [LC-USZ62-95653]; *bottom* Dorothea Lange (1936). Library of Congress [LC-USZ62-58355]; **704** ©Margaret Bourke-White/Time Life Pictures/Getty Images; **705** © Bettmann/Corbis; **706** *top right* The Granger Collection, New York; *left* © Bettmann/Corbis; *bottom right* National Archives and Records Administration (NARA); **707** *Light* (1937), Lester Beall. From the series "Rural Electrification Administration." Lithograph, 101.6 x 76.2 cm (40 x 30 in./Library of Congress Prints and Photographs Division [U.S. B415.3]; **708** *bottom* © Bettmann/Corbis; **709** © Bettmann/Corbis; **710** *center* Espinosa Productions; *top right* © Thomas D. McAvoy/Time & Life Pictures/Getty Images; **711** *top* © Bettmann/Corbis; *bottom, Mary McLeod Bethune* (1875-1955), Educator (Detail) (1943-1944), Betsy Graves Reyneau. National Portrait Gallery, Smithsonian Institution/Art Resource, New York; **712** © Hulton Archive/Getty Images; **713** © Bettmann/Corbis; **714** *right, left* © Bettmann/Corbis; *top right* Poster, chromolithograph (mid-1930s), Ben Shahn. The Granger Collection, New York/© Estate of Ben Shahn/Licensed by VAGA, New York, NY; **715** Carl Linde/Courtesy of the Illinois Labor History Society;.**716** *center* Russell Lee (1941). Library of Congress Prints and Photographs Division [USF34-38814-D]; *top right* © Thomas D. McAvoy/Time & Life Pictures/Getty Images; **717** *top* © MGM/Fred Parrish/Photofest; *bottom* © CBS Radio/Photofest; **718** *top* Photofest; *bottom, Industries of California* (1934), Ralph Stackpole. Collection of the City and County of San Francisco, Calif. Photo courtesy of the San Francisco Arts Commission. Photo by Malcolm Kimberlin; **719** *top, American Gothic* (1930), Grant Wood. Oil on beaver board, 30 11/16" x 25 11/16" (78 cm x 65.3 cm) unframed. The Art Institute of Chicago, Friends of American Art Collection [1930.934]. Photography © The Art Institute of Chicago/All rights reserved by the Estate of Nan Wood Graham/Licensed by VAGA, New York, NY; *bottom* Courtesy of the Woody Guthrie Foundation and Archives; **720** Walker Evans/Library of Congress Prints and Photographs Division [LC-USF342-008138-A]; **721** *center right* © Franklin D. Roosevelt Library/AP Images; *top right* ©

Thomas D. McAvoy/Time & Life Pictures/Getty Images; **723** Dorothea Lange (1936). Library of Congress Prints and Photographs Division [LC-USF34- 009669-E]; **724** Library of Congress Prints and Photographs Division [LC-USZC4-4890]; **725** The Granger Collection, New York; **726** *illustration* Chris Costello/McDougal Littell/Houghton Mifflin Co.; **727** *bottom* Lewis W. Hine (1933)/Courtesy of the Tennessee Valley Authority; *top* Courtesy of the Tennessee Valley Authority; **728** *left* The Granger Collection, New York; *right* National Archives and Records Administration (NARA).

Chapter 24
730–731 *Dawn Patrol of Launching* (1942), Paul Sample. Army Art Collection, Washington DC; **732** *bottom right* Library of Congress Prints and Photographs Division [LC-USE622- D-OA-000067]; *bottom left* © M. Howell/Camerique/Robertstock.com; **732–733** © Corbis; **733** *bottom left* Library of Congress Prints and Photographs Division [LC-USZ62-45002]; *bottom right* © Hulton Archive/Getty Images; **734** *center* © Bettmann/Corbis; *top right* © Hulton Archive/Getty Images; **735** *left* © Three Lions/Hulton Archive/Getty Images; *right* © Archivo Iconografico, S.A./Corbis; **737** *left* © Bettmann/Corbis; *center* © Hulton-Deutsch Collection/Corbis; *right* © Keystone/Hulton Archive/Getty Images; **739** *top* © Keystone/Hulton Archive/Getty Images; **739** *bottom* © Horace Abrahams/Hulton Archive/Getty Images; **740** The Granger Collection, New York; **742** *center* © Bettmann/Corbis; *top right* © Hulton Archive/Getty Images; **743** *all* © Heinrich Hoffmann/Hulton Archive/Getty Images; **745** *right inset* © Hulton Archive/Getty Images; *bottom left* © AP Images; **746** *bottom* © John Topham/Black Star; *top* March of Time/Life Magazine. © Time, Inc.; **747** © Bettmann/Corbis; **748** *center* Courtesy of Gerda Weissman Klein; *top right* © Hulton Archive/Getty Images; **749** *left* © Hulton Archive/Getty Images; *right* Yad Vashem; **750** *Albert Einstein Among Other Immigrants, (Detail, Jersey Homesteads Mural)* (1937-1938), Ben Shahn. Community Center, Jersey Homestead, Roosevelt, New Jersey. Scala/Art Resource, New York/© Estate of Ben Shahn/Licensed by VAGA, New York, NY; **752** *bottom* © Bettmann/Corbis; **752–753** United States Army Military History Institute; **753** *bottom* KZ Gedenkstaette Dachau, courtesy of USHMM Photo Archives. The views expressed in this book, and the context in which the image is used, do not necessarily reflect the views or policy of, nor imply approval or endorsement by, the United States Holocaust Memorial Museum; **754** Main Commission for the Prosecution of the Crimes against the Polish Nation, courtesy of USHMM Photo Archives. The views expressed in this book, and the context in which the image is used, do not necessarily reflect the views or policy of, nor imply approval or endorsement by, the United States Holocaust Memorial Museum.; **755** © Erich Hartmann/Magnum Photos; **756** *center* © Hulton Archive/Getty Images; *top right* © Hulton Archive/Getty Images; **757** National Archives and Records Administration (NARA); **759** *center* National Archives and Records Administration (NARA); **760** © AP Images; **761** *right* The Granger Collection, New York; *left* Library of Congress Prints and Photographs Division [LC-USF34-71206-D]; **762** © Bettmann/Corbis; **765** Vaughn Shoemaker (1935), Chicago Daily News/Library of Congress Prints and Photographs Division [LC-USZC2-6281].

Chapter 25
766 *bottom right* © Corbis; **766–767** © Corbis; **767** *Zoot Suit* © Martha Swope; *Rommel* © Keystone/Hulton Archive/Getty Images; *surrender, tank* © Hulton Archive/Getty Images; **768** *center* Courtesy of Charles Swanson; *top right* © StockTrek/PhotoDisc/Getty Images; **769** *top* © Bettmann/Corbis; *bottom* AL Aumuller/Library of Congress Prints and Photographs Division [LC-USZ62-118263]; **771** Library of Congress Prints and Photographs Division [LC-USW361-295]; **772** *top* Library of Congress Prints and Photographs Division [LC-USW3-11696-C]; *bottom left* US War Department/Photofest; *bottom right* Photofest; **774** *top* © AP Images; *bottom* Printed by the Government Printing Office for the Office of Price Administration NARA Still Picture Branch (NWDNS-188-PP-42); **775** *center right, inset* Courtesy of Adrienne McGrath; *top right* © StockTrek/PhotoDisc/Getty Images; **776** © Corbis; **777** © Bettmann/Corbis; **778** © Bettmann/Corbis; **779** *bottom* © Bettmann/Corbis; *inset* Courtesy of The Red Tail Project; **780** © AP Images; **781** *top left* Robert F. Sargent/Library of Congress Prints and Photographs Division [LC-USZC4-4731]; **782** © Bettmann/Corbis; **783** New York Daily News Photo; **784** *center* © Bettmann/Corbis; *top right*

© StockTrek/PhotoDisc/Getty Images; **785** © Corbis; **787** © AP Images; **788** *top* © Louis R. Lowery/AP Images; *bottom* © Joe Rosenthal/AP Images; **789** *top* © Bettmann/Corbis; **790** *top* © Bettmann/Corbis; *bottom* © Bernard Hoffman/Time & Life Pictures/Getty Images; **792** National Archives and Records Administration (NARA); **794** *top left* © Dan McCoy/Rainbow; *bottom left* © 1999 Russell Munson/The Stock Market/Corbis; **794** *center* © Hank Morgan/Rainbow; **795** *top* © AP Images; *center* © Sovfoto/Eastfoto; *bottom* © Larry Mulvehill/ Rainbow; **796** *center, Twice a Patriot* (1943), unknown artist. Lithograph, 44" x 32-1/4". The Amistad Center for Art & Culture: Simpson Collection, at the Wadsworth Atheneum, Hartford, Connecticut (AF 1987.1.401); *top right* © StockTrek/PhotoDisc/Getty Images; **797** Franklin D. Roosevelt Library, Hyde Park, New York; **798** © Bettmann/Corbis; **799** Library of Congress, Prints and Photographs Division [LC-USZ62-48275]; **800** © Seattle Post-Intelligencer Collection; Museum of History and Industry/Corbis; **803** *inset* © Dennis Cook/AP Images; *top* © Eliot Elisofon/Time & Life Pictures/Getty Images; **804** © AP Images; **805** Michelle Hlubinka/McDougal Littell/Houghton Mifflin Co.; **805 MC1–MC2** Library of Congress, Prints and Photographs Division.

Chapter 26
806 *bottom right* © Bettmann/Corbis; *bottom left* © Jules Frazier/PhotoDisc/Getty Images; **806–807** © AP Images; **807** *bottom center* © Aereo Graphics, Inc./Corbis; **808** *center* © Bettmann/Corbis; *bottom, Destroyed Bridge* Stamp Design © 1995 United States Postal Service. All rights reserved; *top right* © Keystone/Hulton Archive/Getty Images; **809** *left* © Bettmann/Corbis; *right* © Hulton Archive/Getty Images; **811** © Keystone/Hulton Archive/Getty Images; **812** © Hulton-Deutsch Collection/Corbis; **813** © AP Images; **814** *Another Pyramid Party* (1949), Edwin Marcus. By Permission of the Marcus Family/Library of Congress Prints and Photographs Division [LC-USZ62-53089]; **815** *center right* © Pfc. James Cox/Corbis; *top right* © Keystone/Hulton Archive/Getty Images; **816** *right* © Hsinhua News Agency/AP Images; *left* © AP Images; **818** Courtesy of Beverly Scott; **819** © Max Desfor/AP Images; **820** *bottom* © Bettmann/Corbis; *top* © Bettmann/Corbis; **821** © Yonhap/Pool/AP Images; **822** *center* Courtesy of Tony Kahn; *top right* © Keystone/Hulton Archive/Getty Images; **823** *top* © Gordon Parks/Library of Congress Prints and Photographs Division [LC-USF34-013363-C]; *bottom* Photofest; **824** *right* Photofest; *left* © Bettmann/Corbis; **825** *center* © AFP/Getty Images; *left* © AP Images; *right* © Koji Sashara/AP Images; *top* Photofest; **826** A 1947 Herblock Cartoon, copyright by The Herb Block Foundation; **827** A 1954 Herblock Cartoon, copyright by The Herb Block Foundation; **828** *center* © Corbis; *top right* © Keystone/Hulton Archive/Getty Images; **829** The American Civil Defense Association, photo courtesy of Eric Green; **831** © Bettmann/Corbis; **833** *top* © Sovfoto/Eastfoto; *center* © AP Images; **834** © Allied Artists/The Kobal Collection; **835** *top* © AP Images; **837** © Corbis.

Chapter 27
838 *bottom center* © Dorling Kindersley; *bottom left* © Bettmann/Corbis; *bottom right* © George D. Lepp/Corbis; **838–839** *Spring Yardwork* (1957), T. Utz. © 1957 SEPS: Licensed by Curtis Publishing, Indianapolis, IN. All rights reserved. www.curtispublishing.com; **839** *bottom center* National Aeronautics and Space Administraton (NASA); *bottom right* © SuperStock, Inc.; **840** *center* © Harold M. Lambert/Hulton Archive/Getty Images; *top right* © Ken Whitmore/Stone/Getty Images; **841** © J.R. Eyerman/Time & Life Pictures/Getty Images; **843** Culver Pictures; **844** *top left, Wipe Out Discrimination* (1949), Milton Ackoff. Offset lithograph, printed in color, 43 7/8" x 32 3/4". The Museum of Modern Art, New York. Gift of the Congress of Industrial Organizations. Digital Image © The Museum of Modern Art/Licensed by SCALA/Art Resource, New York; *bottom right* © Bettmann/Corbis; **845** *tees* Courtesy of The Ohio Historical Society; *button* 'I like Ike' election badge (20th century), American School. Plastic. Private Collection, Peter Newark American Pictures/The Bridgeman Art Library; *glasses* © David J. & Janice L. Frent Collection/Corbis; **846** © George Silk/Time & Life Pictures/Getty Images; **847** *center* © SuperStock, Inc.; *top right* © Ken Whitmore/Stone/Getty Images; **848** © Bettmann/Corbis; **849** *top* © Lambert/Hulton Archive/Getty Images; *bottom* © Petrified Collection/The Image Bank/Getty Images; **850** © Bettmann/Corbis;

851 *bottom* © Bettmann/Corbis; *top, After the Prom* (1957), Norman Rockwell. Printed by permission of the Norman Rockwell Family Agency. © 1957, Norman Rockwell Family Entities. Photo courtesy of The Norman Rockwell Museum at Stockbridge; **852** © Aldo Torelli/Riser/Getty Images; **853** *background* © PhotoDisc/Getty Images; *top left* © Francis Miller/Time & Life Pictures/Getty Images; *bottom left* © Carl Iwasaki/Time & Life Pictures/Getty Images; *top right* © Alfred Eisenstaedt/Time & Life Pictures/Getty Images; *bottom right* The Granger Collection, New York; **854** *both* The Granger Collection, New York; **855** The Granger Collection, New York; **856** *all* Courtesy of Park Forest Historical Society, Park Forest, Illinois; **857** *bottom, center* Courtesy of Park Forest Historical Society, Park Forest, Illinois; *top right* Dan Weiner: Courtesy Sandra Weiner; **858** *center* © Michael Ochs Archives/Getty Images; *top right* © 2001 Ken Whitmore/Stone/Getty Images; **859** © Photo by William Vandivert/Life Magazine/Time & Life Pictures/Getty Images; **860** *top* © CBS Photo Archive/Hulton Archive/Getty Images; *bottom* © Warner Bros. Pictures/Photofest; **861** © Bettmann/Corbis; **862** *top left, center* © Frank Driggs Collection/Hulton Archive/Getty Images; *bottom right* © Bettmann/Corbis; **863** © Hulton Archive/Getty Images; **864** *bottom right* © Paul Schutzer /Time & Life Pictures/Getty Images; *left* Image courtesy of The Advertising Archives; *center 7 UP®* is a registered trademark of Dr Pepper/Seven Up, Inc. © 2000 Dr Pepper/Seven Up, Inc.; *bottom center* Photo by Sharon Hoogstraten/McDougal Littell/Houghton Mifflin Co.; **865** *bottom* © Paul Schutzer/Time & Life Pictures/Getty Images; *top* Photofest; **866** *center* The Granger Collection, New York; *top right* © 2001 Ken Whitmore/Stone/Getty Images; **868** © William C. Shrout/Time & Life Pictures/Getty Images; **869** Milwaukee (Wisconsin) Journal/Milwaukee Sentinel,1955 © 2007 Journal Sentinel Inc., reproduced with permission.

Chapter 28
872–873 © James Karales; **874** *bottom right* © Keystone/HultonArchive/Getty Images; *bottom left* © Blank Archives/Hulton Archive/Getty Images; **874–875** National Aeronautics and Space Administraton (NASA); **875** *bottom left* © Marilyn Silverstone/Magnum Photos; *bottom right* © Bettmann/Corbis; **876** *center* © 1961 Black Star; **877** © Corbis; **878** Courtesy of the John F. Kennedy Library; **880** *center, Kennedy's Exploding Cuban Cigar* (Apr. 21, 1961), Leslie Gilbert Illingworth. Ink on scraper board; 28.2 x 22.4 cm. By permission of Llyfrgell Genedlaethol Cymru/The National Library of Wales/© Solo Syndication, London; *top* © Burt Glinn/Magnum Photos; **881** *center* © Bettmann/Corbis; *bottom* © MPI/Hulton Archive/Getty Images; **882** *both* © Bettmann/Corbis; **883** *background* © Leonard Freed/Magnum Photos; *inset* © Kreusch/AP Images; **884** *bottom, Cuban Missle Showdown* (1962), Leslie Gilbert Illingworth/© Solo Syndication, London/Library of Congress Prints and Photographs Division [LC-USZ62-70194]; *top* Courtesy of the John F. Kennedy Library; **885** *both* National Aeronautics and Space Administraton (NASA); **886** *bottom* © Bettmann/Corbis; *inset* Photo by Sharon Hoogstraten/McDougal Littell/Houghton Mifflin Co.; **888** *right* © Dan Farrell/New York Daily News Photo; **890** *left* © Roberto Gerometta/Lonely Planet Images/Getty Images; *right* © Bruce Forster/Getty Images; **891** © Tony Savino/Corbis; **892** *center* © AP Images; **893** © MPI/Hulton Archive/Getty Images; **894** *both* Museum of American Political Life, University of Hartford Library, West Hartford, Connecticut. Photograph by Sally Andersen-Bruce; **895** © Paul Conklin/ PhotoEdit; **897** © Bettmann/Corbis; **899** *Sunrise* (1967), John Fischetti. John Fischetti Papers, Midwest Manuscript Collection, The Newberry Library, Chicago. Courtesy of the Estate of Karen Fischetti; **900** © Bettmann/Corbis; **901** *right* © Bob Daemmrich/Stock Boston; *left* Photo by Sharon Hoogstraten/McDougal Littell/Houghton Mifflin Co.; **902** *bottom center* © Paul Conklin/PhotoEdit; *top right, bottom left* © MPI/Hulton Archive/Getty Images; *top left* © 1961 Black Star; **903 MC1–MC2** © Bettmann/Corbis; **903 MC2** *top left* Cold War Civil Defense Museum.

Chapter 29
904 *bottom left* © Joseph Schwartz/Corbis; *bottom center* © Hulton-Deutsch Collection/Corbis; *bottom right* © Bettmann/Corbis; **904–905** © Ivan Massar/Black Star; **905** *bottom right* © Bettmann/Corbis; *bottom left* © Express Newspapers/Hulton Archive/Getty Images/ NewsCom; **906** *center* Courtesy Arthur L. Freeman; *top right* ©

Francis Miller/Time & Life Pictures/Getty Images; **907** *top* Library of Congress, Prints and Photographs Division [LC-USZ62-99293]; *bottom* Library of Congress, Prints and Photographs Division [LC-USZ62-35344]; **908** © Consolidated News Pictures/Hulton Archive/Getty Images; **909** © Bettmann/Corbis; **910** © Gene Herrick/AP Images; **911** Dan Weiner: Courtesy Sandra Weiner; **912** © Flip Schulke/Corbis; **913** © Fred Blackwell; **914** *center* © Carl Iwasaki/Time & Life Pictures/Getty Images; **915** *left* © Bettmann/Corbis; *right* The Granger Collection, New York; **916** *center* © Bettmann/Corbis; *top right* © Francis Miller/Time & Life Pictures/Getty Images; **917** © Bettmann/Corbis; **918** © Bill Hudson/AP Images; **919** *all* © Ernest C. Withers/Courtesy Panopticon Gallery, Boston MA; **921** © 1964 Steve Schapiro/Black Star; **923** *center* © Bettmann/Corbis; *top right* © Francis Miller/Time & Life Pictures/Getty Images; **924** *both* © Bettmann/Corbis; **925** © 1964 John Launois/Black Star; **926** *inset* Photo by Sharon Hoogstraten/McDougal Littell/Houghton Mifflin Co.; *bottom* © Ken Regan/Camera 5; **927** *top* © Black Star; *bottom* © Bettmann/Corbis; **928** © Leif Skoogfors/Corbis; **930** (tr) *The Convalescents* (1861), Marie Francois Firmin Girard. Image © Erich Lessing/Art Resource, NY, (bl) © Peter Casolino/Alamy; **931** Barros & Barros/Getty Images; **932** *top left* © Carl Iwasaki/Time & Life Pictures/Getty Images; *top right* Dan Weiner: Courtesy Sandra Weiner; *center* © 1964 Steve Schapiro/Black Star.

Chapter 30

934 *bottom left* © Louis Fabian Bachrach/Corbis; *bottom right* © SuperStock, Inc.; **934–935** © Tim Page/Corbis; **935** *bottom* © Bob Peterson/Time & Life Pictures/Getty Images; **936** *center right* © Bettmann/Corbis; *top right* © Photomondo/PhotoDisc/Getty Images; **937** © Hulton Archive/Getty Images; **938** The Granger Collection, New York; **939** *bottom right* © Jean-Marie Leroy/Sygma/Corbis; *bottom left* © Corbis; *top right* © Hulton Archive/Getty Images; **940** © AP Images; **941** © Department of Defense/AP Images; **942** *center* © James Pardue/US Army/Hulton Archive/Getty Images; *top right* © Photomondo/PhotoDisc/Getty Images; **943** © Bettmann/Corbis; **946** The Granger Collection, New York; **947** Photo by Sharon Hoogstraten/McDougal Littell/Houghton Mifflin Co.; **948** *top right* © Photomondo/PhotoDisc/Getty Images; **949** *top* © Mark Kauffman/Life Magazine/Time & Life Pictures/Getty Images; *bottom* © 1967 James Pickerell/Black Star; **950** © AP Images; **952** © Burt Glinn/Magnum Photos; **953** *I Want Out* (20th Century). Color lithograph. Private Collection/Peter Newark American Pictures/The Bridgeman Art Library; **954** *center* © Danny Lyon/Magnum Photos; *top right* © Photomondo/PhotoDisc/Getty Images; **956** © Jack Kightlinger/Corbis; **957** © Bill Eppridge/Time & Life Pictures/Getty Images; **958** © Jeffrey Blankfort/Jeroboam; **960** *center* Donald J. Weber; *top right* © Photomondo/PhotoDisc/Getty Images; **962** © David Kennerly/Bettmann/Corbis; **963** © John Filo/Getty Images; **964** © Bettmann/Corbis; **965** © AP Images; **966** *center left* © 1993 Richard Howard/Black Star; *top right* © Chuck Pefley/Alamy; *top left* © Mark Wilson/AP Images; **968** *bottom left* © Peter Power/NewsCom/Toronto Star; **968–969** © Bettmann/Corbis; **969** *center right* Cover illustration © 1988 by Jim Dietz from *Fallen Angels* by Walter Dean Myers. Reprinted by permission of Scholastic, Inc.; *top left* © Henri Huet/AP Images; **970** *top right* © Mark Kauffman/Time & Life Pictures/Getty Images; *center left* © Bettmann/Corbis; *bottom right, I Want Out* (20th Century). Color lithograph. Private Collection/Peter Newark American Pictures/The Bridgeman Art Library; **971** A 1972 Herblock Cartoon, copyright by The Herb Block Foundation.

Chapter 31

972 *bottom left* © Bettmann/Corbis; *bottom center* © AFP/Getty Images; *bottom right* © 1980 Arnold Zann/Black Star; **972–973** © Lisa Law/The Image Works; **973** *bottom left* © Sahm Doherty/Time & Life Pictures/Getty Images; *bottom right* © Bettmann/Corbis; *center right* © Paul Fusco/Magnum Photos; **975** Underwood Photo Archives; **976** © Arthur Schatz/Time & Life Pictures/Getty Images; **977** © John Duricka/AP Images; **978** © Rick Smolan; **980** *bottom* Photograph by Harris (and) Ewing. Collection of the Supreme Court of the United States; **981** *left, right* Information provided by Alabama Department of Archives and History, Montgomery, Alabama; **982** *center left* © Bettmann/Corbis; **984** © Mark Klamkin/Black Star; **985** *top* © Werner Wolff/Black Star; *bottom* © AP Images; **986** *left* Library of Congress Prints and Photographs Division [LC-USZC4-2905]; *right* Reprinted by permission of Ms. magazine, © 1972; **987** *center right* © Bob Fitch/Black Star; **988** *top* Photo by Sharon Hoogstraten/McDougal Littell/Houghton Mifflin Co.; *bottom* © Bettmann/Corbis; **989** © 1967 Hulton-Deutsch Collection/Corbis; **990** *bottom* © AFP/Hulton Archive/Getty Images; *top left* © Danny Lyon/Magnum Photos; *top right* © Bettmann/Corbis; **991** © Bettmann/Corbis; **992** *bottom right* © Joel Axelrad/Michael Ochs Archives/Getty Images; *top right* © AP Images; *bottom left* © Wes Wilson; *center left* Photofest; **993** *top* Photofest; *bottom, Marilyn Monroe* (1967), Andy Warhol. Screenprint on white paper, 36" x 36". © The Andy Warhol Foundation for the Visual Arts/Corbis.

Chapter 32

996–997 Statue of Liberty National Monument/National Park Service/Photograph © Norman McGrath; **998** *bottom center* © Bettmann/Corbis; **998** *bottom left* Photo by Sharon Hoogstraten/McDougal Littell/Houghton Mifflin Co.; **998–999** © AP Images; **999** *fireworks* © Charles E. Rotkin/Corbis; *disco* © Bettmann/Corbis; *Camp David* Courtesy of the Jimmy Carter Library; **1000** *center* © C. Lee/PhotoLink/PhotoDisc/Getty Images; *top right* © C. Lee/PhotoLink/PhotoDisc/Getty Images; **1001** Courtesy of Paul Szep; **1002** National Aeronautics and Space Administraton (NASA); **1003** © Ira Wyman/Sygma/Corbis; **1004** *top* © Bettmann/Corbis; *bottom* © Bettmann/Corbis; **1005** © AP Images; **1006** © Bettmann/Corbis; **1007** © Central Press/Hulton Archive/Getty Images; **1008** *center* © AP Images; *top right* © C. Lee/PhotoLink/PhotoDisc/Getty Images; **1009** *top right, bottom right* © AP Images; *bottom left* © Bettmann/Corbis; *top left* © Hulton Archive/Getty Images; *background* © Robertstock.com; **1010** © 1973 Dennis Brack/Black Star; **1011** *top* © Wally McNamee/Corbis; *bottom* © AP Images; **1012** *bottom* AUTH © 1973 The Philadelphia Inquirer. Reprinted with permission of UNIVERSAL PRESS SYNDICATE. All rights reserved; *top* © National Archives/AP Images; **1013** *top* © 1974 Harry Benson; *center* National Archives and Records Administration (NARA); **1014** *center* © NBC/Photofest; *bottom* © CBS/Photofest; **1015** *top* Photofest; *bottom* © 1977 ABC/Warner TV/MPTV; **1016** *center* © Bill Pierce/Time & Life Pictures/Getty Images; *top right* © C. Lee/PhotoLink/PhotoDisc/Getty Images; **1017** © Time & Life Pictures/Getty Images; **1018** *top* © Owen Franken/Sygma/Corbis; *bottom* Museum of American Political Life, University of Hartford Library, West Hartford, Connecticut. Photograph by Sally Andersen-Bruce; **1019** © Bill Ross/Corbis; **1020** © Alex Webb/Magnum Photos; **1022** Courtesy of the Jimmy Carter Library; **1023** © Alain Mingam/Gamma-Presse; **1024** *center* © Walt Zaboski/AP Images; **1025** © Bettmann/Corbis; **1026** *center* © Bettmann/Corbis; *top right* © C. Lee/PhotoLink/PhotoDisc/Getty Images; **1027** *top* © Erich Hartmann/Magnum Photos; *bottom* © Hulton Archive/Getty Images; **1028** © Leonard Lee Rue III/Stock Boston; **1029** *bottom* © 1994 John McGrail; **1030** *right* © Columbia/The Kobal Collection; *left* © 20th Century Fox/The Kobal Collection; **1031** Library of Congress Prints and Photographs Division [LC-USZ62-102359]; **1032** *left* © Bettmann/Corbis; *center* © Time & Life Pictures/Getty Images; *right* Courtesy of the Jimmy Carter Library.

Chapter 33

1034 *bottom center* © Wally McNamee/Corbis; *bottom right* © Hulton Archive/Getty Images; *bottom left* © MPI/Hulton Archive/Getty Images; **1034–1035** © Robert Maass/Corbis; **1035** *wall* © Owen Franken/Corbis; *tank* © Giles Bassignac/Gamma-Presse; **1036** *center* © 1988 Dennis Brack/Black Star; *top right* © Scott Allen/Corbis; **1037** © Bettmann/Corbis; **1038** © 1991 Dennis Brack/Black Star; **1040** *center* © Wally NcNamee/Corbis; *top right* © Scott Allen/Corbis; **1042** *top* Oliphant © Reprinted with permission of UNIVERSAL PRESS SYNDI-CATE. All rights reserved; *center, bottom* © 1991 Dennis Brack/Black Star; **1043** © Ron Edmonds/AP Images; **1044** © 1987 Dennis Brack/Black Star; **1045** *center* © Peter Morgan/AP Images; *top right* © Scott Allen/Corbis; **1046** © Susan Steinkamp/Corbis; **1047** National Aeronautics and Space Administraton (NASA); **1048** © Wally McNamee/Corbis; **1049** © Christopher Morris/Black Star; **1050** © 1991 Dennis Brack/Black Star; **1051** © Lee Snider/Photo Images/Corbis; **1052–1053** © Bob Rowan/Progressive Image/Corbis; **1054** *center right* © Stephen Jaffe/Reuters/Corbis; *top right* © Scott Allen/Corbis; **1055** © 1989 by National Review, Inc., 215 Lexington Avenue, New York, NY 10016. REPRINTED BY PERMISSION; **1056** *top* © Reuters/Corbis; *bottom* © Jeff Widener/AP Images; **1058** A 1986

Herblock Cartoon, copyright by The Herb Block Foundation; **1060** *bottom left* © John Gaps III/AP Images; *center* © David Turnley/Corbis; **1061** © AP Images; **1062** *left* © 1991 Dennis Brack/Black Star; *right* © 1987 Dennis Brack/Black Star.rack/Black Star; *right* Copyright © 1987 Dennis Brack/Black Star.

Chapter 34

1064 *bottom right* © Steve Helber/AP Images; *bottom left* © Time Life Pictures/US Air Force/Time Life Pictures/Getty Images; **1064–1065** © Nancy Sheehan/PhotoEdit; **1065** *Albright* © Robert Maass/Corbis; *Bush* © Kevin Lamarque/Reuters; **1065** *Dolly* © John Chadwick/AP Images; **1066** *center* © 1993 Jim Stratford/Black Star; *top right* © PhotoDisc/Getty Images; **1067** *top* © Reuters/Corbis; *bottom* © John Duricka/AP Images; **1068** *bottom* © AP Images; *inset* © David Longstreath/AP Images; **1069** © Steve Ludlum/The New York Times/Redux; **1070** © Reuters/Corbis; **1071** © Ken Lambert/Washington Times via Newsmakers/Getty Images; **1072** *left* © Larry Downing/Reuters; *right* Photo courtesy of the White House/Newsmakers/Getty Images; **1073** © AP Images; **1074** © Joe Raedle/Getty Images; **1075** *center* Courtesy of Mike Cavanaugh/UNITE HERE!; *top right* © PhotoDisc/Getty Images; **1076** © Ronald Thomas/Bettmann/Corbis; **1077** © Lou Dematteis/Reuters; **1079** © Mary Altaffer/AP Photo; **1080** © Barron Claiborne/Outline/Corbis; **1081** *top* Copyright © 1989 by Gretchen Schields. Jacket art of *The Joy Luck Club*. Reproduced with permission of the artist and the Sandra Dijkstra Literary Agency; *bottom* © Greg Smith/SABA/Corbis; **1082** *center* Courtesy of Challenged Athletes Foundation/Photograph by Tim Mantoani; *top right* © PhotoDisc/Getty Images; **1083** Courtesy of Gary Brookins/Richmond Times-Dispatch; **1084** © Daily Press/Adrin Snider/AP Images; **1085** © Corbis; **1086** © Bobby Yip/Reuters/Corbis; **1087** *left* © Toby Talbot/AP Images; *right* © Dale Atkins/AP Images; **1088** *center* © Amy Sussman/AP Images; *top right* © PhotoDisc/Getty Images; **1089** *left* Courtesy of Michael Van Valkenburgh Associates, Inc., and Ann Hamilton; *right* Ed Massery; **1090** © Joseph Sohm/Visions of America/Corbis; **1092** © Paul Sakuma/AP Images; **1094** *center* Library of Congress Division of Prints and Photographs [LC-USZC4-4580]; *bottom* © Henry Guttmann/Hulton Archive/Getty Images; **1095** *top* © Sam Shere/Time & Life Pictures/Getty Images; *bottom* National Archives and Records Administration (NARA).

EPILOGUE

1098 *inset* © Wally McNamee/Corbis; **1098–1099** © Steve Kaufman/Corbis; **1099** *top* © Stephen Morton/AP Images; *bottom* © Damian Dovarganes/AP Images; **1100** © AP Images; **1101** © Beth A. Keiser/AP Images; **1102** © Joshua Roberts/AFP/Getty; **1103** © AP Images; **1105** © Scott Nelson/Getty Images; **1107** © Damian Dovarganes/AP Images; **1108** © Dan Loh/Pool/AP Images; **1111** © Jack Sauer/The Day/AP Images; **1113** © Stephen Morton/AP Images; **1114** © Miguel Gandert/Corbis; **1117** © Steve Liss/Time & Life Pictures/Getty Images; **1118** © Wally McNamee/Corbis; **1121** © Mark Foley/AP Images; **1122** © Steve Kaufman/Corbis.

ATLAS AND SKILLBUILDER HANDBOOK

1124–A1 NASA; **R23** © 1964 Steve Schapiro/Black Star; **R24** Culver Pictures; **R37** © 2008 Kindra Clineff.

PRESIDENTS OF THE UNITED STATES; *William J. Clinton and George W. Bush* Patrick Faricy/McDougal Littell/Houghton Mifflin Co.; *Barack Obama* © Ben Baker/Redux Pictures; *all others* Painted exclusively for Main Street Studios/EPCO, "The Oval Office Collection"/McDougal Littell/Houghton Mifflin Co.

NEW YORK PAGES

NY3 © Roman Soumar/Corbis; **NY4–NY5** © Royalty-Free/CORBIS; **NY5** © Photex/Corbis; **NY8** © U.S. Mint/Office of Public Affairs; **NY12** © Tetra Images/Alamy Images; **NY17** © Darren Green/ Alamy Images; **NY20** Library of Congress Prints and Photographs Division, Washington, D.C.; **NY24** Brown Brothers; **NY27** The Granger Collection, New York; **NY28** National Archives and Records Administration; **NY29** The Granger Collection, New York; **NY32** U.S. Naval Institute Photo Archives; **NY37** Cartoon by Paul Conrad. Copyright, Los Angeles Times Syndicate. Reprinted with permission; **NY40** © 2004 Larry Wright, All Rights Reserved, www. caglecartoons.com; **NY46** View of South Street, from Maiden Lane, New York City (1827), William James Bennett. Image © The Metropolitan Museum of Art/Art Resource, New York; **NY47** The Granger Collection, New York, (bl) © SuperStock; **NY48** The Granger Collection, New York; **NY49** (bl) © Francis G. Mayer/ Corbis; **NY50** (bl) The Granger Collection, New York, (bc) Bettmann/CORBIS; **NY51** (bl) Library of Congress Serial and Government Publications Division, Washington, D.C., (bc) The Granger Collection, New York, (br) Bettmann/Corbis; **NY52** (bl) Library of Congress Prints and Photographs Division, Washington, D.C., (br) The Granger collection, New York; **NY53** (bl) © Corbis, (bc) © Corbis, (br) © Joseph Sohm/Visions of America/Corbis; **NY54** (bl) © Bettmann/Corbis, (br) The Granger Collection, New York; **NY55** (bl) The Granger Collection, New York; **NY56** (br) The Granger Collection, New York, (bl) © Underwood & Underwood/ Corbis; **NY57** (bl) © Bettmann/Corbis, (bc) The Granger Collection, New York, (br) Library of Congress Prints and Photographs Division, Washington, D.C.; **NY58** (bl) © Bettmann/ Corbis, (br) The Granger Collection, New York; **NY59** (bl) Photo by Blank Archives/Getty Images, (br) Library of Congress Prints and Photographs Division, Washington, D.C.; **NY60** (bl) Bernd Obermann/Corbis, (br) U.S. Navy Photo by Jim Watson/Getty Images; **NY64** (t) ImageClub/Getty Images, (c) © Royalty-Free/ Corbis, (b) James L. Amos/Corbis

All unlisted photos and illustrations by McDougal Littell/Houghton Mifflin Co.

The editors have made every effort to trace the ownership of all copyrighted material found in this book and to make full acknowledgment for its use. Omissions brought to our attention will be corrected in a subsequent edition.

REVIEWERS (continued)